S0-DNK-295

T. T. Harris

19

1-19-24

University Casebook Series

December, 1981

ACCOUNTING AND THE LAW, Fourth Edition (1978), with Problems Pamphlet (Successor to Dohr, Phillips, Thompson & Warren)

George C. Thompson, Professor, Columbia University Graduate School of Business.
Robert Whitman, Professor of Law, University of Connecticut.
Ellis L. Phillips, Jr., Member of the New York Bar.
William C. Warren, Professor of Law Emeritus, Columbia University.

ACCOUNTING FOR LAWYERS, MATERIALS ON (1980)

David R. Herwitz, Professor of Law, Harvard University.

ADMINISTRATIVE LAW, Seventh Edition (1979), with 1979 Problems Supplement (Supplement edited in association with Paul R. Verkuil, Dean and Professor of Law, Tulane University)

Walter Gellhorn, University Professor Emeritus, Columbia University.
Clark Byse, Professor of Law, Harvard University.
Peter L. Strauss, Professor of Law, Columbia University.

ADMIRALTY, Second Edition (1978), with Statute and Rule Supplement

Jo Desha Lucas, Professor of Law, University of Chicago.

ADVOCACY, see also Lawyering Process

ADVOCACY, INTRODUCTION TO, Third Edition (1981)

Board of Student Advisers, Harvard Law School.

AGENCY, see also Enterprise Organization

AGENCY–ASSOCIATIONS–EMPLOYMENT–PARTNERSHIPS, Second Edition (1977)

Abridgement from Conard, Knauss & Siegel's Enterprise Organization.

ANTITRUST AND REGULATORY ALTERNATIVES (1977), Fifth Edition

Louis B. Schwartz, Professor of Law, University of Pennsylvania.
John J. Flynn, Professor of Law, University of Utah.

ANTITRUST SUPPLEMENT—SELECTED STATUTES AND RELATED MATERIALS (1977)

John J. Flynn, Professor of Law, University of Utah.

BIOGRAPHY OF A LEGAL DISPUTE, THE: An Introduction to American Civil Procedure (1968)

Marc A. Franklin, Professor of Law, Stanford University.

BUSINESS ORGANIZATION, see also Enterprise Organization

BUSINESS PLANNING (1966), with 1981 Supplement

David R. Herwitz, Professor of Law, Harvard University.

BUSINESS TORTS (1972)

Milton Handler, Professor of Law Emeritus, Columbia University.

CIVIL PROCEDURE, see Procedure

CLINIC, see also Lawyering Process

COMMERCIAL AND CONSUMER TRANSACTIONS, Second Edition (1978)

William D. Warren, Dean of the School of Law, University of California, Los Angeles.
William E. Hogan, Professor of Law, Cornell University.
Robert L. Jordan, Professor of Law, University of California, Los Angeles.

COMMERCIAL LAW, CASES & MATERIALS ON, Third Edition (1976)

E. Allan Farnsworth, Professor of Law, Columbia University.
John Honnold, Professor of Law, University of Pennsylvania.

COMMERCIAL PAPER, Second Edition (1976)

E. Allan Farnsworth, Professor of Law, Columbia University.

COMMERCIAL PAPER AND BANK DEPOSITS AND COLLECTIONS (1967), with Statutory Supplement

William D. Hawkland, Professor of Law, University of Illinois.

COMMERCIAL TRANSACTIONS—Text, Cases and Problems, Fourth Edition (1968)

The late Robert Braucher, Professor of Law, Harvard University.
The late Arthur E. Sutherland, Jr., Professor of Law, Harvard University.

COMPARATIVE LAW, Fourth Edition (1980)

Rudolf B. Schlesinger, Professor of Law, Hastings College of the Law.

COMPETITIVE PROCESS, LEGAL REGULATION OF THE, Second Edition (1979), with Statutory Supplement and 1982 Case Supplement

Edmund W. Kitch, Professor of Law, University of Chicago.
Harvey S. Perlman, Professor of Law, University of Virginia.

CONFLICT OF LAWS, Seventh Edition (1978), with 1982 Supplement

Willis L. M. Reese, Professor of Law, Columbia University,
Maurice Rosenberg, Professor of Law, Columbia University.

CONSTITUTIONAL LAW, Sixth Edition (1981), with 1981 Supplement

Edward L. Barrett, Jr., Professor of Law, University of California, Davis.
William Cohen, Professor of Law, Stanford University.

CONSTITUTIONAL LAW: THE STRUCTURE OF GOVERNMENT (Reprinted from CONSTITUTIONAL LAW, Sixth Edition)

Edward L. Barrett, Jr., Professor of Law, University of California, Davis.
William Cohen, Professor of Law, Stanford University.

CONSTITUTIONAL LAW, Tenth Edition (1980), with 1981 Supplement

Gerald Gunther, Professor of Law, Stanford University.

CONSTITUTIONAL LAW, INDIVIDUAL RIGHTS IN, Third Edition (1981), with 1981 Supplement (Reprinted from CONSTITUTIONAL LAW, Tenth Edition)

Gerald Gunther, Professor of Law, Stanford University.

CONTRACT LAW AND ITS APPLICATION, Second Edition (1977)

The late Addison Mueller, Professor of Law, University of California, Los Angeles.
Arthur I. Rosett, Professor of Law, University of California, Los Angeles.

CONTRACT LAW, STUDIES IN, Second Edition (1977)

Edward J. Murphy, Professor of Law, University of Notre Dame.
Richard E. Speidel, Professor of Law, University of Virginia.

CONTRACTS, Fourth Edition (1982)

John P. Dawson, Professor of Law Emeritus, Harvard University.
William Burnett Harvey, Professor of Law and Political Science, Boston University.
Stanley D. Henderson, Professor of Law, University of Virginia.

CONTRACTS, Third Edition (1980), with Statutory Supplement

E. Allan Farnsworth, Professor of Law, Columbia University.
William F. Young, Professor of Law, Columbia University.

CONTRACTS, Second Edition (1978), with Statutory and Administrative Law Supplement (1978)

Ian R. Macneil, Professor of Law, Cornell University.

COPYRIGHT, PATENT, TRADEMARK AND RELATED STATE DOCTRINES, Second Edition (1981), with Problem Supplement and Statutory Supplement

Paul Goldstein, Professor of Law, Stanford University.

COPYRIGHT, Unfair Competition, and Other Topics Bearing on the Protection of Literary, Musical, and Artistic Works, Third Edition (1978)

Benjamin Kaplan, Professor of Law Emeritus, Harvard University,
Ralph S. Brown, Jr., Professor of Law, Yale University.

CORPORATE FINANCE, Second Edition (1979), with 1980 New Developments Supplement

Victor Brudney, Professor of Law, Harvard University.
Marvin A. Chirelstein, Professor of Law, Yale University.

CORPORATE READJUSTMENTS AND REORGANIZATIONS (1976)

Walter J. Blum, Professor of Law, University of Chicago.
Stanley A. Kaplan, Professor of Law, University of Chicago.

CORPORATION LAW, BASIC, Second Edition (1979), with Documentary Supplement

Detlev F. Vagts, Professor of Law, Harvard University.

CORPORATIONS, see also Enterprise Organization

CORPORATIONS, Fifth Edition—Unabridged (1980)

William L. Cary, Professor of Law, Columbia University.
Melvin Aron Eisenberg, Professor of Law, University of California, Berkeley.

CORPORATIONS, Fifth Edition—Abridged (1980)

William L. Cary, Professor of Law, Columbia University.
Melvin Aron Eisenberg, Professor of Law, University of California, Berkeley.

CORPORATIONS, THE LAW OF: WHAT CORPORATE LAWYERS DO (1976)

Jan G. Deutsch, Professor of Law, Yale University.
Joseph J. Bianco, Professor of Law, Yeshiva University.

CORPORATIONS COURSE GAME PLAN (1975)

David R. Herwitz, Professor of Law, Harvard University.

CORRECTIONS, SEE SENTENCING

CREDIT TRANSACTIONS AND CONSUMER PROTECTION (1976)

John Honnold, Professor of Law, University of Pennsylvania.

CREDITORS' RIGHTS, see also Debtor-Creditor Law

CRIMINAL JUSTICE, THE ADMINISTRATION OF, Second Edition (1969)

Francis C. Sullivan, Professor of Law, Louisiana State University.
Paul Hardin III, Professor of Law, Duke University.
John Huston, Professor of Law, University of Washington.
Frank R. Lacy, Professor of Law, University of Oregon.
Daniel E. Murray, Professor of Law, University of Miami.
George W. Pugh, Professor of Law, Louisiana State University.

CRIMINAL JUSTICE ADMINISTRATION AND RELATED PROCESSES, Successor Edition (1976), with 1981 Supplement

Frank W. Miller, Professor of Law, Washington University.
Robert O. Dawson, Professor of Law, University of Texas.
George E. Dix, Professor of Law, University of Texas.
Raymond I. Parnas, Professor of Law, University of California, Davis.

CRIMINAL JUSTICE, LEADING CONSTITUTIONAL CASES ON (1981)

Lloyd L. Weinreb, Professor of Law, Harvard University.

CRIMINAL LAW, Second Edition (1979)

Fred E. Inbau, Professor of Law Emeritus, Northwestern University.
James R. Thompson, Professor of Law Emeritus, Northwestern University.
Andre A. Moenssens, Professor of Law, University of Richmond.

CRIMINAL LAW, Third Edition (1980)

Lloyd L. Weinreb, Professor of Law, Harvard University.

CRIMINAL LAW AND ITS ADMINISTRATION (1940), with 1956 Supplement

Jerome Michael, late Professor of Law, Columbia University.
Herbert Wechsler, Professor of Law, Columbia University.

CRIMINAL LAW AND PROCEDURE, Fifth Edition (1977)

Rollin M. Perkins, Professor of Law Emeritus, University of California, Hastings College of the Law.
Ronald N. Boyce, Professor of Law, University of Utah.

CRIMINAL PROCEDURE, Second Edition (1980), with 1981 Supplement

Fred E. Inbau, Professor of Law Emeritus, Northwestern University.
James R. Thompson, Professor of Law Emeritus, Northwestern University.
James B. Haddad, Professor of Law, Northwestern University.
James B. Zagel, Chief, Criminal Justice Division, Office of Attorney General of Illinois.
Gary L. Starkman, Assistant U. S. Attorney, Northern District of Illinois.

CRIMINAL PROCEDURE, CONSTITUTIONAL (1977), with 1980 Supplement

James E. Scarboro, Professor of Law, University of Colorado.
James B. White, Professor of Law, University of Chicago.

CRIMINAL PROCESS, Third Edition (1978), with 1981 Supplement

Lloyd L. Weinreb, Professor of Law, Harvard University.

DAMAGES, Second Edition (1952)

Charles T. McCormick, late Professor of Law, University of Texas.
William F. Fritz, late Professor of Law, University of Texas.

DEBTOR–CREDITOR LAW, Second Edition (1981), with Statutory Supplement

William D. Warren, Dean of the School of Law, University of California, Los Angeles.
William E. Hogan, Professor of Law, New York University.

DECEDENTS' ESTATES (1971)

Max Rheinstein, late Professor of Law Emeritus, University of Chicago.
Mary Ann Glendon, Professor of Law, Boston College.

DECEDENTS' ESTATES AND TRUSTS, Fifth Edition (1977)

John Ritchie, Professor of Law Emeritus, University of Virginia.
Neill H. Alford, Jr., Professor of Law, University of Virginia.
Richard W. Effland, Professor of Law, Arizona State University.

DECEDENTS' ESTATES AND TRUSTS (1968)

Howard R. Williams, Professor of Law, Stanford University.

DOMESTIC RELATIONS, see also Family Law

DOMESTIC RELATIONS, Third Edition (1978), with 1980 Supplement

Walter Wadlington, Professor of Law, University of Virginia.
Monrad G. Paulsen, Dean of the Law School, Yeshiva University.

DYNAMICS OF AMERICAN LAW, THE: Courts, the Legal Process and Freedom of Expression (1968)

Marc A. Franklin, Professor of Law, Stanford University.

ELECTRONIC MASS MEDIA, Second Edition (1979)

William K. Jones, Professor of Law, Columbia University.

ENTERPRISE ORGANIZATION, Second Edition (1977), with 1979 Statutory and Formulary Supplement

Alfred F. Conard, Professor of Law, University of Michigan.
Robert L. Knauss, Dean of the School of Law, Vanderbilt University.
Stanley Siegel, Professor of Law, University of California, Los Angeles.

EQUITY AND EQUITABLE REMEDIES (1975)

Edward D. Re, Adjunct Professor of Law, St. John's University.

EQUITY, RESTITUTION AND DAMAGES, Second Edition (1974)

Robert Childres, late Professor of Law, Northwestern University.
William F. Johnson, Jr., Professor of Law, New York University.

ESTATE PLANNING, Second Edition (1982), with Documentary Supplement

David Westfall, Professor of Law, Harvard University.

ETHICS, see Legal Profession, and Professional Responsibility

ETHICS AND PROFESSIONAL RESPONSIBILITY (1981) (Reprinted from THE LAWYERING PROCESS)

Gary Bellow, Professor of Law, Harvard University.
Bea Moulton, Legal Services Corporation.

EVIDENCE, Fourth Edition (1981)

David W. Louisell, late Professor of Law, University of California, Berkeley.
John Kaplan, Professor of Law, Stanford University.
Jon R. Waltz, Professor of Law, Northwestern University.

EVIDENCE, Sixth Edition (1973), with 1981 Supplement

John M. Maguire, late Professor of Law Emeritus, Harvard University.
Jack B. Weinstein, Professor of Law, Columbia University.
James H. Chadbourn, Professor of Law, Harvard University.
John H. Mansfield, Professor of Law, Harvard University.
(Supplement edited in association with Norman Abrams, Professor of Law, University of California, Los Angeles and Margaret Berger, Professor of Law, Brooklyn Law School).

EVIDENCE (1968)

Francis C. Sullivan, Professor of Law, Louisiana State University.
Paul Hardin, III, Professor of Law, Duke University.

FAMILY LAW, see also Domestic Relations

FAMILY LAW (1978), with 1981 Supplement

Judith C. Areen, Professor of Law, Georgetown University.

FAMILY LAW AND CHILDREN IN THE LEGAL SYSTEM, STATUTORY MATERIALS (1981)

Walter Wadlington, Professor of Law, University of Virginia.

FEDERAL COURTS, Sixth Edition (1976), with 1981 Supplement

Charles T. McCormick, late Professor of Law, University of Texas.
James H. Chadbourn, Professor of Law, Harvard University.
Charles Alan Wright, Professor of Law, University of Texas.

FEDERAL COURTS AND THE FEDERAL SYSTEM, Hart and Wechsler's Second Edition (1973), with 1981 Supplement

Paul M. Bator, Professor of Law, Harvard University.
Paul J. Mishkin, Professor of Law, University of California, Berkeley.
David L. Shapiro, Professor of Law, Harvard University.
Herbert Wechsler, Professor of Law, Columbia University.

FEDERAL PUBLIC LAND AND RESOURCES LAW (1981)

George C. Coggins, Professor of Law, University of Kansas.
Charles F. Wilkinson, Professor of Law, University of Oregon.

FEDERAL RULES OF CIVIL PROCEDURE, 1980 Edition

FEDERAL TAXATION, see Taxation

FOOD AND DRUG LAW (1980), with Statutory Supplement

Richard A. Merrill, Dean of the School of Law, University of Virginia.
Peter Barton Hutt, Esq.

FUTURE INTERESTS (1958)

Philip Mechem, late Professor of Law Emeritus, University of Pennsylvania.

FUTURE INTERESTS (1970)

Howard R. Williams, Professor of Law, Stanford University.

FUTURE INTERESTS AND ESTATE PLANNING (1961), with 1962 Supplement

W. Barton Leach, late Professor of Law, Harvard University.
James K. Logan, formerly Dean of the Law School, University of Kansas.

GOVERNMENT CONTRACTS, FEDERAL (1975), with 1980 Supplement

John W. Whelan, Professor of Law, Hastings College of the Law.
Robert S. Pasley, Professor of Law Emeritus, Cornell University.

INJUNCTIONS (1972)

Owen M. Fiss, Professor of Law, Yale University.

INSTITUTIONAL INVESTORS, 1978

David L. Ratner, Professor of Law, Cornell University.

INSURANCE (1971)

William F. Young, Professor of Law, Columbia University.

INTERNATIONAL LAW, see also Transnational Legal Problems and United Nations Law

INTERNATIONAL LAW IN CONTEMPORARY PERSPECTIVE (1981), with Essay Supplement

Myres S. McDougal, Professor of Law, Yale University.
W. Michael Reisman, Professor of Law, Yale University.

INTERNATIONAL LEGAL SYSTEM, Second Edition (1981), with Documentary Supplement

Joseph Modeste Sweeney, Professor of Law, Tulane University.
Covey T. Oliver, Professor of Law, University of Pennsylvania.
Noyes E. Leech, Professor of Law, University of Pennsylvania.

INTERNATIONAL TRADE AND INVESTMENT, REGULATION OF (1970)

Carl H. Fulda, late Professor of Law, University of Texas.
Warren F. Schwartz, Professor of Law, University of Virginia.

INTERNATIONAL TRANSACTIONS AND RELATIONS (1960)

Milton Katz, Professor of Law, Harvard University.
Kingman Brewster, Jr., Professor of Law, Harvard University.

INTRODUCTION TO LAW, see also Legal Method, On Law in Courts, and Dynamics of American Law

INTRODUCTION TO THE STUDY OF LAW (1970)

E. Wayne Thode, late Professor of Law, University of Utah.
Leon Lebowitz, Professor of Law, University of Texas.
Lester J. Mazor, Professor of Law, University of Utah.

JUDICIAL CODE and Rules of Procedure in the Federal Courts with Excerpts from the Criminal Code, 1981 Edition

Henry M. Hart, Jr., late Professor of Law, Harvard University.
Herbert Wechsler, Professor of Law, Columbia University.

JURISPRUDENCE (Temporary Edition Hardbound) (1949)

Lon L. Fuller, Professor of Law Emeritus, Harvard University.

JUVENILE COURTS (1967)

Hon. Orman W. Ketcham, Juvenile Court of the District of Columbia.
Monrad G. Paulsen, Dean of the Law School, Yeshiva University.

JUVENILE JUSTICE PROCESS, Second Edition (1976), with 1980 Supplement

Frank W. Miller, Professor of Law, Washington University.
Robert O. Dawson, Professor of Law, University of Texas.
George E. Dix, Professor of Law, University of Texas.
Raymond I. Parnas, Professor of Law, University of California, Davis.

LABOR LAW, Ninth Edition (1981), with Statutory Supplement

Archibald Cox, Professor of Law, Harvard University.
Derek C. Bok, President, Harvard University.
Robert A. Gorman, Professor of Law, University of Pennsylvania.

LABOR LAW (1968), with Statutory Supplement and 1974 Case Supplement

Clyde W. Summers, Professor of Law, University of Pennsylvania.
Harry H. Wellington, Dean of the Law School, Yale University.

LAND FINANCING, Second Edition (1977)

Norman Penney, Professor of Law, Cornell University.
Richard F. Broude, Member of the California Bar.

LAW AND MEDICINE (1980)

Walter Wadlington, Professor of Law and Professor of Legal Medicine, University of Virginia.
Jon R. Waltz, Professor of Law, Northwestern University.
Roger B. Dworkin, Professor of Law, Indiana University, and Professor of Biomedical History, University of Washington.

LAW, LANGUAGE AND ETHICS (1972)

William R. Bishin, Professor of Law, University of Southern California.
Christopher D. Stone, Professor of Law, University of Southern California.

LAWYERING PROCESS (1978), with Civil Problem Supplement and Criminal Problem Supplement

Gary Bellow, Professor of Law, Harvard University.
Bea Moulton, Professor of Law, Arizona State University.

LEGAL METHOD

Harry W. Jones, Professor of Law Emeritus, Columbia University.
John M. Kernochan, Professor of Law, Columbia University.
Arthur W. Murphy, Professor of Law, Columbia University.

LEGAL METHODS (1969)

Robert N. Covington, Professor of Law, Vanderbilt University.
E. Blythe Stason, late Professor of Law, Vanderbilt University.
John W. Wade, Professor of Law, Vanderbilt University.
Elliott E. Cheatham, late Professor of Law, Vanderbilt University.
Theodore A. Smedley, Professor of Law, Vanderbilt University.

LEGAL PROFESSION (1970)

Samuel D. Thurman, Dean of the College of Law, University of Utah.
Ellis L. Phillips, Jr., Professor of Law, Columbia University.
Elliott E. Cheatham, late Professor of Law, Vanderbilt University.

LEGISLATION, Fourth Edition (1982) (by Fordham)

Horace E. Read, late Vice President, Dalhousie University.
John W. MacDonald, Professor of Law Emeritus, Cornell Law School.
Jefferson B. Fordham, Professor of Law, University of Utah.
William J. Pierce, Professor of Law, University of Michigan.

LEGISLATIVE AND ADMINISTRATIVE PROCESSES, Second Edition (1981)

Hans A. Linde, Judge, Supreme Court of Oregon.
George Bunn, Professor of Law, University of Wisconsin.
Fredericka Paff, Professor of Law, University of Wisconsin.
W. Lawrence Church, Professor of Law, University of Wisconsin.

LOCAL GOVERNMENT LAW, Revised Edition (1975)

Jefferson B. Fordham, Professor of Law, University of Utah.

MASS MEDIA LAW (1976), with 1979 Supplement

Marc A. Franklin, Professor of Law, Stanford University.

MENTAL HEALTH PROCESS, Second Edition (1976), with 1981 Supplement

Frank W. Miller, Professor of Law, Washington University.
Robert O. Dawson, Professor of Law, University of Texas.
George E. Dix, Professor of Law, University of Texas.
Raymond I. Parnas, Professor of Law, University of California, Davis.

MUNICIPAL CORPORATIONS, see Local Government Law

NEGOTIABLE INSTRUMENTS, see Commercial Paper

NEGOTIATION (1981) (Reprinted from THE LAWYERING PROCESS)

Gary Bellow, Professor of Law, Harvard Law School.
Bea Moulton, Legal Services Corporation.

NEW YORK PRACTICE, Fourth Edition (1978)

Herbert Peterfreund, Professor of Law, New York University.
Joseph M. McLaughlin, Dean of the Law School, Fordham University.

OIL AND GAS, Fourth Edition (1979)

Howard R. Williams, Professor of Law, Stanford University.
Richard C. Maxwell, Professor of Law, University of California, Los Angeles.
Charles J. Meyers, Dean of the Law School, Stanford University.

ON LAW IN COURTS (1965)

Paul J. Mishkin, Professor of Law, University of California, Berkeley.
Clarence Morris, Professor of Law Emeritus, University of Pennsylvania.

PARTNERSHIP PLANNING (1970) (Pamphlet)

William L. Cary, Professor of Law, Columbia University.

PERSPECTIVES ON THE LAWYER AS PLANNER (Reprint of Chapters One through Five of Planning by Lawyers) (1978)

Louis M. Brown, Professor of Law, University of Southern California.
Edward A. Dauer, Professor of Law, Yale University.

PLANNING BY LAWYERS, MATERIALS ON A NONADVERSARIAL LEGAL PROCESS (1978)

Louis M. Brown, Professor of Law, University of Southern California.
Edward A. Dauer, Professor of Law, Yale University.

PLEADING AND PROCEDURE, see Procedure, Civil

POLICE FUNCTION (1976) (Pamphlet)

Chapters 1–11 of Miller, Dawson, Dix & Parnas' Criminal Justice Administration, Second Edition.

PREPARING AND PRESENTING THE CASE (1981) (Reprinted from THE LAWYERING PROCESS)

Gary Bellow, Professor of Law, Harvard Law School.
Bea Moulton, Legal Services Corporation.

PREVENTIVE LAW, see also Planning by Lawyers

PROCEDURE—Biography of a Legal Dispute (1968)

Marc A. Franklin, Professor of Law, Stanford University.

PROCEDURE—CIVIL PROCEDURE, Second Edition (1974), with 1979 Supplement

James H. Chadbourn, Professor of Law, Harvard University.
A. Leo Levin, Professor of Law, University of Pennsylvania.
Philip Shuchman, Professor of Law, University of Connecticut.

PROCEDURE—CIVIL PROCEDURE, Fourth Edition (1978), with 1981 Supplement

Richard H. Field, late Professor of Law, Harvard University.
Benjamin Kaplan, Professor of Law Emeritus, Harvard University.
Kevin M. Clermont, Professor of Law, Cornell University.

PROCEDURE—CIVIL PROCEDURE, Third Edition (1976), with 1978 Supplement

Maurice Rosenberg, Professor of Law, Columbia University.
Jack B. Weinstein, Professor of Law, Columbia University.
Hans Smit, Professor of Law, Columbia University.
Harold L. Korn, Professor of Law, Columbia University.

PROCEDURE—PLEADING AND PROCEDURE: State and Federal, Fourth Edition (1979)

David W. Louisell, late Professor of Law, University of California, Berkeley.
Geoffrey C. Hazard, Jr., Professor of Law, Yale University.

PROCEDURE—FEDERAL RULES OF CIVIL PROCEDURE, 1980 Edition

PROCEDURE PORTFOLIO (1962)

James H. Chadbourn, Professor of Law, Harvard University.
A. Leo Levin, Professor of Law, University of Pennsylvania.

PRODUCTS LIABILITY (1980)

Marshall S. Shapo, Professor of Law, Northwestern University.

PRODUCTS LIABILITY AND SAFETY (1980), with Statutory Supplement

W. Page Keeton, Professor of Law, University of Texas.
David G. Owen, Professor of Law, University of South Carolina.
John E. Montgomery, Professor of Law, University of South Carolina.

PROFESSIONAL RESPONSIBILITY, Second Edition (1981), with Selected National Standards Supplement

Thomas D. Morgan, Dean of the Law School, Emory University.
Ronald D. Rotunda, Professor of Law, University of Illinois.

PROPERTY, Fourth Edition (1978)

John E. Cribbet, Dean of the Law School, University of Illinois.
Corwin W. Johnson, Professor of Law, University of Texas.

PROPERTY—PERSONAL (1953)

S. Kenneth Skolfield, late Professor of Law Emeritus, Boston University.

PROPERTY—PERSONAL, Third Edition (1954)

Everett Fraser, late Dean of the Law School Emeritus, University of Minnesota.
Third Edition by Charles W. Taintor, late Professor of Law, University of Pittsburgh.

PROPERTY—INTRODUCTION, TO REAL PROPERTY, Third Edition (1954)

Everett Fraser, late Dean of the Law School Emeritus, University of Minnesota.

PROPERTY—REAL PROPERTY AND CONVEYANCING (1954)

Edward E. Bade, late Professor of Law, University of Minnesota.

PROPERTY—FUNDAMENTALS OF MODERN REAL PROPERTY (1974), with 1981 Supplement

Edward H. Rabin, Professor of Law, University of California, Davis.

PROPERTY—PROBLEMS IN REAL PROPERTY (Pamphlet) (1969)

Edward H. Rabin, Professor of Law, University of California, Davis.

PROSECUTION AND ADJUDICATION (1976) (Pamphlet)

Chapters 12–16 of Miller, Dawson, Dix & Parnas' Criminal Justice Administration, Successor Edition.

PUBLIC REGULATION OF DANGEROUS PRODUCTS (paperback) (1980)

Marshall S. Shapo, Professor of Law, Northwestern University.

PUBLIC UTILITY LAW, see Free Enterprise, also Regulated Industries

REAL ESTATE PLANNING (1980), with 1980 Problems, Statutes and New Materials Supplement

Norton L. Steuben, Professor of Law, University of Colorado.

REAL ESTATE TRANSACTIONS (1980), with Statute, Form and Problem Supplement

Paul Goldstein, Professor of Law, Stanford University.

RECEIVERSHIP AND CORPORATE REORGANIZATION, see Creditors' Rights

REGULATED INDUSTRIES, Second Edition, 1976

William K. Jones, Professor of Law, Columbia University.

REMEDIES (1982)

Edward D. Re, Chief Judge, U. S. Court of International Trade.

RESTITUTION, Second Edition (1966)

John W. Wade, Professor of Law, Vanderbilt University.

SALES (1980)

Marion W. Benfield, Jr., Professor of Law, University of Illinois.
William D. Hawkland, Chancellor, Louisiana State University Law Center.

SALES AND SALES FINANCING, Fourth Edition (1976)

John Honnold, Professor of Law, University of Pennsylvania.

SECURITY, Third Edition (1959)

John Hanna, late Professor of Law Emeritus, Columbia University.

SECURITIES REGULATION, Fourth Edition (1977), with 1981 Selected Statutes Supplement and 1981 Cases and Releases Supplement

Richard W. Jennings, Professor of Law, University of California, Berkeley.
Harold Marsh, Jr., Member of the California Bar.

SECURITIES REGULATION (1982)

Larry D. Soderquist, Professor of Law, Vanderbilt University.

SENTENCING AND CORRECTIONS, SANCTIONS (1981)

Nicholas N. Kittrie, Professor of Law, American University.
Elyce H. Zenoff, Professor of Law, George Washington University.

UNIVERSITY CASEBOOK SERIES—Continued

SENTENCING AND THE CORRECTIONAL PROCESS, Second Edition (1976)

Frank W. Miller, Professor of Law, Washington University.
Robert O. Dawson, Professor of Law, University of Texas.
George E. Dix, Professor of Law, University of Texas.
Raymond I. Parnas, Professor of Law, University of California, Davis.

SOCIAL WELFARE AND THE INDIVIDUAL (1971)

Robert J. Levy, Professor of Law, University of Minnesota.
Thomas P. Lewis, Dean of the College of Law, University of Kentucky.
Peter W. Martin, Professor of Law, Cornell University.

TAX, POLICY ANALYSIS OF THE FEDERAL INCOME (1976)

William A. Klein, Professor of Law, University of California, Los Angeles.

TAXATION, FEDERAL INCOME (1976), with 1980 Supplement

Erwin N. Griswold, Dean Emeritus, Harvard Law School.
Michael J. Graetz, Professor of Law, University of Virginia.

TAXATION, FEDERAL INCOME, Third Edition (1981)

James J. Freeland, Professor of Law, University of Florida.
Stephen A. Lind, Professor of Law, University of Florida.
Richard B. Stephens, Professor of Law Emeritus, University of Florida.

TAXATION, FEDERAL INCOME, Volume I, Personal Income Taxation (1972), with 1979 Supplement; Volume II, Taxation of Partnerships and Corporations, Second Edition (1980)

Stanley S. Surrey, Professor of Law, Harvard University.
William C. Warren, Professor of Law Emeritus, Columbia University.
Paul R. McDaniel, Professor of Law, Boston College Law School.
Hugh J. Ault, Professor of Law, Boston College Law School.

TAXATION, FEDERAL WEALTH TRANSFER (1977)

Stanley S. Surrey, Professor of Law, Harvard University.
William C. Warren, Professor of Law Emeritus, Columbia University.
Paul R. McDaniel, Professor of Law, Boston College Law School.
Harry L. Gutman, Instructor, Harvard Law School and Boston College Law School.

TAXATION OF INDIVIDUALS, PARTNERSHIPS AND CORPORATIONS, PROBLEMS in the (1978)

Norton L. Steuben, Professor of Law, University of Colorado.
William J. Turnier, Professor of Law, University of North Carolina.

TAXES AND FINANCE—STATE AND LOCAL (1974)

Oliver Oldman, Professor of Law, Harvard University.
Ferdinand P. Schoettle, Professor of Law, University of Minnesota.

TORT LAW AND ALTERNATIVES: INJURIES AND REMEDIES, Second Edition (1979)

Marc A. Franklin, Professor of Law, Stanford University.

TORTS, Sixth Edition (1976)

William L. Prosser, late Professor of Law, University of California, Hastings College.
John W. Wade, Professor of Law, Vanderbilt University.
Victor E. Schwartz, Professor of Law, American University.

UNIVERSITY CASEBOOK SERIES—Continued

TORTS, Third Edition (1976)

Harry Shulman, late Dean of the Law School, Yale University.
Fleming James, Jr., Professor of Law Emeritus, Yale University.
Oscar S. Gray, Professor of Law, University of Maryland.

TRADE REGULATION (1975), with 1979 Supplement

Milton Handler, Professor of Law Emeritus, Columbia University.
Harlan M. Blake, Professor of Law, Columbia University.
Robert Pitofsky, Professor of Law, Georgetown University.
Harvey J. Goldschmid, Professor of Law, Columbia University.

TRADE REGULATION, see Antitrust

TRANSNATIONAL LEGAL PROBLEMS, Second Edition (1976), with Documentary Supplement

Henry J. Steiner, Professor of Law, Harvard University.
Detlev F. Vagts, Professor of Law, Harvard University.

TRIAL, see also Lawyering Process and Preparing and Presenting the Case

TRIAL ADVOCACY (1968)

A. Leo Levin, Professor of Law, University of Pennsylvania.
Harold Cramer, of the Pennsylvania Bar.
Maurice Rosenberg, Professor of Law, Columbia University, Consultant.

TRUSTS, Fifth Edition (1978)

George G. Bogert, late Professor of Law Emeritus, University of Chicago.
Dallin H. Oaks, President, Brigham Young University.

TRUSTS AND SUCCESSION (Palmer's), Third Edition (1978)

Richard V. Wellman, Professor of Law, University of Georgia.
Lawrence W. Waggoner, Professor of Law, University of Michigan.
Olin L. Browder, Jr., Professor of Law, University of Michigan.

UNFAIR COMPETITION, see Competitive Process and Business Torts

UNITED NATIONS IN ACTION (1968)

Louis B. Sohn, Professor of Law, Harvard University.

UNITED NATIONS LAW, Second Edition (1967), with Documentary Supplement (1968)

Louis B. Sohn, Professor of Law, Harvard University.

WATER RESOURCE MANAGEMENT, Second Edition (1980)

Charles J. Meyers, Dean of the Law School, Stanford University.
A. Dan Tarlock, Professor of Law, Indiana Unversity.

WILLS AND ADMINISTRATION, Fifth Edition (1961)

Philip Mechem, late Professor of Law, University of Pennsylvania.
Thomas E. Atkinson, late Professor of Law, New York University.

WORLD LAW, see United Nations Law

University Casebook Series

CASES AND MATERIALS

ON

DECEDENTS' ESTATES AND TRUSTS

By

JOHN RITCHIE

Emeritus Dean and Wigmore Professor of Law,
Northwestern University

NEILL H. ALFORD, JR.

Percy Brown Professor of Law, University of Virginia

RICHARD W. EFFLAND

Professor of Law, Arizona State University

SIXTH EDITION

Mineola, New York

THE FOUNDATION PRESS, INC.

1982

Printed in the United States of America

Library of Congress Cataloging in Publication Data

Ritchie, John, 1904-
Cases and materials on decendents' estates and trusts.

(University casebook series)
Includes index.
1. Inheritance and succession—United States—Cases. 2. Wills—United States—Cases. 3. Trusts and trustees—United States—Cases. I. Alford, Neill H. II. Effland, Richard W. III. Title. IV. Series.
KF753.A7R5 1982 346.7305'2 82-8675
347.30652 AACR2

ISBN 0-88277-056-X

PREFACE

Much material has been added in this edition without a substantial increase in the length of the book. Principal cases carried over from the Fifth Edition have been further edited in many instances. New cases have been added, and some new cases have been substituted for old ones. The general organization of the former edition is continued but there are, in addition to changes in the principal cases, many changes in the text. The major text changes are the following:

(1) The tax materials are rewritten to reflect changes made by the Economic Recovery Tax Act of 1981. There is further revision of text and notes to reflect numerous statutory and case law changes since publication of the Fifth Edition in 1977, one of the major areas of change being the treatment of illegitimate children in succession matters.

(2) Chapter II is revised to include a dialogue development of an estate plan, followed by a dialogue development of probate and administration. The Chapter can be assigned for student reading to provide an overview of the material in the book at the beginning of the course.

(3) Chapter IV on Limitations Upon Testamentary Power has been rewritten and reorganized to emphasize changes in protective policies caused by changes in domestic relations.

(4) There is new emphasis in the text upon the use of the durable power as a substitute for the trust.

(5) In Chapter IX "Trust Litigation Problems" there is new text treatment of trusts for business purposes. Considered are trusteed employee benefit plans under ERISA; trusts used for business control, such as voting trusts; trusts used in debtor-creditor relations; the "Illinois land" trust and the Massachusetts trust including REITS. The editors recognize that these business trusts, other than employee benefit trusts, figure, if at all, only indirectly in estate planning. Nevertheless they believe it is desirable to have this material available for reading by students when trusts are being discussed in a litigation context. ERISA also receives new consideration in Chapter XVII dealing with the administration of trusts and estates.

When the editors prepared the first edition of this book almost thirty years ago, their primary purpose in integrating teaching materials on wills, trusts and future interests was to prepare students for the private practice of probate and trust law. While this remains a primary purpose of the book, all subsequent editions have emphasized also an examination of the legal system as a means for facilitating and regulating wealth transfers. This emphasis is continued, and increased, in this edition.

It is of paramount importance that a lawyer be sensitive to his ethical responsibilities beyond competence, and the importance of this requirement increases as the bar increases in size and the control by organized bars is complicated by judicial decisions and other factors. These ethical issues are identified for discussion distributively throughout the book in relation to transactions giving rise to them. Attention also is given to malpractice litigation which is likely to increase as professional bar controls become less effective. Of overriding importance is the professional goal of furnishing to the public legal services of consistently high quality at a price reasonably related to the value of the services rendered. The materials in the book emphasize the importance of this objective and the editors believe their organization and combination of materials for law school instruction is conducive to this end.

Lawyers should lead in law reform. This edition continues the emphasis of the editors in earlier editions upon the Uniform Probate Code and upon other suggestions for reform of probate and related laws. While adoption of the Uniform Probate Code as a whole has not increased substantially since publication of the Fifth Edition of this book, the influence of the Code upon law reform in probate matters in the United States and in other countries which share the heritage of the British probate practice has been dramatic. The Uniform Probate Code has had, as the editors predicted in the Fifth Edition, much influence on judicial change on an interstitial basis as courts have reexamined traditional legal doctrines. One excellent example is in the judicial view of "will substitute" transfers. These transfers have enjoyed increased judicial acceptance despite non-compliance with the local wills act. This seems due to a great extent, to the example of the Multiple Party Accounts provisions of the Uniform Probate Code.

In this, as in prior editions, the editors have benefitted from the suggestions of users of the book and other colleagues as well as from the devoted work of student assistants who have checked citations and performed myriad other tasks. These welcomed suggestions and valued student help over the years are, of course, reflected in this Sixth Edition. In particular the editors wish to acknowledge the thoughtful comments of Professors Regis W. Campfield of Southern Methodist School of Law and Joel C. Dobris of the University of California at Davis School of Law, reflected in materials in this Sixth Edition.

JOHN RITCHIE
NEILL H. ALFORD, JR.
RICHARD W. EFFLAND

May, 1982

SUMMARY OF CONTENTS

APPENDICES

*

TABLE OF CONTENTS

CHAPTER IV. LIMITATIONS UPON TESTAMENTARY POWER

CHAPTER V. EXECUTION OF WILLS

CHAPTER VI. REVOCATION, REVALIDATION AND REVIVAL OF WILLS

CHAPTER VII. CONTEST OF WILLS AND RELATED REMEDIES

CHAPTER VIII. THE PRIVATE EXPRESS TRUST

CHAPTER IX. TRUST LITIGATION PROBLEMS

CHAPTER X. TERMINATION

CHAPTER XI. GIFTS TO CHARITY

CHAPTER XII. INTERRELATING TESTAMENTARY AND INTER VIVOS TRANSACTIONS

CHAPTER XIII. FUTURE INTERESTS

CHAPTER XIV. POWERS OF APPOINTMENT

CHAPTER XV. THE EFFECT OF CHANGE ON DISPOSITIVE DESCRIPTIONS AND LIMITATIONS

CHAPTER XVI. SOCIAL RESTRICTIONS ON PERPETUITIES AND ACCUMULATIONS

CHAPTER XVII. ADMINISTRATION

APPENDICES

*

TABLE OF CASES

The principal cases are in italic type. Cases cited or discussed are in roman type. References are to Pages.

*

CASES AND MATERIALS

ON

DECEDENTS' ESTATES AND TRUSTS

*

Chapter I

INTRODUCTION

SECTION 1. THE PATTERN OF PRACTICES FOR TRANSMITTING WEALTH IN VIEW OF DEATH

The editors of this casebook have not attempted to assemble the full range of materials necessary for a single comprehensive course in estate planning. They contemplate instead a "capstone" course in estate planning devoted to an analysis of estates and drafting of the necessary instruments. In a course of this type, the skills and knowledge developed from the study of these materials, materials in related property courses, and tax materials, can be combined, interrelated and applied in the planning context. But the student should keep in mind that the separation of materials dealing with trusts and estates from materials bearing upon the remainder of a complex pattern of practices for the disposition of wealth is simply a "separation" and not a "divorce".

A wit in the Inns of Court once rationalized the peculiar combination of "probate, divorce and admiralty" jurisdiction in one division of the British High Court of Justice (this combination existing between 1873 and 1970) as based on "wrecks"—as he put it, "wrecks of wills, wrecks of marriages and wrecks of ships". By the same token, the organizing theory of these materials might be taken as "the relationship of death to the ownership and control of property". The student will study, for example, the plan provided by the state for the disposition of a man's property when he dies without a will or with a will disposing of only part of his estate—called "intestate succession"; how the man can make a will and alter it; how he can control the use of property after he dies by means of the "trust" and "future interest"; and how his property is required to be managed by others when he establishes a trust or leaves an estate—called "fiduciary administration". But these dispositions and supporting transactions, voluntary or involuntary as the case may be, are simply parts of a larger pattern; they are only some of the many practices applied in the disposition of wealth that relate directly or indirectly to the event of death of the property owner. The law of trusts and estates will, in a real sense, become more meaningful for the student if he will constantly bear in mind that he is considering a fragment of a pattern and will constantly strive to see the working relationships between these fragments and the greater whole.

Assume a hypothetical, Mr. Jones, who has acquired a personal estate of $600,000 and a residence situated on an acre of land. Assume that he is 50 years old and has an income-producing expectancy of about 15 years. As a potential testator or intestate his problems are not unusually complex.

His wealth, during his lifetime, is subject to myriad involuntary transfers that in a time of inflation can exhaust or seriously diminish his estate. The most important of these are taxes:—federal, state and local. These range from taxes on income, usually the most significant, to taxes based simply upon the ownership of property. A state or local government or both may tax him on his ownership of the $600,000 and will almost certainly assess a tax upon his land. If he makes $50,000 per year for the next 15 years he can expect a minimum of 40% of this to be taken in direct taxes by various governments unless he engages in active tax planning. The higher his income goes, the greater percentage of tax loss he must anticipate.

If Mr. Jones is subject to Social Security, he must make involuntary payments up to a stipulated amount of his income. These payments may work to the ultimate benefit of his estate; but the actual amount payable when he dies will depend on his time under the system and the relatives who survive him. If he is survived by a widow and minor child of six, the benefits received by these survivors may ultimately exceed by a great amount his total contributions. If he is survived only by brothers and sisters, these persons will probably receive much less than his total contributions. A retirement system may be operated by Jones' employer; and his union, if he has one, may require contributions to a union fund. While there is greater certainty of repayment of the funds contributed in these private or semi-private arrangements, they are also substantially involuntary.

What avenues are open to Mr. Jones for the voluntary disposition of his estate? He can make absolute gifts of his personal estate. He might be able to make an effective gift causa mortis. He can make a deed of his land creating a future interest in his grantee—for example—retaining a life estate in himself and creating a vested remainder in fee simple in the grantee. Perhaps he can manipulate delivery of the deed by making an absolute delivery to an escrow holder with instructions to deliver the deed after his death to the grantee designated. If the joint tenancy with right of survivorship is recognized in the state, Mr. Jones might set up a title in joint tenancy with the person he desires to take the land as joint tenant; or he might set up a tenancy by the entirety with his wife.

One of the most flexible dispositive devices available to Jones is the inter vivos trust. Flexibility can be developed through broad powers of management conferred upon the trustee. Perhaps Jones will wish to retain powers to revoke or modify the trust to meet future changes in his needs, the needs of his beneficiaries or the tax laws. If the statutes in his state permit, he may declare himself trustee of any or all of his personal property and land for some designated beneficiary and reserve a life estate in himself; he might transfer the property in trust to another and reserve a life estate and perhaps retain a power of appointment over the remainder. He must consider the tax disadvantages of the trust transactions described. To minimize income taxes, he might transfer income producing property on a Clifford or short term trust if he wishes to recover the property after the trust term. He should have no Federal gift or estate taxes if he utilizes fully the 100% gift and estate tax marital deduction by making qualifying transfers to the spouse and, even without these, may pay no tax because of the unified credit.

Contracts of various types are common devices used to dispose of wealth in anticipation of death. The most familiar of these are life insurance policies with various settlement options. Probably more estates of medium size are transmitted by life insurance contracts than by will or the intestate laws. United States Savings Bonds are favored contractual methods of disposing of wealth. These are accrual type bonds which may be issued to joint owners, in which case either owner can surrender the bond for payment, or which may be issued to a named payee but payable on his death to another beneficiary. The interest and principal of these bonds are taxable under appropriate tax laws. Joint bank accounts may contain survivorship provisions; and the courts in some states enforce a trust of a bank account, described as a "Totten" trust. In a valid Totten trust the beneficiary named is entitled to the balance of the account remaining at the death of the depositor. Other contractual schemes, such as partnership survivorship agreements, employment contracts and employment retirement programs have proved popular for inter vivos dispositions, although, as indicated previously, some of these are substantially involuntary.

The circumstances under which inter vivos dispositions of the type mentioned might be used by Mr. Jones, and the particular combinations he might select, should depend upon the tax economy possible, the flexibility which he can retain in managing his estate during his lifetime, and his future personal needs and those of his family prior to his death. Some of these transactions in the particular context in which they are used may be quite similar to a will. If a court should hold the transaction a will, and it lacks testamentary formalities, it will be held ineffective after Mr. Jones' death. The problem of testamentary character is developed in Chapters V and XII, Section 1 hereafter.

If Mr. Jones has property when he dies, his interest is not terminated by his death, and if he either has no will or does not dispose of all of his property by will, his property passes in accordance with a state plan or by "intestate succession". This is an involuntary system for transmitting property. He must dispose of his property by will or it passes by intestacy. Whether he dies with a will or without one, there are further involuntary dispositions for estate and inheritance taxes and administrative expenses. Mr. Jones' widow may be able to claim dower in his land or a "forced share" in his estate. Her forced share may vary from one-third to one-half of the estate or more depending on the local statute. Mr. Jones' children, or some of them may be able to claim as "pretermitted heirs". In this event, even though Jones leaves a will, these children can claim the share that they would have taken if Jones had died intestate.

The emphasis of this casebook upon practices applied in the disposition of wealth relating directly or indirectly to the event of death is not intended to suggest that the disposition of his wealth is the sole or even the primary concern of the property owner. For example, many persons make gifts of all or portions of their bodies for medical purposes. While bodies have been in great demand for medical instruction since the beginning of medical education, more recent advancements in medical transplant techniques have created a demand for hearts, kidneys, blood vessels, eyes, tendons and livers in transplantable condition. There exist organ banks, such as the International Living Bank in Houston, Texas, and the National Eye Bank in Atlanta, Georgia, where such donations may be preserved for potential donees. Mr. Jones may dispose of all or part of his body by will or by some other written statement.

He would not, however, have possessed this power fully until recent times. No property rights in a body were recognized in the early English Common Law. Any direction by the testator to dispose of his body was regarded as only a request by which no one was bound. In the United States, the body was sometimes described as "quasi-property" and the testator allowed to dispose of it. But courts taking this position often permitted, upon various grounds, the wishes of others, particularly the surviving spouse, to prevail over the wishes of the testator.

Today, all states and the District of Columbia have statutes permitting anatomical gifts. The statute usually in force is the Uniform Anatomical Gift Act although some states have variations of the "uniform" terms.

The Uniform Anatomical Gift Act provides that anyone over a specified age and of sound mind may donate any portion or all of his body to certain institutions or individuals for scientific advancement, research, therapy, education or transplantation. Absent a contrary intention expressed by the decedent or certain relatives, the decision to donate may be made by the spouse or others named in the Act. Except for state laws respecting autopsies, the rights of the donee are made paramount to the rights of others. The gift is made by will or other document which must be executed in the presence of two witnesses, the donor and the witnesses signing the instrument. No delivery of the instrument of gift to the donee is required. The gift can be revoked if the requirements of the Act for revocation are met. The Act does not deal with the question of determination of the fact of death, a matter critical in many transplant cases.[1]

1. See Uniform Anatomical Gift Act (1968), 8 U.L.A. 22. Case law prior to adoption of the Uniform Act is summarized in 7 A.L.R.3d 747 (1966) with cases concerning the time, method or place of burial summarized in 54 A.L.R.3d 1037 (1974). On the Uniform Act, see Featherstone, "The Uniform Anatomical Gift Act: The Laws' Approach to a Human Need", 110 Trusts and Estates 468

Not to be confused with the anatomical gift is the so-called "living will" by which a person instructs attending physicians that he does not wish his life prolonged by extraordinary means. As of 1981 ten states had statutes pertaining to this situation and exempting the attending physician and other health professionals from liability for complying with the patient's directives.[2]

SECTION 2. TERMINOLOGY

The words and phrases defined in this section are used in discussing matters arising from the distribution and use of decedents' estates. The definitions are intended to aid the student in reading the historical introduction and the cases and materials which appear hereafter in this book.[3]

We inherited much of our vocabulary of decedents' estates from England. But there was no unified court system in England when this vocabulary was being developed. Jurisdiction over decedents' estates was divided between the common law courts and the ecclesiastical courts. The common law courts, a part of the royal judicial system, decided cases involving the distribution and use of real property. The ecclesiastical courts, a part of the judicial system of the Roman Catholic Church, decided cases involving the distribution and use of personal property.[4] Each group of courts developed a distinct terminology of decedents' estates.[5] Although most of the effects of this ancient division in jurisdiction have disappeared, two sets of words are still used to describe the distribution and use of decedents' estates, one set of words being applied to real property and the other to personal property.

(1971); Smith and Smith, "Kansas and the Uniform Anatomical Gift Act", 19 Kan.L.Rev. 569 (1971); Stanford, "Putting the Anatomical Gift Act to Work: The Story of the Makana Foundation", 111 Trusts and Estates 16 (1972); Comments: "How to Do It: Donations of Bodies or Body Parts under the Texas Anatomical Gift Act", 27 Baylor L.Rev. 141 (1975); "Survey of Legal Aspects of Organ Transplantation", 50 Chi-Kent L. Rev. 516 (1973).

2. See Horan, "Termination of Medical Treatment", 16 Forum 470 (1981).

3. The cases and materials appearing first in this book deal with intestate succession and wills. The language of trusts, future interests and fiduciary administration will be examined in conjunction with the cases and materials bearing principally upon these subjects. The definitions should suggest the need for a critical understanding of the limitations and potentialities of words for communicating ideas. An understanding of semantics, or the "science of meaning", will aid the student in appraising the legal doctrines which he will encounter in this course. Suggested references are: Chase, The Tyranny of Words (1938); Chase, The Power of Words (1954); Hayakawa, Language in Action (1948); Hayakawa, Language, Meaning and Maturity (1954); Ogden and Richards, The Meaning of Meaning (1949).

4. Appeals to Rome from the English ecclesiastical courts were cut off by the Statute of Appeals, 24 Hen. VIII, C. 12 (1533).

5. The common law courts tended to rely for their terminology upon Germanic and feudal sources. The ecclesiastical courts borrowed heavily from the revived Roman Law.

Succession is the fact of becoming beneficially entitled to the property of a decedent. A person becomes beneficially entitled to the property of a decedent by *intestate succession* or by *will*.[6]

If the decedent leaves no valid will, his property passes by *intestate succession* to those of his relatives who are named in a state statute. The statute is called the *intestate law*.[7] The decedent is said to *die intestate* and, whether male or female, is called *the intestate*. Intestate real property passes by *descent* and intestate personal property passes by *distribution*.

The person entitled by statute to the land of an intestate is called the *heir* or *heir at law*. The heir takes by *descent* or by *inheritance*.

Although a living person has no heirs, words have been coined to describe his potential heirs. An *expectant* heir is one who expects to take an inheritance. A *prospective* heir is one who may inherit but who may be excluded. The term *prospective heir* includes an *heir presumptive* and an *heir apparent*. An *heir presumptive* is a person who will inherit if the potential intestate dies immediately, but who will be excluded if relatives closer in relationship to the intestate are born. An *heir apparent* is one who is certain to inherit unless excluded by a valid will.

The word *heir* and the various descriptions of potential heirs are often used to describe the person who is, or may be, entitled to the personal property of an intestate. But the orthodox terms used to describe this person are *distributee* or *next of kin*. The distributee or next of kin *inherits* personal property.

Ascendant or *ancestor* describes a person related to an intestate or to a claimant to an intestate share in the ascending lineal line. *Descendant* describes a person related to an intestate or to a claimant to an intestate share in the descending lineal line. *Collaterals* are relatives who trace relationship to an intestate through a common ancestor but who are not in his lineal line of ascent or descent. Collaterals are said to be in the *collateral line*. Persons related to an intestate through only *one* common ancestor are called *collaterals of the half-blood*. There are no lineals of the half-blood. Relationship by marriage is called relationship by *affinity*. Relationship by blood is called relationship by *consanguinity*.

Intestate property passes to the state or one of its political subdivisions by *escheat* if no relatives of the intestate are entitled to inherit.

6. There are a variety of ways in which a man can exercise posthumous or "dead hand" control over his property, even though the property does not pass by intestate succession or by will. A number of "will substitutes", for example, are considered in Chapter XII, Section 1.

7. An intestate law which applies only to real property is called a *statute of descent*. If it applies only to personal property, it is called a *statute of distribution*. If it applies to land and personal property, it is called a *statute of descent and distribution* or a *uniform table of descent and distribution*.

If the decedent leaves a valid will, his property passes in accordance with the terms of the will rather than by statute.[8] A *will* is a written or oral expression of a person's intention concerning the disposition of his property at his death.[9] A will is effective only when executed with the formalities required by statute. The statutes which prescribe formalities for executing wills and deal with other matters pertaining to wills are called the *wills acts*. The decedent is said to *die testate* when he leaves a valid will. The decedent is called the *testator*, if male, and the *testatrix*, if female.

A clause directing the disposition of real property in a will is called a *devise*. The person who is named to take the real property is called the *devisee*. A clause directing the disposition of money in a will is called a *legacy*. A clause directing the disposition of personal property other than money in a will is called a *bequest*, and the modern tendency is to use the word *bequest* for a gift of any sort of personal property by will. The person who is named to take personal property of any kind is called the *legatee*. The words *devise*, *legacy* and *bequest* are also used to describe the subject matter of a gift by will. A testator is also said to *devise* land and *bequeath* personal property.[10]

An *attested* will is a will signed by witnesses. A *holographic* will is a will entirely in the handwriting of the testator. A *nuncupative* will is an oral will. A *codicil* is a testamentary instrument ancillary to a will.

Probate is the procedure by which a transaction alleged to be a will is established judicially as a valid testamentary disposition. Probate also applies to the act of approving the will after the probate procedure has taken place.

Administration refers to the conduct of the *personal representative* of an *intestate, testator* or *testatrix*, in collecting the assets of the estate, paying the creditors and distributing the residue of the property to those entitled to receive it.[11] Administration is supervised by an appropriate court.

The personal representative of a decedent is the *executor* or *administrator* of his estate. The *executor* is a personal representative named in a will. The *administrator* is a personal representative appointed by a court to administer the estate of an intestate. If a will

8. The will may cover only part of the property which the decedent owns at his death. The decedent dies partially intestate in this case. Of course, there is always the problem of deciding what the decedent meant by certain language in his will, and when a court construes the will it may direct a disposition of the property which the decedent did not intend.

9. Whether a will can be made orally depends upon local statutes. Testamentary character is defined in Chapters V, Section 2 and XII, Section 1.

10. The word *devise* was once used to describe an entire will of real property rather than only a particular clause contained in the will. The word *testament* was used to describe a will of personal property. This terminology is used in the historical introduction in this chapter. The word *will* is now used to describe the entire testamentary instrument.

11. Administration also includes the administration of trusts by trustees and the administration of property of infants and incompetents by guardians and committees.

does not name an executor, or if the executor named does not serve, the court appoints an *administrator cum testamento annexo.* This is abbreviated administrator *c. t. a.* It means administrator "with the will annexed". If the administrator of an intestate fails to complete his administration for some reason, the court appoints an *administrator de bonis non.* This is abbreviated administrator *d. b. n.* It means "administrator of goods not administered". If an executor fails to complete his administration, the court appoints an *administrator cum testamento annexo, de bonis non.*

The Uniform Probate Code, which will be discussed later in this chapter and to which reference will be made throughout the course, has a simplified system of terminology. The Code makes no distinction between real and personal property, thereby eliminating differences in terminology dependent on the kind of property involved. Thus, if decedent died intestate, property passes by *intestate succession* to his *heirs.* If decedent disposes of his estate by will, he *devises* the property and the takers are *devisees,* even though the subject is personal property. In utilizing the Code provisions it is important to remember that the terms are used with their statutory definition and not in their historic connotation.

SECTION 3. HISTORICAL INTRODUCTION

The laws dealing with estates and trusts are a form of community control over the use of wealth. A person who produces or possesses wealth has power to enhance or diminish the security of others. Because of the power wealth carries with it, some form of control by a community over the use of wealth is vital to the welfare of its members.[12]

While facts existing at a particular time and place determine the ends a community seeks through control of wealth and the techniques of control it applies, these facts always include the experience gained by the community from past efforts to control wealth processes.[13] There must be a constant redefinition of the ends of control in the light of community experience. Existing techniques of control

12. Interesting and readable accounts of techniques used by ancient communities for controlling the use of wealth may be found in Maine, Ancient Law (1873) and Seagle, The Quest for Law (1941). A number of wills of early date are collected in Harris, Ancient, Famous and Curious Wills (1912). When a man dies leaving wealth, his loss of control over it stimulates conflicting demands among his survivors. Legal institutions may be used to minimize this conflict within a community, but it is obvious that other forms of control may prove more effective for this purpose under certain circumstances.

13. Legal institutions and other institutions for controlling the use of wealth are ideas, and no idea is entirely original. An invention is always based in part upon ideas formulated in the past.

must be appraised and modified and new techniques must be invented to attain the ends as redefined.

Most American states developed their laws of estates and trusts from English statutes and judicial decisions known to their legislators at the time of the American Revolution, or from English and American statutes and judicial decisions available as models at the times particular states were admitted into the Union. It is important to know something of the background of the English laws in order to understand fully the American laws of estates and trusts we apply today.

Many of the English laws of estates and trusts can be traced to the period between 1066 and 1600. English kings were then engaged in building a strong central government within the English community, and the legal doctrines of estates and trusts which the courts developed reflect the judicial handling of political, economic and social problems that had to be confronted before an effective central government could be created.[14] It was difficult, however, to formulate and apply sound and comprehensive policies in an effort to deal with these problems because policy-making functions were distributed among a number of courts whose activities lacked overall coordination. This diffusion of responsibility is evident in the doctrines of estates and trusts coming down to us from the Medieval English period. The roles of the common law and ecclesiastical courts have been mentioned.[15] In addition, franchise courts, which were courts created by royal grant, heard cases involving the disposition of land and chattels of decedents. Franchise jurisdiction accounts in part for local customs of intestate succession and wills enduring in London, Oxford and other localities until relatively recent times. The lord of a manor in his feudal or "manorial" court directed the disposition of copyhold tenures and chattels of his deceased serfs.[16]

The common law judges were often political craftsmen of exceptional ability, and their decisions in cases involving decedents' freehold estates in land were influenced by considerations of economy and political expediency foreign to the judges of the ecclesiastical, franchise and feudal courts. The ecclesiastical judges, on the other hand, brought to their decisions certain ethical values that had found

14. A number of these problems were created or accentuated by feudalism. The importance of feudalism in England has received undue emphasis. I Pollock and Maitland, History of English Law (2d Ed. 1899) 66 et seq. But feudalism was responsible in part for chronic unemployment and low agricultural production that agitated the English people. The feudal political structure tended to concentrate military power in tenants *in capite* to the king. When a tenant *in capite* could augment his feudal levies with recruits from the disaffected population, he was often encouraged to rebel against the king. While few of these rebellions were successful, they were sufficient to inhibit the process of centralization. The disruptive effects of feudalism were taken into account by the common law judges as they formulated rules for descent of land and collateral restraints upon alienation.

15. The common law courts had jurisdiction in cases involving the politically important freehold tenures. The ecclesiastical courts had jurisdiction in cases involving the distribution and use of decedents' chattels.

16. The common law of descent did not apply to the lands of serfs, nor could a serf make a testament since the lord of his manor could seize his chattels.

no place in the rough and ready administration of the common law, while the decisions of franchise and feudal judges often reflected local demands incompatible with the interests of the English people as a whole.[17]

Beginning in the Seventeenth Century, the patchwork of decisions these courts put together was rewoven into a well-fabricated statutory system by the English Parliament.[18] American states received the benefit of much of this legislation, but also inherited older court-made rules and concepts which must be appraised carefully in order to determine their suitability under modern conditions.

---

(1) ESTATES AND TRUSTS IN ENGLAND BEFORE THE PERIOD OF STATUTORY REFORM

A. The Common Law of Descent, the Devise of Land and the Trust

Blackstone condensed the common law of descent into seven canons as follows:[19]

> "I. * * * Inheritances shall lineally descend to the issue of the person who last died actually seised, *in infinitum;* but shall never lineally ascend.
>
> "II. * * * The Male issue shall be admitted before the female. * * * But our law does not extend to a total exclusion of females * * * for, though daughters are excluded by sons, yet they succeed before any collateral relations. * * *
>
> "III. * * * Where there are two or more males in equal degree, the eldest only shall inherit; but the females altogether. * * *
>
> "IV. * * * The lineal descendants, *in infinitum,* of any person deceased shall represent their ancestor; that is, shall stand in the same place as the person himself would have done, had he been living. * * *

17. Agricultural techniques in Medieval England were primitive and the people lived on the verge of famine. Yet the rules of succession as applied to the land of serfs in the manorial courts tended to divide the land into small and unproductive parcels. In 1066 the Manor of Martham had 63 serfs. In 1292 it had 107 serfs. But in 1292 there were 935 tenures in more than 2,000 strips. Each tenant had about 20 strips, no two of which were probably contiguous. Coulton, Medieval Panorama (1947) 71.

18. The Parliament exercised legislative powers in the modern sense in the Fifteenth Century, but did not legislate frequently in the field of estates and trusts at this early time.

19. II Blackstone, Commentaries (1765) 208 et seq.

"V. * * * On failure of lineal descendants, or issue, of the person last seised, the inheritance shall descend to his collateral relations, being of the blood of the first purchaser; subject to the three preceding rules. * * *

"VI. * * * The collateral heir of the person last seised must be his next collateral kinsman of the whole blood. * * *

"VII. * * * In collateral inheritances the male stocks shall be preferred to the female; (that is, kindred derived from the blood of the male ancestors, however remote, shall be admitted before those from the blood of the female, however near,)—unless where the lands have, in fact, descended from a female."

The common law of descent applied only to freehold estates in land. Life estates, although freehold estates, were not inheritable.

Actual seisin was required before a person could be a stock from whom descent could be traced. A person who took land by descent did not have actual seisin until he made an entry upon the property or performed some other act which indicated that he had taken possession. Seisin was required as evidence of title.

The lineal line of each person who became seised of the land by purchase or descent was traced to exhaustion before resort to his collateral kindred. The rule excluding lineal ascendants from inheritance may have been based upon the feudal technicality that a man could not be lord and heir of the same land. This seems as good an explanation as any that have been offered.[20]

Rules preferring the male stock, including the rule of primogeniture, were applied first to military tenures. Preference for the male stock made it likely that a person who held a military tenure would be fit for military service. It also made more difficult the acquisition of land through marriage.[21] Preference for the eldest male made a single individual responsible to the overlord, prevented frequent partition of land, and provided a family leader with the economic power to hold the family together.[22]

If the eldest male child died without issue, the land passed to the male child next in age. If all male children of the intestate died with-

20. II Pollock and Maitland, History of English Law (2d Ed. 1899) 289 et seq. Glanvil and Bracton said that an inheritance, like an object could fall but not rise.

21. The *mariage de convenance*, which was the normal arrangement in all medieval social classes, was one way by which a tenant *in capite* could build his army. A *mesne* tenant who held land in military tenure owed his overlord personal military service and a certain number of soldiers with equipment. The more *mesne* tenants a tenant *in capite* could acquire, the more feudal levies he would have at his disposal. The policy of the common law courts was to inhibit shifts of land control through marriage.

22. The feudal system was based upon concepts of inter-personal loyalty (between lord and man) that weakened but did not replace the bonds of tribal and family affection that had been the strength of the English community before the Norman Conquest. The medieval Englishman had confused identifications and loyalties, and it was essential that the influence of the central government be thrown behind family and local police organizations in order to maintain a reasonably stable social structure.

out issue, female children inherited in equal shares. The husband of the eldest female child gave homage to the overlord.

The issue of deceased children of the intestate took as representatives. This rule was applied even though it might conflict in particular cases with the rules of preference for the male stock. The rule of primogeniture, however, was applied among the class of representatives. For example, if the eldest son of an intestate predeceased his father but left a male child, the male child took the land so that other children of the intestate (brothers and sisters of the eldest son) were excluded. But if the eldest son left female children and no male children, the female children took in equal shares so that other children of the intestate (brothers and sisters of the eldest son) were excluded. If the intestate was survived by no male children, no issue of male children, and no female children, but was survived by issue of female children, the issue took the shares which their mothers would have taken had they survived the intestate. The eldest son of a deceased daughter of the intestate took the share which his mother would have taken had she lived. Female children divided the mother's share. Representation continued *in infinitum.*

The system of representation is called succession *per stirpes* or "by stocks." In succession *per capita* or "by head" all claimants who are entitled to share in an intestate estate take equally irrespective of the share to which an ancestor through whom they claim would have been entitled.

No collaterals of an intestate inherited if lineal descendants survived him. No collateral of the half-blood inherited in any event. When collaterals did inherit, the land remained within the family into which it had been brought by feoffment.[23] A collateral had to be of the blood of the first purchaser (or feoffee) of the land. Within the collaterals of the blood of the first purchaser, the land remained in the collateral line closest to the intestate. The collaterals had to be heirs of the immediate ascendant last seised of the land. The rules of preference for the male stock and the rule of representation applied among collaterals. The application of the rules concerning inheritance among collaterals is illustrated by the following diagram and examples:

23. A large number of tenants *in capite* were created by feoffments from William the Conqueror after the Norman Conquest. The royal policy thereafter was to prevent any single tenant *in capite* from acquiring large landholdings in any part of England except when required for the defense of the Kingdom. There was a great deal of inter-marriage in the high feudal classes, so that within two centuries after the Conquest many of the more important feudal families were related by blood. The common law courts thus attempted to restrict the shifts in land control that could occur by inheritance among tenants *in capite.* These shifts in control tended to be more pronounced than at the present day since the death rate in England was enormous. It is estimated that the population of Englad increased only 0.147 per cent per annum from the Norman Conquest to the reign of Henry VIII, a period of about 450 years. From 1536 to the beginning of the Nineteenth Century, the population of England more than doubled itself. Coulton, Medieval Panorama (1947) 89.

(U)m

(V)m ——— (T)m

(A)m

(C)m ——— Bm

(R)f ——— (W)f ——— (D)m ——— (E)m ——— (F)f

Sm

(G)m (I)m

Hm Jm ——— Mf

(X)

LEGEND
( )—deceased
m—male
f—female

Assume that X, the propositus, or person from whom descent is to be traced, died seised of Blackacre. Assume that X inherited Blackacre from D and that X has no lineal descendants.

Since there are no lineal descendants of X, the land will pass to collaterals. There are collaterals on the paternal and maternal sides. Assume that A took the land by feoffment from the king. A is the first purchaser of the property. The paternal collaterals inherit and the maternal collaterals are excluded.

To decide which of the paternal collaterals take, it is necessary to trace back to the ascendant of X who was last seised of the land and who also left lineal descendants living at the death of X. D is the immediate ascendant of X but has no lineal descendants living. C has a great grandson, H, who traces through a male, E. C also has a great grandson, J, and a great granddaughter, M, who trace through a female F. By the rule preferring male stock and by the rule of succession per stirpes, H takes the land. If there had been no living lineal descendants of C through E, then J would take the property because the rule of primogeniture would exclude M. M would take the property only if J died without lineal descendants who survived X. If there had been no lineal descendants of C who survived X, then B would take the land. The land would escheat to the overlord if no paternal collateral survived.

If U, instead of A, had been the first purchaser, the land would pass into the maternal collateral line and the paternal collaterals would be excluded. S would inherit.

If X, the propositus, had been the first purchaser of "Blackacre", the land would pass first into the paternal collateral line because of the rule preferring male stock. If there were no paternal collaterals, the land would pass to maternal collaterals.

The scheme of computation used to determine the paternal or maternal collaterals entitled to inherit is known as the *parentelic* method.[24]

A posthumous child could inherit at common law. Illegitimates, aliens and felons could not inherit nor could descent be traced through them.[25]

The common law of descent was a compromise between the desires of common law judges to prevent tenants *in capite* from acquiring excessive military power and the natural desires of feudal tenants to have their lands pass to blood relatives. But shifts in land control among tenants *in capite* could not be minimized if each tenant could dispose of his land as he saw fit. Restraints upon the alienation of land were therefore developed by the courts.[26]

For about a century after the Norman Conquest, extensive use was made by land holders of a rudimentary form of will known as the "post obit gift". The land holder made a gift of his freehold estate to a distributor.[27] It was stipulated that the gift was to take effect at the land holder's death and that the land should then be distributed according to the instructions which the land holder had given. The land holder reserved the equivalent of a modern life estate. The distributor's duties were sometimes enforced by the ecclesiastical courts or by the temporal authorities.[28]

24. Ecclesiastical courts applied a different scheme of computation to determine the next of kin among collaterals who were entitled to inherit personal property. This scheme was known as the "civil law" method. The next of kin were computed by degrees. Each generation between propositus and claimant, counting through their common ancestor, was one degree. The claimant or claimants in nearest relationship to the propositus were entitled to the property. Assuming that X in the diagram is the propositus, H, who took the property under the parentelic scheme, is five degrees removed, counting through C, their common ancestor. But B is four degrees removed from X, counting through A, their common ancestor. S is also four degrees removed from X, counting through T, their common ancestor. B and S would share equally in the personal property. There was a third system of computation used by the ecclesiastical courts to determine prohibited degrees of consanguinity in marriage. This was called the "canon law" method. The number of degrees was counted down from the common ancestor to each collateral. The larger number of degrees was taken as the degree of relationship. If X had survived and desired to marry M, an ecclesiastical court would hold that X was related to M in the third degree.

25. The position was based upon the theory that these parties were lacking in inheritable blood. The common law courts conferred limited rights of inheritance upon illegitimates whose parents later married. The discrimination against aliens appeared after the loss of Normandy in the Thirteenth Century. The fiefs of many Norman nobles were sequestered at that time, and it became the established rule that the king could seize the land of an alien through an "Inquest of Office Found" and that the alien could not recover it. The land of a convicted or outlawed felon escheated to his overlord.

26. A number of restraints upon inter vivos alienation of freehold estates were evolved in the Twelfth Century, but these were disappearing in the Thirteenth Century due to the importation of Roman concepts concerning incidents of land ownership.

27. The distributor was also called a "salman" or "treuhand".

28. The ecclesiastical courts intervened when the *post obit* gift was made on the death bed and a gift was made to the church. Under these circumstances the device was usually called the *verba novissima.* The device was called the *cwide* when temporal authorities enforced it. The temporal authorities

In the Thirteenth Century the common law courts held that a *post obit* gift of a freehold estate was ineffective. The *post obit* gift was regarded as a conveyance which operated to transfer title to the conveyee at the death of the conveyor. Since there was no delivery of possession of the land during the lifetime of the conveyor, the transaction violated the common law rule that required livery of seisin to transfer a freehold estate. A feoffment with livery of seisin to the distributee passed title immediately and no estate was reserved in the feoffor. From the Thirteenth Century until the enactment of the Statute of Wills, 1540,[29] there could be no effective will of a legal freehold estate unless by local custom. Non-freehold estates could be willed as chattels and there could be wills of non-legal freeholds.

The distributor, who had been the essential cog in the *post obit* gift, could be used to confer the benefits of land upon a person who did not have a legal title. A feoffment with livery of seisin could be made to a distributor and the distributor directed to hold the freehold estate to the *use* of the feoffor. The feoffor was called the feoffor *to use.* The distributor was called the feoffee *to use.* The person who enjoyed the *use* was called the *cestui que use.* The feoffor to *use* and the *cestui que use* might be the same person or different persons. If the feoffor reserved the *use* for his own benefit, he could make a will of the *use* despite the common law invalidity of wills of legal freeholds. The *use* of a freehold estate was not regarded as a legal estate that fell within the common law prohibition.

The *cestui que use* of a freehold estate had no action at common law to enforce his claim against the feoffee, although the ecclesiastical courts sometimes enforced covenants by feoffees to hold to the *use* of another.[30] In the Fifteenth Century the Chancellor began to enforce the duties of the feoffee *to use.* Since the value of the *use* depended upon the ability of the *cestui que use* to enforce his claim, the transfer of freeholds to the *use* of the feoffor or a third party became common when the Chancellor enforced the feoffee's duties as a routine matter.[31]

There were applications of the *use* other than for making a "will in equity". Feoffments *to use* were made to avoid the mortmain statutes, incidents of feudal tenures and claims of creditors. The feoffee could be required to manage the land, in which case the *use* was described as "active". If the feoffee served only as a repository of le-

would enforce the *cwide* even though directions as to the disposition of the property were not made on the death bed.

29. 32 Hen. VIII, c. 1 (1540).

30. The common law writs of debt, detinue and account could be used against one who held personal property to the *use* of another. *Uses* which could be enforced in common law actions were called "common law trusts".

31. The *passive use,* a *use* in which the feoffee served only as a repository of legal title, became popular as a means for evading the mortmain statutes. Maitland, "The Origin of Uses", 8 Harv. L.Rev. 127, 130 (1894). The *active use,* a *use* in which the feoffee had active duties of management of the property, may have been employed during the Crusades by landowners who were leaving the country, although there is no evidence that the *active use* was created frequently until the late Fifteenth Century.

gal title, the *use* was described as "passive". Personal property, as well as land, could be transferred upon active or passive *uses*.

The Statute of Uses, 1536,[32] was intended to eliminate the *use* of land as a means for evading the common law and statutory duties that rested upon a holder of legal title. The statute transferred legal title from the feoffee *to use* to the *cestui que use*. If A made a feoffment of "Blackacre" to B to the use of A, the legal title returned to A. If A made a feoffment of "Blackacre" to B to the *use* of C, the legal title passed to C.

The statute did not apply to active *uses* of land or to *uses* of personal property. It was held in Tyrrel's Case [33] that the statute did not apply to a *use* upon a *use*. If A made a feoffment of "Blackacre" to B to the *use* of C to the *use* of D, the statute transferred legal title from B to C, but did not operate a second time to transfer legal title from C to D. C held to the *use* of D even though the *use* was passive.

Uses of personal property, active *uses* of land and passive *uses* upon *uses* were enforced by the Chancellor after the enactment of the statute. The transactions were then called "trusts" and are the origins of the "express trust" which is now enforced in the United States.

Abolition of the "will in equity" was not a principal aim of the Statute of Uses, but the "will in equity" became obsolete after the statute was enacted.[34] In 1540, however, Parliament enacted the Statute of Wills.[35] This statute permitted wills of all lands held in fee simple in socage tenure and two-thirds of lands held in fee simple in military tenure. The will had to be in writing. No other formality was required. The statute did not apply to wills which could be made by local custom. A supplementary statute prohibited wills of land for the benefit of corporations and withdrew power to make wills of land from married women, infants and mental incompetents.[36] Military tenures were changed to socage tenures in 1660.[37] Thereafter, substantially all freehold estates in land were devisable.[38]

---

32. 27 Hen. VIII, c. 10 (1536). For the statutes dealing with *uses* that preceded and followed this statute, see Plucknett, A Concise History of the Common Law (5th Ed., 1956) 579 et seq. The Statute of Uses was the keystone of a thorough system of fiscal reform incident to the centralization of power under the early Tudors. Elimination of the passive *use*, which was an obstacle to the collection of feudal revenues, permitted the Tudors to rely upon funds from this source rather than upon funds appropriated by Parliament. The statute also aided Henry VIII in reaching and confiscating monastic property.

33. Dyer 155 (1557).

34. Tyrrel's Case was decided almost 20 years after the enactment of the Statute of Uses, and although a "will in equity" could have been made after the decision in this case by reserving a *use* upon a *use* in the feoffor, the Statute of Wills then permitted devises of freehold estates.

35. 32 Hen. VIII, c. 1 (1540).

36. The Bill Concerning the Explanation of Wills, 34 & 35 Hen. VIII, c. 5 (1542–43).

37. 12 Chas. II, c. 14 (1660).

38. The Statute of Wills used the words "will" and "devise" to mean a testamentary disposition of land. When the

B. The Testament and Distribution of Intestate Chattels

Before the Norman Conquest, Church officials had sometimes enforced the duties of the distributor of a *post obit* gift.[39] An intestate's chattels were administered by a Church officer called the "Ordinary". In this work ecclesiastical courts developed administrative machinery which common law courts did not possess. The common law courts were in no position to offer serious opposition when, after devises of land were prohibited in the Thirteenth Century, ecclesiastical courts claimed exclusive jurisdiction over testamentary causes and distribution of intestate chattels. This jurisdiction was firmly in ecclesiastical hands by the end of the Fourteenth Century and remained there without substantial impairment for over four hundred years.

Testaments of chattels were developed by the ecclesiastical courts from the *post obit* gift. Legal doctrines related to testaments were influenced by doctrines of the Roman law which had been tempered by the religious views of the Church.[40] A testament was regarded as revocable even though the testator expressly stated that it was not.[41] A testator was subjected to spiritual censure if he took an oath not to revoke his testament but then revoked it. Roman methods of revocation were recognized. Testaments could be revoked by a subsequent instrument, by cancellation, or by a change in the domestic circumstances of the testator. A testament passed no interest in chattels until the death of the testator but could pass chattels acquired by the testator after the testament was executed.[42]

The only formality required for the execution of a testament was naming an executor. This requirement was later abandoned. Most testaments were made orally, and an oral testament could be proved by the testimony of two witnesses.

No person lacked testamentary capacity unless disabled by some special rule of law, by mental incompetence or by infancy. A male could make an effective testament when fourteen and a female could make an effective testament when twelve. A married woman could not make an effective testament because her husband acquired ownership of her chattels. A serf could not make an effective testament because the lord of his manor could seize his chattels. Persons outlawed or convicted as felons could not make testaments.

A testator's title to personal property vested immediately upon his death in the executor of his testament. An executor could not claim

word "devise" is used henceforth in this section, it is used to refer to a "will of land". See this Chapter, Section 2, fn. 10.

39. See fn. 28, supra.

40. The Canon law was influenced by Roman law as taught at Bologna in the Twelfth Century, but ecclesiastical courts in England acquired more jurisdiction than did ecclesiastical courts elsewhere and the ecclesiastical testament, although revealing Roman overtones, was substantially English.

41. This position was based upon the Roman view that a testator could not renounce a power conferred upon him by higher authority.

42. An essential feature of the modern will is its character as a "revocable" and "ambulatory" transaction.

title to the property against third parties in the common law courts unless the Ordinary certified that the testament was valid. This certification was given by the Ordinary in a probate proceeding. There were two types of probate proceedings.

In the "common" or "vulgar" form of probate the executor produced a written testament or established a verbal expression of the testator's wishes and swore that he believed the written or verbal expression to be the last testament of the testator. The testament was probated if the Ordinary accepted the executor's oath. If the Ordinary did not accept the oath, the executor was required to produce affidavits of due execution. The testament was denied probate if these affidavits were not obtained. No notice of the proceeding was given to interested parties, but the proceeding could be reopened at any time within ten years after the testator's death.

If an interested party filed a *caveat* or warning that an invalid testament was to be offered for probate, the Ordinary required a probate in "solemn" form. Probate in solemn form was required even if the *caveat* was filed after the testament had been probated in common form. Notice was given to all interested parties and a full hearing was held by the Ordinary. Judgment was given in the form of an interlocutory decree from which an appeal lay to a higher ecclesiastical court. The validity of the testament was established conclusively unless an appeal was taken and the Ordinary was reversed.

Devises of land permitted by the Statute of Wills, 1540, were not probated. The validity of the devise was determined in a common law action of ejectment against the devisee. If a will contained clauses disposing of real and personal property, probate was not binding upon a common law court as to the validity of the disposition of land.

Ecclesiastical courts developed no clearly defined system for distributing intestate chattels until the Sixteenth Century. Intestacy was rare. The testament was made as a part of the last rites of the Church, and a man died without the last rites of the Church only in exceptional circumstances.

The Statute of Distribution, 1670,[43] purported to define the practices used immediately prior to its enactment by the ecclesiastical courts in distributing intestate chattels. Debts of the intestate were paid first. The residue was then distributed among his spouse and children or next of kin. If a spouse and children survived, the spouse took one-third and the children took two-thirds. If children survived, but no spouse survived, the children took all. If the spouse survived, but no children or issue of deceased children survived, the spouse took one-half and the next of kin took one-half. If no spouse, children or issue of deceased children survived the intestate, the next of kin took all.

Children took in equal shares. Males were not preferred over females. The issue of deceased children took *per stirpes*. Advance-

43. 22 & 23 Chas. II, c. 10 (1670).

ments made to a child were deducted from his share to create equality of distribution among children.

When the next of kin of the intestate inherited, the civil law method of computation was used to determine the next of kin entitled.[44] No representation was permitted among collaterals after brothers and sisters of the intestate. No distinction was made between collaterals of the whole and half-blood.

C. Personal Representatives

The distributor of the *post obit* gift became the executor of the ecclesiastical testament. Ecclesiastical courts identified the executor with the *haeres* of Roman law. The *haeres* was a person who assumed the legal personality of the testator and therefore all of his rights and obligations.[45] Title to the testator's chattels vested absolutely in the executor.[46] An executor could sue in the ecclesiastical courts for debts due the testator and could be sued for debts which the testament expressly required to be paid.

Common law courts, on the other hand, identified the heir to land with the *haeres* of Roman law. An heir could sue or be sued in the common law courts as representative of the intestate. Executors could neither sue nor be sued at common law. The common law courts later abandoned this position for several reasons. Common law judges were anxious to restrict the availability of freehold estates to creditors. Heirs properly objected to liability at common law for all of the debts of an intestate in cases in which they did not also take all of the chattels of the decedent. Executors were therefore permitted to sue in the common law courts for debts due a decedent and could be sued for debts which the decedent owed. Heirs could be sued for specialty debts only.

The Ordinary who distributed the chattels of intestates did not have the representative capacity of the executor. By the Statute of Westminster II,[47] the Ordinary was made liable at common law for a debt owed by the intestate but was given no right of action to recover from the intestate's debtors. In 1387 the power of the Ordinary to administer intestate chattels was divested by statute.[48] The statute directed that an administrator be appointed who could sue and be sued in the common law courts. The administrator was appointed by the Ordinary and, like the executor, was accountable to him. The Ordinary could revoke the appointment of an administrator at his pleasure, but could remove an executor only when the executor was guilty of negligence or misconduct in handling the estate.

44. See fn. 24, supra.

45. This doctrine is sometimes described as "universality of succession".

46. The executor was once entitled to any undistributed residue of the estate. This rule was changed by the Executors' Act, 11 Geo. IV & 1 Wm. IV, c. 40 (1830).

47. 13 Edw. I, St. 1, c. 19 (1285).

48. 31 Edw. III, c. 11 (1387).

Ecclesiastical courts dealt with the problem of administration of estates with primary emphasis upon the claims of legatees and distributees and developed safeguards to protect the interests of these claimants. Personal representatives were required to inventory the estate when administration began, to give bond in particular cases, and to render an account when administration was completed. Rules were developed concerning the authority of the personal representative to purchase from the estate, his acceptance and release of office, and his liability for misappropriation of estate assets. But it became increasingly difficult for ecclesiastical courts to supervise the administration of estates in an adequate way.

Common law courts, having allowed personal representatives to sue and be sued, expanded this jurisdictional bridgehead by allowing actions of account and assumpsit to be used by legatees to recover legacies and bequests from personal representatives. Not content with this, the common law courts also issued writs of prohibition to prevent ecclesiastical courts from inquiring into the truth of an inventory, examining an account, or entertaining an action on a bond to secure the production of an account.[49]

The common law courts were not prepared to supervise the administration of estates, although their attacks brought supervision of administration by ecclesiastical courts to a virtual halt. The procedural machinery of the common law courts had been attuned to the litigation of disputes between the personal representative and debtors or creditors of the decedent. Important doctrines had been developed in this narrow area, but common law courts were unable to supervise the administration of an estate with a full appreciation of the claims of all of the parties involved.

After a period in which the personal representative received little or no official supervision the Chancellor began to use his *in personam* action to enforce the personal representative's duties.[50] By the middle of the Seventeenth Century, the Chancellor had not only devised adequate procedures to supervise the administration of estates but had also held his jurisdiction against attacks by the common law courts. Ecclesiastical courts retained, in substance, only jurisdiction to grant probate and letters of administration.[51]

The Chancellor was able to systematize the rules developed by the ecclesiastical and common law courts, delineate the duties of personal

49. These attacks were part of a general offensive by the common law courts to obtain jurisdiction from the ecclesiastical courts and also from the courts of Chancery, Admiralty, Star Chamber and High Commission. The ecclesiastical courts were far in advance of the common law courts in the maturity and flexibility of most of their procedures. Many of the later common law procedures were ecclesiastical in origin.

50. Perkins said in his "Profitable Booke" (1530) that it was better to give away one's property than to leave it to the caprice of a personal representative. The Statutes of 21 Hen. VIII, c. 5 (1529) and 43 Eliz. c. 8 (1601) dealt with the conduct of personal representatives but were not enforced. The *in personam* action of the Chancellor had been perfected in enforcing the duties of the feoffee *to use.*

51. The ecclesiastical courts continued to examine inventories and accounts until their jurisdiction in matters testamentary was divested, but the main control over the administration of estates was exercised by the Chancellor.

representatives with greater precision, and harmonize the law of administration with changing economic and political conditions in England. The doctrines of marshalling, equitable conversion, satisfaction and election were added to the law of administration by the Chancellor. The concept of the personal representative as a fiduciary was developed in the Chancery Court.

(2) ESTATES AND TRUSTS IN THE PERIOD OF STATUTORY REFORM

Reforms in the English law of decedents' estates were commenced by the Parliament in the late Seventeenth Century.[52] Substantive and procedural distinctions between real and personal property in testate and intestate succession have now been virtually eliminated. Changes by statute in the English law of trusts have been less pervasive.

The early reforms were due in part to disclosures of fraud in the execution and revocation of wills and to the breakdown of judicial procedures for supervising the administration of estates.[53] The reforms of the Nineteenth and Twentieth Centuries were due to widespread discontent with the entire English law of succession to the property of decedents. This discontent was stimulated by criticism of the English law of decedents' estates by Adam Smith, Jeremy Bentham and their followers.

The Statute of Frauds, 1677,[54] brought to an end the special treatment which had been given devises made by local custom. Section V of the statute required that a devise be in writing, signed by the testator or his proxy, and attested by three or four credible witnesses. Section VI provided that a devise could be revoked by specified physical acts to the instrument or by a subsequent instrument executed as a devise was required to be executed. The statute permitted oral testaments of personal property but required in Section XIX many formalities which had to be accomplished before such a testament could be probated.[55] A testament which had been executed in writing could be revoked orally only if the revocation was reduced to writing and read to and acknowledged by the testator.[56]

52. The Statute of Frauds, 1677, is usually considered the first major statute of the reform period.

53. Disclosures of fraud in the case of Cole v. Mordaunt (1675) [stated in note to Mathews v. Warner, 4 Ves.Jr. 186, 31 Eng.Rep. 96 (1798)] are said to have precipitated the enactment of the Statute of Frauds.

54. 29 Chas. II, c. 3 (1677).

55. No formalities were required for a written testament of personal property.

56. Ecclesiastical methods of revocation by operation of law were continued under the statute although they were not mentioned in it.

The Wills Act, 1837,[57] eliminated substantive distinctions between devises and testaments. Except for testaments of soldiers and sailors, all wills of real or personal property were required to be in writing and to be signed by the testator or his proxy. The signature of the testator or proxy had to be made or acknowledged in the presence of two or more competent witnesses present at the same time.[58] The witnesses were required to attest and subscribe the will in the presence of the testator. Identical formalities for revocation were prescribed for wills of real or personal property, and it was provided that marriage of a man or woman revoked a previously executed will. This statute with minor amendments is now in force in England.[59]

Progress in modernizing the law of intestate succession was slow.[60] In 1925, however, the Administration of Estates Act,[61] which consolidated a number of earlier statutory provisions affecting the administration of decedents' estates, also introduced a uniform table of descent and distribution.[62] The common law rules of primogeniture and preference for the male stock and the common law marital estates of curtesy and dower were abolished. As amended by the Intestates' Estates Act, 1952[63] and the Family Provision Act, 1966,[64] the Administration of Estates Act favors the surviving spouse. The surviving spouse takes all of the "personal" chattels of the intestate.[65] In addition, if issue of the intestate survives, the spouse takes a statutory legacy of £8,750 as a charge upon the estate. The charge

57. 7 Wm. IV & 1 Vict., c. 26 (1837).

58. The statute of 25 Geo. II, c. 6 (1752) provided that the interest of a witness to a will should be avoided in order to render him a competent attester at common law.

59. The British Law Reform Committee has recommended a number of changes in the Wills Act, 1837. These included dropping the "signed at the end" requirement; permitting an attesting witness to acknowledge his signature; and modifying in certain cases the strict rule that marriage revokes a will. Cmd. 7902 (1980). As of the time of writing, the Parliament had acted on none of these proposals.

60. The Inheritance Act, 3 & 4 Wm. IV, c. 106 (1833) permitted lineal ascendants to inherit land and abolished the common law rule that an ancestor must have been seised of land before he could be a stock through whom descent could be traced. The Land Transfer Act, 60 & 61 Vict., c. 65 (1897) vested legal title to a decedent's land in his personal representative.

61. 15 Geo. V, c. 23 (1925). In addition to the amendments noted in the text and cited in fns. 63 and 64, infra, the Administration of Estates Act, 1971, 18 & 19 Eliz. II, c. 31, eliminated in most cases the requirement of an administrator's bond and set forth duties in administration once stated in detail in the bonds formerly required. British personal representatives had also enjoyed rights of retainer and preference. These rights were abolished. The right of retainer enabled the personal representative to retain a debt due him from the deceased in priority to other creditors in the same class. The right of preference enabled the personal representative to prefer one creditor over others in the same class. The statute also made it unnecessary to reseal in England grants of representation obtained in the estates of persons domiciled in Scotland or Northern Ireland.

62. A uniform table of descent and distribution was contained in the Law of Property Act, 12 & 13 Geo. V, c. 16 (1922) but the operation of this statute was postponed.

63. 15 & 16 Geo. VI & 1 Eliz. II, c. 64 (1952).

64. 14 & 15 Eliz. II, c. 35 (1966).

65. "Personal" chattels are defined to include furniture, household effects and vehicles but to exclude money, securities and business chattels. For the inheritance system of Scotland, see Succession (Scotland) Act, 1964, 12 & 13 Eliz. II, c. 41.

is increased to £30,000 if no issue survives. These amounts can be fixed from time to time by the order of the Lord Chancellor. The spouse takes the entire estate if the intestate is survived by no issue, parent, brother or sister of the whole blood, or issue of a brother or sister of the whole blood. If issue of the intestate survives, and any residue of the estate remains after the personal chattels and statutory legacy of the spouse are deducted, the spouse takes one-half of the residue in trust for life. The issue takes the remaining one-half in trust and a remainder interest subject to the life estate of the spouse. The spouse may demand that the life interest be redeemed by a capital payment. The statutory trusts for issue of the intestate are contingent upon the issue concerned reaching the age of twenty-one or marrying. The interest does not vest until that time.[66] Distribution among issue is *per stirpes*. If no issue survives, but a parent, brother or sister of the whole blood, or issue of a brother or sister of the whole blood survives the intestate, the spouse takes one-half of the residue absolutely. The other one-half passes absolutely to the parent or, if there is no parent, to the brothers and sisters of the whole blood or their issue.

If the spouse of the intestate does not survive him, the issue of the intestate takes all in statutory trust. If the spouse and issue of the intestate do not survive, the estate is distributed in trust in the following order: parents; brothers and sisters of the whole blood; brothers and sisters of the half blood; grandparents; aunts and uncles of the whole blood; aunts and uncles of the half blood. Inheritance among collaterals is traced no further than children of uncles and aunts. Second cousins of the intestate do not inherit. The property of the intestate escheats to the crown if no one inherits.

The Inheritance (Family Provision) Act, 1938 [67] authorized the courts to provide an allowance for the family of a testator who did not make an adequate provision for them in his will. The Intestate Estates Act, 1952,[68] extended the Inheritance (Family Provision) Act, 1938, to intestate estates. The Inheritance (Provision for Family and Dependants) Act, 1975,[69] replaces the foregoing acts and drastically extends the power of the court to make financial provision for the family and dependants of a deceased person, out of the decedent's estate. In the case of the spouse, provision is not limited to maintenance but can recognize contributions to the marriage; maintenance can be provided for a child regardless of age, for a former spouse who has not remarried, and for any person who was in fact being supported by the decedent at time of his death. Gifts causa mortis, the decedent's share in joint tenancy property, and transfers made by

66. By the English rule, as expressed in Saunders v. Vautier, 4 Beav. 115, 49 Eng.Rep. 282 (1841), the beneficiary of a trust, having an absolute indefeasible interest in it may compel payment to him of the trust corpus when he is competent to give a valid discharge. See Chapter X, Section 3, infra. The *Saunders* rule appears to apply to the statutory trusts required by the Administration of Estates Act since no provision for termination is set forth.

67. 1 & 2 Geo. VI, c. 45 (1938).

68. 15 & 16 Geo. VI & 1 Eliz. II, c. 64 (1952).

69. 1975, c. 63.

decedent during lifetime to defeat the provisions of the statute can be reached.[70]

Under the Family Law Reform Act, 1969,[71] an illegitimate child or issue claiming through an illegitimate child, takes both land and personalty from the mother and father by intestate succession. Each of the parents also may inherit from the illegitimate child but it is not clear whether persons may claim inheritance through the parents from the illegitimate child. To the extent that illegitimacy may still be relevant to some degree in intestate succession matters, the Legitimacy Act[72] provides that children are legitimated by marriage of their parents after their birth.

The Adoption Act, 1958,[73] permits an adopted child to inherit from and through its adopting parents,[74] allowing property to pass as if the adopted child was the natural child of the adopter born in lawful wedlock.

The Court of Probate Act[75] removed jurisdiction to probate testaments and grant letters of administration from the ecclesiastical courts and vested this jurisdiction and jurisdiction to probate wills of land in a statutory Court of Probate. The Supreme Court of Judicature Act[76] merged the statutory Court of Probate into the Probate, Divorce and Admiralty Division of the High Court of Justice, the Chancery Division of this Court retaining jurisdiction over the administration of estates and the Queen's Bench Division hearing various types of actions by and against personal representatives. The Administration of Justice Act, 1970[77] renamed the Probate, Divorce and Admiralty Division the "Family Division" and continued in it jurisdiction over non-contentious or common form probates. Contentious probate matters were transferred to the Chancery Division with admiralty jurisdiction placed in the Queen's Bench Division. The Su-

70. Note, "Family Maintenance: An Inheritance Scheme for the Living," 8 Rutgers-Camden L.J. 673, at 680–686 (1977).

71. 17 & 18 Eliz. II, c. 46 (1969).

72. 16 & 17 Geo. V, c. 60 (1926). The Legitimacy Act, 1959, 7 & 8 Eliz. II, c. 73 legitimates children born in adultery if the parents subsequently marry and children of void marriages when either parent or both believed the marriage valid.

73. 7 & 8 Eliz. II, c. 5 (1958).

74. Disabilities of other classes lacking in rights of inheritance or testamentary power were removed at an earlier date. The Married Women's Property Acts, 45 & 46 Vict., c. 75 (1882) and 56 & 57 Vict., c. 63 (1893) permitted a married woman to dispose of land as if she were sole. The statute of 33 Vict., c. 14 (1870) placed aliens on a par with British subjects as to the ownership and disposition of real and personal property. The statute of 33 & 34 Vict., c. 23 (1870) abolished attainder, corruption of blood, forfeiture and escheat for treason and felony.

75. 20 and 21 Vict., c. 77 (1857). Noncontentious grants of probate are made by the Principal Probate Registry in London or in any of 26 District Probate Registries. For certain small estates application may be made to a customs and excise office. Small Estates (Representation) Act, 1961, 9 & 10 Eliz. II, c. 37. In most estates there are no judicial proceedings after a grant of probate or administration.

76. 36 & 37 Vict., c. 66 (1873).

77. 18 & 19 Eliz. II, c. 31 (1970). County courts have jurisdiction in probate and administration where the value of the estate is below an amount set by statute. See County Courts Act, 1959, 7 & 8 Eliz. II, c. 22, §§ 52, 62, as amended by Administration of Justice Act, 1969, 17 & 18 Eliz. II, c. 58.

preme Court of Judicature (Consolidation) Act established uniform procedures for litigation concerning decedent's estates.[78]

Most of the English law of trusts is still expressed in judicial decisions. The Statute of Frauds, 1677,[79] required that express trusts of land be proved by a writing signed by the party declaring the same,[80] but few comprehensive statutes dealing with the law of trusts were enacted until the Charitable Trusts Act, 1853.[81] This statute was followed by a series of statutes dealing with charitable trusts, culminating in the Charities Act, 1960.[82]

The Settled Land Act, 1925,[83] Law of Property Act, 1925,[84] The Trustee Act, 1925,[85] the Trustee Investment Act, 1961[86] and the Trustee Savings Bank Act, 1969[87] provide a comprehensive code for trust administration. Rigid limitations placed upon the creation of trusts and accumulations of trust income at common law have been greatly alleviated by the Perpetuities and Accumulation Act, 1964.[88]

---

(3) ESTATES AND TRUSTS IN THE UNITED STATES

The English period of statutory reform was well under way when the American colonies achieved their independence. Although English law was winnowed of concepts and practices unsuited to American conditions, state legislatures adopted the substance of English statutes and courts deferred to English precedent in construing the statutes so produced. The statutes of descent and distribution tended to follow the English Statute of Distribution, 1670.[89] Much of

78. 15 Geo. V, c. 45 (1925).

79. 29 Chas. II, c. 3, § VII (1677).

80. Section VIII of the Statute of Frauds excluded from the operation of Section VII trusts arising by operation of law. These include resulting and constructive trusts. These sections are now contained in the Law of Property Act, 15 Geo. V, c. 20, § 53(1) (1925).

81. 16 & 17 Vict., c. 137 (1853).

82. 8 & 9 Eliz. II, c. 58 (1960). This is a general statute relating to the administration and enforcement of charities.

83. 15 & 16 Geo. V, c. 18, as amended.

84. 15 & 16 Geo. V, c. 20, §§ 23–33, as amended.

85. 15 & 16 Geo. V, c. 19, as amended.

86. 9 & 10 Eliz. II, c. 62 (1961). The Judicial Trustee Act, 59 & 60 Vict., c. 35 (1896) and the Public Trustee Act, 6 Edw. VIII, c. 55 (1906) dealt with minor matters of trust administration. The Judicial Trustee Act provided for the appointment of trustees by the court and stipulated that an executor or administrator was a trustee within the meaning of the Act. The Public Trustee Act established the office of public trustee for the administration of small estates and private trusts and set forth the duties and procedures for enforcing the duties of this officer.

87. 17 & 18 Eliz. II, c. 50 (1969).

88. 12 & 13 Eliz. II, c. 55 (1964). A detailed description of English trust and estate administration as currently conducted may be found in Fratcher, "Fiduciary Administration in England", 40 N.Y.U.L.Rev. 12 (1965).

89. 22 & 23 Chas. II, c. 10 (1670). See Comment, "An Analysis of the History and Present Status of American Wills Statutes", 28 Ohio St.L.J. 293 (1967).

the common law of descent was rejected.[90] Wills acts of the states on the Eastern seaboard were patterned upon the Statute of Frauds, 1677,[91] although states which entered the Union in the Nineteenth Century often adopted statutes patterned upon the Wills Act, 1837.[92]

In the colonies, jurisdiction over probate and grants of administration was in courts of general jurisdiction, courts established for the purpose by statute, or in agents of the executive. Ecclesiastical probate procedures were usually followed. After the Revolution, jurisdiction over probate and grants of administration was vested in courts of general jurisdiction or in special statutory courts. These courts also supervised the administration of estates.

The Statute of Uses, 1536,[93] was not re-enacted by most of the state legislatures, although in a majority of states it is considered in force as part of the common law. A majority of states have statutes patterned upon sections VII and VIII of the Statute of Frauds, 1677.[94] A few states have adopted comprehensive trust codes.[95] But for the most part the American law of trusts is to be found in judicial decisions. English cases have had great influence upon the American courts.

American laws of estates and trusts have not progressed to the point reached by English legislation. In intestate succession and wills, for example, a number of states still retain substantive and procedural distinctions between real and personal property that were derived from English law of the Nineteenth Century. There are at least two reasons for this unfavorable comparison.

Reforms were made by state legislatures at an early date and there was no public pressure for change in the laws of estates and trusts comparable to that to which Parliament was subjected. Also, the federal system of government in this country has prevented the uniformity of law which is possible in England. States control to an appreciable extent the transmission of property by will, the devolution of property in intestacy, and grants of probate and letters of administration. In supervising the administration of estates and trusts state courts have almost complete hegemony, although bankruptcy and tax laws provide avenues for Federal intervention.[96]

90. Primogeniture gained a foothold in New York and several of the Southern colonies but was abolished soon after the Revolution. The ancestral property doctrine and the rules preferring male stock to female shared a similar fate in many states. Since many of the colonies had title registration laws before the Revolution, the common law rule that seisin created the stock for descent was never of great importance.

91. 29 Chas. II, c. 3 (1677).

92. 7 Wm. IV & 1 Vict., c. 26 (1837).

93. 27 Hen. VIII, c. 10 (1536).

94. 29 Chas. II, c. 3 (1677).

95. McKinney's N.Y., EPTL (1967); Ga.Code Ann. §§ 108–101 to 108–1005 (1959).

96. There are state and Federal constitutional limitations upon the powers of states in controlling the devolution of property and related matters. As to constitutional limitations upon state disabilities imposed upon illegitimates see Chapter III, Section 2. As to similar constitutional limitations upon state disabilities imposed upon both resident and nonresident aliens, see Chapter III, Section 4(5).

Movements to standardize the American laws of estates and trusts have nevertheless made great headway. The National Conference of Commissioners on Uniform State Laws has adopted a number of proposed uniform laws in the field of wills, trusts, trust and estate administration and related areas. These uniform acts, the dates of their approval by the Commissioners and the number of jurisdictions which have the acts in force are noted below.[97]

By far the most important of the uniform acts in this area is the Uniform Probate Code[98] which was promulgated by the National Conference of Commissioners on Uniform State Laws in 1969. A Model Probate Code had been published in 1946, this being the work of a committee of the Probate Division of the Section of Real Property, Probate and Trust Law of the American Bar Association. The Model Code influenced the revision of probate laws in several states. In 1962, persons within the American Bar Association and the National Conference of Commissioners on Uniform State Laws commenced discussions to update the Model Code. Ensuing studies culminated in promulgation of the Uniform Probate Code (UPC), now in force in eleven jurisdictions and under careful study for possible adoption in at least ten others. Even before the Uniform Probate Code was promulgated officially, drafts of the Code were used in Maryland and Oregon in revisions there in progress. Other states not adopting the Code in its entirety will almost certainly adopt parts of it. The widespread publicity which the Code received, coupled with the generally favorable reaction in those states in which the Code has been tested, is producing a re-examination and modernization of probate laws. Widespread adoption of the Uniform Probate Code will modernize American probate law and will introduce uniformity much needed by a mobile population, the estates of which often contain property in several jurisdictions.

The Uniform Probate Code provides a court of general jurisdiction over all probate and related matters, including trusts in place of the specialized courts with limited jurisdiction now found in many states. By bringing together the best elements of laws and practices in various parts of the United States and in England, and by introducing

97. The numerals following the date of approval indicate the jurisdictions adopting the act, perhaps with amendments, as of 1976: Absence as Evidence of Death and Absentees' Property (1939)(3); Anatomical Gift (1968)(51); Ancillary Administration of Estates (1949) (1); Common Trust Fund (1938)(35); Disclaimer of Property Interests (1973)(0); Disclaimer of Transfer by Will, Intestacy or Appointment (1973)(1); Disclaimer of Transfers Under Nontestamentary Instrument (1973)(0); Disposition of Community Property Rights at Death (1971) (4); Disposition of Unclaimed Property (1954)(12); Disposition of Unclaimed Property (1966)(13); Estate Tax Apportionment (1958)(5); Estate Tax Apportionment (1964)(4); Fiduciaries (1922)(26); Gifts to Minors (1956)(15); Gifts to Minors (1966)(37); Management of Institutional Funds (1972)(13); Interstate Arbitration of Death Taxes (1944)(15); Interstate Compromise of Death Taxes (1944)(17); Principal and Income (1931) (17); Principal and Income (1962)(19); Probate Code (1969)(11); Probate of Foreign Wills (1950)(2); Simplification of Fiduciary Transfers (1958)(37); Simultaneous Death (1940)(50); Supervision of Trustees for Charitable Purposes (1954) (4); Testamentary Additions to Trusts (1960)(44); Trustees' Power (1964)(7).

98. 8 U.L.A. 281; West's Uniform Probate Code (5th Ed.) Official Text with Comments (1977).

concepts borrowed from the law of trusts and the tax laws into the probate field, the Code provides a modern framework for the substantive and procedural law of decedents' estates. The pertinent provisions of the Uniform Code are indicated throughout this casebook as they apply to particular topics under discussion. A more detailed discussion of the provisions of the Code is postponed until the student reads the outline of Administration and Probate in Section 2(2) of Chapter II which follows. When the student understands some of the major problems presented in probate and administrative practices now encountered in various states, he will appreciate fully the benefits which the reforms of the Uniform Probate Code can provide.

The American Law Institute has had great influence upon both the case and statutory law of trusts and trust administration in the United States. The Institute has published a Restatement of Trusts (2d) and a Restatement of Restitution.[99] The Institute also includes materials on future interests in the Restatement of Property[1] which have had great influence upon the courts and legislatures. There is no Restatement of Wills or Intestate Succession, but pertinent extracts from the Restatements of Trusts, Restitution and Property appear throughout this book.

SECTION 4. LAWYERS, DECEDENTS' ESTATES AND TRUSTS—PROBLEMS AND OPPORTUNITIES

Lord Campbell, in his "Lives of the Lord Chancellors", commented upon the many aspersions cast upon the "Temple Corps", a regiment of foot raised by Lord Erskine from lawyers and functionaries of the Inner and Middle Temples during the Napoleonic Wars. Dubbed the "Devil's Own", the regiment boasted greater legal than military talent. Campbell writes: "* * * There were likewise a good many attorneys belonging to us, who brought down many aspersions upon us; among others, that upon the word given 'prepare to charge' they all pulled out pen, ink and paper, and being ordered to 'charge' they wrote down 6s, 8d or 13s, 4d * * *".[2]

Mention any profession, other than the ministry, and the word "fees" flickers in the mind of the layman. The application of the Sherman Anti-Trust Act to bar minimum fee schedules[3] is one more event in a long tug of war between the legal profession and the pub-

99. Restatement, Second, Trusts (3 Vols.); Restatement, Restitution (1937).

1. Restatement, Property [Vol. II (1936); Vol. III (1940); Vol. IV (1944)].

2. 8 Campbell, Lives of the Lord Chancellors (1874) 169, fn. 2.

3. Goldfarb v. Virginia State Bar, 421 U.S. 773, 95 S.Ct. 2004, 44 L.Ed.2d 572 (1975).

lic, a contest illuminated fitfully by such volcanic episodes as the English Peasants' Revolt of 1381 and the Gordon Riots of 1780, in the latter of which even the great Lord Mansfield was roughed up by the vulgar as his coach passed through Parliament Street, his lordship taking his seat upon the woolsack with his robe torn and his wig askew.

Development of a rational relationship between the fee charged and the service rendered, using an index understood and accepted in advance by the lawyer and his client, is one of the major problems of the legal profession today. The Code of Professional Responsibility of the American Bar Association, Ethical Consideration (EC) 2–16 states * * * "[t]he legal profession cannot remain a viable force in fulfilling its role in our society unless its members receive adequate compensation for services rendered, and reasonable fees should be charged in appropriate cases to clients able to pay them. * * *" EC 2–17 and 2–18 deal with determining the "reasonable" fee, EC 2–18 stating that the fees will vary according to many factors, including the time required, the experience, ability and reputation of the lawyer, the nature of the employment, the responsibility involved and the results obtained. Disciplinary Rule (DR) 2–106 prohibits illegal or excessive fees, and states that a fee is excessive when a lawyer of ordinary prudence, after a review of the facts "would be left with a definite and firm conviction" that the fee is in excess of a reasonable fee. The Rule sets forth eight elements which may be included in a determination of reasonableness.[4]

Determining the propriety of a challenged fee certainly will be a difficult task in many situations; but what is even more important is the sense of value received on the part of the many clients who raise no question concerning the fee but whose judgment concerning the fairness of a charge tends to mold the public attitude towards the profession. Thus, in the area of decedents' estates and trusts, a fee may sometimes be based upon the value of the property involved. The services involved may be frequent and difficult to bill individually. It may also be difficult to value a service in the abstract as distinguished from a particular service to a particular client in a specific context. But it is extraordinarily difficult to justify a fee based upon a percentage of the value of property. The American Bar Association has stated principles regarding probate practices and expenses to

4. "* * *

(1) The time and labor required, the novelty and difficulty of the questions involved, and the skill requisite to perform the legal service properly.

(2) The likelihood, if apparent to the client, that the acceptance of the particular employment will preclude other employment by the lawyer.

(3) The fee customarily charged in the locality for similar legal services.

(4) The amount involved and the results obtained.

(5) The time limitations imposed by the client or by the circumstances.

(6) The nature and length of the professional relationship with the client.

(7) The experience, reputation, and ability of the lawyer or lawyers performing the services.

(8) Whether the fee is fixed or contingent.

* * *

[Footnote omitted] * * *."

be used as guidelines for state and local legislatures, courts and bar associations when investigating, evaluating and establishing standards with respect to attorneys' fees and other costs incident to the administration of decedents' estates.[5] The central principle, applied in the Statement to various relationships held by an attorney to a decedent's estate, is that the fee should be measured by the services performed and the responsibility assumed by the attorney. Such studies and statements will be of much assistance in developing greater understanding between lawyers and their clients in fee matters. But no effort to state principles for charges for legal services will go far in ameliorating the severe public relations problem of the bar and enable the bar to "remain a viable force in fulfilling its role in our society", as envisaged by the American Bar Association,[6] *unless the services for which the fee is sought adequately satisfy the requirements of the client.* A client is usually willing to pay for what he gets. For a lawyer dealing with decedents' estates and trusts, a firm grasp of many legal techniques and a pervasive understanding of many legal problems will be necessary to enable him to perform his services adequately. The author of a recent thoughtful article writes:[7]

"* * * In the past, when a lawyer prepared a will for a client, the service may normally have constituted just that and nothing more—no attention to death taxation planning, estate liquidity, income tax planning for the estate and for the family and trusts thereafter, ownership and beneficiary designations for insurance and benefit plans, closely held business problems, lifetime giving, lifetime income tax planning and a host of other legal matters connected with the will. Today, all of these described services should be essential legal services to be performed by the lawyer every time he draws a will or plans an estate, unless they are manifestly inapplicable because of the nature of the client's affairs or unless a special understanding is reached narrowing the area of the lawyer's responsibilities.

"To perform all these services well or indeed even to know whether they should be performed for a particular client, the lawyer must be accomplished in the laws of estate, inheritance, and income taxation, especially of individuals, trusts and estates, as well as the laws of wills, probate and trusts. This is not to say that the services of the lawyer in estate planning are confined to these fields of the law; it is to say that his competence must cover these fields. Other fields the lawyer may encounter in estate planning, requiring him to perform with competence or to obtain competent assistance from another lawyer, include corporate and partnership law, federal income taxation of corporations, partnership and tax-exempt organizations,

5. 62 A.B.A.J. 348 (1976). For an excellent critique of the ABA Statement of Principles and Practices, see Martin, Professional Responsibility and Probate Practices, 1975 Wis.L.Rev. 911.

6. Code of Professional Responsibility, EC 2–16.

7. Eubank, "The Future for Estate Lawyers", 10 Real Prop., Prob. & Tr.J. 223, 224 (1975).

foreign taxation, conflict of laws, litigation and property law. * * * "

For many years, lawyers enjoyed a virtual monopoly of practice in decedents' estates and trusts. They still tend to deal almost exclusively with some of the problems involved. For example, a recent careful and detailed study by the American Bar Association Special Committee to Survey Legal Needs indicates that approximately 85% of the persons with problems concerning wills are consulting lawyers. However 45.5% of those with problems concerning living trusts consulted a "non-lawyer resource".[8] A great part of the administration of estates and trusts is now handled capably by professional corporate fiduciaries. Accountants are dealing with many tax problems. Estate planning is being handled to an appreciable extent by insurance agents and financial counsellors. Clearly, the ancient monopoly of lawyers in decedents' estate and trusts is now much eroded, although litigation, counselling in contentious matters and the drafting of instruments seem securely in the hands of the bar.

The non-lawyer competition in the field of decedents' estates and trusts has been resisted by the bar through efforts to define the practice of law. Canon 3 of the Code of Professional Responsibility states that a lawyer should assist in preventing the unauthorized practice of law. The Code, however, leaves the precise definition of the practice of law to be determined by local courts.[9] Dominating the thinking of the bar has been the importance of securing competent legal service for the public and recognition, shared by non-lawyers concerned with maintenance of a democratic system of government, that the effective functioning of our constitutional system depends upon a properly recompensed, governmentally-independent and responsible legal profession.

Nevertheless, it is becoming apparent that a mere defensive policy of definition of law practice with exclusion of the unlicensed will probably be insufficient to avoid substantial impairment of the work of the profession in any area of practice. This is particularly pertinent in the area of decedents' estates and trusts. The role of the lawyer in decedents' estates and trusts must be redefined and the areas in which legal skills are essential adequately to serve the public should be identified.[10] But it also is especially important that the

8. 3 American Bar Association Consortium on Legal Services and The Public, No. 1, p. 6 (1976).

9. EC 3–5 states: "It is neither necessary nor desirable to attempt the formulation of a single, specific definition of what constitutes the practice of law. Functionally, the practice of law relates to the rendition of services for others that call for the professional judgment of a lawyer. The essence of the professional judgment of a lawyer is his educated ability to relate the general body and philosophy of law to a specific legal problem of a client; and thus, the public interest will be better served if only lawyers are permitted to act in matters involving professional judgment." [footnote omitted]

10. Virginia, for example, has promulgated unauthorized practice rules in estate planning. See Va. UPR 4–101—4–103 reported in 221 Va. 395–97(1980). Other states have left the determination of practice of law in this area to be decided on a case by case basis. See generally, 22 A.L.R.3d 112; 71 A.L.R.3d 1000; Christensen, "The Unauthorized Practice of Law: Do Good Fences Really Make Good Neighbors—or Even Good Sense?", 1980 A.B.F.Res.J. 159; Hyrne, Unautho-

lawyer's services be perfected and expanded.[11] An offensive policy to provide increasingly excellent service to the public at a cost related to the excellence and sufficiency of that service will go far towards eliminating the grievances of ancient standing concerning fees and will deal effectively at the same time with competition by those inadequately trained and less efficient. There are at least three areas of current movement within the profession in this direction.

The reform movement to simplify procedures in decedents' estates and trusts and thus eliminate excessive costs is one example. Canon 8 of the Code of Professional Responsibility states that a lawyer should assist in improving the legal system. Two of the Ethical Considerations stated are as follows:

> **EC 8–1** Changes in human affairs and imperfections in human institutions make necessary constant efforts to maintain and improve our legal system. This system should function in a manner that commands public respect and fosters the use of legal remedies to achieve redress of grievances. By reason of education and experience, lawyers are especially qualified to recognize deficiencies in the legal system and to initiate corrective measures therein. Thus they should participate in proposing and supporting legislation and programs to improve the system, without regard to the general interests or desires of clients or former clients.

> **EC 8–2** Rules of law are deficient if they are not just, understandable, and responsive to the needs of society. If a lawyer believes that the existence or absence of a rule of law, substantive or procedural, causes or contributes to an unjust result, he should endeavor by lawful means to obtain appropriate changes in the law. He should encourage the simplification of laws and the repeal or amendment of laws that are outmoded. Likewise, legal procedures should be improved whenever experience indicates a change is needed.

Although it has been said by some that the bar is inherently conservative, resisting change and thus reform, this characterization is inaccurate. Change (or reform) is not always necessarily to the advantage of the public; and the bar has been deliberate in ascertaining

rized Practice in Estate Planning and Administration: A Wild and Intemperate Dissent", 29 U.Fla.L.Rev. 647 (1977).

11. See Eubank, "The Future for Estate Lawyers", 10 Real Prop., Prob. & Tr.J. 223, 224–226 (1975) where the author suggests the expansion of services to include financial counselling. The author states at 226: "* * * My major concern with financial counselling is that if the lawyer does not engage in it, he will be excluded too much from one of his major, historical roles, namely, counselling the individual client. He can, of course, exercise that function significantly by criticizing the financial counselling report. Is that enough for that role? Aside from counselling by criticism, he may be likened in this situation to an order-taker for documents. With the current development of programmed documents by many lawyers, it may be unrealistic for lawyers to expect substantial fees or high professional standing for simply having an automatic typewriter hammer out a programmed document prescribed by a non-lawyer in a financial counselling report. * * *"

this advantage before the change receives its support. Also, as the American Bar Association points out:[12]

> "* * * Although the organized bar should bear a substantial portion of the responsibility for continually improving the law and its procedures, it must be remembered that lawyers alone are frequently unable to overcome legislative hurdles and selfish opposition, political or otherwise, and that public support is often needed to effect meaningful change. * * *"

As the student may have observed in reading the preceding subsection concerning historical development, more changes have been made in the law of decedents' estates and trusts in the past fifty years than in the preceding eight hundred. Many of these changes have been due not only to public support but also to public demand in response to the enormous economic and social forces unleashed by World War I. But the changes have also been due in part to the presence of leadership within organized bars during this half-century. The American Bar Association was not established until 1878 and was not organized on a federalized basis until 1936. This national organization strengthened local bar organizations, assisting in developing standards for the discipline of lawyers and providing a center for common direction of reform efforts. The state and local bars in the early days of the Republic did not approach in organization, discipline and professional tradition the English bar even of the early Sixteenth Century. The early reshaping of English law to suit American conditions was accomplished by a few outstanding judges, such as Story, Kent, Lumpkin and Shaw and a small number of unorganized lawyers practicing before them. But the well organized bar system in the United States today is suited to reform efforts, with the various uniform laws, including the comprehensive Uniform Probate Code, demonstrating the enormous potential of the bar for the study, planning and execution of reforms. The public expense through these reforms can be reduced, the administration of decedents' estates and trusts can be made more efficient, and the effectiveness of service by lawyers can be enhanced. Routine probate functions by lawyers may be eliminated through reform; but at the same time, new functions in the probate area are in the process of definition.

Another movement which may reduce costs in the field of decedents' estates and trusts and enhance the efficiency of legal services is reorganization of the method of practice. Increasing use is being made of the skills of paraprofessionals to accomplish some of the routine legal tasks, save the lawyer's time and reduce the cost to the client.[13] There is also a pronounced trend towards specialization within the bar which is receiving formal recognition and which may now be brought to public attention through advertising.[14] Recogni-

12. "Statement of Principles Regarding Probate Practices and Expenses," 62 A.B.A.J. 348 (1976).

13. E.g., Mucklestone, "The Legal Assistant in Estate Planning", 10 Real Prop., Prob. & Tr.J. 293 (1975).

14. In Bates v. State Bar of Arizona, 433 U.S. 350, 97 S.Ct. 2691, 53 L.Ed.2d 810 (1977) the United States Supreme Court held that lawyers have a First Amendment right to advertise standardized fees charged for routine legal ser-

tion of a specialty, as in decedents' estates and trusts, will doubtless elicit greater professional discipline among the specialists. There may be some form of professional certification of the specialist and perhaps periodic recertification. Possibly the recertification may be based upon some type of continuing legal education.[15] With these developments, many think the quality of service rendered clients may be enhanced. Whether the cost of service to the client will be more commensurate to the quality and sufficiency of the service is another matter. While it is logical to assume that the experience and skill of the specialist will be considered in fixing a fee for services, there may be increased hidden costs. For example, there is increasing litigation in legal malpractice. Malpractice insurance is now carried by many lawyers, and an increasing cost in malpractice insurance probably would be passed on to clients. The old "privity" rule familiar in legal malpractice cases is being abandoned. Persons injured other than the client have standing to sue the lawyer.[16] Of special importance to lawyers practicing in the area of decedents' estates and trusts is the modern tendency to commence the statute of limitations time period not when the lawyer's negligence occurred but when the injured per-

vices by newspaper. The ABA has interpreted this decision narrowly and has amended its publicity rules accordingly. See DR 2–101, reported in 63 A.B.A.J. 1234 (1977). Approximately 60% of the states have adopted advertising rules similar to that of the ABA. See "The Impact of Advertising and Specialization on Professional Responsibility", 61 Chi. Bar.Rec. 324.325 (1980). Other states have taken a permissive approach, allowing attorney advertising which is not deceptive or misleading. See 4 A.L.R. 4th 306. DR 2–105(A)(2)(3) provides:

> (2) A lawyer who publicly discloses fields of law in which the lawyer or the law firm practices or states that his practice is limited to one or more fields of law shall do so by using designations and definitions authorized and approved by [the agency having jurisdiction of the subject under state law].
>
> (3) A lawyer who is certified as a specialist in a particular field of law or law practice by [the authority having jurisdiction under state law over the subject of specialization by lawyers] may hold himself out as such, but only in accordance with the rules prescribed by that authority.

See as to legal clinics and advertising, Winter, "Clinic Lawyers Oppose Anti-Advertising Ads", 66 A.B.A. 27 (1980); Muris, "Advertising and the Price and Quality of Legal Services: The Case for Legal Clinics", 1979 A.B.F.Res.J. 179; McChesney, "The Effect of Advertising on the Quality of Legal Services", 65 A. B.A.J. 1503 (1979).

15. Approximately 16 states are in the process of implementing specialization programs, 11 with actual certification of specialists. Christensen, "Toward Improved Legal Service Delivery", 1979 A.B.F.Res.J. 277, 280. See Weber, "Why Formal Legal Specialization?", 63 A.B.A. J. 951 (1977).

16. The legal literature on legal malpractice is becoming extensive. One of the early comprehensive articles is Wade, "The Attorney's Liability for Negligence", 12 Vand.L.Rev. 755 (1959). More recent articles of general scope include Gillen, "Legal Malpractice", 12 Washburn L.J. 281 (1973); Haughey, "Lawyers' Malpractice: A Comparative Appraisal", 48 Notre Dame Law. 888 (1973); Rottman and Stern, "The Lawyer Malpractice Problem", 78 Case and Comment 13 (1973); Comment, "Legal Malpractice", 27 Ark.L.Rev. 452 (1973). For malpractice problems in decedents' estates and trusts, see Jackman, "Solicitor's Liability for Negligence in the Drafting and Execution of a Will", 5 Ottawa L.Rev. 242 (1971) (containing good discussion of California cases); Comment, "Considerations of Professional Responsibility in Probate Matters", 51 Neb.L.Rev. 456 (1972); Note, 4 Memphis State U.L.Rev. 188 (1973). On the running of the statute of limitations, see 18 A.L.R.3d 978 (1968). "Attorney's Negligence in Connection with Estate, Will or Succession Matters", 55 A.L.R.3d 977 (1974). On the status of the "privity" doctrine see 45 A.L.R.3d 1181 (1971).

son knew or ought to have known of the negligence.[17] Every instrument a lawyer drafts under such circumstances becomes a continuing basis of potential liability—a problem made particularly acute because of the limited time coverage provided in most malpractice insurance. If the lawyer specializes, will the standard of competence which he must satisfy be greater than if he remains a general practitioner? If he advertises, will he be held to the standard of expertise he represents? If the lawyer uses paraprofessionals to assist him, what standard will be applied to the lawyer in their hiring, training and oversight?[18]

A third movement involves the relations between lawyers and clients, between lawyers and lawyers, and between lawyers and public institutions, matters traditionally described as "legal ethics". These matters are dealt with in detail in the Code of Professional Responsibility and appear to be receiving the most intense attention in the state bars. Such matters as diligence in attention to a client's legal problems, avoidance of conflicts in interest and recognition of the public responsibilities of the lawyer (described by Dean Casner as "Estate Planning Statesmanship" [19]) will be considered in relation to cases and materials examined hereafter. No matters are more critical than strict adherence to standards of legal ethics to instill in the client a sense of fair treatment and to insure public support of the legal profession as an effective institution.

17. See, Joseph, "Commencement of Statute of Limitations for Malpractice of an Attorney", 21 Clev.St.L.Rev. (2) 49 (1972); Solis, "Statute of Limitations in Malpractice Cases; The California Supreme Court Establishes New Guidelines", 7 U.San Francisco L.Rev. 85 (1972). California cases dealing both with "privity" and the statute of limitations are discussed in King, "Legal Malpractice, The Coming Storm", 50 Cal.St. Bar J. 363 (1975).

18. See Wade, "Tort Liability of Paralegals and Lawyers Who Utilize Their Services", 24 Vand.L.Rev. 1133 (1971); Comment, "On the Question of Negligence: The Paraprofessional", 4 U. Toledo L.Rev. 553 (1973).

19. Casner, "Estate Planning Statesmanship", 8 Inst.Estate Planning Ch. 74–12 (1974). See, "The Public, the Practitioner and the Government: A Panel Discussion", 33 Inst. on Federal Taxation (Part 1) 603 (1975) and DeStefano, "The Right of the Government to Know—The Responsibility of the Practitioner to the Client; A Balancing of Rights and Duties", 33 Inst. on Federal Taxation 631 (1975). A good general discussion of ethics in decedents' estates and trusts practice appears in 8 Inst.Estate Planning, Ch. 74–7 (1974).

Chapter II

GENERAL SURVEY OF ADMINISTRATION AND PROBATE

SECTION 1. INTRODUCTION

So the student will appreciate some of the techniques used in planning the estate of a client and then in administering the client's estate when the client dies, the dialogue which follows in Section 2 illustrates planning and administrative procedures and problems. The matters here described will be dealt with in detail in this book. The purpose here is to give the student a simple overview of matters which follow and an awareness of the process involved in estate planning. There are many techniques and approaches which might be used in estate plans for clients, but there are some basic principles in estate planning; and the dialogue between the lawyer and Professor and Mrs. Barton illustrates these. The plan suggested in the dialogue is not the only one that might be formulated for the two estates, but it is one which accomplishes the clients' goals with reasonable tax economy and one which they are willing to accept.

In Section 3 there is a brief discussion of major features of the Uniform Probate Code. The student should consider the extent to which the Uniform Code provisions might affect the plan developed in the dialogue and how it might reduce the complexity and cost of the probate and administrative features discussed.

SECTION 2. THE ESTATE PLAN, PROBATE OF THE WILL AND ADMINISTRATION OF THE ESTATE

(1) PLANNING THE ESTATE

[Myres James Barton, 60, is Alumni Distinguished Professor of Sanskrit in Jefferson University, State of Minor. Barton owns Ramayana Farm in Albercello County, Minor. His principal crop is peanuts. His wife, Desdemona, Chief Librarian in Jefferson City, Minor, has read about the estate planning problems of farmers and suggested to Barton that he consult with Gordon Armistead, a member of the local bar. This conversation ensued:][1]

ATTORNEY: Myres, I'm glad to see you on some matter other than those cows breaking down your fences. Des was right to suggest that you do some estate planning. Many people either do not plan their estates or wait until some of the advantages of estate planning cannot be realized.

BARTON: Maybe I am one of those "waiters" but, after all, I'm going to plan what will be done with my property when I die.

ATTORNEY: You share a common misunderstanding about estate planning with many others. When we plan an estate we are concerned with the most efficient and economical management of your property while you are alive as well as with the disposition of your property at your death in the manner you intend in the most economical fashion. Planning also has to be done after you die, particularly to minimize income taxes upon your estate and upon the persons who take your property. Some of us call this "post mortem estate planning". Post mortem estate planning is facilitated by careful anticipation during your lifetime of problems likely to arise in the administration of your estate after your death.

BARTON: You mean my estate will have to pay income tax! I always thought that when I died I would at least be free of income taxes.

ATTORNEY: Your estate and any trusts you establish are treated as persons for federal and state income taxation. There are federal and state income tax forms for these estate and trust income tax returns.

BARTON: I see that this is going to be a lot more complicated than I thought. What I had in mind was a short will—brief and to the point.

ATTORNEY: I will prepare a will for you. I will also prepare one for Des if she wants one. It may be that wills are the only documents I will have to prepare. But whether these can be simple and short will depend upon the facts of your estate and upon your wishes for the disposition of your property.

BARTON: The facts are simple—except for Ramayana Farm perhaps.

ATTORNEY: To start our planning I want you to fill out this form. I will study the information you supply and determine what other information is needed. Then I will have some proposals for you which we can discuss at our next meeting.

BARTON: Not another form! I have to fill out forms for Jefferson University, the State of Minor, the Federal Government and who

1. The states of Minor and Monroe are common law jurisdictions. If either or both had been a community property jurisdiction, the details of the plan for the Bartons would differ from that suggested by Attorney Armistead in the situation discussed in the text, but the planning process would have been the same.

knows what else. This one looks like an application for a job at the CIA.

ATTORNEY: This will be the most useful form you ever filled out and you must take the time to fill it out carefully. We need accurate information to plan your estate. The plan will be worthless unless the information is accurate. The form will also save me time and you money. Also as you fill out the form you will start doing some thinking of your own about your estate plan. There at the end is a space for you to state your objectives to be attained by the use and disposition of your property. Do the best you can.

It will also be desirable for Des to fill out one of these forms. Information may be duplicated, but we will deal with that in my office. If both of you fill out these forms you will probably discuss your wishes and perhaps reconcile any differences before you see me. I think both husband and wife should participate in developing an estate plan, although some lawyers differ with me concerning the value of joint participation. Joint planning might not be possible if there is domestic disharmony. But you and Des should plan this estate together. A fair and workable plan is likely to be developed. Moreover, Des is likely to survive you. She will then have a right in Minor to elect a statutory share of one-third of your personal property and can claim one-third of your land as dower. She might elect against your will if she does not approve of your disposition of your property. The election against your will would distort and perhaps frustrate your estate plan.

BARTON: I think Des will want to fill out the form. You mentioned something about money. How much is all of this going to cost me?

ATTORNEY: As in those fence breaking cases I handled for you, I prefer to charge by the hour and maintain a careful time record. I think charging by time is fairer to both of us than a set fee. Again, you will find a number of lawyers who differ with me concerning the method of determining the fee.

BARTON: Well, how much per hour and how many hours, for example?

ATTORNEY: It will be on the same basis as for those fence breaking cases except that I have had to go up 20% in the past year. The hours required will depend upon how complicated your estate facts turn out to be.

BARTON: Inflation!

ATTORNEY: Yes, and this is not the only way inflation affects estate planning. You will see more of the impact of inflation as we consider specific aspects of your plan. Values of certain kinds of property are increasing quite rapidly.

[When the Bartons completed their forms and returned them to Armistead's office, Thurlow Blackstone, a paralegal assisting Armistead, examined the forms and prepared the following summary for

Armistead's use. Blackstone also opened an estate planning file for the Bartons. The summary follows:]

MYRES JAMES AND DESDEMONA SMITH BARTON

Date 18 August 1982

FAMILY

Myres James Barton and Desdemona Smith Barton live at Ramayana Farm, Albercello County, Minor. Myres James Barton is Alumni Distinguished Professor of Sanskrit at Jefferson University, Jefferson City, Minor. He was born in the State of Monroe on 22 January 1922 and received his PhD degree at Randolph University. He taught at Randolph University until he joined the Jefferson University faculty in 1959. He is now 60. Desdemona Smith Barton is Chief Librarian of Jefferson City. She was born in Jefferson City on 2 March 1941 and received her B.S. in library science at Jefferson University. She has been employed by Jefferson City since her graduation. She is now 41. Myres James Barton's social security number is 225–48–2482. Desdemona Smith Barton's social security number is 448–21–5293.

The Bartons were married in Jefferson City on 26 June 1959. The marriage certificate, birth certificates of their children, Barton's military papers and other records pertaining to Barton and his family are kept in jointly owned safe deposit box No. 15181 in Fidelity National Bank of Jefferson City.

There are two children by the Bartons' marriage. These are:

1. *Evangeline Barton Jones*, 21, of Greenville, Minor. She married Caleb Jones at age 18 but divorced him and was awarded custody of their child, Caleb, Jr., age 13 months. A support order requiring Jones to pay $200 per month to support Caleb, Jr. was entered in the Circuit Court of Greenville, Minor, but Jones made no payments and has absconded. Evangeline works as a legal secretary in Greenville and makes $10,000 per year. Her monthly expenses are $500 and Barton assists her with payments of $250 per month.

2. *Preston Smith Barton*, 22, of Jefferson City, Minor. He is unmarried and a fourth year college student at Jefferson University. He expects to enter Jefferson University Law School in the Fall. Barton pays all of Preston's expenses which are now about $5,500 per year. Preston obtains summer work, earning $1,500 annually.

Myres James Barton was previously married in 1943 to *Mary Ann Allen Barton* in Randolph City, Monroe. Mary Ann Allen Barton divorced Barton in 1958. A property settlement was incorporated in the divorce decree entered in the Circuit Court of Randolph City, Monroe. No alimony or support was awarded either party. Mary Ann Allen Barton now lives in Randolph City, Monroe.

There is one child by Barton's marriage to Mary Ann Allen Barton. This is *Samuel Arthur Barton,* 34, who lives in Randolph City, Monroe. He is married to *Gail Lawton Barton,* 31. Samuel Arthur Barton is an architect and is advancing rapidly in his profession. His salary is believed by Barton to be about $40,000 per year. Samuel and Gail have one child, *Murgatroyd,* age 7. Murgatroyd is precocious, having entered McGregor School, (a private institution) in Randolph City at age 4 and having made all "A's" since he entered. He has aptitude for languages and Barton has commenced writing him short letters in Sanskrit. Murgatroyd is a disciplinary problem at McGregor and has been expelled twice, having been readmitted each time due to the intervention of his Grandfather Barton, who is an alumnus of McGregor, and his Grandmother Mary Ann Allen Barton, who is the Headmaster's first cousin.

Barton's Mother, Mary Musgrove Barton, 85, resides in Randolph City, Monroe, with Barton's unmarried sister, *Sarah Lawrence Barton,* 54.

Mary Musgrove Barton is life beneficiary in a marital deduction trust established in the will of her husband and Barton's father, *Vanderbilt Carnegie Barton,* in 1965. The trust property, now valued at $1,525,000, is subject to a general testamentary power of appointment in Mary Musgrove Barton. The takers in default in the event this power is unexercised by Mary Musgrove Barton are Myres James Barton and Sarah Lawrence Barton (his sister) in equal shares. The Henry National Bank of Randolph City is trustee of the marital deduction trust. Mary Musgrove Barton now has no will and is incompetent to make one. It is unlikely she will regain testamentary capacity before her death. She has no significant property apart from that in the trust.

Sarah Lawrence Barton is a registered nurse and is dependent upon income received from her employment. She owns her home. This was a gift from Vanderbilt Carnegie Barton twenty years ago.

A second sister, Jane Barton, of whom her father, Vanderbilt Carnegie Barton, disapproved and excluded by his will from participation in his estate, died three years ago. She was a successful artist. Myres James Barton thought his father acted unwisely in excluding Jane from his estate and desired to make a provision for her. He thus took out a $20,000 Benign Life Policy with Jane as beneficiary which remains in force. Myres James Barton served as co-executor with his son, Samuel, of Jane's will in Monroe and his final account as executor has been approved by the Circuit Court of Randolph City, Monroe.

MYRES JAMES BARTON ASSETS

Cash-Bank Balances

Cash	$ 500.00
Checking Account (Fidelity Nat. Bank of Jefferson City—Jointly with Desdemona Smith Barton)	5,500.00
Savings Accounts	
Fidelity Nat. Bank of Jefferson City (5.5%) (Jointly with Desdemona Smith Barton)	$53,000.00
Gibraltar Rock Bank of Randolph City (6%) (Jointly with Desdemona Smith Barton)	1,300.00
Henry National Bank of Randolph City (5.5%)	1,500.00
Total	$61,800.00

Bonds

(*Individually owned by Myres James Barton*)

Name	Yield	Face	Basis	Maturity	Value
(*Acquired by bequest from Vanderbilt C. Barton, 1965*)					
Goliath Tr.	5%	$100,000	$60,000	1993	$ 75,000.00
Minor	9.53%	50,000	50,000	2014	52,000.00
(*Acquired by gift from Mary Musgrove Barton, 1970*)					
Monroe Tpk.	5.8%	$ 50,000	$50,000	2000	51,000.00
Mary's Pies	8%	70,000	40,000	2000	62,000.00
(*Purchased by James Myres Barton, 1975 to date*)					
U. S. Bonds	8.25%	$ 50,000	$50,000	1990	51,000.00
Prestige Nail	9%	30,000	18,000	2005	22,000.00
Total bonds					$313,000.00

(State of Minor and Monroe Turnpike Authority bonds are Federal income tax exempt. Prestige Nail Company bonds are three $10,000 bearer instruments.)

Stocks

(*All individually owned by Myres James Barton and all acquired by bequest from Vanderbilt Carnegie Barton in 1965. All are common shares with average current annual dividend as indicated.*)

Name	Number	Dividend	Basis	Value
Acme Revolver	1,000	$4.50	$11,000	$ 32,000.00
Cons. Dirigible	1,000	——	10,000	90,000.00
Alley Chem. Disp.	1,000	2.15	2,000	20,000.00
Sunset Pub. Co.	1,000	.20	1,000	13,500.00
Sulphur Oil	500	6.00	15,000	25,000.00
Amal. Bolt Cutter	400	3.50	30,000	60,000.00
Canaveral Shuttle Sandwiches	1,000	2.00	1,000	100,000.00
Deliberate Computer	3,000	5.50	60,500	300,000.00
Total stocks				$640,500.00

Real Property

1. Description—Ramayana Farm, 350 acres.
   Location—Albercello County, Minor.
   How owned—Individually.
   Date acquired—1960.
   How acquired—Purchase, Deed Book 153, page 80.
   Cost basis—$175,000.00
   Encumbrances—First Mortgage, Fidelity National Bank of Jefferson City, approximately $60,000 principal remaining.
   Monthly payments—$410.00.
   Insurance—$100,000 on house.
   Premium—$550.00.
   Taxes—$200.00
   Tax value—$100,000.00
   Est. market value—$700,000.00.
   Annual net income—$10,000.00.
2. Description—Timberland, unimproved, 100 acres.
   Location—Baker County, Monroe.
   How owned—Individually.
   Date acquired—1970.
   How acquired—Purchase, Deed Book 352, page 108.
   Cost Basis—$25,000.00.
   Encumbrances—None.
   Monthly payments—None.
   Insurance—None.
   Premium—None.
   Taxes—$150.00.
   Tax value—$150,000.00.
   Est. market value—$150,000.00.
   Annual net income—None.
3. Description—Lake front cottage, 25 acres.
   Location—Yemassee County, Monroe.
   How owned—Individually.
   Date acquired—1965.
   How acquired—Devise from Vanderbilt Carnegie Barton, Wills Book 255, page 143, Circuit Court, Randolph City, Monroe.
   Cost basis—$35,000 (estate value).
   Encumbrances—None.
   Monthly payments—None.
   Insurance—$75,000.00.
   Premium—$360.00.
   Taxes—$120.00.
   Tax value—$125,000.00.
   Est. market value—$125,000.00.
   Annual net income—None.

Total real property $975,000.00

Miscellaneous Personalty

Salary and other income accumulated at death	$______
Furniture in home	5,000.00
Farm equipment	15,000.00
Automobile	18,000.00
Art Objects	10,000.00

Books	2,000.00
Copyright—"Sanskrit Primer"—Sunset Press	1,000.00
Total miscellaneous personalty	$51,000.00

Life Insurance

(All nonparticipating policies)

	A.	B.	C.	D.	E.
Carrier	**Octagon Life**	**Jeff.U.Gp.**	**Benign Life**	**Vet. Adm.**	**Begone Assur.**
Type	Whole	Term	Whole	Whole	Whole
Face	$50,000	$30,000	$20,000	$10,000	$20,000
Int. Ter. Reserve	25,050	—	9,280	5,210	10,280
Age @ Issue	28	60	35	23	25
Div. Accu.	—	—	—	—	—
Death Val.	50,000	30,000	20,000	10,000	20,000
Premium	530	568	290	390	169
Prim. Ben.	M. M. Barton, Mother	D. S. Barton, Wife	J. Barton Sister	M. A. Barton, Wife	M. A. Barton, Wife
Options	Outright	Outright	Outright	Outright	Outright
Sec. Ben.	Children	Children	—	Children	Children
Qual. M/D [2]	No	Yes	No	No	No
Pow.Ch.Ben. Reserved	Yes	Yes	Yes	Yes	Yes
Face value of insurance					$130,000.00

2. "Qual. M/D" means "qualified for marital deduction".

Employee Benefits

Pension Plan: Academic Trust, Plan A (currently $72,160.00) and Academic Trust, Plan B (currently $73,901), payments commencing optionally at age 65 with income now estimated at $20,978 per year. Payments to survivor Desdemona S. Barton at $8,000 per year until principal of funds exhausted and payment in lump sum with other options permitted under terms of contract. Plan is qualified. Premium level currently $4,600 per year, half being paid by Jefferson University until Barton attains 65 and remainder paid by Barton. Plan payments were commenced at Randolph University and data for Barton's total contributions unavailable.

Accident Insurance: $100,000 group, Fireblast Accident and Indemnity Co., premiums paid by Jefferson University until Barton attains 65.

Disability Insurance: Three-fourths salary, premium paid by Jefferson University until Barton attains age 65.

Hospital and Surgical: Blue Cross/Blue Shield, premium paid by Jefferson University until Barton attains age 65.

Income

Salary—Jefferson University	$ 52,000.00
Research grant—Jefferson University	4,000.00
Ramayana Farm	10,000.00
Interest	28,165.00
Dividends	29,750.00
Royalties	500.00
Total income	$124,415.00

Liabilities

General

1.	First mortgage, Ramayana Farm, Fid. Nat. Bk. Jeff. City	$ 60,000.00
2.	Note, $10,000, endorser for Ernest Achiever, student for graduate school expenses	10,000.00
3.	Real property taxes	1,255.00
4.	Personal property taxes	400.00

Income Taxes

(*Based on data for past year. State income taxes 5% of Federal tax. Filing jointly with Desdemona S. Barton.*)

5.	Federal income tax		$ 60,546.00
	Federal gross income	$142,915.00	
	Exclusions	200.00	
	Adjusted gross income	142,715.00	
	Exemptions (3)	3,000.00	
	Deductions	10,000.00	
	Taxable income	$129,715.00	
6.	State income tax		3,027.00
	Total liabilities		$135,228.00

Inter Vivos Transfers

1.	Gift to Sarah Lawrence Barton for new roof on house (1977)	$ 3,000.00
2.	Gift to Samuel Arthur Barton for down payment on home (1978) split between James Myres and Desdemona S. Barton	10,000.00

Will

Executed 1950 in Randolph City, Monroe, entire estate to Mary Ann Allen Barton with nomination of her as executrix.

DESDEMONA S. BARTON ASSETS

Cash-Bank Balances

Cash	$ 300.00
Checking Account (Fidelity Nat. Bank of Jefferson City—Jointly with Myres James Barton)	5,500.00
Savings Accounts	
Fidelity Nat. Bank of Jefferson City (5.5%) (Jointly with Myres James Barton)	53,000.00
Gibraltar Rock Bank, Randolph City (6%) (Jointly with Myres James Barton)	1,300.00
Total	$ 60,100.00

Employee Benefits

Pension Plan: Jefferson City. Currently $130,000, payments commencing optionally at age 65 with income now estimated at $12,000 per year. No survivor designation. Plan is qualified. Premium level currently $2,400 per year, half being paid by Jefferson City until Desdemona attains 65 and the remaining half being paid by Desdemona. All employment under this plan is in Jefferson City.

Accident Insurance: $50,000 group, Bookstack Dependable, premium paid by Jefferson City until Desdemona attains 65.

Disability Insurance: None.

Hospital and Surgical: Blue Cross/Blue Shield, premiums paid by Jefferson City until Desdemona attains age 65.

Miscellaneous Personalty

Furs, Jewelry $10,000.00

Income

Salary, Jefferson City, Chief Librarian $18,500.00

Liabilities

Federal income tax for past year (jointly with Myres James Barton) $60,546.00

State income tax for past year (jointly with Myres James Barton) 3,027.00

Total liabilities $63,573.00

Will

None

PLANNING OBJECTIVES MYRES AND DESDEMONA BARTON

Retirement—Myres James Barton.
- Expected—age 70.
- Minimum income desired—$60,000.00

Retirement—Desdemona S. Barton.
- Expected—age 65.
- Minimum income desired—$50,000.

Desirable income of Desdemona at death of Myres—$50,000.00

Minimum income requirements of family.
- Support daughter Evangeline and grandson Caleb until her remarriage, per year—$8,000.
- Education son Preston through three years of law school—$50,000.
- Education grandson Caleb through three years of graduate school—$100,000.
- Education grandson Murgatroyd through three years of graduate school—$50,000.
- Education other grandchildren—(?).
- Support sister Sarah Lawrence Barton—$6,000.

Charities: Establish Vanderbilt Carnegie Barton Chair of Business Administration at Jefferson University.

[When Armistead completed his review of this summary prepared by Blackstone from information furnished by the Bartons, he called Myres James Barton and this conversation followed:]

ATTORNEY: Blackstone has gone over those forms you and Des filled out and has made up a summary of the information for my use. There are a few more things I will have to ask you for before we meet again. Here they are. Get out your pencil and I will call them off.

First I will need a copy of that divorce decree entered in Monroe. Then I need a copy of your Father's will and copies of the deeds to Ramayana Farm and the timberland with the security agreement on Ramayana Farm. I will need your will, your life insurance policies and fire and casualty insurance policies. Find your Academic Trust contracts so I can examine these. Then go into your tax file and get copies of your last three federal and state income tax returns and any gift tax returns you have filed. It may be necessary for me to examine some other documents as we get into planning—but these will do for now.

BARTON: This is a pretty big order but I think I can get these items to you by the end of the week. I will do my best.

ATTORNEY: If you have any trouble, let me know and I will have Blackstone help.

[A week later, after Barton had furnished the documents requested by Armistead and the latter had gone over them, the Bartons met with Armistead, and they had this conversation:]

ATTORNEY: I am glad both of you are here and may I say that you did an excellent job in filling out these forms. Perhaps before we get into a detailed treatment of your estate plan, I should mention a few factors that we should consider as the plan is developed.

The first of these factors is inflation. Inflation has been present during most of our national life and is likely to continue although there may be episodes of deflation and prices may be level for long periods. But until both of you retire, and for your retirement lives, inflation is likely to be a major problem. There are a number of items among your assets—particularly your land—which are likely to increase in value. The federal estate and gift taxes are on a progressive scale. The top limit as of 1985 will be 50% of amounts in excess of $2,500,000 although the effective estate tax rate will not be this high because the method of computing the state death tax credit was not changed by ERTA in 1981. Between $600,000 and $10,000,000 the effective rate will vary from 33% to 42% and then will be at 34% on amounts over $10,000,000. Of course, to get the state death tax credit the state death tax has to be paid. If your income goes up with inflation, the higher your federal and state income taxes will be. As costs of food and other purchases increase, the greater the cost of living pressure will be upon you, particularly in your retirement years.

DESDEMONA: Anyone who buys groceries can see the impact of inflation.

BARTON: The Hindus had it too. About 300 B.C. they began to depreciate their gold coinage with copper.

ATTORNEY: Well, I don't know what the Hindus did about inflation or about estate planning, but we have some tax and other problems now that they did not have and inflation is going to haunt us.

A second factor which we should consider is the increasing longevity of Americans. Both of you and the members of your family are likely to live about five to ten years longer than your parents. This means that we must give increasing attention to retirement requirements and especially to medical and other expenses associated with old age. We also must consider that women, on the average, live to greater ages than men. This means that the duration of support requirements for women are likely to be greater than for men.

BARTON: I had in mind requiring Des to be burned upon my funeral pyre—suttee, you know.

DESDEMONA: Wrong! I will be looking for a second husband to get the marital deduction for my estate. That's right, isn't it? I would need a second husband to get a marital deduction.

ATTORNEY: We will get to the marital deduction later, Des; but let's be serious, Myres, Des' life expectancy is about age 80. She is likely to survive you. She can earn her own living, but if she wishes to retire at 65 she will have an estimated 15 years of retirement with $12,000 per year from her annuity and with costs probably increasing constantly during that period.

Now I should mention a third factor to be considered, and that is the certainty of changes in our federal and state tax laws. For example, the federal estate and gift tax laws were revised substantially in 1976. Gift taxes were placed on the same rate scale as estate taxes. A new tax, the generation skipping tax, was introduced. And many other significant changes in the tax laws of concern to us were made. Moreover, as in most general revisions of this type, a number of additional changes were required in subsequent years to clarify ambiguities. One major innovation in 1976, the "carryover basis", was later repealed. Then in 1981 in ERTA we moved to a 100% marital deduction, a phased in reduction of the top tax rate through 1985 and a phased in increase of the unified credit through 1987. Other major changes were made. Additional changes in these laws, and in the federal and state income tax laws as well, almost certainly will be made. Some of these will require no changes in estate plans but other shifts in tax policy probably will require changes. Both Minor and Monroe introduced estate taxes in 1977. Formerly both had inheritance taxes and we would have dealt with inheritance taxes if we had been planning your estates a few years ago. The inheritance tax is upon the taker of the property and is based upon the value taken and upon the relationship of the taker to the decedent. The estate taxes in Minor and Monroe now are based upon the federal estate tax "state death tax credit." If there is no adjusted taxable estate for federal purposes you have no state death tax.

BARTON: I'm confused. I never realized that so many taxes had to be considered in planning an estate. Just the number of taxes is bad enough—but to consider possible changes in them also! It's just too much!

ATTORNEY: No one can predict what will happen a number of years hence. We do know that the certain flux in tax policies with changes in Federal Revenue needs, with the factors of inflation and increasing longevity, together with your changing needs and the needs of your family, require us to seek great flexibility in your estate plan. To the extent we can, in a manner consistent with attaining your planning objectives and with reasonable tax economy, you should be able to withdraw from any planning transactions that I recommend and that you decide to execute. But we might not be able to construct this "avenue of retreat" in every instance.

We will want to review your plan periodically. If we find we must abandon parts of the plan because they have become unnecessary or improvident, we want to be able to abandon a particular part without unnecessary cost or inconvenience.

We also want to develop liquidity in your estate. By this I mean that we want to have funds readily available to pay taxes and expenses and satisfy cash legacies without having to sell property which will be costly for tax or other reasons to sell or which you might want to pass without sale to particular persons. Liquidity is related to post mortem estate planning. The greater the availability of funds to pay taxes and expenses, the greater becomes the latitude of your executor to make decisions which will reduce income taxes and other costs to your estate after your death.

BARTON: That makes sense to me. Flexibility and liquidity!

ATTORNEY: Yes, you might think of an estate plan as analogous to a foreign policy. We want to formulate objectives—what you want to do with your assets. Then we engage in an intelligence process. We look at the facts in your case and try to determine how these might impinge upon attaining your desired objectives. Then we formulate various methods by which your objectives can be attained. After that we select methods from among those which we have formulated and execute the plan by drafting the various instruments, such as wills and trusts, and putting these into effect. But then, as soon as we execute your plan this changes the facts in your case. Your objectives may change and the methods which you use in attaining these objectives may change. We should think of an estate plan as a series of successive plans to keep the transactions current. Planning should not cease so long as there is any substantial property or any significant family problems that might be dealt with through the use of property.

BARTON: I believe in keeping things up to date.

ATTORNEY: To give you an idea concerning your estate tax situation as we start, and so you will have some idea as to the improvement in your situation when we finish, I have calculated Myres' tax liabilities and other estate costs upon the assumption he dies tomorrow and Des survives him.

Myres' will was revoked partially by operation of law when Mary Ann divorced him. Under the law of Monroe, where Myres and Mary Ann then resided, divorce revokes the provisions of a will in favor of a divorced spouse. This includes the nomination of the spouse as executrix or executor or as a trustee. I think this is what Myres would have wanted had he thought about the will; but the net effect is that his property will pass by the intestate law unless he makes another will. The intestate law is the statutory statement of state policy prescribing the disposition of a decedent's property which does not pass by will or by some inter vivos arrangement. Des would take one-third of Myres' land in fee simple as "dower". This would be the only interest in land she would take because children have priority as intestate successors to Myres' land. Des would take one-third of Myres' personal property as intestate distributee. She would also take three of the bank accounts by "survivorship" and would take as survivor under the annuity contracts and as designated beneficiary under the Jefferson University Group policy. These interests are passing by inter vivos arrangements and not by the intestate law. Mary Musgrove Barton and Mary Ann Allen Barton would take under their respective life insurance policies. The Benign life policy payable to Jane Barton would pass as part of the intestate estate since Jane is dead and no alternate beneficiary was indicated in the policy.

The situs of land controls its intestate devolution. The domicile of the decedent controls the intestate devolution of personal property. Here the intestate laws and the dower laws of Monroe and Minor are identical and this will simplify my calculations. The law of Monroe will control the intestate succession to the timber land and the summer cottage because both are located in Monroe. The law of Minor will control the intestate succession to the remainder of Myres' property.

DESDEMONA: I told him he needed a will. I didn't realize he still had the old one.

BARTON: You can't teach Sanskrit and remember everything else.

DESDEMONA: I'm not sure I understand all those legal terms, but does Myres have dower in my land if I acquire any?

ATTORNEY: We call his interest "curtesy" but in Monroe and Minor his interest is identical to dower. The difference is in name only.

Well, let's see where we were—yes, I was going to determine Myres' gross estate based upon the current estimates of values of various assets contained in the summary upon the assumption he died intestate.

BARTON: What is this "gross" estate? Sounds like something is wrong with it.

ATTORNEY: This is the estate with which we commence our computation of the federal and state estate taxes. We distinguish the "gross" estate from the "probate" estate.

The "probate" estate embraces the property passing at death by will or by intestate succession. It excludes the property passing by survivorship or by other inter vivos transactions. In both Monroe and Minor the administrator of the intestate estate controls only the personal property passing by intestacy. It is to this personal property that creditors first have recourse to satisfy their claims. But title to land passes directly to the intestate heir in Monroe and Minor. The administrator does not control the land. If the creditors exhaust all of the personal property in the hands of the administrator without satisfying their claims fully, they then can go against the land by a process described as "marshalling". In a broad sense we describe both the intestate personal property and the intestate land as "probate" property. I should note that Des' dower interest in land could not be reached by Myres' creditors unless she waives her claim to dower or unless she is a party to the obligation upon which the creditor's claim is based.

DESDEMONA: Good! I won't waive dower or be a party to an obligation.

ATTORNEY: The probate estate is always part of the gross estate but the gross estate typically includes other property as well. For example, the proceeds of Myres' life insurance will be included in the gross estate because he reserved incidents of ownership over the policies. In fact, as I mentioned a few minutes ago, the Benign life policy, payable to Jane, is included in the probate estate also. Half of those bank accounts which are payable to you jointly are also included in Myres' gross estate although they pass by "survivorship" to Des and are not part of the "probate" estate.

DESDEMONA: Stop right there! A lot of my money is in those joint accounts. In some I may have deposited more than half. Do you mean that Myres' estate will have to pay a tax on my money? I could go down right now and withdraw all of the deposits so none would be in Myres' estate.

ATTORNEY: The money is included in the gross estate as if Myres owned it but it is not taxed because of the marital deduction.

Well, let me mention some other items that would be in the gross estate. How the Academic Trust payments are handled depends upon the election Des makes. If she elects a lump sum settlement, the amount will be included in the gross estate but favorable income tax treatment can be obtained. If she elects instead periodic payments, this being a "qualified" retirement benefit plan, the estate tax would be based upon Myres' contributions only with payments treated as ordinary income, Myres' contributions being recovered pursuant to an exclusion ratio. There are a good many technicalities here that I won't go into and, because of the 100% marital deduction, I assume Des will elect a lump sum settlement. For our present purposes I am going to assume a lump sum settlement election figure at $150,000 includible in the estate for the Academic Trust plans.

We do not have any revocable trusts, trusts with other reserved powers having aspects of retained ownership or general powers of appointment in Myres. If there were any of these, the property subject to the power would be included in the gross estate if the trusts concerned were created by Myres (that is, the powers were reserved by him) and whether the general power was reserved by him or created by someone else. He is a "taker in default" under his Mother's general power, and this interest must be valued and included in the gross estate. Using a table in the Internal Revenue Code, Blackstone determined the value of this interest at $581,387 which I am going to round off for our calculations at $581,000. This is a vested remainder subject to being defeased by Mrs. Mary Musgrove Barton's exercise of her general power, but this possibility is so remote I think the IRS would not make any allowance for it. In any event the figure I state is close enough for our calculations.

You now have a general idea of the "gross" and "probate" estates, so now let's do a little addition. First let's determine the "probate" estate.

The "personal" probate estate (that is, the personal property in the probate estate) will include the bonds ($313,000); the stock ($640,500); cash ($500); miscellaneous personalty ($51,000); the Benign life policy which is now payable to the estate ($20,000); the Henry Bank deposit ($1,500); and the "taker in default" interest ($581,000). We will add a figure, which I am simply estimating, to cover various amounts of income accumulated at death including the proceeds of any casualty insurance ($20,000). This gives us $1,627,500 for the personal probate estate. To this figure I will add the estimated value of the land ($975,000) to give us an estimated probate estate of $2,602,500.

Now let's add the taxable non-probate property to get a gross estate figure. This includes half of the joint bank accounts which pass by survivorship to Des ($29,900); the life insurance (less the Benign policy) ($110,000); and the Academic Trust payments ($150,000). This gives us a non-probate figure of $289,900). The gross estate is the probate plus non-probate included property or $2,892,400.

Now we have to obtain the estimated taxable estate. To obtain this figure, we must estimate deductions. For administrative costs and funeral expenses I use a factor of 3.6% of the gross estate which gives us $104,126. This factor is derived from studies by the IRS of gross estates about the size of this one. Then I add in two-thirds of your federal and state income taxes based on the figure in the summary ($42,382) and two-thirds of your real and personal property taxes ($1,103). We lack a real basis for estimating these because we do not know what Myres' income will be or what the tax will be in future years and state property taxes are spiraling upward. Unpaid taxes for past years would be a deduction. Any interest due would be deductible but I have not added an item for this. $60,000 is a figure I think I might use as the principal amount due on the Ramayana Farm note although hopefully that might be reduced. I assume the worst case on the Achiever note—that Myres will be liable on that for $10,000. This gives us a *very rough* estimate of $217,611. Now to calculate the marital deduction.

There is a 100% deduction for all qualified property which passes to Des either in the probate estate or outside of the probate estate. Thus she takes the $29,900 in the joint accounts as survivor and $30,000 under the Jefferson Group policy. She also takes the $150,000 which we are assuming would be taken as a lump sum settlement under the Academic Trust contracts. In the probate estate she takes one-third of the personal estate under the intestate law ($542,500) plus one-third of the land in fee simple as dower ($325,000) or $867,500 in probate estate. The non-probate property plus the probate property give Des $1,077,400 for which the marital deduction can be claimed. This, added to the general deductions ($217,611) give us $1,295,011 in total deductions. We assume we have no losses or other deductions.

To obtain the taxable estate we now subtract $1,295,011 from $2,892,400 (the gross estate). This gives us a taxable estate of $1,597,389. We have to add $4,000 which is the excess over the split gift amount ($6,000 in 1978) to Samuel. The taxable estate subject to federal estate tax is thus $1,601,389. The tax on this is $601,425, less a state death tax credit of $70,633, and less the unified credit for this year at $62,800. This gives you a federal estate tax payout of $467,992 plus a state death tax payout of $70,633 for a total death tax of $538,625. We would have to take this out of your estate before anything could be distributed. We will have to add to this the $217,611 for administrative expenses, taxes etc., since this in fact would be paid out. That means a total payout of $756,236.

DESDEMONA: Myres, say something!

BARTON: You mean 25% of my gross estate will have to be used for taxes and expenses?

ATTORNEY: It will be about 26%. But let's see what happens as we pay off those obligations during administration of the estate. The death taxes do not fall on the marital property in Minor and Monroe so long as there is any probate property other than marital deduction property available to pay these taxes. Under the federal estate tax law, life insurance passing outside the probate estate, which is being taxed as part of the gross estate, bears its proportionate part of the estate tax. I am assuming that our state law will require this tax paid out of the probate estate if this is available when the life insurance is payable to the surviving spouse. But $80,000 in life insurance here will have to bear its pro rata share of the estate tax. State death taxes are prorated just as is the federal estate tax in Minor and Monroe. Under our apportionment system, I estimate $26,908 payable out of the non-probate life insurance; $198,446 payable out of the land; $311,927 payable out of the probate personal estate; and $1,345 payable out of the $4,000 gift taxable item. As to the latter, we might have difficulty in having this charged against Samuel's share. After all a completed gift was made to him. Indeed, our apportionment system causes nothing but trouble as each estate presents new facts; but my estimates are a fair approximation of how these taxes would be broken down in Minor and Monroe. Expenses of administration and funeral expenses fall on the personal probate estate in Minor and Monroe. Only when the personal probate estate is exhausted do we look to the land. An exception is made for that $60,000 in principal due on the note secured on Ramayana Farm. The creditor can look to the farm for that and probably will demand that the note be paid off when Myres dies. Thus $157,611 will have to be paid out of the personal probate estate, and Des' one-third will have to respond for her share of these expenses. This means $52,537 will have to be deducted from her $542,500 share in the personal estate, leaving her $489,963 in personal estate available for distribution. While Myres' creditors cannot reach her dower interest in land, her dower in Ramayana Farm is subject to one-third of the $60,000 lien, or $20,000 in liability. For our purposes, we will assume she receives $305,000 in land which she might or might not have commuted (or paid in cash). Now let's add up what Des would take. She receives all of the joint accounts, half being from Myres' estate. We will count this for present purposes as $29,900. She receives $30,000 from the group life policy; she takes Academic Trust annuities in a lump sum at $150,000; $489,963 comes to her from the personal estate; and $305,000 in dower from the land. Her total share is $1,004,863.

DESDEMONA: Over a million! Looks good to me!

ATTORNEY: Now let's see what the children get. The probate personalty bears most of the expenses and estate tax. Out of the $1,085,000 of the personal probate estate we deduct $105,074 for expenses and $311,927 for taxes ($417,001) for a balance of $667,999 or $222,666 each. We would have to deduct from Samuel's share an additional amount allocated to his gift; and he probably would resist this. For the real property ($650,000) we deduct $40,000 in principal due on the note on Ramayana Farm and $198,446 in taxes for a balance of $411,554 or $137,185 each.

DESDEMONA: That seems fair enough to me.

ATTORNEY: Now what happens in Des' estate when she dies? I am going to assume a number of facts: (1) Des survives Myres by at least ten years; (2) she does not remarry and leave some or all of her property to a second spouse; (3) she retains all of the property she receives from Myres' estate; (4) this property increases with inflation at 8% per annum; (5) that her other property—her individual interest in the joint accounts, furs, jewelry and $300 in cash does not increase with inflation—(a rash enough assumption)! (6) that she saves an additional $10,000 and has $8,000 in salary and other income due at her death; and (7) she has no will. I notice you have no will right now, Des.

DESDEMONA: I never thought I needed a will. Not until Myres dies anyway.

ATTORNEY: With the value increase I am assuming, the property Des obtained from Myres will be worth about $2,008,722 within ten years. Stocks and bonds can go down as well as up—I know. Then we will assume 3.9% for administrative and funeral expenses ($80,598). We will assume no other deductions. The taxable estate will be $1,986,024. The federal estate tax on this, assuming a $192,800 unified credit and no taxable gifts, is $483,117 and the state death tax is $98,594 for a total death tax of $581,711 or a total payout of $662,309.

DESDEMONA: You are just playing with figures. I might spend all of that money and not have it in my estate. Or I might find a second husband and leave it all to him. Then I would not have a federal estate tax because I would have a 100% marital deduction. Right!

ATTORNEY: Right! My figures are estimates and are based upon many assumptions. What I am attempting to do is to give you a rough picture of your situation now and how it *might* develop in the future.

BARTON: I'm not sure this is what I want. You mean I start with $2,892,400 in my gross estate and by the time Des dies $1,250,000 or thereabouts has been taken out?

ATTORNEY: That's pretty close. But remember some of that property was earned by Des and that we are considering the impact of inflation also.

BARTON: Suppose Des did not remarry. Who would take her property?

ATTORNEY: Evangeline and Preston would take if they survived her. If one of them predeceased her, the children of that child would take in her or his place. That's roughly the picture.

BARTON: Not Sam, or Murgatroyd?

ATTORNEY: No, they will not be Des' intestate successors. She might leave them a share if she had a will. Or perhaps she could adopt Sam. But that would be unlikely.

BARTON: I want my children to share equally in any property that comes from me.

ATTORNEY: There is another potential problem in Myres' assumed intestate estate that we should examine. A comparable problem is likely to be present in Des' estate also. Where is the money going to come from to pay all of those taxes and expenses?

The administrator of the intestate estate is immediately responsible for paying death taxes and must seek contribution from the successors to property which he does not control but from whom part of the death taxes as apportioned is due.

For example, let's take that $26,908 apportioned to life insurance beneficiaries other than Des. Both of the beneficiaries live in Monroe while the estate is being administered in Minor. Suppose they will not contribute to the tax payments. The administrator might be able to reach the money in the hands of the insurance companies before it is paid out. If he could not obtain the money from the insurance companies, you should note that the apportionment of the federal tax is by the Internal Revenue Code but apportionment of the state death tax is by state law. The administrator would probably sue in the appropriate federal district court in Monroe to enforce contribution. That court would apply the federal law as to the federal tax and the state law as to the state tax. You can see how complicated and expensive this can become.

With respect to the land, which is not under the administrator's control in either Minor or Monroe, we have much the same problem that we have with the insurance except that only state apportionment and contribution requirements are involved. The Internal Revenue Service has procedures for collecting the taxes from those who take the land even if the administrator is unable to obtain contribution or is unable to pay all of the taxes from the personal estate. But if the administrator cannot obtain contribution from the heirs to the land, there may have to be litigation to obtain these payments both in Monroe and Minor.

Now let's look at the way in which we handle the personal probate estate. We have estimated that $311,927 in taxes must be borne by the personal probate estate and $157,611 in expenses. Of this latter amount, $52,537 would be paid from Des' one-third share and the rest would fall upon the shares passing to the children. Des' share in personal probate property will not have to respond for any of the federal or state death taxes under our law. Under our law also these taxes and expenses must be paid from principal rather than from income. The only cash available in Myres' estate, as we now see it, will be $500 in cash; $1,500 from the Henry Bank account; $20,000 from the Benign life policy and accumulated income at death, which you remember I assumed would be $20,000. This gives us a total cash element of $42,000 with $157,611 in expenses and $311,927 in taxes to be paid, or a total of $469,538. I am assuming the lienholder will look to the land to satisfy the balance of $60,000 due on Ramayana Farm. What will have to be sold? If Myres had a will, he could state the order in which assets should be sold; but without a will the order of sale of the personal estate would be in the discretion of the administrator. I assume Des would qualify as your administratrix. What would she sell? There is not much in the miscellaneous personalty ($51,000) that she would want to sell. The farm equipment will be needed for the farm. She would not want to sell furniture. The Sunset Press copyright probably is unmarketable. Thus she would probably turn to the stocks and bonds to find the money necessary.

While an experienced administrator will produce 100% of the value of United States bonds, only about 90% of the market value of listed bonds and only 70% to 80% of the estimated value of common stock could be counted on to be available for the payment of estate obligations. Des probably will retain the State of Minor and Monroe Turnpike bonds since these are tax exempt and the market is likely to be down for them. The United States bonds will bring $51,000; the Goliath Trucking bonds about $67,500; and Mary's Pies, a low yield bond, about $55,800. This will give Des $174,300 from the bonds added to the $42,000 in cash or $216,300. A balance of $253,238 is left. Where will this come from? That interest of Myres as "taker in default" under his father's trust is not readily marketable. The Canaveral Sandwiches stock might bring $85,000. The Sunset Publishing stock might bring 75% of its estimated value, or $10,125. The balance could be made up by a sale of the Amalgamated Bolt Cutter stock. While the stock and bonds acquire a new income tax basis at Myres' death, if Des sold stocks or bonds that increased in value between the date of Myres' death and the date of sale, a capital gains item would be produced.

How will those heirs to the land pay the part of the federal and state death tax apportioned to the land? We estimated $198,446 due, with the amount due on the principal of the note secured on Ramayana Farm being $60,000. Des' dower interest would have to respond for a share of that note principal. They might use part of their shares from the personal estate to pay this tax. No doubt Des would want her dower commuted (or paid in cash) in any event. But chances are some of the land would have to be sold, and while the land also acquires a new basis in Myres' estate, the value of land is increasing quite rapidly and a capital gains item might be developed when the land was sold. How this would affect the heirs depends to a great extent upon their income during the year of the sale.

BARTON: You paint a dismal picture, but obviously all those taxes and expenses would have to be paid from some of my assets.

ATTORNEY: By estate planning we can enhance the liquidity of your estate and can also help you achieve the distribution of it that you desire at the least cost.

BARTON: Good!

ATTORNEY: The next thing we should discuss is how both of you want your estates applied. Let's consider your lifetime objectives first. You seem to be living quite comfortably right now. However, it seems to me that your investment portfolio might benefit from professional management. I can see that both of you are too busy to keep an eye on your investments from day to day. But I think we should concentrate upon retirement objectives and examine Myres' objectives first.

Myres states he expects to retire at 70 and that $60,000 in income will be sufficient. Let's see what income items he can count upon.

As to income tax exempt items, he has Social Security which I will estimate at $6,600 per year, although it could be higher when Myres retires or there might be no social security payments. It is difficult right now to make firm judgments concerning the Social Security System. There will be $4,765 from State of Minor bonds and $2,900 from the Monroe Turnpike bonds. We will add to this an estimate of $10,450 from your annuity income until your cost is recovered. This gives us $24,715 for several years after Myres' retirement which will be tax exempt.

As to taxable income, there is $10,450 from the annuity which will increase after Myres' contribution is recovered; $13,300 from bonds; $29,750 from stocks; $10,000 from Ramayana Farm; $3,075 interest from the various savings account; and the royalty of $500. The United States bonds will have matured by the time Myres retires so income from these is not added. Should Des' income be added?

BARTON: Yes.

ATTORNEY: That gives us a total income of $113,290 of which $27,715 for a number of years will not be income taxed, leaving $85,575 as taxable income. It is a bit hard to predict income tax on this. We are not sure whether we are going to receive income tax reductions or income tax increases, this depending considerably on the cost of government, but I am going to assume that by the time Myres retires both of you will file jointly, there will be three exemptions, perhaps $200 as dividend exclusions, and itemized deductions in the neighborhood of $20,000. The adjusted gross income will then be $59,375, the federal income tax will be in the range of $19,372 and the state income tax about $968 for a total income tax of $20,340. These are very rough figures because the income tax rate will probably change. Now let's add your recurring expenses.

If Myres continues the Octagon, Benign, Veterans Administration and Begone policies there will be annual premiums of $1,379. To convert the Jefferson University Group insurance upon retirement will require an additional $568 annually. Myres will not continue the disability coverage upon retirement but probably will wish to retain the accident coverage at $200. The Blue Cross/Blue Shield to supplement medicare will require $634. The real and personal property taxes, assuming they do not increase, which is a rash assumption, will require $1,655. Thus we have recurring expenses of $4,436. The life insurance premiums will not go up, but the taxes, supplementary medicare and accident insurance payments certainly will. Myres, do you contemplate continuing your support of Evangeline at $3,000 per year?

BARTON: I think I will have to do this and probably will have to increase the amount later on.

ATTORNEY: Let's double this amount—putting it at $6,000 by the time you reach 70. You mentioned the cost of educating Caleb and Murgatroyd. How much did you have in mind there?

BARTON: About $10,000 per year each.

ATTORNEY: We will add in $20,000 per year for an indefinite period. I suggest, however, that Samuel might be counted upon to defray most of Murgatroyd's educational costs. Preston, no doubt, will have completed his legal education by the time you retire and will have commenced making his own living.

BARTON: I hope so.

ATTORNEY: Then we will estimate in addition to your income taxes of $20,340 an item of $30,436 recurring annually for an indefinite time after your retirement. This leaves $62,514 available for other purposes. How does this strike you?

BARTON: I don't see how I can finance my Indian archaeological expedition out of that.

ATTORNEY: You didn't say anything about an archaeological expedition in your questionnaire.

BARTON: I go on one each summer.

ATTORNEY: How much do these cost?

BARTON: About $40,000. I use my $4,000 research grant in part for it. I usually get a grant from the National Sanskrit Foundation to help also.

ATTORNEY: You didn't say anything about that either.

BARTON: It also runs about $4,000. It's applied directly in India to pay labor there.

ATTORNEY: Well, when you are 70 you might consider going on these expeditions at two year intervals or, better still, confine your activities to farming. Some of the costs of such an expedition might be deductible for income tax purposes, perhaps all, but when you retire the case will not be so strong for deductions as when you were teaching. You have a good deal of property but you have got to resign yourself to the fact that you cannot maintain the same pace or support all of the activities that you could while you were in active teaching.

BARTON: Nobody is going to hang me out to dry.

DESDEMONA: He didn't say he was going to hang you out to dry. All he said was that after you retired you could not expect to be doing everything you do now.

ATTORNEY: Myres estimated $60,000 in disposable income with Des' income included. I know all of this is a little rough so far as accuracy is concerned, but Myres has about ten years to go before retirement. I think an inflation factor should be built into the estimate to have an income in ten years which could purchase what $60,000 could purchase now. $90,000 would be a reasonable figure in my opinion. Des' salary certainly will increase; the income from investments might go up or down; the annuity income, except for the income from Academic Trust, Plan B, which is a variable annuity, should be relatively stable; the farm income should go up; and we really don't know what the social security will be. But I think you are in a safe retirement income situation if we predict a joint income in the range of $110,000 upon Myres' retirement. Your situation should be reviewed periodically, new facts considered and your objectives reassessed. We don't know how to predict the income tax. Ten years later, when we look back, some of these estimates are going to seem rather ridiculous. But this characterizes any planning. The key to successful planning is constant monitoring and periodic full review.

Now let's look at Des' situation. In her summary, she suggested $50,000 as her desirable income at Myres' death. We should consider first the situation before Des reaches 65, assuming she has not reached 65 when Myres dies.

Until she retires at 65 she will not be getting social security. But we have assumed she will take $1,004,863 from Myres' estate and will have $29,900 from the joint bank accounts representing her own deposits. She may have other assets also but we will assume just these are invested at 11%. This will produce an income before taxes of $113,824. Coupled with her income of $18,500, this gives a total income of $132,324. Let's assume she could develop deductions of about $10,000 with a $100 exclusion for stock and one exemption. By this time the income tax might be indexed to the consumer price index so we can estimate it only roughly, but the federal income tax would be in the range of $60,112 and the state income tax approximately $3,030. She would have recurring expenses for Blue Cross/Blue Shield at $317. Her accident insurance would be about $100 and her pension fund payments will be about $1,200. We should add a third of the real and personal property taxes at $551. This gives us $2,168.00 which, when added to the income taxes, gives her $65,310 in regular outlay. From an income of $132,324 this leaves $67,014.

DESDEMONA: I could live on that.

ATTORNEY: Now let's look at the situation after she retires. Hopefully she will have $6,600 or more in Social Security. She should draw her pension of $12,000 and we will assume this will be free of tax while her contributions are recovered. We will assume her income from investments continues at $113,824. We will assume she files as a single person, has a $100 dividend exclusion, two exemptions and itemized deductions of $8,000. Her federal income tax will be in the range of $51,862 and her state income tax about $2,593. For recurring expenses she would still have the Blue Cross/Blue Shield at $317 with one third of the real and personal property taxes at $551. This gives a recurring outlay of $55,323 from an income of $132,424 for a balance of $77,101.

BARTON: Des, you would never need all that money. What would you ever do with all of it?

ATTORNEY: Well, I suggest with increasing longevity, especially of women, and with the high cost of nursing home care, that income might not be out of line. A husband and wife can look after each other, but a single person can have a rough time of it as they get old. My recommendation is to get all of the income to Des that you feel you can without depriving the children. Federal support for medical and nursing attention under Social Security may diminish and a surviving spouse might be thrown pretty much on his or her own resources.

BARTON: I see your point. I think I had better do that. I can see that Des' estimates of her income needs probably were low.

ATTORNEY: Let's look at some of your other planning objectives.

Preston should be through law school before Myres retires if all goes well with Preston's studies. He may need some help for a few years after graduation but I think his support should not be viewed as a retirement expense for Myres.

The grandchildren other than Caleb and Murgatroyd are unknown quantities. It is uncertain how many of them there will be or what kind of education will be necessary for them. If Myres wishes to provide for them, the best thing is to give a trustee power to make payments as their needs appear.

Now as to the Vanderbilt Carnegie Barton Chair at Jefferson University, this will require about $100,000 to establish. That will take a rather large slice out of Myres' estate. Do you think you might be prepared to make an inter vivos provision for this purpose so some income tax deduction might be obtained?

BARTON: I would be willing to do that.

ATTORNEY: Now what about the farm? Would Des want to live on the farm after Myres' death? Can she manage the farm and carry on her work as librarian? Are any of the children interested in the farm?

BARTON: To take the last question first, none of the children have any interest in farming. Preston will have to spend his full time with law and says he wants to live in a large urban center. Sam will probably continue to live in Randolph City and practice his profession there. Evangeline will probably stay in Greenville—and while I do not know she will stay there for the rest of her life, I do know that she has no interest in farming. Now as to the second question, Des could run that farm and be head librarian as well, but she has never liked that farm and I believe she would move into Jefferson City right now if she had the chance. I would like to stay on the farm for the rest of my life.

ATTORNEY: What do you say about this, Des?

DESDEMONA: If he wants to stay on the farm, I am going to stay there with him. But he is right. I would like to be within walking distance of my work; and if I had my way the only cows and horses I would ever see again would be in those TV westerns that Myres likes to watch.

ATTORNEY: Myres, what do you have in mind for that timber land in Baker County in Monroe?

BARTON: I got that land because I thought I might hunt there; and I have never had a chance to do more than walk over it. The farm takes up all of my extra time. A forestry professor at Randolph University told me the timber was about 50 years old and probably would be infested by borers if I did not cut it soon. I don't know what to do with it. Should I sell it?

ATTORNEY: We will look at that timber land shortly. How about the lake front cottage? What do you have in mind for that?

BARTON: I would like to keep that in the family if I could. The children like to use it at all times of the year.

ATTORNEY: As to the insurance, why do you want the $50,000 Octagon policy paid to your Mother when she is amply supported under your Father's trust?

BARTON: I took out the policy before the trust was set up and failed to change the beneficiary.

ATTORNEY: Is there any reason why the Veterans Administration and Begone insurance policies are still payable to Mary Ann? I see nothing in the property settlement about these, and your divorce does not revoke these beneficiary designations.

BARTON: No, I just forgot to make the change.

ATTORNEY: The same for the Benign life policy in which Jane was beneficiary?

BARTON: Yes, the same thing.

ATTORNEY: Has anyone raised any issues concerning your administration of Jane's estate?

BARTON: No.

ATTORNEY: Do you think that Achiever is likely to pay that note you endorsed? I advised you not to endorse it, but you did anyway—too softhearted I'm afraid.

BARTON: I haven't seen the fellow in eight months. He seems to be avoiding me.

ATTORNEY: I notice you have a military record. Do you have any military retirement pay?

BARTON: No. I was in the Army Reserve for a short time after World War II but could not do that and my archaeological work in India—so I gave up my Reserve status.

ATTORNEY: Do you have any continuing interest in Mary Ann?

DESDEMONA: He had better not!

ATTORNEY: I mean for her support.

BARTON: We get along well, but she got a lot in the property settlement and I think that is enough.

ATTORNEY: Myres, it is my understanding that you want your children to take equal shares in your estate after Des is provided for?

BARTON: Yes, that's the idea—I want to treat them equally. Des should have the primary use of my estate—that is, I want to make sure she is adequately, indeed more than adequately, supported.

ATTORNEY: Myres, I assume you want Des as executrix in your will, and Des, I assume you want Myres as executor in yours?

BARTON: Right!

DESDEMONA: That's the idea!

ATTORNEY: All right, now I am going to make a number of suggestions. I have outlined these for you with a brief summary of the reasons for my recommendations. I want you to study these proposals when you get home and then when you decide what you want to do I can draft the necessary instruments for you. Let me run over these and my reasons briefly for you now. If further questions occur to you, I can answer them by telephone. I'm not trying to rush you about this, but you should give all of my recommendations careful study and perhaps you might want to talk to the children about them and get their views. But I *am* going to rush you about two matters. Both of you need wills, and both of you need durable powers of attorney.

DESDEMONA: What's a durable power? It wears well, I guess.

ATTORNEY: That's about the idea. The durable power is a power of attorney that does not terminate upon disability of the principal. It can be general or special, but I am going to prepare general durable powers for you. For example, Myres will name Des as his attorney in fact in the power he grants. If he has an accident during one of his trips to India, falls off of an elephant for example, and is disabled, Des can conduct his business affairs for him, indeed, could do this at any time. Des will grant a similar power to Myres although I think nothing much is likely to happen to her there at the library.

As to the wills, I have in mind reciprocal wills. Let me describe generally what I propose for Myres. Then I will talk about Des' will. In Myres' will I suggest as to the essential dispositive provisions a marital deduction trust of the "reduce to zero" formula type with a residuary trust which will shelter the exemption equivalent. This sounds very mysterious to you, I am sure, but generally I propose leaving in the will to Des an estate for life, the amount to be determined by a formula which will reduce the estate tax in Myres' estate to zero, taking into consideration credits and any other transfers qualifying for the marital deduction made to Des outside the will. In the residuary or "catchall" clause in the will I recommend setting up a second trust with a sprinkling provision in which the trustee is authorized to make payments of income to Des or to the children or the grandchildren as their need for support and education indicates. Such a power will be discretionary in the trustee. In the residuary trust we would be transferring the amount of the "exemption equivalent" of the unified credit. Right now this is a credit of $62,800 or an exemption equivalent of $225,000. It will go up each year until 1987 when it will be $192,800 or an exemption equivalent of $600,000. The value of your estate probably will be inflating during this time also. Des will be named as executrix and given a power of sale over the land, including Ramayana Farm, in addition to other full powers to deal with the estate. My idea is that she would dispose of the farm promptly after your death by public or private sale. The only specific devise of land I suggest in the will is of the timberland to Jefferson University to be used to establish a chair for your Father, Vanderbilt Carnegie Barton.

Des' life estate in the will should qualify as a Qualified Terminable Interest Property trust. She should have the entire income payable at least annually to her, and the executrix would be directed to elect the marital deduction for the disposition. The remainder following the life estate will be limited to the three children equally, with appropriate provisions substituting their children or, in the case of Samuel, substituting Sarah Gail Lawton, his wife, if Samuel predeceases the life tenant and is survived by no children.

BARTON: That's a good idea. Gail is a great mother. I would like to think that she might get something from my estate one of these days. I have this big bronze statue of Sita, Ramachandra's wife, which I have been saving for her.

DESDEMONA: She doesn't want that statue, Myres. Nobody wants it. It takes three men even to lift it.

BARTON: I meant for her garden.

ATTORNEY: We can save that statue for another time. Perhaps I can help you haul it over to Randolph City one of these afternoons. But even if I don't get around to doing that I will have saved your estate $538,625 in death taxes by getting you to execute this will if you die with it in force. The exemption equivalent is sheltered and bypasses Des' estate (that is, it is not taxable in her estate). The marital deduction can be claimed on her QTIP trust. The charitable deduction can be obtained on the devise of the timberland for the chair. Zero estate tax!—how does that sound to you? The children ultimately take equal shares.

BARTON: That's great! Draft the will that way.

ATTORNEY: I look at this will as a temporary expedient—but an estate plan has got to be made as if the client were going to die the next day. Ultimately, I hope to revise this will to tie it in to a trust that I am going to recommend that you create; but this will serves your immediate purposes. Now let's look at Des' situation. While this will avoids estate tax in Myres' estate, the use of the QTIP trust will mean an estate tax in Des' estate on the QTIP property. Her estate can recover the tax the QTIP disposition produces in her estate from the remainder. But we must find a way to develop funds to pay off this tax, even though anywhere between $225,000 and $600,000 of Myres' estate will bypass Des' estate in that exemption equivalent shelter trust with the sprinkling power in trustee. We have deferred paying any estate tax, thus having the use of the money during Des' lifetime, and the chances are good that the $600,000 exemption equivalent will be operative before Des dies. Just to give you a rough idea of the tax on Des' estate, assuming Myres died tomorrow and Des lived until 1987, using our former figures, Myres' gross estate would be $2,892,400. $150,000 passes by that devise of the timber land in Baker County, Monroc, to Jefferson University for the chair; $225,000 passes in the exemption equivalent trust; you change all beneficiary designations in the life insurance to name Des ($130,000); Des elects a lump sum settlement of the Academic Trust annuities ($150,000); and she takes $29,900 from the joint accounts. If we imposed administrative expenses and other costs upon the QTIP provision ($217,611), this will give us approximately $1,989,889 in the QTIP trust. Des could reduce her estate by making gifts at $10,000 per donee per annum from her non-QTIP property; but I am going to assume that she keeps all she gets from Myres, that she saves $10,000, keeps her $29,900 that she owned in the joint accounts; and has $8,000 in salary due at death. If the amount of $2,329,689 (Des' non-probate acquisitions plus the QTIP amount plus the amount she owned in the joint accounts) is compounded at 8% for five years, we have $3,423,077. Adding $18,000 to this we have $3,441,077 in potentially taxable estate. The administrative costs will be about 3.-9% of this or $134,202. This gives us a taxable amount of $1,465,718 for a federal estate tax of $665,058 and a state death tax of $210,660 or a total tax of $865.718. This looks awful, but what we must do is take steps to reduce Des' estate by a regular program of giving which I shall outline shortly. These can be gifts to members of the family or for charitable purposes. Also we would try to freeze values if we could but I will not take you into possible techniques for this right now. Remember, Des, your estate could recover the tax caused by the QTIP amount from the remaindermen. For present purposes, I suggest a will by Des leaving her property to Myres which we will modify as we develop the plan to contain a "pour over" to the trust which I will propose establishing. If something should happen to Des, I would not want any of her property to pass intestate even though her estate presents no tax problems presently, although she will certainly have these if Myres executes the will I proposed and she survives him.

Now let me turn to this inter vivos trust I have mentioned several times. I hope you will decide to go ahead with my recommendation concerning this trust because it will save a large proportion of the probate and administrative costs in both of your estates. It seems to me that you have been having a good deal of difficulty in managing your securities portfolio and I believe you might benefit from professional management. Thus I am going to recommend that you establish a revocable inter vivos trust, establishing it initially by designating the trustee as beneficiary of those life insurance policies which I recommend temporarily be changed to Des' name. Myres would reserve a life interest in this trust with Des as successor beneficiary to one share, defined as in Myres' will by a reduce to zero formula with a second share sheltering the exemption equivalent as in the will. The children would be designated as beneficiaries in remainder of the QTIP share equally. However, the exemption equivalent share, unlike the will draft, would designate the three children as beneficiaries with power to withdraw annually each an amount not greater than $5,000 or 5% of the value of the total trust share at the date of exercise of the power of withdrawal. In addition to sheltering the exemption equivalent, the purpose of the share ultimately is to permit Des to make additions to it by inter vivos gifts to reduce her non-QTIP estate. The withdrawal power is intended to qualify the gift for the annual exclusion up to the amount of the withdrawal power. I will probably modify this somewhat in drafting but this generally is the way the scheme will work. The trustee will be authorized to make loans from this share, but not from the QTIP share, to the estate. If this trust is established, I will prepare new wills for both of you, making whatever particular dispositions you desire, and then pouring over the residue to this trust. After the trust is established, Myres can commence funding it with stock or bonds to see how the trustee performs. Ultimately virtually all of the securities might be in this trust. One advantage, apart from management, is that these securities would not pass through probate or administration, and while the trustee selected would receive a fee for its work, the overall cost probably should be much less than probate costs. Just as with Myres' will, there should be no death taxes initially, although there would be death taxes when Des dies, hopefully funds being built up in the exemption equivalent share to help pay these. You can think about this trust and we will discuss it further at your convenience. Much care should be taken in selecting a trustee and I can suggest several corporate fiduciaries from which you could select if you decide to proceed with this feature of the plan. If you established the trust and it did not work to your satisfaction, the trust could be revoked and some other technique used. The income will all be taxed to Myres during his lifetime and the trust property will be within his estate although without estate tax.

Now let's look for a bit at the income tax situation. If you establish the trust (and perhaps even if you do not establish it) I will recommend that you make a gift of the timber land in Baker County to Jefferson University inter vivos rather than by will. If you make the gift inter vivos you can then claim a deduction for it, limited generally to 30% of your adjusted gross income although you have a "carry forward" for five years of the excess deduction. If you leave the property by will, as I am having you do as a temporary expedient to carry out your wishes, you lose the income tax advantage of the gift.

Now let's consider your wishes to support Evangeline and Caleb, pay for the educations of Caleb and Murgatroyd and pay for Preston's legal education. Both Preston and Evangeline are over 18 and you owe no legal obligation to support either of them. You also have no legal obligation to support your grandchildren. It does not make any sense for you to receive income, pay taxes on it, and then pay it over to the children or grandchildren. I thus suggest you establish "Clifford" or short term trusts for each, selecting securities to fund the trust which will be sufficient to produce the income. Let's take Evangeline's case for example. You are now paying $3,000 per year to help support her and this cost may go higher. If you established a short term trust for 10 years at least, retained a reversion so you would get the property back after ten years, and had all of the income paid to Evangeline in the interim, you would not have to pay a tax on this income and then pay it to Evangeline. She could pay the tax in her much lower income bracket and then when you are 70 and ready to retire you would be getting the property back and could take a new look at the situation. There is an element of inflexibility in this trust because the property is beyond your reach for ten years. You cannot reserve a power to revoke such a trust and avoid income tax on it. There is a gift tax on these trusts but this should be no inconvenience for you since you and Des could split the gift at $20,000 per annum. It may be that you would prefer a different type of trust for the grandchildren, perhaps accumulating the income for them until the end of the trust term. You and Des can think about this. I should mention that Samuel might prefer to educate Murgatroyd himself, and doubtless will have ample funds with which to do this. I thus hope you will consult with him to obtain his views before a trust for Murgatroyd is established.

You have been very patient. The main thing to do immediately is to execute those powers and wills. Perhaps, Myres, if you can give me a call tomorrow I can let you know how I have progressed with the drafts and we can arrange for a time to have the instruments executed. I will need three witnesses for the wills and it takes a little lead time to assemble them.

[Barton and Desdemona executed the powers and wills. They gave the trust proposals careful study and instructed Armistead to proceed with the necessary drafts. The life insurance policies were changed to Desdemona's name except for the Benign policy payable to Jane, which Barton, for his own reasons, decided to leave as it was. Before the Bartons could proceed further with the plan, Barton was run over by a Marshall laundry truck at a downtown street crossing in Jefferson City, Minor. He died a short time later in Jefferson University Hospital.]

(2) PROBATING THE WILL AND ADMINISTERING THE ESTATE

[Funeral arrangements for Professor Barton were made by Barton's son, Preston. On the afternoon following the funeral, Gordon Armistead, the lawyer who drafted Barton's will, informed the executrix that the will was kept in the safe deposit box. She requested Preston to go with Armistead to obtain the will, giving him a note authorizing his entrance to the box. Preston went with Armistead to the bank, presented the note, and in the presence of a bank officer, Preston used Barton's key to open the box. When the box was opened, Preston, the bank officer and Armistead saw that it contained an undetermined amount in twenty dollar bills and several bearer bonds in addition to the will. They removed the will only, relocked the box and returned with the will to the Barton home at Ramayana Farm. This discussion ensued:]

PRESTON: They certainly were careful at the bank when I opened Dad's safe deposit box. I had the feeling they didn't trust me. It was a little bit embarrassing.

ATTORNEY: They have to be careful. Under our state law the bank has a contract of bailment with the lessee of the safe deposit box and not a simple lease agreement. Under its bailment contract the bank will be liable if property is lost from the box by reason of an unauthorized entry. Your mother, as joint owner of the box and as executrix could have had access to it and under our law the bank would not be liable to any other personal representative of your father for property she took from it. However, even then the bank might have liability under our federal internal revenue law for the tax due on cash or other securities which your mother removed from the box and which should be returned as part of the estate but were not. Some states have a law requiring a bank officer to be present when the box is opened. We have no such law but the bank nevertheless should have an officer present. You should not be sensitive about this. I am counsel to Fidelity National but you notice they still had an officer of the bank there although I accompanied you.

We could have asked your mother to come with us in order to open the box; but I thought we should not bother her with this so soon after your father's death. From the point of view of the bank, although you had a note from your mother who is named as executrix, she might not qualify and administer the estate. If she had come, she could have entered the box as joint owner. But technically we were making an unauthorized entry of the box and some banks in this state are quite uncooperative and will not permit a person claiming nomination as an executor, or any other person, to search for a will or to enter the box unless he or she is joint owner or unless the person seeking entrance has a court order requiring entry. The requirements usually are established in this state by bank rules although you will find that branch banks sometimes differ in their policies relating to entry of the box. I always make a practice of inquiring concerning the bank's policy before I go to the trouble of obtaining a court order for entry. On the other hand, if I think the will might be contested, I usually prefer to obtain the court order and have a deputy clerk of the court go to the bank with me and take the will back to the Probate Court. There have been cases in which a contestant alleged the will was altered between the time it was removed from the box and the time offered for probate. Of course there will be no contest of your father's will so I was not concerned with this problem.

EXECUTRIX: Gordon, I expect to qualify as executrix and I want you to advise me. I am very familiar with that will but, of course, I don't know anything about being an executrix. I have talked the matter over with Samuel and Evangeline and they are agreeable to anything I want to do. I need Preston to help me and, since he is a law student, he can be of real assistance while I am trying to keep up my work at the library. If it is all right with you, I would like him to come over with me tomorrow so we can talk about handling this estate. Fidelity National Bank is trustee of Myres' two trusts in his will, and I think we ought to talk to one of those trust officers also.

ATTORNEY: I will be glad to serve as your lawyer in this matter and will be especially delighted to talk to you and Preston tomorrow. Although we did not get that estate plan fully executed, you and Myres still got enough done so that the estate is not in any trouble. I agree that you ought to talk to the trust officer of Fidelity and I will arrange for an appointment. But I will expect to see you and Preston tomorrow morning at my office.

[The following day, Desdemona and Preston came to Armistead's office and the discussion continued.—]

ATTORNEY: Preston, you have not had a chance to read your father's will. Why don't you go over it while I dictate a few letters to Miss Underwood and then we can talk.

PRESTON: I did get a chance to read it last night, but I'll look over it again. It seems clear to me. Mother and I might discuss the will a bit.

[When Armistead completed his dictation this conversation followed]

PRESTON: Since I am just beginning the study of law, it seems to me that in helping to settle Dad's estate I can learn a lot that will help me in handling estates when I graduate. I hope that you will start at the beginning and explain to me everything that Mother should do.

ATTORNEY: I agree with you. Suppose we start in right now.

In the first place, when a person dies a liquidation must take place which resembles, broadly speaking, that which occurs when a corporation is dissolved. In all states in this country legal machinery has been established to accomplish this liquidation. While the detailed operation of such machinery differs among the states, the overall pattern is much the same. Assets must be collected and debts, including taxes, must be paid. Distribution must then be made of the remaining assets to those persons entitled to them under the will or, if there is no will, according to the intestate laws.

PRESTON: Excuse me, Mr. Armistead, but who performs these functions?

ATTORNEY: A person appointed by the appropriate court which exercises jurisdiction over such matters. In this state the court is called the "Probate Court". In other states it may be known as the Surrogate's Court, the Orphans' Court, or the Prerogative Court. In some states probate jurisdiction is exercised by courts having general trial jurisdiction.

The person appointed to perform the functions that I have mentioned is called a "personal representative". This personal representative is called the "administrator" or "administratrix" if the decedent dies intestate. On the other hand, if the decedent dies leaving a will which nominates a personal representative, and that person is appointed by the court, the personal representative is called the "executor" or "executrix". For instance, your father has named your mother as executrix in his will. She has no authority to act until she is appointed by the court and has qualified. Of course, she will not be appointed by the court until the validity of your father's will has been judicially determined. Our first step is to secure this determination.

PRESTON: Before we get too deeply into that, Mr. Armistead, who took title to the property that Dad owned at this death?

ATTORNEY: By the law of this state, the personal representative by virtue of his or her appointment, takes title to personal property owned by the decedent at this death. But title to freehold real estate passes directly to the heir or devisee, subject only to the widow's dower and the husband's curtesy. In a few states, by statute, title to freehold real estate passes to the personal representative.

You are probably wondering where title is until the personal representative is appointed. There is theoretical difficulty in this situation which the courts bypass by treating title as relating back from the time of the personal representative's appointment to the time of the decedent's death. But if a personal representative disposes of the decedent's property before his or her appointment by the court, this disposition is confirmed by the appointment only to the extent that it would have been proper had it been made thereafter. For this reason, persons are reticent to deal with personal representatives until the latter have been appointed and then only after seeing a certified copy of the court order.

In this state, and in most states, as I told you a moment ago, title to freehold real estate passes directly upon the death of the owner to the heir or devisee. Probate of the will is unnecessary to vest title in the devisee but, of course, is vital in order to prove the title. An adjudication of testacy or intestacy merely evidences title to freehold realty and does not vest the title, although it is often said that probate of the will relates back to the time of the testator's death. In those states in which title to freehold realty passes directly to the heirs or devisees, statutes give to the personal representative the power, upon petition and if the personal estate alone is insufficient to satisfy the claims of creditors, to have the land sold to the extent necessary to discharge the decedent's debts.

Now we must get back to the matter of probating the will. This is the first and vital step in winding up your father's estate.

I can best describe probate as the judicial determination, by an appropriate court, that the instrument produced before the court is the last will and testament of the deceased. The only issue on probate is will or no will. Determination of this issue is in the nature of a declaratory judgment and is of binding force not only upon the parties who have participated in the proceeding but also upon everyone else. The proceeding is *in rem* and is binding upon the world. A decree admitting a will to probate is not subject to collateral attack on the grounds of forgery, improper execution, lack of testamentary capacity, or revocation. These matters can be questioned only in direct proceedings by way of appeal or contest or in some other manner prescribed by statute. The reasons for this doctrine are apparent. In its absence, title to a decedent's estate would be uncertain and a vast amount of time and money might be expended before administration could be completed.

Of course, no court has jurisdiction to probate the will of a living person. Wills, as you know, are freely revocable until the death of the testator and, consequently, no instrument can be determined to be the last will of a person until after that person's death. Death is a jurisdictional prerequisite to probate. It is also a jurisdictional prerequisite to administration of an estate as that of an intestate. These observations seem trite until one considers the occasional Enoch Arden situation and the cases which may arise under the rare civil death statutes. These problems occur infrequently and I will not pause to discuss them.

PRESTON: I can understand that death should be a prerequisite for administration of a person's estate, but what court exercising probate jurisdiction has jurisdiction to admit a particular will to probate? For example suppose that Dad had died while on a visit to Washington, D. C. Should his will be probated in the District of Columbia?

ATTORNEY: In some cases the answer to that question can become rather complicated. You will have questions of this sort in your law school course in Conflict of Laws. Generally speaking, a court exercising probate jurisdiction in a particular state has jurisdiction to probate the will of a decedent who was domiciled within the territorial jurisdiction of the court at the time of his death. The same result will follow if the decedent left property at his death which then had its legal situs within the territorial jurisdiction of the court. Realty and tangible personalty have their legal situs where they are physically situated. A chose in action has its situs wherever the debtor can be served with process. Corporate stock is variously held to have its legal situs where the stock certificate is found, where the corporation is incorporated, or where the corporation does business.

From what I have said, you should be able to see that it makes no difference where the decedent died or where the will was made. Domicile or the situs of property control. The will, however, should first be probated in the jurisdiction where the decedent was domiciled at the time of this death. This is known as the "primary" or "domiciliary" jurisdiction. In fact, a few courts hold that the first probate of the will *must* be by the appropriate court of the decedent's domicile at his death. In most states, however, the absence of domiciliary probate is not an absolute bar to probate of the will for the first time in another jurisdiction so as to permit disposition of local assets.

PRESTON: Does that mean that a will may be probated in more than one jurisdiction?

ATTORNEY: Yes, it is frequently necessary to probate the will in two or more states. This is because the personal representative is in legal contemplation, the "hand of the court" which appointed her. Consequently, your mother has no powers as personal representative in any state other than that of her appointment, except to the extent that statutes in other states permit her to act. Absent such statutes, a personal representative loses her official capacity when she crosses the state line and does not regain it until she returns to the state of her appointment. It is therefore necessary, in the usual case, for a personal representative to be appointed in each state in which the assets of the decedent have their legal situs at his death. This means that the will must also be probated in each state before the personal representative is appointed because it is the will which effects the disposition of the decedent's property. Furthermore, you will remember that it is the probate of the will which proves the title of the devisee of real property who takes thereunder. Probate is a necessary link in the chain of title to real estate. Hence the will must be probated in each state in which the decedent owns real property at his death.

You will recall that the administration at the domicile of the decedent is called the "primary" or "domiciliary" administration. The administration in any other state is called "ancillary" administration. The person conducting the ancillary administration is called the "ancillary administrator", or "administratrix", even though the decedent left a will. "Ancillary executor" or "executrix" is a title unknown in our law.

PRESTON: What does an ancillary administratrix do?

ATTORNEY: It is her job to collect the local assets, pay the local creditors and then transfer the balance of the assets to the domiciliary personal representative for administration and distribution. The chief reason for requiring ancillary administration is to insure payment of the claims of local creditors without undue inconvenience to them. The domiciliary personal representative will usually be appointed ancillary administratrix if she applies for the appointment. A few states require that the personal representative be a resident of that state.

PRESTON: As I understand it then, Dad's will should be probated first before the Probate Court of Albercello County and then should be probated before the courts in the State of Monroe which have probate jurisdiction over the counties in which the summer cottage and the timber land are situated. I suppose that Mother should also apply to a Monrovia court for appointment as ancillary administratrix unless Monroe requires all personal representatives to be residents of the state.

ATTORNEY: That is correct except we would probate the will only once in Monroe. Probably we will probate in Yemassee County where the summer cottage is located and then record a copy of the probated will in the wills book in Baker County where the timber land is located. Now let's discuss what your mother must do to probate your father's will in Albercello County.

In this State wills may be probated in an inter-partes proceeding (solemn form) or in an ex-parte proceeding (common form). Both proceedings are initiated by the executrix, or any interested party, filing a written petition with the probate court. This petition contains a prayer that the will be probated and that a personal representative be appointed. The executrix named in the will is generally recommended in the petition as the proper person for appointment as personal representative. Some states permit the petition to be made orally.

In an inter-partes proceeding notice of hearing on the petition is given to all interested persons by publication. Statutes of some states require personal service on all interested persons who can be reached within the state but make notice by publication sufficient to those who are without the state and cannot be served with process. In an ex-parte proceeding notice by personal service or publication is unnecessary. Some states do not permit the latter form of probate. Where it is permitted, as in the State of Minor, objections to probate are generally made by a petition called a "caveat". In substance, this petition is to set the probate aside and revoke the appointment of the personal representative. In a few states the ex-parte proceeding may be had before the clerk of the probate court. When objections are properly taken to an ex-parte probate in this State, there is a hearing before the court with a jury as in the case of inter-partes proceedings. The advantage of ex-parte probate is that it permits the immediate appointment of the personal representative and thus dispenses, in many cases, with the necessity for appointment of a special administrator to deal with estate matters pending the appointment of the general personal representative. A special administrator is sometimes necessary when probate is by an inter-partes proceeding.

PRESTON: What allegations does the petition for probate contain?

ATTORNEY: In this State we use a printed form of petition for probate with blanks for inserting the following information: the name and residence of the decedent; the date and place of his death; the names and addresses of his heirs; the date of the will that we are asking the court to probate; the name of the executrix appointed in the will; the estimated value of the decedent's real and personal estate, each class of property being itemized separately; and the name of the person to be offered as surety on the executrix' bond, unless the will waives the requirement of a surety, in which event we state that fact.

PRESTON: I see. What does Mother do after the petition is made out?

ATTORNEY: Since we are sure that there will be no contest of your father's will, I think we should use the ex-parte form of probate. Assuming that we do use this form of probate, I will call the clerk of the Probate Court to determine when Judge Blake can hear the petition. We will then arrange to have the witnesses to the will, all of whom are easily available, meet us at the clerk's office shortly before the time set for hearing on the petition. It will not be necessary for your mother to make arrangements for a surety on her bond as executrix because your father has waived that requirement in his will. Your mother and I will meet the witnesses in the clerk's office at the appointed time. We will have with us the petition for probate and the will. We will file the petition with the clerk and then accompany him and the witnesses to the Judge's chambers, where we will inform the Judge of your father's death and prove the execution of the will by the attesting witnesses.

PRESTON: How do we prove the execution of the will?

ATTORNEY: Judge Blake will swear each of the attesting witnesses and, in response to questions by me, they will each testify that your father signed and acknowledged the writing in their presence as and for his last will and testament, they all being present at the same time and in the presence of each other as attesting witnesses. Each of the attesting witnesses will also testify that your father was of sound mind and disposing memory at the time he signed the will.

I will then move that the will be admitted to probate and that your mother be permitted to qualify as executrix. I am sure that Judge Blake will grant these motions and enter an order admitting the will to probate. The Judge will then require your mother to take the prescribed oath and sign her bond. This bond is conditioned upon the faithful performance of her duties as executrix. After she has signed the bond, which will be in a sum twice the estimated value of your father's personal estate, I will move on her behalf that three persons, whom we have agreed upon previously, be appointed to appraise your father's property. The Judge will then enter what is known as an order of "appointment" or "appraisement" directing these persons to conduct the appraisal. Of course, we will secure the consent of these persons to serve as appraisers before we move their appointment. They will be entitled to compensation for their services and your mother, in her capacity as executrix, will pay them from the assets of the estate.

EXECUTRIX: Let me ask a question at this point. Why do I need this appraisal? For the federal estate and state death tax returns that we discussed during the estate plan I am going to need professional appraisals, particularly for the land.

ATTORNEY: Des, this is one of those ancient institutions in our law that we have been trying to abandon for many years. That appraisal is required as the basis for determining the local probate tax. We could do without it and just collect the additional probate tax when federal estate death taxes values are established, but right now we cannot waive that appraisal in the will and we are one of the few states in which appraisers cannot be waived. The procedure is quite antiquated and a probate cost we could do without. The next step after the appointment of the appraisers is to have the clerk issue letters testamentary to you. This is a formal and detailed certificate of your appointment as executrix of Myres' will. You will need only one set of these letters because in this State the clerk will issue a much simpler and less expensive certificate. This form is known as a "certificate of qualification" or "clerk's certificate". I would not even ask for the formal certificate except that you have a power of sale over the land and a purchaser or title insurer might want the formal certificate exhibited if you do sell the land. We will secure a number of the "clerk's certificates" because it will be necessary for you to submit a certificate to each transfer agent when you arrange to have the stocks and bonds sold or when we distribute these to the trustee of Myres' trusts. The banks also are likely to require a display of the certificate and perhaps ask for a copy of it before they pay money to you as executrix or distribute it as you direct.

PRESTON: Excuse me, Mr. Armistead, but suppose Dad had died intestate?

ATTORNEY: Then we would have petitioned for an adjudication of intestacy and for your mother's appointment as administratrix of your father's estate. Otherwise, the procedure would be much the same as I have described, except that her formal certificate of authority would be called "letters of administration" rather than "letters testamentary" and it would be necessary to have a surety on her bond. Of course, there would be no attesting witnesses to be produced before Judge Blake. Your mother would simply testify under oath of your father's death, her diligent search for a will and her inability to find one.

Under our statutes your mother would have the first opportunity to serve as personal representative. The statutes prescribe the classes of persons entitled to appointment as administrator and indicate an order of preference based on kinship by consanguinity or affinity to the decedent. The surviving spouse is first in order of preference. If neither the spouse nor any other relative is interested in serving, or if neither is qualified to serve, our statutes provide that a creditor of the deceased may be appointed administrator.

EXECUTRIX: Preston is getting an excellent law lecture, but I think we had better get back to the things I am suppposed to do.

ATTORNEY: There are several things that must be done immediately after your qualification as executrix. I will first prepare in your name a notice to Myres' creditors of the fact of your appointment as executrix. This notice will call upon the creditors to present their claims to you. I will have this notice published once each week for six successive weeks in the Albercello Bugle, which, as you know, is the only paper of general circulation in this vicinity. Our statutes bar all claims not filed with a personal representative within a year after the date a notice to creditors is first published in a paper of general circulation in the vicinity of the court appointing the personal representative.

I should note at this point that, because the summer cottage and timber land is located in Monroe, we will have to probate the will there and petition that you be appointed ancillary administratrix. To the best of my knowledge the statutes of Monroe do not require a personal representative to be a resident of that state. We will advertise for creditors in Monroe and carry on the administration as in this State. I am sure that Myres owed no money to residents of Monroe, but we will have to go through the procedure in order to clear title to the property. The title would not be marketable otherwise. The ancillary administration should cause no difficulty. Now let's get back to the second step that you must take after your qualification as executrix.

Another thing that must be done is the preparation of an inventory of Myres' personal property. This inventory must be prepared by you, although I will have it typed up. The inventory must list each item of personal property owned by Myres at his death together with the estimated value of each item. Each stock certificate must be separately listed. A description of the real estate owned by Myres in this State and in the State of Monroe must be included. The best way to go about this is to take the summary we used for the estate plan, in which all the property is set forth in detail, and bring the property descriptions up to date. The land is listed for informational purposes and because you have a power of sale over it.

You and I will then meet with the appraisers appointed by Judge Blake, and I, being a notary public, will administer their oaths. They will examine the property and appraise it. The inventory and appraisement will then be filed by me in your name with the clerk of court. The clerk will see that the inventory and appraisement are recorded. The purpose of the inventory and appraisal is to serve as the basis upon which you, as executrix, make your accounts and furnish information concerning the estate to interested persons. However, the appraisal is conclusive upon no one. For example, the federal and state tax authorities are not bound by the appraisal.

This suggests the cause of the principal headache in administering the estate of a decedent. There is a great deal of tax work ahead for the estate, most of which I expect to do for you. There are some minor preliminaries. You will have to give the Internal Revenue Service and the Minor and Monroe Departments of Taxation notice of your fiduciary relationship. There are federal and state forms for this. The notice is given so tax correspondence concerning Myres' past income taxes and other tax matters can be directed to you. You will also want to obtain a taxpayer identification number for the estate and there is an appropriate federal form to obtain this.

I am sure you remember the important details of Myres' will but I will run over these again. The will contains a qualified terminable interest property marital deduction trust (QTIP trust) of which you are life beneficiary. You are to receive all of the income from this trust payable at least annually—and there is going to be a lot of income. There is also an exemption equivalent shelter trust which shelters the "unified credit" or "exemption equivalent". The trustee has power to sprinkle or "spray" the income from this trust to you and the children and the grandchildren as your or their needs for support and education indicate. The three children are remaindermen in equal shares in each trust. Your QTIP trust is in "the reduce to zero" form. Federal estate and state estate tax returns will have to be filed even though there will be no federal estate or state estate taxes payable. We estimated the amount of the gross estate during our estate planning meeting about two months ago as approximately $2,890,000. Since the gross estate exceeds the exemption equivalent at the date of death, the federal return must be filed. The laws of Minor and Monroe require a state return when the federal return must be filed. We would need to file a return in any event if the marital deduction is to be claimed and the state returns are important to clear up any possible questions concerning tax liens on the land.

The federal and state estate tax returns have to be filed within nine months following Myres' death. That gives you a good deal of time but the preparation of these returns should not be delayed until the last minute. Any tax would be payable when the return is filed. For the federal estate tax there is an alternate valuation date six months after Myres' death and we should wait and determine values then before we file a return.

EXECUTRIX: If I am not going to pay any federal or state death taxes in any event, why wait until the alternate valuation date?

ATTORNEY: If the property is then higher in value and you elected this date, there would be a higher basis in this property for capital gains purposes.

The major tax problems of the estate are likely to involve income taxes. You will be required to file a final income tax return for Myres and, as executrix, can elect to file this return jointly with yourself as spouse. I think you will do this because your personal income is lower than that which the estate will produce in its first tax year. This brings us to the fiduciary returns. The estate is a taxable entity and so are the two trusts that Myres established in his will. You will file fiduciary returns for the estate. Fidelity National Bank, as trustee, will file fiduciary returns for the trust. You, as executrix, for the estate, can elect a fiscal tax year for the estate. The trustee can elect a fiscal tax year for the trusts. If the appropriate fiduciary does not elect a fiscal year the return is made on a calendar year. Once you are on a particular system for the returns you remain on that system. The fiduciary also can elect to file for an initial tax year which is less than twelve months when the estate or trust has not been in existence for the whole tax year. When an estate is distributed, that ends its tax year. I feel sure you will decide to elect a fiscal year and I am certain the Fidelity bank will make this election for the trusts. I will give you some examples to show why this is important. Income received in an early part of an estate administration tends to exceed that received in a later part of the administration. Expenses, on the other hand, tend to fall later in the administration. While you must be alert for recurring and non-recurring items, you will find my statement substantially accurate. Thus it will be desirable for you to elect a short fiscal year initially, thus reducing the income taxable. But since the distributee of the income recognizes it as of the end of the tax year of the estate or trust, and the distribution of an estate ends its tax year, care must be taken not to distribute from the estate in the same year in which the fiscal year ends. Income can be bunched in the distributee if this occurs. We will want to activate those testamentary trusts early since they are separate taxpayers. Because you, as beneficiary of that QTIP trust, are going to receive a lot of income which we want to shelter initially as long as we can, your trustee should select a fiscal year which will end one month after the beginning of your calendar year. You, as executrix, should select a fiscal year which will end two months after the beginning of your calendar year. Myres, having died on 10 September 1982, you would select an initial fiscal year ending 28 February 1983. Both your QTIP trust and the exemption equivalent shelter trust will be activated before the end of that fiscal year—commencing 15 February 1983 and, for your QTIP trust, at least, the trustee will elect a fiscal year ending one month after the beginning of your calendar year, that is 31 January 1984. The income would not be exposed to tax on your income tax return as beneficiary of the trust until 15 April 1985. Both the estate and trust act as conduits. All the income is required to be payable to you at least annually and, when the income becomes distributable, you or the trustee deduct this on your fiduciary returns. This is going to require coordination with Fidelity National Bank as trustee of the trusts.

EXECUTRIX: I can see I am going to need a lot of help with this estate.

ATTORNEY: Making the right decisions at the right time is just as important in administration as it is in other situations.

EXECUTRIX: I can see that. Let's get back to this business of collecting the assets of the estate.

ATTORNEY: Your principal function as personal representative will be to collect and preserve the assets of Myres' estate, pay his creditors and those creditors who acquire claims against his estate after his death, and distribute the balance of the personal property according to the terms of his will.

It may be necessary for you to bring actions to recover debts owed to Myres. These actions will be brought in your name in courts of general jurisdiction. If the Marshall Laundry Company does not offer a satisfactory settlement in connection with his death, it will be necessary for you to bring an action as executrix under the Death by Wrongful Act Statute of this State. Any recovery under this statute will be your property and will not be assets of Myres' estate. Our Death by Wrongful Act Statute is fairly typical of those in most states. In some states, however, the recovery becomes part of the assets of the decedent's estate. To the best of my knowledge, Myres was not party to any litigation at the time of his death. If we discover that he was involved in litigation, it will be necessary for you to take appropriate steps to substitute yourself in his place.

I suggest you obtain a safe deposit box for the estate and place all of Myres' securities and other valuable papers in it. It may be that some of these securities will have to be sold to defray expenses of administration and those that are not sold will be distributed to Fidelity National Bank as trustee. When it is necessary for you to transfer any of these securities, transfer agents will probably require a death certificate, a certificate of qualification, an affidavit of domicile, an affidavit that debts have been paid or provided for and a duly certified copy of the will. The stocks will be endorsed in the name of the transferee and submitted to the transfer agents along with the other papers. Much the same procedure will have to be followed with respect to any corporate bonds not payable to bearer. Bearer bonds are freely transferable.

PRESTON: Well, what about the cash and bearer bonds we saw in Dad's safe deposit box? Does Mother take over these assets and inventory them as part of the estate or does Mother just go to the box and withdraw these assets as joint owner or change the box to her own name?

ATTORNEY: It will be necessary for us to look into the facts a bit more before we can answer this one. Under our law the mere deposit of property in a jointly leased or used safe deposit box works no change in title unless there is an express agreement that the contents of the box shall be joint property. There is certainly nothing in the bailment agreement for the box to indicate that all property in it was jointly owned. As we look into the facts we may find that the cash and bearer bonds belonged to your mother at the time they were placed in the box or that these assets were jointly owned property when deposited. If we find no indication that these assets did belong to your mother when deposited or that they actually were joint assets passing by survivorship, we will treat the assets as belonging to your father and will inventory them as part of the estate.

EXECUTRIX: Those bearer bonds were his if the ones you saw were the Prestige Nail Company bonds. I don't remember if Myres ever gave me any bearer bonds and he never said anything about cash in the box. You will have to figure out the ownership and I will agree with whatever you decide. I do get the money in the joint accounts, don't I?

ATTORNEY: There will be no problem about that. Those interests pass to you by survivorship, and while half of the interest in each account will be treated as belonging to Myres for the purpose of determining his gross estate, and will be counted in determining the marital deduction, the assets belong to you personally and are not administered by you as part of the estate. You need do nothing about those joint accounts unless you wish to request now that the respective banks change title to your name. They may ask for a copy of the certificate of death. You should also be able to withdraw the amount in the account Myres held in the Henry National Bank of Randolph City. I assume it still contains close to the $1,500 it had in it when we planned the estate. This deposit, any cash Myres had at his death, and income you receive during administration, until you pay the latter over to the trustee, should be deposited in an estate account which you will open. *All* estate funds that come into your hands should be deposited in this account and all disbursements from the estate should be made by checks signed by you and drawn upon it. Thus, if you have to sell some stock, you deposit the proceeds in this account, keeping a careful record of any expenses that were deducted by a broker from the proceeds of sale. Then when you pay an estate expense, you pay it from this account. Do not get any of these funds mixed up in your own account. Retain all the cancelled checks and other receipts and vouchers which you will receive in the course of administration of the estate because you will need these for your accounting. If you wish, I will keep the estate checkbook and maintain the records for you; but you will have to sign all of the checks. We can talk about this later; but the maintenance of careful records is absolutely essential.

EXECUTRIX: What do I do about the car?

ATTORNEY: Myres left this to you in the will. We will submit to the Division of Motor Vehicles a certified copy of Myres' will, a copy of your certificate of qualification, a copy of the order of distribution, and the registration card and certificate of title previously issued to Myres. A copy of Myres' death certificate will not be necessary. We will accompany these papers with an application for issuance of a new certificate of title to you. This application will show your name and address and will be signed by you as executrix.

EXECUTRIX: What do I do about the insurance policies? All of them were left by Myres naming me as beneficiary except for the policy payable to Jane. I can't imagine why he left that policy as it was when Jane has been dead all this time, especially after you told him he should change the beneficiary. Will I have to reopen Jane's estate—or what?

ATTORNEY: I don't know about Jane's policy. Perhaps Myres just forgot about it. You will not have to reopen Jane's estate. I will have to reread the policy; but, as I recall its terms, the proceeds are payable to Myres' estate when no alternate beneficiary is named. Thus you will collect the proceeds from the insurance company for deposit in the estate account. All of the policy amounts will be recovered from the insurance companies in the same way. You will submit the policy to the company that issued it, or to the Veterans Administration in the case of the VA life insurance. You will send with the policy a certificate of death. In the case of Jane's insurance, you should send one of her certificates of death which Myres should still have in Jane's estate file and should indicate your name and address as executrix of Myres' estate. With the policies payable to you, you will furnish your name and address. In each instance there should be a request for payment. Also you should obtain a form 712 from each insurer. This is a statement by the insurance company concerning the value of the insurance for death tax purposes. All of the insurance is includible in Myres' gross estate, although you will not administer the insurance proceeds payable to you personally as part of the estate assets, the proceeds of these policies belonging to you as beneficiary.

As to the Academic Trust contracts, we will send a copy of the certificate of death to the Trust. You will obtain a valuation of the annuities from the Trust for estate tax purposes. You will have to elect the form of settlement. As we discussed during our estate planning meeting, you will probably elect a lump sum settlement and, if you do, the amount is includible in the gross estate although it will be subject to the marital deduction. The annuity proceeds will belong to you and will not be administered as part of the estate.

EXECUTRIX: Now I think we had better talk about the land. What am I supposed to do about that?

ATTORNEY: The timber land was devised by Myres to Jefferson University to establish the chair for his father. In this state, title to land passes directly to the devisee. As a charitable devise, the value of the land is deductible for federal estate and state estate tax purposes. However, apart from including the amount in the federal estate tax return and in the state estate tax return for Monroe, you will have no duties with respect to this land. The title to Ramayana Farm and the lake front cottage passed to the Fidelity National Bank as trustee. However, you have a power of sale over this land which you will be able to exercise as executrix until the estate is settled and you obtain your discharge. The purpose of the power is to enable you to sell the land if you need funds to pay expenses of administration and to avoid our cumbersome process of marshalling or "calling in" the land to pay creditors if the estate turns out to have a large amount of claims based upon Myres' obligations or obligations of the estate which you develop during administration. There will be no death taxes which require a sale. There is no limit on your power as to the purpose of exercise, only upon its duration. If you decide to sell the farm or cottage or both during your administration you can do this and distribute the proceeds to the trustee. Possibly you will not exercise this power unless the estate turns out to have major claims against it. The trustee will retain the farm or cottage or both or sell them as you wish. I know you do not care to live on the farm and probably it will be best to sell it, but you should take a good deal of time to think about a sale. Myres wanted the lake front cottage kept for the use of the family but at the same time wanted to give you great flexibility in managing the estate and wanted the trustee to enjoy this same flexibility. That is why he did not attempt to "tie up" this property in the will. I should note also that you have dower in this land and if you elect not to take under the will can claim one-third of all of it in fee simple. We should talk further about the benefits you will receive under the will compared with the value to you of dower in the land and forced heirship in one-third of the personal property.

EXECUTRIX: I can tell you right now I am not going to elect against this will. Myres and I planned this estate together and the way Myres disposed of his estate is the way I prefer also. You are right about the farm. I will not exercise the power unless I need to do so to pay claims. Perhaps we ought to talk about the possible creditor claims now. You recall the note Myres endorsed for Ernest Achiever? That note does not mature for fifteen months. I think Achiever will pay the amount due but what should I do if he defaults?

ATTORNEY: That is a $10,000 note. I hope Achiever pays. In this State the holder of the note must present it to you within the time allowed creditors for filing claims. He must also petition the Probate Court to require you to retain assets out of the estate sufficient to pay the claim at maturity in the event Achiever does not pay. I assume the holder of the note will file his claim and petition. The practice with regard to these contingent claims varies from state to state. In some states the practice is to take refunding bonds from the distributees, obliging them to pay the creditor if the claim becomes absolute. In other states the creditor is not required to file his claim with the personal representative but is allowed to assert his claim against the distributees if the claim becomes absolute.

We also have the note with about $60,000 in principal remaining that is secured by a mortgage on Ramayana Farm. It will be desirable to leave that obligation on the farm if the interest rate is low enough and the obligation is assumable by a purchaser. I will check with Fidelity National. Since Fidelity is now trustee of the farm I am sure a satisfactory arrangement can be worked out. However, you must expect Fidelity to present its claim on the note. While it would not be precluded from foreclosing on the land even if it did not present the claim, it would be barred from recovering any deficiency in the foreclosure from the estate. There would not be a deficiency here but this is routine for Fidelity, its officers being quite cautious.

EXECUTRIX: What about the other debts?—What about the funeral expenses and administrative costs?

ATTORNEY: Well, Des, we not only know that Myres was solvent when he died, but also that he left a large net estate. Under these circumstances, I see no reason why you should not pay claims as they are filed with you, provided you are sure that they are valid claims. You should pay administrative costs as they fall due. By all means, pay the funeral expenses promptly.

If you doubt the validity of any claim, you had better talk the matter over with me. If, in fact, the claim is of doubtful legality and the creditor continues to assert it, then we will require the alleged creditor to bring an action against you to establish his claim judicially. I hope that you are aware that you are personally responsible if you overpay a claim or pay an alleged claim that is invalid. If we had any doubts concerning the solvency of Myres' estate, we would pay no claims of creditors until the time for filing claims had elapsed. Then we would get an order from the court directing payment. This would afford you protection; but, since Myres' estate is obviously solvent, I can see no reason for withholding payment.

We will ask creditors to file their claims in the form of an affidavit. You must pay all of these claims by checks drawn on your account as executrix. It will also be wise to require a receipt from each creditor as you pay. In your accounting you will then be able to submit the affidavits as evidence of the claims and the checks and receipts as evidence of their payment.

EXECUTRIX: I understand that. When do I pay your fee, Gordon?

ATTORNEY: The practice on that varies. Under some circumstances the attorney for the executrix asks that his fee be paid in installments in the course of administration. In this particular situation I suggest that you defer paying my fee until just before you make distribution of the estate.

That brings up the question of your fee. In this State an executrix is ordinarily entitled to a fee of five per cent of the value of the assets collected and distributed by her.

EXECUTRIX: I will not charge a fee. I would only be taking money from myself and from the children.

ATTORNEY: I understand how you feel. We won't put in a fee for you.

EXECUTRIX: You have been talking about distribution and my accounting. I'm not sure that I understand exactly what you have in mind.

ATTORNEY: In this State a personal representative is required to file an account within a year after the date of his qualification and annually thereafter until the estate is finally closed. This accounting takes place before the Probate Judge and the account itself is filed with the clerk of the Probate Court. In some states the account is presented to an official known as the "Commissioner of Accounts". This official not only passes upon accounts but also handles other routine matters of administration.

Your account will show in detail your receipts, disbursements and the balance on hand. Affidavits of claims, estate checks in payment of claims and other vouchers and receipts should be presented with the account. They will be returned to you after they have been examined by the Probate Judge. The final account will show the amount available to the testamentary donees. If Myres had died intestate, the final account would show instead the amount available for distribution to the distributees.

It is necessary for you to give notice to all interested persons in advance of the date on which you expect to make an accounting. This will enable interested persons to appear at the accounting and object to any parts of the account not previously approved by the court. After the hearing, the court will either approve the account in toto or surcharge you for items not allowed. I think there will be no disallowed items that you submit as part of your account. After the final account is approved, the Probate Judge will enter an order directing you to distribute the automobile to yourself and the balance of the personal estate to the trustee. In some states, but not in this one, the order also assigns the decedent's real property and thus serves as a muniment of title. In these jurisdictions the personal representative is usually required to record the order of distribution where deeds are recorded.

After you comply with the order of distribution and file receipts with the Probate Court from those to whom distribution has been made, the Probate Court will discharge you from any further obligation to administer the estate. In several states the final accounting does not precede the order of distribution. Where this practice is followed, a petition for distribution is filed and notice is given to all interested parties. A hearing is held if necessary. Upon the final accounting, receipts will be presented from the testamentary donees.

EXECUTRIX: I think Preston and I have a good picture of what I have to do. I know I can count on both of you and I am going to ask you, Gordon, to keep the estate check book and records for me and consider with me the things I do before I do them.

ATTORNEY: That is a good idea. There are many other points which you will pick up as we go through the administration. We will get down to work tomorrow, but now let's call it a day.

SECTION 3. THE UNIFORM PROBATE CODE

You will have observed in your reading of the dialogue between the Executrix, Preston and the Attorney in Section 2(2) that in most of the states when a person dies the administration of his estate is supervised by a probate court in what is conceived to be a single proceeding. The court has continuing jurisdiction. If the will creates a trust, the court often continues to have jurisdiction over the trust until it terminates.

This supervised administration embraces a number of really separate proceedings involving different parties: (1) a determination of the persons beneficially entitled to the estate after debts, expenses and taxes are paid (probate of the will if decedent had one, and determination of his heirs if he left no will); (2) appointment of a personal representative responsible for collection of the assets, management of the assets during administration, payment of claims, expenses and taxes, and ultimately distribution of the net estate; (3) acts of that personal representative in dealing with third parties (the business world) regarding the estate assets, such as sale or lease of property; (4) determination of the claims which should be paid out of the estate and payment accordingly; (5) an accounting by the personal representative at the end of his administration, to reveal his actions and determine whether he has faithfully discharged his responsibilities as a fiduciary managing the property of others; and finally (6) a transfer of formal title to the ultimate beneficiaries, the heirs or devisees (as determined in (1) above), usually accomplished by a formal decree of the court. Careful analysis should convince you that many of these tasks are not proper subjects for a judge but are really administrative in nature, at least if there is no disagreement among the interested persons. In a few states there are existing statutes providing for what is known as "independent administration," permitting the personal representative once appointed by the court to handle the estate without further court orders.

The Uniform Probate Code provides for a flexible system, allowing the parties interested in the estate to follow procedures best adapted to the needs of the particular estate. One procedure would be continuous supervised administration, as at present. The other procedures are premised on the theory that each of the elements of administration listed above can be handled separately and on either a formal (court hearing) or an informal (administrative) basis. Thus, a will can be probated formally, upon notice and hearing before the judge with a decree allowing or disallowing the will; or the will can be probated informally by filing a verified application and the will with an administrative officer of the probate court. If there is a family fight over the will, the parties would probably adopt the formal probate avenue and get the matter settled by the court. But if the family is in agreement, the will could be probated informally; the family would rely on a short statute of limitations to protect against presentation of another will or a claim that the probated will is invalid for any other reason. Similarly, appointment of the personal representative could be handled either formally or informally; usually it would be a routine matter for handling by the administrative officer rather than the judge in a formal hearing. Claims against the estate could be paid by the personal representative without court intervention or, if a dispute arose, the claim could be litigated by the court formally. The personal representative would under the Code have full power to deal with the property of the estate just as a trustee has, and matters such as sale of property would be taken to the court only if the parties are in disagreement. The accounting by the personal representative could be done formally, upon notice and hearing with a formal decree approving the account; or the personal representative could furnish a copy to each interested person and file with the administrative officer of the court and rely on a statute of limitations for protection. Finally, title transfer can be accomplished either by a formal court decree (after notice and hearing); or the personal representative can directly transfer the title by executing documents such as a deed to the distributee entitled to the property. The present law in most states requires fully supervised court administration of the simplest possible estate, such as one where the sole heir is the widow, who is also named executrix and sole beneficiary under the decedent's will, with no debts, and no possible issues requiring a court's attention. Such an estate could be handled by the widow entirely informally under the Code. On the other hand in other estates there may be problems at varying stages of the administration which may require a formal proceedings to adjudicate the matter; at any stage under the Code a party may invoke the court machinery to the extent needed. The route of informal administration would offer not only flexibility but also an opportunity to reduce both the time and cost of the process of transmitting wealth. These have long been targets for critics of the law in this area.

The Uniform Probate Code also contains articles dealing with protection of persons under disability and their property, certain types of nonprobate transfers (notably accounts in financial institutions in the names of several persons), and some aspects of trust administration. These will be noted later in the course.

As of November, 1981, the following states had adopted the Uniform Probate Code, with the effective date indicated for each and with what may be classified as relatively few changes or omissions:

Alaska	Jan. 1, 1973
Arizona	Jan. 1, 1974
Colorado	July 1, 1974
Idaho	July 1, 1972
Maine	Jan. 1, 1981
Minnesota	Aug. 1, 1975
Montana	July 1, 1975
Nebraska	Jan. 1, 1977
New Mexico	July 1, 1976
North Dakota	July 1, 1975
Utah	July 1, 1977

In addition to the above states New Jersey has enacted most of the substantive provisions of the Code by a series of laws enacted from 1971 through 1980. In a number of other states the Code has been partially adopted or has strongly influenced ongoing revision of probate statutes. As of mid-1981 these were Delaware, Florida, Hawaii, Maryland, Michigan, Missouri, Oregon (based on early drafts of the Uniform Probate Code), Pennsylvania and Wisconsin. The Code concept of unsupervised administration is the same as independent administration, which has been utilized for many years in New Jersey, Texas and Washington. It has recently been added as an option to existing probate procedures in Illinois, Michigan and Wisconsin. There is currently support for enactment of the Code in Arkansas, California, Ohio, Tennessee, Vermont and West Virginia; but opposition from groups interested in retaining existing laws makes enactment unpredictable. The Code was adopted in South Dakota in 1974 but repealed early in 1976 shortly after it became effective.

Most states which have adopted the Code have made some changes in substance and procedure which, though minor, nevertheless detract from the objective of uniformity.[3] Although statistical evidence as to operation of the Code in adopting states is still limited,

3. For a critical discussion of variations in the Codes of the adopting states, see Wellman, "The Uniform Probate Code: Article III Analyzed in Relation to Changes in the First Nine Enactments", 1975 Ariz.St.L.J. 477.

there is basis for concluding that the Code has reduced costs and shortened the period of administration.[4]

Courts in states which have not adopted the Uniform Probate Code are using the Code as influential authority in deciding cases on which there is no controlling local precedent.[5] In states which have adopted the Code, if a case presents an issue under prior law (as where decedent died before the effective date of the Code) with no controlling precedent, the courts are likely to be influenced by the legislative policy and decide the prior law to be in accord with the Code.[6]

4. Studies have been made for Idaho, the first state to adopt the Code and hence the state with the longest experience under the Code procedures. Crapo, "The Uniform Probate Code—Does It Really Work?", 1976 B.Y.U.L.Rev. 395; Kinsey, "A Contrast of Trends in Administrative Costs in Decedent's Estates In a Uniform Probate Code State (Idaho) and a Non-Uniform Probate Code State (North Dakota)", 50 N.Dak.L.Rev. 523 (1974).

5. First Church of Christ, Scientist v. Watson, 286 Ala. 270, 239 So.2d 194 (1970); Russell v. Estate of Russell, 216 Kan. 730, 534 P.2d 261 (1975).

6. See Valenzuela v. Anchonda, principal case in Ch. XII, Section 1(5)A.

Chapter III

INTESTATE SUCCESSION

Scope Note

This chapter deals with problems that may arise when a property owner dies without a will, leaves a will which is totally or partially ineffective to pass his property, or by his will directs that his property be distributed according to the intestate laws. The intestate laws of the American states are almost wholly statutory. Illustrative statutes are set forth in Section 1. The materials in Section 2 concern the common problems arising in a determination of the heirs and distributees and their proportionate interests when the share of the surviving spouse of the intestate is not involved. Section 3 deals with the share of the surviving spouse and a few of the factors conditioning the size of the share.[1] Section 4 deals with a variety of miscellaneous matters. Some of the rules considered in Section 4 are applicable not only to intestate but also to testate estates.

Today the bulk of a decedent's wealth may be transmitted to his family and others without becoming part of his "estate" (property subject to administration), by means of property arrangements or contractual provisions, e.g., property owned in joint tenancy with right of survivorship or life insurance payable on death of the insured to a named beneficiary. These "nonprobate" assets are outside the scope of the intestate succession laws and generally are not subject to testamentary disposition. Categorizing these arrangements as nontestamentary leaves us with the need to determine when other doctrines applicable to decedent's estates should apply; in a very real sense these are will substitutes. Interrelation of these assets with the normal estate will be considered in detail in Chapter XIII. However, such assets present problems throughout the course, as in this chapter in applying the doctrine of advancements and the right of a murderer to succeed to his victim's property.

---

1. Elections against a will by the surviving spouse are examined in Chapter IV, Section 2.

SECTION 1. STATUTES

Before looking at several intestate succession statutes, we should consider some of the criteria for such statutes. Certainly the most important criterion ought to be the preference of the average person for disposition of his or her estate. Unless there is a contrary public interest, that preference should be the basis for the pattern of intestate succession. The problem lies in how to determine that preference. A 1978 study sponsored by the American Bar Foundation based its conclusions on a survey of living persons and their preferences;[2] the findings were generally in accord with conclusions of earlier studies based on wills in decedent's estates in limited geographic areas. Some of the conclusions of the Bar Foundation Study are summarized here:

(1) Persons who die intestate do not do so because they rely on the local intestate succession laws; actually the majority of persons do not have accurate knowledge of existing laws.

(2) The surviving spouse should inherit the entire estate in preference to decedent's own children who are also children of the surviving spouse, or in preference to decedent's parents or brothers or sisters. The spouse was preferred regardless of the length of the marriage or the amount of wealth involved.

(3) If surviving children of the decedent are not also children of the surviving spouse, even there the surviving spouse should inherit up to 70% of the estate.

(4) If decedent is survived by parents and siblings (brothers and sisters), siblings should share with parents.

(5) Issue who are of the same generation, such as all grandchildren, should share equally, not by representation of their respective parent (per stirpes).

Because older, wealthier, more educated persons are likely to have a will, the intestate succession statute should be designed primarily to fit the younger person of moderate wealth, often married with minor children. Nevertheless, the American Bar Foundation study concluded that wealth had little to do with the public's preference.

Other factors which may affect the design of the intestate succession statute include: ease of administration, avoidance of division of property ownership into uneconomic shares, avoidance of inheritance by minors with the resulting legal complications and expenses (although the surviving parent would be guardian of the person of the minor child, the parent has no legal authority over the property inher-

2. Fellows, Simon and Rau, Public Attitudes About Property Distribution and Intestate Succession Laws in the United States, 1978 Amer. Bar Foundation Res. J. 319. See Beckstrom, "Sociobiology and Intestate Wealth Transfers", 76 Nw. U.L.Rev. 216 (1981) for a perceptive study of the use of sociobiological method in determining intestate succession goals.

ited by the child; hence a conservator, sometimes called a guardian of property, must be appointed by the court to manage the property) and protection of minors in appropriate cases (particularly where the decedent's children are not children of the surviving spouse who therefore has no duty to support them out of his or her inheritance). Some commentators suggest that merit and need should be factors, e. g., a disabled child or a needy parent should receive a larger share. To accommodate such a criterion would of course require discretionary power in the probate court; fairness competes with ease of administration. Should such factors be embodied in the succession laws or left to the owner of property to embody in a properly executed will, or to the surviving members of the family to provide for by agreement?

How do the following statutes and those of your jurisdiction meet the criteria?

CODE OF ALABAMA § 43–3–1[3]

Course of descents generally

The real estate of persons dying intestate, as to such estate descends, subject to the payment of debts and charges against the estate as follows:

(1) Subject to the widow's dower, to the children of the intestate, or their descendants, in equal parts.

(2) If there are no children or their descendants, then the whole to the husband or wife of the intestate.

(3) If there are no children or their descendants, and no husband or wife, then to the father and mother, in equal parts.

(4) If there are no children or their descendants, no husband or wife, and if there be but one surviving parent, then one half to such surviving parent, and the other half to the brothers and sisters of the intestate, or their descendants, in equal parts.

(5) If there are no children or their descendants, no husband or wife, no brothers or sisters or their descendants, and if there be but one surviving parent, then the whole to such surviving parent.

(6) If there are no children or their descendants, no husband or wife, and no father or mother, then to the brothers and sisters of the intestate, or their descendants, in equal parts.

(7) If there are no children or their descendants, no husband or wife, no father or mother, and no brothers or sisters or their descendants, then to the next of kin to the intestate, in equal degree, in equal parts.

3. Alabama is one of the few states which still differentiates between descent of land and distribution of personal property, with separate sections for each. In recent years most states have either adopted the Uniform Probate Code or modernized the statutory framework. Many of the early state statutes were patterned on the English Statute of Distribution, 22 & 23 Chas. II, c. 10 (1670).

(8) If there are no children or their descendants, no husband or wife, no father or mother, no brothers or sisters or their descendants, and no next of kin to the intestate, then to the next of kin of the intestate's predeceased spouse in the same order of priority as provided for descent to the kin of the intestate.

(9) If there are no children or their descendants, no husband or wife, no father or mother, no brothers or sisters or their descendants, and no kin capable of inheriting, then it escheats to the state.

CODE OF ALABAMA § 43-3-10

Distribution of personal estate

The personal estate of persons dying intestate as to such estate, after the payment of debts and charges against the estate, is to be distributed in the same manner as his real estate, and according to the same rules; except, that the widow, if there are no children, is entitled to all the personal estate, or, if but one child, she is entitled to one half; if more than one, and not more than four children, to a child's part; and if more than four children, to one fifth.

UNIFORM PROBATE CODE [4]

"Section 2-101. [Intestate Estate.] Any part of the estate of a decedent not effectively disposed of by his will passes to his heirs as prescribed in the following sections of this Code." [5]

"Section 2-102. [Share of the Spouse.] The intestate share of the surviving spouse is:

"(1) if there is no surviving issue or parent of the decedent, the entire intestate estate;

"(2) if there is no surviving issue but the decedent is survived by a parent or parents, the first [$50,000], plus one-half of the balance of the intestate estate;

4. The Uniform Probate Code intestate succession scheme has been criticized, principally on grounds of its inflexibility, in Gaubatz, "Notes Toward a Truly Modern Wills Act," 31 U. of Miami L.Rev. 497 (1977) at 547, and Thorson & Samuelson, "A Comparison of Iowans' Dispositive Preferences with Selected Provisions of the Iowa and Uniform Probate Codes," 63 Iowa L.Rev. 1041 (1978) at 1120. The Gaubatz article raises challenging issues related to matters in this and the next two chapters. For a brief summary of the Uniform Probate Code provisions considered in this chapter, see Jones and Wellman, "Intestate Succession Under the Uniform Probate Code," 23 Prac. Lawyer Nos. 3, 23 (1977).

5. The Uniform Probate Code contains a single table for descent and distribution. This accords with preferred modern practice. See N.C.Gen.Stat. §§ 29-1 to 29-30 with comments in McCall, "North Carolina's New Intestate Succession Act", 39 N.C.L.Rev. 1 (1960); Note, "Intestate Succession—Recent Statutory Changes", 40 N.C.L.Rev. 297 (1962). The North Carolina statute adopts a single table for descent and distribution, eliminates the ancestral property and half-blood rules, provides a partial limitation upon succession among collaterals, abolishes the estate of dower and curtesy, makes the surviving spouse a primary statutory heir and accomplishes other desirable changes.

"(3) if there are surviving issue all of whom are issue of the surviving spouse also, the first [$50,000], plus one-half of the balance of the intestate estate;

"(4) if there are surviving issue one or more of whom are not issue of the surviving spouse, one-half of the intestate estate."[6]

"Section 2–103. [Share of Heirs Other Than Surviving Spouse.] The part of the intestate estate not passing to the surviving spouse under Section 2–102, or the entire intestate estate if there is no surviving spouse, passes as follows:

"(1) to the issue of the decedent; if they are all of the same degree of kinship to the decedent they take equally, but if of unequal degree, then those of more remote degree take by representation;

"(2) if there is no surviving issue, to his parent or parents equally;

"(3) if there is no surviving issue or parent, to the issue of parents or either of them by representation;

"(4) if there is no surviving issue, parent or issue of a parent, but the decedent is survived by one or more grandparents or issue of grandparents, half of the estate passes to the paternal grandparents if both survive, or to the surviving paternal grandparent, or to the issue of the paternal grandparents if both are deceased, the issue taking equally if they are all of the same degree of kinship to the decedent, but if of unequal degree those of more remote degree take by representation; and the other half passes to the maternal relatives in the same manner; but if there be no surviving grandparent or issue of grandparent on either the paternal or the maternal side, the entire estate passes to the relatives on the other side in the same manner as the half."[7]

6. An alternative for the spouse's share in a community property jurisdiction is stated in Section 2–102A:

"The intestate share of the surviving spouse is as follows:

"(1) as to separate property

(i) if there is no surviving issue or parent of the decedent, the entire intestate estate;

(ii) if there is no surviving issue but the decedent is survived by a parent or parents, the first [$50,000], plus one-half of the balance of the intestate estate;

(iii) if there are surviving issue all of whom are issue of the surviving spouse also, the first [$50,000], plus one-half of the balance of the intestate estate;

(iv) if there are surviving issue one or more of whom are not issue of the surviving spouse, one-half of the intestate estate.

"(2) as to community property

(i) The one-half of community property which belongs to the decedent passes to the [surviving spouse]."

The provisions for the surviving spouse in the Uniform Probate Code will often permit a substantial Federal Estate Tax marital deduction to be taken in an intestate estate subject to the tax and thus eliminate partially the serious tax consequences now encountered in larger estates when an intestate is survived by a wife and children. Often the wife will take by intestacy not more than one-third of the estate and the marital deduction can thus be claimed only for this one third. The "second tax" problem cannot be avoided by intestate statutes, this requiring a will. These tax matters are discussed in greater detail in Chapter VIII, Section 2.

7. Collateral relatives who can inherit under Section 2–103 are limited to de-

SECTION 2. LINEALS AND COLLATERALS

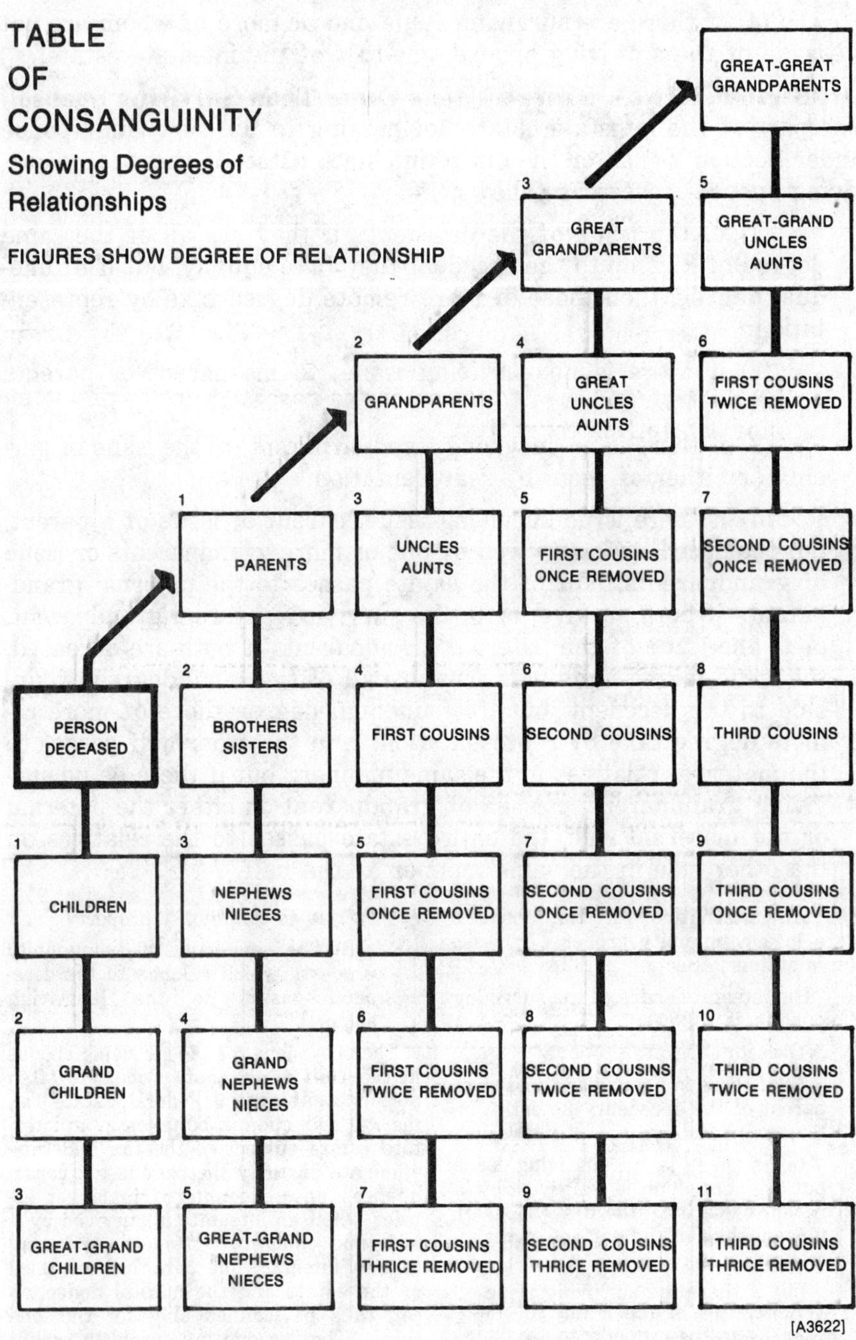

scendants of grandparents of the decedent. This arrangement reflects a modern tendency to exclude remote collaterals from inheritance. This exclusion reduces the expense in locating remote heirs and perhaps eliminates some will contests. For the exclusion of remote relatives under other intestate laws, see Draper v. Draper in Section 2 of this Chapter. The requirement of an interest to contest a will is considered in Chapter VII, Section 1(3).

DRAPER v. DRAPER

Supreme Court of Tennessee, 1939.
174 Tenn. 394, 126 S.W.2d 307.

Edw. J. Smith, Special Justice. R. L. Draper died intestate on February 18, 1935, leaving a considerable estate of real and personal property.

The question presented for decision is whether Smith Cunningham and J. B. Cunningham, surviving uncles of the intestate, take his personal property to the exclusion of the children and grandchildren of seven uncles and aunts, who predeceased him.

From a decree sustaining a demurrer and holding that the surviving uncles are the sole distributees of the personal estate of the intestate, the children and grandchildren of the deceased uncles and aunts have appealed to this court.

Code, Section 8389(6), provides: "If no brother or sister, or their children, to every of the next of kin of the intestate who are in equal degree, equally."

Section 8390 provides: "There is no representation among collaterals, after brothers' and sisters' children."

That the phrase, "the next of kin," in the statute of distribution, is there used in its strict legal sense, and means next in blood, is manifest from the context, and from the provision that the distribution shall be made among persons "who are in equal degree, equally." The words, "who are in equal degree," signify those persons who stand in the same nearness of blood relationship to the intestate. Helms v. Elliott, 89 Tenn. 446, 5 Pickle, 446, 451, 14 S.W. 930, 10 L.R.A. 535; Spofford v. Rose, 145 Tenn. 583, 593, 237 S.W. 68.

Who are the next of kin of an intestate in the distribution of personal property is determined by the rule of the civil law, and in the collateral line the computation is from the intestate up to the common ancestor of the intestate, and the person whose relationship is sought and then down to that person. Kyle v. Moore, 35 Tenn. 183, 3 Sneed, 183, 184.

According to that rule, the intestate, and his uncle, are related in the third degree, and the intestate and children and grandchildren of deceased uncles and aunts are related in the fourth and fifth degree, respectively. * * *

Section 2–105 of the Uniform Probate Code escheats the property to the state if there is no taker under Sections 2–102 and 2–103. In Section 2–104 there is a requirement that a taker under the intestate law must survive the decedent by 120 hours. If it cannot be determined whether or not the person survived the intestate for this time, the person will be presumed to predecease the intestate. Section 2–104 is not applied if it would cause the property to escheat. The survivorship problem as presented in wills is dealt with in Chapter XV, Section 2.

In Penniman v. Francisco, 48 Tenn. 511, 1 Heisk 511, it was held that a grandniece does not take any share in the distribution of an intestate where there are brothers and sisters, nephews and nieces.

In so holding, Chief Justice Nicholson said:

> "The decree as to the distribution of the personal estate of Jacob Burris, deceased, was erroneous. Nancy Smith, being the grandniece of Jacob Burris, could not, under the existing state of facts, be a distributee of his personal estate. By section 2430 of the Code, 'there is no representation among collaterals, after brothers' and sisters' children.'"

By the English statute of distribution (22 and 23 Charles II) it was provided that if there be no children, or their representatives, one moiety of the personal estate of the intestate should go to the widow, and that the residue should be distributed equally among the next of kin, who are in equal degree, and those who represent them; but that no representation should be admitted among collaterals, after brothers' and sisters' children.

While the statute was in force, the English courts uniformly construed the provision which declared that there should be no representation among collaterals after brothers' and sisters' children as meaning the children of brothers and sisters of the intestate. If, therefore, the intestate died without issue, and left surviving him an aunt and children of uncles and aunts, the aunt succeeded to the whole estate. Bowers v. Littlewood, 1 P.Wms. 593, 24 English Reports Reprint 531. * * *

As the chancellor correctly construed the applicable sections of the Code, the decree is affirmed at the costs of the appellant.

NOTE

The three methods for computing kinship among collaterals were discussed in Chapter I.[8] Most of the American states have adopted the "civil law" method of computation used in the principal case.[9] Others have adopted a variety of the "parentelic" method[10] or use the "common" or "canon" law system.[11] The problem of computation arises only when there is no claimant within a class specifically provided for in the intestate law and the property must pass to "the next of kin" of the intestate. The method of computation may be modified by the system of representation since a descendant of a deceased collateral (usually a brother or sister of the intestate) may be permitted to take even though he is not the nearest surviving collateral in degree of relationship to the intestate.

Absent any heirs or next of kin capable of taking the intestate's property, title vests in the state or a sub-division or agency thereof.[12] The intestate

8. See Chapter I, Section 3(1)A, fn. 24.

9. The civil law method has been adopted when no method for computation is set forth by statute. E.g., Thomas v. Marriott, 154 Md. 107, 140 A. 91 (1928).

10. See, White, "Ohio's 'Half and Half' Inheritance Statute", 15 U.Cin.L. Rev. 401 (1941).

11. Ga.Code Ann. § 113–903.

12. E.g., N.C.Gen.Stat. § 29–12; § 116A–2 (escheat to a state Escheat Fund); income of fund to go to the State Education Assistance Authority for loans to worthy and needy resident students enrolled in public institutions of higher education. Id., § 116A–9.)

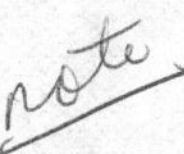

laws are liberal in allowing distant relatives of the intestate to take his property, although representation is sometimes limited to children of brothers or sisters of the intestate[13] and next of kin beyond a specified degree of relationship may be excluded.[14]

The Uniform Probate Code limits succession to descendants of grandparents of the intestate but within this line of descendants establishes no limitation by degree. A relative who traced only through a great grandparent would not be an heir or distributee.[15]

MAUD v. CATHERWOOD

District Court of Appeal, 1st Dist., Div. 1, California, 1945.
67 Cal.App.2d 636, 155 P.2d 111[16]

WARD, JUSTICE. This is an appeal from an interlocutory decree in an action for the partition of real property situated in several counties. An agreed statement constitutes the record on appeal.

The parties appearing in the trial court consisted of plaintiff, Louise C. Maud, a grandchild, and named as defendants, certain grandchildren, the trustees for certain other grandchildren, and two great-grandchildren, descendants of S. Clinton Hastings, deceased, who at one time was Chief Justice of the Supreme Court of Iowa[17] * * *.

In 1874 Judge Hastings set up a trust inter vivos of certain real property for the benefit of himself, his wife Azalea, and their seven children. He provided for the termination of the trust upon the death of the last survivor of the beneficiaries. The last survivor was his daughter Ella, who died about sixty-eight years later. The following clause of the trust indenture then became operative: "Upon the death of the last survivor of all the above enumerated beneficiaries, to wit: the party of the first part, Azalea Hastings, his wife, Marshall, Clara L., Charles F. D., Robert Paul, Flora, Ella, and Lillie, the trust herein expressed shall cease, and all the estate, both real and personal, then in the hands of the Trustee, shall be distributed, partitioned and conveyed to the then living lineal descendants of the party of the first part in fee, each of said descendants taking such parts or portions as they would respectively have been entitled to as heirs at law of the party of the first part had he himself been the last survivor of the said beneficiaries last above enumerated."

Four of Judge Hastings' nine grandchildren and two of his great-grandchildren survived Ella. They are Joseph Fiske Catherwood,

13. The English Statute of Distribution, 1670, did not admit representatives among collaterals after children of brothers and sisters of the intestate, and this provision is found in a number of American statutes. E.g. McKinney's N.Y., EPTL, § 4–1.1.

14. N.C.Gen.Stat. § 29–7 (fifth degree by civil law method, but if no collateral relative within this degree, then collateral succession is unlimited to prevent escheat); Kan.Stat.Ann. § 59–509 (sixth degree by civil law method).

15. Uniform Probate Code, § 2–103, set forth as display statute in Section 1, supra.

16. Noted, 33 Cal.L.Rev. 324 (1945).

17. S. Clinton Hastings was also the first Chief Justice of the Supreme Court of California and the founder of Hastings College of the Law.

great-grandchild, only son of Charles C. Catherwood, deceased, one of the three children born to Clara L. Hastings Catherwood; Louise C. Maud, the only surviving child of Clara L. Hastings Catherwood; Jan Casimir Lewenhaupt, great-grandchild, the only child of Azalea Lewenhaupt, the only child of Flora Hastings Keyes; Ethel H. Crane, grandchild, the only surviving child of three born to Charles F. D. Hastings; Harry C. Hastings and Elizabeth Parker Hastings, grandchildren, the children of Robert Paul Hastings. The attached chart will serve as a convenience.* Thereon the names of the grandchildren are underlined twice; the great-grandchildren thrice.

The trial court divided the estate into four parts and determined the interest of each grandchild and each great-grandchild by representation, so that Louise C. Maud, Joseph Fiske Catherwood, Harry C. Hastings and Elizabeth Parker Hastings or their individual trustee were each decreed an eighth interest and Jan Casimir Lewenhaupt and Ethel H. Crane were each decreed a fourth interest. The plaintiff and all of the defendants, with the exception of Ethel H. Crane and Jan Casimir Lewenhaupt, appear herein as appellants.

The question presented is at what generation the estate should be divided. Appellants contend that it should be divided into six parts; that is, at the level of grandchildren rather than at the level of children, and that the two great-grandchildren should take the shares of their parents by right of representation. Under this method the grandchildren and the great-grandchildren would each receive a like amount, namely, one-sixth.

The question must be determined in accordance with the provisions of the trust instrument, and application of Probate Code, §§ 222 and 250.

The pertinent provision of the trust instrument—the last clause thereof—provides that upon the death of the last beneficiary the trust shall cease and the estate be distributed to the then living lineal descendants of the trustor in such portions as they would respectively have been entitled to "as heirs at law" had the trustor been the last survivor. * * * [The appellants argued that the trustor intended that his grandchildren should take *per capita* since the last clause of the trust indenture excluded any child of the trustor from participating in the trust estate at the time the trust terminated. The court construed the trust indenture as a whole and rejected this argument, holding that the trustor intended his descendants other than children to take by representation unless the statutes in force at the time the trust terminated provided otherwise.] * * *

The statutes directly controlling are Probate Code, §§ 222 and 250, which provide respectively: "If the decedent leaves no surviving spouse, but leaves issue, the whole estate goes to such issue; and if all of the descendants are in the same degree of kindred to the decedent they share equally, otherwise they take by right of representation." "Inheritance or succession 'by right of representation' takes

* [At page 97—ed.]

place when the descendants of a deceased person take the same share or right in the estate of another that such deceased person would have taken as an heir if living. A posthumous child is considered as

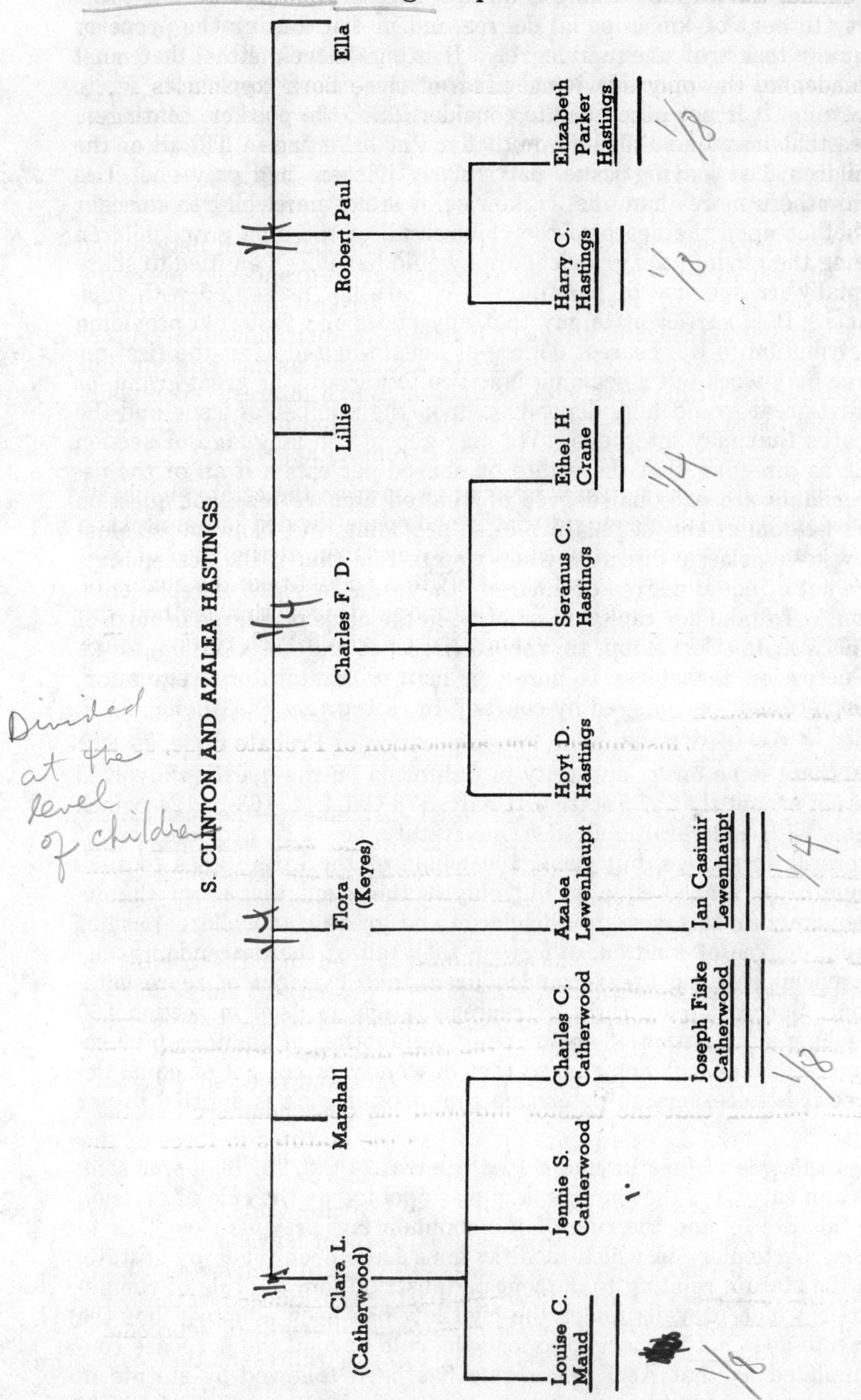

living at the death of the parent." We will first consider appellants' contention that under the above Probate Code sections the grandchildren take per capita. There is quite a difference in distributing property to next of kin in equal degree and in distributing the property equally to kin of unequal degree. It is the latter method that must be adopted as applicable to the facts of this case if appellants are to prevail. It is not necessary to consider all of the possible contingencies that may be suggested or that might have arisen had all of the children died leaving issue, particularly if some had only one child and others more than one. Likewise, it is not necessary to consider whether upon the death of the children all of the nine grandchildren being then living, the grandchildren would have been entitled to share equally irrespective of parentage. We are not presented with such facts. It is sufficient to say that any strict and fast rule providing distribution to the nearest degree of lineal kindred after the first degree may work out a seeming injustice to a grand, or great-grand, or great-great grandchild, depending upon the number of issue and the deaths that may intervene. We may accept the language of section 222 as directing that the estate be shared per capita if all of the descendants are of equal degree of kindred and we may not question the wisdom of the Legislature in so providing, but likewise we must bow to legislative direction when we are told that if the descendants are not of equal degree of kindred "they take by right of representation." To take per capita all must be in the class or degree of next of kin. Am.Jur.Cum.Supp. to Vol. 16 (Descent and Distribution), § 42. "Succession to estates is purely a matter of statutory regulation, which cannot be changed by courts." In re Ingram, 78 Cal. 586, 21 P. 435, 12 Am.St.Rep. 80.

There is no direct authority in California on the question involved herein except that of Estate of Healy, 176 Cal. 244, 168 P. 124, which deals with collateral kindred. Our statute, sec. 222, provides that if there is no spouse, but issue, the whole of the estate goes to such issue to be shared equally, but only in the event that all of the descendants (in this case grandchildren and great-grandchildren) are of equal degree of kindred, otherwise they (all of the descendants, the grandchildren and great-grandchildren) take by right of representation. Succession by right of representation as used in section 250 means a substitution of one or more for another in uninterrupted sequence. Once it is determined that descendants are not of equal degree it is necessary to determine the amount each is entitled to per stirpes.

In People v. Jose Ramon De La Guerra, 24 Cal. 73, 76, it was said: "At an early day the common law was adopted as the rule of decision in this State; and the rule of the common law prevails except as to those particulars in which modifications have been made by statute. In the statute relating to descent and distribution, the rule of computation which prevails under the civil law has been adopted; but the statute does not purport to extend the rule beyond the purposes contemplated by that Act." This rule has been followed by statute in this state. Probate Code, § 252, is specific in presenting a rule to determine the degree of relationship between parent, child and grandchild. It was not contemplated that heirs might hurdle or eliminate a degree for the purpose of obtaining a larger share of an estate. To take per capita all lineal relations should be in the class or degree of next of kin. Per stirpes means taking the share of an immediate ancestor, who in turn takes the share of his next immediate ancestor and so on until a common ancestor is reached. The theory of permitting descendants of the next of kin to inherit is to give such descendants the part which such next of kin would have received if living. If there is more than one descendant the interest of the next of kin's interest is divided among those descendants in appropriate fractional parts. Next of kin has reference to next of kin to the decedent, not to an ancestor or descendant of a decedent. In re Pearsons' Estate, 110 Cal. 524, 42 P. 960; Estate of Way, 29 Cal.App.2d 669, 85 P.2d 563. Let us assume that Ethel Crane, a grandchild of Hastings, should die intestate and without husband or issue. Joseph Fiske Catherwood and Jan Casimir Lewenhaupt are kindred in equal degree to Mrs. Crane but other heirs are not, hence all would take per stirpes and would trace the relationship back to the common root. Upon the death of Ella, a child of Hastings, could it be said that the heirs would take other than as the Judge decreed, by going to the family root and designating each interest in accordance with degree of kindred?

* * *

Referring to the manner in which descendants may share in an estate, section 222 uses the word "they." When read in conjunction with the provisions of section 250, namely, "such deceased person (such child) would have taken as an heir if living," it requires that we start with a child of Judge Hastings. The grammatical propriety of this construction is admitted in the case of Balch v. Stone, 149 Mass. 39, 20 N.E. 322, mainly relied upon by appellants.

California in some statutes provides for equality among next of kin, and in others equality is ignored and relatives by blood or marriage only take by right of representation. The provisions for per capita distribution where the heirs are designated as next of kin appear in Probate Court, §§ 221, 222, 226, and 227. In the above enumerated sections, 226 provides that those who claim through the nearest ancestor must be preferred to those who claim through a remote ancestor. The other sections dealing with a surviving spouse with issue, § 221, and a minor unmarried decedent, § 227, provide that the heirs of the same degree share equally "otherwise they take by right of representation," which is the exact language used in section 222. Where no reference is made to taking per capita, as in the cases of surviving spouse with no issue, § 223, or no surviving spouse nor issue, § 225, or neither issue nor spouse, and the estate is community property, § 228, or under the same conditions and the property is the separate property of the deceased spouse, § 229, no mention is made of those in the same degree of kindred, but the rule of representation is adopted. Under the statutory provisions in this

equality

state, there is no strict rule of equality governing the right of succession to property of a deceased, but where equality is provided for it is limited to all heirs in the same degree of kindred to decedent.

* * *

It appears to have been impossible to devise a statute which would provide for every contingency satisfactorily to the distributees of an estate. Where there is a provision for succession by right of representation, the equality rule has no effect in the application of the statute. It may be conceded that circumstances in the birth or death of the children or grandchildren resulting in all succeeding equally, irrespective of whether the succession should be per capita or per stirpes, could have existed, but that condition did not prevail herein at the time of the death of Ella. One great-grandchild, Joseph Fiske Catherwood, was the son of grandchild Charles C. Catherwood, one of the three children of a child, Clara L. Hastings Catherwood, whereas Jan Casimir Lewenhaupt is the child of Azalea Lewenhaupt, the daughter of Flora Hastings Keyes. Each of the two great-grandchildren is a descendant in a direct line from ancestor S. Clinton Hastings, each is of equal degree of kindred to the common ancestor but not entitled to the same distributive portion for the simple reason that, as shown by the charge in the "agreed statement," Jan, at the time of distribution, is the only child of an only child of a child of Hastings. On the other hand, in the case of Joseph Catherwood, the grandmother, Clara (child of Judge Hastings), left three children: Jennie, deceased without issue; Charles C., with issue (Joseph); and the plaintiff in this case, Louise C. Maud, the aunt of Joseph, who must share with Joseph as the heir of her deceased brother Charles C. the portion represented by Clara. Descendants may be of equal degree as blood relatives, but not on an equality of inheritance when taking by right of representation.

The direct line of lineal consanguinity which connects and determines ascending or descending relationship is measured by generation or degree from the common ancestor. "Thus, the child is, with regard to the parent, in the first [degree]; the grandchild, with regard to the grandparent, in the second [degree]; and vice versa as to the parent and grandparent with regard to their respective children and grandchildren." Probate Code, § 252. If the relationship arises through collateral consanguinity the degree likewise is established by counting the degree from the common ancestor. Section 253.

* * *

Finally, appellants urge that sections 222 and 250 should be construed to make the provision "fair." Undoubtedly appellants mean fair as applied to their view of the facts and the law of this case. If there is unfairness in the rule, we are reminded that "Succession to estates is purely a matter of statutory regulation, which cannot be changed by courts." Estate of Nigro, 172 Cal. 474, 156 P. 1019, 1020.

Death and birth in varying numbers may change the amount of the share to which a relative may succeed to an estate. In view of the possibility of a seeming unfairness, under any rule there should be less claim of injustice if there is followed the requirement that the right of inheritance of a representative descendant should be fixed by reference to the first generation common to each as the criterion to determine the degree of relationship of subsequent relatives in the descending line.

The right to succeed to an interest in an estate of a deceased is not a natural right but one bestowed by law and accordingly subject to statutory authority. Estate of Perkins, 21 Cal.2d 561, 134 P.2d 231. It appears that Judge Hastings adopted the California probate statutes which means that he directed that the trust should be distributed according to the statutes in force at the termination of the trust.

The trust indenture and the statutes in force covering the facts in this case require that the interlocutory decree entered on December 20, 1943, be affirmed. That is the order.

PETERS, P. J., and KNIGHT, J., concur.

NOTE

Uniform Probate Code Section 2–106 provides:

> "If representation is called for by this Code, the estate is divided into as many shares as there are surviving heirs in the nearest degree of kinship and deceased persons in the same degree who left issue who survive the decedent, each surviving heir in the nearest degree receiving one share and the share of each deceased person in the same degree being divided among his issue in the same manner."

Although the Code does not define "degree of kinship," obviously the civil law system embodied in the Table of Consanguinity, supra, applies. How would the estate in Maud v. Catherwood have been distributed under this statute?

The Code's system for representation has been criticized[18] and in 1975 the Joint Editorial Board gave serious consideration to a change. Without full approval, the changes are nevertheless described in the 1975 Code Comment. The changes would consist in altering Sections 2–103(1), (3) and (4) by replacing the wording on representation with the words "to be distributed per capita at each generation as defined in Section 2–106"; the latter would be reworded to read:

> "If per capita at each generation is called for by this Code, the estate is divided into as many shares as there are surviving heirs in the nearest degree of kinship which contains any surviving heirs and deceased persons in the same degree who left issue who survive the decedent. Each surviving heir in the nearest degree which contains any surviving heir is allocated one share and the remainder of the estate is divided in the same manner as if the heirs already allocated a share and their issue had predeceased the decedent."

18. Waggoner, "A Proposed Alternative to the Uniform Probate Code's System for Intestate Distribution Among Descendants," 66 Nw.U.L.Rev. 626 (1971). The American Bar Foundation study cited in fn. 2 supports the Waggoner proposal of "per capita at each generation."

Assume the following family situation, deceased persons being indicated in brackets;

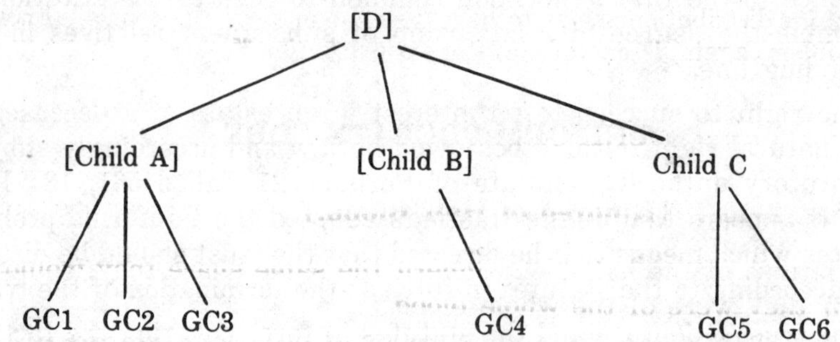

How different would the distribution be under the original version and the alternative version of Sections 2–103 and 2–106? Whether any states which have already adopted the original wording of Sections 2–103 and 2–106 as approved by the Conference in 1969 will amend to follow the alternative form, and how many states considering future enactment of the Code will adopt the alternative remains for future determination. To a limited extent, uniformity will be an important criterion in the choice.

The terms "per capita" and "per stirpes" are used in many older statutes on descent and distribution, by the courts in interpreting such statutes, and by draftsmen of wills and trusts. Unfortunately the terms are not always used with precision nor with complete understanding. The design of an intestate succession statute ought to turn on what the average decedent probably would want, and then appropriate language should be employed. Similarly, some will draftsmen prefer to spell out a pattern for future distribution rather than employ a phrase like "per stirpes." "Per capita" means taking equally. "Per stirpes" refers to taking "by the stocks" with more remote living descendents representing a predeceased ancestor and taking or dividing the share of the ancestor; an heir taking *per stirpes* (or by right of representation) takes directly from the decedent in the sense that his inheritance is free from the claims of creditors of the ancestor whom he represents, by the better view.[19]

Per stirpes distribution among the lineal descendants of an intestate was required by the English Statute of Distribution whether children of the intestate survived or not.[20] *Per stirpes* distribution is required by most American statutes if a child of the intestate survives.[21] But if a child of the intestate does not survive, and the intestate is survived by grandchildren, some courts have construed their statutes as requiring *per stirpes* distribution,[22]

19. Russell v. Bulliner, 370 Ill. 260, 18 N.E.2d 879 (1938); In re Rees' Estate, 204 Iowa 610, 215 N.W. 726 (1927); Johnson v. Huntley, 39 Wash.2d 499, 236 P.2d 776 (1951). The property would, of course, be subject to claims against the intestate estate. See generally, Page, "Descent Per Stirpes and Per Capita", 1946 Wis.L.Rev. 3; White, "Per Stirpes or Per Capita", 13 U.Cin.L.Rev. 298 (1939); Atkinson, Wills (2d Ed. 1953) §§ 16, 17, 18; Rollison, Wills (1939) § 29; 1 Woerner, Administration (3d Ed. 1923) 213.

20. In re Ross's Trust, 13 Eq.Cas. 286 (1871); In re Natt, 37 Ch.Div. 517 (1888).

21. The statutes are collected in Vernier, American Family Laws (1936) § 239; see Wormser, "Per Stirpes or Per Capita", 105 Trusts and Estates 91 (1966).

22. E.g., Crump v. Faucett, 70 N.C. 345 (1874).

while other courts have permitted the grandchildren to take *per capita.*[23] The problem is one of statutory construction and can thus be avoided by a reasonably clear legislative provision.[24] In distribution among collaterals, a *per capita* distribution seems to have been favored by the courts, although the problem, again, is one of statutory construction.[25]

UNIFORM PROBATE CODE

"Section 2–107. [Kindred of Half Blood.]

Relatives of the half blood inherit the same share they would inherit if they were of the whole blood."

"Section 2–108. [Afterborn Heirs.]

Relatives of the decedent conceived before his death but born thereafter inherit as if they had been born in the lifetime of the decedent."

"Section 2–109. [Meaning of Child and Related Terms.][26]

If, for purposes of intestate succession, a relationship of parent and child must be established to determine succession by, through, or from a person,

(1) an adopted person is the child of an adopting parent and not of the natural parents except that adoption of a child by the spouse of a natural parent has no effect on the relationship between the child and either natural parent.

(2) In cases not covered by Paragraph (1), a person is the child of its parents regardless of the marital status of its parents and the parent and child relationship may be established under the [Uniform Parentage Act].

23. E.g., In re Martin's Estate, 96 Vt. 455, 120 A. 862 (1923).

24. E.g., Mich.Comp.Laws Ann. § 702.80; 20 Pa.Stat.Ann. § 2104 (Purdon Supp. 1981). For a critical comment on the Oklahoma statute see Wettengel, "Descent and Distribution: Computing the Representative Share", 10 Okla.L. Rev. 73 (1957).

25. E.g., In re Reil's Estate, 70 Idaho 64, 211 P.2d 407, 19 A.L.R.2d 186 (1949); In re McKeon's Estate, 199 N.Y.S.2d 158, 25 Misc.2d 850 (Surr.Ct., Kings Co. 1960); In re Nunziato's Estate, 202 N.Y.S.2d 39 (Surr.Ct., West. Co. 1960) [Both construing McKinney's Decedent Estate Law § 83(6)(9)]; Estate of Galbraith, 210 Minn. 356, 298 N.W. 253 (1941); Estate of Le Roux, 55 Wash.2d 889, 350 P.2d 1001 (1960).

26. The definition of "child" in Uniform Probate Code Section 1–201 (General Definitions) includes any individual entitled to take as a child by intestate succession; it excludes a stepchild, a foster child, a grandchild or more remote descendant. This definition extends the scope of Section 2–109 throughout the Code.

Alternative subsection (2) for states that have not adopted the Uniform Parentage Act.

[(2) In cases not covered by Paragraph (1), a person born out of wedlock is a child of the mother. That person is also a child of the father, if:

(i) the natural parents participated in a marriage ceremony before or after the birth of the child, even though the attempted marriage is void; or

(ii) the paternity is established by an adjudication before the death of the father or is established thereafter by clear and convincing proof, but the paternity established under this subparagraph is ineffective to qualify the father or his kindred to inherit from or through the child unless the father has openly treated the child as his, and has not refused to support the child.]"

NOTE

Inheritance by, from and through Adopted Persons

Note that under the Uniform Probate Code adoption cuts off inheritance by, from and through the natural parents, except where a child is adopted by the spouse of a natural parent. The exception applies where one natural parent dies (or there is a divorce) and the other parent remarries, the new spouse later adopting the child. The child in such a case becomes the child of the adoptive parent and remains the child of both natural parents, for purposes of inheritance. Prior to 1975 the exception only embraced the natural parent whose spouse adopted the child; the earlier wording of Section 2–109 is in force in states already enacting the Code.

Statutory procedures for adoption exist in all states [27] but many of the state statutes do not deal with matters of inheritance even though an important motive in adoption may be to confer upon the adopted child rights of inheritance from the adoptive parent.

27. There was no adoption at common law. For a history of adoption see Hockaday v. Lynn, 200 Mo. 456, 98 S.W. 585, 8 L.R.A.,N.S., 117, 118 Am.St.Rep. 672, 9 Ann.Cas. 775 (1906); Comment, "Intestate Succession, Sociology and the Adopted Child", 11 Vill.L.Rev. 392 (1966). Summaries of statutory provisions concerning adoption appear in 6 Powell, The Law of Real Property (Rohan Rev.1970) ¶¶ 1004–1007; Vernier, American Family Laws (1936) §§ 262–263; Binavince, "Adoption and the Law of Descent and Distribution; A Comparative Study and a Proposal for Model Legislation", 51 Cornell L.Q. 152 (1966); Kuhlmann, "Intestate Succession by and from Adopted Children", 28 Wash.U.L.Q. 221 (1943); Worthing, "Inheritance and Testamentary Rights with Respect to Adopted Children," 1953 Wis.L.Rev. 38; Fairley, "Inheritance Rights Consequent to Adoptions", 29 N.C.L.R. 227 (1951); "Adoption—The Problems of Descent and Distribution: A Need for Legislation", 31 Notre Dame Law. 451 (1956); "Inheritance By, Through and From an Adopted Child", 9 Ala.L.Rev. 35 (1956); "Property Rights as Affected by Adoption", 25 Brooklyn L.Rev. 231 (1959) (Covering all states and including chart). Contracts to adopt and confer rights of inheritance have been enforced by some courts against the estate of the promisor. E.g., Prince v. Prince, 194 Ala. 455, 69 So. 906 (1915); Wooley v. Shell Petroleum Corp., 39 N.M. 256, 45 P.2d 927 (1935), 49 Harv.L.Rev. 644 (1936). But in most states the procedures prescribed for adoption must be followed with care in order to create rights of inheritance in an adopted child. E.g., Clarkson v. Bliley, 185 Va. 82, 38 S.E.2d 22, 171 A.L.R. 1308 (1946). As to the doctrine of "equitable adoption" see Estate of McConnell, 268 F.Supp. 346 (1967); 6 Powell, The Law of Real Property (Rohan Rev.1970) ¶ 1007.

Unless a statute otherwise provides, an adopted child is permitted to inherit from and through his natural parents.[28] It is also well settled that an adopted child can inherit from his adoptive parents.[29] But there is a sharp division of authority, in the absence of a statutory provision in point, whether or not an adopted child can inherit through his adoptive parents from lineals and collaterals. It has been stated that the prevailing view denies the right of the adopted child to inherit through his adoptive parents, the basis for the view being that an heir cannot be forced upon another without his consent.[30] The modern statutory trend is to permit the adopted child to inherit through the adoptive parents as well as from them.[31]

If an adopted child can inherit from or through his natural or adoptive parents, the child of an adopted child can claim through him in an appropriate case.[32]

The natural parents rather than the adoptive parents inherit from an intestate adopted child unless a statute provides otherwise.[33] A local statute may make the result in such a case depend upon the derivation of the property involved.[34]

28. E.g., In re Sauer's Estate, 216 Wis. 289, 257 N.W. 28 (1934); In re Roderick's Estate, 158 Wash. 377, 291 P. 325, 80 A.L.R. 1398 (1930). See, Comment, "The Adopted Child's Inheritance from Intestate Natural Parents", 55 Ia.L. Rev. 739 (1970).

29. E.g., Bilderback v. Clark, 106 Kan. 737, 189 P. 977, 9 A.L.R. 1622 (1920). An adopted child may be a pretermitted heir, e.g., Hopkins v. Gifford, 309 Ill. 363, 141 N.E. 178 (1923); Alexander v. Samuels, 177 Okl. 323, 58 P.2d 878, 105 A.L.R. 1171 (1936); 94 A.L.R.2d 1200 (1964); and the adoption of a child may revoke a prior will of the adoptive parent if the birth of a child would have that effect. If a child is adopted several times, he is permitted to inherit from all adoptive parents. E.g., Hawkins v. Hawkins, 218 Ark. 423, 236 S.W.2d 733 (1951); Holmes v. Curl, 189 Iowa 246, 178 N.W. 406 (1920). It is arguable that the second adoption annuls the first with all rights of inheritance. In re Klapp's Estate, 197 Mich. 615, 164 N.W. 381, L.R.A. 1918A, 818 (1917), 31 Harv.L.Rev. 488 (1918). As to adopted child taking under antilapse statutes, see Comment, 1962 Duke Law Jour. 558. For discussions of local treatments of adoption pertaining to inheritance, see Comment, "Complete Transplantation of the Adopted Child—A Plan for California", 18 Hastings L.Rev. 377 (1967); Note, "Inheritance Rights of Adopted Child in Kentucky", 55 Ky.L.J. 874 (1967); Comment, "Eligibility of Adopted Children to Take by Intestate Descent and Under Class Gifts in Missouri", 34 Mo.L.Rev. 68 (1969); Note, "Intestate Succession and Adoption in Utah: A Need for Legislation", 1969 Utah L.Rev. 56.

30. Atkinson, Wills (2d Ed., 1953) 89; Hockaday v. Lynn, 200 Mo. 456, 98 S.W. 585, 8 L.R.A.,N.S., 117, 118 Am.St.Rep. 672, 9 Ann.Cas. 775 (1906); Contra, e.g., McCune v. Oldham, 213 Iowa 1221, 240 N.W. 678 (1932).

31. E.g., Va.Code Ann. § 64.1–5.1 (1980). The law in force at the intestate's death determines the inheritance rights of adopted children. Before 1942, an adopted child in Virginia inherited only *from* the *adopting parent.* If an ancestor more remote than a parent, or a collateral relative by adoption, died intestate prior to 1942, the adopted child could not inherit *from* him *through* the adopting parent. Mott v. National Bank of Commerce, 190 Va. 1006, 59 S.E.2d 97 (1950).

32. E.g., Pace v. Klink, 51 Ga. 220 (1874); Williams v. Rollins, 271 Mo. 150, 195 S.W. 1009 (1917); Contra: Harle v. Harle, 109 Tex. 214, 204 S.W. 317, 15 A.L.R. 1261 (1918). For the problems that arise when a blood ancestor, a grandparent for example, adopts a child, see Billings v. Head, 184 Ind. 361, 111 N.E. 177 (1916); Bartram v. Holcomb, 109 Kan. 87, 198 P. 192 (1921); Delano v. Bruerton, 148 Mass. 619, 20 N.E. 308, 2 L.R.A. 698 (1889); Mississippi Valley Trust Co. v. Palms, 360 Mo. 610, 229 S.W.2d 675 (1950).

33. E.g., Russell v. Jordan, 58 Colo. 445, 147 P. 693, Ann.Cas.1916C, 760 (1915); In re Simmons, 121 Me. 97, 115 A. 765 (1922); In re Estate of Frazier, 180 Or. 232, 177 P.2d 254, 170 A.L.R. 729 (1947).

34. For example, Va.Code Ann. § 63–358 (1950), provided that if an adopted child died without issue his property

The problems here considered must be distinguished from those in which the question presented is whether an adopted child satisfies the description of an individual or a class member in a will. The intent of the testator is then the material factor.[35]

Effect of Illegitimacy on Inheritance

Although a bastard cannot inherit from his parents or other ancestors at common law,[36] statutes or judicial decisions generally permit a bastard to inherit from his mother and the mother to inherit from her bastard.[37] A bastard is not an heir in some states unless the father acknowledges the child during the father's lifetime.[38]

passed as if he were the natural child of the adoptive parents; but if he had real or personal property derived by deed, gift, will or inheritance from his natural parents, the property passed as if he had not been adopted. The modern trend is illustrated by the change in the provision to eliminate all possibility of inheritance by the natural parent except in the case in which the surviving natural parent remarried and the child was adopted by a step-parent. Va.Acts 1954, ch. 489. For other statutes illustrating the same trend, see Vernon's Ann.Mo.Stat. § 453.-090; Wis.Stat. § 851.51 (1981 Supp.).

35. See Halbach, "The Rights of Adopted Children Under Class Gifts", 50 Iowa L.Rev. 971 (1965); Note, "Adopted Child as Member of a Class", 11 N.Y.L.F. 522 (1965); Comment, "The Adoptee of Another: Is He a 'Child'?", 26 U.Pitt.L. Rev. 563 (1965); "Adopted Child as Within Class in Testamentary Gift", 86 A.L.R. 2d 12 (1962); "Adoption by Third Person as Excluding One Who Otherwise Answers the Description of a Testamentary Beneficiary", 96 A.L.R.2d 639 (1964). See Chapter XV, Section 2(3) C, Estate of Coe, 42 N.J. 485, 201 A.2d 571 (1964) where the problem is developed.

36. The spouse and issue of a bastard may inherit from him and he may inherit from them. The common law rule was supposedly based upon a policy to discourage illicit sexual intercourse.

37. In Louisiana a bastard child is entitled to alimony (support) payments from his parents if legally acknowledged by them or declared their child by judicial decree but he is heir to neither his mother nor his father. LSA–C.C. arts. 238, 240, 920 (1952). See, Lorio, "Succession Rights of Illegitimates in Louisiana," 24 Loyola L.Rev. 1 (1978); Notes, "Succession Rights of Illegitimates in Louisiana," 27 Loy.L.Rev. 237 (1981); "Illegitimates and Louisiana Succession Law", 55 Tul.L.Rev. 585 (1981). See "The Status of Illegitimates in New England", 38 B. U.L.Rev. 299, 310–313 (1958); "Inheritance by Illegitimate from or through Mother's Ancestors or Collateral Kindred", 97 A.L.R.2d 1101 (1964). In Burris v. Burgett, 16 Del.Ch. 10, 139 A. 454 (1927) it was held that an illegitimate child could not inherit from her maternal grandmother, the statute making no provision for inheritance through the mother as well as from her. In Spencer v. Burns, 413 Ill. 240, 108 N.E.2d 413 (1952), 31 Chi.Kent L.Rev. 268 (1953), 2 De Paul L.Rev. 300 (1953), it was held that Ill. Rev.Stat.1959, c. 3, § 163, providing in part that "an illegitimate child is the heir of his mother and of any maternal ancestor", did not permit inheritance from maternal collaterals. If inheritance is permitted through the mother, it is usually held that maternal ancestors and collaterals can inherit from an intestate bastard. E.g., Henson v. Johnson, 117 Okl. 87, 246 P. 868 (1926); In re Olson's Estate, 54 S. D. 184, 223 N.W. 41 (1929). For an analysis of statutes pertaining to inheritance by bastards see Vernier, American Family Laws (1936) § 249; Vernier and Churchill, "Inheritance by and from Bastards", 20 Iowa L.Rev. 216 (1935). See Note, "The Rights of Illegitimates Under Federal Statutes", 76 Harv.L.Rev. 337 (1962).

38. The formalities required for acknowledgment vary from state to state. The acknowledgment may be treated as a form of legitimation so that the child is permitted to inherit through the father as well as from him. E.g., In re Garcia's Estate, 34 Cal.2d 419, 210 P.2d 841 (1949), 38 Cal.L.Rev. 322 (1950), 2 Stanford L.Rev. 577 (1950). On the other hand, the acknowledged child may not be placed on a par with a fully legitimated child in that he cannot inherit through the father. E.g., Phillips v. Townsend, 223 Ind. 561, 62 N.E.2d 860 (1945), 44 Mich.L.Rev. 661 (1946); Blackwell v. Bowman, 150 Ohio St. 34, 80 N.E.2d 493 (1948). See 33 A.L.R.2d 705 (1969).

There is a strong presumption at common law in favor of the legitimacy of children born in wedlock,[39] and statutes in many states declare that the children of void marriages are legitimate.[40] An illegitimate child may be legitimated by the marriage of his parents, although several states require, in addition, an acknowledgment by the father.[41] A few states have judicial procedures for legitimation. These procedures are in addition to methods of legitimation by marriage and acknowledgment.[42] A legitimated child has the status of any other child of the parents for the purpose of descent and distribution.[43]

In *Trimble v. Gordon*[44] the United States Supreme Court held invalid an Illinois statute which excluded illegitimates as heirs of the father unless the child was legitimated by subsequent marriage of the parents and also acknowledged by the father as his child. The Illinois Supreme Court had upheld the statute on the basis of *Labine v. Vincent*[45] as encouraging marriage and establishing an accurate pattern of intestate succession. Writing for the majority in the United States Supreme Court, Justice Powell indicated that state interest in establishing accuracy in disposition of property at death might justify a stricter standard for proving paternity after death but not total exclusion. However, in *Lalli v. Lalli*[46] the Court sustained the New York probate statute which at that time allowed inheritance by illegitimates from the father only if a court had during the lifetime of the father made an order establishing paternity in a proceeding brought during pregnancy or within two years after birth. Under this statute, the illegitimate was excluded even though recognized by the father; in *Lalli* the father had in fact acknowledged the child as his in a notarized document. The exclusion of acknowledged illegitimate persons does not seem reasonably related to assuring orderly intestate succession, because problems of notice and proof of paternity in such situations are not presented for the probate court. Nevertheless, the majority deemed the State interest in an orderly process of succession to be the objective of the statute and refused to explore the rea-

39. Vernier, American Family Laws (1936) § 241.

40. E.g., Va.Code Ann. § 20–31.1. The statutes do not apply when there has been no marriage agreement but merely a meretricious connection. Vernier, American Family Laws (1931) § 48; Vernier, American Family Laws (1936) § 247; 45 Harv.L.Rev. 933 (1932); 56 Harv. L.Rev. 624 (1943); 84 A.L.R. 499 (1933). For the operation of statutes validating slave marriages and the problems of proof connected therewith see Daniels v. Johnson, 216 Ark. 374, 226 S.W.2d 571, 15 A.L.R.2d 1401 (1950).

41. Vernier, American Family Laws (1936) §§ 242–243.

42. Vernier, American Family Laws (1936) § 245; 68 A.L.R. 129 (1930); 87 A. L.R. 1235 (1933).

43. When a child is legitimated by marriage of its parents, it is usually legitimated for all purposes. In any event the child is legitimated for the purpose of inheritance. Vernier, American Family Laws (1936) §§ 246, 249. If an illegitimate child is adopted by a parent rather than legitimated, the status of the child for inheritance purposes will depend upon the adoption and related statutes.

44. 430 U.S. 762, 97 S.Ct. 1459, 52 L. Ed.2d 31 (1977), noted 91 Harv.L.Rev. 177 (1977), 16 J. Family Law 57 (1977), 38 La.L.Rev. 189 (1977), 52 Tul.L.Rev. 406 (1978).

45. 401 U.S. 532, 91 S.Ct. 1017, 28 L. Ed.2d 288 (1971).

46. 439 U.S. 259, 99 S.Ct. 518, 58 L. Ed.2d 503 (1978), noted 13 Ga.L.Rev. 620 (1979), 57 Denver L.J. 453 (1980), 33 Sw. L.J. 883 (1979), 31 U.Fla.L.Rev. 644 (1979). For a critique of the Supreme Court's treatment of illegitimacy problems, see Maltz, "Illegitimacy and Equal Protection," 1980 Ariz.St.L.J. 831. Constitutionality of the Ohio statute after Lalli is discussed in Comment, 41 Ohio St.L.J. 1037 (1980). The North Carolina statute requiring adjudication during lifetime or a certified written acknowledgment has been upheld under Lalli. Outlaw v. Planters National Bank & Trust Co., 41 N.C.App. 571, 255 S.E.2d 189 (1979).

sonableness of the legislative judgment. The New York statute has subsequently been amended to broaden the inheritance rights of the illegitimate child in that state.[47]

Relatives by the Half-Blood

Persons are related by the whole-blood when they are descended from common ancestors and by the half-blood when there is but one common ancestor. The half-blood did not inherit land at common law.

No distinction is made between the whole and half-blood in matters of inheritance in the United States except as required by statute. These statutes fall into three general categories.

One type of statute merges the ancestral property rule with rules pertaining to the half-blood. The half-blood are excluded from inheritance if not of the blood of the ancestor from whom the property was derived.[48] Another type of statute gives twice as much to the whole-bloods as to half-bloods in the same degree of kinship to the intestate.[49] A third type of statute postpones half-bloods to whole-bloods in the same degree of kinship to the intestate.[50] In no state are the half-blood entirely excluded from inheritance. If there is no statutory provision the half-blood inherit equally with the whole-blood.[51] Equal treatment is required by Section 2–107 of the Uniform Probate Code.

Relatives Born After Death of the Intestate

A posthumous child of an intestate shares in real and personal property as if born in the intestate's lifetime.[52] The same rule is extended by statute in most states to posthumous lineal descendants in any degree of relationship.[53] A majority of jurisdictions now appear to permit posthumous children among collaterals to inherit real or personal property, although such children must have been in embryo at the death of the intestate.[54]

47. N.Y. EPTL § 4–1.2, McKinney's New York Estates, Powers and Trusts Law (1980–81 Supp.) § 4–1.2, as amended L. 1979, c. 139. See also Recommendation of the Law Revision Commission to the 1980 Legislature, McKinney 1980 N. Y. Session Laws, p. 1640, and Note, 49 Ford.L.Rev. 379 (1980).

48. E.g., Ala.Code § 43–3–5. If an intestate inherits land from his mother and is survived by no descendants but one half brother and one whole brother, both will inherit if the half brother traces kinship to the intestate's mother.

49. E.g., Va.Code Ann. § 64.1–2. See Billups v. Bartram, 96 W.Va. 601, 123 S. E. 442 (1924).

50. E.g., Tenn.Code Ann. § 31–208 (1980 Supp.).

51. Gradwohl v. Campagna, 46 A.2d 850 (Del.Ch., 1946). See generally, Atkinson, Wills (2d Ed., 1953) § 19; Rollison, Wills (1939) § 31; Woerner, Administration (3d Ed., 1923) § 70; Atkinson, "Succession Among Collaterals", 20 Iowa L.Rev. 185, 197–202 (1935); Eagleton, "Introduction to the Intestacy Act and the Dower Rights Act", 20 Iowa L.Rev. 241, 256–257 (1935); 42 Yale L.J. 101 (1932).

52. The status of a posthumous child is usually defined by statute. E.g., Ala. Code Ann. § 43–3–6; Ark.Stat.Ann. § 61–142. A posthumous child of an intestate was permitted to inherit land and personal property at common law.

53. E.g., Vernon's Ann.Mo.Stat. § 474.050; Ohio Rev.Code Ann. § 2105.14. The posthumous child must be in embryo at the death of the intestate, otherwise the child will take, if at all, from his ancestor who survived the intestate and not directly from the intestate estate. See "New York Decedent Estate Law, Section 26—Child Born After Making of Will", 24 Fordham L.Rev. 502 (1955); "Distribution to Children Born After the Making of a Will", 26 Fordham L.Rev. 372 (1957).

54. This is the result under Section 2–108 of the Uniform Probate Code. In England, at one time, there was no requirement that the posthumous child in collateral relationship be in embryo at the intestate's death. This gave rise to the doctrine of "shifting" estates. If, for

Ancestral Property Restrictions

The common law rule that a collateral heir had to be of the blood of the first purchaser in order to inherit land was never applied in many states in this country and has been abolished by statute in others.[55] The Uniform Probate Code applies no ancestral property doctrine. A few states continue to apply ancestral property principles in intestate succession to land;[56] but the ancestral property doctrine has no justification under current conditions and gradually is being discarded.[57] Distinctions based on the source from which the intestate acquired title may be found in some of the "half-blood" statutes, collaterals of the blood of the ancestor from whom title was acquired being permitted to inherit.[58] A distinction as to the source of title may be retained when an unmarried infant dies intestate leaving land.[59] When a question of inheritance from an intestate adopted child is presented, the source from which the adopted child acquired title may determine the successor to the property whether real or personal.[60] In at least one state, statutes alter intestate succession from an intestate surviving spouse as to real or personal property derived from a spouse who predeceased.[61]

Children Resulting From Artificial Insemination

One of the problems which may be litigated in the future is status of children born as a result of artificial insemination.[62] Although early drafts of the Uniform Probate Code contained a section dealing with the effect on

example, the intestate died survived by sisters and parents, the parents could not take and the land descended to the sisters in equal shares. But if a male child was born to the parents, although conceived after the death of the intestate, the land passed to the male child by the rule of primogeniture, the interests of the sisters being divested. The doctrine of shifting estates does not appear to be recognized in the United States at the present time.

55. The doctrine is sometimes deemed abolished when the statute makes no mention of ancestral property. Toomey v. Turner, 184 Miss. 831, 186 So. 301 (1939). The current status of the doctrine is discussed in detail in 6 Powell, The Law of Real Property (Rohan Rev. 1981) ¶ 1001. See Atkinson, Wills (2d Ed., 1953) § 21; Rollison, Wills (1939) § 26; Woerner, Administration (3d Ed., 1923) § 73; Pierson, "The Ancestral Status of Personal Property", 16 Geo.L.J. 341 (1928); 42 Yale L.J. 101 (1932); Anno.L.R.A. 1916C, 902; 122 A.L.R. 820 (1939); 141 A.L.R. 976 (1942).

56. In no state does the doctrine now appear to be applied in its full common law rigor.

57. For an almost complete elimination of the doctrine in Arkansas, see Ark. Stat.Ann. § 61–148. Elements of the doctrine are still retained in Arkansas with respect to dower and curtesy.

58. E.g., Ala.Code § 43–3–5. See Caffee v. Thompson, 262 Ala. 684, 81 So. 2d 358, 55 A.L.R.2d 638 (1955); 8 Ala.L. Rev. 384 (1956); 54 Mich.L.Rev. 564 (1956).

59. E.g., Cal.Probate Code, § 227; Minn.Stat.Ann. § 525.16(5). Professor Powell states that these provisions are in force in more than one third of the states. 7 Powell, The Law of Real Property (Rohan Rev. 1981) 676.

60. E.g., Ill.St.Ann. Ch. 3 § 14 (Smith Hurd). As noted previously, there was no adoption at common law and thus the problem dealt with by these statutes was not presented as to personalty. Personal property was distributed under the Statute of Distribution, 1670, to the next of kin of the intestate whether related to the ancestor from whom the property was derived or not.

61. Cal.Probate Code, § 229. A similar statute in Ohio was repealed, effective Jan. 1, 1976. See former Ohio Rev. Code Ann. § 2105.10.

62. See Note, "Artificial Insemination and the Law", 1968 U. of Ill.L.Forum 203. In a case involving need for consent of the husband for adoption of a child born as a result of artificial insemination of the wife, with consent of the husband, by semen of a third party donor, it has been held that the child is the "legitimate" child of the husband and hence the latter's consent is required for later adoption of the child after the couple were divorced. In re Adoption of Anonymous, 74 Misc.2d 99, 345 N.Y.S.2d 430 (Surr.Ct., N.Y.1973).

inheritance, the section was omitted in the Code as promulgated. Section 5 of the Uniform Parentage Act, adopted in 8 states as of 1981,[63] provides that the husband is treated as the legal father of a child resulting from artificial insemination of the wife with the husband's consent. Several other states have adopted specific statutes to govern the problem.[64] Use of a surrogate mother to conceive naturally a child of the father poses the issue of status of the child in relation to the natural mother and the wife of the father for inheritance purposes, as well as the illegitimacy of the child. In both situations wills of both spouses are highly desirable; to the extent that a birth certificate names both spouses as parents of the child the confidential facts concerning conception may never become known.

PROBLEMS

1. Intestate adopted his grandchild, the child of a deceased son. The intestate was survived by four children and the adopted child. In partition proceedings the adopted child claimed two shares, one as representative of her deceased father and the other as adopted child of the intestate. The adoption statute provided that an adopted child was entitled to receive all the rights and interests in the estate of the adoptive parent, by descent or otherwise, that such a child would have been entitled to receive if born to the adoptive parent. How many shares should the adopted child receive? Billings v. Head, 184 Ind. 361, 111 N.E. 177 (1916). Contra, Bartram v. Holcomb, 109 Kan. 87, 198 P. 192 (1921).

2. Plaintiff was adopted by the intestate when she was nineteen months old. When plaintiff was four and one-half years old she was adopted a second time by another person. Thereafter the first adopting parent died intestate survived by a spouse and collateral heirs. The adoption statute provided that an adopted child should be "to all intents and purposes, the child and legal heir of his or her adopter". The plaintiff claims as heir in the estate of the first adopting parent. Should she be permitted to inherit? In re Egley's Estate, 16 Wash.2d 681, 134 P.2d 943 (1943). See In re Leichtenberg's Estate, 7 Ill.2d 545, 131 N.E.2d 487 (1956); 17 Ohio S.L.J. 556 (1956); 44 Ill.B.J. 705 (1956); 16 Md.L.Rev. 178 (1956). Suppose under a statute of the type in *Egley*, the first adopting parent dies before the second adoption. After the second adoption an *uncle* of the *first* adopting parent dies intestate, the general intestate law including among his distributees the descendants per stirpes of the uncle's deceased brothers and sisters. The intestate uncle is unrelated to the second adopting parent. Would you permit the adopted child to inherit from the uncle of the first adopting parent? Evans v. Freter, 20 Ohio App.2d 8, 251 N.E.2d 513 (1969). How would you handle these problems under § 2–109(1) of the Uniform Probate Code: "/A/n adopted person is the child of an adopting parent and not of the natural parents except that adoption of a child by the spouse of a natural parent has no effect on the relationship between the child and either natural parent"? Estate of Luckey, 206 Neb. 53, 291 N.W.2d 235 (1980) (holding that the child is the child of the second adopting parents and not of the first adopting parents).

3. H, owner of an inheritable interest in land, died intestate survived by his wife, W, who was with child at the time of his death, and two daughters, C and M. Two months after the death of the intestate, and before the birth of the child, W, C and M filed a bill for partition and secured a judicial sale of the land to X. The unborn child was not a party to this proceeding by guard-

63. 9A Uniform Laws Ann. (1981 Supp.) 75.

64. E.g., Va.Code § 64.1–7.1.

ian *ad litem* or otherwise. X sold the land to Y, a bona fide purchaser for value. Two months after the judicial sale the child was born and now seeks to recover her portion of the inheritance from Y. Can she recover? Deal v. Sexton, 144 N.C. 157, 56 S.E. 691 (1907).

SECTION 3. THE SURVIVING SPOUSE

(1) PARTICIPATION BY THE SURVIVING SPOUSE IN AN INTESTATE ESTATE

The surviving spouse was not an heir to land at common law but was entitled to dower or curtesy.[65] The widow shared in personal property under the Statute of Distribution, 1670.[66] Under most American intestate laws the spouse is an heir to land, although other classes of heirs may have priority. The spouse is also a distributee of personal property, the modern tendency being to give the spouse the same share in land and personal property of the decedent.[67] The claim of the spouse under statutes of descent and distribution is called "statutory heirship".

Modified versions of the common law marital estates of dower and curtesy or a statutory substitute may be available to the spouse. The common law forms of dower and curtesy have been altered by statute to some degree in all states. In many jurisdictions the common law marital estates have been abolished and a statutory share, usually called "statutory dower", substituted therefor;[68] or "statutory dower" may be provided as an alternative to the common law estates which the spouse can choose. "Statutory dower" may be a fee simple interest in a specified proportion of the decedent's land or it may vary

65. See, American Law of Property (1952) §§ 5.1–5.49, 5.57–5.74; Tiffany, Real Property (3d Ed., 1939) §§ 484–575; Woerner, Administration (3d Ed., 1923) §§ 105–121.

66. No problem arose as to the widower's share since the husband was entitled to the personal property of the wife during her lifetime.

67. E.g., Me.Rev.Stat.Ann., tit. 18, § 851.

68. E.g., McKinney's N.Y., EPTL § 4–1.1(g).

Uniform Probate Code, § 2–113 abolishes both dower and curtesy, substituting therefor in § 2–102 a major share in the intestate estate of the spouse and providing in § 2–201 an elective share of one third of an "augmented" estate which can be claimed against the will. The Code thus continues a "forced heirship" scheme which has presented perplexing problems as courts are required to deal with inter vivos transfers which remove property from the probate estate. The Code meets this difficulty with an "augmented" estate concept which bears an analogy to the "gross estate" used in the Federal Estate Tax law. These matters are discussed in greater detail in Chapter IV.

depending upon the number of children who survive. It may or may not be subject to claims by the decedent's creditors.[69]

When a spouse takes the entire estate of an intestate as heir there is, of course, no problem of election between a share as "statutory heir" and common law dower, curtesy, or a statutory substitute.[70] In some states, however, the spouse may take only part of the estate as heir. The question may then arise whether the spouse can claim as heir and also claim dower, curtesy or "statutory dower". The point is usually covered by a statute which requires election,[71] but in the absence of a statute it would seem that the spouse could take both interests.[72] Where statutory dower exists as an alternative to common law dower or curtesy the spouse is required by statute to elect one or the other.[73]

---

(2) COMMUNITY PROPERTY LAWS

Community property is a system regulating the property rights and obligations of husband and wife during coverture.[74] Its principal characteristic is the common ownership of all property acquired by the individual efforts of either spouse during coverture, each spouse being deemed to have a present and vested interest in one-half of the property so acquired. Each spouse may have an exclusive interest in

69. Common law dower was exempt from the claims of the husband's creditors with some exceptions. The immunity of the statutory substitute will be an important consideration if the estate is insolvent and the widow is put to an election between "statutory" and "common law" dower.

70. A problem sometimes arises when the spouse is an heir, the estate is partially intestate, and the spouse elects statutory dower in lieu of a provision made for her in the will. Can the spouse also take the property that is partially intestate? See Chapter IV, Section 2(2)(B), infra.

71. E.g., Mich.Stats.Ann. (1980) § 27.-5282.

72. See Chapter IV, Section 2(2)(B), infra.

73. See generally, Atkinson, Wills (2d Ed., 1953) § 15; Rollison, Wills (1939) §§ 36, 37; Woerner, Administration (3d ed., 1923) § 121; Sayre, "Husband and Wife as Statutory Heirs", 42 Harv.L.Rev. 330 (1929); Power, "The Law and the Surviving Spouse: A Comparative Study", 39 Ind.L.J. 262 (1964); Chaffin, "A Reappraisal of The Wealth Transmission Process: The Surviving Spouse, Years' Support and Intestate Succession", 10 Ga.L. Rev. 448 (1976) (with emphasis on Georgia law but an excellent general discussion of the problems).

74. Arizona, California, Idaho, Louisiana, Nevada, New Mexico, Texas and Washington have community property laws. Community property laws were enacted in several other states in order to give their citizens the advantage of split income under the Federal Income Tax Law but these laws were repealed after the enactment of the Federal Revenue Act of 1948. There are substantial differences in the statutes of the several states that retain the community property system and a detailed consideration of the operation of these laws in cases of intestacy is not possible here. For a general consideration of the community property laws, see American Law of Property (1952) §§ 7.1–7.36. The one-half interest of the spouse in community property serves the same protective function as dower, curtesy or a statutory form of dower in a non-community property jurisdiction. These laws are discussed in greater detail in Chapter IV, Section 2(3).

separate property, which is property brought into the marriage or property thereafter acquired by descent, devise or gift.

When one spouse dies intestate in a community property jurisdiction, the interest of the survivor must be determined with respect to both community property and separate property. The surviving spouse already owns a half interest in the community property; the decedent's half interest in the community property and decedent's separate property are subject to testamentary disposition and in the absence of a will pass to decedent's heirs. There is no uniformity among the community property states as to the pattern of intestate succession, although a majority give all of the community property to the surviving spouse. Both halves of the community property may in certain circumstances be subject to administration in order to satisfy claims of community creditors.

Currently there is interest in a proposed Uniform Marital Property Act, still in draft form, under consideration by the National Conference of Commissioners on Uniform State Laws. The Act embodies the basic principles of community property. Several common law states have already adopted the concept of marital property in their laws dealing with property division upon dissolution by court decree (divorce);[75] if the marriage ends by death of one spouse, the surviving spouse should be no worse off than if a divorce had occurred. To the extent that present statutes in a particular state already give the surviving spouse the entire intestate estate, the Marital Property Act would not change the pattern of intestate succession but would have its main impact in testate estates as a protection against disinheritance (discussed in the next Chapter).

Where community property rules are applied the common law marital estates of dower and curtesy are not available, nor do such jurisdictions recognize tenancies by the entirety (unless created in another state where such tenancies are permitted).

(3) HOMESTEAD AND EXEMPTION STATUTES

Homestead and exemption statutes are American inventions which have little or no common law background.[76] The primary purpose of statutes of this type is to protect the spouse and family of an insolvent debtor from claims by creditors against his residence and certain items of personal property necessary for his livelihood. This protection is necessary for a spouse and minor children after the death of the debtor and, for this reason, the homestead and exemption stat-

75. These laws are based on the original version of Section 307 of the Uniform Marriage and Divorce Act, which was amended in 1973 to eliminate the concept. See Cain v. Cain, 536 S.W.2d 866 (Mo. App.1976), noted 42 Mo.L.Rev. 479 (1977).

76. See generally, American Law of Property (1952) §§ 5.75–5.120; Woerner, Administration (3d Ed., 1923) §§ 77–104.

utes, in conjunction with statutes providing for allowances to a widow during administration, have been extended in most states to (1) assure the surviving spouse some interest in the estate of the decedent (2) which is protected from creditors.[77]

A homestead statute protects a home or residence from creditors' claims. The householder must comply with the requirements of the statute in order to establish a homestead, although by most statutes the surviving spouse may claim a homestead even though the decedent has not done so.[78] The homestead is not considered an estate in land in many states and does not affect the title to property even though it may last for the life of the widow or during the minority of children.[79] In a few states the title vests in the widow or minor children in fee.[80] Homestead protection is usually limited to a fixed value and, for rural property, to a fixed acreage.

Various types of personal property exemption statutes are in force. These may set forth the value of the personal property that passes to the widow exempt from creditors, enumerate specific items of personal property that are exempt, or give the widow a choice between personal property of a certain value or an equal sum in money.[81] Closely related to the exemption statutes are the family allowance statutes which empower an appropriate court to authorize periodic payments to a widow and her children for their support while an estate is being administered.[82] The court usually has authority to pay in a lump sum or on a monthly basis for a designated period or until the administration is completed. The court may consider the net worth of the estate, the age, health and earning capacity of the family members, and the value of their individual real and personal property, in fixing the amount of the allowance.

Some or all of these statutory provisions may exist in a particular state. The problem sometimes arises whether the surviving spouse must elect between her homestead and exemption rights and her claim to dower or its statutory substitute. It has been held that homestead is in addition to dower when the statute was not clear on the point.[83] Some states require an election by statute.[84] It is proba-

77. All of the states, with the exception of Indiana and West Virginia, have homestead provisions that are available to the surviving spouse. In many states a husband can claim homestead in the property of his deceased wife. E.g., Ky. Rev.Stat.Ann. 427.070.

78. E.g., Va.Code Ann. § 34–11.

79. The interest of the spouse may be regarded as nothing more than a right against creditors and not against heirs, so that its existence is conditional upon the existence of creditors of the decedent or his estate. Robinson v. Baker, 47 Mich. 619, 11 N.W. 410 (1882); Caudle v. Morris, 160 N.C. 168, 76 S.E. 17 (1912); Barker v. Jenkins, 84 Va. 895, 6 S.E. 459 (1888); Comment, "The Wife's Illusory Homestead Rights", 22 Baylor L.Rev. 178 (1970); Note, "Homestead Exemption: What Protection for the Widow and Heirs", 22 U.Fla.L.Rev. 321 (1969).

80. E.g., Utah Code Ann. § 75–2–401.

81. E.g., Ga.Code Ann. tit. 51, § 101–1504 (enumerating items of personal property but limiting claim of spouse to insolvent estate). See Note, "Personal Property Exemptions: A Need for Revision", 17 Baylor L.Rev. 193 (1965).

82. In some states there is a statutory quarantine for the widow until dower is assigned. E.g., Ala.Code, § 43–5–40.

83. E.g., Horton v. Hilliard, 58 Ark. 298, 24 S.W. 242 (1893). Contra, Cook v. Cook, 138 Ga. 88, 74 S.E. 795 (1912).

84. E.g., Va.Code Ann. § 34–12.

ble that the courts will not require a widow to elect between homestead and her share as statutory heiress when the decedent dies wholly or partially intestate;[85] and there is usually no requirement that an election be made between a family allowance and a claim for homestead, dower or intestate share, although the amount of the allowance may be deducted from the shares that the widow eventually takes.

The Uniform Probate Code provides a substantial homestead and exempt property allowance for the surviving spouse which is in addition to the intestate share or elective share.[86] The suggested dollar amount of the homestead allowance is $5,000 and of the exempt property, $3,500, or a total of $8,500.00.[87] The claim can be satisfied from the estate in addition to a testamentary share unless the will otherwise provides. In addition, the surviving spouse is entitled to a reasonable allowance from the estate for maintenance during administration.[88] This can be paid in a lump sum or in periodic payments. This allowance is not chargeable against any benefit passing by intestacy or by elective share or against a share received by will unless the will otherwise provides.

Minor or dependent children, if there is no spouse, are entitled to a suggested total homestead allowance of $5,000.00 (jointly) and to $3,500.00 (jointly) in exempt property.[89] These interests are satisfied just as the interests of a surviving spouse would be satisfied, and also are not charged against ultimate shares in the estate except as a will providing a testamentary share may indicate. There is no special provision for the minor or dependent children of an earlier marriage when the decedent is survived by a later spouse, although such children would be entitled to part of the family allowance during administration.[90]

The homestead allowance is exempt from and has priority over all claims against the estate. The exempt property is defined as "value not exceeding $3,500 in excess of any security interests therein in household furniture, automobiles, furnishings, appliances and personal effects".[91] The right to any assets necessary to make up a deficiency in exempt property abate as necessary to permit prior payment of the homestead allowance and family allowance.[92]

---

85. See Chapter IV, Section 2(2)(B), infra.

86. Uniform Probate Code, §§ 2-401, 2-402.

87. Id. Part 4, "Exempt Property and Allowances, General Comment."

88. Id. § 2-403.

89. Id. §§ 2-401, 2-402.

90. Id. § 2-403.

91. Id. § 2-402.

92. Id.

(4) RELATIVES BY AFFINITY OTHER THAN THE SURVIVING SPOUSE

With the exception of provisions for a surviving spouse, the intestate laws in this country are confined almost entirely to blood relations. Relatives by marriage qualify neither as heirs nor as next of kin,[93] although a few states make provision for stepchildren[94] or stepparents under certain circumstances and others allow relatives by affinity to take property by intestacy in the absence of any blood relations of the intestate.

SECTION 4. SPECIAL SITUATIONS

(1) ADVANCEMENTS

covered 9/9/85

UNIFORM PROBATE CODE

"Section 2–110. [Advancements.]

If a person dies intestate as to all his estate, property which he gave in his lifetime to an heir is treated as an advancement against the latter's share of the estate only if declared in a contemporaneous writing by the decedent or acknowledged in writing by the heir to be an advancement. For this purpose the property advanced is valued as of the time the heir came into possession or enjoyment of the property or as of the time of death of the decedent, whichever first occurs. If the recipient of the property fails to survive the decedent, the property is not taken into account in computing the intestate share to be received by the recipient's issue, unless the declaration or acknowledgment provides otherwise."

93. The definition of "child" in Uniform Probate Code § 1–201(3) specifically excludes a person who is only a "stepchild".

94. E.g., Maryland permits stepchildren to inherit if there are no surviving blood relatives tracing through great-grandparents. Ann.Code of Md., Estates and Trusts § 3–104(e).

NOTE

Transfers during lifetime to a prospective heir may be intended as any one of three legal transactions: (1) a loan with an obligation to repay, which on death of the lender may be an asset of his estate unless barred by a statute of limitation; (2) an outright gift having no relation to the donee's inheritance; (3) an advancement against the donee's share of the donor's estate. The central issue is what the intent of the transferor was, and this determination is controlled in part by the kind of evidence permitted. The Uniform Probate Code section reflects a modern presumption that lifetime gifts normally are not intended to be counted against the donee's share in property passing at death. A problem analogous to the traditional advancement doctrine is presented when property passes to an heir not only by the laws of the intestate succession but also by any of the various arrangements which are used today to avoid the probate courts (joint bank acounts, life insurance payable to a named beneficiary, etc.) and the decedent evidenced his intent that these items be counted as part of the beneficiary's share in the estate. Should these assets be taken into account in dividing the intestate estate even though they are not subject to administration and do not pass under the laws of intestate succession?[95] Would Section 2–110 of the Uniform Probate Code apply? Should a person who wants his probate estate divided differently than under the intestate succession laws because of other transfers have to do so by executing a formal will?

An advancement has been defined and explained as follows:[96]

> "* * * An irrevocable gift *in praesenti* of money or property, real or personal, to a child by a parent to enable the donee to anticipate his inheritance to the extent of the gift * * *. The doctrine is based on the presumption that a parent who dies intestate intends equality among his children in the division of his property, but such presumption is subject to rebuttal by parol evidence."

Almost every state now has some legislation on the subject.[97] Originally, the doctrine was applied only in cases of complete intestacy; and this is the position taken in the Uniform Probate Code.[98] Several states now apply the doctrine in cases of partial intestacy,[99] and a testator may apply the doctrine

95. See Thompson v. Latimer, 209 Ky. 491, 273 S.W. 65 (1925) (charging life insurance proceeds as an advancement); Cazassa v. Cazassa, 92 Tenn. 573, 22 S. W. 560, 20 L.R.A. 178 (1893) (policy taken out in name of son or transferred to him during lifetime). Compare Albers v. Young, 119 Colo. 37, 199 P.2d 890 (1948), 48 Mich.L.Rev. 134 (joint bank account held not an advancement where no intent to make a gift during lifetime); Vinson v. Vinson, 105 La. 30, 29 So. 701 (1901) (insurance proceeds not an advancement). See Atkinson, Wills (2d Ed., 1953) 720.

96. Nobles v. Davenport, 183 N.C. 207, 209, 111 S.E. 180, 181 (1922).

97. The doctrine was incorporated into the English Statute of Distribution, 22 & 23 Chas. II, c. 10, § V (1670). See generally, Atkinson, Wills (2d Ed., 1953) 716; American Law of Property (1952) § 14.-10; 3 Woerner, Administration (3d Ed., 1923) 1879–1898; Elbert, "Advancements", 51 Mich.L.Rev. 665 (1953), 52 Mich.L.Rev. 231 (1953), 52 Mich.L.Rev. 535 (1954); 26 A.L.R. 1178 (1923); 32 A. L.R. 730 (1924); 76 A.L.R. 1420 (1932); 84 A.L.R. 164 (1933); 165 A.L.R. 899 (1946). For an analysis of statutes see Vernier, American Family Laws (1936) § 239.

98. Uniform Probate Code, § 2–110, set forth above. The draftsmen of this section comment that if the decedent leaves a will, evidence of the testator's intent that inter vivos gifts be deducted from his legacies, bequests or devises would be expected to appear in the testamentary instrument. This would seem to be a requirement whether the estate is testate or partially intestate. The matter involves construction of the will and is considered hereafter in Chapter XV.

99. E.g., Va.Code Ann. § 64.1–17.

to a wholly testate estate.[1] The doctrine is regarded in most states as inapplicable to gifts to a surviving spouse or ascending or collateral kin,[2] although there are instances in which the doctrine has been invoked as to lineal distributees other than children.[3]

A substantial gift to a child by a parent raises a presumption of advancement which is rebuttable.[4] The burden of proof is upon the child to show that no advancement was intended by the intestate. The intention of the intestate at the time of the gift usually is the material issue[5] although the intestate may alter the intent to make an advancement before he dies.[6] In most of the states proof of the advancement may be made by parol evidence. Evidence of declarations of intention by the intestate before and after the gift was made is admissible to show his intention.[7] Evidence of the surrounding circumstances,[8] the legal or moral obligation of the intestate to transfer the property,[9] the size and nature of the subject matter of the gift,[10] and similar facts may shed light upon the intention of the intestate. These uncertainties in proof by parol evidence are at least partially eliminated in the Uniform Probate Code.

If a gift is established as an advancement, there is, of course, no obligation upon the donee to account to the donor's estate for its value.[11] But the effect of the advancement is to bar the donee from sharing in the intestate estate unless he is willing to account for what he has received. This accounting is called "bringing the gift into hotchpot".

Suppose an intestate made advancements of $5,000 to son A, $1,000 to son B and gave nothing to son C. Assume that the net estate is $8,000. In order for A and B to receive a share they must bring their gifts into hotch-

1. The doctrine of ademption by satisfaction in testate estates, discussed in Chapter XV, Section 1(2)A, corresponds to advancements in intestate estates.

2. In re Kennedy's Estate, 154 Iowa 460, 135 N.W. 53 (1912); Johnson v. Antriken, 205 Mo. 244, 103 S.W. 936 (1907).

3. The statutes pertaining to advancements usually specify children, children and their issue, or children and other lineal descendants as the donees covered. Vernier, American Family Laws (1936) § 239.

4. E.g., Clements v. Hood, 57 Ala. 459 (1876); Johnson v. Mundy, 123 Va. 730, 97 S.E. 564 (1918). Some states require that evidence of an intention to make an advancement be shown by a writing. E.g., Olney v. Brown, 163 Mich. 125, 128 N.W. 241 (1910); Liesse v. Fontaine, 181 Wis. 407, 195 N.W. 393 (1923). Unless a statutory provision is interpreted to require a writing, parol evidence of intention is admissible. E.g., Page v. Elwell, 81 Colo. 73, 253 P. 1059 (1927).

5. E.g., Nobles v. Davenport, 183 N. C. 207, 111 S.E. 180 (1922).

6. Wheeler v. Wheeler's Estate, 47 Vt. 637 (1874). But an absolute gift cannot be changed to an advancement.

7. Miller's Appeal, 40 Pa. 57, 80 Am. Dec. 555 (1861); Rowe v. Rowe, 144 Va. 816, 130 S.E. 771 (1926); Gaylord v. Hope Natural Gas Co., 122 W.Va. 205, 8 S.E.2d 189 (1940).

8. E.g., Page v. Elwell, 81 Colo. 73, 253 P. 1059 (1927); Trotman v. Trotman, 148 Va. 860, 139 S.E. 490 (1927).

9. Expenditures in discharge of a parental duty, as for the education of a child, may or may not be considered advancements. See Brake v. Graham, 214 Ala. 10, 106 So. 188 (1925); Matter of Denison's Estate, 157 Misc. 385, 284 N.Y. S. 705 (1935); Hill's Guardian v. Hill, 122 Ky. 681, 92 S.W. 924 (1906).

10. Small amounts of money or other property are seldom regarded as advancements. The gift of a pure luxury, such as an automobile to a college student, would probably not be considered an advancement, but might be considered an advancement if intended to be used for profit. Wedding presents have been held advancements in the absence of evidence to the contrary. See Wenbert v. Lincoln National Bank & Trust Co., 116 Ind.App. 31, 61 N.E.2d 466 (1945).

11. An advancement is an irrevocable gift. If a loan rather than an advancement is made, the child is obligated to account for the loan to the estate.

pot. A paper calculation will suffice. The amount of the advancement is added to the estate, in this case $14,000; the estate is then divided into the proper number of shares, in this case three. Each share would then amount to $4,666. Since this sum is less than the amount advanced to A, A would elect not to participate and to retain his gift. A donee cannot be forced into hotchpot. Only B and C would share in the estate, amounting (on paper) to $9,000 or $4,500 each. B, having received $1,000, gets $3,500 more. C receives the full share.

Another method is sometimes used in handling hotchpot. The result is the same. Each heir who has not received an advancement is made equal to those who have received advancements. The balance of the estate, if any, is then distributed equally to each heir. In the preceding example $1,000 would be allocated to C, making him equal to B. Then the remaining assets would be used to make them equal to A. Since this cannot be done with the $7,000 left, B and C would share this amount. The result is $4,500 to C and $3,500 to B as before.

Advancements are usually valued at the time of the transfer of property by the donor.[12] The advancement is deemed to be made, however, at the time the donee obtains possession and enjoyment, so that a donor who retains a life estate in property makes an advancement for valuation purposes at his death.[13] Most of the courts do not compute interest on advancements prior to the death of the donor.[14]

If a child receives an advancement and predeceases the intestate leaving issue surviving, and other children of the intestate survive so that the issue of the deceased child take per stirpes, the value of the advancement is charged against the share of the issue in most states[15] although the Uniform Probate Code provides that the advancement is not taken into account in this situation "unless the declaration or acknowledgement provides otherwise". If all children of the intestate predecease him, and the issue of deceased children take per capita and not per stirpes, advancements to a child are not charged against the shares taken by issue of the child.[16]

---

12. E.g., Smith v. Hood, 212 Ala. 554, 103 So. 574 (1925) (land); Wenbert v. Lincoln National Bank & Trust Co., 116 Ind. App. 31, 61 N.E.2d 466 (1945). The actual value and not the tax value controls. Miller v. Richardson, 85 S.W.2d 41 (Mo. 1935); 1 Mo.L.Rev. 78 (1936). A valid agreement between the donor and donee concerning the value of the property will be enforced against the donee and other heirs. E.g., Home Mixture Guano Co. v. McKoone, 168 Ga. 317, 147 S.E. 711 (1929).

13. Palmer v. Culbertson, 143 N.Y. 213, 38 N.E. 199 (1894); In re Glessner's Estate, 40 D. & C. 271, 57 Montg. 78 (Pa. 1941). Statutes in some states provide that the advancement will be valued at the time of the donor's death in any event. E.g., Iowa Code Ann. § 633.224.

14. E.g., In re Pardee's Estate, 240 Wis. 19, 1 N.W.2d 803 (1942).

15. E.g., Brown v. Taylor, 62 Ind. 295 (1878); Coffman v. Coffman, 41 W.Va. 8, 23 S.E. 523 (1895).

16. E.g., Skinner v. Wynne, 55 N.C. 41 (1854); Person's Appeal, 74 Pa. 121 (1873).

(2) ASSIGNMENT OF EXPECTANCY

SCOTT v. FIRST NATIONAL BANK OF BALTIMORE

Supreme Court of Maryland, 1961.
224 Md. 462, 168 A.2d 349.

[In January, 1948, Wilmer Scott and his wife, Grace, then living in Connecticut, entered into a separation agreement whereby Grace was to have custody of their infant child, Virginia, and Wilmer agreed to pay a stated monthly sum for support. Wilmer also transferred to Grace certain assets and in a separate instrument assigned under seal to Virginia one-half of his expectancy in the estate of his father, Thomas A. Scott, who was then living, "for the consideration of one dollar and other valuable considerations received to my full satisfaction from my wife * * * on behalf of my daughter". Grace obtained a divorce in Connecticut in 1949, the decree incorporating the separation agreement but not mentioning the assignment. Wilmer's father, Thomas A. Scott, died intestate in Maryland in 1958, survived by two children, of whom Wilmer was one, and leaving a personal estate of about $490,000. The Bank, appointed administrator, interpleaded the parties in interest and although the equity court considered evidence that Wilmer had a history of improvidence and instability, living beyond his means, the assignment was declared valid and Wilmer appeals.]

HENDERSON, JUDGE. * * *

The parties agree and concede that the validity and effect of the assignment is to be determined under the law of Connecticut, where it was executed and delivered. That, of course, is the general rule applicable to foreign contracts dealing with personalty. See Restatement, Conflict of Laws § 322, and Baltimore & O. R. Co. v. Glenn, 28 Md. 287, 321. It is also agreed that at common law the transfer of a mere possibility or expectancy, not coupled with an interest, is void. Dart v. Dart, 1928, 7 Conn. 250; cf. Keys v. Keys, 148 Md. 397, 400, 129 A. 504. The parties further agree that under some circumstances, at least, equity will enforce the assignment of an expectancy after the death of an ancestor despite its invalidity at law. It is generally recognized that since the relief sought is in the nature of specific performance of a contract, equity will enforce the contract only where it is fair and equitable and supported by an adequate consideration. Keys v. Keys, supra; 6 Williston, Contracts (Rev. ed.) § 1681A; Pomeroy, Equity Jurisprudence (5th ed.) §§ 953a and 1287; 1 Bogert, Trusts § 112; 1 Scott, Trusts (2d ed.) § 86.1; Restatement, Property § 316. See also Notes, 17 A.L.R. 597, 44 A.L.R. 1465 and 121 A.L.R. 450, and Notes, 25 Colum.L.Rev. 215, and 35 No.Car.L. Rev. 127, 131. The appellant contends that the necessary consideration is lacking in the instant case.

Both parties cite and rely upon the case of Hooker v. Hooker, 130 Conn. 41, 32 A.2d 68, but they place a different interpretation upon it. The facts are strikingly similar to those in the instant case, but the posture of the case was somewhat different. In that case the Hookers executed a separation agreement in Connecticut in which, among other things, Mr. Hooker agreed to pay a certain sum to his wife in lieu of support and to establish two *inter vivos* trusts in favor of the minor children. He further agreed to assign in trust for each child any amounts he might thereafter receive from his mother's estate. It did not appear that any particular consideration passed to the husband in exchange for this agreement. Mrs. Hooker subsequently obtained a divorce in Nevada, and the decree incorporated the terms of the separation agreement by reference; the decree declaring it to be "fair, just and equitable." After the death of the mother the ex-wife sued to enforce the assignment of the husband's interest in his mother's estate.

* * * [T]he court discussed, in connection with the agreement to place additional sums in trust for the children, the husband's claim that the agreement was void as one for the transfer of an expectancy. Citing the case of Brown v. Brown, 66 Conn. 493, 498, 34 A. 490, 491, the court stated that an agreement to assign an expectancy is enforceable in equity and that the rule is supported by the great weight of authority "where the agreement is fairly made upon adequate consideration and without oppression or unjust advantage being taken of the heir." The court discussed authorities, pro and con, as to the necessity that the ancestor have knowledge of the purported assignment but said: "The danger that such an agreement will defeat his intent is not so great as to require that his knowledge of its existence be proved in order to render it valid." The court further said: "We have no statute in this state changing the common law in such a situation as the one before us, and our courts have jurisdiction in equity to enforce the agreement by compelling compliance with it." [130 Conn. 41, 32 A.2d 73].

* * * If the Connecticut court did not discuss the adequacy of the consideration because the point was not raised, as the appellant suggests, and the question was left open, we must still determine, as best we can, what the Connecticut court would hold, were the question presented.

All of the authorities seem to agree that a gratuitous assignment is unenforceable, because there is no contract to enforce. 1 Scott, Trusts, supra at p. 655. Some courts, notably in Kentucky, refuse to enforce any agreements to assign an expectancy because of a public policy against sales to moneylenders and the danger of over-reaching in the case of impoverished prospective heirs. Others enforce agreements to sell, provided the consideration amounts to a fair equivalent. Some of the commentators suggest that the adequacy of consideration is only one element in determining whether equity will enforce and that contracts to assign an expectancy should not be placed in any special category. See the Note, 25 Colum.L.Rev., supra. In this connection we may quote the language of Judge Hammond in Ledingham v. Bayles, 218 Md. 108, 115 145 A.2d 434, 439, a case involving a contract to make a will, where it was said: "As in other contracts, the parties may agree on the surrender or acquisition of any legal rights as consideration, and the adequacy of such consideration is material only as an element of fraud or undue influence or as one of the factors which a court will take into consideration in determining whether or not to grant specific performance." Cf. Sidor v. Kravec, 135 Conn. 571, 66 A.2d 812. In 1 Scott, Trusts, supra at p. 654, the learned author states that the courts uniformly find adequate consideration present in the case of marriage settlements and separation agreements. We find nothing in the Connecticut cases cited to indicate that a property settlement in contemplation of divorce would be unenforceable because lacking in consideration amounting to equivalence. We think the cases cited point in the opposite direction.

We do not suggest that any weight should be attached to the seal or recited consideration. Nor do we suggest that love and affection alone would suffice, although there are cases that suggest a more liberal rule in the case of family settlements. See 6 Williston, Contracts, supra, and Warner v. Warner, 124 Conn. 625, 1 A.2d 911, 118 A.L.R. 1348. Of course, both parties in the instant case were concerned with the welfare of the child Virginia. Grace assumed the burden of the care and education of Virginia, over and above the rather small sum stipulated for her support. It is true that the divorce court could not be bound by the parties' agreement, insofar as it might affect the welfare of the child. But the wife may well have tempered her demands because of the assignment in order to insure that the child would receive a share of the expectancy which might otherwise be frittered away. She also assumed liability for the unpaid bills and loans and the mortgage. We find adequate consideration in these undertakings. There is no claim of fraud or over-reaching and the chancellor found that the agreement was not unfair or inequitable under the circumstances. The bargain was at arm's length and the husband had an opportunity to seek independent advice.

* * *

The passage we have quoted from the Hooker case is a sufficient answer to the appellant's contention that the assignment is invalid because made without the knowledge of the assignor's father. It is true that it was not shown in that case that the mother was unaware of the agreement, although knowledge was not affirmatively shown. But we think the Connecticut court indicated that it would follow the weight of authority to the effect that knowledge is immaterial. See Restatement, Property § 316 comment j, and Keys v. Keys, supra. See also Hofmeister v. Hunter, 230 Wis. 81, 283 N.W. 330, 121 A.L.R. 444, where a conveyance was enforced although the ancestor was insane.

Decree affirmed, with costs.

NOTE

The problem in the principal case may arise whether the assignor has an expectancy as legatee or devisee by will or an expectancy as heir or next of kin of the source of the interest.[17] An assignment of an expectancy must be distinguished from an assignment of an interest in the estate after the death of the source.

The consent of the source is not a condition to enforcement in equity of an assignment of an expectancy,[18] but the source may survive the assignor or disinherit the assignor. In either case the assignor takes no interest and the assignee has no recourse against children of the assignor who take directly from the source,[19] or against the estate of the source.[20]

If an heir purports to release his expectancy to the source, rather than to assign his expectancy to a third party, the release is enforceable in equity if given for fair consideration and binds not only the heir but also his children or other descendants if they take by representation.[21] The consideration required is that necessary to support an action for specific performance.[22]

The theories upon which releases have been enforced are somewhat obscure. It has been suggested that the preferable view is to treat the release as a liquidated advancement, the fair consideration being the property advanced, although a strict application of this theory would seem to bar the children or other descendants of a releasing heir only when the children or other descendants take per stirpes.[23]

17. See Atkinson, Wills (2d Ed., 1953) 729; III American Law of Property (1952) 598; Rollison, Wills (1939) 633, 634; Evans "Certain Evasive and Protective Devices Affecting Succession to Decedents' Estates", 32 Mich.L.Rev. 478, 488–490 (1934).

18. E.g., Gadsby v. Gadsby, 275 Mass. 159, 175 N.E. 495, 74 A.L.R. 434 (1931); Restatement, Property, § 316, Comm. *j.* Contra, McClure v. Raben, 133 Ind. 507, 33 N.E. 275, 36 Am.St.Rep. 558 (1890).

19. E.g., Donough v. Garland, 269 Ill. 565, 109 N.E. 1015, Ann.Cas.1916E, 1238 (1915); Johnson v. Breeding, 136 Tenn. 528, 190 S.W. 545, L.R.A.1917C, 266 (1916).

20. Casady v. Scott, 40 Idaho 137, 237 P. 415 (1925). See, "Effect of Advancements, Debts and Releases when Expectant Distributee Predeceases Intestate", 54 Mich.L.Rev. 984 (1956).

21. See Atkinson, Wills (2d Ed., 1953) 725; III American Law of Property (1952) 594; Rollison, Wills (1939) 631; Evans, "Certain Evasive and Protective Devices Affecting Succession to Decedents' Estates", 32 Mich.L.Rev. 478, 491–498 (1934); Restatement, Property, § 316, Comment *g*.

22. Restatement, Property (1940) § 316, Comment *d*; Restatement, Contracts (1932) §§ 366, 367. The consideration must bear some reasonable relationship to the estimated value of the expectancy relinquished. It is stated in dictum in Price v. Davis, 244 N.C. 229, 93 S.E.2d 93 (1956), 35 N.C.L.Rev. 127 (1956), that if the consideration given for the release is grossly inadequate the consideration might be treated only as an advancement and would not bar the heir from any claim on a theory of estoppel. The consideration also is examined carefully in assignments, especially when the assignment occurs shortly before the death of the intestate. See Mills v. Hendricks, 173 F.Supp. 771 (D.C.Vir.I.1959) (Assignment cancelled when given without consideration and assignor was old and subject to overreaching).

23. See Atkinson, Wills (2d Ed., 1953) 727. When called upon to enforce releases the courts are sometimes troubled by the testamentary aspects of the transactions. A release by an heir may interfere with the operation of the intestate laws upon property in the estate of the intestate. Courts have refused to enforce a release by a devisee of land on the theory that the testator was attempting to evade the formal requirements for revocation of a will. E.g., Burnham v. Comfort, 108 N.Y. 535, 15 N.E. 710 (1888). On the other hand there are a large number of acts by property owners that may serve as will substitutes, the validity of some of these acts as will substitutes being more firmly established than others. The advancement doctrine and the kindred doctrine of ademption by

PROBLEMS

1. An elderly person enters into a contract with a retirement home whereby the home agrees to accept the person as a resident and supply room, board, and nursing services for life, and the person transfers to the home all of his assets and all rights in any property he may thereafter acquire by inheritance. Should the contract be enforceable as to a subsequent inheritance from a person living when the contract was made?

2. A prospective heir assigns for consideration all of his expectancy in his living mother's estate; the estate includes personal and real property. Is this a "conveyance" which should be recorded in order to protect the assignee under the recording statutes against subsequent purchasers from and creditors of the assignor? Lena v. Yannelli, 78 N.J.Super. 257, 188 A.2d 310 (Ch.Div.1963).

---

(3) RENUNCIATION (DISCLAIMER)

COOMES v. FINEGAN

Supreme Court of Iowa, 1943.
233 Iowa 448, 7 N.W.2d 729.[24]

A suit to enjoin the sale of real estate at sheriff's sale under an execution issued on a judgment against an heir of an intestate who died seized of the land, although the heir had filed a renunciation of all interest in the estate. From a decree dissolving a temporary in-

satisfaction, the latter being applied to prevent the operation of a gift by will, are well established devices to evade the intestate laws and wills acts. Consequently the courts have tended to rely upon these doctrines for the enforcement of releases. In Pylant v. Burns, 153 Ga. 529, 112 S.E. 455, 28 A.L.R. 423 (1922), 21 Mich.L.Rev. 100 (1922) a daughter released her interest in the estate of her father for a consideration of $1,000. The father died intestate, leaving no spouse and no child except the daughter. Certain collateral kin of the father claimed his estate. The daughter was permitted to inherit, the court construing the release as an acknowledgment by the daughter of an advancement in full of her intestate share which would not prevent her from inheriting so long as no persons having an equal or preferred claim under the intestate laws survived the intestate. The advancement doctrine has been applied by some courts with such strictness that the release is given effect only to the extent of the consideration furnished. E.g., Weddingdon v. Adkins, 245 Ky. 747, 54 S.W.2d 331 (1932); Ratliff v. Meade, 184 Va. 328, 35 S.E.2d 114 (1945). Other courts have enforced the releases as contracts. E.g., Eissler v. Hoppel, 158 Ind. 82, 62 N.E. 692 (1901); Riddell v. Riddell, 70 Neb. 472, 97 N.W. 609 (1903). In some situations a theory of estoppel may be available as a ground for enforcement as, for example, when it can be shown that the source has changed position in reliance upon the release by failing to make a will. E.g., In re Simon's Appeal, 158 Mich. 256, 122 N.W. 544, 17 Ann.Cas. 723 (1909); Coffman v. Coffman, 41 W.Va. 8, 23 S.E. 523 (1895). The position has been taken that the release extinguishes the heir's right to inherit. Mires v. Laubenheimer, 271 Ill. 296, 111 N.E. 106 (1916).

24. Noted 28 Iowa L.Rev. 700 (1943); 41 Mich.L.Rev. 1201 (1943); 92 U.Pa.L. Rev. 105 (1943).

junction and denying a permanent injunction, the plaintiff, as grantee of all the other heirs, has appealed.

BLISS, JUSTICE. Adda Coomes died intestate on January 26, 1941, seized of about ninety-one acres of land in Carroll County, Iowa, and left surviving, her husband, the plaintiff, seven children, and the children of a deceased daughter. Prior to the death of the intestate, the defendant, Dreesen, had procured a judgment in the District Court of Carroll County against Albert Miller and wife, Lola Miller. The latter was a daughter and an heir of the intestate. On March 18, 1941, Lola Miller filed in the office of the Clerk of said District Court the following instrument:

"I, Lola Miller, do hereby definitely and finally renounce and reject any and all right of inheritance which I might or could have as heir at law of Adda Coomes, deceased; and I renounce and reject any and all right, title or interest which I might or could claim in any property, either real or personal, of which the said Adda Coomes died seized or possessed."

It was executed by Lola Miller on March 14, 1941.

There is no dispute as to the facts. In addition to the facts already stated, it was stipulated that: letters of administration were issued on February 8, 1941; all of the heirs of the intestate except Lola Miller, on April 29, 1941, executed and delivered to the plaintiff a quit claim deed to all of their interest in said real estate, which deed he had recorded about that time; Lola Miller made no affirmative action in any way toward claiming or doing anything with the property involved prior to her renunciation or thereafter; on August 15, 1941, the execution and levy was made upon the alleged one-twelfth interest of Lola Miller in said real estate; and, on September 17, 1941, the injunction was issued and served.

The defendant, Dreesen, alleged that the purported renunciation was made without consideration, with intent to defraud this defendant, and to defeat the collection of the judgment; that it in no way affected his prior and superior right, or the validity of his judgment lien, or execution levy. There is no proof respecting consideration or of any intent to defraud creditors.

The only question presented for determination is whether or not a child who takes an interest in real estate from an intestate parent, under the Iowa statutes of descent, can, by renunciation of that interest, defeat the lien of a prior judgment.

Counsel inform us that this court, so far as they can determine, has never answered the question, and that after long and diligent research they are confident in asserting that the point has not been directly passed upon in the United States and that any reference to this question of law in any case is pure dictum. In quite an extensive search, we have had no better success than counsel. Questions closely akin to this one have been determined in this state and elsewhere.

A testamentary trust, bequest or devise may, prior to any act of acceptance, be renounced by the beneficiary, so long as there is no estoppel, or fraud or collusion for the benefit of the renouncer, and such renunciation when made will revert back to the death of the testator, and will displace the lien, of any personal judgment against the beneficiary existing at that time, or of any levy upon the property made subsequent thereto. Such a renunciation will prevent the testamentary disposition from having any effect to pass any title or interest, and since it relates back to the death of the testator, or the taking effect of the gift, there is nothing to which a lien or levy may attach. Renunciation is not an assignment, contract or conveyance and is not the equivalent of a transfer by a debtor to defeat his creditors. Creditors have no right, and courts have no jurisdiction, to control the right of such beneficiary to accept or to refuse such a gift. It is true that one is presumed to have accepted a gift, testamentary or otherwise, which is beneficial to him, yet he may withhold indicating such acceptance or assent, and upon renunciation the presumption is displaced as of the death of the testamentary donor, or of the time of making the gift.

* * *

In Iowa, and generally elsewhere, the title to a decedent's real estate, whether he die testate or intestate, including the right of dower, vests in the heir, devisee or spouse instantly upon the death of the decedent, subject, of course, to the payment of his debts, and costs of administration, etc. The right or interest of the spouse may be defeasible because of certain elective rights which he or she may take advantage of.

* * *

While the title of a devisee vests immediately on the death of the testator, it is, as we have noted, but a tentative vesting, until there is some definite act of acceptance. Every devise or bequest is optional with the donee. When it is definitely renounced such vesting of title as theretofore existed is divested as completely as though it had never existed, carrying away with it the liens of such personal judgments or levies as may have previously attached.

Under section 11602, Code 1939, the judgment of the appellee, Dreesen, of record, as it was in the District Court of Carroll County, in which county the land was situated, attached eo instante on the intestate's death, and coincident with the vesting of the title to the inheritance in the heir and judgment debtor. Both the lien and the title vested by operation of law. The vesting of the title required no assent or acceptance by Lola Miller. So far as disclosed by the record, that title was indefeasible in her as against any requirements of proper administration of the estate of her mother. Such a title can be lost by prescription, or adverse possession, or perhaps by estoppel. None of which ever took place. She could part with title by intestacy, testamentary disposition, gift, contract, conveyance, and perhaps by other ways. But, none of these ever took place, and even though they had the title would have passed, subject to and burdened with, the lien of Dreesen's judgment.

It is our judgment that the renunciation was not effective to destroy the lien of the judgment and that Lola Miller took her one-twelfth interest in the real estate of her mother subject to and burdened therewith, and that the appellant took no title to Lola Miller's one-twelfth interest by the quit claim deed given by the other heirs.

In support of our conclusion, we call attention to the following language by an eminent authority on the law of real property, Emory Washburn, 3 Washburn, Real Property, 6th Ed., section 1829, to wit: "Heir's Title independent of his own Act.—An heir at law is the only person, who by common law, becomes the owner of land without his own agency or assent. A title by deed or devise, requires the assent of the grantee or devisee before it can take effect. But in the case of descent, the law casts the title upon the heir, without any regard to his wishes or election." The author cites in support of his statement Williams, Real Property, 75 and 2 Blackstone's Commentaries, 201.

* * *

We are satisfied that under our own decisions and the statutes of Iowa, and such authority as we have noted, and the dictates of sound principles of law, that the decree of the trial court should be affirmed. It is so ordered.

Affirmed.

All Justices concur.

NOTE

At common law an heir cannot renounce. Title is vested in the heir by law rather than by "gift" as in the case of the will.[25] Hence the heir cannot refuse the transfer unless the applicable statute governing intestate succession provides for renunciation. The heir can assign his interest at any time after the death of the intestate. As to realty there could be no doubt of this power to assign since title passes to the heir at the moment of death of the owner. As to personalty, even though legal title passes to the personal representative, the next of kin clearly has an assignable interest.

A document purporting to "renounce" the interest of one heir can be treated as a gratuitous assignment in favor of the other heirs. Although this has the same apparent substantive result as a renunciation, it may have different legal consequences for some purposes. If the "renunciation" is really an "assignment", creditors of the heir can reach the property, as in the principal case, on the theory there has been a transfer in fraud of the creditors' rights.[26] Moreover, the "assignment" amounts to a gift which may be subject to a gift tax, as discussed below.

Even in the absence of a statute, a beneficiary under a will may renounce. Renunciation, sometimes called disclaimer, is a refusal to accept the testamentary transfer. The determination of who will get the property as a re-

25. In re Meyer's Estate, 107 Cal. App.2d 799, 238 P.2d 597 (1951). See Howe, Renunciation by the Heir, Devisee or Legatee, 42 Ky.L.Rev. 605 (1953) criticizing the common law rules which permit the beneficiary under a will to renounce but deny the same power to an heir.

26. See Bostian v. Milens, 239 Mo. App. 555, 193 S.W.2d 797, 170 A.L.R. 424 (1946) (allowing the trustee in bankruptcy to set aside an attempted renunciation of an intestate share).

sult of the renunciation depends upon rules of will construction considered later in this course. In some cases the results are plain. Thus, if all the estate is given to A, and A renounces, the estate passes by intestacy. If a devise of specific realty or a pecuniary legacy to A is renounced, and the will contains a standard residuary clause in favor of B, the renounced devise or legacy "falls into" the residuary estate and passes to B.

Similar problems are presented with respect to property passing outside of the decedent's probate estate: Can the beneficiary of life insurance renounce and when? Can a surviving joint tenant renounce (in contradiction of the ancient theory that all joint tenants own the whole and that no interest passes to the survivor on death of the other joint tenant)? Can a beneficiary of a revocable living trust renounce after the death of the settlor if the beneficiary knew of the trust years before at the time of its creation? [27]

All of these problems are important today largely because tax savings can be achieved by renunciation. Renunciation may be made to take advantage of the marital deduction, to qualify a charitable remainder interest for deduction under the federal estate tax, or simply to avoid greater income taxes and later estate taxes for the person renouncing. The tax laws are framed in terminology of "disclaimer," which is merely another label for renunciation. To be effective under the Internal Revenue Code the disclaimer must meet certain requirements in order to be "qualified"; these are set forth in § 2518 of the Code and made applicable to the estate tax by § 2045. A qualified disclaimer is not subject to the gift tax, and property passing by the disclaimer may result in estate tax deductions. There must be an irrevocable and unqualified refusal to accept the property; it must be in writing received by the transferor, his legal representative or the holder of the legal title to the property to which the interest relates, not later than 9 months after the day of the transfer (death of the decedent in the situations considered in this Chapter) or, if the disclaimant is a minor, 9 months after he or she reaches 21. The disclaimant must not have accepted the property or any of its benefits. The disclaimant cannot direct the devolution of the disclaimed property, which is governed by state law. The 1981 amendment to § 2518 allows a person to make a qualified disclaimer by a transfer to a person who would have taken under a valid renunciation by local law even though local law is not complied with, provided that the other requirements for a qualified disclaimer are met.[28] For example, if local law requires renunciation or disclaimer within 6 months, the heir or devisee could transfer within the 9 months for a qualified disclaimer. The main problem, however, is that the disclaimant has no control over who takes as a result of the disclaimer. For example, an heir cannot disclaim in favor of a specific charity; nor can an heir with children disclaim in favor of a parent or brother or sister, because the property passes as though the heir had predeceased, and his children would then take by representation. Nevertheless there are still many situations in which disclaimer will produce tax savings. After 1981, under the Internal Revenue Code as amended by the Economic Recovery Tax Act of 1981, the estate may deduct the full value of property passing to the sur-

27. See Newman and Kalter, "Disclaimers of Future Interests: Continuing Problems and Suggested Solutions", 49 Notre Dame Law. 827 (1974).

28. Economic Recovery Tax Act of 1981, P.L. 97–34, § 426, 26 U.S.C.A. For criticism of the 1976 disclaimer legislation see Martin, "Perspectives on Federal Disclaimer Legislation," 46 U. of Chi.L. Rev. 316 (1979); Roche and Carlson, "The Dynamic Disclaimer", 14 N.Eng.L. Rev. 339 (1979); Wenig, "Recent Developments in Estate and Gift Taxes: Disclaimer—The Proposed Regulations", 15 Real Prop., Probate & Tr. Law Jour. 743 (1980).

viving spouse.[29] If the decedent did not plan his estate properly, sufficient property may not pass to the spouse to achieve the best tax results in both the decedent's and the spouse's estates. In such a situation adult children may be able to disclaim in order to pass to the spouse the amount which will result in maximum tax savings. Similarly, a will may create a trust for a spouse or child with remainder to charity; rules for deductibility of charitable remainders are extremely technical (these will be considered in Chapter XI); if the trust does not qualify, the life tenant may disclaim and the full amount can then be deducted.[30] Or a son who has a large estate of his own may be the heir to a parent's wealth; the additional wealth would only increase the son's income tax to a higher bracket and ultimately result in higher estate taxes at his death; the son could disclaim and have his children inherit in his place.

State law will continue to determine the effect of renunciations or disclaimers for state taxes and for other state purposes.[31] An heir in an intestate estate or a beneficiary under a will may renounce to avoid his creditors, as was attempted in the principal case.[32] Sometimes the person renouncing wants to carry out the decedent's wishes which have been expressed without complying with the formalities for a will; or he may simply feel other family members have greater need or deserve a larger share.

A growing number of states have adopted legislation authorizing renunciation in situations where the common law either does not permit it (as on succession to an heir) or is in doubt (as to power of a surviving joint tenant to renounce on death of the other joint tenant).[33] In 1978 the National Conference of Commissioners on Uniform State Laws promulgated three sets of statutes: the Uniform Disclaimer of Transfers by Will, Intestacy or Appointment Act, the Uniform Disclaimer of Transfers Under Nontestamentary Instruments Act, and the Uniform Disclaimer of Property Interests Act. The first has become proposed Uniform Probate Code § 2–801 (replacing in 1975 an earlier version of that section already adopted in several states, from which it differs in minor respects). The second can be adopted in states which already have the first type and wish to have more complete coverage; the sections on renunciation of nontestamentary transfers and contracts could be added in a statutory title or chapter other than the Probate Code, or perhaps in Article 6 of the Code. The third is simply a comprehensive statute, supplanting the first two. A number of states already have legislation, either limited to intestate and testate succession or applicable to nontestamentary transfers.[34] The statutory provisions specify that renunciation (disclaimer) "relates back for all purposes"; in the case of testate or intestate

29. Internal Revenue Code § 2056, 26 U.S.C.A., as amended by Economic Recovery Tax Act of 1981, P.L. 97–34, § 403(a).

30. For an example see Platt, "Tax Reform 1969: The Estate Tax Charitable Deduction and the Private Charitable Foundation", 31 Ohio St.L.J. 203, 212 (1970).

31. See 27 A.L.R.3d 1354 (1969) (renunciation as affecting *state* inheritance, estate or succession tax).

32. For cases denying relief to creditors of the beneficiary under a will who renounces, see Notes, 133 A.L.R. 1428 (1941) and 27 A.L.R. 472 (1923); an occasional court allows creditors to reach the renounced property even though the renunciation would be valid for other purposes, as in Estate of Kalt, 16 Cal.2d 807, 108 P.2d 401, 133 A.L.R. 1424 (1940). In Hoecker v. United Bank of Boulder, 476 F.2d 838 (10th Cir. 1973), a disclaimer was held not to be a voidable "transfer" within the Bankruptcy Act. See Notes, 49 Ind.L.J. 290 (1974); 20 Wayne L.Rev. 969 (1974); 30 Ala.L.Rev. 595 (1979).

33. Smith-Hurd Ill.Ann.Stat. ch. 3, §§ 16–17; McKinney's N.Y., EPTL, § 2–1.11 (Supp.1980); Wis.Stat.Ann. §§ 852.13, 853.40 (1951 Supp.).

34. Ill.Rev.Stat. ch. 30, § 211–213 (1980 Supp.).

succession, it is to the death of the decedent, and the statutes spell out the time for other types of transfer.[35]

The effect of renunciation is governed by law, whether it is renunciation of a testamentary provision or of an intestate share. A person cannot renounce "in favor of" a named person to whom the property would not pass by law, although he can of course assign to a specific person. Generally, if renunciation is permitted, a person can renounce part of his share or part of a gift under a will, although partial renunciation of a testamentary provision is dependent upon whether the partial renunciation contravenes the testator's intent.[36] Because of tax advantages, most testators would want to permit partial renunciation, and some wills expressly so provide. A beneficiary cannot renounce after he has accepted benefits under the will.[37]

Where the beneficiary under a will (or the heir in a jurisdiction permitting renunciation of an intestate share) is incompetent, there is doubt about the power of a guardian or conservator to renounce; but the modern rule should permit renunciation where the incompetent has no need for the funds and the property will pass to the family of the incompetent upon renunciation.[38]

PROBLEM

Decedent is survived by two children, one of whom was indebted to decedent. That child has children. Can he renounce, go through bankruptcy, and have his share of the estate pass to his children free of the debt if the Uniform Probate Code [§§ 2–110 (advancements), 2–111 (debts to decedent) and 2–801 (renunciation)] is in force? Cf. Matter of Estate of Colacci, 37 Colo.App. 369, 549 P.2d 1096 (1976).

---

35. Newman and Kalter, "The Need for Disclaimer Legislation—An Analysis of the Background and Current Law," 28 Tax Lawyer 571 (1975).

36. Town of Pepperell v. Whipple, 327 Mass. 688, 100 N.E.2d 844 (1951).

37. See Note, 93 A.L.R.2d 8 (1964) as to what constitutes acceptance or renunciation under a will.

38. For factors in the guardian's election, see 3 A.L.R.3d 6 (1965); Uniform Probate Code, § 2–203. Code § 5–408(3) empowers the court on behalf of an incompetent to renounce any interest by testate or intestate succession or inter vivos transfer.

(4) OFFENSES WHICH MAY BAR THE HEIR OR NEXT OF KIN FROM PARTICIPATING IN AN ESTATE

A. HOMICIDE

ESTATE OF MAHONEY

Supreme Court of Vermont, 1966.
126 Vt. 31, 220 A.2d 475.

Before HOLDEN, C.J., and SHANGRAW, BARNEY, SMITH and KEYSER, JJ.

SMITH, JUSTICE. The decedent, Howard Mahoney, died intestate on May 6, 1961, of gunshot wounds. His wife, Charlotte Mahoney, the appellant here, was tried for the murder of Howard Mahoney in the Addison County Court and was convicted by jury of the crime of manslaughter in March, 1962. She is presently serving a sentence of not less than 12 nor more than 15 years at the Women's Reformatory in Rutland.

Howard Mahoney left no issue, and was survived by his wife and his father and mother. His father, Mark Mahoney, was appointed administrator of his estate which at the present time amounts to $3,885.89. After due notice and hearing, the Probate Court for the District of Franklin entered a judgment order decreeing the residue of the Estate of Howard Mahoney, in equal shares, to the father and mother of the decedent. An appeal from the judgment order and decree has been taken here by the appellant widow. The question submitted is whether a widow convicted of manslaughter in connection with the death of her husband may inherit from his estate.

The general rules of descent provide that if a decedent is married and leaves no issue, his surviving spouse shall be entitled to the whole of decedent's estate if it does not exceed $8,000. 14 V.S.A. § 551(2). Only if the decedent leaves no surviving spouse or issue does the estate descend in equal shares to the surviving father and mother. 14 V.S.A. § 551(3). There is no statutory provision in Vermont regulating the descent and distribution of property from the decedent to the slayer. The question presented is one of first impression in this jurisdiction.

In a number of jurisdictions, statutes have been enacted which in certain instances, at least, prevent a person who has killed another from taking by descent or distribution from the person he has killed. 23 Am.Jur.2d Descent and Distribution, § 98, p. 841. A statute of this nature, carefully drawn, is considered by many authorities to be the best solution to the problems presented. See "Acquisition of property by wilfully killing another—a statutory solution," 49 Harvard Law Review 715 (1935–1936).

Courts in those states that have no statute preventing a slayer from taking by descent or distribution from the estate of his victim, have followed three separate and different lines of decision.

(1) The legal title passed to the slayer and may be retained by him in spite of his crime. The reasoning for so deciding is that devolution of the property of a decedent is controlled entirely by the statutes of descent and distribution; further, that denial of the inheritance to the slayer because of his crime would be imposing an additional punishment for his crime not provided by statute, and would violate the constitutional provision against corruption of blood. Carpenter's Estate, 170 Pa. 203, 32 A. 637, 29 L.R.A. 145; Wall v. Pfanschmidt, 265 Ill. 180, 106 N.E. 785, L.R.A.1915C, 328; Bird v. Plunkett et al., 139 Conn. 491, 95 A.2d 71, 36 A.L.R.2d 951.

(2) The legal title will not pass to the slayer because of the equitable principle that no one should be permitted to profit by his own fraud, or take advantage and profit as a result of his own wrong or crime. Riggs v. Palmer, 115 N.Y. 506, 22 N.E. 188, 5 L.R.A. 340; Price v. Hitaffer, 164 Md. 505, 165 A. 470; Slocum v. Metropolitan Life Ins. Co., 245 Mass. 565, 139 N.E. 816, 27 A.L.R. 1517. Decisions so holding have been criticized as judicially engrafting an exception on the statute of descent and distribution and being "unwaranted judicial legislation." Wall v. Pfanschmidt, supra.

(3) The legal title passes to the slayer but equity holds him to be a constructive trustee for the heirs or next of kin of the decedent. This disposition of the question presented avoids a judicial engrafting on the statutory laws of descent and distribution, for title passes to the slayer. But because of the unconscionable mode by which the property is acquired by the slayer, equity treats him as a constructive trustee and compels him to convey the property to the heirs or next of kin of the deceased.

The reasoning behind the adoption of this doctrine was well expressed by Mr. Justice Cardozo in his lecture on "The Nature of the Judicial Process." "Consistency was preserved, logic received its tribute, by holding that the legal title passed, but it was subject to a constructive trust. A constructive trust is nothing but 'the formula through which the conscience of equity finds expression.' Property is acquired in such circumstances that the holder of legal title may not in good conscience retain the beneficial interest. Equity, to express its disapproval of his conduct, converts him into a trustee." See 4 Scott on Trusts (2d ed. 1956) § 402; Bogert, Trusts and Trustees, (2d ed. 1960), § 478. See Miller v. Belville, 98 Vt. 243, 247, 126 A. 590.

The New Hampshire court was confronted with the same problem of the rights to the benefits of an estate by one who had slain the decedent, in the absence of a statute on the subject. Kelley v. State, 105 N.H. 240, 196 A.2d 68. Speaking for an unanimous court, Chief

Justice Kenison said: "But, even in the absence of statute, a court applying common law techniques can reach a sensible solution by charging the spouse, heir or legatee as a constructive trustee of the property where equity and justice demand it." Kelley v. State, supra, pp. 69, 70. We approve of the doctrine so expressed.

However, the principle that one should not profit by his own wrong must not be extended to every case where a killer acquires property from his victim as a result of the killing. One who has killed while insane is not chargeable as a constructive trustee, or if the slayer had a vested interest in the property, it is property to which he would have been entitled if no slaying had occurred. The principle to be applied is that the slayer should not be permitted to improve his position by the killing, but should not be compelled to surrender property to which he would have been entitled if there had been no killing. The doctrine of constructive trust is involved to prevent the slayer from profiting from his crime, but not as an added criminal penalty. Kelley v. State, supra, p. 70; Restatement of Restitution, § 187(2), comment a.

The appellant here was, as we have noted, convicted of manslaughter and not of murder. She calls to our attention that while the Restatement of Restitution approves the application of the constructive trust doctrine where a devisee or legatee murders the testator, that such rules are not applicable where the slayer was guilty of manslaughter. Restatement of Restitution, § 187, comment e.

The cases generally have not followed this limitation of the rule but hold that the line should not be drawn between murder and manslaughter, but between voluntary and involuntary manslaughter. Kelley v. State, supra; Chase v. Jennifer, 219 Md. 564, 150 A.2d 251, 254.

We think that this is the proper rule to follow. Voluntary manslaughter is an intentional and unlawful killing, with a real design and purpose to kill, even if such killing be the result of sudden passion or great provocation. Involuntary manslaughter is caused by an unlawful act, but not accompanied with any intention to take life. State v. McDonnell, 32 Vt. 491, 545. It is the intent to kill, which when accomplished, leads to the profit of the slayer that brings into play the constructive trust to prevent the unjust enrichment of the slayer by reason of his intentional killing.

In Vermont, an indictment for murder can result in a jury conviction on either voluntary or involuntary manslaughter. State v. Averill, 85 Vt. 115, 132, 81 A. 461. The legislature has provided the sentences that may be passed upon a person convicted of manslaughter, but provides no definition of that offense, nor any statutory distinction between voluntary and involuntary manslaughter. 13 V.S.A. § 2304.

The cause now before us is here on a direct appeal from the Probate Court. Findings of fact were made below from which it appears that the judgment of the Probate Court decreeing the estate of Howard Mahoney to his parents, rather than to his widow, was based upon a finding of the felonious killing of her husband by Mrs. Mahoney. However, the appelless here have asked us to affirm the decree below by imposing a constructive trust on the estate in the hands of the widow.

But the Probate Court did not decree the estate to the widow, and then make her a constructive trustee of such estate for the benefit of the parents. The judgment below decreed the estate directly to the parents, which was in direct contravention of the statutes of descent and distribution. The Probate Court was bound to follow the statutes of descent and distribution and its decree was in error and must be reversed.

The Probate Court was without jurisdiction to impose a constructive trust on the estate in the hands of the appellant, even if it had attempted to do so. Probate courts are courts of special and limited jurisdiction given by statute and do not proceed according to common law. While probate courts possess a portion of equitable powers independent of statute, such powers do not extend to the establishment of purely equitable rights and claims. * * *

However, the jurisdiction of the court of chancery may be invoked in probate matters in aid of the probate court when the powers of that court are inadequate, and it appears that the probate court cannot reasonably and adequately handle the question. The jurisdiction of the chancery court in so acting on probate matters is special and limited only to aiding the probate court. In re Will of Prudenzano, supra; Manley v. Brattleboro Trust Co., supra, 116 Vt. p. 461, 78 A. 2d 488.

The Probate Court, in making its decree, used the record of the conviction of the appellant for manslaughter for its determination that the appellant had feloniously killed her husband. If the jurisdiction of the court of chancery is invoked by the appellees here it will be for the determination of that court, upon proof, to determine whether the appellant wilfully killed her late husband, as it will upon all other equitable considerations that may be offered in evidence, upon charging the appellant with a constructive trust. "The fact that he is convicted of murder in a criminal case does not dispense with the necessity of proof of the murder in a proceedings in equity to charge him as a constructive trustee." Restatement of Restitution, § 187, comment d.

The jurisdiction over charging the appellant with a constructive trust on the estate of Howard Mahoney lies in the court of chancery, and not in the Probate Court.

Decree reversed and cause remanded, with directions that the proceedings herein be stayed for sixty days to give the Administrator of the Estate of Howard Mahoney an opportunity to apply to the Franklin County Court of Chancery for relief. If application is so made, proceedings herein shall be stayed pending the final determination thereof. If application is not so made, the Probate Court for the District of Franklin shall assign to Charlotte Mahoney, surviving wife, the right and interest in and to the estate of her deceased husband which the Vermont Statutes confer.

SHANGRAW, JUSTICE (concurring). I concur in the result. It must be acknowledged that it would be inequitable, and unjust, for a person who has intentionally killed another to inherit from the person whose life he has so taken.

I am concerned with the impractical aspects of the constructive trust doctrine applied in this case. In its application the burden and expense of again litigating the criminal issue must be borne by the parties interested. Here, the expense of carrying the burden of proof on this issue by the parents might well be prohibitive.

The amount involved is relatively small. To continue this litigation, even though the parents should ultimately prevail, may well be, at least money-wise, like digging a hole to get the dirt to fill another hole.

Suitable legislation providing for an exception to the usual operation of the statutes of descent and distribution might well eliminate extended and expensive litigation, should similar or like circumstances again be present.

NOTE

Start 9/8/85

A felon forfeits no interest in an estate unless he is guilty of killing the source from whom the estate is inherited or taken by will.[39] A killer forfeits his interest by common law rule or by statute in a great majority of states,[40]

39. Constitutional provisions and statutes in this country have almost eliminated the common law rules of corruption of blood, forfeiture and escheat for conviction of felony. Atkinson, Wills (2d Ed., 1953) 95; III American Law of Property (1952) 567; 1 Woerner, Administration (3d Ed., 1923) 186. A convict subject to a civil death statute usually takes property by will or by inheritance. Avery v. Everett, 110 N.Y. 317, 18 N.E. 148, 1 L.R.A. 264, 6 Am.St.Rep. 368 (1888); Grooms v. Thomas, 93 Okl. 87, 219 P. 700 (1923). Contra, In re Estate of Donnelly, 125 Cal. 417, 58 P. 61, 73 Am.St.Rep. 62 (1899). Cf. In re Lindewall, 287 N.Y. 347, 39 N.E. 2d 907, 139 A.L.R. 1301 (1942), 42 Col.L. Rev. 1208 (1942), 27 Corn.L.Q. 562 (1942), 17 St.John's L.Rev. 46 (1942) (life convict barred from claiming statutory share against will of deceased wife).

40. Uniform Probate Code, § 2–803 sets forth optional provisions concerning the effect of homicide on Intestate Succession, Wills, Joint Assets, Life Insurance and Beneficiary Designations. Subdivision (a) states: "A surviving spouse, heir or devisee who feloniously and intentionally kills the decedent is not entitled to any benefits under the will or under this Article, and the estate of decedent passes as if the killer had predeceased the decedent. Property appointed by the will of the decedent to or for the benefit of the killer passes as if the killer had predeceased the decedent". Subdivision (e) provides: "A final judgment of conviction of felonious and intentional killing is conclusive for purposes of this section. In the absence of a conviction of felonious and intentional killing the Court may determine by a preponderance of evidence whether the killing was felonious and intentional for purposes of this section". Maki and Kaplan, "Elmer's Case Revisited: The Problem of the Murdering Heir," 41 Ohio St.L.J. 907 (1980) contains a complete analysis of current statutes on a state-by-state basis and suggests some modification of the Uniform Probate Code section.

Statutes dealing with forfeiture for homicide are construed strictly. The operation of the statute may be limited to a case of murder so that manslaughter will not bar the killer. E.g., Strickland v. Wysowatcky, 128 Colo. 221, 250 P.2d 199 (1952). Conviction of the killer may be required before forfeiture. E.g., In re Tarlo's Estate, 315 Pa. 321, 172 A. 139 (1934); 20 Iowa L.Rev. 524 (1935), 33 Mich.L.Rev. 446 (1935); 83 U. of Pa.L. Rev. 97 (1934), 44 Yale L.J. 164 (1934); Note, "In re Kravitz' Estate: Conclusive-

but in the absence of a statute dealing with homicide as a ground for forfeiture, most of the courts have been unwilling to imply such a condition in the intestate laws or the wills acts.[41] The same problem is presented when one joint tenant, or tenant by the entirety, murders the other one,[42] or when a named beneficiary of a life insurance policy murders the insured.[43]

If the killer is permitted to take the property, it may be possible to impose a constructive trust and restore the property to the estate of the victim or to his successors in interest.[44] The constructive trust is a remedial device used to prevent a person from retaining title to property if the retention will unjustly enrich him at the expense of another.[45] The trust is imposed by a court exercising equity jurisdiction. The constructive trust decree recites that the respondent is constructive trustee of the property, and must transfer the property to the complainant. The transfer may, in fact, be made by a court officer or the court may purport to vest title by its decree. A decree for an acounting or for a sale of the property may be rendered in conjunction with the trust decree.[46]

ness of a Prior Conviction Under the Slayer's Act," 70 Albany Law Rev. 213 (1966). Certain interests in property may not be subject to forfeiture. E.g., Tyack v. Tipton, 115 N.E.2d 29 (Ohio App.1951) (exempt property passes to spouse convicted of second degree murder); Blanks v. Jiggetts, 192 Va. 337, 64 S.E.2d 809, 24 A.L.R.2d 1114 (1951) (remainder interest passes to murderer of life tenant). If a forfeiture by the killer is required at common law or by statute, innocent heirs who trace inheritance through the killer should be permitted to take. Bates v. Wilson, 313 Ky. 572, 232 S.W.2d 837 (1950). Contra: In re Norton's Estate, 175 Or. 115, 151 P.2d 719, 156 A.L.R. 617 (1944).

41. E.g., Bird v. Plunkett, 139 Conn. 491, 95 A.2d 71 (1953); In re Duncan's Estate, 40 Wash.2d 850, 246 P.2d 445 (1952). See Atkinson, Wills (2d Ed., 1953) 153; Ames, Lectures on Legal History (1913) 310; Rollison, Wills (1939) 61; 1 Woerner, Administration (3d Ed., 1923) 186; Clark "Crime Does Not Pay—Except For Perhaps Homicide: A Comment on Bird v. Plunkett", 27 Conn.B.J. 170 (1953); McGovern, "Homicide and Succession to Property", 68 Mich.L.Rev. 65 (1969); Reppy, "The Slayer's Bounty-History of Problem in Anglo-American Law", 19 N.Y.U.L.Q.Rev. 229 (1942); Wade, "Acquisition of Property by Wilfully Killing Another—A Statutory Solution", 49 Harv.L.Rev. 715 (1936); 46 Dick.L.Rev. 99 (1942); 29 Mich.L.Rev. 745 (1931); 8 N.Y.U.L.Q.Rev. 492 (1931); 22 Temp.L.Q. 443 (1949); 41 Cornell L.Q. 491 (1956); 17 U.Pitt.L.Rev. 494 (1956); 33 N.C.L.Rev. 702 (1955); "Murderer's Interest in His Victim's Property", 9 Ala. L.Rev. 58 (1956).

42. Most states treat the murder as equivalent to a severance of the tenancy, the murderer keeping half but not acquiring the whole by survivorship. Duncan v. Vassaur, 550 P.2d 929 (Okl. 1976); Matter of Estate of Shields, 224 Kan. 604, 584 P.2d 139 (1978). In a few states the murderer loses the entire interest in the property. In re King's Estate, 261 Wis. 266, 52 N.W.2d 885 (1952).

43. Notes, 29 Me.L.Rev. 126 (1977); 54 N.C.L.Rev. 1085 (1976).

44. E.g., Pritchett v. Henry, 287 S.W. 2d 546 (Tex.Civ.App.1955); See V Scott, Trusts (3d Ed., 1967) §§ 492–492.6; Ames, "Can a Murderer Acquire Title by His Crime and Keep It", 36 Am.L. Reg.,N.S., 225 (1897); Restatement, Restitution (1937) § 187. See Waters, "The English Constructive Trust: A Look Into the Future", 19 Vand.L.Rev. 1215 (1966).

45. Restatement, Restitution (1937) § 160. The courts sometimes call a constructive trust a trust "ex delicto", "ex maleficio" or "in invitum" or an "involuntary trust". The constructive trust is classed as a trust "by operation of law" since it does not require an expressed intention by a settlor to establish it. See Chapter VIII, Section 1. Holdsworth refers to applications of the constructive trust rule in the Sixteenth Century. V Holdsworth, History of English Law (3d Ed., Methuen, 1945) 305. No clear cut treatment of the constructive trust as a distinct legal institution appears until Lord Nottingham's famous classification in Cook v. Fountain, 3 Swanst. 586, 36 Eng.Rep. 984 (1676).

46. By the better view, the complainant has an interest in a constructive trust when the duty of restitution arises. The duty arises when the property is acquired wrongfully. The court decree declares and enforces the preexistent duty.

The complainant must come into equity with clean hands[47] and must be willing to do equity.[48] It must be shown that there is property in existence upon which a constructive trust may be imposed,[49] and that the wrongdoer or someone claiming through him has title to it.[50] If these conditions exist, the major difficulty is in determining whether the facts of the case justify the use of the constructive trust device. The burden of proof is upon the complainant to show facts which justify application of a constructive trust by clear and convincing evidence.[51]

The circumstances under which a court will impose a constructive trust upon property in the hands of one other than the wrongdoer are not entirely settled. A bona fide purchaser for value of the legal title will cut off equities in the property of which he had no notice. One who takes as transferee from the wrongdoer with notice of the circumstances giving rise to a constructive trust is required to restore the property to the injured party or to his estate.[52] A constructive trust is also applied to property in the hands of one who, in the very unusual case, takes from the wrongdoer without value but without notice, unless the taker changes his position before notice is received.[53] But if a person acquires property directly from the injured party as a result of wrongful action by another, and is not on notice at the time of acquisition and does not give value [54] or change his position before notice is received, should a constructive trust then be applied? Suppose a wife murders her husband so that their child will take his estate by the intestate law.[55] Should a constructive trust be imposed upon the property in the

47. A constructive trust may be refused when a person has transferred legal title to another on oral trust for the transferor's benefit to avoid creditors and the transferee refuses to perform the oral promise. See Chapter VIII, Section 3.

48. The complainant may be required to reimburse the defendant for expenses incurred by the latter in improving the property before the court will order a reconveyance.

49. A res is required for a constructive trust as for trusts of other types. A person who has been induced to render services cannot avail himself of a remedy by constructive trust although he might secure an equitable lien upon property or have a remedy at law. See Restatement, Restitution (1937) § 160, Comment *i.*

50. Remedies at law are available to secure possession of property that is wrongfully withheld by a person who lacks title. No constructive trust would be imposed upon stolen property in the hands of a thief, although if the thief uses the stolen property to acquire title to other property, he can be held as constructive trustee of the property so acquired.

51. Some courts have used stronger language concerning the quantum of evidence required. E.g., Catherwood v. Morris, 345 Ill. 617, 636, 178 N.E. 487, 494 (1931) ("If the evidence is doubtful or capable of reasonable explanation upon a theory other than the existence of the trust, it is not sufficient to enforce a decree declaring and enforcing the trust"). More than a preponderance of the evidence is required because of the moral stigma attaching to acts that may justify the imposition of a constructive trust, and because the introduction of parol evidence may disturb titles of record by deed or will, or titles evidenced by some other writing such as a bill of sale.

52. Restatement, Restitution (1937) §§ 172–176. A person is on notice if he actually knows or should have known the facts giving rise to a constructive trust, § 174.

53. The change of position must be such that it would be inequitable to require restoration of the property. Restatement, Restitution (1937), § 178, Comment *a.*

54. Value may be furnished either to the transferor or to the third party wrongdoer. If value is furnished to the latter, the situation is the same as if the wrongdoer had acquired title and then transferred it for value to the innocent party. Restatement, Restitution (1937) § 167, Comment *e.*

55. Cases of this sort are, fortunately, rare; but, although as Justice Holmes put the matter in Grigsby v. Russell, 222 U.S. 149, 32 S.Ct. 58, 56 L.Ed. 133 (1911) "The law has no universal cynic fear of the temptation opened by a pecuniary benefit accruing upon a death", the

hands of the child even though the child would have been heir if his father had died naturally and even though the child had nothing to do with the murder other than providing the motive for it? It is probable that in such a case a court would be reticent to raise a constructive trust since normally the constructive trust would be declared for the estate and the child in this case is the heir. The Restatement of Restitution takes the position that no constructive trust should be applied in such a situation; [56] although the Restatement does take the position that innocence of the taker is not a ground for refusing to raise a constructive trust,[57] and there is case and text authority to support the latter view.[58] Except for the homicide cases, little distinction seems to be made between the cases in which an innocent party takes through the wrongdoer and the cases in which the innocent party takes directly from the person injured. Certainly one guilty of bad conduct should not be permitted to frustrate a recovery by having property placed in innocent hands; and it is arguable that a person who acquires property without notice, ratifies or adopts the wrongdoing when notice is received. But many courts seem to view the constructive trust at least partially as a punitive institution; and if it views the trust as "punitive" or "retributive" as distinguished from simply "restitutive", it will no doubt tend to refuse a constructive trust when the innocent party has taken directly from the person injured. This inclination appears to be especially strong when, as in the homicide case suggested, the innocent party takes by operation of the intestate law.[59]

If property is acquired under circumstances giving rise to a constructive trust, and this property is exchanged for other property, the trust may be imposed upon the product of the exchange.[60] But if the wrongdoer transfers the property to one who takes without notice, and who before notice of the facts exchanges the property for other property, the claimant is not entitled to a constructive trust upon the product of the exchange in the hands of the innocent party, although he may enforce an equitable lien to secure his

greater the certainty of devolution of property in a particular manner, the greater the temptation to homicide. Sir Sydney Smith, a distinguished pathologist and figure in British forensic medicine, has commented upon the fact that the Egyptian system of polygamy, coupled with limitations in the Moslem law upon testamentary power in favor of children, produces many child poisonings and ultimately poisoning of the *pater familias* as the various wives maneuver for preference to their own offspring by killing off the offspring of each other. See Smith, Mostly Murder (1959) 75.

56. Restatement, Restitution (1937) § 187, Comment *k*.

57. Restatement, Restitution (1937) §§ 167, 178, 184, Comment *j*.

58. E.g., V Scott, Trusts (3d Ed., 1967) § 469; Bogert, Trusts and Trustees (2d Ed., 1960) § 473. In many of the cases in which a trust has been imposed, the force of the decision is weakened since the facts are sufficient for a finding of notice to the recipient or his actual collusion with the active party. E.g., Bogle v. Goldsworthy, 202 Iowa 764, 211 N. W. 257 (1926). But in other cases the trust has been imposed when such facts were not present. E.g., Pope v. Garrett, 147 Tex. 18, 211 S.W.2d 559 (1948), 3 S. W.L.J. 175 (1949).

59. In Pope v. Garrett, 204 S.W.2d 867 (Tex.Civ.App.1947) Cody, J., remarked at 204 S.W.2d 871: "The fact that the wrongful act caused the non-participating appellants to become vested with undivided interests in the land resulted from the laws of descent and distribution. And what the law gives a party can never be called unjust enrichment." In cases of constructive "fraud" the New Jersey courts have refused to apply a constructive trust when the wrongdoer and the innocent party take as tenants in common. Powell v. Yearance, 73 N.J.Eq. 117, 67 A. 892 (1907). See comment "The Necessity for Unjust Enrichment in a Constructive Trust in California", 19 Hastings L.Rev. 1268 (1968).

60. Restatement, Restitution (1937) § 202.

claim for restitution.[61] In any event, before the product of an exchange can be subjected to a constructive trust the claimant must be able to trace into the product the property wrongfully acquired.[62] He has only a personal claim against the party who injured him if he cannot trace.

As the major equitable device for restitution, the constructive trust will be involved in many situations considered hereafter in this book. In any suitable situation in which a person has been deprived of property by the wrongful act of another, such as fraud, undue influence or duress, the loss to the injured party being accompanied by a commensurate gain to the wrongdoer, the trust will be imposed to restore the property to the injured party or to his estate.[63] The courts are also quick to respond to breaches of confidential relationships; and will impose a constructive trust to remedy an abuse of a confidential position.[64]

The courts have not limited the constructive trust to the facts of these traditional situations. Nor have the courts tried to enumerate the situations in which a constructive trust will be applied. The device is reserved as a flexible means for dealing with bad conduct in whatever shape or form it may appear.

The trust may be applied for the benefit of one who was not deprived of property but was prevented from receiving it. One who obtains the execution or revocation of a will or a part thereof by a fraudulent misrepresentation of extrinsic fact, by a fraudulent representation of the nature or contents of the instrument, by undue influence, or one who prevents the execution or revocation of a will by fraud or duress, may be required to hold the property which he acquires as a result of his wrong for the benefit of the person who would have received it.[65] In Brazil v. Silva,[66] the testator requested his wife to burn his will but she burned an envelope in his presence which did not contain the will but which she said contained it. The will was probated but the heirs of the testator sought to impose a constructive trust upon the property which the widow received as a result of her fraud. The court imposed a constructive trust and in the course of its opinion stated:[67] "* * * We see no real distinction whatever between the present case and those wherein a decedent has either been prevented from making a will by the promise of the heir that he will carry out the decedent's wishes, or has been prevented from revoking a will by a similar promise of the beneficiary. * * * Equity will not, in effect, make a revocation where there was none under the statute merely because the decedent desired or actually attempted to make one. It grants relief only in case and because of a wrong done by

61. Restatement, Restitution (1937) §§ 203, 204.

62. Restatement, Restitution (1937) § 215.

63. Thus, the constructive trust may be a remedy in many of the situations considered in Chapter VII, "Contest of Wills and Related Remedies" when for some reason the person injured has no adequate remedy in the probate court. Likewise, the constructive trust may be used to give a remedy when a contract to make a will has been breached. See Chapter XII, Section 5.

64. The trust is often used to obtain restitution when a fiduciary has taken advantage of his position to reap an improper benefit at the expense of the beneficiary of a trust; or to require an attorney to give up property which he has acquired by breach of his confidential relationship with his client.

65. An objection to the use of the constructive trust in this situation is that it may circumvent the statutes requiring formalities for the execution of wills, or for their revocation or the provisions of the Statute of Frauds which require trusts of land to be proved by a writing. These problems are developed in detail in subsequent chapters.

66. 181 Cal. 490, 185 P. 174 (1919).

67. 185 P. at 177.

the defendant of which he seeks to reap the fruit. In such a case equity will not permit him to have safe shelter under the formal requirements of the law, either statutory or other." [68]

A constructive trust may be impressed upon property when the person for whose benefit the trust is declared does not suffer a loss in the sense of being deprived of property or prevented from receiving it as a result of wrongdoing. For example, a fiduciary who profits through a violation of his duty may be compelled to surrender his profit to the person to whom his duty is owed.[69]

A constructive trust has been imposed even though the acquisition of the property by the constructive "trustee" was not by fraudulent conduct. In these situations the courts have spoken of "constructive" fraud or the "possession of property under circumstances that render its retention unconscionable". If a deed is executed subject to a mutual mistake of fact, as when the deed describes property that the parties did not intend to subject to the bargain, the deed may be rescinded or reformed in equity and a constructive trust imposed to secure the return of the property to the grantor.[70] But if the mistake is unilateral and the conveyance is for consideration, no rescission or reformation may be had and no constructive trust imposed unless the grantee induced the mistake. Nor is a remedy by reformation and constructive trust given when a will or part thereof is executed subject to a mistake of fact.[71] A will cannot be reformed in equity and the courts often state that a constructive trust will be imposed only when the testator's frame of mind was induced by wrongful conduct. But when a will is induced by an oral promise that the promisor will hold a legacy or devise in trust for another, and the promisor repudiates his promise after the will becomes effective, a majority of courts will impose a constructive trust upon the property received by the promisor for the benefit of the beneficiary named in the oral trust, even though the will was not obtained by actual fraud and no confidential relationship existed between the testator and the promisor.[72]

PROBLEMS

1. H and W are married. They own a residence in their joint names as tenants by the entirety (or as joint tenants with right of survivorship). H has stock in the X Company in his name and has given stock in the Y Company to his wife W, in whose name the latter stock is registered. H murders W and commits suicide immediately thereafter. H is survived by his parents and a brother; W is survived by her mother and two sisters. To whom should the above items of property belong? If you represented the heirs of H, would you stipulate that the killing of W was murder or would you allege insanity? On tenancy by the entirety property see National City Bank v. Bledsoe, 237 Ind. 130, 144 N.E.2d 710 (1957), 27 U.Cinc.L.Rev. 135 (1958); cf. In re Foster's Estate, 182 Kan. 315, 320 P.2d 855 (1958). On the insanity issue see Campbell v. Ray, 102 N.J.Super. 235, 245 A.2d 761 (1968); Estate

68. In Dixon v. Olmius, 1 Cox 414, 29 Eng.Rep. 1227 (1787) the court imposed a constructive trust upon a wrongdoer who had prevented republication of a will. For cases involving promises to hold in trust in return for the testator's act of revoking a will or executing a will see Chapter XI, Section 5.

69. Restatement, Restitution (1937) §§ 197, 202, Comment *c*.

70. Restatement, Restitution (1937) § 39, Comment *c*, § 163.

71. See Chapter VII, Section 2(5).

72. See Chapter IX, Section 1(4).

of Wirth, 59 Misc.2d 300, 298 N.Y.S.2d 565 (1969). Assume the following statute is in force:

> "No person who shall be convicted of feloniously killing, or procuring the killing of, another person shall inherit or take by will or otherwise from such other person any portion of his estate".

Will you exclude the husband from taking the property of the wife if she is found to die intestate? If the husband takes the property of the wife by intestacy or survivorship, will you impose a constructive trust upon his successors in interest for the benefit of the successors in interest of the wife? See United Trust Co. v. Pyke, 199 Kan. 1, 427 P.2d 67 (1967).

2. Can a conviction of murder be admitted as conclusive in civil litigation to determine property rights? Can the issue of murder be relitigated? In re Kravitz' Estate, 418 Pa. 319, 211 A.2d 443 (1965).

3. If a wife is murdered by her husband, and by her will leaves her residuary estate to her husband if he survives her and if he does not survive her to his two children by a prior marriage, should the court impose a constructive trust for her heirs or for the alternate beneficiaries under the will? In re Wilson's Will, 5 Wis.2d 178, 92 N.W.2d 282 (1958).

4. § 2–803 of the Uniform Probate Code is phrased in terms of "feloniously and intentionally" killing. If a minor child kills his parents but cannot be charged with a criminal act because of the Uniform Juvenile Court Act provisions, can he be barred from inheriting? Estate of Josephson, 297 N.W. 2d 444 (N.D.1980). Does "intentionally" include an intentional criminal act which unintentionally results in the death? Estate of Kramme, 20 Cal.3d 567, 143 Cal.Rptr. 542, 573 P.2d 1369 (1978) (husband confronted wife and her lover with a shotgun; in the ensuing struggle between the husband and the lover the wife was shot and killed).

covered 9/9/85

B. MARITAL MISCONDUCT AND MISCELLANEOUS GROUNDS FOR DISQUALIFICATION

Marital misconduct may bar a spouse from participation in an estate. The English Statute of Westminster II [73] barred the dower of a wife who deserted her husband and committed adultery.[74] This statute is part of the common law of several states [75] and has been the pattern for statutes in others.[76] Desertion alone or adultery alone will not bar dower unless given that effect by statute.[77] The marital misconduct provision in the Statute of Westminster II does not bar a distributive share in personal property [78] or a share as heir in land.[79]

73. 13 Edw. I, c. 34 (1285).

74. The departure of the wife must have been voluntary. Dower was not barred if her husband permitted her to return to his house after she had committed adultery.

75. E.g., Reel v. Elder, 62 Pa. 308, 1 Am.Rep. 414 (1869).

76. See Vernier, American Family Laws (1935) §§ 202, 221; 1 Woerner, Administration (3d Ed., 1923) 340. The statutes often bar curtesy as well as dower.

77. E.g., Cogswell v. Tibbetts, 3 N.H. 41 (1824); Jarnigan v. Jarnigan, 12 Lea (Tenn.) 292 (1883).

78. E.g., Turner v. Cole, 24 Ala. 364 (1854); Mack v. Pairo, 136 Md. 179, 110 A. 198 (1920).

79. Davis v. Davis' Estate, 167 Wis. 328, 167 N.W. 819 (1918).

Adoption of "no fault" divorce legislation in many states makes it unlikely that marital misconduct will affect intestate succession in the absence of an express statutory provision. If misconduct cannot be considered in division of property at divorce, it should not be a bar at death. Desertion coupled with a subsequent bigamous marriage may, however, bar the deserting spouse by application of the doctrine of equitable estoppel.[80] In a few states desertion alone is enough to bar the spouse who deserts.[81] The situation is obviously one in which a will should be executed to prevent operation of the intestate succession law, although even then the deserting spouse may be entitled to a statutory share (discussed in the next Chapter).

A remedy is usually given at law or in equity for fraud, undue influence or duress practiced upon a testator or intestate. In cases of this type the party guilty of misconduct may be deprived of his interest in the estate.[82] Other forms of misconduct towards the source from whom an estate is claimed by inheritance or by will are unlikely to bar the claimant.

A statute may disqualify a parent who has failed or refused to support his child from inheriting from the child.[83]

(5) ALIENS

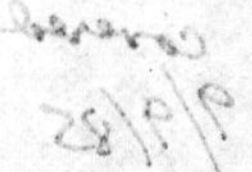

Background

Aliens were subject to major disabilities in intestate and testamentary succession to *land* under the English common law. While these common law disabilities gradually are being eliminated in the United States,[84] new disabilities of aliens as to both land and personalty have

80. No true estoppel arises unless someone acts to his detriment relying upon the validity of the bigamous marriage. E.g., Smith v. Fuller, 138 Iowa 91, 115 N.W. 912, 16 L.R.A.,N.S., 98 (1917).

81. E.g., In re Abila's Estate, 32 Cal. 2d 559, 197 P.2d 10 (1948). For the effect of divorce upon inheritance and marital estates see Vernier, American Family Laws (1932) §§ 96–102.

82. See Chapter VII, Section 2, infra.

83. E.g., McKinney's N.Y., EPTL, § 4–1.4 (1980 Supp.); see also Uniform Probate Code, § 2–109 as to inheritance by the father of an illegitimate child.

84. See "Rights and Restrictions on Interests of Aliens in U.S. Estates: Federal and State Laws Affecting Administration and Distribution of U.S. Estates in Which Aliens Hold Interests", 15 Real Property, Probate and Trust Jour. 659 (1980) for a survey of Federal and state policies concerning aliens in all matters related to estates. The appendix to this article contains a summary of state statutory provisions as of 1980. Uniform Probate Code § 2–112 provides: "No person is disqualified to take as an heir because he or a person through whom he claims is or has been an alien." This section seems sufficiently broad to eliminate disabilities in inheritance by aliens including alien enemies.

been developed. These new disabilities have been limited significantly by Federal constitutional provisions.

An alien *enemy* at common law could neither take nor hold title except by the King's special license. The *enemy* had no effective claim to property by intestacy, will or conveyance. He was disabled as to both land and personalty.

An alien *friend*, by contrast, could take and retain title to *personalty*. The alien friend could be a distributee or legatee. But with respect to *land*, an alien *friend* was almost on the same basis with an alien *enemy*.

An alien *friend* could not take title to land by intestate succession nor could descent be traced through him. He was said to lack "inheritable blood".[85] He could take title to land by will or by conveyance, but his title could then be divested through an "inquest of office found".[86] These rules were generalized into the propositions that alien friends could not take land by "operation of law" but could take land by voluntary transfer.[87]

The land disabilities of an alien friend at common law stemmed from the fact that land tenures were the basis of the medieval English constitutional system. Military support of the King and his revenues depended upon the loyalty and cooperation of his feudal tenants. An alien *enemy* would have no loyalty; and while an alien friend was viewed as having a temporary duty of loyalty while in England, his sovereign might become an enemy of the English King.

The common law disability of the alien *friend* as an intestate heir developed while feudalism was still an important constitutional institution in England. Blackstone wrote that the "defence of the kingdom would have been defeated" had not such a prohibition against alien heirs been enforced.[88] When it became possible to convey and devise land in England, the importance of feudalism as a constitutional institution had diminished, and more liberal rules concerning conveyances and devises to alien *friends* were then developed.

85. II Blackstone, Commentaries (3d Ed., 1768) 249.

86. The land escheats when the alien dies if not divested by the inquest of office found.

87. See 1 Powell, The Law of Real Property (Rohan Rev., 1981) 375.

88. II Blackstone, Commentaries (3d Ed., 1768) 249. Sir Edward Coke in Calvin's Case, 7 Co.Rep. 1a, 18b, 17 Eng. Rep. 377, 399 (1606) commented that if an alien were permitted to inherit: "(1) The secrets of the realm might thereby be discovered. (2) The revenues of the realm (the sinews of war, and ornaments of peace) should be taken and enjoyed by strangers born. (3) It should tend to the destruction of the realm". Calvin's Case involved the status as an alien of a Scot born in Scotland after the accession of James I (James VI of Scotland) to the English throne. The various opinions in Calvin's Case indicate the great difficulty in determining in England who was and who was not an alien, a problem which survives on a less complex scale in the United States today. Pollock and Maitland, whose History of English Law is the best source for a discussion of early English law concerning aliens, assign the common law alien land disabilities to persistent feudal viewpoints and nascent nationalism. These authors point out that aliens were not disabled in land matters in England until King John seized the lands of English nobles who adhered to Philip Augustus of France. I Pollock and Maitland, History of English Law (2d Ed. 1899) 461.

Current Status of Alien Disabilities in Succession

When a lawyer deals with a question concerning title to land, he may find it necessary to inquire into the scope of disabilities imposed upon aliens in land transactions in the state at an early date. This may prove a difficult undertaking in particular states because of uncertainty as to the extent to which common law land disabilities of aliens applied and to piecemeal development of state statutory policy in this area. There are also Federal and state constitutional restraints upon state powers to regulate alien property which have been delineated only gradually by the courts.[89] For example, an exercise of state powers pertaining to alien property may intrude into the conduct of foreign affairs for which the Federal Government has exclusive responsibility. The war and commerce powers may restrict state action. Under the Trading with the Enemy Act of 1917,[90] for example, the alien property custodian vests property owned by alien enemies in time of war. The only way a state can prevent this is to prevent the alien enemy from taking title; and once the property is vested it is withdrawn from the state tax base. Under the Foreign Assets Control Regulations,[91] promulgated under the Trading with the Enemy Act, transactions by aliens who are nationals of listed nations in United States properties are prohibited and any proceeds from these transactions are blocked.[92] Licenses exempting from these restrictions can be obtained from the Treasury but are infrequently granted. If the national of a listed nation takes property by intestate succession or by will, an administrator or executor will not be able to transfer or deal with the property for his benefit without Treasury authorization. A lawyer must be familiar with these regulations in appropriate cases since these regulations supersede conflicting state law.

Discriminations between resident aliens and citizens are vulnerable to attack as violations of the equal protection clause of the Fourteenth Amendment. As decisions are made concerning such constitutional limitations, not only must the time of the decision be considered but it is also possible, although not likely, that the decision will be viewed as having retroactive effect.[93] A treaty pertaining to alien property rights will supersede conflicting state laws on the same subject. A lawyer concerned with the rights of an alien to intestate or

89. The control over succession to real and personal property was thought by many lawyers to be exclusively reserved to the states by the Tenth Amendment. As late as 1849, the revisors of the Virginia Code doubted that a treaty concerning alien property could supersede a conflicting state law. Any questions concerning these matters have now been eliminated by the United States Supreme Court.

90. 50 U.S.C.A.App. § 1 et seq., 40 Stat. 411 (1917).

91. 31 C.F.R. Part 500, et seq. (1980).

92. Countries now on the blocked list are North Korea, Cambodia, North Vietnam, South Vietnam, and Cuba. Rhodesia was on the list but taken off in 1979. China was removed in 1980. Iranian assets were frozen under this authority during the hostage crisis. 31 C.F.R. Part 535.

93. The issue of retroactivity has arisen in connction with the *Levy* decision pertaining to the status of an illegitimate. See Jerry Vogel Music Co. Inc. v. Edward B. Marks Music Corp., 425 F.2d 836 (2d Cir. 1969).

testamentary succession to property must thus inquire whether a treaty concerning these rights is in force. Although a lawyer usually does not have to probe the earlier laws of a state in dealing with the rights of an alien in intestate and testamentary succession to personalty, he will often have to deal with Federal and state constitutional provisions and with treaties bearing upon this subject.

Approximately half of the states impose no disabilities upon aliens, friend or enemy, in intestate or testamentary succession to property.[94] Common law disabilities are eliminated in these states and no new disabilities of significance have been developed. A few of the states in which alien disabilities are retained by judicial decision or by statute, restrict these disabilities to alien enemies in succession to land,[95] the alien enemy succeeding to personalty under an implied license.[96] In other states aliens ineligible for citizenship are disabled in succession to land,[97] while in yet others miscellaneous restrictions are encountered, some extending their disabilities to nonresident aliens[98] and others placing restrictions upon the amount of land the alien can take by devise or descent,[99] the time for which the alien can hold title,[1] or the use the alien may make of the land if he gets it.[2] The policies underlying many of these disabilities are difficult to ascertain. Some of the statutes probably were aimed at specific cases in the past. All, especially those applying to *resident* aliens, are likely to present constitutional issues.[3]

94. Ala.Code § 35–1–1 (1940) (1980 Supp.); Alaska Stat. § 13.11.060 (1962) (1981 Supp.); Ariz.Rev.Stat.Ann. § 14–2112 (1956) (1981 Supp.); Ark.Stat. Ann. § 61–143 (1979 Supp.); Colo.Rev. Stat. § 15–11–112 (1973) (1978 Supp.); Del.Code Ann. tit. 25, §§ 306–308 (1974) (1978 Supp.); Fla.Stat.Ann. § 732.1101 (West); Idaho Code § 15–2–112 (1979 Supp.); Me.Rev.Stat.Ann. tit. 33, § 451 (1981 Supp.); Md. Real Prop. Code Ann. § 14–101 (1974); Mont.Rev.Codes Ann. § 91A–2–111 (1977); N.M.Stat.Ann. § 32A–2–112 (1976); N.D.Cent. Code § 30.-1–04–12 (1976); Pa.Stat.Ann. tit. 20, §§ 2104(8), 2518 (1975) (Purdon Supp.1981); Tenn.Code Ann. §§ 31–401, 31–402, 64–201, 64–202 (1980 Supp.); Tex.Rev. Civ.Stat.Ann. Art. 166a (Vernon); Utah Code Ann. § 75–2–112 (1975); Vermont, Const. Ch. II, § 62 (1873); Wash.Rev. Code Ann. § 64.16.005 (1981 Supp.); W. Va.Code § 36–1–21 (1980 Supp.); Wis. Stat.Ann. §§ 710.01, 710.02 (West Spec. Pamph. 1980); Hawaii appears to have no restrictions and those in Minnesota are negligible.

95. Ga.Code Ann. § 79–303 (1973) (1980 Supp.); Ky.Rev.Stat. § 381.290 (1980 Supp.); N.J.Stat.Ann. § 46:3–18 (West Supp. 1980); S.D.Comp. Laws Ann. Ch. 43–2A (1980 Supp.); Va.Code Ann. § 55–1 (1980 Supp.)

96. The most detailed statement is in Techt v. Hughes, 229 N.Y. 222, 128 N.E. 185, 11 A.L.R. 166 (1920). The implied license is probably that of the Federal Government as an incident to its conduct of economic warfare. When the alien succeeds to the personalty his title then will be vested by the Alien Property Custodian. Trading with the Enemy Act, 50 U.S.C.A. Appendix, § 1 et seq.

97. E.g., Wyoming Const. art. 1, § 29; Wyo.Stat.Ann. §§ 34–15–101 to –103.

98. E.g., Conn.Gen.Stat. § 47–58 (1980 Supp.); Kan.S.A., § 59.511 (1974 Supp.); Miss.Code, § 89–1–23 (1972).

99. Minn.Stat.Ann. § 500.221 (1980 Supp.); S.C.Code § 27–13–30 (1979 Supp.). The land limitations usually are so generous as to impose no significant limitation upon the alien.

1. E.g., Ind.Stat.Ann. § 32–1–8–2 (1979 Supp.); Neb.Rev.Stat. § 76–405 (1976).

2. E.g., Conn.Gen.Stat. § 47–58 (1980 Supp.) (mining, conversion of produce to articles of trade, etc.).

3. Statutes concerning alien enemies may intrude upon the war power of the Congress. Statutes discriminating against resident aliens are subject to attack on due process grounds.

The statutes bearing upon the succession by aliens to real and personal property which appear to have continuing vitality are the "reciprocity" and "retention" statutes. Similar policies may have been developed in some states by judicial decision.[4]

These statutes and court rules were framed to frustrate Nazi confiscation of Jewish property and similar confiscations in occupied territories. After World War II these same statutes and court rules were applied to non-resident aliens in various foreign countries having totalitarian governments and were applied to non-resident aliens in Communist countries with particular vehemence.

"Reciprocity" statutes have been enacted in a number of Western states and in North Carolina.[5] The former California statute is the prototype.[6] These statutes key the right of a non-resident alien to inherit upon the existence of a reciprocal right of an American to inherit in the state of the non-resident alien's nationality. Some states have a further provision that the American must have the right to receive his share of the foreign estate in this country.[7]

The required "reciprocity" appears to differ under the statutes. The statute may require that the foreign state give the same inheritance rights to an American as it gives to its own citizens. Since the alien may have few inheritance rights in his own country, one court has construed the former California statute containing this definition of reciprocity as assuming that the inheritance rights in the foreign country "meet some minimum standard of economic substantiality" and that such rights "are regularly recognized in practice".[8] Statutes in other states extend to non-resident aliens the same inheritance

4. For the extensive literature concerning these problems written shortly before or after *Zschernig* see Fallwell, "State Probate Laws and Alien Heirs—the Zschernig Legacy", 21 Baylor L.Rev. 450 (1969); Snouffer, "Nonresident Alien Inheritance Statutes and Foreign Policy—A Conflict?" 47 Ore.L.Rev. 390 (1968). See Frank, "Alien Inheritance Statutes: An Examination of the Constitutionality of State Laws Restricting the Rights of Nonresident Aliens to Inherit From American Decedents", 25 Syra.L. Rev. 597 (1974) for a survey of New York cases since *Zschernig*. Notes, "The Right of Nonresident Aliens to Participate in the Distribution of American Decedents' Estates", 43 Conn.Bar Jour. 487 (1969); "Alien Inheritance Statutes and the Foreign Relations Power", 1969 Duke L.J. 153; "Alien Heirs—Iron Curtain Statutes as Unconstitutional Invasions of Foreign Affairs", 72 Dick.L.Rev. 675 (1968); "State Statutes Affecting the Inheritance and Distribution of Estates to Foreign Heirs", 1967 U.Ill.L. Forum 141; "Alien Succession Under State Law: The Jurisdictional Conflict," 20 Syracuse Law Rev. 661 (1969); "Reciprocity and Retention Statutes—A New Direction", 22 Rutgers L.Rev. 770 (1968); "The Statutory Regulation of Inheritance by Non Resident Aliens" 13 Vill.L.Rev. 148 (1967). Comments, "Testate and Intestate Succession to Domestic Property by Alien Beneficiaries", 17 De Paul L.Rev. 343 (1968); "In re Estate of Kraemer" 46 North Dakota L.Rev. 465 (1970). There was extensive comment in the law reviews concerning the "reciprocity" and "retention" policies prior to *Zschernig* and these articles, notes and comments are cited in the various opinions in *Zschernig* and in the materials here mentioned.

5. Iowa Code § 567.8 (1979 Supp.); Neb.Rev.Stat. § 4–107 (1974); Nev.Rev. Stat. §§ 134.230–134.250 (1979); N.C. Gen.Stat. § 64–3 (1979 Supp.); Okla.Stat. Ann. tit. 60, § 121 (West Supp.1980); Wyo.Stat.Ann. §§ 34–15–101, 34–15–102.

6. Cal.Prob.Code § 259 repealed by c. 425, p. 1025, § 1 (1974).

7. E.g., Nev.Rev.Stat. §§ 134.230, 134.250 (1979).

8. Estate of Larkin, 65 Cal.2d 60, 65, 52 Cal.Rptr. 441, 442, 416 P.2d 473, 476 (1966); 80 Harv.L.Rev. 675 (1967).

rights which the foreign state of the alien extends to American citizens.[9] Such a statute requires a local probate court to apply multiple standards and make detailed inquiries into foreign legal administration.

The burden of proof of reciprocity, whatever the required reciprocity may be, rests upon the non-resident alien. Reciprocity must be proved as a fact in most of the states having these statutes.[10] A court will take no judicial notice of facts of reciprocity nor will *stare decisis* assist the alien in bearing his burden of proof. If the alien fails to bear his burden of proof, his interest is said to be "divested" so that it passes to other relatives or to the state.

Retention statutes are in force in several Eastern states.[11] Oregon once had a statute containing both reciprocity and retention elements.[12] The New York statute is the prototype.

Retention statutes are premised upon the right of the non-resident alien to inherit. The non-resident alien must bear the burden of proof that if the property is transmitted to him in the foreign country he will be permitted full use, benefit and control of the funds. If he fails to sustain this burden of proof, the property is placed in custody. The ownership by the alien continues but the statute may set a time limit within which the alien must produce the proof required. The fund may or may not draw interest while in the hands of the custodian.

Broad discretion has been conferred upon the courts concerning the evidence to be received upon the retention issue. The court may take judicial notice of the facts or it may raise a virtually irrebuttable presumption that the alien will not have the use, benefit and control of the property if it is transmitted to him.

The reciprocity and retention provisions can be superseded by a treaty of the United States with the state of the non-resident alien. Also the application of these statutes today to the nationals of countries whose legal systems are likely to be unfamiliar to American judges has required minute inquiries by these judges which can be viewed as intrusions into the conduct of foreign policy. This basis for challenging the validity of these statutes has been strengthened by the practice of some judges to emphasize in their opinions the importance of withholding funds from states which they regarded as actual or potential enemies of the United States.

The former Oregon statute was invalidated in Zschernig v. Miller.[13] This statute contained reciprocity and retention provisions with

9. E.g., Okla.Stat.Ann., tit. 60, § 121 (1971) (West Supp.1980).

10. E.g., Estate of Schneider, 140 Cal. App.2d 710, 296 P.2d 45 (1956), construing former Cal.Probate Code § 259.

11. Conn.Gen.Stat.Ann. § 45–278 (1980 Supp.); Mass.Gen.Laws Ann. ch. 206, §§ 27A–27B (West); Mich.Comp. Laws Ann. § 704.55a (1979); N.J.Stat. Ann. § 3A:25–10 (West Supp.1980); N.Y. Surr.Ct.Proc.Act, § 2218 (McKinney Supp.1980); Ohio Rev.Code Ann. § 2113.81 (Page 1976); R.I.Gen.Laws § 33–13–13 (1969).

12. Or.Rev.Stat. § 111.070 repealed by c. 595, § 305 (1969). This was the statute involved in *Zschernig.*

13. 389 U.S. 429, 88 S.Ct. 664, 19 L. Ed.2d 683 (1968). In Clark v. Allen, 331 U.S. 503, 67 S.Ct. 1431, 91 L.Ed. 1633

the additional requirement that American citizens must have the right to receive payments here from foreign estates.

An Oregon resident, probably a citizen, died intestate leaving real and personal property, his sole heirs being non-resident aliens who were nationals of East Germany. The Oregon Supreme Court held that the aliens could take the land of the intestate pursuant to Article IV of the Treaty of 1923 with Germany but held that the aliens could not take the personalty, this not being covered by the treaty. A majority of the Court held the Oregon statute as applied to non-resident aliens an unconstitutional intrusion into the conduct of foreign affairs reserved by the Constitution to the Federal Government. Justice Douglas, for the majority, commented that the earlier Clark v. Allen,[14] in which the California statute had been sustained, seemed to involve no more than a routine reading of foreign laws, but added: [15]

"As we read the decisions that followed in the wake of Clark v. Allen, we find that they radiate some of the attitudes of the 'cold war', where the search is for the 'democracy quotient' of a foreign regime as opposed to the Marxist Theory. The Oregon statute introduces the concept of 'confiscation', which is of course opposed to the Just Compensation Clause of the Fifth Amendment. And this has led into minute inquiries concerning the actual administration of foreign law, into the credibility of foreign diplomatic statements, and into speculation whether the fact that some received delivery of the funds should 'not preclude wonderment as to how many may have been denied the right to receive'."

Reviewing the Oregon decisions applying the statute, Justice Douglas found foreign policy attitudes, "the freezing or thawing of the 'cold war' and the like", the real desiderata. He concluded that it seemed inescapable that "the type of probate law that Oregon enforces affects international relations in a persistent and subtle way". The Oregon law was stated to have "a direct impact upon foreign relations and may well adversely affect the power of the central government to deal with these problems".[16]

It is not clear in the majority opinion in *Zschernig* whether the Oregon statute is considered unconstitutional on its face or whether it is the method of application of the statute that intrudes unduly into the conduct of foreign relations by the Federal Government. The vice in the statute may stem from its application as a cold war weapon, the statute being constitutional if enforced other than as an instrument of economic warfare.

Nevertheless, two Justices (Stewart and Brennan) concurring, considered the statutory statements unconstitutional on their face as necessarily involving a "prohibited voyage into a domain of exclusive-

(1947), the Court had sustained the California reciprocity statute on the ground the California statute had only an incidental or indirect effect in foreign countries and did not enter the forbidden domain of negotiating with a foreign country.

14. See fn. 13.

15. 389 U.S. at 435.

16. Id. 441.

ly federal competence".[17] In the view of these Justices, any realistic attempt to apply the criteria of the statute would involve evaluations, expressed or implied, of the administration of foreign law, the credibility of foreign diplomatic statements and the policies of foreign governments.

Justice Harlan concurred in the result on the ground that the Treaty of 1923 should be applied to supersede the statute as applied to personalty. But he rejected the view of the majority that the application of the statute was an unconstitutional intrusion into the conduct of foreign affairs. He pointed out a number of instances, such as the Uniform Foreign Money-Judgments Recognition Act, under which the judgment does not have to be recognized if rendered under a system not providing impartial tribunals or procedures consistent with due process, in which state courts may make inquiries similar to those under the "reciprocity" and "retention" statutes. He thought the Court would find these intrusions constitutional.

Zschernig has led to the repeal of the Oregon statute involved in that case as well as the repeal of the California statute which was the prototype of the reciprocity provisions.[18] The New York retention statute, under which most of the litigation under retention provisions has occurred, has been modified to require retention in those cases in which the alien is residing or domiciled within a country to which checks or warrants drawn against funds of the United States may not be transmitted by reason of any executive order, regulation or similar determination of the United States government or any department or agency thereof.[19] It is provided that this retention cannot be avoided by assignment.[20] Apparently no hearing is required in those cases in which payment is blocked by the Federal Government or its agen-

17. Id. 442.

18. See In re Estate of Kraemer, 276 Cal.App.2d 715, 81 Cal.Rptr. 287 (1969), where Cal.Probate Code, § 259 was held an unconstitutional intrusion into the conduct of foreign affairs and an East German national was permitted to take personal property of which her son died intestate in California. The 1923 Treaty with Germany was applied to permit the Mother to take land and the rationale of *Zschernig* to permit her to inherit the personalty. Reppy, Associate Justice, in his concuring opinion states: "Zschernig * * * I feel, would not condemn Probate Code Section 259 if, under it, all that could be done by local trial courts, to determine if the other country involved treated its own resident citizens and nonresident United States citizens alike, was to read the applicable written law of that country (presumably through an authenticated translation) and possibly hear expert interpretative testimony where the credibility of the foreign expert was not put into question. However, if, through legislative language or through subsisting court interpretation, trial court inquiry into how the law is administered (such as to learn that officials and the courts of the country do not interpret its inheritance statute literally and sanction discrimination against nonresident United States citizens) is allowed, then the code section is disapproved by *Zschernig*. For example, if our courts hold that Section 259 allows trial court inquiry to determine if distribution to a United States heir turns on the whim or caprice of an official (other, perhaps, than by what the written law says), it is defective. Inquiry into this subject would involve the delicate area of foreign relations and would put into balance the credibility of officials and experts from the foreign countries. * * *" Section 259 was repealed in 1974.

19. N.Y.Surr.Ct.Proc.Act, § 2218 (McKinney Supp.1980). The statute was amended after *Zschernig* by the addition of a new subdivision 1. Laws 1968, c. 998, eff. June 22, 1968.

20. Id., Subd. 1(b).

cies.[21] Apart from this addition, the New York statute remains as it was before *Zschernig.*

Statutes of the "reciprocity" and "retention" types probably can be administered without the "cold war" overtones which proved offensive to the majority of the Court in *Zschernig.* A distinction subsequently may be made between state activity relating to land and similar activity relating to personalty. More of an intrusion may be tolerated into the area of foreign affairs with respect to land than with respect to personalty because of the interest of the state generally recognized in land matters. The efficency with which the Federal Government is prepared to service state requests for information pertaining to foreign aspects of alien property certainly bears on the problem since effective Federal service will reduce the necessity of independent state inquiries in the foreign country concerned.

As pointed out by Justice Harlan, there are numerous instances in which state court decisions impinge upon the foreign relations of the United States. For example, if a testator makes a gift in trust for a purpose in a foreign country, even though no alien is named as beneficiary, the determination of the court whether or not the gift is "charitable" and is effective without a specific beneficiary will have some impact upon foreign affairs and may well involve inquiries in the foreign state. Determining the proper situs for the trust to *administer* the gift also will involve inquiries of a similar nature.[22]

Almost certainly *Zschernig* will deter further experimentation with state laws pertaining to alien property, although probably most of the existing statutes can be administered in a manner consistent with the decision.

21. See Frank, "Alien Inheritance Statutes: An Examination of the Constitutionality of State Laws Restricting the Rights of Nonresident Aliens to Inherit From American Decedents", 25 Syra.L. Rev. 597 (1974). The author states that no hearing is required "if the alien claimant resides in a country to which government checks or warrants may not be transmitted". Nevertheless, the statute in its more stringent form was held constitutional in Bjarsch v. DiFalco, 314 F. Supp. 127 (S.D.N.Y.1970).

22. See Alford, "Voluntary Foreign Aid and American Foreign Policy: The Element of State Control", 46 Va.L.Rev. 477 (1960) where state policies relating to foreign charity matters are discussed.

Chapter IV

LIMITATIONS UPON TESTAMENTARY POWER

Scope Note

Although a testator has broad power to dispose of his property by will, his power is curtailed to a limited degree by the operation of certain statutes and collateral common law rules. A few of the more important of these limitations are discussed in this chapter. The basis and scope of testamentary power are examined briefly in Section 1. A number of important limitations are imposed to protect members of the testator's family. Limitations which protect the surviving spouse, including community property provisions, are considered in Section 2. Section 3 deals with the protection of children and lineal descendants. In Section 4 some miscellaneous limitations are considered which benefit the immediate family of the testator as a whole and which protect other relatives in some instances.

SECTION 1. BASIS AND SCOPE OF TESTAMENTARY POWER

A will usually expresses a plan for the disposition of property after the death of the testator.[1] Whether or not such a plan will be executed as the testator intended depends, among other factors, upon the existence of legal institutions which can be used to carry the plan into effect.[2] Most of the legal institutions which condition the operation of a testamentary plan have a statutory basis. For this reason, it is useful to think of the power to make an effective will as a sub-

1. A will may do nothing more than appoint an executor, appoint a guardian for children or revoke other testamentary instruments. A will is not the only method by which a plan for the disposition of property after the death of the testator may be set forth. A number of will substitutes may be available. See Chapter XII, Section 1.

2. When a man dies leaving property, his loss of control over it is likely to stimulate conflicting demands for its enjoyment among his survivors. Legal institutions are some of the ways in which the power of a community is organized and brought to bear in an effort to reconcile conflicting demands asserted by its members. Legal institutions include legislatures, courts, administrative agencies, the constitutional doctrines that are intended to guide the policies of these organs, the legal formulae or rules by which these policies are expressed, and the various procedures and techniques by which these policies are carried out.

ject of legislative grant which can be divested or regulated by legislative action.[3]

Testamentary power has been granted in plenary fashion in all states and has been curtailed in relatively few major aspects.[4] A testator may exercise considerable caprice. His will is not invalid merely because it contains unjust or unnatural provisions, although provisions of this sort may be evidence of fraud, undue influence or testamentary incapacity.[5]

3. See Atkinson, Wills (2d Ed., 1953) 30; 1 Bowe-Parker: Page, Wills (3d Ed. Rev.1960) § 3.1; Rollison, Wills (1939) 1; Thompson, Wills (3d Ed., 1947) 37. A few courts have taken the position that the power to dispose of property by will is a "natural right" which cannot be taken away or substantially impaired by legislative action. Nunnemacher v. State, 129 Wis. 190, 108 N.W. 627, 9 L.R.A.,N.S., 121, 9 Ann.Cas. 711 (1906); Estate of Beale, 15 Wis.2d 546, 113 N.W.2d 380 (1962).

4. In civil law countries testamentary power has been curtailed sharply. See Bevilaqua, "Legitimate Inheritance Under the Brazilian Code", 20 Iowa L.Rev. 402 (1935); Chang, "Inheritance in China", 20 Iowa L.Rev. 411 (1935); Yadin, "The Proposed Law of Succession for Israel", 2 Am.Jour.Comp.L. 143 (1953); Farrar, "Devolution of Property on Death in Spanish and English Law", 32 Tul.L.Rev. 387 (1958). This trend has been quite marked in countries in which Communist legal codes are in force, although with time the rigid bias against inheritance tends to be relaxed. In the Soviet Union, inheritance was initially abolished except for certain small interests that were allowed to pass to the nearest relatives. Later, inheritance was reinstated with restrictions upon the persons who could take (direct descendants of the decedent, the surviving spouse, and disabled and propertyless persons who were his actual dependents for not less than a year before his death) and upon the amount which could pass (10,000 rubles). In 1926 the limitation of 10,000 rubles was removed, and testamentary power conferred over government bonds and deposits in government banks. In 1943 the inheritance tax was abolished; and in 1945 the heirs were extended to include parents not dependents and brothers and sisters. The testator can will his property to any of these persons although he cannot deprive his minor children or disabled heirs of their shares which they would take in intestacy. If there are no heirs living, the testator can leave his property to anyone. Wills must be written and certified in a notarial office. The heirs must claim their inheritance within six months, although there is no provision for notifying them of the opening of the estate. This would tend to eliminate the "laughing heirs" who are not in contact with the decedent during his lifetime and do not hear of his death. See Guins, Soviet Law and Soviet Society (1954) 124–129; Gsovski, Soviet Civil Law (1948) Vol. I, 130, 618–658; Gsovski and Gryzybowski, Government, Law and Courts in the Soviet Union and in Central Europe (1959) Vol. II, 1163, 1196, 1234, 1268, 1300, 1342, 1348–1352, 1380; Holmes, "The Law of Succession in Soviet Jurisprudence—A Survey", 21 Iowa L. Rev. 487 (1936); Gsovski, "Soviet Law of Inheritance", 45 Mich.L.Rev. 291 (1947); Soloveitchik, "Family Law and Inheritance Law in USSR", 15 U. of Kan.Cit.L. Rev. 83 (1947); Comment: "The About Turn: Soviet Law of Inheritance", 10 Am.J. of Comp.Law 431 (1961). For new trends in the Islamic System, see Anderson, "Recent Reforms in the Islamic Law of Inheritance", 14 Int. and Comp.L.Q. 349 (1965). For trends in the British Commonwealth, see Dainow, "Restricted Testation in New Zealand, Australia and Canada", 36 Mich.L.Rev. 1107 (1938); Dainow, "Limitations on Testamentary Freedom in England", 25 Corn.L.Q. 337 (1940); Keeton and Gower, "Freedom of Testation in English Law", 20 Iowa L. Rev. 326 (1935); Atkinson, "Protection of the Surviving Family: A Foreword to the British System", 35 N.Y.U.L.Rev. 981 (1960). For discussions of limitations upon testamentary power in the United States see, Cahn, "Restraints on Disinheritance", 85 U. of Pa.L.Rev. 139 (1936); McMurray, "Liberty of Testation and Some Modern Limitations Thereon", 14 Ill.L.Rev. 96 (1919); Scott, "Control of Property by the Dead", 65 U. of Pa.L. Rev. 527, 632 (1917); Note, "Protection of the Family Against Disinheritance in American Law", 14 Int. and Comp.L.Q. 293 (1965).

5. Georgia Code § 113–106 provides:

"A testator, by his will, may make any disposition of his property not inconsistent with the laws or contrary to the policy of the State; he may bequeath his entire estate to strangers, to the

The statutory and common law limitations for the protection of the family and the community property laws which are discussed in the remainder of this chapter are some of the most obvious of the legal limitations upon testamentary power. Almost any legal doctrine which conditions the operation of a will to a degree is a limitation upon testamentary power, and there are a host of non-legal limitations which are frequently more effective than limitations imposed by a legislature or court. Certain other legal limitations upon testamentary power, such as the statutory formalities for executing and revoking wills,[6] rules concerning gifts for illegal or immoral purposes,[7] rules concerning restraints on alienation[8] and rules of construction[9] are considered elsewhere in this book. Limitations imposed by the collection of Federal and state succession taxes and the satisfaction of claims of other creditors of the decedent and his estate are touched only briefly in this book and are examined in detail in other courses.

EYERMAN v. MERCANTILE TRUST CO.

Missouri Court of Appeals, 1975.
524 S.W.2d 210.

RENDLEN, JUDGE.

Plaintiffs appeal from denial of their petition seeking injunction to prevent demolition of a house at # 4 Kingsbury Place in the City of St. Louis. The action is brought by individual neighboring property owners and certain trustees for the Kingsbury Place Subdivision. We reverse.

Louise Woodruff Johnston, owner of the property in question, died January 14, 1973, and by her will directed the executor "* * * to cause our home at 4 Kingsbury Place * * * to be razed and to sell the land upon which it is located * * * and to transfer the proceeds of the sale * * * to the residue of my estate." Plaintiffs assert that razing the home will adversely affect their property rights, violate the terms of the subdivision trust indenture for Kingsbury Place, produce an actionable private nuisance and is contrary to public policy.

The area involved is a "private place" established in 1902 by trust indenture which provides that Kingsbury Place and Kingsbury Terrace will be so maintained, improved, protected and managed as to be desirable for private residences. The trustees are empowered to protect and preserve "Kingsbury Place" from encroachment, trespass,

exclusion of his wife and children, but in such case the will should be closely scrutinized, and, upon the slightest evidence of aberration of intellect, or collusion or fraud, or any undue influence or unfair dealing, probate should be refused."

6. See Chapters V and VI.

7. See Chapter VIII, Section 3.

8. See Chapter VIII, Section 5, Chapter XVI.

9. See Chapters XIV and XV.

nuisance or injury, and it is "the intention of these presents, forming a general scheme of improving and maintaining said property as desirable residence property of the highest class." The covenants run with the land and the indenture empowers lot owners or the trustees to bring suit to enforce them.

Except for one vacant lot, the subdivision is occupied by handsome, spacious two and three-story homes, and all must be used exclusively as private residences. The indenture generally regulates location, costs and similar features for any structures in the subdivision, and limits construction of subsidiary structures except those that may beautify the property, for example, private stables, flower houses, conservatories, play houses or buildings of similar character.

On trial the temporary restraining order was dissolved and all issues found against the plaintiffs.

* * *

[In the omitted portion of the opinion, the court upheld the standing of the plaintiffs to maintain the suit, took judicial notice of the need for dwelling units to accommodate increasing population, and then addressed the issue of public policy as grounds for invalidating the provision in the will.]

* * * It becomes apparent that no individual, group of individuals nor the community generally benefits from the senseless destruction of the house; instead, all are harmed and only the caprice of the dead testatrix is served. Destruction of the house harms the neighbors, detrimentally affects the community, causes monetary loss in excess of $39,000.00 to the estate and is without benefit to the dead woman. No reason, good or bad, is suggested by the will or record for the eccentric condition. This is not a living person who seeks to exercise a right to reshape or dispose of her property; instead, it is an attempt by will to confer the power to destroy upon an executor who is given no other interest in the property. To allow an executor to exercise such powers stemming from apparent whim and caprice of the testatrix contravenes public policy.

The Missouri Supreme Court held in State ex rel. McClintock v. Guinotte, 275 Mo. 298, 204 S.W. 806, 808 (banc 1918), that the taking of property by inheritance or will is not an absolute or natural right but one created by the laws of the sovereign power. The court points out the state "may foreclose the right absolutely, or it may grant the right upon conditions precedent, which conditions, if not otherwise violative of our Constitution, will have to be complied with before the right of descent and distribution (whether under the law or by will) can exist." Further, this power of the state is one of inherent sovereignty which allows the state to "say what becomes of the property of a person, when death forecloses his right to control it." McClintock v. Guinotte, supra, at 808, 809. While living, a person may manage, use or dispose of his money or property with fewer restraints than a decedent by will. One is generally restrained from wasteful expenditure or destructive inclinations by the natural desire to enjoy his property or to accumulate it during his lifetime. Such considerations however have not tempered the extravagance or eccentricity of the testamentary disposition here on which there is no check except the courts.

In the early English case of Egerton v. Brownlow, 10 Eng.Rep. 359, 417 (H.L.C.1853), it is stated: "The owner of an estate may himself do many things which he could not (by a condition) compel his successor to do. One example is sufficient. He may leave his land uncultivated, but he cannot by a condition compel his successor to do so. The law does not interfere with the owner and compel him to cultivate his land, (though it may be for the public good that land should be cultivated) so far the law respects ownership; but when, by a condition, he attempts to compel his successor to do what is against the public good, the law steps in and pronounces the condition void and allows the devisee to enjoy the estate free from the condition." A more recent application of this principle is found in M'Caig's Trustees v. Kirk-Session of the United Free Church of Lismore, et al., 1915 Sess.Cas. 426 (Scot.). There, by codicil to her will, testatrix ordered certain statues erected to honor her family in a tower built in the form of an amphitheater on a hill. Balustrades were to be erected so that even the public would have no access inside the tower. Special provision was made for keeping out the public and the ground enclosed was expressly declared to be a private enclosure. There were no living descendants of any member of the family who might, if so permitted, take pleasure in contemplating the proposed statues. The court states at 434: "If a bequest such as in Miss M'Caig's codicil were held good, money would require to be expended in perpetuity merely gratifying an absurd whim which has neither reason nor public sentiment in its favor." In striking down the provisions of the codicil, the court further notes that there is indeed a "difference between what a man, uncognosed, may do at his own hand, and what the law will support under the provisions of his will * * * therefore, without being illegal in the sense of being contrary to any express rule of the common law or contrary to any statute, the principle of public policy will prevent such postmortem expenditure. Whether the act is sufficiently contrary to public policy to warrant the court's interference must depend on the degee to which it is against public policy." The court further observed that the erection of the eleven statues "would be of no benefit to anyone except those connected with the carrying out of the work, for whose interest she expresses no concern." M'Caig's Trustees v. Kirk-Session of the United Free Church of Lismore, et al., supra at 438. In the case sub judice, testatrix similarly expressed no such concern; nothing in the will or record indicates an intent to benefit any razing company called upon to destroy her beautiful home.

In the case of In re Scott's Will, Board of Commissioners of Rice County v. Scott et al., 88 Minn. 386, 93 N.W. 109 (1903), the Supreme Court of Minnesota stated, when considering the provision of a will directing the executor to destroy money belonging to the estate: "We assume, for purpose of this decision, that the direction in the codicil to the executor to destroy all of the residue of the money or cash or evidences of credit belonging to the estate was void." In re Scott's Will, supra at 109. See also Restatement, Second, Trusts § 124, at 267: "Although a person may deal capriciously with his own property, his self interest ordinarily will restrain him from doing so. Where an attempt is made to confer such a power upon a person who is given no other interest in the property, there is no such restraint and it is against public policy to allow him to exercise the power if the purpose is merely capricious." The text is followed by this illustration: "A bequeaths $1,000.00 to B in trust to throw the money into the sea. B holds the money upon a resulting trust for the estate of A and is liable to the estate of A if he throws the money into the sea." Restatement, supra at 267.

* * *

Although public policy may evade precise, objective definition, it is evident from the authorities cited that this senseless destruction serving no apparent good purpose is to be held in disfavor. A well-ordered society cannot tolerate the waste and destruction of resources when such acts directly affect important interests of other members of that society. It is clear that property owners in the neighborhood of # 4 Kingsbury, the St. Louis community as a whole and the beneficiaries of testatrix's estate will be severely injured should the provisions of the will be followed. No benefits are present to balance against this injury and we hold that to allow the condition in the will would be a violation of the public policy of this state.

Having thus decided, we do not reach the plaintiffs' contentions regarding enforcement of the restrictions in the Kingsbury Place trust indenture and actionable private nuisance, though these contentions may have merit.

The judgment is reversed and the cause remanded to the Circuit Court to enter judgment as prayed.

DOWD, P.J., concurs.

CLEMENS, J., dissents in separate opinion. [Dissenting opinion is omitted.] [10]

10. In National City Bank v. Case Western Reserve University, 7 Ohio Op. 3d 100, 369 N.E.2d 814 (Com.Pl.1976) a direction in a will that the family house be razed and the land sold was avoided, although the court stated that the direction was not against public policy. The home had been selected for listing in the National Registry of Historical Places. The drafting attorney testified that the testatrix did not want the home used for non-residential uses; an arrangement to sell the property to a local historical society with restrictions that the property be maintained for the benefit of the public was approved as being within the intent of the testatrix.

If a will directs that a pet animal owned by the testator be destroyed, should the provision be upheld? In a California case where another person was willing to assume care of the animal, the personal representative delayed execution of the will provision until the legislature enacted special emergency legislation declaring the provision invalid and unenforceable. Calif.Stats.1979–80 c. 182.

SECTION 2. PROTECTION OF THE SPOUSE

(1) EXISTING LEGAL PROTECTIONS; SOCIAL AND LEGAL DEVELOPMENTS

Three basic legal systems are designed to protect against intentional disinheritance of the family (the spouse, dependent children, and other dependent relatives such as parents):

(1) the "common law" provisions for a fixed share for the surviving spouse (usually a statutory elective share of one-third, supplanting the old estates of dower and curtesy, supplemented by a right to limited statutory allowances and exempt property);

(2) the community property system;

(3) the English family maintenance system with power in the court to assign as much of the decedent's estate as is necessary to support the surviving spouse and other dependent relatives.

The first system prevails in most of the United States. Eight states have community property and only one state [11] presently has any provision resembling the English system. The system in the "common law" states (non-community) is under strong criticism, particularly from advocates of women's rights. One group favors a version of community property; some favor adoption of the English flexible system. Community property has the advantage of recognizing the contributions of both spouses (including homemaking and rearing of children) to the marital wealth, at the same time allowing testamentary  freedom to dispose of inherited wealth and wealth acquired before the marriage; duration of marriage also becomes part of the equation. These factors are particularly important in remarriages late in life where there are children by the prior marriages.

Commentators favor the English flexible system on the grounds that a testator should no more be free to ignore at death his family responsibilities than he can during lifetime refuse to support his spouse, his minor children, and in many states his dependent adult children and parents.[12] The "upgrading" of the quality of probate judges which has taken place in most jurisdictions in recent years removes one major objection to giving such power to the court. A combination of community property (which recognizes contribution to accumulated wealth and gives each spouse a share to devise) and a flexible maintenance system (which recognizes need) would parallel

11. Maine has adopted the Uniform Probate Code but eliminated from § 2–403 the limitation of the family allowance to the period of administration. 18A Me.Rev.Stat.Ann. § 2–403.

12. Gaubatz, "Notes Toward a Truly Modern Wills Act," 31 U. of Miami L. Rev. 497 (1977); Note, "Family Maintenance: An Inheritance Scheme for the Living," 8 Rut.-Cam.L.J. 673 (1977).

the modern provisions governing termination of the marriage by divorce.

Family law lawyers are more conscious than property lawyers that the American family is undergoing drastic change. How that change will affect the protections discussed in this chapter remains to future developments.[13] The traditional American family (called by sociologists the nuclear family) has consisted of a working husband, a wife who keeps the home and raises the children, and two or three children. This is no longer the norm.[14] There is great diversity in family life style. Often both spouses work, with independent incomes. There are many childless couples. Frequency of divorce has created many families with a single parent who works and raises the children. Remarriage is common, creating marriages with children of one or both spouses by prior marriage; these situations create family tensions over inheritance rights and increase the potential for estate litigation because of the diversity of interest between the nonparent spouse and stepchildren.

There are also increasing numbers of unmarried couples, living together and accumulating property, often without thought to ultimate ownership of the property when the arrangement ends. And the arrangement can end either by death or by a decision by one or both parties. When the arrangement ends during life the law is developing new remedies to compensate for economic loss of one of the parties. When the arrangement ends by death, similar imagination is needed by the lawyer for the surviving party if a fair share of the accumulated property does not pass to the survivor. The survivor is not a "spouse," either within the statutes of intestate succession or within the protections against disinheritance discussed in this chapter. Nor in community property states is the arrangement treated as a community for property purposes. The survivor may of course be lucky; the accumulated property may be owned in joint tenancy, thus assuring the survivor of protection, or the deceased party may have executed a valid will devising property to the survivor. If this is not the case, the survivor may be able to file a claim against the estate on the theory that there was an express or implied contract to share property acquired during the period the couple lived together; sometimes there may be a factual basis for claiming a joint business venture; or if the survivor furnished part of the consideration for property purchased in the name of the decedent, the survivor may claim a purchase-money resulting trust, as explained later in Chapter IX.

Both in the remarriage, often late in life, and in the unmarried couple situation there is great need for the parties to shape their economic future by entering into a contract. Such a contract should provide the protection desired by the parties. The statutory protections

13. Cantwell, "Man + Woman + Property =?—Pondering the Marital Equation," 6 Prob. Lawyer 1 (Summer 1980); Glendon, "Matrimonial Property: A Comparative Study of Law and Social Change," 49 Tul.L.Rev. 21 (1974).

14. Social Indicators III, Bureau of Census (1980); Current Pop. Repts., Special Studies Series P23, No. 100—A Statistical Portrait of Women in the U. S., 1978 (1980); *id.* No. 77—Perspectives on American Husbands and Wives (1980).

considered in this chapter arise out of the marital status. Many lawyers are predicting that in the future the real protection will come from contract rather than status.

Another major development which will impact on this whole area of family protection stems from support by women's groups for legislation which will provide property rights during the marriage as well as on dissolution of the marriage, either by divorce or by death.[15] A proposed Uniform Marital Property Act is being considered by the National Conference of Commissioners on Uniform Laws. The concept is essentially the same as that of community property, that marriage is a partnership giving rise to equal ownership by both spouses of wealth acquired during the marriage other than by gift, devise or inheritance. Similar legislation was introduced in the Wisconsin legislature in 1980 and 1981. If such legislation is adopted in common law states, it would provide substantial protection against disinheritance just as community property does. As under common law, the system would permit the parties to contract regarding their property rights. Whether at death of one spouse the half interest in marital property owned by the survivor would be supplemented by other protections such as family allowances out of the decedent's estate or an elective share in the decedent's separate property (that acquired before marriage or acquired by gift, devise or inheritance) would be decided by individual state legislatures.

(2) THE ELECTIVE SHARE SYSTEM

A. General Nature

In most of the American states, the common law concepts of dower and curtesy form the historical basis for the modern law protecting the surviving spouse. These concepts performed adequately in a culture where most wealth consisted of real property owned by men, and at a time when marriage was a relatively stable institution. As personal property began to be important in the United States, the need to protect the spouse against disinheritance as to such property was recognized by statutes affording the surviving spouse an election to take a statutory share rather than the provision, if any, made in the decedent's will. This share was typically one-third. Today in most states an elective share, supplanting or supplementing dower and curtesy, has evolved.[16] The Uniform Probate Code (Article 2,

15. Bartke, "Marital Property Law Reform: Canadian Style", 25 Amer. Journal of Comp. Law 46 (1977); Prager, "Sharing Principles and the Future of Marital Property Law", 25 U.C.L.A.L. Rev. 1 (1977); Power, "Well Begun Is Half Done: Community Property for Missouri", 21 St.L.Univ.L.J. 308 (1977).

16. McKinney N.Y., EPTL, § 5–1.1 permits the surviving spouse to elect one-half of the net estate if no children survive or, if there are children, one-third of the net estate. Where forced heir statutes are in force, common law dower, its statutory substitute and curtesy are usually abolished. In some states the forced

Part 2) provides for an elective share of one-third for common law states.[17]

B. OPERATION OF ELECTIVE SHARE STATUTES

Because in most states the surviving spouse today is protected by a statutory provision allowing her to elect a forced share (usually one-third) rather than to take the provision under the testator's will, most of the problems turn in large measure on the language of the particular statute. A well-drafted statute should deal with the following kinds of problems; but all too often the problems are left to the courts for solution.

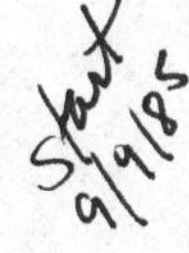

(a) Can the spouse take both a provision for her under the will and the forced share, unless the will specifically indicates that she is not to take both? Because at common law the courts favored dower, the peculiar rule grew up that the widow could claim dower and also take a provision under the will for her unless the will manifested an intent that she not receive both.[18] Usually the modern statutes re-

share is an alternative to dower and the spouse is required to elect. See Stevenson, "Does Dower Still Lurk in Elections to Take Under the Will", 30 U. of Cin.L. Rev. 172 (1962) (Dealing with Ohio Law); Legislative Note, "Protection of Surviving Spouse's Rights under Elective Share Statutes", 18 Vand.L.Rev. 2090 (1965). The share as forced heir may be the same that would be taken if the testator had died intestate or it may be a smaller share. The intestate heir is usually described as a "statutory heir". One who claims a forced share in a testate estate is called a "forced heir". See Vernier, American Family Laws (1935) §§ 188–200, 215–218, 220; Cahn, "Restraints on Disinheritance", 85 U. of Pa.L.Rev. 139 (1936); Freilicher, "The Rights of the Surviving Spouse" 105 Trusts and Estates 107 (1966); Sullivan "Passing of Dower and Curtesy", 19 Geo.L.J. 306 (1931); Sayre, "Husband and Wife as Statutory Heirs", 42 Harv.L.Rev. 330 (1929); Simes, "Protecting the Surviving Spouse by Restraints on the Dead Hand", 26 U.Cinn.L.Rev. 1 (1957); Comments: "Defeating the Inheritance of the Surviving Spouse", 40 Miss.L.J. 286 (1969); "Decedents Estate—Does North Carolina Adequately Protect Surviving Spouses", 48 N.C.L.Rev. 361 (1970) (dealing with N.C. law); "Election by Surviving Spouse," 2 Real Prop.Prob. & T.L. Jour. 310 (1967); "Spouse's Elective Share," Report of Committee on Administration and Distribution of Estates, A.B. A. Section of Real Property, Probate and Trust Law, 12 R.P.P. & T.J. 323 (1977); Chaffin, "A Reappraisal of the Wealth Transmission Process: The Surviving Spouse, Year's Support and Intestate Succession," 10 Ga.L.Rev. 447 (1976).

17. For a general discussion of the Code provisions see Emery, "The Utah Uniform Probate Code—Protection of the Surviving Spouse—The Elective Share," 1976 Utah L.Rev. 771; Kossow, "Probate Law and the Uniform Probate Code: 'One For the Money * * *'," 61 Geo. L.J. 1357 (1973) at 1381.

18. The doctrine of election may have originated in the situation in which a testator makes a gift of property owned by A to B and also makes a gift to A in lieu of the property given to B. A will be required to elect between the gift from the testator and his property which the testator purported to give to B. The analogy of this case to the case in which an election is required between a testamentary gift and community property or dower is amply clear. The testator offers the spouse a testamentary gift in lieu of an existing or inchoate interest which he purports to transfer or to defeat by his will. A spouse who claims as forced heir has an expectancy only, but the transaction may then be regarded as an offer for the release of an expectancy or the election may be predicated simply upon the inconsistency of the claims of the spouse under the will and by statute. For detailed discussions of problems raised by elections of the surviving spouse see, Phelps, "The Widow's Right of Election in the Estate of Her Husband", 37 Mich. L.Rev. 330, 401 (1938–39); Klein, "Recent Developments in the Right of Election of Surviving Spouse," 129 N.Y.L.J. 1604, 1620, 1636, 1654, 1674, 1692 (1953);

verse this presumption, and the surviving spouse cannot take under the will and also receive a statutory share unless the will indicates that the provision under the will is in addition to her legal rights.[19]

A related problem is whether the election against the will results in loss of benefits under the will, or whether the benefits under the will for the surviving spouse are retained and credited against the forced share (with the result that she cannot receive the forced share in addition to the will). Most of the statutes take the first approach, but the Uniform Probate Code adopts the second.[20]

Another related problem arises if the will fails to dispose of all of the testator's property. Can the surviving spouse get an elective share and also take all or part of the intestate property under the laws of intestate succession? Suppose the surviving spouse takes under the will, can she also take the share which the law of intestate succession would give her as heir? Normally the fact that the testator made a provision for his wife does not mean that he intends she should not share in property which he fails to dispose of by his will. But even if the will recites that the provision for the wife is in lieu of any legal rights she may have in his estate, courts may permit her to take both under the will and under the law of intestate succession. This is because the court may take the view that an heir cannot be excluded from succession by mere fiat of the testator. If the testator wishes to disinherit an heir, he can do so only by validly disposing of the property to another person by his will.[21] If the wife elects against the will, however, the court may require the forced share to be satisfied first out of the intestate estate.[22] Thus, if the partially intestate estate is large enough, it will be to her advantage to elect to take under the will if she is also an heir, her testamentary share plus her intestate share exceeding possibly her forced share.

(b) Procedures setting the method of electing and a time period within which the spouse must elect are statutory. Under some statutes the spouse must file an election to take under the will, or an election to take the share provided by law; under other statutes the burden is on the spouse to file an election to take the share provided by law, and if she does not do so within the statutory period she is deemed to take under the will. The time for election is usually geared to expedite settlement of the probate estate; under the Uniform Probate Code the spouse has nine months after date of death or

Sayre, "Husband and Wife as Statutory Heirs", 42 Harv.L.Rev. 330 (1929). For an application of the common law presumption see e.g., Bomar v. Wilkins, 154 S.C. 64, 151 S.E. 110, 68 A.L.R. 501 (1930).

19. Vernier, American Family Laws (1935) § 199.

20. Uniform Probate Code, §§ 2–206(a), 2–207(a). See Schmidt, "Family Protection Under the Uniform Probate Code", 50 Denver L.J. 137 (1973) (comparing prior Colorado law with Code provisions protecting the immediate family).

21. E.g., Coffman v. Coffman, 85 Va. 459, 8 S.E. 672 (1888).

22. See Uniform Probate Code, §§ 2–205, 2–206(a), 2–207(a). Section 2–205 (d) states the Court shall order payment of the elective share "from the assets of the augmented estate or by contribution as appears appropriate under Section 2–207". The augmented estate is described in Section 2–202 and is discussed in greater detail in subdivision 2C of this Section.

six months after probate of the will, whichever is later, within which to file a petition for an elective share, although the court may extend the period for cause.[23] Under some statutes, the period may be as long as one year from filing of the petition for probate.

(c) Is the right to elect personal to the surviving spouse? If she dies without having elected and before the period for election has expired, may her personal representative elect in order to acquire a share for her estate? For example, the testator may have provided by his will a life estate for the wife; if her personal representative elects the statutory share, her estate will receive an inheritable interest. States are divided as to whether or not the personal representative may elect. A comparable problem occurs if the wife is incompetent; may her guardian or conservator elect on her behalf and increase her assets? Under the Uniform Probate Code the result will turn on whether the election is necessary for adequate support of the surviving spouse.[24] If she already has ample assets, no election will be permitted. Presumably this is what she would have intended had she been competent.

(d) What is the effect of an election on the testamentary scheme? Perhaps no problem is more difficult than this, yet most of the statutes are silent on this particular problem. Later we shall see how the courts have attempted to preserve the decedent's testamentary scheme.[25] At common law, dower was an estate for the life of the widow in one-third of the realty of which her husband was seised of an estate of inheritance at any time during coverture. The elective share in personalty came primarily out of the residue, just as would claims of creditors against the estate. But the matter is complicated by the question whether the surviving spouse loses any provision under the will by electing, or whether the provisions under the will for her are retained and counted against the elective share.

(e) Is the elective share available only to the widow, or does the widower have an elective share in the estate of the deceased wife? In the past most wealth has been accumulated by the husband in his name, and husbands are usually survived by their wives (both because of the practice of a man marrying a younger woman, and because of the longer life expectancy of the female). The problem has thus traditionally been one of protecting the widow. However, wealth ownership patterns are changing. Today, both husband and wife often work. For tax reasons, the husband's income may be spent in support of the family and the wife's earnings invested in her name, to the extent they are not required for current needs. Hence, the husband may find at the end of a long marriage that he is at the mercy of his wife if she has unlimited testamentary power. For this reason, the Uniform Probate Code gives the husband the same right to a forced share in the estate of the wife, as she would have in his

23. Uniform Probate Code, § 2–205(a).

24. Uniform Probate Code, § 2–203. For various issues involved in an election for an incompetent see 21 A.L.R.3d 320 (1968) (who may make election); 3 A.L.R.3d 119 (1965) (time within which election must be made); 3 A.L.R.3d 6 (1965) (factors considered in making election).

25. See Chapter XV, Section 4.

estate if he died first.[26] A statute providing an elective share only for widows is probably unconstitutional as a gender-based discrimination with no important governmental objective served by denial of a comparable right in the widower.[27]

(f) Should the surviving spouse be barred for desertion or marital misconduct? As we have already seen,[28] the English Statute of Westminster II barred dower of a wife who deserted her husband and committed adultery; and some states have statutes barring an elective share on a similar principle. In other states the statutes are silent, and the courts take the view that the probate proceeding cannot be turned into a post-mortem divorce trial, with one of the parties deceased and unable to testify; hence, such matters are irrelevant to an elective right. Closely related, however, are the problems growing out of invalid divorces. Because the elective share is available only to a surviving spouse, divorce normally terminates the marital relationship and ends the rights of the surviving spouse to an elective share, as well as to rights under intestate succession laws. In Chapter VI we shall also see that in many jurisdictions divorce operates to revoke a provision in the prior will of one of the parties in favor of the other. But these rules proceed on the assumption that there is a valid divorce. Some divorces may prove not to be valid; yet the parties may have remarried. The complications which can then arise are difficult of solution. The Uniform Probate Code contains one of the few statutory attempts to deal with these situations.[29]

Uniform Probate Code, § 2–301 permits the surviving spouse to claim her intestate share in the estate under specified circumstances if she is not mentioned in the will. This gives her protection similar to that afforded the child who is not mentioned in the will and can claim a share as "pretermitted heir". The Uniform Code provisions, including the provision for the "pretermitted spouse", are considered

26. Uniform Probate Code, § 2–201(a). The election provisions are limited to domiciliaries of the state. If the married person is domiciled outside the state, the law of the decedent's domicile controls.

27. See Orr v. Orr, 440 U.S. 268, 99 S. Ct. 1102, 59 L.Ed.2d 306 (1979) (invalidating a statute requiring only husbands to pay alimony); Kirchberg v. Feenstra, 450 U.S. 455, 101 S.Ct. 1195, 67 L.Ed.2d 428 (1981) (invalidating male management of community property). State courts can avoid the constitutional issue by interpreting any statutory reference to "wife" or "widow" to apply to a spouse of either sex. E.g., Matter of Will of Brooks, 90 N.M. 760, 568 P.2d 596 (1977) (intestate succession statute).

28. See Chapter III, Section 4(4)B. For various forms of misconduct as affecting marital rights by survivor in the estate see 13 A.L.R.3d 446 (1967) (abandonment, desertion, refusal to support); 13 A.L.R.3d 486 (1967) (adultery).

29. Uniform Probate Code, §§ 2–204, 2–802(b). The latter provision states:

"(b) For purposes of Parts 1, 2, 3 & 4 of this Article, and of Section 3–203, a surviving spouse does not include:

(1) a person who obtains or consents to a final decree or judgment of divorce from the decedent or an annulment of their marriage, which decree or judgment is not recognized as valid in this state, unless they subsequently participate in a marriage ceremony purporting to marry each to the other, or subsequently live together as man and wife;

(2) a person who, following a decree or judgment of divorce or annulment obtained by the decedent, participates in a marriage ceremony with a third person; or

(3) a person who was a party to a valid proceeding concluded by an order purporting to terminate all marital property rights."

in greater detail in Subsection (6). It is possible that this provision for the spouse will reduce somewhat the number of elections against wills.

C. Rights In Non-Probate Assets

In non-community property states the most troublesome issue confronting the courts and legislatures arises out of the rapid expansion of a variety of devices for bypassing probate. While a decedent may leave an estate passing under his will, he typically also transfers an accumulation of wealth in different forms, which will pass to named beneficiaries outside of his probate estate. Thus, his life insurance will be paid directly to named beneficiaries. He may have substantial amounts held in a retirement or pension plan set up by his employer and payable to his family, usually as he has designated during his lifetime by agreement with the employer. He may own government bonds in co-ownership or beneficiary designation ("payable on death") form. He usually has some real property (a home) held in joint tenancy with right of survivorship or tenancy by entirety (in a state permitting such an estate); such property passes automatically to the other cotenant. His bank accounts may be payable to himself or another or the survivor. As we shall see later in the course, he may have transferred some of his investment properties during his lifetime to a trustee and retained the income plus extensive powers of control over the trust assets.

Today the proportion of property passing under "probate" is decreasing and the proportion of property passing by such nonprobate methods is increasing. Since the elective share is typically measured only by the probate estate, serious inequities result. Thus, the surviving spouse may be amply provided for by nonprobate methods (life insurance, joint tenancy, etc.) and still elect against the will. Conversely, the decedent may have stripped his probate estate by property arrangements during lifetime, the spouse's elective share being reduced to a nominal amount. Such a scheme to "defraud" the spouse was impossible when wealth consisted of realty, and either inchoate dower or curtesy initiate operated to bar conveyance without consent. Today, however, the inchoate right is gone in many states. In any event, the inchoate right applies only to realty and there is no comparable limitation on transfers of personalty. The effectiveness of such nonprobate transfers to defeat or limit the share of the spouse has usually been left to judicial determination.

The statutory elective share is usually measured in terms of a fraction of "the probate estate", which may be computed with or without deduction of estate taxes. It is thus simple for either spouse to invest wealth during lifetime in forms which do not become part of the probate estate but which pass to other persons on death of the first owner. While the elective share hampers transfer by will, it does not in most states extend to such arrangements set up by lifetime transfer. Absent a statute, the courts have been left to struggle with deliberate attempts to defeat the share of the spouse by such transfers. The analogy of the "fraudulent conveyance" from the creditors' rights field has appealed to some courts, but others consider the issue of "intent" too difficult to administer. Some courts, following the lead of New York, invoked a test whether the arrangement was "illusory", measured in terms of the substance of the arrangement. Later in the course, in connection with revocable living trusts,[30] we shall consider these judicial tests in greater detail. For the present, you might note that if a husband and wife were to obtain a divorce, the property settlement would disregard the form in which the investments were made. If a wife does not sue for divorce and the husband disinherits her by various nonprobate arrangements, why should her legal rights be less after his death than they would have been in the event of divorce during lifetime? Since most of these nonprobate property arrangements are actually included in computing the federal estate tax, and the burden of that tax falls on the probate estate in large measure, the elective share is further reduced in jurisdictions which compute the share on the basis of the net estate after taxes, thus compounding the loss of protection for the spouse.

In recent years there have been various proposals for statutory solution. Two of the most carefully considered statutory solutions offered for the problem appear in the Uniform Probate Code and the New York Estates, Powers and Trusts Law and are set forth in the footnote to give you an idea of the scope of the problem as well as possible patterns for legislation to deal with it.[31]

30. See Chapter VIII, Section 6. For a comparison of the Illinois judicial doctrine of "illusory" transfers and the concept of the augmented estate under the Uniform Probate Code, see Carroll, "The Interplay of Probate Assets and Nonprobate Assets in the Administration of a Decedent's Estate," 25 DePaul L.Rev. 363 (1976).

31. Uniform Probate Code, § 2–202 [Augmented Estate]:

"The augumented estate means the estate reduced by funeral and administration expenses, homestead allowance, family allowances and exemptions, and enforceable claims, to which is added the sum of the following amounts:

"(1) The value of property transferred to anyone other than a bona fide purchaser by the decedent at any time during marriage, to or for the benefit of any person other than the surviving spouse, to the extent that the decedent did not receive adequate and full consideration in money or money's worth for the transfer, if the transfer is of any of the following types:

(i) any transfer under which the decedent retained at the time of his death the possession or enjoyment of, or right to income from, the property;

(ii) any transfer to the extent that the decedent retained at the time of his death a power, either alone or in conjunction with any other person, to revoke or to consume, invade or dispose of the principal for his own benefit;

(iii) any transfer whereby property is held at the time of decedent's death by decedent and another with right of survivorship;

(iv) any transfer made to a donee within two years of death of the decedent to the extent that the aggregate transfers to any one donee in either of the years exceed $3,000.

"Any transfer is excluded if made with the written consent or joinder of the surviving spouse. Property is valued as of the decedent's death except that property given irrevocably to a donee during lifetime of the decedent is valued as of the date the donee came into possession or enjoyment if that occurs first. Nothing herein shall cause to be included in the augmented estate any life insurance, accident insurance, joint annuity, or pen-

The inequity of a forced share measured only by the probate estate may be illustrated by two simplified cases. Assume the wealth

sion payable to a person other than the surviving spouse.

"(2) The value of property owned by the surviving spouse at the decedent's death, plus the value of property transferred by the spouse at any time during marriage to any person other than the decedent which would have been includible in the spouse's augmented estate if the surviving spouse had predeceased the decedent, to the extent the owned or transferred property is derived from the decedent by any means other than testate or intestate succession without a full consideration in money or money's worth. For purposes of this subsection:

(i) Property derived from the decedent includes, but is not limited to, any beneficial interest of the surviving spouse in a trust created by the decedent during his lifetime, any property appointed to the spouse by the decedent's exercise of a general or special power of appointment also exercisable in favor of others than the spouse, any proceeds of insurance (including accidental death benefits) on the life of the decedent attributable to premiums paid by him, any lump sum immediately payable and the commuted value of the proceeds of annuity contracts under which the decedent was the primary annuitant attributable to premiums paid by him, the commuted value of amounts payable after the decedent's death under any public or private pension, disability compensation, death benefit or retirement plan, exclusive of the Federal Social Security system, by reason of service performed or disabilities incurred by the decedent, and the value of the share of the surviving spouse resulting from rights in community property in this or any other state formerly owned with the decedent. Premiums paid by the decedent's employer, his partner, a partnership of which he was a member, or his creditors, are deemed to have been paid by the decedent.

(ii) Property owned by the spouse at the decedent's death is valued as of the date of death. Property transferred by the spouse is valued at the time the transfer became irrevocable, or at the decedent's death, whichever occurred first. Income earned by included property prior to the decedent's death is not treated as property derived from the decedent.

(iii) Property owned by the surviving spouse as of the decedent's death, or previously transferred by the surviving spouse, is presumed to have been derived from the decedent except to the extent that the surviving spouse establishes that it was derived from another source.

"(3) For purposes of this section a bona fide purchaser is a purchaser for value in good faith and without notice of any adverse claim. Any recorded instrument on which a state documentary fee is noted pursuant to [insert appropriate reference] is prima facie evidence that the transfer described therein was made to a bona fide purchaser."

McKinney's N.Y., EPTL, § 5–11.1:

" * * *

"(b) Inter vivos dispositions treated as testamentary substitutes for the purpose of election by surviving spouse.

"(1) Where a person dies after August thirty-first, nineteen hundred sixty-six and is survived by a spouse who exercises a right of election under paragraph (c), the following transactions effected by such decedent at any time after the date of the marriage and after August thirty-first, nineteen hundred sixty-six, whether benefiting the surviving spouse or any other person, shall be treated as testamentary substitutes and the capital value thereof, as of the decedent's death, included in the net estate subject to the surviving spouse's elective right:

"(A) Gifts causa mortis.

"(B) Money deposited, after August thirty-first, nineteen hundred sixty-six, together with all dividends credited thereon, in a savings account in the name of the decedent in trust for another person, with a banking organization, savings and loan association, foreign banking corporation or organization or bank or savings and loan association organized under the laws of the United States, and remaining on deposit at the date of the decedent's death.

"(C) Money deposited, after August thirty-first, nineteen hundred sixty-six, together with all dividends credited thereon, in the name of the decedent and another person and payable on death, pursuant to the terms of the deposit or by operation of law, to the survivor, with a bank-

is owned by the husband. He is survived by his wife and children by a prior marriage. The husband owns $200,000 in stock, life insurance providing for payment of $100,000 on his death, and other assets sufficient to pay taxes and expenses of administration.

Case 1—The husband decides to leave his wife nothing. During his lifetime he changes his stock investments so that the entire

ing organization, savings and loan association, foreign banking corporation or organization or bank or savings and loan association organized under the laws of the United States, and remaining on deposit at the date of the decedent's death.

"(D) Any disposition of property made by the decedent after August thirty-first, nineteen hundred sixty-six whereby property is held, at the date of his death, by the decedent and another person as joint tenants with a right of survivorship or as tenants by the entirety.

"(E) Any disposition of property made by the decedent after August thirty-first, nineteen hundred sixty-six, in trust or otherwise, to the extent that the decedent at the date of his death retained, either alone or in conjunction with another person, by the express provisions of the disposing instrument, a power to revoke such disposition or a power to consume, invade or dispose of the principal thereof. The provisions of this paragraph shall not affect the right of any income beneficiary to the income undistributed or accrued at the date of death.

"(2) Nothing in this paragraph shall affect, impair or defeat the right of any person entitled to receive (A) payment in money, securities or other property under a thrift, savings, pension, retirement, death benefit, stock bonus or profit-sharing plan, system or trust, (B) money payable by an insurance company or a savings bank authorized to conduct the business of life insurance under an annuity or pure endowment contract, a policy of life, group life, industrial life or accident and health insurance or a contract by such insurer relating to the payment of proceeds or avails thereof or (C) payment of any United States savings bond payable to a designated person, and such transactions are not testamentary provisions within the meaning of this paragraph.

"(3) Transactions described in subparagraphs (C) or (D) shall be treated as testamentary substitutes in the proportion that the funds on deposit were the property of the decedent immediately before the deposit or the consideration for the property held as joint tenants or as tenants by the entirety was furnished by the decedent. The surviving spouse shall have the burden of establishing the proportion of the decedent's contribution. Where the other party to a transaction described in subparagraphs (C) or (D) is a surviving spouse, such spouse shall have the burden of establishing the proportion of his contribution, if any. For the purpose of this subparagraph, the surrogate's court may accept such evidence as is relevant and competent, whether or not the person offering such evidence would otherwise be competent to testify.

"(4) The provisions of this paragraph shall not prevent a corporation or other person from paying or transferring any funds or property to a person otherwise entitled thereto, unless there has been served personally upon such corporation or other person a certified copy of an order enjoining such payment or transfer made by the surrogate's court having jurisdiction of the decedent's estate or by another court of competent jurisdiction. Such order may be made, on notice to such persons and in such manner as the court may direct, upon application of the surviving spouse or any other interested party and on proof that the surviving spouse has exercised his right of election under paragraph (c). Service of a certified copy of such order on the corporation or other person holding such fund or property shall be a defense to it, during the effective period of the order, in any action or proceeding brought against it which involves such fund or property.

"(5) This paragraph shall not impair or defeat the rights of creditors of the decedent with respect to any matter as to which any such creditor has rights.

"(6) In case of a conflict between this paragraph and any other provision of law affecting the transactions described in subparagraph (1), this paragraph controls."

* * *

$200,000 is in joint tenancy with his children and makes the life insurance payable to them. His will leaves his entire (probate) estate to his wife. On the given assumption that his remaining wealth is only adequate to pay taxes, claims and expenses of administration, the wife receives nothing. A statute giving her a forced share in the probate estate does not aid her because she receives the entire estate (worth zero) under the will anyway. Nor would common law dower, giving her an inchoate right during the husband's lifetime, help her, for dower applies only to real estate. Of course, in a landed society the concept of inchoate dower afforded the wife protection against inter vivos transfer by the husband without her consent. A limited survival of this is found in many states in the form of statutes requiring conveyances of the homestead to be executed by both husband and wife in order to be valid.

Case 2—During his lifetime the husband makes life insurance payable to his wife and changes his stock investments so that $100,000 is in joint tenancy with the wife. His will recites that he has amply provided for his wife outside the will and that he leaves his (probate) estate in trust for his children. In most states where the widow has an elective share, she can take one-third of the probate estate. Hence the widow receives $233,000 out of the total wealth of $300,000 passing at decedent's death, a result both unintended and unfair.

The need to protect the spouse against inter vivos arrangements to bypass probate and hence the elective share, and the corresponding need to protect the beneficiaries under the will from an election by a spouse who has been amply provided for outside the will led the draftsmen of the Uniform Probate Code in § 2–202 set out above to develop a new concept: "the augmented estate" in which the spouse receives a one-third forced share. The "augmented estate" consists of three elements: (1) the probate estate reduced by funeral and administration expenses, claims, and the various family allowances, (2) the value of property gratuitously transferred during the marriage without the consent of the spouse to third persons by arrangements which are in effect will substitutes (transfers with retained life estate, revocable transfers, joint tenancy or other survivorship forms of ownership), and (3) property acquired by the surviving spouse from decedent (including inter vivos gifts, life insurance proceeds, and joint tenancy assets). As a condition to an election, the surviving spouse must account for her wealth and prove the extent that it was derived from sources other than the decedent. Note that inclusion of the third element operates to reduce rather than increase the elective share.[32]

---

32. On the augmented estate, see Kurtz, "The Augmented Estate Concept Under the Uniform Probate Code: In Search of An Equitable Elective Share," 62 Iowa L.Rev. 981 (1977); Carroll, "The Interplay of Probate Assets and Nonprobate Assets in the Administration of a Decedent's Estate," 25 DePaul L.Rev. 363 (1976); Clark, "The Recapture of Testamentary Substitutes to Preserve the Spouse's Share: An Appraisal of Recent Statutory Reforms," 2 Conn.L.Rev. 513 (1970); Comment, "Widow's Election Under the Augmented Estate," 57 Neb.L. Rev. 147 (1978).

(3) COMMUNITY PROPERTY

Eight states (Arizona, California, Idaho, Louisiana, Nevada, New Mexico, Texas and Washington) have community property laws. There are considerable variations in detail among the community property states. In these states there is no dower, curtesy or elective share in the total probate estate.

The community property system, which was derived from the civil law, proceeds on the assumption that property acquired during marriage (other than by gift or inheritance) is the product of joint efforts of the husband and wife and each therefore has a half share.[33] Property acquired before marriage or by gift or inheritance is classified as the separate property of the respective spouse. Management of community property varies with each state, but usually is either "equal" (either spouse may manage) or "joint" (both must join, as in a conveyance or encumbrance of real property).

Each spouse has a power of testamentary disposition over his half interest in the community property. The surviving spouse is thus assured of a half interest in all community property, but has no rights in separate property which the owner disposes of by will. If the decedent's estate consists entirely of separate property (which may be because it was acquired before the marriage, or because it was inherited wealth) the surviving spouse is dependent on whatever the decedent wishes to provide by will or other transfer. The theory is that the surviving spouse has a right only as to the product of the marital union. If the decedent's wealth is all earned during the marriage, the surviving spouse will get half as her share of community property. But if marriage occurs late in life, and wealth is accumulated before the marriage, or if the wealth is all inherited, the surviving spouse receives nothing, there being no right to separate property.

There are obvious "tracing" problems in determining when and from what source wealth is acquired. The problem is further complicated by the ability of the husband and wife to change property of one kind into the other by agreement or transfer, a process sometimes called "transmutation." The surviving spouse is usually aided by a strong presumption (and judicial attitude) in favor of the property being classified as community.

Movement of families from community property states into common law states, or from common law states into community states, will create increasing problems.[34] Thus, if a husband earns money while the family is domiciled in a community state and as manager

33. See Chapter III, Section 3(2).

34. Lay, Tax and Estate Planning for Community Property and the Migrant Client (1970); Comment, "Community Property in a Common Law Jurisdiction: A Seriously Neglected Area of the Law," 16 Wash.L.J. 77 (1976); Comment, "The Uniform Disposition of Community Property Rights at Death Act," 85 Ky.L.J. 541 (1976).

invests the funds in stock in his name, and then moves to a common law state where he dies, the wife still has an equitable claim to a half interest in the stock as her community property interest. But she will now in many common law states also have an elective share in the deceased husband's half interest![35] Suppose the converse case: The husband earns money in a common law state, retires, and the couple move to a community state. Here the wealth invested in the husband's name would be characterized as "separate" because at the time and place acquired the wife would have no community property right. When the husband now dies domiciled in the community property state, the wife may end up with nothing. She has no community property interest because the property was acquired under a common law system and she has lost the common law protection because the property is now governed by community property law. This result can be avoided only by a statutory provision classifying such property as "quasi-community" (the California approach) and providing the surviving spouse an elective share in such property on death of the spouse who is the owner[36] or by enacting legislation affording some kind of forced share in all separate property.

(4) THE FAMILY MAINTENANCE SYSTEM

The English Inheritance (Provision for Family and Dependants) Act of 1975 vests broad discretionary powers in the court to provide for the decedent's family and persons being maintained by the decedent at the time of his death.[37] Those powers enable the court to vary succession in an intestate estate as well as in a testate estate where the will fails to make adequate provision. The Act goes beyond any American scheme by protecting not only the spouse, but also a former spouse who has not remarried, a child, a stepchild and any person in fact being maintained by the decedent immediately prior to death (for example, a dependent parent or brother or sister, and possibly even a "live-in" companion). The probate court can make a broad range of orders: a lump sum payment, periodic payments over a specified term out of a trust set up for that purpose, transfer of specific property in the estate (such as the family home) and even acquisition of property (such as a smaller home). In the case of the surviving spouse the provision is not limited to maintenance. The

35. Uniform Probate Code, § 2–202 blocks such a double interest. In August, 1971, the Uniform Disposition of Community Property Rights at Death Act was promulgated for adoption in common law states. Uniform Laws Ann., Estate, Probate and Related Laws. The Act has been adopted in 5 states as of the end of 1980. See 5 Real Prop. Prob. & Tr.J. 526 (1970) for the ABA committee report concerning the Act in its draft form.

36. Calif. Probate Code § 201.5; Idaho Code (Bobbs-Merrill) (1979) § 15–2–201 et seq.

37. 1975, c. 63, discussed in Note, 8 Rut.-Cam.L.J. 673 (1977) at 680. For discussion of the earlier provisions, see Crane, "Family Provision on Death in English Law," 35 N.Y.U.L.Rev. 984 (1960).

court can consider duration of the marriage, contribution to the family welfare, and the kind of settlement a court would order had the marriage ended in divorce. The court retains power to vary an order for periodic payments as circumstances change. The court's power is not limited to the probate estate but extends to a variety of nonprobate assets, such as joint tenancy, as well as lifetime gifts made within six years of death with intent to defeat the statutory provision.

(5) AGREEMENTS BARRING RIGHTS

ROSENBERG v. LIPNICK

Supreme Judicial Court of Massachusetts, 1979.
377 Mass. 666, 389 N.E.2d 385.

HENNESSEY, CHIEF JUSTICE.

Charlotte Rosenberg brought this action in the Probate Court against the executors of the estate of Perry Rosenberg, her husband (decedent), seeking invalidation of an antenuptial agreement executed by her and the decedent and a declaration that she is entitled to her statutory share of his estate and a widow's allowance. On the plaintiff's motion, the action was referred to a master. The master made findings of fact and concluded that the agreement is valid and that the plaintiff is not entitled to a statutory share of the estate or to a widow's allowance. The Probate Court judge confirmed the master's report and entered judgment for the defendants. The plaintiff duly appealed.

The plaintiff argues, and the argument finds support in the record, that both the master and the judge viewed this court's decision in Wellington v. Rugg, 243 Mass. 30, 136 N.E. 831 (1922), as controlling. In that case the court held that a husband's simple failure voluntarily to disclose the value of his property prior to executing an antenuptial agreement was not sufficient to invalidate the agreement. Rather, the party seeking invalidation must show fraud.

The plaintiff filed an application for direct appellate review, asking this court to overrule *Wellington*, and hold that (1) an antenuptial agreement which fails to make a full and fair provision for the wife is not enforceable if the husband failed to disclose his assets prior to execution of the agreement, and (2) the representatives of the husband have the burden of proving full and fair disclosure. We granted the plaintiff's application because of the importance of the issues involved.

Although we agree that the *Wellington* principles should be abandoned, we do not think it wise to act retroactively. The *Wellington* decision has remained undisturbed law in this Commonwealth for over a half-century, and numerous agreements have undoubtedly been fashioned in reliance on its rule. Accordingly, we have reviewed this case for error under the law as it existed in 1959. We have discerned none and thus affirm the judgment for the defendants. However, we take this opportunity to delineate new rules that shall apply to antenuptial agreements executed after the publication date of this opinion.

The plaintiff, who was fifty-eight years old, met the decedent, who was sixty-nine years old, in February of 1958. Both were gainfully employed. The plaintiff was a widow, the decedent was a widower, and each had children by previous marriages. After a courtship of approximately eighteen months, the decedent proposed marriage and told the plaintiff that he would like her to sign an antenuptial agreement. The agreement provided that the plaintiff would accept $5,000 from the decedent's estate in lieu of dower or any other rights that she might have were she to survive him.

The plaintiff took the agreement to her brother, a practicing attorney, who asked her whether she had any knowledge of her prospective husband's resources. When she stated that she did not, he told her that he thought the agreement was unfair and called for some explanation. She expressed her desire to sign it, notwithstanding her brother's observations. As he did not want to advise her against the proposed marriage, her brother recommended that she ask the decedent to sign an agreement surrendering any claim against her estate in the event that he survived her. She responded that the decedent had already told her he wanted nothing from her, whereupon her brother drafted a second agreement by which the decedent had no claim to her estate. Both agreements were executed on October 29, 1959. The plaintiff and the decedent were married on November 7, 1959.

At the time of their marriage, the decedent owned a dwelling and a block of stores in Chelsea, Massachusetts. He occupied one of the stores from which he operated his business as an electrician. The block of stores was sold in 1974 for $20,000. The dwelling was sold in 1960; however, no evidence was introduced as to its sale price.

Samuel Shapiro, one of the defendant executors and the decedent's accountant, testified that in 1960, the decedent received dividends from listed companies. Shapiro could not state the amount of such dividends. Neither could he remember whether the decedent received any interest on savings or what the decedent's income taxes were at that time.

The decedent died on July 4, 1976. His estate has an approximate total value of $119,000: $55,000 in stocks and bonds; $51,800 in mortgages, notes and cash; $12,000 in life insurance; and $200 in miscellaneous assets.

During their marriage, the decedent supported the plaintiff, although the plaintiff purchased some of her clothes with her own money. She continued to be employed at the time of the hearing and had assets totalling approximately $45,000, although her living expenses exceeded her income.

The plaintiff contends that the $5,000 to which she is entitled under the antenuptial agreement is grossly disproportionate to the amount to which she would have been entitled but for the antenuptial agreement. The plaintiff further contends that the agreement should have been declared void in the absence of compelling evidence that the agreement was fair when made or that the plaintiff had agreed to take the reduced share with full knowledge of the decedent's assets. The rule in Wellington v. Rugg, supra, is clearly contrary. That case holds that nothing short of proof of fraud will invalidate an antenuptial agreement, irrespective of the unfairness of the agreement's provisions. The following language is controlling: "[T]he allegation that the intestate 'concealed' the amount of his property in the absence of anything to show that he made false representations respecting it or prevented the plaintiff from obtaining whatever facts she desired concerning its character or value is immaterial. The failure on his part to inform her of what he owned falls far short of fraudulent concealment. So far as appears had she so wished, she could have made inquiry of him, and also could have made such investigation as she saw fit before making the contract. Notwithstanding the confidential relations between the parties, the simple failure voluntarily to disclose the amount of his property does not constitute actionable fraud." Id. at 35–36, 136 N.E. at 834. Cf. Anderson v. Anderson, 354 Mass. 565, 238 N.E.2d 868 (1968) (finding fraud in antenuptial agreement purporting to limit the rights of the wife in the event of divorce).

Given our view that *Wellington* governs the rights of the parties now before us, we need not decide whether the agreement's provisions were manifestly unfair to the plaintiff. The master found that the plaintiff failed to establish that the decedent either misrepresented or fraudulently concealed the extent of his assets prior to execution of the agreement. In light of the master's finding, which the judge confirmed and which is supported by the record, the plaintiff cannot prevail under the *Wellington* rule. Accordingly, we affirm the judgment for the defendants.

Massachusetts stands alone in requiring the party seeking invalidation of an antenuptial agreement to show fraud. See 2 A. Lindey, Separation Agreements and Ante-Nuptial Contracts § 90 (rev.ed. 1977); Annot., 27 A.L.R.2d 883–906 (1953 & Supp.1978). The great majority of cases in other jurisdictions hold that the parties to an antenuptial agreement generally do not deal at arm's length. Rather, they occupy a relationship of mutual trust and confidence and as such must exercise the highest degree of good faith, candor, and sincerity in all matters bearing on the proposed agreement. 2 A. Lindey, supra at § 90–42–43. The burden is not on either party to inquire, but on each to inform, for it is only by requiring full disclosure of the amount, character, and value of the parties' respective assets that courts can ensure intelligent waiver of the statutory rights involved. See, e.g., Guhl v. Guhl, 376 Ill. 100, 33 N.E.2d 185 (1941); Megginson v. Megginson, 367 Ill. 168, 10 N.E.2d 815 (1937); Denison v. Dawes, 121 Me. 402, 117 A. 314 (1922); Hartz v. Hartz, 248 Md. 47, 234 A.2d

865 (1967); Kaufmann Estate, 404 Pa. 131, 171 A.2d 48 (1961); McClellan Estate, 365 Pa. 401, 75 A.2d 595 (1950). See Generally Annot., 27 A.L.R.2d 883, §§ 3, 4 (1953 & Supp.1978).

Although the *Wellington* court specifically acknowledged that a confidential relationship exists between parties to an antenuptial agreement, Wellington v. Rugg, supra, 243 Mass. at 36, 136 N.E. 831, its holding treats them as though they stood at arm's length. The decision cites G. S. Bower on Actionable Non-Disclosure § 135 (1915), Potts v. Chapin, 133 Mass. 276 (1882), and Windram Mfg. Co. v. Boston Blacking Co., 239 Mass. 123, 131 N.E. 454 (1921), all of which speak to rights between parties functioning in a commercial context. *Wellington*, supra, 343 Mass. at 35, 136 N.E. 831. Quoting from *Windram*, the *Wellington* court, 343 Mass. at 36, 136 N.E. at 834 stated: "Mere silence on the part of the defendant is all that is charged. But failure to disclose known facts does not amount to fraud, and is not the basis of an action for deceit, unless the parties stand in such relation to one another that one is under legal or equitable obligation to communicate the facts to the other." Although the court chose to view the confidential relationship between the parties in *Wellington* as not giving rise to an obligation to disclose, that case has been cited in subsequent opinions which impose a duty to disclose on parties occupying an obviously less delicate relationship. See, e.g., Goodwin v. Agassiz, 283 Mass. 358, 186 N.E. 659 (1933) (holding that the existence of a fiduciary relationship between corporate director and stockholder may give rise to a duty of disclosure).

While we have, in fairness, followed the *Wellington* case in the instant matter, we think that to the extent that *Wellington* negates any duty of disclosure, we should abandon that precedent in favor of the more enlightened rules of other jurisdictions. Thus, in future cases involving agreements drawn after the publication date of this opinion, we shall feel free to hold that the parties by definition occupy a confidential relationship and that the burden of disclosure rests upon both of them.

In judging the validity of such an antenuptial agreement, other relevant factors which we may consider are whether (1) it contains a fair and reasonable provision as measured at the time of its execution for the party contesting the agreement; (2) the contesting party was fully informed of the other party's worth prior to the agreement's execution, or had, or should have had, independent knowledge of the other party's worth; and (3) a waiver by the contesting party is set forth.[38] It is clear that the reasonableness of any monetary provision

38. [This and the following footnote are by the Court.]

See, e.g., Del Vecchio v. Del Vecchio, 143 So.2d 17 (Fla.1962); Hartz v. Hartz, 248 Md. 47, 234 A.2d 865 (1967); Kaufmann Estate, 404 Pa. 131, 171 A.2d 48 (1961); McClellan Estate, 365 Pa. 401, 75 A.2d 595 (1950). See generally 2 A. Lindey, Separation Agreements and Ante-Nuptial Contracts § 90–36–37 (rev. ed.1977). Cf. Friedlander v. Friedlander, 80 Wash.2d 293, 494 P.2d 208 (1972) (antenuptial agreement made in contemplation of divorce).

As to the burden of proof in cases contesting the validity of antenuptial agreements, see, e.g., Del Vecchio v. Del Vecchio, 143 So.2d 17 (Fla.1962); Guhl v. Guhl, 376 Ill. 100, 33 N.E.2d 444 (1941); In re Estate of Parish, 236 Iowa 822, 20

in an antenuptial contract cannot ultimately be judged in isolation. Rather, reference may appropriately be made to such factors as the parties' respective worth, the parties' respective ages, the parties' respective intelligence, literacy, and business acumen, and prior family ties or commitments.[39]

We add that, even if we were to apply these factors and the "fair disclosure" rule to the instant case, it could be argued that the plaintiff here is not entitled to relief. This result might well be urged from all the circumstances, including the fact that she was advised by counsel that she should request disclosure but decided not to for fear it might result in no marriage. Neither was there the slightest evidence of coercion by the decedent against the plaintiff.

The right to make antenuptial agreements settling property rights in advance of marriage is a valuable personal right which courts should not regulate destructively. Neither should the exercise of that right be looked upon with disfavor. Thus, we recognize that antenuptial agreements must be so construed as to give full effect to the parties' intentions, but we are concerned that such agreements be executed fairly and understandingly and be free from fraud, imposition, deception, or over-reaching.

Judgment affirmed.

NOTE

Marital agreements governing property rights are expected to play an increasing role.[40] Because of changes in the family structure and greater economic independence of working women, an agreement may be desirable in a variety of situations. Marital agreements, whether executed before or during the marriage, may cover one or more of the following property problems:

(1) rights of ownership, management and control during the marriage;

(2) division of property in event of divorce;

(3) rights to property on death of either spouse (our major concern in this course).

Where both spouses are employed, they may want to keep their incomes and investments from those incomes as separate property in community property

N.W.2d 32 (1945); Burns v. Spiker, 109 Kan. 22, 202 P. 370 (1921); Denison v. Dawes, 121 Me. 402, 117 A. 314 (1922); McClellan Estate, 365 Pa. 401, 75 A.2d 595 (1950); Friedlander v. Friedlander, 80 Wash. 293, 494 P.2d 208 (1972); Bibelhausen v. Bibelhausen, 159 Wis. 365, 150 N.W. 516 (1915). See also 2 A. Lindey, Separation Agreements and Ante-Nuptial Contracts § 90–83–85 (rev. ed.1977); Comment, "Husband and Wife—Antenuptial Contracts", 41 Mich. L.Rev. 1133, 1137 (1943), and cases cited.

39. See, e.g., Estate of Nelson, 224 Cal.App.2d 138, 36 Cal.Rptr. 352 (1964); Del Vecchio v. Del Vecchio, 143 So.2d 17 (Fla.1962); Megginson v. Megginson, 367 Ill. 168, 10 N.E.2d 815 (1937); Parker v. Gray, 317 Ill. 468, 148 N.E. 323 (1925); Achilles v. Achilles, 151 Ill. 136, 37 N.E. 693 (1894); Hartz v. Hartz, 248 Md. 47, 234 A.2d 865 (1967); Rocker v. Rocker, 42 Ohio Op.2d 184 (1967); Bauer v. Bauer, 1 Or.App. 504, 464 P.2d 710 (1970); Kaufmann Estate, 404 Pa. 131, 171 A.2d 48 (1961). See generally 2 A. Lindey, Separation Agreements and Ante-Nuptial Contracts § 90–37–38 (rev.ed.1977).

40. Kraushkopf, "Marital and Non-Marital Contracts: Preventive Law for the Family" (1979); Clark, "Antenuptial Contracts", 50 U. of Colo.L.Rev. 142 (1979).

states or to guard against problems if they move to a community property state. An agreement is also desirable for a marriage where there are children by a prior marriage; particularly in marriages later in life each spouse wants freedom to dispose of his or her property to children without any claim by the other spouse. Such contracts not only reduce a source of friction between the spouses but also, where children of the prior marriage are adult, disquiet concern by them over loss of inheritance (an expectation, not a legal right). An agreement is especially important where a husband and wife have decided to separate and obtain a divorce; death prior to the final decree would, in the absence of an agreement, leave the survivor as still the legal "spouse" entitled to allowances, any elective share, and the right to take by intestate succession the spouse's share of any intestate property.[41]

Such agreements require careful drafting.[42] For example, with respect to rights in the estate of the other spouse in event of death, a simple waiver of "all rights" may or may not be construed to include allowances. There is some difference of opinion as to the judicial standards for such agreements, whether validity turns merely on adequate disclosure,[43] or on total "fairness" of the property provisions under all the particular circumstances (and whether that fairness should be judged at the time the contract is entered into or at the time of performance).[44] Fairness would include a consideration of adequacy of support for the surviving spouse. Because of the confidential relation between the parties courts should apply the equitable doctrine against "overreaching." Nevertheless courts tend to uphold such agreements.[45]

Ideally both husband and wife should be represented by separate lawyers. Where both parties retain the same lawyer for economy or other reasons, what ethical problems does the lawyer face in drafting the agreement?

41. Matter of Estate of Loughmiller, 229 Kan. 584, 629 P.2d 156 (1981) illustrates the effectiveness of an agreement in such a situation.

42. Antenuptial and postnuptial property agreements, as well as property settlements incident to a separation or divorce, involve tax pitfalls that are examined in detail in the appropriate tax courses. However, adoption of an unlimited marital deduction in the Economic Recovery Tax Act of 1981, P.L. 97–34, allows interspousal transfers to be made without any federal estate or gift tax. This should simplify most estate planning aspects.

43. Uniform Probate Code, § 2–204 provides that the right of election of a surviving spouse and the rights of the surviving spouse to homestead, exempt property and family allowance may be waived wholly or partially, before or after marriage by a *written* contract, agreement or waiver *signed* by the party waiving *after fair disclosure*. Unless the agreement provides to the contrary a waiver of *all* rights in the agreement *or* a complete property settlement entered into after or in anticipation of separation or divorce is a waiver not only of the rights above specified but also those which would pass by intestate succession or by will. The U.P.C. requirement of "fair disclosure" has been construed to mean that, unlike the commercial transaction, the spouse has no duty to make inquiry merely because he or she has information which would lead a reasonably prudent person to inquire. Matter of Estate of Lebsock, ___ Colo.App. ___, 618 P.2d 683 (1980). On non-disclosure as grounds for setting aside the agreement, see 27 A.L.R.2d 883 (1953).

44. Lindey, Separation Agreements and Ante-Nuptial Contracts (1977) § 90-49.

45. Estate of Borton, 393 P.2d 808 (Wyo.1964); Matter of Estate of Lewin, 42 Colo.App. 129, 595 P.2d 1055 (1979); In re Stever's Estate, 155 Colo. 1, 392 P.2d 286 (1964); Johnston v. Johnston, 134 Ind.App. 351, 184 N.E.2d 651 (1962); In re West's Estate, 194 Kan. 736, 402 P.2d 117 (1965); Lightman v. Magid, 54 Tenn. App. 701, 394 S.W.2d 151 (1965).

Can he faithfully and fairly represent both parties?[46] Consider from the Code of Professional Responsibility:

> **EC 5–15** "* * * On the other hand, there are many instances in which a lawyer may properly serve multiple clients having potentially differing interests in matters not involving litigation. If the interests vary only slightly, it is generally likely that the lawyer will not be subjected to an adverse influence and that he can retain his independent judgment on behalf of each client; and if the interests become differing, withdrawal is less likely to have a disruptive effect upon the causes of his clients.
>
> **EC 5–16** In those instances in which a lawyer is justified in representing two or more clients having differing interests, it is nevertheless essential that each client be given the opportunity to evaluate his need for representation free of any potential conflict and to obtain other counsel if he so desires. Thus before a lawyer may represent multiple clients, he should explain fully to each client the implications of the common representation and should accept or continue employment only if the clients consent. If there are present other circumstances that might cause any of the multiple clients to question the undivided loyalty of the lawyer, he should also advise all of the clients of those circumstances."

If you represent only the husband and have prepared the agreement and know that the wife is not represented, do you owe any duty to her even though she is not your client?[47]

Can there by any question about overreaching if both spouses have independent counsel?[48] In how great detail must the assets of each be disclosed? In some states, including those which have adopted the Uniform Probate Code, the release of prospective rights in the estate of one spouse may be made by the other spouse unilaterally without consideration; should a more strict standard be imposed in such cases?

46. Fisher, What Every Lawyer Knows (Nimrod Press, 1974) p. 44:

"Preparing an antenuptial agreement is a case where separate lawyers are almost always desirable, for example, when a rich widower with children proposes to marry a woman without means under an agreement by which she relinquishes her normal marital rights. In such a case she ought ordinarily to be furnished with a full statement of his assets and have a lawyer of her own who is neither connected with her prospective husband nor selected by him. * * *"

In Whitney v. Seattle-First National Bank, 90 Wn.2d 105, 579 P.2d 937 (1978), the court held that there is no absolute rule that both spouses have independent counsel, although lack of independent advice is one factor to be considered in determining validity of a marital agreement.

47. Daniel Schuyler, participating in a panel discussion on Ethics in Estate Planning, 1974 Institute on Estate Planning (U. of Miami) ¶ 74.700, at p. 7–18:

"It seems to me it is pretty clear, if you are talking about an antenuptial agreement that both spouses must be fully informed, very fully informed as to the assets available and as to what their rights are. And if they are going to enter into an antenuptial agreement, or in some states I take it you can enter into a post-nuptial agreement, not very readily in Illinois, for example, although it can be done, but there you have to have full disclosure. Consequently, it seems to me that you would have to insist on the spouse that you did not represent being separately advised. And I think it would be a great mistake to draft an antenuptial agreement or a post-nuptial agreement for one spouse and then tell the other one 'Okay, this is fine for you to sign.' They ought to be independently represented, and I mean really independently, not just by someone that you select that is going to do it the way you tell him."

48. See Cantor v. Palmer, 166 So.2d 466 (Fla.Ct. of App.1964).

Should the agreement be made before marriage? What problems may arise if the agreement is not formalized until after marriage? In states still adhering to the old rule that the wife cannot contract with her husband, she may be able to elect against the will or claim an intestate share despite the contract; but again the trend is toward upholding postnuptial agreements,[49] even where obsolete statutes codify the common law rules on jointure.[50] If the agreement is made after marriage at a time when the parties may be thinking about going their separate ways, there is danger that the agreement may be held invalid on the grounds that it tends to foster separation.[51]

Some statutes permit a unilateral "release" of the right to elect against a particular will or against any will.[52] In such case the requirement of a formal execution supplants the contractual requirement of consideration in the bilateral agreement.

---

(6) UNINTENTIONAL DISINHERITANCE

Unintentional disinheritance of a spouse occurs when an unmarried testator prepares his will without providing for the contingency that he may later marry (or the testator is married to a wife for whom he provides in his will but who predeceases him, and he later remarries). This problem is dealt with in various ways. Some states have statutes providing an intestate share for the omitted spouse, like Section 2–301 of the Uniform Probate Code;[53] these statutes are similar in operation to the pretermitted heir statutes discussed in the next Section. In some states the later marriage operates to revoke the will, an approach which will be considered in Chapter VI. In a third group of states the spouse must rely on the elective share as protection; this unfortunately equates a spouse to whom the testator would have left a substantial share had he revised his will, with the spouse whom the testator in fact would disinherit if he could.

---

49. McQuate v. White, 389 S.W.2d 206 (Mo.1965).

50. Estate of Beat, 25 Wis.2d 315, 130 N.W.2d 739 (1964).

51. In re Cooper's Estate, 195 Kan. 174, 403 P.2d 984 (1965); compare Ransford v. Yens, 374 Mich. 110, 132 N.W.2d 150 (1965).

52. E.g., McKinney's N.Y., EPTL, § 5–1.1(f).

53. **Section 2–301. [Omitted Spouse.]**

"(a) If a testator fails to provide by will for his surviving spouse who married the testator after the execution of the will, the omitted spouse shall receive the same share of the estate he would have received if the decedent left no will unless it appears from the will that the omission was intentional or the testator provided for the spouse by transfer outside the will and the intent that the transfer be in lieu of a testamentary provision is shown by statements of the testator or from the amount of the transfer or other evidence.

"(b) In satisfying a share provided by this section the devises made by the will abate as provided in Section 3–902."

SECTION 3. PROTECTION OF CHILDREN AND OTHER DESCENDANTS

UNIFORM PROBATE CODE

Section 2–302. [Pretermitted Children.]

"(a) If a testator fails to provide in his will for any of his children born or adopted after the execution of his will, the omitted child receives a share in the estate equal in value to that which he would have received if the testator had died intestate unless:

(1) it appears from the will that the omission was intentional;

(2) when the will was executed the testator had one or more children and devised substantially all his estate to the other parent of the omitted child; or

(3) the testator provided for the child by transfer outside the will and the intent that the transfer be in lieu of a testamentary provision is shown by statements of the testator or from the amount of the transfer or other evidence.

"(b) If at the time of execution of the will the testator fails to provide in his will for a living child solely because he believes the child to be dead, the child receives a share in the estate equal in value to that which he would have received if the testator had died intestate.

"(c) In satisfying a share provided by this section, the devises made by the will abate as provided in Section 3–902."

ESTATE OF GLOMSET

Supreme Court of Oklahoma, 1976.
547 P.2d 951.

BARNES, JUSTICE.

On the 16th day of October, 1972, the deceased, John Larson Glomset, Sr., and the Appellant, Margie V. Glomset, made and signed joint and reciprocal wills leaving each other all of the other's property in case of death of the other, except in the case of a common disaster, in which instance the whole of the estate was to go to John Larson Glomset, Jr., the son of the deceased.

The deceased's 40-year-old daughter, Carolyn Gay Ghan, was not named in the will. On the 15th day of October, 1973, John Larson Glomset, Sr., died, and on the 17th day of October, 1973, his will was filed for probate. On the 9th day of November the will was admitted to probate, but the question of whether Appellee, Carolyn Gay Ghan, was a pretermitted heir was reserved. On February 7, 1974, a hearing was held, in which Appellee's motion for a declaratory judgment that Appellee was a pretermitted heir, as defined by Title 84 O.S. § 132, and entitled to share in her father's estate, was sustained. The Trial Court found:

> "The Court finds, from a complete reading of the will that the Contestant was omitted therefrom, and that said will provides for her in no manner whatsoever. The Court finds that a complete reading of the will discloses no intent to intentionally not provide for said Contestant. No intention to disinherit Contestant affirmatively appears from the four corners of the will. The Court, therefore, finds that Contestant was unintentionally omitted from deceased's said will, and is, therefore, entitled to have the same share in the estate of the decedent as if decedent had died intestate, all as provided in 84 O.S. § 132."

Appellant questions whether this issue can be determined in a summary judgment proceeding, and, if so, Appellant further disputes the Trial Court's finding that Appellee is a pretermitted heir under the provisions of 84 O.S. § 132.

Title 84 O.S. § 132 provides as follows:

> "When any testator omits to provide in his will for any of his children, or for the issue of any deceased child *unless it appears that such omission was intentional*, such child, or the issue of such child, must have the same share in the estate of the testator, as if he had died intestate, and succeeds thereto as provided for in preceding section." (Emphasis added)

There was no dispute concerning the fact the Appellee was a daughter of the deceased. The only question for our determination is whether or not deceased's omission of Appellee appears to have been intentional.

We must first determine if the intent of the deceased must be determined from the will itself, or if extrinsic evidence is admissible. If extrinsic evidence is not admissible, then there is no question of fact still to be determined, and in that event, since there is only a question of law to be determined, a summary judgment by the Trial Court was proper. In deciding if extrinsic evidence is admissible, we must determine whether or not an intention to disinherit Appellee affirmatively appeared from the four corners of the will. We have previously held that if there are no uncertainties appearing on the face of the will, extrinsic evidence is not admissible. See O'Neill v. Cox, 270 P.2d 663 (Okl.1954), and Dilks v. Carson, 197 Okl. 128, 168 P.2d 1020 (1946).

There are no uncertainties on the face of the will in this case. The testator admittedly failed to mention his daughter, Appellee Carolyn Gay Ghan, and also failed to indicate any reason for his failure to mention her.

Thus, if we are to follow previous decisions of this court interpreting 84 O.S. § 132, such as In re Daniels' Estate, 401 P.2d 493 (Okl.

1965), then we must find that Appellee is a pretermitted heir and entitled to inherit her proportionate share of her deceased father's estate.

Appellant has failed to set forth a compelling reason why the interpretation of 84 O.S. § 132 should be changed at this time to permit introduction of extrinsic evidence to show intent of the testator where no ambiguity appears on the face of the will.

The writ of certiorari petitioned for is granted, the decision of the Court of Appeals is vacated, and the judgment of the Trial Court is affirmed.

* * *

HODGES, VICE CHIEF JUSTICE (dissenting).

The majority opinion holds the will is unambiguous on its face and, therefore, extrinsic evidence is inadmissible to determine the intention of the testator. I believe this perpetuates a misinterpretation of the applicable statute, 84 O.S.1971, § 132.

It is generally recognized that pretermitted heir statutes are not intended to limit a testator's power to dispose of his property by will, or to require him to bestow any part of his estate on any child or descendant. The purpose of the statute is to protect such heirs against omission due to *unintentional* oversight, forgetfulness or mistake. Two broad general classifications of such statutes are recognized: (1) The "Massachusetts-type" statutes, which are usually considered to emphasize the intention of the testator as the material factor in determining whether a child or descendant is disinherited; and (2) "Missouri-type" statutes which omit reference to intention and provide for a total or partial revocation of the will if a child is not named or provided for therein.

Our statute, a "Massachusetts-type" statute, was adopted from the Dakotas. Under comparable statutes providing an omitted child or issue of a deceased child should be entitled to a portion of the testator's estate, "unless it appears that such omission was intentional," the courts of North and South Dakota and the majority of jurisdictions, with the exceptions of California and Oklahoma, have consistently held since 1868, that extrinsic evidence was admissible to prove that the testator intended to disinherit an omitted child. The pretermitted heir statute raises the presumption that children are not intentionally omitted from a will. However, the presumption is rebuttable by extrinsic evidence and parol testimony.

The purpose and legislative intent of the statute is to protect children unintentionally omitted from the will. It is not to be construed to alter the testamentary intent of the testator by including children he intentionally excluded from his estate.

I would therefore overrule all cases in conflict with the traditional interpretation of the pretermitted heir statute.

Assuming arguendo, the majority view is correct, I further believe the will is ambiguous on its face, and that the testator's intention to disinherit appears from the will itself. The statute which guides our interpretation of intention, 84 O.S.1971, § 152 permits introduction of extrinsic evidence to show the circumstances under which the will was executed.

This court In Re Adams' Estate, 203 Okl. 377, 222 P.2d 366 (1950) held that the question of the intention to omit may be drawn from inference of the language as well as the face of the will, and that the drawing of such inference is not only within the power of the court, but is the duty of the court. The court held at page 369:

> "In determining whether the omission of a child is intentional or not, no set form of words, indicating testator's intention to omit such child, is requisite. The will is to be taken as a whole; and if it appears from the entire instrument that testator intended to omit such child, the statute does not apply. * * *
>
> "It is not necessary that testator should name his child, or even refer, in terms, to the fact that it is his child."

Extrinsic evidence should have been admissible because by omitting the daughter from the will she thereby is entitled to her statutory share, while the son who was mentioned in the will receives nothing. Thus on the face of the will an uncertainty is created and extrinsic evidence should be allowed. This extrinsic evidence which was offered, but rejected by the trial court, definitely shows the testator intentionally omitted the daughter. She would not visit her father or even allow her child to visit him. They had not seen each other for some time because of their strained relationship.

I believe a construction which permits a child not mentioned in the will to participate in the distribution of the estate while the other child who is mentioned and designated the contingent beneficiary takes nothing, is a tortured interpretation of the will and the Oklahoma Statutes regarding testamentary intent, and reaches a result totally unintended and uncontemplated by the testator or the statute.

The cause should be remanded to the trial court for determination of the factual question of whether the omission of the daughter was intentional.

I, therefore, respectfully dissent.

NOTE

Uniform Probate Code, Section 2–302 and the Oklahoma statute in the principal case are typical of statutes designed to protect children against unintentional disinheritance, although there is considerable variation in the wording of the statutes.[54] Note the differences between the Oklahoma statute and the Uniform Probate Code section. Statutes like the Oklahoma sec-

54. See Rees, "American Wills Statutes", 46 Va.L.Rev. 839, 893 (1960); Dainow, "Inheritance by Pretermitted Heirs", 32 Ill.L.Rev. 1 (1937); Evans, "Should Pretermitted Children be Entitled to Inherit", 31 Calif.L.Rev. 263 (1943); King, "Statutory Status of Pretermitted Heirs", 13 B.U.L.R. 672 (1933); Mathews, "Pretermitted Heirs: An Analysis of Statutes", 29 Col.L.Rev. 748 (1929); Mathews, "Trends in the Power to Disinherit Children", 16 Am. Bar Ass'n J. 293 (1930); Pyle, "How to Beat the Pretermitted Heir Statute", 18 Hastings L.J. 333 (1967); Sweet, "Rights of a Pretermitted Heir in California Community Property—A Need for Clarification", 13 Stan.L.Rev. 80 (1960).

tion, particularly as interpreted in the principal case, tend to provide a share for a child or grandchild omitted under circumstances where it can be reasonably inferred none was intended.[55] In almost all states a testator may intentionally disinherit his children by devising his estate to others with appropriate language showing his intent to disinherit his issue.[56] He cannot, however, disinherit merely by fiat, without disposing of his estate to another. For example, a will stating merely that the testator wishes to disinherit a named child would not bar that child from inheriting under the intestate succession laws.[57] A will disinheriting a child can be contested, of course, on grounds of lack of capacity or undue influence. A will disinheriting all of the testator's children (unless in favor of a surviving spouse) is regarded as "unnatural." This is one of the factors considered in will contests based on lack of testamentary capacity or undue influence and is particularly persuasive if the issue goes to a jury.[58] The concept that a parent may intentionally make no provision or only inadequate provision for minor or other dependent children, whom he is legally obligated to support during lifetime, is being strongly criticized.[59]

Most of the so-called "pretermitted heir" statutes apply to children born or adopted after the execution of the will, although some apply to children born before and some to children in both categories.[60] If a client has children at the time his will is drafted, it is customary to recite his family status, name the children and state that it is the intent of the testator to make no provision in the will for them "or any children I may hereafter have"; another drafting approach where the testator wishes to leave his estate to his spouse is to devise the entire estate to the spouse if he or she survives, with the added statement: "It is my intention to exclude under this paragraph all of my children, whether born or adopted before or after this Will is executed";[61] this would be followed by a gift to the testator's issue if the spouse

55. Crump's Estate v. Freeman, 614 P.2d 1096 (Okl.1980); Armstrong v. Butler, 262 Ark. 31, 553 S.W.2d 453 (1977) ("Our statute * * * operates in favor of the pretermitted child without regard to the real intention of the testator in regard to the omission.")

56. Laube, "The Right of a Testator to Pauperize his Helpless Dependents", 13 Corn.L.Q. 559 (1928). The civil law principle of *legitime* operates in Louisiana. A testator can dispose of two-thirds of his property by will if he leaves one child surviving, one-half if he leaves two children, or one-third if three or more children survive. Ten permissible grounds for disinheritance are prescribed, at least one of which must be set forth and proved before the disinheritance is effective. LSA-C.C., arts. 1493, 1494, 1617–1622 (1952).

For the relationship of the *legitime* to the share of the surviving spouse see Yiannopoulos, "Testamentary Disposition in Favor of the Surviving Spouse and the *Legitime* of Descendants", 28 La.L.Rev. 509 (1968). In Brown v. Drake, ___ S.C. ___, 270 S.E.2d 130 (1980) the court refused to declare against public policy a provision in a will, drafted when testator was contemplating divorce, that if any of his children should be awarded to his wife he willed each child $1. Instead the court reaffirmed the rule that a testator may disinherit his children.

57. Similarly, a child disinherited by a will shares in any intestate property. E.g., In re Martz' Estate, 318 Mich. 293, 28 N.W.2d 108 (1947).

58. See Georgia Code § 113–106 set forth in fn. 5, Section 1, supra.

59. Rein, "A More Rational System for the Protection of Family Members Against Disinheritance: A Critique of Washington's Pretermitted Child Statute and Other Matters," 15 Gonzaga L.Rev. 11 (1979); also the articles cited in fns. 12 & 13 in Section 2(1).

60. A number of pretermitted heir statutes apply only to a child born after the will is executed but distinguish between the case in which a testator has another child living when the will is executed and the case in which the testator has no other child living when the will is executed. E.g., Va.Code Ann. §§ 64.-1–70, 64.1–71.

61. The use of class language, such as "heirs" or "children", may or may not be a sufficient mention of a child in particular states. The result will depend up-

predeceases the testator. Some draftsmen prefer to leave a nominal amount to each child. A generally worded clause ("I have intentionally failed to provide for any person not mentioned herein") is likely to be held not to show the necessary intent to exclude issue.[62]

Whether grandchildren are protected by the statute if their parent is predeceased depends on the wording of the particular statute.[63] In one unusual New York case one afterborn child predeceased the testator, leaving children of the afterborn who survived; the court allowed the grandchildren to take on the principle of representation, even though the statute only made express provision for a "child."[64]

The operation of a pretermitted heir statute does not technically revoke the will,[65] although if the child is the sole heir and takes the entire estate, only the administrative provisions of the will have any effect. Where the pretermitted heir is entitled to only part of the estate under the statute, the methods of satisfying his share raise a problem of abatement, considered hereafter.[66]

Under some circumstances a claim may be filed on behalf of a minor child against the estate of a parent obligated to support the child.[67] Increasingly upon divorce or dissolution of a marriage, the decree may provide for an obligation of support which survives death of the parent.[68] Even in the absence of such an express provision, it is arguable that the child should have a valid claim for support against the estate of a parent who has disinherited him.[69]

on construction of the will as a whole, although if the applicable statute does not require the intention of the testator to appear from the face of the will, parol evidence of his intention to omit a particular child may be admitted.

62. Estate of Gardner, 21 Cal.3d 620, 147 Cal.Rptr. 184, 580 P.2d 684 (1978) (clause held to be too general to show intent to exclude issue, although one phrased in terms of intent to omit "any person claiming as an heir" would be satisfactory.) A comparable problem as to intent to exclude a subsequent spouse is considered in Chapter VI, Section 2(3).

63. The grandchild may be provided for and therefore not be a pretermitted heir if a gift to a child of the testator passes to the grandchild by operation of an antilapse statute. E.g., Miller v. Aven, 327 Mo. 20, 34 S.W.2d 116 (1930). If the parent is mentioned by the testator, some courts permit the grandchild to take as pretermitted heir when the parent is deceased. E.g., In re Ross' Estate, 140 Cal. 282, 73 P. 976 (1930).

64. Matter of Horst, 264 N.Y. 236, 190 N.E. 475 (1934).

65. At common law a will is revoked if the testator marries and has a child after the will is executed. See Chapter VI, Section 2(3).

66. See Chapter XV, Section 1(3)(c).

67. The claim may be sustained when based upon a support provision in a divorce decree. E.g., Creyts v. Creyts, 143 Mich. 375, 106 N.W. 1111, 114 Am.St. Rep. 656 (1906). E.g., contra: In re Moore's Estate, 34 Tenn.App. 131, 234 S.W.2d 847 (1950). Under other circumstances recovery has been denied. E.g., Cissna v. Beaton, 2 Wash.2d 491, 98 P.2d 651 (1940).

68. E.g., Ariz.Rev.Stat. § 25–327C provides that provisions in a decree for support of a minor child do not terminate upon death of the parent obligated to support the child, unless the decree provides otherwise or otherwise agreed in writing.

69. Wisconsin has a unique statute empowering the probate court to make an allowance out of the estate for support of a minor child until he reaches 18. Wis.Stat.Ann. § 861.35 (West Supp.1980). Note also that often the homestead allowance, the exempt property and family allowance (discussed in the next Section) are available to minor or dependent children if there is no surviving spouse and that these statutory provisions cannot be defeated by will.

PROBLEM

A testator executed the following will:

"I, Hiram Coffman, of Rockingham county and State of Virginia, do make and ordain this to be my last will and testament, * * *. It is my will that my son, William H. Coffman, be excluded from all of my estate at my death and have no heirship in the same. * * *" There were no dispositive or administrative provisions in the will.

At the testator's death, William H. Coffman contested the will. Should the will be probated? Coffman v. Coffman, 85 Va. 459, 8 S.E. 672 (1888).

SECTION 4. OTHER PROTECTION OF THE FAMILY

The homestead and exemption statutes and the statutory provisions for family allowances have been examined previously.[70] In a few states homestead and the personal property exemptions are treated merely as a protection against creditors, but in a majority of states the testator cannot defeat the claim of his spouse and minor children to the exemptions provided by statute, although the testator may put the spouse and minor children to an election between a gift by will and their rights at law.[71] Because the purpose of the family allowance is to provide for the family while the estate of the testator is in administration, a substantial minority of courts have refused to permit a testator to put his family to an election between the family allowance and a testamentary gift, but permit the parties entitled to enjoy the family allowance and any testamentary gift made to them.[72]

As in the case of forced heirship,[73] a testator may defeat homestead, the personal property exemption and the family allowance by inter vivos transfers. The testator cannot, however, defeat these claims by general use of his credit. The family allowances are exempt from the claims of most of the testator's creditors although they are subject to claims for expenses of administration, funeral expenses and expenses of the last illness. The homestead is subject to

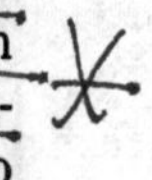

70. See Chapter III, Section 3(3), supra.

71. The homestead and exemption laws and the provisions for election vary a great deal from state to state. See Atkinson, Wills (2d Ed., 1953) 126; 1 Woerner, Administration (3d Ed., 1923) 318; Vernier, American Family Laws (1935) § 228. The Uniform Probate Code Homestead, Exempt Property and Allowance Provisions appear in §§ 2–401 through 2–404. These have been discussed in detail in Chapter III, Section 3(3), supra.

72. E.g., In re O'Shea's Estate, 85 Neb. 156, 122 N.W. 881 (1909). Where elections are permitted there is a strong presumption that a testamentary gift is in addition to the family allowance.

73. See Section 2, supra. The provisions of the Uniform Probate Code also seem to limit homestead, exempt property and the allowance to the probate estate, except that the statutory allowances are effective against survivors on multiple-party accounts (such as joint bank accounts) if the probate assets are insufficient. (Section 6–107).

tax claims, mortgages in which the wife has joined and debts created in the purchase and erection of the home.[74]

An ill or dying person may be disposed or influenced to will too large a proportion of his estate to the church or to charitable causes, at the expense of his family obligations. Statutory restraints upon such dispositions (commonly called "Mortmain" statutes) have been imposed in a limited number of states.[75] These statutes are of several types: (1) invalidating charitable testamentary gifts if the will is executed within a specified period prior to the death of the testator;[76] (2) limiting the proportion of the estate which may be given to charity and invalidating either the entire gift or the excess over the limitation;[77] (3) combining both types of limitations (time of will execution and amount given to charity).[78] Frequently the statutes permit only specified relatives to challenge the gifts;[79] a testator with no close relatives is free to dispose of his entire estate to charity under such a statute. In states which impose a charitable restriction only on testamentary gifts, the revocable inter vivos trust is used to avoid the statute. Several of the Mortmain statutes have been declared unconstitutional in recent years.[80]

Other than the limitations discussed previously in Sections 2 and 3, which provide general protection for the surviving spouse and chil-

74. 1 Woerner, Administration (3d Ed., 1923) 303, 315. See, Lanfer, "Flexible Restraints on Testamentary Freedom—A Report on Decedents' Family Maintenance Legislation", 69 Harv.L. Rev. 277 (1955).

75. Statutes of the mortmain type have virtually disappeared in this country, although there are provisions in a number of states limiting the amount of property which can be held by certain charitable or religious organizations. See Chapter XI, § 1. See "Restrictions on Charitable Gifts" 5 Real Prop.Prob. & T.L.Jour. 290 (1970).

76. Idaho Code § 15–2–615 (120 days).

77. Former Iowa Code Ann. § 633.266 was of this type; it was repealed by Acts 1980, c. 1064, effective Jan. 1, 1981.

78. Ga.Code § 113–107 combines time and amount; it prohibits gifts to charity of more than one-third of the estate to the exclusion of a wife or child, although the limitation does not apply to the excess over $200,000; in all cases the will must be executed at least 90 days before death. Under Ohio Rev.Code § 2107.06 gifts to charity may not exceed 25% of the net probate estate if the will is executed within six months of death.

79. E.g., under the New York statute only issue or a parent may contest a charitable provision and then only if he would benefit by a successful contest as a beneficiary or distributee. McKinney's N.Y., EPTL, § 5–3.3 (1980 Supp.).

80. The Pennsylvania statute which invalidated a testamentary gift if the testator did not survive execution of his will by 30 days was declared unconstitutional as a denial of equal protection in Estate of Cavill, 329 A.2d 503 (1974), cert. den. 421 U.S. 971 (1975), noted 80 Dick.L.Rev. 152 (1975), 37 U. of Pitt.L.Rev. 169 (1975). The Montana Supreme Court held that the general provision in the Uniform Probate Code, that one purpose of the Code is to "make effective the intent of a decedent in distribution of his property" conflicted with the Mortmain Statute; accordingly upon adoption of the Code in Montana there was an implied repeal of the Mortmain Statute. Matter of Estate of Holmes, ___ Mont. ___, 599 P.2d 344 (1979). Subsequently the same Court held that the Mortmain Statute as applied to the will of a testator who died before the effective date of the Code was unconstitutional. Matter of Estate of Kinyon, ___ Mont. ___, 615 P.2d 174 (1980).

The District of Columbia statute has been held unconstitutional. Estate of French, 365 A.2d 621 (D.C.App.1976); appeal to the United States Supreme Court was denied on jurisdictional grounds in Key v. Doyle, 434 U.S. 59, 98 S.Ct. 280, 54 L.Ed.2d 238 (1977). The constitutional issues are analyzed in Note, 52 Notre Dame L.Rev. 638 (1977).

dren of the testator, there are few legal limitations upon testamentary gifts to a mistress or illegitimate children which are intended to protect the spouse and legitimates. In South Carolina,[81] if the testator has a surviving spouse or legitimate children, he can dispose of no more than one-fourth of his estate to his mistress and illegitimates. In Louisiana[82] a testator can will no more than one-tenth of his estate to a woman with whom he has lived in open concubinage. If the parents leave legitimate children, an illegitimate can receive by will only so much as is necessary for his maintenance. But if the mother leaves no legitimate children, an illegitimate can take her entire estate by will, although the amount that an illegitimate can take by the will of the father is limited if the father leaves legitimate ascendants, brothers or sisters or their descendants or other collateral relations surviving.

81. S.C.Code 1962, § 57–310.

82. La.Stat.Ann.—Civ.Code (1981 Supp.) arts. 1481, 1484, 1485. The gift to a concubine under art. 1481 may be of movables only and cannot exceed one-tenth of the estate. If a father has no legitimate children but does have legitimate ascendants or brothers or sisters or their descendents, he can dispose of one-fourth of his property to illegitimate children. If only more remote collateral relations survive, the father can dispose of one-third of his estate to illegitimates.

Chapter V

EXECUTION OF WILLS

Scope Note

Formalities are required for executing wills in all states. This chapter deals with the judicial interpretation of statutes prescribing testamentary formalities and problems that arise from the application of particular statutory provisions. Several statutes prescribing formalities for executing wills are set out as examples in Section 1. In Section 2 the basis and purpose of formal requirements are considered briefly. A specimen will and a suggested procedure for executing an attested will appear in Section 3. Sections 4 through 7 deal with specific formal requirements.

The student will find it helpful to reread Chapter I, Section 2 "Terminology" before examining the materials in this Chapter.

SECTION 1. STATUTES

STATUTE OF FRAUDS

29 Chas. II, c. 3, § V (1677)[1]

"And be it further enacted by the authority aforesaid, That * * * all devises and bequests of any lands or tenements, devisable either by force of the statute of wills, or by this statute, or by force of the custom of Kent, or the custom of any borough, or any other particular custom, shall be in writing, and signed by the party so devising the same, or by some other person in his presence and by his express directions, and shall be attested and subscribed in the presence of the said devisor by three or four credible witnesses, or else they shall be utterly void and of none effect. * * * "

1. Omitted are the provisions of the Statute concerning nuncupative wills (§ XIX) and soldiers' and sailors' wills (§ XXIII). For the background of the Statute of Frauds see Chapter I, Section 3(2). Early drafts of Section 5 of the Statute referred to three "or more" witnesses rather than three "or four" witnesses. The change in language may have been inadvertent. Hening, "The Original Drafts of the Statute of Frauds (29 Car. II c. 3) and Their Authors", 61 U.Pa.L.R. 283 (1913).

WILLS ACT

7 Wm. IV & 1 Vict., c. 26, § IX (1837)[2]

"And be it further enacted, That no will shall be valid unless it shall be in Writing and Executed in manner hereinafter mentioned; (that is to say,) it shall be signed at the Foot or End thereof by the Testator, or by some other Person in his Presence and by his Direction; and such signature shall be made or acknowledged by the Testator in the Presence of Two or more Witnesses present at the same Time, and such Witnesses shall attest and shall subscribe the Will in the Presence of the Testator, but no Form of Attestation shall be necessary. * * *"

TEXAS PROBATE CODE

§ 59. Requisites of a Will

Every last will and testament, except where otherwise provided by law, shall be in writing and signed by the testator in person or by another person for him by his direction and in his presence, and shall, if not wholly in the handwriting of the testator, be attested by two (2) or more credible witnesses above the age of fourteen (14) years who shall subscribe their names thereto in their own handwriting in the presence of the testator. Such a will or testament may, at the time of its execution or at any subsequent date during the lifetime of the testator and the witnesses, be made self-proved, and the testimony of the witnesses in the probate thereof may be made unnecessary, by the affidavits of the testator and the attesting witnesses, made before an officer authorized to take acknowledgments to deeds of conveyance and to administer oaths under the laws of this State. Provided that nothing shall require an affidavit, acknowledgment or certificate of any testator or testatrix as a prerequisite to self-proof of a will or testament other than the certificate set out below. The affidavits shall be evidenced by a certificate, with official seal affixed, of such officer attached or annexed to such will or testament in form and contents substantially as follows:

THE STATE OF TEXAS
COUNTY OF ________

Before me, the undersigned authority, on this day personally appeared ______, ______, and ______, known to me to be the testa-

2. Omitted are Section XI pertaining to soldier's and sailor's wills and Section XIII stating that publication of the will is not required. Revision of the Wills Act, 1837, is now under consideration by the Parliament. Among other recommendations as to the execution of wills, the Law Reform Committee has suggested elimination of the "signed at the end" requirement and has also suggested that a witness signing out of the presence of the testator be permitted to acknowledge his signature to the testator. Cmd. 7902 (1980).

tor and the witnesses, respectively, whose names are subscribed to the annexed or foregoing instrument in their respective capacities, and, all of said persons being by me duly sworn, the said ______, testator, declared to me and to the said witnesses in my presence that said instrument is his last will and testament, and that he had willingly made and executed it as his free act and deed for the purposes therein expressed; and the said witnesses, each on his oath stated to me, in the presence and hearing of the said testator, that the said testator had declared to them that said instrument is his last will and testament, and that he executed same as such and wanted each of them to sign it as a witness; and upon their oaths each witness stated further that they did sign the same as witnesses in the presence of the said testator and at his request; that he was at that time eighteen years of age or over (or being under such age, was or had been lawfully married, or was then a member of the armed forces of the United States or of an auxiliary thereof or of the Maritime Service) and was of sound mind; and that each of said witnesses was then at least fourteen years of age.

____
Testator

____
Witness

____
Witness

Subscribed and acknowledged before me by the said ______, testator, and subscribed and sworn to before me by the said ______ and ______, witnesses, this ______ day of ______ A.D. ______.

(SEAL)

(Signed) ______________
(Official Capacity of Officer)

A self-proved will may be admitted to probate without the testimony of any subscribing witness, but otherwise it shall be treated no differently than a will not self-proved. In particular and without limiting the generality of the foregoing, a self-proved will may be contested, or revoked or amended by a codicil in exactly the same fashion as a will not self-proved.

own handwriting

§ 60. Exception Pertaining to Holographic Wills

Where the will is written wholly in the handwriting of the testator, the attestation of the subscribing witnesses may be dispensed with. Such a will may be made self-proved at any time during the testator's lifetime by the attachment or annexation thereto of an affidavit by the testator to the effect that the instrument is his last will; that he was at least eighteen years of age when he executed it (or, if under such age, was or had been lawfully married, or was then a member of the armed forces of the United States or of an auxiliary thereof or of the Maritime Service); that he was of sound mind; and that he has not revoked such instrument.

§ 64. Capacity to Make a Nuncupative Will

Any person who is competent to make a last will and testament may dispose of his personal property by a nuncupative will made under the conditions and limitations prescribed in this Code.

§ 65. Requisites of a Nuncupative Will

No nuncupative will shall be established unless it be made in the time of the last sickness of the deceased, at his home or where he has resided for ten days or more next preceding the date of such will, except when the deceased is taken sick away from home and dies before he returns to such home; nor when the value exceeds Thirty Dollars, unless it be proved by three credible witnesses that the testator called on a person to take notice or bear testimony that such is his will, or words of like import.

UNIFORM PROBATE CODE (1977)

"**Section 2–502. [Execution.]** Except as provided for holographic wills, writings within Section 2–513,[3] and wills within Section 2–506, every will shall be in writing signed by the testator or in the testator's name by some other person in the testator's presence and by his direction, and shall be signed by at least 2 persons each of whom witnessed either the signing or the testator's acknowledgment of the signature or of the will.

3. The Uniform Probate Code, as does the Texas Probate Code, includes provisions for self-proved wills. The Uniform Probate Code provisions are presented and considered in Section 6(9) of this Chapter and their effect mentioned briefly in fn. 34 at page 206. Section 2–513 substantially relaxes the requirements of testamentary formalities for the disposition of some items of tangible personal property. The section is designed to cover the case of the testator or testatrix who wishes to dispose of tangible chattels of family interest, mementos and the like by informal lists prepared after the will is executed and which will not meet the requirements for incorporation by reference. The section is as follows:

> "Whether or not the provisions relating to holographic wills apply, a will may refer to a written statement or list to dispose of items of tangible personal property not otherwise specifically disposed of by the will, other than money, evidences of indebtedness, documents of title, and securities, and property used in trade or business. To be admissible under this section as evidence of the intended disposition, the writing must either be in the handwriting of the testator or be signed by him and must describe the items and the devisees with reasonable certainty. The writing may be referred to as one to be in existence at the time of the testator's death; it may be prepared before or after the execution of the will; it may be altered by the testator after its preparation; and it may be a writing which has no significance apart from its effect upon the dispositions made by the will."

The Code also applies the doctrine of incorporation by reference in Section 2–510 and the non-testamentary act doctrine in Section 2–512. These doctrines are considered in Chapter XII, Section 3(1) and (2).

"Section 2–503. [Holographic Will.] A will which does not comply with Section 2–502 is valid as a holographic will, whether or not witnessed, if the signature and the material provisions are in the handwriting of the testator.

"Section 2–506. [Choice of Law as to Execution.]

A written will is valid if executed in compliance with Section 2–502 or 2–503 or if its execution complies with the law at the time of execution of the place where the will is executed, or of the law of the place where at the time of execution or at the time of death the testator is domiciled, has a place of abode or is a national."

SECTION 2. THE BASIS AND PURPOSE OF FORMAL REQUIREMENTS

Each state has a statute prescribing formalities for the execution of wills.[4] Formalities prescribed by these statutes exceed in number and complexity those required for any other private dispositive transaction.

A will is void unless executed with *all* of the formalities required by the applicable statute. A will without a required formality is *void* and not merely *voidable*. For example, if the applicable statute requires a will to be signed by two witnesses, and the will is signed by only one witness, the will with a single witness cannot be probated after the testator's death. Such a deficiency could be corrected during the testator's lifetime so long as he had testamentary capacity. But the missing formality cannot be supplied after the testator's death in order to render the will effective.[5]

Why is a testator required to accomplish *each* of the *many* formalities stated in the applicable statute if his will is to be probated? Are some of the required formalities justified? For example, when many wills were death bed transactions, the requirements in many of the statutes that the testator sign the will or acknowledge his or her signature in the presence of two or more witnesses and that the witnesses sign the will in the presence of the testator might minimize

4. Except for the District of Columbia [D.C.Code (1973) §§ 18–103; 18–107] and for the execution of wills by tribal Indians, the federal government prescribes no formalities for the execution of wills, although wills acts have been prepared under federal contracts for adoption by legislatures of territories and in discharge of trust territory responsibilities of the United States. These tend to be based upon state wills acts, the California wills act having been a favored model. See Guam Probate Code § 50; Trust Territories Code, Tit. 13, Ch. 1. The Commonwealth of the Northern Mariana Islands has adopted the Trust Territories Code. The Secretary of the Interior prescribes formalities for the execution of wills by "tribal" Indians disposing of "trust" real and personal property. 43 C.F.R. § 4.26(1978) As to Indian probate matters, including formalities under various tribal codes, see Francisco, Indian Probate Law (1979) (dissertation on file University of Virginia Law Library).

5. An instrument which lacks testamentary formalities may be incorporated by reference into a valid will or codicil. See Chapter XII, Section 3(1).

the opportunity for fraud upon a weakened testator.[6] But are such formalities justified when most wills probably are executed when the testator is in good health and possibly can defend himself against fraud? Perhaps the formalities should be keyed to the most sensitive cases, and death bed wills still are made. These questions have stimulated much comment, the perspectives of the commentators having influenced their definitions of the reasons for and effects of requiring particular formalities as well as their judgments concerning the wisdom of their rigid imposition.

Courts charged with the interpretation and application of these statutes often refer to a "policy of the Wills Act". By "Wills Act", courts usually mean the applicable state statute requiring formalities for the execution of a will although a broader reference is sometimes intended. By "policy", courts usually refer to a legislative intent to "package" the will by wrapping it in a "winding sheet" of testamentary formalities. The testator supposedly is protected to some degree from fraud and undue influence; the search for his intention is restricted to the face of the will unless an ambiguity is found; and various dubious transactions lacking the required formalities can be declared nugatory without prolonged inquiry. In addition to their references to a general "Wills Act policy", the courts sometimes discuss the purposes and effects of particular formalities. Such discussions usually are encountered when a court attempts to determine the meaning of ambiguous formal requirements or attempts to construe a Wills Act liberally in order to probate a particular will.

The search for a general legislative policy in a Wills Act and for legislative intent concerning each formality has proved a difficult undertaking. The Wills Act usually does not state any purpose to be served if the law is obeyed. Also, because legislatures assume laws will be obeyed if enacted, typically omitted is any detailed expression of intent concerning what will be done if the statute is wholly or partially ignored. Often absent are committee reports or reports of debates shedding light on the objectives to be achieved by the requirement of testamentary formalities, although such materials can sometimes be found when formalities of execution were prescribed as part of a general legislative revision of laws pertaining to wills. In many cases legislatures adopted the Wills Act of another state if that "pattern" act seemed to be administered without difficulty. The pattern Wills Act may have been based in turn upon the English Wills Act, 1837[7], upon the earlier English Statute of Frauds, 1677,[8] or upon a combination of the formalities prescribed in these English laws. The courts of the "adopting" state may attribute to their legislature the policy of the legislature of the state from which the "pattern" Wills Act was adopted or the policy of the English Parliament. The process is similar to that found in the interpretation of uniform laws. Explanations of a uniform law, such as the Uniform Probate Code, by its draftsmen, by the Commissioners on Uniform State Laws, and

6. See Section 6(4) this Chapter.

7. 7 Wm. IV & 1 Vict., c. 26 (1837).

8. 29 Chas. II, c. 3 (1677).

constructions of the language by courts in other states, typically carry great weight when a court construes the statute.

There are distinctions in formal requirements made in some of the Wills Acts that are difficult to justify and probably are attributable to local demands. Why, for example, does a legislature insist upon so many formalities for a will that is typed or written in the handwriting of one other than the testator (ordinary attested wills) and allow a will to be probated with few formalities if the will is written in the handwriting of the testator (holographic wills)?[9] The rationale of the distinctive treatment is usually described as the relative immunity of the holographic will to forgery and fraudulent alteration. But the most that can be said for the special treatment accorded the holographic will is that it discourages the inept forger.[10] Or suppose the legislature has given statutory recognition to the host of will substitutes, usually of a contractual nature, such as the "pay on death" (POD) bank accounts. These have been popular devices to avoid probate and estate administration. The statute may state that these transactions are valid without testamentary formalities.[11] Is the chance of fraud less when a bank teller receives and scans the instrument of deposit and later identifies thc payee at death than when only one of the required two witnesses attests a will disposing of the same amount of money? Usually these distinctions will be found based upon some special demands that have been recognized by the legislature. The holographic will in Virginia, for example, introduced in its 1748 Wills Act, was in response to the demand of settlers in the

9. Holographic wills are recognized in twenty-two states as a distinct will type valid without attesting witnesses and several states permit holographic wills in special situations. See Section 1, this Chapter, fn. 59 this Chapter at page 211, and Section 7 of this Chapter, holographic wills being discussed in detail in the latter Section. Holographic wills are recognized in Uniform Probate Code § 2–503. Holographic wills without attesting witnesses could be made in England of personal property and non-freeholds before the Wills Act, 1837 but attesting witnesses were required in that statute for all wills except the special wills of soldiers in actual military service and sailors at sea (these sometimes being offered for probate in holographic form). The English Law Reform Committee recently recommended that the soldiers' and sailors' privilege be retained, citing as one of its reasons the request of the Ministry of Defense. Cmd. 7902(1980), Par. 2.21. For further detail on soldiers' and sailors' wills see Section 4, this Chapter.

10. An expert forger, who can obtain samples of a testator's handwriting, can produce a signature or an entire will with little chance of detection. The controversy surrounding the alleged handwriting of the late Howard Hughes indicates the nature of the problem. Varina Davis, the wife of Jefferson Davis, President of the Confederacy, who wrote many letters for him, could reproduce his handwriting with remarkable exactness—although no one ever asserted that she wrote a holographic will for him. Tom Bell, the notorious impersonator, con-man and forger of Colonial America, who escaped a death sentence in his native Charlestown, Massachusetts, to continue his astounding career well into the 1750's, finally settled as a school teacher in Hanover County Virginia, where he is reputed to have produced both deeds and holographic wills of high quality. Forged holographic wills before the Ecclesiastical Courts were a major problem before the Wills Act, 1837, required attesting witnesses and Dr. Lushington's statement in debate in 26 Hansard 858 (11 March 1835) suggests this difficulty. See Harris, "Genuine or Forged?" 32 Cal.St.Bar.J. 658 (1957). This author states at p. 660 that most bogus wills are holographic.

11. E.g., Uniform Probate Code § 6–106.

Shenandoah Valley who wished to devise land and were not within convenient reach of lawyers.

Commentators concerned with reform of the formality requirements rather than their administration have stressed the "functions" of formalities.[12] This is a combined "purpose-effect" analysis.

But a "functional" analysis of formalities also presents difficulties. Functions of formalities change through time and vary from locality to locality based upon local social and economic structures. Moreover, laws dealing with the devolution of the property at the death of an owner have never been more than marginally effective, depending to a great extent upon the volition of surviving family members to see that they are carried out. Dominating the administration of property devolutions under consideration is the inescapable circumstance that the principal party in the transaction (the testator) is dead and cannot testify in any contentious or non-contentious matter concerning his purported will. There is nothing anyone can do for or to him. The legislative area of will making is one in which the "cutting edge" or sanction of law is of diminished effectiveness. Thus, if one concentrates upon the functions of formalities for executing wills with the expectation that a specific formality will or should produce a demonstrable result, the conclusion of the investigator is likely to be that no formalities currently prescribed are very effective in achieving the goals commonly stated to justify their imposition. It is difficult to verify the impact of a prescribed formality in any event.

For example, formalities for executing wills in their "ritual" or "cautionary"[13] function may well instill in the testator a reflective state of mind. Thus, requiring the will to be in writing and signed by the testator may discourage some heedless dispositions. But the condition of a testator's state of mind cannot be verified after the testator's death.

Formalities may have a "protective" function. The use of witnesses, when these are required, should discourage fraud or undue influence by persons other than the witnesses when the will is executed. The small number of reported judicial decisions involving alleged undue influence or fraud when the will is executed may suggest that the requirement of witnesses does protect the testator during this brief and critical time (or may suggest that the witnesses are not performing a major intended function).[14] But most undue influence is

12. E.g., Gulliver and Tilson, "Classification of Gratuitous Transfers", 51 Yale L.J., 1, 5–15 (1941); Langbein, "Substantial Compliance with the Wills Act", 88 Harv.L.Rev. 489 (1975); Nelson and Starck, "Formalities and Formalism: A Critical Look at the Execution of Wills", 6 Pepperdine L.Rev. 331 (1979). For an excellent recent review of testamentary formalities without primary emphasis upon "functions" see Chaffin, "Execution, Revocation and Revalidation of Wills: A Critique of Existing Statutory Formalities", 11 Ga.L.Rev. 297 (1977). For comment on the Uniform Probate Code formalities see, Gaubatz, "Notes Toward a Truly Modern Wills Act", 31 U. Miami Law Rev. 497 (1977); "Kossow, Probate Law and the Uniform Code: One for the Money * * *", 61 Georgetown L.J. 1357 (1973).

13. See Langbein, fn. 12, 494–496.

14. For one of these rare cases see Pope v. Garrett, 147 Tex. 18, 211 S.W.2d 559 (1948), appearing as principal case in

likely to be exerted before the will is executed. And most fraud probably occurs before the will is executed (as fraudulent misrepresentations of facts to a testator) or after the will is executed (as fraudulent alterations to the will or a fraudulent suppression of the will). The requirement of witnesses may discourage fraudulent suppression of a will or stimulate efforts to find the document. But the requirement is likely to have this effect only if the testator is well known to the witnesses, one or more of them survive the testator, and one or more of the witnesses have sufficient interest in the testator's will to question its whereabouts. In a law office where many wills are executed the witnesses may not know the testator. The protective function in this situation probably is performed by the attorney supervising execution of the will. The attorney is likely to retain a copy of the document and might be alert to note the testator's death and question a failure to offer the will for probate. The executed copy of the will may be in the hands of the attorney or a corporate executor or the attorney may be named as executor or be attorney for the executor. In these situations the production of the will for probate typically presents no problem. The tardy disclosure of holographic wills in states recognizing these as valid although unsigned by attesting witnesses, a problem causing difficulty in the administration of estates and uncertainty in land titles, may be due to the fact that these wills typically are made without the assistance of an attorney who might follow up to see to production of the will and not because witnesses signing the holograph are unnecessary for its validity. Witnessing a will may have a substantial function in discouraging fraudulent suppressions in small communities in which the testator and witnesses are well known to each other. But the increasing urbanization of American society with the increasing anonymity of its members decreases the importance of attesting witnesses in preventing fraud at any time other than when the will is executed, a time not propitious for action by a wrongdoer in any event.

Formalities also have an "evidentiary" function. The writing requirement preserves the expression of the testator's intention. His or her signature links the testator to the expression. If witnesses are required to sign the will, the testimony of these witnesses, if this testimony is available at probate, usually is accorded much weight on the issues of formalities of execution, capacity of the testator, and lack of fraud and undue influence. When the testator is required to sign the will or acknowledge the will or the testator's signature in the presence of witnesses, these requirements provide an affirmation of the will by the testator to which the witnesses can testify.

There are "procedural" functions of formalities for execution, these also having been described as "channelling" functions.[15] A court can reject uncertain informal writings without having to consider elusive issues of fraud or undue influence which might otherwise

Chapter VII, Section 2 (forcible prevention of execution of will).

15. See Langbein, fn. 12, 493–94.

be framed in an effort to disallow the instrument. The expense of litigation and court time is reduced. In uncontested probates, a probate officer, even one without legal training, can readily see whether most of the formalities have been performed or not, these appearing upon the face of the instrument. If two witnesses are required and only one signature appears on the instrument, or if the testator has not signed the will, these matters provoke no argument and the will can be denied probate without further ado. If the formalities are present, most of these will be evident, and the will can be probated quickly. Uncontested probates typically are expeditious procedures.

But there are also "didactic" functions performed by a statutory requirement of formalities of execution of wills although these almost certainly were never consciously intended by the legislatures and occur because of reinforcement of conduct patterns from other statutes, patterns of law practice and professional discipline, and other factors. There is nothing peculiar to legislation concerning formalities for executing wills in this function, since a similar function is associated with all legislation. Yet this is a matter which should not be ignored when major reforms in statutes concerning the execution of wills are proposed. Several dimensions of this "didactic" function of formal requirements can be illustrated by the English experience.

As mentioned in the historical introduction to these materials, the first English statute describing formalities in great detail was the Statute of Frauds, 1677.[16] With a few exceptions, such as Louisiana,[17] this statute established the general pattern for all subsequent Anglo-American statutes prescribing testamentary formalities.

The Statute of Frauds was a judges' statute, intended to relieve the courts of difficult evidential problems as well as to remove cases concerning the validity of wills of freeholds from the hands of juries. The Statute of Frauds "spoke" to lawyers, for whom it proved a bonanza.[18] This was because lawyers were retained in the immense amount of litigation developed under the Statute of Frauds in proof of the transactions to which it related and especially concerning the doctrine of part performance developed in equity, to which the wills

16. There is virtually nothing in Parliamentary materials shedding light on Parliamentary intent respecting particular formalities prescribed by the Statute. Detailed discussions of its background and authorship may be found in Costigan, "The Date and Authorship of the Statute of Frauds", 26 Harv.L.Rev. 329 (1913); Hening, "The Original Drafts of the Statute of Frauds (29 Car. II c. 3) and Their Authors", 61 U.Pa.L.R. 283 (1913); Schouler, "The Authorship of the Statute of Frauds", 18 Am.L.Rev. 442 (1884).

17. La.—LSA—C.C. arts. 1578–1604 (1952). The Louisiana civil law provisions are unique and are not discussed in detail in these materials. See 2 Bowe-Parker: Page, Wills (3d Ed., Rev.1960) §§ 20.31–20.32. A will type similar to the provisions for attested wills found in other states was adopted in Louisiana in 1952 in addition to the will types permitted by the civil code. LSA–R.S. 9:2442–2444 (1980 Supp.); 28 Tul.L.Rev. 288 (1954).

18. Lord Nottingham, who was one of the principal draftsmen of the Statute of Frauds is said to have remarked that "every line was worth a subsidy" by which he meant approximately £50,000; and it was said at Westminster Hall that the Statute had not been *explained* at an expense of less than £100,000. See Costigan, "The Date and Authorship of the Statute of Frauds", 26 Harv.L.Rev. 329, 342, fn. 44 (1913). By any estimate it proved a remarkable source of practice for lawyers and portions of it still do.

formality provisions in Section V and the revocation provisions in Section VI were an exception. But the Statute had the unintended effect of shifting the drafting of wills of freeholds in land to lawyers. Able draftsmen were at work long before the Statute of Frauds was passed, but many wills other than those involved in settlements within major families were prepared by the testators or by other untrained draftsmen. Requiring formalities for execution of wills of freeholds brought prospective testators to lawyers who then prepared the will as well as supervised its execution. The wills these draftsmen produced tended to be more clearly expressed than those prepared by the testators and produced fewer questions as to their meaning after the will was probated. While drafting wills was regarded as a more profitable undertaking then than now, it is probable that legal fees derived from litigation both of formality and constructional issues were reduced so far as wills of freeholds were concerned, while at the same time the seeds for growth of a class of trained professional draftsmen had been planted. But the professional drafting the Statute of Frauds stimulated was, for the most part, still for landed and affluent Englishmen. There were ten ways in which non-freeholds and personal property could be willed in England before the Wills Act, 1837. Nuncupative (oral) wills had been encumbered with so many formalities by the Statute of Frauds that it was difficult to make an effective will of this type. But personal property of any value could be bequeathed by an unwitnessed and unsigned holograph. No formalities were required for a legacy of £30 or under and soldiers in actual military service or sailors at sea could dispose of personal property in any amount without formalities. When the same formalities required for land were extended to personal property in the Wills Act, 1837, Sir Edward Sugden thought the extension of these formalities to small estates "would introduce into the country a sort of pettifogging agent, something between a schoolmaster and an attorney's clerk, either to make wills or to pick flaws in them".[19] But although there was not then, and still is not, a licensing requirement in England for wills draftsmen, the effect of the Wills Act, 1837, was to place the drafting of the wills of "common men" into competent professional hands.

While one cannot state with assurance that the history of will making practices in England (or Germany or France) contain examples of special value for those concerned with the reform of testamentary formalities in the United States, it is evident that about 90% of all litigation concerning wills in states having the holographic will (which was abandoned in the Wills Act, 1837) stems from wills of this type. Wills drafted by attorneys, who also supervise their execution, seldom figure in court other than for probate. Expectations have been generated among property owners that if a lawyer handles the will the chances are good that the owner's intention will be carried out; and the requirement of formalities of execution may discourage

19. 39 Hansard 526 (4 Dec. 1837). Sir Edward sought unsuccessfully to suspend operation of the Wills Act, 1837, for three months to permit the Government to consider amendments that he thought necessary.

home-made wills and channel the drafting of these instruments into the hands of lawyers. Moreover, once the will is in the law office, especially one producing wills in great numbers, the requirement of testamentary formalities provides an event at which the document can be reviewed and the possibility of law office errors minimized. The sanction is the malpractice action if the formalities are not carefully observed and the will is denied probate and, possibly, Bar discipline for careless action.[20]

South Australia[21] and Israel, the former with a full English Wills Act heritage, have abandoned a policy of requiring strict compliance with formalities for making wills, conferring upon their courts a dispensing power to enable them to probate a will without the statutory formalities which is shown to be genuine. Although such a policy was rejected by the English Law Reform Committee on the ground the policy "could lead to litigation, expense and delay, often in cases where it could be least afforded, for it is the home-made wills which most often go wrong"[22] such a policy has been recommended by law reform agencies in British Columbia, Manitoba and Queensland and will have special appeal in the United States at a time when the attractiveness of European (particular French and German) legal models is great and the deregulatory trend pronounced. Professor Langbein describes this relaxation of the strict requirements as a doctrine of "substantial compliance" with Wills Act formalities and considers the application of the doctrine "would not * * * add to the existing stock of probate litigation, but would to some extent substitute one type of dispute for another",[23] perhaps decreasing litigation concerning formalities by bringing to bear upon wills a treatment similar to that applied to life insurance contracts, joint accounts and other contractual will substitutes. An alternative to "substantial compliance" might be reduction in the number of formalities, requiring only those formalities producing demonstrable results.[24] Litigation concerning formalities for execution, even in the states producing most of the wills cases (New York, California, Illinois, Florida and Texas) is now quite slight, in the years between 1969 and 1979 constituting a poor fifth among all subjects of wills litigation. Reforms in

20. See Lewis v. State Bar of California, 28 Cal.3d 683, 170 Cal.Rptr. 634, 61 P.2d 258 (1981), for a suspension for negligently conducting the administration of an estate "without any previous probate experience and without associating or consulting a sufficiently experienced attorney".

21. See In re Graham/1978/ 20 S.A.S. R. 198 for a case arising under this statute.

22. Cmd. 7902 (1980) Par. 2.5. The position the Parliament ultimately will take concerning a dispensing power is uncertain at the time of writing. The recommendation of the Law Reform Commission rejecting a dispensing power has received criticism. See "The Making and Revocation of Wills—I", 125 Sol. Jour. 263 (1981). The substantial compliance proposal is discussed in detail in Miller, The Machinery of Succession (1977) 152. See Manitoba Law Reform Commission, Report on "The Wills Act" and the Doctrine of Substantial Compliance, Report No. 43, 8 Sept. 1980. See also Langbein "Crumblng of the Wills Act: The Australians Point the Way", 65 A.B.A.J. 1192 (1979).

23. Langbein, fn. 12, 525.

24. See Nelson and Starck, "Formalities and Formalism: A Critical Look at the Execution of Wills", 6 Pepperdine L. Rev. 331 (1979) where this approach is advocated and an execution statute is proposed.

formalities which might produce litigation perhaps would produce no great amount and might be worth the experiment, the history of the law of wills being littered with abandoned testamentary formalities, a sure indication that these requirements can be jettisoned and new ones imposed without lasting public damage, although the effects of such changes upon related legal conduct patterns should always be considered.

While variations now exist among the various state statutes prescribing formalities for the execution of wills, it is easy for a lawyer supervising the execution of a will to have the will meet the formalities of any state. The validity of a will of personal property is determined by the law of the state of domicile of the testator *at the time of his death.* The validity of a will of land is determined by the law of the *situs* of the land. In our highly mobile and complex society, a testator may move his domicile to another state after his will is executed or he may acquire real property in another state. The cautious practitioner thus will have the will executed so that it meets any formal requirements, although if the lawyer fails to produce a will meeting the formalities of every state, he or she may be aided in some cases by a "choice of law" statute similar to Section 2–506 of the Uniform Probate Code displayed in Section 1 of this Chapter. Section 2–506 also provides for the unusual case where the testator executes his will while on business or visiting in another state ("the place where the will is executed") or the more frequent case of the foreign national who owns land in the enacting state but executes his will according to the law of his nationality.

As Americans increasingly reside in foreign countries and acquire real estate and other foreign investments, the law of wills for Americans takes on an international aspect. To meet the problem of formalities of execution arising in such situations, an "international will" has been prepared under the auspices of Unidroit (International Institution for Unification of Private Law. A conference meeting in Washington in 1973 produced a "Convention providing a Uniform Law on the Form of an International Will", which was signed by the United States and four other governments, forty-two governments having been represented by delegations and six others by observers. The United States has not ratified the Convention but five ratifications will put the Convention into effect.[25] Formalities in addition to those required by American states would have to be met to qualify a will as an international will to be accepted by the states which might become parties to the Convention. The Uniform Probate Code contains the International Wills Act in Sections 2–1001 through 2–1010. The Commissioners recommend the International Wills Act be enacted by all states whether these states have adopted the Uniform

25. See 12 Int. Legal Materials (1973) 1298–1311 for the Convention; Kearney, "The Washington Diplomatic Conference on Wills: Report of the U. S. Delegation", 9 Real Prop. Prob. & Tr.J. 202 (1974); Nadelmann, "The Formal Validity of Wills and the Washington Convention 1973 Providing the Form of an International Will", 22 Amer.J.Comp.L. 365 (1974); Thomas, "A Uniform Law on the Form of an International Will", 3 Dalhousie L.J. 295 (1976).

Probate Code or not, the Sections, added in the Official 1977 Text of the Uniform Probate Code, being framed as a "free standing act".[26]

Courts, with few exceptions, have not required formalities other than those stated explicitly in the Wills Acts, although a degree of variation occurs when the courts construe the statutes.[27] Nevertheless, as previously noted, the courts do have much latitude in determining the transactions to which the Wills Acts apply. The transaction may be in the form of a deed, contract, inter vivos gift or perhaps a living trust. The court then must deal with the problem whether the dispositive transaction is testamentary and requires testamentary formalities to be effective. Thus, in addition to interpreting the Wills Act, a court must "specialize" the "Wills Act policy" to the various dispositive transactions brought before it. This is a continuing theme in ensuing parts of this book.

The test for "testamentary character" is inexact. If the court desires to sustain the transaction as inter vivos, it can probably find an intent on the part of the transferor to create an interest in property in the transferee during the transferor's lifetime. Perhaps the increasing use of inter vivos transfers, such as the revocable living trust, is producing a trend towards more liberal judicial treatment of devices exhibiting some but not all the aspects of a will. "Will substitutes", such as the Totten Trust, considered in Chapter IX, Section 2, may be excluded from application of the local Wills Act policy by statute as in Uniform Probate Code, Section 6–201. But if not excluded by statute, such devices may nevertheless be excluded as a result of judicial recognition of the local interest in them as a convenient and inexpensive means of disposing of property at death. Gifts *causa mortis,* discussed in Chapter XII, Section 1(3), may be recognized without testamentary formalities because of ancient usage. The economic importance of life insurance may underlie its general treatment as non-testamentary despite certain testamentary features when the right to change the beneficiary is reserved.

The reader should bear in mind that even though a particular dispositive transaction is not required to conform to the Wills Act, the transaction still may be taxed under the federal estate or state estate or inheritance tax laws. These tax laws cover not only transactions which are testamentary in a "Wills Act sense" but also many transac-

26. See Uniform Probate Code (5th ed. 1977) 86.

27. For example, in Virginia, and in several other states recognizing holographic wills as valid without attesting witnesses, the testator's signature found not at the logical end of the holograph is presumed not intended as his final authentication of the will although the Wills Act in these states contains no specific "signed at the end" requirement. The Virginia requirement for holographs stems from the requirement that the will be signed "in such manner as to make it manifest that the name is intended as a signature. Virginia Code § 64.1–49 (1950). E. g. Hall v. Brigstocke, 190 Va. 459, 58 S.E.2d 529 (1950) (evidence from face of will rebutted presumption and indicated name was manifestly intended as a signature). Another formality that seems implied in some cases is a request by the testator to the witnesses that they attest the will. Such a request is usually required for nuncupative (oral wills) in states where these may be made. For the request to witnesses for written attested will see Section 6(6) this Chapter.

tions which are inter vivos yet which are taxed to prevent easy avoidance of the estate and inheritance tax laws.

SECTION 3. DRAFTING AND EXECUTING AN ORDINARY WILL (WITH A SPECIMEN WILL)

(1) PROFESSIONAL RESPONSIBILITY FOR COMPETENT DRAFTSMANSHIP

The lawyer who drafts a will not only has an ethical duty to the client to do so in a competent manner,[28] but also may be liable to disappointed devisees if the will is not drafted to carry out effectively the testator's desires, or if the will is not properly executed.[29] There may, of course, be situations in which a dying person wants a will prepared quickly and the lawyer does not have time to do a thorough preparation. The lawyer must be familiar with taxation as well as the rules and concepts covered in the present book, and must master the art of expressing accurately in the will (or other documents involved in transferring wealth) precisely what the client wants;[30] and part of this process is to foresee the kinds of problems the average testator has never thought about and to assist the testator in deciding what he would want if conditions change. These matters will be developed later in this book.

---

28. Code of Professional Responsibility, Canons 6, 9. If the lawyer is not competent to handle estate planning and will drafting, he should not undertake work in this field. DR 6–101. For a general discussion of the responsibility of the lawyer as draftsman, see Moltzen, The Lawyer and Will Drafting, Ch. 1 in California Will Drafting (1965).

29. Heyer v. Flaig, 74 Cal.Rptr. 225, 449 P.2d 161 (1969) (holding the drafting attorney liable to disappointed devisees where he was informed by client of impending marriage, but failed to draft will to prevent application of California statute revoking the will as to the subsequent spouse unless the will shows an intention not to provide for the spouse, as the client in this case intended; see Chapter IV, Section 2(6) and Chapter VI, Section 2(3) for the substantive rules relating to such a situation). Bar disciplinary action also is possible for negligence in estate cases. See Lewis v. State Bar of California, 28 Cal.3d 683, 170 Cal.Rptr. 634, 621 P.2d 258 (1981), in which a lawyer was suspended for negligence in the administration of an estate.

30. There are a great many excellent books and articles on will drafting. The student will find helpful Shaffer, The Planning and Drafting of Wills and Trusts (2d Ed., 1979); Weinberger, Practical Will Drafting (1975); Martin, "The Draftsman Views Wills for a Young Family", 54 N.C.L.Rev. 277 (1976); Schwartz, "Sins of Omission and Commission in the Drafting of Wills and Trusts", 13 U. Miami Inst. Estate Planning 11.1–.42(1979).

(2) SPECIMEN WILL

[SPECIMEN][31]

I, JAMES MADISON HUNTINGTON, usually known as JAMES M. HUNTINGTON, of Charlottesville, Virginia, hereby revoke my former wills and declare this to be my last will. [Introductory clause and clause of revocation combined.][32]

FIRST: All property which I shall own at my death and all property over which I shall then have any power of appointment, I give and appoint to my wife, MARY ADAMS HUNTINGTON, if she shall survive me. If my said wife shall predecease me, all property which I shall own at my death and all property over which I shall then have any power of appointment, I give and appoint per stirpes to such of my issue as shall survive me, subject to the provision, however, that the share of any minor beneficiary shall be transferred to my trustee in trust and my trustee in its uncontrolled discretion (1) may pay the income therefrom or any part thereof directly to such beneficiary or to a parent or any person standing in the place of a parent or the guardian of the person of such beneficiary and without responsibility on my trustee to see to the application of any such payment, or (2) may expend the whole or any part of the income or principal for the education and comfortable support of such beneficiary, or (3) may retain and invest and re-invest the whole or any part of the income or principal or accumulated income and from time to time pay or expend the whole or any part thereof in the manner hereinabove provided, until such beneficiary attains his or her majority, and thereupon pay the balance then remaining to such beneficiary absolutely.[33]

SECOND: I hereby expressly authorize my executor and my trustee, respectively and successively, to permit any beneficiaries of any and all trusts hereunder to enjoy the specie use or benefit of any household goods, chattels, or other tangible personal property (exclusive of choses in action, cash, stocks, bonds or other securities) which

31. Reprinted in part from Ritchie, "Drafting a Simple Will for a Moderate Sized Estate", 91 Trusts and Estates 724, 725 (1952). The will is not presented as a standard form. Each will must be tailored to the needs of the individual testator. The phrases in brackets are not parts of the will but describe the preceding clauses. The student should observe that Mr. Huntington may not wish to exercise a general power of appointment if it was created on or before 21 October 1942 since a non-exercise of such a power will avoid having the property subject to it included in Mr. Huntington's gross estate for Estate Tax purposes. As to this matter see Chapter XIV, Section 1(4).

32. The introductory clause is often called the "exordium" clause. The clause revoking prior wills occasionally appears near the end of the will.

33. The testator disposes of all of his estate in a single provision. When various specific and general gifts are made in a will, a "catch-all" clause called a "residuary" clause should be included. A residuary clause might read as follows: "All the rest of my estate and all property over which I shall have any power of appointment at my death, I give and appoint to John Doe absolutely."

either my executor or my trustee may receive in kind, and my executor and my trustee shall not be liable for any consumption, damage, injury to or loss of any tangible property so used. The beneficiaries of any trusts hereunder, or their executors or administrators, shall not be liable for any non-negligent consumption, damage, injury to or loss of any tangible personal property so used.

THIRD: I direct that the interests of the beneficiaries of any and all trusts hereunder shall not be subject or liable in any manner to or for their or any of their anticipations, assignments, sales, pledges, debts, contracts, engagements or liabilities, or subject or liable to attachment, execution or sequestrations under any legal, equitable or other process. [Spendthrift provision]

FOURTH: I appoint my wife, MARY ADAMS HUNTINGTON, guardian of the person of each minor child of mine. If she should fail to qualify or cease to act as such guardian, I appoint my brother, HENRY COE HUNTINGTON, guardian in her place.

FIFTH: I appoint RELIABLE TRUST COMPANY of Charlottesville, Virginia, or its successor, guardian of the property of each minor child of mine.

SIXTH: I appoint RELIABLE TRUST COMPANY of Charlottesville, Virginia, or its successor, executor of this, my will, and trustee of any and all trusts hereby created.

Without undertaking to distinguish between the duties and powers of my executor and my trustee, and by way of illustration and not of limitation of its powers, I hereby authorize my executor and my trustee as follows:

(1) To sell any property, real or personal, publicly or privately, for cash or on time, without an order of court, upon such terms and conditions as to it shall seem best, without liability on the part of the purchaser to see to the application of the purchase money.

(2) To retain any of the original investments or other property constituting my estate at the time of my death, regardless of the character of said investments or other property or whether they be such as are authorized by law for investment by fiduciaries, for such time as to it shall seem best and to dispose of any such property by sale or exchange or otherwise as and when it shall deem advisable; and to invest and reinvest funds in such stocks, bonds, notes, mortgages or other property as it shall deem advisable even though they are not of the character expressly approved by law for investment by fiduciaries.

(3) To charge the premiums of securities purchased at a premium either against principal or income or partly against income as it shall deem advisable; and to apply stock dividends and other extraordinary dividends to income or principal or to apportion such dividends between income and principal in its absolute discretion, and its decision with respect thereto shall be conclusive and binding upon all parties in interest.

(4) To vote at corporate meetings in person or by proxy with or without power of substitution.

(5) To hold any or all securities or other property in the name of a duly appointed nominee, with or without disclosing the fiduciary relation.

(6) To make distribution of principal in cash or in kind or partly in cash and partly in kind, not necessarily ratably but on the basis of equal value according to its own judgment.

SEVENTH: I request that no executor, trustee, or guardian hereunder, be required to give any bond, and that if, notwithstanding this request, any bond is required by any law, statute or rule of court, no sureties be required thereon.

This will was signed by me on the 14th day of June, 1982, at Charlottesville, Virginia. [Testimonium clause]

____

JAMES MADISON HUNTINGTON

The foregoing instrument consisting of (four) typewritten pages was signed, published and declared by the testator to be his last will in the presence of us, who, at his request, in his presence, and in the presence of each other have hereunto subscribed our names as witnesses. [Attestation clause]

____________________ of ____________________

____________________ of ____________________

____________________ of ____________________

COMMONWEALTH OF VIRGINIA

CITY OF CHARLOTTESVILLE

Before me, the undersigned authority, this day personally appeared James Madison Huntington, _____, _____, and _____, known to me to be the testator and witnesses, respectively, whose names are signed to the foregoing instrument and, all of these persons being by me first duly sworn, James Madison Huntington, the testator, declared to me and to the witnesses in my presence that the instrument is his last will and that he had willingly signed the same and executed it in the presence of the witnesses as his free and voluntary act for the purposes therein expressed; that the witnesses stated before me that the foregoing will was executed and acknowledged by the testator as his last will in the presence of said witnesses who, in his presence and at his request, and in the presence of each other, did subscribe their names thereto as attesting witnesses on the day of the date of the will, and that the testator was over the age of eighteen years, of sound mind and under no constraint or undue influence.

JAMES MADISON HUNTINGTON
Testator

Witness

Witness

Witness

Subscribed, sworn and acknowledged before me by James Madison Huntington, the testator, and by ______, ______ and ______, witnesses, this 14th day of June, 1982.

(SEAL)

BELLE BOYD
Notary Public

My Commission Expires 7/29/87.

[Self-proved affidavit] [34]

34. This self-proved affidavit is based upon Virginia Code § 64.1–87.1 which, in turn, is patterned generally upon Uniform Probate Code § 2–504(b). While witnesses must sign the attested will, neither the attestation clause added to the specimen will [see this Chapter, Section 6(3)(C)] nor the self-proved affidavit are required for validity. The attestation clause, when signed by witnesses, creates a rebuttable presumption that the formalities of execution recited in the clause in fact have been accomplished. The effect of the self-proved affidavit varies among the states. For example, the Texas self-proved affidavit exhibited in Section 1 of this Chapter dispenses with the testimony of witnesses at probate but otherwise is treated no differently than a will not self-proved. At a minimum where self-proved affidavits are used the proponent of the will (the person offering it for probate) is relieved from the burden of accounting for the whereabouts of the attesting witnesses. Much time may elapse between the time the will is executed and the time the testator dies. The attesting witnesses may then be dead, incompetent or may have changed their residences and be difficult to locate. Although the will can be probated despite the fact that the witnesses are dead, incompetent or cannot be found, the probate officer may wish to be assured that there were indeed persons whose names appear as witnesses to the will and that the names are not fictitious. The self-proved affidavit should assure him on this point and thus save the proponent much time and trouble which might be involved in accounting for the witnesses. Without the self-proved affidavit, a probate officer might want at least one of the attesting witnesses to testify if a witness can be found. When the self-proved affidavit is used, further testimony by a witness concerning a point already sworn to would be redundant and can be dispensed with. In different courts having probate jurisdiction within a particular state there can be found differences in local practice in the use of attesting witnesses at probate. These differences can be avoided when the self-proved affidavit is used.

The self-proved affidavits of the Uniform Probate Code contained in § 2–504(a) and (b) which are exhibited and discussed with a display case in Section 6(9) of this Chapter, have effects in addition to those mentioned in this footnote. When the Uniform Probate Code affidavits are properly executed and appended to the will, in formal testacy proceedings under Uniform Probate Code § 3–406 when the will is contested, compliance with the signature requirements of the Code are *conclusively* presumed and other requirements for execution are presumed subject to rebuttal without the testimony of any witness "upon filing the will and the acknowledgments and affidavits annexed or attached thereto, unless there is proof of fraud or forgery affecting the acknowledgment or affidavit." Uniform Probate Code § 3–406(b). Foreclosed apparently are *all* questions related to the signature such as "whether the witness signed in the presence of the tes-

(3) SUGGESTED PROCEDURE FOR EXECUTING AN ATTESTED WILL

A well-conducted execution is facilitated by a well-prepared document. So that last minute-changes will be unnecessary, the attorney should consider carefully the wishes of the testator and the facts of his case. Conferences with the testator prior to execution of the will should be conducted in private so that there will be no imputation of undue influence.[35]

The will should be drafted on one page if convenient although this is difficult to do if the estate is of such a size or is so complex that its provisions must be drafted to minimize estate, inheritance and income taxes. If several pages are used, the pages should be securely fastened together at the top, each page should be numbered and the number of pages should be recited in the attestation clause.[36]

The will should be typed.[37] There should be no erasures, overstrikes, typographical errors or interlineations. If it is necessary to make a correction without retyping a page, the testator and the witnesses should be required to sign or initial beside each correction before the will is executed.

An attestation clause should be in every will.[38] The clause should recite the formalities required in any state in which it might be necessary to probate the will. Although the attorney must use caution to

tator". Uniform Probate Code § 3–406, *comment.* In a formal testacy proceeding where the petition for probate is unopposed, "[i]f evidence concerning the execution of the will is necessary, the affidavit or testimony of one of the attesting witnesses to the instrument is sufficient", although if this affidavit or testimony is not available, the execution of the will may be proved by other evidence or affidavit. In the *ex parte* or informal probate under Uniform Probate Code § 3–303(c) the testimony of attesting witnesses is not required and thus the significance of the procedural advantage of for a self-proved will is limited to formal testacy proceedings. Uniform Probate Code § 2–504, *comment.*

Whether *both* the attestation clause and the self-proved affidavit should be appended to wills in Uniform Probate Code jurisdictions and non-Uniform Probate Code jurisdictions is discussed in Section 6(9) of this Chapter.

35. It is particularly important that prospective beneficiaries not participate in the preparation of the will. See Chapter VII, Section 2(3); See Allen, "The Will Contest: An Acid Test of Will Drafting" 6 St. Louis L.J. 1 (1960).

36. See Section 5(3).

37. There are certain advantages to be obtained if the will is in the handwriting of the testator. In some states attestation will be unnecessary. Fraudulent alterations of the will are made difficult. But compliance with attestation provisions is fairly simple and it is more convenient for the testator, and usually for those who have to read the will, to have a competent stenographer do the work. In those states in which attestation is unnecessary if the will is holographic, the peril is that a layman is induced to prepare his own will without legal advice. Although the will may then be probated, quite frequently holographic wills present problems in construction, the bulk of litigation in states having holographic wills centering around wills of this type. The assumption in this footnote is that a lawyer will prepare the provisions for the testator and then have him copy them.

38. Whether an attestation clause should be used when the will is executed with a self-proved affidavit is discussed in Section 6(9) of this Chapter.

see that the formalities are performed, the attestation clause raises a presumption of performance of the formalities recited and will thus aid the proponent of the will at probate.[39]

A duplicate copy of the will should be prepared but not executed (signed). The duplicate copy may be useful in proving the contents of the will if the executed copy is lost;[40] a photographic reproduction of the will after it is completely executed is even better for this purpose.

At least three witnesses should be selected before the time set for execution. Three witnesses should be selected because some jurisdictions require that number. If the witnesses have no prior acquaintance with the testator, they should be assembled in advance of the time set for execution so that they can meet the testator and form an opinion concerning his capacity to execute the will. The witnesses should be permanent residents of the locality in which the testator resides so that they may be produced conveniently or accounted for at probate. Unmarried women may change their names by marriage and be difficult to locate. Household servants may be difficult to locate and their handwriting may be difficult to identify. The integrity of the individual should, of course, be a material factor in determining his choice as a witness; but persons who have a pecuniary interest in the establishment of the will should not be used as witnesses because they may be incompetent attesters or may lose their interests by operation of a statute so that they will be competent attesters.[41]

The will should be executed without the presence of the beneficiaries since their presence might give rise to a charge of undue influence. The exclusion of the beneficiaries is of particular importance if future contest of the will is anticipated.

When execution of the will is commenced it should not be interrupted. The testator, witnesses and attorney should be able to observe the acts and hear the words of each other. The attorney should show the will to the testator, ask him if it is his and ask him if he desires to sign it. The testator should be required to answer in a voice audible to the witnesses. The attorney should call the attention of the witnesses to the testator's answer and should then suggest that the testator sign the will. The place for the testator's signature should be indicated to him. As the testator signs, the attention of the witnesses should be directed to his action. The attorney should then ask the testator to declare to the witnesses that the instrument signed by him is his last will and testament. The testator should then request the witnesses by name to attest and subscribe his will.

39. See Section 6(3).

40. The execution of duplicate copies of a will may give rise to difficulty if an executed copy in the possession of the testator cannot be found at his death. See Chapter VI, Section 3(2). It is suggested that the duplicate copy not be executed but rather be kept as a memorandum of the contents of the executed original. The names of the witnesses should be noted on the duplicate copy.

41. See Section 6(2). Under Uniform Probate Code, § 2–505 the interest of a necessary witness does not invalidate the will. There is no Uniform Code provision which "voids" the interest of a necessary witness.

Before the witnesses sign, the attorney should read the attestation clause to them and be sure that they know what it means. The witnesses then sign their names and permanent addresses immediately beneath the attestation clause in spaces provided for that purpose. As the witnesses sign, the signature of the testator should be visible to them.

When the formalities of execution have been completed, the testator should be advised as to the best method of safekeeping of the original copy of the will; see Section 6(11) hereafter.

SECTION 4. ORAL WILLS

Many states provide for probate of oral wills of personal property.[42] The Uniform Probate Code makes no provision for oral wills and § 2–506 of the Code, which declares a will valid if it meets the formalities of its place of execution or the testator's place of abode or nationality, is limited to *written* wills.

There are two types of oral wills, both of which may be found in a particular jurisdiction. There is a nuncupative will which is based upon the nuncupative will authorized by Section XIX of the Statute of Frauds, 1677.[43] There is also a soldiers' and sailors' will which is based upon ancient military and maritime custom.[44] Both types are obsolescent.[45]

42. See, Rees, "American Wills Statutes", 46 Va.L.Rev. 613, 636–37 (1960). A nuncupative will can pass real property in Georgia. Ga.Code Ann. § 113–504 (1959).

43. 29 Chas. II, c. 3, § XIX (1677); Rees, "American Wills Statutes", 46 Va. L.Rev. 613, 636–37 (1960). In almost every instance, American states have added to the requirements of the Statute of Frauds for nuncupative wills. Oral wills of soldiers and sailors were the only exceptions from the writing requirement made by the Wills Act, 7 Wm. IV & 1 Vict., c. 26 (1837).

44. Rees, "American Wills Statutes", 46 Va.L.Rev. 613, 640 (1960). There is evidence of use of these wills in the Roman military establishment. Although there was scattered litigation concerning soldiers and sailors wills before the American Civil War, American policy concerning these wills crystallized in the cases which the war produced. See Alford, "The Influence of the American Civil War Upon the Growth of the Law of Decedents' Estates and Trusts", 4 Am. Jour.Legal Hist. 299, 315–318 (1960); Anderson v. Pryor, 18 Miss. 620 (1848) (Mexican War soldier's will); Hubbard v. Hubbard, 8 N.Y. 196 (1853) (Sailor's will); Ex parte Thompson, 4 Bradf.Surr. 154 (1856) (Sailor's will).

45. The courts have been hostile towards oral wills and there has been a gradual decrease in litigation concerning them during the past century. This may indicate that fewer oral wills are being offered for or admitted to probate. Occasionally a modern decision can be found in which a nuncupative will is probated. See Lee v. Green, 222 Ga. 141, 149 S.E.2d 86 (1966). The British Ministry of Defense has reported an informal soldier's will from Northern Ireland, the soldier having been fatally injured by terrorists and having given oral instructions as to the disposition of his property. The soldiers' and sailors' wills were recommended for retention in the Wills Act, 1837, largely as a result of the request of the Ministry of Defense, which pointed out that "even in peacetime there were occasional cases of servicemen making

The value of personal property which can be transmitted by a nuncupative will is ordinarily limited by statute.[46] The will must be made in the last sickness of the testator[47] and is sometimes required to be made in his dwelling house unless he is taken sick or injured and cannot return.[48] The testator must intend to make a nuncupative will. If he intends to make an attested will, his oral instructions to the draftsman cannot be probated.[49] The testator must request at least one of two competent witnesses to bear witness that his words are his will.[50] The witnesses must be present together at the time of the declaration. It is usually required that the will be probated within six months after the death of the testator unless reduced to writing within six days from the time of the declaration by the testator.[51]

Few formalities are required for a soldiers' and sailors' will.[52] A single witness is sufficient in many states.[53] A soldier is any person who serves the government in a military capacity. A sailor is any person employed on board ship. It is required that the soldier be "in actual military service" and that the sailor be "at sea" in order to make an effective will. These requirements have caused the courts difficulty.

It is generally agreed that for a soldier to be in actual military service there must be a state of war and he must be actively engaged in carrying it on.[54] Efforts to apply this standard to soldiers in the supply services, soldiers in replacement channels in the process of moving to a combat zone, and to military personnel on other duties

privileged wills in the course of certain military operations. Law Reform Committee, Twenty-Second Report, Cmd. 7902 (1980), Par. 2.21. For detailed discussions of oral wills see Atkinson, Wills (2d Ed., 1953) §§ 76, 77; 2 Bowe-Parker: Page, Wills (3d Ed., Rev.1960) §§ 20.-13–30; Rollison, Wills (1939) §§ 172–179, 182; Thompson, Wills (3d Ed., 1947) §§ 30, 32; Comment, "The Nuncupative Will", 18 Baylor L.Rev. 77 (1966). There has been a recent revival of interest in the soldiers' and sailors' wills to avoid age limitations on testamentary capacity. E.g., In re Knight's Estate, 11 N.J. 83, 93 A.2d 359 (1952); N.J.S.A. 3A:3–5.

46. Rees, "American Wills Statutes", 46 Va.L.Rev. 613, 640 (1960). In several states there is no maximum limitation. In most, as in West's Ann.Cal.Probate Code, § 55, the limitation is $1,000. In Indiana and Tennessee, the limitation is $10,000 when a person is in active military, air or naval service. Otherwise the limit is $1,000.

47. "Last sickness" is construed as meaning *in extremis* under such circumstances that the testator has neither the time nor the opportunity to reduce his will to writing. E.g., McClain v. Adams, 135 Tex. 627, 146 S.W.2d 373 (1941). See 8 A.L.R.3d 952 (1966).

48. Rees, "American Wills Statutes", 46 Va.L.Rev. 613, 643 (1960). Six states have this requirement. South Carolina requires the will be made where the testator dies and New Hampshire requires that it be made in his usual dwelling except when he was taken sick from his home and died before returning.

49. E.g., Knox v. Richards, 110 Ga. 5, 35 S.E. 295 (1900); In re Male's Will, 49 N.J.Eq. 266, 24 A. 370 (1892).

50. Rees, "American Wills Statutes", 46 Va.L.Rev. 613, 642 (1960). The request to attest (rogatio testium) need not be in a particular form but must make the witnesses sensible that the testator is making a will and that he wants them to attest it.

51. Rees, "American Wills Statutes", 46 Va.L.Rev. 613, 643–44 (1960).

52. E.g., Virginia Code Ann., § 64.-1–53: "* * * a soldier being in actual military service, or a mariner or seaman being at sea, may dispose of his personal estate as he might heretofore have done; * * *".

53. Gould v. Stafford, 39 Vt. 498 (1866).

54. E.g., Drummond v. Parrish, 3 Curt. 522, 163 Eng.Rep. 812 (1843).

not involving actual contact with the enemy have resulted in much conflict among the decisions.[55]

Although no state of war exists, a sailor is "at sea" if the vessel on which he is employed is in tidal water or is in non-tidal water for a temporary purpose.[56] Much difficulty has been caused by sailors' wills made on inland waters, by wills made by sailor passengers on tidal water, and by wills made by sailors absent from their vessels for some reason.[57]

It is unnecessary that the soldier die in actual military service or that the sailor die at sea in order for the will to be effective. The will is not revoked when the soldier or sailor takes up a new occupation but must be revoked by the means required for the revocation of other wills.[58]

SECTION 5. WRITING AND LANGUAGE

(1) CLASSIFICATION OF WILLS BASED ON WRITING

Wills must be in writing unless a statute authorizes a will of the types mentioned in the preceding section. In twenty-two states[59]

55. E.g., Leathers v. Greenacre, 53 Me. 561 (1866) (soldier in winter quarters in Virginia held in actual military service); Matter of Dumont, 170 Misc. 100, 9 N.Y.S.2d 606 (1938), aff'd 282 N.Y. 606, 25 N.E.2d 388 (1940) (soldier returned from war for demobilization not in actual military service); In re Kapp's Will, 191 Misc. 309, 77 N.Y.S.2d 922 (1947) (prisoner of war in actual military service); In re Sheridan's Estate, 21 N.J.Misc. 473, 34 A.2d 654 (1943), 30 Va.L.Rev. 481 (1944) (soldier inducted but not on active duty not in actual military service); In re Estate of Spark, [1941] Prob. 115, [1941] 2 All E.R. 782 (soldier killed in camp in air raid in actual military service); In re Estate of Gibson, [1941] Prob. 118, [1941] 2 All E.R. 91 (dental officer killed by enemy bomb while residing at home not in actual military service). See Grant and Palmer, "Soldiers' and Sailors' Wills in New York", 12 Albany L.Rev. 68, 13 Albany L.Rev. 10 (1949); Megarry, "Actual Military Service and Soldiers' Privileged Wills", 57 L.Q.R. 481 (1941); Potter, "Soldiers' Wills", 12 Mod.L.Rev. 183 (1949); Powell, "Actual Military Service", 61 Jurid.Rev. 172 (1949); Summers, "Wills of Soldiers and Seamen", 2 Minn. L.Rev. 261 (1918); Wahlen, "Soldiers' and Sailors' Wills—A Proposal for Federal Legislation", 15 U. of Chi.L.Rev. 702 (1948); Weiss, "The Formalities of Testamentary Execution by Service Personnel", 33 Iowa L.Rev. 48 (1947).

56. E.g., In re Gwin's Will, 1 Tuck. (N.Y.) 44 (1865). It is not required that a sailor's will be made in time of war.

57. E.g., In re Gwin's Will, 1 Tuck. (N.Y.) 44 (1865) (captain of gunboat on Yazoo River not at sea); Ex parte Thompson, 4 Bradf. (N.Y.) 154 (1856) (cook on ship tied up at wharf at sea); Warren v. Harding, 2 R.I. 133 (1852) (mariner traveling as passenger to take command of another vessel not a seaman); Matter of McDonald, 179 Misc. 284, 286, 37 N.Y.S.2d 945, 946 (1942) (sailor on unauthorized absence from vessel does not have testamentary privilege).

58. Estate of Beech, [1923] Prob. 46. The will became ineffective one year after discharge under the Roman law.

59. Holographic wills are valid without attesting witnesses in Alaska, Arkansas, Arizona, California, Idaho, Kentucky, Louisiana, Mississippi, Mon-

wills entirely in the handwriting of the testator are probated without attesting witnesses. A will entirely in the testator's handwriting is called a "holographic" will. In the remaining states all written wills, whether holographic or not, are required to be attested by witnesses. Wills of the latter type are described in these materials as "ordinary attested wills".

---

(2) CLARITY AND PERMANENCE OF THE RECORD

A will may be written in any way upon any substance if the record resulting is fairly permanent and legible.[60] Normally, of course, a will is typed upon a good quality of legal-size paper.[61] It is not required that the will be immune to forgery or fraudulent alteration, although a few simple precautions in preparing the instrument can make it reasonably safe from tampering.[62] If the contents of the will were explained to the testator, a will may be written in a language or form of shorthand which the testator could not read.[63]

---

tana, Nevada, North Carolina, North Dakota, Oklahoma, South Dakota, Tennessee, Texas, Utah, Virginia, West Virginia and Wyoming. Holographic wills are permitted in New York and Maryland for testators in military service. Pennsylvania requires attesting witnesses only when the will is signed by mark or by proxy. Holographic wills are permitted by Uniform Probate Code, § 2–503. A holographic will had no special significance in England. One of the major reasons for the preferred treatment given to holographs in some states is the relative immunity of the holograph to forgery and fraudulent alteration. Holographic wills raise unique problems in execution and are considered separately in Section 7.

60. For some wills prepared in bizarre ways see Atkinson, Wills (2d Ed., 1953) 295 et seq.; Harris, Ancient, Curious and Famous Wills (1912) 167 et seq. Freak wills are seldom attested and few are probated. Of course, a lawyer or testator, like a soldier, cannot always pick his time and place for action and must sometimes get by with the materials at hand. See New York Times, 13 Apr. 1965, p. 74, col. 5 for will scratched on fuselage of aircraft by Australian pilot who died of thirst when forced down in desert. Holographic will? Attesting witnesses?

61. The statutes of four states (Louisiana, Ohio, South Carolina and Wyoming) refer to typewriting as a permissible form; but typewriting would seem an ideal form everywhere except with respect to holographic wills which must be entirely in the testator's handwriting. Rees, "American Wills Statutes", 46 Va. L.Rev. 613, 615 (1960).

62. Unnecessary gaps and spaces in the will should be avoided. Some lawyers omit the right margin of the page and have the testator and witnesses initial or sign in the left margin in addition to signing the will. The pages should be numbered and firmly attached together. The number of pages should be recited in the attestation clause.

63. Probate should be denied when the testator did not know the contents of the will. E.g., Debaillon v. Fuselier, 159 La. 1043, 106 So. 559 (1925) (will in English—testator understood French only). There is a strong presumption that the testator knew the contents of his will and this presumption is especially strong when it is shown that the will was read by or to him. See Chapter VII, Section 2(5). If the will is drafted in code, the key to the code may not be admitted to decipher the will unless the key is incorporated into the will by reference. See

(3) JUDICIAL INTEGRATION OF ATTESTED WILLS [64]

ESTATE OF BEALE

14 page will

Supreme Court of Wisconsin, 1962.
15 Wis.2d 546, 113 N.W.2d 380.

The judgment admitted to probate the will of Howard Kennedy Beale dated June 22, 1959. The guardian ad litem of the youngest son, Thomas Beale, has appealed. pending the suit

Howard Beale, about sixty years of age, and a resident of Shorewood Hills, Dane County, Wisconsin, died on December 27, 1959, leaving an estate inventoried at approximately one and one-quarter million dollars. His survivors include:

(1) Georgia Robison Beale, his widow, executrix of Beale's estate and a respondent in this case.

(2) Howard Kennedy Beale, Jr., age 16, his son, and a respondent in this case.

(3) Henry Barton Beale, age 15, his son, and a respondent in this case; and

(4) Thomas Wight Beale, age 10, his son, and appellant in this case.

During his lifetime Beale executed two documents, each of which is presented as his last will. On November 16, 1954, Beale and his wife executed similar wills drafted by an attorney. A short codicil was executed to this document on July 26, 1958. Under these (hereinafter called the "1954" will) all of Beale's children were treated equally.

Chapter VII, Section 2(6); 37 A.L.R.3d 889 (1971).

64. A will must be prepared, established, construed and applied, in the light of existing facts. It is quite obvious that rational action depends upon the conscious or unconscious consideration by the actor of those parts of the environment which he can perceive. He must integrate certain parts of his environment into a plan of action by deciding (1) what things and events exist as "facts", (2) what facts are relevant to his goal or object and (3) to what extent the relevant facts enhance or diminish his chances to attain his goal. In this broad sense most of the materials in this book deal with integration. For example, the incorporation of extrinsic documents into a will by reference (Chapter XII, Section 3(1)); the effect upon the operation of a will of unwritten acts by the testator and others (Chapter XII, Section 3(2)); and the admission of evidence to resolve ambiguities (Chapter VII, Section 2) or to remedy fraud or mistake (Chapter VII, Sections 4, 5), are facets of an all-embracing process of integration. "Integration", as used in this section, refers merely to the process of determining what writings may be probated as physical parts of an attested will. As a rough standard for physical integration the pages are required to have been present when the will was attested. Related problems which arise where unattested holographic wills are valid are considered in Section 7.

A petition for probate of the 1954 will was filed on April 29, 1960, on behalf of Thomas Wight Beale, the appellant. No objections to this will have been filed.

Beale also left a document of 14 typewritten pages not fastened together. These, too, are presented as his last will. The final page, bearing the signatures of the testator and the witnesses is dated June 22, 1959. A petition for probate of this, hereinafter called the "1959" will, was filed April 29, 1960, on behalf of Howard Kennedy Beale, Jr. and Henry Barton Beale, respondents herein. By this one the practical effect is to disinherit Thomas unless the widow makes provision for him from her share.

Objections to the 1959 will were filed June 10, 1960, on behalf of Thomas Wight Beale.

The 1959 will was executed in the following manner:

Beale, a history professor at the University of Wisconsin, planning to take a trip to Russia, dictated the document on either June 16 or June 17, 1959, to his part-time secretary, Mrs. Jessica Burleigh. This dictation took place in the Rathskeller of the Wisconsin Union late in the evening.

Mrs. Burleigh typed the will, 14 pages in all, with three complete carbon copies, and gave them, original and copies, to Beale on June 20, 1959, in his Bascom Hall office. Beale then left for New York with his two eldest sons on his way to Moscow.

On June 21, 1959 Beale attended a party in New York given in his honor at the apartment of a friend who was a history professor at Columbia University. During the festivities he asked three of his friends, all professors at various eastern colleges, one being his host, to witness his will. The four people went into an adjoining room where Beale placed some papers in a "pile" on the table, declaring this was his will. Two of the witnesses testified that they saw Beale sign the last page of the will, while the third remembered only that Beale's signature was on the document when the witness signed. All three testified that they signed the document at the usual attestation clause in the presence of the testator, in the presence of each other and at the testator's request. None of the witnesses were able to identify at the trial any of the pages except the page they had signed. Beale then picked up all the papers and replaced them in his brief-case.

Although the will is dated June 22nd it is undisputed that it was executed June 21st. By letter dated June 21, 1959, Beale sent Mrs. Burleigh pages 12 and 13 of the will, asking her to make certain changes and corrections. The only change affecting the meaning was the substitution of "my friend, Alexander H. McLeod" for "wife, Georgia Robison Beale" as co-executor. The others were corrections of grammar and punctuation. Mrs. Burleigh made the corrections on the original and sent the pages to Beale in Moscow. The envelope inclosing the letter to her and the two will pages has not been found and there is no positive proof of when or where it was mailed. At different times Mrs. Burleigh testified it was mailed to her from New York and at another she testified that she received the two pages in an envelope from Beale in London.

A sealed envelope, postmarked September 7, 1959, from London, was later found among Beale's possessions at his death. The envelope was self-addressed to Beale and contained pages 12 and 13 of a copy of the 1959 will. These pages, along with all other pages of the 1959 will, contained the initials "H.K.B." in the left hand margin.

After returning from Russia, Beale asked Mrs. Burleigh to retype the entire two pages but she testified that she did not do this until after Beale's death and then did it at the later request of Beale's son, Henry. These pages also had the initials "H.K.B" on them.

After Beale's death all the will pages except page 1 were found in his office at the Wisconsin Library. The pages were in looseleaf form and located under other papers on his desk. Underneath these pages was a carbon copy of all the will pages, including a copy of the missing page 1. Then under these copy pages was the 1954 will and the 1958 codicil. The pages of the 1954 will and codicil were stapled together.

The missing first page of the 1959 will was located several months later in Beale's Bascom Hall office among some American History notes.

The trial judge admitted the 1959 will to probate as the will existed before any changes or corrections were typed. The appeal from the judgment was taken by Fred Risser, guardian ad litem for Thomas Wight Beale.

Additional facts will be given in the opinion.

* * *

BROWN, JUSTICE. * * * [omitted is that portion of the opinion dealing with the issue of unnatural character of the will.] * * *

While appellant concedes, or at least does not dispute, that when Professor Beale signed the purported 1959 will he had testamentary capacity and was not subject to undue influence appellant vigorously denies that the 14 pages of the 1959 instrument were legally published and declared to be his will and legally signed and witnessed as such and, in the alternative, that these pages did not constitute his will at the moment of execution.

In this record there are a few indisputable facts. From them there are a number of conflicting inferences reasonably to be drawn.

It cannot be questioned that on June 16 or 17, 1959, Professor Beale dictated a 14 page document in the form of a last will, revoking all prior wills; that his secretary typed the original will, with three carbon copies, and delivered all of them to him in looseleaf form the afternoon of June 20th; that Beale was in New York City at the home of a friend, a professor of Columbia University, on the evening of June 21st and on that evening he exhibited "a pile" of sheets of paper and declared to his three friends that this was his will and desired them to witness his will; that they saw him sign the sheet which was on top of the pile and that immediately thereafter, at his request, they signed as witnesses in his presence and in the presence of each other; that the place where they put their signatures was immediately below the usual testamentary clause declaring this to be Professor Beale's will; that none of the witnesses paid any detailed attention to the number of pages in the pile nor could they identify later any of the pages except the one where they had written their names; that when all four participants had signed, Beale put all papers in his briefcase and the meeting ended.

It is uncontradicted that on the next day, or shortly thereafter, Beale and his two sons left by plane for Moscow; that a few days after June 21st Mrs. Burleigh, Beale's secretary, received a letter from him on Columbia University note paper, bearing date June 21, 1959, mailed in New York or in London on a day not given; that the letter asked Mrs. Burleigh to make several changes in pages 12 and 13 of the will which she had previously typed, to carry out marginal penciled notes in Beale's handwriting on those pages; that enclosed with the letter were the original pages 12 and 13; that Mrs. Burleigh made the alterations as directed and mailed them back to him in Moscow; that these pages were later found in a sealed envelope addressed to Beale in Beale's handwriting and mailed from London, England to him at his Madison address.

There is nothing legally invalid in the execution of a will because the separate pages of the will have not been fastened together. It is a requirement, though, that all the pages be present at the time of execution.

Thompson on Wills (3rd Ed.), sec. 124, page 197, states:

> "* * * It is not necessary that they [the witnesses] see or examine all the pages of the will to see that all the sheets of paper were in place when the will was executed. * * *" Citing In Re Sleeper's Appeal, 129 Maine 194, 151 Atl. 150, 71 A.L.R. 518.

In Sleeper's Appeal, supra, the court stated:

> "* * * nor is it essential that the witnesses should see and examine all the pages of a will at the time of execution, if the court is satisfied, from other evidence or the circumstances surrounding the execution, that all the sheets of paper offered for probate were present at the time of execution. * * *"

2 Page on Wills (Bowe-Parker Revision), sec. 19.147, page 277, is to the same effect, citing Sleeper's Appeal, supra, and 11 B.U.L.Rev. 148; 5 Temp.L.Q. 152; 17 La.L.Rev. 69; and 40 Yale L.J. 144.

In the case at bar the witnesses are unable to say whether or not the 14 pages were on the table before them when, on June 21st, they signed the last page. The determination then, comes down to the reasonable inferences to be drawn from the established facts. Appellant relies on the undisputed fact that two pages of the will were received in Madison within a few days following June 21st, enclosed in a letter dated June 21st. And appellant infers that those two pages had already been sent off to Madison when, late in the evening of June 21st, the testator and witnesses signed the last page.

On the other hand the trial court put weight on the fact that all 14 original pages are clearly identified and legible as they were dictated by Beale before the corrections or amendments. This intact original was handed to Beale by his secretary and was taken by him to New York. The very next day Beale presented "a pile" of papers to his witnesses and declared that such papers were his will. It is not impossible or improbable that Beale was speaking the truth and the pile of pages were the complete 14-page will, as the trial court found. The fact that Beale sent off two pages to Mrs. Burleigh with a letter dated June 21st may raise an inference that Beale did this before he went to the party and he had there only the remaining pages, which he falsely declared to be his will. Certainly that is not the only permissible inference. When Beale and his friends had signed the will and he had gathered up the pages and departed June 21st was not over; Beale could still have written the letter, less than 100 words, on that date after the party and enclosed with it pages 12 and 13. There is no evidence at all of when the letter and the pages were mailed and there is some evidence that they were mailed in London.

The question is one of inference and when the inferences can reasonably go either way the appellate court must adopt the view taken by the trial court.

"It is the function of the trial court, to draw such inferences from the established facts as is deemed proper, and this court is not at liberty to disturb same unless they are against the great weight and clear preponderance of the evidence." Hull v. Pfister & Vogel Leather Co. (1940), 235 Wis. 653, 294 N.W. 18.

* * *

While the present facts permit the inference urged by appellant they do not compel that inference in opposition to the one drawn by the trial court, and the evidence and reasonable inferences sustain the trial court's conclusion that the entire original will, as dictated by professor Beale to his secretary, was before the witnesses and the execution of that will complied with the requirements of law.

* * *

Appellant, however, has other shots in his locker, the first of which is that even if the entire 14 pages of the will, as originally typed, were before the testator and witnesses at the time of execution the fact that Beale so quickly chose to make changes in it must persuade the court that at the moment of execution Beale did not intend this to be his will, no matter what he may have declared. The burden is on appellant to show that although Beale had himself dictated this will in the very recent past and had declared it to his three friends to be his will, he had already changed his mind concerning it.

As before, the court might have drawn that inference but it was not compelled to do so. The trial court considered Beale's express declaration that this was his will as of that moment was entitled to the greater weight. That court said, in its written decision:

> "The objectors contend that the proper *Animus Testandi* is lacking in this case. Such an objection cannot be sustained. It certainly cannot be said that a man who dictates a document consisting of fourteen pages which purports to be his last will and testament, takes the finished typewritten document from Madison, Wisconsin to New York City, secures three personal friends to witness the document, telling them it is his will, all of which takes place shortly before he is to take a long trip to a foreign land, lacks the necessary testamentary intent to make that document his last will. The necessary testamentary intent existed at the time the will was executed, and that is all that is required."

The inference drawn by the trial court is reasonable and we must adopt its conclusion.

* * *

[The portion of the opinion dealing with appellant's contention that the 1959 will had been revoked by Beale and the comments of the court concerning the appearance of Beale's initials upon altered pages 12 and 13 of the will, which had been typed by Mrs. Burleigh after his death, are omitted] * * *

We conclude that the trial court's findings and conclusions are not against the great weight and the clear preponderance of the evidence and the judgment admitting the will to probate as the will existed when it was executed and as Mrs. Burleigh first typed it must be affirmed.

Judgment affirmed.

* * *

CURRIE, JUSTICE, dissented and DIETERICH, JUSTICE, joined in dissenting opinion:—dissenting opinion omitted.

NOTE

An attested will need not be written on one page, prepared by one person, or drafted in one continuous transaction. The proponent of the will must, however, prove that each page offered for probate was (a) present with the page signed by the witnesses at the time of attestation and (b) intended by the testator to be a part of his will.[65] If the proponent can prove that the pages were present at the time of attestation, there is a presumption that the testator intended each page to be a part of his will;[66] and the issue in most

65. E.g., Sleeper v. Littlefield, 129 Me. 194, 151 A. 150 (1930); Evans, "Incorporation by Reference, Integration, and Non-Testamentary Act", 25 Col.L. Rev. 879, 888 (1925). It is stated frequently that the pages in question must have been present at least in the same room at the time of attestation. Bond v. Seawell, 3 Burr. 1773, 97 Eng.Rep. 1092 (1765). There is probably a presumption that the pages offered as part of a will are authentic when compliance with the formalities for execution of the will is shown by the proponent. See Bond v. Seawell, supra. The proponent, however, bears the ultimate risk of non-persuasion.

66. If the proponent proves that the testator intended each page to be a part of his will, there is a presumption that the pages were present at the time of attestation. Evans, "Incorporation by Reference, Integration, and Non-Testamentary Act", 25 Col.L.Rev. 879, 888 (1925).

of the reported cases concerning integration of wills has been whether or not the pages in question were present when the witnesses attested.

Although it is not required that the witnesses see or examine each page of the will at the time of attestation, the witnesses may have signed or initialled each page of the will or may be able to identify a particular page. The proponent should have no difficulty in sustaining his burden of proof when evidence of this sort is available. By the weight of authority, testimony of persons other than attesting witnesses is admissible concerning the circumstances at the time the will was executed.[67]

When extrinsic evidence of sufficient weight is not available, the proponent will have to rely upon rebuttable presumptions raised by intrinsic evidence from the questioned documents. A will is presumed to have been executed in the condition in which it is found at the death of the testator. If the pages are found firmly attached together in a logical order with the page signed by the witnesses, it is presumed that the pages were present when the will was attested.[68] Even though the pages are not physically attached together, there may be a connection in the internal sense of the writing from page to page that will raise the presumption. Consecutive numbering of pages,[69] sentences carried over from page to page,[70] grammatical dependence of parts,[71] or an orderly scheme for the disposition of the estate evident from page to page may furnish the requisite internal connection.[72]

Any presumption raised by the proponent in the process of proof that pages are part of a will is rebuttable by evidence which the contestant may offer.

When an attempt is made to execute an attested will in duplicate the testator may sign one copy of the will and the witnesses sign the other. While several properly executed testamentary instruments are taken as the single will of the testator,[73] the courts have refused to allow two copies of the same will to be integrated in order to make up the requisite formalities of execution[74] unless the duplicate copies are physically attached together at the time of execution.[75]

Perplexing integration problems arise in states in which holographic wills are permitted. Typically, the holographic will is not witnessed and the testimony of witnesses as to the "number of pages" or "size of the pile" is not available. Furthermore there is no requirement that the holographic will be

67. E.g., Sleeper v. Littlefield, 129 Me. 194, 151 A. 150 (1930). In Seiter's Estate, 265 Pa. 202, 108 A. 614 (1919), it was held that extrinsic evidence was not admissible in order to integrate the will but that the evidence must be contained in the papers themselves.

68. E.g., Hitchings v. Wood, 2 Moore P.C. 355, 12 Eng.Rep. 1041 (1841). A reasonable degree of permanence in the attachment is adequate.

69. Sleeper v. Littlefield, 129 Me. 194, 151 A. 150 (1930).

70. E.g., Stanard v. Miller, 212 Ala. 605, 103 So. 594 (1925); In re Swaim's Will, 162 N.C. 213, 78 S.E. 72 (1913).

71. Martin v. Hamlin's Ex'r, 4 Strob. (S.C.) 188, 53 Am.Dec. 673 (1850); Hathaway v. Warren, 277 Mass. 161, 178 N.E. 288 (1931).

72. For collections of cases concerning connection by internal sense and physical attachment see 4 Baylor L.Rev. 211 (1952); 50 Mich.L.Rev. 915 (1952). The order in which the pages of a will should be arranged is often in issue when the governing statute requires that the will be signed by the testator "at the end". See Section 6(1) B, infra.

73. See Chapter VI, Section 3(1). In the event of an inconsistency in the terms of the instruments, the instrument executed last in point of time prevails.

74. E.g., Baldwin's Will, 146 N.C. 25, 59 S.E. 163, 125 Am.St.Rep. 466 (1907).

75. In re Goettel's Will, 184 Misc. 155, 55 N.Y.S.2d 61 (1944).

prepared in a single transaction and the preparation of the instrument may stretch over a period of months or years. The question in dealing with holographs is whether the testator intended each page to be part of his will. This matter is explored further in Section 7 of this Chapter. The issue of testamentary intent as to the entire document, dealt with in *Beale*, receives additional development in Chapter VII, Section 2(2).

SECTION 6. ORDINARY ATTESTED WILLS

(1) SIGNATURE BY THE TESTATOR

A. NECESSITY AND NATURE OF THE SIGNATURE

The wills acts require that the will be signed by the testator. With few exceptions, the wills acts also permit the testator to sign his will by proxy if the proxy signature is made at the direction or request of the testator and in his presence.[76]

The requirement that the testator sign the will is satisfied in almost all states by any visible impression upon the will made by the testator with the intention that it constitute his signature.[77] The testator may sign by his first name,[78] initials,[79] nickname[80] or mark.[81] A

76. Proxy signatures are not permitted in Connecticut, Louisiana, New Jersey and Utah. Except in Pennsylvania, the testator may sign by proxy even though he has the ability to sign himself. Proxy signatures were permitted by the Statute of Frauds, 1677, and the Wills Act, 1837. The Statute of Frauds required an "express direction" by the testator to the proxy signer. The Wills Act required that the signing be at the testator's "direction". The American wills acts usually contain the language of one or the other of these statutes. The proxy signature must be made in the "presence" of the testator. "Presence" includes the elements of consciousness and proximity. The precise tests are discussed in Section 6(4). The proxy signer should write his own name on the will for identification and some of the wills acts require that this be done. See Rees, "American Wills Statutes", 46 Va.L.Rev. 613, 618–19 (1960). Uniform Probate Code, § 2–502 recognizes a proxy signature.

77. See 72 A.L.R.2d 1267 (1960); 98 A.L.R.2d 841 (1964).

78. Knox's Estate, 131 Pa. 220, 18 A. 1021, 6 L.R.A. 353, 17 Am.St.Rep. 798 (1890); Estate of Morris, 268 Cal.App.2d 638, 74 Cal.Rptr. 32 (1968) (Initials "JBM").

79. Quimby v. Greenhawk, 166 Md. 335, 171 A. 59 (1934).

80. Cartwright v. Cartwright, 158 Ark. 278, 250 S.W. 11 (1923); Estate of Guinane, 65 Ill.App.2d 193, 213 N.E.2d 30 (1965) (signature: "Aunt Margaret").

81. In Estate of Williams, 172 So.2d 464 (Fla.1965) subsections (1) and (2) of § 731.07, F.S.A. ["(1) The testator must sign his will at the end thereof, or some other person in his presence and by his direction must subscribe the name of the testator thereto. (2) The testator, in the presence of at least two attesting witnesses present at the same time, must sign his will or cause his name to be signed as aforesaid or acknowledge his signature thereto."] were construed to preclude an effective signature by the testator with an "X" mark. This decision was followed in two cases decided by the same court on the same day. Estate of Zarkey, 172 So.2d 465 (Fla.1965) and Es-

mark is usually made in the form of a cross with the first name of the testator written to the left of the mark and his family name to the right for identification.[82]

The signature by the testator must be the complete act which he intends. If he desists from the act of signing because of weakness or for some other reason, the partial signature may not be the signature which the statute requires,[83] although it has been suggested that the testator may adopt as his signature the marks made in his unsuccessful effort.[84] The testator may be assisted in completing his intended signature.[85]

It is sometimes important to decide whether a testator's signature was made with assistance or by proxy. A signature by assistance must be in the presence of the testator just as a proxy signature must be. But some of the wills acts require an "express direction" by the testator to the proxy signer. Some courts construe this language to require an unambiguous direction to the proxy by words or gesture.[86] On the other hand, there is no requirement that a testator direct by words or gesture that assistance be given him in signing. The signature is effective if he intends to sign and acquiesces in assistance offered. If an "express direction" to a proxy is required by

tate of Levitt, 172 So.2d 466 (Fla.1965). In his dissent in Estate of Levitt, 172 So. 2d 466, 467, Hendry, J. wrote in part: "Many of the authorities which we have examined seem to agree that the testator may use any device to satisfy the requirement of a signature so long as he *intends* for it to be his signature. It may be an 'X' or any other character or representation, and satisfy as a signature so long as the testator intends for this mark to evidence his act of authenticating the document. The purpose of a signature is not to test the person's ability to write, but to evidence his intention to bind himself to whatever legal significance the particular document he is signing represents.

"The statute requires a signing, but it does not specify what manner or combination of writings will constitute a signing. To say that the statute evidences an intent not to permit signing by mark because it provides for the testator's signature to be written at his direction by some other person is too restrictive. We think the fairer interpretation of this section would be that the second portion of § 731.07(1) was included for persons who are physically incapable of putting pen to paper. * * *"

A distinctive seal, Warneford v. Warneford, 2 Str. 764, 93 Eng.Rep. 834 (1727); a fingerprint, In re Romaniw's Will, 163 Misc. 481, 296 N.Y.S. 925 (1937); and a typewritten signature, Zaruba v. Schumaker, 178 S.W.2d 542 (Tex.Civ.App. 1944), 43 Mich.L.Rev. 808 (1945), have been held sufficient signatures when so intended by testator.

82. Most of the wills acts permit the testator to sign by mark even though he has the ability to write his name. When another person writes the name of the testator to identify his mark, the signature is not by proxy and statutory requirements concerning presence and "direction" need not be met.

83. E.g., Knapp v. Reilly, 3 Dem. (N.Y.) 427 (1885).

84. When the testator can "acknowledge" to witnesses a signature not made in their presence, there would seem no reason why a testator could not acknowledge an incomplete signature as his act validating the will. An incomplete signature is not the required signature to the will because the testator did not intend it to be. When the testator's intention is manifested clearly, the intention should be given effect.

85. E.g. In re Kehl's Estate, 397 Ill. 251, 73 N.E.2d 437 (1947); Fraught, "Assistance or Manual Aid in Signing or Affixing Marks to Wills in Pennsylvania", 77 U. of Pa.L.Rev. 741 (1929).

86. E.g., In re Mullin's Estate, 110 Cal. 252, 42 P. 645 (1895); Waite v. Frisbie, 45 Minn. 361, 47 N.W. 1069 (1891).

statute and no "express direction" can be proved, the will fails unless the signature is found to have been made by assistance only.[87]

The testator signs with assistance and not by proxy if he holds the pen while another guides his hand through the letters of his name.[88] The testator also signs with assistance when he touches a pen held by another who is writing the testator's name.[89] But when the testator touches only the hand of the person signing the testator's name it is probable that the signature is by proxy and not by assistance, although the two courts that have had occasion to discuss the matter reached different conclusions.[90]

PROBLEM

Patrick J. O'Neill, weak from illness, tried to sign his will but stopped when he completed the "t" in "Pat", saying that he was too ill to go on. He was given no assistance and died without finishing the signature. The wills act requires that the testator sign his will or that someone else sign it for him at his "express direction". Will or no will? Knapp v. Reilly, 3 Dem. (N. Y.) 427 (1885). Suppose the attending physician held O'Neill's hand and guided it through the remainder of the signature. Same result? In re Clark's Estate, 170 Cal. 418, 149 P. 828 (1915); Boone v. Boone, 114 Ark. 69, 169 S.W. 779 (1914). Suppose the physician asked O'Neill if he would like to have the physician sign O'Neill's name to the will and O'Neill nodded affirmatively, the physician then completing the signature on a table by O'Neill's bed. Same result? Greenough v. Greenough, 11 Pa. 489, 51 Am.Dec. 567 (1849); Waite v. Frisbie, 45 Minn. 361, 47 N.W. 1069 (1891). Suppose O'Neill touched the pen as the physician wrote O'Neill's name. Same result? Ziegler v. Brown, 112 Fla. 421, 150 So. 608 (1933); In re Jernberg's Estate, 153 Minn. 458, 190 N.W. 990 (1922). Suppose no other person attempted to assist O'Neill or make his signature for him, but that O'Neill pointed to the letters "Pat" and said in the presence of the witnesses "This is my will and this is my signature to it." Same result? See 2 Bowe-Parker: Page, Wills (3d Ed., Rev.1960) § 19.52. Suppose the testator directed the attorney to sign his name by proxy but the attorney signed his own name instead of the name of the testator. Same result? In re Estate of McInally, 7 Misc.2d 625, 163 N. Y.S.2d 793 (Surr.Ct.N.Y.Co.1957). Suppose the testator touched the attorney's name written on the will and said: "This is all right". How would this affect your decision?

---

87. The issue may be raised also in those states in which proxy signatures are not permitted. See fn. 76.

88. E.g., Campbell v. McGuiggan, 34 A. 383 (N.J.1896); Brehony v. Brehony, 289 Pa. 267, 137 A. 260 (1927).

89. E.g., Ziegler v. Brown, 112 Fla. 421, 150 So. 608 (1933); Will of Wilcox, 215 Wis. 341, 254 N.W. 529 (1934).

90. See Goldsmith v. Gates, 205 Ala. 632, 88 So. 861 (1921); Waite v. Frisbie, 45 Minn. 361, 47 N.W. 1069 (1891); 2 Bowe-Parker: Page, Wills (3d Ed., Rev. 1960) § 19.53; 98 A.L.R.2d 824 (1964).

B. Location of Signature

STINSON'S ESTATE

Supreme Court of Pennsylvania, 1910.
228 Pa. 475, 77 A. 807, 30 L.R.A.,N.S., 1173, 139 Am.St.Rep. 1014.[91]

BROWN, J. The requirement of the act of April 8, 1833 (P.L. 249), is that "every will shall be in writing, and unless the person making the same shall be prevented by the extremity of his last sickness, shall be signed by him at the end thereof." The question raised on this appeal is whether the paper which was admitted to probate by the register of wills of Montgomery county as the last will and testament of Agnes J. Stinson had been signed by her at the end thereof. On appeal to the orphans' court of the county from the action of the register, the president judge of the orphans' court of Berks county, specially presiding, held, in a well considered opinion, that the will had been so signed. The document admitted to probate consists of a single sheet of legal cap paper, folded in the middle in the usual way along the short dimension, making four pages of equal size. There is no writing on the fourth page. The writing in issue appears upon the first, second, and third pages of the paper. The document is holographic, and the signature of Agnes J. Stinson appears about the middle of the second page, following the usual in testimonium clause, and to the left of her signature are those of two subscribing witnesses.

The learned counsel, who, in the court below, represented the appellant from the decree of the register, admitted with characteristic candor, that the testatrix, after writing the first page, proceeded to the third, then wrote last what appears at the top of the second page, and, after the completed expression of her testamentary intention, signed her name. * * * The question before us, reduced to one of great simplicity, is whether the end of a will is, as counsel for appellants contend, the "physical end of the writing, the point which is spatially farthest removed from the beginning," or is the logical end of the testator's disposition of his property, wherever that end manifestly appears on the paper.

A will is the legal declaration of a man's intention which he wills to be performed after his death. Such declaration must, under our wills act, be in writing and signed at the end thereof by the testator, unless prevented by an absolute inability. His written declaration is his animus testandi. When it is fully expressed, his will is finished, and the end of it is reached. It is there that his signature must appear as evidence that it is his will. What he regards as the end of his

91. Noted 12 Col.L.Rev. 182 (1912); 24 Harv.L.Rev. 247 (1911); 9 Mich.L.Rev. 342 (1911). The present Pennsylvania statute still requires signature "at the end" of the will. Purdon's Pa.Stat.Ann., Title 20, § 2502.

will, and what must be manifestly regarded as the end of it, from an inspection and reading of the writing, is the end of it under the statute, which contains nothing about the spatial or physical end of it. The will before us, admittedly written by the testatrix herself, bears upon its face the unmistakable sequence which she intended to give to her writing. She started on the first page, and when she reached the bottom of it, turning the paper over, skipped to the third, and there continued her writing, at the top of which, on the first line, the unbroken disposition of her property is continued. When the bottom of that page was reached she turned to the second, and, on the first line of it, continued in clear words the clause relating to the provisions on the third page for the Women's Christian Association of Norristown. She then proceeded to appoint her executors, and, having done so, reached the end of her will, and there signed her name. From the beginning of the first page, continuing on to the third, and ending on the second, there is connected internal sense, containing a clear expression of testamentary intention, and the only conclusion to be reached from an inspection of the writing is that the testatrix signed her name at the place which she regarded as the end of her will. She signed her name at the end of her written act, which she intended to be her will; and as it clearly so appears from the paper itself, her execution of it is not to be declared invalid because she failed to follow the sequence of the pages. The sequence of her will is unbroken from the first line on the first page to the place where she signed her name on the second, which was the end.

While no one of our cases where the question in which the sixth section of the Act of 1833 was passed upon is precisely like the one now before us, Baker's Appeal, 107 Pa. 381, 52 Am.Rep. 478, is similar to it, and what was there said is here controlling. In that case a will was written on the first and third pages of a sheet of paper, and signed at the end of the third page. In a devise to A., written on the third page, numbered "4th," certain words describing the property devised were erased, and the words "See next page" were there interlined. On the fourth page of the same sheet of paper was written an unsigned clause, numbered "4th," making a bequest to A., and also additional bequests to other beneficiaries. The scrivener who drew the will testified that the erasure and interlineation were made by him by testator's direction, and he identified the writing on the fourth page as the subject of the said reference in the will, and as having been written by him at the testator's direction prior to the signing by the latter. In holding that the writing on the fourth page was to be read into the will as constituting the fourth clause thereof, and that the entire instrument, with said clause incorporated therein, should be admitted to probate as the testator's will, we said: "Thus the general principle has been clearly established that a will is to be read in such order of pages or paragraphs as the testator manifestly intended, and the coherence and adaptation of the parts clearly require. In writing a will upon the pages of foolscap paper, a testator may or may not conform to the order of the consecutive pages of the folio. There is no law which binds him in this respect. He may begin upon the fourth page of the folio and conclude upon the first, or he may commence upon the first, continue upon the third, and conclude upon the second. In whatever order of pages it may be written, however, it is to be read, as in Wikoff's Appeal, 15 Pa. 281, 53 Am.Dec. 597, according to their internal sense, their coherence or adaptation of parts. The order of connection, however, must manifestly appear upon the face of the will. It cannot be established by extrinsic proof. Whilst, therefore, the end of the writing in point of space may in most cases be taken as the end of the disposition, it does not follow that in all cases the signature must, of necessity, be there written, if it be written at the end of the will, according to such connection and arrangement of the pages or sheets, as the obviously inherent sense of the instrument requires." * * *

It is urged by the learned counsel for appellants that their contention that the end of a will is the physical end of the writing—the point spatially farthest removed from the beginning—has been sustained by the New York Court of Appeals in Will of Andrews, 162 N.Y. 1, 56 N.E. 529, 48 L.R.A. 662, 76 Am.St.Rep. 294. But that case differed in very important particulars from this. There the will was written upon a printed blank, folded in the middle so as to make four consecutive pages, with the attestation clause at the top of the second page. At that point it was signed by the testator and the subscribing witnesses, and the first two pages made a complete will. The third page contained other and complete dispositions of property, in no manner connected with what appeared on the first and second pages, except that the third page was numbered "2nd page" and the second page "3rd page." In addition, the will was not in the handwriting of the testatrix, but in that of a person to whom the bulk of the estate was given as the residuary beneficiary. The case cannot be regarded as authority at all for the question now before us, which was properly disposed of by the court below; and its decree is affirmed, at appellants' costs.

NOTE

The testator or his proxy were not required to sign the will at any particular place by the Statute of Frauds, 1677.[92] In Lemayne v. Stanley[93] a signature by the testator in the exordium clause of his will was held sufficient. No proof was required that the name was intended by the testator as his signature to his will. Lemayne v. Stanley remained the law in England until the Wills Act, 1837.[94] The Wills Act requires that the testator or his proxy sign at "the end" of the will.

A great majority of the American wills acts specify no particular place for the testator to sign his will[95] and the Uniform Probate Code also speci-

92. 29 Chas. II, c. 3, § V (1677).

93. 3 Lev. 1, 83 Eng.Rep. 545 (1681). See Mechem, "The Rule in Lemayne v. Stanley", 29 Mich.L.Rev. 685 (1931); Evans, "Incidents of Testamentary Execution", 16 Ky.L.J. 199, 205–214 (1928).

94. 7 Wm. IV & 1 Vict. c. 26 (1837). The testator or his proxy were required to sign "at the foot or end thereof". The word "foot" is usually dropped in the American wills acts.

95. Rees, "American Wills Statutes", 46 Va.L.Rev. 613, 619 (1960).

fies no place for signing. But the courts require that a signature other than at the end of the will be proved the testator's intended signature,[96] a majority admitting extrinsic evidence of the testator's declarations and circumstances surrounding execution of the will to show intention.[97] A substantial minority of states have adopted the language of the Wills Act, 1837, and require the testator or his proxy to sign "at the end" of the will.[98]

The testator is required to sign at the end in order to eliminate proof of his intention that his signature was to authenticate the will and in order to prevent fraudulent additions to the will.[99] The meaning of "end" caused the courts some difficulty in the past, the New York courts, among others, holding that the physical end of the will was the place intended by the legislature. The "logical end" interpretation given to the statute by the court in the principal case is now the generally accepted view.[1] If the pages of the will are found attached together in an illogical order, they will be arranged in an order suggested by their internal coherence in order to determine whether or not the signature of the testator is at the end.[2]

It is presumed that materials found after the testator's signature were added after the will was executed.[3] If this presumption is not rebutted, the

96. E.g., Thrift Trust Co. v. White, 90 Ind.App. 116, 167 N.E. 141 (1929), 3 Cinn. L.Rev. 489 (1930), 5 Ind.L.Rev. 129 (1929), 25 Ill.L.Rev. 226 (1930); McNair's Estate, 72 S.D. 604, 38 N.W.2d 449 (1949).

97. E.g., Armstrong's Executor v. Armstrong's Heirs, 29 Ala. 538 (1857); Meads v. Earle, 205 Mass. 553, 91 N.E. 916, 29 L.R.A.,N.S., 63 (1910). The Virginia and West Virginia statutes require that the will be signed "in such manner as to make it manifest that the name is intended as a signature". This provision has been construed to require proof that the signature to a holographic will found elsewhere than at the end of the holograph was made "with finality of testamentary intent" and evidence to this effect must be obtained only from the four corners of the instrument. E.g., Hall v. Brigstocke, 190 Va. 459, 58 S.E.2d 529, 19 A.L.R.2d 921 (1950). If the will is attested, a signature found anywhere on the will is presumed to have been made with finality of testamentary intent, evidence to rebut the presumption being admitted only when obtained from the four corners of the instrument. E.g., Murguiondo v. Nowlan, 115 Va. 160, 78 S.E. 600 (1913).

98. As of 1960 Rees listed 13 states as having a requirement similar to that of the Wills Act, with Connecticut requiring the testator to "subscribe" the will. Rees, "American Wills Statutes", 46 Va. L.Rev. 613, 619 (1960). The British Law Reform Committee has recommended that the "signed at the end" requirement be dropped from the Wills Act, 1837, the Committee recommending that the will be admitted to probate "if it is apparent on the face of the will that the testator intended his signature to validate it". In a survey of wills submitted to probate in England and Wales between 4 September to 1 December, 1978, of the 93 rejected for lack of proper formalities only 8 (8.6%) had the testator's signature incorrectly placed. 40,664 wills were probated during this period. Cmd. 7902 (1980) Par. 2.7 and Annex 2. Mississippi requires a holographic will to be "subscribed" but does not extend this requirement to an attested will. Mississippi code, § 91–5–1 (1979 Supp.). The Mississippi construction of "subscribe" is that a signature is required at the logical end of the holograph. As in Virginia and West Virginia, the intent is sought from the four corners of the instrument. Wilson v. Polite, 218 So.2d 843 (Miss.1969). See Finlay v. Hunt, 218 So.2d 858 (Miss.1969) where a signature on an envelope enclosing a will was held not a subscription and it was unsuccessfully argued that the word "signed" written in testatrix' handwriting at the logical end of the will was her signature.

99. See Atkinson, Wills (2d Ed., 1953) 303; 2 Bowe-Parker: Page, Wills (3d Ed., Rev.1960) § 19.57.

1. The "logical end" test seems to have acquired a foothold in New York. See Matter of Field's Will, 204 N.Y. 488, 97 N.E. 881 (1912); Matter of Golden's Will, 165 Misc. 205, 300 N.Y.S. 737 (1937), aff'd 253 App.Div. 919, 3 N.Y.S.2d 886 (1938); In re Reid's Will, 47 N.Y.S.2d 426 (1944). 44 A.L.R.3d 866 (1968).

2. Chandler v. Dockman, 8 Ohio App. 113 (1917).

3. E.g., In re Taylor's Estate, 230 Pa. 346, 79 A. 632, 36 L.R.A.,N.S., 66 (1911). Walsh and Jones, "Instruments Signed

materials fail as an unexecuted codicil. The provisions above the testator's signature are effective. If the presumption is rebutted, it may be argued that the materials following the signature are of a purely formal or non-dispositive nature and should be ignored as surplusage. Thus provisions for the compensation of the executor,[4] for exemption of the executor from bond[5] or for a particular type of burial for the testator[6] which follow the signature may not prevent the will from being signed at the end. There is a division of authority whether a clause appointing an executor can be ignored as surplusage. The prevailing view appears to be that this clause must precede the testator's signature if the will is to be signed at the end.[7] If dispositive provisions or provisions which have a direct relationship to the administration of the estate follow the signature of the testator and were part of the will when the testator signed, the will is invalid as an entirety.[8]

Blanks between the dispositive provisions of the will or between the last dispositive provision and the signature of the testator may result in a finding that the will is not signed at the end and is invalid. If a court considers that the prevention of fraudulent additions or interpolations was a primary aim of the legislature in requiring wills to be signed at the end, a space between the last dispositive provision and the signature of the testator renders the will invalid if the space is of such size that a fraudulent addition or interpolation is facilitated.[9]

---

(2) NUMBER AND QUALIFICATION OF WITNESSES

A will is void unless attested by the number of competent witnesses required by statute.[10] Two witnesses are usually required, although several states require a minimum of three.[11] "Competent" means "qualified to testify in court concerning the material facts of execution".[12]

'at the End Thereof' and the Register of Wills", 71 Dick.L.Rev. 563 (1967).

4. In re McConihe's Estate, 123 Misc. 318, 205 N.Y.S. 780 (1924).

5. Baker v. Baker, 51 Ohio St. 217, 37 N.E. 125 (1894).

6. Goods of Bosanquet, 2 Rob.Eccl. Rep. 577, 163 Eng.Rep. 1419 (1852).

7. E.g., In re Winter's Will, 302 N.Y. 666, 98 N.E.2d 477 (1951); See 21 Corn.L.Q. 351 (1936).

8. E.g., In re Estate of Seaman, 146 Cal. 455, 80 P. 700, 106 Am.St.Rep. 53, 2 Ann.Cas. 726 (1905); see 20 Pa.Stat. § 2502(1) which allows that portion of the will preceding the signature to stand and that portion following the signature to fall.

9. E.g., In re Schroeder's Will, 98 Misc. 92, 163 N.Y.S. 956 (1916). A will has been held signed at the end when there was a space of twenty-three inches between the testimonium clause and the signature. Mader v. Apple, 80 Ohio St. 691, 89 N.E. 37, 23 L.R.A.,N.S., 515, 131 Am.St.Rep. 719 (1909).

10. Use of more witnesses than the statute requires does not invalidate the will but may place an additional burden upon the proponent since it is usually necessary to account for supernumeraries at probate.

11. Rees, "American Wills Statutes", 46 Va.L.Rev. 613, 624 (1960).

12. The Statute of Frauds required "credible" witnesses, but "credible" was construed as "competent". Holdfast d. Anstey v. Dowsing, 2 Strange 1253, 93 Eng.Rep. 1164 (1746). The English construction is adopted when "credible" appears in a wills act in the United States.

A witness offers a species of testimony when he signs the will as an attester. Since it is possible that the will may be probated without additional testimony by the witness,[13] it is held that he is competent within the meaning of the wills act if he is competent according to the standard applicable when the will is executed.[14] If a necessary witness is incompetent when the will is executed, the will is invalid even though the witness is competent at probate.[15]

The common law rules concerning the competence of attesters were derived from the rules concerning the competence of witnesses in litigation. It is possible that a witness may be incompetent by the strict common law standards in force when the wills act was passed but competent in the light of the statutory standards dealing with witnesses in general when the will is executed. Do the wills acts adopt the common law standards of competence in force at their date of passage or the common law standards as altered by statutes dealing with the competence of witnesses in general?[16] The answer lies in the language of the particular statutes involved and, as in other matters of construction, the decisions of the courts are impossible to harmonize.[17] It is wise to choose witnesses who are competent attesters at common law as well as under modern statutory standards applicable to witnesses in litigation.

A direct and immediate pecuniary interest in establishing a will renders a witness incompetent at common law. A witness who is incompetent because of interest when the will is executed cannot render himself competent by releasing his interest thereafter.[18]

The disqualifying interest must be actual and not illusory. A legatee or devisee can witness a will if he takes as much or more as heir if the testator dies intestate.[19] It is probable that a legatee or devi-

E.g., Noble's Estate, 124 Ill. 266, 15 N.E. 850 (1888); Wallace v. Harrison, 218 Miss. 153, 65 So.2d 456 (1953).

13. 3 Bowe-Parker: Page, Wills (3d Ed., Rev.1960) § 29.10.

14. E.g., In re Delavergne's Will, 259 Ill. 589, 102 N.E. 1081 (1913); Wigmore, Evidence (3d Ed., 1940) § 1510. The rule is statutory in some states. Rees, "American Wills Statutes", 46 Va.L.Rev. 613, 627 (1960).

15. E.g., Vrooman v. Powers, 47 Ohio St. 191, 24 N.E. 267, 8 L.R.A. 39 (1890).

16. The statutes are summarized in Wigmore, Evidence (3d Ed., 1940) § 488.

17. There is little judicial authority directly in point. Most of the courts seem to assume that the general procedural law in force at the time the will is executed is the standard by which competence of an attester should be measured. E.g., Kumpe v. Coons, 63 Ala. 448 (1879); Kaufman v. Murray, 182 Ind. 372, 105 N.E. 466, Ann.Cas1917A, 832 (1914). Other courts appear to take the position that the common law standards apply which were in force when the wills act was passed. E.g., Scott v. O'Connor-Couch, 271 Ill. 395, 111 N.E. 272, L.R.A.1916D, 179 (1915), 29 Harv.L.Rev. 795 (1916), 11 Ill.L.Rev. 207 (1916). See 2 Bowe-Parker: Page, Wills (3d Ed., Rev.1960) § 19.84.

18. E.g., Smith v. Goodell, 258 Ill. 145, 101 N.E. 255 (1913); Vrooman v. Powers, 47 Ohio St. 191, 24 N.E. 267 (1890). In a few states a witness can become competent by releasing his interest. E.g., Rockafellow v. Rockafellow, 192 Ark. 563, 93 S.W.2d 321 (1936); Grimm v. Tittman, 113 Mo. 56, 20 S.W. 664 (1892). As to incompetence based on interest see generally Atkinson, Wills (2d Ed., 1953) 312–320; 2 Bowe-Parker: Page, Wills (3d Ed., Rev.1960) § 19.86–107; Evans, "The Competency of Testamentary Witnesses", 25 Mich.L.Rev. 238, 255 et seq. (1927); Winn, "Interested Parties as Witnesses to Wills", 92 Trusts and Estates 786 (1953), 13 A.L.R. 3d 404 (1967).

19. E.g., Smalley v. Smalley, 70 Me. 545, 35 Am.Rep. 353 (1880); Sparhawk v. Sparhawk, 10 Allen (Mass.) 155 (1865);

see who is not an heir can witness a codicil to a will when his testamentary share is not increased by operation of the codicil, although authority on the point is scant and conflicting.[20] An executor is a competent witness by the prevailing view.[21] His commission is earned and is not a gratuity. The attorney who drafts the will and the attorney for the executor are competent witnesses.[22] A creditor of the testator is a competent witness even though the will contains a charge on land for his benefit.[23] The creditor can enforce his claim against the land whether a charge is provided by the will or not.

The interest may be small if it is direct and immediate. It has been held that a stockholder cannot witness a will containing a gift to his corporation;[24] but a taxpayer can witness a will containing a gift to his municipal corporation because his interest in a pecuniary sense is tenuous.[25]

The spouse of an interested party cannot witness the will.[26] The rule is based on the common law fiction of unity of husband and wife

In re Hoppe's Will, 102 Wis. 54, 78 N.W. 183 (1899). Statutes sometimes provide that an heir is a competent witness but cannot take by will more than his intestate share. Rees, "American Wills Statutes", 46 Va.L.Rev. 613, 632–633 (1960); Evans, "The Competency of Testamentary Witnesses", 25 Mich.L.Rev. 238, 251 (1926).

20. See 2 Bowe-Parker: Page, Wills (3d Ed., Rev.1960) § 19.91. Some of the cases which hold the witness incompetent are obsolete in the light of modern legal principles. Thus, in Richardson v. Richardson, Dudley Eq.Rep. (S.C.) 184 (1838) a residuary devisee was held incompetent to witness a codicil which republished the will so that the will operated to pass after-acquired property by the residuary clause. The general view at the present time is that a will operates to pass property acquired before the death of the testator whether a codicil is executed or not.

21. E.g., Bettison v. Bromley, 12 East. 250, 104 Eng.Rep. 98 (1810) (Wife of executor); Meyer v. Fogg, 7 Fla. 292, 68 Am.Dec. 441 (1857). See 74 A.L.R.2d 283 (1960). There are a few cases holding the executor incompetent, although some of these are based on obsolete notions concerning the powers of an executor over an estate. See 2 Bowe-Parker: Page, Wills (3d Ed., Rev.1960) § 19.92. Statutes declare an executor competent in several states. See Rees, "American Wills Statutes", 46 Va.L.Rev. 613, 628 (1960). An executor, of course, may be a devisee or legatee in a will and be incompetent as a witness for that reason. Care should be taken in conferring powers of disposition upon an executor. If the power is so broad as to give the executor virtually unlimited control, he may be held incompetent because of interest. Appeal of Richburg, 148 Me. 323, 92 A.2d 724 (1952) (Statute required witnesses "not beneficially interested". Executor received power to dispose of personal property "as he in his sole discretion may deem best".) Testamentary trustees and guardians are usually regarded as competent witnesses where executors are competent.

22. For the competency of the attorney for the executor as a witness, see 30 A.L.R.3d 1361 (1970).

23. In Holdfast d. Anstey v. Dowsing, 2 Strange 1253, 93 Eng.Rep. 1164 (1746) it was held that a witness could not release a charge made upon the entire estate for his benefit. It was generally assumed that this decision applied to the situation in which a charge upon land was made for the benefit of a creditor since a creditor could not reach the land otherwise. By the Statute 25 Geo. II, c. 6 (1752) a creditor was made a competent witness whether a charge was made upon land for his benefit or not, and statutes in American states often contain a similar provision. It appears, however, that these statutes are now unnecessary since a creditor can reach land as well as personal property in order to satisfy his claim.

24. See 2 Bowe-Parker: Page, Wills (3d Ed., Rev.1960) § 19.99.

25. E.g., In re Marston, 79 Me. 25, 8 A. 87 (1887); Hitchcock v. Shaw, 160 Mass. 140, 35 N.E. 671 (1893).

26. E.g., Fearn v. Postlethwaite, 240 Ill. 626, 88 N.E. 1057 (1909); Sullivan v. Sullivan, 106 Mass. 474, 8 Am.Rep. 356 (1871).

and the policy excluding testimony by one spouse for the benefit of another. On the other hand, the blood relatives of an interested party may witness the will even though they receive a greater benefit from the gift than would a spouse under similar circumstances.[27]

There are grounds of incompetence at common law other than pecuniary interest. Neither a spouse of the testator or testatrix nor a person convicted of felony can witness the will.[28] A person who lacks the physical or mental ability to comprehend or relate facts is incompetent as an attester.

Statutes in the United States tend to correlate the standard of competence to attest a will with the ability of the witness to comprehend and relate facts.[29] There is some doubt, of course, concerning the degree to which statutes aimed at witnesses in general alter the common law requirements concerning attesters to wills. Legislation concerning husband and wife seems to enable one spouse to witness the will of the other.[30] A convicted felon is usually a competent witness by statute, and these statutes may also make him a competent attester, although his conviction may bear upon his credibility if he testifies at probate.[31] By contrast, the statutes dealing with interest as a ground of incompetence have at best superseded in a piece-meal fashion the common law rules concerning attesters.

The English Statute of George II[32] provided that the interest of a witness to a will was void. The witness became a competent attester by losing his gift. The statute did not cover the case of an interested party whose spouse was a witness. The will failed if it was necessary to include the spouse to make up the required number of witnesses. The Wills Act, 1837,[33] added a provision avoiding the interest of a party whose spouse was a witness, but went on to declare that no will should fail because the witnesses thereto were incompetent.

There are statutes in a great majority of American states based substantially upon the Statute of George II.[34] Almost all of these statutes provide for the case of a supernumerary witness.[35] The gift to the witness is effective if it is unnecessary to include the witness

27. In Matter of Ackerina, 195 Misc. 383, 90 N.Y.S.2d 794 (1949) it was held that a statute did not avoid the interest of a witness who took by lapse from a donee named in the will.

28. See Evans, "The Competency of Testamentary Witnesses", 25 Mich.L. Rev. 238, 247 (1927). For the history and policy of the common law doctrines concerning the spouse, see Wigmore, Evidence (3d Ed., 1940) §§ 600, 601.

29. An infant is permitted to attest a will if he has the physical and mental ability to comprehend and relate facts. In a few states a minimum age is set for attesters. Rees, "American Wills Statutes" 46 Va.L.Rev. 613, 629 (1960).

30. Atkinson, Wills (2d Ed., 1953) 318; Wigmore, Evidence (3d Ed., 1940) § 602 et seq.

31. Wigmore, Evidence (3d Ed., 1940) §§ 575, 595, 598, 603. If a court applies the common law standard in force when the wills act was passed, it is likely that the convict will be held an incompetent attester. See O'Connell v. Dow, 182 Mass. 541, 66 N.E. 788 (1903).

32. 25 Geo. II, c. 6 (1752).

33. 7 Wm. IV & 1 Vict. c. 26, § XV (1837).

34. Rees, "American Wills Statutes", 46 Va.L.Rev. 613, 631 (1960). The statute of George II may or may not be part of the common law. See Elliott v. Brent, 6 Mackey (17 D.C. 98) (1887) (That it is); Hudson v. Flood, 28 Del.Ch. 450, 94 A. 760 (1915) (That it is not).

35. Rees, "American Wills Statutes", 46 Va.L.Rev. 613, 631 (1960).

in the number required for validity of the will. A number of the statutes also provide for the case of a witness who is an heir. Although the treatment of the problem differs in various states, the statute may provide that the gift by will is avoided only to the extent that it exceeds the share which the witness would have taken if the testator had died intestate.[36] Few of the statutes provide for the case of the interested party whose spouse has witnessed the will,[37] but statutes designed to qualify one spouse as a witness in litigation involving another may make the spouse a competent attester.[38]

The Uniform Probate Code abolishes interest as a ground of disqualification.[39] It is sometimes difficult to obtain disinterested witnesses, as where testator lives on a farm or ranch, is seriously ill, and only members of the family are available. Moreover, if the law permits persons to execute their own wills without legal advice (and no statute requires employment of a lawyer), the requirement of a disinterested witness is often a trap for innocent persons. Since modern law generally allows interested persons to testify,[40] their interest being a factor in evaluating their testimony rather than a grounds for disqualification, there is reason to adopt the same policy as to wills. If a beneficiary receiving substantially more under the will than he would by intestacy is one of the witnesses, this is of course a factor if the will is contested on grounds of undue influence by the beneficiary-witness. Even in a state having the Uniform Probate Code in force, an attorney would use an interested witness only when absolutely necessary.

Should the lawyer who drafts the will serve as a witness? Consider that, if after death of the testator the same lawyer is retained to represent the estate and if the will is contested, the lawyer would have to testify and he (and his firm) would have to withdraw as counsel for the personal representative and lose the fee for probate of the estate. Code of Professional Responsibility DR 5–102(A). (Is that a proper consideration for the lawyer? Won't the lawyer make a better witness in upholding the will, which is the client's objective?) Also consider the possibility in some jurisdictions that the lawyer who drafts the will cannot testify to communications between him and his client unless the privilege is waived by the client, but that his signing as a witness at the request of the client operates to waive the privilege and permit the lawyer-witness to testify as to client communica-

36. Rees, "American Wills Statutes", 46 Va.L.Rev. 613, 632 (1960).

37. Rees, "American Wills Statutes", 46 Va.L.Rev. 613, 631 (1960).

38. Wigmore, Evidence (3d Ed., 1940) §§ 607, 608, 614, 619, 620.

39. Uniform Probate Code, § 2–505 provides:

"(a) Any person generally competent to be a witness may act as a witness to a will.

"(b) A will or any provision thereof is not invalid because the will is signed by an interested witness."

40. The common law rules concerning the competence of interested witnesses in general litigation have been changed by statute in almost all states. See Wigmore, Evidence (3d Ed., 1940) § 576. It is difficult to determine whether these statutes apply to attesters to wills unless the statute expressly applies to an attester. See 2 Bowe-Parker: Page, Wills (3d Ed., Rev.1960) § 19.84.

tions.[41] Note that these are not problems in the normal estate where probate is uncontested.

PROBLEMS

1. Testatrix, a generous lady, executed her will in 1954, the will including the following clause, among others: "I also request my Executor to pay to each of the signers, as witnesses, of this my last Will, the sum of five dollars each, as a token of appreciation". Three witnesses subscribed the will. The statute in force at the date of execution provides: "* * * and subscribed in his presence by three credible attesting witnesses, not beneficially interested under said will". As counsel for the proponent, what arguments will you make to support the will as valid? See In re Moody's Will, 155 Me. 325, 154 A.2d 165, 73 A.L.R.2d 1225 (1959). Suppose between the date of death of testatrix in 1956 and the date of execution of the will (1954) the following change in the statute was made: "All beneficial devises, bequests and legacies to a subscribing witness are void except that if such interested witness would be entitled to any share of the estate in case the person making the will had died intestate, he shall take only that part of the devise or bequest made to him in the will that equals but does not exceed in value the share of the estate of the person making the will which he would have taken if such person had died intestate". How, if at all, can you use this change in the statute to support your argument for validity of the will? Suppose the change in the statute had been made after the death of testatrix in 1956. Would it then be of any value to you in your argument? See Me.Rev.Stat. Ann., Tit. 18, § 1.

2. T executed a will naming the X bank as executor. A and B subscribed the will as attesting witnesses. A was employed by the bank as a stenographer. B was a stockholder in the bank. Executors are entitled to compensation by statute. Statutes also provide that a will must be attested by "two or more credible witnesses" and that "* * * any beneficial devise, legacy or interest * * * made or given in any will, testament or codicil, as a witness to the execution thereof, * * * shall, as to the beneficiary thereof, and all persons claiming under him, be null and void". Can the X Bank serve as executor? See Scott v. O'Connor-Couch, 271 Ill. 395, 111 N.E. 272, L.R.A.1916D, 179, 29 Harv.L.Rev. 795 (1916); 11 Ill.L.Rev. 207 (1916). But see Meyer v. Fogg, 7 Fla. 292, 68 Am.Dec. 441 (1857); Rucker v. Lambdin, 12 Smedes & M. (20 Miss.) 230 (1849). See 2 Bowe-Parker: Page, Wills (3d Ed. Rev.1960) §§ 19.92, 19.99. For the present Illinois law on the point, see Ill. Ann.Stat. Ch. 3, § 44.

(3) FACTS TO WHICH WITNESSES ATTEST

A. Testator's Authentication

The signature of the testator upon the will is important evidence that the will is his. But the wills acts require additional evidence that

41. See Comment, "Consideration of Professional Responsibility in Probate Matters", 51 Neb.L.Rev. 456, at 458–466 (1972).

the will is authentic. The testator must authenticate the will by some acts which the witnesses can observe and report.[42]

Some states require the testator to indicate to the witnesses that the document executed or to be executed by him is a will.[43] This action is called "publication" and is an American innovation in formalities of execution. No particular form of publication is necessary, but the word or gesture of the testator must indicate to the witnesses with reasonable clarity that the instrument is a will.[44] Disclosure of the contents of the will to witnesses is unnecessary except in Louisiana.[45]

The witnesses need not know that the document is a will where publication is not required.[46] They must, nevertheless, observe acts which indicate that the document is executed by the testator.[47]

Under all of the wills acts the testator's act of signing the will in the presence of the witnesses is a sufficient act of authentication for the witnesses to observe.[48] The witnesses do not have to see the signature in this case. But most of the wills acts provide an alternative means of authentication.[49] If the testator did not sign his will in the presence of the witnesses, he can later acknowledge the will or his signature in their presence. It is this alternative that creates the difficulty. What, precisely, does the testator acknowledge; and what, precisely, do the witnesses have to be able to see?

The Statute of Frauds, 1677,[50] provided in part that "* * * all *devises and bequests* * * * shall be attested and subscribed * * * by * * * witnesses * * *". The Statute did not set

42. The report is made by the act of subscribing the will as witness and, perhaps, by testifying at probate concerning the act. "Attestation" contemplates knowledge of certain facts which are necessary for a valid execution of the will. Wigmore, Evidence (3d Ed., 1940) § 1511.

43. (Arkansas, California, Indiana, New Jersey, New York, Oklahoma, South Dakota, Tennessee, and Louisiana—and possibly in Nevada and Texas) Rees, "American Wills Statutes", 46 Va.L.Rev. 613, 621 (1960). There are decisions in several states which seem to imply a requirement of publication from the statutory requirement that the will be attested. See, e.g., Cone v. Donovan, 275 Mo. 557, 204 S.W. 1073 (1918); In re Ayer's Estate, 84 Neb. 16, 120 N.W. 491 (1909). Publication may precede or follow the signature of the testator if it occurs as part of the same transaction. See Atkinson, Wills (2d Ed., 1953) § 68; 2 Bowe-Parker: Page, Wills (3d Ed., Rev.1960) §§ 19.143–147, 71 A.L.R.3d 877 (1976).

44. E.g., In re Gordon's Estate, 48 Idaho 171, 279 P. 625 (1929). But the communication must emanate from the testator and knowledge from another source does not suffice. E.g., Gilbert v. Knox, 52 N.Y. 125 (1873); Hill v. Davis, 64 Okl. 253, 167 P. 465, L.R.A.1918B, 687 (1917), 18 Col.L.Rev. 96 (1918), 66 U. of Pa.L.Rev. 89 (1917).

45. The "open" or "nuncupative" will in Louisiana must be read to the witnesses. Rees, "American Wills Statutes", 46 Va.L.Rev. 613, 621 (1960).

46. E.g., In re Balk's Estate, 298 Mich. 303, 298 N.W. 779 (1941); In re Estate of Mathews, 234 Iowa 188, 12 N.W. 2d 162 (1943), 43 Mich.L.Rev. 431 (1944); In re Zyck's Will, 251 Wis. 108, 28 N.W. 2d 316 (1947).

47. States which require publication require it as an addition to other acts of authentication (signing in the presence of witnesses or, in most of the publication states, acknowledgment of the signature).

48. See Atkinson, Wills (2d Ed., 1953) 322.

49. Louisiana requires that the signature be made in the presence of the witnesses. Rees, "American Wills Statutes", 46 Va.L.Rev. 613, 620 (1960). An acknowledgment is not permitted by the Louisiana provision for an ordinary attested will. See Section 2, fn. 17, supra.

50. 29 Chas. II, c. 3, § V (1677).

forth any particular acts of authentication by the testator to be seen by the witnesses. The English courts held, however, that the testator could sign the will in the presence of the witnesses; or, if the testator did not sign the will in their presence, he could later acknowledge the will in their presence.[51] It was sufficient that the testator acknowledge the document as one to which he desired to give legal effect, and the witnesses were not required to see the signature because they were attesting "devises and bequests".[52]

The Wills Act, 1837,[53] required, when the testator did not sign in the presence of the witnesses, that "such *signature* shall be * * * acknowledged by the testator" in their presence. The signature appeared to be the subject of acknowledgment, and it was required that the signature be in such a position upon acknowledgment that the witnesses could see it if they looked.[54]

The American courts have tended to follow the English construction placed upon the English statute upon which their wills act was patterned,[55] although some courts have construed wills acts patterned upon the Statute of Frauds as if the *signature* rather than the *will* was the thing to be acknowledged by the testator.[56]

No particular form of acknowledgment is required. The acknowledgment may be by word or gesture.[57] A signature may be acknowledged by making a scroll after it while in the presence of witnesses.[58]

PROBLEM

T executed his will on a blank will form and signed his name at the end of the will and also in a blank in the attestation clause. Later T approached witness A, handed the will to him folded so that both of his names were visible, and said, "Jim, this is my will, I would like to have you sign it." A signed at the bottom of the attestation clause without reading it. T then approached B and handed B the will, folded in such a manner that only his signature in the attestation clause was visible, and said, "John, will you witness this paper for me." B signed, although he was able to see only the signature by T in the attestation clause and not the signature at the end of the will. The applicable statute requires that a will be witnessed by two competent witnesses, that the testator sign the will at the end and that the signature of the testator shall be made.

> "* * * in the presence of each of the subscribing witnesses, or shall be acknowledged by him to have been so made to each of the subscribing witnesses."

51. Ellis v. Smith, 1 Ves.Jr. 11, 30 Eng.Rep. 205 (1754); White v. Trustees of British Museum, 6 Bing. 310, 130 Eng. Rep. 1299 (1829).

52. White v. Trustees of British Museum, supra, fn. 51.

53. 7 Wm. IV & 1 Vict., c. 26, § IX (1837).

54. Hudson v. Parker, 1 Rob.Ecc. 14, 163 Eng.Rep. 948 (1844); Daintree v. Butcher and Fasulo, L.R., 13 Prob.Div. 102 (1888).

55. See Atkinson, Wills (2d Ed., 1953) 323 et seq.; 2 Bowe-Parker: Page, Wills (3d Ed., Rev.1960) § 19.116.

56. E.g., In re Harter's Estate, 229 Iowa 238, 294 N.W. 357 (1940); Tredick v. Bryant, 296 Mass. 50, 168 N.E. 162 (1929); 28 Mich.L.Rev. 780 (1930).

57. See 2 Bowe-Parker: Page, Wills (3d Ed., Rev.1960) § 19.15; 7 A.L.R.3d 317 (1966).

58. In re Halton's Estate, 111 N.J.Eq. 143, 161 A. 809 (1932).

Will or no will? See In re Keeffe's Will, 155 App.Div. 575, 141 N.Y.S. 5 (1913). If witness B had seen T's signature, would the will have been valid if the statute required "publication"?

B. TESTAMENTARY CAPACITY

Numerous courts have stated that the witnesses attest the capacity of the testator to execute the will.[59] This includes his freedom from undue influence, as well as his capacity in age and intellect.[60] On the other hand, it has been stated with equal frequency that the witnesses do not have to know that the instrument is a will unless there is a requirement of publication,[61] and that the witnesses do not have to know the identity of the testator at the time the will is executed.[62] It seems amply clear that the failure of a witness to form an opinion concerning the capacity of the testator does not invalidate the will,[63] although the testimony of witnesses concerning facts bearing upon the capacity of the testator is certainly admissible at probate.

PROBLEM

Testatrix was removed from a hospital to the home of a practical nurse and while in this home executed a will prepared by an attorney who had first had Testatrix examined by a doctor to determine her mental competence. The attorney went over notes concerning the disposition of the property with the testatrix, made some suggestions concerning contingencies he thought should be provided for, and signed the will as one of the witnesses after he had prepared it. Two other witnesses also signed the will, both being residents of the home in which testatrix was receiving care. When testatrix executed this will she was 81. She died about three years later. The pertinent statutes are as follows:

> "* * * [N]o will shall be valid unless proved by the oaths or affirmations of two competent witnesses." "All wills shall be proved by the oaths or affirmations of two competent witnesses, and * * * in the case of a will to which the testator signed his name, proof by subscribing witnesses, if there are such, shall be preferred to the extent that they are readily available, and proof of the signature of the testator shall be preferred to proof of the signature of a subscribing witness". * * * [the wills act requires attestation by witnesses only when the testator signs by proxy or by mark] * * *

The attorney is a competent witness as are the other two witnesses who subscribed the will. However these two witnesses now refuse to sign the affidavit of probate, stating that at the time testatrix signed the will she was senile and was not, in their opinion, competent to execute it. It is contended

59. E.g., Smith v. Young, 134 Miss. 738, 99 So. 370, 35 A.L.R. 69 (1924).

60. See 2 Bowe-Parker: Page, Wills (3d Ed., Rev.1960) § 19.115.

61. See subsection (A), supra.

62. E.g., In re Moxley's Will, 103 Vt. 100, 152 A. 713 (1930).

63. E.g., In re Paradis' Will, 47 Me. 347, 87 A.2d 512 (1952) (two out of three witnesses formed no opinion as to mental capacity at execution); see 69 A.L.R.2d 662 (1960).

that under the statutes set forth a will is not proved unless the subscribing witnesses who attested the execution of the will also attest to the mental capacity of the testatrix. Would you accept or reject this contention as Judge of the Orphans' Court? In re Brantlinger's Estate, 418 Pa. 236, 210 A.2d 246 (1965).

C. MATTERS RECITED IN ATTESTATION CLAUSE

An attestation clause is a certificate signed by the witnesses to a will.[64] The clause recites the performance of formalities of execution which the witnesses purport to have observed. No wills act requires an attestation clause for validity of the will. But, by the prevailing view, a rebuttable presumption arises that the formalities recited were performed if it is shown that the clause was read by or to the witnesses when they signed the will.[65] There is no presumption against the performance of formalities not recited. If some of the facts recited are proved erroneous, there is still a presumption in favor of those remaining.[66]

An attestation clause may be used at probate to refresh the memory of an attesting witness or to impeach the witness if he offers hostile testimony.

(4) PRESENCE

DEMARIS' ESTATE

Supreme Court of Oregon, 1941.
166 Or. 36, 110 P.2d 571.[67]

[George Demaris became ill on 2 April, 1939, and was taken to the office of Dr. Harold B. Gillis. The dimensions of the three front rooms of this office and the location of certain pieces of furniture are shown in the diagram on the following page.

64. See the attestation clause in the specimen will in Section 3(2).

65. E.g., Goff v. Knight, 201 Okl. 411, 206 P.2d 992 (1948); Kittleson's Estate v. Kittleson, 42 S.D. 126, 173 N.W. 161 (1919). See Severns, "The True Function of the Attestation Clause in a Will", 11 Chi.-Kent L.Rev. 11 (1932); Atkinson, Wills (2d Ed., 1953) § 73; see 2 Bowe-Parker: Page, Wills (3d Ed., Rev.1960) § 19.141.

66. E.g., Craig v. Wismar, 310 Ill. 262, 141 N.E. 766 (1923) (erroneous recital that witnesses signed in presence of each other).

67. Noted, 13 Rocky Mt.L.Rev. 345 (1941). For a discussion of the construction of "presence" as involved in the principal case, with particular reference to Nichols v. Rowan, 422 S.W.2d 21 (Tex. Civ.App.1967) (applying a sight test but admitting the will to probate on the strength of an attestation clause signed by the witnesses), and considering several other matters pertaining to attestation developed hereafter in this book see Smith, "Attestation of Wills—An Examination of Some Problem Areas", 11 South Texas L.J. 125 (1969).

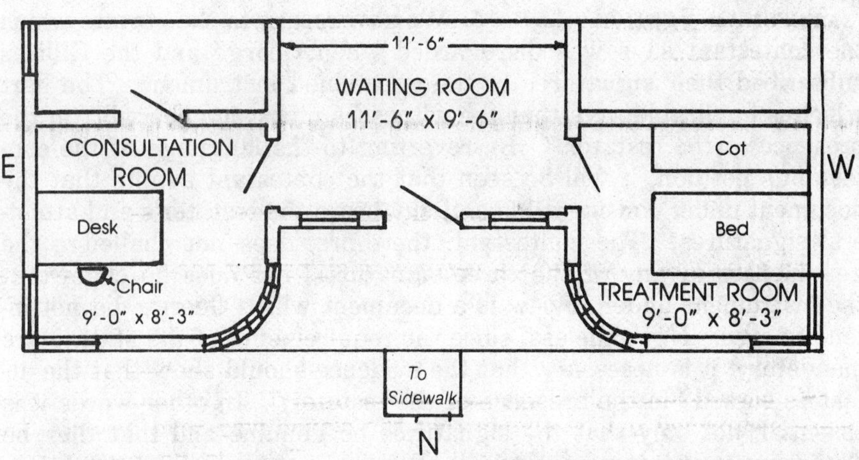

George was placed upon the bed in the treatment room with his head towards the west. At George's request, Dr. Gillis drafted a will which left all of George's property to a sister, Ida Fuller. This will was typed by Dr. Gillis upon a single piece of paper while sitting at his desk in the consultation room. As Dr. Gillis was typing the will, he was visible to a number of George's brothers and sisters who were in the waiting room and requested information from them concerning the spelling of the name "Demaris" and the address of Ida Fuller. Dr. Gillis then carried the will into the treatment room, explained its contents to George and, in a voice audible to the relatives in the waiting room, asked George to sign the instrument. Mrs. Gillis, the wife of Dr. Gillis, was in the treatment room and saw George sign. Dr. Gillis and Mrs. Gillis then returned to the consultation room. The doors to the treatment room and consultation room were open. Dr. Gillis requested Mrs. Gillis to sign the will as a witness. Mrs. Gillis signed the will while standing on the south side of the desk where she would have been visible to George had he looked. Dr. Gillis then signed the will as a witness while seated in his chair at his desk. He was visible to the relatives in the waiting room but was not visible to George. Dr. Gillis placed the will in his desk drawer after signing it. Several days later, George asked Mrs. Gillis if the Doctor had the will and if it was in a place of safekeeping. He also asked Mrs. Gillis if she had witnessed the will. When Mrs Gillis said that she had, George replied: "Yes, I thought you did", and also, "I know Doc did." He did not ask to see the will.

George died on 11 April, 1939. His will was offered for probate by Ida Fuller. Probate of the will was contested by Amos Demaris, the father and heir at law of George. Amos died a short time after the contest was instituted and was succeeded by his son, Arch Demaris, as his executor. One ground of contest was that the will had not been signed by Dr. Gillis in the presence of the testator as required by the Oregon statute. The lower court dismissed the contest. The contestant appeals. Certain additional facts are stated in that part of the opinion of the court which follows.]

ROSSMAN, JUSTICE. * * * We now return to the statute which the contestant says was disregarded when George and the Gillises subscribed their signatures to the questioned instrument. The part which is applicable says that the witnesses must sign the will "in the presence of the testator." By reverting to the language of the contestant's petition, it will be seen that the contestant admits that the document under consideration actually bears the testator's and attesters' signatures. The contestant, therefore, does not challenge the genuineness of any of the three signatures, nor does he claim that the instrument under review is a document which George did not intend to sign. Nevertheless, since the requirements of the statute are mandatory, it is necessary that the evidence should show that the attesters signed "in the presence of the testator." In other words it is essential, not only that the signatures be genuine and that they be found upon an instrument which all three persons intended to sign, but also that the attesters signed in the testator's presence. We shall shortly take note of the reason for the requirement.

The admissions made by the contestant are well justified by the facts. It will be recalled that Mrs. Kelly said that she was alongside the bed within arm's reach of her brother's hand when he signed the will. Harold Biggs, Arch Demaris and the latter's wife described the execution of a paper by George which, it develops, was his will. This is, therefore, a case in which the signatures of all three people are not only admitted, but were made under the very noses of the contestant, his wife, his sister and the latter's employee. Since the will was written upon a single sheet of paper, and since Mrs. Kelly took such careful note of her brother's act in signing the will that she was in a position to comment upon the peculiar slant of the letters, the circumstances afforded no opportunity for the substitution of a spurious copy. Indeed, no one even intimates that a substitution took place. This is a case in which (1) the will was typed in the presence of the contestant and of his witnesses, one of whom says she helped the draftsman by spelling for him the name of the testator; and (2) the will after being typed, was carried by the draftsman openly into the room of the testator where in a voice loud enough to be heard not only by the testator but also by those in the waiting room, he presented it to the testator for his approval and signature.

The meaning of the phrase "in the presence of the testator" has been the subject of much controversy and diversity of opinion. Decisions directly opposite to one another can be readily found. Some of the decisions restrict a testator to his sense of sight in ascertaining whether his attesting witnesses are in his presence when they sign. They hold that if he and the attesters are in the same room all are prima facie in each other's presence, but if the attesting signatures are written in another room, then prima facie the statutory requirement was violated. If a counterpane stretched between the bedposts, to shield the testator from drafts, is between him and the attesters, the attestation is invalid. Reed v. Roberts, 26 Ga. 294, 71 Am.Dec. 210. These strict interpretation courts go further. For instance, in Re Beggans' Will, 68 N.J.Eq. 572, 59 A. 874, and Graham v. Graham, 32 N.C. 219, the courts held that before a finding could be authorized that the attesting witnesses signed in the testator's presence it must appear, not only that the testator could have seen them sign had he chosen to look but that he did actually see the will and the writing of the signatures as the attestation took place. Burney v. Allen, 125 N. C. 314, 34 S.E. 500, 502, 74 Am.St.Rep. 637, represents a slight restriction upon the interpretation just noticed. The court there merely demanded proof that the testator could have seen had he cared to look. It said: "He must have the opportunity, through the evidence of occular observation, to see the attestation." It took pains to point out, however, that if illness rendered it impossible or dangerous for the testator to move his head in order to watch the attesting witnesses, the attestation would be deemed invalid. It will be observed that those courts insist upon the sight test as the medium to be employed in determining the validity of the attestation. Many other decisions to like effect appear in the reports. The courts which insist upon the sight test disregard all others. * * *

The strict interpretation states, confining as they do the test of presence to the element of vision, experience difficulty in determining what the testator must see when he looks. One of the decisions, Graham v. Graham, 32 N.C. 219, which is typical of many others, holds that a view of the attesters' backs is not sufficient; the testator must be able to see the hands and forearms and the paper itself. * * *

The same courts which insist upon the sight test employ a different one—mental apprehension—when they deal with a blind man's will. They hold that if the blind person's intellect and hearing are good and if he is conscious of what is going on around him, attestation made within range of his senses of touch and hearing is valid. See, for instance, In re Allred's Will, 170 N.C. 153, 86 S.E. 1047, L.R. A.1916C, 946, Ann.Cas.1916D, 788.

Other courts adopt a liberal point of view. They speak of the circumstances of the individual case and of the purpose of the statute. One decision says: "This requisite of the statute is designed to prevent substitution and fraud upon an intending testator." In re Beggans' Will, supra (68 N.J.Eq. 572, 59 A. 874). Our court has spoken to like effect in Re Estate of Shaff, 125 Or. 288, 266 P. 630, 632: "The reason of the rule, as before remarked, is to obviate any opportunity of the witnesses committing a fraud upon the testator by changing or altering the document." * * *

The liberal interpretation courts apply to all attestations the test which is employed in strict interpretation jurisdictions to the wills of the blind only: the mental apprehension or conscious presence test. * * * Its essence is thus stated in Healey v. Bartlett, 73 N.H. 110, 59 A. 617, 618, 6 Ann.Cas. 413. "When a testator is not prevented by physical infirmities from seeing and hearing what goes on around him, it is the general, if not the universal rule that his will is attested in his presence, if he understands and is conscious of what the witnesses are doing when they write their names and can, if he is so disposed, readily change his position so that he can see and hear what they do and say. * * * In other words, if he has knowledge of their presence, and can, if he is so disposed, readily see them write their names, the will is attested in his presence, even if he does not see them do it, and could not without some slight physical exertion. It is not necessary that he should actually see the witnesses for them to be in his presence. They are in his presence whenever they are so near him that he is conscious of where they are and of what they are doing, through any of his senses, and are where he can readily see them if he is so disposed. The test, therefore, to determine whether the will of a person who has the use of all his faculties is attested in his presence, is to inquire whether he understood what the witnesses were doing when they affixed their names to his will, and could, if he had been so disposed, readily have seen them do it." * * *

We are, of course, satisfied that the attestation must occur in the presence of the testator and that no substitution for the statutory requirement is permissible. But we do not believe that sight is the only test of presence. We are convinced that any of the senses that a testator possesses, which enable him to know whether another is near at hand and what he is doing, may be employed by him in determining whether attesters are in his presence as they sign his will. Had George been suddenly stricken blind instead of having become afflicted with an abdominal illness, the circumstances determining whether the attestation took place in his presence would have been no different. It is unnecessary, we believe, that the attestation and execution occur in the same room. And, as just stated, it is unnecessary that the attesters be within the range of vision of the testator when they sign. If they are so near at hand that they are within the range of any of his senses, so that he knows what is going on, the requirement has been met.

At least one of the objects of the statute was served in the present instance; that is, two disinterested persons were brought to the testator's bedside to be present while he executed his will. When two disinterested persons, who later tell the truth, are present, the testator has been afforded in our opinion, the best protection against fraud that this statute is capable of yielding. As we have just said, as a result of the demands of this statute, Dr. Gillis and his wife came to George's bedside at the time when he signed. Later, one of the two signed her signature to the will within the testator's range of vision, voice and hearing. All that George had to do to see Mrs. Gillis sign was to look through the two doors which were in alignment between himself and her. A glance would enable him to see Mrs. Gillis, including her hand, while she wrote her signature. It should not be inferred that George was incapable of moving or sitting up; he could do either without assistance. Since the floor covering in all three rooms was linoleum, it seems fair to assume that footsteps in any of the rooms could be easily heard by the testator. The other attesting witness, like Mrs. Gillis, was within 20 feet of George's hand when the attesting signature was written. It is no misstatement of the fact to say that both witnesses were within the immediate nearness and vicinity of the testator. Although Dr. Gillis was not within George's range of vision, he was within his range of voice and hearing. These three small rooms, if combined, would make nothing more than one room of fair length but of narrow width. Present at the time were some of George's brothers, sisters and other relatives. Although George had not told them that the instrument under preparation was his will, he was surely justified in believing that they would not be entirely inattentive to his interests. Those are circumstances which can properly be considered, we believe, in determining whether Dr. Gillis signed in the presence of George. When the doctor signed he was within direct sight and almost within arm's reach of the relatives who were seated upon the waiting room davenport. Since much that was said about the preparation of the paper was heard by those who were in these small rooms, we feel justified in assuming that Dr. Gillis was within the range of George's voice when he signed. These circumstances, together with the fact that both of the Gillises throughout the entire evening were frequently in George's room and were available at all times at his beck and call, convince us that they were in his presence at the time when they signed their attesting signatures.

The question occurs whether George was conscious of the fact that Dr. and Mrs. Gillis were signing their attesting signatures at the moment when they wrote them. Consciousness of the fact that the attesting signatures are being written is an indispensable element of the conscious presence rule. In determining whether George was aware of the fact that the signatures were being written, we may properly take into consideration, we believe, the fact that he had asked that the will be prepared, and that both of the Gillises were present when he signed. Undoubtedly, the request for the preparation of a will, under the circumstances disclosed by the record, carried with it an implied request for an attestation. Therefore, since Dr. Gillis' wife was present with her husband at the moment when George signed, he must have known that those two persons would shortly sign as attesters. We may also take into consideration the fact that two or three days later, while referring to the attestation of the will, he said, "I know that Doc did." Just before making that remark he was assured that Mrs. Gillis had signed and that, in compliance with his request, the will had been deposited in a safe repository. As previously stated, Mrs. Gillis was within the direct range of George's vision when she signed. It seems safe to infer that in a small space of the kind with which we are concerned the attention of a testator, who had just signed a will, would be attracted when he saw his two attesting witnesses go into an office room and there, taking pen in hand, proceed to use it. George lay upon his back at least a part of the time that evening. These circumstances persuade us that George was conscious of the attestation when it took place.

We realize that in having reached these conclusions we have gone as far as any of the precedents. But the circumstances repel any thought of fraud and speak cogently of the integrity of the instrument under review. * * *

In conclusion, we express the belief that if Dr. Gillis and his wife failed to comply with the strict letter of the statute when they attested the will, they, nevertheless, substantially complied with its requirements. To hold otherwise would be to observe the letter of the statute as interpreted strictly, and fail to give heed to the statute's obvious purpose. Thus, the statute would be turned against those for whose protection it had been written. The circuit court in sustaining the will, committed no error. The evidence reviewed above convinces us, as it did the trial judge, that the testator knew the contents of the will before he signed it, and further, that if he did not know the identity of both attesters at the moment when he signed, he discovered the name of the unfamiliar one two or three days later and then expressed his approval.

The above disposes of all issues presented by the contestant. The circumstances, therefore, afford no occasion for an expression of our view upon other matters.

The decree of the circuit court is affirmed.

KELLY, C. J., and RAND and BELT, JJ., concur.

BAILEY, J., dissents.

BEAN and LUSK, JJ., took no part in this decision.

NOTE

All of the courts agree that "consciousness" and "proximity" are elements of "presence". The Oregon definition of "proximity" is a minority position.[68]

"Presence" may appear in a wills act several times. The testator must sign or acknowledge in the *presence* of witnesses and the witnesses must attest in the *presence* of the testator. A proxy signature must usually be made in the testator's *presence*.[69] A number of wills acts require the witnesses "present at the same time" when the testator signs or acknowledges[70] and others require the witnesses to sign in "the presence of each other".[71] The problems involved in determining presence are the same in each instance.

68. See, Atkinson, Wills (2d Ed., 1953) § 72; 2 Bowe-Parker: Page, Wills (3d Ed., Rev.1960) §§ 19.119–126. Rollison, Wills (1939) § 99; Thompson, Wills (3d Ed. 1947) §§ 130, 131; Evans, "Incidents of Testamentary Execution", 16 Ky.L.J. 199, 200–203 (1928); Smith, "Attestation of Wills—An Examination of Some Problem Areas" 11 South Texas L.J. 125 (1969); Winston, "Attestation in the Presence of the Testator", 2 Va.L.Rev. 403 (1915); 27 Ky.L.J. 447 (1939); 16 U. of Detroit L.J. 38 (1952).

69. See Section 6(1)A, fn. 76, supra; 75 A.L.R.2d 318 (1961).

70. New Jersey, Rhode Island, Virginia, West Virginia and England. Rees, "American Wills Statutes", 46 Va.L.Rev. 613, 620 (1960). Under such a provision the witnesses are not required to sign in the presence of each other. Goods of Webb, 1 Deane 1, 164 Eng.Rep. 483 (1855); In re Cook's Estate, 118 N.J.Eq. 288, 179 A. 259, 99 A.L.R. 551 (1935); Parramore v. Taylor, 11 Gratt. (Va.) 220 (1854). Problems raised by the sequence of witnesses' signatures under statutes containing this provision are considered in subsection (5), infra.

71. Iowa, South Carolina, Tennessee, Utah, Vermont, West Virginia and Wisconsin. See Rees, "American Wills Statutes", 46 Va.L.Rev. 613, 624 (1960).

If the statute provides that the witnesses must sign in the presence of the testator (or in the presence of each other) and the witness signs outside the presence of the testator and later acknowledges his signature to the testator, the attempted acknowledgment is generally held to be insufficient.[72] Note that Section 2–502 of the Uniform Probate Code does not require signature of the witnesses in the presence of the testator or of each other; each witness could sign separately and out of the presence of the testator. (Could a witness sign after the death of the testator under such a statute?)[73]

---

72. See 2 Bowe-Parker: Page, Wills (3d Ed., Rev. 1960) § 19.127. In a few cases the witness has been permitted to acknowledge his signature. E.g. Sturdivant v. Birchett, 51 Va. (10 Gratt.) 67 (1853). The British Law Reform Committee also has recommended that the Wills Act, 1837, be amended to permit the witness to acknowledge his signature, this as a result of *Re Colling* [1972] 1 W.L.R. 1440. The Wills Act, 1837, is construed to require both witnesses to subscribe after the operative signature or acknowledgment by the testator. See Subdivision (5) this Section. In *Colling* one witness left before the testator completed his signature but the other witness then signed the will. When the witness returned the testator acknowledged his signature to both witnesses and the witness who signed acknowledged his signature to the testator and to the returning witness but did not sign again. The will was held invalid, the witness who first signed not being permitted to acknowledge his signature. The change recommended by the Law Reform Committee would permit the witness to acknowledge his signature to the testator as well as to the other witness. Cmd., 7902, Par. 2.11.

73. The Real Property Commissioners, whose report formed the basis for the Wills Acts, 1837, recommended that the witnesses not be required to sign in the presence of the testator. The requirement was inserted in the Wills Act, 1837, in the process of passage. The purpose of requiring the witnesses to sign in the presence of the testator probably was to prevent witnesses from substituting a spurious will. See Lord Langdale's presentation of the bill to the House of Lords, 36 Hansard 975–76 (23 Feb. 1837). If a Wills Act does not require the witnesses to sign in the presence of the testator, the execution process tends to become disjointed and casual, there being a tendency to circulate the will from hand to hand for the witnesses' signatures with the consequence that the testator fails to sign the will or acknowledge his signature in the presence of the witnesses with results fatal to the will. Even the presence requirement for the signatures of witnesses does not always avoid a degree of looseness in the execution of wills in busy law offices which in some instances result in failures to satisfy the presence requirement. For example, in Matter of Will of Jefferson, 349 So.2d 1032 (Miss. 1977) the attorney supervising the execution of the will signed as an attesting witness in the presence of the testator but then took the will to his law office where he had his partner sign as a witness, his partner calling the testator by telephone and asking the testator if in fact the instrument presented was his will. The Court applied a "sight test" and refused to probate the will. Suggestions have been made that the requirement that the testator sign the will in the presence of the witnesses also might be eliminated, but it is difficult to see why witnesses should be required if this is done. The Uniform Probate Code and a number of states have no requirement that the witnesses sign in the presence of the testator. The British Law Reform Committee recommended that the requirement that witnesses sign in the presence of the testator be continued in England, although without enthusiasm for the recommendation. Cmd. 7902, Par. 2.13.

(5) SEQUENCE OF SIGNING

The testator should sign the will before the witnesses sign. Although the witnesses sign first, by the weight of authority the attestation is effective if the testator and witnesses sign in one continuous transaction.[74] It is said that there is no true priority between acts that are substantially contemporaneous. There is also little chance of fraud. The English courts and some American courts take the position that the testator must sign first whether the signing is in one continuous transaction or not.[75]

The Wills Act, 1837,[76] states that the testator shall make or acknowledge his signature "in the presence of two or more witnesses present at the same time, and such witnesses *shall* attest and *shall* subscribe the will in the presence of the testator". [Italics added.] The English courts construe the words "shall" in this statute as words of futurity.[77] The witnesses are to attest and subscribe *after* the testator has signed or acknowledged. In applying the requirement that the witnesses be "present at the same time" it has been held that *both* witnesses must sign the will *after* the testator has signed or acknowledged in their mutual presence. Thus, if T signs in the presence of A, who signs as witness, and T then acknowledges the signature in the presence of B and A, not only must B sign, but A must sign again in order to validate the will.[78] Only one American court appears to have adopted the English construction for the purpose of applying the "present at the same time" requirement.[79] On the other hand, the minority American position that the signature of the testator must precede that of the witnesses has a sound basis in theory. If the signature is the thing attested by the witnesses, as required by statutes patterned upon the Wills Act, 1837, the witness-

74. E.g., Gordon v. Parker, 139 Miss. 334, 104 So. 77, 39 A.L.R. 931 (1925). See Atkinson, Wills (2d Ed., 1953) § 71; 2 Bowe-Parker: Page, Wills (3d Ed., Rev. 1960) §§ 19.138, 19.139; Rollison, Wills (1939) § 113; Thompson, Wills (3d Ed., 1947) § 129; Evans, "Incidents of Testamentary Execution", 16 Ky.L.J. 199, 203 (1928); Smith, "Attestation of Wills—An Examination of Some Problem Areas", 11 South Texas L.J. 125 (1969); 39 A.L.R. 933 (1925); 91 A.L.R.2d 737 (1963).

75. E.g., Goods of Olding, 2 Curt.Ecc. 865, 163 Eng.Rep. 611 (1841); Re Colling [1972] 1 W.L.R. 1440; Marshall v. Mason, 176 Mass. 216, 57 N.E. 340, 79 Am.St. Rep. 305 (1900). The will is invalid in all jurisdictions if the testator signs after the witnesses sign in a different transaction. E.g., Duffie v. Corridon, 40 Ga. 122 (1869). The witnesses cannot acknowledge their signatures when the testator signs in order to cure the fatal defect. Hindmarsh v. Charlton, 8 H.L.C. 160, 11 Eng.Rep. 388 (1861). The recommendation of the British Law Reform Committee that a witness be permitted to acknowledge his signature would go far towards eliminating the "sequence of signatures" problem under the English statute. Cmd. 7902, Par. 2.11.

76. 7 Wm. IV & 1 Vict., c. 26 (1837).

77. E.g., Goods of Allen, 2 Curt.Ecc. 331, 163 Eng.Rep. 429 (1839).

78. E.g., Goods of Simmonds, 3 Curt. Ecc. 79, 163 Eng.Rep. 661 (1842); Wyatt v. Berry, L.R. [1893] Prob. 5; Hindmarsh v. Charlton, 8 H.L.C. 160, 11 Eng.Rep. 388 (1861).

79. Will of Sutterlin, 99 N.J.Eq. 363, 132 A. 115 (1926). Contra, Parramore v. Taylor, 11 Gratt. (Va.) 220 (1854).

es cannot very well attest until the signature is made. If the will is the thing attested, as seems to be required by statutes patterned upon the Statute of Frauds, 1677, it can be argued that there is no legal act to be attested until the testator has signed the will, even though the witnesses are not required to see the signature of the testator when they subscribe the will.[80]

PROBLEM

A will was signed by three witnesses in T's presence. T failed to sign through error. On the next day, it was noticed that T had not signed the will. Two of the witnesses who had signed the will, and a third person who had not signed, were summoned to T's room to attest his signature. T signed in the presence of the three persons. The two witnesses who had subscribed on the previous day acknowledged their signatures to T. The third witness subscribed the instrument. The statute provides:

> "All wills, * * * disposing of realty or personalty must be in writing, signed by the party making the same, or by some other person in his presence and by his express direction, and shall be attested and subscribed in the presence of the testator by three or more competent witnesses."

Will or no will? See Duffie v. Corridon, 40 Ga. 122 (1869); Bloechle v. Davis, 132 Ohio St. 415, 8 N.E.2d 247 (1937); Moore v. King, 3 Curt.Ecc. 243, 163 Eng.Rep. 716 (1842); Hindmarsh v. Charlton, 8 H.L.C. 160, 11 Eng.Rep. 388 (1861).

(6) REQUEST TO WITNESSES

A request by the testator to the witnesses to attest and subscribe the will is required expressly by the statutes of a few states.[81] But even though no request is expressly called for by the wills act, a number of courts have stated that a request is required by implication.[82] These holdings appear to be based on the idea that attestation is necessarily by invitation, since otherwise any bystander could intervene to attest the will. Where the courts have stated that no request is required, it is probable that they mean that no formal request is necessary and that acquiescence by the testator in the attestation is sufficient.[83]

80. The arguments for the minority view are discussed in Atkinson, Wills, (2d Ed. 1953) 337; Evans, "Incidents of Testamentary Execution", 16 Ky.L.J. 199, 204 (1928).

81. E.g., Washington. See Rees, "American Wills Statutes", 46 Va.L.Rev. 613, 622–23 (1960); Atkinson, Wills (2d Ed., 1953) § 67; 2 Bowe-Parker: Page, Wills (3d Ed., Rev.1960) §§ 19.130–132.

82. E.g., Moore v. Sanders, 202 Ky. 286, 259 S.W. 361 (1924).

83. E.g., Ritchey v. Jones, 210 Ala. 204, 97 So. 736 (1923).

In the actual application of the "request" requirement, whether statutory or otherwise, the courts have been so liberal that few wills have been denied probate for lack of a request by the testator unless some mental or other incapacity has been manifest.[84] The request need not be by words. Gestures will suffice,[85] and a request by another is sufficient if the testator acquiesces.[86]

PROBLEM

T, in an oxygen tent, read carefully a will prepared for him by A. In the presence of A, B, C, and D, T signed the will. A then placed the will on a table near the foot of T's bed and pointed to a place on the will for B, C and D to sign as witnesses. B, C and D subscribed the will. Neither T nor A verbally requested the witnesses to attest. T seemed mentally alert when the witnesses subscribed. The statute does not expressly require a request by the testator to witnesses to attest and subscribe. Will or no will? Look v. French, 346 Mo. 972, 144 S.W.2d 128 (1940).

(7) INTENTION TO ATTEST

Attestation means bearing witness to the satisfaction of certain requirements for an effective will.[87] Subscription is an act certifying that attestation has occurred.[88] It is required generally that a witness must have the *animus attestandi* or intention to attest when he subscribes the will.[89] The courts have had difficulty in defining precisely what is being required as an intention to attest, but most of the courts appear to be satisfied if a witness signed with the intention to give the document legal effect by virtue of his signature.[90]

84. E.g., In re Lyman's Will, 14 Misc. 352, 36 N.Y.S. 117 (1895) (influence of drugs); In re Cummings' Estate, 92 Mont. 185, 11 P.2d 968 (1932) (mental incapacity).

85. E.g., In re Davis' Will, 172 Or. 354, 142 P.2d 143 (1943) (T handed pen to witness).

86. E.g., Clark v. Crandall, 319 Mo. 87, 5 S.W.2d 383 (1928).

87. For these matters, see Section 6(3), supra.

88. Most of the wills acts require attestation and subscription. Where only the word "attest" and not the word "subscribe" appear in the wills act, the witness is usually required to sign the will. Rees, "American Wills Statutes", 46 Va. L.Rev. 613, 622 (1960).

89. E.g., Baxter v. Bank of Belle, 340 Mo. 952, 104 S.W.2d 265 (1937), 2 Mo.L. Rev. 532 (1937).

90. There has been much discussion of the difference between attestation and subscription in relation to the requirement of *animus attestandi*. The play on words and the choice of *animus attestandi* to describe what is required of the witness is unfortunate. A witness to a will does a number of distinct things. There are a series of mental acts in which the witness observes events occurring when the will is executed, evaluates these events, and attempts to square up his evaluation with the legal standards that he thinks he is to apply. He also signs the will, but his signature reveals nothing of his prior mental processes. All his signature reveals is that the witness was around when the will was signed or acknowledged, although the

The intention of the witness is determined by the attending circumstances and his objective manifestations at the time of signing. If a witness is requested to sign by the testator, and does sign below an attestation clause, he will not be heard to deny that he lacked the intention to attest.[91]

A person may believe that he is signing in a capacity other than as witness, but he may be counted as a witness if he intends to give the document legal effect by his signature. Thus, a person who signs in an official capacity as justice of the peace,[92] notary public[93] or vice consul,[94] or who signs as executor,[95] scrivener[96] or proxy[97] but who also intends to give the document legal effect by his signature, can be used as an attesting witness when that is necessary.[98]

PROBLEM

T, physically weak and confined to his bed, dictated his will to N, a notary public. N prepared the will and added below the place intended for T's mark a certificate to be executed by him as notary public. The certificate stated that T made his mark to the will because he was unable to write his name due to nervousness. T made his mark in the presence of N and A. He did not make his mark in the presence of B who had been called as a witness, nor did he acknowledge the will in the presence of B. N signed the notarial certificate and A and B signed as witnesses. The applicable statute requires that T make his signature or acknowledge the will in the presence of two or more competent witnesses. Will or no will? See Ferguson v. Ferguson, 187 Va. 581, 47 S.E.2d 346 (1948); French v. Beville, 191 Va. 842, 62 S.E.2d 883 (1951); Parham, "Execution of Wills in Virginia", 34 Va.L.Rev. 726, 739 (1948). Accord: In re Montgomery's Estate, 89 Cal.App.2d 664, 201 P.2d 569 (1949); Contra: Baxter v. Bank of Belle of Belle Maries County, 340 Mo. 952, 104 S.W.2d 265 (1935); Matter of McDonough's Estate, 201 App.Div. 203, 193 N.Y.S. 734 (1922).

court may make certain assumptions of fact based upon the signature, particularly when the signature follows an attestation clause. The only way that the subjective action of the witness can be ascertained is to have him give testimony when the will is offered for probate. On the other hand, even though the witnesses do not testify at probate, their signatures are given considerable weight as evidence, not necessarily because the signatures are an iron-clad guarantee that all the formalities of execution were accomplished, but because they give some assurance that enough people were around to discourage fraud or undue influence that might be practiced on the testator at the time of execution. This, after all, is one of the major objectives of the wills acts. If it is shown that these signatures were made with serious intent as part of the execution process, the *animus attestandi* seems to be present.

91. Tilton v. Daniels, 79 N.H. 368, 109 A. 145, 8 A.L.R. 1073 (1920).

92. Tilton v. Daniels, fn. 91, supra.

93. E.g., Tyson v. Utterback, 154 Miss. 381, 122 So. 496, 63 A.L.R. 1188 (1929).

94. Keely v. Moore, 196 U.S. 38, 25 S. Ct. 169, 49 L.Ed. 376 (1904).

95. Griffiths v. Griffiths, L.R. 2 P. & D. 300 (1871).

96. Pollock v. Glassell, 2 Gratt. (Va.) 439 (1846).

97. E.g., Darnaby v. Halley's Executor, 306 Ky. 697, 208 S.W.2d 299 (1948).

98. In any of these cases the signer may not intend to give the will legal force and effect and therefore not qualify as a witness. E.g., In re Jones' Estate, 101 Wash. 128, 172 P. 206 (1918) (Proxy); In re Hull's Will, 117 Iowa 738, 89 N.W. 979 (1902) (Notary). See generally, Atkinson, Wills (2d Ed., 1953) § 69; 2 Bowe-Parker: Page, Wills (3d Ed., Rev. 1960) §§ 19.74, 19.129.

(8) SIGNATURE BY WITNESSES

There is no requirement by a majority of the wills acts that the witnesses sign at any particular place on the will, although a particular wills act may require expressly signing "at the end" or the word "subscribe" may be construed to this effect.[99] The witnesses should sign beneath the attestation clause, or should sign to the left of the testator's signature if no attestation clause is used.

The form of signature required for witnesses is usually the same as that required for the testator.[1] Where the wills acts require the witness to "sign his name" there is conflict whether a mark or the name of another is a sufficient signature. By the better view, a signature by mark is sufficient and the name of another may be regarded as a mark if intended as the signature of the witness.[2]

Some courts have held that the witness must sign the will personally since the wills acts make no provision for a signature by the witness by proxy.[3] A signature by assistance is a signature by the witness. The majority position appears to be that a witness may sign by proxy, just as a principal may have his agent sign for him.[4]

Tenn case

PROBLEM

A and B appeared to witness T's will. B was accompanied by Mrs. B. A subscribed the will as witness. B, who was illiterate, requested Mrs. B to sign his name for him. This Mrs. B did in the presence of B, A and T. The statute requires that the will be attested and subscribed by two competent witnesses and makes no provision for a proxy signature. Will or no will? Goods of Duggins, 39 L.P.J. 24, 22 L.T.R. 182 (1870); Simmons v. Leonard, 91 Tenn. 183, 18 S.W. 280, 30 Am.St.Rep. 875 (1892). Contra: Schnee v. Schnee, 61 Kan. 643, 60 P. 738 (1900); In re Crawford's Will, 46 S.C. 299, 24

99. Signing by the witnesses at the end of the will is required in Arkansas, California, New York, Oklahoma, and South Dakota, Rees, "American Wills Statutes", 46 Va.L.Rev. 613, 623 (1960). In Owens v. Bennett, 5 Harr. (Del.) 367 (1852), the statute required the witnesses to attest and subscribe. It was held that the witnesses must sign at the end, but only the portion of the will following their signatures was invalid. In Soward v. Soward, 1 Duv. (Ky.) 126 (1863) the witnesses were required to subscribe the will. It was held that a gap of two pages between the testator's signature and the witnesses' signatures was not a signing at the end. See Potter v. Ritchardson, 360 Mo. 661, 230 S.W.2d 672 (1950); 10 A.L.R. 429 (1921); 17 A.L.R.3d 705 (1968).

1. See Atkinson, Wills (2d Ed., 1953) § 70; 2 Bowe-Parker: Page, Wills (3d Ed., Rev.1960) §§ 19.133, 19.134, 19.135, 19.136.

2. See 2 Bowe-Parker: Page, Wills (3d Ed., Rev.1960) §§ 19.133, 19.134. If the witness signs the name of another as his signature, he must make the signature with the requisite intent to give the document legal effect.

3. E.g., Simmons v. Leonard, 91 Tenn. 183, 18 S.W. 280, 30 Am.St.Rep. 875 (1892).

4. E.g., Schnee v. Schnee, 61 Kan. 643, 60 P. 738 (1900); In re Crawford's Will, 46 S.C. 299, 24 S.E. 69, 32 L.R.A. 77 (1896).

S.E. 69, 32 L.R.A. 77 (1895); Jesse v. Parker's Administrators, 6 Gratt. (Va.) 57, 52 Am.Dec. 102 (1849).

---

(9) ACKNOWLEDGMENT (SELF-PROVING)

ESTATE OF MACKABEN

Court of Appeals of Arizona, 1980.
126 Ariz. 599, 617 P.2d 765.

HATHAWAY, CHIEF JUDGE.

This is an appeal from orders refusing to admit to probate the purported self-proved will of Bertha Viola Mackaben, dated October 1, 1975, or to grant proponent a new trial. We affirm.

Bertha Viola Mackaben died on May 16, 1979. John P. Sullivan, named in her will as personal representative, offered the document for probate. Eugene Mackaben, decedent's son, filed a contest, alleging undue influence and lack of testamentary capacity.

The contestant was permitted at trial, over objection, to amend his pleadings to introduce the issue that the will had not been executed in accordance with Arizona law. The trial court found in favor of contestant on the latter issue and ruled accordingly in orders merged in the court's order of December 28, 1979. The proponent's motion for a new trial was denied on January 3, 1980.

The decedent's grandchildren, Alice J. Busse, Thomas B. Olson, John Henry Olson, and William E. Olson, filed a petition to vacate orders denying probate of the will and secured an order to show cause why the relief requested should not be granted. Their petition was heard on January 28, 1980, and was ultimately dismissed by the trial court.

The document in question is entitled:

"LAST WILL AND TESTAMENT OF
BERTHA V. MACKABEN"

It is in writing and bears the signature of the testatrix at the bottom of the first and second pages, at the end of the will, and in the self-proving affidavit. It bears the signatures of two witnesses at the end of the will and in the affidavit. The will is dated October 1, 1975, as is the affidavit, which was signed, sealed and stamped with the notary's expiration stamp. The affidavit is in the form then required by A.R.S. Sec. 14–2504, subsequently amended to specifically provide that a will may be simultaneously executed, attested, and made self-proved. The will does not contain an attestation clause preceding the self-proving affidavit. To better visualize the execution portion of the will, it is set forth here:

"IN WITNESS WHEREOF I have hereunto set my hand this 1 day of October, 1975.

/s/ Bertha V. Mackaben
Bertha V. Mackaben—Testatrix
/s/ William A. Carnes III, Tucson, Arizona
/s/ Marcia L. Young, Tucson, Arizona

"STATE OF ARIZONA)
) ss.
COUNTY OF PIMA)

We, Bertha V. Mackaben, William A. Carnes, and Marcia L. Young, the Testatrix and the witnesses, respectively, whose names are signed to the attached or foregoing instrument, being first duly sworn, do hereby declare to the undersigned authority that the Testatrix signed and executed the instrument as her Last Will and that she had signed willingly or directed another to sign for her, and that she executed it as her free and voluntary act for the purposes therein expressed, and that each of the witnesses, in the presence and hearing of the Testatrix, signed the Will as witness and that to the best of his knowledge the Testatrix was at that time eighteen or more years of age, of sound mind, and under no constraint or undue influence.

/s/ Bertha V. Mackaben
Bertha V. Mackaben—Testatrix
/s/ William A. Carnes III, Tucson, Arizona
/s/ Marcia L. Young, Tucson, Arizona

SUBSCRIBED AND SWORN to before me this 1 day of October, 1975.

/s/ Denise Boas
Notary Public

My commission expires:

My Commission Expires Mar. 3, 1977"

Over objection by proponent, the notary and witnesses to the will testified as to details surrounding the signing of the will. Each identified his or her signature and initials on the will. Neither witness remembered signing the will and the notary had no recollection of Mrs. Mackaben coming in, except that the notary did remember taking the will to the witnesses to initial and for signature. Apparently after the testatrix had either signed the will or acknowledged her signature, the notary notarized it and then took it to the adjacent desks of the witnesses to have them initial and sign as witnesses to the will.

The trial court found that the instrument was not entitled to probate for the reason that:

"* * * [T]he Proponent, John P. Sullivan, has failed to sustain his burden of proof that the instrument was '* * * signed by at least two persons each of whom witnessed either the signin [sic] of [sic] the Testator's acknowledgement of the signature or of the Will, * * * "

The formalities required in the execution of wills are set forth in A.R.S. Sec. 14–2502, which provides:

"Except as provided for holographic wills, writings within Sec. 14–2513 and wills within Sec. 14–2506, every will shall be in writing signed by the testator or in the testator's name by some other person in the testator's presence and by his direction, and shall be signed by at least two persons each of whom witnessed either the signing or the testator's acknowledgment of the signature or of the will."

See Estate of Brashear, 54 Ariz. 430, 96 P.2d 747 (1939).

Appellants first argue on appeal that proponent sustained his burden of proof as a matter of law when he filed the self-proved will with acknowledgments and affidavits appurtenant. It is their position that the signature requirements for execution are conclusively presumed under A.R.S. Sec. 14–3406, which provides in part:

"Formal testacy proceedings; contested cases; testimony of attesting witnesses

* * *

B. If the will is self-proved, compliance with signature requirements for execution is conclusively presumed and other requirements of execution are presumed subject to rebuttal without the testimony of any witness upon filing the will and the acknowledgment and affidavits annexed or attached thereto, unless there is proof of fraud or forgery affecting the acknowledgment or affidavit."

We agree with appellants' premise that a self-proved will may not be contested in regard to signature requirements. The difficulty with appellant's position is that the offered document does not meet the self-proved requirements. All authority that has come to our attention on the subject requires that the formal requisites for execution of the will, A.R.S. Sec. 14–2502, supra, appear either preceding the self-proving affidavit or as supplemented in the affidavit. Cases taking the former view are, Matter of Estate of Sample, 572 P.2d 1232 (Mont.1977); Matter of Estate of McDougal, 552 S.W.2d 587 (Tex.Civ.App.1977); Boren v. Boren, 402 S.W.2d 728 (Tex.1966), and McGrew v. Bartlett, 387 S.W.2d 702 (Tex.Civ.App.1965). Taking a more liberal approach allowing proof of attestation to be supplemented in the affidavit is In re Estate of Charry, 359 So.2d 544 (Fla.App. 1978).

The comment to Sec. 2–502 of the Uniform Probate Code provides:

"The formalities for execution of a witnessed will have been reduced to a minimum. Execution under this section normally would be accomplished by signature of the testator and of two witnesses; each of the persons signing as witnesses must 'witness' any of the following: the signing of the will by the testator,

an acknowledgment by the testator that the signature is his, or an acknowledgment by the testator that the document is his will. * * *"

The execution of the will in the instant case does not contain an attestation clause disclosing that the formality of A.R.S. Sec. 14–2502 was met. Nor does the self-proving affidavit disclose that the statutory formality was met in that it does not state that the testatrix signed or acknowledged her signature or the will in the presence of the witnesses. The attempt to self-prove the will was therefore deficient. Testimony from the witnesses did not reveal statutory compliance and the trial court properly refused admission of the document to probate.

Affirmed.

HOWARD and RICHMOND, JJ., concur.[5]

NOTE

Section 2–504 of the Uniform Probate Code[6] provides alternatives for acknowledging the execution of the will before a notary public or other officer authorized to administer oaths. One method is to have the testator and the witnesses execute the will in the presence of the officer, who then completes the acknowledgment. This form is as follows:

> I, ______ the testator, sign my name to this instrument this ______ day of ______, 19__, and being first duly sworn, do hereby declare to the undersigned authority that I sign and execute this instrument as my last will and that I sign it willingly (or willingly direct another to sign for me), that I execute it as my free and voluntary act for the purposes therein expressed, and that I am eighteen years of age, or older, of sound mind, and under no constraint or undue influence.
>
> ______________
>
> Testator
>
> We, ______, ______, the witnesses, sign our names to this instrument, being first duly sworn, and do hereby declare to the undersigned authority that the testator signs and executes this instrument as his last will and that he signs it willingly (or willingly directs another to sign for him), and that each of us, in the presence and hearing of the testator, hereby signs this will as witness to the testator's signing, and that to the best of our knowledge the testator is eighteen years of age or older, of sound mind, and under no constraint or undue influence.
>
> ______________
>
> Witness
>
> ______________
>
> Witness

5. The decision is criticized in Effland, "Self-Proved Wills," 16 Ariz.B.J. 31 (1981).

6. See fn. 34, page 206, this Chapter where the Uniform Probate Code forms and their effect as intended by the Commissioners is discussed briefly.

The State of ______

County of ______

Subscribed, sworn to and acknowledged before me by ______, the testator and subscribed and sworn to before me by ______ and ______, witnesses, this ______ day of ______.

(SEAL) (Signed) ______________________

____

(Official capacity of officer)

The second of the forms set forth in Section 2–504 is the form used in the principal case. Either will is called "self-proved" under the Code. Some states which have not adopted the Code have a provision similar to the second method for a separate acknowledgement or affidavit.[7]

Theoretically the advantage of the self-proved will under the Uniform Probate Code is that no proof as to execution is required after the testator's death, even in the event of a will contest.[8] Unfortunately, some courts as in the principal case are willing to go behind the sworn affidavits and acknowledgment. It should be noted that under the Uniform Probate Code a will with only an attestation clause (not self-proved) can be informally probated without further proof of due execution,[9] and even in formal testacy proceedings proof is relatively simple if there is no contest. The sworn acknowledgment is therefore important only in event of contest or if the will must be probated in a non-Code state which lacks informal probate procedure but recognizes the sworn statements as proof of execution in a formal proceeding. One purpose of the affidavits is to eliminate the expense and delay of locating witnesses after the death of the testator in order to produce their testimony to prove the will.

In the principal case, how should the acknowledgment and affidavits have been worded to avoid the result?

(10) FORMALITIES NOT REQUIRED FOR ATTESTED WILLS

No state requires a seal, date, form of attestation or delivery, for an ordinary attested will.[10] A date should be placed on wills so that if two or more wills, each purporting to revoke all prior wills, are offered for probate, the will executed last in point of time can be determined without undue difficulty.

---

7. These statutes usually provide only for an affidavit of the attesting witnesses. E.g., Nev.Rev.Stat. § 133.050 (affidavit of witnesses written on the will or attached thereto). McKinney's N.Y., SPCA, § 1406 provides for use of an affidavit of the attesting witnesses, which may be made before as well as after the death of the testator; however, the affidavit cannot be accepted if any party objects, so it has value only in the uncontested probate. See the self-proved form used for the specimen will in Section 3(2) of this Chapter.

8. Uniform Probate Code § 3–406(b).

9. Uniform Probate Code § 3–303(c).

10. A seal is required in Louisiana for the execution of a "mystic" will. Rees, "American Wills Statutes", 46 Va.L.Rev. 613, 616 (1960).

(11) SAFEKEEPING OF THE EXECUTED WILL

The testator should be advised to keep the original of the executed will in a "safe" place (where it is unlikely to be lost, or destroyed by fire or by disappointed relatives). The options are: (1) the testator should keep the will in his safety deposit box; (2) the will should be turned over to and kept by the executor named in the will, particularly if the executor is a corporate fiduciary; (3) the will may be deposited with the local probate court in UPC states and other states having statutory provisions for such deposit during lifetime;[11] or (4) the original may be left with the drafting lawyer, and a copy given to the testator. Consider the disadvantages of all except the first in our highly mobile society. Although it has in the past been common practice in some localities for the attorney who drafts the will to suggest that the original be left with him for safekeeping, what are the ethical implications of such a practice? In State v. Gulbankian, 54 Wis.2d 605, 611, 196 N.W.2d 733, 736 (1972) the Supreme Court of Wisconsin disapproved this as a form of solicitation of business (the probate of the will after the testator's death):

> * * * Nor do we approve of attorneys' "safekeeping" wills. In the old days this may have been explained on the ground many people did not have a safe place to keep their valuable papers, but there is little justification today because most people do have safekeeping boxes, and if not, sec. 853.09, Stats., provides for the deposit of a will with the register in probate for safekeeping during the lifetime of the testator. The correct practice is that the original will should be delivered to the testator and should only be kept by the attorney upon specific unsolicited request of the client.

The testator should be cautioned about his making alterations in the will without legal advice (for reasons which will become obvious once the material on revocation in Chapter VI is studied) and informed about methods of revoking the will, again with suitable caution. If the will is kept in a safety deposit box, some states have statutes allowing access to the box to remove the will for probate.

SECTION 7. HOLOGRAPHIC WILLS

Holographic wills are valid in twenty-two states without attestation.[12] The absence of an attestation requirement in these states

11. Uniform Probate Code § 2-901; Wis.Stat.Ann. § 853.09.

12. Alaska, Arizona, Arkansas, California, Idaho, Kentucky, Louisiana, Ma-

eliminates most of the execution problems associated with ordinary attested wills. Unfortunately, however, much litigation is stimulated by other requirements for the execution of holographs, and the difficulty in integrating holographs at probate is particularly acute.[13]

The wills acts require that holographic wills be entirely in the handwriting of the testator.[14] If not entirely in the handwriting of the testator, the will must be attested like any other written will. Is this requirement to be taken literally? Suppose a will is written by the testator upon a printed form. Must the printed provisions be treated as part of the will even though the handwritten provisions are clear and complete? Some courts have ignored the printed provisions as surplusage when the handwritten provisions make sense without them.[15] Even when the printed provisions clouded or contradicted the meaning of the testator, some courts have held that they must be treated as part of the will if the testator intended them to be.[16] Under either view, printed letterheads or addresses which have no direct connection with the provisions in the will are ignored and will not destroy the holographic character of the instrument.[17]

Holographic wills are often found at the testator's death as a series of disconnected papers. The papers may appear to be the product of sporadic effort since there is no requirement that a holographic will be prepared on one day or in one transaction.[18] North Carolina requires that the will be found among the testator's valuable papers

ryland, Mississippi, Montana, Nevada, New York, North Carolina, North Dakota, Oklahoma, South Dakota, Tennessee, Texas, Utah, Virginia, West Virginia, Wyoming. Of these states the holographs permitted in New York and Maryland are for members of the armed forces only. Rees, "American Wills Statutes", 46 Va.L.Rev. 613, 634–636 (1960). See Atkinson, Wills (2d Ed., 1953) § 75; 2 Bowe-Parker: Page, Wills (3d Ed., Rev. 1960) §§ 20.1–20.11; Rollison, Wills (1939) § 171; Thompson, Wills (3d Ed., 1947) § 29; Hansen, "Holographic Wills", 95 Trusts and Estates 875 (1956), Bird, "Sleight of Handwriting: The Holographic Will in California", 32 Hastings L.J. 605 (1981).

13. See Mechem, "Integration of Holographic Wills", 2 N.C.L.Rev. 213 (1933); Closely related to the problem of integration is the issue of testamentary intent with respect to a particular writing. Was it a draft for some later instrument, perhaps only a letter stating what the writer was going to do in the future? These matters are discussed more fully in Chapter VII, Section 2(2).

14. The handwriting of the testator is thought to make the will relatively free from fraudulent alteration so that attesting witnesses need not be used. Uniform Probate Code, § 2–503 and Tenn.Code Ann. § 32–105 require the "material" provisions to be in the handwriting of the testator. The Uniform Probate Code adds that the signature also must be in his handwriting and this is a requirement that, if not mentioned specifically in the holographic will statute, is nevertheless implicit in a requirement that the will be entirely in the testator's handwriting.

15. E.g., In re Will of Parsons, 207 N.C. 584, 178 S.E. 78 (1935); 13 N.C.L.Rev. 524 (1935). The doctrine is called the "surplusage" theory. An integral part of the will cannot be rejected as surplusage. See Pounds v. Litaker, 235 N.C. 746, 71 S.E.2d 39 (1952) (monogram on letterhead cannot be signature of testator since it destroys holographic character); Bird, "Sleight of Handwriting: The Holographic Will in California", 32 Hastings L.J. 605 (1981). See 89 A.L.R.2d 1198 (1963).

16. E.g., In re Bowers' Estate, 11 Cal. 2d 180, 78 P.2d 1012 (1938); In re Wolcott's Estate, 54 Utah 165, 180 P. 169, 4 A.L.R. 727 (1919). The doctrine is called the "intent" theory.

17. E.g., In re Oldham's Estate, 203 Cal. 618, 265 P. 183 (1928); Estate of Lando, 7 Cal.App.3d 8, 86 Cal.Rptr. 443 (1970).

18. E.g., Succession of Cunningham, 142 La. 701, 77 So. 506 (1918).

at his death or have been delivered to another for safekeeping during the testator's lifetime.[19] The requirements in North Carolina provide criteria for integrating the instrument. Since attestation is not required, there is, of course, no requirement that the pages have been present when the witnesses signed the will. The proponent may be able to produce witnesses who can shed some light upon the execution of the will or identify particular pages, but this will be unusual since holographic wills are usually prepared in private.[20] Although the courts have been more liberal in admitting extrinsic evidence for the purpose of integrating holographs than they have for the purpose of integrating attested wills,[21] it is likely that the proponent will have to rely upon evidence appearing in the various pages because sufficient extrinsic evidence may be impossible to obtain. Elements of internal coherence in a holograph are often slight, the handwriting of the testator sometimes being the strongest evidence to support a page as part of the will.

The testator must sign the holograph personally.[22] An unsigned holograph is ineffective. The liberal rules applied to sustain signatures to attested wills apply to holographs so long as the signature is written by the testator.[23]

The wills acts that require attested wills to be signed "at the end" by the testator extend this requirement to holographs. The problems raised in applying this requirement are essentially the same as those raised by applying the requirement to attested wills, although it may be difficult to arrange the disconnected pages of a holograph in order to find the logical end of the will.[24] Where no place of signing is required, the signature may appear at any place on the will if proved by intrinsic or extrinsic evidence to be the signature intended by the testator. In Virginia and West Virginia, where the testator must sign his name "in such manner as to make it manifest that the name

19. N.C.Gen.Stat. § 31–3.4(3). Similar requirements were once made in Tennessee. See Northcross v. Taylor, 29 Tenn.App. 438, 197 S.W.2d 9 (1946); 19 Tenn.L.Rev. 856 (1947); Smith v. Smith, 33 Tenn.App. 507, 232 S.W.2d 338 (1949).

20. It will be necessary to call witnesses to identify the handwriting of the testator in any event. But these witnesses may derive their knowledge of the testator's handwriting from business transactions and have little knowledge concerning his personal arrangements for distributing his estate. On the issue of possible incompetency of these witnesses based on interest, see 13 A.L.R.3d 404 (1967).

21. See Mechem "Integration of Holographic Wills", 12 N.C.L.Rev. 213 (1933). Declarations of the testator's intention are sometimes admitted on the issue of integration. Some courts have presumed that the pages were intended as part of the will if they were found in one place at the death of the testator. But the rules of evidence to be applied in integrating holographs have not reached a stage of crystallization. The integration problem is sometimes presented as an issue of proper signing of the holograph. Thus, in McNair's Estate, 72 S.D. 604, 38 N.W.2d 449 (1949), 48 Mich.L.Rev. 384 (1950), 98 U. of Pa.L.Rev. 272 (1949) the holograph was found on three separate sheets in an envelope. The dispositive provisions ended abruptly on the third sheet and there was no signature at that point. At the top of each page there was a notation, "Will of Ella McNair" or "Will, Ella McNair". The will was held signed as required by the statute. Cf. Succession of Bechtel, 99 So.2d 495 (La. App.1958).

22. A proxy signature or signature by stamp or typewriter is not permitted.

23. See Atkinson, Wills (2d Ed., 1953) 362; 2 Bowe-Parker: Page, Wills (3d Ed., Rev.1960) § 20.7; 75 A.L.R.2d 895 (1961).

24. See Section 6(1)B, supra.

is intended as a signature," a signature not found at the logical end of the will must be proved to be the testator's intended signature by evidence from the face of the instrument.[25]

Several states require that the holograph be dated.[26] An undated and unwitnessed holograph fails in these jurisdictions.[27] The date is required to facilitate a discovery of the capacity of the testator when the will was executed and to aid in determining which of several holographic wills was executed last in point of time. The day, month and year are often required,[28] but an erroneous date does not invalidate the will. The date must be written by the testator since it is an essential part of the will when required by statute.

25. E.g., McElroy v. Rolston, 184 Va. 77, 34 S.E.2d 241 (1945); Hall v. Brigstocke, 190 Va. 459, 58 S.E.2d 529, 19 A.L.R.2d 921 (1950), 2 Mercer L.Rev. 284 (1950), 37 Va.L.Rev. 348 (1950); Black v. Maxwell, 131 W.Va. 247, 46 S.E.2d 804 (1948). See generally as to the place of signing of holographs, Mecham, "Integration of Holographic Wills", 12 N.C.L. Rev. 213 (1933); Mecham, "The Rule in Lemayne v. Stanley", 29 Mich.L.Rev. 685 (1931); 4 Ala.L.Rev. 140 (1952). As to the Mississippi requirement that the testator "subscribe" a holographic will that is unattested, see Section 6(1)(B) fn. 98, supra.

26. E.g., LSA-CC art. 1588; 84 Okl.St. Ann. § 54.

27. E.g., Succession of Buck, 208 La. 556, 23 So.2d 215 (1945) (illegible date). See Bird, "Sleight of Handwriting: The Holographic Will in California", 32 Hastings L.J. 605 (1981).

28. Succession of Sarrazin, 223 La. 286, 65 So.2d 602 (1953) (month and year but no day).

Chapter VI

REVOCATION, REVALIDATION AND REVIVAL OF WILLS

Scope Note

Revocability is a salient characteristic of a will. Revoking a will means taking back or repealing its provisions. The revocation may be total or partial. This Chapter develops the three methods for revocation set forth in state statutes. Several specimen statutes appear in Section 1. The three methods for revocation are considered in Section 2. These are: (1) revocation by subsequent instrument—either by an express clause of revocation or by inconsistent subsequent provisions; (2) revocation by a physical act to the will—either to the paper upon which the will is written or to the writing on the paper; and (3) revocation by operation of law due to a change in the circumstances of the testator. No other kinds of revocation are recognized in the statutes.[1] Problems which may be created when a testator attempts to revoke a will in part are examined in Section 3.

Techniques by which a will may be revalidated or "revived" are considered in Section 4. A revoked will may be revalidated by repetition of the formalities of execution discussed in Chapter V. However, the will may also be revalidated by execution of a codicil to it—"republication by codicil"—considered in Section 4(2). "Revival" of a will by revocation of the revoking will is examined in Section 4(3). Dependent relative revocation, a doctrine permitting probate of the will in some cases of mistaken revocation, and to this extent related to "revival" of the will, is developed in Section 4(4).

1. The classification of certain acts as "revocations" is for the convenience of the legislatures and courts. Statutes regulate acts within this class and the courts apply the statutes to acts which the statutes describe. A revocation, in theory, repeals all or a part of a will. But a testator may prevent his will from operating as a whole or in part by disposing of property described in the will during his lifetime. The net effect is the same in both cases. The will or certain of its provisions do not operate. Inter vivos alterations in the estate of the testator were once called "revocations" by the courts. Because of distinctions made by the legislatures between acts which prevent a will or its provisions from operating, these inter vivos alterations in the testator's estate have been placed in different pigeonholes. See, e.g., Chapter XII, Section 3(2).

SECTION 1. STATUTES [2]

STATUTE OF FRAUDS

29 Chas. II, c. 3, § VI (1677)[3]

"And moreover, no devise in writing of lands, tenements or hereditaments, nor any clause thereof, shall at any time * * * be revocable, otherwise than by some other will or codicil in writing, or other writing declaring the same, or by burning, cancelling, tearing or obliterating the same by the testator himself, or in his presence and by his directions and consent; * * * but all devises and bequests of lands and tenements shall remain and continue in force, until the same be burnt, cancelled, torn or obliterated by the testator, or by his directions in manner aforesaid, or unless the same be altered by some other will or codicil in writing, or other writing of the devisor, signed in the presence of three or four witnesses, declaring the same; any former law or usage to the contrary notwithstanding."

2. For a relatively recent summary of the American statutes, see Comment, "American Will Revocation Statutes: The Need for Change and Uniformity," 8 Cumb.L.Rev. 175 (1977). See generally for a discussion of policies, Chaffin, "Execution, Revocation and Revalidation of Wills: A Critique of Existing Statutory Formalities", 11 Ga.L.Rev. 297(1977).

3. It was settled in ecclesiastical law that testaments of personal property were ambulatory and subject to oral revocation by the testator at any time. Changes in the domestic circumstances of the testator and alterations made by him in his estate had revocatory effect. The common law courts permitted oral revocations of the written devises authorized by the Statute of Wills, 32 Hen. VIII, c. 1 (1540); Brook v. Ward, 3 Dyer, 310b, 73 Eng.Rep. 702 (1572). A devise was revoked by changes in the domestic circumstances of the testator or testatrix or alterations in the estate. Forse & Hembling's Case, 4 Coke 60b, 76 Eng. Rep. 1022 (1589) (Revocation by marriage of woman); Mountague v. Jeoffereys, Moore K.B. 429, 72 Eng.Rep. 674 (1596) (Revocation by alienation). Enactment of the Statute of Frauds was stimulated by the disclosure of perjury in the case of Cole v. Mordaunt (1675) [stated in notes to Mathews v. Warner, 4 Ves.Jr. 188, 31 Eng.Rep. 96 (1798)] in which it had been alleged that a written will was revoked by parol. Section VI covered the devises in writing required by Section V. Section XXII dealt with the revocation of testaments in writing. The common law and ecclesiastical revocations by changes in domestic circumstances and alterations in the estate were recognized by the courts after the enactment of the statute on the ground that the statute dealt with intentional methods of revocation and that the forms of revocation recognized were not based upon the intention of the testator. Section XXII is omitted here because few statutes in the United States have been patterned upon it. Major alterations in the language of Section VI have been made where Section VI is followed in this country. The formalities required by Section VI are extended to personal property. See, Rees, "American Wills Statutes", 46 Va.L.Rev. 856, 872 (1960).

WILLS ACT

7 Wm. IV & 1 Vict., c. 26, (1837)[4]

"XVII. And be it further enacted, That every Will made by a Man or Woman shall be revoked by his or her Marriage (except a Will made in exercise of a Power of Appointment, when the Real or Personal Estate thereby appointed would not in default of such Appointment pass to his or her Heir, Customary Heir, Executor, or Administrator, or the Person entitled as his or her next of Kin, under the Statute of Distributions).

"XIX. And be it further enacted, That no Will shall be revoked by any Presumption of an Intention on the Ground of an Alteration in Circumstances.

"XX. And be it further enacted, That no Will or Codicil, or any Part thereof, shall be revoked otherwise than as aforesaid, or by another Will or Codicil executed in manner herein-before required, or by some Writing declaring an Intention to revoke the same, and executed in the Manner in which a Will is herein-before required to be executed, or by the burning, tearing, or otherwise destroying the same by the Testator, or by some Person in his Presence and by his Direction, with the Intention of revoking the same. * * *

"XXIII. And be it further enacted, That no Conveyance or other Act made or done subsequently to the Execution of a Will of or relating to any Real or Personal Estate therein comprised, except an Act by which such Will shall be revoked as aforesaid, shall prevent the Operation of the Will with respect to such Estate or Interest in such Real or Personal Estate as the Testator shall have Power to Dispose of by Will at the Time of his Death. * * *"[5]

---

4. Section XXI dealt with the effect of interlineations and alterations after the will was executed. Section XXII dealt with revival of a will by revocation of a revoking will and is considered in Section 4, infra. Revision of the revocation provisions of the Wills Act, 1937, is now under consideration in England. See Law Reform Committee, Twenty-Second Report (The Making and Revocation of Wills), Cmd. 7902 (1980).

5. An alienation of devised land revoked the devise at common law. If the testator reacquired the land, the land did not pass by the will because the devise was revoked or because the will did not pass after-acquired property. See Putbury v. Trevilian, 2 Dyer 142a, 143b, 73 Eng.Rep. 310, 313 (1557); Butler & Baker's Case, 3 Coke 25a, 76 Eng.Rep. 684 (1591). By the ecclesiastical rule, the testament passed after-acquired chattels. Section XXIII was intended to abolish the common law rules. Statutes patterned upon Section XXIII are in force in a few states. See, Rees, "American Wills Statutes", 46 Va.L.Rev. 856, 860 (1960). Most of the states have a statute which alters the common law rules, even though the statute is not based on Section XXIII of the Wills Act. After-acquired property passes by will in almost all jurisdictions, but some courts still refer to an alienation of devised land as a revocation. E.g., Laurain v. Ernst, 237 Mich. 252, 211 N.W. 623 (1927), 26 Mich. L.Rev. 124 (1927). An alienation of devised land is treated in most states as an ademption by extinction of the devise. See Chapter XV, Section 1(2) A.

NEW YORK ESTATES, POWERS AND TRUSTS LAW, § 3–4.1

"(a) Except as otherwise provided in this chapter, a revocation or alteration, if intended by the testator, may be effected in the following manner only:

"(1) A will or any part thereof may be revoked or altered by:

"(A) Another will.

"(B) A writing of the testator clearly indicating an intention to effect such revocation or alteration, executed with the formalities prescribed by this article for the execution and attestation of a will.

"(2) A will may be revoked by:

"(A) An act of burning, tearing, cutting, cancellation, obliteration, or other mutilation or destruction performed by:

"(i) The testator.

"(ii) Another person, in the presence and by the direction of the testator; in which case, the fact that the will was so revoked in the presence and by the direction of the testator shall be proved by at least two witnesses, neither of whom shall be the person who performed the act of revocation.

"(b) In addition to the methods set forth in paragraph (a), a will may be revoked or altered by a nuncupative or holographic declaration of revocation or alteration made in the circumstances prescribed by 3–2.2 by any person therein authorized to make a nuncupative or holographic will. Any such nuncupative declaration of revocation or alteration must be clearly established by at least two witnesses; any such holographic declaration, by an instrument written entirely in the handwriting of the testator, although not executed and attested in accordance with the formalities prescribed by this article for the execution and attestation of a will.

"(c) The revocation of a will, as provided in this section, revokes all codicils thereto."

UNIFORM PROBATE CODE (1977)

"Section 2–507. [Revocation by Writing or by Act.] A will or any part thereof is revoked

"(1) by a subsequent will which revokes the prior will or part expressly or by inconsistency; or

"(2) by being burned, torn, canceled, obliterated, or destroyed, with the intent and for the purpose of revoking it by the testator or by another person in his presence and by his direction.

"Section 2–508. [Revocation by Divorce; No Revocation by Other Changes of Circumstances.] If after executing a will the testator is divorced or his marriage annulled, the divorce or annulment revokes any disposition or appointment of property made by the will to the former spouse, any provision conferring a general or special power of appointment on the former spouse, and any nomination of the former spouse as executor, trustee, conservator, or guardian, unless the will expressly provides otherwise. Property prevented from passing to a former spouse because of revocation by divorce or annulment passes as if the former spouse failed to survive the decedent, and other provisions conferring some power or office on the former spouse are interpreted as if the spouse failed to survive the decedent. If provisions are revoked solely by this section, they are revived by testator's remarriage to the former spouse. For purposes of this section, divorce or annulment means any divorce or annulment which would exclude the spouse as a surviving spouse within the meaning of Section 2–802(b). A decree of separation which does not terminate the status of husband and wife is not a divorce for purposes of this section. No change of circumstances other than as described in this section revokes a will."

SECTION 2. REVOCATION OF A WILL IN ITS ENTIRETY

(1) BY SUBSEQUENT INSTRUMENT

MATTER OF McGILL

Court of Appeals of New York, 1920.
229 N.Y. 405, 128 N.E. 194.[6]

[On 23 September, 1916, Margaret McGill executed a will leaving her residual estate to Thomas Hart. J. J. O'Kennedy, who was named executor and a legatee, kept the will in his office safe. Miss McGill became ill, and on 3 July, 1918, requested her cousin, Agnes Thompson, to write a note to O'Kennedy requesting him to destroy the will. Mrs. Thompson wrote the note and Miss McGill signed it in the presence of Mrs. Thompson and Bessie Gilmore, a servant. At Miss McGill's request, Mrs. Thompson and Bessie Gilmore signed the

6. Noted, 20 Col.L.Rev. 715 (1920); 18 Mich.L.Rev. 814 (1920); 19 Mich.L.Rev. 81 (1920); 7 Va.L.Rev. 233 (1920); 29 Yale L.J. 941 (1920).

note on the back since there was not room on the front. The note was as follows:

"July 3, 1918.

"Dr. O'Kennedy—Dear Friend: Please destroy the will I made in favor of Thomas Hart.

"Margaret McGill"

Mrs. Thompson testified that Miss McGill said after signing the note, "I am so glad that it is done." Bessie Gilmore testified that Miss McGill said: "I feel so happy now. * * * I have just done what I wanted to do, what I intended to do." The note was delivered to O'Kennedy on 4 July, 1918, but he was then in the hospital and did nothing to the will in favor of Thomas Hart. Miss McGill died on 5 July, 1918, without attempting any other act of revocation. She left an estate of about $25,000. Her heirs at law and next of kin were thirteen second cousins of the half blood and four third cousins of the half blood. The will of 1916 was offered for probate and some of the heirs at law and next of kin contested. The Surrogate admitted the will to probate. The Appellate Division affirmed this decree. The contestants now appeal.]

CHASE, J. * * * Every last will and testament of real or personal property, or both, shall be executed and attested as provided by statute. Decedent Estate Law (Const.Laws, c. 13) § 21. To revoke or cancel a written will, compliance must be had with the statute. Decedent Estate Law, § 34. Said Section 34 is as follows:

"No will in writing, except in the cases hereinafter mentioned, nor any part thereof, shall be revoked, or altered, otherwise than by some other will in writing, or some other writing of the testator, declaring such revocation or alteration, and executed with the same formalities with which the will itself was required by law to be executed; or unless such will be burnt, torn, canceled, obliterated or destroyed with the intent and for the purpose of revoking the same, by the testator himself, or by another person in his presence, by his direction and consent; and when so done by another person, the direction and consent of the testator, and the fact of such injury or destruction, shall be proved by at least two witnesses." [7]

Concededly the will of September 23 was never burned, torn, canceled, obliterated, or destroyed by Miss McGill or by any other person in her behalf and in her presence. At the time of the execution of the paper of July 3, the will was in a safe in the office of O'Kennedy and remained there until after her death. The question for our consideration resolves itself into the narrow one of determining whether the execution of the paper of July 3 was in and of itself an absolute and unqualified revocation of the will of 1916.

7. McKinney's N.Y., EPTL, § 3-4.1, applying to persons dying on or after 1 September 1967 and set forth in Section 1 of this Chapter uses the words "(B) A writing of the testator *clearly indicating an intention to* effect such revocation or alteration * * *." [Emphasis added—Ed.]

The words used by Miss McGill in the paper of July 3 are not ambiguous except perhaps as to whether she intended to limit the authority of O'Kennedy to a destruction of the will so far as it was "made in favor of Thomas Hart." The testimony relating to its execution and the statements made by her in connection therewith are not contradicted. Her intent in executing the paper, at least so far as such intent is now before us, must be determined by the court as a matter of law.

To revoke a will it is necessary not only that there should be an intent to revoke the will, but the intent must be consummated by some of the acts specified in the statute, or by the execution of an instrument "declaring such revocation". The difficulty with the appellant's position is that the paper writing does not itself declare the revocation. It does not declare an intention to revoke the will except through its destruction, either wholly or so far as Hart is concerned by O'Kennedy.

A revocation to be effective must be made pursuant to the statute. Lovell v. Quitman, 88 N.Y. 377, 42 Am.Rep. 254; Burnham v. Comfort, 108 N.Y. 535, 15 N.E. 710, 2 Am.St.Rep. 462; Delafield v. Parish, 25 N.Y. 9; Matter of Evans, 113 App.Div. 373, 98 N.Y.S. 1042. It is not within the legitimate power of the courts to dispense with the requirements of statute in the execution or revocation of wills and accept even a definite intention to perform the prescribed act in connection therewith for the act itself. Hoitt v. Hoitt, 63 N.H. 475, 3 A. 604, 56 Am.St.Rep. 530.

It is held in Tynan v. Paschal, 27 Tex. 286, 84 Am.Dec. 619, that a letter of a decedent to his attorney in fact directing him to destroy his will does not operate ipso facto as a revocation of it. * * *

It is urged that Miss McGill intended that her will should be destroyed. That may be admitted. Such intention to destroy the will is not a revocation. Her words do not indicate an intention to revoke the will at once or apart from its revocation through a destruction of the will by O'Kennedy. It is further urged that a construction of the paper by which it is held that it does not in itself constitute a revocation is technical and illiberal. The statute relating to the revocation of a will is specific and unqualified. So is the statute regarding the execution of a will. Both are intended for literal compliance. The reason that exists for requiring that a will to be effective must be executed with certain formalities exists to an equal extent for requiring that an instrument revoking a will to be effective must be executed with like formalities. Formalities in the making and in the revocation of a will are necessary to prevent mistake, misapprehension, and fraud. The interests of the people are best subserved by sustaining the statute quoted as it is written.

The ultimate intent of Miss McGill to revoke the will is not sufficient. To make her intent effective, it would be necessary to find as a fact that she intended that the act of signing the paper was in itself a complete revocation of the will. Such a finding would not have any evidence to sustain it.

The order should be affirmed with costs payable out of the estate.

HISCOCK, C. J., and COLLIN, CARDOZO, POUND, CRANE and ANDREWS, JJ., concur.

Order affirmed.

NOTE

Revocation by subsequent instrument is permitted in all American states.[8] With few exceptions the revocation must be made with the formalities required by the state for a written will.[9] By the better view, dispositive provisions in the revoking instrument are not required even when the applicable statute describes the revoking instrument as a "will or codicil."[10] The same formalities usually are required whether the revocation applies to a will of land or a will of personalty.

The courts are in substantial agreement that the testator must have a present intention to revoke at the time the revoking instrument is executed.[11] This requirement has created no difficulty when the revoking instrument contains provisions inconsistent with the prior will.[12] But when the revoking

Intent to revoke

8. See, Atkinson, Wills (2d Ed., 1953) § 87; 2 Bowe-Parker: Page, Wills (3d Ed., Rev.1960) §§ 21.33–21.48; Rollison, Wills (1939) §§ 137–140; Thompson, Wills (3d Ed., 1947) §§ 164–167; Evans, "Testamentary Revocation by Subsequent Instrument", 22 Ky.L.J. 468 (1934); Hoffman, "Revocation of Wills and Related Subjects", 31 Brooklyn L.Rev. 220, 221–230 (1965).

9. In most states a written will cannot be revoked expressly by a nuncupative will, although exceptions are sometimes made as in McKinney's N.Y., EPTL, § 3–4.1(b) where the nuncupative will is similar to the soldiers' and sailors' wills permitted in other states. See EPTL, § 3–2.2. Implied revocations may be possible on the theory that a nuncupative will being executed last in point of time can dispose of property to the extent permitted by statute which otherwise would pass by an earlier attested or holographic will. For an apparent statutory statement of this possibility, see Ind.Ann.Stat. § 29–1–5–4. An attested will can be revoked by a holographic will in states where unattested holographic wills are valid.

10. The wills acts refer to a "will or codicil" as revoking instruments. Most of the acts go further and add that a will may be revoked also by "some other writing declaring the same", "some other writing declaring such revocation", "some declaration in writing" or "some writing declaring an intention to revoke the same". Where a "will or codicil" and also some other writing are authorized means for revocation, the "will or codicil" is sometimes regarded as a reference to a revocation by inconsistent provisions and the "other writing" as a reference to a revocation by an instrument containing a clause of revocation only. But where the statute provides only for a revocation by "will or codicil", the better view is that revocations by inconsistency and express revocations unaccompanied by dispositive provisions are permitted. E.g., Grotts v. Casburn, 295 Ill. 286, 129 N.E. 137, 14 A.L.R. 1015 (1920). Contra: Twilley v. Durkee, 72 Colo. 444, 211 P. 668 (1923). See 22 A.L.R.3d 1346 (1968).

11. E.g., Stratton v. Durham, 191 Miss. 420, 2 So.2d 551 (1941). The extent of this agreement will, of course, depend upon the terms of the applicable statute. Thus, in Luther v. Luther, 211 Ala. 352, 100 So. 497 (1924), the testator used the past tense in referring to the revocation of a prior will. The Alabama statute permitted revocation by "some other will in writing, or some other writing subscribed by the testator and attested". It was held that language of revocation having significance *in praesenti* was unnecessary. For the Alabama problems pertaining to revocation by subsequent instrument, see Holt, "Revocation by Subsequent Instrument in Alabama: The Strange Rule of Bruce v. Sierra", 20 Ala. L.Rev. 66 (1967).

12. The New York courts have distinguished between the "other will in writing" and the "other writing of the testator, declaring such revocation" and have regarded an instrument appointing an executor and containing dispositive provisions as a "will" to which the rule in the principal case did not apply. See Matter of Logasa, 161 Misc. 774, 775, 293 N.Y.S. 116, 119 (1937); Hoffman, "Revocation of

instrument is to have revocatory effect by reason of an expression of intention to revoke contained in it, and contains no provisions inconsistent with those of the prior will, there is a division of authority whether the language of the will can be read in the light of the attending circumstances at the time of execution in order to find that the intention to revoke was "present". Although the English courts have taken the position that directions to destroy wills, such as that contained in the principal case, are *ipso facto* expressions of present intention,[13] the English courts have also read revocatory clauses that were equivocal as to "present" intention in the light of the attending circumstances when the ultimate intention to revoke was clear.[14] Although no American cases support the proposition that a direction to destroy is *ipso facto* an expression of a present intention to revoke,[15] in the few decisions reported, most of the courts, unlike the New York Court, have read the language of the will in the light of the attending circumstances before deciding to accept or reject it.[16]

WOLFE'S WILL

Supreme Court of North Carolina, 1923.
185 N.C. 563, 117 S.E. 804.

* * * [The following will was probated:

> "I, H. W. Wolfe, * * * do make and declare this to be my last will and testament: Item: I will and bequeath all my effects to my brothers and sisters, to be divided equally among them. Witness my hand and seal, this the 14th day of August, 1911.
>
> "H. W. Wolfe. (Seal.)
>
> "R. W. Harris.
>
> "C. L. Harris."

Wills and Related Subjects" 31 Brooklyn L.Rev. 220, 228–230 (1965).

13. Goods of Durance, [1872] L.R. 2 P. & D. 406; Maharajah Pertab Narain Singh v. Maharanee Subhao Kooer, [1877] L.R. 4 Ind.App. 228; In re Spracklan's Estate, 82 Sol.J. 373, 386 (1938).

14. Walcott v. Ochterlony, 1 Curt.Ecc. 580, 163 Eng.Rep. 203 (1837); Goods of Gosling, [1886] L.R. 11 Prob.Div. 79.

15. In Bayley v. Bailey, 5 Cush. (Mass.) 245 (1849), the Massachusetts court, in construing a statute containing the terminology of Section 34 of the Decedent Estate Law, held that the language in a will "It is my wish that the will I made be destroyed, and my estate settled according to law" constituted an expression of present intention to revoke. Primary reliance was placed upon "and my estate settled according to law" as indicating finality of intent. The instrument also contained provisions inconsistent with other wills because it directed a distribution of the property in accordance with the intestate law.

16. In Tynan v. Paschal, 27 Tex. 286, 84 Am.Dec. 619 (1863) a letter containing a direction to revoke a will was considered in the light of the construction placed upon it by the testator and by the witness to whom the letter was directed. In Stratton v. Durham, 191 Miss. 420, 2 So.2d 551 (1941) the testator wrote, "I am revoking my will left to Alto". The statute permitted revocation by "will, codicil, or declaration in writing, made and executed". It was held that the writing did not indicate a present intention to revoke, the determination resting in part upon the attending circumstances.

Thereafter this will was offered for probate but probate was denied:

"I, H. W. Wolfe, * * * do make and declare the following to be my last will and testament: "Item 1: I will and bequeath to Miss Mary Lillie Luffman, a tract of land near Roaring Gap Post Office, on State Road and Southfork, adjoining the lands of J. M. Royal and others, the land bought by me from H. D. Woodruff, and I will that that land in case of my death go into her possession without any further writing whatever. Witness my hand and seal, this 31st day of July, 1911.

"H. W. Wolfe. (Seal.)

his
"T. W. x Luffman.
mark

his
"K. F. x Luffman."
mark

The proponent of the will of July 31, 1911 then appealed to the Superior Court. The Judge thereof instructed the jury, after evidence was heard, that the will of August 14, 1911, which had been probated, was the last will of the testator. His instruction appeared to rest on his construction of the will of August 14, 1911 as revoking the will of July 31, 1911 by inconsistency. The issue of validity of the will apart from possible revocation was not considered by the jury. The proponent of the will of July 31, 1911 appeals, admitting that the will of August 14, 1911 is valid.] * * *

ADAMS, J. * * *

A will may be revoked by a subsequent instrument executed solely for that purpose, or by a subsequent will containing a revoking clause or provisions inconsistent with those of the previous will, or by any of the other methods prescribed by law; but the mere fact that a second will was made, although it purports to be the last, does not create a presumption that it revokes or is inconsistent with one of prior date. C.S. § 4133 et seq.; Gardner on Wills, 266, 271; 1 Redfield on Wills, 350; 1 Jarman on Wills, 186 et seq.; In re Venable's Will, 127 N.C. 345, 37 S.E. 465; Fleming v. Fleming, 63 N.C. 209.

The propounder admits that the instrument dated August 14th (herein for convenience referred to as the second will) is a part of the maker's testamentary disposition, but insists that it does not affect the validity of the instrument dated July 31st, herein designated as the first will. By reason of this admission the appeal presents the single question whether the two wills are so inconsistent that they cannot stand together and whether the first is revoked by the second.

It has often been held that in the construction of wills the primary purpose is to ascertain and give effect to the testator's intention as expressed in the words employed, and if the language is free from ambiguity and doubt, and expresses plainly, clearly, and distinctly the maker's intention, there is no occasion to resort to other means of interpretation. * * *

In the instant case, the language being clear and unequivocal the chief controversy between the parties involves the meaning of the words "all my effects" as used in the second will. The propounder contends that they include only personal property; the respondents insist that the term embraces real as well as personal property, and that the second will revokes the first, the two being necessarily inconsistent.

The observation has been made that the individual cases construing "effects" are of value only for the purpose of illustration, each case being a law unto itself; but there seems to be a practical unanimity of judicial decision, with the exception of certain English cases, that the word "effects" used simpliciter or in a general or unlimited sense, and unaffected by the context, signifies all that is embraced in the words "personal property" but is not sufficiently comprehensive to include real estate. "Effects", however, may include land when used as referring to antecedent words which describe real estate, or when used in written instruments in which the usual technical terms are not controlling, as in Trustees v. Miller, 14 N.C. 188, Graves v. Howard, 56 N.C. 302, and Page v. Foust, 89 N.C. 447. A discussion of these questions with an exhaustive citation of authorities may be found in the following cases with the subjoined explanatory notes: Andrews v. Applegate, 223 Ill. 535, 79 N.E. 176, 12 L.R.A.,N.S., 661, 7 Ann.Cas. 126; Dickson v. Dickson, 180 Ky. 423, 202 S.W. 891, L.R.A.1918F, 765; In Re Molson, 18 Ann.Cas. 279; Gardner v. McNeal, 117 Md. 27, 82 A. 988, 40 L.R.A.,N.S., 553, Ann.Cas.1914A, 119.

In the second will there are no words which ex vi termini import a disposition of real property; there is no residuary clause or clause of revocation; and in these circumstances, as the courts do not favor the revocation of wills by implication, there appears to be no sound reason for holding that the two instruments are so inconsistent as to be incapable of standing together and that the first is necessarily revoked by the second. It is true there is a presumption that the testator intended to dispose of all his estate, and under our construction the testator died intestate as to the land not devised to Mary Lillie Luffman, but, as said in Andrews v. Applegate, supra, such presumption, however strong, will not justify or warrant a construction incorporating in the second will any kind of property which cannot be brought within its terms.

Having admitted that the second will is a valid testamentary disposition of the property therein described, the propounder is entitled to have the jury determine whether the instrument dated July 31, 1911, is any part of the maker's will. The judgment and verdict are therefore set aside and a new trial is awarded.

New trial.

NOTE

A prior will may be revoked entirely or partially by a subsequent will or codicil containing inconsistent provisions. This is described as an "implied" revocation or a revocation "by inconsistency". No express clause of revocation is required.[17]

Whether an implied revocation has occurred depends upon the answers to two questions: (1) Does an inconsistency exist? (2) To what extent does the inconsistency affect the prior will?

The first question is answered by construing the language of the instruments involved. The last valid will of the testator is effective in any event. But a will may consist of several writings executed and attested at different times if the instruments executed earlier in point of time are not inconsistent with or expressly revoked by later instruments.[18] The courts have not favored implied revocations. The fact that a will is titled "last will and testament" does not mean that it revokes earlier wills expressly or impliedly.[19] If a testator gives legacies to the same person by different instruments, it is presumed that the legacy given in the later instrument is in addition to that given in the earlier instrument.[20] But an inconsistency may be found since a court seeks the intention of the testator when it construes a will. To what extent does the inconsistency affect the prior will?

In almost every case the answer will lie in the extent of the inconsistency as determined by construction of the instruments. The wills stand together to the extent that their provisions do not conflict. The provisions of the will executed last in point of time prevail when conflict is discovered. But suppose that the subsequent will does not operate to pass all of the testator's property. Can a prior will operate in part if the subsequent will expresses an essentially different plan of testamentary disposition?[21] The answer may depend upon the rationale deemed by the court to support the implied revocation rule. The rule may be mechanical. If a subsequent will disposes of all that a testator has to give, there is nothing upon which a prior will can operate. The prior will is valid but inoperative.[22] On the other hand, if the im-

17. Neither the Statute of Frauds, 1677, nor the Wills Act, 1837, provided expressly for revocations by inconsistency. The English courts, however, recognized revocations by inconsistency under both statutes. Helyar v. Helyar, 1 Lee 472, 161 Eng.Rep. 174 (1754); Ex parte Hellier, 3 Atk. 798, 26 Eng.Rep. 1265 (1754); Seymor v. Northwortly, Hardres 374, 145 Eng.Rep. 504 (1839); Plenty v. West, 1 Rob.Ecc. 264, 163 Eng.Rep. 1033 (1845). Several of the American wills acts contain express references to revocations by inconsistency. Rees, "American Wills Statutes" 46 Va.L.Rev. 856, 874 (1960). The rule in Illinois was in doubt for some time but was settled in favor of implied revocation in Lasier v. Wright, 304 Ill. 130, 136 N.E. 545 (1922) where the American cases are collected and discussed in detail. The rule in Illinois is now statutory. Smith-Hurd Ill.Ann.Stat. ch. 110½, § 4-7 (1980 Supp.). All of the American states now appear to permit implied revocations whether a statute provides for revocations of this type or not. See 59 A.L.R.2d 11 (1958). For cases dealing with the construction of "belongings", "personal effects" and "effects", as in the principal case, see 30 A. L.R.3d 797 (1970).

18. See Schultz v. Schultz, 10 Gratt. (Va.) 358, 373 (1853). See Holt, "Revocation by Subsequent Instrument in Alabama: The Strange Rule of Bruce v. Sierra," 20 Ala.L.Rev. 66 (1967).

19. E.g., Neibling v. Methodist Orphans' Home Ass'n, 315 Mo. 578, 286 S. W. 58, 51 A.L.R. 639 (1916). The English courts have sometimes given weight to language of this sort. See Plenty v. West, 1 Rob.Ecc. 264, 163 Eng.Rep. 1033 (1845).

20. See Gould v. Chamberlain, appearing as principal case in Section 3, infra.

21. Problems of this type may appear in several forms. When a provision in a will cannot operate for some reason, the issue may be presented as one of dependent relative revocation. See Section 4(3), infra. The question may be one of construction to determine the scope of a residuary clause in the subsequent will. See Atkinson, Wills (2d Ed., 1953) 451.

22. There is an analogy between the mechanical theory of implied revocation and the doctrine of "ademption by extinction" considered in Chapter XV, Section 1(2) (A) (i).

plied revocation is based upon the intention of the testator, the existence of a different testamentary plan may indicate that the testator intended to revoke the prior will for all purposes.[23] If the revocation is simply a matter of mechanics, there seems to be no reason why a prior will should not operate to pass property described by its terms. If the revocation is based upon intention, the prior will might be held revoked for all purposes. It is difficult to determine from most of the cases which rationale the various courts support or what weight is given to an inconsistent testamentary plan as distinguished from a complete disposition of property owned by the testator.[24]

In the event that two testamentary instruments are found to contain conflicting provisions, and the dates of execution of the instruments cannot be determined, both instruments are denied probate.[25]

(2) BY PHYSICAL ACT

THOMPSON v. ROYALL

Supreme Court of Appeals of Virgina, 1934.
163 Va. 492, 175 S.E. 748.[26]

The only question presented by this record is whether the will of Mrs. M. Lou Bowen Kroll had been revoked shortly before her death.

The uncontroverted facts are as follows: On the 4th day of September, 1932, Mrs. Kroll signed a will, typewritten on five sheets of legal cap paper; the signature appeared on the last page duly attested by three subscribing witnesses. H. P. Brittain, the executor named in the will, was given possession of the instrument for safekeeping. A codicil typed on the top third of one sheet of paper dated September 15, 1932, was signed by the testatrix in the presence of two subscribing witnesses. Possession of this instrument was given to Judge S. M. B. Coulling, the attorney who prepared both documents.

23. Can this position be reconciled with the position of the New York courts in Matter of McGill and Matter of Logasa, fn. 12 supra?

24. See, e.g., Plenty v. West, 1 Rob. Ecc. 264, 163 Eng.Rep. 1033 (1845); Gardner v. McNeal, 117 Md. 27, 82 A. 988, 40 L.R.A.,N.S., 553, Ann.Cas.1914A, 119 (1911). When the subsequent instrument is a codicil the courts have been reticent to allow a complete revocation of the will by inconsistency. E.g., Driver v. Driver, 187 Ark. 875, 63 S.W.2d 274 (1933); Joiner v. Joiner, 117 Miss. 507, 78 So. 369 (1918); Evans, "Testamentary Revocation by Subsequent Instrument", 22 Ky.L.J. 468, 476 (1934). Upon the admissibility of extrinsic evidence to show the intention of the testator concerning a complete revocation, see Neibling v. Methodist Orphans' Home Association, 315 Mo. 578, 286 S.W. 58, 51 A.L.R. 639 (1926), 40 Harv.L.Rev. 329 (1926); Kearns v. Rousch, 106 W.Va. 663, 146 S. E. 729 (1929), 15 Iowa L.Rev. 231 (1929); In re Brown's Will, 143 Iowa 649, 120 N. W. 667 (1909).

25. Phipps v. Anglesey, 7 Bro. 443, 3 Eng.Rep. 289 (1751). See In re Westfeldt's Will, 188 N.C. 702, 125 S.E. 531, 535 (1924).

26. Noted, 41 W.Va.L.Q. 172 (1935).

On September 19, 1932, at the request of Mrs. Kroll, Judge Coulling and Mr. Brittain took the will and the codicil to her home where she told her attorney, in the presence of Mr. Brittain and another to destroy both. But, instead of destroying the papers, at the suggestion of Judge Coulling, she decided to retain them as memoranda, to be used as such in the event she decided to execute a new will. Upon the back of the manuscript cover, which was fastened to the five sheets by metal clasps, in the handwriting of Judge Coulling, signed by Mrs. Kroll, there is the following notation: "This will null and void and to be only held by H. P. Brittain instead of being destroyed as a memorandum for another will if I desire to make same. This 19 Sept. 1932.

"M. Lou Bowen Kroll."

The same notation was made upon the back of the sheet on which the codicil was written, except that the name S. M. B. Coulling was substituted for H. P. Brittain; this was likewise signed by Mrs. Kroll.

Mrs. Kroll died October 2, 1932, leaving numerous nephews and nieces, some of whom were not mentioned in her will, and an estate valued at approximately $200,000. On motion of some of the beneficiaries, the will and codicil were offered for probate. All the interested parties including the heirs at law were convened, and on the issue devisavit vel non the jury found that the instruments dated September 4 and 15, 1932, were the last will and testament of Mrs. M. Lou Bowen Kroll. From an order sustaining the verdict and probating the will this writ of error was allowed.

For more than 100 years, the means by which a duly executed will may be revoked have been prescribed by statute. These requirements are found in section 5233 of the 1919 Code, the pertinent parts of which read thus: "No will or codicil, or any part thereof, shall be revoked, unless * * * by a subsequent will or codicil, or by some writing declaring an intention to revoke the same, and executed in the manner in which a will is required to be executed, or by the testator, or some person in his presence and by his direction, cutting, tearing, burning, obliterating, canceling, or destroying the same, or the signature thereto, with the intent to revoke."

The notations, dated September 19, 1932, are not wholly in the handwriting of the testatrix, nor are her signatures thereto attached attested by subscribing witnesses; hence under the statute they are ineffectual as "some writing declaring an intention to revoke." The faces of the two instruments bear no physical evidence of any cutting, tearing, burning, obliterating, canceling, or destroying. The only contention made by appellants is that the notation written in the presence, and with the approval, of Mrs. Kroll, on the back of the manuscript cover in the one instance, and on the back of the sheet containing the codicil in the other, constitute "canceling" within the meaning of the statute.

Both parties concede that to effect revocation of a duly executed will, in any of the methods prescribed by statute, two things are necessary: (1) the doing of one of the acts specified, (2) accompanied by the intent to revoke—the animo revocandi. Proof of either, without proof of the other is insufficient. Malone v. Hobbs, 1 Rob. (40 Va.) 346, 39 Am.Dec. 263; 2 Minor Ins. 925.

The proof established the intention to revoke. The entire controversy is confined to the acts used in carrying out that purpose. The testatrix adopted the suggestion of her attorney to revoke her will by written memoranda, admittedly ineffectual as revocations by subsequent writings, but appellants contend the memoranda, in the handwriting of another, and testatrix' signatures, are sufficient to effect revocation by cancellation. To support this contention, appellants cite a number of authorities which hold that the modern definition of cancellation includes "any act which would destroy, revoke, recall, do away with, overrule, render null and void, the instrument."

Most of the authorities cited that approve the above or a similar meaning of the word were dealing with the cancellation of simple contracts, or other instruments that require little or no formality in execution. However, there is one line of cases which apply this extended meaning of "canceling" to the revocation of wills. The leading case so holding is Warner v. Warner's Estate, 37 Vt. 356. In this case proof of the intent and the act were a notation on the same page with, and below the signature of, the testator, reading: "This will is hereby canceled and annulled. In full this 15th day of March in the year 1859", and written lengthwise on the back of the fourth page of the foolscap, upon which no part of the written will appeared, were these words, "Canceled and is null and void. (Signed) I. Warner." It was held that this was sufficient to revoke the will under a statute similar to the one here under consideration. * * *

The construction of the statute in Warner v. Warner's Estate, supra, has been criticized by eminent text-writers on wills, and the courts in the majority of the states in construing similar statutes have refused to follow the reasoning in that case. Jarman on Wills (6th Ed.) 147, note 1; Schouler on Wills (5th Ed.) § 391; Redfield on the Law of Wills (4 Ed.) 323–325; 28 R.C.L. 180; 40 Cyc. 1173; Dowling v. Gilliland, 286 Ill. 530, 122 N.E. 70, 3 A.L.R. 829; Freeman's notes to Graham v. Burch, 28 Am.St.Rep. 339, 351; Will of Ladd, 60 Wis. 187, 18 N.W. 734, 50 Am.Rep. 355; Howard v. Hunter, 115 Ga. 357, 41 S.E. 638, 639, 90 Am.St.Rep. 121; Sanderson v. Norcross, 242 Mass. 43, 136 N.E. 170; Gay v. Gay, 60 Iowa 415, 14 N.W. 238, 46 Am.Rep. 78; Brown v. Thorndike, 15 Pick. (Mass.) 388; Noesen v. Erkenswick, 298 Ill. 231, 131 N.E. 622.

The above, and other authorities that might be cited, hold that revocation of a will by cancellation within the meaning of the statute contemplates marks or lines across the written parts of the instrument, or a physical defacement, or some mutilation of the writing itself with the intent to revoke. If written words are used for the purpose, they must be so placed as to physically affect the written portion of the will, not merely on blank parts of the paper on which the will is written. If the writing intended to be the act of canceling does not mutilate, or erase, or deface, or otherwise physically come in contact with, any part of written words of the will, it cannot be given any greater weight than a similar writing on a separate sheet of paper, which identifies the will referred to, just as definitely as does the writing on the back. If a will may be revoked by writing on the back, separable from the will, it may be done by a writing not on the will. This the statute forbids. * * *

The attempted revocation is ineffectual, because testatrix intended to revoke her will by subsequent writings not executed as required by statute, and because it does not in any wise physically obliterate, mutilate, deface, or cancel any written parts of the will.

For the reasons stated, the judgment of the trial court is affirmed.

Affirmed.

NOTE

Revocations by physical act are permitted in all states.[27] The acts specified in a particular jurisdiction are usually derived both from the Statute of Frauds, 1677, and from the Wills Act, 1837.[28] Although the language of the applicable wills act must be consulted when an issue of revocation by physical act is presented, certain revocatory acts appear in the statutes with some frequency.[29] "Burning", "tearing", "cutting", "destroying" and "mutilating" are acts done to the paper upon which the will is written. "Cancelling" and "obliterating" are acts done to the writing on the will. It is obvious that a will may be "burned" so that it is "destroyed" and its writing "obliterated". "Tearing" may be the same as "cutting", and either may be a "mutilation".

The words "destruction" and "obliteration" seem to carry with them a notion of degree, "destruction" referring to the degree of annihilation of the paper of the will and "obliteration" to the degree to which the writing on the will is obscured.[30] Except for acts of this character, the only requirement

27. Rees, "American Wills Statutes", 46 Va.L.Rev. 856, 875 (1960); N.Mex. Stat. (1978) § 45–2–507. For revocations by physical act in Tennessee (non-statutory) see Ford v. Ford, 26 Tenn. 92 (1846); Smiley v. Gambill, 39 Tenn. 164 (1858); Billington v. Jones, 108 Tenn. 234, 66 S. W. 1127 (1901). See generally, Atkinson, Wills (2d Ed., 1953) § 86; 2 Bowe-Parker: Page, Wills (3d Ed., Rev.1960) §§ 21.-4–21.32; Rollison, Wills (1939) §§ 127–132; Thompson, Wills (3d Ed., 1947) §§ 154–161; Battle, "Does the Writing of Words Across the Face of a Will Constitute such a Cancellation or Obliteration as Will Revoke the Will", 9 Va.L.Rev. 98 (1922); Evans, "Testamentary Revocation by Act to the Document and Dependent Relative Revocation", 23 Ky.L.J. 559 (1935); 3 A.L.R. 833 (1919); 62 A.L.R. 1375 (1929).

28. Rees, "American Wills Statutes", 46 Va.L.Rev. 856, 875 (1960).

29. Uniform Probate Code, § 2–507 refers to "burned, torn, canceled, obliterated or destroyed".

30. The word "obliteration" appeared on Section XXI of the Wills Act, 1837, coupled with language that might be taken to mean that the "obliteration" was ineffective if the words on the will remained "apparent". In Ffinch v. Combe, [1894] L.R.Prob. 191, the testator pasted strips of paper over certain provisions of his will. Since the words covered by the strips could still be read by placing a piece of brown paper around the passages in question and holding the will against a window pane, the words were held "apparent" within the meaning of the Wills Act, 1837, and were probated with the remainder of the will. Although "obliteration" is a revocatory act described by a number of American statutes and the Uniform Probate Code, the word "apparent" does not appear. The strict English construction has no following in this country, although the language in a few cases suggests that the words are obliterated only when completely illegible. E.g., Townshend v. Howard, 86 Me. 285, 29 A. 1077 (1894); Gardiner v. Gardiner, 65 N.H. 230, 19 A.

seems to be that some visible sign of the act be left upon the paper or its writing. The definition of "cancellation" adopted in the principal case is the prevailing view, although some courts have taken the position that any marks upon the will which show the testator's intention to revoke are sufficient.[31] By the better view, a "mutilation" need not affect the writing on the will.[32] A slight "burning", "tearing" or "cutting" is sufficient and the visible sign need not touch the writing on the will.[33] An act to the cover of the will is not a sufficient act in any event.[34]

651 (1890). The British Law Reform Committee recommended adherence to the view that the words are not obliterated if they are not optically apparent. It rejected the proposal that it would be right to allow the use of chemical processes or infra red photography to decipher obliterations and erasures. It also rejected the view that a court should be given discretionary power to give effect to all partial destructions and obliterations which evince a clear intent on the part of the testator to revoke. Cmd. 7902, 3.44, 3.45 (1980).

31. Warner v. Warner's Estate, 37 Vt. 356 (1864). See 2 Bowe-Parker: Page, Wills (3d Ed., Rev.1960) §§ 21.8–21.9. As used in some statutes, the word "cancel" has been construed as any act of annulling the will and also as a revocation by subsequent instrument. See Blackett v. Ziegler, 153 Iowa 344, 133 N.W. 901, 37 L.R.A.,N.S., 291, Ann.Cas.1913E, 115 (1911), 12 Col.L.Rev. 353 (1912), 21 Yale L.J. 672 (1912); Evans' Appeal, 58 Pa. 238 (1868). By the better view, however, the word "cancel" refers to a physical act to the will and not to a revocation by subsequent instrument. E.g., Harchuck v. Campana, 139 Conn. 549, 95 A.2d 566 (1953). In Estate of Helgert, 29 Wis.2d 452, 139 N.W.2d 81 (1966) the names of the two beneficiaries in the will were lined out and the words "No" written in above both names but not touching the writing. The words "Void" also were written at several places on the will and cover without the writing being touched except for the attestation clause. The Court held that the lines deleting the names of the two beneficiaries were cancellations and when supported by ample evidence from the face of the will that testator intended to revoke the entire will would be taken as a revocation of the whole. The Court states at 139 N.W.2d 87:

> "The general rule is that lines, marks, or written words must be placed across the written portion of the will in order to constitute an effectual cancellation, and that no revocation results when words are merely written in the margin or elsewhere on the will. Nonetheless, it has been recognized that a cancelation, however slight, may constitute a revocation where there is proper intent, particularly where a dispositive provision is affected, or the elimination materially alters the meaning or legal effect of the will".

Statutes may necessitate special local treatments of the act of "cancellation". Thus Smith-Hurd Ill.Rev.Stat. ch. 110½, § 4–7 (1980 Supp.) states that a will may be revoked by "cancelling". But § 4–9 states: "An addition to a will or an alteration, substitution, interlineation, or deletion of any part of a will which does not constitute a revocation of the will under this Article is of no effect, unless made by the testator or by some person in his presence and by his direction and consent and unless the will is thereafter signed and attested in the manner prescribed in this Article for the execution of a will". In Estate of Newell, 119 Ill.App.2d 385, 256 N.E.2d 53 (1970), the testator apparently had made markings by lead pencil through the names of two residuary beneficiaries who would take 98% of his estate. The first nineteen paragraphs of the will, containing eighteen bequests, were intact. The Court found no evidence of an intention to revoke the entire will and concluded that to effect a *partial* revocation by cancellation there would have to be a new attestation (apparently including signing by the testator) to give this attempted partial revocation effect under § 4–9. It was not certain, however, that the will had been in the possession of testator after it was executed.

32. Mutilating means "rendering imperfect". In Indiana, where the testator must "destroy or mutilate" the will, it has been held that mutilation need not render the writing illegible but it is not certain that the mutilation will revoke the will unless if affects the writing to some extent. See Tinsley v. Carwile, 212 Ind. 675, 10 N.E.2d 597 (1937); Ind.Stat. Ann. § 29–1–5–6.

33. E.g., White v. Casten, 46 N.C. 197, 59 Am.Dec. 585 (1853) (Slight burning and singeing but no word destroyed or obliterated).

34. E.g., Doe d. Reed v. Harris, 6 A. & E. 209, 112 Eng.Rep. 79 (1837); In re

Most of the American statutes provide for a proxy revocation by physical act if the act is done in the presence of the testator and by his direction.[35] A testator is not permitted to ratify an act by proxy which was not done in the way required by statute,[36] nor is he permitted to ratify or adopt accidental injuries to his will as acts of revocation by the better view.[37]

The intention to revoke must be concomitant with the act. The will is not revoked if the testator changes his mind while performing the act or if he does not accomplish the full act intended.[38] If the testator does intend to revoke his will at the time the act is done, a later change of mind does not avoid the revocation.[39]

PROBLEMS

1. In 1962, T executed a will which disinherited his children by his first marriage and left his estate to his second wife. He executed a codicil to this will in 1965. In 1966 he executed a will which contained substantially the provisions of the will of 1962 and the codicil, the only material change being the naming of an alternate executor. Thereafter T decided he did not wish to nominate this alternate executor and was told by his attorney that if he revoked his will of 1966, this would revive the will of 1962 and the codicil. While he was in bed, he directed his wife, his stepdaughter and her husband to destroy his will of 1966. They went into the next room, took the will of 1966 from a safe, tore it into pieces and flushed the pieces down a toilet. T's bedroom was separated from the room in which the tearing occurred by a screened terrace. The doors were closed between the decedent and the room and he could not see the destruction. He was subsequently informed that the will had been destroyed and nodded his approval. The applicable statute reads:

> "A will may be revoked by the testator himself or by some person in his presence and by his direction by burning, canceling, defacing, obliterating or destroying the same, with the intent and for the purpose of revocation".

When T dies, his wife offers the will of 1962 and the codicil of 1965 for probate and these are contested by the children of the first marriage on the ground of mental incapacity of the testator and undue influence exercised upon him. Assuming the will of 1966 is not vulnerable to attack on these grounds, can it be probated? Estate of Bancker, 232 So.2d 431 (Fla.1970). Review Chapter V, Section 6(4).

2. In 1964, T executed a will in which he left all his property to his brother, Alphonse and, in the event Alphonse predeceased him, then to his

Silva's Estate, 169 Cal. 116, 145 P. 1015 (1915).

35. Rees, "American Wills Statutes", 46 Va.L.Rev. 856, 877 (1960).

36. E.g., Mundy v. Mundy, 15 N.J.Eq. 290 (1858); Gill v. Gill, [1909] L.R.Prob. 157.

37. In Cutler v. Cutler, 130 N.C. 1, 40 S.E. 689, 57 L.R.A. 209, 89 Am.St.Rep. 854 (1902) it was held that a testator could adopt the mutilation of his will by moths and vermin as a revocation. In Parsons v. Balson, 129 Wis. 311, 109 N.W. 136 (1906) the testator's will was destroyed by fire. It was held that the will was presumed to be revoked, if, after the testator received knowledge of the destruction, he did not take action to reproduce the will within a reasonable time.

38. E.g., Perkes v. Perkes, 3 B. & A. 489, 106 Eng.Rep. 740 (1920); Livelar v. Arnold, 233 So.2d 760 (Miss.1970).

39. The will could be reexecuted by the testator or republished by codicil but is not revived if the testator does not carry out his changed intention by an act that will restore the effectiveness of the will.

brother Allen. The will was prepared on four typewritten pages and stapled in a cover. Two months later, T decided he wanted to change the will. His attorney in his presence and at his direction detached the staples, withdrew page one upon which the dispositive provisions appeared, and then dictated a new page one to his secretary, the new dispositions on this page dividing the estate equally between Alphonse and Allen. He told his secretary to retype the rest of the will and then call his law partner to supervise the execution, the attorney having another appointment. The secretary, instead, typed the new page and restapled this page with the old ones in the same cover, having T initial each page. When T dies, Alphonse and Allen come to you to inquire which pages can be probated. They have the original page one. They would prefer to distribute the estate under the intestate law as they are the only heirs. Advise them assuming the following statute is in force:

> "No will in writing * * * shall be revoked * * * unless such will shall be burnt, torn, canceled, obliterated or destroyed, with the intent and for the purpose of revoking the same, by the testator himself, or by some other person in his presence and by his direction and consent * * *".

Will of Robinson, 26 A.D.2d 306, 273 N.Y.S.2d 985 (1966).

ESTATE OF MARKOFSKE

Supreme Court of Wisconsin, 1970.
47 Wis.2d 769, 178 N.W.2d 9.

* * * [Testatrix executed three wills. The 1959 will left testatrix' estate to her husband and, in the event he predeceased her, then certain specific bequests of $500 and her personal belongings with a bequest of the remainder to Charles M. Cotter, Betty Hanson and Lyle McGwinn. The 1960 will had substantially the same provisions but added specific bequests totalling $450 with the remainder to Charles M. Cotter and Betty Hanson, omitting McGwinn. Testatrix' husband died in 1964 and she then executed the will of 1965 which made no substantive changes in the will of 1960 except for the omission of her deceased husband. Testatrix entered a nursing home in 1967 and died there in 1969. The executed copy of the will of 1959 was found but the executed copies of the wills of 1960 and 1965 were not. The trial court probated the will of 1959, concluding that the wills of 1960 and 1965 had been destroyed by the testatrix with the intention of revoking them since they had been traced to her possession and could not be found at her death. Heirs of the testatrix appeal. Additional facts are stated in the opinion.] * * *

CONNOR T. HANSEN, JUSTICE. * * * [A discussion of jurisdictional issues is omitted] * * *

The initial issue determined by the trial court was that testatrix was presumed to have destroyed the 1965 will:

> "EIGHTH: That the deceased did have in her possession, the Last Will dated February 17, 1959, the Last Will dated April 30, 1960 and the Last Will dated June 17, 1965; that the deceased

knew the contents of the various Last Wills and was faced with a dwindling estate, and therefore, is presumed to have destroyed the Last Will dated June 17, 1965 and the Last Will dated April 30, 1960."

As to the 1965 will, the trial court found that the presumption of revocation had not been overcome; that the will was not destroyed by accident; and that there was no evidence to support a finding that the instrument should be allowed as a lost will and thereupon denied the admission of the will to probate as a lost will.

We consider this case to present a question of whether the trial court was in error in holding that the 1965 will was presumed to have been destroyed. The trial court also made the same finding as to the will of April 30, 1960. Since the material facts are not in dispute, the issue is one on which this court can rule as a matter of law. Will of Donigian (1953), 265 Wis. 147, 60 N.W.2d 732.

In Will of Donigian, supra, pp. 151, 152, 66 N.W.2d p. 734, this court reviewed three cases in which the presumption of destruction had been considered:

> "In Estate of Lambert (1948), 252 Wis. 117, 31 N.W.2d 163, the testator made a will on March 16, 1946, and it was last seen in his possession. He died two weeks later and the will was never found. In the interval he told several people how he had disposed of his property. We held that the presumption of revocation which arises from nonproduction of a will is not so strong in this state as to require the proponent to prove that the testator had no opportunity to destroy the will, and we said 252 Wis. at page 126, 31 N.W.2d at page 167:
>
> > " 'The evidence of the proponent, having established that the deceased made a will and persisted in statements of satisfaction with its contents up to the day of his death, is sufficient to sustain the finding of the trial court that the presumption of destruction was over-come.'
>
> "In Wendt v. Ziegenhagen, 1912, 148 Wis. 382, 134 N.W. 905, the testator made his will in 1900. He died in 1909. He had possession of the will but it was not found after his death. His son who would profit by an intestacy and his widow, who sided with the son, had access to his papers. The court did not consider the question of the possible destruction of the will by interested parties but rested its decision upon the frequent statements of the testator to the effect that he was satisfied with his will and the absence of any change in conditions which would make it likely that he would revoke the will in order to give greater benefits than the son had already received. Such evidence was held to be sufficient to overcome the presumption and to support a finding that the testator did not destroy his will with intent to revoke it.
>
> "In Re Will of Lauberg, 1920, 170 Wis. 502, 175 N.W. 925, the testatrix up to the time of her death made declarations tending to show the existence of her will and that she had no intention of

revoking it. We held that this evidence was strong enough to rebut the presumption and support a finding that the will had not been destroyed by the testatrix with intention of revoking it."

In Will of Donigian, supra, p. 154, 66 N.W.2d p. 735, the presumption of revocation was rebutted:

> "We conclude that undisputed testimony here is sufficient to support a finding that the August 7th will was not revoked by the testator by destruction or otherwise. There is no testimony whatever that he did so revoke it,—nothing but a presumption that he did so arising from the nonproduction of the will,—and that presumption went out of the case when evidence came in that during Donigian's final days he referred to his will with satisfaction, that no change of intent was ever manifested, or cause for such change arose, and that his papers and effects were so situated that others than himself had access to them."

In this case, testatrix entered a convalescent home in September, 1967, and did not again live in the residence she owned prior to that time. The residence was sold in December, 1967, and the furniture, papers, files and other personal belongings were moved to the home of the testatrix's sister, Ann Cotter. Mrs. Cotter testified that at the time her sister's home was vacated, she found negotiable bonds under some newspapers and also found some stock certificates. These were put into the testatrix's safety deposit box by Mrs. Cotter. Mrs. Cotter also testified that she made a search among all the papers, files and insurance policies of the testatrix which were in her possession but she had been unable to find a will; and that she didn't know of anyone other than herself, her son, Charles M. Cotter (respondent-petitioner), or attorney Francis Murphy who would have any papers or personal effects of her sister. Mrs. Cotter also testified that the testatrix had informed her that her son, Charles M. Cotter, was the executor of a will, and that the testatrix told her this at the death of the testatrix's husband in 1964 and again about four or five months before her death.

Charles M. Cotter testified that he did not make any search for the lost will. Attorney Francis Murphy, a witness and scrivenor of the 1965 will, and Wallace Krueger, the other witness, both testified that the original will was executed back near the vault in the Montello State Bank. Their testimony reflects the will was properly executed. Mr. Murphy conformed the copy of the will in the bank after the original was signed. At that time testatrix removed her original will of April 30, 1960, from the lock box in the bank which Mr. Murphy advised her to destroy since she had now signed another will. That was the last time Attorney Murphy discussed the will of June 17, 1965, with her, or saw the original 1960 or the original 1965 wills, and he had no idea as to what had ever been done with them. Wallace Krueger, the other witness, did not know anything about the whereabouts of the original will subsequent to its signing on June 17, 1965.

A comparison of the three wills shows little substantive difference between them, except as to Lyle McGwinn (a nephew of testatrix's husband) and certain comparatively small specific beneficiaries. * * *

There was, therefore, little reason for the testatrix to revoke the 1965 will in the belief she could revive an earlier will.[40]

Most of the personal goods of the testatrix were not in her possession for almost two years before her death. She did not have her bonds and stock certificates with her, and the fact that negotiable bonds were found under newspapers leaves an inference that the testatrix did not make suitable provision for the safekeeping of her important papers. In addition, testatrix made reference to her will four or five months before her death and this fact, coupled with the complete absence of any evidence of intent to revoke or dissatisfaction with the 1965 will, or evidence of destruction, also goes to rebutting the presumption that the lost 1965 will was destroyed with the intention of revoking it.

Finally, no provision was made for the testatrix's sister, Ann Cotter, in any of the three wills. Mrs. Cotter did not contest the admission of any of the wills, nor is there any evidence that she did not make a diligent search for the 1965 will. Nevertheless, her interests would be furthered if no will were found and this is another factor which lessens the impact of the presumption of revocation in this case.

"We consider, further, that the very existence of the presumption we have been discussing depends on the tacit assumption that a diligent search was made for the will by persons trying to find it. We are far from charging that the contestant and his associates did not search in good faith and there is no evidence but what they did; but whatever virtue the presumption created by a failure to find may start with, that virtue is seriously diminished when it must depend on a search made by those whose interests will be impaired by production of the will. As we said in Gavitt v. Moulton, 1903, 119 Wis. 35, 49–50, 96 N.W. 395, 400:

> " 'True, the mere fact that the contestant had an opportunity to destroy the will would not of itself overcome the presumption that it was destroyed by the testator with the intent to revoke it; still it is a circumstance to be considered with other proof.' " Will of Donigian, supra, pp. 153, 154, 60 N.W.2d p. 735.

Therefore, (1) the absence of any testimony that testatrix was dissatisfied with the will, destroyed it, or that she intended to revoke; (2) evidence that she did not have control of her personal papers and files for nearly two years prior to her death; (3) reference by testatrix to her will four or five months before her death; and (4) the manner in which testatrix kept her other important papers such as stocks and bonds, is sufficient to rebut the presumption and support the conclusion that the June 17, 1965 will was not revoked by the testatrix by destruction or otherwise.

40. For the revival of a will by revoking the will which revoked it expressly or by implication, see Section 4(3), infra. [Footnote by the Editors.]

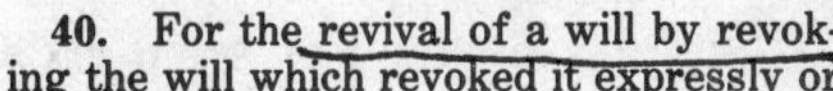

Sec. 310.10, Stats., requires that the petition for probate of a lost will set forth the provisions of the will, which was done in this case by appending a copy of the June 17, 1965 will to the petition. In their brief, appellants state: "It is established that Catherine Markofske properly executed the will of June 17, 1965 as a valid will, and the same was last known to be in her possession." Therefore, the statutory requirements for execution of a will having been met and the presumption overcome, we are of the opinion that the 1965 will should be admitted to probate.

* * * [Discussion by the Court of an argument by the heirs that the trial court had erroneously applied the doctrine of dependent relative revocation, considered hereafter in Section 4(4) of this Chapter, is omitted.] * * * [T]he cause is remanded to the trial court with directions to vacate the order admitting the 1959 will to probate and to proceed with the administration of the estate after admitting the 1965 will to probate as the last will and testament of the decedent.

Judgment reversed and cause remanded to the trial court with directions. * * *

NOTE

A presumption of revocation by destruction is raised when an executed copy of a will is traced to the possession of the testator and cannot be found at his death. The presumption is applied not only in states in which the common law is in force but also in Louisiana and in foreign countries applying the civil law.[41] A similar presumption arises when the executed will is found in mutilated condition in the testator's possession. The presumption when the will is found in mutilated condition is that the entire will is revoked although the character of the mutilation or other evidence may indicate that a partial revocation or no revocation is intended.[42] Extrinsic evidence is admitted freely to show the testator's actual intention, most of the courts admit-

41. E.g., Jones v. Mason, 234 La. 116, 99 So.2d 46 (1958). Noted, 56 Mich.L. Rev. 1036 (1958). In order to raise the presumption the will must be traced to the possession of the testator. E.g., Fletcher Trust Co. v. Morse, 230 Ind. 44, 101 N.E.2d 658 (1951). If the will is not in his exclusive possession, the presumption should be weak if it is raised at all. However, in Citizens First National Bank of Tyler v. Rushing, 433 S.W.2d 741 (Tex. Civ.App.1968) the testatrix, who was ill in bed, lived in a duplex in which her sister had an adjoining apartment. The sister was observed by a nurse on one occasion to have the will in her hand. There was only one witness who had observed this access by the sister and it was not certain that the instrument observed in the sister's hand was the will that was missing. The presumption of revocation was raised, however, and was not rebutted. In Estate of McCue, 254 Or. 259, 456 P.2d 500 (1969) a presumption of revocation of the entire will was raised when the will was found in an office desk drawer in a business school, the room being accessible to others. The name of the principal beneficiary in the will and the name of the executor had been excised with a sharp object.

42. E.g., In re Bakhaus' Estate, 410 Ill. 578, 102 N.E.2d 818 (1951). (Signature cut from will); Estate of McCue, fn. 41, supra.

ting declarations by the testator concerning his intent[43] but some of them limiting these declarations to those that are part of the *res gestae*.[44]

If the presumption of revocation can be rebutted, the proponent faces the issue of proving the contents of the missing original will. If an unexecuted copy (a carbon or a photocopy of the will) is available, it can be useful in proving the contents of the executed will, although contents can be proved by other evidence such as a draft substantiated by the testimony of the draftsman.[45] Although some states have statutes governing the evidence necessary to prove a lost or missing will,[46] the Uniform Probate Code has no express provision;[47] a lost will can be probated only in a formal proceed-

43. E.g., First National Bank of Adams v. Briggs, 329 Mass. 320, 108 N.E.2d 548 (1952) (declarations admitted concerning intention with which pencil marks made on will); In re Kanera's Estate, 334 Mich. 461, 54 N.W.2d 718 (1952) (declarations admitted to rebut presumption of revocation raised by lost will). Even though the testator made no declarations or these are not admissible, there may be evidence intrinsic to the will or in the attending circumstances that will serve to support or rebut the presumption. Interlineations and other marks upon a will may have been made as a guide for preparing a new will which was not executed. See Nelson v. Ratliffe, 137 W.Va. 27, 69 S.E.2d 217 (1952). The English courts and a few American courts treat a cancellation in pencil as tentative and not an indication of final intention to revoke. Francis v. Grover, 5 Hare 39, 67 Eng. Rep. 818 (1845); In re Lord's Will, 106 Me. 51, 75 A. 286 (1909). Contra: e.g., McIntyre v. McIntyre, 120 Ga. 67, 47 S.E. 501, 102 Am.St.Rep. 71, 1 Ann.Cas. 606 (1904); Franklin v. McLean, 192 Va. 684, 66 S.E.2d 504 (1951). The presumption of revocation may be rebutted by the circumstances under which the will is found in the possession of the testator. In Christensen's Will, 197 Misc. 152, 94 N.Y. S.2d 3 (1950) an executed duplicate copy of a will was found with other papers in the attic of the home of testatrix. The will and the papers with it were badly decomposed. A witness testified that the decomposition had been caused by water leaking through the roof. There was no evidence to support a finding that the testatrix intended to revoke the will. The legible copy of the will was admitted to probate.

The equivocal character of the revocation by physical act necessitates that reliance be placed upon unwritten or "parol" evidence in ascertaining the actual intention of the testator; and this has proven one of the greatest embarrassments in judicial attempts to administer the statutes permitting these revocations. See "Will Revocation Cases: More Weight for the Testator's Statement of Intent", 50 Northwestern L.Rev. 691 (1956), in which the policies concerning admission of written and unwritten declarations by the testator are examined.

44. E.g. Will of Bonner, 17 N.Y.2d 9, 266 N.Y.S.2d 971, 214 N.E.2d 154, 28 A. L.R.3d 990 (1966), 28 A.L.R.3d 994 (1969). Testator had cut his will and the envelope containing it in two pieces. Apparently he had then placed this cut envelope with its contents into a larger envelope upon which he had written "My Will". Evidence was offered that testator had stated he had cut his will by mistake while cutting old insurance papers, this statement being made about a year before he died. A witness testified that she had told testator she had a copy of the will and thus it remained in force—and he seemed satisfied with this advice. Another witness testified, however, that testator had repeatedly stated his intention of changing the will and had mentioned that he had cut it. The Court excluded these declarations as not of the *res gestae* and held the presumption of revocation arising from mutilation unrebutted.

45. For the procedure in probating lost wills, see Atkinson, Wills (2d Ed., 1953) § 97; 2 Bowe-Parker: Page, Wills (3d Ed., Rev.1960) §§ 27.1–27.15; Rollison, Wills (1939) § 334; Thompson, Wills (3d Ed., 1947) §§ 204, 205; Evans, "The Probate of Lost Wills", 24 Neb.L. Rev. 283 (1945); 3 A.L.R.2d 949 (1949). If the will was in the possession of the testator and was lost during his lifetime, the presumption of revocation by destruction must be overcome. Until the existence, execution and loss of the will are proved, evidence of the contents is not admissible. When the contents of the will may be proved, the carbon copy may be received in evidence after proper identification. E.g., Forbing v. Weber, 99 Ind. 588 (1885); Tarbell v. Forbes, 177 Mass. 238, 58 N.E. 873 (1900).

46. Ariz.Rev.Stat. § 14–3415; McKinney's N.Y. SCPA § 1407.

47. If a state adopts the Uniform Probate Code and repeals its former code which included an express statute provid-

ing.[48] Note that an unexecuted copy of a will (even a photoprocess reproduction of the executed original) is not the will itself; hence an act done to it will not constitute a revocation.[49] Nor does a presumption of revocation by destruction of an executed copy of a will arise when an unexecuted copy is traced to the possession of the testator and cannot be found or is found mutilated at his death.

But two or more executed copies of a will are all considered as parts of the "will" of the testator. Any executed copy can be probated.[50] A physical act of revocation done by the testator to one copy is presumed to extend to copies not within his possession.[51] This presumption may be rebutted by proof that the testator does not intend the revocation to extend to copies not in his possession.[52] The same presumption is raised when the testator has possession of all executed copies and performs a physical act of revocation to one, although the presumption may be weaker in this case.[53] If an executed copy of the will is traced to the possession of the testator and cannot be found at his death, it is presumed that the testator revoked the executed copy in his possession and intended the revocation to extend to all executed copies not in his possession.[54]

PROBLEM

On March 13, 1926, T executed a will in triplicate. The third executed copy of the will was left in T's possession. This copy could not be found at his death. There was no evidence as to what had happened to the copy. The other two copies can be produced for probate and are executed properly. The applicable statute is McKinney's N.Y. Decedent Estate Law, § 34 (1949). Will or no will? In re Moore's Estate, 137 Misc. 522, 244 N.Y.S. 612 (1930); In re Bates' Estate, 286 Pa. 583, 134 A. 513, 48 A.L.R. 294 (1926). See In re Holmberg's Estate, 400 Ill. 366, 81 N.E.2d 188 (1948) (Copy of will executed in duplicate found in T's pocketbook with "Void" written across both pages

ing for proof of lost wills, there is no implication that lost wills can no longer be proved and probated. Estate of Hartman, 172 Mont. 225, 563 P.2d 569 (1977) (discussing the effect of presumptions and the burden of proof of revocation under the Uniform Probate Code).

48. Uniform Probate Code § 3–301 requires that the original will or an authenticated copy of a will probated in another jurisdiction accompany an application for informal probate.

49. E.g., In re Wehr's Estate, 247 Wis. 98, 18 N.W.2d 709 (1945) (Conformed copy mutilated.). Where the physical act is by writing, such as the language "Null and Void", it may be possible to sustain a revocation of the executed copy as a revocation by subsequent instrument. See In re Kehr's Estate, 373 Pa. 473, 95 A.2d 647 (1953), 3 Buffalo L. Rev. 165 (1953), 32 N.C.L.Rev. 142 (1953), 15 U. of Pitt.L.Rev. 177 (1953).

50. Only one copy need be probated since it would be a useless ceremony to probate the same will twice.

51. E.g., Roberts v. Fisher, 230 Ind. 667, 105 N.E.2d 595 (1952), 50 Mich.L. Rev. 627 (1952) (ribbon copy destroyed, revocation extending to executed carbon in T's possession and executed carbon in possession of attorney); 17 A.L.R.2d 805 (1951).

52. Managle v. Parker, 75 N.H. 139, 71 A. 637, 24 L.R.A.,N.S., 180, Ann.Cas. 1912A, 269 (1908).

53. See Pemberton v. Pemberton, 13 Ves.Jr. 291, 310, 33 Eng.Rep. 303, 310 (1805).

54. E.g., In re Bates' Estate, 286 Pa. 583, 134 A. 513, 48 A.L.R. 294 (1926). But when multiple copies have been executed, even though one of the copies is not in the testator's possession, the presumption of revocation raised by the absence of an executed copy known to be in the testator's possession is a weak one, and possibly may be overcome by the fact that testator preserves an executed copy even though one executed copy which had been in his possession is missing. Jones v. Mason, 234 La. 116, 99 So. 2d 46 (1958).

followed by signature of T. duplicate copy being in possession of another). Same result under McKinney's N.Y., EPTL, § 3–4.1?

(3) BY OPERATION OF LAW

IN RE ESTATE OF BLANCHARD

Supreme Court of Michigan, 1974.
391 Mich. 644, 218 N.W.2d 37.[55]

COLEMAN, JUSTICE.

FACTS

Virginia and Frederick Blanchard were married on November 15, 1949. In 1952, Fred executed a will designating Virginia as executrix and primary beneficiary.

The Blanchards were divorced in 1960. A property settlement was made. Virginia maintains that the couple remained "on close terms" and that she cared for Fred when he was injured in an airplane accident. They were remarried in 1963 and lived together until Fred's accidental death in 1970.

Virginia petitioned for admission to probate of the 1952 will. This was opposed by decedent's children who claimed that the will had been revoked by the divorce. They sought to have Fred's estate pass intestate.

The probate court denied Virginia's petition. The circuit court affirmed as did the Court of Appeals at 43 Mich.App. 752, 204 N.W.2d 730 (1972). In the latter decision, Chief Judge Lesinski recognized that it "gives rise to what might be a harsh result". However, the Court of Appeals held that prior decisions of this Court permitted no other result.

ISSUE

Should the will, executed during the marriage and unaltered at any time after execution, be revoked by implication of law when the parties divorced, remarried and subsequently lived together for seven years until the testator's death?

55. Noted, 21 Wayne L.Rev. 1265 (1975).

STATUTE

This case involves that portion of M.C.L.A. § 702.9; M.S.A. § 27.-3178(79) emphasized below:

> "No will nor any part thereof shall be revoked, unless by burning, tearing, canceling or obliterating the same, with the intention of revoking it, by the testator, or by some person in his presence and by his direction; or by some other will or codicil in writing, executed as prescribed in this chapter; or by some other writing, signed, attested and subscribed in the manner provided in this chapter for the execution of a will; *excepting only that nothing contained in this section shall prevent the revocation implied by law from subsequent changes in the condition or circumstances of the testator.*"

DISCUSSION

The statute above sets forth specific acts which may revoke a will. Further, a revocation may be "implied by law" if "subsequent changes in the condition or circumstances of the testator" warrant such action. "Subsequent changes" do not mandate revocation. The statute provides that the listing of specific acts of revocation does not preclude a finding that "subsequent changes" might also necessitate the court's revocation of the will. The facts of this case demonstrate the validity of the 1952 will.

In Lansing v. Haynes, 95 Mich. 16, 54 N.W. 699 (1893), the testator and his wife executed mutual wills. There was a subsequent divorce accompanied by a property settlement. The Court noted that the "feeling between them, at least upon her part, became bitter". The wife stopped speaking to the husband three months before the divorce. She went out of her way to avoid contact with him.

The testator died without having revoked his will. The Court held that a revocation should be implied by law:

> "By the decree of divorce in this case, the parties became as strangers to each other, and neither owed to the other any obligation or duty thereafter. There was, therefore, a complete change in these relations * * *. It is not * * * the natural presumption that, after the testator had settled with her, had conveyed to her a good share of his property, and they, by agreement, had terminated all their property, as well as their marital relations, the will executed nearly 10 years before should remain in force, and operate upon his death as a conveyance of the remainder of his property to her to the exclusion of his heirs."

The Court then said that the possibility of a different result would be "unusual and contrary to common experience" and that the decision should be controlled by a "reasonable presumption" as to testator's intention.

Lansing established the proper rule for determining whether a revocation should be implied by law, to-wit: such presumption must be reasonable and must take in consideration all of the circumstances. It follows that revocation should not automatically occur by operation of law, but only when the conditions or circumstances warrant such operation.

After the *Lansing* decision, and purportedly based upon that decision, came Wirth v. Wirth, 149 Mich. 687, 113 N.W. 306 (1907) and In re McGraw's Estate, 228 Mich. 1, 199 N.W. 686 (1924). In these latter cases there are statements to the effect that a divorce coupled with a property settlement creates a presumption of revocation which cannot be rebutted by the acts or declarations of the divorced parties. These statements are, in fact, contrary to the decision in *Lansing* which urges a "common sense" and "reasonable" interpretation of the law. An irrebuttable presumption leaves no room for reason to fall upon fact nor for common sense to bring the application of the law into the world of reality.

In cases involving wills probated in Michigan, it is said always to be the court's goal "to effectuate within pertinent precedential and statutory limits" the intent of the testator. Rendle v. Wiemeyer, 374 Mich. 30, 131 N.W.2d 45 (1964) citing Johnson v. Atchinson, 363 Mich. 296, 106 N.W.2d 748 (1961). Justice Sharpe dissenting in the second McGraw case said that the "presumption of revocation is founded upon the inference that, had the testator made a will after the divorce his former wife would not have been provided for as she was in the will he had theretofore made." Such an inference may not be drawn from the instant facts.

It should be noted that under the statute there is no mention of divorce and property settlement as acts of revocation. The only reference is a "revocation implied by law from subsequent changes in the condition or circumstances of the testator".

Each case must be analyzed within the perimeter of its particular facts. The defendants claim that the divorce and property settlement revoked the testator's will. They would not consider as a succeeding condition or circumstance the subsequent remarriage and the maintaining of that relationship until the husband's death.

It is understandable that a man or woman having already written one will—and none subsequently—would see no necessity to republish it or write another if the natural object of his or her bounty were the same after remarriage.

In this case, between the making of the will and testator's death, there was, in addition to the divorce and property settlement, a remarriage of the testator and beneficiary named in the will and seven years of marriage thereafter. At the time of the testator's death, the beneficiary and the testator were not strangers to each other. Each owed the other obligations and duties. The beneficiary named in the will, the testator's wife, was a natural object of his bounty. At the time of death, testator's circumstances in these respects were the same as when he executed his will.

It is not the natural and reasonable presumption from the chain of conditions and circumstances in this case, including divorce, property settlement and remarriage, to imply revocation under the *Lansing* rule. The words "subsequent", "condition" and "circumstances", according to their generally accepted meaning, cannot be restricted to the facts of divorce and property settlement—and no more.

Neither statute nor common law justify a rule that there is an irrebuttable presumption (a conflict of terms) of revocation of a prior will arising upon divorce and property settlement. To the extent that *Wirth* and *McGraw* give credence to such a claim, they are overruled.

If, as in *Lansing*, we draw a reasonable presumption, taking into consideration all of the conditions and circumstances towards the end that the testator's intent be respected and followed, we must reverse the Court of Appeals. Such is our conclusion.

Reversed and remand to the probate court for proceedings consistent with this opinion.

T. G. KAVANAGH, LEVIN and WILLIAMS, JJ., concur.

T. M. KAVANAGH, CHIEF JUSTICE.

* * *

* * * Under the instant facts we only reexamine whether or not a divorce and property settlement falls within the definition of the phrase "subsequent changes in the condition or circumstances of the testator," as our statute uses that phrase. If we decide that it does, then the statute operates automatically by operation of law to revoke the will. If we decide it does not, then the will remains valid. In either case, the intention of the testator as to *the operation of the rule itself* is irrelevant. Our law does not allow such intention to be taken into consideration when statutes of this nature are considered. Either the statute operates upon these *facts* or it does not. While our law permits presumed and *rebuttable fact* situations, it does not countenance rebuttable statutory rules of law. In dealing with a similar issue, this Court made this point very clear in Carpenter v. Snow, 117 Mich. 489, 493, 76 N.W. 78, 80 (1898). In adopting the language of Justice Brewer, the Court stated:

> " 'On the other hand, in Goodtitle v. Otway, 2 H.Bl. 522, Chief Justice Eyre held that, "in cases of revocation by operation of law, the law pronounces upon the ground of a *presumptio juris et de jure* that the party did intend to revoke, and that *presumptio juris* is so violent that it does not admit of circumstances to be set up in evidence to repel it." And in the leading case of Marston v. Roe, 8 Adol. & E. 14, by all the judges in the exchequer chamber, it was finally decided that the revocation of the will took place in consequence of a rule or principle of law, independently altogether of any question of intention of the party himself. Such being the final solution of the question in the English courts, it cannot be that the purpose of the statute in question was to open the door to any other evidence of intention than those expressly named. On

this side of the waters the matter has generally been regulated by statute * * *.'"

The three prior decisions of this Court set forth this Court's reasoning as to why this rule of law is in effect in this State. We reaffirm and adopt their rationale. Further, the Court in In re Bartlett's Estate, 108 Neb. 691, 695, 190 N.W. 869, 870 (1922) adequately set forth my feelings as to the reason "subsequent changes in the condition or circumstances of the testator" should be deemed to include divorce plus property settlement. The Court stated:

> "A full property settlement between husband and wife, either expressed in their agreement or embodied in the divorce decree, is usually arrived at after a consideration of the value and extent of the estate of the husband. The wife upon separation is given an award, its amount influenced to a large degree by the inchoate interest that she then has in her husband's property. Such a settlement, so far as it affects the husband's will, bears to some degree the characteristics of an ademption, and it is the underlying principle of justice which supports the rule as to ademption which no doubt gives strength and reason to the implied revocation in case of a divorce and property settlement between husband and wife."

In the instant case the widow has already received the benefits of a full property settlement. Unless she has conveyed away this property, it remains hers alone. She also is now entitled to her statutory share of her husband's estate. We see no injustice being done in following this Court's prior precedent. The sole fact that the testator remarries the same woman will not suffice to render nugatory the provisions of our statute. Our statute operated on the will and revoked it at the time of the divorce and property settlement. Subsequent action by the testator not fulfilling the statutory requisites for making a will, is necessarily irrelevant.

As to the remaining issue in this case, whether or not the will was revived by the subsequent remarriage of the testator to his prior wife, the law is clear. As stated before in this opinion, the right to make a will is entirely statutory. By virtue of M.C.L.A. § 702.9; M.S.A. § 27.3178(79) this will was revoked by the divorce and property settlement of the parties. Unless the provisions of our Probate Code are followed no new will may come into existence. Any intention of the testator with respect to republication of the will absent the requisite statutory formalities is irrelevant. In re Houghten's Estate, 310 Mich. 613, 17 N.W.2d 774 (1945). Like the provisions dealing with the revocation of a will, our Probate Code sets forth certain definite requirements which must be complied with for a will to be valid. By setting forth these requirements, and by providing for revocation by law only under certain circumstances, our Legislature sought to achieve a certain stability in the probate area of the law. A party should be able to know with certainty whether or not a will is valid, and whether or not it has been revoked. Whenever the answer to one of these questions depends upon the testator's intent at a given point in time, a highly debatable fact situation usually arises. The end result inevitably would be protracted litigation, with the entire costs of this litigation usually being borne by the estate. If this Court were to allow the validity of a will, or the revocation, without the statutory requirement, to be determined by a changing testator's intent, the certainty of our probate law would be lost. The protracted litigation which would follow would create such a drain on all estates, both large and small, as to be unconscionable.

Certainty is needed. The parties and their attorneys need some kind of definite concrete rules, easily determinable, to which the facts of the case might be applied to determine whether a will is, or is not, valid. A rule, based upon an ever changing testator's intent, is not such a rule. The standards set forth by the legislature for the making of a will comprise such a rule and unless these standards are met, this Court holds that no will exists. In the instant case the once valid will was revoked by operation of law. It ceased to exist. It was not reenacted in accordance with our statutory rules. No new will has come into existence.[56]

* * *

NOTE

When the testator destroys his will or otherwise revokes it by act done to the document, the finality of revocation is apparent. However, when the will is "revoked" by change in circumstances but the original document is retained by the testator in its original form, the finality of revocation is far from clear; nor is it clear whether the testator's intent is relevant or whether the revocation occurs regardless of his intent. The problem may be presented in various forms: (1) testator executes a will and later is divorced in a state where divorce revokes the will, but subsequently moves to a state (and dies domiciled there) where divorce is not a revocation;[57] (2) testator executes a will and later is divorced at a time when state law does not make divorce a revocation; still later the Uniform Probate Code is enacted and testator dies.[58] Which law governs, time of revocation or time of death? What light does the principal case shed on this? Some courts apply statutes specifically governing the effect of subsequent marriage or divorce literally,

56. In 1978, Michigan revised its probate code. The present statute Mich. Stat.Ann. § 27.5124(2) [Mich.Comp.Laws Ann. § 700.124(2)], is patterned on Uniform Probate Code § 2–508, set forth on page 261 supra. The result in the principal case would be the same under the statute.

57. See Estate of Garver, 135 N.J. Super. 578, 343 A.2d 817 (1975) (applying law of place of divorce, not decedent's domicile at death, where testator advised by counsel at time of divorce that the will provisions for former spouse had been revoked).

58. The enactment of the Uniform Probate Code poses such a problem in those states which previously had a different statutory rule as to revocation by operation of law. If the revoking event (marriage or divorce) occurred when the old law was in force but the testator died after enactment of the Uniform Probate Code, which law should govern? For a carefully considered opinion and holding that the law in force at testator's death governs, see Matter of Estate of Seymour, 93 N.M. 328, 600 P.2d 274 (1979). See also In re Ziegner's Estate, 146 Wash. 537, 264 P. 12 (1928); Note, 11 Wake F.L.Rev. 527 (1975). For the position that the will has been revoked at time of the divorce or marriage under the law then prevailing, and that intent is immaterial see Will of Mitchell, 285 N.C. 77, 203 S.E.2d 48 (1974), 52 N.C.L.Rev. 949 (1974); cf. De Mars v. Slama, 91 Nev. 603, 540 P.2d 119 (1975).

without regard to testator's intent. In Estate of Spencer,[59] testator's will leaving his entire estate to his fiancee was revoked by his subsequent marriage to her. And in Estate of Montoya [60] where the testator executed a will expressly disinheriting his wife and devising all his estate to his sister and subsequently divorced, then remarried the same wife, the New Mexico court held that the will was revoked by the remarriage so that the wife was entitled to an intestate share. The wording of the statute is crucial.

The Wills Act, 1837,[61] provided that marriage revoked the prior will of a man or woman with certain exceptions. Prior to the enactment of this statute, the English courts held that marriage revoked the prior will of a woman and that marriage coupled with the birth of issue revoked the will of a man which had been executed prior to marriage.[62] A woman lost the capacity to revoke a will when she married, although she could make and revoke wills executing a power of appointment and could dispose of her separate estate if she had made provision therefor in an antenuptial contract. Except in the latter cases, a woman's will would become irrevocable upon her marriage unless the courts elected to treat the will as revoked by operation of law at the time of marriage. The courts regarded the will as revoked by operation of law except to the extent that the will executed a power of appointment, or disposed of the separate estate of the woman when the woman's right of disposition had been reserved by an antenuptial agreement. The rule in the case of a man's will was for the protection of the heir under the common law

59. 60 Haw. 497, 591 P.2d 611 (1979).

60. 89 N.M. 667, 556 P.2d 353 (1976). New Mexico adopted the Uniform Probate Code in 1975; under the present statute the will is not revoked by the marriage nor is the spouse entitled to an intestate share if "it appears from the will that the omission was intentional."

61. 7 Wm. IV & 1 Vict., c. 26, § XVIII (1837); See generally, Atkinson, Wills (2d Ed., 1953) § 85; 2 Bowe-Parker: Page, Wills (3d Ed., 1960) §§ 21.86–21.111; Rollison, Wills (1939) §§ 147–154; Thompson, Wills (3d Ed., 1947) §§ 169–176; Durfee, "Revocation of Wills by Subsequent Changes in the Condition or Circumstances of the Testator", 40 Mich.L. Rev. 406 (1942); Graunke and Beuscher, "The Doctrine of Implied Revocation of Wills by Reason of Change in Domestic Relations of Testator", 5 Wis.L.Rev. 387 (1930); Note, "Implied by Law Revocation of Wills," 42 Notre Dame Lawyer 59 (1966). The reason for revocation of a will by marriage has been speculated upon and was recently considered by the British Law Reform Committee which recommended retention of the revocation with minor modifications. Cmd. 7902, 3.1–3.25 (1980). It is commonly thought that the revocation was for the protection of the family—and it may have been retained for that reason. However the revocation probably originated because the Attorney General, Sir Frederick Pollock did not know the reason for the difference between the rule for revocation of a man's will and revocation of a woman's will at common law and suggested that for uniformity that a single rule of revocation by marriage apply to the will of either—a Victorian gesture towards equality of the sexes. See 26 Hansard 854–855 (11 March 1835). For the probable reason for the distinction at common law read carefully the footnote which follows.

62. The rule relating to the will of a woman probably developed after married women were deprived of the capacity to devise land by the Bill Concerning the Explanation of Wills, 34 & 35 Hen. VIII, c. 5 (1542–43). The rule had nothing to do with the intention of the testatrix. The rule relating to the will of a man was derived in part from the Roman law and was applied by the ecclesiastical courts. The rule was once based upon the presumed change of the testator's intention due to the alteration in his domestic circumstances. In Brady v. Cubitt, 1 Doug. 31, 99 Eng.Rep. 24 (1778), the presumption of revocation was said to be rebuttable by "any sort of evidence". But in order to reconcile the rule with the concluding language of Section VI of the Statute of Frauds, 1677, "any former law or usage to the contrary notwithstanding", the rationale that the rule was based on the testator's intention was abandoned and the rule was treated as an irrebuttable presumption of law. Goodtitle d. Holford v. Otway, 2 H.Bl. 516, 126 Eng.Rep. 679 (1795). The recognized exceptions to the rule reveal its origin in the intention of the testator.

of descent. A man's will was not revoked merely upon marriage because the wife took dower against the will. If the will was executed after marriage and a child was born, it was presumed that the testator contemplated the birth of a child when the will was executed. The will was not revoked for that reason.[63] On the other hand, if the will was executed before marriage and a child was born thereafter, the will was revoked when the child was born. The testator could prevent the operation of the common law rule by a provision by will or other writing for afterborn children. If the testator did not dispose of all of the property that he had when the will was executed, he was presumed to have intended to provide for his afterborn children by operation of the intestate laws.[64] But this presumption was not raised when the testator acquired property after the will was executed and this property passed by intestacy.[65]

The common law doctrines have been superseded by statutory provisions in many American states.[66] As in the Wills Act, 1837, it may be provided that marriage revokes the will of a man or woman.[67] These statutes, like those which do not revoke the will but give the spouse an intestate share as a pretermitted heir,[68] usually provide that the revocation does not operate if the spouse is "mentioned" in the will so as to show an intent not to provide for the spouse, or is provided for by the will or by other transfer.[69] The lawyer who prepares a will for a client planning to marry must draft the will with a clause expressly mentioning the intended spouse by name and stating the client's intent to make no provision for such person, if that is the intent; failure to do so can make the lawyer liable to the devisees whose shares are reduced by a claim of the spouse, either as an omitted spouse under a statute like Uniform Probate Code § 2–301 (supra page 178) or as an heir because the will has been revoked by the later marriage under statute so providing.[70] There is a split of authority as to whether a general clause in the will purporting to make no provision for "any person claiming as an heir by reason of marriage" satisfies the statutory requirement regarding intentional omission.[71]

Divorce revokes the testamentary provision for a divorced spouse in an increasing number of states and Uniform Probate Code, § 2–508 sets forth

63. Doe d. White v. Barford, 4 M. & S. 10, 105 Eng.Rep. 739 (1815).

64. See Doe d. Shelley v. Edlin, 4 A. & E. 582, 111 Eng.Rep. 906 (1836).

65. See Marston v. Roe d. Fox, 8 A. & E. 14, 112 Eng.Rep. 742 (1838).

66. Rees, "American Wills Statutes", 46 Va.L.Rev. 856, 880 (1960).

67. E.g., Conn.Gen.Stat. § 45–162 (1980 Supp.). The will may be revoked only if the spouse survives or if no provision for the spouse is made. E.g., McKinney's N.Y., EPTL, § 5–1.3 (applicable to will executed prior to 1 Sept. 1930). A will made in the exercise of a power of appointment may not be revoked if certain takers in default are named. Mitchell, "The Revocation of Testamentary Appointments on Marriage", 67 L.Q.Rev. 351 (1951). The will of a woman may be revoked by marriage, the death of the husband not reviving the will. E.g., Ala. Code § 43–1–8 (1975). Or the will of a man may be revoked by marriage if his spouse survives him and no provision for the spouse is made by will or antenuptial property agreement.

68. E.g., West's Ann.Calif.Prob.Code § 70.

69. Uniform Probate Code § 2–301. See Chapter IV, Section 2(6).

70. Heyer v. Flaig, 70 Cal.2d 223, 74 Cal.Rptr. 225, 449 P.2d 161 (1969) (also holding that the statute of limitations does not begin to run against the devisees until the testator's death).

71. 2 Bowe-Parker: Page, Wills (3d Ed.Rev.1960) § 21.91; Note (1964) 97 A.L.R.2d 1026. In the following cases such a general clause was construed to show an intent to exclude the subsequent spouse: Estate of Duke, 41 Cal.2d 509, 261 P.2d 235 (1953); Estate of Hall, 159 Wash. 236, 292 P. 401 (1930). Note that clauses intended to exclude afterborn children are necessarily worded in general terms.

divorce as the only ground of revocation by operation of law.[72] The common law rule concerning revocation of a man's will may be enacted in statutory form and extended to the will of a man or woman.[73] A will executed after marriage may be revoked by the birth of issue to the testator or the testatrix.[74] The variations and combinations are numerous. If the statutory methods for revocation by operation of law are exclusive, the common law doctrines are useful only in construing the statute.[75] But a statute may provide no methods for revocation by operation of law,[76] may recognize the common law doctrines expressly,[77] or may recognize the common law doctrines and provide some statutory methods for revocation by operation of law in addition.[78] In these situations the common law doctrines will be applied, although often the doctrines are altered from their English form.

Statutes in this country provide that married women may hold separate property and make or revoke wills. Thus, the common law doctrine that a woman's will is revoked by marriage has been rejected by most of the courts.[79] There is little authority for extending the common law rule applicable to the will of a man to the will of a woman.[80] When the wife is an heir

72. E.g., Ga.Code Ann. § 113–408; Ind.Stat.Ann. § 29–1–5–8; Minn.Stat. Ann. § 524.2–508; McKinney's N.Y., EPTL, § 5–1.4 (1980 Supp.); Pa.—20 P.S. § 2507(2); Wash.Rev.Code Ann. § 11.-12.050. The British Law Reform Committee divided on the issue of divorce as a revocation. The majority favored divorce as a revocation of the provisions for the divorced spouse, treating the situation as if the spouse had predeceased the testator. The minority opposed the inclusion of divorce in the Wills Act, perceiving "no compelling moral or social reason why divorce should have any effect upon a will * * * [it being preferable] * * * that if a testator's true intentions are to fail it should be as a result of his own inaction rather than as a result of some rule of law of which he is ignorant". Cmd. 7902, 3.38, p. 22 (1980). The division was reported in the recommendation.

73. E.g., Md.Code Ann. Estates & Trusts § 4–105(c) (provided child survives the parent). If the testator provides for the afterborn child, the will is not revoked by most statutes of this type.

74. Ga.Code Ann. § 113–408; Tex.—V.A.T.S. Probate Code, § 67(b) (unless the child dies within 1 year after the testator, or unless the principal beneficiary of the will is the surviving spouse and that spouse is the mother or father of all of the testator's children). For the pretermitted heir statutes, which do not revoke the will but allow the child to take an intestate share, see Chapter IV, Section 3. The relationship between pretermitted heir and revocation provisions may become important if it is necessary to argue that a pretermitted heir statute, standing alone, is sufficient to supersede the common law rule of revocation of a will by marriage and birth of issue. See fns. 75 and 78, infra.

75. If statutory methods for revocation by operation of law are provided and no reference is made to the common law doctrines, the statutory methods usually are regarded as exclusive. See In re Sussdorff's Estate, 182 Misc. 69, 43 N.Y. S.2d 760 (1943) (Divorce rejected as ground for revocation when statute specified marriage).

76. If the statute contains the concluding words of Section VI of the Statute of Frauds, 1677, "any former law or usage to the contrary notwithstanding", the English construction of this language as restricted to intentional methods of revocation is usually followed and the common law doctrines are allowed to operate. Pascucci v. Alsop, 147 F.2d 880 (D.C.Cir.1945).

77. E.g., Mich.Stats.Ann. § 27.3178 (79).

78. The common law methods are in force to the extent that the statutory provisions do not work an implied repeal. See Hertrais v. Moore, 325 Mass. 57, 88 N.E.2d 909 (1949), 30 B.U.L.R. 276 (1950), 50 Col.L.Rev. 531 (1950).

79. E.g., Hastings v. Day, 151 Iowa 39, 130 N.W. 134 (1911); Will of Ward, 70 Wis. 251, 35 N.W. 731 (1887). Contra: e.g., Colcord v. Conroy, 40 Fla. 97, 23 So. 561 (1898); Estate of Teopfer, 12 N.M. 372, 78 P. 53 (1904).

80. In Durfee v. Risch, 142 Mich. 504, 105 N.W. 1114 (1905) a woman's will was held revoked by marriage and birth of issue. But birth of issue does not revoke the will executed after marriage of a woman. Masionis v. Kraulikauckas, 103 N. J.Eq. 66, 142 A. 246 (1928).

to the husband a court may be willing to hold that the husband's will is revoked by marriage alone.[81] Due in part to the widespread enactment of pretermitted heir statutes, the majority of the courts have been unwilling to hold that birth of issue alone revokes a will.[82] American statutes provide that an adopted child inherits from his adopting parents.[83] Statutes also provide that an illegitimate child inherits from his mother and, when recognized or acknowledged, from his father.[84] Most of the cases discussing adoption or birth of an illegitimate as grounds for revocation of a will turn upon the construction of statutory provisions for revocation by operation of law.[85] If under the same circumstances the birth of a legitimate child would revoke the will of a parent, it seems that the adoption of a child should revoke the parent's will, that the birth of an illegitimate should revoke the will of his mother, and that recognition or acknowledgment of an illegitimate should revoke the will of his father.

The courts have been in agreement that absent a statute, divorce alone or divorce accompanied by an alimony decree will not revoke provisions in a will in favor of the divorced spouse.[86] But a number of courts have held the provisions in favor of the divorced spouse revoked when the divorce was accompanied by a property settlement,[87] the decisions to the contrary usually resting upon the exclusive nature of prescribed statutory methods for revocation by operation of law.[88]

If the provision in the will for the divorced spouse is revoked, to whom does the property pass? Rarely, if ever, does a will contain an alternative devise for such a situation. If the will contains a substitutionary gift to another person or persons if the named spouse "predeceases" the testator, most courts imply that the testator would want that gift to operate if the

81. E.g., In re Lewis' Will, 41 N.M. 522, 71 P.2d 1032 (1937). Contra: e.g., Hoy v. Hoy, 93 Miss. 732, 48 So. 903 (1908).

82. In Fallon v. Chidester, 46 Iowa 588 (1877), birth of issue was said to revoke the will of a man. No pretermitted heir statute was in force. In Easterlin v. Easterlin, 62 Fla. 468, 56 So. 688 (1911), even though no pretermitted heir statute was in force, it was held that birth of issue did not revoke a man's will.

83. See Chapter III, Section 2.

84. See Chapter III, Section 2.

85. E.g., Thornton v. Anderson, 207 Ga. 714, 64 S.E.2d 186 (1951), 3 Mercer L. Rev. 223 (1951), 5 Vand.L.Rev. 128 (1951). Cases are collected in Atkinson, Wills (2d Ed., 1953) 429–430; 24 A.L.R.2d 1085 (1952). See Evans, "Revocation by Adoption of a Child", 22 Ky.L.J. 600 (1934).

86. E.g., Card v. Alexander, 48 Conn. 492, 40 Am.Rep. 187 (1881); Speroni v. Speroni, 406 Ill. 28, 92 N.E.2d 63 (1950). See Evans, "Testamentary Revocation by Divorce", 24 Ky.L.J. 1 (1935); 18 A.L.R. 2d 697 (1951).

87. E.g., Luff v. Luff, 359 F.2d 235 (D.C.Cir.1966); Lansing v. Haynes, 95 Mich. 16, 54 N.W. 699, 35 Am.St.Rep. 545 (1893); Estate of Bartlett, 108 Neb. 681, 190 N.W. 869 (1922), 23 Col.L.Rev. 404 (1923), 8 Iowa L.B. 281 (1923), 9 Va.L. Rev. 394 (1923), 32 Yale L.J. 627 (1923); Rankin v. McDearman, 38 Tenn.App. 160, 270 S.W.2d 660 (1955); 9 Okl.L.Rev. 112 (1956). The revocation extends only to the provisions in the will for the divorced spouse. The doctrine of "Ademption by Satisfaction" may be applicable in the property settlement cases. See Chapter XV. Although the ecclesiastical courts had jurisdiction to grant a divorce *a mensa et thoro*, there was no judicial divorce completely, severing the marriage relationship in England until 1857. The Wills Act, 1837, had, in the meantime, restricted revocations by operation of law to marriage of a testator or testatrix.

88. E.g., Ireland v. Terwilliger, 54 So. 2d 52 (Fla.1951), 28 N.D.L.Rev. 232 (1952); Hertrais v. Moore, 325 Mass. 57, 88 N.E.2d 909 (1949), 30 B.U.L.R. 276 (1950), 50 Col.L.Rev. 531 (1950); Robertson v. Jones, 345 Mo. 828, 136 S.W.2d 278 (1940); Nenaber's Estate, 55 S.D. 257, 225 N.W. 719 (1929), 5 Wis.L.Rev. 377 (1930). But see Codner v. Caldwell, 156 Ohio St. 197, 101 N.E.2d 901 (1951), 21 U. of Cin.L.Rev. 212 (1952). (No revocation by divorce and property settlement even though statute does not set forth methods for revocation by operation of law.)

former spouse does not take because of divorce.[89] Should the gift be implied if the substituted taker is a child of the divorced spouse but not of the testator (a stepchild)?[90] Note that Uniform Probate Code § 2–508 provides expressly that the property passes "as if the former spouse failed to survive the decedent." If there is no alternative devise, the property devised to the former spouse falls into the residue, or if itself a residuary devise then passes intestate to the heirs.[91]

From time to time the courts have been pressed to extend the common law doctrines of revocation by operation of law to cases in which the donee of a large part of the estate predeceases the testator, grandchildren are born after the will is executed, or there have been fluctuations in the value of property described in the will. In these situations the testator could have changed his will prior to his death if he had desired to do so and the courts are unwilling to hold that there has been a revocation.[92]

The pretermitted heir statutes referred to in this note and considered in Chapter IV should be distinguished from a statute revoking a will by operation of law. A pretermitted heir statute operates as a "forced heirship" provision and does not revoke the will in the sense that part or all of the will is denied probate.

If the pretermitted heir is the only heir, the will passes no estate because the heir takes all of it. The will may be effective in part to nominate an executor and establish the powers and duties of this fiduciary or to set forth other administrative provisions. Some of the pretermitted heir statutes refer to their "effect" as "revocatory"[93] although this description is accurate only to the extent the statute accomplishes the same policy to protect a child accomplished by a statute revoking a will upon birth of children or marriage plus birth of children, this policy being to protect a child against inadvertent exclusion from participation in the estate.

Although statutes providing exclusive methods for revocation by operation of law have seldom been repealed, care should be taken in the event of such a repeal to declare the common law rules of revocation by operation of law inoperative expressly, since by the traditional rule the common law principle is revived when the superseding statute is repealed. Since a pretermitted heir statute may serve the same policy as the repealed statute, an effective argument might be made that the pretermitted heir statute continues to supersede the common law rule.

89. Russell v. Estate of Russell, 216 Kan. 730, 534 P.2d 261 (1975); Jones v. Brown, 219 Va. 599, 248 S.E.2d 812 (1978).

90. In Porter v. Porter, 286 N.W.2d 649 (Iowa 1979), noted 30 Drake L.Rev. 181 (1980–1981), a devise to a stepson if the testator's wife should predecease him was construed to give the devise to the stepson when the wife and the testator were divorced. Some statutes specifically provide that a subsequent divorce also revokes a provision for "any issue of the former spouse who are not also issue of the testator." Ariz.Rev.Stat. § 14–2508.

91. This problem is considered in greater detail in Chapter XV.

92. E.g., Redwood v. Howison, 129 Md. 577, 99 A. 863 (1917) (death of spouse of testator); Ater v. McClure, 329 Ill. 519, 161 N.E. 129 (1923) (major increase in value of estate); Warner v. Beach, 4 Gray (Mass.) 162 (1865). (testator executed will and then became insane, remaining in this condition for 40 years until his death)

93. E.g., McKinney's N.Y., EPTL, § 5–3.2.

SECTION 3. REVOCATION OF A WILL IN PART

(1) NATURE OF THE PROBLEM

Courts speak of a single testamentary instrument and also a series of testamentary instruments which express the intention of a testator as a "will". A "revocation in part" or "partial revocation" may refer to a repeal of some but not all of the provisions of a single testamentary instrument. The reference may be to a repeal of one or more of a number of testamentary writings which set forth a testator's scheme for the disposition of property.

The questions raised by "partial revocation" when used in these two senses are related but are not identical. In this section, three major questions are considered that may arise when it is contended that a single testamentary instrument has been revoked in part. (1) Is it possible to revoke the will in part by the technique used? (2) Has a revocation in part in fact occurred? (3) What is the effect of the revocation on the remaining provisions of the will? When dealing with "partial revocation" as applied to a series of testamentary writings we assume that one or more of the writings have been revoked *in toto*. The major questions which we consider are: (1) how do we show the intention of the testator to extend the revocation to other writings in the series which had not been revoked expressly? (2) to what extent can this intention be given effect?

(2) REVOCATION IN PART OF A SINGLE TESTAMENTARY INSTRUMENT

BIGELOW v. GILLOTT

Supreme Judicial Court of Massachusetts, 1877.
123 Mass. 102, 25 Am.Rep. 32.

MORTON, J. The presiding justice who heard this case has found as facts, that the testator erased the sixth and thirteenth clauses of his will after its execution, and that such erasures were made with the intention of revoking the said clauses, but with no intention of defeating or revoking the other provisions of the will. These findings were clearly justified by the evidence. We need not consider the evidence in detail, as the appellants do not contend that the findings were erroneous, the only questions raised by them being as to the legal effect of such erasures.

The statute provides that "no will shall be revoked, unless by burning, tearing, canceling or obliterating the same, with the intention of revoking it, by the testator himself, or by some person in his presence and by his direction; or by some other will, codicil or writing, signed, attested and subscribed, in the manner provided for making a will," Gen.Sts. c. 92, § 11.[94] This provision is a reenactment of the Rev.Sts. c. 62, § 9, with merely unimportant verbal changes. The Rev.Sts. made material changes in the law as to wills, doing away with the distinctions between wills affecting real, and wills affecting personal, property and putting all upon the same footing. The St. of 1783, c. 24, § 2, permitted the revocation of a devise of land, "or any clause thereof," in the manner pointed out in the statute, which was the same manner now provided for the revocation of a will.

We see nothing to indicate that the legislature, in the revision of 1836, intended to change the law in this respect and to limit the power of revocation to a revocation of the whole will. The power to revoke a will includes the power to revoke any part of it. If we were to hold that under this provision a testator could not revoke a part of a will by canceling or obliterating it, we would be obliged by the same rule of construction to hold that he could not revoke a part by codicil, which would be against the uniform practice in this Commonwealth, sanctioned by numerous decisions.

We are, therefore, of opinion that, in this case, the cancellation by the testator of the sixth and thirteenth clauses of his will, by drawing lines through them, with the intention of revoking them, was a legal revocation of those clauses.

The remaining question is as to the effect of this revocation upon the property affected by the revoked clauses. The appellants contend that the property devised and bequeathed therein is to be treated as intestate property, which goes to the heirs at law or distributees; and the executors and trustees contend that it passes to them under the residuary clause of the will.

It is a clearly settled rule of law that, in a will of personal property, a general residuary bequest carries to the residuary legatee all the personal property of the testator which is not otherwise disposed of by the will, including all lapsed legacies and all void legacies. And in this Commonwealth, since the passage of the Rev.Sts. in 1836, the same rule applies to wills of real estate. Thayer v. Wellington, 9 Allen, 283, and cases cited. It is true that if a special bequest in a will lapses or fails for any reason, the sum bequeathed will not pass to the residuary legatee if it appears from the will that it was the intention of the testator to exclude it from the residuary clause. In Thayer v. Wellington, ubi supra, the court says: "We take the rule to be

94. Now Mass.Gen.Laws ch. 191, § 8 (1981 Supp.)—Ed.

that a general residuary clause passes all the estate of the testator not otherwise disposed of, unless it is manifestly contradictory to the declared purpose of the testator, as found in other parts of the will. There must be a clear intention that in no event it shall pass to the residuary devisee."

In this case, there is nothing to indicate an intention on the part of the testator that the property covered by the revoked clauses should not go to the residuary devisees. The residuary clause is expressed in the broadest terms. "I give, bequeath and devise all the rest, residue and remainder of my estate of every description, of which I shall die seised and possessed." The intention of the testator is clear, to give all his property, not otherwise disposed of by the will, to the trustees named therein, for the support of the charity established by the nineteenth clause. He revoked the sixth and thirteenth clauses, and purposely and intelligently left the other provisions to stand as his will. The only fair inference is that he intended that the property covered by those clauses, and which by his revocation became undisposed of by the other clauses of the will, should fall within the residuary clause. We are of the opinion that this case falls within the general rule, and that the property in question passes to the residuary devisees.

The argument of the appellants, that this view is in conflict with the provisions of law which require that a will disposing of property should be executed in the presence of three witnesses is not sound. It is true that the act of revocation need not be done in the presence of witnesses; but such act does not dispose of the property. It is disposed of by the residuary clause, which is executed with all the formalities required in the execution of a testamentary disposition of property.

Decree of Probate Court affirmed.

NOTE

If the applicable statute contains the language of Section VI of the Statute of Frauds, 1677, "nor any clause thereof" or the language of the Wills Act, 1837, "or any part thereof", or an express provision for partial revocation, the courts have agreed, with some exceptions, that a testator may revoke his will in part by physical act.[95] Where there is no statutory language that supports revocation by physical act in part, most of the courts, unlike

95. Most of the American statutes have language that provides a basis for a construction that the particular statute expressly authorizes partial revocation by physical act. See Rees, "American Wills Statutes", 46 Va.L.Rev. 856, 879 (1960). Uniform Probate Code § 2–507 uses the words: "A will *or any part thereof* * * *" [emphasis added]. The Indiana statute expressly eliminates partial revocations by physical act by providing for partial revocation only by subsequent instrument. Ind.Stat.Ann. § 29–1–5–6. In revocation by operation of law the entire will is usually revoked, although in certain situations, such as divorce, the revocation may extend only to the provisions for the divorced spouse. The courts are agreed that a will may be revoked in part by a subsequent instrument executed with testamentary formalities, although difficulty arises when there is no clause of revocation in the subsequent will and the revocation, if there is one, must depend upon the inconsistency of the provisions of the instruments.

the court in the principal case, have refused to recognize an attempted partial revocation.[96] If partial revocation is not permitted, the provisions purportedly revoked are probated with the remainder of the will.[97] By the better view, the remainder of the will is admitted to probate if the provisions which the testator attempted to revoke cannot be read.[98]

Where partial revocation by physical act is permitted, there can be no partial revocation of the words of a will if the effect is to change the construction of the remainder of a clause or to increase a provision made for someone other than the residuary legatee or devisee. Thus, in Eschbach v. Collins,[99] the testator provided in his will that "the shares of my sons Leo and John E. Eschbach to be held by each of them who may survive me, absolutely. * * * The shares of my other children to be held for their respective lives." The testator then struck out the words "Leo and John E. Eschbach". The testator died survived by sons in addition to Leo and John E. Eschbach and daughters. The deletion of the words was ignored, since to give the deletion effect would be to give all of the sons absolute interests and the daughters life estates.[1] There is no objection to a residuary legatee or devisee taking an increased share because of a deletion in the will.[2] The operation of a residuary clause is essentially prospective in character.

GOULD v. CHAMBERLAIN

Supreme Judicial Court of Massachusetts, 1903.
184 Mass. 115, 68 N.E. 39.

[By will dated March 26, 1900, the Testator made the following bequests and legacies: $5,000 to his housekeeper, Mrs. Whitman;

96. E.g., Board of National Missions v. Sherry, 372 Ill. 272, 23 N.E.2d 730 (1939).

97. E.g., Coghlin v. Coghlin, 79 Ohio St. 71, 85 N.E. 1058 (1908). If the intention is to revoke the entire will by the deletion of several words in it, the entire will should be denied probate. When partial revocation by physical act is not permitted and part of the will is so damaged that the words cannot be read, there is no way in which the damaged material can be probated unless the words can be proved. In Estate of Downie, 213 N.E.2d 833 (Probate Ct. Cuyahoga Co., Ohio, 1966) the will was found in the possession of Testator with the last two bequests on a page torn or cut off. The Court determined that he did not intend to revoke the whole will and could not revoke the will in part. There was, however, a copy of the torn bequests which could be used to prove them. See Estate of McCue, 254 Or. 259, 456 P.2d 500 (1969) in which the name of the principal beneficiary had been excised and one Wood petitioned for probate of the will asserting that his name was the one excised. The Court states that "the parties appear to assume that Wood had been named"; but the entire will was held revoked and the question of proof of the excised provisions was not placed in issue directly.

98. Matter of Enright's Will, 139 Misc. 192, 248 N.Y.S. 707 (1931). Contra: In re Johannes' Will, 170 Kan. 407, 227 P. 2d 148, 24 A.L.R.2d 507 (1951).

99. 61 Md. 478, 48 Am.Rep. 123 (1883).

1. See Nelen v. Nelen, 52 R.I. 354, 161 A. 121 (1932); Pringle v. M'Pherson, 2 Brev. (S.C.) 279, 3 Am.Dec. 713 (1809). The problem is similar to that with which the courts deal when materials are included in a will as a result of a mistake in the factum. See Chapter VII, Section 2(5). If the testator strikes a provision in his will and interlines a substituted provision which cannot be given effect, the courts sometimes deal with the case as a problem in dependent relative revocation and reinstate the deleted provision if that appears to be the intention of the testator as revealed by extrinsic evidence. See Section 4(4), infra.

2. Barfield v. Carr, 169 N.C. 574, 86 S.E. 498 (1915); Brown v. Brown, 91 S.C. 101, 74 S.E. 135 (1912). See Evans, "Testamentary Revocation by Act to the Document and Dependent Relative Revocation," 23 Ky.L.J. 557, 571–575 (1935).

$1,000 to his brother-in-law, Hale E. Crosby; $1,000 each to his brothers, Henry and William Chamberlain; $1,000 to Mattie Fielding, a daughter of a brother-in-law; $1,000 to Sarah W. Fuller, a sister-in-law; $1,000 to Alice W. Putnam, his wife's niece; and $500 each to four friends, Mellen Chamberlain (testator's namesake), Mary A. Jenkins, Elizabeth Porter Gould and Mary F. Colesworthy. Specific bequests and legacies were made to various institutions. The residue of the testator's estate was given to four institutions and five individuals in unequal shares. Thereafter, on May 31, 1900, the testator executed a codicil which read in part:

> "My estate real and personal I bequeath as follows:
>
> "To Mrs. John Whitman my faithful housekeeper, Three thousand dollars to be paid to her out of the first monies that shall come into the hands of my executors or to my estate and without delay for its final settlement and the further sum of two thousand dollars which shall first appear to be a residue thereof.
>
> "To my brother in law, Hale E. Crosby, my brother Henry Chamberlain both of Three Oaks, Michigan, and my brother William Chamberlain of Jackson, said Michigan, eight hundred dollars each,
>
> "To Mrs. Mattie Fielding, daughter of my brother in law, John M. Putnam, to Miss Alice M. Putnam niece of my late wife, and to Mrs. Sarah W. Fuller, sister of my late wife, all of Danvers, Massachusetts, the sum of eight hundred dollars each.
>
> "To Miss Mary A. Jenkins, formerly of the Boston Public Library, to Miss Elizabeth Porter Gould, of Boston, to Miss Mary F. Colesworthy, of Chelsea, the sum of five hundred dollars each.
>
> "To Miss Dora J. Murray, of Revere, the sum of one hundred dollars."

The phraseology of both the will and codicil were similar. Dora J. Murray, who was mentioned in the codicil, was not mentioned in the will.

The testator died on June 25, 1900.]

MORTON, J. This is an appeal from a decree of the probate court for Suffolk county upon a petition for instructions by the executors of the will of Mellen Chamberlain. The single justice who heard the case affirmed the decree, and reported the case to this court for its determination. The questions are whether certain legacies given in the codicil are cumulative or substitutional in respect of legacies given in the will to the same persons, and whether certain evidence admitted subject to the exceptions of the heirs at law was rightly admitted. We take up the question of evidence first.

The evidence objected to was that the testator knew, after August 1898, which was before the date of the will, that he was living on a steadily diminishing income; that subsequent to the execution of the will, and prior to the execution of the codicil, he was told by his attending physician that with good care he would live through the summer of 1900, and probably into the fall, and that he replied that in such case he would make greater inroads upon his principal than he had expected to; and that twice after the execution of the will and before the execution of the codicil he consulted one or more of his executors on the question whether his estate was sufficient to carry out the provisions of the will, and said on these occasions that he doubted whether his estate was sufficient to carry out the provisions of his will. It is well settled that the situation and circumstances of a testator may be shown in order to enable the court to put itself as near as may be in his place and ascertain what he intended to express by the language used. Crocker v. Crocker, 11 Pick. 252, 256; Popkin v. Sargent, 10 Cush. 330; Morse v. Stearns, 131 Mass. 389; Boys v. Williams, 2 Rus. & M. 690; Martin v. Drinkwater, 2 Beav. 215. If every word had only one meaning, and was incapable of being used or understood in any other sense, there would be no occasion for the introduction of such testimony. But language is far from having this certainty, and hence the necessity that, in order to correctly interpret it, the court should understand the circumstances under which and in reference to which it was used. A testator's declarations of his intentions are inadmissible, though logically they would seem to be the best evidence obtainable. They are excluded, however, by reason of the statute which requires wills to be in writing, and also of the rule that forbids the introduction of parol evidence to alter or vary written instruments. In the present case the evidence that was admitted was not evidence of statements by the testator of his intentions, but was evidence tending to show a knowledge and appreciation on his part of his situation and circumstances and as such was clearly admissible.

The question whether the legacies in a codicil are to be regarded as cumulative or substitutional is one of intention. In Wainwright v. Tuckerman, 120 Mass. 232, 238, it is said that: "When legacies are given by different instruments, the general rule is that the second is to be treated as additional to the first, in the absence of anything signifying a different intention; but in this as in all other questions of construction of testamentary instruments the apparent intention of the testator must be the guide of the court." See, also, Bates, Pet'r., 159 Mass. 252, 257, 34 N.E. 266. Taking into account the evidence of the statements of the testator and his knowledge of his circumstances, it seems to us clear that the legacies in the codicil, so far as given to the same persons to whom legacies are given in the will, are to be regarded as substitutional, rather than as cumulative. It is not reasonable to suppose that he could have intended those legacies to be in addition to the legacies already given, when he had, in effect, expressed his doubts whether the estate was sufficient to pay the legacies already given. The more natural interpretation of the codicil is that the testator intended it as the last and final expression of his purposes in regard to the persons named in it, and as taking the place, as far as it went, of the will. The codicil itself, it seems to us, bears out this construction. Although it begins by saying that it is a codicil to his last will and testament, and that is the general character of the instrument, it purports also to be a disposition of the whole estate, real and personal, of the testator, as is shown by the phrase,

"My estate real and personal, I bequeath as follows," which is copied from the will. The reasonable explanation of this language is that the testator intended by it to signify that the legacies which follow were to be all that the several parties named were to receive out of his whole estate. Again, the language of the codicil is copied from corresponding clauses in the will, and this has been held to indicate an intention to substitute in such cases the second legacy for the first. Suisse v. Lowther, 2 Hare, 424, 432. Moreover, the words, "out of the first monies that shall come into the hands of my executors," in the will and codicil, and the words, "which shall first appear to be a residue thereof," in the codicil, which words are used in each instance in regard to the legacy to Mrs. Whitman, and the general scheme of the will, tend to show, we think, that it was the intention of the testator that the savings bank deposits, bonds and other securities should constitute the fund from which the cash legacies should be paid. This intention would or might be defeated, in part at least, if the legacies given in the codicil are regarded as cumulative. It is no doubt true, as the heirs at law contend, that a codicil makes and changes a will only so far as the intention to do so is manifest. But, as already observed, we think that it was the intention of the testator to substitute the legacies given in the codicil for those given to the same persons in the will, and that this is manifest from the will and codicil and the evidence that was admitted. Very likely, if it had occurred to the testator, he would have said in so many words that the legacies given in the codicil were in substitution of those given in the will. But the fact that he did not do so, and that some of the cash legacies given in the will, including one to his namesake, are not referred to in the codicil, does not necessarily show that the legacies in the codicil must be regarded as cumulative in respect to those persons who are named in the will. * * *

The result is that we think that the decree of the probate court should be affirmed.

So ordered.

NOTE

The problem in the principal case does not arise if the testator states clearly in his subsequent instrument that he intends to revoke provisions in a prior instrument and substitute therefor provisions which he sets forth.[3] Nor does the problem arise when the testator makes a specific gift of the same property to the same donee in both instruments.[4] But if the donee is named to receive a general gift in both instruments, or a general gift in one instrument and a specific gift in the other, the courts have presumed that the gift in the subsequent instrument is cumulative, or in addition to, the gift in the prior instrument.[5] The presumption is strong when the prior instrument

3. See generally Rollison, Wills (1939) § 307; Evans, "Testamentary Revocation by Subsequent Instrument", 22 Ky.L.J. 469, 474–475 (1934).

4. For the distinction between "specific" and "general" gifts see Chapter XV, Section 1(1).

5. E.g., Breckinridge v. Breckinridge's Executors, 264 Ky. 82, 94 S.W.2d 283 (1936). See Note, 65 A.L.R.2d 1325 (1975).

is a will and the subsequent instrument is a codicil,[6] but in any case the presumption is rebutted if the testator's contrary intention is shown.[7] The courts look initially to the instruments in question for evidence of intention. If the contents of the two instruments are similar and if the dispositions are made in identical terms, although in different amounts, a court may find that the gift in the subsequent instrument is substitutional and revokes the gift in the prior instrument by inconsistency.[8] Evidence of the circumstances existing when the subsequent instrument was executed, such as whether or not the testator's estate was then sufficient to pay cumulations, is admitted by most courts as an aid in finding his intention.[9] Evidence of declarations by the testator is usually excluded.[10] A number of courts, as did the court in the principal case, have admitted declarations by the testator which tend to show a knowledge and appreciation of his circumstances as distinguished from declarations concerning what he meant by words used in his will.[11]

If general legacies are given to the same donee in different clauses in a single instrument rather than in separate instruments, and the legacies are the same in amount, the courts have presumed that the second legacy appearing in the will is a substitute for the first legacy or is a repetition of the first legacy through mistake.[12] But when the legacies are different in nature or amount the usual presumption is that the gifts are cumulative.[13]

The courts strive to reconcile the provisions when gifts of the same property are made in different clauses to different donees in the same instrument. A court may find, for example, that the donees take the property as joint tenants, as tenants in common, or that one donee takes as life tenant and the other as remainderman.[14] But most of the courts which have considered the point have held that the last provision prevails when the provisions cannot be reconciled.[15] The last provision is sometimes said to "revoke" the

6. See Evans, "Testamentary Revocation by Subsequent Instrument", 22 Ky. L.J. 469, 476–477 (1934).

7. E.g., DeWitt v. Yates, 10 John (N. Y.) 156, 6 Am.Dec. 326 (1813); Third National Bank v. Scribner, 175 Tenn. 14, 130 S.W.2d 126, 123 A.L.R. 1385 (1939).

8. See Leighton v. Leighton, 193 Iowa 1299, 188 N.W. 922 (1922); Wainwright v. Tuckerman, 120 Mass. 232 (1876); Kemp v. Hutchinson, 110 S.W.2d 1126 (Mo.App.1937), 3 Mo.L.Rev. 328 (1938).

9. E.g., Knebelkamp v. Acosta, 272 Ky. 506, 114 S.W.2d 737 (1938); Sondheim v. Fechenbach, 137 Mich. 384, 100 N.W. 586 (1904).

10. E.g., Wilson v. O'Leary, L.R., 7 Ch.App. 448 (1872) (letter of instructions by testator to draftsman inadmissible).

11. E.g., Kemp v. Hutchinson, 110 S. W.2d 1126 (Mo.App.1937), 3 Mo.L.Rev. 328 (1938).

12. Manning v. Thesiger, 3 M. & K. 29, 40 Eng.Rep. 12 (1835); Thompson v. Betts, 74 Conn. 576, 51 A. 564, 92 Am.St. Rep. 235 (1902); Waters v. Hatch, 181 Mo. 262, 79 S.W. 916 (1904). See 1 A.L. R.3d 479 (1965).

13. Curry v. Pile, 2 Bro.C.C. 225, 29 Eng.Rep. 126 (1787); Cunningham v. Spickler, 4 Gill. (Md.) 280 (1846).

14. See, e.g., Paramour v. Yardley, 2 Plow. 539, 541, 75 Eng.Rep. 794, 797 (1579); Atcherley v. Vernon, 10 Mod. 518, 522, 88 Eng.Rep. 834, 835 (1724); Frelinghausen v. New York Life Insurance Co., 31 R.I. 150, 77 A. 98 (1910); Day v. Wallace, 144 Ill. 256, 33 N.E. 185 (1893); Whitlock v. Wardlaw, 7 Rich.L. (S.C.) 453 (1854).

15. Rowland v. Miller, 81 Fla. 408, 88 So. 263 (1921); Estate of Burdin, 282 Ill. App. 511 (1935); Fraser v. Boone, 1 Hill Eq. (S.C.) 360, 27 Am.Dec. 422 (1833). The rule is based upon Sir Edward Coke's dictum that "where there be divers devises of one thing, the last devise taketh place". Coke on Littleton, 112b. At least one court has preferred the earlier provision. Watkins v. Bennett, 170 Ky. 464, 186 S.W. 182 (1916). In other situations the courts have indicated a preference for the earlier language. Thus, a second residuary clause in a will passes property which a first clause is worded too narrowly to pass, and it is often said that a grant of a fee cannot be cut down by doubtful subsequent language. See Evans, "Testamentary Revo-

earlier provision by implication. There is a close analogy, however, to the situation in which a provision included in a will by a mistake in the factum is denied effect.[16] It is possible that a better view would be to ignore both of the conflicting provisions and allow the property to pass by the residuary clause or by intestacy.[17]

---

(3) EFFECT OF REVOCATION BY PHYSICAL ACT OF A WILL UPON A CODICIL AND OF REVOCATION BY PHYSICAL ACT OF A CODICIL UPON A WILL

The Wills Act, 1837, provided that no "will or codicil" could be revoked except in the manner which the statute specified.[18] The English courts construed the statute to mean that a physical act to a will did not revoke codicils to the will.[19] A physical act was required to the written provisions of the codicil or to the paper upon which the codicil was written in order to revoke it.[20] Prior to the enactment of the Wills Act, 1837, the English courts had taken the position that a physical act to a will would revoke codicils to it if the testator so intended. It was presumed that a codicil was dependent upon a will and that the testator must intend to revoke the codicils if he revoked the will. This presumption could be rebutted by showing that the codicil was not in fact dependent upon the will.[21]

The American decisions have been influenced by the English view as expressed prior to 1837. In Youse v. Foreman [22] an executed codicil was found written in the margin of a page of a will that had been revoked by physical act. The codicil was held revoked because dependent upon the terms of the will. In Noke's Estate,[23] the will and codicil were executed on separate sheets. The codicil was held revoked by destruction of the will on the ground that the will and codicil were interdependent.

cation by Inconsistency within the Instrument", 28 Ky.L.J. 45 (1939).

16. See Chapter VII, Section 2(5).

17. See Evans, "Testamentary Revocation by Inconsistency within the Instrument", 28 Ky.L.J. 45, 52 (1939).

18. 7 Wm. IV & 1 Vict., c. 26, § XX (1837).

19. Goods of Turner, L.R. 2 P. & D. 403 (1872).

20. In Goods of Bleckley, L.R. 8 Prob. Div. 169 (1883), the testator cut his signature from his will. A codicil had been executed at the bottom of the same page. It was held that the codicil was revoked, apparently upon the theory that the excision of the signature to the will was an act to the paper upon which the codicil was written and thus satisfied the statute.

21. Medlycott v. Assheton, 2 Add. 229, 162 Eng.Rep. 278 (1824).

22. 68 Ky. (5 Bush.) 337 (1869). See Matter of Francis' Will, 73 Misc. 148, 132 N.Y.S. 695 (1911) (codicil found attached to revoked will by means of seal).

23. 71 Misc. 383, 130 N.Y.S. 187 (1911). See In re Pepper's Estate, 148 Pa. 5, 23 A. 1039 (1892).

A will and codicil are separate instruments for the purpose of execution. It would seem better to require separate physical acts of revocation.[24] The degree to which the codicil is dependent upon the terms of the will can be determined in a proper proceeding for construction of the instrument.

It is well settled in the United States that if a will and codicil are executed upon separate sheets of paper a physical act done to the codicil does not revoke the will even if the testator intended to do so.[25] An act done to the paper with the intention to revoke the will and codicil appears to be sufficient if the will and codicil are on the same sheet. A court may require that the act be one which is directed to the paper upon which the will and codicil are written. "Burning", "tearing" and "cutting" are acts of this type.[26] An act which is directed to the writing of the codicil only, such as "cancellation" or "obliteration", may be insufficient to revoke the will.

PROBLEMS

1. T had six children:—Julia, Clara, Sarah, Louise, Suzanne and Andrew. In 1954, T executed a will revoking all prior wills, containing a bequest of $500 to a former daughter-in-law, with the residue of the estate to Julia (who was incompetent) for her life or her marriage at which time the residue was to be distributed to T's children and grandchildren in stipulated shares. De Paoli, an attorney, was nominated as executor. In 1956 this document was executed by T:

"October 15, 1956

"I, T, add this to my will. Upon my death my daughter, Clara, is to take my place and act in my stead as if it were I. I strongly recommend Julia to her. She and Clara will be the owners of everything I possess. While they live no one will be able to disturb them.

s/T

"*My will is in the possession of De Paoli.* After my death Clara will be the manager because Julia is not good at managing. She is to *take my will from De Paoli* and pay whatever is to be paid.

s/T"

The instrument of 1954 was revoked by burning. The 1956 instrument was found among the valuable papers of T with the words italicized deleted in pencil. A statute in force in the state provides: "The revocation of a will revokes all its codicils". Can the instrument of 1956 be probated? Re Estate of Cuneo, 60 Cal.2d 196, 32 Cal.Rptr. 409, 384 P.2d 1, 7 A.L.R.3d 1132 (1963). See Estate of Steel, 219 N.E.2d 236 (Probate Ct. Cuyahoga Co., Ohio, 1966).

24. See In re Ayres' Will, 43 N.E.2d 918 (Ohio App.1940), 16 U. of Cin.L.Rev. 346 (1942) (Lost will presumed revoked. Codicil held revoked because dependent upon the will).

25. Osburn v. Rochester Trust & Safe Co., 209 N.Y. 54, 102 N.E. 571, 46 L.R.A.,N.S., 983, Ann.Cas.1915A, 101 (1912); Malone's Administrator v. Hobbs, 1 Rob. (Va.) 346, 39 Am.Dec. 263 (1842).

26. See Burton v. Wylde, 261 Ill. 397, 103 N.E. 976 (1913); In re Brookman, 11 Misc. 675, 33 N.Y.S. 575 (1896). Statutes in several states provide that revocation of a will revokes codicils to it. See Rees, "American Wills Statutes", 46 Va.L.Rev. 856, 871 (1960). These statutes do not appear to cover the effect of revocation of a codicil upon a will; 7 A.L.R.3d 1143 (1966).

2. T's will was found revoked by the physical act of tearing. A codicil was written in the margin of the page on which the tearing occurred but none of the writing upon the codicil was touched by the tearing. There is no extrinsic evidence to indicate whether T intended to revoke the codicil. The codicil depends upon the will for interpretation. Should the codicil be probated? Youse v. Foreman, 68 Ky. (5 Bush.) 337 (1869); Same result if the codicil was not dependent upon the will for interpretation and the statute mentioned in problem No. 1 is in force in the state?

SECTION 4. REVALIDATION OF REVOKED WILL

(1) INTRODUCTION

If a testator desires to revive a revoked will, and the revocation was accomplished by a physical act to the paper or writing, the usual procedure is to redraft the will, execute it, and have the will bear the date of its new execution. This avoids any question that might arise from the presence of a mark of revocation upon the paper. The old document is destroyed when the new will is executed.

If the will has not been revoked by a physical act, but the revocation was by subsequent instrument or by operation of law, the usual practice is to execute a codicil to revalidate the revoked will. The codicil is executed with all testamentary formalities and recites that the will is republished and revalidated as of the date of the codicil. This is called "republication by codicil" and is considered in detail in Subsection (2).

It is possible, of course, that a testator and his witnesses might simply repeat the formalities of execution on the original document. This will revalidate the instrument. Reexecution is not recommended. Apart from the fact that reexecuting the same will is often awkward in a physical sense, the practice is so unusual that it might unnecessarily arouse the suspicion of the probate judge or other official who must pass upon the formal validity of the will that the reexecution is fraudulent. The practice is particularly dangerous when the testator is in failing health and his handwriting has changed significantly since the original execution of the will.

These three methods of revalidating the revoked will all necessarily involve a repetition of the formalities of execution directed to the revoked will or its provisions. There are two other ways, however, in which a will which has been revoked, or apparently revoked, ultimately may be given operative effect. These are (1) revival by revocation of a revoking will and (2) dependent relative revocation. Both techniques provoke an interplay of theories concerning the time at which revocation of a will is effective. And both likewise involve presumptions concerning the testator's intention to restore the revoked will and the admissibility of evidence to prove his actual intention.

---

* * * * *

(2) REPUBLICATION BY CODICIL

When a codicil is executed to a will the will is said to be "republished" and "revalidated" as of the date upon which the codicil was executed. The doctrine of "republication by codicil" probably is derived from the doctrine of "incorporation by reference" of extrinsic documents into a will considered hereafter in Chapter XII ("Interrelating Testamentary and Intervivos Transactions").[27] However, certain of the rigid requirements for incorporation by reference of an extrinsic writing into a will are relaxed in republication by codicil due to the special will-codicil context in which the doctrine is applied. An intention to "republish" (or incorporate) and a reference to the will

27. See generally, Atkinson, Wills (2d Ed., 1953) §§ 90, 91; 2 Bowe-Parker: Page, Wills (3d Ed., Rev.1960) §§ 23.1–23.18; Rollison, Wills (1939) §§ 155–159; Thompson, Wills (3d Ed., 1947) §§ 184, 185; Evans, "Testamentary Republication", 40 Harv.L.Rev. 71 (1926). The courts may distinguish between republication and incorporation by reference where the doctrine of incorporation has been rejected or where non-holographic materials are "republished" by a holographic codicil and the physical theory of incorporation by reference is applied. The New York courts, for example, permit republication by codicil but have rejected the doctrine of incorporation by reference. The Arkansas court allows republication of a non-holographic will by a holographic codicil but apparently applied the physical theory of incorporation by reference. See Rogers v. Agricola, 176 Ark. 287, 3 S.W.2d 26 (1928); Kinnear v. Langley, 209 Ark. 878, 192 S.W. 2d 978 (1946). There is a slight historical basis for a distinction. The ecclesiastical courts permitted the validation of revoked wills by parol. But the common law courts appear to have permitted oral republications of devises made under the Statute of Wills, 1540, only for the purpose of passing after-acquired property. Beckford v. Parnecott, Cro.Eliz. 493, 78 Eng.Rep. 744 (1596). But see Duppa v. Mayo, 1 Wms.Saund. 275, 85 Eng.Rep. 336 (1670) (Note 4 by Sergeant Williams, who suggests that a devise revoked expressly or by operation of law could be revived by parol). After the enactment of the Statute of Frauds, 1677, a devise could be republished to pass after-acquired property only if it was reexecuted with all testamentary formalities. See Acherly v. Vernon, 1 Comyns 381, 383, 384, 92 Eng.Rep. 1121, 1122 (1724). Reexecution meant that the will was validated if it was invalid. In a series of cases the common law courts then developed the idea that the execution of a codicil not physically attached to the will was a republication or reexecution of the will which caused it to pass property acquired before the codicil was executed. Sympson v. Hornsby, Prec.Ch. 439, 24 Eng. Rep. 196 (1716); Acherly v. Vernon, 1 Comyns 381, 92 Eng.Rep. 1121 (1724); Potter v. Potter, 1 Ves.Sr. 437, 27 Eng.Rep. 1128 (1750); Barnes v. Crow, 1 Ves.Jr. 486, 30 Eng.Rep. 450 (1792); Pigott v. Waller, 7 Ves.Jr. 98, 32 Eng.Rep. 40 (1802). The Wills Act, 1837, altered the common law rule that a will did not pass after-acquired property. Thereafter the doctrines of republication and incorporation were regarded as identical. Allen v. Maddock, 11 Moore P.C. 427, 14 Eng. Rep. 757 (1858).

"as existing" are implied from the execution of a codicil which describes the will with reasonable certainty.[28] Nevertheless, the will must be in existence when the codicil is executed[29] and the codicil must be a properly executed testamentary writing.[30]

A republished will is validated to the extent that there is no conflict between the provisions of the will and the provisions of the republishing codicil. A revoked will is "revived" by republication.[31] A will which has never been valid or has unexecuted interlineations appearing upon the face of a valid will is validated initially by republication.[32] Thus, in Linnard's Appeal[33] the testatrix revoked a bequest of five hundred dollars by cancellation and interlined a substituted bequest of three hundred dollars. Republication of the will by codicil validated the interlineation. Invalid codicils to a republished will are validated if expressly referred to in the republishing codicil.[34]

28. See Taft v. Stearns, 234 Mass. 273, 276, 125 N.E. 570, 571 (1920). A codicil will sometimes appear which clearly is an ancillary writing but does not clearly describe one of several prior wills. In Estate of Mercer, 207 Misc. 346, 137 N.Y.S.2d 768 (Surr.Ct.1955), aff'd 144 N.Y.S.2d 920, testator had executed three testamentary instruments. His will of January 23, 1951 was revoked by a will executed on May 15, 1951. There was an invalid testamentary writing (lacking in the required formalities) dated June 24, 1952. A writing dated November 28, 1952 was written on the last page of the revoked will of January 23, 1951. This writing altered a legacy to a brother, appearing in the wills of January 23, 1951 and May 15, 1951. The writing was held a codicil to the valid will of May 15, 1951 and not to the revoked will of January 23, 1951 upon which it was written. In a number of cases the testamentary intent with which a supposed codicil is prepared is in doubt, writings which might be memoranda being offered as a testamentary instrument. See, e.g., Pullen v. Pullen, 249 Ark. 489, 460 S.W.2d 753 (1970).

29. A will destroyed with the intention to revoke cannot be republished by codicil. Goods of Steele, L.R. 1 P. & D. 575 (1868); Burge v. Hamilton, 72 Ga. 568 (1884).

30. E.g., Shinn v. Phillips, 8 Ohio App. 2d 58, 220 N.E. 674 (1967). In Georgia a will can be republished by a properly executed codicil or the republication may be oral in the presence of two witnesses who then subscribe the will or the republication may be made in the presence of the original witnesses with no requirement of a repeated subscription. Ga. Code Ann. § 113–409.

31. See "Revival of Revoked Wills", 19 Wyo.L.J. 223, 225–226 (1965) (Comment upon Wilson's Estate, 397 P.2d 805 (Wyo.1964) with collected cases).

32. In New York a will is not validated when republished by codicil if the will was invalid initially because of a failure to perform the required testamentary formalities. See In re Emmon's Will, 110 App.Div. 701, 96 N.Y.S. 506 (1906). McKinney's N.Y., EPTL, § 3–4.6(b)(1) (1967) may permit republication of an initially invalid will, although the section refers to "revival" which suggests a will initially valid but later invalidated. Cf. the rationale in Timberlake v. State Planters Bank of Commerce and Trusts, 201 Va. 950, 115 S.E.2d 39 (1960), appearing as principal case in subsection (3) of this Section.

33. 93 Pa. 313, 39 Am.Rep. 753 (1880). See Shaw v. Camp, 163 Ill. 144, 45 N.E. 211 (1896); In re Hay, [1904] L.R. 1 Ch. 317.

34. Burton v. Newberry [1975] L.R., 1 Ch. 234. Intervening valid codicils to the will are deemed to be republished along with the will even though the last codicil refers only to the will. To the extent that the last codicil is inconsistent with prior ones, it revokes them; otherwise the intervening codicils are construed to alter or modify the original will in spite of the theory that the will is also read as if executed on the date of republication. E.g., In re Johnson's Trust, 435 Pa. 303, 255 A.2d 571 (1969). Validation of an invalid codicil requires a specific reference. E.g. Estate of Erbach, 41 Wis.2d 335, 164 N.W.2d 238 (1969).

Although a will operates at the death of the testator, the language of the will is construed as of the date upon which the will was executed. When a will is republished, the language of the will and of all valid intervening codicils is read as if executed originally at the date of execution of the republishing codicil. In Matter of Champion,[35] the testator executed a will containing a devise of land "now in my occupation". He then acquired additional land which he occupied. After acquiring the additional land the testator republished the will by codicil. The after-acquired land was held to pass by the description contained in the will. In Matter of Hardyman [36] the testator made a bequest to the "wife" of his cousin. The woman who was the "wife" of the cousin died after the will was executed. The testator republished his will by codicil with knowledge of the death. The cousin remarried. The second wife was held entitled to take the bequest. In Knecht's Estate [37] the testator revoked his first will by a second will containing inconsistent provisions. He then executed a codicil to his first will. The first will was republished as of the date of execution of the codicil and revoked the second will by inconsistency. In Goods of Truro [38] the testatrix executed a will referring to certain property stated in an inventory. The inventory was referred to as in existence but was prepared between the date of execution of the will and the date of republication of the will by codicil. The language of the will was read as of the date of the codicil so that the inventory was incorporated by reference.

The courts do not apply the republication doctrine if the application seems to be contrary to the intention of the testator. It has been held that provisions of a will revoked in part or adeemed by satisfaction [39] are not revived unless the codicil expressly indicates the intention of the testator to revive them.[40] A codicil which provides for the

35. [1893] L.R. 1 Ch. 101. See Matter of Reeves, [1928] L.R. 1 Ch. 351.

36. [1925] L.R. Ch. 287.

37. 341 Pa. 292, 19 A.2d 111 (1941).

38. 1 P. & D. 201 (1866).

39. See Chapter XV, Section 1(2)(A)(ii).

40. Powys v. Mansfield, 3 My. & Cr. 359, 40 Eng.Rep. 964 (1837); Tanton v. Keller, 167 Ill. 129, 47 N.E. 376 (1897). A problem concerning the revival of a revoked will as a whole, as well as revival of part of a will by the execution of a codicil to it, is presented under statutes intended to change the common law rule that revocation of a revoking will *ipso facto* revives the revoked will. A statute of this type, such as Virginia Code, § 61.1–60 [now § 64.1–60 (1980 Repl.Vol.)], considered in Timberlake v. State-Planters Bank of Commerce and Trusts, the principal case in Subsection (3) which follows, provides in essence that no will or codicil can be revived except by the reexecution of it or by a codicil executed as a will must be executed "and then only to the extent to which an intention to revive the same is shown". What kind of reference is required in the codicil to satisfy the requirement of an intent to revive? In Kimbark v. Satas, 87 Ill.App.2d 460, 231 N.E.2d 699 (1967), testator executed a will in 1961 which he then revoked by the execution of a one-page printed form will in 1964. In 1965 he executed a codicil to the will of 1961 which disposed of all of his property. The codicil stated in part: "I hereby confirm my said will in all other respects". This was held sufficient as an expression of an intent to revive the will of 1961. In Estate of Barrett, 124 Ill.App.2d 9, 260 N.E.2d 107 (1970) a statement similar to that in *Kimbark* was held an expression of an intent to revive a will of 1948 and supersede an intervening will of 1962 even though the 1962 will contained a more up-to-date estate plan. On the other hand, a reference to an earlier will merely by its date of execution and subscribing witnesses probably is insufficient un-

revival of a will in part does not revive the will in its entirety.[41] If an anti-lapse statute applies to save the gifts of persons living when the will is executed but not the gifts of persons who die before the will is executed, republication of the will by codicil after the death of a legatee should not prevent an application of the statute to save the gift.[42] Where a statute is in force invalidating charitable gifts made within a specified period prior to the death of the testator, republication of the will during the prohibited period should not invalidate the gift.[43]

PROBLEMS

1. Testatrix executed a will in 1945. After the execution of this will she made certain changes in Paragraph 4 which disposed of the residue of her estate. As executed, the residual disposition read: "* * * in equal shares, unto my grandchildren, Lewis Plisch, Nan Plisch, Susan Plisch, John Erbach, Tom Erbach, and Mariana Erbach, and my nephews, Frank J. Hollfelder and Walter Hauboldt, to-wit, each an equal 1/8 share". When the will was found, the names Susan Plisch and Walter Hauboldt were heavily crossed out in ink and practically obliterated. The figure "1/8" was changed to "1/7" and this figure marked out and "1/6" written in. In 1965 the testatrix executed a holographic instrument distributing all of the assets which she controlled, the residual disposition omitting Mariana Erbach who was one of the residuary distributees in the 1945 will. This holographic instrument was not attested and the state requires attesting witnesses for a will even though it is in the handwriting of testatrix. In 1966 shortly before she died, testatrix executed an instrument titled: "Codicil to the Will of Laura Erbach" [her name]. This codicil appointed her stepson as executor, conferred certain powers upon him, exempted him from bond, and stated "All other parts of my Last Will and Testament shall remain the same". The instrument is signed by testatrix and properly attested. Are the residuary dispositions for Susan Plisch and Walter Hauboldt revoked? Is Mariana Erbach excluded as a residuary donee? Can the interlineation of "1/6" in the will of 1945 be given effect? In what shares would you distribute the residuary estate of testatrix? In re Estate of Erbach, 41 Wis.2d 335, 164 N.W.2d 238 (1969).

2. T prepared an unattested and invalid testamentary paper described by its terms as her last will and testament. The paper contained several legacies and named executors. T later executed a valid codicil headed, "This is a codicil to my last will and testament". The codicil contained no other reference to the will and named no executor. The codicil did contain bequests to a servant. After T's death, the unattested testamentary paper was found in a different room from the codicil but sealed in an envelope labelled as containing T's will. No other instrument was found which might meet the

der one of these statutes. The requirement is likely to be applied with particular severity if the will allegedly revised was destroyed with the intent to revoke it. E.g., Clark v. Clark, 280 Ala. 644, 197 So.2d 447 (1967). Of course, if there are no copies of the will, and the court presses the analogy of republication to incorporation by reference, it might be unwilling to declare the will revived even if the intent to revive was clearly stated.

41. Mallory v. Mallory, 72 Conn. 494, 45 A. 164 (1900).

42. Lee v. Lee, 88 Conn. 404, 91 A. 269 (1914). Contra: In re Matthews' Estate, 176 Cal. 576, 169 P. 233 (1917), 6 Cal.L.Rev. 312, 31 Harv.L.Rev. 901 (1918), 16 Mich.L.Rev. 429 (1918), 27 Yale L.J. 852 (1918).

43. In re Moore, [1907] 1 Ir.L.Rep. 315.

description of T's last will and testament. Is the unattested testamentary paper a valid will? Allen v. Maddock, 11 Moore P.C. 427, 14 Eng.Rep. 757 (1858).

3. T executed his will on 1 September 1938. The will was valid in all respects. On 18 December 1941, he executed a codicil which purported to make an additional legacy of $25,000. On 29 September 1943, he executed a second codicil which revoked certain provisions of the will. The second codicil did not refer to the first codicil. Is the will of 1938 republished only as modified by the second codicil or is it republished as modified by the second codicil and supplemented by the first codicil? In re Van Ingen's Estate, 183 Misc. 281, 47 N.Y.S.2d 818 (1944).

---

(3) REVIVAL BY REVOCATION OF A REVOKING WILL

Suppose a testator executes will [A]. He then revokes will [A] by an express clause of revocation or inconsistent provisions contained in will [B]. He then revokes will [B] by (1) a physical act of revocation or (2) will [C] which contains an express clause of revocation referring to will [B] but which does not refer to will [A] or contain provisions inconsistent with those in will [A]. Is will [A] "revived"?

The student should note that the factual situation which gives rise to this "revival" issue is quite limited, there being no issue of "revival" presented by revocation of a revoking will if will [A] has also been revoked by physical act or by operation of law. The limited factual situation in which the issue is presented has encouraged the development of statutes dealing with the problem. A statute may give the answer;[44] but the statute may not provide an answer if the state legislature and courts differ in their theories concerning the time at which revocations by subsequent instrument occur.

TIMBERLAKE v. STATE-PLANTERS BANK OF COMMERCE AND TRUSTS

Supreme Court of Appeals of Virginia, 1960.
201 Va. 950, 115 S.E.2d 39.[45]

Before EGGLESTON, C.J., and SPRATLEY, BUCHANAN, MILLER, WHITTLE, SNEAD and I'ANSON, JJ.

44. Applicable statutes are now in force in England and in about half of the American states. See Rees, "American Wills Statutes", 46 Va.L.Rev. 856, 891 (1960). As to the relevance of these statutes to reviving wills by codicil, see fn. 40, supra.

45. Noted, 10 Kan.L.Rev. 106 (1961); 37 N.D.L.Rev. 128 (1961); 18 Wash. &

BUCHANAN, JUSTICE. The question for decision in this case is whether a will duly executed and in existence when the testatrix died had been revoked by a subsequent will, also duly executed, which contained a revocation clause but which had been destroyed and was not in existence at the death of the testatrix. The answer is in the proper interpretation of § 64–59 of the Code,[46] considered in connection with § 64–60.[47]

The testatrix, Kate Miller Levering, made two wills, both executed and attested in accordance with statute, § 64–51, and left them both in the custody of the Trust Department of a Richmond bank, which was named as executor in both. The first will was dated October 29, 1954. The second was dated January 31, 1955, and in the first clause thereof stated that the testatrix makes "this my last Will and Testament, hereby expressly revoking any and all wills and/or codicils by me at any time heretofore made."

Afterwards, on November 20 or 21, 1956, the testatrix went to the bank and made request to withdraw the 1955 will, giving as her reason that she wanted to make some changes in it and expected to do so by a new will rather than by a codicil. This 1955 will was accordingly delivered to her and was never later found. It is consequently presumed that it was destroyed by her with intent to revoke it. Tate v. Wren, 185 Va. 773, 784, 40 S.E.2d 188, 193. An unsigned carbon copy of it was preserved by the bank and exhibited in evidence.

After the death of the testatrix, which occurred on November 1, 1958, the 1954 will was presented to the chancery court and offered for probate by the beneficiaries and the executor named therein, the parties interested were convened and after hearing the evidence the court held, for reasons stated in a written opinion, that the 1954 will was the true last and testament of Kate Miller Levering, and accordingly ordered it probated and recorded as such. From this order the appellants, heirs at law of the deceased, have appealed and contend that the 1954 will was revoked by the 1955 will and that the deceased died intestate. The holding of the chancery court was based on the proposition that a will is ambulatory, speaks only at the death of the

Lee L.Rev. 166 (1961); 63 W.Va.L.Rev. 86 (1960).

[Footnotes 46 through 48 are by the Court]

46. "§ 64–59. Revocation of wills generally.—No will or codicil, or any part thereof, shall be revoked, unless under the preceding section, or by a subsequent will or codicil, or by some writing declaring an intention to revoke the same, executed in the manner in which a will is required to be executed, or by the testator, or some person in his presence and by his direction, cutting, tearing, burning, obliterating, canceling or destroying the same, or the signature thereto, with the intent to revoke." * * * [Current Virginia Code Ann. § 64.1–58 is the same except for the following added sentence: "The subsequent marriage of the testator or birth of a child to the testator, or both, shall not operate to revoke a will previously executed by the testator." Present § 64.1–59 revokes all provisions in a will in favor of the divorced spouse. —Ed.] * * *

47. "§ 64–60. Revival of wills after revocation.—No will or codicil, or any part thereof, which shall be in any manner revoked, shall, after being revoked, be revived otherwise than by the re-execution thereof, or by a codicil executed in the manner hereinbefore required, and then only to the extent to which an intention to revive the same is shown." * * * [Now Virginia Code Ann. § 64.-1-60.—Ed.] * * *

maker, and the 1955 will having been destroyed in the lifetime of the testatrix, it never had the effect of revoking the 1954 will. The appellants contend that the revocation clause in the 1955 will became effective immediately upon the execution of that will, was not affected by the destruction of it, and hence the 1954 will was without force or effect.

It will be observed that the statute, § 64–59, provides that a will may be revoked (§ 64–58 declaring revocation by marriage was repealed by Acts 1956, ch. 65) only (1) by a subsequent will or codicil, or (2) by some writing declaring an intention to revoke the same executed as a will is required to be executed, or (3) by mutilating or destroying it with the intent to revoke it.

This statute first appeared in the Code of 1849 as § 8 of Chapter 122, Title 33, in the identical words of the present statute, but its prototype has been in the statute laws almost since the birth of the nation. Section 64–60 appeared as § 9 in Chapter 122 of the 1849 Code.

* * *

[In the omitted portion of the opinion, the Court discusses earlier Virginia cases, including Barksdale v. Barksdale, 39 Va. 535 (1842); Rudisill's Ex'r v. Rodes, 70 Va. 147 (1877); and Poindexter v. Jones, 200 Va. 372, 106 S.E.2d 144 (1958).]

* * *

Under § 64–59, so far as we are presently concerned, a will is revoked (1) by a subsequent will or codicil, or (2) by some writing declaring an intention to revoke, executed in the same manner as a will. The first way is a testamentary revocation, the second is a declaratory revocation. The distinction is not formal but essential. The testamentary revocation is made to clear the way for a new disposition of testator's property; the declaratory revocation does not dispose of property but renders the maker intestate. The testamentary revocation would not occur unless the testator intended to change his previous will. The testamentary revocation is thus part and parcel of his new testamentary action. When he destroys the revoking will, how can he do so with any other expectation or belief than that he is destroying it all, the revoking provision along with the disposing provisions, both imbedded in the same document? Barksdale v. Barksdale, supra.

Here we know that Mrs. Levering did not intend to die intestate. The evidence shows it and the chancellor found it to be true. At the bank she asked only for the 1955 will and left the 1954 will intact in the bank where she had placed it. She intended to make some changes in the 1955 will. Instead of doing so she destroyed that will. Then how could we know that she then meant or thought that the revocation would remain effective although she knew the dispositions of her property in the instrument of which it was a part would not be?

In Poindexter we spoke of the paradoxical situation of a testator's dying intestate with an intact will in his hand. As the chancellor said in his opinion in the present case, this testatrix left her will in a better and safer place than if she had died with it in her hand. She died "with a valid, unblemished will in the custody of the executor named therein, upon whose integrity and good faith to propound that will for probate and to carry out its testamentary provisions she had a right to rely."

A will is an ambulatory instrument, not intended or allowed to take effect until the death of the maker. It may be changed during life as often as the mind and purpose of the testator change. While he lives his written will has no life or force, and is not operative or effective for any purpose. 95 C.J.S. Wills § 310, p. 110; Spinks v. Rice, 187 Va. 730, 47 S.E.2d 424. If a testator elects to use the first method provided by the statute and puts a revocation provision in a will which he knows he may change at pleasure and which he knows will not be effective until he dies, it would seem to be wholly illogical to say that if he afterwards destroyed the will with intent to revoke it, he did not thereby destroy all of it, but that, regardless of his intention, the revocation clause, although without physical form or existence, remained alive and vital with power to destroy all the wills he had ever written. Under such a rule the most solemn and deliberate will of a testator may be refused probate on the testimony of a witness, as in Bell v. Timmins, supra, that he saw the testator write and sign a later will which revoked the will now proffered.

We specifically held in Barksdale that a revoking clause in a will is a part and parcel of the will itself, without independent and immediate life or power, and that it survives or perishes with the will. We specifically held in Poindexter that a will which revokes a prior will by being wholly inconsistent with it, does not effect such revocation when executed but may do so only if it subsists when the testator dies. We are unwilling now to turn from the reasoning or the result of those two cases.

Our conclusion is that Barksdale and Poindexter announced the safer and better rule, a rule that keeps in step with the historic character and function of wills and is consonant with the language of the statute; that is, when a revocation of a prior will is made under the statute, § 64–59, by a subsequent will, the revocation clause speaks when the will speaks, not at the time of the execution of the will, but at the death of the testator; and if in the testator's lifetime he destroys or cancels the revoking will with the intent to revoke it, the revocation provision falls with the will and is not effective to revoke the prior will. So far as Rudisill's Ex'r v. Rodes, supra, 29 Grat. 147, 70 Va. 147, is in conflict with this conclusion, it is overruled.

The judgment of the court below establishing and probating the 1954 will is

Affirmed.

SPRATLEY and I'ANSON, JJ., dissenting.

SPRATLEY, JUSTICE (dissenting).

I find myself unable to agree with the opinion of the majority. I think it contrary to the plain provisions of the statutes involved, and to the principles and precepts of Rudisill's Ex'r v. Rodes, 1877, 29 Grat. 147, 70 Va. 147, which have been accepted and approved by eminent jurists, lawyers, legal writers and many courts.[48] The result of the majority opinion is to reverse the decision in the Rudisill case, supra, decided eighty years ago, after the adoption of provisions in Code of 1849, which have remained unchanged to this day.

Here we have a second will dated January 31, 1955, duly executed, wherein testatrix expressly declaring her intention to revoke all former wills by her made. It is clear that she did not intend her former will dated October 29, 1954, to stand, both by that declared intention and by her different property disposals in the two instruments. The execution of the second will was the last testamentary act of the testatrix. Thereafter, she told a friend that she intended to execute a new will, and on some unnamed date she presumptively destroyed the second instrument. She did not later make a new will, undertake to revise, or to re-execute either of the two wills she had made, in any of the methods provided by statute.

The facts present the question: Did the destruction of the second will destroy the declared intent of the testatrix therein to revoke her first will and thereby leave alive and vital the first will as her true last will and testament?

Code §§ 64–59 and 64–60 are so intermingled that it is necessary to give consideration to each of them and to their historical background.

The prototype of Code § 64–59 has been on the statute books of Virginia almost since the birth of the State. Code § 64–60 first appeared as section 9, Chapter 122, Code of 1849, and next as section 9, Chapter 118, Code of 1873.

Prior to the general revisal of the laws of this State in 1849, it was generally held in the common-law courts that the destruction, animo revocandi, of a will containing a revocatory clause, a former preserved uncancelled will was thereby revived, and no proof to the contrary was allowed. In the ecclesiastical courts, the revival or restoration of the former will was made to depend on the intention of the testator and parol evidence was admissible to show the intention. Rudisill's Ex'r v. Rodes, supra, 70 Va. 149.

In the Rudisill case, supra, decided after the enactment of statutes identical with Code §§ 64–59 and 64–60, the testator had executed three wills, the second and third containing clauses revoking former wills, and destroyed the last will with the intent to revoke it. The court held that the second will, though retained uncancelled by the testator "had been revoked by the subsequent will of said decedent

48. See Volume 1, University of Richmond Law Notes, No. 3, page 147, et seq., "Revocation and Revival of Wills in Virginia," by James H. Barnett, Jr.; and cf. Note, "Revocation of Wills by Subsequent Instrument," 46 Virginia Law Review, No. 2, pages 373, et seq.

* * * and was not revived by the destruction, animo revocandi, of the last named will". 70 Va. 152, supra.

* * * [In the omitted portion, Justice Spratley distinguished the other Virginia cases relied upon in the majority opinion.] * * *

In the case before us the trial court gave no consideration to § 64–60, which section was expressly held in the Rudisill case, supra, to have changed the rules of law in effect prior to the revisal of the general laws in force before 1849.

The provisions of § 64–59 and § 64–60 are simple, clear, and positive. Section 64–59 provides how a will may be revoked. Section 64–60 provides how and when a will "in any manner revoked" may be revived. The latter section eliminates any distinction between the effect of a testamentary act of revocation and a separate and independent act.

In § 64–59 no difference is made between a will, or a codicil, or a writing, containing a revocation clause, as to the time when such a clause and either type of instrument becomes effective; and there is no indication that the legislature intended to make a difference. There is no provision that the revocation of a prior will is conditioned upon the existence of a subsequent will containing a revocation clause at the death of the testator, or that the second will be admitted to probate in order that its revocation clause can be made effective. If that condition had been provided, a revival statute such as § 64–60 would be useless because the potential survivor, himself, would be past reviving. The act declaring the intention to revoke is the essence and heart of the revocation process, an act which has immediate effect at the time of commission. In re Will of Bentley, supra, 175 Va. 456, 9 S.E.2d 308.

Moreover, § 64–60, in the employment of the language "in any manner revoked" encompasses all types of revocation in writing, whether by testamentary act or by a separate and independent instrument, duly executed.

A will being ambulatory in its provisions from its very nature constitutes a recognition that a testator may revoke any of its provisions, make a new instrument with new dispositions, or re-execute or republish a former will, in accordance with statutory requirements.

Code, § 64–62 has no application, as I see it, to the question involved in this case. It deals "with reference to the real and personal estate comprised" in a will.

It is all very nice to say that the testatrix here could have destroyed her first will, and that since she did not do so that will remained alive and vital. That she desired the first will to remain alive is contrary to the evidence as declared by her in the execution of the second will, and by her statement that she intended to make a third will. She changed her mind when she made the second will, she changed her mind when she destroyed the second will, and we have no means of knowing whether she subsequently changed her mind again, preferring that her property be disposed of according to the laws of intestacy. May it not be as well presumed that in destroying the subsequent will and in failing to make a new will she elected to die intestate? The intentions of the testatrix with respect to disposal of her property are as ambulatory as are the provisions of a will. I am not inclined to believe that she had any knowledge of the doctrine of dependent relative revocation.

I would reverse the judgment of the trial court and hold that the testatrix revoked her first will on January 31, 1955, when she so declared her intention in her second will. The first will thus became null and void, and there has been no life breathed into it by a revival thereof under the provisions of § 64–60.

Any doubts as to the wisdom of the rules enacted by statute, and adopted in the Rudisill case, supra, are questions for the legislature to resolve.

I'ANSON, J., concurs in this dissent.

NOTE

The Statute of Frauds, 1677,[49] did not deal with the effect upon a prior will of revocation of a revoking will or with the time at which a revocation by subsequent instrument occurred. The ecclesiastical and common law courts developed different views concerning the time at which a revocation by subsequent instrument occurred and, consequently, different views concerning the effect of revocation of a revoking instrument upon a prior will or testament.

The ecclesiastical courts held that a testament was revoked at the time the revoking instrument was executed.[50] The revocation was not contingent upon the operation of the revoking instrument at the death of the testator. But the ecclesiastical courts were liberal in admitting evidence of the circumstances and declarations of the testator to show his intention to revive his first testament.[51] When the testator's intention to revive his first testament by revocation of the revoking testament was shown, the first testament was treated as fully valid. There was a weak presumption against revival, the burden of proof of the testator's intention resting upon the party who alleged that a revival had occurred.[52]

49. 29 Chas. II, c. 3 (1677).

See generally, Atkinson, Wills (2d Ed., 1953) § 92; 2 Bowe-Parker: Page, Wills (3d Ed., Rev.1960) §§ 21.49–21.56; Rollison, Wills (1939) §§ 160–162; Thompson, Wills (3d Ed., 1947) § 183; Evans, "Testamentary Revival", 16 Ky.L.J. 47 (1927); Ferrier, "Revival of a Revoked Will", 28 Cal.L.Rev. 265 (1939); Roberts, "The Revival of a Prior by the Revocation of a Later Will", 48 U. of Pa.L.Rev. 505 (1900); Zacharias and Maschinot, "Revocation and Revival of Wills", 25 Chi-Kent Rev. 185, 271 (1947), 26 Chi-Kent Rev. 107 (1948); 28 A.L.R. 911 (1924); 162 A.L.R. 1072 (1946).

50. E.g., Wilson v. Wilson, 3 Phill.Ecc. 543, 161 Eng.Rep. 1409 (1821); Usticke v. Bawden, 2 Add.Ecc. 116, 162 Eng.Rep. 238 (1824).

51. Sections XIX and XXII of the Statute of Frauds had dealt with formalities for oral wills and formalities for the revocation of written testaments but no formalities were required for the execution of written testaments. The ecclesiastical courts did not hesitate to admit oral evidence concerning the testator's intention when it did not appear in the revoking instrument or when the revocation was by physical act.

52. From time to time, the ecclesiastical cases contain statements that revocation of the revoking will raised no presumption for or against revival. This language is also found in some of the American cases. See Pickens v. Davis, 134 Mass. 252, 45 Am.Rep. 322 (1883); Lane v. Hill, 68 N.H. 275, 44 A. 393, 73 Am.St.Rep. 591 (1895). Since the burden

The common law courts took the position that a will was ambulatory in its revocatory effect.[53] The execution of a revoking will had no effect upon the will purportedly revoked. The revocation occurred only if the revoking will operated at the death of the testator. If the revoking will was revoked in such a way that the first will was not also revoked at the death of the testator, the first will was *ipso facto* revived.[54] Evidence of the testator's contrary intention was not admissible.

Neither the ecclesiastical nor the common law courts distinguished between a revocation by inconsistency and a revocation by an express revocatory clause so far as the time of revocation was concerned. Nor did these courts appear to apply their revival rules when the first will was revoked by physical act or by operation of law even though a revoking instrument was also executed.[55]

The American courts have taken diverse positions concerning revival by revocation of a revoking will when no statute is applicable. A number of courts have applied the common law rule of automatic revival.[56] An almost equal number of courts have applied the ecclesiastical rule or a variation of it.[57] A few courts have distinguished between revocations by inconsistent provisions and revocations by express revocatory clauses so far as the time of revocation is concerned. The distinction is based on the idea that a revocation by inconsistency is mechanical and occurs only if the revoking instrument is in force at the testator's death. The express revocation is a deliberative act and operates as an immediate revocation of the will to which it refers. Thus, the common law rule is applied if the subsequent instrument revokes by inconsistency;[58] and the ecclesiastical rule is applied if the subsequent instrument revokes by an express clause of revocation.[59]

The first statute dealing with revival by revocation of a revoking will was enacted in New York in 1829 and has been the pattern for statutes in many other American states.[60] The New York statute provided in effect that

of proof was on the person alleging revival, the effect was the same as if a weak presumption against revival existed.

53. The common law courts did not treat a devise as ambulatory in the sense that it would pass after-acquired property. See Section 1, fn. 5, supra.

54. E.g., Goodright v. Glasier, 4 Burr. 2512, 98 Eng.Rep. 317 (1770); Burtenshaw v. Gilbert, 1 Cowp. 49, 98 Eng.Rep. 961 (1774).

55. See Burtenshaw v. Gilbert, fn. 54, supra; Moore's Will, 72 N.J.Eq. 371, 65 A. 447 (1907). Revocation by physical act or by operation of law took place immediately. Although the English courts do not appear to have passed upon the matter, it is possible that the ecclesiastical courts would permit parol revivals in these cases as they admitted parol evidence to show the testator's intention to revive a prior will by revocation of a revoking will. The American courts have not extended the doctrine of revival beyond its original confines.

56. E.g., Whitehall v. Halbing, 98 Conn. 21, 118 A. 454, 28 A.L.R. 895 (1922), 32 Yale L.J. 70 (1922).

57. E.g., Bailey v. Kennedy, 162 Colo. 135, 425 P.2d 304 (1967); Pickens v. Davis, 134 Mass. 252, 45 Am.Rep. 322 (1883); Heise v. Earle, 134 N.J.Eq. 393, 35 A.2d 880 (1944). The Maryland court presumes an intention to revive from the act of revocation. Colvin v. Warford, 20 Md. 357 (1863); Rabe v. McAllister, 177 Md. 97, 8 A.2d 922 (1939). The Mississippi court presumes that no revival was intended and admits no evidence to rebut the presumption. Bohanon v. Walcott, 2 Miss. (1 How.) 336, 29 Am.Dec. 631 (1836).

58. Cheever v. North, 106 Mich. 390, 64 N.W. 455, 58 Am.St.Rep. 499, 37 L.R.A. 561 (1895), 9 Harv.L.Rev. 364 (1895).

59. In re Noon's Will, 115 Wis. 299, 91 N.W. 670, 95 Am.St.Rep. 944 (1902). The Iowa court has permitted a revival without a new testamentary act if the testator's intention to revive is shown. Blackett v. Ziegler, 153 Iowa 344, 133 N.W. 901, 37 L.R.A.,N.S., 291, Ann.Cas. 1915E, 115 (1911), 12 Col.L.Rev. 353 (1912), 21 Yale L.J. 672 (1912).

60. McKinney's N.Y.Decedent Estate Law, § 41 (1949) provided as follows: "* * * If, after the making of any

there is no revival unless it appears by the terms of the revocation that the testator intended to revive or unless "he shall duly republish his first will." Statutes of this type are usually interpreted to require that the intention to revive appear in a written and attested instrument or that the first will be reexecuted.[61] Section XXII of the Wills Act, 1837,[62] is followed in part in the

will, the testator shall duly make and execute a second will, the destruction, canceling or revocation of such second will, shall not revive the first will, unless it appear by the terms of such revocation, that it was his intention to revive and give effect to his first will; or unless after such destruction, canceling or revocation, he shall duly republish his first will."

Alabama, California, Indiana, Missouri, Montana, Ohio, Oklahoma, Oregon, and Washington have statutes containing language almost identical to that in § 41. 20 Pa.Stat. § 2506 is patterned in part upon the New York statute but provides expressly that a will cannot be revived by an oral republication.

McKinney's N.Y., EPTL, § 3-4.6 (1967) now provides:

"(a) If after executing a will the testator executes a later will which revokes or alters the prior one, a revocation of the later will does not, of itself, revive the prior will or any provision thereof.

"(b) A revival of a prior will or of one or more of its provisions may be effected by:

"(1) The execution of a codicil which in terms incorporates by reference such prior will or one or more of its provisions.

"(2) A writing declaring the revival of such prior will or of one or more of its provisions, which is executed and attested in accordance with the formalities prescribed by this article for the execution and attestation of a will.

"(3) A republication of such prior will, whether to the original witnesses or to new witnesses, which shall require a re-execution and reattestation of the prior will in accordance with the formalities prescribed by 3-2.1."

Uniform Probate Code, § 2-509 provides:

"(a) If a second will which, had it remained effective at death, would have revoked the first will in whole or in part, is thereafter revoked by acts under Section 2-507, the first will is revoked in whole or in part unless it is evident from the circumstances of the revocation of the second will or from testator's contemporary or subsequent declarations that he intended the first will to take effect as executed.

"(b) If a second will which, had it remained effective at death, would have revoked the first will in whole or in part, is thereafter revoked by a third will, the first will is revoked in whole or in part, except to the extent it appears from the terms of the third will that the testator intended the first will to take effect."

The Uniform Probate Code applies a presumption of no revival which is rebuttable. It would appear fairly easy to rebut the presumption and revive the earlier will when the revocation of the second will has been by physical act. [Subsection (a)]. When the revocation of the revoking will is by a third will, it is unlikely the presumption often will be rebutted. The effect of Subsection (b) is substantially that an intent to revive must be shown from the third (or presumably later) will.

61. E.g., Stickney's Will, 161 N.Y. 42, 55 N.E. 396, 76 Am.St.Rep. 246 (1899); Collins v. Collins, 110 Ohio St. 105, 143 N.E. 561, 38 A.L.R. 230 (1924). The republication in the former New York statute may refer to an oral publication, although probably the language refers to a republication by codicil as distinguished from language of revival in an independent revoking instrument.

62. 7 Wm. IV & 1 Vict., c. 26, § XXII (1837) provides as follows: "* * * And be it further enacted, That no Will or Codicil, or any Part thereof, which shall be in any manner revoked, shall be revived otherwise than by the Re-execution thereof, or by a Codicil executed in manner herein-before required, and showing an intention to revive the same; and when any Will or Codicil which shall be partly revoked, and afterwards wholly revoked, shall be revived, such Revival shall not extend to so much thereof as shall have been revoked before the Revocation of the whole thereof, unless an Intention to the contrary shall be shown." The British Law Reform Committee recommended that the provisions of § XXII be continued without change stating: "We do not think that wills should be altogether incapable of revival nor do we believe that it is the expectation of ordinary people that revocation of a later will

District of Columbia, Kentucky, Virginia and West Virginia.[63] These statutes require reexecution or republication by codicil in order to validate the first will, unless, as in Virginia, the court considers no revocation to occur unless the revoking will is in force at testator's death. In Georgia the statute applies only to the situation in which a will is revoked by an express revocatory clause in a subsequent instrument. The Georgia statute provides that the first will may be republished and the republication proved by parol.[64]

PROBLEM

Assuming the statute cited in footnote 47 (by the Court) in *Timberlake* is in force in your state and the court in your state construes the statute as did the Supreme Court of Appeals of Virginia, how would you redraft your statute to carry out the intention of your legislature that an earlier will revoked by subsequent instrument not become operative merely because the subsequent instrument also has been revoked?

(4) DEPENDENT RELATIVE REVOCATION

CARTER v. FIRST UNITED METHODIST CHURCH OF ALBANY

Supreme Court of Georgia, 1980.
246 Ga. 352, 271 S.E.2d 493.

NICHOLS, JUSTICE.

The caveator, Luther Reynolds Carter, appeals from judgment entered in the superior court in behalf of the propounder, First United Methodist Church, admitting to probate, as the will of Mildred C. Tipton, an instrument bearing the date of August 21, 1963.

The 1963 instrument, typed and signed in the form of and purporting to be the last will and testament of Mildred C. Tipton, was found among Mrs. Tipton's other personal papers in her dining room chest after her death on February 14, 1979. It was folded together with a handwritten instrument dated May 22, 1978, captioned as her will but unsigned and unwitnessed, purporting to establish a different scheme of distribution of her property. Pencil marks had been made diago-

automatically revives an earlier one. The normal presumption of law is that a later document supersedes an earlier document and we think that the ways in which a revoked will may be revived ought to be narrowly circumscribed. * * *" Cmd. 7902, 3.49, p. 25 (1980).

63. D.C.Code, § 18–109(b); Ky.Rev. Stat. § 394.100; Va.Code Ann. § 64.1–60 (1980 Repl.Vol.); W.Va.Code Ann. § 41–1–8 (1980 Supp.)

64. Ga.Code Ann. § 113–403. Revival of a will revoked by inconsistency requires a new testamentary act. See Lively v. Harwell, 29 Ga. 509 (1859); Harwell v. Lively, 30 Ga. 315, 76 Am.Dec. 649 (1860).

nally through the property disposition provisions of the 1963 document and through the name of one of the co-executors.

The superior court found that from time to time prior to her death, Mrs. Tipton had made it known to her attorney that she needed his services in order to change or revise her will, or to make a new will; that at one time she had written out some proposed changes on tablet paper to be suggested to her lawyer when he prepared a new will for her; and that she did not intend to revoke her will by scratching through some of its provisions and by writing out the proposed changes.

* * *

The caveator contends in the remaining enumerations of error that the superior court erred in admitting the will to probate because the propounder did not produce any evidence to rebut the statutory presumption of revocation. Code Ann. § 113–404.

The case was submitted to the trial court on stipulated facts, and under stipulation that the depositions of Mrs. Tipton's attorney and one of her friends, relating to her intentions, be admitted in evidence. There is no transcript, and the record is sparse as to facts. Each party seems to have felt that the burden of proof properly was to be placed upon the other party and, accordingly, neither made much effort to develop the facts. The issue resolves itself, however, if certain presumptions are placed into proper perspective with each other.

"As a general rule, the burden is on a person attacking a paper offered for probate as a will to sustain the grounds of his attack. But by express provision of our statute, where a will has been canceled or obliterated in a material part, a presumption of revocation arises, and the burden is on the propounder to show that no revocation was intended * * * Where the paper is found among the testator's effects, there is also a presumption that he made the cancellations or obliterations * * * It having been shown that the paper offered for probate in this case had been in the custody of the deceased up to the time of his death, the propounder was met with both of the presumptions above alluded to." McIntyre v. McIntyre, 120 Ga. 67, 70, 47 S.E. 501 (1904).

The deposition of Mrs. Tipton's attorney, introduced by stipulation in behalf of the propounder, establishes, without contradiction, that Mrs. Tipton had written out some changes in her will on tablet paper and repeatedly had attempted to get her attorney to change or to revise her will, or to make a new will. The parties stipulated that the two writings, the 1963 will and the 1978 manuscript, were found after her death among her personal effects. No evidence appears in the record, and no contention is made, that Mrs. Tipton did not make the marks on the 1963 will or write the 1978 instrument. The presumption that Mrs. Tipton made the pencil marks and wrote the memorandum of her intentions stands unrebutted. Langan v. Cheshire, 208 Ga. 107, 65 S.E.2d 415 (1951); Porch v. Farmer, 158 Ga. 55, 122 S.E. 557 (1924); Howard v. Hunter, 115 Ga. 357, 41 S.E. 638 (1902). The other presumption, that of absolute revocation, is the focal point of our remaining inquiry.

The statute to which *McIntyre* refers is Code Ann. § 113–404, which provides, in part, that an intention to revoke will be presumed from the obliteration or canceling of a material portion of the will. In Georgia, the drawing of pencil lines through provisions of a will is a sufficient "canceling" *McIntyre,* supra, at p. 70, 47 S.E. 501. The question of whether or not the canceled provision is "material" is one of law. Howard v. Cotten, 223 Ga. 118, 122, 153 S.E.2d 557 (1967). The caveator contends that the propounder introduced no evidence to rebut the statutory presumption of revocation, and the propounder contends that under the doctrine of dependent relative revocation, or conditional revocation, the facts proven give rise to a presumption in favor of the propounder (which the caveator failed to rebut) that Mrs. Tipton did not intend for her 1963 will to be revoked unless her new dispositions of her property became effective in law. The caveator thus contends that the propounder failed to rebut the presumption of absolute or unconditional revocation, and the propounder contends he rebutted that presumption by evidence giving rise to another presumption, that of conditional revocation, which the caveator failed to rebut.

The doctrine of dependent relative revocation (conditional revocation) has been stated by this court as follows: "It is a doctrine of *presumed intention,* and has grown up as a result of an effort which courts always make to arrive at the real intention of the testator. Some of the cases appear to go to extreme lengths in the application of this doctrine, and seem to defeat the very intention at which they were seeking to arrive. The doctrine, as we understand it and are willing to apply it, is this: The mere fact that the testator intended to make a new will, or made one which failed of effect, will not alone, in every case, prevent a cancellation or obliteration of a will from operating as a revocation. If it is clear that the cancellation and the making of the new will were parts of one scheme, and the revocation of the old will was so related to the making of the new as to be dependent upon it, then if the new will be not made, or if made is invalid, the old will, though canceled, should be given effect, if its contents can be ascertained in any legal way. But if the old will is once revoked,—if the act of revocation is completed,—as if the will be totally destroyed by burning and the like, or if any other act is done which evidences an unmistakable intention to revoke, though the will be not totally destroyed, the fact that the testator intended to make a new will, or made one which can not take effect, counts for nothing. In other words, evidence that the testator intended to make or did actually make a new will, which was inoperative, may throw light on the question of intention to revoke the old one, but it can never revive a will once completely revoked." (Emphasis added.) McIntyre v. McIntyre, 120 Ga. 67, 71, 47 S.E. 501, 503, supra. The doctrine has been recognized and applied by the highest courts of many states. Annos. 62 ALR 1401, 115 ALR 721. It has been the subject of considerable discussion by the text writers. 1 Redfearn, Wills And Administration

In Georgia (4th Ed.), p. 188, § 96; Chaffin, Studies In The Georgia Law of Decedent's Estates and Future Interests, pp. 184, 186.

Professor Chaffin is of the opinion that "*McIntyre* represents a sound approach to the doctrine of dependent relative revocation." He writes that in *McIntyre*, "The doctrine was correctly perceived to be a rule of presumed intention rather than a rule of substantive law. The court refused to set aside the revocation until evidence bearing on testator's intent, including his oral declarations, was examined in an effort to discern what he would have desired if he had been aware of the true facts." He also concludes, correctly, this court believes, that "Most courts have taken the position that dependent relative revocation is judged by a stricter standard in a situation involving revocation by subsequent instrument as opposed to physical act." He is strongly of the opinion that "if the purpose of the doctrine is to effect testator's intent, there is no point in distinguishing between revocation by physical act and by subsequent instrument." Chaffin, supra, pp. 186–187. This court agrees. In Georgia, the doctrine is one of presumed intention. The principle is the same whether the revocation is by physical act or by subsequent instrument. As this court said of the doctrine in *McIntyre*, "The matter finally turns upon the intention of the testator, and no mere presumption [that the testator would have preferred the canceled will instead of intestacy] will be allowed to defeat this intention when it has been made to appear." 120 Ga. at 72, 47 S.E. at 504. The reason that the intention of the testator in making the marks or in writing the new instrument is material is that "Joint operation of act and intention is necessary to revoke a will." 120 Ga. at 71, 47 S.E. at 503; Payne v. Payne, 213 Ga. 613, 615, 100 S.E.2d 450 (1957).

In the present case, the testatrix wrote the 1978 instrument which the parties have conceded (by the absence of their contentions) cannot be admitted to probate because it lacks some of the requisites of a will. The propounder says, in effect, if not in express words, that the testatrix would have preferred the property disposition clauses of the 1963 will over the only other alternative—intestacy. The caveator contends, in essence, that the testatrix would have preferred intestacy. How stands the record?

The fact that the old will, with pencil lines drawn by Mrs. Tipton through the property disposition provisions, was found among her personal papers folded together with the 1978 writing, that makes a somewhat different disposition of her property, is some evidence tending to establish that "the cancellation and the making of the new will were parts of one scheme, and the revocation of the old will was so related to the making of the new as to be dependent upon it." 120 Ga. at 71, 47 S.E. at 503. This evidence was sufficient to rebut the statutory presumption of revocation (Code Ann. § 113–404) and to give rise to a presumption in favor of the propounder under the doctrine of dependent relative revocation or conditional revocation. *McIntyre*, supra. The stipulation that these two instruments were found together thus shifted the burden of proof to the caveator to prove, in essence, that Mrs. Tipton would have preferred intestacy.

* * *

Accordingly, the trial court, as finder of the facts, did not err in admitting the will to probate.

Judgment affirmed.

NOTE

Although the courts have refused relief when a will is executed by a testator who makes a mistake of extrinsic fact which is self-induced or unintentionally induced by another, a majority of the courts have been willing to give relief when a will is revoked under similar circumstances.[65] The relief is given upon the ground that the testator's revocatory intention was conditional upon the existence of facts as he believed them to be, and is usually described as "dependent relative revocation".[66] The relief may be given when the will purportedly revoked is offered for probate or when a revoking will is construed.[67]

When a prior will has been revoked by an express clause of revocation in a subsequent instrument, and the dispositive provisions of the subsequent instrument cannot operate for some reason which does not clearly appear upon its face, the courts agree that the mistake must appear upon the face of the revoking instrument before a presumption will be raised that the testator's intention to revoke was conditional or before extrinsic evidence will be admitted on the issue.[68] The courts do not agree whether the mistake

65. See Chapter VII, Section 2(5). See generally, Atkinson, Wills (2d Ed., 1953) § 88; 2 Bowe-Parker: Page, Wills (3d Ed., Rev.1960) §§ 21.57–21.65; Rollison, Wills (1939) §§ 141–146; Thompson, Wills (3d Ed., 1947) § 168; Cornish, "Dependent Relative Revocation", 5 So. Cal.L.Rev. 273 (1932); Dobie, "Dependent Relative Revocation of Wills", 2 Va. L.Rev. 327 (1915); Evans, "Dependent Relative Revocation", 16 Ky.L.J. 251 (1928); Roberts, "Dependent Relative Revocation of Wills", 49 Am.L.Reg. 18 (1901); Warren, "Dependent Relative Revocation", 33 Harv.L.Rev. 337 (1920); 62 A.L.R. 1367, 1401 (1929); 115 A.L.R. 710, 721 (1938).

66. The label is attributed to J. J. Powell, publisher in 1788 of the first text book on wills. See Warren, "Dependent Relative Revocation", 33 Harv.L.Rev. 337 (1920). The leading English case is Onions v. Tyrer, 2 Vern. 742, 23 Eng.Rep. 1085 (1717). Relief is also given for a mistake of law. Thus, dependent relative revocation may apply when a provision is inserted in a revoking will that is void under the Rule against Perpetuities. See Chapter XVI. Dependent relative revocation may apply when a testator revokes a subsequent will upon the mistaken belief that a prior will is revived by revocation of the revoking will. E.g., In re Callahan's Estate, 251 Wis. 247, 29 N.W.2d 352 (1947). While the usual view is that the testator's intention is conditional either (a) presumptively upon a showing of mistake or (b) based upon a finding as to what the testator would have done had he known the facts or law, some courts have taken the position that there is no intention to revoke because of the mistake or that the revocation is intended but will be disregarded.

67. The fact that a provision in a revoking will cannot operate is often not determined until the will is construed as, for example, that a provision is void under the Rule against Perpetuities.

68. In Campbell v. French, 3 Ves.Jr. 321, 30 Eng.Rep. 1033 (1797) the testator executed a codicil modifying a will containing legacies to the grandchildren of a sister in Virginia. The codicil provided "And as to the legacies or bequests given or bequeathed by my will to my sister, Margaret Bell's grandchildren, I hereby revoke such legacies and bequests; they being all dead." It was shown that the grandchildren were not dead and the legacies were held not revoked. Although the mistake and what would have been done in the absence of the mistake appeared upon the face of the codicil, the court placed no reliance upon those facts. The American courts have not insisted that what would have been done in the

must be intrinsic to the document in the sense that the mistake is clear without considering the surrounding circumstances, or whether it is sufficient if the mistake is clear when the surrounding circumstances are considered. The courts disagree as to application of the doctrine where the last will expressly revokes prior wills and contains a residuary gift to charity invalid under a statute prohibiting such gifts if the will is executed within a limited period prior to death of the testator. If the testator had a substantially similar prior will which would have been valid if unrevoked, was the revocation by the later will intentional under the circumstances or was it conditioned on the revoking will being completely effective? In Linkins v. Protestant Episcopal Cathedral Foundation,[69] the United States Court of Appeals applied the doctrine to save the charitable gift; the court affirmed a ruling by the district court allowing for probate both the last will and a prior will to the extent of the residuary gift to religious organizations. Most courts have refused to utilize dependent relative revocation as a device to circumvent the statutory prohibitions.[70] A majority of the courts have distinguished between situations in which a dispositive provision in a will which expressly revokes a prior will fails for some reason *dehors* the instrument and situations in which the reason for the failure of the dispositive provision appears upon the face of the revoking will.[71] In Melville's Estate[72] the testator expressly revoked by codicil a residuary bequest made in his will to his executors. The codicil contained a bequest of his residuary estate to charity but the bequest was not effective because the testator died within 30 days after the codicil was executed. The court allowed the revocation to stand. In Braun's Estate[73] the testator expressly revoked by codicil a bequest made in his will to his daughter but substituted a gift to his daughter in the codicil which was not effective because the amount of the gift was left blank. The court regarded the mistake as intrinsic to the codicil and considered evidence bearing upon the conditional intention of the testator.[74]

If the subsequent instrument contains provisions inconsistent with those in a prior instrument, but contains no express clause of revocation and the provisions in the subsequent instrument are ineffective, the courts are agreed that the provisions in the prior will can operate. This result may be based upon the "mechanical" theory of revocation by inconsistent provisions

absence of the mistake appear from the revoking will, although they do require that the mistake appear. What the testator would have done had the mistake not occurred is presumed or determined from extrinsic evidence.

69. 87 U.S.App.D.C. 351, 187 F.2d 357 (1950), noted, 39 Geo.L.J. 246 (1951); 64 Harv.L.Rev. 686 (1951); 37 Va.L.Rev. 461 (1951). See also Charleston Library Society v. Citizens & Southern National Bank, 200 S.C. 96, 20 S.E.2d 623 (1942); In re Kaufman's Estate, 25 Cal.2d 854, 155 P.2d 831 (1945). When there is no failure of the provision of the courts have shown no disposition to relax the requirement that the mistake appear from a reading of the will. See In re Salmonski's Estate, 38 Cal.2d 199, 238 P.2d 966 (1951).

70. Crosby v. Alton Ochsner Medical Foundation, 276 So.2d 661 (Miss.1973), noted 44 Miss.L.J. 814 (1973).

71. If the revoking will fails to operate because of a defect in formalities of execution, lack of testamentary capacity, undue influence, or because of some other reason which vitiates the entire will, the revocation of the prior will does not take place. Some courts have described this situation as one of dependent relative revocation.

72. 245 Pa. 318, 91 A. 679 (1914).

73. 358 Pa. 271, 56 A.2d 201 (1948).

74. See La Croix v. Senecal, 140 Conn. 311, 99 A.2d 115 (1953), [1953] Wash.U.L.Q. 449 (codicil expressly revoking residuary disposition contained in will but designating same beneficiaries in substituted provision, the interest of one beneficiary under the codicil being void because the husband of the beneficiary was a necessary witness. The provision in favor of the beneficiary in the will was held effective).

or upon the "intent" theory.[75] If the intent theory is applied, it would seem that the same requirements for dependent relative revocation should be made as are made when the revocation is by an express clause.

When the revocation is by physical act to the instrument, rather than by a subsequent instrument, extrinsic evidence is admitted to show the mistake and the conditional intent of the testator. Where a second will is invalidly executed, whether the first will can be probated even though cancelled or destroyed depends upon the similarity of the wills. The issue is whether testator would have wanted the first will probated if the second will is ineffective or would have preferred intestacy. Some courts place upon the proponent of the first will the burden of overcoming the presumption of revocation arising from the destruction.[76] Other courts more readily infer a conditional intent. In Matter of Macomber's Will[77] there were certain marks of cancellation upon the will with a note in the margin "see codicile". An unwitnessed codicil was found. The testator's intention to revoke the will was held conditional upon the validity of the codicil. In Smalley's Estate[78] the testator was caused to execute a second will by undue influence and then tore his signature from the first. It was held that his intention to revoke the first will was conditional upon the effectiveness of the second.

In a number of cases a will has been revoked by physical act and there is no attempt to execute another. If the execution of another will is intended at an indefinite time, the evidence is strong that the testator intended to revoke the first will unconditionally.[79] On the other hand, if the testator intends to revoke the first will and execute a second as part of the same transaction, and succeeds in revoking the first will but is unable to execute the second, a court may find that the intention to revoke the first will was conditional upon the execution of the second.

Where partial revocations by physical act are permitted, a testator may cancel or obliterate a portion of his will and interline an unexecuted provision as a substitute. The interlineation is ineffective unless the will is republished or re-executed.[80] But the original provision may be effective if the testator's intention is found conditional. In Ruel v. Hardy[81] the testatrix struck out the word "five" in a five hundred dollar legacy and interlined the word "one". The court refused to apply the doctrine of dependent relative revocation because the reduction of the legacy by 80% indicated that the testatrix intended to revoke the five hundred dollar legacy unconditionally. Similarly where the testator marked out the names of certain devisees and invalidly attempted to substitute other names, the cancellation has been treated as an unconditional revocation.[82]

75. See Section 2(1), this Chapter, and Subsection 3, this Section.

76. Matter of Estate of Patten, ___ Mont. ___, 587 P.2d 1307 (1979) (also holding that dependent relative revocation can be applicable under the Uniform Probate Code).

77. 274 App.Div. 724, 87 N.Y.S.2d 308 (1949).

78. 131 N.J.Eq. 175, 24 A.2d 515 (1942).

79. E.g., Estate of McKeever, 361 A. 2d 166 (D.C.App.1976); In re Olmstead's Estate, 122 Cal. 224, 54 P. 745 (1898). But revocation may be conditioned on another method of disposition which is ineffective. Board of Trustees of Methodist Church v. Welpton, 284 S.W.2d 580 (Mo. 1955) (devise crossed out and deed to devisee of the devised land executed improperly); Flanders v. White, 142 Or. 375, 18 P.2d 823 (1933) (testator destroyed will and prepared account book which he thought would serve as a valid will substitute).

80. See Subsection 2, this Section.

81. 90 N.H. 240, 6 A.2d 753 (1939).

82. Watson v. Landvatter, 517 S.W.2d 117 (Mo.1974), noted 41 Mo.L.Rev. 477 (1976) (devises to first wife and also to her relatives changed to second wife and her children).

If a revocation is expressly conditioned, and the condition is not against public policy, the condition should be given effect.[83]

PROBLEM

Testator executed will number (1) in 1948. In 1953 he executed will number (2) which contained a clause expressly revoking will number (1). In 1954 the testator took both wills to his attorney and in the presence of the attorney tore will number (2) into pieces and threw the pieces into a wastebasket, saying that he wanted to reaffirm will number (1). If the court applies the common law view of revival by revocation of a revoking will, which will, if any, should be allowed for probate? If the court applies the ecclesiastical rule of revival, which will, if any, should the court allow? If the jurisdiction does not permit revival except by a validly executed will or a republication of the revoked will, could either will be allowed under the doctrine of dependent relative revocation? In re Eberhardt's Estate, 1 Wis.2d 439, 85 N.W.2d 483 (1957).

83. No distinction should be made between a conditional execution of a will and a conditional revocation. See Chapter VII, Section 2(5), infra.

Chapter VII

CONTEST OF WILLS AND RELATED REMEDIES

Scope Note

When probate of a will is contested, the only issue before the court is "will or no will." If the proponent prevails, and the will is established as the valid last will of the testator, disputes concerning what he meant by what he stated in his will are resolved later by appropriate proceedings for construction of the will. It is clear, nevertheless, that a probate court in order to pass upon the issue "will or no will" may have to construe the will.[1] Also it is important that the student become accustomed to think not only of remedies by direct attack upon the validity of a will or its provisions but of ancillary or substituted remedies, such as the constructive trust as an equitable device for restitution, and construction of the will to remedy mistakes in the inducement and in the factum which cannot be remedied conveniently at probate.

This Chapter thus concerns grounds for contest and related remedies. The cases and materials in Section 1 are devoted to a brief résumé of the procedure for probate and contest, the nature and effect of a probate decree, the degree of interest which a party must show in order to be permitted to contest a will, and the effect of agreements and stipulations concerning probate and contest. Certain important grounds for contest and related remedies are considered in Section 2. These grounds for contest are not the only ones upon which objections to the validity of a will may be based. Important grounds for contest, such as failure to comply with the statutory formalities for executing a will and revocation of a will, have been discussed in earlier chapters.[2]

1. A probate court may construe a will for limited purposes. Construction may be necessary when it is alleged that a prior will is revoked by a later inconsistent will. Construction of a will is also necessary during the course of administration of the estate, but administration may or may not be supervised by the probate court. Statutes in some states confer general powers of construction upon probate courts. Uniform Probate Code, §§ 1–302, 3–1001(a) expressly confer upon the court having probate jurisdiction the power to construe wills.

2. See Chapters V and VI.

SECTION 1. PROBATE AND CONTEST—PROCEDURE AND RELATED MATTERS

(1) PROCEDURE AND FUNCTION OF PROBATE AND CONTEST

Probate is the process by which a will is established as the valid last will of a decedent.[3] Neither a legatee nor, in most states, a devisee can establish his rights against third parties until the will under which he takes is probated. Probate of the will and distribution by the personal representative are necessary to vest legal title in the legatee. A devisee of land is usually regarded as receiving his title at the instant of the testator's death. But he cannot prove his title until he probates the will in most of the states. Thus, the devisee might initiate an action, such as an action for ejectment,[4] before the will is probated. But the will must be probated by the time in the proceeding when the devisee must prove title. At common law a devise was regarded as a conveyance and the validity of a devise was determined in an action at law as the validity of a deed was determined. A devise was not probated; and a few states still permit the devisee to prove his title without probate. Uniform Probate Code, § 3–102 permits proof of a devise by an unprobated will if no court proceeding "concerning the succession or administration of the estate has occurred" *and either* the devisee or his successors and assigns pos-

3. See generally Atkinson, Wills (2d Ed., 1953) §§ 93–99; Rollison, Wills (1939) §§ 326–335; Thompson, Wills (3d Ed., 1947) §§ 186–208; Atkinson, "Probate of Wills: Necessity and Effect", 27 N.Y.U.L.Rev. 189 (1952); Basye, "The Venue of Probate and Administration Proceedings", 43 Mich.L.Rev. 471 (1944); Hopkins, "The Extraterritorial Effect of Probate Decrees", 53 Yale L.J. 221 (1944); Levy, "Probate in Common Form in the United States: The Problem of Notice in Probate Proceedings", [1952] Wis. L.Rev. 420; Simes, "Administration of a Decedent's Estate as a Proceeding in Rem", 43 Mich.L.Rev. 675 (1945); Simes, "The Function of Will Contests", 44 Mich.L.Rev. 503 (1946); Simes and Basye, "The Organization of the Probate Court in America", 42 Mich.L.Rev. 965 (1944), 43 Mich.L.Rev. 113 (1944); Lauritzen, "Improvement of Probate Procedure" 94 Trusts and Estates 787 (1955), 96 Trusts and Estates 856 (1957); Chaffin and Barwick, "The Probate and Establishment of Domestic and Foreign Wills: An Analysis of Statutory Requirements," 13 Ga.L.Rev. 133 (1978) (with emphasis on Georgia law); Limbaugh, "Sources and Development of Probate Law", Wash.U.L.Q. 419 (1956) (relative to adoption of Missouri Probate Code of 1955 with good discussion of probate policies); Patton, "Improvement of Probate Statutes—The Model Code", 39 Iowa L. Rev. 446 (1954) (analysis of trends in probate reform with general bibliography); Jaworski, "Preparation and Trial of the Will Contest", 21 Ark.L.Rev. 87, 92–97 (1967); "Procedural Content of Will Contests", 14 Baylor L.Rev. 316, 401 (1962) (clear exposition of Texas practice). As to Uniform Probate Code provisions, see Stroup, "Probate Practice Under the Uniform Probate Code", 46 No.Dakota L. Rev. 289 (1970).

4. E.g., Murphree v. Griffis, 215 Ala. 98, 109 So. 746, 48 A.L.R. 1032 (1926).

sessed the property devised in accordance with the provisions of the will *or* the property devised was not possessed or claimed by anyone by virtue of the decedent's title during the time period for testacy proceedings. This time, under Uniform Probate Code, § 3-108 is, with some exceptions, three years from the decedent's death.

Jurisdiction in probate is statutory and may be vested in courts of special or general jurisdiction.[5] The Uniform Probate Code contemplates a Court with a judge having the same qualifications as a judge of a court of general jurisdiction.[6] The Uniform Probate Code Court is to have jurisdiction over "all subject matter" relating to estates of decedents "including construction of wills and determination of heirs and successors of decedent"; estates of protected persons; protection of minors and incapacitated persons; and trusts.[7] The Court is stated to have "full power to make orders, judgments and decrees and to take all other action necessary and proper to administer justice in the matters which come before it".[8] The Court may try appropriate questions of fact by a jury.[9]

Current state probate procedures also are statutory. There are many procedural variations.

The statutes usually prescribe two forms for probate. These are based upon the ancient English distinction between probate in "solemn" form and probate in "common" form.[10] In the ex-parte proceeding, based upon the English "common" form, no notice to interested parties is required. Only the proponent submits evidence, although prospective contestants may be permitted to cross examine the proponent's witnesses. Unless a contest occurs within a prescribed period of time, an order probating a will in an ex-parte proceeding is final. In the inter-partes proceeding, based upon the English "solemn" form, notice to interested parties is required and the contestant submits evidence against the will.

Probate courts are usually authorized to probate a will in an ex-parte proceeding. In some states the courts of limited or special probate jurisdiction can conduct only ex-parte proceedings. In other states these courts may conduct inter-partes proceedings if the contestant files a *caveat* after the ex-parte proceeding has begun. In a few states only the inter-partes proceeding is permitted, although the court may issue an ex-parte order if there is no contest. Courts of general jurisdiction which also have probate jurisdiction may conduct ex-parte proceedings if these are permitted.

If the proceeding is inter-partes, contest is made before a probate order is issued. Usually, however, a will is contested on an appeal

5. The courts of limited or special jurisdiction frequently have powers in addition to those required for probating wills and supervising the administration of estates. The courts are usually called "probate" courts, although in some states they are called "surrogate's" courts, "prerogative" courts, or "orphans'" courts.

6. Uniform Probate Code, § 1–309.

7. Id., § 1–302(a).

8. Id., § 1–302(b).

9. Id., § 1–306.

10. See Chapter I, Section 3(1)B.

from an ex-parte decision or in a separate statutory action to set aside the order probating the will. The proceeding is inter-partes on an appeal or in a separate statutory action. Except for the fact that the will has been probated, the appellate or statutory proceeding is similar to the English "solemn" form. When an inter-partes proceeding has been conducted the only recourse is an appeal from the decision of the court.

The Uniform Probate Code continues the two forms of probate now used in most of the states. There is an informal probate (a non-adjudicative determination) [11] and a formal probate (a judicial determination after notice to interested parties).[12] The informal probate is before the Registrar. The formal proceeding is only before the Court. The Registrar cannot entertain applications which relate to one or more of a known series of testamentary documents (other than a will and its codicils) the latest of which does not expressly revoke the earlier.[13]

The contest of a will is by the *formal* procedure.[14] This may be invoked to block an informal probate. If the will has been probated informally, a contestant may initiate the formal probate within three years from the decedent's death to set aside the informal probate and either probate another will or have the decedent adjudicated intestate. If the formal procedure is undertaken initially, the contestant states his objections in his pleadings.

In current state probate practice certain facts are jurisdictional. A will cannot be probated unless the testator is dead. Unless a statute provides for probate of the will of an absentee or a convicted criminal, an order probating the will of a living testator is void and is open to collateral attack.[15]

11. Uniform Probate Code, §§ 3-301 through 3-306.

12. Id., §§ 3-401 through 3-413. It is not required that a personal representative be qualified in either type of probate or in an adjudication of intestacy. Notice may also be required in certain informal proceedings before the Registrar. Section 3-306.

13. Id., § 3-304.

14. Id., § 3-401.

15. When the will of an absentee is offered for probate it is required by statute that the absence be in excess of a specified period of time and that notice of the application and distribution of the estate be given to the absentee by publication. If the absentee later appears, the order may be set aside but the personal representative and bona fide purchasers for value from the legatees or devisees are protected.

The statutes pertaining to the probate of the will or an adjudication of intestacy of the estate of an absentee are usually described as "Enoch Arden" statutes. The Uniform Probate Code establishes a presumption of death when the absentee has been missing five years and his absence is not satisfactorily explained after diligent search and inquiry. Section 1-107(3). The finding of death is conclusive only if notice of the hearing on the petition in the *formal* testacy proceeding is sent by registered or certified mail to the alleged decedent at his last known address and the Court finds the search was made. See Section 3-403(b). If the missing person proves not to be dead, despite the care taken to discover him, he can recover assets in the hands of the personal representative and also the estate or proceeds in the hands of distributees or the value of the distributions to the extent "that any recovery from the distributees is equitable in view of all the circumstances." Section 3-412(5).

As between courts in a single state, a statute usually requires that a will be probated by a court having jurisdiction over the domicile of the testator at the time of his death. There is a division of authority as to whether a probate order by a court which has no jurisdiction over the testator's domicile is subject to collateral attack in another court of the same state. It has been held that a decision in favor of jurisdiction by the court before which the petition was first filed excludes from jurisdiction another court in the same state.[16]

As between different states, probate of a will of personal property at the domicile of the testator is usually regarded as conclusive. The view adopted depends upon the application of the common law rule of conflict of laws in the foreign state in which the will is questioned. In any event, the foreign state is not bound by a determination of domicile by the court which probates the will.[17] If the will contains a devise of land, the will must be probated at the situs of the land in order to establish title.[18]

In the probate practice of many states, a will contest commences with the filing of a *caveat* or written objection setting forth the facts upon which the contest is based or with the filing of a bill, complaint or similar pleading. The *caveat* is filed before the will is probated. An answer or demurrer may or may not be permitted by local statutes. In some states the petition for probate is treated as a complaint and the *caveat* as an answer. If the will has been admitted to probate before contest, the contest is commenced as an appeal or by a bill or complaint filed in a separate statutory proceeding. Some responsive pleading is required.

By comparison with the contest procedures now used in many states, the procedure of the Uniform Probate Code is quite simple. As previously noted, only the formal procedure is used for contest. The contestant either initiates this proceeding or the proceeding is initiated by the proponent with the contestant stating his grounds of contest in his responsive pleading.

The only issue upon contest in all states is *devisavit vel non*. The contest may be of the whole will or of a part. Statutes in many

16. E.g., State ex rel. Regan v. Probate Court of Olmstead County, 215 Minn. 322, 9 N.W.2d 765 (1943). Uniform Probate Code, § 3–201 states location of property as the venue if the decedent was not domiciled in the state. Venue for all subsequent proceedings is the place where the initial formal proceeding occurred, although if the initial proceeding was informal the Court, upon finding venue was elsewhere, may transfer the proceeding and file on the application of an interested person and after notice to the proponent in the first proceeding.

17. Uniform Probate Code, § 3–202 stipulates that the state applying the Code must treat the determination of domicile in the proceeding first commenced as the binding determination. Unless the local proceeding was commenced first, if there are conflicting claims of domicile, the Court must stay, dismiss or permit suitable amendment in the local proceeding.

18. Statutes in a majority of states make provision for the probate of foreign wills. See Uniform Probate Code, §§ 3–408 and 3–409. Under Uniform Probate Code, § 2–506 the formalities with which the will is executed do not have to meet the requirements of the formalities required by the state where the land is located if that state has adopted the Code.

states provide for a jury trial in contests, but there is no constitutional guarantee to a jury in contest proceedings.

There has been some interest in a procedure for ante-mortem probate, i.e., a procedure comparable to a declaratory judgment for probate of a testator's will during his lifetime. A few states have adopted statutes authorizing such probate.[19] The procedure may be adversary, on notice to probable heirs with a binding decree in order to foreclose contest after death, or non-adversary for the purpose of officially preserving direct evidence of testamentary capacity and freedom from undue influence.[20]

Will contests tend to receive much publicity but are relatively rare. Although meaningful judicial statistics are not generally available, it seems safe to say that only 1% to 2% of probates are contested, and the ratio of success is not high.[21]

19. Ark.Stats. (1981 Supp.) §§ 62.-2134–2137; N.Dak.Cent. Code (1979 Supp.) § 30.1–08.1; Ohio Rev. Code (1980 Supp.) §§ 2107.081–.085. The Ohio statute is discussed in Comment, 9 Cap.U.L. Rev. 717 (1980).

20. Various "models" for living probate are proposed in Fink, "Ante-Mortem Probate Revisited: Can an Idea Have A Life After Death?" 37 Ohio St.L.J. 264 (1976); Langbein, "Living Probate: The Conservatorship Model," 77 Mich.L.Rev. 63 (1978); Alexander, "The Conservatorship Model: A Modification," 77 Mich.L. Rev. 86 (1978); Alexander and Pearson, "Alternative Models of Ante-Mortem Probate and Procedural Due Process Limitations on Succession," 78 Mich.L.Rev. 89 (1979). For a strong criticism of the concept, see Fellows, "The Case Against Living Probate," 78 Mich.L.Rev. 1066 (1980). The Uniform Probate Code has no such procedure; a proposal for a Uniform Ante–Mortem Probate of Wills Act has been abandoned by the National Conference of Commissioners on Uniform Laws as of 1981. The idea is not new. It was first proposed in the early 1930's. Cavers, "Ante–Mortem Probate: An Essay in Preventive Law," 1 U.Chi.L.Rev. 440 (1933); Kutscher, "Living Probate," 21 A.B.A.J. 427 (1935).

21. For calendar year 1979, the New York Surrogates' Courts had 40,020 petitions for probate of wills. 43 wills were rejected after inquiry, undoubtedly for improper execution. Objections were filed to 408 wills. In 251 of these cases the objections were withdrawn, settled or dismissed before trial; 157 contests went to trial, and in only 89 cases were contestants successful. Report of the Chief Administrator of the Courts for Calendar Year 1979 (N.Y. Legislative Document No. 90, 1980). The low number of successful contests is partially offset by the number of settlements. But note that only 1% of all wills were contested. Unfortunately there is no breakdown as to grounds for contest. In a survey by the Principal Registry of the Family Division of all wills submitted for probate in England and Wales during the period 4 September to 1 December 1978, made for the Law Reform Committee, the total number of wills admitted to proof was 40,664. Of these, 84.3% were professionally drawn. The total number of wills rejected was 97. Of these rejected wills 93.8% were not professionally drawn. See Cmd. 7902 (1980) Annex 2.

(2) NATURE AND EFFECT OF THE PROBATE DECREE

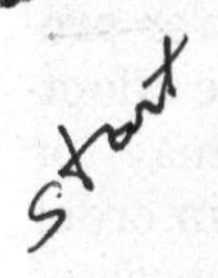

HAAS v. HAAS

Supreme Court of Missouri, 1973.
504 S.W.2d 44.[22]

HIGGINS, COMMISSIONER.

Appeal from dismissal of plaintiff's petition to contest will asserting denial of due process of law under the Fifth and Fourteenth Amendments to the United States Constitution and the presence of questions involving construction of the Constitutions of the United States and of Missouri.

Ervin Frank Haas died testate April 22, 1970, survived by his son, plaintiff Ervin A. Haas, his brother, Albert P. Haas, and his sisters, Ann Martin, Emmie Schrempp, Erma Good, and Augusta Wolf.

On May 1, 1970, a writing purporting to be the last will and testament of Ervin Frank Haas, deceased, naming defendants Albert P. Haas and Melvin Friedman coexecutors, bequeathing $1.00 to plaintiff, stating plaintiff was not testator's son, and distributing the balance of decedent's estate to some thirty-two other beneficiaries, including defendant Shriners' Hospital for Crippled Children, was admitted to probate in the Probate Court of St. Louis County, Missouri.

Schedule B of the Application for Letters Testamentary filed May 1, 1970, by the coexecutors named the beneficiaries, including "Ervin A. Haas, son of decedent [sic] former wife, now deceased, address unknown. Last known confined to Federal Prison."

Letters Testamentary were issued to the coexecutors May 1, 1970; the first publication of notice to creditors was on May 6, 1970; and the proof of publication of the notice was filed May 27, 1970. A stamped unmailed post card addressed to Ervin A. Haas, "address unknown," in the form of the notice of issuance of letters testamentary, was in the probate file.

On October 5, 1971, plaintiff filed his petition to contest the will of Ervin Frank Haas, deceased. Among other things, plaintiff alleged he "was not given proper notice that an estate had been opened for his father"; that coexecutor Albert P. Haas "knew that plaintiff was in Leavenworth penitentiary in Kansas"; and "that plaintiff was entitled to notice reasonably calculated to apprise him of the pendency of the Probate proceeding."

Upon these facts and circumstances defendant Shriners' Hospital moved for dismissal of plaintiff's petition on the ground that Section 473.083, RSMo 1969, V.A.M.S., precluded him from filing his will contest more than six months following probate of the will or six months following first publication of notice of letters testamentary, whichev-

22. Noted 40 Mo.L.Rev. 552 (1975).

er is later. Defendant coexecutors also moved for dismissal of plaintiff's petition asserting their lack of exact knowledge of plaintiff's whereabouts at the time of decedent's death, sufficiency of the notice in accordance with Section 473.017, RSMo 1969, V.A.M.S., and on the ground the suit was barred by Section 473.083, supra, for the reason that it was filed more than six months after first publication of notice of letters testamentary.

After hearing, including evidence, arguments, and briefs, the court sustained the coexecutors' motion to dismiss, ordered plaintiff's petition dismissed with prejudice, and designated the order of dismissal a final order for purpose of appeal.

Appellant contends the court erred "for the reason that the notice to appellant that an estate had been opened for Ervin Frank Haas * * * pursuant to Sections 473.017 and 473.033, RSMo (1959), was inadequate and insufficient and denied appellant due process of law and therefore the special statute of limitations in Section 473.083, RSMo (1959), should not have run against him."

The question thus posed is whether the coexecutors' failure to more adequately advise the probate court of plaintiff's whereabouts in their application for letters testamentary under Section 473.017, if so, or the failure of the notice of letters under Section 473.033 to reach plaintiff, if so, tolled the limitation of time in which to contest a will provided in Section 473.083.

Appellant, relying principally upon Mullane v. Central Hanover Trust Company, 339 U.S. 306, 70 S.Ct. 652, 94 L.Ed. 865 (1950), dealing with quality of notice as a requisite of due process, argues "that absent a requirement for due diligence on the part of the applicant for Letters Testamentary or of the Probate Clerk to ascertain the whereabouts of the heirs and legatees that these statutes [Sections 473.017 and 473.033] are unconstitutional for their failure to require a good faith attempt to give an heir or legatee the notice to which he is entitled under the fifth and fourteenth amendments to the United States Constitution."

The difficulty in appellant's position is that Sections 473.017, and 473.033 are not relevant to the court's action and the issue of this appeal. As recognized by appellant, Section 473.083, unattacked by appellant, "is the statute that sets forth will contest procedures. It is this statute upon which the court relied in dismissing Appellant's petition."

Section 473.083, as applicable to plaintiff, provides: "If any person interested in the probate of a will appears within six months after the date of the probate or rejection thereof, or within six months after the first publication of notice of the granting of letters on the estate of the testator, whichever is later, and, by petition to the circuit court of the county, contests the validity of the will * * *, an issue shall be made up whether the writing produced is the will of the testator * * *. If no person appears within the time aforesaid, then probate or rejection of the will is binding. Whenever it is shown or appears to and is found by the probate court that any person interested in the probate of a will is a minor or person of unsound mind, and that the filing of a contest may be to the interest of the minor or person, the court shall appoint a guardian for the minor or person, who shall file or join in the contest within the time fixed by this section."

As acknowledged by appellant, Section 473.083 is not a statute of limitations in the usual sense but is a special statute of limitations applicable solely to the contest of wills. It is exclusive of the other Statute of Limitations under Section 516.300, RSMo 1969, V.A.M.S., and fraud does not toll the running of the time limit prescribed in Section 473.083 under Section 516.280, RSMo 1969, V.A.M.S., of the General Statutes of Limitations. Section 473.083 is more in the nature of a statute granting jurisdiction than that of a statute of limitations. The right of action to contest a will is purely statutory in that Section 473.083 confers jurisdiction upon the circuit court in derogation of common law, and grants to the persons there named a personal right to contest probate of a will provided the party invokes such jurisdiction within six months after the later of the dates of probate or of first publication of notice of letters. Miller v. Munzer, 251 S.W. 2d 966, 971[7, 8] (Mo.App.1952); State ex rel. Bier v. Bigger, 352 Mo. 502, 178 S.W.2d 347, 350[3, 4] (Banc 1944).

* * *

There is no question that plaintiff failed to file his contest within the time prescribed by Section 473.083, and his failure does not come within any exception provided in such special statute of limitations. Accordingly, the trial court properly dismissed plaintiff's will contest on account of his failure to bring it within the time prescribed.

Judgment affirmed.

WELBORN, C., concurs.

PER CURIAM:

The foregoing opinion by HIGGINS, C., is adopted as the opinion of the court.

SEILER, JUDGE (concurring).

As I understand appellant's claim he contends the statutes under which the probate proceedings were commenced violate due process and are unconstitutional because they do not require executors to exercise due diligence in notifying heirs, legatees and devisees, but are satisfied with only an indifferent effort on the part of the executors. Here, for instance, although the executors presumably could easily have obtained appellant's exact address, they did no more than to say he was in federal prison and gave him notice only by publication. Appellant thus is contending that the procedure followed was insufficient even to confer jurisdiction on the probate court to open the estate and, of course, if appellant is correct in this, the mere passage of six months of time would not serve to cut off his rights despite Sec. 473.083, RSMo 1969, V.A.M.S., as it does not begin to operate until an estate has been validly opened. So I believe we necessarily must address ourselves to the question of whether Secs. 473.017 and 473.033, RSMo 1969, V.A.M.S., violate due process as to notice.

The fourteenth amendment of the U. S. Constitution provides that a person may not be deprived of life, liberty or property without due process of law. "An elementary and fundamental requirement of due process in any proceeding which is to be accorded finality is notice reasonably calculated, under all the circumstances, to apprise interested parties of the pendency of the action and afford them an opportunity to present their objections * * * The notice must be of such nature as reasonable to convey the required information, * * * and it must afford a reasonable time for those interested to make their appearance * * *" Mullane v. Central Hanover Tr. Co., 339 U.S. 306, 314, 70 S.Ct. 652, 657, 94 L.Ed. 865 (1949).

Missouri cases agree that due process sometimes requires more notice than is required by a statute. See State ex rel. Deems v. Holtcamp, 245 Mo. 655, 151 S.W. 153 (1912); Clapper v. Chandler, 406 S.W.2d 114 (Mo.App.1966). And see Maus, Missouri Practice, Probate Law and Practice, Vol. 3, Sec. 514.

Appellant's argument that due diligence in giving notice is essential to due process is the gist of the Mullane decision and would logically seem applicable to probate proceedings. A due diligence requirement would not put a heavy burden on executors nor would it thwart the state's interest in the final settlement of estates, but it would further protect the rights of persons with an interest affected by probate of the will. In this case, for example, it would have required no more than an inquiry by the probate judge as to what efforts the executor had made to locate appellant's address. If no effort had been made the court could direct the executor to make reasonable efforts to determine appellant's whereabouts. On the other hand, were the probate court satisfied that due diligence had been complied with it could proceed.

However, courts of other states have not applied the due process language of Mullane to the notice requirements of probate proceedings. In addition other decisions of the Supreme Court give support to the validity of the notice requirements of our probate code. The court has held that an ex parte probate followed by a one-year period for contest affords due process of law. Farrell v. O'Brien, 199 U.S. 89, 25 S.Ct. 727, 50 L.Ed. 101 (1905). And the Supreme Court has construed the due process provisions of the fourteenth amendment not to overturn aged practices. See Ownbey v. Morgan, et al. Executors of Morgan, 256 U.S. 94, 110, 41 S.Ct. 433, 65 L.Ed. 837 (1921), [although doubt may be cast on this by some of the language in Fuentes v. Shevin, 407 U.S. 67, 91–92, 92 S.Ct. 1983, 32 L.Ed.2d 556 (1972)] and cases cited in "Probate Proceedings—Administration of Decedent's Estates—The Mullane Case and Due Process of Law", 50 Mich.L.Rev. 124 (1952). It is for this reason I concur in the result of the opinion written by Higgins, C.

It should be noted, however, that the concept of due process has changed considerably since 1905 and courts today do not look with favor on ex parte proceedings which affect property rights. See e.g., Fuentes v. Shevin, supra; B-W Acceptance Corporation v. Alexander, 494 S.W.2d 75 (Mo. banc 1973); and State ex rel. Williams v. Berrey, 492 S.W.2d 731 (Mo. banc 1973). The subject of whether our probate statutes should be amended to require executors to exercise due diligence in giving notice would seem, therefore, to be deserving of legislative attention. Even in the absence of more precise statutory requirements, careful executors will no doubt take pains to exercise due diligence in giving notice to interested parties. See annot. Duty and Liability of Executor with Respect to Locating and Noticing Legatees, Devisees, or Heirs, 10 A.L.R.3d 547.

NOTE

Mullane v. Central Hanover Trust Co., discussed in the concurring opinion, involved an accounting in a trust matter. Although the analogy to probate is strong, the United States Supreme Court has to date not decided the issue of adequate notice in probate.[23]

The Uniform Probate Code requires personal or mail notice in formal testacy proceedings and also, because there may be unknown heirs such as an illegitimate child or unknown contestants under a prior or subsequent will, mandates published notice.[24] The effectiveness of publication as a method of notice in modern times is open to serious question but in case of "unknown" persons is the only way yet devised. If there is a defect in notice, however, this does not void the proceeding as to persons who actually receive notice.[25] In informal probate under the Code, no advance notice is generally required;[26] instead the interested persons are allowed a statutory period to contest the informal probate, and in some of the Code states a provision has been added placing a duty on the applicant to inform the heirs and devisees of the informal probate within 30 days.[27] The "information" requirement is a duty, breach making the fiduciary liable but not affecting the validity of the probate. The constitutionality of this approach has been defended.[28]

Similar problems of adequacy of notice may be raised at later stages in administration of an estate, as upon court approval of the accounts of the personal representative. The Uniform Probate Code treats each formal proceeding as independent[29] and requires new notice of each proceeding to interested persons, except in supervised administration and even there notice must be given on formal closing or settlement of the estate.[30] The problem of notice to creditors will be considered later.

---

23. Note, 40 Mo.L.Rev. 552 (1975).

24. Uniform Probate Code § 3–403.

25. Uniform Probate Code § 3–106.

26. Uniform Probate Code § 3–306.

27. Uniform Probate Code § 3–606(b) (optional form—1977 Text).

28. Manlin and Martens, "Informal Proceedings Under the Uniform Probate Code: Notice and Due Process", 3 Prospectus 39 (1969).

29. Uniform Probate Code § 3–107.

30. Uniform Probate Code § 3–505.

IN RE WILL OF SUSAN BENTLEY

Supreme Court of Appeals of Virginia, 1940.
175 Va. 456, 9 S.E.2d 308.

[Susan Bentley died on 28 February 1934. An instrument dated 19 January 1917, offered as her will, was probated *ex parte* on 3 April 1934, before the Clerk of the Chancery Court of the City of Richmond. On 7 July 1939, J. Thomas Hewin offered to the Chancery Court for probate a writing by testatrix dated 7 February 1922. This writing contained provisions inconsistent with those of the instrument of 19 January 1917 and Hewin was named therein as executor. The Chancery Court refused to consider probate of this writing of 7 February 1922, relying upon Virginia Code, § 5259 * * * [Now §§ 64.1–88 through 64.1–90 (1980 Repl.Vol.)] * * * which provided in substance that a will probated *ex parte* could be attacked by a bill in equity to impeach it if the bill was filed within two years from the time of entry of the order probating the will in the court in which the will had been probated.[31] An exception was made as to the time of filing for infants, incompetents and non-residents. If the bill was not filed within the time allowed, the sentence or order was to "be forever binding". Hewin appeals.]

EGGLESTON, J. * * * It will be observed that section 5259 places a limitation on the time within which a suit in equity may be brought "to impeach or establish" a will. It places no limitation on the time within which a will may be probated.

Under Code, section 5263, the title of a *bona fide* purchaser for value of real estate from the heir of a decedent is protected against a devise of the lands by the decedent of which the purchaser had no notice, unless the will be probated within one year of the death of the testator.

Except for this latter section there is no statute in Virginia placing any limitation of time upon the probate of a will. Bliss v. Spencer, 125 Va. 36, 57, 99 S.E. 593, 5 A.L.R. 619.

It is well settled in this State and elsewhere that the judgment of a probate court of competent jurisdiction admitting a paper to pro-

31. At the time of the decision the time for filing had been reduced to one year, and this limit presently remains. The court, however, was applying the time limit in force when the first will was probated in 1934. The Virginia procedure is that the clerk or the court may hear the application for probate *ex-parte*. If the hearing is before the clerk, there is an appeal from his order to his court within six months, and on this appeal the court hears the case *de novo*. This appeal may be *ex-parte* or *inter-partes*. The court may hear the application initially *ex-parte* or *inter-partes*. The clerk cannot probate *inter-partes* and cannot probate the will in a case in which the death of the testator must be presumed. The bill to impeach does not lie if the probate is *inter-partes*. The decision must then be reviewed by the ordinary appellate process. The one year time limit runs from the time of entry of the order probating the will or denying probate as the case may be, whether the order is made *ex-parte* by the clerk or court. Thus, the clerk could deny probate and the applicant appeal from his order to the court within six months. A de novo *ex-parte* hearing could then be held and the will probated. A contestant would then have one year from the time of entry of the court's order to file in the court his bill to impeach the will.

bate is in the nature of a judgment in rem, and as long as it remains in force binds conclusively all parties and all other courts. * * * Such a judgment of probate can not be collaterally attacked and can only be assailed in the manner provided by statute. * * *

But it is equally well settled that the conclusiveness of the judgment of probate of an earlier will does not preclude the probate of a later will for the reason that, as we shall presently see, the probate of the later will is not an attack on the judgment of probate of the earlier will.

The precise question was before this court in Schultz v. Schultz, 10 Gratt. (51 Va.) 358, 60 Am.Dec. 335, decided in 1853, which appears to be a leading case on the subject. In that case a subsequent will was presented to the probate court more than seven years after the first will had been probated. The applicable statute (Code 1819, ch. 104, section 13, p. 378) provided that a person interested might within seven years after the probate of a will file a bill in chancery to contest its validity, and that "no such party appearing within that time, the probate shall be forever binding" with a saving for non-residents and persons under disabilities.

Nevertheless, this court, with full realization of the nature and conclusiveness of the judgment, held that the court by admitting one will of a deceased to probate had not exhausted its jurisdiction over the subject of the testamentary disposition of the decedent's estate and was not precluded by such judgment of probate from passing upon the probate of a later will subsequently propounded.

This court pointed out that a man's last will may consist of several testamentary papers of different dates and that it is not indispensable that they should be probated at the same time. Moreover, it was said that if after the probate of an earlier will a later will is found which "contains an express clause of revocation of former wills, or contains a disposition of the estate incompatible with the provisions of the former, or from its general character may be inferred to be an entire new instrument, intended to supersede the former, the court of probate should receive and admit it to probate, leaving it to have such effect as the law would necessarily attach to it", and that before probating the second will it was not necessary to file a bill in chancery under the statute to set aside the probate of the former will. (10 Gratt. (51 Va.), at page 375, 60 Am.Dec. 335). * * *

But the appellees insist that the offer to probate the later will is in effect a contest of the earlier will, and that it does not conform to Code, section 5259, which prescribes the exclusive method of contesting a will probated *ex parte,* namely, by a bill in equity filed within two years of the order of probate.

Whether the application to probate a later will whose provisions are inconsistent with those of a will previously probated is in effect a contest of an earlier will and may not be heard after the expiration of the statutory period for contesting the first will, is a question on which the courts are divided. The weight of authority seems to be that the offer of probate of a second will is not such a contest within the meaning of a statute similar to Code, section 5259.

In Woerner on The American Law of Administration (Including Wills), 3d Ed., Rev., Vol. II, section 217, p. 719, it is said: "In most States, but not all, a subsequent will may at any time be probated, such proceeding not being considered a contest of the will theretofore probated, though inconsistent with its dispositions".

Those authorities which hold that the probate of a subsequent will is not a contest of an inconsistent will theretofore probated reason thus:

> The order of probate of the first will settles all questions as to the formality of its execution and the capacity of the testator. Upon inquiry the court ascertains and finds that the instrument has been executed and witnessed in the proper manner by one who is capable of making a testamentary disposition of his property.

The probate of the subsequent will does not attack the due execution of the will previously admitted to probate or the testamentary capacity of the testator. It merely establishes that by a testamentary writing of a later date, likewise properly executed by a person of testamentary capacity, the testator has made dispositions of his property which are inconsistent with those found in the will previously probated. It is true that both instruments cannot stand. But the first will is revoked by the act of the testator in executing a subsequent will, and not by the judgment of the court in admitting the later will to probate. The result flows not from any proceeding attacking the probate of the first will, but from the law which gives vitality and force to the last testamentary act of the testator.

On the other hand, a suit in equity to contest a will which has been admitted to probate is a direct attack on the judgment of probate. In such a proceeding if the court ascertains that the will previously admitted to probate is not the true last will and testament of the testator, the judgment of probate is annulled and set aside.

Typical of this line of cases are, In re Moore's Estate, 180 Cal. 570, 182 P. 285, 289; Vance v. Upson, 64 Tex. 266, 269; Murrell v. Rich, 131 Tenn. 378, 175 S.W. 420, 427. See also, 107 A.L.R. 252, note.

There are, however, cases which hold that to probate a later will whose provisions are inconsistent with those of a will previously admitted to probate is in effect a contest of the earlier will within the meaning of a statute similar to Code, section 5259. See Watson v. Turner, 89 Ala. 220, 8 So. 20; Couchman v. Couchman, 104 Ky. 680, 47 S.W. 858, 44 L.R.A. 136; Burns v. Travis, 117 Ind. 44, 18 N.E. 45. See also, 107 A.L.R. 252, note.

In Schultz v. Schultz, supra, this court held that the fact that the time had expired within which a bill in equity could be filed to set aside a will admitted to probate would not preclude the probate of a subsequent inconsistent will. That is to say, the limitation placed on the time for filing a bill in equity under Code, section 5259, does not apply to the probate of a subsequent inconsistent will, for the reason that the offer to probate the subsequent will is not a contest of the first will within the meaning of that section. * * *

Schultz v. Schultz was decided in 1853. It has long been recognized by text writers and by the profession as the settled law in Virginia. * * * [The Court then pointed out that while a time limitation upon probate had been suggested by a distinguished member of the Virginia Bar Association in 1916 in an address, the revisors of the Code of 1919 had adopted some of the suggestions contained in the address but recommended no time limitation on probate; and that there was nothing in section 5259 or its amendments to suggest that the proponent of a subsequent will must offer it for probate only in an equity suit brought to contest a will already probated.] * * *

Our conclusion, therefore, is that to offer to probate the second will in the instant case was not a contest within the meaning of Code, section 5259, of the will previously admitted to probate.

We are not unmindful of the fact that it would greatly promote the stability of titles to real estate if some limitation were placed upon the time within which a will may be probated after the death of the testator, or if the probate of a subsequent will were placed upon the same footing as the institution of a contest of a will already probated. These, however, are matters for the General Assembly and not for the courts.

For the reasons stated we are of opinion that the trial court erred in refusing to hear the application for the probate of the writing dated February 7, 1922.

Accordingly, the order appealed from is reversed and the cause is remanded for further proceedings in conformity with the views here expressed.

Reversed and remanded.

GREGORY, J., dissenting. There can be but one true last will of a testator. In Virginia we have an adequate and all-embracing statutory procedure in Chapter 212 of the Code for the judicial determination of what constitutes the last will of a testator. When the statutory procedure has been carried out and the probate court has finally pronounced the paper or papers offered the last will of the testator, and no contest is instituted within the statutory time (two years in the case at bar), right or wrong that judgment stands binding all persons * * * and it cannot be attacked in any collateral proceedings.

All wills, with very few exceptions, are probated *ex parte*. The admission of a will to probate is conclusive of its validity, which can be drawn into question only on an issue *devisavit vel non* within the time allowed by the statute.

In this case the probate of the first will and the elapse of the time prescribed in the statute for a contest, constituted a final judgment establishing this will as the true will. There must of necessity be a finality to the question of what is the true last will of a testator, and that finality rests in the judgment of probate. To admit another later inconsistent paper to probate after the bar of the statute has fallen would be to permit the impeachment of the former judgment in a collateral proceeding. * * *

[JUSTICE GREGORY then argued that the statement in Schultz v. Schultz relied upon to support the decision of the majority was dictum, and continued:] * * *

The policy of the legislature has been increasingly to narrow the time within which a judgment of probate may be attacked. The time has been gradually whittled down from seven years, the period allowed at the time of the Schultz Case, to one year, the present limitation. This narrowing has been due partly to increased rapidity in the dissemination of information and partly to an increased volume of real estate transfers. As our economic life became more complex, it was found necessary to insist on greater stability of titles, and the legislature kept pace with this need by providing less and less time within which a transfer by will might be attacked.

At the time of the Schultz Case, the speedy settlement of land titles passing by will was not so great a desideratum as it is today; the legislature allowed a leisurely seven year period in which such titles might be attacked, and it is likely that the court felt that no violence would be done to public policy by not treating the expiration of this period as an absolute bar to the displacement of the first will by one turning up subsequently. Since that time, however, the tremendous increase in population and the migration from rural to urban areas has been attended by rapid subdivision of land and an enormous increase in the transfer of real estate titles. Wherever these titles pass by will the legislature has seen fit to safeguard their stability by providing in Section 5259 a one year limitation on the attack of probate. To hold, as the majority does, that an offer to probate a subsequently-appearing will is not a contest of the former will within Section 5259 is to make a distinction in form where none exists in substance. As in the case at bar, to allow the probate of the second will is to destroy the efficacy of the first and is in contravention of the announced public policy of providing stability of land titles. The law must have "stopping places", and I feel that the expiration of the statutory period for the attack on a judgment of probate is just such a necessary stopping place. * * *

[JUSTICE GREGORY then explained why he considered the pertinent statement in Schultz v. Schultz dictum and stated that if it was not dictum the decision should be modified.] * * * We are not bound by the rule of *stare decisis* where to be so bound would upset land titles. It has been the general belief of the profession that after a final judgment of probate it is safe to pass the title of real estate which has been devised. Whether we will be bound by the rule of *stare decisis* is for the court and not the legislature. We may modify our former opinions when changed conditions and compelling reasons demand it.

No doubt we should respect precedent, because to do otherwise would result in confusion and uncertainty, but we should subject precedent to the test of reason. The law must grow and improve in order to meet changing needs, and if an outmoded precedent fails to meet those needs and the test of reason it should be distinguished or disregarded. To follow this ancient rule, unnecessarily announced in the Schultz Case a century ago by a divided court, and to the best of my knowledge never again applied by this court, would result in disastrous consequences to titles passing through devisees. That such titles should remain stable and marketable is the public policy of this state. This is sufficient justification for this court to modify the rule. * * *

NOTE

Statutes in a number of states impose time limits upon the probate of wills or grants of administration which vary from one to twenty-one years. Uniform Probate Code, § 3–108 applies a three year limitation with certain exceptions. If no will is probated within this time the assumption of intestacy is final. Furthermore, if the formal procedure has been invoked to probate a will or obtain an adjudication of intestacy, a later will may be probated only if the proponent was unaware of its existence at the time of the earlier probate or adjudication or was unaware of the earlier proceeding and had no notice of it other than by publication. Section 3–412(1). Even under these circumstances the proponent will still have to probate within the three year period. A still shorter time may apply if the estate has been closed after a formal testacy proceeding.

After the decision in the principal case the Virginia law was changed to protect a *bona fide* purchaser from a devisee or from a personal representative with a power of sale over land unless the will later produced is filed for probate within one year following the testator's death.[32] No special provision is made for personal property.[33] The Uniform Probate Code protects purchasers from the personal representative and from distributees whether or not the three year period has run. The distributee must have received an "instrument or deed of distribution" from the personal representative. The purchaser has no duty of inquiry. The purchaser of land or personalty is protected. Section 3-910.

Statutes protecting *bona fide* purchasers from devisees under wills which are set aside because of subsequent probate of inconsistent or expressly revoking wills must be distinguished from the "Enoch Arden" statutes which protect *bona fide* purchasers from devisees, legatees, heirs or distributees and the personal representative when the supposed "decedent" whose estate has been distributed is found to be alive.[34] As pointed out in subsection (1), death is jurisdictional, and without the aid of the "Enoch Arden" statute no rights could arise under the void decree. Such a decree is subject to collateral attack. But a probate court has inherent power to vacate its order and revoke probate at any time unless constitutional or statutory limitations upon such power are in force.[35] Thus, if the court has jurisdiction, but vacates

32. Va.Code Ann. § 64.1–96.

33. For a commmentary on some of the difficulties arising when there is no time limit on probate, see "Wills—Ghosts in North Carolina—The Haunting Problem of the After-Discovered Will", 47 N.C.L.Rev. 723 (1969).

34. See fn. 15, supra.

35. See In re Estate of Butts, 173 Mich. 504, 139 N.W. 244 (1913) (Where

its order because of probate of an inconsistent will or because of a showing of forgery or fraud upon the court, persons who relied on the vacated order may be protected without the aid of a statute. A debtor who has relied upon the order of a court probating a will and qualifying an executor named therein and who has paid his debt to the executor when called upon to do so will almost certainly be discharged by the weight of authority.[36] The personal representative under the subsequent will must recover the money paid by the debtor from the personal representative he succeeds.

(3) WHO MAY CONTEST

LEE v. KEECH

Court of Appeals of Maryland, 1926.
151 Md. 34, 133 A. 835, 46 A.L.R. 1488.[37]

BOND, C.J. There is one question only raised on this appeal: Whether a judgment creditor of an heir may file and prosecute a *caveat* to a will of the ancestor of that heir, by which real property is devised to other persons. The appellant, Miss Virginia Lee, held a judgment against H. Hobart Keech for $989.15, recovered originally in Baltimore City, in 1914, and later recorded in Harford county. By statute (Code art. 26, §§ 19 and 20), the creditor thus became entitled to a lien on any interest of the debtor in real estate in the latter county. The mother of the debtor, Mrs. Hattie B. Shanahan, of Harford county, owned a farm of 103 acres there, assessed for taxes at $7,755, and valued considerably higher. On the 23rd day of June, 1925, she made a will in which she devised her property to the wife of her son, the debtor, and to his sister, the other heir of the testatrix, in equal shares. The testatrix died on the following December 18, 1925, and letters were granted to her two children as executors. The appellant then filed the *caveat*, as a judgment creditor of the one heir, H. Hobart Keech, and, after a hearing, this was dismissed, because, as stated in the order of the orphans' court, the petitioner had "no right or interest in the property or estate of said testator necessary to maintain a suit to caveat the last will and testament of the said Hattie B. Shanahan." The appeal is taken from that order. * * *

the probate court was held to have no power to vacate its order except to the extent permitted by statute, and the Michigan rule was stated to be a minority position).

36. The leading case is Allen v. Dundas, 3 Term Rep. (K.B.) 125, 100 Eng. Rep. 490 (1789) (In which a debtor was held discharged who paid his debt to the executor under a forged will probated by the Prerogative Court of the Archbishop of Canterbury and the administrator, after the order of probate was vacated, sought to collect the debt again). See Atkinson, Wills (2d Ed., 1953) 502–503; 21 L.R.A. 146–157 (1893); 17 L.R.A.,N.S., 878–879 (1908). With respect to land title problems after probate, see Atkinson, "Title After Probate Action", 3 American Law of Property (1952) 555.

37. Noted, 12 Corn.L.Q. 247 (1927); 36 Yale L.J. 150 (1926).

In all jurisdictions, either by statute or by general principles of law, the right to caveat is limited, as it is in Maryland, to persons who have an interest in the property. Johnston v. Willis, 147 Md. 237, 127 A. 862. And the decision of the question here raised turns on the views taken of the nature of the interest a judgment creditor of the heir has, and of the nature of the interest so required by law for a caveat. Not all interests in the debtor's property will support a caveat; all authorities agree that the interest of a general creditor is not sufficient; that there must be more than the mere right a general creditor has to pursue the property, with a privilege of ultimately requiring payment of his debt from it. In our opinion, the legal requirement is that there must be, in addition, such an interest gained in the property as will give the creditor a part of the sum total rights of ownership. Johnston v. Willis, supra. That this is the general requirement, we understand most, at least, of the authorities cited to agree.

Assuming that a judgment creditor may be said, strictly, to have a lien on the interest of an heir in real property which, in a voidable will, is devised to another (cf. Luhrs v. Hancock, 181 U.S. 567, 573, 21 S.Ct. 726, 45 L.Ed. 1005), it is a general, statutory lien on the property of his debtor, consisting of the right to have any part of that property he may select, or all of it, sold for the payment of the judgment. And this right follows real property into the hands of any subsequent owner. "It gives the judgment creditor no right to the land nor any estate in it." Ahern v. White, 39 Md. 409; Davidson v. Myers, 24 Md. 538, 555. "Such lien secures the creditor neither jus in rem nor jus ad rem." Dyson v. Simmons, 48 Md. 207, 215; Eschbach v. Pitts, 6 Md. 71, 77; Knell v. Green St. Bldg. Assoc., 34 Md. 67. * * * The lien is the same in principle as that of a municipal corporation for taxes. Eschbach v. Pitts, supra. And what the judgment creditor has is rather in the nature of a remedy than of an estate, and as such it is subject to legislative control, and may be changed by statute without violating any constitutional inhibition. * * *

This being the nature of the judgment creditor's interest it is the opinion of this court that it is not such as, under the decisions of the court, would support a caveat. The judgment creditor would not be one upon whom any part of the estate or rights of ownership in the property would devolve if intestacy should be established, and by her caveat she would be seeking, not to clear title to property in which she had gained any estate or property right, but would rather be seeking, in the right of the heir, to procure property for the heir, which might then be sold for payment of the judgment debt. * * *

Order affirmed, with costs to the appellees.

NOTE

The interest of a person to contest a will is usually determined in a proceeding prior to the trial of the contest. The probate court is permitted to construe the will to the extent necessary in the preliminary proceeding.

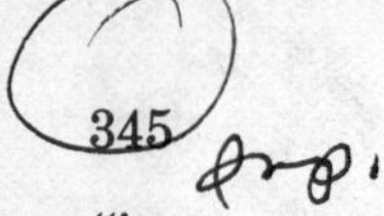

While statutes in various states limit the right to contest to persons "interested", persons "aggrieved", or to "any" person, the statutes are interpreted as limiting the right to contest to persons who have some legal or equitable interest affected adversely by establishment of the will.

The Uniform Probate Code requires interest by the applicant in both informal and formal probate proceedings. Sections 3–303(a)(3); 3–402(a)(2). The Code defines "interested person" in Section 1–201(20) as including "heirs, devisees, children, spouses, creditors, beneficiaries and any others having a property right in or claim against a trust estate or estate of a decedent, ward or protected person which may be affected by the proceeding. It also includes persons having priority for appointment as personal representatives, and other fiduciaries representing interested persons. The meaning as it relates to particular persons may vary from time to time and must be determined according to the particular purposes of, and matter involved in, any proceeding." In Section 3–105 the Code refers to "persons interested in decedents' estates" as those who may apply to the Court for appropriate determinations.

A person who has the same interest under a will as without it is not a proper contestant. General creditors of and purchasers from the decedent are not proper contestants since their interests are the same whether the decedent dies testate or intestate.[38] But an heir who will take property by the intestate laws is a proper contestant unless he receives the same interest by the will or unless he has been disinherited by some means other than the will offered for probate.[39] A beneficiary under a prior will whose share is reduced by a subsequent will is entitled to contest.[40] There is a division of authority when, as in the principal case, a creditor of an heir or devisee under a prior will seeks to contest a subsequent will.[41] A general creditor of an heir, devisee or legatee cannot contest a subsequent will, although the argument may be made that the debtor who takes if the will is set aside will then have property subject to execution for the debt. If a judgment, attachment or lien creditor seeks to contest, a majority of courts have held that he may do so since he has the right to satisfy his claim from the property if the will is set aside.

The widow of the testator may not contest if a statute provides that she can obtain substantially the same benefit by renouncing its provisions and taking her statutory share.[42]

The courts are divided as to whether an administrator or an executor appointed under a prior will can contest a subsequent will. It has been held that the executor has an interest to contest, but an administrator has been denied the right to contest in a substantial minority of jurisdictions.[43]

If a person has a right to contest, a majority of the courts hold that the right survives him and passes to his heirs or personal representative.[44]

38. E.g., Montgomery v. Foster, 91 Ala. 613, 8 So. 349 (1890).

39. See Biles v. Dean, 14 So. 536 (Miss.1893); L.R.A.1918A, 447, 453. An heir has standing to contest even though there are one or more clearly valid earlier wills disinheriting the heir. In re Powers' Estate, 362 Mich. 222, 106 N.W.2d 833 (1961) (heirs located by an heir-hunting corporation had standing to contest despite earlier valid wills; according to the dissenting judge, they had an interest of "only predatory nuisance" value).

40. E.g., Crowley v. Farley, 129 Minn. 460, 152 N.W. 872 (1915).

41. See Note, 50 Notre Dame Law. 309 (1974).

42. See L.R.A.1918A, 447, 462.

43. See 58 A.L.R. 1462 (1929); 88 A.L.R. 1158 (1934); 112 A.L.R. 659 (1938); 94 A.L.R.2d 1409 (1964) (Trustee named in earlier will). 36 Mich.L.Rev. 685 (1938); 37 Mich.L.Rev. 794 (1939).

44. See 129 A.L.R. 324 (1940).

Because only part of a will may be the product of undue influence or an insane delusion, it may be possible to contest only that part of the will, with the balance of the will being allowed for probate if the contest is successful. In states recognizing a doctrine of partial invalidity, the residuary devisee of the will therefore has standing to contest other provisions of the will.[45]

PROBLEMS

1. Attorney drafted a will for Testator which contained a bequest of $10,000 to Attorney. The will was properly executed by Testator. Attorney was unrelated to Testator. Thereafter, Testator thought Attorney was trying to place him in a mental hospital and had another scrivener draft a will in which he left Attorney nothing. This will also was executed by Testator. Attorney now contests the second will on the ground Testator was suffering from an insane delusion when he executed it. A contestant must have a pecuniary interest in order to contest in the State. Should Attorney be permitted to contest the second will? Karabatian v. Hnot, 17 Mich.App. 541, 170 N.W.2d 166 (1969). Suppose Testator's daughter and his only heir qualifies as executrix under the second will. She takes more as *heir* if the first will is probated than if the second will is probated. Attorney persuades her that Testator was suffering from an insane delusion when he executed the second will. Can the daughter contest the second will while she is executrix? See Steinberg v. Central Trust Co., 18 Ohio St.2d 33, 247 N.E.2d 303 (1969).

2. Testatrix died on 20 April 1952. By her will dated 14 April 1952 she gave her estate to her husband and to two sisters in equal shares. The will was probated on 29 April 1952, and notice to creditors filed on that date. This notice expired on 30 October 1952. The state law provides that a surviving husband shall be barred of any share in land or personal property by any devise or bequest in the will unless within thirty days after the expiration of notice to creditors he filed a written renunciation of the will. The law sets forth the shares taken in the event of renunciation and in this case the share would be the same as the intestate share although this would not be true in all cases. On 11 June 1952, the husband filed his caveat and the petition was answered in the same month. In January 1953, the issue devisavit vel non was transmitted by the Orphans' Court to the Circuit Court. In 1956, the executrix of the will moved to dismiss the caveat on the ground that the husband had no interest to contest. The executrix argued that the husband had permitted the period in which he could have renounced to run and thus was barred of any intestate share in the estate. She also argued that his caveat was filed when he could have renounced and taken the same share as if his contest were successful, thus he could not contest. The period for renunciation is approximately seven months from the date of probate of the will. The period in which a caveat may be filed is one year from probate. How would you rule on the motion to dismiss? Senk v. Mork, 212 Md. 413, 129 A.2d 675 (1957). Suppose the period for renunciation and the period within which the caveat could be filed had been the same. Would your ruling be the same? Suppose the husband had released his right of election during the lifetime of the wife. How would you then rule on the motion? In re Alexander's Will, 144 N.Y.S.2d 530 (Sur.Ct., Suffolk Co. 1955).

45. Williams v. Crickman, 81 Ill.2d 105, 39 Ill.Dec. 820, 405 N.E.2d 799 (1980).

3. Testator died survived by a brother, Wilbur, as his only heir and next of kin. Testator left $10.00 to Wilbur; $10.00 to Wilbur's son, William; $1,000.00 to Wilbur's other son, Clifford; $5,000 to a named hospital and the rest to a named Methodist Church. After the death of testator, Wilbur assigned all his right, title and interest in the estate of testator to William and Clifford. The test for interest is the same as that applied in the principal case. Does Clifford have standing to attack the will of testator on the ground testator was subject to undue influence when he executed the will? Yingling v. Smith, 254 Md. 366, 255 A.2d 64 (1968).

BRAKEFIELD v. BALDWIN

Court of Appeals of Kentucky, 1933.
249 Ky. 106, 60 S.W.2d 376.

[Albert Baldwin died testate in 1931. His will provided that his executor should pay to his daughter, Johnnie Brakefield, the sum of $350.00. The remainder of his estate was to be divided equally between two other children, Tom Baldwin and Lizzie Baldwin Carter. The three children survived the testator as his only heirs at law. After the death of the testator, the children executed a written instrument which stated that they agreed not to probate the will, that they had destroyed the will, and that they agreed to divide the estate of the testator equally among them. It was agreed that Tom Baldwin should be appointed administrator. Thereafter, Tom Baldwin offered a copy of the destroyed will for probate, alleging that it had been destroyed unlawfully after the death of the testator. Johnnie Brakefield opposed the petition to establish the will, denying the material allegations of the petition and setting up the agreement in bar of Baldwin's right to offer the will for probate or have the will probated. However, the will was admitted to probate and, without appealing from this decision, Johnnie Brakefield brought an action against Baldwin and Lizzie Baldwin Carter, based on the agreement alleging that the net value of the estate was $4,720 and that she was entitled to $1,573.33 thereof. The defendants contended that the will was destroyed when the parties were in ignorance of its contents and stated that the actual destruction of the will had been accomplished by officers of a bank by mistake "long" before the time that the agreement was made. They also contended that the contract was against public policy, null and void, and without consideration to support it. A demurrer to the petition was sustained and Johnnie Brakefield appeals.]

CREAL, COMMISSIONER. * * * It is first argued by counsel for appellees that the contract entered into between the parties to this action by which they each would share equally in the estate is void because it provided for the destruction of the will in direct violation of section 1226, Kentucky Statutes * * * [this statute is now repealed, Kentucky having a broader statute making it a class "D" felony to tamper with physical evidence believing that an official proceeding is pending or may be instituted, etc. Ky.Rev.Stat. § 524.100 (1975 Repl. Vol.)—Ed.] * * * and also because such agreement is contrary to public policy. That section does provide a severe penalty for the fraudulent destruction of a will, but, without going into the propriety of this agreement, in so far as it provided that the will be destroyed, it is apparent that none of the parties were actuated by fraudulent motives since they were the only parties in interest, and, so far as the pleading discloses, they all stood on an equal footing as to knowledge of the contents of the will if in fact they did not possess that knowledge at the time. It is not made to appear that any one of them took undue advantage of the others. While there is a reference in the contract to the destruction of the will, it is manifest that the sole purpose of the writing was to effect an agreement whereby, in the absence of a provision or provisions in the will making equal distribution of the testator's estate, it would be disregarded and the estate distributed between the parties in interest as in cases of intestacy. These parties had a right to enter into such agreement without regard to whether the will was probated. They were the only parties in interest except the creditors, whose rights were in no way impaired, since they would be paid whether the estate was distributed under the will or in accordance with the statute of descent and distribution.

Notwithstanding the salutary purpose of the statute and the evils it was intended to circumvent, it is apparent that it was never intended to, and it should not be allowed to, operate to invalidate a contract in the circumstances shown here. Appellees do not assume an enviable position in urging this statute against their sister in an attempted avoidance of their contract when in the light of the quoted portion of their answer it is made to appear that the will was actually destroyed by third parties long before the agreement was made.

It is next urged that the contract is entirely without consideration, and therefore cannot be enforced.

In the case of Trimble v. Donahey, 96 Wash. 677, 165 P. 1051, it was held that an agreement between heirs that a will making one of them sole devisee should not be probated but should be treated as destroyed was binding and enforceable; and in Cole v. Cole, 292 Ill. 154, 126 N.E. 752, 757, 38 A.L.R. 719, it is said: "It cannot be doubted that, if it lies in the power of the contracting parties to control all interests given under the will, then such parties have power to supersede the will by a contract that the property shall be treated as intestate property and partitioned as such."

In the foregoing and in many other cases of like tenor it is pointed out that courts look with favor on the settlement of disputes and controversies among members of families by such agreements rather than by resort to litigation. In many of these cases, however, it appears that proceedings had been instituted to set aside the will, and it was held that the agreement to forego litigation with its incident cost and delay was sufficient consideration to support a contract between the heirs to disregard the will and to distribute the estate in the manner provided in the contract. As a matter of course, each of these opinions was rested on the particular facts of the case, and it does not follow that, because a contest was pending and the court held that sufficient consideration for an agreement among the heirs for distribution contrary to the provisions of the will, a contract will be invalid for want of consideration, in the absence of contest proceedings. In fact, contracts of this character have been upheld when no proceedings had been instituted to set aside the will.

In Parker v. Broaddus et al., 128 Miss. 699, 91 So. 394, 395, the testator left his estate to two sons to the exclusion of his other children and attached to the will was a letter to the executor named in the will setting forth the reasons for this discrimination. After the death of testator, the beneficiaries named in the will and his other children entered into an agreement renouncing the provisions of the will and providing that the estate should be equally divided between the children and it does not appear that there was any contest proceeding pending.

In upholding the contract, the court in the course of the opinion said: "It is true the testator, has a right to dispose of his property in the manner that he did dispose of it and to make such disposition not prohibited by law as may suit his purpose. It is equally true, however, that he cannot compel the beneficiaries in his will to accept the will or the property thereunder devised and they have the right to renounce the will where it contains no trust or other limitation upon the property devised or bequeathed by the will, and when a will is renounced the effect of the renunciation relates back to the time the will became effective so as to make it void where, as in this case, the property is devised unconditionally and absolutely to the beneficiaries."

The opinion, after referring to conflict of authority on the subject, quotes with approval from 20 R.C.L. 357, § 359, the following: "Though in some jurisdictions an agreement to dispense with the probate of a will has been declared to be against public policy and void, in a majority of the decisions on the point it has been held that all the persons interested in a decedent's estate may by agreement divide the estate among themselves without probating such decedent's will or administering the estate, and the validity of a contract having for its sole purpose the disposition of property in a manner different from that proposed by testator, even where the contract contemplates the rejection of the will when offered for probate, or its setting aside when admitted to probate, when it is entirely free from fraud, and is made by all the parties in interest, would seem to be freely conceded. Thus it has been held that all the parties in interest may agree to eliminate from a will a clause providing for survivorship among them."

Without further citation, it may be said that the decided weight of authority indicates the validity of the contract, and in the light of these authorities and the circumstances we are constrained to hold that the contract in question is not without sufficient consideration.

Wherefore the judgment is reversed, with directions to overrule the demurrer to the petition and for proceedings in conformity with this opinion.

NOTE

In Tator v. Valden [46] an action was brought on an agreement made by the legatees and heirs to offer a prior will for probate and to suppress a later revoking will. A Connecticut statute required that a will be delivered to the probate court after the death of the testator. The court refused to enforce the agreement as contrary to the policy expressed in the statute and stated in the course of its opinion: [47] "* * * There is a very cogent reason which supports the public policy of the state. If, after a will is destroyed in accordance with such an agreement as the one before us, it should appear for any reason the agreement was invalid, or that all parties in interest did not enter into it, the right of those entitled under the will would be seriously jeopardized if not lost. Such a result is one which should not be made possible by our enforcing an agreement which might bring it about. * * *" In Will of Dardis [48] the will was offered for probate but the executor and eleven children of the testator, eight of whom were devisees or legatees and three of whom were expressly disinherited by the testator, stipulated that the will be disallowed. It was held that this stipulation could not prevent the probate court from establishing the document as a will. The court stated: [49] "* * * The trouble, however, with appellants' position in this case is that no stipulation was presented to the court signed by all parties in interest. The probate of a will is a proceeding in rem to which all the world are in some sense parties. Of course, like any other proceeding it also affects specific individuals. But in addition to its effect upon the rights either of the heirs of the alleged testator or of the legatees, the adjudication of the question whether a given script is or is not the will of the decedent may affect many other rights and interests which cannot be ascertained in advance of such adjudication. Thus, for example, any will devising real estate takes effect at the death of the testator, and may, at the moment of such death, create actual vested rights or liens in judgment creditors of the devisee. * * * Upon probate of the will there is no opportunity to ascertain whether such rights exist, but the holders of them are parties to the proceeding in the sense that they are bound by the adjudication by virtue of the general publication of notice. Indeed, even more remote rights may exist. General creditors of legatees may have a right to question the bona fides by which such legatees surrender any portion of their property after the right to it becomes vested, and no court in which a litigation to that end might be brought has any power to pass on the existence and validity of an alleged will; especially would it not have such right after such will had been adjudicated no testament by the probate court having that jurisdiction, although proceeding upon a stipulation of certain parties in interest. It is for reasons like these that courts have uniformly held that the proceeding to probate a will is a proceeding in rem, binding all the world, and in which even public welfare and policy is involved. * * *

"Apart from the interest of the public there is also recognized by the courts an interest and right of the testator to have the directions of his will carried into effect, at least upon some subjects. His right is recognized to

46. 124 Conn. 96, 198 A. 169, 117 A.L.R. 1243 (1938).

47. 198 A. at 171.

48. 135 Wis. 457, 115 N.W. 332, 23 L.R.A.,N.S., 783 (1908).

49. 115 N.W. at 333.

direct at least the method of management and disposal of his property after his decease, which courts cannot be compelled to disregard to accommodate the wishes of some or even all the parties having pecuniary interest in the property. * * * Whether a will contains any directions of this sort thus protected against modification by the beneficiaries is a question which can only arise after the probate proceeding is complete and the existence of the will has been established. * * * "

Most of the courts have enforced contracts to suppress wills if all of the heirs, legatees and devisees join in the agreement. Usually an action is brought on the contract to enforce the stipulated distribution after the will has been probated. The agreement has been raised as an effective bar to probate in a few states.[50]

When the will has been probated there is nothing to prevent parties in interest from distributing the property among themselves in any way that they see fit.[51] Statutes in some states permit probate courts to make a decree of distribution in accordance with an agreement among the interested parties after probate,[52] and some courts have held that such a decree is proper even though not expressly authorized by statute.

The legatees or devisees sometimes promise to divide the property in return for promises by prospective contestants not to contest. A contract not to contest is not against public policy, although the compromise agreed upon may infringe the rights of parties in interest under the will and be invalid for this reason. When an agreement of this type has been made some of the courts will not permit the contracting party to contest. Other courts permit the contest, the injured party being left to an action at law against the contestant for breach of contract. There is no consideration to support the agreement if the contracting party lacks an interest to contest. If the party has the requisite interest to contest but the grounds for contest are tenuous, good faith on the part of the contestant is probably sufficient to support the contract in most states.[53]

---

50. E.g., Parker v. Broaddus, 128 Miss. 699, 91 So. 394 (1922); Stringfellow v. Early, 15 Tex.Civ.App. 597, 40 S.W. 871 (1897).

51. There is substantial authority to the effect that heirs and devisees cannot terminate a testamentary trust by mutual agreement. E.g., Rose v. Southern Michigan National Bank, 255 Mich. 275, 238 N.W. 284 (1931).

52. The Massachusetts provision is the oldest of this type. Mass.Gen.Laws Ann. c. 192, § 3.

Uniform Probate Code § 3–912 is as follows: "Subject to the rights of creditors and taxing authorities, competent successors may agree among themselves to alter the interests, shares, or amounts to which they are entitled under the will of the decedent, or under the laws of intestacy, in any way that they provide in a written contract executed by all who are affected by its provisions. The personal representative shall abide by the terms of the agreement subject to his obligation to administer the estate for the benefit of creditors, to pay all taxes and costs of administration, and to carry out the responsibilities of his office for the benefit of any successors of the decedent who are not parties. Personal representatives of decedents' estates are not required to see to the performance of trusts if the trustee thereof is another person who is willing to accept the trust. Accordingly, trustees of a testamentary trust are successors for the purposes of this section. Nothing herein relieves trustees of any duties owed to beneficiaries of trusts."

53. See Evans, "Certain Evasive and Protective Devices Affecting Succession to Decedents' Estates", 32 Mich.L.Rev. 478 (1934); 55 A.L.R. 811 (1928); 81 A.L.R. 1187 (1932); 97 A.L.R. 468 (1933); 117 A.L.R. 1249 (1938); 29 A.L.R.3d 8 (1970).

MATTER OF ESTATE OF SEYMOUR

Supreme Court of New Mexico, 1979.
93 N.M. 328, 600 P.2d 274.

PAYNE, JUSTICE.

This dispute arose over the admissibility to probate of Lois Faye Seymour's will. The district court admitted the will to probate over the objections of her son, Jay Lynn Davis, and held that Davis should be disinherited for contesting it. On appeal, the Court of Appeals reversed the district court. We granted certiorari and now reverse in part and affirm in part the decision of the Court of Appeals.

The decedent executed the will at issue in October 1971 while she was married to Dale R. Seymour. Excepting a few specific bequests, the will provided that her estate was to go to her husband, unless he predeceased her, died simultaneously with her, or died within sixty days following her death. In any of those events an alternate disposition provided that Davis, her son, would receive $10,000 plus certain mortgage notes. The alternate disposition also provided that the residue of her estate would go to her stepson, Dale Allen Seymour, an appellee.

After execution of the will, the decedent divorced Dale R. Seymour in September 1975. Lois Faye Seymour died in March 1977. The decedent's former husband makes no claim and asserts no rights under the will. The district court admitted the will to probate over Davis' objections and entered an additional finding that Davis was disinherited under a provision in the will which stated:

> I expressly provide that if either JAY LYNN DAVIS or DALE ALLEN SEYMOUR shall contest the terms and provisions of this Will, making claim that he is entitled to a greater share of my estate than is provided herein, or contesting in any way the terms and provisions hereof, then I direct that said son shall be disinherited.

Davis argues on appeal that his mother's will was revoked on the date of divorce by operation of § 30–1–7.1, N.M.S.A.1953 (Supp.1975) enacted in 1967. He argues that the statute which was in effect on the date of divorce did not prescribe an alternative disposition of the estate following revocation of the primary dispositive provisions.

* * *

Davis therefore argues that the alternative distribution of the estate cannot be given effect, and thus that the alternative distribution of the estate should be distributed under the New Mexico intestacy laws. Davis asserts that the district court order was contrary to the decedent's intention. Davis further asserts that he did not intend to contest his mother's will as such, but only to have a court construe the meaning and effect of the will.

* * *

[In the omitted portion of the opinion the Court decided that the statute in effect at the testator's death—copied from UPC § 2–508, supra page 261—should govern; under that statute the will was not revoked but the divorced spouse is considered to have predeceased the testator. Hence the will was properly admitted to probate and the alternate devises in the will should be given effect.]

* * *

Finally, we address the validity of decedent's no-contest provision and whether appellee Davis is disinherited by its operation. On this issue, we agree with the Court of Appeals and overrule the trial court.

We hold that no-contest provisions are valid and enforceable in New Mexico, but they are not effective to disinherit a beneficiary who has contested a will in good faith and with probable cause to believe that the will was invalid. See Hartz' Estate v. Cade, 247 Minn. 362, 77 N.W.2d 169 (1956). No-contest provisions are valuable will devices. They serve to protect estates from costly and time-consuming litigation and they tend to minimize family bickering over the competence and capacity of testators, and the various amounts bequeathed. However, the function of the court is to effect the testator's intent to the greatest extent possible within the bounds of the law. To strictly construe no-contest provisions in the face of obvious indications of unresolved legal questions, such as were present in this case, could result in complete destruction of a testator's intent. Accordingly, where the circumstances upon which a will is based have changed substantially between the time of its execution and the time of its probate, courts should not discourage contests. The circumstances relative to the Seymour will were sufficiently changed to justify appellee Davis in seeking a judicial determination construing its meaning and effect. We hold that Davis is entitled to share in the estate of his mother under her will.

Whenever a beneficiary contests a will in the face of a no-contest provision, he does so at the peril of his bequest. But, when he does so in good faith and for probable cause, his bequest should not be jeopardized by the contest. The court should infer the existence or absence of good faith and probable cause from the totality of the circumstances. See 80 Am.Jur.2d Wills § 1575 (1975); Annot., 125 A.L.R. 1135 (1940); 5 Bowe-Parker, Page on Wills § 44.29 (rev. 1962); Leavitt, Scope and Effectiveness of No-Contest Clauses in Last Wills and Testaments, 15 Hastings L.J. 45, 67, n. 87 (1963); Note, 23 U.Pitt. L.Rev. 767 (1962); Notes, 43 Marq.L.Rev. 528 (1960).

The case is remanded to the district court for such further action as is necessary to conform to this opinion.

NOTE

The rule of the principal case (except for the judicial requirement of good faith) is embodied in Section 3–905 of the Uniform Probate Code,[54] which provides:

> "A provision in a will purporting to penalize any interested person for contesting the will or instituting other proceedings relating to the estate is unenforceable if probable cause exists for instituting proceedings."

The same rule has been proposed for the Restatement, Second, Property.[55]

The policy behind this section was expressed eloquently by Judge Miller, dissenting in Barry v. American Security and Trust Co.[56] as follows:

> "* * * I join also in believing that the public interest will be better served if, in cases which involve no more merit than is revealed in the present record, those who share the bounty of the testator should be strongly deterred from 'besmirching his reputation or parading the family skeletons after his death.' However, I doubt the wisdom of closing the door completely to contests calculated to reveal the use of fraud, coercion and undue influence in procuring the execution of wills. It seems to me that public policy may well be served by keeping the door a little open for some extreme situations, as where one person or a group of heirs conspire to shut out another; or, perhaps, to prevent the probate of an earlier will containing a bequest for charitable purposes. The object of an *in terrorem* clause may be to protect the family reputation, but it may be to silence a legatee who, otherwise, would be a material witness.
>
> "Where a legatee or devisee is fully competent, armed with adequate legal counsel, and financially able to hazard a contest, public policy may be satisfied by the assumption that fraud or undue influence will be challenged. Under such circumstances a successful contest may break the will and cause a distribution different from the one therein directed. But, while the rule as declared by the majority opinion would,[57] perhaps, be consistent with public policy in such a case, it will not much affect the type of case which it is supposed to affect, or restrain the person whom it purports to restrain, namely, the litigious troublemaker. He will be most apt to take his chances on a successful contest. The person who *will be* discouraged and restrained is just the person whose right to litigate, the public policy should be most concerned to protect: poor, timid people; children, widows, incompetents. It is against the interest of such persons that the schemer, the confidence man and the ruthless rascal are most apt to operate. If fraud, coercion and undue influence—rarely as they now may be used in procuring the execution of wills—can be covered up and made secure by the insertion of a forfeiture condition into a will, then, far from establishing a beneficent rule of public policy, we may, instead, be putting another weapon into the hands of the racketeer. * * *

54. Although New Mexico has adopted most of the Uniform Probate Code, the New Mexico version omits § 3–905. See N.Mex.Stats.Ann. (1978) § 45–3–905 "reserving" this number but omitting the text.

55. Restatement, Second (Tentative Draft No. 4), Property § 9.1.

56. 135 F.2d 470, 473, 146 A.L.R. 1204 (1943), 22 Tex.L.Rev. 361 (1944), 30 Va.L. Rev. 184 (1943).

57. The majority of the court held that a provision for forfeiture is enforceable even though the contest is in good faith and with probable cause.

"Probable cause is a term of well established meaning. An honest, upright person would not act upon a lesser showing of improper conduct. A lawyer would hesitate to advise a client to act on less, in the face of such a rule. * * *"

Some courts give effect to a provision for forfeiture upon contest under all circumstances.[58] A few courts have taken the position that a provision for the forfeiture of a bequest upon contest is *in terrorem* and will not be enforced unless there is a provision for a gift over in case forfeiture occurs.[59]

Whether the action taken by a beneficiary amounts to a contest is complicated by the variety of expressions by which testators set forth the conditions.[60] It has been held that the filing of a caveat and an appeal from a probate decree are not contests if voluntarily abandoned.[61] An objection to the jurisdiction of the probate court has been held not a contest.[62] A bill for construction of a will is not a contest even when a provision is attacked as in violation of the Rule against Perpetuities.[63] If the beneficiary asserts title to property devised to others by the testator, a number of courts have held this action a contest.[64] An objection to appointment of an executor or a petition to remove the executor may technically be a contest of a provision of the will, but it has been held that enforcement of a forfeiture under such circumstances violates public policy; otherwise the assets of the estate could be jeopardized by unchallenged actions of the executor.[65]

Instead of inserting a "no-contest" provision in his will, a testator may secure a release from the expectant heir. The release is enforceable if supported by consideration and will deprive the heir of his interest to contest.[66] An heir or beneficiary under the will may contract with the testator not to contest. A contract of this type is not against public policy and can be en-

58. E.g., Miller's Estate, 156 Cal. 119, 103 P. 842, 23 L.R.A.,N.S., 868 (1909). See generally, Atkinson, Wills (2d Ed., 1953) 408–413; Browder, "Testamentary Conditions Against Contest", 36 Mich.L. Rev. 1066 (1938); Browder, "Testamentary Conditions Against Contest Re-Examined", 49 Col.L.Rev. 320 (1949); Goddard, "Forfeiture Conditions in Wills as Penalty for Contesting Probate", 81 U. of Pa.L.Rev. 267 (1933); Jack, "No-Contest or In Terrorem Clauses in Wills—Construction and Enforcement", 19 S.W. L.J. 722 (1965); Keegan, "Provisions in Wills Forfeiting Share of Contesting Beneficiary", 12 A.B.A.J. 236 (1926); Kenner, "Non-Contesting Clauses in Wills", 3 Ind. L.J. 269 (1928); Kertz, "Contesting a Will in the Face of a Forfeiture Clause" 45 Geo.L.J. 200 (1956); Leavitt, "Scope and Effectiveness of No-Contest Clauses in Last Wills and Testaments", 15 Hastings L.J. 45 (1963); "No Contest Clauses in Wills", 23 U.Pitt.L.Rev. 767 (1962).

59. The rule is derived from a line of English cases and has been applied by the lower courts in New York. The rule was repudiated in Brush's Estate, 154 Misc. 480, 277 N.Y.S. 559 (1935). The rule has not been applied to devises in England or in this country. See Smithsonian Institution v. Meech, 169 U.S. 398, 18 S.Ct. 396, 42 L.Ed. 793 (1898).

60. The testator may require "acquiescence" on the part of the beneficiary. See Smithsonian Institution v. Meech, fn. 59, supra, or the condition may apply to those who express "dissatisfaction" with the will.

61. Drennen v. Heard, 198 F. 414 (N. D.Ga.1912) (caveat); Ayers' Administrator v. Ayers, 212 Ky. 400, 279 S.W. 647 (1926) (appeal from probate decree). Contra: Kayhart v. Whitehead, 77 N.J. Eq. 12, 76 A. 241 (1910), aff'd 78 N.J.Eq. 580, 81 A. 1133 (1911); Restatement, Property (1940) § 428, Comment *d.*

62. In re Hill's Estate, 176 Cal. 619, 169 P. 371 (1917); Maguire v. Bliss, 304 Mass. 12, 22 N.E.2d 615 (1939).

63. In re Harrison's Estate, 22 Cal. App.2d 28, 70 P.2d 522 (1937).

64. Smithsonian Institution v. Meech, fn. 59, supra. But see First Methodist Episcopal Church South v. Anderson, 110 S.W.2d 1177, 1179 (Tex.Civ.App.1937).

65. Estate of Wojtalewicz v. Woitel, 93 Ill.App.3d 1061, 49 Ill.Dec. 564, 418 N. E.2d 418 (1981).

66. See Chapter III, Section 4(2).

forced if valid in other respects. It is usually said that the promise of the contracting party "estops" him from contesting the will.[67] A beneficiary under a will who is not a minor and who acts with full knowledge of the material facts cannot contest a will after he has accepted his bequest, legacy or devise. If the testamentary gift has been accepted because of a mistake of fact, the gift must be returned to the estate before the beneficiary can contest.[68]

SECTION 2. GROUNDS FOR CONTEST

---

(1) TESTAMENTARY CAPACITY

A. Age and Miscellaneous Considerations

All states have an age limit below which a person lacks the capacity to make a will even though the person may be mentally competent.[69] The age limit usually is established by statute, but statutory and common law rules may be in force in the same state.

In the past, the usual age limit established by statute was twenty-one, but the modern trend has been to reduce the age of capacity for both males and females to 18, this having been done in England, for example;[70] the Uniform Probate Code setting forth such an age limitation;[71] and a growing number of states shifting to the lower age limit.[72]

Exceptions to an established age limit are sometimes stated for specific purposes, such as the appointment of a testamentary guardian, or for specific classes of persons, such as members of the armed forces.[73] A variety of other age limitations exist.[74]

Several grounds for incapacity, once important, are no longer significant. Incapacity based upon coverture of a female or conviction

67. Atkinson, Wills (2d Ed., 1953) 527.

68. Atkinson, Wills (2d Ed., 1953) 526. An offer to return has been held sufficient. Dreisback v. Spring, 93 Kan. 240, 144 P. 195 (1914).

69. See Rees, "American Wills Statutes", 46 Va.L.Rev. 613, 653 (1960) where the statutes and common law positions are summarized.

70. Family Law Reform Act 1969 Part I: 1-(2)*b*; 3-(1)*a* and *b*, 17 & 18 Eliz. II, c. 46 (1969).

71. Uniform Probate Code, § 2-501.

72. E.g., Md.Code, Estates & Trusts § 4-101; McKinney's N.Y., EPTL, § 3-1.1; N.C.Gen.Stat. § 31-1.

73. There has been a tendency to permit wills by persons in the armed services at an age lower than that generally established. See Tex.Prob.Code Ann. (Vernon's) § 57. The experience with the military draft probably has been a factor in inducing states to lower age capacity to eighteen for all persons.

74. E.g., Ga.Code Ann. § 113-203 (Fourteen); La.Stat.Ann., Civil Code arts. 1476, 1477 (Sixteen but must be *in mortis causa*).

of a criminal is virtually obsolete. Aliens likewise once labored under certain disabilities. At common law an alien could will personalty and devise land, but the state could seize the land in the hands of his devisee. To the extent that this can be regarded as a species of disability, the problem has been generally eliminated by statute and by treaties of friendship and commerce.[75]

B. Mentality

The standards for testamentary capacity, aside from the minimum age requirement, are left to judicial development. Statutes rarely attempt to define the capacity needed to make a will;[76] most statutes, like the Uniform Probate Code,[77] simply require that the testator be "of sound mind," although it has been suggested that the Code ought to have contained a statutory elaboration of the capacity requirement.[78]

GILMER v. BROWN

Supreme Court of Appeals of Virginia, 1947.
186 Va. 630, 44 S.E.2d 16.[79]

[Rosa Belle Gilmer signed and swore to a petition for the appointment of a committee for her sister, Mary Thomas, who was then between 60 and 80 years of age and appeared to be unable to manage her property. At a proceeding before the Circuit Court of Albermarle County it was adjudged that the infirmities of Mary Thomas did not require the committal of her person to a guardian but that "Mary Thomas by reason of mental and physical infirmity, impaired health and advanced age, is incapable of taking proper care of her property and incapable of handling and managing said estate and has been so for some years." Two attorneys were therefore appointed committees to care for her property. On the same day, and immediately after this proceeding, Mary Thomas executed a will in the pres-

75. See Chapter I, Section 3(1)A, fn. 25; Chapter III, Section 4(5).

76. The Georgia Code § 113–202 contains an unusual provision:

"**Amount of capacity necessary.**—An incapacity to contract may coexist with a capacity to make a will. The amount of intellect necessary to constitute testamentary capacity is that which is necessary to enable the party to have a decided and rational desire as to the disposition of his property. His desire must be decided, as distinguished from the wavering, vacillating fancies of a distempered intellect. It must be rational, as distinguished from the ravings of a madman, the silly pratings of an idiot, the childish whims of imbecility, or the excited vagaries of a drunkard."

77. Section 2–501.

78. Kossow, Probate Law and the Uniform Probate Code: "One for the Money * * *," 61 Georgetown L.J. 1357 (1973).

79. Noted, 5 Nat.B.J. 417 (1947).

ence of two subscribing witnesses by which she left all of her property to Rosa Belle Gilmer upon certain conditions and provided for gifts over to two nieces. After the death of Mary Thomas with this will unrevoked, some of her brothers and sisters filed a bill against the other heirs at law and the committees praying that Rosa Belle Gilmer be compelled to produce the alleged will for probate and that they be allowed to contest it. By agreement the case was referred to a Commissioner of the Court. One of the issues submitted to the Commissioner was whether Mary Thomas was mentally competent to execute the will. In his report, the Commissioner held that the participation of Rosa Belle Gilmer in the proceeding for the appointment of a committee for Mary Thomas estopped her from asserting that Mary Thomas had testamentary capacity on the day that the order was signed and the will was executed. The trial judge approved the report and in his opinion stated that the testimony on mental capacity was in conflict and that the testimony of the family physician convinced him that the proponents of the will had not borne the burden of proving testamentary capacity. The will was not probated.]

HUDGINS, J., delivered the opinion of the court. * * * The precise question presented is whether the issues in a proceeding to appoint a guardian or committee for an adult are the same as the issues in a suit to determine the testamentary capacity of the same adult. * * *

We have repeatedly held that a party may not assume successive positions in the course of a suit, or series of suits, with reference to the same fact or state of facts, which are inconsistent with each other, or mutually contradictory. Burch v. Grace St. Bldg. Corp., 168 Va. 329, 340, 191 S.E. 672, 677.

This court has also held that the appointment of a guardian or committee for the person and property of another is not conclusive evidence as to the mental capacity of such person to execute a deed (Waddy v. Grimes, 154 Va. 615, 153 S.E. 807); nor is a commitment to the insane asylum (Reed v. Reed, 108 Va. 790, 62 S.E. 792; Rust v. Reid, 124 Va. 1, 97 S.E. 324). In each of these cases the deed or will was executed some time after the date of the adjudication. See Wolfrey v. Swank, 184 Va. 922, 37 S.E.2d 17.

These decisions are in accord with the general rule that, in the absence of a controlling statute, the mere fact that one is under a guardianship does not deprive him of the power to make a will. Anno. 8 A.L.R. 1375; Page on Wills, Vol. 1, 2d Ed., sec. 710. Of course, mental capacity must be ascertained as of the date the instrument attacked was executed.

"Mental weakness is not inconsistent with testamentary capacity. A less degree of mental capacity is requisite for the execution of a will than for the execution of contracts and the transaction of ordinary business. One may be capable of making a will yet incapable of disposing of his property by contract or of managing his estate. Greene v. Greene, 145 Ill. 264, 33 N.E. 941. Mental strength to compete with an antagonist and understanding to protect his own interest are essential in the transaction of ordinary business, while it is sufficient for the making of a will that the testator understands the business in which he is engaged, his property, the natural objects of his bounty, and the disposition he desires to make of his property. Ring v. Lawless, 190 Ill. 520, 60 N.E. 881; Greene v. Maxwell, 251 Ill. 335, 96 N.E. 227, 36 L.R.A.,N.S., 418. The condition of being unable by reason of weakness of mind, to manage and care for an estate, is not inconsistent with capacity to make a will. Rice v. Rice, 50 Mich. 448, 15 N.W. 545; Williams v. Robinson, 39 Vt. 267." In re Weedman's Estate, 254 Ill. 504, 98 N.E. 956, 957.

"The adjudications of the probate court establishing facts necessary for the appointment of a conservator of the property of the testatrix were entitled to such weight as the jury saw fit to give them in determining the questions of her susceptibility to improper influence and of her soundness of mind. These adjudications were not decisive but were to be considered in connection with all the other pertinent evidence." McLoughlin v. Sheehan, 250 Mass. 132, 145 N.E. 259, 261.

The converse of this proposition is likewise true. It was held in Emry v. Beaver, 192 Ind. 471, 137 N.E. 55, that a judgment declaring a testator of sound mind in a proceeding for the appointment of a guardian was not conclusive evidence of his testamentary capacity in a subsequent proceeding instituted to determine the validity of his will. * * *

The test of testamentary capacity stated in In re Weedman's Estate, supra, is the test applied in this jurisdiction. "Neither sickness nor impaired intellect is sufficient, standing alone, to render a will invalid. If at the time of its execution the testatrix was capable of recollecting her property, the natural objects of her bounty and their claims upon her, knew the business about which she was engaged, and how she wished to dispose of her property, that is sufficient." Tabb v. Willis, 155 Va. 836, 156 S.E. 556; Redford v. Booker, 166 Va. 561, 185 S.E. 879.

The provisions of the pertinent statutes (Code sections 1017 et seq.) reveal the legislative intent to recognize a distinction between, and to make different provisions for, the insane and the mentally or physically incapacitated. Before a person may be adjudged insane, the statute requires notice and an adjudication by a Commission composed of a judicial officer and two licensed and reputable physicians. "Sanity is the normal condition of the human mind, and every man is presumed to be sane until the contrary is made to appear. After adjudication of insanity, a presumption of insanity continues, but a subsequent adjudication of restoration to sanity by competent authority restores the previous presumption of sanity until the contrary is made to appear." Rust v. Reid, 124 Va. 1, 24, 25, 97 S.E. 324, 331.

The primary object of the pertinent statutes dealing with the insane is the care and custody of the person so afflicted. The primary object of the statutes dealing with mentally or physically incapacitated persons is the management of the property for their benefit.

Persons whose mental powers have been weakened by disease, old age or otherwise are easily influenced, often to their detriment. They become easy prey for the unscrupulous, who may, and sometimes do, fraudulently deprive or strip them of a part or all of their property.

Code 1942 (Michie), sec. 1080a, first enacted in 1932 (Acts 1932, p. 518), was designed to safeguard the property of such persons from dissipation by their own improvidence and to preserve it for their own support and maintenance and, incidentally, for the benefit of the heirs or legatees and devisees. If some protection of this nature were not available, such persons might become charges of the State. The testamentary capacity of persons afflicted with this type of mental disorder is not necessarily destroyed. Such capacity depends upon the degree of mental impairment. * * *

A review of the decisions reveals that the testamentary capacity of such persons is tested by the same formula as in cases of insanity. The test to determine whether a person is capable of properly handling and managing his estate is not the same, as heretofore stated.

The commissioner and the trial court were in error when they declared that the issues in the two proceedings were the same, and that Rose Belle Gilmer was estopped from asserting that Mary Thomas had testamentary capacity.

This eliminates from our consideration the primary reason which caused both the commissioner and the trial court to hold that the will was invalid.

That part of the commissioner's report dealing with mental capacity indicates that, in determining Mary Thomas' testamentary capacity, he placed too much emphasis on the proceeding for the appointment of the committees—he held, in effect, that it was conclusive. * * *

This leads us to an examination and analysis of the testimony tending to show that Mary Thomas possessed testamentary capacity on the date the will was executed.

The issues in the two proceedings, as stated, are not identical. They are strikingly similar in that in each the mental capacity of the same party is involved. The difference is one of degree.

Under these circumstances, it is difficult to understand the action of the experienced and reputable attorneys who, in the forenoon, successfully advocated the appointment of a committee for their client, and who, in the afternoon of the same day, made a contract with her whereby one of them agreed to, and did, prepare her will without notice to or consultation with the trial judge or without taking the precaution of having experts on mental diseases examine their client and advise them of her testamentary capacity. Failure to take either of these precautionary steps has resulted in these attorneys being named as respondents in this suit, and forced them to take the witness stand in their own behalf and on behalf of their client. Notwithstanding these facts, the attorneys have appeared as counsel for the proponent of the will before the commissioner, the trial court and this court.

Rule 19 (171 Va. xxv) of the canons of professional ethics requires that when a lawyer becomes a witness for his client, except to merely formal matters, he should withdraw and leave the conduct of the trial of the case to other counsel. However, the fundamental rights of a litigant should not be prejudiced by the improper conduct of counsel.

The circumstances surrounding the testatrix and her mental condition at the time the will was executed are vital factors in determining testamentary capacity. The fact that the careful and painstaking trial judge determined that Mary's mental deterioration had reached the stage at which it was necessary or expedient that a guardian or committee be appointed for the management of her property, but that it had not reached such stage of deterioration that it was necessary to commit her person to the custody of another, indicates that Mary possessed sufficient mental powers to care for her physical needs. * * *

The only evidence (other than the record of the proceeding for the appointment of committees), which is entitled to any weight, tending to support the allegation that Mary lacked testamentary capacity, is the testimony of the family physician, Dr. George F. Johnson. As his testimony was not transcribed, a summary was made by the commissioner. From this summary, it appears that in the opinion of Dr. Johnson Mary was insane, with no lucid intervals, and that she had been in this condition and incompetent to make a will since her father died in 1937. He does not state how often he saw or treated her. If Mary was insane and had no lucid intervals and her physical condition was such as described by Dr. Johnson, it would appear that the trial judge would not have permitted her, after February 22, 1939, to return to her home and continue to live there alone.

This testimony is in conflict with the testimony of Dr. Edward W. Stratton, Jr., a major in the medical corps of the U.S. Army who had practiced medicine in Charlottesville prior to military service. He said that he examined Mary in April, 1939, at the request of Rosa Belle Gilmer, that she was mentally sound with no evidence of any psychopathic condition. She told this doctor of her relatives, referred to them by name and said that with two or three exceptions they had neglected her and contributed practically nothing to her comfort and happiness.

Elnora B. Sellers, a teacher and a graduate of Columbia University, New York, stated that on Sundays she frequently went out to visit Mary with Rosa Belle Gilmer and found conditions at her home similar to those of the average remote country home. She regarded Mary Thomas as eccentric but mentally sound and logical.

While neither Dr. Stratton nor Elnora Sellers testified as to Mary's mental condition at the time the will was executed, their testimony, if accepted, clearly shows that Mary was not totally incompetent and at times she was normal and in possession of her mental and physical faculties.

The uncontradicted evidence is that Rosa Belle Gilmer was the only one of Mary's relatives who regularly and consistently spent her time and money giving aid and comfort to the testatrix, during her declining years. The other relatives, with the possible exception of Martha Gilmer and Henrietta Brown, paid scant attention to her, making perfunctory visits once, possibly twice, a year until a few months before her death. Under these circumstances, the will itself reflects the normal reactions of a normal person and should be considered as evidence tending to establish testamentary capacity. Page on Wills, Vol. 1, 2d Ed., sec. 692.

The testimony of subscribing witnesses and others present at the factum is entitled to peculiar weight and, unless overcome by other persuasive evidence, settles the issue in favor of testamentary capacity. Thornton v. Thornton's Ex'rs, 141 Va. 232, 126 S.E. 69; Jenkins v. Trice, 152 Va. 411, 147 S.E. 251.

Weighing the evidence with this principle in mind, the irresistible conclusion from the record is that Mary, by reason of advanced age and infirmities, had reached the state of mental deterioration that it was expedient to appoint a committee to manage her property but that she had not reached the stage of mental deterioration which would deprive her of testamentary capacity. She, not her attorney nor Rosa Belle Gilmer, instigated the preparation of her will, remembered her property and named the beneficiaries in the order in which they should take.

* * *

The decree is reversed and the case remanded with directions to the trial court to enter the proper order upholding the validity of the will of Mary Thomas.

Reversed and remanded.

GREGORY, J., dissenting.

NOTE

The two major grounds for testamentary incapacity are non-age, considered in the preceding subsection, and mental disability. Mental disability is the more troublesome of the two grounds because of the obvious difficulties in proof.[80]

80. See generally, Atkinson, Wills (2d Ed., 1953) §§ 50–53; 1 Bowe-Parker: Page, Wills (3d Ed., Rev.1960) §§ 12.1–12.47; Rollison, Wills (1939) §§ 46–66; Thompson, Wills (3d Ed., 1947) §§ 53–72; Epstein, "Testamentary Capacity, Reasonableness and Family Maintenance: A Proposal for Meaningful Reform", 35 Temp.L.Q. 231 (1962). Green, "Public Policy Underlying the Law of Mental Incompetency", 38 Mich.L.Rev. 1189 (1940); Green, "The Operative Effect of Mental Incompetency on Agreements and Wills", 21 Tex.L.Rev. 554 (1943); Green, "Proof of Mental Incompetency and the Unexpressed Major Premise", 53 Yale L.J. 271 (1944); Hulbert, "Probate Psychiatry—the Psychiatric Viewpoint," 25 Ill.L.Rev. 288 (1930); Hutton, "Mental States in Wills", 49 Dick.L.Rev. 67 (1945); Hutton, "Testamentary Capacity and Related Matters", 58 Dick.L.Rev. 100 (1954); Stephens, "Probate Psychiatry—the Legal Viewpoint", 25 Ill.L.Rev. 276 (1930); Slough, "Testamentary Capacity—Evidentiary Aspects", 36 Tex.L.Rev. 1 (1957); Weihofen, "Mental Incompetency to Make a Will", 7 Natural Resources L. J. 89 (1967); "Testamentary Capacity in a Nutshell: A Psychiatric Reevaluation", 18 Stan.L.Rev. 1119 (1966).

A testator may be incapacitated mentally because of mental deficiency or because of mental derangement. Mental deficiency means lack of mentality such as that associated with conditions of idiocy and imbecility. Mental derangement means insane delusions such a those found in cases of paranoia, paresis, senile dementia and senile psychosis. A person may be mentally deficient and mentally deranged.

Some of the major problems now being presented to the courts concerning testamentary mentality are developed from senility of the testator. Between 1900 and 1979 the number of persons over 65 has increased nearly eight times while the total population only tripled. As of 1970 there were roughly 20,100,000 persons over 65; this had increased by 1979 to 24,700,000 of which 9,120,000 were over 75.[81] Problems in geriatric psychiatry have not been well understood by the bar and medical developments in this area have received inadequate attention by the courts.[82]

Not all mental deficiency and mental derangement invalidates a will. While the courts have differed as to the precise test for mental capacity, they are agreed that a testator is mentally deficient for the purpose of making a will if he lacks the ability to understand the general nature of his testamentary act, to know the nature and extent of his property, and the natural objects of his bounty, and to interrelate these factors.[83] If the testator is mentally deficient, the will is wholly invalid. Whether or not the testator is mentally deficient to make a will depends to some extent upon the size of his estate and the number of natural objects of his bounty. He may have the capacity to dispose of a simple estate but lack the capacity to dispose of a complex estate. More capacity may be required to dispose of a complicated estate than to make a simple contract or to transact ordinary uncomplicated business affairs.[84]

Evidence that the testator was eccentric, old, ill, weak, deaf, dumb or blind, or that the provisions of his will are unnatural, is admissible on the issue of testamentary capacity, but proof of one of these facts cannot invalidate the will.[85]

In the principal case, the Court criticizes the attorney who prepared the will under circumstances which made it likely that the will would be contested. Two ethical problems are involved: (1) does the duty to serve the client require the attorney to prepare the will, and (2) does competence re-

81. U. S. Bureau of the Census, Current Population Reports, Special Studies, Series P–23, No. 85 (1979); Series P–25, No. 870 (1980).

82. See Smith and Hager, "The Senile Testator: Medicolegal Aspects of Competency", 13 Cleveland-Mar.L.Rev. 397 (1964).

83. It is the ability to do these things that is material. It is not required that the testator be able to understand the meaning of legal terms or the details of complicated provisions in his will.

84. The courts have said that the capacity to execute a will is less than that required to make a contract or to transact business. This is true in most cases but not true in all. A person may be insane from a medical point of view and still have the capacity to make a will. Mere subnormal mentality does not prevent a person from making a will unless he fails to meet the judicial test.

See "Wills and Contracts—Degree of Mental Capacity Requisite for Each", 34 N.C.L.Rev. 155 (1955).

85. A person who has been deaf, dumb and blind from birth may fail to develop mentally. Blindness alone has no relevance to testamentary capacity, although safeguards must be exercised at probate to prevent proof of a blind testator's will obtained by fraud. Old age alone does not mean senility. In Arnold v. Parry, 173 Ind.App. 300, 363 N.E.2d 1055 (1977) a will executed by a testator at the age of 97 was sustained.

quire that special steps be taken in such a case to preserve evidence of capacity in the strongest possible light?[86]

The answer to the first question is sometimes difficult and involves a judgment by the attorney. Just as the courts invoke a presumption of capacity, the attorney ought to resolve any doubt in favor of capacity in borderline cases, but only after thorough interview of persons (relatives, friends, business acquaintances, family doctor) familiar with the testator and reasonably able to evaluate his capacity; attorneys who have confidence in psychiatric testimony would also ask for examination of the testator by a psychiatrist. Because the standard for testamentary capacity is a legal one, the attorney must make the ultimate decision. If it is clear after careful investigation that the testator lacks capacity, then the attorney should certainly refuse to proceed with drafting the will; courts do rely on the fact that a will has been prepared by an attorney as evidence that the testator has capacity, so preparation of a will for one clearly incompetent is a violation of a duty to the court and may even be participation in a fraud. Often in such situations the attorney is approached by a member of the testator's family and asked to see the testator about preparation of a will; the testator is the client in this situation and the attorney must be careful to see that his loyalty is to the testator, not to the family members. A will which is likely to be successfully contested only results in costly litigation at the expense of the client's estate, so is a disservice to the client.

If the attorney decides to proceed with preparation and execution of the will, then clearly the attorney owes a duty to the client to make the best possible record for upholding the will if it is later challenged. It is important to build a careful written record, preserved in the files of the attorney, with a signed statement from the client's regular physician, allotment of sufficient time when the will is executed for the witnesses to converse with the testator at some length and form an opinion as to his capacity at that time, memoranda of interviews with relatives, friends and business acquaintances, a written opinion of a favorable psychiatrist if one has been consulted, etc. A suggestion was made to the British Law Reform Committee that a statute provide that if medical evidence was obtained from a properly qualified medical practitioner at the time the will was made to the effect that the testator had mental capacity, this should, absent fraud or disqualifying interest, conclude the question. The practice of English solicitors in doubtful cases of capacity to introduce as one of the two witnesses a qualified medical practitioner who is asked in confidence and informally to satisfy himself as to the testator's capacity has been described as the "golden if tactless rule". While the Committee commended the use of the "golden if tactless" rule, it thought the matter should be left to the sound discretion of the solicitor rather than be dealt with by legislation. Adoption of a statutory rule "would put at risk the confidential relations which exist between a solicitor and his client. If a testator were to refuse to submit to such an examination, should the solicitor refuse to act, leaving the testator either to make a will on his own or to seek other advice, which might result in a far less satisfactorily drafted will? The solicitor would find himself in an equally awkward position if the medical evidence was not forthcoming or was qualified in some manner. Further, because a complicated will dealing with large amounts of property requires a greater degree of mental alertness than a simple will dealing with a small estate, the doctor might well have to be told of the terms of the will and

86. See Blinick, "Mental Disability, Legal Ethics and Professional Responsibility", 33 Albany L.Rev. 92 (1968); Miller, "Functions and Ethical Problems of the Lawyer in Drafting a Will", 1950 U. Ill.L.F. 415.

possibly also of the testator's family situation which may be relevant, in order to assess whether or not the testator had sufficient capacity to make the kind of will he in fact made. In our view many testators might well take exception to revealing the contents of their wills or their family circumstances to unknown medical practitioners. * * * ".[87] Some attorneys are now having the execution of the will videotaped along with an explanatory statement by the testator.

IN RE HARGROVE'S WILL

Supreme Court, Appellate Division, First Department, 1941.
28 N.Y.S.2d 571, 262 App.Div. 202.[88]

* * *

TOWNLEY, JUSTICE. The decree appealed from denies probate to the will of Ernest Temple Hargrove. This decree was based upon the verdict of the jury which by a vote of ten to two found the deceased lacking in testamentary capacity. The jury's finding was based upon its conclusion that the testator suffered from an insane delusion that two children born to his wife during their marriage were not his and that as a consequence the testator did not know the true objects of his bounty. The will made no provision for these children, but left all of his property to Mrs. Clement Griscom "as an inadequate acknowledgment of the lifelong kindness shown to me by my business associate and intimate personal friend, her late husband."

With the exception of this claimed delusion about the paternity of his children, there is no serious claim of mental deficiency. The testator appears to have been a very successful business man, capable of managing large interests with conspicuous success and equally successful in the management of many charitable and religious activities in which he became interested. He was active as president and head of the Griscom-Russell Company, manufacturers of heavy machinery, up to within a month of his death on April 8, 1939. The instrument offered for probate was in his own handwriting and executed by him on December 17, 1923. Ten witnesses, all men of importance in New York City, testified that decedent was at all times of sound mind and a man of unusual intelligence and four of these witnesses were called by the contestants.

The only witnesses to the contrary were an alienist who had never seen him and the testator's divorced wife who had not seen him for thirty-one years prior to his death except for an accidental meeting in a book store twenty years prior to his death. As bearing on the credibility of the latter, it is significant that she denied here that the testator prior to his death had ever accused her of being indiscreet, whereas she had obtained a Colorado divorce from the testator in which she alleged that about three years prior to the date of her complaint, the decedent had accused her of being indiscreet in her association with certain persons and that in November, 1905, he had also

87. Cmd. 7902 (1980) p. 8.

88. Aff'd 288 N.Y. 604, 42 N.E.2d 608 (1942).

made similar charges. In that action the jury found the decedent guilty of the matters charged in the complaint.

The law is that assuming the decedent was mistaken in his belief that he was not the father of the children of his divorced wife, that fact would not necessarily establish testator's incapacity. The rule applicable to the determination of the question was clearly stated in Matter of Will of White, 121 N.Y. 406, 413, 24 N.E. 935, 937, as follows: "Delusion is insanity where one persistently believes supposed facts which have no real existence except in his perverted imagination, and against all evidence and probability, and conducts himself, however logically, upon the assumption of their existence. * * * But, if there are facts, however insufficient they may in reality be, from which a prejudiced or a narrow or a bigoted mind might derive a particular idea or belief, it cannot be said that the mind is diseased in that respect. The belief may be illogical or preposterous, but it is not, therefore, evidence of insanity in the person. Persons do not always reason logically or correctly from facts, and that may be because of their prejudices, or of the perversity or peculiar construction of their minds. Wills, however, do not depend for their validity upon the testator's ability to reason logically, or upon his freedom from prejudice."

The question presented, therefore, is whether there is any rational basis, however slight, for the decedent's belief that he was not the father. The story of the married life of the Hargroves may be summarized as follows: The deceased married Aimee Heresheimer in 1899. For the next six years he travelled in Europe, Africa and Australia with her. A son was born in Brussels in February, 1902, and a daughter in Dresden in 1904. In 1905 the decedent and his children returned to the United States and took up a residence in Denver, Colorado. In Denver, the testator became interested in the business of his then father-in-law and in that connection met and became friendly with one Smith, a friend of his father-in-law and his attorney. In the latter part of 1906 the testator's wife asked him for a divorce, claiming incompatibility. This led to many conferences in which the testator's father-in-law and Smith assumed to act as friendly advisors. An action for divorce on the ground of cruelty was brought. The entire proceeding from the service of process to the entry of judgment was accomplished in a single day. Within an hour after the entry of the decree, Smith, whom the decedent had consulted about his divorce, procured a divorce from his own wife and announced that he would marry the wife of the testator.

The conditions surrounding these decrees created a considerable scandal in Denver. Within a month Smith and the testator's wife were married at the alleged insistence of her father. The testator apparently did not discover the remarriage for some months. He then applied to have the divorce set aside on the ground of fraud and alleged that his wife prior thereto had been guilty of improper relations with Smith. This application was denied upon technical grounds. He thereafter left Denver and came to New York where he was befriended by Clement Griscom, became associated with him in business and died the president of his company. Mr. Griscom's wife is named as beneficiary in his will. Neither the divorced wife nor the children communicated with deceased during the thirty-one years intervening before his death.

Decedent left an affidavit with his executor stating that his divorced wife had confessed to him that the children were not his and that he had satisfied himself that this was so. He spoke of this belief only to his intimate friends and then only when necessary. His entire conduct in this connection was that of a dignified, considerate gentleman and there is nothing in connection therewith that justifies the belief that his opinion was based on an insane delusion. All of his reasons for his belief, of course, cannot be known. They relate to the intimate personal affairs incident to the marriage relation. When consideration is given, however, to his unfortunate experiences in connection with his divorce, the fact of his belief in his wife's infidelity certified to by her under oath in her divorce proceeding and confirmed by the formal affidavit left by him with his executor, it cannot be said that his belief on this subject was entirely without reason, although possibly mistaken.

Upon the foregoing facts, the finding that the decedent lacked testamentary capacity cannot be sustained. The conclusion we have reached, however, must not be considered as involving any finding as to the legitimacy of the children involved. * * *

MARTIN, P.J., and CALLAHAN, J., concur.

GLENNON and DORE, JJ., dissent. * * *

[The dissenting opinion by JUSTICE GLENNON is omitted.]

NOTE

In the Chafin Will Case, 32 Wis. 557, 566 (1873), the following judicial analysis of an insane delusion appears: "As a general rule the insane or partially insane do not reason upon the subjects of their hallucinations or delusions. But the peculiar opinions and conduct of Bradley Chafin were the results of processes of reasoning. He argued against the theory of the revolution of the earth by asserting that if a body be projected upwards perpendicularly from the earth it would fall in the place from whence it was projected, which he claimed would not occur if the earth revolved on its axis. His premise was correct but his conclusions therefrom erroneous. * * * "[89]

89. In Will of Riemer, 2 Wis.2d 16, 85 N.W.2d 804 (1957), the Wisconsin court receded from its test in *Chafin* stating at 2 Wis.2d 26: "* * * We conclude that in reviewing the evidence the question before us is not whether there is any evidence on which Mrs. Riemer could base her delusions, but rather whether there is any evidence from which a *sane* person could draw the conclusion which formed such delusions. * * * " For a comment on the Wisconsin change and its significance see Modjeska, "Psychology and Law: An Examination of the Concept of Insane Delusions", [1960] Wis.L.Rev. 54.

A testator has been held not suffering from an insane delusion when he had a narrow escape from an injury and, believing that his escape was due to spirit voices, left his estate to a spiritualist church and library.[90]

Courts have stated that an insane delusion is an extravagant belief to which a person adheres against evidence, argument and reason. It is a belief in facts which do not exist and which no rational person would believe to exist. A belief that arises from known substantial evidence, whatever weight would be given the evidence by a normal mind, and regardless of how faulty the process of reasoning from it may be, is not an insane delusion for testamentary purposes. A belief that the legatee is a steward of the Deity [91] and a groundless hatred of a child [92] have been held insane delusions which vitiate all or part of a will.

Mental derangement invalidates a will to the extent that the provisions of the will are affected. An insane delusion which does not affect provisions of the will may be admitted with other evidence to show mental deficiency or to support a finding that a mental aberration which does affect provisions of the will is in fact an insane delusion.

Testamentary capacity must exist at the time the will is executed. Execution means the time that the testator signs the will in the presence of witnesses or acknowledges the will or signature to them, or the time that he signs a holograph, where holographs are valid without attestation. If the testator lacks the age to make an effective will at the time the will is executed, his later attainment of that age does not automatically validate the will. The testator may have mental capacity before and after the execution of a will but be under the influence of drink or narcotics at the time the will is executed so that he is then a victim of mental deficiency or derangement.[93] When the testator regains mental capacity or reaches the required age to make his will, the will can be validated by re-execution or republication by codicil.[94]

A testator who suffers from insane delusions may have lucid intervals. A will executed during a lucid interval is valid even though the testator never recovers his sanity thereafter.[95]

The authorities are divided as to whether the burden of proof on the issue of testamentary capacity rests upon the proponent of the will or upon the contestant.[96] A minority of courts have placed the risk of non-persuasion upon the contestant. This is due to the construction of statutes relating to the contest of wills, to the presumption of sanity that is usually said to arise

90. Owen v. Crumbaugh, 228 Ill. 380, 81 N.E. 1044, 119 Am.St.Rep. 442 (1907).

91. Ingersoll v. Gourley, 78 Wash. 406, 139 P. 207, Ann.Cas.1915D, 570 (1914).

92. In re Kahn's Will, 1 Con.Surr. 510, 5 N.Y.S. 556 (1889). Compare Dumas v. Dumas, 261 Ark. 178, 547 S.W.2d 417 (1977), where the court denied probate to a will on the ground that it was produced by an insane delusion; testator had disinherited his wife and daughter, on the unfounded belief that they were persecuting him because of an affair with another woman; there was direct testimony of a psychiatrist who had examined testator that the latter suffered from paranoid schizophrenia.

93. The mere fact that the testator is under the influence of drink or narcotics will not incapacitate him unless he fails to meet the judicial test for mental capacity. Evidence of the habitual use of drink or narcotics may be offered to support a contention that the mind of the testator was permanently impaired. See 9 A.L.R.3d 15 (1966).

94. See Chapter VI, Section 4(2).

95. E.g., Tate v. Chumbley, 190 Va. 480, 57 S.E.2d 151 (1950).

96. See Atkinson, Wills (2d Ed., 1953) 545–47.

upon proof by the proponent that the will was executed with the statutory formalities, or to a desire by the courts concerned to divide the burden of proof upon various issues fairly between the parties to the probate proceeding. By the prevailing view, the risk of non-persuasion is upon the proponent who must prove testamentary capacity by a preponderance of the evidence. The burden of going forward with the evidence may be shifted to the contestant if the proponent proves due execution of the will or proves due execution and introduces additional evidence as to the capacity of the testator.[97]

PROBLEM

Testatrix died on December 6, 1944. Her will, dated October 31, 1944, disposed of her entire estate to the National Women's Party. Testatrix had been a member of the New Jersey branch of the party since 1925 and had worked as a volunteer in its New York office from 1939 to 1941. Testatrix was a militant feminist and never married. She was born in 1896 and lived an apparently normal life with her parents until their deaths about 1928. Her heirs contested the will on the ground that the gift to the Party was the consequence of an insane delusion. The evidence offered was as follows. Testatrix' physician, a general practitioner, testified that she suffered from paranoia of the Bleuler type of split personality. From about 1935, when testatrix reached the age of forty, she had kept memoranda and written in the margins of books. These indicated that she looked forward to the day when women would bear children without the aid of men and all males would be put to death at birth. In August 1936, she wrote: "It remains for feminist organizations like the National Women's Party to make exposure of woman's 'protectors' and 'lovers' for what their vicious and contemptible selves are". She also wrote: "My father was a corrupt, vicious, and unintelligent savage, a typical specimen of the majority of his sex. Blast his wormstinking carcass and his whole damn breed." There were many other writings in this same general tone, all clearly written by testatrix. On the other hand, her relationships with her lawyer and bankers, all males, had apparently been normal. On this evidence, will or no will? In re Strittmater's Estate, 140 N.J.Eq. 94, 53 A.2d 205 (1947). Suppose the only evidence offered had been the testimony of the physician. Same result? See Slough, "Testamentary Capacity: Evidentiary Aspects", 36 Tex.L.Rev. 1, 8–16 (1957). Suppose there had been evidence to prove that testatrix had been jilted by a fickle suitor when an impressionable girl. Same result? Suppose testatrix left her

97. As to the burden of proof see Atkinson, Wills (2d Ed., 1953) 545–548; Rollison, Wills (1939) § 345.

The Uniform Probate Code, § 3–407 deals with the burden of proof on testamentary capacity as well as on other issues raised in contest of wills, including execution and revocation, as follows:

"In contested cases, petitioners who seek to establish intestacy have the burden of establishing prima facie proof of death, venue, and heirship. Proponents of a will have the burden of establishing prima facie proof of due execution in all cases, and, if they are also petitioners, prima facie proof of death and venue. Contestants of a will have the burden of establishing lack of testamentary intent or capacity, undue influence, fraud, duress, mistake or revocation. Parties have the ultimate burden of persuasion as to matters with respect to which they have the initial burden of proof. If a will is opposed by the petition for probate of a later will revoking the former, it shall be determined first whether the later will is entitled to probate, and if a will is opposed by a petition for a declaration of intestacy, it shall be determined first whether the will is entitled to probate."

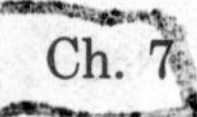

estate to the Republican Party instead of to the National Women's Party. Same result?

(2) TESTAMENTARY INTENT

LISTER v. SMITH

Court of Probate, 1863.
3 Sw. & Tr. 282, 164 Eng.Rep. 1282.

SIR J. P. WILDE: * * * The question raised is whether a certain codicil is or is not entitled to probate. It is regularly executed by the testator, but evidence was given at the trial that the testator never intended it seriously to operate as a testamentary document. It was proved before the jury that the testator wished one of his family to give up a house which she then occupied, and that to force her to do so, he made pretence of revoking by codicil a bequest which he had made by will in favour of this woman's daughter, and that the paper in question was made with that sole object; that the testator gave his attorney instructions to prepare it with that intention, and informed him before it was drawn that he never wished it to operate at all. Further, that the attorney pointed out the folly of executing such an instrument, and would have nothing to do with its execution. It was, however, executed in the presence of the testator's brother, to whom it was then given by the testator with express directions that he was not to part with it, and that it was in no event to operate, or to revoke the bequest made in his will, but to be used only in the manner above described. Similar declarations were made by the testator at the moment of its execution.

A codicil thus duly executed in point of form, and attested by two witnesses, has been directly impeached by parol testimony. It bears all the appearance on the face of it of a regular testamentary act; but on the evidence it has been found by the jury not to have been intended as such by the testator. The momentous consequences of permitting parol evidence thus to outweigh the sanction of a solemn act are obvious. It has a tendency to place all wills at the mercy of a parol story that the testator did not mean what he said. On the other hand, if the fact is plainly and conclusively made out, that the paper which appears to be the record of a testamentary act, was in reality the off-spring of a jest, or the result of a contrivance to effect some collateral object, and never seriously intended as a disposition of property, it is not reasonable that the Court should turn it into an effective instrument. And such no doubt is the law. There must be the *animus testandi*. In Nichols v. Nichols, 2 Phill. 180, the Court refused probate to a will regularly executed, which was proved to have been intended only as a specimen of the brevity of expression of which a will was capable. And in Trevelyan v. Trevelyan, 1 Phill. 149, the Court admitted evidence, and entertained the question whether the document was seriously intended or not. In both cases the Court held that evidence was admissible of the *animus testandi*. And to the same effect is the authority of Swinb. pt. 1, s. 3; and of Shep. Touch. 404. The analogies of the common law point the same way. A deed delivered as an escrow, though regularly executed, is not binding. And in Pym v. Campbell, 6 Ell. and Bl., the Queen's Bench held that a regular agreement signed by the party might be avoided by parol evidence that at the time of its signature it was understood that it should not operate unless a certain event happened. There can therefore be no doubt of the result in point of law if the fact is once established. But here I must remark that the Court ought not, I think, to permit the fact to be taken as established, unless the evidence is very cogent and conclusive. It is a misfortune attending the determination of fact by a jury, that their verdict recognizes and expresses no degree of clearness in proof. They are sworn to find one way or the other, and they do so sometimes on proof amounting almost to demonstration, at others on a mere balance of testimony; sometimes upon written admissions and independent facts proved by disinterested parties, sometimes on conflicting oaths or a nice preponderance of credibility. And it is difficult to impress them with the enormous weight which attaches to the document itself as evidence of the animus with which it was made. This weight it becomes the Court to appreciate, and to guard with jealousy the sanction of a solemn act.

In the present case, however, the Court finds the evidence so cogent that it is prepared to act on the finding of the jury that the codicil was executed as a sham and a pretence, never seriously intended as a paper of testamentary operation. But I am far from saying that the Court will in all cases repudiate a testamentary paper simply because a jury can be induced to find that it was not intended to operate as such. The character and nature of the evidence must be considered, as well as the result at which a jury have arrived, and the Court must be satisfied that it is sufficiently cogent to its end. In this case the Court is so satisfied and it therefore pronounces for the will, and against the codicil; the costs to be paid out of the estate.

NOTE

When an instrument is executed in proper testamentary form and purports to dispose of property at death, the courts are divided as to the admissibility of evidence that the will was executed as a sham or joke and was never intended to take effect. Some American courts have refused to admit such evidence if the will was properly executed by the testator with knowledge of its contents.[98] Other courts have followed the lead of the principal case and have admitted clear and positive extrinsic evidence to show the intention of the testator.[99] Even these courts are reluctant to overturn an

98. E.g., In re Kennedy's Estate, 159 Mich. 548, 124 N.W. 516, 28 L.R.A., N.S., 417 (1910); 23 Harv.L.Rev. 573 (1910).

99. E.g., Vroom v. Curtiss, 18 Cal.2d 512, 116 P.2d 438 (1941). The issue of testamentary intent has been raised in

unambiguous will properly executed and will probate the will unless the evidence of lack of testamentary intent is of a very convincing nature. Such cases are rare. A somewhat similar problem arises when it is alleged that the testator did not intend his will to be effective until additional formalities were accomplished or when it is alleged he intended the will as a specimen for a will later to be executed. The courts have been even less willing to admit parol evidence in these cases and will refuse to do so unless some ambiguity appears upon the face of the written instrument.[1] In a state permitting holographs, an informal writing, such as a letter which does not on its face purport to be a will but may be construed to express the writer's intent to dispose of property at death, may be offered for probate; in such a case the document may be contested on the ground of lack of testamentary intent. Each case depends on the wording of the particular document and surrounding facts.[2]

EATON v. BROWN

Supreme Court of the United States, 1904.
193 U.S. 411, 24 S.Ct. 487, 48 L.Ed. 730.

MR. JUSTICE HOLMES delivered the opinion of the court.

The question in this case is whether the following instrument is entitled to probate:

> "Washington, D. C. Aug. 31"/1901.
>
> "I am going on a Journey and may, not ever return. And if I do not, this is my last request. The Mortgage on the King House, which is in the possession of Mr. H. H. Brown to go to the Methodist Church at Bloomsburgh. All the rest of my properday both real and personal to My adopted Son L. B. Eaton of the life Saving Service, Treasury Department Washington D. C., All I have is my

relation to wills made as part of an initiation into a secret order. See Vickery v. Vickery, 126 Fla. 294, 170 So. 745 (1936); Gooch v. Gooch, 134 Va. 21, 113 S.E. 873 (1922).

1. E.g., Barnewall v. Murrell, 108 Ala. 366, 18 So. 831 (1895); Toebbe v. Williams, 80 Ky. 661 (1883). When the character of the instrument is doubtful, extrinsic evidence of the surrounding circumstances at the time the instrument was executed, including declarations by the testator made before, at the time of, or after the execution of the instrument are admitted to show his intention. In re Kemp's Will, 37 Del. 514, 186 A. 890 (1936), 25 Geo.L.J. 490 (1937). In Taylor's Will, 220 N.C. 524, 17 S.E.2d 654 (1941), an instrument was offered for probate containing the following language: "I am I think sane at this minute but how long it will last I don't know. I may do something, but while I can please give John my land. He had to do and be with me so much I feel he should have what I have for he has been a dear good man and husband to me. This will be a surprise to him. If I last til I can see a lawyer I will will it to him but if not I know you all will give it to him for me." The court stated that the testamentary intent required is more than an intent to execute a will. It is the intent to devise presently by the paper writing being then executed and the language appearing in the instrument indicated no present intent to devise.

2. In Matter of Estate of Webber, 97 Idaho 703, 551 P.2d 1339 (1976), writing on a greeting card sent to a former sweetheart was denied probate on objection by testator's widow; but in Estate of Blake v. Benza, 120 Ariz. 552, 587 P.2d 271 (1978), a postscript on a letter to a niece was allowed even though it operated to revoke a prior will drawn by decedent's lawyer. Other recent cases denying probate to such writings include Dahlgren v. First National Bank, 94 Nev. 387, 580 P.2d 478 (1978); McDonald v. Petty, 262 Ark. 517, 559 S.W.2d 1 (1977). On general requirements for holographs, see Chapter V, Section 7.

one hard earnings and I propose to leave it to whome I please. Caroline Holley."

The case was heard on the petition, an answer denying the allegations of the same, except on a point here immaterial, and setting up that the residence of the deceased was in New York, and upon a stipulation that the instrument was written and signed by the deceased on August 31, 1901, and that she went on her journey, returned to Washington, resumed her occupation there as a clerk in the Treasury Department, and died there on December 17, 1901. Probate was denied by the Supreme Court with costs against the appellant, and this decree was affirmed by the Court of Appeals upon the ground that the will was conditioned upon an event which did not come to pass. * * *

It might be argued that logically the only question upon the probate was the *factum* of the instrument. Pohlman v. Untzellman, 2 Lee, Eccl. 319, 320. But the practice is well settled to deny probate if it clearly appears from the contents of the instrument, coupled with the admitted facts, that it is inoperative in the event which has happened. Parsons v. Lanoe, 1 Ves.Sr. 189; S.C., Ambler, 557; 1 Wils. 243; Sinclair v. Hone, 6 Ves. 607, 610; Roberts v. Roberts, 2 Sw. & Tr. 337; Lindsay v. Lindsay, L.R. 2 P. & D. 459; Todd's Will, 2 W. & S. 145. The only question therefore is whether the instrument is void because of the return of the deceased from her contemplated journey. As to this, it cannot be disputed that grammatically and literally the words "if I do not" (return) are the condition of the whole "last request". There is no doubt either of the danger in going beyond the literal and grammatical meaning of the words. The English courts are especially and wisely careful not to substitute a lively imagination of what a testatrix would have said if her attention had been directed to a particular point for what she has said in fact. On the other hand, to a certain extent, not to be exactly defined, but depending on judgment and tact, the primary import of isolated words may be held to be modified and controlled by the dominant intention to be gathered from the instrument as a whole. Bearing these opposing considerations in mind, the court is of the opinion that the will should be admitted to proof.

"Courts do not incline to regard a will as conditional where it can be reasonably held that the testator was merely expressing his inducement to make it, however inaccurate his use of language might be, if strictly construed." Damon v. Damon, 8 Allen, 192, 197. Lord Penzance puts the same proposition perhaps even more strongly In the Goods of Porter, L.R. 2 P. & D. 22, 23; and it is almost a common place. In the case at bar we have an illiterate woman writing her own will. Obviously the first sentence, "I am going on a journey and may not ever return," expresses the fact that was on her mind as the occasion and inducement for writing it. If that had been the only reference to the journey the sentence would have had no further meaning. Cody v. Conly, 27 Gratt. 313. But with that thought before her, it was natural to an uneducated mind to express the general

contingency of death in the concrete form in which just then it was presented to her imagination. She was thinking of the possibility of death or she would not have made a will. But that possibility at that moment took the specific shape of not returning from her journey, and so she wrote "if I do not return," before giving her last commands. We need not consider whether if the will had nothing to qualify these words, it would be impossible to get away from the condition. But the two gifts are both of a kind that indicates an abiding and unconditioned intent—one to a church, the other to a person whom she called her adopted son. The unlikelihood of such a condition being attached to such gifts may be considered. Skipwith v. Cabell, 19 Gratt. 758, 783. And then she goes on to say that all that she has is her own hard earnings and that she proposes to leave it to whom she pleases. This last sentence of self-justification evidently is correlated to and imports an unqualified disposition of property, not a disposition having reference to a special state of facts by which alone it is justified and to which it is confined. If her failure to return from the journey had been the condition of her bounty, an hypothesis which is to the last degree improbable in the absence of explanation, it is not to be believed that when she came to explain her will she would not have explained it with reference to the extraordinary contingency upon which she made it depend instead of going on to give a reason which on the face of it has reference to an unconditioned gift.

It is to be noticed that in the leading case cited for the opposite conclusion from that which we reach, Parsons v. Lanoe, Lord Hardwicke emphasizes the proposition that under the circumstances of that case no Court of Equity would give any latitude to support such a will. There the will began "in case I should die before I return from the journey I intend, God willing, shortly to undertake for Ireland." The testator then was married but had no children. He afterwards returned from Ireland and had several children. If the will stood the children would be disinherited, and that was the circumstance which led the Lord Chancellor to say what we have mentioned, and to add that courts would take hold of any words they could to make the will conditional and contingent. Ambler, 561; 1 Ves.Sr. 192. It is to be noticed further that in the more important of the other cases relied on by the appellees the language or circumstances confirmed the absoluteness of the condition. For instance "my wish, desire, and intention, now is that if I should not return, (which I will, no preventing Providence)." Todd's Will, 2 W. & S. 145. There the language in the clearest way showed the alternative of returning to have been present to the testator's mind when the condition was written, and the will was limited further by the word "now." Somewhat similar was In the Goods of Porter, L.R. 2 P. & D. 22, where the Lord Penzance said, if we correctly understand him, that if the only words adverse to the will had been "should anything unfortunately happen to me while abroad," he would not have held the will conditional. See In the Goods of Mayd, 6 P.D. 17, 19.

On the other hand, we may cite the following cases as strongly favoring the view which we adopt. It hardly is worth while to state them at length, as each case must stand so much on its own circumstances and words. The latest English decisions which we have seen qualify the tendency of some of the earlier ones. In the Goods of Mayd, 6 P.D. 17; In the Goods of Dobson, L.R. 1 P. & D. 88; In the Goods of Thorne, 4 Sw. & Tr. 36; Likefield v. Likefield, 82 Kentucky, 589; Bradford v. Bradford, 4 Ky.Law.Rep. 947; Skipwith v. Cabell, 19 Gratt. 758, 782–784; French v. French, 14 W.Va. 458, 502.

Decree reversed.

NOTE

If a testator expressly subjects the operation of his will to a valid condition precedent, the condition will be given effect. If the event which is the condition precedent does not occur, the will is valid only if the testator reexecutes it, republishes it by codicil, or incorporates it by reference into another valid testamentary instrument.[3]

The courts have not permitted a condition to be shown if the will is absolute and unambiguous upon its face. Frequently, as in the principal case, language appears which can be read as a condition precedent or as a recitation of a matter of inducement or motive which lead the testator to make the will. The problem is then one of construction, and the courts will examine evidence of the surrounding circumstances at the time the will was executed to find the intention of the testator. A construction that ambiguous language was intended as a recitation of inducement or motive appears to be favored, but the decisions are not harmonious even when similar language is involved.[4]

3. Dougherty v. Dougherty, 4 Metc. (Ky.) 25 (1862); Vickery v. Hobbs, 21 Tex. 570, 73 Am.Dec. 238 (1858). The will is absolute if republished after nonoccurence of the condition. Forquer's Estate, 216 Pa. 331, 66 A. 92, 8 Ann.Cas. 1146 (1907). See generally, Atkinson, Wills (2d Ed., 1953) § 83; 1 Bowe-Parker: Page, Wills (3d Ed., Rev. 1960) §§ 9.1–9.9; Rollison, Wills (1939) §§ 207–209; Thompson, Wills (3d Ed., 1947) § 35; Evans "Conditional Wills", 35 Mich.L.Rev. 1049 (1937); 11 A.L.R. 846 (1921); 79 A.L.R. 1168 (1933).

4. In Poonarian's Will, 234 N.Y. 329, 137 N.E. 606 (1922), 23 Col.L.Rev. 403 (1923) the testator provided that "* * * if anything happen to me in Constantinople or in ocean * * *" a specified disposition was to be made of his property. The contingency did not occur. The court held that the will was conditional and of no effect. In Barber v. Barber, 368 Ill. 215, 13 N.E.2d 257 (1938) the testator stated that he was departing on a journey and "if anything should happen to me I request that everything I own * * * be given to my sister * * *". The testator returned from his journey and died thereafter. It was held that the reference to the journey was a recitation of inducement and not a condition. In Trevaskis' Estate, 345 Pa. 525, 29 A.2d 29 (1942) the testator's language was as follows: "* * * Having made my third will and they were lost in the flood at my office I here make this My last will and testimony If they cannot be found * * *". It was held that the will was contingent upon the finding of the testator's second and third wills.

In Marque's Will, 123 N.Y.S.2d 877 (Sur.Ct., Queens Co.1953), testatrix wrote "I am leaving for N.Y. by Union Pacific Tomorrow March 24th, should anything happen to me please dispose of my holdings as follows". This was held a valid unconditional holograph. Gabriel Pascal executed a holographic instrument which stated: "To Zaya Kingman-Speelman 470 Park Avenue, N.Y. This is my will if I should die on this my trip to India. You are my sol heiress". He did not make the trip to India but died in a New York hospital in 1954. The will was held conditional. In re Pascal's Estate, 152 N.Y.S. 2d 185, (Sur.Ct., N.Y.Co.1956), aff'd 4 A.D.2d 941, 167 N.Y.S.2d 1002 (1957), leave to appeal denied 4 A.D.2d 1021, 169 N.Y.S.2d 419 (1957), 4 N.Y.2d 674, 171 N.Y.S.2d 1027 (1958). See Meszaros v. Holsberry, 84 So.2d 565 (Fla.1956), in which mutual wills of husband and wife were held conditional upon their death in a common disaster.

If a particular provision in a will is conditioned upon the happening of a future event, the non-occurrence of the condition defeats the will only if the provision is the sole material part of the will or the provision is a key part of the testator's scheme for the disposition of his property.

---

(3) UNDUE INFLUENCE

ARNOLD'S ESTATE

Supreme Court of California, 1940.
16 Cal.2d 573, 107 P.2d 25.

[Hobart L. Arnold died leaving what purported to be a holographic will. In addition to a number of miscellaneous dispositions, the will contained a legacy of $1,000 in favor of the testator's nephew and heir at law, Earl W. Peterson. The residual estate was left to Frances Carrington and Vera Logan, and these persons were named as executrixes. When the will was offered for probate, Earl W. Peterson contested upon the grounds of undue influence and unsoundness of mind of the testator. The trial court granted a non-suit on the issue of undue influence and set aside a verdict by the jury in favor of the contestant on the issue of unsoundness of mind. Peterson appeals from the order admitting the will to probate contending that there was substantial evidence to entitle him to a jury verdict on either issue. Only that part of the opinion of the court which relates to the issue of undue influence appears below.]

CURTIS, JUSTICE. * * * In an action to set aside a will of a deceased person on the ground of undue influence, it is necessary to show that the influence was such as, in effect, to destroy the testator's free agency and substitute for his own another person's will. Estate of Motz, 136 Cal. 558, 583, 69 P. 294. Evidence must be produced that pressure was brought to bear directly upon the testamentary act. In re McDevitt's Estate, 95 Cal. 17, 33, 30 P. 101. Mere general influence, however strong and controlling, not to bear upon the testamentary act, is not enough; it must be influence used directly to procure the will, and must amount to coercion destroying free agency on the part of the testator. Estate of Keegan, 139 Cal. 123, 127, 72 P. 828. It is further held that mere opportunity to influence the mind of the testator, even coupled with an interest or a motive to do so, is not sufficient. Estate of Easton, 140 Cal.App. 367, 371, 35 P.2d 614.

"The unbroken rule in this state is that the courts must refuse to set aside the solemnly executed will of a deceased person upon the ground of undue influence unless there be proof of a 'pressure which overpowered the mind and bore down the volition of the testator at the very time the will was made.'" Estate of Gleason, 164 Cal. 756, 765, 130 P. 872, 876.

We will examine the evidence in this case adduced on behalf of this contestant in an effort to ascertain, in the light of the above ruling, whether it was sufficient to require the court to submit to the jury the issue of undue influence.

It is the contention of the contestant that the residuary legatees under said will so unduly and improperly influenced the testator to make said will in their favor as to the residue of this estate as to render the will of no legal effect. The amount of the estate, which the two residuary legatees would receive, is at least $20,000. Neither of these two women was related to the testator either by marriage or consanguinity, while the contestant was his nephew and his only heir at law. Hobart L. Arnold, at the time of his death, was living at the home of the proponent, Vera L. Logan. * * * The will * * * bore date of May 6, 1936, over a year prior to the time of Arnold's death. * * *

[The court then examined the evidence of undue influence allegedly exercised by Mrs. Carrington and found the evidence insufficient to go to a jury.] * * *

Arnold first met Mrs. Logan at her home in Santa Rosa one Sunday in March, 1936. He had been invited by Mr. Logan to have dinner with the Logan family, consisting of Mr. and Mrs. Logan and their nine year old daughter. Sometime later, Arnold spoke to Logan and asked if he could not take his meals at the Logan home. Logan replied that it was all right with him if he could make satisfactory arrangements with Mrs. Logan. As a result of this conversation and after seeing Mrs. Logan regarding the matter, Arnold took his meals at the Logan home, paying therefor $50 a month to Mrs. Logan. Later Arnold sold his own home and arrangements were made with the Logans for Arnold to have a room with them. Arnold was a heavy drinker, and was frequently so badly intoxicated that it was necessary to put him to bed in his room at the Logan home. During these times Mrs. Logan cared for him until he recovered, or until it was necessary for him to be sent to a hospital, which was frequently the case as Arnold suffered a number of attacks of delirium tremens after he began taking his meals with the Logans, both before and after he occupied a room in their home. Afterwards Arnold took a room at the Travelers Hotel and later at the Santa Rosa Hotel. At the direction of the doctor, Mrs. Logan took a room adjoining the room at the hotel occupied by Arnold for the purpose of caring for him during the periods when he was suffering from an over-indulgence in intoxicating liquors. It might be well to here state that Mr. and Mrs. Logan had separated sometime after Arnold became a roomer at their home and it appears they never were legally married.

Mrs. Logan some time before Arnold's death became acquainted with a salesman named Wedell, and shortly after Arnold's death she and Wedell were married. During the later months of Arnold's life he became very lavish in the expenditure of money, especially in behalf of Mrs. Logan. He bought her an automobile and financed the purchase of a saloon for her and Wedell. He signed a power of attorney and delivered it to the Bank of America at Santa Rosa authorizing her to sign and endorse checks, notes and drafts, and conduct other business for him at the bank. Under this authorization she withdrew from the bank various sums of money, a considerable amount of which she evidently appropriated to her own use without any accounting to him. * * *

There is a large amount of evidence of the same character of that recited above respecting the association of Arnold and Mrs. Logan. They were together on numerous occasions. He continued his excessive drinking after suffering attacks of delirium tremens through which she sometimes nursed him and at other times he was sent to the hospital. They were often seen together and sometimes she was seen drinking with him and on at least one of these occasions she was intoxicated. There is no evidence they ever discussed the subject of his will, nor did she ever ask, or even suggest that he make his will in her favor.

From the foregoing the contestant contends that a confidential relation existed between Mrs. Logan and Arnold which caused her to assume the burden of proving that the will was not obtained by her through undue influence and that the testator had the benefit of independent advice.

Conceding, simply for the purpose of argument, that a confidential relation was proved to have existed between Mrs. Logan and Arnold, proof of that fact alone did not cast the burden of proof upon her that the will was not obtained by her through undue influence. Estate of Purcell, 164 Cal. 300, 303, 128 P. 932. In that case it was held that proof of a confidential relationship did not bring into play a presumption of undue influence in the absence of evidence that the beneficiary suggested the terms of the will. In the Estate of Baird, 176 Cal. 381, 384, 168 P. 561, 563, we find the applicable rule stated in the following concise language: "As suggested in Estate of Higgins, 156 Cal. (257) 261, 104 P. (6) 8, a 'presumption of undue influence' arises from proof of the exercise [*sic*–Ed.] of a confidential relation between the testator and such a beneficiary, 'coupled with activity on the part of the latter in the preparation of the will.' The confidential relation alone is not sufficient. There must be activity on the part of the beneficiary in the matter of the preparation of the will." * * *

As the evidence of contestant failed to show any activity on the part of Mrs. Logan in the procurement of the will of decedent, it was inadequate to prove undue influence on her part in the execution of said will. The evidence being insufficient to show that the will of said decedent was the result of the undue influence of either of the proponents, the court properly granted the motion of respondents for a nonsuit.

The judgment is affirmed.

We concur: GIBSON, C. J.; SHENK, J.; EDMONDS, J.; YORK, JUSTICE PRO TEM.; MOORE, JUSTICE PRO TEM.

CARTER, JUSTICE. I dissent.

[Dissenting opinion omitted.]

MATTER OF ESTATE OF SWENSON

Court of Appeals of Oregon, 1980.
48 Or.App. 497, 617 P.2d 305.

WARDEN, JUDGE.

This is a proceeding to contest the will of Grace Swenson brought by Jane Troyer and Urinda Laura Lee "Betty" Russell, daughters of the deceased. They contend that decedent lacked testamentary capacity and that the will was the product of undue influence exerted by the sole beneficiary, Cora Plackett.

The will was admitted to probate on March 20, 1978. Contestants filed objections to probate on July 20, 1978. After a hearing on those objections on July 23, 24 and 25, 1979, the trial court, on September 24, 1979, issued a letter opinion finding that at the time of the execution of the will decedent lacked testamentary capacity and, further, that the will was the result of the undue influence of Cora Plackett. By order entered October 12, 1979, the court made formal findings in accordance with its letter opinion, sustained the objections to probate, declared the will null and void, decreed the order admitting the will to probate set aside and revoked the appointment of Cora Plackett as personal representative of the estate of Grace Swenson. Cora Plackett appeals this order. Our review is de novo. We affirm the trial court, finding that the will of Grace Swenson dated July 21, 1977, was the product of undue influence of Cora Plackett.

We abstain from the usual lengthy recitation of the facts in this type of case. We will recite facts in our discussion of the issue of undue influence which control our decision.

In In Re Reddaway's Estate, 214 Or. 410, 419–20, 329 P.2d 886 (1958), the Supreme Court said:

> "Definitions of undue influence couched in terms of the testator's freedom of will are subject to criticism in that they invite us to think in terms of coercion and duress, when the emphasis should be on the unfairness of the advantage which is reaped as the result of wrongful conduct. 'Undue influence does not negative consent by the donor. Equity acts because there is want of conscience on the part of the donee, not want of consent on the part of the donor.' 3 Modern L.Rev. 97, 100 (1939). Said in another way, undue influence has a closer kinship to fraud than to duress. It has been characterized as a 'species of fraud.' "

The burden of proving undue influence is upon the contestants. In re Southman's Estate, 178 Or. 462, 168 P.2d 572 (1946). A confidential relationship between the testator and a beneficiary, considered together with other suspicious circumstances, may require the beneficiary to carry the burden of proof and present evidence to overcome the adverse inference of undue influence. In Re Reddaway's Estate, supra; In Re Southman's Estate, supra; and Carlton v. Wolf, 21 Or.App. 476, 535 P.2d 119 (1975). Cora Plackett bore a confidential relationship to decedent. She was decedent's "friend"; she bathed decedent, gave her drugs, shopped for her, wrote her checks and transported her.

The factors to be considered in determining whether undue influence is exercised were set out by the Supreme Court in In Re Reddaway's Estate, supra, and reiterated by this court in Carlton v. Wolf, supra.

The first of these factors is procurement, that is, participation of the beneficiary in the preparation of the will. Cora Plackett, after learning that decedent intended to disinherit both her daughters and shortly after being told by decedent that decedent was thinking of leaving her entire estate to her, urged decedent to make a new will. She gave decedent the phone book, made the phone call to the attorney for her, talked to the attorney at the time of his first conference with the decedent and escorted the decedent to the attorney's office for purposes of execution of the will on July 21, 1977. (It is also at least interesting to note that Cora Plackett did not list that date in her diary as one of the days on which she worked for decedent.)

The second factor is independent advice. A beneficiary who participates in preparation of a will and occupies a confidential relationship to the testator has a duty to see that the testator receives independent, disinterested advice. In Re Reddaway's Estate, supra; In Re Estate of Manillus Day, 198 Or. 518, 257 P.2d 609 (1953). Cora Plackett did not seek to have decedent call either Mr. Hammond or Mr. Herbrand, attorneys, each of whom had drawn a will for decedent within ten months immediately preceding the drawing of this will. Instead, she helped the decedent contact a lawyer unknown to decedent. The attorney chosen had been in the practice of law less than two years and he relied in part on misinformation provided him by either decedent or Cora Plackett. The record discloses that he acted as little more than a scrivener. No effort was made by Cora Plackett to communicate with either of decedent's daughters, with other relatives or friends of the decedent, with doctors or with representatives of social agencies serving decedent to secure independent advice.

The third factor is secrecy and haste. No notice was given to the decedent's family members, close friends, or social service personnel. Decedent's true condition was kept from her daughter, Jane Troyer, when she made inquiry of her mother's condition on June 27, 1977, after a cousin, who had visited decedent for a week, phoned Jane telling her that her mother needed help, was being taken advantage of, and was on "dope." The services of an attorney who did not know decedent were sought, rather than those of attorneys to whom she was known. Cora Plackett urged the decedent to change her will and acted to assist her in changing her will within a week after Cora

Plackett learned from decedent that decedent was considering making her her sole beneficiary.

The fourth factor is change in attitude toward others. Decedent had made two wills in the ten months prior to making this will. In September, 1976, she made a will leaving her entire estate to her two daughters to be shared equally. In February, 1977, by a second will, she left her entire estate to both daughters, with one receiving but $5 and the residue going to the other. Though Cora Plackett testified that she did not seek to have decedent leave her entire estate to her, the record is also entirely void of any effort by her to urge upon decedent any reconciliation with her daughter, Jane Troyer, from whom she had become estranged. Jane Troyer was a friend of Cora Plackett's sister and had engaged Cora Plackett's services for the decedent.

The fifth factor is a change in the decedent's plan of disposing of her property. The two prior wills left decedent's entire estate to her daughters. This will disinherited them and gave the estate to a virtual stranger.

The sixth factor is that of an unnatural or unjust gift. The decedent disowned her two daughters, the natural subject of her bounty, and gave her entire estate to an acquaintance of less than two months duration. Decedent's original contact with the lawyer who drew the will was made only 33 days after Cora Plackett entered her home.

The seventh and final factor is susceptibility to influence. Decedent was physically sick, suffering from numerous ailments and injuries. She was unable to walk without help. She could not drive an automobile. She was dependent upon drugs and frequently used alcohol to excess. She had recently lost her husband of 40 years. She mistakenly accused one of her daughters of stealing her property. Her susceptibility to being taken advantage of was amply demonstrated by her dealings with a husband and wife, realtors, who befriended her and then took advantage of her in a series of transactions.

There are substantial conflicts in the testimony in this case. It is apparent from the record and the trial judge's decision that he did not accept the testimony of Cora Plackett as credible. As we have often stated, we give substantial weight to the findings of the trier of fact who saw and observed the witnesses.

We are satisfied from this record that Cora Plackett, the beneficiary of the July 21, 1977 will of Grace Swenson, exerted undue influence in the making of that will. Because we decide the case favorably to contestants on this issue, we do not address the question of the decedent's testamentary capacity. The judgment of the trial court is affirmed.

NOTE

Undue influence is coercion of the mind of the testator.[5] The influence must be such that the testator is deprived of his free agency and the intention of a dominant party substituted for the intention which he would normally exercise. If the testator says, in effect, "this is not my will, but I must do it", he is subject to undue influence.[6] Undue influence need not consist of physical coercion but must amount to more than kindness, advice or persuasion. Fear of a stepmother,[7] threats of violence or criminal prosecution,[8] and a threat to abandon an old and paralyzed testator [9] have been held undue influences. But, as stated in Ginter v. Ginter: [10] "A testator's favor expressed in a will may be won by devoted attachment, self sacrificing kindness, and the beneficent ministrations of friendship and love. These influences are not undue. We expect partiality to accompany them. They bring preferment as their natural reward, and they do not become unrighteous, although they establish a general ascendancy over the testator leading him to find comfort and pleasure in gratifying the wishes and desires of the persons exercising them. Other less worthy influences may make equally strong appeals and may result in the same general dominion and still be sufferable in contemplation of law. Influences to induce testamentary disposition may be specific and direct without becoming undue. It is not improper to advise, to persuade, to solicit, to importune, to entreat, to implore. Hopes and fears may be moved. Appeals may be made to vanity and pride; to the sense of justice and to the obligations of duty; to ties of friendship, of affection and kindred; to the sentiment of gratitude; to pity for distress and destitution. It is not enough that the testator's convictions be brought into harmony with that of another by such means. His views may be radically changed, but so long as he is not overborne and rendered incapable of acting finally upon his own motives, so long as he remains a free agent, his choice of a course is his own choice, and the will is his will and not that of another."

The position expressed in the *Swenson* case, de-emphasizing the coercion element from the standpoint of the testator and emphasizing the conduct of the influencer and the resulting unfairness of the will, is not the usual judi-

5. See generally, Atkinson, Wills (2d Ed., 1953) § 55; 1 Bowe-Parker: Page Wills (3d Ed., Rev.1960) §§ 15.1–15.13; Rollison, Wills (1939) §§ 67–69; Thompson, Wills (3d Ed., 1947) §§ 142–147; Gifford, "Will or no Will? The Effect of Fraud and Undue Influence on Testamentary Dispositions", 20 Col.L.Rev. 862 (1920); Green, "Fraud, Undue Influence and Mental Incompetency", 43 Col.L.Rev. 176 (1943); Hutton, "Undue Influence and Fraud in Wills", 37 Dick.L.Rev. 16 (1932); King, "Undue Influence in Wills in Illinois", 2 U. of Chi.L.Rev. 457 (1935); McKeehan, "Undue Influence and Wills in Pennsylvania", 31 Dick.L.Rev. 123 (1927); Warren, "Fraud, Undue Influence and Mistake in Wills", 41 Harv.L.Rev. 309 (1928); Winder, "Undue Influence and Coercion", 3 Mod.L.Rev. 97 (1939); "Testamentary Undue Influence in Iowa", 18 Drake L.Rev. 255 (1969); 7 Ark. L.Rev. 116 (1953); 16 Marq.L.Rev. 130 (1932); 50 Mich.L.Rev. 748 (1952); 46 W. Va.L.Q. 168 (1940); "Undue Influence—Judicial Implementation of Social Policy" 1968 Wis.L.Rev. 569.

6. Ginter v. Ginter, 79 Kan. 721, 725, 101 P. 634, 636, 22 L.R.A., N.S., 1024 (1909).

7. Ford v. Ford's Estate, 89 N.H. 292, 197 A. 824 (1938).

8. Gay v. Gillilan, 92 Mo. 250, 5 S.W. 7, 1 Am.St.Rep. 712 (1887); In re Brunor, 21 App.Div. 259, 47 N.Y.S. 681 (1897).

9. In re Sickles' Will, 63 N.J.Eq. 233, 50 A. 577 (1901).

10. 79 Kan. 721, 726, 101 P. 634, 640, 22 L.R.A., N.S., 1024 (1909).

cial approach but may more accurately reflect the results of the cases. In Estate of Reddaway, cited in the *Swenson* case, the Court stated: [11]

"* * * Rather than approach the problem from the standpoint of the testator's freedom of will, it would be more profitable to focus the emphasis on the nature of the influencer's conduct in persuading the testator to act as he does. The question is, has the influencer by his conduct gained an unfair advantage by devices which reasonable men regard as improper? The idea is expressed in Morris v. Morris, 1942, 192 Miss. 518, 6 So.2d 311, 312, where the court says that undue influence denotes 'something wrong, according to the standard of morals which the law enforces in the relations of men, and therefore something legally wrong, something in fact, illegal. * * * The nature of the influence can be judged only by its result. It is the end accomplished which colors the influence exerted, and entitles us to speak of it as wrongful, fraudulent, or undue, on the one hand, or as proper or justifiable on the other hand. * * * We are to understand the word "undue" as describing not the nature or the origin of the influence existing, nor as measuring its extent, but as qualifying the purpose with which it is exercised or the result which it accomplishes. * * *'

"It is not expected that all courts would hold to the same moral standard in appraising the influencer's conduct, and further, the consequences of upholding the influenced gift are important. It would be expected that there would be less concern with the influencer's motive in a contest between him and the state claiming an escheat than there would be between him and the donor's deserving spouse."

Undue influence must affect the will in some way. There must be a substantial gift either to the person exercising the influence or to some person in whom the influencing party is interested.[12] If a gift is shown to result from undue influence, the entire will is vitiated if the provision which contains the gift cannot be separated from the rest of the will without defeating the general intent of the testator. If the will is intelligible and complete without the contested provisions, the contested provisions fail and the rest of the will is probated.[13]

Undue influence must operate at the time the will is executed. Undue influence operating before or after the execution of a will does not affect the validity of the instrument, although it is unnecessary to show that the person charged with undue influence was present at the time of execution, since a prior exercise of undue influence may continue to coerce the mind of the testator when the will is executed and thereafter. If the testator was subject to undue influence when the will was executed, the will is not made valid if he becomes free of the influence thereafter, although he may validate the will by re-execution, by republishing it by codicil, or by incorporating it by reference into a valid testamentary instrument.[14]

The evidence available to prove undue influence is likely to be circumstantial. By the prevailing view, the risk of non-persuasion is upon the contestant. The contestant must establish undue influence by a preponderance of the evidence, although some courts have said that the evidence must be

11. 214 Or. at 419, 329 P.2d at 890.

12. Little v. Sugg, 243 Ala. 196, 8 So. 2d 866 (1942) (Presumption of undue influence by son on behalf of mother); 96 A.L.R. 613 (1935); 13 A.L.R.3d 381 (1967).

13. In re Carothers' Estate, 300 Pa. 185, 150 A. 585, 69 A.L.R. 1127 (1930).

14. See 21 A.L.R.2d 821, 831 (1952).

"clear and convincing". The contestant may shift the burden of going forward with the evidence to the proponent by raising a presumption of undue influence. As stated in Burgess v. Bohle:[15] "Before there is imposed upon the proponent of a will the obligation of presenting evidence of volition, and before the question of undue influence becomes one of fact for determination by a jury or the court sitting without a jury, there must be evidence of probative force which establishes (1) the relations between the one charged with exercising undue influence and the decedent, affording an opportunity to control the testamentary act; (2) that the decedent's condition was such as to permit of a subversion of her freedom of will; (3) that there was activity on the part of the person charged with exercising undue influence, and (4) that such person unduly profited as beneficiary of the will. * * * And a presumption against the validity of the will is not created by the existence of any one of the circumtances just narrated, standing alone. It is only when a combination of all these circumstances is present in the evidence that their probative force is sufficient to justify the denial of a non-suit, and place upon the proponent of a will the burden of submitting evidence that the testamentary document was executed free from the taint of undue influence."

This test, or variations of it, appear in numerous decisions.[16] Some courts have not required that evidence be produced by the contestant which indicates that the testator is susceptible to undue influence, although in the cases in which this element of the test has been omitted there has been evidence in the record which indicates that because of age, physical disability, or some other infirmity the testator might have been responsive to coercive action.[17]

The relationships of priest and parishioner,[18] physician and patient,[19] attorney and client,[20] and guardian and ward [21] are frequently described as "confidential" for the purpose of raising the presumption. But business, family and meretricious relationships are not regarded as confidential unless additional evidence showing a relationship of confidence is forthcoming.[22]

A person who drafts the will, controls its drafting, or who participates actively in giving advice and suggestions concerning its contents is "actively concerned" in the preparation of the will. If a substantial gift is made to the testator's attorney, it is advisable to have someone else draft the will. If the draftsman is merely named as executor, no presumption of undue influence will arise since his commission is earned.

The presumption of undue influence is not applied between husband and wife, even when activity by one spouse in the preparation of the will of another is shown and the spouse receives a substantial gift. Influence by one spouse over another is natural and legitimate and undue influence will not be

15. 63 Cal.App.2d 135, 142, 146 P.2d 242, 245 (1944).

16. Cf. Will of Leisch, 221 Wis. 641, 267 N.W. 268 (1936); 66 A.L.R. 228 (1930); 154 A.L.R. 583 (1945).

17. An attack based on undue influence is often coupled with an attack based on testamentary incapacity. The two grounds are consistent. Proof of one does not disprove the other. In some states proof of a confidential relationship and a gift to the party in confidence is enough to raise the presumption.

18. E.g., McQueen v. Wilson, 131 Ala. 606, 31 So. 94 (1901).

19. E.g., In re Bucher's Estate, 56 Cal.App.2d 135, 132 P.2d 257 (1942).

20. E.g., In re Brown's Estate, 165 Or. 575, 108 P.2d 775 (1941); 19 A.L.R.3d 575 (1968).

21. E.g., Limburger v. Rauch, 2 Abb. Pr., N.S. (N.Y.) 279 (1867).

22. A close business association, such as a partnership, may be enough to establish the confidential relationship. As between parent and child, the parent is usually considered the dominant party but it may be shown that the child occupied a position of peculiar trust and influence.

found unless evidence of actual coercion is forthcoming.[23] Courts and juries have not regarded non-marital relationships between two persons, involving illicit sex, with the same sympathy. A devise to a paramour or a homosexual lover is regarded as "unnatural", because it diverts property from legitimate heirs. Nevertheless, the real issue ought to be the extent of the influence over the mind of the testator, not the morality of the relationship.[24]

The nature and weight of the evidence which the proponent must introduce to rebut a presumption of undue influence will depend upon the strength of the presumption in the particular jurisdiction. Evidence of independent advice received by the testator prior to executing the will is sufficient to rebut the presumption in most jurisdictions.[25]

Undue influence may operate with respect to revocation of a valid will, as well as execution of a will.[26] Thus an heir might unduly influence a testator to revoke a valid will in favor of other persons. In such a case revocation of the valid will would be nullified by the undue influence; if the revocation is by physical act, the will can be probated despite destruction of the original if its contents can be proved, as by a copy, as we have previously seen.

The lawyer drafting a will in which the client confers a benefit on the lawyer must be concerned not so much with the legal validity of the provision as with ethical propriety of his conduct. Not only may there be a presumption that the lawyer-draftsman exerted undue influence, but also the lawyer may face disciplinary charges for violation of the Code of Professional Responsibility. Although a provision in the will naming the lawyer as executor, or requiring that the lawyer be retained by the executor to represent the estate, is not regarded as "beneficial" within the undue influence concept (because he is only compensated for services performed), such provisions do raise ethical considerations similar to the outright devise to the draftsman.

If a client wants to make a gift to his attorney under the will, the ethical problems are twofold: (1) the effect this may have on the objectivity of the lawyer's advice to the client about the latter's estate plan, and (2) the public reaction to such a provision in the will (the "appearance of impropriety"). EC 5–5 reads:

> **EC 5–5** A lawyer should not suggest to his client that a gift be made to himself or for his benefit. If a lawyer accepts a gift from his client, he is peculiarly susceptible to the charge that he unduly influenced or overreached the client. If a client voluntarily offers to make a gift to his lawyer, the lawyer may accept the gift, but before doing so, he should

23. An unjust or unnatural will does not raise a presumption of undue influence, although this fact taken in connection with others may support a finding that undue influence exists.

24. See In re Kaufmann's Will, 20 A.D.2d 464, 247 N.Y.S.2d 664 (1964), aff'd 15 N.Y.2d 825, 257 N.Y.S.2d 941, 205 N.E.2d 864 (1965) (will of homosexual lover invalidated as product of undue influence); for a discussion of the few cases involving homosexuality, see Sherman, "Undue Influence and the Homosexual Testator," 42 U.Pitt.L.Rev. 225 (1981). The mere fact that the principal devisee is a paramour is not proof of undue influence. E.g., Parrisella v. Fotopulos, 111 Ariz. 4, 522 P.2d 1081 (1974) (will disinheriting brothers in favor of mistress whom testator had planned to marry). As previously noted a few states have statutes limiting gifts to paramours; see Chapter IV, Section 4.

25. See McQueen v. Wilson, 131 Ala. 606, 31 So. 94 (1901). Proof that the textatrix had independent advice from a reputable attorney at the time the will was executed overcomes the presumption. In re Teller's Estate, 288 Mich. 193, 284 N.W. 696 (1939).

26. Estate of Reddaway, 214 Or. 410, 329 P.2d 886 (1958).

urge that his client secure disinterested advice from an independent, competent person who is cognizant of all the circumstances. Other than in exceptional circumstances, a lawyer should insist that an instrument in which his client desires to name him beneficially be prepared by another lawyer selected by the client.

See Comment, "Considerations of Professional Responsibility in Probate Matters", 51 Neb.L.Rev. 456 (1972). In drafting a will naming the lawyer as fiduciary, or directing that he be employed as attorney by the executor, the ethical considerations are somewhat different. Who suggests the provision? Can the drafting lawyer be independent in advising the client as to whether there is a better selection as fiduciary or attorney for the estate? How can the executor or trustee work with a lawyer not selected by the fiduciary and in whom he may lack confidence?

State v. Gulbankian, 54 Wis.2d 605, 196 N.W.2d 733 (1972) involved disciplinary proceedings against two attorneys on the alleged grounds that they solicited probate of estates by naming themselves as executor or providing that they be employed as attorney. The Wisconsin Supreme Court laid down guidelines:

"It is clear an attorney cannot solicit either directly or by any indirect means a request or direction of a testator that he or a member of his firm be named executor or be employed as an attorney to probate the estate. In those fairly rare cases where a client, because of the unusual familiarity of the attorney with the testator's business or family problems or because of a relationship which transcends the ordinary client-attorney relationship, asks his attorney to act as executor or to provide for his employment to probate the estate, there is no solicitation. A gray area, however, exists when an attorney explains the duties of an executor and the question is reached concerning probate. In preparing a will the attorney must know the identity of the executor. In many cases the testator is unfamiliar with the duties of an executor. It is the lawyer's right and duty to advise the testator what the duties of the executor are, to explain that the executor may hire an attorney to help him probate the estate * * *.

"This problem must be discussed by the attorney and his client objectively and uninfluenced by any desire of the attorney to eventually probate the estate. An attorney should not use a will form which provides for a designation of an attorney for the probate of the estate or executor for submission to the testator on the theory it is properly a part of a standard form of a will; no such form of suggestion may be used. An attorney, merely because he drafts a will, has no preferential claim to probate it. * * *

"We emphasize that while an attorney is discussing the identity and the duties of an executor, he must especially be careful that his conversation does not intimate or suggest or solicit, directly or indirectly, his employment as the possible attorney to assist the executor in the probate of the estate or his appointment as executor. We realize this is an area in which it is difficult to police professional standards, but circumstantial evidence as well as direct testimony may be relied upon to prove that solicitation has occurred."

EC 5–6 states:

EC 5–6 A lawyer should not consciously influence a client to name him as executor, trustee, or lawyer in an instrument. In those cases where a client wishes to name his lawyer as such, care should be taken by the lawyer to avoid even the appearance of impropriety.

Consider, however, the practice of banks in some localities to employ, for each estate in which the bank is named as executor, the lawyer who drafted the will; by advising the testator to name a corporate fiduciary rather than an individual family member as executor, the lawyer is virtually assuring the probate business for himself or his firm.

PROBLEMS

1. Assume you have recently been admitted to practice, and your father, who has helped finance your legal education, wants you to prepare a will for him. You believe the will is "fair" in its provisions for other family members but it does provide a substantial gift for you or your children. Should you draft the will? See State v. Beaudry, 53 Wis.2d 148, 191 N.W.2d 842 (1971).

2. Testatrix, 92 years old, went to Bank to discuss the disposition of her substantial estate. The Bank suggested she establish a revocable trust with income to herself for life, then to various beneficiaries for life after her death with remainder in perpetual trust for charitable purposes with the Bank as trustee. A Bank officer recommended Lawyer, who did extensive work for Bank, to prepare the trust and a will for testatrix. The Bank officer accompanied testatrix to the law office. At that time and thereafter, Lawyer reviewed the plans and prepared the instruments. Testatrix died and Heirs now claim undue influence by Bank and a failure to obtain independent advice from lawyer who did much work for Bank. Do you think a presumption of undue influence can be raised on such facts? Suppose Bank was already trustee for testatrix under a trust established for her benefit by her sister. Would this make any difference in establishing a presumption? If a presumption is raised, in your opinion would the review of the estate plan by the lawyer be the intervening, independent and competent advice necessary to rebut the presumption? See In re Longworth, 222 A.2d 561 (Me.1966).

---

(4) FRAUD

IN RE ROBLIN'S ESTATE

Supreme Court of Oregon, 1957.
210 Or. 371, 311 P.2d 459.

Before PERRY, C. J., and ROSSMAN, BRAND and MCALLISTER, JJ.

ROSSMAN, JUSTICE. This is an appeal by Charles Dana Roblin, contestant, from a decree of the Circuit Court for Marion County which dismissed proceedings he had instituted to contest the will of his father, Charles Ernest Roblin, and which ordered that the will be admitted to probate.

Charles Ernest and Ollie M. Roblin, both now deceased, were the parents of the appellant, Charles Dana Roblin, and of a daughter, Ruth Emily Shantz, proponent and respondent. For convenience we will refer to the elder Charles Roblin as Mr. Roblin and to the younger as Charles.

The family resided for many years in Salem. When Ruth married Carl Shantz they took their residence in Milwaukie, Oregon. Charles became a peripatetic, but during summer months returned to Salem for extended visits in the family home. In 1950 Mr. Roblin left the family home and made his abode in a Salem hotel. Ruth testified that he left in aggravation over his wife's conduct in sending money to Charles and paying his bills. In 1951 Mr. Roblin suffered a stroke and shortly repaired to a nursing home in Salem.

In the fall of 1951, Ruth, at her father's instance, arranged for him to undergo an eye operation in Portland. In that period he resided with Ruth and her husband for seven months. After he had recovered from the operation he returned to the nursing home where Ruth visited him every two weeks. Mrs. Roblin also called upon him from time to time, being driven to the nursing home in the Roblins' car by Charles. The latter, however, did not enter the home. Upon an earlier occasion when he attempted to visit his father, the latter ordered him out of the room in no unmistakable language.

Mrs. Roblin executed a will on July 3, 1953, and died five days later. Her will bequeathed all of her property equally to both children. Its terms were operative on property appraised at $1,581. But Charles received, in addition to his half of that sum, property worth $12,301.06 which was not part of the estate proper. This greater amount represented accounts and chattels the title to which was in Charles and the mother jointly, and to which he survived.

On either the evening of July 8 or the morning of July 9, 1953, Ruth visited her father in the nursing home and informed him, perhaps in response to his inquiry, that her mother had left everything to Charles except a diamond ring. Immediately Mr. Roblin ordered Ruth to obtain for him a lawyer. Ruth suggested a Mr. Steelhammer who was her husband's cousin. The suggestion was acceptable to her father, he having known Mr. Steelhammer through their mutual membership in the Salem Elks Lodge. On the morning of July 9 Mr. Steelhammer went to the nursing home and conversed in privacy with Mr. Roblin, who directed him to prepare a will, leaving Charles one dollar only and the remainder to Ruth. * * *

[The will was prepared as directed and testator died with the will in force. Charles attacked the will, one ground of attack being that the statement by Ruth that she took only a diamond ring from her mother's estate was fraudulent. Other grounds of attack were lack of testamentary capacity and undue influence] * * *

The principal thrust of contestant's attack upon the will is that, according to him, Ruth's statement to her father that she received nothing from her mother but a ring while her brother took all, was knowingly false and fraudulent and that its effect was, as intended, to cause Mr. Roblin to give his entire estate to Ruth. Contestant submits that, though his father may have executed his will voluntarily, the execution resulted from a misunderstanding of fact intentionally created by a false statement made to him.

Courts set aside wills whose provisions reflect the testator's belief in false data arising from fraudulent misrepresentation made to him by a beneficiary. In re Estate of Rosenberg, 196 Or. 219, 246 P.2d 858, 248 P.2d 340.

> "Fraud which causes testator to execute a will consists of statements which are false, which are known to be false by the party who makes them, which are material, which are made with the intention of deceiving testator, which deceive testator, and which cause testator to act in reliance upon such statements."

I Page on Wills, 3d Ed. 347, § 176. Absent any one of the elements of that definition of fraud, no ground for contest is established.

The statement which we are considering, and the consequences of its utterance, must be measured against the elements of fraud which vitiates a solemnly executed will.

The statement must be false and known to be such by the maker. In fact, Ruth's mother did not leave everything, except a ring, to her brother. Ruth was to receive half of $1,581; the other half of which went to Charles along with the $12,301.06 in jointly held property to which Charles survived. After the expenses of administration and taxes were paid by that estate, Ruth received $61.90. Charles received from his mother $12,367.96. The disparity is so great that Ruth may be excused for having been piqued, as is Charles now.

We must distinguish between a belief in the literal truth and falsity of a statement and that type of belief in falsity that underlies the fraudulent misrepresentation. Ruth testified at trial that "The only thing one could say, or I did say, was that Mother had left everything to Charlie." In this context a belief in the falsity of an utterance must be defined with regard to the nature of man and his reactions to an unexpected disappointment. The testimony just quoted demonstrates that at the time of utterance, and indeed at the time of trial, after reflection, Ruth doubted not that the hyperbole fairly described the division of her mother's estate.

The speaker must intend to deceive, and succeed. We are unwilling to decide that even a conscious exaggeration necessarily imports an intent to deceive. Even people of high character often exaggerate in order to express their belief with clarity and force. The purpose in instances of that kind is not to deceive, but better to communicate the belief. We are convinced that the statement made by Ruth is an example of that process. The speaker may in perfect good faith omit what he considers to be a non-material qualification upon his broad statement, thinking that a recital of all the details merely obfuscates the main point.

The misrepresentation must cause the testator to act upon it. In other words, the will must be the fruit of the fraud. In the Roblin family, little family unity or mutuality of attitude toward life bound father and son together. We know that the father emphatically expressed a desire that Charles stay away from the nursing home so that the two would not meet. Evidently, the wanderlust of the son was a canker to the parent. The learned trial judge would have been justified in a conclusion that the statement made by Ruth did not cause her father to rely upon it in the execution of his will, but rather that the statement merely provided an occasion for the taking of a step which the disappointed parent may have independently taken even if the statement had never been uttered.

The testimony of Ruth and of Charles conflicts in that she states, and he denies, that all her information about the division of their mother's estate came from him. If one believes her account, which the judge below may have done, her statement to her father cannot be objectionable. In that event, she merely relayed information which Charles gave her.

Both parties testified on direct and on cross-examination at some length about the amount of money each had received from Mr. and Mrs. Roblin inter vivos. We deem this evidence irrelevant. The statement of Ruth which is objected to refers only to the disposition of her mother's property upon her death. It does not relate to the inter vivos gifts to the children, of which Ruth received the greater share. Consequently the truth or falsity of the statement stands independent of the history of inter vivos donations.

Agreeing, as we do, with the disposition of this matter by the judge below, we affirm his decree.

Affirmed.

POPE v. GARRETT

Supreme Court of Texas, 1948.
147 Tex. 18, 211 S.W.2d 559.

SMEDLEY, JUSTICE.

This suit is by Claytonia Garrett against James Pope and others, the heirs of Carrie Simons, * * * to impress a trust upon property that passed to the heirs on the death of Carrie Simons intestate, after she, during her last illness, had been forcibly prevented by two of the heirs from executing a will devising the property to Claytonia Garrett.

Following trial before a jury the district court rendered judgment awarding to the plaintiff, Claytonia Garrett, the beneficial title to the whole of the property. The Court of Civil Appeals affirmed the trial court's judgment in part and reversed and rendered it in part, holding that a trust should not be impressed upon the interests of those of the heirs who had not participated in the wrongful act. 204 S.W.2d 867.

On October 31, 1944, Thomas J. Green, a neighbor and friend of Carrie Simons, brought to her to be executed a will prepared by him at her request, by the terms of which all of her property was devised to plaintiff, Claytonia Garrett, who was not related to Carrie Simons. Present in the room at the time, besides Claytonia Garrett and Green, were the Reverend Preacher and Jewel Benson, a friend of plaintiff, who had been requested to come as witnesses of the will, and Lillie Clay Smith, sister of Carrie Simons, Mary Jones and Evelyn Jones, nieces of Carrie Simons, and Alberta Justus. The jury made the following findings: That Carrie Simons, some days before her death, requested Thomas Green to prepare a will for her leaving all of her property to Claytonia Garrett; that the will so prepared by Green was read by him to Carrie Simons; that after having heard the instrument read to her, Carrie Simons, in the presence of Reverend Preacher, Jewel Benson and others, declared it to be her last will; that Carrie Simons prepared to sign her name to the will but the defendants, Evelyn Jones and Lillie Clay Smith, by physical force or by creating a disturbance, prevented her from carrying out her intention to execute the will; that Carrie Simons was of sound mind at the time and was not in an unconscious condition; and that shortly after this incident she suffered a severe hemorrhage, lapsed into a semicomatose condition and remained in that condition continuously until her death, which was on November 3, 1944. There is no proof that any of the heirs of Carrie Simons other than those above named were present or were in any way connected with the violence that prevented the execution of the will.

Two questions are presented by the two applications for writs of error that have been granted. First, should a trust be impressed in favor of Claytonia Garrett upon the property described in the will? And, second, if so, should the trust be impressed upon the interests inherited by all of the heirs or only upon the interests inherited by those who participated in the acts of violence that prevented the execution of the will?

We find no difficulty in approving the conclusion reached both by the trial court and by the Court of Civil Appeals as to the interests of the heirs who were guilty of the wrongful acts, that when they acquired, by the inheritance, the legal title to interests in the property, they became constructive trustees for Claytonia Garrett. According to the facts found by the jury, title undoubtedly would have passed to her under Carrie Simons' will but for the acts of violence. The case is a typical one for the intervention of equity to prevent a wrongdoer, who by his fraudulent or otherwise wrongful act has acquired title to property, from retaining and enjoying the beneficial interest therein, by impressing a constructive trust on the property in favor of the one who is truly and equitably entitled to the same. In Binford v. Snyder, 144 Tex. 134, 138, 189 S.W.2d 471, 472, the court quoted with approval the general rule as to the use of the constructive trust thus stated in the Ruling Case Law:

> "It is a well settled general rule that if one person obtains the legal title to property, not only by fraud, or by violation of confidence of fiduciary relations, but in any other unconscientious manner, so that he cannot equitably retain the property which really belongs to another, equity carries out its theory of a double ownership, equitable and legal, by impressing a constructive trust upon the property in favor of the one who is in good conscience entitled to it, and who is considered in equity as the beneficial owner." See also 54 Am.Jur., pp. 167–169, Sec. 218.

It has been said that "The specific instances in which equity impresses a constructive trust are numberless,—as numberless as the modes by which property may be obtained through bad faith and unconscientious acts." Pomeroy's Equity Jurisprudence, 5th Ed., Vol. 4, p. 97, Sec. 1045. * * *

The argument is often made that the imposition of the constructive trust in a case like this contravenes or circumvents the statute of descent and distribution, the statute of wills, the statute of frauds, or particularly a statute which prohibits the creation of a trust unless it is declared by an instrument in writing. It is generally held, however, that the constructive trust is not within such statutes or is an exception to them. It is the creature of equity. It does not arise out of the parol agreement of the parties. It is imposed irrespective of and even contrary to the intention of the parties. Resort is had to it in order that a statute enacted for the purpose of preventing fraud may not be used as an instrument for perpetrating or protecting a fraud. * * *

In this case Claytonia Garrett does not acquire title through the will. The trust does not owe its validity to the will. The statute of descent and distribution is untouched. The legal title passed to the heirs of Carrie Simons when she died intestate, but equity deals with the holder of the legal title for the wrong done in preventing the execution of the will and impresses a trust on the property in favor of the one who is in good conscience entitled to it.

The second question is more difficult. Shall the trust in favor of Claytonia Garrett extend to the interests of the heirs who had no part in the wrongful acts? From the viewpoint of those heirs, it seems that they should be permitted to retain and enjoy the interests that vested in them as heirs, no will having been executed, and they not being responsible for the failure of Carrie Simons to execute it. On the other hand, from the viewpoint of Claytonia Garrett, it appears that a court of equity should extend the trust to all of the interest in the property in order that complete relief may be afforded her and that none of the heirs may profit as the result of the wrongful acts.

There are few decisions in point, and they are conflicting. The New Jersey court has held that a trust, in favor of one excluded from a will by reason of the wrongful act of one of several legatees, will be impressed upon all of the property passing by the will to the legatees, when they take title as joint tenants, but not upon the interests of those who have not been parties to the wrongful act when they take as tenants in common, since such tenants in common do not receive their legacies through the wrongdoer. Powell v. Yearance, 73 N.J. Eq. 117, 67 A. 892; Heinisch v. Pennington, 73 N.J.Eq. 456, 68 A. 233, affirmed 75 N.J.Eq. 606, 73 A. 1181. In Dye v. Parker, 108 Kan. 304, 194 P. 640, 195 P. 599, the husband of Lera Parker, who inherited all of the estate not disposed of by the will, fraudulently induced the testator to omit from her will a clause devising certain real estate to the plaintiff. The opinion was expressed by the court that Lera Parker, the heir, would not take as a constructive trustee since she had not been a party to the deceit. The action, however, was for reformation of the will. Bohannon v. Trotman, 214 N.C. 706, 200 S.W. 852, holds that property in the hands of the beneficiaries of a will is subject to a constructive trust in favor of the plaintiff when the testator was wrongfully induced to exclude the plaintiff from any participation in his estate, although the beneficiaries were not parties to the wrongful act. The same conclusion is expressed in Ruhe v. Ruhe, 113 Md. 595, 77 A. 797, 800, where it may not have been necessary to the decision of the case.

The texts of Scott, Bogert and Perry seem to support this view, that is that the trust should be impressed even though the wrongful conduct because of which the title was acquired is that of a third person. Scott on Trusts, Vol. 3, pp. 2374–2376, Secs. 489.5, 489.6; Bogert's Trusts and Trustees, Vol. 3, p. 1467, Sec. 473; Perry on Trusts, 3d Ed., Vol. 1, pp. 260, 261, Sec. 211. The same is true of the Restatement. See illustrations 17 and 18, under Sec. 184, p. 754, Restatement of the Law of Restitution.

The policy against unjust enrichment argues in favor of the judgment rendered herein by the district court rather than that of the Court of Civil Appeals. But for the wrongful acts the innocent defendants would not have inherited interests in the property. Dean Roscoe Pound speaks of the constructive trust as a remedial institution and says that it is sometimes used "to develop a new field of equitable interposition, as in what we have come to think the typical case of constructive trust, namely, specific restitution of a received benefit in order to prevent unjust enrichment." 33 Harvard Law Review, pp. 420, 421. See also Pomeroy's Equity Jurisprudence, 5th Ed., Vol. 4, p. 95, Sec. 1044; 54 Am.Jur. p. 169, Sec. 219; Restatement of the Law of Restitution, Sec. 160, Subdivisions c and d, pp. 642, 643. Further and in the same trend, it has been said that equity is never wanting in power to do complete justice. Hill v. Stampfli, Tex.Com. App., 290 S.W. 522, 524.

We realize that a constructive trust does not arise on every moral wrong and that it cannot correct every injustice. 54 Am.Jur., p. 169, Sec. 218. It must be used with caution, especially where as here proof of the wrongful act rests in parol, in order that it may not defeat the purposes of the statute of wills, the statute of descent and distribution, or the statute of frauds.

In the instant case the findings of the jury are well supported by the testimony of four disinterested, unimpeached witnesses, although their testimony is contradicted by that of two of the defendants. The will devising the property to the plaintiff, Claytonia Garrett, which Carrie Simons was prevented from executing, was introduced in evidence. In view of the authorities and equitable principles which have been cited and discussed, it is our opinion that the judgment of the district court should be affirmed in order that complete justice may be done.

The judgment of the Court of Civil Appeals is reversed and the judgment of the district court is affirmed.

NOTE

Fraud in the inducement exists when the testator knows the contents of his will but makes the will or inserts a particular provision through reliance upon a false representation of extrinsic fact by one who knows the representation to be false.[27] The representation must be made before or at the time that the will is executed. Except when a fraudulent representation of a single status leads to a void marriage,[28] the representation must be made with the intention of inducing the testator to make or to revoke his will or a part thereof. A testator is not induced by the misrepresentation if he knows the facts,[29] or if the facts misrepresented are immaterial.[30]

Materiality of the facts misrepresented has produced difficulty in some cases. The problem has been particularly acute in cases in which the decedent leaves property to a supposed spouse and it is proved the parties were not married because the supposed spouse lacked the capacity to marry due to an existing marriage. The leading case in which these facts were presented is Kennell v. Abbott [31] in which the Master of the Rolls discussed the civil law test for materiality: "* * * /t/he person giving the legacy would not, if the fraud had been known to him, have given it. * * *" However, the Master of the Rolls in the test actually applied appears to have thought the critical issue was whether the false assumption of status "* * * alone can be supposed the motive of the bounty * * *." The differences in the tests discussed have induced confusion in American cases. A majority of American courts appear to prefer the civil law test. The legacy will fail if the testator would not have made it had he known the facts misrepresented. In Estate of Carson, involving facts similar to those in Kennell v. Abbott, the

27. See generally, Atkinson, Wills (2d Ed., 1953) §§ 56, 57; 1 Bowe-Parker: Page, Wills (3d Ed., Rev.1960) §§ 14.2–14.8; Rollison, Wills (1939) §§ 70–75; Thompson, Wills (3d Ed., 1947) §§ 139–141. Henderson, "Mistake and Fraud in Wills—Part I: A Comparative Analysis of Existing Law" 47 Boston Univ.L.Rev. 303 (1967). Under some circumstances a concealment of facts may have the effect of a misrepresentation. See In re Nutt's Estate, 181 Cal. 522, 185 P. 393 (1919) (Withholding medical opinion that death was imminent).

28. Smith v. DuBose, 78 Ga. 413, 3 S.E. 309 (1887).

29. E.g., In re Donnelly's Will, 68 Iowa 126, 26 N.W. 23 (1885) (Testatrix knew that man with whom she went through marriage ceremony had lived with another woman as his wife); 17 A.L.R. 274 (1920).

30. See In re Janes, 87 Hun. 57, 33 N.Y.S. 968 (1895), aff'd 152 N.Y. 647, 46 N.E. 1148 (1897) (Testator was prejudiced against married women. Servant secured employment by stating that she was unmarried and took good care of the testator until his death two years later).

31. 4 Ves Jun. 802, 31 Eng.Rep. 416 (1799).

court stated:[32] "* * * Now a case can be imagined where, nothing more appearing, as in this case, than that the testatrix had been deceived into a void marriage and had never been undeceived, it might fairly be said that a conclusion that such deceit had affected a bequest to the supposed husband would not be warranted. If, for example, the parties had lived together happily for 20 years, it would be difficult to say that the wife's bequest to her supposed husband was founded on her supposed legal relation with him, and not primarily on their long and intimate association. * * * But on the other hand, a case can be easily imagined where the reverse would be true. If in this case the will had been made immediately after marriage and the testatrix had then died within a few days, the conclusion would be well-nigh irresistible in the absence of some peculiar circumstance, that the will was founded on the supposed legal relation into which the testatrix had been deceived into believing she was entering. Between these two extreme cases come those wherein it cannot be said that one conclusion or the other is wholly unreasonable, and in those cases the determination of fact is one for the jury."

When a will or a part of it has been induced by a fraudulent misrepresentation of extrinsic fact, or when there has been a fraudulent representation concerning the nature of the instrument or its contents, usually described as a fraud in the factum, it is well settled that the will or a fraudulently induced part of a will should be denied probate. In many cases, however, an adequate remedy does not exist at probate. Thus, there may be an omission from the will caused by fraud in the inducement or fraud in the factum. In this case the probate court lacks the power to restore the provision. A refusal to probate an entire will benefits an injured party only if he happens to be an heir or a beneficiary under a prior will which can then take effect. A refusal to probate part of a will benefits an injured party only if he is an heir or residuary legatee. In some cases the injured party may lack an interest to contest. If there is a fraudulent interference with the making of a will, the probate court cannot make a will for the testator.[33] If there is a fraudulent interference with the revocation of a will, the probate court cannot refuse to probate a will which has not been revoked in the statutory form.[34]

There may be a remedy in an action at law against the wrongdoer based on a theory of tort or contract. In Lewis v. Corbin[35] the plaintiff charged that the defendant had caused the testatrix to execute a codicil without the required number of witnesses and had thus by fraud deprived the plaintiff of a legacy as representative of his father under a lapse statute. The court sustained a demurrer to the complaint on the ground that there was no allegation which excluded the possibility that the testatrix had changed her purpose with regard to the legacy prior to her death. It was suggested that had this allegation been made the plaintiff would have stated a cause of action.[36]

32. 184 Cal. 437, 443, 194 P. 5, 8, 17 A.L.R. 239 (1920).

33. See Page, "Of Forbidding or Hindering the Testator to Make Another Testament", [1951] Wis.L.Rev. 474.

34. If the testator intends a revocation by physical act by complete destruction, and fraudulent interference by another prevents him from accomplishing the full act that he intended, a mutilation of the will that meets the statutory requirement is a sufficient revocation if the testator's intention to revoke continues when the mutilation occurs. See Bibb d. Mole v. Thomas, 2 W.Bl. 1043, 96 Eng. Rep. 613 (1775); White v. Casten, 46 N.C. 197, 59 Am.Dec. 585 (1853).

35. 195 Mass. 520, 81 N.E. 248 (1907).

36. See Bohannon v. Wachovia Bank and Trust Co., 210 N.C. 679, 684, 188 S.E. 390, 393 (1936), 22 Corn.L.Q. 440 (1937); 35 Mich.L.Rev. 1033 (1937), 15 N.C.L. Rev. 296 (1937); 23 Va.L.Rev. 614 (1937); Rollison, Wills (1939) 130; 30 Harv.L. Rev. 527 (1917). Cf. Seaver v. Ransom,

If there is no adequate remedy at law,[37] the injured party may have a remedy by constructive trust. The constructive trust is a remedial device imposed to prevent a person from retaining title to property if the retention would unjustly enrich him at the expense of another and has been discussed in detail in connection with the acquisition of property by homicide.[38] If the constructive trust is denied, the usual basis for denial, assuming other equities are present, is that by use of the trust the court would circumvent the statutes requiring formalities for the execution or revocation of wills or the provisions of the Statute of Frauds which require trusts of land to be proved by a writing.[39] When there has been a fraudulent interference with the revocation of a will, some courts have distinguished between an interference with an "attempt" to revoke and an interference with an "intent" to revoke, imposing a constructive trust in the latter case but not in the former. Thus in Moneyham v. Hamilton,[40] the testator sent his daughter for a will which he desired to revoke. She returned and falsely told him that she could not find it. The court refused to impose a constructive trust upon the estate in her hands, stating:[41] "* * * It appears that it is safe to say that the frustration of a mere intent to revoke a will is not sufficient to impress a trust on the devise, while if an interested person by fraud, duress, coercion or deception frustrates an attempt as distinguished from an intent to revoke the will, such person so acting will not be allowed to profit thereby and equity may in such case impress a trust in favor of the heirs at law on the devise which will have the same effect and results as would have been obtained had the will been revoked."

---

(5) MISTAKE REMEDIES AT PROBATE

GIFFORD v. DYER

Supreme Court of Rhode Island, 1852.
2 R.I. 99, 57 Am.Dec. 708.

This was an appeal from a decree of the Court of Probate of Little Compton, proving and approving the last will and testament of Abigail Irish. The will was dated December 4, 1850, and the testatrix

224 N.Y. 233, 120 N.E. 639, 2 A.L.R. 1187 (1918).

37. In addition to an action for damages there may be a quasi-contractual recovery at law. The probate proceeding is treated as a law proceeding. Modern decisions suggest that it is unnecessary to prove an inadequate remedy at law before a constructive trust will be imposed, and this may be the better view. Bogert, Trusts and Trustees (2d Ed. 1960) § 472. But the traditional attitude is to withhold a constructive trust when the remedy at law is adequate unless some other basis for equity jurisdiction exists in the case. The adequacy of the legal remedy is a flexible point for argument, and a constructive trust has been applied in cases in which an adequate remedy seemed to exist. E.g., Fur and Wool Trading Co., Limited v. Fox, Inc., 245 N.Y. 215, 156 N.E. 670, 58 A.L.R. 181 (1927). There are other equitable remedies for restitution in addition to the constructive trust. See Restatement, Restitution (1937) § 161 (Equitable lien), § 162 (Subrogation).

38. See Chapter III, Section 4(4) (A), Note to Estate of Mahoney.

39. See Chapter IX, Section 1(2).

40. 124 Fla. 430, 168 So. 522 (1936).

41. 168 So. at 523.

died December 6, 1850. After several bequests of small sums to the children of Robin Gifford and to others, she gives and bequeaths the rest and residue of her property, one half to John Dyer, who was her brother-in-law, and the other half to her two nephews, Jesse and Alexander Dyer. Robin Gifford, the only child of the testatrix, was not mentioned in the will. It appeared in evidence, that at the date of the will, Robin Gifford had been absent from home, leaving a family, for a period of ten years, unheard from; that all the neighbors considered him dead, and that his estate had been administered upon as of a person deceased. The scrivener who drew the will, testified as follows: "After I had read the will to her, she asked if it would make any difference if she did not mention her son. I asked if she considered him living. She said she supposed he had been dead for years; she said, if it would make any difference, she would put his name in, for they will break the will if they can. I think that was the expression she used. I think she said what she had given to her grandchildren was in lieu of what he would have, but am not positive. I think her son left in 1841, and was not heard of to my knowledge. She was speaking of a home at Mr. Dyer's and said, what she had given him would pay him well. She said her grand-children had not been to see her while she was sick." It appeared that the testatrix had resided with John Dyer for some time previous to her death.

* * *

GREENE, C. J., delivered the opinion of the court. It is very apparent in the present case, that the testatrix would have made the same will, had she known her son was living. She did not intend to give him anything, if living.

But if this were not apparent and she had made the will under a mistake as to the supposed death of her son, this could not be shown *dehors* the will. The mistake must appear on the face of the will, and it must also appear what would have been the will of the testatrix but for the mistake. Thus, where the testator revokes a legacy, upon the mistaken supposition that the legatee is dead, and this appears on the face of the instrument of revocation, such revocation was held void. Campbell v. French, 3 Vesey 321.

MATTER OF SNIDE

Court of Appeals of New York, 1981.
52 N.Y.2d 193, 418 N.E.2d 656.

WACHTLER, JUDGE.

This case involves the admissibility of a will to probate. The facts are simply stated and are not in dispute. Harvey Snide, the decedent, and his wife, Rose Snide, intending to execute mutual wills at a common execution ceremony, each executed by mistake the will intended for the other. There are no other issues concerning the required formalities of execution (see EPTL 3-2.1), nor is there any question of the decedent Harvey Snide's testamentary capacity, or his intention and belief that he was signing his last will and testament. Except for the obvious differences in the names of the donors and beneficiaries on the wills, they were in all other respects identical.

The proponent of the will, Rose Snide, offered the instrument Harvey actually signed for probate. The Surrogate, 96 Misc.2d 513, 409 N.Y.S.2d 204 decreed that it could be admitted, and further that it could be reformed to substitute the name "Harvey" wherever the name "Rose" appeared, and the name "Rose" wherever the name "Harvey" appeared. The Appellate Division, 74 A.D.2d 930, 426 N.Y. S.2d 155, reversed on the law, and held under a line of lower court cases dating back into the 1800's, that such an instrument may not be admitted to probate. We would reverse.

It is clear from the record, and the parties do not dispute the conclusion, that this is a case of a genuine mistake. It occurred through the presentment of the wills to Harvey and Rose in envelopes, with the envelope marked for each containing the will intended for the other. The attorney, the attesting witnesses, and Harvey and Rose, all proceeding with the execution ceremony without anyone taking care to read the front pages, or even the attestation clauses of the wills, either of which would have indicated the error.

Harvey Snide is survived by his widow and three children, two of whom have reached the age of majority. These elder children have executed waivers and have consented to the admission of the instrument to probate. The minor child, however, is represented by a guardian ad litem who refuses to make such a concession. The reason for the guardian's objection is apparent. Because the will of Harvey would pass the entire estate to Rose, the operation of the intestacy statute (EPTL 4–1.1) after a denial of probate is the only way in which the minor child will receive a present share of the estate.

The gist of the objectant's argument is that Harvey Snide lacked the required testamentary intent because he never intended to execute the document he actually signed. This argument is not novel, and in the few American cases on point it has been the basis for the denial of probate (see Nelson v. McDonald, 61 Hun. 406, 16 N.Y.S. 273; Matter of Cutler, Sur., 58 N.Y.S.2d 604; Matter of Bacon, 165 Misc. 259, 300 N.Y.S. 920; see, also, Matter of Pavlinko, 394 Pa. 564, 148 A.2d 528; Matter of Goettel, 184 Misc. 155, 55 N.Y.S.2d 61). However, cases from other common-law jurisdictions have taken a different view of the matter, and we think the view they espouse is more sound (Matter of Brander, 4 Dom.L.Rep. 688 [1952]; Guardian, Trust & Executor's Co. of New Zealand v. Inwood, 65 N.Z.L. Rep. 614 [1946] [New Zealand]; see Wills, 107 U. of Pa.L.Rev. 1237, 1239–1240; Kennedy, Wills-Mistake-Husband and Wife Executing Wills Drawn for Each Other—Probate of Husband's Will With Substitutions, 31 Can.Bar.Rev. 185).

Of course it is essential to the validity of a will that the testator was possessed of testamentary intent (Matter of May, 241 N.Y. 1, 148 N.E. 770; 64 N.Y.Jur., Wills, § 11; see EPTL 1–2.18), however, we decline the formalistic view that this intent attaches irrevocably to the document prepared, rather than the testamentary scheme it reflects. Certainly, had a carbon copy been substituted for the ribbon copy the testator intended to sign, it could not be seriously contended that the testator's intent should be frustrated (Matter of Epstein, Sur., 136 N.Y.S.2d 884, see 81 ALR2d 1112, 1120–1121). Here the situation is similar. Although Harvey mistakenly signed the will prepared for his wife, it is significant that the dispositive provisions in both wills, except for the names, were identical.

Moreover, the significance of the only variance between the two instruments is fully explained by consideration of the documents together, as well as in the undisputed surrounding circumstances. Under such facts it would indeed be ironic—if not perverse—to state that because what has occurred is so obvious, and what was intended so clear, we must act to nullify rather than sustain this testamentary scheme. The instrument in question was undoubtedly genuine, and it was executed in the manner required by the statute. Under these circumstances it was properly admitted to probate (see Matter of Pascal, 309 N.Y. 108, 113–114, 127 N.E.2d 835).

In reaching this conclusion we do not disregard settled principles, nor are we unmindful of the evils which the formalities of will execution are designed to void; namely, fraud and mistake. To be sure, full illumination of the nature of Harvey's testamentary scheme is dependent in part on proof outside of the will itself. However, this is a very unusual case, and the nature of the additional proof should not be ignored. Not only did the two instruments constitute reciprocal elements of a unified testamentary plan, they both were executed with statutory formality, including the same attesting witnesses, at a contemporaneous execution ceremony. There is absolutely no danger of fraud, and the refusal to read these wills together would serve merely to unnecessarily expand formalism, without any corresponding benefit. On these narrow facts we decline this unjust course.

Nor can we share the fears of the dissent that our holding will be the first step in the exercise of judicial imagination relating to the reformation of wills. Again, we are dealing here solely with identical mutual wills both simultaneously executed with statutory formality.

For the reasons we have stated, the order of the Appellate Division should be reversed, and the matter remitted to that court for a review of the facts.

JONES, JUDGE (dissenting).

I agree with the Appellate Division that the Surrogate's Court had no authority to reform the decedent's will and am of the conviction that the willingness of the majority in an appealing case to depart from what has been consistent precedent in the courts of the United States and England will prove troublesome in the future. This is indeed an instance of the old adage that hard cases make bad law.

Our analysis must start with the recognition that any statute of wills (now articulated in this State at EPTL 3–2.1) operates frequently to frustrate the identifiable dispositive intentions of the decedent.

It is never sufficient under our law that the decedent's wishes be clearly established; our statute, like those of most other common-law jurisdictions, mandates with but a few specific exceptions that the wishes of the decedent be memorialized with prescribed formality. The statutes historically have been designed for the protection of testators, particularly against fraudulent changes in or additions to wills. "[W]hile often it may happen that a will truly expressing the intention of the testator is denied probate for failure of proper execution, it is better that this should happen under a proper construction of the statute than that the individual case should be permitted to weaken those provisions intended to protect testators generally from fraudulent alterations of their wills" (64 N.Y.Jur., Wills, § 198, p. 348).

Next it must be recognized that what is admitted to probate is a paper writing, a single integrated instrument (codicils are considered integral components of the decedent's "will"). We are not concerned on admission to probate with the substantive content of the will; our attention must be focused on the paper writing itself. As to that, there can be no doubt whatsoever that Harvey Snide did not intend as his will the only document that he signed on August 13, 1970.

Until the ruling of the Surrogate of Hamilton County in this case, the application of these principles in the past had uniformly been held in our courts to preclude the admission to probate of a paper writing that the decedent unquestionably intended to execute when he and another were making mutual wills but where, through unmistakable inadvertence, each signed the will drawn for the other. Nor had our courts blinkingly invoked a doctrine of equitable reformation to reach the same end. (Nelson v. McDonald, 61 Hun. 406, 16 N.Y.S. 273; Matter of Bacon, 165 Misc. 259, 300 N.Y.S. 920; Matter of Egner, Sur., 112 N.Y.S.2d 568; Matter of Cutler, Sur., 58 N.Y.S.2d 604; subsequently, contra, Matter of Iovino, NYLJ, April 16, 1980, p. 14, col. 5 [an uncontested case].)

On the basis of commendably thorough world-wide research, counsel for appellant has uncovered a total of 17 available reported cases involving mutual wills mistakenly signed by the wrong testator. Six cases arise in New York, two in Pennsylvania, three in England, one in New Zealand and five in Canada. With the exception of the two recent Surrogate's decisions (*Snide* and *Iovino*) relief was denied in the cases from New York, Pennsylvania and England. The courts that have applied the traditional doctrines have not hesitated, however, to express regret at judicial inability to remedy the evident blunder. Relief was granted in the six cases from the British Commonwealth. In these cases it appears that the court has been moved by the transparency of the obvious error and the egregious frustration of undisputed intention which would ensue from failure to correct that error.

Under doctrines both of judicial responsibility not to allow the prospect of unfortunate consequence in an individual case to twist the application of unquestioned substantive legal principle and of *stare decisis,* I perceive no jurisprudential justification to reach out for the disposition adopted by the majority. Not only do I find a lack of rigorous judicial reasoning in this result; more important, I fear an inability to contain the logical consequences of this decision in the future. Thus, why should the result be any different where, although the two wills are markedly different in content, it is equally clear that there has been an erroneous contemporaneous cross-signing by the two would-be testators, or where the scrivener has prepared several drafts for a single client and it is established beyond all doubt that the wrong draft has been mistakenly signed? Nor need imagination stop there.

For the reasons stated, I would adhere to the precedents, and affirm the order of the Appellate Division.

NOTE

The courts have refused relief at probate when a testator has executed a will or part thereof upon a misapprehension of extrinsic fact which is self-induced or unintentionally induced by another.[42] A possible exception to this general rule is that stated in Gifford v. Dyer; the dictum at the end of that case is derived from the treatment of mistakes in revocation, discussed in Chapter VI, Section 4(3) as "Dependent Relative Revocation".

In Matter of Tousey's Will [43] the testatrix stated in her will that she was unmarried and had no direct heirs. A cousin contended that the will was not entitled to probate upon the assumption that the testatrix was in ignorance of his existence when she stated that she had no direct heirs. In rejecting this contention, Surrogate Thomas stated: [44] "In no case which has been brought to my notice has a will been refused probate, or has any attempt been made to correct or change its provisions, on proof extraneous to the document of a mistake by the testator as to a fact which might possibly have led him to do something different from what he has done." [45] In Matter of Shumway's Will [46] the testator provided: "As I have already advanced to Mildred Schulough, daughter of George S. Shumway, deceased, what I consider to be her share of my estate (and she having signed papers to that effect), I do not leave her anything further in my last Will and Testament."

42. See generally, Atkinson, Wills (2d Ed., 1953) §§ 58, 59; 1 Bowe-Parker: Page, Wills (3d Ed., Rev.1960) §§ 13.-2–13.14. Rollison, Wills (1939) §§ 76–79, 83, 86; Thompson, Wills (3d Ed., 1947) §§ 135, 137, 138; Henderson, "Mistake and Fraud in Wills—Part I: A Comparative Analysis of Existing Law", 47 Boston Univ.Law Rev. 303 (1967); Gray, "Striking Words Out of a Will" 26 Harv.L.Rev. 212 (1913); Warren, "Fraud, Undue Influence and Mistake in Wills", 41 Harv.L. Rev. 309 (1928), 5 A.L.R.3d 360 (1966). Uniform Probate Code, § 2–302(b), set forth supra at page 179, is aimed at the type of problem presented in the principal case and for which there would probably be no remedy unless provided by statute. The child receives a share equal in value to that which he would have received if the testator had died intestate. The omission must be "solely" because the testator believes the child is dead.

43. 34 Misc. 363, 69 N.Y.S. 846 (1901).

44. 69 N.Y.S. at 847.

45. See In re Arnold's Estate, 200 Misc. 909, 107 N.Y.S.2d 356 (1951) (Contention that testator was unaware of existence of half-sister. Will probated as written); In re Reidy, 199 Misc. 311, 106 N.Y.S.2d 270 (1951) (Testatrix made gift of $500 to nephew in satisfaction of debt due nephew by brother of testatrix. The contention was made that the debt did not exist, or was barred by the statute of limitations if it ever existed. Will probated as written).

46. 138 Misc. 429, 246 N.Y.S. 178 (1930).

It appeared that the advancement had been made by the wife of the testator. The court probated the will as written, saying: [47] "In the last analysis the testator had an absolute right to divert his property from this contestant; he was under no obligation to assign any reason for so doing, and an inaccurate statement of a reason will not be held to invalidate the free and voluntary testamentary directions of this competent testator."

The dictum in Gifford v. Dyer that relief will be given if the mistake and what would have been done in the absence of the mistake appears upon the face of the will has been approved in dicta in a number of decisions.[48]

Two reasons have been offered for the refusal by the courts to permit mistakes in inducement to vitiate all or part of a will. Inquiries into matters of mistake would impose an undue burden on the courts. The effect of the mistake upon the will is highly speculative unless what would have been done in the absence of the mistake appears in the will.[49]

When the testator does not know the nature of the instrument which he signs or is unaware of its contents, he lacks testamentary intent and the will should be denied probate. The situation is described as one of mistake in the factum.[50] When it can be shown that the testator was unaware of the presence of particular words in his will, and did not intend for them to be there, it may be proper for a court to probate the will without the material mistakenly included.[51] A court cannot, of course, include words which have been omitted by mistake.

Whether or not a court rejects materials at probate which were included by a mistake in the factum should depend upon whether or not the materials are separable from the remainder of the will. The determination of this question should, in turn, rest upon two considerations: (1) Will the deletion alter substantially other provisions in the instrument? (2) If a substantial alteration will occur, whether the intention of the testator will be effectuated

47. 246 N.Y.S. at 184. In Jackson v. Payne, 2 Metc. (Ky.) 567 (1859) the testator provided: "I have made advances to those four children, which advances I deem about equal". Evidence that the advances were not equal was not admitted.

48. E.g., In re Tousey's Will, 34 Misc. 363, 364, 69 N.Y.S. 846, 847 (1901).

49. The refusal of the courts to give a remedy when a person unintentionally induces the mistake and benefits thereby has been subject to particular criticism. E.g., 1 Bowe-Parker: Page, Wills (3d Ed., Rev.1960) 691. In fraud in the inducement and in some cases of mistake in the factum a remedy is given, and in these cases it is necessary to consider some extrinsic matters in order to give an adequate remedy.

50. In Doe d. Small v. Allen, 8 T.R. 147, 101 Eng.Rep. 1314 (1799) the testator having executed one will was induced to sign a second instrument upon being assured that it was the same as his first will. In fact it was not and was denied probate. In Matter of Meyer's Estate, [1908] L.R.Prob. 353, two sisters desired to execute codicils containing similar terms. Each sister signed the codicil written for the other. At the death of one sister the court refused to probate her will. See Hildreth v. Marshall, 51 N.J.Eq. 241, 27 A. 465 (1893) (Testatrix signed will under fraudulently induced misapprehension that it was a burial certificate).

51. No American case is reported in which materials included by a mistake in the factum have been deleted and the remainder of the will allowed to stand. Dicta in a number of cases suggest that part of a will may be denied probate. See, e.g., Ex parte King, 132 S.C. 63, 69, 128 S.E. 850, 852 (1925); Sherwood v. Sherwood, 45 Wis. 357, 362, 30 Am.Rep. 757, 761 (1878). In Burger v. Hill, 1 Bradf. Surr. (N.Y.) 360 (1850), the testator left his personal property to his mistress and his real estate to his mother and sister. The Surrogate found that the testator intended to leave a leasehold interest to his mother and sister and admitted the will to probate with the exception of the leasehold so that it passed by intestacy. The leasehold was not mentioned specifically at any place in the will.

best by probating the will as written or by deleting the materials mistakenly included and the provisions affected by the deletion.[52]

If an entire clause has been included by mistake, a deletion of the clause is unlikely to alter the operation of other provisions in the will.[53] A residuary clause is not altered when the property which it passes is increased by omission of a dispositive clause from the will. But difficulty is likely to be encountered when particular words within a clause have been included by mistake. The English courts have distinguished between the omission of words which change the "meaning" of those which remain and the omission of words which do not change the meaning but do change the "effect". If the "effect" only is changed, the words can be omitted; if the "meaning" is changed the words cannot be omitted.[54] In this connection the following hypothetical cases may be considered: [55]

1. "One hundred dollars to each of my sons, not excepting A." It is proved that the word "not" was inserted by clerical error.

2. "I give $500 to my son William and $100 to my son John." It is proved that the words "to my son William and $100" were inserted by clerical error.

A deletion of the words in either hypothetical would change the "meaning" of the words that remain, in the first hypothetical excluding a beneficiary and in the second hypothetical increasing a gift. In neither case would an English court be likely to delete the language. But the English courts delete words when they serve only to limit or restrict a gift.[56] Viewed from the four corners of the instrument the "meaning" of the remaining words is unchanged, although the words pass a larger amount of property than they did before.

52. This is the separability problem raised in connection with insane delusions, undue influence and fraud. While a court will not hesitate to strike down an entire will if a clause induced by undue influence or fraud or affected by an insane delusion cannot be separated, there will probably be greater reluctance to strike down an entire will because of a clerical error in the insertion of a provision.

53. This would be true of a standard clause revoking prior wills. Goods of Oswald, L.R. 3 P. & D. 162 (1874). It would also be true of a clause appointing an executor. See In re Finn's Estate, 1 Misc. 280, 22 N.Y.S. 1066, 1077 (1892).

54. See Gray, "Striking Words Out of a Will", 26 Harv.L.Rev. 212, 231 (1913); Horrocks v. Kershaw, [1939] 1 A.E.R. 579 (Where the court refused to strike the word "or" in a trust provision for "charitable or benevolent" objects, since that would change the meaning of the remaining words). The difficulty in the test lies in the "meaning of meaning". Words have no intrinsic meaning but acquire meaning only from the context in which they are used. As meaning is used in the English test, it seems to mean "meaning in the limited context of the four corners of the instrument" and not meaning in the light of other relevant circumstances. The test presupposes that the probate court will have to construe the clause before and after the deletion but will ignore the effect of the words upon the testator's estate. "Omission of Mistaken Insertions", 33 Ind.L.J. 556 (1958).

55. Both hypotheticals are borrowed from Gray, "Striking Words Out of a Will", 26 Harv.L.Rev. 212, 227, 228 (1913).

56. In Morrell v. Morrell, L.R. 7 P.D. 68 (1882) the testator desired to leave all his shares in a particular company to his nephews and gave instructions to that effect to his solicitor. The word "forty" was inserted by error before the word "shares". The will was probated without the word "forty". In Vaughan v. Clerk, 87 L.T.R. (N.S.) 144 (1902) the court struck out the word "real" which preceded the word "property" so that the will passed personal property. And see Goods of Bushell, L.R. 13 P.D. 7 (1887); Goods of Boehm, [1891] L.R. Prob. 247; Brisco v. Hamilton, [1902] L.R. Prob. 234.

It appears unlikely that the English distinction between "meaning" and "effect" will be accepted in this country. A court might strike the words mistakenly included and leave the remainder of the clause to be passed upon in an appropriate proceeding for construction of the will.[57] The court might strike the entire clause or probate the clause as written. The course of action should be taken which best effectuates the probable intention of the testator.

Proof of due execution of a will raises a rebuttable presumption that the testator knew and intended to include each part thereof.[58] This presumption is difficult to rebut when it is shown that the will was read by or to the testator, or that the will conforms substantially to the instructions given by the testator to the draftsman.[59]

---

(6) CORRECTION OF SUBSTANTIVE MISTAKES BY CONSTRUCTION

IN RE GIBBS' ESTATE

Supreme Court of Wisconsin, 1961.
14 Wis.2d 490, 111 N.W.2d 413.

[The wills of a husband and wife contained a bequest to "Robert J. Krause, now of 4708 North 46th Street, Milwaukee, Wisconsin, if he survives me * * *". There was a Robert J. Krause living at the address stated in the will but Robert W. Krause who had never resided at the address described but who had been an employee of the husband for 30 years and a friend of the husband and wife filed petitions for construction of the wills alleging he was the Robert Krause intended. At the hearing, Robert W. Krause offered evidence in support of his allegations which was received over objection of Robert J. Krause. Robert J. Krause was not acquainted with testator and testatrix although he recalled a conversation in 1955 with a lady who might have been testatrix. The lower court held the husband and wife intended to refer to Robert *W.* Krause and Robert *J.* Krause appeals.] * * *

FAIRCHILD, JUSTICE. 1. *The intention of the testators as determined from all the evidence.* The evidence leads irresistibly to the conclusion that Mr. and Mrs. Gibbs intended legacies to respondent, and that the use of the middle initial "J." and the address of North 46th street resulted from some sort of mistake.

Respondent testified that he met Mr. Gibbs about 1928. From 1930 to 1949 he was employed as superintendent of a steel warehouse where Mr. Gibbs was his superior. They worked in close contact.

57. This appears to be the position favored by Professor Gray. See Gray, "Striking Words Out of a Will," 26 Harv. L.Rev. 212, 235 (1913).

58. E.g., Downey v. Lawley, 377 Ill. 298, 36 N.E.2d 344 (1941).

59. See L.R.A.1918D, 747, 758, and cases there cited.

Until 1945 the business belonged to the Gibbs Steel Company. In that year the business was sold, but Mr. Gibbs stayed on for four years in a supervisory capacity. Respondent remained with the new company until 1960. After 1949 Mr. Gibbs occasionally visited the plant and saw the respondent when there. From 1935 to 1955 respondent took men occasionally to the Gibbs home to do necessary work about the place. He also visited there socially several times a year and saw both Mr. and Mrs. Gibbs. Mrs. Gibbs had made a few visits at the plant before 1949 and respondent had seen her there. Mr. Gibbs did not visit respondent's home, although on a few occasions had telephoned him at home. Mr. Gibbs always called respondent "Bob."

Miss Krueger, who had been the Gibbs' housekeeper for 24 years up to 1958 and was a legatee under both wills, corroborated much of respondent's testimony. She also testified that Mr. Gibbs had told her he made a will remembering various people including "the boys at the shop," referring to them as "Mike, Ed and Bob."

Miss Pacius, a legatee under both wills, who had been Mr. Gibbs' private secretary for many years while he was in business testified to Mr. Gibbs' expressions of high regard for respondent. Another former employee also testified to a similar effect.

Of the individuals named in the wills as legatees, all except two were shown to be relatives of Mr. or Mrs. Gibbs, former employees, neighbors, friends, or children of friends. The two exceptions were named near the end of the will and proof as to them may have been inadvertently omitted. "Mike," named in the will, was a warehouse employee under the supervision of respondent.

The attorney who drew several wills for Mr. and Mrs. Gibbs produced copies of most of them. They were similar in outline to the wills admitted to probate except that Mr. Gibbs' wills executed before Mrs. Gibbs' death bequeathed his property to her, if she survived. The first ones were drawn in 1953 and each contained a bequest to "Robert Krause, of Milwaukee, Wisconsin, if he survives me, one per cent (1%)." There was testimony that Mrs. Gibbs' will, executed in August, 1955, contained the same language. In the 1957 wills the same bequest was made to "Robert Krause, now of 4708 North 46th Street, Milwaukee, Wisconsin." In several other instances street addresses of legatees were given for the first time in 1957. In the 1958 wills the same bequest was made to "Robert J. Krause, now of 4708 North 46th Street, Milwaukee, Wisconsin." The scrivener also produced a hand-written memorandum given to him by Mr. Gibbs for the purpose of preparing Mr. Gibbs' 1958 will, and the reference on that memorandum corresponding to the Krause bequest is "Bob, 1%." Four bequests (to Gruener, Krause, Preuschl and Owen) appear in the same order in each of the wills and are reflected in the memorandum referred to as "Fred Gruener, Bob, Mike, and Ed." Gruener, Preuschl and Owen were former employees of Gibbs Steel Company, as was respondent. Owen's residence is given as Jefferson, Wisconsin, in all the wills. In the 1953 wills, the residence of Gruener,

Krause and Preuschl was given only as Milwaukee, Wisconsin. A street address was inserted for the first time in each case in the 1957 wills, and repeated in the later ones.

Prior to 1950 respondent had lived at several different locations. From 1950 until April, 1960, he lived at 2325 North Sherman Boulevard. We take judicial notice that this address and 4708 North 46th Street are in the same general section of the city of Milwaukee, and that both are a number of miles distant from the Gibbs' home. We also take judicial notice that the telephone directory for Milwaukee and vicinity listed 14 subscribers by the name of Robert Krause with varying initials in October, 1958, and 15 in October of 1959. The listing for appellant gives his middle initial *J.* as well as his street address.

The only evidence which suggests even a possibility that Mr. or Mrs. Gibbs may have known of appellant may be summarized as follows:

> For a time, appellant had a second job as a part time taxi driver, and he recalled an elderly lady who was his passenger on a lengthy taxi trip in June, 1955. He did not recall where he picked her up. He had driven her across the city, waiting for her while she visited in a hospital, and then driven her back across the city. The place where he let her out, however, was not her home. He did not recall that she had given him her name, but she had inquired as to his. They had conversed about the illness of appellant's wife and his working at an extra job in order to make ends meet. She had expressed sympathy and approval of his efforts. Presumably when he was notified that his name appeared in the Gibbs' wills as legatee, he endeavored to find an explanation of his good fortune and concluded that the lady in question must have been Mrs. Gibbs. The 1955 taxi ride, however, could not explain the gift to Robert Krause in the 1953 wills, and it is clear that the same legatee was intended in the Krause bequests in all the wills. Moreover, appellant's description of his taxi passenger differed in several particulars from the description of Mrs. Gibbs given by other witnesses.

2. *Propriety of considering extrinsic evidence.* As stated above, the county court could reach no other conclusion upon consideration of the extrinsic evidence than that Mr. and Mrs. Gibbs intended to designate respondent as their legatee. The difficult question is whether the court could properly consider such evidence in determining testamentary intent.

Under rules as to construction of a will, unless there is ambiguity in the text of the will read in the light of surrounding circumstances, extrinsic evidence is inadmissible for the purpose of determining intent.[60]

60. Estate of Breese, 1959, 7 Wis.2d 422, 96 N.W.2d 712. [Footnotes 60 through 75 are by the court].

A latent ambiguity exists where the language of the will, though clear on its face, is susceptible of more than one meaning, when applied to the extrinsic facts to which it refers.[61]

There are two classes of latent ambiguity. One, where there are two or more persons or things exactly measuring up to the description in the will; [62] the other where no person or thing exactly answers the declarations and descriptions of the will, but two or more persons or things answer the description imperfectly. Extrinsic evidence must be resorted to under these circumstances to identify which of the parties, unspecified with particularity in the will, was intended by the testator.[63]

Had the probated wills used the language of the 1953 wills "To Robert Krause of Milwaukee," such terms would have described both appellant and respondent, as well as a number of other people. Upon such ambiguity of the first type above mentioned becoming apparent, extrinsic evidence would be admissible in order to determine which Robert Krause Mr. and Mrs. Gibbs had in mind as their legatee.

Had the will said "To my former employee, Robert J. Krause of 4708 North 46th Street," neither appellant nor respondent would have exactly fulfilled the terms. Latent ambiguity of the second type would thus have appeared, and again extrinsic evidence would be admissible to determine what individual testators had in mind.

The wills containing, as they do, similar bequests to a long list of individuals, each bearing some relationship of blood, friendship, or former employment to Mr. or Mrs. Gibbs, come close to implying that every legatee named has some such relationship. Nevertheless the wills do not refer to Krause as standing in any particular relationship.

The terms of the bequest exactly fit appellant and no one else. There is no ambiguity.

> "An ambiguity is not that which may be made doubtful by extrinsic proof tending to show an intention different from that manifested in the will, but it must grow out of the difficulty of identifying the person whose name and description correspond with the terms of the will." [64]

Under the circumstances before us, can a court properly consider evidence showing that some of the words were used by mistake and should be stricken or disregarded? It is traditional doctrine that wills must not be reformed even in the case of demonstrable mistake.[65] This doctrine doubtless rests upon policy reasons. The courts deem it wise to avoid entertaining claims of disappointed persons who may be able to make very plausible claims of mistake after the testator is no longer able to refute them.

61. Will of Frost, 1958, 3 Wis.2d 603, 89 N.W.2d 216; 57 Am.Jur., Wills, p. 676, sec. 10.42.

62. Estate of Pierce, 1922, 177 Wis. 104, 188 N.W. 78.

63. Annotation 94 A.L.R. 26, 47–51.

64. Ward v. Espy, 1846, 6 Humph. 447, 25 Tenn. 447.

65. Estate of Grove, 1959, 6 Wis.2d 659, 95 N.W.2d 788; Will of Hipsch, 1953, 265 Wis. 446, 62 N.W.2d 18; Estate of Gray, 1953, 265 Wis. 217, 61 N.W.2d 467.

Although the courts subscribe to an inflexible rule against reformation of a will, it seems that they have often strained a point in matters of identification of property or beneficiaries in order to reach a desired result by way of construction. In Will of Stack,[66] where the will devised "Block 64," the court included part of block 175 in the provision to conform to the unexpressed intent of the testator. In Will of Boeck,[67] where the will devised the "northeast quarter of the northwest quarter" of a section, which was not owned by the testator, the court held such provision passed the southeast quarter of the northwest quarter, to conform to the misexpressed intent of the testator. In Moseley v. Goodman,[68] where testator bequeathed property to "Mrs. Moseley," the court denied the claim of Mrs. Lenoir Moseley to the gift and held that Mrs. Trimble had been intended by the testator. Mrs. Trimble was known to the testator by the nickname "Mrs. Moseley."

In Miller's Estate,[69] testator left property to "William Wilson's children." Relying on evidence that testator frequently confused William Wilson with his brother Seth, the court held the gift should go to the children of Seth Wilson, who had been intended by the testator. In Groves v. Culph,[70] testator devised a remainder interest in part of lot 15 to his daughter. The court, to conform to testator's true intent, included part of lot 16 in this devise. In Castell v. Togg,[71] and Geer v. Winds,[72] the testator omitted a child from his will by mistake. The court inserted in the will the gift which had been intended for the child by the parent. In Beaumont v. Feld,[73] a bequest to "Catharine Earnley" was proven to have been intended for Gertrude Yardley, and was given to the latter, and in Masters v. Masters,[74] a gift to "Mrs. Sawyer" was given to Mrs. Swopper, because testator knew no one by the former name. In the two cases last mentioned, no one with the name given in the will claimed the gift.

We are also aware of the rule which allows a court in probating a will to deny probate to a provision in the document which was included by mistake. British courts will deny probate to a single word, or part of a sentence, thereby completely altering the provided dispositions.[75]

We conclude that details of identification, particularly such matters as middle initials, street addresses, and the like, which are highly susceptible to mistake, particularly in metropolitan areas, should not be accorded such sanctity as to frustrate an otherwise clearly demonstrable intent. Where such details of identification are involved, courts should receive evidence tending to show that a mistake has been made and should disregard the details when the proof estab-

66. 1934, 214 Wis. 98, 251 N.W. 470, 92 A.L.R. 150.

67. 1915, 160 Wis. 577, 152 N.W. 155, L.R.A.1915E, 1008.

68. 1917, 138 Tenn. 10, 195 S.W. 590, Ann.Cas.1918C, 931.

69. 1904, 26 Pa.Super. 443.

70. 1892, 132 Ind. 186, 31 N.E. 569.

71. (1836), 163 Eng.Rep. 102.

72. 1810, 4 S.C.Eq., 4 Desaus. 85.

73. (1723), 24 Eng.Rep. 673.

74. (1718), 24 Eng.Rep. 454.

75. 1 Bowe-Parker: Page on Wills (1961 ed.), p. 675, sec. 13.7.

lishes to the highest degree of certainty that a mistake was, in fact, made.

We therefore consider that the county court properly disregarded the middle initial and street address, and determined that respondent was the Robert Krause whom testators had in mind.

Orders affirmed.

BROADFOOT and BROWN, JJ., dissenting.

NOTE

A court, in construing a will, tries to find what the testator meant by his words in the will at the time he signed it.[76] The testator's meaning can be discovered from the context in which the words were used. The context includes the written context in which the words appear and the context extrinsic to the will of which the testator was aware when he signed the instrument.

The written context is examined first.[77] The will and valid codicils thereto are construed together. The testator's intention is sought from the relationship of words of doubtful meaning to words of certain meaning.[78] At this stage of construction, and before the court consciously brings to bear extrinsic evidence to clarify the testator's meaning, ambiguous language may be found. When an ambiguity is apparent from the face of the will, it is usually described as a "patent" ambiguity.

Writers and courts have stated that extrinsic evidence is inadmissible to resolve a patent ambiguity.[79] On the other hand, in almost every case, a court must make a conscious or unconscious inquiry into collateral facts before it can safely decide that there is an ambiguity. When extrinsic evidence is examined to define an ambiguity there seems no reason why more extrinsic evidence should not be examined to clarify the testator's meaning if this evidence can be admitted without, in effect, rewriting the will. Thus, in Doe d. George Gord v. Needs,[80] the will contained (1) a devise to "George Gord, the son of George Gord", (2) a devise to "George Gord, the son of Gord", and (3) a bequest to "George Gord, the son of John Gord." The testator's declarations were admitted to show that by "George Gord, the son of Gord", he meant "George Gord, the son of George Gord". On the other hand, a provi-

76. See Henderson, "Mistake and Fraud in Wills—Part I: A Comparative Analysis of Existing Law", 47 Boston Univ.L.Rev. 303 (1967); Power, "Wills, A Primer of Interpretation and Construction", 51 Iowa L. Rev. 75 (1965). A will speaks from its effective date. This is the date upon which the testator dies. It is presumed that the testator intended at the time the will was executed to describe persons and things existing at his death. But this presumption yields to a contrary expression of intention by the testator. Thus, if the testator describes persons or things specifically, it is presumed that he describes persons or things existing when the will is executed. The operation of these presumptions is important when changes in the beneficiaries or the estate occur after execution of the will.

77. The courts often state that a will is construed from "the four corners of the instrument". The statement is accurate to the extent that it describes one stage in construction. Even if the meaning of the testator seems to be clear from the will, some extrinsic evidence will have to be admitted when the provisions of the will are applied.

78. Each part of the will should be construed in relation to every other part. Every provision should be given some effect if possible. If a provision has more than one possible meaning, the meaning is adopted which is in harmony with the rest of the will.

79. The rule seems to have gotten a foothold in Bacon's Maxim, No. 23.

80. 2 M. & W. 129, 150 Eng.Rep. 698 (1836).

sion may be so uncertain in meaning that the use of extrinsic evidence would be tantamount to rewriting the will. If the courts adhere to their traditional position that a will cannot be reformed for mistake, extrinsic evidence should not be admitted when admitting evidence really requires revision of the will. Thus, the will may contain a blank where the name of the beneficiary is to appear,[81] or the amount of property or the name of a beneficiary may appear in code symbols.[82] But if the descriptive language appearing in the will identifies partially the property or the beneficiary, the modern view, held by a minority of courts, permits the introduction of extrinsic evidence to resolve the ambiguity whether the ambiguity is "patent" or "latent".[83] These courts limit the extrinsic evidence to circumstances surrounding the testator at the time the will was executed and do not admit evidence of the testator's declarations.

At the other extreme from the cases of patent ambiguity lie those cases in which the description in the will is clear and fits precisely property which is in the testator's estate or a beneficiary who is a possible object of the testator's bounty. A majority of courts, unlike the Court in the principal case, have been reluctant to admit evidence to show that testator intended to describe property or a person not precisely meeting the description.[84] The likelihood, however, that either the testator or testatrix meant "Robert J. Krause" as the legatee is approximately zero. Sometimes when the described legatee might be an object of testator's bounty some unusual personal usage can be shown. In Moseley v. Goodman,[85] the testator bequeathed $20,000 to "Mrs. Moseley". A Mrs. Moseley, whose husband knew the testator, claimed the legacy. The court admitted evidence to show that the testator habitually referred to a Mrs. Trimble as "Mrs. Moseley" and that Mrs. Trimble had cared for the testator while he was ill.

Between the extremes of "patent" ambiguity and "accurate description" are the cases in which the description is clear from the written context of the will but is found to be uncertain when applied to extrinsic facts. These ambiguities are described as "latent". The courts agree that extrinsic evidence is admissible to resolve a latent ambiguity but are not in agreement as to the kind of extrinsic evidence that can be admitted in every case.

81. In Hunt v. Hort, 3 Bro.Ch.Cas. 311, 29 Eng.Rep. 554 (1791) the will provided: "My other pictures to become the property of Lady ______." Lady Hort was named an executor. Extrinsic evidence was not admitted to show that "Hort" was the name omitted in the bequest. In Estate of Hubbuck, [1905] P. 129, the testator devised "to my granddaughter ______ all my real and personal property". The testator had three granddaughters. Extrinsic evidence was admitted to show which of the three granddaughters was intended, the court finding that "granddaughter" was a partial description.

82. In Kell v. Charmer, 23 Beav. 195, 53 Eng.Rep. 76 (1856) the will provided: "I give and bequeath to my son William the sum of i.x.x. To my son Charles the sum of o.x.x.". Extrinsic evidence was admitted to show that the testator used the symbols to represent certain sums of money in his business. In Clayton v. Lord Nugent, 13 M. & W. 200, 153 Eng. Rep. 83 (1844) the will contained a devise of land "to L, then to M" and recited that a key would be found on a card. The card was not received in evidence on the ground that the ambiguity was patent.

83. E.g., Payne v. Todd, 45 Ariz. 389, 43 P.2d 1004 (1935), 21 Corn.L.Q. 495 (1936).

84. E.g., In re Root's Will, 187 Pa. 118, 40 A. 818 (1898) (Devise to "my nephew, William Root". T had a blood nephew, William Root, and a nephew by marriage, William Root. The blood nephew took the devise.); Orcutt v. Hoyt, 6 N. J. 46, 77 A.2d 227 (1950) (Bequest of "my large diamond solitaire ring". T had two solitaire rings, one large and one small. Extrinsic evidence was not admitted to show that the smaller of the two rings was the subject of the bequest.)

85. 138 Tenn. 1, 195 S.W. 590, Ann. Cas. 1918C, 931 (1917).

The courts do agree that extrinsic evidence of the circumstances at the time the will was executed and evidence of declarations by the testator concerning his intention are admissible to resolve a latent ambiguity in which the description applies equally well to two or more persons or things.[86] Thus in Nicholl v. Bergner,[87] testatrix named "Edward Bergner" as one of her residuary legatees and there were two Edward Bergners who might be natural objects of her bounty—a brother Edward G. Bergner and a nephew Edward C. Bergner. Ambiguities of this nature are usually described as "equivocations" and this is the only case in which courts seem inclined to admit evidence of "direct" declarations of intent by the testatrix. The court held that an "indirect" declaration by testatrix: "* * * [he] won't like it"—"brother Ed. Bergner won't like the will," should have been admitted by the trial court in an effort to resolve the ambiguity.[88]

When the description applies in part to one person or thing and in part to another person or thing but describes neither in full, most of the courts will admit evidence of the surrounding circumstances to resolve the ambiguity but will not admit evidence of the testator's declarations.[89] Evidence of the testator's declarations is admitted by the modern view, and this view is said to be the better of the two.[90] Thus, in Bond v. Riley,[91] there was a bequest to "my grandson, William N. Bond". The testator had two grandsons. One, Boyd C. Bond, was the son of William N. Bond. The other, William H. Bond, was the son of John C. Bond. Extrinsic evidence, including testimony by the scrivener concerning the testator's declarations, was admitted to show that the testator intended Boyd C. Bond as the beneficiary.

A third type of latent ambiguity is that in which a description of a person or thing applies with reasonable certainty in part but is erroneous in part. When the erroneous part of the description is ignored, the part of the description that remains may apply with certainty to a person or thing; or that part of the description that remains may be ambiguous, but may be an ambiguity of a type that can be resolved by extrinsic evidence. When part of the description is certain, or can be made certain by the admission of extrinsic evidence, the courts are agreed that the erroneous part of the descrip-

86. See Wigmore, Evidence (3d Ed., 1940) §§ 2471, 2472. A distinction is made between declarations of the testator that are indicative of his relations with persons or things and his declarations dealing with the contents of the will. The latter are not admitted if they compete with or overthrow the written words. If the declarations merely expand or make certain the words of the will, the declarations are admitted.

87. 76 Ohio App. 245, 63 N.E.2d 828 (1945).

88. The Court nevertheless sustained a decree by the lower Court in favor of "brother" Edward Bergner based on other evidence. The Court quoted Chief Justice Fuller in Coulam v. Doull, 133 U.S. 216, 10 S.Ct. 253, 33 L.Ed. 596 (1890) as follows: "2. Where a devise is, on the face of it, clear and intelligible, yet from extrinsic circumstances an ambiguity arises as to which of two or more things or persons the testator referred to, it being legally certain he intended one or the other, evidence of his declarations, of the instructions given for his will, and of the other circumstances of the like nature, is admissible to determine his intention". (63 N.E.2d at 829)

In Scheridan v. Scheridan, 132 Ga.App. 210, 207 S.E.2d 691 (1974), testator left his entire estate to "Boyd E. Scheridan". Both a stepson and the latter's son were known by that name, and each claimed the property. The Georgia Court of Appeals held that the trial court should have admitted evidence of statements of the testator regarding his relationship with the stepson and statements that the testator intended to "take care of" the stepson's son and had told him to remember what his "true legal name" was after the testator died. Only the name on the birth certificate of the stepson's son corresponded with the name used in the will.

89. E.g., Doe d. Hiscocks v. Hiscocks, 5 M. & W. 363, 151 Eng.Rep. 154 (1839).

90. See Wigmore, Evidence (3d Ed., 1940) § 2474.

91. 317 Mo. 594, 296 S.W. 401 (1927).

tion may be ignored.[92] For example, in Farrell v. Sullivan,[93] the testator made a devise and bequest to Arlene Dwyer, the daughter of James H. Dwyer of Cumberland, and gave one-third of his residuary estate to William Cronin of Pawtucket in trust for his son, Daniel Cronin. James H. Dwyer had no daughter named Arlene but did have a daughter named Helene. William Cronin had no son named Daniel but did have a son named William. The false part of the description was ignored and extrinsic evidence was admitted to show that the testator intended Helene and William as his beneficiaries.

The doctrine has been applied in cases involving misdescription of land. The principal difficulty encountered in these cases is whether the description left after the erroneous portion is ignored can be made certain by extrinsic evidence. The presence of the word "my" in the misdescription, or an expression by the testator that he intends to dispose of all of his estate, is often relied upon in determining that the part of the description remaining is sufficiently definite to be clarified by extrinsic evidence. In Holmes v. Roddy,[94] the will contained language indicating that the testator intended to dispose of all of his estate and contained a devise of "the property known as 3608 Third Avenue". From an examination of the will, the court decided that the testator meant 3608 Third Avenue in Chattanooga, Tennessee. It was discovered, however, that the testator did not own 3608 Third Avenue but did own 3607. The court ignored the false description and admitted evidence to show that the testator intended to devise 3607 rather than 3608.

When the word "my" or words indicating an intent to dispose of the entire estate are lacking, many courts have refused to read these words into the will. In Kurtz v. Hibner,[95] the testator devised to his daughter land in the town of Joliet, Will County, Illinois, described as follows: "the west half of the south-west quarter, section 32, township 35, range 10, containing eighty acres, more or less". The testator owned an eighty acre tract in section 33 but no land in section 32. It was contended that the section number was inserted as a drafting error. It was held that the description was unambiguous and extrinsic evidence of the testator's intention could not be admitted to show the section in which he owned land.[96] A substantial minority of courts apply a presumption against partial intestacy and presume that the testator intends to will property that he owns. These courts admit extrinsic evidence to complete a partial description when the erroneous portion has been deleted.[97] This position is taken even though the description does not contain the word "my" or language indicating that the testator intended to dispose of all of his property.

When a description in a will is meaningless, or when no property or beneficiary fits a description, the gift fails and the property passes by the residuary clause in the will or by intestacy.[98]

92. The doctrine applied is called "falsa demonstratio non nocet".

93. 49 R.I. 468, 144 A. 155 (1929), 38 Yale L.J. 999 (1929).

94. 176 Tenn. 624, 144 S.W.2d 788 (1940); 16 A.L.R.3d 386 (1967).

95. 55 Ill. 514, 8 Am.Rep. 665 (1870).

96. See Wigmore, Evidence (3d Ed., 1940) § 2476.

97. See Wiechert v. Wiechert, 317 Mo. 118, 294 S.W. 721 (1927) (T referred to "all" my land).

98. When a testator describes a nonexistent charity as beneficiary of a charitable trust, a court may apply the *cy pres* power and designate another charity as beneficiary. E.g., In re Tarrant's Estate, 38 Cal.2d 42, 237 P.2d 505 (1951).

In several states there are statutes which provide for the correction of misnomers and misdescriptions in wills.[99] These statutes apply whether the ambiguity is latent or patent.

By the prevailing view, there is no remedy at probate for a mistake of law or a mistake as to the legal effect of language used in a will even though the mistake was unintentionally induced by another.[1] Likewise, there is little opportunity for remedying a mistake of law when the will is construed. If the testatrix gives her property to her heirs at law, thinking that "heirs at law" means her first cousins, when under the applicable statute her aunt is her heir at law, the aunt rather than the cousins takes the property.[2] It has been indicated in an earlier chapter that some mistakes of law in revoking a will are remedied on construction by application of the doctrine of dependent relative revocation.[3]

In England, after a five year study, the Law Reform Committee in 1973 proposed legislation to empower the court to correct mistakes in wills, with a high standard of proof and liberal rules on admissibility of evidence;[4] the Committee recommended that correction ("equitable doctrine of rectification") be available "wherever it can be clearly shown not only that the will does not contain the wording intended by the testator but also what the substance of that wording was."[5] On the interpretation process, the Committee advocated a less rigid approach to establishing special meaning of words and resolving ambiguity, whether latent or apparent on the face of the will; however, the Committee members divided on the issue of admitting direct statements of the testator to establish the meaning of words used in the will. No action has been taken in England on the 1973 report; legislation has been adopted in Ireland.[6]

In recent years some courts have adopted a more liberal approach in admitting extrinsic evidence (including occasionally testimony of the lawyer who drafted the will) to arrive at testator's real intent.[7] The court may admit the evidence to create an "ambiguity" which does not appear by the wording of the will alone and then under the guise of construction resolve the ambiguity in favor of the intent shown by the extrinsic evidence. In dealing with contingencies not specifically covered by the wording of a will,[8]

99. E.g., Ga.Code Ann. § 113–807.

1. E.g., Leonard v. Stanton, 93 N.H. 113, 36 A.2d 271 (1944); 43 Mich.L.Rev. 209 (1944). As to the effect of a fraudulently induced "mistake" of law, see Reed v. Hollister, 44 Cal.App. 533, 186 P. 819 (1919); Lyon v. Dada, 111 Mich. 340, 69 N.W. 654 (1896).

2. Mahoney v. Grainger, 283 Mass. 189, 186 N.E. 86 (1933); 19 Corn.L.Q. 154 (1933).

3. See Chapter VI, Section 4(4).

4. Law Reform Committee, Nineteenth Report (Interpretation of Wills), 1973. For criticism of the present English rules see Lee, "Correcting Testator's Mistakes", 33 Conv.(N.S.) 322 (1969); Poole, "Obscurities in Wills: Some Proposals for a New Approach", 34 Conv.(N.S.) 268 (1970).

5. Id. at p. 23.

6. Irish Succession Act § 90: "Extrinsic evidence shall be admissible to show the intention of the testator and to assist in the construction of, or to explain any contradiction in, a will."

7. For discussion of the modern trends see Smith, "The Admissibility of Extrinsic Evidence in Will Interpretation Cases," 64 Mass. L. Rev. 123 (1979); Stark, "Extrinsic Evidence and the Meaning of Wills in Texas," 31 Sw. L.J. 793 (1977); Comment, "Extrinsic Evidence and the Construction of Wills in California," 50 Cal. L. Rev. 283 (1962); Comment, "Judicial Treatment of Ambiguous, Mistaken, and Uncertain Testamentary Dispositions: An Analysis of Iowa Cases," 24 Drake L. Rev. 409 (1975).

8. In Chapter XV, Section 3, we shall explore the extent to which a court will construe wording of a will to imply a gift in circumstances not expressly provided for to persons named as devisees in other circumstances, but this is done in order to fill a gap in the wording of the will.

the New Jersey Supreme Court has refused to confine its inquiry to the intent expressed by the written instrument and has instead announced a rule of "probable intent" arrived at by consideration of extrinsic evidence. In Engle v. Siegel, 74 N.J. 287, 377 A.2d 892 (1977)[9] a husband and wife had similar wills. In each a common disaster clause divided the residuary estate between the husband's mother and the wife's mother. The husband's mother predeceased her son and daughter-in-law by six years. Under New Jersey statute the residue would pass to the other residuary devisee (the wife's mother) "unless a contrary intention shall appear by the will". The court nevertheless considered testimony of the lawyer who drafted the will, that the couple wanted their property divided between their two families in the event of a common disaster; the court then concluded that half the property should go to the husband's brother and sister in place of the mother. The dissenting judge accused the majority of "rewriting" the will.

In inter vivos transactions, courts freely reform gratuitous transfers on the basis of unilateral mistake by the transferor.[10] Thus a court will even supply an omission in an inter vivos trust instrument,[11] which as we shall see in Chapter VIII is often used as a will substitute. Apparently the absence of the Statute of Wills opens the door to extrinsic evidence even though the same policy objections (prevention of fraud and perjured testimony) are present when the transferor is dead at the time of the reformation.

PROBLEMS

1. Testatrix had two cousins. One, John Carroll Monmonier, was a great, great grandson of his common ancestor with testatrix. The other, Jay Carroll Monmonier, was a great grandson of his common ancestor with testatrix (her second cousin). John works for the B & O Railroad and resides on Birch Drive in Woodlawn. Jay resides on Beechwood Avenue in Catonsville. Testatrix thought both were named "John Carroll Monmonier", both using the first initial "J" and being called "Carroll". The relevant provisions of testatrix' will are as follows:

   a. In Paragraph 2(a) she devises a remainder interest in her home property at Hydes with the furniture contained therein "to my second cousin, John Carroll Monmonier, presently residing on Beech Avenue, Catonsville, Maryland, to have and to hold as his property absolutely".

   b. In Paragraph 3, she devises her "school house" property to "my distant cousin, John Carroll Monmonier (who is presently working for the Baltimore and Ohio Railroad)" in trust for his son, Mark.

   c. In Paragraph 4, testatrix bequeaths $2,000 "to my cousin, John Carroll Monmonier".

Jay Carroll Monmonier claims the devise in Paragraph 2(a). John Carroll Monmonier seeks to introduce evidence by the scrivener that testatrix had

In a sense it is "writing" part of the will, but not "rewriting" it.

9. Noted, 9 Set. Hall L. Rev. 359 (1978).

10. Compare IV Palmer, The Law of Restitution (1978) § 20.1—Mistake in Testamentary Disposition with Chapter 18—Mistake in Inter Vivos Gift Transactions, particularly § 18.5(a) and § 18.9.

11. In Heritage Bank-North v. Hunterdon Medical Center, 164 N.J. Super. 33, 395 A.2d 552 (1978), the entire clause designating charitable remaindermen in a living trust was omitted by a clerical error in the final typing. The trial court allowed reformation to insert the clause, and no appeal was taken on this issue; however, the appellate court in its opinion indicated the reformation was proper.

never mentioned any male Monmonier other than Mark and John Carroll. Should this evidence be admitted for what light it might shed upon testatrix' intention? See Monmonier v. Monmonier, 258 Md. 387, 266 A.2d 17 (1970). Would you admit evidence to show that Jay was the intended legatee in Paragraph 4?

2. Testatrix by her will made a bequest to "The Illinois Industrial Home for the Blind (commonly called Lighthouse for the Blind) 1900 Marshall Boulevard, Chicago 23, Illinois". The testatrix really intended the bequest for The Chicago Lighthouse for the Blind, but the designation of The Illinois Industrial Home for the Blind accurately describes a legal entity and was inserted by the draftsman as a result of a mistake by his secretary in obtaining the "correct" name. Is extrinsic evidence admissible to show which organization was intended? Hays v. Illinois Industrial Home for the Blind, 12 Ill.2d 625, 147 N.E.2d 287 (1958).

3. In 1912, testator made bequests of $10,000 each to Gertrude Byerly and to Julia Byerly, his nieces. Prior to this year, Gertrude had a child which died. In 1916, Gertrude and Julia were living together in Springfield. Julia was married and had one child living. The testator visited Gertrude and Julia in Springfield and thereafter executed a codicil in which he reduced the bequests to the sisters to life estates and gave the remainder to "the child of Gertrude Byerly". Does the child of Julia Byerly take the remainder interest? Borah v. Lincoln Hospital Association, 153 Neb. 846, 46 N.W.2d 166 (1951); 49 Mich.L.Rev. 1262 (1951).

4. Testator executed a will in which he provided in part as follows: "* * * And touching my worldly estate * * * I give, devise and dispose of the same in the following manner and form. * * * I bequeath and give to my dearly beloved brother, Henry Walker, forever, lot numbered six, in square four hundred and three, together with the improvements thereon erected * * *." The testator devised other property and expressed his belief that all of his property was disposed of with the exception of certain lots which he gave to his infant son. The testator did not own lot 6 in square 403 but did own lot 3 in square 406 which was not specifically devised in the will. Should evidence be admitted to show that Walker was to take lot 3 in square 406? Patch v. White, 117 U.S. 210, 6 S.Ct. 617, 29 L.Ed. 860 (1886).

5. The testator's will contained a provision giving to his estranged wife the share of his estate "which she would receive under the law if I died intestate". The residue of the estate was given to the testator's three sisters. No children survived the testator. Under the local intestate law, the surviving spouse takes the entire estate if there are no children. If the surviving spouse elects against the will of her husband, she takes dower and homestead. The draftsman of the will offers evidence of a conversation with the testator in which the testator expressed a desire that the wife take the share which she would take if she elected against the will (dower and homestead) and not the share which she would take if he died intestate without children (all). Does the surviving spouse take all of the estate or only dower and homestead? In re Gray's Estate, 265 Wis. 217, 61 N.W.2d 467 (1953).

Chapter VIII

THE PRIVATE EXPRESS TRUST

Scope Note

In this chapter we examine problems relating to the creation of private express trusts. Why are these trusts frequently a part of plans for the disposition of wealth? What provisions of the tax laws encourage or discourage the creation of particular kinds of express trusts? What are the legal limitations on the purposes for which private express trusts may be created? What are the essential elements of these trusts? What are the legal effects, if any, of the absence of one or more of these elements? How much control over these trusts can be retained by the settlors? In focusing on these questions the opportunity is provided to emphasize the role of the lawyer as draftsman of private express trusts and his role as advocate in litigation in which the issue is whether or not a valid express trust was created.

SECTION 1. TERMINOLOGY AND FUNCTION OF THE MODERN PRIVATE TRUST

The express trust is one of the most useful tools available to the attorney responsible for arranging a suitable disposition of the client's wealth in accordance with the owner's desires. It is the relationship under which one person, called the "trustee", holds legal title to property for the benefit of one or more other persons, each called the "beneficiary" or "cestui que trust". The person creating the trust is called the "settlor" (sometimes the "donor", "trustor" or "creator"). The property held by the trustee is variously referred to as the "corpus", the "subject matter of the trust", the "trust property", the "principal" or the "res". The terms of the trust are spelled out by the creating instrument, which may be a "declaration of trust", a "trust deed" or "trust agreement", or a will. Trusts created by will are "testamentary" trusts. Trusts created by the settlor during his lifetime are called "inter vivos" or "living" trusts.

Since the trustee holds property for the benefit of another, the relationship between the trustee and the beneficiary is said to be "fiduciary". The courts frequently apply this term to transactions in which one party is permitted to exercise extensive control over some or all of the affairs of another. The term is a warning by the court that the person who controls will be held to a high standard of loyalty to the person whose affairs are controlled. Among the relationships described as fiduciary (principal-agent, attorney-client, partners, etc.), the duty of loyalty owed by the trustee to a beneficiary is of the highest degree.

The trust has been treated in almost all states as a property concept. Historically the remedies of the beneficiary for enforcement of the trust terms are in equity.[1] The trustee has legal title to the trust property and each beneficiary is said to have an equitable interest. These property concepts prevail even when the trust is created pursuant to an agreement between the settlor and trustee. There are important procedural consequences.

Suppose a settlor and a trustee both execute a document called a "Trust Agreement," by which the settlor transfers or agrees to transfer certain property to the trustee and the trustee in turn agrees to hold the property according to stated trust terms, and property is either transferred by this document or by concurrent or subsequent methods of transfer. Unless the settlor is also a beneficiary of the trust, or reserves a power to revoke, he has no standing to enforce the trust. Only the beneficiaries can sue to enforce the trust, and their suit is on the theory that they are the beneficial owners of the trust property; they do not sue in contract. Moreover, their suit is in equity. They have a variety of remedies, as we shall see in some detail later when we take up administration problems in Chapter XVII. They can, of course, sue to enforce the trust; they can sue to remove the trustee or to hold him responsible for losses caused by breach of trust or for profits improperly gained by him by reason of his office as trustee; they can sue to get an accounting for his handling of the trust. Because of the equity jurisdiction, the trustee can also turn to the court. He may petition the court for instructions (a type of declaratory relief afforded by equity for many centuries), or for permission to resign his office and have a successor appointed; he may ask the court to approve judicially his accounts, thus adjudicating any issue of responsibility on his part for performance of his duties.

For some understanding of why trusts are created, let us consider a typical trust limitation: settlor by his will leaves certain specified property to a named trustee in trust to pay the income to the settlor's wife for her life, and directs that at her death the trust terminate and the property be transferred to his descendants then living. Why should he utilize the trust rather than make a gift outright to his wife in fee or a gift to her of a legal life estate with a legal remainder in the descendants? One obvious reason is that by carefully selecting the trustee the settlor can provide expert management of the proper-

1. The history of the express trust is considered in Chapter I, Section 3(1)A. Statutory substitutes for the trust have been adopted in Louisiana and in several civil law countries. See LSA–R.S. 9:1731 (1965) et seq. A judicial development similar to the trust in Anglo-American law took place in the Islamic legal system. There the "waghf" is used in much the same fashion as a charitable trust is used in the United States. Some Islamic states have extended the application of the "waghf" by statute to permit the creation of what is essentially a private express trust. E.g., Iranian Civil Code, Ch. 2.

ty, relieving the wife as beneficiary from the duties and responsibilities of management, and at the same time assuring that the property will not be dissipated with little or no inheritance left for the children. Secondly, if you will recall the cumbersome nature of the legal life estate, and the difficulties which arise if a sale of the property becomes necessary, you can appreciate the advantage of having legal title in one person who can, if the settlor so desires, be empowered to sell, with the proceeds being reinvested in other property. The trustee thus is free to change the property which is the subject of the trust, by buying and selling; if the trust consists of securities, such freedom is indispensable in most instances. The modern trustee is therefore a manager and investor. The property placed in trust varies widely: it may be real property, it may be cash, it may be securities, it may be a business interest.

The settlor should confer upon the trustee powers which are broad enough to enable him to handle this property. If you will examine the trust document set forth in Appendix 1 you will see the scope of the trustee's functions, duties and powers as a modern trust instrument is likely to describe them. Since the settlor can specify the duties of the trustee, he can accomplish any special desires he may have with regard to the property placed in trust. For example, if he owns certain real estate which he believes to be a fine long-run investment and which he does not want his family to sell after his death, he can direct the trustee to retain this property rather than empowering him to sell.

Had the property been given to the wife outright, there is the danger that the wife may dissipate the capital fund either through unwise investment or through improvident expenditure. In addition there is the possibility of remarriage, with a second husband not only helping her to spend the funds but also exerting influence (not undue!) to have the wife transfer the wealth to him either during lifetime or at death. The trust therefore serves to "conserv " wealth for the ultimate takers. Moroever, if the owner had chosen to give his property to his wife outright, although it would in normal succession pass to the children, there would be the cost and delay involved in the probate and administration of her estate. If the property is placed in a trust to terminate at the death of the wife, the trustee will pay the principal over to the children directly. The trust is therefore a device to simplify transfer of property from one generation to another.

In addition, the law affords us ample opportunity through careful draftsmanship to keep the trust flexible to meet changing conditions in the future. It will be part of our purpose to explore some of these devices in later chapters. But we should note here that we can confer on the trustee power to make decisions "in his discretion" which the original owner would make if he were still alive. Thus the settlor may feel that the probable income will exceed the needs of the wife; he can empower the trustee to determine the amount needed by her and distribute the excess income to the children, or he can direct accumulation of income. The settlor may be concerned about future emergencies, such as illness, which may create unusual needs beyond current income; he can authorize the trustee to "invade" the principal or corpus of the trust for the benefit of the wife. He can even, if he wishes, direct the trustee to pay portions of the principal to the wife if she makes written demand (so that the real power is in the wife rather than the trustee). In short, the form and content of the trust can be tailored to meet individual family needs.

Since the trust takes management control away from the beneficial owners, it is a protective device by its very nature. But if the beneficiaries can sell their equitable interests, or encumber them by going into debt, the protection is incomplete. We shall see that settlors may try to provide against such loss by inserting additional "protective" or "spendthrift" provisions. Such trusts are often called spendthrift trusts. In Section 5 we shall explore these provisions, which assume a variety of forms, and determine the degree to which they are effective in insulating the beneficiary's interest from his creditors and his own voluntary attempts to convey.

When the trust is created during the settlor's lifetime (a "living" trust), the settlor may expressly retain a power to revoke the trust and take the property back. Such a trust is called a "revocable" trust in contrast to an "irrevocable" trust. The effectiveness of such a trust and the special purposes sought to be accomplished thereby are considered in Section 6 of this Chapter. The power of a settlor to recover the trust property where he has failed to retain such a power of revocation expressly is considered in Chapter X, Termination. In fact, full appreciation of the trust device is gained only after study of that chapter and the circumstances under which the settlor and the beneficiaries can terminate the trust before the time specified in the creating instrument.

The trust which we have been discussing has private individuals as beneficiaries and for this reason is called a "private" express trust. The settlor may create an express trust for a purpose beneficial to the community as a whole, such as a trust to provide scholarships for needy students. This would be a "charitable" trust. Sometimes a settlor may attempt to achieve a purely private objective but without benefit to specified persons, such as a trust to maintain a grave or to care for a pet animal; such trusts are called "honorary" and pose special problems.

All of these are express trusts, that is, trusts which the property owner intentionally creates. There are, however, a variety of situations in which a court raises a trust "by operation of law". Such a trust may be either (1) a resulting trust or (2) a constructive trust. The resulting trust is brought into operation by the court to give effect to what the court presumes is the intention implicit in the transaction. Resulting trusts arise in the following types of transactions:

1.

S conveys property in fee to T in trust for B for life and fails to dispose of the beneficial interest after B's death. A court will presume that S did not intend T to keep the property but that T was to hold the property after B's death for S or his successors in interest. This is a resulting trust arising from failure to make a complete disposition of the equitable interests under an express trust.

2.

S transfers property to T upon terms of an express trust which fails for any of the reasons set forth in this course. The court will return the property to the settlor by imposing a resulting trust.

3.

S purchases property and takes title in the name of X, who pays no consideration and is not so related to S that a gift can be presumed under the circumstances. In many jurisdictions the court will raise what is known as a "purchase money resulting trust", based on the assumption that S intended X to hold for S's benefit. In some jurisdictions this type of resulting trust has been abolished by statute. Since the purchase money resulting trust is based on inferred intent, it is closely akin to the express trust; and we shall explore it briefly as one of the "informal" trust transactions in Section 1(3) of the next chapter.

In contrast to the resulting trust, based on presumed intent, is the constructive trust. This is purely a procedural device imposed by a court on equitable grounds in a wide variety of situations where the court concludes that it is unfair to permit the present owner of property to retain it. For example, we have already seen that some courts utilize this approach to keep the heir who has murdered an ancestor from profiting by his wrongful act.[2] In these cases no one intends a trust, and the court makes the holder of the legal title "trustee" for the benefit of the "rightful" owner solely to prevent unjust enrichment.

In both the resulting and constructive trust situations, the effect of characterizing the legal owner as trustee is to force him to convey legal title to the beneficiary.

SECTION 2. TAX FACTORS IN THE CREATION OF PRIVATE TRUSTS

While trusts are created for many non-tax reasons, Federal and state tax structures have made the creation of certain types of trusts

2. See Chapter III, Section 4(4)A.

of interest to persons with wealth. To understand the relationship of trusts to taxation, rudiments of the tax structure should be examined. This section does not pretend to deal with the details of taxation or estate planning.[3]

---

(1) GIFT AND DEATH (ESTATE AND INHERITANCE) TAXES

Gift, estate and inheritance taxes are imposed upon the transfer of property. Gift and estate taxes are upon the privilege of transferring property. Inheritance taxes are upon the privilege of taking property by transfer. The Federal taxes pertaining to these transfers are gift and estate taxes, although the Federal Government has levied inheritance taxes in the past.[4] All of the states except Nevada have some form of death transfer tax. In most of the states the basic death transfer tax is an inheritance tax. This tax is determined on the basis of the value of the share received. The rate may be based upon the closeness of relationship by the recipient to the decedent. The closer the relationship, the lower the tax rate will be. States having an inheritance tax may combine this tax with an estate tax to use up the credit for state death taxes provided in the Federal estate tax law.[5] Other states have a death transfer tax similar to the

3. The purpose of this Section is only to alert you to some of the tax purposes for which trusts are created rather than to train you in taxation. For a detailed treatment of tax problems you must take the appropriate tax courses and refer to current comprehensive treatises and continuing legal education publications. Tax policy is now in a state of great flux and tax law changes should be anticipated in formulating any estate plan or in the creation of any trust. Among other excellent current references containing an emphasis upon the use of trusts, 4 Powell, The Law of Real Property (Rohan Rev. 1978) pp. 523–530 is regularly supplemented. Farr and Wright, Estate Planner's Handbook (4th Ed., 1979) is updated through the Tax Reform Act of 1976 and no doubt will be revised to reflect the changes by the Economic Recovery Tax Act of 1981 (ERTA). The various current tax services are essential references in this rapidly changing field.

4. There was a duty on receipts for legacies and probates of wills imposed in 1797. In 1862 an inheritance tax was imposed by the Federal Government upon succession to personal property in excess of $1,000. 12 Stat. 485 (1862). The tax was extended to real estate in 1864. 13 Stat. 286, 388–89 (1864). The inheritance tax was repealed in 1870. 16 Stat. 256, 257. In 1894 personal property taken by gift or inheritance was taxed as income. 28 Stat. 509 (1894). The 1894 law was declared unconstitutional in 1895. Pollock v. Farmers' Loan and Trust Co., 157 U.S. 429, 15 S.Ct. 673, 39 L.Ed. 759 (1895). In 1898 a tax was enacted which combined inheritance and estate tax features but this tax was repealed in 1902. 30 Stat. 448; 32 Stat. 96. The present Estate Tax Law was enacted in 1916. 39 Stat. 756, 777 (1916).

5. IRC § 2011, 26 U.S.C.A. The credit is computed based upon the adjusted taxable estate. This is the taxable estate reduced by $60,000. The credit gradually increases, starting with 8/10th of 1% of the amount by which the adjusted taxable estate exceeds $40,000 and moving to a maximum of $1,082,800 plus 16% of the excess over $10,040,000. The state death tax must be paid in order to obtain the credit. The system and rates for computing the credit were not changed by the Economic Recovery Tax Act of 1981. See fn. 28, page 427, infra.

Federal tax; and a few have a death transfer tax designed only to use up the Federal state death tax credit. While there is a trend towards conforming state death taxes to the Federal pattern, there remain many local differences among the states.

In planning an estate (and before establishing a trust) a lawyer should determine which state gift and death taxes apply or are likely to apply to his client's proposed transactions and take these state laws into account in advising his client before a decision is made. State gift and death transfer taxes are likely to become of increased importance. A number of states do not allow a 100% marital deduction for interspousal transfers as does the Economic Recovery Tax Act of 1981 (ERTA).[6] In structuring trusts to take advantage of the Federal tax free interspousal transfers permitted after 31 December 1981, the differences in treatment of these transfers under applicable state laws should be considered. Much wealth also will escape Federal gift and estate taxation in 1982 and thereafter. While the future of Federal gift and estate taxation cannot be predicted, and it is possible that Federal tax rates in the future might be increased and deductions and credits decreased if Federal revenue requirements cannot be satisfied without these changes, it appears that, through 1987 at least, a revenue source of increasing magnitude will become available to the states.[7] At a time when state expenditures are becoming more burdensome, as Federal expenditures for many local purposes are being reduced, state gift and death transfer rates may go up and states may experiment with new techniques for taxing wealth transfers.

The Federal gift and estate tax laws have been developed to a great extent in response to judicial decisions favorable to taxpayers. There also has been great flux in Congressional policies concerning these laws. Shifting social and economic concerns often have dominated the need for revenue. Thus the gift and estate tax amendments of the Internal Revenue Code in the Economic Recovery Tax Act of 1981 (ERTA)[8] reflect the desire of Congress to increase the formation of private capital with the expectation that the increase of private capital will stimulate the economy. But ERTA does not contain the last changes in these laws that we will see. Possible future changes range from abolition of the gift and estate taxes to an increase in rates and reduction in deductions and credits if the revenue requirements of the Federal Government increase. Using one or more trusts in an estate plan assists us in dealing with these uncertainties. The settlor can confer power upon a trustee to make deci-

6. P.L. 97–34 (1981). This Act amends the Internal Revenue Code of 1954, 26 U.S.C.A. The Code hereafter will be abbreviated as IRC.

7. If the need for Federal revenue increases or proves to have been underestimated, there is a chance that the rate reductions and unified credit increases may be changed or delayed. Prior to 1916 the taxation of death transfers was regarded by state officials as an exclusive state revenue source and the repeated Federal dipping into this revenue during emergencies was viewed unsympathetically. By 1916 when the first Federal tax exclusively of an "estate" character was adopted, state resistance had much diminished perhaps because easy evasion of the state taxes had made them a less desirable source of revenue. Ratner, American Taxation (1942) 354–55.

8. P.L. 97–34 (1981) §§ 401–422.

sions to deal with changing tax policies. With a revocable trust, as with a will during the lifetime of the testator, an estate plan can be abandoned and a new plan established to deal with tax changes. Usually, but not always, it is desirable to defer determination and payment of estate and gift taxes when this can be done. A trustee can observe the situation after the death of the settlor and make the necessary decisions to defer determination and payment of the tax when empowered to do this.

For transfers after 31 December 1976, Federal gift and estate taxes are imposed under a unified schedule with a unified credit for the transferor or his estate. The final tax computation is made based on the gross estate of the decedent with taxable gifts cumulated to increase the rate on later gifts and on the estate. Part of the unified credit is used to cover the taxable part of any gift. Any gift tax is then subtracted in the final computation of the estate. The unified rate and unified credit were introduced in the Tax Reform Act of 1976.[9] The Tax Reform Act shifted the emphasis from concern with when the transfer to be taxed was made to how much was transferred in taxable transactions by the transferor. While the taxes, since 1976, are under a unified schedule with a unified credit, and the taxes have a number of parallel provisions, each tax is imposed separately and each has its distinct features, the basic principles for the imposition of both taxes having been established in the years preceding 1976.

The "gross estate" is the figure with which the estate tax computation begins. The gross estate may, and usually does, include more than simply transfers at death. When enacted in 1916[10], the Federal estate tax was imposed upon property subject to administration (usually called "probate property"), upon joint tenancy and tenancy by the entirety property, upon property transferred in contemplation of death within two years of death, and upon transfers intended to take effect in possession or enjoyment after death. Thereafter the gross estate was expanded to embrace certain life insurance,[11] certain general powers of appointment,[12] revocable transfers,[13] and, much later, certain annuities.[14]

9. P.L 94–455 (1976), 90 Stat. 1520.

10. 39 Stat. 756, 777 (1916).

11. Insurance proceeds were first taxed when payable to the estate. Revenue Act of 1918, § 402(f), 40 Stat. 1057, 1098. The "incidents of ownership test" was introduced in statutory form in the Revenue Act of 1942, § 404, 56 Stat. 798, 944. Insurance presently is covered by IRC, § 2042, 26 U.S.C.A.

12. The first Congressional effort to deal with the taxation of powers was in the Revenue Act of 1918 § 402(e), 40 Stat. 1057, 1097; but no comprehensive coverage of powers as attempted until the Revenue Act of 1942 § 403, 56 Stat. 798, 942. The current provisions in IRC §§ 2041, 2514, 26 U.S.C.A are as enacted in the Powers of Appointment Act of 1951, 65 Stat. 91.

13. Revenue Act of 1924 § 302(d), 43 Stat. 253, 304. The present provision is IRC § 2038, 26 U.S.C.A.

14. There was no section specifically applicable to annuities until 1954. Until that time some annuities might be taxable under the "generic section", IRC § 2033, 26 U.S.C.A. Present § 2039 applicable to annuities was enacted as part of the Revenue Code of 1954, 68A Stat. 384.

The gift tax law, enacted in much its present form in 1932,[15] was intended to supplement the estate and income tax laws. Inter vivos transfers to decrease the estate left at death were to be discouraged by taxing them. To be discouraged also were efforts to divide income producing property among a number of trusts, each taxed as an entity, thus reducing the overall tax on the income which the divided property produced. The administration of the gift tax law was attended by many difficulties. The law was fragmentary, having been hurriedly drafted and passed. Inter vivos gifts could be made secretly, making the tax difficult to collect. Moreover, Congress had imposed the gift tax at a rate 1/4 less than the estate tax, allowing also a $50,000 lifetime exemption[16] and a $5,000 per donee per annum exclusion,[17] and later permitting a gift to be split between husband and wife so that $6,000 per donee per annum could be given.[18] A charitable deduction of 100% was allowed and later also a marital deduction of 50% of the value of property transferred to the spouse.[19] Taxable gifts cumulated to increase the tax on subsequent taxable gifts; and would be brought within the estate if made in contemplation of death within the quarantine period.[20] But if the taxpayer was willing to make gifts, it made much sense from a tax point of view to transfer property to members of one's family at a rate 1/4 less than the estate tax. Taking advantage of the major latitude provided by the Congress for tax free gifts, taxpayers experimented with retained life estates, express and de facto, and retained powers considered less than powers of revocation. After litigation pertaining to these trans-

15. A gift tax law was enacted in 1924 but was repealed in 1926. See 43 Stat. 253, 313–16 (1924); 44 Stat. 2015 (1926). The gift tax law in much its present form was enacted as §§ 501–532 of the Revenue Act of 1932, 47 Stat. 169, 245–257. See Turnier, "The Role of Gift Giving in Estate Planning" 59 N.C.L.Rev. 377 (1981) for a thoughtful consideration of gift transfers under the Tax Reform Act of 1976, almost all of the author's observations being pertinent to transfers under the Economic Recovery Tax Act of 1981.

16. 47 Stat. 247, § 505(a)(1). The exemption was reduced to $40,000 commencing in 1939, 53 Stat. 147, § 1004(a)(1) and then to $30,000 commencing in 1943, 56 Stat. 953, § 455 where it remained until superseded by the unified credit in 1976, P.L. 94–455 § 2001(a)(2), (d)(1), (b)(2), (d)(2), currently IRC §§ 2010, 2505 as amended P.L. 97–34 § 401(a)(b).

17. From 1939 to 1942 the exclusion was reduced to $4,000, 53 Stat. 146, § 1003(b)(2) and commencing in 1943 was reduced to $3,000, 56 Stat. 953, § 454 where it remained until increased to $10,000 in the Economic Recovery Tax Act of 1981, P.L. 97–34 § 441(a). The current section is IRC § 2503(a). An unlimited exclusion was granted in 1981 for transfers for certain educational and medical expenses. P.L. 97–34 § 441(b). The new provision appears as IRC § 2503(e), 26 U.S.C.A.

18. Revenue Act of 1948, § 374, 62 Stat. 127.

19. Revenue Act of 1948, § 372, 62 Stat. 125.

20. In the 1916 estate tax law a two year contemplation of death period was established, the presumption that the transfer was in contemplation of death being rebuttable. 39 Stat. 756, 777, § 202(b). The presumption was made conclusive in 1926 in the Revenue Act of that year, 44 Stat. 2007 § 1094(c). But the irrebuttable presumption was held unconstitutional in Heiner v. Donnan, 285 U.S. 312, 52 S.Ct. 358, 76 L.Ed. 772 (1932). The three year contemplation of death period introduced in § 501(a) of the Revenue Act of 1950, 64 Stat. 906, 962 was retained in the Tax Reform Act of 1976 but the contemplation of death standard was dropped and any transfer within three years of death was brought within the gross estate. IRC § 2035 as amended by the Economic Recovery Tax Act of 1981 excludes most inter vivos transfers from the operation of the section. See fn. 44, page 431, infra.

fers, Congress brought the entire transferred property within the gross estate when a life estate was retained,[21] including also transfers in which the interest could be obtained only by surviving the transferor [22] and transfers in which the transferor retained a power to determine directly or indirectly who would enjoy the principal or income from a trust.[23] A gift tax might be payable on these transfers to the extent the transfer was considered complete. If a gift tax was paid or payable a credit was allowed upon the estate tax, the credit being abandoned for a simple subtraction in the Tax Reform Act of 1976. The unified rate and unified credit provided in the latter statute greatly diminished the tax incentive for inter vivos gifts.

The estate tax marital deduction, introduced in 1948 with a similar deduction for the gift tax, was continued by the Tax Reform Act of 1976 as half of the "adjusted gross estate" with a "floor" or minimum amount of $250,000 if the surviving spouse received that much in qualified interests. A typical estate plan to take advantage of the marital deduction involved two trusts. There was a marital deduction trust, established by formula so only one-half of the adjusted gross estate would be included, in which the spouse received a life estate, coupled with a general power of appointment, with the remainder limited to the children. The property of this trust would escape taxation in the estate of the spouse who created the trust but was taxable in the estate of the life tenant because of the general power. A second trust, the "family" or "by-pass" trust, usually contained a life estate for the surviving spouse, perhaps with a special power, and again the remainder limited to the children. The property in this trust would be taxed in the estate of the spouse who created the trust but would escape taxation in the estate of the spouse who was life tenant, the special power not triggering an estate tax on the property subject to it. There would be one overall estate tax for both spouses. So frequently were trusts used in this form that lawyers referred to them as "A" and "B" trusts. Trusts somewhat similar to these, but with major differences in detail, are likely to be used in larger estates to shelter the unified credit "exemption equivalent" in planning estates under the Economic Recovery Tax Act of 1981 (ERTA).

21. Pub.Res. No. 131, 46 Stat. 1516 (1931) in response to May v. Heiner, 281 U.S. 238, 50 S.Ct. 286, 74 L.Ed.2d 826 (1930). Presently substantially IRC § 2036(a). The Revenue Act of 1978, § 702(i) added new § 2036(b) to the effect that the retention of a right to vote directly or indirectly shares of stock in a controlled corporation is considered a retention of the enjoyment of the transferred property. A controlled corporation is defined in subsection (b)(2). This is a corporation in which the decedent owned, or had the right alone or in conjunction with any other person to vote, stock possessing at least 20% of the total combined voting power of all classes of stock. Constructive ownership of stock under IRC § 318 is included. This amendment is to change the rule in United States v. Byrum, 408 U.S. 125, 92 S. Ct. 2382, 33 L.Ed.2d 238 (1972), the Congress having attempted to deal with the point in the Tax Reform Act of 1976, it being then unclear whether the inclusion rule applied when the corporation was not controlled or where the retention of voting rights was indirect.

22. Technical Changes Act of 1949 § 7, 63 Stat. 891, 894. Now with changes IRC § 2037, 26 U.S.C.A.

23. Pub.Res. No. 131, 46 Stat. 1516, 1517 (1931) expanded by 47 Stat. 169, 279 (1932) § 803, presently IRC § 2036 (a)(2), 26 U.S.C.A.

ERTA establishes no basic principles for the imposition of Federal gift and estate taxes, these having been formulated in the Tax Reform Act of 1976 and the detailed tax legislation since 1916. The major amendments made to the gift and estate tax laws by ERTA are a phased in reduction of the top tax rate; a phased in increase of the unified credit; an increase of the marital deduction to 100% for gift and estate transfers; and an increase in the gift tax exclusion.

Of all the provisions of ERTA pertaining to estate and gift taxation, the most important from the aspect of potential trust use is the tax free interspousal transfer.[24] In large estates a trust probably will be used for the marital deduction transfer and a second trust in the amount of the "exemption equivalent" of the tax credit (see the table below) will probably be drafted to be non-deductible in the transferor's estate but by-pass the surviving spouse's estate. There will be no tax in the transferor's estate, because the marital trust is deductible and the tax credit results in no tax payable on the second trust. Leaving the entire estate to the spouse, or in a deductible marital trust, would also result in no tax but potentially would put the amount of the exemption equivalent in the spouse's estate and taxable there; the by-pass trust thus "shelters" the exemption equivalent from taxation in either estate.

In 1981 the top rate for both gift and estate taxes was 70% of amounts in excess of $5,000,000. While there is no indexing for the estate and gift taxes, the top rate is scaled down commencing in 1982 as follows:[25]

1982 ... 65% of excess over $4,000,000
1983 ... 60% of excess over $3,500,000
1984 ... 55% of excess over $3,000,000
1985 ... 50% of excess over $2,500,000

After a period of "phasing in" since 1977, the unified credit had reached $47,000 in 1981 for an exemption equivalent of $175,625. A further phasing in through 1987 is continued under the following table:[26]

Date	Credit	Exemption Equivalent
1982	$62,800	$225,000
1983	$79,300	$275,000
1984	$96,300	$325,000
1985	$121,800	$400,000
1986	$155,800	$500,000
1987	$192,800	$600,000

When the 1987 credit operates no estate tax return will have to be filed unless the gross estate exceeds $600,000. The Treasury estimates that only 3/10th of 1% of the estates of resident decedents will

24. P.L. 97–34 (1981) § 403, currently IRC §§ 2056, 2523, 26 U.S.C.A.

25. P.L. 97–34 (1981) § 402, currently IRC § 2001, 2502, 26 U.S.C.A.

26. P.L. 97–34 (1981) § 401(a)(b), currently IRC §§ 2010, 2505, 26 U.S.C.A.

have to file estate tax returns at this time and far fewer will pay tax because of the 100% marital deduction. Since both husband and wife will have a $600,000 exemption equivalent in 1987, for estates of $600,000 and under there will be no gift or estate taxes for a transfer from one spouse to another or from a surviving spouse to another taker even if the 100% marital deduction is not taken into consideration. Federal and state income tax considerations and perhaps state gift and death taxes will require planning for an estate of this size. Trusts may prove useful devices to execute the plan. Moreover, between 1982 and 1987 a smaller exemption equivalent will be available. Thus there will be some emphasis upon Federal estate and gift tax features for the estates of $600,000 and under during these years. While tax features perhaps have dominated estate plans before 1982, there are many reasons for planning an estate and using trusts to execute the plan other than to minimize taxes. For example, persons receiving assets may need assistance in management or a trust may be used to by-pass the "probate estate" and reduce probate costs.

How should trusts be used under ERTA to take advantage of the 100% marital deduction in estates over $600,000, in very large estates while the reduced rate ceiling is being phased in, and in estates between $225,000 and $600,000 while the unified credit is increased annually through 1987? Certainly we would want to defer determination of the tax by a marital deduction trust until the full $600,000 exemption equivalent was phased in and for estates that will exceed $2,500,000 we would want to delay determination of the tax until the 50% maximum rate took effect in 1985.[27]

Suppose, for example, our taxpayer client has a $3,000,000 estate. His wife has no significant estate. If the taxpayer left the $3,000,000 outright to his wife and died in 1983 there will be no estate tax when he dies. But if the wife retains the $3,000,000 and dies in 1993 without being able to claim a further marital deduction in a second marriage, she would have a $600,000 exemption equivalent and an estate tax of $976,800.[28] If the husband had sheltered his exemption equivalent of $275,000 in 1983 by by-passing the wife's estate, his tax

27. As a general proposition, deferring either the determination or the payment of a tax is desirable but one should keep in mind that when determination of the gift and estate taxes is deferred the tax base tends to expand both through possible accumulation of income and through inflation. If payment of the income tax is deferred there is in effect a tax free or relatively low interest loan from the government and there is no expansion of a tax base since the tax is not an excise tax based on the value of transferred property. Of course there could be a period of deflation and the Federal requirement for revenue might cause rates to go up and unified credits to go down.

28. The state death tax credit is not considered in this statement of the Federal tax. In 1987 the minimum Federal estate tax rate (considering the $600,000 exemption equivalent) will be 37%, although the state death tax credit (assuming the state death tax is paid) will reduce the lowest Federal tax to a 33% effective rate while the highest effective rate will be 42% on estates between $2,500,000 and $2,600,000, the tax on the largest estates being 34%. These differences arise because the method of computing the state death tax credit was not changed by ERTA. Also the reader should observe that between 1983 and 1993 an inflation factor of 8% to 10% per annum should be added to estimate roughly the property in the hands of the spouse by 1993. An inflation factor is not considered in the hypothetical.

would still be zero but the wife's estate tax would be reduced to $842,050, a saving of $134,750. To implement the latter plan, a marital deduction trust could be drafted, stating that the amount to be trusteed is the least amount to result in no tax, taking into consideration property passing to the spouse and qualifying for the marital deduction other than by the will (or inter vivos disposition if such a disposition is used for the transfer) taking into consideration credits, including the unified credit. The residuary clause (if a will is used) would then contain the exemption equivalent shelter trust. The income from this could be "sprinkled" by the trustee among the wife and other beneficiaries. The children of the marriage or others could be designated as remaindermen in both the marital deduction and exemption equivalent trusts. Numerous variations of such a plan might be used. The phasing in of the unified credit is embraced in such a plan, the important feature being the sheltering of the exemption equivalent as it increases through 1987 and the sheltering of the $600,000 exemption equivalent thereafter. Avoiding the tax in the estate of the husband defers the payment on the marital deduction property until the death of the wife.

Prior to ERTA there were three basic forms in which the marital deduction transfer could be made. First, the property could be transferred in fee simple to the surviving spouse. This transfer could be in trust but often was not. Second, the surviving spouse could receive a life estate coupled with a general power of appointment. If the detailed requirements of IRC § 2056(b)(5) were met, the marital deduction could be claimed on this transfer. A trust normally would be used in this transfer but no trust was required. A similar arrangement could be made for life insurance or annuity payments if the requirements of IRC § 2056(b)(6) were satisfied. Third, instead of conferring a general power upon the spouse who received a life estate, a remainder could be limited to the spouse's estate.[29] The third transaction was also usually trusteed but was not required to be. Income tax savings could be developed in an estate trust since income could be accumulated until the spouse's death but there was a significant degree of inflexibility in this transaction and problems existed under local law in the construction of the remainder interest. While each of these transactions can still be used to obtain the marital deduction, ERTA introduced two further marital deduction dispositions.

The first new provision is the qualified terminable interest property transfer, now being described as a "QTIP" transfer or "QTIP" trust.[30] A trust is not required for this transfer although normally a trust would be used. The deduction is permitted if the spouse has only an interest for life if the spouse is entitled to all of the income from the property, payable annually or at more frequent intervals and no person has a power of appointment to appoint any of the property to any person other than the surviving spouse. Thus the spouse

29. Reg. § 20.2056(e)–2(b)(1).

30. P.L. 97–34 (1981) § 403(d)(1)(2), currently IRC §§ 2056(b)(7); 2053(f), 26 U.S.C.A.

can have no power over the property exercisable in favor of anyone but himself or herself, although the spouse could be granted a testamentary special or general power over the remainder. The QTIP trust is proving a popular dispositive form in which to obtain the deduction, particularly in second marriages where there are children by a first marriage for whom the transferor wishes to provide a remainder interest. In these situations the testamentary power is not being conferred. When the spouse dies, the value of the trust property is included in the spouse's gross estate for estate tax purposes.[31] Unless the spouse otherwise directs by will, the estate may recover from the person receiving the property the excess of the estate tax over the tax which would have been paid if the property had not been included in the spouse's gross estate.[32] If the spouse disposes of all of the income interest inter vivos, the transaction is then gift taxable as if the remainder also had been transferred.[33] No exclusion would be allowed for the value of the remainder since the remainder is a future interest.[34] To obtain the marital deduction for the QTIP transfer, the donor must elect the deduction for a gift and the executor elects the deduction for the estate. The election is irrevocable.[35]

The marital deduction also may be claimed for a life interest in the spouse conferred in a charitable deduction annuity trust or unitrust.[36] These trusts are discussed in Chapter XI, Section 3. The transaction must be trusteed and the annuity trust or unitrust must meet all the requirements of IRC § 664. The spouse must be the only noncharitable beneficiary. Inter vivos transactions in this form may have appeal for taxpayers. An income tax deduction may be claimed for the charitable remainder. There will be no gift tax because of the 100% marital and charitable deductions. The property is removed from the estate of the donor spouse and there is no estate tax in the estate of the spouse to whom the transfer of the life interest is made.

Old and new forms for the marital deduction can be combined. For example, a husband having $2,200,000 could transfer $1,000,000 intervivos as a charitable remainder annuity trust or unitrust with the wife as life beneficiary with the income tax and other tax benefits mentioned. A marital deduction, power of appointment trust could be established in his will with the wife as life beneficiary and the children as remaindermen. $600,000 could be put in this trust. He could then shelter his exemption equivalent in his residuary estate, using a trust to by-pass the wife's estate, perhaps giving the trustee discretionary power to pay the income to the wife or children with remainder to the children at the death of the wife. There would be no gift tax for the annuity trust or unitrust; no estate tax in the estate of the husband as of 1987 and no estate tax in the estate of the wife as of 1987.

31. IRC § 2044, 26 U.S.C.A., added P. L. 97–34 (1981) § 403(d)(3)(A).

32. IRC § 2207A, 26 U.S.C.A., added P.L. 97–34 (1981) § 403(d)(4)(A).

33. IRC § 2519, 26 U.S.C.A., added P. L. 97–34 (1981) § 403(d)(3)(B).

34. IRC § 2503(b), 26 U.S.C.A.

35. IRC §§ 2056(b)(7)(B)(v); 2523(f)(4), added P.L. 97–34 (1981) § 403(d)(1)(2).

36. P.L. 97–34 (1981) § 403(d)(1)(2), currently IRC §§ 2056(b)(8); 2523(g).

It is one thing to speculate upon the possibility of large inter vivos charitable transfers and quite another thing to find a client interested in making them. The 100% marital deduction and the large exemption equivalent, becoming progressively larger through 1986, will discourage tax motivated lifetime gifts other than marital gifts, the incentive for these gifts having been much reduced when gift and estate taxes were placed on the same schedule beginning in 1977. If the taxpayer has a spouse, the taxpayer may prefer to have the property pass through his or her estate, thus obtaining a step up in basis for capital gain income tax purposes, use none of the credit in inter vivos transfers but shelter the exemption equivalent as previously described, by-passing the surviving spouse's estate for this amount, and use a power of appointment trust or QTIP trust for the marital deduction, then obtaining another step up in basis in the surviving spouse's estate for that property. If one spouse has no significant estate, the other spouse could build up the estate of the first spouse by tax free inter vivos transfers. If the donee spouse lived for more than a year after the gifts, the property might then come back to the donor spouse with a step up in basis from the donee spouse's estate.[37] There are a number of other income tax reasons for making gifts which will be discussed in relation to the income tax. Gift problems once incident to joint tenancies between husband and wife and tenancies by the entirety are eliminated in 1982 and thereafter by the presumption that each spouse owns one half of the property no matter who contributed the consideration for the transfer[38] and by the unlimited marital deduction. But if a taxpayer does desire to make intervivos gifts other than to the surviving spouse or to a qualified charity, more property can be transferred by gift beginning in 1982 without gift tax than could be transferred without gift tax in 1981 and before. Commencing in 1982, the gift tax exclusion is increased from $3,000 per donee per annum to $10,000 per donee per annum. With a split gift, husband and wife can give $20,000 per donee per annum.[39] When such a gift is to a minor or to any person who needs assistance in the management of the property a trust probably would be used. A gift of a beneficial interest in trust can be characterized as a future interest and the exclusion denied unless the beneficiary is entitled to immediate possession of enjoyment of the property. Thus, if the beneficiary is under 21 an IRC § 2503(c) trust might be created. The income and principal must be expendable by or for the benefit of the beneficiary before he attains 21 and to the extent not so expended must pass to the beneficiary when he attains 21. In the event the beneficiary dies before 21, the principal and accumulated income must be payable to his estate or as he appoints in the exercise of a

37. IRC § 1014(e), 26 U.S.C.A. as amended P.L. 97–34 (1981) § 425.

38. IRC § 2040, 26 U.S.C.A., as amended P.L. 97–34 (1981) § 403(c). Subsections (c), (d) and (e) of IRC § 2040 were repealed as were IRC §§ 2515, 2515A and subsection (c) of § 6019. The automatic inclusion of one-half interest in the estate of the spouse first to die means that the half included will receive a stepped up basis while the part not included will carry over the basis.

39. IRC § 2503(b), 26 U.S.C.A. as amended P.L. 97–34 (1981) § 441(a).

general power of appointment.[40] If the trust does not meet the IRC § 2503(c) requirements, the beneficiary should be given a "Crummey" power to withdraw annually a fixed dollar amount or percentage of the trust principal.[41] This withdrawal power is treated as a general power of appointment. Since the right of withdrawal would be noncumulative, the power lapsing each year to the extent not exercised, the power should be limited to $5,000 or 5% of the value of the principal, whichever is greater. This is to prevent the lapsed power from being taxable as a gift to the beneficiary or from being taxed in his estate.[42] But this limitation also restricts the amount which can be excluded for a transfer to the trust each year. Another frequent gift transaction will be to a "Clifford" or short term trust in which the settlor retains a reversion. The Clifford trust will be discussed in connection with the income taxation of trusts.

The three year quarantine prior to death within which a gift would be brought within the gross estate, taxable at death with the gift tax, paid or payable, "grossed up" to increase the value of the gift, was for most purposes made inapplicable for donors dying on or after 1 January 1982.[43] The three year quarantine was retained for certain gift transfers. These include the retained life estate and retained power transfers under IRC §§ 2036, 2037 and 2038, general power releases or exercises under IRC § 2041 and insurance transfers under IRC § 2042.[44] The exclusion of most gift transfers from the three year quarantine period for most gifts diminishes the importance of valuation of the property. For example, if before 1982, property given within three years of death was within the then exclusion of $3,000 for an individual gift to a donee, the gift was not included in the gross estate. But if the gift was $3,001, so a gift tax return had to be filed, the entire amount was included. After 31 December 1981, whether an individual gift is $10,000 or $10,001 will not cause inclusion of the entire amount in the gross estate, the taxable amount (that exceeding the exclusion) having no effect other than to increase the tax for subsequent gifts and in the estate. Of course the gift might fall within one of the "continued categories" and be included in the gross estate at death value for that reason.

40. In some states there may be a problem concerning the capacity of an infant to exercise a presently exercisable power although legal capacity in most states now commences at age 18. Also age 18 is usually the age for capacity to execute a will and thus to exercise a general testamentary power of appointment. See Stoebuck, "Infants' Exercise of Powers of Appointment", 43 Denver L.J. 255 (1966).

41. Crummey v. Commissioner, 397 F. 2d 82 (9th Cir. 1968); Rev.Rul. 73–405, 1973–2 C.B. 321.

42. IRC §§ 2041(a)(2), (b)(2)(A), (B); 2514(b), (e)(1)(2), 26 U.S.C.A.

43. IRC § 2035(d), 26 U.S.C.A. as amended P.L. 97–34 (1981) § 424.

44. IRC § 2035(d)(2), 26 U.S.C.A. as amended P.L. 97–34 (1981) § 424. The three year rule also was retained for distributions in redemption of stock to pay death taxes (IRC § 303(b), 26 U.S.C.A.); special valuation of farm and closely held business property (IRC § 2032A, 26 U.S.C.A.); for extension of time to pay the estate tax when the estate consists largely of an interest in a closely held business (IRC § 6166, 26 U.S.C.A.) and subchapter C of Chapter 64, 26 U.S.C.A. relating to the lien for taxes. IRC § 2035(d)(3), 26 U.S.C.A. as amended P.L. 97–34 (1981) § 424.

(2) GENERATION SKIPPING TAX

Prior to 1977 the shift of economic enjoyment of property from a life tenant to a remainderman escaped tax unless the life estate was retained by the transferor. Also special powers of appointment escaped taxation unless these were retained powers. However, in the Tax Reform Act of 1976 the Congress imposed a Generation Skipping Tax (GST), sometimes called the "Chapter 13 Tax" to discourage the creation of successive interests and the creation of powers in remote generations.[45] The GST applies gift and estate tax principles to treat the shift in economic enjoyment from the life tenant to the remainderman or other successive taker or the exercise or lapse of the special power just as if the life tenant had owned the property and then had transferred it or as if the power holder had a general (taxable) power rather than a special power over the property. But the GST is calculated upon the prior gifts or estate or both of a deemed transferor who usually will be the holder of a successive interest or power but may not be.[46]

The GST is inapplicable unless there are two generations younger than the grantor of the successive interests and each of these generations has a person with a present or future interest or power or both in the property, as where income is payable from a trust to the transferor's child and on the latter's death the principal goes to that child's children. Husband and wife are treated as in the same generation irrespective of any disparity in ages. A trustee is not regarded as having a power in a trust if the trustee has no interest in the trust, is not a related or subordinate trustee and does not have any present or future power in the trust other than a power to dispose of the corpus of the trust or the income therefrom to a beneficiary or class of beneficiaries designated in the trust instrument.[47]

The taxable event is a taxable "termination" or "distribution." For a taxable termination, a person in a generation younger than the grantor must have a present interest or power which, upon termination, will shift enjoyment to a still younger generation. The termination occurs when the present interest or power terminates by death or lapse of time, exercise or nonexercise or otherwise. For a taxable

45. IRC §§ 2601–2622, 26 U.S.C.A.

46. IRC § 2612, 26 U.S.C.A. As a simple example, if a life estate is limited to a child with a remainder to a grandchild, the child will be the deemed transferor. But the determination of the deemed transferor may be more complex than this since the deemed transferor cannot be determined until the transferee is determined and the transferee is not defined in the Code. Once the transferee is determined, the deemed transferor is the parent of the transferee who is more closely related to the grantor of the trust than the other parent of the transferee or the parent "having a closer affinity to the grantor". If the parent is not a younger generation beneficiary of the trust, but one or more ancestors of the transferee is a younger generation beneficiary related by blood or by adoption to the grantor of the trust, then the deemed transferor is the youngest of such ancestors.

47. IRC § 2613(e)(2), 26 U.S.C.A.

distribution, a person in a generation younger than the grantor must have a present interest or power and there is a distribution to a yet younger generation.

After the deemed transferor is determined, the GST is calculated by adding to other taxable transfers of the deemed transferor the value of the property in the generation skip. A tentative tax is computed on this total value. Then a tax is computed on the deemed transferor's taxable transfers. The GST is the difference between the two taxes as computed. The GST is paid from the property involved in the generation skip and although the GST is applicable to trust equivalents, such as legal life estates and remainders, insurance and annuities and split interests, usually the generation skipping will be by a trust and thus the trustee will pay the tax from the trust property.

There is a $250,000 exclusion from the GST for each child of the transferor for generation skipping transfers to the children of that child.[48] A special power which is limited to lineal descendants of the grantor also does not trigger the tax upon its termination.[49] The GST does not apply to direct transfers to remote descendants. Thus a great-grandparent could establish a trust for a great-grandchild without a generation skipping tax if there are no intervening interests or powers in generations younger than the grantor and senior to the great-grandchild. Successive interests can be created laterally within the same generation and one generation removed without a GST.

The GST is a complicated tax to apply. The facts necessary to compute the tax are difficult to ascertain in many cases. The tax is unpredictable since it is based on the property transfers of a deemed transferor and the high unified credit available by 1987 may render the tax of diminished importance. While the GST will not diminish the frequency of use of trusts it will no doubt discourage the use of successive interests in trusts. If care is used to take advantage of the $250,000 exclusion per child for generation skips to grandchildren and direct transfers in trust are used without interests in intervening generations the GST should create no problems for the trust draftsman.

(3) INCOME TAXES

Depending upon the provisions of the trust, there are three possible persons taxable on the trust income: the settlor (if the trust is a living trust), the trustee in his fiduciary capacity (the trust is an enti-

48. IRC § 2613(b)(6), 26 U.S.C.A.

49. IRC § 2613(e)(1), 26 U.S.C.A.

ty for tax purposes), or the beneficiaries. The choice is narrowed to the trustee or the beneficiaries in a testamentary trust. In a living trust, the settlor may remain taxable on the trust income even though the money does not pass through his hands or end up in his pocket. As in gift and estate taxation, we deal with an income tax with progressive rates, although the income tax rate is more steeply progressive than the gift and estate tax rate under the unified schedule. If we regard the family as an economic unit, not just as between the husband and wife, or the parent and minor child, but also between parents and grown children and grandchildren, transfer of income producing property from the person with large income to the other members of the family in lower income tax brackets will usually effect large savings, although the impact of the generation skipping tax must be considered carefully in this planning.

If the taxpayer creates irrevocable trusts for other members of his family, and retains no interest in either income or principal, he can be taxed on the income only in certain very limited situations, as where the income is being used to discharge his legal obligations: support of his wife or minor children.[50] While no man has a legal obligation to carry life insurance for the benefit of his family, it is realistic to say that if the income from a trust fund is being used to pay premiums on the insurance on the life of the settlor or his wife, the settlor is getting the benefit of the income; hence it is still taxed to him.[51] Nor can the settlor avoid the impact of these rules by not retaining any interest directly but by empowering the trustee to apply income for his benefit.[52]

Where it is clear that the settlor has parted with all right to the income for his own benefit, if he retains control over its distribution among others, this retention of control is still enough to make the income taxable to him.[53]

Often the settlor has no need for the income for a period of years, and is willing to part with all remnants of control during this period, but wishes to retain a reversionary interest in the principal. For example, an executive with a large salary may part with income-producing property during his active years but wish to regain the principal upon retirement. A trust for this objective would be called a "short term" trust in contrast with one in which the settlor retained no right to principal. These short term trusts can within limits be used to transfer income for tax purposes. But to accomplish this the tax law requires that a trust for private beneficiaries last for ten years or the lifetime of the income beneficiary, whichever is shorter;[54] and the settlor may not retain administrative control over the trust which can

50. IRC § 677(b), 26 U.S.C.A., as amended P.L. 91–172 (1969).

51. IRC § 677(a)(3), 26 U.S.C.A. as amended P.L. 91–172 (1969). The same rule is applied if the income may, in the discretion of the settlor or the trustee, be used to pay premiums. It does not apply if the consent of an adverse party (such as the beneficiary who would otherwise receive the income) is required.

52. Regs. § 1.677(a)–1 et seq.

53. IRC § 674, 26 U.S.C.A.

54. IRC § 673, 26 U.S.C.A. as amended P.L. 91–172 (1969).

be manipulated for his own benefit (e.g., he may not retain power to vote stock in a family corporation held in the trust).[55]

Assuming that the income is not taxed to the settlor, the choice is between the trust as an entity and the beneficiary, or beneficiaries, receiving the income. If the income is distributable to the beneficiary, i.e., if he has a right to the income whether or not it is in fact distributed to him, he will be taxed on such income.[56] But often the taxable income is not distributable to the beneficiary, and in such event it is taxed to the trust. The problem frequently occurs because of a difference between the definition of income for tax purposes and for trust purposes. To illustrate, suppose the trustee sells certain assets at a profit. The capital gain normally will be credited to principal under trust law. Nevertheless, under tax law it is "income" which, although accorded special treatment as "capital gain" under that law, is taxable to the trust.

The settlor of the trust may authorize or direct the trustee to accumulate income. Since each trust is a taxable entity, there was once a major income tax advantage in the creation of accumulation trusts, especially multiple accumulation trusts for the same beneficiary, some settlors having created as many as 100 of these for the same person. By creating multiple trusts the impact of the progressive tax rate scale could be minimized. Under the 1954 Internal Revenue Code there was a "five year throwback rule". Income distributed to the beneficiary, but accumulated by the trustee within the preceding five years, was taxed to the beneficiary as if he had received the income during the year in which it was accumulated. He received a credit for the tax paid by the trust on the accumulations. There was no additional tax paid by the beneficiary for amounts accumulated before the five year period and there were also a number of exceptions to the rule. One of the most important of these was that distributions of $2,000 or less per trust were excluded from the application of the throwback principle.

This income tax shelter was almost totally demolished by the Tax Reform Act of 1969, the 1969 provisions having been amended in the Tax Reform Act of 1976.[57] There is now an unlimited throwback except for accumulations while the beneficiary was a minor or before he was born. The tax on the accumulation distribution is computed by first averaging the accumulation distribution over the number of years during which the accumulated income was earned by the trust. This average amount is then included in the beneficiary's income for three of the immediate five prior years, excluding the two years with the lowest and highest income. The average additional tax for the three years selected is then multiplied by the number of years in which the accumulated income was earned. There is a special rule for multiple trusts. Rather than applying a throwback principle for capital gains, if the trust sells property within two years of the time

55. IRC § 675, 26 U.S.C.A.

56. IRC §§ 652, 662, 26 U.S.C.A.

57. IRC §§ 665–669, 26 U.S.C.A. as amended P.L. 91–192 (1969); P.L. 94–455 § 701 (1976).

of transfer to the trust, the built-in gain (if any) is taxed to the trust just as if the settlor had realized the gain and transferred to the trust the net proceeds of sale. The throwback policies are examined in detail in Income Tax courses or courses dealing specially with the Income Taxation of Trusts and Estates.[58]

Some tax advantages can still be developed through accumulation trusts but the administration of these trusts for tax economy requires careful planning and record keeping as well as coordination between the trustee and beneficiary. Payment of income taxes can be deferred until convenient times without the payment of interest on the amount due. The "throwback" tax could produce a lower tax than if the tax was paid currently, depending upon the economic situation of the beneficiary. The beneficiary may be able to obtain a stepped up basis for property distributed in kind, the basis for the property being the fair market value at the date of distribution. There are also non-tax reasons for the use of accumulation trusts, such as the protection of beneficiaries, which will continue to induce the creation of trusts of this type.

(4) TENTATIVE CONCLUSIONS

You should now have some concept of the importance of taxation in the creation of trusts. While "a little learning is a dangerous thing", it is better than no learning. If you have had a tax course or are currently taking one, you know that the tax law is exceedingly complex and requires a great deal of study. Only general outlines of the tax structure in the Estate, Gift and Income tax laws are attempted here.

We can draw certain conclusions under the current law which will remain sound even after you have mastered the tax law details.

(1) Revocable living trusts have tax advantages only to the extent that the power of revocation permits flexibility in an estate plan and thus permits changes in the plan to deal with new tax laws. There is no gift so long as the power of revocation continues but the three year quarantine period of IRC § 2035 applies to a power of revocation renounced during the period so that the property of the trust is included in the estate at death value if the power of revocation is renounced within three years of death. Income of the trust is taxable to the settlor who retains the power.

(2) Irrevocable living trusts which completely dispose of the beneficial interest and leave no control in the settlor are used to distribute

58. See Polasky "Estate Planning in the 70's" 109 Trusts and Estates 568 (1970); "The Trust Throwback Rules of the Tax Reform Act", 5 Real Prop. Prob. & Tr.L.Jour. 171, 185–190 (1970).

tax payments for the convenience of the taxpayer, obtain gift tax exclusions, reduce the base for computing the taxable estate at death under the unified tax by the amount of gift taxes paid on transfers perhaps minimize taxes under state laws and reduce Federal and state income taxes by spreading income among members of the family in lower tax brackets.

(3) Short-term trusts can be created during lifetime to minimize income taxes during the term of the trust but return the principal to the settlor (or his estate) upon termination of the trust.

(4) Testamentary trusts have important tax aspects, both in avoiding future death taxes upon death of the income beneficiaries, consistent with the generation skipping tax, and in minimizing income taxes among the family unit by spreading the income to the beneficiaries who are in the lower tax brackets.

(5) Since the trust is a taxable entity, the trust may be used to defer income taxes by the beneficiary; permit distribution ultimately to be made to beneficiaries in lower tax brackets (as in a sprinkling trust for the benefit of settlor's son and grandchildren, the trustee paying nothing to the son who is in a high income bracket, and delaying payments until the grandchildren who are in lower income brackets are entitled to payments); and may achieve other tax economies consistent with an "unlimited throwback" when a beneficiary receives distributions of the accumulations and with the generation skipping tax imposed in appropriate cases.

Finally we should remember that property law concepts do not always govern in the tax field and vice versa. Not until you have studied the tax field in detail in your tax courses will you be able to pass on the tax consequences of various trust arrangements.

SECTION 3. PROHIBITED TRUST PURPOSES

It is sometimes said that a trust can be created for any purpose that is not illegal. We have noted in Section 1 a number of purposes which a settlor may seek to attain by creating a private express trust, in addition to the tax savings explored in Section 2.

The restrictions on trust purposes are generally of three kinds: (1) general public policy, such as that opposing restraints on marriage; (2) statutory restrictions on trust purposes, which have been amended or judicially construed so that in fact they curtail very few legitimate trust objectives;[59] and (3) the social restrictions against perpetuities and accumulations which are to be studied in Chapter XVI.

59. See Mont. Rev. Codes Ann. § 72–20–106; N.D. Cent. Code § 59–03–02 (1979 Supp.); McKinney's N.Y., EPTL, § 7–1.4 provides simply: "An express trust may be created for any lawful purpose."

While tax statutes operate as an inducement to create certain kinds of trusts, they cannot be said to be restrictive, for the settlor may create the kind of trust he desires if he is willing to accept the tax costs involved. These statutes are, however, a potent force in shaping trust purposes.

When the trust contains an illegal provision, the court is faced with the further issue of the effect of such illegality upon the remaining provisions of the trust. Where the entire trust is motivated by an illegal purpose, and hence fails, there is the issue of disposition of the property in the hands of the trustee: shall the trust property be returned to the settlor by a resulting trust or should some other disposition be made? In the latter type of case, the illegal purpose (such as inducing the beneficiary to live in adultery with the settlor, or defrauding the settlor's creditors) rarely appears on the face of the trust document. Often, in fact, the trust itself is not expressed in writing but arranged orally in order to avoid public knowledge of its existence. Such cases may involve a failure to comply with the Statute of Frauds; and the courts, applying the equitable "clean hands" doctrine, will refuse to grant relief by way of resulting or constructive trust under the principles we shall explore in Chapter IX, Section 1.

MATTER OF LIBERMAN

Court of Appeals of New York, 1939.
279 N.Y. 458, 18 N.E.2d 658, 122 A.L.R. 1.

LEHMAN, J. The testator, Isaac Liberman, provided in his will that after the death of his wife his residuary estate should be divided into six parts or shares. He had two sons and a daughter. To each he bequeathed beneficial interests in two shares. To his son Herman N. Liberman he gave the two shares absolutely. To his daughter Etta L. Baum he gave one share absolutely and a life interest in a second share with remainder to her issue. The testator named his son Herman and his daughter as his executors and trustees. They were both married and had children. The testator's son Harry Liberman had no children. He had married twice. The testator was an orthodox Jew. Harry Liberman had married women of a different faith and the testator had strongly disapproved. Though he bequeathed to Harry Liberman and his issue beneficial interests in the remaining two shares of his residuary estate, he provided that the enjoyment of such beneficial interest—with the exception of a life interest in one share—should be contingent upon the marriage of Harry Liberman with the consent and approval of the executors and trustees named in the will.

The will provides that:

"(d) I give, devise and bequeath one of such shares to my Trustees hereinafter named, in trust nevertheless, to collect the rents, issues and profits thereof and to pay the same to my beloved son Harry Liberman, during his lifetime. Upon his death, should he have during his lifetime married with the consent and approval of my beloved wife and the executors and trustees herein named and/or the survivors or successors of them, and should he be survived by any issue of such marriage, then I give, devise and bequeath the principal of such trust fund to the issue of such marriage; in the event that there shall be no such issue, or should he have married without such consent then I give, devise and bequeath the principal of such trust fund to his brother and sister, him surviving and the issue of any deceased brother and sister, the issue of a deceased brother or sister to take collectively the share their parent would have taken.

"(e) I give, devise and bequeath one of such shares to my trustees hereinafter named, in trust nevertheless, to collect the rents, issues and profits thereof, and to pay the same to my beloved daughter Etta L. Baum and Herman N. Liberman, in equal shares during the lifetime of my son Harry Liberman and/or until the marriage of my said son Harry Liberman as hereafter provided.

"Upon the marriage of my son Harry Liberman if such marriage is with the consent and approval of my beloved wife and the trustees hereinafter named and/or survivors and successors of them, upon such event such income is to be paid to my beloved son Harry Liberman during the term of his natural life, otherwise such income shall continue to be paid to Etta L. Baum and Herman N. Liberman. Should Harry Liberman be survived by an issue of such marriage, contracted as aforestated, then and in that event, I give, devise and bequeath the principal of such trust fund to the issue of such marriage; in the event there shall be no such issue or should he have married without such consent then I give, devise and bequeath the principal of such trust fund to his brother and sister him surviving, and the issue of any deceased brother and sister, the issue of a deceased brother and sister to take collectively the share their parent would have taken.

"In the event of the death of my beloved daughter Etta L. Baum or my son Herman N. Liberman, during the continuance of this trust then and in that event, I give, devise and bequeath the income of this trust fund to which they may be entitled to receive if living to their issue collectively them surviving."

Harry Liberman has asked his brother and sister to consent to his marriage to Margaret Jones. They have refused. Then Harry Liberman brought this proceeding to compel them, or other persons to be appointed in their place as executors and trustees, to give such consent. The courts below have held that the provisions of the will of Isaac Liberman which we have set forth, "insofar as they require the petitioner, Harry Liberman, to obtain the consent of the testator's wife and the trustees thereinafter named, and/or the survivors or successors of them, to a marriage of Harry Liberman, be and the same hereby are declared to be ineffectual and inoperative and in all other respects in full force and effect."

A testator of sound mind may, subject to statutory restrictions, not material here, choose the objects of his bounty. He may exclude a child or other descendant from any participation in his estate for sound reason, or because of whim or prejudice which might seem unreasonable to others. He may prefer a prodigal son or even an unrepentant sinner to a son who has been an exemplar and pattern of virtue. No considerations of public policy affect the validity even of a bequest which others might deem a reward for evil conduct in the past. The courts do, nevertheless, at times deny validity to a condition annexed to a testamentary gift where the condition is calculated to influence the *future* conduct of the beneficiary in manner contrary to the established policy of the State. In this case the courts below have found that the condition attached to full enjoyment of the bequest to Harry Liberman, that he shall marry only with the consent of his brother and sister, is against such public policy.

A condition calculated to induce a beneficiary to marry, even to marry in a manner desired by the testator, is not against public policy. A condition calculated to induce a beneficiary to live in celibacy or adultery is against public policy. "Conditions in general restraint of marriage were regarded at common law as contrary to public policy, and, therefore, void." The rule still prevails in New York. (Matter of Seaman, 218 N.Y. 77, 81). Conditions in partial restraint of marriage, which merely impose reasonable restrictions upon marriage, are not against public policy. Thus a condition annexed to a bequest designed to prevent the marriage of the testator's daughter with a particular individual is valid and enforcible. "Such prohibitions have not only received the sanction of judicial authority but we think may be justified by sound reasoning." (Matter of Seaman, supra.) The court there cited with approval Jarman on Wills: "Conditions not to marry a Papist, or a Scotchman; not to marry any but a Jew * * * have also been held good." Indeed, such conditions seem to have been sustained whenever challenged. (Pacholder v. Rosenheim, 129 Md. 455; Hodgson v. Halford [1879] L.R. 11 Ch.Div. 959; Jarman on Law of Wills [7th ed.], p. 1497.) In this case the evidence leaves no room for doubt that the conditions annexed to the gift to Harry Liberman and his issue were intended by the testator to restrain his son Harry from marrying any but a Jewess. On that ground the appellants urge that the condition is valid.

Even though extrinsic evidence establishes that the *purpose* of the condition, imposed by the testator, was to restrain his son from marrying any but a Jewess, yet the condition as written in the will goes further. Only marriage with the consent of executors and trustees, who under the will of the testator would profit by refusal of consent, constitutes compliance with the terms of the will and there is nothing *in the language of the will* which could be construed as a limitation upon their power to give or withhold their consent in the exercise of an unfettered discretion. The question we must decide is whether such a condition is valid. The question would, of course, be different, if the condition of the will had been different.

In the case of Hogan v. Curtin (88 N.Y. 162, 170) this court approved a condition imposed by the testator that the beneficiary, his daughter, should not marry *during her minority*, without the consent of her mother and the executors named in the will. In an opinion by Andrews, Ch. J., the court there said: "A condition prohibiting marriage before twenty-one without consent, is by the common law valid and lawful. It is otherwise of conditions in general restraint of marriage, they being regarded as contrary to public policy, and the 'common weal and good order of society.' But reasonable conditions designed to prevent hasty or imprudent marriages, and to subject a child, or other object of the testator's bounty, to the just restraint of parents or friends during infancy, or other reasonable period, are upheld by the common law, not only because they are proper in themselves, but because by upholding them the law protects the owner of property in disposing of it under such lawful limitations and conditions as he may prescribe." In the will of Mr. Liberman the restraint was not "during infancy or other reasonable period," it was to continue as long as Harry Liberman should live. Moreover, as we have said, the executors and trustees whose consent is required for compliance with the conditions imposed by the testator are also legatees who under the terms of the will would suffer a detriment by giving their consent.

Authority of weight may be found to support the validity of a condition requiring consent of a specified person or persons without limitation of age. (Thompson on Law of Wills [2d ed.], § 381, p. 469; Schouler on Law of Wills [6th ed.], 1351; Whiting v. DeRutzen, L.R. [1905] 1 Ch.Div. 96; Pacholder v. Rosenheim, supra.) The question has never been decided in this court. Again, there is authority to support the validity of a condition requiring consent of a trustee or other person who might benefit by refusal to give consent (2 Alexander, "Commentaries on Law of Wills," § 1070); and again this court has never directly passed upon the question.

Whether a condition in restraint of marriage is reasonable depends, not upon the form of the condition, but upon its purpose and effect under the circumstances of the particular case. What has been said and decided in other cases may often guide decision in analogous cases; but no rigid rule based upon ancient precedents dictates a decision where the circumstances are different and reason points to another conclusion. In spite of what was said in Hogan v. Curtin (supra) the fact that the legatee is a man of mature age and that the condition that he must obtain consent to any marriage is without limitation of time might not alone and under all circumstances render the condition unreasonable. The fact that if the executors and trustees refuse consent, they or their issue would enjoy the benefits which would otherwise go to Harry Liberman and his issue, might not alone and under all circumstances render the condition unreasonable. We decide in this case only whether the condition in the present case is reasonable and does not contravene our public policy, and we may not ignore any of those factors which determine either the purpose or the extent of the restraint. The fact that the restraint is imposed upon an adult and is to continue during life and is not limited to "reasonable time" is such a factor, and so is also the fact that the executors and trustees would have power to keep the property for themselves or their descendants by withholding their consent. Indeed, so distinguished an equity judge as Chancellor Walworth has indicated that in his opinion, because of that factor alone, the condition "would probably be invalid and inconsistent with the principles of public policy; as it might operate as an inducement to her [them] to withhold her [their] consent to a proper marriage." (Bayeaux v. Bayeaux, 8 Paige Ch. 333, 336.) When the condition is considered in its complete setting it becomes evident that the intention of the testator, *as expressed in his will,* is not merely to prevent the beneficiary from marrying any person other than a Jewess or even from entering into an ill-advised marriage, but to prevent *any marriage* not approved by the very persons who by approval would lose the benefit of a legacy which they might otherwise keep. Both reason and authority dictate the conclusion that such a condition is invalid. Its natural tendency might be to induce the beneficiary to live in either celibacy or adultery.

We reach that conclusion, though in this case it appears that the executors and trustees have given most convincing proof that they withhold consent to their brother's marriage only out of respect for their father's wishes and do not wish to profit at their brother's expense. They have even entered into an agreement to pay to their brother, while he remains unmarried, the income which under the terms of the will they might retain until he marries with their consent. Nonetheless, the natural tendency of the condition contained in the will is to restrain all marriage and for that reason is void.

The question remains, what is the effect of the invalidity of the condition. The testator has annexed the invalid condition to the gift. It is a condition precedent to the vesting of any estate in the beneficiary. Indeed, in paragraph "e" the testator has provided that the estate shall vest in his other children, subject to be divested only upon compliance with the condition. At common law, invalidity or impossibility of performance of the condition would not result in divesting the preceding vested estate. (2 Jarman on The Law of Wills [7th ed.], p. 1339; Manice v. Manice, 43 N.Y. 303, 383; Leonard v. Burr, 18 N. Y. 96, 104.) Courts of equity have, however, given a different effect to conditions in restraint of marriage or other conditions in wills which are void because they have a tendency to induce the beneficiary to adopt a course of conduct contrary to the "common weal and good order of society." The Appellate Division (Second Department) in an earlier case has said: " 'With respect to legacies out of personal estate, the civil law, which in this respect has been adopted by courts of equity, differs in some respects from the common law in its treatment of conditions precedent; the rule of the civil law being that where a condition precedent is originally impossible * * * or is illegal as involving *malum prohibitum*, the bequest is absolute, just as if the condition had been subsequent.' (2 Jar.Wills [6th Am. ed.], 15. See, also, 2 Williams Exrs. [7th Am. ed.] 1264) 'When, however, the illegality of the condition does not concern anything *malum in se*, but is merely against a rule or the policy of law, the condition only is void * * * (1 Roper, Leg. 757.)' " (Matter of Haight, 51 App. Div. 310, 316; Potter v. McAlpine, 3 Dem. 108, 124.) Though the rule there stated has not been authoritatively approved by this State, it is in accord with the weight of authority. (O'Brien v. Barkley, 78 Hun. 609; Matter of Hutchins, 147 Misc.Rep. 462; Drace v. Klinedinst, 275 Penn.St. 266; Brizendine v. American Trust & Sav. Bank, 211 Ala. 694.) The tendency of the courts has been to ignore distinctions between "legacies out of personal estate" and legacies or devises of interests in real property, and to apply the rule of the civil law to conditions precedent and even to conditions creating a limitation upon a precedent estate with respect to all legacies or devises. The beneficiary takes under the will as if no conditions had been annexed to the gift to him or as if he had complied with the void condition. (Cf. 2 Jarman on The Law of Wills [7th ed.], p. 1496.)

The rule in that broad form may not be in accord with common-law principles. We recognize that it is rooted in considerations of practical expediency or necessity rather than logic. To give the rule less force; to declare the condition void without at the same time giving effect to the gift made upon the void condition, would be a mockery of the beneficiary and by indirection would permit a testator to accomplish a result which we hold contrary to the "common weal." Since the condition is void we need not decide whether if valid it would apply to a marriage contracted before the death of the testator.

The order should be affirmed, without costs.

CRANE, CH. J., O'BRIEN, LOUGHRAN, FINCH and RIPPEY, JJ., concur; HUBBS, J. taking no part.

Order affirmed.

NOTE

Several cases sustain the validity of a provision restricting marriage outside of a particular religious faith over the objection that the provision is unreasonable and a violation of constitutional provisions against discrimination.[60] Restatement, Second, Trusts § 62 provides in part:

> "*g. Restraining marriage.* A provision in the terms of the trust may be held invalid on the ground that its enforcement would tend to restrain the marriage of the beneficiary. Thus, a provision in the terms of the trust divesting the interest of a beneficiary if he or she should ever

60. Gordon v. Gordon, 332 Mass. 197, 124 N.E.2d 228 (1955); United States National Bank of Portland v. Snodgrass, 202 Or. 530, 275 P.2d 860, 50 A.L.R.2d 725 (1954).

marry anyone may be invalid. Such a provision with respect to the remarriage of a widow, however, is valid. So also, such a provision is not invalid if it does not impose an undue restraint on marriage. Thus, a provision divesting the interest of the beneficiary if he or she should marry a particular person, or should marry before reaching majority, or should marry without the consent of the trustee, or should marry a person of a particular religious faith or one of a different faith from that of the beneficiary, is not ordinarily invalid. So also, where the settlor manifests an intention not to restrain marriage of the beneficiary but to furnish maintenance to the beneficiary while single, the provision is valid.

"*h. Restraining religious freedom.* A provision in the terms of the trust may be held invalid on the ground that its enforcement would tend to restrain the religious freedom of the beneficiary by offering the beneficiary an improper inducement to change his religious faith. Thus, a provision that the beneficiary should receive a certain sum only if he should change his religious faith, or that his interest should cease if he should not change his religious faith, may be invalid. * * * "

In Girard Trust Co. v. Schmitz, 129 N.J.Eq. 444, 20 A.2d 21 (1941), the court was faced with a provision divesting a gift in trust to named relatives on condition that they have no communication or social relations with a disinherited brother and sister and their families, with an express provision in the will for a different testamentary scheme if the foregoing provision was held invalid. The court held the provision invalid as disruptive of family relations, although the opinion points out the vague nature of "public policy" in this area; but effect was then given to the alternative disposition.

Purely capricious provisions in the terms of a trust are invalid as opposed to public policy. Thus a provision in the instrument creating a charitable foundation that no person could serve as trustee unless his or her spouse was a Protestant was invalid because "There is simply no nexus between settlor's whimsical notion and the competency of trustees to perform their trust duties, always, it must be remembered, under the supervision of the court. In short, the religion of trustees' *spouses* is as irrelevant to the trustee's ability to serve as is the color of their spouses' eyes." In re Estate of Coleman, 456 Pa. 163, 169, 317 A.2d 631, 634 (1974). See also Orloski, "Religious Discrimination in the Selection of Trustees", 36 U. of Pitt.L.R. 325 (1974).

BETTINGER v. BRIDENBECKER

Supreme Court of New York, 1865.
63 Barb.(N.Y.) 395.

MORGAN, J. The plaintiff's complaint charges that prior to February, 1862, she had a just and valid claim against Daniel F. Dygert for damages, which he settled at $500; that he was to pay $50 down, and the residue to be placed in the hands of the defendant for her use and benefit. That Dygert paid her the $50, and paid to, and placed in the hands of, the defendant, $450, for her use and benefit, which sum the defendant agreed to keep and hold as her trustee, and to invest the same for her, and pay over to her annually the interest and income, and to pay her the principal sum on the 15th day of July, 1864; which he neglected and refused to do, although specially requested.

The answer of the defendant alleges that prior to February, 1862, Dygert was arrested and held to bail for the commission of a felony, viz., in aiding the procuring of an abortion of a quick child upon the person of the plaintiff; and that Dygert paid the plaintiff $50, and put $450 in the defendant's hands to be paid to her, in consideration, among other things, that the criminal prosecution then commenced should be abandoned.

On the trial, the plaintiff produced in evidence an agreement in writing, bearing date February 1, 1862, signed by the defendant, by which he acknowledged the receipt of $450 from Dygert to be held by him upon certain trusts therein mentioned, or until the same was revoked. This agreement promised that on the 15th day of July, 1864, the said sum of money should be paid to the said plaintiff as her own, *provided that before that time no prosecution should in any manner and form be instituted against the said Daniel F. Dygert*, on account of any alleged injury to the person or character of the plaintiff, either civil or *criminal*, or in her own behalf, or *in behalf of the people of the State of New York*. And also provided that the plaintiff should also execute a release of all demands.

The plaintiff also proved that she executed a release, and thereupon demanded the money of the defendant, July 15, 1864. The defendant then proved that Dygert was arrested January 2, 1862, and held to bail upon a criminal warrant charging him with the criminal offense of assisting in procuring an abortion of a quick child upon the person of the plaintiff, at Ilion, July 5, 1861. The defendant then proved, by Thomas Richardson, the execution of another agreement by the defendant to Dygert, upon the same subject, written at the same time, which contained a further provision that if any action, either civil or criminal, for the causes aforesaid, should be commenced on or before the 15th of July, 1864, either by the people or the plaintiff, then and in that case the defendant engaged to repay the money to Dygert. The plaintiff objected to the reception of this agreement in evidence, but the objection was overruled, and the plaintiff excepted.

The plaintiff produced as a witness Jacob Wendell, who was present at the execution of the two agreements, and offered to prove by him that the money mentioned in the agreement was not in fact paid to compound a felony, but that the sum was paid in settlement of the plaintiff's claim against the said Dygert, for her private damages, for breach of promise of marriage and seduction. This offer was overruled by the court to which the plaintiff excepted.

The defendant's counsel then moved for a nonsuit, upon the ground that the agreement upon which the action was brought was illegal and void, as against public policy. Which motion was granted by the judge, and the plaintiff's counsel excepted to the decision.

It seems to me that the case is too plain for argument; and that nothing can be necessary to be said to show that one indispensable condition upon which the money is to be paid to the plaintiff, was the successful suppression of criminal proceedings which had already been instituted against Dygert. By the 15th day of July, 1864, it would be too late to indict him, for the three years' limitation would have expired, the alleged offense having been committed at Ilion on the 5th day of July, 1861. This was certainly a contract which tended to obstruct and interfere with the administration of public justice, and of the laws, and it is unnecessary to cite authorities to prove that it is utterly void. No valid trust can be founded upon an interest derived from an illegal contract, or established in contravention of the general policy of the law. Hill on Trustees, 45. The claim that the contract had been executed cannot be supported. This suit is brought to enforce it, and for that reason the court cannot aid the plaintiff, although it would not by any means assist the defendant, if its aid should become necessary to enable him either to execute or to defeat the trust.

It is also quite apparent that the plaintiff could not be permitted to prove, in opposition to the express stipulation of the agreement, that it was not a part of the understanding that criminal proceedings should be abandoned.

In my opinion, it is too plain to require further examination, Porter v. Havens, 37 Barb. 343. There was nothing in the second agreement proved that changed the character of the transaction, and the objection to the reception of that in evidence was a matter of no consequence whatever. Indeed the action cannot be sustained upon any view of it, unless we are prepared to shut our eyes to the clearest evidence of a corrupt agreement to suppress a criminal prosecution.

The motion for a new trial should be denied.

BACON, J., concurred.

[The dissenting opinion of MULLIN, J., is omitted.]

NOTE

Few trusts or trust provisions are invalid for policy reasons. Some of the kinds of trusts which may be invalid because they violate fundamental policies are:

(1) trusts designed to induce criminal or tortious acts, such as a trust to pay the fines of a beneficiary if he commits a criminal act or to reward a beneficiary if he commits perjury;

(2) trusts to encourage immorality, such as a trust to support a woman if she lives in adultery with the settlor;

(3) trusts to encourage divorce, such as a provision that income should be paid to a son if he will divorce his present spouse;

(4) trusts intended to defraud creditors.[61]

The court may refuse to grant any relief to the settlor, as well as the beneficiary, where the trust is created for an illegal purpose. An interesting application of this rule is found in MacRae v. MacRae, 37 Ariz. 307, 294 P.

61. As to trusts to defraud creditors, this problem usually arises on secret oral trusts. A transfer to a trustee can be attacked like any other transfer as a conveyance fraudulent as to creditors when made to defeat existing or future creditors. When the settlor reserves an interest, as in income, we shall see that it cannot be removed from attachment by his creditors (Section 5 of this chapter).

280 (1930)[62] where the husband had conveyed land to his wife to avoid possible creditors on a business deal, and she later, in order to avoid an attachment by creditors of the husband, conveyed to a friend and his wife upon an oral agreement to reconvey. The wife claimed that the reconveyance should be to her rather than the husband. The friend and his wife as trustees filed a disclaimer of any beneficial interest in the property. The court refused relief to either the wife or the husband, and left title in the friends on the grounds that both the wife and the husband had participated in the attempt to defeat creditors. Of course, in the normal situation the trustee is a friend of the settlor and may make a voluntary return of the property.

While the court may refuse to grant relief to the settlor because of the "clean hands" doctrine, this is not a hard and fast rule and depends upon a balance of the equities. Where no fraud is in fact worked on creditors, for example, the court may grant relief by resulting trust for the settlor.[63] Or it may return the property to the settlor where the trustee is in pari delicto. Much depends upon the facts of the individual case.[64]

SECTION 4. ESSENTIALS OF THE FORMAL TRUST

(1) REQUIREMENT OF A PRESENT DECLARATION OR TRANSFER IN TRUST

The methods for creating express trusts depend upon the relationship of the settlor to the property interest designated as the trust res and upon the capacity and power of the settlor to engage in the trust transaction.

If the settlor owns a presently existing and transferable legal or equitable interest in real or personal property, he may create an express trust by declaring himself trustee of the interest for the benefit of another or by transferring his interest to a trustee for his own benefit or for the benefit of another. For example:

1.

S owns 10 shares of stock. S declares himself trustee of the stock for the benefit of B. S is trustee of the stock for the benefit of B.

62. Note, 11 B.U.L.Rev. 282 (1931), 44 Harv.L.Rev. 1143 (1931).

63. Wantulok v. Wantulok, 67 Wyo. 22, 214 P.2d 477 (1950).

64. See Note: "Illegal Trusts: The Resulting Trust Problem", 44 Va.L.Rev. 605 (1958).

2.

S owns "Blackacre". S executes and delivers a deed of "Blackacre" to T. The deed directs that T hold "Blackacre" in trust for B. T is trustee of "Blackacre" for B.

S is both settlor and trustee in the first example. S retains legal title to the stock but creates an equitable interest in B by the trust declaration. In the second example S retains no interest in the property subject to the trust unless he conveys less than a fee simple or unless he retains a power to revoke or modify the trust. The trustee has legal title and B, the beneficiary, has an equitable interest. S can deed "Blackacre" to T in trust for S. S then retains an equitable interest and T has legal title.

When the settlor transfers legal title to a trustee the method of transfer required is that necessary for a transfer of similar property when no trust is involved. Land must be transferred by a deed or will executed with appropriate formalities. Personal property may be assigned or delivered to the trustee. When the settlor retains legal title but declares himself trustee of the property for another an oral declaration is sufficient to transfer an equitable interest in most states, although the declaration must be proved by a writing in most jurisdictions if the trust res is land.[65]

The settlor must have testamentary capacity to create a trust by will. He must have the capacity to make an inter vivos transfer of legal title to the trust property if he declares himself trustee of the property for the benefit of another and, of course, must have the capacity to make a transfer of legal title to a trustee for the benefit of himself or another.

A settlor may create an express trust of property which he does not own by bringing into existence an enforceable obligation against himself which can be held in trust by another or by exercising a power of appointment of which he is donee. For example:

1.

S executes a promissory note for $1,000 payable to T in trust for B. T is trustee of the note for B, if there is consideration for the note or it is binding because under seal.

2.

A devises "Blackacre" to X for life, remainder as S may by will or deed appoint. S appoints the remainder by will to T in trust for B. T is trustee of the remainder for B.

An enforceable promise is property which can be held in trust. But S cannot hold his own promise in trust in the first example because a person cannot have an enforceable obligation against himself. The transaction in the first example differs from the transaction in

65. See Chapter IX, Section 1.

which S declares himself trustee of a promise made by another or transfers the rights of the promisee to another as trustee. The transaction also differs from the transaction in which S promises to create a trust in the future. In the latter case no trust arises unless and until the promisor makes the transfer in trust.

In the second example, S is donee of a general power of appointment over the remainder interest. A is donor of the power. When the donee of a power may appoint to anyone, including himself, the power is general. The donee of a general power may appoint the property in trust for his own benefit or the benefit of another. If the power is "special", that is, the donee is authorized to appoint only within a specified class of persons, the donee may or may not be authorized to make an appointment in trust within the class. This will depend upon the terms of the power conferred upon him. An appointment is void when in excess of the power conferred.[66]

A trust requires a present legal transaction, not a future one. Thus, Restatement, Second, Trusts provides as follows:

"§ 26. No Intention to Create a Present Trust.

"*A manifestation of intention to create a trust inter vivos at some time subsequent to the time of the manifestation does not create a trust.*

"*Comment:*

"*b. Promise to make transfer in trust.* If a person declares his intention or makes an unenforceable promise that he will at a subsequent time transfer property then owned or thereafter to be acquired by him, to another person in trust, no trust arises unless and until he makes the transfer in trust.

"*Illustrations:*

"1. A, the owner of certain securities, tells B that he intends on the following day to transfer the securities to B in trust for C. No trust arises unless and until A transfers the securities to B in trust.

"2. A promises C that if and when A purchases certain shares of stock he will transfer the shares to B in trust for C. No trust arises unless A not only acquires the shares but also transfers them to B in trust. * * *

"*c. Promise to make declaration of trust.* If the owner of property declares his intention or makes an unenforceable promise that he will create a trust of the property by a subsequent manifestation of intention, no trust is created without such subsequent manifestation of intention. It is immaterial whether the property is owned by him at the time of the declaration or promise or is thereafter acquired.

66. See Chapter XIV on Powers of Appointment. Some life insurance trust transactions bear an analogy to the creation of a trust and the exercise of a power of appointment. Methods of creating life insurance trusts will be considered in Chapter XII.

"Illustrations:

"3. A, the owner of certain securities, tells B that he intends on the following day to declare himself trustee of the securities for B. No trust is created unless and until A declares himself trustee.

"4. A promises B that if and when A purchases certain shares of stock he will execute an instrument declaring himself trustee of the shares for B. No trust is created unless A not only acquires the shares but declares himself trustee. * * *

"*g. Postponement of enjoyment.* On the other hand, if the owner of property manifests an intention to create a trust at the time of the manifestation, a trust may arise at that time although by the terms of the trust the interest of the beneficiary is a future interest which is not to take effect in enjoyment until some future time.

"Illustration:

"9. A, the owner of certain securities, declares himself trustee of the securities in trust to pay to B the income accruing after the expiration of ten years, the income during the ten years to be retained by A for his own benefit. A trust is created at the time of the declaration, although B's beneficial interest does not take effect in enjoyment until the ten-year period expires. * * *

"*n. Promisee as trustee.* A promise to create a trust in the future is to be distinguished from the creation of a present trust of a promise to be performed in the future. A promisee of an enforceable promise to be performed in the future can hold his rights as promisee in trust for a third person. See § 17(e). If a person makes an enforceable promise to pay money or to make a conveyance of property to another person as trustee a present trust is created, the rights of the promisee being held by him as trustee, provided that the person creating the trust manifested an intention to create an immediate trust of the promisee's rights, and not merely to create a trust of the money when paid or of the property when conveyed.

"If the promise is made gratuitously and is not under seal, the promisor is not ordinarily bound thereby (see Restatement of Contracts, §§ 19, 95), and the promisee acquires no rights thereunder and no trust arises. If the promise is made gratuitously but is binding because under seal, the promisor is the creator of the trust, and if he manifests an intention that the promisee's rights under the promise shall be held in trust, the promisee immediately becomes trustee of his rights under the promise.

"If the promise is made for consideration paid by the promisee, the promisee is the creator of the trust, and if he manifests an intention that his rights under the promise shall be held in trust, he immediately becomes trustee of his rights under the promise. In the absence of evidence of a different intention, the inference is that the promisee immediately becomes trustee of his rights under the promise.

"Illustrations:

"15. In consideration of a payment of $10,000 made by B to A, A makes a promise in a written instrument signed by him to convey Blackacre to B in trust for C. B thereby acquires a right to recover damages from A if he breaks his promise and a right specifically to enforce the contract. These rights B holds in trust for C.

"16. A signs, seals and delivers to B an instrument whereby he promises B to transfer 1000 shares of the X Company to B in trust for C. The rights upon the contract which B thereby acquires he holds in trust for C.

"17. A, orally and gratuitously, promises to pay B $1000 in trust for C. B acquires no rights upon the promise. No trust is created.

* * *

"§ 30. Consideration for Promise to Create a Trust.

"A promise to create a trust in the future is enforceable, if, but only if, the requirements for an enforceable contract are complied with.

"Comment:

"*a. Manifestation of intention.* Whether an owner of property declares himself trustee of the property or makes a promise to become trustee in the future or to transfer the property in the future to another person as trustee, depends upon the manifestation of his intention. See § 26.

"*b. Promise to create trust.* Whether a promise made by the owner of property to become trustee thereof in the future or to transfer the property in the future to another person in trust creates in the promisee a right to recover damages for breach of the promise is determined by the law governing contracts. See Restatement of Contracts, §§ 148–177. On the question whether such a promise is specifically enforceable, see Restatement of Contracts, §§ 358–380.

* * * [67]

"*c. Promisee as trustee.* If the owner of property makes a promise to another person to transfer property in the future to him as trustee for a third person, the promisee holds such rights, if any, as he thereby acquires in trust for the third person, provided the parties manifested an intention to create a present trust of the promise (see § 26, Comment *n*). * * *."

Consideration is unnecessary to create an express trust. A declaration of trust is today generally treated as a present conveyance of a beneficial interest in the trust property. Interests in property can be transferred gratuitously. Indeed, as pointed out by Professor

67. A valid contract to create a trust is specifically enforceable when related to land or a unique chattel. A remedy for damages is adequate when the promise relates to a non-unique chattel. In those jurisdictions in which a sealed promise is binding, although unsupported by consideration, the contract probably cannot be enforced specifically. It is a general rule that a gratuitous promise, though under seal, is not specifically enforceable. See I Scott, Trusts (3d Ed., 1967) § 30.1.

Scott,[68] a declaration of trust is "* * * the simplest method by which one can give to another an interest in property. If the property is not an interest in land, and if the disposition is not testamentary in character, no formalities are required for a declaration of trust. All that is necessary is that the owner of the property should manifest an intention to hold the property in trust. In the case of a gift of property, delivery or a deed of gift is necessary. In the case of a contract, consideration or a deed is required. But in the case of a declaration of trust neither consideration nor a deed is necessary."

While it is essential for creation of a private express trust that a settlor, possessing the requisite legal capacity, appropriately manifest an intent to create the relationship known to the law as a trust, it is unnecessary that his manifestation be communicated to anyone. It is unnecessary, for example, that the settlor communicate his intention to create a trust to the trustee or to the beneficiary. But failure of the settlor to communicate his intention is evidence that he does not have a final and definitive intention to create a trust, although this evidence is not conclusive upon the point.[69]

NOTE ON FORMALITIES

The requirements for perfecting inter vivos gifts of choses in action represented by so-called indispensable documents are similar to those for perfecting inter vivos gifts of chattels. There must be delivery of either the indispensable document itself, or of a deed of gift of that document, or, possibly, of an unsealed instrument evidencing the intent to make the gift. Illustrations of indispensable documents are corporate bonds, stock certificates, bills and notes, savings bank passbooks, and life insurance policies.

No particular formalities are required for a gift of a chose in action not represented by a so-called indispensable document. All that is necessary is an affirmative manifestation of a present intent to assign the chose in action. A gratuitous assignment of a chose in action not represented by an indispensable document is generally held to be revocable by the donor and terminable on his death. This seems to be the case even though there is delivery to the donee of a deed of gift of the chose in action or delivery to the donee of an unsealed writing affirmatively manifesting an intent to make a present gift. But a gratuitous assignment of a chose in action not represented by an indispensable document is effective in the sense that the obligor cannot set up the gratuitous character of the assignment when sued on the chose in action by the donee. In some jurisdictions it appears that a gratuitous assignment of a chose in action not represented by an indispensable document is irrevocable if evidenced by the delivery of a deed of gift of the chose in action. Possibly in such jurisdictions, an irrevocable gift could also be made by the delivery of an unsealed writing presently manifesting an intent to make such a gift.[70]

Modern statutes provide for the creation and transfer inter vivos of interests in land by delivery of a deed. Inter vivos gifts of land are accomplished by the donor delivering a deed executed by him to the donee.

At common law, because of the fictional unity of husband and wife, one spouse had no power to transfer legal title to property to the other spouse.

68. I Scott, Trusts (3d Ed., 1967) 238.

69. See Restatement, Second, Trusts §§ 24, 35–36.

70. See generally, Restatement, Contracts (1932) § 158; Williston, Contracts (Rev. Ed. 1936) § 440.

Courts of equity, however, held that a husband could effectively declare himself trustee for his wife. The question then arose whether the Chancellor could convert an imperfect gift by a husband to his wife into a declaration of trust. A number of courts held that if a husband made a transfer of property to his wife, which was ineffective solely because of the common law disability of a husband to transfer property to his wife, he became trustee of the property for her. Modern statutes make it possible for a husband to make a direct gift to his wife. Hence the basis for these decisions no longer exists and the rule today should be, and doubtless is, that an imperfect gift of husband to wife does not amount to a declaration of trust for the wife. The same rule should apply to a gift by wife to husband in those states today in which a wife is under no legal disability in making a gift to her husband.[71]

It has been held that where one makes an imperfect gift to a natural object of his bounty and dies believing that he has made an effective gift, a court of equity will effectuate the gift by declaring his heir as constructive trustee. A number of courts refuse to raise a constructive trust in this situation on the ground that the donor himself held the property free of trust. Certainly this should be the result when the donor was aware of the fact that he had not made an effective transfer. If he believes the transfer to have been effective, it may be inequitable to permit his heirs to profit by the circumstance that it was ineffective.[72]

---

(2) INTENT

In the formal express trust it is usual to designate the "trustee" as such and to state that the transfer is "in trust". However, an express trust may be created without using either designation. And the use of the word "trust" or "trustee" is not a conclusive evidence of intent to create a trust in a homedrawn document. In such an informal arrangement the court is concerned with the substance of the transaction intended. The intent which must be manifested by the settlor is an intent to create the juridical relationship known to the law as a trust.[73] An express trust exists only when a settlor appropriately manifests an intention to impose enforceable duties on the trustee to deal with the property for the benefit of another.

Testators frequently annex precatory words to devises or bequests and thus create doubt whether an absolute gift or trust is intended. Is such language a polite testator's manner of imposing a mandatory duty to hold property on trust, or does it express merely a hope or wish, which in no sense is intended to be binding?

71. See Restatement, Second, Trusts § 31; I Scott, Trusts (3d Ed. 1967) § 31.2; Love, "Imperfect Gifts as Declarations of Trust: An Unapologetic Anomaly", 67 Ky.L.J. 309 (1978–79).

72. See V Scott, Trusts (3d Ed. 1967) § 466.2.

73. Distinctions between trusts and debts, bailments and related transactions are examined in detail in Restatement, Second, Trusts §§ 5–16; Bogert, Trusts and Trustees (2d Ed., 1965) §§ 11–38; I Scott, Trusts (3d Ed., 1967) §§ 5–16.

SPICER v. WRIGHT

Supreme Court of Virginia, 1975.
215 Va. 520, 211 S.E.2d 79.

POFF, JUSTICE.

Leila Wilson Spicer died March 22, 1968, survived by her husband, Meade T. Spicer, Jr., her sole heir at law. In her holographic will dated May 20, 1966, admitted to probate, she named her sister, Anne Beecher Wilson as "executor" without bond. Miss Wilson died on June 8, 1970. Russell Alton Wright qualified as Mrs. Spicer's administrator d.b.n.c.t.a. and as such filed a bill seeking aid and guidance in the construction of the will. He named as defendants Meade T. Spicer, Jr.; Archer L. Yeatts, III, Administrator of the Estate of Anne Beecher Wilson, deceased; the heirs at law and distributees of Miss Wilson; and certain parties unknown. John W. Edmonds, III, was appointed Guardian *ad litem* for Meade T. Spicer, Jr.

The third paragraph of the will provided:

> "My estate of every kind and description, personal, real estate, etc., I give to my sister, Anne Beecher Wilson to be disposed of as already agreed between us."

By final decree entered February 7, 1974, incorporating a letter opinion dated December 19, 1973, the chancellor held "that Anne Beecher Wilson acquired a fee simple title to the estate of Leila Wilson Spicer * * * free of and from all trusts". We granted Meade T. Spicer, Jr., by his Guardian *ad litem*, an appeal. By order entered in this Court on November 26, 1974, it appearing that Meade T. Spicer, Jr., died on October 18, 1974, Katharine S. Edmonds, Executrix of the Estate of Meade T. Spicer, Jr., deceased, was substituted as party appellant * * *.

Appellant contends that the language of the will, "to be disposed of as already agreed between us", is imperative and connotes an intent to create an express trust; that such testamentary intent is corrobrated by the extrinsic evidence; and that since the terms of the agreement are unknown and the express trust cannot be enforced, "[t]he property must be held as a resulting trust for Mrs. Spicer's heir and next of kin—her husband."

In Burton v. Irwin, 212 Va. 104, 181 S.E.2d 624 (1971), the testatrix devised her estate by holographic will to her brother whom she named "executor and trustee". The last sentence of the will provided: "My Brother knows my wishes and will carry them out, to the best of his ability." The chancellor held that an express trust was intended, that the trust failed for indefiniteness, and that a "naked trust was created or implied in favor of the heirs at law and distributees" of the testatrix. We said that "[t]he question is whether the testatrix intended to create a trust for undesignated beneficiaries and unspecified purposes which must fail for indefiniteness or whether she intended to leave her entire estate in fee simple to her brother. If she created a void trust then her net estate will be held by Burton as trustee under a resulting trust for the benefit of her heirs at law and distributees." 212 Va. at 105–106, 181 S.E.2d at 626. Reversing the chancellor's decree, we held that "the language found in Mrs. Mallory's will falls short of establishing an intent to create a trust and that it constitutes a devise and bequest of her property in fee simple and absolute estate to her brother William L. Burton." 212 Va. at 110, 181 S.E.2d at 629.

Here, we are faced with essentially the same question. We must decide whether the language of Mrs. Spicer's will, read in context with the extrinsic evidence, is sufficient to establish an intent to create an express trust; if so, that trust fails for indefiniteness and a resulting trust arises in favor of Meade T. Spicer, now deceased; if not, Miss Wilson takes the entire estate in fee simple.

As we said in *Burton* "[p]recatory words are *prima facie* construed to create a trust when they are directed to an executor, * * * [but] no trust is created by precatory language directed to a legatee unless there is testamentary intent to impose a legal obligation upon him to make a particular disposition of property." 212 Va. at 109, 181 S.E.2d at 628.

> "* * * [T]he question in all cases is whether a trust was or was not intended to be created; i.e., looking at the entire context of the will and the facts and circumstances properly admitted into evidence, did the testator intend to impose a binding obligation on the devisee to carry out his wishes, or did he mean to leave it to the devisee to act or not at his own discretion. [Citations omitted]." Smith v. Baptist Orphanage, 194 Va. 901, 905, 75 S.E.2d 491, 494 (1953).

The extrinsic evidence showing the close relationship between Mrs. Spicer and Miss Wilson reinforces the import of the language of the will that, at the time the will was written, the two sisters had "already agreed" how the property of the testatrix was "to be disposed of". But such evidence fails to establish a "testamentary intent to impose a legal obligation * * * to make a particular disposition of property" or to show that the agreement was one designed "to impose duties which are enforceable in the courts." Restatement of Trusts § 25, Comment a at 69 (2d ed. 1959). If the extrinsic evidence had sufficiently identified the beneficiary agreed upon and the terms of the benefits agreed upon, that evidence and the precatory language considered together would be sufficient to establish a testamentary intent to impose a legally enforceable duty, and to create a trust. Since the evidence did not, the precatory language standing alone imposes nothing more than an undefined moral obligation.
* * *

We hold that the language Mrs. Spicer employed is precatory, that the extrinsic evidence is insufficient to render that language imperative or to establish a testamentary intent to impose a legal obligation to make a particular disposition of property, that no express trust was intended or created, and that the language constitutes an absolute testamentary grant to Miss Wilson. Our holding in no way impairs those rights which the parties have agreed vested in the surviving spouse under Code § 64–16 on the date of Mrs. Spicer's death.

Finding no error below, we affirm the chancellor's decree.

Affirmed.

NOTE

In Comfort v. Cantrell,[74] a testator, in the third clause of his will, gave certain property to his wife "to be her absolute estate forever". In the fourth clause of the will appeared these words: "It is my request that upon her death my said wife, Clara Augusta Cantrell, shall give, devise and bequeath * * *" the property given her in the third clause of the will in certain shares to persons named in the fourth clause. The court held that the wife took the property as an absolute gift and not in trust. The opinion reads in part as follows:[75]

"Such being the will before us, we think the case falls under the authority of Smith v. Reynolds, 173 Tenn. 579, 121 S.W.2d 572, 574. In that case the court reviewed earlier decisions and re-affirmed the rule that a clear and certain devise of a fee, about which the testamentary intention was obvious, would not be cut down or lessened by subsequent words which are ambiguous or of doubtful meaning. Although the will said that the estate devised to his wife 'is by my wish returned to my nearest blood kin' at her death, the court held that the wife took the fee, it having been clearly and without ambiguity given to her previously in the instrument. The court said that the testator did not use the word wish as a command. And further that a trust would not be declared on the basis of precatory words where the will showed an intention to leave property absolutely. * * *

"In Scott on Trusts, § 25.2, it is said:[76]

" 'Under the older view the question was whether the testator desired that the legatee should make a particular disposition of the property. If he did and if that disposition was one which could be enforced, the courts held that a trust was created. Under the modern cases the question is: Did the testator not only desire that the legatee should make a particular disposition of the property, but did he intend to impose a legal obligation upon him to make the disposition? Under the earlier rule it was easier to determine whether or not a trust was created than it is under the modern view, which makes the question one of interpretation of each particular will.'

"In 1 Bogert on Trusts and Trustees, § 48, it is said:[77]

" 'The words "request", "desire", and the like do not naturally import a legal obligation. But the early view in England was that such words, when used in a will, were to be given an unnatural meaning, and were held to be courteous and softened means of creating duties enforceable by the courts. According to that opinion words of request prima facie created a trust. But since the beginning of the nineteenth century the English courts have changed their stand upon this question, and now hold that the natural significance of precatory words is not a trust, but that such an obligation may be shown by other portions of the instrument or

74. 177 Tenn. 553, 151 S.W.2d 1076 (1941).

75. 177 Tenn. at 556, 151 S.W.2d at 1077.

76. Currently, I Scott, Trusts (3d Ed., 1967) § 25.2.

77. Currently, Bogert, Trusts and Trustees (2d Ed., 1965) § 48.

by extrinsic circumstances. The American courts have adopted this natural construction of precatory expressions.'

"We find nothing in the record indicating an intention on the part of James G. Cantrell, that his will should be construed otherwise than we have done. It is true that those parties recommended by him to the beneficence of his wife were his relatives, but there is nothing to indicate that they were in need. Moreover, he had remembered them by another substantial devise in his will.

"For the reasons stated, and upon the authorities cited, the decree of the chancellor must be affirmed."

The older rule favoring the finding of a trust from precatory language has been explained as follows: [78] "The wish of a testator, like the request of a sovereign, is equivalent to a command." The basis for the modern attitude is said to be that: [79] "A will is a business document in which the use of diplomatic or courteous language is unnecessary."

As Professor Scott points out in his treatise on trusts: [80] "Since in every case where a testator uses precatory language, it is a question of interpretation of the language used in the light of all the circumstances, and since each will differs from every other will, the decisions are of importance only in showing how somewhat similar situations have been dealt with by the courts. There are numerous cases in which the courts have held that in spite of the precatory language used, the testator intended to create a trust. Still more numerous are the cases in which the courts have held that because of the precatory language used, the testator did not intend to create a trust." Illustrative of the results reached by courts in construing precatory language are the following cases:

1. A legacy to Arthur Garfield Hayes "* * * to use at his discretion in promoting the ends of justice," was held a beneficial gift to Hayes.[81]

2. Testator bequeathed his estate to his sons and in a later paragraph of his will provided: "I have heretofore expressed to my sons my wishes as to certain charitable gifts, and I therefore make no such bequests herein, preferring that my sons shall make such donations within their sole discretion as shall seem to them to be best." Held: An absolute gift to the sons, and their gift to St. Louis University of a million dollars of the estate that they received under their father's will was not exempt from Federal Estate tax as a bequest by the father for charitable purposes.[82]

3. A "request" in the testator's will that the executor pay to each of the attesting witnesses the sum of Five Dollars as a token of appreciation was held to create legacies for the witnesses and therefore they were beneficially interested and consequently under the law of the state the will was invalid.[83]

78. Hill, Trustees (4th Am.Ed., 1867) 116.

79. 2 Jarman, Wills (8th Ed. 1951) 876–77.

80. I Scott, Trusts (3d Ed., 1967) 208–210.

81. Matter of Hayes, 263 N.Y. 219, 188 N.E. 716 (1934). Noted in 19 Iowa Law Rev. 574 (1934), 9 Notre Dame Law 473 (1934), 8 St. John's L.Rev. 308 (1934).

82. Mississippi Valley Trust Co. v. Commissioner, 72 F.2d 197, 198 (C.C.A. 8th 1934), cert. den. 293 U.S. 604, 55 S.Ct. 119, 79 L.Ed. 695, reh. den. 293 U.S. 631, 55 S.Ct. 147, 79 L.Ed. 717 (1934).

83. In Re Moody, 155 Me. 325, 154 A. 2d 165, 73 A.L.R.2d 1225 (1959).

Restatement, Second, Trusts § 25 gives the following illustrations:

"1. A bequeaths $10,000 to B desiring that he should use it for such purposes as he might think the testator would deem wise. In the absence of other evidence, B is entitled beneficially to the money and does not take it in trust.

"2. A devises and bequeaths all his property to B hoping he will continue it in the family. In the absence of other evidence, B is entitled beneficially to the property and does not take it in trust.

"3. A executes a will devising and bequeathing all his property to B, his wife, expressing the wish that she would leave it to our two daughters, C and D. Later a son is born to A and B. A dies. In the absence of other evidence, B is entitled beneficially to the property and does not take it in trust.

"4. A devises and bequeaths all his property to B, his wife, desiring her to give all her estate at her death to my relations. Since the expression of desire applies not only to A's property, but also to B's property as to which A had no power to create a trust, he does not presumably intend to create a trust as to his property. In the absence of other evidence, B is entitled beneficially to the property and does not take it in trust.

"5. A devises and bequeaths all his property to B hoping he will let C have a good part of it. In the absence of other evidence, B is entitled beneficially to the property and does not take it in trust.

"6. A bequeaths all his property to his wife, adding 'I recommend to her the care and protection of my mother and sister, and request her to make such provision for them as in her judgment will be best.' The mother and sister were invalids and needy, and had been for some time supported by A. The testator leaves a large estate. In the absence of other evidence, the wife takes the property in trust to make a reasonable provision for the testator's mother and sister."

SPENCER v. CHILDS

Court of Appeals of New York, 1956.
1 N.Y.2d 103, 150 N.Y.S.2d 788, 134 N.E.2d 60.

FULD, JUDGE. Plaintiff, now 87 years of age, is a sister-in-law of Nellie Childs who died in 1946; defendants are the latter's children who were named by her as executors in her last will and testament. It is a provision of that will, Paragraph Third, which now engages our attention; in it, Mrs. Childs declared:

> "I request my two children, Richard S. Childs and Mary Childs Draper, or the survivor of them, to pay to my sister-in-law, Mary Parker Spencer, now residing at Manchester, Connecticut, the sum of Two hundred and eight dollars and thirty-three cents ($208.33) per month as long as she shall live."

Plaintiff, maintaining that the verb "request," read in context, is to be construed as a direction to pay her the sum specified, sues in contract, see, e.g., Redfield v. Redfield, 126 N.Y. 466, 27 N.E. 1032; Brown v. Knapp, 79 N.Y. 136, 143; Gridley v. Gridley, 24 N.Y. 130,

138, upon defendants' implied promise to pay, a promise implied from their acceptance of the residuary estate.

Mrs. Childs executed her will in 1944, two years before her death. After providing for a number of legacies, including bequests to plaintiff's two sons and to charity, she directed, in Paragraph Ninth, that the residue of her estate be equally divided between the two defendants. The estate consisted of over $2,500,000, the residuary estate, after taxes had been paid, of more than $1,000,000.

Plaintiff had married Mrs. Childs' brother in 1892 and, during their many years of marriage, Mrs. Childs had contributed to their support. In 1928, she made a will, providing for a trust of $100,000, the income—in the neighborhood of $208 a month—to be used for the support of her brother, and, if he predeceased plaintiff, then, for her support for life. After her brother died in 1932, Mrs. Childs gave plaintiff $208.33 a month, and these payments continued until March, 1945. In the meantime, she executed the will before us, which, as we have seen, contained the clause requesting defendants to pay plaintiff the very same sum each and every month as long as she lived. Following his mother's decease, Richard, one of defendants, wrote plaintiff a letter, informing her of the will provision and advising that "monthly checks" would be sent "about the first of each month"; and he added that she should "always endorse the checks for deposit personally, as they will be part of our accounting to the court." The checks were sent for two years—until plaintiff was 79 years old—and then they stopped.

The present action, brought some years later, seeks to recover the amount which has assertedly accumulated. Defendants' motion to dismiss the complaint for insufficiency was denied at Special Term and that decision was affirmed by the Appellate Division, 283 App. Div. 788, 129 N.Y.S.2d 238. Upon the trial thereafter held, there was a verdict for plaintiff, and, upon appeal, the Appellate Division affirmed, one justice dissenting.

Cases such as the present and Matter of Daly, 1 N.Y.2d 100, 150 N.Y.S.2d 785, 134 N.E.2d 58 also decided today, well illustrate the aptness of Judge Learned Hand's wise and trenchant observation that courts should be wary of making "a fortress out of the dictionary", since there "is no more likely way to misapprehend the meaning of language * * * than to read the words literally, forgetting the object which the document as a whole" seeks to achieve. Cabell v. Markham, 2 Cir., 148 F.2d 737, 739; Central Hanover Bank & Trust Co. v. Commissioner, 2 Cir., 159 F.2d 167, 169. "A word * * * may vary greatly in color and content" according to the intent of its author and the circumstances under which it is used. Town v. Eisner, 245 U.S. 418, 425, 38 S.Ct. 158, 159, 62 L.Ed. 372. And so it is with words such as "request," "wish" and "desire." Although ordinarily to be read as precatory (see Matter of Daly, 1 N.Y.2d 102, 150 N.Y.S.2d 787, 134 N.E.2d 59), they will be taken to connote a hope or a command depending on whether the author "meant by them simply to advise or inform a discretion which is vested in somebody or to control or direct a certain disposition." 7 Warren's Heaton on Surrogates' Courts (6th ed., 1951), p. 184. In seeking an answer to the question, the testator's intent and meaning are to be gathered, not alone from the language and terms of the instrument itself, but also from the conditions and circumstances extrinsic to it. See Collister v. Fassitt, 163 N.Y. 281, 286, 57 N.E. 490, 491; see, also, 3 Page on Wills (3d ed., 1941), § 1179.

One circumstance, indicative of a direction, is the degree of clarity and precision employed by the testator in describing the disposition in question—that is, the persons to take, the subject matter or amount of the gift, its terms and duration. See, e.g., Colton v. Colton, 127 U. S. 300, 315, 8 S.Ct. 1164, 32 L.Ed. 138; Matter of Bluestein's Will, 302 N.Y. 760, 98 N.E.2d 886, affirming 277 App.Div. 385, 100 N.Y.S.2d 350; Phillips v. Phillips, 112 N.Y. 197, 204, 19 N.E. 411, 413; see, also, 2 Jarman on Wills [8th ed., 1951], pp. 866–867. A like indication is furnished by the fact that the "request" is addressed to a close relative, for, it has been remarked, "it would be but natural for the testator to suppose that a request, which, in its terms, implied no alternative * * * would be understood and obeyed as strictly as though it were couched in the language of direction and command. In such a case * * * 'the mode is only civility.'" Colton v. Colton, supra, 127 U.S. 300, 319, 8 S.Ct. 1164, 1173; see, also, Notes, 49 A.L.R. 31, 34; 107 A.L.R. 904. And another signpost is found in the circumstance that the bequest, precatory in tone, precedes the clause disposing of the general or residuary estate out of which the gift is to come. See Collister v. Fassitt, supra, 163 N.Y. 281, 287 et seq., 57 N. E. 490.

In Phillips v. Phillips, supra, 112 N.Y. 197, 19 N.E. 411, a leading case, the testator, after providing that the whole of his property should go to his wife, added that, " 'If she find it always convenient to pay my sister Caroline Buck the sum of three hundred dollars a year, and also to give my brother Edwin W. during his life the interest on ten thousand dollars, (or seven hundred dollars per year,) I wish it to be done.' " The court held that the word "wish" was meant to be imperative, and, in reaching that conclusion, the court adverted both to such extrinsic factors as the wife's comfortable circumstances and the absence of children and to the definiteness and clarity of the bequest. "It is perfectly well settled", said the court, "that what are denominated, 'precatory words,' expressive of a wish or desire, may, in given instances, create a trust or impose a charge. Without a detailed consideration of the cases, it is quite clear that, as a general rule, they turn upon one important and vital inquiry, and that is whether the alleged bequest is so definite, as to amount and subject-matter, as to be capable of execution by the court, or whether it so depends upon the discretion of the general devisee as to be incapable of execution without superseding that discretion. In the latter case there can neither be a trust or a charge, while in the former there may be and will be, if such appears to have been the testamentary intention." 112 N.Y. at page 204, 19 N.E. at page 413. And in Matter of Bluestein's Will, supra, 302 N.Y. 760, 98 N.E.2d 886, affirming

277 App.Div. 385, 100 N.Y.S.2d 350, 351, both the language of the testament and the attendant circumstances were said to support the conclusion that, in context, the testator's "request" bespoke a direction, imposing an obligation upon the legatee. By his will, he left his partner " 'any and all interest in' " his accounting practice with the "request" that " 'he continue the same and pay out of such practice' " to his wife Rose the sum of $150 a month " 'for one hundred twenty months, or for her life if she die sooner, immediately following my demise.' " We held that this language amounted to a binding direction, the Appellate Division, whose order we affirmed, writing, "We are of the opinion, construing the will as a whole, that the distinctive language employed by the testator clearly imports an obligation—a legal obligation—by the legatee if he accepts the legacy bequeathed to him to make payment to the widow in the manner therein described. The amount, the duration, the subject matter, and the recipient of the obligation are all clearly and definitely expressed. All this would indicate that the intention of the testator was not to use precatory words expressing desire or hope but to use words giving 'an express, binding direction.' " 277 App.Div. at pages 386–387, 100 N.Y. S.2d at page 351.

Turning to the will under consideration, it is but necessary to observe that the suggested guides and signposts all point to the conclusion, reached by the courts below, that the "request" reflected a direction.

In the first place, the "request" is addressed to "my two children"—which their mother could expect would be understood and obeyed as strictly as if couched in language of command. In the second place, the amount of the gift is given to the penny and the other details are set forth in the most precise and explicit terms. By providing that her son and daughter (or, upon the death of one, the "survivor") were to pay plaintiff $208.33 each and every month during her life, testatrix could not have been more definite or left less to their independent judgment. In the third place, the fact that the provision for plaintiff "[stood] first in the will" and that defendants were to receive the residue only after payments to plaintiff, manifested a design to charge such amounts to defendants. Collister v. Fassitt, supra, 163 N.Y. 281, 287, 288–289, 57 N.E. 490, 492. And, in the fourth place, the further circumstances—the size of the estate left by testatrix, her children's great wealth, in contrast to the comparatively small gift to plaintiff, as well as the testatrix' long-continued practice of giving her $208.33 a month, the identical amount mentioned in the will—render it highly improbable that she intended defendants to be free to disregard the request and discontinue the monthly payments at their pleasure.

The judgment of the Appellate Division should be affirmed, with costs.

DESMOND, DYE and BURKE, JJ., concur with FULD, J.

VAN VOORHIS, J., votes to reverse and to dismiss the complaint upon the ground that the words of the will on which plaintiff's cause of action is based are precatory but not mandatory.

CONWAY, C.J., and FROESSEL, J., taking no part.

Judgment affirmed.[84]

PROBLEMS

1. "I bequeath all tangible personal property which I shall own at the time of my death to my wife, and I hope, but do not require, that out of this property she will give to each of my nieces and nephews some token of my affection for them." Outright gift to wife? See Leach, "Planning and Drafting a Will", 27 B.U.L.R. 157, 172 (1947).

2. "To my son, John, $1,000 with the direction that he use the same for the education of his four children." Outright gift to son? See Matter of Kennedy's Estate, 151 Misc. 193, 271 N.Y.S. 126 (1934).

3. "I bequeath $25,000 to my daughter, Sarah, desiring that she use it for such purposes as she thinks I would deem wise." Outright gift to Sarah? See Restatement, Second, Trusts § 25.

(3) TRUST PROPERTY[85]

Trust property is essential to the creation and continued existence of a trust. Any transferable interest,[86] present or future, vested or contingent, legal or equitable, in any object of ownership, tangible or intangible, may be held in trust. For example, trust property may consist of a life estate in land, a profit *a prendre* to remove minerals, an undivided interest in land as tenant in common, an absolute inter-

84. The relationship created by the testamentary gift in the principal case is not a trust but an equitable charge. This resembles a trust in some respects but not in others. See I Scott, Trusts (3d Ed., 1967) § 10. There may or may not be a personal liability, as was found in the Spencer case. In the equitable charge the beneficiary has only a security interest in the property subject to the charge. A bona fide purchaser of the property without notice of the charge would take free of the encumbrance.

85. The trust res problem in life insurance trusts is considered in Chapter XII, Section 2(1).

86. One has an interest in an object of ownership when he has a right, privilege, power or immunity with respect to it which members of society in general do not have. See Restatement, Property (1936) Ch. I. If the settlor does not declare himself trustee for another, the settlor must transfer the property to the trustee. See Sparkman v. Exchange National Bank of Colorado Springs, 191 Colo. 534, 554 P.2d 1090 (1976) in which the delivery to a bank of unendorsed stock certificates and several stock assignment forms which were blank except for the settlor's signature, with the intent to transfer the shares, conferred upon the trustee a right of specific performance to compel completion of the endorsements to comply with the Colorado statute, the trust being valid.

est in a specific bond or share of stock, or in an identified copyright, patent,[87] or trade secret.

Generally speaking, non-transferable interests in property cannot be held in trust. The interests cannot be transferred to a trustee. A trust cannot be created in such interests by declaration because a declaration, in effect, transfers an equitable interest to the *cestui que trust*. For example, a pension from the government, being non-transferable, cannot be held in trust. One having a non-transferable tort claim cannot create a trust of it. A tortious injury to trust property may give rise to a cause of action which the trustee holds in trust, whether or not it is transferable. But the trust is not *created* in an *existing* non-transferable chose in action. Non-transferable interests in property may, however, be *created* in trust. In jurisdictions in which contingent remainders are non-transferable, a contingent remainder may be created in trust. The trustee cannot transfer the contingent remainder except to a successor trustee. Nor can one owning a previously created contingent remainder create a trust therein by declaration or transfer. To illustrate: X, owning Blackacre in fee simple absolute, conveys Blackacre to T in trust for A for life, and, if A marry B, remainder in trust for B for life, remainder to C in fee. Assuming A and B to be unmarried on the effective date of this conveyance, B has an equitable contingent remainder, which was created in trust for him. B can himself create a trust in his contingent remainder if contingent remainders are transferable by the law of the state in which Blackacre is situated; but he cannot do so if contingent remainders are not transferable.

Trusts can be created only of interests in objects of ownership which are ascertained and definite on the date the trust is created or which are definitely ascertainable from facts then existing. Thus, no trust is created by an artist declaring himself trustee of the next picture he paints or by a person declaring himself trustee of the bulk of his securities or by a person declaring himself trustee of such securities as he may own on July first next. A trust of the residue of a decedent's estate is valid, however, although the amount of this residue cannot be ascertained exactly until the amount of his assets and liabilities has been determined. This determination is made largely from facts existing on the date the trust is created; namely, the date of the testator's death.

Although the object of ownership must be definite, it may change from time to time during the life of the trust. Thus, a trustee by exercising a power of sale and reinvestment may convert a farm into cash, cash into a claim against a bank by depositing the cash in the bank, and the claim against the bank into a government bond by drawing a check in payment for the bond upon the trust account. Hence it appears that the requirement of definiteness of the object of ownership is satisfied if at any given time the then object of owner-

87. But see Hise v. Grasty, 159 Va. 535, 166 S.E. 567 (1932), 1 Duke B.A.J. 94 (1933), 46 Harv.L.Rev. 861 (1933), 17 Minn.L.Rev. 558 (1933), 81 U. of Pa.L. Rev. 636 (1933), 19 Va.L.Rev. 533 (1933) holding that an unpatented invention is not property which can be reached by creditors of the inventor.

ship is definite and ascertained. Although there is some authority to the contrary, it seems to be generally agreed that this requirement is not violated by an authorization to the trustee to withdraw property from the trust at his discretion, despite the fact that this renders uncertain the amount to be received by the beneficiary who is entitled to receive the trust property upon termination of the trust. Similarly a trust will not fail because by its terms an income beneficiary is entitled to receive so much of the principal as he may demand. Nor does the reservation by the settlor of the power to revoke the trust in whole or in part destroy its validity.

Trust property being essential to the existence of a trust, it follows that the trust must end with the destruction of the object of ownership to which the interest held in trust relates. For example, if a trustee of bearer bonds sells them to a bona fide purchaser and squanders the proceeds, there is nothing left for him to hold in trust and the trust ends. For this breach of trust, the trustee is liable to the beneficiary; but, in the event of the trustee's insolvency, the beneficiary of the trust is not entitled to priority over the general creditors unless the wronged beneficiary is able to trace the proceeds of the sale and thus, in effect obtain a priority over general creditors. Nevertheless, although a trust no longer exists, it seems that a fiduciary relationship continues to exist between the former trustee and beneficiary. Hence a release from liability for a breach of trust will be valid only if full disclosure of all relevant circumstances be made by the former trustee and the transaction otherwise be entirely fair and for adequate consideration.

Failure of the settlor to define explicitly the duration of the interest to be held in trust in a definitely identified object of ownership is not fatal to the creation of the trust. When the object of ownership is land, equity will remedy the defect in the description by implying that the settlor intended to invest the trustee with such an estate in the land as he must have to accomplish the trust purpose. When the object of ownership is personal property, on the other hand, equity will imply an intent to invest the trustee with an interest therein of unlimited duration and not one limited to the duration necessary to accomplish the trust purpose. These implications of intent are rules of construction developed in equity. They yield to an intent clearly manifested to the contrary. Why there is a difference between the rule applicable to land and the rule applicable to personal property is not entirely clear. Perhaps it is because the Statute of Uses applied to real property. The Statute executed passive uses.[88] A trust becomes passive when its purposes are accomplished. Thus, the Statute of Uses operated to preclude the trustee from having an estate which would outlast the accomplishment of the trust purpose. Obviously the settlor must have intended the trustee to have an estate which would last that long.

88. For the background and operation of the Statute of Uses see Chapter I, Section 3(1)A.

Confusion exists where the land is transferred to a trustee in trust to pay the income therefrom to A for life and on A's death "to convey" the land to B in fee simple. Does the trustee take an estate in fee simple so that he can "convey" a fee simple to B or does the trustee merely take an estate for the life of A, B taking a legal remainder in fee simple by the transaction creating the trusts? Does the direction to "convey" impose active duties upon the trustee? If not the trust becomes passive on the death of A and is automatically executed by the Statute of Uses. According to the prevailing view in this country, the obligation to convey is viewed as imposing an active duty with the result that the trustee takes a fee simple as trustee and B has an equitable interest as beneficiary of a trust.

One may inquire, as a practical matter, what difference it makes whether the trustee takes an interest of unlimited duration or one limited in duration to the accomplishment of the purposes of the trust. In some jurisdictions it might make a difference in the fees of the trustee.[89] In a limited duration situation the person entitled on termination of the trust requires no transfer of title from the trustee. In an "unlimited duration" situation a transfer of the trustee's title is necessary. But even in the former case a transfer from the trustee is desirable in order to clear title to the property. In both situations equity will compel a transfer.

There are a number of instances, however, in which it is decidedly important to determine the duration of the trustee's interest. Assume Blackacre is transferred to T in trust to pay the income therefrom to A for life and on A's death to convey the land to B in fee simple. If the state in which Blackacre is located recognizes procedural distinctions between actions at law and suits in equity, the forum in which B will seek redress against the trustee or a third party with respect to Blackacre will depend upon whether B's interest is a legal or equitable remainder. That, in turn, will depend on whether the trustee took merely an estate for A's life or a fee simple in Blackacre. Again, if the trustee takes an estate in fee simple, adverse possession by a third party will bar both A and B; whereas if the trustee takes merely an estate for A's life, the statute of limitations will not run against B until A's death. Also, if the trustee has a fee simple, he has power to extinguish the interests of A and B by conveying to a bona fide purchaser; whereas, if the trustee has merely an estate for the life of A, he cannot extinguish B's legal remainder by conveying to a bona fide purchaser. Similarly, if the trustee has merely an estate *pur autre vie*, no fiduciary relationship exists between him and B; whereas, if his estate is a fee simple, a fiduciary relationship does exist.[90]

A debtor cannot be trustee of his own debt because a person cannot be indebted to himself and a trustee is not a juristic entity sepa-

89. See Matter of Chalmers, 62 Misc. 2d 537, 308 N.Y.S.2d 980 (Surr.Ct., Erie Co. 1970) discussed and criticized in Pasley, "Trusts and Administration," 22 Syra.L.R. 227, at 240 (1971).

90. See generally, Restatement, Second, Trusts Ch. 3; Bogert, Trusts and Trustees (2d Ed., 1965) Ch. 7; I Scott, Trusts (3d Ed., 1967) Ch. 3; 3 A.L.R.3d 1416 (1965).

rate and distinct from the individual or corporation serving in that capacity. A, as trustee, is not one person and A, as an individual, another person. If B lends money to A and before the debt is discharged A, B and C enter into an agreement by which A promises to hold his indebtedness to B "in trust" for C, no trust is created because there is no trust property. A cannot be obligated to himself. As trustee, he could not bring an action against himself as an individual. C's only redress against A seems to be in contract on a theory of novation.

If A transfers funds to the B Bank and Trust Company in trust for C, authorizing the Bank to deposit the trust funds pending investment in its commercial department, and immediately after receipt of the funds the Bank deposits them in its commercial department in an account entitled "B in trust for C", the money ceases to be trust property because it is commingled with other funds of the bank. No chose in action takes the place of this money, as would have been the case if it had been deposited in some other bank, because the bank cannot be indebted to itself. The trust property is extinguished and the trust ends. C is simply a general creditor of the bank. A fiduciary relation still exists between the bank and C, and to the extent that the bank invests the amount of the deposit there is a trust res and the trust is reconstituted, assuming always that the bank does not invest in its own obligations. If the bank becomes insolvent pending reconstitution of the trust, C is not entitled to priority over the other depositors.[91]

Assume that B lends A $1,000. Thereafter B dies leaving a will by which he bequeaths his claim against A to A in trust for C. Since A cannot enforce a claim against himself, A's indebtedness to B is extinguished. But a court of equity will not permit A to profit, C to suffer a loss, and B's general intent to benefit C to be frustrated. Although no constructive trust can be raised because there is no trust property, an equitable obligation is recognized co-extensive with the legal duty which was extinguished by B's bequest to A. This means that a court of equity will: (1) appoint a new trustee and compel A to pay the amount of the debt to him for the benefit of C; or (2) compel A to set aside the amount of the debt and hold the money so earmarked in trust for C; or (3) compel A to pay the amount of the debt directly to C, if the trust B purported to create was terminable by C at will.[92]

91. But see Sec. 3(C)(6) of Uniform Trustees Powers Act. Also see Sec. 9.10(b) and the exceptions to Sec. 9.12 of "Regulation 9", which is set out in Appendix II of this book.

92. Most of the courts which have considered the matter and the Restatement of Trusts are believed to support the views expressed in the text. The cases, however, are few in number and, for the most part, cryptic and vague in reasoning. Occasional dicta suggest that a debtor may be trustee of his debt. But this language seems to appear only in cases in which the courts are seeking to evade the application of a rule of law which does not apply to trusts but does apply to other legal institutions. See Restatement, Second, Trusts § 87; Bogert, Trusts and Trustees (2d Ed., 1965) § 114; I Scott, Trusts (3d Ed., 1967) § 87.

PROBLEMS

1. By statute a fraternal organization is authorized to pay a death benefit only to relatives of a member. If the relative designated cannot take, or if no relative is designated, the amount of the death benefit is payable to the next of kin of the member. X, a member of the organization, designated his cousin, B, as the beneficiary of X's death certificate, B agreeing to hold his interest as beneficiary in trust for C, who is not related to X. X dies leaving D as his next of kin. The proceeds of the death benefit are paid to B. Is B entitled to retain this amount or should he pay it to C or to D? O'Brien v. Massachusetts Catholic Order of Foresters, 220 Mass. 79, 107 N.E. 400 (1915); Restatement, Second, Trusts § 79, Comment *g*; 18 Rocky Mt.L.Rev. 415 (1946); 2 A.L.R.2d 489 (1948).

2. Blackacre is located in a state in which a right of action for trespass to land cannot be transferred. T is trustee of Blackacre for B. X trespasses on Blackacre. Does T hold the cause of action for trespass in trust for B? See Breidecker v. General Chemical Co., 47 F.2d 52 (C.C.A.7th 1931); Restatement, Second, Trusts § 81, Comment *b*.

3. May a seat on a stock exchange or a commodity exchange or a board of trade be held in trust? See I Scott, Trusts (3d Ed., 1967) § 82.7.

BRAINARD v. COMMISSIONER OF INTERNAL REVENUE

United States Circuit Court of Appeals, Seventh Circuit, 1937.
91 F.2d 880.[93]

SPARKS, CIRCUIT JUDGE. This petition for review involves income taxes for the year 1928. The question presented is whether under the circumstances set forth in the findings of the Board of Tax Appeals, the taxpayer created a valid trust, the income of which was taxable to the beneficiaries under section 162 of the Revenue Act of 1928.[94]

The facts as found by the Board of Tax Appeals are substantially as follows: In December, 1927, the taxpayer, having decided that conditions were favorable, contemplated trading in the stock market during 1928. He consulted a lawyer and was advised that it was possible for him to trade in trust for his children and other members of his family. Taxpayer thereupon discussed the matter with his wife and mother, and stated to them that he declared a trust of his stock trading during 1928 for the benefit of his family upon certain terms and conditions. Taxpayer agreed to assume personally any losses re-

93. Noted, 26 Ill.B.J. 333 (1938); 36 Mich.L.Rev. 1041 (1938).

94. "§ 162. The net income of the estate or trust shall be computed in the same manner and on the same basis as in the case of an individual, except that—
* * *

"(b) There shall be allowed as an additional deduction in computing the net income of the estate or trust the amount of income of the estate or trust for its taxable year which is to be distributed currently by the fiduciary to the beneficiaries, and the amount of the income collected by a guardian of an infant which is to be held or distributed as the court may direct, but the amount so allowed as a deduction shall be included in computing the net income of the beneficiaries whether distributed to them or not."

sulting from the venture, and to distribute the profits, if any, in equal shares to his wife, mother, and two minor children after deducting a reasonable compensation for his services. During 1928 taxpayer carried on the trading operations contemplated and at the end of the year determined his compensation at slightly less than $10,000 which he reported in his income tax return for that year. The profits remaining were then divided in approximately equal shares among the members of his family, and the amounts were reported in their respective tax returns for 1928. The amounts allocated to the beneficiaries were credited to them on taxpayer's books, but they did not receive the cash, except taxpayer's mother, to a small extent.

In addition to these findings the record discloses that taxpayer's two children were one and three years of age. Upon these facts the Board held that the income in controversy was taxable to the petitioner as a part of his gross income for 1928 and decided that there was a deficiency. It is here sought to review that decision.

In the determination of the questions here raised it is necessary to consider the nature of the trust, if any, that is said to have been created by the circumstances hereinbefore recited. It is clear that the taxpayer, at the time of his declaration, had no property interest in "profits in stock trading in 1928, if any," because there were none in existence at that time. Indeed it is not disclosed that the declarer at that time owned any stock. It is obvious, therefore, that the taxpayer based his declaration of trust upon an interest which at that time had not come into existence and in which no one had a present interest. In the Restatement of the Law of Trusts, vol. 1, § 75 it is said that an interest which has not come into existence or which has ceased to exist can not be held in trust. It is there further said: "A person can, it is true, make a contract binding himself to create a trust of an interest if he should thereafter acquire it; but such an agreement is not binding as a contract unless the requirements of the law of Contracts are complied with. * * *

"Thus, if a person gratuitously declares himself trustee of such shares as he may thereafter acquire in a corporation not yet organized, no trust is created. The result is the same where instead of declaring himself trustee, he purports to transfer to another as trustee such shares as he may thereafter acquire in a corporation not yet organized. In such a case there is at most a gratuitous undertaking to create a trust in the future, and such an undertaking is not binding as a contract for lack of consideration. * * *

"* * * If a person purports to declare himself trustee of an interest not in existence, or if he purports to transfer such an interest to another in trust, he is liable as upon a contract to create a trust if, but only if, the requirements of the law of Contracts are complied with." See, also, Restatement, § 30b; Bogert, Trusts and Trustees, vol. 1, § 112. In 42 Harvard Law Review 561, it is said: "With logical consistency, the courts have uniformly held that an expectancy cannot be the subject matter of a trust and that an attempted creation, being merely a promise to transfer property in the future, is invalid unless supported by consideration." Citing Lehigh Valley R. R. Co. v. Woodring, 116 Pa. 513, 9 A. 58. Hence, it is obvious under the facts here presented that taxpayer's declaration amounted to nothing more than a promise to create a trust in the future, and its binding force must be determined by the requirements of the law of contracts.

It is elementary that an executory contract, in order to be enforceable, must be based upon a valuable consideration. Here there was none. The declaration was gratuitous. If we assume that it was based on love and affection that would add nothing to its enforceability, for love and affection though a sufficient consideration for an executed conveyance, is not a sufficient consideration for a promise. Sullivan v. Sullivan, 122 Ky. 707, 92 S.W. 966, 7 L.R.A.,N.S., 156, 13 Ann.Cas. 163; Fischer v. Union Trust Co., 138 Mich. 612, 101 N.W. 852, 68 L.R.A. 987, 110 Am.St.Rep. 329; Fink v. Cox, 18 Johns. (N.Y.) 145, 9 Am.Dec. 191; Kennedy v. Ware, 1 Pa. 445, 44 Am.Dec. 145.

What has been said, however, does not mean that the taxpayer had no right to carry out his declaration after the subject matter had come into existence, even though there were no consideration. This he did and the trust thereby became effective, after which it was enforceable by the beneficiaries.

The questions with which we are concerned are at what times did the respective earnings which constitute the trust fund come into existence, and at what times did the trust attach to them. It is obvious that the respective profits came into existence when and if such stocks were sold at a profit in 1928. Did they come into existence impressed with the trust, or was there any period of time intervening between the time they came into existence and the time the trust attached? If there were such intervening time, then during that time the taxpayer must be considered as the sole owner of the profits and they were properly taxed to him as a part of his income.

It is said in the Restatement of the Law of Trusts, § 75c: "If a person purports to declare himself trustee of an interest not in existence or if he purports to transfer such an interest to another in trust, no trust arises even when the interest comes into existence in the absence of a manifestation of intention at that time." This we think is especially applicable where as here, there was no consideration for the declaration. It is further stated, however, in the Restatement, § 26k: "If a person manifests an intention to become trustee at a subsequent time, his conduct at that subsequent time considered in connection with his original manifestation may be a sufficient manifestation of intention at that subsequent time to create a trust. * * * the act of acquiring the property coupled with the earlier declaration of trust *may be* a sufficient manifestation of an intention to create a trust at the time of the acquisition of the property." (Our italics, here and hereafter.) In subsection 1 it is said "* * * Mere silence, however, ordinarily will not be such a manifestation. Whether silence is or is not such a manifestation is a question of interpretation." In such interpretation, subsection m is quite pertinent and controlling: "A promise to create a trust in the future is *enforceable*, if * * * the requirements for an enforceable contract are complied with. Whether a promise to transfer property in trust or to become trustee creates in the promisee a right to recover damages for breach of the promise, and whether such a promise is specifically enforceable are determined by the law governing contracts. Thus, if the owner of property transfers the property in trust and agrees to pay a sum of money to the trustee to be held upon the same trust, he is not liable for failing to pay the money if the promise was made gratuitously * * * but if the promise was made for consideration * * * the promisor is liable thereon. So, also, a promise to create a trust of property if thereafter acquired by the promisor imposes no liability upon the promisor if the promise was gratuitous. * * *"

[Omitted is a discussion of Section 112 of Professor Bogert's treatise on Trusts and Trustees.]

* * *

From what has been said we are convinced that appellant's profits in question were not impressed with a trust when they first came into existence. The Board was obviously of the impression that the trust first attached when appellant credited them to the beneficiaries on his books of account. This act, it seems to us, constituted his first subsequent expression of intention to become a trustee of the fund referred to in his original and gratuitous declaration. Prior to that time we think it is clear that the declaration could not have been enforced against him, and that his mere silence with respect thereto should not be considered as an expression of his intention to establish the trust at a time earlier than the credits. The case of Blair v. Commissioner, 300 U.S. 5, 57 S.Ct. 330, 81 L.Ed. 465, is to be distinguished from the present case in that there the corpus of the trust was in existence. The taxpayer was the life beneficiary and had assigned a part of the trust income to his children. The court there held that the taxpayer had an interest in the trust property that he could assign to others. The same may be said of Lowery v. Helvering (C.C.A.) 70 F. 2d 713; Tracy v. Commissioner (C.C.A.) 70 F.2d 93; Copland v. Commissioner (C.C.A.) 41 F.2d 501; Shellabarger v. Commissioner (C.C. A.) 38 F.2d 566; and Byrnes v. Commissioner (C.C.A.) 89 F.2d 243. In the instant case appellant had no property interest, and there was no assurance that it would ever come into existence. * * *

The order of the Board is affirmed.[95]

PROBLEMS

1. A granted and assigned to T the interests in real and personal property to which she might become entitled under the wills or intestacies of her brother, B, and her sister, C, if B or C or both died during her lifetime. C died during the lifetime of A and A delivered to T the property she received

95. The avoidance of income taxes by a short-term trust has been discussed previously in Section 2(3) of this Chapter. This problem is now fully covered by statute, when the settlor succeeds in creating a valid trust. How could the settlor have created a valid trust in the principal case? See, "Creation of Express Trust in Property to be Acquired in Future", 3 A.L.R.3d 1416 (1965).

from C's estate. B died during the lifetime of A but A did not wish to transfer his property to T. Can she be compelled to do so? In re Ellenbrough, [1903] L.R. 1 Ch. 697; In re Bowden, [1936] Ch. 71; 6 Camb.L.J. 251 (1937).

2. A gratuitously executed an instrument by which he declared himself trustee for B of shares of stock of any company that might be formed to operate a mining claim in which A was interested. Subsequently a company was formed for this purpose and A received shares of stock in the company. He refused to hold these shares in trust for B. Can B compel him to do so? Brennon v. Morphett, 6 Comm.L.Rep. 22 (Aust.1908).

(4) THE TRUSTEE

Since the trustee becomes responsible for managing the trust property, it is obvious that choice of a proper person as trustee assumes paramount importance. Normally, this choice will be between an able individual or a corporate fiduciary, or some combination of these (such as the appointment of a bank or trust company as cotrustee with an individual member of the family). Occasionally problems arise concerning the capacity of a person chosen as trustee, and these are considered in this particular section.

Generally speaking, a natural person has the same capacity to take, to hold, and to administer property under a trust as he has to take, to hold and to administer property for his own benefit. Again, generally speaking, a private corporation may be a trustee when it is expressly or impliedly authorized to act in that capacity by its charter or certificate of incorporation or by state statute. Trust companies and banks are the private corporations most commonly made trustees. The Comptroller of the Currency may authorize a National bank to act as trustee. A municipal corporation may act as trustee to carry out the purposes for which it was incorporated. For example, a municipal corporation may act as trustee for such charitable purposes as the promotion of education, the relief of poverty, the protection of health, and the construction and maintenance of public parks. A municipality, however, cannot act as trustee of a private express trust.

The United States or a state may become a trustee, although such a trust can be enforced only with the consent of the National government or the state government concerned because neither the National government nor a state government can be sued without its consent. Thus, the beneficiary cannot enforce the trust against the United States or a state unless authorized to do so by a special act of the legislature or unless a proceeding in a court of claims or other tribunal is provided by statute. This immunity from suit renders enforcement of the trust difficult but does not prevent the United States or a state from acting as trustee.[96]

A married woman at common law did not have the capacity to administer a trust properly.[97] She could not contract and, apart from her husband, could not transfer property. On application by a beneficiary of the trust, a married woman would normally be removed as trustee and she and her husband would be directed by the court to join in a conveyance of the trust property to a new trustee. In some states, by statute, the decree might vest title to the trust property in the new trustee without a conveyance by the wife and husband. Modern legislation giving married women power to take, to convey, and to manage their property as if they were unmarried, removes their disability to act as trustee.

An infant may become trustee since he has the capacity to take and hold property. An infant, however, cannot properly administer a trust because his contracts and conveyances are voidable by him. For this reason, an infant trustee will ordinarily be removed by the court on application by a beneficiary. The court will appoint a competent trustee to fill the vacancy created by removal of the infant. The successor trustee is invested with title to the trust property by operation of a statute or by conveyance from the infant. The infant is restrained from avoiding his conveyance to the new trustee.

A lunatic has the capacity to take and hold title to property and therefore may become a trustee. It is obvious, however, that a lunatic does not have the capacity to administer a trust. He will be removed and a new trustee appointed upon application by a beneficiary. Title is transferred from the lunatic by operation of a statute or his guardian may be compelled to convey title to the new trustee.

Generally speaking, an alien may become trustee of property which he can own beneficially.[98] By statute in some states an alien cannot become a trustee. In other states, by statute, a non-resident alien cannot become a trustee. A court has the power, in the absence of a statute, to deny a non-resident alien the privilege of serving as trustee when, in the judgment of the court, it would be detrimental to the trust to permit the non-resident alien to serve. A typical objec-

96. For an interesting case in which the state court approved appointment of the United States Government as trustee of a trust for relief of indigent American Indians, see Edgeter v. Kemper, 18 Ohio Misc. 143, 136 N.E.2d 630 (Ohio Prob. 1955). The problems include, in such a situation, not only loss of control by state courts but also statutory authorization by the United States Government to act as trustee. See Restatement, Second, Trusts, § 95.

97. A married woman could become trustee at common law because she was capable of taking and holding property, but her husband acquired an interest in her property and held his interest subject to the trust.

98. At common law an alien could not take title to land by descent and title to land taken by devise or inter vivos conveyance was subject to divestment by the Crown in a proceeding of "inquest by office found". The alien was under no disability in taking title to personal property by distribution, testamentary gift or inter vivos transfer. If a state statute provides that an alien cannot take title to land, the alien cannot become a trustee of land. For a discussion of the modern status of the alien as a property owner in the United States see Chapter III, Section 4(5).

tion to allowing a non-resident alien to serve is that the court will have difficulty in supervising his administration.

A natural person,[99] who is a citizen of the United States, but who does not reside in the state in which the trust is created and is to be administered and in which the trust property is situated, may be a trustee. This is true whether the trust be created inter vivos or by will. Some states require by statute a non-resident testamentary trustee to appoint a resident agent upon whom process may be served. Moreover, it seems that a court has the power to refuse to confirm the nomination of a non-resident as testamentary trustee. On the other hand, a statute denying non-residents the privilege of serving as trustees of living trusts might be unconstitutional as an abridgment of the privileges and immunities of citizens of the United States.[1] Statutes providing that executors shall be residents of the state of their appointment are distinguished from statutes denying non-residents the privilege of serving as trustees on the ground that appointment of an executor is a matter within the power of the court making the appointment, the executor being, in effect, an officer of the court. A resident trustee who thereafter becomes a non-resident may be removed from his trusteeship on that ground and a new trustee appointed to take his place.

According to the traditional common law view, an unincorporated association cannot be a trustee because it is not a legal entity and cannot take or hold title to property. The trust will not fail, however, unless the settlor has manifested an intent that the association as such shall alone be trustee. The court will appoint a trustee to keep the trust from failing. A few modern decisions permit unincorporated associations to be trustees on the theory that the association is a legal entity for the purpose of taking and holding title to trust property. This result seems to follow in those states in which there are

99. There is diversity of view whether a foreign corporation may serve in a fiduciary capacity. In most states the matter is handled by statute. See 37 Va.L.Rev. 1119, 1127–1134 (1951); "Administration of Out of State Assets By Corporate Trustees", 103 Trusts and Estates 997 (1964); Switzer, "Common Market for Trusteeship: Removal of Barriers to Non-Resident Trust Institutions," 102 Trusts and Estates 320 (1963). For criteria relating to selection of Trustees see Mulreany, "Foundation Trustees—Selection Duties and Responsibilities", 13 U.C.L.A.L.Rev. 1060 (1966); Bromberg and Fortson, "Selection of a Trustee; Tax and Other Considerations", 19 S.W.L.J. 523 (1965); 26 A.L.R.3d 1019 (1969).

It was held that South Carolina statutes barring a South Carolina Trust Company from acting as executor, administrator, or testamentary trustee because the trust company was controlled by a corporation domiciled in another state was an unconstitutional denial of equal protection of the laws. The court also held that it was not a denial of the due process clause of the 14th Amendment for South Carolina to exclude a foreign corporation (trust company) doing business in the state. The courts further held that "* * * Since South Carolina's ban on foreign testamentary trustees operates equally against state and national banks located in North Carolina, the exclusion of North Carolina National is not an impermissible burden on interstate commerce." American Trust Co. Inc. v. South Carolina State Board of Bank Control, 381 F.Supp. 313 (Col.D.S.C.1974).

1. Ind.Ann.Stat. § 30–4–2–11 (1974); Shirk v. LaFayette, 52 F. 857 (C.C.Ind. 1892); Robey v. Smith, 131 Ind. 342, 30 N.E. 1093 (1892).

statutes authorizing certain unincorporated associations to acquire title in the group name of the association.

Probably the designation of a partnership as trustee will vest title in the trust property in the individual partners as co-trustees.[2] To the extent that today a partnership is recognized as a legal entity, it would seem that the partnership as such could be trustee. If the partnership or its members cannot serve, the trust will not fail unless the settlor's intent is that only the partnership or its members shall serve to administer the trust. If it does not conflict with the settlor's intention, a court will appoint a new trustee to administer the trust.[3]

An owner of property may declare himself trustee of the property for the benefit of another.[4] In this situation the settlor is also trustee. The same situation exists if the owner purports to transfer property to himself as trustee. Obviously, one cannot transfer to himself that which he already has. By purporting to transfer to himself, the settlor manifests an intention to hold in trust property which he previously held free of trust. The transaction is a trust declaration in legal effect.

The owner of a transferable interest in property may create a trust thereof in which he is one of two or more trustees. At common law this could be done only by a transfer by the owner through a straw man to himself and his co-trustees. This was because at common law a joint tenancy could not be created by a transfer by a property owner to himself and others. Such a transaction would lack the essential unities of time and title. Co-trustees have always been deemed to hold the trust property as joint tenants. Today, in most jurisdictions, it is unnecessary for a settlor to convey through a straw man to make himself a co-trustee.

A sole trustee cannot be sole beneficiary of a trust because there would be no one to enforce it. A, as trustee, is not a juristic person separate from A, as an individual. One cannot bring a bill in equity against himself. Hence a trust is created only when a trustee holds property subject to an equitable obligation to deal with it for the benefit of *another*. If the sole trustee acquires the entire interest of the sole beneficiary, the trust is terminated. The legal and equitable titles merge, the trust is extinguished, and the property is held free and clear of the trust.[5]

Where, however, the same person is trustee and also one of several beneficiaries, or where the sole beneficiary is one of several trustees, there is no reason why the legal and equitable titles should

2. A partnership is not recognized as a legal entity at common law.

3. See generally, Restatement, Second, Trusts, §§ 89–99; 4 Powell, The Law of Real Property (Rohan Rev.1970) ¶¶ 561–563; II Scott, Trusts (3d Ed., 1967) §§ 89–99.

4. Under the feudal law, a declaration by the owner of land that he was seised thereof to the use of another was effective only if in the form of a deed of bargain and sale or a covenant to stand seised. A gratuitous declaration of *use* not in one of these forms was unenforceable. These feudal requirements are no longer made.

5. For an apparent exception to this rule in the case of spendthrift trusts, see Chapter X, Section 5. See 7 A.L.R.4th 621 (1981).

merge.[6] Hence it is possible for the settlor to select one of the beneficiaries as trustee or co-trustee.

When property is transferred to A in trust to pay the income to A for life and on A's death to transfer the principal to B, a difficult problem arises in jurisdictions in which it is held that the interest of the trustee in the trust property is limited to the duration of the trust, with the result that the remainderman takes the legal remainder. Thus, the New York courts have held, by applying the doctrine of merger, that such a limitation creates a legal life estate in A, free of the trust, followed by a legal remainder in B.[7] This view has been criticized on the ground that it defeats the intention of the settlor and is not dictated by any reasons of public policy.

In jurisdictions in which the limitation under scrutiny does not create a legal remainder in B, there seems to be no reason for holding that A's equitable life estate is merged in his legal interest with the result that A holds a legal life estate free of trust as well as a legal remainder in trust for B. To so hold would not only defeat the intent of the settlor but would likewise seem to be doctrinally unsound. The settlor has manifested an intent that A hold the entire legal interest in the trust property in trust. The settlor did not divide this legal interest into successive interests. The equitable interests of A and B are divided successively by the settlor. Unlike the sole trustee-sole beneficiary situation, B can always enforce the trust against A.

Occasionally property is transferred to A and B in trust for themselves; is there a merger in such a situation? Since trustees take as joint tenants and the beneficial interests are held in common rather than joint tenancy, the legal and equitable interests are different and no merger should result.[8]

The person named as trustee may accept[9] or disclaim (reject) appointment. His acceptance or rejection may be by words, oral or written, or by conduct. Acknowledgment and delivery to the proper person of a writing signed by the trustee and clearly manifesting his intent to accept or reject the office will, of course, eliminate any doubt as to his decision. Typically, however, acceptance of the trustee is evidenced by the trustee performing some positive act, such as taking possession and control of the trust property. Conversely, the

6. Restatement, Second, Trusts § 99 provides in part as follows: "(1) One of several beneficiaries of a trust can be one of several trustees of the trust. (2) One of several beneficiaries of a trust can be the sole trustee of the trust. (3) The sole beneficiary of a trust can be one of several trustees of the trust. (4) If there are several beneficiaries of a trust, the beneficiaries may be the trustees. (5) The sole beneficiary of a trust cannot be the sole trustee of the trust." See generally, Bogert, Trusts and Trustees (2d Ed., 1965) § 129; II Scott, Trusts (3d Ed., 1967) § 99 et seq.; 151 A.L.R. 1287 (1944).

7. Even New York had indicated it will not apply the rule with "rigidity". Thus, where the life tenant was one of two trustees, and the other trustee died, the court refused a merger on the ground the trust instrument contemplated appointment of successor trustees. Matter of Phipps, 2 N.Y.2d 105, 157 N.Y.S.2d 14, 138 N.E.2d 341 (1956).

8. Morgan v. Murton, 131 N.J.Eq. 481, 26 A.2d 45 (1942).

9. When a trustee accepts he is deemed to have been the owner of the trust property from the time the will or deed creating the trust was effective.

failure of a person named as trustee to do anything to indicate his acceptance of the trust within a reasonable time after its creation will be construed as a disclaimer by him. Acceptance or disclaimer by the person named as trustee is final. He cannot thereafter reverse his decision. If he has once disclaimed, he cannot thereafter accept.[10] If he has once accepted, he cannot thereafter disclaim. A trustee can be relieved of his office only by death, removal or resignation. Resignation is effective only when approved by the proper court, unless the trust terms provide otherwise, or by consent of all the beneficiaries if they are sui juris.

One nominated as trustee is not required to take an oath that he will faithfully discharge his duties as trustee, or to execute a bond with satisfactory sureties conditioned upon the faithful peformance of his duties, or to secure a certificate of authority (letter of trusteeship) from a court, unless he is directed to perform one or more of these acts of qualification [11] by either (1) the provisions of a state statute or (2) the trust terms as prescribed by the settlor or (3) an order of a court of equity issued pursuant to its inherent power to protect the beneficiary of a trust.

In some jurisdictions, the performance of a required act of qualification,[12] such as taking an oath, giving a bond, or securing letters of trusteeship, is a condition precedent to becoming a trustee. Other jurisdictions regard failure to perform a required act of qualification as a breach of trust entitling a court to remove the trustee on application by a beneficiary, but the person nominated as trustee becomes trustee upon accepting the trust.

HILES v. GARRISON

Court of Chancery of New Jersey, 1906.
70 N.J.Eq. 605, 62 A. 865.

* * * BERGEN, V. C. The bill in this case is filed by the complainant, widow of Richard Hiles, deceased, for the construction of his last will and testament and the appointment of a trustee to exe-

10. Possibly a disclaimer can be retracted if the retraction comes before there has been any substantial change of position in reliance upon the disclaimer. See Boehmer v. Silvertone, 95 Or. 154, 174 P. 1176 (1920).

11. Failure of the person named as trustee to accept and qualify does not prevent the creation of the trust unless the settlor has manifested an intent that the trust shall be created only if the person nominated as trustee serves in that capacity. See Chapter IX, Section 3.

12. Statutes sometimes impose one or more of these requirements upon a testamentary trustee. Rarely is an oath or certificate of authority required of a trustee of a living trust; but it is not unusual for such a person to be required to give a bond. When statutes and the trust terms are silent on the matter, a court of equity, on application by a beneficiary, will require a bond if it is convinced that a bond is necessary for the beneficiary's protection. If the trust terms provide that a bond shall not be required of the trustee, the wishes of the settlor will be respected in the absence of a statutory direction to the contrary or extraordinary circumstances unforeseen by the settlor, such as insolvency of the trustee during administration of the trust. A corporate trustee is not required to give a bond when security has already been posted with an appropriate state official.

cute such trusts as may be determined are established by such will. As the relief sought is the appointment of a trustee, and the necessity for such appointment requires the construction of the will as an incident to the relief sought for, the complainant is properly here.

The pertinent part of the will is the second clause, which reads as follows: "I do devise that all my property and bonds and mortgages be put in a trust, and the income be divided equally between my brother, Biddle Hiles and sister, Caroline Garrison, and my wife, as long as she remains my widow, in case of her marriage or deth her share to gowe to my brother Biddle Hiles, and my sister Caroline Garrison." The testator died possessed of considerable estate; the personalty having been appraised at the sum of $54,039.88. His real property consisted of an undivided interest in certain real estate in the county of Salem in this state, such interest being estimated by the parties in interest, at something over $20,000. At the time of his death the only next of kin of the testator was his brother, Biddle, and his sister, Caroline. The will was prepared by the testator, and does not clearly express his desires, and the purpose of this cause is to ascertain whether a trust has been established by the terms of such will, and, if so, that a trustee be appointed to carry out such trust.

While this will is very inartistically drawn, I think the clear intention of the testator was to create a trust by the terms of which the income of his estate was to be divided equally between his widow, brother, and sister, and that this trust shall continue as long as his widow lives or remains unmarried, and on the happening of either such events the trust terminates. As the testator has made no disposition of the corpus of the fund after the expiration of the trust estate, he died intestate as to the residue of his property, and it will go to his next of kin. That the testator named no trustee will not prevent the execution of the trust, for the court will always appoint a trustee wherever necessary to sustain the trust, and a trustee will be appointed. The will contains no power of sale, and therefore the trustee cannot dispose of the land by virtue of any authority contained in the will. It is, in my judgment, however, included in the trust, and, subject to that, will vest in the heirs at law of the testator.

I will advise a decree in accordance with the above.

NOTE

Lack of a trustee may occur in the following situations: (1) as in the principal case, no trustee is named in the document; (2) the trustee named fails to qualify as such (refusal to accept, death of a testamentary trustee before effective date of the trust, refusal of court to confirm the appointment because of incompetence, etc.); (3) the trustee named lacks legal capacity to hold in trust, as an unincorporated association would in some states; (4) death, resignation or removal of the trustee after the trust has been set up. In none of these situations will the court normally let the trust fail on this account.[13] The sole exception occurs where the settlor has manifested an intent that the existence of the trust be dependent upon acceptance of the

13. Restatement, Second, Trusts § 35.

trust by the named trustee, and this rarely occurs. Of course, the doctrine that the court will not let a trust fail for want of a trustee does not save the trust if the trust is testamentary and the will is not valid.

The rule of the principal case has been applied in inter vivos transfers, usually where the trustee refuses to accept or lacks capacity. Here there are two difficulties not present in the testamentary situation: (1) the transfer may fail for want of delivery of the subject matter or the deed of conveyance, although "delivery" effective to pass title may be accomplished through delivery to a third party or through the presumption arising from recording; (2) since legal title has not passed to the trustee, it must remain in the settlor subject to a constructive trust until the court appoints a trustee, and it is clear that the settlor did not intend to make himself trustee. However, the latter conceptual difficulty has not prevented courts from carrying out the intent of the settlor that a trust be established.[14]

When a vacancy arises in the trusteeship by reason of the death of the sole trustee, who has accepted and qualified (if qualification be necessary), title to the trust property passes to the deceased trustee's successor in interest (heir, personal representative or residuary donee) in constructive trust unless a statute or the terms of the trust otherwise provide. As constructive trustee, the successor in interest of the deceased trustee owes a duty to transfer the trust property to the person appointed to the vacant trusteeship. Statutes in a number of states provide that on death of the sole trustee title to the trust property vests in a court or is suspended until a new trustee is appointed, unless the trust terms provide for a successor trustee and he accepts the trust, and qualifies, if that be necessary.

When a trustee resigns, he owes a duty to transfer title to the trust property to a successor trustee, unless by statute or by the terms of the trust the title to the trust property passes to the new trustee without the need for such a transfer. A court will not permit a trustee to resign until a new trustee is appointed and title to the trust property vests in him. Where the terms of the trust permit a trustee to resign *in pais*, it is customary for the provisions of the trust to condition such resignation upon the resigning trustee's transferring title to the trust property to a successor trustee named in the trust instrument, unless the resigning trustee is one of two or more co-trustees. In the latter event, the resigning trustee's title to the trust property passes by operation of law to the trustees who continue the administration of the trust. Similarly, as a practical matter, the beneficiaries of a trust will consent to the resignation of a trustee only if he first transfers title to the trust property to a successor trustee, unless the resigning trustee's title to the trust property will pass by operation of law, on his resignation, to one who was a co-trustee with him and who will continue to administer the trust.

A trustee can be removed from office only by a proper court or by any person who is expressly empowered by the trust terms to remove the trustee. A court in removing a trustee will order him to transfer his title to the trust property to his successor in the trusteeship, unless by statute or the trust terms such a transfer is unnecessary to invest the successor trustee with title. If the trustee is removed *in pais* pursuant to the terms of the trust, he owes a duty to transfer title to the successor trustee.

A court order appointing a trustee does not invest the appointee with title to the trust property unless a statute so provides. Statutes in some states

14. Wittmeier v. Heiligenstein, 308 Ill. 434, 139 N.E. 871 (1923) is the leading case.

give this effect to the appointing order. In other states the court may vest title in the appointed trustee by decree. In still other states the court may designate a person to transfer title to the appointee. Unless one of these methods is authorized by statute, a court must issue an order to the person who holds title directing transfer to the appointed trustee.

When one of two or more co-trustees disclaims, dies, resigns, or is removed from office, his title to the trust corpus passes to his co-trustees by operation of law since co-trustees hold the trust property as joint tenants with right of survivorship.[15]

PROBLEMS

1. Testator left the residue of his property "to the State of Israel, to be used for the relief and resettlement of Jewish scapegoat refugees who have been subject to persecution in Christian, Moslem, Nazi, Fascist or Communist countries". The only residual assets are real property. Assume the residual disposition creates a valid charitable trust. (See Chapter XI, infra). Surrogate's Court Act, Section 94, provides that no person is competent to serve as testamentary trustee who is an alien "not an inhabitant of this state". Can the State of Israel serve as trustee in New York? Will the heirs of testator be able to take the land by intestacy? In re Rose's Will, 48 Misc.2d 475, 265 N.Y.S.2d 91 (1965) discussed in Glasser, "Trusts and Administration", 18 Syra.L.Rev. 337, at 348–349 (1966).

2. X signs, seals and acknowledges a deed purporting to convey Blackacre, which he owns in fee simple absolute, to T in trust for B. X records the deed. Thereafter T learns of the transaction for the first time and promptly repudiates the conveyance and disclaims as trustee. Has a trust been created? See Adams v. Adams, 88 U.S. 185, 22 L.Ed. 504 (1874); I Scott, Trusts (3d Ed., 1967) § 35.

(5) THE BENEFICIARIES

A. Beneficiaries to be Determined in the Future

An identifiable beneficiary is essential to the existence of a private express trust. Otherwise, there is no one in a position to enforce the trust and to prevent the trustee applying the trust property to his own use.

Any person, natural or corporate, who has the capacity to take and hold title to property may be the beneficiary of a private express trust. Married women, infants and lunatics may be the beneficiaries

15. See I Scott, Trusts (3d Ed., 1967) §§ 32, 33, 35, 36, 104, 105, 109. The common law rule that a corporation was not capable of holding as a joint tenant with an individual is not likely to be followed in the situation where a corporate fiduciary is made cotrustee with an individual, Bank of Delaware v. Bancroft, 269 A.2d 254 (Del.1970).

of a trust. A corporation, public or private, may be the beneficiary of a trust to the extent that it has the capacity to take and hold title to property and the purpose of the trust is within its corporate powers. Trusts have been upheld in which the beneficiary was the United States, a state, and a foreign country. An alien may be the beneficiary of a trust to the extent that he is entitled to take and hold title to property.

Since the typical trust involves creation of future interests, the beneficiaries will often be described not by name but rather by a class designation, such as "my grandchildren" or "my issue". When will such a designation be regarded by the courts as too indefinite? We shall see in Chapter XV that, subject to certain rules, such designations are intended to include afterborn persons. Can such unborn persons be treated as beneficiaries on the date the trust is created? These two problems will be explored in the cases which follow.

At common law an unincorporated association was not recognized as a legal entity and lacked the capacity to take legal title to property. The Restatement of Trusts [16] declares that an unincorporated association has the capacity to become the beneficiary of a trust. This view can be explained on the ground that the unincorporated association is treated as an entity in equity even though it is not treated as an entity at law—a rationalization clashing with the slogan "equity follows the law", but adopted because it reaches, with minimum conceptual casualty, what is thought to be a desirable result. Other rationales have been offered in support of the result. Whatever rationale be adopted, it is clear that the trust once recognized as valid may be enforced in a representative suit brought by a member or members of the association for the time being.

There is a minority view in this country of the effect that an unincorporated association as such lacks the capacity to become the beneficiary of a private express trust because it is not a juristic entity at law or in equity, and therefore cannot take or hold title to property.

The identifiable beneficiary requirement is satisfied if the settlor intended as beneficiaries the individual members of the association at the time the trust was created or those individuals who from time to time constitute the membership of the association. A trust for those individuals constituting the membership of the association at the time the trust is created is a trust for an ascertainable group of natural persons. A trust for those individuals who from time to time constitute the membership of the association is also a trust for an ascertainable group. Each change in the membership of the association results, in effect, in a transfer of a beneficial interest in the trust property. For example, if one individual withdraws from the association and another takes his place, there is a transfer of the former's beneficial interest in the trust property to the latter. Again, as membership of the association is enlarged there is a *pro tanto* reduction in the undivided interest of each member in the trust property to the

16. Restatement, Second, Trusts § 119.

extent necessary to give each new member the undivided interest in the trust property to which he is entitled, and the new member is invested with this interest.[17]

A trust for the settlor's "friends" fails for indefiniteness of beneficiaries. As Justice Snow points out in Clark v. Campbell,[18] "The word 'friends' unlike 'relations' has no accepted statutory or other controlling limitations, and in fact has no precise sense at all. Friendship is a word of broad and varied application. It is commonly used to describe the undefinable relationships which exist not only between those connected by ties of kinship or marriage, but as well between strangers in blood, and which vary in degree from the greatest intimacy to an acquaintance more or less casual."

A trust for the benefit of the "relatives" of a designated person will fail for indefiniteness of beneficiaries if the term "relatives" is

17. See generally, Restatement, Second, Trusts Ch. 5; Bogert, Trusts and Trustees (2d Ed., 1965) §§ 161, 167, 168, 172, 173; II Scott, Trusts (3d Ed., 1967) Ch. 5; 35 Va.L.Rev. 1068 (1949). Unincorporated associations as beneficiaries raise special problems under the Rule Against Perpetuities, considered in Chapter XVI.

18. 82 N.H. 281, 286, 133 A. 166, 170, 45 A.L.R. 1433 (1926). But see In re Rowland's Estate, 73 Ariz. 337, 241 P.2d 781 (1952), noted in 6 Okla.L.Rev. 205 (1952), 38 Va.L.Rev. 954 (1952), in which it was held that a testamentary gift of the residue of the decedent's estate to Mr. and Mrs. Hugh Cuthbert "* * * to distribute to any of my close friends. Please give generously to Maria Discombe, who has been my faithful maid * * *," was held to create a special power to appoint to the maid, which was mandatory, and a discretionary special power to appoint among the friends of the decedent. The American decisions seem to draw a distinction between the definiteness required in designating the beneficiaries of a trust and the definiteness required in designating a class of objects of a power of appointment. Thus if A bequeaths property to B for life, remainder to such friends of A as B shall by will appoint and in default of appointment to C, the power of appointment is valid because it will be possible for a court to determine whether or not an appointee is a "friend" of A, and if no appointment is made, A has manifested an intent that the property covered by the power go to C. But if A bequeaths property to B in trust to pay the income to C for his life, remainder to such of A's friends as the trustee shall select, the trust is invalid for indefiniteness of beneficiaries. The reasons usually assigned for this result are: (1) a court of equity will not compel the trustee to make a selection for whether he does so or not is left to his discretion; and (2) if he dies without selecting it is "impracticable to divide the property equally among all members of the class." II Scott, Trusts (3d Ed., 1967) § 122. Section 122 of the original Restatement of Trusts recites, "If property is devised or bequeathed to a person upon an intended trust for such members of an indefinite class of persons as he may select, not only is no trust created but the devisee or legatee has no power by making a selection to carry out the intended purpose but holds the property upon a resulting trust for the estate of the testator." But in the Restatement of Trusts Second it is stated that "if the transferee is authorized or directed to convey the property to such members of the class as he may select, he has power so to convey, unless the selection is authorized or directed to be made at a time beyond the period of the rule against perpetuities, or the class is so indefinite that it cannot be ascertained whether any person falls within it."

Despite the seeming desirability of the position adopted in the Second Restatement, the view of the original Restatement apparently prevails in most American jurisdictions which have considered the matter. For the English position see McPhail v. Doulton (1971) AC 424. Also Baden's Deed Trusts (No. 2) (1972) Ch. 607, aff'd (1973), Ch. 9, noted (1973) Camb.L.J. 36. For definitive discussions of the matters discussed in this note, see: Palmer, "Private Trusts For Indefinite Beneficiaries", 71 Mich.L.Rev. 359 (1972); Palmer, "The Effect of Indefiniteness on the Validity of Trusts and Powers of Appointment", 10 UCLA L.Rev. 241 (1963); Fratcher, "Bequests For Purposes", 56 Iowa L.Rev. 773 (1971).

construed to include all persons who are related, however remotely, to the person named. But if the term is construed to mean those who would take as heirs or next of kin under the statute of descent and distribution, the trust is for a definite and ascertainable class of beneficiaries.[19]

A question of construction arises in the case of a trust for the "family" of a designated person. If the term is construed to mean "relatives", the rules discussed in the preceding paragraph are applicable. It has been said that the term "family" has no exact legal meaning. Thus, a bequest to the brothers and sisters of the testator for the benefit of themselves and their respective families was held to be so indefinite that it manifested no intention to create a trust and the brothers and sisters took absolutely.[20] On the other hand, the Restatement of Property [21] declares in substance that the family of a designated person includes his spouse and issue and no one else absent a contrary indication of intention from additional language or circumstances. The Restatement, Second, Trusts provides in part: [22] "* * * The 'family' of a designated person may be construed to include himself and his wife and children or such children or other relatives or other persons as are living with him or it may include other relatives. In any case it is a definite class within the rule stated in this Section, unless it includes relatives generally, in which case it falls within the rule stated in § 121. * * *"

HASKELL v. STAPLES

Supreme Judicial Court of Maine, 1917.
116 Me. 103, 100 A. 148, L.R.A., 1917D 819.

CORNISH, J. Nathaniel McLellan, of Newfield in the county of York, died testate in 1884, his last will and testament being duly proved and allowed on the first Tuesday of August, 1884. Hall J. Staples was appointed executor thereof. The executor converted all the assets of the estate into cash, paid the indebtedness and the bequests, and filed two accounts which were duly allowed. The last account showed a balance of $3,054.94 in his hands, which balance is

19. See 28 Mich.L.Rev. 944 (1930); 57 A.L.R. 1180 (1928). Restatement, Second, Trusts § 121, Comment *a* provides in part as follows: "* * * A trust for the benefit of the relatives of a designated person, however, does not fail if the trustee has power to select who among them shall take and in what proportions. In such a case the trustee may select any member or members of the class in accordance with the terms of the trust, whether or not they are next of kin of the designated person.

"If the trustee fails to make a selection among the relatives of the designated person, the property will be divided among the next of kin of the designated person in the proportions determined by the statute of distributions, unless the transferor properly manifests a different intention. * * *"

20. In re Hill, [1923] L.R. 2 Ch. 259.

21. Restatement, Property (1940) § 293.

22. Restatement, Second, Trusts § 120. Comment *b*.

on deposit in the Portland Savings Bank and with accrued dividends now amounts to more than $5,000.

Hall J. Staples, being adjudged of unsound mind, was removed from the executorship by the probate court on May 2, 1916, and on June 5, 1916, the plaintiff was duly appointed administrator de bonis non with will annexed.

After providing for the payment of debts and making certain devises and legacies, the concluding paragraph in the will is as follows:

> "Fourth. I give and bequeath to my nephew Hall J. Staples of Buxton in the county of York five hundred dollars, and the residue of my personal estate I leave in trust to said Hall J. Staples to be by him distributed and disposed of as he pleases and I do hereby appoint said Hall J. Staples to be executor of this my last will and testament, hereby revoking all former wills by me made."

What disposition shall be made of the residuum? Does it belong to Staples personally, or was it given in trust, and if so has the trust failed so that the executor is authorized to distribute the same as intestate property among the testator's heirs at law? These are, in substance, the questions propounded to this court, and under well-settled principles of construction it is clear that distribution must be made among the heirs.

That the testator did not intend to give the residue outright to Staples is apparent.

In the first place, in this same paragraph he makes an absolute bequest to Staples of $500. If he had intended to give him the residue also, no reason can be conceived why he should have divided his gift into two parts. The carving out of the $500 and making it an absolute gift, and then leaving the balance to him in trust, makes a sharp distinction between the nature of the two estates intended to be conveyed. When other and separate provision has been made for the legatee, it has been held to indicate an intention on the part of the testator not to bequeath the beneficial interest in other property, the legal title to which is also given to the legatee. Briggs v. Penney, 3 De G. & Sm. 525, affirming 3 McN. & G. 546; In re Keenan, 107 App. Div. 234, 94 N.Y.Supp. 1099; Nichols v. Allen, 130 Mass. 211, 39 Am. Rep. 445.

Again, the words, "I leave in trust," coupled with "to be distributed and disposed of as he pleases," leave no room for doubt as to the testator's intention. They are meant to create a trust, and not to grant an absolute ownership. The legal title is conveyed, but not the beneficial. Perry, Tr. § 158; Fitzsimmons v. Harmon, 108 Me. 456, 81 A. 667, and note 37 L.R.A.,N.S., 400.

The attempted trust, however, must fail for uncertainty and indefiniteness.

> "A trust which by its terms may be applied to objects which are not charitable in the legal sense, and to persons not defined, by name or by class, is too indefinite to be carried out." Nichols v. Allen, 130 Mass. 211, 39 Am.Rep. 445.

The bequest in that case was in these words:

> "To be by them distributed to such persons, societies, or institutions as they may consider most deserving."

The trust was declared void. Other illustrations of the same principle are these:

> "Upon trust to dispose of the same at such times and in such manner and for such uses and purposes as they shall see fit, it being my will that the distribution thereof shall be left entirely to their discretion." Fowler v. Garlike, 1 Russ. & Mylne, 232.

> "Upon trust to pay her debts and legacies and to dispose of the ultimate residue to such objects of benevolence and liberality as the Bishop in his own discretion shall most approve of." Morice v. Bishop of Durham, 10 Ves. 521.

> "To my brother * * * in trust to be disposed of by him as I have heretofore or may hereafter direct him to do," and the beneficiaries were disclosed neither in the will nor in any other document that could be regarded as a part of it. Heidenheimer v. Bauman, 84 Tex. 174, 19 S.W. 382, 31 Am.St.Rep. 29.

> "In trust * * * to expend solely for benevolent purposes in their discretion." Chamberlain v. Stearns, 111 Mass. 267.

> "To distribute the same in such manner as in his discretion shall appear best calculated to carry out wishes which I have expressed to him or may express to him." Olliffe v. Wells, 130 Mass. 221.

> "To divide as seems to her best as I have told her my wishes in the matter, mentioning all relatives including my nephews." Fitzsimmons v. Harmon, 108 Me. 456, 81 A. 667.

The bequest in the will under consideration, "I leave in trust to Hall J. Staples to be by him distributed and disposed of as he pleases," is certainly no less uncertain and indefinite than the illustrations above given. It cannot be upheld as a charitable trust because the fund is not limited to any use that falls within the scope of a public charity as known to the courts and as defined in Jackson v. Phillips, 14 Allen (Mass.) 539. This definition has been followed and applied in this state in the very recent case of Bills v. Pease, 116 Me. 98, 100 A. 146. Clearly, the attempted trust must be held to fail.

Here comes in another well-settled rule that, when a bequest is made in terms clearly manifesting an intention that it shall be taken in trust and the trust is so indefinite that it cannot be carried into effect, the legatee takes the legal title only, and a trust results by implication of law to the testator's residuary legatees or next of kin. Nichols v. Allen, 130 Mass. 211, 39 Am.Rep. 445; Fitzsimmons v. Harmon, 108 Me. 456, 81 A. 667; and the other authorities cited above.

Answering therefore the questions propounded by the executor, we would say: First, that Hall J. Staples is not entitled to the residue of the personal estate bequeathed under clause four in the will of Nathaniel McLellan; and, second, that there is a resulting trust in favor of the heirs at law of said McLellan, and that the balance of the estate, after payment of any remaining expenses of administration, should be divided among them under the laws governing the distribution of intestate property in this state.

Bill sustained with one bill of costs for the plaintiff and one for the defendants. Reasonable counsel fees shall also be allowed by the sitting justice to attorneys on both sides, to be paid from the estate and allowed to the plaintiff in his account.

Decree accordingly.

NOTE

When a testator devises or bequeaths property in trust but fails to name any beneficiary, the general rule is that a resulting trust arises in favor of the decedent's estate. A few cases give the so-called trustee absolute ownership.[23] There are statutes in a few states providing that a deed to a trustee which does not name any beneficiary creates a presumption of absolute title in the so-called trustee which becomes irrebuttable after five years.[24] The purpose of these statutes is to clear records for title searchers.

A resulting trust arises for the benefit of the settlor or his successors in interest when property is transferred gratuitously, either by will or inter vivos, upon a trust which fails for reasons in addition to those in the principal case. It is also presumed where the trust property is in excess of the trust purposes, as where the settlor directs payment of so much of the income as is necessary for the support of the named beneficiary and makes no provision, express or implied, for the excess. Where the settlor is dead when the trust fails or its purpose is accomplished, the trust results to his successors in interest, who will be his heirs at law or next of kin in an intestacy situation, or the residuary devisees or legatees where there is a valid will containing a residuary clause.[25] Where X pays Y to make a declaration of trust or to transfer property in a trust which fails, X is the real settlor and the resulting trust will be in his favor.[26]

The presumption of resulting trust may be rebutted by evidence showing the settlor's intention that there should be no resulting trust. He may, for example, intend that the trustee should keep the property or the surplus. Parol evidence is inadmissible to establish intent,[27] although it would be admissible to show that the transfer was not gratuitous. Establishment of intent is a matter of construing the trust document; and the Restatement, Sec-

23. Reid v. Barry, 93 Fla. 849, 112 So. 846 (1927); Dillage v. Greenough, 45 N. Y. 438 (1871).

24. See Heitkemper v. Schmeer, 130 Or. 644, 275 P. 55, 281 P. 169 (1929).

25. The heirs at law take if the res is land, the next of kin if the res is personal property. The residuary devisees take land and the residuary legatees personal property. If land is the trust res and the settlor has directed by will that the land be converted into personalty by the trustee, and the conversion is not accomplished before the trust fails, the heirs at law or residuary devisees are entitled to the property as if there had been no direction to convert. The same rule is applied when there is a direction to convert personal property into land. Restatement, Second, Trusts § 411, Comment *e*. See 30 A.L.R.3d 1318 (1970).

26. Restatement, Second, Trusts §§ 424, 425.

27. If the trust is testamentary, the local wills act will exclude the evidence unless the settlor's intention is expressed with the formalities required for a will or is incorporated by reference into a valid will. If a written inter vivos trust is established, the parol evidence rule will exclude the evidence, and Section VII of the Statute of Frauds will have the same effect if the subject matter of the trust is land.

ond, Trusts § 431, Comment *c* states that the following circumstances may be important in determining intent:

> "* * * (1) the language used in the trust instrument; (2) the relationship between the transferor and the trustee; (3) whether the trustee is an individual or a corporation, and if a corporation, whether it is a charitable corporation; (4) the certainty or likelihood that there would be a surplus; (5) whether the trust is created inter vivos or by will; (6) whether, if the trust is created by will and there is no disposition of the residue, the testator has made other provision for his heir or next of kin; (7) whether, if the residue is left in trust, the testator has made other provision for the trustee; (8) whether, if the trust is created inter vivos, the settlor has reserved for himself a part of the beneficial interest."

There are several qualifications to the resulting trust presumption which we meet in this course. Where the trust fails for an illegal purpose, the court may on equitable grounds refuse any relief to the settlor by way of resulting trust or otherwise. In the charitable trust situation cy pres operates to prevent failure of most charitable trusts and to dispose of any excess income or surplus trust res.

MOSS v. AXFORD

Supreme Court of Michigan, 1929.
246 Mich. 288, 224 N.W. 425.[28]

FEAD, J. This is a bill to construe the fifteenth paragraph of the will of Caroline M. Girard, made when she was about 77 years of age.

"Fifteenth. I give, devise and bequeath all the rest, residue and remainder of my property to Henry W. Axford with the instructions to pay the same to the person who has given me the best care in my declining years and who in his opinion is the most worthy of my said property. I make him the sole judge and request that his signature with the signature of the person receiving said property shall be a sufficient release for my said executor."

Plaintiffs are sisters of Mrs. Girard and claim as her heirs. Defendant Axford for a long time was attorney and adviser of Mrs. Girard and her husband (who predeceased her), drafted her will, and was named her executor. Defendant Mary E. Piers took care of testatrix from the time the will was made until her death, and was designated by Mr. Axford as the person entitled to the residue of the estate under the above clause. The testimony was undisputed that the designation was proper, if the devise was valid.

Plaintiffs contend that the clause was an invalid attempt to create an express trust, because there was no beneficiary fully expressed and clearly defined upon the face of the will as required by 3 Comp.

28. Noted, 14 Minn.L.Rev. 703 (1930); 4 Notre Dame Law 574 (1929).

Laws 1915, § 11575, subd. 5: [now Mich.Comp.Laws Ann. § 555.11(5) (1981 Supp.)—Ed.]

"Sec. 11. Express trusts may be created for any or either of the following purposes: * * *

> "5. For the beneficial interest of any person or persons when such a trust is fully expressed and clearly defined upon the face of the instrument creating it, subject to the limitations as to time prescribed in this title."

Plaintiffs' argument has its basis in their contention that Mr. Axford was given uncontrolled and unrestrained discretion in designating the beneficiary, and in reliance upon Tilden v. Green, 130 N.Y. 29, 28 N.E. 880, 14 L.R.A. 33, 27 Am.St.Rep. 487, in which the court held void for uncertainty of beneficiaries a charitable trust in which the trustees were given unlimited authority to designate the beneficiaries. They said Axford, not testatrix, selected the beneficiary, and it was his act, not her will, and urged that no court could compel or supervise the execution of the trust, nor substitute a trustee, if Axford failed to act.

While the words used in the residuary clause are precatory, the intent of the testatrix in the disposition of the residue of her property to the person who should care for her is manifest, and the language is mandatory in effect. Trustees of Hillsdale College v. Wood, 145 Mich. 257, 108 N.W. 675; Foster v. Willson, 68 N.H. 241, 38 A. 1003, 73 Am.St.Rep. 581. The devise of the residue to Mr. Axford was not personal, but, if valid, created a trust in him. Cummings et al. v. Corey, 58 Mich. 494, 25 N.W. 481.

We do not read the will as conferring on Mr. Axford unrestrained discretion or right of personal opinion in the designation of a beneficiary. The unmistakable intention of the testatrix, apparent upon the face of the will, was that the residue of her estate should go to the person who should have given her the best care in her declining years. This was to be the basis of selection of the beneficiary as "most worthy" of her property. The duty of designation conferred upon Mr. Axford was a *quasi* judicial power or discretion to pass upon conflicting claims. It arose out of her confidence in him and his interest in her welfare, but it was confined to ascertaining and naming the person who had given testatrix the best care.

The purpose of Mrs. Girard was lawful and should be carried out, "unless there is such an uncertainty that the law is fairly baffled." Tuxbury v. French, 41 Mich. 7, 1 N.W. 904. It is not necessary that a beneficiary be designated by name, or by a description which makes identification automatic. 40 Cyc. 1446. Nor that the testator have in mind the particular individual upon whom his bounty may fall. Bosserman v. Burton, 137 Va. 502, 120 S.E. 261, 38 A.L.R. 767. It is enough if the testator uses language which is sufficiently clear to enable the court by extrinsic evidence to identify the beneficiary. If by such evidence the court can make the identification necessary to give effect to the intention of the testator, the devise will be sustained. Gilchrist v. Corliss, 155 Mich. 126, 118 N.W. 938, 130 Am.St.

Rep. 568; Cook v. Universalist General Convention, 138 Mich. 157, 101 N.W. 217; Gilmer v. Stone, 120 U.S. 586, 7 S.Ct. 689, 30 L.Ed. 734.

The case at bar presents less difficulty of identification than was present in those cited. The undisputed evidence was that Mrs. Piers was the only person who took care of Mrs. Girard from about the time the will was made to the time of her death. But, had there been conflicting claims, they could have been resolved according to the evidence. Will of Mangan, 185 Wis. 328, 200 N.W. 386. While there seem to be no cases in point in this state, direct devises in general language to persons who should care for a testator have been held valid in other jurisdictions. Harriman v. Harriman, 59 N.H. 135; Dennis v. Holsapple, 148 Ind. 297, 47 N.E. 631, 46 L.R.A. 168, 62 Am. St.Rep. 526; Glasgow's Estate, 243 Pa. 613, 90 A. 332; Will of Mangan, 185 Wis. 328, 200 N.W. 386; Bosserman v. Burton, 137 Va. 502, 120 S.E. 261, 38 A.L.R. 767.

A trust is not invalidated by the fact that the trustee is vested with discretion. 39 Cyc. 316. In Lear v. Manser, 114 Me. 342, 96 A. 240, a case closely in point, the residue of the estate was given to the executor in trust,—"to be paid by him to such person or persons, or to such institution as shall care for me in my last sickness, such payment to be made to the person or persons, or institution, or any or all of them as may in the discretion of my said executor be equitably entitled thereto, and the payment by my said executor and receipt taken by him therefor shall be a sufficient voucher and discharge to him under the provisions of this item."

The court held the identification of the beneficiary sufficient, as the testator had "prescribed a rule whereby his beneficiary could be identified with certainty." The Court also pointed out that, although the trustee was invested with discretion, the trust would not perish with him, but "it could be executed by another trustee appointed by the court if necessary, for the duty imposed upon the trustee, and the discretion given to him in the exercise of that duty, are imperative and not optional, they were intended by the testator to be executed at all events."

In re Cawthorpe, 26 Ont.Wkly.Rep. 762, the residuary estate was devised "unto those of my relations who are needy, in such amounts, and to such of the same, as my executors see fit in their discretion." The court held the devise valid and said:

> "It is settled law that when a testator has given a pure discretion to trustees, as to the exercise of a power, the court does not enforce the exercise of the power against the wish of the trustees, but it does prevent them from exercising it improperly. The court says that the power, if exercised at all, is to be properly exercised. * * * 'But, in all cases where there is a trust or duty coupled with a power, the courts will then compel the trustees to carry it out in a proper manner within a reasonable time.' In this case there is * * * a gift which the court would carry into effect if the executors failed to exercise their power over it, but, with

which the court will not interfere if the executors, in good faith, and uninfluenced by improper motive, exercise, within a reasonable time, their power over it."

The ascertainment of testatrix's beneficiary by Mr. Axford was an imperative duty. The test and method were prescribed by the will. He was bound to exercise good faith in the determination, and the honesty of his decision would be reviewable in equity. Chambers v. Chambers, 207 Mich. 129, 173 N.W. 367. Upon his failure or inability to perform the duty, the court could from extraneous evidence ascertain and declare the beneficiary to fully carry out the intention of the testatrix. We think the clause a valid devise in trust, and that the designation of Mrs. Piers by Mr. Axford constituted her the residuary legatee.

Plaintiffs further contend that the devise was void, because it suspended the absolute power of alienation from the death of testatrix until the trustee should make designation of a beneficiary, a period not measured by lives in being. The statute (3 Comp.Laws 1915, § 11532) provides the test, plain and unvexed by complications: * * * "Such power of alienation is suspended when there are no persons in being, by whom an absolute fee in possession can be conveyed."

The will provided no restriction on alienation. The beneficiary, whoever it might be, was in being, and she and the trustee could have conveyed an absolute fee at any time. Moreover, the ordinary delays in the settlement of an estate are not within the reason of the statute. Fitz Gerald v. City of Big Rapids, 123 Mich. 281, 82 N.W. 56.

The decree holding valid paragraph 15 of the will, and the designation of Mary E. Piers as residuary legatee thereunder, and dismissing the bill of complaint, is affirmed, with costs.

NORTH, C.J., and FELLOWS, WIEST, CLARK, MCDONALD, POTTER, and SHARPE, JJ., concurred.[29]

MORSMAN v. COMMISSIONER OF INTERNAL REVENUE

United States Circuit Court of Appeals, Eighth Circuit, 1937.
90 F.2d 18, 113 A.L.R. 441.[30]

[On January 28, 1929, Robert P. Morsman, a bachelor, executed a written instrument, captioned "Trust Agreement," by the terms of which he declared himself trustee of certain identified securities he

29. See Restatement, Second, Trusts §§ 120, 122; Palmer, "Effect of Indefiniteness on the Validity of Trusts and Powers of Appointment", 10 U.C.L.A.L. Rev. 241 (1963). As to drafting problems involved in such grants of broad discretion see, Endacott, "Problems in Drafting and Administering Discretionary Trusts", 46 Neb.L.Rev. 110 (1967). On estate planning and tax problems see Casner, "Trusts Under Which Beneficiaries are to be Determined", 25 The Record of the Association of the Bar of the City of New York 62 (1970).

30. Noted, 38 Col.L.Rev. 195 (1938); 51 Harv.L.Rev. 176 (1937); 22 Minn.L. Rev. 445 (1938); 17 Neb.L.B. 242 (1938); 16 Tex.L.Rev. 270 (1938); 24 Va.L.Rev. 83 (1937).

then owned, to accumulate the income thereon until January 1, 1934, and add it to the principal. Thereafter, the income from the fund was to be paid to Morsman during his life. At his death, the trust property was to be distributed among his descendants, if any, and if none, to his widow, and if none, to his heirs at law. The United States Trust Company was named successor in trust, and it was provided that the trust fund should be turned over to the Trust Company not later than January 1, 1939. On May 3, 1929, Morsman turned the trust fund over to the trust company. Prior thereto a profit had been realized on the sale of certain securities constituting part of the trust fund. This profit was reported by the Trust Company, as trustee, and not by Morsman in his individual income tax return for the year 1929. This is a petition to review a decision of the Board of Tax Appeals which sustained the action of the Commissioner of Internal Revenue in determining that the profits realized by sale of the securities were taxable as income to Morsman individually.]

THOMAS, CIRCUIT JUDGE. * * * First. With respect to the position of Morsman, it is settled that a trust cannot exist where the same person possesses both the legal and equitable titles to the trust fund at the same time. In such a case the two titles are said to merge. Moran v. Cornell, 49 R.I. 308, 142 A. 605, 608; In re Havesgaard's Estate, 59 S.D. 26, 238 N.W. 130, 132; In re Gillespie's Estate, 273 Pa. 227, 116 A. 824, 825; Walton v. Wormington, 89 Colo. 355, 2 P.2d 1088, 1090; Weeks v. Frankel, 197 N.Y. 304, 90 N.E. 969, 971; Trusts, Restatement, §§ 99(5) and 115(5). This principle is not denied. The result, of course, is different where one person conveys property to another who agrees to hold in trust for the grantor, as in the case of Doctor v. Hughes, 225 N.Y. 305, 122 N.E. 221. In such a case there is an immediate severance of the legal and equitable titles and a trust arises at once. In the instant case that provision of the agreement by which the petitioner undertook to hold for himself, standing alone, therefore, contributes nothing toward the creation of a trust. The claim however, is that this provision, coupled with the agreement to hold for the widow, issue, or heirs, effected an immediate severance of the titles and that a trust came into existence immediately upon the execution of the trust agreement. It is further claimed that some importance attaches to the fact that the trust agreement provides that the income was to be accumulated until January 1, 1934, but how a severance of legal and equitable interests results from that fact is not explained and is not apparent.

Second. With respect to the possibility of issue, it will be observed that in designating beneficiaries and providing for the enjoyment of the property the petitioner has looked to the future. In paragraph (6) of the instrument it is provided that, "In the event Robert P. Morsman dies leaving issue, then said income shall be divided annually among such issue. * * *" In other words, he has said that the beneficiaries are to be determined at the time of his death from a class now nonexistent. It is true that the fact that the enjoyment is to be postponed does not go to the validity of the trust where there is a proper manifestation of intent to convey an interest to a present beneficiary, Trusts, Restatement, § 26, Comment g; nor is it at times material that the express beneficiary himself be not in existence, provided he can be ascertained within the period of the rule against perpetuities. Trusts, Restatement, § 112. More specifically it has been held in several cases that a present trust may be created where the beneficiary of an express trust is an unborn child. Folk v. Hughes, 100 S.C. 220, 84 S.E. 713; Heyward-Williams Co. v. McCall, 140 Ga. 502, 79 S.E. 133; Carson v. Carson, 60 N.C. 575 (Winst. 24). The rationale of these cases, however, is not believed to rest on the theory that an unborn child can be the express cestui of an immediate trust. To so hold would violate fundamental principles of trusts which require a present conveyance of the beneficial interest, Eschen v. Steers (C.C.A.8) 10 F.2d 739, 741, and the existence of present enforceable duties, Doan v. Vestry of Parish of Ascension, 103 Md. 662, 64 A. 314, 7 L.R.A.,N.S., 1119, 115 Am.St.Rep. 379. Danforth v. City of Oshkosh, 119 Wis. 262, 97 N.W. 258, 263; Trusts, Restatement, § 2, and it would permit the suspension of the beneficial ownership, a notion repugnant to the requirements of a trust. The rationale of such a case is that the instrument has the effect of creating an immediate resulting trust for the settlor (which will cease if the expected child is born) "with an express trust for the child springing up when and if such child ever materializes." Bogert, Trusts and Trustees, § 163. In such a case, where the trustee is a third person, if no child is born within the period of the rule against perpetuities, the legal and equitable interests both merge in the settlor at the end of the period; but, if the settlor is himself the trustee, the two interests are not severed by the purported declaration. The law of trusts upon this point seems clear. The immediate resulting trust in favor of the settlor is but a specific application of the general rule which recognizes the existence of the resulting trust in favor of the settlor in cases where the legal title is taken by one who is not intended to have the beneficial interest and the beneficial interest is not otherwise effectively disposed of. Blunt v. Taylor, 230 Mass. 303, 119 N.E. 954; Filkins v. Severn, 127 Iowa 738, 104 N.W. 346. So if A, a bachelor, transfers property to B in trust to accumulate the rents and profits and to convey the same to A's eldest son on reaching its majority (Trusts, Restatement, § 112, Illustration 6), a trust will arise at once—B now holding as a resulting trustee for A with the express trust arising if and when the eldest son comes into existence—the resulting trust then to cease. But in that view if A, a bachelor, or any person without issue, declares himself trustee of property for his own eldest son on identical or similar terms, no trust will presently arise. The express trust for the child cannot arise until the child comes into existence, and A cannot hold as a resulting trustee for himself during his lifetime because of the necessary merger in such a case of the legal and equitable interests in the same person. If A should die without issue under these circumstances, the property constituting the so-called trust fund is as much a part of his estate as if he had never made the purported declaration. The distinction thus noted between the case where A declares himself trustee for his unborn issue and where he conveys to B to hold in trust for such issue is vital; and this is the point at which Morsman failed in his attempt to create a present trust. Where the beneficiary is in being, the beneficial interest may be vested in him though its enjoyment be postponed. But by "no distortion of language or legal principles" (Eschen v. Steers (C.C.A.) 10 F.2d 739, 744) can a present severance of legal and equitable titles, an essential element of any completed trust (Dillenbeck v. Pinnell, 121 Iowa 201, 96 N.W. 860, at page 861; Frost v. Frost, 165 Mich. 591, 131 N.W. 60, 61), be spelled out where one makes a purported declaration of trust naming himself as trustee for unborn issue or other nonexistent persons. There are thus limitations to the oft-quoted rule that a present trust may arise although the express beneficiary is not in existence. The application of that rule to every case in which the purported beneficiary is unborn disregards "the perils that are latent in 'a jurisprudence of conceptions.'" Schubert v. August Schubert Wagon Co., 249 N.Y. 253, 164 N.E. 42, 64 A.L.R. 293. "Few formulas are meant to serve as universals." Id. The petitioner may, of course, subsequent to the execution of the trust agreement, have issue, but until such issue come into being, they cannot be said to have the status of existing beneficiaries. The possibility of issue does not of itself have the effect of presently severing the legal and equitable interests. It can operate in futuro at best. It is true that rules governing equitable interests are more flexible than those governing legal interests, but no reason exists for stretching the trust concept to a case where it has no plausible explanation.

It has been said that "If a beneficiary of a trust has not been born or conceived, a suit can be maintained on his behalf by a next friend or guardian to enforce the duties of the trustee." Trusts, Restatement, § 214, Comment a. The rule is illustrated by cases where other members of the class to which the unborn issue belong are already in existence, Trusts, Restatement, § 120, or where the owner has conveyed the property to a third person to hold for such issue, Trusts, Restatement, § 112, Comment d. These cases are instances in which there occurs for other reasons a present severance of the legal and equitable titles thus giving rise independently of any assumed rights of unborn issue to a trust and thereby giving to courts of equity, which traditionally exercise control over trusts, jurisdiction from the beginning; and having acquired jurisdiction the court retains it to protect rights which may later spring up. Trusts, Restatement, § 340, Comment d. In other words, the foregoing rule applies where, apart from the naming of the unborn issue, there is some rational explanation of a present trust. It is true that a guardian may be appointed for an unborn child which is in esse, Utah Copper Co. v. Industrial Commission, 57 Utah 118, 193 P. 24, 13 A.L.R. 1367, but it is difficult to understand how such an appointment can be made for a child not yet conceived where there is no other basis of jurisdiction. It has been held that the existence of a ward is a necessary jurisdictional fact for the validity of an order appointing a guardian, In re Reeve's Guardianship, 176 Wis. 579, 186 N.W. 736, 742. To say that because a guardian may be appointed for an unborn child and that for that reason a present trust exists although the legal and equitable titles be merged in the same person is a plain case of putting the cart before the horse. It is only where there is a present severance of legal and equitable titles, which effect a trust, and which gives equity jurisdiction to act, that a court of equity can appoint a guardian to act in behalf of unborn issue. The creation of the trust is the cause, the power to appoint a guardian is the effect. It is elementary that neither a guardian, a guardian ad litem, nor a next friend can maintain a suit in court on behalf of persons not sui generis [*sic*—Ed.] unless the court has jurisdiction of the subject-matter.

To hold that a *present* trust arises where the owner of property declares that he holds it in trust for himself and other persons who are as yet nonexistent not only lacks a logical explanation but is incapable of practical application. To a creditor seeking to subject the property to the satisfaction of a debt the petitioner would say that it was no longer his, but belonged, in equity, to others who were not yet in existence. But if he sought to dissipate the property, there is no person in being who has such an interest that he may go into a court of equity and prevent the dissipation. To say that the petitioner in this case has an interest in enforcing such an obligation against himself or that the community at large is interested in preserving the rights of issue as yet not conceived is, to say the least, an unwarranted assumption. For the court to regard possible unborn issue as present beneficiaries is to permit the substance and realities of the transaction to be obscured by words and phrases.

It appears in this case that the petitioner has no issue; therefore, no express trust has arisen on behalf of issue who might survive him. This result does not conflict with the rule that the members of a definite class may be the beneficiaries of a trust, Trusts, Restatement, § 120, Comments c and g, as the class was not in existence; nor with the rule that a trustee may be one of several beneficiaries, Woodward v. James, 115 N.Y. 346, 22 N.E. 150, 152; Woodbery v. Atlas Realty Co., 148 Ga. 712, 98 S.E. 472, 473; Trusts, Restatement, §§ 99(2) and 115(3), for the petitioner here was the only present beneficiary.

Third. With respect to the "heirs" as present beneficiaries and to the possible suggestion that petitioner's brother now living may take a present equitable interest under paragraph (8) of the trust agreement, it is observed that one of the elementary rules of law is that "A living person has no heirs." Duffield v. Duffield, 268 Ill. 29, 108 N.E. 673, 675, Ann.Cas.1916D, 859; Moffitt v. Williams, 116 Neb. 785, 219 N.W. 138; Avon State Bank v. Commercial & Savings Bank, 49 S.D. 575, 207 N.W. 654, 656, 44 A.L.R. 1462. For that reason, a son predeceasing his father never becomes his father's heir. Root v. Arnold, 133 Or. 417, 290 P. 1095. Only on death do heirs come into existence, "for the ancestor during his life beareth in his body (in judgment of law) all his heires, and therefore, it is truly said that haeres est pars antecessoris." Co.Litt. 22b. Quoted in Doctor v. Hughes, 225 N.Y. 305, 122 N.E. 221, 222. What has been said with reference to the rights of unborn children applies with equal force to the rights of heirs, two classes equally nonexistent.

"Heirs," therefore, have no present beneficial interest, and cannot be considered beneficiaries.

Under paragraph (8) the interest of the heirs, when they come into existence, is contingent upon failure of a widow and issue. But until they come into existence, through the death of petitioner, they can have no interest either vested or contingent. Reference to the brother and other living relatives as potential heirs adds nothing to their rights under the trust agreement. That instrument recognizes only "heirs," and, as shown above, there are none in existence.

* * * [Omitted is the portion of the opinion in which the court held the instrument ineffective to create any interest in the "heirs" of the grantor, for reasons which will be explored in Chapter XIII, Section 5 hereafter.] * * *

Finally, with respect to the status of a widow as a beneficiary, what has been said in reference to the nonexistence of issue and heirs is applicable here. The record, as pointed out above, does not show the existence of a wife. A widow is, therefore, a mere potentiality without existence and with no one to represent her. As a fiction, she belongs to no class. In case of an hypothetical breach of duty of the trustee, no woman in all the world, upon the record here, has a present right to come forward and enforce any rights under the trust agreement, and no existing person is authorized to enforce her imaginary rights.

We now turn to the consideration of the effect of paragraph (1) of the trust agreement, which provides that on or prior to January 1, 1939, Robert P. Morsman will turn over the trust fund to the United State Trust Company as his successor in trust. The intention of petitioner, so expressed, that the trust company shall hold the property for his benefit during life and after his death for his widow, issue, or heirs does not affect the situation existing before May 3, 1929, for prior to that date the intention was not carried out by a conveyance of the legal title to the trust company. If A makes a gratuitous promise to convey property to B in trust for A and after A's death for A's issue, no trust arises until legal title is actually conveyed to B. If the donee never gets title, he cannot hold for another. Farmers' Loan & Trust Co. v. Winthrop, 238 N.Y. 477, 144 N.E. 686, 688; Brannock v. Magoon, 141 Mo.App. 316, 125 S.W. 535, 536; Barnum v. Reed, 136 Ill. 388, 26 N.E. 572, 574; Warsco v. Oshkosh Savings & Trust Co., 183 Wis. 156, 196 N.W. 829; Cornick v. Weir, 212 Iowa 715, 237 N.W. 245, 248. In McCartney v. Ridgway, 160 Ill. 129, 43 N.E. 826, 835, 32 L.R.A. 555, the rule supported by many authorities is stated as follows:

> "Where the (trust) instrument contemplates that there shall be a transfer of the property to a trustee, the relation of trustee and cestui que trust does not arise until such transfer is made."

Trusts, Restatement, § 26, Comment a, states the rule thus:

> "If a person declares his intention or promises that he will at a subsequent time transfer property then owned or thereafter to be acquired by him to another person in trust no trust arises unless and until he makes the transfer in trust."

Further, the declaration of an intent, unsupported by consideration, to hold and preserve one's own property for the eventual enjoyment of another is no more than a declaration of a purpose to make a gift, and in this case it is ineffective as such for lack of delivery. Farmers' Loan & Trust Co. v. Winthrop, supra. The intent that the property was to be turned over to the trustee does not, therefore, amount to a declaration of trust because that intent had not been carried out at the time of the transactions under consideration. "A declaration (of trust) implies an announcement of an act performed not a mere intention." In re Brown's Will, supra. To the same effect see Trusts, Restatement, § 23.

The trust agreement, therefore, failed to effect the creation of a trust on January 28, 1929. This results from the fact that no existing beneficiaries were named therein and, consequently, there was no present severance of the legal and equitable titles to the property. The question here determined is whether there was a valid declaration of trust operating in praesenti between January 28 and May 3, 1929. That question must necessarily be answered in the negative since there was at that time no person in being who could claim any beneficial interest in the property other than the holder of the legal title. It is true, of course, that in equity a trust may not fail for want of a trustee, nevertheless, the courts cannot supply a private express beneficiary. * * *

Affirmed.

GARDNER, CIRCUIT JUDGE (Dissenting). * * * [JUDGE GARDNER relied on Becker v. St. Louis Union Trust Co., 296 U.S. 48, 80 L. Ed. 35, 56 S.Ct. 78, stating that the record failed to disclose that Morsman was a bachelor without issue in 1929, and arguing that the declaration of trust created a contingent interest in the settlor's brother as prospective heir of the settlor, and that an identifiable beneficiary was in existence on the date of the declaration of trust.]

NOTE

A trust for an unborn beneficiary is not invalid for that reason if the trust is also for a beneficiary or beneficiaries in existence on the date the trust is created. The existing and ascertained beneficiaries can enforce the trust from its inception. For example, if A transfers property to B on an active trust for A's children then living and such children as may later be born to A, the living children can enforce the trust from the date of its creation. After-born children merely add to the number who have an equitable interest in the trust property and can enforce the trust. Similarly, if a testator bequeaths property to a designated trustee in trust for the testator's son A, for his life, and on his death to transfer the property equally among such children of A as are then living, the trust is valid although no child of A is living on the testator's death. A can enforce the trust from its inception and children of A can enforce it as and if they are born.

When no beneficiary is in existence on the date the trust is purportedly created but a beneficiary may be born thereafter, it may become important to determine whether the trust is created by transfer or by declaration. For example, if A transfers property to B on active trust for the eldest child of B, who at the time has no children, it is well settled that B's first born child acquires a beneficial interest in the trust property on birth and that the trust can then be enforced for his benefit. Furthermore, as long as there is a possibility that a child might be born to B, the trust cannot be extinguished even though both the trustor and the trustee desire its extinguishment. Pending the birth of the child, the trustor, A, can enforce the trust as either a resulting or express trust in his favor. If the income is to be paid to A until the child is born, A would seem to be the beneficiary of an express trust. If the income for this period is to be accumulated or the trustee is entitled to it for his own benefit, A would seem to be the beneficiary of a resulting trust because it would seem that the trust corpus should be returned to him on B's death without ever having had a child.

When the only beneficiaries of a trust created by declaration of the trustor are unborn at the time of the declaration there is a diversity of view whether a trust is created. Professor Scott criticizes the holding of the Morsman case. He states that it is immaterial whether the unborn child is the sole beneficiary or merely one of the beneficiaries of the trust. "The question in either case is one of policy, whether it is permissible to tie up property in such a way that even though the settlor, the trustee, and all the world besides should wish to undo what has been done, they cannot do so".[31] The Restatement of Trusts, § 112 provides in part: [32] "A child who has not been born or conceived at the time of the creation of a trust can be a beneficiary of the trust. If the interest is to vest in the child within the period of the rule against perpetuities, the trust is valid if the other requirements for the creation of a trust are complied with. * * *" The illustrations supporting this statement are of trusts created by transfer, but the generality of the language seems to include trusts created by declaration also.

The rules concerning trusts for unborn beneficiaries apply to trusts for corporations to be formed after the declaration or transfer of property by the settlor.[33]

---

31. II Scott, Trusts (3d Ed., 1967) 879. When the settlor declares himself trustee for an unborn beneficiary the difficulty in enforcement might be solved by replacing the trustee pursuant to the settled maxim that no trust fails for want of a trustee. If the trustee is replaced the situation then is much as if the settlor had transferred to a trustee for the benefit of another. Equity might regard as done what should have been done. It is unlikely that such an argument would be viewed favorably in a tax case such as *Morsman* but a court might prove receptive in other situations if the difficulty in enforcement is perceived as the reason for the defect in the declaration. See Section 4(4) of this Chapter.

32. Restatement, Second, Trusts § 112, Comment *d*.

33. See generally, Bogert, Trusts and Trustees (2d Ed., 1965) § 163; II Scott, Trusts (3d Ed., 1967) §§ 112, 112.1, 112.2; Fratcher, "Trustor as Sole Trustee and Only Ascertainable Beneficiary", 47 Mich.L.Rev. 907 (1949).

B. PRIVATE PURPOSES WHICH INVOLVE NO HUMAN BENEFICIARY

Sometimes a testator wishes to set aside a portion of his estate for a private purpose which involves no person as beneficiary.[34] Such purposes are of three types: (1) care of an individual or family burial plot, or the erection of an elaborate monument; (2) care of specified pet animals as long as they live; and (3) saying of masses for the soul of the testator or a designated person. These present theoretical difficulties for a trust arrangement since there is no human being who can enforce the trust. On the other hand, the provision is for a specific purpose and the court should have no difficulty in supervising the trust on grounds of indefiniteness. It should be pointed out that the draftsman may utilize legal concepts other than the trust to carry out the desired purpose. Thus, a contract for care of the burial plot can be entered into; or a sum of money can be given to a named person or institution such as the Humane Society on condition that the pet animal be cared for, with a gift to another person or institution if the condition is broken.[35]

"Trusts" for the saying of masses are now widely sustained as charitable trusts within the rules we shall study in Chapter XI, on the grounds that such trusts benefit the church. Directions for erection of monuments are enforced by the probate courts as part of the directions for burial and allowed as "funeral expenses". There is a split of authority as to how much of an estate can be allocated for this purpose, but the modern view favors a standard of reasonableness. In many states, statutes authorize trusts for care of graves and burial plots.

34. See generally 4 Powell, The Law of Real Property (Rohan Rev.1970 ¶¶ 588, 589; II Scott, Trusts (3d Ed. 1967) § 124; Brennan, "Bequests for Religious Services", 17 Clev.-Mar.L.Rev. 388 (1968); "Bequests for the Erection, Care and Maintenance of Graves, Monuments and Mausoleums", 9 Washburn L.J. 23 (1969). In Perry v. Twentieth Street Bank, 157 W.Va. 963, 206 S.E.2d 421 (1974) it was held that a testamentary trust establishing a fund the net income of which was to be used for flowers to be placed on the graves of the settlor and her parents was authorized by statute and thus was not invalidated by the rule against perpetuities. The statute read in pertinent part "Express trusts may hereafter be created for the perpetual care, preservation, maintenance, improvement and/or embellishment of any cemetery or burial lot, public or private, and of the appurtenances of any such lot, including the erection, repair, preservation, and/or removal of mausoleums, tombs, monuments, gravestones, fences, railings, walks, and/or other structure or structures thereon, and the planting, trimming, watering and/or removing of any tree, shrub or other plant or plants thereon. Any such trust heretofore created shall be valid."

35. Provision can be made for the care and support of pets by a gift of the pets to a person named as beneficiary of a private express trust, stipulating that the beneficiary shall receive the income from the trust only so long as he takes care of the pets and with a gift over if the beneficiary fails to care for the pets. The draftsman of such a trust must be careful not to violate the rule against perpetuities and the rule against unduly prolonging the indestructibility of private express trusts. The income of the trust should exceed the amounts necessary to support the animals by a sum sufficient to offer the beneficiary an inducement to carry out the trust condition. See comment, "Trusts for Animals in New York—Beneficiaries and Perpetuities", 17 Syracuse L.Rev. 705 (1966); Schwartz, "Estate Planning for Animals", 113 Trusts & Estates 376 (1974).

Our problem is thus reduced to finding a way to sustain "trusts" for maintenance of animals, for care of burial plots where there is no applicable statute, and for saying of masses in states which do not treat such a purpose as charitable. The Restatement, Second, Trusts § 124 takes the position that no enforceable trust is created, but the transferee has a power to apply the property to the designated purpose unless this would violate the Rule Against Perpetuities or the purpose is "capricious". Such trusts are often called "honorary trusts". If the transferee does not carry out the power, there is a resulting trust for the donor's estate.[36] Where the amount and purpose are reasonable, the probate court may enforce the "trust" on its own motion in some states.

(6) STATEMENT OF DUTIES AND POWERS

The duties of the trustee, broadly stated, are to manage the property so as to make it productive of income, to pay out the income to the designated income beneficiary, and ultimately on termination of the trust to distribute the trust property or principal in accordance with the trust terms. However, the modern trust document confers upon the trustee by express terms many powers to enable him to carry out his trust function. Sometimes these powers are discretionary; sometimes they are mandatory. Thus, the trustee may be empowered in his discretion to pay principal out to the income beneficiary when the income is inadequate for the needs of the beneficiary. On the other hand, such a power to invade may be imperative in nature and thus become a duty, as where the trustee is directed to pay out principal upon demand of the beneficiary.

36. There is little case authority in this country. Such trusts are recognized in England, In re Dean, 41 Ch.Div. 552 (1889) and by statute in Wisconsin (Wis. Stats. sec. 701.11). In Gold v. Price, 24 N.C.App. 660, 211 S.E.2d 803 (1975), the Court said:

> "In their first assignment of error defendants contend the trial court erred in holding that testatrix did not create a trust for the maintenance of her grave and Tom Gold's grave. We find this assignment of error without merit for several reasons. First, as we pointed out in Starling v. Taylor, 1 N.C.App. 287, 290–291, 161 S.E.2d 204, 207 (1968), '[i]t is well settled in this State that three circumstances must concur in order to constitute a valid trust: (1) sufficient words to raise a trust. (2) a definite subject or trust *res*, and (3) an ascertained object. [Citations omitted.]' Here, testatrix did not provide any funds to maintain the graves. Consequently, the second element necessary to create a trust, a definite subject or res, is missing. Second, even if a trust had been created, which we do not concede, it would be an honorary trust, rather than a charitable trust, since it would not benefit the public as a whole. Such a trust is not enforceable. It may be put into effect or ignored at the option of the person named trustee since he 'has only a power and not a duty to apply the property.' Restatement of Trusts 2d, § 124, p. 264 (1959)."

The effect of a failure to state any duties in the trust document will be considered next.

(7) FAILURE TO IMPOSE ACTIVE DUTIES (PASSIVE TRUSTS)

BELLOWS v. PAGE

Supreme Court of New Hampshire, 1936.
88 N.H. 283, 188 A. 12.[37]

Petition for a declaratory judgment under Laws 1929, c. 86.

* * * WOODBURY, J. The will of the petitioner's aunt, Mary Adams Patterson Bellows, provides merely that the petitioner's share should be held "in trust" for her by her mother. It imposed no duties upon the trustee; it clothed her with no discretionary powers; no action on her part was required in order to effectuate any discernible purpose which the testatrix may have had in mind when she created the trust. The will, therefore, creates a *use*, or, in more modern phraseology, a "dry," "passive," or "naked" trust, and as such it is executed by force of the statute of uses (27 Hen. VIII, c. 10), a statute which has been regarded as in effect in this jurisdiction from the earliest times. New Parish in Exeter v. Odiorne, 1 N.H. 232, 237. See, also, Hening, N.H.Dig. pp. 1473 and 1590.

But the above statute applies only to trusts created upon freehold interests in land. It does not apply to interests in chattels, *choses in action* or other personal property (1 Am.Law Inst., Restatement of Trusts, § 70, Comment c.; Tappan's Appeal, 55 N.H. 317, 322), and the case as transferred, is defective in that it does not indicate whether the trustee under the aunt's will is holding real property, personal property, or both.

This defect does not render it impossible for us to dispose of this phase of the case before us at this time, however, because "modern courts execute passive trusts of personalty, either by analogy to the Statute of Uses, or on the theory that any trust without a purpose is automatically executed." 1 Bogert on Trusts and Trustees, § 207, and cases cited. This section then continues to the effect that: "There are a small number of decisions which apply the Statute of Uses strictly with regard to the trust of chattels, refuse to execute it, and compel the *cestui* to bring a bill to get a conveyance." The cases cited in the footnote appended to this sentence indicate merely that some courts, instead of giving the trust property directly to the beneficiary, require that he bring a bill for its conveyance. They do not indicate that a passive trust of personalty is not executed. In other words, the difference in the decisions noted by Bogert is only a differ-

37. Noted, 17 B.U.L.R. 499 (1937).

ence in technique; it is not a difference in result. In all cases, apparently, the cestui is entitled to hold the trust property free from the intervention of a trustee.

The fact that the rule of law which executes passive trusts is of statutory origin and applies, in terms, only to trusts created upon freehold interests in land, does not prevent us from extending the application of that rule to trusts of personal property. The statute of uses was passed long before the American Revolution. Its authoritative force here is derived from the fact that it was an amendment of the common law suitable to the condition and needs of the inhabitants of this state and in harmony with their institutions. It thus, like other similarly enacted statutes, became part of the body, not of our statutory, but of our common law. (French v. French, 3 N.H. 234, 264; State v. Rollins, 8 N.H. 550, 560), and as such it is susceptible to judicial change under the maxim *cessante ratione cessat lex*. Heath v. Heath, 85 N.H. 419, 422, 159 A. 418.

In sixteenth century England, at the time when the statute of uses was enacted, there may have been good reason for drawing a distinction between passive trusts involving real property and similar trusts involving personalty only, but today, in this country, and under present conditions, we see no valid reason why this distinction should be perpetuated. We approve of the majority rule as enunciated in the cases appearing in the note to the section from Bogert on Trusts and Trustees quoted first above, and it follows that the trust created by the will of the petitioner's aunt is executed and that she is entitled, without further proceedings, to the full legal title to all the property, real or personal, held by the defendant as trustee under that will.

* * * [Omitted is the court's discussion of a trust created for the petitioner's benefit by the will of her father.] * * *

Case discharged.

PAGE, J., took no part in the decision of this case; the others concurred.

NOTE

The Statute of Uses [38] converted the equitable interest of the *cestui que use* into a legal interest and extinguished the legal interest of the *feoffee to use*. This was known as executing the use.[39] The Statute was limited in its operation to passive *uses*. The Statute did not execute an active *use*. A *use* or trust is active when the trust terms impose affirmative duties on the trustee. A trust to preserve contingent remainders is deemed an active trust. Similarly, a trust for the separate *use* of a married woman was deemed an active trust during her coverture. By the prevailing view, a direction to the trustee to convey or transfer the trust property makes the trust active.

38. 27 Hen. VIII, c. 10 (1536).

39. The application of the Statute is discussed in detail in Chapter I, Section 3(1)A.

There is a minority doctrine that such a trust is passive, so that the title vests in the beneficiary without a conveyance by the trustee.

Certain passive trusts (*uses*) were not executed by the Statute. The Statute applied only to trusts of freehold interests in land. Thus, if X conveys an estate for ten years in Blackacre to A to the *use* of B, the Statute is inapplicable and A holds the leasehold estate in trust for B. If X conveys an estate in fee simple to A to the *use* of B for ten years, the Statute of Uses applies because A is seised of a freehold. There is a resulting *use* or trust to X of the interest following the ten year period which is executed by the Statute. The net effect is to leave B with a legal term for ten years with a reversion in X in fee.

When a passive trust is not executed by the Statute, the trustee is under a duty to protect the trust property and to transfer it to the beneficiary, or in accordance with the directions of the beneficiary, on the demand of the beneficiary. The trust being passive, no purpose is served by its continuance.

The Statute of Uses is part of the common law of many American states. In some states there are statutes having an effect similar to the Statute of Uses.[40] In other states, courts of equity, unaided by statute, have held that the title of the passive trustee passes to the *cestui que trust*, with the result that the passive trust is terminated at the moment it arises and the beneficiary of the trust holds the trust property free and clear of the trust. An attempt to create a passive trust in this country usually results in the legal title passing to the trust beneficiary.

A few states have held that the Statute of Uses does not apply to trusts created by devise.[41] Some states hold that a passive trust of personal property is executed by the Statute.[42]

---

40. E.g., McKinney's N.Y., EPTL, § 7–1.2.

41. E.g., Bass v. Scott, 29 Va. (2 Leigh) 386 (1830).

42. Unless the settlor manifests an intent that the trust property passes to the beneficiary upon accomplishment of the trust purpose, and absent a statute executing a passive use of personal property, it seems possible today to create a passive trust of personalty. The trust is not terminated automatically when the purpose is accomplished, but the beneficiary must apply to the proper court for an order compelling the trustee to transfer the property and thus terminate the trust. When the trust is used for business purposes the trustee may be simply a title holder. Thus, when a trust is used as a device to secure a loan (the "deed of trust") the trustees may have no duties unless the borrower defaults and once the secured note is discharged the deed of trust is cancelled with the trustees having done nothing during the life of the trust. In some of the variations of the "land" trust the trustee may have few if any duties, serving only as a title holder. See as to these matters Chapter IX, Section 4.

SECTION 5. VALIDITY OF PROTECTIVE (SPENDTHRIFT) PROVISIONS

(1) NATURE OF THE BENEFICIARY'S INTEREST

Before we can analyze the validity of provisions inserted in the trust document to protect the beneficiary's interest against certain claims, it is necessary to give you some understanding of the normal incidents of such an interest in the absence of special restrictions in the document.

Generally speaking, the same property interests may be created in the beneficiary of a trust that may be created in one who is not the beneficiary of a trust. Thus, the beneficiary's interest in the trust property may be limited to endure for a period of years, or for the beneficiary's life, or for the life of someone other than the beneficiary, or in fee simple. Similarly, the interest of the beneficiary in the trust property may be subject to a condition precedent, or subject to a condition subsequent, or it may be created to terminate automatically upon the occurrence of a specified event. Typically, the interest of the beneficiary in the trust property will not be possessory because ordinarily the trustee will have the right to possession of the trust property in order that he may control and manage it. It is possible, however, for the trustee to direct that the trust beneficiary have possession of the trust property.

If the interest of a trust beneficiary in the trust property is an equitable fee in realty, it passes on his death to his heirs or devisees. On the other hand, if the trust beneficiary's interest in the trust property is personalty, it passes on his death to his administrator or executor. But if the trust beneficiary dies intestate without heirs or next of kin, his interest in the trust property passes to the state. By the terms of the trust, the interest of the beneficiary may terminate on his death.

When the trust beneficiaries are co-owners of the trust property, they ordinarily hold the property as tenants in common. The settlor may make the beneficiaries joint tenants or tenants by the entirety. In any event, a fiduciary relationship exists between co-beneficiaries of a trust and each co-beneficiary owes a duty to the others not to strive for exclusive benefits or advantages.

If the co-beneficiaries are joint tenants or tenants by the entirety of the trust property, the doctrine of survivorship is applicable. Thus, if A and B are co-beneficiaries as joint tenants of an equitable fee simple in the trust property, B, on A's death, will be the sole trust beneficiary and will own the beneficial interest in severalty.

According to the early English common law, the widow of a trust beneficiary was not dowable in the trust property because one could not be seised of an equitable interest in land and dower attached only to an estate of inheritance of which the husband was seised at some time during coverture. This rule has been changed in England by statute. A few American jurisdictions recognizing dower follow the early English rule. But in most states where dower is recognized, dower applies to equitable as well as legal estates and thus attaches to all estates of inheritance in land of which the husband was trust beneficiary during coverture. In a few states the widow has dower only when the husband was trust beneficiary at his death.

The widower of the beneficiary of a trust of land is entitled to curtesy in the beneficiary's interest under the same circumstances under which he would be entitled to curtesy in a corresponding legal interest in land. A few courts have held that when a trust is created for the separate use of a married woman her husband is not entitled to curtesy in her beneficial interest if she transfers that interest by deed or will or if the trust terms provide that the husband shall not be entitled to curtesy. The "forced heir" statutes apply to equitable as well as legal interests and are thus applicable to inheritable interests owned by a deceased spouse as trust beneficiary.

Unless the power is restricted by statute or the trust terms, the beneficiary of a trust may alienate his interest in the trust property as freely as he might alienate a corresponding legal interest in that property. He may also mortgage, otherwise encumber, or dispose by will of his interest in the trust property to the same extent that he might mortgage, otherwise encumber, or dispose by will of a corresponding legal interest in that property. In some states the interest of the beneficiary in the trust property is transferable only by a writing signed by the beneficiary. In other states a signed writing is required only if the trust is of real property. The statutes and decisions of each jurisdiction should be consulted to determine the formal requisites for a valid transfer of a beneficial interest.

A difficult problem arises if the beneficiary makes successive assignments of his beneficial interest. Are the assignments effective in the order made or does the assignee gain priority who first notifies the trustee? There is a division of authority on the issue. The answer depends upon the state in which the problem arises. If B, a beneficiary, transfers his interest to A and thereafter purports to transfer the same interest to C, and C notifies the trustee of the transfer before A gives notice, C can enforce the trust if the issue arises in some states, while A can enforce the trust if the issue arises in other states.

The creditors of a trust beneficiary may realize their claims out of the beneficiary's transferable interests in the trust property. To the extent that by statute or otherwise, a legal interest in property is exempt from the claims of the owner's creditor, a corresponding interest of a beneficiary in a trust is exempt from the claims of his creditors. Homestead exemptions are typical of those types applicable to both legal and equitable interests. Interests of a trust beneficiary in the trust property may be exempt from the claims of the beneficiary's creditors even though a corresponding legal interest is not exempt. Exemptions of the latter type are considered in the section which follows.

The appropriate procedure by which the creditor of a beneficiary reaches the equitable interest is a matter of local law which varies from state to state. A creditor's bill in chancery was originally the only remedy available and is still the only remedy in some states. In many states the beneficiary's interest is subject to execution, attachment and garnishment as if it were a legal interest.[43]

---

(2) DRAFTING TECHNIQUES AND POLICY ISSUES CONCERNING PROTECTIVE CLAUSES

Draftsmen have for years worked to evolve valid and effective clauses which would protect a beneficiary from his own indiscretions. It does little good to create an elaborate trust to provide for the welfare of a member of the family, only to have the beneficiary assign away his equitable interest or incur obligations which can be satisfied by subjecting the beneficiary's interest to payment of those debts. Hence a method of protecting the beneficiary has been sought. The resulting clauses take various forms:

(1) The oldest is a "cesser provision" or "forfeiture" clause which provides that the interest of the beneficiary ceases if he assigns or his creditors attempt to reach his interest by legal process. This is accompanied by a gift over upon forfeiture. Certainly this device affords little "protection" to the beneficiary although it does "protect" the trust property.

(2) A "spendthrift clause" restrains the power of the beneficiary to "anticipate" his right to income or perhaps to principal. There is no restraint upon income or principal once the beneficiary receives payment. Since the beneficiary's power to anticipate is restrained, there is a corresponding restraint upon involuntary transfers by legal process which have the effect of anticipation. A creditor can reach the property once it is paid by the trustee to the beneficiary.

(3) A "discretionary" power in the trustee to pay income, or distribute principal, among several beneficiaries (usually members

43. See generally, Bogert, Trusts and Trustees (2d Ed., 1966) Ch. 11; II Scott, Trusts (3d Ed., 1967) §§ 132–163; Wren, "Drafting Spendthrift, Discretionary, and Support Provisions," 15 Baylor L.Rev. 263 (1963); Kerr, "Discretionary Trusts: Policies for Drafting and Exercise of Powers," 103 Trusts and Estates 116 (1964).

of the same family) enables the trustee, if the interest of any beneficiary is jeopardized, to cease payment to him and pay to other beneficiaries, such as his spouse or children.

(4) A provision that only so much of the income shall be paid to the beneficiary as is necessary for his support is called a "support trust". Here it is the restricted nature of the beneficiary's interest that prevents transfer, rather than any express provision forbidding transfer or imposing a forfeiture.

(5) Combination of several forms may be utilized, particularly in jurisdictions where there is any doubt about the validity of the spendthrift clause.[44] Thus, the trust instrument can provide a spendthrift clause, with a forfeiture clause if creditors attempt to reach the beneficiary's interest followed by a discretionary trust to pay to members of the beneficiary's family.

It is apparent that the arsenal of the draftsman is ample. It remains to be seen how effective these weapons are. In a state which rejects spendthrift clauses for policy reasons, the draftsman must then resort to another type of protective clause.

BROADWAY NATIONAL BANK v. ADAMS

Supreme Judicial Court of Massachusetts, 1882.
133 Mass. 170, 43 Am.Rep. 504.

MORTON, C. J. The object of this bill in equity is to reach and apply in payment of the plaintiff's debt due from the defendant Adams the income of a trust fund created for his benefit by the will of his brother. The eleventh article of the will is as follows: "I give the sum of seventy-five thousand dollars to my said executors and the survivors or survivor of them in trust to invest the same in such manner as to them may seem prudent, and to pay the net income thereof,

44. For an example of such a combination see Duncan v. Elkins, 94 N.H. 13, 45 A.2d 297 (1946). For an interesting discussion of a trust document containing a spendthrift clause, a forfeiture clause and a blended trust see O'Connor v. O'Connor, 141 N.E.2d 691 (Court of Common Pleas of Ohio, 1957).

In an action to have certain lands sold and the proceeds reinvested, the Tennessee court said:

"While there is no case in Tennessee directly passing upon the validity of a restraint upon alienation annexed to a legal life estate, the law generally is clear that any restraint which undertakes to wholly remove the power of a life tenant to alienate his estate is absolutely void. Restatement of the Law of Property, § 405; 6 American Law of Property, § 26.49 (J. Casner Ed. 1952); 6 Powell, Real Property ¶ 844 (1971).

"We can see no reason to depart from this nearly unanimous view of the law. A testator, or the settlor of a nontestamentary trust, if he so desires, may still through the medium of a trust restrict the power of his trustee to sell or otherwise alienate the property which he has devised or given. And, in such a case, the devise or gift is subject to the constant supervision of courts of equity, which are empowered, if conditions so warrant, to decree a sale of the property when necessary to effectuate the intention of the testator. * * *

"The restraint being void, the life tenants are, of course, free to sell their estates." Alsup v. Montoya, 488 S.W. 2d 725, 728 (Tenn.1972).

semiannually, to my said brother Charles W. Adams, during his natural life, such payments to be made to him personally when convenient, otherwise, upon his order or receipt in writing; in either case free from the interference or control of his creditors, my intention being that the use of said income shall not be anticipated by assignment. At the decease of my said brother, Charles, my will is that the net income of said seventy-five thousand dollars shall be paid to his present wife, in case she survives him, for the benefit of herself and all the children of said Charles, in equal proportions, in the manner and upon the conditions the same as herein directed to be paid him during his life, so long as she shall remain single. And my will is, that, after the decease of said Charles and the decease or second marriage of his said wife, the said seventy-five thousand dollars, together with any accrued interest or income thereon which may remain unpaid, as herein above directed, shall be divided equally among all the children of my said brother Charles, by any and all his wives, and the representatives of any deceased child or children by right of representation."

There is no room for doubt as to the intention of the testator. It is clear that, if the trustee was to pay the income to the plaintiff under an order of the court, it would be in direct violation of the intention of the testator and of the provisions of his will. The court will not compel the trustee thus to do what the will forbids him to do, unless the provisions and intention of the testator are unlawful.

The question whether the founder of a trust can secure the income of it to the object of his bounty, by providing that it shall not be alienable by him or be subject to be taken by his creditors, has not been directly adjudicated in this Commonwealth. The tendency of our decisions, however, has been in favor of such a power in the founder. Braman v. Stiles, 2 Pick. 460. Perkins v. Hays, 3 Gray 405. Russell v. Grinnell, 105 Mass. 425. Hall v. Williams, 120 Mass. 344. Sparhawk v. Cloon, 125 Mass. 263.

It is true that the rule of the common law is, that a man cannot attach to a grant or transfer of property, otherwise absolute, the condition that it shall not be alienated; such condition being repugnant to the nature of the estate granted. Co.Lit. 223 a; Blackstone Bank v. Davis, 21 Pick. 42.

Lord Coke gives as the reason of the rule, that "it is absurd and repugnant to reason that he, that hath no possibility to have the land revert to him, should restrain his feoffee in fee simple of all his power to alien," and that this is "against the height and puritie of a fee simple." By such a condition, the grantor undertakes to deprive the property in the hands of the grantee of one of its legal incidents and attributes, namely, its alienability, which is deemed to be against public policy. But the reasons of the rule do not apply in the case of a transfer of property in trust. By the creation of a trust like the one before us, the trust property passes to the trustee with all its incidents and attributes unimpaired. He takes the whole legal title to the property, with the power of alienation; the *cestui que trust* takes the whole legal title to the accrued income at the moment it is paid over to him. Neither the principal nor the income is at any time inalienable.

The question whether the rule of the common law should be applied to equitable life estates created by will or deed has been the subject of conflicting adjudications by different courts, as is fully shown in the able and exhaustive arguments of the counsel in this case. As is stated in Sparhawk v. Cloon, above cited, from the time of Lord Eldon the rule has prevailed in the English Court of Chancery, to the extent of holding that when the income of a trust estate is given to any person (other than a married woman) for life, the equitable estate for life is alienable by, and liable in equity to the debts of, the *cestui que trust,* and that this quality is so inseparable from the estate that no provision, however express, which does not operate as a cesser or limitation of the estate itself, can protect it from his debts. Brandon v. Robinson, 18 Ves. 429. Green v. Spicer, 1 Russ. & Myl. 395. Rochford v. Hackman, 9 Hare 475. Trappes v. Meredith, L.R. 9 Eq. 229. Snowdon v. Dales, 6 Sim. 524. Rippon v. Norton, 2 Beav. 63.

The English rule has been adopted in several of the courts of this country. Tillinghast v. Bradford, 5 R.I. 205. Heath v. Bishop, 4 Rich.Eq. 46. Dick v. Pitchford, 1 Dev. & Bat.Eq. 480. Mebane v. Mebane, 4 Ired.Eq. 131.

Other courts have rejected it, and have held that the founder of a trust may secure the benefit of it to the object of his bounty, by providing that the income shall not be alienable by anticipation, nor subject to be taken for his debts. Holdship v. Patterson, 7 Watts 547. Shankland's Appeal, 47 Penn.St. 113. Rife v. Geyer, 59 Penn.St. 393. White v. White, 30 Vt. 338. Pope v. Elliott, 8 B.Mon. 56. Nichols v. Eaton, 91 U.S. 716. Hyde v. Woods, 94 U.S. 523.

The precise point involved in the case at bar has not been adjudicated in this Commonwealth; but the decisions of this court which we have before cited recognize the principle, that, if the intention of the founder of a trust, like the one before us, is to give to the equitable life tenant a qualified and limited, and not an absolute, estate in the income such life tenant cannot alienate it by anticipation, and his creditors cannot reach it at law or in equity. It seems to us that this principle extends to and covers the case at bar. The founder of this trust was the absolute owner of his property. He had the entire right to dispose of it, either by an absolute gift to his brother, or by a gift with such restrictions or limitations, not repugnant to law, as he saw fit to impose. His clear intention, as shown in his will, was not to give his brother an absolute right to the income which might hereafter accrue upon the trust fund, with the power of alienating it in advance, but only the right to receive semiannually the income of the fund, which upon its payment to him, and not before, was to become his absolute property. His intentions ought to be carried out, unless they are against public policy. There is nothing in the nature or tenure of the estate given to the *cestui que trust* which should prevent this. The power of alienating in advance is not a necessary attribute or incident of such an estate or interest, so that the restraint of such alienation would introduce repugnant or inconsistent elements.

We are not able to see that it would violate any principles of sound public policy to permit a testator to give to the object of his bounty such a qualified interest in the income of a trust fund, and thus provide against the improvidence or misfortune of the beneficiary. The only ground upon which it can be held to be against public policy, is that it defrauds the creditors of the beneficiary.

It is argued that investing a man with apparent wealth tends to mislead creditors, and to induce them to give him credit. The answer is, that creditors have no right to rely upon property thus held, and to give him credit upon the basis of an estate which, by the instrument creating it, is declared to be inalienable by him, and not liable for his debts. By the exercise of proper diligence they can ascertain the nature and extent of his estate, especially in this Commonwealth, where all wills and most deeds are spread upon the public records. There is the same danger of their being misled by false appearances, and induced to give credit to the equitable life tenant when the will or deed of trust provides for a cesser or limitation over, in case of an attempted alienation, or of bankruptcy or attachment, and the argument would lead to the conclusion that the English rule is equally in violation of public policy. We do not see why the founder of a trust may not directly provide that his property shall go to his beneficiary with the restriction that it shall not be alienable by anticipation, and that his creditors shall not have the right to attach it in advance, instead of indirectly reaching the same result by a provision for a cesser or a limitation over, or by giving his trustees a discretion as to paying it. He has the entire *jus disponendi*, which imports that he may give it absolutely, or may impose any restriction or fetters not repugnant to the nature of the estate which he gives. Under our system, creditors may reach all the property of the debtor not exempted by law, but they cannot enlarge the gift of the founder of a trust, and take more than he has given.

The rule of public policy which subjects a debtor's property to the payment of his debts does not subject the property of a donor to the debts of his beneficiary, and does not give the creditor a right to complain, that, in the exercise of his absolute right of disposition, the donor has not seen fit to give the property to the creditor, but has left it out of his reach.

Whether a man can settle his own property in trust for his own benefit, so as to exempt the income from alienation by him or attachment in advance by his creditors, is a different question, which we are not called upon to consider in this case. But we are of opinion that any other person, having the entire right to dispose of his property, may settle it in trust in favor of a beneficiary, and may provide that it shall not be alienated by him by anticipation, and shall not be subject to be seized by his creditors in advance of its payment to him.

It follows that, under the provisions of the will which we are considering, the income of the trust fund created for the benefit of the defendant Adams cannot be reached by attachment, either at law or in equity, before it is paid to him. Bill dismissed. * * *

Held

NOTE

Even in the absence of a statute, spendthrift trusts are permitted in a vast majority of American states.[45] Statutes in a number of states determine the validity of spendthrift trusts.

In jurisdictions sustaining the validity of restraints on alienation of trust income, there is a conflict of authority whether restraints on alienation of principal are valid.

The Restatement of Trusts now recognizes that a restraint on alienation of principal is valid,[46] as do the majority of the modern decisions.

Even though a jurisdiction may recognize spendthrift trusts as valid, judges may differ in their opinions as to the desirability of enforcing spendthrift trusts and thus tend either to strict construction of the clauses or to the recognition of exceptions to their operation. Thus, in Utley v. Graves,[47] Judge Holtzoff regarded a husband who had elected to take under the will of his wife rather than claim forced heirship as the creator of a spendthrift trust in the will of his wife of which the husband was beneficiary. To avoid the operation of the spendthrift clause, Judge Holtzoff invoked the well settled proposition that a person cannot set up a trust and retain the beneficial interest while including a spendthrift clause that will protect him against his creditors. At 258 F.Supp. 960, Judge Holtzoff states:

> "* * * A spendthrift trust is an anomaly and an anachronism. There are many who consider it contrary to their notions of right and wrong that a person should be permitted to live on income that he does not earn and yet that is not subject to the claims of his creditors. It seems incongruous that he should be at liberty to incur pecuniary obligations, free of any duty to fulfill them. That a person should be able to live according to the standards to which he claims to be accustomed and at the same time repudiate any obligation to pay for anything that he purchases on credit, is manifestly inequitable and repugnant to the ideas of right and wrong. That persons who are sufficiently sophisticated and incredulous may decline to extend credit to him, and refuse to sell him anything or render him any service except for current payment in cash, is not an adequate answer. There are numerous small business concerns that are unable to maintain a complete credit department and ascertain the fact that a person, although seemingly affluent, is living on the income of a spendthrift trust. * * *"

Judge Holtzoff's decision was reversed on appeal, the Court rejecting Judge Holtzoff's analysis that the husband was creator of the trust, stating

45. See Bogert, Trusts and Trustees (2d Ed. 1965) § 222; Griswold, Spendthrift Trusts (2d Ed., 1947) Ch. 3; II Scott, Trusts (3d Ed. 1967) § 152.

46. Restatement, Second, Trusts § 153.

47. 258 F.Supp. 959 (D.C.D.C.1966).

that this was a minority view, and quoting with approval the following statement by Professor Scott:[48]

> "On the whole the better view would seem to be that where a husband creates a trust for his wife by will, the mere fact that she surrenders her right to dower or to a distributive share of his estate does not make her the creator of the trust, even to the extent of the value of the interest which she surrendered. If spendthrift trusts are to be permitted at all, it would seem that a husband should be allowed to create such a trust for his widow, even though she may have power to refuse to accept the provisions of his will and take her dower or distributive share in lieu thereof."

Even courts holding that until the time for payment of the principal arises, a restraint on the alienation of the right of the beneficiary to receive principal is effective, agree that when the time for payment does arrive the beneficiary can transfer his interest in the trust capital and his creditors can reach his interest therein. This result is sound when the interest of the beneficiary in the principal is a legal interest because such a restraint on alienation of a legal interest is invalid. The rule is applicable, however, even though the beneficiary's interest is equitable until the trust principal is in fact transferred to him. This seems to be the rule even in those jurisdictions in which the creditors cannot reach trust income in the hands of the trustee due and payable to the beneficiary because the spendthrift provision is applicable until the income is in fact paid over.[49]

No particular form of words is necessary to create a spendthrift trust. It is necessary, however, that the trust terms manifest the settlor's intention to impose a direct restraint on the voluntary and involuntary alienation of the beneficiary's interest. When a settlor expressly imposes a restraint only on voluntary alienation of the beneficiary's interest, a court may conclude that the settlor intended to impose a restraint on involuntary alienation also. Conversely, when the settlor expressly imposes a restraint on involuntary alienation, a court may conclude that he intends to restrain voluntary alienation. The readiness of courts to infer an intent to restrain involuntary alienation from an express restraint of voluntary alienation and, on the other hand, to infer an intent to restrain voluntary alienation from an express restraint of involuntary alienation, stems from the general rule that all transferable interests in property are available for satisfying the claims of the owner's creditors, unless an exemption statute provides otherwise. It is contrary to public policy to permit a settlor directly to restrain involuntary alienation of the beneficiary's interest while permitting voluntary alienation, although there is no policy objection to a restraint on voluntary alienation while permitting involuntary alienation.

When the trust terms as construed in the light of all the attendant circumstances fail to show the settlor's intention to impose a restraint on alienation, and there is no statute imposing such a restraint, the interest of the beneficiary is transferable and can be reached by his creditors.[50]

A contract by the beneficiary of a spendthrift trust to assign his interest is not specifically enforceable. The other party to the contract is entitled to

48. American Security And Trust Co. v. Utley, 382 F.2d 451, 452 (C.A.D.C. 1967). See, 8 U.Balt.L.Rev. 598 (1979).

49. See Bogert, Trusts and Trustees (2d Ed., 1965) § 222; II Scott, Trusts (3d Ed. 1967) §§ 153, 153.2, 153.3. But see Kelley v. Lincoln National Bank, 98 U.S. App.D.C. 264, 235 F.2d 23 (1956).

50. In a few cases the courts have found an intention to create spendthrift trusts although the intention does not appear clearly from the trust terms. E.g., Jones v. Harrison, 7 F.2d 461 (8th Cir. 1925).

restitution of the consideration. If the beneficiary is *sui juris*, the promisee, at his election, may maintain an action for breach of contract. The judgment obtained in such an action can be satisfied out of the interest of the beneficiary in the trust property only to the extent that other creditors can reach his interest in satisfaction of their claims.

If the beneficiary assigns his interest despite a valid spendthrift clause, and the trustee recognizes the assignment and makes payment to the assignee, the trustee will be protected. The assignment is treated by the courts as a revocable order to the trustee to pay the income once accrued to the assignee. Until the beneficiary revokes the order by notice to the trustee, no liability is incurred by the latter in making payments. In Keeler's Estate, the Supreme Court of Pennsylvania stated the rule thus:[51]

> "* * * Even in a spendthrift trust the beneficiary has full ownership and control of the installments of income *after* they respectively accrue, and therefore, after such accrual, the beneficiary may give directions to the trustee to pay such installments to her nominee or assignee. When the beneficiary makes an assignment of future income and directs the trustee to pay such income to the assignee, such an assignment, in the case of spendthrift trusts, is invalid in the sense that it can be revoked at any time by the beneficiary, but, unless and until so repudiated, it constitutes a valid authority to the trustee to make payments of the successively accruing installments of income to the assignee. The direction to the trustee to pay to the assignee is enforceable only as to each installment after it accrues, and then only if the direction has not previously been rescinded."

SHELLEY v. SHELLEY

Supreme Court of Oregon, 1960.
223 Or. 328, 354 P.2d 282.

O'CONNELL, JUSTICE. This is an appeal from a decree of the circuit court for Multnomah county establishing the rights of the parties to the income and corpus of a trust of which the defendant, the United States National Bank of Portland (Oregon) is trustee.

The assignments of error are directed at the trial court's interpretation of the trust. The trust involved in this suit was created by Hugh T. Shelley. The pertinent parts of the trust are as follows:

> "Ninth: All of the rest, residue, and remainder of my said estate, * * * I give, devise, and bequeath to the United States National Bank of Portland (Oregon), in trust, * * * upon the following trusts:
>
> * * *
>
> "(2) I direct that, all income derived from my trust estate be paid to my wife, Gertrude R. Shelley, as long as she lives, said

51. 334 Pa. 225, 231, 3 A.2d 413, 416, 121 A.L.R. 1301 (1939). See 83 A.L.R.3d 1142 (1978).

income to be paid to her at intervals of not less than three (3) months apart;

* * *

"(4) If my said wife, Gertrude R. Shelley, shall predecease me, and my said son is then alive, or upon my wife's death after my death and my son being alive, it is my desire, and I direct, that, the United States National Bank of Portland (Oregon), as trustee, shall continue this estate in trust and pay all income derived therefrom to my son, Grant R. Shelley, as long as he lives, said income to be paid to him at intervals not less than three (3) months apart; Provided, Further, That when my son, Grant R. Shelley, arrives at the age of thirty (30) years, my trustee may then, or at any time thereafter, and from time to time distribute to said son absolutely and as his own all or any part of the principal of said trust fund that it may then or from time to time thereafter deem him capable of successfully investing without the restraints of this trust; Provided, However, That such disbursements of principal of said trust so made to my son after he attains the age of thirty (30) years shall be first approved in writing by either one of my brothers-in-law, that is: Dr. Frank L. Ralston, now of Walla Walla, Washington, or Russell C. Ralston, now of Palo Alto, California, if either of them is then living, but if neither of them is then living, then my trustee is authorized to make said disbursements of principal to my son in the exercise of its sole and absolute judgment and discretion; Provided, Further, That, said trust shall continue as to all or any part of the undistributed portion of the principal thereof to and until the death of my said son.

"(5) I further direct and authorize my trustee, from time to time (but only upon the written approval of my said wife if she be then living, otherwise in the exercise of my trustee's sole discretion) to make disbursements for the use and benefit of my son, Grant R. Shelley, or his children, in case of any emergency arising whereby unusual and extraordinary expenses are necessary for the proper support and care of my said son, or said children.

"(6) If the said Grant R. Shelley shall die, and leave surviving him children, it is my desire that, if my wife be then dead, or upon the death of my wife if she should survive said son, my trustee shall continue said trust for the benefit of said children of my son, Grant R. Shelley, and shall make periodic payments for their benefit at intervals of not less than three (3) months apart, and shall hold said estate in trust to and until the youngest child of Grant R. Shelley shall attain the age of twenty-one (21) years; thereupon, said trust shall terminate, and said estate shall be distributed to the children of my son, share and share alike; If any of said children die before the youngest attains the age of twenty-one (21) years, said distributable estate shall be distributed to the surviving children, share and share alike, or, if there be only one child, to said child.

* * *

"(8) Each beneficiary hereunder is hereby restrained from alienating, anticipating, encumbering, or in any manner assigning his or her interest or estate, either in principal or income, and is without power so to do, nor shall such interest or estate be subject to his or her liabilities or obligations nor to judgment or other legal process, bankruptcy proceedings or claims of creditors or others."

The principal question on appeal is whether the income and corpus of the Shelley trust can be reached by Grant Shelley's former wives and his children.

Grant Shelley was first married to defendant, Patricia C. Shelley. Two children were born of this marriage. Patricia divorced Grant in 1951. The decree required Grant to pay support money for the children; the decree did not call for the payment of alimony. Thereafter, Grant married the plaintiff, Betty Shelley. Two children were born of this marriage. The plaintiff obtained a divorce from Grant in August, 1958. The decree in this latter suit required the payment of both alimony and a designated monthly amount for the support of the children of that marriage.

Some time after his marriage to the plaintiff, Grant disappeared and his whereabouts was not known at the time of this suit. The defendant bank, as trustee, invested the trust assets in securities which are now held by it, together with undisbursed income from the trust estate. The plaintiff obtained an injunction restraining the defendant trustee from disbursing any of the trust assets. Patricia Shelley brought a garnishment proceeding against the trustee, by which she sought to subject the trust to the claim for support money provided for in the 1951 decree of divorce. The defendants, United Adjusters, Inc., and N. J. Campf, obtained judgments against Grant and sought, through garnishment, to reach the trust assets. The latter defendants have not appealed and consequently we are not concerned with their interest in the trust.

The defendant bank finally brought a bill of interpleader tendering to the court for disbursement all of the funds held in trust, praying for an order establishing the respective rights of the interpleaded parties to the trust assets.

The trial court entered a decree subjecting the accrued income of the trust to the existing claims of the plaintiff and Patricia Shelley; subjecting future income of the trust to the periodic obligations subsequently accruing by the terms of the decrees in the divorce proceedings brought by plaintiff and Patricia Shelley; and further providing that in the event that the trust income was insufficient to satisfy such claims, the corpus of the trust was subject to invasion.

We shall first consider that part of the decree which subjects the income of the trust to the claims of plaintiff and of defendant, Patricia Shelley. The trust places no conditions upon the right of Grant Shelley to receive the trust income during his lifetime. Therefore, plaintiff and Patricia Shelley may reach such income unless the spendthrift provision of the trust precludes them from doing so.

The validity of spendthrift trusts has been established by our former cases. Stein v. United States National Bank, 1941, 165 Or. 518, 108 P.2d 1016; Mattison v. Mattison, 1909, 53 Or. 254, 100 P. 4, 133 Am.St.Rep. 829. The question on this appeal is whether the spendthrift provision will be given effect to bar the claims of the beneficiary's children for support and the plaintiff's claim for alimony.

In Cogswell v. Cogswell et al., 1946, 178 Or. 417, 167 P.2d 324, 335, we held that the spendthrift provision of a trust is not effective against the claims of the beneficiary's former wife for alimony and for support of the beneficiary's child. In that case the court adopted the rule stated in 1 Restatement, Trusts, § 157, which reads in part as follows:

> "§ 157. Particular Classes of Claimants.
>
> "Although a trust is a spendthrift trust or trust for support, the interest of the beneficiary can be reached in satisfaction of an enforceable claim against the beneficiary,
>
> "(a) by the wife or child of the beneficiary for support, or by the wife for alimony;"

The defendant bank concedes that the Cogswell case is controlling in the case at bar, but asks us to overrule it on the ground that it is inconsistent with our own cases recognizing the testator's privilege to dispose of his property as he pleases and, further, that it is inconsistent with various Oregon statutes expressing the same policy of free alienation. If we should accept the premise urged by the defendant bank, that a testator has an inviolable right to dispose of his property as he pleases subject only to legislative restriction, the conclusion is inevitable that the testator may create in a beneficiary an interest free from all claims, including those for support and alimony.

But the premise is not sound. The privilege of disposing of property is not absolute; it is hedged with various restrictions where there are policy considerations warranting the limitation. Seidenberg v. Seidenberg, 1955, 96 U.S.App.D.C. 245, 225 F.2d 545, commented upon in 10 S.W.L.J. 228 (1956); England v. England, 1922, 223 Ill. App. 549; Safe Deposit & Trust Co. of Baltimore v. Robertson, 1949, 192 Md. 653, 65 A.2d 292; In re Stewart's Estate, 1939, 334 Pa. 356, 5 A.2d 910; In re Moorehead's Estate, 1927, 289 Pa. 542, 137 A. 802, 52 A.L.R. 1251; Town of Shrewsbury v. Bucklin, 1933, 105 Vt. 188, 163 A. 626, 86 A.L.R. 133; Note, 44 Calif.L.Rev. 615, 618 (1956); Note, 19 Rocky Mt.L.Rev. 87 (1946). Not all of these restrictions are imposed by statute. The rule against perpetuities, the rule against restraints on alienation, the refusal to recognize trusts for capricious purposes or for illegal purposes, or for any purpose contrary to public policy, are all instances of judge-made rules limiting the privilege of alienation. Many others could be recited. Griswold, Spendthrift Trusts (2d Ed.) § 553; Simes, Public Policy and the Dead Hand, passim; Scott, Control of Property by the Dead, 65 U.Pa.L.Rev. 527, 632 (1917). See also Nussbaum, Liberty of Testation, 23 A.B.A.J. 183 (1937); McMurray, Liberty of Testation and Some Modern Limitations Thereon, 14 Ill.L.Rev. 96 (1919); Keeton & Gower, Freedom of Testation in English Law, 20 Iowa L.Rev. 326 (1935). It is within the court's power to impose upon the privilege of disposing of property such restrictions as are consistent with its view of sound public policy, unless, of course, the legislature has expressed a contrary view. Our own statutes do not purport to deal with the specific question before us, that is as to whether there should be limitations on the owner's privilege to create a spendthrift trust.

The defendant bank insists that the legislative intent to vest in a testator the privilege of disposing of his property free from the claims for alimony and support can be found by inference from our statutes. Thus we are referred to ORS 114.020 declaring that a person may dispose of property by will, and to ORS 167.605, 411.410 and 411.425 imposing liability upon parents only for the support of their children and placing no obligation on a grandparent, which was the relationship of the testator to the children for whom support is claimed in the instant case. We do not believe that the statutes to which defendant bank refers, or any other Oregon statute can be construed to evince a legislative intent to bar the type of claim sought to be enforced in the present case.

There remains, however, the question of whether there is a justification in public policy for the recognition of such claims in the face of a spendthrift trust restraint broad enough to bar them.

In holding that a spendthrift trust is subject to claims for alimony and support the court, in Cogswell v. Cogswell et al., supra, did not disclose the reasoning by which it reached its conclusion. This failure to examine the question of public policy in the area of spendthrift trusts is not unusual, for as Griswold, Spendthrift Trusts (2d Ed.), p. 634 points out in discussing the validity of spendthrift trusts, "examination [of public policy] has rarely, if ever, been attempted by the courts," and he admits that "it is obviously a matter difficult to approach and one about which dogmatic conclusions cannot be reached." But once having recognized the validity of spendthrift trusts, which we have and which conclusion defendant bank endorses, the more specific question of the validity of the restraint of such a trust as against the claims of children for support and of the beneficiary's former wife for alimony presents a narrower question of policy which, we believe, is easier to answer. The question is whether a person should be entitled to enjoy the benefits of a trust and at the same time refuse to pay the obligations arising out of his marriage.

We have no hesitation in declaring that public policy requires that the interest of the beneficiary of a trust should be subject to the claims for support of his children. England v. England, supra. Certainly the defendant will accept the societal postulate that parents have the obligation to support their children. If we give effect to the spendthrift provision to bar the claims for support, we have the spectacle of a man enjoying the benefits of a trust immune from claims which are justly due, while the community pays for the support of his children. Wetmore v. Wetmore, 1896, 149 N.Y. 520, 44 N.E. 169, 33 L.R.A. 708. We do not believe that it is sound policy to use the welfare funds of this state in support of the beneficiary's children, while he stands behind the shield of immunity created by a spendthrift trust provision. To endorse such a policy and to permit the spectacle which we have described above would be to invite disrespect for the administration of justice. Seidenberg v. Seidenberg, D.C.Cir., 1954, 126 F.Supp. 19, 21, affirmed 1955, 96 U.S.App.D.C. 245, 225 F.2d 545. One who wishes to dispose of his property through the device of a trust must do so subject to these considerations of policy and he cannot force the courts to sanction his scheme of disposition if it is inimical to the interests of the state. The better reasoned cases in other jurisdictions support this conclusion. Keller v. Keller, 1936, 284 Ill. App. 198, 1 N.E.2d 773, commented upon in 50 Harv.L.Rev. 143 and 14 Chi-Kent L.Rev. 276; Zouck v. Zouck, 1954, 204 Md. 285, 104 A.2d 573, 105 A.2d 214; In re Moorehead's Estate, supra.

The justification for permitting a claim for alimony is, perhaps, not as clear. The adjustment of the economic interests of the parties to a divorce may depend upon a variety of factors, including the respective fault of the parties, the ability of the wife to support herself, the duration of the marriage, and other considerations. Whether alimony is to be granted and its amount are questions which are determined in light of these various interests. It is probably fair to say that the duties created by the marriage relation, at least as they are evaluated upon the termination of the marriage, are conceived of as more qualified than those arising out of the paternal relationship. On the theory that divorce terminates the husband's duty to support his former wife and that she stands in no better position than other creditors, some courts have held that the spendthrift provision insulates the beneficiary's interest in the trust from her claim. Lippincott v. Lippincott, 1944, 349 Pa. 501, 37 A.2d 741. Recognizing the difference in marital and parental duties suggested above, it has been held that a spendthrift trust is subject to the claims for the support of children but free from the claims of the former wife. Eaton v. Eaton, 1926, 82 N.H. 216, 132 A. 10, commented upon in 35 Yale L.J. 1025 (1926). See also, Eaton v. Eaton, 1924, 81 N.H. 275, 125 A. 433, 35 A.L.R. 1034. A majority of the cases, however, hold that a spendthrift provision will not bar a claim for alimony. England v. England, supra; Clay v. Hamilton, 1945, 116 Ind.App. 214, 63 N.E.2d 207; Safe Deposit & Trust Co. of Baltimore v. Robertson, supra; In re Sullivan's Will, 1943, 144 Neb. 36, 12 N.W.2d 148; Corey v. National Bank of Toledo, Ohio Com.Pl.1958, 159 N.E.2d 814, 817; O'Connor v. O'Connor, Ohio Com.Pl.1957, 141 N.E.2d 691; In re Stewart's estate, supra; In re Moorehead's Estate, supra; Dillon v. Dillon, 1943, 244 Wis. 122, 11 N.W.2d 628. See, Buchanan v. National Savings & Trust Co., 1944, 79 U.S.App.D.C. 278, 146 F.2d 13. See also, Griswold, Spendthrift Trusts (2d Ed.) §§ 335, 336; Comment, 21 Calif.L.Rev. 142 (1932); Comment, 10 Md.L.Rev. 359 (1949); Note, 28 Va.L.Rev. 527 (1942).

As we have already mentioned, the case of Cogswell v. Cogswell, supra, is in accord with this latter view. We are of the opinion that the conclusion there reached should be reaffirmed. The duty of the husband to support his former wife should override the restriction called for by the spendthrift provision. The same reason advanced above for requiring the support of the beneficiary's children will, in many cases, be applicable to the claim of a divorced wife; if the beneficiary's interest cannot be reached, the state may be called upon to support her. Cf., Keller v. Keller, supra; Lippincott v. Lippincott, supra; Griswold, Reaching the Interest of the Beneficiary of a Spendthrift Trust, 43 Harv.L.Rev. 63, 68 (1929); Note, 44 Calif.L.Rev. 615 (1956). In a case involving the claim of a deserted wife, In re Moorehead's Estate, 1927, 289 Pa. 542, 137 A. 802, 806, 52 A.L.R. 1251, the basis for this obligation is well described as follows:

> "* * * In every civilized country is recognized the obligation, sacred as well as lawful, of a husband to protect and provide for his family, and to sustain the claim of the husband in the case at bar would be to invest him with a right to be both a faithless husband and a vicious citizen. This case reaches beyond the concern of the immediate parties to it. It affects the status of the family as being the foundation of society and civilization, and hence in a very certain sense is of wide public concern."

Other cases are to the same effect. Tuttle v. Gunderson, 1929, 254 Ill.App. 552; 341 Ill. 36, 173 N.E. 175; Wetmore v. Wetmore, supra. See Audubon v. Shufeldt, 1901, 181 U.S. 575, 577, 21 S.Ct. 735, 45 L. Ed. 1009; Note, 27 Va.L.Rev. 914, 919 (1941). The case of Seidenberg v. Seidenberg, D.C.1954, 126 F.Supp. 19, 23, affirmed 1955, 96 U.S.App.D.C. 245, 225 F.2d 545, contains an excellent review of the problem. In summary the court said:

> "The family is the foundation of society. The duty of a married man to support and protect his wife and children is inherent in human nature. It is a part of natural law, as well as a requirement of the law of every civilized country. It is not an ordinary indebtedness, such as a contractual obligation or a judgment for damages arising out of a tort. It is a responsibility far superior to that of paying one's debts, important as the latter obligation is. No part of a man's property or income should be exempt from meeting this liability, for he is under at least as great a duty to provide shelter, clothing, and food for his immediate family as he is to furnish them for his own person. The law should not regard with complacency any man who repudiates or ignores this obligation, which is instinctive in mankind, and should not permit him to flout it with impunity."

The text writers take the same view and in justifying the rule overriding the spendthrift restraint, generally no distinction is made between the claims of dependent children and the claims of the wife for support or alimony. Thus, 2 Scott on Trusts, § 157.1, states:

> "* * * The claim of a wife and dependent children to support is based upon the clearest grounds of public policy. They are in quite a different position from ordinary creditors who have voluntarily extended credit. It would be shocking indeed to permit a

husband to receive and enjoy the whole of the income from a large trust fund and make no provision for his needy dependents."

Accord: 6 American Law of Property, § 29.130; 1A Bogert, Trusts and Trustees, § 233; Griswold, Spendthrift Trusts (2d Ed.), § 339; Note, 14 Temple L.Q. 229 (1940); Note, 28 Va.L.Rev. 527 (1942).

We hold that the beneficiary's interest in the income of the Shelley Trust is subject to the claims of the plaintiff for alimony and to the claims for the support of Grant Shelley's children as provided for under both decrees for divorce. These claims are not without limit. We adopt the view that such claimants may reach only that much of the income which the trial court deems reasonable under the circumstances, having in mind the respective needs of the husband and wife, the needs of the children, the amount of the trust income, the availability of the corpus for the various needs, and any other factors which are relevant in adjusting equitably the interests of the claimants and the beneficiary. Griswold, Spendthrift Trusts (2d Ed.) § 339; 2 Scott on Trusts, § 157.1; Note, 28 V.A.L.Rev. 527 (1942).

The defendant bank argues that if a policy restricting the permissible scope of spendthrift trusts is desirable, that policy should be declared by the legislature and not by this court. The duty of making a choice of rules in accordance with public interest is shared by both the courts and the legislature. There is nothing about the problem of choosing the policy in this case which makes it any different than most of the cases which come before us. Since the legislature has not spoken, we are free to declare the rule which we think will serve the best interest of the public. This we have done.

In the foregoing treatment of the problem we have assumed that the spendthrift trust provision was intended by the testator to bar the claims of the beneficiary's children and former wife. The language of the spendthrift clause in question is broad, the restraint purporting to free the beneficiary's interest from the "claims of creditors or others." The claims of "others" could be construed to include claims for support and alimony. But with respect to the claims for the support of beneficiary's children, there is a competing thought in the trust provision which permits the invasion of the trust corpus in case of an emergency whereby unusual and extraordinary expenses are necessary for the support of the beneficiary's children. From this obvious solicitude for the welfare of beneficiary's children, it would be reasonable to infer that testator did not intend to make the spendthrift clause a bar to a claim for their support. Buchanan v. National Savings & Trust Co., 1944, 79 U.S.App.D.C. 278, 146 F.2d 13; In re Sullivan's Will, 1943, 144 Neb. 36, 12 N.W.2d 148; Eaton v. Eaton, 1926, 82 N.H. 216, 132 A. 10; Sand v. Beach, 1936, 270 N.Y. 281, 200 N.E. 821; 244 App.Div. 784, 280 N.Y.S. 789. However, we prefer to rest the claims for support of the children on the broader ground that a spendthrift trust is ineffective to preclude such claims.

The question of the claimants' rights to reach the corpus of the trust involves other consideration. For the reasons heretofore stated, the beneficiary's interest in the corpus is not made immune from these claims. But, by the terms of the trust, the disbursement of the corpus is within the discretion of the trustee (or, in some instances subject to the approval of others), and, therefore, Grant Shelley's right to receive any part of the corpus does not arise until the trustee has exercised his discretion and has decided to invade the corpus. Until that time, the plaintiff and Patricia Shelley cannot reach the corpus of the trust because the beneficiary has no realizable interest in it. Mattison v. Mattison, 1909, 53 Or. 254, 100 P. 4, 133 Am.St.Rep. 829. It has been held that a discretionary trust for the "sole benefit" of the testator's son was enforceable by the son's destitute wife and children on the ground that the support of the son's family fell within the terms of the trust. Gardner v. O'Loughlin, 1912, 76 N.H. 481, 84 A. 935, 936. But, assuming without deciding that such an interpretation is reasonable, it has not been extended to a case where there has been a divorce and the wife has ceased to be a member of the family and, therefore, has ceased to be a beneficiary of the trust. Eaton v. Eaton, supra. There is nothing in the trust before us which would indicate the testator's intent to make the plaintiff, either directly or indirectly, the beneficiary of the trust. Patricia Shelley could not be regarded as a beneficiary because the decree under which she claims called only for the payment of support money for the children and not alimony. In some jurisdictions a creditor of the beneficiary of a discretionary trust may attach the potential interest of the beneficiary. Sand v. Beach, supra; Hamilton v. Drogo, 1926, 241 N.Y. 401, 150 N.E. 496; 214 App.Div. 819, 210 N.Y.S. 859, commented upon in 26 Colum.L.Rev. 776 (1926). See Griswold, Spendthrift Trusts (2d Ed.) §§ 367, 368, 357; 2 Scott on Trusts, § 155.1. There is no such procedure in Oregon available to the creditor. And at least with respect to the corpus, ORS 29.175(2) makes the interest constituting the subject matter of the trust free from attachment. It follows that the decree of the lower court in making the corpus of the Shelley Trust subject to the plaintiff's claim for alimony was erroneous.

The claims for the support of Grant Shelley's children, provided for in the two divorce decrees, involve a different problem. The trust directed and authorized the trustee, in the exercise of its sole discretion upon the death of settlor's wife, to make disbursements for the use and benefit not only of Grant Shelley, but also for his children. The disbursements were to be made "in case of any emergency arising whereby unusual and extraordinary expenses are necessary for the proper support and care of my said son, or said children." Here the children are named as beneficiaries of the trust and need not claim derivatively through their father. However, they are entitled to a share of the corpus only if, in the trustee's discretion, it is determined that an emergency exists. The defendant bank contends that the expenses of supporting Grant Shelley's children claimed in this case were for the usual and ordinary costs of support and do not, therefore, constitute "unusual and extraordinary expenses" within the meaning of the trust provision. It is contended that there was no "emergency" calling for "unusual and extraordinary expenses" because there was no proof of an unexpected occurrence or of an unexpected situation requiring immediate action. We disagree with defendant's interpretation. We construe the clause to include the circumstances involved here, i.e., where the children are deserted by their father and are in need of support. We think that the testator intended to provide that in the event that the income from the trusts was not sufficient to cover disbursements for the support and care of either the son or his children an "emergency" had arisen and the corpus could then be invaded. The decree of the lower court would permit the corpus to be employed if the "assets in the hands of the Executor [trustee] and the income cash from said trust shall be insufficient to pay the obligations of Defendant Grant R. Shelley" to plaintiff and Patricia Shelley. The decree is too broad; first because, as we have already indicated, it improperly includes the plaintiff's claim for alimony; second, because it permits encroachment upon the corpus without reference to whether the trustee has exercised his discretion or whether there has been an emergency as contemplated by the testator.

It is to be noted that the children of Grant Shelley are not beneficiaries of the income of the trust; they may reach it only as persons having claims against the beneficiary, Grant Shelley. If, for example, Grant Shelley should decide to support his children out of assets other than income of the trust, the children would have no claim whatsoever against his interest in the trust. The decree, therefore, should have permitted an invasion of the corpus only if it was necessary to first reach the income under the circumstances just mentioned and such income was insufficient. And further, the decree should have made such corpus available only in the event of the trustee's exercise of discretion authorizing the disbursement for the support of the children under the emergency circumstances provided for in the trust. After the entry of such a decree, if the trustee should refuse to exercise his discretion, or if it is claimed that he exercised it unreasonably, relief may be sought in a court of equity by the children.

The decree of the lower court is affirmed and the cause remanded with directions to modify the decree in accordance with the views expressed in this opinion.[52]

NOTE

The Restatement, Second, Trusts provides in part as follows:[53] "Although a trust is a spendthrift trust or a trust for support, the interest of the beneficiary can be reached in satisfaction of an enforceable claim against the beneficiary, (a) by the wife or child of the beneficiary for support, or by the wife for alimony; (b) for necessary services rendered to the beneficiary or necessary supplies furnished to him; (c) for services rendered and materials furnished which preserve or benefit the interest of the beneficiary; (d) by the United States or a State to satisfy a claim against the beneficiary."

52. Statutes in a few states expressly recognize the right of dependents to realize their claims out of the beneficiary's interest under a spendthrift trust. E.g., Mo.Rev.Stats. § 456.080 (1956). See "Spendthrift Trusts—The Public Policy Exception", 45 Mo.L.Rev. 369 (1980).

53. Restatement, Second, Trusts § 157.

A contrary view was adopted by the Minnesota Supreme Court in Erickson v. Erickson,[54] upholding the spendthrift clause as against the claim of the wife for alimony and support money. Commenting on the Restatement position quoted above, the Court said: [55]

> "* * * We are not impressed with the soundness of that doctrine. In the case at bar it would be an attempt judicially to interpret into the language of the donor provisions contrary to his actual intent as expressed. When unrestrained by statute, it is the intent of the donor, not the character of the donee's obligation, which controls the availability and disposition of his gift. The donee's obligation to pay alimony or support money, paramount though it may be, should not, in our opinion, transcend the right of the donor to do as he pleases with his own property and to choose the object of his bounty. Our conclusion does not arise out of any anxiety for the protection of the beneficiary. In the absence of statute and within the limits as to perpetuities, a donor may dispose of his property as he sees fit, and this includes corpus or principal as well as income. First Nat. Bank v. Olufson, 181 Minn. 289, 232 N.W. 337. As a general proposition, when a donor leaves the interest of the beneficiary assignable or transferable it may be reached by creditors. If by appropriate language the right to transfer is completely restrained, then such interest may not be reached by creditors either at law or by equitable proceeding. To hold otherwise would be to defeat the testator's or donor's right and his manifest intent. If alimony or support money is to be an exception to the protection offered by spendthrift provisions, it must be by some justifiable interpretation of the donor's language by which such implied exception may be fairly construed into the instrument of trust. It cannot logically arise out of the character of the obligation, though some cases so hold. The obligation for alimony and support money may be of higher rank than other debts, but it is nevertheless an obligation in the nature of a debt, and if, as here, no assignment could be made, if no title could reach the beneficiary until the actual receipt of the funds, then equity may not enforce claims of any nature against it. This court may not by imputing a constructive intent or by a constructive exception thwart the manifest purpose of the donor."

Professor Scott suggests: [56] "It is possible to take an intermediate view. It may be held that the dependents of the beneficiary cannot be precluded from reaching his interest under a spendthrift trust, but that they can reach only so much of the income as under the circumstances may appear reasonable to the court which has control over the administration of the trust. Much may be said in favor of this view. Under it the beneficiary is not permitted to live in luxury while his dependents starve. On the other hand, they will not be permitted to live in comfort while he starves. * * *"

In those jurisdictions in which creditors are allowed by statute to reach the surplus of the income beyond the sum necessary for the support of the beneficiary there seems no doubt that the claims of dependents for support and the wife for alimony can be enforced at least to the extent of this surplus.

Claims for necessaries furnished to the beneficiary of a spendthrift or support trust may be enforced against his trust interest. Allowing such recoveries seems to advance the purposes for which the trust was created rath-

54. 197 Minn. 71, 266 N.W. 161, 267 N.W. 426 (1936).

55. 197 Minn. at 78, 266 N.W. at 164.

56. II Scott, Trusts (3d Ed. 1967) 1212.

er than to defeat the intention of the settlor. The settlor is usually interested in assuring the beneficiary support despite the beneficiary's improvidence or misfortune. When the necessary goods or services are furnished without the knowledge of the trustee, who is supporting the beneficiary, recovery should be denied on the ground that the person supplying the goods or services is acting officiously. Recovery should be limited, in any event, to the reasonable value of the necessaries furnished rather than the contract price therefor.

Direct authority is lacking on the question whether or not a tort claimant may reach the interest of the beneficiary of a spendthrift or support trust. The recovery should be allowed. Contract creditors can protect themselves by determining the nature and extent of the beneficiary's resources before extending credit to him. Tort creditors are unable to make such an inquiry before their claim arises.

PROBLEMS

1. The beneficiary of a spendthrift trust is suddenly taken ill. A physician who is present at the time renders medical services. Is the physician entitled to compensation out of the beneficiary's interest in the trust property? See Pole v. Pietsch, 61 Md. 570 (1884).

2. The Alien Property Custodian is authorized by Federal statutes and executive orders to seize property belonging to alien enemies. A trust is created for the benefit of certain beneficiaries, some of whom are aliens; it contains a spendthrift clause and also a clause providing for forfeiture of interest and gift over if unable to pay income to the designated beneficiaries. Can the Alien Property Custodian seize the interest of the enemy aliens? Security-First National Bank v. Rogers, 51 Cal.2d 24, 330 P.2d 811 (1958).

3. Can the United States Government assert a claim for income taxes despite a spendthrift clause? What if the trust instrument also contains a forfeiture clause? Leuschner v. First Western Bank & Trust Co., 261 F.2d 705 (9th Cir. 1958).

4. Can a trustee in bankruptcy reach the interest of a beneficiary subject to a spendthrift clause? See 11 U.S.C.A. § 541(c)(2).

5. When a beneficiary of a spendthrift trust commits a tort against a third person, can the latter obtain satisfaction of his claim from the interest of the beneficiary under the trust? See Griswold, Spendthrift Trusts (2d Ed., 1947) § 365.

WARE v. GULDA

Supreme Judicial Court of Massachusetts, 1954.
331 Mass. 68, 117 N.E.2d 137.

WILKINS, JUSTICE. Following the decision in Gulda v. Second National Bank, 323 Mass. 100, 80 N.E.2d 12, 15 A.L.R.2d 605, a hearing on the merits led to a final decree dismissing the bill from which no appeal was taken. The order for decree stated that Louise Gulda had not proved that her ratification of the trust instrument was procured by fraud. In that litigation Louise was represented by the plaintiff, who brings this bill to establish her indebtedness for his legal services, and to reach and apply the trust fund of which the defendant

The Second National Bank of Boston is the trustee. Louise is a resident of California, and personal service was made upon the bank only. The bill was taken pro confesso against her. The plaintiff filed a motion for a final decree. Following a hearing, apparently upon statements of counsel, there was entered a final decree, which (1) established the plaintiff's debt in the sum of $4,050 with interest; (2) ordered execution to issue against Louise in the sum of $4,861.12 and costs; (3) ordered her to pay within sixty days; and (4) in the event of her neglect to do so, ordered the bank "to pay to the plaintiff said sums out of the property, right, title and interest, legal or equitable" of Louise which the bank "had, at the time of service of the bill of complaint and of the temporary restraining order, as successor trustee of the Gulda Family Trust which consists of the proceeds of property formerly belonging to the defendant, Louise Gulda, before she caused it to be placed in said Gulda Family Trust." The only appeal is by the bank, whose argument is confined to item (4).

* * *

The trust instrument provides: "During the lifetime of Louisa [Louise] Gulda * * * the income and/or principal of this trust fund shall be expended for her support and maintenance" (paragraph VI. A). Upon her death the property was to go in varying circumstances to her two daughters and Federico. One contingency was that if both daughters survived, seventy-five per cent of the property was to continue in trust for the benefit of one of them who was not married (paragraph VI. C). The trust was to terminate on the death of the survivor of Louise and her three children (paragraph VII). "Wherever it is provided herein that any payments shall be made or monies expended for the support and maintenance of any person, such payments or expenditures are to be in the sole discretion of the trustee or trustees for the time being" (paragraph VI. F). "The trustees * * * shall have powers * * * to determine who are the distributees hereunder and the proportions in which they shall take * * *" (paragraph IV). "The interest of any beneficiary hereunder shall not be alienated, anticipated nor assigned, nor shall it be subject to the claims of creditors * * *" (paragraph X).

The substance of what happened is this. Louise with her own property created a trust of which she was, for her lifetime, to be the sole beneficiary, if there was to be one at all. The decision as to making or withholding payments, as to both principal and income, was to be entirely in the discretion of the trustee. She was to be incapable of making an assignment of any interest in the trust property, which was intended to be beyond the reach of creditors. At the moment there is no amount which the trustee has exercised its discretion to pay to Louise, although in the past it has made payments to her both of principal and of income.

Merely because the trustee has not exercised the discretionary power conferred upon it by Louise seems to us to be an insufficient ground to distinguish this case in principle from the rule of years' standing we recently restated in Merchants National Bank v. Morrissey, 329 Mass. 601, 605, 109 N.E.2d 821, 823: "The established policy of this Commonwealth long has been that a settlor cannot place property in trust for his own benefit and keep it beyond the reach of creditors. Pacific National Bank v. Windram, 133 Mass. 175; Jackson v. Von Zedlitz, 136 Mass. 342; Taylor v. Buttrick, 165 Mass. 547, 551, 43 N.E. 507; Forbes v. Snow, 245 Mass. 85, 89; 140 N.E. 418."

The rule we apply is found in Restatement: Trusts, § 156(2): "Where a person creates for his own benefit a trust for support or a discretionary trust, his transferee or creditors can reach the maximum amount which the trustee under the terms of the trust could pay to him or apply for his benefit." It has substantial support in authority. Greenwich Trust Co. v. Tyson, 129 Conn. 211, 224, 27 A.2d 166; Warner v. Rice, 66 Md. 436, 8 A. 84; Hay v. Price, 15 Pa.Dist.R. 144; Menken Co. v. Brinkley, 94 Tenn. 721, 728–729, 31 S.W. 92; Petty v. Moores Brook Sanitarium, 110 Va. 815, 817, 67 S.E. 355, 27 L.R.A.,N.S., 800; Scott, Trusts, § 156.2; Griswold, Spendthrift Trusts (2d ed.) § 481. See Am. Law of Property, § 23.18. Although every exercise of the power might take property away from the remaindermen, that is no objection where the trustee could pay the entire principal to the creator of the trust.

The trustee relies upon Crawford v. Langmaid, 171 Mass. 309, 50 N.E. 606, where there was a bill by a judgment creditor against one who by deed had created a trust of real estate, which was all her property. The trustees were to pay the net income semiannually to the defendant, who had a power of appointment by will, and there was a gift in default of appointment. The trustees had power to sell or mortgage the real estate with the consent of the defendant, and the proceeds could be retained by the trustees or paid over in whole or in part to the defendant. The trial judge found that there was no fraud, but nevertheless ordered enough of the trust property to be sold to pay the plaintiff. In reversing his decree, it was said, "This certainly gives her no vested interest in the principal of the estate. * * * The contingency [disposition of the real estate] may never happen. If it happen, the whole matter is in the discretion of the trustees, and cannot be reached by creditors." 171 Mass. at pages 311–312, 50 N.E. at page 607. The decision is contrary to the weight of authority. Scott, Trusts, § 156; Bogert, Trusts and Trustees, § 224; Griswold, Spendthrift Trusts (2d ed.) § 478; Newhall, Future Interests (3d ed.) 167; Am. Law of Property, § 2318. See Shattuck, 26 Boston Univ.L.Rev. 437, 442; 125 A.L.R. 584. The quoted statement with respect to the discretion of the trustees we cannot accept. The cases relied upon in its support all relate to interests of beneficiaries in trusts under wills, and no question of a settlor beneficiary is involved. To the extent of the holding that the discretion confided in the trustees precludes a creditor from reaching the principal, Crawford v. Langmaid is overruled.

There is nothing incongruous in Louise not succeeding in upsetting the trust and in her counsel, the plaintiff, now getting paid out of the trust property. The record makes clear that in her suit she failed to prove fraud. This left her within the principle of such cases as Taylor v. Buttrick, 165 Mass. 547, 43 N.E. 507, and Sands v. Old Colony Trust Co., 195 Mass. 575, 81 N.E. 300, cited by the trustee. The plaintiff here prevails because the policy of our law does not protect the creator of a discretionary trust against the payment of a creditor in the circumstances of this case.

The plaintiff argues that the use of "shall" instead of "may" with the other language of paragraph VI.A indicates a purpose to spend at least the income during the settlor's lifetime; that as matter of law the creditor is entitled to reach the maximum amount which the trustee under the terms of the trust could pay to, or apply for the benefit of, the settlor; that the entry of the final decree imports a finding of every fact essential to its validity; and that this includes a finding that the trustee might pay from the trust the sum of $4,050 with interest and costs. We do not decide that the decree could not be affirmed for these reasons.

Decree affirmed, with costs of appeal.[57]

NOTE

When the beneficiary is not the settlor, support and discretionary trusts are generally held to be valid and effective means of insulating the beneficiary's interest against the claims of creditors.[58]

A discretionary trust is created only when the trustee may in his absolute discretion refuse to pay or to apply any of the trust property to or for the benefit of the trust beneficiary. A discretionary trust is not created when the trustee has discretion merely as to the time or manner of payment, the beneficiary ultimately being entitled to all or part of the trust property. A transferee or creditor of the beneficiary of a discretionary trust cannot compel a trustee to pay over any part of the trust property. If the trustee does pay to the beneficiary or apply for his benefit any part of the trust property with knowledge that the beneficiary has transferred his interest or after the trustee has been served with process in a proceeding by a creditor of the beneficiary to reach his interest, the trustee is personally liable to the transferee or creditor for the amount so paid or applied, unless a spendthrift provision has been validly annexed to the beneficiary's interest in the trust property or the terms of the trust forfeit the beneficiary's interest in the trust property because of his attempted alienation of that interest.[59]

57. The related problem of ability of the settlor's creditors to reach the trust property where he reserves no interest therein but retains control through a power to revoke or a power to amend or to appoint new beneficiaries, is considered in the next Section.

58. Restatement, Second, Trusts §§ 154 (Trusts for Support) and 155 (Discretionary Trusts). Closely related are two types of trusts seldom encountered. In a "blended" trust the interests of several beneficiaries are created in such a way as to be inseparable and thus individually inalienable. Thus, A transfers property to B in trust for "C and his family", intending to give interests to all of C's family. A trust may also be of the "personal" type, such as a trust entitling the beneficiary to occupy a particular room in a designated house. See Restatement, Second, Trusts §§ 160, 161. See, Bird, "Diagnosis: Mental Incapacity Rx: Protective Trust", 116 Trusts and Estates 676 (1977).

59. See Hamilton v. Drogo, 241 N.Y. 401, 150 N.E. 496 (1926), 26 Col.L.Rev. 776 (1926); II Scott, Trusts (3d Ed. 1967) § 155.

SECTION 6. RETENTION OF CONTROL BY THE SETTLOR

When the settlor of a living trust reserves either a life estate in its income or powers over the trust, quite probably he does not have tax economy principally in mind. If he retains a life income interest, he will be taxed on the income, the corpus of the trust will be treated as part of his gross estate for the unified Federal estate tax and he will have to pay a gift tax on the remainder at the unified tax rate which ultimately will be subtracted from the estate tax payable. If he reserves a power to revoke or modify the trust or other extensive authority over the trust administration, he will be subject to taxation on the trust income and the trust corpus will be included in his gross estate.

There has never been any question as to the *validity* of a trust deed in which the settlor reserves the income for life even though such a reservation is accompanied by tax complications. But when the settlor adds a power to revoke the trust, his control approaches that which would exist if he retained legal title and executed a will. Revocability is an essential testamentary feature. When the settlor goes further and, in addition to reserving income and a power of revocation, makes himself trustee during his lifetime or, if there is a third party trustee, reserves a power to approve investments or other powers over trust administration, then it may be argued that the transaction really is testamentary and should not be given effect under the Wills Act unless it is properly executed and probated. This problem is raised in Farkas v. Williams which follows.

With these tax complications and doubt in some instances whether the trust will be given effect unless it is executed with testamentary formalities, why might a settlor reserve control over his living trust?

1. He may seek to avoid claims by his spouse. If the wife has inchoate dower in land transferred in living trust and does not release her dower her dower claim is not avoided. But she may have only forced heirship in land, as discussed in Chapter IV, Section 2(2) (A), in which case it may be possible to limit her forced heirship claim simply to property in the probate estate, reducing the gross estate by inter vivos transfers. Forced heirship generally will be the system used in personal property cases.

2. He may seek to avoid creditors, either those to whom he owes money when the trust is created or contract or tort creditors who may develop claims against him after creation of the trust.

In cases 1 and 2 we return to a policy problem we have examined in Ware v. Gulda in the preceding Section.

There is a settled policy forbidding the retention of extensive control by the owner of property without responding to certain obligations respecting its retention and use—the difficulty being the development of judicial standards by which this settled policy is to be put into execution. The problem is not a difficult one when the only issue is whether a discretionary or spendthrift provision inserted by the settlor to protect his retained beneficial interest will be enforced by a court against his creditors, spouse or children. But, if instead of retaining a beneficial interest in the income of the trust, the settlor retains only a power to revoke or modify the trust—what then? Should a surviving spouse be permitted to reach the trust property in order to subject it to her elective share and, if so, what standards should be applied to distinguish between the degree of control that brings the property within her grasp and the degree of control that places the property beyond her reach? If a surviving spouse attacks the trust on the ground that it is testamentary in character she will be able to subject the trust property to her elective share if her attack is successful—but the trust also fails as a whole, the trust property being brought within the probate estate, the administrative and probate costs being increased and various tax ramifications being invited. The personal representative of the decedent may attack the trust as having testamentary character but it may be unnecessary for the surviving spouse or abused creditor to go this far to satisfy their claims.

There are reasons why powers over the trust might be retained by the settlor other than those set forth in cases 1 and 2. What are some of these?

3. The trust will probably escape probate and administrative costs (unless it is successfully attacked on testamentary grounds) while the settlor still retains indirect benefits from the trust property.

4. The settlor has the benefit of the trustee's managerial service and can observe the wisdom of the trust provisions and the efficiency of the trustee during his lifetime. If the trust proves a mistake or the trustee inept the settlor can exercise his reserved powers to remedy the defects. In a charitable trust, the trustee can insure that the charitable nature of the trust is recognized for tax and state enforcement purposes before it becomes crystallized by his death and subject to variation only by extraordinary equity powers.

5. If a business is placed in trust during the lifetime of its owner, the owner probably will desire to reserve powers permitting his continued participation. If the trust of the business is inter vivos rather than testamentary it will be free from the inventory and accounting procedures of the probate court, privacy will be assured and flexibility in management permitted.

6. If the settlor is threatened by approaching mental incapacity, such as senility, the trust will avoid the publicity of guardianship, which an agency arrangement will not. He can participate in his business, for example, by exercising reserved powers until incapacity overtakes him.

However the "durable" power is an alternative to the trust in this situation. At common law a power granted by a principal to another to act as agent or attorney on behalf of the principal ceases at the subsequent disability (incompetence) of the principal; since the principal can no longer act, his agent has no greater power. However, in recent years many states have enacted statutes legalizing a power of attorney which expressly provides that the power is not affected by the subsequent disability or incapacity of the principal; an alternative form provides that the power becomes effective upon the disability or incapacity of the principal. Such powers are called "durable." Durable powers are authorized by the Uniform Probate Code[60] and by a separate Uniform Durable Power of Attorney Act promulgated in 1979; a majority of the states have adopted such statutes.[61]

The durable power of attorney may be used in some situations as a substitute for an inter vivos trust, particularly where an elderly person has assets which do not make a trust economically feasible, or the owner wishes a trusted relative to manage assets without the complications of a trust if the owner later becomes incompetent or incapacitated. In such a case the instrument will grant the agent very broad powers to act in respect to assets of the principal. The agent is, of course, a fiduciary and accountable to the principal.[62] A durable power may even be granted to make decisions regarding the person of the principal, such as medical decisions, appointment of a guardian, admission to nursing or residential facilities, and withdrawal of life support. In Chapter XII we shall consider how the durable power of attorney may be utilized to effect transfer of assets into a trust, after the principal becomes incompetent.

7. Closely related to case 6 is the high degree of immunity of the living trust from attack based on mental capacity, undue influence or fraud. Living trusts can be attacked successfully on these grounds but until the trust is well established the settlor probably will be around to assist in defending the trust. A will, on the other hand, is only attacked when the testator is dead and issues of fact are likely to be tried before a jury with a possible penchant for rewriting unpopular wills. Novel provisions tend to go unquestioned in a living trust when similar provisions in a will might stimulate a contest.[63]

While these and other advantages of revocable (or perhaps, irrevocable) living trusts may invite attention in a particular situation, assuming the possible losses of tax economy are borne in mind, the legal advisor must also consider the avenues of attack upon living trusts explored in this section. The trust may be adequately armored against attack as a testamentary transaction, but reserved powers less extensive than those upon which testamentary attacks are usual-

60. Uniform Probate Code § 5–501.

61. See "Legal Problems of the Aged and Infirm—The Durable Power of Attorney—Planned Protective Services and the Living Will," 13 Real Prop., Prob. & Tr.J. 1 (1978) (collecting statutes and giving sample forms).

62. Kline v. Orebaugh, 214 Kan. 207, 519 P.2d 691 (1974).

63. See Farr and Wright, Estate Planners Handbook (4th Ed. 1979) Ch. IV. The use of a revocable living trust as a vehicle into which assets can be "poured over" by will, considered in Chapter XII, Section 3(3), increases the utility of a revocable living trust as a basic dispositive device in estate planning. See, Hamana, "The Disposition of Trust Income: Planning and Drafting Considerations for Revocable Trust", 61 Mass.L.Q. 32 (1976).

ly grounded may provide a foothold for a hostile spouse with whom the court may sympathize.

By the prevailing view a trust is irrevocable unless the power to revoke is expressly reserved in the trust instrument.[64] In a few states there is legislation making trusts revocable unless the trust instrument stipulates the trust is irrevocable.[65] In these states draftsmen for a client who seeks to avoid income or estate taxes will insert a statement that the trust is irrevocable. Before taxes became a serious problem, a few other states adopted rules by judicial decision similar to these statutory rules, presuming the settlor omitted a power of revocation by mistake.[66] In these states draftsmen respond as they do when a similar statute is in force. In most states, nevertheless, an expressed power of revocation is required when a revocable trust is intended. We shall consider in Chapter X the special situation in which the trust can be terminated or set aside in the absence of such a revocation clause.

FARKAS v. WILLIAMS

Supreme Court of Illinois, 1955.
5 Ill.2d 417, 125 N.E.2d 600.[67]

HERSHEY, JUSTICE. * * * The plaintiffs asked the court to declare their legal rights, as coadministrators, in four stock certificates issued by Investors Mutual, Inc. in the name of "Albert B. Farkas, as trustee for Richard J. Williams" and which were issued pursuant to written declarations of trust. The decree of the circuit court found that said declarations were testamentary in character, and not having been executed with the formalities of a will, were invalid, and directed that the stock be awarded to the plaintiffs as an asset of the estate of said Albert B. Farkas. Upon appeal to the Appellate Court, the decree was affirmed. See 3 Ill.App.2d 248, 121 N.E.2d 344. We allowed defendants' petition for leave to appeal.

Albert B. Farkas died intestate at the age of sixty-seven years, a resident of Chicago, leaving as his only heirs-at-law brothers, sisters, a nephew and a niece. Although retired at the time of his death, he had for many years practiced veterinary medicine and operated a veterinarian establishment in Chicago. During a considerable portion of that time, he employed the defendant Williams, who was not related to him.

64. See Bogert, Trusts and Trustees (2d Ed., 1965) §§ 992, 993, 998; IV Scott, Trusts (3d Ed. 1967) §§ 330, 331; Stevenson, "Amazing Revocable Trust: A Study in Contradictions", 32 U.Cin.L.Rev. 1 (1963). As to the exercise by will of a testator's reserved power to revoke or modify an inter vivos trust, see 81 A.L.R. 3d 959 (1977).

65. West's Ann.Cal.Civ.Code § 2280 (1954) is typical: "Unless expressly made irrevocable by the instrument creating the trust, every voluntary trust shall be revocable by the trustor by writing filed with the trustee. * * *"

66. E.g., Aylsworth v. Whitcomb, 12 R.I. 298 (1879). For a case in which the Indiana court repudiated earlier case-law and adopted the modern rule against implied revocation, see Colbo v. Buyer, 235 Ind. 518, 134 N.E.2d 45 (1956).

67. Noted, 5 DePaul L.Rev. 153 (1955); 23 U.Chi.L.Rev. 289, 303 (1956).

On four occasions (December 8, 1948; February 7, 1949; February 14, 1950; and March 1, 1950) Farkas purchased stock of Investors Mutual, Inc. At the time of each purchase he executed a written application to Investors Mutual, Inc., instructing them to issue the stock in his name "as trustee for Richard J. Williams." Investors Mutual, Inc., by its agent, accepted each of these applications in writing by signature on the face of the application. Coincident with the execution of these applications, Farkas signed separate declarations of trust, all of which were identical except as to dates. The terms of said trust instruments are as follows:

"Declaration of Trust—Revocable. I, the undersigned, having purchased or declared my intention to purchase certain shares of capital stock of Investors Mutual, Inc. (the Company), and having directed that the certificate for said stock be issued in my name as trustee for Richard J. Williams as beneficiary, whose address is 1704 W. North Ave. Chicago, Ill., under this Declaration of Trust Do Hereby Declare that the terms and conditions upon which I shall hold said stock in trust and any additional stock resulting from reinvestments of cash dividends upon such original or additional shares are as follows:

"(1) During my lifetime all cash dividends are to be paid to me individually for my own personal account and use; provided, however, that any such additional stock purchased under an authorized reinvestment of cash dividends shall become a part of and subject to this trust.

"(2) Upon my death the title to any stock subject hereto and the right to any subsequent payments or distributions shall be vested absolutely in the beneficiary. The record date for the payment of dividends, rather than the date of declaration of the dividend, shall, with reference to my death, determine whether any particular dividend shall be payable to my estate or to the beneficiary.

"(3) During my lifetime I reserve the right, as trustee, to vote, sell, redeem, exchange or otherwise deal in or with the stock subject hereto, but upon any sale or redemption of said stock or any part thereof, the trust hereby declared shall terminate as to the stock sold or redeemed, and I shall be entitled to retain the proceeds of sale or redemption for my own personal account and use.

"(4) I reserve the right at any time to change the beneficiary or revoke this trust, but it is understood that no change of beneficiary and no revocation of this trust except by death of the beneficiary, shall be effective as to the Company for any purpose unless and until written notice thereof in such form as the Company shall prescribe is delivered to the Company at Minneapolis, Minnesota. The decease of the beneficiary before my death shall operate as a revocation of this trust.

"(5) In the event this trust shall be revoked or otherwise terminated, said stock and all rights and privileges thereunder shall belong to and be exercised by me in my individual capacity.

* * *

The applications and declarations of trust were delivered to Investors Mutual, Inc., and held by the company until Farkas's death. The stock certificates were issued in the name of Farkas as "trustee for Richard J. Williams" and were discovered in a safety-deposit box of Farkas after his death, along with other securities, some of which were in the name of Williams alone.

The sole question presented on this appeal is whether the instruments entitled "Declaration of Trust—Revocable" and executed by Farkas created valid *inter vivos* trusts of the stock of Investors Mutual, Inc. The plaintiffs contend that said stock is free and clear from any trust or beneficial interest in the defendant Williams, for the reason that said purported trust instruments were attempted testamentary dispositions and invalid for want of compliance with the statute on wills. The defendants, on the other hand, insist that said instruments created valid *inter vivos* trusts and were not testamentary in character.

It is conceded that the instruments were not executed in such a way as to satisfy the requirements of the statute on wills; hence, our inquiry is limited to whether said trust instruments created valid *inter vivos* trusts effective to give the purported beneficiary, Williams, title to the stock in question after the death of the settlor-trustee, Farkas. To make this determination we must consider: (1) whether upon execution of the so-called trust instruments defendant Williams acquired an interest in the subject matter of the trusts, the stock of defendant Investors Mutual, Inc., (2) whether Farkas, as settlor-trustee, retained such control over the subject matter of the trusts as to render said trust instruments attempted testamentary dispositions.

First, upon execution of these trust instruments did defendant Williams presently acquire an interest in the subject matter of the intended trusts?

If no interest passed to Williams before the death of Farkas, the intended trusts are testamentary and hence invalid for failure to comply with the statute on wills. Oswald v. Caldwell, 225 Ill. 224, 80 N. E. 131; Troup v. Hunter, 300 Ill. 110, 133 N.E. 56; Restatement of the Law of Trusts, section 56.

But considering the terms of these instruments we believe Farkas did intend to presently give Williams an interest in the property referred to. For it may be said, at the very least, that upon his executing one of these instruments, he showed an intention to presently part with some of the incidents of ownership in the stock. Immediately after the execution of each of these instruments, he could not deal with the stock therein referred to the same as if he owned the property absolutely, but only in accordance with the terms of the instrument. He purported to set himself up as trustee of the stock for the benefit of Williams, and the stock was registered in his name as trustee for Williams. Thus assuming to act as trustee, he is held to have intended to take on those obligations which are expressly set out in the instrument, as well as those fiduciary obligations implied by law. In addition, he manifested an intention to bind himself to having this property pass upon his death to Williams, unless he changed the beneficiary or revoked the trust, and then such change of beneficiary or revocation was not to be effective as to Investors Mutual, Inc., unless and until written notice thereof in such form as the company prescribed was delivered to them at Minneapolis, Minnesota. An absolute owner can dispose of his property, either in his lifetime or by will, in any way he sees fit without notifying or securing approval from anyone and without being held to the duties of a fiduciary in so doing.

It seems to follow that what incidents of ownership Farkas intended to relinquish, in a sense he intended Williams to acquire. That is, Williams was to be the beneficiary to whom Farkas was to be obligated, and unless Farkas revoked the instrument in the manner therein set out or the instrument was otherwise terminated in a manner therein provided for, upon Farkas's death Williams was to become absolute owner of the trust property. It is difficult to name this interest of Williams, nor is there any reason for so doing so long as it passed to him immediately upon the creation of the trust. As stated in 4 Powell, The Law of Real Property, at page 87: "Interests of beneficiaries of private express trusts run the gamut from valuable substantialities to evanescent hopes. Such a beneficiary may have any one of an almost infinite variety of the possible aggregates of rights, privileges, powers and immunities."

An additional problem is presented here, however, for it is to be noted that the trust instruments provide: "The decease of the beneficiary before my death shall operate as a revocation of this trust." The plaintiffs argue that the presence of this provision removes the only possible distinction which might have been drawn between these instruments and a will. Being thus conditioned on his surviving, it is argued that the "interest" of Williams until the death of Farkas was a mere expectancy. Conversely, they assert, the interest of Farkas in the securities until his death was precisely the same as that of a testator who bequeaths securities by his will, since he had all the rights accruing to an absolute owner.

Admittedly, had this provision been absent the interest of Williams would have been greater, since he would then have had an inheritable interest in the lifetime of Farkas. But to say his interest would have been greater is not to say that he here did not have a beneficial interest, properly so-called, during the lifetime of Farkas. The provision purports to set up but another "contingency" which would serve to terminate the trust. The disposition is not testamentary and the intended trust is valid, even though the interest of the beneficiary is contingent upon the existence of a certain state of facts at the time of the settlor's death. Restatement of the Law of Trusts,

section 56, comment f. In an example contained in the previous reference, the authors of the Restatement have referred to the interest of a beneficiary under a trust who must survive the settlor (and where the settlor receives the income for life) as a contingent equitable interest in remainder.

This question of whether any interest passed immediately is also involved in the next problem considered, namely the quantum of power retained by a settlor which will cause an intended *inter vivos* trust to fail as an attempted testamentary disposition. Therefore, much of what is said in the next part of the opinion, as well as the authorities cited, will pertain to this interest question.

Second, did Farkas retain such control over the subject matter of the trust as to render said trust instruments attempted testamentary dispositions?

In each of these trust instruments, Farkas reserved to himself as settlor the following powers: (1) the right to receive during his lifetime all cash dividends; (2) the right at any time to change the beneficiary or revoke the trust; and (3) upon sale or redemption of any portion of the trust property, the right to retain the proceeds therefrom for his own use.

Additionally, Farkas reserved the right to act as sole trustee, and in such capacity, he was accorded the right to vote, sell, redeem, exchange or otherwise deal in the stock which formed the subject matter of the trust.

We shall consider first those enumerated powers which Farkas reserved to himself as settlor.

It is well established that the retention by the settlor of the power to revoke, even when coupled with the reservation of a life interest in the trust property, does not render the trust inoperative for want of execution as a will. * * *

A more difficult problem is posed, however, by the fact that Farkas is also trustee, and as such, is empowered to vote, sell, redeem, exchange and otherwise deal in and with the subject matter of the trusts.

That a settlor may create a trust of personal property whereby he names himself as trustee and acts as such for the beneficiary is clear. Restatement of the Law of Trusts, section 17.

Moreover, the later cases indicate that the mere fact that the settlor in addition to making himself sole trustee also reserves a life interest and a power of revocation does not render the trust invalid as testamentary in character. * * *

In the instant case the plaintiffs contend that Farkas, as settlor-trustee, retained complete control and dominion over the securities for his own benefit during his lifetime. It is argued that he had the power to deal with the property as he liked so long as he lived and owed no enforceable duties of any kind to Williams as beneficiary.

* * *

[In the omitted portion of the opinion the court considered prior Illinois cases which, while distinguishable, were found to exhibit a tendency to permit the settlor to retain substantial control over the trust property and then discussed the closely analogous case of United Building & Loan Ass'n v. Garrett, 64 F.Supp. 460 (D.C.Ark.1946) upholding the validity of a similar trust arrangement.]

* * *

That the retention of the power by Farkas as trustee to sell or redeem the stock and keep the proceeds for his own use should not render these trust instruments testamentary in character becomes more evident upon analyzing the real import and significance of the powers to revoke and to amend the trust, the reservation of which the courts uniformly hold does not invalidate an *inter vivos* trust.

It is obvious that a settlor with the power to revoke and to amend the trust at any time is, for all practical purpose, in a position to exert considerable control over the trustee regarding the administration of the trust. For anything believed to be inimicable to his best interests can be thwarted or prevented by simply revoking the trust or amending it in such a way as to conform to his wishes. Indeed, it seems that many of those powers which from time to time have been viewed as "additional powers" are already, in a sense, virtually contained within the overriding power of revocation or the power to amend the trust. Consider, for example, the following: (1) the power to consume the principal; (2) the power to sell or mortgage the trust property and appropriate the proceeds; (3) the power to appoint or remove trustees; (4) the power to supervise and direct investments; and (5) the power to otherwise direct and supervise the trustee in the administration of the trust. Actually, any of the above powers could readily be assumed by a settlor with the reserved power of revocation through the simple expedient of revoking the trust, and then, as absolute owner of the subject matter, doing with the property as he chooses. Even though no actual termination of the trust is effectuated, however, it could hardly be questioned but that the mere existence of this power in the settlor is sufficient to enable his influence to be felt in a practical way in the administration of the trust. * * *

In the case at bar, the power of Farkas to vote, sell, redeem, exchange or otherwise deal in the stock was reserved to him as trustee, and it was only upon sale or redemption that he was entitled to keep the proceeds for his own use. Thus, the control reserved is not as great as in those cases where said power is reserved to the owner as settlor. For as trustee he must so conduct himself in accordance with standards applicable to trustees generally. It is not a valid objection to this to say that Williams would never question Farkas' conduct, inasmuch as Farkas could then revoke the trust and destroy what interest Williams has. Such a possibility exists in any case where the settlor has the power of revocation. Still, Williams has rights the same as any beneficiary, although it may not be feasible for him to exercise them. Moreover, it is entirely possible that he might in certain situations have a right to hold Farkas' estate liable for breaches of trust committed by Farkas during his lifetime. In this regard, consider what would happen if, without having revoked the trust, Farkas as trustee had given the stock away without receiving any consideration therefor, had pledged the stock improperly for his own personal debt and allowed it to be lost by foreclosure or had exchanged the stock for another security or other worthless property in such manner as to constitute gross impropriety and gross negligence. In such instances, it would seem in accordance with the terms of these instruments that Williams would have had an enforceable claim against Farkas' estate for whatever damage had been suffered. Contrast this with the rights of a legatee or devisee under a will. The testator could waste the property or do anything with it he wished during his lifetime without incurring any liability to those designated by the will to inherit the property. In any event, if Farkas as settlor could reserve the power to sell or otherwise deal with the property and retain the proceeds, which the cases indicate he could, then it necessarily follows that he should have the right to sell or otherwise deal with the property as trustee and retain the proceeds from a sale or redemption without having the instruments rendered invalid as testamentary dispositions.

Another factor often considered in determining whether an *inter vivos* trust is an attempted testamentary disposition is the formality of the transaction. Restatement of the Law of Trusts, section 57, comment g; Stouse v. First National Bank, Ky., 245 S.W.2d 914, 32 A.L.R.2d 1261; United Building and Loan Association v. Garrett, D. C., 64 F.Supp. 460; In re Sheasley's Trust, 366 Pa. 316, 77 A.2d 448. Historically, the purpose behind the enactment of the statute on wills was the prevention of fraud. The requirement as to witnesses was deemed necessary because a will is ordinarily an expression of the secret wish of the testator, signed out of the presence of all concerned. The possibility of forgery and fraud are ever present in such situations. Here, Farkas executed four separate applications for stock of Investors Mutual, Inc., in which he directed that the stock be issued in his name as trustee for Williams, and he executed four separate declarations of trust in which he declared he was holding said stock in trust for Williams. The stock certificates in question were issued in his name as trustee for Williams. He thus manifested his intention in a solemn and formal manner.

For the reasons stated, we conclude that these trust declarations executed by Farkas constituted valid *inter vivos* trusts and were not attempted testamentary dispositions. It must be conceded that they have, in the words of Mr. Justice Holmes in Bromley v. Mitchell, 155 Mass. 509, 30 N.E. 83, a "testamentary look." Moreover, it must be admitted that the line should be drawn somewhere, but after a study of this case we do not believe that point has here been reached.

Reversed and remanded, with directions.

BARNETTE v. McNULTY

Court of Appeals of Arizona, 1973.
21 Ariz.App. 127, 516 P.2d 583.

HOWARD, JUDGE.

The appellant-plaintiff in this case disputed the testamentary disposition by her deceased husband of certain property and contended that the property was her sole and separate property upon her husband's death by virtue of an inter vivos trust. This appeal was undertaken when the trial court disagreed with appellant's position and entered judgment in favor of appellee.

Appellant's questions for review revolve around three general areas: (1) Did the deceased create a valid inter vivos trust? (2) Did the deceased revoke the trust? (3) Did the court err in the admission of certain oral testimony?

The facts considered in the light most favorable to upholding the judgment of the trial court are as follows. Appellant and her deceased husband, Wilson M. Barnette, were married on September 17, 1967. They took up residence at the home owned by appellant prior to their marriage. Mr. Barnette was the owner and operator of a moving and storage business incorporated as Van Pack of Arizona, Inc., and appellant was unemployed at the time of the marriage. Appellant was subsequently employed by the corporation and became secretary-treasurer. As such, she kept the books, made the deposits and acted generally as office manager. Her starting salary of $75 per week was raised to $125 per week, which continued until shortly after Mr. Barnette died. Prior to his death, appellant was removed as secretary-treasurer of the corporation even though she continued to receive a salary.

In early March of 1970, Mr. Barnette was hospitalized with high blood pressure and diabetes. On March 12th he executed a power of attorney to appellant so she could continue to run the business. In the spring of 1970, appellant discussed with Mr. Barnette a book that she had read written by a man called Dacy, entitled "How To Avoid Probate". They discussed the book and the creation of a "Dacy Trust" while Mr. Barnette was in the hospital and again when he came home. On March 25, 1970, Mr. Barnette executed a form contained in the book entitled "Declaration of Trust." In this declaration of trust Mr. Barnette declared himself to be the trustee of his shares of the capital stock of Van Pack of Arizona, Inc., for the use and benefit of the appellant. It also provided that upon Mr. Barnette's death, appellant was to be appointed as successor trustee—

the successor trustee was to transfer all of his shares of the trust to the beneficiary. Another provision stated:

> "6. I hereby reserve unto myself the power and right at any time during my lifetime, before actual distribution to the beneficiary hereunder, to revoke in whole or in part or to amend the Trust hereby created without the necessity of obtaining the consent of the beneficiary and without giving notice to the beneficiary. Any-one of the following acts shall be conclusive evidence of such revocation of this Trust:
>
> (a) The delivery to the issuer or transfer agent of the shares by me of written notice that this Trust is revoked in whole or in part;
>
> (b) the transfer by me of my right, title and interest in and to said Shares;
>
> (c) the delivery by me to the issuer or transfer agent of the Shares of written notice of the death of the beneficiary hereunder. * * *"

At the time of the execution of the trust document and up to the time of trial there was issued an outstanding certificate No. 6 dated February 18, 1968, for 201 shares of the capital stock of Van Pack of Arizona, Inc., in the name of Mr. Barnette. The stock was not transferred on the books of the corporation to Mr. Barnette as trustee nor was the assignment on the back of the stock certificate executed by Mr. Barnette.

In June of 1970, appellant became ill and it was not long before marital difficulties arose between the parties. Mr. Barnette filed a divorce action in Cochise County and appellant filed a divorce action on July 15, 1970, in Pima County. On July 9, 1970, Mr. Barnette consulted with his attorney, James F. McNulty, Jr., and discussed both his will and his marital problems. Mr. Barnette told Mr. McNulty that Van Pack of Arizona, Inc., was his corporation, that his efforts had created it, that it was separate property, that his wife owned no interest, and that he wanted his son to succeed to his interest. By Mr. Barnette's explicit direction the will drafted by Mr. McNulty and subsequently executed by Mr. Barnette specifically referred to the Van Pack Corporation as being owned solely by Mr. Barnette.

In July of 1970, Mr. Barnette consulted with Mr. Fred Talmadge, an attorney in Cochise County, concerning his domestic problems and as a result Mr. Talmadge filed on his behalf a divorce complaint in Cochise County on July 17, 1970. Mr. Talmadge testified that in his consultations leading up to the filing of the divorce complaint Mr. Barnette told him that the Van Pack Corporation belonged to him; that he understood the appellant might be filing for divorce herself and that he was sure she would attempt to take his interest in Van Pack from him, they were separated, he was keeping her on the corporation payroll as an employee because she was still his wife and he was under a legal obligation to support her whether he liked it or not.

Mr. Barnette died in the hospital on July 23, 1970 with appellant at his bedside.

WAS A VALID TRUST CREATED?

The essential elements of a trust are: (a) A competent settlor and trustee; (b) clear and unequivocal intent to create a trust; (c) an ascertainable trust res and (d) sufficiently identifiable beneficiaries. Appellee contends that no trust was created in this instance because the settlor, Mr. Barnette, failed to have the stock transferred on the corporation books to himself as trustee and did not execute the assignment on the reverse side of the stock certificates. We do not agree with this contention. The owner of shares of stock in a corporation may make himself trustee of the shares for another by oral or written declaration of the trust without a delivery of any document to the beneficiary or any change in the corporation's records. Bogert, "Trusts and Trustees", 2nd Ed. § 142. Where the settlor is also the trustee, Scott on Trusts, 3rd Ed. § 32.5 states:

> "We have been considering the situation that arises when the owner of property conveys it to another person as Trustee. Where he declares himself Trustee of the property, however, it is obvious that the delivery of the subject matter to the beneficiary is neither necessary nor appropriate. Since his intention is to retain title to the property, although he is to hold it for the benefit of another it is clear that it would be inconsistent with his intention for him to surrender the property."

Further, Restatement (Second) of Trusts, § 17 at 59 states: "A trust may be created by: (a) a declaration by the owner of property that he holds it as Trustee for another person; * * *" The comment on clause (a) states that "if the owner of property declares himself trustee of the property, a trust may be created without a transfer of title to the property." It is therefore clear that Mr. Barnette created a valid trust.

* * *

[In the omitted portion of the opinion, the Court concluded that the provision in the trust instrument that certain specified acts were conclusive evidence of revocation was not exclusive and that the trust had been revoked by the oral statements made to Mr. McNulty prior to execution of the will and to Mr. Talmadge in connection with the divorce action.]

* * *

The judgment is affirmed.

NOTE

Where property is transferred under a formal living trust agreement to a third-party trustee, and the settlor retains various powers of control, the issue is framed in terms of whether the third party is in substance a trustee or a mere agent. However, the basic considerations and arguments are similar to those where the settlor makes himself trustee. While the text writers state that the determining factor is the "degree" of control, the overwhelming modern trend is to sustain the trust as non-testamentary even where the settlor retains the income for life, a power to revoke or amend a power to appoint beneficiaries by will, and some degree of control over administration by requiring the trustee to submit recommendations concerning investments and allowing the settlor to instruct the trustee concerning retention or sale of investments. The courts are careful to emphasize the formal nature of the trust agreement and the fact that, as typically is the case, the agreement expressly confers broad and extensive administrative powers on the trustee.[68]

The use of the revocable living trust as a will substitute for the purpose of avoiding the cost, delay and publicity of probate is widely accepted. In many states it is now expressly sanctioned by statute,[69] in order to eliminate doubt arising from earlier decisions following the famous Massachusetts case of McEvoy v. Boston Five Cents Savings Bank, 201 Mass. 50, 87 N.E. 465 (1909). This case, holding a revocable living trust testamentary and invalid, was followed in several jurisdictions before being overruled in its home jurisdiction in National Shawmut Bank of Boston v. Joy, 315 Mass. 457, 53 N.E.2d 113 (1944).

NEWMAN v. DORE

Court of Appeals of New York, 1937.
275 N.Y. 371, 9 N.E.2d 966, 112 A.L.R. 643.[70]

[Ferdinand Straus executed a will on 5 May, 1934, which contained a trust for his wife for her lifetime of one-third of his property, both real and personal. By Section 18 of the Decedent Estate Law the surviving spouse was given a right to elect her intestate share set forth in Section 83, which was one-third of the estate in the case of Mrs. Straus since the couple had children. But Section 18 also provided at the time of the case that if the testator left a trust of this share with the income payable to the wife for life, then she was deprived of her election.[71] On 28 June, 1934, Straus executed trust

68. See Estate of Steck, 275 Wis. 290, 81 N.W.2d 729 (1957).

69. E.g., Ind.Stat.Ann. § 29–1–5–9 (1972).

70. Noted, 7 Brooklyn L.Rev. 241 (1937); 37 Col.L.Rev. 1219 (1938); 23 Corn.L.Q. 457 (1938); 7 Ford.L.Rev. 115 (1938); 26 Geo.L.J. 784 (1938); 36 Mich. L.Rev. 496 (1938); 12 St. John's L.Rev. 355 (1938); 12 Temp.L.Q. 129 (1937); 5 U. of Chi.L.Rev. 504 (1938); See also Schuyler, "Revocable Trusts—Spouses, Creditors and other Predators", Ch. 74–13, 8th Annual Institute on Estate Planning (Univ. of Miami 1974).

71. Under the current New York Law a revocable trust established after 31 August 1966 can be reached by the surviving spouse to satisfy her elective share. See McKinney's N.Y., EPTL, § 5–1.1 (b)(1)(E). The applicable portion of this statute is set forth in Chapter IV, Section 2(5) supra. Under the new statute the elective share is still 1/3 of the net estate of the decedent if survived by issue and 1/2 if no issue survive, but unlike the provisions at the time of the principal case, a distinction is made between wills executed before 1 September 1966 and those executed thereafter. For wills executed before this date, the statute now requires that to deprive the spouse of her election an absolute gift be made in the will of $2,500 or more and a disposition in trust for the life of the spouse of an amount equal to or greater than the elective share. McKinney's N.Y., EPTL 5–1.1 (a)(1)(D) (1967). For wills executed after this date, the comparable provision barring an election requires an absolute gift by will of $10,000 or more with a provision in trust for the spouse's life of the difference between the gift and the elective share. Idem § 5–1.1(c)(1)(F).

agreements by which he transferred all of his property to trustees for the benefit of a named beneficiary. He died on 1 July, 1934. His widow challenged the validity of the trust agreements of 28 June, 1934, and the beneficiary brought this action to compel the trustees to carry out their terms. The trial court found that the trust agreements were made by Straus to evade New York laws, particularly Sections 18 and 83 of the Decedent Estate Law, and held the transfers ineffective. This decision was affirmed by the Supreme Court, Appellate Division, and the plaintiff appeals.]

LEHMAN, JUDGE. * * * The validity of the attempted transfer depends upon whether "the laws of the State of New York and particularly Sections 18 and 83 of the Decedent Estate Law" prohibit or permit such transfer. If the statute, in express language or by clear implication, prohibits the transfer, it is illegal; if the laws of the state do not prohibit it, the transfer is legal. In strict accuracy, it cannot be said that a "purpose of evading and circumventing" the law can carry any legal consequences. "We do not speak of evasion, because, when the law draws a line, a case is on one side of it or the other, and if on the safe side is none the worse legally that a party has availed himself to the full of what the law permits. When an act is condemned as an evasion what is meant is that it is on the wrong side of the line indicated by the policy if not by the mere letter of the law." Bullen v. Wisconsin, 240 U.S. 625, 630, 36 S.Ct. 473, 474, 60 L.Ed. 830. * * * Under the laws of the State of New York, and particularly sections 18 and 83 of the Decedent Estate Law, neither spouse has any immediate interest in the property of the other. The "enlarged property right" which the Legislature intended to confer is only an expectant interest dependent upon the contingency that the property to which the interest attaches becomes part of a decedent's estate. The contingency does not occur, and the expectant property right does not ripen into a property right in possession, if the owner sells or gives away the property. Herrmann v. Jorgenson, 263 N.Y. 348, 189 N.E. 449; Matter of McCulloch's Will, 263 N.Y. 408, 189 N.E. 473, 91 A.L.R. 1440. Defeat of a contingent expectant interest by means available under the law cannot be regarded as an unlawful "evasion" of the law. A duty imperfectly defined by law may at times be evaded or a right imperfectly protected by law may be violated with impunity, but to say that an act, lawful under common-law rules and not prohibited by any express or implied statutory provision, is in itself a "fraud" on the law or an "evasion" of the law, involves a contradiction in terms.

That does not mean, of course, that the law may not place its ban upon an intended result even though the means to effect that result may be lawful. The statute gives to a spouse a property right. The question is, how far the statute protects that right even while it remains only expectant and contingent. A right created by law may be protected by law against invasion through acts otherwise lawful. A wrong does not cease to be a wrong because it is cloaked in form of law. The test of legality, then, is whether the result is lawful and the means used to achieve that result are lawful. Here, we should point out that the courts below have not based their decision primarily upon the finding that the trust agreements were executed for the purpose of evading and circumventing the law of the state of New York. The courts have also found, and the evidence conclusively establishes, that the trust agreements were made for the purpose of depriving the decedent's widow of any rights in and to his property upon his death. Under the trust agreements executed a few days before the death of the settlor, he reserved the enjoyment of the entire income as long as he should live, and a right to revoke the trust at his will, and in general the powers granted to the trustees were in terms made "subject to the settlor's control during his life," and could be exercised "in such manner only as the settlor shall from time to time direct in writing." Thus, by the trust agreement which transferred to the trustees the settlor's entire property, the settlor reserved substantially the same rights to enjoy and control the disposition of the property as he previously had possessed, and the inference is inescapable that the trust agreements were executed by the settlor, as the court has found "with the intention and for the purpose of diminishing his estate and thereby to reduce in amount the share" of his wife in his estate upon his death and as a "contrivance to deprive * * * his widow of any rights in and to his property upon his death." They had no other purpose and substantially they had no other effect. Does the statute intend that such a transfer shall be available as a means of defeating the contingent expectant estate of a spouse?

In a few states where a wife has a similar contingent expectant interest or estate in the property of her husband, it has been held that her rights may not be defeated by any transfer made during life with intent to deprive the wife of property, which under the law would otherwise pass to her. Thayer v. Thayer, 14 Vt. 107, 39 Am. Dec. 211; Evans v. Evans, 78 N.H. 352, 100 A. 671; Dyer v. Smith, 62 Mo.App. 606; Payne v. Tatem, 236 Ky. 306, 33 S.W.2d 2. In those states it is the intent to defeat the wife's contingent rights which creates the invalidity and it seems that an absolute transfer of all his property by a married man during his life, if made with other purpose and intent than to cut off an unloved wife, is valid even though its effect is to deprive the wife of any share in the property of her husband at his death. Dunnett v. Shields & Conant, 97 Vt. 419, 123 A. 626; Patch v. Squires, 105 Vt. 405, 165 A. 919. The rule has been stated that "while the wife cannot complain of reasonable gifts or advancements by a husband to his children by a former marriage, yet, if the gifts constitute the principal part of the husband's estate and be made without the wife's knowledge, a presumption of fraud arises, and it rests upon the beneficiaries to explain away that presumption." Payne v. Tatem, supra, 236 Ky. 306, at page 308, 33 S.W. 2d 2, 3.

Motive or intent is an unsatisfactory test of the validity of a transfer of property. In most jurisdictions it has been rejected, sometimes for the reason that it would cast doubt upon the validity of all transfers made by a married man, outside of the regular course of business; sometimes because it is difficult to find a satisfactory logical foundation for it. Intent may, at times, be relevant in determining whether an act is fraudulent, but there can be no fraud where no right of any person is invaded. "The great weight of authority is that the intent to defeat a claim which otherwise a wife might have is not enough to defeat the deed." Leonard v. Leonard, 181 Mass. 458, 462, 63 N.E. 1068, 1069, 92 Am.St.Rep. 426, and cases there cited. Since the law gives the wife only an expectant interest in the property of her husband which becomes part of his estate, and since the law does not restrict transfers of property by the husband during his life, it would seem that the only sound test of the validity of a challenged transfer is whether it is real or illusory. That is the test applied in Leonard v. Leonard, supra. The test has been formulated in different ways, but in most jurisdictions the test applied is essentially the test of whether the husband has in good faith divested himself of ownership of his property or has made an illusory transfer. "The 'good faith' required of the donor or settlor in making a valid disposition of his property during life does not refer to the purpose to affect his wife but to the intent to divest himself of the ownership of the property. It is, therefore, apparent that the fraudulent intent which will defeat a gift inter vivos cannot be predicated of the husband's intent to deprive the wife of her distributive * * * share as widow." Benkart v. Commonwealth Trust Co., of Pittsburgh, 269 Pa. 257, 259, 112 A. 62, 63. * * * In no jurisdiction has a transfer in trust been upheld where the conveyance is intended only to cover up the fact that the husband is retaining full control of the property though in form he has parted with it. Though a person may use means lawfully available to him to keep outside of the scope of a statute, a false appearance of legality, however attained, will not avail him. Reality, not appearance, should determine legal rights. Cf. Jenkins v. Moyse, 254 N.Y. 319, 172 N.E. 521, 74 A.L.R. 205.

In this case the decedent, as we have said, retained not only the income for life and power to revoke the trust, but also the right to control the trustees. We need not now determine whether such a trust is, for any purpose, a valid present trust. It has been said that, "where the settlor transfers property in trust and reserves not only * * * a power to revoke and modify the trust but also such power to control the trustee as to the details of the administration of the trust that the trustee is the agent of the settlor, the disposition so far as it is intended to take effect after his death is testamentary. * * *" American Law Institute, Restatement of the Law of Trusts, § 57, subd. 2. We do not now consider whether the rule so stated is in accord with the law of this state or whether in this case the reserved power of control is so great that the trustee is in fact "the agent of the settlor." We assume, without deciding, that except for the provisions of section 18 of the Decedent Estate Law the trust would be valid. Cf. Robb v. Washington & Jefferson College, 185 N.Y. 485, 78 N.E. 359; Von Hesse v. MacKaye, 136 N.Y. 114, 32 N.E. 615. Perhaps "from the technical point of view such a conveyance does not quite take back all that it gives, but practically it does."

That is enough to render it an unlawful invasion of the expectant interest of the wife. Leonard v. Leonard, supra; Brownell v. Briggs, 173 Mass. 529, 54 N.E. 251.

Judged by the substance, not by the form, the testator's conveyance is illusory, intended only as a mask for the effective retention by the settlor of the property which in form he had conveyed. We do not attempt now to formulate any general test of how far a settlor must divest himself of his interest in the trust property to render the conveyance more than illusory. Question of whether reservation of the income or of a power of revocation, or both, might even without reservation of the power of control be sufficient to show that the transfer was not intended in good faith to divest the settlor of his property must await decision until such question arises. In this case it is clear that the settlor never intended to divest himself of his property. He was unwilling to do so even when death was near.

The judgment should be affirmed, with costs.

CRANE, C.J., and HUBBS, LOUGHRAN and RIPPEY, JJ., concur.

FINCH, J., concurs in result.

O'BRIEN, J., takes no part.

Judgment affirmed.

NOTE

The problem in the principal case may arise in some community property states. In other community property states it cannot arise because statute or decision forbids gratuitous transfers by the husband or wife as manager of the community without the consent of the spouse; and in still other community states where statutes require joinder of both to a transfer of community realty, it cannot arise as to realty. However, in other situations the problem is whether the husband or wife as manager of the community property may by creating a revocable living trust do that which he or she could not do by will: control the devolution of the property after the death of both the husband and the wife.

In Land v. Marshall,[72] the husband as manager of community personalty had transferred stock to a trustee to hold in trust to pay the income to the husband for life and after his death to his wife for life, with power in the trustee to invade principal for the beneficiaries, the trust to terminate on the death of both husband and wife and the remaining corpus to belong to named beneficiaries. The husband reserved power to direct payment of principal, power to control various aspects of administration, and a power to revoke. The wife did not learn of the trust until after the husband's death. The widow sued to set aside the trust as to her half interest in the community property transferred into trust. The Texas Supreme Court borrowed the doctrine of illusory trusts as a tool for solution of the problem and held that

72. 426 S.W.2d 841 (Tex.1968). Noted, 20 Baylor L.Rev. 408 (1968). See Bell, "Community Property Trusts-Challenges by the Non-Participating Spouse", 22 Baylor L.Rev. 311 (1970); "The Illusory Trust and Community Property: A New Twist to an Old Tale" 22 Sw.L.J. 447 (1968); Hoft, "Illusory Trusts", 10 So.Tex.L.J. 301 (1968).

the trust in the instant case was illusory. At 426 S.W.2d 846 the Court states:

> "* * * The central question in this case arises out of an apparent conflict in the law and policy of our community property system. The husband, under Texas law, has managerial powers over the wife's community interest. However, the husband's managerial powers do not extend beyond his death so as to allow the husband to dispose of the wife's community interest by his will. The wife, for that reason, has the right to elect to take under or against her husband's will when he undertakes to dispose of her community share upon his death. Thus, the question is whether the husband can accomplish by inter vivos trust what he could not do by a will. The wife contends that her husband could not control the disposition of her community share by the trust instrument. Conversely, the proponents of the trust point out many situations in which it is sound management by the husband to create an inter vivos trust of the wife's community interest even though its disposition is effected upon his death. We believe the paradox can be resolved by the doctrine of illusory trusts. Under the doctrine, the husband has the power to create an inter vivos trust as a part of his managerial powers over the wife's share; but when her community share is involved, the wife can require the trust to be real rather than illusory, genuine rather than colorable. * * *"

In some community property states the problem would be handled by the simple test of "fraud" on the spouse's community rights; but there may not be a definitive rule as to what constitutes such a fraud, just as the courts in a common law state using the "fraud" test avoid a precise test.

NATIONAL SHAWMUT BANK OF BOSTON v. CUMMING

Supreme Judicial Court of Massachusetts, 1950.
325 Mass. 457, 91 N.E.2d 337.

WILKINS, JUSTICE. The plaintiff bank is the surviving trustee under a declaration of trust, dated August 25, 1944, in which the bank and the settlor, William Gray Cumming, of Barre, Vermont, were named as trustees. The settlor died on August 19, 1947. The defendants are the settlor's widow, Cora Mann Cumming, and the mother, brother, and three sisters of the settlor, and constitute all the surviving life beneficiaries under the trust instrument. This bill in equity seeks (1) the removal of a cloud upon the plaintiff's title as trustee to the trust property, as well as upon the beneficial interests of the defendants, the said cloud consisting of a claim asserted by the widow that the trust is invalid: and (2) a binding declaration of the rights of the parties under the trust instrument. G.L. (Ter.Ed.) c. 231A, inserted by St.1945, c. 582, § 1. The answers of the defendants other than the widow admit the allegations of the bill and join in the prayers for relief. The widow's answer sets up that the trust was created in bad faith with intent to defraud her of rights under Vermont law after waiver of the will, and that the validity of the trust is to be determined by the laws of the State of Vermont. The widow (hereinafter called the defendant) appealed from a final decree ad-

judging that the trust is valid, and that she has no claim to the trust property except as a beneficiary under the trust instrument. The judge filed "Findings, ruling and order for decree." The evidence is reported.

We summarize certain facts found by the judge or by ourselves.

The trust agreement provided that the income, and such amounts of the principal as the settlor might direct in writing, should be paid to him for life; and that after his death the income should be paid equally to his widow, his mother, two brothers (one of whom predeceased him), and three sisters, the principal, if necessary, to be used to insure the receipt of $150 monthly by each beneficiary. Upon the death of the settlor and the last survivor of the life beneficiaries, the trust was to terminate and distribution be made to the nieces and nephews of the settlor then living and to the living issue of each deceased niece or nephew by right of representation. The settlor reserved the power to amend, to revoke in whole or in part, and to withdraw principal. The last paragraph reads, "This instrument shall be construed and the provisions thereof interpreted under and in accordance with the laws of the Commonwealth of Massachusetts." Extensive powers of management were reserved to the trustees, but by an amendment of September 26, 1945, the settlor "delegated" his powers as cotrustee to the plaintiff.

The settlor died domiciled in Vermont at the age of fifty-seven. On January 5, 1925, when in Florida, he married the defendant. It was his first marriage. She was "several years" his senior and a widow with three children. The settlor, who until then had lived with his mother, was an eldest son who had assumed the obligations of the head of the family. He took these obligations very seriously, and strong family ties continued throughout his life. His business energies were devoted to the Granite City Tool Company, Inc., in Barre, which he had organized. It had a branch in Georgia and one in Minnesota, each in charge of a brother.

In the summer of 1944 the settlor had accumulated a "sizeable amount" of cash and government bonds, which he kept in Vermont. He was solicited by an employee of the plaintiff, with which his company had an account, to use its facilities as trustee, and went to its offices in Boston, and made arrangements for the creation of the trust. The attorney of the plaintiff drew the trust instrument, which the settlor signed in Vermont on August 25, 1944, and caused to be sent to the plaintiff in Boston, where it was executed by the plaintiff on August 26. The annexed schedule of trust property listed a check for $50,000 of a Barre bank, drawn on a Boston bank and payable to the plaintiff, and $50,000 in Canadian government and United States Treasury bonds. The check had been given to the plaintiff by the settlor on August 16, and the bonds had been sent by the Barre bank, and received by the plaintiff on August 19. Later, on five occasions between March 9, 1945, and August 29, 1945, the settlor delivered or sent, or caused to be sent, to the plaintiff bonds or checks in the total amount of $100,595.25, to be added to the principal. These transfers to the trust were the greater part of his property. On November 12, 1946, there was a withdrawal of $27,000.

The settlor and the defendant "had not gotten along well," and the "rupture became more pronounced in December, 1944, when being quite a sick man physically he made plans to go to Florida for his health, [and] he asked his wife to go with him, but her daughter was sick, and she remained home to take care of her." He returned from Florida on February 15, 1945, lived with her for a brief time in Barre, and about March 1, ceased to do so. In 1946 she brought a petition for a "divorce from bed and board forever," and in 1947 he asked her "to let him have a full divorce."

The judge stated: "I find that the settlor meticulously and designedly arranged his holdings and his business affairs so that his mother, wife, brothers and sisters would share the income, or principal, if necessary, equally after his death. That he knew that but for this arrangement his widow would have been entitled under the laws of Vermont to $4,000 and one half of his estate. But I do not find that in doing what he did * * * he was actuated by bad faith, or that he sought to accomplish something which he under all the circumstances considered to be unjust or unfair to his wife. I do not find that he set up the trust with the fraudulent intent of preventing his wife from obtaining her distributive share of his property. I find and rule that the trust is valid. I find that the settlor intended that the trust be administered in Boston by the National Shawmut Bank as trustee."

* * *

If the settlor had been domiciled in this Commonwealth and had transferred personal property here to a trustee here for administration here, the transfer would have been valid even if his sole purpose had been to deprive his wife of any portion of it. Redman v. Churchill, 230 Mass. 415, 418, 119 N.E. 953; Eaton v. Eaton, 233 Mass. 351, 370, 124 N.E. 37, 5 A.L.R. 1426; Kerwin v. Donaghy, 317 Mass. 559, 571, 59 N.E.2d 299. The Vermont law we understand to be otherwise and to invalidate a transfer made there by one domiciled there of personal property there, if made with an actual, as distinguished from an implied, fraudulent intent to disinherit his spouse. See Thayer v. Thayer, 14 Vt. 107, 39 Am.Dec. 211; Green v. Adams, 59 Vt. 602, 10 A. 742, 59 Am.Rep. 761; Dunnett v. Shields & Conant, 97 Vt. 419, 428, 123 A. 626; Patch v. Squires, 105 Vt. 405, 165 A. 919; In re O'Rourke's Estate, 106 Vt. 327, 331, 175 A. 4.

The plaintiff contends that the validity of the trust is to be determined by the law of this Commonwealth, and, in the alternative, that should the question be determined by Vermont law, the trust would still be valid on the judge's findings. The defendant, on the other hand, contends that the "trust is not valid under either Vermont or Massachusetts law." This argument is founded upon alleged illegality according to the law of Vermont and an assertion that our courts must look to the law of the State of domicil, which determines the right of succession to the settlor's personal property here. Reliance is placed upon Ross v. Ross, 129 Mass. 243, 245, 37 Am.Rep. 321, to which may be added Shannon v. White, 109 Mass. 146, 148; Cheney v. Cheney, 214 Mass. 580, 581, 101 N.E. 1091; Russell v. Shapleigh, 275 Mass. 15, 20, 175 N.E. 100; Hite v. Hite, 301 Mass. 294, 297, 17 N.E. 2d 176, 119 A.L.R. 517, and Phelan v. Conron, 323 Mass. 247, 253, 81 N.E.2d 525. See G.L. (Ter.Ed.) c. 199, §§ 1, 2; Restatement: Conflict of Laws, § 301, comment b. The defendant's brief contains such statements as the "settlor was restricted or prevented by Vermont law from creating such a trust"; "the sole question is: Was the trust created to defraud the widow of the rights she has under Vermont law"; "capacity must be judged in the light of settlor's right to strip his wife of her dower rights, which in the last analysis is judged by Vermont law"; and the "trust property, all having come from Vermont, had its situs in Vermont."

One answer to the defendant's contention is that, wholly apart from what may be the law of Vermont, it was not shown that the trust was created to defraud the wife of statutory rights in Vermont. The judge was not plainly wrong in not making such a finding. There was no evidence which compelled it. The findings which he did make, including the finding that the settlor knew that but for the trust arrangement his wife would be entitled to $4,000 and one half of his estate, meaning, of course, at its then valuation, are not tantamount to findings that the trust was created, or added to, with intent to defraud her, nor are the findings inconsistent with one another.

Another independent and insuperable difficulty is that before death the settlor had effectively disposed of the trust property, which had its situs in this Commonwealth and was not subject here to any equity in favor of a wife or to any similar limitation upon his power of disposition. He had expressed an intent in the trust instrument that it should be construed and interpreted according to the laws of this Commonwealth. Codman v. Krell, 152 Mass. 214, 218, 25 N.E. 90; Greenough v. Osgood, 235 Mass. 235, 237–238, 126 N.E. 461; National Shawmut Bank v. Joy, 315 Mass. 457, 460, 53 N.E.2d 113. See Harvey v. Fiduciary Trust Co., 299 Mass. 457, 464, 13 N.E.2d 299; Amerige v. Attorney General, 324 Mass. 648, 658, 88 N.E.2d 126.

The elements entering into the decision as to the law of which State determines the validity of the trust are, on the one hand in Vermont, the settlor's domicil, and, on the other hand in Massachusetts, the presence of the property or its evidences, the completion of the trust agreement by final execution by the trustee, the domicil and the place of business of the trustee, and the settlor's intent that the trust should be administered by the trustee here. The general tendency of authorities elsewhere is away from the adoption of the law of the settlor's domicil where the property, the domicil and place of business of the trustee, and the place of administration intended by the settlor are in another State. Jackman v. Equitable Life Assurance Society, 3 Cir., 145 F.2d 945, 947; Warner v. Florida Bank & Trust Co., 5 Cir., 160 F.2d 766; Wilmington Trust Co. v. Wilmington Trust Co., 26 Del. Ch. 397, 405–406, 24 A.2d 309, 139 A.L.R. 1117; Kitchen v. New York

Trust Co., 292 Ky. 706, 710, 168 S.W.2d 5; Cutts v. Najdrowski, 123 N.J.Eq. 481, 198 A. 885; Hutchison v. Ross, 262 N.Y. 381, 187 N.E. 65, 89 A.L.R. 1007; Shannon v. Irving Trust Co., 275 N.Y. 95, 9 N.E. 2d 792; Restatement: Conflict of Laws, §§ 294; 46, comment d; 49, comment b; Beale Conflict of Laws, § 294.3; Land, Trusts in the Conflict of Laws, §§ 21–23. 44 Harv.L.Rev. 161, 89 U. of Pa.L.Rev. 360. See Brandeis v. Atkins, 204 Mass. 471, 90 N.E. 861, 26 L.R.A.,N.S., 230; Russell v. Joys, 227 Mass. 263, 267, 116 N.E. 549; Isaacson v. Boston Safe Deposit & Trust Co., Mass., 91 N.E.2d 334. The situation is unchanged by the fact that the one seeking to set aside the transaction is the widow of the settlor. Spicer v. New York Life Ins. Co., 237 Mo.App. 725, 743, 167 S.W.2d 457; Lines v. Lines, 142 Pa. 149, 165–166, 21 A. 809, 24 Am.St.Rep. 487; Roberts v. Chase, 25 Tenn.App. 636, 647, 166 S.W.2d 641. We are of opinion that the question of validity is to be determined by the law of this Commonwealth. There was no error under our law in adjudging the trust to be valid when created, or in omitting to adjudge it to be invalid at the time of the additions to principal made in 1945.

We are not sure whether any contention is made that the trust instrument is illusory on its face apart from alleged fraud toward the widow. The trust is not illusory. National Shawmut Bank v. Joy, 315 Mass. 457, 474–475, 476, 53 N.E.2d 113; Kerwin v. Donaghy, 317 Mass. 559, 572, 59 N.E.2d 299. See O'Donnell v. Commissioner of Corporations & Taxation, 317 Mass. 664, 672, 60 N.E.2d 11.

We have not outlined all the points referred to in the defendant's extended brief, believing that to do so would add nothing to our jurisprudence. Much of her argument seems immaterial to our view of the real issues. We have considered all the questions raised and are of opinion that there is no merit in any of them. These include the exceptions to the exclusion of evidence offered by the defendant as well as the denial of her motion for a new hearing on the ground of newly discovered evidence.

Decree affirmed.

NOTE

Although antenuptial and postnuptial property agreements may bar dower and its statutory substitutes [73] and modify or extinguish the community in a number of community property jurisdictions,[74] these claims by the spouse cannot be defeated by inter vivos transfers of property to which the claim pertains.[75] But in states in which the surviving spouse is made simply a forced heir, with no inchoate or present interest in the property of the husband or wife during coverture, courts have been troubled by efforts to de-

73. See Chapter IV, Section 2(5).

74. Vernier, American Family Laws (1935) § 178 (VII).

75. A transfer of real property prior to marriage with the fraudulent intent to deprive a spouse of dower will be set aside. E.g., Barnett v. Barnett, 209 Ark. 973, 193 S.W.2d 319 (1946). A transfer of personal property with the fraudulent intent to deprive the prospective spouse of a distributive share also has been set aside. E.g., Martin v. Martin, 282 Ky. 411, 138 S.W.2d 509 (1940), 54 Harv.L. Rev. 336 (1940), 30 Ky.L.J. 124 (1941); 11 U.Fla.L.Rev. 321 (1958); 40 Mass.L.Q. 35 (1955); 22 Brooklyn L.Rev. 144 (1955).

feat the claims of the spouse by inter vivos transfers. Frequently these transfers are revocable living trusts or trusts in which the settlor retains some interest or power of modification.

The share of a statutory heir (one taking property if the owner dies intestate as to it) may be defeated by testamentary transfers as well as by inter vivos transfers. Courts have evidenced no special disposition to protect statutory heirs. There is some analogy between the claim of a forced heir and the claim of a statutory heir, the main difference being that a forced heir cannot be defeated by testamentary transfers. However, a court may make a special effort to protect a forced heir against dimunition of her share by inter vivos transfers in states in which dower and its statutory forms have been abolished. It is not clear that the disposition to protect pretermitted heirs, who also take by forced heirship, is equally strong, there being few decisions involving pretermitted heirs who challenge inter vivos transfers by their parents.

A number of courts have held that an inter vivos transfer will be set aside if made for the purpose of defeating the claim of the surviving spouse.[76] This test is objectionable because intention is difficult to prove when the transferor is dead. The prospect of transfers being declared ineffective on this ground may interfere with the alienation of property during coverture. The test proposed in Newman v. Dore, apparently still applicable in New York to transfers made before 1 September 1966 and also applied in other states, is equally objectionable because it turns on the degree of control retained by the surviving spouse and thus places the revocable living trust in jeopardy even though this trust is an important estate planning device.[77] There is uncertainty in the actual amount of retained control necessary to render the transfer illusory, although a trust in which a power of revocation or modification is reserved is a potential target for attack in Newman v. Dore jurisdictions. Some courts, as does the Maryland court in Whittington v. Whittington, discussed in the Note at p. 598, purport to limit their consideration to no single test but examine all aspects of the transaction, including its fairness when the size of the estate and the responsibilities of the transferor are taken into consideration.

It has been suggested that all inter vivos transfers during coverture be subject to the elective claim; that only "testamentary" transfers, as considered in Chapter XII, Section 1 and in Farkas v. Williams be subject to the claim; or that the tests applied under the Federal Estate Tax Law to determine the gross estate of a decedent for taxation should be applied to determine the estate subject to the spouse's claim of forced heirship.[78] Perhaps

76. E.g., Mushaw v. Mushaw, 183 Md. 511, 39 A.2d 465 (1944); Wanstrath v. Kappel, 356 Mo. 210, 201 S.W.2d 327 (1947). This is usually called the "fraud" test.

77. In Matter of Halpern, 303 N.Y. 33, 100 N.E.2d 120 (1951), a tentative savings bank account trust or "Totten" trust was not an illusory transfer even though the depositor could revoke the trust until his death and although the trust had testamentary characteristics. In New York the Totten trust has been brought within reach of the surviving spouse by statute. See McKinney's N.Y., EPTL, § 5-1.-1(b)(1)(B) (1967). In Jeruzal v. Jeruzal, 269 Minn. 183, 130 N.W.2d 473 (1964), 34 U.Cin.L.Rev. 179 (1965), a Totten trust withstood attack by the surviving spouse, the court apparently treating the transaction as not illusory and not in fraud of the spouse's rights. Claims by the surviving spouse against revocable and tentative (Totten) trusts are explored in greater detail in Chapter IX, Section 2.

78. An excellent discussion of the problem with a comprehensive state by state collection of cases may be found in Macdonald, Fraud on the Widow's Share (1960). Periodical materials of value are Haskell, "The Power of Disinheritance: Proposal for Reform", 52 Geo.L.J. 499 (1964) (Covering other members of the family as well as the surviving spouse);

the soundest approach is that taken in Uniform Probate Code, § 2–202 which is set forth in Chapter IV, Section 2(2)(C). The augmented estate as there described is somewhat similar to the "gross estate concept" used in Federal estate taxation. Another approach, taken recently in New York, simply establishes by statute certain categories of inter vivos transfers which will be included in the estate "subject to a surviving spouse's elective right".[79] However, the statute will require much interpretation, conflicts problems will arise under it and attempts will certainly be made to evade the statutory categories. No doubt a question ultimately will be presented whether the doctrine of Newman v. Dore will apply to transactions not clearly within the categories of transactions described as excepted from the net estate, such as life insurance and pension plans,[80] but which might be "testamentary provisions within the meaning of this paragraph" without fitting precisely any of the described categories included in the net estate subject to the elective share. Avoiding the problem presented in National Shawmut Bank of Boston v. Cumming, the New York statute concerning elective shares does not apply to a decedent not domiciled in New York at the time of his death.[81]

MURPHEY v. C.I.T. CORP.

Supreme Court of Pennsylvania, 1943.
347 Pa. 591, 33 A.2d 16.[82]

* * * HORACE STERN, JUSTICE. George Flint and his wife, owners of certain real estate as tenants by entireties, executed a deed of the property to J. Oliver Murphey in trust "to permit the said grantors and or the survivor of them, for and during the term of their natural lives to occupy, use, and enjoy the said premises, the said grantors however, to pay all taxes, water rents, interest on mortgages or other charges against the said premises and to keep and maintain the same in good order and repair, * * * so that neither the said premises nor the income derived therefrom shall at any time be subject to the control of, or liable for the debts and engagements of the said grantors, but the corpus of the said trust shall be held intact to protect the interests in remainder as hereinafter expressed"; upon the death of either of the grantors the survivor was to be per-

Goldman, "Right of the Spouse and the Creditor in Inter Vivos Trusts", 17 U.Cin. L.Rev. 1 (1948); King, "A Reappraisal of the Revocable Trust", 19 Rocky Mt.L. Rev. 1 (1946); Schneider and Landesman, " 'Life, Liberty—and Dower' Disherison of the Spouse in New York", 19 N.Y.U.L. Q.Rev. 343 (1942); Scott, "Revocable Trust and the Surviving Spouse's Statutory Share in Colorado", 36 U.Colo.L. Rev. 464 (1964); Spies, "Property Rights of the Surviving Spouse", 46 Va.L.Rev. 157 (1960); Legislative note, "Protection of Surviving Spouse's Rights Under Elective Share Statutes", 18 Vand.L.Rev. 2090 (1965); Note, "Protection of the Surviving Spouse's Statutory Share Against Inter Vivos Transfers by the Decedent", 52 Yale L.J. 656 (1943).

79. See McKinney's N.Y., EPTL, § 5–1.1(b)(1) (1967), set forth in fn. 31 at pages 166 to 167.

80. McKinney's N.Y., EPTL, § 5–1.-1(b)(2).

81. Idem., (d)(6). Uniform Probate Code, § 2–201 restricts the election and augmented estate concept to the estate of a domiciliary. Section 2–201(b) states: "If a married person not domiciled in this state dies, the right, if any, of the surviving spouse to take an elective share in property in this state is governed by the law of the decedent's domicile at death". If this statute applied, would the result of the principal case be changed?

82. Noted, 42 Mich.L.Rev. 537 (1943); 96 Pa.L.Rev. 216 (1943).

mitted to occupy, use, enjoy or rent the premises for and during the term of the life of the survivor upon the same conditions and subject to the same restrictions as above described; upon the death of both of the grantors, the trustee was to convey the premises to their daughters, Beatrice Flint Collin and Alice Flint Williams, with a contingent grant to grandchildren if the daughters or either of them did not survive the grantors; the grantors reserved the right at any time "to revoke this trust either in part or in its entirety, or from time to time to alter or amend the same in any manner that to them shall seem fit or proper, and this right shall extend to the survivor of the said grantors."

* * * [At the time of the conveyance, C.I.T. Corporation was a judgment creditor of George Flint and a few months thereafter, Mrs. Flint then being dead, attempted to set aside the conveyance as fraudulent but failed in this. The court held the deed valid and C.I.T. Corporation then issued a writ of execution upon its original judgment but the trustee, together with Murphey, Flint and others, brought a bill to restrain C.I.T. Corporation from proceeding further and for a declaration freeing their title from the cloud cast upon it by C.I.T. Corporation's judgment. The court below dismissed this bill and plaintiffs appeal. Justice Stern stated that the issue before the Court was what estate, if any, passed under the conveyance to Flint which could be reached by C.I.T. Corporation as his creditor, and held the spendthrift provision would not protect the reserved life estate in Flint from the creditor's claim. He then continued:] * * * Since property owned by tenants by the entireties is not subject to the debts of either spouse they may alien it without infringing upon the rights of their individual creditors; all claims of the latter, even though reduced to judgment, are subject to extinction in the event of the alienation of the estate by the joint act of the owners: Beihl v. Martin, 236 Pa. 519, 528, 84 A. 953, 956, 42 L.R.A.,N.S., 555. Therefore, since Flint and his wife could have conveyed to their daughters the complete title to the property notwithstanding defendant's judgment, they could, of course, grant them a less estate, namely, the remainder after the life interests which were created by the deed. Nor was the estate given to the remaindermen testamentary in nature; the deed vested in them an immediate, beneficial interest, only the enjoyment and possession being postponed until the death of the grantors; in that connection it is not material that the grantors reserved to themselves the power of revocation or modification: Restatement, Trusts, § 57(1); Dickerson's Appeal, 115 Pa. 198, 210, 8 A. 64, 69, 2 Am.St.Rep. 547; Lines v. Lines, 142 Pa. 149, 167, 21 A. 809, 810, 811, 24 Am.St.Rep. 487; Windolph v. Girard Trust Co., 245 Pa. 349, 367, 368, 91 A. 634, 639, 640; In re Dolan's Estate, 279 Pa. 582, 589, 124 A. 176, 178, 49 A.L.R. 858; Beirne v. Continental-Equitable Title & Trust Co., 307 Pa. 570, 576, 161 A. 721, 722. If the right of revocation is not actually exercised, the validity of the trust remains as unaffected as if the power had not been reserved: Dickerson's Appeal, supra, 115 Pa. 210, 8 A. 69; Lines v. Lines, supra, 142 Pa. 167, 21 A. 810. Although the estate in remainder is subject to the possi-

bility of its being divested by a revocation, "the right to revoke, unexercised, is a dead thing": In re Dolan's Estate, supra, 279 Pa. 589, 124 A. 178. Nor can defendant force Flint to exercise the power. "Unless it is otherwise provided by statute a power of revocation reserved by the settlor cannot be reached by his creditors. If he revokes the trust and recovers the trust property, the creditors can reach the property; but they cannot compel him to revoke the trust for their benefit": Restatement, Trusts, § 330, comment o.

* * *

What we have here, then, is a deed under which (1) Flint has a life interest which is subject to seizure or attachment by defendant under its judgment, and (2) Flint's daughters or their children have an estate in remainder received by them, not as a testamentary gift, but as a present grant, and which, therefore, although subject to being divested if the reserved power of revocation or modification is exercised, is property which cannot be made liable for Flint's debt.

The decree is reversed and the record remanded with direction to enter a decree limiting proceedings in execution by defendant to the life interest of Flint in the premises; the parties to bear their own costs respectively.

NOTE

A creditor can reach the corpus of a trust created by the debtor in fraud of the creditor's claim. Thus if the settlor was insolvent when he created the trust, or the creation of the trust made him insolvent, the corpus of the trust can be reached by the settlor's existing creditors. According to the weight of authority the settlor's creditors can also reach the principal of a trust in which he receives the income and has a general power of appointment over the principal even though a taker in default is designated and the settlor was solvent when he created the trust and its creation did not make him insolvent. Retention of the income and the general power of appointment so closely approximates retention of beneficial ownership that it is thought unsound as a matter of policy to withhold the principal of the trust from the claims of the settlor's creditors. The reserved income can be reached by the settlor's creditors in all jurisdictions.

The Restatement Second, Trusts, § 330, Comment *o*, takes the position that in the absence of statutory provisions to the contrary, the settlor's creditors cannot reach either a power of revocation or the property covered thereby. The privilege of exercising the power is personal to the settlor and the retention of the power is thought not to approximate retention of beneficial ownership of the property subject to the power.[83]

83. In Johnson v. Commercial Bank, 284 Or. 675, 588 P.2d 1096 (1978), the settlor and his wife transferred all of their assets to a bank, reserving a life estate in himself, then in his wife, with successive life estates to their children for their lives and remainder absolutely to their grandchildren. The trust interests were subject to a spendthrift clause applicable to all beneficiaries. The settlor retained a power to revoke the trust or to alter it. A practical nurse cared for the settlor and his wife before their deaths but the estates of the decedents were insufficient to pay her some extra wages agreed upon. The court analogized the situation to that in which a settlor of a trust retains a life estate with a general power of appointment over the principal. In such a situation there is authority that the creditors of the settlor can reach the trust property as if the settlor owned it. See

Although the Bankruptcy Act of 1898,[84] § 70(a)(3) provided that all powers which the bankrupt could have exercised for his own benefit could be reached by the trustee in bankruptcy, such authority is not stated in the Bankruptcy Act of 1978.[85] There is a negative inference in § 541(b) of the 1978 Act that a trustee might reach such a power unless it is exercisable solely for the benefit of an entity other than the bankrupt; but there is no provision in § 541 explicitly conferring this authority upon the trustee. "Entity" is defined in § 101(14) of the 1978 Act as including estates, trusts and governmental organizations as well as natural persons. While there is an indication in the legislative materials that Congress thought the provisions of old § 70(a) were embraced in § 541 of the 1978 Act, the power references in the new legislation are obscure.

There are two types of state statutes relating to the right of a creditor of a settlor to reach a power of revocation reserved in a trust created by the settlor. One type provides in part: "When the grantor in a conveyance reserves to himself an unqualified power of revocation, he is thereafter deemed still to be the absolute owner of the estate conveyed, so far as the rights of his creditors and purchasers are concerned. * * *"[86] The second type provides in relevant part that "* * * where the creator of such trust reserves to himself for his own benefit a power of revocation, a court, at the suit of any creditor of the creator, may compel the exercise of such power of revocation so reserved, to the same extent and under the same conditions that such creator could have exercised the same. * * *"[87] It will be observed that statutes of the first type provide in effect that the settlor is owner of the trust corpus subject to the power of revocation reserved by him in so far as his creditors are concerned; whereas, the second type of statute authorizes creditors of the settlor to compel him to exercise a reserved power of revocation for their benefit to the extent of their claims. Hence it has been held under the second type of statute that creditors of the settlor cannot reach the trust property covered by a reserved power of revocation after the settlor's death for the obvious reason that he could not exercise the power after his death.

There is diversity of view as to whether a reserved power of revocation is property within the meaning of a statute providing that a transfer of personal property in trust for the use of the transferor "shall be void as against his existing or subsequent creditors."[88]

Chapter XIV, Section 4 infra. The court stated:

> "The right to revoke is essentially the same as a general power of appointment since the person having the right to revoke may acquire the property and then appoint or give it to whomever he pleases. There being no practical difference between the right to revoke and a power to appoint, we conclude that the rule stated by the above authorities * * * [that creditors of a settlor can reach property in which he retains a life estate coupled with a reserved general power of appointment] * * * should apply to this case. We conclude that plaintiff was entitled to reach the trust assets to pay her claim".

284 Or. at 681–82, 588 P.2d at 1099.

Holding that the creditor could look to the entire trust to satisfy her claim since the settlor's reserved power extended over the remainder, the court also held that the creditor could reach the trust assets after the death of the settlor, relying upon an Oregon statute. Accord, State Street Bank & Trust Co. v. Reiser, 7 Mass.App. 633, 389 N.E.2d 768 (1979).

84. 30 Stat. 546, 566 (1898) § 70(a)(3).

85. 11 U.S.C.A. § 501(b), P.L. 95–598, 92 Stat. 2549, 2594 (1978).

86. Mich.Comp. Laws Ann. § 556.128 (1981 Supp.).

87. E.g., Ohio Rev.Code, § 1335.01 (Page Repl. Vol. 1979).

88. Van Stewart v. Townsend, 176 Wash. 311, 28 P.2d 999, 92 A.L.R. 275

It seems well settled that the creditor of one who deposits money in a savings account in the name of the depositor as trustee for another, in a jurisdiction in which this transaction creates a so-called "tentative" or "Totten" trust, can reach the deposit in satisfaction of his claims. This is an exception to the general rule that in the absence of statute a creditor of a settlor cannot reach the trust property covered by a power of revocation reserved by the settlor. The reason for the exception is that the depositor has complete control over the deposit during his lifetime and therefore should be treated as the owner of the deposit in so far as his creditors are concerned—a result that might well have been reached, unaided by statute, in all the revocable trust cases, at least in so far as the non-trust assets of the settlor are insufficient to satisfy the claims of his creditors. The "tentative" or "Totten" trust is discussed in Chapter IX, Section 2.[89]

PROBLEM

Settlor established a living trust with a bank as one of the trustees. Settlor reserved the life income and named others as remainder beneficiaries. Both income and principal were subject to a spendthrift clause. A discretionary power was conferred upon the trustees to invade the principal of the trust for the settlor's maintenance or emergencies and to invest not more than 1/4 of the principal of the trust and additions thereto in favorable business ventures open to the settlor. The trust also provided:

> "Settlor reserves the right to change the interests of the beneficiaries as among themselves, to add other beneficiaries and to substitute other beneficiaries for those named herein, by his own act and without the consent of any Trustee or beneficiary, by writing delivered to the corporate Trustee or by will, but Settlor may amend other provisions hereof only with the written approval of the Trustees and he shall have no right to encroach upon or invade the principal of the trust, which shall be irrevocable."

The wife on a claim for maintenance and support and other creditors of the settlor sought to attach the income and principal of the trust. The bank concedes the wife may reach the *income* of the trust on her claim for support and maintenance. May the wife also reach the principal of the trust? May the other creditors reach the income? May the other creditors reach the principal? See Morton v. Morton, 394 Pa. 402, 147 A.2d 150 (1959); Shelley v. Shelley and Ware v. Gulda, appearing as principal cases in Section 5(2) of this Chapter.

(1934); Herd v. Chambers, 158 Kan. 614, 149 P.2d 583 (1944).

89. For discussion of the subject matter of this note see Restatement, Second, Trusts §§ 55–58, 330, I & IV Scott Trusts (3d Ed.1967) §§ 55–58, 330.12.

Chapter IX

TRUST LITIGATION PROBLEMS

Scope Note

In the preceding chapter we examined the essential elements of the private express trust. In this chapter we are concerned with the legal consequences of two types of informal transactions which create trusts and with the application of the trust device for business purposes in which some of the basic doctrines considered in the previous chapter are applied (or not applied) in the process of implementing commercial transactions and relationships. In the first of the informal transactions the declaration of trust or agreement to hold in trust is oral. In the second funds are deposited in a "bank" in trust for another named person. This might be simply a commercial transaction or a trust might have been intended. Then we examine trusts used as an employment incentive, an area in which a federal trust law seems to be developing and federal trust doctrine will be applied in litigation. The trust is also used as a security device and as a device to control other business organizations. Special litigation problems are presented in these contexts with special adaptation of trust law. Last we consider the trust used as a business organization, to operate a mutual fund for example, or to manage or develop land. Many state statutory provisions and federal statutes and regulations are operative in this area and some of the doctrines applied to private trusts in the preceding chapter are not applied in this business context.

SECTION 1. ORAL TRUSTS

In this Section legal problems are considered which are involved where a formal transfer of legal title is made but the trust agreement is oral. Thus, A may convey realty to B by deed which makes no reference to a trust, but the parties may have agreed orally that B is to hold title in trust for either the grantor A or a third party C. Such a transaction comes within the provisions of the English Statute of Frauds, [1] which provides as follows:

> "§ VII. And * * * from and after the said four and twentieth day of June all declarations or creations of trusts or

1. 29 Chas. II, c. 3 (1677).

confidences of any lands, tenements or hereditaments shall be manifested and proved by some writing signed by the party who is by law enabled to declare such trust or by his last will in writing or else they shall be utterly void and of none effect.

"§ VIII. PROVIDED always that where any conveyance shall be made of any lands or tenements by which a trust or confidence shall or may arise or result by the implication or construction of law or be transferred or extinguished by an act or operation of law then and in every such case such trust or confidence shall be of like force and effect as the same would have been if this statute had not been made. Anything hereinbefore contained to the contrary notwithstanding."

Most states have some form of statute either requiring that trusts of land be proved by a writing signed by the appropriate party or requiring that no trust of land be created except by writing.[2] It should be noted that such statutes apply only to real estate; and living trusts of personalty, such as stocks and bonds, can be created orally in all but a few states.[3] A number of jurisdictions have no counterpart to the English statute, and we must decide whether any other rules prevent the beneficiary of an oral trust of land from proving the existence of the trust and its terms. When the transaction is testamentary, as where the testator's will makes a bequest or devise to X with no indication of a trust, and Y alleges that a trust was intended for his benefit, the bar to proof of the oral trust is the Statute of Wills, applicable to both realty and personalty.

It is obvious that this Section presents essentially a litigation problem. Upon what theory can the alleged beneficiary base his case in order to escape the bar of the Statute of Frauds (or Wills)? What must he allege to get past the demurrer stage? How can he prove the facts alleged? There are three possible theories which we shall need to explore. Can the plaintiff sue on the express trust on the basis of any exceptions to the Statute of Frauds, such as part performance? Can the transferor recover on the basis of a resulting trust? (Because this is basic to many of these cases, we shall consider all varieties of resulting trusts at this point.) Can either the transferor or the beneficiary recover on some constructive trust theory,[4] and if so, on what basis? Since constructive and resulting trusts are stated exceptions to the English Statute quoted above, and the American counterparts, such trusts can of course be established by oral evidence.

Such transactions give rise to countless questions, and there is a huge body of case law dealing with these problems.

2. For a summary of the American statutory provisions, see Bogert, Trusts and Trustees (2d Ed. 1965) §§ 62–65.

3. See Ga.Code Ann. § 108–105 (1979 Repl.Vol.), W.Va.Code Ann. § 36–1–6 (1966) (requiring a writing for a declaration of trust but not for a transfer of personalty in trust). See also Andrews, "Creating Secret Trusts", 27 Convey. 92 (1963); Elphinstone, "Mischief of Secret Trusts", 77 L.Q.Rev. 69 (1961).

4. For constructive trusts review Chapter III, Section 4(4)(A), Note to Estate of Mahoney.

(1) STATES HAVING NO STATUTE BASED UPON SECTION SEVEN OF THE STATUTE OF FRAUDS

BRAME v. READ

Supreme Court of Appeals of Virginia, 1923.
136 Va. 219, 118 S.E. 117.

PRENTIS, J. The appellants, claiming under the will of Martha J. Read, filed their bill against the appellees, in which they sought to establish their title as equitable owners of a tract of land which the defendants claim as the heirs at law of Charles F. Read. The legal title is clearly in the appellees under a deed, dated November 18, 1876, whereby Arthur H. Davis, the father of Martha H. Read, reciting a consideration of natural love and affection for his daughter, and $500 due by him to his daughter for money received from her grandfather's estate, conveyed the land to Charles F. Read, her husband. The claim of the appellants is based upon the will of Martha J. Read, dated April 19, 1910, reading:

> "I desire that my husband, Chas. F. Read, shall have the use of the farm upon which we are now living during his life, and at his death, I desire it to go to my niece, Carrie A. Brame and John Arthur Brame equally. I also give to my husband, Chas. F. Read all interest in my sister's (Mary O. Davis) estate that may be coming to me in her personal property."

The case was heard upon the bill, answer and depositions filed by the parties. The trial court adjudged that the appellees were the legal and equitable owners of the property, and dismissed the bill. The appellants are here contending that this decree is erroneous.

One contention is that Charles F. Read took the legal title to the land subject to an express trust in favor of his wife. That an express trust in land may be set up by parol is perfectly well settled in this state. Young v. Holland, 117 Va. 433, 84 S.E. 637; Taylor v. Delaney, 118 Va. 203, 86 S.E. 831; Powers v. Long, 131 Va. 284, 108 S.E. 664; Page v. Page, 132 Va. 63, 110 S.E. 370. It is equally true, however, that in order to establish such a trust the declaration must be unequivocal and explicit, and the evidence thereof must be clear and convincing. In most cases, as in this, there is no longer any reason for debate as to the law, but the question is one of fact.

The facts here relied upon to establish the trust consist of the circumstances stated, and the testimony of several witnesses to the effect that Charles F. Read spoke of the land as his wife's land, as land that he only had a life interest in, and that it was Mr. Brame's children's land, and would go to these children when he died. One witness testified that he (Read) said that he told his wife not to convey it to him, but to let it go back to the house it came from. On the other hand, two witnesses, one of them a justice of the peace, who lived on an adjoining farm, testified that on one occasion Read was asked whether his land did not belong to his wife, and that his reply was, "No sir; Davis didn't believe in women owning land, and deeded the land to me—it is mine;" that, when a contract for the sale of timber on the land was drawn, the name of Read's wife was not mentioned, either in the contract or in the contemporaneous conversation; that he had always heard it called Mr. Read's land; that he never spoke in but one way to him about the land, and that no question about the title or ownership of the timber on the land was raised or suggested. Read made similar statements as to the ownership of the land to another witness. In addition to selling the timber upon the land and taking the proceeds thereof, he on three separate occasions borrowed money and executed deeds of trust securing such indebtedness, recited to be his own. In two of these deeds it was expressly provided that in case of a sale the surplus proceeds should be paid to him, or to his order, and in another that such residue should be "returned to the party of the first part." In addition to this there was a conveyance of 4 acres of the property, in which there was no suggestion that the land belonged to his wife. While one of the witnesses for the plaintiffs, who had been a commissioner of the revenue, testified that the land was listed for taxation in the name of "Pattie J. Read," it was shown conclusively that it was never so listed, but was listed in the names of "Charles F. Read and wife."

It is unnecessary to recite the evidence more in detail. To do so would merely accentuate its unconvincing character. A consideration thereof leads to the conclusion that the appellants have failed to sustain the burden cast upon them by law. The testimony relied on, when considered in connection with the testimony and the circumstances relied upon by the appellees, falls far short of being clear, cogent, and convincing. It doubtless indicates that, because the property was conveyed to Charles F. Read by his wife's father, it was her desire and his purpose to have it go to the appellants after his death. This purpose, however, was not executed by Read, and the title to real estate cannot be transferred by an unexecuted intention. There is no evidence that the grantor in the deed conveying the property to Charles F. Read made any declaration of trust in any way limiting or controlling this conveyance, which is absolute on its face. Such a declaration of a trust, to be effective, must be unequivocal and explicit. The only evidence appearing in this case contradicts such suggestion and excludes such an inference. He purposely conveyed it to the husband, and there is no reason to doubt from his contemporaneous declaration that he fully understood that the effect of his conveyance was to vest the legal and beneficial title in his grantee, Charles F. Read.

Even if the alleged declarations of Charles F. Read subsequent to the conveyance were established by convincing evidence, these alone would be insufficient to establish an equitable title in his wife. While his declarations would be held significant in support of an express trust, which had been impressed upon the land by the grantor when the conveyance was made, they are insufficient of themselves to create such a trust, which was not so impressed by the grantor at the time of the conveyance. To permit such subsequent declarations to have such effect would be to convey an estate in land by parol, which is expressly prohibited by statute. Jesser v. Armentrout's Ex'r, 100 Va. 666, 42 S.E. 681.

[Omitted is that portion of the opinion in which the court discussed and found invalid the appellant's claim that they should succeed on the ground that Charles F. Read had elected to take under the will.]

We find no error in the decree appealed from.

Affirmed.[5]

NOTE

In jurisdictions in which there is no statute explicitly requiring express trusts of interests in land to be created or proved by a signed writing the following situations must be distinguished: first, A conveys Blackacre to B by deed absolute on oral trust for C; second, A conveys Blackacre to B by deed absolute on oral trust for A; third, A orally declares himself trustee of Blackacre for B. In North Carolina it has been held in the second situation above, that the parol evidence rule precludes establishing the trust, although the trust may be shown in the first of the above situations.[6] It should make no difference whether the oral trust engrafted on a deed absolute is in favor of the grantor or a third person. The parol evidence rule either should apply or not apply in both situations. The Virginia court has rejected the dictum in Brame v. Read that the Virginia conveyancing statute (now Virginia Code § 55–5) precludes establishment of the oral trust in the third situation.[7] In both the first and third situations the beneficial interests in land are orally transferred to the beneficiary. If the conveyancing statute precluded establishment of the trust in the third situation it should also preclude establishment of the trust in the first situation—and the Virginia courts have been

5. Restatement, Second, Trusts § 38 states the effect of the parol evidence rule as follows:

"(1) If the owner of property transfers it inter vivos to another person by a written instrument in which it is declared that the transferee is to take the property for his own benefit, extrinsic evidence, in the absence of fraud, duress, mistake or other ground for reformation or rescission, is not admissible to show that he was intended to hold the property in trust.

"(2) If the owner of property transfers it inter vivos to another person by a written instrument in which it is declared that the transferee is to hold the property upon a particular trust, extrinsic evidence, in the absence of fraud, duress, mistake or other ground for reformation or rescission, is not admissible to show that he was intended to hold the property upon a different trust or to take it beneficially.

"(3) If the owner of property transfers it inter vivos to another person by a written instrument in which it is not declared that the transferee is to take the property for his own benefit or that he is to hold it in trust, extrinsic evidence may be admitted to show that he was intended to hold the property in trust either for the transferor or for a third party.

"(4) If the owner of property by a written instrument declares that he holds the property upon a particular trust, extrinsic evidence, in the absence of fraud, duress, mistake or other ground for reformation or rescission, is not admissible to show that he intended to hold the property upon a different trust or to hold it free of trust. * * *"

6. Gaylord v. Gaylord, 150 N.C. 222, 63 S.E. 1028 (1909). See Lord and Van Hecke, "Parol Trusts in North Carolina", 8 N.C.L.Rev. 152 (1929). The adoption of the Uniform Trust Act in North Carolina has been said to change the rule in the Gaylord case. See 17 N.C.L.Rev. 1, 396 (1939).

7. Burns v. The Equitable Associates, 220 Va. 1020, 1032–1033, 265 S.E.2d 737, 744–745 (1980) (citing casebook).

uniformly of the view that the trust can be established by parol evidence in the first situation.

The Restatement of Trusts summarizes the diverse views on these and related matters as follows: [8] "In some States there is no statute like Section 7 of the English Statute of Frauds by its terms applicable to the creation of trusts * * *. In some of these States a statutory provision requiring a writing in the case of a contract as to land is held applicable to the creation of trusts. In some of these Statues a statutory provision requiring a writing in the case of a conveyance of an interest in land is held applicable to the creation of trusts. In some of these States a writing is required where the owner of an interest in land declares himself trustee, but not where he transfers the interest to another in trust. In some of these States a writing is required where the owner of an interest in land transfers it in trust for himself but not where he transfers it in trust for a third person. * * *"

---

(2) IMPACT OF STATUTES OF FRAUDS ON PROOF OF THE EXPRESS TRUST

In a jurisdiction having a statute which is construed to require that an express living trust of an interest in land be manifested and proved by a signed writing, it is necessary that the essential elements of the trust be stated in the writing. Hence, the writing relied upon as satisfying the statute must set forth with reasonable definiteness the trust property, the beneficiaries and the trust purpose. The writing need not be addressed or delivered to anyone. It is unnecessary that the writing be intended to satisfy the requirement of the statute. The intent with which the writing is executed is immaterial. The writing may consist of more than one document but the documents must be connected with each other. This connection may be established by physical attachment; by inclosure in the same receptacle; by incorporation by reference if the incorporating document is signed by the party to be charged; and by the face of each document clearly referring to the same transaction.[9] Oral testimony cannot connect separate documents.

In a few jurisdictions there are statutes which are construed to require that the trust be "created" or "declared" and not merely

8. Restatement, Second, Trusts § 39, Comment *a*. In Stewart v. Damron, 63 Ariz. 158, 160 P.2d 321 (1945), the Court said: "Our statute of frauds does not contain any direct provision pertaining to the creation of trusts. The seventh section * * * was not adopted by our Legislature. * * * (But) this court has held an express trust to be within the statute of frauds. Cashion v. Bank of Arizona, 30 Ariz. 307, 245 P. 360. The holding was approved in MacRae v. MacRae, 37 Ariz. 307, 294 P. 280. Even though the wisdom of those decisions might be doubted, we feel that the matter is foreclosed by the rule: *Stare decisis et non quieta novere.*"

9. The process of integrating a memorandum is analogous to the process of integrating a will. See Chapter V, Section 5(3).

manifested and proved by a signed writing. In these jurisdictions it is possible that the writing itself may be required to contain the declaration of trust. If the trust is created by the owner of an interest in land declaring himself trustee thereof for the benefit of another, the declaration may be required to be set out in a writing signed by the settlor. The owner of an interest in land may transfer it to another in trust by an instrument of transfer containing a statement of the trust. Such an instrument must be signed by the transferor. If the statement of trust does not appear on the face of the instrument of transfer, the requirements of the statute are satisfied if the settlor or trustee signs a separate document containing the statement of trust and prepared at the time of the transfer. In that event the transfer and the signing of the separate document containing the statement of trust must be part of the same transaction.

In a jurisdiction in which the trust is merely required to be manifested and proved, not created, by a signed writing, the problem of when and by whom the writing must be signed is somewhat involved. If the owner of an interest in land declares himself trustee of the interest for the benefit of another, the writing evidencing the trust may be signed by the declarant prior to, at the time of, or subsequent to the declaration. If the writing is signed by the declarant subsequent to the declaration, it will satisfy the statute only if it is signed before the declarant transfers the interest to a third person. After the declarant has transferred his interest to another, he is a stranger to the title and a writing then signed by him would lack the credibility which attaches to what amounts to a declaration against interest. In this connection it makes no difference whether the transferee is a bona fide purchaser for value. For example, X, owning Blackacre in fee simple absolute, orally declares himself trustee of Blackacre for A. Thereafter X conveys Blackacre to B by way of gift. B knows of the oral trust. Subsequently, X signs a writing evidencing the oral declaration of trust. B holds Blackacre free of the trust.

In a "manifested and proved" type jurisdiction, when the owner of an interest in land transfers it inter vivos to another person in trust, a writing properly evidencing the trust will satisfy the statute if it is signed by the transferor prior to, or at the time of, the transfer; or, if it is signed by the transferee, prior to, at the time of, or subsequent to the transfer. But if it is signed by the transferee subsequent to the transfer it must be signed by him before he transfers the interest to another. It makes no difference that the latter is not a bona fide purchaser. But he must be a transferee. For example, X, owning Blackacre in fee simple absolute, conveys Blackacre to A on oral trust for B. Thereafter, C obtains a judgment against A which is docketed so that C acquires a lien on Blackacre. Subsequently, A signs a writing evidencing the oral trust. This writing is duly recorded. The statute is satisfied unless by a recording act or by estoppel C is in the position of a bona fide purchaser.

It has been held that an oral trust of an interest in land is enforceable, although the requirements of the Statute of Frauds are not satisfied if, after the oral trust is created, the beneficiary takes possession of the land with the consent of the trustee and makes substantial improvements or repairs, or pays taxes, or otherwise exercises dominion over the land. Typically, these decisions are explained on the ground of "part performance" of the oral trust by analogy to the doctrine of "part performance" applicable to oral contracts for the sale of an interest in land. The trustee is estopped to deny the enforceability of the trust because, with his consent, the beneficiary has substantially changed his position in reliance upon the trust being enforceable. Courts differ in the liberality with which the doctrine of part performance is applied to oral trusts and in what acts constitute part performance. Where recognized, however, the doctrine is applicable whether the owner of an interest in land declares himself trustee thereof for another or whether he transfers the interest to another in trust for the transferor or a third person. But, by the prevailing view, acts by the trustee rather than the beneficiary do not constitute such part performance as to make the oral trust enforceable. For example, the fact that the alleged trustee turns over the income from the alleged trust property to the alleged beneficiary is not viewed as part performance. The act might be merely a gift. Basically, the question seems to be this: does the act relied upon as constituting part performance sufficiently corroborate the parol evidence of the existence of the alleged oral trust to offset the danger of the fact-finder's being convinced by false testimony that an oral trust was created when in fact no trust was created? If the beneficiary of the trust is in possession of the land prior to the time that the alleged trust is created, the trust does not become enforceable because he continues in possession with the consent of the trustee. Payment of consideration for the creation of the trust is not a sufficient part performance to make the trust enforceable without the required writing.

Although the seventh section of the English Statute of Frauds provides that oral trusts of interests in land "shall be utterly void and of none effect", the statute is construed to render such trusts voidable only by the trustee or a person succeeding to his interest in the trust property. American statutes are similarly construed. Thus, an oral trust of an interest in land is enforceable, despite failure to comply with the signed writing requirement of the statute, unless the trustee or a person succeeding to his interest in the trust property asserts the statute as a defense. Persons succeeding to the interest of the trustee are the following: a person to whom the trustee transfers the trust property by inter vivos conveyance, whether or not consideration is given for the transfer and whether or not the transferee has knowledge, actual or constructive, of the oral trust; those to whom the trustee devises the trust property and the heirs of the trustee who inherit the property from him; attaching and judgment creditors of the trustee; and the trustee in bankruptcy of the trustee of the oral trust. If the beneficiary of a trust of land insures his interest in the trust against loss by fire, his claim on the policy is enforceable against the company even though the trust is oral. The insurance company, being neither the trustee nor his successor in interest to the trust property, cannot escape liability on the ground that the trust is unenforceable and the beneficiary without insurable interest in the trust property, because the insurance company cannot successfully assert the statute.

Since the trustee of an orally created inter vivos trust of an interest in land has the election of asserting or waiving the Statute of Frauds, no one can successfully complain if the trustee performs the trust or signs a writing satisfying the requirements of the statute and thus makes the trust enforceable by the beneficiary or his successor in interest. Thus, the beneficiaries of an oral trust are protected if the trustee performs the trust or signs a written statement of the trust satisfying the Statute of Frauds even though the trustee is insolvent when he performs the trust or signs the written statement. Failure to assert the statute is not a fraud on the creditors or spouse of the trustee. The trust is valid and enforceable until avoided by a person entitled to assert the statute.[10]

When an oral trust is created of an interest in land and the land is thereafter sold by the trustee, is there an enforceable trust of the proceeds of the sale, assuming the land is situated in a state in which a signed writing is required for a trust of land but is not required for a trust of personal property? If the trustee orally declares himself trustee of the proceeds of the sale, an enforceable trust is created at the time of his declaration. But the trust does not become enforceable *merely* because the trustee sells the land and receives the proceeds of sale.

If, however, the owner of land orally declares himself trustee of the land and at the same time orally agrees to sell the land and hold the proceeds in trust, most of the courts have viewed the transaction as separable into two undertakings. The first of these undertakings relates to the land itself and is unenforceable because of the Statute of Frauds. The second of these undertakings relates to the proceeds of sale, personal property, and is not within the Statute of Frauds. The trustee cannot be compelled to hold the land in trust nor can he be compelled to sell the land. But if he does sell the land, the agreement to hold the proceeds in trust is enforceable, provided it is supported by consideration. It seems, however, that a trust of the proceeds does not automatically come into existence on sale of the land. The agreement to hold the proceeds of the sale in trust is, in effect, an agreement to hold after-acquired personal property in trust. In such a situation a trust does not automatically arise when the property is acquired, but there is a contract to hold the property in trust which can be enforced specifically if the subject is a unique chattel or land or made the basis of an action for damages for breach of contract.[11] In the case under consideration, the only remedy of the promisee would seem to be an action at law for damages.

10. For a detailed discussion of the proof of oral trusts, see Bogert, Trusts and Trustees (2d Ed., 1965) ch. 5; I Scott, Trusts (3d Ed., 1967) §§ 39–43, 46–51; Harrington, "Part Performance of Oral Trusts", 30 Mich.L.Rev. 289 (1931).

11. See Chapter VIII Section 4(1) and (2).

It makes little practical difference in most jurisdictions whether there is a trust of the proceeds or a valid contract to hold the proceeds in trust. Some courts discuss the case as though the proceeds of the sale are held in trust. In these jurisdictions the transaction may be an exception to the general rule that a trust does not come into existence automatically at the moment a person acquires property which he has previously agreed to hold in trust. It can be argued that the oral trust with respect to land and the proceeds of sale becomes a present, although unenforceable, trust on the date of the declaration. The bar to enforcement, the Statute of Frauds, is removed when the trust property is converted from realty to personalty. This rationale rejects the view that the transaction is separable into two undertakings. Furthermore, under this rationale, for which there seems to be no judicial support, it would make no difference whether or not a consideration was given for the oral declaration.

The principles applicable to an oral declaration by the owner of a trust of land and the proceeds of its sale apply when the oral trust of land and the proceeds of its sale is created by the owner's transfer of the land to another on oral trust for the transferor or a third party. In this situation, however, under the theory of "separable undertakings" there will always be consideration for the trustee's agreement to hold the property in trust. The transfer of the land to him constitutes consideration to support his promise.

If the trustee of an enforceable oral trust of personal property exchanges the personal property for land or sells the personal property and invests the proceeds in land, the trust continues to be enforceable. When validly created, a trust does not become unenforceable because of a change in the trust property whether or not the conversion of the property into land constitutes a breach of trust.

If the owner of a chose in action secured by a mortgage on land orally declares himself trustee of the chose in action and the mortgage, the trust is enforceable with respect to the mortgage and the note. This is true even though the mortgaged land is in a jurisdiction having a statute requiring a signed writing for the creation of an enforceable trust of an interest in land. The same is true if the owner of the chose in action transfers it and the mortgage to another on oral trust for the transferor or a third party. In the law of mortgages the security follows the debt by operation of law unless a contrary intent is manifested. Thus, in effect, a trust of the mortgage is created by operation of law so that the signed writing requirement is inapplicable to the trust by reason of Section eight of the Statute of Frauds. The justification of the rule that the security follows the debt is that the debt cannot be collected without surrendering the security and the security cannot be redeemed by the debtor without paying the debt. There will be an impasse unless the debt and security are held by the same person.[12]

12. For a discussion of the problems raised by conversion of the res of an oral trust of personalty to land see Restatement, Second, Trusts § 52; I Scott, Trusts (3d Ed., 1967) §§ 52, 52.1.

PROBLEMS

1. X, the owner of Blackacre, orally declares himself trustee of Blackacre for A. Thereafter X conveys Blackacre to B, who is not a bona fide purchaser. Subsequently, and while B holds title to Blackacre, X signs a memorandum of the trust for A. Blackacre is situated in a jurisdiction having a statute similar to Section seven of the Statute of Frauds. Does B hold Blackacre free of the trust? See Restatement, Second, Trusts § 41, Illustration 1.

2. X, the owner of Blackacre, orally declares himself trustee of Blackacre for A. Thereafter X enters into a written contract with B to convey Blackacre to B. Subsequently, X, while still holding title to Blackacre, signs a memorandum stating that he holds Blackacre in trust for A. Blackacre is situated in a state having a statute similar to Section seven of the Statute of Frauds. Can A enforce an express trust? See Restatement, Second, Trusts § 41, Illustration 4.

3. X conveys Blackacre by deed absolute to A on oral trust for B. Thereafter A becomes bankrupt. Subsequently, A signs a memorandum stating that he holds Blackacre in trust for B. Blackacre is situated in a state having a statute similar to Section seven of the Statute of Frauds. Can B enforce an express trust? See Bryant v. Klatt, 2 F.2d 167 (D.C.N.Y.1924) (Since the decision in this case, § 70 of the Bankruptcy Act has been amended by the Chandler Act, 11 U.S.C.A. § 110. This is the basis of current 11 U.S.C.A. § 541(e) which reads: "The estate shall have the benefit of any defense available to the debtor as against an entity other than the estate, including statutes of limitation, statutes of frauds, usury, and other personal defenses. A waiver of any such defense by the debtor after the commencement of the case does not bind the estate.

4. X conveys Blackacre by deed absolute to A, a bachelor, upon an oral trust for B. Subsequently A marries. Thereafter, and while A holds title to Blackacre, he signs a memorandum stating that he holds Blackacre in trust for B. Blackacre is situated in a jurisdiction having a statute similar to section seven of the Statute of Frauds. Common law dower is recognized in the jurisdiction. Does A's wife have a dower interest in Blackacre? See Bartlett v. Tinsley, 175 Mo. 319, 75 S.W. 143 (1903); Jones v. Jones, 281 Ill. 595, 117 N.E. 1013 (1917); I Scott, Trusts (3d Ed., 1967) § 42.3.

5. X, the owner of Blackacre, orally declares himself trustee of Blackacre for A. Thereafter, X enters into a written contract with B to convey Blackacre to B. Subsequently, pursuant to the terms of the oral trust, X conveys Blackacre to A. Blackacre is situated in a state having a statute similar to Section seven of the Statute of Frauds. Is A entitled to keep Blackacre? See Restatement, Second, Trusts § 43, Illustration 3.

6. X, the owner of Blackacre, orally declares himself trustee of Blackacre for A. Thereafter, X conveys Blackacre to B as a gift. B has knowledge of the oral trust. Blackacre is situated in a jurisdiction having a statute similar to Section seven of the Statute of Frauds. May B hold Blackacre clear of the trust? See Moynihan v. Murphy, 253 Mass. 110, 148 N.E. 380 (1925); I Scott, Trusts (3d Ed., 1967) § 51.

(3) RESULTING TRUSTS

After the English Chancellor began to enforce *uses* it was contended that a *use* for the conveyor or the person furnishing the consideration for the conveyance was presumed if no consideration was furnished by the conveyee and no *use* was expressed for the conveyee. The contention was made in three related situations.

1.

A has an estate in fee simple in "Blackacre". A makes a feoffment to B and his heirs. No *use* is expressed and B pays no consideration.

2.

B has an estate in fee simple in "Blackacre". A pays B for a feoffment to C and his heirs. No *use* is expressed and C pays no consideration.

3.

A has an estate in fee simple in "Blackacre". A makes a feoffment to B and his heirs to the *use* of C for life. There is no disposition of the *use* in remainder. Neither B nor C pays consideration for the conveyance.

In medieval England most conveyances were to the *use* of the conveyor or another. When no *use* was expressed, the Chancellor presumed that a gratuitous conveyee of a legal estate was not to enjoy the *use* and concluded that the *use* should "result" to the conveyor or the person who paid consideration for the conveyance.[13] In the first situation, A was presumed to have a resulting *use* of "Blackacre" in fee simple. In the second situation, C was presumed to hold "Blackacre" on a resulting *use* for A because A paid the consideration for the transfer. In the third situation, A had a resulting *use* of "Blackacre" in fee simple subject to the *use* for the life of C.

Enactment of the Statute of Uses[14] and the Statute of Frauds caused no immediate modification of the resulting *use* doctrine. The Statute of Uses executed the resulting *use* by passing legal title to the *cestui*.[15] Section VIII of the Statute of Frauds exempted trusts

13. A feoffment is used in the three examples but the doctrine of resulting *use* applied to fines and recoveries grants and possibly releases. The presumption of resulting *use* was rebutted easily and yielded when a consideration was given by the conveyee or recited in a deed, or when the conveyance was to a natural object of the bounty of the conveyor or payor of consideration.

14. 27 Hen. VIII, c. 10 (1536).

15. The doctrine of resulting use had probably crystallized before the statute was enacted. See I Scott, Trusts (3d Ed., 1967) § 73.

by operation of law from the requirement of a writing made by Section VII, as we have seen previously.

But the influence of the two statutes upon subsequent legal practices narrowed the area within which the resulting *use* doctrine was applied, the presumption of resulting *use* raised in an ordinary gratuitous conveyance being changed to a presumption of gift.[16] The Statute of Uses tended to weaken the custom of conveying land to the *use* of the conveyor which had been the basis for the presumption of resulting use. New forms of conveyance which recited a *use* would rebut the presumption as it was applied originally.[17] The Statute of Frauds influenced the development of the parol evidence rule. This rule gave ground for argument that a recitation of consideration or *use* in a deed could not be contradicted by parol evidence if the operation of the deed would be altered.[18]

In the United States a presumption of resulting trust is raised in three situations only. (1) A purchase money resulting trust is presumed when one person furnishes consideration for the transfer of land or personal property to another. (2) When a gratuitous private express trust fails, a resulting trust is presumed for the benefit of the settlor or his successors in interest. (3) When the *res* of a gratuitous private express trust is excessive for the purpose specified by the settlor, a resulting trust of the excess is presumed for the benefit of the settlor or his successors in interest.[19]

The purchase money resulting trust presumption has been justified on the ground that it conforms to the probable intention of a person who pays consideration for the transfer of property to another. A person who makes a gratuitous conveyance probably intends to make a gift. But a person who pays the purchase price for transfer of property to another may intend to facilitate a resale of the property, secure a debt, impose duties of management upon the

16. The presumption of resulting *use* was applied to a gratuitous conveyance in the Seventeenth Century. Elliott v. Elliott, 2 Ch.Cas. 231, 22 Eng.Rep. 922 (1677). By the middle of the Eighteenth Century a presumption of gift was applied when a consideration not in fact given was recited in the conveyance. Lloyd v. Spillet, 2 Atk. 148, 26 Eng.Rep. 493 (1740). The Law of Property Act, 15 Geo. V, c. 20, § 60(3)(1925) abolished the presumption of resulting trust when the conveyor receives no consideration and no express trust is stated. With the possible exception of Collins v. Collins, 46 Ariz. 485, 52 P.2d 1169 (1935), there are no modern decisions in the United States in which a resulting trust has been presumed in a gratuitous conveyance for the benefit of the conveyor. See Campbell v. Noble, 145 Ala. 233, 41 So. 745 (1906); Champion v. Champion, 110 Colo. 153, 132 P.2d 185 (1942); Restatement, Second, Trusts § 405.

17. Conveyances by bargain and sale and lease and release mention a *use* and usually a consideration furnished by the conveyee. A *use* is mentioned in a covenant to stand seised. Conveyances in the form of grants mention a consideration and *use*.

18. By the operation of the Statute of Frauds and the Statute of Enrollments the principal conveyancing forms that survived the Statute of Uses or were devised after its enactment were required to be written. A grant was always by deed and a release was required to be in writing at common law.

19. See Restatement, Second, Trusts §§ 411, 430, 440. The resulting trust doctrine applies to charitable trusts but may have no effect because of the exercise of the *cy pres* power by a court of equity. Resulting trust presumptions are applied whether the trust res is land or personal property.

transferee or avoid the claims of creditors. A person normally expects some return on his investment.[20]

The legislatures of a number of states have abolished the purchase money resulting trust presumption with certain exceptions.[21] Although a *bona fide* purchaser for value will cut off the equity of the *cestui* of a purchase money resulting trust, the existence of the presumption renders land titles unstable and stimulates litigation. Recitations of consideration and *use* in a recorded deed are not binding upon a complainant who seeks a purchase money resulting trust.[22] The courts have admitted parol evidence to show whose money was used for the purchase and that no *use* for the grantee was intended by the grantor. The evidence is usually admitted without discussion by the court.[23] It has been stated that the evidence is admitted as an exception to the parol evidence rule.[24] The suggestion has been made that the deed recites only that the grantee furnished the consideration and does not recite whose money it was. Hence the introduction of evidence to show the actual source of consideration does not contradict the language of the deed but only rebuts a presumption that the purchase price belonged to the grantee.[25] The evidence does not prevent the deed from operating to pass title even when the language of the deed is contradicted. Professor Bogert has remarked that the recitation of consideration in a deed is a formality and is not adapted to the various facts of different situations [26] and the same observation may be made concerning the recitation of *use* in a deed.

Although apparently not a ground for legislative abolition of the purchase money resulting trust presumption, the objection has been made that the use of the presumption to circumvent the requirement of the Statute of Frauds that an express trust be proved by writing may open the door to the perjured testimony which the Statute of Frauds was intended to prevent. If one person pays consideration for the transfer of land to another and there is an oral agreement that the conveyee will hold the land in trust for the payor, Section VII of the Statute of Frauds prevents proof of an express trust unless there is a writing. But a purchase money resulting trust is a trust

20. See Restatement, Second, Trusts § 440 et seq.

21. E.g., Ind.Stat.Ann. §§ 30–1–9–6, 30–1–9–8 (1972). Kan.Stat.Ann. §§ 58–2406, 58–2408 (1964). The statutes apply to purchase money resulting trusts of land and not to purchase money resulting trusts of personal property. The statutes permit application of the purchase money resulting trust presumption if title was taken by another without the payor's consent or if the title taker purchased with money used in breach of trust. The Indiana and Kansas statutes permit application of the presumption if there was an oral agreement that the grantee would hold the property for the payor of consideration. In several states the purchase money resulting trust presumption is set forth in statutory form.

22. Much the same problem arises when a bill of sale recites payment of consideration by the vendee of personal property.

23. E.g., Brooks v. Union Trust and Realty Co., 146 Cal. 134, 79 P. 843 (1905) (recital of consideration paid by grantee); Stratton v. Dialogue, 16 N.J.Eq. 70, 71 (1863) (recital of use for grantee).

24. Cotton v. Wood, 25 Iowa 43, 47 (1868).

25. Pritchard v. Brown, 4 N.H. 397, 17 Am.Dec. 431 (1828).

26. Bogert, Trusts and Trustees (2d Ed., 1965) § 454.

by operation of law which may be proved without a writing under Section VIII of the Statute. If the payor raises a purchase money resulting trust, the oral agreement is regarded as confirming the presumption or as surplusage. It has been suggested that the public policy to prevent unjust enrichment of the conveyee in this situation outweighs the danger of perjured testimony.[27]

The purchase money resulting trust presumption is applied in a majority of states in spite of the objections made to its application. The courts have required clear and convincing evidence to entitle the complainant to a decree,[28] have been liberal in admitting evidence to rebut the presumption, and have shown a marked reticence to assist the complainant when title has been placed in another for an illegal purpose.[29]

The payor must prove that he furnished the consideration for the transfer in order to raise the presumption.[30] The presumption may then be rebutted by parol evidence of the declarations of the payor before, at the time of, or subsequent to the transfer, or circumstances surrounding the transaction which indicate that the payment was made as a gift, loan, or in payment of a debt. The presumption may be rebutted in part. It may be shown that the payor intended a life estate for his use although he paid consideration for a transfer in fee simple.[31]

The consideration must be the property of the payor at the time of the conveyance. No resulting trust arises if the payment is made as a loan to the conveyee since the money becomes the property of the conveyee by virtue of the loan.[32] The payor has an equitable lien upon the subject matter of the conveyance to secure repayment of the loan if there is an agreement to that effect.[33] Nor is there a resulting trust if the payor furnishes the consideration to satisfy a debt due the conveyee. The situation is the same as if the payor repaid the debt to the conveyee and the conveyee then furnished the purchase price to the conveyor.[34] If the conveyee pays the considera-

27. See V Scott, Trusts (3d Ed.1967) 3325. As to the Missouri practice, see Nelson, "Purchase Money Resulting Trusts in Land in Missouri", 33 Missouri L.Rev. 552 (1968).

28. E.g., Powell v. Race, 151 Fla. 536, 10 So.2d 142 (1942).

29. E.g., Houlton v. Prosser, 118 Colo. 304, 194 P.2d 911 (1948) (illegal cohabitation part consideration for transfer); Culley v. Carr, 137 N.J. Eq. 516, 45 A.2d 850 (1946) (transfer to defeat claim of spouse for separate maintenance for self and children); Harrell v. Fiveash, 182 Ga. 362, 185 S.E. 327 (1936) (transfer in fraud of creditors). See Oyama v. California, 332 U.S. 633, 68 S.Ct. 269, 92 L. Ed. 249 (1948) (avoidance of alien land law).

30. The transferee may have money of the payor in his possession and apply it to the purchase with the payor's consent. The presumption will be raised in this situation, but if the payment is without the consent of the payor, the appropriate remedy is a constructive trust.

31. Larisey v. Larisey, 93 S.C. 450, 77 S.E. 129 (1913).

32. E.g., Pierce v. Harrison, 199 Ga. 197, 33 S.E.2d 680 (1945); Restatement, Second, Trusts § 445.

33. E.g., Leonard v. Duncan, 245 Ala. 320, 16 So.2d 879 (1944); but see Duncan v. Leonard, 251 Ala. 333, 37 So.2d 210 (1948) (evidence held insufficient to establish resulting trust or lien).

34. E.g., McDougall v. Servel, 50 Idaho 9, 292 P. 590 (1930); Restatement, Second, Trusts § 446. There is, of course, no resulting trust if the payment

tion as a loan to another, there is a resulting trust in favor of the person to whom the loan was made.[35] The conveyee holds the property as security for repayment of the loan.[36]

The purchase price must be furnished by the payor, or the payor must assume a binding obligation to furnish it before or at the time legal title is conveyed to the conveyee.[37] The resulting trust arises at the time legal title is transferred or not at all.[38] For example, if the payor agrees to pay a note given to the conveyor by the conveyee, there is no resulting trust in favor of the payor if the agreement to pay the note is made after the conveyee takes title.[39] The payor is subrogated to any lien that the conveyor might have upon the property for payment of the purchase price when the payor exonerates the note of the conveyee.[40] On the other hand, a resulting trust will arise for the payor if he gives his own note to the conveyor or agrees to exonerate the note of the conveyee before or at the time the transfer of legal title takes place.[41] If the conveyee is obligated to pay the purchase price to the conveyor and is compelled to pay, the conveyee has a security interest in the property and cannot be compelled to convey to the payor until he is reimbursed.[42]

Proof that the payor paid part of the consideration for transfer of the legal title gives rise to a presumption of resulting trust in such proportionate interest in the property as the amount of payment bears to the total purchase price.[43] An agreement that the payor

is made as a gift to the conveyee. Restatement, Second, Trusts § 447.

35. E.g., Crain v. Keenan, 218 Ark. 375, 236 S.W.2d 731 (1951); Restatement, Second, Trusts § 448. If the conveyee pays consideration to satisfy a debt due a creditor, there is a resulting trust for the latter. Restatement, Second, Trusts § 449. There is also a resulting trust for a third party if someone other than the conveyee pays consideration as a loan to a third party or to satisfy a debt due to him. Restatement, Second, Trusts §§ 451, 452. But if someone other than the conveyee pays consideration as a gift to a third party no resulting trust arises. Delivery is required for an effective gift. Hence the purchase money never becomes the property of the third party. If someone other than the conveyee purports to make the gift, it may be possible to establish a constructive trust for the purported donor, although this is impossible if the conveyee is the donor in the particular situation. The third party will have a remedy only if an effective express trust has been declared for his benefit. Restatement, Second, Trusts §§ 450–453.

36. Restatement, Second, Trusts § 448, Comment *b*.

37. Restatement, Second, Trusts § 457.

38. Legal title remains in the transferee until the resulting trust is established judicially and a conveyance to the payor ordered. Bona fide purchasers for value are protected, but this does not mean that the beneficial interest does not arise at the time legal title is transferred to the person held as resulting trustee.

39. E.g., Moat v. Moat, 301 Mass. 469, 17 N.E.2d 710 (1938); Restatement, Second, Trusts, § 457, Comment *a*.

40. Allen v. Caylor, 120 Ala. 251, 24 So. 512, 74 Am.St.Rep. 31 (1898), Restatement, Second, Trusts § 457, Comment *a*. The payor is entitled in any event to restitution of his payment by the title holder. Malone v. Romano, 95 N.J.Eq. 291, 127 A. 91 (1923).

41. E.g., Hansen v. Bear Film Co., 158 P.2d 779 (Cal.App.1945) (Note by payor); Watson v. Poore, 18 Cal.2d 302, 115 P.2d 478 (1941) (agreement to exonerate); Restatement, Second, Trusts § 456.

42. Restatement, Second, Trusts § 456, Comment *d*.

43. The presumption is raised even though the consideration is not in money. Restatement, Second, Trusts § 455. When it is shown that part consideration was furnished by the payor two major problems may arise. (1) It may be hard to prove that a definite proportion of the consideration was furnished by the pay-

should take a beneficial interest in excess of that indicated by his payment is unenforceable unless proved by a writing as required by the Statute of Frauds.[44] An agreement that the payor should take an interest less than that indicated by his payment is probably admissible to rebut partially the presumption of resulting trust raised by part payment.[45]

A presumption of resulting trust may be rebutted by evidence other than that relating to the source or character of the consideration. Declarations of intention made by the payor before, at the time of, or subsequent to the time of transfer of title are admissible to show a gift or loan. The relationship between the payor and the transferee of legal title is significant in many cases. If a parent pays consideration for transfer of legal title to his child,[46] or if a husband pays consideration for transfer of legal title to his wife,[47] a gift rather than a trust is presumed. But there is a presumption of trust when the transfer of legal title is to one not a natural object of the payor's bounty, as when a child pays for transfer of legal title to his parent,[48]

or. (2) Payment of a definite *aliquant* part of the purchase price may give rise to a presumption that the payment was made as a gift or loan. Contributions at intervals by the payor to a general fund which has been set aside by the transferee and to which the transferee contributes and from which the transferee withdraws the purchase price may be so indefinite as to raise a presumption of gift or loan. Restatement, Second, Trusts § 454, Comment *c*. Significance has been attached to the fact that the payor did not pay an *aliquot* part of the purchase price or did not have an agreement for an *aliquot* portion of the property as an indication that the payor intended to make a loan or gift. *"Aliquot"* means a fractional part of a whole that can be reduced to a numerator of "1". (1/2, 9/27, 8/32). An *"aliquant"* fraction cannot be reduced to a numerator of "1". (10/27, 19/40). Courts which apply variations of the *"aliquot-aliquant"* rule have said that the words are not used in a mathematical sense. All of the courts agree that a resulting trust is presumed when there is payment of an *aliquot* part of the purchase price and an agreement for a corresponding *aliquot* part of the property. E.g., Young v. Greer, 250 Ala. 641, 35 So.2d 619 (1948). In the usual case there is some agreement between the payor and transferee concerning the payor's interest which cannot be enforced as an express trust because of the Statute of Frauds. If an *aliquot* part of the purchase price has been furnished, most of the courts raise a presumption of resulting trust without corroborating evidence that a trust was intended. E.g., Stayton v. Stayton, 198 Ark. 1178, 132 S.W.2d 830 (1939). Even if an *aliquant* part of the purchase price is paid most of the courts raise a presumption of resulting trust if there is additional evidence that a loan or gift was not intended. E.g., Fox v. Shanley, 94 Conn. 350, 109 A. 249 (1920) (39/55). But in a few states payment of an *aliquant* part will raise a resulting trust only if there is some agreement for an *aliquot* part of the property in favor of the payor. E.g., American Surety Co., Inc. v. Hattrem, 138 Or. 358, 3 P.2d 1109, 6 P.2d 1087 (1932). *"Aliquot-aliquant"* distinctions bearing upon the presumption of resulting trust are rejected by the Restatement. Restatement, Second, Trusts § 454, Comment *b*.

44. Restatement, Second, Trusts § 454, Comment *i*. It may be possible to prove an express trust for the payor if Section VII of the Statute of Frauds is not in force in the state.

45. See Bogert, Trusts and Trustees (2d Ed., 1965) § 462(b).

46. E.g., Daly v. Lanucha, 14 N.J. Super. 225, 81 A.2d 826 (1951). The same presumption arises when the payor is in loco parentis to the transferee. E.g., Mott v. Iossa, 119 N.J.Eq. 185, 181 A. 689 (1935) (stepfather).

47. E.g., Blaine v. Blaine, 63 Ariz. 100, 159 P.2d 786 (1945).

48. E.g., Adams v. Adams, 348 Mo. 1041, 156 S.W.2d 610 (1941).

a wife pays for transfer of title to her husband,[49] or legal title is transferred to a stranger.[50]

The presumption of resulting trust raised by payment of consideration may be corroborated by evidence of an oral agreement between the parties; their acts before, at the time of, and after the transfer; and other circumstances surrounding the transaction which indicate that a gift or loan was not intended. If a husband pays consideration for a transfer to his wife, an admission by the wife after the conveyance that she held the land in trust for her husband, evidence indicating that the husband exercised rights of ownership over the property, and evidence that a gift by the husband would be improvident, has been held to rebut a presumption of gift and confirm a presumption of resulting trust.[51] If a parent pays consideration for a conveyance to a child, the financial condition,[52] age,[53] health and business ability [54] of the parent may be taken into consideration to rebut the presumption of gift and establish a resulting trust for the benefit of the parent.[55]

The decisions are fairly uniform in requiring that the payor prove by clear and convincing evidence that he furnished the consideration and in placing upon him the burden of proof of a resulting trust. Some courts have stated that the evidence necessary to overcome a presumption of gift raised by relationship between the payor and transferee must be of a clear and convincing character,[56] but by the better view the evidence required is no more than that necessary to establish any other fact.[57]

49. E.g., Socol v. King, 36 Cal.2d 342, 223 P.2d 627 (1950). The modern trend may be to raise a presumption of gift in this situation.

50. If the conveyance is to a corporation, the fact that the corporation is charitable may be evidence that a gift rather than a trust was intended. Restatement, Second, Trusts § 441, Comment *b*.

51. Dorman v. Dorman, 187 Ill. 154, 58 N.E. 235, 79 Am.St.Rep. 210 (1900).

52. E.g., Epstein v. Ratkosky, 283 Pa. 168, 129 A. 53 (1925).

53. E.g., Long v. Huseman, 186 Md. 495, 47 A.2d 75 (1946) (age and financial condition).

54. Macias v. Macias, 148 S.W.2d 240 (Tex.Civ.App.1941) (Father could not read or write and transferred property to son for management).

55. There is English authority to the effect that payment by a mother for a transfer to a child raises a presumption of resulting trust. Matter of De Visme, 2 DeG.J. & S. 17 (1863). The natural presumption seems to the contrary and the American courts so hold. E.g., Link v. Emrich, 346 Ill. 238, 178 N.E. 480 (1931). See Whitworth v. Whitworth, 233 Ga. 53, 210 S.E.2d 9 (1975).

56. Powell v. Mackenzie, 137 Md. 266, 112 A. 290 (1920).

57. E.g., Hartley v. Hartley, 279 Ill. 593, 117 N.E. 69 (1917).

(4) CONSTRUCTIVE TRUSTS AND RELATED REMEDIES

HORSLEY v. HRENCHIR

Supreme Court of Kansas, 1937.
146 Kan. 767, 73 P.2d 1010.

ALLEN, JUSTICE. This is an appeal from an order overruling the demurrer of the defendants to the plaintiff's amended petition.

The petition alleges that Benjamin Franklin Bailey died intestate April 11, 1909, leaving as his sole and only heirs at law Margaret A. Bailey, his widow, Mayma Bailey and Paden Bailey, his daughters, and that at the time of his death he was the owner of the real estate in question. Upon the death of Benjamin Franklin Bailey, his widow, Margaret A. Bailey, became the owner of an undivided one-half interest in the real estate, and the daughters, Mayma and Paden, each became the owners of an undivided one-fourth interest therein; that no division of the real estate has ever been had; and that it was occupied by the widow during the remainder of her life. The daughter Mayma Bailey later married W. C. Horsley, and the daughter Paden Bailey later married Permin Hrenchir.

On November 14, 1911, Mayma Bailey Horsley and her husband, W. C. Horsley, conveyed by quitclaim deed the undivided one-fourth interest of Mayma Bailey Horsley to Margaret A. Bailey, which deed was duly filed for record.

The petition further alleged that the conveyance was without consideration and "upon the express oral agreement with the said Margaret A. Bailey that she would hold said interest in trust for Mayma Bailey Horsley, along with the other undivided interests in said real estate until the time of her death, when the whole tract of land above described should descend to her daughters, the said Mayma Bailey Horsley and Paden Bailey Hrenchir"; that on July 25, 1921, without the knowledge or consent of Mayma Bailey Horsley or her husband, W. C. Horsley, and in violation of said trust agreement, Margaret A. Bailey conveyed, by warranty deed, the above-described real estate to her daughter Paden Hrenchir, which deed was filed for record August 14, 1924.

The petition further alleges that the conveyance to Paden Hrenchir was without consideration, and procured by fraud and undue influence exercised upon Margaret A. Bailey by Paden Hrenchir and her husband, Permin Hrenchir, and that on the 3d day of August, 1924, Margaret A. Bailey died intestate, leaving as her sole and only heirs at law, Mayma Bailey Horsley and Paden Bailey Hrenchir; that on August 30, 1931, Mayma Bailey Horsley died intestate, leaving as her sole and only heirs at law her husband, W. C. Horsley, and a son, Franklin G. Horsley, the plaintiff.

The petition then alleges the conveyance, by quitclaim deed, by W. C. Horsley to Franklin G. Horsley, the plaintiff, placing the entire interest, if any there is, arising out of the oral trust agreement, in the plaintiff Franklin G. Horsley. This deed was also filed for record; that on account of the trust agreement, the plaintiff Franklin G. Horsley and the defendant Paden Hrenchir are the absolute owners of the real estate in question, each being the owners of an undivided one-half interest.

For his second cause of action, plaintiff prays for partition.

Section 182 of the Restatement of Restitution and Unjust Enrichment reads as follows:

> "Where the owner of an interest in land transfers it *inter vivos* to another upon an oral trust in favor of the transferor or upon an oral agreement to reconvey the land to the transferor, and the trust or agreement is unenforceable because of the Statute of Frauds, and the transferee refuses to perform the trust or agreement, he holds the interest upon a constructive trust for the transferor, if
>
> "(a) the transfer was procured by fraud, misrepresentation, duress, undue influence or mistake of such a character that the transferor is entitled to restitution, or
>
> "(b) the transferee at the time of the transfer was in a confidential relation to the transferor, or
>
> "(c) the transfer was made as security for an indebtedness of the transferor.
>
> "*Caveat:* The Institute takes no position on the question whether the transferee holds upon a constructive trust for the transferor an interest in land transferred to him *inter vivos*, where he orally agreed with the transferor to hold it in trust for the transferor or to reconvey it to the transferor, except under the circumstances stated in this section."

The Kansas rule is in accordance with the Restatement above quoted. The petition does not allege the transfer from the daughter to her mother was procured by fraud, misrepresentation, duress, undue influence, or mistake. It does not allege that the transferee at the time of the transfer was in a confidential relation to the transferor, nor that the transfer was made to secure a debt. The case therefore falls within the statute of frauds, (G.S.1935, 67–210), according to the settled rule long adhered to by this court. Morrall v. Waterson, 7 Kan. 199; Ingham v. Burnell, 31 Kan. 333, 2 P. 804; Gee v. Thrailkill, 45 Kan. 173, 25 P. 588; Rogers v. Richards, 67 Kan. 706, 74 P. 255; Blackwell v. Blackwell, 88 Kan. 495, 129 P. 173; Clester v. Clester, 90 Kan. 638, 135 P. 996, L.R.A.1915E, 648; Goff v. Goff, 98 Kan. 201, 158 P. 26; Bolin v. Krengel, 116 Kan. 459, 227 P. 266; Mullen v. Hume, 130 Kan. 240, 285 P.2d 626.

Appellee relies upon Smith v. Nyburg, 136 Kan. 572, 16 P.2d 493; Stahl v. Stevenson, 102 Kan. 447, 171 P. 1164, and other cases of similar type. Cases where the owner of property has entered into an agreement to devise property for services rendered are very numerous. In this situation the court is interested in the doctrines of part performance and specific performance. In such cases the promisee may bring an action in the nature of an action for specific performance, and where the proof is ample the court will give relief by impressing a trust on the heirs or devisees of the promisor in favor of the promisee. These cases are not in point in this controversy.

We think the court was in error in overruling defendants' demurrer. The judgment must be reversed. It is so ordered.

ALLEN, JUSTICE (concurring specially). The daughter transferred the property to her mother upon an oral agreement to hold in trust for the daughter and to be returned to the daughter by intestate succession. It is admitted that under the great weight of authority the transferee may retain the property. The majority of the Kansas cases so hold, but we have held that the transferee holds the property upon constructive trust for the transferor. Hunnicutt v. Oren, 84 Kan. 460, 114 P. 1059. Our statute G.S.1935, 67–210, provides that: "Declarations or creations of trusts or powers in relation of real estate, must be executed in the same manner as deeds of conveyance; but this provision does not apply to trusts resulting from the operation or construction of law."

Where land is conveyed on oral trust in favor of the transferor, or upon oral contract to reconvey to the transferor, and where the transferee, relying on the statute of frauds, refuses to perform the trust, the English courts raise a constructive trust in favor of the transferor. Davies v. Otty, 35 Beav. 208. The English court said, "it is not honest to keep the land." (p. 213.)

Few will deny that to allow the transferee to keep the land would result in the unjust enrichment of the transferee.

Where the owner of land transfers it to another as security for a debt, although the deed is absolute on its face, the statute of frauds does not prevent the showing of the oral agreement. Glynn v. Building Ass'n, 22 Kan. 746; Le Comte v. Pennock, 61 Kan. 330, 59 P. 641; Hegwood v. Leeper, 100 Kan. 379, 164 P. 173; Brinkerhoff v. Bank, 109 Kan. 700, 205 P. 779.

"There would seem to be on principle, however, just as much objection to the proof of an oral mortgage as to the proof of an oral trust. Indeed, the unjust enrichment is greater in the case of an oral trust than in the case of an oral mortgage; for if no relief is given in the former case, the whole of the property is lost, while in the latter case only the value above the amount of the debt is lost." (Scott, Conveyances upon Trusts not Properly Declared, 37 Harv.Law Rev., 653, 663.)

Again, if it is shown there was a confidential relationship between the parties as in Silvers v. Howard, 106 Kan. 762, 190 P. 1, the court will compel restitution by raising a constructive trust. The same is true if the transfer was secured by fraud, duress, or mistake. If it is possible to show the oral agreement in such cases, no valid reason has been given why the statute of frauds should forbid showing the oral trust to prevent unjust enrichment.

If A transfers land to B upon an oral trust to hold for or to reconvey to A, or to die intestate so that A could acquire the land by intestate succession, it is clear that A cannot enforce the express trust because of the statute of frauds. But B ought not to be allowed to retain A's land and thus by his breach of faith to enrich himself at the expense of A. If he will not perform the express trust, he should be compelled to reconvey the land to A. Ames, Lectures on Legal History, pages 425, 427. The fact that A would get the same relief by enforcing a constructive trust that he would get by enforcing the express trust is purely an accidental circumstance. There are many cases where the terms of the express trust might be different. (Thus, if A transfers land to B upon an oral agreement to convey to C, the express trust is in favor of C, but should B refuse to perform his agreement the constructive trust should be declared for A.)

In 3 Bogert, on Trusts and Trustees, § 497, it is said: "The party who has made a voidable or unenforceable promise is permitted by the Legislature to set up the statute and avoid performance of his promise. That is a lawful act, which of itself should not be regarded as a basis for any equitable relief. But it does not follow that, because the promisor may avoid performance of his promise by use of the statute, he may also keep what he has received on the strength of a belief that the promise will be performed. To allow him to keep such a payment or other consideration would be giving the promisor something for nothing, would be unjustly enriching him at the expense of the promisee. It would be according to the Statute of Frauds the unnecessarily severe meaning that the promisee not only gets no performance of the promise, but also forfeits as a kind of penalty whatever he may have advanced in order to secure the making of the oral promise." (p. 1607.)

From the caveat to the Restatement of Restitution and Unjust Enrichment it appears the American Law Institute takes no position on the question here presented. To prevent the unjust enrichment of the original grantee, and to those who take under her with notice, it would seem that a constructive trust should be declared. If the agreement relates to personal property of great value, there is no difficulty in enforcing it as an express trust. It seems strange that where twenty-two acres of land is involved, as in this case, a court of equity cannot compel restitution. We cannot enforce the express trust, but we can do justice by raising a constructive trust.

By a long line of cases it seems settled in this state that the transferee can keep the property. One reason given is that "deeds would no longer be valuable as muniments of title." (p. 768.) Silvers v. Howard, supra. The reason given seems unsubstantial, for it would prevent enforcing restitution when a transfer of land was procured by fraud, misrepresentation, mistake, duress, undue influence, or where the transfer was made as a security transaction. But in any view of the question it must be conceded that the rule followed in this case is too firmly established to be departed from at this late day.[58]

NOTE

In Cromwell v. Norton,[59] the Massachusetts court refused to allow the grantor to recover the land conveyed on oral trust but allowed him to recover the value of the land, on the theory that admission of the oral testimony for such purpose did not violate the Statute of Frauds. This is, however, a minority view. But see the Uniform Trusts Act, § 16.

The grantor may recover if he properly alleges and successfully proves actual fraud on the part of the grantee. This is of course extremely difficult to establish by any sort of direct proof, and the burden is upon the plaintiff to establish his case by clear and convincing evidence. The theory will be that the grantee never intended to perform his oral agreement and that he misrepresented the state of his mind at the time of the transfer. Courts differ on the strength of the inference to be drawn from subsequent conduct of the grantee in refusing to perform. More significant are the factors of the situation and relation of the parties and any activity of the grantee in procuring the conveyance.[60]

58. In Patton v. Beecher, 62 Ala. 579, 593 (1878) the court stated: "It is an annihilation of the statute, to withdraw a case from its operation, because of such violation or repudiation of an agreement or trust, it declares shall not be made or proved by parol. There can be no fraud, if the trust does not exist, and proof of its existence by parol, is that which the statute forbids." The English rule is followed in a few American cases. Italiani v. Higbee Coal Mining Co., 331 Mo. 362, 53 S.W.2d 1050 (1932); Chandler v. Georgia Chemical Works, 182 Ga. 419, 185 S.E. 787, 105 A.L.R. 837 (1937). See Uniform Trusts Act, § 16. See generally, Ames, "Constructive Trusts Based Upon the Breach of an Express Oral Trust of Land", 20 Harv.L.Rev. 549 (1907); Costigan, "Trusts Based on Oral Promises to Hold in Trust, to Convey, or to Devise, Made by Voluntary Grantees", 12 Mich. L.Rev. 427, 513 (1914); Costigan, "Constructive Trusts Based on Promises to Secure Bequests, Devises, or Intestate Succession", 28 Harv.L.Rev. 237, 366 (1915); Lauerman, "Constructive Trusts and Restitutionary Liens in North Carolina", 45 No.Car.L.Rev. 424 (1967); McWilliams, "The Doctrine of Constructive Trusts as laid down in Curdy v. Berton", 16 Cal.L.Rev. 19 (1927); Stone, "Resulting Trusts and the Statute of Frauds", 6 Col.L.Rev. 326 (1906).

Also see Guerrieri v. Guerrieri, 13 Ill. App.3d 1043, 301 N.E.2d 603 (1973), holding that relationship of parent and child does not create confidential relationship as a matter of law.

59. 193 Mass. 291, 79 N.E. 433, 118 Am.St.Rep. 499 (1906).

60. See Lipp v. Lipp, 158 Md. 207, 148 A. 531 (1930) allowing recovery of the land on the basis of fraud. Where the transfer is involuntary, as on foreclosure of a mortgage, tax sale, or sale on execution of a judgment, the majority of the courts do not require a showing of actual fraud. Instead they will allow the owner A, who has been induced to refrain from bidding by the oral promise of B to buy in the land and reconvey to A upon reimbursement, to impose a constructive trust on B. See, Brown v. Vick, 23 N.C.App. 404, 209 S.E.2d 342 (1974). Strasner v. Carroll, 125 Ark. 34, 187 S.W. 1057, Ann. Cas.1918E, 306 (1916); Pope v. Depray, 176 Ill. 478, 52 N.E. 58 (1898); Ryan v. Dox, 34 N.Y. 307, 90 Am.Dec. 696 (1886); Jenckes v. Cook, 9 R.I. 520 (1870). A minority of courts apply the same rule to involuntary and voluntary conveyances, allowing a constructive trust only upon a showing of actual fraud or a confidential relation. E.g., Kennerson v. Nash, 208 Mass. 393, 94 N.E. 475 (1911). Of course, no court will grant a constructive trust if the promisee A does not rely on the promise. Wheeler v. Reynolds, 66 N. Y. 227 (1876).

MASINO v. SECHREST

Supreme Court of Wisconsin, 1954.
268 Wis. 101, 66 N.W.2d 740.

[In an action to enforce a constructive trust, the trial court sustained an objection to the introduction of any evidence, and a judgment of dismissal of complaint was entered.]

FAIRCHILD, CHIEF JUSTICE. The questions to be determined on this appeal relate to the sufficiency of the complaint and the admissibility of evidence. Does the complaint state a cause of action, and did the circuit court commit error in sustaining the respondents' demurrer to the offer of evidence by appellants and in granting the respondents' motion to dismiss the complaint?

Appellants assert the existence of a "constructive trust" favorable to them, arising out of the circumstances under which respondents acquired and now hold the legal title to the real estate involved; and contend that such a trust is raised in equity in respect of property which has been acquired originally without fraud and where it is against equity that it should be retained by the persons holding it. The respondents stand on the proposition that where one purchases and pays for land and places the legal title in the name of another by having the seller convey to such other, the title to the land vests in the grantee free from any trust, although he took with the understanding that he was to convey to the purchaser's children.

The trial court bases its decision on Sec. 231.07, Stats., which provides that:

> "When a grant for a valuable consideration shall be made to one person and the consideration therefor shall be paid by another, no use or trust shall result in favor of the person by whom such payment is made; but the title shall vest in the person named as the alienee in such conveyance".

The trial court, in its decision, finds in effect that because it is alleged in the complaint that the mother, Rose Masino, paid the purchase price, and that at her direction the deed was put in the name of the eldest daughter and her husband without consideration, a resulting trust is pleaded; and that since resulting trusts are abolished by Sec. 231.07, Stats., plaintiffs have no cause of action.

It is true that a purchase money resulting trust arises at common law where one person pays the purchase price for land but has it deeded to another who gives him no consideration. Such a resulting trust arises in favor of the payor *merely* because he has paid the purchase price. An inference is made by law from the character of the transaction that the payor did not intend that the grantee should have the beneficial interest in the land. The result is that the beneficial interest springs back to the purchaser of the land. If the grantee refuses to reconvey, the *purchaser* may plead a resulting trust, in which case he has to show merely that he made the payment, in order to benefit from the inference implied by law; and it is for the grantee to prove that there was a gift meant if he wishes to rebut the presumption of law. Purchase money resulting trusts were first abolished in this country by statute in the state of New York; and subsequently some other states have enacted similar statutes derived from the New York statute.

In a New York case, Foreman v. Foreman, 251 N.Y. 237, 167 N.E. 428, 429, Judge Cardozo said: "The statute has put an end to the rule at common law that where a grant is made to one for a consideration paid by another *a trust results inevitably and always, by force merely of the payment,* irrespective of intention. Garfield v. Hatmaker, 15 N.Y. 475, 477; Scott, Resulting Trusts in Purchase of Land, 40 Harv.L.Rev. 653 [675]. The conveyance is operative according to its terms if nothing else is proved. The statute has no effect, however, on trusts constructively imposed as a consequence, not of payment alone, but of payment in combination with other or extrinsic equities. As to this the decisions are uniform and ample. 'It is only the common-law trust for the benefit of an individual from whom the consideration for a grant issues, and resulting from the fact of payment of the consideration, *and having no other foundation,* that the statute abolishes.' * * *"

However, a *resulting trust* can arise only in favor of the *payor* by reason of his payment; it cannot arise in favor of a third party beneficiary. And appellants here do not contend that a trust results in favor of Rose Masino (or her heirs), the person who allegedly paid the purchase price. Appellants make the following allegations (in part):

> "Following her [the mother's] death the said defendants in violation of the trust and confidence placed in them and with intent of unjustly enriching themselves, fraudulently claimed the property herein described to be their own to the prejudice of the plaintiffs herein and contrary to the oral trust imposed by the said Rose Masino prior to her death.
>
> "* * * that said actions of the said defendants in claiming title to said properties are contrary to the intentions of the deceased and the understanding of said defendants and is such an abuse of the confidence reposed in them by the deceased as to constitute unconscionable conduct which in equity and good conscience said defendants should not be permitted or allowed to enjoy; that said defendants should not be permitted to claim the purchase of such lands to their unjust enrichment where another has paid valuable consideration therefor and where said defendants have violated the confidence and duty to perform the trust reposed in them by the said deceased; that such conduct is inconsistent with the character of a purchaser."

It is clear that what is being pleaded here is a constructive trust based on unjust enrichment. In the instant case, the statute of frauds prevents the enforcing of an express trust showing the affirmative intent of the parties because there was no written manifestation of the alleged agreement. From its origin one of the most important uses of the trust has been for the purpose of settling family affairs. Such agreements were often in parol, and where an unenforceable agreement in parol is attended by certain special circumstances, equity resorts to the remedial device of a constructive trust to accomplish justice. The underlying principle of a constructive trust is the equitable prevention of unjust enrichment which arises from fraud or the abuse of a confidential relationship. "A constructive trust arises if, but only if, it is shown that the transferee was guilty of fraud or the abuse of a confidential relationship, or if the transfer was made in contemplation of death, or is in the nature of a mortgage." Scott on Trusts, vol. 3, sec. 481.3, p. 2358. See Krzysko v. Gaudynski, 207 Wis. 608, 242 N.W. 186; Schofield v. Rideout, 233 Wis. 550, 290 N.W. 155, 133 A.L.R. 834. In Popp v. Froelich, 223 Wis. 168, 270 N.W. 38, 39, Mr. Justice Nelson, in discussing a transfer of absolute title to land, said: "If Ernest Froelich claimed absolute title to the lands, equity no doubt would decree a trust." Among other references, he quoted from Restatement, Trusts, p. 140, sec. 45:

> " 'Where the owner of an interest in land transfers it *inter vivos* to another in trust for a third person, but no memorandum properly evidencing the intention to create a trust is signed, and the transferee refuses to perform the trust, the transferee holds the interest upon a constructive trust for a third person, if but only if
>
> " '(a) The transferee by fraud, duress or undue influence prevented the transferor from creating an enforceable interest in the third person, or
>
> " '(b) The transferee at the time of the transfer was in a confidential relation to the transferor, or
>
> " '(c) The transfer was made by the transferor in contemplation of death.' "

The statutes applicable to the instant case are Secs. 240.06 and 240.07 of the Wisconsin Statutes. Sec. 240.06 provides:

> "No estate or interest in lands, other than leases for a term not exceeding one year, nor any trust or power over or concerning lands or in any manner relating thereto shall be created, granted, assigned, surrendered or declared unless by act or operation of law or by deed or conveyance in writing, subscribed by the party creating, granting, assigning, surrendering or declaring the same or by his lawful agent thereunto authorized by writing."

Sec. 240.07 Stats. states the exceptions to that ruling:

> "Section 240.06 shall not be construed to effect in any manner the power of a testator in the disposition of his real estate by a last will and testament nor to prevent any trust from arising or being extinguished by implication or operation of law."

Under the allegations, the daughter, Mary Masino Sechrest, and her husband knew of the mother's wishes and accepted the deed with the understanding that the mother desired to "maintain her property for the benefit of her children." When the mother placed the deed in her eldest daughter's name and that of her husband, she was relying upon more than a bare parol promise made by a grantee to a grantor. The confidence which the mother reposed in her eldest daughter had its origin in their relationship, and that relation was a moving cause in influencing the mother to place the deed in the names of the eldest daughter and her husband for the benefit of all of her children. It is alleged that the daughter admitted that the property herein referred to was the property of the deceased, Rose Masino; and that there was no attempt on the part of Mary Sechrest or her husband to claim said property prior to the death of the mother. However, after her mother's death, Mary Sechrest, and her husband, repudiated the oral understanding under which they received the deed, and claimed the property as their own. Where, in a settlement of family affairs, then, the mother deeded land to her eldest daughter and her husband to be held in trust for "the benefit of her children" under an oral understanding, and where the trustees repudiate the agreement, the children, as beneficiaries, upon the mother's death, have an equitable claim on the *trust res* which they may realize through equity's provision for imposing a constructive trust based on unjust enrichment.

Equity regards as wrongful acts to which it attributes the same or similar effects as those which follow from actual fraud, and grants the same or similar relief as is granted in cases of real fraud. Even if Mary Sechrest and her husband did not actively procure the conveyance, under the allegations their fraud consisted in their holding the property contrary to the terms of the agreement, and they were guilty of constructive fraud upon the mother, Rose Masino, and of tort upon the other children of the family who were the intended beneficiaries.

In Scott on Trusts, vol. 3, sec. 486, p. 2364, it is said that "Where B obtained the land by a promise which he never intended to perform, it is held that the holds the land upon a constructive trust for C. The same result has been reached where B was at the time of the conveyance in * * * confidential relation to A." In the same text, vol. 1, sec. 45.2, p. 268, it is also said:

> "Where A transfers land to B who orally agrees to hold it in trust for or to convey it to C, and at the time of the transfer B is in a confidential relation to A, it is held that B can be compelled to hold the land upon a constructive trust for C * * *. Where, however, B did not obtain the property by undue influence, and is guilty only of an abuse of the confidential relation in subsequently failing to perform his promise, it is more difficult to say that he thereby commits a tort to C. Undoubtedly he should not be permitted to keep the land, since he would be unjustly enriched if he were permitted to keep it; but it is arguable that he should hold it upon a constructive trust for A rather than for C. *It is held*, however, without much consideration for the niceties of the question involved, that C rather than A is entitled to the land." (Emphasis supplied.)

Since a constructive trust, which is based on unjust enrichment, is construed from the circumstances surrounding the transaction, independent of the intention of the parties, parol evidence of the agreement is admissible, not to enforce the agreement, but to prove that the grantee has been unjustly enriched by his repudiation of the agreement. The proving of the contract is incidental. The purpose of the parol evidence is to prove unjust enrichment, and in the instant case, the unjust enrichment is alleged to have arisen from a breach of an agreement arising out of a confidential relationship. "It is not the promise only, nor the breach only, but unjust enrichment under cover of the relation of confidence, which puts the court in motion." Sinclair v. Purdy, 235 N.Y. 245, 253, 139 N.E. 255, 258.

The trial court recognizes the element of confidential relationship existing between Mary Masino Sechrest, the grantee, and Rose Masino, the grantor, where he says: "It [the deed] was placed in their names by the direction or request of Rose Masino, *because of the trust and confidence she reposed in them.*" He then adds: "Such confidential * * * relationship is not essential to establish a constructive trust. The essential element is that the transfer must be induced by fraud, duress or undue influence." But confidential relationship as an element of fraud is one of the grounds for raising a constructive trust based on unjust enrichment; and it is present in the allegations of this case.

With reference to the importance of confidential relation, and because our law has followed enactments of New York, we call attention to a ruling made by the New York Court of Appeals in Goldsmith v. Goldsmith, 145 N.Y. 313, 39 N.E. 1067, in affirming a lower court ruling where a mother conveyed to her son her house and lot, he giving no other consideration than a verbal promise to hold the premises for the benefit of the mother and the other children and to give the latter shares therein. The court said: "It is quite evident that this was an arrangement founded upon the relation of mother and son and brothers and sisters, involving the trust and confidence growing out of that relation, and intended as a settlement of the family affairs."

We are of the opinion that the complaint states facts sufficient to constitute a cause of action for relief in equity under a constructive trust, and that the plaintiffs are entitled to their day in court.

Judgment reversed. Cause remanded for trial of the issues in accordance with this opinion.

STRYPE v. LEWIS

Supreme Court of Missouri, Division No. 1, 1944.
352 Mo. 1004, 180 S.W.2d 688, 155 A.L.R. 99.

[Suit for a declaratory judgment to establish a trust in a two-fifths interest in five parcels of land devised absolutely to the respondent. The statement of facts and a discussion of the Missouri declaratory judgment statutes are omitted.]

VAN OSDOL, COMMISSIONER. * * * It is the contention of appellant that the evidence adduced was such as to compel a decree that the undivided two-fifths interest in the real property should be impressed with a constructive trust in favor of appellant; and that the Statute of Frauds (and Uses) may not be used as a shield for fraud—one acquiring legal title by a verbal promise to hold property for a specific purpose will be deemed to hold title as trustee for the true beneficiary notwithstanding the Statute of Frauds. Respondent urges that facts sufficient to establish a constructive trust were neither pleaded nor proved by appellant, and that the testimony adduced by appellant failed in the degree of proof necessary for relief.

It was the testimony of appellant that there was an agreement between respondent and appellant's father, the elder Lewis, testator, that respondent was to receive the devise of the two-fifths interest in the property and hold the same in trust for appellant until he had recovered physically and mentally from the effects of an automobile accident which he had theretofore suffered, and then to convey the interest in the property to him. Witnesses for appellant testified that the elder Lewis had frequently declared prior and subsequently to the making of his will that he intended to (and had) devised the two-fifths interest in the property unto respondent in trust for appellant upon her, respondent's, agreement to convey the property to appellant upon his recovery from his injuries. Evidence was introduced of the respondent's statements, admissions, that the elder Lewis had devised to her the interest in the property, she to convey to appellant upon the recovery of his physical and mental faculties. It was the testimony of appellant, and of the scrivener of the will, that upon the day of the making of the will respondent reaffirmed to the elder Lewis, testator, her agreement that she would hold the interest in the property devised for appellant and convey to him, as pleaded in the answer of appellant, supra.

It is observed that the appellant did not plead or prove that a relation of confidence existed between the elder Lewis and respondent, nor did the appellant plead or prove that, at the time she gave her assent, respondent did not intend to fulfill her alleged agreement. One of the vexatious problems of the courts is whether equity ought to decree a constructive trust where a donee by deed or will, having received property under an oral promise to hold it for the donor or another, relies upon the applicable section of the Statute of Frauds or statutes regarding the execution of wills, refuses to perform the promise, and retains the property for his own use. Vol. 3, Bogert,

Trusts and Trustees, § 495, p. 1585. In the case at bar, the creation of a trust of the two-fifths interest in the real property was not proved by the will or by any other writing signed by the elder Lewis and so, as an express trust, it was void. Section 3494, R.S.1939, Mo. R.S.A. § 3494.

Cases have been cited by respondent in support of her contention that the appellant did not plead and prove facts entitling him to the remedy, a constructive trust, including the case of Ferguson v. Robinson, 258 Mo. 113, 167 S.W. 447, 452, wherein it is stated, " 'Equity does not pretend to enforce verbal agreements in the face of the Statute of Frauds, and the person holding the legal title to real estate will not be decreed to be a constructive trustee, unless there is something more in the transaction than the mere violation of a parol agreement. Accordingly, the mere refusal of a trustee to execute an express trust, or the denial of the existence of the trust by him, does not make a case for raising a constructive trust. And where a conveyance in trust is made voluntarily, without solicitation or undue influence, and no fraud is shown prior to, or contemporaneous with, the execution of the deed, but consists in denying and repudiating the agreement to reconvey, it will not remove the case from the operation of the Statute of Frauds'. [1 Beach on Modern Equity Jurisprudence, § 234.]" The case is in accord, we believe, with the general ruling of the decisions in this country wherein constructive trusts are sought to be invoked in courts of equity upon real property conveyed by voluntary deed. 26 R.C.L., Trusts, § 85, pp. 1238–9; 65 C.J., Trusts, § 223, pp. 470–2. * * *

In the case at bar, the two-fifths interest in the real property was *devised* to respondent.

Though the establishment of a constructive trust (by oral evidence) in property devised or bequeathed may be had, it is not dependent, upon the pleading and the proof of the exercise of actual intentional fraud prior to or contemporaneously with the making of the will (or the existence of a fiduciary relation); the rule being that, where the testator devises or bequeaths property to a person *in reliance* upon his agreement to hold the property in trust for or to convey it to a third person, the devisee or legatee holds the property upon a constructive trust for the third person. Restatement of the Law of Restitution, Subsection (1), § 186, p. 757; Vol. 3, Scott on Trusts, § 491, p. 2379. See also Vol. I, Restatement of the Law of Trusts, Subsection (1), § 55, p. 160. "The constructive trust which is imposed under the rules stated in this Section (these Sections) arises out of the breach of an intended express trust which is unenforceable because of the failure to comply with the requirements of the Statute of Wills * * *." Comment (a), § 55, Restatement of the Law of Trusts, supra.

The principle so restated if invoked without the proof of actual intentional fraud is not of universal recognition. See Vol. 4, Pomeroy's Equity Jurisprudence, 5th Ed., § 1054; 26 R.C.L., Trusts, § 89, p. 1243. But by the weight of authority the principle is recognized whether the devisee or legatee, when he gave his assent, intended fraud or not. Vol. 3, Scott on Trusts, § 491, supra; 26 R.C.L., Trusts, § 89, supra. The principle rests upon a basis that the disposition of the will was made *in reliance* upon the verbal, or tacit, agreement of the devisee (or legatee); though the acquiring of the property was not wrongful, the testator having relied upon the agreement and consequently disposing of the property to the devisee or legatee, it would be unjust and unconscionable to permit a retention of the property inconsistent with the agreement upon which the testator relied in making the testamentary disposition. Although the agreement cannot be enforced as an express trust, the devisee or legatee would be unjustly enriched if he were permitted to retain the property which he would not have acquired but for his agreement to hold it in trust for or to convey it to a third person. Comment (b), Restatement of the Law of Restitution, § 186, supra.

See the interesting case of Gilpatrick et al. v. Glidden et al., 81 Me. 137, 16 A. 464, 2 L.R.A. 662, 10 Am.St.Rep. 245, wherein many of the early English and American cases upon this question are reviewed. A statement of a basis of the rule by Wood, V. C., in the case of Wallgrave v. Tebbs, Ch. 1855, 2 Kay & J 313, at page 321, is said (Jones v. Badley, L.R., 3 Ch. 362), to be "the clear and felicitous exposition" of the law, "Where a person, knowing that a testator in making a disposition in his favor intends it to be applied for purposes other than his own benefit, either expressly promises, or by silence implies, that he will carry the testator's intention into effect, and the property is left to him upon the faith of that promise or undertaking, it is in effect a case of trust; and, in such a case, the Court will not allow the devisee to set up the Statute of Frauds—or rather the Statute of Wills, by which the Statute of Frauds is now, in this respect, superseded; and for this reason:—the devisee by his conduct has induced the testator to leave him the property; and, as Lord Justice Turner says in Russell v. Jackson (10 Hare 204), no one can doubt, that, if the devisee had stated that he would not carry into effect the intentions of the testator, the disposition in his favor would not have been found in the will. But in this the Court does not violate the spirit of the statute: but for the same end, namely, prevention of fraud, it engrafts the trust on the devise, by admitting evidence which the statute would in terms exclude, in order to prevent a party from applying property to a purpose foreign to that for which he undertook to hold it." * * *

Although the basis of the principle as stated in the sections of the American Law Institute Restatements, supra, and as stated in many of the decisions is not precisely the same, nevertheless the principle is recognized by the great weight of authority in England and this country.

We rule in accordance with the great weight of authority on this question.

It follows that appellant in his answer pleaded facts (and introduced evidence) from which it could be inferred that the elder Lewis devised the interest in the real property unto respondent in reliance upon an agreement of respondent to hold the property in trust for and convey it to appellant; and so, facts were pleaded by appellant sufficient to constitute a cause of action for the establishment of a constructive trust.

But if a court may grant the relief and upon verbal proof declare a constructive trust, notwithstanding the provisions of the statute, such relief should be granted only upon the most clear, positive and definite proof, such as would leave no reasonable doubt in the mind of the chancellor. If the court of equity were to grant such relief upon verbal proof less than that which would remove from the mind of the chancellor a reasonable doubt, the court would permit the practice of the very fraud the statute was intended to prevent. And so, it is held by this court that in order to establish a trust by parol and to engraft it on the legal title to real property, the mere preponderance of the evidence is insufficient, and a higher degree of proof is necessary. The evidence must be so clear, cogent, and convincing as to exclude every reasonable doubt from the chancellor's mind. Purvis v. Hardin, supra.

Attending now again the evidence introduced at the trial of the instant case—testimony of appellant and of appellant's witnesses of the agreement (and its re-affirmance) between respondent and appellant's father that respondent was to receive the devise of the two-fifths interest in the property and hold the same in trust for appellant, and convey the same to him upon his recovery from the effects of his injuries; and of the admissions of respondent that the elder Lewis had so devised the interest in the property to her, she to convey to appellant upon his recovery of his physical and mental faculties, was by the respondent categorically denied. And evidence was introduced by respondent that the appellant had on various occasions, since the death of his father, stated, "he didn't have anything, that everything belonged to her (respondent)." It also appears from the evidence that the elder Lewis held respondent in fatherly esteem, as the appellant expressed from the witness stand, "I will say that he considered her like a daughter. Those were his actual words." And there was testimony of one witness that the elder Lewis had declared to him that "he was leaving part of his property to Lulu (respondent) * * * he thought he could depend on Lulu to take care of it and to make good use of it * * *."

Considering the evidence as a whole, in view of the finding of the chancellor who heard and observed the witnesses and their demeanor as they testified from the witness stand, we are not satisfied that the evidence was so clear, cogent and convincing as to exclude all reasonable doubt of the right of appellant to the relief sought, declaration of a constructive trust.

Although it appears that the trial court ruled the result of the case correctly, the cause should be remanded with directions that the order discharging the respondent with her costs be set aside; and that a judgment be rendered declaring that respondent to be the absolute owner of the legal and equitable title of the two-fifths interest in the land, and that the appellant is not entitled to the relief, a constructive trust.

It is so ordered.

BRADLEY AND DALTON, CC., concur.

PER CURIAM.

The foregoing opinion by VAN OSDOL, C., is adopted as the opinion of the court.

All the Judges concur, except GANTT, J., who concurs in the result only.

NOTE

Assume that A devises Blackacre to B absolutely in reliance upon B's oral promise to hold Blackacre in trust for C. The express trust is unenforceable because of the Statute of Frauds and the Wills Acts.[61] If a confidential relationship exists between A and B, or B procures the devise by actual fraud, duress or undue influence, a constructive trust is raised for C. If there is no confidential relation between A and B, and B is not guilty of actual fraud, duress or undue influence, but intended to perform his promise when he made it and then failed to perform, it would seem to be a violation of both the Statute of Frauds and the Wills Acts to raise a constructive trust for C. But a majority of courts have raised a constructive trust in this situation and the majority view is adopted by the Restatement.[62] To exclude evidence of B's oral promise and allow him to keep Blackacre will result in his unjust enrichment. By the majority view, B holds on constructive trust for C.[63] It has been suggested that a better view would be to receive evidence of B's promise for the purpose of restoring the *status quo* existing before the transfer was made; that is, B should hold on constructive trust for the residuary donee in A's will or, if none, for A's heir at law.[64] When the *status quo* is restored the express trust is not enforced indirectly by means of a constructive trust but unjust enrichment of B is prevented.

It is immaterial whether B's promise is made prior to, at the time of, or subsequent to the execution of the will provided it is made prior to the death of the testator. A promise which induces a testator to refrain from revoking a will may be used as the basis for a constructive trust as well as a promise which induces him to make a will. The promise or agreement by the testamentary donee may be express or may be implied from the donee's conduct. For example, A writes B that A is devising Blackacre to B to be conveyed by B to C. B receives A's letter but does not answer it. Shortly thereafter A dies devising Blackacre absolutely to B. B holds on constructive trust for C.

One to whom property is devised or bequeathed absolutely, without reference to any trust, holds the property free of trust unless he agreed with the testator to hold the property upon trust. It makes no difference that the testator intended the devisee or legatee to hold the property in trust. The testator must communicate this intention prior to his death to the testamentary donee or to an agent of the testamentary donee.

61. "Wills Acts" as here used refers to the statutes requiring formalities for the execution and revocation of wills.

62. Restatement, Second, Trusts § 55.

63. See I Scott, Trusts (3d Ed., 1967) § 55.1.

64. I Scott, Trusts (3d Ed., 1967) 425–426.

If A executes a will devising Blackacre absolutely to B in reliance upon B's promise to hold Blackacre in trust for such persons and purposes as A may thereafter during his lifetime designate, and A dies without making such designation before his death, B will hold on constructive trust for the estate of A. Otherwise B will be unjustly enriched. For example, A executes a will devising Blackacre to B. B agrees with A to hold Blackacre in trust for such person as A may designate in a letter to be found with his will. On A's death a letter is found with his will designating C as beneficiary of Blackacre. The letter is not executed with the formalities required by the Wills Acts. B holds Blackacre upon constructive trust for A's estate, not C.

If A dies intestate relying upon the oral agreement of B, A's sole heir and next of kin, to hold the property inherited from A in trust for C, B will hold on constructive trust for C by the prevailing view. The express trust is unenforceable because of the Wills Acts. A constructive trust for C in this situation is subject to the same criticism that is made when B is testamentary donee instead of heir. The constructive trust is an obvious will substitute and seems to violate the policy underlying the Wills Acts.

It has been assumed thus far that the testamentary gifts were absolute. Suppose, however, that an intention to create a trust but not the identity of the beneficiary appears on the face of the will. For example, A devises Blackacre to B "in trust" or devises Blackacre to B "in trust for such persons and purposes as I shall hereafter designate". If A dies without designating the intended beneficiary, the express trust fails for want of a beneficiary and B holds the property on resulting trust for A's estate. What is the situation, however, when A designates the intended beneficiary to B and B orally agrees to hold the property in trust for that beneficiary? The express trust is unenforceable because of the failure to meet the requirements of the Wills Acts.[65] The intention of A is clear that B shall not be the beneficial owner of the property. Does B hold on constructive trust for C or on resulting trust for A's estate? Most of the courts have declared a constructive trust for the benefit of C, although some declare a resulting trust for A's estate.[66]

A few courts which raise a constructive trust for C when the testamentary gift to B is absolute, raise a resulting trust for A's estate when an express trust is partially declared on the face of the will but the beneficiary is not indicated. Courts drawing this distinction do so on the ground that, unless evidence of the intended trust be received, where the gift is absolute, the testamentary donee will be unjustly enriched. But when the face of the will discloses the testator's intention that the donee hold in trust, oral evidence of the intended beneficiary can be excluded without unjustly enriching the donee named in the will by raising a resulting trust for the estate of the testator. B cannot defeat this resulting trust by conveying the trust property to C. B does not have an election to hold for the estate of A or for C, but holds for one or the other depending upon the rule applied in the particular jurisdiction.

In a few states, when the intention to create the trust appears on the face of the will, but the intended beneficiary is not designated on the face of the will, a distinction is drawn between the case in which the testator designates

65. The beneficiary of the trust may be designated in a writing incorporated by reference into the will or may be ascertained from facts having independent significance. See Chapter XII, Section 3(1), (2).

66. Restatement, Second, Trusts § 55, Comment *h* adopts the view that B holds on constructive trust for C in such a situation.

the intended beneficiary on or before the execution of the will and the case in which he designates the intended beneficiary after the execution of the will. In the former case a constructive trust is raised for the intended beneficiary but in the latter case a resulting trust is raised for the testator's estate. The distinction cannot be justified on any ground.

By the prevailing view, which raises a constructive trust for the intended beneficiary of the express trust in the situations examined in this note, the essential elements are: (1) an expressed or implied promise or agreement by the testamentary donee to hold the property in trust for or to convey the property to the person for whose benefit the constructive trust is raised; and (2) reliance on that promise by the testator or intestate and a change of position accordingly.[67]

PROBLEMS

1. A executes a will making an absolute bequest to B. B orally agrees to hold the bequest for a person to be designated in a letter which A will give B. A dies without giving such a letter to B. A letter designating C as beneficiary is found among A's papers. Does B hold on constructive trust for C? See In re Boyes, 26 Ch.Div. 531 (1884).

2. A executes a will leaving his residuary estate to B, C and D, relying upon B's promise that the residuary donees will hold the property in trust for a fraternal organization. C and D do not learn of the intended trust until A dies. B is not the agent of C or D when he makes the promise. May the fraternal organization enforce a constructive trust against C and D as well as against B? See Meade v. Robertson, 131 Mo.App. 185, 110 S.W. 1095 (1908); Winder v. Scholey, 83 Ohio St. 204, 93 N.E. 1098, 33 L.R.A.,N.S., 995, 21 Ann.Cas. 1379 (1910).

SECTION 2. SAVINGS BANK TRUSTS

WILDER v. HOWARD

Supreme Court of Georgia, 1939.
188 Ga. 426, 4 S.E.2d 199.

DUCKWORTH, JUSTICE. * * * The question presented by this record is whether or not the fact that a deposit was made by Mrs. D. R. Wilder in the Georgia Savings Bank and Trust Company in her name as trustee for Alice Frances Wilder is sufficient to show an intention to create a trust. This exact question has not been decided by this court, and the decisions of the courts of other jurisdictions are somewhat at variance. According to some decisions, the mere fact, standing alone, that a deposit was made by one person in trust for another, creates a presumption that an irrevocable trust was intended, and, unexplained, is conclusive in establishing such trust as of the

67. See generally, Restatement, Second, Trusts § 55; Bogert, Trusts and Trustees (2d Ed., 1965) § 495; I Scott, Trusts (3d Ed. 1967) §§ 55–55.9.

time the deposit was made, thus invalidating any subsequent dealings by the depositor with the funds deposited, except in his capacity as trustee. See Sayer v. Weil, 94 Ala. 466, 10 So. 546, 15 L.R.A. 544; Milholland v. Whalen, 89 Md. 212, 43 A. 43, 44 L.R.A. 205; Connecticut River Savings Bank v. Albee's Estate, 64 Vt. 571, 25 A. 487, 33 Am.St.Rep. 944; Hoboken Savings Bank v. Schwoon, 62 N.J.Eq. 503, 50 A. 490; Merigan v. McGonigle, 205 Pa. 321, 54 A. 994. The weight of authority, however, supports the doctrine that the mere fact of such a deposit, standing alone, does not establish an irrevocable trust, but a tentative trust merely, which is revocable at the will of the depositor until he dies or completes his gift in his lifetime by some unequivocal act or declaration showing an intention to create the trust. Cummings v. Bramhall, 120 Mass. 552, 564; Scrivens v. North Easton Savings Bank, 166 Mass. 255, 44 N.E. 251; Cleveland v. Hampden Savings Bank, 182 Mass. 110, 65 N.E. 27; Marcy v. Amazeen, 61 N.H. 131, 60 Am.Rep. 320; Cunningham v. Davenport, 147 N.Y. 43, 41 N. E. 412, 32 L.R.A. 373, 49 Am.St.Rep. 641; Peoples Savings Bank v. Webb, 21 R.I. 218, 42 A. 874; Re Totten, 179 N.Y. 112, 71 N.E. 748, 70 L.R.A. 711, 1 Ann.Cas. 900. While there are other decisions holding that such a deposit, standing alone, creates neither a tentative nor an irrevocable trust (Brabrook v. Boston Five Cents Savings Bank, 104 Mass. 228, 6 Am.Rep. 222; Clark v. Clark, 108 Mass. 522), in 7 Am.Jur. 309, § 438, the conflict of decisions on this question is recognized, and it is asserted that the weight of authority supports the doctrine that such a deposit, standing alone, establishes a tentative trust, which is revocable at the will of the depositor until he dies or completes the gift by some unequivocal act or declaration showing that the creation of a trust was intended.

In 65 C.J. 293, 294, § 68, it is said: "In some jurisdictions, while it is recognized that a trust in respect of a deposit in bank which is absolute and irrevocable by the donor or depositor may be created, the courts have recognized so-called tentative trusts in respect of such deposits in cases in which usually, if not always, saving deposits or accounts are involved. Whether the trust is tentative or irrevocable depends on the intention of the depositor or donor, determinable as a question of fact. Where the foregoing distinction is recognized, in general a deposit by one person of his own money in his own name as trustee for another, standing alone, creates merely a tentative trust, revocable at the will of the depositor during his lifetime, becoming absolute and irrevocable on the death of the depositor before the beneficiary without revocation or some decisive act or declaration of disaffirmance, and entitling the beneficiary to the balance remaining at the time of the depositor's death, but not to anything more than such balance." In 9 C.J.S., Banks and Banking, p. 1418, § 995, it is said: "Where a deposit is made in the name of the depositor as trustee, the fund presumably belongs to the cestui que trust; but this presumption may be rebutted by evidence showing that the money was that of the depositor who had no intention of giving it to the person named as cestui que trust." In American Law Institute's Restatement of the Law of Trusts, 183, § 58, comment (b), it is said: "A tentative trust of a savings deposit in a bank can be revoked by the depositor at any time during his lifetime, by a manifestation of his intention to revoke the trust. No particular formalities are necessary to manifest such an intention. If he withdraws any part of the deposit during his lifetime, the withdrawal operates as a revocation of the trust to the extent of such withdrawal, and the beneficiary will be entitled only to the amount remaining on deposit at the death of depositor." It is further stated that if the beneficiary should die before the depositor dies, the trust is terminated, although the depositor should subsequently die without manifesting an intention to revoke the trust; and that such a trust can be revoked by the depositor by his will, if he makes a disposition of his property which can not be carried out without using the deposit.

Defendants in error contend that because of the facts that testatrix gave plaintiff in error no notice of the deposit, retained the passbook in her own possession, and made withdrawals from and additions to the deposit, any intent to create a trust is disproved. In 65 C. J. 290, § 65, it is said: "While the fact that the depositor retains possession of the bank-book may, under certain circumstances, show an absence of intention to create a trust, retention of the book or the certificate of deposit, his making subsequent deposits in the account, his retention of the power of withdrawal, or his subsequent withdrawals of deposits or interest, does not necessarily prevent the existence of a trust, or destroy a trust duly executed; such retention of the pass-book, subsequent deposits or withdrawals of deposits or interest, may be consistent with the existence of a trust." In the instant case, the beneficiary was a minor at the time the deposit was made and during the life of the depositor. It was therefore natural and proper that the bank book should not be delivered to her and should be retained by the trustee. In 7 Am.Jur. 310, § 439, it is said: "As regards the creation of a savings-bank trust, retention of the bank-book or pass-book is consistent with any aspect of the transaction, for of course the book would be retained when no trust was intended, and when a trust was intended, the book might be retained by the depositor in the character of trustee of the trust created by himself without parting with the legal title to the fund." In American Law Institute's Restatement of the Law of Trusts, § 58, it is said: "Where a person makes a deposit in a savings account in a bank in his own name as Trustee for another person, intending to reserve a power to withdraw the whole or any part of the deposit at any time during his lifetime and to use as his own whatever he may withdraw, or otherwise, to revoke the trust, the intended trust is enforceable by the beneficiary upon the death of the depositor, as to any part remaining on deposit on his death, if he has not revoked the trust." And in the comment on the above statement, it is said: "If a person makes a savings deposit in a bank in his own name 'as trustee' for another person, his intention may be either (1) to create a revocable trust, or (2) to create an irrevocable trust, or (3) not to create a trust. Evidence may be admitted to show which was his intention. In the absence of evidence of a different intention of the depositor, the mere fact that a deposit is made in a savings bank in the name of the depositor 'as trustee' for another person is sufficient to show an intention to create a revocable trust. To such a trust the rule stated in this section is applicable. Such a trust is called a 'tentative trust.'" In Martin v. Funk, 75 N.Y. 134, 31 Am.Rep. 446, it was said: "S. deposited in a savings bank moneys belonging to her, in trust for M. and K., who were her distant relatives. She retained the pass-books until her death, drawing out only one year's interest, and M. and K. were ignorant of the deposit. *Held,* that the transaction constituted an effectual trust for their benefit, on the death of S." In Re Totten, supra, it was said (179 N.Y. 112, 71 N.E. 752, 70 L.R.A. 711, 1 Ann. Cas. 900): "After much reflection upon the subject, guided by the principles established by our former decisions, we announce the following as our conclusion: A deposit by one person of his own money in his own name as trustee for another, standing alone, does not establish an irrevocable trust during the lifetime of the depositor. It is a tentative trust merely, revocable at will, until the depositor dies or completes the gift in his lifetime by some unequivocal act or declaration, such as delivery of the passbook or notice to the beneficiary. In case the depositor dies before the beneficiary without revocation, or some decisive act or declaration of disaffirmance, the presumption arises that an absolute trust was created as to the balance on hand at the death of the depositor." In the light of these authorities, we hold that neither the retention of the pass-book, the absence of notice to the beneficiary, nor the withdrawals from and additions to the deposit had the effect of disproving an intention on the part of the depositor to create a trust; and we further hold, in harmony with the overwhelming weight of authority, that the deposit here involved is presumptively a tentative trust, and in the absence of evidence to rebut this presumption the beneficiary is entitled to the fund. The evidence for the defendants clearly failed to disprove an intention on the part of the depositor to create a trust, while the evidence for the plaintiff in error tended to prove that the intention of the depositor was to create a trust in her favor.

It is urged by defendants in error that since the trust here relied upon was an express trust, to be valid it must be expressed in writing as required by the Code § 108–105. A sufficient answer is the testimony of an agent of the bank, that at the direction of the depositor a written entry of deposit was made on the records of the bank in the name of the depositor as trustee for the plaintiff in error, that a passbook evidencing such deposit was issued by the bank in favor of the depositor as trustee, and that the depositor signed an identification card as trustee for Alice Frances Wilder. In view of these facts, as well as the decisions of the courts of other States, where the statute of frauds is also of force, this contention of the defendants in error is without merit.

It is further contended that the deposit here involved was testamentary in character, and therefore was void because violative of the wills act, in that it was not executed with the formalities required in the execution of a will. In the first place, the intention of the depositor at the time the deposit is made is, under the authorities, the controlling question as to whether or not a trust is created; and since the deposit here involved, standing alone, is held to be presumptively a tentative trust, unless evidence is produced showing that the depositor had no intention of creating a trust, or that she later revoked the same, it stands as an executed trust as of the time of its creation. Furthermore, in the States where the courts have sustained similar deposits as tentative trusts, (which decisions are cited above) the wills act is of force; and those decisions are adjudication that such a deposit is not testamentary in character. In American Law Institute's Restatement of the Law of Trusts, § 57(3), a number of described intended trusts are said to be testamentary; but § 58 of the same work (heretofore quoted) declares that a deposit made and handled as the one involved in the instant case is a valid trust, is expressly excepted from the rule declaring other trusts testamentary; and in the comment (p. 175) it is said: "Where the owner of property transfers it inter vivos to another person in trust, the disposition is not testamentary merely because the interest of the beneficiary does not take effect in enjoyment or possession before the death of the settlor, or because in addition he reserves power to revoke or modify the trust. In such a case the trust is created in the lifetime of the settlor; and the mere fact that he can destroy it or alter it does not make the disposition testamentary, although if the trust were not to arise until his death the intended trust would be testamentary." Buteau v. Lavalle, 284 Mass. 276, 187 N.E. 628; 1 Bogert on Trusts and Trustees, p. 221, § 47; 68 C.J. 620; § 241; 12 R.C.L. 949, § 24. The deposit here involved was not testamentary.

Judgment reversed.

All the Justices concur.[68]

68. Restatement, Second, Trusts § 58, Comment *c* adds to the provisions discussed in the principal case the following:

> "If the depositor becomes insane, his guardian can apply to the court for permission to revoke the trust and the court will grant such permission if, but only if and to the extent that, the use of the deposit is necessary for the welfare of the depositor."

Most of the courts which have had an opportunity to pass upon the reality of trust intention in a savings bank trust have presumed that a revocable trust is created. Some of the courts which raise a revocable trust presumption hold that a present interest vests in the beneficiary when the deposit is made but is subject to divestment by the depositor's revocation. E.g., Coughlin v. Farmers and Mechanics Savings Bank, 199 Minn. 102, 272 N.W. 166 (1937). Other courts hold that no interest vests until the death of the depositor. E.g., Matter of Slobiansky, 152 Misc. 232, 273 N.Y.S. 869 (1934). Courts in other states have presumed that an irrevocable trust is created at the time of the deposit, Cazallis v. Ingraham, 119 Me. 240, 110 A. 359 (1920), or that no trust is created, Mulloy v. Charlestown Five Cents Savings Bank, 285 Mass. 101, 188 N.E. 608 (1934). In any event, the presumption adopted initially can be rebutted by evidence of a contrary intention by the donor. Thus, where the "Totten trust" presumption is applied notice to the beneficiary or delivery of the passbook to the beneficiary may raise a presumption of irrevocable trust, although the facts may indicate that the acts offered as proof of irrevocable trust intention were in fact conditioned. The delivery of the pass book, for example, may be made for the purpose of safe keeping and not be intended by the depositor to constitute an irrevocable transfer. See generally, Bogert, Trusts and Trustees (2d Ed., 1965) § 47; 4 Powell, The Law of Real Property (Rohan.Rev.1970) Ch. 43; I Scott, Trusts (3d Ed., 1967) § 58; Christopher, "Totten Trust: The Poor Man's Will", 42 N.C.L.Rev. 214 (1963); Estes,

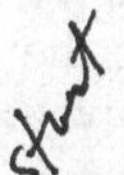

MONTGOMERY v. MICHAELS

Supreme Court of Illinois, 1973.
54 Ill.2d 532, 301 N.E.2d 465.[69]

DAVIS, JUSTICE:

During her lifetime, Bernice D. Montgomery created in certain banks eight savings accounts, which differed somewhat in their terms, but all were essentially the same in that she was named as trustee therein and the accounts were for the benefit of her two children by a prior marriage. All but two of the accounts specifically provided that they were to be paid to the child or children named therein on her death. She retained control over all of these accounts during her lifetime and made deposits in and withdrawals from them.

She died intestate, and her husband, Dr. Earl Montgomery, was appointed administrator of her estate. As administrator and individually, he filed a citation petition in the circuit court of Lake County wherein he alleged that the trusts were a fraud on his marital rights and were illusory, and if sustained would defeat his statutory right to one third of the decedent's personal estate (Ill.Rev.Stat.1969, ch. 3, par. 11), and his right to a widower's award (Ill.Rev.Stat.1969, ch. 3, par. 178). He prayed, among other things, that the court enter an order finding that said trusts are illusory and invalid, that said bank accounts are the property of the decedent, and that the balance of said accounts be turned over to him as administrator of the estate.

The trial court granted a motion to dismiss the petition, except as to the amount of the funeral bill, which was assessed equally against the two beneficiaries of the eight savings-account trusts. It found that the savings-account trusts were not illusory, and that the balances therein should be paid to the named beneficiaries after payment of the funeral bill. The appellate court affirmed (2 Ill.App.3d 821, 277 N.E.2d 739), and we granted leave to appeal.

In In re Estate of Petralia (1965), 32 Ill.2d 134, 204 N.E.2d 1, we upheld the validity of savings-account trusts or "Totten Trusts," so called because of the case entitled In re Totten (1904), 179 N.Y. 112, 71 N.E. 748. In *Petralia* we held that if the settlor is also the trustee and retains complete control over the account during his or her lifetime, such a savings account is not different in substance from other revocable *inter vivos* trusts, which this court has found to be valid; that the declaration of the trust immediately creates an equitable interest in the beneficiaries even though the enjoyment of the in-

"In Search of a Less Tentative Totten", 5 Pepperdine L.Rev. 21 (1977); Ritchie, "What is A Will", 49 Va.L.Rev. 759 (1963); Note, "Savings Account Trusts," 49 Notre Dame L.Rev. 686 (1974). Article 6 of the Uniform Probate Code recognizes the validity of these "trust" accounts, which are presumed to be revocable under § 6–103(c) during lifetime of the depositor; balance at death of the "trustee" belongs to the surviving beneficiary under § 6–104(c) in the absence of clear and convincing evidence of a contrary intent.

69. Noted 23 DePaul L.Rev. 1247 (1974), 50 Chi.Kent L.Rev. 159 (1973), 1973 U.Ill.L.F. 775; also discussed in Carroll, "The Interplay of Probate Assets and Nonprobate Assets in the Administration of a Decedent's Estate", 25 DePaul L.Rev. 363 (1976).

terest is postponed until the death of the settlor and may be completely destroyed by withdrawal from the account of all the deposits made by the settlor during his or her lifetime; and that the destructibility of the interest of the beneficiary does not negate the existence of a valid trust. Farkas v. Williams (1955), 5 Ill.2d 417, 125 N.E.2d 600; Gurnett v. Mutual Life Ins. Co. (1934) 356 Ill. 612, 191 N.E. 250.

In *Petralia*, at page 138, 204 N.E.2d at page 3, we quoted from Restatement (Second) of Trusts, sec. 58: "Where a person makes a deposit in a savings account in a bank or other savings organization in his own name as trustee for another person intending to reserve a power to withdraw the whole or any part of the deposit at any time during his lifetime and to use as his own whatever he may withdraw, or otherwise to revoke the trust, the intended trust is enforceable by the beneficiary upon the death of the depositor as to any part remaining on deposit on his death if he has not revoked the trust."

The question remains, however, whether such a trust is valid for every purpose, and particularly whether it is effective to defeat a surviving spouse's statutory share in the estate of his deceased spouse, and his right to a widower's award. Ill.Rev.Stat.1969, ch. 3, par. 178.

The Probate Act expressed the policy of protecting a surviving spouse in the expectancy which he or she may anticipate from the other's estate. The minimum statutory share of a surviving spouse in the real and personal estate of the deceased spouse is that provided in event of intestacy if there are both a spouse and descendants, namely, a one-third interest therein to the surviving spouse. The surviving spouse takes one half of the estate if there is no descendant. Ill.Rev.Stat.1971, ch. 3, pars. 11, 16.

A surviving spouse may renounce a will, and by doing so will receive this minimum share. (Ill.Rev.Stat.1963, ch. 3, par. 16.) The question in the case at bar is whether a "Totten Trust" is sufficiently testamentary in nature that by analogy the statutory policy of permitting a surviving spouse to renounce under the decedent's will and share in the proceeds of such estate should be applicable to such trust to the same extent as to an estate passing under a will.

Some cases suggest that the answer should depend upon the intent of the deceased spouse in creating the trust. This intent may be revealed by the myriad of attendant circumstances that include the secretive nature in which the decedent acted, what he may have said to others with respect to his intent, the proximity in time between the transfer and death, the size of the estate and the amount otherwise left to the surviving spouse, and, generally, all factors which might be indicative of an intent to defraud the surviving spouse of his or her statutory share. (Rose v. St. Louis Union Trust Co. (1969), 43 Ill. 2d 312, 316, 317, 253 N.E.2d 417.) At the same time, our courts have recognized that one may dispose of his property during his lifetime and thus deprive a spouse of his, or her, statutory share, so long as the disposition was sufficiently effective and complete, unless the transaction is illusory or tantamount to fraud. Holmes v. Mims

(1953), 1 Ill.2d 274, 279, 115 N.E.2d 790; Padfield v. Padfield (1875), 78 Ill. 16, 18, 19.

The infirmities and difficulties in determining the intent of the decedent in connection with an *inter vivos* transfer of his personal property and in ascertaining whether such intent is so tainted with fraud as to cause such transfer to be ineffective in the deprivation of a spouse of his, or her, statutory share in the decedent's estate are readily apparent. Rose v. St. Louis Union Trust Co. (1969), 43 Ill.2d 312, 316, 317, 253 N.E.2d 417.

In the case at bar the settlor was also the trustee. During her lifetime she retained absolute, unqualified control over the bank accounts, and possessed and exercised all incidents of complete ownership, including the right to receive interest payable thereon and withdraw the principal thereof. The enjoyment of the proceeds of the accounts by the beneficiary or beneficiaries named therein would arise only upon the death of the settlor-trustee with the accounts remaining intact.

Under these circumstances, the expressed statutory policy of protecting a surviving spouse's statutory share in the estate should prevail, regardless of the intent of the deceased spouse in creating the savings-account trust. In Blankenship v. Hall (1908), 233 Ill. 116, at page 129, 84 N.E. 192, at page 196, this court stated: "There has been a manifest desire on the part of the lawmakers of this State to provide for the support of the wife, not only during the lifetime of the husband but also after his death, until, as this court said in In re Taylor's Will, 55 Ill. 252, on page 259: 'We do not go too far when we say that it has become a sort of common law in this State that this support shall be in all cases one-third of the husband's real estate for life, and one-third of the personal estate forever, which shall remain after the payment of debts.' "

In Newman v. Dore (1937), 275 N.Y. 371, 379, 9 N.E.2d 966, 968, the court, in considering the right of a surviving spouse in the property of the deceased spouse, stated: "Motive or intent is an unsatisfactory test of the validity of a transfer of property." The court further stated, with reference to the rights of a surviving spouse, that "the only sound test of the validity of a challenged transfer is whether it is real or illusory." (275 N.Y. 371, 379, 9 N.E.2d 966, 969.) The court held that the transfer was illusory and not sufficiently real to deprive the decedent's spouse of her statutory share in his estate. Other cases have reached the same result. Krause v. Krause (1941), 285 N.Y. 27, 32 N.E.2d 779; Steixner v. Bowery Savings Bank (Sup.Ct.1949), 86 N.Y.S.2d 747; MacGregor v. Fox (1952), 280 App.Div. 435, 114 N.Y.S.2d 286.

Text writers have concluded that the control retained over a savings-account trust is so complete that even though the trust is valid, it should not be so as against the surviving spouse. In commenting upon dictum suggesting that a savings deposit in trust for another would be an effective method of cutting out a depositor's surviving spouse, Scott (1 A. Scott, Law of Trusts, sec. 58.5, at 546–547 (3d ed. 1967)) states:

> "It would seem that a strong argument could be made against this result, on the ground that it violates the policy of the statute which gives a distributive share of the decedent's estate to the surviving spouse. It is true that it is generally held that the creation of a revocable trust is sufficient to cut out the surviving spouse, at least if the settlor does not reserve too great a control over the property. In the case of the savings-deposit trust, however, the depositor reserves such complete control that it would seem that, even though the trust is valid as against the personal representative of the depositor, it should not be valid as against the surviving spouse. Certainly the policy underlying the statute protecting the surviving spouse is stronger than the policy underlying the statute providing for certain formalities to evidence a testamentary disposition. It may well be held that the creation of a savings deposit trust is valid but not effective to cut out the surviving spouse."

Also see: Bogert, Law of Trusts and Trustees, sec. 47, at 340–341 (2d ed. 1965).

While we recognize the general validity of "Totten" savings-account trusts for the reasons set forth above, we conclude that the savings-account trusts in question were illusory and invalid as against Dr. Montgomery and that they did not deprive him of his statutory share in his deceased spouse's estate. The trial court order, which was affirmed by the appellate court, provided that the funeral bill of the decedent be paid from the savings bank accounts in question, and that the banks distribute the balance of the said accounts to the beneficiaries named therein. This order properly directed the payment of the funeral bill from said accounts, if such funds were needed therefor. In the event funds from other property are insufficient to pay debts and claims against the decedent's estate, then such trust funds are available for the payment of estate debts and can also be reached for the payment of the expenses of administering the estate if there is not sufficient other property for this purpose, but they are not chargeable with the payment of legacies. In re Will of Morton (Sur.Ct.1969), 61 Misc.2d 624, 305 N.Y.S.2d 555, 557; In re Reich's Estate (Sur.Ct.1933), 146 Misc. 616, 262 N.Y.S. 623, 628. The ALI Restatement of the Law of Trusts (2d ed. 1959), sec. 58, comment d (Creditors of depositor), states: "Although creditors of the settlor cannot reach the trust property merely because he has reserved a power of revocation (see sec. 330, comment *o),* creditors of a person who make a savings deposit upon a tentative trust [Totten] can reach his interest, since he has such extensive powers over the deposit as to justify treating him as in substance the unrestricted owner of the deposit. So also, on death of the depositor if the deposit is needed for the payment of his debts, his creditors can reach it. So also, if it is needed it can be applied to the payment of his funeral expenses and the expenses of the administration of his estate, if he has not sufficient other property which can be applied for these purposes."

In all other respects the order was erroneous. The balances in the savings-account trusts should be treated as the property of the decedent for the purpose of determining Dr. Montgomery's statutory share in his deceased spouse's estate, and, if necessary, he may draw upon the varying amounts in the respective trust accounts on a proportionate basis to the extent required to pay him one third of the net estate remaining after payment of all just claims. Such claims would include a surviving spouse's award, if such an award is appropriate, as well as the costs of administering the estate. (Ill.Rev.Stat.1971, ch. 3, par. 202.) Thereafter the balance remaining in the accounts should be distributed to the beneficiaries named in the trust accounts.

Accordingly, the judgment of the appellate court is reversed in part and affirmed in part, and the cause is remanded to the circuit court for further proceedings not inconsistent with the views expressed herein.

In view of the nature of the proceeding below, we believe it appropriate on remand to specify that respondents be given the opportunity to file an answer to the petition and to present evidence, if there by any, of any defense that might be available to them in view of the conclusions expressed herein.

Affirmed in part and reversed in part and remanded.

NOTE

In Matter of Halpern,[70] the New York Court of Appeals held a Totten trust not illusory and excluded the widow from an elective share in the trust assets. The Court compared the Totten trust to the joint bank account which, at the time of this decision,[71] also could not be reached to satisfy the forced heirship claim. The trusts in Halpern were for the granddaughter of the depositor, a natural object of his bounty, additional deposits were made in each account and there were no withdrawals. The depositor told several persons he wanted his grandchild to have his bankbooks and turned over one of the books to the grandchild's mother. He retained three of the books in his safe deposit box. The American Law Institute in its Restatement, Second Trusts § 58, Comment *e* takes the position that the surviving spouse of the creator of a Totten trust can include the deposit in computing the share to which the surviving spouse is entitled, although the probate assets would have to be applied first in satisfaction of the elective share thus computed.

In Whittington v. Whittington,[72] the Maryland Court adopted a more flexible rule for determining the rights of a surviving spouse in Totten trusts:

> "The subject of fraud on marital rights has recently been carefully reviewed in the Mushaw case and in Allender v. Allender, 199 Md. 541, 87 A.2d 608, and also in an Article entitled "Inter Vivos Transfers in Viola-

70. 303 N.Y. 33, 100 N.E.2d 120 (1951).

71. Inda v. Inda, 288 N.Y. 315, 43 N.E.2d 59 (1942). Both the Totten trust and joint bank account were brought within reach of the surviving spouse by McKinney's N.Y., EPTL, § 5–1.1(b)(1)(B) and (C) (1980 Supp.). These New York provisions are set forth in Chapter IV, Section 2(5).

72. 205 Md. 1, 106 A.2d 72, 49 A.L.R. 2d 513 (1954).

tion of the Rights of Surviving Spouses," by Melvin J. Sykes, Esq. in 10 Md.Law Review 1. Little would be gained by a repetition of the authorities referred to in the cases and article cited.

* * *

"In Maryland, the completeness of the transfer and the extent of control retained by the transferor, the motive of the transferor, participation by the transferee in the alleged fraud and the degree to which the surviving spouse is stripped of his or her interest in the estate of the decedent spouse have all been considered material, and no one test has been adopted to the exclusion of all other tests. As pointed out by Mr. Sykes in his article above referred to, there are several other factors which have been or may be considered as pertinent, such as the relative moral claims of the surviving spouse and of the transferees, other provisions for the surviving spouse, whether or not he or she has independent means and the interval of time between the transfer and the death of the transferor. There is no statute in Maryland comparable to that relating to the inheritance tax, Code 1951, Article 81, Section 150, which sets up any standard by which the effectiveness and treatment of *inter vivos* transfers should be determined insofar as the marital rights of a surviving spouse are concerned.

"In the present case the widow receives a one-third interest in a gross estate appraised at approximately $25,000 of which about $13,000 consisted of realty and about $12,000 of personal property. In addition, she had received during her husband's lifetime $2,000 representing nearly one-fourth of the sale price of a farm, which she had put in a joint bank account in her name and her husband's. The four bank accounts in dispute aggregate roughly $17,000, and one-third of that amount is approximately $5,700. Whether the amount of the bank accounts in dispute should be reduced by $4,000 out of the proceeds of sale of the farm as an offset against the $2,000 from that source already received by the wife, is perhaps a debatable question, which we do not think it necessary to decide. Compare Jaworski v. Wisniewski, 149 Md. 109, 131 A. 40. Assuming that no such reduction should be made, we find that the widow is certainly not completely stripped of her marital rights in her deceased husband's property, even though she does receive approximately forty per cent less than she would have received if the four savings account trusts had not been established.

* * *

"No general and completely satisfactory rule to determine the validity or invalidity of transfers alleged to be in fraud of marital rights has yet been evolved in this State. The test of degree has been recognized, and so have its shortcomings. It remains a very practical consideration among the facts and circumstances to be considered in connection with the completeness and genuineness of a transfer where the transferor, by naming himself as trustee and as a beneficiary, or by means of an agreement with his donees, has retained some control over the subject of the gift or trust under scrutiny. In the light of the family relationships of the parties involved in this case, in the absence of any fraud or undue influence practised by the decedent's sons and in view of the amount and proportion of the property formerly owned by the decedent which the widow will receive, we do not find any basis upon which the trusts created in these savings accounts should be stricken down. Accordingly the decree must be affirmed."

In Jeruzal v. Jeruzal,[73] the Minnesota Court was reluctant to choose between the New York and the Maryland rules. In that case eleven Totten trusts were held to be beyond the reach of a second wife of the depositor, the beneficiaries of each trust being remote relatives of the depositor and relatives of the first wife. There was no evidence that depositor had given any of the beneficiaries notice of the accounts or delivered any of the passbooks to them. In the course of its opinion, the Court analyzed the various positions taken concerning the surviving spouse's claim to Totten trust assets as follows: [74]

* * * "[I]t appears that in Minnesota a motive to deprive one's spouse of the statutory inheritance by inter vivos transfers generally is irrelevant, the only test being whether the transaction is real. This principle, if extended to Totten trusts, would lead to the adoption of the New York rule enunciated in the Halpern case that the balance in a Totten trust cannot be reached by the surviving spouse if the trust is real, that is, if the donor intended the named beneficiary to get the money. There is some suggestion in Smith v. Wold, supra, that the surviving spouse can reach transferred funds if he or she would otherwise be left destitute. This is the rule of Mushaw v. Mushaw, supra.

"We are not satisfied that either the New York or Maryland rule should be adopted. While the Maryland rule is more equitable, it provides no clear standard of application. Under both the New York and Maryland rules, the trust is either good against the spouse or void altogether. We would prefer the Restatement rule, by which the beneficiaries receive what the decedent intended them to have except so far as the trust funds are necessary to satisfy the statutory interests of the spouse after the general assets of the estate have been exhausted. However, in view of the widespread use of Totten trusts in the area of testamentary disposition, we do not feel free to adopt the Restatement rule without first giving the legislature an opportunity to provide for it by statute as was done in Pennsylvania.

"Because of such widespread use of Totten trusts and the reliance which attorneys have doubtless placed on our previous, more general decisions on marital fraud, we will be guided here, and in other cases in which the trust becomes absolute by the death of the depositor before the end of the next session of the legislature, by our previous decisions. In doing so we must affirm the trial court on this issue. It cannot be said that in establishing the trusts in question with the idea of depriving his wife of a share of the money placed in those trusts, decedent was guilty of a breach of legal or equitable duty. He was doing only what our decisions would permit him to do under Smith v. Wold, supra; Balafas v. Balafas, supra; Van Devere v. Moore, supra; and language found in Walso v. Latterner, supra; and Dyste v. Farmers & Mechanics Sav. Bank, supra. Nor do we think that the trial court's decision should be disturbed for equitable reasons because it does not appear from the record, at least within the standard indicated by the Wold and Balafas cases, that the surviving spouse has been left destitute.

73. 269 Minn. 183, 130 N.W.2d 473 (1964). Noted, 34 U.Cin.L.Rev. 179 (1965).

74. 269 Minn. 183, 194, 130 N.W.2d 473, 481 (1964).

"The record fairly establishes that the Totten trusts established by decedent were for the benefit of relatives who would reasonably be expected to be the beneficiaries of his gifts. The record indicates that the trusts were established in good faith with intent to divest himself of ownership.

"However, this court will feel free to follow the Restatement rule hereafter if the legislature declines to act on this matter. The Totten trust is itself a judicial creation, limiting the effect of statutory provisions for the disposition of property by will. It is therefore our duty to subject this judicially-created doctrine to such limitations as are necessary to prevent the defeat of substantive statutory policies. The Restatement rule must recommend itself because it prevents the depositor from leaving the surviving spouse destitute while he retains complete control of the funds during lifetime. The statutory policy against allowing the widow to be left destitute should not be subordinated to the policy of giving broad effect to savings account trusts, however desirable the latter might be. We cannot overlook the danger that lies in the general use of Totten trusts as they may affect the surviving spouse. Actually, a depositor accomplishes nothing by a Totten trust which he could not accomplish by a will. Only the procedure, not the substance, is changed. Moreover, it should be acknowledged that Totten trusts are actually part of the general assets of the estate in the sense that they can be reached for paying funeral expenses and expenses of the estate, if necessary. Matter of Reich, 146 Misc. 616, 262 N.Y.S. 623; Matter of Vetroock, 34 Misc.2d 1073, 230 N.Y.S.2d 485; Restatement, Second, Trusts § 58, Comment *d.* The balance may also be reached by creditors of the depositor. Matter of Reich, supra; Matter of Halbauer, 34 Misc.2d 458, 228 N.Y.S.2d 786, affirmed, 18 App.Div.2d 966, 238 N.Y.S.2d 511; Banca D'Italia & Trust Co. v. Giordano, 154 Pa.Super. 452, 36 A.2d 242; Restatement, Second, Trusts § 58, Comment *d.*

"We feel that the Restatement rule avoids both the inequities of the New York rule and the uncertainties of the Maryland rule. It provides a satisfactory balance of the two policies here involved, namely the policy in favor of protecting the surviving spouse from destitution and the policy of allowing testators full control of the disposition of their estates. * * *"

As mentioned in that portion of Jeruzal here set forth, creditors of the depositor are permitted to reach the balance in a savings deposit trust account regardless of the rule adopted in the state with respect to revocable trusts generally. In New York, creditors of the depositor during his lifetime may reach the account on a "fraud" theory; while estate creditors, such as the undertaker and claimants for administrative expenses, may be permitted to reach the account on the theory that the presumption of the depositor's intent to create an absolute trust at death is "rebutted" to the extent necessary to satisfy their claims.[75]

Under Uniform Probate Code, §§ 6–103 and 6–107 creditors of the "trustee" can reach the beneficial interest of the trustee; and such an account is included in the augmented estate subject to the elective share of a surviving spouse under § 2–202.

75. Various theories concerning creditor claims are discussed in Matter of Reich, 146 Misc. 616, 262 N.Y.S. 623 (1933); See Restatement, Second, Trusts § 58, Comment *d.* If the settlor manifests an intent to make the trust irrevocable it will probably prove difficult for a creditor to reach the account.

SECTION 3. TRUSTS FOR BUSINESS PURPOSES

Trusts are used for a variety of business purposes. Some of these purposes are ancillary to business operations. Examples are trusteed retirement, profit-sharing and welfare plans, used as employment incentives; voting trusts; business life insurance trusts; and trusts used to secure loans or for the protection or satisfaction of creditors. Trusts are also used as business organizations—that is, the trust is used as a substitute for a corporation or partnership.[76]

Trusts for business purposes in many cases have major tax ramifications and are examined in appropriate tax courses. Business trusts also may be considered in courses with a commercial orientation. But it is possible for a student to go through law school without examining trusts in the business context. The American Law Institute, for example, did not deal with business trusts or trusts for security in either of its Restatements of Trusts.[77] Thus, while this book concentrates upon the express trust, private and charitable, as used in dispositive transactions and upon trusts by operation of law used as remedial devices (constructive and resulting trusts) some of the trusts used for business purposes are considered here. The student should observe how some of the doctrines applied with rigidity to private and charitable trusts are relaxed or ignored when trusts are used in a business context; how litigation problems associated with trusts change with the context in which the trust is used; and how new fiduciary doctrines developed in business applications of the trust may influence judicial views in the future pertaining to private and charitable express trusts. We have already observed reciprocal doctrinal influences of private trusts and trusts by operation of law.[78]

(1) TRUSTEED EMPLOYEE BENEFIT PLANS (WELFARE, PENSION, PROFIT SHARING, STOCK BONUS PLANS)

One of the most interesting, and certainly one of the most rapidly expanding, areas of trust law involves the application of the trust and derived fiduciary doctrine to administration of retirement and related plans used by employers as an employment incentive and bargained for by unions in those cases in which employers are reluctant to es-

76. A private express trust or an estate may operate a business. Doctrine concerning this relation of a business enterprise to a trust is considered in Chapter XVII. In the business role here considered the trust is the business organization.

77. See 1 Restatement, Trusts (2d 1959), Introductory Note p. 2, § 1, comment (b). The most useful brief summary of these trusts to be found in a text devoted for the most part to private dispositive trust transactions is in Bogert, Trusts & Trustees (Revised Second Edition, 1977) §§ 247–255.

78. See Chapter III, Section 4; Chapter VIII, Section 1, and this Chapter, Section 1(3) and (4).

tablish them.[79] Payments from these plans also are of importance in the planning of estates and will be briefly considered here.

Prior to 1974, many corporate and other retirement and welfare plans were administered in trust for convenience in management. In this form these plans might qualify for special income tax treatment although other forms of organization might also qualify. However, despite federal legislation concerning these plans based upon the interstate commerce power [80], and even when the plans were trusteed, employees found their remedies, particularly under state law, grossly inadequate to protect their rights. There were instances in which employees received nothing from "tax qualified" plans and there were also instances of abuse of the plans by fund managers and others. Thus, by the Employee Retirement Income Security Act of 1974 (ERISA) (often called the Pension Reform Act of 1974) [81] Congress required trusts for most of the corporate employee benefit plans and imposed major fiduciary responsibilities upon those making decisions concerning these plans even though these persons were not trust-

79. See Bogert, Trusts and Trustees (Revised Second Edition, 1977) § 255; Mamorsky, Employee Benefits Law (1980) (supplemented). The plans assist in attracting able employees, retaining them, and in maintaining good employee relations. From the viewpoint of the employee, the qualified plan serves as a tax shelter; but even when the plan is unqualified, holding out to the employee the prospect of future gain can serve as an incentive to enter employment and remain on the job. See the simple plan used by Farkas to retain his employee, Williams, in Farkas v. Williams, appearing as principal case in Chapter VIII, Section 6.

80. The major statutes under which some protection might be afforded the employees in benefit plans were the Internal Revenue Code, § 401 et seq., 26 U.S.C.A. and the Welfare and Pension Plans Disclosure Act, P.L. 85–836, 72 Stat. 997 (1958), the latter, now repealed, being primarily a disclosure statute to aid plan participants in detecting wrongdoing but being of little help once the wrongdoing was discovered.

81. P.L. 93–406 (1974), 29 U.S.C.A. § 1001 et seq. The major amendment to ERISA has been the Multiemployer Pension Plan Amendments Act of 1980, P.L. 96–364, 29 U.S.C.A. § 1001(a) et seq., pertaining principally to insurance upon termination of multiemployer plans. This Act is usually referred to as "MEPPA". Under ERISA, the Pension Benefit Guaranty Corporation (PBGC), a tax exempt corporation within the Department of Labor, was required to guarantee benefits under most of the single employer plans but had discretion to insure multiemployer plans. Multiemployer plans are those to which more than one employer is required to contribute pursuant to one or more collective bargaining agreements between an employee organization and more than one employer. The amount of contribution by each employer must be less than 50% of the aggregate of contributions for the plan year by all employers and the benefits must be payable with respect to each participant without regard to the cessation of payments by the employer who had employed the participant. ERISA § 3(37). PBGC had elected to insure some of the multiemployer plans but estimated in Fiscal Year 1978 that claims under these plans could reach $4 billion within 10 years. PGBC Report, Fiscal Year 1979, p. 9. This would require premium levels for insurance that would burden other multiemployer plans and induce further terminations. MEPPA was a partial response to this problem, being intended to induce employers not to withdraw from multiemployer plans, initiating a limited insurance requirement, and providing for reorganization of plans in difficulty. Most of the multiemployer plans are trusteed, some embracing several trusts.

Title I of ERISA, the "Labor" title, contains requirements for the employee benefit plans including the fiduciary requirements. Title II contains the Internal Revenue Code amendments. Title III provides for further studies and reports concerning employee benefit plans—which certainly will be needed. Title IV pertains to the Pension Benefit Guaranty Corporation and insurance upon plan termination.

ees.[82] Title I of the Act established detailed requirements for pension, welfare and related plans including a comprehensive federal fiduciary code which is enforced against the trustees and other fiduciaries in federal district courts by the Secretary of Labor.[83] Beneficiaries of the plans can also bring enforcement actions in the federal courts, state courts having concurrent jurisdiction in actions brought by plan beneficiaries. Civil and criminal sanctions are available against the trustees and other fiduciaries. Title II of ERISA contains major amendments of the Internal Revenue Code pertaining to employee benefit plans. The Secretary of the Treasury administers the Internal Revenue Code provisions of ERISA.[84] If the plan is qualified for Federal tax purposes, the employer can deduct its contributions, no income tax is paid by the trust on plan income, and the employee pays no income tax until he receives actual or constructive payment, usually after he retires.

The trusts under ERISA, in their special tax treatment and potential for public enforcement of the duties of trustees and other fiduciaries, resemble to a degree the charitable trusts which we will examine in Chapter XI of this book. The trust must meet the requirements for creation of a trust under state law. In most instances the beneficiaries would be so large a group that the definite beneficiary requirement should be dealt with using the rationale suggested for use when large unincorporated associations are beneficiaries[85] or the

82. There are a number of exceptions to the trust requirement. The Keogh (or HR 10) plans for the self employed and partnerships, which were given special tax treatment in the Self-Employed Individuals Tax Retirement Act of 1962, P.L. 87–792, 26 U.S.C.A., are not required to be trusteed when held in qualified custodial accounts. The Individual Retirement Accounts (IRAs) introduced in ERISA do not have to be trusteed nor do the payments made by employers to these accounts under P.L. 95–600 (1978) (Simplified Employee Pensions) (SEPs). Benefit plans guaranteed by an insurer, "excess benefit plans" and a few others also escape the trust requirement. ERISA § 401, 26 U.S.C.A. § 1103. However, note that the fiduciary obligations imposed in ERISA extend beyond those plans required to be trusteed. The fiduciary obligations extend to any employee benefit plan (including welfare plans) if established and maintained by any employer engaging in interstate commerce or in any industry or activity affecting commerce or by any employee organization or organizations representing employees engaged in interstate commerce or in any industry or activity affecting interstate commerce or by both. ERISA § 4(a), 29 U.S.C.A. § 1003(a). Exceptions are governmental and some church plans; plans to comply with workmen's compensation laws; unemployment compensation or disability insurance laws; unfunded excess benefit plans (in excess of the limitations imposed by IRC § 415, 26 U.S.C.A. on benefits and contributions under qualified plans) [ERISA § 4(b), 29 U.S.C.A. § 1003(b)]; unfunded plans maintained by an employer primarily for the purpose of providing deferred compensation for a select group of management or highly compensated employees or to deferred compensation arrangements solely for the benefit of retired partners or for deceased partners or their successors in interest [ERISA § 401(a)(1)(2); 29 U.S.C.A. § 1101(a)(1)(2)].

83. ERISA §§ 502–506, 29 U.S.C.A. §§ 1132–1136.

84. The principal provisions in the Internal Revenue Code pertaining to employee benefit plans are IRC §§ 401–425. The provisions pertaining to declaratory judgments relating to qualification of retirement plans appear in ERISA, Tit. II, Part 4, 26 U.S.C.A. § 7476, with the establishment of the Office of Employee Plans and Exempt Organizations in the Office of the Commissioner of Internal Revenue in ERISA, Title II, Part 5, 26 U.S.C.A. § 7802.

85. The beneficiary problem is similar to that presented when the members of a large unincorporated association seek to enforce a trust. See Chapter VIII, Section 4(5)(A). The employee benefit trust

trust analogized to a charity since public enforcement is provided. Statutes generally are in force exempting employee benefit trusts from the Rule against Perpetuities or from application of a time limit to the accumulation of income or to the duration of the trust.[86]

Of major interest to lawyers is the federal trust law likely to be proliferated as the ERISA plans are expanded and enforced.[87] State fiduciary law will certainly have a major bearing in the application of fiduciary standards. But federal law will supersede state fiduciary standards when there is a conflict, and it is possible that state law ultimately will be more affected by federal trust law rather than the reverse. There is a great deal of money now in the ERISA plans and the management of these funds should stimulate much litigation. Excluding the welfare plans and the pension plans administered by insurance companies, the SEC in 1980 estimated that more than $297 billion was held in pension and deferred profit sharing plans of corporations, unions, multiemployer groups and nonprofit organizations.[88] These funds have increased on an average of $30 billion per year since 1974. By the date of publication of this book, the plans probably contain $350 billion with an expectation of a similar or perhaps more rapid increase in the future. The Pension Guaranty Corporation (PBGC) which insures most of the plans, becoming trustee if an insured terminated plan does not have sufficient assets to pay the guaranteed benefits, estimates that by 1984 its liabilities under the single employer program *alone* will be $1 billion, $288 million.[89]

The federal trust law of ERISA figures uniquely in four areas. First, there is an extension of fiduciary responsibility to persons who are not trustees and do not deal directly with trustees but nevertheless make decisions relating to the plans. Persons are fiduciaries when dealing with the plans even when the plans are not trusteed. Second, there is a peculiar and often shifting role of trustees in the trusteed plans, quite different from the role of the trustee in a private trust, with an accompanying allocation of responsibilities and delegation of duties, probably predictable features of "bargained" plans which perhaps are products of settled labor disputes. Third are fiduciary standards, including a federal fiduciary code, with special guidelines as to the duty of loyalty (described principally in terms of

has adequate statutory provision for enforcement. The trusts are required by ERISA to be in writing. ERISA § 402(a)(1), 26 U.S.C.A. § 1102(a)(1). Few states require a writing for inter vivos trusts of personal property. See Section 1, this Chapter.

86. E.g., Va.Code § 55–13.1 (1981 Repl. Vol.).

87. There are, of course, many other areas in which federal courts and agencies deal with trust matters. Federal courts handle various trust matters in tax controversies and in diversity jurisdiction. See Chapter XVII, Section 3(3). The trustee in bankruptcy has certain fiduciary responsibilities. The Comptroller of the Currency establishes fiduciary guidelines for national banks. Certain Indian property is held in trust by the Federal Government and administered by the Department of the Interior. But there has not previously been, as in ERISA, an effort to formulate a federal trust administration code applicable to property of such great value, under circumstances likely to provoke such extensive litigation, and under conditions making conventional trust doctrine so difficult to apply.

88. 40 SEC Monthly Statistical Review No. 5 (May 1981) p. 10.

89. PBGC Report Fiscal Year 1979, p. 40.

prohibited transactions), a "federal prudent man rule" and special rules concerning diversification of plan investments. The fourth area involving unique treatment of fiduciaries concerns co-fiduciary responsibility and liability. Each of these areas will be briefly examined.[90]

Fiduciary responsibility is extended to, and fiduciary duties are imposed upon, any person who exercises any discretionary authority or responsibility with respect to the plan or who renders investment advice with respect to the plan or has authority or responsibility to render this advice for a fee or other compensation.[91] A trustee will be a fiduciary but so will others depending on their authority, responsibilities, functions and activities. Much attention has been devoted to the circumstances under which investment advisors will be treated as fiduciaries.[92] The reach of fiduciary responsibility under ERISA is much more extensive than that imposed upon the parties dealing with the trustees of private and charitable trust and may result in gradual extension of third party liability rules applied in the private and charitable trust area.[93]

Each trusteed plan must have at least one trustee [94] but this trustee's functions may range from simply holding title to investment management. The terms of the plan control unless these conflict with the provisions of ERISA. The trustee must be named in the trust or plan document or be appointed by a named fiduciary.[95] While the trustee may be removed by a court there is no provision for court appointment.[96] Unless the plan otherwise provides, the trustee

90. Administrative problems presented in the management of private and charitable trusts are considered in Chapter XVII of this book. The student may wish to reexamine the materials here presented after Chapter XVII is considered.

91. Three fiduciary categories are described in ERISA. In each plan which is required to be in trust there must be at least one trustee. ERISA § 403(a), 29 U.S.C.A. § 1103(a). The trustee is named in the trust or plan instrument or is appointed by a "named fiduciary". The "named fiduciary" is named in the plan instrument or, pursuant to a procedure specified in the plan, is identified as a fiduciary either by the employer or by the employer and an employee organization acting jointly. ERISA § 402(a)(1)(2), 29 U.S.C.A. § 1102(a)(1)(2). For example, the "named fiduciary" might be the president or a vice president of the sponsor company. The "named fiduciary" has authority to control and manage the operation and administration of the plan. Then there are "fiduciaries" not named in the plan. These are persons having discretionary authority or control with respect to the plan. ERISA § 3(21), 26 U.S.C.A. § 1002(2); IRC § 4975(e)(3), 26 U.S.C.A. The elements of discretion or control seem to be critical in determining who is a fiduciary, subject to all of the statutory obligations, and who is not. See DOL Reg. 2509.75–8, 29 C.F.R., Qs D–1 and D–3. A person may wear several fiduciary hats. Thus, a trustee might be the "named fiduciary" and would always be "a fiduciary". The plan sponsor and company directors will be fiduciaries. DOL Reg. § 2509.75–8, 29 C.F.R. Q D–4. There is a comprehensive provision excluding persons from holding fiduciary positions who have been convicted of certain crimes. ERISA § 411(a), 29 U.S.C.A. § 1111. Fiduciary obligations are imposed in plans other than those required to be in trust.

92. DOL Reg. § 2510.3–21, 29 C.F.R.; IRS Reg. 54.1–4975–9, 26 C.F.R.

93. See as to these, Chapter XVII, Section 10(2).

94. ERISA § 403(a), 29 U.S.C.A. § 1103(a).

95. Id.

96. ERISA § 409(a), 29 U.S.C.A. § 1109. The court may remove *any* fiduciary.

controls and manages the plan's assets; [97] but the plan may provide otherwise, and frequently does. The trustee may be subject to the directions of another fiduciary and must follow these directions unless they are in conflict with the terms of the plan or with the provisions of ERISA or other law.[98] Or the "named fiduciary" in the plan may appoint an investment manager or managers.[99] If an investment manager is named, the trustee is not responsible for the manager's actions.[1] The investment manager must acknowledge its, his or her fiduciary responsibilities in writing. The persons to be appointed as investment manager are limited to persons registered as investment advisers under the Investment Advisors Act of 1940 [2], a federal or state bank, or an insurance company qualified to perform investment management services under state law.[3] A typical plan might have the directors of a company with authority to appoint and remove the members of an investment committee and an administrative committee. The directors would have fiduciary responsibility to monitor the work of the committees. The investment committee would appoint the trustee or trustees and the investment manager or managers and would have fiduciary responsibility for reviewing their performance. The administrative committee would have fiduciary responsibility for administration of the plan. Only named fiduciaries can delegate fiduciary responsibilities.[4] Other fiduciaries cannot delegate. But the named fiduciaries (those named in the plan instrument or by a procedure specified in the plan, by an employer or employer organization or by an employer and employee organization acting jointly) [5] might delegate fiduciary responsibilities beyond the committees. The greatest weakness in ERISA, from the point of view of fiduciary administration of the plans, is the ability of those responsible for formulating the plan to limit the fiduciary responsibilities of the named fiduciaries, the trustees and numerous other fiduciaries whose decisions affect the plan. The result is a failure to centralize responsibility for administration of the plans, although the pattern may well influence court decisions in the future concerning the responsibility for administration of private and charitable trusts for which the trustees presently are held accountable. The ERISA diffusion of responsibility and accountability is probably a necessary concession in view of the circumstances under which the pension and related plans are established.

97. ERISA § 403(a), 29 U.S.C.A. § 1103(a).

98. ERISA § 403(a)(1), 29 U.S.C.A. § 1103(a)(1).

99. ERISA § 402(c)(3), 29 U.S.C.A. § 1102(c)(3).

1. ERISA § 405(d)(1), 29 U.S.C.A. § 1105(d)(1). If the trustee knowingly concealed the malfeasance or negligence of the investment manager or participated in the malfeasance or negligence he would, of course, be liable.

2. 15 U.S.C.A. § 80b–3, 54 Stat. 847 (1940).

3. ERISA § 3(38), 29 U.S.C.A. § 1002(38).

4. ERISA §§ 402(a)(1), 405(c)(1), 29 U.S.C.A. §§ 1102(a)(1), 1105(c)(1). But if the plan so provides, a fiduciary designated by the named fiduciary may employ one or more persons to render advice with respect to his or her responsibilities under the plan. ERISA § 402(c)(2), 29 U.S.C.A. § 1102(c)(2).

5. See fn. 99 supra.

Although the responsibility of a particular trustee or other fiduciary may be limited under an ERISA plan, fiduciary standards are set out in ERISA with much detail. As with private trusts, the trustee or other fiduciary must be guided by the terms of the plan but has greater latitude in departure from it than does the trustee of a private trust in deviating from the settlor's expressed intent. If compliance with the terms of the plan would be inconsistent with the "prudent man standard" as set forth in ERISA or any other of ERISA's requirements, the trustee or other fiduciary may deviate.[6] The "prudent man rule" in ERISA states that the fiduciary must act [7]

> "with the care, skill, prudence, and diligence under the circumstances then prevailing that a prudent man acting in a like capacity and familiar with such matters would use in the conduct of an enterprise of a like character and with like aims; * * *"

It should be observed that this standard is not that of "an ordinary prudent man" usually applied to trustees of private and charitable trust but a prudent man "acting in a like capacity and familiar with such matters". This appears to envisage a requirement of expertise on the part of the prudent man and a degree of specialization in employee benefit plans with the special experience that this specialization would be likely to produce. It has been suggested that a corporate fiduciary advertising special expertise might be held to a higher standard than other fiduciaries but this has not been fully established. As the higher standard stated in ERISA is applied to the fiduciaries of the employee benefit plans, the prudent man rule as applied to other fiduciaries might be gradually modified to exact a higher standard of conduct.

The purpose of establishing a federal standard of prudence was to avoid differences in the application of state prudent man rules although cases involving the application of state prudent man standards are likely to have a bearing on the construction of the prudent man rule established by ERISA. With respect to investments under the ERISA rule, the Labor Department has issued regulations [8] containing certain criteria which the fiduciary should consider. If the fiduciary considers these criteria apparently there is a presumption of prudence in the sense that a trustee of a private trust has the advantage of a rebuttable presumption of prudence if he invests in securities on a permissive legal list.[9] An investment manager may rely upon information pertaining to the plan provided by or at the direction of the appointing fiduciary if the information is provided for the stated purpose of assisting the manager in the performance of his investment duties and the manager does not know or have reason to know that the information is incorrect.[10] The fiduciary, unlike the trustee of a private trust, is not charged with information he could have ob-

6. ERISA § 404(a)(1)(D), 29 U.S.C.A. § 1104(a)(1)(D).

7. ERISA § 404(a)(1)(B), 29 U.S.C.A. § 1104(a)(1)(B).

8. DOL Reg. 2550.404a–1, 29 C.F.R.

9. DOL Reg. 2550.404a–1(b), 29 C.F.R. See Chapter XVII, Section 5 infra.

10. DOL Reg. § 2550.404a–1(b)(3), 29 C.F.R.

tained by the exercise of reasonable diligence, but instead is not charged to consider matters outside his designated scope of duties or to make inquiries other than with respect to the particular investment with which he deals.[11] The major points stressed in the Labor Department's guidelines for fiduciary investments are that the investment must be a prudent choice in relation to the plan's objectives and that the overall portfolio will be considered in determining the prudence of an investment. Speculative investments might be proper, although not for the trustee of a private trust unless the settlor has conferred authority to make these investments; and it is probable the fiduciaries might invest in nonproductive assets if this is compatible with the objectives of the particular ERISA plan. The fiduciary under ERISA is required to diversify investments [12] and, with respect to qualifying employer security or employer real property cannot acquire or retain amounts in excess of 10% of the total plan assets,[13] an exception being made for purchases for individual accounts (profit sharing, stock bonus, thrift or savings plans or employee stock ownership plans).[14] There is no effort in ERISA to articulate any general duty of loyalty to which the fiduciaries are required to adhere although it is made clear that they are to act "solely in the interest of the participants and the beneficiaries" [15] and for the exclusive purpose of "providing benefits to participants and their beneficiaries * * * and defraying reasonable legal expenses of administering the plan." [16] There are comprehensive self-dealing rules described as "prohibited transactions" which would appear to put a major strain on fiduciaries administering the stock ownership plans (ESOPS and TRASOPS) for which special rules are provided.[17] The Secretary of Labor may grant exemptions from the prohibited transaction rules and from the percentage limitation on acquiring and holding employer securities and employer real property in the plans upon which this limitation is imposed.[18] Notice is required in the Federal Register of the pendency of the exemption and adequate notice must also be given to interested persons who must be given an opportunity to present their views.[19] A hearing must be conducted with a determination on the record with respect to findings before an exemption is granted under § 406(b) which concerns direct self-dealing.[20]

11. DOL Reg. § 2550.404a–1(b)(1)(2), 29 C.F.R.

12. ERISA, § 404(a)(1)(C), 29 U.S.C.A. § 1104(a)(1)(C).

13. ERISA § 407(a)(2), 29 U.S.C.A. § 1107(a)(2).

14. ERISA § 407(b)(1), 29 U.S.C.A. § 1107(b)(1).

15. ERISA § 404(a)(1), 29 U.S.C.A. § 1104(a)(1).

16. ERISA § 404(a)(1)(A), 29 U.S.C.A. § 1104(a)(1)(A).

17. ERISA §§ 406, 407, 29 U.S.C.A. §§ 1106, 1107. The "parties in interest" prohibitions appear in ERISA § 406(a), 29 U.S.C.A. § 1106(a). "Parties in interest" are defined in ERISA § 3(14), 29 U.S.C.A. § 1002(14). Most of the "parties in interest" also fall within the IRC definition of "disqualified persons". IRC § 4975(e)(2), 26 U.S.C.A. The self-dealing provisions appear in ERISA § 406(b), 29 U.S.C.A. § 1106(b). For the special rules as to acquisition of employer securities, etc., see ERISA § 407, 29 U.S.C.A. § 1107.

18. ERISA § 408, 29 U.S.C.A. § 1108.

19. ERISA § 408(a)(3), 29 U.S.C.A. § 1108(a)(3).

20. Id.

The co-fiduciary rules are of special importance in view of the number of fiduciaries operating in each plan. ERISA § 405 pertaining to co-fiduciary liability [21] contains rules applicable to all fiduciaries and rules specifically applicable to trustees (who are also subject to the fiduciary rules).[22] For all fiduciaries, if by failing to comply with the requirement that they discharge their duties solely in the interest of the plan participants and beneficiaries "in the administration of his specific responsibilities which give rise to his status as a fiduciary", a co-fiduciary is enabled to commit a breach, then the fiduciary is also liable.[23] He is also liable if he has knowledge of the breach and fails to attempt to remedy it by reasonable efforts under the circumstances.[24] If he knowingly participates in or conceals the breach then of course he has joint liability.[25] When a plan permits named fiduciaries to allocate fiduciary responsibilities other than trustee responsibilities the named fiduciary is not liable for the default of the delegate unless he would otherwise be liable under the general rules applied to co-fiduciaries or unless he violates his duty to act in the interest of the participants and beneficiaries with respect to the allocation of duties or designation of the fiduciary, fails to carry out the procedures as described in the plan for allocating responsibility, or is negligent in continuing the allocation or designation.[26] Trustees must use reasonable care to prevent a co-trustee from committing a breach; but if the trust instrument authorizes an agreement to allocate specific responsibilities, obligations or duties among trustees, and such an agreement is properly made, the co-trustee would not be liable for the acts of his fellow in the performance of responsibilities pursuant to this allocation [27] unless one of the general fiduciary rules has been breached. When a named fiduciary has designated an investment manager, the trustee has no liability for the manager's acts unless he participates in or conceals the acts.[28] The very complex structure for management of the employee benefit trusts means that special difficulties are likely to arise concerning failure of a fiduciary to act upon receipt of information concerning misconduct or imprudence in some other area of the plan administration, a potential issue of concealment then being presented unless "the whistle is blown". While the fiduciaries cannot be exonerated from liability in the trust plan [29] they might be able to obtain indemnity from the corporation for which they act under state law when without fault or perhaps should seek insurance coverage for fiduciary liability.

21. 29 U.S.C.A. § 1105.

22. ERISA § 405(b), 29 U.S.C.A. § 1105(b).

23. ERISA § 405(a)(2), 29 U.S.C.A. § 1105(a)(2).

24. ERISA § 405(a)(3), 29 U.S.C.A. § 1105(a)(3).

25. ERISA § 405(a)(1), 29 U.S.C.A. § 1105(a)(1).

26. ERISA § 405(c)(2), 29 U.S.C.A. § 1105(c)(2).

27. ERISA § 405(b)(1)(B), 29 U.S.C.A. § 1105(b)(1)(B).

28. ERISA § 405(d), 29 U.S.C.A. § 1105(d).

29. ERISA § 410(a), 29 U.S.C.A. § 1110(a).

The vesting provisions and new security available for employee benefit trusts under ERISA means that distributions under these plans will become an increasingly important factor in estate planning, with lifetime as well as death transfer features of the plan taken into consideration. How payouts are made depends upon the terms of the plan. ERISA requires that any plan providing benefits in the form of an annuity must also offer the option of a qualified joint and survivorship annuity to married employees, this being a 50% joint and survivor annuity unless he elects some other alternative if the plan provides one. Some plans have lump sum distributions for simplicity. There may be annuities obtained by purchase of annuity contracts or paid directly from the plan assets or perhaps there may be installment payments of the sum due. If the retirement plan makes a lump sum payment this payment can be rolled over to another individual retirement arrangement, less the amount of employee contributions to the plan, and taxes are deferred until distributions are made from the individual retirement arrangement, the distributions being ordinary income.[30] Lump sum payments are included in a decedent's estate although the payments from a qualified plan may be excluded if the beneficiary elects to pay ordinary income tax on the distribution, foregoing ten year income averaging and capital gains treatment.[31] With the tax free interspousal transfer and the large unified tax credit, it may be advisable to allow the lump sum distribution to be included in the estate, treat as long term capital gain that part of the distribution attributable to the participants pre-1974 participation in the plan and treat the balance as ordinary income, using the special ten year averaging election if this is available to the beneficiary.[32] The beneficiary may elect to have the capital gain element taxed as part of the ordinary income element. State income taxes should be considered carefully in this decision. For annuity or installment payments or similar arrangements there is no income tax until payments are made and the tax is then under the annuity rules and treated as earned income. The employee contribution is subtracted in this computation, the taxable portion being that attributable to employer contributions and earnings of the plan.[33] For the annuity type of distribution the value included in the estate is the employee's contributions less income and appreciation, the employer's contributions and any income and appreciation being excluded.[34]

Whether a retirement plan is qualified, so that it receives the treatment above described, or is unqualified, the benefits if payable to a surviving spouse can escape either gift or estate taxation. Thus, the part of an annuity which is qualified that is included in the estate will pass tax free to the spouse if it is otherwise a qualified interest under IRC § 2056. If the whole annuity amount is included because not qualified,[35] that amount also will pass tax free to the spouse if

30. IRC § 402(a)(5), 26 U.S.C.A.

31. IRC § 2039(f), 26 U.S.C.A.

32. IRC § 402(e), 26 U.S.C.A.

33. IRC § 402(a)(1), 26 U.S.C.A. This assumes the plan is "qualified".

34. IRC § 2039(c), 26 U.S.C.A. This assumes the plan is "qualified".

35. IRC § 2039(a)(b), 26 U.S.C.A.

not an unqualified terminable interest. Income tax features of the distributions will have to be considered as will the potential inclusion of the annuity proceeds in the estate of the surviving spouse. As of 1987 the presence of the $600,000 exemption equivalent will tend to diminish the gift and estate tax problems in the estate of the average employee.

(2) TRUSTS IN DEBTOR–CREDITOR RELATIONSHIPS

Trusts are used to secure creditors and have been used to liquidate the estates of debtors and to reorganize ailing businesses. But while the trust as a security device is still much used, the trusts for liquidation and reorganization have been superseded almost entirely by the flexible procedures of the Bankruptcy Act.[36] However, the United States Trustees, appointed by the United States Attorney General, and being used until 1984 in certain pilot districts,[37] and the bankruptcy trustees, appointed by the Bankruptcy Court on an interim basis,[38] appointed by the United States Trustee, or elected by the creditors, are not trustees in the "equity" sense, but have been described as statutory "curators" for the benefit of creditors.[39] Indeed, there is speculation that all bankruptcy trustees will be federal government employees after the Congress reviews the Bankruptcy Act in 1984 and observes the results of its experiment with United States Trustees.[40] The "equity" trusts to liquidate debtors' estates and to reorganize business operations, although certainly obsolescent, nevertheless are considered briefly here and might still be used in cases in which creditors are interested in debt settlements by agreement.

A debtor does not hold his property in trust for creditors. However, a debtor might declare himself trustee of his property for creditors, this perhaps being the required element of a composition in which the creditors agree to discharge the debtor in return for transfer of money or property which they will accept in full discharge of the debt. The trust in such a case would be merely an incident of the transaction, the essence of the composition being its contractual nature, although the trust in this situation might prove particularly val-

36. P.L. 95–598 (1978), 92 Stat. 2549, 11 U.S.C.A.

37. P.L. 95–598 (1978) Title II, § 224, 28 U.S.C.A. § 581 et seq. There are ten pilot districts or groups of districts in which the United States Trustees are being employed on an experimental basis. The United States trustee selects the trustees in the pilot areas, serves as trustee if a trustee cannot be found and supervises their work.

38. The Bankruptcy Court became a court of record under the new legislation with the Judge appointed by the President for term of 14 years. The Judge in the non-pilot districts, appoints an interim trustee in bankruptcy who serves until a trustee is elected by creditors. If the creditors do not elect a trustee then the interim trustee continues to serve. Bankruptcy Act, §§ 701, 702, 11 U.S.C.A.

39. Bogert, Trusts and Trustees (Second Edition Revised, 1977) § 246 pp. 131–132. In the case of the United States Trustee, the comment could be added that this trustee is a Federal administrative officer operating under the supervision of the Attorney General.

40. Cowan, Bankruptcy Law and Practice (Interim Edition, 1980) 25.

uable if the agreement involved an extension of time for the payment of debts.[41] A transaction of much greater frequency was the assignment for the benefit of creditors. The assignment received statutory recognition in many states.[42] Essentially the debtor assigns all of his assets to a trustee who then proceeds to liquidate these for the benefit of creditors. Anything that remained after all of the creditors were satisfied would be returned to the debtor on a resulting trust. Creditors could not object effectively to such an assignment as a fraudulent conveyance. The transfer was for their benefit as beneficiaries and the object of the trust is liquidation. However a creditor might seek involuntary bankruptcy of the debtor by a petition filed within 120 days of the transfer, the transfer of all of the assets being an indication (an irrebuttable presumption) that the debtor cannot pay his debts when due.[43] Assuming there is no involuntary petition, the trustee of the trust has duties very similar to those of the executor of a decedent, liquidating the debtor-settlor's estate for the benefit of his creditors and securing releases from them.

Following the depression of 1929, bondholders' protective committees were formed to coordinate the action of bondholders, perhaps in bidding for the assets at foreclosure; putting up only enough to pay off non-participating bondholders; preserving assets pending reorganization; formulating reorganization plans and the like. Typically a deposit agreement would be framed by a small number of bondholders, bonds deposited would be held by a bank or other depository, with certificates issued to the depositors. The protective committee held title to the bonds.[44] The protective committee might have power to borrow to defray expenses and broad powers to act on behalf of the depositors. Some commentators saw in this transaction only an agency.[45] However the protective committee members held title to the bonds with broad powers and the depositors of the bonds probably were beneficiaries. A fiduciary relationship certainly existed between the protective committee and the depositors. Unfortunately there were abuses of this relationship, and several protective commit-

41. Glenn, Liquidation (1935) Ch. IX. While Professor Glenn's book is now much outdated in its coverage of bankruptcy, it contains the most perceptive treatment available concerning common law composition, assignments for the benefit of creditors and non-bankruptcy creditor transactions.

42. E.g., Ariz. Rev.Stat. §§ 44–1031, –1047.

43. Bankruptcy Act § 303(h), 11 U.S. C.A. The 1978 legislation abandons the "act of bankruptcy" as the criterion for the involuntary case and adopts the "equity insolvency test"—whether the debtor is generally unable to pay his debts as they mature or if the debtor has failed to pay a major portion of his debts as they become due. If a custodian is appointed during the 90 day period preceding the petition, this creates an irrebuttable presumption that the debtor cannot pay his debts as they mature.

44. An excellent description of the various forms of bondholder committees appears in Bogert, Trusts and Trustees (Second Edition Revised, 1977) § 251. A good description of the function of one of the committees with respect to municipal bonds appears in Bullard v. City of Cisco, Texas, 290 U.S. 179, 54 S.Ct. 177, 78 L. Ed. 254, 93 A.L.R. 141 (1933).

45. See Bogert, Trusts and Trustees (Second Edition Revised, 1977), § 251, p. 282. There has been great variation in the organization and functions of the committees and in some situations the transactions resemble agencies rather than trusts. E.g., State ex rel. Lee v. Sartorious, 344 Mo. 912, 130 S.W.2d 547 (1939).

tees might compete for the deposits of bondholders of a single corporation. Statutes were passed in several states in an effort to regulate these committees, the major legislation being in New York.[46] At least some of the functions of the bondholder committees are performed by the creditors' committees in liquidation under the Bankruptcy Code[47] and especially by the creditors' and equity security holders' committees under the reorganization provisions[48].

Unlike the trusts for liquidation and reorganization, the trusts for security are used quite frequently. These range from simple trust transactions securing the payment of a bond for purchase money for land, for example, to the complex trust indentures subject to regulation under the Trust Indenture Act of 1939.[49]

The simple deed of trust for security conveys title to the land used as security for a bond to a trustee or trustees, the condition being stated in the deed that upon notice of default by the bondholder, the trustee or trustees are to sell the land, pay the amount due including interest on the bond, deduct their fees and expenses and pay the balance to the debtor. Judicial procedures attending the mortgage foreclosure are avoided. Usually the attorney who represents the vendor of the land drafts both the deed to the purchaser and the deed of trust. The deed of trust is a deed by the purchaser, usually to the vendor's lawyer and to the purchaser's lawyer, jointly as trustees, with the conditions previously described. The deed of purchase is recorded first and immediately thereafter the deed of trust. The trustees have nothing to do unless there is a default by the purchaser. When the purchaser pays off the loan the bondholder files a release and this is noted in the land record book in the margin of the recorded deed of trust. The states using the deed of trust have extensive legislation concerning the transaction.[50] The student will observe that this trust is passive until default by the debtor and the states using the deed of trust should have a statute stating clearly that the trust is not executed by the Statute of Uses or a parallel judicial rule.[51]

At the other extreme in terms of complexity are the trust indentures used to handle the security interest for bond issues when it would be impractical to have a security instrument for each bondholder. If the property used as security is subject to depletion or obsolesence there should be a sinking fund or serial maturities of the bonds. For debenture bonds unsecured by mortgage, enforcement powers may be centralized in the trustees. In the secured transaction, the security can range from real estate to railroad rolling stock

46. McKinney's N.Y. Real Prop. Law §§ 124–130k. This statute applies principally to trustees under trust indentures, see fn. 52 infra, but applies also to bondholder's committees.

47. Bankruptcy Act § 705, 11 U.S.C.A.

48. Bankruptcy Act §§ 1102, 1103, 11 U.S.C.A.

49. 53 Stat. 1149 (1939), 15 U.S.C.A. §§ 77aaa et seq.

50. E.g. Va.Code Ann. §§ 55–58, –66.-7 (1981 Repl.Vol.).

51. E.g. Va.Code Ann. § 55–17.1 (1981 Repl.Vol.).

to intangibles. The latter is usually described as a "collateral trust", the rolling stock an "equipment trust". There is usually no problem concerning the active duties of trustees in trust indentures. Since most of these are federally regulated, simply filing reports, apart from other duties, can be a demanding task, requiring a substantial administrative staff, and funds to defray administrative expenses. The purpose of the Trust Indenture Act of 1939 was to protect investors and to this end the Act establishes the eligibility of trustees with an effort to preclude conflicting interests. The indentures must contain requirements for information to prospective bondholders and annual reports to bond purchasers. The Securities and Exchange Commission administers the Act. Since the Act applies to securities to be sold to the public through the mails or in interstate commerce, most of the major trust indentures are subject to its provisions, yet there are others subject to state law. New York has the most comprehensive statute dealing with trust indentures; [52] yet even absent a statute the trustees appear subject to the usual state equity doctrines, modified to a degree by the purposes of the trust.[53]

(3) TRUSTS FOR CONTROLLING BUSINESS INTERESTS

The voting shares of a corporation may be trusteed for the specific purpose of having the trustee (or trustees) vote the shares of the corporation. This is called a "voting trust". One of its most frequent uses occurs when a corporation requires money and a lender will not lend it unless the shares are trusteed to be voted to secure, in the lender's view, a sound and economical management of the corporation. At least one distinguished writer was of the view that this creditor situation was one of the few applications in which the voting trust was legal absent specific statutory authorization; [54] and Mr. Justice Douglas, while a Securities Exchange Commissioner, described them "as little more than a vehicle for corporate kidnapping" [55]. The voting trust has been put to nefarious ends—minority stockholders have been abused, monopolies developed, corporations unceremoniously captured or "kidnapped". But these are the matters that have gotten into litigation, the voting trust having been used for over a century for perfectly proper purposes, ranging from such far-flung applications as defensive economic warfare in resisting

52. McKinney's N.Y. Real Prop. Law §§ 124–130k.

53. Bogert, Trusts and Trustees (Second Edition Revised, 1977) § 250 pp. 266–67.

54. Glenn, Liquidation (1935) 145.

55. Quoted from Burke, "Voting Trusts Currently Observed", 24 Minn.L. Rev. 347 (1940). This article contains a clear summary of the history of the voting trust and persuasive arguments for its legality absent statutory sanction. The general validation of voting trusts by statute does not render arguments in favor of or against the legality of voting trusts entirely moot, since questions concerning the validity of the trusts can arise when the statute is not complied with and the purpose of the particular voting trust may be illegal even though voting trusts generally are validated.

German control of a submarine shipyard [56] or control of the assets of an Indian Tribe transferred to it by the Federal Government [57] to the very prosaic purpose of insuring continuity in corporate policy.

The voting trust has had a troubled history. Apart from questions concerning the purposes of the trusts, there have been contentions that they violated the Rule against Perpetuities; were an illegal restraint on the alienation of the stock trusteed,[58] that the trusts were passive, the trustees having insufficient active duties; [59] and as a "general broadside" that they were against public policy because they divided beneficial ownership and control over the corporation. The latter objection was viewed quite seriously in the latter part of the Nineteenth and early Twentieth Centuries.

Underlying the "division" argument was the basic premise in an age in which there was an emphasis upon individual duty and obligation that each stockholder "owes his fellow stockholders a duty in regard to the voting of his stockholdings [60]". This duty should have legal recognition, at least to the extent of not permitting the stockholder to renounce irrevocably for any period his ability to perform his duty. On the other hand the courts did recognize that in particular situations the objection to the abdication of duty should yield to more pressing demands, such as the need of the corporation to borrow money. Yet, despite decisions by a few far-sighted courts, such as the Virginia Court,[61] in which voting trusts were sustained, the general view as of the mid-1920s was accurately stated by Marion Smith as follows: [62]

> "A separation of the voting power of stock from its real or beneficial ownership, irrevocable for a fixed period, is contrary to public policy and void unless: (1) It is coupled with, or to protect, an interest; or (2) Made to carry into effect some determined plan or policy to which the voting trustee is bound; or (3) It is merely a pooling contract under which the real owners reserve the right to direct the voting trustee * * * [in those states in which pooling contracts are sustained] * * *"

While statutes now validate voting trusts, it is doubtful that a court dealing with a trust not complying with the statute would now take so strict a view as that stated by Mr. Smith. The stockholder is

56. Frost v. Carse, 91 N.J.Eq. 124, 108 A. 642 (1919).

57. Tomow v. Menominee Enterprises, Inc., 60 Wis.2d 1, 208 N.W.2d 824 (1973), cert. den. 414 U.S. 1137, 94 S.Ct. 883, 38 L.Ed.2d 763.

58. While the trustee cannot transfer the stock issued by the corporation, the certificate holders can transfer their certificates. Thus, while the trustee does not have a power of sale as the trustee of a private trust usually would have, the restraint on alienation nevertheless seems slight.

59. Deauville Corp. v. Blount, 157 Fla. 322, 25 So.2d 812 (1946).

60. Smith, "Limitations on the Validity of Voting Trusts", 22 Col.L.Rev. 627, 628 (1922). This is a short and very clear presentation of the early view concerning the validity of voting trusts and a view that perhaps might still have application to voting trusts not meeting the statutory requirements.

61. Carnegie Trust Co. v. Security State Life Insurance Co., 111 Va. 1, 68 S. E. 412 (1910).

62. Smith, "The Validity of Voting Trusts", 22 Col.L.Rev. 627, 633 (1922).

no longer thought to have a duty to his fellows or to the corporation to seek a voice in corporate affairs. Stock ownership is an impersonal matter with interest in the welfare of the corporation often so slight that proxies are difficult to obtain. The voting trust tends to encourage participation by stockholders, even though in an indirect manner. Trusteeing the stock tends to centralize responsibility in a trustee or trustees. If there is now no obligation, fiduciary or otherwise, from stockholder to stockholder, there is a fiduciary obligation by the trustee to those transferring voting power to him. Commentators agree that if the purpose of a particular voting trust is illegal a court will not enforce it even though voting trusts generally are validated by statute; and attacks upon voting trusts not meeting the statutory requirements are not likely to be supported effectively by an argument based upon the undesirability of a division between beneficial ownership and control.

It is desirable to follow the terms of the local statute validating voting trusts closely in drafting a voting trust agreement.[63] The terms of the statute may be regarded as mandatory so deviations in the agreement will invalidate the trust irrespective of any policy arguments concerning their general validity.[64]

The New York voting trust provision, the first enacted, has been the prototype for several other statutes.[65] Usually a written agreement is required and the trust must have a limited duration, 10 years being typical.[66] The trust can be reestablished for a new term. After the shares of the stockholder are transferred to the trustee, trust participation certificates are issued to the shareholders and these are transferrable. The corporation issues new shares to the trustee. The trustee is required to keep records and, in particular, a list of the trust certificate holders. The trustee's major duty is to vote the shares. He may have discretion in doing this or be subject to the direction of the stockholders. One feature common to the statutes is the right of all stockholders holding voting shares to participate in the voting trust. If dividends are paid on the trusteed shares, the trustee pays these over to the certificate holders in proportion to their contributed shares after the trustee's commission and expenses are deducted. This duty, in addition to the duty to vote the shares, should be sufficient to resist an argument that the trust is passive. The trust may have funding in addition to the transfer of shares to cover the trustee's commission and other trust expenses. The voting trusts appear to function best when administrative overhead is kept at a minimum.

63. See Note, "The Voting Trust: Drafting Suggestions", 42 N.Y.U.L.Rev. 349 (1967). An appendix to the note sets forth citations to voting trust statutes as of 1966; Woloszyn, "A Practical Guide to Voting Trusts", 4 U.Balt.L.Rev. 245 (1975). With particular reference to the close corporation, see Kessler, "Drafting a Shareholders' Agreement for a New York Close Corporation", 35 Fordham L. Rev. 625 (1967).

64. E.g., Perry v. Missouri-Kansas Pipe Line Co., 22 Del.Ch. 33, 191 A. 823 (1937).

65. McKinney's N.Y. Business Corporation Law § 621.

66. There is no time limit in Indiana and Wisconsin. Ind.Stat.Ann. § 23–3–1–1; Wis.Stat.Ann., § 180.27 (1981 Supp.). The limit in Minnesota is 15 years. Minn. Stat.Ann. § 301.27.

A few states restrict the use of trusts to vote the stock of certain kinds of corporations.[67] Federal restrictions exist on the use of voting trusts. Thus voting trusts might be used illegally in restraint of trade. Restrictions also exist on the use of voting trusts to control two or more carriers without complying with the statutory conditions [68] and upon the use of interstate commerce or the mails to sell voting trust certificates relating to the security of any registered investment company.[69]

Particularly with respect to closely held corporations, another control problem is presented and a trust sometimes is used as a device to deal with it. Similar uses are made of trusts for control purposes in partnerships [70] and sole proprietorships.[71]

In a close corporation there is a constant threat of discontinuity in management and perhaps an end of the corporate life upon the death of a major stockholder. Who will obtain ownership of this stock? The remaining stockholders usually are concerned with the answer to this question. Employees of the corporation, particularly key employees with long service, and creditors of the corporation, who might be affected adversely if the corporation ceased business, are concerned with succession to ownership of the stock and how the stock might be voted. A voting trust might be one technique to deal with the difficulty but in a close corporation, where the stockholders have close contact with the corporate operations, voting trusts often have not proved satisfactory answers. In the case of minority shares, there may be an interest by the majority stockholders to keep these shares out of the hands of potential dissidents who might be disaffected by a failure to pay dividends or some other decision by the directors. How will the survivors of the deceased stockholder obtain benefits from his stock? It is not readily marketable. They may not be capable of assuming managerial positions in the corporation and thus obtain a salary, or they might be incompatible with some of the existing managers and have an insufficient vote to oust them. The death of a partner terminates the partnership. The deceased partner's survivors do not become partners but in certain partnership undertakings might put pressure on the surviving partners to be included in a new partnership. And how should one deal with the deceased partner's interest? Suppose in a sole proprietorship key employees cannot be retained during the proprietor's lifetime unless they have some assurance that the business can be continued after his death. How can they be given this assurance with an incentive to better work?

There are a myriad of potential tax problems presented. One of these is how the close corporation stock will be valued. If there is an

67. In Mississippi the stock of state banks cannot be held in a voting trust. Miss. Code § 81–5–31. In Wyoming there can be no voting trusts for nonprofit corporations. Wyo.Stat. § 17–122.16.

68. 49 U.S.C.A. § 5(4).

69. 15 U.S.C.A. § 80a–20.

70. See Horvitz, "Life Insurance as a Planning Tool: Use of Insurance to Fund Partnership Buy-Sell Agreement", 33 N.Y.U.Inst.Fed.Tax. 867 (1975).

71. Strickler, "Estate Planning and the Sole Proprietor", 36 Minn.Law Rev. 874, 893 (1952).

element of good will in the partnership that can be said to survive the deceased partner, how should good will be valued? If the Internal Revenue Service overvalues the asset, the taxpayer may be without evidence to rebut the presumption of correctness of the assessed value.

There are a number of ways in which some or all of the problems can be dealt with, although techniques must be specialized to the situation confronting the planner, and no method may prove entirely satisfactory. The choice usually will be the technique under the circumstances most likely to be effective, building in sufficient flexibility so other techniques can be used if the circumstances change. Frequently used techniques have been "buy-sell" agreements for the stock of closely held corporations, partnership interests and sole proprietorships and "entity" or redemption agreements for corporations, partnership "buy outs" also sometimes being framed as an "entity" transaction. In the "buy-sell" or "cross purchase" agreements, each stockholder or each partner agrees to sell his interest to the others, the agreement binding the stockholder or partner's estate. In the entity agreement, the corporation agrees to redeem or the partnership to buy out the deceased's interest. Obviously, the buy-sell agreement is complex, involving multiple agreements among stockholders or partners. Moreover, funding of these agreements presents a problem. In the entity transaction funds could be accumulated in the corporation subject to restrictions on this accumulation; but usually the funding is done through life insurance. A closely held corporation with ten stockholders will be used as an example and the pattern illustrated is similar to that which might be used for a partnership.

Each of the ten stockholders will agree with the others that he will not sell his stock during his lifetime without offering it first to the other stockholders at an agreed price. He binds his estate to sell the stock at his death to the surviving stockholders at an agreed price and the other stockholders agree to buy at this figure. The price of the stock usually must be recomputed at intervals to be realistic. Unless the other stockholders agree to buy at the death of the decedent, the latter is not assured that his stock will have a market when he dies; and the commitment to offer the stock to the other stockholders during his lifetime is nothing more than what he would have to do in any event, no one else probably being willing to buy it. The commitment by the surviving stockholders to buy at the death of the deceased stockholder could be financed by assets available to them or by borrowing; but, assuming the stockholder is insurable, the purchase probably will be financed by life insurance taken out by the prospective purchaser upon the life of the prospective decedent. This means that the cross-purchase plan consists not only of a web of agreements but also of a web of life insurance contracts, with promises by each stockholder that his executor will transfer the life insurance contracts that he holds on the lives of the survivors to the surviving shareholders. An agreement in this form, if the transaction is *bona fide* and at arms length, should establish the value of the stock for estate tax purposes.[72] Moreover, the plan will provide for continuity of corporate control as well as liquidity in the estate of the decedent by providing for a market for his stock *if it works.* To provide assurance that the plan will work and to provide a manager of the plan with equal obligations to all stockholders, the plan might be trusteed—although many plans, especially those of small close corporations, are not trusteed. If the plan is trusteed, the life policies can be payable to the trustee, any surplus over that needed to purchase the stock can be retained in the trust. The trustee buys the stock and holds it for the survivors or delivers it to them. Perhaps having the trustee hold all of the stock is desirable to prevent an executor from repudiating the agreement and provoking litigation. The recurrent problem of valuing the stock may be handled by the trustee and he may be given powers to secure payments of the premiums on the life insurance to fund all of the agreements and should hold all of the policies. The use of a trust increases the administrative cost of a buy-sell or entity agreement, and there may be less justification for use of a trust in an entity agreement since the structure of the redemption or buy-out plan in the entity agreement usually is less complex than a "buy-sell" or "cross-purchase" agreement among ten or more stockholders or partners. Nevertheless, the trust may be the necessary element to persuade the parties to agree and any additional cost should be justified if the trust assures execution of the plan. Without a trust the plans often fail.[73]

There are also trust applications in the handling of sole proprietorships, buy-sell agreements having applications to these so the survivors of the proprietor can obtain a suitable market for the business and the proprietor's employees can be assured of their jobs. As one writer has remarked "[W]hat testator, who had bequeathed his wife and family a balanced portfolio of good securities, would direct them to liquidate the bequests and buy a business the day after the death of the man who had built it up?" [74] Also, just as with close corporation stock and partnership interests, a buy-sell agreement which is bona fide and at arms length may be used to establish the tax value of the business. Here the employees agree to purchase the business. The agreement is funded by life insurance on the employer, the premiums being paid as additional compensation to the employees. The employees have a stake in the business and the proprietor's survivors have funds and an established tax value. A trust reassures the employees that the funds will be available to them from the insurance, provides a middleman between the employees and the family and executor of the proprietor to assist in identifying business assets and resolve disputes, and reassures business creditors that the business will continue.

72. IRS Reg. § 20.2031–2(h).

73. For examples of trusts in these applications with drafting suggestions, see Bogert, Trusts and Trustees (Second Edition Revised, 1977) § 253; Farr and Wright, Estate Planner's Handbook (4th Ed. 1979) §§ 56, 60.

74. Strickler, "Estate Planning and the Sole Proprietor", 36 Minn.L.Rev. 874, 893 (1952).

Buy-sell (or "cross-purchase") and "entity" agreement must be drafted with care, tax provisions must be consulted, and each plan must be tailored to the requirements of each corporation, partnership or proprietorship.[75]

(4) TRUSTS AS BUSINESS ORGANIZATIONS

At a time when corporations could not deal in land in Massachusetts, the trust was used as a business organization for this purpose and, having received statutory recognition there in 1909, began to be used in other states, the popularity of the "Massachusetts" trust increasing roughly in proportion to the increasing federal and state regulation and taxation of corporations. The "Massachusetts" trust was used when incorporation was regarded as unnecessarily costly or inflexible, and the trust was used for businesses ranging from the exploitation of oil and gas lands in the Southwest to the organization of express and textile concerns. Although the structure of "Massachusetts" trusts varied (and they were sometimes called "business trusts" or "common law trusts"), Mr. Justice Sanford in Hecht v. Malley[76] described a typical "Massachusetts" as follows:

> "The 'Massachusetts Trust' is a form of business organization, common in that State, consisting essentially of an arrangement whereby property is conveyed to trustees, in accordance with the terms of an instrument of trust, to be held and managed for the benefit of such persons as may from time to time be the holders of transferable certificates issued by the trustees showing the shares into which the beneficial interest in the property is divided. These certificates, which resemble certificates for shares of stock in a corporation and are issued and transferred in like manner, entitle the holders to share ratably in the income of the property, and, upon termination of the trust, in the proceeds."

The essential features of the trust are that the trustees act as principals, the certificate holders do not exercise direct control over the operations of the organization, the certificates issued are transferable, and that the purpose of the trust is business activity for profit.

The enthusiasm with which the "Massachusetts" trust was used in business enterprises ultimately was betrayed by the unsoundness of certain of the assumptions upon which the use of the trust as a business organization was based. It was assumed that the certificate holders could trade with limited liability as beneficiaries of a trust

75. A comprehensive treatment of voting trusts in close corporations appears in Chapter 5 and of cross-purchase and entity agreements in Chapter 7 of O'Neal, Close Corporations (1971) (1981 Supp.) For special emphasis on the use of the trust in close corporation transactions, see Note, "Estate Planning for the Close Corporation", 51 Minn.L.Rev. 725 (1967); Williams, "Continuity and Control in Post-Mortem Planning for Close Corporations", 109 Trusts and Estates 1000 (1970).

76. 256 U.S. 144, 146–147, 44 S.Ct. 462, 463, 68 L.Ed. 949, 953 (1924).

much as stockholders of a corporation enjoyed this protection. In some states limited liability of the certificate holders was recognized;[77] but in others they were held to be partners[78] or that they were sole traders usurping corporate authority. It was assumed the transferable certificates could be traded without compliance with a state's "blue sky" laws; but almost invariably this turned out not to be the case.[79] The trust was to avoid the cost of state regulation of corporations; but when state statutes recognizing business trusts were passed, these subjected the trusts to most of the corporate reporting requirements. The trust was subject to federal regulation as a public utility holding company;[80] as an investment company;[81] and, while there was some doubt whether it was a corporation within the meaning of the former Bankruptcy Act, it is clearly a corporation under the Bankruptcy Act of 1978.[82] The crowning blow came when business trusts were taxed as corporations, and interest in their use declined precipitately when the certificate holders found they were to be subject to the corporate income tax and again to a personal income tax on their distributions from the trust.[83] While use of the "Massachusetts" trust continues, some large business enterprises continuing to operate in this form, the major surviving uses are the "Investment Trusts" and the "Real Estate Investment Trusts".

The "Investment Trust", a business form in which a number of mutual funds are operated,[84] is subject to federal regulation as an investment company and if it elects to be treated as a regulated investment company and qualifies for the taxable year under the Internal Revenue Code[85], it is taxed at corporate rates only to the extent its income is not distributed to the shareholders. Under special conditions also, tax exempt interest acquired by the trust retains that character in the hands of the shareholders.[86] Some of these investment trusts are "closed end" rather than "open end", as in the mutual fund form in which the certificates can be redeemed at any time.

The Real Estate Investment Trust (REIT) in 1960 was given tax treatment similar to that given the investment trust handling securities.[87] There are different kinds of REITs, some specializing in mort-

77. E.g., Greco v. Hubbard, 252 Mass. 37, 147 N.E. 272 (1925).

78. E.g., Thompson v. Schmitt, 115 Tex. 53, 274 S.W. 554 (1925); Note, "Liability of Shareholders in a Business Trust—The Control Test", 48 Va.L.Rev. 1105 (1968).

79. See Bogert, Trusts and Trustees (Second Edition Revised, 1977) § 247(R).

80. 15 U.S.C.A. § 79b(a)–2.

81. 15 U.S.C.A. §§ 80a–2(a)(8), 80a–4(2), 80a–26.

82. Bankruptcy Act § 101(8)(A)(v), 11 U.S.C.A. See Bogert, Trusts and Trustees (Second Edition Revised, 1977) § 247(T).

83. IRC § 7701(a)(3), Regs. §§ 301.-7701–2, 301.7701–4(b)(c).

84. The mutual fund is an "open end" fund. Most of these are in corporate form or a corporation conducts the operations and deposits the stocks or other securities with a trustee which issues the certificates. Roughly a quarter of the mutual funds operate in trust form. Certain "closed end" funds, some of which are in trust, are exempt from the Investment Company Act. 15 U.S.C.A. § 80a–6(d).

85. IRC §§ 851–855, 26 U.S.C.A. Realized capital gains distributed to the shareholders are not taxed to the fund. IRC § 852(b)(3).

86. IRC § 852(b)(5), 26 U.S.C.A.

87. IRC §§ 856–860, 26 U.S.C.A. The REIT regulations are discussed in Grant, "Analysis of New Regulations on Real

gage loans (short and long term), whereupon the income consists of interest and discounts primarily; and "equity" trusts specializing in real property ownership, the income usually being rentals. There also are combinations of these activities. Under the Tax Reform Act of 1976, the REIT also can be organized as a corporation.[88] The REIT must elect to be taxed as a real estate investment trust and must meet the detailed requirements of the Internal Revenue Code to obtain the favorable tax treatment. A number of states have statutes expressly validating REITs [89] and for those that do not have these statutes, or a broader statute validating "Massachusetts" or business trusts, there is a chance that the REIT certificate or share holders might encounter difficulties of the type experienced by the certificate holders of the "Massachusetts" trust.[90]

Unlike the "Massachusetts" trust and its progeny, although perhaps suggested originally by business activity in trust form, are a variety of trusts used for the management or exploitation of land. The "Illinois Land Trust" is perhaps the best known of these and is now being used in a number of states other than Illinois.[91] First used extensively in Cook County, the Illinois Land Trust is established by a trust deed, usually to a corporate fiduciary, which is recorded, and a supplementary trust agreement which is not. The recorded deed recites full powers in the trustee and states that the beneficiary holds no equitable interest in the land, his interest being personalty. The supplementary agreement reserves full control over the trust to the beneficiary, who retains possession and manages or develops the land and receives the income from it. The unrecorded supplementary trust agreement contains an exculpatory clause so the trustee will not be liable for the beneficiary's acts or acts that he directs; and it has been held in Illinois that the trustee of an "Illinois Land Trust" is not liable, even without an exculpatory agreement, for torts arising from the condition, maintenance or use of the land.[92] In a state in which such a trust can be sustained, there are manifest advantages in convenience in creating it. Loans can be obtained using the land as security without a requirement that the beneficiary become an obligor. Judgments against the beneficiary cannot be levied upon the land. Transfers are made simple, especially when there are multiple beneficiaries; and a spouse in a dower and curtesy state, who will not join in a transfer cannot impede the transfer of the title by the trus-

Estate Investment Trusts". 101 Trusts and Estates 730 (1962).

88. IRC § 856(a), 26 U.S.C.A.

89. For a statute dealing expressly with REITs in a state which has no statute dealing generally with "Massachusetts" trusts, see Va.Code Ann. §§ 6.-1-343-351. The trust can last indefinitely. A majority of the trustees are required to be Virginia residents but the statute also states that it is not intended to invalidate a "similar" real estate investment trust created elsewhere operating in Virginia. For a statute of broader scope see Miss.Code §§ 79-15-1, -15-29.

90. See "Modern Status of the Massachusetts or Business Trust", 88 A.L.R.3d 704 (1978).

91. See Kenoe, Land Trusts (1978) (Supplemented); Garrett, "Land Trusts", 1955 U.Ill.L. Forum 655 (with forms).

92. E.g., Brazowski v. Chicago Title and Trust Co., 280 Ill.App. 293 (1st Dist. 1935).

tee at the direction of the beneficiary.[93] If the beneficiary becomes incapacitated, the trustee can transfer the title.

There are instances of abuses of the "Illinois Land Trust", the non-recordation of the supplementary "control" agreement being conducive to this. The trust is also subject to attack on the ground the trustee has no active duties and thus the trust is executed by the Statute of Uses or some parallel judicial rule. Some active duties might be found (at least they are usually specified in the recorded instrument); or perhaps a statute might validate a trust of land even if it is a passive trust.[94] The duration of the trust might be found excessive. If the trust is carefully drafted any corporate income tax problem can be avoided.

On the other hand, if the land trust is elaborated in a more complex land financing transaction with certificates issued, the trust then resembles the "Massachusetts" trust and similarity to a corporation may result in a corporate tax. Thus, entrepreneurs may purchase unimproved land, lease the land to a corporation which will develop it, convey the reversion to a trustee who then issues certificates which the entrepreneurs sell to raise money for improvements. After the apartment building or other structure is completed, the trustee collects the rents, pays the agreed amounts on the certificates, and ultimately applies the residue of the rentals to buy up the certificates and turn over the reversion to the entrepreneurs. The trustee might operate the apartment building. Whether or not this transaction will attract a corporate tax will depend on the skill of the draftsman of the agreement and the care with which the operation is conducted.

There are also applications of trusts to land development bearing an analogy to the "Illinois Land Trust" and also to the trust as a security device previously discussed.[95] For example, the purchaser and seller of land to be subdivided or perhaps to be developed as condominia, might agree to a part payment by the purchaser with transfer of title to a trustee. The seller is beneficiary of the trust, but the trustee agrees to convey title to the purchasers of the lots or condominia as these are developed. The purchaser manages the development, contracting for the improvements, securing purchasers of the developed property and so forth. When the amount agreed upon for the original sale is paid in, the trustee transfers title to the unsold portion of the property to the purchaser-developer. The trustee in these and similar transactions has active duties, although many conditions typically are specified in these agreements and care must be taken that there is no remote vesting of interests which might violate the local Rule against Perpetuities or similar restraint on the duration of the trust.

93. See Bogert, Trusts and Trustees (Second Edition Revised, 1977) § 249, pp. 243–244 for a summary of advantages.

94. See Va.Code § 55–17.1 for a statute intended to eliminate objections founded upon traditional trust doctrine to "Land Trusts". This was the first statute specifically intended to validate land trusts of the "Illinois" type. See Schwind, "Land Trusts—A Real Estate Syndication Device", 101 Trusts and Estates 650 (1962).

95. See subsection (2) supra.

Chapter X

TERMINATION

Scope Note

Herein are discussed the methods by which a private express trust may be terminated prior to accomplishment of the trust purpose when no power of revocation has been reserved by the settlor or granted to the trustee or beneficiaries by the terms of the trust document. This Chapter seeks to answer the following questions: When, if at all, may the settlor set aside a living trust? May a trust be terminated by the trustee acting alone? Can all of the beneficiaries force a termination? Can a trust be terminated by the settlor and beneficiaries acting in unison? Is there any way the trustee and the beneficiaries can effect a termination?

The rules considered in this chapter generally apply also to proceedings to modify the trust terms. In Chapter XVII, Section 5(6), we shall explore the power of the equity court to modify administrative provisions of the trust when, in light of changed conditions, those provisions jeopardize the trust purpose.

SECTION 1. POWER OF SETTLOR TO TERMINATE A TRUST

PERNOD v. AMERICAN NATIONAL BANK & TRUST CO. OF CHICAGO

Supreme Court of Illinois, 1956.
8 Ill.2d 16, 132 N.E.2d 540.

KLINGBIEL, JUSTICE. Nellie Pernod, the settlor of a voluntary *inter vivos* trust, brought suit in the superior court of Cook County to revoke the trust on the ground of mistake. She named as parties defendant the American National Bank & Trust Company of Chicago, a trustee; her daughter, Cleon Murphy, a life beneficiary; her grandson, Pernod Miller, a cotrustee and contingent remainderman; and her minor great-granddaughter, Katherine Miller, a contingent beneficiary. An individual appointed as guardian *ad litem* for the minor defendant and as trustee for persons not yet in being filed his appropriate answer, as did the trust company. The defendants Cleon Murphy and Pernod Miller filed answers admitting the allegations of the complaint and consenting to the entry of a decree in accordance with plaintiff's prayer for relief. After a hearing the court found the trust instrument had been executed through mistake and misunderstanding, and a decree was entered setting it aside and ordering the property reconveyed to the plaintiff. The corporate trustee and the guardian *ad litem* and trustee for persons not yet in being appeal from the decree. Since a freehold is involved the appeal comes directly to this court.

The trust instrument, executed on April 17, 1953, provides that the trustees are to pay to the plaintiff for her life such sums as in their discretion are necessary for her welfare, maintenance and comfortable living. If the plaintiff's daughter, Cleon Murphy, is alive when the plaintiff dies, the trustees are to pay the income, and such part of the corpus as may be necessary, to the daughter for her life. If at the close of these life estates plaintiff's grandson, Pernod Miller, is alive, he is to receive the remainder; but if at that time he is dead the remainder is to go to the then living descendants of the plaintiff. Cleon Murphy is the plaintiff's only child. Pernod Miller is the only child of Cleon Murphy; and Katherine Miller, the minor, is the only child of Pernod Miller. By its terms the trust instrument is declared to be irrevocable and not subject to amendment.

The corporate trustee urges that the evidence is insufficient to support the decree. The record discloses that the plaintiff, a widow eighty years of age, first consulted her attorney on January 15, 1953. At that meeting it was decided to establish a trust of the remainder of her deceased husband's estate, which she no longer desired to manage. On March 5 she again conferred with him about the trust, and a third meeting occurred on April 14. On April 17 another conference was held, at which time the plaintiff executed the instrument. She thereafter placed it in a safe-deposit box which she shared with her daughter, Cleon. When Cleon read the instrument she became highly disturbed and asked her mother to try to have it changed. Cleon was so upset and hysterical about the matter that she went to a hospital. Eighteen months after the trust was established plaintiff brought this suit to set it aside.

She testified that she was not in good health at the time she signed the trust agreement; that she had informed her attorney she wanted her daughter Cleon, after plaintiff's death, "to receive just what I had been receiving a month," and to have everything "just like I had it." She said she wanted her daughter to have everything after she was gone, and if anything was left at her daughter's death it was to go to the grandson. Plaintiff further testified that she did not ask for an irrevocable trust because she did not know anything about one. The question of the trust being revocable, she said, was never discussed. She thought the trust would be "just like a will." Pernod Miller, the grandson, testified that he was present at the final conference; that no one then read the trust instrument aloud; and that as he recalled there was no discussion about it at that time.

The attorney who drafted the trust is a specialist in that field of the law. He testified that during their discussion of the matter he told plaintiff in order to accomplish her purpose the trust should be made irrevocable; that he explained to her an irrevocable trust is one which is fixed and cannot be changed; and that plaintiff thought about the matter and requested him to go ahead and prepare it that way. At the first conference he asked plaintiff whether she wanted her daughter to get the property outright after plaintiff's death, or whether she preferred to have the property held in trust for her daughter's benefit. The plaintiff, he said, then thought about the question and decided it would be better to have the property held in trust for her daughter. At the March 5 meeting a draft of the instrument, substantially the same as that which was ultimately executed, was shown to Mrs. Pernod. They went through it article by article and discussed it as they went along. The witness further testified that as he summarized it for her he thought she understood his explanations, but that "it is possible" she did not understand the provisions.

The rule has long been established that where the grantor has not reserved a power to revoke, a voluntary trust may be set aside only upon a showing that it was induced by fraud, duress, undue influence or mistake, except where all the parties in interest are ascertained, are under no incapacity, and consent to the revocation. Lawrence v. Lawrence, 181 Ill. 248, 54 N.E. 918; 3 Scott, Law of Trusts, sec. 329 A. Since in the present case all the beneficiaries are not in being and *sui juris*, revocation by consent is impossible. To sustain the burden of proving that an instrument was executed by mistake the evidence must be clear and convincing. Lines v. Willey, 253 Ill. 440, 97 N.E. 843; Silurian Oil Company v. Neal, 277 Ill. 45, 115 N.E. 114. In Finucan v. Kendig, 109 Ill. 198, a settlor sought to revoke a trust on the ground that he and his deceased wife had intended to create a revocable arrangement and that a power of revocation had been omitted by mistake. It was further asserted that the settlors had intended the survivor to receive the trust estate in fee, whereas the instrument gave the survivor only a life estate with remainder to the settlors' children. Both the plaintiff and his agent testified that these two mistakes had been made, but this court held the evidence insufficient, saying: "The deed speaks for itself, and it is cogent evidence that it was the instrument, in all its provisions, intended to be prepared. To allow one, at such a distance of time as in this case, to overturn a solemnly executed deed, made by his request and direction, by declaring that his intention was different from what the writing expresses, would be most dangerous to the security of instruments of writing. The evidence in this regard, to have avail, should be of the most satisfactory kind."

In the case at bar not only is there an absence of a power of revocation, but the instrument expressly provides that "The trust created hereunder is hereby declared to be irrevocable and not subject to amendment by any party hereto or by any beneficiary hereunder." Because the testimony of a settlor seeking to revoke a trust is likely to be unreliable, and because solemn written instruments are not to be lightly overturned, strong corroboration of the settlor's testimony is required in order to warrant the granting of relief. Restatement, Trusts, sec. 332(c). In the present case, even if we disregard the testimony of the drafting attorney that there was no mistake, the plaintiff's testimony stands uncorroborated and is clearly inadequate to support the decree. In her search for corroboration plaintiff seizes upon the attorney's statement, on cross-examination, that it is "possible" the settlor did not understand the provisions of the trust agreement. This concession by the witness is obviously no more than a conscientious acknowledgment of the fact that no human being can read the mind of another with certainty. It is of no aid whatever to the plaintiff's case.

It is further argued that it is unlikely an elderly lady in poor health would be capable of understanding a trust agreement several pages long, couched in precise and formal legal phraseology; and that "Few laymen, younger, more vigorous and experienced in business would understand it." The argument proves too much. If such a contention had merit very few modern legal instruments could withstand attacks of the kind made in this case. The general rule is that if the words are written as the parties intended they should be written or supposed they were written when the instrument is signed, then no matter how much they may be mistaken as to the meaning of those words no relief can be granted, either at law or in equity.

Plaintiff finally invokes the rule that findings of the chancellor on conflicting evidence will not be disturbed unless clearly and palpably against the weight of the evidence. In answer to this position it suffices to observe that the requirements of the rule are not fulfilled here. The findings are clearly and palpably against the weight of the evidence. The testimony of the attorney who drafted the trust instrument shows that he painstakingly explained its provisions to the plaintiff and specifically told her that "this document would stand, that it could not be changed." The plaintiff's testimony, on the other hand, is equivocal and contradictory, and is far from being clear and convincing.

Other error is assigned which, in view of our conclusion, it is unnecessary to discuss. The decree of the superior court is against the manifest weight of the evidence and is accordingly reversed.

Decree reversed.

DAILY, JUSTICE (dissenting). I cannot agree with either the reasoning or the result of the majority opinion. It is true that in the absence of reservation of revocatory powers, a voluntary trust may generally be set aside only upon a showing that it was induced by fraud, duress, undue influence, or mistake. However, if it can be shown by clear and convincing evidence that provisions were inserted or omitted because of mistake and that, as written, they did not truly represent the settlor's desires and intention at the time of execution and delivery, the trust may be revoked even though it is, by its express terms, irrevocable. Lawrence v. Lawrence, 181 Ill. 248, 54 N.E.

918; Potter v. Fidelity Ins. Trust & Safe Deposit Co., 199 Pa. 360, 49 A. 85; Restatement of the Law of Trusts, Vol. 2, sec. 333e. Although the statements of the settlor are not, in and of themselves, sufficient ground for revocation, they may suffice when corroborated by other direct or circumstantial evidence. Restatement of the Law of Trusts, Vol. 2, sec. 332c.

The settlor in this case testified that during the several visits which were made to the attorney's office, she was never told that the agreement could not be changed. Her understanding of the instrument was, rather, expressed as follows: "I thought it was like a will, you know. I just could not figure how that could be, that I could not change it. I thought it would be like a will." At other times during her testimony she referred to the fact that she was 79 years of age, had been in ill health for some time prior to the execution of the present trust, and that she was relying upon her attorney to see that the agreement was as she desired.

The drafting attorney testified that after talking with the settlor concerning the management of her property, he suggested either a bank agency account or trust arrangement and that the latter was agreed upon. He further testified that to the best of his recollection he explained various provisions of the agreement to the settlor, including the one pertaining to irrevocability, but did not read the agreement to her nor did he remember her reading it. When asked if he had any doubts that the settlor understood the instrument he replied: "No, I can't say that I did. Quite obviously I never would have had her sign it if I felt that she didn't understand it. That doesn't mean that she did understand." At one point he said, "I told her, I tried to tell her—remember, she's an elderly lady in all of this—but I tried to advise her what each of these meant in order to get her to be answering as to whether or not it measured up as to what she wanted." He also said, "When I recited the substance and tried to explain the provisions of the trust agreement I thought she understood it. I cannot be positive but I made my best efforts, let's put it that way. It is quite possible that I did not get through to her on all these points. It is possible that she did not understand any of the provisions of the trust agreement."

Thus, in the present case, the evidence of mistake is not confined solely to the settlor's testimony but is supported by other proof. The fact that the drafting attorney, upon being advised of her wishes, had advised either a bank agency account or a trust arrangement would indicate that the settlor's primary purpose in creating the trust was not to dispose of her property but rather to reduce the burden of its management. If so, it would be quite reasonable to assume that she intended to retain the power to revoke the trust. As is said in the Restatement of the Law of Trusts, Vol. 2, sec. 332h: "The reasons for which the trust was created may indicate that the settlor intended to reserve a power of revocation, although no such power was reserved in the trust instrument. Thus, if it is shown that the reason of the settlor for creating the trust was to meet a temporary emergency, this is evidence that he did not intend to make the trust irrevocable." This is further supported by the fact that the settlor had managed the property from 1941 to 1953 and had relinquished these duties only because of ill health. In addition, the attorney admitted that he had never read the instrument to the settlor and was not sure whether she even understood his explanation of its provisions. Therefore, it can hardly be said that the settlor's testimony was entirely uncorroborated.

For these reasons, I am of the opinion that the evidence was sufficient to warrant revocation in this case and would affirm the lower court which was in far better position to weigh the demeanor, sincerity and capabilities of the witnesses.[1]

NOTE

Mistake in the creation of a trust may be grounds for rescission. Mistake may be of two kinds:[2] (1) omission of a power to revoke (misunderstanding as to the irrevocable nature of the trust) and (2) mistake as to the tax consequences.[3] In the latter case the settlor may be petitioning for reformation rather than rescission.[4]

When elderly people create inter vivos trusts, as in *Pernod*, there is possibility of misunderstanding despite care on the part of the lawyer in preparing and explaining the trust document. The fact that the beneficiaries are receiving benefits gratuitously should be a factor. The view that "strong corroboration of the settlor's testimony is required" to justify relief, as expressed in the principal case and in Restatement of Trusts, Second, § 332, is criticized by Professor George Palmer as a "thoroughly unsatisfactory position, which courts should reject."[5]

As in the principal case and in some of the cases which follow, objection to termination often comes from a guardian ad litem or a fiduciary acting on

1. In a case where the settlor signed an irrevocable trust on "a misconception" as to the revocability of the trust, the Massachusetts Appeals Court granted rescission for mistake on the grounds that the settlor there was induced to sign by a person standing in a fiduciary relation. Markell v. Sidney B. Pfeifer Foundation, 9 Mass.App. 412, 402 N.E.2d 76 (1980). On the right of the settlor to set aside a trust, see Restatement, Second, Trusts §§ 333, 336. The power of the settlor to revoke or modify the trust where such power is expressly reserved in the trust document, or is implied under the law of some jurisdictions, has been discussed previously in Chapter VIII, Section 6. See Wright, "Termination of Trusts in Pennsylvania—Some Current Trends", 115 U.Pa.L.Rev. 917 (1967).

2. For an excellent discussion of the two types of mistake cases, see 5 Palmer, Law of Restitution (1978) § 18.7.

3. The attorney who prepares a trust document intended to implement his client's purpose of minimizing taxes, but because of negligent drafting fails to prepare the correct provisions to achieve the tax savings, can be held liable to the client or the intended beneficiaries for the amount of the lost savings. Bucquet v. Livingston, 57 Cal.App.3d 914, 129 Cal. Rptr. 514 (1976).

4. Berman v. Sandler, 379 Mass. 506, 399 N.E.2d 17 (1980) (reformation granted where a trust instrument designed to qualify for the marital deduction was altered by an amendment which by a scrivener's error omitted certain words and thereby jeopardized the marital deduction).

5. Palmer, op. cit. supra fn. 2.

behalf of unborn or presently unascertainable beneficiaries, rather than from living beneficiaries. If the trust instrument purports to confer a future interest on persons not presently ascertainable, or not yet even born, two issues are presented: (1) as a policy matter, should the law give recognition to such remote interests with standing to object to termination, and (2) procedurally, how are those interests to be protected? On the first issue, review the *Morsman* case in Chapter VIII, Section 4. In some situations the court may refuse to recognize particular language (such as a limitation to the "heirs" of a life tenant or of the settlor) as creating an interest; we shall explore this problem further in Chapter XIII and will consider related problems in Chapter XV. If the Court must decide whether an interest is to be recognized, as in a group such as "heirs" or future unborn "issue," the potential takers must somehow be represented in court in order that the decision will be binding upon them. How can they be represented? Note that the corporate trustee in *Pernod* took the position that its duty was to protect the trust and hence all potential beneficiaries.[6] The equity court should have inherent power (often confirmed by statute) to appoint a guardian ad litem to protect the future interests of unknown persons. In some situations, existing beneficiaries may "represent" their children, issue or heirs; this is the doctrine of "virtual representation."[7]

The Uniform Probate Code codifies a rule of virtual representation and also authorizes appointment of a guardian *ad litem* if the Court determines that representation otherwise would be inadequate. Section 1–403 reads:

"In formal proceedings involving trusts or estates of decedents, minors, protected persons, or incapacitated persons, and in judicially supervised settlements, the following apply:

"(1) Interests to be affected shall be described in pleadings which give reasonable information to owners by name or class, by reference to the instrument creating the interests, or in other appropriate manner.

"(2) Persons are bound by orders binding others in the following cases:

(i) Orders binding the sole holder or all co-holders of a power of revocation or a presently exercisable general power of appointment, including one in the form of a power of amendment, bind other persons to the extent their interests (as objects, takers in default, or otherwise) are subject to the power.

(ii) To the extent there is no conflict of interest between them or among persons represented, orders binding a conservator bind the person whose estate he controls; orders binding a guardian bind the ward if no conservator of his estate has been appointed; orders binding a trustee bind beneficiaries of the trust in proceedings to probate a will establishing or adding to a trust, to review the acts or accounts of a prior fiduciary and in proceedings involving creditors or other third parties; and orders binding a personal representative bind persons interested in the undistributed assets of a decedent's estate in actions or

6. See In re Curry, 390 Pa. 105, 134 A.2d 497 (1957) holding that representation of unborn and unascertained heirs by the trustee was a matter of discretion for the trial court to determine.

7. See, American Law of Property (1952) §§ 4.82 through 4.90; 2 Powell, the Law of Real Property (Rohan Rev., 1975) ¶¶ 294–296; Rodman and Rodman, "Virtual Representation: Some Possible Extensions", 6 Prop.Prob. & Tr.L.Jour. 281 (1971). In Estate of Evans, 274 Wis. 459, 80 N.W.2d 408, 81 N.W.2d 489 (1957), a will construction was held not to be binding upon subsequently born members of a class who were not represented in the first proceeding.

proceedings by or against the estate. If there is no conflict of interest and no conservator or guardian has been appointed, a parent may represent his minor child.

(iii) An unborn or unascertained person who is not otherwise represented is bound by an order to the extent his interest is adequately represented by another party having a substantially identical interest in the proceeding.

"(3) Notice is required as follows:

(i) Notice as prescribed by Section 1–401 shall be given to every interested person or to one who can bind an interested person as described in (2)(i) or (2)(ii) above. Notice may be given both to a person and to another who may bind him.

(ii) Notice is given to unborn or unascertained persons, who are not represented under (2)(i) or (2)(ii) above, by giving notice to all known persons whose interests in the proceedings are substantially identical to those of the unborn or unascertained persons.

"(4) At any point in a proceeding, a court may appoint a guardian ad litem to represent the interest of a minor, an incapacitated, unborn, or unascertained person, or a person whose identity or address is unknown, if the Court determines that representation of the interest otherwise would be inadequate. If not precluded by conflict of interests, a guardian ad litem may be appointed to represent several persons or interests. The Court shall set out its reasons for appointing a guardian ad litem as a part of the record of the proceedings."

CONNECTICUT GENERAL LIFE INSURANCE CO. v. FIRST NATIONAL BANK OF MINNEAPOLIS

Supreme Court of Minnesota, 1977.
262 N.W.2d 403.

YETKA, JUSTICE.

Appeal from judgment and order denying appellant's motion for amended findings of fact, conclusions of law, and order for judgment. The plaintiff, Connecticut General Life Insurance Co., filed a complaint in interpleader on September 9, 1974. After answers and counterclaims were filed, plaintiff deposited disputed life insurance proceeds with the court and was dismissed from the proceedings. After a trial without a jury, the District Court in Hennepin County determined that the disputed insurance proceeds were to be paid to the First National Bank of Minneapolis, as trustee of the John W. Aughenbaugh Trust. Mrs. Marilyn Aughenbaugh appeals from that determination. We affirm.

On February 2, 1965, Connecticut General Life Insurance Co. (Connecticut General) issued John W. Aughenbaugh a life insurance policy. At that time there was in existence a Last Will and Testament of John W. Aughenbaugh, executed on or about March 16, 1964, which left his estate to Elizabeth Ann Aughenbaugh. On May 4, 1967, John W. Aughenbaugh executed a new will. On the same date he executed an instrument creating the John W. Aughenbaugh Revocable Insurance Trust (the trust). First National Bank of Minneapolis (respondent) was named as trustee. Part of the funding for the trust was to be provided by the Connecticut General policy. The trust was not funded in any respect except by the insurance policies listed. The respondent, First National Bank of Minneapolis, was made beneficiary of the Connecticut General Insurance policy; the trust beneficiaries were Elizabeth Ann Aughenbaugh and three Aughenbaugh children. There were other trusts created in the instrument but they are not in issue in the present case.

In February 1972 the last premium was paid. At that time John W. Aughenbaugh and Elizabeth Ann Aughenbaugh were married and living in Minneapolis. On November 10, 1972, they were divorced, and on February 14, 1973, John W. Aughenbaugh and Marilyn L. Melaas (appellant) were married in Nevada.

In April 1973 Aughenbaugh and his second spouse moved to Arizona. On or about October 16, 1973, John W. Aughenbaugh executed a document entitled "Will." The will purported to "supercede and cancel any previous wills or trusts established by me." It was entrusted by John Aughenbaugh to his wife Marilyn after it was executed. He died on October 21, 1973. The will was probated in Arizona. After several exchanges of documents between Connecticut General and appellant, the present action was instituted raising the issue as to whether the will executed by John W. Aughenbaugh on October 16, 1973, operated to revoke the John W. Aughenbaugh Revocable Insurance Trust, created May 4, 1967. The trial court held in the negative.

Appellant appears to raise five points in her brief, but three of those issues depend primarily upon whether the trust is inter vivos or testamentary in nature. The remaining two issues involve interpretation of the trust agreement itself.

(1) Is a revocable life insurance trust inter vivos or testamentary?

* * *

[In the omitted portion the Court upheld the trust as nontestamentary. For a discussion of this problem see Chapter 12, Section 2(1) infra.]

* * *

(2) Revocation of the trust by will.

It is the general rule that where a settlor reserves the power to revoke a trust by a transaction inter vivos, as for example by notice to the trustee, he cannot revoke the trust by his will. Restatement, Trusts (2d) § 330, comment *j*; Bogert, Trusts and Trustees, § 1001 (2 ed.); IV Scott on Trusts, § 330.8 (3 ed.). The trust involved in the present case includes the following clause:

> "3.1) *Reservations Affecting the Trust.* Donor reserves the right to amend this agreement from time to time in any and all respects; to revoke the trust hereby created, in whole or in part; and to change the identity or number (or both) of the trustee or

trustees hereunder, *by written instrument executed by Donor and delivered to any trustee* (or to Donor's wife if no trustee is acting at a particular time) *during Donor's lifetime*; provided, however, that the duties and responsibilities of the Trustee shall not be substantially increased by any such amendment without its written consent." (Italics supplied.)

The trial court interpreted this clause to mean that the trust could only be *revoked* by written instrument as set forth above. We agree.

Although the clause is not a model of good drafting, appellant concedes that the obvious intent of the section and the requirement of written notice is to protect the trustee. But once this purpose is conceded, any claimed ambiguity in this section of the trust disappears. Maximum protection for the trustee is provided by requiring all major changes to be made by notice to the trustee.

This position, taken by the trial court, appears reasonable because the trustee would wish to know of any major change in its duties; revocation or amendment of the trust would constitute as major a change as an increase or decrease in the number of trustees. The sense of the clause, taken as a whole, is that changes which do not substantially increase the duties and responsibilities of the trustee may be made unilaterally by giving written notice, but that the trustee must concur in substantial increases in its duties.[8]

Affirmed.

WOODRUFF v. TRUST CO. OF GEORGIA

Supreme Court of Georgia, 1974.
233 Ga. 135, 210 S.E.2d 321.

[In 1960 Mrs. Frances Woodruff transferred property to the Trust Company of Georgia as trustee. Item I of the trust agreement provided: "Donor reserves the right to alter, amend, modify or revoke this trust in whole or in part at any time and from time to time by instrument in writing signed by donor and delivered to trustee, but only with the written consent and approval of the trustee. This trust shall be irrevocable except with the written consent and approval of the trustee." Item II of the trust provided that the net income from the trust should be paid to Mrs. Woodruff during her life and upon her death the corpus of the trust should be paid to the personal representative of Mrs. Woodruff. On February 1, 1974 the trustee filed a "petition for Declaration of Rights against Mrs. Woodruff as a defendant asking for direction" on the following question, among others: does Mrs. Woodruff have the right to revoke the trust with-

8. Compare Barnette v. McNulty, 21 Ariz.App. 127, 516 P.2d 583 (1973), which appears as a principal case on page 536 on the issue of validity of a Dacey trust; the Court there found that the terminology of the clause providing for revocation by certain specified acts was not exclusive and that the trust had been revoked orally by statements to the lawyer preparing a later will.

out the consent of the trustee? On February 5, 1974, she wrote to the trustee purportedly revoking the trust. The trial court held as a matter of law that the trust was revocable only with the written consent and approval of the trustee. Mrs. Woodruff appealed, contending that she could revoke the trust without the consent of the trustee.]

JORDAN, JUSTICE.

* * *

[W]e conclude that under the terms of this trust, Mrs. Woodruff occupies the status of settlor-sole beneficiary since at no time during the existence of the trust has she named any beneficiary, contingent or otherwise, of the trust other than herself or her personal representative. The settlor of a trust is "the sole beneficiary where he transfers property in trust to pay the income to himself for life and on his death to pay the principal to his estate * * *" So also, the settlor is the sole beneficiary where he transfers property in trust to pay the income to himself for life and on his death to convey the principal as he may by deed or will appoint. Restatement, Trusts 2d § 127.

The threshold question here is whether such a settlor-sole beneficiary has the right to terminate the trust regardless of the provisions for revocability or irrevocability in the trust instrument itself.

In our opinion this question was answered in the affirmative in Moore v. First National Bank & Trust Co. Of Macon, 218 Ga. 798, 130 S.E.2d 718. In that case we clearly held that a settlor-sole beneficiary of an inter vivos trust could terminate that trust even though the trust was by its terms irrevocable. This right of the settlor-sole beneficiary to terminate his own trust is not a right derived from the terms of the trust agreement, but an inherent right which exists outside of and extraneous to the trust agreement. See Scott on Trusts, (3d Ed.) § 339. The nature of a settlor-sole beneficiary trust embraces this right simply because no one else has any interest in the trust. Who would have any standing to object to the ending of the trust? The trustee has no vested right to insist upon the continuance of the trust, for as we said in *Moore*, supra (p. 802, 130 S.E.2d p. 721), "[t]he incidental benefit which the trustee may derive from future commissions is not of such a character as gives it a vested right to the continuance of the trust." The trustee as such is not the beneficiary of the trust. Restatement, Trusts, 2d, p. 159, § 337, Comment (b).

Because we conclude that *Moore*, supra, is dispositive of this issue we quote, Headnote 3, the relevant portion of that case. "Did Mrs. Moore have a right to terminate the trust she created in 1957 for her own life benefit and for the benefit of 'such other persons after her death as she may by deed or will designate?' The trial judge held that she did not; but, as to this, we think he erred. While it is true that the instrument she executed expressly states that it is irrevocable, it is also true that she is the only person named by it as a beneficiary and the record shows that she has not since the date of its execution designated any other person as a beneficiary of the trust she created. In these circumstances, she is the only person interested in the trust she created (Scott on Trusts, 2d Ed., 908, § 127.1; Restatement, Trusts, 2d Ed., 272, § 127, Comment b); and being such, she, as the settlor thereof, unquestionably had a right to terminate it, even though the trust instrument specifically provides that it shall be irrevocable. Scott on Trusts (2d Ed.), 2481, § 339; Restatement, Trusts (2d Ed.) 171, § 339, Comment a; 89 C.J.S. Trusts § 88e, page 907; Doyle v. Bank of Montclair, 9 N.J.Super. 586, 76 A. 2d 41. Since Mrs. Moore, as the settlor of this trust, and the only person presently interested in it, desires to retake her property and manage it herself, we are of the opinion she should be permitted to do so. The instrument was her voluntary act; it was without consideration; and, as we have said, it presently affects no one but herself * * * If she had a right, as we hold she did, to terminate the trust agreement, she certainly had a right to revoke the declaration that it is 'irrevocable.'" Accordingly, if Mrs. Moore's right to terminate included the right to eliminate the express declaration that the trust was irrevocable, then we must conclude that the appellant's right to terminate her trust includes the right to eliminate the provision prohibiting revocation except with the trustee's consent.

The trial court concluded that *Moore* did not apply in this case because *Moore* dealt with an irrevocable trust while the instant trust was revocable with the trustee's consent. This distinction overlooks the fact that both cases deal with a settlor who is also sole beneficiary and that, with reference to the right to terminate, the terms of a trust agreement relative to revocation become immaterial once it is established that the settlor and the beneficiary are one and the same. The settlor can terminate the trust, if he is not under an incapacity, because he is both the settlor and the sole beneficiary of the trust.

In the present case, so long as the trust was viable, Mrs. Woodruff was bound by the terms of the agreement, under which she could not revoke the trust without the consent of the trustee. Since this consent was not given she was unable to end the trust under the terms of the trust instrument. Subsequently, she had the right as the settlor-sole beneficiary to terminate the trust which she created for her sole benefit.

The appellee vigorously contends that this case is controlled by the law as stated in Restatement, Trusts, 2d, § 330 and Scott on Trusts (3d Ed.) § 330.9, p. 2610. While these sections state general rules dealing with the revocation of a trust by a settlor, we feel, as we did in *Moore*, that the apposite reference is § 339 of the Restatement and Scott which deal specifically with the settlor as sole beneficiary.

For the reasons set forth in this division, the trial court erred in failing to grant Mrs. Woodruff's motion for summary judgment on this issue. * * *[9]

---

9. In a later case the settlor sued the Trust Company for the decline in value of the trust property between the time of her demand for termination and actual

SECTION 2. POWER OF TRUSTEE TO TERMINATE A TRUST

BOYDEN v. STEVENS

Supreme Judicial Court of Massachusetts, 1934.
285 Mass. 176, 188 N.E. 741.

LUMMUS, JUSTICE. Walter H. Edgerly died in 1906, testate, leaving a widow Nathalie A. Edgerly, now Nathalie A. Stevens, and a daughter Madeline who died in 1907, a minor and unmarried. Any interest of Madeline has passed to the widow as her sole heir at law and next of kin.

The will gave the sum of $50,000, and also the residue of the estate, to Roland W. Boyden, "in trust, for the benefit of my wife and children, if any, the income to be paid to my wife during her life. My trustee shall at any time have power in his discretion to pay over to my wife, or to expend for her benefit or for the maintenance and education of my children or any of them, such portion of the principal as he may deem advisable. After the death of my wife, so much of the income as my trustee may deem advisable shall be paid over to, or be expended for the maintenance, education and support of my children, if any, or the issue of any child who may have deceased, until my youngest living child shall reach the age of twenty-five (25) years, or until all of my children shall have deceased, whichever event first occurs. The principal of the trust fund shall then be divided equally among my children then living and the issue of any child who may have deceased, such issue to take such child's share by right of representation. Upon the death of my wife, if no issue of mine survive her, or upon subsequent failure of my issue prior to the time above fixed for distribution of the principal, the trust property shall be distributed as if I had died intestate." Another article of the will provided in part, "The interests of all beneficiaries shall not be subject to attachment or execution, and shall not be anticipated by assignment."

On the death of Mr. Boyden in 1931, the petitioner Albert Boyden was appointed trustee in his stead. He asks to be instructed (1) whether as the successor trustee he may exercise the discretionary power to pay over to Nathalie A. Stevens or to expend for her benefit such portion of the principal as he may deem advisable, (2) whether upon the death of Nathalie A. Stevens the direction that the trust property shall be distributed "as if I had died intestate" gives it to the heirs at the death of the testator (in which case Nathalie A. Stevens owns the entire remainder interest) or to the heirs determined as

termination after the ruling of the Supreme Court in the principal case; recovery was denied. Trust Co. of Georgia v. Woodruff, 236 Ga. 220, 223 S.E.2d 91 (1976). In Johnson v. First National Bank of Jackson, 386 So.2d 1112 (Miss. 1980), where the settlor was the sole beneficiary, she was held to have the right to termination of the trust even though the wisdom of such termination was dubious.

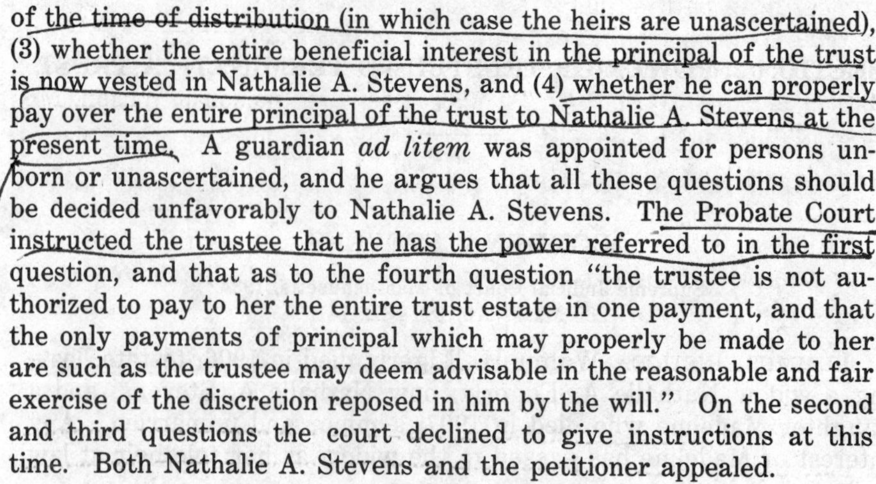

of the time of distribution (in which case the heirs are unascertained), (3) whether the entire beneficial interest in the principal of the trust is now vested in Nathalie A. Stevens, and (4) whether he can properly pay over the entire principal of the trust to Nathalie A. Stevens at the present time. A guardian *ad litem* was appointed for persons unborn or unascertained, and he argues that all these questions should be decided unfavorably to Nathalie A. Stevens. The Probate Court instructed the trustee that he has the power referred to in the first question, and that as to the fourth question "the trustee is not authorized to pay to her the entire trust estate in one payment, and that the only payments of principal which may properly be made to her are such as the trustee may deem advisable in the reasonable and fair exercise of the discretion reposed in him by the will." On the second and third questions the court declined to give instructions at this time. Both Nathalie A. Stevens and the petitioner appealed.

It is not now questioned that the petitioner has succeeded to the discretionary power of the original trustee. In this respect the Probate Court was right. Stanwood v. Stanwood, 179 Mass. 223, 227, 60 N.E. 584; Sells v. Delgado, 186 Mass. 25, 70 N.E. 1036; Shattuck v. Stickney, 211 Mass. 327, 97 N.E. 774. The first question upon which the petitioner asks to be instructed should be answered in favor of his power.

What is his discretionary power? In many of the reported cases a power to pay over principal was conditioned upon a determination by the trustee or other donee of the power that certain facts existed. In Corkery v. Dorsey, 223 Mass. 97, 111 N.E. 795, 796, for example, the power was to be exercised "when in the judgment of said O'Callaghan (the trustee) the said Fay is deserving and in need of aid." See, also, Lovett v. Farnham, 169 Mass. 1, 47 N.E. 246; Allen v. Hunt, 213 Mass. 276, 100 N.E. 552; Wright v. Blinn, 225 Mass. 146, 114 N.E. 79; Lumbert v. Fisher, 245 Mass. 190, 139 N.E. 446; Leonard v. Wheeler, 261 Mass. 130, 158 N.E. 502. But such a power may be given unconditionally. Taft v. Taft, 130 Mass. 461; Kent v. Morrison, 153 Mass. 137, 26 N.E. 427; Burbank v. Sweeney, 161 Mass. 490, 37 N.E. 669; Ford v. Ticknor, 169 Mass. 276, 47 N.E. 877; Woodbridge v. Jones, 183 Mass. 549, 67 N.E. 878; Goodrich v. Henderson, 221 Mass. 234, 108 N.E. 1062; Homans v. Foster, 232 Mass. 4, 6, 7, 121 N.E. 417, and cases cited. Jones v. Old Colony Trust Co., 251 Mass. 309, 313, 146 N.E. 716; Merchants' Trust Co. v. Russell, 260 Mass. 162, 157 N.E. 338. The present will does not make the power conditional upon the actual existence of any tangible facts or the determination by the trustee that any such facts exist. All that is necessary is that the trustee "in his discretion" shall "deem advisable" the payment to Nathalie A. Stevens of the "portion of the principal" that may be under consideration. See Sells v. Delgado, 186 Mass. 25, 70 N.E. 1036. It is true that even so broad a power as that is not an absolute power without limitation. "There is an implication, when even broad powers are conferred, that they are to be exercised with that soundness of judgment which follows from a due appreciation of trust responsibility. Prudence and reasonableness, not caprice or careless good nature, much less a desire on the part of the trustee to be relieved from trouble or from the possibility of making a foolish investment, furnish the standard of conduct." Corkery v. Dorsey, 223 Mass. 97, 101, 111 N.E. 795, 796. See, also, Wilson v. Wilson, 145 Mass. 490, 492, 14 N.E. 521, 1 Am.St.Rep. 477.

There is nothing in the will to prevent the trustee, in a proper exercise of the power, from paying over the entire trust fund at once to Nathalie A. Stevens. The use of the word "portion" does not require that some small fragment of the trust property be retained by the trustee or that the result be accomplished by paying different portions at different times until the whole has been paid over. Cooke v. Farrand, 7 Taunt. 122; Rendlesham v. Meux, 14 Sim. 249, 256, 257; Arthur v. Mackinnon, 11 Ch.D. 385. But the trust must continue during the life of Nathalie A. Stevens, except as the exercise of the power may prevent. Even though she owns the entire remainder, which we do not now decide, Nathalie A. Stevens has no absolute right to have the trust terminated during her life. Claflin v. Claflin, 149 Mass. 19, 20 N.E. 454, 3 L.R.A. 370, 14 Am.St.Rep. 393; Young v. Snow, 167 Mass. 287, 45 N.E. 686; Danahy v. Noonan, 176 Mass. 467, 57 N.E. 679; Welch v. Trustees of Episcopal Theological School, 189 Mass. 108, 75 N.E. 139; Forbes v. Snow, 245 Mass. 85, 93, 140 N.E. 418; Abbott v. Williams, 268 Mass. 275, 283, 167 N.E. 357. The trustee has the right to accomplish a termination of the trust by the exercise of the power only in case, after serious and responsible consideration, he shall deem that such an exercise of the power is advisable. The fourth question upon which the petitioner asks to be instructed should be answered in the affirmative, with the qualification already stated.

The petitioner desires instructions as to the second and third questions, already stated, upon which the Probate Court declined to instruct him. These questions are, in substance, whether the remainder interest is now vested in Nathalie A. Stevens. Ordinarily the court will instruct a trustee only as to questions with regard to which he has a present duty, and will not advise him as to problems of the past or the future. Hill v. Moors, 224 Mass. 163, 165, 112 N.E. 641; Parkhurst v. Ginn, 228 Mass. 159, 117 N.E. 202; Swift v. Crocker, 262 Mass. 321, 328, 159 N.E. 919, 921; Flye v. Jones, 283 Mass. 136, 186 N.E. 64. Occasionally special circumstances have been thought to require a relaxation of this rule. Bowditch v. Andrew, 8 Allen, 339; Old Colony Trust Co. v. Sargent, 235 Mass. 298, 303, 126 N.E. 526. In the present case, the trustee thinks that it would assist him in the exercise of his discretion if the question whether the remainder interest is now vested in Nathalie A. Stevens should be adjudicated now. But on the whole we are of opinion that the ordinary course should be followed, and that the Probate Court was right in declining to answer the second and third questions.

Because of our modification of the answer to the fourth question, the final decree is reversed, and the trustee is to be instructed upon the first and fourth questions in accordance with this opinion. The matter of costs and expenses is to be in the discretion of the Probate Court.

Ordered accordingly.

NOTE

The trustee has no power to modify or terminate the trust unless the power was conferred upon him when the trust was created.

The trust terms may provide that the trustee may in the exercise of his discretion or on the happening of a certain event or events, terminate the trust by transferring the trust *res* to the beneficiaries. The trustee may have power to pay all or part of the principal to the beneficiaries whenever the trustee in his discretion may choose to do so, or when the beneficiary needs the principal or part of it for a purpose named in the trust instrument. The power to pay out corpus necessarily involves a power to terminate the trust in whole or in part. The courts will not interfere with a power exercised in good faith unless the exercise is arbitrary. The trustee's decision is reviewable and may be overruled if arbitrary or in bad faith.[10]

The power to terminate affords flexibility to meet changing tax structures. Kemp v. Paterson, 6 N.Y.2d 40, 188 N.Y.S.2d 161, 159 N.E.2d 661 (1959),[11] is an interesting example of judicial reluctance to recognize this need. Here settlor in 1934 created a trust which, after the settlor's death, provided that the trustees were to pay over to her daughter all of the net income and "so much of the principal sums of the trust from time to time as the Trustees may deem for [her] best interest"; upon the death of the daughter, the corpus was to go to her issue and, if none, to designated persons. The daughter had no need for corpus, but the income from the trust was subject to an income tax of 92½%. In order to enable the daughter to minimize her income taxes and carry out a plan to avoid heavy estate taxes at the daughter's death, the trustees decided that, in her "best interest", they had the power to terminate the trust; however, they brought this action to obtain judicial sanction. The majority of the Court of Appeals of New York held that the trustees did not have this power: "* * * the power to use the principal of the trust may not be enlarged into a power to terminate". The crux of the dissenting opinion lies in the following statement: "In dealing with finances for the benefit of others, the trust apparatus provides many advantages, principal of which is the flexibility and the benefits to be derived from the experienced and untrammeled discretion of dependable trustees to carry out the settlor's intention."

It is not uncommon to find in the modern trust document an express power in the trustee to terminate if the principal sum is reduced below a stated amount, such as $10,000, when administration of the fund in trust is no longer economically justified.[12]

---

10. Bogert, Trusts and Trustees (2d Ed., 1965); IV Scott, Trusts (3d Ed., 1967) § 334.1. See Endacott, "Problems in Drafting and Administering Discretionary Trusts", 46 Neb.L.Rev. 110 (1967).

11. Noted, 26 Brook.L.Rev. 156 (1959), 34 St. Johns L.Rev. 173 (1959).

12. Some courts reach the same result on petition by the beneficiary on the ground that there is no useful purpose served by continuance of the trust. E.g., Dowell's Estate, 270 P.2d 1098 (Okl. 1954).

SECTION 3. POWER OF BENEFICIARIES TO TERMINATE A TRUST

CLAFLIN v. CLAFLIN

Supreme Judicial Court of Massachusetts, 1889.
149 Mass. 19, 20 N.E. 454, 14 Am.St.Rep. 393.

FIELD, J. By the eleventh article of his will, as modified by a codicil, Wilbur F. Claflin gave all the residue of his personal estate to trustees, "to sell and dispose of the same, and to pay to my wife, Mary A. Claflin, one-third part of the proceeds thereof, and to pay to my son Clarence A. Claflin, one-third part of the proceeds thereof, and to pay the remaining one-third part thereof to my son Adelbert E. Claflin, in the manner following, viz.: Ten thousand dollars when he is of the age of twenty-one years, ten thousand dollars when he is of the age of twenty-five years, and the balance when he is of the age of thirty years."

Apparently, Adelbert E. Claflin was not quite 21 years old when his father died, but he some time ago reached that age, and received $10,000 from the trust. He has not yet reached the age of 25 years, and he brings this bill to compel the trustees to pay to him the remainder of the trust fund. His contention is, in effect, that the provisions of the will postponing the payment of the money beyond the time when he is 21 years old are void. There is no doubt that his interest in the trust fund is vested and absolute, and that no other person has any interest in it; and the weight of authority is undisputed that the provisions postponing payment to him until some time after he reaches the age of 21 years would be treated as void by those courts which hold that restrictions against the alienation of absolute interests in the income of trust property are void. There has indeed, been no decision of this question in England by the House of Lords, and but one by a Lord Chancellor, but there are several decisions to this effect by Masters of the Rolls, and by Vice-Chancellors. The cases are collected in Gray, Rest. Alien, §§ 106–112, and appendix II. See Josselyn v. Josselyn, 9 Sim. 63; Saunders v. Vautier, 4 Beav. 115, and on appeal, Craig. & P. 240; Rocke v. Rocke, 9 Beav. 66; In re Young's Settlement, 18 Beav. 199; In re Jacob's Will, 29 Beav. 402; Gosling v. Gosling, Johns.V.C. 265; Turnage v. Greene, 2 Jones, Eq. 63; Battle v. Petway, 5 Ired. 576.

These decisions do not proceed on the ground that it was the intention of the testator that the property should be conveyed to the beneficiary on his reaching the age of 21 years, because in each case it was clear that such was not his intention, but on the ground that the direction to withhold the possession of the property from the beneficiary after he reached his majority was inconsistent with the absolute rights of property given him by the will.

This court has ordered trust property to be conveyed by the trustee to the beneficiary when there was a dry trust, or when the purposes of the trust had been accomplished, or when no good reason was shown why the trust should continue, and all the persons interested in it were *sui juris*, and desired that it be terminated; but we have found no expression of any opinion in our reports that provisions requiring a trustee to hold and manage the trust property until the beneficiary reached an age beyond that of 21 years are necessarily void if the interest of the beneficiary is vested and absolute. See Smith v. Harrington, 4 Allen, 566; Bowditch v. Andrew, 8 Allen, 339; Russell v. Grinnell, 105 Mass. 425; Inches v. Hill, 106 Mass. 575; Sears v. Choate, 146 Mass. 395, 15 N.E.Rep. 786. This is not a dry trust and the purposes of the trust have not been accomplished, if the intention of the testator is to be carried out.

In Sears v. Choate it is said: "Where property is given to certain persons for their benefit, and in such a manner that no other person has or can have any interest in it, they are in effect the absolute owners of it; and it is reasonable and just that they should have the control and disposal of it, unless some good cause appears to the contrary." In that case the plaintiff was the absolute owner of the whole property, subject to an annuity of $10,000, payable to himself. The whole of the principal of the trust fund, and all of the income not expressly made payable to the plaintiff, had become vested in him when he reached the age of 21 years, by way of resulting trust, as property undisposed of by the will. Apparently the testator had not contemplated such a result, and had made no provision for it, and the court saw no reason why the trust should not be terminated, and the property conveyed to the plaintiff. In Inches v. Hill, ubi supra, the same person had become owner of the equitable life-estate and of the equitable remainder, and, "no reason appearing to the contrary," the court decreed a conveyance by the trustees to the owner. See Whall v. Converse, 146 Mass. 345, 15 N.E. 660. In the case at bar nothing has happened which the testator did not anticipate, and for which he has not made provision. It is plainly his will that neither the income nor any part of the principal should now be paid to the plaintiff. It is true that the plaintiff's interest is alienable by him, and can be taken by his creditors to pay his debts, but it does not follow that, because the testator has not imposed all possible restrictions, the restrictions which he has imposed should not be carried into effect. The decision in Bank v. Adams, 133 Mass. 170, rests upon the doctrine that a testator has a right to dispose of his own property with such restrictions and limitations, not repugnant to law, as he sees fit, and that his intentions ought to be carried out, unless they contravene some positive rule of law, or are against public policy. The rule contended for by the plaintiff in that case was founded upon the same considerations as that contended for by the plaintiff in this, and the grounds on which this court declined to follow the English rule in that case are applicable to this; and for the reasons there given we are unable to see that the directions of the testator to the trustees to pay the money to the plaintiff when he reaches the age of 25 and 30 years, and not before, are against public policy, or are so far inconsistent with the rights of property given to the plaintiff, that they should not be carried into effect. It cannot be said that these restrictions upon the plaintiff's possession and control of the property are altogether useless, for there is not the same danger that he will spend the property while it is in the hands of the trustees as there would be if it were in his own.

In Sanford v. Lackland, 2 Dill. 6, a beneficiary who would have been entitled to a conveyance of trust property at the age of 26 became a bankrupt at the age of 24, and it was held that the trustees should convey his interest immediately to his assignee, as "the strict execution of the trusts in the will have been thus rendered impossible." But whether a creditor or a grantee of the plaintiff in this case would be entitled to the immediate possession of the property, or would only take the plaintiff's title *sub modo*, need not be decided. The existing situation is one which the testator manifestly had in mind, and made provision for. The strict execution of the trust has not become impossible; the restriction upon the plaintiff's possession and control is, we think, one that the testator had a right to make; other provisions for the plaintiff are contained in the will, apparently sufficient for his support; and we see no good reason why the intention of the testator should not be carried out. Russell v. Grinnell, 105 Mass. 425; See Toner v. Collins, 67 Iowa 369, 25 N.W.Rep. 287; Rhoads v. Rhoads, 43 Ill. 239; Lent v. Howard, 89 N.Y. 169; Barkley v. Dosser, 15 Lea, 529; Carmichael v. Thompson, 6 A.Rep. 717; Lampert v. Haydel, 20 Mo.App. 616.

Decree affirmed.

NOTE

In Saunders v. Vautier,[13] mentioned in the principal case, the English Chancery Court granted a petition by the sole beneficiary to terminate a trust upon his attaining the age of majority, even though by the terms of the trust the principal was not to be paid to him until he attained the age of 25. This is the rule in England and a minority of the American jurisdictions. The Claflin rule is adopted in a majority of the states: that an active trust may not be terminated if its continuance is necessary to carry out a material purpose of the settlor.

The English view is based on the theory that the sole owners of the entire equitable property interest under the trust are the sole owners of the trust

13. 4 Beav. 115, 49 Eng.Rep. 282 (1841). The concept of "equitable ownership" established by *Saunders v. Vautier* required that all the beneficiaries be in existence and sui juris in order to override the settlor's intent. Chapman v. Chapman, [1954] A.C. 429. In 1958 Parliament enacted the Variation of Trusts Act, 6 & 7 Eliz. 2 429, which gives the court broad power to act on behalf of all beneficiaries incapable of consenting, to modify or revoke the trust. The limitation is that the court cannot act if the proposed arrangement will not be for the "benefit" of those beneficiaries. Usually a cash settlement is arranged to satisfy that limitation, but the benefit does not have to be financial. Primary reasons for varying trust terms in England are said to be altering trust terms which have "disastrous tax consequences", avoiding unduly restrictive investment powers, and facilitating change of trustees where beneficiaries have moved to another locality. See Harris, Variation of Trusts—Modern Legal Studies (1975).

res and should be allowed to enjoy the property as they choose—in trust or not in trust. The view is consistent with the English position that spendthrift trusts should not be permitted because of the restrictions that they impose upon the alienation of property. The English view emphasizes the nature of the beneficiary's interest. The prevailing American view, as expressed in the Claflin Case, emphasizes the intention of the settlor and insists that his intention be executed.

On the other hand, in comparable situations the majority of American courts do not consistently give primacy to the settlor's intent. The donee of an annuity may elect to take the price of the annuity in lieu of the annuity on the ground that he can sell the annuity at once after he obtains it. When realty is given to a trustee to be sold and the proceeds are to be paid to a donee, the donee may choose the realty instead of the sale price.

Extra-judicial terminations of the trust are possible. If the trustee transfers the property to the beneficiaries and obtains releases from them when they are all *sui juris*, the trust is terminated by merger and no one has standing in court to complain of the termination. The Claflin doctrine is applicable when the trustee refuses to terminate or petitions the court for instructions.[14]

ADAMS v. LINK

Supreme Court of Errors of Connecticut, 1958.
145 Conn. 634, 145 A.2d 753.[15]

KING, ASSOCIATE JUSTICE. The defendants Link and the United States Trust Company of New York are the executors and trustees under the will and codicil of Mildred A. Kingsmill, late of Darien. Mrs. Kingsmill left, as her sole heirs at law, two brothers, Orson Adams, Jr., and Alvin P. Adams, and a sister, Ethel A. Martin. This action grows out of, although it is distinct from, an appeal by Orson Adams, Jr., and Alvin P. Adams, two of the three heirs at law, from the admission of the will and codicil to probate.

In the view which we take of the case, only the right to terminate the trust created in paragraph sixth of the will need be considered. This paragraph disposed of the residue by a trust. It provided for the payment of the net income for life, in monthly or quarterly instalments at their written election, to Joan K. Pringle and Mayes M. Foeppel, neither of whom was an heir at law. At the death of the survivor, the trust was to terminate and distribution of the corpus was to be made to the New York Association for the Blind. In fact, Joan K. Pringle predeceased the testatrix, leaving Mayes M. Foeppel as the sole income beneficiary and entitled, under the terms of the trust, to the entire net income for life.

During the pendency of the appeal from probate, a so-called compromise agreement was entered into between Mayes M. Foeppel, party of the first part, the New York Association for the Blind, party of the second part, and the three heirs at law of the testatrix, parties of

14. See generally, Restatement, Second Trusts § 337; Bogert, Trusts and Trustees (2d Ed., 1965) § 1002; IV Scott, Trusts (3d Ed., 1967) § 337; 46 Yale L.J. 1005 (1937).

15. Noted, 39 B.U.L.Rev. 274 (1959).

the third part. The agreement in effect provided that (1) the appeal from the admission of the will and codicil to probate would be withdrawn; (2) 15 per cent of the residuary estate, i.e. the trust corpus, would be paid outright to the three heirs at law in equal shares; (3) 37 per cent would be paid outright to the New York Association for the Blind; and (4) 48 per cent would be paid outright to Mayes M. Foeppel less a deduction of $15,000 which would be used to establish a new trust, the precise terms of which are not material. Basically, it was for the education of a son of Alvin P. Adams, and upon completion of his education the trust would terminate and any unused corpus and interest would be returned to Mayes M. Foeppel. The compromise agreement was by its express terms made subject to the approval of the Superior Court. The defendant executors and trustees refused to participate in the agreement or to carry it out. The present action, the plaintiffs in which include all parties to the agreement except the New York Association for the Blind, which was made a party defendant, seeks in effect (a) the approval of the agreement by the Superior Court, and (b) a decree compelling the defendant executors and trustees to carry it out. Since the provision for the New York Association for the Blind was a charitable gift, the attorney general was made a defendant to represent the public interest, under the provisions of § 212 of the General Statutes. The court refused to approve the agreement, and from this action the plaintiffs took this appeal.

While the parties have extensively argued and briefed a number of questions, one basic proposition is dispositive of, and fatal to, the position taken by the plaintiffs. No corrections of the finding which could benefit them in this view of the case can be made.

The fundamental effect of the compromise agreement, if approved by the court, would be to abolish the trust. Our rule as to the right of the beneficiaries of a testamentary trust to have it terminated has been set forth in a number of cases, including Ackerman v. Union & New Haven Trust Co., 90 Conn. 63, 71, 96 A. 149; De Ladson v. Crawford, 93 Conn. 402, 411, 106 A. 326, and Hills v. Travelers Bank & Trust Co., 125 Conn. 640, 648, 7 A.2d 652, 173 A.L.R. 1419. The rule has also in effect been applied to the right of the beneficiaries to terminate an inter vivos trust. Gaess v. Gaess, 132 Conn. 96, 101, 42 A.2d 796, 160 A.L.R. 432. Here a testatrix, in her will, established a trust in admittedly clear and unambiguous language; she has now died; and the trust beneficiaries and the heirs at law have joined in a plan to set aside the trust and substitute a distribution of the testatrix' estate more to their liking. Such a testamentary trust may be terminated only by a decree of a court of equity, regardless of any stipulation by all parties in interest. Peiter v. Degenring, 136 Conn. 331, 336, 71 A.2d 87. Our rule as set forth in Hills v. Travelers Bank & Trust Co., supra, is: Conditions precedent which should concur in order to warrant termination of a testamentary trust by judicial decree are (1) that all the parties in interest unite in seeking the termination, (2) that every reasonable ultimate purpose of the trust's creation and existence has been accomplished, and (3) that no fair and lawful restriction imposed by the testator will be nullified or disturbed by such a result. "The function of the court [of equity] with reference to trusts is not to remake the trust instrument, reduce or increase the size of the gifts made therein or accord the beneficiary more advantage than the donor directed that he should enjoy, but rather to ascertain what the donor directed that the donee should receive and to secure to him the enjoyment of that interest only." Hills v. Travelers Bank & Trust Co., supra [125 Conn. 640, 7 A.2d 655]; Peiter v. Degenring, supra. The underlying rationale of our rule is the protection, if reasonably possible, of any reasonable, properly expressed, testamentary desire of a decedent. 3 Scott, Trusts (2d Ed.) § 337.

It appears that all the interested beneficiaries have joined in the agreement under consideration. For the purposes of this case only, we will assume, without in any way deciding, that the plaintiffs are correct in their claim that the defendant executors and trustees have no standing to attack the compromise. This assumption is permissible because the compromise was in terms made contingent upon court approval, and this approval could not be compelled by any agreement of the trust beneficiaries among themselves. Peiter v. Degenring, supra. Thus we may assume, without deciding, that the first condition precedent under our rule is satisfied. But see Loring, A Trustee's Handbook (5th Ed.) § 122, p. 316, § 123, p. 318. The second and third conditions precedent have not, however, been satisfied. The obvious objectives of the testatrix were to provide (a) an assured income for life for Mayes M. Foeppel, and (b) at her death an intact corpus for the New York Association for the Blind. In carrying out these objectives, the testatrix took two important steps. In the first place, the management of the trust corpus was committed to trustees selected by her and in whose financial judgment she is presumed to have had confidence. Secondly, expenditure of any principal by the life beneficiary was precluded. Taken together, these two steps would tend to achieve, and in all reasonable probability would achieve, the testatrix' two basic objectives. To abolish the trust and turn over a fraction of the corpus outright to the life beneficiary would be to enable her in a moment to lose the protection of the practically assured life income provided by the testatrix. The two basic objectives of the trust's creation and existence were reasonable and commendable and cannot be fully accomplished prior to the death of the life beneficiary. Peiter v. Degenring, supra, 136 Conn. 337, 71 A.2d 90; 3 Scott, op. cit., § 337.1, p. 2454. Obviously, had the testatrix intended to entrust the life beneficiary with the handling of any part of the corpus, she would have so provided by a simple, outright gift.

The plaintiffs attempt to avoid the impact of our rule by two main claims. The first is that since the protection accorded the life beneficiary could be lost by her voluntary alienation of the income or by its involuntary alienation through attachment or seizure under an order in equity, the testatrix could not have intended to protect the beneficiary. This amounts in effect to a claim that only a spendthrift trust is protected from termination by agreement of all interested beneficiaries. The case against termination under our rule is of course even stronger where a spendthrift trust is involved, as in Mason v. Rhode Island Hospital Trust Co., 78 Conn. 81, 84, 61 A. 57. 3 Scott, op. cit., § 337.2. But the operation of our rule is not restricted to such trusts. The mere fact that the testatrix failed to provide the maximum possible protection for the life beneficiary by creating a spendthrift trust under the terms of what is now § 3195d of the 1955 Cumulative Supplement does not warrant a conclusion that she intended no protection at all, so that we can consider that the trust no longer has any purpose. Id., p. 2454.

There is no merit in the plaintiffs' claim that in Peiter v. Degenring, supra, there was a change in, or a relaxation of, our rule. The facts in that case were peculiar. The testator's brother was seventy-eight years old and under a conservator. The testator created a trust for the payment to the brother or his conservator of "so much of the income and principal of my estate as may be necessary for his support and comfort, using the income first." In other words, the beneficiary was given neither principal nor income except as necessary for his support and comfort. The parties stipulated that the brother owned personal estate the annual income of which was greatly in excess of his needs for comfort and support, that he had not been entitled to receive and had not received any money from the trust, and that there was no possibility that he would be entitled to receive any money from it at any time. The proposal of all interested parties was that the trust be terminated upon the payment to the brother of $10,000, which of course would be under the management of the conservator. We held that a decree terminating the trust could not be granted on any stipulation of the parties but only, if at all, upon the basis of facts found by testimony offered before the court, and that the trust should not be terminated "unless those facts clearly establish that no purpose it was designed to serve would be defeated or jeopardized." Id., 136 Conn. 340, 71 A.2d 91. There is nothing in the decision inconsistent with our rule as set forth in the other cases cited by us. The Peiter case does hold that evidence may be offered of facts, not apparent from the provisions of the trust instrument itself, which, if proved, would warrant a conclusion that the trust does not serve a legal and useful purpose and should be terminated. Ibid. We also held in the Peiter case that if satisfactory proof was made of the peculiar facts therein, it might warrant a conclusion by the court that in all reasonable probability the trust would remain inactive during the beneficary's life and, if so, a termination might be ordered, as in the case of any useless trust. The Peiter case in nowise helps the plaintiffs here.

* * *

The plaintffs also claim that whatever the rule may be in cases involving no will contest, a more liberal rule applies where, as here, the termination of the trust is a part of the settlement of such a contest. Some support for this position may be found in cases cited in 3 Scott, Trusts (2d Ed.) § 337.6. The rationale of our rule as to the power to set aside or terminate a trust is not, however, such that its applicability would be affected by the mere fact that the motivation of a trust termination agreement is the compromise of a will contest. It is true that such contests are not infrequently compromised by agreements involving the transfer of legacies or devises, in whole or in part, by beneficiaries under the will. Where such gifts are alienable this is permissible, since no violence is done to the provisions of the will. But that is not this case. Here the provisions of the will itself are being drastically changed so as to abolish a trust contrary to our rule. This cannot be done. It follows that the court below was not in error in denying approval of the agreement. Indeed, it was the only decision which could properly have been made. This conclusion makes unnecessary the consideration of the other grounds of appeal.

There is no error.

In this opinion the other judges concurred.

IN RE BOSLER'S ESTATE

Supreme Court of Pennsylvania, 1954.
378 Pa. 333, 107 A.2d 443.[16]

HORACE STERN, CHIEF JUSTICE. Newton L. Bosler petitioned the court to decree the termination of a trust under which he was the beneficiary of a life interest with a spendthrift restriction.

Petitioner's mother, Sarah E. Bosler, died in 1916 leaving a will in which she gave her estate to her six children in equal shares. In the case, however, of three of them—two daughters and the petitioner—she created a trust as to a portion of their shares, leaving to each such daughter the income of a fund of $10,000 for life subject to a spendthrift trust, and to the petitioner the income of a fund of $20,000 for life, likewise subject to a spendthrift trust. Upon the death of each of these three children the principal was to go to his or her issue; in default of issue then living each child was to have a general power to appoint the remainder by will; in default of both issue and the exercise of such general power of appointment the remainder was given to decedent's other descendants then living.

There was a clause in decedent's will as follows: "I have made these three bequests in trust, not from any lack of confidence in or affection for my said two daughters and son, but in order that I may feel that I have made provision for them which will assure to each one of them a support throughout his or her whole life, under any circumstances, and for the comfort that I will personally derive from such knowledge."

We are not here concerned with the trust in favor of the two daughters but only with that of petitioner. He is 65 years of age. He seeks termination of the trust on the ground that he has never had any issue and is incapable of having any, and he contends that

16. Noted, 54 Mich.L.Rev. 153 (1955), 28 Temp.L.Q. 310 (1954).

because of his general power of appointment coupled with his life interest he has what is tantamount to an estate in fee and is therefore the only person having an interest in the trust. He presented testimony to the effect that he is a civilian employee of the United States Navy earning between $150 and $160 per month, that by reason of his age he is likely soon to be retired with a probability of not being able then to obtain other employment, and that because, on the one hand, of the shrinkage in the returns from the investments in the trust fund and, on the other, of the rise in living costs, he faces the prospect of inability to support himself and his wife in any degree of comfort. The present annual income from the trust after payment of the trustee's commission and the Pennsylvania Personal Property Tax is approximately $660.

The court below came to the conclusion that it could give partial relief to the petitioner, and accordingly it made an order on the Trustee to pay to petitioner the sum of $1,200 out of the corpus immediately to meet present emergencies, and, in addition to the annual income, the sum of $100 quarterly, also out of corpus. From the court's decree this appeal has been taken by the Farmers Trust Company, Trustee of the trust.

In view of our conclusion on another aspect of the case we shall not discuss the question of petitioner's claim that he is incapable of having children nor his contention that he has, under the trust, what is tantamount to a fee, although it may incidentally be noted that a life estate under a spendthrift trust will not coalesce or merge with an estate in remainder. In re Moser's Estate, 270 Pa. 217, 113 A. 199.

The principles of equity jurisprudence applicable to petitions to terminate trusts have been so often defined by this court as to render extended discussion of the subject wholly unnecessary. If all the parties who are or may be beneficially interested in a trust are in existence and sui juris, if there is no ultimate purpose of any kind requiring the continuance of the trust, and if all the beneficiaries consent, a court of equity may decree its termination. Culbertson's Appeal, 76 Pa. 145, 148; In re Harrar's Estate, 244 Pa. 542, 548, 549, 91 A. 503, 505; In re Stafford's Estate, 258 Pa. 595, 598, 599, 102 A. 222, 223; In re Wood's Estate, 261 Pa. 480, 483, 104 A. 673; In re Bowers' Trust Estate, 346 Pa. 85, 87, 29 A.2d 519, 520; Rest. Trusts § 337. But if the purpose of the settlor in establishing the trust has not been fully accomplished, and if the settlor is deceased and therefore incapable of consenting, the trust cannot be terminated even though all the beneficiaries desire that it should be. In re Bowers' Trust Estate, 346 Pa. 85, 87, 88, 29 A.2d 519, 520, and cases there cited.

Here the settlor *is* deceased and the question therefore is whether her purpose in establishing the trust *has* been fully accomplished. Petitioner contends that because of the statement in her will, hereinbefore quoted, to the effect that her object was to make provision for petitioner and the two daughters which would assure to each of them a support throughout his or her whole life and for the comfort that she would personally derive from such knowledge, her purpose would be defeated if the order of the court below were not sustained, since the income from the trust was not adequate to render the support which the testatrix had in contemplation. Obviously, however, it would be a matter of pure speculation as to whether—whatever the change of conditions since her death—she would now want part of the corpus of the trust turned over to the petitioner, involving, as it would, the pro tanto depletion of the fund from which the income was to be derived and with the future payments ordered out of corpus made available to the claims of creditors and assignees because not subject to the spendthrift trust provision. Since she must have realized that changes might occur both in the amount of the income from the trust and in the varying circumstances of petitioner's life it would have been easy for her, had she so intended, to authorize the trustee in its discretion to advance portions of the corpus to petitioner if conditions at any time so dictated.

The cases are adamant in holding that where the life interest is limited by a spendthrift provision the trust cannot be terminated by the court. Dodson v. Ball, 60 Pa. 492, 496; In re Shower's Estate, 211 Pa. 297, 60 A. 789; In re Moser's Estate, 270 Pa. 217, 113 A. 199; In re Baughman's Estate, 281 Pa. 23, 39, 126 A. 58, 64; Rehr v. Fidelity-Philadelphia Trust Co., 310 Pa. 301, 304, 305, 165 A. 380, 381, 91 A.L.R. 99; In re Harrison's Estate, 322 Pa. 532, 185 A. 766; In re Bowers' Trust Estate, 346 Pa. 85, 88, 29 A.2d 519, 520; In re Heyl's Estate, 352 Pa. 407, 411, 43 A.2d 130, 131, 132; Rest. Trusts, § 337, comment *l*. Certainly there is no appellate authority which holds that a partial reduction in the income of a spendthrift trust constitutes such a failure of the purpose of the trust as to warrant its termination by judicial decree. The principle upon which the cases rest is the protection of the settlor irrespective of the welfare or interests of the beneficiary. It was said in Re Morgan's Estate (No. 1), 223 Pa. 228, 230, 231, 72 A. 498, 499, 25 L.R.A.,N.S., 236: "It is always to be remembered that consideration for the beneficiary does not even in the remotest way enter into the policy of the law. It has regard solely to the rights of the donor. Spendthrift trusts can have no other justification than is to be found in considerations affecting the donor alone. They allow the donor to so control his bounty, through the creation of the trust, that it may be exempt from liability for the donee's debts, not because the law is concerned to keep the donee from wasting it, but because it is concerned to protect the donor's right of property. * * * We repeat, spendthrift trusts are allowed not because the law concerns itself for the donee. He may conserve or dissipate as he pleases. The law's only concern is to give effect to the will of the donor as he has expressed it." So also In re Heyl's Estate, 352 Pa. 407, 411, 43 A.2d 130, 131, 132; In re Borsch's Estate, 362 Pa. 581, 587, 588, 67 A.2d 119, 122.

In short, *if the settlor is alive*, as was the case in In re Bowers' Trust Estate, 346 Pa. 85, 29 A.2d 519, and concurs with all the parties in interest in the trust that it be modified or terminated, the existence of a spendthrift trust provision would not prevent such termination.

Rest. Trusts, § 338(1). But if, as stated in that case, the settlor be deceased and therefore incapable of consenting, such a trust cannot be terminated even though all the beneficiaries desire that it should be. See Rest. Trusts, § 338, comment a.

While the order made by the court below is undoubtedly well intentioned for the purpose of affording some relief to the petitioner's anxieties, it constitutes a modification of the terms of the trust that cannot, in the absence of statutory authorization, be sustained.[17]

The decree is reversed and the petition dismissed.

NOTE

Normally, when a trust is created under which the income is payable to one beneficiary for life and on his death the principal is payable to another, and it does not appear that the settlor had any other purpose in creating the trust than to enable the beneficiaries to enjoy the trust property successively, the beneficiaries can compel termination if both consent and both are *sui juris*.[18] A life beneficiary of a trust who acquires the remainder (or the remainderman who acquires the interest of the life beneficiary) can force termination.[19] But as the preceding cases indicate, a court may find a "material purpose" for the trust other than providing successive enjoyment of the property. The existence of a spendthrift clause is often emphasized as indicating a protective purpose which prevents termination.[20]

A few courts are willing to allow termination where the income beneficiary is suffering hardship. See for example American Security & Trust Co. v. Cramer, where the court allowed termination in favor of the life tenant where the settlor had manifested special affection for the life tenant; this was done on the basis of "assignments" by her children, the presumptive remaindermen, and the furnishing of a bond to protect any unascertained remaindermen.[21]

17. [Footnote by the court.]

The Estates Act of April 24, 1947, P.L. 100, Section 2(a), 20 P.S. § 301.2(a), authorizes the court having jurisdiction of a trust to terminate it, in its discretion, in whole or in part, or make an allowance from principal to an income beneficiary, regardless of any spendthrift or similar provision therein, provided the court is satisfied that the original purpose of the settlor cannot be carried out or is impractical of fulfillment and that the termination, partial termination, or allowance more nearly approximates the intention of the settlor; distributions of principal under the authority thus given were not, however, to exceed an aggregate value of $25,000 from all trusts created by the same settlor. This act, not being retroactive, Section 21, 20 P.S. § 301.21, is, of course, inapplicable to the present case. [Ed. in 1956 the Pennsylvania Legislature amended the statute to make it expressly applicable to trusts previously created. In 1972 the Estates Act of 1947 was repealed in a general recodification and enactment of entire title 20. The same subject matter now appears in 20 P.S. §§ 6101 et seq. A provision similar to former 301.2(a) now appears in 20 P.S. § 6102(a) (Spec. 1973 Pamph.) and applies to trusts "heretofore or hereafter created."]

18. Bogert, Trusts and Trustees (2d Ed., 1965) § 1002; IV Scott, Trusts (3d Ed., 1967) § 337.

19. E.g., Rust v. Rust, 85 U.S.App.D.C. 191, 176 F.2d 66 (1949).

20. Kirkland v. Mercantile-Safe Trust Co., 218 Md. 17, 145 A.2d 230 (1958).

21. 175 F.Supp. 367 (D.C.D.C.1959); Compare Industrial National Bank v. Miller, 86 R.I. 33, 133 A.2d 629 (1957), the court refusing termination on very similar facts.

SECTION 4. POWER OF SETTLOR IN CONJUNCTION WITH TRUSTEE OR BENEFICIARY TO TERMINATE A TRUST

UNDERHILL v. UNITED STATES TRUST CO.

Court of Appeals of Kentucky, 1929.
227 Ky. 444, 13 S.W.2d 502.

* * * STANLEY, C. The appellant Evie Shreve Underhill, on September 20, 1916, executed to the appellee, United States Trust Company, a deed of trust conveying to it considerable real estate for the following purpose: "First, To hold said property for and during the life of Evie Shreve Underhill and with power in the said Evie Shreve Underhill at her death to will same to whomsoever she may see proper and that in the event Evie Shreve Underhill does not leave a will, then to hold the same in trust for and during the life of Sallie Underhill Kemper and on her death to convey same to the child or children of Sallie Underhill Kemper in equal parts, but if the said Sallie Underhill Kemper shall die without leaving child or children surviving her, then the said Sallie Underhill Kemper shall have power by her last will and testament to devise the same to whomsoever she may see proper."

The trustee was given the power to sell and convey the trust estate and reinvest the proceeds thereof in its discretion for the best interest of the trust, and, after maintaining the property and deducting its commission, to pay the net income therefrom to the parties entitled to it under the provisions of the trust, as above stated.

Mrs. Underhill, the settlor of the trust, and Mrs. Kemper, the contingent beneficiary, united in a petition for a declaration of their rights under the deed of trust, specifically asking the court to adjudge whether or not under the circumstances disclosed, Mrs. Underhill was entitled to revoke the trust, or to have the trust terminated by judgment of the court and the property returned to her free of the trust. It is set up in the verified petition that the moving cause for the execution of this trust deed was that the petitioners were then married to men of idle and wasteful habits, and it was feared that the estate, which was the sole property of Mrs. Underhill, might be dissipated, and that its only purpose was to protect herself and her daughter from the habits and conduct of their respective husbands. It is stated that both of the parties have since been divorced. It is averred that Mrs. Underhill was at the time of the filing of the petition over 70 years of age and in bad health, and that Mrs. Kemper, her only daughter, was over 40 years of age and never had any children. It was asserted further that due to Mrs. Underhill's present condition she is in need of more money than the income from the trust estate will provide; and it was claimed that the purpose of the trust having been accomplished, and the necessity therefor no longer continuing, the trust ought to be terminated. The trust company stated in its answer that it could not deny the allegation of fact contained in the petition, but did deny the conclusion of law pleaded, and joined in the prayer for a declaration of the rights of the parties under the deed of trust.

The chancellor was of the opinion that, under the peculiar conditions of this trust deed, neither the settlor nor the court had the power to terminate it; and it was so adjudged.

Except for the provision in this trust deed, giving a life estate to Mrs. Kemper, with a contingent fee to any child or children which she might have or to her devisees, there would be little difficulty in deciding that the trust might be terminated under the authority and for the reasons given in Fidelity & Columbia Trust Co., Trustee, v. Gwynn, 206 Ky. 823, 268 S.W. 537, 38 A.L.R. 937. In that case Gwynn, being subject to epileptic attacks, placed his property in trust for his own benefit, and provided that at his death the principal should pass under his will or under the laws of descent and distribution. The right to cancel the trust was adjudged because it appeared that the cause for its creation no longer existed (Mr. Gwynn having fully recovered his health), and, since he was the sole beneficiary, the consent of no one else was required. The opinion was based on a well-established principle applicable to those facts, namely, the power of the court of equity to terminate a trust when its purpose has been accomplished or the motivating cause has ceased and the consent of both the trustor and cestui que trust is given. The case at bar may be differentiated, as there is a condition not involved in the Gwynn trust, namely, an estate in contingent beneficiaries not in being, or not established, and no other of the same class who might give consent; the contingent beneficiary of a life estate alone joining with the settlor in asking a revocation of the trust.

There should be borne in mind, in considering the case, the conclusive presumption that every one may have children born to them so long as they shall live, regardless of age or condition of health.

The grantor, Mrs. Underhill, parted with all title to the property except the beneficial interest in the net income, and the express reservation of the right in her lifetime to withdraw $2,000 of the principal should she need money for sickness of herself or her daughter's family, which right she has already exercised. She only reserved the power to have the entire trust terminated at her death by testamentary disposition of the capital. If she does not exercise such power in that manner, the trust shall continue throughout the life of her daughter, Mrs. Kemper. No power of revocation whatever was granted the daughter, except that she, too, might withdraw a similar sum for the same use should it become necessary. She was merely given the power to dispose of the corpus by will in case she should die childless. By its express provisions, unless terminated by Mrs. Underhill, in the manner stated, the trust will not determine until the death of Mrs. Kemper, at which time the principal will go to her children or devisees, as the case may be. It is therefore not within the power of the trustor and her daughter together to alter or revoke the instrument, nor within the authority of the court to do so, since by the express terms of the trust others have a contingent right under it.

So far as the desire of Mrs. Underhill is concerned, she is restrained by the rule that it is essential that the mode of revocation specified in the trust deed should be followed, and she has herself provided that mode, namely, by her will, which cannot become effective until after her death. 39 Cyc. 94; Downs v. Security Trust Co., 175 Ky. 789, 194 S.W. 1041.

Having conveyed the estate to ultimate beneficiaries impossible of ascertainment, no other disposition can be made, for these undetermined remaindermen so created cannot consent. * * *

The standard authority of Perry on Trusts, § 104, p. 132, declares the law to be: "A trust once created and accepted without reservation of power can only be revoked by the full consent of all parties in interest; if any of the parties are not in being, or are not sui juris, it cannot be revoked at all." That uniform rule was applied by this court in Beard v. Beard, 173 Ky. 131, 190 S.W. 703, Ann.Cas.1918C, 832, and in cases therein cited. * * *

In Anderson v. Kemper, 116 Ky. 348, 76 S.W. 124, we stated the law thus: "The cestui que trust who was entitled to the whole of the net income of the trust estate during his life may consent, where he is not under legal disability, to a change of the terms of the trust, but not so as to affect the other beneficiaries."

A voluntary deed of trust, as suggested by the learned chancellor in his excellent opinion, is a binding contract between the settlor and the trustee acting for the cestuis que trust, supported by a legal and valuable consideration, namely, the benefits contemplated and resulting to the settlor and the beneficiaries from the creation of the trust. Burton v. Burton's Trustee, 198 Ky. 429, 248 S.W. 1033. As a contract it is, of course, subject to the law applicable to such instruments and, if valid, can be cancelled only with the consent of all the parties. Otherwise, it must be carried into execution. The trustee has not acquired such a title as will enable it to give its consent for and in behalf of the beneficiaries. 39 Cyc. 208–212. Or it may be considered that such a deed is an executed gift and needs no consideration, the acceptance of the trustee being regarded as the acceptance by the beneficiaries, present or ultimate. See 28 C.J. 624; Siter v. Hall, 220 Ky. 43, 294 S.W. 767. We need not take into consideration those cases in which testamentary trusts were involved, some of which are by analogy in point on the question here considered. See Webster v. Bush, 39 S.W. 411, 42 S.W. 1124, 19 Ky.Law Rep. 565; Browning v. Fiklin's Adm'r, 12 S.W. 714, 26 Ky.Law Rep. 470; Carpenter v. Carpenter's Trustee, 119 Ky. 582, 84 S.W. 737, 68 L.R.A. 637, 115 Am.St. Rep. 275; Miller v. Miller, 172 Ky. 519, 189 S.W. 417.

It is earnestly argued by counsel for appellant that where the moving cause for the creation of the trust has been removed, and its purpose has been accomplished, it is not necessary that all the beneficiaries should consent to its termination. Perhaps such an inference may be drawn from statements in some of our opinions. But it is our definite opinion that where the trust deed vests an estate in beneficiaries who do not relinquish or surrender it—either by refusal or incapacity in law—then the trust cannot be terminated.

It is also earnestly contended that these unknown or unborn contingent remaindermen have virtual representation in this case in the person of Mrs. Kemper. The case principally relied upon in support of the proposition is Masonic Widows' and Orphans' Home v. Hieatt Bros., 197 Ky. 301, 247 S.W. 34. We do not think that doctrine may be applied, for it is necessary that the interest of the representative should be identical with the contingent interest of those coming after him. The subject was fully considered in Lowe v. Taylor, etc., 222 Ky. 846, 2 S.W.2d 1042, in which we said: "But in all cases, the doctrine is planted squarely on the ground of identity of interest between the parties to the action and the persons they are held to represent. It being recognized throughout that, if such identity of interest does not exist, such representation cannot be had, and especially is this true where there is a conflict of interest."

The interest of Mrs. Kemper is antagonistic rather than identical. She is given only the net income with the power of testamentary appointment, conditioned upon her dying childless. Those who shall come after will take the principal in fee.

The conclusion which we have reached, that the court is without power to terminate the trust, being premised upon the inability of all of the beneficiaries to consent, there is obviated the necessity of deciding whether parol evidence, or conceded allegations of the petition, may be considered to show that the moving cause for the creation of the trust no longer exists, or that its purposes have been accomplished.

The result may appear harsh and an undue restriction upon these parties in view of the circumstances surrounding them, but it must be remembered that this trust deed was wholly voluntary. Had Mrs. Underhill contemplated the changed conditions or the effect of the instrument, it is not likely the terms of the deed would have been so restricted; but, having made them so, the rights of the parties must under the law be declared in accordance with those terms.

It follows, therefore, that the judgment should be and is affirmed.

NOTE

It appears well settled that an inter vivos trust can be terminated even though its purpose as stated in the trust instrument has not been accomplished if the settlor and *all* of the beneficiaries join in seeking a termination of the trust.[22] The difficult problem is in determining who the beneficiaries are under the trust instrument.[23] If a court recognizes the possibility that

22. See IV Scott, Trusts (3d Ed., 1967) § 338.

23. See Note, "Revocation of Trusts by Consent of the Beneficiaries", 36 Ind. L.J. 76 (1960). In Botzum v. Havana National Bank, 367 Ill. 539, 12 N.E.2d 203 (1937), a wife transferred property to her husband who, in turn, transferred the property to a bank in trust to pay the income to the wife for life. The wife was

equitable interests may be created in unborn beneficiaries, the trust may be difficult or impossible to terminate. Perhaps, if a statute permits the appointment of a guardian *ad litem* for an unconceived child, the guardian *ad litem* can be prevailed upon to consent to the termination of the trust on their behalf. Ancient property principles, such as the Rule in Shelley's Case and the "Conveyor-Heir Rule" or "Worthier Title Doctrine" may have their most important modern application in the elimination of supposed contingent interests that impede the termination of a trust.[24] But in some jurisdictions these doctrines may not be available to assist the settlor.

Thus in Hatch v. Riggs National Bank[25] the settlor had established an inter vivos trust in which she retained the income for life and reserved a general testamentary power of appointment over the remainder. Her "next of kin" under the District of Columbia intestate law were indicated as takers in default of the exercise of the power. No power to revoke was retained and the settlor inserted a spendthrift provision applicable to the income. The cost of living having increased, the settlor desired to *modify* the trust to permit payments to her from the corpus, and claimed that she was sole beneficiary since the limitation of the remainder to her heirs was presumed to be a reversion in her. This is an application of the "conveyor-heir rule" which will be discussed subsequently in this book.[26] But the Circuit Court of Appeals held this rule no longer in force in the District of Columbia (describing it as the "worthier title doctrine", which is the origin of the conveyor heir rule), yet thoughtfully suggested that perhaps a guardian *ad litem* for the heirs or next of kin might be the answer to the settlor's problem. Judge Leventhal, for the Court, states:[27]

> "* * * We think that upon an adequate showing, by the party petitioning to revoke or modify the trust, that those who are, so to speak, the heirs as of the present time consent to the modification, and that there is a reasonable possibility that the modification that has been proposed adequately protects the interests of those other persons who might be heirs at the time the corpus is to be distributed, the District Court may appoint a guardian ad litem to represent the interests of those additional persons.
>
> "Although the question has not been previously discussed by this court we think basic principles of trust law are in accord with appointment of a guardian ad litem to represent interests of unborn or ascertained beneficiaries, for purposes of consent to modification or revocation of a trust. This use of a guardian ad litem is not uncommon in other jurisdictions. In a number of states authority for such appointments is

also given a general testamentary power of appointment over the remainder. A and B were named as takers in default in case the wife did not exercise the power and it was provided that the "heirs at law" of A or B would take the decedent's share if A or B died. The husband and wife then sought to terminate the trust. A and B consented to the termination. The trustee argued that prospective appointees of the wife under her general testamentary power of appointment and the "heirs at law" of A and B were not before the court and that the trust could not be terminated without their consent. The court held that the prospective appointees had no interest and that the use of the term "heirs at law" was a word of limitation creating a fee in the takers in default and was not a word of purchase. Consequently all interested parties had consented to termination of the trust.

24. These rules are examined in Chapter XIII, Section 5. Various rules of construction which have a similar impact in limiting future beneficiaries are examined in Chapter XV. See also Browder, "Trusts and the Doctrine of Estates", 72 Mich.L.Rev. 1509 (1974).

25. 361 F.2d 559 (D.C.Cir. 1966). Noted, 42 Notre Dame Lawyer 542 (1967); 28 Ohio St.L.J. 166 (1967); 42 Wash.L. Rev. 919 (1967).

26. See Chapter XIII, Section 5.

27. 361 F.2d at 565.

provided by statute. These statutes reflect a broad sentiment of the approaches that are consistent with the Anglo-American system of law and adopted to promote the objective of justice. Where it is at least debatable whether rulings must await express legislative authorization, this court must take into account the fact that the legislature for the District of Columbia is primarily concerned with awesome questions of national policy, and we should be more ready to accept our obligation as a court to refine and adopt the corpus of law without waiting for a legislative go-ahead. Here we are certainly in a field where it is not inappropriate for courts to act without statutory foundation, as appears from the well-considered authority cited in the margin. 'Courts of justice as an incident of their jurisdiction have inherent power to appoint guardians ad litem.' The efficacy of a guardian ad litem appointed to protect the interests of unborn persons is no different whether he be appointed pursuant to statute or the court's inherent power. Given such protection, the equitable doctrine of representation embraces the flexibility, born of convenience and necessity, to act upon the interests of unborn contingent remaindermen to the same effect as if they had been *sui juris* and parties.

"The use of guardians ad litem to represent interests of unborn and/or otherwise unascertainable beneficiaries of a trust seems to us wholly appropriate. Though the persons whose interests the guardian ad litem represents would be unascertainable as individuals, they are identifiable as a class and their interest, as such, recognizable.

"The settlor seeking to revoke or modify the trust may supplement his appeal to equity with a quid pro quo offered to the heirs for their consent. In many cases it may well be consistent with or even in furtherance of the interest of the heirs to grant such consent. The case at bar provides a good example. Here the interest of all heirs is contingent, since appellant can defeat their remainder by exercising her testamentary power of appointment. If the modification agreed upon not only increased the annual income of the life tenant but also transferred assets in trust for the benefit of the heirs, without any power of alteration in the settlor, the heirs' remainder interest would be secure, and accordingly more valuable than it is now. The pattern of such a modification is clearly available where the remaindermen of a trust are specific named persons, and, we think, should also be available where the remaindermen are recognizable as a class even though the members of the class are not now individually ascertainable. * * *"

The settlor then secured the appointment of a guardian *ad litem* who agreed to a proposed modification of the trust; and this modification was approved by the District Court, the Court stating that it had authority to appoint a guardian *ad litem* for unborn persons without specific statutory authority and that the majority of jurisdictions and commentators approve of such action.[28]

Some jurisdictions, by legislation,[29] make it possible to terminate a trust with the consent of the settlor and all the *living* beneficiaries.

28. Hatch v. Riggs National Bank, 284 F.Supp. 396 (D.C.D.C.1968). See Notes: "Trusts: Revocation: Doctrine of Worthier Title vs. the Use of Guardian ad Litem", 41 Conn.B.J. 154 (1967); "Trust Termination and Unborn Beneficiaries", 29 Ohio St.L.J. 741 (1968).

29. McKinney's N.Y., EPTL, § 7–1.9 (1980 Supp.) The New York legislation has been liberally construed by the courts to effect the legislative purpose favoring termination. E.g., Matter of Peabody, 5 N.Y.2d 541, 186 N.Y.S.2d 265, 158 N.E.2d 841 (1959); Noted, 5 N.Y.L.F.

Where the settlor reserves a power to change beneficiaries, and he is unable to obtain the consent of the original beneficiaries, the modern view permits him to change the beneficiaries to persons who will consent.[30]

SECTION 5. POWER OF BENEFICIARY ACTING IN CONJUNCTION WITH TRUSTEE TO TERMINATE A TRUST

HAGERTY v. CLEMENT

Supreme Court of Louisiana, 1940.
195 La. 230, 196 So. 330.[31]

[The plaintiff's grandmother created a testamentary trust providing among other things that the income from the plaintiff's share of the trust principal should be paid to him in monthly installments until he attained the age of thirty-one when the principal was to be delivered to him. The trustees named in the will declined to serve, and Mrs. Clement, a daughter of the testatrix-settlor, was appointed by the court. After the plaintiff attained the age of twenty-one, he induced the trustee to transfer his share of the principal to him. Thereafter the plaintiff brought this action seeking to force the trustee to reconstitute the trust and asking for damages for breach of trust. The plaintiff complained that he had lost or otherwise disposed of his entire inheritance and is presently destitute. It is his contention that terminating the trust prior to his thirty-first birthday is void and contrary to public policy. The defendant contends that an agreement to terminate a trust prematurely by consent of the parties is legal or, if not, that plaintiff is estopped from setting aside the transactions without making restitution of that which he had received.]

ROGERS, JUSTICE. * * * The Commissioner found that there was no basis for plaintiff's complaint that he was induced to agree to a termination of the trust through the instigation and supplication of the defendant, Mrs. Clement, or that she had practiced any fraud upon him in connection with the sales and exchanges of the properties that were burdened with the trust. The Commissioner found that plaintiff himself had suggested and insisted upon the termination of the trust. Plaintiff desired more income and he was possessed with the thought that he could manage his share of the property to better advantage than the trustee. Plaintiff's brother and sister, his co-beneficiaries under the trust, were not desirous of terminating it and the trustee, Mrs. Clement, was at first opposed to such termination. She

322 (1959) holding that a child *en ventre sa mere* is not a person in being whose consent is required.

30. 4 Powell, The Law of Real Property (Rohan Rev.1970) ¶ 566.

31. Noted, 3 La.L.Rev. 465 (1941).

was in ill-health at the time and was very much annoyed by plaintiff's complaints that the trust estate was not producing sufficient income and his insistence that it be terminated. Mrs. Clement proposed that she would resign and that some bank could be appointed trustee in her stead. The proposition was not acceptable to plaintiff and finally, Mrs. Clement, yielding to his demands, agreed to a termination of the trust upon being advised by her attorney that this could be done safely by agreement between her and the beneficiaries.

Plaintiff was fully emancipated by judgment of court on April 26, 1931, the judge after the usual examination, certifying that plaintiff was fully capable of managing his own affairs. Plaintiff reached the age of majority on January 11, 1932, and consequently, was of full age and was not suffering from any legal incapacity at the time he brought about the termination of the trust.

In asking that the trust estate be reconstituted, it was impossible for plaintiff to restore to the trust estate any of the propety received by him or its value, and therefore he made no effort to do so. At the time of filing this suit, plaintiff had gambled away or lost by speculation all the property left to him by both his grandfather and grandmother and was dependent for his sustenance upon his sister.

* * *

[A discussion of the applicability of the Louisiana Trust Estates Act is omitted.] * * *

If it be conceded, without so deciding, that the termination of the trust created by the will of Mrs. Wilhelmina Schwartz McCloskey by the agreement between the beneficiary and the trustee was not within the contemplation of the sketchy provisions of Act 107 of 1920, nevertheless, the question persists as to whether the beneficiary, who has demanded and insisted that the trustee breach the trust for his benefit and who has actually reaped the benefit of such breach, can repudiate the act of the trustee and hold her liable therefor. We think he can not.

Plaintiff has squandered his inheritance which he received, in good faith, from his trustee, and he now takes the position that he should be relieved of his folly at the expense of the trustee without offering to restore any of the benefits he has enjoyed. Plaintiff's position is not supported by either law or equity.

The result of the decisions of the courts of many states, in cases arising under trust statutes having a wide scope, has been the formulation of the following general rule relative to the relief of the trustee from liability, viz.—"A cestui que trust may authorize the trustee to perform an act which would otherwise be a breach of trust and thereby estop himself from holding the trustee liable therefor, and even though an act of the trustee is unauthorized and constitutes a breach of trust, it may be so acquiesced in, confirmed, or ratified by the cestui que trust as to estop him from repudiating it and attempting to hold the trustee liable * * *." Verbo, Trust, 65 C.J., § 527, p. 663.

In 2 American Law Institute's Restatement of the Law of Trusts, § 342, subd. e, p. 1055, which is the basis of the Louisiana Trust Estates Act of 1938, appears the following statement of the general rule: "If by the terms of the trust it is provided that the income shall be paid to the beneficiary until he reaches a certain age and that the principal shall be paid to him when he reaches that age and if no other persons have an interest in the trust property and the beneficiary is not under an incapacity, although the beneficiary cannot compel the termination of the trust before he reaches the specified age (see sec. 337, Comment j), yet if the trustee transfers the trust property to the beneficiary before he reaches that age, the trust is terminated and the trustee is under no liability for making the transfer." The practical operation of the rule is set forth in the illustration following its statement, viz.—"A bequeaths property to B in trust to pay the income to C until C reaches the age of forty years, and to pay the principal to C when he reaches that age. There is no other beneficiary who has any interest under the trust, vested or contingent. C is twenty-one years old. B transfers the trust property to C. The trust is terminated. C can retain the property, and cannot hold B liable for breach of trust in making the transfer."

The rule and the illustration thereof set forth in the Restatement of the Law of Trusts, as adopted and promulgated by the American Law Institute, is particularly applicable to the trust under review in this case. If, in the Illustration, Mrs. Wilhelmina Schwartz McCloskey, the testatrix, is substituted for "A", Mrs. Laura McCloskey Clement, the trustee, is substituted for "B", and John B. Hagerty, the beneficiary, is substituted for "C", its analogy to the situation disclosed by this record is perfect. Unquestionably, if plaintiff had retained the trust properties transferred to him, he could not hold the defendant, Mrs. Clement, liable for making the transfer.

The fact that it suited plaintiff's purpose to risk the trust properties or their proceeds in speculative and gambling ventures does not alter the application and effect of the rule and its accompanying illustration. On the contrary, that fact not only brings the case within one of the reasons for the adoption of the rule, but also within the operation of the further rule, that a beneficiary cannot obtain the annulment of a settlement with his trustee who has acted honorably and reasonably in making the settlement, if he is unable to return the trust property. That rule is stated in Bogert on Trusts, Hornbook Series, § 99, p. 336, as follows: "If the cestui has the transaction with the trustee set aside, of course he must return any consideration paid by the trustee to him." Plaintiff has not cited any authority to the contrary, except that he likens a beneficiary under a trust to an incapacitated person and he cites Articles 1793 and 2239 of the Civil Code and the case of Rist v. Hartner, 44 La.Ann. 430, 10 So. 759, as authority for the proposition that an incapacitated person is not required to return any consideration received under a contract afterwards invalidated on account of such incapacity, unless it should appear that the consideration so received was applied to the necessary use or benefit of the incapacitated person. The short answer to that proposition is that a beneficiary under a trust is not such an incapacitated person. See 10 R.C.L., Estoppel, § 85, p. 769; 3 Bogert on Trusts and Trustees, § 544, p. 1731.

In this case, the beneficiary was of full age, not under interdiction, and was not suffering from any incapacity whatever when he demanded and obtained from his trustee a transfer of the property subject to the trust.

If there was ever a case calling for the application of the principles enunciated by the rules to which we have referred, this appeals to us as such a case. There is nothing in the provisions of Act 107 of 1920 authorizing merely the creation of a simplified short-term trust, which was in effect at the time the trust in question here was created, that prohibited its termination by agreement between the beneficiary and the trustee, who were of legal age and competent to act. And, certainly, if the trust authorized by the legislative act was wholly nontechnical in character, which it was, the manner of its termination also should be invested with the same attribute. Moreover, the fact that the framers of the well-prepared piece of legislation, known as the Louisiana Trust Estates Act of 1938, considered it necessary to include among its numerous features a provision forbidding the termination of trusts by consent, clearly indicates their view that the new rule was necessary to make the trust device more effective than the simple instruments of trust drafted under the authority of the previous statute.

Clamoring for the return, or its value, of the property which he had received from his trustee, the plaintiff is now complaining that Mrs. Clement, his trustee, did just what he demanded and insisted she should do. His complaint is ungracious, and manifest injustice would be done Mrs. Clement and her husband, the defendants, if it was maintained and the defendants were judicially compelled to respond to plaintiff's demands.

For the reasons assigned, the judgment appealed from is affirmed.

O'NIELL, C.J., does not take part.

NOTE

The trustee and beneficiary acting together have no power to terminate a trust unless a power of termination was given to one or both of them at the creation of the trust. There are, of course, extrajudicial means of termination.

The trustee may transfer his interest to the beneficiary as in the principal case. A merger of legal and equitable title occurs with full title resting in the beneficiary. The trust is ended whether or not either party could have compelled a judicial termination. If all the beneficiaries are ascertained, *sui juris*, have indefeasibly vested interests and unite in demanding termination, they cannot later hold the trustee liable for a breach of trust to which they consented. If, however, the beneficiary is not *sui juris*, he is not estopped from asserting the breach of trust and may petition a proper court to surcharge the trustee. The beneficiary must account to the trustee for the property remaining in his hands in specie before a surcharge is ordered, but the beneficiary need not account for property which the trustee distributed to him on termination of the trust if the beneficiary no longer has the property.

The beneficiary may also get the trustee's title by operation of law. The trustee may die leaving the beneficiary as his only heir at law who takes title by intestacy. The trust is terminated by merger of the legal and equitable titles in the beneficiary. If the trust was a spendthrift trust, this rule may work a hardship on the beneficiary since the beneficiary cannot create a spendthrift trust for himself which will be effective against his creditor. The *Restatement* solves the problem by allowing the beneficiary to elect to treat the trust as terminated or to secure the appointment of a new trustee.[32] If the state statutes provide that the trustee's title vests in a court or is suspended pending the appointment of a new trustee, then the beneficiary does not inherit the legal title and there is no merger terminating the trust.[33]

If the beneficiary has a transferable interest, he may transfer his interest to the trustee and terminate the trust. The trust will terminate whether or not a judicial termination would be ordered. The transaction is, however, scrutinized by the courts with great care. If the trustee has overreached, the court can set aside the transfer because of the fiduciary relationship between trustee and beneficiary. The trustee must act solely in the financial interest of the beneficiary and has the burden of showing that the beneficiary's interest was acquired after a full and complete disclosure of the facts, for an adequate consideration, and without wrongful acts on the part of the trustee. If the trustee cannot prove these elements of fairness, the court may set aside the transfer even though no over-reaching in fact is shown.

A spendthrift trust may not be terminated by the beneficiary's conveyance to the trustee since the beneficial interest is inalienable voluntarily or involuntarily. Under former McKinney's N.Y., Personal Property Law, § 15 and Real Property Law, § 103, a spendthrift provision was attached by statute to trusts in which the trustee is required to collect and pay over rents and profits. These statutes were construed to preclude estoppel of the beneficiary of such a trust who consented to a breach of the trust by the trustee while *sui juris*. The beneficiary could later successfully seek a surcharge of the trustee.[34] The rationale of the decision is that the beneficiary of the trust cannot indirectly transfer his interest by consenting to a transfer by the trustee and estopping himself from attempting to surcharge when the statute prohibits him from transferring his interest directly. The decision has been criticized on the ground that it encourages dishonesty on the part

32. Restatement, Second, Trusts § 341(2). The trustee may take the title of the beneficiary by operation of law, such as the situation in which the beneficiary is intestate and the trustee is his sole heir. The trustee may also take the beneficiary's interest by devise or bequest unless the trust terms restrict alienation by a testamentary instrument.

33. See Chapter VIII, Section 4(3).

34. Matter of Wentworth, 230 N.Y. 176, 129 N.E. 646 (1920) (Testatrix devised property to her husband in trust for her brother for life with a remainder over. The trustee with the consent of the beneficiary, who was *sui juris*, conveyed the property to X. X borrowed money on the property executing a mortgage as security. The borrowed money was used by X and the beneficiary in a business venture. Then the mortgage was foreclosed and the property lost. The beneficiary then sought to surcharge the trustee who transferred the property to X, and the trustee argued that the beneficiary was barred from seeking a surcharge by equitable estoppel. The court surcharged the trustee.) The case is discussed in detail in 35 Va.L.Rev. 893 (1949).

of the beneficiary.[35] The current New York law permits, unless otherwise provided in the trust instrument, a beneficiary to assign in any year his income above $10,000 to his spouse and certain other named relatives. The assignment must be in writing and delivered to the trustee with an affidavit by the beneficiary that the assignment pertains to the excess over $10,000 of income and that he has not received and is not to receive any consideration in money or money's worth for the transfer. The trustee is protected when he relies upon the affidavit.[36] The Wentworth rule would still seem to operate if he assigns income under $10,000 and no affidavit is given, although the relaxation of the statutory rule may perhaps be taken as a basic change in the policy of the New York legislature to offer less protection to beneficiaries against their extravagance so that an estoppel will now be raised in appropriate cases. New York courts have estopped a consenting beneficiary from complaining of an improper investment of trust funds,[37] and treat the beneficiary's assignment of future income as a revocable order to the trustee which protects him if he pays before notice of revocation of the order by the beneficiary is received by him.[38] The Restatement takes the position that the beneficiary of a spendthrift trust cannot hold the trustee liable for breach of trust in transferring to the beneficiary, nor can he compel the trustee to make restitution to the trust.[39]

If the trustee and all the beneficiaries unite in conveying their respective interests to a third party, and the trust is not a spendthrift trust, a merger of legal and equitable titles takes place and the trust terminates with full title in the third party. Except possibly in New York or a state following the Wentworth doctrine,[40] if all the beneficiaries are ascertained, *sui juris,* have indefeasibly vested interests and unite in the conveyance, they will not be heard later if they seek to surcharge the trustee because they are estopped from objecting. Although there is little authority in point, it is generally recognized that a beneficiary who was not *sui juris* can avoid his transfer to the third party and have the trust reconstituted. A beneficiary who was not *sui juris* or who did not consent to the transfer may surcharge the trustee for breach of trust. In such a proceeding the beneficiary should be required to account for the consideration, if any, that he received as a result of the transfer; but he is usually considered to be under no obligation to account for the consideration if he does not have it in specie or does not have its proceeds.[41]

35. See Griswold, Spendthrift Trusts (2d Ed., 1947) § 526.

36. McKinney's N.Y., EPTL, § 7–1. 5(b) (1980 Supp.).

37. E.g., Matter of Wildenburg's Estate, 177 Misc. 49, 29 N.Y.S.2d 896 (1941).

38. E.g., Matter of Lynch, 151 Misc. 549, 272 N.Y.S. 79 (1934).

39. Restatement, Second, Trusts § 342, Comment *f*.

40. See fn. 34, supra.

41. See generally, Restatement, Second, Trusts §§ 341–344; IV Scott, Trusts (3d Ed., 1967) §§ 341–344.

Chapter XI

GIFTS TO CHARITY

Scope Note

Private wealth may be devoted to selected public purposes through either the charitable trust or the non-profit corporation, sometimes called the charitable corporation. Section 1 provides historical background and points out some of the special rules applicable to charitable trusts. Tax advantages of charitable gifts are briefly explored in Section 2. Section 3 is designed to answer the question: what purposes will be deemed "charitable"? How courts by a doctrine known as "cy pres" deal with trusts which have become outmoded is the subject of Section 4. Extension of trust principles to charitable corporations (Section 5) and problems of enforcement and supervision (Section 6) form the balance of the Chapter. Problems arising out of the Rule Against Perpetuities and limits on accumulation of income are postponed to Chapter XVI, Section 6.

SECTION 1. INTRODUCTION AND HISTORICAL BACKGROUND [1]

The donor who wishes to devote wealth to purposes beneficial to the community may utilize either of two legal structures: the charitable trust or the non-profit corporation.[2] His choice will be determined

1. See generally Bogert, Trusts and Trustees (2d Ed., 1964) Ch. 17; 4 Powell, The Law of Real Property (Rohan Rev. 1970) Ch. 45; IV Scott, Trusts (3d Ed., 1967) Ch. 11. Russell Sage Foundation has published a series of books which should be of interest to the lawyer, particularly if he is faced with establishing a charitable trust or corporation with substantial funds. Among these are Andrews, Legal Instruments of Foundations (1958); Andrews, Philanthropic Foundations (1956); Kiger, Operating Principles of the Larger Foundations (1954); Fremont-Smith, Foundations and Government, State and Federal Law and Supervision (1965).

2. "Charity" embraces a wide variety of organizations performing diverse functions, many of which are beyond the scope of our study. A charitable gift of the type we are considering may range from establishment of a small trust fund to provide a scholarship at a named college, to creation of a foundation. The term "foundation" usually refers to a non-profit corporation (although a foundation may be structured as a trust) which makes grants out of income or principal. Foundations are not necessarily large; many are organized by a particular family or a business corporation to channel private or corporate giving. We are not here concerned with gifts by cor-

by a number of factors: the amount of wealth, the nature of objectives, tax consequences, local legal restrictions upon one or the other device, and the time available to establish the legal structure. When he desires to accomplish a single objective, such as establishing scholarships for students at a particular university, or has only limited funds for charity, he will be likely to use the simpler trust device. The trust can be set up without delay and without organizational expense. When he is channeling a substantial amount of wealth into a broad range of public objectives, with specifics to be determined in the future, he will probably establish a non-profit corporation. He may, of course, simply make a direct gift to an already established entity, either outright or for specified purposes: for example, in our scholarship example, the donor might make a gift to a named college or university with either a request or an express condition that the funds be used for scholarships. As we shall see, such a gift to a charitable organization for a specified purpose is subject to the same rules as a trust, whether or not the court wishes to characterize the relation as a "trust".

A combination of organizations is possible. The donor may set up a charitable trust to receive and hold the property until a corporation is organized; this is often necessary where the gift is by will and the corporation has not been formed during the donor's lifetime.

Since the simpler trust device has more general application, it will receive most of our attention. It also presents more complicated legal problems, partly growing out of its history. The English chancellors had enforced charitable uses for indefinite beneficiaries prior to 1601, when the Statute of Charitable Uses[3] was enacted. The preamble of that statute set forth a comprehensive list of charitable purposes and set up a new method for enforcing charitable trusts by commissioners appointed by the Chancellor for that purpose. In Trustees of Philadelphia Baptist Association v. Hart[4], decided in 1819, Chief Justice Marshall assumed that the Statute of Charitable Uses created charitable trusts and that a court of equity had no inherent power to enforce as a charity a trust without definite beneficiaries. Since a number of states had enacted statutes generally repealing English statutes as part of their jurisprudence, this would result in holding all charitable trust invalid in those states if their courts were to follow the position of the United States Supreme Court. Between 1827 and 1832 the English Record Commissioners published the Calendars of Proceedings in Chancery in the Reign of Elizabeth showing that chancery had prior to 1601 exercised jurisdic-

porations to charity; see Andrews, Corporation Giving (1952) dealing with the special tax and non-tax problems of the business corporation as a donor to charity.

Some charitable organizations perform largely operating functions, although they may receive and manage property as an endowment fund. If the local hospital is not government sustained and operated, it is a charity of this type. Some charities, like the American Red Cross, depend in large part upon periodic public support. Neither operating problems nor public subscription drives are within the scope of our study.

3. 43 Eliz. I, c. 4 (1601).

4. 4 Wheat. (U.S.) 1 (1819).

tion over charitable gifts in perpetuity with indefinite beneficiaries.[5] As a result, the United States Supreme Court in the celebrated case of Vidal v. Girard's Executors[6] held that equity had inherent power over charities and that charitable trusts were not dependent upon the Statute of Charitable Uses. Unfortunately the impact of the earlier decision was already felt in several states and had a lingering effect in others. Three states, for example, which did not regard the Statute of Charitable Uses as part of their common law followed the rule of the Hart case but later enacted statutes which validate trusts for most charitable purposes.[7]

In 1788 New York had repudiated the Statute of Charitable Uses. When the New York Revised Statutes of 1830 were enacted, the chapter on trusts of land provided that all trusts and uses were abolished except as permitted therein and then provided for four classes of express private trusts with no mention of charitable trusts. As a result the New York courts held that charitable trusts could not be created. Gifts to charity could be made only by direct gift to a charitable corporation. In 1891 the provision in Governor Tilden's will leaving property for a public library was held invalid. As a result of the ensuing public indignation, the legislature in 1893 passed the Tilden Act, authorizing the creation of trusts for charitable purposes.[8] A similar experience occurred in the states which had copied the New York legislation, and charitable trusts were jeopardized until amendments to the legislation were enacted.[9]

Assuming we can create a charitable trust, such a trust is often said to have certain advantages over the private trust. (1) Charitable trusts are not subject to the rule requiring definite beneficiaries; on the contrary, of course, the very nature of such a trust is that the ultimate recipients of the income and principal or the persons directly benefited by the charity are to be ascertained in the future (as in a trust to establish scholarships or to add a wing on a hospital). (2) Charitable trusts may last in perpetuity, whereas a private trust in perpetuity would run afoul of the Rule Against Perpetuities. We shall see in Chapter XVI, Section 6, that charitable gifts are subject

5. III Story, Equity Jurisprudence (14th ed., 1918) Ch. XXXV; See Magill v. Brown, Fed.Case No. 8,952 (1833); Jordan, Philanthropy in England 1480–1660 (1959); Jones, History of The Law of Charity 1532–1827 (1969).

6. 2 Howard (U.S.) 127 (1844).

7. Va.Code Ann. § 57–1 et seq. (1980 Supp.); W.Va.Code §§ 35–1–1 to 35–1–13 (1980 Supp.); 1 Md.L.Rev. 105 (1930); 25 Va.L.Rev. 109 (1938).

8. McKinney's N.Y., EPTL, § 8–1.1 (1980 Supp.). See Ames, "The Failure of the 'Tilden Trust' ", 5 Harv.L.Rev. 389 (1892), Ames, Lectures on Legal History (1913) 285.

9. The history of charitable trusts in Michigan, Minnesota, and Wisconsin is similar to that in New York. The legislatures of these states adopted, almost verbatim, the trust provisions of the Revised Statutes of 1830. Thereafter, it was held in Michigan and Minnesota that charitable trusts were invalid. In Wisconsin charitable trusts of realty were invalid, but charitable trusts of personalty were valid. Statutes in these states now authorize creation of charitable trusts. Mich.Comp.Laws Ann. §§ 554.351, 554.-381; Minn.Stat.Ann. § 501.12 (1980 Supp.); Wis.Stat.Ann. § 701.10 (West Spec.Pamph. 1980). Dwan, "Minnesota's Statute of Charitable Uses", 14 Minn.L. Rev. 587 (1930).

to the Rule Against Perpetuities in other respects, although a special exception is made for a gift over from one charity to another on a remote contingency. (3) While private express trusts can accumulate income for only a definite period, income under charitable trusts may be accumulated for the period necessary to accomplish its purpose provided the period is "reasonable" (a qualification which the court can apply with some flexibility). (4) A special doctrine known as cy pres prevents termination of a charitable trust under circumstances which might terminate a private express trust; the court can, upon failure of a specific charitable purpose, apply the funds for similar charities. (5) Under the older decisions trust funds for charity cannot be reached for torts committed by the trustee or his employees or agents even when they are acting within the scope of the trust work. This immunity is rapidly disappearing, however, and has minimal importance today. Special tax advantages will be considered in Section 2 of this Chapter.

We have noted previously in Chapter IV, Section 4, that a few jurisdictions have statutory restrictions upon the power of a donor to dispose of his property by will for charitable purposes. You will recall that these statutes are of two types. One type requires devises and bequests for charitable purposes to be executed not later than a certain period of time before the death of the testator. A second type limits the percentage of the estate which a testator can give to charity if he is survived by certain dependents. These statutes, which are for the protection of the testator's family, do not apply to transfers during lifetime and are relatively easy to evade. The liberality of the courts in allowing various devices to get around these statutes is another manifestation of the judicial favor for charity.[10]

SECTION 2. TAX ADVANTAGES OF CHARITABLE GIFTS [11]

Because charitable expenditures are theoretically of benefit to the public, and much of the charitable work (education, health, welfare, municipal purposes) would otherwise be borne by government if not done privately, governments have encouraged gifts to charity through a number of deductions and exemptions under the tax laws.

10. See "Restrictions on Charitable Gifts", 5 Real Prop.Prob. & Trust L.J. 290 (1970).

11. See Lowndes, "Tax Advantages of Charitable Gifts", 46 Va.L.Rev. 394 (1960); Trautman, "Taxation of Gifts in Trust to Charities Reserving a Life Income Interest", 14 Vand.L.Rev. 597 (1961). Snyder, "Role of Charitable Contributions in Estate Planning", 9 Wake Forest L.Rev. 343 (1973). For changes in the Tax Reform Act of 1969 see Moore, "Estate Planning Under the Tax Reform Act of 1969: The Uses of Charity", 56 Va.L.Rev. 565 (1970); Platt, "Tax Reform 1969: The Estate Tax Charitable Deduction and the Private Charitable Foundation", 31 Ohio St.L.Jour. 203 (1970).

(1) The oldest exemptions are those under the property laws, exempting property held by charitable entities and used for charitable purposes. These laws usually provide that the property cannot be used to produce income, although this may be a matter of degree.

(2) Gift, estate and inheritance tax laws allow the donor to deduct gifts to charities which qualify for deductions under the particular laws involved. The Federal Estate and Gift tax laws currently permit a 100% deduction for gifts to qualifying charities.[12]

(3) The Federal Income tax law exempts from tax the income derived by qualified charitable organizations from invested funds. But the income is not exempt if it is from unrelated business. For example, if a charitable trustee buys stocks or bonds, the income derived from these investments will escape tax. But if the trustee invests in a machine tool factory, the income from this investment will be taxed.[13]

"Private Foundations" were singled out for special treatment in the Tax Reform Act of 1969. The unrelated business income of such a foundation will be taxed just as will the unrelated business income of any other qualified charity. But the Congress responded to criticism of foundations of this type by the Treasury Department by imposing upon them various restrictions having tax sanctions, with these tax sanctions being increased if the foundation neglects to correct discovered abuses. The foundation may lose its exempt status if its abuses are flagrant.

A 2% excise tax is imposed upon the *net investment* income of all private foundations. Striking at various criticized activities of the private foundations, the Congress defined a class of "disqualified" persons (such as a major contributor or the foundation manager) and subjects to tax penalties self dealing by these persons through use of foundations and also imposes a tax upon interests in business corporations in excess of 20% owned by a foundation and all "disqualified" persons or 35% if a nondisqualified person has control of the enterprise. If foundation funds are invested in a manner which jeopardizes the carrying out of the foundation's exempt purpose, there is a tax imposed on this investment. There is also a tax imposed upon funds used for lobbying and similar prohibited activities. One of the most important of the restrictions is a tax of 15% on undistributed income. This is to prevent accumulations by private nonoperating foundations.[14] Their income must be devoted to the charitable purposes which justify their special tax preferences. Reports are re-

12. IRC, 26 U.S.C.A., §§ 2055, 2522.

13. IRC, 26 U.S.C.A., §§ 511–514 as amended 1969, 1976, 1978. See Sugarman and Pomeroy, "Business Income of Exempt Organizations", 46 Va. L.Rev. 424 (1960). An exception was made in 1976 for the income from fairs and expositions of an exempt charitable, social welfare or agricultural organization operating a public entertainment activity meeting specified conditions. IRC § 513, 26 U.S.C.A. as amended P.L. 94–455 § 1305 (1976).

14. The foundation must distribute its minimum investment return which is generally 5% of the foundation's net investment assets. IRC § 4942, 26 U.S.C.A. as amended P.L. 97–34 § 823 (1981). A carefully regulated "set-aside" for specific projects is permitted. IRC § 4942(g)(2), 26 U.S.C.A. as amended P.L. 94–455 § 1302 (1976).

quired to the Internal Revenue Service by most private foundations when exempt status is given; and the foundation will not receive exempt status unless its governing instrument prohibits its engagement in described prohibited activities.[15]

(4) The donor is allowed a deduction from his income for gifts to charity. This, with certain exceptions for gifts to "non 50%" foundations and organizations, is 50% of the adjusted gross income of the taxpayer with a five year carryover of excess contributions subject to adjustments. This deduction can be taken if deductions are itemized. Beginning in 1982 and ending in 1987, when Congress will review the matter, non-itemizers can deduct charitable contributions at 25% of the first $100 for 1982 and 1983, 25% of the first $300 in 1984, 50% of contributions in 1985, and 100% for 1986.[16] The charitable deduction is not allowed if any part of the net earnings of the charity enure to the benefit of a shareholder or individual. The charity also is disqualified if a substantial part of its activities involves carrying on propaganda or otherwise attempting to influence legislation, although a public charitable tax exempt organization (other than churches or affiliated organizations) may elect to submit to a sliding scale limitation on lobbying expenditures.[17]

While the details of planning to minimize taxes by charitable gifts are intricate, and many advantages, especially with respect to the use of private foundations, were precluded by the Tax Reform Act of 1969, there are still possibilities for tax savings.

For example, by placing the property in trust for the life of the spouse, followed by a charitable remainder "annuity trust" or "unitrust", the transfer can be made free of federal tax. There is a 100% marital deduction for the life interest in the spouse and a 100% chari-

15. A private foundation includes either a corporation or a trust. It is described in IRC, 26 U.S.C.A., § 509 as any organization described in § 501(c)(3) (exempt organizations) *except* public charities (churches, educational institutions, hospitals) and semi-public charities (those receiving more than one-third of their support from the public with not more than one-third from gross income); organizations operating for the benefit of and controlled by such charities (second tier charities or community foundations collecting funds for public charities); and organizations testing for public safety. For the semi-public charities the test is the extent to which the organization derives its support from the general public. Private *operating* foundations are singled out for special tax preferences within the category of private foundations and are described in IRC, 26 U.S.C.A., § 4942(j)(3). These would include private foundations operating museums, library associations and learned societies that do not meet the requirements for public or semi-public charities.

The relevant IRC sections applicable to the restrictions mentioned in the text are: IRC, 26 U.S.C.A., §§ 4940 (2% excise tax); 4946 (disqualified persons); 4941 (self dealing); 4943 (excess business holdings); 4944 (investments jeopardizing charitable purpose); 4945 (prohibited expenditures—lobbying, etc.); 4942 (undistributed income); 6056 (reports); 508(e) (governing instrument).

16. IRC § 170(b)(1) and (i) [as added P.L. 94-34, § 121 (1981)], 26 U.S.C.A.

17. IRC § 501(h), 26 U.S.C.A., added P.L. 94-455 § 1307(a) (1976). A distinction is made between lobbying expenditures and "grass roots" expenditures, the latter referring to efforts to influence the public on legislative matters. The line between "education" and "propaganda" or "lobbying" may be a difficult one to draw. See, Bartlett, "Charitable Trusts to Effect Changes in the Law", 16 Cal.L.Rev. 478 (1928); 37 Va.L.Rev. 988 (1951).

table deduction for the remainder. There is no estate tax on this property in the estate of the life tenant spouse and, if the transferring spouse transfers intervivos, he can also claim an income tax deduction for the value of the remainder.

In the annuity trust, a definite amount, not less than five percent of the initial value of the property transferred must be paid to the non-charitable income beneficiary annually. In the unitrust a definite percentage, but not less than five percent of the value of the trust corpus, valued annually is paid annually to the non-charitable beneficiary. When the marital deduction is to be claimed in these transactions, the spouse must be the only non-charitable beneficiary. These arrangements preclude authority in a trustee to invade the corpus for the support of the non-charitable beneficiary even if this power is subject to defined standards in the trust instrument.[18]

As another example, an individual may give his home to a university, reserving a life estate. The value of the remainder interest is a present gift, not subject to the gift tax, and deductible, within statutory limits, from the donor's current income for income tax purposes. The same gift by will would not be subject to estate taxes but would lose the additional income tax benefit. The deduction is not available for gifts of tangible personal property (such as an art collection)[19] and if the subject matter of the trust is in cash or securities, the do-

18. The marital deduction is allowed under IRC §§ 2056(b)(8) and 2523(g) added P.L. 97–34 § 403(1981), 26 U.S.C.A. There is no specific provision covering a remainder to a pooled income fund for the marital deduction although a charitable deduction would be allowed for the value of the remainder. In the pooled income fund each of a number of donors transfers an irrevocable remainder interest to the fund to be used for a public charity, retaining an income interest for the life of a non-charitable beneficiary. The property is commingled and the return to the non-charitable beneficiary is based on the return on the fund for the year. For the Code provisions concerning these charitable remainder interests, see IRC, 26 U.S.C.A., §§ 664(d)(1) (Annuity Trust); 664(d)(2) (Unitrust); 642(c)(5) (Pooled Income Fund). See Regs. §§ 1–664–1 through 1–664–4. The IRS has issued a Ruling setting forth mandatory and optional provisions of unitrusts and annuity trusts and a similar Ruling for pooled income funds. See Rev.Rul. 72–395, C.B. 1972–2, p. 340; Rev.Rul. 72–196, C.B. 1972–1, p. 194. As to the handling of charitable remainders, see Moore, "Estate Planning Under the Tax Reform Act of 1969: The Uses of Charity", 56 Va.L.Rev. 565, 582–585 (1970); Platt, "Tax Reform 1969: The Estate Tax Charitable Deduction and the Private Charitable Foundation," 31 Ohio St.L.J. 203, 205–212 (1970). Wren, "Charitable Remainder Trusts," 8 U.Rich.L.Rev. 25 (1973). The former charitable deduction for the *use* of property by a charity has been eliminated. IRC, 26 U.S.C.A., § 170(f)(3)(A). See Note, "Tax Reform Act: Denial of Charitable Deduction for the Use of Property," 74 Dickinson Law Review 290 (1970). But a donor can give to a charity an undivided interest, in a painting, for example, which would permit the charity to hold the painting for a part of the year proportionate to the interest. IRC, 26 U.S.C.A., § 170(f)(3)(B)(ii). And if a donor sacrifices income by making office space available to a charity, he would not have to report as "constructive income" what he would have made had the office space been leased. Also the deduction for a gift of income to a charity to facilitate the gift of a remainder interest to members of a family has been significantly restricted by the requirement that the income interest be in the form of a fixed annuity or be a fixed percentage of the fair market value of the property to be determined yearly and the income to be distributed yearly. Section 170(f)(2)(B).

19. IRC, 26 U.S.C.A., § 170(f); as amended P.L. 94–455 §§ 1307(c), 2124(e)(1)(c)(1976); P.L. 95–30, § 309 (b)(1)(1978).

nor will have to meet the requirements of the Code by employing an "annuity trust" or "unitrust" for his reserved interest.

Gifts of property in which the donor has had long term capital gains are attractive during the donor's lifetime. If the donor sold the property he would be subject to a capital gains tax on the appreciation. But if he gives the property to charity, his capital gain is not treated as income. Yet he can deduct the full value of the property from his present income subject to the statutory ceiling.[20] There is a reduction from the appreciation if the gift is of tangible personal property to be used by the donee charity in a manner unrelated to the purpose upon which its exemption was based or if it is to a nonoperating private foundation that does not distribute an amount equal to the gift within a stipulated time period.[21]

SECTION 3. NATURE OF CHARITABLE PURPOSES

The notion of the charitable trust has developed over a long period of time. What purposes are regarded as charitable as distinguished from those which serve private objectives can be broadly stated, as was done by Lord Macnaghten in Commissioners v. Pemsel; [22] when he described the categories of charity as "trusts for the relief of poverty; trusts for the advancement of education; trusts for the advancement of religion; and trusts for other purposes beneficial to the community, not falling under any of the preceding heads". But such a broad test evaporates quickly when applied against specific objectives which might come within these general headings but reflect individual notions which may cause more harm than benefit. The task of delimiting particular purposes as charitable or noncharitable falls to the courts, and only by a study of the cases in a particular jurisdiction can one assess accurately whether a donor's particular scheme is likely to meet with judicial approval. Moreover, in many of the states an early history reflecting nineteenth century antagonism towards charitable trusts casts lingering shadows over some trusts which would clearly be held charitable in other states.

On the other hand, the modern non-profit incorporation laws contain virtually no restrictions on purpose: the non-profit corporation can be organized for any purpose not illegal or proscribed by particular statutes.[23] This has not always been true. Before general incor-

20. IRC, 26 U.S.C.A., § 170(e) and (f)(1); Rev.Rul. 55–138, 1955–1, C.B. 223.

21. The reduction from the appreciation is 50% if the gift falls into one of these excepted categories. The private non-operating foundation must disburse the amount received within two and one half months after receipt in order to avoid the restriction. If the sale of the charitable gift subject matter would produce ordinary income, such as a painting produced by the donor, it will not receive special treatment as "long term capital gain" property.

22. [1891] A.C. 531.

23. Boyer, Nonprofit Corporation Statutes (1957); Oleck, Non-Profit Corporations and Associations (1956).

poration statutes were enacted, the charter for each non-profit entity was at least open to scrutiny in the legislature at the time the charter was granted. Because there are no limits on the purposes for which a non-profit corporation may be organized in most states,[24] and because the articles can be broadly drafted to empower the corporation to accomplish objectives which might be dubious for a charitable trust, this form of entity or structure affords greater freedom for donations of substantial amounts of wealth. Moreover, the attack on charitable gifts largely comes from disappointed relatives who believe that charity ought to begin "at home". Thus, if the donor leaves property by his will to a trustee for purposes which can be questioned, the gift may be upset. But if the donor creates a charitable corporation during his lifetime, he can under most circumstances make transfers which will be valid, as against the relatives, whether the transfers are inter vivos or testamentary.

The tightest restrictions imposed on charity are those contained in the taxation statutes. It is of course perfectly possible to make a gift to a valid charitable trust or to a validly organized charitable corporation, but still have the gift not qualify for various tax benefits. Since taxation factors loom so large in modern times, the restrictions in the tax statutes have a heavy impact. To the extent that the tax statutes adopt broad terminology such as "charitable" purposes, the case law in the trusts field will carry over; similarly the tax cases will color the non-tax law in time, even though the former may be based on particular statutory phraseology.

In most cases the court treats the validity of a particular allegedly charitable trust as a legal issue to be decided largely by analytical and historical methods. Is the purpose analogous to those set forth in the preamble of the Statute of Charitable Uses or to language of other trusts held to be charitable in past decisions?[25] Or does it fall within the general categories (health, religion, education, etc.) accepted as charitable? Only rarely does the court seem to consider a factual basis for the ultimate issue: is the particular trust purpose one which has sufficient benefit to the community to justify tying up

24. In most states approval and issuance of the charter by the appropriate official, usually the secretary of state, is a routine matter. In a few states, court approval is required. See Taylor, Public Accountability of Foundations and Charitable Trusts (1953) Ch. 3.

25. The Statute of Charitable Uses, 43 Eliz. I, c. 4 (1601) listed the following charitable uses: "some for relief of aged, impotent and poor people, some for maintenance of sick and maimed soldiers and mariners, schools of learning, free schools, and scholars in universities, some for repair of bridges, ports, havens, causeways, churches, seabanks and highways, some for education and preferment of orphans, some for or towards relief, stock or maintenance for houses of correction, some for marriages of poor maids, some for supportation, aid and help of young tradesmen, handicraftsmen and persons decayed, and others for relief or redemption of prisoners or captives, and for aid or ease of any poor inhabitants concerning payments of fifteens, setting out of soldiers and other taxes." For an example of judicial technique using the statute see Webster v. Sughrow, 69 N.H. 380, 45 A. 139 (1898):

> "The statute of 43 Eliz. I, c. 4 (1601) was the culmination of all prior legislation concerning charities. Since its passage, those objects are considered charitable that are named therein, and many others that are not named, and not within the strict letter of the statute, but which come within its spirit, equity and analogy."

property in perpetuity? Sometimes, when the purpose is borderline, the court at the trial level takes evidence to show whether the project will be beneficial or detrimental to the community. Thus in one case where the testatrix left her home and all of its furnishings together with a personal collection of items as a public museum, the court took testimony to establish that the home and related items had little value as a museum and would only compete with a public project of similar nature but greater worth.[26] Generally, however, the court's approach is on a purely philosophical basis. Does such a judicial technique reflect, perhaps unconsciously, a policy allowing decision-making for private property to rest with the donor?

In the cases which follow, consider whether the court is more concerned about a purpose broadly stated (as a gift "to any charity my trustee may select") or one narrowly stated. How can the court supervise a broadly stated trust like the one above? Is this properly a problem to be considered in determining validity, or more properly a problem of supervision divorced from validity? It must also be remembered that in some states there are vestiges of the last century cases antagonistic to charitable trusts.

SHENANDOAH VALLEY NATIONAL BANK OF WINCHESTER v. TAYLOR

Supreme Court of Appeals of Virginia, 1951.
192 Va. 135, 63 S.E.2d 786.[27]

MILLER, J., delivered the opinion of the court. Charles B. Henry, a resident of Winchester, Virginia, died testate on the 23rd day of April, 1949. His will dated April 21, 1949, was duly admitted to probate and the Shenandoah Valley National Bank of Winchester, the designated executor and trustee, qualified thereunder.

Subject to two inconsequential provisions not material to this litigation, the testator's entire estate valued at $86,000, was left as follows:

"SECOND: All the rest, residue and remainder of my estate, real, personal, intangible and mixed, of whatsoever kind and wherever situate, * * *, I give, bequeath and devise to the Shenandoah Valley National Bank of Winchester, Virginia, in trust, to be known as the 'Charles B. Henry and Fannie Belle Henry Fund', for the following uses and purposes:

"(a) My Trustee shall invest and reinvest my trust estate, shall collect the income therefrom and shall pay the net income as follows:

"(1) On the last school day of each calendar year before Easter my Trustee shall divide the net income into as many

26. Medical Society of South Carolina v. South Carolina National Bank, 197 S.C. 96, 14 S.E.2d 577 (1941).

27. Noted, 23 Miss.L.J. 62 (1951); 20 U. of Cin.L.Rev. 505 (1951); 37 Va.L.Rev. 642 (1951); 9 Wash. & Lee L.Rev. 310 (1952).

equal parts as there are children in the first, second and third grades of the John Kerr School of the City of Winchester, and shall pay one of such equal parts to each child in such grades, to be used by such child in the furtherance of his or her obtainment of an education.

"(2) On the last school day of each calendar year before Christmas my trustee shall divide the net income into as many equal parts as there are children in the first, second and third grades of the John Kerr School of the City of Winchester, and shall pay one of such equal parts to each child in such grades, to be used by such child in the furtherance of his or her obtainment of an education."

By paragraphs (3) and (4) it is provided that the names of the children in the three grades shall be determined each year from the school records, and payment of the income to them "shall be as nearly equal in amounts as it is practicable" to arrange.

Paragraph (5) provides that if the John Kerr School is ever discontinued for any reason the payments shall be made to the children of the same grades of the school or schools that take its place, and the School Board of Winchester is to determine what school or schools are substituted for it.

Under clause "THIRD" the trustee is given authority, power and discretion to retain or from time to time sell and invest and reinvest the estate, or any part thereof, as it shall deem to be to the best interest of the trust.

The John Kerr School is a public school used by the local school board for primary grades and had an enrollment of 458 boys and girls so there will be that number of pupils or thereabouts who would share in the distribution of the income.

The testator left no children or near relatives. Those who would be his heirs and distributees in case of intestacy were first cousins and others more remotely related. One of these next of kin filed a suit against the executor and trustee, and others challenging the validity of the provisions of the will which undertook to create a charitable trust.

Paragraph No. 10 of the bill alleges:

"That the aforesaid trust does not constitute a charitable trust and hence is invalid in that it violates the rule against the creation of perpetuities."

Other heirs and distributees appeared and joined in the cause and asked that the trust be declared void and the estate distributed among testator's next of kin.

The cause was heard upon the bill and a demurrer filed by the executor and trustee. The demurrer was overruled and the contention of the heirs and distributees sustained. From decrees that adjudicated the principles of the cause and held that the trust was not charitable but a private trust and thus violative of the rule against perpetuities and void, this appeal was awarded.

The sole question presented is: does the will create a valid charitable trust?

Construction of the challenged provisions is required and in this undertaking the testator's intent as disclosed by the words used in the will must be ascertained. If his dominant intent as expressed was charitable, the trust should be afforded efficacy and sustained.

But on the other hand, if the testator's intent as expressed is merely benevolent, though the disposition of his property be meritorious and evince traits of generosity, the trust must nevertheless be declared invalid because it violates the rule against perpetuities.

"A charitable trust is created only if the settlor properly manifests an intention to create a charitable trust." Restatement of the Law of Trusts, sec. 351, p. 1099.

Authoritative definitions of charitable trusts may be found in 4 Pomeroy's Equity Jurisprudence, 5th Ed., sec. 1020, and Restatement of the Law of Trusts, sec. 368, p. 1140. The latter gives a comprehensive classification definition. It is:

"Charitable purposes include:

"(a) the relief of poverty;

"(b) the advancement of education;

"(c) the advancement of religion;

"(d) the promotion of health;

"(e) governmental or municipal purposes; and

"(f) other purposes the accomplishment of which is beneficial to the community."

In the recent decision of Allaun v. First, etc., National Bank, 190 Va. 104, 56 S.E.2d 83, the definition that appears in 3 M.J., Charitable Trust, sec. 2, p. 872, was approved and adopted. It reads:

" 'A charity,' in a legal sense, may be described as a gift to be applied, consistently with existing laws, for the benefit of an indefinite number of persons, either by bringing their hearts under the influence of education or religion, by relieving their bodies from disease, suffering or constraint, by assisting them to establish themselves for life, or by erecting or maintaining public building or works, or otherwise lessening the burdens of government. It is immaterial whether the purpose is called charitable in the gift itself, if it is so described as to show that it is charitable. Generally speaking, any gift not inconsistent with existing laws which is promotive of science or tends to the education, enlightening, benefit or amelioration of the condition of mankind or the diffusion of useful knowledge, or is for the public convenience is a charity. It is essential that a charity be for the benefit of an indefinite number of persons; for if all the beneficiaries are personally designated, the trust lacks the essential element of indefiniteness, which is one characteristic of a legal charity." (190 Va. p. 108.)

See also, Collins v. Lyon, 181 Va. 230, 24 S.E.2d 572; Protestant Episcopal Education Soc. v. Churchman, 80 Va. 718.

In the law of trusts there is a real and fundamental distinction between a charitable trust and one that is devoted to mere benevolence. The former is public in nature and valid; the latter is private and if it offends the rule against perpetuities, it is void.

"It is quite clear that trusts which are devoted to mere benevolence or liberality, or generosity, cannot be upheld as charities. Benevolent objects include acts dictated by mere kindness, good will, or a disposition to do good * * *. Charity in a legal sense must be distinguished from acts of liberality or benevolence. To constitute a charity the use must be public in its nature." Zollman on Charities, sec. 398, p. 268. * * *

Appellant contends that the gift qualifies as a charitable trust under the definition in Allaun v. First, etc., Nat. Bank, supra. It is also said that it not only meets the requirements of a charitable trust as defined in Restatement of the Law of Trusts, supra, but specifically fits two of those classifications, viz.:

"(b) trusts for the advancement of education;

"(f) other purposes the accomplishment of which is beneficial to the community."

We now turn to the language of the will for from its context the testator's intent is to be derived. Sheridan v. Krause, 161 Va. 873, 172 S.E. 508, 91 A.L.R. 1067. Its interpretation must be free from and uninfluenced by the unyielding rule against perpetuities. Yet, when the testator's intent is ascertained, if it is found to be in contravention of the rule, the will, in that particular, must be declared invalid. * * *

In clause "SECOND" of the will the trust is set up, and by clause "THIRD" full power is bestowed upon the trustee to invest and reinvest the estate and collect the income for the purposes and uses of the trust. In paragraphs (1) and (2), respectively, of clause "SECOND" in clear and definite language the discretion, power and authority of the trustee in its disposition and application of the income are specified and limited. Yearly on the last school day before Easter and Christmas each youthful beneficiary of the testator's generosity is to be paid an equal share of the income. In mandatory language the duty and the duty alone to make cash payments to each individual child just before Easter and Christmas is enjoined upon the trustee by the certain and explicit words that it "shall divide the net income * * * and shall pay one of such equal shares to each child in such grades."

Without more, that language and the occasions specified for payment of the funds to the children being when their minds and interests would be far removed from studies or other school activities definitely indicate that no educational purpose was in the testator's mind. It is manifest that there was no intent or belief that the funds would be put to any use other than such as youthful impulse and desire might dictate. But in each instance immediately following the above-quoted language the sentence concludes with the words or phrase "to be used by such child in the furtherance of his or her obtainment of an education." It is significant that by this latter phrase the trustee is given no power, control or discretion over the funds so received by the child. Full and complete execution of the mandate and trust imposed upon the trustee accomplishes no educational purpose. Nothing toward the advancement of education is attained by the ultimate performance by the trustee of its full duty. It merely places the income irretrievably and forever beyond the range of the trust.

Appellant says that the latter phrase, "to be used by such child in furtherance of his or her obtainment of an education", evinces the testator's dominant purpose and intent. Yet it is not denied that the preceding provision "shall divide the net income into as many equal parts * * * and shall pay one of each equal parts to such child" is at odds with the phrase it relies upon. The appended qualification, it says, however, discloses a controlling intent that the 450 or more shares are to be used in the furtherance of education, and it was not really intended that a share be paid to each child so that he or she could during the Christmas or Easter holidays, or at any other time, use it "without let or hindrance, encumbrance or care." With that construction we cannot agree. In our opinion, the words of the will import an intent to have the trustee pay to each child his allotted share. If that be true,—and it is directed to be done in no uncertain language—we know that the admonition to the children would be wholly impotent and of no avail.

In construing wills, we may not forget or disregard the experiences of life and the realities of the occasion. Nor may we assume or indulge in the belief that the testator by his injunction to the donees intended or thought that he could change childhood nature and set at naught childhood impulses and desires.

Appellant asserts that literal performance of the duty imposed upon it—pay to each child his share—would be impracticable and should not be done. Its position in that respect is stated thus: "We do not understand that under the law of Virginia a court would pay money for education into the hands of children who are incapable of handling it." It then says that the funds could be administered by a guardian or under sec. 8–751, Code, 1950, (where the amounts are under $500), a court could direct payment to be made to the recipient's parents.

With these statements, we agree. But because the funds could be administered under applicable statutes has no bearing upon nor may that device be resorted to as an aid to prove or establish the testator's intent. We are of opinion that the testator's dominant intent appears from and is expressed in his unequivocal direction to the trustee to divide the income into as many equal parts as there are children beneficiaries and pay one share to each. This expressed purpose and intent is inconsistent with the appended direction to each child as to the use of his respective share and the latter phrase is thus ineffectual to create an educational trust. The testator's purpose and intent were, we think, to bestow upon the children gifts that would bring them happiness on the two holidays, but that falls short of an educational trust.

If it be determined that the will fails to create a charitable trust for *educational purposes* (and our conclusion is that it is inoperative to create such a trust), it is earnestly insisted that the trust provided for is nevertheless charitable and valid. In this respect it is claimed that the two yearly payments to be made to the children just before Christmas and Easter produce "a desirable social effect" and are "promotive of public convenience and needs, and happiness and contentment" and thus the fund set up in the will constitutes a charitable trust. 2 Bogert on Trusts, sec. 361, p. 1090, and 3 Scott on Trusts, sec. 368, p. 1972.

The definition of the word "charity" as it appears in Collins v. Lyon, supra, is relied upon to sustain this position. In that decision the meaning of the word "charity" as given in Wilson v. First Nat. Bank, 164 Iowa 402, 145 N.W. 948, was quoted with approval as follows:

> "The word 'charity', as used in law, has a broader meaning and includes substantially any scheme or effort to better the condition of society or any considerable portion thereof. It has been well said that any gift not inconsistent with existing laws, which is promotive of science or tends to the education, enlightenment, benefit, or amelioration of the condition of mankind or the diffusion of useful knowledge, or is for the public convenience, is a charity."

Numerous cases that deal with and construe specific provisions of wills or other instruments are cited by appellant to uphold the contention that the provisions of this will, without reference to and deleting the phrase "to be used by such child in the furtherance of his or her obtainment of an education" meet the requirements of a charitable trust. Many of those cases are listed below. * * * [Citations omitted.] * * *

Upon examination of these decisions, it will be found that where a gift results in mere financial enrichment, a trust was sustained only when the court found and concluded from the entire context of the will that the ultimate intended recipients were poor or in necessitous circumstances.

A trust from which the income is to be paid at stated intervals to each member of a designated segment of the public, without regard to whether or not the recipients are poor or in need, is not for the relief of poverty, nor is it a social benefit to the community. It is a mere benevolence—a private trust—and may not be upheld as a charitable trust. Restatement of the Law of Trusts, sec. 374, p. 1156:

> "* * * if a large sum of money is given in trust to apply the income each year in paying a certain sum to every inhabitant of a city, whether rich or poor, the trust is not charitable, since although each inhabitant may receive a benefit, the social interest of the community as such is not thereby promoted."

In 2 Bogert on Trusts, sec. 380, we find:

"As previously stated, gifts which are mere exhibitions of liberality and generosity, without regard to their effect upon the donees, are not charitable. There must be an amelioration of the condition of the donees as a result of the gift, and this improvement must be of a mental, physical, or spiritual nature and not merely financial. Thus, trusts to provide gifts to children, regardless of their need, or to make Christmas gifts to members of a certain class, without consideration of need or effect, are not charitable. * * *." (p. 1218).

"Gifts which are made out of mere sentiment, and will have no practical result except the satisfying of a whim of the donor, are obviously lacking in the widespread social effect necessary to a charity." (p. 1219.)

* * * [A discussion of cases from other jurisdictions is omitted.] * * *

Nor do we find any language in this will that permits the trustee to limit the recipients of the donations to the school children in the designated grades who are in necessitous circumstances, and thus bring the trust under the influence of the case styled Appeal of Eliot, 74 Conn. 586, 51 A. 558.

The conclusion there reached was that where a trust is set up and a class is designated as beneficiary which generally contains needy persons, the testator will be presumed to have intended as recipients those members of the class who are in necessitous circumstances.

Payment to the children of their cash bequests on the two occasions specified would bring to them pleasure and happiness and no doubt cause them to remember or think of their benefactor with gratitude and thanksgiving. That was, we think, Charles B. Henry's intent. Laudable, generous and praiseworthy though it may be, it is not for the relief of the poor or needy, nor does it otherwise so benefit or advance the social interest of the community as to justify its continuance in perpetuity as a charitable trust. * * *

[Omitted is that portion of the opinion in which the court held the cy-pres statutes inapplicable because the trust was not for a "charitable, benevolent, or eleemosynary purpose". See Va.Code, 1950, §§ 55–31, 55–32.] * * *

No error is found in the decrees appealed from and they are affirmed.

Affirmed.

NOTE

If the court finds that a trust will aid education, it will be held charitable and valid.

Trusts for the advancement of education include trusts to endow professorships, scholarships, loan funds, primary schools, secondary schools, colleges, universities, public art museums, public libraries and the like; to promote research, to provide for the publication of scholarly treatises or the delivery of lectures on scientific, cultural or legal subjects; and to give training for citizenship, character and leadership.

Trusts for private as well as public educational institutions are charitable even though students are required to pay tuition; but if the institution is conducted for the financial benefit of the owners, and therefore is proprietary in nature, the trust is not charitable.[28]

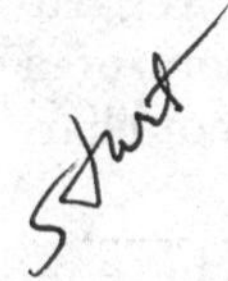

JORDAN'S ESTATE

Supreme Court of Pennsylvania, 1938.
329 Pa. 427, 197 A. 150.

DREW, JUSTICE. Minnie L. Jordan died in 1932, leaving a certain part of her estate "to charity." She appointed no trustee. Because of this fact, and in view of her further omission to specify any particular charities, her next of kin claimed the fund under the Act of July 7, 1885, P.L. 259, 29 P.S. § 196, on the ground that the gift was void for uncertainty. Their contention was rejected by the court below, which, proceeding under the 10th section of the Act of April 26, 1855, P.L. 328, amended by the Act of May 23, 1895, P.L. 114, 10 P.S. § 13 appointed a trustee who subsequently designated certain charitable institutions to share the decedent's bequest. The next of kin have appealed.

The testatrix's obvious intention was the creation of a charitable trust. See Restatement, Trusts, § 397, comment f; Bogert, Trusts and Trustees, § 371. That such a trust shall not fail for want of a trustee has been settled ever since the Act of 1855, supra, under which the duty of supplying a fiduciary is enjoined upon the court. Shand's Estate, 275 Pa. 77, 118 A. 623.

Nor is the gift rendered void because of the testatrix's neglect to specify particular charitable objects. "Indeed, it is said that vagueness is, in some respects, essential to a good gift for a public charity, and that a public charity begins where uncertainty in the recipient begins." Perry, Trusts and Trustees, 7th Ed., § 687. Charities have always been favorites of our law, Daly's Estate, 208 Pa. 58, 57 A. 180, and gifts for such objects have been repeatedly sustained over the objection that they were too uncertain, Murphy's Estate, 184 Pa. 310, 39 A. 70, 63 Am.St.Rep. 802 ("benevolent, charitable, and religious institutions and associations"), Dulles' Estate, 218 Pa. 162, 67 A. 49, 12 L.R.A.,N.S., 1177 ("religious, charitable and benevolent purposes and objects or institutions"); Kimberly's Estate, No. 1, 249 Pa. 469, 95 A. 82 ("charitable uses, objects and purposes"); Thompson's Estate, 282 Pa. 30, 127 A. 446, 447 ("religious and charitable purposes, objects and institutions"). To our minds, the present testatrix's use of the general term "charity" was no more indefinite than

28. Butterworth v. Keeler, 219 N.Y. 446, 114 N.E. 803 (1916), is a leading case.

the language employed by the testators in the cases just enumerated. By confining herself to the use of the generic term, the present testatrix comprehended all of the various religious, educational, benevolent, and humanitarian objects that the single word "charity" connotes. See Fire Insurance Patrol v. Boyd, 120 Pa. 624, 645, 15 A. 553, 1 L.R.A. 417, 6 Am.St.Rep. 745.

The decree is affirmed at appellants' cost.

NOTE

The doctrine of the principal case is followed generally in this country; but it has been held occasionally that a direct testamentary gift to charity is void.[29]

A gift expressly made in trust for such charitable purposes as the trustee shall select creates a valid charitable trust in most states. The Texas Court in upholding a perpetual trust of this type, has said:[30] "Petitioners' contention that the bequest in question is so general, vague and indefinite that it cannot be enforced by the courts has never been directly decided in Texas. But the decisions cited indicate a definite trend in this State contrary to that position, and the weight of authority both in this country and in England, as well as what we consider the better reasoning supports the validity of the bequest. Thus, in the American Law Institute's Restatement of the Law of Trusts, sec. 396, p. 1189, it is declared: 'A charitable trust is valid, although by the terms of the trust the trustee is authorized to apply the trust property to any charitable purposes which he may select, if the trustee is able and willing to make the selection.' In a like vein, it is said in 10 Am.Jur., Charities, sec. 83, that 'if a trustee is appointed by the testator and the will shows that the object of the devise, although expressed in general terms, is for a charitable use, the trust will be declared valid.' The rule is stated and discussed by Professor Scott in his work on Trusts (vol. 3, § 396) as follows:

> " 'A testator may devise or bequeath property in trust for charitable purposes without designating the particular purposes to which he wishes the property to be applied. He may leave the property to trustees for such charitable purposes as they may select. Such a disposition is valid according to the great weight of authority. If the trustee is ready and willing to make the selection, there is no reason why he should not be permitted to do so. This is true where the testator designates the general nature of the charitable purposes to which he desires the property to be applied. It is true also where the trustee is left free to devote the property to any charitable purpose he may select.
>
> " 'There are, indeed, a few cases in which it was held that the trust failed for uncertainty even though the trustee was given authority to select the charitable purposes to which it should be applied and was ready and willing to exercise this authority. In these cases the clear intention of the testator is defeated, and no good reason can be given for defeating it. As long as the purposes to which the property is to be applied are limited to charitable purposes, there is no reason why the trust should not be carried out in accordance with the intention of the testator.' * * * "[31]

29. Norcross' Administrators v. Murphy's Executors, 44 N.J.Eq. 522, 14 A. 903 (1888); Booe v. Vinson, 104 Ark. 439, 149 S.W. 524 (1912).

30. Boyd v. Frost National Bank, 145 Tex. 206, 211, 196 S.W.2d 497, 500 (1946).

31. See Caffrey, "Charitable Bequests: Delegating Discretion to Choose

Sometimes the testator is unfortunate enough to couple the word "charitable" with other words such as "benevolent" which may be given a noncharitable meaning. It seems clear that in context such words are intended as synonyms, but some courts have held that such trusts are invalid because not restricted to charity.[32] Trusts for purposes some of which are considered non-charitable are referred to as "mixed" trusts. Most courts today will uphold a gift to "such charitable, benevolent, religious or educational institutions as my executors may determine" on the grounds that "benevolent" means "charitable".[33] A gift to a trustee to distribute to "charities or causes as he may select" was held limited to charitable causes and thus sustained.[34] Occasionally, however, in a jurisdiction which is historically antagonistic toward charitable gifts the court will seize upon some word as indicating a purpose not within the normal scope of charity. For example, one court invalidated a gift of residue to trustees to pay over "unto such religious, charitable, scientific, literary, educational or fraternal corporations or associations as they may, in their discretion, select" on the grounds that "scientific" institutions were not necessarily charitable![35] Other courts might find "fraternal" to be non-charitable.

If the trust is "mixed", the entire trust fails unless the court finds that the settlor has indicated the proportion to be used for each purpose, in which event the portion for charity can be saved.[36]

YEAGER v. JOHNS

Supreme Court of Missouri, 1972.
484 S.W.2d 211.[36a]

[Miss Sadie Donahoe died in 1968 leaving a will giving her residuary estate "to the Reverend H. J. Lambert, to be used by him at his discretion for religious and educational purposes." The heirs at law of the testatrix contended, and the circuit court held, that the residuary clause was invalid because the beneficiaries " * * * of the pur-

the Objects of the Testator's Beneficience", 44 Tenn.L.Rev. 307 (1977); Wentura v. Kinnerk, 319 Mo. 1068, 5 S.W.2d 66 (1928) (holding invalid a testamentary gift "to such charitable uses and purposes as * * * [the executor] * * * may determine"). 23 Wash.U.L.Q. 556 (1938).

32. Gray, J. in Chamberlain v. Stearns, 111 Mass. 267, 268 (1873), stated the position thus: " * * * The word 'benevolent', of itself, without anything in the text to qualify or restrict its ordinary meaning, clearly includes not only purposes which are deemed charitable by a court of equity; but also many acts dictated by kindness, good will, or a disposition to do good, the objects of which have no relation to the promotion of education, learning or religion, the relief of the needy; the sick or the afflicted, the support of public work or the relief of public burdens, and cannot be deemed charitable in the technical and legal sense."

33. For an important decision in the tax field, often said to be more restrictive than regular property law, see Hight v. United States, 256 F.2d 795 (2d Cir. 1958), holding that "benevolent" meant charitable in light of gifts made by testatrix during life, the drafting of the will, and a list of charities left by testatrix for the guidance of the executors.

34. In re Voegtly's Estate, 396 Pa. 90, 151 A.2d 593 (1959).

35. Goetz v. Old National Bank of Martinsburg, 140 W.Va. 422, 84 S.E.2d 759 (1954).

36. See Restatement, Second, Trusts § 398.

36a. Noted, 39 Mo.L.Rev. 51 (1974).

ported charitable trust * * * are so uncertain that the same cannot be, with certainty as to the intention of the testatrix, carried into effect * * *." The Reverend Lambert, the executrix of the will and the State Attorney General appealed.]

HIGGINS, COMMISSIONER.

Appeal from declaratory judgment that the residuary clause of a will purporting to create a charitable trust was invalid and void, and order of distribution of residuary estate in excess of $50,000 to heirs at law of the testatrix.

* * *

A gift for religious or educational purposes is a gift for charitable purposes under the law in Missouri. Ervin v. Davis, 355 Mo. 951, 199 S.W.2d 366; First Nat. Bank of Kansas City v. University of Kansas City, Mo., 245 S.W.2d 124; Harger v. Barrett, 319 Mo. 633, 5 S.W.2d 1100, 2 Rest.Trusts 2d, §§ 370, 371. No particular words are required to create an express trust; equity need only to ascertain the intention of the creator of the purported trust. Ramsey v. City of Brookfield, Mo., 237 S.W.2d 143. That beneficiaries of a charitable trust are indefinite does not invalidate it since a trust is not a charitable trust where all beneficiaries are definitely ascertained. Buckley v. Monck, Mo., 187 S.W. 31; 2 Rest.Trusts 2d, § 364. Charitable trusts are the favorites of equity and are construed valid where possible and where private trusts would fail. Burrier v. Jones, Mo., 92 S.W.2d 885.

With these principles in mind, the question is stated: Does a devise in trust to a named trustee to be used in the discretion of said trustee for religious and educational purposes create a valid, public charitable trust?

In contending that the language of Article X did create a valid, public charitable trust, appellants rely principally upon authorities construing similar devises in trust to have created valid, public trusts as against charges that they were void for indefiniteness and vagueness, e.g., Chambers v. City of St. Louis, 29 Mo. 543, for "poor emigrants and travelers coming to St. Louis on their way, bona fide, to settle in the west"; Howe v. Wilson, 91 Mo. 45, 3 S.W. 390, "to divide said remainder among such charitable institutions in the city of St. Louis, Mo., as he shall deem worthy"; Powell v. Hatch, 100 Mo. 592, 14 S.W. 49, "to such charitable purposes as my said trustee may deem best"; Sappington v. Sappington School Fund Trustees, 123 Mo. 32, 27 S.W. 356, to "apply the interest of said fund to such other objects of charity in said county as in their judgment may be most needy"; Standley v. Allen, 349 Mo. 1115, 163 S.W.2d 1012, "in trust, for him and charge him with the duty of disposing of said balance of my estate to some worthy charitable organization, in Missouri, and the preference to be given to aged people"; Altman v. McCutchen, Mo., 210 S.W.2d 63 "to the charitable and other institutions devoted to alleviation of human suffering and want"; Sandusky v. Sandusky, 261 Mo. 351, 168 S.W. 1150, "for the general advancement of Christianity"; Irwin v. Swinney, D.C.W.D.Mo., 44 F.2d 172, aff. Gossett v.

Swinney, 8 Cir., 53 F.2d 772, for furtherance and development of various charitable purposes as the trustees should, in their absolute discretion, determine to be in the public interest.

In contending that the court was correct in its declaration that Article X did not create a valid, public charitable trust, respondent Yeager relies principally upon cases where purported charitable trust devises were held void for indefiniteness, e.g., Schmucker's Estate v. Reel, 61 Mo. 592, "to be applied to a specific purpose which I [testator] have explained to him," and "for another and specific charitable purpose which he well understands"; Hadley v. Forsee, 203 Mo. 418, 101 S.W. 59, "to advance the cause of religion, and promote the cause of charity, in such manner as my dearly beloved wife may think will be most conducive to the carrying out of my wishes"; Jones v. Patterson, 241 Mo. 1, 195 S.W. 1004, "to be used for missionary purposes in whatever field he thinks best to use it, so it is done in the name of my dear Savior, and for the salvation of souls." See also Wentura v. Kinnerk, 319 Mo. 1068, 5 S.W.2d 66, "to such charitable uses and purposes as [the executor] may determine."

All parties cite Epperly v. Mercantile Trust and Savings Bank, Mo., 415 S.W.2d 819, and, as suggested by Respondent Love, it reviewed the other cases cited by the parties and enunciated the controlling law on the question presented in this case.

The question in Epperly v. Mercantile Trust and Savings Bank, supra, was stated: Does a devise in trust to unspecified Protestant churches and religious organizations to save souls create a valid, public charitable trust? The answer to, and the ruling of, that question dictate an affirmative answer to the present question. After review of the authorities, the court held: "Where, as here, a trust provision gives to the trustee discretion in applying the trust property to the specified charitable purpose, the rules in Jones v. Patterson, supra [271 Mo. 1, 195 S.W. 1004], and other cases cited by respondents, should not be followed. Although there is conflict in the decisions, the weight of authority is that a charitable trust such as this trust is valid. Annotations, 22 A.L.R. 697 and 115 A.L.R. 1135, covering trusts for religious purposes; 163 A.L.R. 784, 'Charitable Gifts—Definiteness'; 168 A.L.R. 1350, 'Charitable Gift—Discretion of Trustee'; Rest.Trusts 2d, § 396; Bogert, Trusts and Trustees, 2nd Ed., § 376, p. 130 et seq. The class of religious organizations is here sufficiently certain: Protestant churches and religious organizations to be selected in the discretion of trustees. When so selected by the exercise of the trustee's discretion, such class will become fixed and definite, and certainly the purpose 'to save souls' is that of Protestant religious organizations and is charitable, Glidewell v. Glidewell, 360 Mo. 713, 230 S.W.2d 752. The objects of the trust are uncertain—i.e., innumerable persons who may be benefitted. Such is an essential requisite of a charitable gift. 14 C.J.S. Charities §§ 38, 39, pp. 473, 474; Buckley v. Monck, Mo., 187 S.W. 31, 33[1]. While a court of equity cannot undertake to specify what Protestant churches are to be selected, it may compel the trustee to exercise that discretion, and may restrain a diversion or threatened diversion from the religious purpose, and enforce its orders by removal of the trustee. 14 C.J.S. Charities § 49, p. 508; Sandusky v. Sandusky, supra, 265 Mo. 219, 177 S.W. 390, loc. cit. 177 S.W. 394[3]; Howe v. Wilson, supra." 415 S.W.2d 1, c. 822[2–4].

2 Rest.Trusts 2d, § 396, recognized in the foregoing holding, states the rule regarding requisite certainty and definiteness of public charitable trusts succinctly: "A charitable trust is valid, although by the terms of the trust the trustee is authorized to apply the trust property to any charitable purpose which he may select and the trustee is able and willing to make the selection."

Similarly, Miss Donahoe's devise in trust to Reverend Lambert to be used in the trustee's discretion for religious and educational purposes created a valid, public charitable trust. The beneficiaries are sufficiently certain: religious and educational purposes to be selected in the discretion of a named trustee, who is ready, able and willing to act. When so selected by the trustee, such purposes will become fixed and definite, and religious and educational purposes are the very essence of a public charitable trust. First National Bank of Kansas City v. University of Kansas City, supra. Innumerable uses may be benefitted, dependent upon the exercise of the trustee's discretion, an essential element of a charitable gift in trust. The court cannot undertake to specify what religious and educational purposes the trustee shall select; nevertheless, the court may compel the selection and control diversion from the selected purposes. Epperly v. Mercantile Trust and Savings Bank, supra.

It is argued by respondent Love that under Epperly v. Mercantile Trust and Savings Bank, supra, Miss Donahoe's devise did not create a valid, public charitable trust because, in contrast to the devise in that case, "there are no general types * * * of religious or educational organizations named." The possibility of this argument was recognized (and perhaps suggested) in 32 Mo.L.R. 443, 458, that the quoted language "invites more attacks on powers to appoint to charity on the ground that the class of possible appointees is not sufficiently definite."

Such argument is categorically rejected on the premise that both Epperly v. Mercantile Trust and Savings Bank, supra, and this case hold that a devise in trust to unspecified charities creates a valid, public charitable trust even though the instrument creating the trust does not limit in any way the possible charitable appointees. This has long been the law in Missouri, e.g., Chambers v. City of St. Louis, supra (1860), Howe v. Wilson, supra (1887), Powell v. Hatch, supra (1890), favorably construing similar devises as demonstrated by their prior quotation, and which were followed in Epperly v. Mercantile Trust and Savings Bank, supra.

Accordingly, the judgment is reversed, and the cause is remanded with directions to declare that Article X of the will of Sadie Donahoe, deceased, created a valid, public charitable trust, order Marie K. Johns, Executrix, to deliver the residuary estate to the named trustee or his successor, and order that such trustee execute the trust under supervision of the court.

WELBORN, C., concurs.

PER CURIAM:

The foregoing opinion by HIGGINS, C., is adopted as the opinion of the court.

NOTE

Religion is clearly one of the categories of charity. But gifts may be so vaguely phrased that the court is disturbed by the prospect of supervising the trustee in administration of the trust. Thus, in Estate of Small[37] the testator gave the residue of his estate to individual trustees to pay the income to his wife for life, and upon her death:

> "I direct that my said trustees or their successors shall distribute annually or semi-annually as they may see fit, the income thereof to such persons and for such purposes as they may feel is directed by God the Father, Jesus Christ the Son, and Holy Spirit, and as they believe would be acceptable to me and meet my approval were I able to give it, they to be at liberty to choose and change the beneficiaries as said trustees may from time to time unanimously decide, it being my desire, intention and direction that said fund shall continue permanently and forever, and only the income thereof shall be used for the disbursements herein contemplated, and nothing herein shall prevent said trustees from allowing said income to accumulate in the event they do not find a suitable beneficiary as herein stated.
>
> "By way of explanation it is my desire that any disbursements made under this paragraph shall be made to persons who believe in the fundamental principles of the Christian Religion and in the Bible and who are endeavoring to promulgate the same." The gift was finally upheld by a divided court, the majority overruling the objection that the trust was incapable of enforcement. The dissenting justices did not question the proposition that a trust to foster religion is valid as a charity, but questioned whether the will devoted the property to propagation of the faith.

While trusts to promote minority sects are certainly valid, trusts for unorthodox beliefs are likely to meet with difficulty and fail on one technical pretext or another.[38] Would one expect a conservative court to uphold a trust for atheism? On the other hand, the growth of tolerance has had a marked effect. Trusts for the saying of masses were at one time regarded as "superstitious" and void, but are now generally held to be religious and charitable.[39]

---

37. 244 Iowa 1209, 58 N.W.2d 477 (1953).

38. For example, the following gifts were held non-charitable as not being religious or as too indefinite: Zeisweiss v. James, 63 Pa. 465, 3 Am.Rep. 558 (1870) (Infidel Society for free discussion of religion, etc.); Stephan's Estate, 129 Pa. Super. 396, 195 A. 653 (1938) (upkeep of spirtualist camp); Korsstrom v. Barnes, 167 F. 216 (W.D.Wash.1909) (Theosophical Society of India to translate Hieratic Scriptures into English).

39. As typical of the change in judicial attitude see Will of Kavanaugh, 143 Wis. 90, 126 N.W. 672 (1910), overruling earlier cases and sustaining a trust for masses. See Scott, Trusts (3d Ed., 1967) § 371.5.

IN RE PATTBERG'S WILL

Supreme Court of New York, Appellate Division, Second Department, 1953.
282 App.Div. 770, 123 N.Y.S.2d 564.

MEMORANDUM BY THE COURT. In a proceeding by the executor of a decedent's estate for the judicial settlement of his account as such executor, and for a construction of paragraph sixth of decedent's will, objectants, who are the decedent's next of kin, appeal from a decree of the Surrogate's Court of Kings County, which adjudges the bequest in said paragraph to be a valid charitable trust and directs that letters of trusteeship issue.

Decree modified on the law by striking from the first decretal paragraph the words: "terms of said Will" and by substituting in place thereof the following: "purpose and intent of the Unemployment Fund of Local No. 119, Paper Cutters Union." As so modified, the decree is affirmed, with costs to all parties filing separate briefs, payable out of the estate. Findings of fact inconsistent herewith are reversed and new findings are made as indicated herein.

The bequest in question was of the residue of the estate to the respondent executor and trustee "in trust", with direction to turn it over, the entire amount at one time, or in portions from time to time, in his discretion, to the "Unemployment Fund of Local No. 119, Paper Cutters Union." This fund was created by the said trade union local in 1928, at which time the local also adopted certain provisions to govern the fund's administration. According to those provisions, as later changed by amendments to the union's constitution, the source of the monies of the fund are regular assessments upon members of the union and the profits of the union's annual ball; these monies are to be kept separately from other monies of the union, and are to be disbursed to qualifying members of the union during certain periods of unemployment, according to a certain schedule and subject to certain limitations, and to members who have attained the age of sixty-five years and who are no longer able to work at their usual occupation at the trade because of such age, again according to schedules and limitations; and the administrators of the fund are to be five members of the union, two of whom shall be those holding certain stated offices and three of whom shall be "lay members." It was conceded that both the union and the fund are unincorporated associations.

Although generally a bequest to an unincorporated association is void, Owens v. Missionary Society of the M. E. Church, 14 N.Y. 380, 385; Mount v. Tuttle, 183 N.Y. 358, 367, 76 N.E. 873, 875, 2 L.R.A.,N. S., 428; Ely v. Megie, 219 N.Y. 112, 142–143, 113 N.E. 800, 807–808; Fralick v. Lyford, 107 App.Div. 543, 95 N.Y.S. 433, affirmed 187 N.Y. 524, 79 N.E. 1105, this rule was modified by the enactment of chapter 701 of the Laws of 1893 (the so-called Tilden Act; presently section 12 of the Personal Property Law) so as to exempt therefrom bequests to charitable or benevolent uses, and other eleemosynary uses. See Matter of Merritt, 280 N.Y. 391, 399, 21 N.E.2d 365, 369; Baxter v. McDonnell, 155 N.Y. 83, 93, 49 N.E. 667, 668, 40 L.R.A. 670; Murray

v. Miller, 178 N.Y. 316, 321, 70 N.E. 870, 872. Construction of a bequest as being for a charitable or benevolent purpose should be preferred if it "devotes the fund included therein to purposes permitted by law and to the good of humanity". Matter of Robinson's Will, 203 N.Y. 380, 388, 96 N.E. 925, 927, 37 L.R.A.,N.S., 1023. The fact that the persons who are in the class which is intended as the ultimate beneficiary are required, as a condition for inclusion therein, by prescription dehors the bequest itself, to contribute certain sums of money periodically to the fund which is nominally the beneficiary of the bequest does not in itself prevent the bequest from being charitable and benevolent. Cf. Matter of MacDowell's Will, 217 N.Y. 454, 112 N.E. 177, L.R.A.1916E, 1246; Butterworth v. Keeler, 219 N.Y. 446, 114 N.E. 803. Further, as stated in the MacDowell case, supra, "When the purpose accomplished is that of public usefulness unstained by personal, private, or selfish considerations, its charitable character insures its validity" 217 N.Y. at page 460, 112 N.E. at page 178, and "It has often been held that a public charity need have no special reference to the poor." 217 N.Y. at page 463, 112 N.E. at page 179. Classes of beneficiary comparable to the one presently in question, namely, followers of a specified trade or occupation, employees of a named business establishment, or even persons living in a named locality, have been held not to bar characterization of bequests as charitable or benevolent. See Matter of Skuse's Estate, 165 Misc. 554, 556, 1 N.Y.S.2d 202, 205, and authorities there cited. See also Matter of Howells' Estate, 146 Misc. 169, 261 N.Y.S. 859. Moreover, bequests for purposes similar to the instant one, and for the benefit of members of associations of working people, and even members of a trade union have been upheld. Matter of Geller's Estate, 201 Misc. 381, 111 N.Y.S.2d 464; In re Fox's Will, Sur., 123 N.Y. S.2d 562; In re Casper's Estate, Sur., 123 N.Y.S.2d 563. However, since no person has been named trustee to execute the objects of the bequest, we hold that title to the residuary estate is vested in the Supreme Court. Personal Property Law, § 12, subd. 1. The person nominated in the will as trustee to receive the bequest and turn it over to the said fund may serve as trustee to administer the bequest himself according to the purposes and intent of the said fund.

ADEL, WENZEL and SCHMIDT, JJ., concur.

NOLAN, PRESIDING JUSTICE, dissents and votes to reverse and to remit the proceeding to Surrogate's Court for the entry of a decree as prayed for in the objections interposed by appellants, with the following memorandum: Decedent's will provided that his residuary estate should be devised and bequeathed to his executor and trustee, in trust, and directed his executor and trustee, in his discretion, to "turn over" such residuary estate "to the Unemployment Fund of Local 119, Paper Cutters Union". The union is an unincorporated association, and the unemployment fund is maintained by the union, as provided in its by-laws. In my opinion, this bequest was not for a charitable or benevolent use, within the meaning of section 12 of the Personal Property Law. It is not provided that the so-called trust be administered for any particular use. All that is provided or required is that it be turned over to the designated fund, which is sustained by compulsory contributions by the members and the profits of the union's annual ball. Purchase of tickets for the annual ball is required of the members of the union. The purposes for which the fund has been used are unquestionably commendable, and the application of the fund since its creation has conferred substantial benefits upon the unemployed members of the union. It is doubtful, however that the use of the fund has been charitable within the meaning of the statute. The fund was established by the union membership, for their own benefit, and was intended to be sustained by the allocation of dues and by other compulsory contributions. Payments from the fund are not in the nature of charity, but are rather in the nature of unemployment insurance, purchased by the members, in accordance with the union rules. Moreover, there appears to be no limitation, in the constitution or by-laws of the union, which restricts the use of the fund to the relief of unemployment. Pursuant to the by-laws this fund, like all other funds, is the property of the union for its legitimate purposes. Concededly, all of such purposes are not charitable, and since there is no restriction on the use of the fund in the testator's will, there is nothing to prevent the union membership from devoting some part of the fund, at least, from time to time, to such legitimate union purposes as may be considered desirable and proper. Presumably the testator, a member of the union, was aware of this fact, but gave no direction as to the use to be made of the bequest, apparently intending that it might be used for any legitimate purpose that the unemployment fund could be used for, under the constitution and by-laws of the union, even though such purpose might not be charitable.

ESTATE OF ROBBINS

Supreme Court of California, 1962.
57 Cal.2d 718, 21 Cal.Rptr. 797, 371 P.2d 573.[40]

TRAYNOR, JUSTICE. In his will the testator divided his estate into Fund A consisting of "cash, securities and money in the bank" and Fund B consisting of "a parcel of real estate situated in Los Angeles, California, and improved with two (2) single family residences, together with furniture, fixtures, personal belongings and library contained therein." He directed that the assets comprising Fund B be sold and the cash distributed to three named trustees in trust. "The income of said trust, or so much of the principal as in the sole discretion of the Trustees may be deemed desirable or advisable, is to be used for the care, comfort, support, medical attention, education, sus-

40. Noted, 50 Cal.L.Rev. 885 (1962); 12 DePaul L.Rev. 364 (1963); 48 Iowa L. Rev. 1019 (1963); 36 So.Cal.L.Rev. 309 (1963); 8 Utah L.Rev. 152 (1962); 20 Wash. & Lee L.Rev. 85 (1963). See 22 A. L.R.3d 886 (1967).

tenance, maintenance or custody of such minor Negro child or children, whose father or mother, or both, have been incarcerated, imprisoned, detained or committed in any federal, state, county or local prison or penitentiary, as a result of the conviction of a crime or misdemeanor of a political nature." He then set forth illustrative examples of crimes of a political nature for the guidance of the trustees in the exercise of their discretion and stated his reasons for creating the trust.

In this proceeding to determine heirship (Prob.Code, § 1080) the disposition of Fund A is not in dispute, but Lee Mishkin, a grandnephew of the testator, challenges the validity of the Fund B trust. The trial court determined that the trust is invalid. Since the will contained no residuary clause, the court entered an order determining that the property bequeathed to the trustees should pass by the law of intestate succession. The administrator-with-the-will-annexed appeals.

We agree with the contention of the administrator that the testator established a valid charitable trust. The trustees, the beneficiaries, and the trust purpose are all stated. "A bequest is charitable if: (1) It is made for a charitable purpose; its aims and accomplishments are of religious, educational, political or general social interest to mankind. [Citations.] (2) The ultimate recipients constitute either the community as a whole or an unascertainable and indefinite portion thereof. [Citations.]" (Estate of Henderson, 17 Cal.2d 853, 857, 112 P.2d 605, 607.) Provision for the "care, comfort, support, medical attention, education, sustenance, maintenance or custody" of minor children who have been deprived of normal home life by the incarceration of one or both of their parents is unquestionably of social value. Any risk that a parent might be induced to commit a crime he otherwise would not commit because of the possibility that his child might become a beneficiary of this trust is far outweighed by the interests of the innocent children involved and society's interest in them. To hold otherwise would, as stated in another context, "incorporate into the law of the land as legal precepts the sayings that the sins of fathers are visited upon their children (Westbrook v. [Mobile & O.] R. R. [Co.] 66 Miss. [560,] loc. cit. 569, 6 South. 321,) and that the child's teeth must be set on edge because the father has eaten sour grapes. (B[ellefontaine] & I. R. R. Co. v. Snyder, 18 Ohio St. [399], loc. cit. 409)." (Neff v. City of Cameron, 213 Mo. 350, 360, 111 S.W. 1139, 1141, 18 L.R.A.,N.S., 320; see also Zarzana v. Neve Drug Co., 180 Cal. 32, 34–37, 179 P. 203, 15 A.L.R. 401; Reynolds v. Willson, 51 Cal. 2d 94, 102, 331 P.2d 48.)

The testator selected a class of beneficiaries constituting an indefinite part of the community and provided adequate standards to guide his trustees in administering the trust. (Estate of Bunn, 33 Cal.2d 897, 901–904, 206 P.2d 635, and authorities cited.) Like the aged beneficiaries in Estate of Henderson, supra, 17 Cal.2d 853, 112 P.2d 605, Fredericka Home For The Aged v. County of San Diego, 35 Cal.2d 789, 221 P.2d 68, and Estate of Tarrant, 38 Cal.2d 42, 237 P.2d 505,

these children require special care and attention, and it is immaterial that the beneficiaries are not limited to children in financial need. "Relief of poverty is not a condition of charitable assistance. If the benefit conferred has a sufficiently widespread social value, a charitable purpose exists." (Estate of Henderson, supra, 17 Cal.2d 853, 857, 112 P.2d 605, 607; see also Estate of Tarrant, supra, 38 Cal.2d 42, 50, 237 P.2d 505.) "In short, as the word 'charity' is commonly understood in modern usage, it does not refer only to aid to the poor and destitute and exclude all humanitarian activities * * * which are maintained to care for the physical and mental well-being of the recipients, and which make it less likely that such recipients will become burdens on society." (Fredericka Home For The Aged v. County of San Diego, supra, 35 Cal.2d 789, 793, 221 P.2d 68, 71.)

Lee Mishkin contends, however, that the testator's purpose was to encourage the commission of political crimes and that therefore the trust is illegal. The administrator and amicus curiae contend, on the contrary, that the testator's purpose was to encourage constitutionally protected freedom of speech and expression and to protect the right of lawful dissent and that these are valid charitable purposes. They contend that the illustrations the testator set forth in his will, convictions of violating the Smith Act, convictions of contempt of congressional committees, convictions for violating laws dealing with test oaths, convictions for engaging in labor union activities, all involve areas where the lines between constitutionally protected activity and illegal activity are vaguely defined. (Cf., e.g., Dennis v. United States, 341 U.S. 494, 71 S.Ct. 857, 95 L.Ed. 1137, with Yates v. United States, 354 U.S. 298, 77 S.Ct. 1064, 1 L.Ed.2d 1356; Scales v. United States, 367 U.S. 203, 81 S.Ct. 1469, 6 L.Ed.2d 782, with Noto v. United States, 367 U.S. 290, 81 S.Ct. 1517, 6 L.Ed.2d 836; Barenblatt v. United States, 360 U.S. 109, 79 S.Ct. 1081, 3 L.Ed.2d 1115, with N.A.A.C.P. v. Alabama, 357 U.S. 449, 78 S.Ct. 1163, 2 L.Ed.2d 1488.) They assert that the will can reasonably be interpreted as referring only to parents who have been unlawfully convicted for engaging in constitutionally protected activity and that thereby any question of illegality can be avoided.

We need not search for any such limitation in the language of the will to sustain the trust. We may assume that the testator intended to benefit the children of those convicted of even valid laws of which he disapproved and that his motive in part at least was to encourage challenges to such laws by violations of them. It is the purpose for which the property is to be used, however, not the motives of the testator that determines whether a trust is a valid charitable trust. * * * [Citations omitted.]

Assistance to the minor beneficiaries of the trust in this case is a valid charitable purpose. The risk that such assistance may serve to encourage crime is far more remote than that which the Legislature itself may have created by provision for the care of children that extends to those of convicted prisoners. (See Welf. & Inst. Code, § 1500.) The benefit to society offered by the testator transcends whatever criticism there may be of his motives, which have died with him.

The order is reversed. The appeal from the order denying the motion for new trial is dismissed. (Prob.Code, § 1240; Estate of Duke, 41 Cal.2d 509, 515–516, 261 P.2d 235.)

GIBSON, C.J., and PETERS and DOOLING, JJ., concur.

WHITE, JUSTICE. I dissent.

Undoubtedly a valid trust may be created where its purposes are to effect changes in existing laws. (See 4 Scott on Trusts [2d ed.] § 374.4, p. 2677; 2A Bogert on Trusts, § 378, pp. 168–170.)

As was said by this court in Collier v. Lindley, 203 Cal. 641, 650–651, 266 P. 526, 529: "The trend of modern authority has been toward the upholding of trusts which have for their object the creation of a more enlightened public opinion, with a consequent change in laws having to do with human relations and rights in a republic such as ours * * *. To hold that a change in a law is in effect an attempt to violate that law would discourage improvement in legislation and tend to compel us to continue indefinitely to live under laws designed for an entirely different state of society. Such view is opposed to every principle of our government based on the theory that it is a government 'of the people, by the people and for the people,' and fails to recognize the right of those who make the laws to change them at their pleasure when circumstances seem to require. With the wisdom of the proposed change the courts are not concerned."

However, recognition cannot be given to a trust as valid where its purpose is illegal. Therein lies the vice of the trust now engaging our attention. It not only encourages but offers an inducement for violation of the criminal law. In the Restatement of Trusts is found the following cogent statement: "*A trust which tends to induce a breach of the criminal law is invalid.* Thus, a trust of property to be applied to the payment of fines of persons convicted of criminal offenses * * * is invalid." (Emphasis added.) And in 4 Scott on Trusts (2d ed.), section 377 at page 2729, it is said: "A trust cannot be created for a purpose which is illegal. The purpose is illegal if the trust property is to be used for an object which is in violation of the criminal law, or if the trust tends to induce the commission of crime, or if the accomplishment of the purpose is otherwise against public policy. Questions of public policy are not fixed and unchanging, but vary from time to time and from place to place. A trust fails for illegality if the accomplishment of the purposes of the trust is regarded as against public policy in the community in which the trust is created and at the time when it is created. *Where a policy is articulated in a statute making certain conduct a criminal offense, then, of course, a trust is illegal if its performance involves such criminal conduct, or if it tends to encourage such conduct.* Thus, in an early English case a bequest to trustees 'to make seats for poor people to beg in by the highway' was held invalid since such begging was a criminal offense.

"A trust is illegal, even if it does not involve the performance of an illegal act by the trustees, if the natural result of the performance of the trust would be to induce the commission of crime. Thus a bequest to purchase the release of persons committed to prison for nonpayment of fines under the game laws was held illegal." (Emphasis added.)

In my opinion, it would do violence to reason and challenge credulity to say that the object of the trust with which we are here concerned is to bring about a change in the law by lawful and orderly means. On the contrary the testator, with care and precision, undertook to instruct his trustees that those who would violate certain named existing penal statutes, or commit any crime or misdemeanor which the testator terms "of a political nature," and is convicted thereof, were to be rewarded by the furnishing of aid to their children. That the trust property in the case at bar was to be used in the performance of the trust to encourage if not induce the commission of crime, to me seems manifest, and therefore, consonant with the foregoing reasoning and authorities, it cannot be held to be a valid charitable trust.

I would affirm the judgment.

SCHAUER and MCCOMB, JJ., concur.

NOTE

Trusts for the relief of poverty have always been regarded as charitable.

A trust may be charitable although the recipients of the benefits of the trust are to be selected by the trustee from among a limited class of persons, provided the class is large enough to give the community an interest in performance of the trust. The size of the class from which the selection is to be made and not the number to be selected is controlling.

An interesting variant is presented by Estate of Scholler, 403 Pa. 97, 169 A.2d 554 (1961). Settlor by inter vivos deed of trust created the Scholler Foundation "for the benefit of mankind". The deed listed obviously charitable purposes in general—"the alleviation of poverty and destitution", "scientific research", "assistance to persons under disability", "enabling needy students to obtain college educations", "the benefit of colleges, universities, churches, hospitals" and other charitable purposes selected by the Trustees. However, the trust deed added "and specifically for the purpose of providing hospitalization, medical care, and educational, literary, and recreational facilities for employees and/or former employees of Scholler Brothers" and related corporations. Although the United States Treasury Department approved the Foundation for tax exemption,[41] the Canadian authorities questioned the provision for distribution in favor of employees of Scholler Corporation. Although the trust deed was expressly irrevocable and was not amendable, the deed was amended to exclude the specific reference above. The trust was challenged by the settlor's heirs as non-charitable.

41. Compare Watson v. United States, 355 F.2d 269 (3rd Cir. 1965), denying a deduction for federal estate tax purposes where a transfer was made to a trust for retired employees of a corporation founded by the testator, although the state courts had upheld the trust as charitable for purposes of the Rule Against Perpetuities.

The Court upheld the trust and held the amendment effective, not to amend the trust, but to *reform* it on grounds of mistake.

A trust for a fraternal association is not charitable if the purpose of the association is to promote the social interests of the members; but the trust is charitable if the purpose of the association is charitable. If the trust is not created for the general purposes of the association but is for the relief of poverty, the promotion of health, or the advancement of education or religion, the trust is charitable although the recipients of the trust benefits are limited to the members of the association and although the purposes of the association are not charitable.[42]

The line between private and charitable purposes is sometimes difficult to draw. "Pet" schemes of the testator may well be beneficial to the community and sustained. Thus, a trust to acquire land for the production of timber and as bird preserves was recognized as a public conservation measure.[43] But devises of a family homestead and furnishings to be preserved as a memorial to the family may or may not be charitable, depending upon the historic worth of the home.[44] Similarly, a trust to publish documents or writings of a member of the family may be held noncharitable unless the literary or historic value of the writings is established.[45] Clearly, trusts to provide education or medical benefits for one's descendants or relatives are private,[46] although a settlor can create a trust to provide scholarships for needy students of ability and provide that preference be given to descendants who otherwise meet the qualifications without impairing the charitable nature of the trust.[47]

A trust for the promotion of health is clearly charitable. Gifts for hospitals or medical research are easy to sustain under this category. Trusts for municipal purposes are also charitable. Thus a gift to trustees to hold as a perpetual fund to use the income for the use and benefit of a particular town as the trustees shall determine has been upheld.[48] Such trusts are sometimes called "governmental" trusts. Trusts to provide parks are common examples.

The cases we have studied are far from exhausting the kinds of trusts which may be held charitable. Charity is an expanding concept. Thus, a California court sustained a gift to Stanford University in trust to establish a "Foundation of World Relations" and quoted from an earlier opinion as followed:[49]

> "The enforcement of charitable uses cannot be limited to any narrow and stated formula. As has been well said, it must expand with the advancement of civilization and the daily increasing needs of men. New discoveries in science, new fields and opportunities for human action, the differ-

42. See Scott, Trusts (3d Ed., 1967) §§ 375–375.3.

43. Peakes v. Blakely, 333 Mass. 281, 130 N.E.2d 564 (1955) (income also to be used for charitable purposes); see 7 A.L. R.3d 1281 (1966).

44. Compare Smith v. Powers, 83 R.I. 415, 117 A.2d 844 (1955), with Medical Society of South Carolina v. South Carolina National Bank, 197 S.C. 96, 14 S.E.2d 577 (1941).

45. State ex rel. Emmert v. Union Trust Co., 227 Ind. 571, 86 N.E.2d 450 (1949).

46. Hardage v. Hardage, 211 Ga. 80, 84 S.E.2d 54 (1954); Marriner W. Merrill Family Foundation v. State Tax Commission, 3 Utah 2d 244, 282 P.2d 333 (1955) (tax case).

47. See Scott, Trusts (3d Ed., 1967) § 375.3.

48. Peirce v. Attwill, 234 Mass. 389, 125 N.E. 609 (1920).

49. In re Peck's Estate, 168 Cal.App. 2d 25, 28, 335 P.2d 185, 187 (1959), cert. den. 361 U.S. 826, 903, 80 S.Ct. 74, 205, 4 L.Ed.2d 69.

ing condition, character, and wants of communities and nations, change and enlarge the scope of charity, and where new necessities are created new charitable uses must be established. The underlying principle is the same; its application is as varying as the wants of humanity."

PROBLEMS

1. Is a trust for the establishment of an animal home or hospital and for the care, comfort and benefit of dumb animals charitable? Matter of Hamilton, 270 App.Div. 634, 63 N.Y.S.2d 265 (1946), 32 Corn.L.Q. 458 (1947), 21 St. J.L.Rev. 87 (1946).

2. Is a valid charitable trust created by a devise in trust "to be used for missionary purposes in whatever field * * * [the trustee] * * * thinks best to use it, so it is done in the name of my dear Savior and for the salvation of souls."? Jones v. Patterson, 271 Mo. 1, 195 S.W. 1004 (1917). Contra, Hinckley v. Thatcher, 139 Mass. 477, 1 N.E. 840, 52 Am.Rep. 719 (1885). See Newark, "Public Benefit and Religious Trusts", 62 Law Q.Rev. 234 (1946); 22 St. John's L.Rev. 241 (1948); 23 Wash.U.L.Q. 556 (1938).

3. Is a trust to erect a school building on the site of the school which the testator had attended in a named Yugoslavian village a valid charitable trust? Bogdanovich v. Bogdanovich, 360 Mo. 753, 230 S.W.2d 695 (1950).

4. Is a trust for a college fraternity a charitable trust? People v. Phi Kappa Sigma, 326 Ill. 573, 158 N.E. 213, 54 A.L.R. 1376 (1927). Is such a trust charitable for federal tax purposes? See Mott, "Charities, Fraternities and The Income Tax", 44 Taxes 592 (1966).

5. Is a trust to pay the income from the trust property to such highly evolved individuals with much occult knowledge who are ceaselessly working for the advancement of the race and the alleviation of the sufferings of humanity as the trustee might deem worthy a valid charitable trust? In re Carpenter's Estate, 163 Misc. 474, 297 N.Y.S. 649 (1937).

SECTION 4. CY PRES

JACKSON v. PHILLIPS

Supreme Judicial Court of Massachusetts, 1867.
96 Mass. (14 Allen) 539.

Bill in equity by the executor of the will of Francis Jackson of Boston (who died in 1861) for instructions as to the validity and effect of the following bequests and devises:

"Article 4th. I give and bequeath to William Lloyd Garrison, Wendell Phillips, Edmund Quincy, Maria W. Chapman, L. Maria Child, Edmund Jackson, William I. Bowditch, Samuel May, Jr., and Charles K. Whipple, their successors and assigns, ten thousand dollars; not for their own use, but in trust, nevertheless, for them to use and expend at their discretion, without any responsibility to any one, in such sums, at such times and such places, as they deem best, for the preparation and circulation of books, newspapers, the delivery of speeches, lectures, and such other means, as, in their judgment, will create a public sentiment that will put an end to negro slavery in this country; and I hereby constitute them a board of trustees for that purpose, with power to fill all vacancies that may occur from time to time by death or resignation of any member or of any officer of said board. And I hereby appoint Wendell Phillips president, Edmund Jackson treasurer, and Charles K. Whipple, secretary, of said board of trustees. Other bequests, hereinafter made, will sooner or later revert to this board of trustees. My desire is that they may become a permanent organization; and I hope and trust that they will receive the services and sympathy, the donations and bequests, of the friends of the slave.

"Article 5th. I give and bequeath to the board of trustees named in the fourth article of this will, their successors and assigns, two thousand dollars, not for their own use, but in trust, nevertheless, to be expended by them at their discretion, without any responsibility to any one, for the benefit of fugitive slaves who may escape from the slave-holding states of this infamous Union from time to time." * * *

One argument was had in March, 1863, after which the court ordered the attorney general to be made a party, which was done, and he submitted the case without argument, and a second argument by the other counsel was had in November, 1865. While the case was under advisement, the thirteenth article of amendment of the Constitution of the United States was adopted, and the effect of this amendment upon the case was argued in March, 1866. * * *

GRAY, J. * * * [After holding that the gifts in the fourth and fifth articles of the will were valid charities.] * * *

By the thirteenth amendment of the Constitution of the United States, adopted since the earlier arguments of this case, it is declared that "neither slavery nor involuntary servitude, except as a punishment for crime whereof the party shall have been duly convicted, shall exist within the United States or any place subject to their jurisdiction." The effect of this amendment upon the charitable bequests of Francis Jackson is the remaining question to be determined; and this requires a consideration of the nature and proper limits of the doctrine of *cy pres*.

It is contended for the heirs at law, that the power of the English chancellor, when a charitable trust cannot be administered according to its terms, to execute it so as to carry out the donor's intention as nearly as possible—*cy pres*—is derived from the royal prerogative or the St. of 43 Eliz. and is not an exercise of judicial authority; that, whether this power is prerogative or judicial, it cannot, or, if it can, should not, be exercised by this court; and that the doctrine of *cy pres*, even as administered in the English chancery, would not sustain these charitable bequests since slavery has been abolished.

Much confusion of ideas has arisen from the use of the term *cy pres* in the books to describe two distinct powers exercised by the English chancellor in charity cases, the one under the sign manual of the crown, the other under the general jurisdiction in equity; as well as to designate the rule of construction which has sometimes been applied to executory devises or powers of appointment to individuals, in order to avoid the objection of remoteness. It was of this last, and not of any doctrine peculiar to charities, that Lord Kenyon said, "The doctrine of *cy pres* goes to the utmost verge of the law, and we must take care that it does not run wild"; and Lord Eldon, "It is not proper to go one step farther." Brundenell v. Elwes, 1 East 451, 7 Ves. 390. 1 Jarman on Wills, 261–263. Sugden on Powers, c. 9, § 9. Coster v. Lorillard, 14 Wend., N.Y. 309, 348.

The principal, if not the only, cases in which the disposition of a charity is held to be in the crown by sign manual, are of two classes; the first, of bequests to particular uses charitable in their nature, but illegal, as for a form of religion not tolerated by law; and the second, of gifts of property to charity generally, without any trust interposed, and in which either no appointment is provided for, or the power of appointment is delegated to persons who die without exercising it.

It is by the sign manual and in cases of the first class, that the arbitrary dispositions have been made, which were so justly condemned by Lord Thurlow in Moggridge v. Thackwell, 1 Ves.Jr. 469, and Sir William Grant in Cary v. Abbot, 7 Ves. 494, 495; and which, through want of due discrimination, have brought so much discredit upon the whole doctrine of *cy pres*. Such was the case of Attorney General v. Baxter, in which a bequest to Mr. Baxter to be distributed by him among sixty pious ejected ministers (not, as the testator declared, for the sake of their nonconformity, but because he knew many of them to be pious and good men and in great want) was held to be void, and given under the sign manual to Chelsea College; but the decree was afterward reversed, upon the ground that this was really a legacy to sixty individuals to be named. 1 Vern. 248; 2 Vern. 105; 1 Eq.Cas.Ab. 96; 7 Ves. 76. Such also was the case of Da Costa v. De Pas, in which a gift for establishing a *jesuba* or assembly for reading the Jewish law was applied to the support of a Christian chapel at a foundling hospital. Ambl. 228; 1 Swanst. 489 note; 1 Dick. 258; 7 Ves. 76, 81.

This power of disposal by the sign manual of the crown in direct opposition to the declared intention of the testator, whether it is to be deemed to have belonged to the king as head of the church as well as of the state, "intrusted and empowered to see that nothing be done to the disherison of the crown or the propagation of a false religion"; Rex v. Portington, 1 Salk. 162, 1 Eq.Cas.Ab. 96; or to have been derived from the power exercised by the Roman emperor, who was sovereign legislator as well as supreme interpreter of the laws; Dig. 33,

2, 17; 50, 8, 4; Code, lib. 1 tit. 2, c. 19; tit. 14, c. 12; is clearly a prerogative and not a judicial power, and could not be exercised by this court; and it is difficult to see how it could be held to exist at all in a republic, in which charitable bequests have never been forfeited to the use or submitted to the disposition of the government, because superstitious or illegal. 4 Dane Ab. 239; Gass v. Wilhite, 2 Dana, Ky., 176, 26 Am.Dec. 446; Methodist Church v. Remington, 1 Watts, Pa., 226, 26 Am.Dec. 61.

The second class of bequests which are disposed of by the king's sign manual is of gifts to charity generally, with no uses specified, no trust interposed, and either no provision made for an appointment, or the power of appointment delegated to particular persons who die without exercising it. Boyle on Charities, 238, 239; Attorney General v. Syderfen, 1 Vern. 224, 1 Eq.Cas.Ab. 96; Attorney General v. Fletcher, 5 Law Journal, N.S., Ch. 75. This too is not a judicial power of expounding and carrying out the testator's intention, but a prerogative power of ordaining what the testator has failed to express. No instance is reported, or has been discovered in the thorough investigations of the subject, of an exercise of this power in England before the reign of Charles II. Moggridge v. Thackwell, 7 Ves. 69–81. Dwight's Argument in the Rose Will Case, 272. It has never, so far as we know, been introduced into the practice of any court in this country; and, if it exists anywhere here it is in the legislature of the Commonwealth as succeeding to the powers of the king as *parens patriae*. 4 Kent.Com. 508, note; Fontain v. Ravenel, 17 How. 369, 384, 15 L.Ed. 80; Moore's Heirs v. Moore's Devisees, 4 Dana, Ky., 365, 366, 29 Am.Dec. 417; Witman v. Lex, 17 Serg. & R., Pa., 93, 17 Am.Dec. 644; Shields, Attorney General, v. Jolly, 1 Rich.Eq., S.C., 108, 42 Am.Dec. 349; Dickson v. Montgomery, 1 Swan, Tenn., 348; Lepage v. Macnamara, 5 Iowa 146; Bartlet v. King, 12 Mass. 545, 7 Am.Dec. 99; Sohier v. Massachusetts General Hospital, 3 Cush., Mass., 496, 497. It certainly cannot be exercised by the judiciary of a state whose constitution declares that "the judicial department shall never exercise the legislative and executive powers, or either of them: to the end it may be a government of laws and not of men." Declaration of Rights, art. 30.

The jurisdiction of the court of chancery to superintend the administration and decree the performance of gifts to trustees for charitable uses of a kind stated in the gift stands upon different grounds; and is part of its equity jurisdiction over trusts, which is shown by abundant evidence to have existed before the passage of the Statute of Charitable Uses. * * *

The theory that the St. of 43 Eliz. enlarged the discretion of the chancellor to depart from the expressed intention of the founder of a charity is refuted by the words of the statute itself. * * *

In cases of bequests to trustees for charitable uses, the nature of which is described in the will, the chancellor acts in his equity jurisdiction over trusts; and the prerogative of the king finds its appropriate exercise through his attorney general in bringing the case before the court of chancery for a judicial determination. This has been well explained by Lord Eldon. "* * * It is the duty of the king, as *parens patriae,* to protect property devoted to charitable uses; and that duty is executed by the officer who represents the crown for all forensic purposes. On this foundation rests the right of the attorney general in such cases to obtain by information the interposition of a court of equity." * * *

This duty of maintaining the rights of the public, and of a number of persons too indefinite to vindicate their own, has vested in the Commonwealth, and is exercised here, as in England, through the attorney general. Going v. Emery, 16 Pick., Mass., 119, 26 Am.Dec. 645; Parker, County Attorney, v. May, 5 Cush., Mass., 338–340. Gen.St. c. 14, § 20. It is upon this ground that, in a suit instituted by the trustees of a charity to obtain the instructions of the court, the attorney general should be made a party defendant, as he has been by order of the court in this case. President, etc., of Harvard College v. Society for Promoting Theological Education, 3 Gray, Mass., 280. Tudor, 161, 162. The power of the king or Commonwealth, thus exercised, is simply to present the question to a court of justice, not to control or direct its judicial action.

A charity, being a trust in the support and execution of which the whole public is concerned, and which is therefore allowed by the law to be perpetual, deserves and often requires the exercise of a larger discretion by the court of chancery than a mere private trust; for without a large discretionary power, in carrying out the general intent of the donor, to vary the details of administration, and even the mode of application, many charities would fail by change of circumstances and the happening of contingencies which no human foresight could provide against; and the probabilities of such failure would increase with the lapse of time and the remoteness of the heirs from the original donor who had in a clear and lawful manner manifested his will to divert his estate from his heirs for the benefit of public charities.

It is accordingly well settled by decisions of the highest authority, that when a gift is made to trustees for a charitable purpose, the general nature of which is pointed out, and which is lawful and valid at the time of the death of the testator, and no intention is expressed to limit it to a particular institution or mode of application, and afterwards, either by change of circumstances the scheme of the testator becomes impracticable, or by change of law becomes illegal, the fund, having once vested in the charity, does not go to the heirs at law as a resulting trust, but is to be applied by the court of chancery, in the exercise of its jurisdiction in equity, as near the testator's particular directions as possible, to carry out his general charitable intent. In all the cases of charities which have been administered in the English courts of chancery without the aid of the sign manual, the prerogative of the king acting through the chancellor has not been alluded to, except for the purpose of distinguishing it from the power exercised by the court in its inherent equitable jurisdiction with the assistance of its masters in chancery. * * *

The intention of the testator is the guide, or, in the phrase of Lord Coke, the lodestone, of the court; and, therefore, whenever a charitable gift can be administered according to his express directions, this court, like the court of chancery in England, is not at liberty to modify it upon considerations of policy or convenience. President, etc., Harvard College v. Society for Promoting Theological Education, 3 Gray, Mass., 280. Baker v. Smith, 13 Metc., Mass., 34. Trustees of Smith Charities v. Inhabitants of Northampton, 10 Allen, Mass., 498. But there are several cases, where the charitable trust could not be executed as directed in the will, in which the testator's scheme has been varied by this court in such a way and to such an extent as could not be done in the case of a private trust. Thus bequests to a particular bible society by name, whether a corporation established by law or a voluntary association, which has ceased to exist before the death of the testator, have been sustained, and applied to the distribution of bibles through a trustee appointed by the court for the purpose. Winslow v. Cummings, 3 Cush., Mass., 358. Bliss v. American Bible Society, 2 Allen, Mass., 334. * * *

By the Gen.St. c. 113, § 2, this court may hear and determine in equity all suits and proceedings for enforcing and regulating the execution of trusts, whether the trusts relate to real or personal estate, "and shall have full equity jurisdiction, according to the usage and practice of courts of equity, in all other cases, where there is not a plain, adequate and complete remedy at law." The powers usually exercised by the court of chancery in the course of its jurisdiction in equity have thus been expressly conferred upon this court by the legislature. The authority of administering a charitable trust according to the expressed intention of the donor, and, when that cannot be exactly followed, then as nearly as possible, is a part of this jurisdiction, which the court is not at liberty to decline. The only question is, whether the facts of the case show a proper occasion for its exercise according to the settled practice in chancery.

In all the cases cited at the argument, in which a charitable bequest, which might have been lawfully carried out under the circumstances existing at the death of the testator, has been held upon a change of circumstances, to result to the heirs at law or residuary legatees, the gift was distinctly limited to particular persons or establishments. * * *

The charitable bequests of Francis Jackson cannot, in the opinion of the court, be regarded as so restricted in their objects, or so limited in point of time, as to have been terminated and destroyed by the abolition of slavery in the United States. They are to a board of trustees for whose continuance careful provision is made in the will, and which the testator expresses a wish may become a permanent organization and may receive the services and sympathy, the donations and bequests, of the friends of the slave. Their duration is not in terms limited, like that of the trust sought to be established in the sixth article of the will, by the accomplishment of the end specified. They take effect from the time of the testator's death, and might then have been lawfully applied in exact conformity with his expressed intentions. The retaining of the funds in the custody of the court while this case has been under advisement cannot affect the question. The gifts being lawful and charitable, and having once vested, the subsequent change of circumstances before the funds have been actually paid over is of no more weight than if they had been paid to the trustees and been administered by them for a century before slavery was extinguished.

Neither the immediate purpose of the testator—the moral education of the people; nor his ultimate object—to better the condition of the African race in this country; has been fully accomplished by the abolition of slavery.

Negro slavery was recognized by our law as an infraction of the rights inseparable from human nature; and tended to promote idleness, selfishness and tyranny in one part of the community, a destruction of the domestic relations and utter debasement in the other part. The sentiment which would put an end to it is the sentiment of justice, humanity and charity, based upon moral duty, inspired by the most familiar precepts of the Christian religion, and approved by the Constitution of the Commonwealth. The teaching and diffusion of such a sentiment are not of temporary benefit or necessity, but of perpetual obligation. Slavery may be abolished; but to strengthen and confirm the sentiment which opposed it will continue to be useful and desirable so long as selfishness, cruelty, the lust of dominion, and indifference to the rights of the weak, the poor and the ignorant, have a place in the hearts of men. Looking at the trust established by the fourth article of this will as one for the moral education of the people only, the case is within the principle of those, already cited, in which charities for the relief of leprosy and the plague were held not to end with the disappearance of those diseases; and is not essentially different from that of Baliol College, in which a trust for the education at Oxford of Scotch youths, to be sent into Scotland to preach Episcopalianism in the established church there, was applied by Lords Somers and Hardwicke and their successors to educate such youths, although, by the change of faith and practice of the Church of Scotland, the donor's ultimate object could no longer be accomplished.

The intention of Francis Jackson to benefit the negro race appears not only in the leading clause of the fourth article, and in his expression of a hope that his trustees might receive the aid and the gifts of the friends of the slave, but in the trust for the benefit of fugitive slaves in the fifth article of the will, to which, according to the principle established by the house of lords in the case of *Betton's Charity*, resort may be had to ascertain his intent and the fittest mode of carrying it out. The negroes, although emancipated, still stand in great need of assistance and education. Charities for the relief of the poor have been often held to be well applied to educate them and their children. Bishop of Hereford v. Adams, 7 Ves. 324. Wilkinson v.

Malin, 2 Cr. and Jerv. 636, 2 Tyrwh. 544. Anderson v. Wrights of Glasgow, 12 Law Times, N.S., 807. The case of the *Mico Charity* is directly to the point that a gift for the redemption of poor slaves may be appropriated, after they have been emancipated by law, to educate them; and the reasons given by Lord Cottenham for that decision apply with no less force to those set free by the recent amendment of the Constitution in the United States, than to those who were emancipated by act of parliament in the West Indies.

The mode in which the funds bequeathed by the fourth and fifth articles of the will may be best applied to carry out in a lawful manner the charitable intents and purposes of the testator as nearly as possible must be settled by a scheme to be framed by a master and confirmed by the court before the funds are paid over to the trustees. In doing this, the court does not take the charity out of the hands of the trustees, but only declares the law which must be their guide in its administration. Shelford on Mortmain, 651–654. Boyle on Charities, 214–218. The case is therefore to be referred to a master with liberty to the attorney general and the trustees to submit schemes for his approval; and all further directions are reserved until the coming in of his report.

Case referred to a master. * * * [The master reported that the unexpended balance of the bequest in the fifth article was so small that it should be applied by the trustees to the use of necessitous persons of African descent in Boston and vicinity. The master recommended that the sum bequeathed in the fourth article be applied to the support of the New England Branch of the American Freedmen's Union Commission, since the intention nearest to that of emancipating the slaves was education of the slaves to render them capable of self government.] * * *

Final decree accordingly.

NOTE

The courts have developed several techniques for dealing with obsolescence in either the basic purpose of the charitable gift or the detailed plan for carrying out the basic purpose. The cy pres doctrine is the most notable of these techniques to keep the property responsive to changing social needs.[50] In some states, however, the cy pres doctrine was rejected at an early period or severely limited in scope by early decisions.[51] These states resort to a process of "liberal construction" of the trust document to achieve

50. See Fisch, The Cy Pres Doctrine in the United States (1950); 4 Powell, The Law of Real Property (Rohan Rev. 1970) ¶ 587; IV Scott, Trusts (3d Ed., 1967) §§ 395–400; DiClerico, "Cy Pres: A Proposal for Change" 47 B.U.L.Rev. 153 (1967); Peters, "A Decade of Cy Pres" 39 Temp.L.Q. 256 (1966); Comment, "The Girard Trust—Past, Present and Future", 20 Ala.L.Rev. 308 (1968); Chester, "Cy Pres: A Promise Unfulfilled", 54 Ind.L.J. 407 (1979); "Charitable Intent of Trust Settlor—Cy Pres Doctrine", 9 Am. Jur.P.O.F.2d 199 (1976); 67 A.L.R.3d 417 (1975); 67 A.L.R.3d 442 (1975).

51. Johnson v. Johnson, 92 Tenn. 559, 23 S.W. 114, 22 L.R.A. 179, 36 Am.St. Rep. 104 (1893); State Bank & Trust Co. v. Partridge, 198 Ky. 403, 248 S.W. 1056 (1923); Shields v. Harris, 190 N.C. 520, 130 S.E. 189 (1925). In some states cy pres is based on statute. E.g., Ala.Code Ann. § 19–3–301 (1975), Va.Code Ann. § 55–31 (1980 Supp.).

similar results.[52] Where the problem concerns impossible or impractical features of a detailed plan, rather than the basic purpose, there is no need to apply either cy pres or liberal construction, since a court of equity can always alter administrative detail in order to accomplish the basic trust purpose, whether the trust is charitable or private.[53]

Cy pres has been applied not only where the original purpose or scheme becomes outmoded, but also in the following situations:

(1) Where the scheme is impractical at the outset. Thus the settlor has given a sum of money to build a college library, but the sum is clearly inadequate for that purpose. The court may apply the fund cy pres to aid in construction of another building, or to add books to the college library's collection, for example.[54]

(2) Where the funds are in excess of the stated purpose. Thus a trust of real property is established to pay the salary of a minister of a particular church. Subsequently oil is discovered on the property, and income far exceeds the normal salary requirements. The court might accumulate the excess as a business reserve, or apply the excess for other church purposes or to support another minister in the same locality.[55]

(3) Where a gift is made to a charitable organization which either has ceased to exist or refuses to accept the gift. Thus, a testamentary gift is made to a named charitable organization, which for policy reasons refuses to accept the gift. The court should not let the gift fail but should name another oganization operating in the same charitable field.[56]

A court will not apply the doctrine if there is a valid express gift over upon failure of the original purpose,[57] nor is the doctrine applicable if the

52. Potter's Will, In re, 307 N.Y. 504, 121 N.E.2d 522 (1954).

53. First National Bank of Akron v. Unknown Heirs of Donnelly, 96 Ohio App. 509, 122 N.E.2d 672 (1954) (trust fund for establishment of a Catholic orphanage in one county given to Catholic orphanage in adjacent county to care for orphans of first county). See 57 A.L.R. 3d 1044 (1974).

54. See Ford v. Rockland Trust Co., 331 Mass. 25, 116 N.E.2d 669 (1954).

55. Petition of Lewis Pierce, 153 Me. 180, 136 A.2d 510 (1957) (fund for indigent seamen excessive due to successful investment); cf. Estate of Yetter, 183 Kan. 340, 328 P.2d 738 (1958).

56. Estate of Faulkner, 128 Cal.App. 2d 575, 275 P.2d 818 (1954) (gift to Alcoholics Anonymous refused, applied cy pres). Cf. First Portland National Bank v. Kaler-Vaill Memorial Home, 155 Me. 50, 151 A.2d 708 (1959), where gift to a non-existent Memorial Home failed and court refused to admit parol evidence to show intent of testator to establish such a charitable home during lifetime. Some states refused to apply cy pres to this situation and have enacted statutes as a result. See McKinney's N.Y., EPTL, § 8–1.1(d) (1980 Supp.).

57. In Nelson v. Kring, 225 Kan. 499, 592 P.2d 438 (1979), the testator left property in trust for the benefit of a hospital named for him which later ceased to operate. Testator had provided: "Should said Hospital fail to be operated as a hospital for any reason whatever for one year then said entire fund, with any accumulated interest or income from the same shall go and become the absolute property of my friend George Green of Little River, Kansas, or if he be dead then to his legal heirs. * * *" Another clause of the will stated that if any devise or bequest should be adjudged to be void then the sum which otherwise would have been disposed of should go to Green. The gift over to Green and his heirs if the hospital failed was held an executory interest and void under the Rule against Perpetuities. The intent of the testator was held specific, relying upon the character of the hospital gift and the private gift over even though the private gift was void. Treating the gift of void interests to Green as a residuary clause specialized to void or lapsed legacies, the court held that the void gift to Green created a resulting trust for the testator's estate and passed to Green or his heirs under the residuary clause. See, Board of Trustees of York College v. Cheney, 158 Neb. 292, 63 N.W.2d 177 (1954); Re-

court concludes that the settlor intended that the trust funds be used only for the specific purpose indicated.[58]

The few studies that have been made in this field indicate that the courts have been more anxious to adhere to the settlor's plan even when outmoded than to assure that the trust is serving modern social needs and conferring a benefit on the community.[59] Thus it must be virtually impossible to follow the donor's intent before a court will apply cy pres in some jurisdictions. This reluctance is but one facet of the general American policy of carrying out the settlor's intent. In Estate of McKee,[60] involving a testamentary scheme to set up a naval academy for poor colored male orphan children and poor white male orphans, the court refused to apply cy pres but postponed action for 5 years with directions to the trustee to try to gain outside financial support for the contemplated purpose.[61] Moreover, the nature of cy pres—requiring the court to stick "as near as" possible to the donor's intent or specific scheme—keeps the court from exercising free judgment as to a more desirable objective or a more modern scheme. Thus, where testator's will gave to the trustee $25,000 to erect and maintain a public library and the residue to use for organizations that look after the poor of the same city, the court refused to allow the trustee to transfer excess funds from the latter trust to enable the trustee to proceed with the library project, which would cost $75,000.[62]

The careful draftsman ought to foresee the problem of obsolescence, when he is creating an entity to last in perpetuity. He should provide some built-in provisions to keep the trust responsive to current social needs. Several devices are available:

(1) In some large cities a Community Trust has been established to receive and administer gifts from individuals, with control of expenditures vested in a board of trustees selected periodically to represent different interest groups within the community. Unless the donor restricts use of his gifts, the board can select purposes most beneficial to the community from time to time.[63]

statement, Second, Trusts § 399, Comment C; IV Scott, Trusts, sec. 399.2 (3d ed. 1967); Bogert Hornbook, Trusts 528 (5th Ed. 1973).

For an excellent discussion of cy pres see In re Rood Estate, 41 Mich.App. 405, 200 N.W.2d 728 (1972). The opinion in this case states on page 423: " * * * Thus in determining whether testator had a general or specific charitable intent, we must construe testator's will so as to avoid intestacy if at all possible. We must also make this determination in a manner which is consistent with the special favoritism which the law has toward a charitable gift or trust.

"In determining whether Rood's charitable intent is general or specific, the absence of a reverter clause or gift over in the event that the particular purpose fails is evidence of a general charitable intent. Similarly, a general charitable intent will be implied where the bulk of donor's property is given for charitable purposes. * * *"

58. Application of Syracuse University, 3 N.Y.2d 665, 171 N.Y.S.2d 545, 148 N.E.2d 671 (1958) (gift to Syracuse University Medical College held to fail when College was transferred to state university, on grounds that donor, a member of the Syracuse Medical College, intended to benefit only that particular school).

59. See Simes, Public Policy and the Dead Hand (1955) 127–131 and Appendix for an interesting study of the time-lag between social changes and judicial relief under cy pres in the management of the Franklin trust.

60. 378 Pa. 607, 108 A.2d 214 (1954).

61. For a similar case see Moore v. City and County of Denver, 133 Colo. 190, 292 P.2d 986 (1956).

62. First National Bank & Trust Co. v. First National Bank & Trust Co., 35 Del.Ch. 449, 121 A.2d 296 (1956).

63. Bogert, Trusts and Trustees (2d Ed., 1964) § 330.

(2) Where a trust is created, the trust document should state its charitable purpose in the broadest possible terms (unless the local jurisdiction is one of the few that requires a specific purpose) and manifest his general intent to favor charity by appropriate recitals, as well as set forth his specific purpose.[64] If the settlor desires to state a narrow purpose or spell out administrative details, the trustee should be given power to make alterations as to either purpose or detail. While the cy pres doctrine might achieve the same results as such a grant of power, the trustee would have to bring a lawsuit to obtain court approval, the cost to be borne out of the trust assets; and there is the possibility that a conservative court will refuse timely permission for a change.

(3) Where the corporate form is feasible, because the typical articles of incorporation are drawn in broad form, and the board of directors is charged with detail of management, there is no problem of obsolescence.

(4) Some donors, recognizing the limits of foresight and desiring to accomplish a significant impact within the immediate future, require the trustees to expend the principal, as well as the income, within a specified period such as 25 years.[65]

EVANS v. ABNEY

United States Supreme Court, 1970.
396 U.S. 435, 90 S.Ct. 628, 24 L.Ed.2d 634.[66]

* * *

MR. JUSTICE BLACK delivered the opinion of the Court.

Once again this Court must consider the constitutional implications of the 1911 will of United States Senator A. O. Bacon of Georgia which conveyed property in trust to Senator Bacon's home city of Macon for the creation of a public park for the exclusive use of the white people of that city. As a result of our earlier decision in this case which held that the park, Baconsfield, could not continue to be operated on a racially discriminatory basis, Evans v. Newton, 382 U. S. 296, 86 S.Ct. 486, 15 L.Ed.2d 373 (1966), the Supreme Court of Georgia ruled that Senator Bacon's intention to provide a park for whites only had become impossible to fulfill and that accordingly the trust had failed and the parkland and other trust property had reverted by operation of Georgia law to the heirs of the Senator. 224 Ga.

64. Consider the following sample clause: "I recognize that the particular use which should be made of the funds which may be available under this Trust can best be determined upon in view of the conditions existing at the time. I therefore express my present wishes for the use to be made of such fund, but do not make such disposition mandatory."

65. An outstanding example of such a "terminal" provision was the Children's Fund of Michigan established by Senator James Couzens. See Richards and Norton, Biography of a Foundation, 1929–1954 (1957).

66. Noted, 84 Harv. 54 (1970); 2 Loyola L.Rev. 390 (1971); 55 Marq.L. Rev. 511 (1972); 30 Md. 226 (1970); 22 Mercer 493 (1971); 42 Miss.L.J. 246 (1971); 35 Mo.L.Rev. 545 (1970); 16 N.Y. L.F. 448 (1970); 49 N.C.L.R. 148 (1970); 46 N.D. 399 (1971); 32 Ohio St.L.J. 181 (1971); 2 Rutgers, Camden, N.J. 390 (1970); 24 Sw.L.J. 417 (1970); 21 Syra.L. Rev. 1313 (1970); 5 Val.U.L.Rev. 172 (1970); Wash.U.L.Q. 485 (1971).

826, 165 S.E.2d 160 (1968). Petitioners, the same Negro citizens of Macon who have sought in the courts to integrate the park, contend that this termination of the trust violates their rights to equal protection and due process under the Fourteenth Amendment. We granted certiorari because of the importance of the questions involved. 394 U.S. 1012, 89 S.Ct. 1628, 23 L.Ed.2d 38 (1969). For the reasons to be stated, we are of the opinion that the judgment of the Supreme Court of Georgia should be, and it is, affirmed.

The early background to this litigation was summarized by Mr. Justice Douglas in his opinion for the Court in Evans v. Newton, 382 U.S., at 297–298, 86 S.Ct., at 487–488:

"In 1911 United States Senator Augustus O. Bacon executed a will that devised to the Mayor and Council of the City of Macon, Georgia, a tract of land which, after the death of the Senator's wife and daughters, was to be used as 'a park and pleasure ground' for white people only, the Senator stating in the will that while he had only the kindest feeling for the Negroes he was of the opinion that 'in their social relations the two races (white and negro) should be forever separate.' The will provided that the park should be under the control of a Board of Managers of seven persons, all of whom were to be white. The city kept the park segregated for some years but in time let Negroes use it, taking the position that the park was a public facility which it could not constitutionally manage and maintain on a segregated basis.

"Thereupon, individual members of the Board of Managers of the Park brought this suit in a state court against the City of Macon and the trustees of certain residuary beneficiaries of Senator Bacon's estate, asking that the city be removed as trustee and that the court appoint new trustees, to whom title to the park would be transferred. The city answered, alleging it could not legally enforce racial segregation in the park. The other defendants admitted the allegation and requested that the city be removed as trustee.

"Several Negro citizens of Macon intervened, alleging that the racial limitation was contrary to the laws and public policy of the United States, and asking that the court refuse to appoint private trustees. Thereafter the city resigned as trustee and amended its answer accordingly. Moreover, other heirs of Senator Bacon intervened and they and the defendants other than the city asked for reversion of the trust property to the Bacon estate in the event that the prayer of the petition were denied.

"The Georgia court accepted the resignation of the city as trustee and appointed three individuals as new trustees, finding it unnecessary to pass on the other claims of the heirs. On appeal by the Negro intervenors, the Supreme Court of Georgia affirmed, holding that Senator Bacon had the right to give and bequeath his property to a limited class, that charitable trusts are subject to supervision of a court of equity, and that the power to appoint new trustees so that the purpose of the trust would not fail was clear. 220 Ga. 280, 138 S.E.2d 573."

The Court in Evans v. Newton, supra, went on to reverse the judgment of the Georgia Supreme Court and to hold that the public character of Baconsfield "requires that it be treated as a public institution subject to the command of the Fourteenth Amendment, regardless of who now has title under state law." 382 U.S., at 302, 86 S.Ct., at 490. Thereafter, the Georgia Supreme Court interpreted this Court's reversal of its decision as requiring that Baconsfield be henceforth operated on a non-discriminatory basis. "Under these circumstances," the state high court held, "we are of the opinion that the sole purpose for which the trust was created has become impossible of accomplishment and has been terminated." Evans v. Newton, 221 Ga. 870, 148 S.E.2d 329 (1966). Without further elaboration of this holding, the case was remanded to the Georgia trial court to consider the motion of Guyton G. Abney and others, successor trustees of Senator Bacon's estate, for a ruling that the trust had become unenforceable and that accordingly the trust property had reverted to the Bacon estate and to certain named heirs of the Senator. The motion was opposed by petitioners and by the Attorney General of Georgia, both of whom argued that the trust should be saved by applying the *cy pres* doctrine to amend the terms of the will by striking the racial restrictions and opening Baconsfield to all the citizens of Macon without regard to race or color. The trial court, however, refused to apply *cy pres*. It held that the doctrine was inapplicable because the park's segregated, whites-only character was an essential and inseparable part of the testator's plan. Since the "sole purpose" of the trust was thus in irreconcilable conflict with the constitutional mandate expressed in our opinion in Evans v. Newton, the trial court ruled that the Baconsfield trust had failed and that the trust property had by operation of law reverted to the heirs of Senator Bacon. On appeal, the Supreme Court of Georgia affirmed.

We are of the opinion that in ruling as they did the Georgia courts did no more than apply well-settled general principles of Georgia law to determine the meaning and effect of a Georgia will. At the time Senator Bacon made his will and still today, Georgia cities and towns are authorized to accept devises of property for the establishment and preservation of "parks and pleasure grounds" and to hold the property thus received in charitable trust for the exclusive benefit of the class of persons named by the testator. Ga.Code Ann. c. 69–5 (1959); Ga.Code Ann. § 108–203, 207 (1959). These provisions of the Georgia Code explicitly authorized the testator to include, if he should choose, racial restrictions such as those found in Senator Bacon's will. The city accepted the trust with these restrictions in it. When this Court in Evans v. Newton, 382 U.S. 296, 86 S.Ct. 486, 15 L.Ed.2d 373 (1966), held that the continued operation of Baconsfield as a segregated park was unconstitutional, the particular purpose of the Baconsfield trust as stated in the will failed under Georgia law. The question then properly before the Georgia Supreme Court was whether as a matter of state law the doctrine of *cy pres* should be applied to prevent the trust itself from failing. Petitioners urged that the *cy pres* doctrine allowed the Georgia courts to strike the racially restrictive clauses in Bacon's will so that the terms of the trust could be fulfilled without violating the Constitution.

The Georgia *cy pres* statutes upon which petitioners relied provide:

> "When a valid charitable bequest is incapable for some reason of execution in the exact manner provided by the testator, donor, or founder, a court of equity will carry it into effect in such a way as will as nearly as possible effectuate his intention." Ga.Code Ann. § 108–202 (1959).
>
> "A devise or bequest to a charitable use will be sustained and carried out in this State; and in all cases where there is a general intention manifested by the testator to effect a certain purpose, and the particular mode in which he directs it to be done shall fail from any cause, a court of chancery may, by approximation, effectuate the purpose in a manner most similar to that indicated by the testator." Ga.Code Ann. § 113–815 (1959).

The Georgia courts have held that the fundamental purpose of these *cy pres* provisions is to allow the court to carry out the general charitable intent of the testator where this intent might otherwise be thwarted by the impossibility of the particular plan or scheme provided by the testator. Moss v. Youngblood, 187 Ga. 188, 200 S.E. 689 (1938). But this underlying logic of the *cy pres* doctrine implies that there is a certain class of cases in which the doctrine cannot be applied. Professor Scott in his treatise on trusts states this limitation on the doctrine of *cy pres* which is common to many States [67] as follows:

> "It is not true that a charitable trust never fails when it is impossible to carry out the particular purpose of the testator. In some cases * * * it appears that the accomplishment of the particular purpose and only that purpose was desired by the testator and that he had no more general charitable intent and that he would presumably have preferred to have the whole trust fail if the particular purpose is impossible of accomplishment. In such a case the *cy pres* doctrine is not applicable." IV Scott, Trusts § 399, at 3085 (1967).

In this case, Senator Bacon provided an unusual amount of information in his will from which the Georgia courts could determine the limits of his charitable purpose. Immediately after specifying that the park should be for "the sole, perpetual and unending use, benefit and enjoyment of the white women, white girls, white boys and white children of the City of Macon," the Senator stated that "the said property under no circumstances * * * (is) to be * * * at any

67. See e.g., First Universalist Society of Bath v. Swett, 148 Me. 142, 90 A.2d 812 (1953); LaFond v. City of Detroit, 357 Mich. 362, 98 N.W.2d 530 (1959). [Footnotes 67 and 68 are by the Court—Ed.]

time for any reason devoted to any other purpose or use excepting so far as herein specifically authorized." And the Senator continued:

> "* * * I take occasion to say that in limiting the use and enjoyment of the property perpetually to white people, I am not influenced by an unkindness of feeling or want of consideration for the Negroes, or colored people. On the contrary I have for them the kindest feeling, and for many of them esteem and regard, while for some of them I have sincere personal affection.
>
> "I am however, without hesitation in the opinion that in their social relations the two races should be forever separate and that they should not have pleasure or recreation grounds to be used or enjoyed, together and in common."

The Georgia courts, construing Senator Bacon's will as a whole, Yerbey v. Chandler, 194 Ga. 263, 21 S.E.2d 636 (1942), concluded from this and other language in the will that the Senator's charitable intent was not "general" but extended only to the establishment of a segregated park for the benefit of white people. The Georgia trial court found that "Senator Bacon could not have used language more clearly indicating his intent that the benefits of Baconsfield should be extended to white persons only, or more clearly indicating that this limitation was an essential and indispensable part of his plan for Baconsfield." App., at 519. Since racial separation was found to be an inseparable part of the testator's intent, the Georgia court held that the State's *cy pres* doctrine could not be used to alter the will to permit racial integration. See Ford v. Thomas, 111 Ga. 493, 36 S.E. 841 (1900); Adams v. Bass, 18 Ga. 130 (1855). The Baconsfield trust was therefore held to have failed, and, under Georgia law, "[w]here a trust is expressly created, but [its] uses * * * fail from any cause, a resulting trust is implied for the benefit of the grantor, or testator, or his heirs." Ga.Code Ann. § 108–106(4) (1959).[68] The Georgia courts concluded, in effect, that Senator Bacon would have rather had the whole trust fail than have Baconsfield integrated.

68. Although Senator Bacon's will did not contain an express provision granting a reverter to any party should the trust fail, § 108–106(4) of the Georgia Code quoted in the text makes such an omission irrelevant under state law. At one point in the Senator's will he did grant "all remainders and reversions" to the city of Macon, but the Supreme Court of Georgia showed in its opinion that this language did not relate in any way to what should happen upon a failure of the trust but was relevant only to the initial vesting of the property in the city. The Georgia court said:

> "Senator Bacon devised a life estate in the trust property to his wife and two daughters, and the language pointed out by the intervenors appears in the following provision of the will: 'When my wife, Virginia Lamar Bacon and my two daughters, Mary Louise Bacon Sparks and Augusta Lamar Bacon Curry, shall all have departed this life, and immediately upon the death of the last survivor of them, it is my will that all right, title and interest in and to said property hereinbefore described and bounded, both legal and equitable, including all remainders and reversions and every estate in the same of whatsoever kind, shall thereupon vest in and belong to the Mayor and Council of the City of Macon, and to their successors forever, in trust etc.' This language concerned remainders and reversions prior to the vesting of the legal title in the City of Macon, as trustee, and not to remainders and reversions occurring because of a failure of the trust, which Senator Bacon apparently did not contemplate, and for which he made no provision." 165 S.E. 2d 160, 165 (1968).

When a city park is destroyed because the Constitution required it to be integrated, there is reason for everyone to be disheartened. We agree with petitioners that in such a case it is not enough to find that the state court's result was reached through the application of established principles of state law. No state law or act can prevail in the face of contrary federal law, and the federal courts must search out the fact and truth of any proceeding or transaction to determine if the Constitution has been violated. Presbyterian Church in United States v. Hull Church, 393 U.S. 440, 89 S.Ct. 601, 21 L.Ed.2d 658 (1969); New York Times v. Sullivan, 376 U.S. 254, 84 S.Ct. 710, 11 L.Ed.2d 686 (1964). Here, however, the action of the Georgia Supreme Court declaring the Baconsfield trust terminated presents no violation of constitutionally protected rights, and any harshness that may have resulted from the State court's decision can be attributed solely to its intention to effectuate as nearly as possible the explicit terms of Senator Bacon's will.

Petitioners first argue that the action of the Georgia court violates the United States Constitution in that it imposes a drastic "penalty," the "forfeiture" of the park, merely because of the city's compliance with the constitutional mandate expressed by this Court in Evans v. Newton. Of course, Evans v. Newton did not speak to the problem of whether Baconsfield should or could continue to operate as a park; it held only that its continued operation as a park had to be without racial discrimination. But petitioners now want to extend that holding to forbid the Georgia courts from closing Baconsfield on the ground that such a closing would penalize the city and its citizens for complying with the Constitution. We think, however, that the will of Senator Bacon and Georgia law provide all the justification necessary for imposing such a "penalty." The construction of wills is essentially a state-law question. Lyeth v. Hoey, 305 U.S. 188, 59 S.Ct. 155, 83 L.Ed. 119 (1938), and in this case the Georgia Supreme Court, as we read its opinion, interpreted Senator Bacon's will as embodying a preference for termination of the park rather than its integration. Given this, the Georgia court had no alternative under its relevant trust laws, which are long standing and neutral with regard to race, but to end the Baconsfield trust and return the property to the Senator's heirs.

A second argument for petitioners stresses the similarities between this case and the case in which a city holds an absolute fee simple title to public park and then closes that park of its own accord solely to avoid the effect of a prior court order directing that the park be integrated as the Fourteenth Amendment commands. Yet, assuming *arguendo* that the closing of the park would in those circumstances violate the Equal Protection Clause, that case would be clearly distinguishable from the case at bar because there it is the State and not a private party which is injecting the racially discriminatory motivation. In the case at bar there is not the slightest indication that any of the Georgia judges involved were motivated by racial animus or discriminatory intent of any sort in construing and enforcing Senator Bacon's will. Nor is there any indication that Senator Bacon in drawing up his will was persuaded or induced to include racial restrictions by the fact that such restrictions were permitted by the Georgia trust statutes. *Ante,* at 630. On the contrary, the language of the Senator's will shows that the racial restrictions were solely the product of the testator's own full-blown social philosophy. Similarly, the situation presented in this case is also easily distinguishable from that presented in Shelley v. Kraemer, 334 U.S. 1, 68 S.Ct. 836, 92 L. Ed. 1161 (1948), where we held unconstitutional state judicial action which had affirmatively enforced a private scheme of discrimination against Negroes. Here the effect of the Georgia decision eliminated all discrimination against Negroes in the park by eliminating the park itself, and the termination of the park was a loss shared equally by the white and Negro citizens of Macon since both races would have enjoyed a constitutional right of equal access to the park's facilities had it continued.

Petitioners also contend that since Senator Bacon did not expressly provide for a reverter in the event that the racial restrictions of the trust failed, no one can know with absolute certainty that the Senator would have preferred termination of the park rather than its integration, and the decision of the Georgia court therefore involved a matter of choice. It might be difficult to argue with these assertions if they stood alone, but then petitioners conclude: "Its [the court's] choice, the anti-Negro choice, violates the Fourteenth Amendment, whether it be called a 'guess,' an item in 'social philosophy,' or anything else at all." We do not understand petitioners to be contending here that the Georgia judges were motivated either consciously or unconsciously by a desire to discriminate against Negroes. In any case, there is, as noted above, absolutely nothing before this Court to support a finding of such motivation. What remains of petitioners' argument is the idea that the Georgia courts had a constitutional obligation in this case to resolve any doubt about the testator's intent in favor of preserving the trust. Thus stated, we see no merit in the argument. The only choice the Georgia courts either had or exercised in this regard was their judicial judgment in construing Bacon's will to determine his intent, and the Constitution imposes no requirement upon the Georgia court to approach Bacon's will any differently than it would approach any will creating any charitable trust of any kind. Surely the Fourteenth Amendment is not violated where, as here, a state court operating in its judicial capacity fairly applies its normal principles of construction to determine the testator's true intent in establishing a charitable trust and then reaches a conclusion with regard to that intent which, because of the operation of neutral and non-discriminatory state trust laws, effectively denies everyone, whites as well as Negroes, the benefits of the trust.

Another argument made by petitioners is that the decision of the Georgia court holding that the Baconsfield trust had "failed" must rest logically on the unspoken premise that the presence or proximity of Negroes in Baconsfield would destroy the desirability of the park for whites. This argument reflects a rather fundamental misunderstanding of Georgia law. The Baconsfield trust "failed" under that law not because of any belief on the part of any living person that whites and Negroes might not enjoy being together but, rather, because Senator Bacon who died many years ago intended that the park remain forever for the exclusive use of white people.

Petitioners also advance a number of considerations of public policy in opposition to the conclusion which we have reached. In particular, they regret, as we do, the loss of the Baconsfield trust to the City of Macon, and they are concerned lest we set a precedent under which other charitable trusts will be terminated. It bears repeating that our holding today reaffirms the traditional role of the States in determining whether or not to apply their *cy pres* doctrines to particular trusts. Nothing we have said here prevents a state court from applying its *cy pres* rule in a case where the Georgia court, for example, might not apply its rule. More fundamentally, however, the loss of charitable trusts such as Baconsfield is part of the price we pay for permitting deceased persons to exercise a continuing control over assets owned by them at death. This aspect of freedom of testation, like most things, has its advantages and disadvantages. The responsibility of this Court, however, is to construe and enforce the Constitution and laws of the land as they are and not to legislate social policy on the basis of our own personal inclinations.

In their lengthy and learned briefs, the petitioners and the Solicitor General as *amicus curiae* have advanced several arguments which we have not here discussed. We have carefully examined each of these arguments, however, and find all to be without merit.

The judgment is affirmed.

MR. JUSTICE MARSHALL took no part in the consideration or decision of this case.

[Dissenting opinions of MR. JUSTICE DOUGLAS and MR. JUSTICE BRENNAN are omitted.]

NOTE

For many years there was no questioning of features of charitable gifts which restricted the benefits to a limited group, thereby excluding those who did not qualify for the group. Thus it was common to find trusts for scholarships to persons of a particular ethnic or racial group or to persons belonging to a particular religious faith. Currently such restrictions are being widely challenged as discriminatory. The problem is not easily solved. The discrimination may be viewed as "benign" discrimination and sustained on this basis. Thus in Trustees of University of Delaware v. Gebelein, 420 A.2d 1191 (Del.Ch.1980) a trust providing a scholarship fund restricted to women was held designed to assist financially poor women who would otherwise be denied equal educational opportunity at the college level and compensation for past discrimination. The Trustees of the University were permitted to administer the trust with the restriction to females.

Since the ruling in Shelley v. Kraemer[69] extended the scope of the Fourteenth Amendment to embrace certain state action which may be involved in enforcement of private kinds of discrimination, there has been a slow growth in the scope of the constitutional doctrine. Is a college or university which is not supported by state funds but which receives the benefits of state tax exemption and is accredited and regulated by state educational authorities a "private" or a "public" entity? Are its acts in excluding enrollment of a Black "state action" within the constitutional prohibition? Is every charitable trust within the scope of the constitutional limitation because a state officer, the Attorney General, is the enforcing party? Or are certain kinds of charities more public than others, requiring inclusion of the entire public within the scope of their benefits in order to be considered charitable?

In the cases in which a private trustee has been substituted for a city or other public instrumentality in administering a charitable trust to avoid the Fourteenth Amendment prohibition based on state action, this method of avoidance has proven unsuccessful.[70] Indeed, there is an open question whether some or all charitable trusts are part of the public sector of our economy and involve state action through their enforcement.[71]

Often the managing body of the charitable entity voluntarily reaches a policy decision against discriminatory provisions.[72] This then presents a problem of trust law. Does refusal to enforce discriminatory provisions nullify prior transfers of property which were given to the charity subject to such conditions? Can the condition itself be excised from the gift on the theory that it is an "illegal" condition, leaving the gift itself valid, as was done in Matter of Liberman, in Chapter VIII, Section 3? Can cy pres be used to permit continued use of the trust property for the general charitable purpose (education, public recreation, etc.) but without the specific discriminatory provision? Some courts have indicated a willingness to find a general charitable intent and apply cy pres if the donor has not made the discriminatory provision an express condition or very clearly manifested his intent that the property be applied solely in the discriminatory manner.[73]

69. 334 U.S. 1, 68 S.Ct. 836, 92 L.Ed. 1161, 3 A.L.R.2d 441 (1948); See 25 A.L. R.3d 736 (1969).

70. For a history of the course of the litigation concerning the provision in the will of Stephen Girard, see Commonwealth of Pennsylvania v. Brown, 392 F. 2d 120 (3d Cir. 1968), cert. den. 391 U.S. 921 (1968).

71. See the reasoning of Mr. Justice White concurring in Evans v. Newton, 382 U.S. 296, 86 S.Ct. 486, 15 L.Ed.2d 373 (1966), noted 14 Kan.L.Rev. 613, 10 St.L. U.L.J. 576, 19 Vand.L.Rev. 939 (1966). But see First National Bank of Kansas City v. Danforth, 523 S.W.2d 808 (Mo. 1975), noted 1975 Wash.U.L.Q. 1111; cert. den. 421 U.S. 992 (1975).

72. See Comment, 1963 Wis.L.Rev. 254.

73. Howard Savings Institution v. Trustees of Amherst College, 61 N.J. Super. 119, 160 A.2d 177 (Ch.Div.1960), 61 Colum.L.Rev. 111 (1961) (where testator made a gift to Amherst College as a scholarship fund "for deserving American born, Protestant, Gentile boys of good moral repute" and the College adopted a resolution refusing to accept the gift if restricted in use on such a discriminatory basis, held that cy pres could be applied to give the fund to the College without the limitation, rather than to another school to administer according to the discriminatory restriction). In LaFond v. City of Detroit, 357 Mich. 362, 98 N.W.2d 530 (1959), the Supreme Court of Michigan divided on application of cy pres to save a testamentary gift to the city for a playfield for white children," the city having agreed to accept the gift if the court construed the will to permit operation of the playfield without regard to race, color, or creed; since the lower court had refused to apply cy pres, the divided vote in the Supreme Court sustained the lower court. See, DiClerico,

Where the trustees decide to eliminate a discriminatory feature contary to the original trust document, and no objection is made by the Attorney General, there may well be no one with standing to raise the issue.[74] See the discussion of this problem in Section 6.

SECTION 5. CHARITABLE CORPORATIONS

ST. JOSEPH'S HOSPITAL v. BENNETT

Court of Appeals of New York, 1939.
281 N.Y. 115, 22 N.E.2d 305, 130 A.L.R. 1092.[75]

FINCH, J. This is an appeal from an order of the Appellate Division of the Supreme Court, fourth department, affirming a declaratory judgment of the Supreme Court at Special Term, Onondaga county, granting the relief prayed for in the complaint. The Supreme Court denied defendant appellant's motion for a dismissal of the complaint after issue had been joined, and granted plaintiff's motion for judgment on the pleadings.

Plaintiff is a charitable corporation which operates a hospital in Syracuse. It received and accepted a bequest under the following clause of the will of one George Doheny, deceased: "*Seventh:* All the rest, residue and remainder of my estate, both real and personal, I give, devise and bequeath to St. Joseph Hospital, the Syracuse Memorial Hospital, the House of Providence, St. Vincents Asylum and School (Madison St.), the Syracuse Free Dispensary, the Syracuse Homeopathic Hospital, St. Mary's Maternity Hospital and Infants Asylum, the Onondaga Orphans Home and the Syracuse Home Associa-

"Cy Pres: A Proposal for Change, 47 B.U.L.Rev. 153 (1967); Nelkin, "Cy Pres and the Fourteenth Amendment: A Discriminatory Look at Very Private Schools and Not so Charitable Trusts", 56 Geo.L.J. 272 (1967); Comment, "Trusts: Application of Cy Pres to Remove Discriminatory Racial and Religious Restrictions from a Charitable Trust", 20 Okla.L.Rev. 101 (1967); 25 A.L.R.3d 736 (1968).

74. In Coffee v. William Marsh Rice University, 387 S.W.2d 132 (Tex.Civ.App. 1965), a group of alumni of Rice University opposed admission of applicants without regard to color; they were denied standing to object either as beneficiaries under the original trust indenture or as contributors to the University endowment fund. In Coffee v. William Marsh Rice University, 408 S.W.2d 269 (Tex.Civ.App.1966), noted 10 So.Tex.L.J. 52 (1968), the action of a lower court in applying the cy pres power to allow the charging of tuition and the acceptance of qualified applicants without regard to color was sustained. Can the state Attorney General constitutionally oppose admission of students without regard to race if the trust contains a discriminatory provision but the trustees propose to adopt a different policy?

75. Noted, 19 B.U.L.R. 655 (1939); 18 Chi.-Kent L.Rev. 325 (1940); 40 Col.L. Rev. 550 (1940); 53 Harv.L.Rev. 327 (1939); 23 Minn.L.Rev. 670 (1939); 17 N.Y.U.L.Q.Rev. 275 (1940). See Blackwell, "The Charitable Corporation and the Charitable Trust", 24 Wash.U.L.Q. 1 (1938); Lincoln, "A Question on Gifts to Charitable Corporations", 25 Va.L.Rev. 764 (1939); Taylor, "A New Chapter in the New York Law of Charitable Corporations", 25 Corn.L.Q. 382 (1940); 64 Harv.L.Rev. 1168 (1951).

tion (commonly known as the Old Ladies Home) all of Syracuse, N. Y., share and share alike, one-ninth to each to be held as an endowment fund and the income used for the ordinary expenses of maintenance."

Plaintiff's share has been kept separate and intact and, at the time of this action, consisted of personal property valued at $147,932.93. The income from the fund has been used to meet "the ordinary expenses of maintenance" of the institution. The real estate of plaintiff is encumbered by a mortgage of $175,000. By this action, plaintiff sought authorization to apply the fund in partial payment of the mortgage debt or in its judgment to use the principal of the fund for objects within its corporate powers other than meeting the ordinary expenses of maintenance. The Attorney-General opposed on the grounds that the bequest was a gift in trust, that the intention of the testator was to create a perpetual fund, the income from which was to be used for the ordinary expenses of maintaining the plaintiff institution, and that any use of the principal or any other use of the income would be a violation of the testator's intention and of the fiduciary duties of plaintiff. The declaratory judgment, which was affirmed by a divided court in the Appellate Division, held that the bequest to plaintiff did not create a trust but an absolute gift, and that the plaintiff need not maintain the gift intact as an endowment fund but that it could use the income and principal of said fund for any of its corporate purposes, in particular toward the discharge of the mortgage on its property.

In the case at bar it is practically conceded that the language of the bequest shows the intention of the testator that his gift be held as a permanent fund. The testator has coupled in one sentence gifts to charitable corporations and a statement that each gift is "to be held as an endowment fund and the income used for the ordinary expenses of maintenance." The gift and the statement of its purpose cannot be separated, one from the other. Not only was there an express direction that the principal be held, but this direction was fortified by the use of the words "endowment fund." The term "endowment" has been defined as the bestowment of money as a permanent fund, the income of which is to be used in the administration of a proposed work. In still further restriction, direction is given to use only the income. Giving to these plain words their ordinary meaning, the intention of the testator is clear to direct the holding of a permanent fund, the income of which is to be used in the administration of the work. Though these words may not avail to create a legal trust, they furnish a direction and restriction upon the use of the gift. No different result is reached through the application of the rule of construction that where language employed in a will looks in the first place towards a gift without restrictions, such gift cannot be cut down by later words unless these later words express as clear an intention to cut down the gift as the former do to make the gift. In this case the later words are of equal force with the former and are free from ambiguity.

The question here presented is whether the clearly expressed direction of the testator must be obeyed. The answer to that question does not depend upon whether the gift was absolute or created a trust, or whether the testator annexed a direction or a technical condition to the gift. The authorities sustain the validity of the direction of the testator, and equity will afford protection to a donor to a charitable corporation in that the Attorney-General may maintain a suit to compel the property to be held for the charitable purpose for which it was given to the corporation. Restatement of the Law of Trusts, vol. 2, ch. 11, p. 1093. Nothing in authority, statute or public policy has been brought to our attention which prevents a testator from leaving his money to a charitable corporation and having his clearly expressed intention enforced. In the case at bar, no question is raised as to the reasonableness or propriety of the restriction.

The Legislature, many years ago, enacted statutes providing for the incorporation of charitable corporations and permitting such corporations to hold funds in perpetuity. The statute against perpetuities never applied to gifts to such corporations. "The corporate body is legally immortal; and it is the very nature of contributions to it, to withdraw the subject of them from every kind of circulation; their manifest object being to sustain continually the charitable or religious institutions, in carrying out their pious or benevolent designs." Williams v. Williams, 8 N.Y. 525, 534. In the same case it was also held that the statute of perpetuities did not apply to gifts to individuals upon charitable trusts, and that courts of equity might give effect to a devise or bequest for charitable uses, although defective, for the want of a grantee or donee capable of taking. That doctrine was later rejected by this court in Holmes v. Mead, 52 N.Y. 332, but the principle that a charitable corporation might take an absolute gift to be held in perpetuity for purposes prescribed by its charter was expressly approved.

In considering the effect of the cases thereafter decided by this court, the distinction drawn in Holmes v. Mead must be kept in mind. Gifts in perpetuity to a corporation, the income to be applied to any of its corporate purposes, were valid, though such gifts to a corporation upon a general charitable trust and not for its own benefit, were invalid. The courts thereafter gave to wills whenever possible a construction which would sustain the charitable gift rather than render it invalid. In the absence of language requiring other construction, a gift to a charitable corporation was construed as a gift to the corporation not in trust for others but a gift in perpetuity for a corporate purpose. The rule of construction has been followed even after the Tilden Act (L.1893, ch. 701, now Real Property Law, Consol.Laws, ch. 50, § 113, Personal Property Law, Consol.Laws, ch. 41, § 12) would have saved the charitable gift. We should not now abandon that rule, but even when the courts found that a gift to a charitable corporation for a corporate purpose was an "absolute" gift and not a trust, they also indicated that directions in regard to the manner in which the gift was to be held and used would be enforced.

* * * [Omitted is the court's discussion of earlier New York cases.] * * *

It is submitted that when the opinions in these cases are read as a whole, they merely decided that gifts to a charitable corporation, though subject to enforceable restrictions, do not create a trust in the legal sense. In Bird v. Merklee, supra, the gift was attacked on the ground that it was invalid because it created a trust with no defined beneficiary, and the court held only that it was not a trust but a gift to a corporation for a single corporate purpose which the corporation *must* carry out. In Matter of Griffin, 167 N.Y. 71, 60 N.E. 284, the only question was whether a gift to a corporation of a fund with instructions to maintain the principal intact and to use the income for a specific purpose within the corporate powers, but which the corporation promoted through a subsidiary or related corporation, created a trust for the subsidiary corporation or whether the corporation which received the principal might use the income if it saw fit to carry out that purpose itself. Though the court held that no trust for the subsidiary corporation was created, the reason for the holding is that the instructions might be carried out without creating a trust. The question in the case of Matter of Durand, 194 N.Y. 477, 87 N.E. 677, was similar. The gift there was to the trustees of the University of Rochester and their successors, to be held by them as a "perpetual fund" and the income to be used for "female education of high grade in the city of Rochester, and under the management of the Trustees of said university" 194 N.Y. at page 479, 87 N.E. at page 677. The decision of the court was that the gift was intended as a gift to the University of Rochester for one of its corporate purposes. It is noteworthy that far from intimating that the university was not bound to carry out the direction, the court reached its decision that the gift was intended as a gift to the corporation and not as a trust because, it is clear, so the court said, that the testator "had in mind the university itself as the *lasting and unchanging beneficiary*, which would receive his property and carry out his purposes, which were of no *temporary* character." 94 N.Y. at page 484, 87 N.E. at page 678. (Italics not in original.) The testator in his will required that there be express acceptance of the terms of the gift. The court said that the terms of the bequest would be binding without express acceptance. The testator "was a layman, and erroneously he may have deemed it necessary that the beneficiary, being a corporation, should signify that acceptance which the law implied in order to make his bequest effective, or he may have desired to procure from the university a formal, though unnecessary, acceptance of his bounty, in order that it might seem the more fully to be bound by the wishes which accompanied such bounty." 194 N.Y. at page 485, 87 N.E. at page 679.

The case of Sherman v. Richmond Hose Co., 230 N.Y. 462, 130 N.E. 613, again illustrates the same rule. The gift was absolute for a corporate purpose. It was not a trust in a technical sense. None the less the court held that the corporation could not divert the fund from its purpose. No authority has been brought to our attention that a gift to a charitable corporation with the express direction that it be applied to a specific corporate purpose in a specific manner may be accepted by the corporation, and then used for a different corporate purpose in a different manner. No trust arises, it is true, in a technical sense, from such a gift for trustee and beneficiary are one. The charitable corporation is not bound by all the limitations and rules which apply to a technical trustee. It may not, however, receive a gift made for one purpose and use it for another, unless the court applying the cy pres doctrine so commands.

It follows that the judgments should be reversed and judgment directed for the defendant, without costs.

* * * [The dissenting opinion of HUBBS, J., is omitted.]
* * * [76]

IN RE LOS ANGELES COUNTY PIONEER SOCIETY

Supreme Court of California, in Bank, 1953.
40 Cal.2d 852, 257 P.2d 1.

TRAYNOR, JUSTICE. Los Angeles County Pioneer Society and Harry Lelande, a member thereof, appeal separately from an order appointing the Historical Society of Southern California trustee of all property in the possession of Pioneer. The order was entered after the trial court determined that Pioneer held its property for charitable purposes, that Pioneer had repudiated its trust, and that appointment of Historical as trustee was necessary to carry out the purposes of the trust. We have concluded that the order is amply supported by the evidence and must be affirmed.

Pioneer was founded in 1897 as an unincorporated association of pioneers living in Los Angeles County, with about 600 members. In 1910 the members incorporated as a non-profit corporation. Over the years membership decreased until in 1941 there were less than 100 members. In that year and later years Mrs. Emma Stoltenberg, a member of Pioneer, made substantial gifts to Pioneer and on her death in 1946 left additional sums to Pioneer by will. Her gifts amounted to about $53,000. The money was used to purchase a building that was used for meetings of Pioneer and rented for commercial purposes. The membership continued to decrease and in 1948 the members decided to dissolve the corporation, distribute the assets among themselves, and continue the organization as an unincorporated association to carry out the purposes of the articles of incorporation.

To determine whether its assets were impressed with a trust, Pioneer filed an action for declaratory relief against a member of the society. On June 1, 1949, judgment was entered declaring that no

76. Accord that a gift to a nonprofit corporation for a charitable purpose is enforceable by the Attorney General although the gift does not create a trust in the technical sense: Estate of Berry, 29 Wis.2d 506, 139 N.W.2d 72 (1966).

trust of any kind was impressed upon the assets. Thereafter the membership, by a petition signed by 53 of the 58 members, agreed to dissolve the corporation. The assets were converted to cash and, since the property owned by the corporation had greatly appreciated in value, $95,243.54 was realized. Pioneer then petitioned the superior court for judicial supervision of the dissolution. Corp.Code § 4607. Several members of Pioneer objected to the dissolution. Pursuant to stipulation of the parties, the Attorney General filed a petition in intervention, alleging that Pioneer held its assets in trust and praying that a new trustee be appointed on the ground that Pioneer had abandoned its trust. The court ordered that the assets be impounded. On May 19, 1950, the court entered judgment that Pioneer was a charitable corporation, that its assets were dedicated to charitable purposes, that it had abandoned its trust and was threatening to divert the assets to the private benefit of its members, and that appointment of a new trustee was necessary. The judgment was entitled "interlocutory judgment" and the court retained jurisdiction to make such further orders as were necessary to a complete determination of the action. Pioneer did not appeal. On October 18, 1950, after a further hearing, the court appointed Historical trustee and ordered the impounded assets turned over to it. The present appeals are from this order.

The first question presented is whether the trial court correctly determined that all of the assets of Pioneer were given and received for charitable purposes and held by Pioneer for those purposes.

Pioneer contends that the declaratory relief judgment is res judicata as to the question whether Pioneer holds its assets for charitable purposes, and characterizes the opposition to the dissolution proceedings as a collateral attack on the former adjudication, relying upon City of San Diego v. Superior Court, 36 Cal.2d 483, 224 P.2d 685. Historical, on the other hand, contends that the declaratory relief action was collusive and a fraud on the court, pointing out that all evidence therein was presented by stipulation, that Pioneer paid the attorneys' fees for both plaintiff and defendant in that action, and that the two opposing attorneys subsequently joined forces and together represented Pioneer at the trial of the dissolution proceedings. See Guardianship of Jacobson, 30 Cal.2d 326, 333, 182 P.2d 545. It is unnecessary to pass upon Historical's contention, since the declaratory relief judgment is res judicata only against persons who were parties or in privity with parties thereto. Restatement, Judgments, § 77; Bernhard v. Bank of America, 19 Cal.2d 807, 813, 122 P.2d 892; City and County of Denver v. Denver Land Co., 85 Colo. 198, 201, 274 P. 743. The Attorney General was not a party to the declaratory relief action and was not in privity with parties thereto and, accordingly, he was not bound by that adjudication and was free to contend in the dissolution proceedings that Pioneer held its assets for charitable purposes.

* * *

Since neither the declaratory relief judgment nor the May 19th judgment settled the issue whether Pioneer held its assets for chari-

table purposes, the determinative question is whether subtantial evidence supports the order of October 18th. The articles of incorporation of Pioneer provide: "That the purpose for which this corporation is formed is to cultivate social intercourse and friendship among its members, to collect and preserve data touching the early history of Los Angeles County and the State of California, to collect and preserve articles, specimens and material things illustrative or demonstrative of the customs, modes and habits of the aforesaid times in said State; to perpetuate the memory of those who, by their labors and heroism, contributed to make the history of said County and State; and in furtherance of said purpose [to do all acts] necessary and convenient for the promotion of the aforesaid purpose; and to exist as a social corporation under the provisions of the laws of the State of California, covering such corporations, and not for pecuniary profit." In Pioneer's answer to the petition in intervention it is alleged that between 1945 and 1950 Pioneer engaged in acquiring material concerning the pioneers and founders of Los Angeles County and the State of California; that Pioneer perpetuated the memory of those who by their labors and heroism contributed to make the history of the County and the State; that the members attended a meeting at the Biltmore Hotel in 1948 to honor the memory of the dead pioneers during the discovery of gold in California; that Pioneer participated in the erection of a plaque at Inglewood, California, to mark the site of the first school building in Inglewood; that Pioneer held four picnics at which time the memory of the former pioneers and founders of Los Angeles County were commemorated; that in 1947 Pioneer celebrated the 166th anniversary of the founding of the City of Los Angeles and the members dressed in costumes of the Spanish period; that at the monthly meetings talks and discussions were held recollecting the activities and labors of the pioneers and their memories were perpetuated and honored; and that many further and additional activities were engaged in pursuant to the purposes set forth in the articles of incorporation.

The commemoration of historical events and the collection and preservation of data of historical interest are for the educational and recreational benefit of the community as a whole and are recognized charitable purposes. Restatement, Trusts, § 374; Estate of Butin, 81 Cal.App.2d 76, 81, 183 P.2d 304; Centennial & Memorial Association of Valley Forge, 235 Pa. 206, 211, 83 A. 683; Steenis v. Appleton, 230 Wis. 530, 533, 284 N.W. 492; Missouri Historical Society v. Academy of Science, 94 Mo. 459, 466, 8 S.W. 346, 12 A.L.R.2d 888–896. By the allegations in its answer, Pioneer conceded that it was actively engaged in carrying out such objectives. Even if the concessions in the answer are disregarded, the articles of incorporation supply sufficient evidence to sustain the action of the trial court. It may be assumed that if the only purpose of Pioneer were "to cultivate social intercourse and friendship among its members" it would not be a charitable corporation, see 2 Bogert, Trusts and Trustees, § 380, and cases cited therein, but it is clear from a reading of the articles as a whole that the social purposes of Pioneer are incidental to its public and charitable purposes. Since members of a charitable organization often participate in its activities with the object of making new friends and participating in pleasurable group activities in the course of carrying out the charitable purposes of the organization, the incidental social activities of Pioneer do not deprive it of its charitable character. See Young v. Boy Scouts of America, 9 Cal.App.2d 760, 764, 51 P.2d 191; Estate of Wirt, 124 Cal.App. 7, 11, 12 P.2d 95. * * *

Pioneer contends that the gifts of Mrs. Stoltenberg were for the benefit of the members of Pioneer personally and were not received for charitable purposes. Her will provided: "the Balance of my estate to be given to the Pioneer Society Meeting at the Biltmore Hotel." The gifts during her lifetime were subject to an oral understanding that the money would be used to purchase a permanent home for the society. Pioneer erroneously assumes that the gift could not be for charitable purposes unless the instrument of gift expressly so provided. "[A] devise to a society organized for a charitable purpose without a declaration of the use to which the gift is to be put is given in trust to carry out the objects for which the organization was created." Estate of Clippinger, 75 Cal.App.2d 426, 433, 171 P.2d 567, 572; Estate of McDole, 215 Cal. 328, 332, 10 P.2d 75. Similarly, in the present case the gift of Mrs. Stoltenberg in her will was for the purposes expressed in Pioneer's articles, and the gifts during her lifetime were for a building to be used to carry out those purposes.

The conclusion that Pioneer held its assets for charitable purposes disposes of Pioneer's contention that the trial court should not have allowed the Attorney General to become a party to the dissolution proceedings. The Attorney General is a necessary party to proceedings affecting the disposition of assets of a charitable trust, People ex rel. Ellert v. Cogswell, 113 Cal. 129, 136, 45 P. 270, 35 L.R.A. 269; Society of Cal. Pioneers v. McElroy, 63 Cal.App.2d 332, 342, 146 P.2d 962; Restatement, Trusts, § 391; cases collected in 14 C.J.S., Charities, § 62b, and when assets are held by a charitable corporation, as here, the duty to protect such assets is expressly placed upon the Attorney General by the Corporations Code. Section 10207. Accordingly, it was not error to allow the Attorney General to intervene in the dissolution proceedings and challenge the claim of Pioneer that the assets could be distributed for the personal benefit of its members.

The next question to be determined is whether the trial court was justified in appointing a successor trustee. Pioneer contends that the only remedy available to the Attorney General was an order of the trial court directing Pioneer to comply with its articles. As previously pointed out, substantial evidence supports the finding of the trial court that Pioneer held its assets for charitable purposes. Under the Corporations Code a charitable corporation is subject to the same supervision by the Attorney General as is a nonprofit corporation holding its assets subject to a charitable trust, sections 9505, 10207; see, 26 So.Cal.L.Rev. 80, and deviations from the purposes stated in Pioneer's articles are thus subject to the same corrective measures that would be taken against a trustee of a charitable trust that similarly refused to carry out its duties.

Pioneer amended its by-laws to close its membership and provide that existing members had a proprietary interest in its assets; it brought a declaratory relief action to obtain a ruling that the assets were not held in trust, paying the attorney fees for both parties thereto; it sold its assets and reduced its property to cash; it commenced dissolution proceedings; and it maintained in the trial court, in a petition for writs of prohibition and mandate, and on this appeal that its assets are not held for charitable purposes. Pioneer's course of conduct throughout these proceedings thus demonstrates that it has abused and abandoned its trust and amply supports the determination of the trial court that a new trustee should be appointed. Corp.Code § 10207; Estate of Grblny, 147 Neb. 117, 131, 22 N.W.2d 488; Attorney General v. Armstrong, 231 Mass. 196, 214, 120 N.E. 678; Restatement, Trusts, §§ 387, 399. "If the trustees abandon, or in any way abuse, their trust, equity will correct the abuses, and remove the offenders." People ex rel. Ellert v. Cogswell, supra, 113 Cal. 129, 141, 45 P. 270, 273, see Scott on Trusts, § 387.

Pioneer invokes cases where the evidence showed that the corporation involved was a nonprofit corporation that existed for the private benefit of the members thereof and that the assets were not held for charitable purposes. In such cases it is properly held that the assets are distributed among the members upon dissolution. Corp. Code § 9801; see Brown v. La Societe Francaise, 138 Cal. 475, 477, 71 P. 516; Abalian v. Townsend Social Center, 112 Cal.App.2d 441, 449, 246 P.2d 965; 168 A.L.R. 956, but those decisions are not controlling here, since substantial evidence supports the determination of the trial court that Pioneer holds its assets for the charitable purposes expressed in its articles of incorporation.

Pioneer points out that in 1948 its by-laws were amended to provide that active members "shall have exclusive proprietary rights in the property and assets of the corporation." Whatever may have been the prospective effect of this amendment, it does not appear from the record that any donations were received by Pioneer after the amendment and, of course, the members of Pioneer could not appropriate to themselves the assets previously acquired by the device of renouncing the purposes expressed in its articles.

Pioneer contends that upon dissolution the assets must be distributed among its members and any holding allowing the assets to be transferred to another charitable corporation would be a confiscation of the members' property in contravention of the Fourteenth Amendment. The contention is without merit, since the members of Pioneer have not at any time had any right to receive the property. A charitable corporation cannot dissolve and distribute its assets among its members. See Ashton v. Dashaway Association, 84 Cal. 61, 69, 22 P. 660, 23 P. 1091, 7 L.R.A. 809; Zollmann, American Law of Charities, § 476. Thus in a case apposite to the present case, the Centennial and Memorial Association of Valley Forge, a charitable corporation, received contributions to perpetuate and preserve the site upon which George Washington had encamped in winter quarters. Upon dissolution, a member contended that the funds should be distributed among the members of the corporation, but the court held that no individual right to the funds existed and that the property should go to another charitable corporation with purposes akin to those of the dissolved corporation. Centennial & Memorial Association of Valley Forge, supra, 235 Pa. 206, 213, 83 A. 683; see In re Mt. Sinai Hospital, 250 N. Y. 103, 113, 164 N.E. 871, 62 A.L.R. 564.

Pioneer contends that in proceedings under Section 10207 a charitable corporation must be given an opportunity to correct its deviation from its articles, as it would if the proceeding were in quo warranto. Section 4691. Pioneer's contention comes too late. * * *

Pioneer contends that even if it is held that neither Pioneer nor its members may receive the assets, the trial court should have distributed the assets to the heirs of Mrs. Stoltenberg and not to Historical. We will assume that Pioneer is entitled to raise this point. In cases where property is conveyed to a trustee with an express declaration of a charitable purpose by the donor, a court of equity will appoint a successor trustee to carry out the charitable purpose expressed by the donor upon failure of the original trustee, Fay v. Howe, 136 Cal. 599, 603, 69 P. 423; Estate of Upham, 127 Cal. 90, 94, 59 P. 315; 14 C. J.S., Charities, § 27, and Historical contends that these cases govern here. But in cases where, as here, property is conveyed without restriction to a charitable corporation and the charitable intent of the donor is ascertained by reference to the charitable purposes of the donee, the courts have had more difficulty. Some decisions state that upon dissolution of the corporation the property reverts to the donor or his heirs, see Mormon Church v. United States, 136 U.S. 1, 47, 10 S.Ct. 792, 34 L.Ed. 481; Mott v. Danville Seminary, 129 Ill. 403, 416, 21 N.E. 927, and a dictum in an early case indicates that that rule would be followed in this jurisdiction, at least as to real property. People v. President & Trustees of College of California, 1869, 38 Cal. 166, 174; cf. Victoria Hospital Ass'n v. All Persons, 169 Cal. 455, 464, 147 P. 124. Pioneer contends that the Constitution of the United States compels us to follow here the dictum in the College of California case; it is settled, however, that judicial decisions may be overruled and dicta disapproved without violating either the due process clause or the contract clause of the United States Constitution. Tidal Oil Co. v. Flanagan, 263 U.S. 444, 450–451, 44 S.Ct. 197, 68 L.Ed. 382; Alferitz v. Borgwardt, 126 Cal. 201, 208–209, 58 P. 460. Accordingly, we are free to re-examine the dictum in the College of California case.

Decisions holding that gifts to charities revert to the donors upon dissolution have been subjected to severe criticism (See Simes, The Law of Future Interests, § 185; Gray, The Rule Against Perpetuities [4th ed.] § 51.1; Turrentine, Suggestions for Revision of Provisions of the California Civil Code Regarding Future Interests, 21 Cal.L. Rev. 1, 14), and other states reach a contrary result. In re Centennial

& Memorial Association of Valley Forge, supra, 235 Pa. 206, 213, 83 A. 683; McAlhany v. Murray, 89 S.C. 440, 446, 71 S.E. 1025, 35 L.R. A.,N.S., 895; see also Wilson v. Leary, 120 N.C. 90, 94, 26 S.E. 630, 38 L.R.A. 240; Hopkins v. Crossley, 138 Mich. 561, 566, 101 N.W. 822. We have concluded that the latter rule should be followed and that a court of equity should appoint a successor trustee to carry out the charitable intent of the donor whether the charitable purpose is found in the terms of the conveyance to the corporation or in the articles thereof, or whether the failure of the corporation is through dissolution or other disqualification. The policy of the law in favor of charitable gifts requires a court to carry out the dominant purpose of the donor to make a charitable gift for the purposes expressed in the articles of the original corporate donee. See Estate of Tarrant, 38 Cal.2d 42, 49, 237 P.2d 505, 28 A.L.R.2d 419; Estate of Loring, 29 Cal.2d 423, 436, 175 P.2d 524; Estate of Scrimger, 188 Cal. 158, 166, 206 P. 65. If the donors of property to a charitable corporation wish the property to revert upon dissolution, they may insert clauses to that effect in their gifts. See Estate of Randall, 341 Pa. 501, 19 A.2d 272; Bogert, Trusts and Trustees, § 419. If the right of reverter is not expressly reserved, recognition of a right of reverter by the courts would amount to a mere windfall since by the original gift the donors indicated that they preferred the property to be used to carry out the charitable purposes of the donee rather than go to themselves or to their heirs. A transfer of the assets to the donors or their heirs would thus conflict with the policy that the expressed purpose of the donors should be carried out so far as possible. See Estate of Lefranc, 38 Cal.2d 289, 296, 239 P.2d 617. Finally, recognition of the right of reverter presents grave practical difficulties, since in many cases dissolution of the charitable corporation will occur many years after the death of the donors of its assets and it will be extremely difficult or impossible to determine the heirs entitled to the property. For the foregoing reasons, the dictum in People v. President & Trustees of College of California, supra, is disapproved. The trial court therefore properly appointed a trustee in the present case.

* * *

The order is affirmed. The motion by appellant Los Angeles Pioneer Society to remand the case to the trial court, the motion by appellant Lelande to dismiss the appeal of appellant Los Angeles Pioneer Society, and the motion of appellant Los Angeles Pioneer Society to dismiss the appeal of appellant Lelande, are, and each is, denied.

GIBSON, C.J., and SHENK, EDMONDS and SPENCE, JJ., concur.

[CARTER, J. dissented [77] on the grounds that the purposes and activities of Pioneer were primarily social and not charitable and that if

77. On petition for rehearing, which was denied, Justice Carter again dissented and stated in part:

"The record in this case presents one of the most outrageous examples of legalized larceny which has come under my observation."

Pioneer was a charitable organization it should be allowed to correct its deviation from its articles and to revoke its petition to dissolve the corporation.]

SECTION 6. ENFORCEMENT AND SUPERVISION[78]

The problem of establishing effective enforcement machinery for charitable gifts is not a new one. The primary purpose of the Statute of Charitable Uses in 1601 was to prevent abuses and establish an administrative system to see that charitable gifts were devoted to the purposes for which they had been given. In recent years the problem has once again received attention. In a private trust, self-interest on the part of definite beneficiaries will prompt them to require accounting by the trustee and to assure that the trustee is fulfilling the terms of the trust. In a charitable trust, on the other hand, where the beneficiaries are necessarily indefinite, there must be some other administrative machinery.

Under present law, enforcement proceedings may originate from several sources:

(1) Traditionally it is the Attorney General in each state who has standing to enforce charitable trusts [79] and also to enforce limitations on gifts to charitable corporations. But standing to sue is not sufficient to bring about effective enforcement. There must be a procedure for keeping track of charitable gifts through regular reporting, so that deviations from the trust purpose can come to the attention of the Attorney General. Too often that office is burdened with other diverse duties which have political importance, and there is no demand by any interested segment of the public for supervision of the work of charitable organizations. However, steps have been taken in some states to establish a public registry of charitable gifts and to regularize reporting by such organizations.

78. For a thorough analysis of the problems in this Section see Taylor, Public Accountability of Foundations and Charitable Trusts (1953); Fremont-Smith, Foundations and Government, State and Federal Law and Supervision (1965).

79. Obviously the standing of the Attorney General ought to extend not only to enforcement but also to protection of the charitable gift in the first instance. A decision such as Commonwealth ex rel. Ferguson v. Gardner, 327 S.W.2d 947 (Ky.1959), 14 Vand.L.Rev. 428 (1960), that the Attorney General has no standing to intervene in a will contest to protect a charitable gift, is clearly erroneous. In re Quinn's Estate, 156 Cal.App. 2d 684, 320 P.2d 219 (1958). Dealing with enforcement issues see, Fremont-Smith, "Duties and Powers of Charitable Fiduciaries: The Law of Trusts and the Correction of Abuses", 13 U.C.L.A.L. Rev. 1041 (1966); "Regulating Charitable Trusts", 103 Trusts and Estates 845 (1964); Gray, "State Attorney General—Guardian of Public Charities???" 14 Clev.Mar.L.Rev. 236 (1965); Taft, "Control of Foundations and other Non-Profit Corporations", 18 Clev.Mar.L.Rev. 236 (1965); Forer, "Relief of the Public Burden: The Function of Charities in Pennsylvania", 27 U.Pitts.L.Rev. 751 (1966); "Standards for Supervision of Charitable Trusts", 3 Real Prop.Prob. & T.L.J. 154 (1968); Notes, "The Enforcement of Charitable Trusts in America: A History of Changing Social Attitudes", 54 Va.L. Rev. 436 (1968); "Charitable Trust Enforcement in Virginia", 56 Va.L.Rev. 716 (1970).

(2) The settlor (or after his death his family) would seem logically to have both the motivation and the legal standing to enforce charitable restrictions. However, in the absence of statute[80] or resort to one

80. An excellent statute permitting flexibility in administration and defining techniques for enforcement has been operative in Wisconsin since 1971. This is Wis.Stat.Ann. § 701.10 (West Spec. Pamph.1980) as follows:

"**Charitable trusts**

"**(1) Validity.** A charitable trust may be created for any of the following charitable purposes: relief of poverty, advancement of education, advancement of religion, promotion of health, governmental or municipal purposes or any other purpose the accomplishment of which is beneficial to the community. No gift to charity, in trust or otherwise, is invalid because of indefiniteness. If a particular charitable purpose is not indicated and the trustee is not expressly authorized by the creating instrument to select such a purpose, the trustee has an implied power to select one or more charitable purposes. If a particular charitable purpose is not indicated and no trustee is named in the creating instrument, the court may appoint a trustee with such an implied power to select or may direct that the property be transferred outright to one or more established charitable entities.

"**(2) Modification and termination.** (a) If a purpose of a charitable trust is or becomes impractical, unlawful or impossible, the court may order the trust continued for one or more other charitable purposes designated by the settlor or, in the absence of such designation, order the property devoted to one or more other charitable purposes either by continuing the trust or by distributing the property to one or more established charitable entities. In determining the alternative plan for disposition of the property, the court shall take into account current and future community needs in the general field of charity within which the original charitable purpose falls, other charitable interest of the settlor, the amount of principal and income available under the trust and other relevant factors. The provisions of this subsection do not apply insofar as the settlor expressly provides in the creating instrument for an alternative disposition if the original trust fails; nor do they apply to gifts by several persons to a charitable entity on a subscription basis if the court finds that the donors intended their gifts to be limited to the original purpose and such purpose fails initially.

"(b) If any administrative provision of a charitable trust or part of a plan set forth by the settlor to achieve his charitable purpose is or becomes impractical, unlawful, inconvenient or undesirable, and a modification of such provision or plan will enable the trustee to achieve more effectively the basic charitable purpose, the court may by appropriate order modify the provision or plan.

"(c) If a charitable trust is or becomes uneconomic when principal and probable income, cost of administration and other relevant factors are considered, or in any event if the trust property is valued at less than $5,000, the court may terminate the trust and order outright distribution to an established charitable entity in the general field of charity within which the charitable purpose falls.

"(d) It is the purpose of this subsection to broaden the power of the courts to make charitable gifts more effective. In any situation not expressly covered the court shall liberally apply the cy pres doctrine.

"(e) The settlor if living, the trustee and an established charitable entity to which income or principal must be paid under the terms of the trust shall be made a party to any proceeding under this subsection.

"**(3) Enforcement; notice to attorney general.** (a) A proceeding to enforce a charitable trust may be brought by:

"1. An established charitable entity to which income or principal must be paid under the terms of the trust;

"2. The attorney general in the name of the state upon his own information or, in his discretion, upon complaint of any person;

"3. Any settlor or group of settlors who contributed half or more of the principal; or

"4. A cotrustee.

"(b) In a proceeding affecting a charitable trust, notice must be given to the attorney general.

"**(4) Established charitable entity.** As used in this section, 'established charitable entity' means a corporation

of the following drafting devices the settlor has no standing in court to sue.[81] If the settlor desires to keep control over the administration of the charitable gift, he may at the time the gift is made achieve his objective by one of the following: (a) he can insert a condition subsequent or reverter clause, requiring return of the property for breach of condition (unfortunately this may serve to keep the fund narrowly confined to the original purpose and perhaps to promote litigation by heirs unsympathetic to the charitable purpose); or (b) if the funds justify the corporate form, the settlor can provide in the bylaws (or articles of incorporation) that he or a member of his family will be one of the directors, or even have control over selection of successor directors.

(3) It might seem that interested organizations in the particular charitable field and potential beneficiaries of the charity would also have standing to enforce the purpose. Unfortunately the courts have taken a narrow view of standing to sue on the grounds that control of litigation in this field should be exclusively in the Attorney General.[82]

If the interest of the beneficiary is "direct", then the beneficiary may sue, joining the Attorney General as a necessary party to the suit. Thus, a trust in perpetuity to use the income to pay the salary of the minister of a particular church may be enforced by any minister of that church. Or a trust for a charitable corporation may be enforced by the corporation. But where the charitable purpose is broader, members of the public are not entitled to sue since the Attorney General can sue on their behalf. They can bring a suit as relators in the name of the Attorney General, but this is not always a practical remedy; not only do the relators bear the cost of the suit, the conduct of the litigation is controlled by the Attorney General.

(4) Voluntary public reporting by charitable organizations has assumed substantial proportions.[83] While this may in part be prompted by the desire to avoid more stringent governmental supervision, the practice is also a commendable recognition of the public interest, on the part of responsible trustees and directors. This kind of self-policing is extremely helpful, but it must be remembered that the trustees and directors who may be guilty of mismanagement or who are not

or trust operated exclusively for a charitable purpose defined in sub. (1)."

81. Amundson v. Kletzing-McLaughlin Memorial Foundation College, 247 Iowa 91, 73 N.W.2d 114 (1955). There is contrary authority allowing the settlor standing. See Scott, Trusts (3d Ed.1967) § 391. It has been proposed that the heirs of the settlor should be able to sue to get the property back, so that self-interest may be the motivation for effective enforcement, at least until there is more effective government enforcement. See Alford, "The Disposition of Assets Upon Failure of a Charitable Trust or Corporation: Policy Relationship to Enforcement of Charities", 9 Utah L.Rev. 217 (1964).

82. In Art Institute of Chicago v. Castle, 9 Ill.App.2d 473, 133 N.E.2d 748 (1956), testator had left a large trust fund with the income to be paid to the Art Institute to be used for the erection and maintenance of statuary and monuments, and the term "monuments" was construed to include an art building. The court refused to allow The National Sculpture Society to intervene. See "Standing of Minister or Member of Religious Society to Seek Enforcement, Termination or Proper Administration of Charitable Trust", 94 A.L.R.3d 1204 (1979).

83. See Andrews, Philanthropic Foundations (1956) Ch. 12.

making the most effective use of the funds in their trust are not likely to follow the practice.

(5) The Internal Revenue Service is charged with guarding against use of the tax-exempt status of charitable organizations to further private objectives. Under the 1950 Revenue Act, the Service instituted an elaborate system of annual reports by exempt organizations.[84] Part of these reports are available for public inspection. This may well prove the most potent force in public supervision, both because it opens records to the public and because the Government's financial interest through tax collection is substantial enough to justify an enforcement staff.

The unprecedented growth of charitable trusts and corporations in recent years, both in terms of numbers and in amounts of wealth, has brought increased interest in methods of enforcement.[85] There is general concern that the traditional method of enforcement through the Attorney General acting on complaint of interested persons is inadequate to supervise the variety of activities and potential abuses. Although the Treasury Department has a more direct motivation in policing charities because of the tax exemptions and deductions, it is questionable whether such control is a proper activity of the Treasury. The heart of supervision is both effective legislation to obtain reporting and an adequate staff to implement the legislation. A number of states have now adopted the Uniform Supervision of Trustees for Charitable Purposes Act or variants of legislation setting up a registry of charitable entities.[86] Although the original Uniform Act is defective in applying only to trusts, several states have amended the act to include charitable corporations.[87] Proof of the economic benefits of providing adequate staff is found in the recent California history.[88]

HOLT v. COLLEGE OF OSTEOPATHIC PHYSICIANS & SURGEONS

Supreme Court of California, 1964.
61 Cal.2d 750, 40 Cal.Rptr. 244, 394 P.2d 932.[89]

TRAYNOR, JUSTICE. Plaintiffs appeal from a judgment of dismissal entered after the sustaining of a demurrer to their complaint

84. IRC §§ 6033, 6034, 6104, 26 U.S.C.A. As to the reporting requirement for private foundations see Section 2 fn. 15.

85. See "Foundations, Charities and the Law: The Interaction of External Controls and Internal Policies," Symposium Issue, 13 U.C.L.A.L.Rev. 933–1133 (1966).

86. See Fremont-Smith, Foundations and Government, State and Federal Law and Supervision (1965); Kutner and Koven, "Charitable Trust Legislation in the Several States," 61 N.W.L.Rev. 411 (1966).

87. E.g., West's Ann.Cal.Government Code § 12581 (1963); Ore.Rev.Stat. § 128.630 (1969).

88. Howland, "The History of the Supervision of Charitable Trusts and Corporations in California," 13 U.C.L.A.L.Rev. 1029 (1966); Bell and Bell, "Supervision of Charitable Trusts in California", 32 Hastings L.J. 433 (1981).

89. Noted 16 Hast.L.J. 479 (1965); 40 Notre Dame Law 349 (1965); 13 U.C.L.A. L.Rev. 1123 (1966).

without leave to amend in an action to enjoin the breach of a charitable trust and for declaratory relief.

Plaintiffs are three trustees of defendant College of Osteopathic Physicians and Surgeons (hereinafter COPS), a California charitable corporation. The other defendants are the twenty-three remaining trustees on the COPS board of trustees and the Attorney General. The complaint alleges in substance that COPS holds assets in excess of $1,500,000 in trust for charitable purposes, and that defendant trustees have acted contrary to these purposes and threaten other such acts. By their first cause of action plaintiffs seek to enjoin these acts, and by their second cause of action they seek a declaration of their and defendants' rights and duties with regard to the operation of COPS.

The Attorney General filed an answer to the complaint denying for want of information and belief the allegations that defendant trustees were diverting the assets of COPS from its charitable purposes. As an affirmative defense the Attorney General stated that "The matter of proposed changes in the operation of said College was reviewed by the Attorney General to determine whether such changes would constitute a violation of a charitable trust warranting institution of a suit by this office to remedy the situation. It has been concluded that the changes to be made in the operation of said College would not be detrimental to the public interest and do not warrant legal action by this office to prevent such changes." The Attorney General also stated that he had not granted "relator status" to plaintiffs and had not consented to their bringing this action. Defendant trustees demurred to the complaint and the trial court sustained the demurrer on the grounds that plaintiffs have no capacity to bring this action and that the complaint does not state facts showing a threatened breach of a charitable trust.

The first issue is whether plaintiffs, as minority trustees of a charitable corporation, can sue the majority trustees to enjoin their allegedly wrongful diversion of corporate assets in breach of a trust for charitable purposes. Defendants contend that only the Attorney General can bring such an action.

The prevailing view of other jurisdictions is that the Attorney General does not have exclusive power to enforce a charitable trust and that a trustee or other person having a sufficient special interest may also bring an action for this purpose. This position is adopted by the American Law Institute (Rest.2d Trusts, § 391) and is supported by many legal scholars. (Karst, The Efficiency of the Charitable Dollar: An Unfulfilled State Responsibility, 73 Harv.L.Rev. 433, 443–449; 4 Scott, Trusts (2d ed.) § 391; 4 Pomeroy, Equity (5th ed.) 287, n. 13; see also Note 62 A.L.R. 881; 4 Witkin, Summary of California Law (7th ed.) 2918–2919.)

In accord with the majority view, this court has stated that "* * * the only person who can object to the disposition of the trust property is one having some definite interest in the property—he must be a trustee, or a *cestui*, or have some reversionary interest in the trust property." (O'Hara v. Grand Lodge I.O.G.T., 213 Cal. 131, 140, 2 P.2d 21, 24; see also People ex rel. Ellert v. Cogswell, 113 Cal. 129, 136, 45 P. 270, 35 L.R.A. 269; Pratt v. Security Trust & Sav. Bank, 15 Cal.App.2d 630, 640–641, 59 P.2d 862; cf. St. James Church v. Superior Court, 135 Cal.App.2d 352, 360, 287 P.2d 387.)

Defendants invoke Corporations Code, sections 9505 and 10207 for the proposition that only the Attorney General can bring an action for the enforcement of a charitable trust administered by either a nonprofit or charitable corporation. These sections provide that if there is a failure to comply with a charitable trust "* * * the Attorney General shall institute, in the name of the State, the proceedings necessary to correct the noncompliance or departure." Nothing in these sections suggests that trustees are precluded from bringing an action to enforce the trust. The Uniform Supervision of Trustees for Charitable Purposes Act (Gov.Code, §§ 12580–12595) similarly authorizes the Attorney General to supervise charitable trusts, and likewise fails to preclude suits by trustees.

The foregoing statutes were enacted in recognition of the problem of providing adequate supervision and enforcement of charitable trusts.[90] Beneficiaries of a charitable trust, unlike beneficiaries of a private trust, are ordinarily indefinite and therefore unable to enforce the trust in their own behalf. (E.g., People ex rel. Ellert v. Cogswell, 113 Cal. 129, 136–137, 45 P. 270, 35 L.R.A. 269; Pratt v. Security Trust & Sav. Bank, 15 Cal.App.2d 630, 639–641, 59 P.2d 862.) Since there is usually no one willing to assume the burdens of a legal action, or who could properly represent the interests of the trust or the public, the Attorney General has been empowered to oversee charities as the representative of the public, a practice having its origin in the early common law. (See generally Scott, supra, § 391, pp. 2753–2756.)

In addition to the general public interest, however, there is the interest of donors who have directed that their contributions be used for certain charitable purposes. Although the public in general may benefit from any number of charitable purposes, charitable contributions must be used only for the purposes for which they were received in trust. (O'Hara v. Grand Lodge I.O.G.T., supra, 213 Cal. at pp. 140–141, 2 P.2d 21; Pacific Home v. County of L. A., 41 Cal.2d 844, 854, 264 P.2d 539; see also Estate of Faulkner, 128 Cal.App.2d 575, 578, 275 P.2d 818.) Moreover, part of the problem of enforcement is to bring to light conduct detrimental to a charitable trust so that remedial action may be taken. The Attorney General may not be in a position to become aware of wrongful conduct or to be suffi-

90. [Fns. 90–92 are by the Court. Ed.]

This problem has been extensively discussed in recent years. (See Karst, The Efficiency of the Charitable Dollar: An Unfulfilled State Responsibility, 73 Harv. L.Rev. 433; Bogert, Proposed Legislation Regarding State Supervision of Charities, 52 Mich.L.Rev. 633; Bogert, Recent Developments Regarding the Law of Charitable Donations and Charitable Trusts, 21 U.Chi.L.Rev. 118; Note, State Supervision of the Administration of Charitable Trusts, 47 Colum.L.Rev. 659; Note, The Charitable Corporation, 64 Harv.L.Rev. 1168.)

ciently familiar with the situation to appreciate its impact, and the various responsibilities of his office may also tend to make it burdensome for him to institute legal actions except in situations of serious public detriment. (See Karst, supra, 73 Harv.L.Rev. at pp. 478–479; Bogert, Proposed Legislation Regarding State Supervision of Charities, 52 Mich.L.Rev. 633, 634–636; Scott, supra, § 391, pp. 2754–2756.)

The present case illustrates these difficulties. The pleading filed by the Attorney General stated that he had no information or belief as to the plaintiffs' allegations that trust assets were being diverted from their charitable purpose. Yet the pleading also stated that the Attorney General determined that legal action by his office was not warranted because the changes in the operation of COPS "would not be detrimental to the public interest. * * *" The test applied by the Attorney General in deciding not to take legal action is clearly incorrect, for the assets of COPS as a charitable institution can be used only for the purposes for which they were received in trust. The trust is not fulfilled merely by applying the assets in the public interest.[91]

Although the Attorney General has primary responsibility for the enforcement of charitable trusts, the need for adequate enforcement is not wholly fulfilled by the authority given him. The protection of charities from harassing litigation does not require that only the Attorney General be permitted to bring legal actions in their behalf. This consideration "* * * is quite inapplicable to enforcement by the fiduciaries who are both few in number and charged with the duty of managing the charity's affairs." (Karst, supra, 73 Harv.L.Rev. at pp. 444–445.) There is no rule or policy against supplementing the Attorney General's power of enforcement by allowing other responsible individuals to sue in behalf of the charity.[92] The administration of charitable trusts stands only to benefit if in addition to the Attorney General other suitable means of enforcement are available. "The charity's own representative has at least as much interest in preserving the charitable funds as does the Attorney General who represents the general public. The cotrustee is also in the best position to learn about breaches of trust and to bring the relevant facts to a court's attention." (Karst, supra, 73 Harv.L.Rev. at p. 444.) Moreover, permitting suits by trustees does not usurp the responsibility of the Attorney General, since he would be a necessary party to such litigation and would represent the public interest. (See In re L. A. County Pioneer Society, 40 Cal.2d 852, 861, 257 P.2d 1.)

91. We are not presented with the applicability of the cy-pres doctrine, which permits change of charitable purposes under some circumstances. (See, e.g., Estate of Loring, 29 Cal.2d 423, 436, 175 P.2d 524; O'Hara v. Grand Lodge I.O.G. T., supra, 213 Cal. at 140–141, 2 P.2d 21.)

92. Defendant trustees' reference to the safeguards afforded in the area of private corporations (Corp.Code, § 834) is inapplicable, since trustees as fiduciaries have a special interest wholly unlike that of a private corporate shareholder. We do not reach the question whether minority directors of a private corporation can bring an action in behalf of the corporation. (Cf. Sealand Inv. Corp. v. Emprise, Inc., 190 Cal.App.2d 305, 12 Cal.Rptr. 153.) The differences between private and charitable corporations make the consideration of such an analogy valueless.

Defendant trustees urge that a distinction should be made between trustees of a charitable trust and the governing board of a charitable corporation. They apparently concede that a minority trustee of a charitable trust has the capacity to sue, but contend that members of a governing board of a charitable corporation are not truly trustees and that a different rule applies to them. The Attorney General takes the position that he is the only one empowered to bring suit in either situation. Corporations Code, Section 10205 states that the powers of a charitable corporation shall be vested in a "board of trustees." Defendant trustees contend, however, that this title does not disclose their true status, that it is the corporation as a legal entity that is properly designated the trustee of the assets held in trust for charitable purposes, and that the members of the board are merely employees of the corporate trustee.

It is true that trustees of a charitable corporation do not have all the attributes of a trustee of a charitable trust. They do not hold legal title to corporate property (see Corp.Code, § 10206, subd. (d)) and they are not individually liable for corporate liabilities (Corp. Code, § 9504). The individual trustees in either case, however, are the ones solely responsible for administering the trust assets (Corp. Code, § 10205), and in both cases they are fiduciaries in performing their trust duties. (St. James Church v. Superior Court, 135 Cal.App. 2d 352, 361, 287 P.2d 387.) Rules governing charitable trusts ordinarily apply to charitable corporations. (Karst, supra, 73 Harv.L.Rev. at pp. 435–436; Rest.2d Trusts, supra, § 348, p. 212; Scott, supra, § 348.1, p. 2559; Comment, Trusts—Gifts to Charitable Corporations, 26 So.Cal.L.Rev. 80, 85.) There is no sound reason why minority directors or "trustees" of a charitable corporation cannot maintain an action against majority trustees when minority trustees of a charitable trust are so empowered.

The rules governing private trusts also support plaintiffs' position with respect to the enforcement of a charitable trust. It is settled that one trustee of a private trust may sue a cotrustee to enjoin conduct by him that violates the trust, notwithstanding the right of the beneficiaries to bring an action in their own behalf. (E.g., Estate of Hensel, 144 Cal.App.2d 429, 438, 301 P.2d 105; Stanton v. Preis, 138 Cal.App.2d 104, 106, 291 P.2d 118; Rest.2d Trusts, § 200, comment *e*.) It follows a fortiori that a charitable trust should be enforceable by one or more of its trustees, since its indefinite class of beneficiaries is ordinarily not able to protect its own interest by legal action.

Plaintiff trustees therefore have the capacity to bring an action in behalf of COPS against the majority trustees to enjoin any breach of trust that is threatened. To the extent it is contrary to this opinion, George Pepperdine Foundation v. Pepperdine, 126 Cal.App.2d 154, 271 P.2d 600, is disapproved.

* * * [The Court then took up the question of the sufficiency of the complaint and held that it did state a cause of action.]

* * *

The judgment is reversed.

[The dissenting opinion of Justice McComb is omitted. He would have ruled that only the Attorney General could bring an action to correct noncompliance with a trust assumed by a charitable corporation; his opinion was based on the fact that the California statutes dealing with charitable corporations expressly authorize the Attorney General to sue and nowhere mention suit by minority trustees.]

NOTE

For a comparison of the liabilities of directors of charitable corporations and trustees of charitable trusts see Stern v. Lucy Webb Hayes National Training School for Deaconesses and Missionaries, 381 F.Supp. 1003 (D.D.C. 1974). In the opinion in that case Judge Gesell says, at page 1013:

> "* * * The charitable corporation is a relatively new legal entity which does not fit neatly into the established common law categories of corporation and trust. As the discussion below indicates, however, the modern trend is to apply corporate rather than trust principles in determining the liability of the directors of charitable corporations, because their functions are virtually indistinguishable from those of their 'pure' corporate counterparts.
>
> "Both trustees and corporate directors are liable for losses occasioned by their negligent mismanagement of investments. However, the degree of care required appears to differ in many jurisdictions. A trustee is uniformly held to a high standard of care and will be held liable for simple negligence, while a director must often have committed 'gross negligence' or otherwise be guilty of more than mere mistakes of judgment. 1 Hornstein, Corporation Law and Practice § 446 (1959); Ballantine, Corporations § 63(a) (Rev.Ed.1946); Bishop, 'Sitting Ducks and Decoy Ducks: New Trends in the Indemnification of Corporate Directors and Officers,' 77 Yale L.J. 1078, 1101 (1968). See also Mann v. Commonwealth Bond Corp., 27 F.Supp. 315, 320 (S.D.N.Y.1938).
>
> "This distinction may amount to little more than a recognition of the fact that corporate directors have many areas of responsibility, while the traditional trustee is often charged only with the management of the trust funds and can therefore be expected to devote more time and expertise to that task. Since the board members of most large charitable corporations fall within the corporate rather than the trust model, being charged with the operation of ongoing businesses, it has been said that they should only be held to the less stringent corporate standard of care. * * *"

Chapter XII

INTERRELATING TESTAMENTARY AND INTER VIVOS TRANSACTIONS

Scope Note

We saw in Chapter I that today the transmission of wealth is achieved by a variety of legal devices. These depend in some measure on the type of property involved. But the day when an estate consists solely of real and personal property transmitted by will has disappeared. Often the bulk of an owner's wealth is transmitted by devices other than the will. In the larger estates, the living trust which we have discussed in Chapters VIII through XI is a principal channel for transmitting wealth in such a way that it does not become part of the probate estate—and this is so whether the trust is revocable or irrevocable. There are numerous other devices discussed in Section 1 of this Chapter. For example, jointly owned assets pass to the surviving owner. These jointly owned assets may be real property, stocks, bank accounts or government bonds. Gifts, such as stock during the owner's lifetime, are attractive means for reducing the size of the estate subject to estate taxes. None of these assets, if effectively settled during the lifetime of the owner, will pass through the probate estate of the owner under the terms of his will. Many of these devices when properly integrated into a maturely considered estate plan may result in substantial savings in taxes and costs of administration. But if these transactions are used by laymen without competent legal advice, the tax costs and costs of litigation may prove catastrophic to the family or other beneficiaries of the decedent.

Thus in Section 1 we consider the specialization of certain policies, such as those underlying the Wills Acts (discussed in Chapter V) and those for protecting the surviving spouse (discussed in Chapter IV, Section 2 and Chapter VIII, Section 6) to various inter vivos transactions. The supposedly inter vivos transaction will be ineffective if the court decides it is, in reality, a will and must have the formalities for the execution of a will in order to be valid. What policies bear upon these determinations of testamentary character? The lawyer must understand these policies to advise his client. Or the transaction may be regarded as "inter vivos" for Wills Act purposes and yet be subject to the forced heirship claim of the surviving spouse. As mentioned in Chapter VIII, Section 2, certain inter vivos transfers will not escape estate or inheritance taxation when the transferor dies and the transferor may continue to have income tax liability on income produced by the transferred property during his lifetime.

These various difficulties place a premium on the ability of the estate planner to coordinate transfers by his client to reduce the overall tax burden and to avoid administrative complications and cost. One of the mechanical problems is achieving unity of assets, non-probate and probate, into a single trust for purposes of administration. He may, for example, wish to add life insurance to a trust set up during his lifetime. Problems associated with this transaction are examined in Section 2 (Interrelating Inter Vivos Transactions). Perhaps he wishes to make a gift by will to the trustee of a living trust to have the administration of the property conducted with the freedom from court control associated with living trusts. The techniques involved are considered in Section 3 (Interrelating Testamentary and Inter Vivos Transactions). The doctrines of incorporation by reference and nontestamentary acts, both potentially involved in "pour-overs" from wills to living trusts, are considered here with modern statutes designed to permit "pour-overs" without complications produced by the Wills Acts.

Occasionally a draftsman uses a will in an effort to control the disposition of non-probate assets. He might, for example, attempt to change the beneficiary of a life insurance contract by will or dispose of an interest in a joint tenancy which passes by survivorship. While these attempts usually stem from ignorance of the proper method by which these non-probate assets should be transferred, the case presented in Section 4 suggests arguments by which these efforts to control non-probate assets may be accomplished. In Section 5 the reverse of this situation is examined. In these transactions the owner of property agrees to dispose of his probate assets in a particular way. He might contract to make a will or to die intestate as to his property. While most of the cases presented involve attempted breaches by the property owner of his agreement, the judicial remedies provided in effect allow him to control the distribution of probate assets by contract.

The donation of property during the life of the donor should of course be integrated with gifts by will to the same persons. Study of the legal consequences of failure to observe this rule is postponed to Chapter XV, Section 1(1) (ii), on the Effect of Change on Dispositive Descriptions and Limitations.

SECTION 1. WILL SUBSTITUTES

A property owner may create rights in others by contract, deed, living trust or gift in such a way that he achieves the same ultimate distribution of his estate that he could have made by will. The use of these devices has become common because of the efforts by property owners to avoid inheritance and estate taxes and to eliminate the expense and other difficulties of probate and administration. In applying the legal doctrines of wills, intestate succession and administration, the courts must specialize the legislative or judicial policies which these doctrines express to the entire complex of acts by which a property owner can dispose of his property.

In this process of specialization the courts have not been concerned with the effect of the questioned transaction upon the ultimate distribution of the decedent's estate. The courts have confined their attention to the analogy between the mechanics of the questioned transaction and the mechanics of the conventional will. Dispositive transactions have been categorized as "inter vivos" and "testamentary". If the transaction is held "testamentary", the legislative and judicial policies concerning wills, intestate succession and administration will be brought to bear. If the transaction is held "inter vivos", the policies relating to contracts, deeds, living trusts or gifts are applied as the circumstances require.

The ambulatory character of a will is accepted as the distinguishing feature of a testamentary transaction. The courts look to the time that the transferor intends to create an "interest" or "property right" in the transferee. A court will, in all likelihood, hold that a transaction is testamentary if it finds that the transferor intended to create no "interest" or "property right" in the transferee until the death of the transferor. The degree of control which the transferor retains over the property carries great weight in determining his intention and may be considered independently as a criterion of testamentary character by analogy to a testator's power of revocation of a will.

A transaction may be held testamentary for one purpose and not for another. The question may be whether the property transferred is subject to succession taxes. A doubtful transaction may be held taxable as a testamentary disposition. On the other hand, the same transaction may not be required to be executed with the formalities for a will in order to pass a property interest. The terms "interest", "property right" and "control" are terms of a high order of abstraction and can be manipulated by the courts to satisfy equities in particular cases. The common law doctrine of survivorship, which operates as an exception to the statutory requirement that property owned by a decedent must pass at his death by will or intestacy, may be infused into a transaction such as a partnership agreement or joint bank account.

For these reasons, among others, there are no rules of thumb by which categorization of a transaction as "inter vivos" or "testamentary" can be predicted with any degree of assurance. Despite the apparent uniformity of the tests applied by the courts, the results produced have been chaotic and conflicting. As general references pertinent to the materials which follow it is suggested the student read Bordwell, "Testamentary Dispositions", 19 Ky.L.Rev. 283 (1931); Gulliver and Tilson, "Classification of Gratuitous Transfers", 51 Yale L.J. 1 (1941); Ritchie, "What Is a Will?", 49 Va.L.Rev. 759 (1963); and Browder, "Giving or Leaving—What Is a Will?", 75 Mich.L.Rev. 845 (1977).

(1) LIVING TRUSTS

The living trust figures in almost every estate plan because of its flexibility and service as a convenient device to integrate the various dispositions which have been made before the plan was undertaken and which will be undertaken as the plan is executed. While such a trust may be irrevocable,[1] the probability is that a revocable trust will be the "integrating" institution in most plans.[2] When life income in such a trust is reserved by the settlor and especially when he serves as trustee or reserves extensive powers over the administration of the trust, attacks based on the testamentary character of the transaction may be stimulated. The student should refer at this point to Farkas v. Williams, which appears as the first principal case in Chapter VIII, Section 6 and should review the features of that trust which stimulated the unsuccessful arguments by the co-administrators that the trust was testamentary.

1. See Walsh, "The Irrevocable Living Trust: Income and Estate Tax Consequences to the Donor and the Trustee", 4 Duquesne U.L.Rev. 303 (1966). See also, Sacher, "Estate Planning and the Partially Irrevocable Trust, Another View of United States v. Byrum," 48 Notre Dame Lawyer 581 (1973).

2. See Bostick, "The Revocable Trust: A Means of Avoiding Probate in the Small Estate?" 21 U.Fla.L.Rev. 44 (1968); Huff, "An Aspect of Estate Planning in Colorado: The Revocable Inter Vivos Trust", 43 Denver L.J. 296 (1966); Winkelman, "Living Trusts", 108 Trusts and Estates 346 (1969); Schuyler, "Revocable Trusts—Spouses, Creditors and Other Predators," Chapt. 74–13, 8th Annual Institute on Estate Planning (Univ. of Miami, 1974).

(2) DEEDS

BUTLER v. SHERWOOD

Supreme Court of New York, App.Div., 1921.
196 App.Div. 603, 188 N.Y.S. 242.[3]

WOODWARD, J. Ella F. Sherwood, being about to undergo an operation for a cancer, made and executed an instrument in writing, in form a quitclaim deed, of all her real estate and personal property, to her husband. This instrument bears date of January 25, 1916. The plaintiff is the brother and only heir at law of Ella F. Sherwood, and brings this action to set aside the said instrument, on the ground that it was procured by undue influence, and that there was never any transfer of the property under the instrument. Upon the trial of the action there does not appear to have been any serious contention of conduct amounting to fraud, and there is little room for doubt that Ella F. Sherwood intended to place her property where it would be vested in her husband, this defendant, upon her death. If she has failed in this purpose, it is because she has sought to accomplish an entirely legal result by an illegal method—because she has attempted to accomplish by an instrument in the form of a deed that which could be accomplished only by a will. The learned court at Special Term has found that the instrument relied upon by the defendant was of a testamentary character, and did not comply with the statutory requirements of a will, and that it was therefore void. 114 Misc. 483, 186 N.Y.S. 712. See Decedent Estate Law (Consol.Law, c. 13) § 21. The defendant appeals.

The instrument in question provides that it is between Ella Francis Sherwood and Edward H. Sherwood, and that—

> "the said party of the first part, in consideration of the sum of one dollar, love and affection, and other good and valuable considerations," does hereby "remise, release and forever quitclaim unto the said party of the second part, his heirs and assigns forever," all of the real estate of the said Ella F. Sherwood, wherever situate, "to have and to hold the same unto the party of the second part, his heirs, executors and administrators and assigns forever," and "for the same considerations, I do hereby sell, assign, transfer, convey and set over unto the party of the second part, all personal property, bills, notes, deposits in bank, certificates of stock, and all choses in action, evidences of indebtedness due me, and all my personal property of whatever name or kind the same may be and wheresoever situate, to have and to hold the same unto the party of the second part, his executors, administrators and assigns forever."

If the instrument had ended here, and had been executed and delivered, it would, of course, have operated to divest Ella F. Sherwood

3. Noted, 31 Yale L.J. 106 (1921).

of her property and to have vested it in Edward H. Sherwood. But this would not have accomplished the purpose which Ella F. Sherwood had in mind; she wanted to hold the ownership and possession of her property until her death, and then to vest it in her husband. She had, however, been through a will contest in connection with the estate of a former husband, and, as she told her friends, she had no faith in wills; she wanted to fix her property where it would be disposed of without a contest, and, of course, invited one. She provided that—

> "this conveyance and transfer are made upon the condition that the party of the second part, my husband, survive me, and the same is intended to vest and take effect upon my decease and until said time the same shall be subject to revocation upon the part of the party of the first part."

This instrument was delivered to the defendant, but what did it convey? It could not be determined at any time prior to her death whether her husband survived her, and unless he survived her there was clearly no intention of conveying to him. Moreover, she provided that the conveyance and transfer "are intended to vest and take effect only upon my decease"; so that there was no time prior to her death when the instrument could have any effect, and when that event took place the law determined the disposition to be made of her estate in the absence of a valid will. There was no moment from the time of making the instrument down to the very instant of dissolution when any rights could vest under the intent or language of this deed, and beyond this it was provided that "until said time, the same shall be subject to revocation upon the part of the party of the first part"; so that the supposed grantor was in full control of the property during all of her life subsequent to the making of the deed, with the right reserved to revoke the instrument itself. No right whatever passed to the defendant under the terms of the deed; it was not to take effect until the decease of the party of the first part, and then only upon the condition that the defendant survived her. This is not the case of a deed executed and delivered to a third party, with instructions not to record or deliver the same until the death of the grantor. Such a deed, absolute in form and to take effect immediately, divests the grantor of his interest in the property, making its enjoyment to depend upon the date of his death; but here the instrument is, by its terms, to take effect only upon the decease of the grantor, and at a time when the law operates to prevent a transfer otherwise than by a last will and testament.

It is impossible to sustain this transaction as an executed gift of the personal property, for that was subject to the same conditions and limitations as the real estate.

"It is an elementary rule," say the court in Young v. Young, 80 N. Y. 422, 435 (36 Am.Rep. 634), "that such a gift cannot be made to take effect in possession in futuro. Such a transaction amounts only to a promise to make a gift, which is nudum pactum. Pitts v. Mangum, 2 Bailey (S.C.) 588. There must be a delivery of possession with a view to pass a present right of property. 'Any gift of chattels which expressly reserves the use of the property to the donor for a certain period, or (as commonly appears in the cases which the courts have had occasion to pass upon) as long as the donor shall live, is ineffectual.' Schouler on Pers.Prop. vol. 2, p. 118, and cases cited; Vaas v. Hicks, 3 Murphy (N.C.) 494. This rule has been applied, even where the gift was made by a written instrument or deed purporting to transfer the title, but containing the reservation."

In the case here under consideration the instrument itself is limited to take effect upon the death of the donor if the donee shall survive her, and there is no pretense that any of the personal property itself was ever delivered to the defendant. Delivery by the donor, either actual or constructive, operating to divest the donor of possession of and dominion over the thing is a constant and essential factor in every transaction which takes effect as a completed gift. Instruments may be ever so formally executed by the donor, purporting to transfer title to the donee, or there may be the most explicit declaration of intention to give, or of an actual present gift, yet, unless there is a delivery, the intention is defeated. Beaver v. Beaver, 117 N.Y. 421, 429, 22 N.E. 940, 6 L.R.A. 403, 15 Am.St.Rep. 531.

While there is a recital of a consideration of $1, and every legal mode of acquisition of real property except by descent is denominated in law a purchase, and the person who thus acquires it is a purchaser, there is no doubt that the transaction here under consideration possesses all of the essential qualities of a gift, as distinguished from a valuable consideration supporting a bargain and sale. (Ten Eyck v. Whitbeck, 135 N.Y. 40, 44, 45, 31 N.E. 994, 31 Am.St.Rep. 809, and authorities there cited; Real Property Law, Consol.Laws, c. 50, § 246); and as this gift was not to take effect until the death of the grantor, upon the survival of the named grantee, and even the instrument itself might be revoked, it must be clear that Ella F. Sherwood undertook to accomplish by deed what the law requires to be done by will, and, of course, she has failed. The judgment appealed from should be affirmed.

Judgment affirmed without costs. All concur.

NOBLE v. FICKES

Supreme Court of Illinois, 1907.
230 Ill. 594, 82 N.E. 950.[4]

[John Noble executed an instrument in the form of a statutory warranty deed whereby he purported to convey certain land to his son, Thomas Noble. The instrument was attested by two credible witnesses. Thereafter, John Noble executed a will which purported to dispose of his residual estate to Thomas Noble and two other sons.

4. Noted, 21 Harv.L.Rev. 451 (1908).

The will specifically excepted from its operation the land purportedly conveyed to Thomas Noble in the deed. The deed in question, another deed and the will were placed in an envelope and delivered by John Noble to J. S. Miles. At the direction of John Noble, Miles wrote on the envelope that the deeds were to be delivered to the grantees after the death of the grantor and that the will was to be delivered to the proper officers "all of the said property to be held subject to the order of John Noble." After the death of John Noble the deed in question was delivered by Miles to Thomas Noble. Two heirs of John Noble contended that the deed was void for want of delivery. Their contention was sustained in Noble v. Tipton, 219 Ill. 182, 76 N.E. 151 (1905), where the court said at 219 Ill. 182, 186 "The deed was intended as a testamentary disposition of the farm to take effect at the death of the grantor and such a disposition can only be effected by an instrument in writing executed in conformity with the statute of wills." However the court did not pass upon the validity of the instrument as a will. Thomas Noble then offered the instrument for probate as a will and probate was denied by the circuit court. This is an appeal from that decision.]

VICKERS, J. * * * A will is an instrument by which a person makes a disposition of property to take effect after his death. * * * [The court then set forth the formalities of execution required for a will in Illinois, Hurd's Rev.Stat.1905, c. 148. Among these requirements was the attestation of the will by two or more credible witnesses] * * * Proof of the foregoing facts, in the absence of any proof of fraud, compulsion, or other improper conduct will make a prima facie case entitling the will to probate. * * * There is no prescribed form for a will, either under our statute or by the common law. If the intention of the maker to dispose of his estate after death is sufficiently manifested, and this intention be lawful in itself, and the instrument is executed in conformity to the statute, it will operate as a will regardless of its form. Jarman on Wills, 34; 1 Redfield on Wills (4th Ed.) c. 6, div. 7–9; Robinson v. Brewster, 140 Ill. 649, 30 N.E. 683, 33 Am.St.Rep. 265. * * *

After an exhaustive examination of all the authorities accessible to us, we think the rule may be laid down that any writing, however informal it may be, made with the expressed intent of giving a posthumous destination to the maker's property, if executed in accordance with the statutory requirements, will be a good testamentary disposition. We have not been able to find a case in this state where a testamentary disposition in the form of an ordinary deed of bargain and sale has been sustained, although a number of cases are to be found where such instruments have been declared testamentary in character and void because not executed in compliance with section 2 of our statute of wills. Where such deeds have been actually delivered to the grantee during the lifetime of the grantor, they have been sustained as a present grant of a future interest. Thus, in Schackelton v. Sebree, 86 Ill. 616, a deed containing the words, "this deed not to take effect until after my decease—not to be recorded until after my decease" which had been delivered to the grantee in the lifetime of the grantor, was held to pass a vested remainder in fee to the grantee. Livery of seisin having been abolished by our statute, no intermediate life estate is necessary to support a remainder. In Harshbarger v. Carroll, 163 Ill. 636, 45 N.E. 565, the words in the deed were: "This indenture, made this seventeenth day of March, in the year of our Lord eighteen hundred seventy-one, between Samuel Harshbarger, Sr., party of the first part, and Sylvia Harshbarger and her heirs (only to take effect at the death of the grantor)," etc. It was held that such a deed, duly executed and delivered in the lifetime of the grantor, vested a remainder in the grantee. Bowler v. Bowler, 176 Ill. 541, 52 N.E. 437, is another case of the same class. There the words of the deed were: "Not to be of any force and effect until after the death of the grantor." The deed was upheld as a good conveyance in praesenti of a future estate in fee. Other cases of the same class no doubt might be found, but these are sufficient to illustrate the rule established by them. In all of these cases it is to be noted that there was an actual delivery of the deed to the grantee in the lifetime of the grantor. Had there been no delivery, the instruments could not have been upheld as deeds, and whether they could have been supported as testamentary dispositions would have depended upon whether the statutory requirements relating to the attestation of wills had been complied with. * * *

Cline v. Jones, 111 Ill. 563, a case much relied on by the appellant in the case at bar, is a case where a father executed a deed to one of his children, but did not deliver it. The evidence showed that the grantor retained control of the deed and did not intend it to take effect until after his death. In disposing of that case, this court said (page 569): "The deed, by its purport, was absolute, conveying the grantor's entire interest, to operate immediately. But the evidence shows the deed was not intended to be absolute, but to be qualified in its effect; that it was not intended to convey the grantor's whole interest, but that he meant to have a life estate unless the grantee should move upon the land, which she never did; that the deed was not intended to operate presently, but only upon the grantor's death or going upon the land to reside. The evidence shows the distinct intention not to create a present estate in the grantee. As, then, there was never any actual delivery of the deed, but the grantor ever kept it in his own possession, and as it never was his intention that the deed should presently take effect and become operative according to its terms, there was no delivery of instrument as the deed of the grantor, and it was not valid as a deed. As Mrs. Jones never moved on the land, this made the deed one to take effect at the grantor's death, which was a disposition of property of a testamentary character, and invalid because not in compliance with the statute of wills." Many other cases are to be found where this court has held deeds and other instruments disposing of property at the death of the maker invalid because they were testamentary in character and not executed in strict conformity with the statutory enactments regulating the making of wills. * * * In many of these cases, and perhaps others of the same class, the instrument under consideration has been freely spoken of by this court as testamentary in its character and therefore invalid because not executed in accordance with the statute of wills; but none of these cases can be regarded as an authority holding that the instruments under consideration would or would not be sustained as valid testamentary dispositions if such instruments had been properly executed under the statute of wills. The case in hand is therefore, so far as we are advised, the first one to come before this court involving the validity of an ordinary deed of bargain and sale as a testamentary disposition.

Upon the general proposition that a valid will may be made in the form of an ordinary deed of bargain and sale, we entertain not the slightest doubt, where the formalities of the statute are properly observed, and it clearly appears on the face of the instrument that it is not to take effect until the death of the maker. The inherent difficulty with the instrument involved in this case is that there is nothing in the writing itself which imparts to it a testamentary character. To give it this character a resort must be had to extrinsic facts depending on parol evidence. The admissibility of such evidence for the purpose of establishing the animo testandi when offered for the purpose of supporting the writing as a testamentary disposition, is, in our opinion, the most serious question involved in this case. It is a well-established rule that parol evidence is inadmissible to add to, alter, vary, or contradict the terms of a valid written contract or other instrument of a solemn and conclusive nature. Elliott on Evidence, § 568; Rigdon v. Conley, 141 Ill. 565, 30 N.E. 1060. The rules for the admission and exclusion of parol evidence in regard to wills are essentially the same which prevail in regard to contracts generally. Such evidence is not receivable to show the intention of the testator except to enable the court, where the question arises, to give the language such an interpretation as, from the circumstances in which he was placed, it is reasonable to presume the testator intended it should receive, or, as it is sometimes expressed, to put the court in the testator's place. 1 Redfield on Wills (4th Ed.) p. 496. * * *

In Clay v. Layton, 134 Mich. 317, 96 N.W. 458, the question arose as to the admissibility of parol evidence to show the testamentary intention in the making of a deed which was unambiguous on its face. That court in a well considered and exhaustive opinion, held that such evidence was not admissible, and expressed its conclusion as follows: "We have had difficulty in finding a case in which the exact point before us is raised, but it seems manifest that the same rule that forbids the contradiction of an established will should forbid the contradiction of the same instrument as a means of establishing it as a will, when its terms plainly show it to be a deed conveying a present interest. It is only when the writing is of doubtful import that interpretation by the aid of extrinsic evidence becomes necessary, and in such case interpretation—not contradiction—is permissible. We are reluctantly driven to the conclusion that we cannot give effect to the deceased's manifest desire—a desire so well established and so apparently well grounded and just as to merit our approbation—but we fear that the trite saying that 'hard cases make bad law' would be applicable should we sustain the complainant's contention. To do so would be to override established rules and principles essential to the protection of the rights of heirs." There are very strong reasons why this rule should be applied in this state. Our statute requires wills to be in writing. If an unambiguous deed, which on its face purports to convey a present interest, can be converted into a will by proving an animo testandi in the maker by parol evidence, the effect is not only to change the legal character of the instrument, but to engraft upon it one of the essentials of a will by parol, in the face of our statute, which requires all wills to be in writing.

This case is clearly distinguishable from Cline v. Jones, supra, and other cases in line with it, including the case between these parties decided in 219 Ill. 182, 76 N.E. 151, 3 L.R.A.,N.S., 1645, where the question at issue was whether a deed had been delivered. Delivery is largely a question of intention and may be shown by any competent evidence. Evidence on that point does not contradict or vary the terms of the instrument, but bears on the question whether the instrument, in fact, ever had a legal existence. It would be a strange result if the same evidence which destroyed the instrument as a deed should bring it to life as a will.

Our conclusion is that it would be an unsafe rule to hold that an undelivered deed, which by chance happened to be attested by two witnesses, could be converted into a will by parol evidence.

The decree of the circuit court of Carroll county is affirmed.

Decree affirmed.

CARTWRIGHT and CARTER, JJ., dissent [Dissenting opinion omitted].

NOTE

Questions relating to the testamentary character of deeds have been presented frequently in two classes of cases:[5] (1) as in Butler v. Sherwood, when the deed is delivered to the grantee but there is language in the deed which may indicate that the grantor intended no interest to pass to the grantee until death;[6] (2) as in Noble v. Fickes, when the deed is absolute in form but the delivery of the deed is manipulated for testamentary effect.[7]

5. See generally, Atkinson, Wills (2d Ed., 1953) § 43; 1 Bowe-Parker: Page, Wills (3d Ed., Rev.1960) §§ 6.9–6.14; Rollison, Wills (1939) § 196; Ballantine, "When are Deeds Testamentary", 18 Mich.L.Rev. 470 (1920); Garvey, "Revocable Gifts of Legal Interests in Land", 54 Ky.L.J. 19 (1965); Gulliver and Tilson, "Classification of Gratuitous Transfers", 51 Yale L.J. 1, 18–21 (1941); "Use of Deeds to Effectuate Transfer at Death of Grantor", 32 Notre Dame Law 300 (1957); 10 Miss.L.J. 183 (1938); 18 Notre Dame Law 281 (1943); 32 Va.L.Rev. 148 (1945). Note, "The Issue of Delivery Raised by 'Dispositive' Conveyances", 18 Drake L.Rev. 67 (1968); Comment, "Proof of Deed by Circumstantial Evidence", 20 Baylor L.Rev. 167 (1968).

6. See 11 A.L.R. 23 (1921); 76 A.L.R. 636 (1932); 31 A.L.R.2d 532 (1953).

7. 52 A.L.R. 1222 (1928); 56 A.L.R. 746 (1928); 141 A.L.R. 305 (1942).

The will-deed relationship has been described as follows: [8]

"A will is essentially a tentative nomination of successors to take effect at death. If the devisee dies before the testator the devise lapses, as he has nothing to transmit. A will is ambulatory up to the testator's death, so that by its execution he has parted with no rights and divested himself of no incident of his estate. A deed, on the other hand, must convey some right, present or future, vested, contingent or executory in some specific property then owned by the grantor to some existing grantee. The grantee even in a deed deposited in escrow has an inheritable right. A deed is essentially a present conveyance of some interest, present or future. It is sometimes said that it must pass a present interest, but one should say rather presently pass an interest on its execution. The creation of a future or executory interest is to be contrasted with the future creation of an interest. A deed is not rendered testamentary because of reservations respecting the use of property during the grantor's life, or by provisions that 'title' shall pass at the grantor's death, or even by a power of revocation; but it must divest the grantor to some extent of his title, at least to the extent of creating a liability to have it drawn out of him without further act on his part. If an instrument is intended to become presently binding and nothing is left for the grantor to do to complete the transaction, then it need not be regarded as of a testamentary character. It is sufficient if it appears that the maker intended to convey any estate or interest whatever, though it be future or contingent."

It is well settled that a grantor can convey land and reserve a life estate in the property. Upon delivery of the deed a vested remainder is created in the grantee, his enjoyment of the property being postponed during the lifetime of the grantor.[9] When the deed contains no express reservation of a life estate but postpones the grantee's possession and enjoyment until the grantor's death, it is a matter of construction whether the deed creates a present or future interest in the grantee or whether the grantor intended to pass no interest until his death. In the latter event the deed is testamentary. Thus, the language in the deed may state that the deed is to "take effect and be in force",[10] "become absolute" [11] or "commence" [12] at the grantor's death. Or it may state that the grantor reserves "control, use, possession and enjoyment" of the property.[13] The deed may provide for some contingency, such as survival of the grantor by the grantee before it is to be effective,[14] or the grantor may reserve a power of revocation of the deed or a power of sale over the property.[15] The deed may contain only one such provision or various provisions may appear in combination.

The courts rely primarily upon the language in the instrument in reaching a decision concerning the grantor's intention, but if the language is considered ambiguous, extrinsic evidence is admitted to clarify the grantor's meaning. Each decision concerning the testamentary character of a deed is *sui*

8. Ballantine, "When are Deeds Testamentary", 18 Mich.L.Rev. 470, 482–483 (1920).

9. E.g., Johnson v. Seely, 139 Miss. 60, 103 So. 499 (1925).

10. Shaull v. Shaull, 182 Iowa 770, 166 N.W. 301, 11 A.L.R. 15 (1918), 2 Minn.L.Rev. 467 (1918).

11. Sutton v. Sutton, 141 Ark. 93, 216 S.W. 1052 (1919), 18 Mich.L.Rev. 564 (1920).

12. O'Day v. Meadows, 194 Mo. 588, 92 S.W. 637, 112 Am.St.Rep. 542 (1906).

13. Marsh v. Rogers, 205 Ala. 106, 87 So. 790 (1920).

14. Young v. O'Donnell, 129 Wash. 219, 224 P. 682 (1924).

15. Ellis v. Pearson, 104 Tenn. 591, 58 S.W. 318 (1900); Wright v. Huskey, 592 S.W.2d 899 (Tenn.App.1980).

generis since the language and extrinsic evidence differs in each case, but a majority of the courts tend to construe the language of the grantor liberally in order to give effect to his probable intention that the instrument should take effect as a deed and not fail as an unexecuted will.

When the language indicates that the deed is to be in force or take effect upon the grantor's death, many courts have regarded the language as an expression of intention to convey a vested remainder with a reservation of a life estate in the grantor.[16] A similar result has been reached when the language indicated that the deed was "to become absolute" [17] or was "to commence" [18] upon the death of the grantor, or when the grantor reserved "control" of the property.[19] A deed has been held non-testamentary when the grantor provided that the deed was not to take effect and operate until his death and that the grantee should not take unless she survived him.[20] A substantial minority of the courts have held that language similar to that discussed above expresses the grantor's intention that no interest is to be created until his death.[21]

When language of survivorship alone appears, a probable majority of the courts have held that the testator intends to create a present interest in the grantee, the enjoyment and possession of the property being contingent upon his survival of the grantor.[22] It is probable that these courts treat the language as a reservation of a fee simple in the grantor with a springing executory interest in the grantee, although the rationale of most of the decisions is unclear.[23] An almost equal number of courts hold that no present interest is created by language of survivorship.[24]

If the grantor reserves a power of revocation of the deed or a power of sale over the property the prevailing view appears to be that the deed is testamentary.[25]

Instead of inserting provisions in the deed with the intention of postponing possession and enjoyment of the property by the grantee, the grantor may execute a deed in absolute form and attempt to manipulate delivery in order to achieve the same effect. The grantor may deliver the deed to a third party depository with instructions to deliver it to the grantee at the death of the grantor. In most states this will operate as an immediate transfer of the property but will, in substance, reserve a life estate in the grantor.[26] In some states the conveyance creates no immediate interest in the grantee but is held good as an escrow to create an interest in the grantee at the grantor's death.[27] By either theory there must be an effective delivery of the deed. This means that the grantor must part with all dominion and

16. E.g., Kelley v. Shimer, 152 Ind. 290, 53 N.E. 233 (1899).

17. E.g., White v. Willard, 232 Ill. 464, 83 N.E. 954 (1908).

18. O'Day v. Meadows, fn. 12, supra.

19. Marsh v. Rogers, fn. 13, supra.

20. Abbot v. Holway, 72 Me. 298 (1881).

21. E.g., Kisecker's Estate, 190 Pa. 476, 42 A. 886 (1899); Donald v. Nesbitt, 89 Ga. 290, 15 S.E. 367 (1892).

22. E.g., Thomas v. Williams, 105 Minn. 88, 117 N.W. 155 (1908).

23. See Ballantine, "When Are Deeds Testamentary", 18 Mich.L.Rev. 470, 480 (1920).

24. E.g., Aldridge v. Aldridge, 202 Mo. 565, 101 S.W. 42 (1907).

25. E.g., Cunningham v. Davis, 62 Miss. 366 (1884). See Garvey, "Revocable Gifts of Legal Interests in Land", 54 Ky.L.J. 19 (1965).

26. E.g., Fine v. Lasater, 110 Ark. 425, 161 S.W. 1147, Ann.Cas.1915C, 385 (1913).

27. Stone v. Duvall, 77 Ill. 475 (1875); Ballantine, "When Are Deeds Testamentary", 18 Mich.L.Rev. 470, 474 (1920).

control over the instrument.[28] If he reserves a right of revocation or recall of the deed the delivery is ineffective.[29] No one can deliver the deed at the grantor's death if the grantor failed to deliver it during his lifetime.

The grantor may retain no unconditional power to revoke or recall the deed but may provide that the deed is to be delivered by the depository to the grantee upon the happening of some uncertain event. Thus, the grantor may direct the depository to deliver the deed to the grantee only if the grantee survives the grantor. Most of the courts have held that if the contingency is survival of the grantor by the grantee the delivery is ineffectual even though the condition is fulfilled.[30] This position is based upon the assumption that the condition is tantamount to a reservation of control by the grantor.[31] On the other hand, if the condition is to be performed after the death of the grantor, such as a payment of money by the grantee to another, the weight of authority is that the delivery is effective.[32] This view may be justified on the theory that title passes to the grantee immediately, subject to a life estate reserved in the grantor and subject to a further condition of divestment upon non-performance by the grantee.

If an attempt to sustain an instrument as a deed fails because provisions in it indicate testamentary intention on the part of the grantor, or if delivery of the deed is held to be ineffective, an attempt may be made to probate the instrument as a will. The instrument can be probated if it is executed with proper testamentary formalities and if the language of the instrument expresses testamentary intent or is so ambiguous that extrinsic evidence is admitted to show testamentary intent. But if the language in the deed is clearly non-testamentary the deed cannot be probated even if it is executed with testamentary formalities.

---

(3) GIFTS INTER VIVOS AND CAUSA MORTIS [33]

SCHERER v. HYLAND

Supreme Court of New Jersey, 1977.
75 N.J. 127, 380 A.2d 698.

PER CURIAM.

Defendant, the Administrator, *ad litem*, of the Estate of Catherine Wagner, appeals from an Appellate Division decision, one judge dis-

28. See 56 A.L.R. 746 (1928); 52 A.L.R. 1222 (1928); 141 A.L.R. 305 (1942); 54 L.R.A. 865 (1902); 9 L.R.A.,N.S., 224 (1907); 38 L.R.A.,N.S., 941 (1912).

29. E.g., Johnson v. Fleming, 301 Ill. 139, 133 N.E. 667 (1921).

30. E.g., Stone v. Daily, 181 Cal. 571, 185 P. 665 (1919).

31. See Ballantine, "When are Deeds Testamentary", 18 Mich.L.Rev. 470, 476 (1920).

32. E.g., Jackson v. Jackson, 67 Or. 44, 135 P. 201, Ann.Cas.1915C, 373 (1913).

33. Elements of gift transactions are developed here only to the extent necessary to delineate the relationships of gifts inter vivos and causa mortis to the will. For detailed considerations, see 1 Bowe-Parker: Page, Wills (3d Ed., Rev., 1960) Ch. 7, § 6.16; Brown, Personal Property (3d Ed., 1975) Ch. VII. Oppenheim, "The Donation Inter Vivos", 43 Tulane L.Rev. 731 (1969); Note, "Wills—

senting, affirming a summary judgment by the trial court holding that Ms. Wagner had made a valid gift *causa mortis* of a check to plaintiff. We affirm.

The facts are not in dispute. Catherine Wagner and the plaintiff, Robert Scherer, lived together for approximately fifteen years prior to Ms. Wagner's death in January 1974. In 1970, the decedent and plaintiff were involved in an automobile accident in which decedent suffered facial wounds and a broken hip. Because of the hip injury, decedent's physical mobility was substantially impaired. She was forced to give up her job and to restrict her activities. After the accident, plaintiff cared for her and assumed the sole financial responsibility for maintaining their household. During the weeks preceding her death, Ms. Wagner was acutely depressed. On one occasion, she attempted suicide by slashing her wrists. On January 23, 1974, she committed suicide by jumping from the roof of the apartment building in which they lived.

On the morning of the day of her death, Ms. Wagner received a check for $17,400 drawn by a Pennsylvania attorney who had represented her in a claim arising out of the automobile accident. The check represented settlement of the claim. Plaintiff telephoned Ms. Wagner at around 11:30 a. m. that day and was told that the check had arrived. Plaintiff noticed nothing unusual in Ms. Wagner's voice. At about 3:20 p. m., decedent left the apartment building and jumped to her death. The police, as part of their investigation of the suicide, asked the building superintendent to admit them to the apartment. On the kitchen table they found the check, endorsed in blank, and two notes handwritten by the decedent. In one, she described her depression over her physical condition, expressed her love for Scherer, and asked him to forgive her "for taking the easy way out." In the other, she indicated that she "bequeathed" to plaintiff all of her possessions, including "the check for $17,400.00 * * *." The police took possession of the check, which was eventually placed in an interest-bearing account pending disposition of this action.

Under our wills statute it is clear that Ms. Wagner's note bequeathing all her possessions to Mr. Scherer cannot take effect as a testamentary disposition. N.J.S.A. 3A:3–2. A *donatio causa mortis* has been traditionally defined as a gift of personal property made by a party in expectation of death, then imminent, subject to the condition that the donor die as anticipated. Establishment of the gift has uniformly called for proof of delivery.

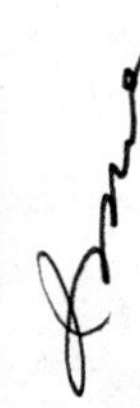

The primary issue here is whether Ms. Wagner's acts of endorsing the settlement check, placing it on the kitchen table in the apartment

Will Substitutes in Mississippi", 41 Miss. L.J. 177 (1969); Engle, "Making Gifts from the Estate of an Incompetent: The Substitution of Judgment Doctrine," 9 Wake Forest L.Rev. 199 (1973); Temple, "Gifts Effected by Written Instrument: Faith Lutheran Retirement Home v. Veis," 35 Mont.L.Rev. 132 (1974). See also Bradbrook, "Reassessment of the Scope of the Gift Causa Mortis," 17 McGill L.J. 567 (1971). As to arguments that ineffective gifts are trust declarations, see Love, "Imperfect Gifts as Declarations of Trust: An Unapologetic Anomaly", 67 Ky.L.J. 309 (1978–79).

she shared with Scherer, next to a writing clearly evidencing her intent to transfer the check to Scherer, and abandoning the apartment with a clear expectation of imminent death constituted delivery sufficient to sustain a gift *causa mortis* of the check. Defendant, relying on the principles established in Foster v. Reiss, 18 N.J. 41, 112 A.2d 553 (1955), argues that there was no delivery because the donor did not unequivocally relinquish control of the check before her death. Central to this argument is the contention that suicide, the perceived peril, was one which decedent herself created and one which was completely within her control. According to this contention, the donor at any time before she jumped from the apartment roof could have changed her mind, re-entered the apartment, and reclaimed the check. Defendant therefore reasons that decedent did not make an effective transfer of the check during her lifetime, as is required for a valid gift *causa mortis.*

The majority and dissenting opinions in Foster v. Reiss contain thorough analyses of the evolution of the delivery requirement of the gift *causa mortis.* See also Mechem, "The Requirement of Delivery in Gifts of Chattels and of Choses in Action Evidenced by Commercial Instruments," 21 Ill.L.Rev. 341, 457, 568 (1926); Burton, "The Requirement of Delivery as Applied to Gifts of Choses in Action," 39 Yale L.J. 837 (1930). For commentary on Foster v. Reiss, see Bordwell, "Testate and Intestate Succession," 10 Rutgers L.Rev. 293, 297 (1955); Note, 10 Rutgers L.Rev. 457 (1955); Note, 54 Mich.L.Rev. 572 (1956). We see no need to retrace that history here.

There is general agreement that the major purpose of the delivery requirement is evidentiary. Proof of delivery reduces the possibility that the evidence of intent has been fabricated or that a mere donative impulse, not consummated by action, has been mistaken for a completed gift. Since "these gifts come into question only after death has closed the lips of the donor," the delivery requirement provides a substantial safeguard against fraud and perjury. See Keepers v. Fidelity Title and Deposit Co., 56 N.J.L. 302, 308, 28 A. 585 (E. & A.1893). In *Foster*, the majority concluded that these policies could best be fulfilled by a strict rule requiring actual manual tradition of the subject-matter of the gift except in a very narrow class of cases where "there can be no actual delivery" or where "the situation is incompatible with the performance of such ceremony." 18 N.J. at 50, 112 A.2d at 559. Justice Jacobs, in his dissenting opinion (joined by Justices Brennan and Wachenfeld) questioned the reasonableness of requiring direct physical delivery in cases where donative intent is "freely and clearly expressed in a written instrument." Id. at 56, 112 A.2d at 562. He observed that a more flexible approach to the delivery requirement had been taken by other jurisdictions and quoted approvingly from Devol v. Dye, 123 Ind. 321, 24 N.E. 246, 7 L.R.A. 439 (Sup.Ct.1890). That case stated:

> [G]ifts *causa mortis* * * * are not to be held contrary to public policy, nor do they rest under the disfavor of the law, when the facts are clearly and satisfactorily shown which make it appear

that they were freely and intelligently made. Ellis v. Secor, 31 Mich. 185. While every case must be brought within the general rule upon the points essential to such a gift, yet, as the circumstances under which donations *mortis causa* are made must of necessity be infinite in variety, each case must be determined upon its own peculiar facts and circumstances. Dickeschild v. Bank, 28 W.Va. 341; Kiff v. Weaver, 94 N.C. 274. The rule requiring delivery, either actual or symbolical, must be maintained, but its application is to be militated and applied according to the relative importance of the subject of the gift and the condition of the donor. The intention of a donor in peril of death, when clearly ascertained and fairly consummated within the meaning of well-established rules, is not to be thwarted by a narrow and illiberal construction of what may have been intended for and deemed by him a sufficient delivery * * *.

The balancing approach suggested in Devol v. Dye has been articulated in the following manner:

Where there has been unequivocal proof of a deliberate and well-considered donative intent on the part of the donor, many courts have been inclined to overlook the technical requirements and to hold that by a "constructive" or "symbolic" delivery is sufficient to vest title in the donee. However, where this is allowed the evidence must clearly show an intention to part presently with some substantial attribute of ownership. [Gordon v. Barr, 13 Cal.2d 596, 601, 91 P.2d 101, 104 (Sup.Ct.Cal.1939)]

In essence, this approach takes into account the purposes served by the requirement of delivery in determining whether that requirement has been met. It would find a constructive delivery adequate to support the gift when the evidence of donative intent is concrete and undisputed, when there is every indication that the donor intended to make a present transfer of the subject-matter of the gift, and when the steps taken by the donor to effect such a transfer must have been deemed by the donor as sufficient to pass the donor's interest to the donee. We are persuaded that this approach, which does not minimize the need for evidentiary safeguards to prevent frauds upon the estates of the deceased, reflects the realities which attend transfers of this kind.

In this case, the evidence of decedent's intent to transfer the check to Robert Scherer is concrete, unequivocal, and undisputed. The circumstances definitely rule out any possibility of fraud. The sole question, then, is whether the steps taken by the decedent, independent of her writing of the suicide notes, were sufficient to support a finding that she effected a lifetime transfer of the check to Scherer. We think that they were. First, the act of endorsing a check represents, in common experience and understanding, the only act needed (short of actual delivery) to render a check negotiable. The significance of such an act is universally understood. Accordingly, we have no trouble in viewing Ms. Wagner's endorsement of the settlement check as a substantial step taken by her for the purpose of effecting

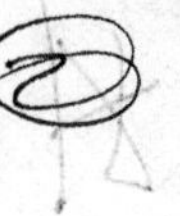

a transfer to Scherer of her right to the check proceeds. Second, we note that the only person other than the decedent who had routine access to the apartment was Robert Scherer. Indeed, the apartment was leased in his name. It is clear that Ms. Wagner before leaving the apartment placed the check in a place where Scherer could not fail to see it and fully expected that he would take actual possession of the check when he entered. And, although Ms. Wagner's subsequent suicide does not itself constitute a component of the delivery of this gift, it does provide persuasive evidence that when Ms. Wagner locked the door of the apartment she did so with no expectation of returning. When we consider her state of mind as it must have been upon leaving the apartment, her surrender of possession at that moment was complete. We find, therefore, that when she left the apartment she completed a constructive delivery of the check to Robert Scherer. In light of her resolve to take her own life and of her obvious desire not to be deterred from that purpose, Ms. Wagner's failure manually to transfer the check to Scherer is understandable. She clearly did all that she could do or thought necessary to do to surrender the check. Her donative intent has been conclusively demonstrated by independent evidence. The law should effectuate that intent rather than indulge in nice distinctions which would thwart her purpose. Upon these facts, we find that the constructive delivery she made was adequate to support a gift *causa mortis*.

Defendant's assertion that suicide is not the sort of peril that will sustain a gift *causa mortis* finds some support in precedents from other jurisdictions. E.g., Ray v. Leader Federal Sav. & Loan Ass'n, 40 Tenn.App. 625, 292 S.W.2d 458 (Ct.App.1953). See generally Annot., "Nature and validity of gift made in contemplation of suicide," 60 A.L.R.2d 575 (1958). We are, however, not bound by those authorities nor do we find them persuasive. While it is true that a gift *causa mortis* is made by the donor with a view to impending death, death is no less impending because of a resolve to commit suicide. Nor does that fixed purpose constitute any lesser or less imminent peril than does a ravaging disease. Indeed, given the despair sufficient to end it all, the peril attendant upon contemplated suicide may reasonably be viewed as even more imminent than that accompanying many illnesses which prove ultimately to be fatal. Cf. Berl v. Rosenberg, 169 Cal.App.2d 125, 336 P.2d 975, 978 (Dist.Ct.App.1959) (public policy against suicide does not invalidate otherwise valid gift *causa mortis*). And, the notion that one in a state of mental depression serious enough to lead to suicide is somehow "freer" to renounce the depression and thus the danger than one suffering from a physical illness, although it has a certain augustinian appeal, has long since been replaced by more enlightened views of human psychology. In re Van Wormer's Estate, 255 Mich. 399, 238 N.W. 210 (Sup.Ct.1931) (melancholia ending in suicide sufficient to sustain a gift *causa mortis*). We also observe that an argument that the donor of a *causa mortis* gift might have changed his or her mind loses much of its force when one recalls that a *causa mortis* gift, by definition, can be

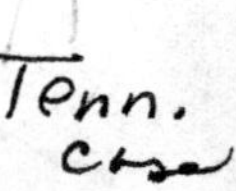

revoked at any time before the donor dies and is automatically revoked if the donor recovers.

Finally, defendant asserts that this gift must fail because there was no acceptance prior to the donor's death. Although the issue of acceptance is rarely litigated, the authority that does exist indicates that, given a valid delivery, acceptance will be implied if the gift is unconditional and beneficial to the donee. See, e.g., Sparks v. Hurley, 208 Pa. 166, 57 A. 364, 366 (Sup.Ct.1904); Graham v. Johnston, 243 Iowa 112, 49 N.W.2d 540, 543 (Sup.Ct.1951). The presumption of acceptance may apply even if the donee does not learn of the gift until after the donor's death. Taylor v. Sanford, 108 Tex. 340, 344, 193 S.W. 661, 662 (Sup.Ct.1912) (assent to gift of deed mailed in contemplation of death but received after grantor's death should be presumed unless a dissent or disclaimer appears). A donee cannot be expected to accept or reject a gift until he learns of it and unless a gift is rejected when the donee is informed of it the presumption of acceptance is not defeated. See id. at 344, 193 S.W. at 662. Here the gift was clearly beneficial to Scherer, and he has always expressed his acceptance.

Judgment affirmed.

NOTE

A gift inter vivos may be made of land or personal property. A gift causa mortis may be made of personal property only.[34] At common law there is no limitation upon the proportion of a donor's estate or the value of the property that can be the subject of a valid gift.[35]

The requisites for an effective gift inter vivos of personal property and an effective gift causa mortis are the same for the most part. A property owner who has the mental capacity to make a gift[36] must, gratuitously[37] and during his lifetime, make an actual or symbolical delivery[38] of the property to the donee or a third party on the donee's behalf, accompanied by a manifested intention[39] to make a present[40] gift of the property by the act of delivery. The donee must accept the gift, although acceptance of a beneficial gift will be presumed.[41] A gift causa mortis must be made when the

34. E.g., Gordon v. Clark, 149 Ark. 173, 232 S.W. 19 (1921). A gift causa mortis cannot be a substitute for a devise. Rood, Wills (2d Ed., 1926) 12–13. But see the principal case, Scherer v. Hyland, 75 N.J. 127, 380 A.2d 698 (1977).

35. The amount may be limited by the claims of creditors or the surviving spouse or there may be statutory limitations.

36. E.g., LaMar v. Bank of America National Trust & Savings Association, 218 Cal. 252, 22 P.2d 689 (1933). Capacity to make a gift is usually defined as mental capacity sufficient to understand the nature of the transaction. Cf. Rood, Wills (2d Ed., 1926) 20.

37. The transaction is a sale if consideration is received.

38. Aubrey v. Kent, 292 Ky. 740, 167 S.W.2d 831 (1943), Delivery is not required if a person gratuitously declares himself trustee of property for another. For a possible distinction between "symbolical" and "constructive" delivery, see Brown, Personal Property (3d Ed. 1975) §§ 7.5, 7.6.

39. E.g., Henley v. Live Stock National Bank, 127 Neb. 857, 257 N.W. 244 (1934).

40. E.g., Hart v. Ketchum, 121 Cal. 426, 53 P. 931 (1898).

41. E.g., Ammon v. Martin, 59 Ark. 191, 26 S.W. 826 (1894). See, Annot. "Unexplained Gratuitous Transfer of Property from One Relative to Another as Raising Presumption of Gift", 94 A.L.R.3d 608 (1979).

donor is in imminent peril of death and under such circumstances that the gift would not be made were it not for the peril.[42]

The courts have established no precise test for the delivery required in a gift inter vivos or causa mortis. The nature of the property and the circumstances of the parties are considered in determining whether the requisites for delivery are satisfied. If the property is in a safety deposit box, delivery of the key as a symbol of control over the property may be sufficient.[43] If a writing, such as a pass book to a savings account, evidences a chose in action, the chose in action may be given by delivery of the writing.[44] If the chose in action is not embodied in a writing or evidenced thereby, delivery must be by a written assignment.[45]

The test for imminence of death which is required for an effective gift causa mortis is equally indefinite. It is not the same as that required for a nuncupative will.[46] The donor must anticipate more than the general mortality of man.[47] Yet he need not be *in extremis.*[48] The courts have seemed more willing to regard a peril as imminent when the donor is suffering from a physical infirmity than when he is threatened by some external peril. There is some authority to support the proposition that peril need be only in the mind of the donor, so that the donor may make a gift causa mortis even if no peril exists.[49] A majority of the courts do not require that the donor die from the particular peril that he anticipates.[50]

A gift inter vivos is irrevocable and the donor must intend to create an immediate interest in the donee at the time delivery is made. A gift to take effect in the future is ineffective. If no interest is created at the time of delivery, there is only a gratuitous promise to make a gift in the future. If no interest is created until after the donor's death, the transaction is testa-

42. E.g., Williams v. Guile, 117 N.Y. 343, 22 N.E. 1071, 6 L.R.A. 366 (1889).

43. See Winder, "Delivery of a Donatio Mortis Causa", 3 Mod.L.Rev. 310 (1940); Mechem, "The Requirement of Delivery in Gifts of Chattels and of Choses in Action Evidenced by Commercial Instruments", 21 Ill.L.Rev. 341, 457, 568 (1926). Minor distinctions may be made between the delivery required for a gift inter vivos and the delivery required for a gift causa mortis. See Brown, Personal Property (3d Ed. 1975) § 7.16. For an interesting case on failure of a gift *causa mortis* for want of delivery see Rust v. Phillips, 208 Va. 573, 159 S.E.2d 628 (1968). See Annot. "Joint Lease of Safe-Deposit Box as Evidence in Support or Denial of Gift Inter Vivos of Contents", 40 A.L.R.3d 462 (1971); "Creation of Joint Savings Account of Savings Account or Savings Certificate as Gift to Survivor", 43 A.L.R.3d 971 (1972); "Issuance of Stock Certificate to Joint Tenants as Creating Gift Inter Vivos", 5 A.L.R. 4th 373 (1980).

44. E.g., In re Estate of Hanson, 205 Iowa 766, 218 N.W. 308 (1928). There is a conflict of authority whether there must be compliance with the rules of the bank regulating the transfer of accounts. Brooks v. Mitchell, 163 Md. 1, 161 A. 261, 84 A.L.R. 547 (1932); Grigonis's Estate, 307 Pa. 183, 160 A. 706 (1932), 12 B.U.L. R. 711 (1932), 81 U. of Pa.L.Rev. 224 (1932). There was a similar dispute whether United States Savings Bonds might be the subject of a gift under the applicable statutes and treasury regulations. Marshall v. Felker, 156 Fla. 476, 23 So.2d 555 (1945), 30 Marq.L.Rev. 208 (1946); Fidelity Union Trust Co. v. Tezyk, 140 N.J.Eq. 474, 55 A.2d 26 (1947), 61 Harv.L.Rev. 542 (1948); note, 27 Sw.L.J. 561 (1973). In United States v. Chandler, 410 U.S. 257, 93 S.Ct. 880, 35 L.Ed.2d 247 (1973), the U. S. Supreme Court held that gifts inter vivos could be made only by reissuance, as required by Treasury Regulations.

45. See, Brown, Personal Property (3d Ed., 1975) § 8.4.

46. See Nicholas v. Adams, 2 Whart. (Pa.) 17 (1836).

47. E.g., Taylor v. Harmison, 79 Ill. App. 380, aff'd 179 Ill. 137, 53 N.E. 584 (1898).

48. E.g., Grymes v. Hone, 49 N.Y. 17 (1872).

49. See Brown, Personal Property (3d Ed. 1975) § 7.18.

50. E.g., Ridden v. Thrall, 125 N.Y. 572, 26 N.E. 627, 21 Am.St.Rep. 758, 11 L.R.A. 684 (1891).

mentary and ineffective unless executed with the formalities required for a will. The donee's possession and enjoyment of the property may be postponed if an immediate interest is created in him.

A gift causa mortis is revocable by the donor during his lifetime [51] and is revoked automatically by the cessation of the peril which inspired the gift.[52] There is some support for the proposition that the gift is revoked if the donor survives the donee.[53] The gifts are sustained as non-testamentary in a majority of jurisdictions on the ground that an interest is created immediately in the donee subject to being divested by the cessation of the peril or the donor's revocation. Some courts have regarded an interest in the donee as subject to a condition precedent of the donor's death, and the gift causa mortis as an exception to the requirements made by statute for testamentary formalities.

A gift causa mortis need not be probated. The property is subject to the claims of creditors of the donor after the assets of the estate have been exhausted and to the forced share of a surviving spouse if the remaining estate is inadequate to satisfy it.[54] A gift causa mortis cannot be revoked by the donor's will,[55] but there is a division of authority whether the gift is revoked by the birth of a child after the gift is made or whether it is subject to the claims of a pretermitted heir. The courts which adhere to the theory that a vested interest subject to being divested is created in the donee during the lifetime of the donor deny the claims of the children.[56] The courts which treat the gift causa mortis as a variety of will sustain the claims of the children.[57]

The Economic Recovery Tax Act of 1981 made death-bed gifts attractive in large estates which are likely to exceed the exemption equivalent of the estate tax credit (recall the tax material in Chapter VIII, Section 2). Gifts of property such as cash, stocks and bonds (but not life insurance) may be made to family members or friends, provided that the amount given to each donee does not exceed $10,000. Such gifts are no longer reportable for gift tax purposes and are not required to be included in the gross estate for estate tax purposes. Such amounts may have to be eliminated from the estate of a taxpayer by "last minute" planning. Because such gifts are likely to be made to persons named as devisees in the donor's will, care must be taken to be sure that the gift causa mortis will be subtracted from any general devise to the same person; see the materials on ademption by satisfaction in Chapter XV, Section 1(2)(ii).

51. E.g., Parker v. Marston, 27 Me. 196 (1847).

52. E.g., Ellsworth v. Cornes, 204 Ark. 756, 165 S.W.2d 57 (1942).

53. See Brown, Personal Property (3d Ed. 1975) § 7.19.

54. The gift inter vivos is ineffective when made in fraud of creditors but probably is effective in most states against the claim of the surviving spouse. See Chapter IV, Section 2. See Schwartz Estate, 449 Pa. 112, 295 A.2d 600 (1972), noted in 12 Duquesne L.Rev. 125 (1973) on whether or not the surviving spouse of the custodian of a gift to a minor may, under the Uniform Gift to Minors Act, reach the gift on electing to take against the will of the deceased custodian.

55. E.g., Moore v. Shifflet, 187 Ky. 7, 216 S.W. 614 (1920).

56. See McCoy v. Shawnee Building & Loan Association, 122 Kan. 38, 251 P. 194, 49 A.L.R. 1441 (1926), 75 U. of Pa.L. Rev. 569 (1927).

57. Bloomer v. Bloomer, 2 Bradf.Surr. (N.Y.) 339 (1853).

PROBLEM

H, after learning that he had cancer, assigned in blank certain shares of stock, signed a typewritten memorandum that the stock and a certain bond were the property of W, put the stock, bond, and memorandum, in an envelope addressed to W and locked the envelope in a drawer in his office safe. Thereafter, H told W and others that he had given W the stock. After being confined to his bed, H gave W a bunch of keys, among which was the key to the drawer in the safe, and told her to take good care of them as they would mean a great deal to her if anything happened to him and that they opened the box in which there were private papers for her. Thereafter, W retained the keys in her possession and had access to the locked drawer at any time. When H died, his executor contended that the facts showed an intention to make a testamentary disposition of the property. Should the bond and stock pass to W or to the estate of H? Thomas v. First National Bank, 166 Va. 497, 186 S.E. 77 (1936).

---

(4) JOINT INTERESTS AND TENANCIES BY THE ENTIRETY [58]

FREY v. WUBBENA

Supreme Court of Illinois, 1962.
26 Ill.2d 62, 185 N.E.2d 850.

HOUSE, JUSTICE. This cause originated as an action to partition real estate. The complaint was filed by plaintiffs, Leona Frey and Rosanna Dietmeier, daughters by a prior marriage of Herman E. Wubbena, against Martha Wubbena, Herman's widow, and the executor of his estate. The widow filed a counterclaim to determine the rights and interests of the parties in certain securities, accounts and notes. An amicable agreement for sale of the real estate was reached, and it was stipulated that the issues were limited to ownership of such other assets. The trial court entered a decree finding that certain United States savings bonds belonged to plaintiffs, but

58. Joint tenancies and tenancies by the entirety are considered in detail in courses on real and personal property and are developed here only to the extent necessary to delineate their relationship to the will. For detailed considerations see American Law of Property (1952). §§ 6.1–6.4, 6.6; Tiffany, Real Property (3d Ed., 1939) §§ 418–425, 430, 436. For some of the problems created in estate planning by joint interests see Hines, "Real Property Joint Tenancies: Law, Fact and Fancy", 20 Okla.L.Rev. 462 (1967); "Personal Property Joint Tenancies: More Law, Fact and Fancy", 54 Minn.L.Rev. 509 (1970); Riecker, "Joint Tenancy: The Estate Lawyer's Continuing Burden", 64 Mich.L.Rev. 801 (1966); Warner, "Tenancies by the Entirety—An Estate Planner's Dilemma or (A Study of Unintended Result)", 23 Ark.L.Rev. 44 (1969). Note, "Donee Beneficiary Contracts as Applied to Joint Survivorship Accounts", 21 Sw.L.J. 323 (1967). Comments, "Joint Bank Accounts: The Survivor's Right to Payments Due to the Account", 1968 U. of Ill.L.F. 410 (1968); "Personal Property: Joint Accounts with Right of Survivorship", 20 Okla.L.Rev. 462 (1967); "Requirements for Certificates of Deposit and Bank Accounts Held in Joint Tenancy with Right of Survivorship in Indiana," 8 Val.U.L.Rev. 140 (1973); Harris, "Will Substitutes", 41 Ala. Lawyer 235 (1980).

that all other items were property of the estate and directed that they be assigned to the executor. Upon appeal to the Appellate Court, Second District, the decree was affirmed. (32 Ill.App.2d 374, 177 N.E.2d 724.) We granted leave to appeal.

Herman and Martha were married on February 11, 1941. They lived together until his death on August 31, 1957, except for about six weeks early in 1944 when she left him and instituted a separate maintenance action. Investments were made by Herman from his sole funds without the knowledge of his wife or daughters. He managed his own affairs and collected rents and income until his death. He left a will by which he gave his wife only so much of his estate as she was entitled to under the statute and the remainder to his daughters.

The assets in question are described in the opinion of the Appellate Court and need not be again detailed here. They consisted of corporate stocks, savings accounts in various banks and savings and loan associations, checking accounts, bank certificates of deposit, notes, and a certificate evidencing an interest in an elevator partnership. Stocks were registered on the books of the several corporations in the name of Herman E. Wubbena and one or the other of his daughters as joint tenants. Checking and savings accounts were opened in the name of Herman and his two daughters in joint tenancy. The agreements with the depositaries were signed by Herman and his daughters. Two certificates of deposit were purchased payable to the father and two daughters, and $500 was placed in an investment trust in the name of each daughter. Loans were made to individuals and notes taken as evidence thereof in their three names as joint tenants, and another note was made payable only to the two daughters. He also issued a certificate in a partnership in which he was a 1/4 owner declaring that interest belonged to him and his two daughters "jointly or either survivor."

This case involves a wide variety of personal property interests and brings into sharp focus most of the troublesome problems which the concept of survivorship with respect to personalty has presented to the courts. As was said in In re Estate of Schneider, 6 Ill.2d 180, 127 N.E.2d 445, the relationships contemplated "do not fit readily into common-law categories." Thus the unities which characterize the common-law joint tenancy, the notion of an undivided moiety in each joint tenant, and the difficulties of applying the common-law concept of joint tenancy to a fluctuating *res*, prevent the traditional joint tenancy estate from providing a logical solution. (See Mr. Justice Thompson's dissents in Illinois Trust and Savings Bank v. Van Vlack, 310 Ill. 185, 141 N.E. 546, and Reder v. Reder, 312 Ill. 209, 143 N.E. 418.) We are faced with the further problem of fitting the foot of modern day use and understanding of gifts of intangible personal property through survivorship arrangements into the rigid shoe of common-law principles.

However troublesome the strict application of these common-law principles may be, the concept of survivorship with respect to personal property has grown until it has become an established fact of present day life. Joint bank and savings and loan accounts, with the balances payable to survivors, are widely used. Government savings bonds commonly contain survivorship provisions. Many stock certificates have been and are being issued daily in the names of two or more persons as joint tenants with rights of survivorship and issuing corporations and their transfer agents are continually acting in reliance upon the effectiveness of the survivorship provisions. The legislature has recognized the realities of this situation by enacting statutory provisions (hereafter more particularly referred to) relative to joint bank accounts, joint accounts in savings and loan associations, and corporate stocks and bonds or other evidences of indebtedness in the names of two or more persons as joint tenants with right of survivorship.

In 1953, when the common-law requirement with respect to the four unities in the case of a joint tenancy in real estate was relaxed by the statutory provision that an estate with all the effects of a common-law joint tenancy could be created through a conveyance from a grantor directly to himself and another, without the intervention of a third party (Ill.Rev.Stat.1961, chap. 76, par. 1b) the legislature passed a similar enactment relative to transfers of tangible or intangible personal property. (Ill.Rev.State.1961, chap. 76, par. 2.1.) Public policy would seem to require the adoption by the courts of a more liberal and practical view of these common transactions. With these preliminary observations in mind, we proceed to consider the several categories of securities here involved.

Section 2(a) of the statute on joint rights and obligations (Ill.Rev. Stat.1961, chap. 76, par. 2(a)) expressly provides that "When a deposit in any bank * * * has been made or shall hereafter be made in the names of two or more persons payable to them when the account is opened or thereafter, such deposit or any part thereof or any interest or dividend thereon may be paid to any one of said persons whether the other or others be living or not, and when an agreement permitting such payment is signed by all said persons at the time the account is opened or thereafter the receipt or acquittance of the person so paid shall be valid and sufficient discharge from all parties to the bank for any payments so made." This statute was enacted in 1919, and while there have been some amendments, the basic provisions have remained in substance the same.

It has been suggested that this enactment does no more than protect the bank. That point was made in the dissent in the Van Vlack case but the majority opinion there construed the statute as having a broader application in that it also provided a statutory method by which a right of survivorship could be created as between the parties themselves. * * *

* * *

Section 4–10 of the Illinois Savings and Loan Act, (Ill.Rev.Stat. 1961, chap. 32, par. 770), which became effective July 5, 1955, contains broad and comprehensive provisions for the creation of rights of survivorship in the case of savings and loan association capital accounts, and makes the signing of an agreement among the parties mandatory. * * *

The right to create a joint tenancy in corporate stock is also recognized by Section 2 of the statute on joint rights and obligations. (Ill. Rev.Stat.1961, chap. 76, par. 2.) * * *

A statutory right of survivorship exists and we think it unnecessary to follow the principles of common-law joint tenancy whether an agreement has been signed by the parties or not. The registration of stock ownership upon the books of the corporation in appropriate statutory language is sufficient to vest legal title, subject to divestment if the circumstances surrounding the transaction warrant it. This view may seem at odds with our approval of the holding in the Doubler case that an agreement must be signed by the parties to effectuate survivorship rights in a bank account. Aside from the differences in the several statutory provisions, we think there is ample justification in the very nature of the property. Corporate stock is issued in fixed units of ownership (shares of stock) and remain fixed, whereas a bank account is a fluctuating *res*, subject to daily change in amount by any of the joint owners. Joint tenancy in such an unstable atmosphere as a shifting bank account should be created by contract of the parties detailing their rights and duties under existing statutory authority. Bank accounts are in this respect similar to saving and loan capital accounts, and a joint account in the latter is not recognized by the Illinois Savings and Loan Act unless there is an agreement in writing.

Promissory notes when drawn in appropriate language, are instruments in writing within the meaning of Section 2 (Ill.Rev.Stat.1961, chap. 76, par. 2,) and constitute exceptions to the section abolishing joint tenancy in personal property.

What we have said with respect to creation of joint tenancies in intangible personal property in the language of the statutes amounts to a holding that legal (as differentiated from equitable) title is vested in the holders with right of survivorship by force of the statutes, and compliance with the appropriate statutory requirements dispenses with the necessity of applying common-law principles governing creation of joint tenancies. We do not mean to imply that where joint ownership is set up in conformity with the statutory provisions, a court of equity is thereby foreclosed from looking behind the form of the transaction and determining questions of real and beneficial interest as between the parties. In In re Estate of Schneider, 6 Ill.2d 180, 127 N.E.2d 445, Schneider, who was the owner of funds in a savings and loan association, established a joint account with one Ralston (who was not related to him) and both of the parties signed an agreement purporting to establish a joint tenancy with right of survivorship. After Schneider's death, his executor claimed the account as a part of Schneider's estate. The executor established by parol evidence that Ralston's name had been used on the account solely for Schneider's convenience so that in case of Schneider's illness Ralston could get funds for him, and that it was never contemplated by the parties that Ralston should have any beneficial interest in the account. Such evidence was held admissible to show the true ownership of the account as between the parties. It was there pointed out, however, that the deposit agreement was sufficient to establish ownership in the survivor by virtue of the contract upon the death of the original owner, in the absence of evidence to the contrary. The opinion further makes it clear that the court was concerned only with the rights of the depositors between themselves and, irrespective of the equities between them, the association would be protected in making payments in accordance with the terms of the deposit agreement.

There is no contention by the daughters that they contributed any funds for the investments in the joint tenancy personalty, but they rely upon the gift theory. There is a presumption that the taking or placing of title by a father in a child is a gift or advancement, and the burden is upon one questioning the gift to overcome the presumption by clear and convincing proof. (Moore v. Moore, 9 Ill.2d 556, 138 N.E.2d 562; Kraft v. Kretchman, 17 Ill.2d 71, 160 N.E.2d 806). There is a further presumption of acceptance of a gift beneficial to the donee. Healy v. Stevens, 347 Ill. 202, 179 N.E. 535; Fonda v. Miller, 411 Ill. 74, 103 N.E.2d 98; Maciaszek v. Maciaszek, 21 Ill.2d 542, 173 N.E.2d 476.

Defendants contend that the placing of title to the various assets in joint tenancy did not create valid *inter vivos* gifts. This is predicated primarily upon the theory that there was lack of donative intent and that the purpose was to use joint tenancy as a device for testamentary disposition. Secondarily, it is asserted that the donor did not part with control over the property and hence there was no irrevocable delivery.

Evidence tending to rebut the presumption of donative intent is meagre. Only four witnesses testified, each called by the plaintiffs. Two were farmers to whom Herman had loaned money. The essence of Herman's statements to them when he took the notes in the three names was that he wanted the money to go to his daughters when he died. Another witness, the secretary-treasurer of one of the savings and loan associations, testified that Herman wanted his daughters "to go on the account with him" so that the proceeds would be paid to his daughters. The only other witness, an employee of the elevator partnership, said that he was fixing it so that the girls would get his interest in the partnership. No testimony was offered as to the circumstances surrounding the placing of the other items in joint tenancy. This evidence, taken in conjunction with the surrounding circumstances as disclosed by the stipulation of facts, is far short of the clear and convincing proof necessary to rebut the presumption of donative intent. We think the record affirmatively shows that the father by his actions intended to make gifts to his daughters through survivorship arrangements. His conversations with the witnesses regarding his desires and intentions did not make the gifts void as testamentary dispositions. As was aptly said in the case of In re Estate of Mueth, 33 Ill.App.2d 449, 179 N.E.2d 695, where similar expres-

sions of intentions were made: "This is the essence of joint tenancy, and if such thoughts of the contingencies make the contract void as testamentary, then there is no such thing as a joint tenancy in a bank account in this state, * * *."

We turn to the question of whether the acts of the intended donor amounted to consummation of his intent to make *inter vivos* gifts. In addition to donative intent, other elements must be present. The donor must part with exclusive dominion and control over the subject of the gift and there must be delivery. The decedent surrendered his exclusive right to the several items when he voluntarily placed ownership in himself and others. The rights of the co-owners were equal to his own and by the transfer of his funds into joint-tenancy obligations he gave up exclusive dominion and control. Each of the co-owners has an equal right to possession of the evidence of title (passbook, note, certificate, etc.) and, since they cannot both have manual possession at the same time, possession by one is possession for the benefit of both. (Illinois Trust and Savings Bank v. Van Vlack, 310 Ill. 185, 141 N.E. 546.) We think it follows that delivery by the issuer or maker to one of the joint owners is delivery for the benefit of all and satisfies the requirement of delivery where, as here, there is donative intent. Cf. Maciaszek v. Maciaszek, 21 Ill.2d 542, 173 N.E.2d 476.

* * *

It is finally contended by the defendants that the creation of the joint tenancies amounted to fraud upon Mrs. Wubbena and was contrary to public policy. As was said in Hoeffner v. Hoeffner, 389 Ill. 253, 260, 59 N.E.2d 684, 687: "It has long been settled that a husband enjoys the absolute right to dispose of his property during his lifetime, independently of the concurrence and exonerated from the claim of his wife, provided, of course, the transaction is not merely colorable and is free from circumstances of fraud upon the rights of the wife". Defendants concede this to be the law, and concede that when actual fraud is alleged the one alleging it must substantiate the charge by clear and convincing evidence, but attempt to avoid the burden of proof thus placed upon them by advancing the theory that the facts themselves, regardless of the intent of the perpetrator, amount to fraud *per se* for the reason that they violate public policy and good conscience. This is a novel theory, particularly under the facts before us.

This second wife was well provided for. Herman's entire estate, including the securities in question, was about $229,000. The value of the joint securities is about $78,500, so the amount here actually involved is $26,200, leaving in excess of $150,000. The widow will receive 1/3 of that amount. While the husband was creating joint tenancies for the benefit of his daughters, he was at the same time building up the value of the farm chattels, which were inventoried at $22,850.29. During the same period he took out life insurance policies in favor of his wife with benefits of $9900. The mere fact that he created the joint tenancies after the separation with his wife is not clear and convincing proof of intent to defraud, if it can be said to be proof at all. This claim is wholly untenable.

We apply what has heretofore been said to the various intangible assets which are the subject of this litigation. The savings account in the Ogle County National Bank was carried in the names of Herman E. Wubbena or Leona Frey or Rosanna Dietmeier. This does not indicate an intention to create the right of survivorship nor was there a deposit agreement providing for joint tenancy. The deposit agreements covering the remaining bank checking accounts and the three savings and loan accounts were in apt language to create the rights of survivorship and they should have been held to be the property of the respective survivors. Thirty shares of preferred stock of Quality Milk Company were issued in the names of Herman E. Wubbena or Rosanna Dietmeier and likewise failed to create joint tenancy ownership. All of the remaining stocks were in appropriate language to create joint tenancy and became the property of the surviving joint tenants upon the death of Herman. Certificate of deposit No. 15251 issued by First State Bank of Shannon was issued to Herman E. Wubbena and/or Leona Frey and/or Rosanna Dietmeier and also failed to create joint tenancy ownership. Certificate of deposit No. 77055 issued by Forreston State Bank was in apt language and should have been held to be the property of the surviving daughters.

The notes of Harvey Wubbena, Harley and Ardis M. Motter, and Cornelius F. and Ethel Hayenga, were payable to Herman and the two plaintiffs in language appropriate to create rights of survivorship and should have been declared the property of the survivors. A note from Aril L. Barton was payable to Herman Wubbena and another was signed by Lillian G. and Helen M. Spratler and was payable to Leona Frey and Rosanna Dietmeier. There was neither loss of dominion and control nor a delivery of the Barton note, and there was no delivery of the Spratler note, and they were properly held to be the property of the estate. Their mere presence in a safety deposit box rented jointly in the names of the decedent and his daughters did not make the contents joint tenancy obligations. There was no proof of delivery of the savings accounts in Investor's Mutual issued to Herman E. Wubbena "for" each of his daughters and the trial court properly held them to be the property of Herman's estate.

The savings account in the Ogle County National Bank, the shares of stock in Quality Milk Company and certificate of deposit No. 15251 should have been declared to be the property of the respective parties designated as owners in equal shares as tenants in common. Engelbrecht v. Engelbrecht, 323 Ill. 208, 153 N.E. 827; Harvey v. United States, (7th Cir.) 185 F.2d 463.

The certificate of interest in the partnership which Herman issued attempting to place it in joint tenancy with his daughters was wholly ineffective under the Uniform Partnership Act. (Ill.Rev.Stat.1961, chap. 106½.) The very nature of a partnership is such that joint tenancy between one of the partners and a stranger to the partnership would be abhorrent to the act. The interest in the partnership was properly held to be the property of the estate.

The trial court was right in holding the United States savings bonds to be the property of the survivors. This is in conformance with the statute (Ill.Rev.Stat.1961, chap. 76, par. 2(d) as well as Federal regulations. It was recently held in Free v. Bland, 369 U.S. 663, 82 S.Ct. 1089, 8 L.Ed.2d 180, that if a conflict arises, Federal law prevails over State law. Thus, no issue remains with respect to the government obligations.

For the reasons assigned, the decree of the trial court and the judgment of the Appellate Court, Second District, is affirmed in part and reversed in part, and the cause is remanded to the circuit court of Carroll County, with directions to enter a decree consistent with this opinion.

Affirmed in part and reversed in part and remanded, with directions.

NOTE

A devise or conveyance of land to two or more persons jointly, without a direction concerning the share that each will have, at common law is presumed to create a joint tenancy. A devise or conveyance to a husband and wife during coverture, which does not require them to hold the property in some other form of tenancy, at common law creates a tenancy by the entirety. The tenancy by the entirety is a form of joint tenancy based upon the common law theory that husband and wife are one person. Upon the death of one joint tenant or tenant by the entirety, the remaining tenant takes the interest of the deceased tenant by survivorship unaffected by his will.

Traditional common law required "four unities" for creation of a joint tenancy or tenancy by the entirety: the title of the owners must be created by the same act, the interests vest at the same time, the interests be of the same quantity and duration, and the owners hold the same (undivided) possession. If the owner of property wished to create a joint tenancy in that property with another, the owner had to convey to a third person (called a "strawman") who then conveyed back to the original owner and the other person as joint tenants, so that they took at the same time and by the same instrument. Any destruction of one of the unities terminated ("severed") the joint tenancy and destroyed the right of survivorship. Thus a conveyance by one joint tenant of his interest to another person would make the latter a tenant in common rather than a joint tenant; however, a different rule governed tenancies by the entirety and a conveyance by one tenant could not destroy the survivorship right of the other tenant by the entirety. Upon death of one joint tenant or tenant by the entirety the surviving tenant became the sole owner, not on a theory that he succeeded to the deceased tenant's interest but on the concept that both owned the whole and the deceased tenant's interest ceased at death. This is why the deceased tenant's will could not devise his interest, and his unsecured creditors could not pursue claims against the property now owned solely by the survivor.

The present status and requirements for creation of joint tenancies and tenancies by the entirety vary widely from state to state.[59] Tenancies by the

59. See, "Property Owned with Spouse: Joint Tenancy, Tenancy by the Entireties and Community Property," 11 Real Prop., Prop. & Tr.J. 405 (1976).

entirety cannot be created in community property states; some common law states no longer permit their creation, either because of Married Women's Property Acts or by application of general statutes governing joint tenancy, or as an obsolete incident of marriage. In other states the common-law characteristics of tenancies by the entirety are deemed modified by the Married Women's Property Acts. The four unities for creation of joint tenancies and tenancies by the entirety have been eliminated in many states, either by statute or court decision; in creating joint ownership of stocks, bonds and other forms of personal property modern courts often dispense with the requirement of four unities. On the other hand, some states still have statutes, enacted in the last century, which purport to abolish either joint tenancies or the right of survivorship. In still other states the old common law presumption in favor of joint tenancies has been eliminated by statute; instead, these statutes require that there be a clear expression of the intent to create a joint tenancy, some statutes requiring specific wording such as "with right of survivorship" or "as joint tenants and not as tenants in common." Moreover, these statutes sometimes impose different rules for creating joint tenancies between husband and wife and those between persons not husband and wife. Thus it is still important to check local technicalities in creating joint ownership and in determining whether assets which appear to be in joint tenancy are legally owned in joint tenancy or in tenancy in common; if the latter, the decedent's interest is an asset of the probate estate.

Upon death of one joint tenant, in most states there is no court proceeding comparable to probate. "Title" to land can be established in the survivor by a certified copy of the death certificate, an affidavit of the survivor that there has been no severance of the joint tenancy, and proof of payment or exemption from death taxes or a waiver of tax liens from the proper tax authority. Stocks and bonds registered in joint tenancy form can be reissued in the name of the survivor upon furnishing the transfer agent similar proof. In a few states a court proceeding is provided;[60] aside from a check on payment of death taxes to the state, the value of such proceeding is questionable because it is not on notice.

The joint estate rationale in bank deposits is often based upon a statute which makes a deposit of money in the joint names of the owner and another in an account payable to either or the survivor presumptive or conclusive evidence that the depositor intended to make a gift of an interest during his lifetime.[61] The application of a joint estate theory to the bank deposit as in the principal case may prove difficult if no statute of this type is in force. Joint estates in land with rights of survivorship may have been abolished so that the wisdom of applying the doctrine to personal property is doubtful. The statute may require that the intention to create a joint estate with right of survivorship appear by express language. In some states where the bank is authorized by statute to pay the balance in the account to the survivor, the statute may be construed to be simply for the protection of the bank and not to dispose of the claim of the personal representative against the survivor to whom the bank makes payment.[62] But even when statutes of this type are construed to be for the protection of the bank, the statute may nevertheless be construed to implement some other theory, such as a theory of contract,

60. Calif.Prob.Code §§ 1170–1175; Wis.Stat.Ann. (1971) § 867.04. The California procedure is apparently rarely used because title companies will insure on the basis of affidavit. 1 Calif.Decedent Estate Administration (C.E.B.1981) § 4.15.

61. E.g., Wright v. Smith, 235 Mich. 509, 209 N.W. 576 (1926), 46 A.L.R.2d 523 (1956).

62. See Godwin v. Godwin, 141 Miss. 633, 107 So. 13 (1926).

discussed in the next subsection, so as to avoid a holding that the transaction is testamentary. Thus, in Estate of Michaels [63] the statute provided: (Wis. Stat.Ann. § 221.45)

> "When a deposit has been made or shall hereafter be made, in any bank, trust company bank or mutual savings bank transacting business in this state in the names of 2 persons, payable to either, or payable to either or the survivor, such deposit, or any part thereof, or any interest or dividend thereon, may be paid to either of said persons whether the other be living or not; and the receipt or acquittance of the person so paid shall be a valid and sufficient release and discharge to the bank for any payment so made."

A mother made a joint deposit with her husband; following her husband's death, she added her son by the same name as joint owner. The son did not learn of the deposit until after the mother's death; she retained the passbook and alone made withdrawals. The Court sustained the claim of the son against the administrator of the mother's estate, stating in the course of its opinion:

> "* * * The thoughtful analyses of the problems arising in the field of joint bank accounts contained in the article by Professor Richard W. Effland, Estate Planning Co-Ownership, 1958 Wisconsin Law Review, 507; and those by Professor Kepner, The Joint and Survivorship Bank Account—A Concept Without a Name, 41 California Law Review (1953), 596, and Five More Years of the Joint Bank Account Muddle, 26 University of Chicago Law Review (1959) 376, commend themselves to this court. Both authors advocate that the survivorship feature of these accounts be enforced by the courts even though the surviving donee named as codepositor has had no right of withdrawal during the lifetime of the donor. We quote their views as follows:
>
> > " 'It is submitted that frank judicial recognition of an account which confers no rights during lifetime (or as to a checking account, rights which are revocable), but carries survivorship rights, is justified, serves the modern policy of carrying out intent, and is no more a violation of the Statute of Wills than presently exists.' Effland, supra, 1958 Wisconsin Law Review, 507, at page 520.
> >
> > " 'The fact that the donee cannot make withdrawals may be evidence of the donor's intention, but it should not be conclusive on the question of whether or not a gift was made. The joint bank account gift is actually not intended to be a donation of an unrestricted right to make withdrawals, but is a present gift of the balance of the account, with the donee's enjoyment postponed until the donor's death. It is intended to be a form of a testamentary disposition of property in that the gift is not perfected until the donor's death. The gift should not be invalidated because the donee cannot make withdrawals.' Kepner, supra, 26 University of Chicago Law Review (1959), 376, at page 388.
>
> "However, in order for this court to achieve this socially desirable result here and not overrule Tucker v. Simrow (1946), 248 Wis. 143, 21 N.W. 2d 252, it will be necessary to ground it upon sec. 221.45, Stats., rather than the contract between Helen Michaels and the bank. In the Tucker Case, the owner of a savings account and a checking account signed a written direction to the bank that, upon her death, the bank pay one-half

63. 26 Wis.2d 382, 132 N.W.2d 557 (1965).

of these accounts to the depositor's husband, and one-fourth thereof to each of her two children. The bank accepted this written direction and it became part of the deposit contract. Both the trial court and this court held that there was an ineffective testamentary disposition. The court distinguished Estate of Staver [218 Wis. 114, 260 N.W. 655 (1935)], on the ground that in the latter case a present interest had been created in the person alleged to be a joint tenant while in the Tucker Case the depositor had retained complete control until death. We deem a better basis for distinguishing the two cases to be that in the one there existed a statute which vested legal title to the account in the named surviving donee depositor while in the other there is no such statute covering bank accounts standing in the sole name of the depositor but payable on death to another. Young v. McCoy (1950), 152 Neb. 138, 40 N.W.2d 540, is in accord with Tucker v. Simrow, supra. See also Kepner, 41 California Law Review (1953), 596, at page 615.

"This court has on occasion stated that sec. 221.45, Stats., was enacted for the protection of the banks and does not determine the rights of the named payees of a joint bank account as between themselves. Estate of Schley (1955), 271 Wis. 74, 80, 72 N.W.2d 767, and Estate of Kemmerer, supra, 16 Wis.2d at page 488, 114 N.W.2d 803. This does not mean, however, that this statute may not be pertinent on the issue of whether the attempted conferral of survivorship rights on the surviving donee payee is an ineffective testamentary disposition. It is this statute which implements the deposit contract and causes legal title to vest in the survivor payee even though equity in a proper case may intervene to impress a trust against such survivor payee. The passing of legal title is irreconcilable with the concept that such an attempted transfer is an ineffective testamentary disposition because of failure to comply with the requirements of the Statute of Wills. Thus it necessarily follows that sec. 221.45 is a statutory exception to sec. 238.06, Stats., the same as is sec. 215.14, Stats., which we were called upon to construe in Estate of Fucela, Wis., 132 N.W.2d 553. * * * "

There is indication that the rationale of the bank account cases will be extended to corporate stock held in joint names. In Blanchette v. Blanchette,[64] stock purchased by a husband had been issued in the names of both the husband and wife as joint tenants, as an admitted device to avoid probate. In connection with a divorce of the couple, the wife petitioned for a determination of her rights in the stock. The Supreme Judicial Court of Massachusetts, Justice Braucher writing the opinion, held that there was not a completed gift of a half interest in the wife and affirmed a lower court ruling that the husband was the sole owner of the stock. Analogizing the registration of the stock to the joint bank account, the court indicated that it would have upheld the rights of the survivor upon death, however. Justice Braucher wrote: "We recognize that under the cases cited the arrangement of the parties provides a substitute for a will. But we see no harm in that."

Uniform Probate Code, Art. VI, Part I (§§ 6–101 through 6–113) sets forth detailed rules concerning multiple party accounts. Such accounts may appear in any of the following forms: "A or B"—the "joint account"; "A in trust for B"—the Totten Trust which we considered in Chapter IX, Section 2; and "A payable on death to B"—a POD or beneficiary account which probably requires specific statutory authorization in most states and without this

64. 362 Mass. 518, 287 N.E.2d 459 (1972).

authorization may be held testamentary and void without testamentary formalities. The Uniform Probate Code sets forth rules governing rights of the parties named on the account during the lifetime of the depositor; rights of survivorship on the death of a party; and the protection of the bank if it makes payment in accordance with the form of the account. By separately treating these problems, the Uniform Code provides workable rules to accord with the intent of the original depositor or depositors. A rigid conceptual approach dictated by traditional concepts of "joint tenancy", "trust" and the like is avoided.[65]

(5) CONTRACTS

stop 10/21/85

A. APPLICATION OF CONTRACT THEORIES

SPINKS v. RICE

Supreme Court of Appeals of Virginia, 1948.
187 Va. 730, 47 S.E.2d 424.[66]

[A holographic will, dated 14 July, 1939, which purported to dispose of the entire estate of Mary Jane Steele was admitted to probate. Thereafter, C. J. Spinks, who was not named as a legatee in the will, instituted a chancery suit against the administrator c.t.a. and the legatees. In this bill of complaint he set forth the following agreement upon which he based his claim to the entire estate subject to the payment of the debts and funeral expenses of the decedent and the expenses of administration:

> "This Agreement made this 12th day of December, 1945, between C. J. Spinks and Mary Jane Steele,
>
> "WITNESSETH: that whereas the said parties hereto being desirous of making arrangements concerning the future, it is hereby agreed as follows,
>
> "In the event that said C. J. Spinks should die before the said Mary Jane Steele, any and all property he may have is to be her sole and separate property.

65. See generally, Atkinson, Wills (2d Ed., 1953) §§ 39, 40, 44; Bowe-Parker: Page, Wills (3d Ed., Rev.1960) §§ 6.1, 6.17–6.19; Rollison, Wills (1939) §§ 190–192; Gulliver and Tilson, "Classification of Gratuitous Transfers", 51 Yale L. J. 1 (1941); Effland, "Estate Planning: Co-Ownership", 1958 Wis.L.Rev. 507; Barber and Segatto, "Joint Tenancy Property and Estate Planning", 1959 U. of Ill.L.F. 1022; "Joint Tenancies and Wills", 1959 U. of Ill.L.F. 1043; "The Joint and Survivorship Bank Account", 1957 U. of Ill.L.F. 655; 1 A.L.R.2d 1178 (1948). Volkmer, "Multiple Party Accounts Under the Nebraska Probate Code", 9 Creighton L.Rev. 519 (1976); Harris, "Will Substitutes", 41 Ala.Lawyer 235 (1980); Note, "Multiple Party Accounts: Does Virginia's New Law Correspond With the Expectations of the Average Depositor?", 14 U.Rich.L.Rev. 851 (1980).

66. Noted, 34 Va.L.Rev. 741 (1948).

"It is also agreed that in the event the said Mary Jane Steele die first, then she desires and hereby directs that the said C. J. Spinks shall have the same without any claim of any other person.

"This is the 12th day of December, 1945."

The instrument was signed by Mary Jane Steele and C. J. Spinks and notarized. Rice, one of the legatees named in the will of 14 July, 1939, demurred to the complaint, the substance of the demurrer being that the instrument upon which Spinks relied was of no legal force or effect. The judge of the trial court concluded that the writing was not a deed, valid will, or enforceable contract and dismissed the complaint. The appeal is from this decree.]

MILLER, J., delivered the opinion of the court. * * * The writing obviously contains none of the attributes of a deed. It fails to measure up to a will, however, solely because of insufficiencies in its formal execution. It is ambulatory, dispository, and testamentary in character. Fundamentally and intrinsically it bears and has all the necessary qualities of a will and falls short of full recognition as such not because of inherent insufficiency, but only due to lack of formal execution.

The instrument contains no promise to execute a deed or will and is not intended as a contract to make a deed or will. They call it an agreement, but its name does not necessarily make it such. It is simply what it appears to be, i.e., an ambulatory, dispository, reciprocal testamentary undertaking between two people to pass, upon the death of the maker first to die, his or her property to the survivor. It has been finally executed by the parties signatory and is, in and of itself, supposed to pass property only upon death. It contemplates no further action and is obviously the first and last instrument intended to be executed by the makers to carry into effect their wishes by testamentary operation, the purpose and will of the makers being that the property of the one first to die pass at his or her death as he or she directs by and under that instrument, and that it, by its terms, necessarily ceases to operate as to the estate of the survivor.

Being a will in substance, but lacking in the necessary formalities of execution, no property can pass thereunder as a will. In attempting to have it function, appellant contends that it is a contract between the parties that each shall have the other's property upon the death of the one who is first to die. * * *

[Omitted is a discussion of Virginia cases] * * *

Pure testamentary disposition of property must be by will and cannot be made by contract. The inherent and intrinsic characteristics of the two undertakings are repugnant. But difficulty often arises in distinguishing a will from a contract. The fundamental difference is well expressed by the following authorities:

"The essential characteristic of a will is, that it operates only upon and by reason of the death of the maker. Up to that time it is ambulatory and revocable. By its execution the author has parted with no rights nor divested himself of no interest in or control over his property, and no rights have accrued to, and no estate has vested in, any other person. The death of the maker for the first time establishes the character of the instrument. It then ceases to be ambulatory, acquires a fixed status, and operates as a transfer of title. An instrument which is to operate in the lifetime of the donor, and to pass an interest in his property before his death, even though its absolute enjoyment by the donee is postponed till the death of the donor, or even if it is contingent upon the survivorship of the donee, is a deed, contract or gift, and not a will. It is essential to a will that it should be made to depend upon the death of the maker to consummate it, up to which time it is inoperative and revocable." (Citing cases.) 89 Am.St. Rep. 487. * * *

"In general the test of testamentary character is * * *, does the paper show an intention to presently create an interest in another though enjoyment is postponed, or does it create no such interest but merely direct what shall be done after the maker's death, being entirely ambulatory until that time? This is frequently a fine and difficult distinction to draw, but is often vital to the success of the instrument. Thus, if the court decides that the document is testamentary, it can be valid only as a will and if it lacks the required formalities of the latter, it will be of no effect. On the other hand, if the instrument is non-testamentary in character, its execution with testamentary formalities will not sustain it, but it is invalid for all purposes unless it has all the requirements necessary for some sort of *inter vivos* transaction." Atkinson on Wills, Sec. 64, p. 151. * * *

There are but two conduits or cables, the statute of wills, and of descents and distributions by which the Grim Reaper may at the moment of and by the stroke of his scythe flash the transfer and transmission of property and estate to the quick from the dead. A gift *causa mortis* is the next nearest approach to this accomplishment. But even there death does not spark the transmission. It is but the final seal upon an existing intent to donate coupled with a previously executed act of delivery. There death precludes revocation of a thing already done.

Those two statutes are, for the purpose intended, all inclusive, self-sufficient and stable. Equity may not be used to stretch and extend them. But here, by the application of equitable principles, an attempt is made to effectually by-pass the statute of wills. * * *

Wills, as such, simply cannot be made solely by mutual agreement. If the instrument is fundamentally testamentary, it must comply with the statutory formalities. * * *

If the validity of this instrument be established, it would accomplish a clear evasion of the statute of wills. And of equally serious results, it would, not until, but at the death of one maker effectually nullify or revoke a previously made will. That result would inevitably follow though this instrument is not executed as required by Section 5233 of the Code. * * *.

The instrument here sued upon was and is actually a joint and mutual will, in substance, dressed in the clothes of a contract—an old will with a "new look". But by the aid of equity, upon and at the death of one of the parties signatory, effort is made to transform it into a contract, in substance, enforceable by the surviving co-maker. And it is sought to have it so operate as to effectually nullify or revoke a previous will of the party who died, and lapse, nullify itself and cease to function as a valid instrument of any character as to the estate or property of the survivor. Upon the death of one, it is to spring into life and operate upon the estate of the dead, but it is to die and be inoperative as to any estate of the survivor.

We find no such hybrid instrument, with its dual personality, self-executing and shifting gears, chameleon characteristics and Phoenix-like qualities as yet known to the law.

Due to its conflicting features, inherent infirmity, and external insufficiency, it died aborning.

The decree appealed from is therefore affirmed.

Affirmed.[67]

VALENZUELA v. ANCHONDA

Court of Appeals of Arizona, 1974.
22 Ariz.App. 332, 527 P.2d 109.

HATHAWAY, CHIEF JUDGE.

This appeal is from the trial court's entry of summary judgment in favor of appellees-defendants, quieting title to certain real property in them, and against appellant-plaintiff.

On or about February 20, 1970, appellees, as purchasers, and Jose Gallegos and Elvira V. Gallegos, husband and wife, as sellers, entered into an agreement for the sale of real estate for a total purchase price of $9,500, payable $2,000 in cash at the time of purchase and the balance of $7,500 to be paid at the rate of $125 per month, with the first payment due on April 15, 1970. The contract provided:

> "That all payments are to cease upon the death of both of the sellers herein, and at that time, the property being sold herewith will be deemed to have been paid in full."

Both sellers are deceased. Jose Gallegos, the second to die, died on October 1, 1972. On that date there was a balance due and owing on the purchase price of the real property in the sum of $3,750.

The plaintiff, executor of the Estate of Jose M. Gallegos, deceased, sued for the unpaid balance and the defendants counterclaimed for slander of title, seeking damages and attorneys' fees.

67. In Virginia National Bank v. Harris, 220 Va. 336, 257 S.E.2d 867 (1979), the Virginia Supreme Court applied contract principles to uphold P.O.D. financial accounts; there was, however, an express statute providing that the bank "may" pay to the named survivor on the death of the depositor, which was construed to create an exception to the Statute of Wills.

Both parties moved for summary judgment. The court entered summary judgment in favor of the defendants and against the plaintiff, hence this appeal.

We are called upon to determine the validity of an agreement providing that a debt or legal obligation contemporaneously incurred be cancelled by the death of the creditor. Appellant first contends that the provision in question was invalid since it was an attempt to effect a testamentary disposition of property through a document that is not a valid will of the decedent, and secondly, if it were an attempt to make a gift, it was ineffective since the gift would take effect only after the death of the donor. McNabb v. Fisher, 38 Ariz. 288, 299 P. 679 (1931). Appellees submit that the provision is sustainable as a valid contractual provision pointing out that nearly thirty jurisdictions having occasion to consider the question have upheld the validity of such a provision. See Annot. 11 A.L.R.3d 1427. This position also finds support in 17 Am.Jur.2d, Contracts § 487, pp. 957–958:

> "Moreover, the prevailing view is in favor of the validity of an agreement contemporaneous with a debt or legal obligation that such obligation shall be extinguished or terminated by the death of the creditor or obligee. While the validity of such an agreement is sometimes predicated on the theory that a valid gift is made thereby, more often such validity has been predicated on the theory that the agreement constitutes a valid and enforceable contract. Under either theory of validity the courts have repeatedly denied the testamentary character of such an agreement." [Footnotes omitted]

We hold that the provision in question is a valid and enforceable part of the contract.

* * *

Affirmed.

NOTE

A contract is seldom held testamentary in character merely because it is performable after the death of one of the parties. Thus, contracts of life insurance which are payable by the insurance carrier to a named beneficiary upon the death of the insured are generally held not testamentary even though the right to change the beneficiary is reserved.[68] Special problems pertaining to life insurance are considered in the next subdivisions and in Section 3. Promissory notes which are given for consideration but which are performable after the death of the maker have been held non-testamentary.[69]

68. Kansas City Life Insurance Co. v. Rainey, 353 Mo. 477, 182 S.W.2d 624, 155 A.L.R. 168 (1944); Vance, Insurance (3d Ed., 1951) 679–681.

69. Occasionally the decedent has utilized a promissory note payable out of his estate or a check, as a will substitute. These cases usually involve a moral or legal obligation which the decedent has recognized: Smith v. Gentilotti, 371 Mass. 839, 359 N.E.2d 953 (1977) (postdated check drawn by a father in favor of a son born out of wedlock, with an endorsement that if the drawer "should pass away" the amount of the check should be taken from his estate) (Justice Braucher reasoned that the check was a negotiable instrument and that the defense of want of consideration had not been established; he added that an argument that the instrument was testamentary would not prevail, because

But a gratuitous promise that the executors or administrators of the promisor will do certain acts after his death creates no present interest in the promisee and must be executed with the formalities required for a will.[70]

The Uniform Probate Code provides in Section 6–201: [71]

"(a) Any of the following provisions in an insurance policy, contract of employment, bond, mortgage, promissory note, deposit agreement, pension plan, trust agreement, conveyance or any other written instrument effective as a contract, gift, conveyance, or trust is deemed to be nontestamentary, and this Code does not invalidate the instrument or any provision:

(1) that money or other benefits theretofore due to, controlled or owned by a decedent shall be paid after his death to a person designated by the decedent in either the instrument or a separate writing, including a will, executed at the same time as the instrument or subsequently;

(2) that any money due or to become due under the instrument shall cease to be payable in event of the death of the promisee or the promissor before payment or demand; or

(3) that any property which is the subject of the instrument shall pass to a person designated by the decedent in either the instrument or a separate writing, including a will, executed at the same time as the instrument or subsequently.

(b) Nothing in this section limits the rights of creditors under other laws of this state."

The use of contracts, rather than creation of joint tenancy, to achieve survivorship may become increasingly important. In community property states community property cannot be held in joint tenancy, the right of survivorship (a common law concept) being inconsistent with the testamentary power of each spouse over half of the community property (a civil law concept). Nevertheless, community property has tax advantages.[72] Two community property states therefore have special statutes which permit a husband and wife to contract that all property acquired during the marriage (even though normally separate property) shall be community property and shall pass to the survivor on death of either.[73] The same result seems possi-

"a valid contract may properly serve as a substitute for a will"); Hackmeyer v. McConnell, 336 So.2d 1107 (Ala.1976) (a promissory note payable to a woman with whom decedent had a close relationship was placed in a sealed envelope addressed to the woman, which in turn was put in a sealed envelope marked "My Last Will and Testament" and deposited in the decedent's brother's safety deposit box; held, a "completed gift"); Estate of Tulley, 86 Wis.2d 593, 273 N.W.2d 329 (1979) (a check payable to a neighbor-friend who had assisted the decedent, delivered to the payee along with a note saying "I am leaving a check for you rather than putting you in the will," not presented to the bank until after death of the drawer, held an invalid testamentary transfer; the court reasoned that the claimant had rendered the services gratuitously and that the note accompanying the check clearly showed the testamentary nature of the transaction).

70. Hamor v. Moore's Administrator, 8 Ohio St. 239 (1858).

71. Comment, "Non-Probate Transfers—Provisions Relating to Effect of Death: Will UPC § 6–201 Be 'Effective' in Nebraska", 12 Creighton L.Rev. 1173 (1979).

72. Both halves of community property receive a "stepped-up" basis at death for capital gain purposes upon later sale, under Internal Revenue Code § 1014; community property put in joint tenancy has a stepped-up basis only for the half included in decedent's taxable estate.

73. Wash.Rev.Code (1979) §§ 11.02.-090, 26.16.120; Idaho Code (1979) § 15–6–201(c) (a modified version of the U.P.C. section). The Washington experience is discussed in Price, "The Trans-

ble under Uniform Probate Code Section 6–201. Because decedent's interest passes at death pursuant to contract, unlike joint tenancy where decedent's interest ceases, the interest should be subject to rights of creditors even in the absence of statutory provision to that effect. The proposed Uniform Marital Property Act contains provisions expressly permitting spouses to contract regarding classification of their property (e.g., that all property would be marital) and also to contract that marital property shall pass on death of either spouse to a person (or trust) designated in the agreement, to be effective as a nontestamentary disposition.[74] Another likely area for use of contract is the situation where an unmarried couple live together and want to share property; they may want to contract that all acquisitions of either or both shall, in event of death, belong to the survivor.

Even though a technical consideration to support the contract is shown, the courts have ignored the inter vivos interests created by the contract and have held the transaction testamentary when the circumstances of the case reveal that the contract was used in a flagrant attempt to evade the wills acts.[75] In some states the courts have tended to regard contracts performable after the death of one party as testamentary even though there is no strong indication that the transaction was used consciously as a will substitute. In American University v. Conover[76] a charitable subscription to "become due upon the day of my decease" and "to be paid one year thereafter by my administrator or executor out of the proceeds of my estate" was held testamentary even though a consideration could be shown in the mutual promises of other subscribers.

As we have seen in Frey v. Wubbena, a theory of joint tenancy may be used to support the survivorship feature of a joint bank account, although as pointed out in the note to that case, the most satisfactory way in which the matter can be handled is by statute, the Uniform Probate Code offering an excellent example of a comprehensive statute covering multiple-party accounts.

Without such a statute some courts have avoided a joint estate theory in multiple party accounts and have disposed of their cases using contract, gift or trust theories. These theories share with the joint estate the limitations of any older concept applied to relatively new and flexible transactions.

But, as to bank accounts, a theory of contract has obvious application in view of the circumstances under which most deposits are made. If both parties sign the deposit agreement, it can be held that a joint estate was created by contract between the depositor, the survivor, and the bank.[77] If the survivor does not sign the deposit agreement during the lifetime of the deposi-

mission of Wealth at Death In a Community Property Jurisdiction", 50 Wash.L. Rev. 277 (1975) at 282–285; Bell, "Statutory Survivorship Contracts in the State of Washington", 1 Comm.Prop.J. 239 (1974); see also Comment, "Property—Probate Law & Procedure—No More Probate? ", 51 Wash.L.Rev. 451 (1976).

74. Proposed Uniform Marital Property Act, Jan. 1, 1982, draft, §§ 15, 29, (modeled on UPC § 6–201). The Act would also permit an optional "survivorship marital property" title form which would add survivorship to normal incidents of community property. Draft § 19.

75. See McCarty v. Waterman, 84 Ind. 550 (1882); Imthurn v. Martin, 150 Kan. 906, 96 P.2d 860 (1939); Reynolds v. Chase, 87 N.H. 227, 177 A. 291 (1935); Needles v. Needles, 7 Ohio St. 432, 70 Am.Dec. 85 (1857); In re Knisely, 27 Ohio Op. 216, 12 Ohio Supp. 140 (1943).

76. 115 N.J.L. 468, 180 A. 830 (1935), 36 Col.L.Rev. 834 (1936), 5 Ford.L.Rev. 374 (1936), 16 B.U.L.R. 269 (1936).

77. Holt v. Bayles, 85 Utah 364, 39 P. 2d 715 (1934).

tor, it can be argued that the survivor is a third party beneficiary of a contract between the depositor and the bank, his interest being vested subject to being divested by a partial or total withdrawal of funds by the depositor.[78]

A number of courts have sustained the transactions on theories of gift or trust.[79] The evidence which is available to support an application of these theories is often meager. The control which a depositor retains over the account by retention of the pass book or by a reservation of the right to withdraw funds is inconsistent with the intention and delivery required for a gift.[80] The depositor usually manifests no trust intention and exercises control which is incompatible with the existence of a beneficial interest in someone else during his lifetime.

Problems similar to those in joint accounts have arisen in applying the "co-ownership" and "beneficiary" provisions of United States Savings Bonds.[81] These bonds have been issued under treasury regulations payable to not more than two persons—the survivor being recognized as sole owner of the bond—or payable to a named beneficiary on the death of the person to whom the bond is issued. In the "co-ownership" form, surrender of the bond by either co-owner extinguishes the interest of the other. In the "beneficiary" form, surrender of the bond by the person in whose name it is issued extinguishes the interest of the beneficiary.

In Free v. Bland,[82] the United States Supreme Court held that Treasury Regulations creating a right of survivorship in co-owner defense bonds preempted under the Supremacy Clause any inconsistent Texas community property law. In its opinion the Court stated: [83]

> "The success of the management of the national debt depends to a significant measure upon the success of the sales of savings bonds. The Treasury is authorized to make the bonds attractive to savers and investors. One of the inducements selected by the Treasury is the survivorship provision, a convenient method of avoiding complicated probate proceedings. Notwithstanding this provision, the State awarded full title to the co-owner but required him to account for half of the value of the bonds to the decedent's estate. Viewed realistically, the State has rendered the award of title meaningless. Making the bonds security for the payment confirms the accuracy of this view. If the State can frustrate the parties' attempt to use the bonds' survivorship provision through the simple expedient of requiring the survivor to reimburse the estate of the deceased co-owner as a matter of law, the State has interfered directly

78. Although a right of withdrawal to defeat completely the rights of the survivor seems inconsistent with the notion of a joint tenancy in land, joint tenancies in bank accounts have received special treatment so far as a right of withdrawal is concerned. See McLaughlin v. Cooper, 128 Conn. 557, 24 A.2d 502 (1942).

79. E.g., Mississippi Valley Trust Co. v. Smith, 320 Mo. 989, 9 S.W.2d 58 (1928) (Gift theory); Halsted v. Central Savings Bank, 36 Cal.App. 500, 172 P. 613 (1918) (Trust theory).

80. Garland's Appeal, 126 Me. 84, 136 A. 459 (1927).

81. See McElwain, "The Application of the Law of Wills and of Gifts to War Bonds", 4 Mont.L.Rev. 61 (1943); Milne, "The Applicability of Contract and Trust Theories to War Bonds", 4 Mont.L.Rev. 70 (1943); 36 Va.L.Rev. 381 (1950); 168 A.L.R. 245 (1947). McGovern, "The Payable on Death Account and Other Will Substitutes," 67 Nw.L.Rev. 7 (1972). Uniform Probate Code, § 6–201 [Provisions for Payment or Transfer at Death] will cover POD provisions in bonds not supported by the "preemption" theory. A contract theory is adopted in this section; and many transfers are permitted that might otherwise fail for lack of testamentary formalities.

82. 369 U.S. 663, 82 S.Ct. 1089, 8 L.Ed.2d 180 (1962).

83. 369 U.S. at 669, 82 S.Ct. at 1093.

with a legitimate exercise of the power of the Federal Government to borrow money. * * *"

To what extent the Regulations will be interpreted as superseding state law under the Supremacy Clause is currently uncertain[84] but there is little doubt that the Regulations will be construed to supersede state Wills Acts whether co-ownership or beneficiary forms are used. Most of the state courts have given effect to these provisions when the question has been presented without requiring testamentary formalities either on the ground the provisions reasonably relate to the borrowing or war power of the Congress or that the contracts are "federal," and "federal" rather than state law must apply.[85] In the few cases in which the provisions have been held testamentary and thus ineffective the state legislatures have passed statutes giving effect to the provisions.[86] It may be argued, however, that the Treasury Regulations protect the Federal government against suits or controversies but do not supersede state laws concerning the devolution of a decedent's property. If this view is accepted, it seems, nevertheless, that the "co-ownership" form can be sustained on a theory of third party beneficiary contract. The third party beneficiary theory has been applied in several cases to sus-

84. See Yiatchos v. Yiatchos, 376 U.S. 306, 84 S.Ct. 742, 11 L.Ed.2d 742 (1964), where husband bought U. S. Savings Bonds with community assets and had beneficiary (POD) provision in favor of his brother. The Court held it would not contravene federal law as expressed in the applicable regulations to require the bonds to bear the same share of the debts that they would have borne if they had passed to petitioner as a specific legacy rather than by the survivorship provisions of the bonds. As to the claim by the widow for her share of the community the Court stated in its opinion: "* * * Under the federal regulations petitioner * * * [the brother named as beneficiary] * * * is entitled to the bonds unless his deceased brother committed fraud or breach of trust tantamount to fraud. Since the construction and application of a federal regulation having the force of law * * * are involved, whether or not there is fraud which will bar the named beneficiary in a particular case must be determined as a matter of federal law * * *. But in applying the federal standard we shall be guided by state law insofar as the property interests of the widow created by state law are concerned. It would seem obvious that the bonds may not be used as a device to deprive the widow of property rights which she enjoys under Washington law and which would not be transferable by her husband but for the survivorship provisions of the federal bonds." Holding that the brother was entitled to at least one-half of the bonds, the Court remanded the case to the Washington Court to determine whether the widow had consented to a gift of the community property to her husband's brother or if she did not give her consent whether she had a one-half interest in each community asset. In Free v. Bland, 369 U.S. 663, 82 S.Ct. 1089, 8 L.Ed.2d 180 (1962), the Court held the issue of fraud was not properly before it but stated at 369 U.S. 670, 82 S.Ct. 1094, concerning the regulations:

"While affording purchasers of bonds the opportunity to choose a survivorship provision which must be recognized by the States, the regulations neither insulate the purchasers from all claims regarding ownership nor immunize the bonds from execution in satisfaction of a judgment. The Solicitor General, appearing as *amicus curiae*, acknowledges that there is an exception implicit in the savings bond regulations, including the survivorship provision, so that federal bonds will not be a 'sanctuary for a wrongdoer's gains'. With this, we agree. The regulations are not intended to be a shield for fraud, and relief would be available in a case where the circumstances manifest fraud or a breach of trust tantamount thereto on the part of a husband while acting in his capacity as manager of the general community property. * * *"

See also United States v. Chandler, discussed in fn. 44 supra, ruling that the Regulations superseded state gift law.

85. E.g., Ervin v. Conn., 225 N.C. 267, 34 S.E.2d 402 (1945).

86. E.g., McKinney's N.Y. Personal Property Law, § 24, now McKinney's N.Y., EPTL, § 13-3.1 (1967).

tain the "beneficiary" form.[87] The successful application of gift or trust theories is difficult for the reasons mentioned in the discussion of joint accounts. It may be possible to prove a purchase money resulting trust if the "co-owner" or "beneficiary" furnishes the funds for purchase of the bond.[88]

B. LIFE INSURANCE CONTRACTS AND OPTION SETTLEMENTS

There are four fundamental forms of life insurance contracts.[89]

The cheapest and simplest kind of life insurance is "term" insurance. As the name indicates, "term" insurance is insurance protection for a specified period of years. The premiums paid are for insurance coverage and no cash value in the policy is created. Most term insurance policies are convertible so that the insured may convert into straight life or endowment policies at any time before the end of the term without a medical examination. Term insurance is not an investment since there is no value in the contract when the term expires.

The most common type of insurance policy is "ordinary life" insurance. Premiums are paid during the life of the insured and on the death of the insured the face amount of the policy is paid to the designated beneficiary. A cash surrender value is built up from year to year as premiums are paid. The insured may withdraw against the cash surrender value (thereby reducing the face amount of the policy), borrow against it, or have it converted into paid-up insurance in a lesser amount than the original contract.

"Endowment" insurance contracts have increased in popularity in the last twenty years. "Endowment" contracts provide that the insured pay premiums until he reaches a certain age at which time the face amount of the policy becomes available to him or may be converted into an annuity. The proceeds are paid to a designated beneficiary if the insured dies before reaching the age designated in the policy. This type of policy is often used to provide for the education of children or funds for the insured's retirement. It is the most expensive of the "life" contracts.

An "annuity" is insurance against living too long. Typically, an annuity involves the deposit of a sum of money with an insurance company, the company agreeing to pay the insured a specified monthly income for life. The variations of this "simple" type of annuity are too numerous for treatment here.

Payment of the face amount of a life insurance policy may be made in several different ways. These methods of payment are called "settlement options". The options are usually exercised by the beneficiary after the death of the insured but may be exercised by

87. E.g., Mitchell v. Edds, 181 S.W.2d 323 (Tex.Civ.App.1944), aff'd 184 S.W.2d 823, 158 A.L.R. 470 (1945).

88. Makinen v. George, 19 Wash.2d 340, 142 P.2d 910 (1943).

89. See Crandell, What a Lawyer Needs to Know About Life Insurance (Practising Law Institute, Estate Planning and Administration, Course Handbook, Series 9) (1969); Huebner & Black, Life Insurance (Eighth Ed.1972) II where the types of contracts are discussed in detail; Vance, Insurance (2d Ed.1951) §§ 7, 8.

the insured during his life if he so chooses. The usual forms in which options are available in life insurance contracts are five in number.[90]

1. *Outright Payment of the Principal to the Beneficiary.* The normal procedure is payment to the beneficiary in a lump sum unless the beneficiary elects one of the four following forms for settlement.

2. *The Interest Option.* The proceeds of the policy are held at interest by the insurance company and interest is paid monthly, quarterly, semi-annually, or annually to the designated payee. A specified interest rate is guaranteed in the policy and, depending upon the investment earnings of the company, excess interest is paid in amounts voted by the company. Older policies have a comparatively high guaranteed interest rate, some as high as 4 or 4½ per cent. Some of the newer contracts have a minimum guaranteed rate as low as 2.5 per cent, although the typical rate is 3 per cent.

3. *The Fixed Payment Option.* This arrangement provides for regular payments in a specified amount, these payments to continue as long as the principal plus interest will last. For example, $10,000 paid out at 2½ per cent interest in installments of $100 per month will last 9 years and 3 months.

4. *The Fixed Period Option.* This option is the actuarial equivalent of the fixed payment option. The payee elects payment for a specified number of years rather than for a fixed periodic payment. For example, $10,000 paid out over a 10 year period would pay $93.90 a month at 2½ per cent.

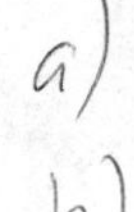

5. *The Annuity Option.* Election of this option usually provides for payments over the future lifetime of the beneficiary in amounts determined by actuarial tables. This option may be presented in a number of variations: (a) the "life annuity" which ends at the death of the annuitant; (b) the 5, 10, 15 or 20 year "certain" annuity which guarantees payments to the annuitant for life, but with the additional covenant that if death occurs before the end of the certain period, the balance of the certain payments will be paid to a named beneficiary; and (c) the "survivorship annuity" in which the age and sex of two beneficiaries establish the amount of annuity payments and such payments are then made to the two beneficiaries jointly, and for the life of the survivor of them.

---

90. See Krueger and Waggoner, The Life Insurance Policy Contract (1953) 104–165; Farr and Wright, An Estate Planner's Handbook (4th Ed., 1979) Chs. III, X.

ZIMMERMAN v. MUTUAL LIFE INSURANCE CO. OF NEW YORK

United States District Court, N.D. Alabama, S.D., 1957.
156 F.Supp. 589.

[Mary G. Ragsdale became entitled to payment of $20,000 as proceeds of endowment life policy (No. 3,192,051) upon the life of her husband. $12,000 of this amount was paid to Mary G. Ragsdale under an optional mode of settlement contained in the policy and is not in dispute. As to the remaining $8,000, Mary G. Ragsdale elected to exercise an option contained in a form (No. 4241) furnished her by the Company after the death of insured. This option, which appears to have contained minor variations from a similar option stated in the policy, but which seems assumed by the parties to be the same as the policy option, is in part as follows:

> "The proceeds of this Policy, if payable in a single sum, may, if so elected by the person entitled to such proceeds, be settled by one of the following optional Modes of Settlement instead of being paid in one sum or being settled by any Mode of Settlement provided for in this Policy.
>
> "The terms 'payee' and 'payees' as used herein shall refer to the person or persons on the continuance of whose life the Mode of Settlement elected depends."
>
> "Option 1.
>
> "By the Company's holding the proceeds as a principal sum payable at the death of the payee, the Company meanwhile paying monthly interest (with a final interest payment to the date of such death) at three per cent a year plus participation in excess interest at such rate as the Company may determine for each year."

Exercising Option 1, contained in the form, Mary G. Ragsdale elected:—" * * * Semi-annual payments of interest" * * * to herself * * * *"if living if not to Dorothy R. Meloy daughter in a like manner"*. The Company then issued its Supplementary Contract (S.N. 8737) providing for the payments of interest to Mary G. Ragsdale for her life, *then to Dorothy R. Meloy if she survived Mary G. Ragsdale with the principal to the executors or administrators of the survivor.* The contract provided Mary G. Ragsdale could surrender her rights under the Supplementary Contract. This she did in part, receiving $500 in cash in 1936, reducing the principal to $7,500. Mary G. Ragsdale died in 1953 leaving a will naming Dorothy R. Meloy (now Zimmerman) as sole devisee and legatee. The Company is paying the interest on the principal amount of $7,500 to Dorothy R. Meloy (Zimmerman) but she brought an action for a declaratory judgment against the Company in an Alabama Court which is removed to the Federal District Court by the Company, a New York corporation.]

* * * LYNNE, CHIEF JUDGE. * * *

Plaintiff, her mother's sole legatee and devisee, asserts that she is entitled to the aforementioned $7,500 outright because defendant's Supplementary Contract No. S.N. 8737 with the beneficiary constituted an attempted testamentary disposition by the beneficiary, void for want of compliance with the Statute of Wills. Defendant, to the contrary, contends that the relationship between its underlying Policy No. 3,192,051 and S.N. 8737 is such that the validity of S.N. 8737 is established by reference to the Policy under the law of life insurance, and that the Statute of Wills has no application. These contentions pose the only issue in the case.

* * *

Having considered the authorities, the court concludes and holds that a "supplementary contract" prescribing the disposition of policy proceeds pursuant to agreement between an insurer and a beneficiary must be sustained as valid and non-testamentary if its provisions are sufficiently close to those contemplated by the underlying insurance policy to warrant the conclusion that the "supplementary contract" is indeed "supplementary" to that policy, and not merely a totally unrelated document reflecting an agreement that could not reasonably be carried out under the terms of the policy. The plaintiff herself concedes as much, for her brief says that:

> "There is no doubt that where the supplementary contract is made pursuant to the terms of the original policy and one or more of the options are adopted as provided for in the policy of insurance; there can be no insistence, that a new contract has been effected, in violation of the Statute of Wills, and many supplementary contracts have been upheld * * *."

The court is aware that the issue herein might be resolved, perhaps not unjustly, by invoking various highly refined and technical subtleties that have evolved in the law pertaining to real and personal property, deeds, trusts, and gifts. Such an approach, not adopted by either side in this case, was rejected by the Appellate Division in the Hall case,[91] supra (see 122 N.Y.S.2d at page 243), apparently because that court believed, as this court does, that the issue should be decided in the light of the public interest inherent in the insurance system, the continued general use of optional modes of settlement, the high probability that they do not present an evil at which the Statute of Wills is aimed, and the fact that seemingly settled and long comatose dispositions, many of which may aptly be labeled matters of property, should not be irrevocably unsettled by retroactive action. In this case, therefore, the issue was posed and argued, whether S.N. 8737 was "supplementary" to the Policy as a matter of substance.

Defendant concedes that it need not prevail merely because the money, held under S.N. 8737 came from the Policy, and plaintiff concedes that not every difference between the Policy and S.N. 8737 will destroy the necessary connection between them. However, Plaintiff insists that S.N. 8737 disposes of the $8,000 in a manner not contem-

91. The Court's reference is to Hall v. Mutual Life Ins. Co. of N. Y., 282 App. Div. 203, 122 N.Y.S.2d 239 (1953), aff'd 306 N.Y. 909, 119 N.E.2d 307 (1954).

plated by the Policy because, as she contends, the strict wording of option No. (1) in the Policy forbids the continuation of that optional mode of settlement beyond the life of Mary G. Ragsdale. Defendant, conceding that S.N. 8737 does not strictly comport with the Policy in all respects, nevertheless contends that the import of Policy option No. (1), read in the light of certain applicable modifying language also contained in the Policy, is consistent with S.N. 8737. Defendant also contends that S.N. 8737 comports strictly with the terms of the beneficiary's election upon defendant's above-mentioned printed form, which the court finds as and to be a fact; that such form made available to the beneficiary, among other options, all of the identical options set out in the Policy, which the court also finds as and to be a fact; and that the beneficiary's choice on the printed election form of an option whose very deviation, if any, from the corresponding policy option is doubtful, should not be construed as an attempted testamentary disposition in the light of a claimed deviation that comes to be the subject of a close controversy between lawyers long after the fact.

Upon consideration of the facts, the documents, the briefs, and the oral arguments, the court is of the opinion that the provisions of Supplementary Contract No. S.N. 8737 must be regarded as sufficiently close and similar to the optional modes of settlement necessarily contemplated by the option clauses in the Policy that S.N. 8737 must be held to be a valid extension of the Policy within the contemplation of the Policy provisions, and the court so finds and holds. * * *

[The Court gave judgment on the merits for Defendant Insurance Company, concluding in part that Supplementary Contract No. S.N. 8737 was a valid and subsisting contract and] * * *

[N]either the execution and delivery to the defendant by Mary G. Ragsdale of the defendant's form No. 4241.7–34 (Ex. E attached to Stipulation), nor the making by Mary G. Ragsdale of the election evidenced therein, nor the issuance by defendant of its Supplementary Contract No. S.N. 8737 to Mary G. Ragsdale, nor her acceptance of the same, constituted an attempt by Mary G. Ragsdale to make a testamentary disposition of the residue of the insurance proceeds.

* * * Let judgment be entered in accordance with this opinion.

C. Application of Trust and Will Principles to Life Insurance

---

PIEROWICH v. METROPOLITAN LIFE INSURANCE CO.

Supreme Court of Michigan, 1937.
282 Mich. 118, 275 N.W. 789.

CHANDLER, JUSTICE. The appellee, on September 15, 1931, issued a policy of life insurance on the life of Dan Pierowich, in which his wife was named beneficiary. Subsequently the parties were divorced and during the pendency of the proceedings the insured changed the policy and named his two minor sons, Alex and James, age ten and eight respectively, as the beneficiaries. On November 23, 1934, the insured executed and delivered to appellee the following:

"Policy No. 7288571—A

"Amount of Insurance $2,000.

"To the Metropolitan Life Insurance Company, New York, New York.

"I hereby direct that in the event either of my sons, Alex Pierowich, born 5/9/1924, and James Pierowich, born 2/1926, the beneficiaries of record, shall survive me but shall not have attained the age of 21 years at the time of my death, the amount payable under the said policy upon my death, to such son, shall be retained by the Company and interest thereon at the rate which the Company may each year declare on such funds (but at no less rate than three and one-half per centum per annum) shall be compounded annually at the end of each year until such child shall have attained the age of 21 years when his share, together with the interest then accumulated thereon, shall be paid at once in one sum to him.

"Provided, however, in the event that either of my said sons shall survive me but shall die before attaining the age of 21 years, his share, together with the interest then accumulated thereon, shall be paid at once in one sum to the executors or administrators of such deceased son.

"And I hereby further direct that neither of my said sons shall have the right to withdraw any of the amount retained by the Company, except as hereinbefore provided, nor the right to assign or incumber any payment hereunder.

"Provided, however, that the foregoing directions shall not apply to the share of either of my said sons who shall predecease me or who shall not be a beneficiary of record at the time of my death or who shall have attained the age of 21 years at the time of my death.

"The right to cancel the foregoing directions by written notice to the Home Office of the Metropolitan Life Insurance Company of New York, New York, is reserved. Dated at Hamtramck, Mich. Nov. 23, 1934.

"Insured Dan Pierowich.

"Witness

"L. M. Locianoures."

Dan Pierowich died on June 18, 1935, and thereafter appellee, upon surrender of the policy, delivered to each of the beneficiaries a supplemental contract providing for payment of the proceeds of the policy in exact accordance with the directions given by the insured in his lifetime and set forth above.

The mother of Alex and James filed her bill in equity as guardian of said minors alleging that she is without sufficient funds with which to maintain and educate the children properly, and prayed for a decree ordering appellee to pay her for this purpose such sums from the proceeds of the policy as the court found necessary. The trial court dismissed the bill.

Whether or not a trust was created must depend upon the intention of the insured in providing for the disposition of the proceeds of the policy in the manner which he instructed and whether the necessary requisites to the creation of a trust were observed. In Equitable Trust Co. v. Milton Realty Co., 261 Mich. 571, 246 N.W. 500, 502, we held that: "To create a trust, there must be an assignment of designated property to a trustee with the intention of passing title thereto, to hold for the benefit of others. There must be a separation of the legal estate from the beneficial enjoyments."

We are unable to find from an examination of the evidence the essential element of intent to create a trust. Although not decisive, the provision for the payment of interest on the fund held by appellee, together with the fact that there was no designation or segregation of any particular fund from which payment was to be made, are of interest in determining the intent, and are not indicative of the trust relationship. The supplemental agreements executed by appellee which in terms specifically incorporate the insured's directions appear to be no more than contracts containing a promise to pay the proceeds of the policy in such a manner as the contingencies therein expressed shall command. We fail to find that the fund was assigned from the appellee as debtor to the appellee as trustee as is contended by appellants. The relationship existing is that of debtor and creditor rather than that of trustee and *cestui que trust*.

The case is not unlike that of McLaughlin v. Equitable Life Assurance Soc. of the U. S., 112 N.J.Eq. 344, 164 A. 579, 580, where the policy contained an agreement that, in the event of the death of the insured prior to the beneficiary attaining the age of 18 years, the proceeds thereof should be held by the insurer and be paid in installments upon the beneficiary reaching the mentioned age. It further provided for the payment of interest and that any payments due during the minority of the beneficiary should be paid to the insured's wife as trustee. A bill was filed to reach a portion of the fund in question for the support, education, and maintenance of the beneficiary. In denying relief, the court said:

> "The defendant below appeals to this court on the ground that the policy of insurance and the claim which resulted thereunder by reason of the death of the insured did not create a trust and that the relation of the parties to the suit was not that of trustee and *cestui que trust,* and also for the reason that there was no evidence before the vice chancellor which justified him in decreeing that the defendant should pay the guardian of the infant $25 a week. We are of the opinion that the court below erred in respect to the construction which it placed upon the contract of insurance. The policy of insurance was a contract, and under its terms the insurance company was bound to carry out its provisions. The intention of the insured was to provide a fund for the education, support, and maintenance of his son, John F. McLaughlin, in the event that the insured died before his son attained the age of eighteen years and that he should not have access to such fund except as provided in the contract of insurance until he attained the designated age. This fund, therefore, did not become a trust fund until it was paid over by the insurance company under the terms of the contract of insurance to the trustee, and this was not to take place until the beneficiary arrived at the age of eighteen years, when it should be paid in installments covering a period of four years.
>
> "We are of the opinion that the court could not change the terms of this contract and that the insurance company cannot be compelled to agree to any other terms than the terms set forth therein. It is, therefore, not necessary to consider the other point raised by the appellant.
>
> "The decree below is, therefore, reversed."

Appellant further contends that, even though no trust relationship appears, the facts are such as to warrant the interference of a court of equity to grant the desired relief. In support of this position, testimony was introduced establishing the indigent circumstances of the family and the lack of funds claimed necessary to provide properly for the support and education of the beneficiaries. Although in certain circumstances an advancement will be allowed from a trust fund for such purposes as are relied upon in the instant case, Post v. Grand Rapids Trust Co., 255 Mich. 436, 238 N.W. 206, we do not find this rule to be applicable here. The disposition of the property has been fixed by contract, and this court cannot alter the terms thereof even in view of the changed, now existing conditions.

The decree is affirmed, with costs to appellee.

FEAD, C. J., and NORTH, WIEST, BUTZEL, BUSHNELL, SHARPE, and POTTER, JJ., concurred.

NOTE

In many respects the ordinary life insurance contract is like a will, and the settlement options resemble a trust. Yet life insurance occupies a unique position with a law of its own. While life insurance may be classified as "non-testamentary" in the sense that the contract does not have to comply with the Statute of Wills and the proceeds are not part of the probate estate, it is obvious that many of the wills problems may occur with regard to life insurance contracts. Suppose insured has his life insurance payable to his mother. Subsequently he marries and has a child. This might revoke a will executed before marriage, but it does not revoke the beneficiary designation under the life insurance contract. Or he has the insurance payable to a named beneficiary, his wife. A subsequent divorce will not operate to revoke this designation.[92] The formalities required for change of beneficiary are those imposed by the insurance company embodied in the terms of the insurance contract and must be complied with.[93] Within some limits the provisions for payment of proceeds may be tailored to meet the individual needs of the insured. If a beneficiary predeceases the insured, he cannot take, just as a beneficiary under a will cannot take.[94] Insured may name contingent beneficiaries if the first-named (primary) beneficiary predeceases the insured. Clauses for payment of proceeds often resemble similar clauses found in wills.

Retention of the proceeds by the insurance company under one of the settlement options also resembles the testamentary trust, except that the forms of payment available are more restricted. The beneficiary can be given what amounts to a power of appointment over the balance of the proceeds remaining at the first beneficiary's death, or it can be made payable to

92. See Couch, Insurance (2d Ed., 1960) §§ 27:111, 29:4. The rule that divorce does not change the right of a spouse as a beneficiary designated by insured is subject to certain exceptions: in a few jurisdictions the beneficiary must have an insurable interest in the insured and this is lost by the divorce; in some states, statutes have been enacted which divest the divorced wife of any rights as beneficiary of a policy on her husband's life (see Couch, § 27:112); a separation agreement may affect the divorced wife's rights (Couch, § 27:116); some contracts provide for a termination of the beneficiary's rights upon divorce.

93. Contract provisions concerning the formalities for change of beneficiary vary. Some companies require a formal request on a form provided by the company, properly witnessed; some require that the policy be surrendered to the company for indorsement. Most courts require substantial compliance with such provisions. See Couch, Insurance (2d Ed., 1960) ch. 28. For an example of insistence upon formal compliance see Scherer v. Wahlstrom, 318 S.W.2d 456 (Tex.Civ.App.1958). There insured had named as beneficiary a young lady, "fiancee", if living, with his father as beneficiary if she predeceased insured. Later, while insured was in the service, he received a letter from the fiancee notifying him that she was marrying another. Deceased wrote to the insurance company and asked them to change the beneficiary to name his father. The company sent him the necessary forms on June 19. He was killed in an accident on July 13; the forms were found among his effects. The former fiancee claimed the proceeds as designated beneficiary. The father also claimed and asked the court to impose a constructive trust. The court held that the proceeds were payable to the former fiancee. Would the result have been the same if she had been named beneficiary under decedent's will executed while they were still engaged and describing her as "fiancee"?

94. Under the older policies where insured did not reserve the right to change the beneficiary, if the policy failed to specify that the beneficiary must survive insured, the beneficiary had a vested right which passed to his representative if the beneficiary predeceased insured. Present policies always reserve the right to change the beneficiary, and commonly name a contingent beneficiary. See Couch, Insurance (2d Ed., 1960) § 27:129 et seq.

named beneficiaries who are like "remaindermen". The interest of the beneficiaries can be protected from the claims of their creditors by "spendthrift" clauses. Under the interest option, the beneficiary may be given power to withdraw all or limited amounts of principal, similar to a power of invasion under a trust.

Technically, the insurance company is not a trustee.[95] An insurance company cannot undertake to exercise the personalized discretion characteristic of the modern trust. No assets are segregated to meet the obligations under the particular insurance contract. The company has contractual obligations, and cannot be a trustee of its own debt. However, statutes in some states treat the transaction whereby the company retains proceeds under the settlement options as a trust without a duty to segregate the trust property from the company's general assets.[96] Even in the absence of statute, the issue should be whether principles similar to trust law are to be applied.

SECTION 2. INTERRELATING INTER VIVOS TRANSACTIONS

---

(1) LIFE INSURANCE TRUSTS

The owner of life insurance has several choices with regard to the proceeds of life insurance.[97] As we have just seen, he may have the proceeds retained by the insurance company under one of the settlement options in the policy, rather than have the proceeds payable outright to named beneficiaries or to his estate. But he may prefer to

95. See Bogert, Trusts and Trustees (2d Ed., 1964) § 240. Nevertheless, the courts recognize the close analogy between the trust and the settlement options. Thus, in Prudential Insurance Co. v. Heyn, 139 F.Supp. 602 (S.D.Cal.1956), where the issue was whether proceeds under an installment option settlement were payable directly to children as beneficiaries or were to be paid to a trustee as part of a trust set up for the children, the court argued that this would be a trust upon a trust and said: "This beneficiary provision virtually established a trust in favor of the children, with the Company as trustee, and there was no necessity for the interposition of the Bank as a further trustee."

96. E.g., Conn.Gen.Stat.Ann. § 38–162 (1969).

97. See Friedman, "The Irrevocable Life Insurance Trust", 107 Trusts and Estates 717 (1968); Haskell, "Testamentary Trustee as Insurance Beneficiary: An Estate Planning Gimmick", 41 N.Y.U. L.Rev. 566 (1966); Kamers, "Using Life Insurance for Estate Planning", 107 Trusts and Estates 983 (1968); Lesar, "The Use of Life Insurance in Estate Planning", 1958 W.U.L.Q. 379 (1958); Poole, "Life Insurance Uses in Trusts", 106 Trusts and Estates 631 (1967); Rabin, "The Life Insurance Trust—A Basic Technique in Estate Planning", 105 Trusts and Estates 691 (1966); Wasserman, "Leased Life Insurance", 105 Trusts and Estates 110 (1966); Wren, "The Role of Life Insurance in Estate Planning", 41 St. Johns Law Review 6 (1966); Wright, "Life Insurance and Its Use in Estate Planning", 23 Okla.Law Rev. 125 (1970); Notes, "The Testamentary Life Insurance Trust", 51 Minn.L. Rev. 1118 (1967); "Life Insurance Trusts in Estate Planning", 10 So.Dak.L.Rev. 128 (1965).

utilize the trust device. If so, he will normally set up a trust of the life insurance policies during his lifetime. Such a trust may be revocable or irrevocable. The revocable life insurance trust has been attacked as testamentary, and we shall consider this objection in Gordon v. Portland Trust Bank hereafter. The "transfer" of the insurance in this type of trust is usually effected by a deposit of the policy and designation of the trustee as beneficiary under the policy. If the trust is irrevocable, the transfer will consist of both a present assignment of all interest in the policy to the trustee and designation of the trustee as beneficiary.

The trust may be "funded" or "unfunded". In a "funded" insurance trust, not only is the policy transferred, but the settlor also transfers securities or cash to the trustee in an amount sufficient to pay the premiums. The trustee covenants to hold, manage and invest the securities and apply the income to premium payments. Since the active duties of the trustee begin at once, he is entitled to compensation from the creation of the trust. His obligations with regard to collection, management and ultimate disposition of the insurance proceeds are spelled out in the trust agreement.

A revocable trust is normally "unfunded", and the settlor retains full control over the policies and pays the premiums. The insurance trust agreement in such a case, signed by the insured (settlor) and the trustee, provides that upon death of the insured the trustee will collect the proceeds of the insurance and administer this fund in accordance with the terms of the agreement. No compensation is paid the trustee until the death of the insured because the trustee has no substantial duties until that time, although the usual agreement provides for a cancellation fee in case the trust is revoked before the death of the insured.[98]

One of the main advantages of a life insurance trust is that it provides for the special requirements of beneficiaries and allows the exercise of discretion in applying insurance proceeds. For example, the trustee of an insurance trust can be authorized to make larger payments during times of inflation and emergency, smaller payments when the funds are not needed or when purchasing power of the dollar is high.

Another advantage of the life insurance trust lies in its ability to provide needed cash for estate requirements. Since the main burden of taxes, debts and administration expense falls on the probate estate, there may in larger estates be heavy demands for cash. This often makes necessary the sale of assets which are not readily marketable, such as stock in a closely held family corporation, unless

98. A typical "accumulative" insurance trust stands more or less midway between the funded and unfunded type of insurance trust agreement. The insurance policy is made payable to the trustee or is assigned to him. The insured agrees to pay the trustee a definite sum each month. The trustee uses the monthly payments to pay the premiums and invests any balance remaining. Income on the balance accumulates at compound interest. The accumulative insurance trust provides an estate for the insured's family at his death or may be used to provide a retirement fund for the insured if he lives until a designated age.

there is a ready source of cash. Life insurance is ideal in this respect since it provides immediately after death a determined amount of cash. If the probate assets have to be liquidated, the forced nature of the sale often means that full value will not be realized and may result in loss of control in the corporate situation. While life insurance can be made payable to the executor to meet this need, such a method results in subjecting the insurance proceeds to the executor's fees. The same result can be achieved by use of the insurance trust with a provision authorizing the trustee to purchase securities or other assets from the general estate of the decedent at prevailing prices and to make loans to the estate.

On the other hand, in certain situations, the settlement options offered by the insurance companies may be better than a trust. Under the annuity option the beneficiary may be assured of a fixed income for life; the installment options offer the same guarantee for a fixed period. The disadvantage of course lies in the lack of flexibility. However, the insurance trust involves trustee's fees and is not suited to an individual with a small estate. The annuity and installment options with the wife as beneficiary also offer income tax savings under the present law, since each year $1,000 of the interest element payable to the surviving spouse is exempt from tax when those options are selected.[99]

GORDON v. PORTLAND TRUST BANK

Supreme Court of Oregon, 1954.
201 Or. 648, 271 P.2d 653.[1]

LUSK, JUSTICE. This is an action at law brought by Leotta Belle Gordon as executrix under the last will and testament of Albert Leslie Gordon, deceased, to recover the sum of $26,352.75 from the Portland Trust Bank, a banking corporation. Judgment for defendant was entered after a demurrer to the complaint had been sustained. Plaintiff appeals.

As the complaint discloses, the money involved is the proceeds of fifteen policies of insurance upon the life of Albert Leslie Gordon, deceased, which he delivered to the bank pursuant to the terms of an instrument in writing, executed by Gordon as trustor and the bank as trustee. Gordon caused the bank to be designated beneficiary under the insurance policies, and after his death the bank collected the proceeds of the policies, which it claims the right to hold and to distribute in accordance with the provisions of the trust agreement.

It is the theory of the plaintiff that the trust agreement is actually a "testamentary disposition or Last Will and Testament", and that it

99. IRC, 26 U.S.C.A., § 101(d).

1. Noted, 27 Rocky Mt.L.Rev. 240 (1955), 2 U.C.L.A.L.Rev. 151 (1954).

was revoked by a will executed by Gordon four days later under which Mrs. Gordon has been appointed executrix.

The trust instrument, a copy of which is made an exhibit to the complaint, is dated August 3, 1942. It recites that the parties, Gordon as trustor and the bank as trustee, have agreed that the bank has been designated beneficiary as trustee under the policies of life insurance enumerated in an attached schedule for the uses and purposes thereinafter stated. The bank agreed:

> "To hold said insurance policies during the life of the Trustor without any duties of any nature in respect thereto other than the safekeeping thereof; it being expressly agreed that the said Trustee shall not in any event be obliged or required to pay any premium, assessment or other sum that may become due or payable on any of the said policies. In no event is it the intention of the parties hereto that this agreement should restrict the rights of the Trustor under any policy contained in this trust, the Trustor reserving the right to obtain loans under any policy or to surrender any policy for the cash surrender value, or to exercise any other right or option under the said insurance policies, this trust becoming effective only insofar as the said insurance policies are concerned upon the death of the Trustor.
>
> "Upon the Trustee receiving proof of the death of the Trustor, it is agreed that it will use its best efforts to collect and receive any and all sums of money payable thereunder, the receipt of said Trustee to be a full and complete release to any insurance company for any and all funds paid to the said Trustee as beneficiary under the said insurance policy or policies which may be hereafter deposited."

Other pertinent provisions follow: After paying the expenses incurred in managing the trust estate and deducting the same from the gross income, the trustee shall distribute the net income of the trust estate in quarterly installments to the trustor's wife, Leotta Belle Gordon, until her death or remarriage, and, upon the happening of either of those events, the trustee shall distribute the corpus equally between the trustor's two daughters, with further provisions for the contingencies of the death of either or both daughters before the death or remarriage of the widow:

> "The Trustor shall have power at any time during his life by an instrument in writing delivered to the Trustee to modify, alter or terminate this agreement, in whole or in part, provided, however, that the duties, powers and liabilities of the Trustee hereunder shall not be substantially changed without its written consent."

The trustee shall not in any event be obliged or required to pay any premiums, assessment or other sum that may become due or payable on any of the said policies; and it shall not be obliged to bring suit to collect the principal amount on any of the policies unless properly indemnified, the sole obligation and liability of the trustee being to receive, manage and dispose of such money as may be paid to it under the said policies:

> "In the event that the said Trustor shall at any time after having designated said Trustee as beneficiary under said policies, subsequently cause such designation to be changed so that another beneficiary be named or other payment of the proceeds of such policies provided, this trust, and all rights and obligations hereunder, shall as to such policy or policies thereupon become null and void for every purpose, and said Trustee shall as to such policy or policies be released from all liability and obligation."

The agreement also contains a section entitled "Open Trust Clause" under which the trustor was authorized to deposit with the trustee securities, personal property and sums of money, and to deed to the trustee real property, which would become part of the trust res, but there is nothing to show that any property of any kind was ever added to the trust res in pursuance of this authority.

The question raised by this appeal is before this court for the first time, though it has been extensively litigated in other jurisdictions and has been the subject of a good deal of discussion by textwriters and commentators. See, e.g., Hanna, "Some Legal Aspects of Life Insurance Trusts" (1930), 78 Univ.Pa.L.Rev. 346; Scott, Trusts 345 et seq.; 2 Bogert, Trusts and Trustees §§ 238, 239; Grahame, "The Insurance Trust as Non-testamentary Disposition" (1934), 18 Minn.L. Rev. 391. A brief historical account will aid to an understanding of the problem.

It should be noted that life insurance, and its natural concomitant, the insurance trust, did not become popular in the United States until the latter half of the nineteenth century. At that time the doctrine of the third-party beneficiary had not developed as yet and the status of the beneficiary under an insurance policy was defined in several early cases, notably in Central Nat. Bank of Washington v. Hume, 128 U.S. 195, 9 S.Ct. 41, 44, 32 L.Ed. 370, as follows:

> "It is indeed the general rule that a policy, and the money to become due under it, belong, at the moment it is issued, to the person or persons named in it as the beneficiary or beneficiaries; and that there is no power in the person procuring the insurance, by any act of his, by deed or by will, to transfer to any other person the interest of the person named."

In other words, the beneficiary was held to be the recipient of the benefits of an irrevocable trust. To the same effect see, Mutual Benefit Life Ins. Co. v. Cummings, 66 Or. 272, 285, 126 P. 982, 133 P. 1169, 47 L.R.A.,N.S., 252, Ann.Cas.1915B, 535. Several prior state court decisions in New Jersey, Connecticut and Louisiana had already established the rule that a donee-beneficiary held a vested interest which could not be defeated by the insured, who was the promisee under the insurance contract. These cases are collected and exhaustively analyzed by Professor Vance in his article, "The Beneficiary's Interest in a Life Insurance Policy" (1922), 31 Yale L.J. 343. The early cases were soon buttressed by many others which followed in quick succession. See cases cited in 4 Cooley, Briefs on Insurance (2d ed.) 3755; 3 A. & E.Enc.Law (2d ed.) 980. Whether the beneficiary was looked upon as the recipient of a trust, or whether the policy was considered a gift of a chose in action, the important thing in these early cases is that the beneficiary was declared to be the owner. This view is entirely understandable in the light of the provisions of life insurance contracts then written. There were no loan or cash values, no extensive powers of assignment or change of beneficiary.

The older rule which gave a vested interest to the beneficiary does not, of course, square with the modern notions of life policies. In modern times, the real incidents of ownership are undisputably vested in the insured and it was only logical that many courts should take the position that the beneficiary, where he is subject to divestment at the mere whim of the insured, takes only a contingent interest or an expectancy. Thus, today there is considerable authority for the view that the beneficiary gets a vested right only as his expectancy or contingent interest matures on the death of the insured. Grosz v. Grosz, 151 Or. 438, 450, 50 P.2d 119; Grimm v. Grimm, 26 Cal.2d 173, 157 P. 2d 841; Shay v. Merchants Banking Trust Co., 335 Pa. 101, 6 A.2d 536; 46 C.J.S., Insurance, § 1173(2), notes 15, 16, pages 62–63; 27 Am.Jur. 952, Insurance, § 1276. But the courts are by no means in accord on the issue. Many hold that the beneficiary takes a vested interest subject to divestment upon change of beneficiary in accordance with the provisions of the policy. Roberts v. Northwestern Life Nat. Ins. Co., 143 Ga. 780, 85 S.E. 1043; Indiana Nat. Life Ins. Co. v. McGinnis, 180 Ind. 9, 101 N.E. 289, 45 L.R.A.,N.S. 192; Metropolitan Life Ins. Co. v. Woolf, 138 N.J.Eq. 450, 47 A.2d 340; Wodell v. John Hancock Mut. Life Ins. Co., 320 Mass. 1, 67 N.E.2d 469. Where this view obtains, there is no problem concerning the testamentary aspect of the transaction, for the vested right of the beneficiary is without doubt a proper subject for a trust. Restatement, Trusts § 57, comment f, p. 178; § 84, comment b; Fidelity Title & Trust Co. v. Graham, 262 Pa. 273, 105 A. 295.

Under the general view that the beneficiary has no more than an expectancy, it is more difficult to find the necessary res for a present trust. Rather, the transaction appears to be a contract with the trust-beneficiary to create a trust at the insured's death. The courts, however, have not felt constrained to arrive at this conclusion, and the cases are legion which have upheld the usual form of unfunded insurance trust even where the court had previously announced that the beneficiary has no more than a mere expectancy. In some of the earlier cases, the rationale appeared to be that, since a life insurance policy payable to an ordinary third-party beneficiary is not testamentary, then neither is one wherein the third-party beneficiary is also trustee, for in both cases the legal title to the proceeds is in the beneficiary according to the doctrine of the third-party beneficiary as it has developed in the law of contracts. In the insurance trust device, the trustee-beneficiary takes a divided interest in the property, but this is specifically a trust problem and has no bearing on the testamentary character of the device. This view was adopted by the New

Jersey court in the well-known case of Bose v. Meury, 112 N.J.Eq. 62, 163 A. 276, and also by the Illinois court in Gurnett v. Mutual Life Ins. Co., 356 Ill. 612, 191 N.E. 250. We observe, therefore, that both under the old view, where the beneficiary is considered the owner, and under the new view where he has only an expectancy, the result is the same, for even in the new view, the third-party beneficiary has a present right to fulfillment of the insurer's promise to pay. There is no inconsistency in this position. A right of revocation of the trust deed in the case of any trust cannot really be distinguished from the power reserved by the insured to change the beneficiary. The extent of control reserved to the donor and the insured is the same in both cases, and the vested interest of the beneficiary of the ordinary trust is not open to question, despite the fact that the donor might revoke the trust at his pleasure. See, Allen v. Hendrick, 104 Or. 202, 224, 206 P. 733. A close analogy is found in the so-called "Totten" or tentative savings bank trust, under which complete control is likewise reserved by the donor during his lifetime, but the beneficiary is permitted to take the money on his death. See, Matter of Totten, 179 N.Y. 112, 71 N.E. 748, 70 L.R.A. 711.

This court, having carefully reviewed the cases, is of the opinion that the insurance trust attacked in this case can be sustained without deciding that the beneficiary-trustee has either vested rights or a mere expectancy. We perceive that some courts have taken steps to avoid the pitfalls of this particular aspect of the insurance trust problems. Some have resolved the problem by calling the right of the beneficiary a contingent interest which is something more than a mere expectancy, yet something less than a vested interest. See, e.g., Hirsch v. Auer, 146 N.Y. 13, 40 N.E. 397; Kerr v. Crane, 212 Mass. 224, 98 N.E. 783, 40 L.R.A.,N.S., 692. These cases, it should be noted were decided at a time when the life policies in question had none of the modern features such as cash rights, borrowing, reserves, etc. Our own view is that the ownership of the modern policy is actually divided between the beneficiary and the insured. The various marketing or sales features, such as the loan and cash surrender values, are clearly the property of the insured. On the other hand, the beneficiary is the owner of a promise to pay the proceeds at the death of insured, subject to insured's right of revocation. It seems to us that the right of the beneficiary is actually the primary right under the policy, whereas the insured's rights are secondary and have nothing to do with the basic purpose of life insurance. It has been pointed out that a life policy is an anomalous thing when it is separated from its primary object and obligation, namely, to pay the beneficiary the amount of the policy at the death of the insured. See, Boughton, "Creditors and Surrenders" (1926), 3 Association of Life Insurance Counsel Proceedings 311.

The rule that the beneficiary takes rights of his own rather than those of the settlor-insured was recognized in Bose v. Meury, supra

[112 N.J. 62, 163 A. 277]. In answer to the claim that the insurance trust was testamentary, the court said:

> "The proceeds are the fulfillment of promises by the insurance company to the Montclair Trust Company, trustee, to pay the stipulated sums, upon the death of the insured. The insured paid the consideration for the promises and he had the right, under the terms of the policies, to change the promises at will, but when the day came—the insured's death—the obligations of the insurance company were due to the Montclair Trust Company, trustee. *Its source of title was the promise in the policies, not the trust agreement.*" (Italics added.) Under the above language the trust was sustained. The court also held, and we are in agreement, that actually the beneficiary is the one who declares the trust where he has been named trustee. This view is supported by several other cases. See, Lashley v. Lashley, 212 Ala. 255, 102 So. 229; Makowiec v. Prudential Life Ins. Co., 83 N.H. 547, 145 A. 269.

It follows from the foregoing analysis of the nature and incidents of an insurance trust that Mr. Gordon intended to, and did, transfer to the bank a present interest in the insurance policies. Allen v. Hendrick, 104 Or. 202, 225, 206 P. 733, and that the plaintiff's contention that the instrument is testamentary in character, rather tha[n] a trust, must fail.

The judgment is affirmed.[2]

NOTE

There are certain drafting problems peculiar to a life insurance trust. Set out hereafter are some drafting suggestions.

1. All insurance policies whose proceeds are to form the trust should be set out in detail in a schedule which is made part of the trust agreement.

2. The unfunded trust should expressly relieve the trustee of any responsibility to pay the premiums on the insurance and place the responsibility for paying premiums, assessments and other charges upon the settlor. If the trust is funded or accumulative, the trustee must pay the premiums and other charges on the policies. The instrument should define the trustee's duty if the income is more than sufficient to pay the premiums and charges. The action to be taken by the trustee if the income is insufficient to pay the premiums and charges should be stipulated clearly.

2. Some courts recognize very frankly that the life insurance trust is no more testamentary than life insurance itself. Thus, in In re Albert Anderson Life Ins. Trust, 67 S.D. 393, at 399, 293 N.W. 527, at 530 (1940), the Supreme Court of South Dakota concluded an opinion sustaining a life insurance trust by saying:

"* * * But appellants' arguments in support of their contention that the trust agreement is invalid would equally, we believe, support the view that the naming of a beneficiary in a life insurance policy, wherein the right to change the beneficiary is reserved, would in itself constitute a testamentary disposition of property. Quite obviously such view could not be sustained."

3. The trust agreement should indicate the rights reserved by the insured. The typical unfunded trust agreement reserves to the insured the following rights:

(a) to add other insurance to the trust by making other policies payable to the trustee;

(b) to receive dividends, disability benefits or matured endowments;

(c) to obtain loans on the policies;

(d) to exercise options, rights or privileges, granted by the policies;

(e) to pledge, assign or sell a policy;

(f) to change the beneficiary of a policy;

(g) to withdraw policies covered by the trust agreement;

(h) to change the beneficiaries under the trust agreement; and

(i) to revoke, amend or modify the trust agreement.

4. The trustee's duties related to collection of the policy proceeds should be set out in detail. In general, a trustee of life insurance should have the same power of compromising and adjusting claims against the insurance company that an executor should have with respect to claims in favor of, or against, the general estate.

5. The agreement should give the trustee power to purchase securities from the general estate of the settlor at prevailing market prices and to make loans to the executor of the settlor's estate. The will of the settlor should give the executor authority to sell securities to, or borrow money from, the trustee of the life insurance trust.

6. When the insurance contract allows it, the trustee should be given power to exercise options available to the beneficiary of the policy.[3]

(2) RIGHTS OF SURVIVING SPOUSE IN REVOCABLE LIFE INSURANCE TRUST

Life insurance proceeds payable directly to a named beneficiary do not pass through the estate and hence are not part of the "net personal estate" under election statutes affording the surviving spouse a share of that estate.[4]

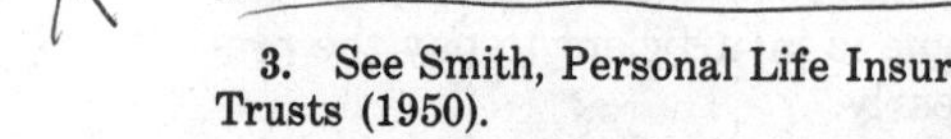

A revocable unfunded life insurance trust is, as we have just seen, generally regarded as valid and non-testamentary. Should the an-

3. See Smith, Personal Life Insurance Trusts (1950).

4. For an interesting application of this rule under the Pennsylvania Estates Act, see In re Henderson's Estate, 395 Pa. 215, 149 A.2d 892 (1959). The Act now specifically exempts life insurance and life insurance trusts. 20 P.S. § 6108 (spec. 1973 Pamph.) Under McKinney's N.Y., EPTL, § 5-1.1(b)(1)(E) and (b)(2)(B)(1967), a revocable life insurance trust appears subject to the election by the surviving spouse under the statutory conditions set forth. See Lipnick, "Estate Planning and the Widow's Election", 43 Taxes 313 (1965); Scott, "The Revocable Trust and the Surviving Spouse's Statutory Share in Colorado", 36 U.Colo. L.Rev. 464 (1964); Note, "Revocable Inter Vivos Trusts Versus The Statutory Share", 45 Neb.L.Rev. 603 (1966); Schuyler, "Revocable Trusts—Spouses, Creditors and Other Predators," Ch. 74-13, 8th Annual Institute on Estate Planning (Univ. of Miami, 1974).

swer be any different if the trust is attacked by the surviving widow? There are, of course, different policy considerations present here. The cases indicate that the courts may be more willing to hold the trust "testamentary" when attacked by the widow. The problem is in essence one we have already encountered in Chapter VIII, Section 6, dealing with revocable trusts generally; and the result will depend upon the tests used in the particular jurisdiction. The revocable unfunded insurance trust has less substance during lifetime than a revocable trust containing property such as stocks and bonds. It is therefore easier for a court to hold that the life insurance trust is illusory or lacks substance during lifetime, and allow the widow her share.

If the husband creates a life insurance trust in favor of his spouse, in some states he should provide in the trust agreement that if she elects against his will, her benefits under the trust shall be reduced or eliminated; otherwise she may accept the trust benefits and still elect against his will in those states giving her an elective share in the probate estate.[5] In this respect an insurance trust is the same as any inter vivos trust. Note that under the Uniform Probate Code, either life insurance payable to the spouse or an insurance trust in her favor will be counted against her share in the augmented estate. See Chapter IV, Section 2(2)(C).

In community property states the right of the spouse in life insurance taken out by the husband and made payable to someone other than the spouse depends on the rule followed in the particular state. In some states the right depends on the manner of initial purchase of the policy (inception of title theory); if before the marriage, or out of separate property after the marriage, the policy is separate property; if after the marriage and out of community funds, the insurance is community property. In other states the right depends on source of payment of premiums. If all or part of the premiums are paid out of community funds, the spouse may either get the portion of the proceeds attributable to her share in such funds or recover the amount of premiums paid out of her half of the community funds. The same rules would apply if the insurance proceeds were made payable to a trustee.

---

5. The trust should indicate unequivocally that it is to operate if the settlor dies intestate. For the testamentary character problem presented in an unfunded life insurance trust intended to force the wife to accept the will but with no provision for intestacy, see Bickers v. Shenandoah National Bank, Executor, 197 Va. 145, 88 S.E.2d 889 (1955). 31 N.Y.U.L.Rev. 967 (1955), 17 U.Pitt.L.Rev. 513 (1956), 42 Va.L.Rev. 256 (1956); 13 Wash. & Lee L.Rev. 117 (1956).

SECTION 3. INTERRELATING TESTAMENTARY AND INTER VIVOS TRANSACTIONS

(1) INCORPORATION BY REFERENCE INTO A WILL

BRYAN'S APPEAL

Supreme Court of Errors of Connecticut, 1904.
77 Conn. 240, 58 A. 748.

[Philo S. Bennett executed a will dated 22 May 1900 in New York. Clause twelve of the will provided:

> "I give and bequeath unto my wife, Grace Imogene Bennett, the sum of fifty thousand dollars ($50,000) in trust, however, for the purposes set forth in a sealed letter which will be found with this will."

When Bennett died the will was found in his safe deposit vault in the Wool Exchange Bank in New York City. With the will was found a letter in a sealed envelope. The envelope bore the following indorsement in the testator's handwriting: "Mrs. P. S. Bennett. To be read only by Mrs. Bennett and by her alone, after my death. P. S. Bennett. (Seal.)" The letter was dated "New York, 5/22/1900", was in the handwriting of the testator and was signed by him. The letter referred to "my will just executed", recited clause twelve of the will, and directed Mrs. Bennett to pay over the $50,000 to William Jennings Bryan for his financial aid. Among the testator's private papers there was found a typewritten copy of the same letter in an envelope subscribed in the testator's handwriting: "Copy of letter in Safe Deposit Company vault Wool Exchange." The typewritten copy was unsigned. The evidence indicated that a draft of the will and the typewritten copy of the letter had been prepared by Bennett and Bryan about ten days before the will was executed; that the letter in the handwriting of the testator had been drawn from the typewritten copy; and that both the executed will and the handwritten letter had been placed in the safe deposit vault by Bennett and had remained in his custody until his death. The will was offered for probate in the Probate Court of New Haven as Exhibit A. The handwritten letter was offered for probate with the will as Exhibit B and the typewritten letter was offered as Exhibit C. Neither letter was executed with the testamentary formalities required in Connecticut. The will was admitted to probate but both letters were rejected. Bryan then appealed to the Superior Court of New Haven County, offering Exhibits B and C in evidence and offering parol evidence to show that Exhibit B was the letter referred to in clause twelve of the will. This evidence was excluded and the court directed a jury verdict that Exhibits B and C were not part of the testator's will and entered judgment accordingly. Bryan appeals "individually and as trustee under the will" from this decision.]

TORRANCE, C. J. * * * From the opinion of the trial court, which is made part of the record, the rulings of the court seem to have been based upon several distinct grounds, which may be briefly indicated in this way: (1) Apparently upon the ground that the doctrine of incorporation by reference does not prevail as to wills, under our statute relating to their making and execution; (2) that, even if that doctrine prevails here, no paper in the present will is by reference made a part of it, according to the rules universally applied in jurisdictions where the above doctrine prevails; and (3) that the letter Exhibit B shows on its face an intent on the part of the testator that it should not constitute a part of his will. As we think the rulings of the court below can be vindicated upon the second of the grounds above mentioned, it will be unnecessary to consider the other two grounds; but, in thus resting our decision upon the second ground, we do not mean to intimate that it could or could not be made to rest upon the first or third.

Before considering the second ground, a word or two regarding the first ground may not be out of place. Under the rule prevailing in England, an unattested document may, by reference in a will, under certain conditions and limitations, become by reference incorporated in the will as a part of it, and that, too, whether the document referred to is or is not a dispositive one; and one of the leading cases upon this subject is that of Allen v. Maddock, 11 Moore's P.C.C. 427, decided in 1858. This is known as the "doctrine of incorporation by reference," and the principle upon which it rests does not differ essentially from that which is applied in incorporating unsigned writings in a signed instrument, so as to constitute a memorandum in writing under the statute of frauds. The English rule appears to prevail in many of our sister states, but the question whether it prevails in this state, and, if so, with what limitations and under what conditions, was left undetermined in Phelps v. Robbins, 40 Conn. 250, and has never been passed upon since. In the present case we find it unnecessary to decide those questions, but, for the purposes of the argument, we shall assume, without deciding, that the doctrine of incorporation by reference in a will prevails here. Two of the conditions without the existence of which the English rule will not be applied are concisely, but we think correctly, stated in Phelps v. Robbins, 40 Conn. 250, as follows: "First, the paper must be in existence at the time of the execution of the will; and, secondly, the description must not be so vague as to be incapable of being applied to any instrument in particular, but must describe the instrument intended in clear and definite terms." In a California case upon this subject this language is used: "But before such an extrinsic document may be so incorporated, the description of it in the will itself must be so clear, explicit, and unambiguous as to leave its identity free from doubt." Estate of Young, 123 Cal. 342, 55 P. 1012. In an important and well-considered English case, decided in 1902, the court uses this language upon this subject: "But it is clear, that, in order that the informal document should be incorporated in the validly executed document, the latter must refer to the former as a writing existing—that is, at the time of the execution—in such terms that it may be ascertained." "The document which it is sought to incorporate must be existing at the time of the execution of the document into which it is to be incorporated, and there must be a reference in the properly executed document to the informal document as an existing one, and not as a future document." In the Goods of Smart, L.R.P.D. 238. Tested by the rules as thus laid down in the cases above cited, and in numerous others that might be cited, the will in the present case fails to comply with the required conditions under which incorporation by reference can take place in the case of wills. In clause 12 of the will in question here, a large sum of money is given to Mrs. Bennett, "in trust, however, for the purposes set forth in a sealed letter which will be found with this will." There is not in the language quoted, nor anywhere else in the will, any clear, explicit, unambiguous reference to any specific document as one existing and known to the testator at the time his will was executed. Any sealed letter, or any number of them, setting forth the purposes of the trust, made by anybody at any time after the will was executed, and "found with the will," would each fully and accurately answer the reference; and, if we assume that the reference calls for a letter from the testator, it is answered by such a letter or letters made at any time after the will was drawn. The reference is "so vague as to be incapable of being applied to any instrument in particular" as a document existing at the time of the will. "The vice is that no particular paper is referred to." Phelps v. Robbins, 40 Conn. 250, 273. Such a reference as is made in the present will is in fact, as well as in law, no reference at all. Certainly it is not such a reference as the rules, under the doctrine of incorporation by reference, require in the case of wills. A reference so defective as the one here in question cannot be helped out by what is called "parol evidence," for to allow such evidence to be used for such purpose would be practically to nullify the wise provisions of the law relating to the making and execution of wills.

We know of no case, and in the able and helpful briefs filed in this case have been referred to none, where a reference like the one here in question has been held to incorporate into the will some extrinsic document. Assuming, then, without deciding, that the doctrine of incorporation prevails in this state, as claimed by the appellant, we are still of the opinion that the rulings of which he complains were correct.

There is no error. The other Judges concurred.

NOTE

In Bryan v. Bigelow,[6] the unincorporated letter was held testamentary and not admissible in evidence to rebut a resulting trust in favor of the resid-

6. 77 Conn. 604, 60 A. 266 (1905).

uary estate. Connecticut subsequently rejected the incorporation doctrine.[7] The Connecticut view is shared by Louisiana[8] and possibly New Jersey.[9] New York applies the doctrine subject to limitations.[10] The doctrine is adopted expressly by the Uniform Probate Code.[11] Courts rejecting the doctrine have done so on the ground it opens the door to the fraud the Wills Acts were designed to prevent.[12]

If the written document representing the transaction in question was present when the will was executed, it may be argued that the document is a physical part of the will.[13] But when the document cannot be integrated as part of the will, the party seeking to give the transaction effect must rely upon the incorporation doctrine, the non-testamentary act theory (considered in subsection 2 of this Section) or upon some special statute which authorizes interrelationship of the will and inter vivos transactions under the conditions such as those discussed hereafter in subsection 3 of this Section.

If one of the statutes mentioned or the non-testamentary act theory cannot be applied effectively then the party arguing that effect be given to the extrinsic transaction in conjunction with the will probably must rely upon the incorporation doctrine. In those states in which the incorporation doctrine

7. Hatheway v. Smith, 79 Conn. 506, 65 A. 1058 (1907). A Connecticut statute subsequently permitted the incorporation of living trust provisions into a will and Connecticut now has the Uniform Testamentary Additions to Trusts Act. Conn. Gen.Stat.Ann. § 45–173a (1980 Supp.). The current trend is to enact pour-over statutes among the states, forty-three and the District of Columbia having the Uniform Act by 1982 and others having pour-over statutes containing different terms. The Uniform Act is set forth in Subsection 3 hereafter. Other pour-over statutes are analyzed in Rees, "American Wills Statutes", 46 Va.L.Rev. 613, 651 (1960).

8. See Succession of Ledet, 170 La. 449, 128 So. 273 (1930); Hessmer v. Edenborn, 196 La. 575, 199 So. 647 (1940); 40 Mich.L.Rev. 492 (1942).

9. See Murray v. Lewis, 94 N.J.Eq. 681, 121 A. 525 (1923); Swetland v. Swetland, 100 N.J.Eq. 196, 134 A. 822 (1928); First Mechanics National Bank of Trenton v. Norris, 134 N.J.Eq. 229, 34 A.2d 746 (1943). New Jersey now has the Uniform Testamentary Additions to Trusts Act with minor changes. N.J.Stat.Ann. 3A:3–16.1 to 3A:3–16.5 (1981 Supp.).

10. The New York courts have permitted republication of a will by codicil except when the will was invalid initially because improperly executed. Cook v. White, 43 App.Div. 388, 60 N.Y.S. 153 (1901), aff'd 167 N.Y. 588, 60 N.E. 1109; McKinney's N.Y., EPTL, § 3–4.6(b)(1) (1980 Supp.) apparently continues this view, referring to "revival" of the will by a codicil "which in terms incorporates by reference such prior will or one or more of its provisions". McKinney's N.Y., EPTL, § 3–3.7 (1980 Supp.) permits "pour-overs" into amendable inter vivos trusts and is a reenactment of D.E.L. 47–g. For cases and comment concerning these transactions see Matter of Fowles, 222 N.Y. 222, 118 N.E. 611, Ann.Cas.1918D, 834 (1918) (possible incorporation of will of spouse); Matter of Rausch's Will, 258 N.Y. 327, 179 N.E. 755, 80 A.L.R. 98 (1932); Matter of Hull, 37 A.D.2d 325, 325 N.Y.S.2d 340 (1971). 6 U. of Cin.L.Rev. 295 (1932); 32 Col.L. Rev. 917 (1932); 17 Minn.L.Rev. 564 (1933); 9 N.Y.U.L.Q.Rev. 505 (1932) (unamendable and irrevocable trust deed); In re Ivie's Will, 4 N.Y.2d 178, 173 N.Y.S.2d 293, 149 N.E.2d 725 (1958); 45 Corn.L.Q. 135 (1959); 33 St. John's L. Rev. 169 (1958) (amendable trust deed, amended three times, but right to amend relinquished before death of settlor); "Incorporation by Reference and Independent Legal Significance in the New York Law of Wills", 29 Fordham L.Rev. 143 (1960).

11. Uniform Probate Code, § 2–510.

12. The incorporation doctrine originated before extensive formalities for the execution of wills were required by the Statute of Frauds, 1677. See Molineux v. Molineux, (1603) Cro.Jac. 144, 145. Application of the doctrine was seldom questioned in England until the Wills Act, 1837, added the requirement that wills be "signed at the end". It was held in Allen v. Maddock, 11 Moore P.C. 427, 14 Eng.Rep. 757 (1859), that a will was signed at the end even though other writings were incorporated by reference.

13. See Chapter V, Section 5(3).

has been applied the requirements for incorporation have been imposed rigidly by the courts and an attempted incorporation not meeting these requirements fails.

Only writings can be incorporated [14] and only valid testamentary instruments can incorporate[15] where the doctrine is applied. The courts are in general accord that there can be no incorporation unless five conditions are satisfied. (1) The incorporating document must describe the writing with reasonable certainty. (2) The writing must be described as in existence when the incorporating document is executed. (3) The testator's intention to incorporate the writing must appear from the incorporating document. (4) The writing must conform to the description contained in the incorporating document. (5) The writing in fact must have been in existence when the incorporating document was executed.[16]

Requirements (1) and (2) are closely related. The writing must be described as "in existence" so that the search can be limited to documents in existence when the incorporating instrument was executed. Words of futurity used in describing the writing are fatal to incorporation [17] and some courts have refused incorporation when the words could be construed as referring to either a future or a past writing.[18] The sufficiency of the description in other respects depends upon the type of writing which the testator seeks to incorporate. A deed, contract or note may be described adequately by date and parties. A will should be described by the date and witnesses.[19] A description by location of a holographic memorandum has been held sufficient.[20]

A testator who intends to incorporate by reference usually makes his intention clear in the incorporating instrument. The intention would be clear if the writing was described and language in the incorporating instrument indicated that the described writing was to be a part of the testamentary plan.[21] Most of the courts do not admit parol evidence to show an intention to incor-

14. Except in a few states in which non-holographic materials cannot be incorporated into a holographic will or codicil, the character of the writing is immaterial. The writing need not be dispositive in nature nor need it be executed with testamentary formalities.

15. A writing cannot be incorporated into a nuncupative (oral) will. The incorporating instrument must be a valid written will or codicil.

16. See generally, Atkinson, Wills (2d Ed., 1953) § 80; 2 Bowe-Parker; Page, Wills (3d Ed., Rev.1960) §§ 19.17–19.36; Rollison, Wills (1939) § 122; Thompson, Wills (3d Ed., 1947) § 106; Dobie, "Testamentary Incorporation by Reference", 3 Va.L.Rev. 583 (1916); Evans, "Incorporation by Reference, Integration and Non Testamentary Act", 25 Col.L.Rev. 879 (1925); Evans, "Nontestamentary Acts and Incorporation by Reference", 16 U. of Chi.L.Rev. 635 (1949); Malone, "Incorporation by Reference of an Extrinsic Document into a Holographic Will", 16 Va.L.Rev. 571 (1930); Mechem, "The Integration of Holographic Wills", 12 N.C. L.Rev. 213, 225 (1934); 6 John Marshall L.J. 72 (1949); 46 Mich.L.Rev. 77 (1947); 17 Minn.L.Rev. 527 (1933); 16 Tenn.L. Rev. 741 (1941); 6 U. of Cin.L.Rev. 295 (1932); 15 Wyo.L.J. 58 (1960).

17. E.g., Goods of Smart, [1902] L.R. Prob. 238 ("to give to such of my friends as I may designate in a book or memorandum that will be found with this will"); Lawless v. Lawless, 187 Va. 511, 47 S.E.2d 431 (1948) (property to "be used as I shall later request").

18. E.g., Magnus v. Magnus, 80 N.J. Eq. 346, 84 A. 705 (1912), 26 Harv.L.Rev. 278 (1912) (To be disposed of by niece "in accordance with my instructions to her").

19. A reference to "my last will and testament" in a codicil has been held a sufficient description when the testator had only one will. Allen v. Maddock, 11 Moore P.C. 427, 14 Eng.Rep. 757 (1859).

20. Estate of Miller, 128 Cal.App. 176, 17 P.2d 181 (1932) ("There is another paper in my pocket book which will explain * * *").

21. See Estate of Hopper, 90 Neb. 622, 134 N.W. 237 (1912).

porate when the intention does not appear from the face of the incorporating instrument.[22]

If the will contains a distinct reference to an existing writing, and the testator's intention to incorporate is plain, parol evidence of the circumstances surrounding the testator at the time the incorporating document was executed is generally held admissible to aid in identifying the writing incorporated.[23] But parol evidence is not admitted to formulate a description when the terms of reference are so vague as to be applicable to any writing.[24]

The fact that the incorporating document contains a reference to a writing as in existence cannot support an incorporation if the writing was prepared after the incorporating instrument was executed.[25] The rule is applied strictly. The writing cannot be incorporated if it is prepared immediately after the execution of the incorporating document. A testator would be permitted to make a will without the legislative safeguards if any writing prepared after the execution of a will was permitted to alter its operation.

Incorporation by reference of a writing, by the better view, does not make the writing a physical part of the incorporating instrument. The writing is read with the incorporating document for the purpose of construction. It is not required that the incorporated document be probated with an incorporating will.[26] The writing is incorporated metaphorically and not physically.

Distinctions between metaphorical and physical theories of incorporation are immaterial in most states. But where a will must be "signed at the end" by the testator, a reference may be made preceding the signature to a dispositive provision following the signature. In a "logical" end jurisdiction the provision would be read at the place intended by the testator.[27] Assuming that the reference is sufficient to incorporate, it might make a difference in a "physical" end jurisdiction whether the incorporation was physical or metaphorical. Where holographic wills are valid without attestation, a number of courts have refused to permit the incorporation of non-holographic materials into unattested holographic instruments on the ground that the incorporation was physical.[28] Other courts have permitted incorporation on the theory that the non-holographic materials are read as a part of the holographic instrument but do not become a physical part of it.[29]

22. Most of the cases reported involve an attempt to incorporate an undelivered deed into a will which contains a reference to the deed. E.g., Witham v. Witham, 156 Or. 59, 66 P.2d 281, 110 A.L.R. 253 (1937). But see Estate of Dimmitt, 141 Neb. 413, 3 N.W.2d 752, 144 A.L.R. 704 (1942), 37 Ill.L.Rev. 425 (1943), 41 Mich.L.Rev. 751 (1943), 22 Tex.L.Rev. 87 (1943).

23. Estate of Hopper, fn. 21, supra; Baker's Appeal, 107 Pa. 381 (1884).

24. E.g., Young's Estate, 123 Cal. 337, 55 P. 1011 (1899) ("The two deeds".); Phelps v. Robbins, 40 Conn. 250 (1873) ("Written instructions in my handwriting to be left with my will").

25. Shillaber's Estate, 74 Cal. 144, 15 P. 453, 5 Am.St.Rep. 433 (1887).

26. E.g., Tuttle v. Berryman, 94 Ky. 553, 23 S.W. 345 (1893). An integrated paper is part of the will in a physical sense and must be probated with it. See Chapter V, Section 5(3).

27. See Chapter V, Section 6(1)(B).

28. Sharp v. Wallace, 83 Ky. 584 (1886); Hewes v. Hewes, 110 Miss. 826, 71 So. 4 (1916).

29. Estate of Soher, 78 Cal. 477, 21 P. 8 (1889); Gooch v. Gooch, 134 Va. 21, 113 S.E. 873 (1922), 21 Mich.L.Rev. 485 (1923). The Arkansas court also permits incorporation but seems to proceed on the theory that the incorporated writing becomes a physical part of the incorporating instrument. See Kinnear v. Langley, 209 Ark. 878, 192 S.W.2d 978 (1946).

There is an apparent trend towards liberalization of the requirements for applying the incorporation doctrine in those states which recognize it. General acceptance of the doctrine of republication by codicil, considered in Chapter VI, Section 4(2) is indicative of this trend. The public interest in facilitating the interrelationship of wills and living trusts in estate planning certainly contributes to tacit relaxation of certain elements of the doctrine—most significantly the requirement stressed in Bryan's Appeal that the will *refer* to the extrinsic writing as an *existing* writing.[30] The enactment of "pour-over" statutes may result in decreased reliance upon the doctrine of incorporation by reference; but at the same time may induce the courts to become more liberal in applying the doctrine since the "pour-over" statutes reflect a legislative judgment that the policy to prevent fraud thought to underlie the Wills Acts is of diminished importance in the current estate planning context.

But there is, nevertheless, interest among draftsmen and estate planners in avoiding the incorporation doctrine. The property described in the incorporated instrument may be treated as part of the probate estate.[31] If a testamentary gift is made to the trustee of an inter vivos trust subject to the trust terms, the trust being incorporated by reference, an attempt might be made to require a bond of the trustee as a testamentary trustee;[32] or the terms of the trust might have been changed after execution of the will so that the reference would be made to an obsolete document. These difficulties have suggested the development of other theories which might be employed to sustain these attempted interrelationships, the most important of these being the doctrine of "non-testamentary acts".

PROBLEM

An instrument was offered for probate as the will of T. The instrument consists of a single sheet of paper upon which appear three typewritten dispositive paragraphs. The typewritten materials are not dated, signed or attested. At the end of the page in the handwriting of T appears:

> "To my brother James I give ten dollars only. This will shall be complete unless hereafter altered, changed or rewritten. Witness my hand this April 6th, 1947—Easter Sunday, 2:30 P.M.
>
> [s] T"

There is evidence to prove that the typewritten provisions were prepared before the holographic material at the bottom of the page. The state recognizes holographic wills and codicils without attesting witnesses, but requires the testator's signature and attestation if the instrument is non-holographic. Can the typewritten provisions be probated as part of the will of T? Can the holographic provisions be probated as the will of T or as a codicil? Can any of the writing on the paper be probated as part of T's will? Johnson v. Johnson, 279 P.2d 928 (Okl.1954). But cf. Hinson v. Hinson, 154 Tex. 561, 280 S.W.2d 731 (1955). For comments and decisions on Johnson see 24 Kansas Bar Assoc.J. 193 (1955); 30 N.Y.U.L.Rev. 1456 (1955); 9 Okla.L.Rev. 225 (1956);

30. E.g., Smith v. Weitzel, 47 Tenn. App. 375, 338 S.W.2d 628 (1960); Noted 28 Tenn.L.Rev. 593 (1961), Cf. In re Estate of Foxworth, 50 Cal.Rptr. 237 (Dist. Ct. of Appeal, 1966) (Where requirement of present reference not made but will apparently satisfied general test); Contra: Phelps v. La Moille Ill. Lodge No. 270, 52 Ill.App.2d 164, 201 N.E.2d 634 (1964) (where incorporation failed upon ground among others that no reference to incorporated document as existing).

31. See e.g., Smith v. Weitzel, 47 Tenn.App. 375, 338 S.W.2d 628 (1960).

32. See York's Estate, 95 N.H. 435, 65 A.2d 282 (1949); 63 Harv.L.Rev. 543 (1950); 48 Mich.L.Rev. 244 (1949).

17 U. of Pitts.L.Rev. 312 (1956); 8 Vanderbilt L.Rev. 924 (1955); 44 Ky.L.J. 130 (1955); 7 Hastings L.J. 225 (1956); 23 U. of Chi.L.Rev. 316 (1956). For comment on Hinson, see 1956 Wash.U.L.Q. 260. For a discussion of both Johnson and Hinson see 34 Tex.L.Rev. 148 (1955).

---

(2) NON-TESTAMENTARY ACTS

HASTINGS v. BRIDGE

Supreme Court of New Hampshire, 1933.
86 N.H. 247, 166 A. 273.

* * *

Petition for instructions, by the executors of the will of Caroline G. B. Cooksey.

Clause 4 of the will reads as follows:

> "Fourth: All my wearing apparel, jewelry and all other articles of personal use or adornment, except those mentioned in paragraph First of this will, all of my linen, silver, books, pictures and household effects, except those mentioned in paragraph First of the will, I give and bequeath to Florence M. Hastings, wife of Russell Hastings, 16 Emerson Street, Brookline, Massachusetts, and request her to distribute them to the persons named in a letter or memorandum of instructions which I shall leave addressed to her. Any of the articles not mentioned in said letter or memorandum of instructions I give and bequeath to the said Florence M. Hastings personally and if she is not living to her children. If the said Florence M. Hastings does not survive me I direct the person who administers my estate to distribute them to the persons named in the letter addressed to said Florence M. Hastings."

A memorandum subsequently prepared by the testatrix, and enumerating about fifty different gifts, was denied probate as a part of the will, and no appeal was taken.

The assets of the estate are not sufficient to pay the pecuniary legacies in full.

The executors ask whether the articles mentioned in the memorandum go to Mrs. Hastings, or "become part of the general estate or pass as intestate to Harrison G. Bridge, sole heir at law."

* * *

PEASLEE, CHIEF JUSTICE. All testamentary acts must be evidenced as the statute requires. It is true that in many ways a testator may alter the effect of his will by acts done subsequently to its execution. A gift of all his lands in the town of A, or of all his stock in a certain corporation may be increased or diminished by purchases or sales of the described property. But such transactions are not testamentary acts. They merely place certain property within the description contained in the will.

This theory has frequently been given application to extreme cases. Bequests, for example, of the contents of a certain box, have always been sustained. While there has been frequent contest over the issue whether mere evidences of title, like notes, bonds, and certificates of stock, would pass under such description, the difficulty encountered has not been found in the matter of location, but in the nature of the documents. Being mere evidences of title rather than property in the more tangible sense, it has frequently been held that they did not pass in the absence of further evidence that such was the testator's intent. But as to tangible personal property, described in this way, the bequests appear to have always been upheld. The authorities are collected in 40 Cyc. 1552.

It is manifest that such holdings give a testator a wide range of power to alter the destination of property passing under his will without doing any testamentary act. If he had ten boxes numbered consecutively, and willed the contents of each to a different legatee, he could cut down or increase their respective takings at pleasure. In this way the purpose of the statute of wills can be evaded to a large degree.

This objection to the validity of such acts has, however, rarely been noticed. It is commented on in but two cases which have come to our attention. Both are of comparatively recent date. In one of them the bequest was upheld, despite the court's view of the dangerous nature of the procedure. In re Robson, (1891) 2 Ch. 559. In the other the case was disposed of on different grounds. Parrott v. Avery, 159 Mass. 594, 35 N.E. 94, 22 L.R.A. 153, 38 Am.St.Rep. 465.

We have no cases in this state indorsing this doctrine. This may be due to the idea that no lawyer "has been bold enough to risk the experiment." Phelps v. Robbins, 40 Conn. 250. The only one found approaching the question takes care to state both in facts and opinion, a compliance with a much narrower rule. The note was indorsed and put in the trunk before the will was made. Lock v. Noyes, 9 N. H. 430.

Granting that the theory of the cases is good law, it should be kept within bounds. Where some act of the testator, in itself testamentary in character is required to complete a gift by will, that act should be evidenced in the manner prescribed by the statute of wills. Such a situation is presented here. It is not a question of description of property by kind, location, ownership, or other characteristic. The description relates to what the testator has done with it in a testamentary way. The will plainly contemplated that the memorandum was to be a valid disposition of property—a part of the will. Since there is no such document, a less formal one cannot supply the deficiency in the will nor affect the disposition made by the will. It is plain that a bequest could not be either created or increased by such a document. No more can an incomplete gift be made complete thereby. Had the testatrix provided that Mrs. Hastings have all the testatrix' personal belongings except such as she should by word of mouth direct should be otherwise disposed of after her death, such direction would not complete the will.

The distinction lies between future acts which may or may not affect the location, etc., of property, and words which are by the terms of the will made necessary to its completion. In the latter class the subsequent verbal act is testamentary.

A valid testament includes two essential elements. There must be a sufficient designation of the beneficiary and of the property given to him. If either is in terms left to future designation, the will is incomplete and ineffective. While future acts may determine what is within the designation contained in the will, the designation cannot be altered or created in that way, unless the provisions of the statute of wills are complied with. It is for this reason that it is uniformly held that a document referred to in the will for further direction as to the disposition of the estate must be in existence when the will is made, and must be made a part thereof by a sufficient identifying description contained therein; "for a testator cannot reserve to himself the power to modify a will by a written instrument subsequently prepared and not executed in the manner required by the statute of wills." 28 R.C.L. 113; Bryan's Appeal, 77 Conn. 240, 58 A. 748, 107 Am.St.Rep. 34, 1 Ann.Cas. 393, 68 L.R.A. 353; and note extensively reviewing the authorities.

In the present case the description of what is to go to Mrs. Hastings is incomplete. If no memorandum had been made, it could not be ascertained what the testatrix intended to give her. Manifestly there was no intent to give her the whole, and no separation having been made, the whole clause would be ineffective. Unless some further act of designation were performed, there was no gift.

The case for Mrs. Hastings rests solely upon the testatrix' declaration, made subsequently to the execution of the will, that certain property was the portion she gave to others. Nothing was done to or with any property to bring it within a description contained in the will. The whole case comes to this: The testatrix said in her will, "I give Mrs. Hastings that part which I do not give to some one else," or, as more directly applying to her, "such part as I do not subsequently say she shall not have." The designation is incomplete. It could not be completed by any dealing with property, by buying, selling, changing location, or the like so as to bring it within terms stated in the will. It seems illogical to say that, while such a memorandum as that involved here cannot be used to prove a testamentary gift, it may be used to show what is not so given, and thus make the gift valid.

The law relating to cancellation of items in a will has no application. That relates solely to dealing with the will in a physical way. If it be undertaken through a separate document, there must be an execution according to the statute of wills. P.L. c. 297 § 13; Morey v. Sohier, 63 N.H. 507, 3 A. 636, 56 Am.Rep. 538.

The argument advanced against these conclusions is ingenious and logical. But its logic is only an argument against the desirability of the statute of wills. The cases as to location, etc., of property have gone quite far enough in undermining that statute. A line must be drawn somewhere; and a limit which excludes subsequent words, which stand alone, from the category of descriptive acts is fully as far as we ought to go. The description must be in the will. That contained in this will is on its face insufficient. By its very terms it is incomplete. Nothing could complete it except subsequent words uttered by the testatrix.

The matter is well summed up by Professor Evans in an excellent article dealing with this subject. This is his test for the validity of subsequent identification: "The means so provided should not be any act whose sole or chief purpose is that of complementing the will. It should have the force and effect of an independent legal transaction." 25 Col.Law Rev. 902.

The executors are advised that Mrs. Hastings takes nothing under the paragraph of the will involved in this controversy, and that all of the property therein described becomes a part of the general estate not specifically bequeathed.

Case discharged.

All concurred.

NOTE

The courts have accepted the influence upon testamentary dispositions of acts and events extraneous to the will without, in most instances, a detailed examination of the testamentary character of the acts or events involved. If the testator makes a bequest to the "woman whom I may marry", he is able to designate a beneficiary by the act of marriage, but the problem is discussed ordinarily as a matter of sufficiency of description.[33] If the gift is to be effective only if some other person does a specified act, the courts usually discuss the matter as one of "condition".

Because of the increasing interest in the last forty years in techniques for making testamentary gifts to the trustee of an inter vivos or living trust to be distributed in accordance with the trust terms, and for making testamentary gifts to the trustee designated in a testamentary trust of another to be distributed in accordance with the terms of the second trust, there has been much discussion among the text writers of a theory upon which these "pour overs" may be sustained when the terms of the extrinsic writing cannot be integrated or incorporated by reference into the will in question or sustained as the exercise of a power of appointment. In Langdon v. Astor's Executors, Denio, J., stated: [34] "I concede that a testator cannot prescribe in his will that an act to be performed by him, indifferent in itself and having no pertinency except its effect upon his testamentary dispositions, shall change

33. See generally, Atkinson, Wills (2d Ed., 1953) § 81; Evans, "Incorporation by Reference, Integration and Non-Testamentary Act", 25 Col.L.Rev. 879 (1925); Evans, "Nontestamentary Act and Incorporation by Reference", 16 U. of Chi.L. Rev. 635 (1949).

34. 16 N.Y. 9 (1857).

such dispositions." This statement has since been reformulated as follows:[35]

> "Beneficiaries may be pointed out generally in a will and may be limited and more precisely defined by a subsequent non-testamentary act. The will should (a) purport to dispose of the property; and (b) provide directions for determining the identity of the beneficiaries by giving a general description of them; but (c) the means so provided should not be any act whose sole or chief purpose is that of complementing the will. It should have the force and effect of an independent legal transaction." The same rule may be applied to a general description of property subject to testamentary disposition.

Gifts dependent upon past un-written acts of the testator, such as a bequest to "my present wife"[36] or a bequest of "$50,000 par value U. S. Government bonds now in my safety deposit box",[37] seem clearly valid. Gifts by location which can be altered in amount by the testator after the will is executed may invite difficulty. If the testator bequeaths "my old mahogany desk with the contents thereof",[38] the contents of a specified trunk,[39] or the "contents of my bank box in the Whitney Bank",[40] the testator may increase or diminish the contents of the receptacle after the will is executed. If the contents are not readily marketable, it may be argued that the alterations were solely to modify the will. But the changes may be made for a business purpose, such as a sale of marketable securities.

The act may be one done by the testator in conjunction with others. Bequests have been upheld to the co-partners of the testatrix at her death,[41] "to such persons as shall be in my employ at my death",[42] and to the employees of the O. J. Lewis Mercantile Company who have been employed ten years prior to the death of the testator.[43] In Dennis v. Holsapple,[44] the testatrix provided in her will: "Whoever shall take good care of me, and maintain, nurse, clothe, and furnish me with proper medical treatment at my request, during the time of my life yet when I shall need the same, shall have all of my property of every name, kind and description left at my death * * *. The person or persons whom shall be selected by me to earn my estate * * * shall have a written statement signed by me to that effect." The testatrix by letter directed Ella Holsapple to care for her and stated that Ella should receive all of her property. Ella furnished the care requested. It was argued that the testatrix had left the object of her bequest to depend upon her future volition and that the subsequent acts were testamentary in nature. The court relied upon the analogy of a *feme sole* who makes a bequest to her surviving husband, saying that the subsequent exercise of volition could not be deemed testamentary in a "legal" sense.

If the subsequent act is not within the control of the testator the courts treat the act as satisfaction of a condition. In Bate v. Amherst[45] the testa-

35. Evans, "Incorporation by Reference, Integration and Non-Testamentary Act", 25 Col.L.Rev. 879, 902 (1925).

36. Parker v. Oliver, 52 R.I. 117, 158 A. 146 (1932).

37. Nuttle's Estate, 1 Cal.App.2d 678, 37 P.2d 200 (1934).

38. In re Robson, [1891] L.R. 2 Ch. 559.

39. Magoohan's Appeal, 117 Pa. 238, 14 A. 816 (1887).

40. Succession of Maginnis, 158 La. 815, 104 So. 726 (1925).

41. Stubbs v. Sargon, 3 Myl. & Cr. 507, 40 Eng.Rep. 1022 (1838).

42. Metcalf v. Sweeney, 17 R.I. 213, 21 A. 364 (1891).

43. Abbot v. Lewis, 77 N.H. 94, 88 A. 98 (1913).

44. 148 Ind. 297, 47 N.E. 631 (1897).

45. 1 T.Raym. 81, 83 Eng.Rep. 45 (1663).

tor devised land to "one of my cousin Nicholas Amherst's daughters that shall marry with Norton within fifteen years". The daughter who married Norton within fifteen years took the devise. The independent significance of the act of marriage seems clear.

Although as will be seen in the following subsection, the "independent significance" test has been used to sustain a "pour over" into an inter vivos trust, the increasing interest in the test which its application to "pour overs" has stimulated may forecast restrictions upon the kinds of extrinsic acts and events that are permitted to supplement a will and thus serve, to a limited extent, as substitutes for codicils.

Uniform Probate Code, § 2–512 expressly allows references to acts and events having independent significance. Furthermore, Uniform Probate Code, § 2–513, also set forth in Chapter V, Section 1, fn. 3, provides:

> "Whether or not the provisions relating to holographic wills apply, a will may refer to a written statement or list to dispose of items of tangible personal property not otherwise specifically disposed of by the will, other than money, evidences of indebtedness, documents of title, and securities, and property used in trade or business. To be admissible under this Section as evidence of the intended disposition, the writing must either be in the handwriting of the testator or be signed by him and must describe the items and devisees with reasonable certainty. The writing may be referred to as one to be in existence at the time of the testator's death; it may be prepared before or after the execution of the will; it may be altered by the testator after its preparation; and it may be a writing which has no significance apart from its effect upon the dispositions made by the will."

How would Hastings v. Bridge have been decided if this section of the Uniform Probate Code had been in force in New Hampshire?

---

(3) CREATION OF SINGLE TRUST BY SEVERAL KINDS OF TRANSFERS:—"POUR-OVER"

In an era when several transfers are often made as part of an integrated estate plan, it will be desirable to merge control of administration under a single trust with a single dispositive plan. This may arise in the following kinds of situations:

(1) Owner has during lifetime created a living trust, which may be revocable or irrevocable depending upon his objectives, and wishes to add to that trust by the terms of his will (this is commonly called a "pour-over");

(2) The living trust may consist of no assets other than rights as beneficiary under a life insurance policy, and the owner wishes

to add his probate estate to that trust, again by a pour-over clause;

(3) Testator desires to set up the trust by his will and to make life insurance payable to the testamentary trustee without subjecting it to the perils surrounding probate assets (election by the surviving spouse or claims of creditors);

(4) Occasionally testator wishes to add part of his probate estate to a trust established or to be established by the will of another person.

What legal doctrines are available to accomplish these objectives? If jurisdiction over trusts is divided beween a probate court having jurisdiction over testamentary trusts and another court having jurisdiction over living trusts, which court has jurisdiction over a trust composed partly of assets transferred during life and partly by will, or do both courts? Since in many states, there is a considerable difference over the amount of control exercised by the probate court over administration, requiring annual court accounting for testamentary trusts for instance, this involves more than just determining jurisdiction when a party wishes to bring suit against the trustee or the trustee wishes instructions or court approval of some action.

SECOND BANK–STATE STREET TRUST CO. v. PINION

Supreme Judicial Court of Massachusetts, 1960.
341 Mass. 366, 170 N.E.2d 350.

WHITTEMORE, JUSTICE. Each of the wills of Richard W. Symons and his wife Edna H. executed April 27, 1955, gave the residue to the trustees under a revocable and amendable inter vivos trust established by them under date of "September 13, 1945, as amended." On November 19, 1955, Richard and Edna as settlors, and Richard as one of the trustees, signed and acknowledged an instrument purporting to amend the trust by altering the disposition of the trust property to be made after the death of both settlors. The trust provided for amendment by a written instrument signed and acknowledged by the settlors and the trustees. The other trustee, Second Bank-State Street Trust Company, signed and acknowledged the amending instrument on November 23, 1955. Richard and Edna, also on November 19, 1955, executed codicils to their wills to name a coexecutor and each codicil ratified and confirmed the will in all other respects.

Following the death of Edna on November 20, 1956, and of Richard on March 13, 1958, the bank, as executor, asked to be instructed, under each will, whether the residue passed to the trustees to hold under the trust as amended, or, if not, then subject to the terms of the unamended trust, or, alternatively, how it should be distributed. The probate judge consolidated the cases, and, the facts being admitted and found, reserved and reported the cases under G.L. c. 215, §

13. We hold for reasons stated below that under each will there was, as all the respondents contend, an effective residual gift to the trustees to hold under the trust as amended on November 19, 1955.

It is to be observed at the threshold that the doctrine of incorporation by reference is inapplicable. Any intent to incorporate into the wills the dispositive provisions of the trust and thus to make them dispositive parts of the wills was expressly negatived. Each of the residuary clauses provided that the fund paid to the trustee was "to be held, administered, and distributed solely under the provisions of such indenture, and in no way as trustee under this will nor as a trustee subject to appointment by or jurisdiction of any probate or other court." See Restatement 2d: Trusts, § 54, comment k. It is therefore immaterial that at the time of the execution of the codicils the terms of a proposed, but incompleted, amendment to the trust were set out in writing. Compare Newton v. Seaman's Friend Soc., 130 Mass. 91; Bemis v. Fletcher, 251 Mass. 178, 187–188, 146 N.E. 277, 37 A.L.R. 1471; Restatement 2d: Trusts, § 54, comment c.

No amendment to the trust existed until November 23, 1955, when the second trustee executed and acknowledged the instrument as required by the trust indenture. Phelps v. State St. Trust Co., 330 Mass. 511, 115 N.E.2d 382. If attestation under the statute of wills was required to give effect to the trustee's disposition, under the amended trust, of assets received from the executor, it could not be supplied by the attestation of the codicil prior to the effective execution of the trust amendment. Old Colony Trust Co. v. Cleveland, 291 Mass. 380, 382, 196 N.E. 920. Scott, Trusts (2d ed.) § 54.3, pp. 375–376. Restatement 2d: Trusts, § 54, comment i. The doctrine of incorporation by reference, even if applicable at all where an intent to incorporate in the usual sense is negatived (In re Estate of York, 95 N.H. 435, 437, 65 A.2d 282, 8 A.L.R.2d 611; Lauritzen, Can a Revocable Trust be Incorporated by Reference, 45 Ill.L.Rev. 583, 600; Polasky, "Pourover" Wills and the Statutory Blessing, 98 Trusts & Estates, 949, 954–955; compare Old Colony Trust Co. v. Cleveland, 291 Mass. 380, 196 N.E. 920; Bolles v. Toledo Trust Co., 144 Ohio St. 195, 58 N.E.2d 381, 157 A.L.R. 1164; Restatement [2d]: Trusts, § 54, comments e–j, 1), could not import the nonexistent amendment.

We agree with the suggestion that such a gift as this "stand[s] on its own merits, to be compared to a gift to a corporation or any other entity, and as such wholly distinguishable from an attempted incorporation into the will of the terms of the trust as to additional property." Annotation, 21 A.L.R.2d 223. Shattuck, Inter Vivos Trusts in Massachusetts, 26 B.U.L.Rev. 437, 458. Such a gift is no less valid because of the reservation in the settlor of the power to amend or revoke the trust. Old Colony Trust Co. v. Cleveland, 291 Mass. 380, 196 N.E. 920.

The Cleveland opinion, however, states (291 Mass. at page 382, 196 N.E. at page 921) that "the will * * * could not, give the residue in trust for purposes which * * * remained to be defined by a later amendment of the trust deed." We have recently noted

(Loring v. Clapp, 337 Mass. 53, 65, n. 10, 147 N.E.2d 836, 843) that this statement is "inconsistent with present legal thought," and, for the reasons stated in the following paragraphs, we do not rule in accordance with it.

It is to be noted that the issue was not squarely raised in the Cleveland case. The underlying controversy was whether the beneficiaries under the trust deed should be paid twice, "once out of the original trust fund * * * and again out of the fund passing under the will" (291 Mass. at page 382, 196 N.E. at page 921). The briefs in the Cleveland case show no contention that the subsequent amendment was effective under the will.

We agree with modern legal thought that a subsequent amendment is effective because of the applicability of the established equitable doctrine that subsequent acts of independent significance do not require attestation under the statute of wills. Scott, Trusts (2d ed.) § 54.3. McClanahan, Bequests to an Existing Trust, 47 Cal.L.Rev. 267, 287, 292–294, and articles cited note p. 267. Palmer, Testamentary Disposition to the Trustee of an Inter Vivos Trust, 50 Mich.L.Rev. 33, 55–59. Compare Lauritzen, Can a Revocable Trust be Incorporated by Reference, 45 Ill.L.Rev. 583, 600–609. This is the view of the Restatement 2d: Trusts, § 54, comment i, and reporter's note.

The decided cases disclose a "confused and confusing area of the law." 47 Cal.L.Rev. 267, 291. Some of the decisions, however, give support to the doctrine of independent significance. In Swetland v. Swetland, 102 N.J.Eq. 294, 297, 140 A. 279, although the trust was not amended subsequent to the will, the court, in sustaining a pour-over provision, approved the lower court's statement that "[t]he trust to which this bequest is added is not theoretical, nebulous, intangible, or incapable of identification, but exists in fact, and the trustee legatee is as distinct and definite an entity as would have been an individual or corporation legatee." Likewise, the court in In re Estate of York, 95 N.H. 435, 437, 65 A.2d 282, 283, where also there was no subsequent amendment, held that a gift from a will to a trust "is equally sustainable according to the view that the inter vivos trust is a fact 'having significance apart from the disposition of the property bequeathed.'" See In re Ivie's Will, Sur., 155 N.Y.S.2d 544, but compare with it President & Directors of Manhattan Co. v. Janowitz, 260 App.Div. 174, 954, 21 N.Y.S.2d 232. See also Matter of Rausch's Will, 258 N.Y. 327, 332–333, 179 N.E. 755, 80 A.L.R. 98.

The creation and amendment of an amendable, revocable inter vivos trust were necessarily recognized as facts of independent significance in National Shawmut Bank of Boston v. Joy, 315 Mass. 457, 469–478, 53 N.E.2d 113. See 26 B.U.L.Rev. 437, 447, 453. In the Joy case it was held that such a trust, which upon stated contingencies disposed of trust property after the settlor's death, is valid even though not executed with the formalities required by the statute of wills. A purpose to avoid making a will or to evade the statutory requirements for a will was held immaterial.

Dispositions to persons employed at the testator's death have been held valid in our decisions without reference to the possible objection of action of testamentary significance subsequent to the will. White v. Massachusetts Ins. of Technology, 171 Mass. 84, 97, 50 N.E. 512; Frazer v. Weld, 177 Mass. 513, 59 N.E. 118; Murphy v. Lawrence, 218 Mass. 39, 105 N E. 380; Anderson v. Stone, 281 Mass. 458, 183 N. E. 841; In Gaff v. Cornwallis, 219 Mass. 226, 106 N.E. 860, a gift of the contents of a drawer in a safe was sustained. Acccord, Old Colony Trust Co. v. Hale, 302 Mass. 68, 71, 18 N.E.2d 432, 120 A.L.R. 1207. The court in Holmes v. Coates, 159 Mass. 226, 228–229, 34 N. E. 190, sustained a gift of whatever sum should be necessary to add to gifts made by the testator in his lifetime for the benefit of a class of disabled soldiers and seamen to cause the total to equal $500 per year up to his decease despite the contention that the gift was void because dependent upon the contents of books of account not in existence when the will was made. We are unable to distinguish these cases in applicable principle from the cases at bar.

Scott, Trusts (2d ed.) § 54.3, pp. 376–377, observes, "It is true that the testator is thereby enabled to change the testamentary disposition without executing codicils to his will. This is, however, what he does where he bequeaths the contents of a room or of a safe-deposit box, since he can modify the contents from time to time by removing or adding articles. The same thing is true where he bequeaths property to persons in his employ at the time of his death * * *. Indeed, there seems to be no greater objection than there is to the whole doctrine which permits a testator originally to make a disposition by reference to a living trust, the terms of which are not stated in the will. The test is not whether the facts are subject to the control of the testator, but whether they are facts which have significance apart from the disposition of the property bequeathed."

The reasons for adoption of the rule of the Restatement are persuasive. The pour-over device is important in modern estate planning. Casner, Estate Planning (2d ed.) pp. 83–106. The underlying purpose of the statute of wills against frauds is secured in the formalities attendant upon the execution of trusts and the solemnity of the actual transfer of property to trustees. 47 Cal.L.Rev. 267, 293–294. 98 Trusts & Estates, 949, 950–951. Contrast Thayer v. Wellington, 9 Allen 283; Olliffe v. Wells, 130 Mass. 221; Wells v. Hawes, 122 Mass. 97.

The growing acceptance and approval of the device are shown by the enactment in eighteen States of statutes which authorize it in some form. It is particularly significant that in sixteen of these States (all save Connecticut and Oregon) the statutes validate gifts by will to trusts which have been amended after the will was executed.

The long established recognition in Massachusetts of the doctrine of independent significance makes unnecessary statutory affirmance of its application to pour-over trusts.

In each case a decree is to be entered in the Probate Court that the trustee is to administer and distribute the funds received from the executor in accordance with the terms of the amended trust.

So ordered.

NOTE

As the principal case indicates, there are two theories upon which a pour-over into a living trust can be sustained: (1) the theory that the living trust is an entity to which a testamentary gift can be made or (2) incorporation by reference.[46] Since the purpose of pouring-over is sometimes to minimize probate control over the trust, the former theory has distinct advantages. Moreover, incorporation by reference raises questions as to the independent validity of the living trust as against the widow's election. Often the draftsman therefore makes his theory explicit by pointing the way for the court, as was done in the principal case.[47] The difficulty is that many of the older cases adopted the theory of incorporation by reference, which at most would allow incorporation of a revocable and amendable trust document only as it read at the time of execution of the will; this has forced attorneys to execute a codicil referring to the trust as amended after each amendment to the trust. Some courts even refused to allow any reference to a document which was subject to change. The tide has now turned.

Many states now have statutes permitting pour-overs into amendable living trusts.[48] Forty-three states and the District of Columbia as of December 31, 1981 had adopted the Uniform Testamentary Additions to Trusts Act approved by the Commissioners on Uniform State Laws. Section 1 of the Uni-

46. See Flickinger, "The 'Pour-Over' Trust and the Wills Statutes: Uneasy Bedfellows", 52 Ky.L.J. 731 (1964); Leal, "The Revocable Trust and Pour Over Wills", 1 Real Prop.Prob. & T.L.J. 286 (1967); Kajan, "The Pour Over Trust", 13 Clev.Marsh.L.Rev. 544 (1964); Marcus, "Pour Over Provisions and Estate Planning", 70 Dickinson L.Rev. 158 (1966); McClanahan, "Bequests to an Existing Trust—Problems and Suggested Remedies", 47 Cal.L.Rev. 267 (1959); "The Pour Over Device Comes of Age", 39 So.Cal.L.Rev. 163 (1966); Polasky, "'Pour Over' Wills and the Statutory Blessing", 98 Trusts and Estates 949 (1959); Robinson, "The Developing Use of the Revocable Trust and Pour Over Will—Some Functional Problems During the Executorial Period", 21 Ark.L.Rev. 499 (1968); Scott, "Pouring Over", 97 Trusts and Estates, 189 (1958); Shipper, "Possible Problem Areas with Pour Over Wills", 1 Real Prop.Prob. & T.L.J. 366 (1967); Note, "Trusts-Pour-Over from a Will to an Inter-Vivos Trust", 8 Washburn L.J. 81 (1968).

47. In Estate of Steck, 275 Wis. 290, 81 N.W.2d 729 (1957), a living trust was sustained against the contention of the widow that the trust was testamentary, in part because it was "tied in" with the will by a pour-over clause. The will there specifically provided: "It is not my intention that 'my residuary estate' shall be received by said * * * Bank as a testamentary trustee or upon a testamentary trust, but the devise and bequest of 'my residuary estate' is made to the aforesaid trust of September 17, 1951 as a distinct legal entity already in existence at the time of the execution of this will." In commenting on the argument, the court said: "Appellant contends that because the will bequeaths the residue of Vincent Steck's estate to the trustee, the trust was incorporated in the will by reference. This is exactly what the testator did not do, expressly stating in his will that it was not his intention that the residue should be received by the trustee as a testamentary trustee but as the trustee of a 'distinct legal entity already in existence.' To apply the doctrine of incorporation by reference in this situation would be to ignore that expressed intent." 275 Wis. at 299, 81 N.W.2d at 734.

48. For citations to these statutes see I Scott, Trusts § 54.3 (3d Ed. 1967 and Supp.1981). See also Uniform Laws Ann. Estate, Probate and Related Laws (1972) 629. Note, "The Desirability of Pour Over Legislation", 44 Minn.L.Rev. 131 (1959).

form Act is incorporated in the Uniform Probate Code, § 2–511. The Uniform Act provides in part:

"§ 1. Testamentary Additions to Trust.—A devise or bequest, the validity of which is determinable by the law of this state, may be made by a will to the trustee or trustees of a trust established or to be established by the testator or by the testator and some other person or persons or by some other person or persons (including a funded or unfunded life insurance trust, although the trustor has reserved any or all rights of ownership of the insurance contracts) if the trust is identified in the testator's will and its terms are set forth in a written instrument (other than a will) executed before or concurrently with the execution of the testator's will or in the valid last will of a person who has predeceased the testator (regardless of the existence, size, or character of the corpus of the trust). The devise or bequest shall not be invalid because the trust is amendable or revocable, or both, or because the trust was amended after the execution of the will or after the death of the testator. Unless the testator's will provides otherwise, the property so devised or bequeathed (a) shall not be deemed to be held under a testamentary trust of the testator but shall become a part of the trust to which it is given and (b) shall be administered and disposed of in accordance with the provisions of the instrument or will setting forth the terms of the trust, including any amendments thereto made before the death of the testator (regardless of whether made before or after the execution of the testator's will), and, if the testator's will so provides, including any amendments to the trust made after the death of the testator. A revocation or termination of the trust before the death of the testator shall cause the devise or bequest to lapse.

"§ 2. Effect on Prior Wills.—This Act shall have no effect upon any devise or bequest made by a will executed prior to the effective date of this Act. * * * "[49]

Absent applicable statutes there are recent decisions recognizing that formalities surrounding the amendment of trust documents accomplish the basic purpose of the Wills Act in reducing the opportunity for fraud.[50] The practice is, of course open to question in states where no applicable legislation or decisions exist. The Restatement, Second, Trusts § 54 Comment *i* supports a testamentary gift to be added to a trust even as amended after execution of the will. Where the settlor revokes the living trust after execution of the will, the pour-over fails unless incorporation by reference is used.

On the jurisdictional question, there is growing support for the position that the probate court loses jurisdiction over the property under the will after it is paid over into the living trust.[51] This is easier to rationalize if the court adopts the theory that the testamentary gift is to a valid entity, than under the doctrine of incorporation by reference.

The theory of treating the living trust as an entity, having significance independently of the will, to which testamentary gifts may be made, is easy

49. See Osgood, "Pour Over Will, Appraisal of Uniform Testamentary Additions to Trust Act", 104 Trusts & Estates 768 (1965).

50. In Matter of Ivie, 4 N.Y.2d 178, 173 N.Y.S.2d 293, 149 N.E.2d 725 (1958), 45 Corn.L.Q. 135 (1959), 33 St.J.L.Rev. 169 (1958), the New York Court of Appeals sustained a pour-over into an amendable living trust which had been amended after execution of the will as to administrative provisions of the trust. See Trachtman, "Pour Overs", 97 Trusts & Estates 416 (1958).

51. York's Estate, 95 N.H. 435, 65 A. 2d 282 (1949), 63 Harv.L.Rev. 543 (1950), 48 Mich.L.Rev. 244 (1949).

to sustain where there are assets in the living trust and the trustee has been actively managing property during the settlor's lifetime. Suppose, however, that the trust is a revocable unfunded life insurance trust; here the trustee has no active duties during lifetime and there may be a serious doubt whether the living trust has independent significance during life. To avoid this many attorneys insist upon funding the trust with at least a small amount of assets, other than the usual deposit of the life insurance policies. However, there would seem to be no different policy reasons for objecting to a pour-over into such a trust. This seems to be only a logical combination of the recognition of validity of such a revocable life insurance trust as nontestamentary in the first instance plus acceptance of the principle of the pour-over clause. In State ex rel. Citizens National Bank v. Superior Court, 236 Ind. 135, 138 N.E.2d 900 (1956), the Supreme Court of Indiana sustained the trust and the pour-over and held that the probate court had no jurisdiction over the life insurance trust as increased by the will.

Can the life insurance policy be made payable to the trustee under a will to be held and administered under the terms of the testamentary trust, without subjecting the insurance proceeds to probate court control, claims of creditors, and election by the wife? The existing case law indicates this is impossible.[52] The practice may, of course, be authorized by statute.[53]

Sometimes two persons, typically husband and wife, wish to draw wills providing for a single trust. Here if the trust terms are set forth in the will of the one expected to die first (the husband) and the will of the other provides for a pour-over into that trust, the same kind of problems are presented. Which theory is applicable? Suppose the one expected to die first survives the other, so that there is no trust to pour into.[54] Another possibility is to set forth two identical trusts in the two wills, with the same trustee, and a clause authorizing the trustee to administer the assets as one trust.[55]

PROBLEM

In Article II of her will, T devised and bequeathed her estate of over $1,000,000 to the trustees of "The Houston Foundation" if at the time of her death her brother, Robert, was living. In Article III she provided:

> "If at the time of my death my said brother shall have died leaving a will, duly probated, by which property is devised and bequeathed to trustees for charitable purposes, then it is my will and I so direct that in lieu of the devise and bequest contained in the preceding Article II all of said

52. Frost v. Frost, 202 Mass. 100, 88 N.E. 446 (1909); In re Kenin's Trust Estate, 343 Pa. 549, 23 A.2d 837 (1942) (creditors can reach proceeds).

53. McKinney's N.Y., EPTL, § 13–3.3 (1980 Supp.); Wis.Stat. § 701.09(3) (1981). See generally Schipper, "Designating Trustee Under Will as Beneficiary of Insurance Policy—Legal Problems", 94 Trusts & Estates 819 (1955); Lawthers, Same—"Home-Office Problems", id. at 826; Cooper, "Testamentary Trust for Insurance?" 97 Trusts & Estates 113 (1958) (Penn. law).

54. In re Brandenburg's Estate, 13 Wis.2d 217, 108 N.W.2d 374 (1961), involved a gift by testatrix of half of a remainder interest "to my son's trust estate, which is willed to charities, including those of my choosing"; at the time of preparation of this will the son also drafted a will making certain charitable gifts. The son's will was executed a day after the mother's will. After the death of the mother, the son executed a new will with no provisions for charities. The court upheld the gift under the mother's will to the charities by holding that her will incorporated by reference the charitable beneficiaries named in the son's will even though the latter will was only in draft form at the time the mother's will was executed.

55. See Kay, "From One Will to Another", 97 Trusts & Estates 524 (1958).

rest and residue of my property shall be devised and bequeathed to said trustees named in my said brother's will upon the same terms and conditions, for the same uses and purposes, and subject to the same limitations and restrictions as if the language in my said brother's will creating said trust and setting forth said terms and conditions, said uses and purposes and said limitations and restrictions, were copied at length herein with appropriate changes to make them a part of my will".

Robert, T's brother, predeceased her. His will and several codicils establishing "the Houston Foundation", now "The Robert A. Welch Foundation" and naming trustees were probated. Assuming validity of T's will at her death and that no statute sustaining "pour overs" is applicable, does Article III contain an effective disposition to the trustees of the Robert A. Welch Foundation? South Carolina National Bank of Charleston v. Copeland, 248 S.C. 203, 149 S.E.2d 615 (1966).

SECTION 4. FUNDING REVOCABLE TRUSTS BY DURABLE POWERS OF ATTORNEY

In Chapter VIII we noted the growing importance of "durable" powers of attorney which remain effective despite subsequent incompetence of the principal, as substitutes for creation of a living trust to protect property of an elderly person. But such powers may also be used to fund a revocable living trust. Sometimes a client recognizes the importance of having a revocable living trust in the event of later incapacity but is not quite willing to give up present ownership and management to a trustee. In such a case a revocable living trust agreement can be executed between the settlor and the trustee, but no assets transferred to the trustee; at the same time the settlor can execute a durable power of attorney naming a relative or friend as agent with limited power to transfer any or all assets into the living trust. Until the transfer is made, the trust can be unfunded. If the transfer is made into the trust and the principal is legally competent, he can of course still exercise his power to revoke. Consider whether the client's will can "pour over" testamentary assets by a devise to the trustee under such an agreement if the trust is still unfunded at the time of the client's death; would it be safer to transfer nominal assets such as a $1000 bond into the trust when first agreed upon?

This combination of a durable power of attorney, a revocable living trust, and a pour-over will has the advantage of providing a complete vehicle for the client's estate plan as well as protection against incompetency. A broad durable power of attorney alone ends at death of the principal; because it is a new concept its legal limits are not as carefully defined as the trust with its centuries of equity jurisprudence. The trust can last beyond the death of the settlor and provide for a surviving spouse, children, and other desired beneficiaries.

The durable power to transfer assets into the trust may be supplemented by a broader durable power to accomplish still other estate planning objectives, as well as to handle problems relating to the person of the principal.[56]

Another method of achieving the objectives of an elderly person who does not wish to give up control operates as follows: the owner transfers stocks and bonds to a fiduciary such as a bank under an agreement to hold the stocks and bonds registered in the name of the fiduciary or its nominee but as agent subject to full direction of the transferor so long as he is competent (despite legal title in the fiduciary the arrangement is an agency rather than a trust, see Restatement Second, Trusts (1959) Comment *i*); upon the subsequent incompetence of the transferor the fiduciary is then to hold as trustee upon the terms set forth in the agreement, with full trustee powers (the arrangement now converts to a trust; transfer of legal title has taken place before incompetence and is therefore fully effective); similarly, if the transferor does not become incompetent, on his death the fiduciary may be given power to hold the assets as trustee. What starts out as an agency becomes a trust upon certain events.

SECTION 5. CONTROL BY WILL OVER DISPOSITION OF NON-PROBATE ASSETS

IN RE SCHAECH'S WILL

Supreme Court of Wisconsin, 1948.
252 Wis. 299, 31 N.W.2d 614.

[Testator's will, written in his own handwriting on a printed form, was duly executed and admitted to probate. It provided as follows:

"Last Will and Testament

"Know all men, That I, Andrew J. Schaech of Milwaukee County of Milwaukee, State of Wisconsin, being of sound and disposing mind and memory, but mindful of the uncertainty of life, hereby revoking any and all wills and codicils heretofore by me made, do make, publish and declare this my Last Will and Testament.

"All personal property etc. unless otherwise stipulated to my wife Florence L. Schaech.

"Prudential Insurance Policy #3674243

"N. W. Mutual Life Insurance Policy #1331994

56. Huff, "The Power of Attorney—Durable and Nondurable: Boon or Trap?" 11 Inst.Est.Plan. 300 (1977); Moses and Pope, "Estate Planning, Disability and the Durable Power of Attorney", 30 S.C.L.Rev. 511 (1979). The durable power can apparently be utilized in anticipation of the principal's death to purchase at discount "flower bonds" (a particular series of federal bonds which can be redeemed at par in payment of federal estate taxes). Estate of Watson v. Simon, 442 F.Supp. 1000 (S.D.N.Y. 1977), rev'd on other grounds 586 F.2d 925 (2d Cir.1978); Silver v. United States, 498 F.Supp. 610 (N.D.Ill.1980).

"N. W. Mutual Life Insurance Policy #1359515

"Connecticut Mutual Life Ins. Policy #836709

"Travelers Accident Ins.

"St. Josephs Benevolent Society

"All to be paid to my wife Florence L. Schaech

"Cash in Second Ward Branch—First Wis. National Bk.

"Shares in Milwaukee Journal Employees Thrift Ass'n. to my wife Florence L. Schaech.

(One paragraph crossed out.)

"To my daughter Carol Margaret Schaech

"My one half interest in home at 2815 N. Hartung Ave.

"Prudential Ins. Policy #6750767

"Milwaukee Journal Group Insurance

"My diamond ring, watch and other jewelry

"500.00 to Theresa Schaech, 2172 N. 55th St.

"500.00 to Carolyn Schaech, 2172 N. 55th St.

"This amount is to be paid out of Prudential Insurance Policy #3674243 of which my wife is beneficiary.

"This is for assistance in raising my daughter Carol.

"300.00 to the Mission Procure, Techny, Ill. for Holy Masses for myself.

"I do hereby constitute and appoint George P. Schaech and Carolyn Schaech—2172 N. 55th St., Milwaukee to be Executors of this my Last Will and Testament.

"In Testimony Whereof, I have hereunto subscribed my name and affixed my seal, this 24th day of June, in the year of our Lord, one thousand nine hundred and thirty five." The daughter Carol petitioned to require the widow to elect whether to take under the will or at law, and the executor and widow petitioned for construction of the will. The County Court denied the daughter's petition. Other facts appear in the opinion.]

FOWLER, JUSTICE. The case involves two appeals. One is by a daughter of the testator from a judgment of the county court of Milwaukee county denying her petition to require the widow of the testator to elect whether she will take under the will of the testator and renounce whatever right she may otherwise have or "whether she shall renounce said will and take apart therefrom." The widow and the daughter are the only heirs. The other appeal is by two aunts of the daughter of the testator who claim that had the court as it should have required the widow to elect and she had elected to take under the will they would be entitled to awards of $500 each under the will. The widow made no election but by petition requested for construction of the will to declare (1) "what property passes" to the widow by the provision—"all personal property, etc., unless otherwise stipulated, to my wife"? (2) Can decedent, by his will dispose of four designated insurance policies in which his wife is named as beneficiary? (3) Can decedent dispose of the joint bank account of himself and wife? (4) Can decedent dispose of his interest in the homestead of the testator and his wife in the name of the two as joint tenants? (5) What becomes of the bequests to the two aunts payable out of a designated insurance policy payable to the widow when there are no monies from the company to pay the bequest? (6) For an order and judgment determining what property belongs to the estate and to whom decedent's property is to be distributed.

The property here in question under which the parties claim their respective rights consists of insurance policies and property held in joint tenancy by a husband and wife. As to the insurance policies the court held that they or the money due thereon at the testator's death did not belong to his estate but to the wife, and therefore the testator could by will transfer no claim thereunder to the aunts of the daughter of the testator. The bequests by their terms were to be paid out of a designated insurance policy not belonging to or payable to the estate of the testator but belonging to and payable to the wife of the testator. That the insurance belonged to the wife and the testator's estate had no interest therein and therefore no interest under the policy could be passed to the widow against her will is unquestionably correct. Christman v. Christman, 163 Wis. 433, 157 N.W. 1099. But it does not follow that the widow could not take under the will if compelled to make her election, and that if she elected so to take all beneficiaries would also take according to the provisions of the will.

The three insurance policies first named in the will were of $1,000 each, each payable by its terms to the widow of the testator and were in force at the death of the testator. The policy of the St. Joseph Benevolent Society for $250 was also payable to the widow. There are four policies named in question (2) of the widow's prayer for relief. The Connecticut Mutual Insurance Company policy named in immediate connection was not in force at decedent's death and the other policy there named was an accident policy on which nothing was payable.

The Milwaukee Journal group insurance policy of the Prudential Insurance Company for $6,000 was by its terms payable to the daughter of the testator and $6,000 was due her thereon.

The real estate of the decedent was not only in the joint names of the testator and his wife but the wife had contributed from her own funds a large part of the consideration therefor.

The inventory of the deceased shows that besides the insurance and other property named in the will the deceased owned at his death one hundred twenty units of Milwaukee Journal stock appraised at $8,271.60 and other items of personal property aggregating with this stock $10,174.80. The first item of gift in the will is: "All personal property, etc., unless otherwise stipulated to my wife, Florence L. Schaech." The first request of the widow in her petition is for construction of this provision. The county judge construed it as meaning what it said—including all personal property, intangible, as well as

tangible, and as giving all items above referred to to the widow. This is in effect a finding of fact that the testator intended by the first provision of the will that these items should all go to his widow and this finding can not be disturbed.

As to the appeal of Theresa and Carolyn Schaech we think the case is plainly ruled by Allen v. Boomer, 82 Wis. 364, 52 N.W. 426. In that case a wife gave to her husband by will certain of her property and also gave certain of his property to a third person. This put it up to Allen to elect whether to take her property under the will. If he took her property under the will he must surrender his property given by his wife's will to the third person. So here. The widow can not take the units of the Milwaukee Journal stock, worth $8,000, and not give up her rights to the $1,000 under the life insurance policy which the testator wished to be paid to his sisters-in-law. There is no escape from the ruling of the Allen case. We must adhere to it or overrule it. The rule of that case is well established. Page on Wills, Life Ed., sec. 1355, says of it:

> "A testator frequently attempts by will to dispose of the proceeds of life insurance policies, payable to certain designated beneficiaries, and not subject to his disposition by will. In such a case if testator makes some other provision by his will for the beneficiaries under the life insurance policy, a case for election is created, and the beneficiaries under the will have their choice between taking the life insurance and accepting the benefits of the will, and their election of either waives their right to the other."

See 2 Pomeroy, Eq.Juris., 5th Ed. sec. 461.

The county judge based his ruling as to the policies of insurance wholly on the Christman case, supra, which does not involve any fact which invokes the doctrine of election. The testator in that case attempted to will insurance due on a policy payable to his divorced wife to his father and nieces, without willing anything to her, except an amount due at his death to her by the terms of another policy of insurance. Thus the ex-wife received nothing by the terms of the will that belonged to the deceased and was thus not charged with the duty of disposing of the insurance according to the will.

Counsel for the respondent lay stress upon two statutes, secs. 238.01 and 238.05, which declare what property, real and personal, may be passed by will. But these statutes were in force as far back as R.S.Stats.1849, ch. 66, secs. 1 and 4, and were as effective when the Allen case was decided as now. They did not then serve to render the bequest involved nugatory under the circumstances. No more do they now.

No Wisconsin case expressly covers the devise of the testator's joint interest in the real estate to the daughter by his will, but the nature of the interest in the property involved makes no difference in applicability of the principle of election. In Page on Wills, Life. Ed., sec. 1358, it is said:

> "A tenant in common, joint tenant, or tenant by the entirety, who devises the whole of such real estate to some one other than the other tenant, and then gives to such other tenant other property by will, puts such other tenant to an election between retaining his original interest in such real estate or accepting the benefits of the will."

The following cases will be found to support the contention that the widow must elect whether to take under the will, and if she so takes the daughter will take the testator's half interest in the joint real estate: Young v. Biehl, 1906, 166 Ind. 357, 77 N.E. 406; Smith v. Butler, 1892, 85 Tex. 126, 19 S.W. 1083; Waggoner v. Waggoner, 1910, 111 Va. 325, 68 S.E. 990, 30 L.R.A.,N.S., 644; Colden v. Alexander, 1943, 141 Tex. 134, 171 S.W.2d 328; Morrison v. Fletcher, 1905, 119 Ky. 488, 84 S.W. 548; Thurlow v. Thurlow, 1944, 317 Mass. 126, 56 N.E.2d 902; Penn v. Guggenheimer, 1882, 76 Va. 839; Job Haines Home v. Keene, 1917, 87 N.J.Eq. 509, 101 A. 512.

* * *

[In the omitted portion of the opinion the court discussed the effect of statutory sections giving the widow one year within which to elect her rights at law against the provisions of the will.]

* * *

The judgment of the county court construing the first paragraph of the will to pass all personal property possessed by the testator at his death to his widow except as otherwise stipulated in his will is affirmed; and the other provisions of the judgment are vacated and set aside; and the court is directed to enter judgment declaring the widow to have elected to take under the will; adjudging the will valid in all its terms; directing the executor to pay appellants Schaech each $500 out of the funds in his hands as executor; and to all other beneficiaries named in the will the amounts of their several legacies and deliver to them their specific legacies; directing that the judgment assign to Carol Mickowski the half interest of the testator in the real estate held jointly by the testator and his wife; and directing concluding the administration and distribution of the estate as required by the terms of the will and the law.[57]

57. In a sequel to this case, State ex rel. Schaech v. Sheridan, 254 Wis. 377, 36 N.W.2d 276 (1948), it was held that the probate court could by its judgment pass title to a share of the joint tenancy realty and, if the widow refused to pay over the portion of the insurance proceeds disposed of by the will, deduct that amount from the widow's share of the estate. See also Wis.Stat.Ann. § 853.15 for the present Wisconsin rule.

NOTE

Aside from the doctrine of equitable election, the power of a testator to change the normal disposition of nonprobate assets passing by survivorship or contract provisions is extremely narrow. (1) If the property is owned in joint tenancy with right of survivorship the joint tenant's interest theoretically ceases at death, so there is nothing he can devise. (2) If the property consists of multiple-party financial accounts in joint, trust or payable-on-death form, the form of the account can only be changed during lifetime under the Uniform Probate Code.[58] However, at common law Totten trust accounts can be changed by express provision in a will executed after the account is opened.[59] (3) Government bonds in co-ownership and beneficiary forms cannot be changed by will. (4) A living trust which the settlor reserves the power to revoke or amend usually provides for revocation or amendment by a written instrument delivered during lifetime to the trustee, and such a provision must be complied with. Hence it cannot be revoked or amended by will. The settlor may also reserve a power to appoint by will, in which case he can change the beneficiary by proper exercise of the power. (5) In most states the beneficiary designation on a life insurance policy can be altered only during lifetime by compliance with the insurer's rules on change of benéficiary. Only if the rules expressly permit change by will or if the insurer does not insist on compliance with its rules, can the will designate a new beneficiary.[60]

There has been some professional interest in developing a "blockbuster" will which, under statutory authorization, could by an express provision override the devolution of all or specific nonprobate arrangements. However, to date, the special committee of the Real Property, Probate and Trust Law Section of the American Bar Association has made no progress on formulating the necessary legislation. The ideal course, if possible, is to alter the nonprobate arrangements during lifetime by severing the joint tenancy and destroying the survivorship right,[61] by changing the form of multiple-party accounts or reregistering the government bonds, by properly amending the

58. Uniform Probate Code Section 6–104E.

59. Restatement Second, Trusts, § 58, Comment *c*; Jones v. First National Bank of Rome, 142 Ga.App. 18, 234 S.E.2d 794 (1977); the rule is codified in New York EPTL § 7–5.2(2).

60. 2A Appleman, Insurance Law and Practice (1966) §§ 1072–1074; 5 Couch on Insurance 2d (1960) §§ 28:59–28:64; 1 Page on Wills (Bowe-Parker, 1960) § 16.3. For a statutory rule see Wis.Stat.Ann. (1971) § 853.17. In Connecticut General Life Insurance Co. v. Peterson, 442 F. Supp. 533 (W.D. Mo. 1978), the federal court, applying Missouri law, held that testator's will effectively changed the beneficiary of life insurance devised by the will to another, the insurer having by its bill of interpleader waived its right to insist on contract provisions for change of beneficiary; as an alternate grounds the doctrine of election could reach the same result, the opinion notes.

61. Since a person could not at common law convey to himself, a joint tenant who wished to terminate the joint tenancy in order to devise his interest had to convey to another person who then conveyed back (a "strawman" comparable to that used by one owner to create a joint tenancy with another). Just as some jurisdictions have dispensed with the four unities in the creation of a joint tenancy, some modern courts permit a unilateral severance by a conveyance from one joint tenant to himself as tenant in common. Riddle v. Harmon, 102 Cal.App.3d 524, 162 Cal.Rptr. 530 (1980) (deed reciting a purpose "to terminate those joint tenancies formerly existing between the Grantor * * * and * * her husband"); Hendrickson v. Minneapolis Federal Savings & Loan Association, 281 Minn. 462, 161 N.W.2d 688 (1968) ("declaration of election to sever survivorship of joint tenancy").

living trust agreement, or by executing the necessary forms to change the insurance beneficiary and sending them to the insurer.

Equitable election is the only doctrine available to accomplish a change by will, and it has obvious limitations. The election doctrine may be deliberately employed by the testator. In community property states, either spouse can execute a will expressly providing for a trust of both halves of the community property, even though the spouse technically has power of testamentary disposition over only his or her half of the community; the will typically creates a trust with income for life to the surviving spouse and a broad power in the trustee to invade principal for that spouse, the corpus to go on death of the spouse to designated beneficiaries (often a further trust for issue of the testator); finally, the will provides an alternative disposition with little or no provision for the surviving spouse in the event the latter elects to claim his or her share of community property outside the will.[62] Whether or not there are tax advantages to such an election will, the will can achieve unified management of community assets, often important if business property or voting control of stock in a closely held corporation is involved. As in *Will of Schaech*, the doctrine also operates when the testator, mistakenly believing that he can dispose of nonprobate assets, executes a will which purports to make such disposition and also devises other property to the person entitled to the nonprobate assets by survivorship, beneficiary designation or other legal doctrine.[63] In other words, the doctrine does not depend on knowledge by the testator that he cannot devise the property. In community property states an election issue is created if the testator makes a specific devise of described property which the testator mistakenly believes to be separate property when the property should be classified as community or mixed community-separate (such as separate property improved with community funds.) [64]

If the devisee wishes to take under the will, he must abide by its terms. The doctrine in effect operates to preserve the testamentary plan. What if the devisee elects to take the nonprobate assets outside the will? Suppose real property in which X owns a life estate and Y the remainder interest. X's will purports to devise the realty to Z and the same will devises $100,000 to Y. If Y elects to come under the will and take the $100,000 devise he must convey the realty to Z. But if Y elects to keep the realty, Z will receive compensation for the value of the realty out of the $100,000 (the equitable doctrine of sequestration considered in Chapter XV, Section 4). If the realty were worth less than $100,000, the remainder of that amount, after paying Z the value of the realty, would still pass to Y.

62. Such wills are commonly called "widow's election" wills, although the wife can include a similar election provision in her will because of her power of testamentary disposition over her half of the community property. For tax consequences see Brown, "The Widow's Election: Recent Developments and an Examination of Alternatives," 1973 So. Cal. Tax Inst. 567; Johanson, "Revocable Trusts, Widow's Election Wills, and Community Property," 47 Tex.L.Rev. 1247 (1969). A leading treatise on community property disapproves of the doctrine of election as applied to community property. DeFuniak and Vaughn, Principles of Community Property (2d ed. 1971) § 217.

63. Note, 38 Mo.L.Rev. 533 (1973).

64. E.g., Wolfe's Estate, 48 Cal.2d 570, 311 P.2d 476 (1957); Chace v. Gregg, 88 Tex. 552, 32 S.W. 520 (1895); Estate of Patton, 6 Wash.App. 464, 494 P.2d 238 (1972). General devises of "all of my property" are interpreted to refer only to the decedent's half of the community and hence do not force an election. LaTourette v. LaTourette, 15 Ariz. 200, 137 P. 426 (1914).

SECTION 6. CONTROL BY CONTRACT OVER DISPOSITION OF PROBATE ASSETS: CONTRACTS TO MAKE OR NOT TO MAKE WILLS

A promisor may contract to exercise or to refrain from exercising his testamentary power. He may contract to make a will, to make a will and not to revoke it, to refrain from revoking a will that is already made, to refrain from making a will, or to revoke a will that is already made. The contracting parties may stipulate for any combination of these acts. Except when a promisor agrees to exercise a testamentary power of appointment,[65] the courts agree that a valid contract can be enforced even though its enforcement limits or frustrates an exercise of the promisor's testamentary power by determining an ultimate disposition of his probate property in accordance with the terms of his prior agreement.[66]

---

(1) LEGAL REQUIREMENTS, PROOF AND EFFECT OF CONTRACT

There are no basic differences in legal requirements between contracts to make or revoke wills and other contracts. The parties must have the capacity to contract.[67] There must be an offer and acceptance and a consideration. The terms of the contract must be certain. The contract may be rescinded, modified or abandoned as other contracts may be. The rules of construction are the same as those ap-

65. E.g., O'Hara v. O'Hara, 185 Md. 321, 44 A.2d 813 (1945).

66. See Drake, "The Public Policy of Contracts to Will Future Acquired Property", 7 Mich.L.Rev. 318–329 (1909). A thorough and thoughtful examination of contracts to make wills may be found in Sparks, Contracts to Make Wills (1956). See generally, Atkinson, Wills (2d Ed., 1953) § 48; Rollison, Wills (1939) §§ 187–189; Thompson, Wills (3d Ed., 1947) §§ 13, 14, 16; Cook, "The Contractual Will: Invitation to Litigation and Excess Taxation", 48 Texas L.Rev. 909 (1970). "Contracts to Devise and Bequeath in New England", 39 Bost.U.L.Rev. 62 (1959) (Mass., Conn., Maine, R.I., N.H., Vt.); Note, "Separation Agreements to Make Mutual Wills for the Benefit of Third Parties", 18 Hastings L.J. 423 (1967).

67. The capacity to contract and the capacity to make a will may differ. See Chapter VII, Section 2(1) (B).

plied to contracts generally. A contract to make a will does not have to be executed with testamentary formalities.

O'CONNOR v. IMMELE

Supreme Court of North Dakota, 1950.
77 N.D. 346, 43 N.W.2d 649.[68]

[The plaintiff, Mable M. O'Connor, brought an equitable action in the nature of specific performance against the defendants, Frances Immele and another, to enforce an alleged contract to make a will. The action was brought in a state district court which had no jurisdiction in probate matters. The plaintiff alleged that on 5 October, 1936, pursuant to a contract, Ella C. Sweeney and Daniel F. Sweeney, husband and wife, executed mutual wills containing identical provisions. These wills left the entire estate of each testator to the survivor. The residue of the estate remaining at the death of the survivor was devised and bequeathed to the plaintiff and the defendant, nieces of Ella C. Sweeney and Daniel F. Sweeney respectively. In the event of the death of either of the named beneficiaries, their heirs were to succeed to their shares and take per stirpes and not per capita. Ella C. Sweeney died on 17 February, 1945, leaving an estate valued at approximately $20,000. Her will was probated and Daniel F. Sweeney took the property in accordance with its provisions. Thereafter, on 11 July, 1945, Daniel F. Sweeney revoked his reciprocal will and executed a new will in which he named his niece, Frances Immele, as his sole beneficiary. Daniel F. Sweeney died on 2 September, 1946. His new will was probated and Frances Immele qualified as executrix. During the course of administration of the estate, the plaintiff filed no proof of claim with the executrix. Distribution of the estate was ordered. The plaintiff now demands that the contract of Daniel F. Sweeney to make a will be recognized, that she be decreed to be the owner of one-half of the property of which he died possessed, that Frances Immele be declared a trustee of such property and required to account, and that conveyance and payments to the plaintiff by Frances Immele be ordered in accordance with the facts disclosed upon the accounting.

The defendant, Frances Immele, denied that the wills were made pursuant to a contract and contended that the plaintiff's claim was barred because she had filed no proof of claim during the course of administration as required by the non-claim statute of the jurisdiction. She also contended that the district court had no jurisdiction because the issues raised by the complaint were matters of probate jurisdiction alone and that his jurisdiction rested exclusively in the county courts; and that the plaintiff had at all times a plain, speedy and adequate remedy at law.

The district court found that the wills had been executed pursuant to a contract and that Daniel F. Sweeney after receiving the property

68. Noted, 27 N.D.L.Rev. 69 (1951).

under his wife's will had breached the contract by revoking his reciprocal will and executing a new one. However, the court held that under the non-claim statute the plaintiff was required to present a proper proof of claim for money damages to the executrix of the will of Daniel F. Sweeney. Having failed to do this, her claim was forever barred. She was not entitled to specific performance or other equitable relief inasmuch as she had an adequate remedy at law. The plaintiff appealed from this judgment and the case came to the Supreme Court of North Dakota for a trial de novo upon all the issues.]

BURKE, JUDGE. * * * The first question is whether the reciprocal wills of Ella C. Sweeney and Daniel F. Sweeney were made in accordance with an agreement or contract to make such wills. It is undisputed that the wills in question were made at the same time and place; that at that time the testator and testatrix were each individually possessed of a substantial amount of property; that they had no children of their own, that each had heirs who were not heirs of the other and that the residuary legatees in both wills were the nieces of the testator and testatrix respectively. These facts are exceedingly persuasive of a conclusion that the wills were made in accordance with an agreement. However, since they do not exclude an hypothesis that the reciprocal provisions in the wills may have been due to a coincidental common intent, they are not in themselves sufficient evidence of a contract. The direct evidence of the existence of a contract consisted entirely of parol evidence, the testimony of relatives of the plaintiff, one of whom was an attorney who drafted the wills. * * *

The testimony of the witnesses was unequivocal. They all said that Ella and Dan Sweeney had declared the reciprocal wills of October 5, 1936 were made as the result of a mutual agreement. * * *

The trial judge who saw and heard the witnesses for the plaintiff considered their testimony credible. There is nothing in the record which tends to impeach them. We therefore adopt his finding that the wills were mutual as well as reciprocal.

Defendants also urge that if there was an agreement between the Sweeneys to execute reciprocal wills, it was not solemnized by a memorandum in writing and is therefore invalid under the statute of frauds. The oral agreement was fully performed by Ella Sweeney. She executed her will in accordance therewith. This will remained unrevoked at the time of her death. Daniel Sweeney presented the will for probate and accepted its benefits. In equity this is a sufficient performance to remove the contract from the operation of the statute of frauds. * * *

The next question for consideration concerns the remedy available to the plaintiff. The defendants contend that this action, in the nature of specific performance, will not lie because plaintiff has or had an adequate remedy at law. A decision upon this contention requires an examination into the nature of plaintiff's claim. Her claim rests upon the oral agreement of Ella and Dan Sweeney to make reciprocal wills and upon the acceptance by Dan Sweeney of the benefits of that agreement upon Ella Sweeney's death. It is well settled that the survivor of the parties to such a contract may not, after accepting its benefits, repudiate it. Anno. 169 A.L.R. 48, Mosloski v. Gamble, 191 Minn. 170, 253 N.W. 378; Stewart v. Todd, 190 Iowa 283, 173 N.W. 619; 180 N.W. 146, 20 A.L.R. 1272; Doyle v. Fischer, 183 Wis. 599, 198 N.W. 763, 33 A.L.R. 733. A will made in accordance with such an agreement, however, may be revoked and the revoking will admitted to probate. Fuller v. Nelle, 12 Cal.App.2d 576, 55 P.2d 1248; In re Higgins' Will, 264 N.Y. 226, 190 N.E. 417; In re Burke's Estate, 66 Or. 252, 134 P. 11; Sumner v. Crane, 155 Mass. 483, 29 N.E. 1151, 15 L.R.A. 447. Despite revocation of the will, the contract to make the will remains effective and it may be enforced. In Doyle v. Fischer, 183 Wis. 599, 606, 198 N.W. 763, 765, 33 A.L.R. 733, it was said: "It should be borne in mind that it is the contract, and not the will, which is irrevocable. The authorities generally hold that the will may be revoked, but that the contract stands, and will be enforced by equity if it be a valid contract, and such enforcement is necessary for the prevention of fraud." See also 69 C.J. 1302, Sec. 2726, 57 Am.Jur. 488, Sec. 718, Anno. 169 A.L.R. 55 et seq.

Plaintiff's claim therefore is one which arises upon contract. It is not, however, a claim against the estate of Dan Sweeney. Rather it is a claim of a property right in that estate which is itself subject to claims against the estate. Fred v. Asbury, 105 Ark. 494, 152 S.W. 155; McCullough v. McCullough, 153 Wash. 625, 280 P. 70; Furman v. Crane, 18 Cal.App. 41, 121 P. 1007; Brickley v. Leonard, 129 Me. 94, 149 A. 833; Oles v. Wilson, 57 Colo. 246, 141 P. 489.

By this action plaintiff is seeking to be placed in the position in which she would have been had Dan Sweeney not revoked the will making her his heir. Section 56–0525, NDRC 1943 provides: "Testamentary dispositions, including devises and bequests to a person on attaining majority, are presumed to vest upon the testator's death."

Thus if the contract to make the will is given effect, plaintiff, upon Dan Sweeney's death, became vested with equitable title to an undivided one-half interest in all of the property of which he died possessed. It is clear that an action to have this title established, to have the executrix and devisee of the testator declared a trustee for the plaintiff to the extent of her interest, and to have the executrix and devisee of the testator directed to make the conveyances and payments necessary to convert plaintiff's equitable title into a legal title, will, if it lies, give plaintiff complete justice. Without mentioning the question of whether an adequate remedy at law was available we have held that rights similar to those of the plaintiff in this case may be enforced by actions in the nature of specific performance. Torgerson v. Hauge, 34 N.D. 646, 159 N.W. 6, 3 A.L.R. 164; Brock v. Noecker, 66 N.D. 567, 267 N.W. 656; Klein v. Klein, 69 N.D. 353, 286 N.W. 898; Heuer v. Kruse, 67 N.D. 552, 274 N.W. 863. In the syllabus in Torgerson v. Hauge, supra, it is said: "Equity will grant relief equivalent to specific performance and fasten a trust upon the property for the benefit of the heirs of the beneficiary under the contract, as against any transferee or devisee."

The fact that a plaintiff may have a remedy at law by an action for damages does not prevent equity from assuming jurisdiction if the equitable remedy is better adapted to render more perfect and complete justice than the remedy at law. 49 Am.Jur. 21, 58 C.J. 853. Of the more complete efficacy of equity in the instant case, we have no doubt. Here, because the contract was not in writing, and because the estate of Dan Sweeney has been distributed in accordance with his subsequent will, made in violation of his agreement, plaintiff's right and ability to recover depend upon removing the contract to will from the operation of the statute of frauds by part performance, and upon impressing a trust upon the distributed property in the hands of the defendant devisee.

Decision of these issues is primarily, if not exclusively, within the jurisdiction of equity. * * *

What we have said above disposes of the remaining issues in this case. Defendants' contentions that the case is one exclusively within the jurisdiction of the county court and that plaintiff's claim is barred by the statute of non-claim, are disposed of by our conclusion that plaintiff's claim is not a claim against the estate of Dan Sweeney but a claim, arising out of contract, of a property right in that estate. In Muhlhauser v. Becker, 74 N.D. 103, 20 N.W.2d 353, 359, and Goodwin v. Casselman, 51 N.D. 543, 200 N.W. 94, we have stated the rule that "the jurisdiction of the probate court does not extend to the determination of rights in property left by a deceased, where such right does not depend upon heirship or will, but upon contract."

Defendants' claim that plaintiff's right is barred by the distribution of the estate of Dan Sweeney is eliminated by our adherence to the prior decisions of this court in Torgerson v. Hauge, 34 N.D. 646, 159 N.W. 6, 3 A.L.R. 164 and Klein v. Klein, 69 N.D. 353, 286 N.W. 898. In each of these cases it was held that in equity the beneficiary of a contract to make a will may enforce the contract against devisees as well as against the personal representative of the testator.

The judgment of the district court is therefore reversed and upon remand judgment in favor of the plaintiff is ordered.

NUESSLE, C. J., and BURKE, MORRIS, CHRISTIANSON and GRIMSON, JJ., concur.

RIGBY v. POWELL

Supreme Court of Georgia, 1974.
233 Ga. 158, 210 S.E.2d 696.

JORDAN, JUSTICE.

This is an appeal from the order of the trial court dated April 24, 1974, granting the appellees' motion to dismiss and for summary judgment.

Appellant, Ralph A. Rigby, and Doris Wynn were married in 1957 and lived together as husband and wife until her death in Lowndes County, Georgia on September 16, 1971. Both had children by previous marriages and the appellees are the two sons of Doris Wynn Rigby by a previous marriage. Anthony Powell, named as executor of his mother's will, petitioned the Court of Ordinary of Lowndes County for the probate in solemn form of the will of his mother dated March 30, 1965. Notice was given to the appellant who acknowledged due and legal notice of the petition to probate in solemn form the will of said Doris Wynn Rigby. On October 4, 1971, the Ordinary of Lowndes County entered an order admitting to record said will and issued letters testamentary to Anthony Powell. Ralph A. Rigby was a legatee under the provisions of this will, having been devised an interest to certain real property until his death or remarriage and fee simple title to certain items of personalty including a checking account. All other property, both real and personal, was given to her two sons, the appellees herein.

The appellant remarried on April 20, 1972, and in January 1973, was notified to vacate certain real property under the terms of the will due to his remarriage.

In July, 1973, the appellant filed his petition in Barrow Superior Court against the appellees in which he asserted that in August, 1962, he and his wife Doris Wynn Rigby entered into an agreement whereby both would make and execute companion or mutual wills by which each would leave all of their estate to the other, but that his wife secretly violated the terms of their agreement and executed a different will. He prayed that the court enter a decree declaring the will of Doris Wynn Rigby void and inoperative as to him and that the appellees be ordered and directed to pay over to him the entire assets of the estate of Doris Wynn Rigby.

To this petition the appellees filed timely defensive pleadings and a motion to dismiss for failure to state a claim and for summary judgment which was granted by the trial court. * * *

The terms of the contract between the appellant and his deceased wife, as shown by the allegations and affidavit, were essentially as follows: The appellant and his wife agreed that they would execute mutual wills, by which each would leave to the other the respective properties of which each died seized and possessed, giving to their respective sons the sum of one dollar each, except that the wife would leave the sum of $1,000 to her stepdaughter; all of the appellant's earnings as a trader would be deposited in a bank selected by them, out of which all their joint living expenses were to be paid, and any surplus would be invested in income-producing real estate; the wife's earnings would be deposited in a savings account to be used only for emergencies.

The appellant's affidavit stated that from the date of their marriage he had purchased several parcels of real estate out of his surplus earnings and caused the title thereto to be placed in the name of his wife, in keeping with the terms of their agreement. He further stated that it was not until after the death of his wife that he learned that she had failed to perform her part of the agreement to make mutual wills.

This court has held that: "Where mutual wills are the result of a contract based upon a valid consideration, and *where, after the death of one of the parties, the survivor has accepted benefits under the will of the other, which was executed pursuant to an agreement,* equity will, where the facts are fully proved, interpose to prevent fraud, and will compel the execution of such agreement by the survivor." Clements v. Jones, 166 Ga. 738(2b), 144 S.E. 319; C. & S. National Bank v. Leaptrot, 225 Ga. 783, 786, 171 S.E.2d 555.

That is not the situation in the present case. The wife, who breached the contract, died first, and she had not accepted any benefits under the appellant's will.

There is a conflict of authority in other jurisdictions as to whether there is sufficient consideration for a contract to make a mutual will where the party breaching the contract predeceases the party performing the contract. See 169 A.L.R. 45.

During the wife's lifetime she had the benefit of the possibility of taking under the appellant's will, which will remain unrevoked at her death. Furthermore, the whole plan of their joint acquisition of property was a part of their agreement to make mutual wills, and the appellant placed property in his wife's name under the mistaken belief that she had performed her contract and made a will leaving all of her property to him. The present case made an issue of fact as to the right of the appellant to equitable relief.

Since there are material issues of fact which must be determined in the trial court, it was error to grant the appellees' motion to dismiss for failure to state a claim and the motion for summary judgment.

Judgment reversed.

All the Justices concur.

NOTE

Promises to make or not to revoke wills are made frequently in return for support and maintenance of the promisor, a promise to release a claim against the promisor's estate, a promise to refrain from contesting provisions in the promisor's will or, as in the first principal case, in connection with the execution of mutual wills.[69]

Wills are "mutual" when two or more persons execute separate wills containing reciprocal provisions. A will is "joint" when two or more persons execute the same instrument as their respective wills. A "joint and mutual" will is when two or more persons execute the same instrument which contains reciprocal provisions. It should be noted that the court in the principal case uses the term "reciprocal" to refer to "mutual" wills in the usual sense; while it reserves the term "mutual" to refer to reciprocal wills made pursuant to a contract. Courts once referred to a will that was simply joint as "mutual" or "conjoint" but this terminology is now obsolete.

The English and American courts once held that a joint will was invalid. The decisions turned upon the idea that an instrument signed by two testators could not be treated as the separate will of each. As stated in Clayton v. Liverman: [70] "An insuperable objection in the way of pronouncing this the several will of either of the parties is, that is does not *purport* to be the separate will of either. It is wholly a joint act, and in no respect a several act. It is a joint declaration of a joint purpose as to the disposition of joint property, after the death of both parties, by joint executor, appointed to carry into effect this arrangement; but it contains no declaration of the separate intentions of either in regard to her property, to be executed at her death, nor the constitution of any executor to carry into effect her intention. To pronounce for it as a separate will is to adjudge it to be what it is not". The court refused to probate the instrument as the single will of both parties. "If conjoint, it is to take effect after the death of both, not upon the death of one. If conjoint, then it is either irrevocable except by the act of both—which would deprive each testator of the power of altering his intentions in regard to the disposition of his own property—or it is revocable by the act of either, which would give to one the power of changing the disposition of another's property." [71]

By the modern view, a joint will may be drafted so that it can be probated at the death of each testator or revoked as the will of either of them.[72] But a joint will which provides expressly that it shall not be effective until the death of the surviving testator, or which disposes of property owned in common, or which treats the separate property of each testator as a common fund, has been held invalid.[73] The main objection to wills of the latter type

69. The principles applicable to contracts to make or not to revoke wills are applicable to all of the contracts relating to testamentary power which are mentioned in this section. See Note, "Separation Agreements to Make Mutual Wills for the Benefit of Third Parties" 18 Hastings L.J. 423 (1967).

The doctrine has been extended to inter vivos revocable trusts used as will substitutes. Reznik v. McKee, 216 Kan. 659, 534 P.2d 243 (1975) (implying a contract where husband and wife executed reciprocal inter vivos revocable trusts as will substitutes, and amendments during lifetime of both settlors were always made with consent or joinder of the other spouse).

70. 19 N.C. 558, 561 (1837). Overruled by In re Davis' Will, 120 N.C. 9, 26 S.E. 636, 38 L.R.A. 289, 58 Am.St.Rep. 771 (1897). See generally, Atkinson, Wills (2d Ed., 1953), § 49; Bowe-Parker: Page, Wills (3d Ed., Rev.1960) §§ 101–107; Rollison, Wills (1939) §§ 183–185; Thompson, Wills (3d Ed., 1947) § 34.

71. 19 N.C. at 561.

72. E.g., Lewis v. Scofield, 26 Conn. 452 (1857); Bright v. Cox, 147 Ga. 474, 94 S.E. 572 (1917); Frazier v. Patterson, 243 Ill. 80, 90 N.E. 216, 27 L.R.A.,N.S., 508 (1909); 169 A.L.R. 15 (1947).

73. E.g., Hershy v. Clark, 35 Ark. 17 (1879); Epperson v. White, 156 Tenn. 155, 299 S.W. 812, 57 A.L.R. 601 (1927). In Palmer v. Riggs, 209 Miss. 127, 46 So.2d 86 (1950), 22 Miss.L.J. 120 (1950) two grantors executed identical deeds and

rests upon the difficulties that are invited when probate of the will of the testator first to die is postponed until the death of the survivor. Serious questions may be presented as to how the estate of the first decedent is to be administered, how his debts will be paid, and how the will is to be construed as to questions of lapse, ademption, abatement and similar matters. It may be possible to find a dominant intention on the part of each testator that his will operate as a disposition of his property. This should prevail over a subsidiary intention that the will should not operate or be subject to probate until the death of the survivor.[74]

If a will is joint and wholly mutual, the will need be probated only at the death of the first testator; but if there is a gift over upon the death of the surviving testator, the will should be probated upon the death of the survivor.

But by far the greatest problem produced by the execution of a mutual or joint and mutual will at the present time is the contractual implication that tends to arise from the obvious co-ordination that has occurred in the execution by the testators. Of course, contracts to make wills are not confined to wills in this form.

A great majority of the courts have refused to imply a contract to make wills from the execution of mutual or joint and mutual wills.[75] The contract must be proved as other contracts must be proved. A minority of the courts have implied a contract to make and not to revoke from the valid execution of a will that is joint and mutual.[76] Several courts have been willing to imply a contract when the wills are mutual but not joint.[77]

The doctrine of implied contract not to revoke mutual wills has been applied by some courts to revocable living trusts in a single trust document set up by husband and wife, so that after the death of one spouse, the other cannot revoke or amend the trust created by the survivor.[78]

Contracts to make wills have not been favored by the courts because of the opportunities for fraud in proving them. Clear and convincing evidence of the existence of the contract and its terms is usually required.[79] The burden of proof is upon the party alleging the existence of the agreement.

The contract and its terms may appear upon the face of the will. In this case the language of the will may be sufficient evidence of the contract, at least when supported by some other evidence which indicates the existence of an agreement.

provided that the deeds should not be delivered to the grantee until the death of the surviving grantor. In a prior proceeding the instruments were held testamentary and inoperative as deeds. It was held that the instruments were not valid as a will because a will must take effect at the maker's death.

74. E.g., Collins v. Stroup, 71 N.D. 679, 3 N.W.2d 742 (1942). See Note, "The Interim Nature of Property Passing Under Joint and Mutual Wills", 20 Baylor L.Rev. 102 (1967); 4 Vand.L.Rev. 185 (1950).

75. E.g., Plemmons v. Pemberton, 346 Mo. 45, 139 S.W.2d 910 (1940). If these courts are willing to imply a contract to make wills, they are unwilling to imply a contract not to revoke them, and in the absence of the latter implication the former implication is illusory. See 61 Harv. L.Rev. 675, 677–79 (1948). See generally, Bailey, "Contracts to Make Wills—Proof of Intent to Contract", 40 Tex.L.Rev. 941 (1962).

76. E.g., Frazier v. Patterson, 243 Ill. 80, 90 N.E. 216 (1909).

77. Hermann v. Ludwig, 186 App.Div. 287, 174 N.Y.S. 469 (1919); Nye v. Bradford, 144 Tex. 618, 193 S.W.2d 165 (1946).

78. Reznik v. McKee, 216 Kan. 659, 534 P.2d 243 (1975). See Annot. 85 A.L.R.3d 8 (1978).

79. See, Plemmons v. Pemberton, fn. 75, supra.

If the contract is oral, a writing signed by the promisor evidencing the agreement may be required for proof. Statutes in several states require that all contracts to make wills be in writing or proved by a written memorandum signed by the promisor.[80] In other states the contract may be subject to section four or section seventeen of the Statute of Frauds.[81]

Uniform Probate Code, § 2–701 contains a comprehensive requirement pertaining to proof of contracts of the nature here considered. This section operates as a limited Statute of Frauds and, if adopted, would appear to reduce litigation based on promises to make wills, not to revoke them or to die intestate. The section is as follows:

> "A contract to make a will or devise, or not to revoke a will or devise, or to die intestate, if executed after the effective date of this Act, can be established only by (1) provisions of a will stating material provisions of the contract; (2) an express reference in a will to a contract and extrinsic evidence proving the terms of the contract; or (3) a writing signed by the decedent evidencing the contract. The execution of a joint will or mutual wills does not create a presumption of a contract not to revoke the will or wills."

Most of the courts have held that contracts to devise land are subject to the provision of Section four relating to contracts for the sale of land, and that contracts to bequeath personal property are subject to the provision of the same section relating to contracts made in consideration of marriage. A contract to make a will is not subject to the provision of Section four concerning contracts not to be performed within one year. Some courts have held that a contract to bequeath personal property is subject to Section seventeen, but the language of this section seems applicable to contracts to engage in inter vivos transactions and not to contracts to make wills.[82] If the contract concerns both devises and bequests, by the prevailing view it is "indivisible" and must be proved as an entirety by the required writing.

An informal memorandum signed by the promisor will satisfy the Statute of Frauds. The memorandum must indicate an intention to contract and the essential terms of the agreement. Whether the execution of mutual or joint and mutual wills may satisfy the memorandum requirement without an express reference to the oral agreement depends upon the willingness of the court concerned to imply a contract from the transaction. Most of the courts have refused to make this implication.[83]

If a substantial part performance of a contract to make a will has taken place, the part performance may be sufficient to raise the bar of the Statute in equity. A majority of courts have held that the execution of mutual or joint and mutual wills is not a sufficient part performance.[84] But if one party dies with his will in force so that the contract is fully performed on his

80. E.g., McKinney's N.Y., EPTL, § 13–2.1 (1980 Supp.). See Note, 58 Va.L. Rev. 1363, 1370 (1972) on When An Oral Contract to Devise is Specifically Enforceable.

81. See Hirsch, "Contracts to Devise and Bequeath", 9 Wis.L.Rev. 388 (1934); Peterson, "Effect of the Statute of Frauds on Contracts for Testamentary Disposition", 17 Ind.L.J. 399 (1942); Schnebly, "Contracts to Make Testamentary Dispositions as Affected by the Statute of Frauds", 24 Mich.L.Rev. 749 (1926); Stubbs, "Oral Contracts to Make Wills", 9 Yearbook of the Selden Soc. (U. So.Car.) Part III, 10 (1948); 52 Mich.L. Rev. 319 (1953); "The Need of a Writing for an Enforceable Contract to Will Personalty", 1957 Wis.L.Rev. 506 (limited to the Wisconsin cases).

82. See Schnebly, fn. 81, supra.

83. See 61 Harv.L.Rev. 675, 681 (1948).

84. E.g., Hale v. Hale, 90 Va. 728, 19 S.E. 739 (1894); Allen v. Dillard, 15 Wash.2d 35, 129 P.2d 813 (1942).

side, there is a substantial part performance which will remove the contract from the operation of the Statute.

A contract to make a will should take effect when the offer is accepted in accordance with the conditions prescribed by the offeror. Nevertheless, a number of courts, without determining whether the offeror contemplated a promise or an act as an acceptance, have held that there is no contract until there is a substantial performance by the offeree. The offer may be revoked at the whim of the offeror until this substantial performance has occurred. In Stone v. Hoskins [85] a husband and wife executed mutual wills pursuant to a contract. The wife revoked her will secretly during the lifetime of the husband. The husband offered her revoked will for probate after her death. The court refused probate on the ground that the "arrangement" was revocable during the lifetime of the parties without notice to the survivor. The survivor could not complain because he could revoke his will after the death of the decedent and would not be injured. The court stated in dicta that if one party died with his will in effect, the "arrangement" was binding and the survivor could not depart therefrom.

A majority of the American courts have taken a position similar to that of the court in Stone v. Hoskins, although most require notice of the revocation during the lifetime of the parties.[86] If one party dies with his will in effect, the contract is binding upon the other. If the survivor probates the will and receives its benefits, he cannot repudiate the agreement, and in some jurisdictions the contract may not be binding until that time.[87] The language in a few cases suggests that the contract is binding when the mutual wills are executed.[88]

A will made pursuant to a contract to devise or bequeath is as ambulatory and revocable as any other will. But once the contract becomes effective it is binding on the parties and cannot be revoked unilaterally. A will revoked in violation of a contract must be denied probate. A will executed in breach of a contract must be probated if valid.[89]

85. [1905] L.R.Prob. 194.

86. E.g., Frazier v. Patterson, 243 Ill. 80, 90 N.E. 216 (1909). See Comment, "Wills: Made Pursuant to a Contract: When Parties Bound" 50 Marquette L. Rev. 549 (1967).

87. See Tooker v. Vreeland, 92 N.J. Eq. 340, 112 A. 665 (1921).

88. See Schramm v. Burkhart, 137 Or. 208, 2 P.2d 14 (1931).

89. A number of courts have suggested that a will made pursuant to a contract is irrevocable. This position may be taken because it is considered efficient to raise the contractual issue at probate. Often no suggestion is intended but the court uses loose language. Much of this language can be traced to the leading case of Dufour v. Pereira, 1 Dick. 419, 421, 21 Eng.Rep. 332, 333 (1769), where Lord Camden said: "The defendant * * * hath taken the benefit of the bequest in her favour by the mutual will; and hath proved it as such; she hath thereby certainly confirmed it; and therefore I am of opinion, the last will of the wife, so far as it breaks in upon the mutual will, is void." The case was later explained as one of a contract to make a will enforceable in equity and as decided upon that theory. Walpole v. Orford, 3 Ves.Jr. 402, 30 Eng.Rep. 1076 (1797). In other decisions the courts have confused a contract with a will. The contract is inter vivos and irrevocable. The will is testamentary, unilateral and ambulatory and revocable until the death of the testator. As to the problem of revocability in joint and mutual wills see Evans, "Concerted Wills—A Possible Device for Avoiding the Widow's Privilege of Renunciation", 33 Ky.L.J. 79, 88 (1945); Evans, "Concerted Wills—Again", 35 Ky.L.J. 214 (1947); Goddard, "Mutual Wills", 17 Mich.L.Rev. 677 (1919); Partridge, "The Revocability of Mutual or Reciprocal Wills", 77 U. of Pa.L.Rev. 357 (1929); Young, "The Doctrinal Relationships of Concerted Wills and Contract", 29 Tex.L.Rev. 439 (1951); 19 Minn.L.Rev. 95, 101 (1934); 1 Syracuse L.Rev. 480 (1950). A detailed and clear discussion may be found in Sparks, Contracts to Make Wills (1956) 101–134.

The tax consequences of contracts to make wills or not to revoke mutual or joint wills between husband and wife are highly uncertain. Suppose a husband and wife simultaneously execute similar wills, each giving all of his or her estate to the other spouse if the latter survives and providing for an agreed pattern of disposition if the spouse does not survive (typically half to the husband's named relatives and half to the wife's named relatives). Upon the death of the first spouse does his or her will qualify for the marital deduction or has the surviving spouse been given a disqualified terminable interest (on the theory that the spouse has only a life estate because the named relatives can impose a trust on the property if the spouse breaks the contract and devises the property to others)?[90] If the surviving spouse leaves his or her will unrevoked in accordance with the contract, and then dies, can his or her personal representative now use the "equitable life estate-remainder" concept against the government to claim that the decedent's interest ended at death and hence none of the property should be included in the gross taxable estate?[91] Or if the surviving spouse does revoke the will and makes a different disposition at death, either by a new will or by arranging nonprobate substitutes like joint tenancy with right of survivorship, and the beneficiaries under the contract successfully claim the entire estate either as damages for the breach or by way of a constructive trust, can the personal representative then reduce the gross taxable estate by a deduction for the claim?[92] The very uncertainty surrounding the substantive legal nature of these arrangements invites tax litigation. Tax answers may be affected by the characterization of the property interests under local state law. To minimize such tax complications Uniform Probate Code § 2–701, set forth above, provides that the execution of a joint will or mutual wills does not create a presumption of a contract not to revoke.

(2) BREACH AND REMEDIES FOR BREACH OF THE CONTRACT

The injured party may have an action for damages during the lifetime of the testator for an unconditional anticipatory breach of a contract to make or not to revoke a will.[93] Proof of damages during the

90. The Internal Revenue Service has successfully denied a marital deduction for a transfer by will subject to a contract by the surviving spouse to will it to specific persons. See, e.g., Estate of Opal v. Commissioner, 450 F.2d 1085 (2d Cir. 1971); Estate of David A. Siegel, 67 T.C. 662 (1977). On the other hand, if the property passed to the surviving spouse by survivorship arising out of joint tenancy, or by beneficiary designation on life insurance, the Service treats the restriction as one imposed by the surviving spouse rather than by the first decedent; hence the interest passes from the surviving spouse to the contract beneficiaries and the marital deduction is allowed. Rev. Rul. 71–51, 1971–1 Cum. Bull. 274.

91. In the Revenue Ruling described in the preceding footnote, the Service ruled that the surviving spouse made a transfer with a retained life estate and therefore the property was includible in her gross estate under I.R.C. § 2036. In the transfer by will of the first spouse, however, the issue would be different.

92. The deduction was denied in Bank of New York v. United States, 526 F.2d 1012 (3d Cir. 1975).

93. E.g., Smith v. Long, 183 Okl. 441, 83 P.2d 167 (1938). See generally, Costigan, "Constructive Trusts Based on Promises Made to Secure Bequests, Devises, or Intestate Succession", 28 Harv. L.Rev. 237 (1915); Hirsch, "Contracts to Devise and Bequeath", 9 Wis.L.Rev. 388 (1934); 61 Harv.L.Rev. 675 (1948); 34 Va.

testator's lifetime is difficult.[94] A quasi contractual action is available in most states for the recovery of consideration furnished to the testator.[95] A declaratory judgment to establish the rights of the contracting parties during the lifetime of the testator may be had in some states.[96] The judgment may then serve as a basis for an action to recover the promised property after the death of the testator. An injunction may be secured against an attempted conveyance of specific realty which the testator promised to devise.[97] An executed conveyance to one not a bona fide purchaser for value may be set aside.[98] A court of equity will not compel the execution of a will during the lifetime of the testator or enjoin his revocation of a will.[99] An order of this sort would require constant supervision by the court. It is always possible that a testator may execute a will pursuant to a contract or republish a will revoked in violation of a contract. A will is not effective until his death and, technically, the contract cannot be breached until that time.

After the death of the testator, the injured party may bring an action for damages against his estate or may obtain a quasi-contractual recovery of consideration. The usual remedy, however, is a constructive trust upon property passing from the testator in violation of his agreement for the benefit of the injured party, commonly described as *quasi* specific performance.[1] The features of the remedy have been discussed as follows: [2]

> "* * * Thus, when the courts grant relief in terms of constructive trust, they are met with theoretical objections that lack of intent not to perform at the time of the promise is fatal; that a constructive trust requires that the recovery be measured by the enrichment derived from the promisee, while here it is measured by the promise given in exchange for that agreement; and that the strict theory of constructive trusts requires that equity give the defendant an election to perform or reimburse the plaintiff, while in these cases an election is usually unsatisfactory and performance is required. The court that grants 'specific performance' is met with the argument that the term is a misnomer when used in this context, for the court will not compel the execution of a will during the promisor's lifetime nor can it force a dead man to make a will.

L.Rev. 590 (1948); "Two Problems in Contracts to Make a Will", 57 Col.L.Rev. 1151 (1957); Sparks, Contracts to Make Wills (1956) 135–166; Note, "Enforcement of Contracts to Make Wills", 21 Baylor L.Rev. 411 (1969).

94. The agreement may be that the testator is to will the property which he has at his death so that his estate will be diminished by inter vivos transfers.

95. In some states only the quasi contractual recovery is available at law. See, e.g., Cramer v. McKinney, 355 Pa. 202, 204, 49 A.2d 374, 375 (1946).

96. E.g., Hagerman v. Hagerman, 160 Kan. 742, 165 P.2d 431 (1946).

97. E.g., Cagle v. Justus, 196 Ga. 826, 28 S.E.2d 255 (1943).

98. E.g., Lawrence v. Ashba, 115 Ind. App. 485, 59 N.E.2d 568 (1945).

99. DeMattos v. McGovern, 25 Cal. App.2d 429, 77 P.2d 522 (1938).

1. See, Chapter III, Section 4(4) (A), Note to Estate of Mahoney.

2. Read, "The Contractual Will and Some Consequences of its Breach," 34 Va.L.Rev. 590, 592 (1948).

"Since, strictly speaking, specific performance seldom secures the precise thing bargained for, and since these very arguments apply equally to the specific performance granted against anyone not an original party to the contract enforced, the courts have shown little tendency to quibble over the precise doctrinal basis of the relief * * *. Their greatest concession to the objectors seems to be to denominate the remedy 'relief in the nature of specific performance' or 'quasi specific performance'.

"Of course, here as in other instances, it is generally held that equity will not lend its aid unless there is a substantial consideration and lack of an adequate remedy at law * * *. As always, the injunction and specific performance are granted as a matter of discretion and will not be employed to inflict hardship on the innocent. This discretionary power to preserve essential fairness has been considered a major argument in favor of the use of equitable remedies in preference to those available at law. The fact that these contracts are particularly susceptible to the pressure of unforeseen circumstances involving intimate family details makes the creation of undue hardship especially likely and the exercise of an equitable discretion particularly appropriate." [3]

3. For the effect of a contract to make a will upon the share of the surviving spouse of the promisor, see Sparks, Contracts to Make Wills (1956) 167–178; Hirsch, "Contracts to Devise and Bequeath", 9 Wis.L.Rev. 388, 389–391 (1934); 61 Harv.L.Rev. 675, 684–685 (1948); 34 Va.L.Rev. 590, 595–596 (1948). For the effect upon shares of pretermitted heirs see Burkhart v. Rogers, 134 Okl. 219, 273 P. 246 (1928), 42 Harv.L. Rev. 966 (1929); Estate of McLean, 219 Wis. 222, 262 N.W. 707 (1935), 21 Iowa L. Rev. 653 (1936). A third party beneficiary is permitted to sue on a contract to make a will if third party beneficiaries are permitted to sue on other contracts.

Chapter XIII

FUTURE INTERESTS

Scope Note

This Chapter develops some of the basic concepts in the field of future interests. Chapters XIV–XVI take up in detail powers of appointment, construction problems and social restrictions on perpetuities and accumulations. As will be evident when these chapters have all been studied, the future interests material is a closely knit whole. In the immediate chapter the student will learn the meaning of the term "future interest", will review the historical development of such interests in land and the complex classification system set up at common law, and will see how these interests can be created in personal property. Some of the general characteristics of such interests are then explored.[1]

SECTION 1. THE MEANING OF THE TERM "FUTURE INTERESTS"

A devise of Blackacre to B for life, then to C and his heirs, creates a present interest in B and a future interest in C. B's interest is present because he is entitled to the immediate beneficial enjoyment of the land. C's interest is future because he or his successor will be entitled to the beneficial enjoyment of the land at some time in the future; that is, on the termination of B's estate. Certainty of future beneficial enjoyment is not, however, essential to the creation of a future interest. It is sufficient that there is a possibility of beneficial enjoyment at some time in the future. Thus a devise to B for life, then to C for life, creates a future interest in C, although he be an infirm octogenarian and B be a robust 21-year-old with a long life expectancy. Again a devise to B for life, then to C and his heirs on a condition precedent which may never occur or subject to a condition

1. Suggested references for a review of matters considered in this chapter and succeeding chapters dealing with future interests are Bergin and Haskell, Preface to Estates in Land and Future Interests (1966) and Simes, Handbook on the Law of Future Interests (2d Ed., 1966). See Bostick, "Loosening the Grip of the Dead Hand: Shall We Abolish Legal Future Interests in Land?", 32 Vand.L.Rev. 1061 (1979).

subsequent which may preclude C or his successors ever becoming entitled to the beneficial enjoyment of the land, creates a future interest in C.

At least the possibility of future beneficial enjoyment is an essential characteristic of the future interest. Likewise, a future interest is always a portion of total ownership measured in terms of duration. In the words of the Restatement of Property.[2]

> "Ownership regarded as potentially infinite in duration can be subdivided into chronologically successive segments, each having a duration of its own. A future interest exists only when the interest is one of these segments of ownership."

A future interest in land, then, can be described as one which will or may entitle the owner thereof to the beneficial enjoyment of the land at some time in the future and is a portion or segment of total ownership measured in terms of duration.

A future interest exists as a legally recognized and enforced relationship from the moment it is created. It does not spring into existence for the first time on the future date when the owner thereof becomes entitled to the beneficial enjoyment of the land. Futurity is annexed to the beneficial enjoyment of the land, not to the existence of the interest itself. The word present or future immediately preceding the word interest refers to the time of beneficial enjoyment, not to the existence of the legal relationship. Thus a devise of Blackacre to B for life, then to C and his heirs creates a future interest in C the moment the testator dies. This existing future interest may be disposed of by C and he is afforded redress against B for any use of the land by B, actual or threatened, which will impair the value of C's privilege of beneficially enjoying the land upon the termination of B's life estate.

The foregoing description of present and future interests must be modified when applied to trusts. A trustee is deemed to have a present interest in the trust res when he is entitled to the immediate control and management of the trust res. He has a future interest as trustee in the trust res when he or his successor as trustee will or may become entitled to the control and management of the trust res at some time in the future. If, as is typically the case, the beneficiary of a trust is entitled merely to the beneficial enjoyment of the proceeds of the trust, the beneficiary is deemed to have a present interest in the trust res when he is entitled to the immediate beneficial enjoyment of the proceeds of the trust and a future interest in the trust res when he or his successor will or may become entitled to the beneficial enjoyment of the proceeds of the trust at some time in the future. The present interest of a trustee in the trust res stands in contrast to the future interest of the person who, at some time in the future, will or may become either successor trustee of the trust res or become entitled to the beneficial enjoyment thereof. The present interest of the beneficiary of a trust stands in contrast to the

2. Restatement, Property (1936) § 9, Comment *c*.

future interest of the person, who, at some time in the future, will or may become entitled either to the beneficial enjoyment or to the trust res itself. By way of illustration, assume a devise of Blackacre to B as trustee, to receive the rents, issues and profits thereof and to apply them to the use of C for his life, the remainder on C's death to D as trustee in perpetuity for the E University. B and C have present interests. D and E have future interests.

A future interest, being an existing relationship between persons with respect to a subject matter of ownership, cannot, strictly speaking, be created by a limitation in favor of an unborn person. Thus, if Blackacre is devised to B for life, then to B's first born child in fee simple and B's first child is born some years after the testator's death, the future interest in favor of the child is not created until his birth. Yet, for many purposes, this future interest is treated as if it had been created at the testator's death. Courts and lawyers typically so refer to it. For example, it is believed that most members of the Bar would say that the limitation under scrutiny created, as of the testator's death, a present life estate in B and a remainder (a type of future interest) in favor of B's first born child. Where it does not make the context ambiguous, the practice of referring to a limitation in favor of an unborn person as if it created a future interest from the effective date of the limitation will be followed in this section.

Reference has been made only to future interests in land. As we shall later learn future interests analogous to those in land may now be created in tangible and intangible personal property. Father's portrait may be given to the eldest son for his life and then to the eldest grandchild absolutely. Corporate stocks and bonds, as the res of an express trust, are presently the most typical of all subject matters of future interests. And, as suggested by our discussion of trusts, future interests today may be legal or equitable. But much of the modern law of future interests was formalized by the law courts of England during the 13th, 14th and 15th centuries in developing the land law of that country. That future interests were first recognized in land is understandable. Relative permanency and economic value have always been characteristics of subject matters of ownership in which future interests are ordinarily created. Throughout the 13th, 14th, and 15th centuries English wealth consisted chiefly of land and other then-recognized subject matters of ownership lacked the quality of permanence.

The fact that the modern law of future interests has its origins in the land law of feudal England accounts for many of its peculiarities of both terminology and content. Hence it is that an historical survey of the development of future interests in the land law of England is essential to an understanding of the contemporary law of future interests.

SECTION 2. HISTORICAL DEVELOPMENT OF FUTURE INTERESTS IN LAND

Three basic doctrines of the medieval land law of England contributed to the development of the concept of future interests. These were the doctrines of tenure, estates, and seisin.

According to feudal theory land was owned absolutely (allodially) in the sense that one owns a horse, for example, only by the King. Others held their lands mediately or immediately of the King. Thus A, the farmer in possession of Blackacre, held of B, who held of C, who held of the King. Each person in this hierarchy was thought of as having an interest in Blackacre. Here then is the genesis of the idea that present and future interests may exist in the same land at the same time.

When the King allotted Blackacre to C a legal relationship known as tenure from the word *tenere,* to hold, was created between the King and C. Thereafter C held his interest in Blackacre as tenant of the King. When C in turn allotted Blackacre to B a new tenurial relationship was created in which B was tenant and C lord. And B's parcelling out of Blackacre to A created still another tenurial relationship in which A was tenant and B lord. Landholding thus assumed the form of a pyramid, with the King at the apex and those in actual possession of the land at the base. Each tenurial relationship involved the rendition of some type of service by the tenant to his immediate overlord. Also various incidents, such as wardship, marriage, and relief, were attached to each of these relationships.

Performance of the services and incidents was essential to the preservation of the feudal society. Military service provided the overlord with his armies. Relief, wardship, and marriage enriched his purse. Conversely, it was to the overlord that the tenant looked for military protection and the discharge of many responsibilities which we now associate with the obligations owed by a government to its citizens. Lord and tenant were thus bound together in the feudal structure by mutual self interest.

During the 13th Century the feudal theory of landholding was modified by the emergence of the modern conception of the fee simple as an estate of potentially infinite duration out of which might be created estates of finite duration. From this conception evolved the future interests which we know of today as the possibility of reverter, the reversion and the remainder.

An estate is an interest in land measured in terms of duration, which entitles the owner thereof to the possession of the land or which will or may entitle him to the possession thereof at some time in the future. Originally mere possibilities of future possession were not thought of as estates, but as possibilities of becoming estates. Over the centuries, however, the meaning of the term estates has expanded to include these possibilities. Excluded are non-possessory interests, such as easements and profits, and interests in things other than land. Interests analogous to estates may be created in personal property and in easements, profits, rents and the like; but they are not denominated estates. The essential characteristics of an estate, then, are three in number. First, an estate is always an interest in land; second, an estate is always an interest that is, will, or may become possessory; and third, the term always connotes ownership measured in terms of duration.

Implicit in the conception that estates of finite duration may be part of an estate in fee simple was the thought that someone always had to have the fee simple itself. It could not be in abeyance in the sense that it was extinguished, even for the time being. The fee simple itself was not carved up and killed off in creating lesser estates in point of duration. Always there had to be someone entitled to the land when the lesser estates terminated; otherwise there might be no tenant of a tract of land to whom the overlord could look for the performance of the feudal services and incidents. Thus, however many life estates and fee tails were created to take effect in enjoyment successively, their total would not equal the fee simple in the land.

Estates came to be classified as either freehold or non-freehold. Freehold estates were, and are today, the various types of the fee simple, the fee tails, and the life estates. Over the centuries tenancies for years, periodic tenancies, tenancies at will, and tenancies at sufferance (to the extent that they are regarded as estates) achieved recognition as non-freehold estates. The freehold estates were the normal feudal tenures. The feudal law had little regard for the non-freehold estates. Indeed, originally the term for years, certainly the most important of the non-freehold estates, was merely a contract right and not an estate at all. It was only the freehold estates which enjoyed the dignity of full recognition and protection by the medieval courts. And only the freeholder could be seised of a tract of land. The non-freeholder could have possession but not seisin.

Seisin was a feudal concept of vast significance in the shaping of the law of medieval England. It was responsible for the development of a number of the peculiar and arbitrary rules applicable to the future interest known as the remainder. And the term is widely used in contemporary judicial opinions and other legal writings as well as in statutes currently in effect in this country. What then is its meaning?

A person who has a freehold estate in land in his possession or to the possession of which he or his successor will be entitled immediately upon the expiration of the non-freehold estate of the person in possession, is seised of the land. For example, A, holding a possessory fee simple in Blackacre, is seised of Blackacre. Furthermore, A retains seisin even though he leases Blackacre to B for ten years and B goes into possession. Not having a freehold estate, B cannot be seised. As owner of the fee simple out of which B's estate is created, A has a freehold estate in the land which will entitle him to possession of the land immediately upon the expiration of B's estate for years. Hence A is seised. Thus we have a situation in which one person is seised and another person has possession. Moreover it is possible for the person who owns no estate in a tract of land to be seised thereof. If A, owning a possessory fee simple estate in Blackacre, is wrongfully ousted of his possession by B, who claims ownership of Blackacre in fee simple, B and not A is seised of Blackacre. It is for this reason that B is called the disseisor. Legal redress is of course available to A to regain possession and re-acquire seisin.

The feudal law seems to have assumed that the performance of the services owed by the person seised to his overlord was essential to the preservation of the feudal system. Apparently it was feared that default by the person seised of a tract of land in performing the services he owed would lead those above him in the hierarchy of landholding to default in performing the services owed by them. In other words, if those at the base of the feudal pyramid defaulted in performing the services owed by them the entire structure would collapse. Like a modern skyscraper, the feudal pyramid of landholdings was no stronger than its foundation or base. And so little regard did the feudal law have for the non-freehold estates, that this base was deemed to be composed solely of those seised.

Bearing in mind the vital importance which the feudal law attached to the concept of seisin we can readily understand why the doctrine developed that seisin could never be in abeyance and the person seised must always be ascertainable. A corollary of this doctrine was the rule that livery of seisin was essential to the creation of a present freehold estate. Otherwise the largely illiterate members of the community might not know of the transaction and hence there would be difficulty in ascertaining the person who was seised. Remember that in feudal times only a few could read and write and recording acts were unknown.

Livery of seisin was accomplished by the transferor and the transferee going on the land where the transferor symbolically delivered possession of the land to the transferee by handing to him a twig or clod of turf. Alternatively, livery of seisin could be accomplished by a statement of the transferor made in view of the land to the effect that possession was given to the transferee, followed by entry of the transferee on the land.

SECTION 3. THE CLASSIFICATION OF FUTURE INTERESTS IN LAND

The common law developed an elaborate system of classification for future interests in land. You may well become impatient with the refinements and subtleties differentiating the various types of future interests. Many of these differentiations are historical hangovers from the rigid, inflexible formalism of the medieval land law. And there is danger of overemphasizing their contemporary significance. Often the same rule applies indiscriminately to two or more future interests. Thus in many jurisdictions today it makes no practical difference whether a future interest is classified as a remainder or as an executory interest. But courts, lawyers, and text-writers still distinguish between them. Furthermore, vitally important consequences frequently result from the classification of a future interest. For example, the Rule against Perpetuities applies only to certain types of future interests. Studying the classification of future interests, therefore, is not a mere exercise of semantics. Nor is it of value only in providing an historical background. Rather, a thorough understanding of each type of future interest is part of the essential professional equipment of one engaging in an estates practice. It is believed that this understanding can best be gained by studying a step by step analysis presented in outline form.

A. First Step in Classification

The first step in classifying a future interest is to determine the persons in whom the interest will or may become possessory.

1. Creator or His Successors in Interest

The creator of the interest is the person who brings it into existence. The term therefore describes the grantor or devisor. His successors in interest are his heirs, devisees or alienees. If the interest will or may become possessory in the creator or his successors in interest, it will be one of the following:

a. Possibility of Reverter;

b. Right of Entry for Condition Broken (called a Power of Termination by the Restatement, Property, § 155);

c. Reversion.

2. Someone Other than Creator or His Successors in Interest

If the interest will or may become possessory in someone other than the creator or his successors in interest, it is one of the following:

a. Remainder

(Common Law Sub-Classification) [3]

(1) Vested Remainder

(2) Contingent Remainder

3. The Restatement of Property (1936) sub-classifies remainders as follows:

(a) Indefeasibly vested (§ 157 f–k);

(b) Vested subject to open (§ 157 *l*–n);

(c) Vested subject to complete defeasance (§ 157 o–t);

(d) Subject to a condition precedent (§ 157 u–x).

Under the Common Law Sub-Classification indefeasibly vested remainders, remainders vested subject to open and remainders vested subject to complete defeasance are vested remainders. The remainder subject to a condition precedent at Common Law is called a contin-

b. Executory Interest

(1) Shifting Executory Interest

(2) Springing Executory Interest

B. Second Step in Classification

The second step in classifying a future interest is to determine the precise future interest involved by the process of elimination as follows:

1. Possibility of Reverter

A possibility of reverter is the future interest left in one who creates a fee simple conditional or a fee simple determinable.

Examples:

A fee simple conditional is created, in the few states in which it is recognized, by language which would create a fee tail in England under the Statute De Donis enacted in 1285. Thus if X conveys Blackacre, which he owns in fee simple absolute, to A and the heirs of his body, a fee simple conditional is created in A, provided Blackacre is situated in a state recognizing this type of estate. X, in that event, retains a possibility of reverter.

A conveys Blackacre to B and his heirs so long as the premises are used for residential purposes. The limitation to B and his heirs subject to the provision for automatic termination creates a fee simple determinable. A has a possibility of reverter.

2. Right of Entry for Condition Broken (called a Power of Termination by the Restatement)

A Right of Entry for Condition Broken is the interest retained in the creator of an estate defeasible upon a condition subsequent.

Example:

A conveys Blackacre to B and his heirs but upon the express condition that if the property is used for nonresidential purposes, A may enter and terminate the estate thereby conveyed. B takes a fee simple subject to a condition subsequent. A has a right of entry for condition broken.

3. Reversion

All future interests left in one who has disposed of less than his entire interest in land measured from the point of view of du-

gent remainder. The Restatement subclassification is illustrated by the following examples:

Examples:

A conveys Blackacre to B for life, remainder to C and his heirs. C has an indefeasibly vested remainder.

A conveys Blackacre to B for life, remainder to the children of B. When this interest is created, assume that B has a child C. C has a vested remainder subject to open to let in afterborn children of B.

A conveys Blackacre to B for life, remainder as B shall by will appoint, and in default of appointment, remainder to C and his heirs. C has a vested remainder subject to complete defeasance by B's exercise of the power of appointment conferred upon him by A.

A conveys Blackacre to B for life, remainder to C and his heirs, if, but only if, C shall attain the age of 21. C is ten years old when the interest is created. He then has a remainder subject to a condition precedent or a contingent remainder.

ration, which are not possibilities of reverter or rights of entry for condition broken are reversions.

Example:

A conveys Blackacre to B for life. B has a life estate. A has a reversion.

4. Remainder

A remainder is a future interest that will or may become a present interest in someone other than the creator or his successors in interest immediately upon the natural expiration of a prior particular estate created by the same instrument.

a. Meaning of Particular Estate

A particular estate is an estate other than a fee simple. The fee simple estates are as follows: (1) fee simple absolute, (2) fee simple conditional, (3) fee simple determinable, (4) fee simple subject to a condition subsequent. A fee tail is not a fee simple. If the interest does not follow a particular estate it is an executory interest rather than a remainder.

Examples:

A conveys Blackacre to B for life, then to C and his heirs. B has an estate for life. This is a particular estate. C has a vested remainder.

A conveys Blackacre to B and his heirs, but if no children of B are living at B's death, then to C and his heirs. B has a fee simple defeasible on condition subsequent. This is not a particular estate. C has a shifting executory interest.

b. Must Take Effect Immediately

The interest must become a present interest, if at all, immediately upon the expiration of the prior particular estate. If it does not become a present interest immediately, it is an executory interest and not a remainder.

Example:

A conveys Blackacre to B for life and one year after his death to C and his heirs. B has an estate for life. A has a reversion. C has a springing executory interest and not a remainder.

c. Upon the Natural Expiration of the Prior Particular Estate

If the interest is limited to take effect in derogation of a prior particular estate rather than upon its natural expiration, it is an executory interest rather than a remainder.

Examples:

A conveys Blackacre to B during widowhood, then to C and his heirs. B has an estate for her widowhood. C has a vested remainder. When B dies or remarries the particular estate will terminate naturally.

A conveys Blackacre to B for life, but if B remarries then to C and his heirs. B has a life estate subject to a condition subsequent. A has a reversion. C has a shifting executory interest.

d. Created by the Same Instrument

It is essential that the particular estate and the remainder be created by the same instrument.

Example:

A conveys Blackacre to B for life. Thereafter A conveys his reversion to C. C has a reversion and not a remainder.

5. Common Law Sub-Classification of Remainders

a. Vested

A remainder is vested when throughout its continuance the owner's right to possession of the land is subject to no condition precedent except the termination of the prior particular estate or estates.

Example:

A conveys Blackacre to B for life, then to C and his heirs. C has a vested remainder.

b. Contingent

A remainder is contingent at the time it is created if at that time the remaindermen are (a) unborn, (b) though born are unascertained, (c) though born and ascertained, the remainder is subject to some condition precedent other than the termination of a prior particular estate or estates. All remainders that are not vested are contingent.

Examples:

A conveys Blackacre to B for life, remainder to B's first born child and his heirs. Assume B has no child at the time of the conveyance. At that time the remainder is contingent upon the birth of the child. When the child is born, the remainder is vested.

A conveys Blackacre to B for life, remainder to B's children him surviving in fee simple. Assume that B has children at the time of the conveyance. The children have a contingent remainder until the death of B since they cannot be ascertained as survivors until that time.

A conveys Blackacre to B for life, and if C is living at B's death, then to C and his heirs. Assume that B and C are alive at the time of the conveyance. C is ascertained but the remainder is subject to the condition precedent that he survive B.

6. Executory Interest

An executory interest is a future interest that will become a present interest, if at all, in someone other than the creator or his successors in interest and which does not satisfy the definition of remainder. Consider in this regard the examples set forth in 4 b, c and d. Otherwise put: an interest that will not become a present interest, if at all, immediately upon the natural termination of a prior particular estate is an executory interest. Executory interests are classified as (a) springing and (b) shifting.[4]

a. Springing Executory Interest.

A springing executory interest is one that divests only an interest left in the creator or his successors in interest.

Examples:

A conveys Blackacre to B and his heirs twenty years from the date of this deed. B has a springing executory interest.

A conveys Blackacre to B for life and one year after the death of B then to C and his heirs. C has a springing executory interest which divests the reversion in A.

b. Shifting Executory Interest

A shifting executory interest is one that divests an interest created in someone other than the creator or his successors in interest.

Example:

A conveys Blackacre to B for life but if B remarries then to C and his heirs. Technically there is here a reversion in A subject to the condition that B not remarry. But if B does remarry the estate limited to C will operate to divest B's particular estate and is therefore a shifting executory interest.

c. Strict Rule of Construction Concerning Executory Interests

Executory interests were made legal interests by the Statute of Uses and the Statute of Wills. Prior to the enactment of these statutes executory interests were not considered legal interests at Common Law. Since these statutes are in derogation of the Common Law they are strictly construed. Thus the rule is now applied that no limitation in a deed or will is ever considered an executory interest if, at the time it is created, and disregarding the Rule Against Perpetuities, it could possibly take effect as a Common Law remainder.[5]

4. If a conveyor sets up a fee simple determinable and makes no disposition over upon automatic termination of the estate he retains a possibility of reverter. But if he provides for an executory interest following the automatic expiration of the estate he cannot be said to have a possibility of reverter. Thus there can be no interest in the creator which is divested. Furthermore there is no divestment of the fee simple determinable since that estate expires naturally. Nevertheless the disposition over in this case is called a shifting executory interest since there can be no contingent remainder following a fee simple.

Example:

A conveys Blackacre to B and his heirs until B marries C, then to C and her heirs. C has a shifting executory interest even though this interest does not operate in derogation of the prior fee simple estate in B.

5. Limitations creating alternative future interests frequently present difficult problems of classification. If X conveys Blackacre to A for life, remainder to B and his heirs, but if B dies before A, then to C and his heirs, B has a vested remainder subject to complete defeasance and C has a shifting executory interest. On the other hand if X conveys Blackacre to A for life, and if B survive A, then to B and his heirs; but if B does not survive A then at A's death to C and his heirs, B and C have alternative contingent remainders, or, as they are sometimes called, contingent remainders with a double aspect. Language less clear than that in the foregoing illustrations may be

7. Distinguishing Reversions, Remainders and Executory Interests in Certain Cases

The student should observe that the system of classification of future interests set forth, while apparently arbitrary, becomes less so when actual instruments are considered. The intention of the grantor or testator is of importance in the case of a deed or will and, especially when dealing with contingencies, cases can easily go either way. It is especially difficult at times to distinguish in practice between vested and contingent remainders and sometimes between remainders and other interests.

Assume X devises Blackacre to A for life. In a subsequent clause of the same will, he devises the residue of his estate to B in fee. By the definition of remainder in Part B(4) of the text on classification at page 844, B has a remainder and not a reversion. The interests are created by the same instrument.[6]

But suppose X devises Blackacre to A for life and if B marries C, then to D and his heirs. In his residuary clause X devises his residuary estate to E. Since the contingency might not occur, X would have had a reversion or reversionary interest if he had disposed of the contingent interest by deed. But since he disposed of the estate by will, the interest not disposed of in the contingency provision passes by the residuary clause (the same instrument) and satisfies the definition of remainder. Is this a vested remainder following a contingent remainder? While there could be no contingent remainder following a vested remainder in fee, the interest in this situation being an executory interest, there was dictum in Loddington v. Kime[7] that a vested remainder could not follow a contingent remainder. But the interest in D could be an executory interest with a vested remainder in the residuary devisee. Or there could be alternate contingent remainders in D or in the residuary devisee, E. Or perhaps it is correct to have a vested remainder "following" a contingent remainder. Could E have received a "reversion" by the residuary devise?

According to the definition of remainder on Part B(4) of the text on classification at page 844, the interest would be a remainder or might be an executory interest depending upon the intent found in the particular will as to the time the interest is to take

construed by some courts as creating alternative contingent remainders and by other courts as creating a vested remainder subject to a shifting executory interest. Probably there is a constructional preference for the latter interpretation. It is a recognition of the policy favoring a vested over a contingent construction. It is a denial, however, of the preference for construing a limitation as creating a remainder rather than an executory interest. See Rabin, "The Law Favors the Vesting of Estates. Why?" 65 Colum. L.Rev. 467 (1965). The problem is discussed in American Law of Property (1952) § 4.36; Restatement, Property (1940) §§ 277, 278; Simes and Smith, Future Interests (2d Ed., 1956) §§ 204, 206. Schuyler, "The Art of Interpretation in Future Interests Cases", 17 Vand.L.Rev. 1407 (1964); "The Art of Interpretation of Wills", 104 Trusts and Estates 971 (1965).

6. See Restatement, Property (1936) § 156; Id. (1940) § 278, *comment* (d).

7. 1 Salk. 224, 91 Eng.Rep. 198 (1695). Approved in Fearne, Contingent Remainders *225.

effect if it does take effect. Nevertheless, in Egerton v. Massie,[8] on facts somewhat similar to those in the hypothetical, the interest was held a reversion. X had devised Blackacre to A for life, remainder to such of A's children as A should by deed or will appoint. In default of appointment, the remainder was devised to such of A's children and the issue of deceased children who survived her. If no child or issue of a deceased child survived A, then Blackacre was devised to B and his heirs. X also devised her residuary estate to A. A was thus life tenant with a special power of appointment and also was residuary devisee. A conveyed all of her interests in Blackacre to C. A then died unmarried and without children or issue of deceased children surviving her. The Court of Common Pleas held a reversion was devised to A in X's residuary clause, and when A conveyed her interests to C, the interests merged in C, destroying the contingent remainder in B under the doctrine of destructibility of contingent remainders.[9] Un-

8. 3 C.B. (N.S.) 338, 140 Eng.Rep. 771 (1857).

9. Under the English common law, a contingent remainder fails if the contingency does not occur on or before the termination of the preceding particular estate. The "Doctrine of Destructibility of Contingent Remainders" is founded on the medieval concept of "seisin". The freehold estate in remainder is invalid unless the instant the preceding possessory freehold terminates seisin passes to an identified remainderman. If there is no such remainderman, seisin returns to the transferor or his heirs and the remainder fails.

The destructibility doctrine applies when the contingency fails to occur prior to the formal expiration of the prior particular estate. Suppose X conveys Blackacre to A for life and then to the heirs of B. There are no heirs of the living. If A dies and B survives the remainder is destroyed because it had not vested by the time of A's death. The remainder also is destroyed if the preceding estate terminates by merger. If X conveys Blackacre to A for life remainder to the heirs of B and, while B is still living, X conveys his reversion to A, A's life estate and the reversion merge, destroying the intervening contingent remainder. The doctrine of merger does not apply when the two estates to be merged are created by the same deed or will and no subsequent transfer of the interests occurs. In *Egerton* the life tenant conveyed her life tenancy with her residuary interest to a third party thus destroying the intervening interest (which the court classified as a contingent reminder). If a vested interest had intervened no merger would occur until the intervening interest terminated.

The destructibility doctrine applies only to contingent remainders and not to executory interests. Thus, suppose X devises Blackacre to A for life with remainder to the heirs of B and A renounces his life interest, B being alive at the time of the renunciation. The renunciation (or disclaimer) relates back to the death of the testator. B thus takes by springing executory interest rather than by remainder and the destructibility doctrine is inapplicable. Moreover, the doctrine applies only to legal freehold estates in land. It is inapplicable when the contingent remainder is equitable; and trusts to preserve contingent remainders were once used to avoid application of the doctrine. The doctrine is inapplicable to contingent remainders in chattels real and chattels personal. Stemming from the desire of the English courts to preserve family settlements, if a contingent remainderman was conceived but unborn on termination of the supporting particular estate, and ascertainment of the remainderman is the only contingency, the remainder was not destroyed if the remainderman thereafter was born alive.

The destructibility doctrine has been abolished by statute in England and has also been abolished by statute or by judicial decision in a great majority of American states or was never recognized. For example, in ABO Petroleum Corp. v. Amstutz, 93 N.M. 332, 600 P.2d 278 (1979), the doctrine was held not in force, the court describing it as a relic of the feudal past. See Note, "Property—Contingent Remainders—Rule of Destructibility Abolished in New Mexico", 10 New Mex. L.Rev. 471 (1980). The seisin concept, upon which the doctrine is based, has little current relevance other than as an aid to understanding common law classifica-

like the hypothetical, the contingent interests in *Egerton* were "closed" contingencies, one of the contingent interests devised being certain to vest; but even in this situation X retained some interest under the older view. So shadowy and evanescent was this "interest" in *Egerton* it is doubtful that there should have been a merger to destroy a contingent remainder; and the interest in B might reasonably have been classified as an executory interest to which the destructibility rule did not apply. But the major controversies concerning *Egerton* have centered on the classification of the interests created. There is support for the classification of A's residuary interest as a reversion.[10] According to the Restatement of Property, the interests in A and B are alternate contingent remainders.[11] Some writers have described the interest in B as an executory interest and the interest in A as residuary devisee as a remainder;[12] while others find no objection to a contingent remainder being followed by a vested remainder in fee.[13]

NOTE

A few states, which have patterned their property legislation on the New York Revised Statutes of 1830, have a statutory classification of estates.[14]

In New York this classification of the 1830's has now been abandoned, in Estates, Powers and Trusts Law §§ 6–3.1 through 6–4.10 the New York Legislature returning to classification very similar to that at common law. The former New York classification was intended to remove the "subtleties and refinements" of the English law, particularly by abolishing the distinction

tion of future interests. The doctrine of destructibility of contingent remainders is important as an aid to understanding early English decisions and American decisions which applied it. Currently, the doctrine appears to be in force in Florida, Oregon, Pennsylvania, and Tennessee. See Smith, "Destructibility of Contingent Remainders in Florida", 3 U.Fla.L.Rev. 319 (1950); Note, "Present Status of the Rule of Destructibility in Pennsylvania", 27 Temp.L.Q. 207(1953); Jones & Heck, "Destructibility of Contingent Remainders in Tennessee"; 42 Tenn.L.Rev. 761 (1975); Note, "Remainders—Contingent Remainders—Destructibility Doctrine in Oregon", 23 Ore.L.Rev. 138 (1944). In some states there is doubt whether the doctrine is still in force. See McCall, "The Destructibility of Contingent Remainders in North Carolina", 16 N.C.L. Rev. 87 (1937); Fetters, "Destructibility of Contingent Remainders", 21 Ark.L. Rev. 145 (1967). Arkansas embraces the destructibility principle in its fee tail statute, allowing the interests of unborn contingent remaindermen to be destroyed so a fee simple can be conveyed. Ark.Stat. Ann. § 50–405.1 (1971 Repl. Vol.). By destroying contingent remainders the doctrine does remove restraints on alienation; but the Rule against Perpetuities also has this function and the general application of the common law Rule against Perpetuities may account in part for the decline of the destructibility doctrine. For general discussions of the destructibility doctrine, see American Law of Property (1952) §§ 84.59–84.63; Simes and Smith, The Law of Future Interests (2d Ed. 1956) § 193 et seq.; Powell, The Law of Real Property (Rohan Ed. 1977) § 314; Restatement, Property (1936) § 240.

10. Gray, The Rule Against Perpetuities (4th Ed. 1942) § 113.1.

11. 3 Restatement, Property (1940) § 278, comment (d).

12. E.g. Kales, Estates and Future Interests (2d Ed. 1920) § 95.

13. Tiffany, The Law of Real Property (3d Ed., Jones 1939) § 333; Warren "The Progress of the Law, 1919–1920: Estates and Future Interests, 34 Harv.L. Rev. 508, 515–18 (1920). See Holt, "The Testator Who Gave Away Less Than All He or She Had: Perversions in the Law of Future Interests", 32 Ala.Law Rev. 69 (1980).

14. Mich.Comp.Laws Ann. §§ 554.9–554.13 (1980 Supp.); Minn.Stat.Ann. § 500.06 et seq. (1980 Supp.).

between legal and executory interests. Where the old New York classification has been the model for legislation on this subject, this variant classification, "modern" in 1830, and creating a partially new terminology, has stimulated certain problems. For example: (1) other statutory sections use terms, such as "future estates", with the statutory rather than the common law meaning; (2) the statutory definition may be construed by courts to change the accepted construction of certain limitations with resultant confusion, as we shall see in a case like Moore v. Littel; and (3) the statute may draw lines which have outlived their usefulness and could be discarded by a court acting under common law principles today. This is not to suggest that statutory reform in classification will not be useful; and interesting and carefully conceived programs for reform have been suggested.[15] It is possible that states adopting a statutory classification from the old New York legislation will now also modernize their statutes as New York has done or will follow some modern recommendation for simplified classification.[16]

The *old* (1830) New York classification divides estates into two categories: a present possessory estate becomes "an estate in possession", and a future estate of any variety is called "an estate in expectancy". How would the various future interests we have just defined at common law in this section fit, if at all, under the following statutory classifications and definitions, within the category of expectant estates?

(1) Enumeration of estates in expectancy

"All expectant estates, except such as are enumerated and defined in this article, have been abolished. Estates in expectancy are divided into,

1. Future estates; and
2. Reversions."

(2) Definition of future estates

"A future estate is an estate limited to commence in possession at a future day, either without the intervention of a precedent estate, or on the determination, by lapse of time or otherwise, of a precedent estate created at the same time."

(3) Definition of remainder

"Where a future estate is dependent on a precedent estate, it may be termed a remainder, and may be created and transferred by that name."

(4) Definition of reversion

"A reversion is the residue of an estate left in the grantor or his heirs, or in the heirs of a testator, commencing in possession on the determination of one or more particular estates granted or devised."

(5) When future estates are vested and when contingent

"A future estate is either vested or contingent. It is vested when there is a person in being, who would have an immediate right to the possession of the property, on the determination of all the intermediate or precedent estates. It is contingent while the person to whom or the event on which it is limited to take effect remains uncertain."

15. Waggoner, "Reformulating the Structure of Estates: A Proposal for Legislative Action", 85 Harv.L.Rev. 729 (1972); Bostick, "Loosening the Grip of the Dead Hand: Shall We Abolish Legal Future Interests in Land?" 32 Vand.L. Rev. 1061 (1979).

16. Wisconsin changed from its statutory classification to the common law pattern in 1971. Wis.Stat.Ann. §§ 700.-03–700.05 (West Spec. Pamph. 1980).

The case of Moore v. Littel, 41 N.Y. 66 (1869), illustrates the confusion introduced by statutory definition. In 1832 one Samuel Jackson had conveyed a farm which he owned in fee simple absolute to "John Jackson for and during his natural life, and after his decease to his heirs and their assigns forever." The issue in the case was whether or not the remainder created by the limitation in John Jackson's "heirs" was alienable during John Jackson's lifetime by his children, who were his heirs apparent. The case could have been decided on the basis of a New York statute then in force which made all expectant estates, including contingent as well as vested remainders, alienable; see Section 6 infra. But Justice Woodruff speaking for a majority of the Court of Appeals of New York, also based the decision that the remainder was alienable on the grounds that it was vested. Such a classification of the remainder as vested conflicts with the generally accepted maxim that no one is heir to the living. From time immemorial Anglo-American courts have declared that a limitation to the heirs of a living person is a limitation to unascertained persons. Death of the ancestor is a condition precedent to ascertaining his heirs. Hence it is held uniformly that a limitation to A for life, then to the heirs of B, a living person, creates a contingent remainder, which becomes vested on B's death. And in most jurisdictions like New York in which the Rule in Shelley's case is not in force (see Section 5 infra), a limitation to A for life, then to the heirs of A, would create a contingent remainder during A's lifetime. In holding otherwise in Moore v. Littel, Justice Woodruff asserted that a remainder is vested under the statutory definition "If you can point to a human being and say as to him, 'that man or that woman, by virtue of a grant of a remainder would have an immediate right to the possession of certain lands if the precedent estate of another should now cease' * * *."

Justice Woodruff failed to recognize the distinction between the primary meaning of the word heirs and the words heirs apparent and heirs presumptive. He vested the remainder in heirs apparent subject to being divested if and as they respectively predeceased their ancestor. But the gift was to heirs, not heirs apparent, and a person's heirs, within the primary meaning of that term, cannot be acertained until his death. Under what would seem to be the better view, therefore, a remainder to the heirs of a living person is contingent.[17]

---

17. For a discussion of Moore v. Littel types of limitations see Restatement, Property (1940) § 249; American Law of Property (1952) § 4.36; Simes and Smith, Future Interests (2d Ed., 1956) §§ 154–163.

SECTION 4. FUTURE INTERESTS IN PERSONAL PROPERTY

(1) CHATTELS REAL

Limitations of space preclude tracing the evolution in England of recognition of the power to create legal future interests in chattels real. Under the early feudal law future interests could not be created in a term for years. A life estate was considered larger than a term for years regardless of its duration. Hence a purported transfer of a term of years for life was held to constitute an assignment of the entire term. In time the English courts recognized that a future interest similar to an executory interest could be created in terms for years. For example, X, the owner of a term for years, could transfer his term "to B from and after the death of A". By a subsequent transaction X could transfer the interest left in him to A, or to anyone else. Thus by two transactions X could in effect transfer his term for years to A for life, then to B. This modification of the ancient doctrine denying that future interests could be created in terms for years was followed by the English courts holding that a devise of a term for years "to A for life, remainder to B" would be given effect as the two transactions previously mentioned. B thus acquired an executory interest, not a remainder. The executory devise would take effect in possession on the death of A and A had the term only for his life. This conclusion assumes, of course, that A died before the term expired. Apparently, the English courts did not allow the result described above to be achieved by a single inter vivos transaction. Indeed the recognition of the power to create an executory devise in a term seems to be as far as the English common law went in permitting future interests to be created in terms for years.

American courts have been much more liberal than the courts of England in recognizing future interests in chattels real. According to the Restatement of Property all five varieties of the common law future interests in land may be created in chattels real.[18] What little authority there is in this country bears out the view of the Restatement. In this connection it should be noted that, when the residue of an estate includes a chattel real, a testamentary residuary gift of a life estate with remainder over is usually construed as manifesting an intent that the legatee of the life estate should not receive the leasehold itself. Rather an implied duty is imposed on the executor to sell the leasehold, invest the proceeds of the sale, pay the income to the life tenant and transfer the corpus to the remainderman on the death of the life tenant.

18. Restatement, Property (1936) §§ 153–156, 158.

It will be remembered that a fee tail estate cannot be created in an estate for years. An attempt to do so is held to constitute an assignment of the term.[19]

---

(2) CHATTELS PERSONAL

Chattels personal may be consumable or nonconsumable, tangible or intangible. Whatever be their nature they lack the elements of permanence, indestructibility and immovability which are characteristic of land. For obvious reasons the creation of a legal future interest in a particular bushel of wheat, or hundred dollar bill or corporate bond would be impractical. Equitable future interests, on the other hand, are constantly created in corporate stocks, bonds, and other types of securities, through the medium of the trust. Indeed, to make a gift of a future interest in intangible personal property without the intervention of a trust would be an inexcusable oversight by the draftsman.

Occasionally, as in the case of heirlooms, it may be desirable to create legal future interests in nonconsumable tangible personal property. If this is done it is wise to provide expressly in the instrument creating the interest whether or not the owner of the present interest is to give security against loss or injury. Otherwise courts will require security if there is proved to be danger of such loss or injury. Futhermore, if the owner of the present interest is expressly empowered to convert the subject matter into other forms of property many jurisdictions will require security without any showing of danger. However, absent an express provision to the contrary in the instrument creating the future interest, security will not be required when the owner of the present interest is empowered to destroy the future interest for his own benefit.

By the weight of authority in this country today the same types of legal future interests may be created in nonconsumable chattels personal as may be created in land.[20] It seems, however, that legal future interests cannot be created in consumables. For example, a transfer purporting to give a consumable for life is held to pass the absolute interest to the transferee. This result is regarded as a positive rule of law and not merely a rule of construction in most jurisdictons which have passed upon the matter. To this rule, however,

19. For a full discussion of the matters outlined in this subsection see Simes and Smith, Future Interests (2d Ed., 1956) Ch. 11.

20. Neither a fee tail nor a fee simple conditional can be created in chattels personal. Language appropriate to create such estates in land passes an absolute interest in personal property. See Williamson v. Daniel, 12 Wheat. 568, 6 L.Ed. 731 (1827); Cooke v. Bucklin, 18 R.I. 666, 29 A. 840 (1894); Note "The Fee Simple Conditional in South Carolina," 18 S.C. Law Rev. 476 (1966).

there is a well recognized and important exception. An absolute interest does not pass and a future interest is created if the transferee for life has either an express or implied power to sell and convert the consumables into nonconsumables, to which the future interests are to attach. Moreover, as in the case of chattels real, such a power is implied in the case of a testamentary residuary gift, which includes consumables. In that event it is presumed that the testator intended the transferee for life to receive the income arising from investing the proceeds realized on selling the consumables, rather than to enjoy the consumables in specie.[21]

Distinguishing between consumables and nonconsumables sometimes presents difficulty. Tangible personal property that is necessarily destroyed in the physical sense through its normal use, such as grain and hay, is a consumable. Probably most perishable goods are consumables. Household goods, farm machinery and livestock are generally held to be nonconsumables. But a printing press has been held to be a consumable, apparently because it would wear out and become obsolete in normal use.[22] So broad an interpretation of the term consumable would probably not be recognized in most jurisdictions. If the physical identity of the goods will not be destroyed in normal use most jurisdictions would classify the goods as nonconsumable.[23]

In states which have court-supervised administration of a decedent's estate, if a will does not manifest an intent to create a trust but leaves personal property to a life tenant with a remainder over, the court may assign the personalty to the life tenant or a third per-

21. There are statutes in a number of states requiring the recordation of certain instruments creating future interests in chattels personal in order to protect the owner of the future interests from the effect of a transfer by the owner of the present interest to a bona fide purchaser. The Virginia statute is typical. It reads:

"Loans and reservations of a use or property to be recorded.—When any loan of goods or chattels is pretended to have been made to any person with whom, or those claiming under him, possession shall have remained five years without demand made and pursued by due process of law on the part of the pretended lender, or when any reservation or limitation is pretended to have been made of a use or property by way of condition, reversion, remainder or otherwise in goods or chattels the possession whereof shall have so remained in another as aforesaid, the absolute property shall be taken to be with the possession and such loan, reservation or limitation void as to creditors of, and purchasers from, the person so remaining in possession, unless such loan, reservation or limitation be declared by will which, or a copy of which, or by deed or other writing which, is duly admitted to record within such period of five years in the county or corporation in which the goods or chattels may be." Va. Code Ann., § 55–87 (1975 Supp.)

A Georgia statute provides in substance that any estate can be created in personalty that can be created in realty. Ga.Civ.Code § 85–104 (1975 Supp.). And there are statutory provisions elsewhere making certain rules of real property law applicable to personal property. However, these various statutory provisions seem to have been construed in conformity with the rules set out in the text. See Simes and Smith, Future Interests (2d Ed. 1956) § 371.

22. Seabrook v. Grimes, 107 Md. 410, 68 A. 883, 16 L.R.A.,N.S., 483, 126 Am. St.Rep. 400 (1907).

23. See Simes and Smith, Future Interests (2d Ed., 1956) Ch. 12 for detailed discussion of the matters covered in this subsection.

son as trustee.[24] The purpose of this approach is to obtain the security provided by the trust concept, typically in the form of continuing court supervision over the testamentary trust, with an inventory, bond and annual accounting. Such a court-created trust is sometimes referred to as a "trust for convenience".[25] In a sense the court is doing what the good will draftsman always does, since the trust is a far better device for handling creation of future interests in most kinds of personalty. For example, if the testator leaves his farm and all the livestock, equipment and personalty thereon to his wife for life, with remainder to his children, the creation of successive interests in specific personalty such as the equipment is cumbersome while creation of future interests in livestock poses a problem as to whether such livestock should be classified as consumable, not to mention the problem of obvious consumables such as feed, seed and fertilizer on hand. Although the legal life estate and successive future interests in land would be workable because the land stays constant, is readily identifiable and cannot be removed from the jurisdiction, it is apparent that the farm personalty constitutes a form of business asset which will change in content during the "life estate". Appointing the life tenant as "trustee" permits the kind of reasonable business decisions in trading in equipment, replacing livestock, and sale of individual items which a trustee has power to make. Where the court assigns the personalty to an independent trustee, such as a corporate fiduciary, there is additional protection afforded.

---

24. See Note, 46 A.L.R.2d 502 (1954); Vaughn v. Vaughn, 238 Miss. 342, 118 So.2d 620 (1960); Miller's Estate, 160 Ohio St. 529, 117 N.E.2d 598, 46 A.L.R.2d 493 (1954).

25. See Estate of Martin, 21 Wis.2d 334, 338, 124 N.W.2d 297, 300 (1963):

"Defendant argues he was a 'trustee for convenience,' relying on the Estate of Lenahan (1951), 258 Wis. 404, 46 N.W.2d 352. A trustee for convenience in Wisconsin is a unique concept and apparently is applied to both real and personal property. When a life estate with the remainder over is created in property, especially personal property of the nature which may be transferred or appropriated, a risk exists that the remainderman might not receive the property the testator intended he should have. The problem of securing a future interest in personal property has long been a problem confronting the courts and there is historic authority for a court's requiring security of the life tenant by way of a bond in cases involving intangibles, money, or quasi-negotiable personalty. The trust device has also been used to protect the owner of a future interest in personalty. Apparently a judicial trust is a more modern approach and finds sanction in the hazard to the owner of the future interest in personalty or on the basis of an implied intent as the trust will not be established by the court if the will manifests a contrary intent. The trust device or the requirement of security did not apply to a life estate involving land because such property was not destructible, could not be removed from the jurisdiction, or secreted. At common law there were remedies to protect the remainderman from waste by the life tenant and the recording acts protected him against rights arising in third parties. We do not approve of keeping a probate proceeding open for the duration of the life of the life tenant in order to insure some protection to the owner of the future interest. This procedure is impracticable and inevitably leads to more difficulties than it solves. * * *"

SECTION 5. RULES RESTRICTING CREATION OF REMAINDERS TO HEIRS

(1) THE RULE IN SHELLEY'S CASE

Shelley's Case is a decision by Sir Edward Coke in 1581 [26] and the Rule is derived from a discussion by Sir Edward in that case of the arguments of counsel. Due to the authority of Coke's Reports and the popularity of Blackstone's Commentaries, the Rule at one time was in force as a rule of law in virtually all of the American states. The Rule is now abolished by statute or judicial decision in a great majority of states, probably now having significance in less than a quarter of them.[27]

The usual statement of the Rule is that when a freehold estate in land is conveyed or devised to a person and in the same instrument a remainder is limited immediately or mediately to the heirs of that person or to the heirs of that person's body,[28] and both estates are legal or both estates are equitable, the word "heirs" or the words "heirs of the body" are read as a word or words of limitation rather than purchase, the conveyee or devisee of the freehold estate also taking a remainder in fee simple, fee tail or fee simple conditional, as the case may be. If there is no intermediate estate or estates and the remainder is vested the remainder and freehold estate will merge. Thus, if a person is conveyed a life estate in Blackacre and a remainder is limited to his heirs, the Rule in Shelley's Case being in force, the conveyee has a fee simple absolute after the merger occurs. The freehold estate is usually a life estate but might be a fee tail if a fee tail is recognized in the jurisdiction, there being little authority upon the point.[29]

The Rule is confined to real estate, thus eliminating any application to trusts of personalty. It is, however, a rule of law where applied and thus applies irrespective of the transferor's actual intention. The Rule is not applied when the first estate is a non-freehold (an estate for years, for example), when the estate limited over is an executory interest, or when one estate is legal and the other is equita-

26. 1 Co. Rep. 93b at 104a. The date might be as early as 1579 and the case may have been in the moots in the Inns of Court. A comprehensive discussion of the origin and modern application of Shelley's Rule may be found in Simes and Smith, The Law of Future Interests (2d Ed. 1956) Ch. 45.

27. For the current status of the Rule, see Simes and Smith, The Law of Future Interests (2d Ed. 1956) §§ 1563–1569 (1979 Supp.)

28. E.g., Sybert v. Sybert, 152 Tex. 106, 254 S.W.2d 999 (1953). Following this case the Rule was abolished in Texas. Vernon's Ann.Tex.Civ.Stat. art. 1291a (1980 Repl. Vol.)

29. If the freehold was a fee tail the early view was that the Statute De Donis prevented a merger. Wiscot's Case, 2 Co. Rep. 60b (1599).

ble. A court wishing to avoid the rule may construe the trust instrument to create an equitable life estate with a legal remainder to the heirs of the life beneficiary. Thus in Elsasser v. Elsasser[30] the will became effective two months before the effective date of a statute abolishing the Rule. The Florida court avoided the Rule by construing the life estate as equitable and the remainder legal despite a direction to the trustee to convey to the remaindermen. On the other hand, the Rule might be useful when a life tenant seeks to terminate a trust and there is a remainder limited to the life tenant's heirs. The Rule could, in effect, eliminate the heirs so their consent would not be required in a trust termination.

In cases in which the Rule might be applied, there is frequently a preliminary construction problem to determine whether the word "heirs" is used in a restricted sense "children" or "issue" or in the sense of heirs in indefinite succession or in the sense of a class which would take on the death of the ancestor intestate. If the remainder to heirs is intended in either of the latter two senses, the Rule should apply. If the first sense is intended, the Rule is inapplicable. For example, in Cahill v. Cahill[31] the devise was to the testator's nephew and upon the death of the nephew "said described property to become the property of his Heirs of Blood." Under Illinois law the widow, under certain conditions, and adopted children are heirs. Is the Rule in Shelley's Case applicable? A term other than heirs, such as "children", may have been intended as synonymous with heirs.

Suppose both the life estate and the remainder are future interests. For example, A conveys to B for life, remainder to C for life, remainder to the heirs of C. Does C take a fee simple in remainder if Shelly's Rule is in force?[32] Suppose the limitation is to A and B for life remainder to the heirs of A? Would the Rule apply? If it did apply would A's interest as life tenant merge with his interest as remainderman?[33]

The Rule was applied in England for at least two centuries before Shelley's Case but the reasons for it were not understood, there probably being little to the Rule other than an expression of a general policy found in administering the common law of descent to move the title back towards its source in an effort to keep title to land as closely as possible in the family which took it by subinfeudation. No satisfactory explanations of the Rule were offered in Coke's day and there certainly are no reasons for its application today to defeat the intent of a conveyor or testator.[34]

30. 159 Fla. 696, 32 So.2d 579 (1947).

31. 402 Ill. 416, 84 N.E.2d 380 (1949).

32. See Simes and Smith, The Law of Future Interests (2d Ed. 1956) § 1555.

33. Id. § 1559.

34. For a discussion of the many reasons offered to support the Rule, see Simes and Smith, The Law of Future Interests (2d Ed. 1956) § 1543. Simes and Smith state that the only rationale supporting the Rule today is that it increases the alienability of land. Id. 430. See Webster, "A Relic North Carolina Can Do Without—The Rule in Shelley's Case", 45 No.Car.L.Rev. 3 (1966).

PROBLEMS

Assume the Rule in Shelley's Case is in force in the jurisdiction. To which of the following cases would it apply:

1. X conveys Blackacre to A for life, remainder to the heirs of A, and states "under no circumstances is more than a life estate to vest in A". Wilson v. Harrold, 288 Ill. 388, 123 N.E. 563 (1919).

2. X conveys Blackacre to A for 5 years, remainder to the heirs of A. See Tyndale v. McLaughlin, 84 N.J.Eq. 652, 95 A. 117 (1915).

3. X bequeaths his antique writing desk to A for life, remainder to A's next of kin. Simes and Smith, The Law of Future Interests (2d Ed. 1956) § 367.

4. X devises Blackacre to A for life, remainder to the heirs of A's body. Sybert v. Sybert, 152 Tex. 106, 254 S.W.2d 999 (1953).

5. X devises Blackacre to A for life and if A survives B, remainder to the heirs of A. Starnes v. Hill, 112 N.C. 1, 16 S.E. 1011, 22 L.R.A. 598 (1893).

6. X devises Blackacre to trustee for the life of A to manage the property and pay the net profits to A for life and at the death of A the trust to terminate and the principal then to be transferred by the trustee to the heirs of A. Simes and Smith, The Law of Future Interests (2d Ed. 1956) § 1552.

7. X devises Blackacre to A for life, remainder to the issue of A. Mylin v. Hurst, 259 Pa. 77, 102 A. 429 (1917).

8. X conveys Blackacre to A for life, remainder to the heirs of B. A conveys his life estate to B. 1 Fearne, Contingent Remainders and Executory Devises 71.

9. X devises Blackacre to A for life and in the same will devises his residuary estate to A's heirs, not elsewhere in the will disposing of the remainder interest in Blackacre. See Simes and Smith, The Law of Future Interests (2d Ed. 1956) § 1551.

10. X conveys Blackacre to A for life, remainder to the heirs of X.

---

(2) THE CONVEYOR-HEIR RULE: WORTHIER TITLE

MATTER OF BURCHELL
WORM v. UNITED STATES TRUST CO.

Court of Appeals of New York, 1949.
299 N.Y. 351, 87 N.E.2d 293.

Proceeding in the matter of the estate of Celestine A. Gardner, (Formerly Celestine A. Burchell), deceased, on the application of Celestine A. Thomson, under Civil Practice Act, § 1307 et seq., for an order requiring the Lawyers Trust Company, as successor trustee under a trust indenture executed by decedent June 22, 1891, to account, directing successor trustee to distribute the corpus of the trust between the four children of the settlor in equal shares as remaindermen and for a determination that surviving spouse of settlor had no interest in trust fund whether as an heir at law, next of kin, surviving spouse, or otherwise, opposed by Frank P. Nohowel, executor of decedent's estate, and others, and Josephine M. Burchell and others. From an order of the Appellate Division, 85 N.Y.S.2d 300, 274 App. Div. 925, affirming an order of the Supreme Court at special term, Schreiber, J., entered in New York County, granting the application, Frank P. Nohowel, as executor and others appeal.

Submission of controversy upon agreed statement of facts pursuant to Civil Practice Act §§ 546–548 by Alice Macy Beers Worm, against the United States Trust Company of New York. From a judgment of the Appellate Division, by a divided court, 86 N.Y.S.2d 632, 274 App.Div. 637, in favor of defendant, plaintiff appeals. The appeals were heard together.

BROMLEY, JUDGE. We are again asked to determine whether a limitation over to the heirs of the grantor in an inter vivos conveyance created a remainder in the heirs or left a reversionary interest in the grantor.

The instrument of conveyance in each case is a trust agreement. In Matter of Burchell the question arises in the course of the administration of the estate of the deceased settlor. In Worm v. United States Trust Co. the settlor has attempted to revoke the trust instrument under Section 23 of the Personal Property Law, Consol.Laws, c. 43, by a notice of revocation executed by her alone.

The provisions in each of the two instruments are similar. The settlor conveyed property to trustees who were directed to pay income therefrom to the settlor during her life and upon her death to convey the principal of the trust estate to the persons whom the settlor should appoint in her will, or, in default of appointment, to the settlor's next of kin as in intestacy. In the Burchell case the trust instrument further provided that the settlor, as evidence of her consent and approval, should join in the execution of any conveyance or mortgage of any of the property, or of a lease for a period of more than three years, or of the appointment of a successor trustee or trustees.

The trustees, however, were authorized and empowered to sell, convey or mortgage the real estate and to invest and reinvest the trust funds. In the Worm case the trustee was given full power to manage, invest and reinvest the trust property, except that approval of the settlor's father was required during his lifetime. No power of revocation was reserved in either agreement nor was there any provision for withdrawal of any of the principal of the trust fund.

In each case we reach the conclusion that the future interests limited in the instrument resulted in the creation of valid remainders.

In Richardson v. Richardson, 298 N.Y. 135, 81 N.E.2d 54, decided only last year, we reaffirmed the rule, first announced in Doctor v.

Hughes, 225 N.Y. 305, 122 N.E. 221, that the nature of the future interest where an estate is limited to heirs of the grantor is dependent upon the intention of the settlor as expressed in the trust agreement. We stated, 298 N.Y. page 139, 81 N.E.2d page 56: "Thus direction to transfer trust property to one's next of kin is insufficient in and of itself to create a remainder. There must be additional factors, i.e., other indications of intention in order that there may be found 'sufficient' or 'clear expression' of intention on the part of the settlor to create a remainder to his next of kin." We tabulated certain additional factors which had been considered of significance in earlier cases in pointing the intention of the grantor to create a remainder. The reservation of only a testamentary power of appointment, together with " 'full and formal disposition of the principal of the trust estate' ", 298 N.Y. page 141, 81 N.E.2d 57, and the failure to reserve a power to grant or assign an interest in the property, led us to conclude that the interest limited in that case was a remainder and the settlor's attempt to revoke the instrument was ineffective since presumptive remaindermen were not parties to the revocation.

The trust agreement in the Richardson case, supra, differed only slightly from those now before us. There the settlor, then unmarried and her mother, her sole next of kin, directed the trustees named to pay the income to the settlor for life and at her death to pay over the corpus to such person or persons as the settlor should appoint by will, and in default of appointment the principal should be paid over to her mother, but should her mother predecease her the principal was to be paid to her next of kin as in intestacy. Settlor's mother predeceased her and settlor attempted to revoke. The immediate power of appointment followed by a limitation to a named person rather than a designation of a remainder followed by a power of appointment, cf. Engel v. Guaranty Trust Co. of New York, 280 N.Y. 43, 19 N.E.2d 673, was not deemed significant enough to warrant an opposite conclusion from that reached in the Engel case.

In the instant cases it is true there was no grant of a remainder interest to a named individual and the limitation to the heirs was only upon default in the exercise of the power of appointment. But whether a remainder is created or a reversion left in the grantor is not dependent upon the number of contingent or vested limitations created. A valid gift may be made to a designated class; so also may a valid remainder be created subject to be divested by a reserved power of appointment; and a valid remainder interest may be created though the naming of specific takers is reserved for future announcement under a testamentary power of appointment.

Confusion as to the nature of an estate when that estate is limited to heirs of the grantor arises because of the existence in our modern jurisprudence of remnants of the ancient doctrine of worthier title (46 Harv.L.Rev. 993). Prior to our decision in Doctor v. Hughes, 225 N.Y. 305, 122 N.E. 221, supra, a conveyance by a grantor with a limitation over to his heirs was said to be governed by that doctrine, under which a limitation over to a grantor's heirs resulted in an automatic reversion in the grantor and nullified the limitation over.

The doctrine had its origin in the feudal custom of awarding certain valuable incidents to the overlord upon the descent of property held by a feoffee. These incidents did not accrue if the property was acquired through purchase, and, in order to obviate this means of curtailing the payment of incidents, title by descent was declared to be more worthy than title by purchase. If a gift over might pass to an heir by descent rather than by gift, he took his title through inheritance. Although the reason for the rule disappeared with the disappearance of feudal customs, the rule itself remained as part of the common law. Its effect was to deny the intent of the grantor and to cut out entirely the limitation to the heirs, thus accelerating the reversion which remained in the grantor. See Warren, A Remainder to the Grantor's Heirs, 22 Tex.L.Rev. 22; Matter of Brolasky's Estate, 302 Pa. 439, 153 A. 739. The doctrine was abolished in England in 1833 by a statute which allowed an heir to take title as purchaser where property passed to him by devise (3 & 4 Wm. IV, ch. 106, § 3). In this country the doctrine remained as part of the common law but has been principally applied where a limitation is made to heirs under an inter vivos conveyance. The intent of a grantor is said to be the controlling element and the common-law rule is not applied where the grantor clearly indicated his intention to grant a remainder to his heirs (3 Restatement, Property, § 314). Doctor v. Hughes, 225 N.Y. 305, 122 N.E. 221, supra, announced that such was the rule of this State. We said in that case, 225 N.Y. pages 311–312, 122 N.E. page 222: "in the absence of modifying statute, the rule persists to-day, at least as a rule of construction, if not as one of property. * * * We do not say that the ancient rule survives as an absolute prohibition limiting the power of a grantor. * * * There may be times, therefore, when a reference to the heirs of the grantor will be regarded as the gift of a remainder, and will vest title in the heirs presumptive as upon a gift to the heirs of others. * * * But at least the ancient rule survives to this extent: That, to transform into a remainder what would ordinarily be a reversion, the intention to work the transformation must be clearly expressed."

The use of the old doctrine as a rule of construction results in either (1) a shift from an absolute rule against remainders to heirs of grantors to a rule that the grantor must expressly indicate his intention to create a remainder in his heirs; or (2) a presumption in favor of reversions which may be rebutted by indication of the grantor's contrary intent gathered from the instrument as a whole. The practice adopted in the majority of States falls into the second classification. Some few States have entirely dispensed with the doctrine, allowing the gift of the grantor to take effect as a remainder. This has been accomplished by applying a statute abrogating some other ancient rule of property. For instance, a statute abrogating the rule in Shelley's case, 1 Coke Rep. 93b, 76 Eng.Rep. 206, has been said to apply to a situation involving the doctrine of worthier title. Gray v. Union Trust Co., 171 Cal. 637, 154 P. 306; Bixby v. California Trust

Co., Cal.App., 190 P.2d 321. In other States the doctrine has on occasion been rejected. Mills v. Mills, 275 Ky. 431, 121 S.W.2d 962; Kennedy v. Rutter, 110 Vt. 332, 6 A.2d 17; Norman v. Horton, 344 Mo. 290, 126 S.W.2d 187, 125 A.L.R. 531. It has been said that the doctrine is "more quaint than sensible" and has "no place under other than a feudal system" (Nossaman, Trust Administration and Taxation, § 303, p. 285). Under the proposed Uniform Property Act, not yet adopted by any State, the doctrine is completely dispensed with by providing that a conveyance to heirs or next of kin operates by purchase and not by descent (Proposed Uniform Property Act, § 15; 9 U.L.A. 613, 616).

It is clear from the cases in this State since Doctor v. Hughes, 225 N.Y. 305, 122 N.E. 221, supra, as admirably analyzed in Richardson v. Richardson, supra, that, despite the language in that opinion that a reversion exists unless there is clear evidence to the contrary, the rule has been less limited in application. Where a clear intent exists, there is no problem in construing the instrument, since the doctrine no longer exists as a rule of property. But where the grantor's intent is not expressed in unmistakable language, the rule comes into play. Then we look to the instrument for those indicia deemed significant in arriving at the intent of the grantor. In the first of the line of cases following Doctor v. Hughes, supra; Whittemore v. Equitable Trust Co. of New York, 250 N.Y. 298, 165 N.E. 454, we applied the rule of construction in the manner indicated in the second interpretation above. We discovered the intent of the grantor from other factors, as shown by the instrument, in order to give full effect to the words of limitation.

While we have not yet adopted a rule, either by statute or judicial construction, under which language limiting an interest to heirs is unequivocally given its full effect, the presumption which exists from the use of the common-law doctrine as a rule of construction has lost much of its force since Doctor v. Hughes, supra. Evidence of intent need not be overwhelming in order to allow the remainder to stand. Whether the rule should be abrogated completely is a matter for the Legislature.

The instant cases furnish sufficient additional indications of the settlor's intent to justify our giving effect to the language of the instrument limiting an estate to the grantor's heirs. Not the least among those indications was the reservation of a testamentary power of appointment as the sole control over the subsequent disposition of the corpus of the trust estate. We do not think that the reservation of a veto power over certain conveyances, as provided in the trust instrument in Matter of Burchell, was sufficient to give the settlor control over the trust property where the trustees otherwise had full power to invest and reinvest the trust funds. The fact that the trust agreement reserved a power of appointment is evidence that the settlor believed she had created an interest in the property on the part of others and reserved the power in order to defeat that interest or to postpone until a later date the naming of specific takers. Whittemore v. Equitable Trust Co. of New York, 250 N.Y. 298, 165 N.E. 454, supra; Engel v. Guaranty Trust Co. of New York, 280 N.Y. 43, 19 N.E.2d 673, supra; Sands v. Old Colony Trust Co., 195 Mass. 575, 81 N.E. 300, 12 Ann.Cas. 837; Fehr Brewing Co. v. Johnston, Ky., 97 S.W. 1107, 30 Ky.Law Rep. 211. Where we have held that a reversion was intended although a testamentary power of appointment was reserved, the instruments have provided that the trust principal would revert to the grantor upon some contingency. Berlenbach v. Chemical Bank & Trust Co., 235 App.Div. 170, 256 N.Y.S. 563, affirmed 260 N.Y. 539, 184 N.E. 83; City Bank Farmers Trust Co. v. Miller, 278 N.Y. 134, 15 N.E.2d 553, or that the grantor retained control over the principal. Guaranty Trust Co. of New York v. Armstrong, 294 N.Y. 666, 60 N.E.2d 757.

In analyzing an instrument and attempting to explore the almost ephemeral qualities which go to prove the necessary intent, many single factors may be considered. Some considered significant in one case may be deemed minimal in another, since their effect may be counteracted by the presence of other factors. It is impossible to set up absolute criteria to serve as a measuring standard for all cases. In the last analysis, the ultimate determination rests on the particular instrument under consideration, aided by the rule which has grown out of the old common-law doctrine and developed over a long line of cases as a rule which allows the language of the instrument creating a remainder to take effect provided some additional evidence pointing the intent of the grantor is present to buttress the language which would create the remainder.

The order in Matter of Burchell should be affirmed, with costs to all parties appearing separately and filing separate briefs, payable out of the fund; the judgment in Worm v. United States Trust Co. should be affirmed, without costs.

LOUGHRAN, C.J., and LEWIS, CONWAY, DESMOND and DYE, JJ., concur with BROMLEY, J.

FULD, J., dissents in opinion

Order and judgment affirmed.

FULD, JUDGE (dissenting). In each of these cases, the trust agreement provided, in essence, that the trustees to whom the property had been conveyed were to pay the income to the settlor for life, and that, upon her death, the principal was to be paid over by the trustees to such persons as the settlor might appoint by will, or, in default of such appointment, to the settlor's heirs at law and next of kin as in intestacy. In addition, in Matter of Burchell, the settlor reserved to herself the right and power to approve and join in the execution of any conveyance or mortgage of the property, of any lease for a period of more than three years or of the appointment of a successor trustee or trustees.

The rule has long been established that "to transform into a remainder what would ordinarily be a reversion, the intention to work the transformation must be clearly expressed." Doctor v. Hughes,

225 N.Y. 305, 312, 122 N.E. 221; see, also, Richardson v. Richardson, 298 N.Y. 135, 139, 81 N.E.2d 54, 56; Matter of Scholtz v. Central Hanover Bank & Trust Co., 295 N.Y. 488, 68 N.E.2d 503; City Bank Farmers Trust Co. v. Miller, 278 N.Y. 134, 15 N.E.2d 553.

Had the agreement not reserved to the settlor a power to appoint by will, no one would question or dispute that a reversion had been created. To find, in the retention of such a power—to appoint by will—the "clearly expressed" intention which is essential to transform a reversion into a remainder, impresses me as illogical and unreal. Even without such a reservation, the property would have passed, upon the settlor's death, to whomever she had designated by will or to her heirs and next of kin as upon intestacy, see e.g., City Bank Farmers Trust Co. v. Miller, supra, 278 N.Y. at page 145, 15 N.E.2d at page 555, the circumstance that the settlor specifically reserved a power to appoint a taker means, if it means anything, that she wanted to affirm and emphasize that she desired to retain control of her property up to the time of her death and to direct its devolution thereafter.

We carry form and the accident of language too far if we conclude that the insertion of such a power can accomplish the transformation of that reversion into a remainder. Certainly, nothing held or said in the Richardson case, 298 N.Y. 135, 81 N.E.2d 54, supra,—wherein the settlor had provided for an intervening contingent remainder in fee to her mother—requires that result. I cannot believe that the court ever meant, in listing the criteria that usually attend the creation of a remainder, 298 N.Y. at pages 140, 144, 81 N.E.2d at pages 56, 59, to express an inflexible rule or an inexorable juridical formula by the use of which we would be able to derive an automatic answer in all cases. Just as before the Richardson case, so today—unless the court by its present decision is overruling what has long been settled law—the interest created depends upon the intention of the settlor as expressed in the trust indenture as a whole. In my view, the language employed in the agreements before us plainly points a reversion: entirely lacking is any "clear expression" to justify changing it into a remainder. See Doctor v. Hughes, supra, 225 N.Y. at page 312, 122 N.E. at page 222.

Reversion or remainder, however, the volume of litigation on the subject, the diversity of opinion, not to mention the difficulty, frequently, of decision, point of advisability, if not the urgency, of clarifying legislation.

In my opinion, the determination in each case should be reversed.

NOTE [35]

How would the following provisions of McKinney's New York Estates, Powers and Trusts Law affect the result in Matter of Burchell?

35. For a comprehensive study see Johanson, "Reversions, Remainders and the Doctrine of Worthier Title," 45 Tex. L.Rev. 1 (1966); Verrall, "The Doctrine of Worthier Title: A Questionable Rule of Construction", 6 U.C.L.A.L.Rev. 371 (1959); Morris, "The Inter Vivos Branch of the Worthier Title Doctrine", 2 Okla.L.

"§ 6–5.9 Heirs or distributees of creator take as purchasers

"Where a remainder is limited to the heirs or distributees of the creator of an estate in property, such heirs or distributees take as purchasers."

"§ 7–1.9 Revocation of trusts

"(a) Upon the written consent, acknowledged or proved in the manner required by the laws of this state for the recording of a conveyance of real property, of all the persons beneficially interested in a trust of property, heretofore or hereafter created, the creator of such trust may revoke or amend the whole or any part thereof by an instrument in writing acknowledged or proved in like manner, and thereupon the estate of the trustee ceases. If the conveyance or other instrument creating a trust of property was recorded in the office of the clerk or register of any county of this state, the instrument revoking or amending such trust, together with the consents thereto, shall be recorded in the same office of every county in which the conveyance or other instrument creating such trust was recorded.

"(b) For the purposes of this section, a disposition, contained in a trust created on or after September first, nineteen hundred fifty-one, in favor of a class of persons described only as the heirs, next of kin or distributees (or by any term of like import) of the creator of the trust does not create a beneficial interest in such persons."

Recent legislation in as yet only a few states [36] is eliminating the impact of the Doctrine of Worthier Title.

Statutes intended to eliminate the doctrine are not always viewed sympathetically by the courts and may be narrowly construed. In Stewart v. Merchants National Bank of Aurora [37] the settlor established a ten year trust in 1967, retaining the beneficial interest for the term and the reversion in fee. The trust provided that upon the beneficiary's death during the term, or upon the exhaustion of principal and income during the term, the trust would terminate. If the beneficiary died during the term, after payment of claims, expenses and taxes the remainder was to be distributed pursuant to the settlor-beneficiary's will "or to the beneficiary's heirs-at-law in equal shares if the beneficiary leaves no valid will." The trust was expressly irrevocable

Rev. 133 (1949); Comments, "The Doctrine of Worthier Title in Arkansas", 21 Ark.L.Rev. 394 (1968); "The Doctrine of Worthier Title", 16 Baylor L.Rev. 429 (1964); "The Iowa Doctrine of Worthier Title—Why Perpetuate the Testamentary Branch", 66 Iowa L.Rev. 439 (1981); Note "The Doctrine of Worthier Title as a Rule of Construction in Illinois", 67 Nw.U.L.Rev. 773 (1973); American Law of Property (1952) § 4.19; 3 Powell, The Law of Real Property (Rohan Rev., 1975) p. 381; Simes and Smith, Future Interests (2d Ed., 1956) §§ 1601–1613; Restatement, Property (1940) § 314; 16 A.L.R.2d 691 (1951).

36. West's Ann.Cal.Civ.Code, § 1073 (1980 Supp.): "The law of this State does not include (1) the common law rule of worthier title that a grantor cannot convey an interest to his own heirs or (2) a presumption or rule of interpretation that a grantor does not intend, by a grant to his own heirs or next of kin, to transfer an interest to them. The meaning of a grant of legal or equitable interest to a grantor's own heirs or next of kin, however designated, shall be determined by the general rules applicable to the interpretation of grants. This section shall be applied in all cases in which final judgment has not been entered on its effective date."

The statute was enacted in 1959. Previously California followed a very strong preference for a reversion. Bixby v. California Trust Co., 33 Cal.2d 495, 202 P.2d 1018 (1949).

37. 3 Ill.App.3d 337, 278 N.E.2d 10 (1972); Noted, 87 Nw.U.L.Rev. 773 (1973).

and contained a spendthrift clause. After three years, the settlor-beneficiary desired to terminate the trust. The trial court held that contingent interests were created in the "heirs-at-law" so their consent would be required to revoke the trust. Since such heirs would include minors and perhaps unborn heirs, this consent could not be obtained. It was agreed that the settlor could terminate the trust if he had capacity and the full beneficial interest. On appeal, the settlor was permitted to terminate the trust, the Court applying May v. Marx, 300 Ill.App. 144, 20 N.E.2d 821 (1939) which antedates the Illinois Statute which attempts to abolish the Rule. The opinion reads in part: (278 N.E.2d 10, 13–14)

"* * * Appellee * * * [Merchants National Bank] * * * has objected strenuously to authorities such as the *May* case herein on the ground that they are merely applications of the now obsolete 'Doctrine of Worthier Title' which has been done away with by statute in Chap. 30, Sec. 188, Ill.Rev.Stat. (1955). We are aware that this statute provides that:

> 'Where a deed, will or other instrument purports to create any present or future interest in real *or personal* property in the heirs of the maker of the instrument, the heirs *shall take*, by purchase and not by descent.' (Emphasis supplied.)

Imperative as that language may seem, we refuse to believe that it would require a trust to be construed in such a way as to override the expressed intent of the maker of such an instrument. It is important to note that in the *May* case, supra, the court stated:

> 'The determination in each case depends on the intent of the settlor as disclosed in the language used in the instrument.'

And in our view, that court's determination of the settlor's intent was a correct interpretation thereof. * * *

"Having concluded that the *May* case is valid law, we next determine whether the trust in our case discloses an intent to dispose of the trust property similar to the disposition in *May*. The present trusts differs from *May* concerning the relevant language regarding 'heirs' only in that it provides the property shall pass to such heirs 'in equal shares.'

"In McKeown v. Pridmore, 310 Ill.App. 634, 35 N.E.2d 376 (1941) an extremely complicated case, some clarity was cast on this issue by way of a statement from Griswold on Spendthrift Trusts, appearing at page 653, 35 N.E.2d at page 384 of *McKeown:*

> 'The chief justification of spendthrift trusts should be found in the protection they furnish to the beneficiary. He cannot be protected if he has died, and the restraint should accordingly be allowed only during his lifetime. After his lifetime his property should be held liable for debts.'

This statement is applicable to the instant case. Since according to the trust instrument, appellant intended, if he died without a will, to pass his property to his heirs, this constituted, in our view, a general intention to keep the remaining corpus within his estate upon this contingency. This, we believe, means that he intended the trust to remain 'his property' to quote the language of *Griswold* above, a conclusion buttressed by the fact that considerable expenditures were contemplated under the trust for payment of expenses in the event of his death, and further under the trust he could designate such legatees he might desire. In our view, it would be unjust, merely by virtue of the fact that the heirs took equal shares rather than shares in accordance with the rules of intestacy, for that property not to 'be liable for his debts.' We therefore hold that the consent of the heirs would not be required to revoke this trust as the appellant did not intend to vest such an interest in them. * * *." [38]

If a settlor of a living trust provided that income would be reserved to the settlor for his life, thereafter to his wife for life, with principal to be paid to his heirs, would a statute like the following one nullify the doctrine of worthier title? [39]

> "When a remainder is limited to the heirs, or heirs of the body, of a person to whom a life estate in the same property is given, the persons who, on the termination of the life estate, are the successors or heirs of the body of the owner for life, are entitled to take by virtue of the remainder so limited to them, and not as mere successors of the owner for life."

The worthier title or "conveyor-heir" rule should apply only when the limitation is to the "heirs", "next of kin" or some other description referring to those persons who take the property on the death intestate of the conveyor. Suppose the limitation is to the "executors" of the conveyor or to his "estate." [40] Will such a description bring the doctrine into operation? Suppose the "heirs" are referred to as the heirs of the conveyor at the time of the conveyance? Will the doctrine then apply?

In Bottimore v. First & Merchants National Bank of Richmond,[41] the settlor created a living trust which was expressly made irrevocable; income was to be paid to the settlor during her life. Corpus was payable under the following clause: "Article IV. On the death of the Trustor the corpus and accumulated income, if any, of the Trust Fund shall pass as the Trustor shall direct by will, and, if the Trustor shall die intestate as to the Trust Fund, it shall be divided among her children who survive her and the lawful issue, *per stirpes*, of those children who predecease the Trustor leaving such issue who survive her, but the shares or parts of shares of all minor beneficiaries shall be held by the Trustee who shall expend on the several minor beneficiaries the net income and so much of the corpus of their respective shares or parts of shares as the Trustee in its absolute discretion shall deem necessary for their maintenance, support and/or education and/or for any emergency sufficient in the opinion of the Trustee to warrant such action, until each shall in turn reach the age of twenty-one years, when the corpus or so much as remains thereof shall be paid over outright and free of all trusts. The shares of any of the children of the Trustor who take under this Article but die before becoming twenty-one years of age, unmarried and without

38. See Note, "The Doctrine of Worthier Title as a Rule of Construction in Illinois", 67 Nw.U.L.Rev. 773 (1973) where the decision is criticized and alternative methods to handle the trust termination issue are suggested. Stewart the beneficiary had his attorney create the trust but the court held that Stewart was settlor since he had furnished the consideration for the trust, apparently money received in settlement of a personal injury action. The case and the worthier title doctrine are discussed in Browder, "Trusts and the Doctrine of Estates", 72 Mich.L.Rev. 1509, 1512–17 (1974). On the Illinois cases, see Schuyler, "Future Interests in Illinois: Current Maturities and Some Futures", 50 Nw.U.L.Rev. 457 (1955).

39. See Doctor v. Hughes, 225 N.Y. 305, 122 N.E. 221 (1919); EPTL § 6–5.9 set forth in full in the note above is intended to change the case law of Doctor v. Hughes.

40. See Browder, "Trusts and the Doctrine of Estates", 72 Mich.L.Rev. 1509, 1512–17 (1974); 10 A.L.R.3d 483 (1966).

41. 170 Va. 221, 196 S.E. 593 (1938). Virginia applies the conveyor-heir rule. Braswell v. Braswell, 195 Va. 971, 81 S.E.2d 560 (1954).

lawful issue, shall revert to the Trust Fund and pass under the terms of this agreement. If, however, there be a widow, or widower, and/or lawful issue surviving, the said shares shall pass according to the provisions of the Virginia Statutes for Descents and Distribution as then in effect. (Code 1936, § 5264 et seq.) If the Trustor shall die intestate and without leaving lawful issue who survive her, then whatever remains of the Trust Fund shall be equally divided among those sisters of the Grantor who survive her and the lawful issue, *per stirpes,* of those sisters who predecease her leaving lawful issue who survive her, absolutely and free of all trusts."

The settlor filed a bill in equity seeking revocation of the trust agreement and alleging that she had no children and that four sisters were the only persons now in being described in Article IV; and that the settlor was the sole beneficiary under the trust agreement and as such entitled to revocation. The trustee and the four sisters were made parties defendant; the sisters filed an answer consenting, in so far as their interests were concerned, to a revocation. The Supreme Court of Appeals of Virginia held that the settlor was entitled to revocation, on the grounds that no persons acquired any interest under Article IV but "merely an expectancy or possibility of an estate", and that the settlor had a reversion.

The doctrine of worthier title may create unexpected tax repercussions: a settlor may believe that he has divested himself of all interest in property, only to have a reversion under the doctrine.[42] For this reason some draftsmen expressly provide in the living trust, in an appropriate case, that the settlor reserves no right, title or interest or power over the trust. How would such a clause affect the doctrine?

SECTION 6. ALIENABILITY, DEVISABILITY AND DESCENDABILITY [43]

The English common law permitted alienation of reversions and vested remainders. On the other hand, the contingent remainder was not considered alienable, and the same rule was applied to executory interests. The objection was partly theoretical (the early notion that a contingent remainder was not an interest at all until the contingency took place) and partly practical (fear of profiteering and confusion of land titles). If this appears inconsistent with the basic policy of the common law favoring free alienability, it should be remembered that such contingent interests by their very nature were not really

42. See Beach v. Busey, 156 F.2d 496 (C.C.A.6th, 1946), cert. den. 329 U.S. 802, 67 S.Ct. 493, 91 L.Ed. 685 (1947).

Not only will the value of the reversionary interest be included in the settlor's estate under Internal Revenue Code § 2033, 26 U.S.C.A., under some circumstances but the existence of the reversion, if of substantial value, may result in including the value of the entire trust corpus in the settlor's taxable estate under § 2037; this is, however, a complex issue to be studied in your Tax Course.

43. On the problem of transferability of future interests generally see American Law of Property (1952) §§ 4.64–4.77; 2 Powell, The Law of Real Property (Rohan Rev., 1975) ¶¶ 280–284.

marketable anyway, and also that there were other devices available to achieve free alienation. The contingent remainder was destructible at common law; it could also be released to the person whose interest would be divested if the contingency occurred.

The majority rule today is that a future interest may be transferred even if contingent. In some states this is the result of express legislation, such as Section 6–5.1 of McKinney's New York Estates, Powers and Trusts Law, which reads:

> "Future estates are descendible, devisable and alienable, in the same manner as estates in possession."

In still other states more generally worded statutes have been construed to include contingent future interests.[44] Such statutes exist in almost three-fourths of the states.

In the remaining jurisdictions, the same result has been reached by judicial decision, and the Restatement takes the position that contingent interests are alienable.[45] In a few states, the old rule prevails,[46] although the number is diminishing.[47] Even in those states, the same objective can be obtained by proper conveyancing techniques.[48] Just as "estoppel" may operate to pass title where the grantor has no interest at all, but later acquires it, so a warranty deed by the person holding a contingent interest may estop him if the contingency occurs. Again, even the expectant heir, who has no interest at all, may make a valid and specifically enforceable contract to convey for an adequate consideration; similarly the holder of a contingent interest may for a valuable consideration contract to convey, and his deed may in equity be treated as such a contract. It is also possible for a court to achieve the same result by construing doubtful limitations as being vested subject to divestment, rather than contingent.

One objection to the modern rule is that it operates to defeat the intent of the creator of the interest, who normally wants a particular person to have the interest. As a practical matter, the seeming freedom of the present law may be avoided by (1) greater care in spelling out the persons who are to take at time of distribution of trust principal, and (2) inserting a spendthrift clause restraining alienation by the trust beneficiary, which as we have seen is valid (in some states even as to a restraint on the interest of the principal beneficiary).

44. For example, Section 442.020 RSMo (1980), V.A.M.S. (1980 Supp.) reads: "Conveyances of lands, or of any estate or interest therein, may be made by deed * * *." This has been construed to include contingent future interests. Grimes v. Rush, 355 Mo. 573, 197 S.W.2d 310 (1946).

45. Restatement, Property (1936) § 162.

46. Some states have gone part way by recognizing as alienable a future interest contingent as to event, although not when contingent as to person—a rather fine distinction. This has been enacted into statute in New Jersey. N.J.S.A. 46:3–7 (West Supp. 1981).

47. E.g., New Hampshire abandoned the rule in 1953; see Merchants National Bank v. Curtis, 98 N.H. 225, 97 A.2d 207 (1953).

48. Illinois clings to the old rule; the intricacies of local conveyancing statutes in achieving a transfer despite the rule are considered in Carey and Schuyler, Illinois Law of Future Interests (1949) §§ 62, 63.

There is greater diversity in holdings on the transferability of possibilities of reverter and of the rights of entry for condition broken (power of termination).[49] The right of entry has been considered personal and not transferable unless it is incident to a reversion, in which case it can be alienated with the reversion. Statutes may make the right of entry alienable.[50] Some courts have held that a right of entry is forfeited for attempted alienation,[51] although the American Law Institute takes the position that the right of entry is not forfeited when the owner attempts to alienate it.[52] Possibilities of reverter are generally considered alienable either by judicial decision or by statute.[53] This more liberal position concerning the possibility of reverter may be due to its similarity to a reversion.

A right of entry may be released to the person owning the interest subject to the right,[54] the general rule being that any future interest can be released to the owner of the interest to be divested if the contingency occurs.

Today, with very minor exceptions, one can say that all future interests pass on death in the same manner as possessory interests and that they are devisable. Historically, however, the doctrine of seisin required that a taker by descent had to be an heir of the person last seised. If A conveyed to B for life and then predeceased B, leaving a son C as his heir, C had an incomplete interest until B's death. If C died before B, the taker of the reversion would have to qualify not as C's heir but as A's heir. C was said to "represent" A. This was subject to the important qualification that C might convey or devise the interest (the reversion in our example being alienable). This notion of representation survives in a few jurisdictions as to possibilities of reverter and rights of entry only. At least one court has held that a right of entry is descendible while stating in dictum that the right of entry was not devisable or alienable inter vivos.[55]

49. American Law of Property (1952) §§ 4.68–4.70; 2 Powell, The Law of Real Property (Rohan Rev. 1977) ¶¶ 281, 282.

50. E.g., New York, Estates, Powers and Trusts Law, §§ 6–3.2(a)(1)(C); 6–4.6; 6–5.1 (1980 Supp.). See Pasley "Future Interests", 17 Syra.L.Rev. 257, 260–261 (1965).

51. The leading case is Rice v. Boston & Worcester R. R., 12 Mass. (Allen) 141 (1866).

52. Restatement, Property (1936) § 160 (1948 Supp.). The earlier position of the American Law Institute supported forfeiture upon attempted transfer except in special cases set forth in § 161.

53. Simes and Smith, Future Interests (2d Ed. 1956) § 1860. See Dunham, "Possibility of Reverter and Powers of Termination—Fraternal or Identical Twins?" 20 U.Chi.L.Rev. 215 (1953).

54. See Simes and Smith, Future Interests (2d Ed., 1956) § 1862.

55. Polette v. Williams, 456 S.W.2d 328 (Mo.1970). See Fratcher, "Exorcise the Curse of Reversionary Possibilities", 28 Jour.Mo.Bar 34 (1972); Note, "Classification of Reversionary Possibilities", 37 Mo.L.Rev. 94 (1972). The Rule Against Perpetuities will not apply to interests retained in the grantor unless the Rule is extended to these interests by statute or unless the Common Law Rule is altered radically by judicial decision. Thus, to prevent possibilities of reverter and rights of entry from becoming clogs on alienation some states have imposed time limits on the duration of the interests. See Hiddleston v. Nebraska Jewish Education Society, 186 Neb. 786, 186 N.W.2d 904 (1971) where such a statute was held constitutional as applied to preexisting interests. The case is noted in 5 Creighton L.Rev. 140 (1971) and 38 Mo.L.Rev. 140 (1973). See Fratcher, "A Modest Proposal for Trimming the Claws of Legal Future Interests", (1972) Duke L.J. 517. For special local treatments see

When a future interest is purportedly created inter vivos (as in a living trust beneficial interest) or when it is created by will, and when an existing future interest passes from the owner thereof by intestate succession, the designated taker of the future interest may renounce or disclaim the interest. Disclaimer is distinguishable from "release" and this distinction has important tax ramifications.[56] In a "release" the owner of the future interest has accepted it and is releasing it (actually transferring it) to the holder of the interest which might be defeased. If the release is without adequate consideration in money or money's worth, the transfer may be gift taxable under the unified rate schedule.[57] If the person to whom the future interest purportedly is transferred has not accepted the interest, he is permitted to disclaim for Federal tax purposes. The disclaimer must be in writing and received by the transferor, his legal representative or the holder of the legal title to which the interest relates, not later than nine months after the date of the transfer or the date the purported transferee attains twenty-one.[58] For state tax and property matters, the effect of the disclaimer depends upon state law, the state law usually being that if the disclaimed interest passes by will, the disclaimer relates back to the death of the testator, whereas if the interest passes by intestate succession, the disclaimant retransfers the property, this transfer being gift taxable and possibly estate taxable.[59] Some states have statutes permitting the disclaimer to "relate back" in either situation and there are uniform laws available for state adoption which have this effect.[60]

While there seems to be general agreement for state law purposes that the time for disclaimer should not run until the disclaimant has knowledge or should have had knowledge of his interest, there is a persuasive argument that he should not have to decide whether to disclaim until his interest vests in interest. The Uniform Probate Code deals with this problem, Section 2–801(b)(2) stating: "An instrument renouncing a future interest may be filed not later than [9]

Carter, "Recent Developments Relating to Devolution and Descent of Future Interests in Maryland", 11 Md.L.Rev. 187 (1950); Core, "Transmissibility of Certain Future Interests", 5 Ark.L.Rev. 111 (1951); Chaffin, "Descendible Future Interests In Georgia: The Effect of Preference for Early Vesting", 7 Ga.L.Rev. 443 (1973); Hancock, "Descendibility of Remainder Interests in New York", 36 Corn.L.Q. 97 (1950); Reno, "Alienability and Transmissibility of Future Interests in Maryland", 2 Md.L.Rev. 89 (1938); "Further Developments as to the Alienability and Transmissibility of Future Interests in Maryland", 15 Md.L.Rev. 193 (1955); Comment, "Transmissibility of Future Interests in Pennsylvania", 42 Dick.L.Rev. 92 (1938); Note, "Inheritability of Possibilities of Reverter and Rights of Entry", 37 Va.L.Rev. 123 (1951).

56. Lentz, "Income and Gift Tax Effect of Renunciation of a Bequest or Inheritance", 21 N.Y. Inst. on Federal Taxation 313 (1963).

57. IRC §§ 2001, 2502(a), 26 U.S.C.A., as amended P.L. 94–455, § 2001 (1976), P.L. 97–34 § 402 (1981).

58. IRC §§ 2518, 2045, 26 U.S.C.A., added P.L. 94–455 § 2009 (1976), amended P.L. 95–600 § 702(m)(1) (1978), P.L. 97–34 § 426 (1981).

59. See Chapter III, Sec. 4(3) supra, note to Coomes v. Finegan, 233 Iowa 448, 7 N.W.2d 729 (1943), where the disclaimer rules are discussed fully.

60. Uniform Probate Code (1977 text) § 2–801; Uniform Disclaimer of Property Interests (1973) (8 U.L.A. pocket part, p. 12); Uniform Disclaimer of Transfer by Will, Intestacy or Appointment (1973) (8 U.L.A. pocket part, p. 18); Uniform Disclaimer of Transfers Under Nontestamentary Instrument (1973) (8 U.L.A. pocket part, p. 23).

months after the event determining that the taker of the property or interest is finally ascertained and his interest is indefeasibly vested". There is no comparable provision for future interests in the Federal law.

Of course, the nature of the future interest, and of any contingency upon which it is limited, qualifies its transferability inter vivos or at death. Assume a conveyance to A for life, remainder to B and his heirs if he survives A, but if B does not survive A, then to the children of B living at the death of A. During the lifetime of A, B can convey his interest to C. However, if B subsequently predeceases A, C's contingent interest fails. Nor could B devise his remainder during the lifetime of A. The ability of the creator of an equitable future interest to impose express restraints upon the power of the beneficiary to convey has been discussed in Chapter VIII, Section 5. To the extent that the modern trust instrument expressly requires survival to the time of distribution and contains valid spendthrift provisions, the issue of transferability is thus eliminated.

Chapter XIV

POWERS OF APPOINTMENT

Scope Note

The scope of this Chapter is determined largely by professional usage of the term "power of appointment". It does not include powers relating to administration of an estate, such as the power of sale given to an executor or trustee, or the power of a beneficiary of a trust to appoint successor trustees. However, some of these administrative powers may, in substance if not in form, come close to being powers of appointment. For example, a trustee who has discretion to augment payments of income out of principal or who has discretion to pay to any of several beneficiaries is in a position to determine the persons who will take property, or the amount which they will take. The power of revocation reserved to the settlor is also excluded from this chapter, although it may have the same practical effect as reservation of a general power of appointment.

The historical background, the modern classification, the influence of statutes and taxation factors are briefly explored in Section 1. When has the donee manifested sufficiently his intention to exercise the power? What sort of appointments can he make, and to whom? Can he release the power or make a contract to exercise it in favor of a particular person? Do the creditors of the donee have any rights in property over which he has a power of appointment? Who will take the property if the power is not exercised? These are explored in the remaining Sections of the Chapter. The application of the Rule against Perpetuities to powers of appointment is postponed to Chapter XVI.

SECTION 1. NATURE AND CLASSIFICATION OF POWERS

---

(1) BACKGROUND INFORMATION

The power of appointment originated prior to the Statute of Wills of 1540. To avoid the general rule of the law courts that land could not be devised, it became common practice to make a feoffment to the use of the feoffor for life and then to such uses as he might designate by his will; equity recognized and enforced the uses which he then appointed. The will was thought of as operating not to pass the land but merely to point out the persons who would have the use under the original feoffment. Essentially the will was merely an event upon which the use shifted to the designated persons. Apparently it was believed that the Statute of Uses blocked this method, for popular pressure resulted in the enactment of the Statute of Wills of 1540. However, draftsmen found new functions for the old concept. For example, in order to afford a married woman power to convey or will when under common law as owner she would have no such legal capacity, it was possible to give her a power to appoint by deed or will. To a very limited extent the power may still be employed by draftsmen to avoid legal rules; e.g., to avoid marital rights of a wife. Early in the twentieth century the concept afforded a large loophole in estate and inheritance taxes, and even today tax considerations are an important factor in the creation of powers.

The modern significance of the power of appointment lies primarily in the flexibility which it affords to an estate plan.[1] For example, assume a devise to the testator's wife for life, remainder in equal shares to their children. This plan may be excellently conceived in the light of facts at the time the will was drafted, but may not be what the testator would want if later events leave one of the children in dire need while the others have gained independent wealth. Now revise the plan by inserting a simple power of appointment: to the wife for life, at her death to such one or more of the children as she shall appoint by her will, and if she makes no appointment, then in equal shares to the children. Here we have basically the same plan, but the testator is relying on his wife to make decisions for him in the light of developments after his death. One incidental benefit of this scheme, of course, is that the children will be more mindful of their treatment of the widow in her old age. Or the testator may have such a large estate and such complete confidence in his wife's decisions that he will broaden the power given her: "to my wife for life, at her death to such person or persons as she shall appoint by her

1. For discussions of the use of powers of appointment in estate planning see Allen, "How to Achieve the Greatest Benefits From Powers of Appointment in Estate Planning," 26 Jour. of Taxation 306 (1967); "Use of Trusts and Powers of Appointment in Estate Planning", 21 Ark.L.Rev. 15 (1967); Bolich, "The Power of Appointment: Tool of Estate Planning and Drafting" 1964 Duke L.J. 32; Casner, "Legal Life Estates and Powers of Appointment Coupled with Life Estates and Trusts", 45 Neb.L.Rev. 342 (1966); Coleman, "The Special Power of Appointment in Estate Planning", 109 Trusts and Estates 920 (1970); Fratcher, "Powers of Appointment to Unspecified Charities", 32 Mo.L.Rev. 443 (1967); Lenoir and Messinger, "Powers of Appointment", 8 Ariz.L.Rev. 276 (1967); Lowndes, "Tax Consequences of Limitations Upon the Exercise of Powers", 1966 Duke L.J. 959 (1966); Jones, "The Rule Against Perpetuities and Powers of Appointment: An Old Controversy Revived" 54 Iowa L.Rev. 456 (1968); Rusoff, "Powers of Appointment and Estate Planning", 10 Jour.Fam.Law 443 (1971); Wormser, "Powers of Appointment—Special Uses, Problems and Pitfalls", 7 Inst. Estate Planning, Ch. 73–16 (1973); "Use and Drafting of Powers of Appointment" 1 Real Prop.Prob. & T.L.J. 307 (1966); Comment, "Power of Appointment in Alabama: A Plea for Reform", 26 Ala.L.Rev. 355 (1974); Note, "Life Estate with Power of Appointment: An Exception to the Terminable Interest Rule" 17 West.Res.L.Rev. 863 (1966); Halbach, "Powers of Distribution, Invasion and Appointment", 32 So.Calif. Tax Inst. 14 (1980).

will, but if she makes no appointment, then to our children in equal shares." Then if she wishes to appoint the property out of the family, e.g. to charity, she may do so; or she may make the appointment within the family as seems desirable; or she may refrain from any appointment and let the property go according to the original plan.

In the above examples, the creator of the power would be called the "donor"; the person having the power the "donee"; and the provision for disposition in event the power is not exercised a "gift in default of appointment" (the persons would be "takers in default"). The persons in favor of whom the power may be exercised (such as the children) are referred to as the "permissible appointees" or "objects" of the power. The property which can be appointed under the power is often referred to as the "appointive assets", or the "property covered by the power".

(2) MODERN CLASSIFICATION

The most useful classification of powers of appointment is made with respect to (a) the time when the power is exercisable and (b) the scope of permissible appointment under the power.[2] In the examples heretofore given the donee was empowered to appoint by will only; these are testamentary powers. Had the donee been given power to appoint by deed, the power would have been presently exercisable. In our first example, where the wife was given a power to appoint among the children—a limited group of persons which did not include her or her estate, the power is special. In the second example, where the wife could appoint to anyone including her creditors and her estate, the power was general. The line between these is frequently stated in terms of the ability of the donee to appoint to himself or his estate. However, the special power is usually confined to a still narrower group, typically a class such as "children" or "issue". A power to appoint "to any person except the donee or his creditors" is a

2. Historically a cumbersome classification grew up in England, for reasons now outmoded. Since this terminology is sometimes encountered in the case law relating to release, it is given here for reference purposes. Where the donee of the power had no other interest in the property, the power was "collateral" (to B for life, remainder as C shall appoint). Where the donee has an interest, with power to appoint another interest, the power was "in gross" (to B for life, remainder as B shall appoint). A third type of power, called "appendant", arose where the power operated to divest the estate of the donee (to A in fee simple, with power to appoint by deed or will). In England such a power was used after the Statute of Wills in order to effect a testamentary transfer of all land held in knight's service, although under the Statute of Wills one-third of such land could not be devised. Sir Edward Clere's Case, 6 Co.Rep. 17b, 77 Eng.Rep. 279 (K.B. 1599). American courts do not recognize such a power appendant, the fee simple obviously encompassing the power itself. Browning v. Blue Grass Hardware Co., 153 Va. 20, 149 S.E. 497 (1929); Restatement, Property (1940) § 325.

hybrid; the Restatement of Property does not recognize this as either general or special.[3]

In the case of the special power one additional differentiation is made. The special power may be so drafted that the donee must appoint some share to each object if the donee exercises the power at all. An example would be a gift of a remainder "to my children in such shares as my wife may appoint". Such a power is called non-exclusive. Or the special power may be drafted to empower the donee to appoint to one or more of the objects, as in a gift of the remainder "to such one or more of my children, and in such amounts, as my wife may appoint". The latter would be an exclusive power.

As we have seen, the early English law treated the exercise of the power as merely an event upon which the interest shifted to the appointees. The power itself was not an interest in the property. Once the donee exercised the power by appointing, the appointees took directly from the donor. It was almost as though the donee were an agent acting for the donor. Suppose A devised land to B for life, remainder as B should appoint by will. B subsequently dies, having executed a will reading: "I hereby exercise the power given me by the will of A by appointing to C for life, remainder to D." This limitation would be "read back" into A's will, as though A had directly devised to B for life, then to C for life, remainder to D.

The present American law is based in part on a logical development of this technical concept of the power, and in part on a realistic approach to general and special powers. The donee of a general power of appointment is in a position tantamount to ownership. If the power is presently exercisable, he can appoint to himself and make himself the owner. Even if the general power is testamentary, the donee can appoint to his estate or to his creditors. On the other hand the donee of a special power is more like a trustee. He is to act not for his own benefit but for the benefit of the objects of the power. However, strictly speaking, the donee is not a trustee. He does not have legal title or any of the management functions of the trustee. The trust is merely an analogy, useful but not controlling. As we shall see in Section 5, there is a difference of opinion whether a special power which the donor has directed the donee to exercise ought to be treated as a power "in trust".

Throughout this chapter, we shall see illustrations of the conflict between logical application of the traditional concept of the power to appoint and the modern approach based on the analogies of the general power to ownership and of the special power to a trust. In many areas the traditional concept prevails because of long-standing precedent. In others it has given way by force of judicial opinion or statute. We shall meet the same conflict in Chapter XVI in applying the Rule against Perpetuities to limitations created by exercise of powers of appointment.

3. Restatement, Property (1940) § 320, Comment *a*.

In Chapter XVII we shall consider the liability of a trustee for breach of trust when he acts with the consent of the beneficiaries. One of the problems which the trustee encounters if he finds it necessary to take action which might be construed as a breach of trust is that of obtaining consent when potential beneficiaries of the trust are unborn. This frequently will be the case when the principal is to go to the surviving issue of an income beneficiary. Can the trustee act if he has the consent of the income beneficiary who also has a general power of appointment? Such a beneficiary can appoint to himself and thus defeat the interests of any unborn takers. The trustee would argue that a beneficiary, having such power, should be able to consent for the takers in default. Uniform Probate Code, § 1–108 permits the holder of a presently exercisable general power, including one in the form of a power of amendment or revocation, to act for beneficiaries whose interests are subject to the power in consenting to a modification of the trust or a termination or deviation from its terms.

PROBLEMS

The following problems are intended to illustrate some of the areas in which the traditional concept of the power of appointment has prevailed:

1. X devises land to a son A for life, remainder to such person or persons as A may appoint by deed or will, in default of appointment to A's heirs. The Rule in Shelley's Case is not in force in the jurisdiction. A appoints by will to one of his children. Can A's widow elect to take against the will and claim a statutory share of the appointed land? Kate's Estate, 282 Pa. 417, 128 A. 97 (1925); Restatement, Property (1940) § 332. What result under Uniform Probate Code, § 2–202 set forth in Chapter IV, Section 2(5) fn. 31 supra? See Mahoney, "Elective Share Statutes: The Right to Elect Against Property Subject to a General Power of Appointment in the Decedent", 55 Notre Dame Law 99 (1979).

2. X establishes an inter vivos trust to pay the income to himself for life, at his death to distribute the principal to such person or persons as he shall appoint by will, in default of appointment to his issue. X makes an appointment to B by his will. Are the appointive assets part of X's estate so as to be subject to fees of the executor and other probate expenses? Nicols v. Estate of Nicols, 181 Md. 582, 31 A.2d 326 (1943).

3. X establishes a trust for his wife for life, then to convey the trust property to such person or persons as she may appoint by her will. The wife appoints by her will in favor of her sister. Is the appointment subject to a state inheritance tax which does not expressly tax exercise of powers of appointment but imposes a tax on property passing by the will of the decedent? Emmons v. Shaw, 171 Mass. 410, 50 N.E. 1033 (1898). See American Law of Property (1952) § 23.24; 3 Powell, The Law of Real Property, (Rohan Rev.1977) ¶ 392; Restatement, Property (1940) § 333. About half of the states have adopted legislation expressly taxing the exercise and non-exercise of powers of appointment in the estate of the donee.

(3) STATUTES GOVERNING POWERS

The statutory ingredient in the American Law of Powers is not substantial. The New York Revised Statutes of 1830 contained an elaborate chapter on powers, which was copied in 7 states in whole or in part.[4] The chapter on powers was prepared against the English background of powers with its cumbersome and confusing classification. The Revisers attempted a new classification, which encompassed not only powers of appointment but also powers of revocation and administrative powers of executors and trustees. California repealed its chapter almost as soon as it had been enacted; Minnesota followed suit in 1943. New York [5] and Wisconsin [6] adopted completely new versions of their chapters effective in 1965. Michigan also revised its chapter on powers in 1967; and California in 1969 enacted a chapter similar to New York's.[7] In the last five states there are statutory provisions on much of the law of powers but the balance is left to the common law.

On several specific problems, notably that of manifestation of intent to exercise the power (considered in Section 2(1) of this Chapter) and the problem of release (taken up in Section 3), there is more widespread legislation.

Whether the growing litigation resulting from increased use of powers will produce satisfactory results or whether other states will feel the need to enact comprehensive legislation in the field of powers remains to be seen.

(4) TAXATION FACTORS

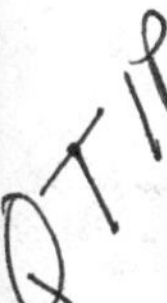

Prior to 1982, the federal gift and estate tax laws stimulated the creation of general powers of appointment by a property owner in the surviving spouse. A general power, as described in IRC §§ 2056 and 2523, was necessary to obtain the marital deduction if the spouse was to have a life estate. But beginning in 1982, two life estate dispositions will qualify for the marital deduction without the use of general powers. In the qualified terminable interest property transfer

4. E.g., N.D.Cent.Code, ch. 59–05 (1975 Supp.). See Rarick and Henry "Oklahoma Powers of Appointment Act of 1977", 32 Okla.L.Rev. 787 (1979).

5. McKinney's N.Y. EPTL, art. 10 (1980 Supp.). See Powell, "The New Powers of Appointment Act", 103 Trusts and Estates 807 (1964); Comment, "Powers of Appointment—The New York Revision", 65 Col.L.Rev. 1289 (1965).

6. Wis.Stat.Ann. Ch. 702 (former Ch. 232). See Effland, "Powers of Appointment—The New Wisconsin Law," 1967 Wis.L.Rev. 583 (1967).

7. Calif.Civil Code, §§ 1380–1392.1 (1971); Mich.Comp.Laws, §§ 556.111–556.133 (1981 Supp.).

(QTIP) the deduction can be obtained if the spouse has only a life estate without a power if the spouse is entitled to all of the income payable at least annually and the executor elects the deduction. The spouse can have a general power exercisable at the spouse's death (a testamentary power). But no one can have a power to appoint any part of the property to any person other than the spouse, although such a power could be conferred to appoint the property at or after the spouse's death. The marital deduction also can be obtained if the spouse is the only noncharitable beneficiary of a charitable remainder annuity trust or unitrust. In neither of these trusts could a power be conferred upon the spouse or anyone else to appoint the property. Both the QTIP transaction and the life interest in the charitable remainder trust have been discussed in Chapter VIII, Section 2. The life interest in the spouse, coupled with the general power, will be used after 1981 but probably not with the frequency as before. When the general power is presently exercisable, additional flexibility is injected into the plan since the spouse can appoint the principal during his or her lifetime if this appears desirable. This same opportunity is presented when the transfer is made to the spouse in fee simple; and it is possible that after 1981 in estates which do not exceed the exemption equivalent ($600,000 by 1987) many estates of this size or smaller will be transferred in this manner.

Tax laws will have a great impact on the types of powers employed by draftsmen to obtain flexibility in estate plans. In enacting tax statutes, legislators tend to ignore property technicalities to get at economic realities. Hence they frequently impose a tax on the transmission of property subject to a general power of appointment by the donee just as if the donee owned the property and the appointive assets passed to the appointee or taker in default from the donee and not from the donor of the power. Currently, a general power is defined in the Internal Revenue Code as one in which the donee can appoint to himself or herself, his or her creditors, his or her estate or the creditors of his of her estate.[8] Such a power created on or before 21 October 1942 (when it also was defined with minor differences) is not taxed unless it is exercised.[9] If the power is created after 21 October 1942, the property subject to the power is included in the gross estate of the donee whether it is exercised or not.[10] The exercise of a power created on or before 21 October 1942 is also subject to gift taxation but the release of it is not.[11] On the other hand, the release of a "post 1942" power is subject to gift taxation; [12] but the power can be disclaimed within nine months from the time it was conferred upon the donee without adverse tax consequences to the donee.[13]

8. IRC §§ 2041(b)(1), 2514(c), 26 U.S.C.A.

9. IRC §§ 2041(a)(1), 2514(a), 26 U.S.C.A.

10. IRC § 2041(a)(2)(3), 26 U.S.C.A.

11. IRC § 2514(a), 26 U.S.C.A.

12. IRC § 2514(b), 26 U.S.C.A.

13. IRC § 2518, 26 U.S.C.A., added P.L. 94–455, § 2009 (1976), amended 95–600, Title VII, § 702(m)(1) (1978), P.L. 97–34, § 426 (1981).

Powers not meeting the definition of "general" power in the federal gift and estate tax laws escape these taxes; but a "special" power not limited to the lineal descendants of the grantor may be the basis of a generation skipping tax under the federal law. Some states also tax property subject to special powers.

SECTION 2. EXERCISE OF THE POWER OF APPOINTMENT

(1) THE INTENT TO EXERCISE THE POWER

The materials in this section deal with problems frequently met in practice concerning the exercise of powers of appointment. The first issue is whether the donee intended to exercise his power. The donee should clearly indicate his intent to exercise any power conferred upon him which he intends to exercise. If he intends not to execute a power, he should make that intention clear. Thus, if he has a general testamentary power and after careful consideration of tax and other consequences has decided to exercise the power, the donee's will may be drafted to read: "I have a power of appointment under the will of my father [naming him] dated August 1, 1972. It is my intention by this will to exercise the said power, and I hereby appoint as follows * * *."

A blanket clause purporting to exercise all powers is sometimes inserted in the donee's will. The following is an example: "By this will, I intend to dispose of all property which I may own at my death or over which I have any power of appointment." Such a clause is a dangerous one unless the draftsman knows with precision the powers which the donee holds. For example, if he holds a special power, he might appoint outside the class to which the power is limited. If his power is general and created on or before 21 October 1942, he might bring the property subject to the power within his gross estate for federal estate tax purposes. Such a clause, however, would make the intent of the donee to exercise his powers amply clear. The cases which follow deal with situations when there is no such express declaration.

If the power has been exercised, can the donor later revoke his exercise of the power? He could certainly revoke a will containing an exercise of the power—and after his death the exercise would be irrevocable if the will containing the exercise was effective at the donee's death. But what of a power exercised inter vivos? Can such an exercise be revoked and the power be exercised again?

In deciding whether to exercise the power or not, a great many factors must be weighed. One of the most important of these, tax impact or possible tax savings, is left to the course in Taxation.

Others will appear as you become familiar with the materials which follow. Who will take the property if the power is not exercised? Can litigation to determine who will take in default be eliminated by a careful exercise of the power? Can the donee, within the scope of his power, make the type of appointment he desires? Will he subject the property to claims of his own creditors if he exercises the power?

BANK OF NEW YORK v. BLACK

Supreme Court of New Jersey, 1958.
26 N.J. 276, 139 A.2d 393.

WACHENFELD, J. As testamentary trustee under the will of William Byrd, deceased, the Bank of New York brought this action principally for the purpose of having the court determine to whom it should distribute some $334,000 in trust funds now that the trust in question has expired. Various relatives of the settlor, William Byrd, and his wife, Julia Byrd, were joined as parties-defendant.

The Chancery Division of the Superior Court decided Julia Byrd did not intend, by her last testament, to exercise the general testamentary power of appointment which she had over the subject personalty and, further, that the fund now constituted intestate property which should be equally divided among William Byrd, Jr., Lucy Carter Bredin and the estate of Julia Byrd.

Mary Martin Black appealed and Anne Syfret and Mark Bredin cross-appealed. On our own motion, we granted certification to the Appellate Division.

William Byrd died on August 6, 1952 while domiciled in Short Hills, New Jersey. His will was admitted to probate in the Essex County Surrogate's Court on August 19, 1952, and letters of trusteeship were issued thereunder to the plaintiff Bank of New York. The testator left surviving his wife, two children (William Byrd, Jr., and Lucy Carter Bredin), two grandchildren (Anne Syfret and Mark Bredin), and his stepdaughter (Mary Martin Black).

The residuary clause of William Byrd's will provided:

> "Eleventh: I give, devise and bequeath all the rest, residue and remainder of my estate, real and personal and wherever situated as follows:
>
> "If my wife, Julia Kingsbury Byrd shall survive me, one third thereof to Bank of New York and Fifth Avenue Bank, a corporation of New York, having its principal office at 48 Wall Street, New York City, duly qualified to act in the State of New Jersey, In Trust to invest and reinvest the same and to pay the net income thereof to my wife so long as she shall live and upon her death to pay the principal as my wife shall appoint by her last Will and Testament. In the event that my wife shall die before me I give, devise and bequeath said one third share absolutely to my step-

daughter Mary Martin Black. If both my wife and Mary Martin Black die before me, I give such share to my issue per stirpes. I give to my wife, if she shall survive me, full power and authority to withdraw the whole or any part of the capital of said trust during her lifetime and to use the same for her own benefit.

"One third thereof to my son William Byrd, Jr., absolutely and forever. If my said son shall die before me I give his share to his issue me surviving per stirpes.

"One third thereof in equal shares to my daughter Lucy Carter Bredin of 21 Camden Crescent, Bath, England, my granddaughter Anne Syfret of Wolverley near Kidderminster, Worcestershire, England, and my grandson Mark Bredin. If my said grandson has not attained the age of twenty-five years at the time of my death I direct my Executors to pay him the income of his share until he attains that age and then to pay him the principal. If my said daughter or either of my said grandchildren shall die before me, I give, devise and bequeath the share of the one so dying to her or his issue me surviving per stirpes, and in default of such issue to the survivor or survivors of them."

Julia Byrd died on January 10, 1956 while domiciled at Mary Martin Black's home in Warrenton, Virginia. Mrs. Black is Mrs. Byrd's daughter by a marriage antedating her union with William Byrd in 1941. The last will and testament of Mrs. Byrd was admitted to probate by the Circuit Court of Fauquier County, Virginia. It did not by exact and specific words exercise the general testamentary power of appointment which Mrs. Byrd had over the trust fund established by William Byrd's will, and thus is provoked the present controversy among the defendants over who is entitled to the trust principal now that the trust itself has terminated.

Mrs. Byrd's will was drawn by a Virginia practitioner two months after her husband's demise. It is short and in so far as relevant provides:

"Second: I give, bequeath and devise all of my estate, both real and personal, or mixed, wheresoever situated, whether in being or in expectancy, to my daughter Mary Martin Black of Warrenton, Virginia. Should my said daughter Mary Martin Black predecease me, I give, bequeath and devise all of my estate, both real and personal and mixed, in equal share to my grandsons, namely Josiah Macy, Jr., Archer Martin Macy, and Noel Everit Macy, and I hereby request said grandsons to equally share the responsibility of the care and maintenance of Aubrey Henry Martin, Jr."

Aubrey Henry Martin, Jr., is another grandson of Mrs. Byrd's. William Byrd, Jr., Lucy Carter Bredin, Anne Syfret, Mark Bredin and Mary Martin Black all survive the testatrix.

During the course of this litigation, the defendants have made various concessions and reached certain accommodations respecting the principles of law which they deem relevant to their claims. A brief résumé of these will serve to illuminate the import of the parties' several contentions.

Initially, we are not confronted with the necessity to resolve any problems in conflict of laws because defendants agreed in the trial court that New Jersey law should completely govern the disposition of this case. During oral argument we requested the respective attorneys to submit authorities on the question of whether the existence of an intent to execute the power should be gauged by Virginia or New Jersey law, but in reaching our decision we abide by the parties' original understanding that New Jersey law applies. It is conceded that under the statutory law of Virginia a general residuary clause is presumed to exercise a general power of appointment, but that New Jersey observes the converse of this rule.

Mary Martin Black first contends that an intention to appoint the *corpus* of the trust to her is implicit in the residuary clause of her mother's will. Failing this, she urges us to overrule our previous cases holding that a general residuary clause is not presumed, *ipso facto*, to exercise a general testamentary power of appointment. If she does not succeed on either of these two points, she then proposes that William Byrd's will be construed to establish an implied gift of the trust principal to her in default of appointment by Mrs. Byrd.

Anne Syfret and Mark Bredin oppose all of Mrs. Black's contentions and argue that the trust fund held by the bank should be divided among the residuary beneficiaries under the will of William Byrd in proportion to their respective shares in the residue of his estate, citing N.J.S. 3A:3–14, N.J.S.A. This statute provides that when a residuary devise or bequest cannot take effect due to lapse or some other cause, it shall thereupon vest in the remaining residuary beneficiaries, if any.

William Byrd, Jr., and Lucy Carter Bredin, who were successful below, deny the validity of Mrs. Black's arguments and also contest the applicability of N.J.S. 3A:3–14, N.J.S.A., maintaining that the trust fund has now become intestate property belonging to William Byrd's next of kin under N.J.S. 3A:4–2, N.J.S.A.[14]

In order to elucidate the dispositive intentions of William and Julia Byrd, evidence was adduced of the circumstances which probably motivated them at the times when they executed their respective testaments. As a result of examining the terms of Julia Byrd's will in the revealing context of her personal relationships with the parties involved and other extrinsic circumstances, we are persuaded that the relevant factors adequately combine to demonstrate an intention by the testatrix to appoint the trust property to her daughter Mary Martin Black. This conclusion makes it unnecessary to adjudicate the further conflict between the claims of Anne Syfret and Mark Bredin, on the one hand, and William Byrd, Jr., and Lucy Carter Bredin, on the other.

14. This statute is repealed and is replaced by N.J. Stat.Ann., §§ 3A:2A–34, 3A:2A–35 (West)—Ed.

The general rule in our jurisdiction is that a residuary clause, general in its nature, will not ordinarily suffice to exercise a power of appointment. E.g., Lippincott v. Haviland, 93 N.J.Eq. 585, 117 A. 147 (Ch.1922); Farnum v. Pennsylvania Co., 87 N.J.Eq. 108, 99 A. 145 (Ch.1916), affirmed 87 N.J.Eq. 652, 101 A. 1053 (E. & A. 1917).

The testator must in some way express or indicate a conscious intention to execute it. In many instances the intention exists and, although imperfectly expressed, is aided and supported by surrounding circumstances and their reasonable and logical implications, while in other cases the intention is not expressed at all. * * * [discussions of New Jersey cases omitted] * * *

Ultimately, of course, each case must be determined upon its own facts and circumstances, but the fundamental purpose of the inquiry always remains. Our primary desire is to effectuate the wishes of the deceased if they are reasonably and lawfully discoverable and adequately proven.

Mary Martin Black raises a preliminary question concerning the *quantum* of proof needed to establish an intent to exercise a power of appointment, arguing that the standard exacted by the Chancery Division was unwarrantably high. In disposing of appellant's contention that the terms of the will and the circumstances surrounding testatrix when it was executed conjoined to reflect an intention to exercise, the lower court determined: "* * * it cannot be said that the circumstances are so clear that one must inevitably draw the conclusion that she intended to exercise the power," and concluded that "Singly and collectively they do not compel the conclusion that Mrs. Byrd exercised the power of appointment * * *."

* * * [discussion of various formulae postulating standards of proof omitted] * * *

We do not think it is necessary for the appellant to present so forceful and compelling a case that it is impossible to form a rational supposition contrary to her contention. The object of our investigation is to determine the probable intent of the testatrix by a preponderance of the evidence and to carry it out in accordance with her wishes even though they be imperfectly expressed. We do what elemental justice and fundamental fairness demand under the necessitous circumstances. Mrs. Byrd's testament is final beyond reprieve. She cannot return to illuminate or to modify its terms. Therefore, we put ourselves in her position in so far as possible, endeavoring to accomplish what she would have done could she have envisioned the present inquiry. Certainties are seldom attainable in this realm, and probabilities should customarily be sufficient. See Restatement, Property, § 343, comment (a).

* * * [discussion of English standard of proof as compared with standard of proof in New Jersey omitted] * * *

A minority of jurisdictions, most notably Massachusetts, has held, even in the absence of a statute, that a general dispositive clause alone exercises a power of appointment, and one of the foremost authorities on future interests finds logic in this view. Boston Safe Deposit & Trust Co. v. Painter, 322 Mass. 362, 77 N.E.2d 409 (Mass.Sup. Jud.Ct.1948); Amory v. Meredith, 7 Allen, 89 Mass., 397 (Sup.Jud.Ct. 1863); Simes, Future Interests (Handbook), 208–209 (1951).

Many states have enacted statutes accomplishing this same end. See Restatement Property, § 343, comment (d) (1948 Supp.). There is no danger of doing violence to the law of wills in holding that the intent to exercise a power of appointment need be proven only by a preponderance of the evidence which makes the existence of such an intent probable, and, in fact, all of the litigants so concede.

Respondents direct us to the classic statement of Mr. Justice Story that:

> "Three classes of cases have been held to be sufficient demonstrations of an intended execution of a power: (1) Where there has been some reference in the will, or other instrument, to the power; (2) or a reference to the property, which is the subject, on which it is to be executed; (3) or, where the provision in the will or other instrument, executed by the donee of the power, would otherwise be ineffectual, or a mere nullity; in other words, it would have no operation, except as an execution of the power." Blagge v. Miles, 3 Fed.Cas. pages 559, 566, No. 1,479, (1 Cir. 1841).

They argue that the case *sub judice* does not fall within any of the three categories enumerated in Blagge and that therefore the lower court was correct in concluding Mrs. Byrd had not exercised the power donated by her husband.

The fallacy of this reasoning lies in its assumed premise that Mr. Justice Story was attempting to describe all of the instances in which an intent to exercise could be found. The author of the opinion himself refuted this proposition, however, and only one or two later cases have considered the categorization above to be all-inclusive. See Annotation 91 A.L.R. 436 (1934). They failed to recognize that the basic endeavor is to ascertain the testator's intent and that the classification adopted in Blagge was only a synthesis of the fact patterns in earlier cases where the requisite intent had been found. * * *

A multiplicity of considerations persuade us to the conclusion that Mrs. Byrd probably desired to appoint the trust fund for the benefit of her daughter.

It is undisputed that Mrs. Black enjoyed an extremely close and affectionate relationship with both her mother and stepfather. She had known William Byrd for some 40 to 50 years prior to his death. The existence of a gratifying rapport among these parties is persuasively demonstrated by the fact that the Byrds journeyed from New Jersey to Virginia on the day of their wedding to spend the first ten days of their married life with Mrs. Black in her home. After visiting a brother of Mr. Byrd's, they returned to Warrenton for another stay before assuming permanent residence at Mr. Byrd's home in Short Hills.

This strong mutual esteem and devotion never waned and continued to flourish throughout the lives of William and Julia Byrd. Mary Martin Black was with her mother and William Byrd quite frequently. The Byrds and the Blacks invariably celebrated Christmas together, either in New Jersey or in Virginia. They jointly vacationed each summer in Edgerton, Massachusetts, where the Blacks had a cottage.

When her mother became ill, Mrs. Black stayed at the home in Short Hills for two months. Subsequently, Mrs. Byrd was removed to a hospital in New York, and Mrs. Black thereupon established a residence in that city journeying back and forth to Short Hills with Mr. Byrd. She was also in attendance at Short Hills during the last illness of Mr. Byrd.

Following her husband's demise, Mrs. Byrd accompanied Mrs. Black to Edgerton, where they stayed until September of 1952. Then, Mrs. Byrd went to her daughter's home in Virginia, where she spent the remainder of her life. Mrs. Black cared for her mother, who was almost 82 years of age when she died, and wrote all of Mrs. Byrd's correspondence since the latter was afflicted with palsy.

This close companionship, accompanied by constant and dedicated consideration, created a profound gratitude which deepened the natural maternal love of the mother for her only daughter. Incontrovertibly, Mary was the logical object of Mrs. Byrd's bounty.

Although it is asserted there is no proof the testatrix was cognizant of the contents of her husband's will, any reasonable hypothesis, we think, reflects quite definitely that she knew its provisions. When the sustaining head of a household departs this life, those who have been and still are dependent upon him naturally inquire as to their present financial status and the extent of the provisions made for them. Human nature prompts the inquiry; self-preservation stimulates it. Additionally and undisputedly, Mary was familiar with the terms of her stepfather's will, and it was she who suggested that her mother see a lawyer to have her own affairs put in order.

Surely, nothing yet revealed in these developments sustains the thought that Mrs. Byrd, as suggested below, willfully refrained from exercising the power of appointment in favor of the daughter who meant so much to her.

The purpose and pattern of Mr. Byrd's testamentary plan were logical, intelligent and lucid. He divided his estate into three parts. Two were given to his children and grandchildren; the other was placed in trust for his wife, she to receive the income therefrom during her life with unlimited power to invade the *corpus* if she so desired. If Mrs. Byrd predeceased her husband and daughter, Mrs. Black was to receive her mother's share. It is evident that the testator wanted one-third of his residuary estate to go to his wife's family.

In this setting, certainly Mrs. Byrd had no occasion to entertain compunctions about unfairly depriving William Byrd's own children of a portion of their father's estate. It had been granted to her and her daughter. Testator was demonstrably fond of his stepdaughter since, in the event that Mrs. Byrd predeceased him, he placed Mary on an equal footing with his son and gave her more than his daughter.

Nor is it reasonable, by virtue of considerations pertaining to the independent financial status of herself or Mary Martin Black, to impute to Mrs. Byrd an inhibition against following the common human impulse. Her net estate, aside from the appointive fund, amounts to approximately $25,000. It is described by the respondents as "substantial and consequential" while the appellant terms it "inconsequential," signifying the importance which both sides attribute to its size as bearing upon the intent of the testatrix. When Mrs. Byrd's estate is compared with the sum subject to the power, one cannot logically deem it to be a legitimate surmise that the testatrix thought her daughter was amply provided for by the gift of $25,000 without the appointive property. Certainly the net worth of the estate flowing to Mary directly from her mother would have to be classified as small in comparison with the amount involved in the appointment. Moreover, Mrs. Black is not so affluent that it might deter her mother from appointing to her a fund containing over $300,000. The court below found that "Mrs. Black had received a fund which yielded her an income of $12,000 per year." This is not factually so. The fund was not hers; she merely received the income from a trust with no power of disposition over the *corpus*.

Mary and her mother were as close as human affection and esteem could bind them, and one searches in vain for a cause why, under these circumstances, without explanation, the mother, at the infirm age of 82 years, stricken with palsy and leaning more heavily upon her daughter for comfort and physical aid, should intentionally deprive her of the only sizable inheritance involved.

To the contrary, in sweeping language Julia Byrd endowed Mary Martin Black "with all my estate, both real and personal, or mixed, wheresoever situated, whether in being or in expectancy * * *." Although she had the full power and authority to withdraw the whole or any part of the capital of the trust in question, she never reduced it to possession or converted it to her enjoyment. Could the fund as it thus existed be termed or regarded by her as an expectancy? Regardless of the strict legalistic definition of the phrase, the possibility that she used it to refer to the trust fund contributes something to the composite of various factors ultimately portraying the testatrix' intention.

The scrivener of Mrs. Byrd's will was a Virginia lawyer located in Warrenton. He drew the residuary clause, which by Virginia statute was sufficient to execute the power donated to the testatrix. The rule that the law of the donor's domicile governs the determination of whether the donee of a power intended to exercise it, despite the fact that the donee has a different domicile, is, to say the least, abstruse. It is said by some authorities to run contrary to legitimate expectation and has been condemned as illogical. Goodrich, Conflict of

Laws, § 177 (1949); 2 Beale, Conflict of Laws, § 288.1 (1935); 5 American Law of Property, § 23.3 (1952). Withholding our judgment on the merits of this controversy over which is the more seemly choice of the law, it is enough to say that we can appreciate, at least in part, why a Virginia lawyer might regard the residuary clause in question as fully complying with Mrs. Byrd's desire to exercise her power of appointment in favor of her daughter.

Then, too, we are mindful of the plausible inferences to be drawn from the terms of Mrs. Byrd's contingent gift to the Macy grandchildren in the event Mrs. Black should predecease her. She specifically requested these grandsons "to equally share the responsibility of the care and maintenance of Aubrey Henry Martin, Jr." He is another grandson of the testatrix and is mentally retarded as a result of a forceps injury suffered at birth. His father does not contribute to his support and his mother is confined to a mental institution. During his formative years, he was sent to various schools for special training at the expense of Mrs. Byrd. His aunt, Mrs. Black, shared the responsibility of his care, and he lived with her during vacation periods. Since he has become of age, he has worked erratically at various positions and for a time was an usher in a movie theater. Because of his physical and mental difficulties, he is not self-supporting, and previous to her death Mrs. Byrd regularly gave him for his maintenance as much as $1,200 a year even when he was employed.

Considering Mrs. Byrd's obvious solicitude for the welfare of her unfortunate and handicapped grandchild, who was only 18 years of age when her will was executed and had a probable life expectancy of 40 to 50 years, and interested as she was in the future security and maintenance of Aubrey, is it reasonable to assume she would leave only $25,000 from which this could be accomplished when she had a fund of over $300,000 at her disposal?

The history and past experience of the family's existence demonstrate beyond doubt that she could trust her daughter Mary to care for Aubrey since Mary had already, in part, assumed that obligation, but in the event her daughter predeceased her, she cautiously inserted the precatory request in the will as to the joint responsibility of the other grandsons to assume this burden. $25,000 would hardly be sufficient to support Aubrey comfortably with the things which he required for the rest of his life, and his cousins could not be expected, because they were all young men, to supply his wants from their personal resources. Mrs. Byrd surely wanted the Macys also to have some financial benefit from her gift after the moral obligation to Aubrey had been discharged, and a reasonable inference is that she intended to dispose of the trust fund through her testamentary bequest.

It may well be that none of the incidents related above is adequate in and of itself to prove the required intention. Yet the combination of all the circumstances in their aggregate, as they integrate with one another and reflect upon the problem as a whole, is sufficient to sustain the appellant's burden of proof in the case *sub judice*.

Essential justice does not permit "a discernible intention of the testator" to be defeated. The *quantum* of proof may be supplied by logical inferences if they are sufficiently persuasive to carry the necessary conviction. We accordingly, from the whole record, conclude that Mrs. Byrd intended to and did appoint the trust fund to her daughter.

The judgment below is reversed and the cause is remanded for further proceedings consistent with the views expressed in this opinion.

For reversal: CHIEF JUSTICE WEINTRAUB and JUSTICES WACHENFELD, BURLING, JACOBS, FRANCIS and PROCTOR.

[The dissenting opinion of JUSTICE HEHER is omitted.]

NOTE

With the principal case compare Carlisle v. Delaware Trust Co., 34 Del. Ch. 133, 99 A.2d 764 (1953), holding that the will of the donee did not exercise the power of appointment. Each case will invite litigation if the donee's will fails to express clearly an intent to exercise or not to exercise the power, as may be his desire. The careful draftsman always recites intent and makes explicit reference to the power. If he fails to perform his job adequately, and litigation results, there are two kinds of problems: what kind of evidence is admissible, and what factual elements are important in proving or disproving intent? How strong must the evidence be to meet the burden of proof in the local jurisdiction?

Consider the following factual elements: suppose the donee is the person who created the power, by reserving a power to appoint in a living trust; the personal relations between the donee and the persons who will take in default; the absence of an express gift in default, as in the principal case; the amount of property in the donee's estate and its adequacy to accomplish the donee's estate plan.

Undoubtedly the weight of authority is that, in the absence of statute, a residuary or other clause referring generally to "my estate" or "my property" does not operate sufficiently to manifest intent to exercise even a general power of appointment unless other facts establish intent. A few states, including until recently Massachusetts, take the view that a general residuary clause is presumed to exercise a general power to appoint by will, unless the opposite intent is shown; this is because of the tendency of the donee to think of a general power as equivalent to ownership, and the same courts will not extend the rule to a special power.[15]

15. Fiduciary Trust Co. v. First National Bank, 344 Mass. 1, 181 N.E.2d 6 (1962) Massachusetts has adopted the majority view by statute. Mass.Gen. Laws Ann (1981 Supp.) Ch. 191 § 1A. See French, "Exercise of Power of Appointment: Should Intent to Exercise be Inferred From General Disposition of Property", 1979 Duke L.J. 747; Gallo, "Drafting and Exercising Powers of Appointment", 120 Trusts and Estates 41 (1981); Pennell and Stansfield, "Inadvertent Exercise of Powers of Appointment in Oklahoma", 33 Okla.L.Rev. 565 (1980); 15 A.L.R.3d 346 (1967); 16 A.L.R.3d 911 (1967); 16 A.L.R.3d 951 (1967).

ESTATE OF SMITH

Colorado Court of Appeals, 1978.
41 Colo.App. 266, 585 P.2d 319.

Opinion by JUDGE VAN CISE.

The Colorado Springs National Bank, as the personal representative of the estate of Helen J. Smith, deceased (the wife), petitioned the district court, sitting in probate, to determine whether the decedent, in the residuary clause of her will, had validly exercised a general testamentary power of appointment conferred upon her by the trust provisions of the will of her late husband, Willard A. Smith. Marjorie K. Thompson, who was named as a residuary legatee in the husband's will and who is a taker in default of appointment, brings this appeal from an order of the trial court which determined that the wife had validly exercised the power of appointment. We reverse.

The relevant provisions of the husband's will read as follows:

> "Upon the death of my wife all property then belonging to Trust A shall be paid to such persons and corporations, including her estate, her creditors and the creditors of her estate, in such amounts, shares and interests as my wife may, by her last will have appointed, *but only if such will specifically refers to this power.*" (emphasis added)

By the above-quoted language, the husband conferred upon his wife a general power of appointment by will. See § 15–2–103(1) and (3), C.R.S.1973.

In the residuary clause of the wife's will, she provided in pertinent part as follows:

> "I give, devise and bequeath the rest, residue and remainder of my estate (*including any property in which I hold a power of appointment*, appointing said property to my residue) as follows: * * *." (emphasis added)

The trial court held that whether a general testamentary power of appointment has been validly exercised depends upon the intention of the donee of the power, and found that here the donee intended to exercise the power of appointment conferred upon her by her husband's will. Thus, the court determined that the power had been validly exercised.

The issue presented on this appeal is whether the attempted exercise of the power by the donee was fatally defective because she did not make specific reference to the power as required by the donor. For a general discussion of the issue presented here, see Rabin, Blind Exercises of Powers of Appointment, 51 Cornell L.Q. 1 (1965). See also 5 American Law of Property § 23:44 (A.J. Casner ed. 1952).

A donor of a power of appointment may effectively restrict the manner in which that power may be exercised, by requiring a specific mention of the donor's will by the donee. See generally 5 W. Bowe and D. Parker, Page on the Law of Wills, § 45:12 (1962); 4 A G. Thompson, Real Property § 2028 (J. Grimes Repl.1961). These specific reference clauses have a well reasoned purpose, which is to insure a considered and intentional, rather than an inadvertent exercise of the power. Inadvertent and blind exercise of unknown powers may and often have led to adverse results such as incurring unnecessary estate taxes, giving the property to the wrong people, and making invalid dispositions of the property. See 2 J. Appleman, Basic Estate Planning 714.

Contrary to the ruling of the trial court, the question of whether a power of appointment has been validly exercised depends not on the intent of the donee of the power, but on whether the power was exercised in the manner prescribed by the donor, i.e., by making specific reference in her will to this power. See Holzbach v. United Virginia Bank, 216 Va. 482, 219 S.E.2d 868 (1975); Leidy Chemicals Foundation, Inc. v. First National Bank, 276 Md. 689, 351 A.2d 129 (Md.App. 1976); In re Estate of Schede, 426 Pa. 93, 231 A.2d 135 (1967); Shine v. Monahan, 354 Mass. 680, 241 N.E.2d 854 (1968). Where the controlling requirements are clearly stated in the donor's will, the donee's intent is irrelevant if she fails to comply with those requirements. Holzbach, supra.

Here, the donor did restrict the manner in which the power could be exercised by specifying that it could only be exercised if the donee of the power, his wife, specifically referred to the power in her will. Since the wife's will does not make specific reference to her late husband's will or to the power conferred therein, the power was not exercised in the manner prescribed, and therefore was not validly exercised. As stated in Holzbach v. United Virginia Bank, supra:

> "Pursuing his right to dispose of his property as he saw fit, donor created a power of appointment and selected the conduit through which it should pass. Upon the exercise of that power, he imposed a lawful requirement that his donee manifest on the face of her will an intent to exercise the power by making specific reference to the power created in his will. While donee's will makes general reference to powers of appointment, it makes no specific reference to donor, to his will, or to the power created by his will. We hold that donee's will failed to comply with donor's requirement and, therefore, failed to make an effective appointment of donor's property."

The order of the trial court is reversed and the cause remanded for further proceedings consistent with the views expressed herein.

JUDGE RULAND concurs.

* * *

JUDGE PIERCE dissents:

I agree with the majority that the question of whether the power of appointment here was validly exercised depends on whether the power was exercised in the manner prescribed by the donor. However, I would hold that the donee's exercise of the power was effective, and would therefore affirm the judgment.

As the majority points out, the donor's purpose in requiring specificity is to "insure a considered and intentional rather than an inadvertent exercise of the power." The question then becomes whether the donee exercised the power in a manner consistent with this purpose.

The evidence established that the power of appointment conferred on Helen by her late husband was the only power she possessed at the time she executed her will. Under the circumstances here, the manner in which she exercised the power should satisfy her donor's requirement of specificity. See Cross v. Cross, 559 S.W.2d 196 (Mo. App.1977); First Union National Bank v. Moss, 32 N.C.App. 499, 233 S.E.2d 88 (1977). See also Restatement of Property § 347.

The tax advantages which donors enjoy by conferring powers of appointment should not be a one-edged sword. By creating the power of appointment in Helen, Willard ran the risk that she would exercise it. He should not be permitted to reduce that risk by imposing hypertechnical and unrealistic conditions on the exercise of the power.

I would affirm the judgment of the district court.

MATTER OF SMITH

Appellate Division of the Supreme Court of New York, 1st Dept., 1951.
279 App.Div. 140, 108 N.Y.S.2d 290.[16]
Affirmed 304 N.Y. 612, 107 N.E.2d 92 (1952).

SHIENTAG, JUSTICE. The Chase National Bank of the City of New York, as executor of the estate of Ann Hughes Smith, deceased, appeals from a final order in an Article 79 proceeding settling the accounts of Bank of New York and Fifth Avenue Bank, as trustee, under an inter vivos trust set up by Alfred Holland Smith, and directing distribution of the trust corpus as follows: two-thirds to Ann Charlotte Emery Smith Waterous, respondent, and one-third to the Chase Bank, respondent-appellant. Chase Bank appeals from so much of the order below that awards to it as executor of the estate of Ann Hughes Smith only one-third of the corpus of the trust and fails to award to it the entire corpus.

There is no dispute as to the facts. On August 2, 1922, Alfred H. Smith, now deceased, as grantor, created an irrevocable trust, appointing as trustee the Fifth Avenue Bank of New York (predecessor of Bank of New York and Fifth Avenue Bank). The corpus of the trust consisted of various stocks and bonds, including 600 shares of a company which had been formed to hold title to a large estate owned by the settlor.

Under the terms of the agreement of trust, the income of the trust was to be paid to the grantor's wife, Maude Emery Smith (later Mrs. Maude Emery LeBaron) during her lifetime, and upon the death of Mrs. LeBaron, the principal of the trust was to be paid to the gran-

16. Noted, 16 Alb.L.Rev. 261 (1952), 3 Syr.L.Rev. 386 (1952).

tor's son, Emery Holland Smith, or, should he not then be living, as he should have appointed by will duly admitted to probate or, in default of appointment, to Emery Holland Smith's intestate distributees. Emery Smith predeceased Mrs. LeBaron and died on January 28, 1927, leaving a last will and testament dated May 11, 1917, which was admitted to probate by the Surrogate's Court of New York County on March 16, 1927. In this will, dated some five years prior to the creation of the Alfred Smith trust, there appears the following pertinent provision: "Third. I hereby give, devise and bequeath all of my property, real and personal, of every kind and description whatsoever, and wheresoever situate, to my wife, Ann Hughes Smith."

Ann Hughes Smith died on August 9, 1946, leaving a last will and testament under which letters testamentary and letters of trusteeship were granted and issued by the Surrogate's Court of New York County to respondent-appellant, The Chase National Bank of the City of New York.

Mrs. LeBaron, the life income beneficiary of the trust, died on September 12, 1949, thus making the principal of the trust distributable.

It should be noted that Emery Smith, prior to his death, knew of the existence of the power of appointment granted to him by the agreement of trust, but executed no will subsequent to his will dated May 11, 1917.

At issue in this proceeding is the ownership of the principal of the trust created by Alfred Smith. Its disposition turns squarely on the question whether or not the will of Emery Holland Smith, the pertinent provision of which was quoted above, constitutes an exercise of the power of appointment conferred upon him by the trust agreement. If the power is deemed to have been exercised, the entire principal of the trust, upon the death of Mrs. LeBaron, became payable to the estate of Ann Hughes Smith. If the power was not so exercised, the principal of the trust became distributable, upon Mrs. LeBaron's death, to Emery Smith's distributees—his widow, Ann Hughes Smith, and his daughter, respondent Ann Charlotte Emery Smith Waterous. The court below determined that the will of Emery Smith did not execute his power of appointment, and accordingly directed the trustee, in the final order, to distribute the principal of the trust, one-third to respondent-appellant and two-thirds to respondent Ann Charlotte Emery Smith Waterous.

Section 176 of the Real Property Law, derived originally from part 2, ch. 1, tit. 2, Section 126 of the Revised Statutes of New York, provides: "Real property embraced in a power to devise passes by a will purporting to convey all the real property of the testator, unless the intent that the will is not to operate as an execution of the power, appears, either expressly or by necessary implication."

Section 18 of the Personal Property Law is to the same effect.

By his will, Emery Smith quite plainly undertook to devise all of his property. Under the above Sections, it would seem to follow automatically that he must be deemed to have exercised his power of appointment as to the trust principal unless a contrary intent appears either expressly or by necessary implication.

* * * [Omitted is the portion of the opinion in which the court held that the above statutory sections were not qualified by Section 175 of the N.Y. Real Property Law.]

In Section 176, however, the Legislature, by language clear and unequivocal, undertook to change, with respect to wills purporting to devise all of the donee's property, the fundamental common-law rule of construction. Lockwood v. Mildeberger, 159 N.Y. 181, 185, 53 N. E. 803, 804. With respect to this particular kind of testamentary provision, the Legislature has ordained that it is no longer necessary that a donee clearly manifest an intent to exercise a power of appointment. As the Court of Appeals put the matter in the Lockwood case 159 N.Y. at page 188, 53 N.E. at page 805, "It was not necessary, as we have seen, that she should have had an intent to execute it, for the statute steps in and sends the property, subject to the power, in the same direction as that in which the testatrix has sent her own property." Since the so-called power-plus-interest rule has significance only as an application of the principle that intent to exercise a power must be clearly manifested, that principle having been abolished by statute with respect to wills purporting to dispose of all the testator's property, the power-plus-interest rule no longer has significance with respect to such instruments.

* * *

The only question still remaining for determination is whether or not an intent not to execute his power of appointment appears in Smith's will, either expressly or by necessary implication. Certainly no such intent appears expressly, nor in our opinion does it appear by any implication, necessary or otherwise. It is well settled that an intent not to exercise the power cannot be implied from the fact that the will of Emery Smith was executed prior to the date of creation of the power. County Trust Company v. Quencer, Sup.Ct. Westchester Co., 1944, 183 Misc. 922, 54 N.Y.S.2d 29, affirmed without opinion 2d Dep't, 1945, 269 App.Div. 861, 56 N.Y.S.2d 542, affirmed without opinion 1946, 296 N.Y. 559, 68 N.E.2d 864. Not only is there no evidence of an intention not to exercise his power of appointment but, on the contrary, from all the facts and circumstances set forth, it seems plain that Emery Smith, by his will, intended to benefit his wife to the fullest possible extent. We find that he did so effectively.

The order so far as appealed from should be reversed and the entire principal of the trust is transferred and paid over to the Chase National Bank as executor of the estate of Ann Hughes Smith, with costs to all parties appearing herein and filing briefs payable out of the trust. Settle order in accordance with this opinion. * * *

All concur.

NOTE

A number of states have statutes identical with or similar to that in Matter of Smith.[17] Some of these statutes are applicable to special as well as general powers; other statutes are confined to general powers.[18]

Since the principal case was decided, the New York statute has been changed to read as follows: [EPTL]

"§ 10-6.1 Exercise of a power of appointment; manifestation of intention of donee

"(a) Subject to paragraph (b), an effective exercise of a power of appointment does not require an express reference to such power. A power is effectively exercised if the donee manifests his intention to exercise it. Such a manifestation exists when the donee:

"(1) Declares in substance that he is exercising all the powers he has;

"(2) Sufficiently identifying the appointive property or any part thereof, executes an instrument purporting to dispose of such property or part;

"(3) Makes a disposition which, when read with reference to the property he owned and the circumstances existing at the time of its making, manifests his understanding that he was disposing of the appointive property; or

"(4) Leaves a will disposing of all of his property or all of his property of the kind covered by the power, unless the intention that the will is not to operate as an execution of the power appears expressly or by necessary implication.

"(b) If the donor has expressly directed that no instrument shall be effective to exercise the power unless it contains a specific reference to the power, an instrument not containing such reference does not validly exercise the power."

Under this statute would the result in the principal case be the same? New York law also provides that a power to appoint by deed only may be exercised by a will of the donee—McKinneys' N.Y., EPTL, § 10-6.2(a)(3). Suppose the donee of a power to appoint by deed executes a will making no mention of the power, on the assumption that his will could not exercise a power to appoint by deed only: what result? Could testimony of the attorney who drafted the will be admitted to show he advised the donee that his will would not exercise the power?[19]

Wisconsin, which originally copied the New York statute, in 1965 amended its statute and reverted to the common law rule that a general re-

17. 3 Powell, The Law of Real Property (Rohan Rev. 1979) ¶ 397. See 16 A.L. R.3d 911 (1967).

18. Many of these statutes are patterned upon § 27 of the English Wills Act of 1837. Such statutes are interpreted to apply only to general powers. Wachovia Bank & Trust Co. v. Hunt, 267 N.C. 173, 148 S.E.2d 41 (1966). See Rabin, "Blind Exercises of Powers of Appointment", 51 Corn.L.Q. 1 (1965); Sherrin, "Exercise of Testamentary Powers of Appointment", 121 New L.J. 41 (1971); "Exercise of Powers of Appointment", 121 New L.J. 808 (1971). For a state by state survey of the law as to when a will effectively exercises a power of appointment see "When Does a Will Effectively Exercise a Power of Appointment," 104 Trusts and Estates 814 (1965).

19. Holding such testimony inadmissible: Estate of Carter, 47 Cal.2d 200, 302 P.2d 301 (1956); Matter of Deane, 4 N.Y. 2d 326, 175 N.Y.S.2d 21, 151 N.E.2d 184 (1958). Similarly a letter by the donee stating his intent not to exercise the power is excluded because the statute requires the intent to appear by the will. Washington Trust Co. v. Dyer, 98 R.I. 79, 200 A.2d 1 (1964).

siduary clause does not operate to manifest intent to exercise a power of appointment.[20] The basis of this change was twofold: the donor would prefer to have the property pass in default unless the donee really intends to exercise the power, and the statutory presumption that a general residuary clause operates to exercise the power unless a contrary intent is manifested often results in unintentional exercise of the power.[21] Uniform Probate Code, § 2–610 also sets forth the common law rule.

Do these statutes require the party claiming under the gift in default to show that the donee "had no intention to exercise the power" or that the donee "intended not to exercise the power"?

Suppose, having exercised the power effectively, the donee later purports to exercise the power again for different appointees. The power could be exercised in part at one time and in part at another; but, if the power has been exercised fully and effectively, has the power been exhausted so it cannot be exercised again by the donee? Can the donee expressly or impliedly subject his appointment to a power of revocation? One of the major reasons for creation of a power is to generate flexibility in the disposition of property. What effect should be given to the donor's statement that an appointment may be revoked when the donee does not reserve a power of revocation?

A power exercised by will is certainly revocable so long as the donee-testator lives and possesses the mental capacity to revoke and is, with equal certainty, irrevocable when the donee-testator dies, the will being effective at the donee-testator's death.[22] Problems concerning implied and express revocations of powers are limited to revocations of inter vivos exercises although the purported revocation of the inter vivos exercise might be by will.

When the donee exercises his power to create a trust and reserves no power of revocation, his trust should be irrevocable unless an intent to revoke could be implied from the trust terms. If he reserves a power to revoke the trust, there would seem no difficulty in his revocation of his exercise of the power so long as he adhered to the terms upon which the power of revocation was reserved. Nevertheless, the authorities also appear to support the effectiveness of a power of revocation reserved in a deed exercising the power of appointment even though the appointment was not in trust, the general position being that if no such power is retained, then the exercise of the power of appointment is irrevocable.[23] The power of revocation can be reserved by the donee whether or not the donor conferred authority upon him to reserve the power, although in the case of a special power the donor

20. Wis.Stat.Ann. § 702.03 (West Spec. Pamph. 1980).

21. For two cases in which the donee did not intend to exercise the power, and was erroneously advised by legal counsel that a will not mentioning the power would not exercise the power, see footnote 19 above. In both cases the result of the statutory presumption was that the donee's will operated as an exercise of the power although this was the opposite of the donee's intent.

22. In re Bauer's Trust, 251 N.Y.S.2d 23, 14 N.Y.2d 272, 200 N.E.2d 207 (1964). Noted: 29 Alb.L.Rev. 115 (1965); 31 Brooklyn L.Rev. 145 (1964); 65 Col.L. Rev. 348 (1965); 50 Corn.L.Q. 523 (1965); 40 N.Y.U.L.Rev. 793 (1965); 10 N.Y.L.Forum 402 (1964); In re Estate of Conreid, 59 Misc.2d 593, 299 N.Y.S.2d 885 (Surr. 1969), aff'd 33 A.D.2d 992, 308 N.Y.S.2d 286.

23. Wilmington Trust Co. v. Wilmington Trust Co., 21 Del.Ch. 102, 180 A. 597 (1935), mod. 21 Del.Ch. 188, 186 A. 903 (1936); Central Trust Co. v. Watt, 22 Ohio Ops. 18, 139 Ohio St. 50, 38 N.E.2d 185 (1941), noted, 9 U.Chi.L.Rev. 499 (1951); Restatement, Property (1940) § 366; Simes and Smith, Future Interests (2d Ed., 1956) § 985; 60 A.L.R.3d 143 (1974).

could provide that it could *not* be exercised by a revocable appointment,[24] such a restriction being futile in a general power because the donee could appoint to himself and then reserve such powers as he wished.

Possibly when the donor reserves a power of appointment and states in his reservation that the power to revoke an appointment is reserved, the donor will be permitted to revoke a particular exercise of the power of appointment even though the power of revocation was not expressly retained when the power of appointment was exercised.[25] This, however, was the fact situation in Hele v. Bond,[26] the early English case from which the rule of "irrevocability" or "exhaustion" is traced, and the rule of which has been substantially adopted by the American Law Institute as applied to revocations of exercises of powers of appointment generally. In State Street Trust Co. v. Crocker [27] the donor-settlor's intent to create a series of powers of amendment of his trust in his wife, his children and the issue of children was sufficient to sustain a second amendment (which was the equivalent of exercise of a power of appointment) even though a power to revoke a first amendment of similar character had not been reserved. The settlor had two children, a son and daughter. After the death of the settlor and his wife, the children exercised their power to amend the trust by substituting a distribution of three-fourths of the son's share to his widow with the remaining one-fourth of the share to his issue in place of the original trust provision. No power to alter this amendment was reserved by the children. After the death of the son, his sister and the son's issue exercised a power to revoke the first amendment and distribute the entire share of the son to his issue. This exercise was sustained by the Court.

The intent to retain a power of revocation when a power is exercised may be implied. In Estate of Wood [28] a testator conferred a general power exercisable by deed only upon his widow, this power being over a remainder interest following her life estate in trust. The widow purported to exercise his power by four inter vivos instruments. In the first two purported exercises (1967 and 1969) the widow reserved no powers of revocation. Some of the appointees were the same in these instruments and others differed. In 1970 she purported to revoke these earlier exercises and appoint to her companion and later in the same year again purported to appoint to the companion. The Court relied upon the words "devise and bequeath" in the 1967 instrument as indicating no intent to make a present gift but a gift only at her death. Although the 1969 instrument did not contain these words, the instrument did direct distribution upon the widow's death and, having been drawn by an experienced draftsman, the Court considered that if an immediate gift of the remainder had been intended, that intent would have been made clear. Making an analogy to a testamentary transaction (an intent to create no property interest until death) the Court viewed the 1967 and 1969 exercises as impliedly revocable. The distinction made by the Court is between a present gift of a future interest (the remainder) and a future gift of a future interest. In the latter situation the intent to retain a power of revocation when the power to appoint is exercised is being implied.

24. Restatement, Property (1940) § 366, comm. (d).

25. Goodell's Estate, 53 Pa. D & C 13 (1945); First National Bank & Trust Co. of Oklahoma City, Okl. v. Foster, 346 F. 2d 49 (10th Cir. 1965).

26. Prec. Ch. 474, 24 Eng.Rep. 213 (1717).

27. 306 Mass. 257, 28 N.E.2d 5, 128 A.L.R. 1166 (1940), noted, 41 Col.L.Rev. 155 (1941).

28. 32 Cal.App.3d 862, 108 Cal.Rptr. 522, 60 A.L.R.3d 123 (1973), noted, 14 Santa Clara L.Rev. 429 (1974). Comment, "Powers of Appointment in California: Revocability of an Appointment", 8 Calif.Western L.Rev. 439 (1972).

The uncertainties generated by the cases concerning revocations of exercises of powers of appointment make statutes dealing with the issue desirable.[29] Similar difficulties are produced by a donor's attempt to revoke the power after he has conferred it upon the donee and a donee's revocation of his release or renunciation of a power to appoint.[30] The California statute deals with the problem of revocation of release of a power.[31]

(2) SCOPE OF THE POWER

Assuming the donee wants to exercise the power, the second issue is whether he can make the type of appointment he desires. When can he appoint? To whom? Can he create new trusts and new powers of appointment? These questions may (and should) be answered by the terms of the creating instrument. The first two (time and person) are almost always answered to a large degree. Thus, under a simple limitation "to such person or persons as A may appoint by will", A may not appoint during his lifetime but only by will. He may, however, appoint by will to any person without limit; except for one state,[32] he may appoint in favor of his own estate or his creditors.

29. See West's Ann.Cal.Civ.Code § 1392.1 as follows:

"**Authority to revoke or release**

(a) Unless the power to revoke is reserved in the instrument creating the power or exists pursuant to Section 2280, the creation of a power of appointment is irrevocable.

(b) Unless made expressly irrevocable by the creating instrument or the instrument of exercise, an exercise of a power of appointment is revocable if the power to revoke exists pursuant to Section 2280 or so long as the interest to the appointive property, whether present or future, has not been transferred or become distributable pursuant to such appointment.

(c) Unless the power to revoke is reserved in the instrument releasing the power, a release of a power of appointment is irrevocable."

Section 2280 makes all voluntary trusts revocable by the settlor in writing filed with the trustee unless the trust is made irrevocable expressly by the instrument creating it. For comment upon Section 1392.1 see Powers of Appointment in California: Revocability of an Appointment, 8 Calif.Western L.Rev. 439 (1972).

30. See Manville v. Dresselhuys, 181 Misc. 290, 43 N.Y.S.2d 658 (1943), in which the donee attempted to revoke a release and renunciation of the power.

31. Fn. 29, supra.

32. In Maryland a power to appoint to "any person" does not include authority to appoint to the creditors or estate of the donee unless this is expressly mentioned by the donor. Connor v. O'Hara, 188 Md. 527, 52 A.2d 33 (1946). Conferred upon a surviving spouse, a power so limited would not be the basis for a marital deduction in the estate of the decedent conferring the power unless the deduction is taken in the qualified terminal interest (QTIP) form. IRC § 2056 (b)(7), 26 U.S.C.A. However, in Guiney v. United States, 425 F.2d 145 (4th Cir. 1970), noted 31 Md.L.Rev. 157 (1971), the marital deduction trust contained the usual expression that the testator intended to take full advantage of the marital deduction. Although bound by the Maryland law concerning powers, the Court considered this language beyond any considered in the Maryland cases and was of the view that the Maryland Supreme Court would construe the statement as sufficient to permit the spouse to appoint to herself or to her estate. The marital deduction was allowed.

On the issue of capacity to exercise a power, see Stoebuck, "Infants' Exercise

On the other hand, the donee may be restricted in his choice by the terms of the original limitation. Thus, if the donor had given a remainder interest "to such of A's children as he may appoint by will" (a special power), A may appoint only to children living at his death, and not to grandchildren or to the spouse of a deceased child. Under some forms of special powers, there may also be a question whether A has only a power to designate the shares or amounts which the objects of the power are to receive, rather than a power to select one or more of the persons to the exclusion of others. Again, since most powers are created today in trust documents, the donee is likely to be aware of the advantages of the trust. What more natural than that he should think in terms of continuing the present trust, or creating a new one, and perhaps also creating new powers of appointment? Can he do so?

The draftsman for the donor must anticipate these problems and make careful provision in advance. The draftsman for the donee, on the other hand, operates only within the limits already set for him by the donor and the law. Thus the donee's lawyer should have in front of him the creating instrument at the time he drafts a deed or will intended to exercise the power. He is, of course, further limited by restrictions, such as the Rule against Perpetuities, consideration of which is postponed to Chapter XVI.

HARLAN v. CITIZENS NATIONAL BANK OF DANVILLE

Court of Appeals of Kentucky, 1952.
251 S.W.2d 284.[33]

SIMS, JUSTICE. This declaratory action was brought by the Citizens National Bank of Danville, as trustee of George L. Harlan, deceased, against his surviving brother and sister, Jay W. Harlan and Mrs. Sue Robinson, to determine whether a power of appointment the will of their mother, Mrs. Annie S. Harlan, gave George was exclusive or nonexclusive. The chancellor in an exhaustive and well-reasoned opinion held the power to be nonexclusive, which we think was an erroneous conclusion as we will attempt to show.

For the sake of brevity and to avoid confusion, since all persons involved in this litigation, except Mrs. Robinson, have the same surname, we will refer to Mrs. Annie S. Harlan as Annie; to Mrs. Sue Robinson as Sue; to Messrs. Jay W. Harlan and George L. Harlan as Jay and George.

Annie died in February, 1939, after executing her will on March 1, 1938. She was survived by three children, Jay, George and Sue. George never married but Jay and Sue married and each have two children. After making certain specific bequests to each of her three

of Powers of Appointment", 43 Denver L.J. 255 (1966).

33. Noted, 51 Mich.L.Rev. 936 (1952).

children, to her grandchildren and to the wife of Jay, testatrix in the third article of her will devised the residue of her estate to George in trust for life and then provided:

"At the death of said George L. Harlan, said share and his entire interest in my estate, in whatever manner acquired, shall pass to and vest in equal shares in his descendants, per stirpes, and his widow if any, said widow to share and be regarded as one of his children, provided, however, that said George L. Harlan may devise his interest to his widow, his descendants or my descendants.

"In the event George L. Harlan leaves no descendants nor widow nor makes no testamentary disposition of his said interest as above provided, then one-half thereof shall pass to and vest in Jay W. Harlan or his descendants, per stirpes, and his widow, if any, said widow to be regarded and share as one of his children, and the other one-half thereof shall pass to and vest in my daughter Sue Lee Robinson, but if Sue Lee Robinson does not survive George L. Harlan, the said other one-half shall pass to and vest in Jay W. Harlan or his descendants per stirpes, and his widow, if any, said widow to share as one of the children of said Jay W. Harlan."

George died in 1951, and in the third paragraph of his will he devised all of his property to Jay "absolutely and in fee simple".

It is insisted by Sue that the power of appointment given George in their mother's will was nonexclusive, therefore when he excluded her, his will was void and she inherited from him the same as if he had died intestate. Jay contends that the power was exclusive and he took George's entire estate under his will.

We think it may help to set out the distinction between an exclusive and nonexclusive power. 41 Am.Jur., Powers, § 63, page 852, says:

"Powers of appointment are necessarily either exclusive or nonexclusive, according to the reasonable import of the language creating them. A power is 'exclusive' when there is granted the right to exclude from the distribution any of the designated objects of the power; 'nonexclusive' when no such right of selection or exclusion is conferred. In the case of 'nonexclusive' powers, the exclusion of any member of the designated class in making the appointments invalidates the attempted exercise of the power. But if the donor expressly provides that there may be exclusions, there is no objection to the execution of a power in favor of less than all of the class. There can be no doubt that where a donee is given a power to appoint to all or any one or more of a class, he may appoint to one or more to the exclusion of the others."

Dealing with the same subject "exclusive and nonexclusive power," 69 C.J. § 1949, p. 842 states the rule:

"A power to appoint, divide, or distribute property 'to' or 'among' designated persons, or a specified class, is nonexclusive; * * * the donee's authority extending only to determining what portion each shall receive. Where, however, the power to appoint or distribute the property among 'any of' designated persons, or members of a designated class, or 'such of' them as the donee may wish or direct, * * * it is an exclusive one, and may be exercised by appointing to such one or more of the designated persons, or the members of the designated class, as the donee may choose, to the exclusion of another or others, * * * except where a contrary intention appears in the will."

The more modern rule, and we think the better one, appears in the Restatement, "Property and Future Interest," § 360, p. 1985, in these words:

"The donee of a special power may, by an otherwise effective appointment, exclude one or more objects of the power from distribution of the property covered thereby, unless the donor manifests a contrary intent.

"The nature and scope of the discretion given to the donee depends upon the intent of the donor. When the donor creates a power of appointment it is inferable that he intends the donee to be unrestricted in its exercise except as restrictions are affirmatively imposed. Unless the contrary is indicated, it is to be inferred that the donee is intended to have as broad a power of selection among the objects, including the power to exclude one or more, as the donor would have had at the time of creating the power or as the donee has with reference to his owned (own) property."

In a nutshell, the Restatement says that the donee may exclude one or more objects unless the donor forbids him to do so.

* * *

It was argued orally before us that the power only allowed George three alternatives in his appointment—to his widow, to his descendants or to his mother's descendants. We do not see it that way. Certainly children are descendants, although descendants are not necessarily children, and if we follow the narrow construction given by the chancellor, George could have appointed to his widow or to his children, but not to both groups, despite the fact that in this same sentence his mother wrote the "said widow to share and be regarded as one of his children". Under this construction George had no discretion and could not have devised a portion of the estate to his widow, had he married and not been survived by children, and then divided the balance of the estate between his brother and sister. Manifestly, testatrix did not intend to so restrict George in disposing of the property she devised him. Rather her purpose was to limit the disposition to her family or to George's family as he might "pick and choose".

"Descendants" in Webster's New International Dictionary (2nd Edition) is defined as "one who descends as offspring, however remote; opposed to ancestor and antecedent." This was the meaning given to "descendants" in Moore v. Emery, 137 Me. 259, 18 A.2d 781, at page 789.

Jay has children and grandchildren, Sue likewise has children and grandchildren, all descendants of Annie. It is admitted George was given power to appoint to Annie's descendants. Does Annie's will mean he must appoint to each and every one of her descendants? We think not. Had George lived to a great age and had Jay's and Sue's grandchildren themselves borne children by the time of George's death, these great-grandchildren would have been descendants of Annie. And under the construction of the chancellor, George would have had to devise the estate among all of Annie's descendants and could have excluded none, else his appointment would have been void. This leads to an unreasonable, if not absurd, conclusion.

The first paragraph in article 3 of the will provides if George did not appoint, then his estate vested one-half in Jay or "his descendants, per stirpes, and his widow, if any, said widow to be regarded and share as one of his children," and the other one-half pass to Sue; but if she did not survive George, then the whole of George's estate shall vest in Jay in the manner just quoted. There would be some force in the argument that the words "per stirpes" prevent the estate of George from being appointed by him to all of Annie's descendants had these words been included in the power. But "per stirpes" were not used in the phrase granting the power of appointment, they were only used in disposing of the property if George died intestate. Neither "per stirpes" nor "descendants" were used in reference to the part of the estate Sue would get had George died intestate. Had Sue predeceased George, could he have appointed to her children and grandchildren? There is nothing in the will intimating he could not and certainly Sue's children and grandchildren are descendants of Annie.

The chancellor seems to have bottomed his opinion on Barrett's Ex'r v. Barrett, 166 Ky. 411, 179 S.W. 396, L.R.A.1916D, 493. There the power was in Lewis Barrett to appoint "to his wife and heirs-at-law". Lewis had no children and was survived by his widow, one sister and two brothers. There, the parties agreed that this was a nonexclusive power, and this court so held. But the real question was whether Lewis made an illusory appointment to his sister and his brothers out of a $150,000 estate when he devised $147,000 to his widow and $1,000 to each of his heirs-at-law. We held that such an appointment was an illusory one. The Barrett opinion is of no help here.

The chancellor in his opinion in the instant case quoted what the Barrett opinion said in reference to McGaughey's Adm'r v. Henry, 15 B.Mon. 383, 54 Ky. 383, "that the power of appointment is nonexclusive where there is no express power of selection or exclusion". We are not willing to follow this rule and think the correct one is as set out in Restatement, "Property and Future Interest," § 360, p. 1985:

> "Unless the contrary is indicated, it is to be inferred that the donee is intended to have as broad a power of selection among the

objects, including the power to exclude one or more, as the donor would have had at the time of creating the power or as the donee has with reference to his owned (own) property."

There are two other cases cited in the chancellor's opinion, where he quoted from the Barrett case, which we think are wrong. In the case of Degman v. Degman, 98 Ky. 717, 34 S.W. 523, the power to appoint reads, "among my children as she may think best", which we held to be nonexclusive; and in Clay v. Smallwood, 100 Ky. 212, 38 S. W. 7, the power to the donor's daughter was to appoint to donor's "other children as she may direct". There, it was erroneously held, so we now think, that this was a nonexclusive power. Manifestly, in both the Degman and Clay cases the donee was given the power to "pick and choose" which we held in Shaver v. Ellis, 226 Ky. 806, 11 S. W.2d 949, was an exclusive power.

Perhaps, Moore v. Emery, 137 Me. 259, 18 A.2d 781, is regarded by the text writers as the leading case in America on the question now before us. Specific trusts created in the will of John J. Emery were to terminate at the death of each daughter, who was given the power of appointing "provided it be bequeathed to my descendants". In holding that the powers given the daughters were exclusive ones, the court illustrated that if the power were nonexclusive, each daughter would have to give a substantial amount of her estate to each brother and sister and to each of their issue, since they were all descendants of Mr. Emery, to the great detriment of her own children. We lift this from the opinion, 18 A.2d at pages 791, 792:

> "If he had intended to bind the daughters by such a rigid rule, he could just as well have settled himself how the remainder would go after the death of a life tenant. That he did not do so shows that he trusted to the unfettered judgment of the daughters to dispose of the principal of the trusts to his descendants in the light of events which he could not anticipate."

Applying these words to the case at bar, Annie might as well not have given George the right to appoint and have disposed of the remainder herself as she did in the words just preceding the power. That she did not do so shows she trusted to George's unfettered judgment the disposition of his estate among his descendants or her descendants in the manner he desired.

On page 790 of 18 A.2d, the Moore opinion says: "Strangely enough the inclination of courts has been in cases of doubt to construe powers as non-exclusive". We adhered to this erroneous rule in McGaughey's Adm'r v. Henry, 15 B.Mon. 383, 54 Ky. 383; Clay v. Smallwood, 100 Ky. 212, 38 S.W.2d 7; Degman v. Degman, 98 Ky. 717, 34 S.W. 523, and perhaps others. We now overrule those cases and adopt the modern rule set out in Restatement, "Property and Future Interest," § 360, p. 1985, which has been copied heretofore in this opinion.

The judgment is reversed with directions to enter one that Annie's will gave George an exclusive right of appointment which he has exercised by devising his entire estate to Jay.

NOTE

A donor may clearly manifest an intention that some share should be left to each member of a group: to B's children in such shares or amounts as B shall appoint by will. Moreover, if he intends that a minimum amount go to each member of the group, it is a simple matter to make direct gifts of that amount to each and give the donee power to appoint the remainder: one-half of the principal to be divided in equal shares among B's children, the other half to such one or more of B's children as B may appoint by will. Where a donor creates a non-exclusive power and fails to indicate any minimum amount, can the donee validly exercise the power by making merely nominal appointments to some of the group and substantial appointments to others? The English cases held that such an appointment was "illusory" and ineffective, but left open to litigation in each case what constituted the minimum amount which would be regarded as substantial enough within the intent of the donor. Although the Restatement of Property recognizes the doctrine in Section 361, there is substantial American authority rejecting it.[34]

The donor's draftsman can and should prevent any problem of interpretation as to whether a special power is intended to be exclusive or non-exclusive. Since the purpose of creating powers is to provide flexibility, the donor usually wants an exclusive power. Drafting to achieve this end may utilize a variety of language: "to such of his issue, and in such shares or amounts, as [the donee] may appoint" or "with power to appoint by will as he sees fit to any one or more of his issue, and in such shares or amounts as he may designate". Litigation is invited when the draftsman is not explicit. Consider the ambiguity inherent in the following choice of words: "with power to appoint to his children" or "to his children as he may appoint by will" or "with the principal to be divided among his children as [the donee] may appoint by his last will and testament." [35]

A few states have statutes relevant to this problem. Compare the following statutes as applied to the ambiguous language just set forth above:

McKinney's N.Y., EPTL—[36]

"§ 10–6.5 Exercise of exclusive and non-exclusive power of appointment

"(a) Unless the donor expressly provides otherwise:

"(1) The donee of an exclusive power may appoint all or any part of the appointive property to one or more of the appointees to the exclusion of the others.

"(2) The donee of a non-exclusive power must appoint in favor of all of the appointees equally."

Wisconsin Statutes Annotated—

"§ 702.07 Powers to be Construed as Exclusive

"The donee of any power may appoint the whole or any part of the appointive assets to any one or more of the permissible appointees and exclude others, except to the extent that the donor specifies either a minimum share

34. Hawthorn v. Ulrich, 207 Ill. 430, 69 N.E. 885 (1904); Hodges v. Stegall, 169 Tenn. 202, 83 S.W.2d 901, 100 A.L.R. 339 (1935).

35. Restatement, Property (1940) § 360, Illustration 4 treats such a power as non-exclusive.

36. See also the New York definitions in McKinney's EPTL, § 10–3.2(d) and (e) (1980 Supp.).

or amount to be appointed to each permissible appointee or to designated appointees, or a maximum share or amount appointable to any one or more appointees."

HORNE v. TITLE INSURANCE & TRUST CO.

United States District Court for the Southern District of California, Central Division, 1948.
79 F.Supp. 91.[37]

Action for declaratory judgment by Gwendolyn Smith Horne against Title Insurance & Trust Company, a corporation, and others.

Judgment for plaintiff.

MATHES, DISTRICT JUDGE. Plaintiff, a citizen of the State of Washington, seeks a declaratory judgment pursuant to 28 U.S.C.A. § 400. She invokes the jurisdiction of this court under 28 U.S.C.A. § 41(1), alleging that the matter in controversy exceeds the $3,000 minimum and is between citizens of different states. Defendant Title Insurance and Trust Company is a California corporation, defendant Day a citizen of Ohio, and defendant Miller a citizen of Illinois.

As appears from admissions in the pleadings, stipulations made at pre-trial and evidence adduced upon the trial, the controversy arises from the following facts: In 1940 defendant Title Insurance and Trust Company received certain properties from one George E. Day to be held in trust for the benefit of certain named beneficiares in accordance with the provisions of a declaration of trust known as Trust No. P–10453, and then executed by the title company as "Trustee" and by the trustor's son, William H. Day, as "co-trustee."

The trustor declared the trust to be irrevocable, and, so far as of interest here, the declaration further provided:

(1) that monthly payments of $833.33 be made to the co-trustee, William H. Day, during his lifetime, "in the payment of which the Trustee shall resort firstly to income and secondly to corpus";

(2) that monthly payments of $250 be made to "Frances Day (wife of William H. Day)" during the life of the trust following death of the co-trustee if "said Frances Day" survive him;

(3) that the remainder of the net income, if any, "shall be added to the principal of the trust estate * * * ";

(4) that the trust shall terminate "upon the death of the survivor of * * * William H. Day and the said Frances Day (wife of William H. Day)", or upon remarriage of Frances Day if she be the survivor;

37. Noted 47 Mich.L.Rev. 848 (1949).

(5) that upon such termination of the trust, the entire net trust estate "shall pass and vest and thereupon be delivered by the Trustee," except 40% thereof not involved here, as follows:

(a) "20% thereof shall be distributed to [defendant] Walter S. Day";

(b) "20% thereof shall be distributed to [defendant] Richard Miller";

(c) "20% thereof shall be distributed to Gwendolyn Smith * * * ", now Horne, plaintiff at bar; and

(6) that "as to the distributions to be made under the provisions * * * [just stated under (5)], William H. Day, during the * * * time * * * he shall be acting as co-trustee * * *, shall have the absolute right and power, with the approval of the Trustee, to prescribe and direct the Trustee that the distribution shall be made in different proportions than those provided; and in the event the said William H. Day, as such co-trustee, shall have exercised this discretionary power, with the approval of the Trustee, the Trustee shall make the distributions in accordance therewith. * * * "

Prior to 1946, Frances Day, the wife of William H. Day named in the declaration of trust, died. On May 17, 1946, the attorney for co-trustee William H. Day wrote plaintiff:

"As you know, Mr. Day recently remarried, and under the terms of Trust No. 10453, Mrs. Ruth Day does not and would not participate in any of the principal or income of said Trust at the time of Mr. Day's death.

"It is the desire and request of my client that separate agreements be entered into as between yourself and the present Mrs. Day, * * * whereby out of the 20% interest which you are entitled to under the terms of said Trust at the * * * death of Mr. Day, that you personally agree to pay * * * 7½% of your amount [to the present Mrs. Day].

"Similar requests are being made to Mr. Walter S. Day and Mr. Richard Miller. * * * "

Plaintiff replied requesting further information. On June 2nd co-trustee William H. Day himself wrote plaintiff at length of his wishes, stating in part: "Dad * * * drew up TR–10453 for my exclusive benefit but we both overlooked the possibility that Frances would precede me in death. * * * Now at my death Ruth gets nothing whatever except my own private estate. * * * Since Frances' share of 10453 was to have been 40% and since I do not wish to wreck the trust * * * I am trying to so arrange it that at my death Ruth can have something more. * * * Richard Miller and Walter Day each have agreed to give up 7½% or about ⅓ of the 20% they will receive. * * * If you now agree, then Ruth will receive at my death 3 × 7½%. * * * "

Plaintiff replied on June 10th declining to agree, saying: "Will, I don't see any reason why I should take any * * * actions in changing your Father's trust. * * *" On July 2nd, the cotrustee's attorney again wrote plaintiff enclosing a proposed agreement between Ruth Day and plaintiff, whereby the latter agreed to pay to the former 37½% * * * of the total amount received by plaintiff "as her distributive interest under the terms of said Trust. * * *"

Plaintiff declined to execute the agreement, and on August 8th, co-trustee William H. Day wrote again at length urging plaintiff to consent to the proposal, adding: "Now Gwen I am going to be frank and say your letter to me hurt me so I simply could see no reason to reply. * * * I planned this trust myself and do not wish to change it to the detriment of anyone. * * * Now Gwen I have gone to great lengths in this letter to have peace and understanding. I cannot go any farther. * * *" Plaintiff did not reply; nor did she execute the requested agreement.

On November 26th, William H. Day, as co-trustee, wrote defendant Title Insurance and Trust Company, as trustee, that "the undersigned, by reason of the authority vested in him as co-trustee, and subject to the approval of your company as Trustee, hereby directs that the provisions [of the Trust] be changed * * *" so that upon termination, instead of 20% each, the distributive shares in question would be as follows:

(a) "28% thereof * * * to Walter S. Day";

(b) "28% thereof * * * to Richard Miller";

(c) "4% thereof * * * to [plaintiff] Gwendolyn Smith * * *."

On the same date the trustee acknowledged receipt of the co-trustee's requested amendment, and certified that "said amendment and modification be, and the same is hereby accepted and approved." On November 29th, the trustee wrote plaintiff informing her of the "direction from William H. Day, co-trustee * * * changing the distributable percentages * * * of said trust." The letter concludes: "Said direction has been accepted and approved by this company as trustee, in accordance with the terms of said trust."

On November 30th, William H. Day wrote plaintiff: "Your refusal to join Richard Miller * * * and Walter Day in assenting to any change has forced me to go through a very expensive legal process."

"In accordance with original terms of the trust * * * you would have received 20% of the principal * * * at my death, whereas now you will receive but 4% as you will note. * * *

"I tried to arrange this in a friendly way but your uncompromising attitude made it impossible.

"I deeply regret being forced to do this. * * *"

On December 6th, plaintiff wrote the trustee: "Referring to your approval of the transfer of percentages from trust P–10453 in the amount of 16% of my 20% to Richard Miller and Walter S. Day. * * * This transaction involves the loss to me of roughly $16,000 and without just cause. Please send me at once all the information and reason why you sanctioned such a drastic change in this trust."

Defendant Title Insurance and Trust Company replied to plaintiff on December 9th: "The change in the distributive percentages * * * was made in accordance with the terms of the trust and upon the written direction of William H. Day, co-trustee. * * * Upon receipt thereof, the matter was submitted to our trust officer and trust counsel, neither of whom could find any valid reason why we should not accept and approve such direction. It was, therefore, accepted and approved in accordance with the terms of the trust."

On December 17, 1946, William H. Day died, and Trust No. P–10453 ipso facto terminated.

Plaintiff contends "that the purported exercise by said William H. Day of his power to effect such change in the distributive shares under said Declaration of Trust was invalid and ineffective and that it was not bona fide and in furtherance of the Declaration of Trust but was fraudulent and intended by means of said separate agreements to accomplish in substance distribution of a portion of the trust estate to a stranger to the trust, Ruth Day," who was not an object of the power of appointment reposed in William H. Day by the trustor.

As set forth in the pre-trial stipulation, "It is the position of Title Insurance and Trust Company that the co-trustee, William H. Day, was vested with the absolute right and power, with the approval of said Title Insurance and Trust Company, to prescribe and direct said Title Insurance and Trust Company that distribution be made in any proportions which said co-trustee, William H. Day, might desire, and that there was vested in William H. Day the discretionary power, with the approval of Title Insurance and Trust Company, to make distributions in accordance therewith and that when said direction is once made and said power exercised, that same cannot be collaterally or otherwise attacked by a beneficiary."

Plaintiff concedes that a trustee holding an absolute power to appoint within a limited class may be even arbitrary or capricious in its exercise, but urges that the power may not be exercised in bad faith or with an intent to benefit a non-object of the power, as plaintiff maintains was done here.

* * *

The rule has long been settled at common law that "If a donee of a special power makes an appointment to an object of the power in consideration of a benefit conferred upon or promised to a non-object, the appointment is ineffective to whatever extent it was motivated by the purpose to benefit the non-object * * *." [Restatement, Property, § 353]. Such an exercise of a special power is held to be a fraud upon the power and hence void. [Matter of Carroll, 1937, 274 N.Y. 288, 8 N.E.2d 864, 115 A.L.R. 923; Chenoweth v. Bullitt, 1928, 224 Ky. 698, 6 S.W.2d 1061; Degman v. Degman, 1896, 98 Ky. 717, 34 S.W. 523; Pitman v. Pitman, 1943, 314 Mass. 465, 50 N.E.2d 69, 150 A.L.R. 509.] Decisions of the courts of England have added the reverence of antiquity to this principle [Lee v. Fernie, 1 Beavan 483, 48 Eng.Repr. 1027 (1839); In re Marsden's Trust, supra, 4 Drewry 594, 62 Eng.Repr. 228; In re Kirwan's Trusts, L.R. 25 Ch.Div. 373 (1883)], and in the absence of California decisions or statutes to the contrary, the law of California must be presumed to be in accord with the common law of England [Cal.Pol.Code, § 4468].

The manifest purpose of the rule is to insure that the intention of the donor of the power be effectuated. An appointment to a non-object, by direction or indirection, patently negatives the donor's intent, is technically a fraud on the power, and a breach of trust. Such action by a trustee in fraud of a power necessarily defeats at least in part the purpose of the trust. When such a circumstance exists, a court of equity should declare the appointment void. [In re Kirwan's Trusts, supra, L.R. 25 Ch.Div. 373 (1883); Chenoweth v. Bullitt, supra, 1928, 224 Ky. 698, 6 S.W.2d 1061.]

* * *

It is my opinion, therefore, that the challenged exercise by the trustees of the power of appointment conferred under Trust No. P–10453 was ineffective to change the distributive shares. It follows that plaintiff is entitled to 20% of the net trust estate available for distribution.

Counsel for plaintiff will submit findings of fact, conclusions of law and judgment pursuant to local rule 7 within ten days.

NOTE

In the principal case did the lawyers for William H. Day and for the trust company view Day's special power as "exclusive" or "non-exclusive"? Suppose Day had appointed directly to his second wife? Would the case be handled differently? [38] Can there be a fraudulent or excessive exercise of a general power? In Delaware, and perhaps in a few other states, it is possible to create a general power which can be exercised only to appoint an absolute interest (sometimes described as special as to the estate).[39] There is a presumption that the donor of the general power did not intend to impose such a limit in states in which this limitation is recognized and it has been stated that the presumption of no limitation stands "unless the language of the power or other provisions of the instrument involved compel a contrary construction".[40] If the intent to impose such a limitation upon general powers was found in a jurisdiction which recognized the limitation, a fraudulent or excessive issue might be presented, but there are no decisions on these points. The American Law Institute takes the position that a donor cannot restrict a general power so an appointment cannot be made by the donee in trust and this is the general rule.[41]

In addition to creating new trust limitations, the donee of a general power may also attempt to create further powers of appointment. Suppose A conveys to trustees in trust for B for life, then as B shall appoint by his will. B leaves a will appointing to C for life, remainder as C shall appoint by his will.

38. See Simes and Smith, The Law of Future Interests (2d Ed. 1956) § 981.

39. See Equitable Trust Co. v. James, 29 Del.Ch. 166, 47 A.2d 303 (1946).

40. Id. 29 Del.Ch. at 178, 47 A.2d at 309.

41. 3 Restatement, Property (1940) § 356.

This is subject to two objections: (1) that the donor A has special confidence in B and did not intend B to "delegate" to someone else the power conferred upon him, in other words that the power was personal to B; and (2) that the second power is void under the Rule against Perpetuities. Obviously these are separate objections, and the possibility that the second one is sound has no bearing on the first. In Lamkin v. Safe Deposit & Trust Co.,[42] the settlor established a trust for his wife for life, with directions to the trustee upon the death of the wife "to transfer and deliver the rest and residue of my estate to such person or persons as she may limit, nominate and appoint by her last will and testament." The wife appointed in trust for certain named relatives and gave them power to dispose of their shares of the corpus by will. The court held this valid, stating:

> "It is said in Simes, Law of Future Interests, Section 264, where that author is discussing powers of appointment generally, that 'The exercise of the power cannot be delegated.' Further, in the same section is the statement 'It is also held that the donee of a general power may exercise his power by appointing a partial estate, and creating another power' and also '* * * the creation of the second power is explainable, *not as a delegation of the first power*, but as an appointment of the property, to shift on an event, namely, the exercise of the second power.' (Emphasis supplied.) In Restatement, Property, Future Interests, Paragraph 357, it is stated: 'The donee of a general power can effectively exercise the power by creating a new power.' In the case of Mays v. Beech, 114 Tenn. 544, 86 S.W. 713, 714, 4 Ann.Cas. 1189, where a testator left his estate to his daughter, with power to her (in the absence of children, which was the case) to dispose of it by her will. She left the income from it to her husband, and empowered him to dispose of it by his will. It was contended in that case, as here, that this was a delegation of the power given the daughter, but the court said 'The power * * * is not a delegation of the power vested in the testatrix by her father's will, but the creation of a distinct and original power appurtenant to the life estate given the devisee for life, to appoint the property in question, and is valid. * * * This is a less estate than she was authorized to create by the will of her father, and is within the power therein vested in her.' The Supreme Court of Tennessee cited as authority for its conclusion three English cases, Bray v. Bree, Clark & Finley's House of Lords Reports, Vol. 2, p. 453, Phipson v. Turner; 9 Simons' English Chan.Rep. 287 and Moses v. Martin, 34 Beavan's Rep. 500.
>
> "The same conclusion has been reached in Pennsylvania, McClellan's Estate, 221 Pa. 261, 70 A. 737; Lawrence's Estate, 136 Pa. 354, 20 A. 511, 11 L.R.A. 85, 20 Am.St.Rep. 925; Lewis' Estates, 269 Pa. 379, 112 A. 454. See note on the last case in 13 A.L.R. 1055. A similar opinion was expressed in Massachusetts. Thayer v. Rivers, 179 Mass. 280, 60 N.E. 996; Garfield v. State Street Trust Co., 320 Mass. 646, 70 N.E.2d 705, 169 A.L.R. 719. And in New York it was stated 'The decisions in our State have held that it is within the authority of the donee of a general power to give a further and secondary power of appointment to some other person.' In re Wildenburg's Estate, 174 Misc. 503, 21 N.Y.S.2d 331, 337, citing four earlier New York decisions."

Care should be taken in attempting to apply these same rules to a special power, however. The very nature of the special class to whom appointment

42. 192 Md. 472, 64 A.2d 704 (1949), 48 Mich.L.Rev. 129 (1949).

may be made makes it likely that appointments by the donee which create future interests and additional powers of appointment will be in favor of non-objects. Suppose A gives property in trust for B for life, then to such of B's issue as B may appoint by will. B appoints to a son C for life, then to such of C's issue as C may appoint by his will, in default to C's issue per stirpes. The New York court has taken the position that only the life estate appointed to C is within the objects of the original power, since A contemplated as objects of the power a class composed of B's issue determined at the time of B's death.[43] However, it has been held that the donee of a special power may appoint in favor of an object a life estate with a general power of appointment, since this is tantamount to a full appointment.[44] And the Restatement takes the position that he may appoint a life estate with a special power to appoint among the objects of the original power.[45]

SECTION 3. RELEASE AND CONTRACT TO APPOINT

---

(1) RELEASE

The ability of the donee of a power of appointment to release it assumed great importance because of tax advantages which could be gained in some situations. It also affords flexibility to the donee. The only objection is that it may run counter to the intention of the donor. Since the donee of a power presently exercisable could presently make an appointment, there is no objection to his making a release. On the other hand, a testamentary power could not be exercised by a deed. Is it subject to release? This and the related problem of presently contracting to make a particular appointment are closely allied to the preceding Section.

DISTRICT OF COLUMBIA v. LLOYD

United States Court of Appeals for the District of Columbia, 1947.
160 F.2d 581.

WILBUR K. MILLER, ASSOCIATE JUSTICE. The District of Columbia exacted from the respondent an inheritance tax calculated on the

43. Matter of Kennedy's Will, 279 N.Y. 255, 18 N.E.2d 146 (1938).

44. Stone v. Forbes, 189 Mass. 163, 75 N.E. 141 (1905).

45. Restatement, Property (1940) § 359. See American Law of Property (1952) § 23.49. See, McCoyd, "Exercising Powers of Appointment by Creating New Trusts and New Powers: Extent of the Donee's Authority", 111 Trusts and Estates 272 (1972).

value of certain property which it claimed had passed to the respondent's ward, Tangley C. Lloyd, at and because of the death of her father, Demarest Lloyd, Jr. Its Board of Tax Appeals having held the tax inapplicable and having ordered a refund, the District of Columbia appeals.

On January 23, 1932, Tangley's grandfather, Demarest Lloyd, then the owner of the property, placed it in an irrevocable trust. The instrument provided that the income, subject to certain restrictions, should be expended for or paid to the donor's son, Demarest Lloyd, Jr. Provision was also made for the corpus of the estate to be distributed to the son, one portion at the age of 25 years, another at 35, and the remainder at 45.

In the following terms, the declaration of trust gave Demarest Lloyd, Jr., a general power of appointment with respect to the corpus: "6. If the said Demarest Lloyd, Jr., dies after attaining the age of twenty-one years, all of the trust property which has not been distributed to said Demarest Lloyd Jr., shall upon the death of the said Demarest Lloyd Jr., be assigned and transferred as he may by his will appoint, or in default of such appointment by the said Demarest Lloyd Jr., shall be paid and transferred to the persons who would be entitled to distribution of his personal estate as of the date of his death according to the laws of the District of Columbia."

Demarest Lloyd, Jr., executed a will on October 11, 1943, which contained the following paragraph: "Nothing contained in this, my Will, is intended to be or operate as an exercise in any respect whatsoever of any right or power of appointment which now vests or may be vested in me under any declaration of trust or testamentary instrument whatsoever."

On January 24, 1944, Demarest Lloyd, Jr., executed under seal an instrument by the terms of which he released and surrendered all power or powers of appointment conferred upon him under the declaration of trust of January 23, 1932. The text of the release is shown in the margin.[46]

46. [Footnote by the Court. Other Judicial footnotes have been eliminated—Ed.]

"I, Demarest Lloyd, formerly Junior, beneficiary named in a declaration of trust by my father, Demarest Lloyd, dated January 23, 1932, for the benefit of Demarest Lloyd, Jr., et als., of which the Harvard Trust Company of Cambridge, Massachusetts, and my mother, Katharine Nordel Lloyd, are at present the Trustees, do hereby, in consideration of one dollar and other valuable considerations which I acknowledge to have received from each of the persons who would be entitled to distribution of my personal estate as of the date of my death, according to the laws of the District of Columbia, and from the Trustees aforesaid for the benefit of such persons, release and hereby surrender all power or powers of appointment conferred upon me under paragraph 6 as to 'Distribution of Principal' under said declaration of trust or elsewhere in said trust, so that I may henceforth be absolutely precluded from exercising said power, and for the consideration aforesaid I, the said Demarest Lloyd, hereby make (a) with said Trustees and their successors as such, and (b) with each of the persons who would be entitled to distribution of my personal estate as of the date of my death, according to the laws of the District of Columbia, a covenant in the terms following, namely, that I, the said Demarest Lloyd, will not exercise said power or powers of appointment conferred upon me in said declaration of trust.

Young Lloyd was a naval reserve officer in active service and was killed in action on June 12, 1944, at an age or more than 21 and less than 45 years. His will as admitted to probate in the District of Columbia on June 29, 1944. Nancy T. Lloyd, his widow, and an infant daughter, Tangley C. Lloyd, survive and are "the persons who would be entitled to distribution of his personal estate as of the date of his death according to the laws of the District of Columbia."

Except for the provisions of the will and the instrument of release, there would be no question of the petitioner's right to the inheritance tax which it claims. Section 1601(j) of Title 47, District of Columbia Code 1940,[47] provides that an appointment made under a power such as that involved here shall be deemed to be a transfer taxable as though the property transferred by the appointment had belonged absolutely to the donee of the power. Moreover, by the terms of the same section of the statute, if the person possessing the power omits or fails to exercise it within the time provided for, nevertheless a taxable transfer results as though the power had been exercised.

The petitioner asserts that the release of the power attempted to be made by the decedent in this case did not destroy the power of appointment, but amounted to no more than an assertion of an intention not to exercise it. Hence, the petitioner argues, there was a taxable transfer under § 1601(j) because of the nonexercise of a general power of appointment. The petitioner further contends that the tax is justified under § 1601(a), which applies it to the transfer of property from any person who dies "seized or possessed" thereof or of any interest therein.

The two contentions of the District of Columbia are so intertwined with respect to the factual situation, and indeed the statutory provisions as well, that they may be considered together. The petitioner says that Demarest Lloyd, Jr., died seized or possessed of the corpus, within the meaning of § 1601(a), for three reasons, viz., (a) he had the right to the income from the corpus up to the date of his death; (b) had he lived to the age of 45 years he would have become the legal owner of the corpus; (c) he had the power to dispose of the property by will. The right to the income during his life gave Demarest Lloyd, Jr., an equitable interest in the corpus, but that interest terminated with death. Although he would have become seized and possessed of the corpus had he reached the age of 45, that fact is without significance for the reason that he never attained that age. The petitioner's third contention that Demarest Lloyd, Jr., died seized or possessed of the corpus because he had the power to dispose of the property at death assumes the very fact upon which the case turns and this brings us then to the decisive question at issue: Did the release destroy the power of appointment, or was the release no more than a

"In witness whereof, I, the said Demarest Lloyd, set my hand and seal hereunto and to two other instruments of like tenor and date and make delivery of the same to said Harvard Trust Company, Trustee, for itself and as Trustee for each and every the said covenantees, on the 24th day of January 1944."

47. Amended in 1971. See D.C. Code § 47–1601 (1979 Supp.).—Ed.

covenant not to use the power with the result that until death the right of appointment, though not exercised, still existed?

No statutory provision in this jurisdiction answers the question, for the Congress, in legislating for the District of Columbia, has not expressly authorized the donee of a general power of appointment to release it, as have the legislatures of at least sixteen states. Nor is the answer to be found in judicial decisions, as the problem posed in this case as a matter of first impression in this jurisdiction.

The American Law Institute announces in 3 Restatement, Property § 334, that "all general powers of appointment can be released by the donee." To be sure, the Institute admits American case law on powers of appointment to be "distinctly thin in quantity," but the practical unanimity of the available cases impelled it to the statement contained in § 334. The conclusion reached, in so far as it embraces testamentary powers, is, as Randolph E. Paul says, "apparently tinged with a note of regret because releasability seems to violate the donor's desire that the power be held until the final moment of the donee's death. * * *" Mr. Paul adds that, while the Restatement's views are not conclusive, "it is highly significant that with one lone exception all commentators on the question have agreed that a general testamentary power is releasable."

The power with which we are now concerned is not one which can be said to be in trust; that is to say, the donee was not under an active duty to exercise it. Moreover, the donor clearly contemplated that the donee might not exercise the power. In that situation, we see no reason why the donee may not extinguish the power if he desires and it seems that no serious or material frustration of the donor's wish can be said to result. Accordingly we hold that Demarest Lloyd, Jr., could release his general power of appointment.

* * *

It remains to consider whether the instrument of release executed by Demarest Lloyd, Jr., was in form sufficient to accomplish his purpose. We deem it enough to refer to 3 Restatement, Property § 336(1), which is as follows: "When the donee of a releasable power delivers, to some person who could be adversely affected by an appointment, an instrument, by consideration or under seal, declaring that he releases the power, the power is thereby released."

The carefully considered opinion of the Board of Tax Appeals and the decision pursuant thereto seem to us to be correct.

Affirmed.

NOTE

The modern doctrine favoring free release of general and special powers was given great impetus by the Federal Revenue Act of 1942 which taxed the exercise or non-exercise of all except a restricted type of special power defined in the Act and permitted donees to release their powers without incurring a gift tax. As the principal case illustrates, there may be advantages under other tax statutes. Commencing in 1943, the legislatures of more than half the states adopted statutes which vary in detail but all of which were designed to permit donees freely to release powers and avoid the unexpected impact of the federal estate tax.[48] Almost all of these cover special as well as general powers, sometimes even "trust" powers.

Many of the tax advantages attendant upon release of powers in the 40's have been eliminated under the present tax laws. A partial release achieves no tax savings; a complete release is subject to the gift tax[49] and under many circumstances may still leave the appointive property in the taxable estate of the donee for estate tax purposes (as where the donee retains the right to income from the property for his life).[50] Undoubtedly the widespread adoption of legislation permitting free release and the liberal attitude of the courts demonstrated in the principal case can be attributed to the desire to permit flexibility to achieve tax savings. Now that these savings are less dramatic under present tax laws, some commentators are beginning to question the desirability of permitting release of a testamentary power, on the ground that release violates the intent of the donor that the donee retain his power until the time of his death.

The English common law, influenced by the notion that a life tenant could make a tortious feoffment which barred subsequent exercise of the power, permitted release of all except a power simply collateral (where the donee has no other interest in the land).

The Restatement of Property (1940) § 335 originally expressed the view that a special testamentary power could not be released unless the donor had manifested an intent that the power should be releasable. The 1948 Supplement reversed this position, leaving in essence only so-called trust powers non-releasable.

The formalities of executing a valid release (necessity of consideration or seal, delivery, recording, etc.) are discussed in 46 Mich.L.Rev. 106 (1947).

---

(2) CONTRACT TO APPOINT

Occasionally the donee of a power wishes to contract to appoint in favor of a specific person. In most of these cases the donee resorts to a contract as a legal device to accomplish an objective impossible

48. E.g., Ill.Rev.Stat. c. 30, §§ 177–182, 1965; M.G.L.A. c. 204 §§ 27–33 (1975 Supp.).

49. IRC § 2514 (26 U.S.C.A.). A complete release of a general power of appointment created on or before Oct. 21, 1942 is not subject to gift tax; but the release of such a power achieves no tax savings since the failure to exercise the power would not result in any estate tax on death of the donee under § 2041(a)(1). The release of a special power is not subject to the gift tax; but the release of a present special power held by a "deemed transferor" will be a taxable termination resulting in a generation skipping tax unless the power is one limited to the lineal descendants of the grantor. IRC § 2613(b)(1), (d)(2), (e), 26 U.S.C.A. added P. L. 94–455 § 2006 (1976).

50. IRC § 2041(a)(2) (26 U.S.C.A.) includes in the donee's estate property with respect to which the donee released a general power "by a disposition which is of such nature that if it were a transfer of property owned by the decedent, such property would be includable in the decedent's gross estate" under other provisions of the Code.

under the terms of the power itself. It should be obvious that the courts will not enforce such an arrangement when it infringes the intent of the donor. For example, as we saw in Horne v. Title Insurance & Trust Co., where a special power is involved, the donee cannot contract with a permissible appointee to appoint to him in consideration of benefit to a non-object, any more than the donee could appoint directly to the non-object. If the power is general and presently exercisable, no conceivable purpose of the donor can be thwarted by enforcement of a contract to appoint. On the other hand, if the power is testamentary, even though general, a present contract to appoint—if enforceable either by specific performance or by a suit for damages—would violate part of the purpose of the donor. The Supreme Court of Illinois states the judicial position well in Northern Trust Co. v. Porter: [51]

> "The donor, in giving a general power of appointment by will only, intends that the donee shall retain his discretion as to who shall receive the property subject to appointment, until the time of his death. The purpose of giving such power is to allow the exercise of such power to represent the final judgment of the donee. To permit a contract to appoint in a certain way to be binding would be, in effect, to change the power from a general testamentary power to a power to appoint by deed or will. The intention of the donor must not be thus circumvented. This holding, of course, in no way implies that an appointment in compliance with a contract to appoint will be set aside.
>
> "If the defendants' claim for damages be allowed, it would indirectly be allowing performance of the settlement contract and the defendants would become creditors of the estate of Mrs. Porter. Since Mrs. Porter's individual estate is very small, the McWilliams fund would have to be retained as part of the donee's estate in order to satisfy creditors, who take in preference to appointees or takers in default after a defective appointment. Gilman v. Bell, 99 Ill. 144.
>
> "Moreover, the knowledge that damages would be given in case she did not comply with the contract would make the donee reluctant to breach the contract and thus to exercise her freedom of choice up to the last moment of her life—a thing which the donor intended. In other words, if damages are allowed against the estate of the donee, it has the effect of exerting coercion of a threatened judgment to compel voluntary performance of an act which could not be judicially enforced by specific performance. For this reason, damages may be recovered from neither the individual estate of the donee nor from the appointive fund. In so holding, we do not depart from Gilman v. Bell, supra. What was said there applies to creditors of the donee other than the promisee of a contract to appoint property subject to a power of appointment. In the instant case, the contract to appoint is entirely void,

51. 368 Ill. 256, 266–267, 13 N.E.2d 487, 492–493 (1938).

and, as a result, the defendants are not creditors of the donee, so as to come under the rule of Gilman v. Bell, supra.

"Our view is in accord with that of the reporters of the American Law Institute, who state, in the Restatement of Property, tenative draft No. 7, § 463, comment (a): 'By giving a testamentary power or a power otherwise not presently exercisable, the donor expresses an intent that the discretion as to the exercise of the power shall be retained until the donee's death or such other time as is stipulated. To specifically enforce a promise to appoint under such a power would be to permit the donor's intent as to disposition of his property to be directly defeated. Moreover, to allow the donee to render himself liable in damages for breach of such promise would be to permit the donor's intent to be defeated by indirection; for the compulsion of a prospective suit for damages would be sufficient to eliminate any practical freedom of choice after the making of the contract. These considerations are especially strong where the power is special and consequently the duty to postpone the exercise of discretion is one of the fiduciary duties owed to the objects of the power; but even where the power is general the fulfillment of the donor's lawful wishes is a sufficient reason for denying validity to promises to appoint.' The reporters evidently preferred not to follow the case of In re Parkin, 3 L.R. (Ch.Div.1892) 510, 1892 Probate 591, and with them we agree."

Unlike an appointment to the object of a special power, pursuant to a contract to benefit a non-object, a testamentary appointment under a general testamentary power pursuant to contract is valid even though the contract itself is not enforceable.

Suppose X, deceased, left property in trust to pay the income to his widow for life, the principal to go at her death to such person or persons as she might appoint by her will, in default to their children equally. The widow is about to remarry, and the children are apprehensive that she may appoint to the second husband. To eliminate this possible source of friction, the widow wants to reassure the children that they will receive the trust fund on her death. She can, of course, release the power as we have seen; and a release is the proper legal method of achieving this result. If the widow executes a document which is in form "a contract" to appoint in favor of the children (who are the takers in default), there is authority that this should be treated as a release and hence effective.[52]

---

52. American Law of Property § 23.-36 (1952).

SECTION 4. CREDITORS OF THE DONEE

STATE STREET TRUST CO., TRUSTEE v. KISSEL

Supreme Judicial Court of Massachusetts, 1939.
302 Mass. 328, 19 N.E.2d 25.

DOLAN, JUSTICE. This is an appeal from a decree entered in the Probate Court, instructing the petitioner as to its duties with relation to a certain trust estate, held by it as trustee under the fourth and residuary clause of the will of Julia Emma Bradford, late of Boston, deceased (hereinafter described as the testatrix), for the benefit of Samuel Dexter Bradford, who is now deceased.

* * *

[The full statement of facts by the court is omitted, and only an abbreviated statement is given here. Julia Emma Bradford died in 1886. Her will left half of her residuary estate to trustees to pay the income in equal shares to the three children of her deceased son; upon the death of each grandchild the trustees were directed to "pay over and distribute such portion of the principal of said trust fund as such grandchild dying was entitled to the income of, during its life, to such person or persons as such grandchild by its last will and testament directs and appoints to receive the same, but in no event shall any part of said trust funds be liable for, or be paid or appropriated to or for any debts or liabilities of such grandchildren"; there followed a detailed gift over in default of appointment. One of the grandchildren, Samuel D. Bradford, died May 18, 1935. His will dated October 22, 1934, specifically exercised the power by appointing $30,000 in favor of Thelma Cooper, $5,000 to Jacob Rosenberg and the remainder to Percy D. Atherton. Other facts appear below.]

The petition was heard on the facts therein alleged, statements and stipulations of counsel, and certain exhibits, all of which appear in the record. The judge filed a report of facts in substance as follows: At the time of the execution of the will of Samuel D. Bradford, hereinafter described as the donee, he was indebted to the appointee Rosenberg in the sum of $5,000; to the appointee Cooper in the sum of about $30,000, and to the residuary appointee Atherton in the sum of $23,490.50 and interest. The provisions for them were made by the donee in consequence of agreements made by him so to satisfy their claims. The judge specifically found that the relation of debtor and creditors existed between the donee and them at the times of the execution of the will of the donee and of his death.

After hearing, the judge entered a decree to the effect that the power of appointment conferred upon the donee by the will of the testatrix was a general one; that it was validly exercised by the donee, and that the provision in the fourth clause of the will of the testatrix "that after the exercise of the above mentioned power of appointment, no part of the trust property shall be appropriated for the payment of the debts of the donee of the power, is invalid as an improper limitation upon the general power of appointment," and that the appointed property be paid to the executors in Massachusetts of the will of the donee of the power.

The respondent Mary J. Kissel appealed from this decree and now contends "that the provision in the clause of the will of Julia Emma Bradford granting a power of appointment to her grandchildren—'*but in no event shall any part of said trust funds be liable for, or be paid or appropriated to or for any debts or liabilities of such grandchildren*'—was a limitation upon the power prohibiting an appointment by Bradford to creditors for the purpose of paying his debts to them, that the persons to whom Bradford appointed the trust property were creditors and that the appointment was made for the purpose of satisfying his debts to them, that accordingly no appointment within the scope of the power was made, and that in accordance with the terms of the will the trust fund was to be continued in trust for the benefit of this respondent."

It has long been settled in this Commonwealth that "when there was a general power of appointment, which it was absolutely in the donee's pleasure to execute or not, he might do it for any purpose whatever, and might appoint the money to be paid to his executors if he pleased, and, if he executed it voluntarily and without consideration, for the benefit of third persons, the money should be considered part of his assets, and his creditors should have the benefit of it." Clapp v. Ingraham, 126 Mass. 200, 202. While reference is made in the case just cited to an execution of the power "voluntarily and without consideration," it is also established in Vinton v. Pratt, 228 Mass. 468, 117 N.E. 919, L.R.A.1918D, 343, a case which in the facts closely resembles the case at bar, that, where the donee of a testamentary power exercised it for the purpose of discharging his obligations upon a guaranty in writing, by the exercise of the power the property, if necessary, could be applied in satisfaction of the donee's debts. In that case, at page 470, 117 N.E. at page 920, it is said that this "has become a rule of property, and having been unchallenged for nearly 40 years, we cannot agree with the defendant, that it should be overset." We think that the rule is the same whether the appointment be made voluntarily as a benefaction, or upon a consideration.

The intention of the testatrix is to be gathered from a reading of her will as a whole considered in the light of the material circumstances known to her at the time of its execution. When thus ascertained, her intent must be given effect unless some positive rule of law forbids. Ware v. Minot, 202 Mass. 512, 88 N.E. 1091. Thus considered, it appears that the will was executed and allowed over fifty years ago. Its provisions for the children of her son Samuel are identical. The will contains a specific spendthrift provision applicable to the shares of all the grandchildren during their respective lives, which embraces both the trust fund and the income therefrom. It is established in this Commonwealth that such a provision is valid. Broadway National Bank v. Adams, 133 Mass. 170, 43 Am.Rep. 504;

Boston Safe Deposit & Trust Co. v. Collier, 222 Mass. 390, 111 N.E. 163, Ann.Cas.1918C, 962. We see no reason for departing from the principles set forth in those cases, and followed in Bucknam v. Bucknam, Mass., 200 N.E. 918, 104 A.L.R. 774. See also Burrage v. Bucknam, Mass., 16 N.E.2d 705. Immediately following this spendthrift provision effective during the lives of the grandchildren, the testatrix provided that "upon the death of each of such grandchildren * * * [the trustees] shall pay over and distribute such portion of the principal of said trust fund as such grandchild dying was entitled to the income of, during its life, to such person or persons as such grandchild by its last will and testament directs and appoints to receive the same, but in no event shall any part of said trust funds be liable for, or be paid or appropriated to or for any debts or liabilities of such grandchildren. * * *" Then follow the provisions in case, not of an exercise of the power by the donees in favor of creditors, but of default of appointment without qualification.

We are of opinion that it is manifest that the dominant intention of the testatrix was that, as during the lives of the respective donees, neither the trust fund nor the income therefrom should be liable for any debts contracted by them, so also the testatrix intended that upon their respective deaths, notwithstanding the general power conferred upon them to appoint their shares by will, the appointed property should not be paid to their creditors nor appropriated to the satisfaction of their creditor's claims. We think that her intent was the same whether the appointment was exercised indirectly or expressly to creditors of the donees, or was exercised to volunteers as pure benefactions, and that her clear purpose was to extend the rules established by our decisions relating to spendthrift trusts during the lives of the beneficiaries, beyond, notwithstanding the general power to appoint by will conferred upon them. She was concerned not with whom the appointees should be, but rather that in no event should the creditors of the donees reach the trust estate in satisfaction of their claims. The power was a general one; the subsequent provision, that the property appointed should not be appropriated to or for any debts or liabilities of the donees, we think was a direction to the trustees, who would be the only persons who could "pay," and a restriction upon them rather than a limitation upon the power to appoint. Such an intent cannot be given effect. The testatrix could not effectually thus give with one hand and take away with the other.

In the case of Hill v. Treasurer & Receiver General, 229 Mass. 474, 118 N.E. 891, L.R.A.1918D, 337, in the course of a careful analysis of the nature of general powers of appointment, at page 476, 118 N.E. at page 892, the court said: "The doctrine that appointed property shall be regarded as assets of the estate of the donee who has exercised a general power of appointment is purely equitable. It rests on the fundamental idea that a man ought to pay his debts when he has the power to do so, rather than to give property to those who are not his creditors. It is not founded on the actual intent of the one who has exercised the power. This principle of equity disregards the desires of the donor in creating the power, deprives the donee of the untrammelled authority conferred upon him in terms, and to the extent of its scope does violence to the manifest design of the donee in exercising the appointment. It would operate even in the face of his testamentary declaration to the contrary. Equity seizes the property on its way from the donor to the appointee, and applies it to the satisfaction of the obligations of the appointor." We think that these principles are decisive of the question before us; that the desire of the donor in the case at bar to place a subsequent limitation on the general power once given must be disregarded. In like manner, the actual intent of the donee who has exercised the power to satisfy in that manner certain of his creditors must be set aside, and they must take their places with the other creditors of his estate, which is insolvent, and must take their pro rata shares, not as appointees, but just as creditors.

The appointees in the case at bar have not appealed from the decree under consideration, and thus have evidenced their acceptance of what we have just said, although it sets at naught the intent of the donee. See Am.Law.Inst.Restatement: Property, § 452 and comment c, where, after stating the general equitable doctrine (which is the law of this Commonwealth), it is said: "The rule * * * applies in spite of the manifestation of a contrary intent by the donor or the donee or both. Thus it is immaterial that the donor provides in the instrument creating the power that the property covered thereby shall in no circumstances be appointed to the donee's creditors or subjected to their claims. It is also immaterial that the donee provides in the instrument of appointment that the property shall not be subjected to the claims of his creditors." Thus both attempts are condemned in this statement. Without intimating that all that is there said is not a correct statement of the law and one that would follow from what has been said by this court in such cases as Hill v. Treasurer & Receiver General, 229 Mass. 474, 118 N.E. 891, L.R.A.1918D, 337, it goes further, we think, than we are required to go in the instant case, where the provision is not a specific one that the property shall not be appointed to the donee's creditors, but is one which follows the grant of the general power, and which provides against the payment or appropriation of the appointed property to or for any debts or liabilities of the grandchildren, the donees. In its essence, however, the comment in the restatement, before referred to, includes the facts in the case at bar, and is consistent with the rule, which we have often repeated and have here followed, that the general power once given by the testatrix may not be limited by her so as to defeat the equitable doctrine that the property appointed shall be dealt with as assets of the donee's estate for the satisfaction of his debts, in so far as his individual estate is insufficient therefor. See Tuell v. Hurley, 206 Mass. 65, 91 N.E. 1013.

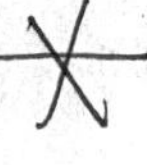

Nothing is said in the decisions of this court sustaining spendthrift trusts as effective during the life of the beneficiary to whose interests as to either principal or income they applied, from which it may be inferred that such provisions, following the grant of a general power to appoint, are valid. "The purpose of a spendthrift trust, however phrased, is to provide a secure living for the beneficiary." Bucknam v. Bucknam, Mass., 200 N.E. 918, 921, 104 A.L.R. 744. Such provisions were effectively made by the testatrix in the case at bar affecting the interests in the trust fund which the donees of the power were to enjoy during their respective lives. We are of opinion that the testatrix could not thereafter, having conferred upon them a general power of appointment, legally make another form of spendthrift trust, to the end that the power having been exercised, the appointed property should still remain beyond the reach of the creditors of the donees. The purpose of the testatrix in this respect must be disregarded.

* * *

The decree entered in the Probate Court instructing the petitioner to pay the appointed property involved to the executors in Massachusetts of the donee is correct. Olney v. Balch, 154 Mass. 318, 28 N.E. 258; Lovejoy v. Bucknam, Mass., 13 N.E.2d 23. It is affirmed, and costs and expenses of this appeal as between solicitor and client are to be in the discretion of the Probate Court.

Ordered accordingly.

NOTE

The policy issue here is similar to that in the spendthrift trust cases generally: can a donor (settlor) confer upon a donee (beneficiary) the practical benefits of ownership without corresponding liability to creditors? See Chapter VIII, Section 5(2). Only where the power is general is this a real issue, since the donee of a special power is more like a trustee than an owner. The cases dealing with the power of appointment have in the past turned largely on the technical property notion that the power of appointment is not itself property. Thus, if the donee of a general power of appointment does not exercise the power, his creditors cannot reach it. Bankruptcy Act,[53] § 541(b) excludes from the estate "any power that the debtor may only exercise solely for the benefit of an entity other than the debtor". By negative inference powers other than these excluded can be reached by the trustee, but the Bankruptcy Act, unlike the superseded Bankruptcy Act § 70–a–3,[54] has no provision extending expressly to powers, although it was apparently thought by the draftsmen that the provisions of former § 70–e were being carried over in the new provision. It thus remains for determination by the courts, unless the statute is amended to cover powers specifically, whether the trustee in bankruptcy can reach an unexercised presently exercisable power which the bankrupt can exercise for his own benefit. Under old § 70–a–3 a testamentary power could not be reached by the trustee since the bankrupt could not exercise it for his own benefit and the new Act probably will be so construed.[55] Special powers seem clearly excluded under the Act. If the presently exercisable general power, whether exercised or not, can be reached under local statutes by creditors the trustee in bankruptcy should be able to reach these powers also unless they fall within the specific federal exemption.

53. 11 U.S.C.A.

54. Former 11 U.S.C.A. § 110(a)(3).

55. Montague v. Silsbee, 218 Mass. 107, 105 N.E. 611 (1914); In re Peck's Estate, 320 Mich. 692, 32 N.W.2d 14 (1948), 47 Mich.L.Rev. 424 (1949).

Just as a spendthrift clause is not effective to protect the interest of a settlor who reserves a life interest, or a power of revocation, so creditors of a settlor may reach the appointive assets when the settlor reserves to himself a general power of appointment, even though it is not exercised.[56]

Where the general power is exercised by the donee, the technical doctrine (if adhered to) that the property passes from the donor and not the donee would again prevent creditors from reaching the property. Here most courts depart from the doctrine and allow creditors to proceed in equity and reach the appointive assets when appointment is made to a "volunteer" and the donee's individual assets are insufficient. Since most general powers are testamentary, and a contract to appoint is void as to a testamentary power, the appointee under a will is almost always a volunteer.

The minority view is stated by the Colorado Supreme Court in Johnson v. Shriver:[57]

> "Fourth: *In this jurisdiction is the rule to be adopted that, where a general power of appointment is exercised by the donee in favor of a volunteer, the appointive property becomes assets in equity for payment of the donee's debts?*
>
> "In paragraph second of the will here involved, there appears to have been an exercise of the power of appointment to beneficiaries who were volunteers. While an answer to the question is not essential to an affirmance of the judgment, for the reasons already stated, the question is presented by this record, and we deem it advisable to give the answer for the guidance of counsel in determining possible future action with relation to those who took property as volunteers under the terms of paragraph second of the will. Our considered opinion is that the rule stated in the question should not be adopted in Colorado. We believe that better reasoning is to be found in the cases from jurisdictions which do not recognize the rule. * * *
>
> "For a discussion of the opposite view see United States v. Field, 255 U.S. 257, 41 S.Ct. 256, 65 L.Ed. 617, 18 A.L.R. 1461.
>
> "In volume 3, Tiffany, Real Property, 3d Ed., at page 86, we find the following comment: 'The doctrine has been criticized as operating to defeat the intention of the donor of the power and of the donee as well, and as ignoring the distinction between powers and property, and has been repudiated or questioned in a steadily increasing number of jurisdictions.'
>
> "We recognize the right of the donor of a power of appointment to condition his bounty as he sees fit, and the creditors of the donee of the power have no reason to complain that the donor did not give his bounty to them."

The early New York legislation which was copied in several other states contained complicated provisions for rights of creditors.[58] Although the basic intent of the New York Revisers in 1828 was to afford creditors access to property over which the debtor had a general power of appointment,[59] this intent was frustrated by judicial interpretation.[60] McKinney's New York Estates, Powers and Trusts Law appears at first glance to give creditors

56. In re Mogridge's Estate, 342 Pa. 308, 20 A.2d 307 (1941).

57. 121 Colo. 397, 216 P.2d 653 (1950), 23 Rocky Mt.L.Rev. 212 (1950).

58. E.g., D.C.Code Ann. §§ 45–1001 to 45–1019.

59. Reports of the Revisers, N.Y.Rev. Stat. (2d Ed. 1836), vol. 3, p. 589.

60. Cutting v. Cutting, 86 N.Y. 522 (1881) (holding that the statute replaced the common law equity rule and afforded no relief if the donee had a life estate under a trust, by an extremely technical in-

greater rights.[61] However, it is inapplicable if the general power is testamentary only;[62] and can be avoided initially by creating a power to appoint to any person except the donee, his creditors, his estate or the creditors of his estate (which is a special power under the New York statutory classification).[63] Four other states have modernized their law on rights of creditors of the donee of a general power.[64]

PROBLEM

Your client is donee of a general testamentary power given him by the will of his father, which contains a gift in default to your client's children or the issue of any deceased child. Because of risks incident to your client's business, there is a possibility that he may die insolvent. In the light of the case-law dealing with rights of creditors, and the materials in Section 2(1), how will you draft the residuary clause of his will?

---

terpretation of the old statute); see also In re Peck's Estate, 320 Mich. 692, 32 N.W.2d 14 (1948), 47 Mich.L.Rev. 424 (1949) (holding the statute inapplicable if the donee has a general testamentary power).

61. McKinney's N.Y., EPTL (1980 Supp.).

"§ 10–7.1 Creditors of the donee; special power

"Property covered by a special power of appointment is not subject to the payment of the claims of creditors of the donee, his estate or the expenses of administering his estate.

"§ 10–7.2 Creditors of the donee; general power presently exercisable

"Property covered by a general power of appointment which is presently exercisable, or of a postponed power which has become exercisable, is subject to the payment of the claims of creditors of the donee, his estate and the expenses of administering his estate. It is immaterial whether the power was created in the donee by himself or by some other person, or whether the donee has or has not purported to exercise the power.

"§ 10–7.3 Creditors of the donee; power subject to a condition

"A general power of appointment may be created subject to a condition precedent or subsequent, and until the condition is fulfilled, it is not subject to the provisions of 10–7.2.

"§ 10–7.4 Creditors of the donee; general power not presently exercisable

"(a) Property covered by a general power of appointment which, when created, is not presently exercisable is subject to the payment of the claims of creditors of the donee, his estate and the expenses of administering his estate, only:

"(1) If the power was created by the donee in favor of himself; or

"(2) If a postponed power becomes exercisable in accordance with the terms of the creating instrument, except in the case of a testamentary general power."

62. See a criticism of the N.Y. law in Comment, "Powers of Appointment—The New York Revision", 65 Col.L.Rev. 1289 (1965).

63. McKinney's N.Y., EPTL, § 10–3.2 (b) and (c) (1975 Supp.).

64. Calif.Civ.Code § 1390.3 (1971); Mich.Comp.Laws § 556.123 et seq. (1981 Supp.); Minn.Stat.Ann. § 502.70 (1980 Supp.); Wis.Stat.Ann. § 702.17 (West Spec. Pamph. 1980). See, Note, "Creditor's Ability to Reach Assets Under a General Power of Appointment", 24 Vand.L.Rev. 367 (1971) (containing discussion of the statutes).

SECTION 5. DISPOSITION UPON INEFFECTIVE EXERCISE AND NON-EXERCISE

TALBOT v. RIGGS

Supreme Judicial Court of Massachusetts, 1934.
287 Mass. 144, 191 N.E. 360, 93 A.L.R. 964.[65]

RUGG, CHIEF JUSTICE. This is a petition by the trustee under the will of Emma C. F. Keller, late of Boston, for instructions as to the disposition to be made of a trust fund remaining in his hands after the death of all the life tenants. A power of appointment over this fund was given by the will to Thomas H. Talbot. The trustee seeks instructions on two points: (1) Whether there has been a valid exercise of the power of appointment by the donee, and (2) if there has not been such valid exercise of the power, whether distribution of the fund shall be made to the next of kin and heirs at law of the testatrix, the donor of the power, or to the representative of the deceased donee of the power.

There is no dispute concerning the material facts. The testatrix, the donor of the power, died in 1900. By her will duly allowed in 1904, she gave all her property to her brother, Thomas H. Talbot, upon certain trusts. The income was to be paid to certain of her kindred; the last of these beneficiaries died in 1931. The will also directed that, upon the termination of all the life estates, the principal sum of the trust fund with its accumulations "shall * * * go to such use as he [her brother] shall, by will or other writing, appoint at any time before or after my decease. * * *" He left a will which was allowed in 1907. It consists of ten clauses aside from an unnumbered one appointing an executor and trustee. The first seven clauses deal with his own property. By clauses eighth, ninth, and tenth he attempted to exercise the power of appointment given him by the will of the testatrix. The eighth clause is in these words: "Further, the preceding dispositions do not affect any estate or property, which may come, during my life, to me, or after my death, to my representative, under the will of my sister, Emma C. F. Keller, except that, my said wife surviving me, the same is hereby devised, given and bequeathed to said William Richardson Billings in trust to pay the income" to beneficiaries who did not survive the termination of the life estates in the fund created by the will of the testatrix. It is conceded that this clause was ineffective to the extent that none of the persons therein named could, in the events which have come to pass, receive any benefit thereby. By clause ninth it was provided that the trust created by clause eighth "not taking effect at my decease, or thereafter being fully discharged," as has happened, the "property coming under the will of my sister Mrs. Keller" was given "to my

65. Noted 2 U.Chi.L.Rev. 156 (1934); 19 Minn.L.Rev. 127 (1934); 15 B.U.L. Rev. 404 (1935).

nephew Thomas Lincoln Talbot * * * in trust to use the income thereof for the benefit and assistance of any legitimate descendant of my parents * * * who shall, for the time being, need the same for support, education or comfort, as long as any such descendant shall continue to be." By clause tenth it was provided that, "Failing all such descendants, said estate or property shall go to the Congregational Society of East Machias, Maine," in trust for the erection of a church building.

* * *

[The court held the appointments under clauses nine and ten invalid under the Rule Against Perpetuities.]

The will of the testatrix contains no direction as to the disposition of the trust fund in these circumstances. Therefore the remaining question is whether the trust fund shall be distributed to the heirs at law and next of kin of Emma C. F. Keller, the donor of the power, or of Thomas H. Talbot, the donee of the power.

This point is expressly covered by Dunbar v. Hammond, 234 Mass. 554, on page 558, paragraph 6, 125 N.E. 686. It was there held that the trustee named in the instrument whereby the power of appointment was exercised held the fund for heirs at law and next of kin of the donee of the power. In Bundy v. United States Trust Co., 257 Mass. 72, 80, 81, 153 N.E. 337, 340, the case of Dunbar v. Hammond was cited with approval and it was said that, although where property was appointed under a general testamentary power on "a trust which failed for want of a cestui que trust, the property passed by a resulting trust to the next of kin of the donee," the rule was "limited to the case where the donor has made no provision for the donee's default of appointment, or for the event of his intestacy."

There is no sound distinction between Dunbar v. Hammond and the case at bar. An urgent argument has been made to the effect that Dunbar v. Hammond ought to be overruled. The point there decided was one relating to that kind of property which passes by the execution of a power. Stability of rules of law is as important in this as in other branches of the law. Mabardy v. McHugh, 202 Mass. 148, 152, 88 N.E. 894, 23 L.R.A.,N.S., 487, 132 Am.St.Rep. 484, 16 Ann. Cas. 500. Decisions ought not to be lightly overruled. The case of Dunbar v. Hammond was fully argued upon ample briefs. The rule adopted in that case is the one prevailing in the English courts, where the question has often arisen.

The question to be decided in cases of this nature is one of intention. If the donee of the power had made no attempt to dispose of the trust fund, it would be plain that the design was to leave its devolution entirely to the law governing the estate of the donor of the power. If, however, the donee of the power makes an appointment, the further inquiry arises whether the intent was to take the property dealt with out of the instrument conferring the power for all purposes, or only for the limited purpose of giving effect to the particular disposition expressed. In re De Lusi's Trusts, 3 L.R.Ir. 232, 237. In re Boyd, [1897] 2 Ch. 232, 235. An additional indication of intent is that a testamentary appointment, under a general power, to a trustee upon trusts which lapse as to the beneficial interest, nevertheless operates as a good appointment to the trustee who holds it upon the same trusts as if it had been the property of the one exercising the power. In re Davies' Trusts, L.R. 13 Eq. 163, 166. The trust fund in the case at bar was appointed in unmistakable terms by the donee of the power to a trustee specially named by him for that purpose. The fund was thus by the donee taken entirely out of the instrument conferring the power and appointed to his trustee. Since the particular beneficiaries cannot take the fund, that trustee holds it upon a resulting trust for the benefit of the heirs at law and next of kin of the donee of the power. In re Marten, [1902] 1 Ch. 314. Coxen v. Rowland, [1894] 1 Ch. 406. In re Pinede's Settlement, 12 Ch.D. 667. In re Van Hagan, 16 Ch.D. 18, 31, 33, 34. In re Vander Byl, [1931] 1 Ch. 216. 2 Jarman on Wills (7th Ed.) 792, 793.

This rule bears some analogy to the one not infrequently applied where appointed property is held for the payment of the debts of the donee exercising the power of appointment in favor of named beneficiaries, provided his own estate is insufficient for payment of such debts. Clapp v. Ingraham, 126 Mass. 200. Shattuck v. Burrage, 229 Mass. 448, 118 N.E. 889.

The conclusion is that a decree should be entered ordering the entire trust fund now in the hands of the trustee under the will of Emma C. F. Keller, the donor of the power, to be turned over to the administrator with the will annexed of the estate of Thomas H. Talbot, the donee of the power, for distribution as property of his estate. Olney v. Balch, 154 Mass. 318, 28 N.E. 258. Costs as between solicitor and client out of the fund are to be in the discretion of the single justice.

Ordered accordingly.

NOTE

The rule of the principal case applies only where the donee has attempted to exercise the power by an instrument which is itself effective but the appointment is ineffective for some reason, such as the prior death of the appointee or the Rule Against Perpetuities. The rule has now been extended to the situation where there is an express gift in default.[66] It has been suggested that the same result will be reached even if the gift in default is worded to take effect "in the event the donee shall fail to make an effective appointment" or any similar wording which seems to require a valid appointment; the reasoning is that the donee has made a valid appointment, an implied appointment in favor of his own estate if the express appointment fails.[67] For an able exposition of the contrary view, see Jones, "Consequences of an Ineffective Appointment—Capture", 18 Ala.L.Rev. 229 (1966). The rule is confined to general powers, since the donee of a special power could not appoint to his estate, expressly or impliedly. A similar result is reached in any case where the court finds that the donee intended to "blend"

66. Fiduciary Trust Co. v. Mishou, 321 Mass. 615, 75 N.E.2d 3 (1947). See Jones, "Consequences of an Ineffective Appointment—Capture," 18 Ala.L.Rev. 229 (1966). As to the application of anti-lapse statutes see French, "Application of Antilapse Statutes to Appointments Made by Will", 53 Wash.L.Rev. 405 (1978).

67. See 5 Amer.Law of Prop. 637 (1952).

the appointive property with his own assets. For example, the donee's will may start with a general recital: "By this will I intend to dispose of all property which I own at my death or over which I have any power of appointment"; an invalid provision in such a will would leave the appointive property as part of the donee's estate. Old Colony Trust Co. v. Allen[68] is an illustrative case. Here the donor A established a trust to pay the income to himself for life, then to pay the income to B, with general power to dispose of the principal by will; there was no gift in default. B left a will giving "all the rest and residue of her property" in equal shares to two named sisters, one of whom predeceased B without issue. Under applicable Massachusetts law the residuary clause operated to manifest intent to exercise the power. Even though, because of lapse, the residuary clause was not effective as an appointment of the property, it was effective to "blend" the appointive property with the individual property of the donee and to make it part of the donee's (B's) estate, to pass by intestacy.

DANIEL v. BROWN

Supreme Court of Appeals of Virginia, 1931.
156 Va. 563, 159 S.E. 209.

HUDGINS, J. This case involves the construction of the fourth clause of the will of Joseph S. Jackson, dated August 28, 1895, wherein power of disposition of certain property was given to his wife, Jane C. Jackson, and the third and fourth clauses of the will of Jane C. Jackson, wherein she attempted to execute this power.

The will of Joseph S. Jackson disposed of his property in three paragraphs, as follows:

> "Second: After the payment of all my just debts, I give and bequeath all my personal estate of every kind and description to my beloved wife, Jane C. Jackson, absolutely.
>
> "Third: I give and devise to my brother, Philip M. Jackson, the small lot or piece of land on the east side of the Marquis' Road, leading to Unionsville, said land adjoins the lands of said Philip M. Jackson and contains about one and one-half acres.
>
> "Fourth: All the rest and residue of my real estate, I give and devise to my said wife, Jane C. Jackson, for life, with power to her to give, by last will, said real estate, to such of my nephews and nieces, and in such proportions as she may choose."

Jane C. Jackson, by will dated February 23, 1917, attempted to execute the power given her under the fourth clause of the will of Joseph S. Jackson in the following manner:

> "Third: All the real estate of which my late husband, Joseph S. Jackson, died seized and possessed, and which by last will and testament he gave and devised to me for life with power to me to give by my last will the said real estate to such of his nieces and nephews and in such proportions as I may choose, I give, devise and bequeath to Clarinda J. Daniel, William R. Brown and Charles

68. 307 Mass. 40, 29 N.E.2d 310 (1940).

J. Brown, in equal proportions absolutely and in fee simple; the said Clarinda J. Daniel, William R. Brown and Charles J. Brown being the children of Jane Brown, who was the sister of my said husband, Joseph S. Jackson:

"Fourth: In the event that either the said Clarinda J. Daniel, William R. Brown or Charles J. Brown should die before my death, leaving lawful issue of his or her body them surviving, I give and devise to said issue the share that the parent would have taken hereunder if living."

Clarinda J. Daniel, William R. Brown and Charles J. Brown died intestate prior to the death of Jane C. Jackson. Josephine J. Brown was the only child of William R. Brown. Neither Clarinda J. Daniel nor Charles J. Brown left issue.

The heirs at law of Joseph S. Jackson were a brother, Philip Jackson, a sister, Mildred A. Daniel, and the children of Jane C. Brown, a deceased sister. Philip Jackson and Mildred A. Daniel predeceased Jane C. Jackson. This controversy is between the nieces and nephews of Joseph S. Jackson and the grandniece, Josephine J. Brown.

The learned judge of the trial court decreed that Josephine J. Brown took one-third of the land as issue of her father, William R. Brown, one of the appointees of Jane C. Jackson, aided by sections 5226 and 5238 of the Code, that the devises to Clarinda J. Daniel and Charles J. Brown failed by reason of the death of the appointees in the lifetime of Jane C. Jackson, and that as to this two-thirds interest Joseph S. Jackson died intestate. From this decree an appeal was granted.

It is admitted that the fourth clause of the will of Jane C. Jackson is invalid because she was limited in her appointment to the nieces and nephews of her husband, and this clause attempts to leave the property to the issue of the nieces and nephews named by her in the third paragraph, in the event that any of them should predecease her. * * * [The court held that the Virginia lapse statute was inapplicable to enable the donee of a special power to appoint to issue of the objects of the power.] * * *

There being no valid exercise of the power, the court is confronted with two possible courses of action. One is to hold that there was no valid devise of this land after the life estate, and in the absence of a residuary clause it would pass under the statute of descent to the heirs at law, in which event the property would have to be divided per stirpes, as there were a brother, sister, and the children of a deceased sister living at the time of the testator's death. Such is not the testamentary disposition of his property which the testator evidently had in mind.

The other course is to hold that the will disposes of all the property owned by the testator at the time of his death. When a party executes a will, the presumption is reasonable and natural that such party intends to dispose of his entire estate.

The testator in the second paragraph of his will made an absolute gift of all his personal estate to his wife; in the third paragraph he devised to his brother, Philip, certain real estate in fee, describing it minutely; in the fourth paragraph he gave in express terms the real estate in question to his wife for life, with power by will to select from a certain class of his relations the particular objects of his bounty. No provision was made in case there was a failure to exercise the power. The court is unable to say which of the nephews and nieces the donee of the power would have selected, and if the devise of the remainder should fail it must fail for this reason. For aid in the solution of this problem we turn to the authorities.

In Morris v. Owen (1801) 2 Call (6 Va.) 520, personal property was given the wife for life, with power to divide it at her discretion among the testator's children. The wife gave some of the property to a grandchild and died without disposing of the balance. It was held that the gift to the grandchild was void because the grandchild was not in the class mentioned in the testator's will, and the property undisposed of by the donee was distributed under the statute of descent and distribution.

A similar will was before this court in 1820, in Knight v. Yarbrough, Gilmer (21 Va.) 27, where the testator gave his wife certain lands and other property, in the following language: "* * * To live upon, pay my debts, and dispose of among my children and grandchildren, as she pleases, and should she find it necessary to sell, all or either of the lands, to convey and make titles thereto, to any person or persons whatsoever, which title so made shall be valid to all intents," etc.

The wife, under this provision, undertook to give certain property to a son-in-law; the court held the appointment void, and further held that the will of the donor created a trust in the wife for the children and grandchildren of the testator, and hence there was no intestacy growing out of the void appointment.

Since the above case, it has been uniformly held in Virginia that where the language of the will confers a nonexclusive power of disposal among a certain class, the members of that class take a vested remainder, or, as it is sometimes put, if the gift is in express terms to the class, with power in another to determine the proportion or share that each member of the class shall take, then there is a vested remainder in all members of the class. Hudson v. Hudson, 6 Munf. (20 Va.) 352; Carrington v. Belt, 6 Munf. (20 Va.) 374; Thrasher v. Ballard, 35 W.Va. 524, 14 S.E. 232; Minor on Real Property, Vol. 2, § 1330. Such was the holding in the case of Lantz v. Massie, 99 Va. 709, 40 S.E. 50, where the power was expressed in the following language:

> "I will and bequeath to my beloved wife, Elizabeth Virginia Massie, all of my estate, of every description, real, personal, and mixed, to have and to hold during her natural life, and then *to be divided among my children* by will or otherwise, as she may deem best and right." (Italics supplied.)

* * *

Perry in his admirable work on Trusts and Trustees (7th Ed.) Vol. 1, § 250, quoting from Lord Cottonham in Burrough v. Philcox, 5 My. & Cr. 72, states the general rule thus:

> "When there appears a general intention in favor of a class, and a particular intention in favor of individuals of a class to be selected by another person, and the particular intention fails from that selection not being made, the court will carry into effect the general intention in favor of the class. When such an intention appears, the case arises, as stated by Lord Eldon in Brown v. Higgs, of the power being so given as to make it the duty of the donee to execute it; and, in such case, the court will not permit the objects of the power to suffer by the negligence or conduct of the donee, but fastens upon the property a trust for their benefit."

Jarman on Wills, 549, states that under such circumstances the gift to the class is implied, and that the testator could not have intended the objects of the power to be disappointed of his bounty by the failure of the donee to exercise such power in their favor.

Applying the general principle to the facts in the instant case, the court will not permit the devise of the remainder to fail because of its inability to say which members of the class the donee of the power would have selected. The will gives it no guide by which it can distinguish or prefer one member of the class over another. Under such circumstances, equity will decree an equal distribution of the property among all of the nephews and nieces.

This case presents another point which has given the court some difficulty, that is, when does the gift take effect, at the death of the testator or at the death of the donee of the power? Between the death of the testator, Joseph S. Jackson, and the death of the donee, Jane C. Jackson, several of the nieces and nephews died, one leaving issue. Whether or not any nephews or nieces were born during that time does not appear. The donee could execute this power only by will. She was limited in her selection to the members of a certain class, who were to take only at her death. If all the objects of the power had died in the lifetime of the donee there could have been no valid appointment by the donee. Inasmuch, therefore, as the donee was confined in her appointment by the will to the nieces and nephews living at the time the appointment should take effect, the court is likewise so confined. Perry on Trusts and Trustees, Vol. 1, Section 238, states "that when it appears that the donee is to have his whole life to make the selection or distribution, or if the donee is to have the use of the fund for his life, then the court will distribute it to the parties entitled living at the death of the donee," and cites a great number of English cases supporting the text. To the same effect, see Minor on Real Property, § 1330, and Jarman on Wills, 551.

It is admitted that the donee could not select grandnieces and grandnephews under the power given her. It would be inconsistent to hold that they could take in default of appointment when no appointment could be made to them direct. Suppose that the property had been given to Jane C. Jackson for life and at her death "with power in B to give to such of my nieces and nephews and in such proportions as B may choose." Is there any question of the fact that in such a case B, if living at the death of Jane C. Jackson, would have been confined in his selection to the nieces and nephews living at that time? Does it make any difference that the power is given the owner of the life estate? We think not. It follows that the court in enforcing the trust will be confined to the nieces and nephews living at the death of Jane C. Jackson. The record discloses that the property will have to be sold for division among the parties entitled thereto, and that a final order cannot be entered in this court.

For the reasons stated, the decree herein complained of is reversed, and the case remanded for further proceedings not in conflict with the views herein expressed.

Reversed.

NOTE

Where the donee fails to exercise a power of appointment, expressly or by implication, and the power is general, the choice is between the donor and the donee. Here the courts hold that the failure of the donee to exercise the power, coupled with the lack of an express gift in default, results in a reversion (to the donor, his residuary devisee or his heirs, as the case may be). For example, A by his will leaves property in trust for B for life, then as B shall appoint by his will. B dies leaving no will or one which does not exercise the power. The property will be part of A's estate. Where the power is special, however, a new alternative is introduced: the persons to whom appointment might have been made. Thus, if B had been given a power to appoint among his children, the very nature of the special power indicates that the donor intended to benefit the children. As seen in the principal case, two theories have been used by the courts, sometimes concurrently, to reach the obvious result.

The "property" approach is to treat this as a problem of reading between the lines of the donor's creating instrument to find what his intent would have been and to fulfill that intent by implying a gift in default accordingly. The other approach is to treat the special power like a "trust", especially if the wording appears mandatory ("as the donee shall appoint"), with the permissible appointees as "beneficiaries" of the power; when the donee dies without exercising the power, the court invokes trust law so that the "trust" devolves upon the court, with the court exercising the power in favor of the beneficiaries equally. The 1830 New York Revised Statutes adopted the trust theory, and in the few states which still have legislation based on the old New York Statutes the trust theory is frozen into statute.[69] The present New York Estates, Powers and Trusts Law retains this approach, although it departs from the "trust" terminology in favor of classifying powers as "imperative" or "discretionary" and giving the court authority to exercise an imperative power on death or incompetence of the donee.[70] On the other hand, Wisconsin drafted its recent powers legislation on the implied gift theory.[71] In the vast majority of cases there is no practical difference in result between the trust and property theories. Occasionally, however, the theory adopted (or used by the advocate) may make a difference. For example, rarely a donor specifies that the appointment be made to only one of the

69. E.g., N.D.Cent.Code §§ 59–05–12, 59–05–54.

70. McKinney's N.Y., EPTL, § 10–6.8. (1980 Supp.).

71. Wis.Stat.Ann. § 702.15 (West Spec.Pamph.1980).

group and the donee fails to select one. What difference can theory make in that situation? [72]

See Restatement, Second, Trusts § 27, Comment *b* and the Reporter's Notes, adopting the implied gift theory.

You should remind yourself that the careful draftsman should always anticipate that the donee may not exercise the power, whether it is general or special, and provide an express gift in default.

Suppose a special power is expressly subject to a trust to exercise it. Does the class within which the power must be exercised have to meet the requirement of a definite beneficiary for a private trust? [73] Suppose the power is not subject expressly to a trust to exercise it, but the court implies a duty to exercise the power from the donor's failure to name a taker in default—describing the power as "imperative" or "mandatory." How definitely must the class be described in this situation, assuming the court can make a distinction between this case and a power expressly in trust? [74] If a definite beneficiary is lacking for a trust expressly declared, we have seen that the trust fails with a resulting trust back to the settlor or his successors in interest. But if the donor has indicated no taker in default and the class of appointees is indefinite, should the court simply construe the power as *general* or *hybrid* with no duty imposed upon the donee to exercise it? The absence of definiteness in the class of appointees might overturn any presumption of duty to exercise derived from the lack of a named taker in default.

Few American cases deal with these problems but the various issues have perplexed the British Courts. In Inland Revenue Commissioners v. Broadway Cottages Trust,[75] the Court of Appeal held that if the power was "imperative," the whole range of class members must be ascertainable at any particular time. It was not enough that a particular individual could be identified as a member of the class. Following the rationale of Brown v. Higgs,[76] cited in the principal case, the Court of Appeal assumed that "equity was equality" and equal distribution among all class members was required if the donee failed in his duty to exercise his power. This equal distribution among all could not be ordered unless the entire class was ascertainable. Enforcement of the duty apparently would be possible by any person who could prove that he was within the class.

A different test for a class was applied when the power was not imperative. The power in this situation is often described as "discretionary". In Gulbenkian's Settlement Trusts,[77] the House of Lords held the power valid if it could be said with certainty whether any given member was or was not a member of the class. It was not required that every class member be ascertained or ascertainable. Suppose one could not say with certainty whether any given member was or was not a member of the class? Has not the donor created a general power or hybrid very close to a general power in such a situation? Problems of attempted void or fraudulent appointments would require ascertainment of class membership even if there is no duty to exercise the power, but these problems in turn arise only when the power is treated as a *special* power.

72. Compare Waterman v. New York Life Insurance & Trust Co., 237 N.Y. 293, 142 N.E. 668 (1923), with Bridgewater v. Turner, 161 Tenn. 111, 29 S.W.2d 659 (1930).

73. See Chapter VIII, Sec. 4(5)A. Moss v. Axford, 246 Mich. 288, 224 N.W. 425 (1929), principal case in section cited.

74. See Simes and Smith, Future Interests (2d Ed., 1956) § 1033.

75. [1954] 3 All E.R. 120; [1955] Ch. 20.

76. 8 Ves. 561 (1803).

77. [1968] 3 All E.R. 785; [1968] 3 W. L.R. 1127.

In Baden's Deed Trusts [78] a divided House of Lords applied the *Gulbenkian* rule to an imperative power. Lord Wilberforce, for the majority, rejected an invariable application of the principle "equity is equality" in a court ordered distribution to a class. The court, he stated, should act in a manner best calculated to give effect to the donor-settlor's intent. This might require new trustees to exercise the power who would then prepare a plan for distribution in which the shares might be unequal or a plan in which some class members might be excluded. The beneficiaries might be required to draw up a plan. It was enough to sustain an imperative special power (and presumably a power expressly in trust) if it could be determined with certainty whether any given individual was a member of the class. With an imperative power a wider and more comprehensive range of inquiry concerning class members was required than when there was no duty to exercise the power.

The *Baden* test was applied in *Manisty's Settlement* [79] to sustain an imperative power in which the trustees could add to the class of appointees, there being excluded as permissible appointees only the settlor, his wife for the time being, or any other person settling property upon the trust.

When the court follows a "property" approach as distinguished from a "trust" approach in dealing with the special power for which there is no specified taker in default, the difficulties in defining the class of potential appointees who would receive distribution as takers in default seem the same, although the court would not become enmeshed in trust beneficiary requirements.

In charitable trusts, if the donee-trustee has power to designate takers to accomplish the charitable purpose, the "class" of takers is defined by the purpose of the trust.[80] It is clear also that powers (including those of distributive character) conferred upon a trustee are usually of a discretionary rather than of an imperative character, the trustee being obliged only to use reasonable prudence in determining whether the powers should be exercised or not.[81]

78. Sub nom. McPhail v. Doulton, (No. 1) [1967] 1 W.L.R. 1457; [1967] 3 All E.R. 159; [1969] 2 Ch. 388; [1969] 3 W.L. R. 12; [1969] 1 All E.R. 1016, C.A.; [1971] A.C. 424; [1970] 2 W.L.R. 1110; [1970] 2 All E.R. 228, H.L.(E.). (No. 2) [1972] Ch. 607; [1971] 3 W.L.R. 475; [1971] 3 All E.R. 895; [1973] Ch. 9; [1972] 3 W.L.R. 250; [1972] 2 All E.R. 1304, C.A. See Davies, "Distinction Between Powers of Appointment and Trust Powers—Certainty of Object—The Saga of Re Baden's Deed Trust", 50 Can.Bar. Rev. 539 (1972); Harris, "Trust, Power and Duty", 87 L.Q.Rev. 31 (1971); Hopkins, "Certain Uncertainties of Trusts and Powers", 29 Camb.L.J. 68 (1971); Note, 30 Camb.L.J. 41 (1972).

79. [1974] Ch. 17.

80. See Jordan's Estate, 329 Pa. 427, 197 A. 150 (1938) and Matter of Durbrow, 245 N.Y. 469, 157 N.E. 747 (1927), appearing as principal cases in Chapter XI, Section 3.

81. See Boyden v. Stevens, 285 Mass. 176, 188 N.E. 741 (1934), appearing as principal case in Chapter X, Section 2.

Chapter XV

THE EFFECT OF CHANGE ON DISPOSITIVE DESCRIPTIONS AND LIMITATIONS

Scope Note

A skillful draftsman of a will, deed or trust indenture, cannot describe persons and things with absolute certainty; nor can he describe with complete accuracy the conditions and circumstances under which persons described in a dispositive instrument are to take and enjoy property. Not only are written words awkward means for communicating ideas; but descriptions in dispositive instruments have an inherent vice of almost immediate obsolescence. This difficulty is particularly striking in the case of a will. Twenty years may elapse between the execution of a will and the death of the testator. In this interval, he may buy and sell property and the condition and status of persons described in the will may alter. Descriptions in the will when the draftsman composed them may be slightly out of date when the will is executed and may present thorny problems of construction when the testator dies.[1] The same kind of problem may be present in a deed. The transferor may create by deed a life tenancy in land with a contingent remainder over to a class following the death of the life tenant. If the life tenant happens to die a short time after delivery of the deed, the class description may convey rather accurately what the transferor had in mind. But if the life tenant lives for fifty years, alterations in the potential class membership may occur. A serious question may then be presented concerning who is and who is not a member of the class.

A transferor's state of mind, assuming he is dead when the question arises, can be determined only from the words he used, the writ-

1. Courts and text writers sometimes distinguish between interpretation and construction, interpretation being described as a quest for the actual intention of the maker of the instrument involved, and construction being described as the application of canons of construction if the actual intention of the maker cannot be discovered. The words "interpretation" and "construction" are used interchangeably in these materials.

A will cannot be reformed or rescinded after the testator's death. It is possible to rescind or reform a deed under some circumstances. The courts are comparatively strict in construing wills, limiting their search into extrinsic matters to circumstances existing when the will was executed, although sometimes they consider declarations that shed light upon his intention when he executed the will. The courts have been fairly liberal in examining extrinsic evidence in construing deeds. See Becker, "Future Interests and the Myth of the Simple Will: An Approach to Estate Planning", [1972] Wash. U.L.Q. 607; [1973] Wash.U.L.Q. 1. Schuyler, "The Art of Interpretation of Wills", 104 Trusts and Estates 971 (1965); "The Art of Interpretation in Future Interest Cases" 17 Vand.L.Rev. 1407 (1964); McGovern, "Facts and Rules in the Construction of Wills," 26 UCLA Law Rev. 285 (1978).

ten context in which the words were used, and those parts of the extrinsic context apart from the writing which can be admitted in evidence to shed light upon the transferor's intention. Accordingly, when a court construes a will, deed or other dispositive instrument, two major questions may be presented: (1) What parts of the context extrinsic to the words in question may be considered in trying to determine the intention of the transferor; and (2) assuming his intention cannot be discovered with reasonable certainty, what should the court presume that he intended? With respect to the latter question, postulates or canons of construction have been developed by the courts. Most of the postulates or canons operate as rebuttable presumptions of intention and yield when the actual intention of the transferor can be shown from admissible evidence. Some are "conclusive" presumptions of intention and apply even though a contrary intention of the maker is shown.

The cases and materials in Section 1 deal with the question of proof of intention when uncertainty has been created by changes in the property of a testator after his will has been executed but before his estate has been distributed. The courts are more reticent in considering extrinsic evidence to construe a will than to construe an inter vivos transfer; and it is one of the purposes of this Section to delineate the purpose and ambit of this policy. The cases and materials in Section 2 concern problems of change common to all dispositive transactions, testamentary and inter vivos. The changes examined are those in the condition and status of persons as descriptions and limitations in dispositive instruments are affected. Many property changes in inter vivos transactions are not vital in the construction of the instrument, although one of these, the allocation of expenses and income between life tenants and remaindermen in trusts, will be considered in detail in Chapter XVII, discussion being reserved until a consideration of the powers and duties of fiduciaries.[2]

In Section 3 we shall consider the task of the court when the will or trust instrument expressly provides for one contingency but fails to provide for the opposite contingency which in fact occurs.

Section 4 deals with the disposition of property when a limitation fails. This area is also touched upon in the consideration of Lapse in Section 2(1).

Throughout the Chapter, the student should ask himself how the limitation or description concerned could have been drafted to avoid the problem of construction raised by the writing in question. While absolute certainty is impossible in drafting, a high standard of exactness is expected; and certain obvious pitfalls exist which any careful draftsman is expected to avoid.

2. A will is ambulatory and revocable until the testator dies and has no immediate effect upon the maker's estate when it was executed. Hence, changes in the estate of the testator and the death of beneficiaries may disturb the effect of provisions in the will. Changes in beneficiaries before a deed is delivered (the effective date) may have some bearing upon its construction, although the principal problems arise from changes which occur after delivery.

SECTION 1. CHANGES IN TESTAMENTARY PROPERTY AFTER EXECUTION OF THE WILL

(1) CLASSES OF LEGACIES, DEVISES AND BEQUESTS

The courts construe legacies, bequests and devises, as "specific", "general", "demonstrative" and "residuary".[3] The classification is based upon the estate source from which the testator intends the gift in question should be satisfied. The intention of the testator is found by construing the will as a whole.

This system of classification is employed for convenience in describing the effect upon the operation of provisions in the will caused by changes in property constituting the estate after the will is executed.[4]

A specific legacy, bequest or devise is a gift of property which can be distinguished with reasonable accuracy from other property which is part of the testator's estate. The testator must intend that the gift be limited to the particular item. A legacy to be paid only from a particular fund is specific. A gift of a described watch or picture is a specific bequest. A devise of "my farm, Blackacre" is a specific devise.

A general legacy or bequest is a gift of personal property which the testator intends to be satisfied from the general assets of the estate. The testator does not intend the gift to be satisfied from a particular source. A legacy of a specified sum of money is general if there is no designation of a fund from which the legacy is to be paid. A gift of a specified sum in bonds, stocks or mortgages is a general bequest if there is no direction that these be selected from securities which are part of the estate. A gift of all, or an aliquot portion, of the testator's estate is general.

All devises were once regarded as specific. This position was based upon the common law rule that a will did not pass after-acquired land. This rule has been changed in England and in the United States.[5] As a result of statutory changes in common law rule, it is well settled in the United States that a devise can be general, al-

3. There are, of course, many other terms used to describe legacies, bequests and devises. The terms considered in this Chapter are those used by the courts in dealing with the constructional problems examined hereafter in this Chapter.

4. There are statutory definitions of classes of legacies in several states. E.g., West's Ann.Cal.Probate Code, § 161 (1980 Supp.).

5. The statutes differ in phraseology, but all provide in effect that after-acquired property may pass by will. E.g., Va.Code Ann. § 64.1–62; Uniform Probate Code, § 2–604.

though the English courts still treat all devises as specific.[6] A devise of "one-third of my real estate" is classified as a general devise in the United States.[7]

A legacy is demonstrative if the testator intends that it be paid from a particular source, but if this source is insufficient to satisfy the legacy, then out of the general assets of the estate. Thus, the testator may bequeath a certain sum of money with a direction that specified shares of stock be sold and the proceeds of sale applied to pay the legacy. The legacy is demonstrative if the court finds that the testator intended the legacy to be paid from the general assets of the estate if the proceeds of sale are insufficient. A bequest of personal property other than money may be demonstrative.

A residuary legacy or bequest is a gift of the estate remaining when claims against the estate and specific, general or demonstrative legacies and bequests have been satisfied. A residuary devise is a gift of the testator's land remaining when claims against the estate and specific, general or demonstrative devises have been satisfied.

A true residuary gift is general in nature. But a testator may make a specific or demonstrative gift in a residuary clause if the requisite language appears. If the description is in general terms, the presence of the description in the residuary clause is evidence that a general gift and not a specific or demonstrative gift was intended by the testator.

PROBLEMS

[Classify the following legacies, bequests or devises.]

1. "I give and bequeath to my son, X, the money now due and owing to me from Y." Cf. Hayes v. Hayes, 45 N.J.Eq. 461, 17 A. 634 (1889).

2. "I give and bequeath to my son, X, all the horses, mules, cows, hogs, farming implements, household and kitchen furniture, on my farm Blackacre." McFadden v. Hefley, 28 S.C. 317, 5 S.E. 812, 13 Am.St.Rep. 675 (1887).

3. Devise of "my residence property on which I now reside, situated on Love Street in Mexico, Missouri". National Board v. Fry, 293 Mo. 399, 239 S.W. 519 (1922).

4. Devise of "the residue of my land in Sampson County". Morisey v. Brown, 144 N.C. 154, 56 S.E. 704 (1907).

5. The testator owned 10 shares of Leed's stock when his will was executed. His will contained the following bequest: "I give and bequeath 10 shares of Leed's stock to X." Robinson v. Addison, 2 Beav. 515, 48 Eng. Rep. 1281 (1840).

6. E.g., Hensman v. Fryer, 3 Ch.App. Cas. 420 (1867); Lancefield v. Iggulden, 10 Ch.App.Cas. 136 (1874).

7. See Haslem v. de Alvarez, 70 R.I. 212, 214, 38 A.2d 158 (1944) (devise of "all real estate owned by me or in which I may have an interest" held specific).

6. Suppose the bequest in Problem 5 had read: "I give and bequeath my 10 shares of Leed's stock to X"? Kearns v. Kearns, 77 N.J.Eq. 453, 76 A. 1042 (1910).

7. "I bequeath to my daughter, X, five thousand dollars ($5,000) in cash out of my interest in the Baker estate." Waters v. Selleck, 201 Ind. 593, 170 N.E. 20 (1930).

8. "To my son, X, the sum of fifteen hundred dollars, to be paid to him first out of my personal estate on hand and before any division shall be made of said personal property." Hibler v. Hibler, 104 Mich. 274, 62 N.W. 361 (1895).

9. "I give and bequeath absolutely to my nephew, X, the sum of $4,000 to be paid by my personal representative to said legatee by turning over any of my bonds, notes, or other evidences of debt at their market value, and if these are not sufficient, then the balance of said $4,000 to be paid in money." Baptist Female University v. Borden, 132 N.C. 476, 44 S.E. 47 (1903).

10. "I give and bequeath all of my cash and personal property as follows" (equal shares to named persons). Matter of Estate of Murray, 579 P. 2d 203 (Okla.App.1978).

(2) CHANGES IN PROPERTY BETWEEN THE EXECUTION OF THE WILL AND TESTATOR'S DEATH

A. ADEMPTION

If property specifically described by the testator in his will is not in his estate at his death, the bequest or devise is said to be *adeemed by extinction.* Suppose a testator makes a specific devise of "Blackacre" to X in his will. Testator then sells "Blackacre". The devise is said to be adeemed. It is obvious that this is a way by which a testator can prevent his will or part of it from being effective; yet in Chapter VI it was stated that a testator could revoke his will only by the methods stated in the statutes. In a case of ademption, the will can be probated—but it does not operate to pass the property adeemed because there is no property meeting the description in the will. The testator may be permitted, on the other hand, to adeem a provision in the will *by satisfaction.* This was once treated by the courts as a type of revocation. In ademption by satisfaction the testator makes an inter vivos gift of property to a devisee in the will with the intention of rendering the testamentary gift inoperative. *Ademption by satisfaction* is related to the doctrine of advancements in intestacy.

(i) Ademption by Extinction

McGEE v. McGEE

Supreme Court of Rhode Island, 1980.
___ R.I. ___, 413 A.2d 72.

WEISBERGER, JUSTICE.

This is a complaint for declaratory judgment, in which the plaintiff administrator, Richard J. McGee (Richard), sought directions from the Superior Court in respect to the construction of certain provisions of the will of his mother, Claire E. McGee, and instructions relating to payment of debts and distribution of assets from the testatrix's estate. The sole issue presented by this appeal concerns the question of the ademption of an allegedly specific legacy to the grandchildren of the decedent and the consequent effect of such ademption upon payment of a bequest in the amount of $20,000 to Fedelma Hurd (Hurd), a friend of the testatrix. The provisions of the will pertinent to this appeal read as follows:

"CLAUSE ELEVENTH:

I give and bequeath to my good and faithful friend FEDELMA HURD, the sum of Twenty Thousand ($20,000.00) Dollars, as an expression to her of my appreciation for her many kindnesses.

"CLAUSE TWELFTH:

I give and bequeath all of my shares of stock in the Texaco Company, and any and all monies standing in my name on deposit in any banking institution as follows:

> (a) My Executor shall divide the shares of stock, or the proceeds thereof from a sale of same, *with all of my monies, standing on deposit in my name, in any bank*, into three (3) equal parts and shall pay 1/3 over to the living children of my beloved son, PHILIP; 1/3 to the living children of my beloved son, RICHARD and 1/3 over to the living children of my beloved son, JOSEPH. Each of my grandchildren shall share equally the 1/3 portion given to them." (Emphasis added.)

At the time of the execution of the will and up until a short time before the death of the testatrix, a substantial sum of money was on deposit in her name at the People's Savings Bank in Providence. About five weeks prior to his mother's death, Richard, proceeding pursuant to a written power of attorney as modified by an addendum executed the following month, withdrew approximately $50,000 from these savings accounts. Of this amount, he applied nearly $30,000 towards the purchase of four United States Treasury bonds, commonly denominated as "flower bonds," from the Federal Trust Company in Waterville, Maine (Richard then resided in that state). His objective in executing this transaction was to effect an advantageous method of satisfying potential federal estate tax liability.[8] The bonds, however, did not serve the intended purpose since at the time of Mrs. McGee's death her gross estate was such that apparently no federal estate tax liability was incurred. The remainder of the monies withdrawn from the savings accounts were deposited in Claire McGee's checking account to pay current bills and in a savings account in Richard's name to be transferred to his mother's account as the need might arise for the payment of her debts and future obligations. The sole sum that is now the subject of this appeal is the approximately $30,000 held in the form of United States Treasury bonds.

The complaint for declaratory judgment sought instructions concerning whether the administrator should first satisfy the specific legacy to the grandchildren from the proceeds of the sale of the flower bonds or whether he should first pay the $20,000 bequest to Fedelma Hurd, since the estate lacked assets sufficient to satisfy both bequests.

After hearing evidence and considering legal memoranda filed by the parties, the trial justice found that the bequest to the grandchildren contained in the twelfth clause of the will constituted a specific legacy. He held further, however, that Rhode Island regarded the concept of ademption with disfavor and he sought, therefore, to effectuate the intent of the testatrix. He proceeded to determine that since there is an assumption that one intends to leave his property to those who are the natural objects of his bounty, rather than to strangers, the administrator "should trace the funds used to purchase the Flower Bonds and should satisfy the specific legacy to the grandchildren" under the twelfth clause of the will. Consequently, the trial justice held that the legacy to Fedelma Hurd under the eleventh clause of the will must fail. This appeal ensued.

The McGee grandchildren suggest that the principal design of the testatrix's estate plan, ascertainable from a contemplation of the testamentary disposition of her property, was to benefit her family rather than "outsiders." They urge us to consider her intentions—which they assure us were concerned, in part, with protecting the family interests from an anticipated reduction of the estate's value by taxes—in determining whether the transfer of the funds in her accounts did in fact work an ademption. In addition, Richard points out that the decedent did not herself purchase these bonds. On the contrary, Richard acquired them in order to help discharge anticipated tax obligations of the estate and informed his mother of them only subsequently to the purchase. He argues, furthermore, not only that the funds with which he purchased the flower bonds originated in his mother's accounts, but also that since these bonds "are as liquid as cash" they are indeed monies standing in the decedent's name on deposit in a banking institution. He suggests that this description con-

8. [This and the following footnote are by the Court.]

Although not otherwise redeemable before maturity, flower bonds may be redeemed at par value, plus accrued interest, upon the owner's death for the purpose of paying the federal taxes on his estate. See Girard Trust Bank v. United States, 602 F.2d 938, 940 n. 1 (Ct. Cl. 1979).

forms in every respect to the formula drafted into the twelfth clause of her will. Merely the form of the legacy has changed, according to Richard, not its essential character, quality, or substance.

In response, appellant asserts that an ademption occurred by the voluntary act of the testatrix during her lifetime, since her son withdrew the funds as an authorized agent operating under a lawful power of attorney. There is evidence, moreover, that the testatrix subsequently ratified the purchase of the bonds when Richard afterwards told her of his actions and their intended effect upon estate taxes.[9] As a consequence, Hurd asserts that there was no longer any money standing on deposit in the name of the testatrix in any bank with which to discharge the specific legacy to the grandchildren. These transactions resulted in an extinction of the subject matter of the legacy. Hurd argues, in addition, that the intention of the testatrix, even if discernible, is irrelevant to the question of the ademption of the bequest. She therefore contends that her general legacy should be payable from the proceeds of the sale of the flower bonds.

At the outset, we recognize that the instant case concerns specifically the concept of ademption by extinction, a legal consequence that may attend a variety of circumstances occasioned either by operation of law or by the actions of a testator himself or through his guardian, conservator, or agent. Gardner v. McNeal, 117 Md. 27, 82 A. 988 (1911); In re Wright, 7 N.Y.2d 365, 165 N.E.2d 561, 197 N.Y.S.2d 711 (1960). In particular, a testamentary gift of specific real or personal property may be adeemed—fail completely to pass as prescribed in the testator's will—when the particular article devised or bequeathed no longer exists as part of the testator's estate at the moment of his death because of its prior consumption, loss, destruction, substantial change, sale, or other alienation subsequent to the execution of the will. In consequence, neither the gift, its proceeds, nor similar substitute passes to the beneficiary, and this claim to the legacy is thereby barred. Atkinson, Handbook of the Law of Wills § 134 at 741, 743–44 (2d Ed. 1953); 6 Bowe & Parker, Page on the Law of Wills § 54.1 at 242, § 54.9 at 256–57 (1962); Note, Wills: Ademption of Specific Legacies and Devises, 43 Cal.L.Rev. 151 (1955).

The principle of ademption by extinction has reference only to specific devises and bequests and is thus inapplicable to demonstrative or general testamentary gifts. 6 Page, supra § 54.3 at 245, § 54.5 at 248. In Haslam v. de Alvarez, 70 R.I. 212, 38 A.2d 158 (1944), we prescribed the criteria for determining the character of a legacy, relying on the earlier case of Dean v. Rounds, 18 R.I. 436, 27 A. 515 (1893), wherein we held that "[a] specific legacy, as the term imports, is a gift or bequest of some definite specific thing, something which is capable of being designated and identified." Id. When the testator intends that the legatee shall receive the exact property bequeathed rather than its corresponding quantitative or *ad valorem* equivalent, the gift is a specific one, and when "the main intention is

9. Richard testified his mother "was pleased that [he had] done this because there would be more money available for the children and grandchildren."

that the legacy be paid by the delivery of the identical thing, and that thing only, and in the event that at the time of the testator's death such thing is no longer in existence, the legacy will not be paid out of his general assets." Hanley v. Fernell, 54 R.I. 84, 86, 170 A. 88, 89 (1934). In particular, the designation and identification of the specific legacy in a testator's will describe the gift in a manner that serves to distinguish it from all other articles of the same general nature and prevents its distribution from the general assets of the testator's estate. 6 Page, supra § 48.3 at 11–12.

In the case at bar, the trial justice construed the twelfth clause of Mrs. McGee's will as bequeathing a specific legacy to her grandchildren. While it is true that the party who contends the legacy is a specific one must bear the burden of proof on this issue, DiCristofaro v. Beaudry, 113 R.I. 313, 320 A.2d 597 (1974), and appellant, in her brief, characterized the twelfth clause as a bequest of a particular residuary gift, the trial justice apparently found that petitioner's contentions met the burden and that the testatrix clearly considered the bequest a specific one.

Without a doubt, the trial justice properly interpreted the McGee grandchildren's bequest, primarily because of the tone of the other provisions, the tenor of the entire instrument, see Hanley v. Fernell, 54 R.I. at 86, 170 A. at 89; Gardner v. Viall, 36 R.I. 436, 90 A. 760 (1914), and the specificity with which the testatrix described that portion of the twelfth clause relative to the Texaco stock. Additionally, money payable out of a fund—rather than out of the estate generally—described with sufficient accuracy and satisfiable only out of the payment of such fund, Haslam v. de Alvarez, or a bequest of money deposited in a specific bank, Hanley v. Fernell, is, as a rule, a specific legacy. When a will bequeaths "the money owned by one which is on deposit" in a designated bank, although the amount remains unspecified, the gift is nevertheless identifiable and definite, apart from all other funds or property in the testator's estate; and the legacy is specific. Willis v. Barrow, 218 Ala. 549, 552, 119 So. 678, 680 (1929); Prendergast v. Walsh, 58 N.J.Eq. 149, 42 A. 1049 (Ch.1899). Despite the fact that Mrs. McGee did not name any particular bank in the twelfth clause of her will, she bequeathed all the money in her name "in any bank." In view of the fact that she expected all of her money remaining at her death to go to her grandchildren and, further, the money to be payable from a particular source—that is, accounts in her name in banking institutions—we conclude that the legacy was sufficiently susceptible of identification to render it a specific one.

Accordingly, since the bequest to the grandchildren is specific, we must now determine whether or not it was adeemed by the purchase of the bonds. Note, Ademption and the Testator's Intent, 74 Harv.L. Rev. 741 (1961). In connection with the early theory of ademption, the courts looked to the intention of the testator as the basis of their decisions. 6 Page, supra § 54.14 at 265. But ever since the landmark case of Ashburner v. MacGuire, 2 Bros.C.C. 108, 29 Eng. Rep. 62 (Ch.1786), wherein Lord Thurlow enunciated the "modern theory," courts have utilized the identity doctrine or "in specie" test. This test focuses on two questions only: (1) whether the gift is a specific legacy and, if it is, (2) whether it is found in the estate at the time of the testator's death. Atkinson, supra § 134 at 742; Note, 74 Harv.L.Rev. at 742; Comment, Ademption in Iowa—A Closer Look at the Testator's Intent, 57 Iowa L.Rev. 1211 (1972). The extinction of the property bequeathed works an ademption regardless of the testator's intent. In re Tillinghast, 23 R.I. 121, 123–24, 49 A. 634, 635 (1901); Humphreys v. Humphreys, 2 Cox Ch. 184, 30 Eng.Rep. 85 (Ch.1789); 6 Page, supra § 54.15 at 266.

The legatees of the twelfth clause argue that the subject matter of the specific bequest, although apparently now unidentifiable in its previous form, actually does exist in the estate of their grandmother but in another form as the result of an exchange or transfer of the original property. But there is a recognized distinction between a bequest of a particular item and a gift of its proceeds, see generally Annot., 45 A.L.R.3d 10 (1972); and the testatrix, in the instant case, did recognize the distinction in the twelfth clause of her will by bequeathing the Texaco stock "or the proceeds thereof from a sale of same" but omitting to include similar provisions regarding proceeds in connection with the language immediately following which described the bank-money legacy. It appears that the testatrix's intention, manifest on the face of her will, was that her grandchildren receive only the money in her bank accounts and not the money's proceeds or the investments that represent the conversion of that money into other holdings. Atkinson, supra § 134 at 743–44; 6 Page, supra § 54.9 at 256–57, § 54.16 at 268–70; see Gardner v. McNeal, 117 Md. 27, 82 A. 988 (1911).

In accordance with the generally accepted "form and substance rule," a substantial change in the nature or character of the subject matter of a bequest will operate as an ademption; but a merely nominal or formal change will not. In re Peirce, 25 R.I. 34, 54 A. 588 (1903) (no ademption since transfer of stock after consolidation of banks without formal liquidation was exchange and not sale); Willis v. Barrow, 218 Ala. 549, 119 So. 678 (1929) (no ademption by transfer of money from named bank to another since place of deposit was merely descriptive); In re Hall, 60 N.J.Super. 597, 160 A.2d 49 (1960) (no ademption by transfer of the money from banks designated in will to another one since location was formal description only and did not affect substance of testamentary gift).

Since the money previously on deposit in Mrs. McGee's bank accounts no longer exists at the time of her death, the question arises whether the change was one of form only, rather than substance. We have determined that the change effected by Richard was not merely formal but was substantial. There is no language in the will that can be construed as reflecting an intention of the testatrix to bequeath a gift of bond investments to her grandchildren. The plain and explicit direction of the twelfth clause of the will is that they should receive whatever remained in her bank accounts at the time of her death. Since no sums of money were then on deposit, the specific legacy was adeemed. Clearly, this case is dissimilar to those in which the fund, at all times kept intact, is transferred to a different location, as in *Willis* and *Prendergast,* where the money merely "changed hands," not character. See also In re Tillinghast, 23 R.I. 121, 49 A. 634 (1901) (no ademption by mere act of transferring mortgages to own name since they were in specie at the time of testatrix's death). The fact that Mrs. McGee did not herself purchase the bonds is not significant. Disposal or distribution of the subject matter of a bequest by an agent of the testator or with the testator's authorization or ratification similarly operates to adeem the legacy. Gardner v. McNeal, 117 Md. 27, 82 A. 988 (1911); In re Wright, 7 N.Y.2d 365, 165 N.E.2d 561, 197 N.Y.S.2d 711 (1960); Glasscock v. Layle, 21 Ky. Law.Rep. 860, 53 S.W. 270 (Ky.1899).

The petitioner improperly relies upon the case of Morse v. Converse, 80 N.H. 24, 113 A. 214 (1921). In that case the testatrix voluntarily placed her property into the hands of a conservator to care for and use for her support. The conservator purchased a Liberty bond out of bank deposits bequeathed in the testatrix's will, and the legacies were not adeemed thereby. But, contrary to the case at bar, the testatrix in *Morse* neither knew about nor consented to the conservator's acts; therefore, the court explained, the change "furnishes no evidence of an intentional revocation by her." Id. at 26, 113 A. at 215. But see In re Wright, citing Matter of Ireland's Estate, 257 N. Y. 155, 177 N.E. 405 (1931) (specifically bequeathed stock adeemed even though sold by conservator after testator had become incompetent).

Moreover, under the principles enunciated by Lord Thurlow in *Ashburner v. MacGuire,* and more fully expressed in the case of *Humphreys v. Humphreys,* only the fact of change or extinction, not the reason for the change or extinction, is truly relevant. The vast majority of jurisdictions adhere to this rule. See Atkinson, supra § 134 at 741–42; 6 Page, supra § 54.15 at 266–68. This "in specie" theory of ademption, although it may occasionally result in a failure to effectuate the actual intent of a testator, has many advantages. Significant among these advantages is simplicity of application, as opposed to ad hoc determination of intent from extrinsic evidence in each particular case. This theory further has the advantages of stability, uniformity, and predictability. The argument in support of Lord Thurlow's rule is well expressed in 6 Page, supra § 54.15 at 266:

> "If the sale or collection of the bequest works an ademption or not depending upon testator's intention as inferred from the surrounding circumstances, many cases will arise in which it is difficult or impossible to ascertain what testator's intention was; and probably, in many cases, testator did not think of the consequences which would follow from his conduct. If the sale or collection of the bequest operates as an ademption or not, depending upon his intentions, and such intention may be shown by his oral declarations, then the controlling evidence in the case will consist

of the written will, executed in accordance with statute, together with testator's oral declarations. This violates both the letter and the spirit of state wills statutes, which insist on the formalities of writing and execution in order to avoid opportunities for perjury. For these reasons, it is now held that the sale, destruction, or collection, of the bequest or devise, adeems it without regard to the actual intention of the testator."

Accordingly, we hold that the trial justice erred in allowing the admission of extrinsic evidence regarding Mrs. McGee's intent. We further hold that the specific legacy in the twelfth clause of the testatrix's will is adeemed and the legatees' claim to this bequest is thereby barred. We direct the trial justice to order the petitioner to satisfy the general pecuniary legacy bequeathed in the eleventh clause of the will from the sale of the flower bonds, with the excess to pass under the residuary (fourteenth) clause of the will.

The respondent's appeal is sustained, the judgment below is reversed, and the cause is remanded to the Superior Court for proceedings consistent with this opinion.

NOTE

A specific legacy, bequest or devise may be adeemed by extinction.[10] A general or demonstrative gift cannot be adeemed by extinction.

A testator may provide in his will for the disposition of proceeds of the sale of property specifically devised or bequeathed or for the disposition of insurance paid when such property is lost or damaged and may stipulate in his will the action which is to be taken by his executor in the event of other changes in his property which the testator can foresee. When this intent is not expressed and the devise, legacy or bequest is determined by the court to be "specific", the devise, legacy or bequest is adeemed by extinction when there is no property in the testator's estate at his death answering the description.

Thus, the doctrine of ademption by extinction has been applied when the described property is transferred by the testator,[11] when an executory contract for sale of the property is in force at the testator's death,[12] when a specifically bequeathed debt is discharged during the testator's lifetime,[13] and when the property is destroyed.[14]

10. See Paulus, "Ademption by Extinction: Smiting Lord Thurlow's Ghost", 2 Texas Tech.L.Rev. 195 (1971); Comments, "Ademption and the Testator's Intent," 74 Harv.L.Rev. 741 (1961); "Ademption by Extinction in California", 18 Hastings L.J. 461 (1967); "Ademption in New York: The Identity Doctrine and the Need for Complete Abrogation by Legislation", 25 Syra.L.Rev. 978 (1974); 45 A.L.R.3d 10 (1972); 65 A.L.R.3d 541 (1975).

11. E.g., Gardner v. McNeal, 117 Md. 27, 82 A. 988, 40 L.R.A.,N.S., 553, Ann. Cas.1914A, 119 (1911).

12. On unpaid proceeds of an executory contract of sale of specifically devised property, compare Matter of Estate of Hills, 222 Kan. 231, 564 P.2d 462 (1977) (applying equitable conversion and hence ademption) with Newbury v. McCammant, 182 N.W.2d 147 (Iowa 1970) (declaring equitable conversion applicable but then refusing to apply ademption to any unpaid proceeds).

13. E.g., In re Estate of Jepson, 181 Cal. 745, 186 P. 352 (1919).

14. E.g., Brady v. Brady, 78 Md. 461, 28 A. 515 (1894).

The ademption may be *pro tanto*. The testator may convey part of the land which is specifically devised, or part of a debt which is specifically bequeathed may be discharged.

The doctrine is not applied, by the better view, when the testator transfers the property but reacquires it before he dies.[15]

Uniform Probate Code, § 2–608(a) eliminates ademption by extinction in several of the cases in which this doctrine is now frequently applied in many states. The subsection is as follows:

"(a) A specific devisee has the right to the remaining specifically devised property and:

"(1) any balance of the purchase price (together with any security interest) owing from a purchaser to the testator at death by reason of sale of the property;

"(2) any amount of a condemnation award for the taking of the property unpaid at death;

"(3) any proceeds unpaid at death on fire or casualty insurance on the property; and

"(4) property owned by testator at his death as a result of foreclosure, or obtained in lieu of foreclosure, of the security for a specifically devised obligation."

If this statute had been in force, how would the court have decided the principal case?

Most courts do not apply the doctrine of ademption by extinction when the guardian or conservator of the estate of an insane testator transfers property specifically devised or bequeathed.[16] This position is adopted in Uniform Probate Code, § 2–608(b) as follows:

"(b) If specifically devised property is sold by a conservator, or if a condemnation award or insurance proceeds are paid to a conservator as a result of condemnation, fire, or casualty, the specific devisee has the right to a general pecuniary devise equal to the net sale price, the condemnation award, or the insurance proceeds. This subsection does not apply if subsequent to the sale, condemnation, or casualty, it is adjudicated that the disability of the testator has ceased and the testator survives the adjudication by one year. The right of the specific devisee under this subsection is reduced by any right he has under subsection (a)."

The ademption by extinction doctrine is not applied to acts done by the executor which change specific legacies, bequests and devises after the death of the testator.[17]

15. This should be the result under statutes providing that a will can pass after-acquired property. The leading case to the contrary is Phillippe v. Clevenger, 239 Ill. 117, 87 N.E. 858, 16 Ann.Cas. 207 (1909).

16. A number of cases taking this position seem to assume that ademption by extinction depends upon the intention of the testator to adeem the devise or bequest. This may be due to a Roman Law heritage in states once subject to Spanish or French law and in other cases the result stems from a confusion of ademption by extinction with ademption by satisfaction. As to the latter, see Bryson v. Turnbull, 194 Va. 528, 74 S.E.2d 180 (1953). The point may be covered by statute.

17. The doctrine of ademption by extinction is not brought into operation by any change in the estate after the testator dies. In Shymer's Estate, 136 Misc. 334, 242 N.Y.S. 234 (1930), the Mixed Claims Commission made an award for the loss of specifically bequeathed property which was lost when the testatrix died in the Lusitania disaster. It was held that the award passed to the legatee because the property was not lost during the lifetime of testatrix. Statutes in a number of states deal with the doctrine

Ademption by extinction is ameliorated in some situations by two modern constructional preferences. One is the modern rule that a will is to be construed "to speak" as of the date of death, rather than the date of execution.

Thus, in Lusk's Estate, 336 Pa. 465, 9 A.2d 363, 125 A.L.R. 787 (1939), the will devised "my house and lot in which I now reside, situated in the Second Ward, City of New Castle"; after execution of the will, testator sold his residence and bought a new one, fortunately also located in the Second Ward of New Castle. Because of a statute allowing the court to construe the will as if executed immediately before the death of the testator, the language was held to refer to the after-acquired property. Some courts would adopt the same construction without statute, even though the devise is "specific".

The second avenue open to a court is to construe language to create a "general" devise or bequest if broadly phrased, even though probably intended by the testator to refer to specific property. Thus where testator owned two hundred shares of X Company stock at the time of drafting of the will and the will contained two bequests of "one hundred shares of X Company stock", classification of the bequests as general prevents ademption even though the two hundred shares had been sold by testator between the execution of the will and his death; the executor is required to purchase stock to satisfy the general bequests.[18] Of course, these constructional preferences have limited scope and do not apply if the description is so detailed and specific as to foreclose such construction.

Some modern courts are willing to reject a mechanistic "identity" approach to ademption in favor of an "intention" test. But if direct evidence of testator's statements regarding the change in the property is held inadmissible, "probable" intention may override "real" intention.[19]

GOODE v. REYNOLDS

Court of Appeals of Kentucky, 1925.
208 Ky. 441, 271 S.W. 600, 63 A.L.R. 631.[20]

[This was an action brought by an executor of the will of Col. L. P. Tarlton for construction of the will. Among other provisions, the first item of the will contained a bequest to the testator's stepdaughter, Christine H. Reynolds, of "four (4) shares of my eighteen (18) shares in the stock of the Farmer's Bank of Frankfort, and the five (5) shares of stock in the Third National Bank of Lexington * * *." The third item of the will contained the following provision: "I wish the ten (10) shares of my stock in the Farmer's Bank of Frankfort set aside for the permanent endowment of a Meta Westfeldt Tarlton room in the King's Daughters' Hospital in Frankfort * * *." The remaining facts are set forth in the opinion. Only

of ademption by extinction. E.g., Ga. Code Ann., § 113–817 (1975 Supp.) ("A legacy is adeemed or destroyed, wholly or in part, whenever the testator delivers over the property or pays the money bequeathed to the legatee, either expressly or by implication, in lieu of the legacy given; or when the testator conveys to another the specific property bequeathed, and does not afterward become possessed of the same, or otherwise places it out of the power of the executor to deliver over the legacy. If the testator attempts to convey and fails for any cause, the legacy is still valid.")

18. Will of Blomdahl, 216 Wis. 590, 257 N.W. 152, 258 N.W. 168 (1935).

19. See Notes, 11 Ind.L.Rev. 849 (1978); 23 Drake L.Rev. 478 (1974).

20. Noted, 11 Corn.L.Q. 271 (1926); 14 Ky.L.J. 182 (1926).

that part of the opinion relating to the mentioned provisions is included.]

DIETZMAN, J. The first question which is presented concerns the bequests of the stock in the Farmers' Bank of Frankfort and the Third National Bank of Lexington to Miss Reynolds and the King's Daughters' Hospital. After Col. Tarlton's will was executed, but before his death, the Farmers' Bank mentioned in his will consolidated with the Deposit Bank of Frankfort; the combined institutions being known thereafter and at the time of Col. Tarlton's death as the Farmers' Deposit Bank. In the consolidation, the stockholders of the old Farmers' Bank were given an equal number of shares in the consolidated organization. They were likewise allowed to retain their certificates in the old company, which in the consolidation reserved certain assets to be liquidated and distributed among its old stockholders. It appears that during Col. Tarlton's life there was paid as a liquidating dividend on these old certificates $120 per share, and that there will be still further liquidating dividends to come, although they will not exceed probably $30 per share. At the time of his death, Col. Tarlton had on hand the old certificates and the certificates in the consolidated company, but had disposed of the cash liquidating dividends. With regard to the Third National Bank of Lexington, after Col. Tarlton wrote his will and before his death, it consolidated with the Phoenix National Bank of Lexington, and in the consolidation Col. Tarlton was issued, for the 5 shares of stock he then owned in the old Third National Bank, 5 shares of stock in the consolidated bank, and also 5 shares of stock in a realty company organized to take over certain real estate holdings owned by the old Third National Bank, and which did not go into the consolidation.

The appellant claims with reference to these bank stocks that the change in the character of the securities worked an ademption of the legacies, and that Miss Reynolds is not entitled to take anything under these bequests in the will. On the other hand, Miss Reynolds claims there was no ademption, and she is entitled, not only to the stock in the consolidated corporations, but, also, in the case of the Farmers' Bank, to the old certificates, which carry with it future liquidating dividends, and the liquidating dividends paid Col. Tarlton, and further, in the case of the Lexington bank, to the 5 shares of stock in the realty corporation.

Regarding this matter of ademption, one theory is that the ademption of specific legacies depends upon intent. The other theory is that, whenever the specific thing devised has ceased to belong to the testator, the bequest is adeemed. Despite this, however, it is held that a legacy is not adeemed if the alteration be purely formal. Such is the case where there is a mere subdivision of a company's shares. In re Greenberry, 55 Sol.J. 633. And this principle has been extended to cover the substitution of shares in a consolidated company for shares in an old company. Thus in Re Clifford's Estate, 56 Sol.J. 91, we find that a testator bequeathed 23 shares which he owned in the London & County Bank Company. Before his death that company consolidated with another; the new company going under a different name and having enlarged capital. Each stockholder of the old company received 4 shares in the new. The court held that the bequest passed 92 of the new shares. To the same effect is In re Leeming (1912) 1 C.H. (Eng.) 828.

In Pruyn v. Sears, 96 Misc.Rep. 200, 161 N.Y.S. 58, the testator bequeathed 30 shares of the S. & P. Corporation, which did business at Rome and Watertown. Later all the assets of this corporation were transferred to a new corporation, known as S. & P., Inc., which did business only at Watertown. The stockholders of the old company received shares in the new company for their old stock. The court held that the new shares passed under the bequest, and that the same was not adeemed. In Ford v. Ford, 23 N.H. 212, the court held that renewal of notes by less than all of the original signers did not adeem a specific legacy of the original notes.

In Pope v. Hinckley, 209 Mass. 323, 95 N.E. 798, it was held that, where stock in a New Jersey corporation was bequeathed, and later this company became defunct, whereupon a Connecticut company was organized to take over the assets of the New Jersey company, pending which transfer the stock in the old company was surrendered for voting certificates to be later exchanged for the Connecticut stock, and then the testator died, the legacy was not adeemed, and the legatees were entitled to the voting certificates in lieu of the New Jersey stock.

In Re Thomas Peirce, 25 R.I. 34, 54 A. 588, stock in a consolidated bank and a small cash payment were given for stock in one of the consolidating banks. It was held that a legacy of stock in such consolidating bank was not adeemed by the exchange. To the same effect are Spinney v. Eaton, 111 Me. 1, 87 A. 378, 46 L.R.A.,N.S., 535; Hill's Adm'r v. Hill, 127 Va. 341, 103 S.E. 605. See, also, 28 R.C.L. 341.

In 40 Cyc. 1921, we find:

> "A change in the form of a security bequeathed does not necessarily work an ademption. So there is no ademption where notes bequeathed are renewed, where stock bequeathed is exchanged for notes of the company, where stock in a consolidated corporation is accepted by testator in lieu of stock in a component corporation which he had bequeathed, or where a state bank, stock in which has been bequeathed, is changed to a national bank."

We believe the rule laid down by these authorities to be the correct one. The likeness of the new shares to the old is more important than their differences. Applying this rule, we think it plain that Miss Reynolds is entitled to the securities given in the consolidation for the securities surrendered. Hence the lower court correctly adjudged her the 5 shares of stock in the new Lexington bank and the 5 shares of stock in the realty company. It also correctly adjudged her and the King's Daughters' Hospital the shares of stock in the Farmers' Deposit Bank, and also the certificates in the old Farmers' Bank on which future liquidating dividends are to be paid; but it erred in giving to them the liquidating dividends which were paid to Col. Tarlton in his lifetime, since he disposed of these himself, and they are no longer in existence. To this extent at least an ademption was worked.[21] * * *

PROBLEMS

1. The testator devised specified real property to X. After the will was executed, the property was taken by the city in an eminent domain proceeding. The award was placed on deposit in the testator's name. After T's death, X, the devisee, claims that she is entitled to the fund received by T as a result of condemnation of the property. Is X entitled to the fund? Ametrano v. Downs, 170 N.Y. 388, 63 N.E. 340 (1902). Suppose the testator had been insane at the time of the condemnation proceedings and his guardian was permitted by court order to accept an agreed sum for the land taken. Same result? See Bryson v. Turnbull, 194 Va. 528, 74 S.E.2d 180 (1953). What result under Uniform Probate Code, § 2–608(b)?

2. The testator provided in his will: "I give to X nine thousand dollars in war bonds of the following description". Testator then described the bonds. At the time the will was executed, the testator owned the bonds described. When the testator died, $6,000 in war bonds were in his estate. He also had $2,021 in a bank account and a $1,000 note which represented the proceeds of sale of $3,000 in war bonds. To what part of the estate is X entitled? Taylor v. Hull, 121 Kan. 102, 245 P. 1026 (1926).

3. The testator directed that the balance of the money due to his estate under his life insurance policies in the Northwestern and Penn Mutual Insurance Companies be added to a testamentary trust of one-half of his residuary estate created for the benefit of his daughter, X. The testator surrendered the policies and obtained their cash value after the will was executed. He invested the cash value in mortgage notes which he held at his death. His will contained a residuary clause in which he directed that half of his residuary estate should pass to his wife and that the other half should constitute a trust fund for X. Is the trustee entitled to all of the mortgage notes for the benefit of X or only half of them? See American Trust and Banking Co. v. Balfour, 138 Tenn. 385, 198 S.W. 70 (1917).

21. See 39 Va.L.Rev. 1085 (1953). Ga.Code Ann. § 113–818 provides:

"If the testator exchanges the property bequeathed for other of like character, or merely changes the investment of a fund bequeathed, the law deems the intention to be to substitute the one for the other, and the legacy shall not fail." See, Paulus, "Special and General Legacies of Securities—Whither Testator's Intent", 43 Iowa L. Rev. 467 (1958); Notes, 27 Md.L.Rev. 745 (1972); 8 Suffolk U.L.Rev. 1266 (1974); 22 A.L.R.2d 457 (1952); 16 A.L. R.2d 1404 (1951); 46 A.L.R.3d 7 (1972). Uniform Probate Code, § 2–607(a) assists in meeting the problem posed in the principal case as follows:

"(a) If the testator intended a specific devise of certain securities rather than the equivalent value thereof, the specific devisee is entitled only to:

(1) as much of the devised securities as is a part of the estate at time of the testator's death;

(2) any additional or other securities of the same entity owned by the testator by reason of action initiated by the entity excluding any acquired by exercise of purchase option;

(3) securities of another entity owned by the testator as a result of a merger, consolidation, reorganization or other similar action initiated by the entity; and

(4) any additional securities of the entity owned by the testator as a result of a plan of reinvestment if it is a regulated investment company. * * * "

4. The testatrix made a specific bequest of her automobile to X. The automobile was insured against damage by collision. The testatrix had a collision in which the automobile was severely damaged. The testatrix died from injuries which she sustained. The insurance company paid $1,000 to the executor for the automobile, $800 of this amount representing the loss caused by the collision and $200 representing the value of the damaged vehicle. Is X entitled to $1,000 or $200? See In re Barry's Estate, 208 Okl. 8, 252 P.2d 437 (1952), 53 Col.L.Rev. 885 (1953), 38 Corn.L.Q. 630 (1953), 31 N.C. L.Rev. 517 (1953). What result under Uniform Probate Code, § 2–608(a)(3)?

(ii) Ademption by Satisfaction

A testator may adeem by satisfaction a general or residuary legacy or bequest by a gift to the donee during the lifetime of the testator and after the will is executed. In ademption by satisfaction, as distinguished from ademption by extinction, the testator's intention to adeem must exist before the legacy or bequest is rendered inoperative. The intention to adeem must exist when the inter vivos gift is made. A statement in the will that subsequent advancements are to be deducted from the shares of legatees is usually taken to indicate that later gifts are made with the intention to adeem. Typically, however, the testator's intention is obscure and the courts tend to rely upon rebuttable presumptions of intention.

In a majority of states, if the testator stands in *loco parentis* to the donee, the inter vivos gift is presumed to be intended in satisfaction of the testamentary provision.[22] And a similar presumption arises if the testator made a testamentary gift to accomplish a specified purpose and then accomplishes the purpose by a gift during his lifetime. For example, if the testator makes a bequest to X to pay X's debt to Y, and the testator then pays X's debt to Y during his lifetime, it is presumed that payment of the debt was intended to satisfy the bequest. Likewise, a presumption may arise that the testator did not intend to adeem his testamentary gift. Thus, if the testator makes a gift of property which is of a different nature than the property bequeathed, an application of the doctrine *ejusdem generis* gives rise to a presumption that he did not intend to adeem.

The presumptions of intention are rebuttable and most courts admit parol evidence to sustain or rebut the presumptions.[23] Thus, evi-

22. The presumption may not be applied by some courts in favor of a stranger against a child. In re Heather, [1906] L.R. 2 Ch. 230. There is no presumption that the testator did not intend to adeem when it is shown that the testator did not stand in *loco parentis* to the donee.

23. In several states the intention of the testator must be expressed in writing or there must be a written acknowledgment by the donee. E.g., West's Ann. Cal.Probate Code, § 1050 ("A gift before death shall be considered as an ademption of a bequest or devise of the property given; but such gift shall not be taken as an advancement to an heir or as an ademption of a general legacy unless such intention is expressed by the testator in the grant or otherwise in writing, or unless the donee acknowledges it in writing to be such.")

In Trustees of Baker University v. Trustees of Endowment Association, 222

dence of the circumstances at the time the alleged adeeming gift was made and declarations by the testator at the time are admitted to show his intent. In a few states, evidence of the testator's declarations prior to and after the inter vivos gift is made is admissible upon the issue of intention to adeem. There may be a *pro tanto* ademption by satisfaction if the evidence indicates that the testator so intended.

Uniform Probate Code, § 2–612 presumes no ademption by satisfaction and limits the sources of evidence of the testator's intent to adeem to three sources. These are the will, which must provide for the deduction of the inter vivos gift; a contemporaneous writing by the testator expressing the intent to adeem; or a written acknowledgment by the devisee that the gift is in satisfaction. The latter writing is not required to be contemporaneous. The Code does not require the "contemporaneous" writing to be signed by the testator. Presumably evidence of the circumstances would be admissible to identify an unsigned writing, although in many instances if such a writing could be produced, it might be in the handwriting of the testator which could be identified by witnesses. With these evidential restrictions, the Code substantially precludes litigation based on ademption by satisfaction, most of which stems from uncertainties concerning the intent with which the inter vivos gift was made.

There is little authority to support the application of the doctrine of ademption by satisfaction to specific or demonstrative legacies or bequests,[24] although there is no reason why specific or demonstrative gifts should be exempt if the testator intends to satisfy them. Usually, however, if specific property is transferred inter vivos to a specific legatee, the gift is adeemed by extinction since there is no property meeting the description in the estate of the testator at his death. The doctrine of *ejusdem generis* may be applied with particular force when the gift to the specific legatee is of a different nature than the property given in the will.

By the weight of authority, a devise cannot be satisfied by a conveyance of land or a gift of personal property.[25] The rule appears to have been based at one time upon an analogy between ademption by satisfaction and revocation.[26] Modern applications of the rule may

Kan. 245, 564 P.2d 472 (1977), testatrix left a will with a bequest of $20,000 to the Endowment Association of Kansas State College of Pittsburgh to endow a scholarship fund; later she asked her lawyer to arrange for establishment of the scholarship fund during her lifetime; this was done and $40,000 given. Subsequently testatrix prepared a new will omitting the College, but she failed to execute the will. The Court held evidence regarding the new will should be admitted to show intent in making the gift as a satisfaction.

24. In Weston v. Johnson, 48 Ind. 1, 7 (1874), it is stated that a specific legacy cannot be adeemed by satisfaction. In Jones v. Mason, 26 Va. 577, 16 Am.Dec. 761 (1827), a specific bequest of slaves was adeemed by an inter vivos gift of other slaves.

25. Statutes in several states provide expressly for ademption of devises by satisfaction. E.g., Va.Code Ann. § 64.1–63.

26. No formalities were required by the Statute of Frauds, 1677, for revocation of a testament of personal property. Formalities were required by the Statute for revocation of a devise. Since there is a close analogy between ademption by satisfaction and revocation, there was once some basis for distinguishing be-

increase the stability of land titles. A conveyance to the devisee of property specifically devised will adeem the devise by extinction.[27]

PROBLEMS

1. The testator's will provided: "All of the remainder of my personal estate I give and bequeath to my three daughters, X, Y and Z, share and share alike." After the will was executed, the testator conveyed to X land valued at $14,000 and to Y land valued at $10,000. There was evidence that the testator also intended to convey land to Z but did not do so. The testator had a personal estate of $75,000 when he died. Z contended that the conveyances to X and Y were ademptions of their respective legacies. To what share of the estate is Z entitled? Carmichael v. Lathrop, 108 Mich. 473, 66 N.W. 350 (1896).

2. The testator's will contained a legacy of $600 to his niece. The testator gave the niece $400 after the will was executed. When the gift of $400 was made, the niece executed a receipt in which she stated that she released all claims against the testator's estate. The testator was not indebted to his niece. Was the legacy of $600 adeemed? Johnson v. McDowell, 154 Iowa 38, 134 N.W. 419 (1912).

3. Testatrix bequeathed $1,000 to X for the purpose of "making her home comfortable according to her wishes". After the will was executed, X, who was then building a new home, appealed to the testatrix for help. The testatrix borrowed $1,000 from a bank and paid it to X. Testatrix gave her note to the bank for $1,000, the note also being signed by X. The cashier of the bank heard the testatrix mention the legacy in her will at the time the loan was made, the testatrix stating that the legacy to X would take care of the note if it was not paid at her death. The note was unpaid when the testatrix died and was paid by her executor. Is the legacy of $1,000 adeemed by satisfaction? Grogan v. Ashe, 156 N.C. 286, 72 S.E. 372 (1911).

4. The testator devised certain land to his brother for life and after the death of the brother, to his daughter in fee simple. The testator's son, Oliver, was named residuary devisee. After the will was executed, the testator paid his daughter $500, for which she gave a receipt as follows: "Received of Oliver Comfort five hundred dollars, which money I receive as part of my father's estate up to this time, and all such other property as he may accumulate up to his decease". After the testator's death, Oliver, the residuary devisee, claimed the daughter's remainder interest. Does Oliver take the remainder as residuary devisee? Burnham v. Comfort, 108 N.Y. 535, 15 N.E. 710 (1888).

5. In each of the preceding problems, assume the following statute is in force in the state:[28] "Property which a testator gave in his lifetime to a per-

tween a legacy and a devise for the purpose of applying the doctrine of ademption by satisfaction, applying the doctrine in the case of a legacy but not in the case of a devise for which a formal revocation was required.

27. See generally as to ademption by extinction and satisfaction, Barstow, "Ademption by Satisfaction", 6 Wis.L. Rev. 217 (1931); Evans, "Effect of Corporate Transformation Upon Ademption, Lapse and Fiduciary Appointments", 88 U. of Pa.L.Rev. 671 (1940); Mechem, "Specific Legacies of Unspecified Things—Ashburner v. Macguire Reconsidered", 87 U. of Pa.L.Rev. 546 (1939); Page, "Ademption by Extinction: Its Practical Effects", 1943 Wis.L.Rev. 11; Smith, "Ademption by Extinction", 6 Wis.L.Rev. 229 (1931); Warren, "History of Ademption", 25 Iowa L.Rev. 290 (1940); 26 A.L.R.2d 9 (1952) (Ademption by Satisfaction).

28. Uniform Probate Code, § 2–612 (1977 Text).

son is treated as a satisfaction of a devise to that person in whole or in part, only if the will provides for deduction of the lifetime gift, or the testator declares in a contemporaneous writing that the gift is to be deducted from the devise or is in satisfaction of the devise, or the devisee acknowledges in writing that the gift is in satisfaction. For purpose of partial satisfaction, property given during lifetime is valued as of the time the devisee came into possession or enjoyment of the property or as of the time of death of the testator, whichever occurs first."

How will this statute affect your result?

B. EXONERATION

ASHKENAZY v. ASHKENAZY'S ESTATE

District Court of Appeal of Florida, 1962.
140 So.2d 331.

* * * [Decedent, Saul Ashkenazy, in 1952 purchased real property which was conveyed to him and his wife Jeanne, subject to a mortgage. In 1957 Saul and his wife were divorced; pursuant to a separation agreement the wife conveyed to the husband her interest in the real estate and he assumed and agreed to pay the mortgage. On June 6, 1960, the decedent executed a valid will providing in part as follows: * * *

"SECOND: I instruct my hereinafter named Executrix and Executor to pay all of my just debts as soon after my death as shall be practicable.

"TENTH: Unto my former wife, JEANNE ASHKENAZY, I give, devise and bequeath my house, located on Douglas Road in Coral Gables, Florida, to do with as she sees fit; unto my said former wife I likewise give, devise and bequeath my cemetary lots in Mount Sinai Far Band Cemetary in Miami to do with as she sees fit.

"TWELFTH: I give, devise and bequeath unto my friend, LILLIAN CONROY FINE of Miami, Florida, all of my shares in The Wellington Fund, the property legally described as:

"Lots 1 and 2 in Block 1 of LAKE LETTA ESTATES, according to the Plat thereof, recorded in Plat Book 1, Page 70–B of Highlands County, Florida

and my automobile.

"FOURTEENTH: All of the rest, residue and remainder of my estate, whether real, mixed or personal, wheresoever situate, I give, devise and bequeath to my beloved nephew, DAVID B. ASHKENAZY, absolutely."

* * *

Later in 1960 decedent obtained a loan of $4,000 from a bank and encumbered the shares in the Wellington Fund referred to in clause Twelfth of the will as security for the loan. Decedent died in February 1961 and his will was admitted to probate. No claim was filed in the estate by the mortgagee of the real property, although a balance of approximately $5,000 was still owing. However, the bank filed a claim in the estate. Jeanne Ashkenazy filed a petition to require the executors to exonerate the real property devised to her under clause Tenth; and the executors filed a petition for instructions. The county judge held that the devise of the real property was subject to the mortgage, so that Jeanne Ashkenazy is obligated to make payments in order to protect her interest; the judge also held that the bequest of shares in the Wellington Fund was free of liens and that the executors were authorized and directed to pay the claim of the bank out of the residuary estate.] * * *

HENDRY, JUDGE. * * *

The first question is presented by the appellant, Jeanne Ashkenazy, who asserts that she is entitled to have the real property free and clear from the lien of the mortgage encumbering such property. The second question is presented by the appellee, David Ashkenazy, the residuary legatee, who urges, by cross-assignment of error, that the court erred in holding that the shares of stock "to Lillian Conway Fine is free and clear of liens and encumbrances".

It is the appellant's contention as to the initial question that the law is that the testator's intent controls only where the will specifically provides either for or against exoneration; that the instruction in the will for payment of debts (under paragraph "Second" above) is evidence that the intent of the testator was to have the real property exonerated from the mortgage lien; that, in the absence of the testator's intent to the contrary, the specific devisee of real property has a common law right of exoneration; and that the facts and surrounding circumstances herein, show that the testator intended that the appellant take the real property free and clear of the mortgage lien.

* * *

We hold that since no statute has been passed changing the common-law rule of exoneration,[29] the common-law rule remains in full force and effect by reason of § 2 of Article XVIII of the Constitution of Florida, 26 F.S.A. The decisive determination therefore is the application of the common-law rule to the situation at hand. We find the common-law rule to be that the specific devisee of real property is entitled to have the mortgage on the devised property paid at the expense of the residue of the estate[30] unless the will expressly shows a

29. [Footnotes 29–33 are by the Court; some of the Court's footnotes have been omitted. Ed.]

For a recent judicial determination of the applicability of the common-law rule of exoneration, see In re Budd's Estate, 11 Wisc.2d 248, 105 N.W.2d 358.

30. King v. King, 3 P.Wms. 358, 361, 24 Eng.Rep. 1100 (Ch.1735); Bartholomew v. May, 1 Atk. 487, 26 Eng.Rep. 309 (Ch.1737); Cope v. Cope, 2 Salk 449, 1 Eq.Ca.Abr. 269, 21 Eng.Rep. 1038 (Ch. 1707); Hill v. Bishop of London, 1 Atk. 618, 26 Eng.Rep. 388 (Ch.1738); In re Fo-

contrary intent[31] or an implied intent not to exonerate can be extracted from the provisions of the will as a whole when viewed in light of the surrounding circumstances.[32]

In the case at bar, we find that the deceased, Saul Ashkenazy, did not expressly signify any intention not to exonerate the property here involved from the mortgage lien. In so finding, we fully concur with the lower court that the general direction in paragraph "Second" of the decedent's will, i.e., "to pay all of my just debts as soon after my death as shall be practicable" does not of itself, indicate a positive intent to exonerate the real property.[33] Hence, unless an implied intent not to exonerate can be elicited from the entire will when scrutinized in the light of the surrounding circumstances, the appellant, Jeanne Ashkenazy, is entitled to have the real property exonerated.

The lower court, in concluding that it was the intent of the deceased not to exonerate the specific devise of real property, stated that the grounds for such a conclusion were:

"1. The land was encumbered when the will was made.

"2. The testator intended to devise the property he then owned, which was the equity in the property.

"3. The mortgage was a long term obligation which might not be paid in the lifetime of the testator."

While we are in accord that the above-quoted grounds were indicative of an implied intent not to exonerate, we feel that the lower court failed to take into consideration other factors which, at the very least, counterbalanced those indicators that there was an implied intent not to exonerate. These factors were:

1. The fact that as part of the separation agreement between the decedent and the appellant, the decedent assumed payment of the mortgage in return for the appellant-wife's conveying such property to the decedent. It is our belief that this evinced an intention to exonerate. This is so, because the failure to exonerate the real property from the mortgage lien would put the appellant in almost the same position as before the separation agreement and would, in effect, nullify the obvious gift intended to the former wife by the devise in question.

2. The will and the entire record reveal that the deceased, Saul Ashkenazy, was a very benevolent man who was in the habit of making charitable gifts all over the world. An interpretation of paragraph "Tenth" (which is the provision in favor of appellant, Jeanne Ashkenazy) as the executors so interpret it, would leave

garty's Estate, 165 Misc. 78, 300 N.Y.S. 231; Annot., 19 A.L.R. 1421.

31. Galton v. Hancock, 2 Atk. 424, 26 Eng.Rep. 656 (Ch.1742); Annot., 5 A.L.R. 488; 3 American Law of Property § 14.-25 (Casner Ed.1952); Thompson, Wills § 484.

32. Taylor v. Broadway Methodist Church, 269 Ky. 108, 106 S.W.2d 69; Howell v. Ott, 182 Miss. 252, 180 So. 52, 181 So. 740; Savings Trust Co. v. Beck, Mo.App.1934, 73 S.W.2d 282. See 97 C.J.S. Wills § 1316(b)(1), p. 221.

33. Savings Trust Co. v. Beck, Id.; In re McNulta, 168 Wash. 397, 12 P.2d 389; In re Budd's Estate, 11 Wisc.2d 248, 105 N.W.2d 358; see Annot., 5 A.L.R. 488 at 505 and cases cited therein.

the deceased's former wife little, if anything. This is in contravention of the will read as a whole in that the applicable provisions show that there was still some closeness of relationship between the decedent and his former wife.

3. The fact that the mortgage is not of such size in relation to the residuary estate that application of the common-law rule of exoneration would operate to deprive the residuary legatee of most of his estate and thus prevent, to a large extent, the testamentary plan of disposition.

It is our belief that these further factors divulge an intention by the decedent, Saul Ashkenazy, to exonerate the real property in question. Assuming arguendo, however, that these factors do no more than counteract the aforesaid findings of the lower court, we would still reverse the order appealed as to this question because the common-law rule was that a specific devisee was entitled to exoneration absent an intent to the contrary. In other words, the burden of proof in such a situation is on the residuary legatee.

We hold that the common-law rule as to the right of exoneration is here controlling and there being no contrary testamentary intent shown, either express or implied, the appellant, Jeanne Ashkenazy was entitled to have the real property exonerated from the mortgage lien.

As to the second question, i.e., the right of the specific legatee, Lillian Conroy Fine, to have the shares of stock (under paragraph "Twelfth") exonerated from all liens thereon, we affirm the lower court's holding that it was the intention of the testator that this legacy be exonerated from all liens. We concur with the lower court that the factors which evince an intention of exoneration as to the shares were:

"1. The shares of stock were not encumbered when the will was made.

"2. The testator intended to bequeath the property he then owned, which was free and clear.

"3. The bank loan was a short term obligation which the testator expected to pay in his lifetime."

We have reviewed the other contentions of the parties and have found them to be without merit.

It follows, therefore, that the order appealed is in all respects affirmed except that it is reversed so that the appellant, Jeanne Ashkenazy, shall have a right to have the real property in question exonerated from the mortgage lien.

Affirmed in part and reversed in part.

NOTE

The courts have presumed in some cases that a lien upon particular property was intended by the testator to be discharged from his general personal estate.[34] The debt which the lien secures must be the personal obligation of the testator. Thus he may incur the obligation initially or assume the obligation, as when he purchases land with a mortgage lien upon it and assumes the mortgage debt.[35] The basis of the presumption is that the general personal estate was benefited because of the debt assumed by the testator, the assumption being that the personal estate would have been less had the debt been discharged. Only liens on land devised and property specifically bequeathed are subject to exoneration; and the source of the fund for exoneration usually is limited to intestate and residuary personalty. Some courts have used general pecuniary legacies for this purpose.[36]

The presumption that the testator intended to exonerate property is rebuttable and yields to a contrary expression of the testator's intention. The modern trend is to confine the presumption within its common law limits or to abolish the presumption by statute as is done in Uniform Probate Code, § 2–609.[37] Consider whether the statute should differentiate the following situations:[38] (1) testator has a mortgage or other lien on the specifically devised property when he executes his will; (2) testator has no incumbrance on the property when he executes the will (or pays off the existing incumbrance later), and subsequently mortgages the specifically devised property in order to finance purchase of other property which passes under the residuary clause; (3) after execution of the will, testator encumbers the specifically devised property in order to finance improvements to such property; (4) as in the principal case, testator encumbers the property on a short-term obligation.

Exoneration problems may arise with regard to nonprobate assets. If decedent has assigned his life insurance policies to a bank or other lending institution to secure a loan, can the named beneficiary on the policies (typically the spouse) require the personal representative to pay the loan out of the probate estate? Should it make any difference that the will contains the

34. See Note 4 A.L.R.3d 1023 (1965); Paulus, "Exoneration of Specific Devises: Legislation vs. The Common Law" 6 Willamette L.Rev. 53 (1970); Ryan, "Exoneration of the Specific Devise at the Expense of the Residue", 44 Marq.L.Rev. 290 (1960–61).

35. See Higinbotham v. Manchester, 113 Conn. 62, 69, 154 A. 242, 79 A.L.R. 85 (1931).

36. E.g., Brown v. Baron, 162 Mass. 56, 37 N.E. 772, 44 Am.St.Rep. 331 (1894).

37. Uniform Probate Code, § 2–609 provides:

> A specific devise passes subject to any mortgage interest existing at the date of death, without right of exoneration, regardless of a general directive in the will to pay debts.

McKinney's N.Y., EPTL, § 3–3.6(a) reads:

> "Where any property, subject, at the time of decedent's death, to any lien, security interest or other charge including a lien for unpaid purchase money, is specifically disposed of by will or passes to a distributee, or where the proceeds of any policy of insurance on the life of the decedent are payable to a named beneficiary and such policy is subject to any lien, security interest or other charge, the personal representative is not responsible for the satisfaction of such encumbrance out of the property of the decedent's estate except as provided in SCPA 1811, unless, in the case of a will, the testator has expressly or by necessary implication indicated otherwise. A general provision in the will for the payment of debts is not such an indication."

38. Compare Vernon's Ann.Mo.Stat. § 474.450.

usual clause directing the personal representative to "pay my just debts out of the residue of my estate"? [39] If the insured borrows from the insurer, this operates to reduce the amount payable on the policy and there is no personal obligation, hence no "debt" and no right to exoneration.[40] Testator may of course expressly provide in his will that the beneficiary should receive out of the estate an amount equal to any indebtedness by which the insurance proceeds are reduced.

PROBLEM

The testator purchased land from A and B for $1,000, assuming a mortgage in the amount of $500 which had been given by the grantors. The grantors retained a lien upon the property for payment of the amount of the mortgage. A tax lien of $13.10 was upon the property at the testator's death. The testator devised the land to C. There was a provision in the will that the testator's debts should be paid from his notes and accounts. The will contained no residuary clause and the personal estate was intestate except for certain minor legacies and bequests. C contends that the mortgage and tax liens should be exonerated from the intestate personalty. Should either of these liens be exonerated? Barlow v. Cain, 146 Ark. 160, 225 S.W. 228 (1920).

C. INTER VIVOS ACCESSIONS

HICKS v. KERR

Court of Appeals of Maryland, 1918.
132 Md. 693, 104 A. 426, 10 A.L.R. 1323.

URNER, J. The eighth paragraph of the will of Ella J. Kerr, late of Baltimore city, deceased, is as follows:

> "To my daughter, Ella K. Hicks, wife of R. Randolph Hicks, of Norfolk, Virginia, I give and bequeath the forty-two (42) shares of stock in the Northern Central Railway Company, now registered in my name. I further provide with reference to said legacy that, in the event my said daughter predeceases me without children or descendants of children surviving her, the same shall become the absolute property of her husband, R. Randolph Hicks."

The will was executed July 1, 1913, and the testatrix died on the 17th day of March, 1917. During the period between the execution of the will and the death of the testatrix, her daughter, Mrs. Hicks, died without leaving any children or descendants, but survived by her husband, to whom the 42 shares of stock specifically bequeathed by the clause of the will we have quoted have been transferred in due course of administration. At the time of her death the testatrix was also the owner of 16 additional shares of stock of the Northern Central Rail-

39. Estate of Cohen, 469 Pa. 29, 364 A.2d 888 (1976) (direction requires payment from estate).

40. Faris v. Faris, 76 Ind.App. 336, 130 N.E. 444 (1921).

way Company, which she had received, by virtue of her existing share holdings, as her proportion of a 40 per cent. stock dividend declared by the company in July, 1914, on account of surplus earnings appropriated to improvements or otherwise invested. The 16 shares which thus accrued to the testatrix are claimed by her son-in-law, Mr. Hicks, as the substituted legatee, under her will, of the 42 shares therein bequeathed, upon the theory that the dividend stock subsequently issued bore such a relation to the original shares as to follow the course of their testamentary disposition. This claim is contested by the two surviving sons of the testatrix, who assert that the 16 shares in question have passed to them as residuary legatees. The appeal is from a decree by which the latter view was sustained.

The descriptive terms of the bequest are clear. The property intended to be bequeathed was plainly designated by the testatrix as "the forty-two (42) shares of stock in the Northern Central Railway Company now registered in my name." It was the only stock of that company owned by her when she executed her will, and it was readily identified by the description quoted when the will took effect at her death. So far as the specific terms of the bequest are concerned, they are completely gratified by the delivery to the legatee of the 42 shares precisely described. It is only because the stock dividend represented assets which previously formed elements of value of the stock already issued that the dividend stock is claimed by the legatee of the original shares.

When the 16 shares of dividend stock were issued to the testatrix, she also received her due proportion of a cash dividend, likewise declared on account of accumulated earnings of the corporation. It is, of course, not suggested that this cash dividend would pass under the bequest of the stock, even if the money thus derived could be identified at the period when the will became operative. The railway company might have distributed its surplus earnings wholly in the form of cash dividends, instead of using a part of such funds for improvements on account of which stock dividends were declared. If the former course had been pursued, it would not be contended that the bequest of the 42 shares should be treated as carrying with it such part of the proceeds of the cash dividends as the testatrix may not have expended in her lifetime. The fact that the dividends were declared partly in stock, instead of entirely in cash, does not affect the principle of the question now being determined. Northern Central Dividend Cases, 126 Md. 16, 94 A. 338; Miller v. Safe D. & T. Co., 127 Md. 612, 96 A. 766.

The ordinary rule is that dividends and income accruing prior to the death of the testatrix, from stock or other property which is the subject of a specific bequest under the will, do not follow the legacy, but form part of the general estate. 40 Cyc. 1549; Thompson on Corporations (2d Ed.) vol. 4, § 4292; Wethered v. Safe Deposit & Trust Co., 79 Md. 153, 28 A. 812. In the application of that rule no distinction can properly be made between stock and cash dividends of corporate earnings received by a testator under such circumstances as those shown by this record.

In the case of In re Brann, 219 N.Y. 263, 114 N.E. 404, L.R.A. 1918B, 663, a testatrix had bequeathed the 30 shares of stock of the Standard Oil Company owned by her at the time of the execution of her will, to be held in trust for her brother for life and for certain charities in remainder. The will was executed in 1908 and the testatrix died in 1912. About a year prior to her death she received from the Standard Oil Company a number of shares of the stock of its various subsidiary oil companies, which it distributed to its stockholders under a decree of the United States Supreme Court requiring it to dispose of its holdings in corporations under its control. The question in the case was whether the shares of the subsidiary companies, thus accruing to the testatrix in her lifetime, passed with her bequest of the primary shares, on account of which they were distributed, or were included in the portion of the estate to which the residuary legatee was entitled. The Court of Appeals of New York, adopted the latter theory, and in the course of its opinion said:

> "The new shares are, in effect, an extraordinary dividend declared during the life of the testatrix. * * * The case stands the same as if the Standard Oil Company has sold the shares, and distributed the proceeds. It is hardly denied that a voluntary dividend, whether paid in money or in stock, would be separate from the primary shares."

A different rule could not be invoked, the court said, merely because the dividend in that case was compulsory. Due consideration was given to the fact that the subsidiary shares, while held by the parent company, contributed to the value of its stock, but it was held that the reduction which their distribution caused in the value of the bequeathed shares was analogous to a partial ademption of the legacy.

If, in the present case, the dividend shares had been received by the testatrix before her will was executed, it is obvious that they could not be held to be embraced in the specific bequest of the original 42 shares of which she was the owner. In such a situation the omission of the testatrix to mention the additional shares in connection with the legacy would be accepted as a plain indication of her intention that they were not to be included in the bequest. They would certainly not be attached to the legacy by judicial action, simply because they represented assets from which the bequeathed stock had formerly derived a part of its value. While the dividend stock with which we are now dealing had not been received by the testatrix at the time of the execution of her will, it was in her possession for more than two years prior to her death; but no change was made in her will to include the new stock within the terms and effect of the bequest under consideration. If it had been the desire of the testatrix to have the legacy include the 16 shares of Northern Central stock issued to her in 1914, as well as the 42 shares specified in the bequest, it may well be supposed that, in the ample time available, she would have made the simple alteration in her will necessary to accomplish that result.

Decree affirmed, with costs.[41]

NOTE

The disposition of accessions occurring during the lifetime of a testator to property specifically described in his will has been a matter of much difficulty. The devisee clearly takes the property with any increased market value; and the devisee takes land with improvements made upon it. Income from the property collected by the testator passes as a part of the general estate. The testator's intention should control the disposition of uncollected income. Thus, a legacy of a sum due on a debt indicates the testator's intention that the interest accrued during his lifetime should not also pass with the principal sum.[42] On the other hand, a specific gift of a mortgage or debt, instead of a sum of money represented by a mortgage or debt, has been held to pass the uncollected interest thereon.[43] A specific bequest of a bond has been held to pass an overdue coupon which was physically attached to the bond at the testator's death.[44] Since in the absence of statute the common law does not apportion rent over the rent-paying period, but treats rent as due on the day when payable, rent which covers a period extending before and after the testator's death, but which is payable after death, belongs to the devisee; conversely, if the rent were due and payable in advance prior to the testator's death, even though for a period extending after death, the personal representative would be entitled to the entire rent.[45] Of course, the will may manifest an intention that rent be apportioned regardless of when due and payable.[46] The common-law rule has justification only in that it avoids separate actions by the devisee and the personal representative against the tenant for rent for a single period. Statutes providing for apportionment of rent in certain situations usually do not provide for the present situation.

41. Where the additional shares result from a stock split, rather than a dividend, the shares have been held to pass with the specific bequest of the original stock. Fisher v. Paine, 210 Or. 429, 311 P.2d 438 (1957); Note, 27 Md.L.Rev. 745 (1972).

Uniform Probate Code, § 2–607, which deals in part with accessions to specific gifts of securities, excludes in subsection (b) all distributions prior to death as part of the gift except the accessions mentioned in subsection (a) which are:

"* * * (2) any additional or other securities of the same entity owned by the testator by reason of action initiated by the entity excluding any acquired by exercise of purchase options;

"(3) securities of another entity owned by the testator as a result of a merger, consolidation, reorganization or other similar action initiated by the entity; and

"(4) any additional securities of the entity owned by the testator as a result of a plan of reinvestment if it is a regulated investment company. * * *"

See comment, "The Creation of General and Specific Bequests of Securities and The Rules for the Distribution of Accessions to Securities", 52 Marquette L.Rev. 271 (1968). Note, 46 A.L.R.3d 7 (1972).

42. Roberts v. Kussin, 2 Atk. 112, 26 Eng.Rep. 470 (1740).

43. Fleming v. Carr, 47 N.J.Eq. 549, 22 A. 197 (1891); Alford v. Bennett, 279 Ill. 375, 117 N.E. 89 (1917).

44. Ogden v. Pattee, 149 Mass. 82, 21 N.E. 227, 14 Am.St.Rep. 401 (1889).

45. Holliday v. Price, 146 Ga. 782, 92 S.E. 533 (1917); Estate of Jensen, 225 Iowa 1249, 282 N.W. 712 (1938). See generally on apportionment of rent, American Law of Property (1952) § 9.44; 126 A.L.R. 12, 42 (1940).

46. Estate of Hemphill, 157 Wis. 331, 147 N.W. 1089 (1914).

A gift of the testator's entire estate, a designated portion of it (as for example a specified percentage), or the residue of the estate will pass accessions not otherwise disposed of or necessary to pay claims against the estate.

PROBLEMS

1. Testator bequeathed to X a described bond of the Boston and Albany Railroad Company. When the testator died, his executors clipped an overdue interest coupon from the bond and cashed it. Is X entitled to the interest represented by the coupon? Ogden v. Pattee, 149 Mass. 82, 21 N.E. 227, 14 Am.St.Rep. 401 (1889).

2. A will provided: "I give and bequeath to my brother, X, a bond and mortgage of six thousand five hundred dollars which I now hold against him." At the testator's death, interest had accrued on the bond in the amount of $217.46. The interest had not been collected by the testator. Is X entitled to the interest? Fleming v. Carr, 47 N.J.Eq. 549, 22 A. 197 (1890).

3. How would you decide problems 1 and 2 if Uniform Probate Code, § 2–607, stated in part in fn. 41, supra, was in force in the state?

4. The testator devised his farm, Blackacre, to X in fee simple absolute. When the testator died, there were growing crops on the farm. Is X entitled to the growing crops? Cheshire v. Keaton, 184 Ga. 29, 190 S.E. 579 (1937).

(3) CHANGES IN PROPERTY AFTER TESTATOR'S DEATH

A. Post Mortem Accessions

The amount of a specific legacy, bequest or devise, is increased by all accessions that occur after the death of the testator unless the testator provides otherwise. Stock or cash dividends which are declared after the testator's death pass to the specific legatee of the stock even though the dividends were earned during the lifetime of the testator. Rent or royalties from land for the period following the testator's death pass to the specific devisee.

B. Interest on Legacies

A general legacy bears interest at the legal rate from the date upon which it is payable to the legatee. By the common law rule, a legacy is payable one year after the testator's death. There are three exceptions to the general rule. A general legacy bears interest from the testator's death: (1) if it is in favor of a minor to whom the testator stood in *loco parentis* and for whose maintenance the testator made no other provision; (2) if it was made to satisfy a debt due at the testator's death; and (3) in some states, if it is in lieu of the dower of the widow. In any event, the testator's expressed intention is controlling. The testator may designate a date upon which general legacies are payable and the amount of interest, if any, that the legacies will bear if not paid at the time directed.

Statutes in several states modify the common law rules concerning interest, but the statutory rules also yield when in conflict with the testator's expressed intention.[47]

Interest upon general legacies is paid from the residuary estate. Residuary legacies do not bear interest because there is no other fund from which the interest can be paid and because the amount of a residuary legacy cannot be determined until the estate is settled.

There is a division of authority whether a will contest or other estate litigation excuses payment of general legacies and stops the interest from accruing. Some courts have taken the position that the executor must pay the general legacies when proper security is given for his protection. Other courts have held that the legacies are not payable and interest does not begin to run until the litigation is settled.

The common law and statutory rules concerning interest are usually applied to demonstrative legacies since these are ultimately payable out of the general assets of the estate. A specific legacy does not draw interest, although the legatee receives the accessions and accretions after the testator's death.

C. ABATEMENT

ESTATE OF KRAFT

Supreme Court of Iowa (1971).
186 N.W.2d 628.[48]

RAWLINGS, JUSTICE.

Testator's surviving widow filed objections to accounting by executors abating residuary bequest for payment of debts and expenses. Decedent's children resisted and petitioned for declaratory judgment. Trial court sustained the widow's objections. Executors and all but two adversely affected children appeal. We reverse.

47. E.g., West's Ann.Cal.Probate Code § 162 (1980 Supp.) ("General pecuniary legacies, including general pecuniary legacies in trust, if not paid prior to the first anniversary of the testator's death, bear interest thereafter at the rate of 4 percent per annum. Annuities commence at the testator's death and are due at the end of the annual, monthly or other specified period. * * *"); Uniform Probate Code, § 3–904 requires that general pecuniary legacies (the term "devises" being used in the Code) bear interest at the legal rate beginning one year "after the first appointment of a personal representative" unless the will indicates a contrary intent.

48. Noted 57 Iowa L.Rev. 1394 (1972).

The instant will, executed June 4, 1965, by Fred W. Kraft, decedent, provides in material part:

> "1. I give, devise and bequeath to my wife, Joyce E. Kraft, the Northwest Quarter (1/4) of Section 33, Township 94, North, Range 26, West of the 15th P.M., Iowa, and I also bequest to Joyce E. Kraft, my homestead located at 206 South Kirkwood Avenue, Eagle Grove, Iowa, or any homestead that I may own at the time of my death.
>
> "2. I give, devise and bequeath to Dale E. Kraft and Everett L. Kraft, share and share alike the following real estate towit: West 120 acres of the South One-Half (1/2) of Section 5, Township 93 North, Range 26, West of 5th P.M., Iowa.
>
> "3. I give, devise and bequeath to my following children, Joyce L. Meyer, William P. Kraft, Julie M. Kraft and Vicki Jo Kraft, share and share alike the following described real estate towit: Northeast Fractional Quarter of Section 6, Township 93 North, Range 26, West of 5th P.M., Iowa.
>
> "4. Subject to the foregoing I give, devise and bequeath all my property both real and personal to my wife, Joyce E. Kraft."

It is contended by decedent's widow, the foregoing bequests must stand abated in accord with The Code 1966 Section 633.436.

The appealing executors and children assert that does not conform with decedent's testamentary plan, The Code 1966, Section 633.437 is applicable, and trial court erred in holding to the contrary.

Our review is de novo. The Code 1966, Section 633.33; In re Estate of Miguet, 185 N.W.2d 508 (Iowa), opinion filed March 11, 1971; Zion Lutheran Church v. Lamp Executors, 260 Iowa 363, 366, 149 N.W.2d 137.

Code §§ 633.436 and 633.437, both comparatively new, have been heretofore considered by this court on relatively few occasions. See In re Estate of Miguet, supra; In re Estate of Twedt, 173 N.W.2d 545 (Iowa); Bergren v. Estate of Mason, 163 N.W.2d 374 (Iowa); Zion Lutheran Church v. Lamp Executors, supra; In re Estate of Tedford, 258 Iowa 890, 140 N.W.2d 908.

Since the cited statutory enactments are vital to a determination and understanding of the instant case they are here set forth at length.

> "633.436. Except as provided in section 633.211, shares of the distributees shall abate, for the payment of debts and charges, federal and state estate taxes, legacies, the shares of children born or adopted after the making of a will, or the share of the surviving spouse who elects to take against the will, without any preference or priority as between real and personal property, in the following order:
>
> "1. Property not disposed of by the will;
>
> "2. Property devised to the residuary devisee, except property devised to a surviving spouse who takes under the will;

"3. Property disposed of by the will, but not specifically devised and not devised to the residuary devisee, except property devised to a surviving spouse who takes under the will;

"4. Property specifically devised, except property devised to a surviving spouse who takes under the will;

"5. Property devised to a surviving spouse who takes under the will.

"A general devise charged on any specific property or fund shall, for purposes of abatement, be deemed property specifically devised to the extent of the value of the property on which it is charged. Upon the failure or insufficiency of the property on which it is charged, it shall be deemed property not specifically devised to the extent of such failure or insufficiency.

"633.437. If the provisions of the will, the testamentary plan, or the express or the implied purpose of the devise would be defeated by the order of abatement stated in section 633.436, the shares of distributees shall abate in such other manner as may be found necessary to give effect to the intention of the testator."

In support of their position the appealing executors and children presented extrinsic trial evidence upon the theory it was admissible and should be considered because "subject to the foregoing", found in paragraph 4 of the will, supra, is ambiguous, or in any event proper under Code § 633.437, supra, for the purpose of determining decedent's testamentary plan.

It is neither necessary nor do we rest our holding infra on any such testimonial showing.

In re Estate of Twedt, 173 N.W.2d 545 (Iowa), involved a problem similar to that here presented.

The *Twedt* case was submitted on pleadings and a stipulation disclosing decedent left an estate worth about $700,000, including joint tenancy property having a value of approximately $90,000. The remainder consisted of real and personal property wholly owned by testator. His will directed, (1) payment of all debts and costs of administration (2) a specifically described farm be sold and proceeds distributed to eleven designated charitable beneficiaries, (3) all residue pass to the widow.

In holding Code § 633.437 applicable we quoted this from trial court's decree, loc. cit., 173 N.W.2d 548:

" '* * * this is one of those unusual cases. Consider "the testamentary plan" alone. Here was a man possessed of substantial resources to provide for his widow. With the joint tenancy property and the property in the estate, even after all taxes are paid and the charitable gift is fulfilled, abundant assets still exist for the widow. Testator selects his favorite charities and sets aside a farm for them. He makes his will and gives them the proceeds of the farm, and the balance to the widow. He had legal counsel and no doubt knew that the charitable gift was deductible.

" 'Now what would application of regular abatement do? It would wipe out the charitable gift, just contrary to testator's expectations and his testamentary plan. If he had possessed any notion that such result would ensue, he would not have gone to the bother of inserting the charitable gift in the will; to do so was a completely idle act. * * *

" 'The Court concludes in this particular situation that application of regular abatement would frustrate the testamentary plan so substantially that the estate taxes should fall on the residuum in order to effectuate testator's intention. * * *.' "

As stated in 20 Drake L.Rev. 288, 328: "The *Twedt* situation was held * * * to be a proper case for amelioration of the abatement which would otherwise have entirely defeated the charitable gift." In the case at bar no such showing is made regarding specific bequests contained in the will. Briefly stated, Code § 633.436, supra, must here control unless an exception is disclosed, invoking application of § 633.437, in which event testamentary intent would be controlling.

In the case of In re Estate of Miguet, 185 N.W.2d 508 (Iowa), opinion filed March 11, 1971, we said:

"Inceptionally it is well settled, in cases such as this, (1) testator's intent is the polestar and if expressed must control; (2) that intent must be gleaned from a consideration of, (a) all language contained within the will, (b) the scheme of distribution, (c) circumstances surrounding testator at time the will was executed, (d) existing properly established facts; and (3) technical rules of construction should be resorted to only if the will is clearly ambiguous, conflicting, or testator's intent is for any reason uncertain."

See also In re Estate of Thompson, 164 N.W.2d 141, 146 (Iowa).

The first question posed is whether the phrase "subject to the foregoing" as employed in paragraph 4 of decedent's will is ambiguous or testator's intent for any reason uncertain.

Trial court found the will free from ambiguity, concluded the foregoing phrase merely limited all residue bequeathed to property not previously described, and ordered abatement pursuant to Code § 633.-436.

We concede the will is unambiguous, but for reasons set forth infra cannot agree with the foregoing conclusion and order.

It is to us evident trial court improperly attributed to the subject phrase a meaning too limited or restricted.

Black's Law Dictionary, Revised Fourth Ed., page 1594, defines "subject to" as, "Liable, subordinate, subservient, inferior, obedient to; governed or affected by; * * *."

To the same effect is this statement in 83 C.J.S. Subject page 554:

"The term 'subject,' which is frequently employed with the preposition 'to,' is variously defined as meaning to bring under control, power, or domination; to make subservient; to make liable; to make subject; to subordinate; to cause to become subject or subordinate; to subdue; also to become servient, subservient, or subordinate to."

See also Bulger v. McCourt, 179 Neb. 316, 138 N.W.2d 18, 22; Renner v. Crisman, 80 S.D. 532, 127 N.W.2d 717, 721.

Absence in the will of any provision for payment of debts and charges is of no particular significance.

"When a will provides, as most wills do, that the executor shall pay the just debts and funeral expenses, it merely recites the duty which every executor or administrator would have under the law * * *." Luckenbill v. Bates, 220 Iowa 871, 875, 263 N.W. 811, 813. Accord, In re Estate of Tedford, 258 Iowa, 890, 895–896, 140 N.W.2d 908. The same rule unquestionably applies to estate charges as defined by The Code 1966, Section 633.3(4). See The Code 1966, Sections 633.425, 633.426, 633.435, 633.449.

Stated otherwise, a testamentary provision for payment of all debts and charges is prefatorily impressed by law upon every will.

It is also assumed testator was aware of this rule, or in any event knew that all just debts and expenses attendant upon administration of his estate must be paid.

In that regard this court has said: "It is true, we cannot make a new will or substitute one provision for another, *but we have the right, in determining the intent, to consider what the testator must have known,* * * *." (Emphasis supplied). In re Estate of Ritter, 239 Iowa 788, 799, 32 N.W.2d 666, 672. Accord, In re Estate of Tedford, supra.

Mindful thereof we look again to the paragraph 4 phrase, "subject to the foregoing". Surely, in the absence of a clearly expressed qualification, testator did not thereby mean the residual estate should stand *partially* subordinate or subservient to "the foregoing". In other words, it is apparent testator intended the paragraph 4 residuary bequest stand totally or entirely subordinate to all impressed debts, charges and prior bequests specifically declared.

Resultantly it can only be concluded, decedent here manifested a testamentary plan to the effect the residual bequest should be subject or subordinate to, (1) payment of all his just debts and estate charges, (2) those bequests specifically set forth in paragraphs 1, 2 and 3 of his will. Under these circumstances Code § 633.436, supra, is not instantly applicable or controlling.

The foregoing conclusion is accorded more than minimal support by paragraph 1 of the will under which testator specifically devised to his wife, the present widow, a described farm, and the homestead. Upon electing to take under the will she accepted that, with the paragraph 4 residual bequest, in lieu of dower. This beneficiary is therefore instantly deprived of no right under the interpretation heretofore accorded decedent's will. See In re Estate of Hartman, 233 Iowa 405,

9 N.W.2d 359. Accord, In re Estate of Twedt, 173 N.W.2d 545, 547–548.

We are satisfied the above holding appropriately reflects decedent's testamentary plan as evidenced by his will.

This case must be accordingly reversed and remanded for entry of a decree consistent herewith.

The instant action was neither improperly nor unnecessarily commenced and pursued. Costs attendant upon this appeal are therefore taxed to the estate to be assessed as part of administration expenses. See Court Rule 23; In re Estate of Miguet, 185 N.W.2d 508 (Iowa), opinion filed March 11, 1971.

Reversed and remanded.

MOORE, C.J., and MASON, BECKER and REES, JJ., concur.

LEGRAND, STUART and UHLENHOPP, JJ., dissent.

REYNOLDSON, J., takes no part.

LEGRAND, JUSTICE (dissenting).

I must dissent from the conclusion reached by the majority because, despite protestations to the contrary, I believe the opinion *does* remake decedent's will by determining—unjustifiably—that section 633.436 of The Code should be shunted aside in favor of section 633.437.

In doing so the majority not only circumvents the clear legislative purpose set out in the abatement statutes but also defeats the testator's expressed intent. The legislature provided that section 633.436 should govern the order of abatement unless "the provisions of the will, the testamentary plan, or the express or the implied purpose of the devise would be [thereby] defeated." In other words, abatement under 633.436 is to be the rule and the application of section 321.437 the exception. In my opinion the majority completely reverses this priority.

I agree with the majority's statement that the language of the will is unambiguous. I agree, too, that the testator undoubtedly knew all debts and charges must be paid from the assets of his estate whether he so specified or not; but that is not the point. The issue is not whether he knew those items must be paid, but rather his intention as to the source from which payment should come.

Actually when the majority refers to the testator's knowledge of the law concerning the liability of his estate to pay existing debts and charges, it is making an argument *against* the result reached rather than *for* it. Once it is assumed he knew these items must be paid out of his estate, his failure to make the residuary bequest subject to them, while at the same time being careful to state what that provision *was* subject to, strongly suggests the omission was not inadvertent.

The majority disregards the preference which the legislative plan gives the surviving spouse in each step of the abatement statute. In re Estate of Twedt, Iowa, 1970, 173 N.W.2d 545, 547. Such preference is not dependent alone on the fact that ordinarily a testator's first desire is adequate provision for his surviving spouse above all others, but results also from the rule that the terms of a will in favor of a surviving spouse are not gratuitous. The survivor gives up the statutory dower right by consenting to take under the will and is considered a purchaser for value. In re Estate of Hartman, 233 Iowa 405, 409, 9 N.W.2d 359, 362; Nolte v. Nolte, 247 Iowa 868, 880, 76 N.W.2d 881, 888; In re Estate of Twedt, Iowa, 1970, 173 N.W.2d 545, 548.

We are considering here a *residuary bequest to a surviving spouse*. Under the plain provisions of section 633.436 this abates last. The statute provides that "shares of the distributees shall abate * * * in the following order:

"1. Property not disposed of by the will;

"2. Property devised to the residuary devisee, *except property devised to a surviving spouse who takes under the will*;

"3. Property disposed of by the will, but not specifically devised and not devised to the residuary devisee, *except property devised to a surviving spouse who takes under the will;*

"4. Property specifically devised, *except property devised to a surviving spouse who takes under the will*;

"5. Property devised to a surviving spouse who takes under the will." (Emphasis added.)

It seems indisputable that *all* the property described in subsections two, three and four (which specifically exclude property devised to a surviving spouse who takes under the will) must be exhausted before property devised to the surviving spouse abates under subsection five. There is simply nothing in this will to indicate the testator intended this statutory preference in favor of his widow should not apply. To hold, as the majority does, that section 633.437 controls is to emasculate, if not virtually repeal, the provisions of subsection two of section 633.436.

The insurmountable difficulty, it seems to me, is that the testator explicitly sets out what the residuary bequest was subject to—the specific bequests in favor of his children and *nothing else*. The majority says that because his debts and charges must be paid he must have intended payment to come from the residuary bequest. This is a non sequitur arrived at by doing violence to well established principles of testamentary construction.

The majority spends some considerable time in defining the meaning of "subject to" as used in Paragraph 4 of the will; but that isn't what causes the trouble. "Foregoing", not "subject to", is what requires explanation.

Simply stated, "foregoing" means that which has gone before. The Random House Dictionary (1966); Webster's International Dictionary (Third Ed.). The majority, however, enlarges its meaning to include a provision *which is not in the will at all*; and, having judicially supplied the missing language, it then goes on to decide what the testator *would* have meant had he used it in the first place. I find it impossible to agree with such a free interpretation of this will.

Specifically, I cannot accept the conclusion of the majority that "it is apparent testator intended the paragraph 4 residuary bequest stand totally or entirely subordinate to all impressed debts, charges, and prior bequests specifically declared."

None of the authority cited by the majority supports this view. In re Estate of Twedt, supra, mentioned in both the majority opinion and in this dissent is easily distinguishable on its facts. There the provision in favor of certain charitable beneficiaries would have been nullified from the very moment the will was prepared if the abatement rules of section 633.436 were applied. We held that under those circumstances the testator must be presumed not to have intended a useless and futile bequest. Zion Lutheran Church v. Lamp, 260 Iowa 363, 149 N.W.2d 137, held there was insufficient evidence to defeat the abatement provisions of section 633.436. If anything, it is helpful to this dissent. The other cases do not touch the particular problem facing us here.

I would affirm the trial court.

STUART and UHLENHOPP, JJ., join in this dissent.[49]

NOTE

An estate may be insufficient to satisfy all legacies, bequests and devises. The testator may have disposed of part of the estate after he executed the will. Claims superior to those of legatees or devisees, such as claims for expenses of administration, inter vivos debts of the testator, or for statutory shares asserted by the surviving spouse or a pretermitted heir, may sharply reduce the size of the estate available for distribution pursuant to the testator's will. It may then be necessary to "abate" some or all of the legacies, bequests and devises in order to satisfy superior claims.

The testator's intention concerning the order in which legacies, bequests and devises shall abate is controlling. His intention is determined by construing the will as a whole in the light of the surrounding circumstances. The legatee or devisee who claims that his gift is preferred has the burden of showing that the testator intended a preference.

49. Subsequent to this case, in 1975 and 1977 § 633.437 was amended and now reads:

"1. When provisions of the will, trust or other testamentary instrument of the decedent provide explicitly for an order of abatement contrary to the provisions of section 633.436, the provisions of the will or other testamentary instrument shall determine the order of abatement.

"2. Except as provided in subsection 1 of this section, if the provisions of the will, the testamentary plan, or the express or the implied purpose of the devise would be defeated by the order of abatement as provided in section 633.436 then upon application to the court by a fiduciary or a distributee, and after notice to all interested parties, the court shall determine the order for abatement of the shares of distributees in such other manner as may be found necessary to give effect to the intention of the testator. In order to change the order of abatement as provided in section 633.436, it will be necessary for the court to find it clear and convincing that the provisions of the will, the testamentary plan, or the express or implied purpose of the devise would be defeated by the order of abatement stated in section 633.436."

If the amended statute had been in force when the testator died, would the result in this case have been different?

If the testator's intention as to an order of abatement cannot be discovered, a statute in the jurisdiction may prescribe the order.[50]

If there is no statute applicable, two basic views with variations have been taken by the courts. By the older basic view which probably represents a majority position, legacies and bequests are abated before devises are taken.[51] By the modern view, devises, legacies and bequests of the same nature abate ratably.[52] States following the old view will sometimes abate personalty first, if it is intestate, residual or the subject of a general bequest or legacy, before land is taken; but will then abate specific devises and bequests ratably. Another variation of the older view is that intestate personalty and intestate land are taken before any property disposed of by the will is touched.

These hybrid approaches are indicative of a general judicial trend towards the same treatment for devises, legacies and bequests in abatement. The most satisfactory way to handle the matter is by statute, rather than having an abatement doctrine developed piecemeal by the courts. Abatement cases, not involving forced heirship or similar claims against an estate, are infrequent; and the development of a full scheme of abatement by judicial decision in any state will require much litigation and many years. Statutes establishing abatement doctrines usually adopt the modern judicial view, as previously described, handling land and personal property alike.

The modern view seems more likely to be in harmony with the intention of the average testator. The older view stems from the ancient common law rules that a decedent's personal estate was the only source from which

50. E.g., West's Ann.Cal.Probate Code, §§ 750 through 754 (1980 Supp.); Ga.Code Ann., § 113–821.

Uniform Probate Code, § 3–902 establishes this order of abatement:

"(a) Except as provided in subsection (b) and except as provided in connection with the share of the surviving spouse who elects to take an elective share, shares of distributees abate, without any preference or priority as between real and personal property, in the following order: (1) property not disposed of by the will; (2) residuary devises; (3) general devises; (4) specific devises. For purposes of abatement, a general devise charged on any specific property or fund is a specific devise to the extent of the value of the property on which it is charged, and upon the failure or insufficiency of the property on which it is charged, a general devise to the extent of the failure or insufficiency. Abatement within each classification is in proportion to the amounts of property each of the beneficiaries would have received if full distribution of the property had been made in accordance with the terms of the will.

"(b) If the will expresses an order of abatement, or if the testamentary plan or the express or implied purpose of the devise would be defeated by the order of abatement stated in subsection (a), the shares of the distributees abate as may be found necessary to give effect to the intention of the testator.

"(c) If the subject of a preferred devise is sold or used incident to administration, abatement shall be achieved by appropriate adjustments in, or contribution from, other interests in the remaining assets." For community property states an additional subdivision would be added to the abatement statute as follows: (§ 3–902A)

"(c) If an estate of a decedent consists partly of separate property and partly of community property, the debts and expenses of administration shall be apportioned and charged against the different kinds of property in proportion to the relative value thereof.

"[(d) same as (c) in common law state.]"

51. E.g., Edmunds' Administrator v. Scott, 78 Va. 720 (1884). See Note, "Wills—Abatement of Wills", 41 Miss.L. Rev. 346 (1970) where abatement systems are discussed and the non-statutory "old method" of Mississippi is described.

52. E.g., O'Day v. O'Day, 193 Mo. 62, 91 S.W. 921, 4 L.R.A.,N.S., 922 (1906); May v. Burns, 222 Ala. 68, 131 So. 232 (1930).

non-specialty debts could be satisfied, and that land could be reached to satisfy specialty debts only when the personal estate was exhausted and when the heir had been bound expressly by the terms of the obligation or when a devise had been expressly charged with payment of a debt. A creditor can reach land in the hands of an heir or devisee today whether or not his claim is based on a specialty debt. The major justification for applying the older view is the convenience in having the creditor file his claim with the personal representative and be paid by him from the personal assets.

In aspects other than the relative priority of devises, legacies and bequests, the older and modern views are similar. Intestate personalty and realty, if any, will abate before legacies and devises are taken.[53] The order of abatement of legacies and bequests is usually as follows: (1) residuary legacies and bequests; (2) general legacies and bequests; (3) specific and demonstrative legacies and bequests. If the specific property upon which a demonstrative legacy is charged is not part of the estate at the testator's death or is insufficient to pay the legacy, the legacy, or a part thereof, will abate with general legacies and bequests.[54] Within particular classes of legacies and bequests, certain gifts may be given priority. General legacies for the maintenance of close relatives of the testator,[55] in lieu of dower,[56] or in payment of a debt[57] have been given priority over other general legacies. It is probable that specific gifts for such purposes will also be given priority within that class. It has been held that a testamentary gift in lieu of dower has priority over all other testamentary gifts.[58] Devises abate in the order of: (1) residuary devises; (2) general devises; and (3) specific devises. A demonstrative devise probably abates with specific devises.

Except for gifts given priority, legacies, bequests and devises in the same class abate ratably. One class is exhausted before the next class is taken. By the modern view, for example, general devises, legacies and bequests abate together, and all general gifts abate before specific gifts are touched.

When a surviving spouse elects to take a statutory share or when a pretermitted heir claims his intestate share, testamentary gifts may abate ratably to satisfy these claims without priority based upon the classification of legacies, bequests or devises. Statutes conferring the right of election upon the surviving spouse and pretermitted heir statutes often provide the manner in which testamentary gifts are abated to satisfy the claims to which the statutes give rise.[59]

If the testator has charged property with the payment of debts, the property so charged abates after intestate property. For example, if devised land is charged with the payment of debts, the legatees may have the estate marshalled so that their legacies and bequests may be exonerated from payment. When a legacy is charged upon a devise, the devised realty must respond to exonerate the legacy and prevent its abatement. An intention to

53. E.g., Verdier v. Verdier, 12 Rich. Eq.(S.C.) 138 (1860). In those states in which title to intestate real property passes directly to their heir and not to the personal representative, it is probable that intestate real property cannot be reached until the entire personal estate is exhausted.

54. O'Day v. O'Day, 193 Mo. 62, 91 S.W. 921, 4 L.R.A.,N.S., 922 (1906).

55. E.g., In re Neil's Estate, 238 N.Y. 138, 144 N.E. 481, 34 A.L.R. 1245 (1924).

56. E.g., Security Co. v. Bryant, 52 Conn. 311, 52 Am.Rep. 599 (1884).

57. E.g., In re Shaaf's Will, 120 Misc. 292, 199 N.Y.S. 284 (1923).

58. Steele v. Steele's Administrator, 64 Ala. 438 (1879).

59. See Section 4 infra; Va.Code Ann. §§ 64.1–70, 64.1–71.

charge a legacy upon realty may be implied when there is no discrimination between land and personal property in a residuary gift. Under the older view, general and specific legacies may be regarded, in many cases, as charged upon residuary realty. The residuary realty abates first under the modern view in any event. A few courts have implied a charge upon residuary realty when the testator's legacies exceeded the value of his personal estate when the will was executed.

Closely akin to the abatement problem, and much more common, is that of determining where the burden of Federal estate taxes and local inheritance taxes should fall.[60] Inheritance tax burden is relatively simple; since inheritance taxes are on the right to receive, each recipient is primarily liable for the tax on his share. But the Federal estate tax burden is much more intricate. Consider two different situations: (1) All of the assets in the taxable estate pass under the will. The common law rule is that the estate tax comes out of the residue, in the absence of a clause directing a different method of payment. Statutes in a number of states require that the burden of the tax be apportioned among the various beneficiaries under the will.[61] (2) Some of the taxable estate consists of probate assets passing under the will, and some passes outside the will. Non-probate assets which are taxable as part of the decedent's estate for Federal estate tax purposes may, as you will recall from Chapter VIII, Section 2, include life insurance as to which decedent had the incidents of ownership at the time of his death, property over which decedent had a general power of appointment, joint tenancy assets for which decedent furnished the consideration, and certain inter vivos transfers by decedent such as revocable living trusts. As to life insurance and property over which decedent had a general power of appointment, the Internal Revenue Code itself provides that the portion of the estate tax attributable to those assets be borne by them.[62] But the Code is silent as to other non-probate assets and the allocation of burden becomes a matter of state law. Here the case law is in conflict. Some states again place the entire burden of the estate tax on the residue under the will; others require the non-probate assets to bear a portion of the tax (this would always be true in jurisdictions having the apportionment statutes mentioned previously).

Fluctuation in value of assets, especially securities in small corporations, may involve drastic impact on the residue under the common law rule. To put an extreme case, assume testator executes a will leaving XYZ Company stock, valued at the time the will is drawn at less than $5,000, to his business partner with a residuary clause leaving the residue of his estate, consisting of stable assets worth $75,000, in trust for testator's family. Later the corporation stock rises spectacularly until it is worth $300,000 at testator's death. The burden of the estate tax can wipe out the residue in such a situation. It is the task of the draftsman to guard against such consequences.

The burden of any of these taxes can be shifted by appropriate direction of the relevant documents. For example, the living trust agreement may provide that the trustee shall pay a portion of the estate taxes as well as the inheritance tax attributable to interests created under the trust. Or the will may direct that all estate and inheritance taxes, including those attributable to non-probate assets, be paid out of the residue. It is especially important

60. See Bowe, Estate Planning and Taxation (1957) § 5.19; 4 Powell, The Law of Real Property (Rohan Rev.1978) ¶ 529.

61. McKinney's N.Y., EPTL, § 2-1.8. Uniform Probate Code, § 3-916 incorporates the Uniform Estate Tax Apportionment Act.

62. IRC §§ 2206, 2207, 26 U.S.C.A.

where the marital deduction is availed of, to direct payment of taxes out of a portion of the estate other than that which is intended to qualify for the deduction; otherwise, the amount passing to the surviving spouse is reduced by taxes (at least the inheritance taxes in almost all jurisdictions, and often the estate taxes as well) and hence the amount eligible for the marital deduction itself is reduced.[63] It is obviously important that the draftsman explore the general problem of tax burden with the testator and carefully draft an appropriate provision if the normally applicable rules are not in accord with testator's wishes. Broadly phrased clauses merely directing the executor to pay taxes are not helpful and only lead to litigation.[64]

PROBLEM

The testator gave a legacy of $1,000 to X. The testator also devised "all my real estate now had by me wheresoever the same may be located" to his four sons, and devised the residue of his estate, real and personal, to the same four sons. The testator had sufficient personal property to pay the legacy to X when the will was executed. He had no personal estate at his death. When the will was executed, testator owned an equity of redemption in the land and house where he lived valued at $4,000. He still owned this equity of redemption when he died. Assuming that there is no statute in force concerning abatement, is X entitled to the legacy (1) by the older view concerning abatement? (2) by the modern view concerning abatement? See Kaplan v. Leader, 297 Mass. 145, 8 N.E.2d 344 (1937). Under Uniform Probate Code, § 3–902 set forth in fn. 50, supra?

SECTION 2. CHANGES IN THE CONDITION OR STATUS OF A BENEFICIARY OR DONEE AFTER EXECUTION OF A WILL, DELIVERY OF A DEED OR CREATION OF A TRUST

---

(1) LAPSE

ESTATE OF MANGEL

Supreme Court of Wisconsin, 1971.
51 Wis.2d 55, 186 N.W.2d 276.

CONNOR T. HANSEN, JUSTICE.

The testator died on March 6, 1967, leaving a will executed on June 1, 1951, in which he bequeathed his estate as follows:

63. IRC § 2056(b) (4) (A), 26 U.S.C.A.

64. For example, in Will of Cudahy, 251 Wis. 116, 28 N.W.2d 340 (1946), a general clause providing "I direct that my just debts, funeral expenses and all inheritance, estate and succession taxes be paid by my executors" was held to shift the burden of inheritance taxes on specific devises and general legacies from the recipients to the residue, but not to require payment of inheritance taxes on non-probate assets out of the residue.

"2. I hereby give, devise and bequeath all of my property, both real and personal, of whatsoever kind or character and wheresoever situated, to my beloved wife Irene E. Mangel and to her heirs and assigns forever, who has been a constant source of comfort and inspiration to me and to whom I owe all my worldly success."

The testator married Irene E. Mangel in 1931. Mrs. Mangel had been previously married and had one son by that marriage, Daniel Torsrud, born July 18, 1915. Irene Mangel predeceased testator, having died four days earlier on March 2, 1967.

The trial court held that by paragraph two of his will, the testator intended to dispose of his estate by leaving his property to his wife's son, Daniel, in the event his wife predeceased him.

It is well settled that where a bequest is made to a named beneficiary who dies before the testator, the bequest lapses, unless the anti-lapse statute, sec. 238.13, is applicable. Sec. 238.13 provides:

"*Rights of issue of deceased legatee.* When a devise or legacy shall be made to any child or other relation of the testator and the devisee or legatee shall die before the testator, leaving issue who shall survive the testator, such issue shall take the estate so given by the will in the same manner as the devisee or legatee would have done if he had survived the testator unless a different disposition shall be made or directed by the will."

It is also well settled that when a bequest is made to the testator's wife, and the wife predeceases the testator, sec. 238.13 does not prevent a lapse of the bequest, a wife not being a relative within the meaning of sec. 238.13. Cleaver et al. v. Cleaver et al. (1875), 39 Wis. 96; Estate of Dodge (1957), 1 Wis.2d 399, 84 N.W.2d 66.

The question raised on this appeal is whether the testator intended the words "and to her heirs and assigns forever" to be words of limitation or words of substitution. Appellants contend that these are words of limitation rather than substitution, and that the legacy lapsed when Irene Mangel predeceased the testator.

At common law, a devise to a person and his heirs and assigns created an estate in fee simple. The words "and to his heirs and assigns" were held to be words of limitation rather than substitution. Without the use of these words, a general devise passed only a life estate, unless an intention to pass a fee simple estate appeared in the will. In this state the necessity of using words of inheritance to devise an estate in fee simple has been abandoned. By sec. 238.02, Stats., a general devise creates an estate in fee simple unless a contrary intention appears in the will.

However, the meaning of the words of inheritance has not been changed by statute even though the necessity for the use of such words has been removed. The general rule is that the words "and to his heirs" or "and to his heirs and assigns forever," when used in a will are merely words of limitation and not of substitution, and hence do not prevent a lapse of a gift upon the death of the donee in the testator's lifetime, unless an intention to make a substitution can be gathered from other language in the will. See 96 C.J.S. Wills § 809, p. 234; Annot., *Devise or bequest to one "or his heirs" or to one "and his heirs" as affected by death of person named before death of testator.* 78 A.L.R. 992, supplemented at 128 A.L.R. 94.

* * * [In the omitted portion the Court discussed earlier Wisconsin cases.]

This court has held that a will is to be construed to ascertain the intent of the testator; the intent of the testator is to be determined from the words of the will and the surrounding circumstances at the time of its execution. Estate of Boerner (1970), 46 Wis.2d 183, 174 N.W.2d 457.

> "* * * Language in a will is used by a testator in reference to known surrounding circumstances. Specific words and phrases used by one testator in view of particular circumstances may have a materially different or at least a different shade of thought content or of meaning than the same phrases or words used by another testator under different circumstances.
>
> "Words are but arbitrary verbal or written containers carrying such thought or meaning as is placed therein by their user. The construction of a will by a court is the ascertainment of that content or the meaning of the words, i.e., the intention of the testator. To do this the court attempts to place itself in the position of the testator when he made his will and to consider the use of the words in relation to the surrounding circumstances. In re Will of Ehlers, 1913, 155 Wis. 46, 143 N.W. 1050; see also In re Will of Klinkert, 1955, 270 Wis. 362, 71 N.W.2d 279. * * * " Estate of Breese (1959), 7 Wis.2d 422, 426, 96 N.W.2d 712, 716.
>
> "When the surrounding circumstances have been considered and an ambiguity appears or remains, then only may there be a resort to extrinsic evidence. This is the clear rule in Wisconsin. The reason that we first look to surrounding circumstances is pointed out by McCormick in his text, Evidence (hornbook series), sec. 220, p. 448. He states that, unlike a contract, a will is a unilateral transaction consisting of words whose meaning is to be ascertained subjectively. The question is not what the usual usage of a word may be or the dictionary usage, but the testator's individual meaning." Estate of Gehl (1968), 39 Wis.2d 206, 210, 211, 159 N.W.2d 72, 73–74.

Extrinsic evidence of the testator's intent may be resorted to only after the surrounding circumstances have been considered and an ambiguity appears or remains. Estate of Gibbs (1961), 14 Wis.2d 490, 111 N.W.2d 413; Estate of Gehl, supra.

An affidavit of prejudice was filed against the County Judge of Oneida county and Donald E. Schnabel, County Judge of Lincoln county, was assigned this case. In his decision granting respondent's petition for construction of the testator's will, Judge Schnabel held that the words "and to her heirs and assigns forever," were sufficiently ambiguous in the light of the surrounding circumstances to permit consideration of extrinsic evidence of the testator's intent.

The trial court found an ambiguity existed on the basis of several factors. It found that paragraph two of the testator's will in which he disposed of his entire estate constituted a residuary clause, and if the words were construed in the technical sense, the planned distribution of the testator's estate was no different than if he had died intestate.

> "The presumption of the law is against an intended intestacy as to any part of an estate because the will indicates a contrary general intention. This presumption is strengthened by the presence of a residuary clause, one obvious purpose of which is to preclude the occurrence of intestacies by unforeseen contingencies. * * * " Estate of Britt, supra, 249 Wis. p. 34, 23 N.W.2d p. 500.

Second, the court relied on the testimony of the attorney who drafted the will taken at the proof of the will. The attorney stated he had drafted the will "with the understanding of the terms that [the testator] wished to have." The court found this was a surrounding circumstance creating an ambiguity because it indicated the scrivener had not necessarily used the words in their technical or legal sense.

> "Atkinson, Wills, supra, p. 811, sec. 146, says:
>
> " 'It is practically necessary that the testator's intent should be identified with that of the agent whom he employed to express the intent.' " Estate of Gehl, supra, 39 Wis.2d p. 215, 159 N.W.2d p. 76.

The third factor relied on by the court in finding an ambiguity was the testator's acknowledgement of the contribution of his wife by the use of the words, "to whom I owe all my worldly success." The court found that by using that phrase the testator recognized his indebtedness to his wife, "which proprietary interest, if assumed to exist, might again serve to refute the thought that he was limiting such interest to her alone and not her son in event of her prior death."

Relying on these three factors, the trial court found that the language used in paragraph two of the will that contained words, which presumptively have the technical meaning of limitation, were in this case ambiguous and permitted consideration of extrinsic evidence of the testator's intent. We agree with this determination of Judge Schnabel.

After determining that an ambiguity existed, an evidentiary hearing was ordered. Judge Schnabel was unable to conduct the hearing because of illness, and Frank W. Carter, Jr., County Judge of Vilas county, was then assigned to the case.

The attorney who drafted the will testified at the hearing. He stated that he had graduated from law school in 1949 and had practiced law from 1949 to March or April of 1951. He stated he had drafted about 15 wills before drafting the testator's will on June 1, 1951. He testified that in drafting the will, he had used the words that he felt would do what the testator wanted to do, and that he had attempted to convey in the language of the will that which he felt was appropriate to accomplish the things the testator wanted. He testified that he did not know the difference between the words "and heirs and assigns" and "or heirs and assigns." He testified that the words were not used in their technical or legal sense.

Hazel Schoenfelder, who had been a friend of Otto and Irene Mangel, testified that she had observed Daniel Torsrud working at the testator's resort from 1932 to 1951. In 1947, she had observed Dan working around the resort and had heard the testator say, "Why shouldn't he; some day it will be his any way." She also testified that in July or August 1951, the testator told her that he had made his will and that if everything went as it had been going that neither Dan nor Irene would have any worries in later life. She further testified that on more than one occasion she had heard the testator state that his property would never go to the Mangels.

Anita Bliesner, who was also acquainted with Otto and Irene Mangel, testified that the testator had a friendly relationship with his stepson, and that in 1948, she had heard him introduce Daniel Torsrud as his son.

Marrian Doughty testified that she had been a friend of Irene Mangel, and that in the spring of 1951 she overheard the testator in a conversation with his wife, tell her, "You don't need to worry. The Mangel's [sic] * * * will not get anything. It's yours and Dan's." She also heard the testator say that the Mangels were not going to get any part of his resort. She testified that Daniel Torsrud had worked around the resort; that the testator had had a friendly relationship toward him; and that this relationship continued to the time of his death.

Gertrude Mangel, the testator's sister, testified that sometime in 1963, the testator told her that he should make a new will, and that he had a will but it did not provide for disposition of the property in the event both he and his wife died at one time.

Following the taking of testimony as to the testator's intent, Judge Carter held that it was the intent of Otto Mangel to leave his property to the son of Irene Mangel in the event of her prior death. In so holding, he relied on the making of the will as evidence of an intent not to die intestate. Estate of Britt, supra; Estate of Hoermann, supra.

He also relied on the testimony of the attorney who drafted the will that he was not aware of the strict legal meaning of the words, "and to his heirs and assigns forever," and that he had attempted to draft a will in accordance with the intent of the testator. While testimony of an attorney, as to statements made to him by the testator, is not considered a surrounding circumstance in determining whether words used in the will are ambiguous, Estate of Breese, supra, once it has been determined that the words of the will are ambiguous in the light of the surrounding circumstances, the attorney who drafted the will may testify as to the testator's intent.

> "* * * [T]his court has several times held that communications between an attorney and a client concerning a last will and testament, the transactions which led to the execution of the will, and the circumstances surrounding the execution of the will, do not enjoy the status of privileged communications after the client's death in a suit between the testator's heirs, devisees, legatees or other parties who claim through him.
>
> "* * * [T]he testimony of the attorney as to statements made to him by the testator are admissible on the question of intent, once such extrinsic evidence became admissible. * * *"
>
> Estate of Boerner, supra, 46 Wis.2d p. 192, 174 N.W.2d p. 461.

Finally, Judge Carter relied on the addition of the clause, "who has been a constant source of comfort and inspiration to me and to whom I owe all my worldly success," and the testimony offered at the hearing concerning the testator's intent. He held that by this clause the testator recognized the part his wife had played in helping him accumulate his property, and that this, together with the testimony of witnesses that the testator had stated the property would belong to Dan, showed that the intent of the testator was to leave his property to Daniel Torsrud in the event his wife predeceased him.

We conclude that the will was properly construed. Also, we do not consider the determination made in this case to be a modification, extension, or change of the existing case law in this state. It is a decision based primarily upon the authority of Estate of Hoermann, supra, and Estate of Britt, supra.

Judgment affirmed.[65]

ESTATE OF ULRIKSON

Supreme Court of Minnesota, 1980.
290 N.W.2d 757.

YETKA, JUSTICE.

In this contest over the construction of a residuary clause of a will, the Hennepin County Probate Court held the anti-lapse statute, Minn.Stat. § 524.2–605 (1978), to be applicable. A three-judge panel appointed by the Chief Judge of the district court for the Fourth Judicial District affirmed. This court granted appellants' application for leave to appeal. We affirm.

The sole issue in this case is whether Minn.Stat. § 524.2–605 (1978), the anti-lapse statute, applies where the residuary estate is

65. Compare Niemann v. Zacharias, 185 Neb. 450, 176 N.W.2d 671 (1970) where the residue was devised to named persons "and to their heirs, devisees and legatees as set forth in their Last Wills and Testaments, to be theirs absolutely"; the court held that on the death of a named beneficiary prior to the testator the gift lapsed, that the language could not create a power of appointment in a dead person, and that the quoted wording constituted only words of limitation, describing a fee simple.

given to a brother and sister, "and in the event that either one of them shall predecease me, then to the other surviving brother or sister," but in fact both brother and sister predecease the testatrix, the brother leaving issue.

This case is before the court on stipulated facts which can be summarized as follows: Bellida Ulrikson died testate in 1976 with a will drafted in 1971. The will made specific bequests of $1,000 each to nine nieces and nephews and two nieces by marriage; each respondent and appellant received one of these bequests. The residue is to be distributed as follows:

> SIXTH, All the rest, residue and remainder of my property of whatever kind or character, I give and bequeath to my brother MELVIN HOVLAND, and my sister, RODINE HELGER, share and share alike, and in the event that either one of them shall predecease me, then to the other surviving brother or sister.

Melvin Hovland and Rodine Helger were both alive when the will was drafted. Melvin Hovland died in 1974 and left surviving two children, Annabelle Erickson and Mavis Barth. Rodine Helger died in 1975 without issue. If the anti-lapse statute is applied to the residuary clause, the residue passes in equal shares to respondents Annabelle Erickson and Mavis Barth. Both lower courts so ordered.

In 1971, two other siblings of Bellida Ulrikson were deceased; namely, Sena Olson and Louis Hovland. These two siblings had seven surviving children in 1971, and the will gives $1,000 to each. Before 1976, three of these nieces and nephews died without issue, and one died leaving issue. Under the laws of intestacy, therefore, the residue would be divided into six shares among Tillman Olson, Leonard Olson, Guy Olson (appellants), Annabelle Erickson, Mavis Barth (respondents), and the issue of Eleanor Yankowiak by right of representation. Minn.Stat. § 525.16(4)(d) (1978).

The applicable Minnesota statutes, which incorporate portions of the Uniform Probate Code, contain the following provisions:

> 524.2–603 *Rules of construction and intention.* The intention of a testator as expressed in his will controls the legal effect of his dispositions. The rules of construction expressed in the succeeding sections of this part apply unless a contrary intention is indicated by the will.

> 524.2–604 *Construction that will passes all property; after acquired property.* A will is construed to pass all property which the testator owns at his death including property acquired after the execution of the will.

> 524.2–605 *Anti-lapse; deceased devisee; class gifts.* If a devisee who is a grandparent or a lineal descendant of a grandparent of the testator is dead at the time of execution of the will, or fails to survive the testator, the issue of the deceased devisee who survive the testator take in place of the deceased devisee and if they are all of the same degree of kinship to the devisee they take equally, but if of unequal degree then those of more remote de-

gree take by representation. One who is a grandparent or a lineal descendant of a grandparent of the testator and who would have been a devisee under a class gift if he had survived the testator is treated as a devisee for purposes of this section whether his death occurred before or after the execution of the will.

Minn.Stat. §§ 524.2–603 to 524.2–605 (1978). Upon reading these statutes together, it is apparent that the law prefers testacy over intestacy and that the anti-lapse statute applies unless a contrary intention is indicated by the will.

The appellants argue that Bellida Ulrikson expressed an intention contrary to the application of the anti-lapse statute by the words "and in the event that either one of them shall predecease me, then to the other surviving brother or sister." They contend the testatrix intended to establish an absolute condition of survivorship to receive any residue.

It is far more likely, however, as respondents contend, that Bellida Ulrikson simply did not contemplate that both her younger brother and sister would predecease her. The residuary clause in fact contains no instructions for the circumstances which occurred. In this case, we hold the words of survivorship to be effective only if there are survivors. Since there are no survivors in this case, the anti-lapse statute is free to operate.

The appellants further argue that by making a thousand-dollar bequest to each of her nieces and nephews, the testatrix expressed an intention to treat her legal heirs equally, and thus contrary to the anti-lapse statute. This argument loses sight of the fact that Melvin Hovland and Rodine Helger are preferred in the residuary clause of the will. The argument is further negated by the fact that two persons outside the testatrix's bloodline, the two "nieces by marriage," were also given thousand-dollar specific bequests.

In summary, this case appears to be precisely the type of case that our statutory scheme was designed to solve. Accordingly, the decision of the three-judge district court review panel is affirmed.

ESTATE OF BUTTON

Supreme Court of Washington (1971).
79 Wash.2d 849, 490 P.2d 731, 47 A.L.R.3d 352.

* * *

ROSELLINI, ASSOCIATE JUSTICE.

This action was instituted by the Old National Bank of Washington, asking the Superior Court for Whitman County to determine its obligations under two sets of trust instruments and the applicable Washington law.

The evidence presented at the hearing of the matter showed that in 1940, Robert H. Button executed a revocable trust, covering certain real property located in Whitman County, retaining a life estate, and naming the Old National Bank of Washington as trustee. The trust provided that it could be revoked or modified upon execution of an instrument in writing, duly signed by the trustor and delivered to the trustee, and, in case the trustee's duties were altered, upon its approval of the change. The trust contained the following provision:

> Upon the death of the Trustor without having withdrawn the entire fund, the balance of investments and cash remaining in the trust fund shall be delivered to the Trustor's mother, Audrey A. Burg, and her receipt for the residue of said trust fund shall thereupon release the Trustee from any further responsibility therefor.

There was no provision for the disposition of the trust property in the event the trustor's mother should predecease him.

* * * [Audrey A. Burg died intestate on 15 November 1966. The settlor, Button, died on 28 November 1966 leaving a will disposing of his property in California but making no mention of his property in Washington. Certain instruments had been delivered by the settlor to his attorney in 1964 which purported to revoke the trust of 1940 and create a new trust of which settlor's niece, Stefanie Button, and Washington State University were beneficiaries. Both the Trial Court and the Court of Appeals held the 1940 trust unrevoked, the 1940 trust requiring delivery of the revoking instrument to the trustee, which Button had never instructed his attorney to do. There was also evidence that Button considered the Trust of 1940 in force after 1964. The Supreme Court affirmed the Court of Appeals on this point. The Trial Court had held the trust of 1964 inoperative but had been reversed on this point by the Court of Appeals, the latter court holding that Button had intended to give the 1964 trust operative effect to the extent that it benefitted Stefanie and Washington State University. The Supreme Court reversed the Court of Appeals on this point, holding the trust of 1964 wholly inoperative. The Trial Court held the interest of Audrey A. Burg lapsed upon her death, reverted to the estate of the settlor and passed on his death under the intestate laws of Washington, the California will having not disposed of Button's Washington property. The Court of Appeals reversed the Trial Court, holding that Audrey's interest had not lapsed because her interest had vested. That part of the opinion of the Supreme Court pertaining to the interest of Audrey follows.] * * *

We are thus brought to the question of the proper disposition of the trust property, the only named beneficiary of the 1940 trust (other than the trustor himself) having died prior to the death of the trustor.

It was the rule at common law that a gift in trust lapsed upon the death of the beneficiary prior to the death of the trustor. Restatement (Second) of Trusts § 112, comment f at 245 (1959); A. Scott, The Law of Trusts § 112.3 (3d ed. 1967). And in this state, if the named legatee in a will is not a relative by consanguinity, the common law rule that the gift lapses is still in effect. In re Estate of Smith, 49 Wash.2d 229, 299 P.2d 550 (1956) (where the testator's gift of the residue of his estate to his wife was held to have lapsed upon her death prior to the testator's) and In re Estate of Sims, 39 Wash. 2d 288, 235 P.2d 204 (1951) (where a wife's bequest to her husband was held to have lapsed when he failed to survive the testatrix).

However, by the terms of RCW 11.12.110, when an estate is devised or bequeathed to any child, grandchild, or other relative of the testator, and the devisee or legatee dies before the testator, leaving lineal descendants, such descendants shall take the estate.

The act declares that under the provisions of that section a spouse is not a relative. It does not, however, exclude a parent from the definition of "relative."

Of course, the gift to Audrey A. Burg was not made by will, but by inter vivos trust. If it were made by testamentary trust, we do not think that it could be seriously suggested that this statute was not meant to affect it, and the only difference between such a gift and that involved here is that the inter vivos trust disposes of property upon the death of the settlor without the necessity of complying with the statute of wills. Similar statutes do indeed apply to trusts. Restatement (Second) of Trusts § 112, comment f (1959); A. Scott, The Law of Trusts § 112.3, n. 3 (3d ed. 1967). Courts in other jurisdictions which have considered the question also have held that similar statutes apply to beneficiaries of testamentary trusts. See Annot., Statute to prevent lapse in event of death of devisee or legatee before testator as applicable to interest of beneficiary under trust who dies before testator, 118 A.L.R. 559 (1939).

A gift to be enjoyed only upon or after the death of the donor is in practical effect a legacy, whether it is created in an inter vivos instrument or in a will. RCW 11.12.110 declares the policy of the law of this state, and that policy is against the lapsing of gifts to relatives of the deceased. This does not mean that a testator or trustor cannot provide for a different disposition. If he does, of course, the statute has no application.

Where a statute (RCW 11.12.180) applied by its terms to devises of real estate, we held that it declared the policy of the state applicable to a trust covering personal property as well. Abbott v. Everett Trust & Savings Bank, 50 Wash.2d 398, 312 P.2d 203 (1957). By the same principle, there being no conflicting statutory provision, a statute covering gifts by will which would lapse in the absence of the statute, applies to gifts provided in a trust.

We conclude that the gift to Audrey A. Burg did not lapse, and that the trustee holds the residue for her descendants.

The Court of Appeals reached the same result on this question, but based its conclusion upon a rationale that the gift to Audrey A. Burg had vested. We do not examine the propriety of the conclusion that her interest had vested, since we are of the opinion that that conclusion does not answer the question whether that interest was intended to pass to her heirs upon her death. The case cited in support of the rationale was Seattle First Nat'l Bank v. Crosby, 42 Wash. 2d 234, 254 P.2d 732 (1953). There the trust instrument provided that if the principal beneficiary should die before attaining the age of 35, the trustee should distribute his share to his heirs at law. Since the trustor expressly provided for the disposition of the named beneficiary's share in the event of his death, no question of lapse was involved in the case.

Whether or not the interest of Audrey A. Burg had vested prior to the death of the trustor, it was subject to be divested if she died before the trustor died, under the rule as it existed prior to the enactment of RCW 11.12.110. That statute alone, interpreted to apply to trusts as well as to wills, saves her interest for her heirs.

The judgment of the Court of Appeals is reversed in part and the cause is remanded to the Superior Court for Whitman County with directions to enter an order in conformity with the views expressed herein.

HAMILTON, C. J., FINLEY, HUNTER, HALE, STAFFORD and SHARP, JJ., and OTT, J. pro tem., concur.

NEILL and WRIGHT, JJ., did not participate.

NOTE

The devise or legacy fails or lapses at common law if the devisee or legatee dies after execution of the will but before the testator. The devise or legacy is void if the devisee or legatee is dead when the will is executed.

The testator's intention controls when it can be found. The testator may prevent a lapse by providing a substituted beneficiary or by making a gift to a class or to several persons as joint tenants. It has been held that a legacy to discharge a debt does not lapse if the legatee dies before the testator.[66] The courts have been reluctant to prevent lapses unless the testator's intention is expressed clearly in his will. Most courts do not admit extrinsic evidence to show intention.[67]

The common law rules concerning lapse have been altered by statute in almost all states. These statutes are often construed to extend to cases in which the named donee dies before the will is executed, although this situation is not technically a lapse.[68] If the statute does not provide that a contrary intention expressed by the testator controls, the courts usually read in such a limitation.[69]

66. Ballard v. Camplin, 161 Ind. 16, 67 N.E. 505 (1903).

67. Estate of Pierce, 177 Wis. 104, 188 N.W. 78 (1922). See comment, "Disinheritance and the Anti-Lapse Statute", 26 Wash. & Lee U.L.Rev. 105 (1969).

68. If the statute uses the word "lapse", a minority of courts have held that the statute applies to a lapse in the technical common law meaning of the word. The anti-lapse statute in force at the death of the testator will usually control the disposition of the property although problems concerning the provisions applicable are sometimes raised by amendments of the statute between the date of execution of the will and the testator's death with language in the statute making the amendments applicable to wills *executed* after a specified date. See Note, "The Anti-Lapse Statute", 14 Washburn L.Rev 361 (1975).

69. Wallace v. Diehl, 202 N.Y. 156, 95 N.E. 646, 33 L.R.A.,N.S., 9 (1911). A contrary intention is indicated by a gift to a devisee "if he survives me".

The statutes pass the property to the representative of a deceased legatee or devisee as if the legatee or devisee had died immediately after the testator died. By the prevailing view, the property does not pass into the estate of the legatee or devisee and thence to his heirs or in accordance with his will, but passes instead to his representatives by operation of the testator's will. There is a division of authority whether creditors of the deceased legatee or devisee can reach the property.[70]

Some of the statutes operate only if the legatee or devisee is a child or relative of the testator. The statutes are usually construed to apply to a devisee or legatee who is a member of a class and who predeceases the effective date of the will and thus dies before the earliest time at which the class membership can be determined.[71] The courts in England and in some American states take a contrary position.[72] Some lapse statutes are expressly applicable to class gifts.[73] A lapse statute is usually applied to a testamentary exercise of a general power of appointment in which the appointee dies before the donee, the appointed property passing to the representatives of the appointee.[74] There is authority supporting the proposition that a lapse statute does not apply to the case in which a member of a class appointed by a testamentary exercise of a special power of appointment predeceases the donee if the representatives of the appointee are not members of the class indicated by the donor of the power.[75]

The representatives of the deceased legatee or devisee are his "heirs" by some statutes. Other statutes limit the representatives to "lineal descendants", "children" or "issue" of the decedent. Some statutes make no definition of representatives.

Uniform Probate Code, § 2–605 sets forth the following comprehensive anti-lapse provision applicable to individual and class gifts:

> "If a devisee who is a grandparent or a lineal descendant of a grandparent of the testator is dead at the time of execution of the will, fails to survive the testator, or is treated as if he predeceased the testator, the issue of the deceased devisee who survive the testator by 120 hours take in place of the deceased devisee and if they are all of the same degree of kinship to the devisee they take equally, but if of unequal degree then those of more remote degree take by representation. One who would

70. E.g., Courtenay v. Courtenay, 138 Md. 204, 113 A. 717 (1921) (creditors have no claim); In re Estate of Rueschenberg, 213 Iowa 639, 239 N.W. 529 (1931) (creditors have a claim).

71. There is a different result if the devisee or legatee predeceases the execution of the will. White v. Massachusetts Institution of Technology, 171 Mass. 84, 50 N.E. 512 (1898).

72. E.g., In re Harvey's Estate, [1893] L.R. 1 Ch. 567; Martin v. Trustees of Mercer University, 98 Ga. 320, 25 S.E. 522 (1896).

73. E.g., Va.Code Ann., § 64.1–64.

74. See Restatement, Property (1940) § 350; Simes and Smith, Future Interests (2d Ed., 1956) § 984.

75. See Daniel v. Brown, 156 Va. 563, 159 S.E. 209 (1931), appearing as principal case in Chapter XIV § 5 supra. Query, whether the decision in that case is correct. Had the donor of the power made an express gift in default to the class of appointees ("my nephews and nieces"), most courts would have construed the gift as "vested", with no implied requirement that the members of the class survive the donee of the power; see the materials immediately following in Section 2(2) and (3). It is also arguable that, under the doctrine that the exercise of the special power relates back to the creating will and is "read back" into that instrument, the appointee only has to be alive when the donor dies and the donee can appoint by will to a person even though the appointee predeceases the donee, the property passing to the appointee's estate (thence to his heirs or devisees). Wis.Stat.Ann. § 853.27 embodies the contrary rule stated in the text above.

have been a devisee under a class gift if he had survived the testator is treated as a devisee for purposes of this section whether his death occurred before or after the execution of the will."

Testamentary gifts may lapse for reasons other than the death of the legatee or devisee. The donee may renounce his gift or the donee may fail to perform a condition precedent. Likewise, testamentary gifts may be void for reasons other than the fact that the legatee or devisee was dead when the will was executed.

When a general, specific or demonstrative gift lapses—and this may occur even though a lapse statute is in force—the property usually passes by the residuary clause in the will or by intestacy if there is no residuary clause or if the residuary clause is not sufficiently broad. If a residuary gift to one of a number of residuary donees lapses, there is a division of authority whether the lapsed gift passes by intestacy or passes to the remaining residuary donees. Some courts have held that the gift passes by intestacy on the theory that there can be no residue of a residuum.[76]

Uniform Probate Code, § 2–606 covers the situation in which one or more residuary provisions lapse but at least one residuary donee is available to take the residue:

"(a) Except as provided in Section 2–605 if a devise other than a residuary devise fails for any reason, it becomes a part of the residue.

"(b) Except as provided in Section 2–605 if the residue is devised to two or more persons and the share of one of the residuary devisees fails for any reason, his share passes to the other residuary devisee, or to other residuary devisees in proportion to their interests in the residue."

The problem of death of a beneficiary is one which the will draftsman should always anticipate and provide for in accordance with the testator's wishes. If this were the sole problem, it would be simple to provide as to any devise or bequest that if the named beneficiary predeceases the testator, his gift shall go to his issue, or another named person, or shall become part of the residue (depending on the testator's wishes). However, modern life involves frequent auto or airplane trips during which several members of the same family can be killed in a common accident. The Uniform Simultaneous Death Act provides for the devolution in such event if the will does not expressly provide otherwise.[77] However, the Uniform Act applies only if there is no proof that the persons died otherwise than simultaneously.

76. See Aitken v. Sharp, 93 N.J.Eq. 336, 115 A. 912 (1921) (Where the doctrine is followed but criticized). Contra: Hedges v. Payne, 85 Ind.App. 394, 154 N.E. 293 (1926), 23 Ill.L.Rev. 300 (1928). Other problems raised by the disposition of an interest which fails are examined in Section 4, infra.

77. "§ 1. **No Sufficient Evidence of Survivorship**—Where the title to property or the devolution thereof depends upon priority of death and there is no sufficient evidence that the persons have died otherwise than simultaneously, the property of each person shall be disposed of as if he had survived, except as provided otherwise in this act.

"§ 2. **Survival of Beneficiaries**—If property is so disposed of that the right of a beneficiary to succeed to any interest therein is conditional upon his surviving another person, and both persons die, and there is no sufficient evidence that the two have died otherwise than simultaneously, the beneficiary shall be deemed not to have survived. If there is no sufficient evidence that two or more beneficiaries have died otherwise than simultaneously and property has been disposed of in such a way that at the time of their death each of such beneficiaries would have been entitled to the property if he had survived the others, the property shall be divided into as many equal portions as there were such beneficiaries and these portions shall be distributed respectively to those who would have taken

Suppose a husband, with a wife but no children, wishes his entire estate to go to his wife if she survives him but to certain of his relatives if she predeceases him. If they die in a common accident, the wife's relatives may try to prove that she survived the husband. They need only prove that she outlived the husband by a minute or second. If they can carry this burden of proof, they will take the property from the wife's estate. If the couple has children, whether the wife survives or not, the property will go to the children, either under the will of the husband, assuming he has provided for them, or through the wife's estate;—but, if the wife outlives the husband, it will be necessary in most states to have probate and administration in two estates, the husband's estate and the wife's estate.

There is an attempt to deal with problems such as this in Uniform Probate Code, § 2–601 which requires a devisee to survive the testator for five days ("120 hours") in order to be treated as a survivor unless "the will of decedent contains some language dealing explicitly with simultaneous deaths or deaths in a common disaster, or requiring that the devisee survive the testator or survive the testator for a stated period in order to take under the will". Many draftsmen would nevertheless prefer to insert a more detailed or different provision. Furthermore, even if a state adopts this provision of the Uniform Probate Code as a supplement to or in place of the Uniform Simultaneous Death Act, there is a chance that the testator will not be domiciled in the state. Thus, to meet the common accident problem, and the related problem where the beneficiary is known to have a short life expectancy, draftsmen have developed a variety of clauses.

It should be noted that the draftsman seeks to attain either or both of two objectives by such clauses: to prevent the property from passing as part

in the event that each of such beneficiaries had survived.

"§ 3. **Joint Tenants or Tenants by the Entirety**—Where there is no sufficient evidence that two joint tenants or tenants by the entirety have died otherwise than simultaneously the property so held shall be distributed one-half as if one had survived and one-half as if the other had survived. If there are more than two joint tenants and all of them have so died the property thus distributed shall be in the proportion that one bears to the whole number of joint tenants.

"The term 'joint tenants' includes owners of property held under circumstances which entitled one or more to the whole of the property on the death of the other or others.

"§ 4. **Community Property**—Where a husband and wife have died, leaving community property, and there is no sufficient evidence that they have died otherwise than simultaneously, one-half of all the community property shall pass as if the husband had survived [and as if said one-half were his separate property,] and the other one-half thereof shall pass as if the wife had survived [and as if said other one-half were her separate property.] As amended 1953.

"§ 5. **Insurance Policies**—Where the insured and the beneficiary in a policy of life or accident insurance have died and there is no sufficient evidence that they have died otherwise than simultaneously the proceeds of the policy shall be distributed as if the insured had survived the beneficiary, [except if the policy is community property of the insured and his spouse, and there is no alternative beneficiary, or no alternative beneficiary except the estate or personal representatives of the insured, the proceeds shall be distributed as community propery under Section 4.] As amended 1953.

"§ 6. **Act Does Not Apply If Decedent Provides Otherwise**—This act shall not apply in the case of wills, living trusts, deeds, or contracts of insurance, or any other situation where provision is made for distribution of property different from the provisions of this act, or where provision is made for a presumption as to survivorship which results in a distribution of property different from that here provided. As amended 1953."

* * * [§ 7 (Uniformity of Interpretation); § 8 (Short Title); § 9 (Repeal); § 10 (Severability) are omitted.] Uniform Laws Ann., Estate, Probate and Related Laws (1972) 605–627. (In force in 49 jurisdictions in 1981, some having made changes).

of the estate of the beneficiary to persons whom the testator has no desire to favor and to prevent the additional cost and possible added taxes if the property were to pass through the beneficiary's estate. These objectives are in fact also attained by a carefully drafted trust document giving the primary beneficiary only income for life and requiring survival of principal beneficiaries to the time of distribution of corpus. For example, in our childless couple situation, if the will created a trust to pay the income to the wife for life, with a gift of corpus to the husband's relatives, no additional clause is required to prevent either administration of the property in the wife's estate or passage of the property to ultimate recipients not desired by the testator.

If a trust is not desired, the most effective clause [78] is one which requires that any beneficiary under the will survive the testator by a stated period of time, such as 90 days; the following is typical:

> "For the purpose of this will a legatee or devisee shall not be deemed to have survived me if such legatee dies within 90 days of my death."

Such a clause would, of course, be accompanied by an express gift over if the legatee or devisee fails to survive the testator. Another clause which covers only the situation where the testator and the beneficiary die "simultaneously" is inadequate; for example, courts have interpreted such a clause not to apply where the beneficiary outlives the testator by a day or even an hour.[79] Equally poor are the clauses, worded in terms of the testator and the beneficiary dying "as a result of a common disaster", since this may invoke litigation as to cause of death and, besides, the cause of death is immaterial to the objective sought in such clauses.[80]

Anti-lapse statutes are not applicable expressly to inter vivos transactions, although two states have statutes dealing with the effect of death of the owner of a future interest before his estate becomes possessory which are applicable to such interests whether created inter vivos or by will.[81] In its usual form an anti-lapse statute is applicable only to a will. The will is ambulatory, no interest being created in any legatee or devisee until the

78. See generally, Bowe, "Draftsmanship: Wills and Trusts", 94 Trusts & Estates 797 (1955); Lauritzen, "Simultaneous Death—Tax and Other Problems", 94 Trusts & Estates 787 (1955); McGorry, "Survivorship Clauses in Wills", 104 Trusts and Estates 118 (1965); Monroe, "The Simultaneous Death Problem in the Drafting of Estate Plans", 7 Inst. on Estate Planning, Ch. 73–4 (1973); Note, "Use of Survivorship Clauses in Wills," 8 Vand.L.Rev. 627 (1955); 40 A.L.R.3d 359 (1971).

79. In larger estates where the will is drafted to take advantage of the marital deduction, the draftsman may require that the spouse survive the testator by a period not exceeding six months (or only if it occurs as a result of a common disaster resulting in the death of both, or only if it occurs in either event) and still obtain the marital deduction unless the spouse dies within the period. I.R.C. § 2056(b) (3). If the estate is substantial (over $600,000 after 1986), it may be desirable to have a share of the estate pass to the surviving spouse even if he or she dies shortly after the testator, in order to utilize the credit of the surviving spouse to transmit another $600,000 without estate tax; in such cases a reverse clause presuming that the spouse of the testator survives in the event of simultaneous death is commonly used. It will be given effect for tax purposes. Treas.Reg. § 20.2056(e)–2(e).

80. White v. Taylor, 155 Tex. 392, 286 S.W.2d 925 (1956) (beneficiary survived testator by one hour—death held not to be simultaneous under clause); cf. American Trust & Safe Deposit Co. v. Eckhardt, 331 Ill. 261, 162 N.E. 843 (1928) (clause phrased in terms of death "approximately" at the same time held to apply where beneficiary died a day after testator).

81. Mich.Comp.Laws Ann. § 554.101 (1981 Supp.); Tenn.Code Ann. § 32–305. The Tennessee section is limited to class gifts.

Illinois has an anti-lapse statute applicable expressly to future interests. See Note, p. 1002.

death of the testator. Does the Washington Supreme Court in Estate of Button imply a condition of survivorship:—that Audrey A. Burg is required to survive the settlor Button for her remainder to vest? There is an implied condition at common law that all legatees and devisees must survive the testator. Could the Washington Supreme Court have avoided an application of the anti-lapse statute to a living trust by construing the interests involved as a life estate in Button followed by a vested equitable remainder in fee in Audrey subject to being defeased by Button's revocation of the trust in the manner prescribed prior to his death?[82] Would such an "undefeased" vested remainder pass to her heirs under the intestate law of Washington without an application of the anti-lapse statute? If Button's trust of 1940 is so similar to a will that the anti-lapse statute should apply, should the trust be effective without testamentary formalities?[83]

PROBLEM

Suppose H and W enter into a contract not to revoke mutual wills, each devising all his or her estate to the surviving spouse, and if the other spouse predeceases, then half to named relatives of H and half to named relatives of W. W survives H; H's named relatives predecease W. Who should take? Cf. Graham v. Patton, 231 Ga. 391, 202 S.E.2d 58 (1973).

(2) EXPRESS AND IMPLIED CONDITIONS OF SURVIVORSHIP[84]

CLOBBERIE'S CASE

Court of Chancery, 1677.
2 Vent. 342, 86 Eng.Rep. 476.

In one Clobberie's Case it was held, that where one bequeathed a sum of money to a woman, at her age of twenty-one years, or day of marriage, to be paid unto her with interest, and she died before either, that the money should go to her executor; and was so decreed by my Lord Chancellor Finch.

But he said, if money were bequeathed to one at his age of twenty-one years; if he dies before that age the money is lost.

82. See Estate of Button, 4 Wash. App. 773, 483 P.2d 1290 (1971); Randall v. Bank of America, National Trust & Savings Association, 48 Cal.App.2d 249, 119 P.2d 754 (1941); First National Bank of Cincinnati v. Tenney, 60 O.O. 481, 165 Ohio St. 513, 138 N.E.2d 15, 61 A.L.R.2d 470 (1956); 30 A.L.R.3d 1318 (1970); 47 A.L.R.3d 358 (1973).

83. See Chapter VIII, Section 6, supra; I Scott, Trusts (3d Ed., 1967) §§ 56–57.2.

84. See Simes and Smith, The Law of Future Interests (2d Ed.1956) §§ 164, 575–594; Halbach, "Future Interests: Express and Implied Conditions of Survival", 49 Cal.L.Rev. 297, 431 (1960–61); Trautman, "Class Gifts of Future Interests: When is Survival Required", 20 Vand.L.Rev. 1 (1966); 26 A.L.R.3d 407 (1969); 54 A.L.R.3d 280 (1974).

On the other side, if money be given to one, to be paid at the age of twenty-one years; there, if the party dies before, it shall go to the executors.

IN RE MANSUR'S WILL

Supreme Court of Vermont, 1925.
98 Vt. 296, 127 A. 297.

SLACK, J. This is an appeal from a decree of the probate court within and for the probate district of Orleans dismissing a petition brought by appellant, as administrator of the estate of Sallie Storrs Tate, for the purpose of effecting a final settlement, and distribution of the assets, of the estate of the late Zophar M. Mansur, on the ground that appellant, as such administrator, has no interest in the Mansur estate because the legacy bequeathed to the said Sallie by the said Mansur did not vest in the legatee, but lapsed at her death.

The agreed facts in the case, so far as material to the question before us, are these: Zophar M. Mansur died March 28, 1914. He was survived by one son, Arthur G., and two grandchildren, John D. Storrs and Sallie L. Storrs, children of a daughter who died December 1, 1911. Mr. Mansur left a will bearing date January 15, 1914, which was allowed by the probate court in said district April 21, 1914, which contained the following provision:

> "I give to my granddaughter, Sallie L. Storrs, the sum of thirty thousand dollars, to be placed in the hands of a trustee, the income thereof to be paid to the said Sallie L. Storrs semiannually, one-half of the principal to be paid to the said Sallie L. Storrs when she shall become thirty years of age and the remaining one-half when she shall become thirty-five years of age."

It contained a like provision for the grandson, John D. Storrs. The granddaughter, Sallie L., was born November 18, 1894, she married the appellant August 4, 1920, and died intestate November 23, 1921. She was survived by one daughter, the fruit of said marriage, born October 29, 1921, who is still living. The appellant is the duly appointed administrator of Sallie's estate. Mr. Mansur's son, Arthur G., is executor of the Mansur will and, as such, has in his hands a large amount of property that belongs to the Mansur estate. No part of the legacy bequeathed to the said Sallie has ever been paid.

Whether the court erred in dismissing the petition depends, entirely, upon whether the provision in the Mansur will, above quoted, created a vested or a contingent legacy, and this, in turn, depends upon whether the contingency, namely, the attainment of a certain age by the legatee, attached to the substance of the gift or to the time of payment thereof.

In construing wills, the first and chief object is to ascertain the intention of the testator since, so far as it may be legally carried out, that governs. Harris et al. v. Harris' Estate, 82 Vt. 199, 72 A. 912. To aid in ascertaining this fact certain well recognized rules have been established. One is that the law favors the vesting of estates on the death of the testator when the will becomes operative, and if the language used is consistent with an intention to postpone the enjoyment only such will be presumed to have been the testator's intention. This presumption is so favorably regarded that no estate will be held contingent unless positive terms are employed in the will indicating that such is the intention. In re Robinson's Estate, 90 Vt. 328, 98 A. 826; Harris et al. v. Harris' Estate, supra; Burton v. Provost, 75 Vt. 199, 54 A. 189; Jones' Adm'r v. Knappen, 63 Vt. 391, 22 A. 630, 14 L.R.A. 293; In re Tucker's Will, 63 Vt. 104, 21 A. 272, 25 Am.St. Rep. 743; Weatherhead v. Stoddard, 58 Vt. 623, 5 A. 517, 56 Am.Rep. 573. Another rule is that when futurity is annexed to the substance of the gift the vesting is postponed; but if annexed to the time of payment only the legacy vests immediately. Perhaps this rule is nowhere better stated than by Blackstone; he says:

> "And, if a contingent legacy be left to anyone, as when he attains, or if he attains, the age of twenty-one, and he dies before that time, it is a lapsed legacy. But a legacy to one to be paid when he attains the age of twenty-one years, is a vested legacy; an interest which commences in praesenti, although it be solvendum in futuro, and if the legatee dies before that age, his representatives shall receive it out of the testator's personal estate, at the same time it would have become payable in case the legatee had lived." 2 Bl.Comm. 513.

See, also, 2 Williams on Executors (11th Ed.) 973.

In the first instance, futurity being annexed to the substance of the gift, the vesting is postponed; in the latter instance, futurity being annexed to the time of enjoyment only, the legacy vests immediately. Regardless of its origin, or the reason for its adoption, this rule is now recognized by the great weight of authority both in this country and in England. * * *

[Omitted is the Court's discussion of cases from other jurisdictions.] * * *

Applying the rules of construction already referred to, in the light of the application given them in the cases cited, to the case at bar, it would seem that but one conclusion could be reached. Other provisions of the bequest aside, the language, "I give to my granddaughter, Sallie L. Storrs, the sum of thirty thousand dollars, * * * one-half of the principal to be paid to the said Sallie L. Storrs when she shall become thirty years of age and the remaining one-half when she shall become thirty-five years of age," would seem to leave no doubt of the testator's intention to create a vested legacy with postponed enjoyment.

But the provision that the legacy shall be placed in the hands of a trustee, and the income thereof paid to the legatee semiannually, makes the intent of the testator doubly certain. Under this provision not only is the legacy to be segregated instanter from the rest of the testator's estate, but the legatee receives an immediate beneficial interest therein. Similar provisions have been before the courts in other jurisdictions. See Eldridge v. Eldridge, supra; Equitable Guarantee & Trust Co. v. Bowe, 9 Del.Ch. 336, 82 A. 693; Warner v. Durant, 76 N.Y. 133; Gifford v. Thorn, 9 N.J.Eq. 702 and Reed's Appeal, 118 Pa. 215, 11 A. 787, 4 Am.St.Rep. 588.

In Eldridge v. Eldridge, Shaw, C. J., said:

> "But it is a decisive circumstance, in the present case, that the legacy is charged with the support of the legatee during her minority. In the first clause, he directs his son, James, the executor and residuary devisee, to pay to his grand-daughter, Sarah Malvina, $1,000, at twenty-one years of age, and proceeds to direct that she be supported out of it during her minority. If it stood upon this clause alone, it appears to us that the intent would be quite clear, because it creates an immediate beneficial interest in the legatee, and the payment only is postponed."

In Equitable Guarantee & Trust Co. v. Bowe, the testator gave to a trustee $10,000 for each of his grandchildren to hold as a trust fund, and "to pay over the net income for the maintenance and education of said grandchildren until they arrive at the age of thirty years, and as they respectively arrive at the age of thirty years to pay over to them the share of the principal sum to which they are entitled, free and discharged from all trusts." One of the grandchildren died at the age of 14 years, and it was held that the gift vested and that the administrator of the deceased child was entitled to the legacy. Speaking to this point the court said:

> "The principles of law applicable to such a gift are clear and well settled. In bequests of personal estate, a gift of the whole interim interest to or for the benefit of the legatee prima facie vests the principal, though if such words had not been used the legacy would not have been treated as vested."

* * *

Other circumstances are called to our attention by the appellant which it is claimed are indicative of the testator's intention to create a vested legacy but it is needless to consider them, since, notwithstanding the ingenious argument of appellee, we are satisfied from what has already been said that no other conclusion is warranted.

We hold, therefore, that the legacy of $30,000 vested in Sallie Storrs Tate immediately upon the death of the testator and, consequently, that the appellant, as her legal representative, is entitled to receive the same out of the testator's estate.

The appellant insists that since the legatee had the entire beneficial interest in the legacy, he is entitled to recover the full amount of the principal at once, and calls attention to numerous authorities that seem to support this view, but the disposition of the petition below was such that the court was not called upon to, nor did it, pass upon this question; hence, it is not before us.

Decree of the probate court reversed and cause remanded for further proceedings, and decree not inconsistent with the views herein expressed. Let the appellant recover his costs in this court. To be certified to the probate court.[85]

ESTATE OF FERRY

Supreme Court of California, 1961.
55 Cal.2d 776, 13 Cal.Rptr. 180, 361 P.2d 900, 90 A.L.R.2d 300.

DOOLING, JUSTICE. These are appeals from a decree settling a trustee's final account and distributing the property of the estate of J. S. Ferry, who died testate in 1951.

By a will executed on June 13, 1942, decedent J. S. Ferry left $1 to each of his three daughters, Isabelle Lucas, May Ferry and Rose Murphy, and left an unrestricted gift of the residue to his son Joseph J. Ferry. On May 5, 1949, decedent executed a codicil partially revamping his testamentary scheme by establishing, in lieu of the outright residual gift, a trust for the benefit of his son Joseph. This codicil, after confirming the original bequest of $1 to each of the three daughters "and no more," provided that the trust was to terminate upon alternative events: either twenty years from the date of the codicil's execution or upon the son Joseph's death, whichever occurred first. If the son Joseph was living at the termination of the trust he was to receive possession of the residue but if he died before the twenty-year period elapsed, then the residue was to go to the son's wife and issue, but if "no wife or issue, then * * * to [decedent's] sister, Mary Silva." The testator died with this codicil in effect. Among those surviving him were Joseph Ferry, the decedent's three daughters, and Mary Silva, decedent's sister. Decedent was also survived by his wife who is not involved here because by a separation agreement she renounced any claim to the estate of J. S. Ferry.

* * *

85. The presumption against a condition of survivorship applies even though the executor or trustee is authorized merely to apply so much of the income as is necessary or appropriate for the maintenance of the testamentary donee. Equitable Guarantee & Trust Co. v. Bowe, 9 Del.Ch. 336, 82 A. 693 (1912). And even though a part of the income is to be paid to the executor or trustee to compensate him for his services provided the residue of the income is to be paid to the testamentary donee. Steinway v. Steinway, 163 N.Y. 183, 57 N.E. 312 (1900). However, the presumption against a condition of survivorship does not arise if the will provides that the income is to be applied for the maintenance of a class of beneficiaries and there is no provision that any one of the beneficiaries is to receive a stipulated share of the income. In re Parker, 16 Ch.Div. 44 (1880). In the latter case there was a bequest in trust to pay the income, or such part thereof as the trustee should deem expedient, for the maintenance of the children of the testatrix until they should attain their respective ages of 21 years; and from and immediately after their attaining their respective ages of 21, to transfer the said fund to them in equal shares, if more than one, and if but one, then to such child. Held: that survivorship to date of distribution was a condition precedent to vesting.

[The reference to "the decree" in the portion of the opinion which follows is to the decree of distribution of testator's estate, which is almost a verbatim excerpt from the codicil.] * * *

* * *

On December 18, 1953, Mary Silva died intestate survived by her daughter and son, Mamie and Harry Silva, her sole heirs. Thereafter, on January 14, 1957, decedent's son, Joseph J. Ferry, died testate leaving neither wife nor issue but devising whatever interest he had in the trust property to Joseph and Clarence Telles. Joseph and Clarence Telles are not related to the testator. Thus the principal issue of this case arises from the fact that Mary Silva, the ultimate possible taker, predeceased Joseph J. Ferry, the first-named taker under the decree and codicil.

After the death of Joseph, the trust beneficiary, the trustee petitioned the court for instructions. The court entered its decree concluding that by reason of "non-fulfillment of conditions precedent imposed by the codicil of J. S. Ferry, deceased, and the failure of decedent to otherwise dispose of the residue of his estate, J. S. Ferry died intestate as to the [remaining] trust property." The court then ordered distribution of the residue of the trust property in shares of one-fourth to each of decedent's three daughters and one-fourth to Joseph's devisees, Joseph and Clarence Telles. It is implicit in this decree that the court determined that Mary Silva would have had to survive Joseph in order for her interest to be inheritable by Mary's heirs.

Mary Silva's two children, Harry and Mamie Silva, have appealed from the decree. The distributees of Joseph's estate have filed a cross-appeal from so much of the decree as orders distribution of three-fourths of the trust estate to decedent's three daughters. The three daughters of decedent are respondents and ask that the court's determination of intestacy be upheld.

This discussion leads to the principal question of the case: whether the testator intended that Mary Silva must survive the trust beneficiary, Joseph J. Ferry, before her interest could be transmissible to her heirs. It is noteworthy that the decree and codicil attached express conditions of survivorship to the interests of Joseph and to any wife or child of Joseph but do not add any words of that character to the limitation describing Mary Silva's interest. Thus if a condition of survivorship attaches to Mary Silva's interest it must be implied from the terms of the codicil and decree; and if such a condition was intended, Mary Silva's heirs could take no interest in the trust property.

The difficulty with the arguments seeking to imply Mary Silva's survival of Joseph as a condition is that they would result in holding that because it is *express* that Joseph must survive until the period of distribution to take an inheritable interest, a similar contingency should be *implied* as to Mary. Although the limitations describing the nature of their interests do have in common the effect of Joseph's death before the termination of the twenty-year trust period, that fact alone cannot mean that common conditions and contingencies were intended to prevail throughout the entire devise. The "precise contingency" effecting her interest in possession is not her survival but Joseph's death. (Cf. Prob.Code, § 143.) "Certainly there is no rule of law that a condition precedent of survivorship is implied wherever a gift is subject to another condition precedent." (Simes and Smith, Future Interests, supra, § 594, p. 44; see supporting this rule as to contingent remaindermen: Tapley v. Dill, 358 Mo. 824, 217 S.W. 2d 369, 373–374; In re First National Bank of Ithaca, 2 A.D.2d 292, 153 N.Y.S.2d 857, 862; Colony v. Colony, 97 N.H. 386, 89 A.2d 909, 911–912; Fulton v. Teager, 183 Ky. 381, 209 S.W. 535, 538; Fisher v. Wagner, 109 Md. 243, 71 A. 999, 1000–1003, 21 L.R.A.,N.S., 121; Loring v. Arnold, 15 R.I. 428, 8 A. 335, 336. To draw a contrary conclusion would produce the result that very few contingent interests of this type would be descendible or devisable. Thus here, as in other instances, a finding that Mary had to survive Joseph in order that her interest might be descendible to her heirs requires a "literal basis" or a clear intent deducible from the particular words employed in the instrument. Estate of Haney, supra, 174 Cal.App.2d 1, 11, 344 P.2d 16. "Where the requirement of survival is found to exist, it is usually applicable only to the first name takers. *The persons who are the alternative takers* need not survive unless such a requirement is specifically expressed." (Simes and Smith, Future Interests, supra, § 581, p. 24; emphasis added.) Section 255 of the Restatement of Property, Future Interests, supports the propriety of this construction. Section 255 reads: "In a limitation purporting to create a remainder or an executory interest in a person, which is ambiguous as to whether such interest is, or is not, subject to a requirement of survival to some particular time, the absence, with respect to such particular time, of both an alternative and supplanting limitation tends to establish that such interest is free from any requirement of survival to such time whenever such construction results in more interests being disposed of than would otherwise be disposed of by the conveyance in question." To here imply a condition of survivorship of Mary Silva beyond the death of Joseph would result in the remainder interest being undisposed of, and this quoted rule of the Restatement therefore supports the conclusion that the requirement of Mary's surviving Joseph should not be implied. Thus, absent a clear intent deducible from the words of the codicil or decree we are unwilling to imply a condition that Mary, as executory devisee or alternative contingent remainderman, must survive Joseph, the first-named and primary taker under the instrument.

The fact that the decree and codicil did not append the word "heirs" after the limitation devising an interest to Mary does not preclude her interest's descendibility. Probate Code Section 107 provides: "The term 'heirs,' or other words of inheritance, are not requisite to devise a fee, and a devise of real property passes all the estate of the testator, unless otherwise limited." (See Civ.Code, § 1072.)

* * *

Nor is the argument convincing that the words "then to Mary Silva" mean that Mary must be alive at Joseph's death to assure her an interest which her heirs could take. In the case of Hall v. Wright, 17 Cal.App. 502, 120 P. 429, the court was referring to the time for *identifying a class* of takers by reason of the limitation of "then to the heirs of her body," and held that in such a context "then" meant the expiration of the preceding life estate. Hall v. Wright, supra, 17 Cal. App. at page 506, 120 P. at page 431. Clearly the case and framework in which the word "then" was there interpreted is distinguishable and inapplicable here.

We conclude that Mary Silva did not have to outlive Joseph in order for her heirs to take the trust property on Joseph's death. Since Joseph's interest terminated on his death, the devise to Joseph and Clarence Telles passed no interest to them; and since the property passed to Mary's heirs upon Joseph's death, the testator's three daughters can take no interest therein. This result carries out the testator's expressed intention that his three daughters should each receive $1 "and no more."

The decree is reversed with directions to order distribution to Mary Silva's heirs, Harry and Mamie Silva.[86]

IN RE GAUTIER'S WILL

Court of Appeals of New York, 1957.
3 N.Y.2d 502, 169 N.Y.S.2d 4, 146 N.E.2d 771.

FULD, JUDGE. In this proceeding, brought to settle their accounts, the successor trustees under the will of Dudley G. Gautier requested and obtained a construction of the will. The controversy revolves about the term "surviving" as used in paragraph Ninth, subdivision (b), and calls upon us to say whether the essential survivorship refers to survival merely to the death of the testator, as the courts below held, or as the two dissenting Appellate Division justices concluded, to the death of the life beneficiary.

Paragraph Ninth of the will disposes of the testator's entire residuary estate. By subdivision (a) of that paragraph, he gave one half of such residue in fee to his sister Annie Witherbee if, as happened, she survived him. Subdivision (b), with which we are concerned, deals with the disposition of the other half of the residuary estate.

86. Contra: Schau v. Cecil, 257 Iowa 1296, 136 N.W.2d 515 (1965) (devise to son Everett but if he should not survive the testator or die without issue, then to son Cecil; held, that Cecil must survive Everett to take); criticized in 65 Mich.L. Rev. 203 (1966), 20 Ark.L.Rev. 190 (1966); Comment, "The *Schau v. Cecil* Survival Requirement: Consequences for Iowa Property Law," 63 Iowa L.Rev. 924 (1978) (recommending a statute to reverse the *Schau* rule). For a similar case where the court implied survivorship because the gift was subject to another contingency (to testator's son, "his heirs and assigns", if a prior life tenant died without heirs of her body) see Fletcher v. Hurdle, 259 Ark. 640, 536 S.W.2d 109 (1976), noted and criticized in 31 Ark.L. Rev. 134 (1977).

The testator directed that that half be divided into eight shares, of which four were to be in trust for his sister Clara Bird for life and, after her death, each of said four shares was to be held as a separate trust for the benefit of her four children, his nephews and nieces, Oliver Bird, Claire Bird Lewis, Dudley Bird and Marie Louise Bird, during the life of each of them. On his or her death, the will continues, "the one share held in trust for the one so dying shall cease and the share of such nephew or niece shall be paid to his or her children, if any, and in the event that the nephew or niece dies leaving no children the share shall be divided equally amongst his or her brothers and sisters surviving." The other four shares were given directly, that is, without the intervention of any other life estate, in trust for Oliver, Claire, Dudley and Marie Louise during the life of each, with a provision, identical with that quoted above, as to the disposition of the corpus upon the death of any one of such life beneficiaries.

The testator's sister Clara, the primary life beneficiary as to four shares, died some years after her brother. Upon her death, trusts were set up for the benefit of each of her children, the named Oliver, Claire, Dudley and Marie Louise. On the death of Oliver and Claire, the corpus of each of the trusts set up for them went to their respective children. Marie Louise died in 1955 leaving no issue and is survived only by Dudley who is still alive. As already indicated, the sole question involved—and it is presented on appeals from two orders, one relating to the trust for Marie Louise and the other to the trust for Dudley—is the meaning to be accorded the word "surviving" in subdivision (b) of paragraph Ninth.

The testator's intention as gathered from the will is, of course, controlling and, in seeking it, we must give to his words their natural and ordinary meaning. When so read in this case, there can be no doubt what the testator had in mind. Upon the death of any nephew or niece, he explicitly stated, the share of the one who died was to be paid over to his or her children and, if such nephew or niece died leaving no children, then, that one's share was to be divided among "his or her brothers or sisters surviving". Neither this language nor any provision of the will is in the slightest ambiguous. There was a primary remainder to "children", a class determinable solely on the death of the life beneficiary and, if that class failed, the beneficiary's "brothers or sisters surviving" were substituted. Just as determination of the class, the children who would share in the primary remainder, had to await the time of division and distribution, that is, the death of the childless nephew or niece, so determination of the brothers and sisters, who were to share in the substitution remainder, had to be postponed until such time. The testator, thus indicating a clear-cut intention to postpone vesting until the termination of each trust, created a remainder contingent upon survival of the life beneficiary.

We would strain language and do violence to the meaning of words were we to read the provision otherwise and ascribe to the decedent a different intention. As cases very like the present demonstrate, absent language pointing a contrary intention, words of survivorship refer to the time of the testator's death "only in the case of an absolute devise or bequest to one and in case of his death to another"; they carry no such implication where, as in the will under consideration, the first devisee or legatee takes a life estate. Mullarky v. Sullivan, 136 N.Y. 227, 231, 32 N.E. 762, 763; see, also, Matter of Parsons' Estate, 242 N.Y. 246, 250, 151 N.E. 441, 442; Matter of Buechner, 226 N.Y. 440, 123 N.E. 741; Matter of Pulis, 220 N.Y. 196, 204, 115 N.E. 516, 518; Lyons v. Ostrander, 167 N.Y. 135, 140, 60 N. E. 334, 336; Restatement Property, § 251, p. 1266. The Restatement sums up the subject in this way (loc. cit.): "In a limitation purporting to create a remainder or an executory interest, a description of the intended takers as persons 'who survive,' or who are 'living,' or by other language of the same import, but which fails to designate the time to which such takers must survive, tends to establish the time of the termination of all preceding interests as the time to which survival is required".

If there could be any doubt as to the meaning which the testator desired to attach to the word "surviving" in subdivision (b) of paragraph Ninth, it is entirely dissipated by a consideration of subdivision (a). The meaning intended for the term in that subdivision is plain beyond all peradventure, its reference to the date of death of the life beneficiaries, rather than to the testator's unmistakable. When he wished distribution to depend on mere survival of himself, he said so in so many words; he gave one half of the residue to his sister Annie if "she survives *me*," and then created trusts for the life of each of her children if "she shall not survive *me*." The scheme of subdivision (a), the pattern of the trusts there created, is the same as that in subdivision (b). The life beneficiaries are his sister's son and daughter and, as in (b), it is provided that, on the death of his nephew or niece the share of the one dying shall be paid to his or her children, if any, and if the nephew or niece dies leaving no children, the share shall be given to "the nephew or niece surviving." Such a provision unquestionably reflected an intention on the part of the testator that, if either his nephew or niece died childless, the other, if still living, was to enjoy the whole trust estate. There just cannot be any question that the testator intended that the remainderman, in order to share in the corpus of the trust, outlive the life beneficiary, not himself. Since, then, the term "surviving" in subdivision (a) relates to the time of the life beneficiary's death, it must be given the same meaning in subdivision (b).

It is quite true that, in ascertaining the testator's intention, the will should be considered in its entirety. And, as bearing on that, the respondents point to paragraph Twelfth wherein the testator declared, "I have not made any provision" for Charles Gautier, a nephew. If the will be read as we have read it, that nephew (or, more precisely, since he is dead, his estate) will realize an intestate share in Dudley's trust if Dudley happens to die without children. But that circumstance cannot possibly affect the meaning of the word "surviving" found in paragraph Ninth. The testator did not, of course, expect that any of his estate would pass as if he had died intestate. As a general proposition, one who executes a will believes that the testament covers all contingencies that might eventuate. At any rate, if the language employed by the testator is plain and his meaning clear, a court may not rewrite the will in order to avoid intestacy. Cf. Matter of Disney's Will, 190 N.Y. 128, 131–132, 82 N.E. 1093; Matter of Englis' Will, 2 N.Y.2d 395, 161 N.Y.S.2d 39, 141 N.E.2d 556; also, 3 Jessup-Redfield, Surrogates' Law and Practice [rev. ed., 1949], § 1929, p. 100. Although the testator may not have intended that Charles share as legatee or devisee under his will, he evinced no intention that he was to be excluded as next of kin, through operation of the laws dealing with intestacy, if the last survivor of Clara's children were to die childless and the share of such survivor distributed as intestate property. Consequently, the happenstance that nephew Charles (or his estate) may participate in Dudley's trust as one of the testator's next of kin, when the word "surviving" is given its natural and normal meaning, cannot warrant giving it a strained and unreasonable meaning or justify a contrary judicial construction solely to prevent such result.

In sum, then, since, of the four nephews and nieces, only Dudley survived the childless Marie Louise, it is he who is entitled to the entire corpus of the trust set up for her benefit and, if Dudley dies without children, the corpus of his trust will pass as in intestacy.

The orders appealed from should be reversed and the matter remitted to the Surrogate's Court for further proceedings in accordance with this opinion, with costs to all parties appearing separately and filing separate briefs, payable out of the estate.

CONWAY, C. J., and DESMOND, FROESSEL, VAN VOORHIS and BURKE, JJ., concur with FULD, J.

DYE, J., dissents and votes to affirm.

In each proceeding: Order reversed, etc.

NOTE

Where there is a gift by will to one person for life, with a gift over to others accompanied by words of survivorship, a minority of courts relate survivorship to death of the testator, the earlier date.[87] Thus a testamentary gift "to my widow for life, then to my surviving children" is considered to involve an ambiguity: surviving whom, the testator or the widow? The preference for "early vesting" expressed in the minority view is predicated on two factors: (1) promoting alienability of property where the gift creates legal estates in realty, and (2) preserving a share for children of a deceased child, which is presumed to be what the testator would have intended. The

87. Porter v. Porter, 50 Mich. 456, 15 N.W. 550 (1883). In a few states there are statutory provisions applicable to limitations of this type. Thus, a Georgia statute states that: "In construing wills, words of survivorship shall refer to the death of the testator in order to vest remainders, unless a manifested intention to the contrary shall appear". Ga.Code Ann. § 85–708. To the opposite effect is the following statutory provision in California: "Words in a will referring to death or survivorship, simply, relate to the time of the testator's death, unless possession is actually postponed, when they must be referred to the time of possession". West's Ann.Cal.Probate Code, § 122 (1980 Supp.).

careful draftsman should avoid any question (and resulting litigation) by specifically stating what he means: "to my widow for life, then to my children who survive her" if that is the intent; usually this will be accompanied by a substitutional gift to children of a deceased child if the children survive the life tenant.

There has been little legislative effort to cope with the problem of survivorship in the field of future interests, unlike the anti-lapse statutes which apply to death before the testator. In 1969 Illinois amended its anti-lapse statute to extend its operation to future interests, both as to individual and as to class gifts when these interests are created by will as follows:[88]

"§ 49. (Prob.Act § 49). Devise or Legacy to a Deceased Devisee or Legatee

"Unless the testator expressly provides otherwise in his will, (1) when a devise or legacy of a present or future interest is to a descendant of the testator who dies before or after the testator, the descendants of the devisee or legatee living when the devise or legacy is to take effect in possession or enjoyment, take per stirpes the estate so devised or bequeathed, (2) when a devise or legacy of a present or future interest is to a class and any member of the class dies before or after the testator, the members of the class living when the devise or legacy is to take effect in possession or enjoyment, take the share or shares which the deceased member would have taken if he were then living, except that if the deceased member of the class is a descendant of the testator, the descendants of the deceased member then living take per stirpes the share or shares which the deceased member would have taken if he were then living, and (3) except as provided in (1) and (2), when a devise or legacy lapses by reason of the death of the devisee or legatee before the testator, the estate so devised or bequeathed shall be included in and pass as part of the residue under the will, and if the devise or legacy is or becomes part of the residue, the estate so devised or bequeathed shall pass to and be taken by the legatees or devisees, or those remaining, if any, of the residue in proportions and upon estates corresponding to their respective interests in the residue. The provisions if (1) and (2) do not apply to a future interest which is, or becomes, indefeasibly vested at the testator's death or at any time thereafter before it takes effect in possession or enjoyment.

"This amendatory Act of 1969 applies to all wills of decedents dying on and after January 1, 1970."

We shall return to the problem of survivorship in the material hereafter dealing with the decrease of classes in class gifts.

88. See Waggoner, "Future Interests Legislation: Implied Conditions of Survivorship and Substitutionary Gifts Under the New Illinois 'Anti-Lapse' Provision", 1969 U.Ill.L.Forum 423. The author criticizes the statute as amended but suggests at p. 436 that the statute should be extended to inter vivos transactions if the amendments are retained. See the Michigan and Tennessee statutes cited at fn. 81 supra.

(3) CLASS GIFTS

The essence of planning is to think in terms of the future. This involves change not only in property but also in terms of the persons to whom the property is to go. In thinking of one's own family in the future, one must take account of possible increase by births and decrease by death in the group of persons to whom property should pass. The simplest way to provide for such change is by reference to a class or group of persons described not by name but by some common characteristic. The ordinary example is a gift to "my children". Thus if a testator wants a simple will with a gift of $10,000 to each of his children and he now has two sons John and James, he might make a gift of $10,000 to John and $10,000 to James by name; or he might simply provide: "I give and bequeath $10,000 to each of my children". When he employs this latter approach, he does not confine the gift to his existing children but includes children born (or adopted) after the will is executed. As the limitation postpones distribution to a more remote date, the advantage of such an approach becomes even greater. If the client wants to set up a trust for a son or daughter for life, it is probable that he would want the trust principal to go to the child's descendants; obviously that group can change between the present and the death of the child. Again the draftsman will resort to a group designation, probably some variant of a gift to "issue" of the child and with a provision for the property to go to the client's other "heirs" if the child dies without any surviving issue. Such gifts are called class gifts, and they create special problems. When you have finished with these materials, you will have a better idea of the drafting difficulties presented by the relatively simple group designations presented above. It is of course possible that a person may use a generic word and be thinking of individuals. If I refer to my "brothers and sisters", I may mean specific individuals, particularly if my parents are deceased. However, in some contexts it will make a difference how the court treats such a gift, whether to individuals or to a class. Some gifts are even more confusing as to the intent, as where a gift is made to "John Jones and my own children"; whether this means that the testator thought of the named person as one of his own children and hence all as one class is a tough problem we shall explore only briefly. The essence of the class gift is what is sometimes called "group-mindedness". In most of the cases the presence of the class gift is obvious from the language used in the will or trust document; the issue to be decided is the legal consequence of the class gift on the given facts.

A. Increase of Class

LOOCKERMAN v. McBLAIR

Court of Appeals of Maryland, 1847.
6 Gill's Rep. 177.

MAGRUDER, J., delivered the opinion of this court.

The late Jeremiah T. Chase, died in the year 1828. He made a will dated in 1824, to which several codicils were added. One of the devises is in these words: "I will, devise and give to my dear grandchildren, my lots on Whetstone Point, Nos. 10, 11 and 12, to them, and their heirs forever, to be equally divided among them."

At the time of executing the will, the testator had several grandchildren in being. Others were born after the will was executed, but before his death; and the son of the testator had three children born after the death of the latter; the eldest of them was born in 1830.

An application having been made in behalf of the last three grandchildren to be considered among the devisees, (each entitled to an equal interest in the devised premises with each of the older children) the Chancellor so decided, and the single question now to be determined is, whether those three children born since the death of Mr. Chase, have, in the premises devised to his grandchildren, the interest which the Chancellor has allowed to them.

If the property is not to vest immediately after the death of the testator, but the vesting of it in possession is postponed, then such grandchildren as are born before the property does vest in possession, may take. In this case, however, the devise is immediate. Those who are entitled to the devised premises became entitled to the land, so soon as the testator died—the description of the persons to take is general, and only those, who at the time of the testator's death came within that description can take.

In 3 Bro.Chan.Cases, 404, note A, to Andrews and Partington, it is said that the testator's intent must prevail. This is not always the case. Lord Eldon, in Walker vs. Shore, 15 Vez. 125, said, "the construction I am obliged to make in this cause, may break in upon the actual intent of the testator: this rule, we are told by the master of the rolls, 11 Vez. 238, is a rule of necessity, and as soon as any became entitled to a vested interest in possession, after-born children," (of course, grandchildren), are excluded.

But we discover nothing in this clause of the will, nor in all the clauses of the will taken together, from which can be inferred a manifest intent that all the children of his children, no matter when born, should have a portion of the estate devised.

The will itself (if we knew nothing of the testator), furnishes abundant evidence that it was written by a man able to express whatever was his intention. If indeed a doubt could exist in regard to the intent here, the question to which it might give rise could only be made by a different class of these claimants. Those born at the time of the execution of the will, might, with some reason, insist that the intent could not be to give to any who might be born afterwards, an interest in the devise, and might refer to the expression, "my dear grandchildren," as not used in reference to children, who possibly may—but possibly may not—ever be in esse, and certainly not to those of whose existence, of course, he would not have any knowledge. This is the case, however, of a general devise to grandchildren, as a class, and in such a case the authorities collected in the note to which reference has already been given in 3 Brown, show the devise "comprehends all persons answering the description at the time of the testator's death."

A decree will be signed reversing the Chancellor's order, and in conformity to this opinion.

The costs in chancery and in this court to be a charge upon the fund.

Decree Reversed.

ROGERS v. MUTCH

High Court of Justice, Chancery Division, 1878.
10 Ch.Div. 25.

Elizabeth Hill, widow, by her will, dated the 3rd of June, 1873, bequeathed "the sum of £100 to each of the children of my niece Eliza Mutch, who shall live to attain the age of twenty-one years."

The testatrix died on the 31st of October, 1873.

Eliza Mutch was still living, and she and her husband were defendants in this action, which was for the administration of the estate of the testatrix. Mrs. Mutch had not yet had any children. In distributing the estate the question arose whether any, and, if so, what amount should be set apart to answer the legacies to the "children" of Mrs. Mutch.

JESSEL, M. R. As I understand the rule, its object is simply one of convenience.

In the old case of Ringrose v. Bramham, the gift was of £50 to every child of Joseph Ringrose and Christopher Rhodes by their present wives who came of age, and the Master of the Rolls says this: "Here there are distinct legacies of £50 to each of the children, and therefore if I am to let in all the children of these two persons born at any future time, I must postpone the distribution of the testator's personal estate until the death of Joseph Ringrose and Christopher Rhodes, or their wives, for I can never divide the residue until I know how many legacies of £50 are payable." And he distinguishes the case of Gilmore v. Severn, 1 Bros.C.C. 582, by saying that in that case a gross sum of £350 was given to the children of Jane Gilmore, to be paid to them in equal shares at twenty-one, and that there was no inconvenience in postponing the vesting of those shares until some one of them attained that age, so as to let in the children born in the meantime, because there was nothing to do but to set apart the sum of £350, and the residue of the testator's personal estate might be immediately divided. So that the rule is a rule of convenience; unless you adopt it you cannot divide the estate.

In Ringrose v. Bramham, 2 Cox, 384, there were children living at the death of the testator, but the same rule applies, where, as in the present case, there are no children living at the testator's death. If, in such a case, you are to let in children born after the death, the estate is no more divisible in the one case than in the other; and so Lord Hatherley, when Vice Chancellor, points out in Mann v. Thompson, Kay, 638. He says this (Id. 642): "The next case is not a bequest of a sum to be divided among a class, but a gift of a certain sum to each individual of the class, where no time is fixed by the will at which the class is to be ascertained. I do not find any decided case in which the point has arisen, which occurs here with regard to children, who were neither in esse at the date of the will, nor at the testator's death." He then refers to Ringrose v. Bramham, 2 Cox, 384, and says: "The reason which he (the Master of the Rolls) gave for excluding them (the afterborn children) seems to be very sound, namely, the extreme inconvenience of postponing the distribution of the testator's personal estate until all the children who might be born should be ascertained, which would not happen until the death of their respective parents." The actual point in this case did not arise in Ringrose v. Bramham, but still the ratio decidendi clearly applies. * * *

It appears, therefore, that the Vice Chancellor approves of the decision in Ringrose v. Bramham, and also of the reason for that decision, and would have applied it to the case before him but that the language of the will was sufficient to shew the testator contemplated those children only who should be living at his death.

Then I find the rule is laid down in Mr. Hawkins' well-known and valuable book, where he says (page 73): "The rule which admits objects born after the testator's death and before the period of distribution, to share in the bequest, only applies where the total amount of the gift is independent of the number of objects among whom it is to be divided, and is therefore not increased by the construction adopted. But a gift of a certain sum to each of a class of objects at a future period is confined to those living at the testator's death." He then illustrates the rule by referring to the two authorities I have mentioned, and proceeds: "The reason given is, that in the latter case, if afterborn children were admitted, the distribution of the personal estate of the testator would have to be postponed till it could be ascertained how many legacies of the given amount would be payable." So he obviously takes the same view as has been taken by the authorities, namely, that no children born after the testator's death

can be admitted unless the total amount of the gift is independent of the number of objects.

So I apply the rule in this case, and hold that no child Mrs. Mutch may have can take under this bequest.

IN RE EVANS' ESTATE

Supreme Court of Wisconsin, 1957.
274 Wis. 459, 80 N.W.2d 408.[89]

[The third clause of decedent's will provided as follows:

" 'Third, I give, devise and bequeath to my grandchildren the sum of Fifty Thousand Dollars ($50,000), said sum to be placed in trust by my executor in a trust company or a bank exercising trust powers, the income from the principal being allowed to accumulate until said grandchildren shall respectively become of age. After each grandchild becomes of age he is to receive the income which accumulates on his share, said income to be paid to him annually until he reaches the age of thirty years. After each grandchild reaches the age of thirty years he is to be paid his full share of the principal sum of this bequest together with the interest which has accumulated thereon. * * *' " At the time of his death, decedent left six grandchildren, four of whom were born prior to the execution of the will and two of whom were born after the execution. In the probate proceedings the court entered a final judgment assigning the sum of $50,000 to the six grandchildren by name. Subsequently but before the eldest of the six attained the age of 30, three additional grandchildren were born. The trustee, having been advised of the birth of such additional grandchildren and being concerned as to whether they might be beneficiaries, brought the present proceedings to construe the final judgment and the will. The lower court held that the final judgment was not binding upon the grandchildren born after the death of the testator, because not adequately represented in that proceeding, and construed Article Third of the Will to create a gift vested in the six grandchildren living at the time of death of testator subject to being reopened to admit additional grandchildren, the trust to be divided each time a grandchild reaches the age of 30 on the basis of the number of grandchildren then actually living. The trustee appeals.]

FAIRCHILD, CHIEF JUSTICE. Before taking up the question of whether or not the judgment entered April 17, 1942, is *res judicata* as to grandchildren born after the date of death of the testator, it seems well to pass upon the nature and inclusiveness of the bequest. If the gift grant in Article Third is to a class, and that class is so

89. Noted, 41 Marq.L.Rev. 205 (1957), 1958 Wis.L.Rev. 150. Motion for rehearing was denied: 81 N.W.2d 489 (1957). See Sherrin, "The Meaning of Class Gift", 120 New L.J. 938 (1970).

fixed by the terms of the bequest that there may be an interval of time during which the class may increase, then the gift is one which vests in the existing number of the class and such other persons as thereafter become members of the class. That interval continues to the point of time or event which is specified and certain. The gift we are considering is to "my grandchildren," and because of the absence of an alternative gift over or reversion in favor of the testator's heirs, it bespeaks an intention of a vested gift. The grandchildren living at the death of the testator are members of the class, but the class is subject to a change by addition of after-born grandchildren who came into being before the coming of the event which closes forever the membership in the class.

The time fixed for closing the class is set in the bequest: "After each grandchild reaches the age of thirty years, he is to be paid his full share of the principal sum of this bequest together with the interest which has accumulated thereon." This controls the increase in membership in the class. The time of the distribution of the *corpus* settles the question of maximum membership. In the absence of words in the will indicating a contrary intent, a testator would naturally desire to include all grandchildren born at the time of the distribution of the *corpus*. In Simes, The Law of Future Interests, we find the following recognition of rules of construction:

> "The maximum membership in the class is determined when the time for distribution has arrived. The class may increase until that time, and persons born thereafter are excluded." Sec. 634, p. 69.
>
> "The time for distribution arrived when the first member of the class attained the designated age." Sec. 644, p. 89.

In 5 American Law of Property, the following rules are recognized:

> "When a class gift is postponed until the occurrence of some event, such as the attainment of age twenty-one, the class does not normally close until the first member of the class attains the designated age." Sec. 22.44, p. 372.
>
> "It must be kept in mind that the probable desire of the average transferor, when he describes his transferees by a group designation, is to benefit as many persons who comply with the description as he can, without at the same time causing too much inconvenience." Sec. 22.43, p. 364.

The gift may be so made that the class may either increase or decrease after the death of the testator until the arrival of the fixed point of time or the happening of the specified event. It may be so worded that there may be an interval of time during which the class may increase but during which it cannot decrease. The most common example of this kind of gift is one which vests in the existing members of a class and in such other persons as thereafter become members of the class up to the point of time or event which is specified. Page on Wills, sec. 1052. It is considered that the three grandchildren born after the death of the testator and before the distribution of the *corpus* are members of the class and inherit as such.

* * *

[In the omitted portion of the opinion the court held that the final judgment in the original probate proceedings was not binding on the afterborn grandchildren, because not represented therein by either a guardian ad litem or the existing members of the class (grandchildren already born who had antagonistic interests); hence the defense of res adjudicata was without merit.]

* * *

Inasmuch as and because the trial court erroneously held that membership in the class opened up each time a new grandchild is born, until such time as the entire trust *corpus* was distributed, the order must be modified to correct this error.

We do not continue a discussion of other questions not necessary for a determination of the material issues.

Order modified so as to provide that membership in the class permanently closed when the oldest grandchild arrived at the age of thirty years, and as so modified it is affirmed. Cause remanded for further proceedings according to law.[90]

90. In Carter v. Long, 181 Mo. 701, 81 S.W. 162 (1904) a testator devised property in trust to T for the children of A. One child of A was alive at the time of the testator's death. Two more children were born to A subsequent to the death of the testator. Held: that the child alive on the testator's death took to the exclusion of the other children. The trust created was a dry trust with the result that it had the same effect as if the property were devised directly to the children of A.

Where property is transferred by will or deed to "A for life, remainder to the children of B", and A and B are alive on the effective date of the instrument, the general rule is that the class does not close until the date of the life tenant's death. Wherefore all the children of B living on the effective date of the instrument and all the children of B born prior to the death of the life tenant, and all of the children of B in gestation at the life tenant's death who are born alive thereafter, are included in the class. If B's first child is born after the death of the life tenant and was not in gestation at the time of the life tenant's death, all of B's children, whenever born, are included in the class. The foregoing conclusions are applications of the "rule of convenience". It will be recalled that this rule is merely a rule of construction. Thus, it is not applied when it conflicts with the express intention of the transferor. For example, in Buckner v. Buckner, 255 Mo. 371, 164 S.W. 513 (1913) a testator devised property to A for life, remainder to B's children with an alternative devise to B's child, Q, if B should die without having any other issue. Q was born prior to the testator's death. R and S, children of B, were born after the testator's death but prior to the death of the life tenant, A. T, B's fourth child, was born more than 10 months after the death of the life tenant. At the time the case arose, B was alive and capable of having more children. The court held that all children of B, whenever born, were included in the class and that the class would not close until B's death. Although recognizing that the "rule of convenience" would close the class at the death of the life tenant, the court refused to apply that rule because it concluded that the testator had manifested an intention that all children of B, whenever born, should be included within the class. The court reached this conclusion because the alternative devise to Q could not take effect until B's death. The court held that the children of B born prior to the death of

IN RE WENMOTH'S ESTATE

Chancery Division, 1887. 37 Ch.Div. 266.

William Wenmoth, who died in February, 1871, by his will, dated the 19th of April, 1870, after certain pecuniary and specific bequests gave all the residue of his property upon trust to pay to his daughter Eliza (Mrs. M'Kever) an annuity, and directed his trustees during the life of his said daughter to pay and apply the surplus of the rents, dividends, interest, and annual proceeds, and after her death to apply the whole of such income "unto and equally between my grandchildren (being the children of my son Joseph and my said daughter Eliza) on their respectively attaining the age of twenty-one years, during their respective lives, share and share alike." On the death of any grandchild (except the last survivor) who should die leaving issue the share of such income and annual proceeds of such grandchild so dying to be paid unto and equally between his or her children who being sons should attain twenty-one or being daughters should attain that age or marry. After the death of the last surviving grandchild the residuary estate to be converted, and the proceeds of the conversion to be divided equally amongst testator's great grandchildren living at the death of his last surviving grandchild and attaining twenty-one. The share of any grandchild in the said rents and annual proceeds to be invested by the trustees during the minority of any such grandchild and form part of the trust. The trustees were also empowered to apply all or any of the share of the income or capital of any minor for his or her maintenance, education, or advancement.

Mrs. M'Kever had two children, both of whom died in the testator's lifetime.

Joseph Wenmoth had eleven children, of whom eight were now living.

Of these eight grandchildren of the testator five were born in the testator's lifetime, and the eldest attained twenty-one on the 25th of March, 1883. Two were born after the testator's death and before the eldest grandchild attained twenty-one; one was born in February, 1887.

The question, raised by originating summons, was whether the trusts of the will for the benefit of grandchildren were confined to such grandchildren as were living at the testator's death, or extended

the life tenant took vested remainders subject to an executory devise in favor of the children of B born thereafter who would become co-tenants with those born prior to the life tenant's death.

In Austin's Estate, 315 Pa. 449, 173 A. 278 (1934) there was a devise to "A for life, remainder in trust to the children of B until they shall attain the age of 21." A survived the testator. At A's death only one child had been born to B. This child was over 21 on the date of A's death. B was then still capable of having children. The court held that the class closed on the death of the life tenant since B's child would then be entitled to demand his share of the gift. That share could only be determined by then closing the class to after-born members. See, Simes and Smith, The Law of Future Interests (2d Ed.1956) §§ 634–659; Focht, "Class Gifts: Increase in Class Membership and the Rule of Convenience", 2 Wm. & Mary L.Rev. 254 (1959); 6 A.L.R.2d 1342 (1959); 61 A.L.R. 2d 212 (1958).

(a) to grandchildren born after his death, before the eldest grandchild attained twenty-one or (b) to all grandchildren whenever born. A further question was whether the grandchildren who for the time being had attained twenty-one were entitled to the whole of the net income, subject to Mrs. M'Kever's annuity; and if not, to what part of such income they were entitled, and whether the plaintiff (the surviving executor) could apply any and what part of such income for the maintenance, &c., of such of the grandchildren as for the time being were under twenty-one.

CHITTY, J. An immediate gift of personal estate to the children of A. is free from doubt, and those children only take who are living at the testator's death. A gift to the children of A. who shall attain the age of twenty-one, is also one on which no question can arise. The class of children in either case remains open until the period of distribution and then closes, and all those children who may be born before the death of the testator, or before the eldest of them has attained twenty-one, are admissible, while those born after the period of distribution are excluded. This rule, excluding as it does from the class to be benefited any child born after the period of distribution, may be explained by the attempt of the court to reconcile two inconsistent directions, viz., that the whole class should take and also that the fund should be distributed among them at a period when the whole class could not possibly be ascertained. The rule, which was intended as a solution of the difficulty, may be said to be a cutting of the knot rather than an untying, and, though it has been called a rule of convenience, must be very inconvenient to those children who may be born after the period of distribution. In Gillman v. Daunt, 3 K. & J. 48, Lord Hatherley, when Vice-Chancellor, said that a child "who has attained twenty-one cannot be kept waiting for his share; and if you have once paid it to him, you cannot get it back." Where, however, as in this will, the distribution is of income and not of corpus there is nothing which requires the application of the rule, and the difficulty does not arise.

In the case of the distribution of corpus, the trustees cannot ascertain what is the aliquot share of a member of the class until the class is closed, but in the case of a distribution of income the distribution is periodical. Each member of the class, as soon as he becomes entitled, takes his share of the income, and there is no reason why the rule should be applied beyond each periodical payment. I have no difficulty, therefore, upon principle in holding that in the case of a bequest of income among a class of children to be paid on their attaining twenty-one years, the date of the first attaining twenty-one years was not the date of the ascertainment of the class, and that any child at any time attaining twenty-one years will be entitled to a share of the income. Mogg v. Mogg, 1 Mer. 654, appears to me to be an authority for my decision as to the distinction between a gift of corpus and a gift of income. In the two cases cited in support of the contention that the grandchildren living at the testator's death were the only objects to take under the bequest (Elliott v. Elliott, 12 Sim. 276; In re Coppard's Estate, 35 Ch.D. 350), there was a question in

each as to the rule against perpetuities, and although in neither case was remoteness made the actual ratio decidendi such a construction was adopted as avoided an intestacy by the operation of the law of remoteness, and the decision in each case saved the will. The general law on this point is stated by Lord Selborne in Pearks v. Moseley, 5 App.Cas. 719: "You do not import the law of remoteness into the construction of the instrument, by which you investigate the expressed intention of the testator. You take his words, and endeavour to arrive at their meaning, exactly in the same manner as if there had been no such law, and as if the whole intention expressed by the words could lawfully take effect." If I thought those two cases in point I should have to consider them very carefully, but I do not. I decline to decide the question as to the interests of the great grandchildren as being premature.[91]

PROBLEMS

1. Bequest in trust for "B, C, and D, children of A and such other children as A may have, the sum to accumulate until the youngest surviving of these children shall attain the age of 21 years." B, C, and D were born prior to the execution of the will. A's children, E, F, and G, were born after the testator's death. Who is entitled to share in the gift? See In re McBride's Estate, 152 Pa. 192, 25 A. 513 (1893).

2. Testamentary gift in trust to the children of B "until the time arrives when there shall be no child of B living and under 21 years of age". At the testator's death two children of B were living, age 4 and 9 respectively. No other child was born to B on the date the youngest child of B living at the testator's death attained the page of 21 but B was then still capable of having children. Does the class then close? See Dawson v. Akers, 127 Md. 585, 96 A. 806 (1915).

B. DECREASE OF CLASS (SURVIVORSHIP REVISITED)

The cases which follow deal with problems we have previously explored—what effect does death before the testator or before termination of a preceding interest such as a life estate have upon the gift? But the problems of lapse and implied or express survivorship have a different dimension in the class gift situation. Because the membership of the class is determined at a date later than execution of the will, through increase in the class under the rules studied in the just preceding materials, does this mean that the class can decrease through death of one of the members prior to that date? Moreover, unlike the gift to an individual with no provision for a gift over in event of the individual's death, the class gift by its nature contains within it a gift over to the other members of the class. Should this make any difference in either application of the anti-lapse statute or willingness of the court to imply survivorship? Although you may well conclude that the same rules should apply to the class gift as to

91. See In re Powell, [1898] L.R. 1 Ch. 227; In re Carter, 30 New Zealand L.R. 707 (1911); Pippin v. Sams, 174 S.C. 444, 177 S.E. 659 (1934); Restatement, Property (1940) § 295.

the individual gift, these cases afford an opportunity to add experience in applying those rules to new factual situations.

DRAFTS v. DRAFTS

District Court of Appeal of Florida, 1959.
114 So.2d 473.

CARROLL, DONALD, JUDGE. This appeal is from a declaratory decree construing the provisions of a will. There being no dispute as to the facts, no evidence was taken. The case was submitted to the chancellor for decision on the issues of law made by the complaint and answer.

The testatrix had seven brothers and sisters, three of whom died leaving lineal descendants prior to the execution of the will, and two of whom died leaving lineal descendants after the will was executed but prior to testatrix's death. The will itself is simple and uncomplicated. After making a specific bequest to two of testatrix's nephews, it concluded with the following provision:

> "I will, devise and bequeath all the residue of my property, both real and personal, to my brothers and sisters, share and share alike."

The question presented for the chancellor's decision was two-fold. First, were the lineal descendants of the three brothers who died prior to the execution of the will entitled to take as members of the class under the quoted residuary clause of the will? Second, were the lineal descendants of the brother and sister who died after the execution of the will, but prior to testatrix's death, entitled to take as members of the class under the residuary clause of the will? In resolving these issues the chancellor answered both questions in the negative, and decreed that only the brother and sister who survived the testatrix were entitled to share the residuary estate.

Under the common law a testamentary gift is void if made to one who was deceased at the time the will was executed. Redfearn on Wills and Administration of Estates in Florida, (3rd Ed.) Vol. 1, Section 149; 57 Am.Jur. 954, Section 1424; In re Hutton's Estate, 106 Wash. 578, 180 P. 882, 3 A.L.R. 1673. It is also a settled common law principle that a testamentary gift lapses if made to one who dies after the execution of the will but before the death of the testator, or before the time for the estate to vest. Redfearn on Wills and Administration of Estates in Florida, (3rd Ed.) Vol. 1, Section 149; Williams v. Williams, 152 Fla. 255, 9 So.2d 798; Williams v. Williams, 149 Fla. 454, 6 So.2d 275; Sorrells v. McNally, 89 Fla. 457, 105 So. 106; 57 Am.Jur. 957, Section 1426. The above-stated principles are applicable unless a contrary intention appears from the provisions of the will. It is further provided at common law that if the testamentary gift is to a class, and a member of the class dies before the death of the testator or before the time fixed for the vesting of the estate, his interest goes to the surviving members of the class unless the testator has expressed a contrary intention in his will. Dean v. Crews, 77 Fla. 319, 81 So. 479; Redfearn on Wills and Administration of Estates in Florida, (3rd Ed.) Vol. 1, Section 157.

In the will now under consideration the testamentary gift of the residuary estate, being to the brothers and sisters of the testatrix, was a class gift within the meaning of the applicable law. There are no provisions in the will which could be construed to indicate an intention on the part of the testatrix that her estate should be shared by anyone other than those entitled to take under the applicable provisions of law.

Under the common law, which is in force and effect in Florida unless otherwise changed by statute, it clearly appears that the lineal descendants of the brothers and sisters who predeceased the testatrix are not entitled to share in the residuary estate under the terms and provisions of the will in question.

The common law relating to lapsed or void legacies or devises has been modified by statute in this state (Section 731.20, Florida Statutes, F.S.A.) as follows:

> "(1) If a devisee or legatee dies during the lifetime of the testator, the testamentary disposition to such devisee or legatee lapses, unless an intention appears from the will to substitute another in his place; but, when any property is devised or bequeathed to an adopted child or blood kindred of the testator, and when such devisee or legatee dies before the testator, leaving lineal descendants, or is dead at the time the will is executed, leaving lineal descendants who survive the testator, such legacy or devise does not lapse, but such descendants take the property so given by the will in the same manner as the devisee or legatee would have done had he survived the testator."

Unquestionably the foregoing statute applies to testamentary gifts made to named beneficiaries. However in the will now under consideration the brothers and sisters of testatrix were not named therein, but were designated as a class. Our decision must therefore necessarily turn on the question of whether the foregoing statute applies to testamentary gifts made to a class as well as gifts made to named beneficiaries. This question has not been squarely presented to, or passed upon by, our Supreme Court, so we must look to decisions of other jurisdictions as a guide in reaching our conclusion.

Non-lapse statutes such as the one now in effect in Florida have been adopted by most states of this country. A majority of the states have held that a non-lapse statute does not apply to a member of a class who was dead at the time of the execution of the will. Such holding is based upon the common-law principle that a gift to any beneficiary who is dead at the time the will is executed is void, and no question of lapse arises. On the other hand, a majority of the states hold that non-lapse statutes will apply to members of a class who die after the execution of the will, but prior to the death of the testator, or the date on which the estate vests in the class. Such holding is justified on the premise that a lapse of a testamentary gift is thereby prevented, and the gift will pass to those whom the testator would most likely have wished to be substituted for the deceased member of the class. The states which hold to a contrary view justify their position on the basis that a gift to members of a class cannot lapse so long as any member of the class survives the testator, which rule is followed in this jurisdiction. Redfearn on Wills and Administration of Estates in Florida, (3rd Ed.) Vol. 1, Section 157; Arnold v. Wells, 100 Fla. 1470, 131 So. 400. These decisions further reason that there is no more logic in assuming that the testator intended for lineal descendants of deceased members of a class to share in his estate than it is to assume the contrary.

In view of the difference which has arisen in the several jurisdictions of this country as to whether a non-lapse statute such as the one now under consideration should be applied to class gifts as well as to gifts made to named beneficiaries, five states have adopted non-lapse statutes which by clear and unmistakable terms apply to gifts made to a class. Florida has not yet seen fit to adopt such a statute. The decisions on this subject have been collected and reported in 56 A.L.R.2d 948.

We acknowledge the settled rule in this jurisdiction that statutes which are in derogation of the common law must be strictly construed. But even strictly construing the antilapse statute quoted above, it seems to us clear that the legislature intended that statute to be applied to class gifts where the class consists of blood relatives, at least to the members of such class who were living at the time of the execution of the will. It will be noted that the quoted statute provides that the antilapse provisions will apply "when any property is devised or bequeathed to an adopted child or *blood kindred* of the testator". (Emphasis supplied.) It appears clear that when the Florida Legislature enacted this law it manifested its intention that the antilapse provisions should be applied to that class of persons comprising "blood kindred" or, to use a synonymous expression "blood relatives". In the present appeal the testatrix devised and bequeathed the residue of her property to "my brothers and sisters" and these brothers and sisters were certainly blood relatives or, to use the statutory words, "Blood kindred".

This conclusion is consonant with the rule prevailing in the majority of jurisdictions as set forth in an annotation entitled "Applicability of Anti-lapse Statutes to Class Gifts", wherein the annotator states on page 950 of 56 A.L.R.2d:

> "In a majority of the jurisdictions where the courts have considered the question it has been held that antilapse statutes are, in the absence of language indicating a contrary intention on the testator's part, applicable to a gift to a class so as to preserve a share of the gift in favor of heirs or descendants of persons falling within the class description and alive at the date of execution of the will, but predeceasing the testator."

The statutes in most jurisdictions do not appear to include such language as "blood kindred", which language seems to us as clearly establishing the intent of the legislature to embrace gifts to classes composed of blood relatives. Our conclusion, therefore, is that the Florida antilapse statute applies to gifts to a class composed of blood relatives, such as brothers and sisters, as here, as to such relatives who are living at the time of the execution of the will.

A more difficult question is whether the statute should be applied as to the brothers and sisters who were deceased at the time of the execution of the will. It will be remembered that at common law a gift to one already deceased was void, and hence no question of lapse was presented. The antilapse statute being directly in derogation of this principle of the common law, the statute must be strictly construed. The intention of the testator as expressed in the testamentary instrument is always the pole star in the interpretation of the will. In the instant appeal the testatrix devised and bequeathed the residue of her property "to my brothers and sisters". There is nothing in her will to indicate that the testatrix wanted to provide for her then deceased brothers and sisters or their lineal descendants. We think it would be more logical construction to hold that when a testator provides for his brothers and sisters, he normally intends to include only his living brothers and sisters, unless elsewhere in his will he indicates that he intends to include already deceased brothers and sisters or their descendants. We therefore align ourselves with the courts which have held that antilapse statutes do not apply in favor of members of a class who die before the execution of the will in question, unless the testator in his will expresses an intention that such members should be included.

For the foregoing reasons we hold that the chancellor was correct in decreeing that the lineal descendants of the testatrix's brothers and sisters who were deceased at the time of the execution of her will were not members of the class described in the residuary clause of the will and were therefore not entitled to share in that estate; but was in error in decreeing that the lineal descendants of the testatrix's brothers and sisters who predeceased her after she executed her will were not members of the class described in the residuary clause and therefore not entitled to share in that estate. The decree appealed from is therefore affirmed in part and reversed in part, and the cause is remanded for further proceedings consistent with the views herein.

STURGIS, J., concurs.

WIGGINTON, CHIEF JUDGE (concurring in part and dissenting in part).

I am in thorough accord with that part of the majority opinion which holds that the non-lapse statute in effect in Florida is not applicable to the lineal descendants of the members of a class who die before the execution of a will. I must respectfully dissent, however, from that part of the opinion which holds that the statute is applicable to the lineal descendants of those members of a class who die after the will is executed, but before the death of the testator.

The majority opinion agrees that the bequest contained in the will now under consideration which reads "to my brothers and sisters, share and share alike", is a class gift. Non-lapse statutes are enacted for the sole purpose of preventing the lapse of testamentary gifts. It is universally recognized that a gift to a class is legally incapable of lapsing so long as any member of the class survives the testator's death. It is for this reason that non-lapse statutes have been held not to apply to class gifts unless made so by clear and unambiguous language.

It is manifest from no more than a cursory examination of our statute that it is not expressly made applicable to beneficiaries as a class. In fact, an objective interpretation of the statute impels the conclusion that it was never intended to apply to class gifts. I am convinced that by use of the language "when any property is devised * * * to *an adopted child* or *blood kindred* of the testator, and when such *devisee* or *legatee* dies before the testator * * *" the legislature intended by the use of the singular noun to make the non-lapse provision of the statute applicable only to named individuals as devisees and legatees, and not to beneficiaries as a class.

A will is ambulatory in character and subject to change at any time. I cannot bring myself to hold that an average testator of reasonable intelligence would not be justified in assuming that a brother or sister who predeceases him would no longer be considered a brother or sister at the time of testator's death. Knowing of the death of his brother or sister, a testator is free to amend his will to include such lineal descendants of the deceased brother or sister as he may care to share in his estate. Failure to do so should be construed as evidencing a testamentary intent to confine class gifts to those members of the class who might survive the testator.

* * * [92]

---

92. The English lapse statute is inapplicable to class gifts. In re Harvey's Estate, [1893] L.R. 1 Ch. 567; Sherrin, "Class Gifts and Lapse", 120 New L.J. 963 (1970) (British cases). A lapse statute is construed to yield to a contrary intention of the testator. The English construction of a testamentary gift "to the children of A" is that the testator refers to the children of A living when the testator dies. Hence children who die before the testator were not intended by him to be within the class. Some American courts follow the English view, particularly when the statute contains the word "lapse". E.g., Trenton Trust & Safe Deposit Co. v. Sibbits, 62 N.J.Eq. 131, 49 A. 530 (1901). Most courts, however, hold their lapse statutes applicable to class gifts provided the gifts would be subject to the statute if made to the donees as individuals. E.g., Rudolph v. Rudolph, 207 Ill. 266, 69 N.E. 834, 99 Am.St.Rep. 211 (1904). In American jurisdictions where the lapse statutes are applicable to class gifts there is a division of authority whether the statute applies to a person who otherwise meets the class description but who, known to the testator, died before the will was executed. See Pimel v. Betjemann, 183 N.Y. 194, 76 N.E. 157, 2 L.R.A.,N.S. 580, 5 Ann.Cas. 239 (1905) (holding statute inapplicable; Hoverstad v. First Nat. Bank & Trust Co., 76 S.D. 119, 74 N.W.2d 48, 56 A.L.R.2d 938 (1955), 9 Vand.L.Rev. 577 (1956) (holding statute applicable). If a testator devises Blackacre "to the children of A living at my death" a lapse statute will not be applied to save the gift to a child of A pre-

HOFING v. WILLIS

Supreme Court of Illinois, 1964.
31 Ill.2d 365, 201 N.E.2d 852.[93]

SCHAEFER, JUSTICE. This case calls for the construction of two warranty deeds conveying interests in separate tracts of property.
* * *

On February 24, 1904, Michael Wittlinger held fee-simple title to a 40–acre tract of land in Sangamon County and an adjoining 160–acre tract in Menard County. On that date he and his wife Anna executed warranty deeds to both tracts. One deed conveyed the 40–acre tract to their son "Geo. Wittlinger and Edna Wittlinger his wife," and the other deed conveyed the 160-acre tract to "George Wittlinger and Edna Wittlinger, his wife during their natural lives," reserving to Michael and Anna "the use of two rooms in the house in which they now live during the remainder of their lives." Each deed also contained the following provision: "It is expressly understood that at the death of the said George Wittlinger and Edna Wittlinger his wife the said lands herein described shall revert to the heirs of the body of the said George Wittlinger. In case there be no heirs then the said lands shall revert to the sisters of the said George Wittlinger and to their heirs and assigns forever."

When the deeds were executed, Michael and Anna Wittlinger had five living children—their son George and four daughters. No more children were born to them. Michael died intestate in 1905, and Anna in 1928. George Wittlinger, the son, survived his wife who devised her entire estate to him, and he died testate on January 3, 1961. His only child and his four sisters predeceased him. One sister, Amelia, devised her estate to George and some of the plaintiffs. By his will George devised all his property "to my friends, Howard Willis and Mary Willis," who are the defendants in this action.

The plaintiffs are the living children of the sisters of George, or, in the case of a deceased child of a sister, the living children of that deceased child. They brought this action for partition, claiming title by inheritance or devise through the sisters of George. Their complaint prayed for a construction of the two deeds, an accounting, and the appointment of a trustee. The defendants filed a counterclaim, asserting title to the property under George's will.

The trial court held that the deed to the 160-acre tract conveyed a joint life estate to George and his wife, followed by a contingent remainder to the heirs of the body of George and an alternative contingent remainder, in case George died leaving no heirs of the body, to his sisters as a class. And relying on Drury v. Drury, 271 Ill. 336,

deceasing the testator because the statutes always yield to the testator's expressed intention. In some states the statutes now expressly apply to class gifts. E.g., Smith-Hurd Ill.Ann.Stat. ch. 110½, ¶ 4–11; Va.Code Ann. §§ 64.1–64. See Uniform Probate Code, § 2–605, set forth in Section 2(1), supra this Chapter, which applies expressly to class gifts. See, Note "Class Gifts in Iowa", 21 Drake L.Rev. 167 (1971); 54 A.L.R.3d 280 (1974).

93. Noted, 1965 U.Ill.L.F. 141.

111 N.E. 140, the court adopted the view that the latter remainder was contingent on survivorship and that since all of George's sisters predeceased him, no interest in the 160-acre tract passed as a part of their estates. The court then held that since neither contingency had occurred, the reversion that remained in the grantor descended to George Wittlinger and his four sisters as the heirs of the grantor.

As to the 40-acre tract, the trial court held that George and his wife took a fee subject to alternative executory devises, first to the heirs of George's body and, if none survived him and his wife, then to his sisters. Again relying on the Drury case, the court held that both executory devises failed and that the fee in George and his wife therefore became absolute at his death.

* * * [In the omitted portion of the opinion, the Court held that both deeds created life estates only in George and Edna Wittlinger.] * * *

This brings us to the issue of the descendibility of the interests that the deeds conveyed to George's sisters. The defendants, who claim under George, argue that the alternative gifts over to George's sisters were class gifts and that they were contingent not only upon the death of George and his wife without leaving heirs of the body of George surviving them, but contingent also on the sisters' surviving George and his wife. Since the sisters all predeceased George, the defendants assert that the alternative gifts over failed. This result, they say, is the necessary consequence of this court's decisions in Drury v. Drury, 271 Ill. 336, 111 N.E. 140, Blackstone v. Althouse, 278 Ill. 481, 116 N.E. 154, L.R.A.1918B, 230, and Farmer v. Reed, 335 Ill. 156, 166 N.E. 498. The defendants also refer to Golladay v. Knock, 235 Ill. 412, 85 N.E. 649, and Continental Ill. Nat. Bank & Trust Co. of Chicago v. Eliel, 17 Ill.2d 332, 161 N.E.2d 107, in support of their position.

In the Drury case, this court said that where "a gift to a class is postponed pending the termination of a life estate, those members of the class, and those only, take who are in existence at the death of the life tenant." (271 Ill. at 341, 111 N.E. at 142.) Plaintiffs contend first, that the gifts over to George's sisters were not class gifts, and that the Drury case therefore does not apply, and second, that the Drury case should be overruled or distinguished.

Plaintiffs' contention that the sisters were to take as individuals rather than as a class emphasizes that the gift over mentioned only sisters and not brothers, (George had no brothers at the date of the deed or later), that the grantor was probably of such an age that he did not expect additional children, and that the grantor and his wife reserved the use of two rooms in a house located on the 160-acre tract. Plaintiffs assert that these facts show that the grantor did not contemplate additional children and that the sisters "were as definitely ascertained as if they were specifically named." (Cf. Blackstone v. Althouse, 278 Ill. 481, 489, 116 N.E. 154, 157.) Defendants, on the other hand, invoke the presumption that the capacity to bear children continues until death. They also cite authorities tending to support

the view that the word "sisters" should be construed to include half-sisters, thus suggesting that even if the grantor was too old to contemplate more children, his wife might have remarried after his death and have had additional daughters who would fall within the class of George's "sisters."

It may be, as the plaintiffs urge, that by the references in the deeds to "the sisters of the said George Wittlinger", the grantor intended to point to the four sisters who were living when the conveyances were made. But there is no evidence in the record as to the age of the grantor or his wife when the deeds were executed, or as to the age of George and his sisters. Nor is there any evidence as to the grantor's health or financial circumstances. The absence of such evidence makes it difficult to say with conviction that the grantor, in framing the gifts over to the sisters, had only the four daughters in mind, and had singled them out as effectively as though he had named them. The difficulty appears clearly if we assume that the grantor had another daughter after he executed these deeds. Absent a more compelling record it could hardly be supposed that by the words he used the grantor intended to exclude such a daughter. Upon the record before us it is more reasonable to conclude that the grantor referred to the sisters of George as a class, and we are thus brought to a consideration of the effect of Drury v. Drury, 271 Ill. 336, 111 N.E. 140.

Read in context, the statement in the Drury case seems to assert a rigid rule of construction to the effect that a gift to a class of a future interest, contingent on an event unrelated to survivorship, is also contingent on survivorship. The two earlier Illinois decisions that the court relied upon in announcing this rule do not support it. One of them, Brewick v. Anderson, 267 Ill. 169, 107 N.E. 878, construed a will containing an express condition of survivorship; the other, Handberry v. Doolittle, 38 Ill. 202, was concerned with the time when a particular class should close and did not involve the question of whether all members of the class must survive in order to take.

The Drury rule has been vigorously condemned. (See Kales, Future Interests, pp. 382–385, 609 (2d ed., 1920); Carey & Schuyler, Illinois Law of Future Interests, pp. 341–345 (1941); Simes and Smith, The Law of Future Interests, pp. 113–14, 116–117 (2d ed., 1956); Restatement, Property, secs. 261, 296(2).) No reasons have been advanced in its support. On the facts of the Drury case itself, the rule operated to keep the property in the testator's line of descent, but whether that result would follow in any other case is entirely fortuitous, and it may be that such a result was not intended.

We therefore disapprove the Drury case and others purporting to follow it insofar as they announce as a mechanical and universal rule of construction that a class gift of a future interest which is contingent on an event other than survivorship is also contingent on survivorship. Subject to statutory prohibitions and considerations of public policy, the owner of property should be able to create such interests in his grantees as he wants them to have. There are no statutory prohibitions or policy considerations that militate against the creation of a transmissible interest in the sisters of George Wittlinger if that is what the grantor intended.

The question thus becomes one of determining, free from the compulsion of any artificial rule of construction, what kind of an interest the grantor intended to transfer by his deeds. The language is: "It is expressly understood that at the death of the said George Wittlinger and Edna Wittlinger, his wife, the said lands herein described shall revert to the heirs of the body of the said George Wittlinger. In case there be no heirs then the said lands shall revert to the sisters of the said George Wittlinger and to their heirs and assigns forever."

The right of the first remaindermen, the heirs of the body of George, to take the property, is expressly conditioned upon survival of George. The grantor attached no similar condition of survival to the right of the alternate remaindermen, the sisters of George, to take the property. On the contrary the gift over is "to the sisters of the said George Wittlinger and to their heirs and assigns forever." In determining the effect of the deeds, we see no justification for completely rejecting the last seven words in each deed, "and to their heirs and assigns forever", thus refusing to give effect to all of the words of the instrument.

While there is some support for the proposition that the phrase "and to their heirs" could be considered as words of purchase by reading the word "and" as "or," (see Kales, Future Interests, pp. 172–175 (2d ed., 1920); cf. Golladay v. Knock, 235 Ill. 412, 85 N.E. 649), the presence of the words "and assigns" makes such a construction unacceptable. If the word "and" is read "or", the language creates a substitutionary gift in favor of the "heirs and assigns" of George's sisters, who would take as purchasers. That a deceased sister's heirs should take as purchasers by way of substitution would be quite reasonable. But it is hardly reasonable to suppose that the grantor would create a substitutionary gift and at the same time designate the assigns of the named takers to take by way of substitution.

Despite the fact that the words "heirs and assigns" were unnecessary to create a fee, those words need not be treated as having no effect whatever. In fact, our decisions in Smith v. Grubb, 402 Ill. 451, 84 N.E.2d 421, and Noe v. Moseley, 377 Ill. 152, 36 N.E.2d 240, are authority for the point that words of inheritance, though surplusage in a sense, are not always to be disregarded. In their ancient usage the words "heirs and assigns forever" indicated an intent to grant a fee-simple estate—the largest known to the law and one of inheritable quality. We believe that those words, as used in these deeds, combined with all the other circumstances of this case, indicate that the interests of George's sisters should be considered to be of an inheritable quality. We therefore hold that the sisters' interests were not contingent on survivorship but were descendible and passed as a part of the sisters' estates The defendants have no interest in the two parcels of land except to the extent that George acquired an interest therein, in addition to his life estate, under the will of his sister Amelia.

The decree is reversed and the cause is remanded, with directions to proceed in accordance with the views herein expressed.

Reversed and remanded, with directions.

WILL OF WALKER

Supreme Court of Wisconsin, 1962.
17 Wis.2d 181, 116 N.W.2d 106.[94]

[In 1924 testatrix executed a will which made certain specific bequests followed by a residuary clause which provided:

> "The remainder of my estate is then to be held in trust until such time as the youngest of my great nephews and nieces is fifty (50) years old. The interest from it to be divided among them every year. At the time the youngest great nephew or niece is 50 years old the residue of my estate is to be divided among them all share and share alike."

It is evident that testatrix used the term "great" as synonymous with "grand". At the time she had two living sisters, two nephews and five grandnephews and grandnieces. When she died in 1947, testatrix was survived by her two nephews (aged 56 and 62) and seven grandnephews and grandnieces, ranging in age from 17 to 41. In the probate proceeding the court entered a judgment stating that the gift was to a class which would include those born after the death of testatrix but before the time fixed for distribution, which would be the time when all members of the class living at any one time should have attained the age of 50 years; however, the judgment stated that no adjudication was made as to whether the class gift was contingent upon survival until the time of distribution. In 1952 the residue was assigned to the trustee. In 1960 grandniece Mrs. Louise Crow died intestate, survived by her husband and two daughters. The trustee petitioned for construction, and the lower court ruled that the heirs of Louise Crow did not share in distributions of income and principal on the grounds that the will limited distribution to persons who were either grandnephews or grandnieces.]

CURRIE, JUSTICE. The sole issue before us is whether the bequest of the trust corpus to the grandnephews and grandnieces is conditioned upon their survival until the date of distribution. This date has previously been determined to be the time when the youngest living member of the class arrives at the age of fifty years. * * *

94. Noted 47 Marq.L.Rev. 548 (1964), 1963 Wis.L.Rev. 494. In Chapter XVI we shall consider application of the Rule Against Perpetuities to a limitation such as the one in the *Walker* case; Wisconsin has a special statutory rule which permits delayed vesting under a trust in which the trustee has a power of sale.

It is well established that all rules of construction yield to the cardinal rule that the language of a will should be so construed as to give effect to the intention of the testator, if that intention may be ascertained from the language of the will itself, considered in the light of the surrounding circumstances. Will of Emmerick (1954), 268 Wis. 186, 189, 67 N.W.2d 374. When testatrix made her will in 1924 there was every likelihood that, had she died shortly thereafter, the final date of distribution of the trust corpus would not have arrived for more than 50 years. This is because of the probability of further children being born to her two nephews. Even when she died in 1947 there was still the possibility that distribution might occur more than 50 years hence. However, the youngest living grandnephew and grandniece was then seventeen years old, and, thus, the probability was that final distribution would not take place for approximately 33 years. Another probability existing at the time of testatrix' death was that one or more of the grandnephews and grandnieces might die prior to the distribution date. From these facts it is quite evident that testatrix intended a long-term trust, the specific beneficiaries of which were not then determinable.

Moreover, this conclusion as to testatrix' intent is fortified by the actual words used in her will. She directed that "At the time the youngest great nephew or niece is 50 years old the residue of my estate is to be divided among them all share and share alike." The pronoun "them" refers only to "great nephews and nieces." This would seem to exclude a division among persons who are neither grandnephews or grandnieces. Completely absent from this will is any provision for substitution of the issue, heirs, or estates of any deceased grandnephew or grandniece. Furthermore, the words "share and share alike" import a *per capita* and not a *per stirpes* distribution. Will of Bray (1951), 260 Wis. 9, 17, 49 N.W.2d 716. Therefore, to construe this provision so as to entitle the issue, heirs, or estate of a deceased grandnephew or grandniece to their decedent's share in the corpus would be inconsistent with the language of the will itself, and to entitle such parties, as individual persons or entities, to a share of the corpus equal to that of the surviving members of the class would appear to be contrary to the intention of the testatrix.

Furthermore, if the will were construed as not requiring survivorship until the date of distribution, then the next of kin or legatees of a deceased grandnephew or grandniece would receive a share of the trust estate. Thus, persons not of testatrix' blood line, or even corporate institutions, might be the ultimate distributees under this construction. 5 American Law of Property, pp. 131–132, sec. 21.3, states that, when faced with problems of construction to arrive at donative intent, courts invoke a preference for keeping property among blood relatives. We quote from this text as follows (p. 132):

> "In some cases this preference should work against a finding that an interest given to a blood relative is vested prior to the time set for enjoyment of the interest in possession because as a vested

interest it may descend to the transferee's heirs, who may not be related by blood to the transferor, whereas if the interest is contingent on the survival of the initial transferee, his failure to meet the requirement of survival will normally cause the property to go back to the blood relatives of the transferor."

In Will of Latimer (1954), 266 Wis. 158, 173, 63 N.W.2d 65, this court gave expression to this same principle of favoring a construction which would insure the transmission of the trust estate to blood relatives. Application of that principle here would favor a construction that the bequest to the grandnephew and grandniece beneficiaries was conditioned upon their survival until the date of distribution.

There is another principle of construction which favors requiring the beneficiaries of the instant bequest to survive until the date of distribution. This principle is stated in 4 Page, Wills (Lifetime Ed.), p. 176, sec. 1421, as follows:

> "If testator has made a gift to a class, and one of the class dies before testator, or even after testator, while the class is not yet determined there is no lapse or failure of any part of such gift; but, in the absence of statute, no interest under such gift passes to the heirs or next of kin of the deceased beneficiary. The entire gift passes to the members of the class who were in existence at the time that the class was determined."

This same paragraph from Page was quoted with approval by this court in Will of Friend (1951), 259 Wis. 501, 510, 49 N.W.2d 423, 33 A.L.R.2d 234. Since the instant will has been previously construed as permitting new born grandnieces and grandnephews to enter the class, the composition of the class has not yet been finally determined and will not be determined until the possibility of new arrivals in the class is extinguished, or until the youngest member of the class reaches age fifty, whichever event occurs first. Therefore, because membership in the class is still open, the above quoted rule is fully operative.

Furthermore, this construction requiring survival is supported by the following statement from II Simes & Smith, The Law of Future Interests (2d ed.), p. 120, sec. 656:

> "* * * as a fact and not as a rule of law, the existence of a class which may increase or decrease may well have a tendency, when coupled with other facts, to show that a testator intended to imply a condition precedent that the members of the class survive the period of distribution."

Thus far we have considered two rules of construction which favor the county court's determination that survivorship until the date of distribution is required. Appellant relies upon two rules of construction which favor the opposite result. The first of these is that where a gift of income accompanies a gift of corpus the law favors a construction that the gift of corpus is a vested interest. The second is that the law favors a construction which results in an absolutely vested interest rather than a defeasibly vested one.

In support of the first of these rules, appellant cites Restatement, 3 Property, p. 1297, sec. 258, which states:

> "In a limitation which does not purport to create a prior interest but purports to create a springing executory interest in a person 'at 21,' or 'when 21,' or 'if he attains 21,' or by other language similarly connoting the condition precedent of survival to a stipulated future date, the inclusion of a gift of the income produced by the thing up to such future date, *tends to establish* that such interest, after such income payments are to begin, is free from the condition precedent of survival." (Emphasis supplied.)

We deem the phrase "tends to establish" to be significant. This intimates that the rule may not be conclusive in all cases.

The reason for this rule is set forth in comment *a* to this section of the Restatement, as follows (p. 1299):

> "When an interest postponed as to possession or control is coupled with a gift of the economic benefits produced meanwhile by the thing, the conveyor thereby indicates an intent to have the postponement operate solely as a protection of the taker against his possible intermediate unwisdom, rather than as a condition precedent of his interest."

However, in the present case the postponement of possession and control was deliberately made to continue until the youngest of the grandnieces and grandnephews reached the age of fifty. At the time the will was made, the youngest was seven years old and the oldest was eighteen. The testatrix was not guarding against immaturity or unwisdom of these grandnieces and grandnephews. Rather, the inference is fairly strong that she desired a long-term trust extending over a great many years during which time her estate was to be kept intact. To attribute to her, because she directed annual disposition of the trust income, an intent that each grandniece and grandnephew should have a vested interest in the corpus by reason solely of the gift of income, is to apply a purely artificial rule to a situation in which it has no rational application.

Moreover, appellant has cited no Wisconsin cases holding that the gift of the income, during the period of the trust, to the same class that is designated to take the corpus at the close of the trust, creates any vested interest in any member of the class prior to the time that the composition of the class has become fixed. The only Wisconsin cases cited involve either a gift to a class whose composition is already completely fixed and closed (Patton v. Ludington (1899), 103 Wis. 629, 279 N.W. 1073; Will of Prasser (1909), 140 Wis. 92, 121 N. W. 643; Will of Fouks (1931), 206 Wis. 69, 238 N.W. 869), or a determination by the court as to what the vesting situation will be *after* the class becomes completely fixed and closed (Benner v. Mauer (1907), 133 Wis. 325, 113 N.W. 663).

We turn now to the second rule of construction relied upon by appellant, viz., the law favors an absolutely vested interest, rather than a defeasibly vested one. Will of Colman (1948), 253 Wis. 91,

100, 33 N.W.2d 237. The effect of the construction determined by the county court is to make the beneficial interest of the grandnephews and grandnieces in the corpus of the trust a defeasibly vested interest. This is because, although the beneficial interest in the corpus is vested in the class, death of a member of the class prior to the date of distribution causes a defeasance.

The preference for absolute vesting originated in connection with conveyances of interests in land, and at the time in feudal England when contingent interests in land had not attained a dignified stature. 5 American Law of Property, p. 130, sec. 21.3. It was based upon the desirability of a definitely ascertained placement of an interest as opposed to a suspension thereof pending some contingency. This rationale is still appropriate to support a preference for a vested, rather than a contingent, interest. However, because of the wide use of the trust device, this rationale does not lend any support to the preference for absolute rather than defeasible vesting. Therefore, it is doubtful if this rule should continue to have vitality when applied to beneficial interests in a trust where title is at all times vested in the trustee. This is in accord with the view expressed in the above-cited text that adherence to this preference in modern times "is at least of doubtful validity in many situations." Furthermore, this court has previously stated that the rule of construction in favor of an absolute vested interest is not to be resorted to where a contrary intent of a testator may be gathered from the language employed in a will. Will of Latimer, supra, 266 Wis. at page 172, 63 N.W.2d 65; Will of Friend, supra, 259 Wis. at page 510, 49 N.W.2d 423.

In light of the rules of construction and the language of the instant will the problem of the proper construction is a difficult one. However, after a careful weighing of the various conflicting rules of construction, and considering the particular language used by testatrix in light of the long period of postponement of the date of distribution, we determine that it was testatrix' intent that survival of a member of the class to the date of distribution is a requisite condition to sharing in such distribution.

This conclusion is also applicable to the entitlement to distributions of trust income. The will provision that the interest was to be divided among "them" every year—"them" referring to the grandnephews and grandnieces—necessitates the construction that testatrix intended the gift of income also to be subject to defeasance by not surviving until the respective dates of distribution.

Judgment affirmed.

NOTE

Most authorities take the position that the rule favoring early vesting applies to class gifts as well as to individual gifts.[95] However, some commentators are beginning to question seriously the preference for early vesting.[96] The court in the principal case suggests several reasons for this departure

95. See Simes and Smith, Future Interests (2d Ed., 1956) § 656.

96. Rabin, "The Law Favors Vesting of Estates. Why?", 65 Col.L.Rev. 467

from the settled rule, especially where there is a terminal distribution of principal under a trust.

Is a gift impliedly contingent on survivorship if it is in the form of a direction to a trustee to pay over to members of a class or to be distributed among them? Most courts reject the contingent preference, which is commonly called the "divide and pay over" rule. Matter of Crane, 164 N.Y. 71, 58 N.E. 47 (1900), is frequently cited as a leading case announcing the rule. There the Court of Appeals said: "Where the only words of gift are found in the direction to divide or pay over at a future time the gift is future, not immediate; contingent and not vested." The courts almost always state as an exception to the rule that the rule does not apply if the distribution is postponed for the purpose of letting in an intermediate estate. Since a limitation to A for life and at his death to divide the property among his children would fall within the exception, the exception is as broad as the rule itself. It has been suggested that the results in the cases would be the same without regard to the rule. The American Law Institute in the Restatement of Property [97] denies that the rule is a material factor in determining a requirement of survival to date of distribution, and the text writers have criticized the rule.[98]

Suppose in the principal case the will had read: "Upon the termination of the trust the property to be divided among my grandnephews and grandnieces and the issue of any deceased grandnephew or grandniece by right of representation." On a similar limitation, the Supreme Judicial Court of Massachusetts in Old Colony Trust Co. v. Clemons [99] adopted the early vesting rule and held that a member of the class who died after the testator but before the life tenant had a vested, hence transmissible interest; actually in that case the limitation appeared in a trust indenture setting up a revocable living trust, and the Court adopted the date of death of the settlor as the crucial date for vesting on the grounds that such a trust was analogous to a will. In view of the express substitutional gift to issue, would you prefer the rule of the Massachusetts court or that in the principal case?

C. SPECIAL PROBLEMS

ESTATE OF COE

Supreme Court of New Jersey, 1964.
42 N.J. 485, 201 A.2d 571.[1]

WEINTRAUB, C. J. The testatrix executed her will in 1897 and died in that year. In the will she provided for Theodora Margery Coe, "who has been living with me nearly all her life and has been main-

(1965); But see Trautman, "Class Gifts of Future Interests: When is Survival Required", 20 Vand.L.Rev. 1 (1966) (Emphasizing importance of searching for transferor's intent and deemphasizing rule of presumptions).

97. Restatement, Property (1940) § 260.

98. 2 Powell, The Law of Real Property (Rohan Rev.1977) § 333; Simes and Smith, Future Interests (2d Ed., 1956) §§ 657, 658; Note, 16 A.L.R.2d 1383 (1951).

99. 332 Mass. 535, 126 N.E.2d 193 (1955); compare DeFord v. Coleman, 348 Mass. 299, 203 N.E.2d 686 (1965).

1. Noted, 10 Vill.L.Rev. 192 (1965).

tained and educated by me and has become as a daughter to me, for whom I feel the affection of a mother to a daugher." Theodora was an infant when she came to the decedent and was ten years old at decedent's death. Decedent never formally adopted Theodora. Theodora married, had no natural children, but did adopt two daughters. The question is whether they take a bequest to "lawful children" of Theodora. The trial court held the adopted daughters of Theodora were not her "lawful children" upon the authority of In re Wehrhane, 23 N.J. 205, 128 A.2d 681 (1957). In re Estate of Coe, 77 N.J.Super. 181, 185 A.2d 696 (Ch.Div.1962). We certified their appeal before the Appellate Division acted upon it.

Our first adoption law was enacted in 1877 (c. 83). Its pertinent provisions appeared in R.S. 9:3–9 (since superseded by N.J.S.A. 9:3–30, enacted in 1953, c. 264, § 14), in these terms:

> "Upon the entry of a decree of adoption, * * * the child shall be invested with every legal right, privilege, obligation and relation in respect to education, maintenance and the rights of inheritance to real estate, or the distribution of personal estate, on the death of such adopting parent or parents, as if born to them in lawful wedlock; subject, however, to the limitations and restrictions hereinafter in this section set forth.
>
> The adopted child shall not be capable of taking property expressly limited to the heirs of the body of the adopting parent or parents, nor property coming from the collateral kindred of such adopting parent or parents by right of representation.
>
> * * *
>
> If the adopting parent or parents shall have other child or children, the children by birth and by adoption shall, respectively, inherit from and through each other, as if all had been children of the same parents born in lawful wedlock."

In Wehrhane the testatrix provided for a gift over upon her daughter's death "to the issue of my * * * daughter per stirpes." A bare majority of the court held that the adopted son of the daughter could not take. One member concurred on other grounds, and another dissented. The majority said in part (23 N.J., at p. 208, 128 A.2d at p. 682):

> "All parties are in accord respecting the decisional law of our State that a provision for a 'child,' 'children' or 'issue' of another is presumed not to include an adopted child or children. See, e.g., In re Fisler, 131 N.J.Eq. 310, 25 A.2d 265 (Prerog. 1942), affirmed 133 N.J.Eq. 421, 30 A.2d 894 (E. & A. 1943); Fidelity Union Trust Co. v. Potter, 8 N.J.Super. 533, 73 A.2d 625 (Ch.Div.1950). The rule has general acceptance. 5 American Law of Property (1952), secs. 22.34, 22.36. The same authorities invariably recognize that the presumption may be sufficiently contradicted in the total context of the instrument or the circumstances surrounding and existent at its execution or the death of the testator."

The reference to "child" and "children" was dictum since the will spoke of "issue * * * per stirpes," but nonetheless as a trial court the court below in the present case quite properly felt it should abide by the quoted statement.

I.

The pertinent decisions in this State are reviewed at length in the majority and dissenting opinions in Wehrhane and we see no benefit in repeating the discussions in detail. It will suffice to speak in terms of the broad concepts involved.

The majority opinion viewed the quoted provision of the adoption law to establish a rule of inheritance as between the adopting parent and the adopted child, and not "a rule of testamentary construction" (23 N.J., at p. 209, 128 A.2d 681). It held the statute cannot control and indeed is not relevant in the interpretation of a will except, we assume, where the testator is the adopting parent, in which event words such as "issue" would be found to include the adopted child in light of the relationship created by the adoption act. But as to instruments executed by "strangers to the adoption," meaning anyone other than the adopting parent, the majority held such words mean only descendants of the blood unless it appears from the instrument or attendant circumstances that adopted children were intended to be included.

As the majority opinion in Wehrhane points out, its result prevails in a majority of the states. Litigation has been prolific, see Annotations, 86 A.L.R.2d 12 (1962) and 86 A.L.R.2d 115 (1962) and perhaps the very volume suggests the prevailing rule runs so against the common grain that adopted children will not abide by it until a court holds there is no escape. Indeed our Legislature was moved to reverse that rule of construction as to instruments executed after January 1, 1954 by c. 264, L.1953, to which we will later refer, and the legislature of Rhode Island did so too. Prince v. Nugent, R. I., 172 A.2d 743, 750 (Sup.Ct.1961).

We are unable to accept Wehrhane's view of the adoption statute of 1877. We think the statute goes beyond merely prescribing a right of inheritance between the adopting parent and the adopted child. It expressly provides for cross-inheritance between natural and adopted children of the adopting parent. Further, the second paragraph of the statute, quoted above, by providing that an adopted child may not take by representation property coming from collateral kindred of the adopting parent, inferentially contemplates the child may so take from lineal kin. And the provision in the same paragraph of the statute that the adopted child shall not be capable of taking property "expressly limited to the heirs of the body of the adopting parent" plainly relates to the interpretation of some instrument and nothing in the statute limits it to the will or deed of the adopting parents.

At any rate, it is not important whether the adoption statute directly controls the interpretation of instruments. The important point is that the statute reflects the feeling and attitude of the average man and hence its policy should be followed unless the benefactor explicitly reveals a contrary purpose. In this regard Wehrhane observed (23 N.J. at p. 210, 128 A.2d 681) that society's view of an adopted child has changed since 1877 when the adoption law was enacted. We must disagree. Adoption "was known to the ancients of Greece and Rome, and probably to other ancient peoples, and has been practiced among many of the continental nations under the civil law from the remotest antiquity." 2 Am.Jur.2d, Adoption § 2, p. 861; In re Holibaugh, 18 N.J. 229, 233, 113 A.2d 654, 52 A.L.R.2d 1222 (1955). True there was no legally recognized right to adopt at common law and hence the right as such depends upon statute as the authorities just cited point out, but our statute did not generate that familial or social phenomenon. Rather our statute belatedly recognized relationships which men have always assumed, and translated into a rule of law what the Legislature found to be their common expectation and wish.

Hence even if the quoted provisions of the adoption statute were thought to speak only of intestacy, they should nonetheless be accepted as a reflection of a common expectation and wish and hence as a guide to proper interpretation of a gift:

> "Where the construction of a gift is doubtful after all extrinsic assistance is afforded, the leaning of the court should be to that course of disposition for which public policy pronounces in the statutes of descent and distribution; and this maxim may serve for particular words and phrases of uncertain tenor." 2 Schouler, Wills, Executors and Administrators (6th ed. 1923), § 959, p. 1111.

As Judge Fuld said in In re Upjohn's Will, 304 N.Y. 366, 107 N.E.2d 492, 495 (Ct.App.1952): "Wills, too, must be read and construed in harmony with the legislative policy of placing adopted children on a level with natural born offspring." The same thought had been expressed in Haver v. Herder, 96 N.J.Eq. 554, 558–559, 126 A. 661 (Ch. 1924). To the same effect are Estate of Heard, 49 Cal.2d 514, 319 P. 2d 637, 640 (Sup.Ct.1957), and Ansonia National Bank v. Kunkel, 105 Conn. 744, 136 A. 588, 591 (Sup.Ct.Err.1927).

The trouble in our State began in 1925 with Ahlemeyer v. Miller, 102 N.J.L. 54, 131 A. 54 (Sup.Ct.1925), affirmed 103 N.J.L. 617, 137 A. 543 (E. & A. 1927), which introduced the stranger-to-the-adoption concept, an unwarranted assumption that when one who is not a party to the adoption makes a gift to a class consisting of children of the adopting parent, he probably intends to benefit only natural children.

* * *

We cannot believe it probable that strangers to the adoption would differentiate between the natural child and the adopted child of another. Rather we believe it more likely that they accept the relationships established by the parent whether the bond be natural or by adoption and seek to advance those relationships precisely as that parent would. None of us discriminates among children of a relative or friend upon a biological basis. See In re Patrick's Will, 259 Minn.

193, 106 N.W.2d 888, 890 (Sup.Ct.1960); In re Trusteeship Agreement with Nash, 265 Minn. 412, 122 N.W.2d 104, 109 (Sup.Ct.1963). We ought not impute to others instincts contrary to our own. Nor should we think we are different from our ancestors of 1877. As we have said, the adoption act of that year did not amend human nature; it yielded to it.

Finally, it is suggested that to depart from the stranger-to-the-adoption view would invite fraud by permitting a person to adopt someone solely to enable him to take under the will of another. In this connection we are referred to a New York statute (Domestic Relations Law, § 115, McK.Consol.Laws, c. 14) which provides that an adopted child shall not be deemed the child of the adopting parent so as to defeat a gift over upon the death of the adopting parent without heirs. It seems to us that the prospect of fraud is quite remote and can be dealt with upon equitable principles if the circumstances are truly compelling. Obviously this prospect did not disturb our Legislature when it adopted L.1953, c. 264, discussed later in this opinion, whereby it rejected the canon of testamentary construction Fisler had applied and provided without exception that in the construction of any document thereafter executed an adopted child shall be deemed lawful issue unless the document shall otherwise provide.

For these reasons we will not assume Mrs. Coe intended to deny her beneficence to a child her foster daughter might one day embrace and adopt as her own. If that intent affirmatively appeared, we of course would enforce her wish. But no such purpose can here be found and hence we are satisfied that the adopted daughters of Theodora are "children" within the meaning of the will.

II.

As already noted, Wehrhane involved "issue per stirpes" and not "children." We have disapproved Wehrhane's dictum that "children" presumptively means only natural children in the will of one other than an adopting parent. Our basic approach of course implicates the soundness of Wehrhane with respect to "issue" or "issue per stirpes" and the question is whether we should decide now whether Wehrhane can stand even as to its actual holding.

Some authorities do suggest that "issue," unlike "children," has a biological connotation. The Vice Chancellor in Herder, supra, 96 N.J. Eq., at pp. 558–559, 126 A. 661, posed the question and left it unanswered. In McEwan, supra, 128 N.J.Eq., at p. 145, 15 A.2d 340, the Vice Ordinary thought issue would include adopted children. In Fisler, as we have already said, the Court of Errors and Appeals held that issue meant "heirs of the body," and while Wehrhane rejected that view of the statutory phrase, it nonetheless found that issue inherently signified the blood line, saying (23 N.J., at pp. 208–209, 128 A.2d, at p. 682):

> "* * * The term in its normal usage connotes progeny to the remotest degree, Stickel v. Douglass, 7 N.J. 274, 277, 81 A.2d 362 (1951), or descendants, In re Fisler, supra, 133 N.J.Eq., at

page 423, 25 A.2d at page 895, and because it is not confined in this sense to one generation it emphasizes the thought of kinship or blood relationship."

Thus, although Wehrhane opened with a statement in which children and issue were treated as equivalents, yet at the point of actual decision, it stated a rationale upon which the words could be readily distinguished. Elsewhere, too, there is some authority which would differentiate children from issue on the basis of the peculiar "biological flavor" of issue. See 3 Powell, Real Property § 360, p. 132 (1952); Oler, "Construction of Private Instruments Where Adopted Children Are Concerned," 43 Mich.L.Rev. 705, 727 (1945).

And it may be noteworthy that when our Legislature undertook to correct "these unfortunate rules of construction," 5 N.J.Practice (Clapp, Wills and Administration) (3d ed. 1962) § 213, p. 358, it spoke only of issue, perhaps thereby suggesting that that word (and that word alone) had acquired a signification in our cases disqualifying an adopted child. We refer to the statute already mentioned. L.1953, c. 264, § 14 (N.J.S.A. 9:3–30), effective January 1, 1954, which reads:

> "* * * In the construction of any testamentary or other document executed subsequent to the effective date of this act, an adopted child shall be deemed lawful issue of the adopting parent unless such document shall otherwise provide."

Frankly we would not, as an original matter, distinguish among issue, descendants, children, and heirs, since ordinarily the word is not selected by the testator but rather by the scrivener, who, if he were conscious of the question whether adopted children should be in or out, would elicit the testator's wish and express it unequivocally. The cases at most attributed but *prima facie* meaning to such words, and a competent draftsman would not deliberately pick a word which instead of controlling the context is easily colored by it. The caveat against that course has been unmistakable. Annotation, 86 A.L.R.2d 12, 19 (1962).

But the immediate question is whether an equity might be shown in some circumstances with respect to the word "issue" in light of our prior cases and perhaps also in light of the fact that L.1953, c. 264 which we just quoted overturned the judicial view of issue prospectively only. As to the effect of prospective legislation upon the judiciary's responsibility for pre-existing situations, see In re Arens, 41 N.J. 364, 384–387, 197 A.2d 1 (1964). We think the sound course is to leave the question open so that the possible equities may be weighed in a specific setting.

In summary, then, we will not extend Wehrhane and if that case is to be followed at all, it will be confined to its precise holding.

The judgment is therefore reversed and the matter remanded for proceedings not inconsistent herewith.

JACOBS, J., concurring in result.

For reversal: CHIEF JUSTICE WEINTRAUB and JUSTICES JACOBS, FRANCIS, PROCTOR, SCHETTINO and HANEMAN.

For affirmance: JUSTICE HALL.

HALL, J. (dissenting). It seems to me that, in resolving the kind of will construction problem presented in this case where there is nothing in the language of the instrument or in competent evidence to demonstrate a contrary intent of the testator, a court must be governed by the law at the time of execution. 5 N.J.Practice (Clapp, Wills and Administration) (3d ed. 1962) § 193, p. 287. In other words, since we cannot know whether the particular question was ever discussed between testator and scrivener and therefore actual intent can never be disclosed, the only proper and safe thing to do is to assume conclusively that the testator intended the scrivener's language to be construed in accordance with the law at that time. Conversely, we also must presume that the scrivener knew what that law was and that the language he used was deliberately chosen to express it. He cannot be criticized or his intent questioned where he used terminology entirely proper and consistent with the law of his time, even though we today might feel it desirable to be more explicit.

At the time this will was drawn, the common law was well settled generally, and well understood to be such by New Jersey lawyers, that an adopted child could not take as a "child" under the will of a stranger to the adoption. I am equally confident that such understanding has in fact continued without doubt until this very moment. See concurring opinion of Justice Jacobs and authorities there cited in In re Wehrhane, 23 N.J. 205, 211, 128 A.2d 681 (1957), taking the same point of view with respect to the testamentary language there present which I am now espousing as to slightly different words. I think it also clear that the majority's view of the meaning and effect of our 1877 adoption statute was not that of lawyers in 1897 or indeed that of our courts until now. It seems improper to say at this late date, as the majority opinion in effect actually does, that the common law of New Jersey was wrong for sociological or any other reasons where the result is to change substantially and retroactively those who are to take under a probated will, no matter how we in 1964 may feel about its legal correctness or overall desirability. Apparently the Legislature was proceeding along this line of thought when it adopted L.1953, c. 264 (N.J.S.A. 9:3–30), effective January 1, 1954 as to future executed wills only. This is not the situation of a modification of a mere rule of estate administration like that which was held in In re Arens, 41 N.J. 364, 386–387, 197 A.2d 1 (1964), to be capable of retroactive change.

I would affirm the judgment of the Chancery Division.

NOTE

As the court in the principal case states, the problem whether a class gift to "children", "issue", "descendants" or the like includes an adopted person is currently much litigated.[2] Clearly the trend is to include the adopted person,[3] although the older cases presumed that the testator did not intend to include any except blood relations within the class. The modern presumption is based partly on the adoption statutes which are generally given a liberal construction. A few states have enacted legislation that such class gifts are presumed to include adopted persons unless the will expresses a contrary intent.[4] This is done in Uniform Probate Code, § 2–611 which adopts a rule of construction favoring inclusion of the half blood, adopted children and children born out of wedlock in class gift terminology. The person born out of wedlock is not treated as the child of the father unless the person is openly and notoriously so treated by the father. This section of the Uniform Probate Code, however, is limited to the construction of wills and would not be applicable to the construction of class gifts in inter vivos transactions—although the court might use the statute by analogy. There are state statutes which extend the preference to all types of instruments.[5]

To be effective such legislation should be applicable to existing instruments, just as was the court-made rule in the principal case;[6] however, courts may construe the statute to be prospective only in order to avoid what some feel to be unconstitutional retroactivity.[7]

If the children are adopted at the time the will is executed, it is easier to find that the testator intended to include them.[8] The more difficult problem arises where the adoption takes place after the execution of the will or even after the death of the testator.[9] In some jurisdictions statutes permit adop-

2. See Halbach, "The Rights of Adopted Children Under Class Gifts", 50 Iowa L.Rev. 971 (1965); Fetters, "The Determination of Maximum Membership in Class Gifts in Relation to Adopted Children: In re Silberman's Will Examined", 21 Syracuse L.Rev. 1 (1969); Comments, "The Dilemma of Adoptees in the Class Gift Structure—The Kentucky Approach: A Rule Without Reason", 59 Ken.L.J. 921 (1971); "Eligibility of Adopted Children to Take by Intestate Descent and Under Class Gifts in Missouri", 34 Mo.L.Rev. 68 (1969).

3. Most recent cases include adopted persons within class gifts in both wills and inter vivos trusts. McCaleb v. Brown, 344 So.2d 485 (Ala.1977) ("descendants"); Zimmerman v. First National Bank of Birmingham, 348 So.2d 1359 (Ala.1977) ("children"); Chichester v. Wilmington Trust Co., 377 A.2d 11 (Del. 1977) ("issue"); Warner v. First National Bank, 242 Ga. 661, 251 S.E.2d 511 (1978) ("descendants"); Elliott v. Hiddleson, 303 N.W.2d 140 (Iowa 1981) ("lineal heirs"); In re Trusts of Harrington, 311 Minn. 403, 250 N.W.2d 163 (1977) ("issue of the body"); Estate of Sykes, 477 Pa. 254, 383 A.2d 920 (1978) ("issue" under gift in default even though power was to appoint to "blood relatives"); Wheeling Dollar Savings & Trust Co. v. Hanes, ___ W.Va. ___, 237 S.E.2d 499 (1977) ("children"). In many of these cases, the court had to overrule contrary precedent.

4. E.g., Smith-Hurd Ill.Ann.Stat. ch. 110½, ¶ 2–4; McKinney's N.Y., EPTL, § 2–1.3.

5. See Wis.Stat.Ann. § 851.51(3) (Limited to adopted children).

6. Prof. Halbach argues persuasively that the "reliance interest" has been over-emphasized in perpetuating rules of construction. See the article cited above in footnote 2 and his article on "Stare Decisis and Rules of Construction in Wills and Trusts", 52 Cal.L.Rev. 921 (1964).

7. Wachovia Bank & Trust Co. v. Andrews, 264 N.C. 531, 142 S.E.2d 182 (1965).

8. Estate of Breeze, 7 Wis.2d 422, 96 N.W.2d 712 (1959).

9. In Estate of Tafel, 449 Pa. 442, 296 A.2d 797 (1972), noted 77 Dick.L.Rev. 415 (1973), the Pennsylvania Supreme Court permitted children adopted after the death of the testator to take within a class of "issue" of his son. The Court stated in dictum that the presumption including adopted children who were adopted after the death of the testator did not

tion of adults; should the class gift include persons adopted as adults?[10] Can a person be deliberately adopted for the sole purpose of qualifying as a member of the class? In one case a man was permitted to adopt his wife in order that she might share in a trust fund created by his mother's will.[11]

Although the trend is to include an adopted child of another person within the description "children", there is no equally well defined trend to include illegitimates within the description even when the testator refers to his own children.[12] However, in a 1976 landmark case the New York Supreme Court, Appellate Division, overruled longstanding precedent to hold that an illegitimate child was within the meaning of the word "issue" in a testamentary gift. Will of Hoffman, 53 A.D.2d 55, 385 N.Y.S.2d 49 (1976).[13] The Court reasoned that such a construction was more in accord with modern social mores and legislative trends and that the old rule restricting the meaning to legitimate children involved discrimination which might well violate the equal protection requirements of the Constitution.[14] In many wills the testator's intent to include illegitimate children within a class of his own children may be found expressly or impliedly stated.[15] An illegitimate child inherits from the mother and there is usually no problem of identification of the parent. Consequently a reference to the children of a female might reasonably include her illegitimate children.[16] If an illegitimate child lives as a member of a family, the word "children" may be construed as embracing children as

include adults at the time of adoption. At 296 A.2d 803 the Court states the reason: "* * * By the restriction of this rule of construction to minor adoptions we serve and effectuate the purpose of preventing an adult adoptee or adoptees from being considered a testamentary 'child' or 'children' where such adoption is undertaken by a person other than the testator to prevent a gift over in default of a natural 'child' or 'children' and thus, in effect, rewrite the testator's will. * * *" The rule announced in *Tafel*, including a qualification for adoption of adults, was embodied in a 1976 amendment to the Pennsylvania statute. 20 Purdon's Penn.Stat.Ann. § 2514(7) (1981 Supp.).

10. In Estate of Stanford, 49 Cal.2d 120, 315 P.2d 681 (1957), an adopted person was included within the term "children" of a named beneficiary, even though adopted as an adult in another state although such an adoption would not have been possible under the law of California by which the will was construed. See 31 S.Cal.L.Rev. 441 (1958). In Matter of Estate of Fortney, 5 Kan. App.2d 14, 611 P.2d 599 (1980), devisee under a will, at age 90, adopted his wife's 65 year-old nephew, who was held entitled to take under a provision giving the property to the devisee's children ("by birth or by adoption") even though adoption of an adult was not possible when the will took effect the statute being amended later to permit such adoption. Wis.Stat.Ann. § 851.51(3) includes adopted persons in class gifts but requires that the person, if adopted as an adult, have been raised as a member of the household by the adoptive parent from the age of 15 or before.

11. Bedinger v. Graybill's Executor, 302 S.W.2d 594 (Ky.1957) (will left property to son for life, then to his "heirs at law"; wife was adopted in order to make her an "heir").

12. See Simes and Smith, Future Interests (2d Ed., 1956) § 724. Under the Family Law Reform Act, 17 & 18 Eliz. II, c. 46(15) a reference to a child or children in a deed or will is presumed to include an illegitimate child. A contrary expression of intention by the transferor controls.

13. Noted 5 Hofstra L.Rev. 697 (1977).

14. Compare Lalli v. Lalli, discussed in Chapter III Section 2. *Hoffman* involved a gift to issue of a male cousin; there had never been an order of filiation, but the Surrogate determined that the claimants were in fact children of the cousin. Note that under New York law at that time the children could not have inherited directly from their own father; the United States Supreme Court in *Lalli* sustained that discrimination.

15. E.g., Gardner v. Heyer, 2 Paige (N.Y.) 11 (1829) (Bequest to "each of my daughters". Testator had only two children, both daughters and both illegitimate.)

16. E.g., Eaton v. Eaton, 88 Conn. 269, 91 A. 191 (1914).

"family members" whether illegitimate or not.[17] If the testator intends to include or exclude illegitimate children of his own or of another, this intent should be stated in the will.

IN RE PARANT'S WILL

New York Surrogate's Court, 1963.
39 Misc.2d 285, 240 N.Y.S.2d 558.[18]

ROBERT W. BASCOM, SURROGATE. Clause Fifth of the will of Helen C. Parant, which was executed August 17, 1960 and admitted to probate May 29, 1962, reads as follows:

> "I give, devise and bequeath all of my real property located on the Vaughn Corners Road in the Town of Kingsbury, New York and the contents of the house and barn, excepting the above bequeathed articles mentioned in the Fourth clause of this will, to my niece MARY ESTHER CRONKHITE WOODWARD and to her children."

Both on the date of the execution of the will and on the date of death of the testatrix, Mrs. Woodward had two living children.

A determination is sought as to whether the quoted clause vested a fee simple absolute in the named legatee or whether any interest was vested in her children, and if so, the nature of the respective estates and the respective proportions in which Mrs. Woodward and her children share. There appears to be a paucity of law on the subject in this jurisdiction and the precise question, as far as the interpretation of a devise and bequest to a named person and her children is concerned, seems not to have been entertained by the courts of this state for a hundred twenty years.

Three possible interpretations of this particular language are suggested, namely (a) that Mary Esther Cronkhite Woodward takes a fee simple absolute to the exclusion of her children, either on the theory that the words "and to her children" are words of limitation, or that the word "or" was intended for the word "and" and that the gift to the children was substitutional; (b) that Mrs. Woodward takes a life estate with remainder on her death to her children, as similar devises or grants have been interpreted in other jurisdictions, notably Pennsylvania; and (c) that Mrs. Woodward and her two children are tenants in common, each having an undivided one-third interest in the property.

We must collect the intent of the testatrix from within the four corners of the will, if the document as a whole reveals this intent. We must not confuse intention with meaning (Sams v. Garlick, 14 M.

17. In re Trust of Parsons, 56 Wis.2d 613, 203 N.W.2d 40 (1973); Noted, 57 Marq.L.Rev. 173 (1973).

18. Noted, 15 Syracuse L.Rev. 95 (1963); see Pasley, "Future Interests", 15 Syra.L.Rev. 306, 308–309 (1963) where *Parant* is discussed.

& W. 698, 701). Although perhaps susceptible of differing interpretations, the words under consideration are not ambiguous in and of themselves. If they have or have acquired a technical meaning in the field of devises, grants or bequests we must apply that meaning unless we discern a different design of the testatrix from the whole document.

In support of her contention that she takes an absolute fee to the exclusion of her children, petitioner contends that the word "and" was intended to be "or" and was inadvertently used by the draftsman, with the result that the gift to the children was meant to be substitutional in the event of Mrs. Woodward's predeceasing testatrix. To bolster her contention of inadvertence, she points to the residuary clause which follows the one in question, where the residue is given to Mrs. Woodward and to two other named persons, in equal shares, and provides that in the event of Mrs. Woodward's prior death, her share is given and bequeathed to her children in equal shares; that having demonstrated her ability to create a substitutional gift of the residue, it is improbable the testatrix intended other than that in devising real estate in such a manner that it would be held by an unknown number of infant co-owners, thereby rendering the title inalienable except by order of court. The argument, though plausible, is not elevated to the plane of conviction. To conclude that simply because testatrix made a substitutional or alternative gift in the residuary clause, she must have intended a like gift in another clause, is purely speculative and capricious. When a testator in one part of his will demonstrates his ability to make a certain variety of gift by apt terms, the use of a different mode of expression in another direction raises the inference that he had a diverse disposition in mind (Matter of Corlie's Will, 150 Misc. 596, 599, 269 N.Y.S. 890, 894).

There being nothing else in the will from which to glean an indication of testatrix' intent, and the will having been prepared by an experienced draftsman, we must take the words "and to her children" as we find them and give to them "their usual and accepted meanings without enlargement and without restriction * * * and when particular or technical terms are used, particular or technical interpretation or construction follows as of course, in the absence of all clear intent to the contrary" (Matter of Barrett's Estate, 141 Misc. 637, 638–639, 253 N.Y.S. 658, 660, 661; Graves v. Deterling, 120 N.Y. 447, 457, 24 N.E. 655, 657).

In its usual and commonly accepted meaning "and" is a connective, while "or" is a disjunctive. "And" is not correctly or generally used to express an alternative, unless followed by words which clearly indicate that intent. "Or" is correctly and generally used for that purpose (Matter of Barrett's Estate, supra, 141 Misc. p. 640, 253 N.Y. S. p. 663). As the court said in the last cited case (p. 641): "It seems to me that it must be assumed that an experienced lawyer would have used the word 'or' rather than the word 'and' to express a gift intended to be in the alternative, and that, having made use of the word 'and,' he would have added thereto words clearly indicating that it was intended to be used in the alternative sense if that was the testator's intention. There were no such words added here." We must therefore reject the theory that an alternative or substitutional gift to the children was intended.

The word "children" in its primary and natural sense is always a word of purchase and not of limitation * * *. As used in a will, "children" is a word of personal description. It points to individual acquisition. It is limited to persons standing in the same relations and has the same effect as if all the names had been given (Rowley v. Currie, 94 N.J.Eq. 606, 120 A. 653; Balcom v. Haynes, 96 Mass. (14 Allen) 294). It is not a word of limitation. It does not point to hereditable succession. It is employed in contradistinction to the term "issue" (Crawford v. Forest Oil Co., 3 Cir., 77 F. 534, aff'd. 77 F. 106). As was said by the Court of Appeals in Chrystie v. Phyfe (p. 354): "There is one class of cases, and one only, in which the term 'children' is considered as a word of limitation; that is, where there is a present devise to one and his children, when he has no children at the time. There if the word 'children' should be interpreted as words of purchase, future children could not take at all, and in order that the will of the testator may operate favorably to them and not confine the gift to the parent for life, 'children' is then deemed a word of limitation."

We conclude, therefore, that Mrs. Woodward and her children living at the death of testatrix (Campbell v. Rawdon, 18 N.Y. 412) all took some interest in the real and personal property devised and bequeathed by the clause of the will in question. It remains to determine their respective interests.

* * *

Wild's Case, decided in 1599, expresses the common-law on the subject and from it evolved the so-called Rule in Wild's Case. This was in the form of two "resolutions", both of which were dicta. Under the first, if A devises his lands to B and to his (B's) children or issues, and he (B) has not any issue at the time of the devise the same is an estate-tail. (This of course would be a fee simple absolute today). Under the second "resolution", with which we are here concerned, if A devises his lands to B and to his children, and B has children at the death of A, the parent and children take equal and concurrent estates. The rule has been subject to some criticism and although generally accepted, has not been uniformly adopted. In Pennsylvania, for example, a life estate is found in the named devisee, with remainder to the children, as witness Crawford v. Forest Oil Co., 77 F. 534, affd. 77 F. 106, supra, where there was a devise to son Matthew and his children. Matthew had six children living when the will was made and seven at testator's death, and the court found that by the use of the term "children" the testator vested an estate in remainder in a specified class of persons and a precedent life estate in Matthew the father. In Hague v. Hague, 161 Pa. 643, 29 A. 261, a grant by deed was to Sarah Hague and her children, and the court said that if they were strangers it would constitute them all tenants in common, but the weight of authority holds the mother to be only a tenant for life. Likewise, in Coursey v. Davis, 46 Pa. 25, the words of a grant were to Mildred Ann Davis and her children exclusively, and their heirs and assigns, and it was held that the words vested in Mildred Ann Davis a life estate with remainder in fee to the children as a class, so that those in being at the date of the deed, as well as those subsequently born, would be entitled to take in the distribution on the termination of the life estate.

In re McCullough's Estate, 272 Pa. 509, 116 A. 477 is in the same vein, but on the other hand, In re McIntosh's Estate, 158 Pa. 528, 527 A. 1044 holds to the contrary, as there a devise to James and his children was held to give the children equal distributive rights with their father.

Kentucky seems to follow the majority of the Pennsylvania cases, as witness Smith v. Smith, 119 Ky. 899, 902, 85 S.W. 169, 170, where there was a devise "to my son and his children" and it was held that the son took a life estate, with remainder to the children. See also Bowe v. Richmond, 33 Ky.L.Rep. 173, 109 S.W. 359. Indiana is in the same category (Edwards v. Bates, 79 Ind.App. 578, 139 N.E. 192, supra.) * * *

Other jurisdictions, however, follow the Rule in Wild's Case. A sampling of such decisions would include In re Utz's Estate, 43 Cal. 200, where a devise to testator's daughter and her children, entitled the children to share in the devise, and it passed to the daughter and her children as tenants in common. Also Jones' Executors v. Jones, 13 N.J.Eq. 236, wherein a devise to a woman and her children, she having children living at the time of the devise, the word "children" was said to be a word of purchase to be taken according to its natural import, and the children took a joint estate with the mother in the land devised. Moore v. Ennis, 10 Del.Ch. 170, 87 A. 1009, where the testator gave two of his sons and their children bequests of money, is to the same effect and it was held that the children took jointly and in equal shares with the parents. In Davis v. Sanders, 123 Ga. 177, 51 S.E. 298, testator directed his property be divided "equally between my wife * * * my daugher-in-law * * * and her children, my daugher * * * and her children * * * now or hereafter born", and it was held that the children took equally with the parents.

North Carolina takes the same position, for there it is held that in a deed to A and his children, if A has children when the deed is executed, he and his children will take as tenants in common (Boyd v. Campbell, 192 N.C. 398, 135 S.E. 121; Cullens v. Cullens, 161 N.C. 344, 77 S.E. 228, 5 L.R.A.1917B, 74).

Thus it appears that Wild's Case is followed more often than rejected and we apprehend it is the law in this state, insofar as the factual situation now before us is concerned.

There is, however, another basis upon which to rest our determination, and that is, absent a showing of a contrary intent, the devise and bequest here involved is a class gift and the named parent is treated as a member of the class composed of herself and her children. If Mrs. Woodward had predeceased testatrix, or if the gift to her had been revoked by codicil, the gift would have gone to those who were members of the class at the time for distribution, namely her children. In the absence of facts showing a different intent of the testatrix, the members of the class receive undivided interests as tenants in common in an estate in fee simple absolute as to the realty, and fractional shares in undivided complete ownership as tenants in common of the personalty (3 Restatement, Property, Ch. 22, § 283). Clause Fifth of Helen C. Parant's will is construed accordingly.

NOTE

Where there is a gift to A and his children, and A has no children at the time the instrument takes effect, the first rule in Wild's Case would result in holding that A takes a fee tail (in many jurisdictions converted by statute into a fee simple today). Some American courts follow this rule.[19] However the Restatement takes the position that in such a case the gift is to be construed as creating a life estate in A with a remainder to his children.[20] This construction comes closer to intent in modern times and is followed in a number of jurisdictions.[21]

If there is a gift to A and his children, and A has children at the time the instrument takes effect, the second rule in Wild's Case results in holding that A and the children take as cotenants. Although at common law they would take as joint tenants, in most jurisdictions today the statutory presumption of a tenancy in common would control. Moreover, because of the modern rules preferring a fee simple construction in the absence of manifestation of a contrary intent, A and his children take a fee simple.

A minority of jurisdictions in this country reject the second resolution in Wild's case and hold that A takes an estate for his life with a remainder to his children.[22]

The second resolution in Wild's case has been applied to deeds as well as to wills, and to personalty as well as to realty.[23] If the gift is by deed, there is more reason for preferring the construction of a life estate in A with remainder to the children since this permits afterborn children to share; and even states favoring the majority rule use this circumstance to find that a life estate in A with remainder to his children was intended.[24]

A somewhat similar problem arises if there is a gift to A and the children of B. For example, In re Moss, [1899] L.R. 2, Ch. 314, involved a gift by will in trust for the testator's wife for life and after her decease upon trust for a niece Elizabeth Jane Fowler "and the child or children of my sister Emily Walter who shall attain the age of twenty-one years equally to be divided

19. Ewing v. Ewing, 198 Miss. 304, 22 So.2d 225, 161 A.L.R. 606 (1945); Larew v. Larew, 146 Va. 134, 135 S.E. 819 (1926).

20. Restatement, Property (1940) § 283, comment *b*.

21. Chambers v. Union Trust Co., 235 Pa. 610, 84 A. 512 (1912); Stahr v. Mozley, 284 Ky. 552, 145 S.W.2d 40 (1940); Note, "Judicial Construction of 'To A and His Children'", 75 West Va.L. Rev. 296 (1973). See Link, "The Rule in Wild's Case in North Carolina," 55 N.C. L.Rev. 751 (1977) (with a proposed statute).

22. Elliott v. Diamond Coal & Coke Co., 230 Pa. 423, 79 A. 708 (1911).

23. For a full discussion of the resolutions in Wild's case see Simes and Smith, The Law of Future Interests (2d Ed., 1956) §§ 691–702; American Law of Property (1952) §§ 22.16–22.25.

24. United States v. 654.8 Acres of Land, 102 F.Supp. 937 (E.D.Tenn.1952), 36 Marq.L.Rev. 191 (1952).

between them as tenants in common". At the time the will was drafted, there were living the niece Elizabeth Jane Fowler (who was then almost 21), the sister Emily Walter, and five children of Emily. Elizabeth Jane predeceased the testator, who was survived by the sister and her five children. Was this an individual gift to Elizabeth Jane Fowler, in which case it would have lapsed on her death, or was she intended to be a member of the same class as the children of Emily? Since Elizabeth was a niece and the children of Emily were also nephews and nieces, it is probable that testator thought of them all as a class; and the Court of Appeal so held. It would also be possible to construe a gift to A and the children of B as creating a gift of one-half to A and one-half to the children of B as a class; or to hold that A and each child of B take individual gifts.[25]

The good draftsman will never draft a document which merely gives property to "A and his children" or to "A and the children of B" or, for that matter, to any individual coupled with a class; he will determine more precisely the intent of his client and spell it out expressly in the document.

IN RE LATIMER'S WILL

Supreme Court of Wisconsin, 1954.
266 Wis. 158, 63 N.W.2d 65.

CURRIE, JUSTICE. The sole question presented upon this appeal is whether the heirs of James F. Latimer (the deceased husband of testatrix), who were to take one-half of the trust residue upon the death of Mary Widney (the life beneficiary), are to be determined as of the date of the death of the testatrix or as of the date of the death of the life beneficiary.

The general rule is that when a will provides for a limitation over to the "heirs" of the testator or of some other person already deceased, to be determined by a statute governing the intestate succession of property, following the expiration of a life estate, the determination of the class of persons who qualify as such heirs is to be made as of the date of the death of the testator *unless an intent of the*

25. The following constructions have been placed on the limitation to "A and the children of B":

(1) A and the children of B take as a single class, A taking the same share as each child of B. Manier v. Phelps, 15 Abb.N.C. 123 (1884). In Matter of Estate of Kalouse, 282 N.W.2d 98 (Iowa 1979), a gift to "my first cousins * * * and to Frank Nespor, in equal shares, share, alike, with the share going to Frank Nespor to be equal to that of my other first cousins" was held to be a gift to a class composed of the surviving cousins and Frank Nespor, the Iowa anti-lapse statute not being applicable to class gifts.

(2) A takes one-half and the children of B one-half, but for purposes of lapse the gift to A is treated as a gift to an individual and the gift to the children of B as a gift to a class. Cf. Estate of Pierce, 177 Wis. 104 188 N.W. 78 (1922). In Bradley v. Estate of Jackson, 1 Kan.App.2d 695, 573 P.2d 628 (1977), a gift of the residue to an unrelated named devisee "and to my lawful heirs" was held to be a gift of half to the named devisee and half to the class of heirs.

(3) A takes one-half and the children of B the other half but for purposes of lapse all gifts are treated as a class gift. Palmer v. Jones, 299 Ill. 263, 132 N.E. 567 (1922). Theoretically another construction is possible. A and the children of B might be held to take as individuals. See Restatement, Property (1940) § 284.

testator to have such determination made as of the death of the life tenant "is found from additional language or circumstances." 3 Restatement, Property, p. 1706, sec. 308.

We, therefore, must turn our inquiry to resolving the issue of whether there is additional language in the will or other circumstances present in the instant case which would establish an intent on the part of the testatrix that the heirs of her deceased husband should be determined as of the death of the granddaughter, Mary Widney. In the absence of any such additional language or circumstances so establishing such an intent, the general rule would apply that such heirship must be determined as of the date of testatrix's own death, which latter result was the one reached by the learned trial court.

Counsel for the appellant rely on several provisions in the will and other circumstances as establishing an intent on the part of testatrix that the persons, who are to take as heirs of her deceased husband, were to be determined as of the death of the life beneficiary. However, we find it necessary to consider only two of such points so advanced, they being:

(1) Mary Widney, the life beneficiary, was the sole heir at law of James F. Latimer, deceased husband of testatrix, as of the date of the death of testatrix; and

(2) The remainders provided for by the testatrix, after the death of the granddaughter, Mary Widney, to the children of Mary Widney, or to the issue of such great-grandchildren, or upon said great-grandchildren failing to reach age twenty-one to their issue, and for the gift over upon failure of issue of Mary Widney to the heirs of testatrix and her deceased husband, are alternative remainders and thus necessarily contingent remainders.

Inasmuch as Mary Widney was the sole heir at law of her grandfather, James F. Latimer, at the time of the death of testatrix, Mary L. Latimer, in 1923, there would be an incongruity if the will were to be construed as requiring the heirs of James F. Latimer to be determined as of the date of the death of testatrix instead of at the date of death of Mary Widney. If such heirship were determined as of date of death of testatrix, the only person who would qualify as being an heir of James F. Latimer under our statutes governing the descent and distribution of intestate property was Mary Widney, the life beneficiary. Respondents contend that such incongruity is avoided if the words of the will "*heirs of said James F. Latimer*" be construed as "*heirs of said James F. Latimer excluding Mary Widney.*" However, to reach such result a reformation of the language of the will is necessary. Furthermore, such construction attempts to make persons heirs at law of James F. Latimer who never were such heirs.

On the other hand, if the will should be construed as requiring the determination of the class of persons, who are to take as heirs at law of James F. Latimer, to be made as of the date of the death of the life beneficiary, there is no incongruity present and therefore no necessity of reforming the language of the will.

This aspect of the case is one of first impression in this court. The courts of other jurisdictions are divided on the question, and from the decisions of these other courts we are provided with ample precedent for deciding the issue either way. However, the Restatement has adopted the rule that an incongruity is present, if the gift over to heirs following a life estate to the sole heir at law is to be construed as requiring the heirship to be determined as of date of death of the testator. 3 Restatement, Property, p. 1715, sec. 308, comment k., states:

> "If a person to whom a prior interest in the subject matter of the conveyance has been given is the sole heir of the designated ancestor at the death of such ancestor, there is some incongruity in also giving such person all the interest under the limitation to 'heirs' or 'next of kin'. The incongruity is especially great when a will conveys property 'to B and his heirs but if B dies without issue to my heirs' and B is the sole heir of A. The incongruity is almost as great when A, by will, conveys property 'to B for life then to my heirs' and B is the sole heir of A. *Thus, the fact that in such cases, B is the sole heir of A at the death of A tends to establish that A intended his heirs to be ascertained as of the death of B,* so that B is prevented from sharing in the limitation to the heirs of A." (Emphasis supplied.)

Professor Lewis M. Simes, author of The Law of Future Interests, and one of the advisors on Property to the American Law Institute, is in agreement with the principle adopted by the Restatement. See 2, Law of Future Interests, p. 234, sec. 422; wherein Simes states:

> "Where the donee of the possessory interest is the sole heir of the testator and there is a future interest to the testator's heirs, the situation is more difficult of solution. Here the heir cannot be excluded if we determine the testator's heirs as of the testator's death, since, if that were done, there would be no one but the sole heir to take the future interest; and, if he is excluded, no one is left. The only way to exclude him is to determine heirship as of a time subsequent to the testator's death and thus include a different group of persons in the class."

We take cognizance of the fact that the framers of the Restatement on Property were specialists in this field of the law and were selected for such task because of their recognized ability as the leading authorities in the nation on this particular subject. Undoubtedly they fully considered the existing conflict in the decisions and framed comment k., sec. 308, 3 Restatement, Property, in the light of that which they thought the correct rule ought to be. We, therefore, adopt such principle enunciated by the Restatement, and hold that it is directly applicable to the fact situation of the case at bar.

Respondents cite the decisions in Brown v. Higgins, 1923, 180 Wis. 253, 193 N.W. 84, and In re Cowley's Will, 1904, 120 Wis. 263, 97 N. W. 930, 98 N.W. 28, as requiring that the class of persons who take as heirs of James F. Latimer be determined as of the death of testatrix rather than upon the death of the life beneficiary. A study of the facts in such two cases, however, discloses that they are readily distinguishable from those of the instant case. In neither case were the life beneficiaries the sole heirs at law of the testator. In the first mentioned case testator was survived by a wife and seven children, and one son was the life beneficiary, while in the second case testator was survived by a wife and eight children, and two daughters were the life beneficiaries. Therefore, by determining heirship as of the date of the death of testator in those two cases there was not present the incongruity of the remaindermen not being heirs at law of the testator as of the date of testator's death. In commenting on this fact situation, 3 Restatement, Property, p. 1717, sec. 308, comment k., states:

> "When the taker of a prior interest is one of several heirs of the designated ancestor at the ancestor's death, no constructional tendency is sufficiently definite to be capable of statement."

* * *

However, there is another circumstance present in the instant case, in addition to the fact that Mary Widney, the life beneficiary, was the sole heir at law, which tends to establish that the heirship of James F. Latimer was intended by testator to be determined as of the date of the death of Mary Widney rather than that of testatrix. Such circumstance lies in the alternative remainders provided in the will. These alternative remainders which were to be effective upon the death of Mary Widney for disposition of the trust residue were as follows:

> (1) In equal parts to Mary Widney's issue provided such issue lived to age twenty-one;
>
> (2) If any such great-grandchildren of testatrix died before age twenty-one, leaving issue, the share of such great-grandchild was to go to his or her issue, time of distribution to be as of the date the deceased great-grandchildren would have reached age twenty-one, if living;
>
> (3) If any such great-child died without issue, then his or her share was to go to the surviving great-grandchildren or great-grandchild;
>
> (4) If there should be no surviving great-grandchild, or if the granddaughter, Mary Widney, should have died without issue surviving, then one-half of the residue was to go to the heirs of testatrix and the other one-half to the heirs of her deceased husband, James F. Latimer.

The New York courts in numerous cases have held that, where there are alternative remainders of this kind created by will so that the ultimate gift over to heirs or next of kin is contingent upon the beneficiary of a prior estate not being survived by issue, the determination of those who take as heirs or next of kin is to be determined as of the time of the ending of the life estate which results in the gift over to heirs or next of kin becoming operative, and not as of the date of the death of the testator. * * *

* * *

While we are not prepared to lay down a hard and fast general rule that, where a will provides for an alternative remainder to heirs contingent upon whether or not the life beneficiary is survived by issue, such heirs are always to be determined as of the death of the life beneficiary, we do conclude that such circumstance may well indicate an intent to postpone determination of the class of persons who are to take as heirs until the happening of the contingency which converts such a contingent remainder into a vested one. This would seem to be particularly true in those cases where the occurrence of the contingency would be likely to occur a long time in the future, with the further likelihood that the contigency might never occur. In such cases there obviously would be no intent on the part of the testator that any persons alive at the death of testator would benefit from the contingent gift over.

Turning to the facts of the instant case, we have a situation that when testatrix made her will in 1920 her granddaughter, Mary Widney, was but twenty-one years old and recently married. Her life expectancy according to the American Experience Table of Mortality was forty-one and one half years, and, in addition to that factor, there was every likelihood that she would have children and be survived by them or their issue. There was only a remote possibility that the gift over to her heirs and those of her husband would ever occur. Furthermore, if such a contingency did occur it was unlikely that the nephews and nieces of her husband living at the time of the making of the will, who were then of middle age or beyond would survive such event. For example, his niece, Alice Latimer, was then sixty-two years of age. Any intent to benefit heirs then living of her husband or herself would seem to be entirely lacking. On the contrary, the clause providing for the remainder over to heirs was most likely inserted with the intent that in the event of the happening of such contingency the undistributed balance of the trust should go to those persons who then constituted the heirs of her husband and herself. The court in its opinion in the New York case of Matter of Brewster's Estate, supra, emphasized somewhat the same argument based upon the young ages of the two daughters who by the will in that case were named as life beneficiaries.

In those cases in which a vesting of a contingent remainder to heirs is likely to take place many years after the death of testator, and after the death of testator's living collateral relatives, there are great practical difficulties if heirship is to be determined as of the date of testator's death, instead of the date of the happening of such uncertain future contingency. For example, the estates of at least four of the nephews and nieces of James F. Latimer were probated in Walworth county subsequent to the death of testatrix, and no interest in the trust estate was inventoried in those estates or assigned in the final decrees. If the heirs of James F. Latimer who are now to take a half of the residue were to be determined as of the date of the death of testatrix, all of these estates would have to be opened up. If a testator or testatrix were to give any thought to these possibilities occurring, would he or she not seek to avoid this by having the class of persons who are to take as heirs determined as of the date of the occurrence of such contingency?

* * *

To summarize, the fact that the life beneficiary, Mary Widney, was the sole heir at law of James F. Latimer, both at the time testatrix made her will, and at the time she died, would cause an incongruity if the determination of the class, who were to take as the heirs of James F. Latimer, were to be made as of the death of testatrix, which result would be avoided by determining such heirship as of the death of Mary Widney. Added to this, we have the additional circumstance of the alternative remainders, the particular one under which the heirs of James F. Latimer were to take being contingent upon whether the life beneficiary, a young married woman of an age when the birth of children to her was to be expected, was survived by issue. Under the authorities cited these circumstances are such as to manifest an intent on the part of testatrix that the heirs of James F. Latimer who were to take under the will be determined as of the death of Mary Widney. We, therefore, are constrained to conclude that the will should be so construed.

Counsel for respondents contend that this result will work an injustice in the instant case because one-half of the residue will be distributed in accordance with the will of Alice Latimer, she being the only heir at law of James F. Latimer living at the time of the death of Mary Widney, so that the descendants of the other nephews and nieces of James F. Latimer will take nothing because of the provisions of section 237.01(4), Stats. There are several obvious answers to this contention. One is that this is an unexpected result which it is unlikely testatrix could have contemplated because the respective ages of Mary Widney and Alice Latimer were such that the former would have normally outlived the latter by many years, Mary Widney having been born in 1898, while Alice Latimer was born in 1858, and was ninety-four years old when she died. Another is that if testatrix had given any thought at the time of making her will as to which of the two dates the heirs of James F. Latimer should take would bring about the most equitable result (which we doubt that she did) it might well have occurred to her that the better result might well be obtained by having the class of heirs determined as of the date of the occurrence of the contingency that would enable them to take. This is so because, if such determination of heirs were made as of her own death, persons who were no blood relatives of James F. Latimer might be the ones to ultimately come into enjoyment of part of the estate, by reason of the possibility of husbands of nieces of James F. Latimer inheriting from their wives. Lastly, the best answer is that the intent of testatrix must be construed from the language of the will as of the time it was drafted in the light of the then surrounding circumstances, and not in the light of what developed many years later.

That part of the judgment appealed from is reversed and cause remanded for further proceedings consistent with this opinion.[26]

NOTE

As ambiguous as gifts to "heirs" are testamentary gifts to "issue". According to the early English law a testamentary gift to the "issue of A" was construed to be a gift per capita to all legitimate lineal descendants of A of whatever degree. Thus if A predeceased the testator and left surviving the testator a child, B, and two grandchildren, C and D, the offspring of a child E who predeceased the testator, B, C, and D would share equally in the property, each taking one-third. Under similar facts most American courts would decree a stirpital distribution. Thus B would take one-half and C and D would take one-fourth each. Again, assume a testamentary gift "to the issue of A". Assume further that A predeceases the testator leaving children, B and C, who survive the testator, and grandchildren D and E, the offspring of C, who also survive the testator. Do D and E share in the gift? The answer to this question would be in the affirmative under the early English law but the modern tendency is to answer the question in the negative. Courts of today tend to construe a testamentary gift to the issue of a person predeceasing the testator as referring to those descendants of that person who would take under the applicable statute of distribution.[27] In a testamentary gift to the issue of A, grandchildren of A may be the only descendants of A living at the testator's death and A may then be dead. Assume that there are three grandchildren. Two are descendants of one child of A and one is a descendant of another child of A. Do all the grandchildren take equally with the result that each takes one-third or is the property divided into halves and one-half given to the grandchild who is the only child and the other half divided equally between the other two grandchildren? Probably most courts of today would follow the plan of distribution adopted by the appropriate statute of distribution.

In the event of a devise to A for life, remainder to A's "issue", the usual rules concerning the opening and closing of the class would seem to be applicable but it would appear that there is an implied condition that donees meeting the primary meaning of the class description survive A.[28]

---

26. For a discussion of the meaning of the words "heirs", "heirs of the body", "next of kin", and "relatives", see Restatement, Property (1940), § 308; 37 A.L.R.3d 9 (1971).

27. For a case adopting the modern view despite local precedent favoring the English view, see Clarke v. Clarke, 222 Md. 153, 159 A.2d 362 (1960).

28. See Restatement, Property (1940) § 249, Comment *k*. For a full discussion of this and the other matters examined in this Note see Simes and Smith, Future Interests (2d Ed., 1956) §§ 721–747; Trautman, "Class Gifts of Future Interests: When is Survival Required", 20 Vand.L.Rev. 1 (1966).

(4) "DEATH WITHOUT ISSUE" AND RELATED LIMITATIONS

An apparently simple devise to a named person with a gift over "if he die without issue" (or comparable wording) gives rise to some bizarre construction problems, as the following cases illustrate. Without historical background one would not suppose that such language could result in creation of a fee tail, the phrase being construed to mean "if his line of issue ever fail" (known as an indefinite succession construction). The modern struggle to avoid such a construction still leaves us with a second ambiguity: "if he die [when? before the testator? either before or after the testator?] without issue." Did the testator intend an absolute gift to the first taker if he survived the testator and a substitutionary gift if the first taker die before the testator? Is there a further ambiguity: "if he die without [ever having had? leaving surviving?] issue"?

HAYES v. HAMMOND

Supreme Judicial Court of Massachusetts, 1957.
336 Mass. 233, 143 N.E.2d 693.

CUTTER, JUSTICE. This is a petition for registration under G.L. (Ter.Ed.) c. 185, as amended, of title to land in Marblehead (hereinafter called the locus). The petition was filed September 27, 1954, and, as amended, has been prosecuted by seven petitioners. Answers filed in behalf of numerous respondents deny the title of the petitioners and claim that the respondents hold title of record to the locus. The trial judge held that the respondents have a good title of record to the locus and ordered that the petition be dismissed. The petitioners duly saved exceptions to the denial of certain requests for rulings (discussed below). The case is before us upon the petitioners' substitute bill of exceptions, from which the following pertinent facts are summarized.

In 1830, John Girdler gained title to the Girdler Farm, which included the locus. He died on May 25, 1855, still owning the Girdler Farm. His will was dated March 23, 1855. Then (and at his death) he had a wife Betsey, three children (Lucy, through whom the petitioners claim, Deborah, and Rachel) and a granddaughter, Elizabeth, child of a son, who had theretofore died. By this will (after a life estate to his wife for her support and maintenance) he provided: "After the decease of my said wife Betsey, my will is that whatever remains of my Estate not expended by her, shall descend in four equal parts: to wit one part to my daughters, Lucy Ann Harris, one part to Deborah, one part to Rachel and the other part to Elizabeth Girdler, the child of my late son John B. Girdler, now deceased: To hold the same to them, their respective heirs, administrators and assigns forever: But if either of my said daughters or grand daughter should die without issue, then in such case my will is that such respective part or parts should descend in equal proportions to said surviving legatees or to their legal representatives."

Betsey Girdler, John's widow, died prior to 1871 when the three daughters and the granddaughter named in John Girdler's will, all of whom survived Betsey, filed a petition for a partition in the Probate Court "alleging [that] they held as heirs equal * * * shares in the estate of John Girdler, taking an one-fourth part each. The petition was assented to by the four petitioners and their husbands." In 1874 the Girdler Farm was separated by the partition into four lots of about thirteen acres each, the locus then being assigned to Lucy A. Harris. Lucy died without issue in 1885 leaving the residue of her estate to her husband, who died in 1900. It is indirectly under this will that the petitioners claim. In their claim of alleged title (which need not be summarized), it does not appear that the locus had been mentioned of record from 1874 to 1953 in any conveyance or in any probate inventory.

In 1908 various persons, through whom the respondents claim, namely (1) Elizabeth Bessom, the last survivor (who died in 1914) of the persons named in the residuary article of John Girdler's will, (2) the grandchildren of Rachel Girdler High (one of John Girdler's daughters, who died in 1897, leaving issue), and (3) the heirs of Deborah Hooper, another daughter (who died in 1907, leaving issue) of John Girdler, joined in deeds, separating the locus into thirds, which by the several grantees (and certain successors in title) have since been conveyed and reconveyed, with the consequence that, by such conveyances (which need not be set forth in detail) of parts of the locus subsequent to 1908, the respondents, in the aggregate, claim title to the whole locus, directly or indirectly, under one or more of the parties to the 1908 partition deeds. The premises have been improved from time to time by persons for the time being so claiming title to parts of the locus.

The trial judge held (1) that, under the residuary article of John Girdler's will (quoted above), upon his death, each of his daughters and his granddaughter, Elizabeth Bessom, "took a fee tail in expectancy and upon the death of the wife Betsey a fee tail in possession"; (2) that the 1871 partition proceeding in the Probate Court operated to make "the daughters and granddaughter * * * tenants in tail in severalty of separate portions of the Girdler Farm"; and (3) that upon Lucy Harris's death in 1885 without issue the "locus vested in fee tail in the three others, namely" Rachel High, Deborah Hooper, and Elizabeth Bessom.

The residue of John Girdler's estate after the life interest of Betsey was to "descend" in four equal parts, to Lucy, Rachel, Deborah, and Elizabeth, and their respective heirs. Each would then have taken an undivided one-fourth interest in fee simple in the Girdler Farm, were it not for the further provision that if any one (or more) of them "should die without issue, then * * * such respective part * * * should descend in equal proportions to said surviving legatees or to their legal representatives."

The will took effect on the death of John Girdler in 1855, prior to the enactment of St.1888, c. 273 (now found in G.L.[Ter.Ed.] c. 184, § 6), which as to limitations effected by deed or will after April 30, 1888, provides that the words "die without issue" "shall, unless a contrary intention clearly appears by the instrument creating such limitation, mean a want or failure of issue in the lifetime or at the time of the death of such person, and not an indefinite failure of his issue." The statute is not applicable to instruments executed prior to 1888. Gilkie v. Marsh, 186 Mass. 336, 338, 71 N.E. 703; Lyman v. Sears, 283 Mass. 404, 413, 186 N.E. 56. Accordingly, John Girdler's 1855 will must be construed in accordance with principles of construction in effect prior to 1888.

The Massachusetts authorities, construing pre-1888 limitations applicable to land, have followed the common law view, that (in the absence of clear controlling provisions in the governing instrument showing a contrary intention), a gift over if A shall die without issue following a gift to A and his heirs, means that the gift over is to take effect upon the indefinite failure of A's issue. Nightingale v. Burrell, 15 Pick. 104, 109–115; Wheatland v. Dodge, 10 Metc. 502, 505; Terry v. Briggs, 12 Metc. 17, 22–23; Malcolm v. Malcolm, 3 Cush. 472, 481–482; Hall v. Priest, 6 Gray 18, 20–21; Allen v. Trustees of Ashley School Fund, 102 Mass. 262, 264; Brown v. Addison Gilbert Hospital, 155 Mass 323, 325–326, 29 N.E. 625, 626 (where the rule is said "to have become a rule of property"). Gilkie v. Marsh, 186 Mass. 336, 337–339, 71 N.E. 703. See Swain, Crocker's Notes on Common Forms (7th ed.) §§ 908–909.

With respect to real estate, such a gift over, in the event of the indefinite failure of the issue of the first taker, was construed to cut down and limit the interest of the first taker (even if expressed as a gift in fee simple) to an estate tail, so that the person entitled to the devise over has "a remainder in expectancy after the estate tail, and not an executory devise." Brown v. Addison Gilbert Hospital, supra, 155 Mass. at page 326, 29 N.E. at page 626, and cases cited. With respect to personal property, a gift to A and his heirs and personal representatives, but if A shall die without issue, then to B, was construed to be an absolute gift to A. There cannot be an estate tail in personal property, and "the limitation over, being on an indefinite failure of issue, is too remote * * * and is * * * void." Hall v. Priest, 6 Gray 18, 22. In Hall v. Priest it was said, with respect to a residuary clause making by a single provision gifts of realty and personalty, "* * * the words are to be construed in the same manner, as applicable to both species of property * * * the same words [importing a gift over upon an indefinite failure of issue] which, applied to real estate, will create an estate tail, when applied to personal property, will give an absolute interest." Compare Restatement: Property, § 269, comment h; Powell, Real Property, § 343, at page 46. Accordingly, even if the residue of John Girdler's estate included personal property (as it probably did), as to his real estate it gave to his three daughters and his granddaughter an undivided remainder interest in fee tail in the locus after the life interest in the widow in the absence of some substantial showing that the testator intended (a) a result different from that of the well settled pre-1888 rule declared in Brown v. Addison Gilbert Hospital, 155 Mass. 323, 326, 29 N.E. 625, and cases cited, or (b) that the gift over should take effect only in the event of an indefinite failure of issue either at or prior to (1) his own death or (2) the death of his widow.

We find in John Girdler's will no evidence of either intention. Obviously, the "construction of a will is to be ascertained by careful consideration of the entire document" and "too much weight must not be given to cases involving * * * other wills different in their content" (see Old Colony Trust Co. v. Shackford, 291 Mass. 361, 365, 197 N.E. 32, 34). However, the residuary article of the Girdler will is in form closely similar to provisions which had been held to create estates tail in the earlier cases, some of which already have been cited (see, for example, Nightingale v. Burrell, 15 Pick. 104, 105, 114–115, decided before 1855 when John Girdler's will was made; Hall v. Priest, 6 Gray 18, 19–20; Hayward v. Howe, 12 Gray 49, 51–52). There is some indication in the will of an intention to keep the property (dealt with by the residuary article) in the family, a result which perhaps would be facilitated by the interpretation (that estates tail were created) adopted by the trial judge. There is no express provision in the will (and one could easily have been included if such a result had been intended) requiring that the indefinite failure of issue must take place either (a) prior to the death of the testator or (b) prior to the death of the widow, Betsey, in order for the gift over to take effect.

The modern trend, with respect to instruments executed after the enactment of statutes like St.1888, c. 273, may be to find that testamentary gifts over, upon the death without issue of a first or subsequent taker, were intended to take effect only if such taker should die without issue prior to the death of either the earlier taker or of a life tenant (if one is named). That trend does not appear to have been given effect in this Commonwealth (to the extent that it has been recognized) as early as 1855. Accordingly, in construing this 1855 instrument, we should not be guided by modern authorities expressing views greatly influenced by post-1855 developments.[29] The existence of the life estate in the widow, Betsey, under our earlier

29. [The following footnote by the court is retained; others have been omitted. Ed.]

Restatement: Property, § 266, gives a narrower, construction of "death without issue" than prevailed in Massachusetts in 1855, in the absence of a contrary intention exhibited in the particular instrument under consideration. Similarly, §§ 267, 268, and 269 do not state the common-law rules in this Commonwealth, but are designed reasonably to reflect the supposed consensus of modern authority in this area, which obviously has been much influenced by statutory enactments in the several States. See Restatement: Property, c. 20, Introductory notes, pages 1317–1319, 1336; § 266, comments a, b (also 1948 sup.), c; Proc.Am.Law Inst. vol. XV, pages 236–241. For comprehensive discussions of this whole area of the law and its historical development, see the thorough article of Professor Joseph Warren, Gifts Over on Death Without Issue, 39 Yale L.J. 332, and Am.Law of Property, §§ 21.49–21.53; Powell, Real Property, §§ 340–343; Simes and Smith, Future Interests (2d Ed.) §§ 521–539.

decisions, does not imply (in the absence of some real indication that the testator had such an intention) that the indefinite failure of the issue of any one of John Girdler's daughters (or granddaughter) must take place prior to Betsey's death, in order for the gift over to take effect. There were initial life estates in the instruments considered in Hall v. Priest, 6 Gray 18, 19–21, in Hayward v. Howe, 12 Gray 49 (semble), and in Allen v. Trustees of Ashley School Fund, 102 Mass. 262. In none of these cases did the existence of the prior life estate lead to any suggestion by this court that the gift over on the death of the first subsequent taker without issue could not take effect unless that indefinite failure of issue occurred prior to the death of the life tenant. We think that there is nothing to the contrary in Boynton v. Boynton, 266 Mass. 454, 459, 165 N.E. 489 (where with respect to a gift in trust, apparently of personal property, the court held that, under the particular instrument executed in 1911, the death "without issue" which would give rise to a gift over must take place prior to the final distribution of the trust, if the gift over was to take effect). We hold that at the death of John Girdler's widow, Betsey, his three daughters and granddaughter held undivided equal estates tail in the locus.

* * *

There appears to have been no conveyance by Lucy Girdler Harris, prior to her death in 1885, which would bar her estate tail. She could not dispose of her estate tail by will. Hall v. Priest, 6 Gray 18, 24. Gen.Sts. c. 92, § 1, now G.L. (Ter.Ed.) c. 191, § 1. Accordingly, Rachel High, Deborah Hooper, and Elizabeth Bessom (all of whom survived Lucy) took in possession and in fee simple, as the result of Lucy's death without leaving any issue, a one-third undivided interest in the locus. By the division by deeds of the locus in 1908, it was divided among the respective parties to those deeds, through whom the respondents claim. The petitioners (whose claim is under Lucy Harris' will) have no title to the locus.

* * *

Exceptions overruled.[30]

30. According to the American Law Institute the definite failure of issue construction is preferred in this country both as to limitations of real and of personal property. See Restatement, Property (1940), § 266. Indeed, a majority of states have enacted statutory provisions declaring a preference for the definite failure of issue construction. Simes and Smith, Future Interests (2d Ed., 1956) § 526 lists thirty states in which statutes of this type are in effect. Although the indefinite failure of issue construction has been applied to personalty as well as to realty, it was easier to show that a definite failure of issue was intended when the subject matter of the gift was personal property. This was because a fee tail estate could not be created in personal property and therefore the limitation over on failure of issue would be an executory interest. Thus, a limitation "to A but if A die without issue then to B" would be construed as though it read to A but when A's line of lineal descent runs out, then to B; since A's line of lineal descent might run out beyond the permissible period under the rule against perpetuities, the gift over to B would be invalid and A would have an absolute interest. The reluctance of courts to apply the indefinite failure of issue construction to personal property is illustrated by a limitation containing the words, "if A die without leaving issue". These words were presumed to refer to a definite failure of issue if the subject matter were personal property and an indefinite fail-

GOLDBERGER v. GOLDBERGER

Court of Chancery of Delaware, 1954.
34 Del.Ch. 237, 102 A.2d 338.

BRAMHALL, VICE CHANCELLOR. Testator under Item Second of his last will and testament provided as follows:

> "Second: I give, devise and bequeath all my property and estate of whatsoever nature whether real, personal or mixed and wheresoever situate, unto my two beloved children, Saul Harold Goldberger, and Frances Estelle Shore, absolutely and in fee simple, share and share alike; should either of my said children die leaving issue, then the share of such child so dying shall go to his or her issue; should either *my* my said children die without issue, then the share of the child so dying shall go to the survivor."

Saul Harold Goldberger and Francis Estelle Shore are children of testator. Michele Lois Shore, Joseph Theodore Shore, and Saul Samuel Shore are children of Frances Estelle Shore. Joanne D. Goldberger and Lenora J. Goldberger are children of Saul Harold Goldberger. Michele Lois Shore, Lenora J. Goldberger and Joanne D. Goldberger are minors and are represented by their guardian ad litem.

It will be noted that testator under Item Second of his will gave his estate to his two children Saul Harold Goldberger and Frances Estelle Shore "absolutely and in fee simple, share and share alike". In the same item he further provided that should either of said children die "leaving issue", then the share of that child should go to his or her issue. Testator also provided that should either of his children die "without issue" the share of such child should go to the survivor of his two children.

It will be conceded that, standing alone, testator in his gift to his children created, in terms an absolute fee simple estate. The question is: Is the estate to the two children affected, and, if so, in what manner, by the subsequent clauses in which testator provided for contingencies relating to the death of any child leaving issue and the death of any child without issue.

The cardinal rule in construing a will is to ascertain from its language the intention of the testator. That intention, when found, must prevail unless it runs counter to some positive rule of law. Farrell v. Faries, 25 Del.Ch. 404, 22 A.2d 380; Carrow v. Thropp, 29 Del. Ch. 201, 48 A.2d 379. Here testator has used the words "absolutely and in fee simple". They are technical words, having a definite technical meaning, and in the absence of anything in the will indicating a contrary intention, they will be given their technical meaning. I find in the will no explanatory or qualifying expressions indicating that

ure of issue if the subject matter were real property. Tenny v. Agar, 12 East 253 (1810). See, comment, "Death Without Issue is Not a Dead Issue in New York", 18 Syracuse Law Review 751 (1967); Note, "Time to Which Condition of Remainderman's Death Refers Under Gift or Grant to One for Life or Term of Years and Then to Remainderman, But if Remainderman Dies Without Issue Then Over to Another", 26 A.L.R.2d 407 (1969).

these words were not used with technical accuracy or that their import is plainly contrary to testator's intention.

In this state, following the common law, a gift to A and her heirs forever, "except she should die without heirs born of her body" with a remainder over in that event to B, creates an estate tail in A with a vested remainder in B. Caccamo v. Banning, 6 Terry 394, 75 A.2d 222; Caulk's Lessee v. Caulk, 3 Pa. 528, 52 A. 340; Roach v. Martin's Lessee, 1 Harr. 548, 28 Am.Dec. 746. It has also been held in this state that a devise to A and her heirs, but should she die leaving no issue surviving her, then to B and his heirs, created a fee simple defeasible estate. Mock v. Goldstein, 18 Del.Ch. 71, 156 A. 221; Delaware Trust Co. v. Elliott, 17 Del.Ch. 14, 147 A. 244. The decision in the Caccamo case as well as other cases cited therein was predicated upon the presumption of an indefinite failure of issue construction. Apparently the decisions in the Mock and Elliott cases were based upon a definite failure of issue construction.

An indefinite failure of issue means a general failure of issue, that is, a failure of issue whenever it shall happen, even in the remotest generation without any fixed or certain time within which or at the end of which it must happen. Farrell v. Faries, supra. I do not have to deal here with any possible presumption that testator intended that an indefinite failure of issue construction should be given to his will because the language of the will clearly shows testator's intention that a definite failure of issue construction should be applied. Even at common law a devise over on the failure of issue may be shown by the context to refer to a definite failure of issue, and in such case the estate created will be a fee simple or a life estate according to the form of the limitation of the devise, without reference to the devise over. Farrell v. Faries, supra. The tendency of the courts today is to adopt upon slight indication of intention a construction which refers to words importing a failure of issue to the death of the first taker. Farrell v. Faries, supra.

Several provisions of testator's will show a preference for a definite rather than an indefinite failure of issue construction. Any provision of testator's will changing the expressly granted fee simple estate in the first taker to a lesser estate would have to be at least as clear as the provision creating the fee simple estate. James, Administrator v. James, 16 Del.Ch. 34, 36, 139 A. 787, 788; Craven v. Wilmington Teachers Association, 29 Del.Ch. 180, 47 A.2d 580; Carrow v. Thropp, supra.

The fact that the gift over upon failure of issue is to the survivor of living persons, also indicates testator's preference for a definite failure of issue construction. Restatement of Property, Vol. 3, Sec. 267, Comment "K". Testator's provision for the issue of his children, in the event that they should die leaving issue, clearly relates to the then known issue of testator's children. If testator used the word "issue" in one instance as referring to the immediate issue of his children, in the absence of any indication in the will to the contrary, the same word used in another clause of the same Item of the will would be given the same construction. Equitable Trust Co. v. Johnson, 28 Del.Ch. 45, 36 A.2d 257. The gift over is inconsistent with the estate "absolutely and in fee simple" given to the two children of testator. Whatever interpretation may be given to such inconsistency, it certainly does not indicate a preference for the indefinite failure of issue construction.

I conclude that testator sufficiently indicated his preference for the definite failure of issue construction to overrule any presumptive preference which might have existed for an indefinite failure of issue construction.

Having rejected the indefinite failure of issue in favor of the definite failure of issue construction, the case of Rickards v. Gray, 6 Houst. 232, becomes controlling. The Rickards case as authority for the proposition that where a limitation gives in terms an absolute interest with gifts over to the issue on the death with issue of the first taker and to another person on the death without issue of the first taker, the inconsistency between the absoluteness of the gift to the first taker and the all-inclusiveness of the gifts over is resolved by regarding the gift to the first taker and the gifts over as alternative or substitutional. The conclusion reached by the Court of Errors and Appeals in the Rickards case in supported by Restatement of Property, Vol. 3, Sec. 267, Comment "G", and Page on Wills, Vol. 3, Sec. 1113, p. 363. The children of testator, having both survived testator, took an absolute fee simple estate under Item Second of Testator's will.

This construction is in accord with testator's intention as I understand it. The dominant purpose of testator was to give to his two children a fee simple estate. His attempt to provide a gift over was subordinate to the main purpose and was to take effect only in the event of the death of the first takers during the lifetime of testator. The only way in which, having accepted the definite failure of issue construction, the will of testator can be given effect as written is by interpreting the gifts over as alternative or substitutional; otherwise, the gifts over conflict with the absolute fee simple estate provided by testator for his two children.

I conclude that the children of testator, Saul Harold Goldberger and Frances Estelle Shore, take an absolute fee simple estate under the provisions of Item Second of testator's will.

An order will be signed on notice in accordance with this opinion.[31]

PYNE v. PYNE

United States Court of Appeals, District of Columbia, 1946.
154 F.2d 297.

PRETTYMAN, ASSOCIATE JUSTICE. The trustee under the will of Elizabeth A. Pyne, deceased, filed its petition in the District Court for instructions as to the distribution of a trust fund. Answers were

31. See Sherrin, "Substituted Gifts", 121 New L.Rev. 680, 703 (1971).

filed and, upon motion, judgment was entered upon the pleadings. From that decree the guardian ad litem of an infant defendant appeals.

The question arises upon the Fourth paragraph of Mrs. Pyne's will. The persons whose names appear in the proceeding are relatives of the testatrix as follows: her sister, Caroline L. Frailey; her daughter, Caroline C. F. Pyne; her three sons, John, Charles L. and Henry R. Pyne; her grandson, John Pyne, Jr., and her great granddaughter, Jennifer Pyne.

The Fourth paragraph of the will is:

> "Fourth. I give, devise and bequeath to my sister Caroline L. Frailey all my right, title and interest in house and lot numbered 1315 New York Avenue, in the city of Washington, District of Columbia, known as lot numbered three (3), in Square numbered two hundred and fifty-one (251), in said city and District, for and during her natural life; and after her death, or in case she die before me, I give, devise and bequeath the same to my daughter Caroline C. F. Pyne, for and during her natural life; and after her death, I give, devise and bequeath all my right, title and interest in the aforesaid land and premises to my three other children, John Pyne, Charles L. Pyne, and Henry R. Pyne, and the issue of my said daughter, if she leave any surviving her, in fee simple, said issue to take a one-fourth ($^1/_4$) part; and if my said daughter die without issue, then I give and devise the same to my three children aforesaid, John Pyne, Charles L. Pyne, and Henry R. Pyne, their heirs and assigns forever, share and share alike. And in any case, if any one of my said three children, John Pyne, Charles L. Pyne, and Henry R. Pyne, should die leaving a descendant or descendants, said descendant or descendants to take the share his, her or their parent would have taken had he lived."

The will was executed in 1897. In 1905 the testatrix died. In July, 1914, Caroline L. Frailey died. In November, 1914, John Pyne assigned all his right, title and interest in the estate to his brother, Henry, for one dollar and other valuable considerations. In 1935 John Pyne died. In 1943 John Pyne, Jr., died, leaving a daughter, Jennifer. In 1944 Caroline C. F. Pyne died without issue.

Jennifer Pyne, appellant by her guardian ad litem, is the sole descendant of John Pyne.

The trustee asked the District Court for instructions as to the distribution of funds which are the proceeds of the sale of the real estate devised in the paragraph above quoted. The ultimate question is which of two persons takes the share of John Pyne: his assignee, Henry, or his descendant, Jennifer. The answer depends upon whether John Pyne's interest was absolute or was defeasible.

Caroline Pyne had a life estate. John, Charles and Henry had remainders. The remainders in one-fourth of the property to each of them were vested. The remainders in the other one-fourth (i.e., one-twelfth to each son) were contingent, dependent upon Caroline Pyne's death with or without issue. Whether vested or contingent, John Pyne's interests were assignable, but he could assign only that which he had. If his vested interest was defeasible, his assignment was subject to the same defeasance, and likewise his assignment of his contingent interest was subject to the conditions upon which he had the interest.

The difficulty arises because of the last sentence of the pertinent paragraph of the will, which reads as above-quoted except that we now italicize the key phrases, "*And in any case, if* any one of my said three children, *John Pyne,* Charles L. Pyne, and Henry R. Pyne, *should die leaving a descendant* or descendants, said descendant or descendants to take the share his, her or their parent would have taken *had he lived.*"

In the provisions of the Fourth paragraph which precede this last sentence, the testatrix unmistakably devised the fee. She used the words "in fee simple" and "their heirs and assigns forever," which are distinctive descriptions of fee conveyance. In those provisions no qualification appears as to the remainders in three-fourths of the property, and the remainders in the other fourth are upon the contingency of issue vel non of Caroline Pyne. So that, if the testatrix had not added the final sentence, the vested remainders would have been absolute, and the contingent remainders would have been certain in point of ownership in the three sons. But the last sentence in the paragraph was added. That it was not an inadvertence or mere tautology is clear from the fact that in devising other property in the Second paragraph in her will, the testatrix devised in fee simple absolute and added no sentence such as this last one in the Fourth paragraph. The sentence must have had some purpose and must be given meaning in accordance with its intent.

The language to be construed is the language of contingency. It is "if any one of my said three children should die leaving a descendant". Thus, an event which might or might not have happened is described, and upon that event, if it happened, another devisee was to take in place of the first-named devisee. But the *time* when that event must occur in order to have that result is not specified. The key to the problem in the case is the time as of which the last sentence in the Fourth paragraph of the will speaks.

There are four possibilities of time, (1) the death of the remainderman before the death of the testatrix; (2) the death of the remainderman during the lifetime of the life tenant; (3) the death of the remainderman at any time, and (4) the death of the last descendant of the remainderman, i.e., the final extinction of his line.

Variations of provisions in wills relating to the death of legatees or devisees without specification of time have led to much confusion and uncertainty in the authorities. Generally speaking, the variations are classed in four groups, (1) where there is a devise to A and if A should die, then to B; (2) a devise to A and if A should die without issue (or with issue surviving), then to B; (3) a life estate to X with remainder to A, and if A should die, then to B; (4) a life estate

to X, a remainder to A, and if A die without issue (or with issue surviving), then to B. It is unnecessary that we venture into the field of controversy about the effect of the first three of these types of provision, because we have before us one of the fourth type.

The first possibility is that the time to which the sentence in the present case refers is the death of the remainderman before the death of the testatrix. She might have had in mind the possibility that one of her sons would die before she did, and thus have meant that in such event the descendant, if any, of such son should take his share. If such be the meaning, then, upon the death of the testatrix with the three sons living, the possibility of substitution of devisee expired, and the remainders thereupon became absolute. Such, in effect, is the contention of the appellee-assignee.

The second possibility is that the sentence before us refers to the death of the sons, leaving descendants, at any time before the death of the life tenant. If that be the meaning, then upon the death of the testatrix each son took a vested remainder in fee subject to being divested if he should die, leaving a descendant, before the death of his sister, Caroline. Such, in effect, is the contention of appellant-descendant.

The third possibility is that the sentence before us refers to the death of the sons, leaving descendants, at any time. If such be the meaning, then the nature of the interest of each son must await his death for determination, because, if he should die without issue, his interest would be a remainder in fee simple absolute, but if he left issue surviving, his interest would be a life estate only. Grave questions are raised by such a construction, into which, however, we need not go in this case because remainderman John Pyne died leaving issue and his descendant would take under this construction as she would under the second possibility of construction above discussed. The case at bar, therefore, does not depend upon any distinction between the second and third possible constructions.

The fourth possibility is that the critical sentence refers to the final extinction of the descendants of any son. At the common law, when estates tail were favored, this last possibility would have been of importance. But fee tail estates were abolished in this jurisdiction long ago, and words purporting to convey them are to be construed as conveying in fee simple. So, in the present case, if the last sentence in paragraph Fourth be given this meaning, John Pyne would have taken, by it, a fee simple absolute; and thus the sentence would have no meaning whatever, coming, as it does, after expressions already devising the fee. Under this construction, the appellee would be sustained, because, by it, the controversial sentence would, in effect, be stricken from the will.

The basic, always controlling, rule in the construction of wills, is the intent of the testator. If that intent can be discerned in the language of the will, read, of course, in the light of the surrounding circimstances, there is an end to the matter. If it cannot be so discerned, the testator must be presumed to have intended the result which the law has theretofore attached to the language which he chose to use.

In the case at bar, the intention of the testatrix in the controversial sentence is not indubitably certain, but there are signs which are helpful. In the first place, in this same Fourth paragraph, in providing for the life estate of Caroline Pyne in succession to or in substitution for the life estate of Caroline Frailey, the testatrix used the term "or in case she die before me". It is reasonable to assume that if she had meant to restrict the substitution provided by the last sentence of the paragraph to the death of her sons before her own death, she would have used the words with which she was obviously acquainted and had just used. In the second place, as we have pointed out, in the Second paragraph of the will she devised other real estate to her four children, their heirs and assigns forever, share and share alike, and stopped there. It is a reasonable assumption that if, as she wrote her will, she had in mind the possibility of the death of any of her children prior to her own death, and desired to provide for that contingency, she would have provided for it in the Second paragraph as well as in the Fourth. Or, viewing the two paragraphs together from another viewpoint, it appears that when this testatrix made a direct devise to her children, she provided no substitute devisee, but when she interposed a life estate, she specified a substitute, and the fact of this difference indicates that the substitution in the latter provision was coupled with the idea of the life estate, and was intended to be effective throughout the term of that estate. In the next place, we note that in the sentence preceding the last, the testatrix provided that if Caroline Pyne should die leaving issue, each son should take one-fourth, but if Caroline Pyne should die without issue, each son should take one-third. Then she proceeds, "And in any case," etc. It is a reasonable inference that by the expression "And in any case," she meant to refer to the immediately preceding possibility that each son might take one-fourth or might take one-third. If such was her intent, the last sentence clearly relates to the death of a son at any time prior to the death of Caroline Pyne.

If these indicia of intent within the will be not conclusive, we must ascertain the meaning which the law attaches to the provision in controversy.

The only cases in which we find the authorities in agreement in fixing the lifetime of the testator as the time of the effectiveness of a clause relating to the death of a devisee, are those in which the devise is directly to A and if A die (or should A die), then to B. There no contingency is stated, and no life estate intervenes. The clause is construed, for many reasons, to mean that the descendant is designated as an alternate, or substituted, devisee in the event that A should die before the will takes effect. Only one other construction of such a provision is possible, and that is that the descendant should take whenever A should die. The effect of such a construction would be to give A a life estate only, and where words conveying a fee, without contingency, are first stated, the law will not permit later indefinite language to reduce that estate. So, where no life estate intervenes and no contingency is added to the possibility of death, the construction of a sentence naming an alternate devisee is simple.

When a contingency is added to the reference to the death of the devisee—as "Blackacre to A and if he die without issue, to B"—a different situation is presented, because, whereas "if A dies" is not a contingency, "if A dies without issue" is a contingency. At common law the latter clause was held to refer to the indefinite failure of issue of A at any time, i.e., the running out of his line. That rule was changed by the Statute of Wills in 1838. Under that statute, failure of issue is to be construed as referring to the death of the named devisee. When a life estate intervenes, an additional consideration is introduced, because another possibility of time is involved, the death of the life tenant. At first the English courts held, in Edwards v. Edwards, 1852, 15 Beav. 357, 21 L.J., Ch., 324, that death of a remainderman refers to his death during the life of the life tenant, whether or not the contingency "without issue" is stated, but later the House of Lords overruled that case and held that reference to the death of a remainderman refers to his death at any time. 3 Jarman on Wills (7th ed. 1930) 2083 et seq., 2102 et seq. The learned authors of the later editions of Jarman's work on Wills, id., at 2102–3, point out that although the rule has been settled in England by the last-named case, almost any context evidencing an intention of the testator that the alternative designation is to be ineffective upon the first estate vesting in possession, is sufficient to lift the case from the general rule. In the case at bar, as we have already said, we need not go into that basic dispute, because either of those two rules sustains appellant here.

In this country the cases are somewhat in confusion, but the great weight of authority supports the rule that, absent a statute, where a will refers to the death of a remainderman survived by issue, without specification as to time, his death prior to the death of the life tenant is meant. * * *

[Omitted is the court's discussion of cases from other jurisdictions.] * * *

We have examined with great care the cases cited to us by appellee, given in the annotation at 109 A.L.R. 56 as supporting the proposition that a remainder given by a will containing a direction that the children of a deceased remainderman should take their parent's share, is vested not subject to be divested. But upon examination it appears that in many of these cases there was a definitive phrase fixing the time, and that in almost all the states from which cases are cited, there is a line of authority to the contrary where a contingency, such as "leaving issue surviving", is expressed and a life estate intervenes. The two Supreme Court cases mentioned are not helpful in the problem before us, because both of them contained phrases definitive of the time. The language in the will in McArthur v. Scott was "if any grandchild aforesaid shall have died before said final division," and in Johnson v. Washington Loan & T. Co., the language was "among my daughters living at my death." Other cases cited by appellee relate to the time of vesting in interest and are not pertinent to the problem before us.

The expression in the will before us is not death "without issue" but death "leaving a descendant", and the vast majority of the reported cases in this field concern limitations upon failure of issue. The learned framers of the Restatement of the Law of Property, Future Interests treat the expressions "die without issue" and "survived by issue" equally as contingencies and apply the same rule in determining the effective time of such expressions, and we agree with them to the extent of believing that the basic principles of "without issue" cases are helpful in construing limitations upon death leaving descendants surviving.

We think it clear that the testatrix in the present case did not intend by the last sentence in paragraph Fourth of her will to refer to the death of her sons during her own lifetime only. In the first place, it may reasonably be supposed that the testatrix would contemplate taking care of events before her death by a new will, or a codicil, but at the same time provide for events after her death but before the time when the devise in fee became possessory. Moreover, it hardly seems reasonable that if she had meant to limit the substitution of devisees to her own lifetime she would have placed such general language after provisions for two successive life estates and a remainder clearly successive to the life estates. The placement of the sentence in the paragraph and the generality of its terms negative the idea that it was intended to be of effect only if the sons died before the testatrix. Again, as we have already said, the fact that the testatrix used the expression "or in case she die before me" in referring to the substitution of Caroline Pyne in place of Caroline Frailey as life tenant, indicates that she would have used the same words if she had meant to restrict to her own lifetime the substitution provided in the last sentence of the paragraph.

We do not think the sentence in controversy can be construed as referring to the final extinction of the line of descendants. To do so would be to construe it as devising an estate tail, which, in this jurisdiction, must be translated into a fee simple. The fee simple having already been devised in the preceding sentence, the result would in effect be to strike the last sentence. We do not think that the testatrix intended to do that which she must be presumed to have known was a nullity.

It is our view that the sentence under consideration was intended to refer to the death of the sons at any time prior to the death of their sister, Caroline Pyne. In our view, this construction fits such internal evidence of intention as we can glean from the will itself, and is also in accord with the great weight of authority upon the point.

We, therefore, conclude that by the last sentence of paragraph Fourth, the testatrix intended to, and did, provide that upon the death of John Pyne, leaving a descendant, during the lifetime of Caroline C. F. Pyne, the descendant of John Pyne should become the remainderman in his stead. In the language of future interests, as to three-fourths of the property we hold that upon the death of the testatrix, each designated remainderman took a vested remainder in fee simple subject to be divested in the event of his death, leaving a descendant, prior to the death of the life tenant; that upon the event of divestment, the substituted remainderman took the remainder. Since John Pyne's assignment to Henry Pyne carried John Pyne's interest only, it was ineffective as against Jennifer Pyne upon the death of John Pyne prior to the death of Caroline C. F. Pyne. As to the one-fourth of the property in which John Pyne's interest was contingent, his assignment was subject to the same limitations as his vested interest; his descendant became a substituted remainderman when he died before the event which constituted the contingency upon which his interest depended. As the District Court held that John Pyne's interests were indefeasible, it follows that the decree must be reversed.

Reversed.[32]

PROBLEMS

1. Bequest in trust to A for life with remainder to B and C "but in the event of the death of either B or C without issue the deceased's share to go to the survivor." A survived B and C, both of whom died without issue. Who is entitled to the corpus of the trust on the death of A? See Easterday's Estate, 45 Cal.App.2d 598, 114 P.2d 669 (1941).

2. Devise "to A for life, remainder to B but if B dies without issue then to B's wife for life, remainder to C and his heirs." Classify the estate created in B after the death of A. See Scanlin v. Peterson, 105 Conn. 308, 135 A. 394 (1926).

3. Devise "to A and his heirs but if A dies without issue, then to B and his heirs". A dies after the testator leaving a wife enceinte. The wife later gives birth to A's child. Has A died with or without issue? See Restatement, Property (1948 Supp.) § 266.

4. Devise "to A and his heirs but if A dies without issue then to B and his heirs". A survives the testator and has a child who predeceases A. No descendant of A is alive at A's death. Has A died without issue? See Kendall v. Taylor, 245 Ill. 617, 92 N.E. 562 (1910); Drummond v. Drummond, 146 S.C. 194, 143 S.E. 818 (1928).

32. Footnotes by the court are omitted. See 33 A.L.R.2d 242 (1954).

SECTION 3. IMPLIED GIFTS TO FILL GAPS

SMITH v. USHER

Supreme Court of Georgia, 1899.
108 Ga. 231, 33 S.E. 876.

SIMMONS, C. J. Sarah A. Smith, as widow and sole heir at law of Michael H. Smith, brought suit against Savannah Usher for a one-half undivided interest in a certain tract of land, claiming it under an item in the will of Michael Mixon, deceased, which was set out in her petition as follows: "I give and devise my Mixon place * * * to my two daughters, Savannah and Amelia, to be used and enjoyed by them during their natural lives, subject to their own control, and to be managed by them as femes sole; and should my said daughters, Savannah and Amelia, have lawful children, then at their decease I give and devise said plantation to said heirs, forever. But should both of said daughters die childless, I give and devise said Mixon place to my grandson, Michael Smith, to his heirs and assigns, forever." The petition alleged that the daughter referred to as Amelia had died, leaving no child or children, and that the daughter referred to as Savannah, the defendant in the suit, had married Usher, and was living upon the property, and refused to recognize petitioner's rights to an interest therein. There was also in the petition an allegation that by the item of the will above set out the testator "intended that, in the event of the death of one of said daughters without issue, or leaving no child, an undivided half interest in said property should go to and vest in said Michael H. Smith; and said testator, at the time of the execution of said will, so stated, and repeatedly afterwards said that such was his understanding and construction and intention." The defendant demurred to the petition on several grounds, among them that it set out no cause of action; that it showed that the plaintiff had no "present interest" in the land; that it sought by extraneous testimony to show an interest other than that given by the will; that it showed that under the will the defendant had a life estate in all the land, and that no remainderman had any present interest until the termination of the life estate. The judge sustained the demurrer, and the plaintiff excepted.

* * * [In the omitted portion of the opinion of the court ruled that the parol evidence could not be used to vary the meaning of the words in the will.] * * *

We will now proceed to a consideration of the item of the will under which plaintiff claims. The testator clearly expressed his intention that, in the event both daughters had lawful children, such children should take, and also his intention that, in the event both daughters died childless, the estate should go to the grandson named; but the will failed to provide for one contingency, viz. where one daughter died childless and the other had children. The grandson cannot take under any express provision of the will until both daughters die childless, for his interest is so expressly restricted in the will. The testator, therefore, made no express disposition of the land in the event one daughter died childless and the other had children, and this is the condition that has now arisen. To prevent a partial intestacy and a lapse in the limitations of the estate, and to give effect to the manifest intention of the testator, the law will in such a case raise by implication cross remainders between the two daughters and their issue; for, while in a deed cross remainders are created only by express words, it has long been settled that they may in a will be raised by implication. We think therefore, that the effect of the item of the will under discussion was a devise to the two daughters for life, with remainder to their lawful children if both have such children, with remainder to plaintiff's husband in the event both the daughters die childless, and with implied cross remainders between the two daughters and their children in the event that one of the daughters has lawful children while the other dies childless. "Where a devise is of black acre to A., and of white acre to B. in tail, and, if they both die without issue, then to C. in fee, here A. and B. have cross remainders by implication, and, on the failure of either's issue, the other or his issue shall take the whole, and C.'s remainder over shall be postponed till the issue of both shall fail." 2 Bl.Comm. p. 381. In the case of Doe v. Webb, as stated in the opinion by Lord Mansfield, the testatrix gave her interest in certain lands "to her three daughters, and the heirs of their bodies, as tenants in common, and not as joint tenants; and, in default of such issue (not meaning thereby her daughters, for to them she gave estates respectively, but the heirs of their bodies) she [gave] the same to her own right heirs." The court held that none of the property went to the heir at law unless the issue of all the daughters should fail, when he took the whole, and that it was a case in which cross remainders were to be implied. 1 Taunt. 238. Where the testator devises certain lands "unto my two daughters, Elizabeth and Anne Meynel, and their heirs, equally to be divided betwixt them, and, in case they happen to die without issue, then I give and devise all the said lands to my nephew, Francis Meynel, * * * and to the heirs male of his body," "* * * Francis takes nothing upon the death of Anne, but * * * her part remains to her sister by way of a cross remainder." Holmes v. Meynel, T. Raym. 452. "Devise by testator * * * to his two daughters A. and B., to them, their heirs and assigns, but, in case they should die without issue, that the same should go to, and vest in, their two sisters, C. and D., held, * * * that the estate to C. and D. was a vested remainder, to take effect upon the death of both A. and C. [*sic*] without issue; that cross remainders in tail were to be implied between A. and B." Lillibridge v. Adie, 1 Mason, 223, Fed.Cas.No.8,350. See, also, Taaffe v. Commee, 10 H.L.Cas. 64; Pierce v. Hakes, 23 Pa.St. 231; Allen v. Trustees, 102 Mass. 262; Atherton v. Pye, 4 Term R. 710; Dow v. Doyle, 103 Mass. 489; Mackell v. Winter, 3 Ves. 536;

note to Green v. Stephens, 12 Ves. 418; 29 Am. & Eng.Enc.Law, p. 394 et seq.; 2 Jarm. Wills, 1339 et seq.

As is shown by the case of Fenby v. Johnson, 21 Md. 106, and the authorities there cited, there is a distinction "between devises in tail and in fee, as affecting the doctrine of cross remainders by implication." Where the devisees held the land as tenants in common in fee, with a limitation over upon a named contingency, the share of one who dies devolves upon his representatives, subject to be defeated by the happening of the contingency. There is, therefore, no lapse of the estate, and no necessity for the implication of cross remainders. The present case is, we think, not affected by this doctrine, for the estate of the testator's daughters is by the will limited to their lives, with remainder over upon their death. In the event of the death of one of the daughters without issue, her representatives could not take, because her interest, being for life only, would have been terminated by her death, and there would be nothing for her representatives to take. Her interest being at an end, and the ultimate devise not taking effect until the death of both daughters without children, an implication of cross remainders is necessary, in order to prevent a "chasm in the limitations," and a consequent partial intestacy.

For these reasons, we think that the trial judge did not err in sustaining the demurrer filed by the defendant to the petition of the plaintiff. Judgment affirmed. All the justices concurring.[33]

SPATHARIOTIS v. SPATHAS' ESTATE

Supreme Court of Colorado, 1965.
156 Colo. 131, 398 P.2d 39.[34]

McWILLIAMS, CHIEF JUSTICE. This writ of error involves the construction to be given a will and the precise issue is whether the will contains a devise by implication.

33. The dictum in the principal case to the effect that cross-remainders will not be implied where the incomplete limitation appears in a deed, is supported by English authority. See Edwards v. Allisston, 4 Russ. 78, 6 L.J.Ch. 30, 23 Eng.Rep. 118 (1827). However, there is American authority declaring that cross-remainders will be implied in a deed as well as in a will. Restatement, Property (1940) § 115, Comment *a*. Cross-remainders are not implied if the life tenants or tenants in tail take as joint tenants or as tenants by the entireties. In such cases the doctrine of survivorship precludes any gap in successive enjoyment and there is no need to imply remainders. See Kemp v. Sutton, 233 Mich. 249, 206 N.W. 366 (1925).

A limitation reading "to B and C as tenants in common for their lives and after the death of the survivor to D" has given rise to diverse interpretations if B dies during the lifetime of C. In that event some courts have implied a cross-remainder in favor of the surviving tenant C for his life. Addicks v. Addicks, 266 Ill. 349, 107 N.E. 580 (1914). Also it has been held that B's estate is entitled to receive B's share until C's death. Anderson v. Simpson, 214 Ky. 375, 283 S.W. 941 (1926). A third view holds that D, the remainderman, is entitled to receive B's share at B's death. New Jersey Title Guaranty & Trust Co. v. Elsworth, 108 N.J.Eq. 229, 154 A. 602 (1931).

34. Noted 42 Denver L.C.J. 52 (1965).

James Spathas died on August 15, 1960, leaving a last will and testament which contained the following provisions, among others:

* * *

"II. I give, devise and bequeath to my trustee hereinafter named, in trust nevertheless, the business properties known and numbered 828, 830, 832 and 834 Santa Fe Drive, located in the City and County of Denver, State of Colorado, to hold, manage and control in accordance with the authority hereinafter conferred upon it.

"III. All the rest, residue and remainder of my estate of every kind and description, wherever situate, I give, devise and bequeath to my beloved wife Eleni * * *.

"IV. If I am survived by my wife, my trustee shall accumulate the sum of Two Thousand Five Hundred Dollars ($2500) out of the income from the properties listed in Paragraph 2 and shall maintain the above sum at all times for the payment of real estate taxes, current expenses, major repairs and other emergencies; all income received after giving due effect to the above shall be paid to my wife so long as she shall live.

"V. In the event that my wife shall predecease me then I devise and bequeath all my property, real and personal, or mixed, to the First National Bank of Denver in trust nevertheless, and I direct my trustee to pay the entire net income from my trust estate to my nephew Georgi Spathariotis, Athens, Greece, (Carare 17—Athen) for so long as he shall live. Upon his death my trustee shall pay the entire net income from my trust estate to the surviving issue of my nephew Georgi Spathariotis, for a period of twenty years. At the end of said twenty year period the trustee shall distribute all of the corpus of the trust to the surviving issue of my nephew Georgi Spathâriotis, share and share alike."

This will was duly admitted to probate on September 2, 1960 in the County Court of the City and County of Denver. On April 17, 1961 the duly qualified executor of the estate of James Spathas filed a petition in the aforementioned County Court asking for a "construction and clarification of the last will and testament of James Spathas," averring that the will "presents certain inconsistencies and problems in that * * * said will makes no disposition of the legal remainder of the business properties known and numbered as 828, 830, 832 and 834 Santa Fe Drive."

Thereafter, James' widow, Eleni, and his nephew, Georgi, appeared by counsel and participated in the hearing held in connection with the petition for "construction and clarification" theretofore filed by the executor.

It was the basic position of Georgi in the trial court, as it is here, that though there is no *express devise* to him of any interest in the business properties situate on Santa Fe Drive, there is nonetheless a *devise by implication* of the remainder interest in said properties, in trust, to himself and his surviving issue.

Contrarily, it was Eleni's contention in the trial court, as it is here, that there was no devise, be it express or implied, of this remainder interest in the aforementioned business properties to any person whatsoever and that such being the case under applicable Colorado law this interest passes as intestate property to the heirs of James Spathas, namely herself, there being no surviving issue of James.

Upon hearing, the trial court decreed that the remainder interest in the business properties "is not devised or bequeathed to any person, the will being silent with respect thereto, * * * the remainder descends and must be distributed in the same manner as intestate property, * * * [and] under Colorado law the wife, Eleni * * * is the sole and only heir of testator and is entitled to take the fee of the 'business properties' as intestate property, and her life estate merges in the fee." By writ of error Georgi now seeks reversal of this judgment.

A "devise by implication" is a well-recognized concept in the general field of will construction, though Colorado authority bearing on this point is quite limited. The general rule concerning it is not difficult of statement, but a problem frequently arises when the rule is sought to be applied to a particular will. By way of a background, 57 Am.Jur. p. 782 reads as follows:

> "A bequest or devise may be made by mere implication, unless the implication violates public policy or some established rule of law, but to raise such implication it must be necessary to do so in order to carry out a manifest and plain intent of the testator which would fail unless the implication is allowed. Gifts by implication are not favored, and cannot rest upon conjecture. Such a gift will not be inferred from mere silence, but must be founded on expressions in the will, and is only admitted as a means of carrying out what the testator appears on the whole to have really meant, but failed somehow to express as distinctly as he should have done. It has been said that the probability of an intention to make the implied gift must be so strong that an intention contrary to that which is imputed to the testator cannot be supposed to have existed in his mind. On the other hand, it is not required that the inference be absolutely irresistible; it is enough if the circumstances, taken together, leave no doubt as to the testatorial intention, and in some cases it is said that the implication may be drawn from slight circumstances appearing in the will."

* * *

In Blatt v. Blatt, 79 Colo. 57, 243 P. 1099, 57 A.L.R. 221, the testator disposed of his property as follows: "I give, devise and bequeath to my wife * * * all my property, real, personal and mixed, and wherever situate, so long as she shall live", and there was no disposition whatsoever of the remainder. Under this circumstance this court held that the remainder was intestate property and in so holding stated:

> "* * * Though the intention of the testator is a paramount rule, that intention is to be derived from some expression of the

will itself and not mere silence. A devise by implication is never inferred by silence. It must rest on some language in the will which the testator has employed and not upon some language which the testator might have had in mind at the time but did not use. * * * "

Eleni, the surviving widow, argues that Blatt v. Blatt, supra, is the complete answer to the present controversy. Georgi on the other hand, contends that the instant case is quite readily distinguishable from the Blatt case in that the will of James Spathas is not "silent", but does contain language which would clearly justify and indeed require a devise by implication. The language relied upon by Georgi is that contained in paragraph V to the effect that "in the event my wife shall predecease me then I devise and bequeath all my property * * * to the First National Bank * * * in trust * * * and I direct my trustee to pay the entire net income from my trust estate to my nephew Georgi * * *." In other words, it is Georgi's position that but for paragraph V in the will, as the same has been set forth, supra, the Blatt case would be controlling and the remainder interest in the business properties would pass as intestate property, but that the presence of paragraph V in the will clearly indicates that it was the intention of James Spathas that his will create a remainder interest in his business properties, in trust, to Georgi and then to his surviving issue. Eleni, by way of reply, minimizes the importance of paragraph V, pointing out that by its very terms it is inoperative unless she predeceased James, which she did not.

In our view the Blatt case is not controlling, as we find language in the will which clearly supports a devise by implication of the remainder interest in the Santa Fe business properties, in trust, to Georgi and his surviving issue.

A somewhat analogous factual situation is to be found in Ussher v. Mercantile Trust Co., Mo., 328 S.W.2d 699. There, as here, the testator directed that certain property be held in trust with the income to be given to his wife, "as long as she shall live", and there was no express devise of the remainder interest. In the Ussher case there was also a paragraph number V, similar to paragraph V in the Spathas will, to the effect that "In the event my wife shall predecease me I hereby will and direct that the property be transferred and delivered to my two cousins * * *." (We recognize that in the Ussher case the paragraph numbered V contained a further proviso to the effect that "the same disposition shall be made of any of my property remaining which has not been disposed of under my will.") There, as here, the wife survived the testator, and a dispute arose as to whether the widow took the remainder interest by way of intestacy, or was there a devise by implication of said interest in favor of the two cousins. In the Ussher case, as here, the surviving widow argued that paragraph number V was "wholly conditional upon the testator's wife predeceasing him and, since she survived him, conveys no interest in the estate." The Supreme Court of Missouri rejected this contention and held that under the circumstances there was a devise by implication. It is to be observed that in the Ussher case, as in the Russell case, a devise by implication was grounded upon an express devise which was to take effect in the event of a particular contingency, *which contingency did not occur.*

* * *

[In omitted portions of the opinion, the Court reviewed the facts and holdings in Russell v. Russell, 16 N.J.Super. 589, 85 A.2d 296 (1951) and In re Selner's Estate, 261 App.Div. 618, 26 N.Y.S.2d 783 (1941), aff'd 287 N.Y. 664, 39 N.E.2d 287 (1941).]

The foregoing authorities afford ample precedent for holding in the case now before us that the remainderman's interest in the business properties on Santa Fe Drive is not intestate property, and that there is a devise by implication of this interest, in trust, in favor of Georgi and his issue. James Spathas by his last will and testament solemnly declared that if his beloved wife should predecease him all of his property—be it business or non-business property—should go to a named trustee with a direction that the income therefrom should go first to his nephew Georgi, and then to Georgi's issue. He further provided that if his wife should outlive him, then his nonbusiness property should go outright to his wife, but that his business property should go to the same trustee with the direction that the income therefrom go to his wife, but only "so long as she may live." There is no contention that there was by any provision of the will a devise of these business properties to Eleni, and under the terms of the will she is entitled only to the income therefrom for her lifetime. Eleni was not given any power of appointment, nor did the will permit any invasion of the corpus of the trust by the trustee. Under such circumstances, the argument that James intended that Eleni take the remainderman interest in said property by intestacy is not very convincing. See Simes and Smith, The Law of Future Interests, Second Edition, § 842, p. 328. For all these reasons it is abundantly clear to us that James Spathas did *not* intend that his beloved wife Eleni should take the remainder interest in the South Santa Fe Drive Business properties.

Having thus established that there was no intent that this remainder interest should go to Eleni, by testacy or intestacy, is there any language in the will which could form the basis for a devise by implication of this interest? We find such language in paragraph V of the last will and testament of James Spathas. There, in clear and unequivocal language he directed that "in the event * * * my wife shall predecease me * * * I devise and bequeath all my property * * * to the First National Bank of Denver in trust * * * to pay the entire net income to my nephew Georgi * * * for so long as he shall live * * * [and] upon his death my trustee shall pay the entire net income to the surviving issue of my nephew Georgi for a period of twenty years * * *." This language is more than adequate to form the basis for implying a devise of the remainder interest in the South Santa Fe business properties, in trust, to Georgi and his issue. In so holding we are not making a new will but "merely giving effect to testamentary intention limited to language within the four corners of the will" by doing that which was done in the Russell, Ussher and Selner cases, i.e. using an express devise which was to take effect only in the event of a particular contingency, *which contingency did not occur*, as the basis for implying a like devise in a contingency which did occur but was not fully covered or provided for by the will.

The judgment is reversed and the cause remanded for further proceedings consistent with the views herein expressed.[35]

PROBLEMS

1. Testatrix's will left her entire estate to her husband if he survived her and further provided that if she and her husband died in a common disaster, the estate was to go to named devisees. She and her husband did not die in a common disaster, but her husband predeceased her. Should the estate go intestate or to the named devisees? In re Estate of Wood, 226 So.2d 46 (Fla. App.1969).

2. Testator's will devises his estate to his wife and in the event she "predeceases" him then to a named devisee. Testator and his wife are later divorced. If the governing statute simply provides that divorce revokes the provision for the former spouse, should the court imply a gift to the alternate devisee in such a situation? See Chapter VI Section 2(3).

35. A devise to "B for life and if B dies without issue, to C and his heirs" fails to provide expressly for the disposition of the property if B dies with issue. According to the limitation C will take only if B dies without issue. Some courts have created a gift by implication in favor of the issue of B, if B dies survived by issue.

The attitude of courts toward implying gifts where the limitation is incomplete in failing to provide for a contingency which actually occurs, varies a great deal. Thus in In re Blake's Estate, 157 Cal. 448, 466, 108 P. 287, 295 (1910) the court says: "Bequests by implication have from remote times been sustained where no direct language in a will is found to support them, but where from informal language used such reasonable construction can be placed on it as implies an intention to make a bequest." The Illinois court in Bond v. Moore, 236 Ill. 576, 580, 86 N.E. 386, 387 (1908) expresses a reluctance to imply gifts, in the following language: "Devises by implication have been recognized but they can only be given effect in cases of such clear necessity that from the will itself no reasonable doubt of the intention can exist. * * * The implication must be so strong that an intention contrary to that imputed to the testator cannot be supposed to have existed in his mind." For a discussion of gifts by implication, see Simes and Smith, Future Interests (2d Ed., 1956) §§ 841–845; Note, "Implied Gifts of Remainders", 76 W.Va.L. Rev. 217 (1974).

Since the inter vivos trust performs the same function as a will, the modern view is that a court can imply gifts to fill gaps in the trust document. E.g., DuPont v. Equitable Security Trust Co., 35 Del.Ch. 514, 122 A.2d 429 (1956); A. B. v. Wilmington Trust Co., 41 Del.Ch. 191, 191 A. 2d 98 (1963).

A court will not imply a gift if there is any possibility that the testator did not intend a gift. Thus, where the will devised "furnishings and personal effects" to a spendthrift son outright, but "if my son should predecease me, then the home, furnishings and personal effects" were to be added to the residue, the court refused to imply a gift of the home to the son; the same clause appeared in an earlier will which did specifically devise the home to the son outright whereas the last will created a spendthrift trust for the son during lifetime. Seattle-First Nat. Bank v. Tingley, 22 Wash.App. 258, 589 P.2d 811 (1978).

SECTION 4. EFFECT OF FAILURE OF AN INTEREST

SELLICK v. SELLICK

Supreme Court of Michigan, 1919.
207 Mich. 194, 173 N.W. 609, 5 A.L.R. 1621.

FELLOWS, J. This case involves the construction of the will of William J. Sellick, late of Paw Paw, Van Buren county, and the effect as between certain of the legatees of the election of the widow to take under the statute. Mr. Sellick left real estate inventoried at $8,500 and personal property inventoried at upwards of $176,000. He left a widow, Caroline Sellick, and one son, William R. Sellick, the plaintiff, now grown to manhood, who was the child of a former wife. He also left collateral kindred, including the defendants Arthur F. Sellick, a nephew, and Gertrude Sellick, a niece. To his collateral kindred other than defendants he gave varying sums aggregating $15,000. By the second clause of his will he gave to each of the defendants $5,000. The first clause of his will is as follows:

> "I give, devise and bequeath to my wife, Caroline Sellick, twenty-five thousand dollars ($25,000), to be used and enjoyed by her during her life and at her death to be equally divided between my nephew, Arthur F. Sellick, and my niece, Gertrude Sellick."

The residue of his estate he gave to his son, the plaintiff. The widow elected to take under the statute. The trial judge construed the first clause of the will, when taken in connection with the second clause, which gave each defendant $5,000, and the residuary clause, as giving the widow absolutely $25,000 and accordingly held that the defendants took nothing under such clause. This rendered unnecessary the determination, of the other questions involved. From a decree in accordance with these views the defendants appeal, and it is here urged by their counsel that the first clause of the will gave the widow a life estate, with remainder over to them; that by the election of the widow to take under the statute her life estate is at an end, and that, applying the doctrine of acceleration of remainders, they are now entitled to said sum of $25,000. On the other hand, it is insisted by counsel for the appellee that the bequest to the widow gave her an absolute estate; that the bequest falls within that class of bequests controlled by Jones v. Jones, 25 Mich. 401, and kindred cases, and that the decree should be affirmed. It is further insisted by appellee's counsel that if we decline to follow this contention and accept the view that a life estate only was given the widow, still we should not apply the doctrine of acceleration of remainders, but that such life estate, given to the widow by the will, should be sequestered to reimburse the plaintiff in part for the depletion of his bequest occasioned by the payment out of it of the sums necessary to make up the widow's statutory share. In short, that he is known in the law as a disappointed legatee, and that the doctrine of acceleration of remainders should not be adopted at the expense of disappointed legatees.

We are not disposed to take time or space in differentiating between the instant case and Jones v. Jones, supra, and kindred cases. Under the repeated decisions of this court the clause of Mr. Sellick's will above quoted gave the widow the use of $25,000 for her life, a life estate, and it gave her no more. Glover v. Reid, 80 Mich. 228, 45 N.W. 91; Gadd v. Stoner, 113 Mich. 689, 71 N.W. 1111; Farlin v. Sanborn, 161 Mich. 615, 126 N.W. 634, 137 Am.St.Rep. 525; In re Moor's Estate, 163 Mich. 353, 128 N.W. 198; Bateman v. Case, 170 Mich. 617, 136 N.W. 590; Laberteaux v. Gale, 196 Mich. 150, 162 N.W. 968. The opinions in these cases, together with the authorities cited in them, established beyond doubt that under the language found in this clause Caroline Sellick took but the life use of $25,000. While it is true that the entire will must be considered, we find nothing at variance from this conclusion in any of its provisions. The fact that the testator gave each of the defendants $5,000 to be paid presently in no way modifies the plain, unambiguous language of clause 1 by which he gave them $25,000, to be paid upon the death of his wife.

This brings us at once to the interesting and novel questions in the case. It must be conceded at the outset that the decisions of the court of last resort of the state of Pennsylvania sustain the contention of defendants' counsel unequivocally. Coover's Appeal, 74 Pa. 143; Ferguson's Estate, 138 Pa. 208, 20 Atl. 945; Vance's Estate, 141 Pa. 201, 21 Atl. 643, 12 L.R.A. 227, 23 Am.St.Rep. 267. Is the rule laid down by the Pennsylvania court supported by the weight of authority and by equitable principles? Should the doctrine of acceleration of remainders be applied where by its application the remainderman gets more than the will gave to him and legatees either specific or residuary get less? To these questions we shall now direct our attention.

Some support is given defendant's contention by the holding of the Court of Appeals of Kentucky in Trustees Church Home v. Morris, 99 Ky. 317, 36 S.W. 2. But in that case it was said:

> "There is no reason whatever, in this case to depart from the direct command of the testator to distribute this estate in the manner in which he directs it to be done. It might be different if an intention was apparent to benefit certainly the residuary legatees, and the bulk of the estate was expected to be left for them. In such event they, and not others, could be said to be the chief objects of the testator's bounty, and they would be protected, not because it would be equitable or just, but because such was the intention of the testator."

And Sherman v. Baker, 20 R.I. 446, 40 Atl. 11, 40 L.R.A. 717, Dean v. Hart, 62 Ala. 308, Slocum v. Hagaman, 176 Ill. 533, 52 N.E. 332, and Adams v. Gillespie, 55 N.C. 244, give color to defendants' claim. But some of these cases only consider the general doctrine of acceleration of remainders and do not determine that such doctrine should be applied where by an election not to take under the will other legacies to other legatees are diminished.

That the determination of the life estate by act other than the death of the life tenant is as effective to let the remainderman into possession as the death of the life tenant, that the time of taking possession is accelerated by such act, is generally recognized in this country and in England. Thus in Jull v. Jacobs, 35 L.T.R. 153, the testator gave a life estate to his daughter, with remainder over to her children on their becoming of age. The daughter witnessed the will, thus incapacitating her from taking the life estate. The life estate having failed from this fact, it was held that the children who took the fee should be let into possession at once, Vice Chancellor Malins remarking:

> "Then, taking away her life estate, does that cause an intestacy as to the life, or an acceleration of the estate in remainder? It is clear that the children are postponed because of the mother's life estate, but if she does not take the life estate why should they be postponed? It is a mere accident, through ignorance on the part of the testator, and I think that, as the tenant for life cannot take, the reason for postponing the children ceases."

In the case of Lainson v. Lainson, 18 Beav. 1, the testator gave an estate for life to A., and on his decease to B. in tail. By a codicil he revoked the devise to A. It was held that the estate of B. was accelerated, and that he took at once. A similar result was reached on a similar state of facts in Eavestaff v. Austin, 19 Beav. 591. But it has also been held in England that where the heir takes against the will under which he received considerable benefit, those devisees and legatees disappointed by such election may not have a lien upon the estate, but may require such heir to account for the whole amount received by him under the will. Greenwood v. Penny, 12 Beav. 403.

This court has recognized the doctrine of acceleration of remainders upon the termination of the life estate of the widow by her election to take under the statute. In re Schulz's Estate, 113 Mich. 592, 71 N.W. 1079. But that was a case where none of the legatees were in any way harmed by the application of the doctrine. By the election of the widow to take under the statute their bequests were proportionately diminished, and by the acceleration of their remainders they were proportionately reimbursed.

The Supreme Court of Ohio in Millikin v. Welliver, 37 Ohio St. 460, has also recognized the doctrine of acceleration of remainders. But that case, like the Schulz Case, did not involve a disappointed legatee whose legacy was depleted to make up the sum paid to the widow for her statutory right. This was pointed out by that court in the later case of Holdren v. Holdren, 78 Ohio St. 276, 85 N.E. 537, 18 L.R.A., (N.S.), 272, where the court quoted from the former case and said:

> "This holding is based upon the doctrine of acceleration, but it must be understood as limited to cases in which that doctrine is applicable; otherwise it is too broad. In that case there was no disappointed legatee, but all of the estate went to the remainder-

man. It is well settled, when a widow elects not to take under a will, but to take under the law, her portion under the will will be sequestered to compensate those beneficiaries under the will whose shares, are cut down by her election."

* * * [Omitted is the court's discussion of other cases establishing the same principle.] * * *

Mr. Pomeroy in his work on Equity Jurisprudence (1 Pomeroy, Eq. Jur. [4th Ed.] § 517), says in considering the question of elections:

> "The other parties interested as donees under the instrument creating the necessity for an election are affected by it, when made, in the following manner: If the person on whom the duty of electing rests elects to take in conformity with the will or other instrument of donation, he thereby relinquishes his own property, and must release or convey it to the donee upon whom the instrument had assumed to confer it. If he elects against the will or other instrument of donation, he thereby retains his own property, and must compensate the disappointed donee out of the estate given to himself by the donor. A court of equity will then sequester the benefits intended for the electing beneficiary, in order to secure compensation to those persons whom his election disappoints. This rule is applied in many of the American cases cited below to elections made by widows in favor of their dower and against the testamentary provisions, whereby the interests of other devisees were disturbed. Such disappointed devisees are held entitled to compensation out of the benefits intended to be conferred by the will on the widow, but which she had rejected." * * *

We are persuaded that under the great weight of authority the contention of plaintiff's counsel in this regard must prevail. While the doctrine of acceleration of the time of taking effect of the remainder upon the termination of the life estate by act other than the death of the life tenant (i.e., by the election of the widow to take under the statute) must be recognized and applied in proper cases, such doctrine should not be applied where by the election a portion only of the legacies are diminished in order to make up the amount required by the statute to satisfy the widow's statutory rights. And that this should be true whether the legacy diminished be a specific or a residuary one. Under such circumstances the disappointed legatee may in a court of equity compel the sequestration of the legacy to the refractory legatee for the purpose of diminishing the amount of his disappointment.

Manifestly this is in consonance with equitable principles. In the instant case the residuary fund given to the plaintiff has been diminished by many thousand dollars in order to discharge the claim of the widow resulting from her election. To adopt defendants' claim would give to them the $25,000 many years before the time fixed by the testator for its payment. They would not only receive the amount given them by the will, but they would also receive the widow's life estate renounced by her to the disadvantage of the plaintiff. Equitable principles do not require that this should be done.

We are asked to fix the present worth of the widow's life use of the $25,000 with a view of finally closing the estate and disposing of all matters at once. The parties interested are all of age, and may make such adjustment as they may desire, but we do not feel empowered to fix the present worth of the widow's use and direct its present payment. We see no occasion, however, to longer hold the estate open. A trustee may be appointed to handle this fund of $25,000. He shall annually pay the income thereon to the plaintiff during the life of the widow, and upon her death pay the corpus to defendants in equal shares.

It follows that the decree must be reversed, and one here entered in conformity with this opinion. The defendants will recover costs of this court. Neither party will recover costs of the circuit court.[36]

KILCOYNE v. REILLY

United States Court of Appeals, District of Columbia Circuit, 1957.
101 U.S.App.D.C. 380, 249 F.2d 472.

BURGER, CIRCUIT JUDGE. Emma F. Shepley died in August 1955, leaving an estate consisting of stock and secured notes valued at about $124,000. Her husband, Belmar H. Shepley, survived her; there were no children. The District Court admitted to probate a longhand will dated June 25, 1955 by which the husband was bequeathed a life interest in the entire estate. Upon his death ten named legatees were to receive certain personal effects and cash legacies totaling $53,000, the balance of the estate "to be divided among the children of my [deceased] brother Albert E. Berry."

36. The life estate may fail for a variety of reasons, although the most common is election by the life tenant-spouse to take against the will. If the failure does not diminish other interests under the will, acceleration of the remainder interests is usually the result; this would be the case where there is a simple renunciation by the life tenant, for example. Even if the future interest is expressly contingent upon the remainderman's surviving the life tenant, some courts will accelerate on the theory that the testator intended to benefit remaindermen living at the time their interests become possessory and that the time is accelerated by the failure of the interest, just as if the life tenant died.

If the life estate fails and as a result other interests under the will are diminished, the problem has a new dimension. This is the case where the spouse elects to take a statutory share of the estate and gives up a life estate under the will, or where the life tenant renounces in exchange for a settlement out of the estate. Here the choice is between acceleration or sequestration of the life estate for the benefit of those persons whose interests in the estate are most diminished by the life tenant's action. The function of the court is essentially a salvage operation—to prevent distortion of the testamentary scheme. Rarely does a testator indicate what his intent would be in such an event, although a draftsman should give attention to the problem in any case where there is a strong possibility of election by the surviving spouse. See Aberg v. First National Bank in Dallas, 450 S.W.2d 403 (Tex.Civ.App. Dallas, 1970), Noted, 2 Tex.Tech.L.Rev. 132 (1970) (where acceleration was denied and the problem and cases are discussed in detail at 450 S.W.2d 407); Cunningham v. Cunningham, 230 Ga. 463, 197 S.E.2d 731 (1973), Noted, 8 Ga.L.Rev. 502 (1974) (Problem raised by assignment by life tenant to alternative contingent remainderman); Prichard, "Acceleration and Contingent Remainders", 32 Camb.L.J. 246 (1973).

For an interesting case with an excellent discussion of the law but reaching a questionable result, see In re Nixon's Estate, 71 N.J.Super. 450, 177 A.2d 292 (1962), Noted, 61 Mich.L.Rev. 1007 (1963).

The surviving husband renounced the provisions of the will and elected to take under the statute which granted him one-half of the net estate. The executor petitioned the District Court for instructions as to the effect of the election upon the bequests contained in the will.

Appellants, the residuary legatees and heirs-at-law of decedent, claimed that the renunciation so distorted the testamentary scheme that the altered distribution no longer effectuated the testatrix' wishes. In the District Court, and now here, appellants urge in the alternative (1) that the distribution of the whole estate should be made as though the testatrix died intestate, or (2) that the husband's one-half share be charged wholly against legatees other than appellants or ratably against all the legacies made in the will, or (3) that the life estate renounced by the husband, i.e., one-half of the estate remaining after he receives his elective one-half, be sequestered until the husband's death with income therefrom paid to appellants for diminution of their remainder share.

The District Court, upon the motion of the executor, granted summary judgment, and ordered the executor to (1) deliver to the surviving husband one-half of the net assets of the estate, (2) deliver and pay to the specific and general legatees the items and sums bequeathed to them in accordance with the will and (3) divide the residuum among the residuary legatees. The residuary legatees appeal.

In support of their first contention appellants rely on Pascucci v. Alsop, 79 U.S.App.D.C. 354, 147 F.2d 880, certiorari denied 1945, 325 U.S. 868, 65 S.Ct. 1406, 89 L.Ed. 1987, in which this court held that marriage and birth of issue subsequent to execution of a will operated as a revocation of the will. But there the "change in circumstances" occurred *before* the will became operative and was, of course, known to the testator. Neither the will nor the surrounding circumstances warrant the inference in this case that decedent would have preferred intestacy to the adjustment of the legacies caused by the husband's election.

The question to be resolved, therefore, is whether the general rules of abatement control an alteration affecting one-half of the estate under a will executed two months before death and operating to reduce the residue designated for next of kin from $50,000 to $60,000 to between $4,000 and $7,000.

The general rules governing the abatement of legacies were developed to meet the situation where the net distributable assets of a decedent were insufficient to satisfy in full the testamentary gifts. This general rule provides that residuary legacies abate first, followed by general legacies and then specific and demonstrative legacies, which give way together ratably. This order of abatement rests on an arbitrary presumption of law as to the probable intent of the testator where the will does not anticipate the necessity for abatement.[37] The present validity of an assumption that testators tend to

37. [Footnotes by the court have been eliminated, except the following. Ed.] Cases have applied the conventional order of abatement to satisfy the elective

use specific and general legacies as a means of providing for those to whom or for whom they desire a priority is questionable. While there are few absolutes in this area, we can notice judicially, if we need, that contemporary wills more often than not use the residuary clause to carry out the most important provisions. It is impossible to say flatly that any pattern of disposition is controlling: each will must be examined in the light of the entire background and fact situation and only the most general guides can be formulated.

Some jurisdictions, notably New York, have attempted to solve this problem by applying more flexible and equitable standards, keyed essentially to a *substantial* distortion of the testamentary scheme caused by an election hostile to the interests of the named beneficiaries. A leading case in this regard is In re Byrnes' Estate, 1933, 149 Misc. 449, 267 N.Y.S. 627, in which a net estate of $180,000 remained after expenses and debts. After providing legacies and trusts of $40,000 to three non-profit institutions, the will bequeathed the residue to the widow in trust for life or until remarriage. Under the terms of the residuary trust the remainder, upon the death or remarriage of the widow, went to children of the testator's brother living at the termination of the life estate, or their issue. The widow effectively elected to take under the statute. Her election depleted the net estate by one-half, leaving only $90,000 in place of an anticipated $140,000 balance after satisfaction of the $40,000 in charitable gifts.

The New York court was confronted with the question of whether the widow's elective share of $90,000 should be charged wholly out of the residue or equally apportioned out of the cash legacies, charitable trusts and the residue. The court adopted the second alternative: "By apportioning the withdrawn share [of the surviving spouse] against all the beneficiaries, the general plan of the will may be, to a great extent, preserved and the balance maintained between the respective preliminary and residuary beneficiaries."

The relevant New York statute provided: "Where any such election [by a spouse] shall have been made, the will shall be valid as to the residue remaining after the elective share provided in this section has been deducted *and the terms of the will shall as far as possible remain effective.*" (Emphasis added.) While no comparable statute exists in this jurisdiction, it seems clear to us that the New York statute was simply declaratory of the broad equitable powers of a court dealing with the construction of wills. Courts have always endeavored to ascertain the probable intention of the testator and to carry that into effect with a minimum disturbance to the general testamentary plan. The New York statute, at most, represents a negation in certain circumstances of the arbitrary presumptions (1) that the average testator prefers specific and general legatees to those mentioned in the residuary clause and (2) that a testator is presumed to contem-

share of a renouncing spouse upon the theory that "residuary" contemplates that which is left after payment of all other bequests. See cases collected in 1954, 36 A.L.R.2d 299.

plate and provide for a renunciation by the spouse. Instead, the courts, using inherent equity powers, are authorized to shape a presumption providing for a more equitable adjustment of the estate. Of course, even this rule of abatement gives way where the will itself indicates its application would be inappropriate or contrary to the testator's intentions.

Some state statutes now contain more explicit provisions for the apportionment of a depletion resulting from reduction of the distributable estate as a consequence of an election by a surviving spouse. Even under such statutes, however, courts have recognized that "Irrespective of statute, it is a general rule applicable to cases of this type that a widow's election to take against the will defeats the testator's intention in part and the court will try to ascertain his primary intention and carry it into effect as nearly as possible." In re Maske's Estate, 1952, 243 Iowa 1394, 55 N.W.2d 474, 476, 36 A.L.R. 2d 285.

Recourse to the history of the development of the general rules of abatement of legacies shows that they were evolved by courts over a period of time to deal with practical problems. The same source of judicial power by which courts formulated what might be called general rules of abatement of legacies empowers us to deal with the problem here presented. The testatrix in this case prepared her will in longhand, apparently with the benefit of a will professionally drawn a few years prior. The dispositive provisions of the two wills are nearly similar, the testatrix making certain cash legacies and bequeathing the remainder to appellants. Such inferences as can be drawn from this comparison support the conclusion that testatrix at all times intended the appellants to be the recipients of a substantial portion of her estate. The fact that appellants were her next of kin also supports this conclusion.

Furthermore the will was prepared only two months before testatrix' death. Testatrix must have been aware that her assets were sufficient to satisfy all administration expenses and still insure appellants a sum in excess of $50,000. It is equally plain that by reason of the surviving spouse's election the distribution affirmed by the District Court's summary judgment operates so that there will be substantially less than $9,000 available for the residuary legatees. That this is a substantial distortion of the testamentary plan there is no doubt. The presumption that a testator realizes the spouse may elect against a will carries little weight where, as here, decedent prepared her own will and had no reason to believe that her husband, then in his 80's, would renounce a life estate in the whole and elect to take one-half absolutely.

Considering these circumstances we adopt the rule applied by the New York courts and hold, in this case, the general pecuniary legacies should abate pro rata with the residuary legacies. We think this is the sound and equitable approach, and one which more nearly conforms to the presumed intention of the testator, where the diminution of assets in an estate results (1) from election by a surviving spouse

(2) in circumstances where this clearly produces a substantial distortion of the testamentary scheme (3) as it applies to blood relatives or others similarly situated who have a natural claim on the bounty of the testator, (4) where there is no discernible evidence that the election was foreseeable and (5) where there is no contrary intent manifested in the will as to the order of abatement and none appears from the circumstances of the parties.

We next come to the specific nonpecuniary legacies. In this case they are a ring and a silver dish of nominal value only but sometimes such legacies are of substantial value and represent a significant proportion of a whole estate. There is no logical basis for treating these legacies in any way different from general pecuniary legacies and in the application of the above rule a charge in the nature of a burden or lien attaches to the specific legacy and this "must be satisfied either from the subject matter of the several gifts or by exoneration by the donees, in a manner identical with that practiced in respect of any other lien. * * *." In re Topazio's Estate, 1940, 175 Misc. 132, 22 N.Y.S.2d 847, 851; 1954, 36 A.L.R.2d 302.

Appellants also urge that the remaindermen's shares should not be accelerated and that the renounced portion of the estate, i.e., the husband's life interest, should be sequestered for the benefit of appellants during the life of the husband. "It is not possible to lay down a hard and fast rule of acceleration applicable under all circumstances to the distribution of estates wherein the [spouse] has declined to take under the will. But it may be said that it is the duty of courts to accomplish as near as may be done equitably the same result between the beneficiaries as would have resulted from distribution of the estate in accordance with the terms of the will." In re Povey's Estate, 1935, 271 Mich. 627, 261 N.W. 98, 99–100, 99 A.L.R. 1183. See also McDonnell v. McDonnell, 1940, 72 App.D.C. 317, 114 F.2d 478.

Under D.C.Code, 1951, § 45–812, the pecuniary and residuary legatees took a vested interest in the portion of the estate bequeathed them. Absent manifestation of a contrary intent, it is generally accepted that "Where the remainder is vested, in title and interest, as of the date of the death of the testator under the terms of the will, acceleration is desirable and should be enforced." In re Byrnes' Estate, supra, 267 N.Y.S. at page 632. See also, Mayhew v. Atkinson, D.C.D.C.1950, 93 F.Supp. 753. Moreover, where, as here, the pro rata abatement will remove the substantial distortion among the dispositions, the equitable considerations favoring sequestration disappear, and the attendant expenses and delays are avoided. See Restatement, Property § 234 (1936).

The case is remanded for modification of the judgment to conform with a distribution not inconsistent with our holding. This does not alter the District Court's order accelerating the remainder interests.

Affirmed in part; reversed in part and remanded.[38]

NOTE

Section 2–207 of the Uniform Probate Code (1975) provides:

"(a) In the proceeding for an elective share, values included in the augmented estate which pass or have passed to the surviving spouse, or which would have passed to the spouse but were renounced, are applied first to satisfy the elective share and to reduce any contributions due from other recipients of transfers included in the augmented estate. For purposes of this subsection, the electing spouse's beneficial interest in any life estate or in any trust shall be computed as if worth one half of the total value of the property subject to the life estate, or of the trust estate, unless higher or lower values for these interests are established by proof.

"(b) Remaining property of the augmented estate is so applied that liability for the balance of the elective share of the surviving spouse is equitably apportioned among the recipients of the augmented estate in proportion to the value of their interests therein.

"(c) Only original transferees from, or appointees of, the decedent and their donees, to the extent the donees have the property or its proceeds, are subject to the contribution to make up the elective share of the surviving spouse. A person liable to contribution may choose to give up the property transferred to him or to pay its value as of the time it is considered in computing the augmented estate."

The original (1969) version of § 2–206(a) and § 2–207 of the Code would have permitted the spouse to renounce (including for example limited interests as beneficiary of a testamentary trust) provided the renunciation was expressed in the petition for the elective share, and not have the renounced gift counted against the elective share as sub. (a) above requires. The 1975 change operates to preserve the estate plan, but also leaves difficult problems in valuing interests of the spouse under complicated trusts. Under the 1975 provisions there is little reason for an electing spouse to also renounce.

Compare the Code sections on effect of the claim of a pretermitted heir: Section 2–301(b) and 2–302(c), discussed in Chapter IV.

38. See 24 Iowa L.Rev. 714 (1939); 1942 Wis.L.Rev. 312; 36 A.L.R.2d 291 (1954).

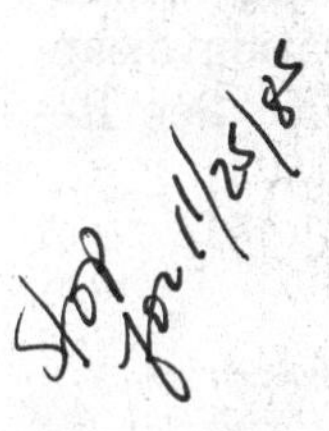

Chapter XVI

SOCIAL RESTRICTIONS ON PERPETUITIES AND ACCUMULATIONS

Scope Note

This chapter deals with the Rule against Perpetuities and restrictions upon accumulations of income. The common law Rule and the related statutory rule against suspension of the power of alienation are considered in application to class gifts and powers of appointment, the two most troublesome problems in the estate field. The application of these rules to areas other than the estate field is only briefly mentioned. Direct restraints on alienation are not within the scope of this chapter; we have already encountered the specialized restraint on the interest of a trust beneficiary in Chapter VIII.

SECTION 1. HISTORY AND SUMMARY OF THE RULE AGAINST PERPETUITIES [1]

The average practitioner regards the area covered by this Chapter as a "specialty". Yet the fundamentals of what we have come to call

1. There is an abundance of valuable literature in this field. Professor Leach's "Perpetuities in a Nutshell", 51 Harv.L.Rev. 638 (1938) and "Perpetuities: The Nutshell Revisited", 78 Harv.L.Rev. 973 (1965) are highly recommended. The classic work is Gray, The Rule Against Perpetuities (4th Ed., 1942). See also American Law of Property (1952) Vol. VI, Part 24; Bergin and Haskell, Preface to Estates in Land and Future Interests (1966) 183–229; 5 Powell, The Law of Real Property (Rohan Rev.1975) Chs. 71–73; Simes and Smith, Future Interests (2d Ed., 1956) Ch. 39.

For a discussion of policy issues, see Simes, Public Policy and the Dead Hand (1955); Grimes, "Runnymede Revisited", 6 Val.L.Rev. 135 (1972); Van Doren, "Redistributing Wealth by Controlling Inheritance: The Community Interest in the Rule Against Perpetuities and the Estate Tax", 3 Fla.State U.L.Rev. 33 (1975). For a summary of legislation concerning perpetuities, see Perpetuity Legislation Handbook, 2 Real Prop.Prob. & Tr.J. 176 (1967). Legislative trends are considered in Eckhardt, "Perpetuities Reform by Legislation," 31 Mo.L.Rev. 56 (1966); Leach, "Perpetuities: What Legislatures, Courts and Practitioners Can Do About the Follies of the Rule," 13 Kan.L.Rev. 351 (1965); Lynn, "Perpetuities Reform: An Analysis of Developments in England and the United States," 113 U.Pa.L.Rev. 508 (1965); Comment, "Further Trends in Perpetuities", 5 Real Prop.Prob. & Tr.J. 333 (1970); Note, "Perpetuities Reform: Approaches and Reproaches", 49 Notre Dame Law 611 (1974). On state developments, see Bostick, "The Tennessee Rule Against Perpetuities: A Proposal for Statutory Reform", 27 Vand.L.Rev. 1153 (1974); Dukeminier, "Perpetuities Revi-

the Rule against Perpetuities can be mastered with certainty and should be part of the professional equipment of every will or trust draftsman, so that its pitfalls may be avoided. Most of the future interests held invalid under the Rule could have been valid if the creating instrument had been properly drafted. Since local statutes [2] and decisions vary the picture given in this chapter in degree at least, the student will want to learn with precision the local law. Yet the mobility of modern society, and increasing probability of clients who own property in several states, make appreciation of the national picture more than academic.

Like most property rules, the modern form of the Rule can be best understood by study of its historical development. That history begins with the struggle to make land freely transferable under the feudal system. Only the landmarks are here reviewed. The decision in D'Arundel's Case (1225) that the present holder of the fee could defeat the claim of his heirs by conveyance was the first of a series of judicial efforts to make land freely alienable by the present holder. The Statute of Quia Emptores in 1290 eliminated the fine imposed by the overlord for transfer. The attempt of the courts to prevent limitations which would keep land in a family for future generations (to "B and the heirs of his body") was temporarily halted by the Statute De Donis in 1285, permitting creation of the fee tail. But the judicial invention of the common recovery as a means of barring the reversion and the entail, in Taltarum's Case (1472), made it possible once again for the present holder of the fee tail to convey a fee simple. Even after recognition of contingent remainders the law courts facilitated present transfer of the fee simple. Under the doctrine of destructibility the holder of the life estate could defeat the contingent remaindermen by a tortious feoffment or by effecting a merger with the reversioner. The application of the Rule in Shelley's Case where

sion in California: Perpetual Trusts Permitted," 55 Cal.L.Rev. 678 (1967); Logan, "Oklahoma Perpetuities and Such," 7 Tulsa L.J. 5 (1971); Lynn, "The Ohio Perpetuities Reform Statute," 29 Ohio St.L.J. 1 (1968); Powell, "The Rule Against Perpetuities and Spendthrift Trusts in New York: Comments and Suggestions", 71 Col.L.Rev. 688 (1971); Schuyler, "The Statute Concerning Perpetuities", 65 Nw.U.L.Rev. 3 (Illinois) (1970); Smith, "Perpetuities in New Jersey: A Plea for Judicial Supremacy", 24 Rutgers L.Rev. 80 (1969); Comment, "New York's Two-Part Statutory Substitute for the Common Law Rule Against Perpetuities", 38 Alb.L.Rev. 570 (1974); Notes, "Perpetuities—Cy Pres Invades Oklahoma", 25 Okl.L.Rev. 139 (1972); "Perpetuities—Texas Enacts Cy Pres Statute", 49 Tex.L.Rev. 181 (1970); "The Rule Against Perpetuities—Statutory Reform" (Ohio) 20 West.Res.L.Rev. 295 (1968); Kurtz, "Iowa Rule Against Perpetuities: A State of Little or No Law", 65 Iowa L.Rev. 177 (1979); Note, "Rule Against Perpetuities in Kansas", 19 Washburn L.J. 284 (1980); Link, "Rule Against Perpetuities in North Carolina", 57 N.C.L.Rev. 727 (1979). For excellent suggestions concerning drafting, see McGovern, "Perpetuities Pitfalls and How Best to Avoid Them", 6 Real Prop.Prob. & Tr.J. 155 (1971).

2. A number of states have constitutional or statutory provisions dealing with perpetuities in very general terms. Such provisions usually have little significance although they may impel the court to enforce the common law rule. For example, see Estate of Sahlender, 89 Cal. App.2d 329, 201 P.2d 69 (1949), where former California Constitution Art. XX, § 9 (repealed in 1969) led the Court to invalidate future interests in a trust even though the trust met the requirements of a statutory rule against suspension of the power of alienation.

there was a conveyance to B for life, remainder to his heirs enabled the present holder freely to alienate the full interest in fee. These and other court-made rules made it possible to defeat the interests of future generations by favoring the present holder of the land in his efforts to transfer.

The development of springing and shifting uses, recognized first in Chancery and then foisted upon the law courts by the Statute of Uses in 1536, disrupted this neat judicial pattern, as did the Statute of Wills in 1540, permitting creation of new future interests by will. Draftsmen were quick to seize upon these new weapons to further private plans for tying up land for future generations. When these new types of future interests were held to be indestructible as to an estate for years (Manning's Case, 1609) and then when created on a fee (Pells v. Brown, 1620), the whole policy favoring free transferability was threatened—unless the courts would impose a new rule limiting the length of time for which these indestructible interests might tie up land. The momentous decision in which the Rule began to take shape was the famous Duke of Norfolk's Case in 1682.[3]

The Earl of Arundel, anticipating that the title and estates of Arundel would pass not to descendants of his eldest son Thomas (who was mentally defective) but to his second son Henry, wished to provide for Henry until he took over the family estates and upon that contingency for a younger brother Charles. Hence the 200 year term in controversy was conveyed to trustees for the use of Henry and the male heirs of his body so long as Thomas lived, and if Thomas should die without issue in the lifetime of Henry or if Henry became Earl, then to Charles and the heirs male of his body (with admittedly invalid gifts in remainder to other children in succession). As events proved, the limitation was soundly planned. Thomas died without issue and Henry became Earl of Arundel and later Duke of Norfolk. Henry, now in possession of the family estates, also claimed the term in controversy on the ground that the gift to Charles "tended to a perpetuity". Some idea of what this meant to the bench and bar of that day may be gathered from the opinion of Lord Nottingham, which discussed valid and invalid interests in a term for years (employed by draftsmen because such interests were indestructible). A gift of a long term to A and the heirs of his body, then to B was described as a "direct perpetuity". A gift to A and his issue, and if his issue die without issue, then to B was said to involve a void remainder because it "looks toward a perpetuity". On the other hand a large number of successive life estates to living persons were said to be all good "because they produce no inconvenience, they wear out in a little time." Hence, Lord Nottingham concluded that the gift to Charles, since it must take effect if at all within the lifetime of Henry, did not involve a perpetuity. Although subsequent history almost resulted in a reversal, the ruling was eventually sustained by the House of Lords. It is interesting to note that the original statement

3. See Barry, "The Duke of Norfolk's Case", 23 Va.L.Rev. 538 (1937); Haskins, "Extending the Grip of the Dead Hand: Reflections on the Origins of the Rule Against Perpetuities", 126 U.Pa.Law Rev. 19 (1977).

of the doctrine was highly flexible. Asked where he would stop in upholding these new contingent interests, Lord Nottingham replied:

> "Now the ultimum quod sit, or the utmost limitation of a fee upon a fee, is not yet plainly determined, but it will be soon found out, if men shall set their wits on work to contrive by contingencies, to do that which the law has so long labored against, the thing will make itself evident, where it is convenient, and God forbid, but that mischief should be obviated and prevented."

Later cases over a century and a half extended the period and crystallized the form of the Rule until we find Professor Gray's classic statement as follows: [4]

"NO INTEREST IS GOOD UNLESS IT MUST VEST, IF AT ALL, NOT LATER THAN TWENTY-ONE YEARS AFTER SOME LIFE IN BEING AT THE CREATION OF THE INTEREST."

The modern rule applies to legal and equitable interests, to real and personal property. Although the original rule arose from judicial concern over private plans to keep large aggregations of land within the family circle for generations and hence out of commerce, the modern rule is no longer designed merely to promote free transfer of land. Although a trust to retain specific land still occurs, the common subject-matter of the trust is intangible wealth in the form of corporate stocks and bonds, and the trustee is usually given full power to sell and reinvest, so that specific assets are not tied up. Nevertheless there ought to be some limit upon the power of the present owner to project his desires into the future, to tie the hands of future generations; the American doctrines recognizing spendthrift trusts and the indestructibility of certain trusts increase the importance of such a restriction. The modern Rule thus imposes a limit on the "dead hand". Note that this is a rule against "remoteness of vesting". As we shall see in Section 4, the early New York attempt to embody the rule in statutory form phrased it as a rule "against suspension of the power of alienation." A conveyance to "B and his heirs, but if Puerto Rico becomes a state, then to C and his heirs," involves an invalid gift to C under the common-law Rule since the event may not occur within the period of the Rule; it would not violate a rule "against suspension of the power of alienation" because B and C may presently join in a conveyance of the full fee simple. Nevertheless, it should be noted that the existence of the contingent interest in C substantially restricts any sale by B and also jeopardizes useful development of the land by B or any purchaser from him.

Since the Rule operates with almost mathematical precision, it can be mastered by learning a series of corollaries:

(1) It requires that the future interest "vest" in interest, rather than possession, within the period of the Rule. A transfer to B for 100 years, then to C and his heirs is valid although C's interest will not become possessory for longer than the permissible period.[5] In

4. Gray, Rule Against Perpetuities (4th Ed., 1942) 191.

5. This assumes the construction is that C and his heirs take a vested remain-

general, it should be noted that some constructional preferences, such as the preference for vesting, operate to save limitations which on their face might be considered to violate the Rule.

(2) The permissible period may be extended to include all of the following: (a) lives in being, (b) periods of gestation, and (c) twenty-one years.[6] The "lives in being" are called the "measuring lives".[7] They may be specified as such in the creating instrument, and need not be persons given any interest thereunder; in one case the English court sustained a 1926 gift to "my descendants who shall be living 21 years after the death of all lineal descendants of Queen Victoria now living". On the other hand, the group must be such that the deaths may be ascertained and proved without too great inconvenience or cost; thus it is probable that the above limitation would be invalid in a will drafted today. The measuring lives need not be designated as such in the instrument. Thus a gift by will to "those of my grandchildren who attain the age of 21" would be valid, since there will be lives in being at the death of testator, namely those of his children, by which to measure the limitation. Periods of gestation may be part of the period. Thus in the above gift, even though a child of the testator might be born after his death and a grandchild born after the death of the last surviving son, the gift would be valid. Finally, the courts admit an additional period of 21 years added onto the measuring lives, as in the above illustration, or standing alone. Arising originally out of provisions for minority, the period of 21 years became permissible even when unrelated to an actual minority (then called a "period in gross").

(3) In order to be valid, the future interest, judged in the light of facts at the time the instrument becomes effective, must be *certain* to vest within the period, if at all. It is not enough that it probably will vest, or in fact does vest, within the period. In other words, if there is *any possibility* of the interest vesting beyond the permissible period, the interest is invalid under the Rule. The possibilities are to be determined from the terms of the instrument and the facts at the time the instrument becomes effective. In the case of a will that is the date of death; in the case of a deed, it is the date of delivery. However, a revocable deed of trust, for purposes of the rule, is not objectionable so long as the power of revocation lasts; hence, unless the power were released during life, the limitations would be judged as of the date of death of the settlor. For example, assume a gift to the "children of B who attain the age of 25". If B is dead at the time the instrument becomes effective, the limitation is valid as the gift would have to vest within lives in being, namely those of the children

der in fee following a term of years. Professor Gray states that remainders after long terms are objectionable. See Gray, The Rule Against Perpetuities (4th Ed., 1942) § 201, fn. 3; § 210; Pasley, "Perpetuities in the Pentagon", 5 Catholic U.L.Rev. 10, 22 (1955).

6. See Soled, "Effect of Reduction of the Age of Majority on the Permissible Period of the Rule Against Perpetuities", 34 Md.L.Rev. 245 (1974) (The author concludes that the reduction has no effect upon the 21 year period).

7. See Note, "Understanding the Measuring Life in the Rule Against Perpetuities", (1974) Wash.U.L.Q. 265.

of B who are then in existence; if B is alive, however, there is the possibility that he may have additional children, so that the measuring life in being would become that of B and the gift may not vest for more than 21 years after his death. On the other hand, the courts have refused to judge limitations in the light of what we might call "the facts of life". In the above limitation it is probable most courts would invalidate the gift even though B had, at the time the instrument became effective, passed the age where medically it would be considered possible to have additional children. This unscientific approach was entrenched by the famous decision in Jee v. Audley (1787), holding a woman of 70 still capable of having children so that a gift upon an uncertain event to her daughters "then living" was too remote under the Rule. Now that Biblical notions of fertility have been replaced by medical data, the approach has been criticized but seems to have judicial adherence. It is at this point in the operation of the Rule that advocacy can make or break a limitation by approaching the problem in terms of construction.[8]

The notion that a limitation is to be judged in the light of possibilities, not actual events, is the traditional rule. We shall shortly see the birth of a modern trend which advocates judging a limitation in the light of events as they actually occur.

(4) The Rule applies to future interests but not per se to the duration of a trust.[9] Thus, if all the equitable interests of the beneficiaries are certain to vest within the period, the fact that the trust itself is created to last beyond the period will not invalidate the interests. Commonly, it is the remainder or principal interests under the trust which are invalid because not certain to vest within the period, with a resulting trust to the settlor. Two qualifications to this generalization are worth remembering. A non-administrative power in the trustee, i.e., one which directly affects the beneficiaries' interests, may be invalid because it may be exercisable beyond the permissible period; for example, a discretionary power is sometimes given a trustee to withhold income or principal from a beneficiary when the beneficiary's creditors threaten his interest by legal process and to pay or apply the income or principal to or for the beneficiary's family. Secondly, while the authority is meager, a trust probably becomes destructible by the beneficiaries at the end of the permissible period of the Rule; in other words, the beneficiaries can force termination after lives in being and 21 years despite efforts of the settlor to tie up the property in trust longer.[10] Thus the policy against fettering

8. E.g., Gettins v. Grand Rapids Trust Co., 249 Mich. 238, 228 N.W. 703 (1930).

9. In Kelly v. Womack, 153 Tex. 371, 268 S.W.2d 903 (1954), the court avoided the issue by construing the trust to last only for a "reasonable" period of time, hence within the period of the Rule. Only North Carolina holds a private trust void if limited to last longer than the permissible period. However, the Rule is applied to so-called "honorary trusts" and, with some qualifications, to non-charitable trusts for unincorporated associations. Restatement, Property (1944) §§ 379, 380. See Downing "The Duration and Indestructibility of Private Trusts", 16 Western Res.L.Rev. 350 (1965); Comment, "Trusts for Animals in New York—Beneficiaries and Perpetuities", 17 Syracuse L.Rev. 705 (1966).

10. American Law of Property (1952) § 24.67; Simes, Handbook on Future Interests (2d Ed. 1966) Ch. 26. Restatement, Property (1944) §§ 378–381.

alienability for too long a period constitutes an important qualification upon the Claflin doctrine.[11]

(5) While the Rule normally operates to strike down only the remote contingent interest, this interest may be so integral a part of the plan of distribution that the settlor or testator would have preferred a complete failure of the entire transfer. Particularly in the case of a testamentary trust, this affords an avenue by which persons who have perfectly valid interests may seek to attack the entire disposition as a means of terminating the trust and taking the entire property outright, thus avoiding the indestructibility doctrine. Unless a clause expressly provides for separability, this issue, since it involves essentially a fact question, becomes vital in litigation.

There are two areas outside the estate field where the Rule may have important impact. One is the land use area, where the right of entry and possibility of reverter have for centuries been employed as devices for private control of land use. For example, A conveys to B "so long as the premises shall be used exclusively for residential purposes". Traditionally, B has a determinable fee and A has a possibility of reverter contingent upon an event which may take place far beyond the period of the Rule. The American courts, adopting the view that such interests reserved to the grantor are "vested", have in general not applied the Rule; and thus the grantor in effect may reserve power over the use of land beyond the period specified in the Rule.[12] This is not the English view, and the American position has been ably criticized on both policy and theory grounds.[13]

The other area involves the commercial option. Must an option to buy be limited to the period of the Rule? Since options normally would be drawn in terms of a period in gross, this means a maximum period of 21 years. Of greater practical importance, does the Rule apply to an option to buy (or to renew) contained in a long-term lease for years? Since the Rule is based on a policy favoring maximum present utilization of land, and the existence of an option encourages the lessee to make such maximum utilization, the Rule ought not to apply. The policy factors involved in these non-estate problems can best be explored in other courses.

---

11. See Chapter X, Section 3 for Claflin v. Claflin.

12. E.g., Yarbrough v. Yarbrough, 151 Tenn. 221, 269 S.W. 36 (1925). See Boyer and Spiegel, "Land Use Control: Pre-Emptions, Perpetuities and Similar Restraints", 20 U.Miami L.Rev. 148 (1965).

13. Leach, "Perpetuities in Perspective: Ending the Rule's Reign of Terror," 65 Harv.L.Rev. 721 (1952).

COOK v. HORN

Supreme Court of Georgia, 1958.
214 Ga. 289, 104 S.E.2d 461.

[In 1929 O. J. Massee, Jr., created a revocable inter vivos insurance trust. He transferred to the trustee Bank certain insurance policies made payable to the Bank. The trust instrument provided that the trustee would collect the proceeds of the policies and hold them in trust for certain purposes: the income was payable to the widow for life; on her death (or if she predeceased the settlor, then on his death) the principal was to be divided into as many shares as the settlor had children then living and deceased children whose issue were then living; the income from the share of a living child was payable to him for life, and at his death the principal distributable to his issue, provided that the share of any such issue under 21 should be retained in trust until such issue reached 21; there were detailed gifts over to the other children or their issue if a child died without issue; there was also a provision for distribution, on the death of the widow or settlor, to the issue of a deceased child if the issue had attained 21 and for holding in trust the share of issue of the deceased child not then 21 until the issue reached 21. The trust instrument reserved to the settlor the usual powers, including a power to change beneficiaries of any insurance policy and to amend or revoke the trust agreement in whole or in part.

The children of the settlor petitioned the court to terminate the trust; they contend that remainder interests beyond theirs are void under the Rule. The lower court sustained a demurrer to the petition. The portion of the opinion construing the document and disposing of other contentions is omitted.]

WYATT, PRESIDING JUSTICE. * * * It is next contended that the instrument in question violates the rule against perpetuities, and that since the limitations beyond the petitioners are void, they are entitled to have the property delivered to them. In order to determine this question, it is necessary first to determine when this instrument took effect, whether at the time it was executed and delivered, or at the death of the settlor. This question is settled by the decision of this court in Wilson v. Fulton National Bank, 188 Ga. 691, 4 S.E.2d 660, where an instrument similar in all material respects to that here under consideration was held to create a valid trust, to convey a present interest, and not to be testamentary in character.

It is contended that, if the trust instrument is effective to convey a present interest at the time it was executed and delivered, as is held above, then the limitations beyond the petitioners are void as violative of the rule against perpetuities, because there was a possibility at that time that the settlor would have additional children born to him thereafter, by whose life the duration of the trust would be limited. This result does not necessarily follow. While there is a scarcity of authority on this question, and none that we have found in Georgia, the prevailing opinion by both the courts of other jurisdictions and recognized text writers is that, when a settlor has the power during his lifetime to revoke or destroy the trust estate for his own exclusive personal benefit, the question whether interests, or any of them, created by an instrument or deed of trust are void because in violation of the rule against perpetuities, is to be determined as of the date of the settlor's death and not as of the date the instrument is executed and delivered. See Ryan v. Ward, 192 Md. 342, 64 A.2d 258, 7 A.L.R.2d 1078; Mifflin's Appeal, 121 Pa. 205, 15 A. 525, 1 L.R.A. 453; Goesele v. Bimeler, 14 How. 589, 14 L.Ed. 554; Manufacturers Life Insurance Company v. von Hamm-Young Co., 34 Haw. 288; Pulitzer v. Livingston, 89 Me. 359, 36 A. 635; City Bank Farmers Trust Co. v. Cannon, 291 N.Y. 125, 51 N.E.2d 674, 157 A.L.R. 1424; Equitable Trust Co. v. Pratt, 117 Misc. 708, 193 N.Y.S. 152, affirmed on opinion below 206 App.Div. 689, 199 N.Y.S. 921; Gray, Rule Against Perpetuities, (4th Ed.) 510, par. 524; 45 Harv.L.Rev. 896; 51 Harv.L.Rev. 638; 86 Univ. of Pa.L.Rev. 221; Restatement of Property, § 373 and comments (c) and (d), and Ryan v. Ward, 192 Md. 342, 64 A.2d 258, 7 A.L.R.2d 1078.

While none of these authorities is binding upon this court, the conclusion reached by them is in accord with the aim of and reason for the rule against perpetuities, which is to prevent the tying up of property for an unreasonable length of time and to prohibit unreasonable restraint upon the alienation of property. So long as the settlor of an inter vivos trust has the absolute right to revoke or terminate the trust for his own exclusive personal benefit, there is no tying up of property and no restraint upon the alienability of the property in the trust fund, and thus no reason to include this time during which the trust is so destructible in determining whether a limitation is violative of the rule against perpetuities. Restatement, Property, sec. 373 states: "The period of time during which an interest is destructible, pursuant to the uncontrolled volition, and for the exclusive personal benefit of the person having such a power of destruction is not included in determining whether the limitation is invalid under the rule against perpetuities." We conclude that this rule is a sound one, which does no violence to the rule against perpetuities, but is in complete accord with its aim and purpose.

In the instant case, the settlor, during his lifetime, had an absolute right to revoke or terminate the trust, to change the beneficiaries in the policies, and to receive any and all benefits under the policies. Therefore, under the rulings above made, the time from which it will be determined whether any of the limitations in the trust agreement are void for remoteness is the date of the settlor's death. When so considered, it is apparent that none of the limitations in the instrument violate the rule against perpetuities, since all limitations under the instrument will end and all interests vest within twenty-one years after the death of the settlor's children plus the usual period of gestation, and, of course, no children can be born to the settlor after his death plus the usual period of gestation. It follows, the limitations over to the issue of the children of the settlor are valid, and the petitioners are not entitled to have the trust terminated for any reason alleged. The judgment of the court below dismissing the petition on general demurrer was therefore not error.

Judgment affirmed.

All the Justices concur.[14]

IN RE LATTOUF'S WILL

Superior Court of New Jersey, Appellate Division, 1965.
87 N.J.Super. 137, 208 A.2d 411.

[Testator died in 1962. He was survivied by three sisters and 41 nephews and nieces. His will, prepared shortly before his death, created a trust of all the residue of his estate and directed the trustees as follows:

"As To Income

To establish a fund, from which, in their absolute discretion, they may pay for or provide the reasonable necessities of life of any of my nephews or nieces or their or any of their issue in their several stations or situations in life; to pay for or provide for the higher education or specialized training in any craft or profession, of any of, or such of, my grand-nephews and nieces as may in my said Trustees absolute discretion, have need for such assistance and have displayed the capacity, ability and talent to utilize and benefit from such higher education or specialized training.

* * *

As To Principal or Corpus

When the youngest child of my niece, Marie Endress shall have attained, or would have attained the age of twenty-five (25) years, then the trust hereby created shall end, and the principal thereof, together with all accumulated and undisbursed interest or income thereon and therefrom shall be equally disbursed and divided among my then living grandnephews and grandnieces. The expense of administering this trust shall be charged to and paid from the income so far as possible."

The will was duly probated, but one of the decedent's nephews moved to have the probate set aside. Among other grounds for contest, he alleged the invalidity of the trust. The county judge held that the trust did not violate the rule against perpetuities. Portions of the

14. In Fitzpatrick v. Mercantile-Safe Deposit & Trust Co., 220 Md. 534, 155 A. 2d 702 (1959), 20 Md.L.Rev. 142 (1960), a settlor reserved the power, in the event of death or resignation of the trustee, to revoke or appoint a successor trustee. The trustee died during the settlor's lifetime, and a new trustee was appointed. The court held that interests were to be measured not from the creation of the trust but from appointment of the successor trustee. How does this differ from the principal case?

opinion dealing with the other objections to the will have been omitted.]

The opinion of the court was delivered by GOLDMANN, S.J.A.D.

* * *

This brings us to defendants' contention that the residuary trust violated the rule against perpetuities. The county judge held it did not, and in doing so fell into error.

The rule against perpetuities is in force in this State as a part of the common law. McGill v. Trust Co. of N. J., 94 N.J.Eq. 657, 664, 121 A. 760, 764 (Ch.1923), affirmed as modified, 96 N.J.Eq. 331, 125 A. 108 (E. & A. 1924). The rule requires that "all future interests, legal or equitable, in realty (except dower and curtesy and rights of entry for conditions broken) or personalty, which are contingent and indestructible, must be such as necessarily to vest, if at all, within the term measured by the life or lives of a person or persons in being at the time of the creation of the interest and 21 years thereafter." Otherwise, they are invalid and void. Ibid.; Litcher v. Trust Co. of N. J., 11 N.J. 64, 79, 93 A.2d 368 (1952); Gray on Perpetuities (4th ed. 1942) 191; 6 N.J.Practice (Clapp, Wills and Adminstration) (3d ed. 1962), § 611, p. 130. To satisfy the requirements of the rule, a gift to a class must not only vest within the period prescribed by the rule, but the number of members of the class sharing in the gift and the size of each member's share must be fixed within that period. Thus, "if the maximum number of members who are to take may not be determined within the period of the rule, the gift to the class is void; or in other words, if the size of each member's share may be diminished by an increase in the membership of the class after the expiration of the period, the gift violates the rule." 6 N.J.Practice, above, § 614, p. 139; McGill v. Trust Co. of N. J., above, at page 665, 121 A. 760.

The trial judge held that testator had failed to designate expressly an event or time period at or within which the various interests created by the trust were to vest. Not so; vesting was to occur when the "youngest child of my niece, Marie Endress shall have attained, or would have attained the age of twenty-five (25) years." Not until then would the class of grandnephews and grandnieces close and their identity and number be determined. However, the trial judge considered this language ambiguous and proceeded to construe it as meaning the youngest child living at the time of testator's death, and not the last-born child of Marie Endress. We find no ambiguity in the language employed.

We must look at the *corpus* provision of paragraph Seventh as of the date of testator's death. Would the trust *corpus* vest within a life in being plus 21 years? The answer is clearly no.

Marie Endress had sometime prior to the execution of the will undergone a complete hysterectomy. The parties by stipulation agreed that she was incapable of bearing children when the will was executed and the testator died. The record reveals that testator knew of the hysterectomy when he executed his will.

Defendants-contestants rely upon the ancient legal presumption, often mentioned in our cases, that a woman is presumed legally capable of bearing children at any age. Oleson v. Somogyi, 93 N.J.Eq. 506, 115 A. 526 (E. & A. 1921); 2 Blackstone's Commentaries 125. If one were to follow through on contestants' argument that Marie Endress could still have children, there exists the possibility that she might die and leave a child under four years of age. Since the vesting of the trust *corpus* among the "then living grandnephews and grandnieces" is to take place when that child "shall have attained, or would have attained" the age of 25, this possibility would violate the requirement of vesting within the period of the rule.

However, we are unwilling to follow the contestants in their reliance upon the ancient presumption. As was said in Trenton Banking Co. v. Hawley, 7 N.J.Super. 301, 307–308, 70 A.2d 896 (Ch.Div.1950), the presumption should not, merely because of its antiquity, blind us to present realities and conceal demonstrable truth. And see Sevel v. Swarzman, 33 N.J.Super. 198, 203, 109 A.2d 685 (Ch.Div.1954). The hysterectomy, involving complete removal of Marie Endress' procreative organs, rendered her permanently sterile. It logically follows that she could bear no children other than the only child she had when testator died. That child, Linda, it has been stipulated, was just short of three years and ten months old when Lattouf expired.

The rule would be violated were we to take Linda as the measuring life. The trial judge did so, but assumed she was 4½ years old when testator died. This was error. Linda was born December 1, 1958; Lattouf died September 26, 1962, so that the child, as noted, was at least two months short of age 4. Accordingly, had she died immediately after the execution of the will and Lattouf's death, more than 21 years would expire before she "would have attained" age 25.

So, too, were we to take Marie Endress as the measuring life. Had she died immediately after Lattouf, the trust would not have vested within her life and 21 years thereafter.

As our cases have uniformly held, a future interest must vest, if at all, within a period measured by a life in being when the interest was created, plus 21 years. The nine-month period tacked on in case of an existing pregnancy (6 N.J.Practice, above, § 611, p. 130, citing Randolph v. Randolph, 40 N.J.Eq. 73 (Ch.1885), and Hewitt v. Green, 77 N.J.Eq. 345, 77 A. 25 (Ch.1910); Simes, Future Interests, 373 (1951) has no application in the circumstances of this case. Marie Endress was not pregnant. She could not be, nor, of course, could the infant Linda. Although plaintiffs' counsel claimed at oral argument that consideration should be given to this extra term of gestation, he has now abandoned the argument, and necessarily so.

Accordingly, we conclude that the trust failed because it was in violation of the rule.

* * *

The matter is remanded to the County Court, Probate Division, for the entry of a judgment in accordance with this decision * * *.

PROBLEMS

(1) In light of the decision in Estate of Coe, Chapter XV, Section 2(3)C, Marie Endress could have adopted a child after testator's death and such adopted person presumptively would be her child for purposes of the testator's will: moreover, such child could have been born after testator's death. If so, how material in any case would the medical testimony be that Marie could no longer bear children? Does not the inclusion of adopted children force the court back to the old rule of Jee v. Audley?

(2) The will in the principal case was prepared by an attorney. What is his liability for defective draftsmanship? Suppose the trust were for persons who do not take as a result of the judicial holding that the trust is invalid. Can disappointed beneficiaries sue him? Who took the property in the principal case as a result of the holding that the trust was invalid? Compare the opinion of the California Supreme Court in Lucas v. Hamm, 56 Cal.2d 583, 15 Cal.Rptr. 821, 364 P.2d 685 (1961) [15] with the opinion below in the same case, reported in 11 Cal.Rep. 727 (1961). Should an attorney hold himself out to the public as qualified to draft wills creating trusts if he does not understand the rule against perpetuities? [16]

(3) How could the trust in the principal case have been worded to be valid?

(4) If the court in the principal case had followed the precedent of the next case, what would the result have been?

MERCHANTS NATIONAL BANK v. CURTIS

Supreme Court of New Hampshire, 1953.
98 N.H. 225, 97 A.2d 207 [17]

[The statement of facts is abbreviated here. Margaret A. Harrington, owning an undivided seven fifty-fourths interest in certain realty, died in 1902. Her will, which was duly probated, gave her son Edward Harrington and her daughter Delana B. Curtis a life estate in this real estate, and the remainder "to my granddaughter Margaret May Curtis and her heirs forever." The will further provided:

> "Fifth: In the event of either of my children having other heirs of their body, surviving them such heir or heirs shall share equally with Margaret May Curtis, and in that event I give, bequeath and devise my estate to them, and their heirs, on the death of my children.

15. Cert. den. 368 U.S. 987, 82 S.Ct. 603, 7 L.Ed.2d 525 (1962); noted 14 Stan. L.Rev. 580 (1962).

16. See Simes and Smith, Future Interests (2d Ed., 1956) § 1298 (1975 Supp.). For an excellent critique of *Lattouf* and implications in the problem see Fetters, "Perpetuities Period in Gross and the Child en Ventre Sa Mere in Relation to the Determination of Common-Law and Wait-and-See Measuring Lives: A Minor Heresy Stated and Defended", 62 Iowa L.Rev. 309, 313–21(1976).

17. Noted, 33 B.U.L.Rev. 528 (1953); 53 Col.L.Rev. 1158 (1953); 67 Harv.L. Rev. 355 (1953); 52 Mich.L.Rev. 305 (1953); 38 Minn.L.Rev. 679 (1954).

"Sixth: If my Grand Daughter Margaret May Curtis or other grand children shall survive both of my children and shall have and leave no heirs of her or their body, then and in that event, I give, bequeath and devise all my estate unto my brothers and sisters then living and to the representatives of those not living, and to my late husband's niece, Almeda S. Goyscan formerly Almeda S. Harrington, in equal shares * * *."

The said Almeda S. Goyscan predeceased the testatrix leaving no issue. The testatrix' son, the said Edward W. Harrington, survived the testatrix and died leaving no issue. The testatrix' daughter, the said Delana B. Curtis, also survived the testatrix and died leaving no children other then her said daughter, Margaret. Margaret was twice married and, at the time of her death without issue, on January 16, 1951, her name was Margaret May Curtis Reynolds Vreeland.

The testatrix, Margaret A. Harrington, had three sisters and three brothers, who were living or who had issue living at the time of her death, namely: Abigail Bond Chandler, Nancy Bond Corliss, Maria Bond Hill, James B. Bond, Jonathan Bond and John R. Bond. All of these brothers and sisters left representatives in interest in this case, with the exception of Nancy Bond Corliss, who died on July 1, 1910, leaving an only child, George W. Corliss, who died unmarried and without issue on September 6, 1922. Accordingly, the parties to this proceeding are the representatives in interest of five brothers and sisters of Margaret A. Harrington, who were living at the death of Margaret May Curtis Reynolds Vreeland on January 16, 1951. The representatives of these brothers and sisters have been stipulated by the parties.

As a result of a partition petition in 1914 the premises were sold, and approximately $38,000 was set aside to represent the interests of the Margaret A. Harrington estate. This sum was administered by a court-appointed trustee to pay the income to the assignee of the surviving life tenant Delana Curtis. Upon the death of Margaret May Curtis Reynolds Vreeland in 1951 the Superior Court transferred to the Supreme Court the question of distribution of the trust moneys.]

KENISON, CHIEF JUSTICE. The question transferred in effect asks us to decide who is entitled to how much of what trust moneys. This question depends in part on whether clause sixth of the will violates the Rule against Perpetuities.

* * *

The Rule against Perpetuities, hereinafter called the rule, prevails in this state, Gale v. Gale, 85 N.H. 358, 159 A. 122, but it has never been "remorselessly applied" as advocated by Gray in "The Rule against Perpetuities" (4th Ed.) § 629. The genesis of the modified rule in New Hampshire began in 1891 with Edgerly v. Barker, 66 N.H. 434, 31 A. 900, 28 L.R.A. 328, when a gift of a remainder interest to grandchildren reaching forty years of age, which offended the rule, was cut down to a gift to grandchildren reaching twenty-one years of age so as to not offend the rule. This decision was bitterly assailed by Gray in his treatise (appendix G) since he thought it was a dangerous thing to tamper with this ancient English rule "which is concatenated with almost mathematical precision". Gray, supra, § 871. Nevertheless, Edgerly v. Barker, supra, has been followed in subsequent decisions in this state and continues to remain in good standing here. Wentworth v. Wentworth, 77 N.H. 400, 92 A. 733; Flanders v. Parker, 80 N.H. 566, 120 A. 558; Gale v. Gale, supra; Amoskeag Trust Company v. Haskell, 96 N.H. 89, 91, 70 A.2d 210, 71 A.2d 408. See Quarles, The Cy Pres Doctrine; Its Application to Cases Involving the Rule against Perpetuities and Trusts for Accumulations, 21 N.Y.U.L.Q.Rev. 384 (1946). In England the same result has been achieved by legislation. Laws of Property Act, 1925, 39 & 40 Geo.V., c. 98, Sec. 163.

The rationale of the Barker case was that, wherever possible, a will should be construed to carry out the primary intent to accomplish a legal testamentary disposition even though the will may have inadvertently exposed a secondary intent to accomplish the testamentary disposition in an ineffective manner. That rationale has been applied in many recent will cases that have not involved the rule itself. "Traditionally, the courts of this jurisdiction have shown a signal regard for the intent of the testator * * * at times at the expense of other recognized principles deemed less cogent in their application. Cf. Edgerly v. Barker, 66 N.H. 434, 31 A. 900, 28 L.R.A. 328." Petition of Oliver Wolcott, 95 N.H. 23, 26, 56 A.2d 641, 643, 1 A.L.R.2d 1323. The same thought received expression in different language in Burtman v. Butman, 97 N.H. 254, 258, 85 A.2d 892, 895: "Probably no jurisdiction has stood more steadfastly for giving effect to the intention of the testator rather than to arbitrary rules of law than New Hampshire." The refusal of this court to apply in unmodified form common law principles which defeat normal and reasonable estate plans has not been limited to wills but applies to conveyances as well. Therrien v. Therrien, 94 N.H. 66, 46 A.2d 538, 166 A.L.R. 1023.

The rule is a technical one, difficult of application and is often enforced to frustrate testamentary intent although the policy of the rule may not require such enforcement in a particular case. It is not surprising, therefore, that there has been an increasing tendency to avoid the application of the rule by various judicial techniques. There is a constructional preference for considering interests vested rather than contingent. Upton v. White, 92 N.H. 221, 29 A.2d 126. "The public interest in keeping *the destructive force of the rule against perpetuities within reasonable limits* is a considerable present factor supporting the public interest in that construction which accomplishes the earlier vesting." 3 Restatement, Property, § 243 comment i. (Emphasis supplied.) If a gift is made upon alternative contingencies, one of which might be remote, while the other is not, the gift is valid where the second contingency actually happens. This doctrine is used to prevent the application of the rule in many cases. Annotation 64 A.L.R. 1077. "Essentially this represents a revulsion against the rule requiring absolute certainty of vesting as viewed from the creation of the interest * * * Courts have a strong tendency to 'wait and see' wherever possible." 6 American Law of Property (1952) § 24.54. These techniques have the salutary effect of avoiding the punitive and technical aspects of the rule but at the same time confirming the policy and purpose of the rule within reasonable limits. Wentworth & Co. v. Wentworth, 77 N.H. 400, 92 A. 733.

Clause sixth of the will is capable of at least two possible constructions. The first construction is that clause sixth created two contingencies upon which it would take effect; one to occur, if at all, on the death of Margaret May Curtis; the other to occur, if at all, on the death of unborn grandchildren. Since the first contingency actually occurred and is within the period of perpetuities, the gift may be considered valid. A closely parallel case is Springfield Safe Deposit & Trust Co. v. Ireland, 268 Mass. 62, 167 N.E. 261, 64 A.L.R. 1071. Under this construction the event occurs at the death of Margaret May Curtis, a life in being, and clause sixth would not be considered violative of the rule.

The second possible construction of this sixth clause is the one urged by the Bean-Quirin interests. They argue that the will gives the brothers and sisters an executory interest upon a single contingency which may occur at the death of as yet unborn grandchildren. While this is not the only construction that the clause is susceptible of, it is not a labored one. There is no doubt that, if there had been another grandchild who died after Margaret May Curtis without leaving heirs of his body, this event would have occurred beyond the period allowed by the rule against perpetuities.

Assuming this second construction to be permissible, we come to the crucial question whether we are justified in deciding the perpetuities issue on the facts which actually occurred rather than on facts that might have happened viewed as of the death of the testator. There is little case authority for deciding upon facts occurring after the testator's death in a case such as the one before us. However, recognized modern commentators present convincing arguments for doing so. Leach, Perpetuities in Perspective: Ending the Rule's Reign of Terror, 65 Harv.L.Rev. 721 (1952); 6 American Law of Property (1952) § 24.10; and a full study by a Pennsylvania law revision commission resulted in a statute that permits such events to be considered. Pa.Estates Act of 1947, § 4, Pa.Stat.Ann. (Purdon, 1947) tit. 20, § 301.4. There is no precedent in this state that compels us to close our eyes to facts occurring after the death of the testator.

In the present case we are called on to determine the validity of a clause of a will that did not in fact tie up property beyond the permissible limit of lives in being plus twenty-one years. There is no logical justification for deciding the problem as of the date of the death of the testator on facts that might have happened rather than the facts which actually happened. It is difficult to see how the public welfare is threatened by a vesting that might have been postponed beyond the period of perpetuities but actually was not. The recent decision in Sears v. Coolidge, 329 Mass. 340, 108 N.E.2d 563, allows the court to take a "second look" under powers of appointment. While this is not direct authority for doing the same thing with a devise or bequest, it is bottomed on the same proposition that the glacial force of the rule will be avoided where the interests actually vest within the period of perpetuities. 6 American Law of property, § 24.35. When a decision is made at a time when the events have happened, the court should not be compelled to consider only what might have been and completely ignore what was. Analogy may be found in cases where the validity of a remainder interest is not considered until the facts existing on the death of the life tenant can be established. See Orr v. Moses, 94 N.H. 309, 52 A.2d 128; B. M. C. Durfee Trust Co. v. Taylor, 325 Mass. 201, 89 N.E.2d 777.

At the death of the survivor of the life tenants, Edward Harrington and Delana B. Curtis, both of whom were lives in being at testatrix' death, it became certain that no grandchildren of the testatrix would be born after her death. This in turn made it certain that the gift in clause sixth of the will would in fact vest at the death of Margaret May Curtis Reynolds Vreeland, also a life in being at testatrix' death. Consistent with the principles above stated, the facts existing at the death of the two life tenants are taken into consideration in applying the rule.

We therefore conclude that clause sixth does not violate the rule against perpetuities. The individuals who are entitled to participate in the distribution of the trust moneys and the extent of their interests are to be determined under this clause.

Since Almeda S. Goyscan predeceased the testatrix leaving no issue and since the testatrix' sister, Nancy Bond Corliss and her only child George died without issue before the death of Margaret, the division is to be made among the representatives in interest of five brothers and sisters of the testatrix as stated in In re Harrington's Estate, 97 N.H. 184, 187, 84 A.2d 173.

* * *

[Omitted is the balance of the court's opinion, determining who the representatives of deceased brothers and sisters are and deciding that their contingent interests were transferable.] * * *

Case discharged.

All concurred.[18]

18. See Fetters, "Perpetuities: The Wait and See Disaster—A Brief Reply to Professor Maudsley, With a Few Asides to Professors Leach, Simes, Wade, Dr. Morris, et al.", 60 Corn.L.Rev. 380 (1975); Fletcher, "A Rule of Discrete Invalidity: Perpetuities Reform Without Waiting," 20 Stan.L.Rev. 459 (1968); Maudsley, "Perpetuities—Reforming the Common Law Rule—How to Wait and See", 60 Corn.L.Rev. 355 (1975); "Measuring Lives Under a System of Wait-and-See", 86 L.Q.R. 357 (1970); Schwartz, "Mr. Justice Kenison and Creative Continuity in Perpetuities Law," 48 Bost.U.L.Rev. 207 (1968); Comment, "Wait and See Revisited", 51 Chi-Kent Law Rev. 738 (1975); Note, "Doctrine That Gift Which Might be Void Under Rule Against Perpetuities Will be Given Effect Where Contingency Actually Occurs Within Period of Rule," 20 A.L.R.3d 1094 (1968). For a consideration of possible problems arising from the *possibility* of postponing lives through the application of modern biological techniques, see Schuyler, "The New Biology and the Rule Against Perpetuities," 15 U.C.L.A.Law Rev. 420 (1968); Sappideen, "Life After Death—Sperm Banks, Wills and Perpetuities", 53 Aust.L.J. 311 (1979).

NOTE

Although the Rule has for almost a century operated rigidly to invalidate contingent future interests which violated the limits of the Rule, the principal case marks the beginning of a modern trend to "reform" the Rule. The change in many jurisdictions is now marked. In some states various judicial techniques have been innovated to lessen the harsh effects of the Rule. The "wait and see" doctrine of the principal case is one of those. The American Law Institute has adopted the "wait and see" doctrine for its Restatement, Property (2d) in the following terms: [19]

> **"§ 1.4 The Vesting Requirement with Respect to Donative Transfers**
>
> Except as provided in § 1.6, * * * [this section applying to charities * * *] a donative transfer of an interest in property fails, if the interest does not vest, if it ever vests, within the period of the rule against perpetuities."

The statement is stated by the Institute to reflect a minority view.[20]

Construction of the document to avoid invalidity is another ameliorating technique. This is analogous to construing legislation to avoid unconstitutionality. The traditional view is to construe first without regard to the Rule. Other ameliorating doctrines will appear in Industrial National Bank of Rhode Island v. Barrett and Sears v. Coolidge in Section 3 hereafter. These changes have cumulatively had an impact on the entire judicial outlook in some states.[21] There are, however, limits. Some judges are properly reluctant to overturn long lines of precedent in the property field.[22] Thus, few courts are likely to follow the old New Hampshire doctrine of Edgerly v. Barker, described in the principal case, by which the court "cuts down" an offending age limitation by rewriting the limitation to the permissible limit.[23] For example, in the Lattouf case, under such precedent the New Hampshire court could have made the corpus distributable when the youngest child of

19. Restatement of the Law Second, Property (Donative Transfers, Tentative Draft No. 2, 15 March 1979) p. 66.

20. Id. Comm. (*a*) See Note, "Rule Against Perpetuities: The Second Restatement Adopts Wait and See", 19 Santa Clara Law Rev. 1063 (1979).

21. Estate of Freeman, 195 Kan. 190, 404 P.2d 222 (1965), summarizes the various doctrines available to a court willing to curtail application of the Rule.

22. See American Security & Trust Co. v. Cramer, 175 F.Supp. 367 (D.C. 1959). Principal case in Section 2, infra.

23. In Estate of Chun Quan Yee Hop, 52 Haw. 40, 469 P.2d 183 (1970), 84 Harv. L.Rev. 738 (1971), 28 W. & L.L.Rev. 184 (1971) the trust was to cease on the death of testator's wife or 30 years after his death. The court cut down the time to 21 years by cy pres or, as the Court described it, "equitable approximation" to best effectuate the testator's intent. See Carter v. Berry, 243 Miss. 321, 140 So.2d 843 (1962).

In Berry v. Union National Bank, ___ W.Va. ___, 262 S.E.2d 766 (1980), the court cut down a 25 year limitation to 21 years to effectuate the testator's general intent. The court stated at 262 S.E.2d 771: "We support the underlying policies of the rule against perpetuities and will deny validity to an interest which vests beyond the time limit permitted by the rule. However, before a testamentary scheme is totally obliterated by application of the rule, we will determine whether the testamentary disposition can be equitably modified to comport with the rule's underlying policy.

"A non-charitable devise or bequest which violates the rule will be modified if the following conditions are met: (1) The testator's intent is expressed in the instrument or can be readily determined by a court; (2) The testator's general intent does not violate the rule against perpetuities; (3) The testator's particular intent, which does violate the rule, is not a critical aspect of the testamentary scheme; and (4) The proposed modification will effectuate the testator's general intent, will avoid the consequences of intestacy, and will conform to the policy considerations underlying the rule."

the niece would have attained 21 years of age and thereby saved the trust. Other courts even feel constrained to reject the "wait and see" approach and prefer to leave the task of reform to the legislature.[24]

The modern importance of trusts with contingent future interests intended to save taxes under state laws and to minimize Federal income and estate taxes (to the extent a generation skipping tax can be avoided in the particular transaction) [25] and the fact that many of the limitations invalidated under the traditional Rule do not involve attempts to create perpetual trusts but merely involve oversight by the draftsman in wording the will or trust, have resulted in enactment of legislation to modernize the Rule and prevent invalidity of seemingly innocent provisions in wills.

Such legislation is of various types.[26] One type adopts the "wait and see" approach:

24. See "Reform of Rule Against Perpetuities—A Panel Discussion," Proceedings of Probate and Trust Law Divisions, A.B.A. (1953) pp. 83–96.

25. See Bloom, "Transfer Tax Avoidance: The Impact of Perpetuities Restrictions Before and After Generation Skipping Taxation", 45 Albany L.Rev. 261 (1981).

26. See "Perpetuity Legislation Handbook", 2 Real Prop.Prob. & T.L.J. 176 (1967); McClean, "British Columbia Perpetuities Act: A Primer", 13 U.B.C.Law Rev. 240 (1979); Sappideen and Butt, "Rendering the Rule Against Perpetuities Less Remote", 8 Sydney L.Rev. 620 (1979). See also the Illinois Perpetuity Statute as follows:

ILL.ANN.STAT. CH. 30 (1980 Supp.)

¶ 191. Title

§ 1. Title. This Act shall be known and may be cited as the "Statute Concerning Perpetuities".

¶ 192. Purpose

§ 2. Purpose. This Act modifies the common law rule of property known as the rule against perpetuities, which, except as modified by statutes in force at the effective date of this Act and by this Act, shall remain in full force and effect.

¶ 193. Definitions and Terms

§ 3. Definitions and Terms. As used in this Act unless the context otherwise requires:

(a) "Trust" means any trust created by any written instrument, including, without limitation, a trust created in the exercise of a power of appointment.

(b) "Trustee" includes the original trustee of any trust and also any succeeding or added trustee.

(c) "Instrument" means any writing pursuant to which any legal or equitable interest in property or in the income therefrom is affected, disposed of or created.

(d) "Beneficiary" includes any person to whom any interest, whether vested or contingent, is given by an instrument.

(e) Any reference in this Act to income to be "paid" or to income "payments" or to "receiving" income includes income payable or distributable to or applicable for the benefit of a beneficiary.

(f) Words importing the masculine gender include the feminine and neuter, and words importing the singular number include the plural and words importing the plural number include the singular.

¶ 194. Application of the Rule Against Perpetuities

§ 4. Application of the Rule Against Perpetuities. (a) The rule against perpetuities shall not apply:

(1) to any disposition of property or interest therein which, at the effective date of this Act, does not violate, or is exempted by statute from the operation of, the common law rule against perpetuities;

(2) to powers of a trustee to sell, lease or mortgage property or to powers which relate to the administration or management of trust assets, including, without limitation, discretionary powers of a trustee to determine what receipts constitute principal and what receipts constitute income and powers to appoint a successor trustee;

(3) to mandatory powers of a trustee to distribute income, or to discretionary powers of a trustee to distribute principal prior to termination of a trust, to a beneficiary having an interest in the principal which is ir-

PURDON'S PENNSYLVANIA STAT. ANN.

Tit. 20, § 6104 (1978).

"(a) General.—No interest shall be void as a perpetuity except as herein provided.

revocably vested in quality and quantity;

(4) to discretionary powers of a trustee to allocate income and principal among beneficiaries, but no exercise of any such power after the expiration of the period of the rule against perpetuities is valid;

(5) to leases to commence in the future or upon the happening of a future event, but no such lease shall be valid unless the term thereof actually commences in possession within 40 years from the date of execution of the lease;

(6) to commitments (A) by a lessor to enter into a lease with a subtenant or with the holder of a leasehold mortgage or (B) by a lessee or sublessee to enter into a lease with the holder of a mortgage; nor

(7) to options in gross or to preemptive rights in the nature of a right of first refusal, but no option in gross shall be valid for more than 40 years from the date of its creation.

(b) The period of the rule against perpetuities shall not commence to run in connection with any disposition of property or interest therein, and no instrument shall be regarded as becoming effective for purposes of the rule against perpetuities, and no interest or power shall be deemed to be created for purposes of the rule against perpetuities as long as, by the terms of the instrument, the maker of the instrument has the power to revoke the instrument or to transfer or direct to be transferred to himself the entire legal and equitable ownership of the property or interest therein.

(c) In determining whether an interest violates the rule against perpetuities:

(1) it shall be presumed (A) that the interest was intended to be valid, (B) in the case of an interest conditioned upon the probate of a will, the appointment of an executor, administrator or trustee, the completion of the administration of an estate, the payment of debts, the sale or distribution of property, the determination of federal or state tax liabilities or the happening of any administrative contingency, that the contingency must occur, if at all, within the period of the rule against perpetuities, and (C) where the instrument creates an interest in the "widow", "widower", or "spouse" of another person, that the maker of the instrument intended to refer to a person who was living at the date that the period of the rule against perpetuities commences to run;

(2) where any interest, but for this subparagraph (c) (2), would be invalid because it is made to depend upon any person attaining or failing to attain an age in excess of 21 years, the age specified shall be reduced to 21 years as to every person to whom the age contingency applies;

(3) if, notwithstanding the provisions of subparagraphs (c) (1) and (2) of this Section, the validity of any interest depends upon the possibility of the birth or adoption of a child, (A) no person shall be deemed capable of having a child until he has attained the age of 13 years, (B) any person who has attained the age of 65 years shall be deemed incapable of having a child, (C) evidence shall be admissible as to the incapacity of having a child by a living person who has not attained the age of 65 years, and (D) the possibility of having a child or more remote descendant by adoption shall be disregarded.

(d) Subparagraphs (a) (2), (3) and (6) and paragraph (b) of this Section shall be deemed to be declaratory of the law prevailing in this State at the effective date of this Act.

¶ 195. Trusts

§ 5. Trusts. (a) Subject to the provisions of paragraphs (e) and (f) of this Section, a trust containing any limitation which, but for this paragraph (a), would violate the rule against perpetuities (as modified by Section 4) shall terminate at the expiration of a period of (A) 21 years after the death of the last to die of all of the beneficiaries of the instrument who were living at the date when the period of the rule against perpetuities commenced to run or (B) 21 years after that date if no beneficiary of the instrument was then living, unless events occur which cause

"(b) Void interest; exceptions.—Upon the expiration of the period allowed by the common law rule against perpetuities as measured by actual rather than possible events, any interest not then vested and any interest in members of a class the membership of which is then subject to increase shall be void.

This subsection shall not apply to:

(1) Interest exempt at common law. Interests which would not have been subject to the common law rule against perpetuities.

an earlier termination in accordance with the terms of the instrument and then the principal shall be distributed as provided by the instrument.

(b) Subject to the provisions of paragraphs (c), (d) and (e) of this Section, when a trust terminates because of the application of paragraph (a) of this Section, the trustee shall distribute the principal to those persons who would be the heirs at law of the maker of the instrument if he died at the expiration of the period specified in paragraph (a) of this Section and in the proportions then specified by statute, unless the trust was created by the exercise of a power of appointment and then the principal shall be distributed to the person who would have received it if the power had not been exercised.

(c) Before any distribution of principal is made pursuant to paragraph (b) of this Section, the trustee shall distribute, out of principal, to each living beneficiary who, but for termination of the trust because of the application of paragraph (a) of this Section, would have been entitled to be paid income after the expiration of the period specified in paragraph (a) of this Section, an amount equal to the present value (determined as provided in paragraph (d) of this Section) of the income which the beneficiary would have been entitled to be paid after the expiration of that period.

(d) In determining the present value of income for purposes of any distribution to a beneficiary pursuant to paragraph (c) of this Section:

(1) when income payments would have been subject in whole or in part to any discretionary power, it shall be assumed (A) that the income which would have been paid to an individual income beneficiary would have been the maximum amount of income which could have been paid to him in the exercise of the power, (B) if the income would or might have been payable to more than one beneficiary, that (except as hereinafter provided) each beneficiary would have received an equal share of the income, unless the instrument specifies less than an equal share as the maximum amount or proportion of income which would have been paid to any beneficiary in the exercise of the power, in which event the maximum specified shall control, and (C) if the income would or might have been payable to the descendants of the maker of the instrument or of another person, that, unless the instrument provides otherwise, the descendants would have received the income per stirpes;

(2) (A) present value shall be computed on an actuarial basis and there shall be assumed a return of 5%, at simple interest, on the value of the principal from which the beneficiary would have been entitled to receive income, and (B) where the interest in income was to be for the life of the beneficiary or for the life of another, the computation shall be made on the expectancy set forth in the most recently published American Experience Tables of Mortality and no other evidence of duration or expectancy shall be considered;

(3) if the trustee cannot determine the present value of any income interest in accordance with the provisions of the instrument and the foregoing rules concerning income payments, the present value of the interest shall be deemed to be zero.

(e) This Section applies only when a trust would violate the rule against perpetuities as modified by Section 4 and does not apply to any trust which would have been valid apart from this Act.

(f) This Section does not apply when a trust violates the rule against perpetuities because the trust estate may not vest in the trustee within the period of the rule.

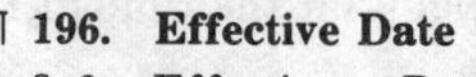

¶ 196. Effective Date

§ 6. Effective Date. This Act shall apply only to instruments, including instruments which exercise a power of appointment, which become effective after the effective date of this Act.

(2) Cemetery trusts. Interests which are directed to be used for the maintenance, care, or adornment of any cemetery, churchyard, or other place for the burial of the dead, or any portion thereof, or any grave therein or any improvement on or about the same, and which are subject to no condition precedent at the end of the period described in subsection (b).

(3) Pension or profit-sharing plans. Interests created by a bona fide trust inter vivos primarily for the benefit of business employees, their families or appointees, under a stock bonus, pension, disability or death benefit, profit-sharing or other employee-benefit plan.

(4) Administrative powers. Powers which contribute to the effective management of trust assets, including powers to sell, mortgage, or lease trust assets, powers relating to investment of trust assets, powers to determine what is principal and what is income, and powers to name successor trustees.

"(c) Time for beginning period.—The period allowed by the common law rule against perpetuities under subsection (b) of this section shall be measured from the expiration of any time during which one person while living has the unrestricted power to transfer to himself the entire legal and beneficial interest in the property."

"(d) Applicability.—The provisions of this section and of section 6105 (relating to rule against perpetuities; disposition when invalidity occurs) shall apply to all interests heretofore or hereafter created." [27]

A second legislative approach follows the pattern of Edgerly v. Barker, empowering the court to reduce age contingencies: [28]

McKINNEY'S NEW YORK ESTATES, POWERS AND TRUSTS LAW (1980 SUPP.)

"§ 9–1.2 Reduction of age contingency

"Where an estate would, except for this section, be invalid because made to depend, for its vesting or its duration, upon any person attaining or failing to attain an age in excess of twenty-one years, the age contingency shall be reduced to twenty-one years as to any or all persons subject to such contingency."

A third variant proceeds along the line of construction to avoid invalidity:

McKINNEY'S NEW YORK ESTATES, POWERS AND TRUSTS LAW (1980 SUPP.)

"§ 9–1.3 Rules of construction

"(a) Unless a contrary intention appears, the rules of construction provided in this section govern with respect to any matter affecting the rule against perpetuities.

"(b) It shall be presumed that the creator intended the estate to be valid.

"(c) Where an estate would, except for this paragraph, be invalid because of the possibility that the person to whom it is given or limited may be a person not in being at the time of the creation of the estate, and such person

27. See Levin, "Section 6104(d) of the Pennsylvania Rule Against Perpetuities: The Validity and Effect of the Retroactive Application of Property and Probate Law Reform", 25 Vill.L.Rev. 213 (1980).

28. See Fratcher, "Missouri Perpetuities Act", 45 Mo.L.Rev. 240 (1980).

is referred to in the instrument creating such estate as the spouse of another without other identification, it shall be presumed that such reference is to a person in being on the effective date of the instrument.

"(d) Where the duration or vesting of an estate is contingent upon the probate of a will, the appointment of a fiduciary, the location of a distributee, the payment of debts, the sale of assets, the settlement of an estate, the determination of questions relating to an estate or transfer tax or the occurrence of any specified contingency, it shall be presumed that the creator of such estate intended such contingency to occur, if at all, within twenty-one years from the effective date of the instrument creating such estate.

"(e)(1) Where the validity of a disposition depends upon the ability of a person to have a child at some future time, it shall be presumed, subject to subparagraph (2), that a male can have a child at fourteen years of age or over, but not under that age, and that a female can have a child at twelve years of age or over, but not under that age or over the age of fifty-five years.

(2) In the case of a living person, evidence may be given to establish whether he or she is able to have a child at the time in question.

(3) Where the validity of a disposition depends upon the ability of a person to have a child at some future time, the possibility that such person may have a child by adoption shall be disregarded.

(4) The provisions of subparagraphs (1), (2) and (3) shall not apply for any purpose other than that of determining the validity of a disposition under the rule against perpetuities where such validity depends on the ability of a person to have a child at some future time. A determination of validity or invalidity of a disposition under the rule against perpetuities by the application of subparagraph (1) or (2) or (3) shall not be affected by the later occurrence of facts in contradiction to the facts presumed or determined or the possibility of adoption disregarded under subparagraphs (1) or (2) or (3)." [29]

A fourth technique permits a flat period in gross, so that draftmen may safely utilize this period as the basis for termination of the trust: [30]

WEST'S ANN.CAL.CIVIL CODE (1980 SUPP.)

"§ 715.6. No interest in real or personal property which must vest, if at all, not later than 60 years after the creation of the interest violates Section 715.2 of this code."

The most drastic statute of all is that in Washington, adopted in 1959, which combines "wait and see" with power to excise the invalid portion and dis-

29. Compare West's Ann.Cal.Civil Code § 715.5 (1980 Supp.):

"No interest in real or personal property is either void or voidable as in violation of Section 715.2 of this code if and to the extent that it can be reformed or construed within the limits of that section to give effect to the general intent of the creator of the interest whenever that general intent can be ascertained. This section shall be liberally construed and applied to validate such interest to the fullest extent consistent with such ascertained intent."

See also § 715.7 of the same Code.

30. The English Perpetuities and Accumulations Act of 1964 permits the instrument by which the disposition is made (such as a will) to specify a period not exceeding 80 years for the duration. The English Act also contains elaborate provisions for admitting evidence that a person will not be able to bear children, for utilizing as the measuring lives those of persons in existence, for reducing the age limitations as necessary to save the disposition, and for determining validity at the end of the period. 12 & 13 Eliz. II, ch. 55.

tribute on a private *cy pres* basis.[31] Under this unique statute the trust limitations would not be held invalid during the period of the rule; if the interests all in fact vested within the period of any measuring lives and 21 years, they would be valid; and if at the end of the period, any trust assets have not then become vested, they would be distributed under order of the court to give effect to "the general intent of the creator of the trust".

The traditional common law Rule still has great vitality in a majority of the states. You must therefore be thoroughly acquainted with its ramifications. As to limitations affected by the law of states adhering to the common law Rule, the careful draftsman may resort to standard clauses for "saving" the interests under a trust from possible invalidity by reason of the Rule.[32] Unfortunately these saving clauses are not always well drafted, as the next case illustrates.

PROBLEM

The Model Rule Against Perpetuities Act[33] provides as follows:

> "No interest in real or personal property shall be good unless it must vest not later than twenty-one years after some life in being at the creation of the interest and any period of gestation involved in the situation to which the limitation applies. The lives selected to govern the time of vesting must not be so numerous nor so situated that evidence of their deaths is likely to be unreasonably difficult to obtain. It is intended by the enactment of this statute to make effective in this State the American common law rule against perpetuities."

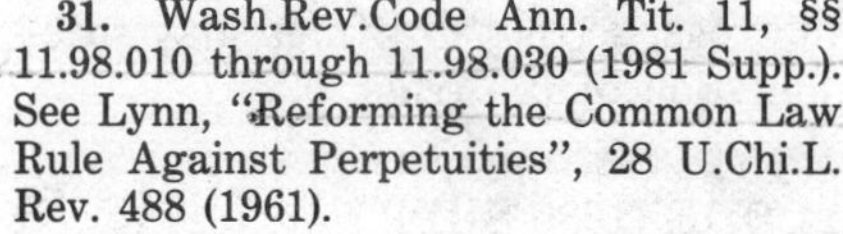

Under this statute could a court follow the doctrine espoused in Merchants National Bank v. Curtis?

31. Wash.Rev.Code Ann. Tit. 11, §§ 11.98.010 through 11.98.030 (1981 Supp.). See Lynn, "Reforming the Common Law Rule Against Perpetuities", 28 U.Chi.L. Rev. 488 (1961).

32. For a discussion of the function of "saving clauses" and a proposed standard clause see Leach and Logan, "Perpetuities: A Standard Saving Clause to Avoid Violations of the Rule", 74 Harv.L. Rev. 1141 (1961).

33. 9C Uniform Laws Ann. (1957). Adopted in Wyoming (Wyo.Stat.Ann. § 34–1–139); California (West's Ann.Cal. Civ.Code § 715.2 (1980 Supp.)) with modifications and additions.

SECTION 2. APPLICATION TO CLASS GIFTS

IN RE LEE'S ESTATE

Supreme Court of Washington, 1956
49 Wash.2d 254, 299 P.2d 1066.[34]

ROSELLINI, JUSTICE. This appeal from a decree of distribution involves the construction of the trust provisions of a will. The pertinent provisions are as follows:

"*Fifth*: Upon the death of my said son, Fairman Burbidge Lee, my trustee, Seattle-First National Bank is authorized to pay to each of my said grandchildren so much from the income and/or principal of my said estate as my said trustee shall deem necessary and proper for the maintenance, health and education of such grandchild until he shall have completed his education, but not after he shall have attained the age of twenty-five (25) years. Thereafter, my said trustee shall pay to each of my said grandchildren after he shall have completed his education, as aforesaid, the sum of Twenty-Five and No/100 Dollars ($25.00) per month from the income and/or principal of my said estate, until the youngest of my said grandchildren shall have attained the age of forty (40) years, at which time my said estate shall be distributed to my grandchildren then living at said time, share and share alike; provided further that in the event none of my said grandchildren shall live to attain the age of forty (40) years, then upon the death of my last grandchild prior to attaining the age of forty (40) years, the trustee shall then distribute my estate to my great-grandchildren.

"*Sixth*: If all of my grandchildren shall die prior to attaining the age of forty (40) years, without issue, then all of the remainder of the estate in the hands of my trustee shall be used by my trustee to endow beds in the Children's Orthopedic Hospital of Seattle, Washington, in the names of Anna Williams Lee, Chester Fairman Lee and Fairman Burbidge Lee.

"*Eighth*: If any provisions of this Will should be void on account of the rule of perpetuities or any other rule of law pertaining to such trusts, then the trusts herein provided shall continue in force for the full period permitted by law and on the day prior to the expiration of such full period, trustee shall make distribution of any remainder of the trust estate to the persons herein named who would be entitled to take distribution thereon upon termination of the trust.

"*Tenth*: I direct that if any part or provision of this, my Will, shall be declared illegal or void by any court, such illegality or invalidity shall not affect any other portion of this instrument and

34. Noted, 32 Wash.L.Rev. 136 (1957).

that all other parts thereof shall remain in full force and effect the same as if no part thereof had been declared void, and also that this instrument be construed under the laws of the State of Washington, and that notwithstanding the date of its execution, so far as the administration of the trust is concerned and the provisions for the beneficiaries, it shall be construed as becoming effective as to the date of my death for all purposes."

In the fourth paragraph of her will, the testatrix provided a life estate for her son, which is concededly valid. It was also conceded in the trial court that the remainders provided in the fifth and sixth paragraphs violate the rule against perpetuities; and the only question which the trial court was asked to decide was whether the trust was saved by the eighth and tenth paragraphs. The trial court concluded that the provision for distributing the estate to the "persons herein named who would be entitled to take distribution thereon at the termination of the trust" was sufficiently definite to enable the court to ascertain to whom distribution was to be made upon termination of the trust one day before the expiration of the full period permitted by law. It is the contention of the appellants that the provision is too indefinite to be enforced, that if this paragraph is ineffective, the dispositive scheme is destroyed and the entire trust has failed. Consequently, they say, Mrs. Lee died intestate and the estate should be distributed immediately to her only heir at law, her son, Fairman Burbidge Lee.

The respondents devote a considerable portion of their brief to a theory that the remainders to the grandchildren when and if they reach age forty, and to the great-grandchildren if no grandchild lives to attain age 40, are not contingent but vested remainders, even though they are gifts to a class, and therefore do not violate the rule against perpetuities. No argument was made on this point in the trial court; however, since we are asked to construe the will, which involves only a question of law, we will dispose of the theory presented. Three cases are cited from other jurisdictions which have held that if a beneficiary is to receive the income from a trust and, upon the happening of a named contingency, he is to receive the corpus, the gift of the corpus is not contingent but is vested, subject to divestment. Insofar as these cases are contrary to the rule which has been laid down by this court, they do not express the law which controls our decision here. The question raised by the respondent was discussed at length in Betchard v. Iverson, 35 Wash.2d 344, 212 P.2d 783, 787 the authorities were reviewed, and the rule was recognized as follows:

"A class which includes after-born children is subject to fluctuation; the number of its members may increase or decrease, and the size of the gift to each is determined by the ultimate membership of the group. It is this peculiarity of gifts to a class, as contrasted with gifts to individuals, that has led to the rule that, for the purposes of the rule against perpetuities, a class gift is not regarded as vested until the maximum and minimum membership of the class is determined. As long as the class may increase by the birth of additional members, or decrease by the death of members, there can be no vesting. See Denny v. Hyland, 162 Wash. 68, 297 P. 1083; 2 Simes, Law of Future Interests, 399, § 526 and 400, § 528."

The rule against perpetuities prohibits the creation of future estates which, by possibility, may not become vested within a life or lives in being at the time of the testator's death and twenty-one years thereafter. If, by any conceivable combination of circumstances, it is possible that the event upon which the estate or interest is limited may not occur within the period of the rule, the limitation is void. Betchard v. Iverson, supra.

Under these rules, it is clear that the gifts of the remainders to the grandchildren are void, for they will vest only if one or more grandchildren survive until the youngest reaches age forty; and since grandchildren may be born after the death of the testatrix, and within the gestation period after the death of her son (the measuring life in being at the time of the testatrix' death), the youngest may reach age forty more than twenty-one years after the death of the son. By the same token, the gifts over to the great-grandchildren and to the hospital are void, for they are contingent upon events which may occur more than twenty-one years after the death of the son.

Since the remainders are void, by the expressed intent of the testatrix, the eighth paragraph of the will applies, and the trust is to terminate one day before the expiration of the full period allowed by law, that is, twenty-one years after the death of the son. The question to be decided is, whom did the testatrix intend to receive distribution at that time. The words of the testatrix are ambiguous and subject to two interpretations. It is the position of the appellant that the phrase "persons herein named who would be entitled to take distribution thereon at the termination of the trust" means those persons who would be entitled to take distribution of the corpus if the trust were terminated under the provisions of the fifth and sixth paragraphs of the will. Consequently, they say, it will be impossible to determine the beneficiaries at the termination of the trust; and for this reason, the provision is too indefinite to enforce. The respondents, on the other hand, argue that the obvious intent was to provide for distribution of the corpus to those persons named in the preceding paragraphs who would be entitled to take distribution thereof if those paragraphs provided for the termination of the trust at the end of the lawful period rather than at the time designated in the invalid provisions of the will.

If the interpretation placed upon the phrase by the appellants is adopted, the clause is unenforceable, for the persons entitled to take distribution under the fifth and sixth paragraphs cannot be determined until the youngest grandchild has reached age forty, or all of the grandchildren have died before reaching age forty. It is exactly these contingencies which violate the rule against perpetuities, and it was just such a violation which paragraph eight was designed to guard against. Although she expressed herself ineptly, it is plain that the testatrix, in paragraph eight, intended to substitute a valid disposition for any invalid disposition which she may have made in the earlier paragraphs.

The eighth paragraph can be given effect only if the persons entitled to receive the corpus can be ascertained at the time of the termination of the trust—one day before the expiration of the period allowed by law. The law presumes that a valid disposition is intended. Atkinson, Wills, 815, § 146.

A court is bound to give that construction to a will which will effectuate the intention of the testator if such intention can be gathered from the terms of the will itself; and the intention is to be gathered from everything contained within the four corners of the instrument. O'Shaughnessy v. Brooks, 153 Wash. 247, 279 P. 591; In re Peters' Estate, 101 Wash. 572, 172 P. 870. When a court is faced with two possible constructions, one which will accomplish the evident ends sought by the testator and another which will not, the former construction should be adopted if the language used will admit of such construction. In re Peters' Estate, supra.

Applying these rules of construction to the will in question, it is clear that the testatrix did not intend to substitute an invalid disposition for a prior invalid disposition. It is true that the language which she used is subject to the interpretation placed upon it by the appellants; but, viewed in the light of the purpose which paragraph eight was meant to serve and the other language contained therein, it is also subject to the interpretation placed upon it by the respondents. Under the latter interpretation, a valid disposition is provided and the will can be given effect; but if the meaning assigned by the appellants is adopted, the provision cannot possibly be carried out.

This court is disposed to as liberal a construction as possible to effect the carrying out of the intention of a testator, when it is possible to determine the testator's intention from all the surroundings and context of a devise. In re Peters' Estate, supra.

We conclude that the testatrix intended by the language used in paragraph eight to provide for the acceleration of the date on which distribution was to be made if the prior dispositive clauses should prove invalid; and for the distribution of the corpus on that date to her grandchildren if any were then living, otherwise to her great-grandchildren; and if all of her grandchildren had died without issue, to the Children's Orthopedic Hospital. As the trial court noted in its decree of distribution, an intestacy would occur if the grandchildren had issue but no great-grandchild survived to the date of distribution, since the testatrix failed to make provision for this contingency.

The trial court, in its decree of distribution, provided that the trust should continue until the youngest grandchild reached age forty, or until the death of the last surviving grandchild prior to reaching age forty, or until twenty-one years, less one day, after the death of the son, whichever event should occur first. Such a disposition goes beyond any expressed intent of the testatrix. The will provides that in the event any provision of the will should be void, the trust should terminate one day before the end of the full period allowed by law, not that the trust should terminate in accordance with the provisions contained in paragraphs five and six or one day before the end of the full period allowed by law, whichever date was earlier.

The cause is remanded, with direction to modify the decree accordingly. In all other respects, the judgment is affirmed.

MALLERY, HILL, and WEAVER, JJ., concur.

AMERICAN SECURITY & TRUST CO. v. CRAMER

United States District Court, District of Columbia, 1959.
175 F.Supp. 367.

YOUNGDAHL, DISTRICT JUDGE. Six of the eleven defendants before the Court have moved for summary judgment. A hearing has been held and memoranda of points and authorities have been submitted. Plaintiff, trustee of a testamentary trust, is a stakeholder in this controversy among competing heirs. Since all the material facts have been stipulated, the Court is free to render summary judgment.

Abraham D. Hazen, a resident of the District of Columbia, died in the District on December 4, 1901. His will, executed on October 16, 1900, was admitted to probate on March 11, 1902.

Testator was survived by Hannah E. Duffey, who is referred to in his will as his "adopted daughter". At the time of the testator's death, Hannah had two children: Mary Hazen Duffey [now Cramer], born November 12, 1897, and Hugh Clarence Duffey, born July 11, 1899. After the testator's death, Hannah gave birth to two more children: Depue Hazen Duffey, born October 9, 1903, and Horace Duffey, born July 8, 1908.

The will provided for the payment of debts and certain specific bequests and then provided that the residue of the estate be put in trust for the benefit of testator's wife for life. At her death, one-half of the corpus was to be, and has been, given to testator's sister and brothers; the other half, composed of realty, remained in trust for Hannah for life. At Hannah's death, the income was to go to the children of Hannah "then living or the issue of such of them as may then be dead leaving issue surviving" Hannah, and then "upon the death of each the share of the one so dying shall go absolutely to the persons who shall then be her or his heirs at law according to the laws of descent now in force in the said District of Columbia".

Testator's widow died on October 31, 1916; Hannah died on May 21, 1915.

On October 5, 1917, the heirs of the testator brought an action in equity to have the provisions of the seventh paragraph of the will stricken as being in violation of the rule against perpetuities. The Supreme Court of the District of Columbia held that the interests of Hannah's children under the will were valid and the Court of Appeals affirmed. Hazen v. American Security & Trust Co., 1920, 49 App.D.C. 297, 265 F. 447. The validity of the remainders over, after the death of each child, was expressly not ruled upon as the life estates were not "so intimately connected with the gift over as to require us now to determine the validity of such gifts."

Hugh, one of the four life tenants after the death of the widow and Hannah, died on December 19, 1928 and shortly thereafter the trustee brought a bill for instructions; this time the validity of the remainder over to Hugh's heirs was in issue. On January 2, 1930, Judge Bailey ruled that "the remainder provided by the will after his [Hugh's] death to the persons who shall then be his heirs at law became vested within the period prescribed by law and is valid."

On December 13, 1954, Depue died and for the fourth time a suit concerning this trust was started in this court. The trustees desired instructions as to the disposition of Depue's one-sixth share. While this action was pending, on December 18, 1957, Horace died. A supplemental bill was then filed, asking for instructions as to the disposition of this one-sixth share as well. The remainder over after the death of the sole living life tenant, Mary, cannot yet take effect; however, due to the request of all the parties concerned, and in order to save both the time of this court and the needless expense it would otherwise cost the estate, the Court will also pass on the validity of this remainder.

The law that governs the questions here involved is the law in effect at the time of the testator's death: December 4, 1901.

The common-law rule against perpetuities, as stated by Professor Gray, is as follows:

> "No interest is good unless it must vest, if at all, not later than twenty-one years after some life in being at the creation of the interest."

The effect of the rule is to invalidate *ab initio* certain future interests that might otherwise remain in existence for a period of time considered inimicable to society's interest in having reasonable limits to dead-hand control and in facilitating the marketability of property. The policy of the law is to permit a person to control the devolution of his property but only for a human lifetime plus twenty-one years and actual periods of gestation. With careful planning, this period could be as long as one hundred years—and this is long enough.

A gift to a class is a gift of an aggregate amount of property to persons who are collectively described and whose individual share will depend upon the number of persons ultimately constituting the class. Evans v. Ockershausen, 1938, 69 App.D.C. 285, 292, 100 F.2d 695, 702, 128 A.L.R. 177. The members of the class must be finally determined within a life or lives in being plus twenty-one years and actual periods of gestation, or the gift will fail. Put another way, the class must close within the period of the rule against perpetuities, if the class gift is to be valid. Unless a contrary intent is indicated by the testator, the class will close when any member of the class is entitled to immediate possession and enjoyment of his share of the class gift. Applying these basic principles to the trust here involved, it is seen that the life estates to Hannah's children had to vest, if at all, at the termination of the preceding life estates of the widow and Hannah. Since Hannah's children had to be born within Hannah's lifetime, and since Hannah was a life in being, the class (Hannah's children) physiologically had to close within the period of the rule. This has already been so held. Hazen v. American Security & Trust Co., supra, at note 6. Furthermore, the remainder over at Hugh's death has been held valid. The Court now holds that the remainder limited to the heirs of Mary is valid. Both Hugh and Mary were lives in being at the testator's death; the remainders limited to their heirs had to vest, if at all, within the period of the rule. Horace and Depue were born after the testator died; the remainders over at their deaths are invalid.

In applying the rule against perpetuities, it does not help to show that the rule might be complied with or that, the way things turned out, it actually was complied with. After the testator's death, Hannah might have had more children; one of these might have lived more than twenty-one years after the death of all the lives in being at the testator's death. The vesting of the remainder in this after-born's heirs would take place after the expiration of lives in being and twenty-one years, since the heirs could not be ascertained until the after-born's death and an interest cannot be vested until the interest holder is ascertained. Consequently, because of the possibility that this could happen, even though, in fact, it did not,[35] the remainders limited to the heirs of Horace and Depue (both after-borns) are invalid as a violation of the rule against perpetuities.

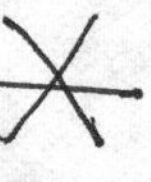

Counsel have not argued the point of whether the invalidity of the remainders to the heirs of Horace and Depue serves to taint the otherwise valid remainders to the heirs of Mary and Hugh. Of course, the remainder after Hugh's life estate has already been distributed and is not properly in issue. Nevertheless, as shall be demonstrated, it (and the remainder to the heirs of Mary) are not affected by the two invalid remainders, since the four remainders are to subclasses and stand (or fall) separately.

35. Mary, a life in being at testator's death, is still alive. Therefore, the heirs of Horace and Depue would *actually* be taking within the period of the rule, but in this area of imagination-run-wild, actualities do not count; what could happen is all that matters.

In this case, the above suppositions are not unreasonable since Hannah was in her middle thirties when the testator died. But cf. the cases of "the fertile octogenarian", "the unborn widow" and "the magic gravel pit" in Professor Leach's classic article, "Perpetuities in a Nutshell", 51 Harv.L.R. 638, 642–645 (1938).

[The foregoing is by the court. Other footnotes have been eliminated; in one of these the court noted the "wait and see" doctrine but stated that a statute would be necessary to effect this change in local law. Ed.]

Beginning with Jee v. Audley, 1 Cox Eq.Cas. 324 (1787) and flowering with Leake v. Robinson, 2 Mer. 363, 35 Eng.Rep. 979 (Chancery 1817), there has been the curious anomaly in future interests law that if the interest of any potential member of a class can possibly vest too remotely, the interests of all the members of the class fails. In other words, the rule is that a class gift is inseparable. For example, T creates a trust to pay the income to A for life and then to pay the corpus over to such of A's children as attain the age of twenty-five. When A dies he might have a child who is not yet four years of age and who was not in being at T's death; this child, would not take a vested interest until he satisfied the contingency of reaching the age of twenty-five; since a child under four could not become twenty-five within twenty-one years, the child's interest is void by virtue of the rule against perpetuities. While this much may be sound, the rule in Leake v. Robinson goes on to invalidate the *entire* class gift. That is, even if the child under four has two brothers who are over twenty-five when A dies, these two brothers take nothing because the invalid interest of their little brother (who, remember, may only be imagined) is contagious—so says Leake. Unless the testator intended to have *all* of the twenty-five-year-old sons take, or none at all (and this is difficult to imagine in the absence of an express provision in the will), the rule is a dubious one. Fortunately, the Court need not apply it in this case because of the limitation put on it by a long line of cases beginning with Catlin v. Brown, 11 Hare 372, 68 Eng.Rep. 1318 (Chancery, 1853).

In Catlin, the devise was of mortgaged property to A for life, then to the children of A in equal shares during their lives, and after the death of any such child, his share to his children and their heirs. Some of A's children were in being at the time that the testator died; some were born after his death. Counsel conceded that the remainders over to the heirs of those children of A born after the testator's death were invalid. The question was whether those concededly invalid remainders tainted the otherwise valid remainders and rendered them invalid. The Court held that they did not; the remainders to the heirs of the children in being at the testator's death were valid. Leake was distinguished on the ground that it concerned remainders to *one* class (A's children that reach twenty-five) while the remainders involved in Catlin were to a group of subclasses (the heirs of each of A's children was a subclass). In other words, the limitation placed on Leake by Catlin is that if the ultimate takers are not described as a single class but rather as a group of subclasses, and if the share to which each separate subclass is entitled will finally be determined within the period of the rule, the gifts to the different subclasses are separable for the purpose of the rule.

In the instant case, the language of the will compels the Court to read it as a devise of remainders to subclasses and within the rule of Catlin. The provision in issue reads, in part:

> "* * * and *each* of the children of said adopted daughter shall take only for and during the terms of their *respective* lives

and upon the death of *each* the share of the *one* so dying shall go absolutely to the persons who shall then be *her or his* heirs at law * * *" (Emphasis supplied).

The Court deems it advisable to mention that it thoroughly explored the possible applicability here of the Rule in Shelley's Case. Prior to January 2, 1902, this ancient principle of law was in force in the District of Columbia. Noyes v. Parker, 1937, 68 App.D.C. 13, 92 F.2d 562. If it could be utilized in the case at hand, the remainders limited to the heirs of each of Hannah's children would be converted into a remainder in the child himself. This, for one thing, would save the two remainders found invalid and prevent their defaulting to the heirs of the testator.

Assuming, without deciding, that the remainders here are equitable (because the trust is active), nevertheless the rule does not apply because the remainders were not limited to "heirs" but instead went to "her or his heirs at law according to the laws of descent now in force in the said District of Columbia".

When a remainder in fee after a life estate fails, there is no enlargement or diminution of the life estate; rather there is then a reversion in the heirs of the testator. Hilton v. Kinsey, 1950, 88 U.S. App.D.C. 14, 17, 185 F.2d 885, 888, 23 A.L.R.2d 830; Simes and Smith, supra, at note 10, § 1263, and numerous cases cited. The two one-sixth shares held invalid shall pass to the successors in interest to the heirs of Abraham D. Hazen.

* * *

Counsel will submit an appropriate order.[36]

PROBLEMS

Although a more thorough knowledge of the intricacies of the Rule may be necessary to attack a particular will or trust instrument, you should have sufficient knowledge to determine whether the following provisions can be validly employed by the draftsman implementing an estate plan for the client who wishes to exercise some control over the future.

1. Which of the following would be valid in a trust created by will, where the testamentary disposition is in favor of the testator's family:

(a) "To pay the income to my wife for life, then to pay the income to my children for life, and on the death of my last child to distribute the principal in equal shares to my grandchildren then living."

(b) "To pay the income to my son John for life, after his death to pay the income to his widow, and upon the death of the survivor of my said son and his widow to distribute the principal among his then living issue per stirpes."

(c) "To pay the income to my son John for life, and on his death to divide the principal into as many shares as he has children then living, the share of any child under 21 to be held in trust for him until he reaches 21

36. See Lynn and Carpenter, "Applying the Rule Against Perpetuities to Class Gifts: The Influence of Leach", 43 Tex.L.Rev. 37 (1964); Note, "Separability and the Rule Against Perpetuities", 77 Dick.L.Rev. 277 (1973).

and if he dies before reaching 21 his share to be added to the shares of then surviving children of my son John."

(d) Same provisions as the preceding problem (c) but with the age of 30 specified.

(e) "To pay the income from the trust fund semi-annually to my issue per stirpes for a period of twenty-five years from my death, then to terminate the trust and distribute the principal to my issue then living per stirpes."

(f) "To accumulate the income during the life of my wife Jane, and to pay over the principal and accumulated income to the executor or administrator of my wife's estate." (Assume the validity of the provision for accumulation.)

2. Which of the foregoing would be valid in an irrevocable inter vivos trust? In a revocable inter vivos trust?

3. Which of the following provisions in the will of a testator who wishes to provide for collateral relatives or friends would be valid:

(a) "The rest, residue and remainder in trust to pay the income to my sister Jane for life, then to pay the principal to her issue who survive her, per stirpes."

(b) "To pay the principal to my nieces and nephews who reach the age of 21 in equal shares."

(c) "To pay the income to my sister Jane for life, then to pay the income to her children for life, and at the death of the survivor of them, to distribute the principal to their issue per stirpes."

4. If the testator's sister in 3(c) is 65 at the death of the testator, would your answer be the same? Would the limitations be valid if you included the names of the nieces and nephews (John, Mary, Jean, and Ralph) in the will? If you described the class as "my nieces and nephews living at my death"?

5. A will gives a number of devises and legacies to named relatives if each survives the testator, followed by a clause reading: "If any beneficiary under this will shall die prior to the final distribution of this estate, his interest shall pass under the terms of this will as though he had predeceased me." The will also contains a general residuary clause. What is the effect?

SECTION 3. APPLICATION TO POWERS

As we have seen, powers of appointment are frequently created as an integral part of an estate plan. The Rule against Perpetuities applies both to powers of appointment and to the property interests created in the exercise of such powers.

In applying the Rule to powers of appointment and to interests created in the exercise of such powers, a distinction is drawn between general presently exercisable powers on the one hand, and special powers and general testamentary powers on the other. This distinction is based on the fact that a general presently exercisable power closely approximates ownership of the property covered by the power.

In testing the validity of powers of appointment and of interests created in their exercise, one should first classify the power of appointment to determine whether it is a general presently exercisable power, or a special or general testamentary power. After this classification is made, the validity of the power under the Rule may be tested. If the power be valid and if it has been exercised, then the validity of the appointed interests under the Rule may be tested.

In testing the validity of the power itself, the following rules are applied: (1) If the power is general and presently exercisable, it is invalid if, in view of the circumstances existing on the date that the power is created, there is then any possibility of the power's being *acquired* beyond the permissible period under the Rule against Perpetuities. (2) If the power is special, or is general but testamentary, the power is invalid if, in view of the circumstances existing on the date that it is created, there is then any possibility of the power's being *exercised* beyond the permissible period.[37] These rules arise because the power itself introduces a contingency as to the persons who will take under the power.

Assuming the power is valid, we may still find that interests created in its exercise are invalid under the Rule. We have seen in Chapter XIV, Section 2(3), that property rules normally enable the donee to make an appointment creating new future interests and new powers of appointment. How are these appointed interests to be judged? If the power is general and presently exercisable, the authority is unanimous that the interests created under such a power are measured from the date of its exercise in the light of circumstances then existing.[38] Since the donee of such a power has full power to transfer, such a power does not violate the policy of the Rule. On the other hand, if the power is general testamentary, or is special, a different rule is usually applied. The cases which follow deal particulary with the general testamentary power, which causes the greatest difficulty in practice.

Suppose A transfers property in trust to pay the income to B for life, then to transfer the principal to such person or persons as B may by will appoint, in default to C. B by his will appoints to D for life, then to such person as D may by will appoint, in default to E. Because the power created in B is general but not presently exercisable, under the traditional rules such a power ties up the property for B's lifetime and it must be certain that the power can be exercised only within the permissible period. So long as B is alive at the time the power is created, it is certain that the power would be exercised, if at all, at the end of a life in being and hence the power itself would be valid. If, on the other hand, B were not a person in being at the time the power was created, the power would be void under the traditional Rule against Perpetuities because there is a possibility that it might be exercised beyond lives in being and 21 years. Some jurisdictions

37. Camden Safe Deposit & Trust Co. v. Scott, 121 N.J.Eq. 366, 189 A. 653, 110 A.L.R. 1442 (1936), 36 Mich.L.Rev. 146 (1937).

38. Mifflin's Appeal, 121 Pa.St. 205, 15 A. 525, 1 L.R.A. 453 (1888).

having modern variants of the rule, either by statute or judicial decision, would approach the problem differently; and the creating instrument might have a savings clause applicable even under the traditional Rule.

Next we must test the appointment by B (a life estate in D, a new testamentary power in D, and a gift in default to E); how does the Rule apply here? In the first place, when does the period of the Rule commence to run? Do we read the appointment back into the original limitation and measure from the *creation* of the power? If so, can we consider circumstances existing as of the date of *exercise* in judging validity? Suppose, for example, D is unborn on the date the power is created but is in fact born within a life then in being.[39]

If the validity of an appointment is measured from date of creation, the attempt to create a new power of appointment in D makes the issue concerning validity of this power more complicated. Assuming the power is either special or testamentary, it is not enough that D be in existence when the first power is exercised; he must have been in existence when the first power was created. Otherwise the second power of appointment in D is void.

If an appointment is invalid under the Rule, there remain several troublesome issues. If only one of several appointed interests are invalid, are the remaining interests (such as the life estate to D) separable? Do the assets which B has invalidly attempted to appoint pass in default to C under the original limitation, or do they become part of B's estate?

Finally, if no appointment had been made by B at all, does the presence of a valid power of appointment have any effect in judging the validity of the original gift in default to C?

MARX v. RICE

Superior Court of New Jersey, Chancery Division, 1949.
3 N.J.Super. 581, 67 A.2d 918.

Suit by Abram D. Marx and others against Alexander S. Rice, individually and as surviving administrator cum testamento annexo of the estate of Bernard Strauss, etc., and others, wherein Robert Herzog and others filed a counterclaim raising the issue whether the exercise of a testamentary power of appointment violated the rule against perpetuities.

FREUND, J. S. C. The defendants, Alexander S. Rice, individually and in his representative capacity on behalf of the estates of Bernard Strauss and Florence R. Strauss, and others moved for summary judgment in their favor on the counterclaim filed by the defendants-counterclaimants, Robert Herzog et al. With the exception of the

39. In addition to the cases which follow, see American Law of Property (1952) § 24.30 et seq.; Gray, The Rule Against Perpetuities (4th Ed., 1942) §§ 473–561; Simes and Smith, Future Interests (2d Ed., 1956) §§ 1271–1277; Jones, "The Rule Against Perpetuities and Powers of Appointment: An Old Controversy Revived", 54 Iowa L.Rev. 456 (1968).

question of perpetuities, the counterclaim sets up the same allegations and seeks the same relief as did the complaint filed by the plaintiffs. The complaint was stricken by orders of the Court of Chancery, Marx v. Rice, 142 N.J.Eq. 315, 60 A.2d 61 (Ch.1948), affirmed on appeal by the Supreme Court, 1 N.J. 574, 65 A.2d 48, 52 (1949). On the appeal, the defendants-counterclaimants petitioned and were granted leave to intervene, argue and file a brief. The present motion to strike the counterclaim was initiated while the appeal was pending, and because of the identity of issues I deferred decision until after the Supreme Court had made its determination. The defendants have renewed their motion to strike and the counterclaimants have moved to amend in particulars hereafter to be discussed.

The remaining issue raised by the counterclaim to be determined on this motion concerns the rule against perpetuities. The facts are detailed in the opinion of the Supreme Court. For the purposes of this decision, the following are pertinent: Bernard Strauss died July 5, 1906, survived by his widow Florence, who died January 31, 1918, and their son, Irving, who died October 9, 1947, without issue. By his will, Bernard bequeathed and devised one-half of his estate to his widow absolutely and the other one-half to his son, Irving, for life. He provided that if Florence should predecease their son and if he died without issue, which happened, then he bequeathed and devised the remainder "to such person or persons as my said wife, Florence, shall by her last will and testament appoint and, in case she shall fail to make such appointment", then to his heirs and next-of-kin. By her will, Florence Strauss exercised the power of appointment, by appointing her executors upon certain trusts. The Supreme Court declared her power of appointment to be general and that, although exercised by placing the property in trust, it was, nevertheless, valid, because "unless the donor manifests a contrary intent, the donee of a general power of appointment may make appointments in trust. * * * We perceive no manifestation of a contrary intent in the will presently before us."

The counterclaimants argue, however, that the exercise of the power by Florence R. Strauss was in violation of the rule against perpetuities because the life in being specified in the will of Bernard Strauss was that of his son, Irving; that all interests must vest within twenty-one years after his death and that Florence Strauss extended the vesting of the estate beyond the life of Irving and twenty-one years thereafter. The defendants argue that Irving's is not the sole life to be considered in measuring the period under the rule; and that all the interests in Bernard's estate will necessarily vest before the expiration of the period interdicted by the rule against perpetuities.

The familiar rule against perpetuities is that all future interests, legal or equitable, must vest, if at all, within the term measured by the life or lives of a person or persons in being at the time of the creation of the interest and twenty-one years thereafter. It is the possibility that the period may be exceeded, and "not the certainty or even probability that it will be exceeded, in a given trust, which calls for the application of the rule." * * *

The nature of a power of appointment is thus described in Restatement, Property, Introductory Note, Topic 2, Chapter 27, Page 2294: "The power of appointment is a hybrid between concepts of agency and concepts of property. To the extent that a power of appointment has been thought of as a mere authority to act for the donor in the completion of a disposition initiated by the donor, the agency factor has dominated and the doctrine of 'relation-back' has been applied. To the extent, however, that a power of appointment has been thought of as giving to the donee a control over the appointive assets which is the substantial equivalent of ownership, the property factor has dominated, and the validity of an attempted exercise of a power has been determined as if it had been a disposition by the donee of his owned assets."

Whenever such a power is in fact exercised, the validity of the appointment is determined by precisely the same rule as if the original testator, who created the power, had in his own will the same provision in favor of the same appointee. The donee of the power takes from the donor, the original testator, from the date of his death. With reference to the rule against perpetuities, the remoteness of an appointment depends on its distance from the creation and is to be measured or computed from the date of the death of the testator, and not from the exercise of the power. * * *

In the application of the rule to a general testamentary power, Restatement, Property, Sec. 392, declares:

> "An appointment under * * * a general testamentary power * * * is invalid, because of the rule against perpetuities, only to the extent, that its limitations
>
> "(a) construed in the light of the circumstances existent when the power is exercised, but
>
> "(b) measured for the purpose of applying the rule against perpetuities, from the time when the power was created, violate that rule."

The affidavits on the motion for summary judgment disclose that all of the cestuis of the trust established under the exercise of the power of appointment by Florence R. Strauss were alive at the time of the death of the donor. Mrs. Strauss set up two funds, one for $10,000 and the other for $24,000. With respect to the $10,000 fund, she directed that the income be paid to Marian D. Marx for life and upon her death the fund be distributed between her two daughters, Paula and Fannie, with a proviso that if Paula should not be married, then two-thirds was to be paid to her and one-third to Fannie; but if Paula were married, then the fund was to be shared equally between them. Marian D. Marx died on September 15, 1946, having predeceased Irving. At the time of her death, both her daughters were married; they are still living. The counterclaimants contend that the contingency of the marriage of Paula invalidates the bequest. The contention is without merit because the fact of marriage did not affect the vesting of the interest in the appointees, but merely the extent of the interest.

The fund of $24,000 was thus disposed of: income to be paid to Moses Strauss for life and upon his death, the corpus to his children, Isidore, Daniel and Paula, in equal shares. Moses, the life tenant, predeceased Irving, having died September 25, 1926. He was survived by his three children, who are still living.

The residue of the property Florence R. Strauss directed to be sold and the proceeds divided into four equal shares, to be held in trust as follows: One share was set aside for the benefit of Bertha J. F. Rice and Joseph Rice, her son; one-third of the income was to be paid to Bertha and the remaining two-thirds to Joseph, and upon the remarriage or death of Bertha, the corpus of said share with accumulations thereon was to be paid to Joseph. Bertha died in 1942, survived by her son, Joseph, who is still living. As to the other three shares, the net income to Alexander S. Rice, Rose R. Siegel and Leah R. Fuld so long as they may live and until the death of the last survivor of them; and upon the death of the last survivor, the trust estate to be distributed in equal proportion among the children of Rose and Leah per capita. Alexander S. Rice and Leah R. Fuld are living. Rose R. Siegel died on November 9, 1933, survived by two daughters, Helen S. Simpson and Alice R. Hannoch, who are still living. Leah R. Fuld, a widow, now about 76 years of age, has two children Abram L. Fuld and Florence F. Vogel. Abram absconded about December 20, 1928 and his present whereabouts are unknown. Florence F. Vogel is living. All of the foregoing persons were living when Bernard Strauss, the donor, died.

The counterclaimants urge that the exercise of the appointment as aforesaid is violative "of the rule against perpetuities because of the possibility of children being born to * * * Leah beyond the period measured by the life in being (Irving Strauss) and twenty-one years. It is also violative of the rule because there is no vesting of the interest until the death of the survivor of Alexander, Rose and Leah, and there is no certainty that this will happen within a period measured by twenty-one years after the death of Irving." The fallacy of the contentions lies in the fact that the Supreme Court has construed the power to be a general, and not a special or limited, power. The provisions of the will of Bernard creating the power are to be read together with the will of Florence exercising the power. Applying the standard that the exercise of a general testamentary power should be "construed in the light of the circumstances when the power was exercised" but "measured for the purpose of applying the rule against perpetuities from the time when the power was created", there is no violation of the rule. Irving who was the life tenant under Bernard's will and all of the persons appointed by Florence under her will were living at the date of death of the donor. Measured by all those lives in being at and from the time of the creation of the power, there will be an absolute vesting within the prescribed period. Thus, reconstructing the provisions, we have the following: Income to A (Irving) for life; thereafter, income to B, C and D (Alexander Rice, Rose Siegel and Leah Fuld) during their lives, and upon the death of the last survivor of them, corpus to be divided among the children of C and D (Rose and Leah) in equal shares. A, B, C and D being alive at the death of the testator, there must necessarily be a vesting within the period measured by their lives in being, and twenty-one years thereafter. Rose being dead, the only person whose heirs may be increased is Leah, who is a widow, 76 years of age. While in theory and contemplation of law, the possibility of issue is always supposed to exist, 2 Bl.Com. 125, In re Smith, 94 N.J.Eq. 1, 118 A. 271 (Ch. 1922); Graves v. Graves, supra; Schumacher v. Howard Savings Institution, 126 N.J.Eq. 325, 8 A.2d 908 (Ch.1939); Byers v. Fidelity Union Trust Company, 132 N.J.Eq. 416, 28 A.2d 655 (Ch.1942), the appointment in the particular instance is not invalidated because such issue would necessarily be born in the lifetime of Leah and would share in the ultimate distribution of the estate.

The defendants further argue that even if the exercise of the power in trust in some respects violates the rule against perpetuities, which they deny, the counterclaimants cannot benefit because they are heirs-at-law and next-of-kin of Bernard Strauss, the donor, and not related to Florence R. Strauss, the donee. The defendants' contention is in this respect well-founded. The recognized principle is thus stated by Professor Scott in Trusts, Sec. 426, Page 2208: "Where a person upon whom a general power of appointment is conferred makes an appointment to a trustee upon a trust which fails, the trustee holds the property upon a resulting trust for the estate of the donee of the power, unless it was otherwise provided in the instrument by which the power was created or unless the donee of the power manifested a different intention." See, also, Restatement, Trusts, Chapter 12, Sec. 426; Fidelity Trust Co. v. Mishou, supra; Gray, Perpetuities, Sec. 540.1. The donor provided that only in case the donee should fail to appoint was the property to be given to his heirs and next-of-kin. However, the donee did not fail to appoint. According to the general rule, therefore, if in the exercise of the power the trust or some part of it should fail for remoteness, there is nothing in the donor's or donee's will to manifest an intention that the property should not become part of the donee's estate.

The defendants are entitled to summary judgment on the counterclaim.

* * *

Judgment will be entered in accordance with the foregoing conclusions.

INDUSTRIAL NATIONAL BANK OF RHODE ISLAND v. BARRETT

Supreme Court of Rhode Island, 1966.
101 R.I. 189, 220 A.2d 517.

PAOLINO, JUSTICE. This is a bill in equity brought by the Industrial National Bank of Rhode Island, executor and trustee, and Aline C. Lathan, co-executor, under the will of Mary M. Tilley, deceased, for construction of the latter's will and for instructions to the executors and trustee thereunder. The adult respondents have filed an answer to the bill and all minor and contingent interests and those of persons unascertainable or not in being are represented by a guardian ad litem appointed for that purpose by the court. The guardian has filed an answer neither admitting nor denying the bill's allegations and submitting the interests of his respective wards to the court's care and protection.

After the cause was heard in superior court and was ready for hearing on the final decree it was certified to this court for our determination under G.L.1956, § 9–24–28.

There are no factual issues in dispute, all the allegations of fact contained in the bill in equity and the answers of respondents having been admitted by the parties either in the pleadings or at the certification hearing. In addition the parties have filed an agreed statement of facts concerning the value of stock given by the testatrix to respondents Lathan and Barrett and includible in her gross estate for federal estate tax purposes, the value of the marital trust created under Arthur H. Tilley's will, and the value of Mrs. Tilley's gross estate and her taxable estate.

It appears that Arthur H. Tilley, husband of the deceased, died January 28, 1959. Under the eighth clause of his will, admitted to probate February 5, 1959, he devised the property, which qualified for the full marital deduction, to the Industrial National Bank, in trust, with directions to pay the net income at least quarterly to his wife for life and such amounts of the corpus annually or at more frequent intervals as she should in writing request, for her comfort and support, and without being accountable to any court or remainderman therefor. He also conferred upon her a general testamentary power of appointment over the corpus remaining at her death.

Mary M. Tilley died October 28, 1963. Under the fourth clause of her will, admitted to probate November 7, 1963, she exercised her general testamentary power of appointment to the Industrial National Bank, in trust "to pay over the net income thereof to and for the use and benefit of my granddaughters, Aline C. Lathan and Evelyn M. Barrett * * * equally for and during the term of their natural lives, and upon the death of either of them, to pay over said net income to her issue, *per stirpes* and not *per capita*." The trustee was also given uncontrolled discretion to pay over to either of said grandchildren, or the issue of any deceased grandchild, for specific purposes, portions of the principal. Finally, the testatrix provided the trust would terminate "twenty one (21) years after the death of the last survivor of the younger grandchild or issue of either grandchild of mine living at my death * * *."

On the date of Arthur H. Tilley's death, Aline C. Lathan and Evelyn M. Barrett and one great-grandchild were in being. On the date of Mary M. Tilley's death the aforesaid respondents plus six additional great-grandchildren were in being. One great-grandchild was born subsequent to her death.

* * *

The complainants contend that Mrs. Tilley's exercise of the power of appointment created under her husband's will does not violate the rule against perpetuities on two alternative grounds.

First, they say, in clause eighth of his will, Arthur H. Tilley manifested a clear intent to bestow upon his wife an unlimited power to consume the trust principal giving her in effect a general power of appointment exercisable during her lifetime.

* * * [The Court held that the power to withdraw, even though broad and even though the trustee was not accountable for such withdrawals, was not equivalent to a general power of appointment.]

* * *

The complainants next contend that even if Mrs. Tilley had only a general testamentary power of appointment, the better-reasoned authorities hold the perpetuity period should be counted from the date of the power's exercise rather than its creation, which would make the gift here vest within the prescribed time.

Before reaching complainants' contention there is an initial problem we feel necessitates some discussion here. Clause fourth of Mrs. Tilley's will provides the trust created thereunder will terminate "twenty one (21) years after the death of the last survivor of the younger grandchild or issue of either grandchild of mine living at my death * * *." It is clear the testatrix set out the measuring lives alternatively as "the last survivor of the younger grandchild" or the "issue of either grandchild * * *." Since both are modified by the phrase "living at my death" the rule is satisfied on that point.

The difficulty arises in determining what person the testatrix designated when she used the word "survivor." After reading the clause as a whole we believe that this was but an inartistic reference by her draftsman to one of her grandchildren's issue. For a general discussion of this problem, see Perpetuities: A Standard Saving Clause To Avoid Violations Of The Rule, by W. Barton Leach and James K. Logan, 74 Harv.L.Rev. 1141 (1961).

Since this provision was manifestly intended as a savings clause to obviate any violation of the rule, we will give effect to the testatrix' obvious intent that this trust be created and will adopt the above interpretation, thereby removing any initial impediment to complainants' contention on this point. See Gray, The Rule Against Perpetuities (4th ed.) § 633, p. 601, where Gray said "When the expression which a testator uses is really ambiguous, and is fairly capable of two constructions, one of which would produce a legal result, and the other a result that would be bad for remoteness, it is a fair presumption that the testator meant to create a legal rather than an illegal interest."

* * *

It is fundamental law that when the free alienation of a future interest in property is limited, the interest must vest within lives in being plus twenty-one years from the date of the creating instrument. When the persons who will take or the extent of their interests are to be determined by the exercise of a subsequent power of appointment, the rule against perpetuities requires that the vesting time be computed as if the appointment were a part of the instrument creating the limitation, because until it is exercised the limitation is incomplete.

Nevertheless as the primary concern behind the rule is to prevent restraint on alienation, a distinction is made between general and special powers. In the case of a general power of appointment by deed and will, all courts hold that since the donee has absolute disposing power over the property and may bring it into the market place at any time, he has what is tantamount to a fee. Therefore, since whatever estates may be created by one seized in fee may be also created under a general power, the commencement of the limitation is computed from the time of the power's exercise and not its creation.

In the case of a general power of appointment by will, however, the weight of authority counts the perpetuity period from the date of creation on the ground that since the donee cannot freely alienate the property during his life, he is not the practical owner thereof. A minority view disagrees with this position on the theory that the concept of actual ownership clouds the substance of the matter, which is that if the person having the power without the ownership may appoint to whomsoever he pleases at the time he exercises it, he is in the same position *in respect to the perpetuity* as if he were actually the owner. Thorndike, General Powers And Perpetuities, 27 Harv.L.Rev., pp. 705, 717. Also see Northern Trust Co. v. Porter, 368 Ill. 256, 13 N.E. 2d 487, for leading citations on both positions.

Since this is a case of first impression, we have read with interest the authorities supporting the above positions. See Gray, General Testamentary Powers And The Rule Against Perpetuities, 26 Harv.L. Rev., p. 720; Thorndike, General Powers And Perpetuities, supra; Annot., 1 A.L.R. 374; and Northern Trust Co. v. Porter, supra. From this reading it appears that the early English cases in counting the perpetuity period did not distinguish between a general power to appoint by deed and will and a general power to appoint by will only and we think the cases following this position are the more persuasive.

In essence the majority jurisdictions characterize a general power of appointment by will as being in the nature of a special power, and, as such, a part of the creating instrument of the donor. They reach this result solely on the ground that because the donor has tied up ownership of the property until the donee's death, the restraint on alienation is sufficient to count the perpetuity period from the power's creation.

We think that this position misapprehends the fundamental concepts involved here. The law does not prohibit an estate being tied up for the life of any one individual, but prohibits only restraint beyond lives in being plus twenty-one years. See Thorndike, supra. When the donee exercises his power, he is *at that time* the practical owner thereof, *for the purposes of the rule*, as he can appoint to anyone of his choice as well as his own estate. Furthermore when he exercises the power he can create, unlike the case of a special power, estates entirely independent from those created or controlled by the donor, and so, as to the donee, the power is a general one. See Perpetuities In Perspective: Ending The Rule's Reign Of Terror, by W. Barton Leach, 65 Harv.L.Rev. 721.

Consequently, we hold the trust created by clause fourth of Mrs. Tilley's will pursuant to her general testamentary power of appointment is valid. We arrive at this conclusion not only because logic favors its adoption but also because we believe it is in line with the trend to obviate the technical harshness of the rule against perpetuities and decide cases on the substance of things. 6 American Law of Property § 24.45 (1952), p. 118; 3 Restatement, Property § 343 (1940), p. 1913; Union & New Haven Trust Co. v. Taylor, 133 Conn. 221, 50 A.2d 168. For a learned discussion of this problem, see Perpetuities In A Nutshell, 51 Harv.L.Rev. 638, and Perpetuities: The Nutshell Revisited, 78 Harv.L.Rev. 973, both being articles by W. Barton Leach.

* * * [40]

40. Accord: Miller v. Douglass, 192 Wis. 486, 213 N.W. 320 (1927). See Delaware Code Ann., Tit. 25, § 501 (1974) as follows:

"Every estate or interest in property, real or personal, created through the exercise, by will, deed or other instrument, of a power of appointment, irrespective of—

(1) whether such power is limited or unlimited as to appointees;

(2) the manner in which such power was created or may be exercised;

(3) whether such power was created before or after the passage of this section, shall, for the purpose of any rule of law against perpetuities, remoteness in vesting, restraint upon the power of alienation or accumulations now in effect or hereafter enacted be deemed to have been created at the time of the exercise and not at the time of the creation of such power of appointment. No such estate or interest shall be void on account of any such rule unless the estate or interest would have been void had it been created at the date of the exercise of such power of appointment otherwise than through the exercise of a power of appointment."

As to the situation in Ohio, where there has been legislation reforming the common law rule, adopting a "wait and see" coupled with "cy pres" approach, but there remains ambiguity in the statute as to its application to general testamentary and special powers, see Johnson and Williams, "Application of the Rule Against Perpetuities to Powers of Appointment: Ohio Style", 5 U. Dayton L. Rev. 39 (1980).

FIDUCIARY TRUST CO. v. MISHOU

Supreme Judicial Court of Massachusetts, 1947.
321 Mass. 615, 75 N.E.2d 3.[41]

QUA, CHIEF JUSTICE. This is a petition by the remaining trustee under the will of Martha S. Parker, late of Beverly, for instructions as to the distribution of the principal of a trust created by her will.

The testatrix died March 12, 1878. Her will was dated March 8, 1864. A codicil made in 1872 is not here material. In 1851 Martha S. Parker, the testatrix, married Richard T. Parker and immediately after the marriage, under date of October 2, 1851, she and her husband, as parties of the first part, entered into an indenture with James Parker, the elder of that name, party of the second part, in the nature of a marriage settlement, wherein the husband and wife conveyed to James certain property of the wife, who was then a minor, including all the personal property held by her guardian for her benefit and of which she or her husband was entitled to receive a transfer from her guardian. This conveyance was expressed by the indenture to be in trust to pay the income to the wife to her separate use during the marriage and to pay the entire fund to her if she should survive her husband, but if he should survive her, as actually happened, to dispose of the entire trust fund "as she, whether of full age or not, may have directed by any last will and testament in writing by her executed in the presence of three witnesses, or by any instrument of appointment by her so executed in the nature of a last will and testament, and in default of any such will or appointment," to pay the income to the husband, Richard T. Parker, during his life and at his death to dispose of the fund as he "may have directed by any such last will and testament or instrument of appointment in the nature thereof; and in default of any such will or appointment," then to the persons who would be the heirs at law of the wife if she had then died intestate and a widow.

Mrs. Parker by her will of 1864 attempted to dispose of all her property and estate "and of all property over which * * * [she had] any power of appointment, and especially" of all property held in trust for her under the indenture of 1851 "over which property and estate by the terms of the said Indenture * * * [she had] a full and absolute power of appointment." She gave her husband, Richard T. Parker, a life estate in the family plate belonging to her, with remainders over after his decease. She also bequeathed to him her jewelry, and her articles of personal use and ornament and household furniture. She then bequeathed the residue of her estate, without any express distinction between property owned outright by her and property over which she had a power of appointment under the indenture of 1851, to trustees in trust to pay certain legacies and thereafter to make out of income certain payments for the use, support and

41. Note, 61 Harv.L.Rev. 715 (1948), 28 B.U.L.Rev. 251 (1948), 47 Mich.L.Rev. 93 (1948).

education of her living children and when each should arrive at the age of twenty-one to pay him or her "yearly and in each year during life that portion of the said net income to which on an equal division of the same among all my children then living and the issue of any deceased child by right of representation, such child would be entitled * * * and from and after the decease of such child to pay the said share or portion [of income] to his or her issue living (if any) until the decease of my last surviving child and the division of the trust estate to be then made as hereinafter provided." The will then provided that upon the decease of the last surviving child the trustees should distribute the fund among the issue of the deceased children by right of representation, but that if no issue of any deceased child should be living at the decease of the last surviving child the fund should be distributed among the sisters of the testatrix then living and the issue of any deceased sister by right of representation, and if no sister or issue of a deceased sister should then be living to the testatrix's heirs at law. This is the trust with reference to which the petitioner as sole present trustee now seeks instruction. The testatrix named her husband, Richard T. Parker, as executor of her will. He assented in writing to the will and acted as executor.

Upon her death in 1878, the testatrix, Mrs. Parker, was survived by her husband, Richard T. Parker, and by her three children, James Parker, the younger of that name, Charles T. Parker, and Mary Martha Parker (later Taylor). All three children had been born after the execution of the indenture of 1851. Charles T. Parker died in 1912, leaving no issue. James Parker the younger died in 1930, leaving no issue. Mary Martha Taylor died in 1943, leaving as her only surviving issue two illegitimate daughters, Aimee Henry Mishou and Martha Sakrausky. The testatrix's husband, Richard T. Parker, died in 1904, leaving a will wherein, after exercising in Article Five a power of appointment under his father's will (not here involved), he gave his residuary estate including "all property over which I may have any power of appointment other than given me in the will of my father, and exercised in Article Five of this will," to his three children James Parker (the younger), Charles T. Parker, and Mary Martha Parker (Taylor) in the proportions respectively of eleven undivided twentieths, three undivided twentieths, and six undivided twentieths. None of the sisters of the testatrix was living at the death of the testatrix's last surviving child (Mrs. Taylor in 1943), but certain of the sisters did leave issue then surviving.

The trust fund now in controversy was received in 1878 by the original trustees from the executor of the will of Mrs. Parker without distinction between property owned outright by Mrs. Parker and property derived by virtue of her exercise of her power of appointment under the indenture of 1851. The fund, during the period of the trust, has been administered "as one fund, no division or distinction having been made at any time with regard to the source of said property whether derived from property owned by the said Martha S. Parker in her own right or whether derived from said trust of October 2, 1851." At least the greater part of the original fund came from the 1851 trust and not from property owned outside that trust by the testatrix, Mrs. Parker. Some of the parties contend that all of the present fund is proceeds of the 1851 trust.

Facts in addition to those hereinbefore stated will be mentioned hereinafter as occasion requires.

There are three sets of claimants to the principal of the existing fund. They may be identified and the general nature of their claims may be summarized as follows: (1) The respective executors or administrators with the will annexed of the husband and of the three children of Mrs. Parker contend that the period of time within which, under the rule against perpetuities, future interests in property derived from the 1851 trust must vest is to be calculated from the creation of the 1851 trust from which the testatrix's power of appointment sprang and not from the attempted exercise of that power at the death of the testatrix in 1878; that the limitations in her will of principal after the death of the last survivor of her children (none of whom was a life in being in 1851) to the issue of those children and in the event of failure of such issue to the sisters of the testatrix or their issue are too remote; that to that extent there was a failure on Mrs. Parker's part to make a valid appointment under the 1851 indenture; that in default of such valid appointment the power of appointment given by the 1851 indenture to the husband, Richard T. Parker, became operative; that by his will he made a valid appointment under that power to the three children in the proportions hereinbefore mentioned; and therefore that the estates of these children are entitled to share in the principal of the trust fund under Mrs. Parker's will in those proportions in so far as that principal is derived from the 1851 trust fund. (2) Mrs. Mishou, an illegitimate daughter of Mrs. Parker's daughter Mary Martha Taylor, and the Attorney General of the United States as presently entitled to the share of Mrs. Sakrausky, the other illegitimate daughter, an alien enemy, contend that the time when future limitations must vest under the rule against perpetuities is to be calculated from the death of Mrs. Parker, who attempted to exercise her power, and not from the creation of the power in 1851; that the limitations of principal to the issue of Mrs. Parker's children at the death of the last survivor of such children, such children being lives in being at the death of Mrs. Parker, was not too remote but was valid; and that the illegitimate children were "issue" of Mrs. Parker's daughter within the meaning of the word issue in the will and were entitled to take notwithstanding illegitimacy. The Attorney General of the United States makes the further claim that Mrs. Mishou has formally and effectually renounced all interest in the fund and that the entire fund must be distributed to him as claiming under Mrs. Sakrausky. (3) The issue of the deceased sisters of Mrs. Parker contend that the illegitimate daughters of Mrs. Taylor are not entitled to take as "issue" of a child of Mrs. Parker within the meaning of the word issue in the will; that the time under the rule against perpetuities began to run from the death of Mrs. Parker; that the limitation to the issue of Mrs. Parker's sisters is not too remote but is valid; and that such issue living at the death of

Mrs. Parker's last surviving child (Mrs. Taylor) are entitled to take the entire fund by right of representation.

The judge of the Probate Court accepted the view last above stated and ordered the entire principal of the trust, whether derived from the 1851 trust fund or from Mrs. Parker's own property, to be distributed among the surviving issue of Mrs. Parker's sisters. The other interested parties appeal.

1. Any consideration of the questions presented in this case must begin with the rule laid down in Minot v. Paine, 230 Mass. 514, 523, 120 N.E. 167, 1 A.L.R. 365. In that case, after elaborate consideration, it was settled as the law of this Commonwealth that "the remoteness of an appointment, made in the exercise of a power to appoint by will alone, so far as affected by the rule against perpetuities must be measured from the time of the creation and not the exercise of the power" (230 Mass. at page 523, 120 N.E. at page 171, 1 A.L.R. 365), but that "the words of the rule are satisfied if it appears that in the light of facts as to relationship and longevity existent when the appointment is exercised, the estates created in truth will vest and take effect within the period limited by the rule, although this may not have been certain at the death of the donor of the power." 230 Mass. at page 522, 120 N.E. at page 170, 1 A.L.R. 365. The Restatement is in accord with Minot v. Paine, Restatement: Property, § 392. In the case at bar Mrs. Parker's power of appointment under the indenture of 1851 was a testamentary power and did not include a power to appoint by deed in her lifetime. If the rule of Minot v. Paine applies, and if consequently the period fixed by the rule against perpetuities for the vesting of future interests must be calculated from 1851 when Mrs. Parker's power was created and not from 1878 when she exercised it, the result will be that the limitation of principal in Mrs. Parker's will, in so far as derived from property embraced in the 1851 trust, upon the decease of her last surviving child to the issue of her deceased children by right of representation and the alternative limitation to the issue of her deceased sisters will be too remote, since even with the aid of all facts as to relationship and longevity existing in 1878 these gifts might not finally vest in ascertained persons within any life or lives in being in 1851 and twenty-one years thereafter. Minot v. Paine, 230 Mass. 514, at page 522, 120 N.E. 167, 1 A.L.R. 365, and cases cited. Restatement: Property, §§ 374, 383. Greenough v. Osgood, 235 Mass. 235, 242, 126 N.E. 461 (as to limitation to children of Robert T. Osgood).

2. It is argued that the rule of Minot v. Paine does not apply where the power is "reserved" by the donor to himself rather than granted to another, that is to say, where the donor and the donee of the power are the same person. No authority for such a distinction is cited from any jurisdiction in which the rule of Minot v. Paine is adopted. The rule against perpetuities is a rule of public policy resting upon the view that it is socially undesirable that the alienation of property be fettered for long periods of time. So far as that object is concerned it would seem to be immaterial whether in the beginning

the power was granted or merely "reserved." The validity of the indenture of 1851 is not challenged. Under the indenture Mrs. Parker had no power of appointment by deed inter vivos. From the moment the indenture of 1851 took effect her right of alienation was appreciably restrained. See Crawford v. Langmaid, 171 Mass. 309, 50 N.E. 606; Vinton v. Pratt, 228 Mass. 468, 471, 117 N.E. 919, L.R.A. 1918D, 343; Gorey v. Guarente, 303 Mass. 569, 573–575, 22 N.E.2d 99. If the appointments contained in her will are held wholly valid, the result will have been that at no time from 1851 until 1943 could any one have conveyed a fee in the beneficial interest of the property included in the 1851 trust. When tested by the facts in this case, this period would far exceed that permitted by the rule. As to the applicability of the rule of Minot v. Paine in the case of a "reserved" power see Genet v. Hunt, 113 N.Y. 158, 21 N.E. 91. Moreover, it can hardly be correct to assume, as the argument under examination does assume, that Mrs. Parker was the sole creator of the power. Before her marriage the indentured property was hers, but the indenture of 1851 was executed after her marriage. Her husband joined her in it as a grantor. Even at that time the greater part of this property was personalty. In 1851 the rights of the husband in his wife's personal property were so extensive that his joining as a grantor was certainly more than a mere form. See Hayward v. Hayward, 20 Pick. 517; Smith v. Chandler, 3 Gray 392.

3. Since originally the greater part at least of the trust fund in controversy was composed of property over which Mrs. Parker had a testamentary power of appointment under the 1851 indenture, it may be convenient to deal first with the devolution of that appointive property.

It is a recognized principle in the law of property that where the donee of a general power attempts to make an appointment that fails, but where, nevertheless, the donee has manifested an intent wholly to withdraw the appointive property from the operation of the instrument creating the power for all purposes and not merely for the purposes of the invalid appointment, the attempted appointment will commonly be effective to the extent of causing the appointive property to be taken out of the original instrument and to become in effect part of the estate of the donee of the power. And where, as in this instance, the invalid appointment is in trust there will be a resulting trust to the estate of the donee of the power. It is unnecessary to restate the reasons for these rules. They originated in a series of decisions of the English courts and have been applied in our own cases of Dunbar v. Hammond, 234 Mass. 554 (see particularly page 558, paragraph 6), 125 N.E. 686; Talbot v. Riggs, 287 Mass. 144, 191 N.E. 360, 93 A.L.R. 964, and Old Colony Trust Co. v. Allen, 307 Mass. 40, 29 N.E.2d 310, where many of the English cases are collected. They are adopted in Restatement: Property, § 365, and Trusts, § 426. We think that they apply in this case, and that the complete blending by Mrs. Parker in her will of the appointive property with any property owned by her outright shows her intent to capture the appointive property for her own estate (Restatement: Property, §

365, comment d), if indeed it is necessary that any such intent of the donee be shown affirmatively where the appointment is in trust and therefore technically valid to the extent of the bare legal title. See Restatement: Property, § 365(2); Scott on Trusts, § 426; Talbot v. Riggs, 287 Mass. 144, 148, 191 N.E. 360, 93 A.L.R. 964.

We have not overlooked the case of Bundy v. United States Trust Co., 257 Mass. 72, at page 81, 153 N.E. 337, at page 340, where this court said, "We are of opinion that Dunbar v. Hammond is limited to the case where the donor has made no provision for the donee's default of appointment, or for the event of his intestacy." No authority was cited for this statement. If this means that the principle of Dunbar v. Hammond; Talbot v. Riggs, and Old Colony Trust Co. v. Allen can never apply in any instance where the donor of the power has made a gift over in default of appointment, we think it is based upon a misapprehension of Dunbar v. Hammond and that it goes too far. * * * It may be that the fact that the donor of a power has made explicit provision for the devolution of the property in the event of nonexercise of the power, taken in connection with other circumstances, will sometimes have some tendency to indicate an intent of the donor that the donee shall not appropriate the appointive property to his own estate, but there are no circumstances in this case indicating such intent.

4. For the reasons stated, Mrs. Parker's exercise by her will of the power of appointment given her by the indenture of 1851 had the effect, by way of a resulting trust, of making the appointive property assets of her own estate. But it did not have the effect that some of the parties assume it had of subjecting that property to the terms of the trust under the residuary provisions of her will and therefore of making valid again the invalid limitations contained in those provisions on the theory that such limitations would not have been too remote and would have been valid, if made by Mrs. Parker at her death in 1878 as to her own property not governed by any power of appointment. It would be reasoning in a circle and a mere evasion of the rule of Minot v. Paine, 230 Mass. 514, 120 N.E. 167, 1 A.L.R. 365, to say that because those limitations were invalid and could not take effect there was a resulting trust to Mrs. Parker's Estate and then to say that because of such resulting trust the appointive property must go under the residuary provisions according to the invalid limitations. The same consequence must follow in this instance that commonly follows when future limitations of property are declared invalid because of the rule against perpetuities; and that consequence is that "the will is to be construed as if no such provision or clause were contained in it; and the person or persons otherwise entitled to the estate or property will take it wholly discharged of the devise, bequest and limitation over." Fosdick v. Fosdick, 6 Allen 41, 43. Since in the case before us the invalid limitations were the final limitations of the residuary clause itself and not in some other part of the will, the consequence was that the equitable fee in the principal of the appointive property, which by 1878 was all personalty, went as intestate property to the person or persons who by law would be entitled to

Mrs. Parker's personal property in case of intestacy. Fosdick v. Fosdick, 6 Allen 41, 47; Lovering v. Worthington, 106 Mass. 86; Andrews v. Lincoln, 95 Me. 541, 50 A. 898, 56 L.R.A. 103; Greenland v. Waddell, 116 N.Y. 234, 245, 22 N.E. 367, 370, 15 Am.St.Rep. 400; Gray, Rule Against Perpetuities (4th Ed.) § 540.1. As the statute of distributions stood in 1878, Richard T. Parker, husband of the testatrix, was her sole distributee. Gen.Sts. c. 94, § 16, Fourth. A vested equitable estate in the principal of the appointive property therefore went, upon Mrs. Parker's death, by resulting trust to Richard T. Parker in fee, subject to Mrs. Parker's valid appointments of income from the appointive property to her children, and upon Richard T. Parker's death in 1904 his interest in the principal went by his will, as his own property and not by virtue of his attempted exercise of his power of appointment under the indenture of 1851, to his three children, who were also Mrs. Parker's children, namely James Parker, the younger, Charles T. Parker, and Mary Martha Parker (Taylor) in the respective proportions hereinbefore stated.

* * *

[In the omitted portion of the opinion, the court held that Mr. Parker's acceptance of appointment as executor and of legacies under Mrs. Parker's will did not constitute an election estopping those claiming under him; that, as an issue of fact, the appointive assets could be traced and distinguished from Mrs. Parker's individual property; and that the illegitimate daughters of Mrs. Taylor were not "issue" as that term was used in Mrs. Parker's will.] * * *

The decree is reversed and the cause is remanded to the Probate Court for the entry of a decree in accordance with this opinion. Costs and expenses of appeal are to be in the discretion of the Probate Court.

So ordered.

NOTE

In the case of a special power of appointment (such as a power to appoint to issue of the donor) whether testamentary or presently exercisable, similar rules are applicable. The paucity of cases dealing with application of the Rule to special powers may be accounted for by two other legal rules considered heretofore in the Chapter on Powers of Appointment: while the donee may appoint new future interests and create new powers, he is severely limited by the scope of the power and secondly, a special power is less likely to be exercised by implication. We start from the premise that a special power by its nature ties up property. (1) Interests appointed under a special power are measured from the date of creation of the power, not the date of exercise.[42] (2) However, they are to be judged in the light of facts at the date of exercise. (3) Some slight mitigation of the Rule may be found in the doctrine of marshalling. Suppose A leaves property in trust for his son B for life, then to such of A's lineal descendants as B shall by will appoint. B executes a will which attempts to dispose of his own and the appointive assets indiscriminately, half to B's children outright and the other half in trust for B's

42. Greenough v. Osgood, 235 Mass. 235, 126 N.E. 461 (1920).

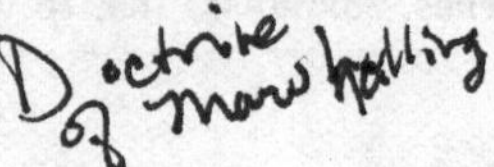

children for life and thereafter to his grandchildren. The appointive assets could be used validly to satisfy the outright gift and would be so allocated. Then B's individual assets could be used to set up the trust for grandchildren without violating the Rule.[43] But this doctrine of marshalling is limited, of course, to valid objects of the special power; obviously the appointive assets could not be used to pay debts, taxes or specific legacies to non-objects such as B's wife or charity, as would be true if the power were general. Note also that, in the case of a special power, the donee rarely "blends" the appointive assets with his individual assets; the draftsman usually sets out a separate paragraph purporting to exercise the power for a specific purpose, further reducing the opportunity to use the marshalling approach. (4) In the event of an invalid appointment, the appointive assets go in default rather than as part of the donee's estate. The donee could not have appointed to his estate, as in the case of a general testamentary power.

SEARS v. COOLIDGE

Supreme Judicial Court of Massachusetts, 1952.
329 Mass. 340, 108 N.E.2d 563.[44]

WILKINS, JUSTICE. These two petitions under G.L.(Ter.Ed.) c. 231A seek binding declarations as to the validity of the provisions relating to income and to gifts of principal by way of remainder in a deed of trust executed by Thomas Jefferson Coolidge, late of Manchester, under date of February 12, 1913. The settlor died on November 17, 1920. In each case a decree was entered declaring that the life interests are valid; but that the gifts over of principal are invalid and void, and upon the termination of the trust the personal representatives of the settlor's estate are to receive the principal and any unpaid accumulated income. The petitioners, the trustees, and numerous other persons interested in the trust or in the settlor's estate appealed.

The net income of the trust was payable one third semi-annually to "such of the issue of my deceased son as shall be living at the time of each such semi-annual payment," and two thirds, divided into three parts payable semi-annually, one part each to Marian A. Sargent and to Sarah L. Newbold and after their death to their respective issue, and one to the living issue of Eleonora R. Sears, who were the petitioners Eleonora R. Sears and Frederick R. Sears.

The appeals relating to the life interests have been "waived and withdrawn." We are now concerned only with the decrees in so far as they affect the remainder interests. Whenever we refer to the appellants, we shall mean all or some of those who are seeking to establish the validity of the remainder interests. The facts are undisputed and, for the most part, are embodied in a written stipulation in the Probate Court. The evidence is reported.

43. Stone v. Forbes, 189 Mass. 163, 75 N.E. 141 (1905).

44. Noted, 33 B.U.L.Rev. 119 (1953), 66 Harv.L.Rev. 937 (1953), 22 U. of Cin.L. Rev. 26 (1953).

The fundamental issue is whether the remainder interests violate the rule against perpetuities. Paragraph 5 of the trust instrument provides that the capital of the trust is to be distributed "in equal shares to and among my issue living" at the time of distribution. Distribution is to take place upon "whichever shall first happen" of two events: (1) "the death of the last survivor of those of my children, grandchildren and great grandchildren who shall be living at my death"; or (2) "the attainment of fifty years by the youngest surviving grandchild of mine who shall be living at my death." The second event first happened. William A. Coolidge, the youngest grandchild living at the settlor's death, attained the age of fifty years on October 21, 1951.

Where a trust instrument contains two alternative conditions, of which the first might be too remote and the second, which actually occurs, is not too remote, the rule is not violated. Jackson v. Phillips, 14 Allen 539, 572–573; Stone v. Bradlee, 183 Mass. 165, 171–172, 66 N.E. 708; Gray v. Whittemore, 192 Mass. 367, 372, 78 N.E. 422, 10 L.R.A., N.S., 1143; Springfield Safe Deposit & Trust Co. v. Ireland, 268 Mass. 62, 67–68, 167 N.E. 261, 64 A.L.R. 1071. Accordingly, the appellants contend that the attainment by the youngest grandchild of the age of fifty years was certain to occur within the period required by the rule, and that as matter of construction the reference in paragraph 5 to "the youngest surviving grandchild of mine who shall be living at my death" must be read as if "grandchild" were qualified by "now living" or similar words. In support are adduced various facts in the settlor's family situation obvious to him when he executed the deed of trust. He was then eighty-one years of age and had been a widower for twelve years. At that time he had two living children, Marian A. Sargent, who was aged fifty-nine and had been a widow for twenty years, and Sarah L. Newbold, who was then fifty-five years of age. During the preceding year there had died two of his children, T. Jefferson Coolidge and Eleonora R. Sears. The settlor then had ten living grandchildren. Four were the minor sons of his deceased son. Two were the children of his deceased daughter, one being the petitioner, Eleonora R. Sears, and the other Frederick R. Sears, the administrator of whose estate is the petitioner Fiduciary Trust Company. One was the child of Marian A. Sargent, and three were the children of Sarah L. Newbold. The oldest grandchild was thirty-five and the youngest was seven. No further grandchildren were born in the settlor's lifetime, but the youngest of the ten died before the settlor.

The appellees argue, on the other hand, that it is not permissible thus to qualify the clause in paragraph 5, and for present purposes we accept their position on this point, and assume that the phrase "the youngest surviving grandchild of mine who shall be living at my death" is not to be interpreted as excluding grandchildren who might be born after the trust instrument was created.

The appellants make the contention that the settlor in the trust deed reserved a power which was at least equivalent to a special power of appointment, and that the validity of the remainders must in any event be determined in the light of the facts existing at his death when it was known that his only grandchildren had been lives in being at the time the trust was created. This has been referred to in the arguments as "a second look."

Paragraph 9 reads: "I reserve to myself power at all times to make any additions to the trust property, to change and alter any or all of the trusts herein set forth and to declare new uses and trusts of the property in any way or manner except such as will vest in myself the trust property or any beneficial interest therein, to name and appoint any other persons than those above specified or hereafter appointed as beneficiaries, whether by way of addition or substitution, and to appoint other trustees instead of or in addition to any or all of those above named. Every such change, alteration, nomination and appointment shall be made by my deed and shall take effect immediately upon the delivery thereof to any person who shall at the time be acting as a trustee under the provisions of these presents."

The point, which, so far as appears, has not been pressed upon an appellate court before, is based upon the analogy of Minot v. Paine, 230 Mass. 514, 120 N.E. 167, 1 A.L.R. 365. The theory is that at the settlor's death the expiration of the power to divert the property from the takers in default was the same in effect as an appointment of the remainders by the settlor's will.

The reserved power is, at the very least, akin to a power of appointment. National Shawmut Bank v. Joy, 315 Mass. 457, 474, 53 N.E.2d 113; Restatement: Property, § 318, comment i. See Saltonstall v. Treasurer & Receiver General, 256 Mass. 519, 524, 153 N.E. 4; Boston Safe Deposit & Trust Co. v. Commissioner of Corporations & Taxation, 294 Mass. 551, 554, 3 N.E.2d 33, 109 A.L.R. 854; State Street Trust Co. v. Crocker, 306 Mass. 257, 262, 28 N.E.2d 5, 128 A.L.R. 1166. And, for present purposes, we treat it as having attributes of a special power to appoint by deed.

In Minot v. Paine, the power to appoint was, in fact, exercised and there was presented a question as to the effect of the language used by the donee of the power, who had become, in law, the agent of the donor for the purpose. At page 522 of 230 Mass., at page 170 of 120 N.E., it was said: "The donee in exercising the power is in effect writing the will of the donor respecting the appointed property. * * * The words used by the donee in exercising the power are to be construed and interpreted as to their meaning in the light of the facts as they are at the time the power is exercised. The will of the donor is projected forward to the time of the exercise of the power so as to receive the benefit of the facts which have appeared since his decease. * * * As applied to the exercise of a power of appointment the words of the rule are satisfied if it appears that in the light of facts as to relationship and longevity existent when the appointment is exercised, the estates created in truth will vest and take effect within the period limited by the rule, although this may not have been certain at the death of the donor of the power."

In the present instance, no appointment having been made, there were no words expressed by the holder of the reserved power to be read back into the deed of trust. That fact, however, should not be decisive. In every case where there is a power, whether it be exercised or not, there is the common feature that until the opportunity for its exercise ceases to exist, there will persist uncertainty as to the ultimate disposition of the property. Until then nothing final can be known as to what are the provisions for the vesting of the future interests, and it is with such vesting the policy of the rule is concerned.

* * *

Since it is permissible to make use of the circumstances known when a power, which is special or testamentary, is exercised to determine validity under the rule, it seems reasonable to afford the same opportunity in cases where such a power is not exercised. In the case of the trust instrument under consideration until it became too late for the settlor to exercise the reserved power no one could tell what might be the ultimate disposition of the trust property. As long as there remained a right to change, alter, and make new appointments, no instructions to the trustees or declaratory decree would ordinarily have been given as to the validity of the settlor's limitations. See National Shawmut Bank v. Morey, 320 Mass. 492, 497–500, 70 N.E.2d 316, 174 A.L.R. 871; Young v. Jackson, 321 Mass. 1, 7, 71 N.E.2d 386; Burn v. McAllister, 321 Mass. 660, 662, 75 N.E.2d 114. Upon his death it could be learned for the first time what definitely were to be the terms of the trust. It then could be seen for the first time that there was to be no failure to vest within the period limited by the rule. No further grandchildren had been born. In these precise circumstances there is no compelling decision which prevents taking advantage of facts known at the moment when the power ceased to be exercisable. American Law of Property, § 24.36. We are unwilling to apply the rule so as to invalidate the trust instrument.

The appellees strongly urge that the doctrine of "a second look" has no place in reading the original limitations in default of appointment, which were capable of examination when created, and which should retain the same meaning throughout. They argue that its adoption would be a nullification of the rule "that executory limitations are void unless they take effect ex necessitate and in all possible contingencies" within the prescribed period. Hall v. Hall, 123 Mass. 120, 124. But this rule, while recognized, was assuaged as to the exercise of a power of appointment in Minot v. Paine, 230 Mass. 514, 522, 120 N.E. 167, 1 A.L.R. 365. It was there deemed wise not to apply unmodified a remorseless technical principle to a case which it did not fit. That principle seems equally inappropriate here.

The decrees are reversed and the causes are remanded to the Probate Court for the entry of decrees in accordance with this opinion. Costs and expenses of appeal are to be in the discretion of the Probate Court.

So ordered.

PROBLEMS

A's wife having predeceased him, A left his estate by will in trust "to pay the income to my daughter (B) for life, then to pay the principal to such persons, in such shares and upon such trusts, as my said daughter may by her will appoint, in default of appointment to such of her children as shall attain the age of 25." At A's death, B has one child C. Subsequently a second child D is born.

1. B's will reads as follows: "I hereby exercise the power of appointment conferred upon me by my father's will, by appointing as follows: One half of the property to be held in trust for my son C to pay him the income for life, at his death to pay the principal to such persons, in such shares and upon such trusts, as my said son C may by his will appoint, in default of appointment to his issue living at his death; the remaining one-half to be held in trust to pay the income to my daughter D for life, then to pay the principal to such of her children, and in such shares, as she may appoint by will, in default of appointment to her children living at her death equally." How much, if any, of the appointment is valid?

2. If the above appointment were part of a residuary clause ("All the rest, residue and remainder of the property which I own at my death, including any over which I have any power of appointment, to the XYZ Trust Company in trust as follows: * * * ") and the value of the residue of B's individually owned assets is equal to or greater than that of the appointive assets, would the doctrine of "marshalling" assets save the invalid portion? See American Law of Property (1952) § 23.59.

3. Assuming B has no individually owned assets, does the property invalidly appointed pass in default under A's will or become part of B's estate?

4. Suppose B's will contained as its first clause the following: "I hereby exercise the power conferred upon me by the will of my father A by appointing all of the assets subject to said power to my estate and direct that they be paid over to my executor." The residuary clause then attempted to set up the foregoing trust for C and D. What result? Cf. Union & New Haven Trust Co. v. Taylor, 133 Conn. 221, 50 A.2d 168 (1946) (donor established by will a trust to pay the income to a son Paul for life and to pay the principal at his death "to the Executor of his will to become and be administered as a part of his estate in accordance with the provisions of his will"; held that the interests created under the son's will should be measured from the son's death, not the donor's).

5. B makes no appointment. At B's death her children C and D are aged 8 and 5 respectively. Is the gift in default in A's will valid?

SECTION 4. STATUTORY RULE AGAINST SUSPENSION OF THE POWER OF ALIENATION

Although minor statutory variations or codifications of the common-law Rule against Perpetuities have been previously noted, the New York statutes which formed the prototype for legislation in 13 other states constitute a basic departure.[45] Because the New York legislation was first drafted (1825–1828) at a time when the common-law Rule was still in the process of formulation, the statute took the form of a rule "against suspension of the power of alienation", although it had the same objective as the modern common-law Rule against "remoteness of vesting".

A thorough understanding of the New York rule can come only through experience in working with all the related property and trust sections of the statutes, and with numerous decisions of the New York courts filling in the gaps. However, the salient features are set forth here for comparison with the common-law Rule:

(1) The statutes prohibit the suspension of "the absolute power of alienation", which occurs whenever there are no persons in being by whom an absolute fee in possession can be conveyed.[46] A limitation to B and his heirs, but if the land shall ever be used for certain purposes, then to C and his heirs would not suspend the power of alienation, as B and C can presently join in a conveyance of the full fee; the gift to C would, however, violate a rule against remoteness since it might not vest for an indefinite time. This leaves an open question in jurisdictions having the statutory rule whether the rule against remoteness of vesting is also in force. New York held that its rule also embraced remoteness of vesting in the famous case of Matter of Wilcox.[47]

The 1966 New York revision of the Estates, Powers and Trusts Law expressly enacted a statutory version of the Wilcox rule.[48] The Wilcox case has been followed in some of the other states [49] having the original New York statute but is rejected in others, such as Wisconsin.[50]

45. See American Law of Property (1952) §§ 25.2–25.82; 5 Powell, The Law of Real Property (Rohan Rev. 1980) Chs. 74–75; Simes and Smith, Future Interests (2d Ed., 1956) Ch. 41.

46. McKinney's New York, EPTL, 1980 Supp.):

"§ 9–1.1 Rule against perpetuities

"(a) (1) The absolute power of alienation is suspended, when there are no persons in being by whom an absolute fee or estate in possession can be conveyed or transferred.

"(2) Every present or future estate shall be void in its creation, which shall suspend the absolute power of alienation by any limitation or condition, for a longer period than lives in being at the creation of the estate and a term of not more than twenty-one years. Lives in being shall include a child conceived before the creation of the estate but born thereafter. In no case shall the lives measuring the permissible period be so designated or so numerous as to make proof of their end unreasonably difficult.

"(b) No estate in property shall be valid unless it must vest, if at all, not later than twenty-one years after one or more lives in being at the creation of the estate and any period of gestation involved. In no case shall lives measuring the permissible period of vesting be so designated or so numerous as to make proof of their end unreasonably difficult."

47. 194 N.Y. 288, 87 N.E. 497 (1909).

48. See the text of the statute at footnote 46 supra.

49. This result was reached in California under its counterpart to the New York statutes. See Estate of Sahlender, 89 Cal.App.2d 329, 201 P.2d 69 (1949). By legislation in 1959 California repealed all references to a suspension rule and returned to the common law rule against remoteness of vesting.

50. Miller v. Douglass, 192 Wis. 486, 213 N.W. 320 (1927).

(2) The permissible period was originally reduced to two lives in being under the New York statute. There was no period of 21 years in gross. A single exception was made permitting a gift by remainder to a minor (after one or two life estates) with a contingent gift over if the minor died under 21 or on any other contingency by which the estate of the minor might be determined before reaching full age: this was commonly referred to as the "restricted minority" provision. The concept that only two lives could be used in creating future interests influenced separate statutory provisions that not more than two successive life estates could be created.[51]

The two-life rule was unduly restrictive and was abandoned in other jurisdictions as experience proved its harsh nature. Finally, New York amended its statute in 1958 to lives in being, and in 1960 added a period in gross of 21 years, so that its period is now the same as that of the common law rule. Since these amendments were prospective only, the two-life rule will continue to take its toll of dispositive limitations drafted prior to the effective dates of the amendments.[52]

(3) The statutes have been construed to invalidate a trust for more than the permissible period.[53] You will recall that the New York statutes make the interest of the beneficiary of a trust to receive the income from realty or personalty inalienable; most trusts thus become indestructible. Even though the trustee is given a power of sale, so that specific assets are not removed from commerce, the beneficiary's interest is inalienable; nor can all the beneficiaries join together and force termination of the trust, at least without the consent of the settlor. In this sense, the courts hold that a trust suspends the power of alienation. Thus, a gift to a trustee to hold in trust for A and his heirs for twenty-five years would be void.

(4) The common law rule that interests created by exercise of a power of appointment are measured from the date of creation of the power was retained by express statutory provision. However, the New York statute was amended in 1960 and presently the statutes governing the application of the statutory Rule to interests created by the exercise of powers of appointment are similar to the prevailing common law doctrine we have already studied.[54]

The combination of a permissible period limited to two lives in being and of holding void any trust which might last beyond that period results in a rule much more restrictive than the common law Rule

51. The legislature no doubt was influenced by the importance of consistency between the rules but otherwise the rules are not connected. See Pasley, "Future Interests: Successive Life Estates: New York Real Property Law Secs. 42, 43", 21 Corn.L.Q. 466, 469–470 (1936); Comment, "New York's Two-Part Statutory Substitute for the Common Law Rule Against Perpetuities", 38 Alb. L.Rev. 570 (1974).

52. See Powell, "Changes in the New York Statutes on Perpetuities and Accumulations", 58 Col.L.Rev. 1196 (1958); "The Rule Against Perpetuities and Spendthrift Trusts in New York: Comments and Suggestions", 71 Col.L.Rev. 688 (1971).

53. Leading cases are Coster v. Lorillard, 14 Wend. 265 (N.Y.1835) and Hawley v. James, 16 Wend. 61 (N.Y.1836).

54. McKinney's New York, EPTL, §§ 10–8.1 through 10–8.3 (1980 Supp.).

against Perpetuities. Only a willingness on the part of the courts to construe limitations as valid and to separate invalid provisions without condemning the remaining provisions has made the statutory rule "liveable". The practice of the New York courts goes beyond the common law "separability" doctrine and is self-described as a process of "excision", cutting out invalid provisions in order to save the remaining provisions.[55]

However, the modern desire to create trusts has resulted in a wholesale abandonment of the old two-life rule against suspension in states which borrowed the New York legislation. A number of states have in recent years repealed their statutes against suspension of the power of alienation and substituted the common law rule: Indiana in 1945, Michigan in 1949, California in 1959, and Arizona in 1963. The few states which have retained the statutory rule have either expanded its period (Idaho has lives in being and 25 years;[56] Wisconsin has lives in being plus 30 years)[57] or virtually destroyed its impact by judicial construction (Minnesota limits the statute to realty and holds that the power of alienation is not suspended by a trust if the trustee has power of sale.)[58]

55. A leading case is Matter of Horner, 237 N.Y. 489, 143 N.E. 655 (1924).

56. Idaho Code § 55–111 (1979 Repl. Vol.).

57. See Wis.Stat.Ann. § 700.16 (West Spec. Pamph. 1980) as follows:

"(1) (a) A future interest or trust is void if it suspends the power of alienation for longer than the permissible period. The permissible period is a life or lives in being plus a period of 30 years.

"(b) If the settlor of a living trust has an unlimited power to revoke, the permissible period is computed from termination of such power.

"(c) If a future interest or trust is created by exercise of a power of appointment, the permissible period is computed from the time the power is exercised if the power is a general power as defined in s. 702.01(4) even if the power is exercisable only by will; in the case of other powers the permissible period is computed from the time the power is created but facts at the time the power is exercised are considered in determining whether the power of alienation is suspended beyond a life or lives in being at the time of creation of the power plus 30 years.

"(2) The power of alienation is suspended when there are no persons in being who, alone or in combination with others, can convey an absolute fee in possession of land, or full ownership of personalty.

"(3) There is no suspension of the power of alienation by a trust or by equitable interests under a trust if the trustee has power to sell, either expressed or implied, or if there is an unlimited power to terminate in one or more persons in being.

"(4) This section does not apply to limit any of the following:

(a) Transfers, outright or in trust, for charitable purposes;

(b) Transfers to literary or charitable corporations;

(c) Transfers to any cemetery corporation, society or association;

(d) Transfers, outright or in trust, to the state society of physicians and surgeons incorporated under the law of this state, when the transfer is for the advancement of medical science;

(e) Transfers to any person pursuant to ch. 703; or

(f) Employes' trusts created as part of a plan as described in s. 272.18(31).

"(5) The common-law rule against perpetuities is not in force in this state."

58. Congdon v. Congdon, 160 Minn. 343, 200 N.W. 76 (1924) (Statutory rule against suspension for longer than two lives held not to apply to personalty). A separate section in the trusts statutes seems to limit duration to lives in being and 21 years: M.S.A. § 501.11(6) West Supp. 1980. Even a trust of realty is held valid beyond the statutory period of two lives if there is a power of sale, on the theory (counter to the New York view) that the power of alienation is not

Since the 1960 amendments to the New York statute, not only is the common law period embodied in the statutory rule in New York, but the impact of the rule is softened by statutory presumptions and provisions for reducing age contingencies.[59]

SECTION 5. SOCIAL POLICY TOWARDS ACCUMULATIONS OF INCOME

The amassing of a vast amount of wealth by accumulation of income over an extended period of time may have been attractive to some of the landed gentry of England of a century or more ago who sought to perpetuate family fortunes in the feudal tradition, unhampered by income or estate taxes. Not many settlors today wish to deprive their immediate family of the benefits of income by directing the trustee to accumulate income at some remote future date. Whatever attraction there may be is deterred by our tax structure. As the reader will recall from Chapter VIII, Section 2 the Tax Reform Act of 1969 and the Tax Reform Act of 1976 adopted an unlimited throwback rule except for accumulations before the beneficiary was born or while the beneficiary is a minor. Earlier exceptions made to the limited throwback are abandoned. When accumulated income is paid to a beneficiary, the average amount of the accumulation is included in the beneficiary's income for three of the immediate five prior years, the years of lowest and highest income being excluded, and the additional tax is determined by multiplying the additional average tax by the number of years of accumulation. The "generation skipping tax" imposed in 1976 will also militate to a degree against accumulations for successive generations but this tax is not imposed when the skipped generation has no present interest in or power over the property. Restriction on the accumulations of income by private foundations (discussed in Chapter XI, Section 2) will make costly any delays in foundation distribution. The requirement that fixed dollar amounts be paid to noncharitable income beneficiaries in charitable remainder trusts (5% of initial value of property transferred or 5% of value of trust corpus valued annually) will restrict the power of a trustee to accumulate in gifts of this type nor could there be an accumulation when the marital deduction is claimed in the life interest of the spouse in a charitable remainder annuity trust or unitrust disposition.

Social policy may be reflected not merely in rulings on validity of directions to accumulate or in the tax laws, but also in judicial han-

suspended in such a trust. See Atwood v. Holmes, 224 Minn. 157, 28 N.W.2d 188 (1947) (restricted power of sale of stock).

59. For the New York Statutes see note to Merchants National Bank v. Curtis, Section 1, supra.

dling of construction problems which arise from failure of the draftsman to make disposition of surplus income in two fairly common situations. Suppose a settlor creates a trust to pay $5,000 per year out of income to his daughter for life, remainder to her issue; he transfers what he conservatively estimates to be ample capital to produce that amount of income. What happens to income in excess of $5,000 for any given year? Again, the same settlor, desiring greater flexibility, provides that the trustee shall pay or apply out of income and principal such amounts as the trustee may deem necessary for the daughter's support and maintenance. If the income of the trust exceeds the daughter's needs, what disposition should the trustee make of the surplus?

STEMPEL v. MIDDLETOWN TRUST CO.

Connecticut Supreme Court of Errors, 1940.
127 Conn. 206, 15 A.2d 305, 157 A.L.R. 657.

[By her will, testatrix gave the residue of her estate in trust for the following purposes:

> "So much of both the income and principal of such trust fund as is necessary in the discretion of said Abigail Thompson and Joseph Seiferman or their successors to provide for the comfortable support of my daughter, Mary B. Donovan during the term of her natural life shall be expended or paid over by said trustees for said purpose and further when and if my sister, Mrs. John Hoar shall have expended all of her own property said trustees shall use and expend so much of the income and principal of said trust estate as is necessary for her comfortable support during the term of her natural life. Upon the death of the last of said Mary B. Donovan and said Mrs. John Hoar to survive, said trustees shall pay over to my daughter, Olive D. Stempel all of the income of said trust fund then remaining during the term of her natural life and upon her death or in the event that she predecease either said Mary B. Donovan or said Mrs. John Hoar, then upon the death of the last survivor of them, all of the principal of my estate then remaining shall be divided by said trustees equally among the issue of the body of her the said Olive D. Stempel who then survive, equally as nearly as may be per stirpes, provided however, that if no issue of her body then survive, then all of the principal of said estate then remaining shall be divided among my heirs-at-law in proportion to their heirship and upon the principal of said fund being distributed in accordance with the directions of this clause, then said trust shall cease and determine."

The daughter Mary was incompetent. The will was probated in 1920. During the years 1923–1936 the trustees expended for the support of Mary an average of $1,917.73 per year. Through 1927 the income was either under or somewhat over the amount necessary for

Mary's support. During the years 1928 through 1936, however, it varied from a low of $7,165.51 in 1930 to a high of $10,719.70 in 1936, the average per calendar year being $9,081.79. This was due largely to a fortuitous sale of real estate by the trustees in 1927. The original trust fund of $76,781.84 has been increased to an inventory value of $175,990.31 as of the end of 1936. In the meantime the other daughter Olive and her two children were in dire financial need, without even some of the necessities of life. This action was brought by Olive individually and as guardian for her children, alleging that the surplus income either was given by the will to Olive or passed by intestacy because undisposed of. Details of a compromise agreement entered into in the original probate proceedings, under which Olive received up to $1,000 per year out of surplus income, and of a further agreement in this proceeding have been omitted. The trial court held that the net income in excess of amounts expended for Mary's support constituted intestate estate and that all funds in the hands of the trustees representing accumulations of such net income are distributable forthwith.]

BROWN, JUDGE. [The court's statement of the facts is omitted.]

* * *

The fundamental question for determination is whether surplus income in any calendar year during the life of the survivor of Mary and Mrs. Hoar constitutes intestate estate currently distributable to Olive and Mary, the testatrix' heirs. The answer lies in the determination of the intent of the testatrix as evidenced by the will. In a case of this nature "the question whether the excess shall accumulate and be added to the principal or shall be otherwise disposed of depends primarily upon the intent of the testator." New Haven Bank v. Hubinger, 117 Conn. 417, 420, 167 A. 914, 915. In the opinion in that case after reviewing our decisions dealing with this question as presented in its varying aspects, 117 Conn. at page 423, 167 A. at page 916, we summarized the result by this statement of the rules of interpretation involved: "It may be stated, therefore, generally speaking, that, where the will discloses an intent that excess income shall accumulate, or its distribution as it accrues will be contrary to the scheme of the will, it should be permitted to accumulate, unless, indeed, such an accumulation would be invalid, Hoadley v. Beardsley, supra, 89 Conn. [270] 280, 93 A. 535; Belcher v. Phelps, supra, 109 Conn. [7] 18, 144 A. 659; Wilson v. D'Atro, 109 Conn. 563, 567, 145 A. 161; Colonial Trust Co. v. Waldron, 112 Conn. 216, 222, 152 A. 69; Moeller v. Kautz, 112 Conn. 481, 152 A. 886; that, where the will discloses an intent that there shall be no accumulation of excess income or such an accumulation would be contrary to the scheme of the testator, or where the will discloses no intent either way, the excess income should be distributed to those entitled to it as it accrues."

It remains to apply these principles in this case. There is no reference in the will to surplus income to indicate the testatrix' intent. From its provisions it is clear that she was primarily concerned with making provision for the support for life of her incompetent daughter

Mary or her sister Mrs. Hoar should she become destitute. That she failed, however, to anticipate the possibility that there would be income in excess of the amount required for their support, and instead contemplated that it would be insufficient for this purpose, is evidenced by the authorization to the trustees to use "so much of the income and principal" for their support, and more particularly by her language used in directing the disposition of the income and principal after the death of the survivor. It is the income from the "trust fund then remaining" that is given to Olive until her death, and the "principal of my estate then remaining" that is given to the remainder beneficiaries. Assuming, as we may, that when she executed her will making these dispositions, the testatrix had in mind the value, character and probable income possibilities of her estate, she undoubtedly conceived that the support provided by it for Mary and Mrs. Hoar would require the use of at least a part of the principal, while there is nothing to warrant the assumption that the sudden substantial increase in value of the estate which occurred seven years after her death could have been in her mind at that time. Had she contemplated the possibility of substantial surplus income, being on intimate and friendly terms with Olive and her family and fully conversant with their acute financial need, as the finding shows she was, the conclusion is practically inescapable that she would have given it to Olive, to whom she did give all of the income upon termination of the necessity of providing for the support of Mary and Mrs. Hoar. In the words of the trial court, the testatrix "never conceived the possibility of accumulated surplus income, but rather foresaw a likely shrinkage of the principal of the trust fund and, hence, completely overlooked the necessity of providing for any disposition of surplus income," and its conclusion that under the Hubinger case the surplus income is intestate is correct.

Except for the fact that the Hubinger case involved a trust to provide payment of an annuity instead of one to provide support as here, the two cases are practically on all fours. That in one the testator fixes the amount of income to be paid over to the beneficiary, and in the other leaves the amount to be determined by the latter's need for support as ascertained by trustees, is not a difference sufficient to distinguish them as contended by the appellants. The court's determination that the surplus income is intestate, effectively avoiding, as it does, tieing up and so depriving Olive and her children of the enjoyment of it for what might prove a long term of years "during the period of their lives, when it would mean most to their careers and position in life," is a result which fortifies its conclusion. Belcher v. Phelps, 109 Conn. 7, 20, 144 A. 659, 664. The case of Jaretzki v. Strong, 98 Conn. 357, 119 A. 353, chiefly relied upon by the appellants as authority that the surplus income should not be held intestate, is clearly distinguishable from this case. In that case the trusts instead of being for life, as here, were until the beneficiaries had reached certain ages, and in the event one died before the termination of the trust the money was not to be paid to his estate but he was given a power of appointment. We held that under the terms of the will the beneficiary of each of the trust funds was given the net income, with a restriction limiting the power of the trustees to pay it to him before the termination for any other purpose than his maintenance, education and support, and with power in them to withhold income in any year and use the amount so withheld in any future year for the purposes specified; with the result that the income would not become a part of the principal and that at the termination of the trust the beneficiary would be entitled to receive any balance in the hands of the trustee. The distinction between that case and the one before us lies in the fact that in the Jaretzki case there was a gift to the beneficiary of the entire net income, though enjoyment might be postponed to the termination of the trust, whereas here there was no gift of income beyond that required for the necessary support of Mary and Mrs. Hoar.

The judgment in the present case correctly provides that the individual trustees in the calendar years after 1938, in determining the amount required for Mary's support, "may properly include a reasonable reserve represented by a sum in excess of that required for [her] proper care and comfortable support" in such year. Colonial Trust Co. v. Brown, 105 Conn. 261, 278, 135 A. 555. This provision in the judgment, in connection with the results to be realized from others therein, looking to the restoration to Mary's conservator of her portion of the intestate income for the years 1923 to 1938 inclusive, provides a substantial safeguard for her future support. It also affords a practical answer to the appellant's claim that this support is endangered by the court's decision, as well as to the claim that the determination of what constitutes "so much of * * * the income * * * as is necessary (in the trustees' discretion) * * * for the * * * support of Mary," essential to fixing the surplus income, can only be properly ascertained as of the date of her death. The court's determination that after 1938, surplus income must be determined and distributed on the basis of calendar years is in accord with our rule. New Haven Bank v. Hubinger, supra, 117 Conn. 428, 167 A. 914. The contention that the surplus income should not be held to be intestate because to do so may result in substantial payments of intestate income to Mary's conservator by reason of the fact that she is an heir of the testatrix, and so in large measure in substituting his discretion as to expenditures for her, for that of the trustees as provided by the testatrix in the will, is not of great weight. Even of less weight is the possible further claim that to so hold would violate the will by depriving the trustees of their discretion to conserve the principal. Since the testatrix contemplated only the necessity of drawing upon principal for the support of Mary and Mrs. Hoar because of lack of sufficient income, no such discretion with relation to surplus income could have been within her testamentary intent.

That in determining the amount of net income to be expended for Mary's support in any calendar year after 1938, her personal estate and income from sources other than by the provisions in her favor in the will must be taken into account, is indicated by the context of the will and is supported by authority. The provision is that the trustees shall expend for Mary "so much * * * as is necessary * * * to provide for [her] comfortable support." The intent so expressed limits the payments to those required for such support by reason of her own inability to provide it. In so far as she receives from some other source personal estate which enables her to make such provision, the necessity essential to taking under the will disappears. Accordingly her personal estate, her share of accrued past intestate surplus income, as well as intestate surplus income currently received by her, are to be taken into account by the trustees in future payments to her. Hull v. Holloway, 58 Conn. 210, 217, 20 A. 445; Bridgeport-City Trust Co. v. Beach, 119 Conn. 131, 138, 174 A. 308.

* * * the case is remanded with direction to enter judgment in accordance with this opinion.

In this opinion the other Judges concurred.[60]

NOTE

Consider the difference in attitude in the principal case between allowing reasonable reserves and simply accumulating income for no purpose other than adding it to principal to be conserved for a future taker. See IV Restatement, Property (1944) § 439, providing in effect that no accumulation exists when retention of income is "in the course of judicious management of the trust". Note also that once the court decides against allowing the income to accumulate and directs its immediate distribution, the court is faced with a constructional problem as to the proper person to whom the undisposed of income should be distributed. Courts have variously, depending on the facts of the individual case, decided that the undisposed of income should go: (1) to the current income recipient (for example, Mary in the principal case; (2) to the remainderman or, if the remainder is contingent, to those presumptively entitled to the remainder; or (3) under the residuary clause or by intestacy.

GERTMAN v. BURDICK

BURDICK v. BURDICK

United States Court of Appeals for the District of Columbia, 1941.
123 F.2d 924, 152 A.L.R. 645.

VINSON, ASSOCIATE JUSTICE. These three appeals are concerned with certain provisions of a testamentary trust. Willard L. Lalor, the deceased, made a number of bequests. Then he directed that the remainder of his estate be put in trust until 21 years after the death of the survivor of Ruth and Esther Lalor (nieces). Trust income is to pay several annuities. The remainder of the trust income "is to be reinvested by the Trustee for the increase and benefit of this trust fund". At the expiration of 21 years after the two lives in being, the

60. Where the trust provides for an annuity, such as $10,000 per year, to be paid to a beneficiary, and fails to provide that it can be paid out of principal as well as income, the trustee can set aside reserves of surplus income as appears reasonably necessary to meet future deficiencies in income. Smith Trust, 385 Pa. 416, 123 A.2d 623 (1956).

trust is to cease, and the principal and accumulations are to be divided into five parts; a part is to go to the lawful issue of each of the named nieces, and a part to each of three named relatives, or if deceased, to their lawful issue.

The trustees asked for a construction of, and instructions under, the will. The adults interested in the testamentary disposition were named defendants. The District Court appointed a guardian ad litem to represent the infants and unborn issue. The Court found three main questions timely. (1) Do the future interests created violate the rule against perpetuities, i.e., will any of the future interests remain "unvested" 21 years after lives in being? The District Court said no. That answer has not been questioned upon appeal; we believe that the conclusion reached is clearly sound. (2) Does the will creating the future interests violate the statutory provision limiting the period for which the power of alienation may be suspended? The District Court said no. We believe that this answer is correct and a brief discussion will follow. (3) In this jurisdiction, is the provision that this amount of income be accumulated for lives in being plus 21 years valid? The District Court said no. Most of our discussion will be devoted to this question. * * *

[The court then discussed the contention that the limitation might suspend the power of alienation beyond the statutory period of lives in being and twenty-one years because one of the takers at the end of the trust might be a minor incapable of alienating an absolute fee; the court held that suspension of the power of alienation in such an event would not be due to any provision of the will but to the taker's legal status.]

* * *

We now come to the important question for decision. It is the question raised in Gertman, Guardian, et al. v. Trustees et al. (No. 7773), and Trustees v. Anna Lalor Burdick et al. (No. 7775). In the first, the guardian ad litem is the appellant, and the appellees are the trustees and adult beneficiaries. In the second, the trustees have appealed to be sure that all issues are before this court; the adult beneficiaries and the guardian ad litem are the appellees. The question: is the provision of this trust directing the accumulation, through reinvestment, of a rather large amount of income, for a period of lives in being plus 21 years, valid?

We have no statute on the subject. The case law offers some guides, some persuasive ideas, and some helpful history, but there is no holding that we must accept within the meaning of stare decisis.

The English common law on the subject is generally regarded as the Thellusson case which maintained the validity of such a provision. There were two other questions in the case, but the Lord Chancellor's opinion to the House of Lords was devoted precisely to the problem before us. The Lord Chancellor made it clear that the question was to be answered under law and equity, not legislative policy. He pointed out that alienation could be postponed for any number of lives and then said, "If the law is so as to postponing alienation, another question arises out of this will; which is a pure question of equity: whether a testator can direct the rents and profits to be accumulated for that period, during which he may direct, that the title shall not vest, and the property shall remain unalienable; and, that he can do so, is most clear law." Upon his motion the decree was affirmed. Subsequently, this has been such clear law that no court on its own has ever fixed a period limiting accumulations other than the one that equalled the rule against perpetuities. It has been such clear law that, apparently, no court before the action in this case has ever knocked down a provision accumulating income for lives in being plus 21 years.

When England wanted a shorter period, it acted through its legislature. In fact, Parliament passed a statute in 1800 between the High Court of Chancery's opinion in 1799 and the House of Lords' affirmance in 1805. Parliament set four alternative maximum periods. The Act is not entirely a happy one. The period to be applied to any individual case is the one most fitting.

The Thellusson case came too late to be a part of the common law that this jurisdiction adopted.

* * * Thus the common law of the District clearly does not embrace an English case of 1799 or 1805. One does not reach the point of applying the repugnant-to-our-conditions test to ascertain whether this particular case is a part of our common law.

It is even clearer that the Thellusson Act is not a part of our common law. Acts of Parliament had to become a part of the judicial heritage to be taken over as part of the English common law. Maryland's original declaration of rights and its present constitution set the critical date for statutes even more specifically than for court decisions, clearly excluding an act of Parliament 14 years after the Declaration of Independence.

Two significant guides, however, are afforded us by the Thellusson case and statute. The British common law for Britishers was that a testamentary provision for accumulating income for as long as future estates could remain not vested was good. When the people desired a shorter period for accumulations, it was the legislative body that took action.

These two propositions have been repeated in this country's legal history. Here, however, because of our 48 states, and dependencies, we are not limited to one case and one statute.

It has been generally, if not universally assumed, that the common law in the United States permitted accumulations for 21 years after lives in being. This was certainly the assumption of 13 state legislatures which passed statutes creating a shorter period. This assumption is supported by the tenor of the case law. True our attention has been called to no case which directly held and applied a rule of lives in being plus 21 years. Undoubtedly this is largely due to the accepted-in-practice common law which deterred litigation on the point. Likewise, our attention has been called to no case which, in the absence of statute, directly rejected a rule allowing a period of lives in being plus 21 years. Obviously, then, the courts have never adopted a rule prescribing another period of time.

The tenor of our case law is well illustrated by the case of Fitchie v. Brown. The testator, living in Hawaii, made a will which gave certain pecuniary legacies; the will directed that the residue of the estate was to be put in trust "for as long a period as is legally possible" under the statute; trust income was to go to some forty odd annuitants and then to their heirs with three exceptions; at the termination of the trust, the trust fund was to go over equally to those then entitled to the annuities. As it turned out, there was surplus income over the annuities for which the will made no provision. The Supreme Court of Hawaii held the trust valid. The Court directed the trustees to pay the annuities during the respective lives of the annuitants and thereafter to their heirs until 21 years after the death of the survivor, then to divide the trust fund and its accumulated income as provided by the will. There was an appeal to the United States Supreme Court. Its opinion began, "In the view we take of the case there are but two questions necessary to be noticed, and they involve the validity of the trust and the disposition of the surplus income." The Court proceeded to hold the trust valid, deciding that while there was no statute applicable to the length of trusts in Hawaii, as the testator suggested, he intended it to exist as long as legally possible which under the common law is lives in being plus 21 years. The lives in being that are to be used in this case are the annuitants; forty odd is not too large for a valid limitation. Thus the trust fund is to be distributed 21 years after the survivor of forty odd annuitants. Meanwhile, "we think the surplus, after paying annuities, must accumulate as part of the trust estate until the time arrives for the distribution of that estate, and that such accumulation must then be distributed as a part thereof to those who will then have the right to take the estate as provided for in the will."

The case which most fully addresses itself to the problem before us, Moeller v. Kautz, held accumulations for lives in being good and stated that the general rule for accumulations was identical in length to the rule against perpetuities. It further stated that this general rule was to be applied except in the most unusual situations. It is not clear that the instant case would be one of those unusual situations.

In view of the common understanding, and the judicial acceptance, including this court (albeit not in fully discussed direct holdings) of a rule permitting accumulations for as long as the period of the rule against perpetuities, we have no hesitation in saying that has been the common law of this country and of this jurisdiction.

Our discussion cannot stop here, however. The common law is imbued with reason, sound policy, and a capacity for growth. It is claimed that the old law on accumulations is repugnant to the public policy of the 5th decade of the 20th century. It is argued that the accumulation in the instant case is so big and is to last so long that it should be invalidated. We are told that under the force of logic, of history, of custom, of justice, of morals, of social welfare, we must declare the common law for today differently than it was declared for Britishers in the Thellusson case. We are told that this is a model case for bold action on the part of a court, that we should free ourselves from the stinted legalistic reasoning of the 18th century. On this challenge further considerations are relevant.

Let us assume for a moment that we are to set some limitation on the size and length of accumulations on realty and personalty. What are our standards? We must turn to the statutes, for the courts have used no period other than the rule against perpetuities. A survey of the statutes reveals that in spite of the crystallized existence of this problem for a century and a half and with the New York Act to serve as a lead for 110 years only 12 other states have placed any statutory limitation on accumulations.

First, what limit should be set on the amount of the accumulation? The statutes give no suggestion whatsoever as to where the line should be drawn, for while they have not been highly uniform in general, there has been uniformity in legislative non-action as to size.

Second, should our limit on accumulations apply both to realty and personalty? In respect of the ten "New York Acts" five apply to both, four to realty alone, and one to personalty alone. The two "Thellusson Acts" apply to both. The unique Alabama Act applies to property in trust for accumulation only.

Third, for what period should accumulations be good? Originally all "New York Acts" used a minority period. Two "New York Act" states, however, have had a significant history in regard to length. California in her Civil Code of 1872 followed the minority period of New York. In 1929 the Code provision was amended so as to allow accumulations for the same length of time that alienation might be suspended, which is lives in being or in the alternative 25 years in gross. Montana has a similar history. Her Code of 1895 followed those of California and New York. Ten years after California's action, Montana likewise amended her Code to provide that income might be accumulated so long as the power of alienation might be suspended, which in this state is lives in being. Thus we find a lengthening of the time for permitted accumulations, and a period set which coincides with another critical time limit in the field of future interests. Illinois uses the four periods of the Thellusson Act. Pennsylvania has altered to ambiguity the English Act. The Alabama Trusts-for-accumulations-only Act allows ten years or a minority.

Fourth, when we choose, as a legislature would, a permissible period, shall we hold the accumulation bad only in respect of the excess? It has been uniformly held that an accumulation is bad only as to such excess where there is a statutory permissible period, whereas an accumulation that violates the common law of lives in being plus 21 years is void in its entirety; the latter remains the law even when you have a statutory period.

Fifth, what exceptions shall we adopt? The thirteen states with statutes have differing exceptions. The list includes charities, debts, portions, stock dividends, insurance trusts.

Thus far we have assumed that we were to set some period. The difficulties outlined have been those of choosing *a* period. But has it been established that *we* should set *any* period? If we set no period, yet hold this trust bad, is it because it is too long, too big, or both? What guide will the next testator have in respect of what is good? It would not be a very happy policy to require each testator to write knowingly an uncertain will to be passed upon when it is too late to express further intentions.

Nonetheless it is insisted that this will is so incompatible with sound public policy that it should be voided. What are some of the elements of that public policy?

It is argued that this will injures government financing because much of our revenue today comes through wealth in circulation—excise taxes, income taxes. At the outset it would seem that if there is some place today where taxes are not large enough or do not come often enough, it would be better for the revenue law makers to solve the problem specifically than for us to correct it through indirection. It could be that the trustees are paying larger taxes than the revenue would be if the income were dispersed among the heirs or beneficiaries.

It is argued that the amount involved in this accumulation ties up too much wealth, and that it lowers the country's purchasing power which is already too small. A picture of the future size of this accumulation can be painted with gigantic lines. Such a prognostication is not without precedent. Realization has yet to approach these anticipations.[61] It is, moreover, highly dubious whether size should be relevant in the courts on the issue of good or bad accumulations. In keeping with the general attitute of the law which for the most part avoids such distinctions, none of the states have made size rele-

61. [This and fn. 62 are by the court; the other footnotes accompanying the original opinion have been omitted. Ed.]

All figures and statements are estimates or approximations. In this case there is $1,600,000 in trust, earning $80,000 per year; $50,000 is now being accumulated; the expectancy of the younger life in being plus 21 years equals 55 years. The principal of the trust is figured to reach around $10,800,000. The rate of return, the investment gains or losses, the costs of administration and litigation, the length of the lives, are important but imponderable factors. With this in mind consider the Thellusson history. The value of the trust estates was something over £600,000. The predicted life of the trusts was 75 to 80 years. The predicted ultimate value ranged from £23,000,000 to £34,500,000. The trusts continued for 60 years and grew but little. Powell, Cases on Future Interests, (2d ed., 1937) p. 729, fn. 30; Barry, Mr. Thellusson's Will (1936) 22 Va.L.Rev. 416.

The estate in Moeller v. Kautz (112 Conn. 481, 152 A. 886) was something over $1,000,000. During the first year the amount of accumulated income was $42,000, for the second, $37,000, for the third, $23,000, and for the fourth, $123,000. Then the income shrunk; one year there was none to accumulate for it did not pay the expenses of administration and the annuities. At the time of the decision the trust had been in existence some 14 years. The accrued income was only a little over $350,000. Thus the last ten years had netted $125,000, a little more than was realized in the fourth year alone. The length of this trust is measured by nine lives.

vant in their legislative action. As to the repercussions of a large accumulation it might be that we are not sufficiently well versed in economic cause and effect to know how much of what will lead us to spend all of our days in prosperity. As an example of the rapidity of change of emphasis in this field, consider the effort that has been made to keep purchasing power down to prevent inflation since these briefs have been written. This trust, moreover, directs that the income is to be reinvested. This trust estate is no Fort Knox.[62] We are not prepared to say how much better or worse is the use of this money by a trustee to buy a security than by an heir or beneficiary to purchase a topcoat.

It is argued that this accumulation is against principles of ethics. Posthumous avarice leading to disherison is bad. Living greediness is bad too. We are told that this will is a carry over from feudal days and is diametrically opposed to the principles of democracy. We presume that is because this trust is a large estate, a modern security-landed gentry. Yet the whole system of inheriting is a carry over from the past. That does not necessarily make it good or bad. It is contended that balance between security and frontier resourcefulness is needed. Today we do not feel the omniscience to promulgate the balance that will make us a race of supermen.

This discussion has not been an attempt to state exhaustively the questions that must be answered to establish a period for accumulations that would be good policy, much less to answer them. Nor are any of the observations that we have made to be applied to the parties of this litigation. We have given this synopsis to show, in spite of the well written Brandeis-like briefs before us, that this is not the proper forum to consider and establish the limitations on accumulations if they are to be other than those of the common law.

Under the accepted, established common law to date, this accumulation is good. Even though the common law is organic, the rule for this case should not be changed. Only 13 states have seen fit to change that rule by statute. The changes have not been uniform. There is a serious question as to whether the changes represent any improvement. Changing the rule by holding the accumulation in this case bad would not make for any orderly improvement in our law. Any change made in the rule for accumulations should be correlated to other problems and periods in future interests. A court does not have as good facilities to study these problems, nor does it represent as directly the people, as the legislative body. We therefore hold the accumulation provision of this testamentary disposition valid.

62. Counsel quotes in italics these words from Bogert's Treatise: "It is possible that accumulation provisions are subject to further restrictions based on public policy. If they are useless, wasteful, and arbitrary the courts may refuse to enforce them, even though the period and beneficiaries are satisfactory." Bogert's next sentence is: "Thus, a trust to keep the money received as income in a box in specie for a certain period, without investment, might well be stricken down as unreasonable and contrary to good economic policy." Bogert, Trusts and Trustees (2d ed. 1964) § 215, p. 372. [See "Distribution of Income Released by Declaration of Invalidity of Express Direction for Accumulation", 17 A.L.R.3d 231 (1968). (Ed.)]

The decree of the District Court is reversed and the cause remanded for whatever further proceedings are necessary not inconsistent with this opinion.

Reversed.[63]

NOTE

The concern expressed by Justice Vinson in the Burdick case as to whether a court should pattern a judicial rule on the statutes then in force appears in retrospect to have been more than well-founded. Since this decision, almost all of the jurisdictions have abandoned their restrictive rules in favor of a rule permitting accumulations for the period allowed for vesting of estates. This wholesale abandonment of the principle embodied in the Thellusson Act and similar American statutes makes any consideration of the impact of such statutes relatively unimportant. Indicative of this sweeping trend were the changes in Michigan in 1952, Illinois in 1953, Pennsylvania in 1956, Wisconsin in 1957, and New York in 1959. Wisconsin went the farthest of any state by authorizing accumulations for any period specified in the trust document. Problems may still arise as to trusts created prior to the effective dates of the repealing acts in the respective jurisdictions, but the draftsman is free to provide for discretionary or mandatory accumulation for the same periods allowed under the rule for vesting or suspension. In the few states still retaining restrictions, the legislation has very limited scope: the Alabama statute applies to trusts for "accumulation only" and not where the trustee has discretionary power to pay out income; the Minnesota statute applies to trusts of real estate only, not to trusts of personalty.[64]

SECTION 6. TREATMENT OF CHARITABLE TRUSTS UNDER RESTRICTIVE RULES

In this section we shall study two questions: (1) must gifts to charity "vest" within the period of the Rule? (2) can the donor provide for an accumulation of income for a charitable purpose beyond the period of the Rule and if so for how long? Since these are obviously "policy" issues, some preliminary thought should be given to the kinds of questions courts and legislatures should ask in deciding on policy. The pitfalls for the draftsman are relatively easy to discover and to avoid.

We have previously seen in Chapter XI numerous judicial and legislative examples of public policy favoring gifts to charity. Preferential treatment is reflected in the holdings that charitable trusts may be created for indefinite beneficiaries, not to mention the lengths that courts go under the cy pres doctrine to prevent failure of a charitable gift, and in the statutes affording liberal tax advantages to charitable

63. See, Keeton, "The Thelluson Case and Trusts for Accumulations", 21 No. Ire.Legal Q. 131 (1970).

64. For a state by state summary see American Law of Prop. (1952) Ch. XI; Simes and Smith, Future Interests (2d Ed., 1956) § 1466 (Supp. 1975).

organizations. One might expect corresponding dispensations for charity in the various rules just studied in this chapter. Nevertheless, countervailing policy considerations have been evident ever since the Statutes of Mortmain, restricting the amounts of wealth which may be transferred out of the normal channels of social organization. This conflict is evident in legislative struggles over extension or restriction of tax privileges for charitable organizations. It is present whether the charity takes the corporate or trust form. Here, as with many policy issues, there is little factual information available upon which to judge.[65]

There is no doubt but that a trust for charity may last in perpetuity, just as a charitable corporation may. This means, since there are no beneficiaries who can alienate the equitable interest or petition for termination, that an amount of wealth is removed from the field of private enterprise indefinitely. This also enables a man to perpetuate his ideas and his name (simply by designating the trust as such).

Furthermore a charitable foundation continues to have use in maintaining the role of a family in business. Prior to 1969 foundations were manipulated for this purpose in two ways: (1) A donor contributes voting stock controlled by his family to a charitable foundation also controlled by his family. He obtains an income tax deduction for the contribution; eliminates the estate tax upon the value of the contributed stock; and by shifting control of the foundation to the younger members of his family, thus shifts to their control the voting stock of the business corporation without tax. (2) The donor recapitalizes his corporation, issuing voting and non-voting common stock. He contributes the non-voting stock to the foundation and obtains an income tax deduction on the value of this transfer. When the voting stock passes at the death of the owner, or if it is given during his lifetime to younger members of the family, the gift or estate tax is minimized because a diminished proportion of the equity in the corporation is transferred.

These techniques are not proscribed by the Tax Reform Act of 1969 but their usefulness is limited by restrictions upon accumulations by the foundation and by stringent limitations upon excess business holdings with a five year grace period, with exceptions, for the disposition of excess holdings acquired by gift or bequest. The disposition of the excess holdings has the sanction of a heavy tax but the period of grace may mean that the transfer of closely held corporation stock to a foundation will be an effective "short term" estate planning device. Not uncommonly a settlor desires to accumulate income in a charitable trust in order to amass sufficient wealth to carry out a program of charity beyond his present means, so that the double problem of a perpetuity and an accumulation is involved.

65. For discussions of policy issues see, Lynn, "Perpetuities: The Duration of Charitable Trusts and Foundations", 13 U.C.L.A.Law Rev. 1074 (1966); Najarian, "Charitable Giving and the Rule Against Perpetuities" 70 Dick.L.Rev. 455 (1966); Simes, Public Policy and the Dead Hand (1955) Ch. V. Note, "Rule Against Perpetuities—Charitable Trusts—Influential Factors in the Determination of Vestiture", 43 Tenn.L.Rev. 166 (1975).

Consider also the following:

(1) If an accumulation is involved, what does experience demonstrate as to whether income accumulates according to expectations of the settlor or not? (2) To whom are the trustees accountable? Is such an accounting likely to be as closely examined as one to a private beneficiary? (3) If a business is involved, are trustees likely to be aggressive in management over a long period? Are they as responsive as a board of directors of a business corporation answerable to the stockholders? (4) If the trustees have broad discretion as to the public or charitable purposes for which funds are expendable, will trustees have the same breadth of vision as the donor who has amassed the wealth? (5) Should society foster large accumulations of wealth controlled by individuals free to encourage research, education, and other charitable areas in manners which government would never undertake? (6) Is a charitable trust which is tied down to one narrow purpose more objectionable than one which gives the trustees broad discretion as to charitable purposes? Or does cy pres assure sufficient flexibility if social conditions change and outmode the narrow purpose?

ASCHE v. ASCHE

Court of Chancery of Delaware, 1964.
41 Del.Ch. 481, 199 A.2d 314.

[Ruby R. Vale, an attorney, died in 1961. His will created a marital deduction trust of half of his adjusted gross estate for the benefit of his widow; the other half of the estate, after payment of taxes, was given in trust to invest and reinvest "until there has been accumulated by the Trustees the sum of Two Million ($2,000,000) Dollars, as artificial principal, at which time the said Trustees shall irrevocably assign, transfer and pay over the said sum of Two Million Dollars * * *" to a corporation to be known as the Ruby R. Vale Foundation "* * * for educational uses and purposes, which perpetual foundation shall be caused to be set up and established by my Trustees solely for said purposes * * *". After the accumulation of the two million dollars for educational purposes, the trust was to provide for the testator's descendants "during the period of time valid under the law of the State of Delaware for lawful issue born after my death" on a complex scheme set forth in detail. The executors of the estate sought instructions. Certain members of the family contended that the charitable trust violated the Rule on the grounds that the gift to charity was effective only after the sum of $2,000,000 had been accumulated.]

MARVEL, VICE CHANCELLOR: * * *

The basic point sought to be made is apparently that on such theory the gift to charity may not vest within the period allowed by the rule against perpetuities and is accordingly void. The point of distinction between a vested gift to be paid in futuro and a contingent gift to be paid to a person only upon reaching a certain age is made by Chief Justice Booth in the case of Carey v. Pettyjohn, 5 Har. 296, as follows:

> "* * * if a legacy be given to a person, *payable*, or *to be paid*, at, or when he shall attain the age of 21 years; or at or upon any other definite period or event; the legacy becomes vested immediately on the testator's death; and is transmissible to the executors or administrators of the legatee, although he dies before the time of payment. But if the words *'payable'* or *'to be paid'* are omitted, and the legacy is given at 21; or at or upon any other future period or event; the interest is contingent, and depends for its vesting on the legatee being alive at the period or event specified."

On the basis of this principle it is also contended that the gift here in issue is contingent for another reason, it being additionally argued in disregard of the fact that the cy pres doctrine is recognized in Delaware that at the time of Vale's death the corporation contemplated by the testator as the recipient of the ultimate accumulation of $2,000,000 of income was not in existence.

In the first place, while a legacy made to an individual at twenty-one years of age is contingent because of the possibility of the legatee's death prior to reaching such age, here we are dealing with a charitable gift to a perpetual foundation, the purposes of which exist continuously and do not come of age, as it were, in futuro. However, apart from this practical distinction, the language here used is not, in my opinion, susceptible to the narrow interpretation advanced by the guardian ad litem for the Asche children and their issue. The object of Mr. Vale's bounty is not "* * * a corporation to be created for the purpose of giving effect to the gift * * *" but the educational purposes which the testator wished to advance. Compare Ingraham v. Ingraham, 169 Ill. 432, 48 N.E. 561, 49 N.E. 320. In other words, I have no doubt but that the charitable bequest made by the testator became vested on his death, the enjoyment of the gift merely being postponed until the stipulated amount of income had been raised, and I fail to see why the absence of a direction that principal as well as income ultimately be paid over to a perpetual foundation makes any substantial difference in arriving at a proper interpretation and implementation of the testator's plan. In short, he clearly intended that the designated moneys should be applied to educational uses and purposes in perpetuity, and there is no acceptable possibility of the nonexistence of such uses and purposes at the time such payment is ready to be made and applied to such ends pursuant to the specific design to be set up by the trustees. Finally, the language of the will gives no indication that the testator had any intention of making the gift in question contingent on the happening of any intervening prior event, and, if course, as will be noted later, the permissible length of the period during which moneys may be accumulated for charitable purposes is not governed by the strict terms of the rule against perpetuities.

There is apparent agreement on the fact that the principal sum here involved exceeded $1,900,000 at the time of testator's death and that the will provided for no estate prior to the charitable uses and purposes contemplated by the testator. The sum to be devoted to such purposes, which had appreciated to the sum of $2,150,000 at the time it was turned over to the trustees, has at least since such date been devoted to the testator's charitable purpose of endowing a $2,000,000 educational foundation incorporated under the name of the Ruby R. Vale Foundation. In my opinion, the facts and circumstances surrounding Mr. Vale's gift are closely analogous to those found in the charitable gift case of Girard Trust Company v. Rectors, Wardens etc. of St. Anne's Church, 30 Del.Ch. 1, 52 A.2d 591. In the cited case, the will in question provided:

> "All the rest, residue and remainder of my estate * * * I give * * * IN TRUST * * * to accumulate the income therefrom until, in the opinion of trustee, a sufficient amount has been accumulated, both as to principal and income, to build a small Chapel of Ease and a Parish House in connection with St. Anne's Protestant Episcopal Church at Middletown, Delaware, whereupon the corpus or principal of my said residuary estate, together with the accumulations thereon, shall be paid over for the erection of such Chapel and Parish House * * *."

In upholding such bequest, the Chancellor, invoking will construction principles which favor early vesting as well as an avoidance, if possible, of violations of the rule against perpetuities and against unreasonable accumulations, stated:

> "Nothing in the language of the will providing for the accumulation of income suggests that such accumulation is to be a condition precedent to the vesting of the Church's interest. Even if it should be said that there is some doubt, this doubt is to be resolved in favor of a conclusion which will result in the early vesting of the estate. * * * Moreover, as Professor Gray states in his work on The Rule Against Perpetuities (4th Ed.) § 673: 'The tendency of the courts being to construe limitations as vested, the arrival of the period fixed for, or needed for, the accumulation will not be deemed a condition precedent to the gift of the accumulated fund, unless the language employed requires such a construction.' "

See also Ingraham v. Ingraham, supra, Webster v. Wiggin, 19 R.I. 73, 31 A. 824, 28 L.R.A. 510, and Brigham v. Peter Bent Brigham Hospital (C.A.1) 134 F. 513.

Furthermore, as noted above, the fact that the period during which $2,000,000 of income is to accumulate in the hands of the trustees prior to being applied to educational uses and purposes may conceivably exceed the time specified in the rule against perpetuities does not, of course, affect the legality of such accumulation. As stated in the case of Girard Trust Co. v. St. Anne's Church, supra:

> "* * * the validity of provisions for accumulation of income in charitable trust cases seem to have been tested in most cases by the reasonableness of the period of time during which the income is to be accumulated, rather than by the rule against perpetuities."

See also Simes and Smith, Future Interests § 1467 where it is stated:

> "If a trust for charity is vested, a provision for accumulation of income is valid and will be effectuated so long as it is not unreasonable. * * * 'In the case of gifts to charities, the ordinary rule against accumulations does not apply, the only limitation being in the power of the court to take remedial measures should an unreasonable condition result.' The argument for this position is about as follows: Charities are favored by the court. The charitable trust is subject to the directions of the court of equity; and, if the accumulation should become unreasonable, the court has power to direct the trustee to disregard it. Thus the charitable trust will be sustained, and objectionable features will be prevented by subjecting it to the control of the court."

Here, even on the hypothesis of a minimal return of income earned by the trust property turned over to the trustees of the trust here in issue, the stipulated amount of artificial principal contemplated by the testator should be realized within a reasonable time even though such period might conceivably run beyond the time allowed by the rule against perpetuities. Cases to the contrary such as Girard Trust Company v. Russell, (C.A.3) 179 F. 446, and Murphy v. Johnston, 190 Ga. 23, 8 S.E.2d 23, are concerned with situations negativing a finding of a present gift. In other words, because of conditions precedent, reciprocal covenants, unreasonable periods of accumulation, and in the latter case, preceding gifts for non-charitable purposes, a vested gift in such cases could not be established. A significant element in each case was, I believe, that the money to be deposited pursuant to the terms of a brief, inconclusive inter vivos trust agreement in the Russell case was a mere $377.35 and in the Murphy case the money to be accumulated for ultimate charitable uses (after being applied to certain noncharitable purposes) was approximately $1,700, an amount referred to by the court as "* * * a small sum of money". This sum was directed to be held until, with additions it had reached the sum of $600,000. However, on the same day on which the Murphy case was decided, the same court (The Supreme Court of Georgia) in a factual situation more closely analogous to that found in the case at bar held that a will provision for the accumulation of income prior to the application of moneys for charitable purposes did not create a condition precedent to a charitable gift, Perkins v. Citizens and Southern National Bank, 190 Ga. 29, 8 S.E.2d 28. I conclude that the better reasoned cases, in which not only the amount involved in relation to a reasonable accumulation period is

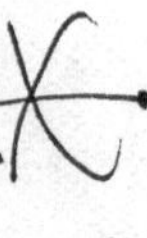

realistic but the intention of the testator to make a present gift is clear and uncomplicated, control in the case at bar. Here, I am satisfied that the testator not only intended a present gift to charity, the enjoyment whereof was merely postponed until the stipulated sum had been accumulated but that the time reasonably needed for the accumulation of $2,000,000 of income for payment over to a charitable foundation is entirely within proper limits.

* * * [In the balance of the opinion, the court held the provisions for the testator's family, following the accumulation for charity, invalid under the Rule Against Perpetuities on the grounds that such provisions were contingent on the accumulation which might, under the rules discussed above, take place beyond the period of the Rule; hence the corpus of the trust, after the accumulation, was directed to be distributed as intestate property.] [66]

NOTE

It would have been doctrinally possible in the principal case to hold the gift to charity invalid. The Rule against Perpetuities clearly applies to charitable gifts and invalidates remote contingent gifts to charity,[67] with an exception where a gift is made to charity within the period of the Rule followed by a gift over to a second charity upon the happening of an event which may take place beyond the permissible period.[68] The court would have to find that the gift in the principal case was contingent, either on the grounds that it was to a corporation to be formed (which might take place beyond the period of the Rule) [69] or on the concept that the gift did not vest in the chari-

66. On appeal the Delaware Supreme Court sustained the holding of the lower court as to validity of the charitable gift but reversed the lower court as to the provisions for the family. 210 A.2d 306 (1965). This result was reached by construing the will in a manner which would uphold the family provisions; because of the reference in the will to "the period of time valid under the law," the Supreme Court held that testator intended accumulation to be completed within the period of the Rule, even though it might not possibly reach the $2,000,000 goal. This is another example of the tendency of modern courts to stretch construction doctrine to uphold validity. Chief Justice Wolcott dissented on the grounds that the language requiring accumulation of $2,000,000 was clearly a prerequisite to the family provisions; he would have affirmed the lower court. A "wait and see" approach would have undoubtedly saved the whole limitation, since it appeared likely that the goal of accumulation would be completed in 17 years. However, the case was remanded to determine which of the private interests following the accumulation would vest within the Rule, on the basis of the Supreme Court's interpretation. For the sequel, see 216 A.2d 272 (1965). See, Phelps v. Shropshire, 254 Minn. 777, 183 So.2d 158, 20 A.L.R.3d 1086 (1966) where the gift over was to the family if the charity declined, which it did within the time period. The court took a wait and see approach, sustaining the private gift. 20 A.L.R.3d 1094 (1968).

67. See Lynn, "Perpetuities: The Duration of Charitable Trusts and Foundations", 13 U.C.L.A.L.Rev. 1074 (1966); Najarian, "Charitable Giving and the Rule Against Perpetuities", 70 Dick.L. Rev. 455 (1966).

68. E.g., Dickenson v. City of Anna, 310 Ill. 222, 141 N.E. 754, 30 A.L.R. 587 (1923) (devise of land to an academy, with a provision that if the land should ever be alienated, then to the city).

69. Usually the court will hold that formation of a corporation is not a condition precedent to the gift to charity but rather an administrative provision for implementation of the charitable plan. See Henderson v. Troy Bank & Trust Co., 250 Ala. 456, 34 So.2d 835 (1948). A direct testamentary gift to a charitable corporation to be formed after death of the testator is valid in many states. Hoenig v. Lubetkin, 137 Conn. 516, 79 A.2d 278 (1951) (reasonable time limit implied); Maynard v. Farmers' Loan & Trust Co., 119 Misc. 503, 197 N.Y.S. 526 (1922), aff'd 208 App.Div. 112, 203 N.Y.S. 83

ty until the accumulation had taken place (which again might be beyond the period of the Rule).[70] As the principal case illustrates, a modern court will attempt to find the gift vested. Compare First Camden National Bank & Trust Co. v. Collins [71] where the trust provided for accumulation for lives of three named grandchildren plus 21 years, to be paid over to a corporation to be formed at the end of that period, with additional accumulation until the principal should reach $327,000,000; the "charitable" nature of the entire plan was nebulous, and the testator had left his family with a pittance; the court held the gift contingent on formation of the corporation after the period and hence invalid.

It should also be noted that the Rule against Perpetuities may work in favor of charity. This occurs when there is a valid gift to charity, defeasible by a gift over to a private person on a contingency too remote under the Rule; the Rule operates to invalidate the gift over and leaves the charity with an absolute interest. A classic illustration is found in the situation where real property is conveyed to a church entity A with a limitation over to B and his heirs if the church ever ceases to use the property for church purposes. If later community development makes the site no longer desirable for church purposes, application of the Rule invalidates the gift over to B, leaving the church free to sell and convey the realty in order to finance purchase of a new site.[72] Some courts imply a possibility of reverter in the grantor and his heirs, which under the traditional American view is not subject to the Rule.[73]

The second feature of the principal case deals with the permissible limit of accumulation. Review Gertman v. Burdick in Section 5. Why should there be a different rule on accumulations for charitable trusts? Suppose the court finds that the period for accumulations as set up in the will or trust instrument is unreasonably long. What are the consequences? How do you determine what is a reasonable period?

ESTATE OF JAMES

Supreme Court of Pennsylvania, 1964.
414 Pa. 80, 199 A.2d 275.

ROBERTS, JUSTICE. Frank James died testate on March 22, 1960. In his will, admitted to probate by the Register of Wills of Philadel-

(1924), aff'd 238 N.Y. 592, 144 N.E. 905 (1924) (administrative delay not within statute prohibiting suspension of power of alienation). Cf. Litcher v. Trust Co., 18 N.J.Super. 101, 86 A.2d 601 (Ch.Div. 1952).

70. Girard Trust Co. v. Russell, 179 F. 446 (C.C.A.3d 1910) (settlor established a trust of $20,000 to invest principal and income in bonds of the State of Pennsylvania, to accumulate the fund until equal to the debt of the state, at which time the fund was to be paid to the State Treasurer in discharge of the indebtedness; held, contingent and invalid).

71. 114 N.J.Eq. 59, 168 A. 275 (1933).

72. Starr v. Starr Methodist Protestant Church, 112 Md. 171, 76 A. 595 (1910); Proprietors of Church in Brattle Square v. Grant, 69 Mass. (3 Gray) 142, 63 Am.Dec. 725 (1855).

73. Pruner's Estate, 400 Pa. 629, 162 A.2d 626 (1960), 109 U.Pa.L.Rev. 433 (1961). The Rule does not invalidate an express possibility of reverter after a gift to charity. Institution for Savings v. Roxbury Home for Aged Women, 244 Mass. 583, 139 N.E. 301 (1923); Brown v. Independent Baptist Church of Woburn, 325 Mass. 645, 91 N.E.2d 922 (1950).

phia County, he created a life estate, in trust, of certain real estate and personalty, at the termination of which he directed sale of the assets and the addition of the proceeds to the principal of his residuary trust. He set aside a fund for the maintenance of the real property and directed that any balance from this fund also be added to the residuary trust. The unique terms of the residuary trust, which give rise to this litigation, provide as follows:

> "SECOND: All the rest, residue and remainder of my estate, of whatsoever kind and wheresoever situate, I give, devise and bequeath unto my Trustee, hereinafter named, and its successors, IN TRUST NEVERTHELESS, to hold, invest, and reinvest the same, to collect the income therefrom, and after paying all expenses incident to the management of the trust, to accumulate and to pay over the net income to THE RIGHT WORSHIPFUL GRAND LODGE OF FREE AND ACCEPTED MASONS OF PENNSYLVANIA, for the use of the Masonic Homes at Elizabethtown, Pennsylvania as follows:
>
> "(A) At the expiration of twenty years from the date of my death, 50 per cent of the net income received to date. The remaining 50 per cent of net income shall be added to the principal of this trust to be invested and reinvested in accordance with the terms hereof. Upon the receipt of this first payment of income, it is my request that an appropriate memorial tablet be erected by The Right Worshipful Grand Lodge of Free and Accepted Masons of Pennsylvania at the Masonic Homes in Elizabethtown, Pennsylvania, in honor of ELIZABETH STOTT JAMES and FRANK JAMES.
>
> "(B) Thereafter every twenty years on the anniversary date of the date of my death, Trustee shall pay over 50 per cent of the net income received since the last payment date and the remaining 50 per cent shall be added to the principal of this trust to be invested and reinvested in accordance with the terms hereof. This manner of payment shall continue until two hundred twenty years have elapsed from the date of my death.
>
> "(C) Two hundred twenty years from the date of my death, my Trustee is to increase the percentage of income payable to 75 per cent, and the other 25 per cent shall be added to the principal of this trust to be invested and reinvested in accordance with the terms hereto. This manner of payment shall continue every twenty years on the anniversary date of the date of my death until four hundred years have elapsed from the date of my death.
>
> "(D) Four hundred years from the date of my death this trust shall terminate, and the principal of this trust and any accumulated and undistributed income shall be paid over to THE RIGHT WORSHIPFUL GRAND LODGE OF FREE AND ACCEPTED MASONS OF PENNSYLVANIA, for the use of the Masonic Homes at Elizabethtown, Pennsylvania, absolutely."

The Masonic Grand Lodge filed a petition for leave to deviate from the administrative terms of the trust, asserting that the provision for accumulation of income is unreasonable and illegal, and seeking annual distribution of income. The Commonwealth, as *parens patriae* in charitable trusts, appeared by the Attorney General in support of the petition. Fidelity-Philadelphia Trust Company, Executor, filed an answer. On October 9, 1961, the estate came on for audit.[74]

The auditing judge dismissed the petition of the Grand Lodge. Exceptions filed by the Attorney General were dismissed by the court en banc (three of the six members agreeing). That court affirmed the adjudication of the auditing judge directing distribution in exact compliance with the terms of the will and in accord with the literal wording of the Estates Act of 1947, April 24, P.L. 100, § 6(b) (1), added Feb. 17, 1956, P.L. (1955) 1073, § 3, 20 P.S. § 301.6(b) (1) (Supp. 1963). This appeal by the Commonwealth followed.

The concept of what constitutes a charitable trust is a continually expanding one. On the record before us, and under applicable law, there is no question but that testator established a charitable trust.

The basic issue for determination is the proper construction of the legislative direction that the statutory provisions under which accumulations of income are declared void shall not apply to accumulations of income for charitable purposes. Estates Act of 1947, April 24, P.L. 100, § 6(b) (1), added Feb. 17, 1956, P.L. (1955) 1073, § 3, 20 P.S. § 301.6(b) (1) (Supp.1963). Interpretation of this provision must be in accord with the presumption "[t]hat the Legislature does not intend a result that is absurd, impossible of execution or unreasonable." Statutory Construction Act, May 28, 1937, P.L. 1019, § 52(1), 46 P.S. § 552(1).

The majority below observed, "That the instant record discloses no present absurdity in the prospective growth of this prescribed accumulation does not close the door to proof of such fact (if it should become a fact) in the future." To the contrary, as our determination here indicates, we are in complete accord with the observation of the concurring and dissenting opinion that "it is not necessary for the Court to await future events to determine whether the accumulation provisions of this trust prove absurd or unreasonable. The inevitability of such result is now apparent."

Furthermore, the court interpreted the statute in its strict, literal sense and held that it was without authority to pass on the reasonableness of the accumulations directed. In doing so, the court erred. We may not view the statute as the mere utilization of words em-

74. On October 3, 1961, the executor filed an "Analysis of Projected Principal and Income." The approximate corpus of the residuary trust was $41,500. With the expected increase from the life estate in trust, the residuary trust corpus was estimated at $52,500. Under the formula for accumulation provided in the will, compounding interest at 3%, and without considering profits or losses in the administration of the trust, the estimated value of the trust in March, 2360, would be $14,411,000. (This is the figure given in appellee's brief. According to the dissenting opinion, the figures at various rates are: 3%—$16,270,940; 4%—$150,414,516; 5%—$1,595,511,171; 6%—$19,242,724,745.)

[This footnote is by the court; others by the court have been omitted. Ed.]

ployed in an exclusively literal sense without regard to the social circumstances, charitable needs and public policy surrounding the legislation. So considered, its provisions require the application of a doctrine of reasonableness.

The concurring and dissenting opinion persuasively commented:

"The division in the Court arises because the Auditing Judge and those of our colleagues who agree with him appear to have concluded that Section 6(b) (1) of the Estates Act of 1947, as amended 1956–1957, P.L. 1073, 20 P.S. § 301.6(b) (1) must be interpreted strictly and literally regardless of how unreasonable the direction to accumulate income may be. Such a construction could easily lead to an absurd result, which the Legislature obviously did not intend as for example, a direction to accumulate the income on a trust principal of $10,000 for a period of 10,000 years.

* * *

"Charitable trusts are favorites of the law because they are in relief of the public burden. * * * It follows necessarily from this legislative favoritism that the legislative intent inherent therein is that the benefits flowing from such gifts in trust should directly, currently and reasonably perform their function and not be unduly postponed. Therefore, it is the duty of this Court, in the furtherance of its visitorial powers over charitable trusts, to implement this intent. The adjudication and the majority opinion overlook this basic aspect of the case.

* * *

"The principal of charitable trusts may be held for any period of time even in perpetuity. A literal reading of this statute would authorize the perpetual accumulation of *income* as well as of principal. Obviously, this was not the legislative intent. Such gifts would be ineffectual, would achieve no charitable purpose and would consequently be void as charitable gifts, since no direct benefit would flow from them; their term would be uncertain: Girard [Trust] Company v. Russell [3 Cir.], 179 Federal 446. We must imply that the legislative intent was to further charitable purposes and not to void them. It would, therefore, appear that if income cannot be accumulated perpetually, there must be some stage during the operation of a trust short of perpetuity when the accumulation of income shall cease. At what stage of its operation such event shall occur must be a judicial function in the absence of any legislative direction relating thereto.

"* * * Therefore, the Act must be *liberally* construed; such construction should be consistent with the Pennsylvania legislative intent of its tax exempting statutes and thus brought into line with the law in practically all of the other states of the union, all of which subscribe to the 'reasonableness doctrine'. * * *"

The dissenting opinion appropriately noted:

"The majority makes reference to Benjamin Franklin's famous will. It is probably the most extreme illustration of accumulation of income in the books. This will has been sustained in Benjamin Franklin's Estate, 27 W.N.C. 545 and 150 Pa. 437 [24 A. 626]; Benjamin Franklin Administratrix v. City of Philadelphia et al., 2 D.R. 435; City of Boston v. Doyle et al., [184 Mass. 373, 68 N.E. 851] 68 N.E.2d 662. However, none of these cases specifically ruled upon the point now at issue. Moreover, in Benjamin Franklin's Estate, supra, 27 W.N.C. 545, 548, the illustrious Judge Penrose quoted with approval Gray on Rule Against Perpetuities, [§ 678 (4th ed. 1942)] viz.:

" ' "And where there is an unconditional gift to charity, the gift will be regarded as immediate and good, although the particular mode of carrying out the charity which the donor has indicated is too remote. Consequently, in such a case, *if a direction for accumulation is too remote, the only result is that the income is immediately distributable in* charity; the heirs or next of kin are not let in." ' " (Emphasis supplied) [Emphasis indicated in opinion below.]

"It is notable that the corpus and the accumulated income in Dr. Franklin's trust were to be put to work immediately and continuously throughout the 200 years of its existence to afford assistance to young and impecunious artificers by providing them with loans at 5% interest, which was less than the current rate, and without collateral security. How different the instant case, where a portion of the accumulations is to lie idle for 400 years! * * *

"* * * [T]he 'reasonable' test is generally accepted and applied throughout the United States. It is approved by text writers. Analysis of the Pennsylvania statute and cases fails to disclose clear legislative or judicial policy to set the law of Pennsylvania apart from that of the other states on this subject. It follows that this court has the power and the duty to apply the 'reasonable' test to charitable accumulations. This historic court, founded by Penn on the pattern of the famous Court of Orphans in London and grounded in the application of equitable principles, is not impotent to vary a trust which will continue until the accumulations reach astronomical size 400 years from now."

See 4 Scott on Trusts § 401.9, at p. 2886 (2d ed. 1956).

The will of Frank James supplies no indication of purpose for the 400 year accumulation provision, nor does it, either by express language or by implication, reveal any particular plan or need for retaining accumulations over such an extended period of time. We are satisfied, however, that the settlor intended to benefit the charity rather than to demonstrate by the device of a lengthy charitable accumulation the effect of accumulation of income and the compound interests tables. In reality, were we to sustain the accumulation of wealth in the amount and manner contemplated, we would demonstrate the latter effect rather than implement the settlor's primary charitable intention. We are reluctant to ascribe to testator the paramount desire merely to turn an approximately $50,000 trust fund into a final gift of almost $15,000,000, at the expense of immediate social needs.

No case has been cited to us, nor have we been able to locate any authority, which appears to recognize the validity of a proposed gift whose enjoyment is delayed for a period of four centuries without apparent reason.

We hold, therefore, that the provisions for accumulation of income are unreasonable and void as being unnecessary, charitably purposeless and contrary to public policy as well as to testator's primary charitable intention.

We turn now to the issue of what is to be done with the income. We are unable to agree with the conclusion of the concurring and dissenting opinion that all the income be accumulated for twenty successive periods of twenty years and that the income accumulated during such period be distributed at the end of each period. Although this distribution pattern would follow that established in testator's will, on this record, such an accumulation of income for 20 twenty-year periods has no apparent practical or reasonable purpose.

Had the will provided some guide as to testator's plan or purpose, there might be some basis for that scheme of distribution. But testator did not point to capital improvements or to any other needs of the charitable institution which ordinarily could not be met by drawing on current funds, nor did he indicate any other motivation for his plan. The projected scheme of delayed distribution prevents practical, effective use of the fund in question, and, as such, is unreasonable.

It is, however, clear that testator's plan of accumulation was merely incidental to his primary charitable intention to create a source, perhaps in the nature of an endowment fund, which would provide continuing income over the 400 year term for the maintenance of the Masonic Homes. The result we reach is in harmony with his primary and controlling charitable objective.

We are not without some guide as to the proper disposition of the income. Section 7 of the Estates Act of 1947, April 24, P.L. 100, § 7, added Feb. 17, 1956, P.L. (1955) 1073, § 3, 20 P.S. § 301.7 (Supp. 1963), requires, in those situations controlled by it, that "[i]ncome subject to a void direction or authorization to accumulate shall be distributed to the person or proportionately to the persons in whom the right to such income has vested by the terms of the instrument or by operation of law." While this charitable trust is not governed specifically by this provision, it is pertinent to observe that in Section 7, the Legislature has approved immediate distribution.

Even though our laws favor the accumulation of income and wealth for philanthropy, nevertheless, gifts and the accumulation of income for unreasonably long periods offer many opportunities for disservice to immediate charitable needs as well as to those of remotely future generations.

It has been prophetically observed that no human being, no matter how wise or experienced, is able to foresee the special needs of society, even one or two generations away, let alone 400 years hence. Shifting and advanced social concepts, programs and concerns emphasize the hazards of seeking to correct or alleviate social problems so distantly removed from testator's generation. We conclude, therefore, that the testator's primary charitable intention is best attained by making available to the beneficiary the income of the trust on a current basis.

Accordingly, the decree below is vacated, and this matter is remanded for the entry of a decree consistent with this opinion. Costs upon the estate.

BELL, C. J., dissents.

NOTE

In both of the preceding cases the testator attempted to set up a charitable scheme which merely called for accumulation without a concrete objective such as financing a library or hospital building. How can the court test the "reasonableness" of the accumulation except against a definite charitable plan? Or is there a social interest in allowing accumulation of income in order to provide substantial capital for future benefit of charity?

A private non-operating foundation may obtain IRS permission to set aside income for a long range project of up to five years on a showing that the project can better be accomplished by accumulation than by immediate payment; and can set aside without permission for a project not to be completed before the end of the taxable year if requirements as to payouts for designated periods in the law are met. If it does not meet these conditions, the foundation must distribute its entire adjusted net income not later than the end of the following year. This income includes investment income, exempt interest and net short term capital gains. If the income is not so distributed, that which is undistributed is subject to a 15% tax which is increased to a 100% tax after a "correction period".[75]

McKinney's New York Estates, Powers and Trusts Law contains two interesting provisions relating to accumulation of income in charitable trusts. One of these makes any such accumulation subject to the court as to "reasonableness, amount and duration" and empowers the court to prohibit or limit accumulation despite an otherwise valid direction or authority.[76] The other feature of the New York statute empowers the court to authorize an accumulation despite the absence of a direction in the trust instrument and also grants the trustee implied authority to accumulate income "to the extent necessary to carry out the purpose of the trust."[77]

PROBLEM

After small legacies the testator left the residue of his estate to a trustee to invest and accumulate the income until the principal and accumulated income amount to one million dollars, to be held as a permanent fund for the benefit of the local hospital with income to be paid to the hospital semi-annually thereafter. The gross value of the estate is $117,000. Is the accumulation provision valid? See Frazier v. Merchants National Bank of Salem, 296 Mass. 298, 5 N.E.2d 550 (1936).

75. IRC § 4942, 26 U.S.C.A. as amended P.L. 94–455 § (a)(b) 2002 (1976).

76. McKinney's N.Y., EPTL, § 8–1.-1(e) (1980 Supp.). See Glasser, "Trusts, Perpetuities, Accumulations and Powers Under the Estates, Powers and Trusts Law," 33 Brook.L.Rev. 551 (1967).

77. Ibid. § 8–1.7.

Chapter XVII

ADMINISTRATION

Scope Note

The materials in this Chapter focus upon major problems in fiduciary administration. The functions, powers and duties of trustees and personal representatives are compared in an effort to emphasize common fundamentals in legislative and judicial policies applicable to them. At the same time, these statements of legislative and judicial policy are episodic, tending to be made in large numbers after economic depressions have dragged fiduciaries to disaster. Many cases are thus used in this chapter to emphasize the importance of considering the social and economic environment when a decision in fiduciary law is being developed. The corporate professional fiduciary, for example, as a part of this new environment, is exercising influence that is often decisive over the development of the new fiduciary law. In no area of property law are practices changing so rapidly and in few areas do social and economic facts loom so large in decisions by courts, legislatures and administrative officers.

Section 1 compares functions of various types of fiduciaries—the personal representative, the trustee, the guardian or conservator, the custodian for a minor—and evaluates the modern role of the corporate fiduciary. Section 2 considers reasons why administration of a decedent's estate may be required and statutes dispensing with administration in small estates. In Section 3 are developed various problems relating to jurisdiction of courts in the administration of estates and trusts (ancillary administration, trusts involving a foreign element, and federal jurisdiction over administration). Section 4 explores the fiduciary office: appointment, qualification, removal and the all-important determination of compensation. Section 5 looks at the fiduciary in his primary role, that of manager of property and investor. The fiduciary duty of loyalty and the duty not to delegate are covered in Sections 6 and 7. Distribution problems, including rules for determination of principal and income, are examined in Section 8. Accounting problems are studied in Section 9, and the chapter concludes with Section 10, exploring remedies of the beneficiary for breach of trust and defenses of the fiduciary.

SECTION 1. INTRODUCTION

Procedural Law

The law governing the administration of a decedent's estate is to a large extent concerned with procedure. What documents must be filed in probate court and when? How many days' notice to heirs and creditors must be given? Must it be given personally, or will publication be sufficient? Almost all of this is regulated by statutes with wide variation in detail, and even within a single state there may be local "practice" differences from county to county. On the other hand, the administration of a trust is much less subject to continual court supervision; an inter vivos trust is free from any court supervision until one of the interested parties seeks some form of judicial relief. But in most states the testamentary trust remains subject to the probate court jurisdiction even after the estate proceedings are "closed". However, even in trust administration, statutory regulation is increasingly important and, except for uniform legislation, differs from state to state.

This variation in detail should not obscure common fundamentals; and an understanding of common fundamentals by the student facilitates his training in the legal skills required in fiduciary administration. The lawyer deals with problems in fiduciary administration primarily in three contexts—each requiring different techniques. The lawyer may draft the basic instrument (will or trust agreement). He may serve as counsel to the fiduciary, advising him relative to a safe course of conduct (or as counsel for someone dealing with the fiduciary, such as a purchaser). He may serve as an attorney for one of the parties in litigation, usually in a suit by the beneficiaries against the fiduciary. Of course the lawyer may participate in fiduciary administration in other contexts—perhaps serving in this position or serving as a draftsman preparing new fiduciary legislation. In examining fundamentals of judicial and legislative policies concerning fiduciary administration we must also be alert to the "skill lessons" to be derived from the cases and materials. The cases, for example, can teach draftsmen not only problems to be provided *for* but also court attitudes to be guarded *against*. A careful analysis of a case in the context in which it was decided can suggest the probable reshaping in the future of the problem with which it deals and probable changes in judicial attitudes that will take place by the time the reshaped problem is presented for decision. These considerations are relevant both to the task of the draftsman and to the task of the counsellor. Cases also show, usually by the unhappy display of bad examples, the desirable ways to handle litigation and harsh lessons in relevancy of evidence and techniques of presentation.

The traditional text emphasizes the contrast between the personal representative and the trustee, rather than the similarities. It is true that the historical background is to an extent different, and legal theory reflects these differences.

The personal representative is thought of as appointed by the court, even though named by will as executor; the trustee is usually selected by the settlor. The personal representative is subject to probate court jurisdiction, the trustee to equity jurisdiction. The personal representative has title only to the personalty, whereas the trustee has legal title to realty as well. The stated function is different. The function of the personal representative is to take possession of the personal property of the deceased, to liquidate the property so far as necessary to pay expenses, claims and taxes and then to distribute the balance to those entitled under the will or, in case of intestacy, to the next of kin; it is a liquidating function, winding up the affairs of the deceased. The normal period for this function is one year, but it may run more or less. The trustee, on the other hand, has a continuing function, that of managing the property over the duration of the trust. That will normally be for the period of the life or lives of the income beneficiary or beneficiaries; but it may, as in the case of the charitable trust, run indefinitely.

Yet, impressive as the dissimilarities are, the likenesses are even greater in modern law. The executor derives his powers just as much from the testator as the trustee does from the settlor; while the administrator is court-appointed, so is a successor trustee where the trust instrument provides no machinery for appointment. The testamentary trustee cannot act in many states until formally appointed by the probate court any more than can the personal representative. The scope of the fiduciary's power will be fixed by court where the instrument is silent, but the same powers may be conferred expressly on either a trustee or a personal representative. Under the Uniform Probate Code, the personal representative is a fiduciary subject to the same standard as a trustee,[1] and derives his powers from a statutory grant.[2] His power over title is "in trust" for creditors and others interested in the estate.[3] Except in supervised administration the personal representative is as free from court control as is a trustee of an inter vivos trust. In Code states the probate court has jurisdiction over all trust matters,[4] though not continuing control and supervision. In non-Code states a testamentary trust is often thought of as an extension of the administration of the decedent's estate, with the probate court appointing the testamentary trustee, requiring annual accounting, and retaining control as well as jurisdiction over the testamentary trust; in such states only the inter vivos trust remains the concern of the equity court.

Moreover, the problems faced by the executor and the trustee are similar. They are both fiduciaries and subject to the duties imposed upon those who deal with property belonging to another (whether they hold legal title or merely a power of sale); these common duties are discussed in the next section. What property shall be retained in specie and what liquidated for distribution, either at the end of the estate or at the end of the trust? Which receipts shall be treated as

1. Uniform Probate Code § 3–703(a).

2. Uniform Probate Code § 3–715.

3. Uniform Probate Code § 3–711.

4. Uniform Probate Code § 7–201.

income and which as principal? Both the personal representative and the trustee face these problems.

Consider the "blending" of functions in the following typical situation. A will devises the residue of the estate to a trustee in trust to pay the income to the widow for life, at her death to turn the principal over in equal shares to the testator's children then living, and the will names the same individual (or trust company) as both executor and trustee. Here the fiduciary performs both functions, and frequently is given expressly identical powers by the will in both capacities. Although the period of administration will be formally terminated with a final accounting after creditor's claims have been determined and paid, expenses and taxes paid, and legacies and bequests set aside, it is not easy to draw a clear-cut line between the functions of the fiduciary during this period. Obviously the purpose of the trust is in a sense to prolong the ultimate distribution of the residue, thus partially transferring this function from probate to the trust. During probate is the function of the fiduciary to liquidate, or should he commence, at least in part, his management functions?

Although this chapter is primarily concerned with the personal representative and the trustee, a third type of fiduciary whose function partially resembles estate administration and partially the trust is the guardian. The law with respect to guardians is today almost wholly statutory, although there are historical antecedents in common law.[5] A guardian may be appointed with respect to the person or property, or both, of a minor or a mental incompetent. The terminology varies widely from state to state; in some states the guardian of an incompetent is called a "committee"; elsewhere the guardian of property may be referred to as a "conservator".

The parent is, of course, natural guardian of his or her minor child. However, he is only guardian of the child's person, not his property; a court appointment is necessary to give a parent management and control of the minor's property. Often a common concern of a young married couple with children is to be able to designate a particular relative or friend to act as guardian of minor children if both parents are killed in a common accident or die otherwise. Such a designation may in most states be made by will; [6] in states adopting the Uniform Probate Code the appointment is achieved by probate of the will of the parent and acceptance by the named guardian; court confirmation is unnecessary.[7] The will should of course also provide for management of property left for care of the children; this

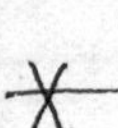

5. The standard American text is Woerner, American Law of Guardianship (1897) now quite out of date. Short treatments of value are Mackay, Law of Guardianships (3d. Ed. 1980); Mathiasen (Ed.), Guardianship and Protective Services for Older People (1963); Weissman, Guardianship as a Way of Fulfilling Public Responsibility for Children (1949).

6. Wren, Creative Estate Planning (1970), Vol. 1 at 232–237.

7. Uniform Probate Code § 5–202; if the minor is 14 years or older he may block the appointment, or force termination, under § 5–203 simply by filing a written objection with the probate court. There are similar provisions for testamentary appointment for a retarded adult child or an incompetent spouse in § 5–301.

should be done by testamentary trust with any life insurance proceeds payable to the testamentary trustee, unless an inter vivos trust has already been set up.

Obviously the guardian of property is somewhat similar to a trustee. He is subject to most of the fiduciary duties. He manages property over an extended period, with both income and expenditures. There are significant differences, however. The guardian has no title and acts only under court authority; his function is almost that of an agent of the court. His accounting to the court is more like that of the personal representative, but the court will raise issues on its own motion to protect the ward. As to investment powers, dependent on local statutes, the guardian generally lacks the discretion available to the trustee. Jurisdiction over guardianship today is usually vested in the probate courts, although in a few states concurrent jurisdiction is in the equity courts on the basis of English precedent (the English Court of Chancery at an early date assumed jurisdiction to appoint guardians of the property of minors).[8]

Often judicial proceedings may involve the property rights of a minor. The court will then appoint a guardian ad litem, whose sole function is to protect the interests of the minor during the course of the particular proceedings; by practice or statutory requirement the court will appoint only an attorney. However, if there is a general guardian of the minor's property, that person will represent the minor unless he has an adverse interest in the litigation; remember, however, that the parent is not such a guardian without court designation. For instance, X has been judicially appointed guardian of the property of his minor child Y. X's wife dies and X is appointed administrator of her estate. Since X's interests as administrator conflict with Y's interests as heir, a guardian ad litem would have to be appointed to represent Y in the administration proceedings. The function of the guardian ad litem is limited to the course of the litigation. Thus, if a minor were given a pecuniary legacy under the terms of a decedent's will, a guardian ad litem would be appointed to protect the minor's interests during the course of probate; upon distribution a guardian of the minor's property would have to be appointed to

8. The relative importance of guardianship is indicated by the following statistics which are believed to be representative of the situation throughout the United States. For the calendar year 1978 Arkansas Probate Courts had 1,871 guardianships, compared with total probate filings of 9,934 and pending decedents' estates of 14,797 at the end of the year. Fourteenth Annual Report of the Judicial Department of Arkanas, page 72. In Iowa during 1979 there were 3,197 guardianships and conservatorships opened compared with 19,484 decedents' estates. 1979 Annual Statistical Report by the Court Administrator of the Judicial Department of Iowa, Table 5(a) page 77. In Ohio for the fourth quarter 1980 (October 1 to December 31), 2,277 guardianships were filed compared to 14,724 decedents' estates. Report of the Administration Director of the Supreme Court of Ohio for the fourth quarter of 1980 at page 35. During the calendar year 1979 in Oregon 2,027 guardianships were filed compared with 4,846 decedents' estates. Twenty-sixth Annual Report relating to Judicial Administration in the Courts of Oregon, 1979, at page 55. For the year 1979 the New York Surrogates' Courts granted letters of guardianship in 5,911 proceedings compared with 55,144 letters in decedents' estates. Report of the Chief Administrator of the Courts for Calendar Year 1979 (N.Y.Legis. Doc. No. 90, 1980), Table 48.

receive the legacy. Statutes frequently allow limited amounts to be deposited in a bank in the name of a minor without appointment of a guardian, to be turned over to the minor upon attaining majority.

Article 5 of the Uniform Probate Code, where adopted, completely changes the basic concept of property guardianship. The person appointed to protect property of a minor or of a person unable to manage his property effectively is called a "conservator." The conservator is given the title to the property which a trustee would have (Section 5–420). He is granted specifically by the Code broad powers of management which can be exercised without court order (Section 5–424). In other words the Code takes the conservator out from under the tight court supervision which now prevails and in effect makes him a trustee. Moreover, the court may authorize by order limited acts without appointment of a conservator; for example, if a person aged 20 is still under disability as a minor but wishes to mortgage or sell realty, a protective order to that effect could be entered by the same court which handles probate (Section 5–409). The court also has powers which go far beyond the traditional concept of conserving property; thus the court may exercise or direct the exercise of any powers which the protected person could exercise if not under disability, except the power to make a will. For example, the court could authorize creation of a revocable trust for the protected person, or the making of gifts, or the release of a power of appointment (Section 5–408). The conservator may also expend income or principal without court order for the support, education, care or benefit of the minor or incapacitated person and his dependents (Section 5–425). The Code should therefore remove the disadvantages of guardianship or conservatorship which prevail in many states today.

Another feature of the Code should result in less need for creation of inter vivos trusts or appointment of a conservator, as a means of providing management for property. This is the Code provision for a power of attorney which recites: "This power of attorney shall not be affected by disability of the principal"; under the Code such a power is exercisable by the agent notwithstanding subsequent disability of the principal or later uncertainty as to whether he is alive or dead (Section 5–501). Even ordinary powers of attorney (without such a recital) can be exercised by an agent despite the disability or death of the principal if the agent has no actual knowledge of the disability or death (Section 5–502). These provisions of the Code are, of course, contra to the common law rules which have discouraged use of powers of attorney. Powers of attorney therefore become a much more effective device, particularly to handle management of affairs of a person for a temporary period.

The fact that courts, zealous in their self-appointed role of protector of minors, have interpreted statutory provisions strictly against guardians and the scarcity of case authority on many guardianship issues have made attorneys cautious of this as a device for handling property of a minor. If substantial amounts of property are being willed to a minor, the trust device is more popular. The limits of the trust are known, and its flexibility permits almost any family objective. A grandparent X wishes to leave $10,000 for the support and education of a minor grandson Y; his will is accordingly drawn to leave the $10,000 to a trustee in trust to pay or apply the principal and income for the support and education of the beneficiary Y until he reaches 21 and then to turn over to him any unexpended balance. If the amount is small, so that the trust is uneconomical, some lawyers prefer to avoid guardianship complications by leaving the property to a close relative with precatory language. Thus X wishes to leave small amounts of $500 to each of his grandchildren to be used for their education; his will is drawn to leave the appropriate amount to X's children with the request that it be used for the education of the respective grandchildren. Section 5–103 of the Uniform Probate Code is designed to facilitiate payment to minors; payment of $5,000 per annum due to a minor can be paid to the minor if he is married, or to a person having care and custody of the minor (normally a parent) or to any guardian, or by deposit in the name of the minor in a federally insured savings account. Small cash legacies for minors can be handled under this provision in Code states; in some states it is common practice to insert in the will a clause authorizing the personal representative to make payment of the legacy to a parent on behalf of the minor and providing that receipt of the parent is a discharge of the obligation of the personal representative.

To facilitate inter vivos gifts to minors without using a trustee or guardian, all American states now have statutes permitting delivery of types of personal property to a "custodian", the minor having absolute title. The minor is prevented from wasting the property and its transfer is simplified. The gift is viewed as a present gift for federal gift tax purposes, permitting the donor to take the $10,000 annual exclusion.[9] There are two Uniform Acts for Gifts to Minors which are in force, most of the states having the Uniform Gifts to Minors Act (1956) [10] with several having the Revised Uniform Gifts to Minors Act (1966).[11] The Uniform Act of 1956 permits gifts of money for investment and permits any adult person or a trust company to serve as custodian. There are differences in the two acts relative to the powers of the custodian as to distribution. The Uniform Gifts to Minors Act (1966) extends the description of permissible depositories of funds by custodians; it includes life insurance contracts and annuities as possible subjects of gifts; and it has provisions for facilitating the appointment of successor custodians. Forms for the gifts are prescribed in all of the Acts and the powers and duties of the custodian are set forth. These powers and duties parallel many of those associated with trustees and guardians. It cannot be determined, however, until these statutes are extensively construed by the courts, which will take many years, to what degree the courts will be pre-

9. If a spouse makes the gift to a third party, it may with consent of the other spouse be "split" between them, so that $20,000 may be given with no federal gift tax consequences. I.R.C. § 2513, 26 U.S.C.A. Prior to 1982 the exclusion was $3,000 so a split gift then would have been $6,000.

10. Uniform Laws Ann., Estate, Probate and Related Laws 225 (1972).

11. Id. at 181.

pared to "read into" the acts powers and duties developed by analogy from those of trustees or guardians.

Corporate professional fiduciaries, serving as trustees or in other fiduciary capacities, are having a decisive role in the current development of fiduciary law. Although corporations were specially chartered with power to exercise trust functions more than a century ago, the concentration of trust business in the hands of corporations is a phenomenon of the present century. These trust institutions are of three types: the trust company (which is organized under state law), the state bank authorized to do trust business, and the national bank granted a permit by the Comptroller of the Currency to act in fiduciary capacities.

The following general statistics for all federally insured commercial banks, savings banks and certain trust companies reporting to the Federal Reserve Board illustrate the phenomenal volume of business conducted by corporate fiduciaries; for the calendar year 1980 these institutions were administering 871,084 personal trust accounts with assets of $210.8 billion, 97,447 estates with assets of $18.1 billion, 290,623 employee benefit trusts with assets of $175.2 billion, and 125,918 agency accounts (other than employee benefit) with assets of $113.2 billion. The average size of personal trust accounts was $242,000 but varied widely according to the size of the trust department.[12]

While many trusts in rural areas are still managed by individual trustees, the urban trust business has largely passed into the hands of the trust institutions. Although some trust institutions have been reluctant to serve as co-trustees with individuals, it is possible to name an individual and trust company as co-trustees, thereby combining the features of continuity, specialized experience, and expert personnel of the trust company, with the advantage which an individual better acquainted with the personal needs of the beneficiaries may enjoy in dealing with the beneficiaries.

The rise of the corporate fiduciary has introduced a fundamental issue: should the standards developed historically for the individual serving as trustee be applied equally to the trust institution? A definite difference in legislative treatment is apparent, and the development of dual standards by the courts is beginning to be noticeable. On the one hand, the trust institution by its advertising holds itself forth to the public as possessing specialized skills, hence may be properly charged with having that skill. On the other hand, the trust institution is subject to periodic inspection by public officials, and to other safeguards such as deposit of securities to protect against defalcation;[13] this makes it possible to relax some of the normal legal

12. "Trust Assets of Banks and Trust Companies—1980," Report of the Board of Governors of the Federal Reserve System, Federal Deposit Insurance Corporation, and Office of the Comptroller of Currency: Federal Financial Institutions Examination Council (1981), Trust Assets, Tables 1, 3.

13. See Part 9, Fiduciary Powers of National Banks and Collective Investment Funds set forth in Appendix 2, infra. ("Regulation 9")

safeguards set up to protect beneficiaries against mishandling by individual trustees.

In recent years rapidly rising costs have discouraged corporate fiduciaries in acceptance of trusts having small amounts of capital, which they can only operate at a loss to them, or with reduced services, or at a heavy fee to the customer.[14] This has led to interest in creation by state legislation of the Office of Public Trustee.[15]

In decedents' estates, trusts and conservatorships (guardianships of property) the fiduciary usually employs a lawyer as legal counsel. Fees for the lawyer are paid out of the estate, however. Whom does the lawyer represent? Is only the fiduciary his client to whom he owes a duty of loyalty? Or does the lawyer have a duty to the beneficial owners? If the lawyer knows of breach by the fiduciary of the duties considered in this chapter, can and should he inform the beneficial owners (or the court) if the fiduciary refuses to follow the lawyer's legal advice? Is the lawyer liable to the beneficial owners in negligence if he should with reasonable diligence have known of the breach? Historically lawyers in this role have thought of themselves as representing only the fiduciary. However, the fiduciary's duties run to the beneficial owners, and there may be a derivative duty on the lawyer for the fiduciary. There is little law to date.[16]

---

14. Gelfand, Trusts Without Trustees, 115 T. & E. 8 (1976).

15. "The Public Trustee—Is It the Answer for Modest Sized Estates, Trusts and Conservatorships?", 10 R.P.P. & T.J. 321 (1975). For a discussion of the English system, see Fratcher, Probate Can Be Quick and Cheap (1968), p. 11. A few states already have authorized such a public office, intended to handle estates and conservatorships which would not be accepted by anyone else. See Ariz.Rev. Stat. § 14–5601 (Public Fiduciary); West's Ann.Cal.Welf. & Inst. Code § 8000 (Public Guardian).

16. The California courts have apparently as a policy matter taken the opposite position that only the fiduciary can be sued for his breach of duty; the lawyer is the fiduciary's lawyer. Estate of Lagios, 118 Cal.App.3d 459, 173 Cal.Rptr. 506 (1981); Baldock v. Green, 167 Cal. Rptr. 157, 109 Cal.App.3d 234 (1980) (here there was no negligence by the attorney; cash was distributed to the person who was personal representative but in his capacity as life tenant under the will; the wrongful act was by the life tenant in depositing the funds in a joint account with only one of the remaindermen; the distribution itself was proper). In Fickett v. Superior Court, 27 Ariz.App. 793, 558 P.2d 988 (1976), the court took the view that the lawyer for a conservator could be liable for negligence in failing to discover and disclose that the conservator was misappropriating funds and making improper investments. The case involved an incompetent beneficial owner. Whether the same rule would apply to decedents' estates and trusts with competent beneficiaries is a matter of opinion. The New York Surrogate's Court has recently held that trust beneficiaries may not sue the lawyer for the trustee for negligently counseling the trustee to make an improper trust investment. Matter of Will of Newhoff, 107 Misc.2d 589, 435 N.Y.S.2d 632 (1980).

SECTION 2. REASONS FOR ADMINISTERING A DECEDENT'S ESTATE

The need for court intervention in the disposition of an owner's wealth at his death arises in modern times from several factors: (1) settlement of family disputes over succession (probate of a will or determination of heirs); (2) protection of the commercial world (financial institutions and purchasers) in dealing with decedent's property; (3) formal transfer of title from decedent's name to the heirs or devisees; (4) provision for creditors to collect claims against the decedent and for assuring the successors that they receive title free of the threat of such claims; and (5) establishing responsibility for payment of taxes—federal and state death and income taxes.

There are simple estates in which these problems do not arise. A man dies intestate; his probate estate consists solely of $100,000 in cash and bearer bonds; his wife is dead and his two adult children constitute his sole heirs. The only probable creditor claims are outstanding medical bills and, of course, the funeral expenses. The children take possession of the cash and bonds, pay the bills and funeral expenses, and divide the remainder. Because the greatly increased credit on the federal estate tax removes estates of this and even larger size from its scope, there is no federal estate tax concern. If the state has a death tax reaching the smaller estates, it may be possible to settle the tax problems administratively with the state tax authority.

As soon as the property is the kind that involves "title" considerations, third persons may be unwilling to deal directly with the heirs concerning the property unless they are protected by court proceedings. Suppose the property is not in the form of readily available cash and bearer bonds but part is in a savings account. Would the bank pay out to the children? Or suppose $10,000 is in the form of stock registered in the name of the decedent. How could the heirs obtain a transfer of the stock into their names or the name of a purchaser from them? This problem of title is basic to administration. It involves determinations of the fact of death, which is jurisdictional, the presence or absence of a validly executed will, or, in the absence of a will, the persons who are heirs.

Of equal importance is the machinery for presenting and paying claims against the estate. Historically real property was not subject to claims of unsecured creditors on death of the owner; this is now universally changed by statute. While court proceedings protect creditors, they can also protect those acquiring the property from later assertion of claims. This second goal is accomplished by "nonclaim" statutes. These are short statutes of limitations and bar claims which could be but are not presented in the required time.[17]

The use of the administration proceedings as part of the tax collection machinery of government is a modern afterthought. The determination of the value of the decedent's various property interests is already necessary for various reasons. For example, filing fees and in some states fees of the personal representative are generally based on value of the estate assets set by appraisal. It is possible to utilize that same valuation process for tax purposes. And the personal representative is a readily available person on whom to impose responsibility for filing tax returns and for paying the tax due. However, it should be noted that tax problems can be handled administratively, without court intervention. The federal estate tax is administered by the Internal Revenue Service; the government is protected by tax liens on decedent's property; appraisals in the probate court proceedings do not bind the Service. Nor is the Service generally bound by rulings of the local probate court on substantive matters.[18]

As to personalty common law vested title in the personal representative. Hence anyone dealing directly with the next of kin or legatees ran the risk that a personal representative might be appointed later and bring suit to recover the assets for the estate. Even today if heirs sue to obtain decedent's personalty, as on a promissory note payable to the decedent, some courts will dismiss the suit on the theory that only a duly appointed personal representative has title; other courts allow the heirs to proceed if they prove that all debts have been paid and no administration is necessary. If all estate assets are exhausted in payment of debts and funeral expenses, proceedings serve no purpose and a court will not appoint a personal representative on petition of an heir.[19]

Real property poses special problems, largely because of the complexities of title transfer in American law and the inherent conservatism of the industry engaged in assuring land titles, whether title insurance companies or lawyers who perform title examination in states where title insurance does not prevail. At common law an estate of inheritance in land passed directly to the heirs or devisees, free of claims of unsecured creditors; a personal representative had no right, even to possession of the land; and a will could be proved in any action involving an issue of title. In modern times, real property is subject to creditor claims and usually any personal representative has at least the power to sell realty to satisfy creditor claims and taxes; possible death taxes may result in tax liens; unknown heirs or devisees are a potential threat; and realty is easy to pursue even in the hands of a good faith purchaser. Hence court proceedings become a practical necessity to clear title in most estates involving real

17. For the nonclaim statutes, see Section 5(8), infra.

18. Commissioner v. Estate of Bosch, 387 U.S. 456, 87 S.Ct. 1776, 18 L.Ed.2d 886 (1967).

19. Waterhouse v. Churchill, 30 Colo. 415, 70 P. 678 (1902).

property. Affidavits to prove succession and freedom from claims and taxes necessarily involve risk for a purchaser of the land.[20] Local title standards or insurance company practice may accept affidavits to establish marketable title for realty of small value or after lapse of several years from death of the decedent owner when creditor claims are barred or unlikely, or when adverse possession provides additional title assurance.

There is a definite statutory trend toward reducing administration, either eliminating it altogether in certain kinds of estates or reducing it to a summary proceeding.[21] The trend is manifest in several developments: (1) widespread adoption of an affidavit procedure for collecting personal property in small estates, (2) summary (shortened) administration in other small estates, (3) statutory provisions to shore up title in successors after several years, and (4) recent proposals to adopt the civil law system of universal succession. Note also that nonprobate assets are not subject to administration and, as we have seen throughout the course, the variety of arrangements recognized as nontestamentary as well as the volume of assets passing through such arrangements is increasing. Creditor groups have not presented opposition to the enactment of these statutes.[22] There are a variety of possible reasons: (1) institutional lenders rely on security interests which are not affected by the changes; (2) many institutional creditors carry insurance against death of their debtors; (3) the small estate is probably exempt anyway and the creditor can write the loss off on his income tax return; and (4) tort claimants, even when represented by an organized group like the College of Trial Lawyers, rely primarily on collecting against the decedent's liability insurance rather than estate assets.

Statutes in many states now provide for collecting personal property[23] of the decedent as well as money owed to the decedent by affi-

20. Siedel v. Snider, 241 Iowa 1227, 44 N.W.2d 687 (1950). For a general discussion of this problem see Report of Comm. on Admin. & Dist. of Decedents' Estates, Clearing Titles of Heirs to Intestate Real Property, 10 Real Prop., Prob. & Tr.J. 454 (1975).

21. See Atkinson, Wills (2d Ed., 1953) § 103; "Recent Statutes—Streamlining the Administration of Small Estates", 49 Mich.L.Rev. 111 (1950).

22. For example, when Virginia Code (1950) § 46.1–94, permitting the transfer by affidavit of title to a motor vehicle owned by a decedent was being considered by a legislative committee during a general revision of the Virginia Motor Vehicle Code in 1958, it was suggested that the value of the vehicle so transferred be limited, or else that such transfers be permitted only when the total estate was below a designated value. There was no interest in the Committee whatever concerning such a limitation, although "creditor" interests were certainly represented in its membership, the major concern being with the difficulties the Commissioner of Motor Vehicles might have in administering the section. This appears to be typical of the adoption of proposed small estate laws. Delay in adopting them is produced more by the pressure of other legislative business than by opposition to the proposed laws as such.

23. The UPC does not provide for transferring title to realty by affidavit. A Model Small Estates Act approved by the National Conference of Commissioners on Uniform State Laws in 1951 did provide a procedure for recording an affidavit of title to realty without appointment of a personal representative, but required published notice to any person having a claim to commence administration within a specified period [three months]. The affidavit could be used only if the total estate was small in value. Some states modeled their affidavit statutes on the Model Small Estates Act and

davit presented to the person holding the property or owing the debt, the latter being protected if he acts on the basis of the affidavit. Sections 3–1201 and 3–1202 of the Uniform Probate Code provide an affidavit procedure if the value of the entire estate is $5,000 or less, and a number of Code states have increased the amount to $10,000.[24] In a few non-Code states the amount is substantial.[25] In some states a limited version of the affidavit procedure can be used as to bank accounts. Statutes may also protect an employer owing wages and other compensation to a deceased employee if the employer makes payment to the surviving spouse; these statutes have been enacted at the request of employers, who are anxious to clear their books of such obligations.[26] Summary administration, in some states called "set aside" provisions, shortens regular administration when the estate assets are only sufficient to meet exempt property and allowances passing to the family and priority claims such as administration expenses, funeral expenses and expenses of last illness; there being no property for general creditors, further proceedings would be meaningless, the assets can be distributed, and the administration be closed. The Uniform Probate Code provisions for summary administration are found in Sections 3–1203 and 3–1204. As the Code suggests a homestead allowance of $5,000, exempt property of $3,500 and a family allowance of $6,000 without necessity of a court order (totalling $14,500), many smaller estates can be settled quickly and simply, even if realty is involved.

The Uniform Probate Code contains provisions to minimize need for administration when nothing has been done about opening administration for several years after the decedent's death: (1) title to both real and personal property passes directly to heirs or devisees (Sections 3–101, 3–901),[27] (2) administration is barred unless commenced within 3 years after death (Section 3–108), (3) unsecured creditors are likewise barred 3 years after death because they can only pursue

permit real property to be transferred, with dollar limits and protection such as filing a bond. See Vernon's Mo.Ann. Stat. § 473.077 (1981 Supp.) (limited to $10,000, requires bond but no publication); Vernon's Ann.Texas Stat.Prob. Code §§ 137–142.

24. E.g., Ariz.Rev.Stat. § 14–3971B; Colo.Rev.Stat. § 15–12–1201; Utah Code Ann. § 75–3–1201.

25. West's Ann.Calif.Prob. Code § 630 ($30,000 plus $5,000 salary); Vernon's Ann.Tex.Stat.Prob. Code § 137 ($50,000 plus homestead and exempt property). The statutory limits are deceptive if decedent's assets are partially nonprobate (e.g., joint tenancy) and if all or part of the property is community property (only half being included in decedent's estate). By contrast New York's procedure for settling estates without administration is limited to $5,000 and requires a filing with the Surrogate Court. McKinney's N.Y. SCPA §§ 1301–1312 (1981 Supp.).

26. E.g., Ariz.Rev.Stat. § 14–3971A (compensation not exceeding $5,000); Ga. Code Ann. § 66–103 (wages payable to spouse or minor children not exceeding $2,500); Wis.Stat.Ann. § 109.03(3) (full amount).

27. Uniform Probate Code § 3–901 reads:

"In the absence of administration, the heirs and devisees are entitled to the estate in accordance with the terms of a probated will or the laws of intestate succession. Devisees may establish title by the probated will to devised property. Persons entitled to property by homestead allowance, exemption or intestacy may establish title thereto by proof of the decedent's ownership, his death, and their relationship to the decedent. * * *"

their claims through a personal representative (Section 3–104; see also 3–803). If there has been no administration, and there is a will, a devisee who has taken possession under the will can prove his title without probate (Section 3–102); in other cases the will would have to be probated within 3 years after death (Section 3–108), but the Code permits formal or informal probate (proof of the will) without appointment of a personal representative (Section 3–107). Proof of death would be necessary to show succession, but can be made without court proceeding, as is done in joint tenancy in most states.

A proposed Uniform Succession Without Administration Act at the time of writing is being drafted by a committee of the National Conference of Commissioners on Uniform State Laws. The Act is patterned on the civil law system now in force in Louisiana and Quebec. The heirs in an intestate estate, or the residuary devisee under a will, would be able to take over the decedent's property as "universal successor" by assuming liability for payment of debts and taxes, and in the testate estate by also assuming responsibility for satisfying general and specific devises under the will. A simple court procedure would give the applicant the necessary title.[28] A limited version of this system has recently been adopted in California; the surviving spouse, if entitled to the decedent's half of community and quasi-community property by intestate succession or by will, can elect to dispense with administration of such property.[29] The spouse becomes personally liable for debts chargeable against the community and quasi-community property. Unlike the civil law system where liability for decedent's debts is unlimited,[30] the liability of the spouse is limited to the amount of the nonexempt community and quasi-community property. A simple proceeding to confirm title results in a court order determining that the described property is community or quasi-community property passing to the surviving spouse.

The lawyer owes his client a duty to minimize the expense of handling any estate. In many jurisdictions there are now one or more of the above options available which the lawyer must consider. It may well be that administration is necessary, or it may be desirable under the circumstances of the particular estate, not only for legal reasons (the estate is a separate entity for federal income tax purposes and tax savings may be important in larger estates) [31] but also for practical reasons (to provide emotional assurance to the family). Two situations in which administration is almost always desirable are (1) estates in which there are many creditor claims, as where an unincorporated sole proprietorship business is involved, and (2) es-

28. Compare Ga.Code Ann. § 113–1232 which provides for dispensing with administration by petition to the probate court, stating that there are no debts and the heirs have agreed upon a division of the estate; there is publication of notice to creditors to show cause why an order should not be entered dispensing with administration. This procedure does not apply to testate estates, but there is no stated dollar limit.

29. West's Ann.Calif.Prob.Code §§ 650–657 (1981 Supp.).

30. Atkinson, Wills (2d Ed. 1953) pp. 562–3.

31. Moore, "The Advantages of Probate," 10 Inst.Est.Plan. ch. 4 (U. Miami 1976) (discussing mainly tax considerations but also noting use of probate to cut off creditors claims).

tates with valuable real property. As the value of the realty increases, so does reluctance of title examiners and title insurance companies to assure buyers of the marketability of a title based on any procedure other than an administration which will bar creditors and determine succession.

PROBLEM

Your client is the widow and sole heir of decedent and has paid the funeral expenses and expenses of the last illness. There are no outstanding debts. Assume the decedent was domiciled in your jurisdiction and determine how the following assets could be transferred to your client without the necessity of administration; you should check local statutes for any relevant provisions, since the references given are general.

(1) A few shares of stock listed on the New York exchange, registered in the name of decedent. See Christy, The Transfer of Stock (5th Ed. 1972) § 145.

(2) United States Government bonds of $500 denomination issued in the name of the decedent. See 31 Code Fed.Reg. § 306.65 et seq.

(3) A small bank account in decedent's name.

(4) An automobile with certificate of title in name of decedent.

(5) Wages due decedent from his employer.

(As to 3, 4, 5, check your local statutes for provisions authorizing payment or transfer if the amount involved is small.)

(6) A promissory note of a third party, who is unwilling to pay on the basis of an agreement of your client to indemnify any loss. Compare McBride v. Vance, 73 Ohio St. 258, 76 N.E. 938 (1936) representing the majority rule, with Metropolitan Life Insurance Co. v. Fitzgerald, 137 Ark. 366, 209 S.W. 77 (1919).

(7) An insurance policy with no beneficiary designated but with a "facility of payment" clause reading:

> "The Company may make payment * * * to the Executor or Administrator of said Insured or to any relative by blood or connection by marriage, or to any person appearing to the Company to be equitably entitled thereto by reason of having incurred expense in any way on behalf of the Insured for burial or for any other purpose; and the receipt of any such payee shall be conclusive evidence that * * * all claims under this policy have been fully satisfied."

See 2A Appleman, Insurance Law and Practice (1966) ch. 69; Dickin v. John Hancock Mutual Life Insurance Co., 254 N.Y.S. 607, 142 Misc. 452 (Mun.Ct. 1931).

Would your answer be the same if there were children who are all competent and over twenty-one and who have signed a "family settlement" agreement assigning all of their interests to the widow? See Brown v. Baxter, 77 Kan. 97, 94 P. 155, 574 (1908).

You will note that no additional transfer problems are created if there are unlimited amounts of property in joint tenancy, United States bonds payable on death to the widow, or insurance with designated beneficiaries. However, such property is included in an estate for inheritance and estate tax purposes, so that administration may be necessary to remove tax liability. Hence, if real estate is held in joint tenancy, the survivor may be unable to transfer to a purchaser until tax clearance is obtained; similarly, a bank may be unwilling to release funds in a joint bank account to the survivor because of statutes imposing liability on the bank under such circumstances. The same is true of stocks registered in the name of decedent and another as joint tenants, as the transfer agent may be liable for the transfer. Here again, if the total amount of probate and nonprobate assets is not large, there is no problem of a federal estate tax (the credit of $62,800 in 1982 means there is no tax unless the taxable estate exceeds $225,000; the credit escalates until 1987, with the result that there will be no tax in that year unless the estate exceeds $600,000). State death taxes vary widely. If the probable amount of the taxable estate does not exceed exemptions (reasonably substantial for a widow and minor children), state tax authorities usually will issue a waiver or a consent to the particular transfer.

SECTION 3. JURISDICTION OVER ADMINISTRATION

---

(1) ANCILLARY ADMINISTRATION OF DECEDENTS' ESTATES

LEVE v. DOYLE

Supreme Court, Special Term, New York County, Part I, 1958.
13 Misc.2d 274, 177 N.Y.S.2d 617.[32]

WM. C. HECHT, JUSTICE. This is a motion to vacate a warrant of attachment and the levy thereunder on various grounds.

Plaintiff is ancillary administrator in this State of the will of Denis P. S. Conan Doyle, who died a resident of Switzerland. The defendant is admittedly a nonresident of this State, who has not been served with process in this jurisdiction. This is not an action to recover assets of the decedent located in the State of New York. Defendant accordingly contends that the plaintiff, as New York ancillary administrator, does not possess a cause of action against him to collect his alleged indebtedness to the decedent.

It is well settled that the power of the Surrogate's Court of this State to appoint an ancillary administrator is dependent upon the existence in the State of assets of the decedent (In re Rogers' Will, 225 App.Div. 286, 232 N.Y.S. 609, affirmed 254 N.Y. 592, 173 N.E. 880). In that case Mr. Justice Proskauer, writing for the Appellate Division, said (225 App.Div. at page 289, 232 N.Y.S. at page 613):

> "A proceeding for ancillary administration is directed against assets within the state * * * so in the case of ancillary administration the decree can have no effect, except as it may be satisfied by property within the reach of process of our courts * * *. An ancillary administration in this state, without assets

32. Aff'd 6 A.D.2d 1033, 178 N.Y.S.2d 1017 (1958).

presently here for administration, would be mere *brutum fulmen*".

That an ancillary administrator is limited to the collection of assets of the deceased located in this State is the view taken in leading texts (5 Warren's Heaton on Surrogates' Courts, p. 459, subds. 1b and 1c; 2 Jessup Redfield Surrogates Law and Practice, Rev.Ed., p. 1639).

In Fox v. Carr, 16 Hun 434, the court declared that if the claim in suit did not constitute an asset of the decedent within this State, the plaintiff, as ancillary administrator appointed in this State, could not maintain the action. The court upheld the action only on the theory that the defendant, who had been personally served in this State, had brought into this State the decedent's chose in action against him, the situs of a debt following the debtor.

In Dempsey v. Guaranty Trust Co. of New York, 138 F.2d 663, certiorari denied 321 U.S. 785, 64 S.Ct. 781, 88 L.Ed. 1076, the Circuit Court of Appeals, of the Seventh Circuit, held that a grant of ancillary letters gave the ancillary administrator only the limited authority to act in collecting and disposing of personal property within the confines of the State where he was appointed.

In Lockwood v. United States Steel Corp., 153 App.Div. 655, 138 N.Y.S. 725, 728, an ancillary administrator appointed in New York, for the estate of a decedent who died while domiciled in Bermuda, sued to compel the defendant, a New Jersey Corporation, which had a transfer office in New York, to transfer to a nominee of the plaintiff the shares of stock of defendant which had come into the plaintiff's hands. The Appellate Division dismissed the complaint on the ground that "The authority of the ancillary executor is * * * strictly limited to personal property within the jurisdiction of his appointment". The court held that the situs of the stock was in New Jersey and not in New York. The Court of Appeals reversed (209 N.Y. 375, at pages 384–385, 103 N.E. 697, at page 700, L.R.A.1915C, 471), holding the existence of defendant's transfer office in New York State constituted New York as the domicile of the corporation "to some extent at least * * * so far as the registry and transfer of shares thereunder are concerned". It is true, as plaintiff points out, that the court in an earlier portion of its opinion had said (209 N.Y. at page 380, 103 N.E. at page 698): "We do not perceive that it makes any essential difference *in this case* whether the letters of the plaintiff executor are ancillary or domiciliary. Ancillary administration in this State is regulated by statute, and an ancillary executor or administrator has the same general powers as a domestic executor or administrator * * *". (Italics supplied.) The fact that the court used the words "in this case" and that it went on to devote the major portion of its opinion to the proposition that the situs of the stock was in this State indicates, however, that the court did not mean to hold that an ancillary legal representative may collect assets of the decedent which are not situated within the State. What the court appears to have intended by the language previously quoted was merely that for the purpose of compelling a transfer of stock certificates physically within the possession of the ancillary administrator within this State, his powers are the same as those of a domiciliary legal representative. Apart from the fact that the quoted language was only dictum and limited to "*this case*", the observations made therein must be deemed overruled by the subsequent affirmance by the court of the holding of the Appellate Division in Matter of Rogers' Will, supra, that ancillary administration is limited to assets of the decedent physically located within the ancillary jurisdiction.

The statute referred to by the Court of Appeals was the present Section 166, Surrogates' Court Act, which, in the same language, had formerly been Section 2636 of the Code of Civil Procedure. That section appears to have been intended to refer only to the powers of ancillary representatives *in matters coming within their jurisdiction.* To interpret it as broad enough to confer jurisdiction upon them without the presence in this State of assets of the decedent would be utterly irreconcilable with the reasoning of the Rogers case, supra.

To permit an ancillary administrator to enforce collection of a debt due to the estate of a nonresident decedent from a nonresident, not present or served in the ancillary jurisdiction, could possibly subject the debtor to a double liability since the domiciliary legal representative might not be bound by the judgment in the action. The only case cited by plaintiff, in support of his right to sue here, was decided in Delaware and is contrary to the authorities above referred to, as well as to the text writer heretofore cited.

The motion to vacate the attachment and the levy thereunder is, accordingly, granted. It is therefore unnecessary to consider the other grounds of the motion.

NOTE

Death, domicile and assets are the three touchstones for jurisdiction to administer a decedent's estate. Death as a jurisdictional prerequisite to probate of a will has been considered in Chapter VII, Section 1. A determination of death is likewise important in an adjudication of intestacy.

Assuming the property owner is dead, the primary situs for administration of his estate is his domicile—usually described as the *domiciliary* administration. Administration may be had in the domicile of the decedent without a showing of assets. Each state, however, is entitled to make its own determination of domicile; and for this reason two or more domiciliary administrations may be conducted at the same time—although this is unusual.[33] If a decedent has assets in a state other than his domicile, it may be necessary to conduct an *ancillary* administration in the foreign state. If an ancillary administration is necessary, the domiciliary administrator or executor usually receives the ancillary letters, although the local law may require a domestic personal representative, serving alone or with the domiciliary ad-

33. E.g. Colvin v. Jones, 194 Mich. 670, 161 N.W. 847 (1917); See 2 Beale, Conflict of Laws (1935) § 450.9.

ministrator.[34] Foreign trust companies may not be permitted to receive ancillary letters.[35]

An ancillary administration is conducted in the same manner as a domiciliary administration. The assets of the decedent are collected, local taxes and creditors are paid. When the obligations of the decedent are satisfied in the state of ancillary administration, the assets are usually then remitted to the state of domiciliary administration to be applied to the debts of the decedent there and then distributed in accordance with his will or the domiciliary intestate law.[36] The ancillary representative is considered an officer of the court which appoints him, just as the domiciliary representative is considered an officer of his court. If the same person holds both offices, he is an official representative of the courts in both states. But if the representatives are different persons, there is said to be no privity between them; and an action by one administrator is not barred by an action by the other in which there is a decision for the defendant,[37] and there is no *res judicata* in an action against one representative when the action is brought against the other in the second state.[38]

Problems in ancillary administration sometimes arise when the total estate is insufficient to pay all creditors in both states but the ancillary assets are sufficient to pay the local creditors. What should the court in the ancillary jurisdiction do? See that the local creditors are paid in full or try to insure that the creditors in both states are paid an equal proportion? It has been suggested that a preference of local creditors over creditors in the domicile is a violation of the privileges and immunities clause.[39] The court in the ancillary administration should withhold the assets until it assures that local creditors will be treated as well as creditors in the domicile. A reciprocal responsibility exists in the domiciliary jurisdiction. At best a difficult problem in coordination is presented.

It may be possible to secure assets in a foreign state without ancillary administration. Avoiding ancillary administration often proves desirable for a number of reasons. The overall cost of administering the estate is reduced and accounting problems involving administration expenses in the foreign state are avoided at decedent's domicile. The chance that a foreign state will

34. E.g., Virginia Code § 26–59.

35. Statutes of this type usually are obtained by local trust companies to reduce foreign competition for estate business. Although there might be difficulty in obtaining jurisdiction over the foreign company, there would be none if the company was permitted to qualify as ancillary administrator.

36. In a few cases the ancillary property has not been delivered. E.g. In re Lane's Estate, 199 Iowa 520, 202 N.W. 244 (1925); In re De Lano's Estate, 181 Kan. 729, 315 P.2d 611 (1957); Comment, "Jurisdiction Over Administration of Intangibles in Light of the De Lano Decision," 6 Kan.L.Rev. 439 (1958). In some states, statutes authorize the court to either direct distribution to the successors or deliver the residue to the domiciliary personal representative. In re Estate of Radu, 35 Ohio App.2d 187, 301 N.E.2d 263 (1973).

37. Ingersoll v. Coram, 211 U.S. 335, 29 S.Ct. 92, 53 L.Ed. 208 (1908). Restatement, Conflict of Laws 2d (1971) § 353 (but suit is barred if the same person sues as executor in both states). Contra: Peare v. Griggs, 8 N.Y.2d 44, 167 N.E.2d 734 (1960).

38. Brown v. Fletcher's Estate, 210 U.S. 82, 28 S.Ct. 702, 52 L.Ed. 966 (1906); Restatement, Conflict of Laws 2d (1971) § 356. But a judgment in favor of a representative in one state precludes a claimant from suing on the same claim against a representative in another state. Id. § 357.

39. In re Braun's Estate, 276 Mich. 598, 268 N.W. 890, 106 A.L.R. 889 (1936). See, "Possibilities of a Claimant Barred by Nonclaim Statute of Domiciliary Jurisdiction Recovering Against an Ancillary Administrator", 41 Iowa L.Rev. 271 (1956); 34 A.L.R.2d 1270 (1954).

impose taxes on property found there will be reduced if there is no foreign administration. Uncertainties in conflict of laws doctrines may be avoided.

On the other hand, ancillary administration may be desirable or necessary in a particular estate. If it is necessary to sue in a foreign state, the personal representative usually will have to qualify there as an ancillary administrator. Often property of a decedent which comes under federal control may be paid over to a relative named in a federal statute or regulation. If this payee is in a state other than the domicile of decedent, the personal representative may have to sue in a foreign state and thus have to qualify there. Exceptions to this general rule are made as, for example, when the asset to be recovered is not subject to creditors' claims—such as recoveries under a death by wrongful act statute.[40]

A domiciliary personal representative who is to collect debts in a foreign state without exact knowledge of the creditors of the decedent there may seek ancillary letters for his own protection. Knowledge of the decedent's activities in the foreign state may be obscure so that ancillary administration may produce information vital to the proper administration of the estate. Some domiciliary fiduciaries are not sufficiently skilled to be permitted to collect assets in another state without judicial supervision there. There may be foreign land to be cleared of creditor claims by administration of the personal estate at the situs of the land.[41]

In large commercial centers, such as New York, banks by their own rules may pay over small deposits to foreign domiciliary personal representatives without local administration, although the representative must agree to exonerate the bank from liability for subsequent claims to the deposit. An increasing number of statutes provide for withdrawing assets without ancillary administration after certain formalities are accomplished, such as publication of notice to creditors.[42] In foreign countries other than those applying the common law there usually will be no administration of the estate in the sense here discussed. Complicating factors in foreign countries are diverse conflict of laws problems—concerning the domicile of the decedent, for example—local demands for public revenue and currency controls. The usual pattern of liquidation is for the heir to receive the assets and pay the debts without formalities. In certain areas in which the civil law applies but which have also been influenced by common law traditions it may prove virtually impossible to escape without ancillary administration especially when dealing with funds already in the hands of trustees. In Scotland, for example, where many American personal representatives seek to recover assets, all ancillary administrations are handled by the Commissary Court (Sheriff's Court) of Edinburgh. The letters of administration issued by the American court must also be under the seal of the Secretary of State of the American State and under the seal of the Consular Section, British Embassy. The so-

40. See Atkinson, Wills (2d Ed., 1953) 586.

41. For a survey of these problems see Alford, "Collecting a Decedent's Estate Without Ancillary Administration", 18 S.W.L.J. 332 (1964); Currie, "The Multiple Personality of the Dead: Executors, Administrators, and the Conflict of Laws", 33 U. of Chi.L.Rev. 429 (1966) (Emphasizing actions by and against foreign personal representatives); Report of Subcommittee on Administration of Out-of-State Assets by Corporate Trustees of Committee on Trust Administration and Accountability of Trustees of American Bar Association, 103 Trusts and Estates 997 (1964). See "Ancillary Administration—Procedures and Expenses" 1 Real Prop.Prob. & T.L.J. 498 (1966); "Estate Administration: Current Practices and Proposed Uniform Probate Code" 3 Real Prop.Prob. & T.L.J. 143 (1968); Note, "Executors and Administrators: Estate Necessary to Support Ancillary Administration", 20 Okla.L.Rev. 448 (1967).

42. E.g., Virginia Code, § 64.1–130.

licitor retained to collect the assets must have a power of attorney to yield up the Inland Revenue Inventory and collect and remit the assets.

Uniform legislation relating to ancillary administration is highly desirable. Nevertheless, early attempts by the National Conference of Commissioners on Uniform States Laws (the Uniform Probate of Foreign Wills Act, the Uniform Powers of Foreign Representatives Act, and the Uniform Ancillary Administration of Estates Act) did not meet with wide success.[43] Article IV of the Uniform Probate Code is a comprehensive effort to deal with the problem.[44] It is set forth below. You will note that it offers three possible approaches to facilitate handling of assets located outside the domiciliary jurisdiction: (1) a facility of payment provision to protect persons voluntarily making payment or transferring personalty on the basis of an affidavit by the domiciliary personal representative; (2) an administrative proceeding whereby the domiciliary representative may file in the probate court of the ancillary jurisdiction an authenticated copy of his appointment and acquire the same powers (including power to sue) as if he were appointed by the ancillary probate court; and (3) a provision giving the domiciliary representative priority if appointment of an ancillary administrator is sought, as when local creditors seek an ancillary administration to protect their rights (Section 3–203(g), not reproduced here). To protect local creditors the Code also provides that the foreign personal representative subjects himself to suit in the ancillary state by utilizing the payment or filing provisions, (1) and (2) above. And of course the local creditors can always institute a formal proceeding for administration and foreclose use of the payment or filing provisions. Other Sections of the Code not reproduced here are also relevant to the problems of inter-state estates: (1) once a will is probated formally in the domicile, the matter cannot be relitigated in the ancillary administration (Section 3–408); (2) if an ancillary administrator is appointed first, the domiciliary personal representative can insist on taking over the ancillary administration (Section 3–611(b)); (3) claims barred in the domiciliary jurisdiction before the first publication of notice to creditors in the ancillary jurisdiction are barred in both places (Section 3–803(a)(1)); (4) some unity of treatment of claims in the insolvent estate is achieved (Section 3–815); and (5) the ancillary administrator, upon completion of administration, must generally turn over assets to the domiciliary personal representative (Section 3–816).

43. 9 Uniform Laws Ann. 62 (1957). See Atkinson, "The Uniform Ancillary Administration and Probate Acts", 67 Harv.L.Rev. 619 (1954). Useful references bearing upon ancillary administration are III Beale, Conflict of Laws 1444–1597 (1935); McDowell, Foreign Personal Representatives (1957); Basye, "Dispensing with Administration", 44 Mich.L.Rev. 329, 394–419 (1945); Beale, "Voluntary Payment to a Foreign Administrator" 42 Harv.L.Rev. 597 (1929); Cheatham, "The Statutory Successor, the Receiver and the Executor in Conflict of Laws, 44 Colum.L.Rev. 549 (1944); Goodrich, "Problems of Foreign Administration", 39 Harv.L.Rev. 797 (1926); Hopkins, "Conflict of Laws in Administration of Decedent's Intangibles", 28 Iowa L. Rev. 422, 613 (1943); Mersch, "Voluntary Payment to Foreign Administrator," 18 Geo.L.J. 130 (1930); Stimson, "Conflict of Laws and the Administration of Decedents' Personal Property," 46 Va.L.Rev. 1345 (1960); "Conflict of Laws—Wills and Administration—Ancillary Administration of Decedent's Stock," 31 N.Y.U.L. Rev. 1092 (1956).

44. Wellman, "How the Uniform Probate Code Deals With Estates That Cross State Lines", 5 Real Prop., Prob. and T.L. J. 159 (1970); Vestal, "Multiple-state Estates Under the Uniform Probate Code", 27 Wash. & Lee L.Rev. 70 (1970); Comment, "The Need for Reform in Multistate Estate Administration," 55 Tex.L. Rev. 303 (1977) (outlining the wide variation in procedures for handling local property of non-domiciliaries and urging a flexible, uniform system such as the Uniform Probate Code).

Uniform Probate Code, Article IV [Foreign Personal Representatives: Ancillary Administration—§§ 4–101 through 4–401] is as follows:

"PART 1

"DEFINITIONS

"Section 4–101. [Definitions.]

"In this Article

"(1) 'local administration' means administration by a personal representative appointed in this state pursuant to appointment proceedings described in Article III.

"(2) 'local personal representative' includes any personal representative appointed in this state pursuant to appointment proceedings described in Article III and excludes foreign personal representatives who acquire the power of a local personal representative pursuant to Section 4–205.

"(3) 'resident creditor' means a person domiciled in, or doing business in this state, who is, or could be, a claimant against an estate of a non-resident decedent."

"PART 2

"POWERS OF FOREIGN PERSONAL REPRESENTATIVES

"Section 4–201. [Payment of Debt and Delivery of Property to Domiciliary Foreign Personal Representative Without Local Administration.]

"At any time after the expiration of sixty days from the death of a nonresident decedent, any person indebted to the estate of the nonresident decedent or having possession or control of personal property, or of an instrument evidencing a debt, obligation, stock or chose in action belonging to the estate of the nonresident decedent may pay the debt, deliver the personal property, or the instrument evidencing the debt, obligation, stock or chose in action, to the domiciliary foreign personal representative of the nonresident decedent upon being presented with proof of his appointment and an affidavit made by or on behalf of the representative stating:

"(1) the date of the death of the nonresident decedent,

"(2) that no local administration, or application or petition therefor, is pending in this state,

"(3) that the domiciliary foreign personal representative is entitled to payment or delivery."

"Section 4–202. [Payment or Delivery Discharges.]

"Payment or delivery made in good faith on the basis of the proof of authority and affidavit releases the debtor or person having possession of the personal property to the same extent as if payment or delivery had been made to a local personal representative."

"Section 4–203. [Resident Creditor Notice.]

"Payment or delivery under Section 4–201 may not be made if a resident creditor of the nonresident decedent has notified the debtor of the nonresident decedent or the person having possession of the personal property belonging to the nonresident decedent that the debt should not be paid nor the property delivered to the domiciliary foreign personal representative."

"Section 4–204. [Proof of Authority-Bond.]

"If no local administration or application or petition therefor is pending in this state, a domiciliary foreign personal representative may file with a Court in this State in a [county] in which property belonging to the decedent is located, authenticated copies of his appointment and of any official bond he has given."

"Section 4–205. [Powers.]

"A domiciliary foreign personal representative who has complied with Section 4–204 may exercise as to assets in this state all powers of a local personal representative and may maintain actions and proceedings in this state subject to any conditions imposed upon nonresident parties generally."

"Section 4–206. [Power of Representatives in Transition.]

"The power of a domiciliary foreign personal representative under Section 4–201 or 4–205 shall be exercised only if there is no administration or application therefor pending in this state. An application or petition for local administration of the estate terminates the power of the foreign personal representative to act under Section 4–205, but the local Court may allow the foreign personal representative to exercise limited powers to preserve the estate. No person who, before receiving actual notice of a pending local administration, has changed his position in reliance upon the powers of a foreign personal representative shall be prejudiced by reason of the application or petition for, or grant of, local administration. The local personal representative is subject to all duties and obligations which have accrued by virtue of the exercise of the powers by the foreign personal representative and may be substituted for him in any action or proceedings in this state."

"Section 4–207. [Ancillary and Other Local Administrations; Provisions Governing.]

"In respect to a non-resident decedent, the provisions of Article III of this Code govern (1) proceedings, if any, in a Court of this state for probate of the will, appointment, removal, supervision, and discharge of the local personal representative, and any other order concerning the estate; and (2) the status, powers, duties and liabilities of any local personal representative and the rights of claimants, purchasers, distributees and others in regard to a local administration."

"PART 3

"JURISDICTION OVER FOREIGN REPRESENTATIVES

"Section 4–301. [Jurisdiction by Act of Foreign Personal Representative.]

"A foreign personal representative submits himself to the jurisdiction of the Courts of this state by (1) filing authenticated copies of his appointment as provided in Section 4–204, (2) receiving payment of money or taking delivery of personal property under Section 4–201, or (3) doing any act as a personal representative in this state which would have given the state jurisdiction over him as an individual. Jurisdiction under (2) is limited to the money or value of personal property collected."

"Section 4–302. [Jurisdiction by Act of Decedent.]

"In addition to jurisdiction conferred by Section 4–301, a foreign personal representative is subject to the jurisdiction of the courts of this state to the same extent that his decedent was subject to jurisdiction immediately prior to death."

"Section 4–303. [Service on Foreign Personal Representative.]

"(a) Service of process may be made upon the foreign personal representative by registered or certified mail, addressed to his last reasonably ascertainable address, requesting a return receipt signed by addressee only. Notice by ordinary first class mail is sufficient if registered or certified mail service to the addressee is unavailable. Service may be made upon a foreign personal representative in the manner in which service could have been made under other laws of this state on either the foreign personal representative or his decedent immediately prior to death.

"(b) If service is made upon a foreign personal representative as provided in subsection (a), he shall be allowed at least [30] days within which to appear or respond."

"PART 4

"JUDGMENTS AND PERSONAL REPRESENTATIVE

"Section 4–401. [Effect of Adjudication for or Against Personal Representative.]

"An adjudication rendered in any jurisdiction in favor of or against any personal representative of the estate is as binding on the local personal representative as if he were a party to the adjudication."

---

(2) TRUSTS INVOLVING A FOREIGN ELEMENT

BOONE v. WACHOVIA BANK & TRUST CO.

United States Court of Appeals, District of Columbia, 1947.
82 U.S.App.D.C. 317, 163 F.2d 809.

WILBUR K. MILLER, ASSOCIATE JUSTICE. [Footnotes are omitted.]

These appeals involve the validity of a judgment removing a testamentary trustee which was entered, pursuant to the application of the beneficiaries, by a North Carolina Court which had admitted the will to probate, established the trust thereunder and appointed the trustee, and was exercising supervision over the administration. The order of removal is attacked by the deposed trustee because process on the application for removal was not served on him in North Carolina and he did not appear or answer.

Prior to 1940, Frances M. Lightner died testate, a resident of and domiciled in North Carolina. She nominated her son-in-law, Daniel F.

Boone, as executor of her will and as trustee thereunder. Boone was also a North Carolinian at that time. The will was duly admitted to probate in the Superior Court of Polk County, North Carolina, and Boone qualified as executor and trustee. Later he sued in the Superior Court for a construction of the will with respect to the trust imposed upon certain personalty and, having obtained the court's opinion, proceeded with the administration of the trust.

In the same court, on November 25, 1942, the beneficiaries of the trust filed a complaint against the trustee, seeking his removal. Boone had left North Carolina in 1940 and had taken the trust assets with him to the District of Columbia. Service was had on him in the removal proceeding by publication and, in addition, a summons was served on him in the District of Columbia by a United States marshal, both notifications being authorized by North Carolina statutes. He was not served in North Carolina, however, and did not appear or plead in response to the removal petition; but, more than a year after the filing of that petition, Boone filed in the court in which it was pending his fourth annual accounting as trustee.

The Superior Court entered judgment on February 7, 1944, removing Boone as trustee and appointing Wachovia Bank & Trust Company as his successor. As a basis for its decree, the court found as facts that Boone's misconduct in handling the trust fund had resulted in a loss of $11,490.56, for which judgment against him personally had theretofore been rendered by the Superior Court, and affirmed by the Supreme Court of North Carolina and the Supreme Court of the United States; that without the approval or authority of the court or any court he had removed the trust fund to the District of Columbia; and that in other respects he had acted improperly. It was determined that he was an unfit, unsuitable and improper person to act as trustee. The successor trustee was expressly authorized and directed to institute and prosecute in any jurisdiction such actions as might be necessary to obtain possession of the trust assets.

Pursuant to that authority, the successor trustee sued Boone on April 2, 1945, in the District Court of the United States for the District of Columbia to recover all assets of the trust estate and to obtain an accounting. He answered, stating that he was testamentary trustee under the will of Frances M. Lightner, and that the proceedings in North Carolina to remove him as trustee had been instituted after he had moved his domicile from that state to the District of Columbia, and after he had brought the trust assets to the District. He pleaded that he had not appeared in the removal proceeding and he had not been served in North Carolina with respect thereto; that, therefore, the alleged successor trustee had no power or authority to maintain in any jurisdiction an action for recovery of the trust assets.

Summary judgment was granted to Wachovia, and Boone was ordered to surrender to it all assets which he held as trustee. The action having also been referred to the District Court's auditor, Boone filed with him on July 29, 1946, a verified account. Later the District Court confirmed the auditor's report, which disallowed commissions claimed by Boone, without prejudice to his right to claim them in the North Carolina court.

The appellant assigns as error the District Court's refusal to dismiss the complaint, its grant of summary judgment to Wachovia, and its denial of commissions.

It is thus seen that we are called upon to decide whether the North Carolina removal judgment was entitled to full faith and credit in the District Court, as the appellee contends, or was not so entitled because, as the appellant argues, he was denied due process of law.

If a judgment of a state court is to be accorded full faith and credit by a court of the United States, it must have been rendered by a tribunal competent by the law of its creation to pass upon the subject matter. The Superior Court of Polk County, North Carolina, being a court of equity, had the inherent power to establish and supervise trusts, to appoint and remove trustees. Such power is not dependent upon statutory authorization nor upon a direction of the instrument of trust, and is as broad and comprehensive as the exigencies of any case may require. Consequently, the Superior Court had the basic right to deal with such a situation.

A court's power to pronounce judgment depends not only on its constitutional authority to deal with cases such as that before it, but also upon its actual jurisdiction over the particular subject matter involved; and, in actions not strictly in rem, upon having the defendant before it by appearance or by service of process, either actual or constructive, as the nature of the proceeding may require or permit.

The Superior Court initially had complete control of the trust relationship, the trust assets, the trust beneficiaries and the trustee. Had the status remained unchanged, there could be no challenge here of its judgment removing the trustee. It did remain unaltered except for Boone's act of establishing a domicile in the District of Columbia and taking the assets with him without authority to do so, either from the will or from an order of the appointing court. Such removal of the assets was wrongful. It was the trustee's duty to administer the trust according to the law of North Carolina, and under the supervision of the court of that state which had established the trust and appointed him as trustee.

The Superior Court of Polk County, having exercised its inherent power as a court of equity to establish a trust over assets subject to its control, and being engaged in supervising the administration thereof by its appointed trustee, did not lose jurisdiction over the trust or the trust assets merely because the trustee wrongfully removed the assets to his new domicile in the District of Columbia nor did the trustee's absence from North Carolina impair or destroy such jurisdiction. Boone's contention that he had deprived the Superior Court of Polk County of jurisdiction over the trust assets by carrying them to the District of Columbia is thus seen to be unsound.

We turn to consider the appellant's argument that his absence from North Carolina had rendered the appointing and supervising court powerless to remove him; for such is the effect of his assertion that, in the circumstances, the order of removal is invalid because he did not appear and was not personally served in North Carolina.

In examining this argument it is of prime importance properly to classify the removal judgment as to whether it was in personam, in rem or quasi in rem. The necessity of determining the form of the action in that respect, in a case such as this, was pointed out by the Supreme Court in Grannis v. Ordean, 234 U.S. 385, 392, 34 S.Ct. 779, 782, 58 L.Ed. 1363, where it was said: "In determining what is due process of law within the meaning of the 14th Amendment, a distinction is to be observed between actions in personam and actions in rem or quasi in rem. In Pennoyer v. Neff, 95 U.S. 714, 733, 24 L.Ed. 565, 572, it was held that by force of the Amendment a judgment rendered by a state court in an action in personam against a nonresident served by publication of summons, but upon whom no [personal] service of process within the state was made, and who did not appear to the action, was devoid of any validity, either within or without the territory of the state in which the judgment was rendered; it being, however, conceded that a different rule obtains, where, in connection with initial process against a person, property in the state is brought under the control of the court and subjected to its disposition, or where the judgment is sought as a means to reach such property or affect some interest in it; in other words, where the action is in the nature of a proceeding in rem. * * *"

Appellant quotes to us, in support of his theory that the judgment removing him is in personam, an excerpt from Parker v. Kelley, C.C., 166 F. 968, 970, and heavily relies upon that case. In the Parker case, a proceeding brought for the sole purpose of removing a trustee was held to be strictly in personam, and a judgment removing him was refused full faith and credit in another sovereignty because the trustee had not been before the removing court by appearance or by personal service. The decision seems to us to be correct, but the present case is distinguishable because of its different factual and legal aspects.

In the cited case, Kelley was named as trustee in a written instrument executed in Massachusetts, and removed the trust assets to New York with the consent of the trustor. No Massachusetts court had asserted or exercised jurisdiction over the trust. The beneficiary instituted in Massachusetts a proceeding to remove the trustee under a statute of that state which provided that a trustee under a written instrument may be removed by the court after notice to him and all interested persons, and after he has been afforded an opportunity to be heard and to show cause why he should not be removed. Kelley appeared specially to challenge the jurisdiction, did not plead to the merits and was not served in Massachusetts. Nevertheless, a judgment of removal was entered. Parker was appointed successor trustee and sued Kelley in the New York federal court to recover the trust assets. Kelley's defense was that the removal judgment was not entitled to full faith and credit. The New York court held that the sole purpose of the Massachusetts proceeding was to remove the trustee, and so that the judgment was in personam.

But in this case, the North Carolina court, prior to its order removing the trustee, had jurisdiction of the trust and was supervising its administration by Boone; he had sought its construction of the trust and had made accounting reports to the Superior Court, one such having been filed by him as we have seen, more than a year after the beneficiaries petitioned that he be removed.

In Parker v. Kelley, the only purpose was to induce a court, theretofore a stranger to the trust, to remove a trustee. Here the trust res was already in the court's hands and under its control, and the question of what trustee should administer it was collateral to the jurisdiction over the res, and the trustee's right to continue to act was at most a right in or to the res, or one which arose therefrom. The distinction which we have pointed out between that case and the present situation is recognized by Freeman in his work on Judgments, where Parker v. Kelley is cited in support of the following textual statement: "Where a trust is created under a written instrument, an action to remove the trustee is a proceeding in personam rather than in rem, and while it might be transformed into a proceeding quasi in rem as to the trust property if that were brought within the jurisdiction of the court, so that constructive service would be sufficient as to the res, yet if both the property and the trustee are in another state when the action is instituted, a judgment of removal upon constructive service is ineffective and not entitled to full faith and credit". [3 Freeman on Judgments 3124] Freeman's consciousness of the factual situation in the Parker case is shown by the fact that he was careful to point out that the removal proceeding there involved might have become quasi in rem had the trust property been brought within the court's jurisdiction; in which event he says constructive service would have been sufficient to cause the judgment of removal to be entitled to full faith and credit.

The Superior Court judgment was, therefore, not in personam. We think it properly falls within the classification known as judgments quasi in rem. The Supreme Court has said that judgments in personam, in rem, and quasi in rem cannot be defined but must be classified as they are encountered. Yet definition has been attempted. A judgment quasi in rem has been described as a judgment against a person with respect to property as distinguished from one against property only, or a person only.

It may be said also that judgments quasi in rem, which lie between the extremes of those strictly in rem or strictly in personam, are so denominated because they affect not only the status of or title to the res, but likewise rights of individuals in or to the res, or arising from it. Such an adjudication is binding and obligatory on the defendant in any court of any state, if he were properly before the court by constructive service of process.

It has been expressly held that the court which appoints a trustee has power to remove him and appoint another in his stead when he goes out of the jurisdiction, and that a proceeding to remove such a trustee is in rem, so that notice to him by constructive process is sufficient. [Letcher's Trustee v. German National Bank, 134 Ky. 24, 119 S.W. 236, 20 Ann.Cas. 815] Our own decisions are to the effect that the court which is supervising the administration of a trust and has jurisdiction of the trust res has power to remove, for cause, a trustee who has been notified of the application for removal only through constructive service of process. D.C.Code (1940), Title 13, § 108; Green v. Brophy, 71 App.D.C. 299, 305, 110 F.2d 539, 545.

In Buchanan v. National Savings & Trust Company, 79 U.S.App. D.C. 278, 146 F.2d 13, 14, a wife sued to have it adjudged that her husband, who was beneficiary of certain trusts established by his father received the income therefrom as a trust fund for the support of his wife and children. The husband, being absent from the District of Columbia, was proceeded against by publication under Title 13, § 108. He made no defense and entered no appearance. We held that the immediate object of the wife's suit to establish the husband's trust income as being also in trust was "to enforce or establish a lawful right, claim or demand against property within the jurisdiction of the court; hence it becomes within the meaning of § 13–108." We further held that the absent husband was not only a beneficiary but a trustee as well; that if he defeated the purpose of the settlor by failing to provide for his child, a court of equity could require the carrying out of the trust and, if necessary, appoint a new trustee for that purpose. See also Morgenthau v. Fidelity & Deposit Company, 68 App.D.C. 163, 94 F.2d 632.

On reason and authority, it is our view that procedure by the appointing court, which already has jurisdiction of a trust and the assets subject to it, to remove an absent trustee who has wrongfully taken the trust assets with him and done other acts justifying his removal, is a proceeding quasi in rem, and that notice by constructive service is sufficient to satisfy the requirements of due process.

In addition to what has been said, for yet another reason due process did not require that a summons issued on the removal petition be personally served on Boone in North Carolina to enable the court to remove him as trustee. The Supreme Court of the United States has held that a petition for the removal of an executor, and for an accounting for the unadministered residue of the estate, is so far a part of the original probate proceedings that the executor is not denied due process of law by a personal judgment for the amount of the unadministered assets, which was rendered against him by publication on account of his absence from the state. [Michigan Trust Co. v. Ferry, 1913, 228 U.S. 346, 33 S.Ct. 550, 57 L.Ed. 867.] The principle is applicable here. It was doubtless in Mr. Pomeroy's mind when he wrote that "a court of equity * * * may and will remove a trustee who has permanently changed his residence to another country, or has absconded." [III Pomeroy's Equity Jurisprudence 2504 (1918 ed.).]

Recognition is given by the Restatement of the Law of Conflict of Laws to the principle that removing an unfit or unsuitable trustee is a part of the general supervisory proceeding in the court in which the trust is being administered, so that the trustee already before the court in the general proceeding, is entitled to no more than constructive notice when his absence from the state makes necessary that form of service. Section 76 of the Restatement is as follows:

> "If a court obtains jurisdiction over a party to an action, that jurisdiction continues throughout all subsequent proceedings which arise out of the original cause of action." * * *

Boone was not denied due process of law, because he had the benefit of its essential elements which are notice and an opportunity to be heard. Process may be adapted to the nature of the case, and of necessity there must be some form of constructive notice. Notice was actually brought home to the appellant by personal service in the District, so the essential elements of due process were accorded to him. * * *

With respect to other questions not heretofore disposed of, we hold: (a) that after Boone's removal and upon its appointment and qualification as successor trustee, Wachovia became automatically vested with title to the trust assets, and entitled to sue for their recovery; (b) that it was proper for the District Court to require Boone to state his accounts so that it might be assured of a complete disclosure of the trust assets; (c) that it was also proper for the court to refuse to pass on the question of commissions, as that is an administrative problem of the North Carolina court.

It cannot be that a testamentary trustee acting under court supervision can step across the state line with the portable trust assets in his pocket and then defy the supervising court to remove him, on the ground that his wrongful removal of the assets and his own absence had rendered the court powerless. Equity is not so weak as that. The District Court's rulings were correct.

Affirmed.

NOTE

Professor Beale states: "All matters of administration are determined by the law of situs or seat of the trust. The situs of a trust must be determined by an interpretation of the words by which the trust is created. No rule of law can be laid down for the purpose of interpretation. As has been seen, all indications are considered, such as the intention of the parties, the place of business or domicile of the trustee, the location of the trust res, and other similar matters. The seat of the trust having been determined, the law of the state in which the trust is located will apply to its administration".[45] The student should re-examine at this point National Shawmut Bank of Boston v. Cumming, 325 Mass. 457, 91 N.E.2d 337 (1950), appearing as a principal case in Chapter VIII, Section 6, supra. Professor Beale also states that only one court can supervise administration of the trust and this court should be the

45. II Beale, Conflict of Laws (1935) 1023.

one at the situs of the trust.[46] Mr. Land rejects the concept of a single governing law and jurisdiction and suggests a clear distinction be made between the law applicable to a trust and the court which asserts jurisdiction over it.[47]

The administration of a trust often involves the performance of acts in more than one state and these acts must be performed in a manner consistent with the laws of the states concerned. However, this multi-state aspect of performance of the trust does not determine the state exercising primary jurisdiction (the situs of the trust) and the general law applicable to its administration.

Nothing in Shaffer v. Heitner, 433 U.S. 186, 97 S.Ct. 2569, 53 L.Ed. 683 (1977), should affect the established law in this area. Clearly the state where the trust is administered has sufficient contacts to base jurisdiction over a nonresident trustee or beneficiary. The state in which the trustee resides and is personally served would have in personam jurisdiction.

The situs of the trust can be shifted if this is necessary for the proper discharge of the trustee's duties. Such shifts usually are unnecessary in a private trust. But the non-residence of a principal beneficiary whose needs can be determined only by close surveillance and when these needs must be determined to discharge trust duties, or, perhaps, the location of the bulk of the trust property in another state may require a change of situs. The trustee at the original situs of the trust may be handicapped in the use of agents in another state by the rules concerning delegation of trust powers. A number of states have statutes dealing with these changes.[48] Others handle the matter by court rule.[49] Courts usually are reticent to supervise administration of charitable trusts the purpose of which is to be accomplished wholly in another state or foreign country. This position in part stems from enforcement of the trust by a public officer of the state of situs who presumably cannot enforce without ability to find facts or cannot act for a "non-state" purpose. The assets usually are transferred to the state or country in which the charitable purpose is to be accomplished to a trustee or public officer there who can conduct the administration effectively.[50] When a foreign trustee is named and the beneficiaries and trust property are at the situs of the trust, a proper administration may be difficult and the trustee may be removed, as in the principal case, on the ground of his non-residence. The

46. Idem, p. 1026.

47. Land, Trusts in the Conflict of Laws (1940) 199.

48. E.g., Mich., M.C.L. §§ 706.4–706.6 (limited to transfer to state in which beneficiary resides and to trustee or trustees lawfully appointed there). Uniform Probate Code § 7–305 facilitates transfer to another state and places the trustee under a duty to administer the trust at "a place appropriate to the purposes of the trust and to its sound, efficient management." See Hendrickson, "Change of Situs of a Trust" Parts I–X, 118 Trusts and Estates 19 (1979) *passim*.

49. Maryland Ann.Code 9B, Maryland Rules V80.

50. See Alford, "Voluntary Foreign Aid and American Foreign Policy: the Element of State Control", 46 Va.L.Rev., 491–498 (1960). For due process requirements in service upon non-resident beneficiaries in trust accountings, see Mullane v. Central Hanover Bank & Trust Co., 339 U.S. 306, 70 S.Ct. 652, 94 L.Ed. 865 (1950); Fraser, "Jurisdiction by Necessity—An Analysis of the Mullane Case", 100 U. of Pa.L.Rev. 305 (1951). Suggested general references on conflict of laws problems raised in this note are II Beale, Conflict of Laws (1935) 1018–1026; Currie "The Multiple Personality of the Dead: Executors, Administrators, and the Conflict of Laws," 33 U. Chi.L.Rev. 429 (1966); Land, Trusts in the Conflict of Laws (1940); Capron, "Situs of Trusts in Conflict of Laws", 93 Trusts and Estates 878–888 (1954); Scott, "What Law Governs Trusts" 99 Trusts and Estates 186 (1960). Shriver, "The Multi-State Estate", 3 Real Prop.Prob. & T.L.J. 189 (1968); Note, "The Extraterritorial Authority of Executors and Administrators to Sue and Collect Assets", 52 Iowa L.Rev. 290 (1966).

trust will not fail for want of a trustee, a local fiduciary then being appointed.

Article 7 of the Uniform Probate Code will revolutionize some aspects of the law in this area. The Code does away with the concept of continuing jurisdiction over testamentary trusts and allows the settlor to select a trustee and a place of administration outside the place of creation of the trust. It institutes a system of registration for all trusts. Under the Code the trustee is under a duty to register the trust with the probate Court at the principal place of administration of the trust (Section 7–101). The probate Court is given exclusive jurisdiction over internal affairs of the trust (appointment and removal of trustees, matters of administration, ascertainment of beneficiaries, and fees) (Section 7–201). There are penalties for failure to register, including removal and denial of fees (Section 7–104). Registration is a simple filing procedure (Section 7–102). The consequence of registration is that the trustee submits personally to jurisdiction of the court in any proceeding relating to the trust, and the beneficiaries in the trust also become subject to the jurisdiction of the court to the extent of their interests (Section 7–103). Thus the court of registration is in a position to handle litigation of any aspect of the trust. If the trustee leaves the jurisdiction, he may be served by mail. If it becomes appropriate to change the place of administration, as where a trust involves personal discretion and the beneficiaries have moved to another state, the Code provides for releasing registration at the initial place and appointment of a trustee in the other state and registration there (Section 7–305).

To the extent that the law relating to duties of the trustee becomes uniform, differences between the states as to problems of administration (proper investments, determination of principal and income, etc.) will no longer create choice of law issues.

---

(3) FEDERAL JURISDICTION OVER ADMINISTRATION

The jurisdiction of federal district courts in matters involving fiduciary administration is for the most part concurrent with that of state courts. This jurisdiction is based upon Article III of the United States Constitution and is defined and limited by Congress. Fiduciary administration cases brought before federal district courts usually are based upon diversity of citizenship. Less frequently, a federal question is involved. In some instances, federal courts will have exclusive jurisdiction, as in cases arising under the internal revenue laws. In cases resting upon diversity of citizenship, and in some cases involving a federal question, the requisite jurisdictional amount or value ($10,000) must be claimed and the burden of establishing the amount is upon the plaintiff.

When the requisites for jurisdiction are present, federal district courts may exercise substantially the equity powers enjoyed by the English High Court of Chancery in 1789. In diversity cases, this power is limited by the doctrine of Erie Railroad v. Tompkins [51] to the extent that a federal court cannot withhold a remedy which the state makes available or give a remedy which the state denies; [52] although the mere fact that the state limits a remedy to a particular state court will not preclude the federal court from exercising its equity power.[53]

With respect to the administration of inter vivos trusts and other fiduciary transactions not involving the custody of the *res* by a state court, when the federal court takes custody of the *res* it has exclusive jurisdiction necessary to achieve the objects of the suit and may enjoin a state court proceeding which interferes. State proceedings which do not interfere with custody of the *res* may not be enjoined. If, however, a state court has custody of the *res* of an inter vivos trust for an accounting or other proceeding to which this control is requisite, a federal district court will not entertain an action interfering with this custody. Thus, in Princess Lida of Thurn and Taxis v. Thompson [54] a state court in Pennsylvania had assumed control of a trust *res* of a living trust for an accounting and thereafter several beneficiaries sued the trustees in a federal district court in Pennsylvania alleging mismanagement, and praying for an accounting, restitution and other relief. Each court enjoined proceedings before the other. The United States Supreme Court held the Pennsylvania state court gained jurisdiction *quasi in rem* upon filing of the account and was entitled to proceed without interference by the federal court. Speaking for the Court, Mr. Justice Roberts summarized the principles established in earlier cases as follows: [55]

> "* * * /I/t is settled that where the judgment sought is strictly in personam, both the state court and the federal court, having concurrent jurisdiction, may proceed with the litigation at least until judgment is obtained in one of them which may be set up as res judicata in the other. On the other hand, if the two suits

51. 304 U.S. 64, 58 S.Ct. 817, 82 L.Ed. 1188, 114 A.L.R. 1487 (1938). See Barron & Holtzoff (Wright), Federal Practice and Procedure § 43. The federal court could not grant a remedy available in a state which Congress has forbidden, nor can a state by characterizing a particular remedy as equitable defeat a jury trial guaranteed by the Seventh Amendment.

52. See, Comment, "The Equitable Remedial Rights Doctrine", 55 Yale L.J. 401 (1946).

53. E.g., Beach v. Rome Trust Co., 269 F.2d 367 (2d Cir. 1959), Noted 34 St. John's L.Rev. 339 (1960).

54. 305 U.S. 456, 59 S.Ct. 275, 83 L. Ed. 285 (1939). See McComas, "Surcharge Litigation—Jurisdiction and Procedural Considerations", 16 Real Prop., Prob. & T.J. 733 (1981).

55. 305 U.S. at 466, 59 S.Ct. 280. In Donovan v. City of Dallas, 377 U.S. 408, 84 S.Ct. 1579, 12 L.Ed.2d 409 (1964), the Supreme Court in holding a state court could not enjoin an *in personam* action before a federal court to restrain the issuing and selling of municipal bonds, distinguished *Princess Lida,* stating in its opinion at 377 U.S. 412, 84 S.Ct. 1582. "* * * Early in the history of our country a general rule was established that state and federal courts would not interfere with or try to restrain each others proceedings. That rule has continued substantially unchanged until this time. An exception has been made in cases where a court has custody of property, that is, proceedings *in rem* or *quasi in rem.* In such cases this Court has said that the state or federal court having custody of such property has exclusive jurisdiction to proceed. * * *"

are in rem, or quasi in rem, so that the court, or its officer, has possession or must have control of the property which is the subject of the litigation in order to proceed with the cause and grant the relief sought the jurisdiction of one court must yield to that of the other. We have said that the principle applicable to both federal and state courts that the court first assuming jurisdiction over property may maintain and exercise that jurisdiction to the exclusion of the other, is not restricted to cases where property has actually been seized under judicial process before a second suit is instituted, but applies as well where suits are brought to marshal assets, administer trusts, or liquidate estates, and in suits of a similar nature where, to give effect to its jurisdiction, the court must control the property. The doctrine is necessary to the harmonious cooperation of federal and state tribunals. While it has no application in a case in a federal court based upon diversity of citizenship, wherein the plaintiff seeks merely an adjudication of his right or his interest as a basis of a claim against a fund in the possession of a state court, this is not such a case. No question is presented in the federal court as to the right of any person to participate in the res or as to the quantum of his interest in it. The contentions are solely as to administration and restoration of corpus. * * *

"The Common Pleas Court could not effectively exercise the jurisdiction vested in it, without a substantial measure of control of the trust funds. Its proceedings are, as the court below held, quasi in rem, and the jurisdiction acquired upon the filing of the trustees' account is exclusive. * * *"

The custody of the *res* by state courts and the federal jurisdiction relating to this *res* is most often placed in issue when testamentary trusts or the administration of a decedent's estate are involved. Since federal courts have no probate jurisdiction,[56] the *res* in a dece-

56. In most of the states, probate (the determination "will or no will") is a proceeding *in rem* and is not part of the general jurisdiction of a court of equity. Thus probate and proceedings which are so ancillary or incidental to probate that they are a continuation thereof are not within federal jurisdiction. Sutton v. English, 246 U.S. 199, 38 S.Ct. 254, 62 L.Ed. 664 (1918). Quite probably, if the Congress desired, it could constitutionally confer probate jurisdiction on federal district courts with respect to wills of persons under federal supervision or protection or perhaps could confer general probate jurisdiction under the interstate commerce power. If state statutes regulating the contest of wills provide adversary proceedings which are not merely incidental or ancillary to probate but in which the validity of the will may nevertheless be put in issue, a federal court has jurisdiction if the requisites for jurisdiction such as diversity of citizenship and jurisdictional amount are present. Gaines v. Fuentes, 92 U.S. 10, 23 L.Ed. 524 (1875); Ellis v. Davis, 109 U.S. 485, 3 S.Ct. 327, 27 L.Ed. 1006 (1883). In Foster v. Carlin, 200 F.2d 943 (4th Cir. 1952), an action was brought in a federal district court to declare a trust fraudulent and void in its inception and to declare the deceased had died intestate as to certain stock that was part of the trust res. It was held the court had jurisdiction to determine the trust issue but could not declare the decedent intestate because that was a probate matter. The mere fact that the method of attack upon the validity of a will has some features of an equity proceeding does not mean that the state legislature has made this a part of general equity jurisdiction. Eyber v. Dominion National Bank of Bristol Office, 249 F.Supp. 531 (D.C.Va.1966). Concerning "probate jurisdiction" of federal courts see Atkinson, Wills (2d Ed.1953) 594–5; Barron and Holtzoff, Federal

dent's estate will probably be under the control of a state court.[57] The administration of a testamentary trust probably will be under close court supervision with *quasi in rem* jurisdiction in a state court. Litigants may nevertheless be tempted to invoke federal aid, rather than pursue their remedies in state courts, with the thought of avoiding possible local bias or with an eye to the appeal as a matter of right to the Court of Appeals.

Invoking federal jurisdiction may not be advantageous to the litigant in the long run. Apart from the fact that federal dockets may be crowded and that federal district judges do not possess the experience in property cases often found among the state judiciary, difficulties may arise concerning the jurisdiction of the court, the discretion of the court to abstain from taking jurisdiction pending an outcome of the state decision, and the nature of the decree it can render if it takes jurisdiction.

The federal court in such a case may entertain *in personam* proceedings or actions *inter partes* against personal representatives and other parties as, for example, to establish a right to a share in the estate,[58] a debt due from the decedent,[59] or a lien on a distributee's share.[60] It may construe the will or testamentary trust.[61] If the court has jurisdiction, the decision will be binding in the state proceeding; but the federal court cannot order actual distribution of the property, although it probably can exercise its power to require the trustee of a charitable trust to apply the property *cy pres*, at least when this does not interfere with accomplishment of the purpose for which the state court holds control of the *res*.[62]

Practice and Procedure (1960) § 51.1; 3 Bowe-Parker: Page, Wills (3d Ed.1961) § 26.21; Woerner, "Probate Jurisdiction of Federal Courts" 4 St. Louis L.Rev. 69 (1919); Notes and comments 10 Col.L. Rev. 166 (1910); 23 Harv.L.Rev. 225 (1910); 43 Harv.L.Rev. 462 (1930); 41 Ill. L.Rev. 424 (1946); 15 Okl.L.Rev. 462 (1962); 158 A.L.R. 9 (1945); 45 Ind.L.J. 387 (1970).

57. There is an exception for estates of Indians. If the will relates to land held in trust by the United States Government or other trust property, probate is conducted by hearing examiners of the Department of Interior, with appeal to the Secretary. 25 C.F.R. § 15.0 et seq. Tribal courts also have jurisdiction over probate, based on tribal membership. See Canby, "Civil Jurisdiction and the Indian Reservation", 1973 Utah L.Rev. 206; Cohen, Handbook of Federal Indian Law (1982) Ch. 6, Sec. B3. State courts may have concurrent jurisdiction as to estates of tribal members domiciled off the reservation or owning property off the reservation.

58. E.g., Waterman v. Canal-Louisiana Bank Co., 215 U.S. 33, 30 S.Ct. 10, 54 L.Ed. 80 (1909).

59. Hess v. Reynolds, 113 U.S. 73, 5 S.Ct. 377, 28 L.Ed. 927 (1885).

60. Ingersoll v. Coram, 211 U.S. 335, 29 S.Ct. 92, 53 L.Ed. 208 (1908).

61. Construction of a will or trust is a settled part of general equity jurisdiction and will seldom be construed as merely incidental or ancillary to probate, a probate court construing wills only to a very limited extent necessary to determine the issue "will or no will".

62. See Smith v. Moore, 343 F.2d 594 (4th Cir. 1965), in which the court directed an application of the funds based upon the "doctrine of approximation" although apparently for a purpose in which the *cy pres* power normally would be applied. An order to apply the property *cy pres* would operate *in personam* upon the trustee and would not interfere with the custody or supervision of the *res* by a state court. In Smith v. Moore the doctrine of approximation was adopted in order to avoid passing upon the issue of retroactivity and scope of the Virginia *cy pres* statute. In Schell v. Leander Clark College, 10 F.2d 542 (D.C.Iowa, 1926), the District Judge appeared to have doubts about the application of *cy pres* but was spared the necessity of ruling upon this

Even though the federal court may have jurisdiction in a case based upon diversity of citizenship or the presence of a federal question, the court may abstain from exercising this jurisdiction to await the outcome of state court proceedings. This is a limited judicial discretion and the federal court should decline to exercise jurisdiction only in exceptional cases.[63] The discretion to abstain should not be exercised merely because a case involves state law or because the law is difficult to determine. An exceptional case might be presented when the case turns upon a statute which has not been construed by a state court but which is of critical importance to the effective operation of the state government.[64]

PROBLEM

Testatrix left real and personal property and one half of the residue of her estate to her son, Samuel, absolutely. The other half of the residue of her estate and stock in a closely held corporation, she left in trust for her daughter, Priscilla, for life, remainder to Priscilla's issue, but if Priscilla died without issue, then to Samuel or his issue. The X Trust Company was named trustee and directed to vote the stock as directed by Samuel. While the estate of testatrix and the trust were in process of administration in the Surrogate's Court, Priscilla brought this action in a Federal District Court of the state, seeking an accounting of the estate and trust, removal of the trustee, damages from it for breach of trust, adjudication and declaration of title to the shares in the closely held corporation and an order turning them over to plaintiff, and such other further relief as is proper. Assuming diversity of citizenship and the requisite jurisdictional amount, should the Federal District Court take jurisdiction? If so, what relief can it give? Beach v. Rome Trust Co., 269 F.2d 367 (2d Cir. 1959); Noted 34 St. John's Law Rev. 339 (1960).

---

issue since joining the attorney general as a necessary party would have eliminated diversity of citizenship. In United States v. 263.5 Acres of Land, More or Less, Marin County, Cal., 54 F.Supp. 692 (D.C.Cal.1944), the District Judge seemed prepared to apply *cy pres*, although the issue presented was whether a change of the trust subject matter defeated the trust purpose.

63. Meredith v. City of Winter Haven, 320 U.S. 228, 64 S.Ct. 7, 88 L.Ed. 9 (1943).

64. Louisiana Power and Light Co. v. City of Thibodaux, 360 U.S. 25, 79 S.Ct. 1070, 3 L.Ed.2d 1058 (1959). For general references concerning the problems raised in this note, see 3 Bowe-Parker: Page, Wills (Rev.Ed.1961) § 26.21; Barron & Holtzoff (Wright), Federal Practice and Procedure §§ 43, 46.1, 51.1; 1A Moore's Federal Practice (2d Ed. 1981) §§ 0.214–0.216, 0.219–0.226.

SECTION 4. THE FIDUCIARY OFFICE

(1) APPOINTMENT, QUALIFICATION AND REMOVAL

We have already dealt with appointment of trustees in Chapter VIII. Principal focus in the present section is on the personal representative. The personal representative is appointed by the probate court. How is he selected and what are his qualifications? Must a bond be posted to protect creditors, heirs or devisees?

UNIFORM PROBATE CODE

"Section 3–203. [Priority Among Persons Seeking Appointment as Personal Representative.]

"(a) Whether the proceedings are formal or informal, persons who are not disqualified have priority for appointment in the following order:

(1) the person with priority as determined by a probated will including a person nominated by a power conferred in a will;

(2) the surviving spouse of the decedent who is a devisee of the decedent;

(3) other devisees of the decedent;

(4) the surviving spouse of the decedent;

(5) other heirs of the decedent;

(6) 45 days after the death of the decedent, any creditor.

"(b) An objection to an appointment can be made only in formal proceedings. In case of objection the priorities stated in (a) apply except that

(1) if the estate appears to be more than adequate to meet exemptions and costs of administration but inadequate to discharge anticipated unsecured claims, the Court, on petition of creditors, may appoint any qualified person;

(2) in case of objection to appointment of a person other than one whose priority is determined by will by an heir or devisee appearing to have a substantial interest in the estate, the Court may appoint a person who is acceptable to heirs and devisees whose interests in the estate appear to be worth in total more than half of the probable distributable value, or, in default of this accord any suitable person.

"(c) A person entitled to letters under (2) through (5) of (a) above, and a person aged [18] and over who would be entitled to letters but for his age, may nominate a qualified person to act as personal representative. Any person aged [18] and over may renounce his right to nominate or to an appointment by appropriate writing filed with the Court. When two or more persons share a priority, those of them who do not renounce must concur in nominating another to act for them, or in applying for appointment.

"(d) Conservators of the estates of protected persons, or if there is no conservator, any guardian except a guardian ad litem of a minor or incapacitated person, may exercise the same right to nominate, to object to another's appointment, or to participate in determining the preference of a majority in interest of the heirs and devisees that the protected person or ward would have if qualified for appointment.

"(e) Appointment of one who does not have priority, including priority resulting from renunciation or nomination determined pursuant to this section, may be made only in formal proceedings. Before appointing one without priority, the Court must determine that those having priority, although given notice of the proceedings, have failed to request appointment or to nominate another for appointment, and that administration is necessary.

"(f) No person is qualified to serve as a personal representative who is:

(1) under the age of [21];

(2) a person whom the Court finds unsuitable in formal proceedings;

"(g) A personal representative appointed by a court of the decedent's domicile has priority over all other persons except where the decedent's will nominates different persons to be personal representative in this state and in the state of domicile. The domiciliary personal representative may nominate another, who shall have the same priority as the domiciliary personal representative.

"Section 3–601. [Qualification.]

"Prior to receiving letters, a personal representative shall qualify by filing with the appointing Court any required bond and a statement of acceptance of the duties of the office.

"Section 3–602. [Acceptance of Appointment; Consent to Jurisdiction.]

"By accepting appointment, a personal representative submits personally to the jurisdiction of the Court in any proceeding relating to the estate that may be instituted by any interested person. Notice of any proceeding shall be delivered to the personal representative, or mailed to him by ordinary first class mail at his address as listed in the application or petition for appointment or as thereafter reported to the Court and to his address as then known to the petitioner.

"Section 3–603. [Bond Not Required Without Court Order, Exceptions.]

"No bond is required of a personal representative appointed in informal proceedings, except (1) upon the appointment of a special administrator; (2) when an executor or other personal representative is appointed to administer an estate under a will containing an express requirement of bond or (3) when bond is required under Section 3–605. Bond may be required by court order at the time of appointment of a personal representative appointed in any formal proceeding except that bond is not required of a personal representative appointed in formal proceedings if the will relieves the personal representative of bond, unless bond has been requested by an interested party and the Court is satisfied that it is desirable. Bond required by any will may be dispensed with in formal proceedings upon determination by the Court that it is not necessary. No bond is required of any personal representative who, pursuant to statute, has deposited cash or collateral with an agency of this state to secure performance of his duties.

* * *

"Section 3–611. [Termination of Appointment by Removal; Cause; Procedure.]

"(a) A person interested in the estate may petition for removal of a personal representative for cause at any time. * * *

"(b) Cause for removal exists when removal would be in the best interests of the estate, or if it is shown that a personal representative or the person seeking his appointment intentionally misrepresented material facts in the proceedings leading to his appointment, or that the personal representative has disregarded an order of the Court, has become incapable of discharging the duties of his office, or has mismanaged the estate or failed to perform any duty pertaining to the office.

* * *

"Section 3–701. [Time of Accrual of Duties and Powers.]

"The duties and powers of a personal representative commence upon his appointment. The powers of a personal representative relate back in time to give acts by the person appointed which are beneficial to the estate occurring prior to appointment the same effect as those occurring thereafter. Prior to appointment, a person named executor in a will may carry out written instructions of the decedent relating to his body, funeral and burial arrangements. A personal representative may ratify and accept acts on behalf of the estate done by others where the acts would have been proper for a personal representative."

NOTE

The Uniform Probate Code differs from existing law in most other states in many respects. Usually the statutes are more explicit in enumerating disqualifications. Some states are reluctant to allow appointment of a non-resident.[65] Although the latter is often explained on the grounds that the appointing court would lack power over the non-resident, that this need not be

65. E.g., Pennsylvania law allows the register to refuse letters to a non-resident. Purdon's Penn.Stat.Ann. tit. 20, § 3157 (1981 Supp.).

the case is demonstrated by the Uniform Probate Code Section 3–602, set forth above.[66] Corporate professional fiduciaries are not within the protection of the privileges and immunities clause of the United States Constitution; hence a state can exclude foreign corporations from serving as fiduciary. This rule may be avoided by incorporating a subsidiary locally.[67]

Traditionally the personal representative has been thought to derive his power from the appointing court, even when he is an executor named in a will which expressly confers broad powers on him, and he is also treated as an "officer" of the appointing court. The court will normally appoint the executor named in the will unless there is some special reason for disqualification.

In most non-Code states a bond is required before a person can qualify as either executor or administrator, although statutes commonly permit the testator to waive the bond by provision in his will.[68] The result is that the expense of the bond is saved for wealthier persons, who usually have executed wills drawn by competent lawyers.

The Code concept that title or powers of a personal representative relate back to the date of decedent's death is usually followed in non-Code states; however, the judicial relation-back concept tends to be applied when it is to the advantage of the estate and ignored when it is to the disadvantage of the estate.[69] The explicit Code rule, coupled with the possibility of obtaining informal appointment of a personal representative five days after decedent's death, obviates the need for appointment of a special administrator (in ex parte proceeding) to handle estate assets pending appointment of the regular personal representative (as where an unincorporated business is involved, or other assets need prompt management or protection).

Personal representatives of special types may be involved in the administration of estates. Many states now provide a Public Administrator for estates when there are no applicants for letters of administration. In Texas a testator may make his representative an "Independent Executor", freeing him to an extent from judicial supervision, and thus simplifying the administration of his estate.[70] Special administrators may be appointed to manage an estate during litigation as, for example, during a will contest. A person who intervenes and takes possession of the estate of a decedent without qualification may be subject to limited responsibilities as a personal representative. He is sometimes described as an "executor de son tort". The tendency today is to move away from this concept and treat the intervenor as a converter of the estate from whom the duly qualified personal representative is bound to recover it.[71]

66. Some non-Code states achieve the same result by conditioning appointment of a non-resident on his designation of a local agent to receive process. Vernon's Ann.Tex.Stat. Probate Code, § 78; Wis. Stat.Ann. § 856.23.

67. American Trust Co., Inc. v. South Carolina State Board of Bank Control, 381 F.Supp. 313 (D.C.S.C.1974).

68. See Atkinson, Wills (2d Ed.1953) 576–584, 602–603 for a detailed discussion of these matters.

69. A collection of cases in which the "relation back" doctrine has been in issue may be found at 26 A.L.R. 1359 (1923).

70. Vernon's Ann.Tex.Stat. Probate Code § 145: Independent administration is achieved automatically under the Uniform Probate Code, unless the court orders supervised administration under Section 3–501 et seq.; independent administration is the normal way of proceeding and is available in an intestate estate or a testate estate, i.e., it is not dependent on a clause in the will directing it. The same concept, but called "settlement without court intervention," prevails in Washington. Rev.Code Wash. Ann. § 11.68.010 et seq.

71. See Evans, "The Intermeddler and the Fraudulent Transferee as Execu-

Testamentary trustees are treated in many states like executors and are required to give bond and make periodic accountings.[72] The trustee of a living trust, on the other hand, derives his authority from the trust indenture or deed. Usually no bond is required and he administers the trust from its inception to its termination without judicial intervention. It is possible that he may find himself in need of instructions from a court of equity, or a beneficiary may complain of his breach of trust, or it may be necessary to replace him as trustee.[73]

IN RE ESTATE OF WEAVER

Supreme Court of Kansas, 1974.
214 Kan. 550, 520 P.2d 1330.[74]

[Gordon L. Weaver died intestate in June, 1973. He left an estate consisting of stocks, bonds and other personal property worth approximately $2,400,000 and 53½ quarter sections of Kansas wheat land. Decedent's wife had predeceased him, and he was survived by 39 next of kin. Two of decedent's in-laws petitioned to have four in-laws appointed as co-administrators, on the grounds that they were best acquainted with his business and farm interests; they were represented by Mr. Kite as their attorney. The next of kin (under leadership of a cousin, Mrs. Reed) petitioned for the appointment of Edgar Robertson, a banker who owned farm land, did decedent's tax returns, and had administered several estates; the next of kin were represented by Mr. Postlethwaite as attorney. The probate court appointed all four in-laws and Robertson; this was appealed to the district court and the matter tried de novo. The district court in its findings stated that the actual controversy concerned who should be selected as attorney for the administrator. The in-laws objected to Mr. Postlethwaite on the grounds that the decedent disliked him and had discharged him as attorney for the estate of decedent's father. The district court appointed two of the in-laws and Edgar Robertson as co-administrators. The in-laws had an apparent conflict of interest because one farmed estate land on leases and partnership basis, and the other had a claim against decedent. The district court found that the estate was too large to be administered by a single administrator. The next of kin appeal.]

SCHROEDER, JUSTICE:

* * *

tor", 25 Geo.L.J. 78 (1938); McGovney, "Executor of His Own Wrong", 6 Iowa L.Bull. 65 (1920); Atkinson, Wills (2d Ed., 1953) 570–572. The institution of "executor de son tort" is incompatible with the modern notion of the orderly settlement of creditor's claims. The "executor de son tort" bears some analogy to the chicken who finds a worm and is then pursued in a disorderly rout by his barnyard comrades.

72. No bond for the trustee is required under Uniform Probate Code § 7–304.

73. See Bogert, Trusts (5th Ed. 1973) § 33.

74. Noted, 14 Washburn L.J. 673 (1975).

Our statute governing the appointment of administrators is K.S.A. 59–705, which reads:

"Administration of the estate of a person dying intestate shall be granted to one or more of the persons hereinafter mentioned, suitable and competent to discharge the trust, and in the following order:

"(1) The surviving spouse or next of kin, or both, as the court may determine, or some person or persons selected by them or any of them.

"(2) If all such persons are incompetent or unsuitable, or do not accept, administration may be granted to one or more of the creditors, or to a nominee or nominees thereof.

"(3) Whenever the court determines that it is for the best interests of the estate and all persons interested therein, administration may be granted to any other person, whether interested in the estate or not."

The above statute pertaining to the granting of administration of an estate establishes three classifications in the order in which they shall be considered for the appointment of a suitable and competent person or persons to discharge the trust. The court has no power or authority to appoint any person falling under a lower classification, unless it first finds that the person or persons designated by a prior classification are nonexistent, incompetent or unsuitable to discharge the trust or do not accept the trust. (In re Estate of Paronto, 163 Kan. 85, 180 P.2d 302; and In re Estate of West, 165 Kan. 483, 195 P. 2d 616.)

Statutes regulating the order in which administration may be granted are ordinarily construed as mandatory and as leaving the courts no discretion in the matter, save where there are two or more persons equally entitled under the statute, or where a question arises as to the fitness or qualifications of the person or persons primarily entitled to the appointment. (33 C.J.S. Executors and Administrators § 34, p. 924.)

Values of substance inhere in the right to letters of administration and those upon whom the right has been conferred by statute should not be deprived of it, except as the statute has provided. (Williams v. Williams, 24 App.D.C. 214, 217 [1904].)

Here detailed statutory provision has been made for the issuance of letters of administration under 59–705, supra, and an explicit system of priorities as between next of kin and others has been established; hence, if the next of kin in the first classification have submitted a nominee for appointment as administrator, who is not barred under a specific statutory disqualification, a creditor under the second classification or other person not in any preferred classification may not be appointed.

The appellees in their petition for the appointment of an administrator alleged Edgar Robertson to be a "proper and suitable person to whom to grant letters of administration"; their attorney, Mr. Kite, admitted into the record that the appellees conceded Edgar Robertson was a fit and suitable person to serve as administrator in every way; and none of the appellees filed any written defense to the allegations of the next of kin in their petition that "Edgar Robertson is a proper and suitable person to whom to grant letters of administration."

Furthermore, the next of kin who were the owners of this estate indicated their unanimous desire to have Edgar Robertson appointed as the administrator and objected to the appointment of anyone else.

There is no dispute that Edgar Robertson is a competent person to serve as administrator of this estate. The controversy concerns his suitability to serve as sole administrator. The trial court did not find him unsuitable. It merely found him unsuitable to serve as the sole administrator. The trial court by appointing Edgar Robertson as one of the administrators clearly found him suitable to serve as administrator.

* * *

There is no evidence to support the trial court's conclusion that administering the estate would be an "undue burden" upon Robertson. It is undisputed Robertson is president of a bank, farms some land, and is a trustee in a two million dollar trust, but there is nothing to show these activities would prevent him from ably administering the estate. While this is a large estate, there is no evidence it is too large for Robertson to properly administer. Robertson's uncontradicted testimony was that he could administer the estate. If anything, his access to the bank's facilities and personnel together with his attorney will assist him in administering the estate rather than hinder it.

The other basis for the court's finding that Robertson was unsuitable is that he was not familiar with the operation of some of Weaver's land. The evidence was, and Robertson was aware, that all the land was farmed on a landlord-tenant basis with written leases, except some land on an oral partnership-custom-farming basis by the Lindstens and an oral lease with one of the tenants. The record discloses the tenants are all good farmers and work independently, so that it would not be necessary for Robertson to closely supervise the farming operations. Also, Robertson is familiar with the local farming methods since he farms some land of his own. Robertson's lack of specific knowledge of the decedent's farming operations is irrelevant. One of the purposes of administration is to inventory the assets and determine these facts. It would be an unusual situation for any one person to know all the facets of a decedent's business interests.

* * *

The trial court had before it the nominee of the next of kin whom they designated to be appointed administrator of the estate. The record discloses their nominee was competent and suitable for the position, and falling within the first classification of 59–705, supra, their nominee was eligible for the appointment. Accordingly, the trial court's refusal to appoint Edgar Robertson as the sole administrator of the estate of Gordon Weaver, deceased, was error.

The trial judge improperly injected himself into this case as evidenced by his own remarks in the record that he was ready to appoint Edgar Robertson sole administrator of this estate, provided Mr. Kite and Mr. Postlethwaite would agree that both represent the estate as its attorneys. Mr. Kite and Mr. Postlethwaite had no authority whatever to make such an agreement and bind the fiduciary to it. Under Kansas law it is the sole province and responsibility of the fiduciary to choose and employ his attorney. (In re Estate of Bertrand, 188 Kan. 531, 542, 363 P.2d 412; and In re Estate of Eyth, 157 Kan. 268, 139 P.2d 378.)

The trial judge also improperly stated:

> "* * * I hoped I could get them [Kite and Postlthwaite] to go in and work together on the estate because I think that probably this is a large enough estate they probably could merit the allowance of fees for two attorneys. * * *"

The district court had no authority to dictate who should be the attorney for the fiduciary in this matter, or to force the employment of multiple attorneys upon the next of kin who are the owners of the property in this estate.

The judgment of the lower court is reversed with directions to appoint Edgar Robertson the sole administrator of the estate.[75]

---

(2) COMPENSATION OF FIDUCIARY

The cost of estate and trust administration is of vital interest to the public (the consumers), the Bar and corporate fiduciaries.[76] Excessive cost has been a common complaint of the public. Closely related are the charges of the fiduciary and the attorney, particularly in probate and estate administration. In the past many states have by statute fixed the compensation of the personal representative (executor or administrator) according to a schedule of fees computed as a percentage of the estate, with provision for allowance of additional

75. In a number of cases the lower courts refuse to follow the statutory priority but are reversed on appeal. In State ex rel. First National Bank & Trust Co. v. Skow, 91 Wis.2d 773, 284 N.W.2d 74 (1979) the devisees under the will sought to have one of them (a daughter) appointed as personal representative although the will named the Bank as executor. The devisees contended that the Bank was "unsuitable" because of its fees, whereas the daughter who petitioned would serve without fee. The trial court appointed the daughter. The Supreme Court of Wisconsin reversed on the grounds that the statutory priority governed appointment and that charging a fee did not disqualify the Bank.

76. The materials in Chapter I, Section 4, should be reviewed at this point.

compensation for extraordinary services.[77] The charge for services of the lawyer for the estate has often been fixed by minimum bar fee schedules, now outlawed as a form of price fixing and violation of the antitrust laws.[78] These fee schedules often paralleled the statutory percentages for personal representatives, regardless of the work done by the lawyer in the particular estate. However, there was usually an additional charge based on the nonprobate assets (joint tenancy, life insurance, living trusts, etc.) which occasioned work for the attorney, largely in preparing federal estate tax returns and local estate or inheritance tax returns.[79]

The Uniform Probate Code abandons a fee schedule and provides "reasonable compensation" both for the personal representative[80] and for the lawyer for the estate.[81] In the past the probate courts have "policed" fees (both in terms of maximum and minimum fees) at the time of formal approval of accounts. The Code puts the burden on the heirs or devisees to question fees if they believe the charges unreasonable. The American Bar Association in 1973 approved a Statement of Principles Regarding Probate Practices and Expenses to guide the profession. The abolition of fee schedules opens to litigation the issue of reasonableness of fees, especially in probate.[82]

In living trusts the compensation of the trustee is usually set by the terms of the trust agreement.[83] Corporate fiduciaries have established fee schedules, but are willing to negotiate in individual cases; the type and amount of fees vary in different localities.

MATTER OF ESTATE OF TIERNEY

Supreme Court of Wisconsin, 1975.
70 Wis.2d 438, 234 N.W.2d 357.

HEFFERNAN, JUSTICE.

Upon the filing of the final account in the estate of Patrick Tierney, the probate judge found the attorney's fees in the amount of

77. For a summary of state laws on fees as of 1980, see Bell, "Fees of Executors, Administrators and Testamentary Trustees," American College of Probate Counsel Study No. 5 (1980). For an earlier survey, see Jack, "Fiduciary Fees—Variations and Complexities," 112 Trusts & Estates 622 (1973).

78. See "Fiduciary and Probate Counsel Fees in the Wake of Goldfarb," 13 Real Prop., Prob. & Trust J. 238 (1978) (discussing the demise of minimum fee schedules, relevant fee statutes, judicial review of fees, inclusion of nonprobate assets in the fee base, and fees for an attorney acting in the capacities of both personal representative and lawyer for the estate).

79. See Report of Subcommittee of Committee on Administration Expenses, ABA, Fiduciary Compensation and Legal Fees with Respect to Nonprobate Assets, 8 Real Prop., Prob. & Tr.J. 1 (1973).

80. Uniform Probate Code, Section 3–719.

81. Uniform Probate Code, Section 3–721.

82. It has been suggested that the proper role of the lawyer needs more careful delineation. Martin, "Professional Responsibility and Probate Practices," 1975 Wis.L.Rev. 911. If the attorney personally does work which the personal representative should do, or which a paraprofessional can do, he should not charge at professional rates for this kind of work.

83. In the absence of an agreement, the trustee is entitled to reasonable compensation. Bogert, Trusts and Trustees (2d Ed. 1962) § 975.

$6,964.75 to be unreasonable, and he reduced the fees to $2,650. The attorney for the estate has appealed, claiming that fees should be allowed in the full amount. We conclude that the fees as submitted in the final account were excessive and that a reduction was proper. However, we conclude that the appropriate fee to be allowed is $4,500.

In this case Attorney Crawford furnished all the legal services from the commencement of the probate proceedings to the preparation of the final account, which was filed on August 13, 1973. The record shows that the work usually done by an executor was performed by the attorney. The executor limited his services to the deposit of checks to his account. The inventoried assets of the estate were slightly in excess of $200,000. The attorney's fees were based on the suggested fee schedules of the Douglas County Bar Association. They were computed as follows:

5% on first	$ 15,000.00	=	$ 750.00	
4% on next	30,000.00	=	1,200.00	
3% on balance	156,529.35	=	4,759.75	
				$6,709.75
Preparing Federal Estate Tax Return	$ 90.00			
Serving as witness on proof of will	15.00			
Legal services in Special Administration	150.00			
				255.00
	TOTAL			$6,964.75

The executor of the estate, who is not a beneficiary under the will, did not enter into any agreement for attorney's fees. He made no objection to Attorney Crawford's charges in the final account. However, upon the filing of the final account, objections were made by the residuary beneficiaries. * * *

The trial judge asked that the attorney support his charges by an itemization of the time spent on each of the proceedings and matters considered during the course of the probate. The attorney did not keep time charges during the course of the probate but prepared an estimate which purported to show that 140 hours had been spent in the course of the probate.

The trial judge concluded that these estimates were too high. For example, he pointed out that the attorney's estimate of 32 hours for the preparation of the final account was unrealistic and that 6 hours would have been appropriate and that only 16 hours, rather than 32 hours, should have been allocated to the preparation of the Federal Estate Tax Return. He also noted that some of the charges on an hourly rate were duplicated by lump sum charges allowed for the same work. He found that, in some instances, the attorney had allocated an hour of time for the dictation of letters which were extremely brief. The trial judge concluded:

> "There are a substantial number of additional weaknesses in the time estimate and it is my conclusion that I can give no weight to the time estimate * * *.
>
> "Mr. Crawford, having kept no time records in this matter, having submitted no reconstruction of the time involved acceptable or helpful to me, and having offered no other testimony or evidence of the time reasonably required for a reasonably experienced and efficient lawyer to perform services such as those involved in this matter, I have no alternative but to rely on my own knowledge of and experience in probate practice."

Judge Larsen proceeded to do just that and, in reliance upon his own experience, he said:

> "[I]t is my best judgment that an experienced efficient and prudent lawyer neither should nor would expend more than eighty hours in the performance of all legal services required in this proceeding from beginning to end. That allowance of time is sufficient to cover the special administration proceeding, the work involved with respect to the Federal Estate Tax Return and the appearance as a witness on the proof of the will."

During the course of the hearing, Attorney Crawford produced two witnesses, both practicing lawyers in Douglas county, one of whom had been the public administrator for many years. Both had extensive experience in probate practice, and both had reputations as skillful and experienced lawyers.

The public administrator, Axel B. Peterson, testified that, "The fees are in line with the usual charges by Douglas County attorneys with the size of the estate and the work involved." He further stated that the normal charges made by attorneys in the area were those set forth in the schedule of fees adopted by the Douglas County Bar Association. His basic conclusion was that he felt that the fees were in an amount that could reasonably be allowed for inheritance tax purposes.

Attorney James C. McKay, Sr., the other witness, testified that he did not keep a log of the time spent in the handling of probate matters and that his fees were determined by the county bar schedule. He testified that the hourly rate for attorney's fees at the time of the hearing was $40 per hour. He said that, in the determination of fees, the amount of time an attorney must spend on the probate of the estate that should have been done by the personal representative should also be considered.

Attorney Crawford stated that $40 per hour was a normal fee for him to charge in other types of work. He acknowledged that his reconstruction of time charges could not be totally accurate and that it merely represented his best estimate of the time spent on the various phases of the probate proceeding.

On the basis of this evidence and taking judicial notice of his own experience in the handling of probate matters, the trial judge concluded that the chargeable time should not exceed eighty hours and that the appropriate rate per hour was $35. From this figure of $2,800, he subtracted $150 which had been approved as an additional fee for the special administration proceedings. In this manner he determined that the appropriate fee was $2,650.

Although there was some evidence to sustain the findings and conclusions of the trial judge, this court is not bound by the great-weight-and-clear-preponderance-of-the-evidence test in the matter of reasonable attorney's fees. Touchett v. E Z Paintr Corp. (1961), 14 Wis.2d 479, 111 N.W.2d 419.

As we said in Giffin v. Tigerton Lumber Co. (1965), 26 Wis.2d 327, 132 N.W.2d 572, a trial court conclusion in respect to attorney's fees is subject to this court's determination of what is reasonable, because this court has firsthand knowledge of the value of legal services. We are obliged, therefore, to review independently attorney's fees whenever they are challenged on appeal. Herro, McAndrews & Porter v. Gerhardt (1974), 62 Wis.2d 179, 184, 214 N.W.2d 401, 404. In *Herro*, we said:

> " 'The things to be taken into consideration in determining the compensation to be recovered by an attorney are the amount and character of the services rendered, the labor, the time, and trouble involved, the character and importance of the litigation, the amount of money or value of the property affected, the professional skill and experience called for, and the standing of the attorney in his profession; to which may be added the general ability of the client to pay and the pecuniary benefit derived from the services.' "

The record shows without dispute that, although the amount involved in the estate was substantial, and therefore the proper handling of the litigation was of considerable importance to the beneficiaries and to the Wisconsin tax authorities, the problems presented were of a rather routine nature. The assets were substantially placed in trust and no unusual services in transferring securities were required of the attorney in the probate proceedings.

Although the attorney involved in this litigation is, according to the record, a highly skilled and competent practitioner, the services required were not of a particularly challenging nature. On the other hand, there is nothing to show that the estate was not handled expeditiously, and there is no evidence that any assets were wasted or allowed to dissipate in the course of the proceedings. The record indicates that the probate proceedings were well handled.

We said in the Will of Willing (1926) 190 Wis. 406, 415, 209 N.W. 602, that it is improper to charge a lump sum based almost entirely on the value of the estate. Nevertheless, that case recognizes that it is a factor to consider. It is, to some extent, the measure of the attorney's responsibility in the proceedings. We do not believe that the value of the estate should be used as a measure of ability to pay, for we have long ago come to the conclusion that legal services are just as valuable to the impoverished as they are to the rich although certainly indigency and poverty must be considered in setting fees. Accordingly, we do not consider the gross inventory as evidence of ability to pay but rather as an index of the responsibility entrusted to the lawyer. This responsibility was substantial. However, as we said in the Will of Willing, consideration must be given to the difficulties that are encountered in the numerous steps that make up an entire probate proceeding. The record indicates that there were no contests of any sort, and the entire process went on without any controversy or legal difficulties. Nevertheless, we should not place a premium upon contested litigation, for a skillful lawyer may well avoid litigation that might ensue in the hands of a blunderer. We will not allow additional compensation merely because a contest ensues. The question in such instance must be whether the additional contested proceedings were reasonably necessary. In this case, all went smoothly—the mark of a good lawyer in proceedings of this kind.

The time involved in the probate was sharply disputed. The trial judge concluded that no more than eighty hours should properly have been allowed, while the appellant and his two witnesses estimated the time charged was not unreasonably excessive. The most that we can say, on the basis of the record, is that the actual time properly to be allocated to the probate of this estate lies somewhere between the estimate of the appellant and the estimate of the judge.

The appellant originally based his fee upon the schedule adopted by the Douglas County Bar Association. If such schedules are considered as minimum fees, they may well be in violation of the anti-trust laws of both the State of Wisconsin and of the United States. This was the position taken by the United States Supreme Court under the facts of Goldfarb v. Virginia State Bar (1975), 421 U.S. 733, 95 S.Ct. 2004, 44 L.Ed.2d 572. The evidence in this case is nowhere near as strong as it was in *Goldfarb* to prove that the bar schedule was indeed a minimum fee. On the contrary, the trial judge stated that in Douglas county the fee schedule was considered as a maximum allowance, and on this appeal the appellant does not contend that he should be compensated on the basis of the original computation in accordance with the fee schedule. The constitutionality of the Douglas county minimum fee schedule is not before us. We note in passing, however, that the State Bar Association has abandoned its state minimum fee schedule because of anti-trust reservations that were apparent to it even prior to the United States Supreme Court's decision in *Goldfarb*.

We also note that this court recently, in State v. Sidney (1975), 66 Wis.2d 602, 609, 225 N.W.2d 438, 442, took judicial notice of the problems of economics that face the bar and said:

> "* * * the court recognizes that the cost of managing a legal office has increased and that the prevailing average rate now charged by attorneys in this state is $45 per hour."

The legislature has, by sec. 857.05, Stats., set the compensation for personal representatives at the rate of two percent of the inventoried value of the property. That fee is, of course, subject to the approval of the court and may be modified and increased in the event that there are unusual or extraordinary services rendered by the personal representative. Sec. 857.05(3) provides that, where a personal representative is also the attorney for the decedent's estate, the court may allow him either the executor's commissions or the attorney's fees and may allow both the executor's commissions and the attorney's fees in some instances.

While, in the instant case, neither the attorney nor any member of his law firm acted as a personal representative, the record indicates that, with a single minor exception, the personal representative's function was performed by the lawyer. That statutory executor's fee alone would have amounted to more than $4,000, almost $1,500 in excess of the amount allowed Attorney Crawford in this case. It is apparent to us that the $2,650 fee awarded by the trial judge was inadequate when measured against the statutory guideline of sec. 857.05(1) and (2), Stats.

Bearing in mind the nature of the services, the amount of the estate, the present prevailing rate charged by lawyers in the State of Wisconsin, and the approximate time involved in the probate of the estate, we conclude, on the basis of the record and reaching our conclusions *ab initio*, that the sum of $4,500 should be awarded for attorney's fees. Such sum shall also be in payment of any further services that may be required in the preparation of an amended final account, amended tax returns, and other steps necessary to close the proceedings.

Since there was no contract in this case, we do not decide whether an attorney can in advance contract with the personal representative for the fee to be charged. Nevertheless, it seems apparent that some understanding should be reached prior to the inception of legal work, so that parties concerned, either in a probate case or in other types of litigation, will have a clear idea of the factors to be involved in setting the fee and, unusual contingencies aside, the approximate amount of the fee that will be charged. In probate matters, by statute, it is the probate judge's function, and ultimately this court's function, to determine the reasonableness of the fee. To the extent that that is possible, the basis for future fees should be clearly understood.

Order vacated and cause remanded with directions to allow attorney's fees consistent with this opinion.[84]

NOTE

The burden of administration expenses in a decedent's estate falls on the heirs in an intestate estate and normally on the residue in a testate estate (see Chapter XV, Section 1(3)C for abatement rules). One vexing problem is whether any part of the fees can be recovered from recipients of nonprobate assets when they benefit from the services performed by the lawyer. The ABA Statement of Principles Regarding Probate Practices and Expenses reads:

> "7. When a personal representative or any attorney is required to render services with regard to nonprobate property, he should be reasonably compensated for such services and a determination should be made with respect to the amount to be charged and the property against which the charge should be made. The fact that the owner of such property did not request the services should be immaterial where it is the duty of the personal representative to consider such property in order to settle the estate properly. Such determination should be made, if feasible, by the interested parties themselves, otherwise by the court having jurisdiction of the decedent's estate applying general principles of equity.
>
> "*Comment*: (1) Examples of the indicated work, required primarily because of the complexity of the federal tax laws, are (a) the proper valuation and tracing of property passing outside the will, such as jointly held property or property held in an inter vivos trust; and (b) the determination of whether a gift has been made in contemplation of death.
>
> "(2) Specific legislation assessing charges against nonprobate assets appears to be rare and incomplete, and in most jurisdictions legislation may be indicated to assure the desired result."

84. For a general discussion of fees based on a percentage of the estate and factors to be considered if an hourly rate is used, see Kabaker, "Probate Fees—Where Are We Headed?", 46 N.Y.State Bar Jour. 577 (1974); "Fees of Executors, Administrators and Testamentary Trustees," Amer.Coll.Prob.Counsel Study No. 5 (1980). In adopting the Uniform Probate Code, Colorado added the following provision to the section corresponding to 3–721, Colo.Rev.Stat. § 16–12–721:

"(2) Factors to be considered as guides in determining the reasonableness of a fee include the following:

(a) The time and labor required, the novelty and difficulty of the questions involved, and the skill requisite to perform the service properly;

(b) The likelihood, if apparent to the personal representative, that the acceptance of the particular employment will preclude the person employed from other employment;

(c) The fee customarily charged in the locality for similar services;

(d) The amount involved and the results obtained;

(e) The time limitations imposed by the personal representative or by the circumstances;

(f) The nature and length of the relationship between the personal representative and the person performing the services;

(g) The experience, reputation, and ability of the person performing the services."

Recovery may be predicated on an unjust enrichment theory; legislation is sparse.[85]

If the personal representative also serves as lawyer for the estate, should he be entitled to collect in both capacities? The answer is determined by a composite of the law relating to compensation generally and the duty of loyalty (see Section 6 of this Chapter) which normally forbids the fiduciary to profit from the estate, i.e., to sell his own services to the estate any more than he as fiduciary can purchase property from himself personally. The ABA Statement provides:

> "4. Even if he is the sole personal representative, an attorney may serve both as a personal representative of a decedent's estate and as counsel to the personal representative, and he may receive reasonable compensation for his aggregate services and responsibilities.
>
> "*Comment*: In a few jurisdictions it is either illegal for an attorney to serve in both capacities or impossible for him to be adequately and fairly compensated for his services when he so acts. As the rule in the overwhelming number of jurisdictions is to the contrary, and as there are a great many estate situations where service in both capacities by the attorney may be the most efficient and economical way to settle the estate, the above statement seems clearly to be in the public interest."

The economic unfairness of a double commission is minimized under the Uniform Probate Code, where both the compensation of the personal representative and the compensation of the lawyer are determined on a flexible basis rather than a percentage of the estate; "reasonableness" obviously includes the amount of work in hours and value of services performed. If the same person serves as personal representative and lawyer, the total compensation should be less than when two individuals perform the functions separately. The non-Code states vary: some allow double fees, some allow the personal representative additional compensation for the legal work, some allow no additional compensation when the personal representative also does his own legal work[86] and may even forbid compensation to a law firm of which the fiduciary is a member unless there is an agreement under which the fiduciary does not share in such revenues.[87] (Do you believe the last qualification really serves to avoid "the appearance of professional impropriety"—Canon 9?).

If the same person serves as both executor and trustee under the will, and there is no specific agreement on compensation, a similar problem may arise as to double commissions when the duties overlap. Some courts have allowed the double fees when double work is done.[88] Other courts authorize only a single fee when the functions of the dual offices cannot be distinguished.[89]

When two or more persons serve as co-representatives or as co-trustees, should they receive separate fees or divide one fee?[90] The problem often

85. McKinney's N.Y. EPTL, § 2–1.8 (h) provides for allocation of fees to non-probate assets, for legal services in connection with tax apportionment. For a brief summary see "Fiduciary and Probate Counsel Fees in the Wake of *Goldfarb*", 13 Real Prop., Prob. & Tr.J. 238, at 248–249 (1978).

86. Lightner v. Boone, 221 N.C. 78, 19 S.E.2d 144 (1942).

87. Estate of Parker, 200 Cal. 132, 251 P. 907, 49 A.L.R. 1025 (1926). See Atkinson, Wills (2d Ed., 1953) 655–656.

88. E.g., In re Armour's Will, 61 N.J. Super. 50, 160 A.2d 160 (1960).

89. E.g., Johnson v. Lawrence, 95 N. Y. 154 (1884).

90. See, Bogert Trusts (5th Ed.1973) 515; III Scott, Trusts (3d Ed.1967) §§

arises where a corporate fiduciary and an individual serve together; the corporate fiduciary will perform the same services normally performed if it alone served and will in addition have the burden of informing the individual co-fiduciary and obtaining his concurrence; hence its work is actually increased. The corporate fiduciary therefore justifiably wants its normal fee without sharing. If the compensation is set by a statutory schedule, the corporate fiduciary may ask the co-representative (usually a family member) to waive any share of the fee. When compensation is on a "reasonable basis" there is less need for such a practice. On living trusts, the trust agreement usually provides expressly for this problem, and of course a will also may attempt to do so.

SECTION 5. THE FIDUCIARY AS MANAGER AND INVESTOR

Although the express trust is used for a wide variety of purposes, such as business organization and security, the modern trust is primarily a device for managing property. It has evolved from the ancient use, where the function was purely passive, through the active trust to pay the rents and profits of specific realty, into the present-day trust where the res is normally invested and reinvested in bonds and stocks.[91] Since the Statute of Uses, the trustee has been under a

242–243; co-trustees are usually entitled to one commission only in the absence of statute and the same is true of co-executors. See 85 A.L.R.2d 537 (1962).

For special problems concerning compensation, see McRitchie, "Trustees' Fees—Then and Now", 93 Trusts and Estates 300 (1954) (Comparison of fees before and after growth of corporate fiduciary institutions); Pope, "Fee Schedules as Remedy for Inadequate Executor Compensation", 98 Trusts and Estates 442 (1959); Huffaker, "The Principles Relating to Compensation and Selection of Fiduciaries" 33 Temple L.Q. 293 (1960).

91. For the year 1980 the asset distribution of personal trusts and of decedents' estates administered by federally insured commercial and mutual savings banks, and by trust companies which are members of the Federal Reserve or by holding companies under supervision of the Federal Reserve, *in percent*:

	Trusts	Estates
Non-int. bearing deposits—own bank	0.7	1.4
Non-int. bearing deposits—other	0.1	0.0
Int. bearing deposits—own bank	0.9	3.1
Int. bearing deposits—other	1.2	2.1
U.S. Gov't & Agency obligations	8.9	13.6
State, County, Municipal oblig.	9.6	4.7
Other short-term obligations	6.0	9.6
Other notes and bonds	5.5	2.6
Preferred stocks	0.9	0.7
Common stocks	56.1	35.7
Real estate mortgages	1.6	3.0
Real estate	7.0	19.7
Miscellaneous	1.6	3.8

"Trust Assets of Banks and Trust Companies—1980," Report of the Board of Governors of the Federal Reserve Sys-

duty to make the property productive, unless otherwise directed. In the simplest situation it means that the trustee cannot let funds sit idle; he must make them produce income by investing them and will be liable for the normal rate of return on trust investments if he leaves the funds uninvested. Similarly he must take possession of the trust property promptly, and will be liable if loss results from his failure to do so.[92] A necessary corollary to the duty of management is that the trustee has the powers necessary or appropriate to proper management; and these will be implied when not expressly conferred by the trust instrument. While the function of the personal representative in decedent estate administration has been to liquidate, the modern cases reflect a trend towards requiring the representative to invest idle funds when administration is extended beyond the normal period.[93] In the case of a testamentary trust it is the personal representative who manages the trust res until the period of probate administration is over and letters of trusteeship issued to the trustee. Where an estate is held open for a long period, the representative is really performing the functions of a trustee.

In the course of his administration of a trust or estate, the fiduciary must as to each proposed act answer three questions:

(1) Can I do this act within the authority given me by the terms of the instrument or by law?

(2) Must I do it, or do I have a choice; and if the latter, how much choice?

(3) Assuming I have a choice, is the act a wise one in the interests of the beneficiaries?

The first question is traditionally treated as one of "power" on the part of the fiduciary. If the act affects a third person, as where the act is a sale of the trust property to the third person, the latter is interested only in the trustee's power. The beneficiary is also interested in this issue, since an act in excess of the trustee's powers is a breach of trust. For example, if the trustee has no power to sell, a sale would be a breach of trust.

The second question is traditionally treated as one of "duty", or of the "mandatory" versus "discretionary" nature of the power. A power which the trustee must exercise is called mandatory, and we say he has a duty to exercise the power. One which he may or may not exercise is called discretionary, and there is no duty. But this is not strictly accurate, for a trustee may be guilty of a breach of duty in the exercise or nonexercise of a so-called discretionary power; this is accomplished by judicial classification of the act as an abuse of discretion. Fundamentally the problem is how much leeway the settlor

tem, Federal Deposit Insurance Corporation, and Office of the Comptroller of Currency: Federal Financial Institutions Examination Council (1981), Trust Assets, Table 2. While a much higher percentage of real estate holdings will be likely for individually held trusts, these statistics clearly indicate that the trust is no longer primarily a landholding device.

92. See Section 5(2), infra.

93. See Section 5(3), infra; Uniform Probate Code, § 3–715(e).

intended to give the trustee in his administration of the trust, and there are infinite variations in such leeway.

The answers to these questions the trustee or executor, as the case may be, will find by first looking at the trust agreement or will. The trust agreement or will can and usually does spell out in detail the powers of the fiduciary. The present widespread practice is to insert in a trust instrument a detailed expression of powers,[94] but where this is not done modern courts are willing to imply powers either by interpretation of the instrument or because reasonably necessary to the management function inherent in the trust. In such case the trustee must either rely on prior court decisions or seek specific guidance from a court having jurisdiction by a bill for instructions or by petition for a court order authorizing the act. As to how much "discretion" or leeway a trustee has in the exercise of his powers, he will again resort primarily to the instrument setting up the trust, although here more is likely to be left to interpretation. Again cases and statutes may provide answers in specific situations. The courts also are prepared to imply powers of an executor from language in a will, but implication is less important in the case of an executor, because powers, such as a power of sale, not always implied in the case of a trustee, are taken for granted as a necessary part of the executor's functions, while powers such as authority to borrow money and mortgage the estate property are not normally exercised in the process of liquidating a decedent's estate.

But assuming the power and discretion in the fiduciary, the judicial control over the wisdom of an act is imposed through the basic duties and their corollaries considered in this section. Even then, the settlor of a trust, or sometimes the maker of a will, may desire to confer on the fiduciary authority to do acts which would not meet the normal standards of reasonable care and skill. In any event the fiduciary must obtain all the relevant facts and pass judgment on the soundness of any proposed action. The current practices of corporate fiduciaries will provide some guidance.

Unlike the trustee and executor, the administrator can look only to the court or the law for his powers and duties. These are generally set out by statute, but he may have to obtain court orders for exercise of some of the powers (such as sale of realty). The Uniform

94. A Uniform Trustees' Powers Act, suggested by Professor William B. Fratcher in "Trustees' Powers Legislation", 37 N.Y.U.L.Rev. 627 (1962), was approved by the Commisioners on Uniform State Laws in 1964. See Uniform Laws Ann., Business and Financial Laws (1970). Powers are recited in the Act which may be incorporated by reference into a will or trust instrument. As of 1980, 10 states had adopted the act with variations being adopted in other states. E.g. Minn.Stat.Ann. §§ 501.64–501.67; Va.Code Ann., § 64.1–57. The Act is discussed in Horowitz, "Uniform Trustees' Powers Act", 41 Wash.L.Rev. 1 (1966), and criticized in Hallgring, "The Uniform Trustees' Powers Act and the Basic Principles of Fiduciary Responsibility", 41 Wash.L.Rev. 801 (1966). See Haskell, "Some Problems With the Uniform Trustees' Powers Act", 32 Law and Contemp.Prob. 168 (1967).

See the powers conferred on the Trustee in the trust instrument set forth in Appendix I, at pp. 1404, 1405.

Probate Code, § 3–715, grants the administrator broad powers to act without court order.

Powers may be "personal" if the settlor or testator intends them to be exercised only by a particular person as fiduciary. Normally the settlor or testator intends the powers to be incidents of the office, so that a successor trustee may exercise them. If this is not his desire, he may specify that only the original trustee, naming him, can exercise the power. The management powers will seldom fall in the personal category, but it is not uncommon to make powers to invade principal personal.

The issues to be considered will arise most frequently upon an accounting by the fiduciary, either voluntary or compulsory. If there is an objection to the account, the fiduciary has the burden of showing that his actions were within his powers and that he has fulfilled all of his fiduciary duties. Because he has this burden, it is important that he carefully preserve throughout his administration a record of his activities. If he is unable to explain or justify his acts, he may be liable.

Although most of the law governing this area is made by state courts and legislatures, two bodies of federal law are relevant. Regulation 9, issued by the Comptroller of the Currency, Department of the Treasury, governs trust administration by national banks; it appears as Appendix II of this casebook at page 1408. Whenever a national bank is serving in a fiduciary capacity, you should look at Regulation 9 for applicable provisions; it contains rules not only on internal bank operations but also on investment of fiduciary funds, self-dealing, earmarking, and common trust funds. The Employment Retirement Security Act of 1974 (ERISA) set up fiduciary standards for administration of qualified retirement plans.[95] Because the statute includes the prudent man rule and a requirement of diversification, regulations under the Act and cases elaborating and applying the rule to pension trusts are likely to influence general trust law.

---

(1) THE DUTY TO USE REASONABLE CARE AND SKILL

The American Law Institute states that the trustee "is under a duty to the beneficiary in administering the trust to exercise such

95. See Chapter IX, Section 3(1) for a general treatment of fiduciary responsibility under ERISA. See also Canan, Qualified Retirement Plans, ch. 16; Kroll and Tauber, "Fiduciary Responsibility and Prohibited Transactions Under ERISA," 14 Real Prop., Prob. & Trust J. 657 (1979) (discussing Labor Department Regulations for investments under ERISA); Note, "Fiduciary Standards and the Prudent Man Rule Under the Employment Retirement Income Security Act of 1974," 88 Harv.L.Rev. 960 (1975). Little & Thrailkill, "Fiduciaries Under ERISA: A Narrow Path to Tread," 30 Vand.L.Rev. 1 (1977).

care and skill as a man of ordinary prudence would exercise in dealing with his own property; and if the trustee has or procures his appointment as trustee by representing that he has greater skill than that of a man of ordinary prudence, he is under a duty to exercise such skill."[96] The standard as stated is generally accepted, although variations in statement may be found. Thus in Estate of Allis,[97] the court states:

> "A trustee occupies a position of peculiar responsibility. A trustee is selected because of confidence in his diligence, prudence and absolute fidelity, as well as in his ability to so administer the trust as to protect those who, through infancy or other cause, are not able to protect their own interests. The performance of the duties of a trustee requires the exercise of a high degree of fidelity, vigilance, and ability. Especially is this true when the trustee is a company organized for the purpose of caring for trust estates, which holds itself out as possessing a special skill in the performance of the duties of a trustee, and which makes a charge for its services which adequately compensates it for a high degree of fidelity and ability in the administration of a trust estate."

In order to convey the concept that a trustee must comply with an external rather than a personal standard of care, the Uniform Probate Code modifies the traditional language slightly. Section 7–302 states the following standard of care and skill, which is also applicable to personal representatives by reason of Section 3–703(a):

> "Except as otherwise provided by the terms of the trust, the trustee shall observe the standards in dealing with the trust assets that would be observed by a prudent man dealing with the property of another, and if the trustee has special skills or is named trustee on the basis of representations of special skills or expertise, he is under a duty to use those skills."

The statement of the standard of prudence also tends to vary with the special context in which the issue of prudence is raised.[98] Thus,

96. Restatement, Second, Trusts § 174.

97. 191 Wis. 23, 29, 209 N.W. 945, 947, 210 N.W. 418 (1926). Note also the following from a footnote by Justice Stern, dissenting in Casani's Estate, 342 Pa. 468, 491, 21 A.2d 59, 60 (1941): "When it is said that a trustee must exercise common prudence and caution there is obviously meant the prudence and caution rightly demandable of one who *is* a trustee and is therefore not dealing with his own property. In other words, a trustee must act not merely as a prudent *man*, but as a prudent *trustee*."

98. A problem of growing importance is whether the board members of a charitable nonprofit corporation are to be held to the standard of a trustee or that of the corporate director. See Note, page 733, supra. The Uniform Management of Institutional Funds Act, promulgated in 1972 and adopted in 26 states and the District of Columbia as of 1982, resulted from a Ford Foundation study of investment of endowment funds of colleges and universities; see Cary and Bright, The Law and the Lore of Endowment Funds (1969). 7A Uniform Laws Ann., Business and Financial Laws (1978) 405. The Uniform Act applies to nonprofit charitable corporations as well as colleges, universities, hospitals and other institutions of eleemosynary nature. The Act among other provisions not only grants the governing board broad investment powers (§ 4) and permits delegation (§ 5), but also embodies as the standard of care for governing boards "ordinary business care and prudence under the facts and circumstances prevailing at the time of the action or decision" (§ 6).

with respect to *investments* the American Law Institute states that the trustee "is under a duty to the beneficiary (a) in the absence of provisions in the terms of a trust or of a statute otherwise providing, to make such investments and only such investments as a prudent man would make of his own property having in view the preservation of the estate and the amount and regularity of the income to be derived * * * ".[99]

Although an administrator and executor usually have limited investment functions, their actions must also be guided by the general standard of prudence for fiduciaries.

Whether the standard has been crystallized in detailed rules, as in the legal lists for investments, or whether it is a general judicial standard for guidance, the standard applies to all fiduciary action. Furthermore, if special skill is advertised—and this is done as a routine matter by professional corporate trustees, a higher standard may be applied commensurate with the skill represented.[1]

When the prudent man standard was first used in the United States, the use was by courts in instructing trustees and other fiduciaries. Judicial dockets were not crowded and fiduciaries obtained instructions readily—even as to matters of contemplated investments—which today are considered well beyond the ambit of judicial responsibility.[2] Today, however, the prudent man standard is applied by a court after the fact: when a beneficiary complains that some imprudent action by the trustee, executor or administrator has produced financial loss. While the court will tend to consider the facts as the fiduciary at the time should have seen them, and will attempt to exclude the wisdom of hindsight from its decision, the standard is so loosely framed that a careful fiduciary must be sure that his conduct more than meets it.

The application of the prudent man standard will be demonstrated repeatedly in the materials which follow.[3] A consideration of these materials should make clear that a "generalized" prudent man is involved and an incompetent trustee may breach the prudent man standard even though he uses all of the care and skill of which he is capable. Likewise the trustee's ignorance of the trust terms or of the existence of the standard will not preserve him from liability if the standard is breached.

99. Restatement, Second, Trusts § 227.

1. In Estate of Killey, 457 Pa. 474, 326 A.2d 372 (1974), noted 21 Vill.L.Rev. 151 (1975), the lower court was reversed for failure to apply a higher standard to a corporate fiduciary advertising "expert" skills; the advertisement used by the fiduciary was set forth as an appendix to the concurring opinion.

2. See, Alford, "The Influence of the American Civil War Upon the Growth of the Law of Decedents' Estates and Trusts", 4 Am.Jour. of Legal History 299, 349–354 (1960).

3. See, Stevenson, "Why the Prudent Man", 7 Vand.L.Rev. 74 (1953); Barclay, "Why the Prudent Man Rule", 99 Trusts and Estates 127 (1960); Note, "Trusts—Fiduciary Administration—Prudent Man Rule", 1960 Wis.L.Rev. 142. Fremont-Smith, "Duties and Powers of Charitable Fiduciaries: The Law of Trusts and the Correction of Abuses", 13 U.C.L.A.L. Rev. 1041 (1966).

Because the standards imposed by law upon the fiduciary are sometimes considered too strict, particularly for the individual as a fiduciary, it may be desirable to insert in some trust instruments a clause protecting the fiduciary. This may take the form of a broad "exculpatory" or "exoneration" clause reading as follows:

> "I direct that my executor and trustee shall not be liable except for loss caused by willful neglect or default."

There is evidence that courts will construe such clauses strictly against the trustee. For example, a court could easily find a particular breach of trust to be "willful" default by construing the phrase to include any intentional act of the trustee, such as purchase of securities not conforming to the legal standard, even though done in good faith.[4] The same judicial technique can be used where the clause exempts the trustee from all liability except for "bad faith" or "gross negligence". No court would enforce a clause to protect the trustee guilty of bad faith or gross negligence. This is not to say that such clauses are not effective to afford some protection to a fiduciary, particularly where the breach is a pure technicality. The corporate fiduciary will seldom rely on such a clause, as a matter of policy.[5]

A less sweeping clause such as the following is more likely to be given full effect by a court:

> "The trustee shall not be liable for any act taken upon advice of legal counsel."

Another indirect, and highly effective, method of protecting the fiduciary is to confer upon him broad powers, such as powers of sale and investment. The average trustee or executor has no desire to avoid the general fiduciary standards of reasonable care and loyalty, but to be protected against liability for acts done in good faith in the belief that he has authority to act under an interpretation of the will or trust document, or the applicable law, only to find later that a court interprets the will or trust differently or takes a different view of the law.

---

4. Compare New England Trust Co. v. Paine, 317 Mass. 542, 59 N.E.2d 263 (1945) with Tuttle v. Gilmore, 36 N.J.Eq. 617 (1883).

5. On exculpatory clauses generally, see Report of Committee on Trust Administration and Accounting, Exculpatory Clauses—Their Legal Significance, 1 Real Prop., Prob. & Tr.J. 530 (1966), reproduced in Probate in Midcentury (1975) 179–197; Report of Committee on Investments by Fiduciaries, Investments by Personal Representatives, 8 Real Prop., Prob. & Tr.J. 465 (1973) at 478–480. Normal policy reasons for opposition to exculpatory clauses seem inappropriate in a "directory" trust (where the trustee is directed by the terms of the trust to invest in accordance with instructions of a third person). Comment, "Directory Trusts and the Exculpatory Clause", 65 Col.L. Rev. 138 (1965); Report of Committee on Investments by Fiduciaries, Responsibility of Trustee Where Investment Power is Shared or Exercised by Others, 9 Real Prop., Prob. & Tr.J. 517 (1974) at p. 529.

(2) ACQUISITION OF ESTATE OR TRUST PROPERTY

A fiduciary must take possession of the estate of which he is to have custody within a reasonable time. The personal representative of a decedent must proceed to collect debts due the decedent, and may compromise these claims when the compromise is reasonable.[6] Usually it is advisable to obtain court sanction before a claim is compromised or abandoned. The personal representative may sue in his official capacity to collect debts due the decedent during his lifetime; [7] and may assert causes of action personally or in his official capacity for claims that arise after the decedent's death.[8] The personal representative is personally liable for assets lost due to his bad faith or imprudence in collecting them. The same principle of prudence in acquiring the assets of a trust applies to a trustee. Thus a testamentary trustee must require the executor to turn over the trust assets to him within a reasonable time and can be held liable personally for a loss resulting from his failure to make such a demand upon the personal representative.[9] Of course the trust terms may provide that personal estate of some special nature shall remain in the possession of the beneficiary; and while the trustee in this case is required to obtain possession of the property from the executor, he would then be expected to deliver it to the beneficiary in accordance with the trust terms. If land is leased, the trustee is not required to take possession, but should notify the lessee to pay the rent to him.[10]

The most difficult problem relating to the fiduciaries' duty of acquisition is identification of assets in a decedent's estate.

Since realty at common law was not subject to payment of debts generally and title passed directly to the heirs or devisees, realty was not an asset of the estate. Statutes now provide for sale of realty when necessary to pay debts and expenses of administration; if a sale is necessary, the representative can sue to set aside a fraudulent conveyance made by decedent during lifetime. In many states statutes also confer upon the representative the power or the duty to take possession during probate.[11] Absent such a statute, or a will devising realty to the executor in trust, the representative is not entitled to rents and profits accruing after decedent's death.[12] A claim for rent accruing before death is personalty to which the representa-

6. See, Atkinson, Wills (2d Ed., 1953) 645–6; Shaffer, "Fiduciary Power to Compromise Claims", 41 N.Y.U.L.Rev. 528 (1966); 72 A.L.R.2d 191, 243, 285 (1960). See Uniform Probate Code § 3–715(17).

7. E.g., Kent v. Bothwell, 152 Mass. 341, 25 N.E. 721, 9 L.R.A. 258 (1890). See Uniform Probate Code, § 3–703(c).

8. Thurmond v. Guyan Valley Coal Co., 85 W.Va. 501, 102 S.E. 221 (1920).

9. See, Bogert, Trusts (5th Ed., 1973) § 97; II Scott, Trusts (3d Ed.1967) § 175; Comment, "Duties of a Trustee in the Acquisition of the Corpus", 6 St. Louis L.J. 562 (1961).

10. See, Restatement, Second, Trusts, § 175, Comments *a*, *b*.

11. See Uniform Probate Code, § 3–709.

12. Lockridge v. Citizens Trust Co. of Greencastle, 110 Ind.App. 253, 37 N.E.2d

tive is entitled. By the doctrine of equitable conversion, realty under some circumstances may be treated as personalty. Thus, the personal representative may be entitled to the proceeds of a contract for the sale of land. Most states now have statutes requiring real property to be included in the inventory and decree of distribution.

The personal representative will not take possession of certain items. These include: property transferred by the decedent during his lifetime in some cases, proceeds of life insurance owned by deceased but payable to named beneficiaries, property held in joint tenancy, United States bonds registered in the name of deceased payable on death to another designated individual and property held in a revocable trust created inter vivos by the decedent. In addition, property over which the decedent had a general power of appointment is not considered his property. However, these items may all be included as part of the decedent's "taxable estate" for purposes of Federal estate taxes. Some of them can also be reached by decedent's creditors if his probate estate were inadequate; and in some cases the spouse may establish a claim to an elective share. Thus, when we refer to these as not being assets of the estate, we mean here for purposes of administration; this is sometimes called the "probate estate". Since in many instances there may be reasonable doubt whether an effective legal arrangement has been completed inter vivos, the task of litigating this issue falls to the personal representative. Thus if decedent has attempted gifts causa mortis, but delivery is questionable, the representative may bring suit to obtain possession of the assets from the alleged donee. Where decedent has a joint safety deposit box with another person (spouse, child, friend), there is sometimes a dispute as to respective ownership of contents of the box. Usually the agreement with the bank does not purport to create a joint ownership in the contents of the box, but merely provides access to the box by either "joint tenant." Obviously the personal representative owes a duty to the estate to claim all property which belonged to the decedent at the time of death.[13]

---

728 (1941). Even the "possession" of the personal representative conferred by statute is not regarded as a possessory interest beyond the period of administration. Suppose an owner of realty during lifetime leased to a tenant with option to renew: to whom does the tenant give notice of intent to renew while the estate is still in process of administration? O'Connor v. Chiascione, 130 Conn. 304, 33 A.2d 336 (1943).

13. If the agreement is silent, most courts will hold that no right of survivorship arises out of the mere fact that there is a joint safety deposit box. California Trust Co. v. Bennett, 33 Cal.2d 694, 204 P.2d 324 (1949); Estate of Wilson, 404 Ill. 207, 88 N.E.2d 662 (1949). Contra: Lilly v. Schmock, 297 Mich. 513, 298 N.W. 116 (1941) (oral statement by decedent to banker that he wanted survivor to have contents). In some states the survivor will not be granted access to the box after death of the other party until clearance is obtained from the appropriate state taxing official; for example, until the local public administrator is present to make an inventory of the contents of the box. Even where the box is in the name of decedent alone, a similar procedure may have to be followed in order to obtain a will from the box, if placed there for safekeeping. Dacey, How to Avoid Probate (1965) at p. 11 suggests that a better way to avoid administrative snags is for a husband and wife to have two boxes, the husband's box containing the wife's property and the wife's box containing the husband's property. This avoids only the delay in opening the box

IN RE FIRST NATIONAL BANK OF MANSFIELD

Supreme Court of Ohio, 1974.
37 Ohio St.2d 60, 307 N.E.2d 23.

[Testator's will created a trust for the benefit of the widow, with full power in her to invade principal and a general power of appointment of principal and undistributed income, with a gift in default to their daughter. The will named the Bank as both executor and trustee. The state inheritance tax return was prepared by counsel for the executor; a mistake was made involving a substantial overpayment, which was not refundable. In 1966, the account of the Bank as executor was approved. Following the death of the widow in 1967, the counsel for her executrix (the daughter) raised the propriety of the overpayment; an objection to the account of the Bank as trustee ensued. The trial court overruled the objection, and the Court of Appeals affirmed.]

CORRIGAN, JUSTICE.

Appellant's propositions of law, as presented here, are (1) that the trustee of a testamentary trust owes to trust beneficiaries a duty to collect and preserve the assets of the trust estate, and (2) that the beneficiary of a testamentary trust is not barred from asserting a claim against the trustee to redress a breach of the trustee's duties by failure on the part of the beneficiary to assert a claim against the executor.

As noted in the opinion of the Court of Appeals, appellant did not file exceptions to the final account of the executor, First National Bank. The question, then is whether this forecloses appellant's present action excepting to the account filed by the First National Bank, as trustee.

It is settled trust law that a "* * * trustee owes a duty to the cestui on taking over property from the executor to examine the property tendered and see whether it is that which he ought to receive." 6 Bogert, Trusts and Trustees (2 Ed.), 226, Section 583. "A successor trustee is liable for breach of trust if he neglects to take proper steps to compel his predecessor to deliver the trust property to him." 3 Scott on Trusts (3 Ed.), 1782, Section 223.2.

The scope of the trustee's duty to enforce claims upon assuming responsibility for management of trust property is summarized in 1 Restatement of the Law, Trusts 2d, 383, Section 177, as follows:

> "The trustee is under a duty to the beneficiary to take reasonable steps to enforce any claim which he holds as trustee against predecessor trustees * * * or in the case of a testamentary trust against the executors of the estate, to compel them to trans-

if one dies; it will not achieve transfer of registered securities in decedent's name and, if used to evade death taxes, would only result in fraud penalties upon discovery. Another practice is to put cash or bearer securities in a sealed envelope marked "property of" a named beneficiary, with the envelope kept in the decedent's box; this too can lead to litigation. Valentine v. St. Louis Union Trust Co., 252 S.W.2d 167 (Mo.1952).

fer to him as trustee property which they are under a duty to transfer, or to redress any breach of duty committed by them."

The foregoing principles of trust law make it clear that, upon assumption of administration of the trust, the bank, as trustee, had an obligation to redress the breach of duty which occurred when the executor overpaid the inheritance tax. Failure by the trustee to discharge that obligation constituted a breach of duty on the part of the bank in its capacity as trustee.

However, the trial court and Court of Appeals refused to impose liability on the bank, as trustee, because of appellant's failure to file exceptions to the final account made by the bank in its capacity as executor.

In the case of Dickerson v. Camden Trust Co. (1949) 1 N.J. 459, 464, 64 A.2d 214, upon the allowance of their final account as executors the defendants turned over to themselves as trustees all the assets of the estate including investments which should have been disposed of under the terms of the will because they were not "legal securities" which the fiduciaries were directed to invest in. Several of the cestuis sought to surcharge the fiduciaries for losses resulting from the "decline in value of the non-legal investments." The court held the fiduciaries liable despite a prior court approval and allowance of the executor's account, reasoning, at page 467, 64 A.2d at page 218, as follows:

> "The liability of these defendants as executors for their breach of duty in failing to dispose of the improper investments within a reasonable time, however, is dependent upon the effect to be accorded the Orphans' Court decrees approving and allowing their two accounts. Each of the accounts as filed had annexed a statement of assets upon which were listed all of the investments held by the estate and the corresponding values of each, which were in fact in most instances the same values set up in the original inventory. In these circumstances, both the executors and the beneficiaries are concluded by the decree of the Orphans' Court approving and allowing the accounts, and the executor's administration of the estate may not be challenged in the present proceedings either with respect to the propriety of the investments or as to the value thereof as stated in the accountings. * * *
>
> "But as trustees whose power of investment was restricted to legal securities and who had no authority to continue non-legal investments of the testator, the defendants were under an unqualified duty upon assuming the administration of the trust to accept for the trust estate only cash or legal securities valued at the then market value. * * * Instead, the trustees took over all of the assets held by themselves as executors, consisting in large part of non-legal investments, accepting them at the original inventory value of the estate. Having accepted the securities at inventory value in breach of their trust they are charged with and required to account for the assets at the values at which they received

them. As stated in 3 Bogert, Trusts and Trustees, § 583, pp. 15, 16:

"'* * * The trustee owes a duty to the cestui on taking over property from the executor to examine the property tendered and see whether it is that which he ought to receive. If the executor is under a duty to deliver money to the trustee, and tenders corporate stock in which the executor has wrongfully invested the funds of the estate, the trustee may render himself liable to the cestui by accepting such a tender. * * *'

"This principle would be applicable whether the trustee accepts securities in which the executor has wrongfully invested or whether he accepts securities which the executor has improperly retained. The fiduciary obligation which is breached is the same in each instance—the acceptance of improper assets. And where, as in the present cause, the trustees take over non-legal securities at values in excess of actual worth, they are liable to surcharge for the difference between the values at which the securities were accepted and the amounts realized upon the disposition of such securities. It follows as a necessary consequence that the trustees are liable also for the loss of income to the estate resulting from their breach of trust."

We agree with the reasoning of the court in the *Dickerson* case, and apply the principles expressed in the Restatement, supra, that a successor fiduciary is obliged to compel his predecessors "to transfer to him as trustee property which they are under a duty to transfer, or to redress any breach of duty committed by them." Thus, the First National Bank, as trustee, was under an unqualified duty, upon acceptance of the trust property from itself, as executor, to take action to recover for the benefit of the beneficiaries that portion of the trust property which had been wrongfully disbursed by the bank while acting as executor.

Inasmuch as appellee's liability is based upon its failure to discharge its responsibilities as trustee, the failure of appellant to file exceptions to the final account of the executor does not preclude her from filing exceptions to appellee's account in its capacity as trustee.

Therefore, the judgment of the Court of Appeals is reversed and the cause is remanded to the Probate Division of the Court of Common Pleas for further proceedings according to law.

Judgment reversed.

* * *

STERN, JUSTICE (dissenting).

Although I have no quarrel with the broad, legal principles relied upon by the majority, those principles must be recognized for what they are, i.e., guidelines that give only *general* direction to a judicial inquiry. The fiduciary duty of a trustee, or executor, is usually couched in terms like "reasonable" and "prudent," and therefore, in a particular case, a more meticulous examination of the facts is required.

The controversy in this case centers about a testamentary trustee's failure to redress an alleged breach of duty by the executor. Appellant claims that appellee, in its capacity as executor, negligently overpaid the Ohio inheritance tax due on decedent's estate, and that appellee, in its capacity as trustee, was subsequently negligent in failing to recover that overpayment from itself as executor. Appellant's entire case is premised upon the conclusion that the executor was personally liable for what is admitted by both parties to be an overpayment of taxes. I disagree with that conclusion.

It is undisputed that the inheritance tax form was prepared by William A. Calhoun, counsel for the executor. There is substantial support for the concept that an executor who reasonably relies upon the advice of counsel, in an area peculiarly requiring legal expertise, is not personally responsible for his attorney's mistakes. See 31 American Jurisprudence 2d 117, Executors and Administrators, Section 218; Annotations, 47 A.L.R.3d 507, and 28 A.L.R.3d 1191. Paragraph two of the syllabus in In re Estate of Butler (1940), 137 Ohio St. 96, 28 N.E.2d 186, contains general language to the contrary, but that case is readily distinguishable, on its facts, from the instant case.

The error made by Mr. Calhoun was judgmental, not arithmetic or accounting. It involved a failure to appreciate the consequences of a contingent interest in computing the decedent's inheritance tax. As such, the executor would not have been personally liable for the resultant tax overpayment. In relying upon its attorney, the executor acted reasonably.

Having determined that appellee, in its capacity as executor, was not negligent, it necessarily follows that appellee, in its capacity as trustee, breached no fiduciary duty in failing to recover the tax overpayment.

---

(3) INVESTMENTS [14]

Here, as elsewhere, historical background is helpful in understanding modern law, as well as putting cases in proper perspective.

14. On the duties of the trustee with respect to investments see Bogert, Trusts and Trustees (2d Ed., 1960) §§ 641–664; Bogert, Trusts (5th Ed.1973) Ch. 12; Curtis, The Modern Prudent Investor—How to Invest Trust Funds (1961); Loring, A Trustee's Handbook (6th Ed.—Farr, 1962) Ch. 8; 4 Powell, The Law or Real Property (Rohan Rev. 1981) ¶¶ 542–546; III Scott, Trusts (3d Ed.1967) §§ 227–231; Farr and Wright, "An Estate Planner's Handbook (4th Ed. 1979) §§ 32, 33; Restatement, Second, Trusts §§ 227–231; Comments, "The Prudent Investment Theory in Trust Administration", 9 Rutgers L.Rev. 130 (1947); "Prudent Trustee's Investment in Common Stock—Permissive or Mandatory?", 52 Northwestern Law Rev. 788 (1958); "Trusts—Trustees—Investment Duties of Trustees and the Problem of Unduly Conservative Trust Investments", 61 Mich.L.Rev. 1545 (1963);

The original pattern, set first by court decision and later by statute is a conservative one. Most trusts in England in the formative period of the law were trusts of a specific res, land. There was no problem of investment as we know it today. It is only as wealth shifts to personalty, principally in the last century, that the trustee is faced with decisions as to how the funds of the trust are to be made productive. In England, absent a provision in the trust instrument authorizing other investments, the Chancellor considered only government securities proper. In 1859 legislation authorized investment in first mortgages on land in the United Kingdom and stock in the Bank of England or Ireland, or the East India Company. In this country, the Massachusetts court in 1830 adopted a much more flexible rule in Harvard College v. Amory: [15]

> "All that can be required of a trustee to invest, is, that he shall conduct himself faithfully and exercise a sound discretion. He is to observe how men of prudence, discretion and intelligence manage their own affairs, not in regard to speculation, but in regard to the permanent disposition of their funds, considering the probable income, as well as the probable safety of the capital to be invested." New York in 1869 in King v. Talbot [16] seemingly adopted the same approach:
>
> "* * * the just and true rule is, that the trustee is bound to employ such diligence and such prudence in the care and management, as in general, prudent men of discretion and intelligence in such matters, employ in their own like affairs.
>
> "This necessarily excludes all speculation, all investments of an uncertain and doubtful rise in the market, and, of course, everything that does not take into view the nature and object of the trust, and the consequences of a mistake in the selection of the investment to be made."

Seemingly both courts were adopting a "prudent man" standard; but the test was in the results, not the verbal formula. Massachusetts courts drew no line as to types of permissible investments. New York prohibited investment in stocks, thus drawing a line between "legal investments" and those which a trustee might not make except at his peril. This was later carried a degree further by statutes setting up "legal lists". Recently there is a legislative trend back to the more flexible approach.[17]

"Common Stocks in Trusts", 113 U.Pa.L. Rev. 228 (1964).

15. 26 Mass. (9 Pick.) 446, 461 (1830).

16. 40 N.Y. 76, 85–86 (1869).

17. A majority of the states have statutes adopting the Prudent Man Rule. See Bogert, Trusts and Trustees (2 Ed., 1960) Ch. 30 for a collection of the investment statutes for each state. The legal list states are a distinct minority, and many of them have in recent years adopted amendments permitting investment of a stated percentage in preferred and common stocks. Investments are governed by the statute in force at the time the investment is held rather than at the time the trust instrument becomes effective. In re Flynn's Estate, 205 Okl. 311, 237 P.2d 903 (1951). For constitutionality of such an application of the statutes, see Goodridge v. National Bank of Commerce of Norfolk, page 1282, infra.

States are usually classified, for investment purposes, as "prudent man rule" or "legal list" states. The "legal list" is sometimes mandatory, making the fiduciary liable for all investments not complying with the list unless the trust instrument gives him broader powers; but it may be permissive, placing the burden on the trustee of justifying any investments not on the list but protecting him if he stays within the list. To the extent that legal lists have in recent years been amended to permit investment in common and preferred stocks, the difference between the two classes of states is lessened. The prudent man rule remains a more flexible standard.

The trust instrument may confer on the trustee discretion to make investments which would not be proper under common law or statute. However, such a provision should be explicit. Particularly in legal list states, a clause giving the trustee power to "invest as he deems proper" or "invest in sound securities" can be narrowly construed by a court to mean "within the legal list". It is therefore desirable to draft a clause dealing with investment powers explicitly to authorize investments without regard to statutory requirements as to kinds or amounts of investments.

Even in a legal list state, the fiduciary may be liable for failure to exercise due care in making an investment within the list, although the burden is cast on the beneficiary to prove that the trustee failed to exercise care. Note also that the statutes in particular states may or may not include personal representatives and guardians, as well as trustees.

The following investment factors must be considered by the trustee in the light of the purpose and terms of the particular trust which he is administering:

(1) *Safety of principal.* There is an obvious difference in the certainty of recovering the full dollar amount invested, between a United States government bond and a share of stock in a speculative venture. *Security* is also closely associated with safety, and secured obligations (first mortgages and corporate bonds) have generally ranked as proper investments. *Diversification* also aids safety by spreading risk, and has therefore been required in one degree or another by the courts and legislatures. However, in an inflationary period safety in terms of dollars is likely to be attained at the expense of purchasing power, since maintaining a constant dollar amount of principal means a loss of purchasing power; settlors have been more conscious of this than the courts.

(2) *Liquidity* (marketability). An investment may be perfectly "safe" in the long-run but not immediately saleable for its full cash value. A trustee may be under a duty to obtain cash, as where principal is payable to a beneficiary and is not distributable in kind (specific assets); this is impossible if he cannot readily convert the investment into cash. Even where the trustee is authorized to distribute principal assets in kind under the terms of the trust, a common provision arising from experience during the depression when market conditions made it undesirable to liquidate

many kinds of assets, the trustee must be concerned with liquidity.

(3) *Rate of return.* The amount of income received annually, in the form of interest and dividends, in relation to the principal invested is obviously important. The purpose of investment is to produce income. Yet rate of return reflects safety inversely; the surest investments carry the lowest rate. The trustee's problem is to strike a balance. The draftsman's problem is to implement the decision of the settlor as to whether safety or return is more important, by giving the trustee appropriate authority and direction as to investments. Note that the return here considered is not capital gain, the excess of sale price over purchase price. In some forms of investment, however, the excess may properly be considered income; [18] for example, in the familiar United States Government bonds Series EE there is no annual interest payment but rather an increase in redemption value.

Continued inflation and the devastating impact of high interest rates on both the bond and the stock markets in recent years have presented serious problems for trustees.[19] Unless the trust instrument gives them broad discretion in making investments, they are forced to operate under the traditional rule formulated in a different era with a stable economy. New forms of investments provide both opportunities and risks for trustees. Can the trustee invest in real estate investment trusts (REITs), supposedly designed to spread risk in investment in productive real estate which could appreciate more rapidly than inflation? [20] Can the trustee invest in market funds? [21] When, if ever, are nonincome producing items such as gold and silver,

18. Will of Wehner, 238 Wis. 557, 300 N.W. 241 (1941) (trustee holding United States bonds series D, purchased for ¾ths of face value and redeemable at an increasing amount each year, may properly pay the annual increase in redemption price as interest to the life tenant, taking this amount out of principal funds and restoring the principal by retaining the full amount on maturity or redemption).

19. See Melfe, "Investment Responsibilities of Professional Trustees," 15 Inst. of Est. Plan. (U. Miami, 1981) Ch. 4; Fleming, "Prudent Investments: The Varying Standards of Prudence," 12 Real Prop., Prob. & Trust J. 243 (1977) (criticizing the statutory codifications of the prudent man rule as obsolete under modern investment conditions); Note, "Investment and Management of Trust Funds in an Inflationary Economy," 126 U.Pa.L.Rev. 1171 (1978); "Current Investment Questions and the Prudent Person Rule," 13 Real Prop., Prob. & Trust J. 650 (1978); Blair & Heggestad, "The Prudent Man Rule and Preservation of Trust Principal," 1978 U.Ill.L.F. 79 (1978) (applying modern portfolio theory in assessing the effectiveness of the prudent man rule).

20. In Matter of Will of Newhoff, 107 Misc.2d 589, 435 N.Y.S.2d 632 (1980), investment in REITs was held to be improper because REITs were new forms of investment with no record of experience. But in Hoffman v. First Virginia Bank of Tidewater, 220 Va. 834, 263 S.E. 2d 402 (1980), the trustee was held not liable for holding original investments 38% of which were REITs under a will authorizing retention so long as considered "wise and expedient" and which also was construed to waive the prudent man rule.

21. Langbein and Posner, "Market Funds and Trust-Investment Law," 1976 A.B.F.Res.J. 1; Humbach and Dresch, "Prudence, Information and Trust Investment Law," 62 A.B.A.J. 1309 (1976); Langbein and Posner, "Market Funds and Trust-Investment Law II," 1977 A.B. F.J. 1.

diamonds, and works of art prudent investments for a trust portfolio? [22]

How far can a trustee, especially an institutional trustee administering charitable trust funds or a corporate fiduciary administering a pension trust, pursue nonfinancial goals within the parameters of the prudent man rule? Such goals might be positive (encouraging low-cost housing development or restoring local industry) or negative (avoiding investments in nuclear power companies, enterprises which endanger the environment, or corporations operating in a particular foreign country which has a discriminatory racial policy). If the primary purpose of the trust is to maximize income and principal growth, yet retain safety of principal, can this objective be met along with a policy involving nonfinancial goals? Professors Langbein and Posner have concluded that such goals tend to reduce diversification and increase administration costs and are therefore questionable under the existing prudent man rule.[23] A contrary argument has been made.[24]

RAND v. McKITTRICK

Supreme Court of Missouri, Division Two, 1940.
346 Mo. 466, 142 S.W.2d 29.

WESTHUES, COMMISSIONER. * * * [A hospital was established pursuant to a trust contained in the will of Robert A. Barnes. The res consisted of about $2,000,000 in land, cash, stocks and bonds. The trustees had a duty to invest the funds. During the year 1936 about one-half of the fund was invested in stocks of private corporations and the other one-half in bonds. During this year the stocks produced income of about $24,000 and the bonds $18,000. The total income for the year was over $505,000 and the total expense, including depreciation was about $680,000. The deficit was about $175,000, although about $79,000 was received from the community fund. About 11% of the patients paid their bills in full. This action was filed by the trustees to determine the propriety of investments in common and preferred stocks of private corporations and for the approval of investments already made. The Attorney General of the State was made a party defendant and contends such investments are not sanctioned by the greater weight of authority and do not coincide with the highest possible regard for preservation of the trust res.]

The question for determination * * * is: May trustees of a charitable trust, in the absence of statutory inhibition or restrictions

22. Sieling, "Personal Trusts: The Prudent Man Rule and Collectibles," 120 Tr. & Est. 48 (1981).

23. Langbein and Posner, "Social Investing and the Law of Trusts," 79 Mich. L.Rev. 72 (1980).

24. Ravikoff and Curzan, "Social Responsibility in Investment Policy and the Prudent Man Rule," 68 Calif.L.Rev. 518 (1980).

imposed in the grant, invest trust funds in stocks of private corporations? No case from Missouri is cited in the briefs which directly involved this question. The authorities from other jurisdictions are to some extent in conflict. There are two lines of authority which will be briefly noticed. One of these, often referred to as the New York rule, does not permit trustees to invest in stocks of private business corporations. The other rule, referred to as the Massachusetts rule, permits such investments to be made. A collation of the cases illustrating the two theories may be found in the annotations to the case of Walker v. Buhl, 211 Mich. 124, 178 N.W. 651, 12 A.L.R. 569, loc. cit. 575, 580. In a number of these states trustees' investments in private corporate stocks are regulated by statute or constitutional provisions. As a rule they prohibit such investments. See People's State Bank & Trust Co. v. Wade, 269 Ky. 89, 106 S.W.2d 74; White v. White, 230 Ala. 641, 162 So. 368, loc. cit. 371, 372(6)(7); In re Taylor's Estate, 277 Pa. 518, 121 A. 310, loc. cit. 311(2), 37 A.L.R. 553. In other states the rule prohibiting investments of trust funds in stocks of private corporations was established by the courts. See In re Grotenrath's Estate, 217 Wis. 109, 258 N.W. 453; Sellers v. Milford et al., 101 Ind.App. 590, 198 N.E. 456; King v. Talbot, 40 N.Y. 76. Courts of other states have held that a trustee may invest trust funds in stocks of private corporations. See Harvard College v. Amory, 9 Pick., Mass., 446; Morris Community Chest v. Wilentz, 124 N.J.Eq. 580, 3 A.2d 808, loc. cit. 810(4); Marshall v. Frazier, 159 Or. 491, 80 P. 2d 42, loc. cit. 58(23), 81 P.2d 132 (by statute enacted 1929, Code Or. 1930, § 32–803); Walker v. Buhl et al., supra; Fox v. Harris et al., 141 Md. 495, 119 A. 256, 26 A.L.R. 806. In Restatement of the Law, on Trusts, sec. 227, page 651, the rule is stated as follows: "The purchase of shares of preferred or common stock of a company with regular earnings and paying regular dividends which may reasonably be expected to continue is a proper trust investment if prudent men in the community are accustomed to invest in such shares when making an investment of their savings with a view to their safety."

As to the duty of a trustee in making investments, see sec. 227, page 645, of the same book, where we find the rule as follows:

> "In making investments of trust funds the trustee is under a duty to the beneficiary.
>
> "(a) in the absence of provisions in the terms of the trust or of a statute otherwise providing, to make such investments and only such investments as a prudent man would make of his own property having primarily in view the preservation of the estate and the amount and regularity of the income to be derived."

This latter statement is the yardstick generally used by the courts of the union in determining the duties of a trustee. Courts following the New York rule, as well as those following the Massachusetts rule, are in perfect harmony on this question. It is also the rule in this state. See Cornet v. Cornet, 269 Mo. 298, 190 S.W. 333, loc. cit. 339(5).

An analysis of these cases will disclose that the courts of the land have required trustees of trust funds to exercise a greater degree of care and caution when investing such funds than prudent men ordinarily exercise when investing their own funds. Investments which are speculative in nature have been universally tabooed, by the courts of the union, as proper investments for trust funds. Yet prudent men may and do invest in speculative enterprises. Wild v. Brown, 120 N. J.Eq. 31, 183 A. 899. Hence the rule is well stated, Restatement of the Law, on Trusts, supra, that trustees may "make such investments and *only* such investments as a prudent man would make of his own property *having primarily in view the preservation of the estate and the amount and regularity of the income to be derived.*" The part we have italicized is important. If that rule is adhered to, does it become necessary, or is it expedient or advisable for a court to arbitrarily declare any particular class of securities as unfit for trust investments? We think not. An examination of the cases will demonstrate that trust funds, in those states where the courts, legislature, or the people by constitutional provision have prohibited the investment of trust funds in stocks, have fared no better than have the trust funds in the states following the Massachusetts rule. We think this demonstrates that the preservation of trust estates depends more upon the integrity, honesty and business acumen of the trustees than it does upon arbitrary legal classification of securities wherein trust funds may be invested. Changed economic conditions often play havoc with the best laid plans. For example, a favorite investment, that is, first mortgage security on farm lands and other real estate, due to a changed economic condition, was the cause of many banks closing their doors in recent years. * * *

Turning our eyes to the present case we find from the evidence given by Mr. Rand that he had been one of the trustees since the year 1916; that the trustees always carefully investigated the securities in which the trust funds were to be invested. There was no charge or even a suggestion of any neglect of duty on the part of the trustees. We may say in passing that could the donator of the trust speak he would say to the trustees, "Well done." It may be interesting to quote from the evidence of Mr. Rand to get the viewpoint of the trustees:

> "If we meet to discuss the best interests of the hospital and the investment of certain funds that we have, and we reach the conclusion that a definite kind of investment should be made, and then if we have placed on us the restraint that this may be a technical violation of a law, then we are turned from what I consider the high purposes of the Trustees, and we have a warped judgment—that our judgment indicates one thing, but we are turned off of our course by the restriction which we have to follow * * *.
>
> "I am suggesting that it would be helpful to this hospital, if the Trustees felt that they could make an investment in what they believed to be a sound preferred stock or a sound common stock—

sound because of the history behind it of continuous success and the reputation for integrity and uprightness—that if we felt free and privileged to make the latter investment, that the hospital would receive greater benefit than from putting its money—making investments in government bonds at a yield that is nominal."

The purpose of the trust was to establish and maintain a hospital. The demands upon the service of this charitable institution were so great that the expense of operation far exceeded the income. It was the desire of the trustees to derive as much income as possible from the funds on hand compatible with the safety of the principal. As Mr. Rand testified, the purpose of the trust would fail if no substantial income were derived from the endowment fund. Therefore the trustees were of the opinion that all of the fund should not be invested in government securities because of the low income it would produce. In this theory the trustees are supported by a number of well reasoned cases. See Walker v. Buhl, supra; People's State Bank & Trust Co. v. Wade, 269 Ky. 89, 106 S.W.2d 74; Morris Community Chest v. Wilentz, 124 N.J.Eq. 580, 3 A.2d 808, loc. cit. 810(4). In the latter case the court approved the action of the trustees in changing a trust investment from governmental securities to stocks in business enterprises, when it was shown that the governmental securities proved non-productive. * * *

We therefore rule that where trustees exercise that degree of care and prudence, when making investments of trust funds, as is required by the courts in the cases above cited, and make investments in accordance with the rule as stated in the Restatement of the Law, on Trusts, Sections 227, 228, they have discharged their duty. We think the better rule to be that courts should not arbitrarily classify securities as proper or improper for investment of trust funds.

The judgment of the trial court is therefore affirmed.

MUELLER v. MUELLER

Supreme Court of Wisconsin, 1965.
28 Wis.2d 26, 135 N.W.2d 854.[25]

L. J. Mueller, the sole stockholder of L. J. Mueller Furnace Company, died in 1931. By the THIRD article of the will he left 4,450 shares of Mueller stock in trust, the income to go to his widow, respondent Jean Mueller, and the remainder to this children, respondents Robert W. Mueller and Elizabeth Mueller Ellis. Under the FOURTH article, 1,112½ shares were left in trust for the benefit of Ruth Mueller and Patricia Mueller Maslowski, the children of a deceased son. Appellant Harold P. Mueller, another son, received 3,337½ shares outright. Appellant and respondent Jean Mueller (and another now deceased) were named co-trustees of both trusts. Ap-

25. Noted, 49 Marq.L.Rev. 642 (1966).

pellant was president and managing director of Mueller Furnace Company.

In 1938 appellant put 1,156 shares of Mueller stock in an *inter vivos* trust with the income to go to Jean Mueller for life and the remainder to Robert W. Mueller and Elizabeth Mueller Ellis. Appellant named himself as trustee.

In 1954 the Mueller Furnace Company was merged into the Worthington Corporation. Pursuant to the reorganization plan, the Mueller stock held under the THIRD article, FOURTH article and *inter vivos* trust, was exchanged for 6,527½, 1,632⅔, and 6,782⅕ shares of Worthington common stock respectively. Appellant Mueller was appointed a vice-president and director of Worthington. Stock dividends were declared in 1957 and 1958, adding to the corpus of each trust.

In 1958, the county court approved the accounts of the trustees of the article THIRD and FOURTH trusts. In early 1963, appellant suggested to respondent Jean Mueller that the Worthington stock, which was the sole asset of the trusts since the reorganization of the Mueller company in 1954, be sold. During the year all the Worthington stock was sold at average prices of $29.59, $29.71, and $34.00 per share for the THIRD, FOURTH, and *inter vivos* trusts respectively.

Thereafter, appellant Mueller petitioned the court for allowance of accounts from November 8, 1938, to December 31, 1962, for the *inter vivos* trust, and from January 1, 1958, to December 31, 1962, for the THIRD and FOURTH article trusts. Objections were filed, and appeal is taken from a judgment which (1) surcharged appellant Harold Mueller and respondent Jean Mueller, as trustees, the sum of $116,299.12 plus interest and $30,555.84 plus interest under the THIRD and FOURTH article trusts respectively; (2) rendered Mueller liable to idemnify Jean Mueller in full for her liability; and (3) surcharged appellant Mueller, as trustee, the sum of $100,499.18 plus interest under the *inter vivos* trust.

Further facts will be stated in the opinion.

WILKIE, JUSTICE.

Three major issues are presented on this appeal:

1. *Did the trial court err in determining that the co-trustees had a duty to diversify the single asset of the trusts, the Worthington stock, and that this duty was breached by the failure to sell in October or November of 1961?*

* * *

Diversification of the Trusts

The trial court concluded first that the trustees should have diversified the investments of the three trusts within a reasonable time after October 18, 1958, when the THIRD and FOURTH article trust accounts were approved, and second, that the trustees should have disposed of 80 percent of the Worthington stock in October or November of 1961.

We first consider the trustees' duty to diversify.

A basic rule of trust administration is that a trustee should diversify investments so as to minimize the risk of loss. The Restatement, 2 Trusts (2d), p. 541, sec. 228, provides:

> "Except as otherwise provided by the terms of the trust, the trustee is under a duty to the beneficiary to distribute the risk of loss by a reasonable diversification of investments, unless under the circumstances it is prudent not to do so."

Appellant first turns to the terms of the trust instruments and argues that the trustees had the power, under these instruments, to retain the Worthington common stock. However, the *inter vivos* trust instrument did not authorize the retention of any stock whatsoever and only Mueller common stock could have been retained under the express terms of the article THIRD and FOURTH trusts.

As to both the article THIRD and FOURTH trusts the will provided:

> "[Article FIFTH] (c) Said trustees may in their discretion participate in and make any payments required by any proceedings for the reorganization, refinancing, dissolution, or other transactions, including the acquisition of stock rights when offered, *and may accept substituted or distributed stocks and securities,* in respect of any corporate securities subsisting in said trusts." (Emphasis added.)

Article 6 of the *inter vivos* trust contained an identical provision. Thus the trust instrument authorized the acceptance of substitute stock (Worthington), but contained no express authorization to retain the substituted stock.

While there is no express provision authorizing the trustees to retain the substituted stock, if the Worthington stock was substantially equivalent to Mueller, the trustees under both the article THIRD and FOURTH trusts (but in no event under the *inter vivos* trust) could have retained the Worthington Stock once it was received in the exchange for Mueller.[26] But as appellant himself admitted, Worthington was a considerably different corporation in terms of size, variety of products, and ownership. Accordingly, the stocks were obviously different and it cannot be seriously contended that the stocks were substantially equivalent.

26. [Footnote by the Court; other footnotes of the Court have been eliminated.]

Restatement, 2 Trusts (2d), p. 553, sec. 231, comment *f*; 3 Scott, Trusts (2d ed.), p. 1740, sec. 231.4, which states in part: "Substitution of new securities. Where a trustee is authorized to retain certain securities but is not authorized to purchase similar securities, and owing to a merger or other change in the corporate organization new securities are issued in place of the old securities, the question arises whether the trustee can properly receive and retain the new securities. It has been held that he can properly do so if the new securities are substantially equivalent to the old ones. On the other hand, if the new securities are substantially different from the old ones the trustee is under a duty to sell them. * * * "

As a further contention in support of his position that the express terms of the testamentary trust instrument (as distinguished from the *inter vivos* trust instrument) authorized the trustees to hold onto the Worthington stock, appellant cites another provision of the will, to-wit article FIFTH, par. (b), which provides:

> "My trustees *shall have power in their discretion* to take, receive, hold, administer, collect, *invest, and reinvest the assets of said trust estates*, with full power to bargain, sell, and convey at such prices and upon such terms as to them may seem best, or to exchange or otherwise realize upon any or all of the assets of said trust estates *as and when said trustees, in their discretion, deem it advisable.* * * *" (Emphasis added.)

Relying on In re Allis's Estate, Estate of Allis, and Welch v. Welch, appellant contends that this language, while not specifically sanctioning retention of the substituted stock, was broad enough to have permitted the trustees to do so without regard to any statutory limitations. In these three cases, this court held that where sweeping powers are given in regard to investing and reinvesting the trust assets, the trustees are not bound to comply with specific statutory limitations on retention of particular investments. But even with such broad powers, this court held that the trustees are still required to act as prudent and provident persons would act under similar circumstances.

In Allis the will granted the trustees:

> "full power and authority in their discretion to invest, reinvest and employ said real estate and generally manage the same; to continue the same as it is invested at the time of my death—and especially as invested in the E. P. Allis Company, or to change such investments; to receive and collect such profits and income thereof, and to dispose of the net income as follows."

In Welch the trust deed provided that:

> "Said trustees, their survivors and successors, shall have full power and authority to grant, bargain, sell, convey and otherwise dispose of the whole or any part of said property and to invest and re-invest the proceeds of any sales thereof, and to convert personal property into real property and real property into personal property as they may deem for the best interests of the trust estate, * * *."

A comparison of the above-quoted provisions of the Mueller will (Article FIFTH (b)) discloses that the trustees (as to the article THIRD and FOURTH trusts) may well have been empowered to retain the Worthington stock without complying with statutory regulations in regard to the type or class of security retained. However, in the last analysis, and as the Allis and Welch cases held, regardless of the trust provisions the ultimate question as to the two testamentary trusts and the *inter vivos* trust is whether or not the trustees acted prudently in retaining the Worthington stock.

Therefore, we now turn from a consideration of the effect of the terms of each trust instrument to an analysis of whether the action of the trustees in not diversifying each of the three trusts was prudent. The late Andrew Carnegie once admonished: "Put all your eggs in one basket and watch the basket." This may be good advice for some investors, but it is not the prevailing rule governing the investment practices of trustees. The rule is diversification. The exception is to retain the stock.

Is there any guide in the statutes as to what is prudent? Ch. 320, the trust-fund-investment chapter, was amended on August 2, 1959, to adopt the "prudent man" investment rule.[27] To begin with this statute provides:

> "Executors, administrators, guardians and trustees may invest the funds of their trusts in accordance with the provisions pertaining to investments contained in the instrument under which they are acting, or in the absence of any such provision, then within the limits of the following standards:"

Then follow subsections (1) and (2). Sec. 320.01(1) provides that the fiduciary shall:

> "exercise the judgment and care under the circumstances then prevailing, which men of prudence, discretion and intelligence exercise in the management of their own affairs, not in regard to speculation but in regard to the permanent disposition of their funds, considering the probable income as well as the probable safety of their capital. * * *"

Sec. 320.01(2) qualifies (1) by limiting (with certain qualifications not relevant here) the holdings in common stock to 50 percent of the total market value of the fund. Thus, in trusts subject to the provisions of sec. 320.01(2), the statutes themselves forbid investment of common stock in excess of 50 percent of the fund. This is true of the *inter vivos* trust.

It appears that the standards set forth in secs. 320.01(1) and (2), Stats., do not apply to the two testamentary trusts in the instant case in view of the authority vested in the trustee by the provisions above cited. On the other hand these standards do apply to the *inter vivos* trust where there was no similar provision in the trust instrument.

* * *

Since the trial court concluded that the stock in all three trusts should have been diversified to the extent of 80 percent of the holdings of Worthington, the statutes, even as to the *inter vivos* trust, do not control what is prudent, and the determination as to whether or not the conduct of the appellant was prudent, in the last analysis, is governed as to all three trusts by the fundamental rules regarding diversification. The basic rule of diversification applies to both the making of investments and the retention of investments. In re Re-

27. This is now Wis.Stat. § 881.01.

statement, 2 Trusts (2d), p. 548, sec. 230, comment i, it is stated, in part:

> "*Diversification.* Except as otherwise provided by the terms of the trust, the trustee is under a duty to the beneficiary to distribute the risk of loss by disposing of investments included in the trust at the time of its creation which, although otherwise proper investments for the trustee to retain, are improper because not properly diversified. Compare § 228. Thus, if a testator bequeaths all his property in trust and more than half of his estate consists of the bonds of a particular railroad, the trustee is ordinarily under a duty to sell some of the bonds and to invest the proceeds in other securities, so that the estate will not include an undue proportion of the securities of a single corporation."

The trial court picked October 16, 1958, the date of the approval of the trustees' accounts in the article THIRD and FOURTH trusts, as the date when the trustees' duty arose to diversify by selling the Worthington stock in all three trusts. In essence the court's conclusion is based entirely on the application of the fundamental rules requiring diversification of trust investments.

There is no point in considering whether the duty to diversify actually arose back in 1954 when the Worthington stock was first received. The objectors concede that the "Order of October 18, 1958, approving prior accounts had the effect of relieving the trustees from their *prior* duty to diversify." (Emphasis added.) It is the duty arising thereafter that the objectors contend for and which the trial court found. Once the duty to diversify arises the trustees should perform that duty as soon as they can reasonably do so. Fixing the exact deadline for diversification is an extremely difficult task and the general rule guiding the court in making that determination is set forth in 2 Scott, Trusts (2d ed.), sec. 209, at page 1548, where it is stated:

> "* * * it is ordinarily impossible to fix that moment [of the period within which he should have sold] with any exactness, at least where no time within which the trustee must sell the property is fixed in the trust instrument. Probably the only rule is that the court will use its common sense and determine what under all the circumstances it is fair to say that the trustee ought to have received if he had done his duty in selling the property within a reasonable time. * * *"

The trial court concluded that it was mandatory for the trustees to dispose of 80 percent of the stock no later than October or November of 1961. In arriving at this conclusion the trial court made certain findings of fact, which on review will be sustained unless against the great weight and clear preponderance of the evidence.

As a director of Worthington, appellant was aware of antitrust actions within the electrical industry. The status of certain treble damage suits against Worthington was discussed at a directors' meeting on October 18, 1961. Appellant attempts to minimize this knowledge by maintaining that he did not feel that Worthington would become involved in a significant number of suits. It may well be that

Worthington's ultimate involvement in the suits was negligible. But the trial court's decision (Findings No. 10 and No. 11, and Conclusion No. 2) did not rest on this alone; it was not unreasonable for the trial court to have concluded that this information had at least a small bearing on the question of whether and when it was prudent to sell Worthington.

In addition, by virtue of his corporate office, appellant was aware that Worthington was in a profit squeeze. (Findings No. 10 and No. 11, and Conclusion No. 2.) The percentage of income before taxes to billings had dropped from 7.18 percent in 1960 to 4.87 percent in 1961. Earnings dropped from $4.42 in 1960 to $3.40 in 1961. Dividends were also cut and the price of Worthington stock dropped approximately 50 percent between September, 1961, and December, 1962. Appellant counters that it was not only Worthington but the whole capital-goods industry that was involved in a profit squeeze. But this analysis ignores the possibility of investing in another segment of the market. Appellant also points out that the backlog of Worthington's unfilled orders was greater in 1961 than in 1960. But this is no particular advantage if profits are down.

Commencing on October 18, 1961, the date of the Worthington board of directors' meeting, the appellant resumed the sale of his personally held Worthington stock. (He had sold 20,500 shares from 1954 through 1958 with no sales after that date until those in 1961.) All told, in the months of October and November of 1961, he sold 13,000 shares so that by the end of these sales he had disposed of 53.-2 percent of his total holdings of 62,850 shares, leaving 29,380 shares. He received an average price of approximately $51 per share on these 1961 sales. No trust shares of Worthington were sold until 1963.

Appellant maintains that the corpus of the trust would have been significantly reduced by the payment of the state and federal income taxes on any sales of Worthington (in 1961 or otherwise), and that the trial court ignored these tax consequences in arriving at its two-fold conclusion: the duty to diversify and the mandatory sale date of 1961. The Mueller Furnace Company stock had a tax basis of zero in the THIRD and FOURTH article trusts, and five cents a share in the *inter vivos* trust. The respective bases were transferred to the Worthington stock under the tax-free reorganization in 1954. Although the tax factor is one which can be properly considered in passing on the prudence of the trustee's actions, the trial court not only made no mention of it in its conclusions, findings, or decision, but expressly indicated during the trial that "the tax angle has nothing to do with the propriety of the accounts." However, the failure of the trial court to consider any income tax ramifications is not grounds, of itself, for reversal in this case. This is because the trial court could still have properly concluded, relying on the general rule calling for diversification in connection with appellant's knowledge of Worthington's financial condition, that it was imprudent to retain the stock even if he had considered the possible tax implications. This is not to say that the tax aspect is unimportant; rather it is to say that under the circumstances any tax advantages gained by not diversifying were outweighed by the factors requiring the sale of part of the Worthington stock.

At the trial, appellant introduced many investment digests, analyses, and bulletins he had received which indicated, in somewhat glowing terms, that Worthington was a sound investment. But a trustee cannot ignore the rule requiring diversification merely because a particular stock is a prudent investment in terms of quality.

It is apparent from its decision and findings, that the trial court placed much emphasis on the fact that appellant Mueller disposed of a considerable block of his personal holdings of Worthington in the fall of 1961, while not making similar disposals of the stock in the trusts. However, although appellant did sell 13,000 shares in October and November, he retained 29,380 shares, or 46.8 percent of his original holdings in the company. No further sales were made until August of the next year. In addition, the mere fact that appellant sold some of his own Worthington stock does not mean that retaining the stock in the trusts was imprudent *per se*. The sale has a bearing on the present case only if the same reasons which prompted it would also dictate a diversification of the trusts. Because he was in a 90 percent tax bracket, appellant claims that he sold the Worthington stock, upon the suggestion of his financial adviser, in order to invest in municipals. Even assuming, then, that it was to his advantage to dispose of his Worthington holdings, this does not mean that it was not to the advantage of the beneficiaries to sell. Mrs. Mueller, the income beneficiary of the THIRD article and *inter vivos* trusts, was in the 65 percent bracket herself. Arguably, it would have been equally as sound to invest in municipals to give her a tax break also. But this is somewhat conjectural.

* * *

The trial court found as a matter of fact (Finding No. 13) that appellant retained the Worthington stock in the trusts primarily for voting control purposes. But since there were over 1,600,000 shares of Worthington stock outstanding, of which only a little more than 15,000 were held by the trust, this could hardly have been a "paramount consideration." In addition, the fact that he had disposed of over half of his personal holdings is inconsistent with this purportedly avowed purpose. Furthermore, there was no evidence adduced which affirmatively demonstrated that voting control played any part in his decision. Therefore, this particular finding is against the great weight and clear preponderance of the evidence.

However, keeping in mind that diversification is the general rule, it cannot be said, in light of the information possessed by appellant concerning the financial affairs of Worthington, that the trial court erred in concluding that 80 percent of the stock should have been sold in the fall of 1961.

* * * [In the omitted portion of the opinion, the Court held that none of the beneficiaries were estopped from objecting to failure to diversify, and that appellant was not more negligent than Jean

Mueller and hence that he was entitled to contribution from her, although she relied on him to actually manage the trust.] * * * [28]

NOTE

At the inception of the trust, a trustee may receive an investment portfolio which does not comply with normal standards for trust investments, either because some of the investments would be imprudent for a trustee to make or, as in the principal case, because of the lack of diversification. He is then under a duty to sell improper investments with reasonable diligence, unless the trust instrument authorizes retention. What is a reasonable time for conversion to proper investments depends on many factors, including current market price upon sale, prospects for an improved price, and tax considerations.[29]

If there is express authority to retain, this does not relieve the trustee from his duty to use reasonable care in reviewing continued holding of the improper investments, in the same manner that prudence requires continuous review of all trust holdings.[30] Care must be taken to distinguish a trust instrument which *directs* (rather than merely authorizes) the trustee to retain; in such a case the trustee has a duty not to sell and will be liable for breach if he sells, except upon court order in the special circumstances discussed in Subsection (6), infra.

Note that the Court in the principal case says: "The basic rule of diversification applies to both the making of investments and the retention of investments." Should the Court have given weight to the following Wisconsin statute (then § 230.05, now § 881.05)?

> "(1) Unless the trust instrument or a court order specifically directs otherwise, a trustee shall not be required to dispose of any property, real or personal or mixed, in the estate or trust, however acquired, until the trustee determines in the exercise of a sound discretion that it is advisable to dispose of the same; but nothing herein contained shall excuse the trustee from the duty to exercise discretion at reasonable intervals and to determine at such times the advisability of retaining or disposing of such property."

---

28. Compare Baldus v. Bank of California, 12 Wash.App. 621, 530 P.2d 1350 (1975) (holding trustee not liable for failure to diversify where the trustee retained stock in one corporation amounting to 80–90% of corpus, the trust instrument not only authorizing but expressing the desire that the trustee retain the stock if in its judgment it was desirable).

29. During the great depression of the Thirties the courts were reluctant to impose liability on trustees who retained improper investments in expectation of improved prices. See Casani's Estate, 342 Pa. 468, 21 A.2d 59 (1941) where trustees retained investments not on the state legal list for 8 years and were not surcharged for breach of duty.

30. Bogert, Trusts and Trustees (2d Ed. 1960) §§ 683–686; III Scott, Trusts (3d Ed. 1967) § 230.1; Stirling's Estate, 342 Pa. 497, 21 A.2d 72 (1941) ("The authority to retain investments does not justify holding without attention.")

ESTATE OF BEACH

Supreme Court of California, 1975.
125 Cal.Rptr. 570, 542 P.2d 994.

WRIGHT, CHIEF JUSTICE.

Seth G. Beach died on August 4, 1968, leaving an estate valued at over $2.4 million. His will, after making a number of smaller dispositions, placed the bulk of his estate in a testamentary trust for the benefit of his four children and named the Bank of California as both executor and trustee. The estate included 27,700 shares of Reserve Oil and Gas Company (Reserve) common stock appraised at $391,-262.50, or $14.125 per share. In June 1969 the executor sold 3,000 shares of the stock for approximately $16 per share to raise funds toward the payment of claims, taxes and expenses of administration. By the time the remaining 24,700 shares were distributed to the testamentary trustee in September 1970, their value had declined to little more than $6 per share.

Three of the four residuary trust beneficiaries filed a contest of the executor's first account (Prob.Code, § 927) claiming the estate was entitled to damages from the executor for the latter's alleged negligence in not selling the stock while its market price was above its appraised value at the date of death. After discovery proceedings and a six-day nonjury trial, the trial court found that the executor had exercised due care in retaining the stock and accordingly rendered judgment rejecting the exceptions to the account and declaring the account settled. Appealing from the judgment, objectors (hereafter contestants) assert that the trial court applied an incorrect standard of care in exonerating the executor from negligence and that in any event the finding of no negligence is unsupported by the evidence. We conclude that the executor was not negligent if it exercised ordinary care in applying the skills and knowledge ordinarily possessed by banks engaged in the trust business under similar circumstances to the administration of the present estate, and that the evidence sufficiently shows that the executor met this standard. We reject the contestants' contention that the bank can be called to account for performance of its duties as *trustee* in the present proceeding for settlement of its account as *executor* even though it might have to give due consideration to the existence and terms of the trust and the circumstances of the beneficiaries of the trust in order to properly carry out its duties as executor in the probate administration of the estate.

With regard to other contentions on appeal, we conclude that the trial court committed no error in denying contestants' demand for a jury trial, in allowing the executor extraordinary compensation for defending against the contest, and in making an order subsequent to the judgment (separately appealed from) allowing the executor's attorneys extraordinary fees for such defense. However, such compensation and fees should have been charged against the entire estate instead of against only the contestants' shares, and the executor should not have been allowed interest based on deferral of some of its compensation. With modifications to eliminate these errors, we affirm the judgment and the order.

Bank's Alleged Liability as Executor for Retention of Stock in Estate

An executor is not liable for losses suffered by the estate without his fault (§ 920) but may be required to reimburse the estate for losses proximately resulting from his failure to exercise the requisite duty of care in its administration (Estate of Guiol (1972) 28 Cal.App. 3d 818, 105 Cal.Rptr. 35). The standard of care generally applicable to executors is "that degree of prudence and diligence which a man of ordinary judgment would be expected to bestow upon his own affairs of a like nature." (Estate of Moore (1892) 96 Cal. 522, 525, 31 P. 584. Estate of Barbikas (1959) 171 Cal.App.2d 452, 457–458, 341 P.2d 32, 37.) However, as a bank engaged in the business of acting as a fiduciary for estates and trusts (see Fin.Code, §§ 106–107, 1502), the executor could be held liable for negligence if it failed to exercise the skill and knowledge ordinarily possessed by such professional fiduciaries. (Gagne v. Bertran (1954) 43 Cal.2d 481, 489, 275 P.2d 15; Rest. 2d Torts, § 299A.)

Contestants claim that the judgment is not supported by the evidence. To consider this contention, we review the facts, viewing the evidence in the light most favorable to the executor and indulging in all reasonable intendments and inferences that tend to sustain the judgment. * * *

Under the decedent's will the residue of the estate left in trust was to be divided into four shares, one for each of the testator's children. One third of each child's share was to be distributed to him or her at age 25, one third at age 30, and the remaining third at age 35, with periodic distributions of income from the part of the share held in trust. The decedent's four children were: Marianne Beach Edwards, born June 1, 1939; Joette Beach Carter, born January 1, 1942, and twins named Scott Gregory Beach and Schuyler Jean Beach, born November 19, 1952. Thus, upon the decedent's death both Mrs. Edwards and Mrs. Carter were eligible to receive one third of their trust shares, and Mrs. Edwards became eligible for an additional third nine months thereafter. Only Mrs. Carter and the twins are contestants in the present proceeding.

The principal assets of the estate and their appraised values as of the date of death were 27,700 shares of Reserve common stock ($391,262.50); Reserve convertible debentures ($117,625); Mother Lode Bank common stock ($300,600); government and public utility bonds ($691,238); real estate ($387,000); a lumber business which was liquidated during administration ($299,389); and cash, notes, insurance and miscellaneous items ($235,680).

The Reserve stock was listed on the American Stock Exchange. The company's main activity was the exploration for and production of oil. The stock paid no dividend, and the company's earnings were "flat," lacking any significant increase or decrease. The principal attraction of the stock was the prospect of capital growth through oil exploration activities.

Donald T. Dooling, the bank's trust officer immediately in charge of the estate, testified that when administration commenced in August 1968 he was concerned about the size of the Reserve holding and discussed the matter with Roger Newell, head of the bank's portfolio management section, who replied within a week or two that no immediate steps were necessary. Newell testified that on receiving Dooling's inquiry he went to the securities research section to read available information concerning Reserve and discuss the stock with the section's security analysts, whose function was to analyze individual securities and industries as well as general economic conditions. Newell concluded there was no reason to recommend immediate sale of the stock because he found no apparent "deterioration" in the company's balance sheet, management, or other "fundamentals."

The following December, the bank's trust investment committee (T.I.C.), responsible for portfolio management decisions, made an "initial review" of the estate's assets and decided to retain the stock because of the absence of deterioration in the company. In January 1969 the same committee considered what assets should be sold to raise cash needed for administration and decided "to continue with the program to sell the real estate assets and to defer sale of Reserve." The reasons for this decision were (1) that the real estate required current expenditures from the estate and was not as readily marketable as a listed stock, which could be sold later if and as needed, and (2) the absence of any evidence of deterioration in Reserve.

In February 1969 the bank's trust *securities* committee (T.S.C.) recommended that holdings of Reserve stock be sold. However, the T.S.C.'s recommendation was based on information furnished by the securities research section concerning the stock itself, without regard to the nature of the trust or estate in which the stock might be held. Despite the T.S.C.'s recommendation, the T.I.C. decided to retain the Beach estate's holding of the stock because of the continued absence of any sign of deterioration in the company.

In May 1969, Dooling reported to John Pierson of the portfolio management section that the estate required $390,000 of additional cash to conclude administration and suggested consideration of a sale of part of the Reserve holding for this purpose. About this time it was learned that the Reserve convertible debentures held by the estate would be called for redemption on July 16th at a price below the current market price. To avoid a loss through redemption the estate would have either to sell the debentures or to convert them into some 7,600 shares of common stock thereby increasing its stock holding to some 35,300 shares. Under these circumstances the T.I.C., on advice from the portfolio management section, decided to raise the needed cash by selling the debentures, 3,000 shares of the stock, and certain short-term government bonds. Based on court authorization received on June 24, 1969, the executor sold the debentures for $119,500 and the 3,000 shares of stock for $47,607, reducing the estate's holding of the stock to 24,700 shares. Newell testified that in recommending this sale the portfolio management section felt that "some reduction of Reserve was in order," that the "one-third reduction" (35,300 to 24,700 shares) was "appropriate," and that the remaining Reserve stock was acceptable for distribution into the trust because the company remained fundamentally sound and the stock had "some long-term potential for increase in value."

In July and August of 1969 the stock's market price commenced a gradual decline which continued into the following May and was followed by a moderate rise until distribution to the trustee in the fall. The bank's security analysts interpreted this decline as a reflection of a downward trend in stocks generally which was particularly pronounced in oil stocks and not as indicating any deterioration in Reserve's operations or prospects.

In determining that the Reserve stock was suitable for inclusion in the trust, the bank's portfolio management section considered the circumstances and resources of the trust beneficiaries and determined that the tentative objectives of the trust should include not only the production of income but also long-term capital growth as a protection against inflation. None of the beneficiaries or their families had any special problems of ill health or disability which would require unusual amounts of income. The twins in addition to having interests under the trust were the beneficiaries of a settlement agreement between their mother and the decedent under which the estate was paying $500 per month for their benefit in child support and was obligated to pay the expenses of their college educations. Assets distributable to the trust other than the Reserve stock were producing substantial amounts of income. Under these circumstances the growth potential of Reserve was deemed to make it a desirable trust asset despite the fact that it paid no dividends.

On the other hand, the portfolio management section did not base its decision to retain the 24,700 shares of Reserve stock on any standard of diversification. Its practice was not to attempt to diversify particular investment holdings during probate because of the restrictions on the executor's power to reinvest. Thus the retention of the stock in the estate was based on the executor's determination that Reserve was not in a deteriorating condition, that no further cash was needed to complete administration of the estate, and that the stock was a suitable asset for inclusion in the trust.

The bank concedes that as a professional fiduciary its liability must be determined by more stringent standards than would the liability of a lay executor. Those undertaking to render expert services in the practice of a profession or trade are required to have and apply the skill, knowledge and competence ordinarily possessed by their fellow practitioners under similar circumstances, and failure to do so subjects them to liability for negligence. * * *

The bank contends we should accept the findings of its freedom from negligence simply for lack of testimony by qualified experts sufficient to prove its noncompliance with the relevant professional standards. Plaintiff called three expert witnesses who gave reasoned opinions that the bank should have sold more or all of the Reserve stock during the administration of the probate estate. One of these witnesses was president of an investment management firm; another had been in charge of the trust department of a title company from 1952 to 1966; and a third was director of research for a stock brokerage firm. It is unnecessary for us to consider the sufficiency of these witnesses' expert qualifications or testimony because the findings are fully supported by the testimony of the *bank's* expert witnesses, who included not only those of its employees already mentioned but also an independent securities analyst and a senior trust officer of a competing bank with 38 years of banking experience. The latter witness testified in answer to a hypothetical question that in his opinion and based on his professional experience, the executor's retention of the 24,700 shares of Reserve stock in the estate was prudent and did not deviate from any investment standard in California known to the witness.

It is suggested that the trial court's findings and memorandum decision show that it failed to give proper weight to the requirement that the bank use the skills and knowledge ordinarily possessed by professional fiduciaries in similar circumstances. However, the memorandum decision refers to the last mentioned expert as "[t]he most persuasive witness produced * * * who had excellent qualifications, vast experience, vast knowledge and who impressed the Court as being totally impartial" and further commends the bank's "committee set-up of checks and balances and review within [its] trust department" as "excellent." The findings uphold the bank's exercise of due care "in the manner in which it utilized all of its available relevant internal banking services and procedures" in making the decisions for which contestants seek to impose liability. * * * Under these circumstances we are satisfied that the trial court properly judged the bank's conduct by professional rather than lay standards.

Contestants claim that the trial court erred in determining the bank's liability according to its exercise of care as an executor rather than as a testamentary trustee. They contend that because the bank received title to the trust assets upon the decedent's death by operation of his will, subject only to probate administration (§§ 28, 300; Estate of Lefranc (1952) 38 Cal.2d 289, 297, 239 P.2d 617; Estate of Muhammad (1971) 16 Cal.App.3d 726, 733, 94 Cal.Rptr. 856), the bank acted during probate administration in a dual capacity as executor and trustee, and that its supposed capacity as trustee subjected the bank's decisions concerning the retention or disposition of the Reserve stock in the probate estate to the "prudent investor" rule of Civil Code section 2261. Contestants are particularly concerned with the requirement implicit in the rule that investments be diversified (Mandel v. Cemetery Board, supra, 185 Cal.App.2d 583, 587, 8 Cal. Rptr. 342) and argue that by judging the bank solely on its performance as executor the trial court erroneously failed to consider whether the retention of the unsold shares of Reserve stock in the estate violated this diversification requirement. Although contestants recognize that apart from sections 584.5–584.6 (see fn. 10, ante) the executor could not have invested the proceeds from any sale of Reserve stock in anything but savings accounts or government securities (§§ 584, 584.1, 585), they argue that even those forms of interest-bearing investments would have been preferable to retention in the estate of a disproportionately large holding of a "speculative" stock yielding no dividends.

In making this argument contestants overlook or misconceive basic distinctions between the bank's duties as executor and its duties as trustee. In the first place, the fact that the same bank was named as both executor and trustee in the will is immaterial. Even though the executor in handling estate assets may sometimes be required to take into account the fact that all or part of the net estate will be distributed to a testamentary trust with particular terms and beneficiaries, the executor's duty in this regard does not vary according to whether the executor and trustee are the same or different entities. The present bank's powers and duties as executor were just as distinct from its powers and duties as trustee as if the will had named another bank as trustee. * * *

Moreover, the anticipation that the bulk of the estate would be transferred to a testamentary trustee, which in this case happened to be the same bank, did not require the executor to manage the estate assets as if they were already being held under the terms of the trust. The executor has numerous functions and obligations not normally imposed upon a testamentary trustee, such as presenting the will for probate (§§ 320, 323, 324), locating assets (§§ 571, 581), locating beneficiaries (§ 326, subd. 3), handling creditors' claims (§§ 700–719, 730–738), providing for any immediate needs of the decedent's family through a family allowance (§ 680), preparing returns for and paying estate and inheritance taxes (Int.Rev.Code, § 2002 (26 U.S.C.A. § 2002); Rev. & Tax Code, § 14101) as well as income taxes of the decedent and the estate (Int.Rev.Code, §§ 641(b), 6012(b) (26 U.S.C.A. §§ 641(b), 6012(b)); Rev. & Tax Code, § 18405) and distributing the remaining assets to the beneficiaries (§§ 1000–1003, 1020–1029). The executor holds and manages the estate assets incidentally to performance of the various duties of administering the estate, in contrast to the testamentary trustee, whose primary mission is to serve the trust beneficiaries under the terms of the trust. Usually, as in the instant case, such management by the executor concerns the interests of the trust beneficiaries only through its effect on the nature and value of the property distributed to the trustee and the timing of such distribution or distributions. * * *

The present record reveals that in handling the Reserve stock in the probate estate the executor made three kinds of decision affecting the contestants' interests as trust beneficiaries and supports the trial court's conclusion that in all three areas the executor applied the requisite skills and knowledge and exercised the requisite degree of care. These decisions related to (1) preservation of the estate assets, (2) selection of assets to sell for needed cash and (3) timing of distributions to the trust. Each area of decision will be considered in turn.

A primary duty of the executor is to take reasonable steps to preserve the assets of the estate. (Estate of King (1942) 19 Cal.2d 354, 358, 121 P.2d 716; Estate of McSweeney (1954) 123 Cal.App.2d 787, 793, 268 P.2d 107; Estate of Smith (1931) 112 Cal.App. 680, 685, 297 P. 927.) The duty of preservation may require the executor to take affirmative steps to prevent deterioration in value. (Estate of Porter (1900) 129 Cal. 86, 61 P. 659 (sale of vineyard-orchard to avoid maintenance expenses pending escheat proceeding); Estate of Fernandez (1898) 119 Cal. 579, 585, 51 P. 851 (care of livestock until sold); Estate of Smith (1897) 118 Cal. 462, 50 P. 701 (maintenance of vineyard); cf. § 770, authorizing executor's sale without notice of "[p]erishable property and other personal property which will depreciate in value if not disposed of promptly.") However, an executor or administrator is not liable for any decreases in the value of estate assets on account of his acts or omissions done in good faith and without negligence. (§ 920 ("He shall not * * * suffer loss by the decrease or destruction without his fault, of any part of the estate"); Estate of Armstrong (1899) 125 Cal. 603, 604–606, 58 P. 183; cf. Estate of Fraysher (1956) 47 Cal.2d 131, 138–139, 301 P.2d 848.)

Contestants argue that the executor's duty of preservation required it in the exercise of due care to sell the Reserve stock before it depreciated in market value, but the authorities upon which they rely indicate that such liability has rarely been imposed. The executor normally is not held to account for failure to anticipate fluctuations in the price of a publicly traded stock arising from general market conditions, as distinct from conditions peculiar to the company in which the stock is held. (Estate of Kent (1936) 6 Cal.2d 154, 164–165, 57 P.2d 901; cf. Day v. First Trust & Sav. Bank (1941) 47 Cal.App.2d 470, 479, 118 P.2d 51.) There was evidence that the decline in the value of the Reserve stock reflected a decline in the market price of oil stocks generally * * * and that the executor used reasonable care to become informed about any special circumstances that might affect the value of the stock. Thus, the evidence showed that during the initial two weeks of probate administration and periodically thereafter until distribution the executor ascertained through the research facilities of its investment department, staffed by security analysts and other experts, that there was no deterioration in the financial condition or management of Reserve which would indicate the existence or prospect of a substantial loss of intrinsic value. This evidence supported the trial court's finding that "Reserve Oil & Gas Company was not in a deteriorating condition at any time during the probate of this estate and the [executor] so determined in the course of considering whether to retain any shares of the common stock of said corporation in the estate."

In addition to the executor's duty to preserve the estate assets, a second area of its responsibility necessarily affecting the contestants' interests in the trust was its selection of which assets to sell to raise the cash needed by the estate and which to retain for distribution into the trust. Contestants attack the executor's sales of short term government bonds authorized by the probate court in June 1969 along with the sale of part of the Reserve holdings. They argue that the executor was negligent in not obtaining the needed cash entirely from a larger disposition of Reserve instead of partly from Reserve and partly from the bonds. To have retained the bonds for distribution to the trust would have been nearly equivalent to retaining cash for this purpose as the maturity dates of the bonds made it probable that some and perhaps all would be converted to cash before administration of the estate was completed. As previously stated, there was evidence that the executor in deciding not to obtain cash from selling additional shares of Reserve took into account the suitability of that stock for inclusion in the trust, based on the trust's terms, the circumstances and resources of the beneficiaries, the income produced by trust assets other than Reserve, the propriety of capital growth as one of the trust objectives, and a judgment that Reserve stock had long-term potential for increase in value. This evidence supports the trial court's finding * * * that the executor exercised due care in deciding to retain the stock for distribution to the trust.

A third area of the executor's responsibilities having at least a potential effect on the contestants' interests as trust beneficiaries was the timing of the distribution of particular assets from the probate estate into the trust. Upon such distribution the management of the Reserve stock was freed from the restrictions imposed by the executor's multifarious duties and limited powers and became subject to the broad powers conferred upon the trustee by the terms of the trust. "It is the established policy of this state, implemented by sections 1000 and 1001 of the Probate Code, to encourage the distribution of property to legatees as soon as can be done without jeopardizing the rights of others interested in the estate. [Citations.]" * * * However, there was no evidence that earlier distribution of the Reserve stock would have resulted in its being sold by the trustee at any price higher than its market value at the time it was in fact distributed.

Right to Jury Trial

Contestants claim the trial court erred in not ordering a jury trial of the factual issues raised by the contest. The executor asserts contestants waived any right to a jury trial by failure to make timely demand therefor. We need not pass on the waiver issue in view of our conclusion that even if the jury trial claim was effectively asserted it was properly denied on its merits.

There is no right to a jury in probate proceedings unless that right is granted by statute. (Estate of Van Deusen (1947) 30 Cal.2d 285, 291, 182 P.2d 565; Estate of England (1931) 214 Cal. 298, 300, 5 P.2d

428.) Thus there are express statutory provisions for the right in will contests before probate (§ 371) and after probate (§ 382), contests of allowed claims (§ 928), determinations of rights to distribution (§ 1081), and hearings on restoration of "incompetent" persons to capacity (§ 1471) and termination of conservatorships (§ 1755).

* * *

Contestants point out that the early *Moore* decision was based in part upon the impracticability of requiring "a jury to wade through, comprehend, and disentangle a long account, or to express an intelligent judgment upon each item" (72 Cal. at p. 338, 13 P. at p. 882) and argue that the issues in the instant case of whether the executor was negligent in retaining the Reserve stock and if so the amount of resultant damages to the estate were relatively clearcut and as fully appropriate for jury consideration as the fact issues in regular civil actions for negligence or professional malpractice. However, there is another characteristic of claims for mismanagement of a probate estate which makes jury resolution inappropriate. Such claims, unlike ordinary claims for negligence or malpractice, are necessarily based on conduct that is subject to the independent control and supervision of the very court before which the claim must be asserted. As we said in Estate of Sanderson, supra, 74 Cal. 199, 208, 15 P. 753, 757: "There may be a manifest propriety in requiring, at the request of a party, issues of fact such as ordinarily arise in the contest of the probate of a will, (was the testator of unsound mind? was he subjected to undue influence?) to be tried by a jury.

But the proceeding in probate for the settlement of an account is *sui generis,* bearing but a distant and incomplete analogy to the procedure for an accounting in equity. The executor or administrator derives his power to act as such from the will, or order of the court, but in his conduct of the affairs of the estate he is subjected largely to the discretion and control of the court. The court is bound to protect the estate, and, as far as may be, the rights of all concerned. Publication is had that all interested may have an opportunity, by written exceptions, to call the attention of the court to alleged errors or defects; but, in the absence of exceptions, the court may and should inquire into any matter which may seem to the court objectionable, and pass judgment thereon, and, in the presence of specific objections, the court is not limited to the specific objections." (See also Estate of Randall (1922) 188 Cal. 329, 335, 205 P. 118.) In short, to subject the court's determination of the propriety of an executor's acts in the course of administering the estate to contradiction by a jury verdict would tend to dilute and undermine the court's ongoing responsibility for detecting and correcting executorial mismanagement.

* * *

The judgment of August 1, 1972, is modified by striking therefrom the provisions for (1) charging extraordinary compensation of the executor and its attorneys "against the principal share of the Contestants' trusts" and (2) allowing interest on the withheld amounts of executor's statutory and extraordinary compensation allowed in the order of September 28, 1970. As so modified, the judgment is affirmed. The order for payment of attorney's fees for extraordinary services, dated and filed on November 17, 1972, is affirmed. Each party shall bear its own costs on appeal.

McComb, Tobriner, Mosk, Sullivan and Clark, JJ., and Taylor, J., Assigned, concur.

NOTE

On intermediate appeal, the Court of Appeal, Third District, had reversed the trial court. It reasoned that the applicable standard was that of a trustee, as the Bank was both executor and trustee, and that a sharp line should not be drawn between the two functions.[31] The Supreme Court vacated the opinion of the Court of Appeal. Consider how the principal case would have been treated under the Uniform Probate Code: the personal representative has *power* to "retain assets owned by the decedent pending distribution or liquidation including those * * * which are otherwise improper for trust investments"; he also has power to sell assets and to invest liquid funds in "prudent investments which would be reasonable for use by trustees generally" (Section 3–715). On the other hand, he is a fiduciary "who shall observe the standards of care applicable to trustees" (Section 3–703). The real issue is whether the executor has a different function when he is also trustee, a function which in turn affects how he should exercise his powers.

If active trust functions are expressly conferred by the terms of the will on the executors, even though there is no designation as "trustee", trust standards will be applied.[32]

The power and duty of a personal representative to invest surplus funds is reasonably clear; the power and duty to change from one investment to another is not so clear.[33] Where the same person is both executor and testa-

31. 116 Cal.Reptr. 418, at 420: "The contrast between the comparative obligations of executor and testamentary trustee represents a false issue here. According to convention, the executor conserves, the trustee manages and the decree of distribution sharply marks a transition from one function to the other. However suitable to the quiet past, this dogma is unfit for the urgencies of the contemporary marketplace. In real life, business management problems do not await the switch of hats from executorship to trusteeship. They often exist at the testator's death, demand prompt attention by the executor and persist into trusteeship. Cash coming into the executor's hands may and should be invested. (See Prob.Code, §§ 584–586.1, 920.3.) Market fluctuations call for early review of the decedent's investment portfolio. The desideratum is continuity of management among the decedent, the executor and trustee, not sharp breaks. There is little realism in legal generalizations which tolerate a comparatively depressed standard of management during probate administration. It is said that the executor of an estate has the obligation to collect, preserve and protect the assets. (Prob.Code, § 571; Estate of Turino, 8 Cal.App.3d 642, 647, 87 Cal.Rptr. 581.) That sort of description expresses only a minimum set of expectations. To say that an executor must conserve but need not manage is unrealistic. The present case may not be decided in terms of the contrast between executorship and trusteeship."

32. Matter of Estate of Wiese, 257 N.W.2d 1 (Iowa 1977) (where will directed executor to convert residue "into cash within a reasonable time after my death, having regard to economic conditions * * * so that said property will not be liquidated at a loss", the Trust Company named as executor was held not liable for losses incurred in holding investments for 9 months in a falling market, even though sale at the end of 4 months would have been at higher prices).

33. For a thorough discussion see Report of Committee on Investments by Fiduciaries, Investments by Personal Rep-

mentary trustee, some courts insist on a sharp line being drawn between actions as personal representative and actions as trustee; the line is usually the final account and discharge as personal representative.[34] other courts are more lenient.[35] The problem is complicated because in non-Code states the personal representative often lacks power to invest, although the will usually grants broad powers in both capacities, as executor and as trustee. If the rule is that the executor must dispose of improper investments during administration of the estate, approval of his final account may foreclose raising the issue later; but then the same person as trustee may be surcharged for breach of his duty to use reasonable care in accepting the assets for the trust.[36]

MECHANICKS NATIONAL BANK OF CONCORD v. D'AMOURS

Supreme Court of New Hampshire, 1957.
100 N.H. 461, 129 A.2d 859, 64 A.L.R.2d 260.

[A national bank, qualified to act as fiduciary, petitioned for instructions whether it could invest the assets of a testamentary charitable trust in a common trust fund. The will contained no provisions concerning permissible investments by the trustee. Questions of law were reserved and transferred to the Supreme Court.]

KENISON, CHIEF JUSTICE. The first question transferred reads as follows: "1. Subject to the limitations contained in said plan for the establishment and maintenance of said common trust fund, may all of the assets of said residuary trust lawfully be invested in interests in said common trust fund by virtue of the provisions of RSA ch. 391 and notwithstanding the provisions of RSA 564:18?" This requires a determination of whether, notwithstanding the more general provisions of RSA 564:18 relating to investments by trustees, the Hall trust may be invested in the Common Trust Fund by virtue of the Uniform Common Trust Fund Act, RSA ch. 391, which allows a bank qualified to act as fiduciary to establish a common trust fund.

Although the Uniform Common Trust Fund Act was promulgated by the National Conference of Commissioners on Uniform State Laws

resentatives, 8 Real Prop., Prob. & Tr.J. 465 (1973).

34. See Baker, "The Executor-Trustee", 13 Okl.L.Rev. 408 (1960); Note, "Trusts: Executor Distinguished From Trustee," 52 Marquette L.Rev. 303 (1968).

35. In Springfield National Bank v. Couse, 288 Mass. 262, 192 N.E. 529 (1934), objection was made to purchases and sales of securities by the bank which resulted in a loss to the estate; the bank had qualified as trustee as well as being appointed executor. The court refused to surcharge the Bank as executor, on the grounds that the bank was really acting in its function as trustee.

36. In Dickerson v. Camden Trust Co., 1 N.J. 459, 64 A.2d 214 (1949), the executors held certain estate assets, which were not proper trust investments, throughout administration of the probate estate, filed a final account with the probate court, and turned over to themselves as trustees the depreciated assets, accepting them at inventory value. The will directed the executors-trustees to "invest said estate in legal securities." The accounts as executors having been approved by the probate court, the executors could no longer be charged for the loss: but the same persons could—and were—charged as trustees for wrongfully accepting the improper securities at inventory value.

in 1938 and has been adopted in at least twenty-six states,[37] it has not been the subject of judicial interpretation. 9 Uniform Laws Annotated 148 and 1956 Supp. pp. 67–69. The New York decisions concerning common trust funds are of limited value since they involve a statute, N.Y.Banking Law, McKinney's Consol.Laws, c. 2, § 100–c, which is more inclusive and differs in many particulars from the Uniform Act. Bogue, Common Trust Fund Legislation, 5 Law & Cont.Probs. 430. See Restatement, Trusts, § 227, comment j in 1948 supplement. "Common trust funds have become increasingly important since 1930, as a device by which small trusts can have the benefit of a diversified investment, while a corporate fiduciary incurs a lower operating cost". 4 Powell, Real Property (1954) § 546, p. 283. In practice as well as theory it has been said "that the beneficiaries of smaller trusts have gained a protection against capital loss and a continuing yield of income which would have been impossible without pooled management of this sort". Shattuck & Farr, An Estate Planner's Handbook (2d Ed. 1953) § 33, p. 191. See Survey of Common Trust Funds, 1955, 42 Federal Reserve Bulletin, p. 800 (1956). The authority for a trustee to invest in common trust funds is generally recommended in estate planning. Stephenson, Drafting Wills and Trust Agreements, Administrative Provisions (1952) § 19.19.

New Hampshire adopted the Uniform Common Trust Fund Act in 1953 with certain additions which are not material to the issues in this case. RSA ch. 391, Laws 1953, c. 109. The establishment of common trust funds is permitted by RSA 391:1, the pertinent part of which reads as follows: "Establishment of Common Trust Funds. Any bank or trust company qualified to act as fiduciary in this state may establish common trust funds for the purpose of furnishing investments to itself as fiduciary, or to itself and others as co-fiduciaries; and may, as such fiduciary or co-fiduciary invest funds which it lawfully holds for investment in interests in such common trust funds, if such investment is not prohibited by the instrument, judgment, decree or order creating such fiduciary relationship, and if, in the case of cofiduciaries, the bank or trust company procures the consent of its cofiduciaries to such investment. * * *" RSA 391:2 embodies the 1952 amendment to the original uniform act which was drafted to overcome the constitutional difficulties of notice by publication which was condemned in Mullane v. Central Hanover Bank & Trust Co., 339 U.S. 306, 70 S.Ct. 652, 94 L.Ed. 865. See Handbook, National Conference of Commissioners on Uniform State Laws (1952) p. 433; Note, Accounting for Common Trust Funds: A Statutory Scheme, 64 Harv. L.Rev. 473. RSA 391:3 relates to exemption from state taxability and is not in the uniform act as drafted. The remaining sections of RSA ch. 391 follow in substance the uniform act including RSA 391:7, which provides that all acts or parts of acts which are inconsistent with the Uniform Trust Fund Act are thereby repealed.

37. 7 Uniform Laws Ann., Business and Financial Laws (1978) 86 (34 states and D.C. as of 1982).

It will be noted that a Common Trust Fund is nowhere defined in RSA ch. 391 or elsewhere in our statutes. However, it had a well defined meaning prior thereto. An authority in this field has said that a common trust fund in its technical sense means "(1) a fund composed of funds contributed by estates, trusts and guardianships, (2) established, maintained and operated by a bank or trust company for the exclusive use of its own estates, trusts and guardianships, (3) under authority or permission of the law of the state in which the bank or trust company is located, (4) according to rules and regulations promulgated by the Board of Governors of the Federal Reserve System." Stephenson, Participating Investments—The Common Trust Fund Device, 12 Ohio St.L.J. 522, 526 (1951).

The life blood of any common trust fund is its exemption from federal income tax which can be obtained only by compliance with Regulation F of the Federal Reserve System.[38] Internal Revenue Code of 1954, 26 U.S.C.A. § 584; Bogert, Cases on Trusts (2d Ed.) 525. "Thus these funds operate within a double framework, fixed in part by state legislation, and, in part, by Federal regulations which must be met if the fund is to be practically possible." 4 Powell, Real Property (1954) § 546, p. 281. To the same effect is the Commissioners' Prefatory Note to the Uniform Common Trust Fund Act: "The reason for not covering * * * the details of the operation of such a common trust fund is that as a practical matter such details are covered by the regulations issued by the Federal Reserve Board * * *" 9 Uniform Laws Annotated, 148, 149. See 1 Bogert, Trusts and Trustees, § 134.

In considering whether RSA ch. 391 was intended by the Legislature to have a broad or restrictive effect, attention may be directed to other statutes in which certain specified corporate and public trustees have been authorized to establish common trust funds or allowed to have collective investments. Prior to allowing banks qualified to act as fiduciaries to have common trust funds the Legislature had granted that privilege to state agencies administering state trust funds, RSA 11:5; to town and city trustees of trust funds, RSA 31:27, 31:30; to cemetery corporations, RSA 289:14, 289:15. More recently the privilege to establish common trust funds has been granted to charitable corporations, RSA 292:18 Supp. * * * Likewise a public trustee for small charitable trusts may establish common trust funds and make collective investments, RSA 564:2–a. * * * These statutes evidence a clear legislative intent to give certain corporate and public trustees privileges that are not granted to testamentary trustees in general under RSA 564:18.

A well established and salutary principle of the law of trusts is that a trustee cannot commingle trust funds with his own funds or with other trust funds. * * * We have continued to follow this rule except where the Legislature has made selective exceptions to it. Note, The Common Trust Fund Statutes—A Legalizing of Commin-

38. Superseded by Part 9, Fiduciary Powers of National Banks and Collective Investment Funds ("Regulation 9") 12 C.F.R. 9. See Appendix II.

gling, 37 Col.L.Rev. 1384. "Until fairly recently, courts were able to see only the bad side of mingling trust funds * * * Many states have authorized what have come to be called common trust funds. But as a general rule they have extended the privilege of mingling trust funds only to corporate fiduciaries." 3 Prentice-Hall, Wills, Estates and Trusts Service (1950) par. 10,000. Although diversification of investments is not an absolute and inflexible requirement of trust law, it has come to be recognized that commingling of trust funds under legislative authority for collective investment was a practical necessity in certain smaller trusts and is desirable in other trusts when managed by public or corporate trustees. Dicus, The Trustee's Dilemma: Retention or Diversification of Investments, 95 Trusts and Estates 1130 (1956). In other words common trust funds have been created and encouraged by legislative enactments although commingling of trust funds is inevitable when common trust funds are created. 3 (part 2) Bogert, Trusts and Trustees, § 677 and 1956 Supp.

RSA 564:18 provides for investments for trustees generally. This statute, which was last amended in 1949, provides that trustees of estates may make investments in four general categories only. The section is detailed but these categories may be explained in oversimplified summary as follows: The first category is certain mortgages, the second is deposits in certain banks, the third is stocks and bonds which are legal investments for savings banks, the fourth is stocks and bonds and other securities which may be invested in, under the prudent man rule, provided that fifty per cent of the trust estate is invested in the first three categories. There is nothing in this statute which authorizes investments in common trust funds. It has been argued that investments of the Common Trust Fund are securities within the meaning of RSA 564:18(IV) and that therefore participation of any underlying trust in a common trust fund must be limited to fifty per cent of the assets of the trust. This argument overlooks the extensive legislative authorization of collective investments and common trust funds which has steadily increased since RSA 564:18 was last amended in 1949. Considering this legislative history we conclude that the Common Trust Fund Act was not intended to be thus restricted by the general statute governing investments by trustees. The answer to the first transferred question is yes, and, notwithstanding the provisions of RSA 564:18, all or any part of the Hall trust may be invested in the Common Trust Fund by virtue of the Uniform Common Trust Fund Act.

It is our opinion that any trust which does not expressly or impliedly prohibit investment in common trust funds may be invested by a bank qualified to act as fiduciary in this state in its common trust fund when, as in this case, that fund is operated under a plan subject to federal and state law governing common trust funds and investments by trustees. Any other conclusion would be inconsistent with the legislative history of collective investment in this state, would be impractical of operation if limited to an investment of fifty per cent of the underlying trust under RSA 564:18(IV), and would impair the benefits of diversification and reasonable income in the case of small trusts. Inasmuch as the common trust fund in this case is being administered under severe and detailed federal and state regulations, there is no danger that the underlying trusts will be dissipated or subverted in their purposes by participation in the Common Trust Fund. See III Scott, Trusts (2d Ed., 1956) § 227:9, pp. 1683–1687. * * *

[In answer to the second question transmitted, the court stated that new investments for the common fund in accordance with the plan of the Bank would not preclude continued investments of the charity funds in the Common Trust Fund.] * * *

It is our conclusion that the present law allows qualified banks to set up common trust funds from the assets of particular trusts which contain no prohibition against investments in common trust funds, and that the plaintiff's plan for the operation of its common trust fund is consistent with state law. The plan also appears to comply with the regulations of the Federal Reserve System, although that is a matter upon which we are not required to pass. However, this does not relieve a trustee of a common trust fund from the overriding duty of loyalty and the requirement of making investments prudently even though it may have privileges not granted individual trustees. * * *

Remanded.

All concurred.

NOTE

The common trust fund, authorized by statute, is the device widely used by corporate fiduciaries to achieve diversification in investments.[39] Funds of individual trusts are pooled; investments are then made with the total fund, and the individual trusts are credited with a proportionate share of income and capital. Such funds must be authorized by statute; the Uniform Common Trust Fund has been adopted in 34 states and the District of Columbia. In the case of national banks, Regulation 9, § 9.18 governs collective investment in common funds.[40] Because the investment objectives of individual trusts vary, larger banks now make available a variety of common trust funds: equity, diversified balanced, fixed income, municipal bond, real estate equity, short-term investment, mortgage, foreign equity, foreign fixed income, index equity, and index fixed income. A 1980 survey of collective investment funds administered by national banks, all federally insured banks, and trust companies which are members of the Federal Reserve System or are members of bank holding companies showed that 891 institutions administered 2,350 such funds available for personal trusts with total assets of $34 billion; in addition 46 funds were available for charitable trust investment with assets of $1 billion.[41]

39. For a thorough analysis of the common trust fund law and practice, see Report of Committee on Investments by Fiduciaries, Investments by Fiduciaries in Common Trust Funds, 11 Real Prop., Prob. & Tr.J. 28 (1976).

40. See Appendix II at page 1414.

41. "Trust Assets of Banks and Trust Companies—1980," Report of the Board of Governors of the Federal Reserve System, Federal Deposit Insurance Corporation, and Office of the Comptroller of Currency: Federal Financial Institutions Examination Council (1981), Collective Investment Funds, Table 1.

Such funds are not available to the individual trustee. In order to achieve diversity in investing limited amounts, he must invest in mutual funds.[42] A special type of mutual fund, called a "market" or "index" fund, holds a portfolio of securities of many companies, designed to approximate an index of market performance. The composition of the portfolio remains unchanged over a long period. The managers make no attempt to select a limited number of investments expected to be superior, but effect economies in transfer costs and investment analysis, and achieve great diversification. The legality of trustee investment in such a fund has been defended.[43]

PROBLEMS

1. Assuming no provision in the trust instrument relating to investment powers, what would you advise a trustee in your jurisdiction relative to his investment powers? If he were also executor, what would you advise him concerning investments during probate?

2. If the trust instrument provided that "the trustee may invest and reinvest in such securities as he deems wise", would your advice be any different? Compare Babbitt v. Fidelity Trust Co., 72 N.J.Eq. 745, 66 A. 1076 (1907); Wilmington Trust Co. v. Worth, 19 Del.Ch. 314, 167 A. 848 (1933); and Hale Estate, 347 Pa. 177, 32 A.2d 20 (1943). See Bogert, Trusts (2d Ed., 1960) § 682; III Scott, Trusts (3d Ed.1967) § 227.14.

3. If you were advising a settlor creating a trust, in the light of the cases studied, what sort of investment powers would you suggest that the trustee be given?

4. If you were preparing to defend a trustee being sued by a beneficiary for improper investments in a state having the prudent man rule, what sort of evidence would you offer? In view of this, what sort of records would you like a client-trustee to maintain?

---

(4) OTHER MANAGEMENT POWERS

A. SALE OF REALTY AND CHATTELS

Just as the fiduciary must decide whether to sell or retain securities, so he is faced with the same decision as to any property he receives. If he is performing the function of administrator or executor, his decision is the product of several factors: (1) must he sell assets of the estate to satisfy debts, taxes, expenses of administration and general pecuniary legacies, and (2) should he distribute remaining assets in kind or liquidate them and pay out in cash? Of course, specifi-

42. On the operation of such a company see Redden and Thelen, The Lawyers Investment Manual (1952) §§ 67–69; Stevenson, Shares in Investment Funds (1946).

43. For an excellent analysis of, and argument for, use of "market" funds as a prudent method of diversification, see Langbein and Posner, "Market Funds and Trust-Investment Law", 1976 A.B.F. Res.J. 1.

cally devised items would not be sold unless absolutely necessary under the principles of abatement previously studied in Chapter XV, in order to pay claims. Assuming the estate includes enough cash to meet claims, what kind of distribution should be made of realty and chattels not specifically devised? In case of intestacy, distribution will be made in kind unless such distribution is impractical; for example, a diamond ring is not readily divisible among several heirs. As to residuary property under a will, the law is not always clear whether distribution is to be made in cash or in kind. In any case the personal representative ought to consult with the heirs or residuary distributees. Sale by the personal representative, even to meet claims and expenses, is complicated by historical distinctions between real and personal property. At common law title to realty passed directly to heirs or devisees while title to personalty passed to the personal representative and then ultimately he distributed to the next of kin or legatees the personalty not sold to pay claims and expenses. Although statutes now make realty liable for debts, the old concept remains in some states in the form of a statutory preference for sale of personalty before realty in order to pay claims and expenses. In most states realty may be sold only on order of the probate court, or the sale must be confirmed by the probate court, unless power of sale is expressly conferred on the personal representative by the terms of the will. On the other hand, the power of the personal representative to sell personalty arose from the legal title which the law vested in him; hence no court order is necessary to authorize sale of personalty, unless a statute requires it. However, a personal representative is often unwilling to sell even personalty without court order, as an added protection to him and to the purchaser; so that it is desirable to confer on the executor an express power to sell without court order, by the terms of the will.

These distinctions are removed in a state where the Uniform Probate Code has been enacted. Although generally assets may be distributed in kind, the Code recognizes a number of situations in which distribution must be in cash (Section 3–906), and of course cash is required to pay debts, claims and expenses. The Code does not give legal title to the personal representative but does confer on him broad powers, including the specific power to sell or lease real and personal property (Section 3–715(6) and, (9)). No court order is necessary (Section 3–704). In fact the Code specifically gives the personal representative a broad grant of powers similar to that usually expressed by the careful will draftsman. Similarly the Uniform Trustees' Powers Act accomplishes the same objective for trustees. However, the careful draftsman cannot presently rely on those statutes because they have not yet been widely adopted, and there is always the chance that the testator's will may be governed at his death by the law of a state where those statutes are not in force.

The decision of the trustee to sell or retain is colored by his function. Since his primary duty is to make the trust res productive, he must sell non-productive property, including realty, unless specifically authorized to retain it. Thus a vacant lot would have to be sold unless the trustee is given power to improve it in order to make it productive or has an opportunity to rent it unimproved at a rate commensurate with that on normal trust investments. It is this reason which normally makes it undesirable to include in the trust the home and furnishings, not to mention personal effects. If the home and furnishings are put in the trust, the trustee should be given express authority to retain them and allow the widow or family to use them, and to pay expenses of upkeep such as repairs and taxes. As to investments, we have already noted the trustee's duty to convert to legal trust investments. However, productive realty such as an apartment building or other rental property has traditionally occupied a unique position in trust law, just as it has in the administration of a decedent's estate. Because the trust originated as a device for holding specific land, the presumption was that the original land was to be retained, with no power to sell. Certainly the trustee had no power to sell and invest in other land, and for many years he had no power to sell in order to invest in legal trust securities. Modern American law takes a more liberal view toward implying a power in the trustee to sell land. Sometimes this is predicated on language in the trust instrument; thus if the trustee is directed to divide the corpus of the trust among a number of beneficiaries on termination of the trust, it can be implied that land is to be sold because undivided interests held by the beneficiaries after termination are not readily marketable.[44] But most American courts will assume the intent was to empower the trustee to sell, unless of course the trust instrument interpreted in light of all the circumstances manifests an intent that the land be retained.[45] Even where there is an express power to sell, no case holds that the trustee has a duty to sell productive realty and convert to other trust investments unless there is an express direction to do so.

If the fiduciary is authorized (either by the terms of the instrument or by a court order) to sell at private sale "subject to court confirmation," and the fiduciary enters into a contract to sell, what is the scope of the judicial function at the confirmation hearing? What if a higher offer is received prior to the hearing, or made in open court at the time of the hearing? Some courts limit their review to determining whether the contract was a fair and reasonable one at the time it was made and will confirm the contract if it was, despite the subsequent higher offer.[46] Other courts in effect hold that the contract binds the purchaser but not the selling fiduciary and will "auction off" the property at the time of hearing.[47] Involved here are complex

44. E.g., Smith v. Mooney, 5 N.J.Misc. 1087, 139 A. 513 (1927). See Atkinson, Wills (2d Ed.1953) 667, 799.

45. E.g., Walker's Will, 258 Wis. 65, 45 N.W.2d 94, 23 A.L.R.2d 991 (1950).

46. Gilden v. Harris, 197 Md. 32, 78 A. 2d 167 (1951).

47. Some courts have held that the fiduciary has a duty to refuse to perform the contract to sell if he receives a higher offer. Kane v. Girard Trust Co., 351 Pa. 191, 40 A.2d 466 (1945) (sale of realty by trustee); Bowdry v. Stitzel-Weller Distillery, 200 Okl. 213, 192 P.2d 279 (1948) (sale of personalty by executor). The Illinois court has said that the duty does not apply if the sale is by virtue of an express power conferred by the will, as distinguished from a sale on court order. Evans v. Hunold, 393 Ill. 195, 65 N.E.2d 373 (1946). See, 23 A.L.R.2d 1000 (1952).

issues: whether public or private sale brings the highest price, whether the private market place should be protected (commissions of real estate agents), whether the fiduciary has incurred personal liability for damages to the purchaser, etc.

If a fiduciary has power to sell, either under a statutory grant or under the express terms of the will or trust instrument, and enters into a binding contract to sell at an inadequate price, the remedy of the beneficiaries is to sue the fiduciary for damages for breach of fiduciary duty; the contract is enforceable and the purchaser is entitled to specific performance.[48]

PROBLEM

Your client is interested in purchasing realty held by a trustee. The trust instrument contains no express grant of power to sell realty. On the other hand, it does not direct the trustee to retain the realty. Will you advise your client that he will obtain marketable title on the basis of an "implied" power? Would you be satisfied on the basis of a court order instructing the trustee that he has a power of sale under the above case? Would you be satisfied by a deed signed by the trustee and all the beneficiaries, assuming them to be sui juris?

B. Power to Manage Realty

The courts have been liberal in implying powers to manage realty retained in a trust.

(1) *Power to lease.*[49] This power is easily implied, even if the trust instrument is completely silent, in order to make realty productive. However, the trustee may not enter into a lease extending beyond the probable duration of the trust. Thus if a trust is to last for the life of W, with a fee in the trustee, the trustee would not enter into a lease for longer than W's life expectancy. If a long-term commercial lease were desirable from the standpoint of all beneficiaries, because of higher rental and improvements to be made by the lessee, a court might authorize such a lease or the trustee might obtain the consent of all beneficiaries. The trustee should beware of clauses granting the lessee the option to purchase or even to renew the lease, since these impinge on the trustee's own freedom of action and duty to protect the beneficiaries.

48. Wittick v. Miles, 274 Or. 1, 545 P. 2d 121 (1976) (personal representative had statutory power to sell; even though contract was at an inadequate price, successor personal representative could not refuse to perform). Note that if a conflict of interest were involved, then the contract itself would be voidable.

49. Bogert, Trusts and Trustees (2d Ed.1960) Ch. 37; Bogert, Trusts (5th Ed. 1973) § 139; 4 Powell, The Law of Real Property (Rohan Rev. 1981) ¶ 538; III Scott, Trusts (3d Ed.1967) § 189; 67 A.L. R.2d 978 (1954).

(2) *Power to improve.*[50] Whether the trustee has power to make improvements in the absence of express authority is essentially a question of business judgment. If the improvements are additions to or replacements of existing buildings, and are necessary to modernize them to obtain tenants, there should be no question of the power. New ventures, however, would be doubtful, to say the least, since they would involve the investment of funds which ought to be put into legal trust fund investments. If no funds are available, the improvement would require borrowing by the trustee.

(3) *Power to borrow.*[51] Borrowing may be necessary to proper management of the trust. To put the extreme case, suppose the trust consists of realty and the buildings are in need of repair in order to preserve them. The trustee's legal duty is to repair, but he has no available funds. Clearly a court would find an implied power to borrow and even to mortgage under such circumstances. But courts are reluctant to imply such a power normally, since there is possible loss of the entire trust estate. Thus, before asking a court for such power the trustee will explore the alternative of sale of the realty. Although the court of equity has inherent power over such cases, statutes commonly authorize the court to grant a power to sell, lease or mortgage.

At common law the representative did not have a right to possession of realty, title passing directly to the heirs or devisees. Hence there was no problem of leasing, etc. Even in states where statutes give the representative possession of realty, his function is limited to collection of rents and would not extend to long-range management decisions.[52] In older wills, the testator sometimes directed that his estate be held open for a period of years, that realty be leased out, and that rent be paid to the family or to creditors; in such cases the executor was really acting as a trustee with corresponding powers.

---

50. Bogert, Trusts and Trustees (2d Ed.1960) § 601; III Scott, Trusts (3d Ed. 1967) § 188.2.

51. Bogert, Trusts and Trustees (2d Ed.1960) Ch. 36; Bogert, Trusts (5th Ed. 1973) § 136; 4 Powell, The Law of Real Property (Rohan Rev.1981) ¶ 538; III Scott, Trusts (3d Ed. 1967) § 191.

52. But see the broad powers conferred on the personal representative by Uniform Probate Code, § 3–715.

C. OPERATING A BUSINESS [53]

IN RE ESTATE OF KURKOWSKI

Supreme Court of Pennsylvania, 1979.
487 Pa. 295, 409 A.2d 357.

EAGEN, CHIEF JUSTICE.

Appellant-administratrix, Ellen Kurkowski Simon, appeals from a decree of the Court of Common Pleas of Westmoreland County, Orphans' Court Division, dismissing exceptions to the court's decree nisi surcharging her for improper administration of the estate of her husband, Carl J. Kurkowski, upon consideration of objections to the final account.

Carl J. Kurkowski died intestate on November 22, 1973, survived by his wife, the administratrix, and two minor sons from a prior marriage, Carl W. and Wayne Kurkowski. At the time of his death, decedent was president and sole shareholder of Monroe Cycle Center, Inc. which was in the business of selling and servicing motorcycles. The business was valued in the estate inventory by administratrix at $43,797.88. Decedent also owned a home valued at $75,000.00, subject to a mortgage, in addition to furniture, fixtures, and tools. Further, the decedent's life was insured for approximately $90,000.00 of which approximately $75,000.00 was paid to Monroe Cycle Center, Inc. as beneficiary. The administration of the estate was undertaken by Ellen Kurkowski Simon in January 1974 upon the posting of a $500.00 bond.

After her husband's death, Ellen Kurkowski Simon was elected president, secretary, and treasurer of Monroe Cycle Center, Inc. Prior to his death, she had served as a corporation's vice-president and had worked part-time in the business. Shortly after her election, the two other members of the Board of Directors, including the attorney for the estate, resigned. Thereafter, the administratrix ignored corporate procedures and formalities. The administratrix paid herself a salary in excess of $33,000.00 during the twenty-month period she continued to operate the business. One of decedent's sons worked part-time in the business as a mechanic and received compensation of $1,148.86. Administratrix utilized a car titled in the corporate name for her personal use and subsequently traded it in on a new car which she titled in her own name without any accounting to the corporation for the value of the car. She paid the decedent's funeral bill from the corporate assets and subsequently included the bill in her final account as an expense of the estate without having repaid the corporation the cost of the funeral.

53. See generally, Atkinson, Wills (2d Ed.1953) § 121; Bogert, Trusts and Trustees (2d Ed.1960) §§ 571–579; 4 Powell, The Law of Real Property (Rohan Rev.1981) ¶ 546; III Scott, Trusts (3d Ed.1967) § 230.4; Krasnowiecki, "Existing Rules of Trust Administration: A Stranglehold on the Trustee Controlled Business Enterprise", 110 U.Pa.L.Rev. 506 (1962). Comment "Operation of Business By Trustees", 1967 Duke L.J. 321.

The business operated at a continuing loss for the entire twenty-month period. During this period, administratrix made no attempt to sell the business or its assets. She testified she intended to operate it indefinitely. The record indicates some attempts to sell were made after administratrix closed the business. However, when these efforts were not successful, administratrix made no provision for disposition or liquidation of the corporate assets or for payment of the corporate debts. At the time administratrix closed the doors of the business, the corporate accounts reflected over $120,000.00 in assets.

In June 1976, nine months after it ceased operating, the corporation was placed into state receivership to avoid the landlord's execution on a judgment for past due rents. Several months later, all of its assets were sold by the receiver for $22,759.00. This fund was exhausted after the payment of administrative expenses and priority claims including $5,783.25 to the estate for reimbursement of rents advanced. In the interim, the house was sold and administratrix posted an additional bond.

In October 1976, decedent's sons petitioned for an accounting of the estate which was filed by administratrix in January 1977. Objections to the accounting were sustained in part and the court entered a decree directing administratrix to perform certain administrative tasks and surcharging her $119,000.00 for having continued to operate the solely owned corporation, which was the principal asset of the estate, without court approval as required by the Pennsylvania Probate, Estates and Fiduciaries Code, 20 Pa.C.S.A. § 3314 (1975). The amount of the surcharge was determined by the value of the capital stock of the corporation at the time of decedent's death—viz. $43,000.00—and the $76,000.00 paid into the corporation from insurance proceeds which resulted in total assets in the corporation of $119,000.00 at the time of death. Exceptions to the decree were dismissed and administratrix appealed.

The court below concluded administratrix should not have continued to operate decedent's solely owned corporation without first securing the court's authorization as required by 20 Pa.C.S.A. § 3314 (1975).[54] In this appeal, administratrix argues the court's application

54. 20 Pa.C.S.A. § 3314 provides as follows:

"3314. Continuation of business

"The court, aided by the report of a master if necessary, may authorize the personal representative to continue any business of the estate for the benefit of the estate and in doing so the court, for cause shown, may disregard the provisions of the governing instrument, if any. The order may be with or without notice. If prior notice is not given to all parties in interest, it shall be given within five days after the order or within such extended time as the court, for cause shown, shall allow. Any party in interest may, at any time, petition the court to revoke or modify the order. The order may provide:

"(1) for the conduct of business, by the personal representative alone or jointly with others, or, unless restricted by the terms of the governing instrument, as a corporation to be formed;

"(2) the extent of the liability of the estate or any part thereof, or of the personal representative, for obligations incurred in the continuation of the business;

"(3) whether liabilities incurred in the conduct of the business are to be chargeable solely to the part of the estate set aside for use in the business or to the estate as a whole;

of section 3314 to a corporation was error. We need not decide this question. Even assuming the statutory procedures contained in section 3314 were not applicable to decedent's business, administratrix nevertheless breached her common law fiduciary duty in failing to liquidate the estate for purposes of distribution to decedent's heirs and, therefore, is chargeable with the losses incurred.

A decedent's personal representative is under a duty to take custody of the estate and administer it in such a way as to preserve and protect the property for distribution to the proper persons within a reasonable time. In re Wallis' Estate, 421 Pa. 104, 218 A.2d 732 (1966); Miller's Estate, 345 Pa. 91, 26 A.2d 320 (1942). In the discharge of this duty, he is regarded as a fiduciary and is held to the highest degree of good faith. Moreover, he will be required to exercise the care and diligence which prudent persons ordinarily exercise in their own affairs. A personal representative who fails to use common skill and ordinary business caution may be held liable for losses to the estate which result therefrom. Miller's Estate, supra; Istocin's Estate, 126 Pa.Super. 158, 190 A. 382 (1937). See also 33 C.J. S. § 184; 31 Am.Jur.2d, Executors and Administrators, §§ 216–218. *Cf.* Scott on Trusts, Vol. 2, § 201 et seq. (1939); Restatement of Trusts 2nd § 205 (1959).

The personal representative's duty to settle the estate must be viewed with reference to the situation of the assets at the time of decedent's death. Thus, he has no duty to carry on a business conducted by the decedent. On the contrary, a personal representative breaches his trust if he continues to operate a trade or business on behalf of an estate in the absence of testamentary direction. * * *. If he does so, he will be liable for any loss thereby resulting to the estate. * * *

This general rule is subject to the limitation that the personal representative may continue operating a business of the decedent for a limited time without liability for the purpose of selling the business as a going concern or winding up the business by converting the assets into cash or performing existing contracts of the decedent. See Shane Estate, 63 Pa.D. & C.2d 177 (Mont.Co.1973); Branagan's Estate, 78 Mont.Co.L.R. 51 (1961); Jurkowitz v. Jurkowitz, 44 Lack.Jurist 266 (1940). See generally, 33 C.J.S. §§ 193–197; 31 Am.Jur.2d 318, Executors and Administrators, §§ 220–226; 58 A.L.R.2d 365; Bogert, Trusts & Trustees 2d Ed. §§ 571–579.

In this case, administratrix clearly breached her fiduciary duty as personal representative of the decedent by continuing to operate the business at a loss for a period of twenty months after decedent's death while realizing personal gain in the form of salary and fringe benefits and by eventually abandoning the business without making provision for disposition or liquidation of its assets or payment of the corporate debts.

"(4) the period of time the business may be conducted; and

"(5) such other regulations, including accountings, as the court shall deem advisable."

Administratrix argues she should not be liable to the heirs for any loss sustained by continued operation of the business since they consented both expressly and implicitly to the continuance. A personal representative relying on consent for authority to continue a business must show the consent of all interested parties was procured or given after full information and a fair representation of the risks involved was communicated to them. See 31 Am.Jur.2d § 222. Neither the express nor implied consent of decedent's minor sons was established in this case. * * *

Decree affirmed. Costs on appellant.

IN RE GIBSON'S ESTATE

Surrogate's Court, Nassau County, New York, 1965.
46 Misc.2d 954, 261 N.Y.S.2d 550.

* * * JOHN D. BENNETT, SURROGATE. The decedent died on October 14, 1960 leaving a will wherein Seymour M. Litman was named executor. Objections to the probate of the will were filed by an alleged son of the decedent and letters testamentary were not issued to Mr. Litman until March 2, 1962. He served as temporary administrator from January 26, 1961 until he was appointed executor.

The decedent's estate included a wholly owned corporation known as Gibson's Fish and Chips, Inc. Objections were filed by the special guardian to the final accounting of the temporary administrator and his intermediate accounting as executor on the grounds that he continued to conduct the business of the corporation and used general assets of the estate in that business.

A temporary administrator has no authority under section 127 of the Surrogate's Court Act to continue a business and must liquidate same (Matter of Dennis' Estate, Sur., 136 N.Y.S.2d 84), except where an order pursuant to section 127 (Matter of Dennis, supra) has been issued authorizing the continuation of the business for such time as fixed by the surrogate. No order has been requested to continue said business.

However, unlike a non-incorporated business, a temporary administrator for an estate of a decedent who wholly owned a corporation is not required to obtain authorization to continue said business (Matter of Dix, 34 Misc.2d 421, 226 N.Y.S.2d 111).

The executor contends he had authority to conduct the business by provisions set forth in the decedent's will. Paragraph "Sixth" provides: "When my daughter, Gail Lou Gibson, attains the age of twenty-five years, she shall become general manager of the restaurant heretofore managed by me and licensed by the State of New York. Said position shall be retained solely by my said daughter until my son, Bennie Gibson, Jr., shall attain the age of twenty-five years, at which time the general management and supervision thereof shall be exercised jointly by my said children. It is my wish that Charles Hudson and Shirley Fields shall remain as employees of said licensee for as long as they shall continue to work for the benefit of said restaurant, provided they are so employed at my death."

* * *

The court finds that in reading paragraph "Sixth" of the will, the intent is clear that the decedent wished to have his children carry on his business and it would, therefore, be necessary to have the executor carry on the business until the trustees and said children could take over the business.

However, even when a fiduciary continues a decedent's business with authority, he is individually liable for all contracts and obligations incurred in the operation of the business, and although he may be entitled to reimbursement if he acted prudently, obligations are primarily his (Matter of Blaszkiewicz, supra; Matter of Munzor, 4 Misc. 374, 25 N.Y.S. 818). The special guardian in his objections of June 10, 1963, objects to some of the expenses of the temporary administrator and executor in conducting the business. An executor can be held liable to the estate for losses to the estate in the operation of a business due to his fault (Matter of Horowitz, 297 N.Y. 252, 78 N.E.2d 598). A hearing will be necessary to determine the validity of said objection.

The question remains whether or not the accounting party, first as temporary administrator and later as executor, had the right to use general estate assets in conducting the business. The accounting submitted indicates that the business had suffered losses and that rental income of the estate property and other funds of the general estate were loaned or turned over to the corporation.

"It seems also to be a well established rule that at least in the absence of a testamentary provision to the contrary where a business is carried on by executors under authority conferred by decedent's will they can use only such assets of the estate as were already invested in the business at the time of decedent's death" (3 Warren's Heaton on Surrogates' Courts, § 245.2b, p. 263; see Willis v. Sharp, supra; Matter of Hickey, 34 Misc. 360, 69 N.Y.S. 844; Matter of Blaszkiewicz, supra; Matter of Gorra, supra; Thorn v. De Breteuil, 179 N.Y. 64, 71 N.E. 470; Third Report of the Temporary State Commission on the Modernization, Revision and Simplification of the Law of Estates, N.Y.Legis.Doc., 1964, No. 19, Appendix E, pp. 301–303 [889–891]). Only debts incurred by the business during the decedent's lifetime may be paid by general assets after business assets are exhausted (In re Aboff's Will, Sur., 142 N.Y.S.2d 817).

The executor contends that the testator intended the continuation of the business and when the will is read as a whole, there is authority to use general estate assets to continue the business. He further contends that paragraph "Sixth" quoted heretofore, and the powers to "hold, invest and reinvest" as set forth in paragraph "Ninth" of the last will and testament support his position.

The court has determined from reading the last will and testament in its entirety, that the executor could continue the operation of the business, but no authority can be inferred from reading said will that general assets of the estate could be used to continue the business. Such an authorization cannot be inferred from a construction that the business could be continued. Authority to use said assets must be authorized by the testator (Willis v. Sharp, supra; Matter of Hickey, supra; Matter of Gorra, supra). No such authority exists.

* * *

As for paragraph "Ninth", a testamentary trustee may invest and reinvest in nonlegal investments only when the will explicitly provides for same (3 Warren's Heaton on Surrogates' Courts, § 266, p. 486; see In re Walbridge's Estate, Sur., 138 N.Y.S.2d 847). Authorization to permit a testamentary trustee to retain testator's nonlegal investments does not constitute authority to make new investments in nonlegal securities (In re Gillis' Will, Sur., 117 N.Y.S.2d 454; Matter of Taylor, 6 Misc.2d 60, 162 N.Y.S.2d 393, aff'd 6 A.D.2d 756, 174 N.Y.S.2d 456; Matter of Westerfield, 193 Misc. 443, 82 N.Y.S.2d 766, mod. on other grounds and affd. 278 App.Div. 153, 103 N.Y.S.2d 973, aff'd 303 N.Y. 916, 105 N.E.2d 497).

The court, therefore, holds that the temporary administrator and now executor had the power to continue the business prudently but did not have authority to use general estate assets to run the business. A hearing will be necessary to determine if the business was conducted prudently as set forth heretofore, and also to establish what funds of the general estate were used to continue the business without authority.

* * *

NOTE

Frequently the most valuable asset in an estate is the decedent's unincorporated business. Immediate liquidation of the business may result in severe loss. Continuation of the business by the representative may be on one of the following bases: (1) temporary continuation for the purpose of liquidating stocks and winding up the business, clearly within the power and function of the executor or administrator, (2) continuation over a longer period, several years if necessary, in order to sell as a going concern rather than piece-meal, and (3) continuation in order to preserve the business intact for ultimate distribution to the family and to realize income in the meanwhile. Since the representative is often a member of the family, having a personal interest in the decision, the temptation towards the last type of continuation is strong. However, it is not even clear under existing case law that the representative has power to continue a business for any considerable length of time in order to make a sale, although this ought to be a consequence of his duty to preserve the assets and obtain the best price under all the circumstances. Even the third type of continuation might be justified on the basis of preserving specific assets for distribution. The danger is that the operation of the business may result in a loss, affecting creditors and legatees. Although incorporation by the representative may be a sound business step, it is not a complete answer; for the business assets may still decline in value or be dissipated in continuance of the business.

That continuance of the business during probate or administration should be a matter for sound business judgment, rather than the announced rule against continuance, is illustrated by the following from the opinion of the California District Court of Appeal in Riedy v. Bidwell: [55]

> "By virtue of the carrying out of the terms of the contract in the instant case the estate stood to receive a very considerable benefit: First, in the fact that the business would be more presentable to any intending or prospective purchaser as a 'going concern,' and hence more salable and at a higher price than though it were 'closed down'; secondly, as a 'going concern,' and by reason of its reasonable use the various machinery, equipment, and property generally would not deteriorate and therefore depreciate in value to the same extent as though standing idle; and thirdly, there was a possibility not only of having the taxes and general upkeep bills paid by reason of the operation of the business, but as well a net profit to the estate of 6 per cent. on the investment. The contract was not illegal in itself. Having been made by the executor presumably for the purpose of preserving the property of the estate, as well as with the expectation of earning a profit therefrom, it would have been within the power of the court to make allowance to the executor in his account for his proper and necessary expenses in connection therewith. * * *"

Four classes of persons are interested in the decision to carry on the business: (1) existing creditors of the decedent who have claims against the estate for which they want prompt payment, (2) subsequent creditors whose claims arise out of the operation of the business by the representative, (3) the legatees whose property interests may be jeopardized if the business is operated at a loss, and (4) the representative who may have to stand the loss personally. The representative is the person who must take the initiative in carrying on the business, so we shall look at the problem primarily from his viewpoint.

Express authority in the will to carry on the business serves to dispense with the need for a court order authorizing continuance; but it provides only limited protection to the personal representative, who is still held to the prudent person standard. In the absence of such authority in the will, the personal representative will become liable for losses in the business operation unless he obtains a court order or the consent of all interested parties. Statutes in most states empower the probate court to grant authority for continuance of the business.

The Uniform Probate Code, § 3–715(24) confers on the personal representative a power to continue the business, without obtaining a court order, if he acts reasonably for the benefit of the interested persons, within the following limitations:

> "(24) continue any unincorporated business or venture in which the decedent was engaged at the time of his death (i) in the same business form for a period of not more than 4 months from the date of appointment of a general personal representative if continuation is a reasonable means of preserving the value of the business including good will, (ii) in the same business form for any additional period of time that may be approved by order of the Court in a formal proceeding to which the per-

55. 70 Cal.App. 552, at 559, 233 P. 995, at 998 (1925), 13 Cal.L.Rev. 495 (1925).

sons interested in the estate are parties; or (iii) throughout the period of administration if the business is incorporated by the personal representative and if none of the probable distributees of the business who are competent adults object to its incorporation and retention in the estate".

This power is supplemented by power to borrow under subsection (16) of the same section and to incorporate any business under subsection (25).

As we shall see in Subsection (7) infra, even where the representative has authority by terms of the will, consent or court order, he still may incur personal liability to third parties having claims arising out of operation of the business, although he may be able to recover from the estate in proper cases.

Existing creditors may object to continuation of the business, even if all the other parties agree and the court is willing to authorize continuation. However, if the existing creditors consent to continuation, their claims will be subordinated in priority to those of subsequent creditors as to assets used in the business.[56]

If the business is operated as a partnership, the problem is further complicated by the presence of a surviving partner or partners.[57] The law of partnership provides for dissolution of the partnership on death of a partner, and the surviving partners have a duty to wind up the affairs of the partnership very analogous to that of the representative in a sole proprietorship. However, a common practice in drafting partnership articles is to provide expressly for continuation of the business on death of one partner.[58] Another modern method of anticipating this problem is for the partners to enter into a "buy-sell agreement", providing that the surviving partner will purchase the partnership interest of the deceased, funding of the purchase price being accomplished by cross-insurance on the lives of each partner.

The courts purport to apply the rule against continuance of the business to operation of a farm. Of course, at common law realty passed directly to the heirs or devisees, who were free to carry on the farming. Today personalty in the form of livestock and equipment is a major part of the farming operation in some areas. To require the representative in possession to cease the farming operation is unrealistic. In fact continuance of the regular course of farming would seem to be a consequence of the duty to preserve the assets. The tendency of courts is to protect, on one ground or another, the representative who tries to hold the farm together as an economic unit.[59]

56. III Scott, Trusts (3d Ed.1967) § 268.4; Note, "Continuation of a Decedent's Business; Rights of Subsequent Creditors", 35 Va.L.Rev. 358 (1949).

57. For an example of the difficulties which may arise where the personal representative and the surviving partner continue to operate the business, see Spivak v. Bronstein, 367 Pa. 70, 79 A.2d 205 (1951).

58. See Reuschlein & Gregory, Agency and Partnership Ch. 23; Volz and Berger, The Drafting of Partnership Agreements (6th ed. 1976) 26.

59. Hardy & Co. v. Turnage, 204 N.C. 538, 168 S.E. 823 (1933) (administrator carrying on farming operation under court order not liable for losses due to excessive rain); Re Estate of Bethel, 111 Or. 178, 209 P. 311, 226 P. 427 (1924) (expenses of operation of dairy farm for three years allowed as proper in winding up estate); Lelek v. Hemshorn, 184 Or. 364, 198 P.2d 597 (1948) (estoppel by acquiescence).

The testator desiring to authorize or direct continuation of an unincorporated business ought to make express provision in the will for the following matters:[60]

(1) What assets are to be used in the business. Courts take a narrow view of this issue, unless explicitly spelled out.[61]

(2) Whether the personal representative or trustee is to receive additional compensation for management functions. There is still some judicial support for the view that the fiduciary, because of the duty of loyalty, is not entitled to additional compensation if he personally performs the management duties although he might hire others for compensation.

(3) What special powers the fiduciary is to have, such as the power to borrow and mortgage. While these may be implied, a lawsuit to establish the implied power may be costly and involve delay which would endanger the business.

(4) Whether the fiduciary is to incorporate the business in order to attain limited liability.

(5) Certain other problems considered in detail hereafter, such as protection of the fiduciary against personal liability for torts and contracts and determination of income.

If the business is incorporated, a somewhat different problem is presented. One purpose of incorporation is to provide continuity at death, the corporation being a different "person" from the decedent. If the decedent owned all or a controlling interest in the stock, many courts nevertheless apply the rule against continuance of the business to such cases. Note that both principal cases did involve an incorporated business. Certainly the only safe course is to provide expressly in the will for authority to continue or, if that is lacking, to obtain court approval in advance. Probably the issue ought to be in terms of the duty of a fiduciary to convert to proper trust fund investments.[62] Thus, while a representative might be safe in holding the stock for the normal period of administration, in the absence of expressed authority to retain the stock a trustee would have to sell, since stock in a closely held corporation lacks liquidity, violates the requirement of diversification and may involve a speculative element contrary to reasonable prudence.

Until recently trust companies have been reluctant to assume management of even an incorporated business, since it involves skills beyond those of investment. However, there is increasing recognition of the need for development of new techniques of management to meet this problem. Most estates of size will include stock in a family business; most testators would want such stock retained under conditions of inflation because of its income-producing qualities. In the case of the inter vivos trust, the problem is likely to receive detailed attention if the stock is transferred to the trustee. There is more danger that it will be neglected in the will, particularly under a pour-over clause.

In addition to authority to retain the stock, some direction as to the extent to which the fiduciary is to participate in direct management of the corporation is advisable. Under the duty of loyalty, can a fiduciary voting a

60. In general on drafting, see Stephenson, Drafting Wills and Trust Agreements—Administrative Provisions (1952) ch. VII; Shaffer, The Planning and Drafting of Wills and Trusts (2d Ed. 1979). See also Handling Businesses in Trust (1959).

61. See Estate of Britt, 249 Wis. 602, 26 N.W.2d 34 (1946) (accounts receivable and firm bank account held not part of the business).

62. Blauvelt v. The Citizens Trust Co., 3 N.J. 545, 71 A.2d 184 (1950).

controlling interest in the corporation elect himself a director and officer at the usual salary? Here there is in theory a threefold division of interest. The fiduciary must remain loyal to the trust; as a director he owes a duty to the corporation; and as an individual he derives a benefit from the salary. Since there is a conflict of authority on the right of the fiduciary to retain the salary in addition to his compensation as trustee, the draftsman of the trust instrument should anticipate this problem. The real fear here is that the trustee will elect himself to office for the salary, rather than the good of the estate. Actually in many cases it is obvious the trustee was selected because he was already an officer of the company or familiar with the business and selected in anticipation that he would participate actively in the operation of the business. Clearly the normal fiduciary duties carry over into the operation of an incorporated business by a personal representative or trustee.[63]

(5) SAFEGUARDING PROPERTY (EARMARKING)

When a fiduciary acquires custody of property, he must take measures to keep it safely. Securities and other easily stolen items should be kept in a safe or safe deposit box. The fiduciary must use reasonable prudence in selecting a bank for deposit of the estate or trust funds.[64] He must take reasonable care of tangible personal assets, such as farm equipment and motor vehicles; and must insure buildings against loss by fire and other hazards if reasonably prudent men insure under the same circumstances.[65] He must defend actions which might result in loss to the estate or trust if he has a reasonable defense; although, as with respect to claims by the estate or trust, he may arbitrate or compromise if under the circumstances arbitration or compromise is reasonable.[66]

A difficult problem that often arises concerning security of the estate or trust is a tendency by personal representatives and trustees to permit the estate or trust assets to become merged for long or short intervals with their own. Since the fiduciary is handling funds and property which are not his, he is under a duty at all times to keep such property separate from his individual property and clearly identified. Likewise, where he administers several estates or trusts, he must keep property of each separate to prevent confusion or deliberate juggling of accounts. The most obvious application of the rule is

63. Jennings v. Speaker, 1 Kan.App. 2d 610, 571 P.2d 358 (1977); Matter of Hubbell, 302 N.Y. 246, 97 N.E.2d 888 (1951) (duty of loyalty); Matter of Auditore, 249 N.Y. 335, 164 N.E. 242 (1928) (administrator liable for diversion of corporate funds); Estate of Stephen L. Baldwin, 442 A.2d 529 (Me.1982) (citing casebook). See Cahn "Estate Corporations", 86 U. of Pa.L.Rev. 136 (1937).

64. Restatement, Second, Trusts § 176. II Scott, Trusts (3d Ed.1967) § 176.

65. Restatement, Second, Trusts § 176, Illustration 3. The trustee should make repairs necessary to maintain the property but is not required to make permanent improvements. If the money is not available in the trust for repairs, he should notify the beneficiaries, but he is not required to pay for repairs out of his own pocket.

66. Restatement, Second, Trusts, § 178. II Scott, Trusts (3d Ed.1967) § 178.

the requirement that cash funds of an estate or trust must be deposited not in the fiduciary's individual bank account but in a separate account identified as a fiduciary account. Many courts carry this to the point that it is insufficient to label the account "John Jones, Executor" or "John Jones, Trustee". The identity of the particular estate or trust must be added: "Mary Jones Estate, John Jones, Executor" or "John Jones, Trustee for Mary Jones Estate". Similarly, the documents of title such as a stock certificate should reveal the existence of the fiduciary relation. This rule has a two-fold purpose. It serves not only to identify the estate or trust property as against individual creditors of the fiduciary but also to prevent unauthorized transfer. For example, a trustee as holder of legal title might transfer unearmarked trust property to a good faith purchaser for value and thereby cut off the equitable claim of the beneficiary to the property; when the documents of title reveal the existence of the trust, any purchaser is put on notice and must inquire into the power of the fiduciary to make the particular transfer.

The older cases enforced this duty rigorously and imposed strict liability for failure to earmark fiduciary assets. However, the requirement of earmarking creates practical difficulties in the modern business world, particularly as to securities. If bonds or stocks are registered in the name of the individual as representative or trustee, their transfer upon sale is held up or hampered by requirements of transfer agents who insist upon voluminous documentary evidence of authority of the fiduciary to make the particular transfer. This insistence stems from concern over lawsuits based on the rule of law making the agent and the corporation liable for participation in breach of trust and requiring the transfer agent to inquire into the power of the fiduciary to make the transfer.[67] The Uniform Act for Simplification of Fiduciary Security Transfers [68] approved by the Commissioners on Uniform State Laws and adopted by 37 jurisdictions as of 1982 tends to eliminate this problem and the Uniform Probate Code also contains sections protecting third persons dealing with a personal representative (Section 3–714) or a conservator (Section 5–423). But other statutes designed to protect the transfer agent and the corporation, including the Uniform Fiduciaries Act,[69] have generally not been regarded as adequate protection by the transfer agents.[70] The desire to avoid this "red-tape" has led to various practices: (1) the purchase of securities in unregistered or bearer form; (2) the purchase of securities in the name of a nominee who indorses the certificate and

67. Bogert, Trusts and Trustees (2d Ed. 1960) § 902; IV Scott, Trusts (3d Ed. 1967) § 325.

68. 7A Uniform Laws Ann., Business and Financial Laws, 709.

69. 7A Uniform Laws Ann., Business and Financial Laws (1978) 127 (25 jurisdictions as of 1982). See Christy The Transfer of Stock (5th Ed. 1972) Ch. XVII. Adoption of the Uniform Commercial Code has also simplified transfers by fiduciaries. See Sections 8–401, 8–402, 8–403.

70. Efforts to change the practices of transfer agents to recognize transfer of a registered security upon assignment by the fiduciary may eventually make such securities readily marketable. For recent developments, see Report of Special Committee on Simplification of Security Transfers to and by Fiduciaries, 9 Real Prop., Prob. & Tr.J. 611 (1974).

leaves it in the possession of the fiduciary (in effect making it a bearer document); and (3) the purchase of securities in the name of the individual without disclosing the fiduciary relation, with a separate record of the estate or trust for which the securities are held. The first practice has been upheld by the courts even as to securities which are available in registered form; the only explanation for such a holding is the long-standing practice.[71] However, not all securities are available in unregistered form, and the other two devices may be resorted to.

Despite the comparatively wide adoption of the Uniform Simplification of Fiduciary Security Transfers Act, the problem of rapid transfer of securities registered in the name of the fiduciary in his representative capacity has not been resolved to the satisfaction of the marketplace. Hence there is a growing movement to adopt statutory authorization for registration of securities in the name of a nominee or other form, in order to facilitate transfer. Statutes commonly permit a corporate fiduciary to use the nominee form.[72] The Uniform Probate Code empowers the personal representative to use the nominee or another form without disclosure of the interest of the estate (Section 3–715(14)), with a similar provision for a conservator (Section 5–424(c)(16)). As for individual trustees, the same practice is authorized in the few states which have adopted the Uniform Trusts Act (Section 9) and in the eleven states which have the Uniform Trustees Powers Act (Section 3(c)(16)). Under all of these statutes the fiduciary is absolutely liable if loss is due to act of the nominee. In addition, the trust instrument frequently contains an express provision permitting the trustee to carry securities without earmarking. In the situations not covered by these statutory or other express authorization, the fiduciary may register the investment in his own or "street" name and keep a careful written record of the fact that the particular security is held for the estate or trust and show the investment in his periodic accounting to the beneficiaries. How the courts will treat such a practice in modern times is illustrated by the case which follows.

Since no practical inconvenience results from full earmarking of bank deposits and real estate holdings, there is not the same reason for relaxation of the old rule.

BUCKLE v. MARSHALL

Supreme Court of Appeals, Virginia, 1940.
176 Va. 139, 10 S.E.2d 506.

[Testatrix died in 1918. Her will gave her property in trust to pay the income to her daughter Sallie Martin Buckle for life and at the death of the daughter to divide the estate into four parts, one to go to

71. In re Dommerich's Will, 191 Misc. 893, 74 N.Y.S.2d 569 (Sup.Ct.1947).

72. E.g., Ariz.Rev.Stat. § 14–7308.

each of Sallie Martin Buckle's daughters. On the death of the sole original executor in 1921, Frank Marshall was appointed administrator d.b.n., c.t.a. and after giving bond and qualifying entered into performance of his duties. Among other investments, he purchased between April 1, 1929 and April 1, 1930 $5000 in bonds issued by the Grace Securities Corporation, payable to bearer. One of these bonds for $500 was paid before April 1, 1930. The remaining $4,500 in bonds purchased were called in as of October 1, 1931 because of the necessity, occasioned by the depression, of securing an extension of the time of their payment. These bonds were issued by a reputable bond investment house. They were sold to many of the banks in Virginia, and were approved by state bank examiners as sound and satisfactory investments in the portfolios of securities of banks.

In 1931, when the coupon bonds, payable to bearer, were exchanged for registered bonds, it was impossible to dispose of them without loss because of the financial depression. Marshall had the bonds registered in his name individually, rather than as administrator. In 1937 the present suit was brought by Sallie Martin Buckle and others against Frank Marshall to surcharge his accounts as administrator and to hold him personally liable for losses incurred through investments and to deprive him of compensation for his services as administrator. Marshall testified that he had the bonds registered in his name to avoid delay, costs and difficulties in making a transfer or sale of them, since if they were sold as belonging to an estate, it would be necessary for him to acquire, produce and show authority to make the sale. He also testified that, when the bonds were received, he wrote on each of them that they belonged to the estate of Mrs. Martin; that he kept them so earmarked in an envelope separate from other assets in his possession; and that payments made thereon were deposited in the bank to the credit of his account as administrator of Mrs. Martin's estate. From an adverse decree, the plaintiffs appeal. Only the portion of the opinion dealing with the issue of liability for failure to earmark the Grace Securities Corporation bonds is reprinted here.]

SPRATLEY, JUSTICE. * * * We are not unmindful of the sound and salutary rule, and of the obvious reasons and logic therefor, that a trustee who keeps trust assets in his individual name and without any trust earmarks, bears the risk of any loss of such property. Mitchell v. Moore, 95 U.S. 587, 590, 24 L.Ed. 492; Ammon's Adm'r v. Wolfe et al., 26 Grat. 621, 67 Va. 621; 3 Bogert, Trusts and Trustees, § 596.

In the case of Ammon's Adm'r v. Wolfe et al., supra, it was held that a guardian was liable for the investment of the trust estate in Confederate bonds. The holding was based upon the fact that there was not sufficient evidence to show that the investment, when made, was intended for the ward, and the further fact that the guardian had no right to invest the money in Confederate bonds.

The facts in the instant case are not similar to those in the above case. Here the uncontradicted evidence was that the administrator purchased bonds, regarded by prudent investors as sound, for and with money of the trust estate for the trust estate, and that he earmarked the said bonds in a manner to identify them as the property of the estate for which they were purchased.

We do not approve of any departure from the general rule requiring a trustee or fiduciary to exercise the utmost good faith and reasonable diligence in preserving a trust estate in his care, to keep complete and accurate records, to make, state and report his accounts as required by law, and to distribute such estate only to the persons entitled thereto.

The instructions in the will of Mrs. Martin directing that special care be taken to secure safe and profitable investments and to keep a clear, concise and separate record of all transactions are but an expression of the general principles of a trustee's duty and are in accord with the requirements of the law. They furnish no ground for an extended liability.

We find no error in the refusal of the trial court to deny commissions to the administrator, under the particular circumstances of this case. He has honestly accounted for all of the assets coming into his hands and has by diligent efforts brought additional funds to those assets. He invested the funds of the estate in investments which prudent and cautious business men deemed to be sound and safe. The depreciation in the value of those investments was due to circumstances not only beyond the control of Marshall, but also beyond the control of any known human agency. He stood ever ready to make a statement of his accounts. No loss was suffered by the failure to make or state any of his accounts, or by his method of making the statements. The interested beneficiaries for many years silently acquiesced in the manner in which the accounts were stated.

* * *

We are unable to say that the discretion of the Chancellor has been arbitrarily exercised. The quality of his decision tempering the requirements of law with justice and fair play brings no reproach upon our legal institutions and violates no principle of equity. We are, therefore, of opinion to affirm the decree of the trial court.

Affirmed.[73]

CAMPBELL, CHIEF JUSTICE (dissenting). I cannot concur in the opinion of the court, insofar as it holds that Frank Marshall should not be charged with the loss sustained by the estate of his decedent, in his unwarranted investment in the Grace Security Bonds.

Here we have a fiduciary admittedly purchasing bonds in his own name, and not until there was default in the payment of the bonds, do we find that he reported them as assets of the estate. The record clearly shows that the first Grace Security Bonds purchased by Marshall were coupon bonds purchased in the year 1931, and that he did

73. Accord: Miller v. Pender, 93 N.H. 1, 34 A.2d 663, 150 A.L.R. 798 (1943).

not make any report to the commissioner of accounts between the period beginning 1931 and ending 1935. * * *

The question of the wisdom of his investment, which the majority opinion defends at length, may be conceded. The vice in his action was in purchasing the bonds in his own name and in receiving checks for interest on the bonds and curtailment thereof which checks were made payable to Marshall individually. The fact that he ear-marked the bonds *in pencil* and placed them in an envelope, should not relieve him of liability if we are to adhere to the rule adopted in Ammon's Adm'r v. Wolfe et al., 26 Grat. 621, 67 Va. 621. * * *

The overwhelming weight of authority is to the effect that it is a breach of trust for a fiduciary to invest trust funds in his own name and that he is liable for losses resulting from such investment. See 106 A.L.R. 271.

In Morris v. Wallace, 3 Pa. 319, 45 Am.Dec. 642, the prevailing rule is thus succinctly stated:

> "Granting that Mr. Morris [the Trustee] acted bona fide, which I am not disposed to deny, yet this is a practice which we unequivocally condemn, and have always done so; and if persisted in, it must be at the peril of the trustee. The rule which makes them personally liable is intended to prevent fraud, avoiding the temptation to put the profits of the investment in their own pockets, and throw the loss, if any, on others; a temptation, to which those who act in a fiduciary character are exposed, and producing an injustice which may be perpetrated, if allowed, almost without the possibility of detection. It is said, that guardians frequently purchase stock in their own names, with the money of their wards, intending it, at the time, for the exclusive benefit of the latter. If so, the sooner there is an end put to the practice, the better, as it may lead to fraud, and can answer no good purpose whatever. It does not deserve the countenance of a court of justice, for another reason. When the funds of the cestui que trust are invested in the name of the trustee, there is always a difficulty, sometimes insurmountable, in tracing the money to the benefit of the cestui que trust; the consequence of which is, that the funds of the cestui que trust are taken to pay the debt of an insolvent trustee. As this is contrary to every principle of equity, it should be avoided, if possible; we therefore wish it to be distinctly understood, that we regard such an investment as a legal fraud, liable to all the consequences as such, without regard to the intention, or integrity of the trustee, or the honesty and good faith of the particular transaction."

See, also, Groves' Estate v. Groves and others, 120 W.Va. 373, 198 S.E. 142; 26 R.C.L. 1313, 21 Am.Jur., Section 273.

For the reasons stated, I am unwilling to place the stamp of my approval upon the conduct of a fiduciary who engages in the beneficial game of "heads I win, tails you lose".

NOTE

Funds received by a lawyer on behalf of a client are held by him in trust for the client. The rule requiring earmarking applies rigorously to bank accounts, and a separate Client Trust Funds Account (or several such Accounts) should be set up. Deposit of clients' funds in the lawyer's personal account, even for a short period, is a serious violation of Canon 9 and will subject the lawyer to discipline even if no loss occurs.[74]

---

(6) CHANGING CONDITIONS AND ADMINISTRATIVE FLEXIBILITY

Changes in circumstances during administration of an estate or trust may be accommodated to an extent by implications of powers not expressly granted by a testator or settlor. But there is a limit to which powers can be implied reasonably—a point at which implication really becomes permissible deviation. Powers may also be needed which have been expressly denied to the fiduciary. An administrator of an intestate estate cannot benefit from implications of power from an instrument. His authority is based on statutes and judicial decisions. Consequently, to provide an administrator additional freedom of action, his powers must be enlarged by a legislature or court.

There may be constitutional obstacles to the exercise of legislative power to permit deviations from the terms of a will or trust. A century ago there was much private legislation concerning the administration of particular trusts and wills. Today constitutional provisions concerning special legislation eliminate many laws of this type.[75] Even general laws enlarging the powers of fiduciaries to meet new conditions sometimes encounter constitutional obstacles. A retroactive statute may adversely affect vested rights and prove constitutionally objectionable.[76] Apart from constitutional problems, courts tend to construe statutes in substantive property matters as prospective in operation rather than retrospective unless the contrary clearly appears by the terms of the statute in question.

The power of a court to order a fiduciary to deviate from the terms of his instrument is more flexible. The power exercised is akin

74. Code of Professional Responsibility, DR 9–102.

75. See 2 Sutherland, Statutory Construction (Sands, 4th Ed. 1973) §§ 40.01 et seq.

76. See 2 Sutherland, Statutory Construction (Sands, 4th Ed., 1973) §§ 41.03, 41.05, 41.06. Compare In re Allis's Will, 6 Wis.2d 1, 94 N.W.2d 226 (1959), 69 A.L.R.2d 1128 (1960) with In re Warden's Trust, 382 Pa. 311, 115 A.2d 159 (1955), in which divergent views were expressed concerning the constitutionality of retroactive provisions of the Uniform Principal and Income Act. See, King, "Uniform Principal and Income Act, § 5: Constitutionality of Its Retroactive Application", 1960 Wash.U.L.Q. 339; 69 A.L.R.2d 1137 (1960).

to the cy pres power exercised with respect to some charitable trusts.[77]

The cases which follow are intended to provide a basis for comparison of legislative and judicial powers to authorize deviations when circumstances occur unforeseen by a testator or settlor.

GOODRIDGE v. NATIONAL BANK OF COMMERCE OF NORFOLK

Supreme Court of Appeals of Virginia, 1959.
200 Va. 511, 106 S.E.2d 598.

[Goodridge created two trusts, one by indenture in 1940 in which the National Bank of Commerce was named trustee, and another by his will dated 6 February 1951 which was effective in 1952 and which named the National Bank of Commerce and another as trustees. Both trusts conferred upon the trustee or trustees authority to invest in "bonds, stocks, notes, mortgages or other securities that are eligible for the investment of fiduciary funds under the statute laws of the State of Virginia". At the effective date of both trusts, Virginia had a permissive legal list.[78] In 1956 a statute was passed permitting investments generally subject to the prudent man rule. This statute is set forth in the footnotes.[79] Upon the assumption that the provi-

77. See generally, Alexander, "Court Control of Trusts" 33 U. of Mo. at K.C. Law Rev. 1 (1965); Haskell, "Justifying the Principle of Distributive Deviation in the Law of Trusts" 18 Hastings L.J. 267 (1967); "Enlargement of Administrative Powers of a Trustee" 3 Real Prop.Prob. & T.L.J. 273 (1968). Wentworth, "Deviations from Terms of a Will", Proceedings of Probate and Trust Law Section, American Bar Association (1953) 10; "Deviations from the Distributive Terms of the Trust", 53 Northwestern U.L.Rev. 268 (1958); "Deviation from the Terms of the Trust", 17 Mod.L.Rev. 420 (1954) (Discussion of English cases). Dobris "Equitable Adjustments in Postmortem Income Tax Planning: An Unremitting Diet of *Warms*", 65 Iowa L.Rev. 103 (1979).

78. Virginia Code § 26–40 sets forth a "permissive legal list".

79. Va.Code Ann. § 26–45.1 is as follows:

"(a) Except with respect to the securities described in §§ 6–184 and 26–40, trustees or other fiduciaries in selling and managing property and making investments, shall exercise the judgment and care, under the circumstances then prevailing, 'which men of prudence, discretion and intelligence exercise in the management of their own affairs, not in regard to speculation but in regard to the permanent disposition of their funds, considering the probable income as well as the probable safety of their capital.' Within the limitations of the foregoing standard, a trustee or other fiduciary is authorized to acquire and retain every kind of property and every kind of investment, including debentures and other corporate obligations and stocks, preferred or common, and other described securities, which men of prudence, discretion and intelligence acquire or retain for their own account; and within the limitations of the foregoing standard, an executor, administrator, trustee or other fiduciary, both individual and corporate, may retain property properly acquired, without limitation as to time and without regard to its suitability for original purchase.

"(b) Nothing contained in this section shall be construed as authorizing any departure from, or variation of, the express terms set forth in any will, agreement, court order, or other instrument creating or defining an executor's, administrator's, trustee's or other fiduciary's duties and powers, but the terms 'legal investment' or 'author-

sions in the indenture and will limited them to investments on the legal list, the trustees sought instructions concerning the effect of the 1956 statute, which expressly applied to instruments "now existing or hereafter made", upon their authority. The lower court held the new statute constitutionally unobjectionable and that investments pursuant to the new statute would not constitute a variation from the express terms or limitations of the indenture or will. The guardian ad litem for certain infants and unborn beneficiaries appeals.]

BUCHANAN, JUSTICE. * * * The guardian ad litem appealed and assigned error under which he contends that if § 26–45.1 is applied to the trusts here involved, both of which were created before that section was enacted, then it is unconstitutional. He argues with respect to the *inter vivos* trust that the settlor made a contract with the trustee which was governed by the statutes in effect at the time of its execution; that it is not to be presumed that the settlor anticipated that the statutes regarding investments might be afterwards changed from time to time and therefore acquiesced in the type of investments which might later be permitted by statute; but that the presumption should be that the settlor had in mind only the "legal lists" of investments for fiduciaries which the statutes at that time enumerated. Hence, he says, to permit the prudent man statute to apply would impair the obligation of the contract, which is forbidden by both State and Federal Constitutions.

He concedes that the will was not a contract, but he says that under it the beneficiaries of the trust took vested rights; that the application of the subsequently enacted prudent man statute changes the effect of the will and divests the beneficiaries of their vested rights in violation of the Fourteenth Amendment.

Similar arguments were made and rejected in Fidelity Union Trust Co. v. Price, 11 N.J. 90, 93 A.2d 321, 324, 35 A.L.R.2d 980, in which the New Jersey prudent man investment statute was construed and applied. The New Jersey statute authorized fiduciaries to invest up to 40 per cent of the corpus of the estate according to the prudent man rule, and § 12 of that statute, N.J.S. 3A:15–29, N.J.S.A., made it applicable to "trust instruments heretofore and hereafter made," just as paragraph (d) of the Virginia statute makes it applicable to trust "instruments now existing or hereafter made." In the opinion by Chief Justice Vanderbilt it was said that the prudent man statute had the effect of expanding the types of investments which a fiduciary

ized investment' or words of similar import, as used in any such instrument, shall be taken to mean any investment which is permitted by the terms of paragraph (a) hereof.

"(c) Nothing contained in this section shall be construed as restricting the power of a court of proper jurisdiction to permit an executor, administrator, trustee or other fiduciary, both individual and corporate, to deviate from the terms of any will, agreement, or other instrument relating to the acquisition, investment, reinvestment, exchange, retention, sale or management of fiduciary property.

"(d) The provisions of this section shall govern executors, administrators, trustees or other fiduciaries, both individual and corporate, acting under wills, agreements, court orders and other instruments now existing or hereafter made."

might legally make and that now as heretofore a trustee in making investments of whatever type must exercise that degree of care and judgment which persons of ordinary prudence and reasonable discretion exercise in the management of their own affairs. As to the constitutionality of the retrospective provision of the statute he wrote:

> "Further, it is plain that the provision of the statute making it applicable to prior created trusts is not constitutionally objectionable. The statute as thus applied in no way impairs the obligation of any contract or interferes with or alters any vested right or legal remedy that antecedently existed. * * * Unless the trust instrument provides otherwise, it is presumed that the trustor intended that his trustee should have the power to make such investments of the corpus of the trust as the Legislature in its wisdom might from time to time permit. * * *."

Then from the earlier case of Reiner v. Fidelity Union Trust Co., 126 N.J.Eq. 78, 8 A.2d 175, 178, where the trust agreement gave the trustee power to invest the proceeds from the redemption of certain stock " 'in such securities as are by the laws of the State of New Jersey designated as legal investments for trust funds,' " he took this quotation which is equally applicable to the present case:

> " 'To interpret the language of this trust instrument as requiring that the trust funds should be invested only in securities which were legal investments for trust funds at the time of the creation of the trust is to attribute to the creator of the trust a complete lack of ordinary intelligence. * * * it is absurd to assume that the creator of the trust did not contemplate situations would arise from time to time, which would induce the legislature to change the types of legal investments because of changes in economic conditions which would render investments safe at one time, unsafe at another time. What the creator of this trust (who undoubtedly was possessed of ordinary common sense) must have believed, was that investments which were approved by the legislature or by the courts for trust funds would be more likely to be safer investments than other investments.' "

"Where the intention of the creator of the trust," adds Judge Vanderbilt, "is thus carried out quite obviously there is no interference with the vested rights of the beneficiaries."

In the Annotation to the Price case, 35 A.L.R.2d beginning at page 991, it is pointed out that courts have generally held that the propriety of a trust investment is to be determined by the terms of the statute in effect at the time when the investment is made, and not at the time when the trust was created, except where the language of the trust instrument limited the trustee to certain investments; and it is said:

> "In the rare instances in which the question was raised it has been held that provisions making a trust investment statute applicable to trusts created prior to its enactment are not violative of the constitutional prohibition against impairment of the obligation of a contract."

It is common knowledge that economic conditions and property values change frequently and what was a safe investment in 1940 or 1951 may be an unsafe and unwise investment in 1959. It is not to be presumed, in the absence of such a purpose expressly stated in or necessarily to be inferred from the trust instrument, that a trustor intended that the trustee should invest only in securities permitted by the statutes in effect at the time the trust was created. There is nothing in the trust instruments in the present case to indicate, as could readily have been done if desired, that the trustor intended to restrict investments to those enumerated in the statutes in effect at the time of the execution of the instruments. In such case it is the natural and legal presumption that the trustor intended that the trustees could make such investments as were lawful and proper under the statutes in effect at the time the investments were made.

To give effect to such intention impairs no contract and takes away no vested property right.

The decree appealed from correctly decided the question and it is therefore

Affirmed.

STANTON v. WELLS FARGO BANK & UNION TRUST CO.

District Court of Appeal of California, First Appellate District, Division 1, 1957. 150 Cal.App.2d 763, 310 P.2d 1010.[80]

[A testamentary trust was created in 1931, distribution of the estate to the trustees being made in 1936. The trust provided that the trustees "shall have full power and authority * * * to invest and reinvest any of the trust property * * * as to the trustee shall deem fit and proper", subject to the limitation that "investments by the trustees shall be made only in bonds of the United States Government, in bonds of the States of the United States, and municipalities thereof, and in such other bonds (the bonds of foreign governments or foreign municipalities excluded) as shall be rated at least 'AA' by Moody Investor's service, or in the event such service shall no longer be in existence, by such first class service as such trustees shall deem best." The income of the trust was given to certain beneficiaries for life with a general testamentary power of appointment in them over the remainders following their respective life estates with issue of the life tenants designated as takers in default. In 1951 the life beneficiaries petitioned that the trustees be authorized to deviate from the terms of the trust concerning investments and invest in accordance with the "prudent man rule" as provided in Section 2261 of the California Civil Code. The trial court permitted the deviation and one of the trustees appeals.]

* * *

PETERS, PRESIDING JUSTICE. * * * The trial court made findings generally in accord with the allegations of the petition. Respon-

80. Noted, 15 Wash. & Lee L.Rev. 108 (1958).

dent points particularly to findings to the effect that it was the intent of the settlor to secure an income for the life beneficiaries in as large amount as possible commensurate with reasonable safety; that the sole purpose of the restrictions was to protect the corpus; that because of changes in the general economy this purpose is "being defeated and thwarted; * * * [a] result the testator could not have foreseen prior to his death". It was also found that the settlor was influenced by investment conditions existing at the time he planned the trust, but "was not adverse to investing in common and/or preferred stocks, or real estate, which fact is evident by the large number of preferred and common stocks and the real estate which constituted a part of the residue of the decedent's estate distributed to the trustees, the defendants herein, under the decree of final distribution."

The sole question presented is whether, under this state of facts, the trial court was justified in exercising its admitted equitable powers by authorizing deviation from the trust terms relating to investments.

Appellant concedes, of course, that since 1931 economic conditions have changed, but argues that such change alone does not warrant a court in authorizing the trustees to deviate from the terms of the trust. It is argued that to warrant deviation some emergency endangering the main trust purpose must exist, and it is contended that there is no evidence of such an emergency. Appellant considers it significant that since the inception of the trust the estate has been substantially invested in common stocks and realty, with bonds, as late as December 31, 1954, comprising only 17.4% of the estate. Appellant argues that respondent seeks the deviation solely because the bond investment provision is inflexible, and believes that flexibility would be preferable, and contends such fact alone did not warrant the court in authorizing the deviation. * * *

The main contention of respondent in answer to these arguments is that if the trustees are compelled to adhere to the terms of the trust the settlor's intent and his main trust purpose would be frustrated. It is argued that all of the interested beneficiaries, including the living remaindermen, have consented to the deviation, and all will benefit by the proposed modification. Respondent refers specifically to the evidence showing a marked decline in the purchasing power of the dollar, and to the return on bonds as compared to the return on stocks. It is urged that since the settlor drafted this trust the following unanticipated events have occurred: The depression of the thirties; World War II and the cold war; the current defense program; the increase in income taxes; and the government controls on capital. In order to keep the record straight, it is obvious that respondent erroneously refers to the depression as an unanticipated event. The trust was drafted in the middle of the depression and undoubtedly the depression was one of the reasons that motivated the trustor to insert the provision in question.

The problem of when a court may permit a deviation from the provisions of a trust has been discussed by many commentators and text writers (See 23 Cal.L.Rev. 86; 34 Cal.L.Rev. 453; 28 Cal.L.Rev. 785; 21 So.Cal.L.Rev. 433; 170 A.L.R. 1219; 168 A.L.R. 1018; 4 Pomeroy's Equity Jurisprudence, §§ 1062, 1062b, 1073a; 2 Scott on Trusts, § 167, p. 836; 3 Bogert on Trusts and Trustees, §§ 561, 562; Restatement, Trusts, § 167.)

The power to permit deviation from the terms of private trusts is analogous to the cy-pres doctrine applicable to charitable trusts. In re Estate of Loring, 29 Cal.2d 423, 175 P.2d 524. A few generalizations can be made. Normally, of course, the trust instrument constitutes the measure of the trustee's powers. Bryson v. Bryson, 62 Cal. App. 170, 216 P. 391. Except in unusual or emergency situations the courts will limit the trustees to the powers conferred. But the courts will not permit the main purpose of a trust to fail by compelling slavish adherence to the administrative limitations of the trust instrument. Where the main purpose of the trust is threatened the courts will and should grant permission to deviate from restrictive administrative provisions. But the court should not permit a deviation simply because the beneficiaries request it where the main purpose of the trust is not threatened and no emergency exists or is threatened. It must be remembered that it is the theory of this rule that, by the exercise of this power, the court is not defeating the trust, but in fact is furthering it. The equity court is simply doing what the testator, presumably, would have done had he anticipated the changed conditions. In other words, the specific intent of the testator is disregarded in order to enforce his general intent.

In the instant case all persons interested in the trust except one trustee, and unlikely unborn contingent remaindermen request that the modification be made. This is a factor to be considered. Also, the requested modification concerns only the method of administration of the trust and does not affect any rights of the beneficiaries between themselves. This, too, is important. It should also be mentioned that the objecting trustee concedes that the existing restriction is ill advised. No doubt economic changes have occurred since 1931.

On the other hand, the considered conclusions of the settlor regarding what should constitute appropriate investments cannot be lightly disregarded. He had managed to preserve a large fortune during a terrible depression. He had seen stock investments wiped out overnight. He knew that in the past there had been recurring periods of inflation and deflation. He, the man who had accumulated this fortune, whose property it was, wanted to protect his niece and her children from such vicissitudes, and to provide them with an adequate income. He decided that this could best be done by limiting the trustee's reinvestment powers to the purchase of certain types of bonds. While the equity court has power in an emergency to disregard these directions, the express and considered wishes and desires of the settlor should not be cavalierly disregarded. In the instant case the judgment of the settlor, to date, has not proved devastatingly erroneous. The trustees received assets in 1936 of the value of $2,323,718.50. By December 31, 1954, these assets were worth $2,860,687.21. The distributable annual income was $88,890.60 in 1938, and by 1954 this had increased to $109,942.84. There is no evidence that any beneficiary is in want or that the distributable income is not sufficient to supply the reasonable needs of all beneficiaries. No emergency exists. The existing inflationary cycle has continued for some years. The government has adopted many economic measures to try to control and stop this inflationary trend. Some economists predict an era of deflation and others warn us of a depression. These matters are mentioned to indicate that, while the settlor might not have been omniscient, neither are the beneficiaries nor the courts, omniscient. No one can forecast, with any certainty, future events. Certainly, it is true that misguided restrictions imposed by a settlor should not be permitted to defeat his fundamental trust purpose, but it is equally true that the court should not try to guess what economic conditions may be in a few years by permitting deviations when no real emergency exists or is threatened.

These general conclusions are supported by the decided cases both in California and in other states. One of the leading California cases is Adams v. Cook, 15 Cal.2d 352, 101 P.2d 484. A business trust there conveyed certain real property to trustees with instructions to sell such property at a named price, or at a lesser price if the trustees considered this in the best interest of the beneficiaries. The trustees were given power to lease the property but only "subject to the sale of the property under the conditions of the trust." 15 Cal.2d at page 354, 101 P.2d at page 486. Oil was found on nearby property and application by drillers was made for an oil lease of the premises. They would not accept a lease subject to the trust conditions of sale, and the trustee refused to execute a lease under any other circumstances. Ninety percent of the beneficial interests sought declaratory relief, requesting permission to lease the property for drilling; one of the beneficiaries objected. The court affirmed a judgment authorizing the trustee to enter into oil leases without inserting the trust condition of sale. This was based on findings that the intent of the trustors was to secure the largest return possible on the investment; that they did not at the time of the creation of the trust know the property contained oil; that the highest purpose for which the property was adapted was the production of oil and gas; and that the drilling of other wells on contiguous properties would seriously deplete the corpus.

It was stated as well settled that "a court of equity has the power to change the method of administering a trust estate when it is shown that such a change is necessary to prevent loss or destruction of the trust property * * * 15 Cal.2d at page 358, 101 P.2d at page 487.

At page 360 of 15 Cal.2d, at page 488 of 101 P.2d the court made the following comments: "It seems only reasonable to assume that had the trustors, at the time the trust was created any knowledge that oil and gas could be produced from the trust property, they would have had the declaration of trust provide for a lease thereof for that purpose. In giving to the trustee this right to lease the trust property for the production of oil and gas, the court is only doing what the trustors would have done had they had the same facts before them then that were before this court at the trial of this action."

At page 361 of 15 Cal.2d, at page 489 of 101 P.2d the applicable rules were summarized as follows: "It is perfectly clear from the above authorities that the rule against courts modifying the terms of a contract, and that they should construe it precisely as the parties had made it, does not apply to declarations of trust, where the primary purpose of the trust would not be acomplished by a strict adherence to the terms of the declaration of trust and that when it is made to appear in a court of equity, as was shown in the present case, that the benefits and advantages which the trustors desired to confer upon the beneficiaries would not accrue to them by a 'slavish adherence to the terms of the trust' the court may modify the terms of the trust to accomplish the real intent and purpose of the trustors".

Another interesting California case is Security-First Nat. Bank of Los Angeles v. Easter, 136 Cal.App. 691, 29 P.2d 422. There a trust consisted, in part of a group of houses called Catalina Court. The decedent-settlor's wife was given the use for life of one of the houses rent free together with the sum of $300 per month out of the net income from the corpus. The balance of the income was to go to the heirs at law of the deceased, who were also the remaindermen. The trustee was prohibited from selling or in any manner disposing of Catalina Court. Because of the depression the value and income from the real property was so reduced that the trustee was unable to make the payments in full to the beneficiaries. The trustee brought an action to secure permission to sell the property. This was resisted by the remaindermen. The trial court made findings that the purposes of the trust would be frustrated without such sale and directed a sale for the best price obtainable. This was reversed, emphasis being placed on the absence of any showing that a reasonable price or any sum whatever could be obtained for the real property, and on the fact that there was no evidence to support a finding that, if a sale were permitted and the proceeds reinvested, there would be sufficient income to carry out the purposes of the trust. While the factual situation is different from the one here presented, the case was dealing with an attempted modification claimed to be justified by changed economic conditions. In that case the income had decreased over 40 per cent because of the depression. The court had the following comments to make, 136 Cal.App. at page 697, 29 P.2d at page 425: "In view of the seriousness of interfering with the express declarations of an express trust prohibiting the alienation of property for a limited time, a court of equity should not order the property to be sold except upon clear and satisfactory proof that it is necessary to do so to preserve the estate and carry out the intention and purpose of the testator. A court has no right to speculate upon the mere probability that such a sale will ultimately inure to the benefit of the beneficiaries.

In the present unsettled financial condition of affairs, it is generally conceded that all investments are highly speculative. Real property may not ordinarily be sold only at a ruinous sacrifice. It is a perplexing problem to determine what investments might be fairly safe or reasonably profitable." * * *

The cases cited by respondent involved real emergencies. Thus, in Lambertville Nat. Bank v. Bumster, 141 N.J.Eq. 396, 57 A.2d 525 * * * the settlor, who died in 1945, prohibited the trustees from selling any of the securities in the trust estate. Seventy-seven per cent of these securities were highly speculative. The market value of the estate by 1948 had already declined 19 per cent. The chancellor held that, had the settlor envisaged the changed circumstances, he would have permitted the deviation. All the parties interested requested the deviation, including the trustee.

In Citizens' Nat. Bank v. Morgan, 94 N.H. 284, 51 A.2d 841, 170 A.L.R. 1215, the income of the trust had been halved since the creation of the trust. The court granted relief from the restrictive investment provisions of the trust.

These cases involved real, not imagined emergencies. It is not the function of courts to remake the provisions of trust instruments. Generally, it is the duty of courts to enforce the provisions of the trust instrument. A court should not presume to remake a trust instrument even though the court believes that it could do a better job. The court's power to permit a deviation exists so that the settlor's main trust purpose will not fail, and to take care of grave emergencies. That is not this case. The trial court should not have permitted the deviation.

Respondent also argues that Section 2261(5) of the Civil Code supports the action of the trial court. That subdivision reads as follows: "The provisions of this section shall apply to all trusts now existing or hereafter created. Where, in trusts now existing or hereafter created, the term 'investments permissible by law for investment of trust funds,' or 'authorized by law for investment of trust funds,' 'legal investments' or 'authorized investments', or other words of similar import are used in defining the powers of the trustee relative to investments, such language, in the absence of other controlling or modifying provisions of the trust instrument, shall be construed as authorizing any investment permitted by the terms of subdivision (1) of this section [establishing the Prudent Man Rule of Investment]."

Respondent argues that the provision of the trust restricting the trustees to reinvesting in bonds is no different than if the testator had limited the trustees to such investments as were then permitted by law for the investment of trust funds. In that event, of course, the rules established by Section 2261 would apply.

The obvious answer to this contention is that the settlor did not state that the trustees were to be limited by what the law provided were legal investments for trustees. He specified certain types of securities regardless of what the statute then provided and without reference to the statute. The quoted provision of the statute is only applicable where the testator limits investments to statutory approved investments. It has no application where the settlor himself specifies particular investments that are prohibited.

The judgment appealed from is reversed.

BRAY and FRED B. WOOD, JJ., concur.

Hearing denied; MCCOMB, J., dissenting.

---

(7) CONTRACT AND TORT LIABILITY OF FIDUCIARIES

VAUGHN v. JONES

Supreme Court of Oklahoma, 1937.
179 Okl. 545, 66 P.2d 504.

HURST, JUSTICE. Byron Arthur Vaughn, plaintiff in error, is executor of the last will and testament of his father. The deceased owned a farm, which, after his death, the executor leased to the plaintiff, C. E. Jones. This action was filed to recover for certain work that the plaintiff claims he did on said farm under an agreement with the defendant. In all the pleadings the defendant is named "Byron Arthur Vaughn, Executor of the Estate of Thomas Arthur Vaughn, deceased." The court instructed the jury that if they returned a verdict for the plaintiff, it must be against the defendant individually, and not against him as executor of the estate of his father. The jury returned a verdict for the plaintiff and against the defendant individually, on which the trial court rendered judgment, from which this appeal was taken.

The defendant urges but one proposition for reversal, and that is that the court committed error in instructing the jury that they could return a verdict against him individually and in rendering such judgment against him. In support of this proposition he cites Sterrett v. Barker (1898) 119 Cal. 492, 51 P. 695; Hines v. Bacon (1922) 86 Okl. 165, 207 P. 93; Youst v. Willis (1897) 5 Okl. 413, 49 P. 1014. The Sterrett Case is authority against the defendant's contention that he is not individually liable. It was agreed in that case that it was against the estate, and the court held that the complaint could not be amended so as to constitute an action against the executor individually. It is further held that an executor is individually liable for breach of contract made by him in connection with the administration of the estate, and the estate is not liable unless such contract is expressly authorized by will or statute. The Hines Case and the Youst Case do not touch upon this point.

The law is well settled that an executor or administrator is individually liable for contracts made by him in the course of the administration of the estate, unless he stipulates against personal liability. 11 R.C.L. 166; 24 C.J. 63; Brown v. Quinton (1909) 80 Kan. 44, 102 P. 242, 25 L.R.A.,N.S., 71, 18 Ann.Cas. 290; Riedy v. Bidwell (1925) 70 Cal.App. 552, 233 P. 995; Judy v. Guaranty Trust Co. (1936) 186 Wash. 637, 59 P.2d 745. See, also, Drinker v. Kepley (1914) 43 Okl. 686, 144 P. 350. The defendant does not contend that he stipulated against personal liability.

The defendant, however, contends that he was sued only in his representative capacity, and that for that reason no personal judgment can be rendered against him. The petition alleges that the defendant is liable "both individually and in his capacity as such executor." The reference to the defendant as executor should be treated as descriptive of the person, and may be rejected as surplusage. 24 C.J. 825; Brown v. Quinton, supra; Blair v. Hall, Mo.App., 201 S.W. 945; Hanson v. Blake, 63 W.Va. 560, 60 S.E. 589. See, also, Allen v. Clover Valley Lumber Co. (1935) 171 Okl. 238, 42 P.2d 850.

This rule does the defendant no injustice. Under section 1330, O. S.1931 (58 Okl.St.Ann. § 525), on the settlement of his accounts as executor, he is "allowed all necessary expenses in the care, management and settlement of the estate," if the county court deems it proper. Affirmed.

NOTE

Since the representative or trustee has a right to indemnity for all expenses properly incurred in the course of administration, he will normally pay routine contract claims out of estate assets. It is only where he disputes the amount or the liability, or where there are no cash assets available for payment, that the contract creditor will be forced to sue. If the fiduciary pays, his right to pay may be contested upon accounting, to determine whether the expense has been properly incurred.

Two remedies of the creditor forced to sue must be carefully distinguished: (1) suit against the fiduciary personally, and (2) suit to reach the assets of the estate or trust. As to the former, suit at law will lie unless there has been an express contract against personal liability. A common illustration is the personal liability of the representative who arranges for burial of the deceased.[81] Even if the contract provides that the fiduciary is not personally liable, the creditor may have a remedy against him for breach of implied warranty if it develops that the contract was unauthorized and there is no remedy against the estate. Suit to reach the assets of the estate or trust, i.e., against the fiduciary in a representative capacity, is always a secondary remedy. Since the fiduciary would be entitled to indemnity in equity if his action relative to the contract were within his authority, this right of indemnity is an equitable asset which his creditors may reach. Hence, in the contract cases, the creditor may maintain a single suit in equity to try the breach of contract and the right to indemnity if he (a) joins the beneficiaries as necessary parties and (b) shows that his remedy at law is inadequate, as where the fiduciary is personally insolvent. Two exceptions should be noted: (1) Where the third party confers a benefit upon the estate, there ought to be a direct recovery against the estate to that extent, on an unjust

81. E.g., Smolka v. Chandler, 41 Del. 255, 20 A.2d 131 (1941).

enrichment theory; this should take care of many of the cases involving sale of goods to a fiduciary carrying on a business. (2) The contract which stipulates no personal liability may expressly or by implication create an equitable lien on the estate assets; the issue then becomes whether the fiduciary has authority to make such a contract.

Three types of contract claims are common: (1) attorney's fees and burial expenses, (2) debts incurred in the course of running a business, and (3) suit for breach of contract by a party who has contracted to purchase realty from the fiduciary, the latter claiming prior breach by the purchaser. Burial expenses and attorney's fees incurred in the course of administration of a decedent's estate are frequently made part of the expenses of administration by statute and hence chargeable against the estate assets. However, increasing attention seems to be given to burial expenses that appear excessive and excessive amounts may be disallowed in the personal representative's account.[82] As to business debts, many courts treat the estate as an entity chargeable with debts properly incurred in the course of running it.[83] Many of the third class involve claims for improvements made by the purchaser, which could be solved on the unjust enrichment theory of benefit conferred on the estate.[84]

If a personal representative or trustee borrows funds (we have already considered the power to borrow in Section 5B), he will normally execute a promissory note in his representative capacity. This particular type of contract falls under the provisions of the Uniform Commercial Code, and Section 3–403 of the Code provides that a person signing in a representative capacity "is personally obligated if the instrument neither names the person represented nor shows that the representative signed in a representative capacity." To avoid personal liability, the fiduciary therefore should be careful to sign in the proper manner, such as: "Mary Smith, personal representative for the Estate of William Smith".

JOHNSTON v. LONG

Supreme Court of California, 1947.
30 Cal.2d 54, 181 P.2d 645.

TRAYNOR, JUSTICE. Defendant appeals from a judgment entered in favor of plaintiff for damages for personal injuries sustained by the latter when an overhead door fell on him as he was entering a garage of the C. A. Gray automobile agency in San Diego. The ga-

82. In DiNezzo's Estate, 49 Misc.2d 237, 267 N.Y.S.2d 67 (1966), the funeral bill was $4,253.25. Testator's will made no provision for the type of funeral but had stated to the executor and others that he desired a "bronze box * * * a good funeral". Payment for a bronze casket and the sum of $145 for a funeral reception was approved by the Court but the Court considered $500 could have been saved and surcharged the executor for this amount, deducting it from his commission. At 267 N.Y.S.2d 69 the Surrogate states: "* * * In complying with testator's expressed wishes, nevertheless the executor has some duty to conserve the assets of the estate. His attitude herein was one of apparent abandon and he stated he merely 'left everything up to the funeral director'. The court believes that an executor should conduct himself in the performance of his duties as a careful reasonable businessman and conserve the assets wherever possible" * * *.

83. Moore v. McFall, 263 Ill. 596, 105 N.E. 723 (1914); Roberts v. Hale, 124 Iowa 296, 99 N.W. 1075 (1904).

84. An excellent summary of common law doctrine and statutory modifications concerning contract liability may be found in Johnston, "Developments in Contract Liability of Trusts and Trustees," 41 N.Y.U.L.Rev. 483 (1966).

rage was owned and operated by C. A. Gray during his lifetime. At the time of the accident it was operated as part of his estate according to the terms of his will and pursuant to section 572 of the Probate Code by Ralph C. Long and A. J. Verheyen as executors. In accordance with the wishes of the decedent as expressed in the will, the actual operation of the business was left in the hands of John Berger, who had been manager of the business during decedent's last illness. Plaintiff's injuries occurred when he was opening the door to make a delivery of gasoline before the premises were opened for business. The door was of the overhead type, operated by means of counterweights connected to the door by a wire cable. While plaintiff was opening the door the cable pulled from its fastening, and the door in falling shut cut off the end of plaintiff's nose.

Eight months after the accident occurred, the assets of the estate were distributed to J. O. Miller, as trustee, the estate was closed and the executors were discharged. Four months later plaintiff brought this action naming as defendants, J. O. Miller, the trustee; the San Diego Planing Mill Company, the company that had installed the door and put in a new cable before the accident; and Long and Verheyen, both as individuals and as executors of the estate of C. A. Gray. A demurrer filed by Miller, the trustee, was sustained without leave to amend. A demurrer was also sustained in favor of the San Diego Planing Mill and judgment was entered for that defendant but, on appeal, the ruling and judgment were reversed. (Johnston v. Long, 56 Cal.App.2d 834, 133 P.2d 409). Demurrers filed by defendant Long were overruled. A. J. Verheyen, the coexecutor, died before the trial, and the action was dismissed as to him. Defendant, at the opening of the trial, objected to the introduction of any testimony against him in his representative capacity, but the objection was overruled and the case went to trial against Long, as an individual, Long, as an executor, and the San Diego Planing Mill Company. Throughout the trial, Long also made several motions that the case be dismissed as to him in his capacity as executor, including motions for nonsuit and directed verdict, but all such motions were denied.

The jury returned a verdict for $87,575 "against defendant Ralph C. Long, an individual acting as executor of the estate of C. A. Gray, deceased," and a special verdict in favor of the defendant planing mill that there was no negligence on its part or on the part of its employee who had repaired the door. Defendant Long appeals on the grounds that an executor may not be sued in his representative capacity after the estate has been closed, the assets distributed, and he has been discharged as executor; that the verdict is indefinite and uncertain in that it does not disclose whether the jury intended to find against Long as an individual or against him as an executor; that after an estate has been closed and the executor discharged, the executor may not be held personally liable for the negligence of an employee in a business conducted by the executor pursuant to Section 572 of the Probate Code; and that the manner in which the trial was conducted and the issues presented to the jury so prejudiced the defendant as to deprive him of a fair trial on the issue of his personal liability.

A basic issue in this case is whether an executor is personally liable for torts committed by employees of a business operated by him pursuant to Section 572 of the Probate Code. An executor has always been liable for any torts committed by him in the administration of the estate. (Eustace v. Jahns, 38 Cal. 3, 21; see Nickals v. Stanley, 146 Cal. 724, 727, 81 P. 117; Rapaport v. Forer, 20 Cal.App.2d 271, 278, 66 P.2d 1242, cases collected 44 A.L.R. 637, 640.) Before the 1929 Amendment, St.1929, p. 157, to Section 1581 of the Code of Civil Procedure (now Section 572 of the Probate Code), if an executor elected to carry on decedent's business without authorization in the will (see Estate of Ward, 127 Cal.App. 347, 353, 15 P.2d 901), he did so at his own risk and his liability for anything that occurred in the course of conducting the business was a personal one, with no right of reimbursement from the estate. Estate of Burke, 198 Cal. 163, 166, 244 P. 340, 44 A.L.R. 1341.

Section 572 of the Probate Code provides:[85] "After notice to all persons interested in an estate, given in such manner as may be directed by the court or a judge thereof, the court may authorize the executor or administrator to continue the operation of the decedent's business to such an extent and subject to such restrictions as may seem to the court to be for the best interest of the estate and those interested therein."

Defendant contends that since an executor authorized under this section to operate a decedent's business no longer does so at his own risk, he is not liable for torts committed in the course of business operations when he is free from fault, and that to construe the section otherwise would impose too heavy a burden on executors who must operate businesses. This contention overlooks not only the fact that the executor is not required to operate the business, but must petition the court for permission to do so, but the fact that the rule as to the personal liability of an executor for torts committed during the course of his administration is not confined to cases in which the executor carries on operations that are outside the scope of his authority. (See Nickals v. Stanley, supra; Rapaport v. Forer, supra; 44 A.L. R. 637, 640.) Personal liability for torts committed during operations that are otherwise within the proper scope of the executor's authority is not a new burden. There is nothing in Section 572 to indicate that any change in the rule as to personal liability was intended. The principal effect of the 1929 amendment was to provide an authorization, should the will fail to provide one, for the executor to carry on the decedent's business. Estate of Ward, supra; Estate of King, 19 Cal.2d 354, 359, 121 P.2d 716.

* * *

85. [This statutory provision was amended in 1971, to add special provisions relating to continuation of a partnership. See Cal.Prob. Code § 572 (West 1980 Supp.).—Ed.]

With regard to obligations incurred in the operation of businesses under Section 572, it has been held that while the administration continues, contractual obligations are properly chargeable against the estate but do not become liens on the assets of the estate. Estate of Allen, 42 Cal.App.2d 346, 348, 108 P.2d 973; Estate of Smith, 16 Cal. App.2d 239, 241, 60 P.2d 574. Defendant relies, however, on California Employment Stabilization Commission v. Hansen, 69 Cal.App.2d 767, 770, 160 P.2d 173, in which the court stated that the obligations incurred in managing the decedent's business pursuant to Section 572 are charges against the estate and that after a final decree of distribution the executor is not liable for contributions under the Unemployment Insurance Act when the claimant has failed to file a creditor's claim against the estate. Not only was that case concerned with the construction of the Unemployment Insurance Act, but there was no issue of fault on the part of the executor. Nor is it applicable if the plaintiff has no provable and liquidated claim against either the executor or the estate at the time the estate is closed.

Under the doctrine of respondeat superior, except where the rule may have been changed by statute, torts committed by employees of a trustee in the course of administration of the trust estate subject the trustee to personal liability. (Rest.Trusts, sec. 264, comment (b); cases collected, Vol. 3, Part 2, Bogert, Trusts and Trustees, § 731, p. 532; 2 Scott on Trusts, § 264; 43 Harv.L.Rev. 1122, 1124.) Most cases have recognized that the same rules determine the personal liability of an executor for torts committed in the course of administration. (See Kirchner v. Muller, 280 N.Y. 23, 28, 19 N.E.2d 665, 127 A. L.R. 681; Clauson v. Stull, 331 Pa. 101, 103, 200 A. 593; cases collected 43 Dick.L.Rev. 143; 44 A.L.R. 637, 640; Vol. 3, Part 2, Bogert, op. cit. supra, § 731, p. 533.) Except for the Oregon case of Fetting v. Winch, supra, the cases hold that the doctrine of respondeat superior is applicable to an executor and that he is personally liable for the torts of employees. (Fischer v. McNeely, 110 Wash. 283, 284, 188 P. 478, 14 A.L.R. 369; Guatti-McQuade Co. v. Flynn, 79 Misc. 430, 431, 140 N.Y.S. 135; Kalua v. Camarinos, 11 Haw. 557, 558; see Bogert, loc. cit. supra.)

The rule of personal liability of a trustee or executor for the torts of his agents in the course of administration is now generally qualified by giving the executor or trustee a right to reimbursement aainst the assets of the estate when he is personally without fault. (Rest.Trusts, sec. 247; cases collected Vol. 3, Part 2, Bogert, op. cit. supra, § 734; Scott, op. cit. supra, sec. 247; 44 A.L.R. 637, 676.) The Restatement also provides that when the claim against the trustee is uncollectible because his personal assets are insufficient, the plaintiff may reach the trust assets to the extent that the trustee would have had a right of reimbursement. (Rest.Trusts, § 268; see also, Scott on Trusts, § 268; Stone, A Theory of Liability of Trust Estates for the Contracts and Torts of the Trustee, 22 Col.L.Rev. 527.) A few cases have gone further and allowed the trustee to be sued in his representative capacity in order to avoid circuity of action. (In re Raybould, 1900, 1 Ch. 199, 201; Ewing v. Wm. L. Foley, Inc., 115 Tex.

222, 234, 280 S.W. 499, 44 A.L.R. 627; contra, Kirchner v. Muller, supra.) None of these authorities, however, holds that the trustee is absolved from personal liability (see Stone, loc. cit. supra), and it is clear that any right of action that the plaintiff has against the estate is purely a derivative one.

When the executor carries on the decedent's business with proper authorization, there is no doubt that contractual obligations properly incurred are chargeable against the estate and that tort liability, where the executor is not personally at fault, should ultimately be borne by the estate. If Section 572 has any effect on the question of tort liability of the estate, the purpose of that section as well as the purpose of any authorization in the will for the carrying on of the business may be fully carried out by applying the rules of the Restatement of Trusts in regard to such liability as well as the representative's right of reimbursement out of the assets of the estate.

It has been contended, however, that the doctrine of respondeat superior should apply directly against the executor in his representative capacity and not subject him to personal liability when he is without fault. Although this precise question has never previously been decided by the California courts, there are good reasons for not departing from the general rule. To hold the estate rather than the executor primarily liable for the torts of the agents of the estate, it would be necessary to apply the rules governing the liabilities of a corporate officer and to abandon those governing a trustee, which have heretofore been held applicable to executors. It is clear that an officer of a corporation is not liable under the doctrine of respondeat superior for the torts of corporate employees except where the officer is at fault. The liability falls upon the corporation. Unlike a corporation, however, an estate is not a legal or corporate entity (Tanner v. Best, 40 Cal.App.2d 442, 444, 104 P.2d 1084), and cannot be a principal. Nor can the executor properly be regarded as the agent of the heirs or distributees, for his authority is derived from the will, and the control that is exercised over him is the control exercised by the probate court. (Eustace v. Jahns, 38 Cal. 3, 22.) His position is more nearly that of a trustee or of the decedent himself than that of an agent. The employees are thus regarded as his employees and his liability for their actions should be that of any employer. (Kalua v. Camarinos, 11 Haw. 557, 558.)

Moreover, even if it be assumed possible by some procedure to hold the estate directly liable for the torts of employees without any right against the executor personally, where the executor is not personally at fault, there are practical objections to such a procedure. Under the existing system of administration such a procedure would not afford the heirs adequate protection. The only method available for reaching the assets of the estate is an action against the executor in his representative capacity. (Golden Gate Undertaking Co. v. Taylor, 168 Cal. 94, 99, 141 P. 922, 52 L.R.A.,N.S., 1152, Ann.Cas.1915D, 742; Tanner v. Best, supra.) If the plaintiff could recover directly from the estate in an action against the executor in his representative capacity, the heirs would have no assurance that the question of the personal fault of the executor would be properly tried. It would not be to the interest of either the plaintiff, who would be attempting to recover out of the assets of the estate, or the defendant, whose interest as an individual and as an executor would be in conflict (see Kirchner v. Muller, 280 N.Y. 23, 28, 19 N.E.2d 665, 127 A.L.R. 681), to show personal fault on the part of the executor. Under the general rule that the executor is personally liable for the torts committed by him or his agents in the course of administration, the plaintiff may recover a judgment against the executor personally and the question of the executor's fault is determined in the probate court, where the interest of the heirs may properly be protected. (See Atkinson on Wills, 611.)

It is contended that this application of the respondeat superior doctrine may have harsh results if the executor is not able to recover against the estate and his own property is subject to execution under the judgment. Ordinarily, if the executor is without fault he is protected by his right of reimbursement out of the assets of the estate. Moreover, this application of the doctrine of respondeat superior is no harsher than its usual application to a principal who may gain no profit from the actions of his agent (Silva v. Providence Hospital, 14 Cal.2d 762, 775, 97 P.2d 798) and there is no estate from which he can get reimbursement. The principal justification for the application of the doctrine of respondeat superior in any case is the fact that the employer may spread the risk through insurance and carry the cost thereof as part of his costs of doing business. (See Smith, Frolic and Detour, 23 Col.L.Rev. 444, 456 et seq.) Under the broad power granted to the probate court under Section 572 of the Probate Code, the court may require, as a condition to the right to continue decedent's business, the executor to insure against any tort liability arising out of the conduct of the business, with the premiums for such insurance payable out of the assets of the estate as a proper expense of the business.

In the present case, even if there were either a direct or derivative right against the executor in his representative capacity, defendant Long could not be held liable in that capacity, for he was no longer an executor and there was no estate for him to represent at the time of the suit. The purpose of such a suit is to reach the assets of the estate under the executor's control. Golden Gate Undertaking Co. v. Taylor, supra; see Sterret v. Barker, 119 Cal. 492, 494, 51 P. 695. Where the executor has been discharged and the estate distributed, the executor is therefore no longer subject to suit in his representative capacity. (Union Savings Bank v. De Laveaga, 150 Cal. 395, 398, 89 P. 84.) There would be no purpose in such a suit, for the executor has no assets of the estate under his control. Similarly, after an executor has been removed, his connection with the estate is severed and a judgment against him does not bind the estate. More v. More, 127 Cal. 460, 462, 59 P. 823.

In this case, therefore, the plaintiff could proceed directly against the assets of the estate only by suing the distributee. This action was originally instituted against the distributee as well as against the executors, but a demurrer was sustained without leave to amend, and a judgment, which has now become final, was entered in favor of the distributee. Since the distributee is not a party to this appeal, it cannot be decided in this case whether the executor has a right of indemnity against the distributee to the extent of the assets distributed. (See Rest.Trusts, §§ 249(2) and 279 for the Restatement rules as to the trustee's right of indemnity after distribution and the derivative rights of a tort plaintiff.) The suggestion that a plaintiff should have only a direct right against the distributee after an estate has been closed and the assets distributed is completely unsupported by authority. Moreover, such a rule would impose a considerable burden on the plaintiff in a case in which the assets are widely distributed among many legatees, who may all be residents of other jurisdictions and have no property within this state. There are not, therefore, sufficient reasons for deviating from the general rule of personal liability of the executor for the torts of himself and his agents in the course of administration, and it is clear that in closing the estate an executor does not thereby cut off his personal liability for such torts.

* * *

[The balance of the opinion, which is omitted, dealt with various contentions of defendant relating to rulings and instructions of the trial court; the court held that the jury had not been misled as to the personal nature of defendant's liability.] * * *

The judgment is affirmed. * * *

[The dissenting opinions of Justice Edmonds and Justice Schauer are omitted. Justice Edmonds dissented on the grounds that the jury believed they were awarding damages against the estate for which Long would be indemnified, hence the award was prejudicial to Long. Justice Schauer would have given a "liberal construction" to Section 572; he reasoned that the estate was an entity which, like a corporation, could be sued, that court authorization to carry on the business was not intended to make the non-negligent executor personally liable for torts of employees of the estate, and that a right of reimbursement may in reality be worthless.] [86]

NOTE

The Uniform Probate Code changes the law in this area. Section 3–808 provides:

"[Individual Liability of Personal Representative.]

"(a) Unless otherwise provided in the contract, a personal representative is not individually liable on a contract properly entered into in his fiduciary capacity in the course of administration of the estate unless he

86. See Bogert, Trusts and Trustees (2d Ed., 1960) §§ 731–735; III Scott, Trusts (3d Ed.1967) §§ 264–265; Midgett, "Trustee Liability to Third Persons", 102 Trusts and Estates 157 (1963).

fails to reveal his representative capacity and identify the estate in the contract.

"(b) A personal representative is individually liable for obligations arising from ownership or control of the estate or for torts committed in the course of administration of the estate only if he is personally at fault.

"(c) Claims based on contracts entered into by a personal representative in his fiduciary capacity, on obligations arising from ownership or control of the estate or on torts committed in the course of estate administration may be asserted against the estate by proceeding against the personal representative in his fiduciary capacity, whether or not the personal representative is individually liable therefor.

"(d) Issues of liability as between the estate and the personal representative individually may be determined in a proceeding for accounting, surcharge or indemnification or other appropriate proceeding."

The same rules prevail under the Code as to the conservator of an incompetent's property (Section 5–429) and as to a trustee (Section 7–306). Also relevant are Section 3–715(26) specifically empowering a personal representative to provide for his exoneration from personal liability in any contract entered into on behalf of the estate and Section 3–803(b) limiting recovery against the estate on all claims to four months after performance by the personal representative is due on a contract or after the claim arises in non-contract matters.

PROBLEMS

1. Is the liability of the trustee limited to the value of the trust assets? See McLaughlin v. Minnesota Loan & Trust Co., 192 Minn. 203, 255 N.W. 839 (1934).

2. Can the trustee properly carry insurance to protect himself and charge the premiums against the estate? See Bogert, Trusts and Trustees (2d Ed.1960) § 599; 4 Powell, The Law of Real Property (Rohan Rev.1981) ¶ 536.

3. In Smith v. Rizzuto, 133 Neb. 655, 276 N.W. 406 (1937), an apartment house was devised to a trustee. A tenant was injured three days after death of the decedent, before the trustee had qualified; the injury was allegedly caused by "negligence" in permitting an accumulation of ice on a porch of the apartment house. Is the trustee personally liable? Would he be liable if he renounced his appointment upon learning of the trust? Who would be liable if the accident occurred after death of the sole trustee and before appointment of a successor, assuming a statute provides that in such event title vests in the court until a successor is appointed and qualified?

---

(8) HANDLING CLAIMS AGAINST AN ESTATE

The machinery for handling claims against the estate is largely statutory. These statutes vary in detail on such matters as: what type of claims must be presented; whether the claim must be presented to the personal representative or filed with the court; what date (appointment of the personal representative or publication of notice to creditors) commences the period within which claims against the estate must be filed; whether the length of the period is fixed by the statute itself or determined by court order; whether the claim must be verified and generally how formal it must be; how objections by the personal representative or the heirs are made; whether the court has power to extend the period in cases of hardship. Once the claim is presented or filed, the personal representative must decide whether to pay the claim or not. In some states he may not make payment until the claim is formally passed on (allowed) by the probate court. In others he may either obtain court allowance or proceed to make payment, subject to disallowance by the probate court on final accounting. He has of course a duty to determine whether there is a valid defense, such as lack of consideration for a promissory note, or the statute of limitations; and he will be liable if he does not protect the estate by using reasonable care in raising the defense.[87]

At common law the personal representative has power to compromise claims against the estate, and frequently the executor is expressly given a power to compromise by the terms of the will. Even where he has the power, he may ask for court approval for his own protection; and statutes sometimes require court authorization or approval.[88]

Many wills start with the provision: "I direct that my executor pay all my just debts as soon as convenient." Does such a clause authorize payment without presentment and allowance? [89]

The Uniform Probate Code provisions on claims are substantially different from those presently in force in most states, although publication as a method of notice to claimants is basically the same (Section 3–801). The Code provisions cover all claims, whether contract, tort or other, and whether the claim is one which arose before death or one which arose against the estate after death (those which we considered in the preceding section of the Casebook). In line with the philosophy of the Code that the estate can and normally should be administered outside of court except where there is a genuine controversy, claims may be presented directly to the personal representative (Section 3–804), who may allow or disallow the claim (Section 3–806). If the personal representative wishes, he may petition the probate court on a doubtful claim (Section 3–806(b)); or he may simply disallow the claim and force the claimant to sue for recovery. The personal representative may pay a just claim with or without formal presentation, but if the estate is insolvent he may become personally liable to other claimants injured thereby (Section 3–807). The basic period of limitations, within which claims must be presented, is 4

87. For example, see In re Taylor's Estate, 251 N.Y. 257, 167 N.E. 434 (1929).

88. See, Shaffer, "Fiduciary Power to Compromise Claims", 41 N.Y.U.L.Rev. 528 (1966).

89. See, Foster v. Featherston, 230 Ala. 268, 160 So. 689 (1935); Estate of Boyd v. Thomas, 162 Minn. 63, 202 N.W. 60 (1925).

months, running from the date of first publication of notice to creditors as to claims arising before death, or from the time the personal representative is due to perform in case of breach of contract after death or from the time the claim itself arises in tort or other non-contract matters (Section 3–803). The short period of limitations as applied to torts such as auto accidents has been criticized.[90] The personal representative has ample power to compromise claims (Sections 3–715(17); 3–813). And he may waive the defense of limitations with the consent of all successors of the decedent (Section 3–802).

Secured claims require a brief word. The person holding a secured claim, such as the mortgagee or pledgee, need not present his claim in order to realize on the security. If he wishes a deficiency judgment, however, the claim must be presented. Where the estate is insolvent, by the better view the secured creditor must resort to his security first and then present a claim for the balance.[91] One other word about secured claims: where the property subject to lien is realty, or is the subject matter of a specific bequest, we have seen in Chapter XV, Section 1(2)B that the doctrine of "exoneration" may require the representative to use the general assets of the estate to pay off the encumbrance. This would be true even though no claim has been presented and is most obvious in cases where the will devises or bequeaths the property "free of any incumbrances thereon", indicating an intention on the part of the testator that other assets be used to pay off any liens. But the common law required exoneration where the will was silent, and the doctrine was even applicable where realty passed by intestacy to the heir. Where property is subject to mortgage, it may therefore be desirable for the draftsman of the will expressly to provide either that the burden of payment should be on the devisee or legatee or that the mortgage should be paid out of general assets.

Ordinarily the estate is sufficient to satisfy all obligations and claims, and order of payment is immaterial. Where the estate is insolvent, it becomes necessary to determine priority of payment.[92] Compare the statutory priority in your local jurisdiction with the following from the Uniform Probate Code:

"Section 3–805. [Classification of Claims.]

"(a) If the applicable assets of the estate are insufficient to pay all claims in full, the personal representative shall make payment in the following order:

(1) costs and expenses of administration;

(2) reasonable funeral expenses;

(3) debts and taxes with preference under federal law;

90. See, Langrock, "Uniform Probate Code: What Price Certainty", 6 Trial 23 (1970).

91. See, Uniform Probate Code, § 3–809.

92. See Wellman, "Bankruptcy Proceedings for Insolvent Decedents' Estates", 6 U.Mich.J.L.Ref. 552 (1973), advocating extension of the bankruptcy laws to decedents' estates.

(4) reasonable and necessary medical and hospital expenses of the last illness of the decedent, including compensation of persons attending him;

(5) debts and taxes with preference under other laws of this state;

(6) all other claims.

"(b) No preference shall be given in the payment of any claim over any other claim of the same class, and a claim due and payable shall not be entitled to a preference over claims not due."

NOTE

Although this section is concerned mainly with procedural aspects of handling creditor claims, it should be pointed out that claims may afford the court an opportunity to make an equitable distribution of the estate contrary to the law of intestate succession or the provisions of a will. Thus where a family member, friend or neighbor has taken care of the decedent during the last illness or over a period of years, a claim may be presented for the value of the services rendered. The decedent may even have promised to devise property to the claimant in recognition of the services but the promise was oral and hence unenforceable under the law we considered in Chapter XII, Section 5(1). The claimant can recover the reasonable value of the services, although the presumption that services rendered by a family member are intended as gratuitous must be overcome. Claims therefore serve as a possible avenue to introduce some flexibility and counter to some extent the criticism of some commentators that intestate succession laws are inflexible. In Chapter IV, Section 2(1), we raised the problem of the unmarried cohabitor for whom no provision is made by will or a nonprobate arrangement (life insurance or joint tenancy). One remedy is to file a claim for services rendered to the decedent on either an express contract or an implied contract. Although the illicit relationship was, and in some jurisdictions still is, a bar to any recovery, modern courts are applying in the decedents' estates field the same theories applied during lifetime. In Matter of Estate of Steffes, 95 Wis.2d 490, 290 N.W.2d 697 (1980), the claimant was allowed to recover for a variety of services rendered even though she had been living in an adulterous relationship with decedent. The court upheld a finding of an implied contract to pay for the nonsexual services, in spite of the "illegal or illicit arrangement" which the court treated as separable. It is necessary to establish that the claimant expected compensation (not always an easy task) for services performed at the decedent's request.[93]

93. See also Green v. Richmond, 369 Mass. 47, 337 N.E.2d 691 (1975) (quantum meruit, allowed for value of services based on unenforceable oral promise to make a will in favor of the survivor); Lawrence v. Ladd, 280 Or. 181, 570 P.2d 638 (1977) (denying claim where evidence failed to overcome presumption that services were gratuitous). There may be a property claim to assets in the name of the deceased cohabitor based on a purchase money resulting trust. Cf. Edwards v. Woods, 385 A.2d 780 (D.C.App. 1978). The Washington Supreme Court has even indicated that "if warranted by the facts of a particular case, the court could apply the community property law by analogy to determine the rights of the parties." Latham v. Hennessey, 87 Wash.2d 550, at 554, 554 P.2d 1057, at 1059 (1976). Other theories (such as implied partnership or joint business venture) developed in suits where the nonmarital relationship is terminated

GILMAN v. TAYLOR

Supreme Judicial Court of Massachusetts, 1929.
266 Mass. 346, 165 N.E. 494.

CROSBY, J. This is an appeal from an order of the probate court allowing a petition, filed under G.L. c. 197, § 13, and directing the respondent to retain in his hands sufficient assets to satisfy an alleged claim set forth in the petition.

The judge of probate made the following findings of fact: Levi L. H. Taylor died September 12, 1927, intestate, and Henry L. Taylor was appointed administrator of his estate, October 10, 1927, and duly qualified by giving bond which was approved on the same day. The estate has not been fully administered. The petitioner owns a tract of land in Haverhill on which there is a brick block. On January 1, 1919, she leased the premises to the intestate. The lease is for a term of fifteen years beginning January 1, 1919, the rent for the first ten years of the term being $1,800 a year, payable in monthly installments of $150, and for the last five years, $2,100, payable in monthly installments of $175. The lessee covenants "to pay the lessor taxes on alley-ways, land, and buildings, and any additions thereto above the present tax bill of $555. * * *" The lessor has the right to terminate the lease for neglect or failure of the lessee "to perform and observe any of the covenants" contained in the lease, which are to be performed by the lessee, or if the estate created by the lease shall be taken on execution or other process of law, or if the lessee shall be declared bankrupt or insolvent, and in certain other specified cases; "* * * and the Lessee covenants in case of such termination to indemnify the Lessor, against all loss of rent and all costs which the Lessor may incur by reason of such termination during the residue of the time first above specified for the duration of the said term." The lease also provides that the expression "lessee" shall include, among others, administrators of the lessee.

The petition alleges, among other things, that under the terms of the lease and the covenants therein the lessee is to pay rent and taxes above the present tax bill of $555; that the petitioner is a creditor of the deceased and herewith presents her claim; that his estate is not fully administered; and prays that if upon examination thereof the

during lifetime could be applied where the relationship is terminated by death. See Note, 59 Ore.L.Rev. 277 (1980).

States which refuse relief during lifetime, on the grounds that the nonmarital sexual relation is illegal and that the state must protect the institution of marriage by denying relief in the meretricious relationship, will similarly deny relief at death. McCall v. Frampton, 99 Misc.2d 159, 415 N.Y.S.2d 752 (1979). For a discussion of the broader social and legal issues, see Fineman, "Law and Changing Patterns of Behavior: Sanctions on Non-Marital Cohibitation," 1981 Wis.L.Rev. 275, especially pp. 316–332; Bruch, "Property Rights of De Facto Spouses Including Thoughts on the Value of Homemakers' Services," 10 Fam.L.Q. 101 (1976). In 1970 there were 523,000 unmarried couples living together in the United States; by 1977 this had increased to 957,000 households and by 1980 to 1,560,000; the majority of the couples (63%) were under 35 years of age. "Marital Status and Living Arrangements: March 1980"; Bureau of the Census, Current Population Reports, Series P-20, No. 365 (1981), Table F.

court shall find that her several claims, or any of them, are or may become justly due from said estate, it shall order the administrator to retain in his hands sufficient assets to satisfy the same. A citation issued on the petition returnable July 30, 1928, and a hearing was held on September 12, 1928. On September 24 the probate court found that a claim against the estate of the deceased may become justly due to the petitioner, said claim not exceeding $13,500, and ordered the administrator to retain in his hands sufficient assets to satisfy said claim. The court further found that at the time of the hearing all rent due under the lease was paid up to and including September 1, 1928, and the amount due for taxes above $555 on alleyways, land and buildings for the year 1928 has not been determined; that all amounts due for such taxes in the years before 1928 had been paid; that in the years since the date of the lease the annual amount due from the lessee for said taxes had averaged $500. No evidence was offered in support of any claim under the lease other than for such taxes and the rent. Since the death of the decedent the rent has been paid by his administrator.

The statute under which this petition is brought provides that "a creditor of the deceased, whose right of action does not accrue within one year after the giving of the administration bond, * * * may present his claim to the probate court at any time before the estate is fully administered; and if, upon examination thereof, the court finds that such claim is or may become justly due from the estate, it shall order the executor or administrator to retain in his hands sufficient assets to satisfy the same. * * *"

* * *

It is the contention of the respondent that, as nothing was due and payable to the lessor at the time the petition was filed, it cannot be maintained as the petitioner was not then a creditor of the deceased, and that to authorize the maintenance of such petition it must appear that a debt is owed to constitute the petitioner a creditor; that as nothing was due under the terms of the lease when the petition was filed the relation of debtor and creditor did not exist. The word "creditor" is defined in Boston v. Turner, 201 Mass. 190, at page 193, 87 N.E. 634, 635. It was there said that the word " 'creditor' is ordinarily used as the antonym of 'debtor' and involves a debt and a credit. It commonly signifies one who holds some contractual obligation against another." Hammond v. Granger, 128 Mass. 272, was a petition brought under Gen.Sts. c. 97, § 8. It was said by Gray, C. J., at page 275, of 128 Mass.: "These provisions in terms cover every claim, the right of action upon which does not accrue within the period of the special statute of limitations, and which now appears to be 'justly due from the estate,' and include every debt arising out of a contract of the deceased which becomes 'justly due' before the estate is settled, even if it was neither debitum nor solvendum within the two years." Gen.Sts. c. 97, § 8, was amended by St.1879, c. 71, which extended the application of the previously existing law to claims which "may become" justly due. The statute took effect February

28, 1879, and is embodied in G.L. c. 197, § 13, under which the petition in the case at bar is brought. The cases decided under statutes existing before the enactment of St.1879, c. 71, are not decisive of the question raised in the case at bar. The rent and taxes under the lease to the decedent, which will become due and payable after the expiration of the special statute of limitations, do not depend upon any contingency or uncertainty as to whether these claims may become justly due, and the obligation of the lessee to pay them is definitely and specifically required by the terms of the lease.

The contract which the deceased signed in Ames v. Ames, 128 Mass. 277, Bowditch v. Raymond, 146 Mass. 109, 15 N.E. 285, and similar cases, is not analogous to that in the case at bar. It cannot be doubted that promissory notes, bonds and certain other obligations not then due of a deceased person were within the terms of the statute even before the enactment of the amendment, provided the holder presented his claim to the probate court in conformity with the terms of the statute. Pratt v. Lamson, 128 Mass. 528; Bassett v. Drew, 176 Mass. 141, 57 N.E. 384, and cases cited; Thompson v. Owen, 249 Mass. 229, 234, 144 N.E. 216. Although the precise question of a lessor's rights under the statute respecting the retention of assets does not appear to have been heretofore passed upon by this court, we are of opinion that under the statute as amended it was intended that covenants in a lease to pay rent, and to perform other acts therein stipulated that are capable of a reasonably definite estimate, the amount of which may become due, are claims of creditors which may be presented to the probate court for the retention of assets. The cases cited by the respondent are not at variance with what is here decided.

Decree of probate court affirmed.[94]

NOTE

The nature of a particular claim may cause trouble because it is: (a) unliquidated, (b) unmatured, or (c) contingent. The first requires merely a procedure for trying the issue of amount. The second is primarily a matter of computing present value. Thus Smith-Hurd Ill.Ann.Stat. ch. 3 § 193 reads:

> "A claim against a decedent's estate, that is not due, may be filed and allowed and paid out of the estate as other claims; but interest which has been included as a part of the principal obligation, computed from the time of the allowance of the claim to the time when it would have become due, shall be deducted."

Moreover, the almost universal use of acceleration clauses permitting the creditor to declare the entire unpaid balance of an obligation immediately

94. The personal representative must decide whether to retain a lease as a valuable asset or to abandon the leasehold or negotiate a surrender. In the event of abandonment, the estate remains liable either for future rent or for damages, depending on the local law of landlord-tenant. Where the lessor has a duty to mitigate damages by re-renting, the amount of the estate's liability is uncertain. If the lease is retained, the personal representative may have a personal liability to the landlord to the extent of rent collected on subleases for the estate. See Miller v. Knox, 48 N.Y. 232 (1872). If he enters into a new lease, liability is governed by the principles covered in subsection (7), supra.

due and payable on death of the debtor minimizes this as an important problem. The contingent claim, on the other hand, requires special machinery or procedure to handle properly. Determine how an unmatured claim and a contingent claim would be handled under your local practice and under the following section of the Uniform Probate Code:

"Section 3–810. [Claims Not Due and Contingent or Unliquidated Claims.]

"(a) If a claim which will become due at a future time or a contingent or unliquidated claim becomes due or certain before the distribution of the estate, and if the claim has been allowed or established by a proceeding, it is paid in the same manner as presently due and absolute claims of the same class.

"(b) In other cases the personal representative or, on petition of the personal representative or the claimant in a special proceeding for the purpose, the Court may provide for payment as follows:

"(1) if the claimant consents, he may be paid the present or agreed value of the claim, taking any uncertainty into account;

"(2) arrangement for future payment, or possible payment, on the happening of the contingency or on liquidation may be made by creating a trust, giving a mortgage, obtaining a bond or security from a distributee, or otherwise."

MATTER OF ESTATE OF LECIC

Court of Appeals of Wisconsin, 1981.
101 Wis.2d 713, 305 N.W.2d 194.

MOSER, PRESIDING JUDGE.

The issue in this appeal is whether the trial court properly extended the time for filing claims against an estate in a probate proceeding on the ground that the personal representative of the estate, and the attorney for the estate, committed passive fraud on certain creditors. We agree with the trial court's determination on this issue and affirm, although we modify the claim amount in one of the orders.

George Lecic (George), owner and operator of a furniture store called George's Shopping Center, died on April 30, 1978. Dobrila Lecic (Dobrila), George's widow, was appointed special administratrix of George's estate. An order was filed on May 4, 1978, in which the court set a date for a hearing on a petition for administration for George's estate and ordered that all creditors' claims be filed on or before August 4, 1978. The order further set a date for a hearing on the creditors' claims and commanded that notice of the time for filing claims and the hearing be given by publication in The Daily Reporter. Notice was published on May 9, 16, and 23, 1978. On June 12, 1978, Dobrila was appointed personal representative of George's estate.

On May 5, 1978, prior to the publication of the notice to creditors to file claims, Dobrila wrote a letter to George's suppliers advising them of George's death, of her appointment as special administratrix "responsible for the continuation of the business and the payments of all accounts payable," and of the name and address of the attorney she had retained to handle George's estate. On July 13, 1978, The Lane Co. (Lane), one of George's creditors, sent a mailgram to George's Shopping Center stating that it was "imperative we receive payment." The attorney retained by Dobrila to handle George's estate replied to Lane in a July 17, 1978, letter which simply stated: "It is our intention to pay the delinquent account as soon as money becomes available. We shall keep you advised." In a July 28, 1978, letter Lane's credit manager, Vince J. Grytko (Grytko), wrote to the estate's attorney regarding the status of George's Shopping Center's account, and attached an itemized statement of delinquent account. On August 18, 1978, Grytko wrote the estate's attorney again, asking: "Will you please advise when we can expect a payment?" The estate's attorney responded on August 23, 1978: "We wish to state that as soon as money becomes available in the estate, we shall pay the invoices." The debt owed Lane was never paid. On February 23, 1979, Schweiger Industries (Schweiger), another creditor, petitioned the court for an extension of time to file claims on the ground that Dobrila and the estate's attorney acted fraudulently in representing to Schweiger and others that their claims would be paid.

On July 12, 1979, Lane filed a petition with the trial court requesting that the court extend the time for filing creditors' claims until ten days beyond the court's decision on the petition. As a basis for this request, Lane alleged that through their repeated statements to various creditors of their intention to pay the delinquent accounts, Dobrila and the estate's attorney had fraudulently prevented Lane and other creditors from filing claims against George's estate. Lane attached a statement of its claim for $6,119.03 to the petition.

On July 30, 1979, the trial court held a hearing on that petition and a decision was filed September 5, 1979, in which the court said "that a creditor who can satisfy the court by clear and convincing testimony that his failure to file his claim within the time limit was induced by fraud committed by the personal representative or her attorney acting for the estate is entitled to have his claim considered by the court; that in such a case the failure to file timely would not be a bar." The court then said that creditors should file their claims asserting fraud to avoid the automatic late-filing bar, and then "proceed to hearing in the usual manner to determine whether the alleged fraud was such as to excuse the late filing."

On January 31, 1980, Schweiger filed its claim for $5,610.85. On February 21, 1980, Lane filed its claim for $6,119.03 with a notation that it was filed late because of "alleged fraud on the part of the personal representative and her attorney."

A hearing on the late-filed claims of Lane and Schweiger was held on June 25, 1980. At the hearing, Robert Louis Short (Short), the treasurer for Lane, testified regarding the procedure generally followed by Lane when the operator of a store that is doing business with Lane dies. He explained that usually, within thirty days, the unpaid account of the deceased operator is turned over to a collection agency. Because of the letters from Dobrila and the estate's attorney assuring payment, Short said he did not turn George's Shopping Center's account over to a collection agency.

At the end of Short's testimony the court rendered an oral decision saying:

> Time for filing claims expired August 4, 1978. The court is of the opinion that Dobrila Lecic at the time she wrote the letter of May 5, 1978 to the creditor had a duty to inform the creditor that the time for filing claims expired on August 4, 1978. Her failure to notify the creditor constituted passive fraud. A person acting in the capacity of Dobrila Lecic at the time had not only a duty not to misrepresent but she had a duty not to remain silent under these circumstances. That duty was emphasized by further correspondence which merely put her upon notice that the creditor was acting in reliance upon her previous statement and expected the claim to be paid without anything further being done on the creditor's part.
>
> The court is convinced by clear and convincing testimony that the creditor was mislead [*sic*] by the letter of May 5, 1978 and subsequent letters up to the date of August 4, 1978, the last date for the filing of claims. That the creditor was mislead [*sic*]; that as a result of this misleading by failure to speak, the creditor acted in reliance upon the statement and representations made by Dobrila Lecic, and the attorney [for the estate] and did not file its claim, and that but for such statement so made the creditor would have taken appropriate action through its collection agency and would have filed its claim within the time limited.
>
> Accordingly, the court extends the time for filing claims to permit the filing of this claim, and the claim as filed is in the amount of $7,136.04

The court then indicated that it would proceed to hear the claim of Schweiger. Dobrila's trial counsel indicated that the proof would be the same and that he was willing to let the testimony in the Lane case stand also for the Schweiger claim. The court then ruled that Schweiger's claim could be filed.

An order filed July 8, 1980, ordered that Schweiger's claim of $5,835.85 "shall be deemed to have been filed * * * prior to August 4, 1978, and shall be accorded its statutory rights and distribution as allowed by appropriate Wisconsin Statutes forthwith." A similar order was filed on July 9, 1980, ordering that Lane's claim in the amended amount of $7,136.04 was to be deemed properly and timely filed. This appeal is from those orders.[95]

95. Footnotes by the court citing authorities and explaining the discrepancies in the amounts of the claims have been omitted.

STATUTES INVOLVED

859.01 Limitation on filing claims against decedent's estates. (1) Except as provided in sub. (3) and s. 859.03, all claims against a decedent's estate including claims of the state and any subdivision thereof, whether due or to become due, absolute or contingent, liquidated or unliquidated, are forever barred against the estate, the personal representative and the heirs and beneficiaries of the decedent unless filed with the court within the time for filing claims.

859.05 Time to file. Upon the filing of an application for administration, the court or the probate registrar under informal administration proceedings shall by order fix the time within which claims against the decedent shall be presented or be forever barred. The time shall be 3 months from the date of the order.

859.07 Notice; publication. Notice of the time within which creditors may present their claims and of the time when the claims, as set by the court or probate registrar under informal administration proceedings, will be examined and adjusted by the court shall be given by publication, under s. 879.05(4), and may be given with the notice for granting letters. No date for examination and adjustment need be given in informal administration proceedings. The first insertion shall be made within 15 days of the date of the order setting the time. In addition to the foregoing, if the decedent was at the time of death or at any time prior thereto a patient or inmate of any state or county hospital or institution, notice in writing of the time within which creditors may present their claims and of the time when the claims will be examined, shall be sent by registered or certified mail to the department of health and social services and the county clerk of the county of legal settlement not less than 30 days before such examination, upon such blanks and containing such information as the department may provide.

On appeal, Dobrila argues that the time limit set in secs. 859.01(1) and 859.05, Stats., for filing claims against an estate are absolute and that the trial court was without authority to permit claims to be filed later. We disagree with this unduly restrictive view of the trial court's power. Our supreme court long ago affirmed that probate courts have "all * * * jurisdiction, both legal and equitable, unless expressly reserved, necessary to the due administration of the estates of deceased persons * * *." "While the county courts derive their powers from the statutes, they have plenary jurisdiction in all matters of administration, settlement, and distribution of estates of decedents, and their jurisdiction is in considerable part concurrent with that of courts of equity." Accordingly, we determine that the trial court in this probate proceeding had the requisite equitable power to extend the time for filing claims where justice so required.

We also determine that where there is fraudulent conduct on the part of the personal representative which induces the creditors to forego the proper filing of their claims, the personal representative is estopped from asserting the notice of claim statute to bar those creditors' claims.

A personal representative of an estate is similar to a trustee of a trust, and owes fiduciary duties to the creditors as well as the beneficiaries of the estate. A personal representative is not required by statute, nor by his or her fiduciary duties, to personally contact all of the creditors of an estate and inform them of the time limit for filing claims against the estate. However, where a personal representative takes it upon himself or herself to contact creditors and assure them of his or her intention to satisfy delinquent claims as soon as possible, as was done here, it is incumbent upon the personal representative to also inform the creditors of the need, nevertheless, to file their claims against the estate and the deadline for such filing. This duty arises as a result of the personal representative's own act of contacting creditors and informing them that their claims would be paid. The failure to inform the creditors of the need to file their claims within the time limit constituted, as the trial court concluded, passive fraud and estopped the personal representative from asserting the deadline for filing claims as a bar to the claims of the defrauded creditors.

Our holding in this case is rooted in the broad principle that a wrongdoer should not be permitted to benefit from his or her own wrong. Technical arguments and factual distinctions between cases should not obscure the applicability of this basic maxim. This principle has been applied to foreclose the assertion of the statute of limitations defense:

> One cannot justly or equitably lull his adversary into a false sense of security, and thereby cause his adversary to subject his claim to the bar of the statute of limitations, and then be permitted to plead the very delay caused by his course of conduct as a defense to the action when brought.

Passive or constructive fraud exists when there is suppression of a fact that should have been disclosed.

> In ordinary situations one may, legally if not morally, keep silent and profit by his adversary's ignorance. * * * But where there is a solemn duty to speak independently of coercion, and in judicial controversy as well, whether asked to speak or not, and there is a failure to speak, resulting in the enrichment of the wrongdoer and the impoverishment of the one to whom that duty is owing, there is a fraud of most serious nature * * *.

Passive or constructive fraud has been utilized as a basis for modification or reversal of a prior order of a probate court, and statutory time limits have not prevented a probate court from vacating an order induced by such fraud. We believe this type of fraud should also estop the assertion of the deadline for filing claims in circumstances such as we have here.

Dobrila also argues that there was insufficient evidence to establish passive fraud. Passive fraud is established if there is a duty to disclose certain information, a failure to disclose, and detrimental reliance by the defrauded person.

We have already explained that by virtue of the personal representative's duties, a duty to inform of the deadline for filing claims arose when Dobrila and the estate's attorney contacted the creditors and informed them that their claims would be paid. The other elements, failure to disclose and reliance, were established by the testimony of the only witness in this case, Short, Lane's treasurer.

Short testified about the letters sent by Dobrila and the estate's attorney assuring him that Lane's claim would be paid. At the time these letters were written, the deadline for the filing of claims against the estate had ready [*sic*] been set. However, no mention of that fact is made in any of the letters. Short also testified that relying on Dobrila's and the estate's attorney's assurances that the claim would be paid, he did not pursue Lane's customary collection practice. The court found, based upon this evidence, that there was clear and convincing proof of fraud. This finding is not against the great weight and clear preponderance of the evidence and, therefore, will not be upset on review.

The finding of fraud was sufficient to warrant the application of estoppel principles to prevent Dobrila from raising the defense of nonfiling of a claim within the time limit.

July 8, 1980 order regarding Schweiger modified to show a claim of $5,610.85 instead of $5,835.85, and, as modified, affirmed. July 9, 1980 order regarding Lane, affirmed.[96]

NOTE

Statutes bar claims of creditors if the claims are not presented within the time set by statute.[97] The period varies; but the three months period set by the Wisconsin statute and the four months period set by Section 3–801 of the Uniform Probate Code are representative time periods, which have in recent years been reduced in order to facilitate earlier settlement of estates. Notice to creditors is given by publication. Although it is arguable that Mullane v. Central Hanover Trust Co., 339 U.S. 306, 70 S.Ct. 652, 94 L.Ed. 865 (1950), requires actual notice to known creditors, that case dealt with notice to known trust beneficiaries of a court proceeding resulting in adjudication; the creditor claim statutes are statutes of limitation triggered by the publication, (compare Haas v. Haas, on page 332). Publication has been consistently sustained against such constitutional attack.[98] Once a claim has been presented, however, the creditor is then an interested party until his claim is

96. Does the principal case present a case for estoppel or for fraud? Contrary to this case, many courts refuse to apply either doctrine to avoid the bar of the nonclaim statute. E.g., Vanderpool v. Vanderpool, 48 Mont. 448, 138 P. 772 (1914).

97. In Texas failure to present a claim within the statutory six months period is not a complete bar, but merely results in postponement of payment until claims presented within the period and allowed are first paid. Vernon's Ann.Tex. Stat. Probate Code §§ 298, 327.

98. For the most recent cases see Matter of Estate of Fessler, 100 Wis.2d 437, 302 N.W.2d 414 (1981); Gano Farms, Inc. v. Estate of Kleweno, 2 Kan.App.2d 506, 582 P.2d 742 (1978).

paid, and he is entitled to personal notice of subsequent adjudications affecting his claim.[99]

The nonclaim statutes are not to be confused with the general statutes of limitations. In many states, if the statute of limitations has not yet barred the claimant at the time of the debtor's death, the general statute continues to run even though a personal representative has not been appointed and there is no one to sue. In such states the claimant must be alert and initiate appointment of a special administrator against whom action can be commenced, if there is any possibility that the statute may bar his claim before appointment of a personal representative in normal course. In other states the statute of limitations is held not to run during the interval from death to appointment of a personal representative, on the theory that there is no available defendant during this period. In still other states the statute of nonclaim is deemed to control and to extend the period during which the claim may be presented. As to whether the personal representative may waive the defense of the statute of limitations, there is a conflict of authority. Since the representative who pays a claim on which the statute has run will be personally liable in a state where waiver is not permitted, he must carefully investigate the possible bar of claims under the general statute of limitations. Since the answer to these problems depends in large degree on statutory provisions, they are not pursued here; but the student should examine statutes and practice in his local jurisdiction.

Uniform Probate Code, Section 3–802 deals with the interrelation between regular statutes of limitations and the process of administration; it provides:

"Section 3–802. [Statutes of Limitations.]

"Unless an estate is insolvent the personal representative, with the consent of all successors whose interests would be affected, may waive any defense of limitations available to the estate. If the defense is not waived, no claim which was barred by any statute of limitations at the time of the decedent's death shall be allowed or paid. The running of any statute of limitations measured from some other event than death and advertisement for claims against a decedent is suspended during the 4 months following the decedent's death but resumes thereafter as to claims not barred pursuant to the sections which follow. For purposes of any statute of limitations, the proper presentation of a claim under Section 3–804 is equivalent to commencement of a proceeding on the claim."

PROBLEMS

1. Must tort claims be presented? At common law personal injury actions did not survive the death of the tort-feasor, but statutes generally modify this rule. In such states can the claimant proceed independently in suit against the representative or must he present a claim in the probate court? See Mueller v. Shacklett, 156 Neb. 881, 58 N.W.2d 344 (1953), for interpretation of a statute imposing on the probate judge the duty "to receive, examine, adjust and allow all lawful claims and demands of all persons against the deceased". The nonclaim statutes often specifically include or exclude tort claims.[1] See 87 A.L.R.2d 1231 (1963); Comment, "Filing Tort Claims

99. Estate of Engbrock, 90 N.M. 492, 565 P.2d 662 (1977) (constructive notice to known creditor by publication of a hearing on the final account is insufficient to meet due process requirements).

1. The Ohio statute, for example, expressly refers to claims "arising out of tort". Ohio Rev.Code Ann. § 2117.06 (Page 1978). Uniform Probate Code, § 3–803 covers all claims, including tort.

Against Decedent's Estates Within Non-Claim Statutes: A Survey", 47 Marq.L.Rev. 230 (1963).

2. Must claims of the state be presented? Or is the statute of nonclaim like the statutes of limitations, which generally do not run against the government? This has modern significance because of the claim of the state for refund of old age assistance benefits. See Donnally v. Montgomery County Welfare Board, 200 Md. 534, 92 A.2d 354 (1952).

3. Must claims against the estate of the decedent be presented? See Estate of Kelly, 183 Wis. 485, 198 N.W. 280 (1924) (funeral expenses). As to personal liability of the representative for such items, see Subsection (7), supra.

4. Must a claim for ownership of assets held by the personal representative be presented? See Hawkey v. Williams, 72 Wyo. 20, 261 P.2d 48 (1953) (two daughters had conveyed their interest in father's estate to mother, who agreed to leave the property to them equally at her death; when the mother left all the property to one daughter, the other sought to impose a constructive trust without having presented the claim); Padula v. Padula, 138 Conn. 102, 82 A.2d 362 (1951) (suit to set aside deed to decedent on grounds of fraud).

5. Can suit be brought after the period of nonclaim on a cause of action for breach of trust not discovered until after the period has expired? Compare First National Bank v. Connolly, 172 Or. 434, 138 P.2d 613, 143 P.2d 243 (1943) with Davis v. Shepard, 135 Wash. 124, 237 P. 21, 41 A.L.R. 163 (1925). The former case also considers the remedies available after the estate has been closed and the assets distributed, if the court decides that the claim is not barred.

SECTION 6. THE DUTY OF LOYALTY

The nature of the fiduciary relation requires the fiduciary to act only for the benefit of the real owner. He may not deal with the property so as to benefit himself directly or indirectly. His sole concern must be the carrying out of the testator's or settlor's intent and the welfare of the beneficiaries. Because of the likelihood of inside knowledge about property values, because human nature is frail, and because it is often difficult for the beneficiary to prove profit to the fiduciary, this duty of loyalty becomes a flat prohibition against any transactions involving self-dealing.[2]

Assuming the claim must be presented, there is the further problem of the appropriate forum in which to try the claim, the probate court itself or a court of general jurisdiction. If the probate court has exclusive jurisdiction, the constitutional right to a trial by jury may necessitate trial de novo on appeal to the court of record, unless a jury trial is available in the probate court.

2. See Report of Committee on Trust Administration and Accounting, The Trustee's Duty of Loyalty, 6 Real Prop., Prob. & Tr.J. 528 (1971); Restatement II, Trusts § 170.

The simplest application of the duty comes in sale by the fiduciary of his own property to the trust, or the converse, the purchase of estate or trust property by the fiduciary. The beneficiary has the right to disaffirm or avoid such a transaction; of course, if it is to his advantage he may affirm it. Proof of good faith or lack of personal profit on the part of the fiduciary is immaterial. It should be apparent that a sale to the fiduciary's spouse or to a strawman who conveys back to the fiduciary stands on no better footing.

The duty of loyalty may in practice come into conflict with other duties of the trustee. For example, it is the duty of the fiduciary to use reasonable efforts to obtain the highest price possible. Frequently the fiduciary is a member of the family and the person willing to bid the most for family realty or business interest. How can the purchase be arranged without violating the duty of loyalty? The courts have invalidated purchase by the fiduciary even when made at a public sale under court order, or when the price is fixed by an impartial person. However, the fiduciary may seek a court order permitting him to bid or confirming a sale to him, after notice to all parties, and this order would protect him against later objection by all parties. Statutory authority for this procedure in decedents' estates exists in some jurisdictions, and Uniform Probate Code, § 3–713 permits purchase by the representative subject to court approval. Another means, if all parties are sui juris, is to obtain from the interested parties consent to purchase by the fiduciary.[3]

---

3. In Estate of Scheibe, 30 Wis.2d 116, 140 N.W.2d 196 (1966), the executor was given full power to sell without court order, under the terms of the will. He sold estate property at private sale to his sister, at less than the assessed value and at about half the appraised value; the trial court found that the sale was made in good faith. The Supreme Court of Wisconsin reversed; the will was not intended to relieve the executor of his duty of loyalty to the beneficiary, nor of the duty of reasonable care.

For special comment on the problems considered in this section, see Van Aartsen, "Conflict of Interests of Corporate Fiduciaries", 103 Trusts and Estates 379 (1964); Niles, "The Divided Loyalty Rule, Caveat to Draftsman to Avoid Absolute Liability of Trustee", 91 Trusts and Estates 734 (1952); Fletcher, "Divided Loyalty and Self Dealing: What Courses of Fiduciary Conduct are Indicated by Cases", 94 Trusts and Estates 234 (1955); Hoover, "Basic Principles Underlying Duty of Loyalty", 5 Cleveland-Marshall L.Rev. 7 (1956); Prochnow, "Conflict of Interest and the Corporate Trustee", 22 Business Lawyer 929 (1967); Niles, "A Contemporary View of Liability for Breach of Trust", 114 Trusts & Estates 12, 82 (1975); Becker, "Conflicts of Interest, Parts I & II", 116 Trusts & Estates 111, 187 (1977) (discussing unique problems of corporate fiduciaries); As to the duty to act impartially with respect to the beneficiaries in allocating receipts and expenditures during the administration of an estate, see Dobris, "Equitable Adjustments in Postmortem Income Tax Planning: An Unremitting Diet of *Warms*", 65 Iowa L.Rev. 103 (1979); "Limits on the Doctrine of Equitable Adjustment In Sophisticated Postmortem Tax Planning", 66 Iowa L.Rev. 273 (1981).

MATTER OF ESTATE OF ROTHKO

Court of Appeals of New York, 1977.
43 N.Y.2d 305, 401 N.Y.S.2d 449, 372 N.E.2d 291.

COOKE, JUDGE.

Mark Rothko, an abstract expressionist painter whose works through the years gained for him an international reputation of greatness, died testate on February 25, 1970. The principal asset of his estate consisted of 798 paintings of tremendous value, and the dispute underlying this appeal involves the conduct of his three executors in their disposition of these works of art. In sum, that conduct as portrayed in the record and sketched in the opinions was manifestly wrongful and indeed shocking.

Rothkos' will was admitted to probate on April 27, 1970 and letters testamentary were issued to Bernard J. Reis, Theodoros Stamos and Morton Levine. Hastily and within a period of only about three weeks and by virtue of two contracts each dated May 21, 1970, the executors dealt with all 798 paintings.

By a contract of sale, the estate executors agreed to sell to Marlborough A.G., a Liechtenstein corporation (hereinafter MAG), 100 Rothko paintings as listed for $1,800,000, $200,000 to be paid on execution of the agreement and the balance of $1,600,000 in 12 equal interest-free installments over a 12-year period. Under the second agreement, the executors consigned to Marlborough Gallery, Inc., a domestic corporation (hereinafter MNY), "approximately 700 paintings listed on a Schedule to be prepared", the consignee to be responsible for costs covering items such as insurance, storage restoration and promotion. By its provisos, MNY could sell up to 35 paintings a year from each of two groups, pre-1947 and post-1947, for 12 years at the best price obtainable but not less than the appraised estate value, and it would receive a 50% commission on each painting sold, except for a commission of 40% on those sold to or through other dealers.

Petitioner Kate Rothko, decedent's daughter and a person entitled to share in his estate by virtue of an election under EPTL 5–3.3, instituted this proceeding to remove the executors, to enjoin MNY and MAG from disposing of the paintings, to rescind the aforesaid agreements between the executors and said corporations, for a return of the paintings still in possession of those corporations, and for damages. She was joined by the guardian of her brother Christopher Rothko, likewise interested in the estate, who answered by adopting the allegations of his sister's petition and by demanding the same relief. The Attorney-General of the State, as the representative of the ultimate beneficiaries of the Mark Rothko Foundation, Inc., a charitable corporation and the residuary legatee under decedent's will, joined in requesting relief substantially similar to that prayed for by petitioner. On June 26, 1972 the Surrogate issued a temporary restraining order and on September 26, 1972 a preliminary injunction enjoining MAG, MNY, and the three executors from selling or otherwise disposing of the paintings referred to in the agreements dated

May 21, 1970, except for sales or dispositions made with court permission. The Appellate Division modified the preliminary injunction order by increasing the amount of the bond and otherwise affirmed. By a 1974 petition, the Attorney-General, on behalf of the ultimate charitable beneficiaries of the Mark Rothko Foundation, sought the punishment of MNY, MAG, Lloyd and Reis for contempt and other relief.

Following a nonjury trial covering 89 days and in a thorough opinion, the Surrogate found: that Reis was a director, secretary and treasurer of MNY, the consignee art gallery, in addition to being a coexecutor of the estate; that the testator had a 1969 *inter vivos* contract with MNY to sell Rothko's work at a commission of only 10% and whether that agreement survived testator's death was a problem that a fiduciary in a dual position could not have impartially faced; that Reis was in a position of serious conflict of interest with respect to the contracts of May 21, 1970 and that his dual role and planned purpose benefited the Marlborough interests to the detriment of the estate; that it was to the advantage of coexecutor Stamos as a "not-too-successful artist, financially", to curry favor with Marlborough and that the contract made by him with MNY within months after signing the estate contracts placed him in a position where his personal interests conflicted with those of the estate, especially leading to lax contract enforcement efforts by Stamos; that Stamos acted negligently and improvidently in view of his own knowledge of the conflict of interest of Reis; that the third coexecutor, Levine, while not acting in self-interest or with bad faith, nonetheless failed to exercise ordinary prudence in the performance of his assumed fiduciary obligations since he was aware of Reis' divided loyalty, believed that Stamos was also seeking personal advantage, possessed personal opinions as to the value of the paintings and yet followed the leadership of his coexecutors without investigation of essential facts or consultation with competent and disinterested appraisers, and that the business transactions of the two Marlborough corporations were admittedly controlled and directed by Francis K. Lloyd. It was concluded that the acts and failures of the three executors were clearly improper to such a substantial extent as to mandate their removal under SCPA 711 as estate fiduciaries. The Surrogate also found that MNY, MAG and Lloyd were guilty of contempt in shipping, disposing of and selling 57 paintings in violation of the temporary restraining order dated June 26, 1972 and of the injunction dated September 26, 1972; that the contracts for sale and consignment of paintings between the executors and MNY and MAG provided inadequate value to the estate, amounting to a lack of mutuality and fairness resulting from conflicts on the part of Reis and Stamos and improvidence on the part of all executors; that said contracts were voidable and were set aside by reason of violation of the duty of loyalty and improvidence of the executors, knowingly participated in and induced by MNY and MAG; that the fact that these agreements were voidable did not revive the 1969 *inter vivos* agreements since the parties by their conduct evinced an intent to abandon and abrogate these compacts. The Surrogate held that the present value at the time of trial of the paintings sold is the proper measure of damages as to MNY, MAG, Lloyd, Reis and Stamos. He imposed a civil fine of $3,332,000 upon MNY, MAG and Lloyd, same being the appreciated value at the time of trial of the 57 paintings sold in violation of the temporary restraining order and injunction. It was held that Levine was liable for $6,464,880 in damages, as he was not in a dual position acting for his own interest and was thus liable only for the actual value of paintings sold MNY and MAG as of the dates of sale, and that Reis, Stamos, MNY and MAG, apart from being jointly and severally liable for the same damages as Levine for negligence, were liable for the greater sum of $9,252,000 "as appreciation damages less amounts previously paid to the estate with regard to sales of paintings." The cross petition of the Attorney-General to reopen the record for submission of newly discovered documentary evidence was denied. The liabilities were held to be congruent so that payment of the highest sum would satisfy all lesser liabilities including the civil fines and the liabilities for damages were to be reduced by payment of the fine levied or by return of any of the 57 paintings disposed of, the new fiduciary to have the option in the first instance to specify which paintings the fiduciary would accept.

The Appellate Division, in an opinion by Justice Lane, modified to the extent of deleting the option given the new fiduciary to specify which paintings he would accept. Except for this modification, the majority affirmed on the opinion of Surrogate Midonick, with additional comments. Among others, it was stated that the entire court agreed that executors Reis and Stamos had a conflict of interest and divided loyalty in view of their nexus to MNY and that a majority were in agreement with the Surrogate's assessment of liability as to executor Levine and his findings of liability against MNY, MAG and Lloyd. The majority agreed with the Surrogate's analysis awarding "appreciation damages" and found further support for his rationale in Menzel v. List, 24 N.Y.2d 91, 298 N.Y.S.2d 979, 246 N.E.2d 742. Justice Kupferman, in an opinion styled "concurr[ing] in part and dissent[ing] in part", stated that, although he had "expressed reservations with respect to various factors to be considered in the calculation of damages", he concurred "in the basic conclusion and, therefore, in order to resolve the matter for the purpose of appeal" voted to modify as per the *Lane* opinion 56 A.D.2d 499, 505–506, 392 N.Y.S.2d 870, 875. Justices Capozzoli and Nunez, in separate dissenting in part opinions, viewed *Menzel v. List* as inapplicable and voted to modify and remit to determine the reasonable value of the paintings as of May, 1970, when estate contracts with MNY and MAG had their inception in writing.

Since the Surrogate's findings of fact as to the conduct of Reis, Stamos, Levine, MNY, MAG and Lloyd and the value of the paintings at different junctures were affirmed by the Appellate Division, if there was evidence to support these findings they are not subject to question in this court and the review here is confined to the legal issues raised (CPLR 5501, subd. [b]; Simon v. Electrospace Corp., 28

N.Y.2d 136, 139, 320 N.Y.S.2d 225, 227, 269 N.E.2d 21, 22; Matter of City of New York [Fifth Ave. Coach Lines], 22 N.Y.2d 613, 620–621, 294 N.Y.S.2d 502, 505–506, 241 N.E.2d 717, 719–720).

In seeking a reversal, it is urged that an improper legal standard was applied in voiding the estate contracts of May, 1970, that the "no further inquiry" rule applies only to self-dealing and that in case of a conflict of interest, absent self-dealing, a challenged transaction must be shown to be unfair. The subject of fairness of the contracts is intertwined with the issue of whether Reis and Stamos were guilty of conflicts of interest. Scott is quoted to the effect that "[a] trustee does not necessarily incur liability merely because he has an individual interest in the transaction * * * In Bullivant v. First Nat. Bank [246 Mass. 324, 141 N.E. 41] it was held that * * * the fact that the bank was also a creditor of the corporation did not make its assent invalid, *if it acted in good faith and the plan was fair*" (2 Scott, Trusts, § 170.24, p. 1384 [emphasis added]), and our attention has been called to the statement in Phelan v. Middle States Oil Corp., 220 F.2d 593, 603, 2 Cir., cert. den. sub nom. Cohen v. Glass, 349 U.S. 929, 75 S.Ct. 772, 99 L.Ed. 1260 that Judge Learned Hand found "no decisions that have applied [the no further inquiry rule] inflexibly to every occasion in which the fiduciary has been shown to have had a personal interest that might in fact have conflicted with his loyalty."

These contentions should be rejected. First, a review of the opinions of the Surrogate and the Appellate Division manifests that they did not rely solely on a "no further inquiry rule", and secondly, there is more than an adequate basis to conclude that the agreements between the Marlborough corporations and the estate were neither fair nor in the best interests of the estate. This is demonstrated, for example, by the comments of the Surrogate concerning the commissions on the consignment of the 698 paintings (see 84 Misc.2d 830, 852–853, 379 N.Y.S.2d 923, 947–948) and those of the Appellate Division concerning the sale of the 100 paintings (see 56 A.D.2d, at pp. 501–502, 392 N.Y.S.2d, at pp. 872–873). The opinions under review demonstrate that neither the Surrogate nor the Appellate Division set aside the contracts by merely applying the no further inquiry rule without regard to fairness. Rather they determined, quite properly indeed, that these agreements were neither fair nor in the best interests of the estate.

To be sure, the assertions that there were no conflicts of interest on the part of Reis or Stamos indulge in sheer fantasy. Besides being a director and officer of MNY, for which there was financial remuneration, however slight, Reis, as noted by the Surrogate, had different inducements to favor the Marlborough interests, including his own aggrandizement of status and financial advantage through sales of almost one million dollars for items from his own and his family's extensive private art collection by the Marlborough interests (see 84 Misc.2d, at pp. 843–844, 379 N.Y.S.2d at pp. 939–940). Similarly, Stamos benefited as an artist under contract with Marlborough and, interestingly, Marlborough purchased a Stamos painting from a third party for $4,000 during the week in May, 1970 when the estate contract negotiations were pending (see 84 Misc.2d, at p. 845, 379 N.Y.S. 2d at p. 941). The conflicts are manifest. Further, as noted in Bogert, Trusts and Trustees (2d ed.), "The duty of loyalty imposed on the fiduciary prevents him from accepting employment from a third party who is entering into a business transaction with the trust" (§ 543, subd. [S], p. 573). "While he [a trustee] is administering the trust he must refrain from placing himself in a position where his personal interest or that of a third person does or may conflict with the interest of the beneficiaries" (Bogert, Trusts [Hornbook Series—5th ed.], p. 343). Here, Reis was employed and Stamos benefited in a manner contemplated by Bogert (see, also, Meinhard v. Salmon, 249 N.Y. 458, 464, 466–467, 164 N.E. 545, 547–548; Schmidt v. Chambers, 265 Md. 9, 33–38, 288 A.2d 356). In short, one must strain the law rather than follow it to reach the result suggested on behalf of Reis and Stamos.

Levine contends that, having acted prudently and upon the advice of counsel, a complete defense was established. Suffice it to say, an executor who knows that his coexecutor is committing breaches of trust and not only fails to exert efforts directed towards prevention but accedes to them is legally accountable even though he was acting on the advice of counsel (Matter of Westerfield, 32 App.Div. 324, 344, 53 N.Y.S. 25, 39; 3 Scott, Trusts [3d ed.], § 201, p. 1657). When confronted with the question of whether to enter into the Marlborough contracts, Levine was acting in a business capacity, not a legal one, in which he was required as an executor primarily to employ such diligence and prudence to the care and management of the estate assets and affairs as would prudent persons of discretion and intelligence (King v. Talbot, 40 N.Y. 76, 85–86), accented by "[n]ot honesty alone, but the punctilio of an honor the most sensitive" (Meinhard v. Salmon, 249 N.Y. 458, 464, 164 N.E. 545, 546, supra). Alleged good faith on the part of a fiduciary forgetful of his duty is not enough (Wendt v. Fischer, 243 N.Y. 439, 443, 154 N.E. 303, 304). He could not close his eyes, remain passive or move with unconcern in the face of the obvious loss to be visited upon the estate by participation in those business arrangements and then shelter himself behind the claimed counsel of an attorney (see Matter of Niles, 113 N.Y. 547, 558, 21 N.E. 687, 689; Matter of Huntley, 13 Misc. 375, 380, 35 N.Y.S. 113, 116; 3 Warren's Heaton, Surrogates' Courts [6th ed.], § 217, subd. 3, par. [b]).

Further, there is no merit to the argument that MNY and MAG lacked notice of the breach of trust. The record amply supports the determination that they are chargeable with notice of the executors' breach of duty.

The measure of damages was the issue that divided the Appellate Division (see 56 A.D.2d, at p. 500, 392 N.Y.S.2d at p. 872). The contention of Reis, Stamos, MNY and MAG, that the award of appreciation damages was legally erroneous and impermissible, is based on a principle that an executor authorized to sell is not liable for an increase in value if the breach consists only in selling for a figure less than that for which the executor should have sold. For example, Scott states:

> "The beneficiaries are not entitled to the value of the property at the time of the decree if it was not the duty of the trustee to retain the property in the trust and the breach of trust consisted *merely* in selling the property for too low a price" (3 Scott, Trusts [3d ed.], § 208.3, p. 1687 [emphasis added]).
>
> "If the trustee is guilty of a breach of trust in selling trust property for an inadequate price, he is liable for the difference between the amount he should have received and the amount which he did receive. He is not liable, however, for any subsequent rise in value of the property sold". (Id., § 208.6, pp. 1689–1690.)

A recitation of similar import appears in Comment *d* under Restatement, Trusts 2d (§ 205): "*d.* Sale for less than value. If the trustee is authorized to sell trust property, but in breach of trust he sells it for less than he should receive, he is liable for the value of the property at the time of the sale less the amount which he received. If the breach of trust consists *only* in selling it for too little, he is not chargeable with the amount of any subsequent increase in value of the property under the rule stated in Clause (c), as he would be if he were not authorized to sell the property. See § 208." (Emphasis added.) However, employment of "merely" and "only" as limiting words suggests that where the breach consists of some misfeasance, other than solely for selling "for too low a price" or "for too little", appreciation damages may be appropriate. Under Scott (§ 208.3, pp. 1686–1687) and the Restatement (§ 208), the trustee may be held liable for appreciation damages if it was his or her duty to retain the property, the theory being that the beneficiaries are entitled to be placed in the same position they would have been in had the breach not consisted of a sale of property that should have been retained. The same rule should apply where the breach of trust consists of a serious conflict of interest—which is more than merely selling for too little.

The reason for allowing appreciation damages, where there is a duty to retain, and only date of sale damages, where there is authorization to sell, is policy oriented. If a trustee authorized to sell were subjected to a greater measure of damages he might be reluctant to sell (in which event he might run a risk if depreciation ensued). On the other hand, if there is a duty to retain and the trustee sells there is no policy reason to protect the trustee; he has not simply acted imprudently, he has violated an integral condition of the trust.

* * *

[Omitted is the Court's discussion of the computation of appreciation damages in light of the difficulties in valuing works of art, and the trial record of evidence to support the computation.]

Accordingly, the order of the Appellate Division should be affirmed, with costs to the prevailing parties against appellants, and the question certified answered in the affirmative.[4]

NOTE

There are degrees of conflict of interest. A direct conflict is involved where there is self-dealing—the fiduciary buying from or selling to the estate or trust. Here the courts have developed a "no further inquiry rule", making the transaction voidable even though the fiduciary may have acted fairly under the circumstances. A purchase of property from the trust or estate by the fiduciary may in fact have been at the best price then obtainable; however, if the property later appreciates the beneficiaries can recover either the property if still in the hands of the fiduciary or the profit realized by the fiduciary if the property has been sold. Even if the sale is by public auction, the fiduciary cannot purchase; his self-interest might conflict with his duty to avoid the sale if possible or to see that the sale is held under maximum conditions for obtaining the highest price. The rule is a strong deterrent, and can be avoided only by obtaining consent from the beneficiaries (or in an estate the heirs or the residuary devisee) or by petitioning the court for permission to buy. As the *Rothko* case illustrates, where self-dealing is not involved, there still may be a conflict of interest in a less direct sense. Here the rules are not as rigid. There is not a flat prohibition, but the fiduciary has the burden of showing that the transaction was completely fair to the beneficiaries, despite the taint of possible conflict.

The duty of loyalty to the beneficiaries of an estate or trust applies directly to the situation where the fiduciary wants to obtain consent or release from the beneficiaries to a proposed action by the fiduciary, such as a sale, an investment, approval of accounts, etc. Because the fiduciary has a self-interest in protecting himself from liability, he must be especially careful to make a full disclosure. Sometimes the fiduciary also occupies a position as a beneficiary. If so, he may not favor himself as beneficiary over other beneficiaries.[5] An illustrative case is In re James' Estate, 86 N.Y.S.2d 78 (Surr. Ct.1948), where the executors of decedent's will were also acting as trustees for a charitable Foundation which was the residuary devisee under the will;

4. For criticism of the *Rothko* case, see Wellman, "Punitive Surcharges Against Disloyal Fiduciaries—Is *Rothko* Right?" 77 Mich.L.Rev. 95 (1978); Note, "Trustee Liability for Breach of the Duty of Loyalty, Good Faith Inquiry and Appreciation Damages", 49 Ford.L.Rev. 1012 (1981). See also Harrow, "Reflections on Estate of Rothko: The Role of the Legal Advisor in Relation to the Artist," 26 Clev.St.L.Rev. 573 (1977) (more detailed exposition of facts by one of the lawyers involved in the litigation).

5. This frequently arises where the widow is executrix or administratrix and a family settlement is made under which she is assigned all the interests of the other beneficiaries. See for an example, Zuercher v. Zuercher, 245 Iowa 1105, 65 N.W.2d 452 (1954) (applying the presumption of overreaching where the widow was appointed administratrix in the afternoon and later the same day she obtained her mother-in-law's signature to a deed quitclaiming all the latter's interest in the estate to the widow).

The fiduciary may not favor one of the beneficiaries at the expense of others, as by selling estate or trust assets to one at an inadequate price. See McCarter v. McGregor, 1 N.J. 558, 64 A.2d 449 (1949). In after death tax planning fiduciary problems of special difficulty are presented in the administration of tax burdens and benefits with respect to multiple beneficiaries. For able discussions of these see Dobris, "Equitable Adjustments in Postmortem Income Tax Planning: An Unremitting Diet of *Warms*", 65 Iowa L. Rev. 103 (1979); "Limits on the Doctrine of Equitable Adjustment in Sophisticated Postmortem Tax Planning", 66 Iowa L. Rev. 273 (1981).

the same law firm acted as counsel for the estate and the Foundation. A proposal for distribution of the estate was made to other devisees under the will, who accepted the proposal and executed releases to the executors. The executors did not disclose that they had considered three possible methods of apportioning the burden of estate taxes among beneficiaries under the will; the method embodied in the proposal favored the Foundation. The New York Surrogate's Court set aside the releases and reopened the accounting. The fiduciary always has the burden of proving full disclosure in dealing with beneficiaries and, in the situation where the fiduciary is also a beneficiary, the further burden of showing that the transaction is fair to the other beneficiaries.

Where the fiduciary is expressly granted discretionary powers under the will or trust instrument, and the person named as fiduciary by the testator or settlor is also an income or principal beneficiary, may he exercise those express powers to favor himself? Thus if the surviving spouse is both trustee and income beneficiary, and the trust instrument expressly grants the trustee discretionary power "to allocate receipts between principal and income" (a problem considered later in Section 8 of this Chapter), can the trustee allocate questionable items to income? Does the duty of loyalty apply to limit the express power to allocate? The testator or settlor has created the conflict by his choice of fiduciary and may have intended to exempt the fiduciary from the normal duty of impartiality. This is essentially a problem of construing the trust instrument to determine the intent.[6]

Because the corporate fiduciary usually performs many functions other than fiduciary administration, including banking, marketing of securities, and mortgage financing, the issue is often presented whether its trust activities must be rigidly segregated from these other activities, in terms of barring the trust department from taking advantage of the facilities offered by other departments of the same institution. For a simple illustration, if there are idle funds available in a trust, it is clearly the duty of the trustee to provide safekeeping. Can the trust department place these idle funds on temporary deposit in the commercial banking department, or must they be deposited in another bank? If there were a national bank involved, Part 9-Fiduciary Powers of National Banks and Collective Investment Funds [Revised] ("Regulation 9")[7] would apply. If a state bank or trust company were involved, state legislation may permit a regular deposit with security similar to that provided by "Regulation 9". In the absence of statute the authority is in conflict. In deciding the propriety of such a course of dealing, it must be remembered that the corporate fiduciary is often selected for the very reason that it has such specialized services available.[8]

6. Bank of Nevada v. Speirs, 95 Nev. 870, 603 P.2d 1074 (1979) (rule against self-dealing modified in such cases to exempt fiduciary if he acts in good faith). Compare Matter of Estate of Gaylord, 552 P.2d 392 (Okla.1976) (statute forbidding self-dealing held not to apply because will created an inherently conflicting situation because of existing contractual right in a corporation controlled by the executor). These cases involve individual family members named as fiduciary. Where a corporate fiduciary is involved, courts have been strict in construing trust provisions as not relieving the fiduciary from the rule against self-dealing. In re Anneke's Trust, 229 Minn. 60, 38 N.W.2d 177 (1949) (express authority to pay commission or underwriting profits on securities "held" by it did not extend to bonds "owned" by the Bank).

7. See 12 C.F.R. (1976) § 9.10, App. II, infra. The general section on self-dealing is 9.12.

8. An unusual conflict of interest problem may be presented if a bank officer or employee acquires "inside" information adversely affecting the value of securities held in a trust account by the Bank; does its fiduciary duty require it

Where the trustee is trustee of two or more trusts, the "conflict of interest" rule does not prohibit him from selling from one trust to another. Such a practice may be advantageous to the beneficiaries as to certain securities, notably mortgages or mortgage participations, which are not readily marketable. For example, trust no. 1 in which a real estate mortgage is held as an investment provides for distribution in cash; in order to make distribution the mortgage must be sold. If the market is slow, and the trustee is administering trust no. 2 in which there are funds available for investment in such a mortgage, it will assist trust no. 1 if the mortgage can be transferred to trust no. 2 in exchange for cash. However, the trustee has the burden of justifying such a transaction as being fair to each trust.[9] There is possible temptation in such cases to make the transfer at full inventory value, even though the true value is less at the time of transfer, in order to make a good showing on accounting for the first trust, with the hope that the security will regain its transfer valuation by the time it matures or is sold in the second trust.

A lawyer in dealing with his client's property should be especially careful to avoid any self-dealing or conflict of interest. Breach of his duty of loyalty not only is subject to the rules applicable to all fiduciaries, but also violates his professional obligations and can result in disciplinary proceedings with serious consequences for his license to practice. In addition to abstaining from self dealing, the trustee must deal impartially with the beneficiaries. Special problems in this area are created in postmortem tax planning. For an excellent treatment dealing with the handling of estate expenses in postmortem tax planning see Dobris, "Equitable Adjustments in Postmortem Income Tax Planning: An Unremitting Diet of *Warms*", 65 Iowa L.Rev. 103 (1979).

PROBLEMS

1. Would the duty of loyalty extend to an attorney of the fiduciary, so as to bar him from purchasing estate or trust assets from the fiduciary? Matter of People (Bond & Mtge. Guar. Co.), 303 N.Y. 423, 103 N.E.2d 721 (1952).

2. Could the fiduciary sell to an employee, such as his secretary? Cf. Noonan Estate, 361 Pa. 26, 63 A.2d 80 (1949). 12 CFR (1976), § 9.12 states that, unless authorized by the trust instrument, by court order or by local law, national banks exercising fiduciary powers cannot invest in stock, obligations or property acquired from a director, officer, employee of the bank or "individuals with whom there exists such a connection, or organizations in which there exists such an interest, as might affect the exercise of the best judgment of the bank in acquiring the property, or in stock or obligations of, or property acquired from, affiliates of the bank or their directors, officers or employees." Similar restrictions are placed upon sales of property subject to additional exceptions stated in the Regulation.

to sell the securities at the best price, or is there a paramount duty to the public to disclose material facts prior to sale or retain the security? See Schuyler, From Sulphur to Surcharge?—Corporate Trustee Exposure Under SEC Rule 10b–5, 67 N.W.U.L.Rev. 42 (1972).

9. II Scott, Trusts (3d Ed.1967) § 170.16; see Prochnow, "Conflict of Interest and the Corporate Trustee", 22 Business Lawyer 929 (1967) "Corporate Trustees Conflict of Interest", 25 U. of Chi.L.Rev. 382 (1958), Comment, "Trusts—The North Carolina Fiduciary Powers Act and the Duty of Loyalty", 45 N.C.L.Rev. 1141 (1967).

3. Is an exercise of a general power of appointment by a beneficiary-donee in favor of a trustee subject to the rules on fiduciary loyalty? See Kenney v. Citizens National Trust & Savings Bank, 269 P.2d 641 (Cal.App.1954).

4. Testatrix devised all her property to her sisters, X and Y, and expressed the "desire that my said two sisters shall use a substantial part of the proceeds therefrom for the benefit of" Z. In litigation, Z established a trust against X and Y who then set aside $1,000 out of a net estate of $4,144.02, they to determine "how and when the fund was to be used depending on the 'needs', [of Z] and what would 'contribute to his welfare and well being' ". Assuming X and Y have not abused their discretion by setting aside the $1,000, and have testified they will carry out the trust, should they be removed if they are residuary beneficiaries of the undistributed residue of the trust fund, are hostile towards Z's attorneys because of the litigation and perhaps hostile towards Z because the trust was established against them for his benefit? Would a case for removal be weaker if they were not residuary beneficiaries of the trust fund? Would the case for removal be stronger if they had been named trustees by a court rather than by the settlor-testatrix? If a removal is ordered, what basic duty would the Court probably conclude X and Y could not properly perform? See Reed v. Ringsby, 156 Neb. 33, 54 N.W.2d 318 (1952) (Where the elements of animosity were not disclosed by the trial record). To what extent should the degree of discretion which a trustee must exercise to administer the trust be material on the issue of removal? See Matter of Townsend, 73 Misc. 481, 133 N.Y.S. 492 (1911).

5. Attorney is named as executor in will of Husband and also as trustee of testamentary trust for Wife. Wife seeks removal of Attorney as trustee alleging: [He] "was the opposing attorney to me in involved litigation in which he represented the decedent during his lifetime. He is the opposing attorney to me in presently pending involved litigation in which title to the ownership of assets is involved as between me and my late husband. He was the attorney for businesses and corporations, title and ownership of which is the subject of past and pending litigation between decedent and myself. He may be a witness in discovery proceedings thereunder. His office represented the complainant in a proceeding to have me arrested on a criminal charge. He and his office have exhibited personal hostility towards me." Should the court remove the attorney? In re Miller's Estate, 48 Misc.2d 815, 265 N.Y.S.2d 999 (1965). As trustee, can Attorney represent the estate in litigation pending against Wife?

6. A trustee resigned under fire. His attorney was appointed by a lower court as one of two successor trustees over objection of some of the beneficiaries. The attorney promptly resigned as counsel for the prior trustee with litigation still pending to surcharge the latter. Was the appointment proper in view of the duty of a successor trustee to proceed against a prior trustee for breach of trust? See Stone v. Baldwin, 414 Ill. 257, 111 N.E.2d 971 (1953).

SECTION 7. DELEGATION OF FUNCTIONS

The fiduciary is selected for his position of responsibility. He may be an executor or trustee selected by the testator. He may be an administrator or successor trustee appointed by the court upon appropriate petition. In either event, he is selected or appointed to a position in control of property belonging to someone else because of his personal integrity, because confidence is imposed in his ability and character. Hence he may not delegate his powers to others. Obviously this principle is subject to practical limitations. A corporate fiduciary must of necessity act through its officers and employees, but correspondingly is liable for their acts. The fiduciary must, in the modern business world, utilize the services of specialists; for example, to accomplish a sale of listed stock belonging to the estate it is far more efficient to deal through a broker than to find a direct buyer, even if that were possible. What sort of a test shall be used in deciding where to draw the line? The traditional test is in terms of discretionary vs. ministerial powers. If the power involves discretion, it may not be delegated, and the trustee who does delegate is in effect absolutely liable for any loss resulting. Ministerial powers may be delegated, but the trustee still must use reasonable care in selecting his agents and in supervising their activities.

Where there are two or more fiduciaries, the need for power on the part of one or of a majority to act in certain situations is apparent. The rule is that trustees of a private express trust must act unanimously,[10] unless the trust instrument provides that a majority may act. A majority of the trustees of a charitable trust can act, however, probably on analogy to the board of a charitable corporation. Obviously unanimous action may be difficult as to certain functions, such as custody of assets. It may also be complicated by absence of one of the individual trustees from the jurisdiction. To meet these problems some delegation between co-trustees of a private trust is indispensable. Nevertheless, such delegation is subject to the general rules.

The law dealing with co-representatives has anticipated some of these difficulties by allowing one co-representative to act for all in matters which are ministerial, without an express delegation. As to more important matters, however, one co-representative cannot act alone, and unanimous action is required.[11]

Hence, where three or more fiduciaries are appointed, it is usually desirable to provide that a majority can act. It may also be desirable to provide that certain powers can be exercised by a particular fiduci-

10. See American Security & Trust Co. v. Frost, Section 8(1), infra.

11. Atkinson, Wills (2d Ed.1953) 582–4. Uniform Probate Code, § 3–717 requires concurrence of all co-representatives with certain exceptions. The exceptions allow limited delegation in certain situations when reasonable, but not "blanket delegation." See Official Comment to the section.

ary alone, such as management of realty and custody of investments by the corporate fiduciary. Such a provision relieves the other fiduciary from responsibility for action of the one having the power.[12] A clause permitting delegation to a co-trustee, particularly during periods of absence, should be considered by the draftsman.

KOHLER ESTATE

Supreme Court of Pennsylvania, 1943.
348 Pa. 55, 33 A.2d 920.

PATTERSON, JUSTICE. This appeal is from the refusal of the court below to surcharge an executrix for the alleged improper investment of the proceeds from a sale of principal real estate.

Martin Luther Kohler died August 20, 1916. By his will his daughter, Ruth K. Bates, appellee, was appointed executrix. She was empowered, but not directed, to convert decedent's real estate and directed to "pay all moneys received by her to The Philadelphia Trust, Safe Deposit and Insurance Company of Philadelphia [now the Fidelity-Philadelphia Trust Company] in trust to invest the same and keep the same invested * * *." A spendthrift trust was created for his two daughters, the executrix and Else Campbell, during their lives. Their issue were the remaindermen. Letters testamentary were issued to appellee on August 25, 1916, and in 1917 a first account was filed, audited and confirmed. The auditing judge awarded $2,629.05 to appellee for the purpose of preserving the unproductive real estate until a sale thereof could be effectuated. A period of twenty years was required for the conversion of all real estate, the last tract being sold in 1937. The estimated cost for maintaining the real estate was $2,000 yearly.

To prevent an unnecessary impairment of principal, appellee, pursuant to advice of counsel, retained and invested a portion of the proceeds received from the sale of real estate. By 1924 the amount so invested was $25,000. That sum was invested in government securities for the executrix by T. E. Frame, vice-president of the Fidelity-Philadelphia Trust Company. Appellee was advised and urged by the Trust Company to open an agency account, and on October 2, 1924, executed an agency agreement prepared by the company. By this agreement the Trust Company became the agent and attorney-in-fact for the executrix, formally received all securities, agreed to collect the income, make such investments as she should authorize and "to suggest suitable investments for any principal moneys in hand, without assuming any responsibility for the value or safety of such investments", and was to receive a commission of three per cent on all income collected.

12. Matter of Langdon, 154 Misc. 252, 277 N.Y.S. 581 (Surr.Ct.1935). See Note "Delegation of Fiduciary Duties" 46 Iowa L.Rev. 127 (1960).

On May 16, 1938, on motion of appellants, Else Campbell, a life tenant, and Dorothy Miller and Robert Campbell, remaindermen, a citation was issued directing the trustee to show cause why an account should not be filed. The trustee thereupon caused a similar citation to be directed to the executrix. On November 4, 1938, twenty-one years after the testator's death, separate accounts were filed by the executrix and the trustee. Only the account of the executrix is here involved. To this account appellants filed exceptions, urging that the investments were improperly made and, in the alternative, that if the executrix had the power to so invest, there had been an unlawful delegation of that power. The trustee was awarded the investments at their face value. Appellants contend that the true value of these investments is far less than their face value and, therefore, they should have been replaced with cash, measured by the present market value, with interest thereon from the date of investment. Exceptions to the adjudication were dismissed and this appeal followed.

The duty of an executor generally is not to retain and invest, but to liquidate and terminate. Restatement, Trusts, section 6. If, however, a valid reason exists for the retention of a fund by the executor, it is incumbent upon him not to permit such fund to remain idle, but to invest it, and if there is a default in this regard he is chargeable with lawful interest thereon. In re Henry's Estate, 341 Pa. 439, 19 A.2d 66; In re Dick's Estate, 183 Pa. 647, 39 A. 2; Burner's Appeal, 57 Pa. 46; Yundt's Appeal, 13 Pa. 575, 53 Am.Dec. 496. See, also, Landis v. Scott, 32 Pa. 495.

In investing a portion of the principal the executrix acted as a reasonable and prudent person under the circumstances. Counsel was consulted before the reserve was created, a sum for maintaining the unproductive real estate was awarded to her by the auditing judge when the first account was confirmed, and she endeavored to preserve the principal of the estate. There was a valid reason for the retention of the fund, and all investments were legal investments. Whether her counsel was correct in assuming that the trustee had no power to hold the real estate under the will is a question not here involved. Suffice it to say that she relied upon advice of competent counsel in retaining the fund for investment purposes. "Where a guardian or other fiduciary acts in good faith, under the advice of a competent lawyer, he is not liable for mistakes of law, if such there be, or for errors in judgment." In re Dempster's Estate, 308 Pa. 153, 158, 162 A. 447, 448. See, also, Riebel's Estate, 321 Pa. 145, 149, 184 A. 118; In re Henry's Estate, supra, 341 Pa. 447, 19 A.2d 66; In re Kline's Estate, 280 Pa. 41, 44, 124 A. 280, 32 A.L.R. 926.

Having acted properly in making the investments, has the executrix breached her fiduciary duty to the beneficiaries by delegating this power to invest? That the power to invest the funds of an estate is a personal one, to be exercised by the one to whom the testator entrusted such power, is admitted. See Restatement, Trusts, Section 171. Appellee relies upon the agency agreement and maintains that, on its face, it cannot be construed to have delegated to the trustee-agent the broad power complained of, for the reason that there has been given only the right to "suggest" suitable investments and the investments were made as agent and only with the principal's consent and at her direction. Appellants contend, however, that the power was in fact delegated.

That a fiduciary may not delegate to another the performance of a duty involving this discretion and judgment is well settled. In re Clabby's Estate, 338 Pa. 305, 12 A.2d 71; In re Seaman's Estate, 333 Pa. 358, 5 A.2d 208, 122 A.L.R. 793; In re Iscovitz's Estate, 319 Pa. 277, 179 A. 548; In re Bohlen's Estate, 75 Pa. 304; Restatement, Trusts, section 171(H). This is true even though the one to whom the power is delegated is a co-fiduciary. Bohlen's Estate, supra. That the agency agreement by its terms delegated no authority to invest must be conceded. If, however, there has been a delegation in fact the Court is not powerless to act. It may, and should, charge the fiduciary with any loss resulting from the breach of his fiduciary duty. Appellee relies upon In re Clabby's Estate, supra. In that case this Court said (338 Pa. at page 315, 12 A.2d at page 76): "This instrument, on its face, could not have the broad effect attributed to it by the court below. It merely empowered the attorney-in-fact to hold the trust assets for safekeeping, to collect income and to distribute it under the terms of the will. The agent was given no power over investments, and the actual management of the trust remained at all times in the hands of the trustee. * * * " The record before us, however, shows that the agent did not limit itself solely to the exercise of purely ministerial duties. The manner in which the agency agreement operated is the criterion by which the scope and extent of delegated power must be determined.

A delegation of duties, as shown in Re Iscovitz's Estate, and In re Seaman's Estate, both supra, does not appear here. In those cases the funds had been turned over to an agent with privileges to invest and manage as the fiduciary should direct. The fiduciaries, however, seem to have believed they were "relieved of the duty of keeping a watchful eye on the situation." [333 Pa. 358, 5 A.2d 212, 122 A.L.R. 793.] Here the executrix maintained constant contact with her agent; she had numerous conversations with Mr. Frame; and, she knew of all transactions and approved them. At the same time she was endeavoring to liquidate the remaining unproductive real estate. What Scott on Trusts (p. 916) says with regard to the delegation of duties in Re Bohlen's Estate, supra, is applicable here: "It was the duty of the [executrix] to exercise [her] own discretion in determining whether the securities should be sold and at what price. The result would be different if [the executrix] had exercised [her] discretion in determining to sell the specific securities and in fixing the price, or if the sale had been reported to [her] and in the exercise of [her] discretion [she] had ratified it."

The evidence fails to disclose an improper delegation of discretionary duties, for the breach of which the executrix could be surcharged for loss, if any, occasioned thereby.

The decree of the court below is affirmed. Costs to be paid out of the estate.

NOTE

Investment by an individual trustee, particularly when the trust fund is not large, poses special problems. Use of an agency account, with investment advice of a bank or trust company, is permitted within the limits prescribed in the principal case. Investment in shares of mutual funds, selected prudently in accordance with the normal standard of care, which achieves diversification of investments, is also sometimes attacked as improper delegation but upheld.[13] Where the individual is not a professional, it is the essence of prudence to employ professionals for advice.[14]

Both the Uniform Probate Code and the Uniform Trustees' Powers Act empower the fiduciary to "employ persons, including attorneys, auditors, investment advisors, or agents, even if they are associated with the personal representative, to advise or assist the personal representative in the performance of his administrative duties; act without independent investigation upon their recommendations; and instead of acting personally, employ one or more agents to perform any act of administration, whether or not discretionary." [15]

Trustees of charitable foundations face a similar problem of delegation in reliance on investment advisors. With increasing scope of liability of directors of non-profit corporations, even corporate directors should be concerned.[16] How far can and should the trustees and directors rely on expert investment counsel? [17]

KAUFMAN v. KAUFMAN'S ADMINISTRATOR

Court of Appeals of Kentucky, 1942.
292 Ky. 351, 166 S.W.2d 860, 144 A.L.R. 866.

STANLEY, COMMISSIONER. The principal question is the liability of an administrator and the sureties on his bond for the embezzlement of funds of the estate by an attorney to whom they were entrusted. A cross-appeal questions the time from which interest allowed in the judgment began and the power of the court to decree that it should bear 3% interest instead of the legal rate of 6%.

Upon the insistence of his brothers and sisters Henry Kaufman qualified as administrator of the estate of his recently deceased father, Peter Kaufman, in January, 1933. Kaufman is a farmer with little schooling or experience in financial matters and was reluctant to

13. In re Rees' Estate, 53 Ohio L.Abs. 385, 85 N.E.2d 563 (1949).

14. White, "Prudent Delegation of Trustees' Responsibilities to Professionals," 29 Lab.L.J. 586 (1978) (delegation under ERISA).

15. Uniform Probate Code § 3–715(21) (personal representative), § 5–424(c)(23) (conservator); Uniform Trustees' Powers Act § 3(c)(24). For a comparison of these provisions and the American common law rules with the English law, see Note, "Trustee's Power to Delegate: A Comparative View", 50 Notre Dame Law. 273 (1974).

16. Stern v. Lucy Webb Hayes National Training School for Deaconesses and Missionaries, 381 F.Supp. 1003 (D.C. D.C.1974).

17. Report of Committee on Charitable Trusts and Foundations, Delegation of Investment Responsibility by Trustees of Charitable Trusts and Corporations, 9 Real Prop., Prob. & Tr.J. 583 (1974).

undertake the responsibility; but it was agreed that he should employ an attorney and some of the heirs suggested that the lawyer would attend to the business. The personal estate consisted principally of notes, many of which were secured by mortgages. Kaufman retained W. L. Doolan, Sr., as his attorney and placed in his hands the entire management of the estate. At that time Doolan was a highly respected and reputable lawyer. It is not contended that the administrator was negligent in retaining him as counselor. The National Surety Corporation was engaged by Doolan to become surety on Kaufman's bond in the sum of $10,000.

When Peter Kaufman's widow died eighteen months later, Henry Kaufman qualified as the administrator of her estate also, with the New Amsterdam Casualty Company as surety, in the sum of $1500. Her estate consisted of her distributable share of her husband's property.

In 1938 it was developed that Doolan had systematically embezzled the Kaufman and other estates and funds of his clients, and nothing was recoverable of him. Shortly before this discovery Doolan had filed a suit to settle the father's estate. It is believed now that this was done to obtain further time and avoid an earlier settlement required by the county court. When the situation had been developed, Kaufman employed other counsel and endeavored to salvage something. They filed an amended petition on July 31, 1938, consistent with the developments. Kaufman was removed in August and the estates placed in the hands of the public administrator. He intervened in the suit, brought in the two sureties and sought to recover the sums lost to both estates. In a clear and exhaustive manner the master commissioner by his deputy reported his findings of facts and recommendations. The chancellor adjudged a recovery as on a devastavit against Henry Kaufman in the sum of $12,162.63 with interest from the date of the judgment at the rate of 3% per annum. Judgment was also rendered against the National Surety Corporation for $10,000 and the New Amsterdam Casualty Company for $1,500, both being included in the judgment against their principal, Kaufman. They join in the prosecution of this appeal.

The honesty and good faith of the administrator is not questioned. His inexperience and reliance upon the dishonest lawyer is what got him into trouble. Kaufman kept no records or bank account as administrator, but turned everything over to Doolan, including collections he made himself. The attorney deposited the funds in his individual account and gave personal checks for disbursements, including some to the heirs. The administrator testified that he was kept busy during the time collecting rents, and supposed he had conferred with his lawyer on an average of once a week. Doolan advised there should be a joint control of the funds of the estate, but that he would take care of them. On one occasion Kaufman issued a check for $12.50, signed "Henry Kaufman, Administrator," in refund of interest paid by his sister to the estate, and it went through all right. It was developed in the trial that Doolan had given the bank his check for that sum, marked "for Kaufman check," and it was cleared with Doolan's check attached. He testified he issued a check for about $500 for his father's funeral expenses. It appears that Doolan simply did not use that check but gave his own to cover the bill. Kaufman had no knowledge of these manipulations and supposed he could issue checks for the estate just as Doolan could, but he never made any inquiry about it. From time to time he and some of the others asked Doolan about a settlement and he gave some plausible excuse and said the money was drawing interest. Judge Gilbert Burnett, as attorney for one of the heirs, talked with Doolan several times over a period of three years before his exposure and was told that the estate was complicated, requiring the collection of a number of lien notes, which Judge Burnett realized did take time. He testified he and everyone else had confidence in Doolan and his investigation showed the administrator to have a sound surety and he so advised his client. Thus, Doolan lulled the administrator, the heirs, and the attorneys of one of them into inaction for five years.

It is not always easy to describe or discern the liability of executor or administrator or other fiduciary for loss resulting from the negligence or fault of agents or attorneys properly employed or retained by him. The question is essentially one of good faith and reasonable diligence. Where that appears, the acts are treated with indulgence. Mistaken judgment is not enough to impose liability. There is a vague distinction, in general, between the functions and duties of an executor or administrator and a trustee. Bogert on Trusts and Trustees, Sec. 12. But in relation to conditions like the present, there appears to be no distinction within the limitations of fiducial duties of a personal representative. Cf. Thompson v. Fraley, 279 Ky. 323, 130 S.W.2d 793. Those duties are to collect and distribute the estate among creditors and heirs in accordance with the statutes or will. The administration involves all that may be done rightfully in the collection and preservation of the assets and the management of the same, with that prudence and diligence which is observed in regard to private affairs by men of reasonable prudence and fair, average capacity. Barth v. Fidelity & Columbia Trust Co., 188 Ky. 788, 224 S.W. 351; Melheiser v. Central Trust Co. of Owensboro, 237 Ky. 757, 36 S.W.2d 377; Schouler on Wills, Executors and Administrators, Section 3362. For losses resulting from the failure to exercise that care the representative is personally liable. Schouler, Sections 2480, 2490. But this degree of prudence obviously calls for the exercise of administrative discretion, which, in turn, often requires the use of agents and assistants, particularly in the performance of duties of a ministerial nature or of a type the executor or administrator could not reasonably be expected to perform personally. In the instant case there is no doubt that prudence and discretion required the employment of a lawyer as counselor, and, in respect to some of the assets, to his services as an attorney to collect and reduce the same to cash. And it is the generally accepted view that an administrator is not personally liable for loss through his lawyer's misconduct, negligence or nonfeasance if he exercised due prudence in the selection of the lawyer.

24 C.J. 126. But this necessary authority cannot extend to the surrender of all the duties of the trust or the delegation of all functions without becoming responsible to distributees for any loss sustained. Schouler, Section 2258; 24 C.J. 126. "The trustee is under a duty to the beneficiary not to delegate to others the doing of acts which the trustee can reasonably be required personally to perform." Thus, he cannot properly commit the entire administration of the trust to an agent or other person unless he is permitted to do so by the terms of the trust. Restatement of Law of Trusts, A.L.I., Sec. 171. If he does that without such permission and loss results he is responsible for it.

Under similar states of fact, it is generally held that an administrator permitting an attorney to retain for several years money of the estate collected by him without any effort to recover it from the attorney is liable for its loss to the estate. * * *

In the case at bar the evidence fully developed the situation and disclosed facts which bring it fully within the rulings declared in the original opinion in the Carneal Case to constitute culpable negligence. As in that case, so it is here. The negligence is not confined simply to the act of employing the attorney to collect the notes but in permitting him to assume exclusive control and retain the proceeds and other funds and then by reason of the administrator's supine inaction apply the money to his own use. It is the administrator's course of conduct or the negative violation of his duty in remaining passive and in letting the attorney handle the funds of the estate, commingled with his own, as if they were his own property, and not requiring an accounting and settlement. While Kaufman was not familiar with his duties in respect to managing and settling the estate himself, and rested upon his confidence in the lawyer, he is to be judged by the standard of the average prudent and diligent man in handling his personal affairs. We cannot conceive of such man going along for five years without requiring an accounting from anyone. We concur in the chancellor's decision that the administrator did not, in the language of his bonds, "faithfully perform and discharge all the duties" of his trust. The failure to make the accounting is the essential liability. The defense was properly adjudged insufficient.

* * *

On the direct appeal, the judgment is affirmed except as to the failure to make an allowance for compensating the former administrator's attorneys. On the cross-appeal, it is affirmed except in respect to the rate of interest it should bear.

Whole court sitting.

NOTE

Reliance on the advice of a lawyer in legal matters is not improper delegation if reasonable care is used in selection of the attorney. But even this is not always a protection for the fiduciary, as we have already seen in First National Bank of Mansfield on page 1227.

Just as the principal case penalizes complete delegation by the fiduciary, one fiduciary cannot delegate administration of his trust to a cofiduciary.[18] When an individual person and a corporate fiduciary serve together, some separation of functions is inevitable. The trustee who relies on another co-trustee may be liable for contribution if the co-trustee is guilty of breach of trust. In Mueller v. Mueller, supra, page 1237, where a mother relied entirely on a son as co-trustee to look after investments, she was held to be as much at fault as he and hence liable to contribute to losses incurred; a minority of the court would have held the son more at fault and not entitled to contribution under the circumstances. If it is intended that certain powers be exercised only by one (the individual or the corporate fiduciary), the will or trust should explicitly so state and relieve the other from any liability to oversee the exercise of such powers.[19]

SECTION 8. DISTRIBUTION PROBLEMS

(1) DETERMINATION OF PRINCIPAL AND INCOME

The normal trust pattern consists of a trust to pay the income from the trust to a named beneficiary (frequently the settlor's wife) for life and to turn the principal of the trust over to one or more beneficiaries (typically the settlor's issue) upon the death of the income beneficiary. Such a pattern requires the trustee to make an allocation of receipts and expenses between income and principal. A century ago the problem was simple; the res of the trust would most likely be realty, the rents and profits would constitute the income, current charges such as taxes and repairs would be charged against income to determine net income; and the principal remained easily ascertainable—the realty itself. The shift of the trust res from realty to stocks and bonds, or a going business, has introduced new complications. Are stock dividends principal or income? When are cash dividends realized as income, when declared or when payable? Should some of the expenses of administration (the trustee's fees) be charged against principal since the services benefit the principal beneficiary as well as the income beneficiary? If the trust consists of a

18. Report of Committee on Trust Administration and Accounting, The Co-Trustee Relationship—Rights and Duties, 8 Real Prop., Prob. & Tr.J. 9 (1973).

19. Cohan, "Splitting Powers Between Fiduciaries", 8 Real Prop., Prob. & Tr.J. 588 (1973) explores the problems ably. In the "directory pension trusts" where the bank trustee is required to follow the direction of an investment advisor or an investment committee, there is reason not to apply the normal trust rules. Comment, "Separable Liabilities of Trustees in Directory Trusts", 60 Cal. L.Rev. 1151 (1972). See also Report of Committee on Investments by Fiduciaries, Responsibility of Trustee Where Investment Power is Shared or Exercised by Others, 9 Real Prop., Prob. & Tr.J. 517 (1974).

going business, can reserves be set up out of current gross income even though they may ultimately benefit the principal beneficiaries?

Fundamental is the issue of appropriate *method* of determining income and principal. Is "income" a legal or economic concept? Who is to determine its specific content, the lawyer or the accountant? Can the settlor effectively spell out its content or "delegate" the power to the trustee to do so? What influence will concepts of income developed in other impinging fields of law, notably taxation, have?

The allocation of receipts and expenditures to the principal and income accounts is one of the most difficult problems facing a fiduciary today.[20] This is commonly called "apportionment" and arises both in the course of administering a decedent's estate and in the administration of a trust. For example, the executor must pass on such questions as whether pecuniary legacies carry interest and from what date or whether rent due decedent before his death but not paid until later is an asset of the estate or income which goes to the devisee. The trustee inherits some of these problems. If there is a residuary trust, the trust usually will not be set up until administration of the estate is completed; what is to be distributed to the income beneficiaries as delayed income for that period? Are trustee's fees charges against income or principal or both? Where there are successive income beneficiaries under the trust, there is the further problem of determining which beneficiary is entitled to receipts which cover a period during which the right to income shifts from one beneficiary to the other. These are only some of the problems which may arise.

A settlor or testator may anticipate these problems by an express provision. More than two-thirds of the states have adopted the Uniform Principal and Income Act, either in its 1931 form or as revised in 1962.[21] These Acts should be consulted to determine how problems raised in this section would be answered where one of the Acts is in force.

Absent a satisfactory trust provision or legislation such as one of the Uniform Acts, the courts have built up methods of handling the

20. In general, see Bogert, Trusts (5th Ed. 1973) Ch. 13; Bogert, Trusts and Trustees (2d Ed., 1960) §§ 801–860; 4 Powell, The Law of Real Property (Rohan Rev.1981) ¶¶ 551–556; III Scott, Trusts (3d Ed.1967) §§ 232–241; Flickinger, "A Trustee's Nightmare: Allocation of Stock Dividends between Income and Principal", 43 Bost.U.L.Rev. 199 (1963); Machen, "The Apportionment of Stock Distributions in Trust Accounting Practice", 20 Md.L.Rev. 89 (1960); Scott, "Principal or Income?", 100 Trusts and Estates 180 (1961); Walker, "Trustee's Dilemma in the Distribution of Dividends", 7 S.Tex.L.J. 294 (1964); Comment, "Probate and Trust Accounting Problems", 46 Marq.L.Rev. 458 (1963); Comment, "Trust Administration-Apportionment and other Remedies of an Income Beneficiary When the Trustee's Retention of Unproductive Property Causes a Loss or Termination of Income", 58 Mich.L.Rev. 1049 (1960). For clear discussions of the apportionment of tax benefits and burdens, see Dobris, "Equitable Adjustments in Postmortem Tax Planning: An Unremitting Diet of *Warms*" 65 Iowa L.Rev. 103 (1979); "Limits on the Doctrine of Equitable Adjustment in Sophisticated Postmortem Tax Planning", 66 Iowa L.Rev. 273 (1981).

21. 7A Uniform Laws Ann., Business and Financial Laws, (1978) 429, 461. 23 states are listed as having adopted the 1962 Act and 13 as having adopted the 1931 Act as of the end of 1981.

problem, partly based on legal notions and partly based on recognition of sound practices of the accounting profession.

To give you some idea of the problems and common solutions, we shall briefly consider a simple case. Testator died on March 2, 1982. His will provided that $10,000 was to be paid to his daughter Jane outright; certain common stock in the XYZ corporation was specifically bequeathed to a son John; realty consisting of a commercial building and land under lease for five years to a tenant was devised to his wife Mary for life, then to his daughter Jane; and the residue of the estate was left in trust to pay the income to his wife for life, then to pay the principal over to their then surviving issue. His executor was appointed March 10, 1982. (1) Part of the estate consists of corporate bonds with interest payable semi-annually on January 15, and July 15. When the executor receives the interest payment on July 15, 1982, is this to be treated as principal or income? Since we consider interest as an item which accrues daily, part of the payment attributable to the period from January 15 to date of decedent's death, March 2, would be principal and included as an asset in the inventory of the estate. The balance would be income, and would be held by the executor and turned over to the trustee for ultimate distribution to the wife Mary as income beneficiary of the trust, assuming the bonds are not sold to pay the $10,000 legacy, debts, taxes, or expenses of administration. (2) The executor receives a check for rent for the realty for the month of March. Under the existing lease on the property rent was due and payable on the first of each month in advance. Since the March rent was due before date of death, this is a claim decedent had at death and is a capital asset of the estate, included in the original inventory. Unlike interest, rent has historically been considered as accruing on its due date, not spread over the entire rent paying period. Statutes in some states provide for apportionment. (3) The executor receives a dividend check from the XYZ corporation. The dividend was declared Feb. 26, payable March 14 to stockholders of record as of March 1; it is a quarterly cash dividend out of current earnings. Here the critical date is that on which stockholders of record become payees. This dividend is therefore a capital item since the stock was in the name of decedent on March 1. Had it not specified stockholders of record as of a given date, the date of declaration, Feb. 26, would have controlled. All subsequent dividends would belong to the person to whom the stock was specifically bequeathed, since a specific bequest carries income with it. Thus, even though the executor received later dividends in the course of administration, these would ultimately be distributed to the son John.[22] (4) If the legacy of $10,000 is not paid to Jane until June 3, 1983, is she entitled to any interest? Since the normal period of administration is one year, a fact which the testator presumptively foresaw, the general pecuniary legacy would only carry interest after one year from date of death, at the legal rate. There are exceptions, however, and statutes sometimes set a different date from which interest runs.

22. Review Chapter XV, Section 1(3)(A).

Assume the executor in our problem makes his final account and distributes the residue to the trustee on July 18, 1983. (5) The trustee sells stock in August at a profit of $500 over the inventory value; is this credited to income or principal? Profit is always treated as capital gain, not income. The same would be true if the trustee bought any investment and sold at a profit. (6) The trustee invests the proceeds from sale of the stock in corporate bonds. Although each of the bonds has a maturity value of $1,000, the trustee pays a price of $1,010 because the particular bonds carry a 9% interest rate, which is higher than the rate at which similar bonds are then being issued. Is the $10 premium a charge against principal or income? Since the price reflects a greater return than normal, the entire purchase price would normally be charged to principal now but the premium of $10 would be amortized out of receipts from the bond over the period to maturity, since only $1,000 will be recovered as principal when the bond is paid at that time. To simplify our problem, if the bond had ten years to run to maturity, $1 each year would be deducted from current receipts and credited to capital, the balance being paid as income to the income beneficiary. (7) If the income beneficiary Mary dies on July 3, 1984, is her estate entitled to any of the interest on corporate bonds which is payable subsequently on July 15, or does the entire interest payment belong to the principal beneficiaries? Here we apply our notion of accrual from (1) above, now benefiting the income beneficiary, and Mary's estate is entitled to interest for the period from January 15th to the date of her death. However, the trust instrument should be read carefully. It often provides that on the death of the life beneficiary, "the principal *and* any undistributed income" shall go to the principal beneficiaries; this avoids adding the undistributed income to the probate estate of the income beneficiary.[23] (8) Would the daughter Jane, the legal remainderman as to the realty, be entitled to any of the rent for the month of July? Again our concept that rent is not apportionable means that rent for July all belongs to Mary or her estate. (9) Should the annual compensation of the trustee for the period of the trust all be charged against income? If a fee for setting up or terminating the trust were charged, it would be paid out of principal; but many corporate fiduciaries feel annual fees also reflect services benefiting principal as well as income beneficiaries. While an inter vivos trust will commonly provide for some apportionment of fees, the annual fee has otherwise been charged against income; a few states have adopted statutes apportioning the annual fee.

23. Such a clause may have adverse tax consequences which must be considered. It is permissible in a marital deduction power-of-appointment trust because the spouse has a power over the undistributed income, but it may disqualify a qualified terminable interest trust under the Economic Recovery Tax Act of 1981, which requires that the spouse receive all of the income for life.

IN RE CATHERWOOD'S TRUST

Supreme Court of Pennsylvania, 1961
405 Pa. 61, 173 A.2d 86.[24]

* * * Before CHARLES ALVIN JONES, C. J., and BELL, MUSMANNO, BENJAMIN R. JONES, COHEN, BOK and EAGEN, JJ.

BENJAMIN R. JONES, JUSTICE. These appeals present three problems arising under the so-called Pennsylvania Rule of Apportionment.

The factual background of these problems is relatively simple. On June 9, 1924, Mr. Catherwood created an inter vivos trust under which the First Pennsylvania Banking and Trust Company was named trustee. To this trust Mr. Catherwood transferred 1896.72 shares of the common stock of American Gas and Electric Company, now American Electric Power Company. The trust provided that the trustee hold the res, collect the income and distribute the net income in equal shares to Mr. Catherwood's two children for life and remainder over at their death to their descendants per stirpes. Mr. Catherwood is dead but his two children (the appellants) are living.

At the audit of the trustee's third account by the Orphans' Court of Philadelphia County three apportionment problems were presented.

These problems of apportionment were:

Problem I.

When this trust was created, the *book value* of the stock was $11.76 per share and its *market value,* i.e. the value at which the stock was carried in the trustee's account was $71.77 per share. On July 16, 1948 the trustee sold 200 shares of this stock. When sold, the *book value* (i.e., *intact value*) of these 200 shares was $2,352.94 and the proceeds of the sale were $7,808.18 ($39.04 per share). The proceeds of the sale ($7,808.18) exceeded the *intact value* ($2,352.94) by $5,455.24. However, the sale of this stock resulted in an actual loss to the trust of $6,546.90, i.e. $14,355.08 (the *carrying value* at $71.77 per share) less $7,808.18 (the proceeds of the sale). Under such circumstances should an apportionment take place of *any* part of the proceeds of the sale? The court below answered in the negative and directed the retention of the entire proceeds of the sale in principal.

Problem II.

The trustee received four stock dividends—a 5% dividend in 1951, a 2½% dividend in 1952, a 2% dividend in 1955 and a 2½% dividend in 1957. Do such small dividends belong to the life tenants or should

24. Noted, 7 Vill.L.Rev. 497 (1962).

they be apportioned? The court below held the dividends should be apportioned.

Problem III.

On July 5, 1956, a 50% stock dividend amounting to 800 shares was received by the trustee and labeled by the Company as a "$1^1/_2$ for 1" split. The Company issued 6,555,540 shares of common stock having a $10 share value and $65,555,400 was transferred to the capital stock account of which $40,551,060 (61.9%) was transferred from earned surplus and $24,999,480 (38.1%) from capital surplus. When the Company issued stock dividends in 1951, 1953 and 1955, $27,600,000 was transferred from earned surplus to capital surplus. The court below held that this 50% stock dividend did not constitute an apportionable event. The auditing judge (President Judge Charles Klein), joined by Judges Lefever and Saylor, in addition to determining the three apportionment problems adversely to the life tenants, urged upon us a re-examination of our decision in Crawford Estate, 362 Pa. 458, 67 A.2d 124 looking toward the relaxation of the rigidity of the rule therein enunciated so as to permit the retroactive application of the Principal and Income Act [25] to trusts created prior to its passage. With the disposition of the apportionment problems, the court en banc was unanimous.

Our initial attention is given to the suggestion that we re-examine and overrule Crawford which, if concurred in, would mean the abolishment and extinction of the so-called Pennsylvania Rule of Apportionment, a Rule consistently applied by this Court since Earp's Appeal, 28 Pa. 368, decided in 1859. That Rule was an equitable one which at the time of its conception and for many years thereafter—under vastly different economic conditions than those of the last several decades—strove to balance the equities between life tenants and remaindermen with the aim of protecting the interests of both.

In Nirdlinger's Estate, 1927, 290 Pa. 457, 462, 463, 464, 465, 139 A. 200, 202, 56 A.L.R. 1303, this Court pointed out that "[w]hen the earnings [of a corporation whose stock forms part of the trust] have been permitted to accumulate by a corporation and their proceeds invested in corporate property, in working capital, or retained as cash or its equivalent, and an extraordinary dividend is declared in stock or cash, the respective rights of life tenants and remaindermen" were adjudicated under three rules—the Massachusetts, Pennsylvania and Kentucky rules. Under the Massachusetts rule—one of convenience—all cash dividends are awarded to the life tenant and all stock dividends to the remainderman. Minot v. Paine, 99 Mass. 101.[26] Under the Kentucky rule, a "dividend, whether of stock or cash goes to

25. [Footnotes 25 through 30 are by the Court. Ed.] Act of July 3, 1947, P.L. 1283 which substantially reenacted the Act of May 3, 1945, P.L. 416 (repealed), 20 P.S. § 3470.1.

26. This rule was then followed by Connecticut, Georgia, Illinois, Maine, North Carolina, Rhode Island, West Virginia and the U.S. Supreme Court. See 24 A.L.R. 29. It was also the English rule.

the person entitled to receive the income at the time the dividend is declared, without regard to the time when it was earned". Nirdlinger's Estate, supra, 290 Pa. 465, 139 A. 203. Under the Pennsylvania rule "the rights of the life tenant and the remainderman to an extraordinary cash or a stock dividend declared during the life tenancy are determined by a division of the dividend between the claimants so as to preserve intact the book value of the devised property (the corpus) as it existed at testator's death [or in the case of an intervivos trust, at the time of its creation]" and the "effect of the rule is to give to the life tenant the income which has been earned since the trust came into being, but, at the same time, to preserve the value of the corpus as it was * * *, or, * * *, to preserve the intact value of the estate." Nirdlinger's Estate, supra, 290 Pa. at page 464, 139 A. at page 203.

The so-called Pennsylvania Rule was followed for many years in a majority of the jurisdictions in this country.

This Rule recognized an "apportionable event" to occur in four situations: (1) the distribution by a corporation of an extraordinary cash or stock dividend; (2) the liquidation of the corporation; (3) the sale of the stock by the trustee; (4) the issuance of stock rights. Cunningham Estate, 395 Pa. 1, 7, 149 A.2d 72; Jones Estate, 377 Pa. 473, 476, 105 A.2d 353; Buist's Estate, 297 Pa. 537, 147 A. 606.

In 1931, the National Conference of Commissioners on Uniform State Laws promulgated a Uniform Principal and Income Act which was enacted by the Legislature of this Commonwealth on May 3, 1945. That Act rejected the Pennsylvania Rule and adopted the Massachusetts Rule.[27] Therefore, as to *all* trusts created since May 3, 1945, the Massachusetts Rule is now applied.

Both the 1945 and 1947 Acts provided that their provisions should become effective upon enactment and should apply to *all* trusts "*theretofore* or thereafter made or created". (Emphasis supplied.)

In Crawford Estate, supra, this Court was called upon to determine whether the Act of 1945 could constitutionally receive a retroactive application to trusts created prior to its enactment. In Crawford, a testator, who died in 1935, placed his residuary estate in trust to pay the income, under spendthrift provisions, to his daughter for life and provision was made for distribution of the corpus after the daughter's death. *The testator directed that all stock dividends should constitute principal.* After the effective date of the 1945 Act but prior to the effective date of the 1947 Act, the trustees re-

27. In a Prefatory Note to the Uniform Principal and Income Act the Commissioners stated: "When the first draft of the act was presented, the Conference voted to follow the so-called Massachusets rule of awarding cash dividends on corporate stock to income and share dividends to principal, thereby rejecting the Pennsylvania rule, or one of the several variations of it, requiring some apportionment between the two funds. Experience has shown that, however praiseworthy the intent, the latter rule is unworkable, since neither trustee nor court has the means to value the corporate assets in such way as to secure the fair adjustment aimed at. Consequently the majority of the large commercial states have already favored the former and more convenient rule * * *"

ceived stock dividends from three corporations and sold other corporate stock and subscription rights. The court below held that, under the Pennsylvania Rule, the life tenant had a *vested right* to receive, as income, an apportionment of the stock dividends and the gains from the sale of the stock and subscription rights.[28] On appeal, the remaindermen contended that the interest of a life tenant in accumulated unpaid corporate earnings and profits, under the Pennsylvania Rule, was a contingency and expectancy which the legislature could constitutionally modify or extinguish: the life tenant maintained that, by reason of the Rule, her interest in accumulated unpaid corporate earnings and profits was a vested property right which was beyond the power of the legislature to constitutionally alter or extinguish. This Court held that the decisional law embodied in the Pennsylvania Rule established in the life tenant a *vested property right* and that the provisions of the 1945 Act providing for its retroactive application to trusts created prior to the Act were constitutionally inhibited by Article I, sections 1 and 9 of the Pennsylvania Constitution, P.S., and the 14th Amendment to the U. S. Constitution.[29] In support of its position that a retroactive application would be violative of the Pennsylvania Constitution, reliance was placed on three decisions. Brown v. Hummel, 6 Pa. 86; Palairet's Appeal, 67 Pa. 479; Willcox v. Penn Mutual Life Insurance Co., 357 Pa. 581, 55 A.2d 521, 174 A.L.R. 220. An examination of those decisions reveals their inapposition to this type situation. In Brown, we held that will-appointed trustees had vested rights and that a statute which summarily removed them and appointed other trustees was invalid. In Palairet, we held that a statute which provided for the extinguishment of ground rents effected a deprivation of vested property rights for a nonpublic use and was, therefore, invalid. In Willcox, the Community Property Law of July 7, 1947, P.L. 1423 was held unconstitutional because, inter alia, it effected a deprivation of vested property rights for a non-public use. The rights therein held vested and beyond the reach of legislative interference were rights in property, whereas the right claimed in Crawford was to a rule of law and a method of interpretation.

28. Because such items constituted "income" under the Pennsylvania Rule, the direction of testator that stock dividends be treated as principal was ignored on the ground such direction violated the statute against accumulation of "income".

29. Section 1. Article I, of the Pennsylvania Constitution—extremely general in nature—provides: "*Section 1. Natural rights of mankind:* All men are born equally free and independent, and have certain inherent and indefeasible rights, among which are those of enjoying and defending life and liberty, of acquiring, possessing and protecting property and reputation, and of pursuing their own happiness."

Section 9 of Article I of the Pennsylvania Constitution applies to criminal prosecutions: "*Sec. 9. Rights of accused in criminal prosecutions:* In all criminal prosecutions the accused hath a right to be heard by himself and his counsel, to demand the nature and cause of the accusation against him, to meet the witnesses face to face, to have compulsory process for obtaining witnesses in his favor, and, in prosecutions by indictment or information, a speedy public trial by an impartial jury of the vicinage; he cannot be compelled to give evidence against himself, nor can he be deprived of his life, liberty or property, unless by the judgment of his peers or the law of the land."

The Fourteenth Amendment to the United States Constitution states, inter alia: "No State shall * * * deprive any person of * * * property, without due process of law * * *."

In Crawford, no federal cases were cited to support the assertion that a retroactive application of the Act would be in violation of the 14th Amendment to the U. S. Constitution. Tidal Oil Co. v. Flanagan, 263 U.S. 444, 450–451, 44 S.Ct. 197, 68 L.Ed. 382 and cases therein cited would indicate the contrary.

On the same day Crawford was handed down by this Court, Pew Trust, 362 Pa. 468, 67 A.2d 129 was decided. In Pew, relying on Crawford, we held that the retroactive provisions of *both* the 1945 and 1947 Acts were unconstitutional when applied retroactively to trusts created prior to their passage. References to our holdings in Crawford and Pew were later made in and affirmed in Steele Estate, 377 Pa. 250, 103 A.2d 409; Jones Estate, 377 Pa. 473, 105 A.2d 353. Finally, in Warden Trust, 382 Pa. 311, 115 A.2d 159, we decided that a life tenant had a vested property right in extraordinary dividends declared on stock *acquired after* the effective date of the 1947 Act and that such Act could not be constitutionally applied to stock acquired by trusts created prior to the Act even though the acquisition of such stock took place after passage of the Act.

The present situation of the law constitutes an "apportionment morass" as President Judge Klein so aptly stated. If a trust was created prior to May 3, 1945, the Pennsylvania Rule of Apportionment now governs: if a trust was created thereafter, the Massachusetts Rule, codified by the legislature, governs. Orphans' courts *now* have three different sets of apportionment formulas to apply: (1) for trusts created prior to May 3, 1945; (2) for trusts created between May 3, 1945 and before July 3, 1947; (3) for trusts created after July 3, 1947.[30] Under the present state of the law the Pennsylvania Rule *must* be applied to all trusts created prior to May 3, 1945: its application will continue until the last of such trusts terminates, conceivably many, many years in the future.

In determining whether the Principal and Income Act can be applied retroactively to trusts created prior to May 3, 1945, we must consider solely the *legality* from a constitutional viewpoint of so doing: if no constitutional barrier interposes to prevent such retroactive application, we must carry out the legislative mandate which made the provisions of the Act applicable to trusts "theretofore", i.e. prior to the effective date of the Act, created. The constitutionality of a retroactive operation of the Act will depend on the existence or nonexistence of any vested property right in the life tenants or remainderman subject to interference by the legislative enactment.

Certain principles of law are beyond dispute: (1) a gift of an equitable life estate in income or of an estate in remainder does constitute

30. If the legislature should amend (or repeal) the Principal and Income Act of 1947, the Orphans' courts would then have four different sets of apportionment formulas to apply, depending upon the creation dates of various trusts. If, over a period of years, the legislature should amend the Principal and Income Act of 1947 five times, the Orphans' courts would have seven differing apportionment formulas to keep straight and apply; if the Act were amended 10 times, they would have twelve differing formulas to understand and apply. The situation is bound to get worse; it can never get better. Unless, that is, Crawford Estate is overruled.

a grant of a vested property right of which the recipients cannot be divested by legislative action; (2) a vested property right cannot exist in a rule of law, although a rule of law may establish a vested property right; (3) where an interest is declared vested by this Court, such interest cannot be altered or extinguished by the retroactive effect of any statute. That these life tenants have a vested property right in the *income* from this trust cannot be questioned. Stated otherwise, if there be *income* arising from the trust, in such *income* the life tenants have such a property right that brooks no legislative interference. The present Act in nowise alters or extinguishes a right to the income arising from the trust.

It does not follow, however, that these life tenants have any vested interest in the accumulated unpaid earnings of a corporation, the stock of which is held in the trust or a vested interest in any particular apportionment formula for the ascertainment of such earnings. Even though a corporation be highly successful, its earnings may never reach either the dividend stage or an earned surplus account. Corporate earnings may be siphoned off in innumerable ways: in salaries, bonuses, advertising, plant expansion, research, building up of inventory, and through a myriad of other expenses and investments. Reserves may be set up for countless objects and these reserve accounts credited instead of the earned surplus account. How great a corporation's accumulated earnings on its books are and, indeed, whether the corporation shows any accumulated earnings at all is a function of the particular accounting procedure employed by the corporation. It would be just as logical to reason that the life beneficiary of a trust has a vested interest in the particular accounting procedure employed by a corporation at the date that one or more of its shares become a part of the trust corpus as to reason that the life beneficiary has a vested interest in a particular apportionment formula to ascertain the accumulated earnings of the corporation.

In In re Allis' Will, 1959, 6 Wis.2d 1, 94 N.W.2d 226, 232, 69 A.L.R.2d 1128, the Supreme Court of Wisconsin expressly rejected the whole rationale of Crawford Estate, stating:

> "It is fundamental that the life beneficiary possessed no vested property right in the earnings of a corporation, shares of whose stock constituted part of the portfolio of investments of the trust at the time of the enactment of the Wisconsin Uniform Principal and Income Act, prior to a declaration of a dividend by the board of directors payable therefrom. In re Estate of Gerlach, 1922, 177 Wis. 251, 256, 188 N.W. 94. We consider it to be equally clear that she also has no vested property right in the rule with respect to the allocation of corporate stock dividends, which had been established by court decision and was in effect at the time of the death of the testatrix. Therefore, it is our considered judgment that the legislature could change such rule with respect to any stock dividends subsequently declared without violating the due process clause of the Fourteenth Amendment."

This reasoning appears eminently sound.

* * *

While *expediency* can furnish no reason or basis upon which to determine the constitutionality of the retroactive operation of the Act, we cannot refrain from noting the unworkability of the Rule under present day economic conditions. In Cunningham Estate, supra, 395 Pa. at page 14, 149 A.2d at page 78, noting the unworkability of the Rule, we refused to extend its application to events other than those recognized as apportionable prior to the effective date of the 1945 Act, and we therein stated: "Present day economic conditions, particularly in the corporate field, present a drastic contrast to the economic conditions in existence at the inception of and during the formative years of the Rule, and corporate practices plus multiplication and extension of taxes has made the application of the Rule even more difficult and often unworkable. The complexities, the uncertainties, and the difficulties which are inherent in the application and administration of the Rule have too often in these modern times created confusion, injustices and glaring inconsistencies. The essential fairness and equity of the Pennsylvania Rule was beyond question. The basis for its rejection and abandonment by legislation is the fact that changes in corporate practice have, in many instances, rendered unworkable the Rule. In recent years the ingenuity of corporate management, seeking to achieve various ends such as broadening or enhancing the market for its stock, effect tax savings, etc., has produced a complexity of corporate transactions which involve the transfer on corporate books of earnings, earned surplus, etc., from one account to another. Earnings, under modern corporate practice, no longer retain the simplicity of meaning of the earnings considered by this Court in Earp's Appeal, supra [28 Pa. 368], and other decisions." Other reasons, such as the prevalence of common stocks in trust portfolios, the unprecedented boom during the last decade which resulted in the issuance of "more stock dividends and offerings than our economy has ever experienced before", etc., have added to the practical difficulty of applying the Rule.

In his adjudication, the able auditing judge well stated: "The apportionment picture in Pennsylvania has, indeed, degenerated into a sorry state, in spite of the lofty ideals of the many sincere and scholarly jurists who contributed to its development over the years. The fantastic growth of business structures in this country in the past one hundred years, with its myriads of corporate complexities and resulting astronomical apportionment calculations, has made the Pennsylvania Apportionment Rule practically unworkable today. It is described as an equitable doctrine, but it frequently produces results which are not only completely unforeseen and unpredictable, but actually harsh, inequitable and often contrary to the intentions of the creator of the trust. * * * Because recent amendments to our laws permitting fiduciaries to invest in common stocks, most estates, even the smaller ones, now have shares of the nation's largest corporations in their portfolios. The apportionment problems which confront trustees today, as the result of such holdings, create administrative problems of such complexity as to make the management of trust estates a truly nightmarish experience. It is utterly unrealistic to expect trustees to be compelled to analyze the intricate financial statements of mammoth multi-million dollar corporations, every time a stock dividend is declared, or a share of stock sold. The entire subject of apportionment should be carefully reviewed and the rule simplified by the Courts which created the existing burdensome situation."

Pennsylvania, of all the states which adopted the Uniform Principal and Income Act, stands alone in having held that retroactive application of the Act is unconstitutional. In the original Restatement of Trusts, Section 236(6) promulgated in 1935, the American Law Institute adopted the Pennsylvania Rule: in the 1948 Supplement to the Restatement of Trusts the Pennsylvania Rule has been abandoned in favor of the Uniform Principal and Income Act.

Over a century ago the Pennsylvania Rule of Apportionment was created: great and distinguished jurists contributed to its creation and the formulation of its principles. The purpose and aim of the Rule was commendable: it sought, and was generally acknowledged to have achieved, an equitable adjustment of the rights of both life tenants and remainderman. Over sixteen years ago, faced with drastic changes in our economy and other factors which rendered unworkable the Rule, the legislature in its wisdom abolished the Rule and substituted a new Rule in its place. Our only task is to determine whether the legislative enactment can constitutionally apply to trusts created prior to its passage. Crawford found it could not and Pew and Warden followed Crawford. We have re-examined these decisions and disagree with the results reached. The legislative enactment did not modify or extinguish any vested property rights. There is no vested property rights in a court-made rule of apportionment. The experience under the Crawford rule teaches us it cannot justly be applied and, therefore, we overrule Crawford followed in Pew and Warden.

In overruling these decisions, we are keenly aware of the fact that distributions have been made in many estates in reliance on these decisions and the vitality of the Pennsylvania Rule of Apportionment. *Such distributions are not affected in any manner by our present ruling.*

In the case at bar, the court below, in reliance on Crawford, Pew and Warden, applied the Pennsylvania Rule of Apportionment to the solution of the three problems presented to it.

As to the second question of apportionment we believe the decree of the court below was in error. While we have never held that ordinary small stock dividends should be considered as income payable to the life tenant, we have not held to the contrary; our prior decisions dealt with stock dividends, extraordinary in nature. If a total stock distribution for the current year is payable at the rate of 6% or less of the corporation's outstanding shares before such distributions were made such distribution in stock of the distributing corporation should be treated as income.

As to the first and third questions of apportionment, the decree of the court below was correct.

In holding valid the retroactive provisions of the Principal and Income Act and, in effect, abolishing the Pennsylvania Rule of Apportionment, we do so prospectively. Great Northern Ry. Co. v. Sunburst Oil & Refining Co., 287 U.S. 358, 53 S.Ct. 145, 77 L.Ed. 360. *In all audits now pending and henceforth,* distributions shall be made under the provisions of the Principal and Income Act of 1947.

Decree, as modified, affirmed. Each party pay own costs.

BELL, JUSTICE (concurring in part and dissenting in part).

I enthusiastically agree with that part of the majority Opinion which holds that small stock dividends which do not exceed 6% in that particular year belong to the life tenant and are not subject to apportionment. However, I would not restrict stock dividends to that of the issuing corporation or require them to be of the same class. I said in Cunningham Estate, 395 Pa. 1, at page 34, 149 A.2d 72, at page 89 and I repeat:

> " '[a] Ordinary cash or scrip [or stock] dividends coming to [the trustee] belong to life tenants regardless of how soon after testator's death they are declared by the company whose stock is held in the corpus. * * * '
>
> "In order to avoid costly, vexatious, 'de minimis' litigation, and to eliminate conflict and confusion, and to comply with the requests of Bench and Bar to make clear and definite the rules with respect to various situations that frequently arise, I would add: An ordinary cash dividend and an ordinary stock dividend belong to the life tenant, irrespective of when earned and irrespective of whether the intact value is or is not thereby impaired. Ordinary cash dividends include small extra cash dividends which are paid currently or irregularly (usually at year's end). Ordinary stock dividends would include stock dividends [of any class] which are paid quarterly, semi-annually or annually, currently or irregularly, and do not exceed 6% in any one year."

Not once in over 100 years has this Court ever heretofore declared or required a small stock dividend—irrespective of what kind or class is issued—to be apportioned. The reasons are obvious and cogent. In the first place the primary object of testator's bounty is his widow or occasionally his children, in preference to his often unknown or unseen or unborn issue. To require that small stock dividends of another class or another corporation belong to principal vitiates testator's dominant intent. To hold that these and all small stock dividends should be apportioned between the life tenant and the remainderman (as appellee urges) is ridiculous. They have a market value (sometimes) of $2 or $5 or $19 a share. Such an apportionment rule would multiply litigation; it would be so costly, vexatious and wasteful that it would deplete large estates and virtually ruin small estates; and to express it mildly, it would be obviously impractical, unrealistic and unwise!

The majority opinion declares that an extraordinary stock dividend of 50% is not an apportionable event and therefore the dividend belongs to principal, even though 62% of the dividend represented earnings which had accumulated since the acquisition of the stock by the trustee. In this conclusion the majority is supported by their majority opinion in the very recent case of Cunningham Estate, 1959, 395 Pa. 1, 149 A.2d 72. However, they have now repudiated and impliedly overruled Cunningham Estate. I pointed out in great detail in my concurring and dissenting opinion in Cunningham Estate, 395 Pa. at pages 15 to 62, 149 A.2d at pages 80–103 that where, as here, an extraordinary stock dividend is paid out of accumulated applicable earnings which were earned and accumulated since the acquisition of the stock (in the instant case 62% of the stock dividend was legally authorized and issued by virtue of a transfer *from earned surplus* to the capital stock account and only 38% of the capital surplus was applied to support the stock dividend), that part which represents accumulated and paid out earnings, (viz., 62% of the dividend) belongs to the life tenant. I cited therein a myriad of cases which supported this proposition. I am convinced that this was and should be the law and since Cunningham Estate has been overruled, I would award 62% of the stock dividend to the life tenant.

The majority further affirms that the life tenant is not entitled to any portion of the proceeds of sale of the stock of the American Gas Company which was sold at a market value loss, even though part of the proceeds included in the sale price were due to and represented accumulated capitalized applicable earnings.

The majority reach their conclusion in re the 50% stock dividend and the proceeds of sale, by expressly overruling Crawford Estate, 362 Pa. 458, 67 A.2d 124; Pew Estate, 362 Pa. 468, 67 A.2d 129; and Warden Trust, 382 Pa. 311, 115 A.2d 159; and impliedly and necessarily their most recent opinion in Cunningham Estate, 1959, 395 Pa. 1, 149 A.2d 72 supra. The rationale of the majority decision—"convenience"—is something I cannot appreciate or approve. The majority not only repudiate the 100 year old Pennsylvania rule of apportionment which was unanimously reaffirmed approximately one year ago, but they further declare that what this Court repeatedly said was unconstitutional, was constitutional and vice versa. The Pennsylvania rule of apportionment which often is difficult to work out or apply practically, has always been an equitable rule intended to favor the life tenant (widow or children) who are almost always the primary objects of the testator's bounty. The rule says, in substance, that when an *extraordinary* stock dividend is paid or a *sale* is made which represents, in part, earnings which had accumulated from the time the stock was acquired—the earnings, no matter in what form they are given by a corporation or are hidden in a sale, belong to the life tenant. Every year, since Crawford Estate was decided in 362 Pa. (1949) the Supreme Court has been asked to overrule it, and every year the Supreme Court has rejected all such pleas, arguments and contentions. It rejected it in Steele Estate, 377 Pa. 250, 103 A.2d 409; it rejected it in Warden Trust, 382 Pa. 311, 115 A.2d 159; it rejected it in Jones Estate, 377 Pa. 473, 105 A.2d 353; and within the last two years it again rejected it in Cunningham Estate, 395 Pa. 1, 149 A.2d 72, supra. Each of these cases, as well as many others which were cited or quoted in my Cunningham opinion, reaffirmed the equitable rule of apportionment which, I repeat, has been the law of Pennsylvania for over 100 years. Every member of the present Court (except the recently elected Justice Eagen) who is now voting to repudiate Cunningham Estate, voted in that recent case in favor of the Pennsylvania rule of apportionment and rejected all pleas to change the rule and overrule the prior decisions of this court. Justice Benjamin R. Jones, speaking for the majority, and on this point for the entire Court, decreed that *there should be an apportionment* between principal and income in the following four situations:

> "* * * '(1) the distribution by the corporation of an *extraordinary* cash or *stock dividend*, or (2) the liquidation of the corporation, or (3) a *sale* of the stock by the trustees, or (4) the issuance of stock rights [citing cases].' In re Jones Estate, 377 Pa. 473, 476, 105 A.2d 353, 354."

Since Crawford Estate in 1949, and certainly in the last two years since Cunningham Estate in 1959, there has been no change of circumstances; not even a change of personnel in the Court; nothing, absolutely nothing, has occurred except a change of mind. Once again I plaintively ask: Stare Decisis—"Quo Vadis?"

MUSMANNO, J., joins in this concurring and dissenting opinion.

TAIT v. PECK

Supreme Judicial Court of Massachusetts, 1963.
346 Mass. 521, 194 N.E.2d 707, 98 A.L.R.2d 503.[31]

[Settlor established a living trust in 1935, naming his wife (Letitia M. Tait) as life beneficiary with remainder over to others. He transferred to trustees 100 shares of Linden Associates, a mutual investment trust, stating that if Linden was liquidated the trustees were to receive the distributive share in the assets "properly allocable to them" to pay over the net income therefrom monthly to his wife. Settlor died in 1940 and in 1961 all of the assets of Linden were sold to Broad Street Investment Corporation, a mutual investment trust subject to the operation of the Investment Company Act of 1940 as amended and so classified for tax purposes under the Internal Revenue Code. Linden was liquidated following this sale. Trustees received 55,434 shares of Broad Street in exchange for their Linden shares. Thereafter Broad Street paid the trustees two cash dividends from income and then in December 1961 delivered to trustees 1,463 additional shares of Broad Street as "distributions of gain" as distin-

31. Noted, 16 Baylor Law Rev. 79 (1964); [1964] Duke L.J. 650.

guished from "dividend from income" on the shares the trustees then held. Under I.R.C.(1954) § 852 (26 U.S.C.A.), trustees must pay a Federal capital gains tax on these shares.[32] Trustees paid to the life beneficiary the dividends from income paid by Broad Street but refuse to transfer to her the 1,463 shares. The 1,463 shares were paid to the trustees at their request and at their option they could have received these shares in cash. The life beneficiary now seeks a declaratory decree that the distribution of capital gains is to be treated as income of the trust.] [33]

* * * Before SPALDING, WHITTEMORE, CUTTER and REARDON, JJ.

CUTTER, JUSTICE. * * * No party contends that the inter vivos trust shows what the settlor's intent was with respect to capital gains dividends. There are no special provisions concerning the allocation of receipts as between principal and income. Cf. Dumaine v. Dumaine, 301 Mass. 214, 222–224, 16 N.E.2d 625, 118 A.L.R. 834. Because the original trust fund consisted of shares of Linden, there may be (wholly apart from the usual investment powers of a trustee in Massachusetts) special indication of the settlor's approval of investment trust shares as a trust investment. See Loring, Trustee's Handbook (Farr Rev.) § 81. The settlor included in the trust no discretionary power to expend principal for the widow, which would have been a natural provision for him to make if he had intended that she be given more than the normal benefits afforded to a life beneficiary. Beyond these slight indications of the settlor's views, interpretation of the trust instrument seems to us to be of no assistance. See Scott, Trusts (2d ed.) § 236.3, pp. 1819–1821.

The usual Massachusetts rule for the allocation of dividends was stated in Minot v. Paine, 99 Mass. 101, 108, "A trustee needs some plain principle to guide him; and the cestuis que trust ought not to be subjected to the expense of going behind the action of the directors, and investigating the concerns of the corporation, especially if it is out of our jurisdiction. A simple rule is, to regard cash dividends,

32. By IRC § 852(b)(3) (26 U.S.C.A.) as amended P.L. 94–455 § 1402 (1976) a capital gain dividend is treated by shareholders of an investment company as a gain from the sale or exchange of a capital asset if held more than 1 year.

33. Each share in the mutual investment trust represents a share in the ownership of a number of diversified companies so that the investor has a broad spread of risk and the benefit of general investment management of the fund. The trust derives earnings from net income on dividends and interest and from net profits realized on the sale of investments. Broad Street pays its dividends from net income quarterly and distributions of gain realized on sale of investments are paid at the end of each year. Since 1945, except for 1949, Broad Street paid dividends from income. It has paid distributions of capital gain to its shareholders, either in stock or in cash at their option except in 1936, 1937 and 1944. In these years capital gain distributions were paid in cash. On 5 December 1961 there was a distribution of 14¢ per share as "dividends from income" and a distribution of "distributions of gain" of the equivalent of 39¢ per share. Prior to the distribution the bid price of a share was $15.32. Immediately thereafter the bid price was $14.77. The bid price per share is obtained by dividing the net assets of the company by the number of outstanding shares. A roughly comparable decrease was experienced in the asking price. The asking price is determined by adding to the bid price 7½% of the offering price.

however large, as income, and stock dividends, however made, as capital." See Lyman v. Pratt, 183 Mass. 58, 60, 66 N.E. 423. This simple rule, in practice, has come to be based in some degree, in certain instances, upon the substance, rather than the form alone, of the transaction as carried out by the entity declaring the dividend. See Newhall, Settlement of Estates (4th ed.) §§ 446–447; Scott, Trusts (2d ed.) §§ 236, 236.3, 236.4, 236.5, 236.7, 236.10, 236.11, 236.14; Bogert, Trusts and Trustees (2d ed.) §§ 846, 850; Loring, Trustee's Handbook (Farr Rev.) §§ 100, 103, 104. See also Third Natl. Bank & Trust Co. v. Campbell, 336 Mass. 352, 354–355, 145 N.E.2d 703; Flickinger, A Trustee's Nightmare: Allocation of Stock Dividend between Income and Principal, 43 B.U.L.Rev. 199. Dividends in cash in substance paid out of capital or in liquidation have been treated as belonging to principal. See Heard v. Eldredge, 109 Mass. 258, 260; Anderson v. Bean, 272 Mass. 432, 441–444, 172 N.E. 647, 72 A.L.R. 959. See also Restatement 2d: Trusts, § 236(e) and (f), and comments w and x. Cf. Hemenway v. Hemenway, 181 Mass. 406, 410–411, 63 N. E. 919; Lannin v. Buckley, 256 Mass. 78, 84, 152 N.E. 71. The substance of a transaction has been examined to determine whether it was equivalent to a stock dividend. D'Ooge v. Leeds, 176 Mass. 558, 565, 57 N.E. 1025. See Coolidge v. Grant, 251 Mass. 352, 354–355, 146 N.E. 719. Cf. Gray v. Hemenway, 212 Mass. 239, 241–242, 98 N. E. 789; Gray v. Hemenway, 268 Mass. 515, 518–519, 168 N.E. 102. Where the trustee, as shareholder, is given the option to receive a dividend in stock or in cash, the later cases, in effect, treat the dividend as a cash dividend and as income. Smith v. Cotting, 231 Mass. 42, 48–49, 120 N.E. 177. See Newhall, Settlement of Estates (4th ed.) § 447, pp. 164–168 (but cf. Daland v. Williams, 101 Mass. 571, 573–574; Rand v. Hubbell, 115 Mass. 461, 476–478). See also Restatement 2d: Trusts, § 236(c) and comment u; Scott, Trusts (2d ed.) § 236.4, pp. 1821–1822; Bogert, Trusts and Trustees (2d ed.) § 846. We look at the substance of the capital gain distribution made by Broad Street in December, 1961, against the background of these authorities. No prior Massachusetts case has presented the question whether such a distribution, received by a trustee, is to be treated as capital or income.

Decisions outside of Massachusetts have generally treated such capital gain dividends as income rather than principal. See Rosenburg v. Lombardi, 222 Md. 346, 350–353, 160 A.2d 601; Briel v. Moody, 77 N.J.Super. 306, 309, 186 A.2d 314; Matter of Byrne, 192 Misc. 451, 81 N.Y.S.2d 23; Matter of Bruce, 192 Misc. 523, 527–528, 81 N.Y.S.2d 25; Lovett Estate (No. 2), 78 Pa.Dist. & Co. 21, 25. See also Coates v. Coates, 304 S.W.2d 874, 876 (Mo.); Matter of Appleby, 15 Misc.2d 200, 204–208, 175 N.Y.S.2d 176. Cf. Re Whitehead's Will Trusts, [1959] 1 Ch. 579, 591–592. The Maryland case to a considerable extent (see 222 Md. pp. 349, 353, 160 A.2d p. 603) turns upon "analysis of previous decisions of" that court, not relating to regulated investment companies, holding that "moneys arising from the sale of corporate property * * * and distributed as a cash or stock dividend are income if they arise from a sale of property made by the corporation in the ordinary course of its business, when it sells only such property as it is its regular business to sell." The force of the New York cases, as a precedent for out of state guidance, has been somewhat diminished by the recent statutory reversal of the rule announced in those decisions. See N.Y.Sess.Laws, 1963, c. 1005, § 3, effective June 1, 1964.[34] The other cases do not give comprehensive consideration to the novel problems presented by the capital gains distributions of regulated investment companies.

Some commentators have felt that dividends from net capital gains from the sales of securities held in a mutual fund's portfolio are income from the ordinary conduct of the fund's business, that the portfolio holdings are bought and sold like inventory or other corporate property of a business corporation, and that distributions from such gains, at least where there is opportunity to receive the distribution in cash, should be treated as income.[35] Weight is given by these commentators to the circumstance that investors in investment companies rely on both income and capital gains as a part of the expected yield. It is suggested by at least one author (Professor Bogert) that to invest in mutual funds would be a breach of trust, about which the life beneficiary could complain, unless the investment produced a normal trust investment yield. The contrary view [36] is that the sale of a security in an investment company portfolio involves the sale of a capital item, so that, if the gain is distributed the capital is necessarily reduced. In some years such a company may experience net losses. It is argued that if capital gain distributions of other years have been paid to the income beneficiary, the trust principal will inev-

34. New York has adopted the Uniform Principal and Income Act (1962). McKinney's N.Y., EPTL, § 11–2.1(e)(7 and 8) now provide:

"(7) Distributions made from ordinary income by a regulated investment company or by a trust qualifying and electing under federal law to be taxed as a real estate investment trust are income. All other distributions made by such company or trust, including distributions from capital gains, depreciation or depletion, whether in the form of cash or an option to take new shares or cash or an option to purchase additional shares, are principal.

"(8) If the distributing corporation or association gives a shareholder an option to receive a distribution, whether in the form of cash or its own shares or cash or an option to purchase new shares, the distribution chosen is income."

[Footnotes 35 through 39 are by the Court.]

35. See Bogert, Trusts and Trustees (2d ed.) § 858; Cohan and Dean, Legal, Tax and Accounting Aspects of Fiduciary Apportionment of Stock Proceeds: The Non-Statutory Pennsylvania Rules. 106 U. of P.L.Rev. 157, 181–183; Putney, Capital Gain Dividends, 95 Trusts and Estates 22; Young, A Dissent on Capital Gain Distribution, 88 Trusts and Estates 280, More About Capital Gains, 88 Trusts and Estates 467. Cf. Rogers, Capital Gain Dividends—A Suggestion for Draftsmen, 20 Fordham L.Rev. 79, who proposes meeting the problem by appropriate drafting of trust instruments, see also 90 Trusts and Estates 300.

36. Shattuck, Capital Gain Distributions, Principal or Income? 88 Trusts and Estates 160, 429. See discussion of Revised Uniform Principal and Income Act, in which Professor Scott participated, 101 Trusts and Estates 894, 897. He there is quoted as saying that it is unknown whether capital gains distributions of regulated investment companies "are income or principal under the present [a]ct," i.e. the uniform act prior to the 1962 revision * * *, but he went on to say, "The revised draft has adopted the proper rule." See doubts expressed about some of the cases from other jurisdictions cited above, Scott, Trusts (2d ed.) § 236.14 at pp. 1844–1845. The need of a clear rule is obvious. See Loring, Trustee's Handbook (Farr Rev.) § 100, pp. 258–259.

itably suffer in years of losses, which must be expected even in an era generally inflationary, so that, in effect, the investment company shares may become a wasting investment. It is also urged that a trustee's investment in an investment company is in substance nothing more than a fractional ownership in a diversified portfolio of securities, as to which the trustee should account as if he held the portfolio securities directly. The special character of regulated investment companies and their specialized tax treatment under the Internal Revenue Code also have some tendency to give capital gains distributions the aspect of principal.

If the dividends and distributions of a regulated investment company should be regarded as inherently the same as those of an ordinary industrial company, then the rule of Smith v. Cotting, 231 Mass. 42, 48–49, 120 N.E. 177, should be applied to Broad Street's 1961 capital gain distribution, which the trustees, at their option, could have received either in cash or in shares. It seems to us, however, that, when a fiduciary invests in investment company shares, he is entering into an arrangement more closely like participation in a common trust fund (see G.L. c. 203A) than like an investment in the shares of an industrial company. His purpose generally will be to obtain for his trust beneficiaries (usually of a small trust) the same type of spread of investment risk which the trustee of a common trust fund can obtain for its participating trusts, or which the trustee of a large trust fund can obtain by a well conceived program of diversified direct investment.[37]

The arguments against the soundness of the analogy between investments in mutual funds and in a common trust fund (see e.g. Bogert, Trusts and Trustees [2d ed.] § 858, pp. 557–558, and The Revised Uniform Principal and Income Act, 38 Notre Dame Lawyer, 50, 54–55) are to us unconvincing. It may be a sound reason for a trustee to refrain from investing in investment company shares that the return from dividends paid from ordinary income of such companies is low, so that the life beneficiary will suffer unless he receives also the capital gain distribution. It may be also that appropriate downward adjustment in the rate of trustee's fees should be made, if he invests substantially in investment company shares (because he is not burdened with investment management), with the consequence that the income return to the life beneficiary will be improved pro tanto. See discussion in Scott, Trusts (2d ed.) § 227.9A; Bogert, Trusts and Trustees (2d ed.) § 679, pp. 311–313. These matters we need not determine. The possible meager return does not change the substance of the investment as a reasonable attempt at risk diversification similar to that of the common trust fund. To say that the realized gains of a common trust fund are not distributed to the participating trust,

37. Broad Street as of December 31, 1962, is reported by a standard manual to have had $249,079,948, invested in the common shares of 99 companies, in the preferred shares of seven companies, and in the bonds of twenty-four companies, plus some government bonds. See Wiesenberger, Investment Companies (1963 ed.) part 5, p. 12. Such an investment diversification could not possibly be directly achieved by any trustee unless the trust res was extraordinarily large.

whereas those of an investment company are distributed (primarily for tax reasons) to fiduciaries who are shareholders, is merely to state the obvious fact that a common trust is administered by the trustee itself, whereas the regulated investment company is a separate entity from the trustee who invests in its shares. If a trustee elects to take shares of the investment company in payment of any distribution made to him of capital gains, he will be able to achieve the same substantive result as that achieved by the common trust fund.

The method of determining the purchase and sale prices of investment company shares [fn. 33 supra—Ed.], in relation to the net asset value of shares, is consistent with the concept that the trustee is obtaining diversification by an indirect participation in the investment company's portfolio. It is apparent that if a fiduciary were to redeem his shares at a profit just before a capital gain distribution, he would necessarily allocate any gain to principal. No practical reason requires treating the capital gain distribution, when made, in any different way, or prevents retaining it as a part of the principal of the trust.

One major virtue of our Massachusetts rule for allocation between principal and income has been its simplicity as a rule of convenience. See Minot v. Paine, 99 Mass. 101, 108; Third Natl. Bank & Trust Co. v. Campbell, 336 Mass. 352, 354–355, 145 N.E.2d 703. To treat capital gains distributions of registered investment companies as principal will not impair the simplicity of our rule, for no inquiry need be made as to the source of the distribution. The source must be announced,[38] as it was in respect of Broad Street's capital gain distribution in December, 1961.

Since no binding precedent controls our decision, we are guided by the substance of the situation. We adopt the rule that distributions by a regulated investment company, from capital gains (whether made in the form of cash or shares or an option to take or purchase new shares), are to be allocated to principal. This is essentially the view adopted by the Commissioners on Uniform State Laws in 1962 after full deliberation. The Commissioners' action can be taken as reflecting a considered current view of what is in the public interest.[39] In effect, we think that the regulated company, from the standpoint of a trustee investing in its shares, is merely a conduit of

38. Section 19 of the Investment Company Act of 1940, 15 U.S.C. § 80a–19 (1958), makes it unlawful for any registered investment company to make any distribution from any source other than—"(1) such company's accumulated undistributed net income, determined in accordance with good accounting practice *and not including profits or losses realized upon the sale of securities or other properties;* or (2) such company's net income *so determined* for the current or preceding fiscal years; unless such payment is accompanied by a written statement which adequately discloses the *source* * * * of such payment * * *" (emphasis supplied).

39. Because there has been reasonable doubt until this decision of what our rule was, it is probable that trustees' allocations in good faith of such distributions to income, if already completed, cannot fairly be said to have been improper or to constitute a breach of trust. It is not necessary for us to decide this question on this record.

its realized gains to the trust fund and that, in the hands of the trustee, the gains should retain their character as principal.

A decree is to be entered in the Probate Court (a) that the distribution of capital gains by Broad Street in December, 1961, in the hands of the trustees of the settlor's trust is to be treated as principal and not as income, and (b) that future similar distributions to the trustees of capital gains by Broad Street also are to be allocated to principal. Costs and expenses of this appeal are to be in the discretion of the Probate Court.

So ordered.

AMERICAN SECURITY & TRUST CO. v. FROST

United States Court of Appeals for the District of Columbia, 1940.
73 App.D.C. 75, 117 F.2d 283.
Cert. den. 312 U.S. 707, 61 S.Ct. 829, 85 L.Ed. 1139.

Before GRONER, CHIEF JUSTICE, and STEPHENS and RUTLEDGE, ASSOCIATE JUSTICES.

GRONER, C. J. The appeal is from a decree of the District Court construing a will and ordering distribution of certain proceeds of testatrix' estate as "income" to the life beneficiaries of a residuary trust rather than as principal to be added to the corpus.

The will, executed December 30, 1935, is that of Mary Harlan Lincoln, who died March 31, 1937, leaving two daughters, two grandsons, and one granddaughter. After various specific provisions, the will created a residuary trust with three trustees, the income to go to the children and grandchildren for life, and the corpus ultimately to be distributed to any direct descendants of the testatrix living at the time specified for its final distribution to them. If there were no such descendants at that time, the corpus was to be divided among the First Church of Christ Scientist in Boston, the American Red Cross, and Iowa Wesleyan College. Item Eleventh of the will authorized the executors and trustees "To retain as part of the principal of the trust estate hereby created any shares of stock or bonds or other investments of which I may be possessed at the time of my demise; to decide finally any question that may arise as to what constitutes income and what principal,—it being my wish, however, that whenever feasible their decision be in favor of the life beneficiaries named herein; * * *." The issues relate to the applicability of this provision to two items of assets of the estate, consisting of "administration income" and stock dividends.

To pay funeral expenses, debts, legacies, taxes and costs of administration, the executors sold during the course of administration securities which yielded $835,715.28. Prior to sale, these securities produced an income of $38,018.84. During the administration the estate also received 500 shares of new common stock in the Continental Illinois National Bank and Trust Company as a 25 per cent dividend on the 2,000 shares of the bank's common stock held by testatrix at the time of her death.

The testatrix nominated the American Security and Trust Company, Norman B. Frost, and Frederic N. Towers, as executors and trustees under the will, and they have qualified and are acting as such. The corporate trustee is the appellant, and the individual trustees are appellees.

The two individual executors and trustees, Frost and Towers, decided that the $38,018.84 and the 500 shares of stock were income which should be distributed to the life beneficiaries. The trust company disagreed, and contended that the property should be added to the corpus of the trust. As the trust company declined to join in a proceeding to obtain instructions from the court, it was made a defendant in this action in which the individual trustees ask that the court construe the will with particular reference to the power therein conferred upon the executors thereof and trustees thereunder to decide finally any question that may arise as to what constitutes income and what principal. A special master found that the $38,018.84 was "income," but that the 500 shares of stock were "principal." The trial court approved the master's findings as to the $38,018.84, but held that the 500 shares of stock also should be distributed to the life beneficiaries. The trust company is the only appellant.

The question is whether, considered in connection with the whole will, Item Eleventh empowers the trustees to allocate the funds and stock in question to the life beneficiaries as income.

When the will is entirely silent on what shall constitute corpus and what income, contains no provision as to how that question shall be determined, and merely directs that income be distributed in one manner and corpus in another, the question is determined in accordance with rules of construction established by law. Thus, in such a case, it has long been the established law of the District of Columbia that stock dividends shall be distributed as corpus. Gibbons v. Mahon, 136 U.S. 549, 10 S.Ct. 1057, 34 L.Ed. 525; Lanston v. Lanston, 53 App.D.C. 340, 290 F. 315. And since Proctor v. American Securities & Trust Co., 69 App.D.C. 70, 98 F.2d 599, it has been settled that "administration income" shall be disposed of likewise.

While it is true these are rules of construction, it is also true they are rules which affect the disposition of property by will in the District of Columbia and as such must control whenever appropriate in the interest of certainty. Testatrix was a resident of the District, and her will was prepared by experienced counsel. She is presumed to have been familiar with the fact that certain rules had been announced and would be adopted from time to time with respect to the disposition of various items in the administration of trusts. She is also presumed to have intended these rules to govern in the interpretation of her will unless she expressed a contrary intention.

The conceded facts demonstrate that the particular stock dividend in question, as well as the administrative fund, under the settled rules to which we have just referred, constitute corpus and not income unless a contrary intention appears from the whole will or unless the language in paragraph 11 is held to confer on the trustees discretionary power to reach a different result. We are of opinion neither of these conditions exists. * * *

There is nothing in any of these clauses which even suggests an intention to depart from the rules which we have shown to exist in the District of Columbia. Whatever contrary intent exists—if it exists at all—must be found in Clause 11, and we shall, therefore, confine ourselves to considering the effect of the words of that paragraph, which gives the trustees power "to decide finally any question that may arise as to what constitutes income and what principal".

The learned trial judge was of opinion that the quoted language was sufficiently broad to permit, in the discretion of the trustees, the distribution of the "fund" and the "dividend" among the life beneficiaries. He conceded that to do this would involve a determination contrary to a local rule of construction, but was of opinion the rule should yield to the expressed intention of the testatrix. While without doubt that view would be correct in a proper case, we nevertheless think that his interpretation of the language of the paragraph is too broad. To say that Clause 11 empowers the trustees to "decide" contrary to local "rules of construction", proves too much. In a sense, every item of property is controlled by a "rule of construction." E.g., bonds received from the original estate would be corpus, the interest on those bonds, income. This is a "rule of construction" derived from the customs of the community. Surely, it would not be said that under the power given in Mrs. Lincoln's will, the trustees could override this rule. And yet if they may override some rules of construction and not others, there would be complicated questions of degree, e.g., whether one rule or another was so certain that the trustees must not overstep it. We think the will was intended to be more certain than this. It does not empower the trustees to decide what is income and what is principal, but only to decide "any question" that may arise in that respect. Doubtless a question may arise in respect to many items on the borderline, but a "question" should not and cannot arise except where there is a reasonable doubt. Where, as in the instant case, the exact status of the "fund" and of the dividend has been determined by judicial decisions, no question can arise because there is no proper place for doubt. To say in such circumstances that the trustees are authorized to assume a doubt where there is none and thus to declare something to be income which under judicial decisions is principal, would open the whole will to such revision and change as they might think wise or desirable. The correct rule to be followed is stated by a New York court in Matter of Talbot's Estate, 170 Misc. 138, 9 N.Y.S.2d 806, 812. In that case power was given the trustees "to determine" whether any moneys, stocks, or securities received by them were to be considered as capital or income. The purpose of the trust was to maintain a farm as a vacation spot for children. The corpus was insufficient to maintain the project. The trustees held $14,000 cash "conceded to be income as a matter of fact and law". They desired instructions on whether they could "determine" this sum to be capital and so increase the corpus and carry out the project. In answering this, the court said: "In the first paragraph of clause 'twelfth' the trustees were given authority 'to determine all questions and matters of doubt arising in the execution of the trusts'. These words indicate what the testator had in mind, when in the forepart of the same paragraph he authorized his trustees to determine whether any moneys, stocks or securities are to be considered as capital or income. In other words, we cannot assume that this testator intended to violate any of the settled rules of law in giving this authority to his trustees, but rather to authorize them to come to a conclusion upon matters of doubt, whether in the characterization of receipts of money, stocks or securities as capital or income, or in any other connection, and this determination by the trustees upon any question about which there could be reasonable doubt, arrived at genuinely and not arbitrarily [cases], would be binding upon all persons interested; * * *."

In short, the reasoning in that case was that the right to determine arises only when there is a genuine *question* as to the category in which the fund or stock, as the case may be, properly falls. In such a case under a provision like the one here the trustees might very reasonably and properly decide it, on the ground that, lacking a positive and definite guide, there is difference of opinion requiring the exercise of discretion. Numerous illustrations might easily be given of cases in which a question might properly arise, and in those instances the grant of discretion in the will would apply, but since in this jurisdiction the answer is established—in the absence of a contrary intent expressed in the will—so far as the particular fund and the particular shares of stock are concerned, obviously no proper ground is left on which to base a question and consequently no ground for the exercise of a discretion. See, also, In re Matthews' Will, 255 App. Div. 80, 5 N.Y.S.2d 707, 712.

The rule on stock dividends was established long before the transactions now involved. The rule on "administration income" was not settled by this court until about six weeks after the bill in the present case was filed. However, the logic of the decision in the Proctor case is so inescapable that we think no question could have arisen. The testatrix provided that the residue be kept intact as corpus and that only income *of the residue* be given to the life beneficiaries. Since the amount used to pay debts and legacies is not and cannot be considered part of the residue, the income thereof cannot be considered income of the residue.

Cases relied on by appellees, while interesting, are distinguishable because the power given to trustees was either expressed in terms specifically applicable to the item involved or expressed so broadly as to be practically a power of appointment.

Since we hold that the trustees had no discretion in the premises, we have not discussed the further question whether a majority of the trustees could make a binding determination, but if the question were still in the case, we should feel disposed to say that all three trustees must concur in the exercise of the power given. Winslow v. Baltimore & O. R. Co., 188 U.S. 646, 23 S.Ct. 443, 47 L.Ed. 635; Wilbur v.

Almy, 12 How. 180, 13 L.Ed. 944; Ubhoff v. Brandenburg, 26 App.D. C. 3; Colburn v. Grant, 16 App.D.C. 107, affirmed 181 U.S. 601, 21 S. Ct. 737, 45 L.Ed. 1021; Cooper v. Federal National Bank of Shawnee, 175 Okl. 610, 53 P.2d 678; Kramme v. Mewshaw, 147 Md. 535, 128 A. 468; Matter of Johnson's Will, Sur.Ct., 123 Misc. 834, 207 N.Y.S. 66; 2 Scott on Trusts, § 194; Restatement of Trusts, § 194.

Reversed; costs to be paid by the estate.

RUTLEDGE, ASSOCIATE JUSTICE (dissenting). The question is whether the testatrix intended by Item Eleventh to confer upon her trustees a narrowly limited discretion to decide only unsettled legal questions or, on the contrary, to give them a broader and more discretionary power which would permit them, to some extent, to distribute as income what would otherwise go as principal and vice versa. I think the latter was her expressed wish, from the language of the clause, its context in Item Eleventh and the will as a whole, the circumstances in which it was executed, the purposes the testatrix had in mind, and the more nearly applicable authorities. As presented here, the question is whether the testatrix intended to bind her fiduciaries' discretion by the rules of construction concerning stock dividends and administration income which would be applied if her will had been entirely silent.

These rules are not "thou shalt nots." They merely create presumptive declarations of intent when the testator omits to disclose his own. They give way to his contrary intention when he sufficiently expresses or indicates it. They afford no help as to what constitutes a sufficient expression or indication of contrary intention. That must be determined from the will and the circumstances of its execution as must any other question of intention. The will here is not silent, but the question remains whether Item Eleventh discloses an intention to permit the fiduciaries to disregard the rules of construction.

When the will directs that stock dividends or "administration income" or any other fund or property specifically described, which under the presumptive rules would go as corpus or as income, shall be distributed in a manner contrary to them, the direction is given effect. That is true also when the will empowers trustees to determine whether funds specifically designated shall be distributed as income or as principal. It is not necessary for the testator to make the decision himself. He may delegate that to others. This is analogous to what is commonly done under powers of appointment and of interpretation. So long therefore as the testator specifies the particular funds which shall or may be distributed contrary to the rules of presumption, the will rather than the rules controls.

But when the will omits to specify the particular assets, and makes the direction or creates the power generally, there is more difficulty. No doubt the testator might direct that all income, except specified funds, be distributed as corpus, or vice versa, and thus achieve a form of generality which would be effective. But if no funds or property are specifically described, whether by way of direction or of exception to it, the generality of the power raises difficulties like those which appear in Boyden v. Stevens, 1934, 285 Mass. 176, 188 N.E. 741. However, under the more persuasive and conclusive authorities, these difficulties do not nullify the power or require that it be whittled down to the narrowest possible scope.

* * *

The case which most closely resembles the present one in its facts, including the language of the empowering provision and issues of law, is Dumaine v. Dumaine, 1938, 301 Mass. 214, 16 N.E.2d 625, 626, 118 A.L.R. 834. The provision of the will in issue was: "The trustee under this instrument shall have full power and discretion *to determine* whether *any money or other property* received by him *is principal or income* without being answerable to any person for the manner in which he shall exercise that discretion." (Italics supplied.) The trustee, under power granted by another provision, had sold certain shares of stock at a profit over their cost. He sought instructions whether he could distribute this profit, under the quoted provision, to the life beneficiaries under the trust. By the established law of Massachusetts, gains resulting from the purchase and sale of securities composing the corpus of a trust were accretions belonging to the principal of the trust fund, rather than income, for purposes of distribution as between life beneficiaries and remaindermen. As stated by the court, the remaindermen did not "argue that a settlor has no power to confer a discretion upon his trustees to determine what is income and what is principal, but do contend that, under the trust instrument in question, the trustee has no power to determine, contrary to established rules of law in this Commonwealth, what money or other property received by him as trustee is principal or income." 16 N.E.2d at 628–629.

The argument, identical with that made here, was rejected. The court said: " 'Full power and discretion' to determine whether any money or other property received by the trustee is principal or income, in the light of attendant circumstances and the language of the trust instrument as a whole, would have little significance if construed to mean a discretion so to determine *only in cases where there is no settled law to guide.* * * * The court may properly have in mind that, when a settlor reposes a discretion in a trustee, he does so because *he desires the honest judgment of the trustee, perhaps even to the exclusion of that of the court.*" (Italics supplied.) 16 N.E.2d 629.

It is clear from these authorities that specification of particular funds or property is not necessary to rebut the presumptions applied when the will is entirely silent and make the power effective as to assets within the presumptive rules. The testator or settlor indicates his intention that they shall not apply by a general power to distribute principal as income and vice versa, to decide what is principal or income, or to determine whether any money or property is principal or income. If therefore Item Eleventh created a power of this general character, the presumptions prevailing in the District concerning stock dividends, and "administration income" have no application. In my judgment, it had this effect.

As the majority note, the will was drawn by experienced and able attorneys. They have become the testatrix' individual fiduciaries. She directed that they also be employed as counsel during the administration of her estate and of the trusts created by the will because they "through long and intimate knowledge of my affairs and those of my family are best fitted to undertake this responsibility," and carry out the terms of her will. The language of the clause is not narrow. It nowhere limits the "question" committed to the fiduciaries to questions of law. Had this been intended, it would have been simple and obvious to say so. The language is: "to decide finally any question that may arise as to what constitutes income and what principal." It is general, not limited or particular. It is coupled with a precatory direction that the question be decided "whenever feasible * * * in favor of the life-beneficiaries." These are words of broad discretion, not of narrow limitation.

This appears also from the context of the clause in Item Eleventh. The Item confers on the fiduciaries highly discretionary powers—to mortgage and sell real estate, and the whole or any part of the residuary estate; to fix the terms and conditions of sale "as they may think fit and proper"; to invest and reinvest the proceeds; and "to do all other acts and things whatsoever that may be necessary and proper in carrying out the terms" of the will. These broad powers were given by their author "not intending, however, by the giving of specific powers to limit those of a general nature." They involved matters of high business judgment, not merely technical or doubtful legal questions. In the midst of them, the clause in question appears. It is in strange company, if unlike them in scope. It marches as a pygmy among giants or as an equal with them. In my judgment, it is with comrades.

Purpose and circumstance also point to the same conclusion. Two things the testatrix had in mind when she included this clause with the others: (1) to avoid litigation; (2) to favor her life beneficiaries so far as possible. The latter was dominant throughout the will. The life beneficiaries were the primary objects of the testatrix' bounty, as shown by the facts surrounding the will's execution, the general scheme of bequests and devises, and her expressed favoritism for them. All were children or grandchildren, of middle age or beyond and without direct descendants capable of taking the corpus, and possibility of issue was remote though not absolutely extinct. The corporate remaindermen were only contingently so. The testatrix was not attempting to protect them to the utmost extent. The exact contrary was the case. They were not the natural or nearest objects of her bounty. When the will was executed, it was highly probable that the corpus of the trust would go eventually to them. In these circumstances it is more consonant with the testatrix' emphatically expressed preference for the life beneficiaries and her desire to avoid litigation to construe the broad language of the clause to mean, not the narrow power to decide merely unsettled questions of law, but the discretionary one to make effective as wide a favoritism to her nearest kin as could be accomplished without undue injury to the estate and destruction of the general scheme of gifts. So construed, the clause would confer upon the exercise of the trustees' discretion the finality intended by the testatrix, since litigation could be successful only by showing an abuse of their discretion. On the other hand, the opposite construction leaves open the possibility of litigation, since the question whether there is an unsettled legal question is not one upon which disagreement is either impossible or infrequent. And it leaves little which the clause can accomplish by way of favoring the life beneficiaries.

The broader construction would not give the fiduciaries power to destroy the trust by converting income to principal and vice versa in their uncontrolled desire or whim. Such an argument was advanced and rejected in Dumaine v. Dumaine, supra. The court refused to infer that the power was so unlimited, but it also declined to emasculate the trustee's authority by bounding it with the settled rules of presumption. It found the limitations upon the trustees' discretion, not in the rules applicable when the will is silent, but in their obligation "to exercise a 'sound judgment and a reasonable and prudent discretion,' Appeal of Davis, Appellant, 183 Mass. 499, 502, 67 N.E. 604, 605; that kind of 'power and discretion which inheres in a fiduciary relation and not that illimitable potentiality which an unrestrained individual possesses respecting his own property * * *.'" 16 N.E.2d 629. It is not necessary to state the ultimate limits of reasonableness beyond which the fiduciaries may not go; but their discretion must be exercised in a manner consistent with their fiduciary obligation, which requires not only informed and considered judgment rather than caprice, but due consideration for the preservation of the estate and of the general scheme of gifts, the interests of all concerned in the distribution, and the testatrix' wishes in relation to particular funds or property, as determined in the light of their long familiarity with her affairs and desires. These conditions being fulfilled, the courts consistently refuse to interfere with the decisions made by the trustees,[40] when as here the direction is that their decision shall be final, recognizing that the very purpose of the settlor is to substitute their discretion for that of the courts.

40. [The following is part of a footnote by Justice Rutledge; other footnotes to his dissenting opinion have been omitted.]

It may be that under no circumstances could the fiduciaries distribute the original shares of stock as income or cash dividends as corpus. No question has arisen concerning such items. In the absence of specific enumeration in the will some things are and always have been so clearly corpus or income that no course of litigation has been needed to establish presumptive rules concerning them. On the other hand, other assets, including stock dividends, "administration income," and gains made on the sale of securities, have required long courses of litigation to establish their presumptive character, often with diverse results in different jurisdictions. Possibly the line could be drawn reasonably between these two groups of assets, if it were necessary to hold that what may be called basic corpus could not be distributed as income, though that which by adjudication has become presumptively such could be.

I think, therefore, that the broader construction, which gives the fiduciaries discretionary, but not unlimited, power is the one intended by the testatrix, and this view seems to me to be supported by the language of the clause, its context in Item Eleventh and in the will, its paramount purposes of avoiding litigation and favoring the life beneficiaries, by the circumstances surrounding the execution of the will, and by the more pertinent authorities. The opposite view emphasizes the words "question * * * may arise" at the expense of the remaining language of the clause, disregards the testatrix' expressed confidence in the business judgment of her individual fiduciaries, narrowly restricts their discretion under the clause, and thereby defeats both her purpose of favoring the life beneficiaries widely, and that of avoiding litigation. It may be added also that it is more than questionable whether the testatrix intended to bind her fiduciaries by a rule of construction (that relating to "administration income") which was not settled in this jurisdiction until long after her will became operative and her estate was in course of administration.

The view which I have taken, if accepted, would require consideration of the further question whether, upon the facts disclosed, the fiduciaries have exercised their discretion. I think there could be little doubt that they have done so as to the fund derived from "administration income," since the corporate trustee has indicated that it would exercise its discretion in favor of the life beneficiaries if it should be held that it has such discretionary power.

As to the stock dividends, however, it has indicated no such concurrence and the question would remain whether the trustees' discretion can be exercised by a majority of them or requires the concurrence of all. I do not regard Ubhoff v. Brandenburg, 1905, 26 App.D.C. 3, as foreclosing or deciding this question, since in that case all of the trustees had concurred in the action taken and the statement that less than all could not act was purely dictum. The formerly prevailing rule in other jurisdictions requiring unanimous action, except where modified by the terms of the trust or by statute, has been changed by statute in some jurisdictions, and the Uniform Trusts Act, § 11, adopted in 1937 by the National Conference of Commissioners on Uniform State Laws and since then by two states, provides that "unless it is otherwise provided by the trust instrument, or an amendment thereof, or by court order, any power vested in three or more trustees may be exercised by a majority of such trustees." The old rule has been criticized as a survival of "medieval land law relating to joint tenancy," not "necessary or convenient in modern conditions." I therefore regard this question as undetermined for this jurisdiction, and express no opinion concerning it.

But in my judgment Item Eleventh by clear implication modifies the rule of unanimity, if it exists, both in specifying that the trustees' decision shall be final and that "whenever feasible" it shall be exercised "in favor of the life-beneficiaries." These directions are more clearly consistent with action of the majority than with requiring unanimity, subject to the right of the dissenting trustee to show that the majority have acted in abuse of the trustees' discretion. In the absence of such a showing, to require unanimous action would create the litigation which the power was designed to avoid, in order to escape from a stalemate or from making the minority's decision controlling; and, in that event, the discretion of the court would be substituted for that of the trustees, a consequence not consonant with the testatrix' evident intention.

I think the judgment should be affirmed.[41]

NOTE

Some corporations finance plant expansion by "ploughing back" current earnings; they adopt a deliberate dividend policy of paying low current dividends and using the accumulated cash to buy new equipment or expand physical plant. After several years, the accumulated surplus item of the balance sheet becoming unduly large, the directors convert it into capitalization by declaring a stock dividend. In essence this may be nothing but a paper transaction. For instance if it is a 100% stock dividend, the trustee holding 80 shares of stock in the corporation would receive a certificate evidencing ownership of an additional 80 shares. This is to be carefully distinguished from a dividend payable in shares of another company, since such a dividend is a distribution of assets. The directors may also convert the surplus into stock of another type than that presently held, as by declaring a dividend of preferred stock on common. In either event the income beneficiary who has been deprived of current income by the dividend policy of the corporation feels that the stock dividend received ought to be treated as income. Ideally this is true; practically it is costly and administratively difficult to determine how much of the stock dividend should be retained to keep the original capital of the trust intact and how much should be allocated to income. A classic example of this is the case of King Estate,[42] which was appealed to the Supreme Court of Pennsylvania three times before a precise application of the rule of apportionment could be worked out. The state which led in the attempt to work out equitable apportionment, Pennsylvania, abandoned it in 1947 by adopting the Uniform Principal and Income Act with some modifications. A few states still attempt apportionment. Others have held to the view that certainty and ease of administration are more important than ideal justice. The prevailing view is the so-called Massachusetts rule which treats dividends payable in newly issued shares of the corporation entirely as principal. The American Law Institute originally favored the Pennsylvania rule

41. Whether a discretionary power in the trustee to allocate items of receipts and expenditures between principal and income permits the trustee to depart from normal rules, see Note, "Principal and Income: The Discretionary Allocation Clause," 30 Baylor L.Rev. 343 (1978). Draftsmen and courts should be conscious that too much discretion may have serious tax repercussions. Thus, after a clause in a charitable remainder trust was interpreted in Estate of Gardiner, 5 Ariz.App. 239, 425 P.2d 427 (1967), to permit the fiduciary to allocate capital gain to income, the charitable deduction was denied in Gardiner v. United States, 458 F.2d 1265 (9th Cir.1972). A reverse problem exists as to a marital deduction trust where the surviving spouse must be entitled to all the income and the danger is that normal income items will be credited to capital; see Estate Tax Regs. § 20.2056(b)–5(f)(4). In Englund v. First National Bank, 381 So.2d 8 (Ala.1980), the majority held that none of capital gain could be allocated to income under a discretionary power to allocate receipts; there was a strong dissent.

42. 349 Pa. 27, 36 A.2d 504 (1944); 355 Pa. 64, 48 A.2d 858 (1946); 361 Pa. 629, 66 A.2d 68 (1949).

of apportionment in the Restatement of Trusts (1935) § 236, but it has now adopted the Massachusetts rule.[43]

This is a very brief summary of a very complex and still troublesome issue. If you are forced to litigate the issue, you will want to explore it in detail.

Liquidating dividends are, of course, distributions of capital even though payable in cash; likewise rights to subscribe to stock or other securities of the corporation are treated as principal.

American Security and Trust v. Frost also involves the disposition of certain items of probate income. The income beneficiary of a testamentary trust is entitled to receive any income actually earned by the trust corpus during the period of administration, from the date of death of the testator. When such corpus and income are turned over by the personal representative to the trustee, he is therefore charged with the duty of paying the income to the income beneficiary. Where the trust is a residuary trust, the trustee will also receive what is called "administration" or "probate" income, income earned by property subsequently used to pay legacies, debts, administration expenses and taxes. Since such income is not earned by property which clearly falls in the residue, an ambiguity exists as to whether such receipts when turned over to the residuary trustee should be allocated to corpus or income; the will of course could expressly provide for their disposition but usually does not. Although the early cases treated such receipts as properly allocable to corpus, the trend in the last decade is to treat them as payable to the income beneficiary. See Restatement, Second, Trusts § 234, Comment *g*. The Uniform Principal and Income Act (1962) § 5(b) states that income from the assets of an estate after the death of testator and before distribution shall be distributed as follows unless the will otherwise provides:[44]

> "(1) to specific legatees and devisees, the income from the property bequeathed or devised to them respectively, less taxes, ordinary repairs, and other expenses of management and operation of the property, and an appropriate portion of interest accrued since the death of the testator and of taxes imposed on income (excluding taxes on capital gains) which accrue during the period of administration;
>
> "(2) to all other legatees and devisees, except legatees of pecuniary bequests not in trust, the balance of the income, less the balance of taxes, ordinary repairs, and other expenses of management and operation of all property from which the estate is entitled to income, interest accrued since the death of the testator, and taxes imposed on income (excluding taxes on capital gains) which accrue during the period of administration, in proportion to their respective interests in the undistributed assets of the estate computed at times of distribution on the basis of inventory value.
>
> "(c) Income received by a trustee under subsection (b) shall be treated as income of the trust. * * * "

43. See, Restatement, Second, Trusts § 236.

44. 7A Uniform Laws Ann., Business and Financial Laws (1978) 429, 442. A similar provision (§ 3A) was added to the Uniform Principal and Income Act (1931) in 1958. Idem, 461, 474.

IN RE BAILEY'S TRUST

Supreme Court of Minnesota, 1954.
241 Minn. 143, 62 N.W.2d 829.

DELL, CHIEF JUSTICE. Appeal from an order of the district court allowing the accounts of trustees from January 1, 1947, to December 31, 1950, in proceedings under M.S.A. § 501.34. This matter came to the writer recently on reassignment.

The trustees who prepared and submitted the accounts in question are Vincent K. Bailey, Gordon Bailey, and Elizabeth Fritz, sons and daughter of John Vincent Bailey, deceased. The trust involved was created in and by the last will and testament of the decedent. The objectors to the accounting of the trustees are Elizabeth Anna Bailey, widow, and Virginia M. Bailey and Margaret J. Scott, daughters, of John Vincent Bailey.

For many years the above-named decedent was the sole owner and operator of a successful unincorporated wholesale nursery business at Newport, Minnesota. His will, dated August 23, 1938, after certain specific devises and bequests, placed the residue of his estate, consisting of the assets of the business, in trust for the benefit of the above-named members of his family. His sons, Vincent K. and Gordon, were named as executors in the will. The will provided for three trustees at all times. Vincent, Gordon, and Margaret were named in the original will as trustees, but Elizabeth Fritz later was substituted for Margaret under a codicil to the will. Under the terms of the will, the trustees were directed to carry on the nursery business during the lifetime of testator's wife and for a period not to exceed 20 years after her death. Under paragraph VI(10) of the will it was directed that, after the payment of the expenses of the nursery business, replenishment of emergency funds, care and maintenance of the widow, payment of indebtedness of the business, investment of earnings or capital in the business, and payment of debts left by decedent and all other disbursements deemed necessary or advantageous by the trustees, the remaining net income, if any, be paid by the trustees from time to time during the lifetime of the widow as follows: One-fifth or 20 percent to the widow and the remaining four-fifths to his five children in equal shares of 16 percent.

The will provided that upon the death of the widow the remaining net income should be paid from time to time during the continuance of the trust to decedent's five children in the following proportions: One-third each to his sons, Vincent and Gordon, and one-ninth each to his daughters, Virginia, Elizabeth, and Margaret. At the termination of the trust the assets were to be distributed one-third to each son and one-ninth to each daughter.

Other provisions, which it is not necessary to discuss here, were made for the event that any of testator's children predeceased him or died during the lifetime of the widow.

At the outset, we must try to determine the testator's intentions and wishes. After a careful examination of the will and the trust provisions in their entirety, it is our opinion that his primary wish and intention was to provide that the nursery business—his apparent lifework—would be carried on, expanded, developed, and improved principally under the management and direction of his sons, Vincent and Gordon, or the survivor. It is also apparent from the document that he reposed great confidence in the managerial ability, as well the personal industry, of his sons. Under paragraph IX of the will he said that, while he had equal affection for all his children, his sons were responsible in a large measure for the property he had accumulated and that as a reward for their excellent service and co-operation and in keeping with a promise made to them previously, which was not fulfilled because of change in plans, he had given them each a larger share of his estate than he had given his daughters.

Throughout the entire document he has evidenced his faith and confidence in his sons by making them executors of the will and by naming them as two of the three trustees. He then directed, authorized, and empowered the trustees to manage, operate, control, and carry on the business, investing them with all the powers, rights, and privileges which may be exercised by natural persons. He authorized and empowered them, as a necessary incident to the successful management of the nursery business, to buy, sell, and rent land and personal property, construct buildings, borrow money, and manage real estate; to establish a special fund, not in excess of $15,000, to be kept for emergency use in the business and replenished from time to time from income or capital; to cultivate, develop, improve, sell, and remove nursery stock; and to use a part of the net income from the business if they deemed it advantageous to the business. He expressed a wish that his sons would devote their full time to the business, in the capacity of managers, providing for a monthly salary or such larger salary as the trustees deemed commensurate with the business done, such salary to be a part of the running expenses of the business. He also expressed a wish and desire that his sons ultimately would become the owners of the business. He authorized the trustees, after the death of his wife or at any time during the continuance of the trust if she predeceased him, to sell the nursery business and all real and personal property in the trust for fair value to his sons or, if one of them were dead, to the survivor of them. He requested that a fair and conservative appraisal of the property be made by disinterested persons before such sale and that favorable terms of sale be made so as to enable his sons, or the surviving son, to purchase the trust property from profits of the business and apply their or his beneficial share in part payment.

No one can fail to recognize upon a perusal of the entire document that, while the testator was concerned about the care and support of his surviving spouse and desired to have all his children share in the net income from the business, if any, he firmly desired to have his sons carry on the business and eventually own it, since he acknowledged that they were responsible in a large measure for the property he had accumulated.

The trial court made no findings and issued no memorandum in connection with its order allowing the accounts.

Although numerous objections have been filed, they have been listed and discussed in the briefs under four basic headings: (1) Issues primarily involving accounts; (2) questions concerning compensation of the trustees in their capacity as managers; (3) issues primarily involving accumulation of income; and (4) widow's support and maintenance.

1. The first of the four categories into which the issues presented by this appeal have been classified deals with the propriety of certain accounting practices used to determine the net income of the nursery. A number of questions are raised. First, appellants contend that the trustees' accounts are neither on a cash basis nor on an accrual basis; that inventories are not valued and certain liabilities are not reported; and that, therefore, it is impossible to determine the true status of the income and capital accounts.

It is true that the duty of a trustee to make annual accounts requires a complete disclosure of the financial transactions affecting trust property. To fulfill this duty, the trustee is required to keep records which will provide a complete and accurate foundation for the report. Whether or not a particular system of bookkeeping reasonably fulfills this obligation ordinarily is a fact question for the trial court.

The record here contains testimony of a certified public accountant to the effect that, for a business of the nature of the one under consideration, a cash system, using no inventory of growing crops, does permit an accurate and conservative determination of income. Determining the income for a given period of a business of the type and magnitude of the one before the court is not a simple matter of addition and subtraction, and the proper method of determining income cannot be considered a matter of law. There are a number of questions affecting the final determination which must be decided in the light of the expert opinion of persons having knowledge of good and current accounting practice. There was evidence which, in our opinion, would sustain a finding that the accounting system used here was adequate under the circumstances.

Appellants contend also that it was improper for the trustees to charge depreciation on fixed assets to the annual income of the business. They rely on the rule that the beneficiary entitled to receive the income from a trust may not be required to suffer a deduction from the income by way of a charge for depreciation of the trust assets. We do not consider this a proper case for the application of that rule. It seems clear from a reading of the instrument that the testator considered the nursery business as a whole the *res* of the trust created. In the instant case, the business as a whole, not any particular part or asset of it, is the source of income. It is also clear that the testator desired and intended that the business be continued in the hands of his sons, initially as trustees and, after the termination of the trust, as beneficial owners. Paragraph VI(10) of the will provides for distribution of the net income of the business "After the payment of the expenses of the nursery business." Since depreciation is as much an expense as any of the other business expenses, we consider it proper, under the circumstances of this case, to make a charge for asset depreciation according to good business usage in arriving at the income of the business.

The principle that the trustees may rely on recognized accounting practices also controls the issue raised by appellants regarding the action of the trustees in charging off the value of a patent determined to be useless and in charging against income in 1947 taxes for the year 1946. There was testimony by a qualified accountant that the patent item was charged off in conformance with good business practice. While the record is not complete on the tax item, it appears that the payments and the method of accounting, at least in part, were compelled by adjustments made by the internal revenue department.

Appellants contend that the accounts filed by the trustees do not discharge their duty to make a full and complete disclosure of the trust affairs since the accounts do not contain segregated principal and income accounts. The first account filed covered the period from the commencement of the trust to December 31, 1946. It listed an inventory consisting of one item of real estate and one item of personal property. The account then listed the receipts of the business for each year and the disbursements for the same year, including the disbursements made to the income beneficiaries. The difference between the receipts and disbursements for the year was listed as an "increase" for that year. The inventory and increases were totaled and labeled "TOTAL TRUST ESTATE DECEMBER 31, 1946." The account also contained an inventory of the assets of the trust, which equaled the amount of the total trust estate. The later accounts filed were made out in much the same manner. Appellants argue that, if the accounts properly segregated income and principal, certain improper charges would be revealed.

In passing upon an account of a trustee, much must be left to the sound judicial discretion of the trial court. While there are some deviations from the required statutory requirements in the preparation of these accounts, we are satisfied that, if they are corrected in the future, the rights of all parties can be adequately protected.

2. Appellants question the amount of compensation paid to the two trustee-managers by way of salaries and bonuses for services in managing the business. The instrument creating the trust provided that the trustees shall take as salary "$200.00" per month "or such larger salary as my trustees deem commensurate with the business done." The trustee-managers have followed the practice in recent years of paying themselves a base salary of $8,400 per year. In addition, they have taken a bonus amounting to 25 percent of the net income after taxes. It must be agreed that the method of computation of the bonus of the trustees makes it appear that such payments amounted to a distribution of income. However, in our opinion, the

testimony is sufficient to support a finding that the amounts paid are reasonably commensurate with the business done. The volume of business has increased significantly in recent years. There is ample testimony by experienced nurserymen to the effect that $22,000 was a fair compensation for a manager having the experience and ability of the two trustees and producing the results which they did. In the will the trustees were given authority to take a salary which *they* deemed commensurate with the business done. Although no finding was made, it appears to us that the evidence would sufficiently support a finding that the payment of the amounts by the trustees was a fair exercise of the powers granted.

* * *

[In the omitted portion the Court dealt with appellants' third contention, that the trustees had built up substantial cash reserves out of income, far in excess of the $15,000 special fund specifically authorized by Paragraph VI (3) of the will. The Court relied on wording in other clauses (referring to net income after expenses, taxes and "investment of earnings or capital in the business" and authorizing use of part of the income in the business).]

* * * Over and above the possible need of a business for an "emergency" fund, it may be determined that the business requires an adequate working capital to meet the regularly recurring business expenses. In addition, liquid assets on hand provide a source from which it is possible to expand the fixed assets of the business. There is no reason to suppose that the testator did not intend that the business should be allowed to carry liquid assets sufficient to provide adequate working capital.

Implicit in the court's order approving the account is a finding that amounts withheld from income were not more than was reasonable for working capital under the circumstances of this case. Such determination involves a question of fact. The evidence sustains such finding so it must be affirmed. However, we must point out that § 501.34 requires the annual account of a trustee to segregate principal and income. That requirement is mandatory and must be followed in submitting future accounts in order that we may know, when the proper time comes for determining who is the owner of the accumulated income, what is income and what is principal.

* * *

Affirmed.

THOMAS GALLAGHER, JUSTICE (dissenting). The testamentary trust here under consideration authorizes the trustees to carry on the nursery business conducted by the testator prior to the time of his death.

Testator died March 1, 1943. Trustees Gordon Bailey, Vincent K. Bailey, and Elizabeth Fritz took over as of December 27, 1943.

1. The first account of the trustees was filed for the period to December 31, 1946. It contained no itemization of salaries or bonuses for the trustees. While substantial distributable income had been ac-

cumulated by that time, it was not set forth as a separate item in this account but was lumped together with principal and designated "net worth." This income thus accumulated has never been distributed to the beneficiaries but has been added to the corpus of the trust. There is nothing in this report to indicate that it was not to be distributed or that the life tenants had lost their respective rights thereto.

2. Subsequent to 1946 no annual accounts were filed by the trustees until April 22, 1950, when the accounts for the years 1947, 1948, and 1949 were filed. They likewise did not separate income from principal but again lumped the two items together under the heading "net worth," and the income thus accumulated is still retained as part of the principal of the trust.

* * *

4. The trust authorizes the trustees to establish a special fund not in excess of $15,000 to be kept for emergency use in the business. The accounting of December 31, 1946, listed bonds and securities held in the trust in excess of $60,000. By December 31, 1949, this account had an accumulation of over $75,000, and during 1950 for several months it exceeded $100,000. In some of the accounts these investments were designated as "reserve accounts." It is clear that the sums held therein far exceeded $15,000 authorized for this purpose by the trust.

During the year 1950, $25,000 of the amount so held was transferred from the reserve account to cash. Later it was reduced to $56,000, while the cash on hand was increased to over $42,000. These reductions were made after it appeared that a controversy might arise with reference to the management of the trust. The conclusion is inescapable that the sums thus held constituted distributable income to which the beneficiaries were entitled by virtue of the trust, no part of which was ever received by them.

5. Under the trust Gordon Bailey and Vincent K. Bailey were to act as managers of the business and were to be paid each month a salary of $200 or "such larger salary as my trustees deem commensurate with the business done, such salary to be * * * paid regularly as other salaries and wages in the usual course of business." Under this provision, the two trustees took salaries for the years 1944 through 1950 of $8,400 each per year. In addition, they took bonuses of $1,000 each in the years 1944, 1945, and 1946. In 1947 they took a bonus of $3,500 each. In 1948 and 1949 they each took a bonus of $5,000, and in 1950 each took a bonus of $13,068. These bonuses were in addition to their salary, which remained unchanged at $8,400 per annum.

While it is true that the gross sales of the business increased substantially during this period, had the basic salary of $200 provided for by the trust been increased in proportion to the increased sales for the years 1947 to 1950, inclusive, it would have been as follows:

1947	$ 9,024 to each
1948	10,464 to each
1949	11,088 to each
1950	11,856 to each

This would have meant a salary of $42,432 for each of the trustees, as against the $60,168 which each of them withdrew during this four-year period.

While some increase in the business, no doubt, was due to the efforts of the manager-trustees, we cannot fail to note that perhaps the greatest increase thereof may be attributed to the general business increase experienced by all industry during this period due to conditions brought about as an aftermath of World War II.

6. Since the commencement of the trust, the trustees have accumulated income in excess of $91,000. If the bonuses over and above their salaries as above described had not been withdrawn, the distributable income would have reached a total of $180,372 by 1950.

The disbursements to the beneficiaries, other than the widow, since the inception of the trust have been extremely meager, notwithstanding the substantial amount of income accumulated as above set forth and notwithstanding the substantial increase in sales of nursery products shown as follows:

	Receipts from sales, etc.	**Disbursements to beneficiaries (each)**
1944	$111,829.48	$ 800.00
1945	129,336.10	800.00
1946	143,901.11	800.00
1947	189,181.74	1,600.00
1948	220,851.78	800.00
1949	232,520.77	1,200.00
1950	243,520.42	2,400.00

Since by the terms of the trust each of the manager-trustees is entitled to 16 percent of the income during the lifetime of testator's widow, and subsequent to her death, such percentage is to be increased to 33⅓ percent each, it is obvious that it is to their advantage to withhold distribution of income until subsequent to the widow's death. Likewise, if the transfer of accumulated income to the corpus of the trust be approved, the manager-trustees will each be entitled to one-third thereof when the principal of the trust is ultimately distributed as against the smaller percentage they would now receive were the income paid over to the beneficiaries as required by the terms of the trust.

* * *

For the reasons set forth, I am of the opinion that the trustees' accounts as submitted should not be allowed; that the trustees should be required to submit full, complete, and detailed accounts of their transactions; that all improper charges for expenses, reserve account, depreciation, bonuses, and other like items should be disallowed; and that the trustees thereafter should be directed to distribute to the beneficiaries the net income derived from the trust as then determined, whether previously accumulated or otherwise.

CHRISTIANSON, JUSTICE (dissenting in part). The will in question is devoid of any reference to a charge for depreciation. It refers only to *payment* of expenses and other disbursements prior to the distribution of the remaining net income. Depreciation, although an operating expense of a business, requires neither a payment nor disbursement of any kind; it is nothing more than a bookkeeping entry representing the gradual exhaustion of tangible assets during the usual course of business. Although this court has never had the occasion to pass upon the question, the often-repeated rule is that, unless the settlor has manifested a contrary intention, an income beneficiary is entitled to all the income of a trust without regard to the exhaustion or wear and tear of the trust assets. However, there is authority supporting an exception to the general rule when the trust assets consist of a business. Despite the inherent difficulties in defining *business*, I am of the opinion that this distinction is sound in principle. For this reason, I concur in the majority's holding that an allowance for depreciation was proper in the instant case.

The majority rely on an accountant's statement that writing off the entire book value of a worthless patent against 1950 income was proper. While this may be proper for some purposes, it is not proper in the case of a trust where the rule is well established that income beneficiaries are not responsible for losses to the corpus. In re Trust Under Will of Koffend, 218 Minn. 206, 15 N.W.2d 590. The patent in question, which was originally a part of the decedent's estate, was written off because it was determined to be a total loss and, therefore, the total assets of the trust were overstated by the book value of the patent. This situation should be carefully distinguished from the amortization of a patent over the period of its useful life. I would disallow the loss on the patent as not a proper charge against income.

The majority have approved the trustees' accounts for the period from January 1, 1947, to December 31, 1950, with the admonition that income be segregated from principal in all future accounts filed. M.S.A. § 501.34 provides in part as follows:

> "* * * such trustee shall render to such court at least annually a verified account containing a complete inventory of the trust assets and itemized principal and income accounts."

Regardless of the basis used for reporting income, this section makes the filing of a complete inventory of the trust assets and the filing of segregated principal and income accounts mandatory. The majority agree that these provisions are mandatory and not merely directory. They concede that the trustees have failed to comply with either requirement of the statute and that it is impossible to determine the true status of the principal and income accounts of the trust from the accounts as filed. Moreover, they recognize the necessity of having income segregated from principal because of the large accumulations of income that have been made in this trust. Yet, the majority in effect hold that the requirements of the statute will be satisfied if the principal and income of the trust are segregated in all future accounts filed. To me, this conclusion is not sound in principle particularly in view of the clear and mandatory language of the statute. Moreover, as a precedent it may have the effect of closing the barn door after the horse is gone, which certainly would be contrary to all principles of justice. I find no justification whatsoever for the failure of the trustees to comply with the requirements of the statute. Their failure to do so in the past has had the effect of concealing such flagrant violations of trust-accounting principles as charging the decedent's personal income taxes against the income of the trust. In my opinion the accounts as filed are inadequate and improper and the trustees should be required to file corrected accounts for the period now in question.

For the foregoing reasons, I respectfully dissent in part from the majority opinion.[45]

NOTE

Bailey's Trust poses several issues which you should consider. (1) Should general accounting principles (which may be designed to minimize income for tax purposes and to maximize principal for market sale or stock issuance purposes) govern in the field of trust accounting when a business is involved? (2) In trusts administered by a remainderman-trustee chosen by the settlor, should the inherent conflict of interest be a factor in court review? Did the settlor intend the trustee to favor himself when he conferred powers to affect determination of income and principal? (3) What lesson does this case teach you about using a family member with conflicting interest as trustee with broad power to affect income determination? Would the case have arisen if a corporate fiduciary had been trustee or co-trustee? (4) Would the result in the case have been any different if the jurisdiction had established standard forms for reporting principal and income? (See the next Section on Accounting.)

Some assets originally transferred to the trustee may produce either much less or much more than the rate of return which could be obtained on normal trust investments. Thus, if unproductive property is included in the estate, its carrying charges may exceed any slight income produced by such property. Currently such charges must be either taken out of income from other trust assets or paid out of principal; and the general rule favors the income beneficiary by charging such expenses against principal. If the settlor has not directed retention of the unproductive asset, the trustee must sell within a reasonable time. By the very nature of such assets, they may not have a ready market. Until sale the income beneficiary is deprived of income which normally would be his. Should the proceeds of sale be appor-

45. The Bailey trust was again before the courts in a later case. Under an interpretation of language in the trust instrument authorizing the trustees in their discretion to "use" in the business part of the business income, earnings of the business reinvested by the trustees in the business were held to be capital, and not undistributed income, upon death of an income beneficiary. 261 Minn. 521, 113 N.W.2d 505 (1962).

tioned to make up for this loss of income in the interim? Most courts hold that expenses of carrying the property until sale should first be deducted and credited to capital, to restore the capital account, and the balance than apportioned between principal and income accounts on the basis of the following formula:

Principal + income = net proceeds (a known figure).

Although principal is an unknown amount to be ascertained, the other unknown, income, can be translated into terms of the first unknown, since income is merely principal times the normal rate of return on trust investments times the period during which the trustee held the asset under a duty to sell. It is then a simple matter of mathematics to work out the apportionment. Suppose, for example, the trustee receives unproductive realty which, because of market conditions, he is unable to sell for five years. He then sells and realizes a net of $52,000. During the same period the normal rate of return on trust investments was 6% (a matter established by expert testimony). Letting P represent our unknown principal amount, our formula reads:

$$P + (P \times 6\% \times 5) = \$52{,}000.$$

This becomes:

$$P = \frac{\$52{,}000}{1.30} \text{ or } \$40{,}000$$

The balance of $12,000 is the income item. You will find other helpful examples in the Restatement, Second, Trusts § 241, Comments (e) through (i). Compare Uniform Principal and Income Act (1962) § 12; Uniform Principal and Income Act (1931) § 11.

A similar problem is encountered when assets productive when acquired subsequently cease to produce an adequate return. The common example is the real estate mortgage, long an accepted trust investment. During a period of depression, the mortgagor may default. Foreclosure proceedings take time, and the trustee may be forced to buy in at the foreclosure sale in order to protect the investment. He may even have to sell the realty at a loss, after several years during which no return has been realized. The income beneficiary will assert a claim to a portion of the proceeds as delayed income. A substantial body of case authority built up during the depression of the 1930's apportions the ultimate proceeds of the mortgage investment between principal and income, using substantially the same formula given above, with local variations.

Other assets included in the original estate may produce a greater than normal return because the return reflects a partial return of capital; these are called wasting assets. Typical are copyrights, patents, leaseholds, and mineral rights. The trustee normally has a duty either to dispose of such assets or apportion the current receipts into an amount representing normal return on the investment as income and the balance representing the depletion or depreciation of the asset as capital, to be credited to income and principal respectively. The settlor can provide, if he so desires, that all of the current return of such assets shall be paid as income to the income beneficiary; and the court may find such an intent from a direction to the trustee to retain such an asset, along with other circumstances.

(2) INVASION OF PRINCIPAL OF A TRUST

ESTATE OF VAN DEUSEN

Supreme Court of California, 1947.
30 Cal.2d 285, 182 P.2d 565.

TRAYNOR, JUSTICE. Florence Lenore Van Deusen by her will dated June 20, 1932, left the residue of her estate to American Security and Trust Company of Washington, D. C., as trustee, for the following purposes: "* * * to pay over the net income arising therefrom, in equal shares, unto my aforesaid daughters, Gladys Van Deusen Bright and Hazel Van Deusen Lee, during the period of their joint lives, and in case of the death of either of them, then all of said net income unto the survivor, for and during the natural life of the survivor. Upon the death of the survivor of my said daughters, this trust shall finally cease and determine, and my trustee shall thereupon transfer, assign and pay over the entire trust fund, including any undistributed income, absolutely and in fee simple, in equal shares unto those of my grandchildren who may then be living, the then surviving issue, however of any of them who may then be dead, to take, per stirpes, the same part or share the deceased ancestor would have taken if living."

The testatrix died on April 10, 1944, and the will was admitted to probate on June 13, 1944. The named trustee declined to act, and Bank of America National Trust and Savings Association was appointed administrator-with-the-will-annexed. On March 22, 1945, the daughters of the testatrix, the life beneficiaries of the trust, filed a "Petition for Directions to Trustee" with the probate court. The purpose of the petition was to have the trustee, when appointed, instructed to pay each of the life beneficiaries at least $200 a month, out of income, if that was sufficient, but if not, out of the corpus of the trust. It is alleged in the petition that the provision made by the testatrix for her daughters was intended to provide them with enough income to take care of their needs, that it was contemplated at the time the will was executed that the net income from the trust investments would be at least $400 a month, and that the testatrix intended that not less than $200 a month would be available for each daughter under the trust. It is also alleged that since the creation of the trust one of the daughters has been afflicted with a disease believed to be incurable and needs special medical care and that the other daughter must rely entirely upon the income from the trust for the necessities of life.

On April 3, 1945, Bank of America Trust and Savings Association was appointed trustee, and by order for ratable distribution a part of the residue of the estate was distributed to the trustee. On the same day the "Petition for Directions to Trustee" was denied. The order for ratable distribution provides: "The Trustee shall pay in equal shares to Gladys Van Deusen Bright and Hazel Van Deusen Lee during the period of their joint lives, and in case of the death of either of them then to the survivor for and during the natural life of said survivor, all of the net income arising from said trust estate.

"Upon the death of both of decedent's daughters, said trustee shall distribute the corpus of the trust estate in equal shares to the grandchildren of decedent who may then be living, or, in the event of any of said grandchildren not surviving, then his or her share shall be distributed to his or her surviving issue in equal shares and per stirpes, and thereupon this trust shall cease and terminate."

On September 12, 1945, the probate court made its order of final distribution, distributing the balance of the residue to the trustee "in trust for the uses and purposes set forth in the Order for Ratable Distribution, dated April 3, 1945. * * *" No appeal was taken from either order of distribution. Some time after April 3, 1945 (the record does not disclose the date of the order) a new trial was granted on the "Petition for Directions to Trustee" and another hearing was held on the petition on February 14, 1946. On the basis of the record at the original hearing on the petition, the court entered its order granting the petition of the life beneficiaries for directions to the trustee to pay each of them at least $200 a month, after a showing that the net income of the trust at that time was sufficient to pay each beneficiary from $100 to $125 a month only. This order was based on a finding by the probate court "that the main benefits under said trust were intended for the petitioners herein who were the primary objects of the testatrix's solicitude and that the primary purpose of the trust could not be accomplished by a strict adherence to the terms of the declaration of the trust * * * and that it is the purpose of said trust that the said petitioners herein receive the sum of $200 each per month." From this order the trustee, who appeared at the hearing in opposition to the petition, appeals.

The trustee contends that the probate court was without jurisdiction to make the order on the grounds that respondents' petition was not a proper petition under Section 1120 of the Probate Code, that the new trial on the petition after the final decree of distribution constituted a collateral attack on the final decree of distribution, that the probate court was without jurisdiction to modify the trust pursuant to Section 1120, and that if the probate court had jurisdiction and the matter was not conclusively determined by the final decree of distribution, the probate court erred in ordering an invasion of the corpus of the trust contrary to the express terms of the decree of distribution and of the will itself.

* * *

[In the omitted portion of the opinion, the court held that any question of construction of the will should have been determined either at the time of the order for ratable distribution or the decree of final distribution; that, on the theory that the petition was filed to obtain a modification of the trust, appeal should have been taken from the original order of denial; and that the probate court had no jurisdiction to grant a new trial under the relevant provisions of the California Probate Code.] * * *

Even if it be assumed that the probate court had jurisdiction to grant a new trial on respondents' petition for instructions to the trustee, the order appealed from is erroneous on its merits. The theory of the order, and the only basis for granting it after the decree of distribution, was to allow a modification or deviation from the trust to carry out the purpose of the testatrix in view of changed conditions. A court of equity may modify a trust on a proper showing of changed conditions occurring after the creation of a trust if the rights of all the beneficiaries may be protected. Whittingham v. California Trust Co., 214 Cal. 128, 134, 4 P.2d 142; Adams v. Cook, 15 Cal.2d 352, 358, 101 P.2d 484; Moxley v. Title Insurance & Trust Company, 27 Cal.2d 457, 466, 467, 165 P.2d 15, 163 A.L.R. 838; see Rest.Trusts §§ 167, 168; Scott on Trusts, §§ 167, 168. If it is assumed that a probate court has the same power under Section 1120, the order appealed from is nevertheless erroneous, since it provides for an invasion of the corpus of the trust contrary to the express provisions of the decree of distribution without any attempt to protect the interests of the residuary beneficiaries in that corpus.

The only interest given respondents in either the will or the decree of distribution is the net income from the corpus. The grandchildren of the testatrix, children of the respondents, are entitled to distribution of the corpus on the death of the surviving respondent. To allow an invasion of the corpus without the consent of the residuary beneficiaries contrary to the provisions of the trust instrument is to take property from one without his consent and give it to another. (See 3 (pt. 1) Bogert, Trust and Trustees, 504.) As stated in the Restatement of Trusts (sec. 168, comment d.) "The court will not permit or direct the application of the principal to the support or education of one beneficiary where by the terms of the trust income only is to be so applied, if the result would be to deprive another beneficiary of property to which he is or may become entitled by the terms of the trust, whether the interest of such other beneficiary is vested or contingent, or unless such other beneficiary consents to such application." See also Hughes v. Federal Trust Co., 119 N.J.Eq. 502, 504, 183 A. 299; Scott on Trusts, sec. 168.

In Whittingham v. California Trust Co., 214 Cal. 128, 134, 4 P.2d 142, the claimant, a beneficiary of a testamentary trust, was the only person interested in the estate. It was held that a court of equity could modify the trust to allow distribution of part of the corpus to the beneficiary on a proper showing of the beneficiaries' need therefor and of changed circumstances occurring since the execution of the will. In the present case, the respondent life beneficiaries are not the only persons interested in the trust, and the rights of the residuary beneficiaries must be protected. The respondents contend, however, that the probate court did not have to protect the interests of the residuary beneficiaries, and that the trustee had no right to attempt to do so, since the living residuary beneficiaries were all served with notice of the filing of the petition and two of them, who appeared through counsel, stated that they had no objection to increasing the payments to $150. This can hardly be considered consent by all the residuary beneficiaries to an invasion of the corpus of the trust to provide each of the life beneficiaries with at least $200 a month.

Moreover, in Estate of Markham, 28 Cal.2d 69, 74, 168 P.2d 669, it was held by this court that where the trust instrument provides for payments to a life beneficiary out of net income, there may be no invasion of the corpus or of accumulated income in the absence of "a clear expression to the contrary in the trust instrument." The respondents contend that the rule of the Markham case is confined to a situation where there is a fully expressed plan or purpose set forth in the trust instrument and that in the present case there was no plan or purpose shown by the will itself. Even if this limitation of the rule might be applied in a proper case, respondents have failed to show by parol evidence or otherwise that the testatrix clearly intended an invasion of the corpus, if necessary, to provide each of the daughters with an income of $200 a month.

The conditions as to the health and need of the respondents were stipulated to by the trustee at the hearing. The only other evidence of changed conditions after the execution of the will in 1932 is that the income from the securities that were distributed as the corpus of the trust decreased some time between 1932 and the date of the original hearing on the petition. The evidence introduced by respondents consisted only of the testimony of the husband of one of the life beneficiaries that he was the financial adviser of the testatrix, that at the time of the execution of the will in 1932, the testatrix received $400 a month income from the securities in question; that at that time she told the witness that she expected that her daughters would receive a similar income therefrom under the trust. The witness also testified that in 1943, the testatrix stated in a letter that "I *will arrange it* so that it will be used to the advantage of Gladys and Hazel [the respondents], no others." (Italics added.) He also testified that the testatrix did make a statement "with respect *to seeing* that her children were not impoverished as a result of illness or any unforeseen contingencies." (Italics added.) This evidence, whether admissible or not, shows only that in 1932 the testatrix expected the income from her securities to remain at approximately $400 a month after her death and that in 1943 she contemplated changing her will to provide solely for her daughters. Nevertheless the will admitted to probate provided for her grandchildren as well as her daughters. She died without changing her will and the court did not have power to remake the will on the basis of the fact that at one time some 11 years after making the will she had an intention, which she failed to act upon, to change her will.

Sympathy for the needs of the respondents does not empower the court to deprive the residuary beneficiaries of their interests in the corpus of the trust without their consent, nor does it enable the court to construe the non-testamentary declarations of the testatrix into an expression of her plan or purpose in providing for the trust some 11 years previous thereto. If the courts could increase the payments under testamentary trusts without the consent of all the beneficiaries merely because the income therefrom is not what it was at the time the will was executed and because at one time or another the testator expressed the desire to provide adequately for the beneficiaries, there would be no stability to any testamentary trust in this state.

The order is reversed.

NOTE

In order to achieve flexibility in meeting an uncertain future the modern trust instrument frequently confers discretion upon the trustee in making distributions of principal and income. Thus the trustor may expressly empower the trustee to "invade" (pay out) principal to an income beneficiary in order to assure the latter enough funds to maintain a customary standard of living in an inflationary economy. Or a "sprinkling trust" in which income is to be spread among several members of the family will vest discretion in the trustee to decide the amounts and the recipients. Such powers are also created for tax reasons.[46] These powers relate directly to distribution. Note that discretionary powers of management may also substantially affect distribution, e.g., a power to determine principal and income or a power to invest in high-income property without regard to risk.

The form of a power to invade principal varies all the way from a direction to the trustee to pay over principal whenever requested by the income beneficiary, to an absolute and uncontrolled discretion in the trustee to pay over principal when he alone deems it necessary;[47] and there are hundreds of shades of difference in phraseology employed by the draftsmen. These clauses have led to considerable litigation in recent years, by trustees desiring instructions from the court as to what factors they should consider in deciding whether to invade, by income beneficiaries unhappy because the trustees have not exercised their power when the beneficiaries thought they ought to have, and finally by the principal beneficiaries who have challenged the use of the power by the trustees. Judicial review of these discretionary powers is customarily phrased in terms of "abuse" of the discretion,[48] and is limited in scope.[49]

The grant of discretionary powers to the trustee in administration matters, such as sale or investments, is designed to give him greater freedom in his usual management function. On the other hand, the grant of power affecting disposition of principal thrusts upon the trustee wholly new problems, sometimes involving delicate relations with the interested beneficiaries. He now has to make decisions affecting beneficial ownership. He takes on a

46. Halbach, "Another Look at Discretionary Trusts; Income Tax Avoidance Under the 1969 "Reform" Act", 5 Inst.Est.Plan. Ch. 71–5 (1971); Price, "Trustee's Discretionary Powers", 4 Real Prop., Prob. & Tr.J. 643 (1969).

47. In Estate of Miller, 41 Cal.Rptr. 410, 230 Cal.App.2d 888 (1965), the trustee was ordered to make payments of principal to maintain the beneficiary's standard of living even though the trust instrument granted the trustee "sole discretion" to determine the amounts necessary to provide for the support of the beneficiary (textatrix' daughter); the discretion was not unlimited but must be exercised to carry out the purpose of the trust.

48. Restatement, Trusts 2d (1959) § 187.

49. Halbach, "Problems of Discretion in Discretionary Trusts", 61 Col.L.Rev. 1425 (1961) is the classic article.

totally new function. While his normal duty is to be impartial between beneficiaries, the essence of his new power is to favor the income beneficiary.[50] The fact issues are endless. Does the income beneficiary really need the money requested? In how much detail should the trustee go into the monetary affairs of the beneficiary in order to exercise his discretion? What standard is he to employ in judging need? Can principal be invaded to enable the beneficiary to make gifts to other family members or charity? These and other questions should be anticipated by the draftsman. If the trustee has power to invade principal "if the income is insufficient to meet the needs" of an income beneficiary, the trust instrument should expressly provide the trustee with guidance as to whether to consider other income and assets of the beneficiary, including income of a married beneficiary's spouse. In the absence of such a provision, litigation is invited.[51] The result again depends on a construction of the entire trust document in light of the circumstances to arrive at the settlor's intent, and on the scope of the discretion given the trustee (which may range from "in his discretion" to "in his sole and uncontrolled discretion, not subject to court review"). Litigation is not often successful but always expensive.

PROBLEMS

1. Does it make any difference if the income beneficiary is also entitled to the principal, and the invasion merely gives him principal at a date earlier than that specified in the trust instrument? How would the Claflin doctrine be distinguished? Cf. In re Solomon, 149 Misc. 551, 267 N.Y.S. 767 (N.Y. Surr.Ct.1933).

2. Does an express provision that, if a share of income payable to the wife is inadequate, she be given additional amounts from income payable to children, justify an inference that no principal may be used where total income becomes inadequate? In re Cosgrave's Will, 225 Minn. 443, 31 N.W.2d 20, 1 A.L.R.2d 175 (1948).

3. If all the beneficiaries are sui juris and consent to a distribution different from that provided by the trust instrument, does the trustee have a right to refuse an invasion or should he be neutral in the controversy except to assure protection of his own interests? Cf. Altmeier v. Harris, 335 Ill.App. 130, 81 N.E.2d 22 (1948).

4. What is the likely court attitude where the income beneficiary is receiving adequate income by normal standards but inadequate because of his standard of living? Estate of Boyle, 252 Wis. 511, 32 N.W.2d 333 (1948).

5. If the settlor directs payment of an annual amount such as $5,000 "out of income" and the income becomes insufficient to produce that amount, should principal be invaded to make up the deficiency? Arkansas National Bank of Hot Springs v. Mayer, 216 Ark. 255, 225 S.W.2d 331 (1950); In re Pusey's Estate, 370 Pa. 572, 88 A.2d 750 (1952).

50. Where a power to invade principal is expressly conferred and either the income beneficiary or the principal beneficiary is a trustee, there is a potential conflict of interest. See Section 6 of this Chapter. The draftsman ought to foresee this conflict and make some provision against it.

51. See In re Ferrall's Estate, 41 Cal. 2d 166, 258 P.2d 1009 (1953), the third in a series of suits involving the same trust; the lower court construed the trust to require invasion of principal if the trust income alone was insufficient to meet needs of the beneficiary; the Supreme Court reversed, holding that the trustees did not abuse their discretion in considering the community assets and income of the husband. There was a sharp dissent.

6. What effect has a statute such as Purdon's Statutes Annotated (Pa.) Tit. 20, § 6102:

"(a) Failure of original purpose. The court having jurisdiction of a trust, heretofore or hereafter created, regardless of any spendthrift or similar provision therein, in its discretion may terminate such trust in whole or in part, or make an allowance from principal to a conveyor, his spouse, issue, parents, or any of them, who is an income beneficiary, provided the court after hearing is satisfied that the original purpose of the conveyor cannot be carried out or is impractical of fulfillment and that the termination, partial termination, or allowance more nearly approximates the intention of the conveyor, and notice is given to all parties in interest or to their duly appointed fiduciaries. But, distributions of principal under this section, whether by termination, partial termination, or allowance, shall not exceed an aggregate value of $100,000 from all trusts created by the same conveyor.

"(b) Distribution of terminated trust. Whenever the court shall decree termination or partial termination of a trust under the provisions of this section, it shall thereupon order such distribution of the principal and undistributed income as it deems proper and as nearly as possible in conformity with the conveyor's intention.

"(c) Other powers. Nothing in this section shall limit any power of the court to terminate or reform a trust under existing law."

For a statute empowering the court to make an allowance out of principal for any income beneficiary if his support is not sufficiently provided for, see Wis.Stat.Ann. § 701.13 (made retroactive by § 701.24).

7. Under a trust instrument empowering the trustees to pay from principal "as in their absolute discretion may be needed for the comfortable support and maintenance" of the income beneficiary, do the trustees have a duty to investigate requests by the income beneficiary? In re Murray, 142 Me. 16, 45 A.2d 636 (1946).

8. What is the duty of the trustee in passing on requests from the income beneficiary (widow of settlor) under the following clause: "If the income from such trust fund shall not be sufficient to maintain and care for my said wife comfortably, then it is my will and wish and I hereby authorize and direct my said trustees or trustee, as the case may be, to pay to her from time to time out of the corpus of the trust estate such additional sums as she may desire and request for her comfort, due consideration being given to her age, condition of health and position in society. Such payments shall not exceed $2,500." Estate of Curtis, 253 Wis. 119, 33 N.W.2d 193, 864 (1948). Compare In re Morse's Will, 280 App.Div. 171, 112 N.Y.S.2d 392 (1952).

9. Can the trustee terminate a trust by paying over all of the principal under a clause authorizing him to pay to the income beneficiary such portion of the corpus "as in his sole and uncontrolled discretion he may deem wise, whether because of insufficiency of income, personal need or otherwise"? In re Bisconti's Estate, 306 N.Y. 442, 119 N.E.2d 34 (1954).

SECTION 9. ACCOUNTING [52]

The fiduciary has a duty to render an account of his activities to those whose interests are involved (the beneficiaries in the case of the trust, the distributees and unpaid creditors in the case of the decedent's estate). This account must be rendered at reasonable intervals. The degree of formality attending it varies. In the case of the decedent's estate the representative must render a final accounting to the probate court, after proper notice to all interested persons; he must also render intermediate accounts if the estate is held open for longer than the usual period, as at the end of each year. These accounts are normally approved by the court after hearing and are res judicata on all issues which might be raised on the basis of the facts disclosed. After the testamentary trust is set up, statutes often require an annual account to be filed with the court. This is not necessarily a full accounting upon notice and hearing, however. As to the inter vivos trust, the trustee normally renders an account at regular intervals directly to the beneficiaries, without court action. The period varies from triennially to quarterly, but is usually on an annual basis. If the trustee fails to account, however, the beneficiaries may petition the court for an order directing him to account and for other appropriate action (such as removal or denial of compensation). The trustee may take the initiative in both testamentary and inter vivos trusts and petition for court approval of his accounts; to be binding this must be upon notice to all beneficiaries and hearing. This would normally be done at least upon final distribution and closing of the trust, but there may also be intermediate accounts upon the same basis. Since the cost of such court proceedings must be borne by the trust estate, the trustee must exercise a reasonable judgment as to how often a full court accounting is necessary, considering the amount of property involved and the amount of activity during the period. If there were any change in the fiduciaries, as upon death or resignation, an accounting of this nature would be necessary; and it would be the duty of a successor to ask for an accounting. In some states the intermediate account is not considered conclusive, and the same matters may be raised upon the final accounting. If the trustee renders an informal accounting directly to the beneficiaries, he may protect himself by securing their written approval of all acts disclosed by the account, with a release of any liability on the part of the

52. See Browning, "Problems of Fiduciary Accounting", 36 N.Y.U.L.Rev. 931 (1961); Niles, "Trustee Accountability in the Absence of Breach of Trust". 60 Col.L.Rev. 141 (1960). Zaloom, "Accounting for Decedent's Estates", 106 Trusts and Estates 528 (1967); Note, "Waiver of Accounting in Estate Administration—A Legislative Proposal", 6 Santa Clara Lawyer 59 (1965); Whitman, "Searching for a Reasonable and Balanced Fiduciary Accounting System", 9 Inst.Est.Plan. Ch. 6 (1975). See II Scott, Trusts (3d Ed.1967) § 172; III Scott, Trusts (3d Ed.1967) § 220; IV Scott, Trusts (3d Ed.1967) § 379.

trustee.[53] Even if approval is not obtained, the beneficiaries may be barred after a lapse of time by the equitable doctrine of laches. It is therefore desirable for the trustee to make a full disclosure by making the account as full as possible.

The "account" is a means by which the beneficiary or distributee can judge the administration of the fiduciary. It must therefore show the disposition of assets held at beginning of the accounting period and of income received, as well as assets on hand and expenditures during the period. The exact form of the account in the case of the probate account is sometimes set by statute or standard forms; otherwise it is a matter of local practice. The importance of careful records has been intensified by the obligation of the fiduciary to make tax returns.

In addition, the fiduciary is under a duty to supply the distributees or beneficiaries with information in accordance with reasonable request. Thus, if a trustee accounts on an annual basis and a beneficiary is concerned about the status of the trust in the middle of the year, he may request such information from the trustee; if the request is reasonable and compliance does not unduly burden the trustee, he would have to comply.

The content of specific items of the account vitally affects the beneficiaries. Thus the designation of "income" to be distributed to the beneficiaries entitled to receive it, and the expenses to be charged to income and principal—both problems already considered in Section 8(1)—are derived from the account of the fiduciary.

The Uniform Probate Code imposes on the personal representative a duty to keep heirs and devisees informed. Within 30 days of his appointment, he must inform them of his name and address, whether bond has been filed, and the court where estate papers are on file (Section 3–705). He must send a copy of the inventory to interested persons who request it (Section 3–706). When the personal representative closes the estate, he may either do so by formal proceedings on notice to interested parties and with a final account (Section 3–1001), or close informally by furnishing each distributee a full written account and by filing a verified statement (Section 3–1003). Because the Code would remove testamentary trusts from continuing supervision of the probate court, there is a single section (Section 7–303) imposing a duty on every trustee to keep beneficiaries informed:

"Section 7–303. [Duty to Inform and Account to Beneficiaries.]

"The trustee shall keep the beneficiaries of the trust reasonably informed of the trust and its administration. In addition:

"(a) Within 30 days after his acceptance of the trust, the trustee shall inform in writing the current beneficiaries and if

53. On informal accounting practices see Fleming, "Settlement of Trustee's Account Without Court Proceedings", 5 U.Miami 1971 Inst. Estate Plan., Ch. 71–6; Westfall, "Nonjudicial Settlement of Trustees' Accounts", 71 Harv.L.Rev. 40 (1957); Report of Subcommittee, Committee on Trust Administration and Accountability of Trustees, Settling Trustees' Accounts, 102 T. & E. 979 (1963).

possible, one or more persons who under Section 1–403 may represent beneficiaries with future interests, of the Court in which the trust is registered and of his name and address.

"(b) Upon reasonable request, the trustee shall provide the beneficiary with a copy of the terms of the trust which describe or affect his interest and with relevant information about the assets of the trust and the particulars relating to the administration.

"(c) Upon reasonable request, a beneficiary is entitled to a statement of the accounts of the trust annually and on termination of the trust or change of the trustee."

A few states have adopted the Uniform Trustee's Accounting Act. Under the Uniform Probate Code a conservator must account to the court (Section 5–419).

The fiduciary's duty is normally to protect his beneficiary (the heirs or devisees of a decedent's estate, the incapacitated person in the conservatorship, the beneficiaries of a trust). Yet at the point of obtaining private or judicial approval of accounts the fiduciary's personal interest is in conflict. He wants his accounts approved without question; he no longer represents the beneficiary and the latter must look out for himself. The problem is how the beneficiary can best be protected in an accounting proceeding. Should the court exercise a supervisory role and actively audit the account? Should the beneficiary be expected to retain his own legal counsel? Does the lawyer retained by the fiduciary but paid out of the estate owe a duty to the beneficiaries or only to the fiduciary? (At present there is a surprising diversity of professional opinion on this point; see Whitman, Report of the National Fiduciary Accounting Study (1972) pp. 59–67.) If the lawyer learns from the fiduciary that the latter has prepared a fraudulent account, can he reveal this to the court? If the lawyer merely realizes that the account includes questionable items, can and should he inform the beneficiary? Should there be a requirement that every account be approved by a court-appointed CPA? If the beneficiary is incompetent (as usually is the case in guardianship or conservatorship), should a guardian ad litem be appointed to protect the incompetent's interest? Protection may be costly and unnecessry. There is no simple answer. The Uniform Probate Code is drafted on the premise that the beneficiary should look after his own interest except in conservatorships; the court is not expected to exercise a supervisory function.

The following is from a summary of a group discussion at a 1974 Seminar on "The Future for Estate Lawyers," sponsored by the ABA Real Property, Probate and Trust Law Section: [54]

"Although no definite conclusions were reached, there did seem to be a general feeling that, since the accounting usually provides the basis on which a fiduciary is released from liability, it

54. "A Bakers' Dozen Topics", 10 Real Prop., Prob. & Tr.J. 243, at 259–261 (1975). (Copyright 1975 American Bar Association; reprinted with permission from Spring 1975 Real Property, Probate & Trust Journal.)

should provide an effective opportunity for reviewing his performance. In only a very few instances is a fiduciary's handling of an estate or trust being critically reviewed. This is partly because there is no one to do the job and partly because the accounting does not provide sufficient information for this to be done.

"In the typical situation, the accounting is looked at by beneficiaries and probate judges or surrogates and in a few cases by specially appointed guardians ad litem. It is safe to say that the overwhelming majority of beneficiaries are totally unqualified to review an accounting in a meaningful way. Moreover, the form of most accountings is sufficiently incomprehensible that even the most astute beneficiaries have difficulty in understanding them. Of course, a beneficiary is free to turn the accounting over to a qualified attorney for review. However, he may be reluctant to incur this additional expense and, furthermore, the attorney in whom he has the most confidence is most likely to be the legal counsel for the fiduciary.

"In those states in which an accounting is presented to the court for allowance (mandatory in some states and optional in others), it comes under the supposed scrutiny of a surrogate or probate judge. Almost universally these judicial officers give little more than a superficial review of the accounting and for the most part their concern is whether the local form requirements have been observed and whether the commission and fee requests are in line. In some instances, the judges reviewing accounts have a general jurisdiction and are not expert in probate matters.

"In some cases, a guardian ad litem may be appointed to represent the interest of minors or unknown beneficiaries. In those states having adopted the rule of virtual representation this number will be very small indeed. In some instances, a thorough, in-depth, qualitative analysis of the fiduciary's performance will be made by the guardian ad litem. In other instances, this will not happen because the person appointed is not qualified or is unwilling to devote the necessary time, or has a conflict of interest. It is not unusual for the accountant or his attorney to suggest the person to be appointed as guardian ad litem.

"As for the accounting itself, it is inadequate in two respects. First, the form is complex and difficult to understand. This is compounded when the accounting is produced by computers which print out massive and intimidating reams of paper comprehensible only by a computer programmer. Secondly, the accounting itself does not contain much of the information which is necessary for qualitative review. For instance, there is usually no indication as to tax elections made by the fiduciary, such as whether to take expenses on Form 706 or Form 1041, or whether the election was even considered. There is no information that would assist in determining whether a reasonable valuation of assets was made. It is ironic that the lower a valuation obtained by a fiduciary in a federal estate tax proceeding, the lower will be his compensation.

"While the group found much to criticize in the present system of accounting, it had a more difficult time coming up with solutions. One obvious reform is a simplification and national standardization of the form of an accounting. This matter is under consideration by the Section's Committee on Accounting and Accountability. It is also felt that additional information should be provided on such matters as whether tax elections were considered and, if so, the basis on which they were made, the basis for the valuation of assets and other such matters."

Local court rules often prescribe the form in which accounts should be submitted. In 1974 the National Center for State Courts, the American College of Probate Counsel and the Real Property, Probate and Trust Law Section of the American Bar Association sponsored a study of fiduciary accounting standards. This resulted in 1978 in proposed Uniform Fiduciary Accounting Principles and Model Account Formats, for adoption by state courts.[55] The object was to achieve some uniformity in this field by establishing standard guidelines. Computerized accounting systems are of course utilized by corporate fiduciaries; corporate fiduciaries generally appreciate the need to inform beneficiaries by summary statements which are understandable to lay people.

SECTION 10. REMEDIES OF A BENEFICIARY FOR BREACHES OF TRUST

(1) GENERAL PRINCIPLES [56]

The essence of the fiduciary relation is that the fiduciary must deal with property for the benefit of another. From this, certain basic duties flow: (1) the fiduciary must act reasonably; (2) he must act solely for the benefit of the other person, never for his own benefit; (3) he may not delegate his powers to others; (4) he must prevent any chance that the property will be confused with his own, with resulting loss to the beneficial owner; and (5) he must account for his activities.

For breach of these duties there are a variety of remedies available, depending upon the gravity of the danger to the relationship, ac-

55. "Proposed Uniform Fiduciary Accounting Principles and Model Account Formats," 13 Real Prop., Prob. & Trust J. 941 (1978).

56. See generally, Bogert, Trusts (5th Ed. 1973) §§ 153–160; Bogert, Trusts and Trustees (2d Ed. 1960) §§ 861–867; III Scott, Trusts (3d Ed. 1967) §§ 197–226; Restatement, Second, Trusts §§ 197–226.

tual loss resulting, the good or bad faith of the fiduciary, and the chance of repetition of the breach. The beneficiary may frequently elect more than one of these, where not inconsistent: (a) a "surcharge" forcing the fiduciary personally to make up a loss resulting to the estate; (b) avoidance of the transaction, except in case of a sale where the legal title has passed into the hands of a bona fide purchaser for value; (c) specific performance of the duty where feasible; (d) constructive trust or accounting for profits made by the trustee personally; (e) removal of the fiduciary; (f) a penalty in the form of refusal of all or part of the normal compensation of the fiduciary.

The fiduciary may incur liability because he has exceeded the powers conferred upon him by the terms of the instrument under which he is acting, or by "the law". This is not an issue of violation of any of the fiduciary standards or duties discussed in this chapter. For example, if the fiduciary is directed to retain certain assets, their sale by him would be unauthorized and a breach of his duties. Even if there were no direction to retain, he may legally have no power to sell without a court order, and a sale would again be unauthorized. But if he has the power to sell by express terms of the instrument or by implication, or by law (statute or decision), then a sale is measured by the general standards set forth here. Again, if statutory or case law specifies the type of investments he may make, he may act reasonably in believing the will or trust instrument authorizes him to invest in other securities, as when he obtains advice of legal counsel to that effect, and still be liable if the court finds no such authority under the instrument. Since a fiduciary may seek instructions from the court when in doubt as to his powers, he is likely to want such instruction for his own protection; he may not carry this to the absurd point of running to the court at every turn for advice on matters of business judgment, however, for those decisions are his responsibility in the first instance.

The fiduciary may obtain protection through the consent of all interested parties. In the case of the personal representative this would be the unpaid creditors as well as the persons taking under the will or the laws of intestacy. In the case of the trustee, it would be the beneficiaries. Since there may be minors or even unascertained beneficiaries, as where there is a gift of the remainder to heirs of a living person, it is not always possible for the fiduciary to obtain consent. One very important qualification is that the trustee will be protected if he obtains the consent of the settlor who has a power to revoke,[57] or the consent of a life tenant who has a general power of appointment, even if testamentary;[58] in such cases the other beneficiaries cannot question the acts of the trustee. As we have seen in Section 6, the transaction by which the fiduciary obtains consent is itself subject to judicial scrutiny.

57. City Bank Farmers Trust Co. v. Cannon, 291 N.Y. 125, 51 N.E.2d 674 (1943).

58. Perkins' Trust Estate, 314 Pa. 49, 170 A. 255 (1934). But cf. Uniform Probate Code, § 1–108.

(2) REMEDIES AGAINST THIRD PARTIES: DEFENSES AND RELATED MATTERS[59]

KING v. RICHARDSON

United States Circuit Court of Appeals, Fourth Circuit, 1943.
136 F.2d 849.[60]

[Lunsford Richardson, founder of the Vick Chemical Company, died in 1919 leaving a will executed in 1917 by which, among other dispositions, he gave 8/100ths of the shares of the company to his wife for life with a remainder over of 3/100ths to the trustees of the First Presbyterian Church of Greensboro, North Carolina, the "profits or dividends" therefrom to be used for the benefit of Home and Foreign Missions and other benevolent purposes of the Church as the trustees deemed best. The remaining 5/100ths was divided among his children equally in fee simple. At the time the will was executed, testator owned 51/100ths of the Vick Company, then a partnership, and his two sons J. H. Smith Richardson and Lunsford Richardson, Jr. owned the remaining 49/100ths. By other provisions in his will, testator disposed of his remaining interest to members of his family so that only members of the Richardson family had an interest in the Company. The Company was incorporated during his lifetime in North Carolina and was afterwards incorporated in Delaware. In 1923, Mrs. Richardson, in order to aid the First Presbyterian Church in a building program, made an agreement with her children that they would pay her $45,000 for a fee simple interest in the 3/100ths interest held in remainder by the Church Trustees. She, in turn, arranged to purchase the remainder interest from the Church Trustees for the same amount. This was done. The Vick Chemical Company transferred the stock and issued new certificates. The will was on file in the records of the Company. One of the children was President of the Company. All of the stockholders were members of the Richardson family. All concerned knew all the facts. The Trustees used part of the $45,000 to buy a lot for a new church and part for a contribution to Davidson College. Mrs. Richardson died in 1940. Representatives of various corporations engaged in the benevolent purposes of the church and representatives of Home and Foreign Missions then discovered the diversion of trust funds and these, with the Church Trustees, now sue the Vick Chemical Company and the two Richardson sons, as surviving executors and trustees under the will of their father, to have the trust reconstituted. The District Court allowed the plaintiffs to

59. See Bogert, Trusts (5th Ed. 1973) §§ 160–170; Bogert, Trusts and Trustees (2d Ed., 1960) §§ 868–871; III Scott, Trusts (3d Ed. 1967) §§ 280–329; Restatement, Second Trusts §§ 280–329; Scott, "Participation in a Breach of Trust", 34 Harv.L.Rev. 454 (1921); Smith, "Remedies in Surcharge Action", 16 Real Prop., Prob. & T.J. 775 (1978).

60. Cert. den. 320 U.S. 777, 88 L.Ed. 466, 64 S.Ct. 91 (1943).

815 — 872 for 10/28/85

Note p. 811 — + ~~Pinion~~ on p. 807; 2 theories upon which a Pour-Over into a living trust — is sustained;
(1) — theory P / living trust, an entity P which a testamentary gift — (— δ; (2) incorporation by reference.

R.A.P, p. 1107

Class Gifts — p. 1110

recover on the basis of increased value of the stock but allowed a setoff of the $45,000 received by the Trustees with interest from the date of sale. Cross appeals are taken from that decision.]

PARKER, CIRCUIT JUDGE. * * * We may assume, as defendants argue, that the trustees were vested with a power of sale with respect to the corpus of the trust estate; but this becomes entirely immaterial under the admitted circumstances of the case. Granting that the trustees had a power of sale with respect to the trust property, it was a power which they could exercise lawfully only for the purposes of the trust; and when it was exercised in derogation thereof to the knowledge of the purchasers, the latter took the property subject to the trust. There can be no question but that the sale was made, in breach of the trust, to obtain funds for the new church building, that it was made pursuant to a prior arrangement that the proceeds of the sale should be used for that purpose, and that Mrs. Richardson and her children to whom the stock was transferred were parties to the arrangement. The Vick Chemical Company in making the transfer on its books was, likewise, chargeable with knowledge of the trust and that the transfer was in violation thereof; for testator's will had been made a part of its records and all of its officers and stockholders, who at the time consisted of the members of the Richardson family, knew that the transfer was being made in violation of the trust created by the will. That they had no fraudulent intent and honestly believed that they were acting lawfully does not affect the matter. The rule is thus stated by Professor Pomeroy, Equity Jurisprudence, 4th Ed., Vol. 3, § 1048: "Wherever property, real or personal, which is already impressed with or subject to a trust of any kind, express or by operation of law, is conveyed or transferred by the trustee, not in the course of executing and carrying into effect the terms of an express trust, or devolves from a trustee to a third person, who is a mere volunteer, or who is a purchaser with actual or constructive notice of the trust, then the rule is universal that such heir, devisee, successor, or other voluntary transferee, or such purchaser with notice, acquires and holds the property subject to the same trust which before existed, and becomes himself a trustee for the original beneficiary. Equity impresses the trust upon the property in the hands of the transferee or purchaser, compels him to perform the trust if it be active, and to hold the property subject to the trust, and renders him liable to all the remedies which may be proper for enforcing the rights of the beneficiary. It is not necessary that such transferee or purchaser should be guilty of positive fraud, or should actually intend a violation of the trust obligation; it is sufficient that he acquires property upon which a trust is in fact impressed, and that he is not a bona fide purchaser for a valuable consideration and without notice."

A.L.I. Restatement of the Law of Trusts states the rule as follows:

"Sec. 288. Transferee with Notice. If the trustee in breach of trust transfers trust property to a person who takes with notice of the breach of trust, the transferee does not hold the property free of the trust, although he paid value for the transfer.

"Comment: (a) The interest of the beneficiary in the trust property is not cut off by a transfer by the trustee in breach of trust to a third person who at the time of the transfer has notice that the transfer is in breach of trust, although he paid value for the transfer; and the beneficiary can in equity compel the third person to restore the property to the trust. The third person holds the interest which he acquires by the transfer upon a constructive trust for the beneficiary of the trust.

"The rule stated in this Section is applicable where the transferee has notice that the trustee is committing a breach of trust, whether the breach is intentional or negligent or results from a misinterpretation of the trust instrument." * * *

As the suit is concerned with a remainder interest in stock which was not available to the trust until the termination of the life estate, and as the life estate was not terminated until the year 1940, less than three years before the suit was instituted, we think it clear under the law of North Carolina that the suit was not barred by the statute of limitations. * * * The reason for this is well stated by the Supreme Court of Appeals of Virginia in Stewart v. Conrad's Adm'r, 100 Va. 128, 135, 40 S.E. 624, 627, in a passage quoted with approval by the Supreme Court of North Carolina in Pritchard v. Williams [175 N.C. 319, 95 S.E. 570] as follows: "The remaindermen under the terms of the will creating the trust fund are not entitled to the possession of any part of it until the death of the life tenant, who was a party to this suit, and who, so far as this record shows, is still living. Until her death the appellants would have no standing in a court except to ask a court of equity to prevent or remedy a violation of the trust and to preserve the trust fund. They had the right to invoke the aid of a court * * * for those purposes, but they were under no legal obligation to do so, and the objection of laches or acquiescence will not lie for their failure to assert rights which have not yet accrued."

Here the $^{3}/_{100}$ths interest in controversy was given to Mrs. Richardson for life. Not until her death did it go to the trustees for the benefit of the trust, and not until then did a cause of action arise in their favor for its recovery. * * * [61]

It is suggested that the conveyance by the trustees to Mrs. Richardson resulted in the merger of the life estate and remainder interest so that the life estate fell in at that time and the statute of limitations began to run immediately. What occurred, however, was not a surrender or conveyance of the life interest to the trustees for the benefit of the trust but a sale of the remainder by the trustees to the holder of the life interest under such circumstances as to constitute a breach of the trust and impress a constructive trust upon the remainder in the hands of the holder of the life interest and her transferees.

61. See Bogert, Trusts (5th Ed. 1973) § 170.

Under such circumstances it is well settled that a merger of the estates does not result. "To constitute a merger, it is necessary that the two estates be in one and the same person, at one and the same time, and in one and the same right." 19 Am.Jur. p. 588. Here the remainder interest was not held by Mrs. Richardson or her transferees in the same right as was the life estate, but was held subject to the trust imposed by the will. * * *

The same facts which preclude the bar of the statute of limitations are applicable to the plea of laches.[62] As said by Judge Sanborn in Kelley v. Boettcher, 8 Cir., 85 F. 55, 62, and quoted with approval by this court in Fretwell v. Gillette Safety Razor Co., 4 Cir., 106 F.2d 728, 730, 731: "In the application of the doctrine of laches, the settled rule is that courts of equity are not bound by, but that they usually act or refuse to act in analogy to, the statute of limitations relating to actions at law of like character. * * * The meaning of this rule is that, under ordinary circumstances, a suit in equity will not be stayed for laches before, and will be stayed after the time fixed by the analogous statute of limitations at law; but if unusual conditions or extraordinary circumstances make it inequitable to allow the prosecution of a suit after a briefer, or to forbid its maintenance after a longer period than that fixed by the statute, the chancellor will not be bound by the statute, but will determine the extraordinary case in accordance with the equities which condition it. * * * When a suit is brought within the time fixed by the analogous statute, the burden is on the defendant to show, either from the face of his bill or by his answer, that extraordinary circumstances exist which require the application of the doctrine of laches; and when such a suit is brought after the statutory time has elapsed, the burden is on the complainant to show by suitable averments in his bill, that it would be inequitable to apply it in his case."

There is nothing in the pleadings or in the evidence showing any special circumstances which would require a holding that suit by the plaintiffs would be barred by anything less than the period of limitation prescribed by statute. There is nothing to show that the beneficiaries of the trust knew of the sale of the remainder interest prior to the death of the holder of the life estate or that the defendants have been prejudiced in any way by the fact that suit was not brought earlier. On the contrary, it appears that an enforcement of the trust at this time will result in nothing more than that the beneficiaries will receive what was intended by the will of the testator and what would unquestionably now be theirs if the conveyance by the trustees had not been made.

And we see no merit in the plea of estoppel.[63] As pointed out above, beneficiaries of a trust are not bound by a sale made by trustees in violation of the trust to purchasers who take with knowledge of the violation. It would hardly occur to anyone to suggest an estoppel against the trust if the suit were being prosecuted by other

62. See Bogert, Trusts (5th Ed. 1973) § 169.

63. See Bogert, Trusts (5th Ed. 1973) 455–456.

trustees appointed to conserve it; but the fact that two of the three trustees who are plaintiffs joined in the conveyance which they are attacking makes no difference. They are acting as trustees, not as individuals, and it is their duty to preserve the trust estate and recover any property improperly diverted from it, even though they themselves may have participated in the diversion. The rule is thus stated in A.L.I. Restatement of Trusts, 294(c): "c. Suit by trustee. Not only can the beneficiary maintain a suit against a transferee of trust property who is not a bona fide purchaser, but the trustee himself can maintain a suit against the transferee. Although the trustee if he held the property free of the trust would have no cause of action against the transferee, he is permitted to maintain a suit for the benefit of the trust estate. Although the trustee bases his cause of action upon his own voluntary act, and even though the act was knowingly done in breach of his duty to the beneficiary, he is permitted to maintain the action, since the purpose of the action is to recover money or other property for the trust estate, and whatever he recovers he will hold subject to the trust." * * *

The suit is against the executors, as such, against the trustees under the Richardson will and against the Vick Chemical Company, the Delaware corporation, which succeeded to the rights and liabilities of the North Carolina corporation that made on its books the transfer which deprived the trust of the stock in question. Under the North Carolina decisions, there can be no doubt as to the liability of the corporation for the loss thus sustained by the trust. * * * The corporation is liable, also, on the theory that the stock constituting the trust estate was acquired by a corporation which the defendant corporation has succeeded in a process of corporate reorganization.

And we think it equally clear that the executors, too, are liable for the value of the stock. As executors, they held it as trustees for those to whom it was devised; they have never delivered it to the trustees of the trust; and, for reasons heretofore stated, they are not protected by the conveyance made by the trustees to the holder of the life interest, who was one of their number. The fact that the executors filed an account is immaterial. It is well settled that the filing of such an account does not discharge them of their trust as to property remaining in their hands. * * * Only after final account is filed or after the lapse of two years, the time allowed by law for filing it, could a suit for the legacy be maintained. N.C.Code of 1939, sec. 147.

The executors never delivered the stock certificates to Mrs. Richardson, the holder of the life interest. After the transfers to the children, the executors permitted certificates to be issued in the name of the children by the corporation, taking no steps to protect the remainder devised to the trust, although fully advised of the circumstances under which the conveyance was made by the trustees. The fact that the person taking the conveyance from the trustees was one of the executors, that the other two received transfers of the stock from her and that all were parties to the plan by which the stock was being diverted from the purposes of the trust, means that the transfer amounted to nothing, since all parties were charged with notice that the remainder was subject to the trust just as though the transfers had not been made. As trustees holding the stock for the legatees, the executors can defeat liability only by showing that they properly discharged their trust, and this they are unable to show.

As we have noted, the decree of the court below requires the defendants to restore to the trust the shares of stock diverted therefrom or their equivalent. The defendants include the trustees of the trusts created by the Richardson will. It does not appear that these trusts participated in or profited from the violation of the trust with which we are here concerned; and consequently the decree should not run against the defendants in their capacity as trustees under the trusts expressly created by the will, and since the executors are not sued in their individual capacities, the decree does not of course run against them as individuals.

As to the extent of liability, we think that the court below correctly held that the corporation and the executors are bound to account for all the property in the corpus of the trust in whatever form it may now be. * * *

This is undoubtedly the rule to be followed in cases where it is sought to impress a constructive trust on property in possession of a defendant. We see no reason why the same rule should not be followed in a suit to recover a legacy in stock from executors, where it appears that the stock has been converted into other stocks. Whether this is the rule to be followed in measuring the liability of the corporation making the wrongful transfer upon its books, we need not stop to inquire, since the defendant Vick Chemical Company not only assumed the liabilities of the corporation making the transfer but also, through its various corporate reorganizations, acquired its rights and assets, including the interest in that corporation represented by its stock subject to the trust. * * *

The question remains as to the correctness of permitting the deduction from the recovery of the $45,000 received by the trustees from Mrs. Richardson with interest thereon from its receipt. The payment to the trustees was not used for the purposes of the trust, but was diverted to other purposes, viz., the building of a new church and the payment of a subscription by the Richardson family to Davidson College; and, as heretofore stated, the persons making the payment knew at the time that it was to be thus diverted. The trust certainly cannot be charged with the payment made to the trustees under such circumstances. It is true that ordinarily a purchaser from a trustee is not required to look to the application of the purchase money to the purposes of the trust; but this rule has no application where the purchaser knows at the time of purchase "of the trustee's violation of trust, committed or intended". 65 C.J. 782–783. * * * The rule applicable is thus stated in A.L.I. Restatement of Trusts 291 (*o*): "*o*. Credit for purchase price. If the trustee in breach of trust transfers trust property to a person who takes with notice of the breach of trust and who pays value for the trust property, and the beneficiary compels him to restore the property to the trust or to account for its value or for the proceeds, the transferee is entitled to credit for the amount which he paid for the trust property to the extent to which the trust estate has the benefit thereof. If, however, the purchase price has been misappropriated by the trustee and the trust estate has therefore not received a benefit therefrom, the transferee is not entitled to credit therefor."

For the reasons stated the decree appealed from will be affirmed as to the liability of the corporate defendant and of the executors under the will and will be reversed as to the liability of the trustees under the will and as to the deduction of the $45,000 received by the trustees from Mrs. Richardson and will be remanded for further proceedings with respect to the extent of liability, with leave to the parties to take additional testimony if they so desire.

Affirmed in part, reversed in part and remanded.

SOPER, CIRCUIT JUDGE (dissenting). [Dissenting opinion omitted.] [64]

64. The Uniform Probate Code contains a short statute of limitations to protect a trustee who has furnished a final account to a beneficiary; as to matters fully disclosed, the suggested period is 6 months after receipt of the account; as to matters not disclosed by the account, the period is 3 years if the trustee has informed the beneficiary of the location and availability of trust records for examination by the beneficiary. Section 7–307. A personal representative is protected if his account is adjudicated, after notice and hearing, in an order of complete settlement (formal closing) under Section 3–1001; or if he files an informal closing statement under Section 3–1003, action must be commenced against him within 6 months after the filing (Section 3–1005), except for a cause of action based on fraud (2 years after discovery, Section 1–106), or nondisclosure.

APPENDICES

Appendix I

TESTAMENTARY TRUST PROVISIONS[1]

[The testamentary trust provisions here presented should be preceded by an appropriate definitions article similar to that which follows. The definitions article is unnumbered here, since it might be preceded by an article identifying the members of the testator's family and perhaps by an article dealing with the source of funds for the payment of debts, with the exoneration of liens on property specifically devised and bequeathed, or with similar matters. However, the definitions article should precede all dispositive provisions and also all major administrative provisions. The reader should understand the meaning of special terms used in drafting before these terms are read. The trust provisions exhibited might be preceded by articles disposing of real and personal property which the testator desires to deal with specifically.]

* * *

ARTICLE —

In construing this will: "children", "grandchildren" and "issue" mean lawful children, grandchildren and issue and include legally adopted children, grandchildren and issue. Words which import one gender shall be applied to any gender where appropriate. "Trustee" includes any person or corporation from time to time holding that office. "Executor" includes any person or corporation from time to time holding that office and also an Administrator with the Will Annexed.

[This article defines certain terms and thereby eliminates any question concerning the meaning of those terms. Successor fiduciaries would normally have all powers of the original fiduciary, since powers are not construed as personal unless that is the expressed intent; see Boyden v. Stevens, page 637]

* * *

1. Generations of law students have been warned about the limitations of forms. Thoughtless use of any form is dangerous. Each form has been developed for use in a particular state and may reflect peculiarities of local law. If the subject matter of the trust were a business interest, special provisions would have to be added for the problems raised in Chapter XVII, Section 5(4)C. Any form must be tailored to fit the client's special situation. In these days of all-important tax factors, careful thought must be given to the ultimate tax impact.

[Trust provisions for the marital deduction and "shelter" dispositions are illustrated although non-trust transfers might also be used. The form provides two trusts. In inverse order of sequence below there is an "exemption equivalent shelter" trust, described in the form as a "family trust" because it is for the benefit of the surviving spouse and family, and sometimes described by draftsmen simply as the "shelter" trust or "Trust 'B' ". This trust is designed to include the exemption equivalent of the unified credit available in the year in which the testator dies. This credit increases annually with an exemption equivalent in 1982 of $225,000, reaching $600,000 by 1987. The "sheltered" amount is taxable in the testator's estate but there is no tax on this amount payable because the amount in trust does not exceed the exemption equivalent. The trust "bypasses" or "shelters" the trusteed property, the surviving spouse having a life income interest but no powers which would cause inclusion of the property in the surviving spouse's estate for federal estate tax purposes. A special power could be conferred upon the surviving spouse without causing the property to be included in that spouse's estate; but a special power is not used in the form because such a power might produce a tax under some state tax laws. The trustee is given a "sprinkling" or "spraying" power to permit it to pay income from the trust to the spouse and to other family members in its discretion. Such a fiduciary power might be useful when the spouse has income from sources other than the trusts created by the testator. If, during a particular year, the surviving spouse received high income from other sources, the trustee could exercise its discretion to pay trust income to other family members, thus reducing the income tax of the surviving spouse for that year. The other trust, which appears first in order, is a marital deduction trust. The initial marital deduction trust form exhibited is a power of appointment trust. If the testator did not wish the spouse to have a general power of appointment, a qualified terminable interest property trust (QTIP trust) might be used instead of the power of appointment form. A QTIP trust provides only a life estate in the surviving spouse and a suggested form for such a trust is exhibited as an alternative. These and other marital deduction dispositions are discussed in Chapter XII, Section (2)(1). The QTIP form is likely to become increasing popular to provide for a spouse when there are children by an earlier marriage or marriages. Both the power of appointment trust and the QTIP trust employ a formula designed to put the smallest amount in the marital trust consistent with full utilization of the unified credit (or exemption equivalent) in the testator's estate, thus minimizing any increase in the spouse's taxable estate at the spouse's death.[2] The marital deduction property will be taxable in the estate of the surviving spouse but can be offset by the spouse's unified credit (or exemption equivalent). The forms indicate the pecuniary formula marital deduction trust and the "family" or "shelter" trust framed as part of the residuary article. Some draftsmen prefer to establish the pecuniary formula marital deduction trust as a separate article and the "family" or "shelter" trust in the residuary article. The formula

2. The executor of the estate of a spouse who is beneficiary of a power of appointment marital deduction trust may recover from the person who takes property by the exercise, nonexercise or release of the taxable power part of the estate tax paid by the estate of the donee of the power proportionate to the property subject to the power. IRC § 2207, 26 U.S.C.A. Under IRC § 2207A the executor of the life beneficiary of the QTIP trust may obtain from the remaindermen the proportionate part that the QTI property contributes to the estate tax on the estate of the beneficiary.

clause in the residuary estate might provide for a fractional interest in the residuary estate. Each type of clause has advantages and disadvantages. With the pecuniary formula clause here exhibited, if the testator's taxable estate does not exceed the exemption equivalent, nothing will pass under the marital trust, all of the property in the residuum of the estate passing in the "family" or "shelter" trust.

While the provisions here set forth reduce the testator's federal estate tax to zero, there may be a federal estate tax on the estate of the surviving spouse. Moreover, state death taxes may not be minimized by these drafts. Some states have estate taxes based upon the amount of the state death tax credit allowed on the federal estate tax. These state estate taxes would be avoided. But other states have estate taxes not linked to the credit. The marital deduction in these states might not be 100% and the credits or exemptions might differ from the federal credit. If the state has an inheritance tax, this tax would be affected only to the extent that it might combine an estate tax feature, using up the federal state death tax credit if this credit exceeds the total inheritance tax imposed on the testator's transfers.

Before any of the forms presented are used, the tax laws at the time of use should be considered carefully.]

* * *

ARTICLE VI.

The residue of my property, real and personal, tangible and intangible, wherever situated and however held, I devise[3] as follows:

Clause 1: If my wife, Mary Doe, survives me, my Executor shall distribute to my Trustee as my Marital Trust the smallest pecuniary amount which, if allowed as a Federal estate tax marital deduction, would result in the least possible Federal estate tax payable by reason of my death. In determining the pecuniary amount, my Executor shall consider the credit for state death taxes only to the extent those taxes are not thereby incurred or increased, and shall assume that all payments and devises under the preceding articles of this will have been made or satisfied in full. My Executor shall select and distribute to the Trustee the cash, securities and other property, including real estate and interests therein, which shall constitute the pecuniary amount, employing for this purpose values current at the time or times of distribution. No asset or proceeds of any asset shall be selected as to which a marital deduction is not allowable. If my estate depreciates in value after the applicable Federal estate tax valuation date and as a result is insufficient to satisfy in full all pecuniary devises under this will, those devises shall share proportionately.

The remainder of my residuary estate shall be distributed by my Executor to my Trustee as my Family Trust. My Marital Trust and Family Trust shall be disposed of as provided in Clauses 4 and 5 hereof.

Clause 2: If my wife, Mary Doe, predeceases me or survives me and elects not to take the provisions for her in this will, then all property given, devised or bequeathed to her in this will, including the property directed to be allocated in Clause 1 of this Article to my Marital Trust and passing by

3. The draftsman here uses the term "devise" to refer to any testamentary disposition of property, whether land or personal property. This is in accordance with Uniform Probate Code § 1–201(7). If the terms "bequest" or "legacy" are used for dispositions of personal property under local practice, the draftsman should use these terms.

this will, shall be held, administered and distributed as part of my Family Trust as provided in Clause 4 upon her death.

Clause 3: If my wife, Mary Doe, and I die under circumstances such that there is no sufficient evidence that we have died otherwise than simultaneously she shall, for purposes of this Will, be deemed to have survived me.

[Clause 1 provides for creation of two trusts, the Marital Trust, funded by a pecuniary formula amount and a Family (or "Shelter") Trust to reduce to zero federal estate taxes on the testator's estate. The special provisions relating to funding of the Marital Trust are shaped by tax law. Although use of values at the time of distribution to fund the Marital Trust meets the requirements of Revenue Procedure 64–19, there is concern among will draftsmen that the reasoning underlying this Procedure may be extended. The sentence providing for abatement of all pecuniary devises in the event of severe post death depreciation of asset values has been inserted as a precaution against such a tax development. Clause 2 eliminates the constructional problem which might otherwise arise if the wife elected against the will. See Chapter XV, Section 4. It also avoids any possible claim that the wife retains the powers of appointment conferred upon her despite her election not to take under the will, on the theory that the power is not property passing to her under the will but merely an event for designating the beneficiaries under the donor's will. See Chapter XIV, Section 1. Clause 3 is designed to assure the marital deduction for testator's estate when his death and that of his wife are substantially simultaneous. Normally, were it not for the tax advantages in this particular instance, the testator would want the reverse presumption.]

Clause 4: My Trustee shall hold, administer and distribute my Marital Trust as follows:

A. The net income from the time of my death shall be distributed to my wife, Mary Doe, at least quarterly during her life and shall not be subject to assignment, alienation, pledge, attachment or claims of creditors.

B. My Trustee in its discretion may distribute to my said wife or apply for her benefit such amounts of principal as it considers appropriate for her care, comfort, maintenance and general welfare, taking into account all other resources available to her. In its discretion, it may also distribute principal to her for other purposes, including the making of gifts, upon her request.

C. Upon the death of my said wife, the assets then held in the trust, or any part thereof, including accrued and undistributed income, shall be distributed to her appointee or appointees, including her estate, in trust, or otherwise, as she shall appoint by her will specifically referring to this power. To the extent that my wife fails to exercise this power effectively, the assets of the trust, including accrued and undistributed income, shall be added to my Family Trust herein created.

D. It is intended to qualify my Marital Trust for the marital deduction allowable under the Federal Internal Revenue Code and any amendments thereto and this instrument is to be construed accordingly. Notwithstanding any provision of this instrument, my Executor and Trustee shall have no discretion or power in the administration of this trust the existence or exercise of which would disqualify it for the marital deduction, including, without limitation, any power to invest in unproductive property or to retain such property for more than a reasonable time during the lifetime of my wife without her written consent, or any power to so allocate receipts and disbursements as between principal and income as to deny to my said wife all the net income of the said trust to which she would be entitled under applicable rules of law.

[Clause 4 contains the terms of the marital deduction trust, largely dictated by the provisions of the Internal Revenue Code, § 2056, and the relevant Regulations. For example, compare paragraph A as a spendthrift clause under the marital deduction trust with Clause 5(L) under the family trust below. The latter clause is more effective but would disqualify the entire marital deduction since the wife would not be entitled to the income and would have a terminable interest. Notice the broad power of invasion of principal embodied in paragraph B; this avoids the problems presented in Chapter XVII, Section 8(2). Paragraph C contains the necessary general power of appointment, testamentary in this case (although the tax law would permit a power to appoint by deed if the testator so desired); see Chapter XIV on Powers of Appointment. Notice that this trust document requires specific reference to the power for an effective exercise although there still may be litigation as Estate of Smith on page 890 illustrates. It is also explicit that the donee of the power (the wife) may make appointments in trust. There is an express gift in default, here to the family trust, in event the power is not exercised "effectively". Paragraph D is again a tax clause, to overcome possible interpretation of some of the trustee's powers under Article VII below as so broad as to affect the substance of the wife's right to income in all events and thus result in the loss of the marital deduction. Where taxes are not the primary consideration, as in the family trust, the trustee is given the widest possible latitude in the management powers.]

[Alternative Clause 4 (Qualified Terminable Interest Property (QTIP) Trust).]

Clause 4: My trustee shall hold, administer and distribute my Marital Trust as follows:

A. The net income from the time of my death shall be distributed to my wife, Mary Doe, at least quarterly during her life, and shall not be subject to assignment, alienation, pledge, attachment or claims of creditors.

B. Upon the death of my wife, Mary Doe, my Trustee shall pay over the then principal of this trust to be held and administered as part of my family trust as provided in Clause 5.

C. I intend to qualify my Marital Trust for the marital deduction allowable under the Internal Revenue Code and any amendments thereto and this instrument is to be construed accordingly. Notwithstanding any provision of this instrument, my Executor and Trustee shall have no discretion or power in the administration of this trust the existence or exercise of which could disqualify this trust for the marital deduction and no person shall have any power to appoint any of the property of this trust to any person.

D. I direct my Executor to elect the marital deduction provided in this ARTICLE.

[Under IRC § 2056(b)(7) the marital deduction can be obtained for a life estate in the surviving spouse if the surviving spouse is entitled to all of the income, payable at least annually and there is no power in any person to appoint any of the property to any person other than the surviving spouse. The form suggested excludes any power of appointment. The deduction is available only if the executor elects it. The form suggested requires the executor to elect the deduction. This is to protect the executor and the estate from litigation. If the executor elects the deduction

the property is then taxable in the surviving spouse's estate. The spouse usually will accept the marital deduction provision but a clause might be included giving her power to renounce the trust while accepting other provisions for her benefit.]

Clause 5: My Trustee shall hold, administer and distribute my Family Trust as follows:

A. The net income from the time of my death shall be accumulated or distributed to, or applied for the benefit of, any one or more of the group consisting of those of my wife, Mary Doe, and my issue, living from time to time, in such amounts and at such times as my Corporate Trustee in its absolute discretion may determine, until the principal is divided into shares as provided in Paragraph B(1) of this Article. I anticipate that the needs of the beneficiaries may be unequal and that since distributions may be related to needs they may also be unequal.

[Clause 5 contains the dispositive provisions for the family trust. The "sprinkling" provision will enable the trustee to apply the income to those beneficiaries which need it but under the current unlimited throwback rule the beneficiary will be taxed on accumulated income as if he had received it during the year in which it was received by the trust. Thus the value of deferring income is greatly reduced by the unlimited throwback principle, although the beneficiary would be taxed on the accumulations only if he received them. While the power vested in the trustee by this clause is not strictly classified as a power of appointment as the term is used in Chapter XIV or in the Restatement of Property, Ch. 25, it is closely akin to a power of appointment and presents some of the same construction problems as to scope of the power. Here it is clearly expressed that the trustee may distribute all the income to "any one or more" of a group of persons; compare the exclusive interpretation of the power in Harlan v. Citizens National Bank, *page 899. When the class includes the wife and issue living from time to time, a changing group, the beneficiaries are sufficiently identified within the rules laid down in Chapter VIII, Section 4(5).]*

B. (1) At the time after the death of my said wife when there are no living children of mine under the age of 21 years, the principal and any accumulated income shall be divided into equal shares so that there will be one share for each of my children who is then living and one share for each of my children who is then deceased and is survived by then living issue.

(2) Each share for a living child of mine shall constitute a separate trust to be administered in accordance with the provisions of Paragraph C of this Article.

(3) Each share for a deceased child of mine shall be divided into separate parts for his then living issue by right of representation. The part allocated to each of my grandchildren shall constitute a separate trust to be administered as provided in Paragraph D of this Article. The part allocated to each of such issue more remote than my grandchildren shall be distributed.

[Paragraph B provides for creation of separate trusts for children and issue of deceased children. Note that throughout the trust document—here and in C(3), D(3) and F below—no beneficiary has a "vested" interest but must survive to the time of distribution of either income or principal in order to take. Thus there are no construction problems such as the cases in Chapter XV, Section 2(2), on Implied Survivorship involve. By substituting the next generation for a deceased beneficiary the costs of transmitting the interest through his estate are avoided. Nor will there

be a generation skipping transfer (there being no taxable distribution or termination) when the generation skipped has no more than a future interest or future power. If, however, the younger generation representative has a present interest or power there is a taxable transfer upon distribution or termination. This particular document is designed to implement an estate plan calling for a per stirpital distribution, and not containing a special power of appointment in the wife. Whether the wife should be given a special power to appoint among the issue depends upon the desires of the testator and the circumstances of the particular estate; see Chapter XIV generally.]

C. Each trust for a child of mine shall be held, administered and distributed as follows:

(1) The net income shall be distributed to my child at least quarterly until the principal is distributed.

(2) The principal shall be distributed to my child: one-third when he has reached the age of 25 years, one-half of the remainder when he has reached the age of 30 years and the balance when he has reached the age of 35 years.

(3) If my child dies before the principal of his trust is fully distributable, the remaining principal shall be distributed to his then living issue by right of representation, (except that the shares of my grandchildren shall be held, administered and distributed as separate trusts in accordance with Paragraph D of this Article), and, if there be none, to my then living issue by right of representation.

[C requires distribution of income from each trust to the child and postpones payment of principal in stated installments. The problem dealt with in In re Mansur's Will, *page 992, which would be presented if the child were to die before he reached 35, is eliminated by subparagraph (3), since an express disposition of the principal is made in that event.]*

D. Each trust for a grandchild of mine shall be held, administered and distributed as follows:

(1) Until my grandchild reaches the age of 21 years, my Trustee in its discretion may accumulate the net income in whole or in part or may distribute such income to him or apply it for his benefit.

(2) When my grandchild reaches the age of 21 years, the principal and all accumulated income shall be distributed to him.

(3) If my grandchild dies before the principal of his trust is distributable, the remaining principal shall be distributed to his then living issue by right of representation; and, if there be none, to his brothers and sisters then living and to the then living issue of his brothers and sisters then deceased by right of representation; and, if there be no such issue, brothers, sisters, or issue of a deceased brother or sister, to my then living issue by right of representation.

[The generation skip from children to grandchildren will give rise to a generation skipping tax subject to an exclusion of $250,000 for each child. The skip from grandchildren to great-grandchildren is fully taxable without exclusion. The future interest here created involves the most remote generation permissible under the Rule Against Perpetuities (Chapter XVI) but is valid since at the end of the testator's life, when the will becomes effective, his children will have been born or conceived and thus become the measuring lives under the Rule. At the end of those lives, all grandchildren will be born or conceived, and vesting may be postponed an additional 21 years under the common law Rule.

Note the draftsman has a saving clause as a precautionary measure in N(2) below; compare the clause in the case on page 1105, In re Lee's Estate.]

E. Principal distributable under the Preceding Paragraphs C(3) and D(3) of this Article to a person who is an income beneficiary of a trust hereunder shall be added to his trust; and if there has been a principal distribution from his trust pursuant to Paragraph C(2) of this Article, there shall be a proportionate distribution from the addition.

[E is almost self-explanatory; it is to prevent premature distribution where there is a gift over.]

F. If at any time there is no person in existence to whom the principal or income of a trust is distributable, the remaining assets shall be distributed according to the *[name of state]* law of intestacy to those who would be my next of kin if I had then died intestate.

[F provides for the unlikely possibility of a failure of issue. The phrasing of the dispositive language reaches the same result as the court does by construction in the Latimer *case on page 1041 but without the necessity of costly litigation.]*

G. My Corporate Trustee in its discretion may distribute to a beneficiary of a trust then eligible to receive income, or for whom income is being applied or accumulated, such amounts of the principal of his trust as it considers appropriate for the care, comfort, maintenance, education or general welfare of the beneficiary or his dependents, or it may distribute such amounts of principal to a friend or relative or to his legal guardian, if any, to be applied for such purposes, or may itself make such applications. My Corporate Trustee shall not be responsible for the application by other persons of distributions. In exercising its discretion under this paragraph, my Corporate Trustee shall take into account all other resources available to the beneficiary. No distribution of principal shall be made to my wife until the principal of my Marital Trust has been exhausted.

[This is a broad power of invasion in the trustee, to provide liberally for the current income beneficiaries. As Section 8(2) of Chapter XVII illustrates, the courts have been unduly zealous in protecting remaindermen whereas the normal desire of a settlor is to favor those closest to him (wife and children) rather than the remote generation of issue or collateral relatives. This power allows the trustee to use principal for the income beneficiaries when income is inadequate for their comfortable living. Note that the trustee is directed to take account of other resources; while this is the same result the court would probably reach (see the Note on page 1379) there is a split of authority and the expressed intent would avoid any litigation of the issue. The trustee is directed to invade for the benefit of the wife only after the principal of the marital deduction trust has been exhausted under the provisions of Clause 4 B previously discussed. This is because the marital deduction trust will be taxable in the wife's estate but the family trust will not; thus if any invasion for the wife is desirable, it should come first from the assets which will be taxed on her death.]

H. If principal becomes distributable to a person under legal disability and there is no provision for adding it to a trust for the distributee, my Trustee, in its discretion, may postpone the distribution until the disability is removed. In any such case the assets shall be administered as a separate trust in accordance with the provisions of this instrument and the net income and principal shall be applied for the benefit of the beneficiary at such times and in such amounts as my Trustee considers appropriate. If the beneficiary dies before the removal of his disability, the remaining assets shall be distributed to his estate.

I. At the termination of an income beneficiary's interest, unless otherwise provided, all income then undistributed attributable to his interest, including accruals, shall be distributed as though it had been received after such termination.

[Normally income would be apportioned in event of death of an income beneficiary, under the rules set forth in Chapter XVII, Section 8(1), and income earned or accrued during the life of the income beneficiary would be payable to the beneficiary's estate. Since this merely results in increased administration expenses and death taxes, the above clause disposes of undistributed income to the next beneficiary in line. The provision is important under the unlimited throwback rule to avoid unnecessary income taxation based on accumulations. The beneficiary would be taxed only on accumulations paid to him. The applicable legal rules on income apportionment, of course, yield to such an expressed intent. This is true under the Uniform Principal and Income Acts (1931) and (1962).]

J. If an income beneficiary is a minor or, in the opinion of my Trustee, is unable properly to administer his affairs, income distributable to him may, in my Trustee's discretion, be applied directly by it for the care, comfort, maintenance, education or general welfare of the beneficiary or his dependents, or be distributed to a friend or relative or to his legal guardian, if any, to be applied for such purposes. My Trustee shall not be responsible for the application by other persons of distributions.

K. My Trustee, in the absence of any provision to the contrary, may transfer to principal and hold for distribution as such, income accumulated in any trust pursuant to the terms thereof, and re-transfer to income any amount so transferred for distribution to income beneficiaries pursuant to the terms of such trust.

L. The interests of the beneficiaries are created for their personal enjoyment, protection and welfare and shall not be susceptible of assignment, anticipation, hypothecation or seizure by legal process. If my Trustee believes that the interest of a beneficiary is threatened to be diverted from the purpose for which it was created, my Trustee shall withhold any income and principal which it is authorized to distribute to the beneficiary and shall apply it in such manner as it considers advisable for the care, comfort, maintenance, education or general welfare of the beneficiary or his dependents. Such distributions to the beneficiary may be resumed when my Trustee considers the diversion is no longer effective or threatened. This provision shall not be construed to extend the term of any trust.

[L is a carefully constructed protective clause, a composite of several of the various types considered in Chapter VIII, Section 5(2). Like any good clause which may be challenged on policy grounds, it recites first its purpose and ties the spendthrift provisions with the very nature of the private trust itself: protection of the beneficiaries chosen by the settlor as the objects of his bounty. The clause not only attempts directly to insulate the interests of the beneficiaries against creditors, as well as prohibiting voluntary assignment, but also includes forfeiture and discretionary provisions to further discourage attack by creditors through any court proceedings.]

M. My Trustee in its discretion may pay the expense of the last illness and funeral of a beneficiary or of a member of his immediate family, including purchase of a cemetery lot, provision for its perpetual care and erection of a suitable marker.

N. Notwithstanding any other provision of this Article:

(1) Whenever the principal of a trust has a market value of less than $20,000, my Trustee may distribute the principal to the beneficiaries then entitled to receive the income of the trust in proportion to their income shares, or by right of representation if the income is not distributable in shares, and thus terminate the trust.

(2) At the expiration of the period limited by applicable law for the duration of a trust, it shall terminate and the remaining assets shall be distributed as provided in subparagraph (1) of this paragraph.

[N(1) gives the trustee power to terminate any trust when it becomes uneconomical to administer the corpus. As to N(2) see the explanation after D above.]

ARTICLE VII

Clause 1: My Executor and Trustee is empowered to do all things necessary or convenient for the orderly and efficient administration of my estate and the trusts hereunder and generally to have, manage and control my said estate and trusts as fully as I might, if living, do myself with respect to my own property. Without limiting this general grant of power by the following enumeration, my Executor and Trustee shall possess the discretions and powers:

A. To retain assets owned by me at the time of my death for as long a period as it may think proper in the exercise of its absolute discretion without regard to statutes or rules of law (including any requirement of diversification) regulating investments by executors and trustees, and without liability for any decrease in the value thereof.

B. To invest and reinvest in property of any kind without regard to statutes or rules of law (including any requirement of diversification) regulating investments by executors and trustees; to invest in any Common Trust Fund maintained by my Corporate Executor and Trustee; to invest in insurance on the life of any person; and to permit assets to be temporarily uninvested.

C. To carry assets in its own name without disclosure of trust or in the name of a nominee.

D. To borrow money for such period of time and upon such terms and conditions as it may think proper and to mortgage and pledge assets as security for any such loan.

E. To sell at public or private sale, exchange for like or unlike property, convey, assign, lease for longer or shorter terms than the trusts hereunder, and otherwise dispose of or option any property, real or personal, for such price and upon such terms and credits as it may think proper.

F. To pay, compromise, contest or abandon claims in favor of or against my estate or any trust, upon such terms as it may think proper.

G. To make distribution or division of principal in cash or in kind, or both, at values current at a date of distribution fixed by it, without any requirement that each item be distributed or divided ratably. To determine upon allocations, charges or credits as between principal and income where there is no provision made therefor by statute; but regardless of any statute, the Trustee may charge its customary annual fee to income.

H. To engage in or discontinue any business or commercial enterprise, including farming; to delegate management thereof; and to do all things appropriate in the prosecution of any such business or enterprise, including, without limitation, participation in the management of any corporation in which stock may be held, the organization of corporations and the formation of limited partnerships. To employ agents or servants upon such terms as it may think proper.

I. To participate in or oppose any plan of reorganization, merger, consolidation or dissolution or similar plan involving assets; to deposit or withdraw securities under any such plan and to accept and retain substituted securities. To exercise conversion, subscription, voting and other rights involving securities through delegation of its powers or by limited or unlimited proxies.

J. To maintain such reserves for expenses and depreciation as it may think proper.

K. To erect, repair, alter or demolish buildings or other structures; to plat, improve, maintain and develop real estate.

L. To effect fire, rent, title, liability, casualty or other insurance of such nature and in such form and amount as it may think proper.

M. To exchange assets with, borrow from, loan to, and sell assets to itself acting as a fiduciary or co-fiduciary under this will, or under a trust established by me during my life, or otherwise.

N. To accept from a minor or incompetent legatee or beneficiary his receipt for a distribution of principal or income, and such receipt shall be as effective for all purposes as it would be if the distributee were adult and competent.

O. To rely upon a court order admitting to probate the will of a holder of a power hereunder or finding that he died intestate; to assume that the holder of a power died intestate unless it has actual notice to the contrary within ninety days after his death; all without prejudice to any right which an appointee or a beneficiary in default of appointment may have against distributees.

P. To accept deposits in a trust by will or otherwise from any person but my Trustee shall accept all deposits which I may make. Assets which I have made or shall make payable to my Trustee, whether from insurance proceeds, employee benefit plans or otherwise than under this will, without specific reference to my Marital Trust or my Family Trust, shall be allocated by my Trustee as follows: (a) assets not qualifying for the marital deduction (including those excluded from my gross estate for federal estate tax purposes) shall be allocated to my Family Trust; (b) the remaining assets shall be allocated to my Marital Trust and my Family Trust in such amounts as my Trustee shall determine, but in no event shall assets in excess of the amount needed to satisfy the amount specified in Clause 1 of ARTICLE VI of this Will be allocated to my Marital Trust; and (c) no employee benefit payments shall be devoted to any use which would disqualify them for the federal estate tax exemption under the Federal Internal Revenue Code or any amendments thereto.

[Article VII sets forth the powers of the fiduciary. Note that the same powers are conferred on the fiduciary in both his capacities, executor and trustee, thus preventing any challenge that the fiduciary is acting in one capacity under powers pertinent to his other office. The opening paragraph is a broad grant of powers; some draftsmen use only this grant, without the following enumeration, in what is professionally known as

the "short form" of powers. However, most draftsmen prefer to elaborate and state specifically all the powers on which problems commonly arise. This prevents any argument by beneficiaries or by third parties who might question the power of a trustee to enter into a specific transaction. Consider whether the following cases would have been litigated if the trustee had been operating under a grant such as the one in this trust:

Mueller v. Mueller, *page 1237*	(A) *on retention of assets.*
Rand v. McKittrick, *page 1234*	(B) *on investment powers.*
Buckle v. Marshall, *page 1277*	(C) *on earmarking.*
American Security & Trust Co. v. Frost, *page 1354*	(G) *on determination of principal and income.*
Estate of Kurkowski, *page 1266*	(H) *on power to continue business.*
Bailey's Trust, *page 1365*	(J) *on business reserves.*

The other powers eliminate any need for "implied" powers, which might require court action to verify; see Chapter XVII. Section 5(4). Special consideration should be given to 1(G), second sentence, above, on determination of principal and income. This was drafted for a jurisdiction having the Uniform Principal and Income Act. The empowering clause does not give the trustee as much freedom as might be desirable in some jurisdictions or under some circumstances. Of course, when the trustee has ample power to use principal for income beneficiaries, the need for a liberal definition of trust income is no longer so vital; and as we have already seen above, clause 5(G) of this trust document does give the trustee ample power to invade. An alternative clause on determination of income might read: "to determine upon allocations, charges or credits as between principal and income without regard to rules of law relating to trust accounting". Some draftsmen also prefer to recite that the settlor's chief concern is the comfort and welfare of the income beneficiary (wife or child), who is to be favored in making this determination. The clause on power to determine income is also interrelated with the power to invest. If the investment program contemplates investments in common stocks, it has been suggested that the trustee be given express power to pay over part or all of the net capital gains to the income beneficiary. See Curtis, The Modern Prudent Investor (3d Ed. 1961) 111.

Note that 1(P) above authorizes addition of assets to the trust, either by the testator himself from non-probate sources such as life insurance, or by other donors; for example, the wife may wish to add some of her individual assets by pour-over from her will. See Chapter XII, Section 2, 3(3) on the problems involved in such an arrangement and consider your local law to determine how valid such transfers may be and what problems they present.]

Clause 2. My Executor and Trustee shall not be liable for any loss or damage resulting from decisions made or actions taken by it in good faith under the provisions of this Article. All discretions and powers under this Article shall be continuing and may be exercised without leave of court.

[Clause 2 is a typical exoneration clause. How much actual protection it affords the fiduciary varies with judicial interpretation of "good faith". See Chapter XVII, Section 5(1). The best protection to the trustee will be found in the specific powers granted in Clause 1, which eliminate the possibility that he will exceed his powers unintentionally. For an example, reread clause 1(O) which gives the trustee absolute protection in a specific situation.]

ARTICLE VIII

In addition to the powers conferred by Article VII of this will, my Corporate Executor is empowered in its absolute discretion:

A. To determine, when a choice is available, whether deductions shall be taken against income tax or estate tax, and whether any adjustment shall be made as between income and principal as a consequence of such determination.

B. To select a date for the valuation of property in my gross estate for estate tax purposes.

C. To join with my spouse or her personal representative in gift tax returns and income tax returns for any period prior to my death and to agree with my spouse or her estate as to distribution of burdens, refunds or credits growing out of joint income tax returns or declarations filed by or on behalf of my spouse and myself or our estates.

D. To allocate income to the trusts under this will according to its best estimates and distribute it to the beneficiaries according to the terms of such trusts during the period of probate of my estate.

[Article VIII is again a product of our complex tax structure, and gives the executor freedom to deal freely with the tax problems, income and estate, which he will encounter in the course of administration. Note D allows distribution during the period of administration of the estate, so that distribution to trust income beneficiaries does not have to be postponed until the final decree settling the estate.]

* * *

Appendix II

PART 9 ("REGULATION 9") FIDUCIARY POWER OF NATIONAL BANKS AND COLLECTIVE INVESTMENT FUNDS, 12 C.F.R. (1981).[4]

PART 9—FIDUCIARY POWER OF NATIONAL BANKS AND COLLECTIVE INVESTMENT FUNDS

AUTHORITY: Sec. 1, 76 Stat. 668; 12 U.S.C. 92a; and R.S. 5240, as amended (12 U.S.C. 481) unless otherwise noted.

SOURCE: 28 F.R. 3309, Apr. 5, 1963, unless otherwise noted.

§ 9.1 Definitions.

For the purposes of this part, the term:

(a) "Account" means the trust estate or other fiduciary relationship which has been established with a bank;

(b) "Equity security" means any stock; or similar security convertible, with or without consideration, into such a security; or carrying any warrant or right to subscribe to or purchase such a security; or any such warrant or right; or any other security which the Comptroller of the Currency shall deem to be of similar nature and considers necessary or appropriate to treat as an equity security in the public interest;

(c) "Fiduciary" means a bank undertaking to act alone or jointly with others primarily for the benefit of another in all matters connected with its undertaking and includes trustee, executor, administrator, registrar of stocks and bonds, guardian of estates, assignee, receiver, committee of estates of lunatics, managing agent and any other similar capacity;

4. Regulation 9 is being revised at the time this book is published.

(d) "Fiduciary powers" means the power to act in any fiduciary capacity authorized by the Act of September 28, 1962, 76 Stat. 668, 12 U.S.C. 92a. Under that Act, a national bank may be authorized to act, when not in contravention of local law, as trustee, executor, administrator, registrar of stocks and bonds, guardian of estates, assignee, receiver, committee of estates of lunatics, or in any other fiduciary capacity which State banks, trust companies, or other corporations which come into competition with the national bank may exercise under local law;

(e) "Fiduciary records" means all matters which are written, transcribed, recorded, received or otherwise come into the possession of a bank and are necessary to preserve information concerning the acts and events relevant to the fiduciary activities of a bank;

(f) "Guardian" means the guardian or committee, by whatever name employed by local law, of the estate of an infant, an incompetent individual, an absent individual, or a competent individual over whose estate a court has taken jurisdiction, other than under bankruptcy or insolvency laws;

(g) "Investment authority" means the responsibility conferred by action of law or a provision of an appropriate governing instrument to make, select or change investments, review investment decisions made by others, or to provide investment advice or counsel to others;

(h) "Local law" means the law of the State or other jurisdiction governing the fiduciary relationship;

(i) "Managing agent" means the fiduciary relationship assumed by a bank upon the creation of an account which names the bank as agent and confers investment discretion upon the bank;

(j) "State bank" means any bank, trust company, savings bank, or other banking institution, which is not a national bank and the principal office of which is located in the District of Columbia, any State, commonwealth, or territorial possession of the United States;

(k) "Trust department" means that group or groups of officers and employees of a bank organized under the supervision of officers or employees to whom are designated by the board of directors the performance of the fiduciary responsibilities of the bank, whether or not the group or groups are so named.

(*l*) "Bank" shall include two or more banks which are members of the same affiliated group with respect to any fund established pursuant to § 9.18 of which any of such affiliated banks is trustee, or two or more of such affiliated banks are co-trustees.

(m) "Custodian under a uniform gifts to minors act" means an account established pursuant to a state law which is substantially similar to the Uniform Gifts to Minors Act as published by the American Law Institute and with respect to which the bank operating such account has established to the satisfaction of the Secretary of the Treasury that it has duties and responsibilities similar to duties and responsibilities of a trustee or guardian.

[28 F.R. 3309, Apr. 5, 1963, as amended at 37 F.R. 24161, Nov. 15, 1972; 39 F.R. 28145, Aug. 5, 1974; 41 F.R. 47937, Nov. 1, 1976]

§ 9.2 Applications.

A national bank desiring to exercise fiduciary powers shall file an application with the Comptroller of the Currency pursuant to 12 CFR 4.7b.

(12 U.S.C. 1 et seq.)

[14 F.R. 47937, Nov. 1, 1976]

§ 9.3 Consideration of applications.

In passing upon an application to exercise fiduciary powers, the Comptroller of the Currency will give consideration to the following matters and to any other facts and circumstances that seem to him proper:

(a) Whether the bank has sufficient capital and surplus to exercise the fiduciary powers applied for, which capital and surplus in no case shall be less than that required by State law of State banks, or other institutions exercising such powers;

(b) The needs of the community for fiduciary services and the probable volume of such fiduciary business available to the bank;

(c) The general condition of the bank, including the adequacy of its capital and surplus in relation to the character and condition of its assets and to its deposit liabilities and other corporate responsibilities, including the exercise of fiduciary powers;

(d) The general character and ability of the management of the bank;

(e) The nature of the supervision to be given to the fiduciary activities, including the qualifications, experience and character of the proposed officer or officers of the trust department;

(f) Whether the bank has available legal counsel to advise and pass upon fiduciary matters wherever necessary.

* * *

§ 9.7 Administration of fiduciary powers.

(a)(1) The board of directors is responsible for the proper exercise of fiduciary powers by the bank. All matters pertinent thereto, including the determination of policies, the investment and disposition of property held in a fiduciary capacity, and the direction and review of the actions of all officers, employees, and committees utilized by the bank in the exercise of its fiduciary powers, are the responsibility of the board. In discharging this responsibility, the board of directors may assign, by action duly entered in the minutes, the administration of such of the bank's fiduciary powers as it may consider proper to assign to such director(s), officer(s), employee(s) or committee(s) as it may designate.

(2) No fiduciary account shall be accepted without the prior approval of the board, or of the director(s), officer(s) or committee(s) to whom the board may have designated the performance of that responsibility. A written record shall be made of such acceptances and of the relinquishment or closing out of all fiduciary accounts. Upon the acceptance of an account for which the bank has investment responsibilities a prompt review of the assets shall be made. The board shall also ensure that at least once during every calendar year thereafter, and within 15 months of the last review, all the assets held in or for each fiduciary account where the bank has investment responsibilities are reviewed to determine the advisability of retaining or disposing of such assets.

(b) All officers and employees taking part in the operation of the trust department shall be adequately bonded.

(c) Every national bank exercising fiduciary powers shall designate, employ or retain legal counsel who shall be readily available to pass upon fiduciary matters and to advise the bank and its trust department.

(d) The trust department may utilize personnel and facilities of other departments of the bank, and other departments of the bank may utilize the personnel and facilities of the trust department only to the extent not prohibited by law. Every national bank exercising fiduciary powers shall adopt written policies and procedures to ensure that the Federal securities laws are complied with in connection with any decision or recommendation to purchase or sell any security. Such policies and procedures, in particular, shall ensure the national bank trust departments shall not use material inside information in connection with any decision or recommendation to purchase or sell any security.

[28 F.R. 3309, Apr. 5, 1963, as amended at 43 F.R. 6759, Feb. 16, 1978]

§ 9.8 Books and accounts.

(a) Every national bank exercising respect thereto as may be required by fiduciary powers shall keep its fiduciary records separate and distinct from other records of the bank. All fiduciary records shall be so kept and retained for such time as to enable the bank to furnish such information or reports with respect thereto as may be required by the Comptroller of the Currency. The fiduciary records shall contain full information relative to each account.

(b) Every such national bank shall keep an adequate record of all pending litigation to which it is a party in connection with its exercise of fiduciary powers.

§ 9.9 Audit of trust department.

A committee of directors, exclusive of any active officers of the bank, shall at least once during each calendar year and within 15 months of the last such audit, make suitable audits of the trust department or cause suitable audits to be made by auditors responsible only to the board of directors, and at such time shall ascertain whether the department has been administered in accordance with law, this part and sound fiduciary principles. The board of directors may elect, in lieu of such periodic audits, to adopt an adequate continuous audit system. A report of the audits and examination required under this section, together with the action taken thereon, shall be noted in the minutes of the board of directors.

§ 9.10 Funds awaiting investment or distribution.

(a) Funds held in a fiduciary capacity by a national bank awaiting investment or distribution shall not be held uninvested or undistributed any longer than is reasonable for the proper management of the account.

(b) Funds held in trust by a national bank, including managing agency accounts, awaiting investment or distribution may, unless prohibited by the instrument creating the trust or by local law, be deposited in the commercial or savings or other department of the bank: *Provided,* That it shall first set aside under control of the trust department as collateral security:

(1) Direct obligations of the United States, or other obligations fully guaranteed by the United States as to principal and interest; or

(2) Readily marketable securities of the classes in which state banks exercising fiduciary powers are authorized or permitted to invest trust funds under the laws of the state in which such national bank is located; or

(3) Other readily marketable securities that qualify as investment securities pursuant to the Investment Securities Regulation of the Comptroller of the Currency, 12 CFR, Chapter I, Part 1. The securities so deposited or securities substituted therefor as collateral shall at all times be at least equal in face value to the amount of trust funds so deposited, but such security shall not be required to the extent that the funds so deposited are insured by the Federal Deposit Insurance Corporation. The requirements of this sec-

tion are met when qualifying assets of the bank are pledged to secure a deposit in compliance with local law, and no duplicate pledge shall be required in such case.

§ 9.11 Investment of funds held as fiduciary.

(a) Funds held by a national bank in a fiduciary capacity shall be invested in accordance with the instrument establishing the fiduciary relationship and local law. When such instrument does not specify the character or class of investments to be made and does not vest in the bank, its directors or its officers a discretion in the matter, funds held pursuant to such instrument shall be invested in any investment in which corporate fiduciaries may invest under local law.

(b) If, under local law, corporate fiduciaries appointed by a court are permitted to exercise a discretion in investments, or if a national bank acting as fiduciary under appointment by a court is vested with a discretion in investments by an order of such court, funds of such accounts may be invested in any investments which are permitted by local law. Otherwise, a national bank acting as fiduciary under appointment by a court must make all investments of funds in such accounts under an order of that court. Such orders in either case shall be preserved with the fiduciary records of the bank.

(c) The collective investment of funds received or held by a national bank as fiduciary is governed by § 9.18.

(d) As a part of each examination of the trust department of a national bank and as provided by the Comptroller's Handbook for National Trust Examiners, the Comptroller of the Currency will examine the investments held by such bank as fiduciary, including the investment of funds under the provisions of § 9.18, in order to determine whether such investments are in accordance with law, this regulation and sound fiduciary principles.

[28 F.R. 3309, Apr. 5, 1963, as amended at 42 F.R. 65139, Dec. 30, 1977.]

§ 9.12 Self-dealing.

(a) Unless lawfully authorized by the instrument creating the relationship, or by court order or by local law, funds held by a national bank as fiduciary shall not be invested in stock or obligations of, or property acquired from, the bank or its directors, officers, or employees, or individuals with whom there exists such a connection, or organizations in which there exists such an interest, as might affect the exercise of the best judgment of the bank in acquiring the property, or in stock or obligations of, or property acquired from, affiliates of the bank or their directors, officers or employees.

(b) Property held by a national bank as fiduciary shall not be sold or transfered, by loan or otherwise, to the bank or its directors, officers, or employees, or to individuals with whom there exists such a connection, or organizations in which there exists such an interest, as might affect the exercise of the best judgment of the bank in selling or transferring such property, or to affiliates of the bank or their directors, officers or employees, except:

(1) Where lawfully authorized by the instrument creating the relationship or by court order or by local law;

(2) In cases in which the bank has been advised by its counsel in writing that it has incurred as fiduciary a contingent or potential liability and desires to relieve itself from such liability, in which case such a sale or transfer may be made with the approval of the board of directors, *Provided,* That in all

such cases the bank, upon the consummation of the sale or transfer, shall make reimbursement in cash at no loss to the account;

(3) As is provided in § 9.18(b)(8)(ii);

(4) Where required by the Comptroller of the Currency.

(c) Except as provided in § 9.10(b), funds held by a national bank as fiduciary shall not be invested by the purchase of stock or obligations of the bank or its affiliates unless authorized by the instrument creating the relationship or by court order or by local law: *Provided*, That if the retention of stock or obligations of the bank or its affiliates is authorized by the instrument creating the relationship or by court order or by local law, it may exercise rights to purchase its own stock or securities convertible into its own stock when offered pro rata to stockholders, unless such exercise is forbidden by local law. When the exercise of rights or receipt of a stock dividend results in fractional share holdings, additional fractional shares may be purchased to complement the fractional shares so acquired.

(d) A national bank may sell assets held by it as fiduciary in one account to itself as fiduciary in another account if the transaction is fair to both accounts and if such transaction is not prohibited by the terms of any governing instrument or by local law.

(e) A national bank may make a loan to an account from the funds belonging to another such account, when the making of such loans to a designated account is authorized by the instrument creating the account from which such loans are made, and is not prohibited by local law.

(f) A national bank may make a loan to an account and may take as security therefore assets of the account, provided such transaction is fair to such account and is not prohibited by local law.

[28 F.R. 3309, Apr. 5, 1963, as amended at 37 F.R. 24161, Nov. 15, 1972]

§ 9.13 Custody of investments.

(a) The investments of each account shall be kept separate from the assets of the bank, and shall be placed in the joint custody or control of not less than two of the officers or employees of the bank designated for that purpose by the board of directors of the bank or by one or more officers designated by the board of directors of the bank; and all such officers and employees shall be adequately bonded. To the extent permitted by law, a national bank may permit the investments of a fiduciary account to be deposited elsewhere.

(b) The investments of each account shall be either:

(1) Kept separate from those of all other accounts, except as provided in § 9.18, or

(2) Adequately identified as the property of the relevant account.

[28 F.R. 3309, Apr. 5, 1963, as amended at 37 F.R. 24161, Nov. 15, 1972]

§ 9.14 Deposit of securities with state authorities.

Whenever the local law requires corporations acting as fiduciary to deposit securities with the state authorities for the protection of private or court trusts, every national bank in that state authorized to exercise fiduciary powers shall, before undertaking to act in any fiduciary capacity, make a similar deposit with the state authorities. If the state authorities refuse to accept such a deposit, the securities shall be deposited with the Federal Reserve Bank of the district in which such national bank is located, and such securities shall be held for the protection of private or court trusts with like effect as though the securities had been deposited with the state authorities.

§ 9.15 Compensation of bank.

(a) If the amount of the compensation for acting in a fiduciary capacity is not regulated by local law or provided for in the instrument creating the fiduciary relationship or otherwise agreed to by the parties, a national bank acting in such capacity may charge or deduct a reasonable compensation for its services. When the bank is acting in a fiduciary capacity under appointment by a court, it shall receive such compensation as may be allowed or approved by that court or by local law.

(b) No national bank shall, except with the specific approval of its board of directors, permit any of its officers or employees, while serving as such, to retain any compensation for acting as a co-fiduciary with the bank in the administration of any account undertaken by it.

* * *

§ 9.18 Collective investment.

(a) Where not in contravention of local law, funds held by a national bank as fiduciary may be invested collectively:

(1) In a common trust fund maintained by the bank exclusively for the collective investment and reinvestment of moneys contributed thereto by the bank in its capacity as trustee, executor, administrator, or guardian or custodian under a uniform gifts to minors act.

(2) In a fund consisting solely of assets of retirement, pension, profit sharing, stock bonus or other trusts which are exempt from Federal income taxation under the Internal Revenue Code.

(b) Collective investments of funds or other property by national banks under paragraph (a) of this section (referred to in this paragraph as "collective investment funds") shall be administered as follows:

(1) Each collective investment fund shall be established and maintained in accordance with a written plan (referred to herein as the Plan) which shall be approved by a resolution of the bank's board of directors and filed with the Comptroller of the Currency. The Plan shall contain appropriate provisions not inconsistent with the rules and regulations of the Comptroller of the Currency as to the manner in which the fund is to be operated, including provisions relating to the investment powers and a general statement of the investment policy of the bank with respect to the fund; the allocation of income, profits and losses; the terms and conditions governing the admission or withdrawal of participations in the fund; the auditing of accounts of the bank with respect to the fund; the basis and method of valuing assets in the fund, setting forth specific criteria for each type of asset; the minimum frequency for valuation of assets of the fund; the period following each such valuation date during which the valuation may be made (which period in usual circumstances should not exceed 10 business days); the basis upon which the fund may be terminated; and such other matters as may be necessary to define clearly the rights of participants in the fund. A copy of the Plan shall be available at the principal office of the bank for inspection during all banking hours, and upon request a copy of the Plan shall be furnished to any person.

(2) Property held by a bank in its capacity as trustee of retirement, pension, profit sharing, stock bonus, or other trusts which are exempt from Federal income taxation under any provisions of the Internal Revenue Code may

be invested in collective investment funds established under the provisions of subparagraph (1) or (2) of paragraph (a) of this section, subject to the provisions herein contained pertaining to such funds, and may qualify for tax exemption pursuant to section 584 of the Internal Revenue Code. Assets of retirement, pension, profit sharing, stock bonus, or other trusts which are exempt from Federal income taxation by reason of being described in section 401 of the Code may be invested in collective investment funds established under the provisions of paragraph (2) of paragraph (a) of this section if the fund qualifies for tax exemption under Revenue Ruling 56–267, and following rulings.

(3) All participants in the collective investment fund shall be on the basis of a proportionate interest in all of the assets. In order to determine whether the investment of funds received or held by a bank as fiduciary in a participation in a collective investment fund is proper, the bank may consider the collective investment fund as a whole and shall not, for example, be prohibited from making such investment because any particular asset is nonincome producing.

(4) Not less frequently than once during each period of 3 months a bank administering a collective investment fund shall determine the value of the assets in the fund as of the date set for the valuation of assets. No participation shall be admitted to or withdrawn from the fund except (i) on the basis of such valuation and (ii) as of such valuation date. No participation shall be admitted to or withdrawn from the fund unless a written request for or notice of intention of taking such action shall have been entered on or before the valuation date in the fiduciary records of the bank and approved in such manner as the board of directors shall prescribe. No requests or notice may be canceled or countermanded after the valuation date.

(5)(i) A bank administering a collective investment fund shall at least once during each period of 12 months cause an adequate audit to be made of the collective investment fund by auditors responsible only to the board of directors of the bank. In the event such audit is performed by independent public accountants, the reasonable expenses of such audit may be charged to the collective investment fund.

(ii) A bank administering a collective investment fund shall at least once during each period of 12 months prepare a financial report of the fund. This report, based upon the above audit, shall contain a list of investments in the fund showing the cost and current market value of each investment; a statement for the period since the previous report showing purchases, with cost; sales, with profit or loss and any other investment changes; income and disbursements; and an appropriate notation as to any investments in default.

(iii) The financial report may include a description of the fund's value on previous dates, as well as its income and disbursements during previous accounting periods. No predictions or representations as to future results may be made. In addition, as to funds described in paragraph (1) of paragraph (a) of this section, neither the report nor any other publication of the bank shall make reference to the performance of funds other than those administered by the bank.

(iv) A copy of the financial report shall be furnished, or notice shall be given that a copy of such report is available and will be furnished without charge upon request, to each person to whom a regular periodic accounting would ordinarily be rendered with respect to each participating account. A copy of such financial report may be furnished to prospective customers. The cost of printing and distribution of these reports shall be borne by the bank. In addition, a copy of the report shall be furnished upon request to any person for a reasonable charge. The fact of the availability of the report for any fund described in paragraph (1) of paragraph (a) of this section may be given publicity solely in connection with the promotion of the fiduciary services of the bank.

(v) Except as herein provided, the bank shall not advertise or publicize its collective investment fund(s) described in paragraph (1) of paragraph (a) of this section.

(6) When participations are withdrawn from a collective investment fund, distributions may be made in cash or ratably in kind, or partly in cash and partly in kind: *Provided,* That all distributions as of any one valuation date shall be made on the same basis.

(7) If for any reason an investment is withdrawn in kind from a collective investment fund for the benefit of all participants in the fund at the time of such withdrawal and such investment is not distributed ratably in kind, it shall be segregated and administered or realized upon for the benefit ratably of all participants in the collective investment fund at the time of withdrawal.

(8)(i) No bank shall have any interest in a collective investment fund other than in its fiduciary capacity. Except for temporary net cash overdrafts or as otherwise specifically provided herein, it may not lend money to a fund, sell property to, or purchase property from a fund. No assets of a collective investment fund may be invested in stock or obligations, including time or savings deposits, of the bank or any of its affiliates: *Provided,* That such deposits may be made of funds awaiting investment or distribution. Subject to all other provisions of this part, funds held by a bank as fiduciary for its own employees may be invested in a collective investment fund. A bank may not make any loan on the security of a participation in a fund. If because of a creditor relationship or otherwise the bank acquires an interest in a participation in a fund, the participation shall be withdrawn on the first date on which such withdrawal can be effected. However, in no case shall an unsecured advance until the time of the next valuation date to an account holding a participation be deemed to constitute the acquisition of an interest by the bank.

(ii) Any bank administering a collective investment fund may purchase for its own account from such fund any defaulted fixed income investment held by such fund, if in the judgment of the board of directors the cost of segregation of such investment would be greater than the difference between its market value and its principal amount plus interest and penalty charges due. If the bank elects to so purchase such investment, it must do so at its market value or at the sum of cost, accrued unpaid interest, and penalty charges, whichever is greater.

(9) Except in the case of collective investment funds described in paragraph (a)(2) of this section:

(i) No funds or other property shall be invested in a participation in a collective investment fund if as a result of such investment the participant would have an interest aggregating in excess of 10 percent of the then market value of the fund: *Provided,* That in applying this limitation if two or more accounts are created by the same person or persons and as much as one-half of the income or principal of each account is payable or applicable to the use of the same person or persons, such accounts shall be considered as one;

(ii) No investment for a collective investment fund shall be made in stocks, bonds, or other obligations of any one person, firm, or corporation if as a result of such investment the total amount invested in stocks, bonds, or other obligations issued or guaranteed by such person, firm or corporation would aggregate in excess of 10 percent of the then market value of the fund: *Provided,* That this limitation shall not apply to investments in direct obligations of the United States or other obligations fully guaranteed by the United States as to principal and interest;

(iii) Any bank administering a collective investment fund shall have the responsibility of maintaining in cash and readily marketable investments such part of the assets of the fund as shall be deemed to be necessary to provide adequately for the needs of participants and to prevent inequities between such participants, and if prior to any admissions to or withdrawals from a fund the bank shall determine that after effecting the admissions and withdrawals which are to be made less than 40 percent of the value of the remaining assets of the collective investment fund would be composed of cash and readily marketable investments, no admissions to or withdrawals from the fund shall be permitted as of the valuation date upon which such determination is made: *Provided,* That ratable distribution upon all participations shall not be so prohibited in any case.

(10) The reasonable expenses incurred in servicing mortgages held by a collective investment fund may be charged against the income account of the fund and paid to servicing agents, including the bank administering the fund.

(11)(i) A bank may (but shall not be required to) transfer up to 5 percent of the net income derived by a collective investment fund from mortgages held by such fund during any regular accounting period to a reserve account: *Provided,* That no such transfers shall be made which would cause the amount in such account to exceed 1 percent of the outstanding principal amount of all mortgages held in the fund. The amount of such reserve account, if established, shall be deducted from the assets of the fund in determining the fair market value of the fund for the purposes of admissions and withdrawals.

(ii) At the end of each accounting period, all interest payments which are due but unpaid with respect to mortgages in the fund shall be charged against such reserve account to the extent available and credited to income distributed to participants. In the event of subsequent recovery of such interest payments by the fund, the reserve account shall be credited with the amount so recovered.

(12) A national bank administering a collective investment fund shall have the exclusive management thereof. The bank may charge a fee for the management of the collective investment fund: *Provided,* That the fractional part of such fee proportionate to the interest of each participant shall not, when added to any other compensations charged by a bank to a participant, exceed the total amount of compensations which would have been charged to said participant if no assets of said participant had been invested in participations in the fund. The bank shall absorb the costs of establishing or reorganizing a collective investment fund.

(13) No bank administering a collective investment fund shall issue any certificate or other document evidencing a direct or indirect interest in such fund in any form.

(14) No mistake made in good faith and in the exercise of due care in connection with the administration of a collective investment fund shall be deemed to be a violation of this part if promptly after the discovery of the

mistake the bank takes whatever action may be practicable in the circumstances to remedy the mistake.

(c) In addition to the investments permitted under paragraph (a) of this section, funds or other property received or held by a national bank as fiduciary may be invested collectively, to the extent not prohibited by local law, as follows:

(1) In shares of a mutual trust investment company, organized and operated pursuant to a statute that specifically authorizes the organization of such companies exclusively for the investment of funds held by corporate fiduciaries, commonly referred to as a "bank fiduciary fund."

(2)(i) In a single real estate loan, a direct obligation of the United States, or an obligation fully guaranteed by the United States, or in a single fixed amount security, obligation or other property, either real, personal or mixed, of a single issuer; or

(ii) On a short-term basis in a variable amount note of a borrower of prime credit: *Provided,* That such note shall be maintained by the bank on its premises and may be utilized by it only for investment of moneys held in its trust department accounts: *Provided further,* That the bank owns no participation in the loans or obligations authorized under paragraphs (c)(2)(i) or (ii) of this section, and has no interest in any investment therein except in its capacity as fiduciary.

(3) In a common trust fund maintained by the bank for the collective investment of cash balances received or held by a bank in its capacity as trustee, executor, administrator, or guardian, which the bank considers to be individually too small to be invested separately to advantage. The total investment for such fund must not exceed $100,000; the number of participating accounts is limited to 100, and no participating account may have an interest in the fund in excess of $10,000: *Provided,* That in applying these limitations if two or more accounts are created by the same person or persons and as much as one-half of the income or principal of each account is presently payable or applicable to the use of the same person or persons, such account shall be considered as one: *And provided,* That no fund shall be established or operated under this subparagraph for the purpose of avoiding the provisions of paragraph (b) of this section.

(4) In any investment specifically authorized by court order, or authorized by the instrument creating the fiduciary relationship, in the case of trusts created by a corporation, its subsidiaries and affiliates or by several individual settlors who are closely related: *Provided,* That such investment is not made under this subparagraph for the purpose of avoiding the provisions of paragraph (b) of this section.

(5) In such other manner as shall be approved in writing by the Comptroller of the Currency.

[37 FR 24161, Nov. 15, 1972, as amended at 40 F.R. 18771, Apr. 30, 1975; 40 F.R. 20612, May 12, 1975; 41 F.R. 26679, June 29, 1976; 41 F.R. 47938, Nov. 1, 1976]

* * *

INDEX

References are to Pages

†